1989/43rd Annual Edition

EDITED BY KEN WARNER

DBI BOOKS, INC.

ABOUT OUR COVERS

Celebrating their 40th year of gunmaking, Sturm, Ruger & Co. graces the covers of this 43rd Edition, 1989 GUN DIGEST, with three new guns and we're proud to be the showcase for these exciting offerings.

Our front cover depicts the still-new Ruger GP-100 revolver on the left, only with a new twist—instead of the usual adjustable rear sight, they've added this model with a groove rear sight that won't snag on clothing or holster. This sighting arrangement will be available with 3-inch or 4-inch barrel only, in both blue or stainless steel models. Grip options will be either round butt or square butt Cushion Grip live rubber with Goncalo Alves inserts.

On the right is the all-new small-frame SP-101 five-shot revolver, introduced initially in 38 Special, with plans for 22 Long Rifle, 32 H&R Magnum, and possibly others in the future. In 38 Special, barrel lengths will be 2¼ or 3 inches and, like its larger GP-100 brother, the gun will be offered with non-adjustable rear sight (adjustable rear sight may be added to the line later). Stocks will be round butt design only and of the Cushion Grip configuration. It is planned that the gun will be made only in stainless steel. This is the first true snub-nose revolver to come from the Ruger factory.

Our back cover shows the latest in M-77 rifles, the new short-action M-77 Mk II, initially chambered for the 223 Remington (5.56 NATO). It has the three-position safety of the M77/22 rimfire rifle. The new rifle has a stainless steel bolt, fixed ejector and weighs 6¾ to 7 pounds, and in this caliber will come without iron sights. All the metal on this gun except the bolt is blued steel. Barrels will include a 22-inch standard weight tube and a heavy 24-inch varmint-weight. The new rifle will have all the quality and features that have made the M-77 line a major factor in today's hunting rifle market.

Cover paintings by James M. Triggs.

GUN DIGEST STAFF

EDITOR-IN-CHIEF
Ken Warner
SENIOR STAFF EDITOR
Harold A. Murtz
EDITORIAL/PRODUCTION ASSISTANT
Maria L. Connor
ASSISTANT TO THE EDITOR
Lilo Anderson
CONTRIBUTING EDITORS
Bob Bell
Doc Carlson
Dean A. Grennell
Rick Hacker
Clay Harvey
Edward A. Matunas
Layne Simpson
Larry S. Sterett
Hal Swiggett
D.A. Warner
J.B. Wood
EUROPEAN CORRESPONDENT
Raymod Caranta
GRAPHIC DESIGN
Jim Billy
Mary MacDonald
MANAGING EDITOR
Pamela Johnson
PUBLISHER
Sheldon L. Factor

DBI BOOKS, INC.

PRESIDENT
Charles T. Hartigan
VICE PRESIDENT & PUBLISHER
Sheldon L. Factor
VICE PRESIDENT—SALES
John G. Strauss
TREASURER
Frank R. Serpone

Arms and Armour Press, London, G.B. exclusive licensees and distributor in Britain and Europe; New Zealand; Nigeria, South Africa and Zimbabwe; India and Pakistan; Singapore, Hong Kong and Japan. Capricorn Link (Aust.) Pty. Ltd. exclusive distributors in Australia.

ISBN 0-87349-025-8 Library of Congress Catalog #44-32588

Winchester Bows Out But Not Quite

The Winchester Division of Olin Corporation had, apart from its exciting cartridge developments, two recent announcements of interest:

The first, in November of 1987, held the somewhat startling comment, "The sale of our interest in O.K. Firearms Co. in Japan completes Olin's exit from the firearms manufacturing business," made by John Johnstone Jr., president of Olin. That's the end of about six decades or so of building guns.

The second shoe dropped in April, 1988, when Olin announced Browning S.A. is to be exclusive worldwide distributor of Winchester-marked guns made by U.S. Repeating Arms Co., although USRAC hangs onto the U.S. and Canada and Olin, for whatever arcane reason, keeps Oceania (the Pacific area). This arrangement was preceded by other arrangements between USRAC and Browning and, no doubt, Olin, since Olin now may sell Browning-marked shotshells worldwide, except Spain, Turkey, Nigeria and the Benelux nations.

All Winchester-Olin guns are fully backed for future service, and the new Classic Japan Ltd. will be selling its versions of the former Winchester 101 and such. USRAC is a lot healthier. And Winchester is not quite gone, which is a relief.

The Maxine and Sharon Show Gets Good Reviews

Everybody over at the National Muzzle Loading Rifle Association is happy. Maxine Moss is a whole lot glad to be retired; Sharon Cunningham, she once of Dixie Gun Works, is even happier to have so nice an editorial challenge as running *Muzzle Blasts*. And the NMLRA Board and members and all are right pleased to have pulled it off so slick.

If You Can't Join 'Em, Invite 'Em

At the 1989 Custom Gun Show (January 20-22 in the Nugget, Reno, NV) the Gunmaker's Guild and the Engravers Guild plan to show off fine guns besides theirs. They have decided to invite high-class commercial exhibitors.

During their 1988 show in Las Vegas, they were able to see fine stuff with names like Purdey, Westley Richards, Merkel and such over at the Safari Club International Convention. So it's a match made in Las Vegas.

Penguin Presents 1,000,000th Ruger

The first Ruger Standard Automatic Pistol since 1951 to carry a red eagle is No. 1,000,000 and you can see it in the National Firearms Museum in Washington, 10 AM to 4 PM, 7 days a week. The gun was presented to NRA's museum by Warren E. Moser, president of Penguin Industries, this past year as a contribution to the Museum's educational efforts.

SHOT Show Numbers Up Again

The National Shooting Sports Foundation uses a factor of four now to discuss this 10-year-old national institution: in Las Vegas in 1988, there were about four times as many exhibitors showing to more than four times the visitors in well over four times the space as that first show in 1979 in St. Louis. And what do they do with this money? Lots—pro-hunting ads, new ideas in conservation and competition, positive events like National Hunting And Fishing Day and more are all funded by NSSF.

NRA's tough-talk ads seemed to shooters a welcome switch in communication technique but won few friends, the experts say.

A $300,000 Colt

Sixty-three years ago in New England, Fred P. L. Mills paid a widow lady $4 for a Colt revolver. Last year, the U.S. Historical Society paid dealer Greg Martin $300,000 for that same revolver, no doubt influenced by a fact not in evidence during the 1925 transaction: This is No. 1. And with it in hand, the Society is issuing (they call it that, which means *selling* in Societese) 6-inch miniatures which are cute as hell.

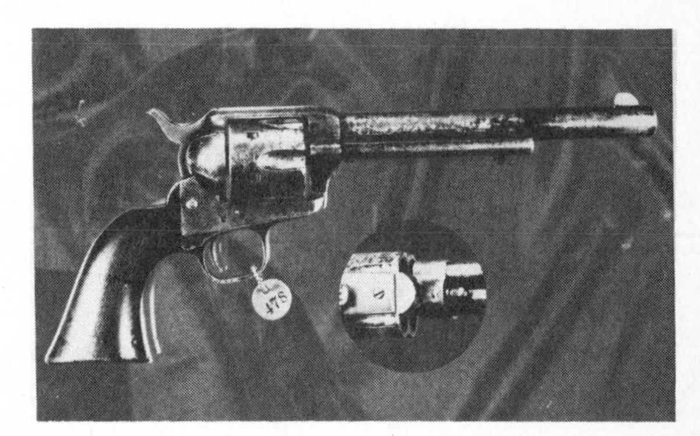

The $300,000 Peacemaker Number 1 will be replicated in miniature by U.S. Historical Society.

Remington Recall

If you bought a Remington bolt-action centerfire—a Model 700, a Model Seven, a Sportsman 78, or either a Model 40X-B or 40-XC—after July 29, 1987, write down the serial number and call, toll-free, 1-800-634-2459. You might need a new trigger assembly, which Remington will furnish and install at no charge. There is a slight possibility of parts breakage, perhaps an accidental firing, so do it if you have such a bolt-action rifle.

The Skeeter Fund

Skeeter Skelton's final illness was financially catastrophic and Mrs. Skelton has serious problems. Those who got more than their money's worth from Skeeter's writings over the years (and are maybe now fixed better than they were) could spend some of that old profit now. Just send it to Mrs. Skeeter Skelton, care of United New Mexico Mimbres Valley Bank, P.O. Box 1050, Deming, NM 88031. Be generous.

CONTENTS

FEATURES

DEPARTMENTS

MOST BIG game hunters would be perfectly served by 2½x or 4x scopes. The reasons are simple: These magnifications give precise aiming capabilities on the game being hunted at the ranges where it's normally shot, and they come in sizes and weights appropriate to the rifles they're mounted on.

However, there are a few specialists, riflemen who habitually do their shooting at long range, often under truly adverse light conditions, who need more magnification and/or more brilliant target images than the traditional big game scopes give. Typical of these are the whitetail shooters of South Carolina, Alabama, and other parts of the Deep South, and pronghorn hunters. The latter rarely are bothered by lack of light, but deer hunters often are. In the South, a great percentage of deer shots come just before full dark, when natural movement brings whitetails out of the swamps to feed. The typical target now is a ghostly image, the bottom half perhaps hidden by weeds or crops, at the far side of a wide field. The hunter's job is to find that image in his scope, get the reticle on a vital area, and squeeze off a shot. The kill must be instantaneous, or nearly so, if the animal is to be recovered before it gets into impenetrable cover. Many rifle/cartridge combinations have accuracy and power to do the job if the bullet is properly placed; the trick is to use a scope that will permit such placement under such conditions.

"Long range" is a relative thing. To someone who grew up snapshooting deer in frozen cedar swamps, 85 yards is a long shot, while Pennsylvania's 1000-yard benchrest competitors feel a deer at ½-mile is too close. The former is best served by iron sights or a small variable at the 1½x setting, while the latter might prefer a 2-inch Unertl 24x fitted with a series of Lee Dots. Most hunters do not fall into either of those extremes. In our lingo here, a couple of hundred yards is a long chance in the gloom, and 400-500 yards is as far as even a better-than-average rifleman should shoot at any time. I know a few super-experts will scoff at these limits, but most of us don't fall into their category. As a general statement, I don't believe any big game hunter should try a shot he is not at least 85 percent certain of making; it isn't fair to the game. When I use this as a criterion, things seem to fall into place.

So, assuming we have a cartridge which delivers ballistics appropriate to our needs and a rifle which can take advantage of the load's efficiency, and we can shoot, the question becomes: For such an outfit, which scope is best? Note that we said *best.* Many scopes are good, but some are better than others and a few are best of all for these specialized needs.

A jumper to a quick conclusion might say a medium-size variable would be top choice. A 3-9x offers a fully adequate power spread in reasonable bulk and weight. However, most variables have minor weaknesses in this regard. Fields at a given power are usually smaller than in straight powers, reticles are rarely ideal for dim light use, and they are less weatherproof than single-power scopes, due to the slot in the tube for the connecting unit between power selector ring and inner mechanism.

This brings us to the medium-power scopes, the 6x and 8x models. That shouldn't be surprising. Middle Europeans reached the same conclusion long ago, at least insofar as the bad-light requirements went, and we have followed their lead for generations,

WHY BIG SCOPES MAKE THE DIFFERENCE

It's high school physics that causes it.

by BOB BELL

P. J. Bell tries the ol' man's Ultimate Illuminator from Redfield. She says 7mm Mags don't kick that much, and big optics give the reach.

introducing variations and improvements as needed for better solutions to our specific problems.

Scope literature from reputable manufacturers pretty much indicates what will work best in any given situation. However, it's always more satisfying to have first-hand experience, so we decided to testfire a number of models. There's never time to exhaust the possibilities, but we assembled a dozen representative models to work with. The 6xs included the Kassnar Beta 3, Leupold M8, Redfield Five Star, Schmidt & Bender, Swarovski ZFM, Zeiss Diatal AZ, and my pre-WWII Zeiss Zielsechs.* The 8xs were the Kahles, Schmidt & Bender, Weaver 856, and Zeiss Diatal ZA. So the variables would be represented, we added a Leupold Vari-X-III 3.5-10x.

The testing was simple. We wanted to know how such scopes would perform in bad light, so we took them out and used them from near sunset until after dark. I recruited hunting pal Bob Wise and his son Dave, so more than one pair of eyes would be involved, and in late November and early December we spent numerous evenings on their farm, looking at assorted targets at various distances. Results were enlightening, if you don't mind a bad pun.

First, I might mention that the scopes were routinely tested for field, eye relief, adjustment value, etc., though we've learned over the years that such effort is mostly wasted. Good manufacturers meet their advertised specs so closely that a significant variation is rarely found. It's worth noting that European scopes often have adjustment values different from the normal quarter-minutes of American models, and that sometimes those values are different in scopes of different powers from the same maker. For instance, adjustments in the Kahles line are 12mm/100m in the 2½x, then 7, 6 and 4 millimeters, respectively, in the 4x, 6x and 8x. Literature accompanying all these scopes lists such information, so it pays to read it. One other thing should be checked and remembered—adjustment dialing direction in European scopes is often opposite that of American models. To raise point of impact, we normally turn the dial counter-clockwise—like raising (unscrewing) a jar lid. Some European models work that way, others just the opposite, so don't go twisting without checking unless you like surprises.

We did most of our looking across a cut hayfield that slopes gently to a thickly grown creek bottom flanked on one side by a narrow woods. Alongside the woods is an alfalfa field. Many times over the years we've checked the distance to the end of the hayfield with a Barr & Stroud military rangefinder and by stepping it off—it's 475 yards. That means anything we can see in the adjoining alfalfa field is at just about 500 yards. A number of hay bales were scattered around the cut field. They were similar in color and texture to whitetails, and because the bottom half of one some 250 yards away was concealed by a hump in the field, it looked about the same size as a deer's body. This

GD Editor Ken Warner has threatened to bash me with an ax if I ever mention this old Zeiss again (it has cropped up often in my Scope Reviews, as it was the first good scope I ever owned), but it obviously belongs here as it is an early representative of this class, so gives us a starting point and lets us see how things have advanced.** ***(Actually, I'm going to hit him with the scope. It's heavier than an ax. KW)

was convenient when there were no deer to look at.

Luckily, though, deer often came out to feed in the alfalfa in late afternoon. Bedded down on solid rests, Bob, Dave and I studied them through one scope after another, trading the assorted models back and forth among us. The binocular-type adjustment of the European models' ocular lenses was handy here as it allowed instantaneous reticle focusing to accommodate to different eyesight, after each of us had determined his optimum setting. Normally, a scope will be used by one person only, so the American screw-type adjustment is no big problem, despite its comparative slowness. Once adjusted for an individual's eyes, it rarely requires any change.

In late afternoon, aiming was no problem at any range, even with a 4x Swarovski we had along. But after the sun had been down awhile, working with only the glow from a cloudy sky, more power and bigger lenses were necessary. At this point the modern 6xs were still usable, but my old Zeiss Zielsechs couldn't hack it any longer. Its 1.75-minute Lee Dot was part of the problem (dots have so little total area, compared with other reticles, that they're not at their best in poor light); however, its big weakness was lack of coating. This Zielsechs was built in the early '30s, before even single coating came along, and that lack is a severe handicap. Many new models are not only coated, but multi-coated, and the difference is striking. Most of today's shooters have never used a scope with uncoated lenses, so can't realize what an improvement those few millionths of an inch of applied material make.

At this time, whitetails feeding in the alfalfa field 500 yards away could still be aimed at with all the other 6xs, and the job was even easier with the 8xs. European-type duplex reticles helped. These have three or four posts (the 12 o'clock one is sometimes missing) that are significantly heavier than American duplex posts. (Posts of the 6x42 Leupold are thicker than normal but not as heavy as in European scopes.) The inner crosswire permits precise aim at long range, of course. Reticles in some of the big European scopes were the style intended for short-range shooting in very bad light—three posts which almost meet in the middle, the bottom one being pointed. These do not give the long-range capabilities of the duplex design as they conceal the target with a high hold. This has nothing to do with scope optics, but rather reflects a deliberate choice to satisfy a specific need. Either style reticle can be had in any of the European scopes we used. Most American hunters would be best served by the duplex version.

The 3.5-10x Leupold and the Weaver 856 both had American duplex reticles. The Leupold variable did not have a big enough objective to make its top power usable at long range in early evening, but it did very well at a setting of 6x or 7x. The Weaver had enough lens for its power, but its American reticle faded at about this point. All other 8x56s were still fully usable.

One evening we stayed out until it was truly dark. The unaided eye could not see hay bales at fairly close range in the cut field. I was searching the far end with Swarovski 8x56 binoculars. These are even better than the big scopes under such conditions, probably because they have a separate optical unit for each eye. Not a lot better, but enough that the user can tell the difference.

I picked up three deer as they drifted out of the woods into the alfalfa. There was something otherworldly about being able to see those small whitetails in utter gloom, five football fields distant. I mean, it was *dark*. It felt even stranger to pick up my old 7x61 Sharpe & Hart Magnum, which now wore the 8x56 Kahles, or a 700 Remington with the 8x56 Zeiss, and see the crosswires sharp against the shoulders of one deer after the other. When I looked above either scope, everything—the fields, the far-off creek-bottom, the woods—was murky shades of gray and black. But using that big Kahles or Zeiss, and then the Schmidt & Bender in turn, it was—though it seems incredible—easy to aim at a deer 500 yards away.

It would not have been possible to aim at a deer in cover at that distance, or even against a background which did not give some silhouette effect. But under the conditions stated, which could duplicate chances offered at occasional whitetails during hunting season, a shot could have been taken.

We also tried the 6xs on the same deer at the same time, passing those and the 8xs back and forth, squinting and muttering and trying to decide if any one of them was clearly superior to the others. We looked until we ran out of light completely—there comes a time when you can't see a bull moose in a field at 100 yards, let alone a deer at 500. Some conclusions were easy:

- Optically the 8x56mms were definitely the best.
- The 6xs couldn't cut it at our maximum range when it was this dark, though they still did well against half a hay bale at half the distance.
- The European duplex reticle was

(Above and opposite page) Bell rigs M700 Remington in 25-06 with Zeiss 8x56mm for deer hunting in farm country. It works.

COMMON OPTICAL SPECS

Power	Objective Diameter	Exit Pupil	Relative Brightness	Twilight Factor
1½x	20mm	13.3mm	177	5+
2½x	20mm	8.0mm	64	7
4x	32mm	8.0mm	64	11+
6x	42mm	7.0mm	49	16−
8x	56mm	7.0mm	49	21+
12x	38mm	2.4mm	6−	21+

best for long-range aiming under the worst light conditions, usable several minutes longer than the American design.

- The three heavy German-style posts would doubtless be best of all at short distances in the woods.
- A variable power chosen specifically for such shooting should have a duplex reticle heavy enough for good visibility at 6x or 7x as no available objective lens is big enough to deliver the light required to make 10x usable (that would necessitate a 70mm objective, which couldn't be mounted by any practicable means).

We probably should mention that the 8x56 is also significantly heavier, bulkier and more expensive than the others—factors which might be highly important when selecting a scope.

Why should the 8x56 be the top choice?

A little background on hunting optics might be helpful here.

For decades, American scope specifications listed relative brightness (RB) as a means of comparing the amount of light transmitted by different scopes. This is a numerical rating related to the area of the scope's exit pupil. It is calculated by squaring the diameter of the exit pupil in millimeters. For example, a 6x42 scope with a 7mm exit pupil had an RB of 49, while a 2½x20 with an 8mm exit pupil had a relative brightness rating of 64, suggesting the 2½x was better in poor light. Yet simple observation showed that the 2½x scope was not as bright as the 6x. Obviously, something was out of kilter.

European makers took a different approach. They rarely listed relative brightness figures. Rather, they went with a "twilight factor." This was a rating determined by multiplying the objective lens diameter in millimeters by the scope's magnification, then taking the square root of the product. The table nearby gives pertinent figures for some common scope designs, and perhaps shows the weakness of both the RB and TF systems.

I included the 1½x there as it is typical of the bottom power setting of a small variable, and because the large exit pupil gives an extremely high relative brightness figure. However, as the pupil of the human eye never exceeds 7mm in diameter, it cannot accommodate a beam of light greater in diameter than that so the 1½x's RB figure is irrelevant and the twilight factor gives a more useful rating.

At the other extreme, the 12x is representative of a target scope with 1½-inch objective. Here, the TF equals that of an 8x56mm, yet anyone who has tried to use a target scope in bad light knows it's a pointless effort. You simply have a large dark image. In this case, the RB rating is more indicative of reality. The gloomy image is a result of the scope's small exit pupil—much smaller than the eye's entrance pupil when ambient light is bad.

Thus, although I've never seen it mentioned in scope literature, the twilight factor obviously is most useful when the scope creates an exit pupil at least equal in diameter to the eye's entrance pupil at the moment of use. This diameter varies tremendously, depending upon the intensity of the ambient light, from about 2mm in bright sunlight to 7mm in darkness. Therefore, in order to perform as well as possible under the worst light conditions, a scope must have an exit pupil of 7mm. That's why in binocular design the most common so-called night glass is a 7x50mm. That's why the German/Austrian scopes and some of their American derivatives intended for early morning and late evening use have objectives that give a 7mm exit pupil. (The new 6x Leupold and the old Weaver 856 meet this specification; the Redfield Five Star's objective is slightly smaller at 1.58 inches or 40mm.)

A 7mm exit pupil gives a relative brightness figure of 49, no matter what the magnification. But as noted in our testing and as indicated by the twilight factor, the 8x56mm models were definitely superior to the 6x42mms for aiming at distant targets in near darkness, despite identical RB figures of 49. Why?

I've wondered about that for a long

time, but have never heard nor read a suitable explanation. Then a short time ago a statement I'd memorized from a physics book when I was a high school freshman popped into my mind. (That was in 1939, incidentally; don't ask me where it was buried in my head all those years.) It said: *"The intensity of light varies inversely as the square of the distance from the source."*

That, if true, obviously would account for many things of interest to scope users. But was it true? Was my memory correct? I didn't know. I'm no optical engineer. So I called one of the country's leading scope designers and asked. He said the statement is true.

That put a whole new perspective on things. Instead of talking about the cross-sectional area of the light beam which enters the eye, this law dealt with the intensity or brilliance of the light making up that area, and with the way that intensity decreases as it travels through space.

For example, light from a given source has only one-hundredth the intensity at 10 yards as it has at 1 yard (the inverse relationship of the square of these distances). This helps explain why nearby objects are fairly visible even in bad light but rapidly vanish as the distance grows.

I then asked if a scope affects light intensity because it reduces distance according to its power. That is, an object at 600 yards, when viewed through a 6x scope, appears approximately as it would at 100 yards to the naked eye. (Not exactly, as the scope invariably has imperfections, there is much more "dirty" atmosphere to be looked through at the longer range, etc.). I was told this is simplistic, but as a general comment has considerable validity. So I worked out a few examples. Even assuming some error is involved, this approach seems to explain the intensity or brilliance of a scope image better than either the relative brightness or twilight factor methods.

Consider those deer at 500 yards. In good light they'd have been visible to the naked eye, but not in the evening; they were literally invisible then because it was simply too dark. But that's another way of saying that the light reflected from them, so far as the eye was concerned, was only one quarter-millionth what it would have been if they were at 1 yard (500 squared equals 250,000). At 1 yard they'd have been easily visible at that same moment in time, but at 500 everything was simply "dark."

How did the scopes change things? And why was there a difference in image brilliance among the different scopes? Remember that all had 7mm exit pupils, which meant all had a relative brightness rating of 49, and all would equal the eye's entrance pupil under the worst light conditions.

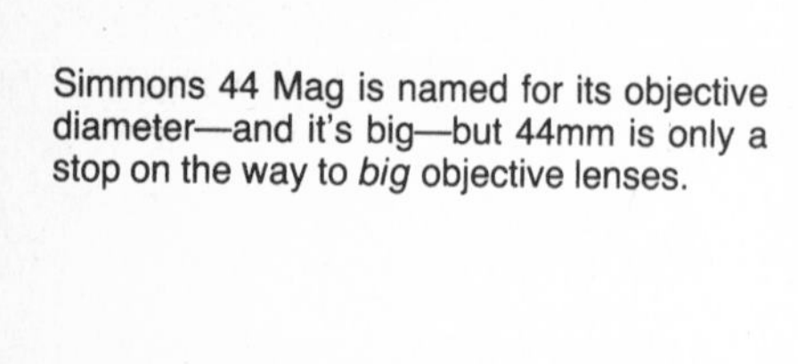

Bushnell's Banner line now has a large objective variable, a 3-9x56mm, which is probably going to have a lot of competition soon.

Simmons 44 Mag is named for its objective diameter—and it's big—but 44mm is only a stop on the way to *big* objective lenses.

Dividing that 500-yard range by 6x gives an apparent range of 83.3 yards. Squaring 83.3 gives 6940, and as the variation is inverse, we get a fraction of $\frac{1}{6940}$. In other words, the intensity of the light striking the eye from a target at 500 yards when using a 6x42mm scope is $\frac{1}{6940}$ what it would be at 1 yard. The same procedure with an 8x56mm gives an apparent range of 62.5 yards. Squaring this gives 3900, for an intensity of $\frac{1}{3900}$ of the 1-yard reading.

These through-the-scope numbers might seem small, but they're awfully impressive when compared to the unaided eye's performance—36 times better with the 6x42mm, 64 times better with the 8x56mm. The numbers also show why the 8x56mm is the top choice when the light is bad: It gives an intensity some 1.78 times that of a 6x42mm, though both have the same size exit pupil.

It should be remembered that no matter what the situation, all of the light which reaches the scope's objective lens does not emerge from the ocular lens and enter the eye. That never happens. A certain percentage is always reflected away, absorbed by the lenses, or whatever. With today's coated—or multicoated—lenses, something between 75 and 90+ percent of the light which reaches the objective lens actually emerges from the scope and reaches the eye. Even allowing for such loss, a medium-power, large-objective scope creates a brighter image than the unaided eye because the eye is working with the full target distance while the scope's magnification essentially decreases this, as discussed.

Thus, the law from that old physics book seems to explain why higher magnification gives a more brilliant image, so long as the objective lens is big enough to provide all the light the eye can admit. Its significance is most important when ambient light is bad, for that's when the eye pupil opens to its maximum.

And it therefore explains why the big-eye scopes are the best choice for the bad-light specialists. That's what those deer in alfalfa were saying, too. ●

Back in the '50s, this 7x61 S&H Magnum accounted for a large truckload of deer. Dave Wise, who's using it here, figures Bell would have gotten even more if he'd had this big Kahles on it back then.

Seven of the scopes mentioned: 6x42 Redfield, 6x42 and 8x56 Zeiss, 4x32 Swarovski, Swarovski ZFM 6x42, 6x42 and 8x56 Schmidt & Bender.

Noted novelist Hamilton marked his return to rifle hunting with this nice YO Ranch whitetail.

The *Easy* Whitetail

by DONALD HAMILTON

If you are very lucky,
you can almost go home again.

IT TOOK less than an hour to find my deer. Before daybreak, Hal Swiggett knocked on the door of my room at the fabulous YO Ranch just west of Kerrville, Texas. I had time for a generous breakfast at the Chuckwagon, as they call their dining hall. Then we set out to cruise the little ranch roads in Hal's pickup looking for a suitable whitetail buck.

Hal Swiggett is a compact, energetic gent who doesn't show his 60-odd years. He's a triple-threat man. A Baptist minister, he's also an outdoor writer of some renown, and, having been associated with the YO Ranch for years, he will upon occasion help out a clumsy fellow-writer like me by acting as a guide there. As we drove, he gave me a history of the ranch: Founded in 1880 by one Charles Armand Schreiner, it's at present managed by his great-grandson, Charles Schreiner IV, known as Charley Four, each of whose three brothers has responsibility for a different phase of the big operation. The ranch covers over 40,000 acres and supports longhorn cattle, sheep, elk, whitetail deer, wild turkeys, and numerous varieties of exotics—everything from addax to zebra. (For information: YO Ranch, Mountain Home, Texas 78058, 512-640-3222.)

Located in the south central portion of the Lone Star State, these are not the endless flat plains of western Texas. I believe they call it their Hill Country, but that's Texas exaggeration. Hills they aren't, to amount to anything, but it's a pleasantly rolling landscape covered with various kinds of thorny vegetation, and occasionally shaded by the twisty low trees that Westerners call oaks although an Easterner familiar only with the great white oak would never recognize them.

We prowled slowly along various dirt tracks waiting for good shooting light. Hal pointed out some exotics—a band of white-spotted axis deer, and a spectacular blackbuck with, he said, a near-trophy head. How he could tell, in the early-morning grayness, I had no idea. The sky gradually turned red in the east and the sun made a dramatic appearance. We covered some more slow miles and saw some more strange game from distant continents. At last Hal stopped the pickup and reached for his binoculars. A nearby hillside displayed a small group of honest-to-Pete, U.S.-type deer, the first we'd seen.

After a little, he shook his head. "They're all does," he said. "But there ought to be some bucks around . . . what did I tell you? Look down there to the right! Three of them, coming into the open now. Get out carefully; don't slam the door. The middle one, the nearest one, is the one you want . . ."

You'll say it was too easy. I mean, we hadn't been out a full hour and there was my whitetail buck, less than 100 yards away. However, I couldn't help remembering the last easy shot I'd had, at an antelope with a magnificent head. I'd worked much harder for that shot, scouting a considerable amount of desolate New Mexico real estate on wheels and finally scrambling up to a high roadless mesa on foot. At the top, while I was still puffing from the climb, I found my antelope waiting. Well, he was walking slowly across in front of me with a bunch of others, at just about the same easy range—but I'd missed him completely even though I'd dropped to one knee for steadiness. I could still see the massive black horns on that pronghorn buck, and the dirt spraying up between his feet. How can a man, even a man who's slightly out of breath, shoot almost 2 feet low at point-blank range?

It's a question I never answered. The ridiculous miss had, somehow, taken the fun out of big-game hunting for me. I don't mean that I never missed ordinarily—there are few marksmen who can say that—but I'd always considered myself a tolerable rifle shot. That extraordinary goof was just too much to bear. I'd hung up my old 308 deer rifle in disgust.

That had been some 15 years ago and until recently I hadn't taken it down again except to clean it. Maybe the missed antelope hadn't been the real reason; maybe I'd just been ready to call it quits as far as big-game hunting was concerned; it's always a lot of work for, if you do your part, just one shot.

In any case, from that time on, all my hunting had been done with a shotgun. However, an event that comes to everyone who lasts long enough had brought a change in attitude: I'd passed my 70th birthday. Somehow it made a difference; and that spring, making bird-hunting plans for the fall, I'd found myself taking down from the rack, instead of the Remington 1100 I'd intended to inspect, the venerable Winchester Model 70 Featherweight that had been my first hunting rifle and had stayed with me while others came and went.

Blowing the dust from it, checking the chamber, and holding it to my shoulder to peer through the 2½x Lyman scope, I'd felt a stirring of the old excitement, remembering the fine hunts we'd shared. I found myself recalling the special pleasure of putting one precise bullet in exactly the right place with a good rifle. Maybe, I thought, maybe I should give it another try while I was still getting around okay in the field. I reminded myself that I never had taken a respectable antelope. The pronghorns seemed to have my number. The hunt already described had been my second; and the first had also been a fiasco at the end of which, having missed a fairly good buck—although not as good as the one I missed later—I'd had to settle for a small (legal) doe.

I discovered that I had, at this late date, developed a sudden desire to redeem myself, antelope-wise. However, before going after those jinxed pronghorns again, I felt I should have at least one easy hunt under my belt, preferably after game I'd never encountered in my younger hunting days. . .whitetail! That was the answer. Living in mule deer country most of my hunting life, I'd never even seen a whitetail deer except in a zoo. It would be interesting to hunt a brand new species; and I'd heard there were some fairly easy whitetails to be had in nearby Texas.

I cautioned myself that no hunt is ever really easy, and that while I was making the arrangements for an autumn Texas deer hunt, I'd better sight in my old gun carefully and spend the summer getting some intensive practice. After 15 years of nothing but shotgunning, it was possible that my shooting eye and trigger finger had lost a little of the delicate coordination required for accurate rifle shooting. I headed for the rifle range, therefore, settled down at the benchrest for a sighting-in session, and got an unpleasant shock.

I discovered that I couldn't cope with the 308 any longer. At least my slightly arthritic shoulder couldn't. Oh, by using a PAST recoil-absorbing shoulder pad (I'd bought it for patterning my shotguns) I could get the old gun sighted in after a fashion, although it didn't seem to be shooting quite as well as it used to, and I could probably tolerate its kick for a few shots at game, but the warning signs—well, pains— were there; the same signs that had led me to switch from 12-gauge to 20-gauge shotguns. No way would I take the risk of extensive practice with this fairly hard-kicking caliber. I might knock my vulnerable shoulder out and find myself unable to hunt next fall. I had a choice between giving up my big-game plans or buying a new gun.

Hamilton had to get serious and suit up his old Mossberg with a big Bushnell to get his eye back.

It took 2000 rounds fired through the Mossberg on the lonely weekday range to come back from 15 years of shotgunning.

As any hunter could have predicted, I bought a new gun. Well, a new old gun. What the hell, I told myself, it was really just an experiment. Shotgunning was my true love, after all; I didn't want to put too much money into this rifle project. I settled on 243 Winchester because it was the smallest caliber generally legal for big game; besides, I'd worked with it in the past and found it accurate, reasonably effective, and easy on the shoulder. To make it even easier, I decided on a gas-operated semi-automatic action. Since I'd had good luck with my Remington 1100 shotguns (I currently own three), I looked for that brand, and found one: a rather beat-up Model 742, no longer manufactured. Of course, it needed a scope. Still trying to keep this a shoestring project, I looked for an inexpensive one, but I came across a Leupold 2x-7x on sale. Even at a bargain, it cost more than the full price of many others, but it was such a beautiful optical instrument that I couldn't resist it.

With my fine new scope mounted on my battered second-hand gun I repaired to the rifle range and found that the recoil was practically non-existent, but the clunker wouldn't shoot worth a damn. I tried to convince myself that 4-inch to 6-inch groups at 100 yards were actually good enough; after all, I wasn't planning on picking mountain goats off the tall peaks. However, there really isn't any pleasure to be had in owning a rifle that won't put its bullets reasonably close to where you point it. Besides, the ancient autoloader didn't always function properly; so I took it back to Max, my dealer, and traded for a secondhand bolt-action rifle I'd noticed on his rack: a handsome little Mannlicher-style Ruger in the same 243 caliber.

Back on the range, with the Leupold switched over to my latest acquisition, I found that the recoil was still insignificant; I hadn't needed the help of the gas-operated auto action. This rifle worked all the time, and its 100-yard groups were a considerable improvement. However, they were still up in the 3-inch to 4-inch bracket. I tried to tell myself that was really good enough. But really. I wasn't planning to enter any benchrest competitions, was I? I was just going to shoot a deer and later maybe, just maybe, an antelope. I didn't *need* a tack-driving rifle. Did I?

But by now I was hooked. I'd forgotten that the search for accuracy can become compulsive. I took the sawed-off little rifle back to Max and traded for a new 243 Ruger M77 with a longer, heavier barrel and a standard stock. The Leupold scope endured one more transfer. And in the meantime, I'd ordered another piece of optical equipment. My legs, not as young as they used to be, were complaining about all this 100-yard hiking back and forth; and I'd never owned a good spotting scope. There were all kinds to be had, at all prices, but I picked Bushnell because I'd kept a pair of their 7x50 binoculars on a small cruising sailboat I'd owned many years. They'd been fine, sharp glasses and, equally important, when they took a quick trip to leeward in a squall and got badly damaged, the repair service had been fast, efficient, and very reasonable.

With my new Bushnell spotting scope (a 12x-36x zoom), and with my new Leupold telescopic sight mounted on my brand-new Ruger rifle (so much for economy), I returned to the range figuring that now I had it made. Well, maybe. There was some improvement. The groups averaged 2 to 3 inches. There was an occasional hopeful 1½-incher; but then there'd be a real disaster at 4 inches or worse. I

Writer shot so much he bought a spotting scope to save on shoe leather and time.

had a consultation with a local gunsmith who found that the stock was binding badly on one side; he recommended free-floating the barrel completely. Ruger's instruction manual sternly forbade such tinkering. But Ruger's instruction manual wasn't shooting the gun, I was, and I'd had good results from this technique in the past. As a matter of fact, years ago with advice from Winchester, I'd free-floated the barrel of my old 308 myself—the marks of my amateur gunsmithing are still visible—and brought the groups down from over 2 inches to 1¼ inches.

George, my gunsmith, relieved the barrel channel carefully and also took a little off the magazine box that was binding and keeping the action from settling properly into the stock. Hopeful, I headed out to the range, but I found no significant improvement. There'd be an occasional fairly respectable group followed by one that looked as if it had been shot with a blunderbuss. I'm no reloader so I couldn't experiment that way, but as I'd done with the two rifles I'd already checked out, I tried the 100-grain bullets suitable for deer in all available

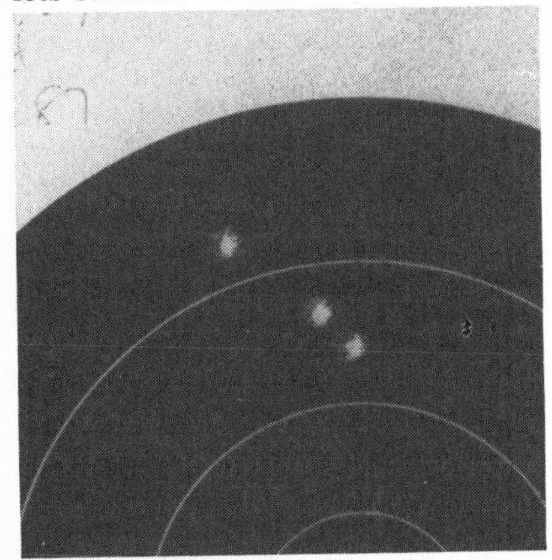

Eventually, it came together—1⅛-inch groups.

brands of factory ammunition (Federal, Remington, and Winchester; Norma 105-grain loads were ordered but never arrived). The exact location of the group varied a bit with the brand, but the size of the group seemed unaffected, so I settled on the Winchester Powerpoints simply because they'd killed deer for my offspring and me in years past and could be found practically everywhere. But no matter what the ammunition, the gun wouldn't group consistently.

I went back to George. He scratched his head when he looked at the targets, and reached for his headspace gauges. The rifle bolt closed when it shouldn't, on a No-Go gauge. I called Ruger and they weren't impressed; there were lots of weird gauges around, they said. Had I monkeyed with the stock? I had? Couldn't I read instruction manuals? But send the gun along, and they'd see what they could do for me.

That left me without a rifle to practice with; and summer was moving right along towards autumn. Well, when there's nothing else to shoot with, grab a 22. I got down from the rack my ancient Mossberg 144 target rifle, another gun from my earliest rifle-shooting days. It carried a little ¾-inch Redfield 4x scope that used to work well on jackrabbits. On an impulse, seeing that our club was holding a small-bore silhouette match that weekend, I fired a few shots from the bench at the required 40, 60, 77, and 100 meters to see roughly how much holdover was required. Sunday, I entered the competition. It was, of course, a slaughter. I won't even mention my score; I'll just state that I didn't hurt my back much bending over to set up my fallen targets.

However, it did seem like a fun way to get my practice for the hunting season (serious silhouette shooters please forgive me); but the little scope, although clear and sharp, obviously wouldn't do, since it wasn't designed for target-type adjustments. I referred once more to the Bushnell Bible, and soon was the proud owner of a 6x-18x target/varmint scope, a very impressive optical device, particularly when mounted on a $30 rifle (at least that was what it had cost when I bought it, more years ago than I cared to remember.)

At the benchrest, I got my equipment calibrated for the four silhouette ranges, and then sighted it in for 25 yards, a handy distance for offhand practice. The convenient knobs and precise adjustments were a revelation, as was the ease with which the powerful glass with its enormous objective picked out the bullet holes as they appeared, even in the black. Standing up, I fired five shots at each of the five bulls of a standard target. (With that much scope, I found, a 50-foot target gave a suitable aiming point at 25 yards.)

In the short time since I'd picked up a rifle again, this was the first offhand shooting I'd done at a paper target that let me see exactly where my shots were going. It was a very humiliating experience. I mean, I used to be a pretty fair hand with a pistol, and not too bad at small-bore rifle (all positions), but when I walked up to that target, I found it looking as if I'd fired a load of buckshot at it—no wonder I'd missed all those little silhouettes! I wouldn't have known which bullet holes were intended for which bulls if I hadn't watched them through the big scope sight. I tried again, but my second target was just as bad as the first. Clearly, I had two problems: 1.) My elderly, untrained muscles simply couldn't hold the 9-pound target rifle steady enough; and 2.) Trying to outwit those wildly waving crosshairs, I was yanking at the trigger, shotgun-fashion whenever the sight picture looked halfway respectable. To put it more succinctly: in the 15 years that had passed, I'd simply forgotten how to shoot a rifle offhand.

That was bad enough, but driving home I had a very disturbing thought: *Can one yank a trigger even when shooting from a benchrest*? Maybe there hadn't been anything wrong with any of the rifles I'd tested, in-

Deer hunt outfit included 2-7x Leupold, a heavy-barreled Ruger 243, and Hal Swiggett's pickup.

cluding my old 308 Winchester which, I now remembered, hadn't shot as well for me as its past record indicated it should have. Maybe it was just me.

Well, if it was, I had a cure for it, I hoped. Max was happy to sell me a brick containing 1000 rounds of Remington 22 target loads. There was no word from Ruger, so I concentrated on relearning the basics of rifle marksmanship. Club events monopolize the range most weekends, but I was out there every weekday afternoon, weather and social obligations permitting. (I had important engagements with some doves, some ducks, and one large Canada goose, that couldn't be canceled.)

The first lot of 22 ammo didn't bring much improvement. I fired another silhouette match and got a magnificent score of 8 out of 40. I bought another brick of 22s. By the time I'd shot up most of that, I could at least tell which bull I'd been shooting at. I entered another match and scored a 12, nothing to write to the newspapers about; but the improvement was a hopeful sign. I might make it yet.

But time was getting short. Asking around, I'd been referred to Hal Swiggett, and he'd been kind enough to arrange this December hunt for me at the YO. I called Ruger. It turned out that the boys and girls had been on vacation, but they'd get around to my gun any day now. It arrived the following week. There was no charge, and no description of any repairs, but when George stuck his No-Go gauge into the chamber this time, the bolt behaved as it should, refusing to close. There was a target in the box with the gun, and a note to the effect that, since I'd messed with my own stock, returned herewith, they'd used one of theirs for the test firing, which showed barrel and action to be within limits. The group was 1¼ inches, which looked terrific until I read the fine print which said it had been fired, not at 100 yards, but at 50.

Well, I suppose 2½ inches at 100 yards will pass for adequate hunting accuracy; in any case, this late in the fall, I was obviously stuck with it. I put the scope back on the gun and headed off to sight it in, doing a little better with my stock than Ruger's test marksman had done with theirs. At 100 yards, I got groups around 2 inches; but the important thing was the improved consistency: While there were no pretty little cloverleaf groups, there weren't any wild spreads either. Whether this was due to the adjustments Ruger had made, whatever they were, or to the recent intensive education received by my trigger finger, is anybody's guess.

I continued to practice with the 22. The week before the hunt, in early December, I shot another small-bore silhouette match, and scored 13. Not as much improvement as I'd hoped. I was still way down in the cellar with the other Class B shooters, but I consoled myself with the thought that even when I missed those little 100-yard metal rams, I was coming close enough to make a full-sized, flesh-and-blood deer very nervous. A few days later I took the M77 to the range for a final check. I'd cleaned it carefully, of course, in preparation for the hunt; and the first group, out of the oily barrel, was. . .well, let's just call it discouraging.

I let the gun cool and tried again. The first two shots, seen through the fancy new spotting scope at my elbow, were within an inch of each other. Well, that happens occasionally, even with the worst rifles. I sent a third bullet out there, and leaned over to see where it had gone. It was right with the others. Even just looking through the scope from 100 yards away, I could tell that this was the best group I'd fired with the gun to date. When I got down there with the tape, it measured 1¼ inches. The group was a little too high. Back at the bench, I made the adjustment, and fired another careful three-shot group. It was in the right place, about 3 inches high, and it measured a glorious 1⅛ inches, which I feel is as good a group as you have a right to expect from any standard hunting rifle and factory ammunition. (We can dream of minute-of-angle guns, but I've only had one in my life.)

Swiggett performs the official "local count" ceremony, pronounces the Hamilton buck an 11-pointer.

Don't ask me what happened. Did Ruger actually fix the rifle but a little shooting was needed to settle it down? Or did those weeks—actually a couple of months—of 22 practice enable me in the end to get its full potential from a rifle that had been basically pretty accurate from the start? I suppose the moral of the story, if there is one, is that you have to get acquainted with any rifle to make it shoot well, and even more important, that just because you knew how to shoot 15 years ago doesn't mean you can shoot today. In any case, when I headed south and east from my home in New Mexico, destination Texas, I had a lot more confidence in my equipment than I might have had, and maybe even a little more confidence in myself. Now, with the bright Texas sun just starting to climb into the blue Texas sky, and a whitetail buck before me, I was about to learn if that confidence was justified. . .

Trying to be quiet, I was a little slow getting out of the pickup and getting a round chambered. The deer, moving from right to left, was already heading into some heavy brush when I picked him up in the variable scope, which I'd set at 2x in case I'd have to make a dawn shot in poor light. It was plenty of magnification at this range, and I swung the duplex crosshairs onto the target, that seemed very large after all those tiny silhouettes. The gun fired—and I knew immediately that I'd put my bullet a little too far back, afraid of hitting the stout saplings behind which the buck was about to disappear. He hunched up briefly but didn't run; instead he turned and moved deliberately back the way he'd come, reaching another patch of cover before I was ready to shoot again. However, the scope showed me a small, clear window in the brush through which I could aim, and the months of offhand practice paid off. With the second sharp crack of the 243 he went down, dead when we reached him, a handsome buck with a total of 11 antler points by local count.

So I had my easy whitetail. All it had taken was 6 months, five rifles counting my 308 and 22, five scopes of one persuasion or another if you include the Lyman and Redfield I'd already owned, about 20 boxes of 243s, and 2000 rounds of 22s. Not to mention some friendly help from Hal Swiggett and the YO Ranch.

Now bring on that antelope. I'm ready. I think. ●

The HMS John Ericsson looked like this model and held the guns now standing guard at Filipstad. (Photo: National Maritime Museum, Stockholm)

DAHLGREN GUNS AND ERICSSON SHIPS. . . . they changed our world

by GAD RAUSING

FOR NEARLY A century, two heavy naval guns have stood in the churchyard of inland Filipstad, in Sweden, eternally pointing over the still lake and the 1000-mile forest. A cast-iron plate records:

> *John Ericsson skänkte Sverige dessa kanoner år 1865 till bestyckning av dess första Monitor. Svenska Staten överlämnade dem är 1897 till Filipstads och Färnebo församlingars kyrkoråd som lät uppställa dem här. (In 1865 John Ericsson presented these guns to Sweden as*

armament for that country's first Monitor. In 1897 the Swedish Government gave them to the parish councils of Filipstad and Färnebo, who had them mounted here.")

These are the only two 15-inch Dahlgren guns, muzzle-loading rifles named for their designer, to survive, or at least the only ones to have survived on land. Some must lie in the submerged wrecks of such monitors as the *Weehawken* and the *Patabsco*, in Charleston harbor, and in the *Tecumseh*, in Mobile Bay.

Most 15-inch guns used in the Civil War were designed by Brevet Brigadier General Thomas J. Rodman, U.S.A., (1815-71). Rodman's barrels, although tapering, have some stretches along which the external diameter is constant, whereas Dahlgren's gun barrels show continuous curvature, reflecting the internal pressure curve. Both Dahlgren's and Rodman's guns were made by casting iron round a chilled core which, as the first part of the piece to cool, was compressed and strengthened by the subsequent, controlled contraction of the outer layer.

The first reference to the obese monsters now guarding John Ericsson's tomb at Filipstad is a record of their having been, "Sold to J. Ericsson for Swedish Govt., Mar '65."

McClurg, Cuthbert & Cuddy; McClurg, Wade and Co; Freeman, Knap & Totten; Knap, Wade & Totten; Knap & Co; Knap and Wade; Charles Knap's Nephews. All this time it was also called Pennsylvania Penn Foundry as well as Fort Pitt Foundry, the name by which the company is generally known.

The letter P. signified Navy proofing by Captain John M. Berrien, USN.

Only two series of 15-inch Dahlgren guns are recorded as having been manufactured, all within the same number sequence, numbers 11 through 34 by Fort Pitt Foundry for the PASSAIC class of monitors, which were most probably originally designed for 13-inch Dahlgren guns. The 15-inch Dahlgrens were too short to protrude from the turrets, these being filled with smoke upon each discharge, which led to the introduction of smoke boxes. The remaining 15-inch Dahlgrens, serial numbers 35-70 and 81-87, manufactured by Fort Pitt Foundry, and serial numbers 71-79 by Cyrus Alger and Co., and serial numbers 91 and 92 by Seyfert, McManus and Co., were of a "new Model," introduced in November, 1863, 16 inches longer, but slimmed to weigh the same. These were long enough to protrude from the gun-tower and to discharge their smoke outside.

FILIPSTAD GUN MARKINGS

(On breech)	Gun No. 1.	F.P. NO 20 41875 lbs.
(On left trunnion)		P. J.M.B.
(On right trunnion)		15 in. 1863.
(On breech)	Gun No. 2.	F.P. NO 21. 41790 lbs.
(On left trunnion)		P. J.M.B.
(On right trunnion)		15 in. 1863.

How and why have these Civil-War-period American naval guns found their way here? There is an answer.

The letters F.P. signify that the guns were made at Fort Pitt Foundry in Pittsburgh, PA, an arsenal which produced very many of the heavy guns used by the Union forces, but one which changed names frequently, as new partners were brought in, presumably with funds averting bankruptcy. It appears in the records as Joseph McClurg, in turn both father and son, Alexander McClurg; William T. McClurg; McClurg and McKnight;

The guns at Filipstad are of the older, shorter type.

The mean weight of the projectiles (called "shells") used in these guns was 330 pounds empty and 352 pounds filled and saboted. The weight of the propellant charge was 35 pounds for close and intermediate range and 50 pounds for long range.

Monitor embrasures were so small and the turret so crowded that carriage elevation was limited. The 1866 Navy Ordnance Instructions tabulate a range of 2100 yards with the 350-pound shell and 35 pounds propellant charge. The elevation was 7 degrees and the time of flight 7.7 seconds. The "practical" range was given at 1700 yards, with the heavy charge and an elevation of 5 degrees. The time of flight was then 5.7 seconds.

These figures might be compared with those of the last 15-inch guns used, those arming British battleships in both the World Wars: gun weight was 100 tons; shell weight was 1970 pounds and range was 29,000 meters.

Rarely, indeed, is it granted to any one man so to steer technical and, consequently, also economic, military and political development not only of his own country but of the whole world, as it was to John Ericsson and to his less well-known brother, Nils. To do so on no less than three occassions is probably unique, but John Ericsson was unique.

Most Americans know that Colt's revolvers and Winchester's rifles won the West but comparatively few know anything about Admiral Dahlgren and his guns or about Captain Ericsson and his steam engine, his propeller and his battleship, in spite of the fact that these were the two men who made certain that the U.S. remained the *United* States, that they determined world history for a century. There was a greater technical break between the last sailing ships of the line, such as Sir Charles Napier's flagship in 1856, the 131-gun Duke of Wellington, and the Monitor of 1862 than there is between the latter and the battleships of WWII.

John Ericsson was born on July 1, 1803, at Långshyttan, some 20 km north of Filipstad in central Sweden. As a young man he moved to England in order to find a wider scope for his genius as an inventor. There, he designed one of the first forced-draft steam engines, of a type later widely used on early locomotives, and also the propeller which was first used widely in the U.S.

In military history, some battles stand out as milestones, marking the introduction of revolutionary changes of one kind or another, such as new tactics, new offensive or defensive weapons or the application of new strategic concepts. In the 19th century, technical development accelerated, affording belligerent states ever newer possibilities.

One such revolutionary breakthrough was the development of rifled cannon throwing explosive shells, which overnight made the smooth bore cannon, shooting cast-iron balls, obsolete. Although French General Paixhans, in his great work *Nouvelle Force Maritime*, Paris 1822, had sug-

They called it "hot work," but these Yankee gunners happily served Dahlgrens in the relative safety of a revolving Ericsson Monitor turret.

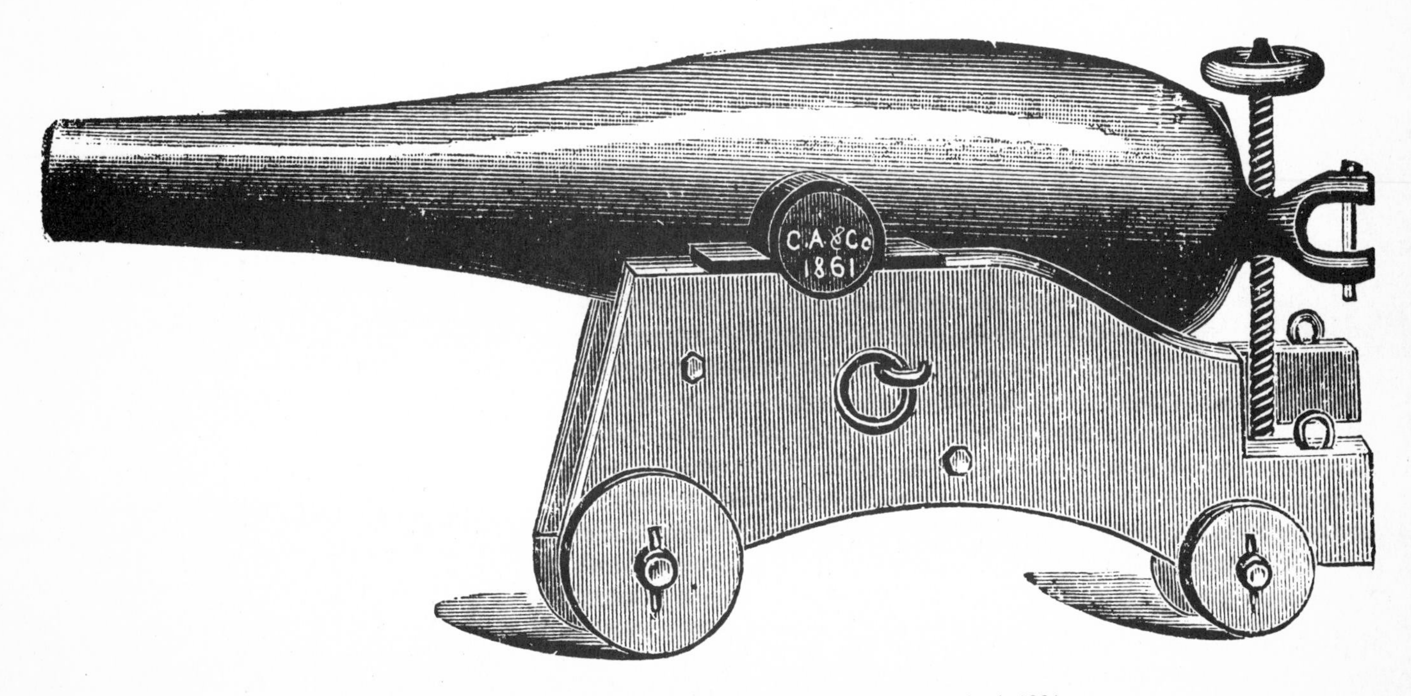

Bannerman pictured this Cyrus Alger & Co. Dahlgren, but the woodcut's 1861 date is a puzzler unless this is a smaller Dahlgren. See text.

Dahlgren and Dahlgren-type guns shot over land, too, as this Harper's Civil War-report woodcut showed.

gested the use of explosive shells in cannon and designed the first rifled guns suitable for the purpose, it was not until the 1850s that explosive shells were generally adopted and even longer before these were rifled cannon.

At Sinope in the Black Sea, in November, 1853, two fleets of otherwise fairly evenly matched wooden ships of the line met; the Turkish with smooth bore guns and solid shot, the Russians with rifled guns and explosive shells. In a short, sharp action the Turkish squadron was completely annihilated. The outcome showed that no wooden ship stood the slightest chance of surviving a broadside, or even a few hits, from the new guns. The conclusion, which had actually been drawn much earlier, was obvious: Ships had to be armored and they had to be steam-powered.

Steam power was first used in battle by the British, in Burma, as early as 1824. Ever since, steam had been used in wooden ships, but only as an auxiliary to sail. Even the large paddle-steamers of the 1850s still had square-rigged masts to use in favorable winds. In men-of-war, steam was practically useless, the paddle-wheels being extremely vulnerable even to cast-iron balls. Thus, paddle-wheel propulsion was not generally adopted by any navy, although it did have one special advantage: it could be used in ships of very shallow draught. As late as WWII, the Royal Navy used diesel-powered paddle-wheel minesweepers in shallow coastal waters.

By 1829 John Ericsson had designed a tubular steam boiler with artificial draught and a surface condenser, a revolutionary new concept. The principle underlying that of the screw propeller had long been known, but Ericsson was the first to apply power directly to the propeller shaft, building the tiny steamer *Francis B. Ogden* in 1836-37 and the first ship with a direct-acting screw propeller, the *Robert F. Stockton* in 1838.

His first man-of-war, the *USS Princeton*, was an iron frigate, launched in 1844, before Sinope. In her way and in her day she was quite as revolutionary as the *USS Monitor* was to become 18 years later, since she was the first man-of-war of any navy not to be built of wood, to be independent of wind propulsion and with her entire machinery below the waterline, protected against enemy fire. The ship carried 12-inch guns designed by Ericsson, one of which now stands in the park of the U.S. Naval Academy at Annapolis. On May 14, 1858, Congressman Stephen R. Mallory of Florida, the chairman of the Naval Committee, wrote that, "the *Princeton* is the foundation of our present steam marine. It is the foundation of the steam marine of the whole world . . ."

The last British wooden ship of the line was launched as late as 1858, after the end of the Crimean War. However, in 1859 the first armored, as opposed to iron-built, ship was launched in France, the frigate *Gloire*, designed by Dupuy de Lôme. She was built of wood, but partly protected by 12 cm armor. Britain immediately countered with the all iron armored frigate *Warrior*. However, even armored ships like the *Gloire* and the *Warrior* suffered from weaknesses inherited from the sailing ships of the line. The guns were mounted on deck and could fire in one general direction only.

Still, these were infinitely superior to all unarmored ships. One of the first to draw the practical conclusion was Stephen Mallory, Confederate Secretary of the Navy. On May 8, 1861, he wrote to the Confederate Congress that, "invulnerability might compensate for inequality in numbers. It would be both economical and wise to fight with iron against wood."

His recommendation was accepted and the *CSN Merrimac* was built, the last great ship of John Ericsson's *Princeton* lineage, only to be defeated by the first ship of his new and greater lineage.

Since, in the days of solid shot, the "weight of the broadside" was of paramount importance, a ship was to carry as many guns as possible — which meant guns on superimposed decks, where the lowest deck had to be high enough above the waterline not to be swamped through the gun-ports when the ship heeled to a breeze. The introduction of explosive shells changed all this. Now, one or two big-bore guns could knock out any sailing ship in the world and the new efficient steam engine and the propeller meant that ships could be propelled by engines protected even against these new guns.

The first man to draw the obvious conclusion was John Ericsson, the father of the already existing navy. He mounted two 11-inch muzzle-loading Dahlgren guns in a revolving armored turret, set on the flush deck of an armored hull with a freeboard of no more than 2 feet. The *Monitor*, as she was called, was expressly designed to meet the most extreme armored ship yet built, the *CSN Merrimac*.

The Confederate shipwrights had neither time nor means to design an entirely new concept, but they went the *Gloire* and the *Warrior* one further in dispensing altogether with masts and rigging. Within their means they did brilliantly, cutting down the burnt-out wreck of the *USS Merrimack* (which *was* spelled with a final *k*) to within less than 3 feet above the waterline, where an entirely new battery deck was installed. Above this they erected an armored deckhouse, pierced for 10 guns. She was commissioned, and went into battle, as the *CSS Virginia*, but is usually remembered under her old name, erroneously spelled *Merrimac*. Her rate of fire has been reported as one broadside every 15 minutes.

In the battle to come the armor of both ships proved adequate against the projectiles of the enemy's guns, but the guns of the *Merrimac* being mounted in deck batteries it was necessary to turn the entire ship in order to bring one-half of the guns to bear.

The Confederate gun crews were exposed during the critical minutes of sponging out, loading and running out.

Ericsson had mounted two guns in a rotating tower on the *Monitor*, from which they could be fired in any direction, no matter the heading of the ship, and which could be turned away from the enemy immediately upon the discharge of the guns, thus not exposing the gun crews to enemy fire during the lengthy process of reloading. The rate of fire has been stated to be one volley every 7 minutes, so the *Monitor* was actually superior in artillery to the *Merrimac*, firing four rounds in 14 minutes, and doing so on any course, as against five rounds in 15 minutes, and doing so only when broadside on to the target.

Although Hampton Roads was one of the decisive battles in naval history, no lives were lost in the duel between the two battleships, because such we must call them, but one result was the immediate appreciation of the revolving turret, which had made any pre-*Monitor* ship, of any design, obsolete overnight. The *Monitor* was the precursor of all battleships of all nations. As Swedish Major Ernst von Vegesack, serving with the Union Army and an eyewitness to the battle of Hampton Roads, reported to Stockholm: "These two ships give occasion to a total subversion of the navies of all nations."

And what of the designer of the guns, those guns which assured the U.S. Navy of supremacy over that of the Confederacy? That can be answered also.

John Adolf Dahlgren was born in Philadelphia on November 13, 1809. His father, Bernhard Ulrich Dahlgren, was the scion of a distinguished Swedish family of scientists and physicians. He had come to the U.S. in 1806, to settle in Philadelphia where he eventually became the consul of the United Kingdoms of Sweden and Norway.

John Dahlgren joined the U.S. navy as a midshipman in 1826, to become a lieutenant in 1837. By 1834, his knowledge of mathematics had led to his being employed on the coast survey, but in 1847 he was transferred to the Ordnance Department, where he designed that type of gun, at first smoothbore but later rifled, which is usually called by his name. He was the first to measure pressure at different points of the gun barrel and to design the barrel to stand this pressure without being unnecessarily heavy. He also designed gun sights, and he may be regarded as one of the fathers of modern ordnance and gunnery. Dahlgren's guns were first mounted in a ship which he commanded between 1857 and 1859, but the design was an immediate success and most of the ships, both of the Union Navy and of that of the Confederacy were armed with Dahlgren guns, as were many heavy artillery regiments of both armies.

In 1862, after many years in command of the Washington Navy Yard, where all but three officers had resigned because of Confederate sympathies, Dahlgren became Chief of the Bureau of Ordnance. In 1863 he became a rear admiral, taking over the command of the blockading South Atlantic Fleet. In the autumn of 1864, he helped Sherman take Savannah. After the war, he commanded the South Pacific Fleet and later became, once again, Chief of Ordnance. Finally, at his own request, he was, for a time, head of the Washington Navy Yard, where he had once designed his guns. He died in Washington on July 12, 1870.

After the end of the Civil War, John Ericsson drew up the specifications for a similar type of ship for the Swedish navy, without charging anything for his work, and he also gave the two Dahlgren guns now standing before his tomb, to arm the first of these ships to be launched, the *HMS John Ericsson*. She was designed by Lieutenant J.C.A. d'Ailly, and built at Motala Verkstad. Her displacement was all of 1500 tons, i.e. considerably more than that of the original *Monitor*, which was one of 1000 tons.

Apparently d'Ailly solved the problems caused by the short, early-type, Dahlgren guns when mounted in turrets. Contemporary photos and drawings show their muzzles as protruding about 10 inches when the guns were in firing position and a very well-made model of one of these guns in its carriage, as mounted in the *John Ericsson*, shows the very long distance the gun could be advanced after loading. It is not known whether this model represents the original American mount, but no such is mentioned in the original deed of gift. It seems more likely that the guns were placed in Swedish-designed and Swedish-made mounts.

The *John Ericsson* was rapidly followed by *Thordön*, *Tirfing* and *Loke*, all of the same size and all launched between 1868 and 1875, as well as by the "baby monitors" *Garmer, Sköld, Fenris, Hildur, Gerda, Ulf, Björn, Berserk, Söve* and *Folke*, all launched in the same years. Of these, *Garmer, Sköld* and *Fenris* were experimental vessels, of 350 tons and 6 knots, whereas the others were of 460 tons and 8 knots.

Thordön, Tirfing and *Loke* each carried two 24 cm breech-loading rifled guns of Swedish design and manufacture. The "baby monitors" each carried one gun of the same type, except for the Garmer, which carried one 23.7 cm smooth bore muzzle-loader designed by Swedish Captain von Feilitzen "to the American pattern."

Their low free-boards made the *Monitor*-type vessels extremely unsuitable and dangerous for use in the open sea. Very soon, naval designers realized a fighting ship must also be a sea-going ship, and learned to arm an all-iron, armored hull, more or less of the *Warrior's* type, with a small number of very heavy guns, mounted in pairs in one or more of revolving turrets. The modern battleship or, rather, the battleship of yesteryear, was born.

John Ericsson died in New York on March 8, 1889. Although he had become an American citizen in 1848, he had requested he be buried at Filipstad, near the place of his birth. His body was brought to Sweden on a U.S. cruiser and to Filipstad on the railway built by his almost equally famous brother, Nils. Eight years later, the guns he had once given to his native country were mounted before his tomb, a latter-day parallel to the old Norse custom of burying his weapons with the warrior. ●

Free Pistols For Collectors?

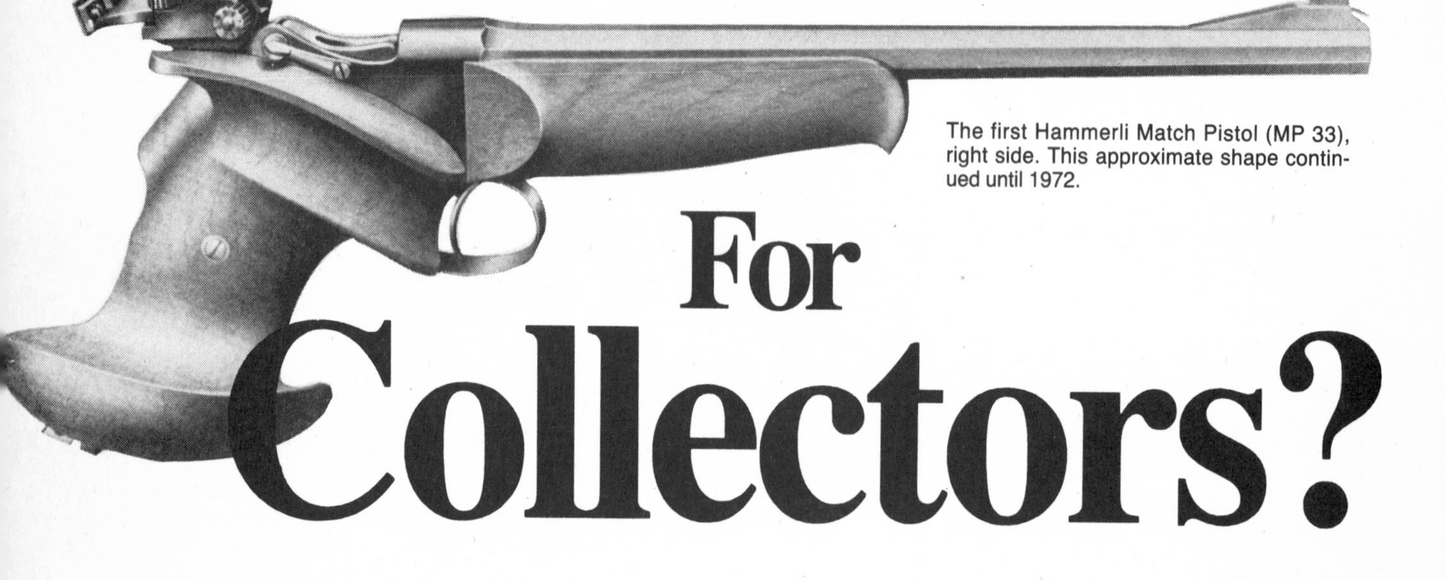
The first Hammerli Match Pistol (MP 33), right side. This approximate shape continued until 1972.

Writer-collector believes the genre has potential and Hammerli has impact.

by WILFRID WARD

SOMEHOW NOBODY can avoid using that horrible pun, so I put it in the title. Everyone knows that Free Pistols cost a great deal, probably more than any currently manufactured pistol. They are the Rolls Royces of the pistol world. What freedom they have is from the restrictions in the rules of the International Shooting Union (U.I.T.). Free pistols provide a magnificent and largely unexplored field for the collector. To understand the gun itself one must understand both the rules which govern its construction and of the competitions in which it is used.

When compared to the restrictions applying to other pistol disciplines in international competition, the Free Pistol rules are delightfully simple. This is refreshing, not only for the normal attractions of simplicity, but because the very lack of restrictions has encouraged ingenuity, sometimes to a remarkable degree. Human nature being what it is, freedom has been whittled away. Nonetheless the traditional definition has been largely maintained:

1.) Any rimfire pistol

2.) Which has open sights without optical lenses
3.) The grip of which does not support the wrist joint
4.) Firing one 22 round (N.B. Not necessarily a 22 LR round).

There is no need for me to describe the prohibitions. Whilst the comparison cannot be carried too far, the Free Pistol can to a degree be likened to the Match Rifle, so popular amongst our Victorian ancestors, for with that arm, too, it was hoped that an almost total absence of restrictions would lead to an optimum performance being obtained from the cartridge. Apart from the limitation imposed by a nominated caliber, both have maintained their freedom today.

I have begun by defining the pistols because the Free Pistol is a working, and above all a developing firearm, which may be encountered at any major pistol meeting in Europe, and at a good many in the United States.

Free pistol targets are exceptionally difficult. They are the 100-meter rifle target used for pistol at 50 meters. Their difficulty can be gauged by the fact that the 10-ring is 1.968 inches, the Standard American nine-ring 3.94 inches, and so on. There is no beginner's margin incorporated into the UIT target. All wild shots are glaringly reflected in one's score.

The origins of the Free Pistol can be traced back to the dueling pistols of the 19th century, and their closely related contemporaries, percussion target pistols. With the rising popularity of target shooting, the use of Flobert-type pistols, firing a 22 bulleted cap, followed. It was but a short step from these to the blackpowder 22 rimfire cartridge.

My illustrations reveal the similarity between the later full-bore dueling/target pistols and the earlier 22 target pistols. How late dueling continued in Europe is uncertain. Whatever the truth, there is no doubt that there were dueling pistols being made at the same time as the early Free Pistol.

This discipline was an almost entirely European form of sport, and Europeans were the sources of the highly specialized pistols required. Pistol competitions have been held for many years, certainly since the second half of the 19th century, but though some form of Free revolver shoot was held at the first Olympic Games in 1896, it was not until 1912 that the competition was firmly established at 50 meters, where 60 shots were fired to count. It has continued in roughly the same form ever since.

The first "Free" competition was won by Sumner Paine of the United States, with a score of 442 from 30 shots at 30 meters. It was, however, in the nature of an "any revolver" match and as such was not the true beginning of the Free Pistol. The foundation of the International Shooting Union in 1907 also gave encouragement to the event, and it is now one of the best established in the Union's program.

Some single shot pistols made in the United States, such as the Smith & Wesson Perfected, and the Harrington & Richardson United States Revolver Association Model, were far more suited to this type of shooting than the revolver. Perhaps because of the popularity of the NRA's conventional pistol course, the ISU-style match has never been so popular in the United States as in Europe, nor were the specialized European Free Pistols used to start with. Indeed, Bill Toney, writing in the 1959 edition of *Gun Digest*, reveals that as late as 1948 the U.S. team set out for the London Olympics thinking that 22 automatics would yield results as good as single shot pistols in that competition.

It was Huelet E. Benner, one of America's finest shooters, who first dissented from this view, and changed to a 22 single shot belonging to Karl Frederick. The pistol, fitted with a 10-inch Pope barrel, already had Olympic experience for Frederick had won the 1920 Olympic Free Pistol competition with it with 489 points. This was a wise decision, and Benner came second in score (539), though he was counted out to fourth place. The winner, Vasquez-Cam of Peru, obtained 545 points.

By the 1952 Olympics, Benner had established his superiority, and won the Gold Medal with 553 points using

Xu Haifeng of China won the Gold Medal with a score of 566 using a Model 150 at the Los Angeles Olympics. Skanaker (Sweden) got a score of 565 using his electronic trigger Model 152.

a Hammerli. This not only secured the medal for the United States, but firmly established the position of the single shot hair-triggered pistol as the only realistic match winner.

It will come as no surprise to my older readers to know that as early as 1934, that great gun thinker, Major (later Major General) Julian S. Hatcher, had been examining the European Free Pistols in order to evaluate the effect of hair triggers. In his *Textbook of Pistols and Revolvers* he describes his own interest in Free Pistols, and the current competitions provided by the USRA and NRA, under the rules of which it was possible to have up to a 20-inch barrel, and there was no specified trigger weight. More important was Hatcher's declared desire to use his pistols to, "try out the advantages of the set trigger and unlimited sighting radius." He goes on to relate how the latter was even longer than the barrel because of late the practice had arisen, "of mounting the sights on an extension which curves back over the hand so as to extend the sight radius."

Though perhaps he lacked the uncanny gift of prophecy in pistol matters of his countryman, Walter Winans, the future General, having dissected the nature of a Free Pistol's grips, summed up the whole matter in the following sentence: "When you take hold of one of these guns, with the grip properly fitted in your hand, *you only have to extend your arm and the pistol very nearly holds itself.*"

He also illustrates three pistols which he observed at the International Matches at St. Gallen in 1925, a Stutzer Perfekt, his own single shot Smith & Wesson, the grips of which he had altered, and to which he had added a weight, and his Widmer pistol with a Buchel action. Hatcher's pistols are typical of the range of high-grade pistols from which a would-be international shot of the time might have chosen his arms.

Prior to 1914 the majority of Free Pistols had top-break actions, and many were fitted with double-set triggers. Sometimes one encounters a hair trigger operated on the single trigger, as on a dueling pistol. Though it is impossible to be dogmatic in classification of devices so free from rules for their construction, one can generalize to the extent of saying that the actions of models made after 1920 are likely to fall into one of three categories:

a.) Falling block
b.) Martini action
c.) Bolt operated.

All had hair triggers. (*Hair trigger* is a label British people insist on when describing set triggers: *Editor.*) Other falling block pistols are illustrated with line drawings, and their actions are sufficiently simple to be followed without explanation. I also show a Tell pistol, belonging to a friend of mine. It was one of a group of four which came to England after the 1939 war, and also included a Flobert type pistol (presumably for indoor practice) and two other Free Pistols. The muzzlebrake was added later. This outfit can be said to be typical of that of the reasonably prosperous Continental shooter between the wars.

The well-known names of Ideal, Tell and Luna were products of Buchel of Suhl. Haenel produced the Aydt falling block action, whilst the Venus, Frohn and Kommer had Martini actions. In Switzerland Weber and Tschudi produced a number of different models with either top-break or Martini actions. These were equipped with either set triggers or two-stage pulls. Widmer of St. Gallen (Hatcher owned one) and Hauptli of Solothurn also produced these pistols in the '30s. In 1931 another name, destined to rise to the highest pinnacles of pistol-making fame, was becoming known. It was that of Rudolph Hammerli et Cie. Fabrique d'Armes of Lenzbourg, Switzerland, long famed as makers of Free Rifles.

In the 1950s, a British Free Pistol was developed by a Polish immigrant, Dr. Jurek of Birmingham. This weapon doubled for use in ordinary 22-caliber competitions by the use of an al-

(Above) Stutzer Perfekt falling block Free Pistol with 15-inch barrel by Pope and double triggers similar to those of a sporting rifle. Back sight is in front of chamber. Action is shown open at right.

ternative lock mechanism, and can still be obtained today. An example of the Stutzer Perfekt is illustrated. This comes from the NRA's collection. The 15-inch barrel is by Pope. The falling block action is operated by forward pressure on the trigger guard. As can be seen, the workmanship is of the highest grade with a limited non-adjustable palm support at the base of the grip. The hair trigger mechanism might have come from a high-grade hunting rifle. It is cocked by pressure on the back trigger. When the moment comes to fire, the lightest pressure on the front trigger discharges the hair trigger action, which in turn fires the pistol itself. The sights are simple, and are operated both for windage and elevation by means of a key similar to that of an old-fashioned watch. The foresight is guarded by a protector. The designer has used a very long round barrel, and so has had to sacrifice weight.

The bolt-action type of pistol is exemplified by the Schultz-Larsen from Denmark. This form was not frequently encountered, but has regained popularity more recently. A current example is the Pardini Free Pistol from Italy.

Prior to the 1939 war, another firm of rifle makers held the highest place in Free Pistol making—Udo Anschutz from Germany. Their pistol was of very similar appearance to the later Hammerlis, and combined the collector's ideals of fine finish, handsome decoration, and small production.

To these qualities can be added that common to all the top makes of Free Pistol, the capacity to trace some of the pistols to the actual events which they won, and the shooters who owned them. I well remember the late William M. Locke emphasizing to me the high significance of properly established personal connections between a distinguished man and your gun, which is a vital attribute of any "postgraduate" collection.

When the Anschutz was in its prime, the evolution of the weapon had advanced sufficiently that it was a purpose-built pistol devoted solely to the Free Pistol discipline. It is true that some examples exist with additional mechanisms giving a 2-pound pull, but the pistols were what might be termed "classic" Free Pistols. The sights were fully adjustable. The foresight blades were interchangeable. The width of the backsight aperture could be altered by merely revolving the inlet circle of metal into which they were cut. Delicate carving often embellished grips, with scroll engraving and color hardening upon the action of the pistol. Sometimes inlaid silver lines surround the work or the name of the maker. The grips themselves were fitted to the hand measurements of the shooter, and the heel of the hand supported by an adjustable palm shelf. At first instance this might seem to be unnecessary in a custom built pistol, but this capacity to release or tighten the pressure of the grip on the hand was useful, as the measurements of the hand will sometimes vary with weather conditions or the degree of fatigue of the shooter.

The Anschutz pistol had many successes, particularly in the hands of that great Swedish shooter Torsten Ullman. Ullman's shooting achievements must rank with the greatest in the world, for in 1933, 1935, and 1937 he won the World Championships, with an outstanding 559 at the Berlin Olympic Games in between. This latter score, which took the Gold Medal for Free Pistol, remained the Olympic Record until it was broken at the Rome Olympics by Guschtchin of Russia some 24 years later. Ullman himself had not been wasting his time, for meanwhile he had won two more World Free Pistol Championships in 1947 and 1952 (not to mention World Center Fire Championships in 1947 and 1954).

At the end of hostilities in 1945, the manufacturers of Free Pistols in Germany were not only forbidden to make arms, but were largely destroyed. This left Switzerland in the ideal situation for the production of a high-grade target weapon; and Ham-

The Stutzer has a duelling pistol-type spur on trigger guard, key operated rear sight, and thumb rest. (Photos courtesy NRA Museum Service)

Tell falling block Free Pistol. Trigger guard is fixed; action opens by raising lever set in grip. The muzzlebrake is a later (useless) addition. (Author photo)

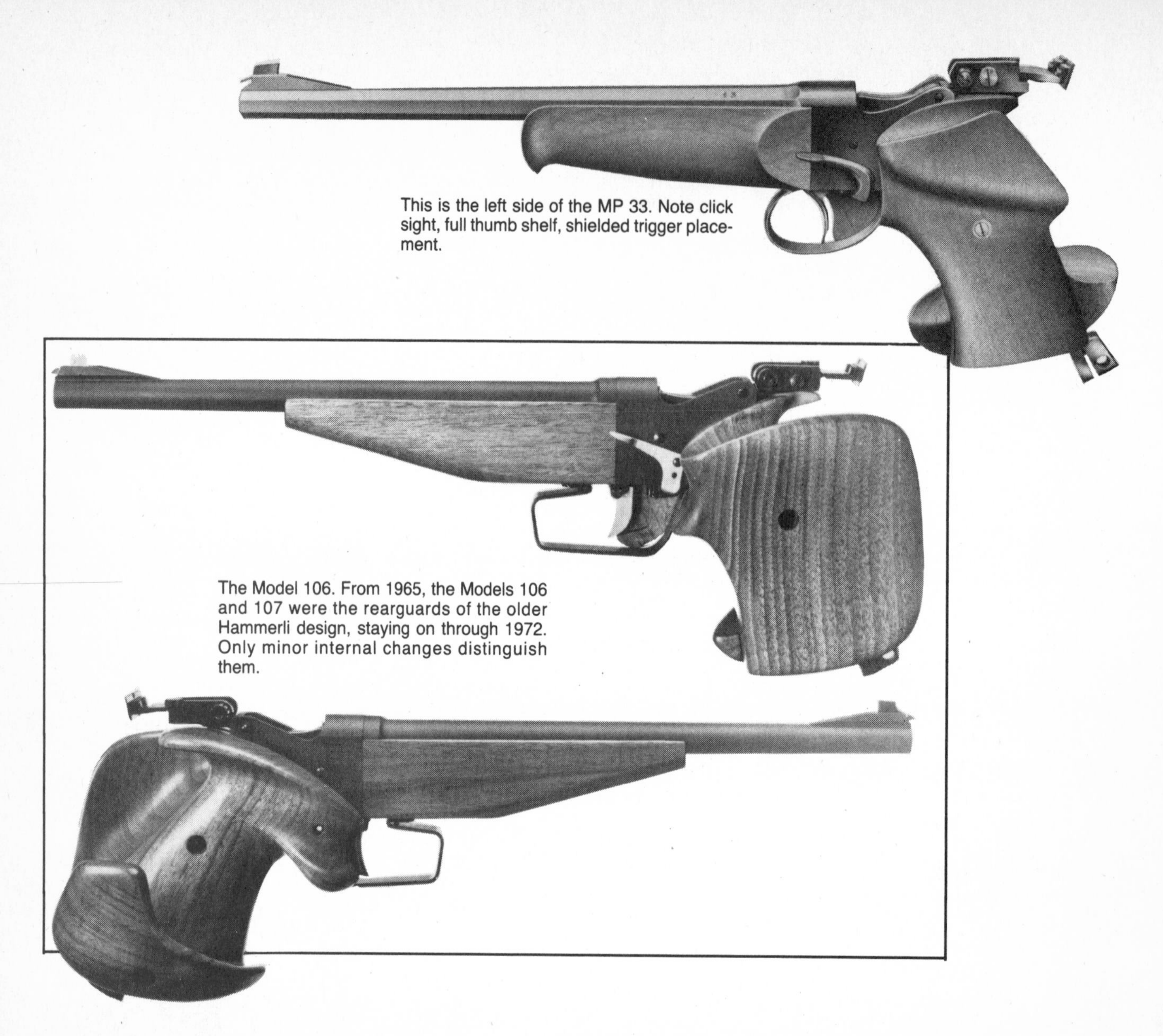

This is the left side of the MP 33. Note click sight, full thumb shelf, shielded trigger placement.

The Model 106. From 1965, the Models 106 and 107 were the rearguards of the older Hammerli design, staying on through 1972. Only minor internal changes distinguish them.

merli was not slow to appreciate the opportunity. Because of developments which followed, this marque is unique, not only because of the quite exceptional series of awards won with the company's weapons, but by virtue of the long period of manufacture, which gives the collector opportunity to trace the evolution of the pistol through its various phases. As such, the Hammerli Free Pistols can be regarded as a distinct sub-group within the general class of Free Pistols, and as such deserve particular attention.

The earliest of the Hammerli Free Pistols was designated the MP 33, or to give it its full name the Hammerli Martini Match Pistol. Although it was not an original design, it was a top-grade target pistol, produced with a high percentage of handwork. The pistol was based on consultations with Swiss National team members, who had been highly successful in this discipline during the period following the 1914 war.

Traditional gunmaking design was reflected in the wooden forend which culminated in the *schnabel* often found on Continental sporting rifles. The wood was walnut, and an integrated palm shelf was incorporated in the design. A glance shows how, even in the 1930s, some of the shape of the dueling pistol was still present.

The left side of the pistol incorporates an almost spoon-like thumbrest, enabling the shooter to fire with a straight thumb, thereby attaining a more relaxed shooting position. The cocking lever for the action is visible at the bottom of the frame. In the first production batch of the MP 33, the hair trigger assemblies were bought from a contractor in Suhl. The sights were based on the design of the Hammerli Free Rifle sight, and were adjustable for both windage and elevation. Figures 1-8 mark the positions available on one complete revolution of the sight.

The shapes of backsight notches were variable as were the elements for foresights. As will be seen from the illustration, Hammerli also produced a backsight offering different sizes of notches which could be changed without recourse to the screwdriver. Because the rules did not insist upon the use of a screwdriver for all sight adjustments, (as in most British and U.S. competitions) fingertip sight adjustment was possible by use of a knurled screwhead. It will also be noted that the grip extends to a point almost level with the trigger, which is curved in a backward sweep coinciding with that of the woodwork. Indeed apart from minor alterations, the only striking external differences between the MP 33 and its immediate successors were the shape of the thumbrest,

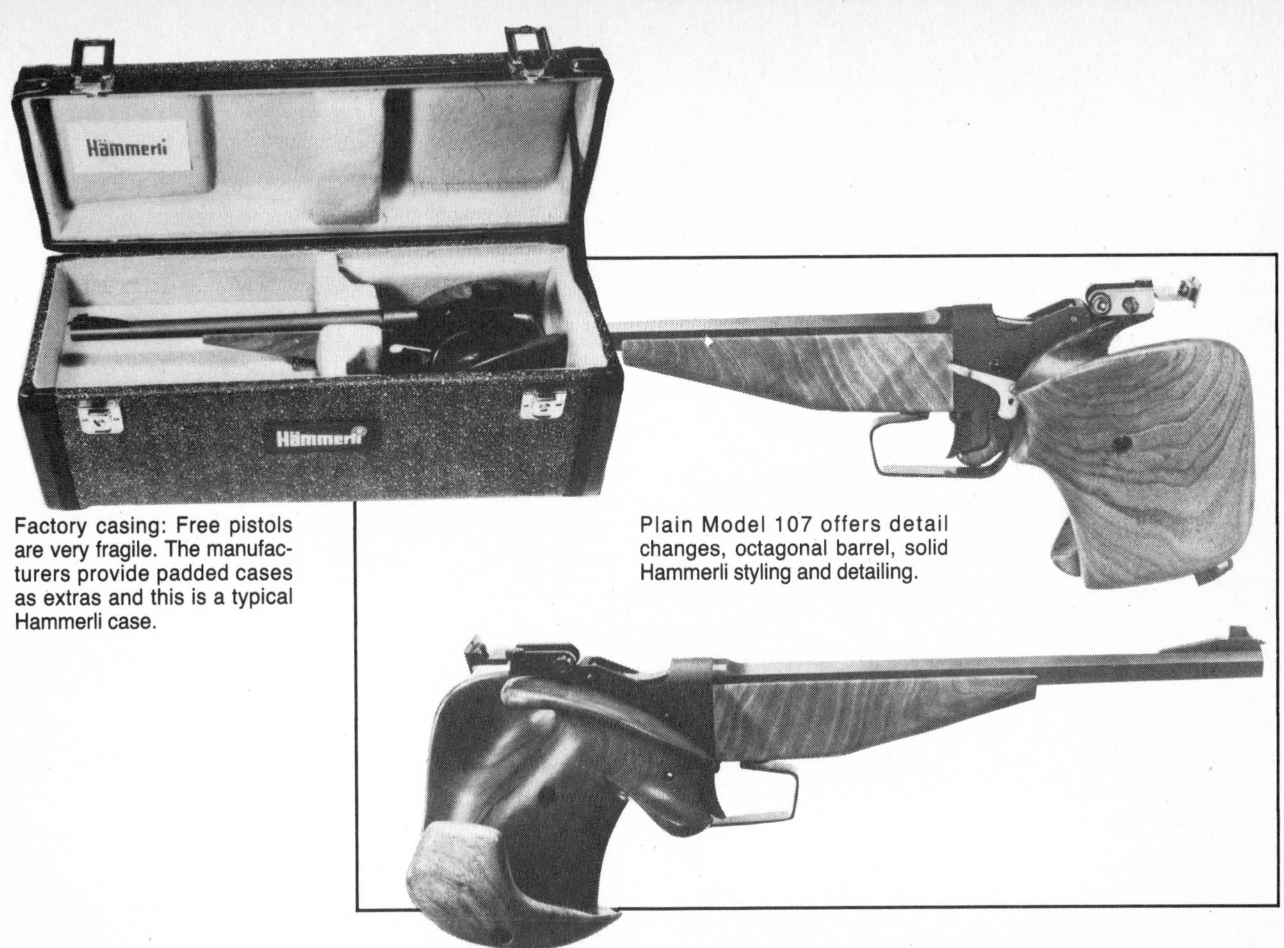

Factory casing: Free pistols are very fragile. The manufacturers provide padded cases as extras and this is a typical Hammerli case.

Plain Model 107 offers detail changes, octagonal barrel, solid Hammerli styling and detailing.

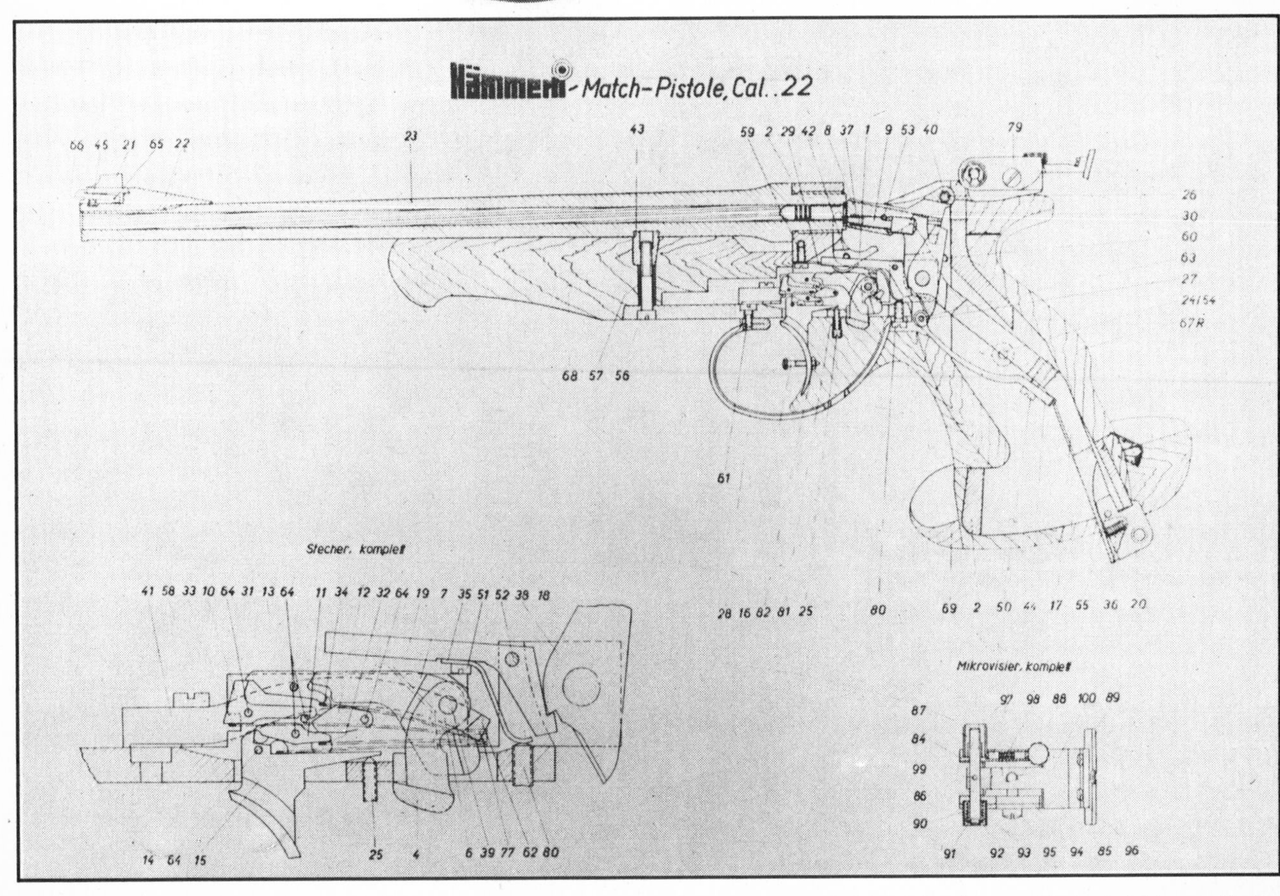

Spare parts drawing of late Model 100 or Model 103, its trigger and its backsight reveal that a free pistol is quite complex, and not simple at all.

Skanaker. Note the plastic wood for detailed adjustments on grips. The Free Pistol is an entirely personalized weapon. It may take a shooter months of adjustments to get one to his exact requirements.

Mr. F. Hediger, Sales Manager of Hammerli, with one of his most successful customers. (Photo courtesy Mr. K. Skanaker)

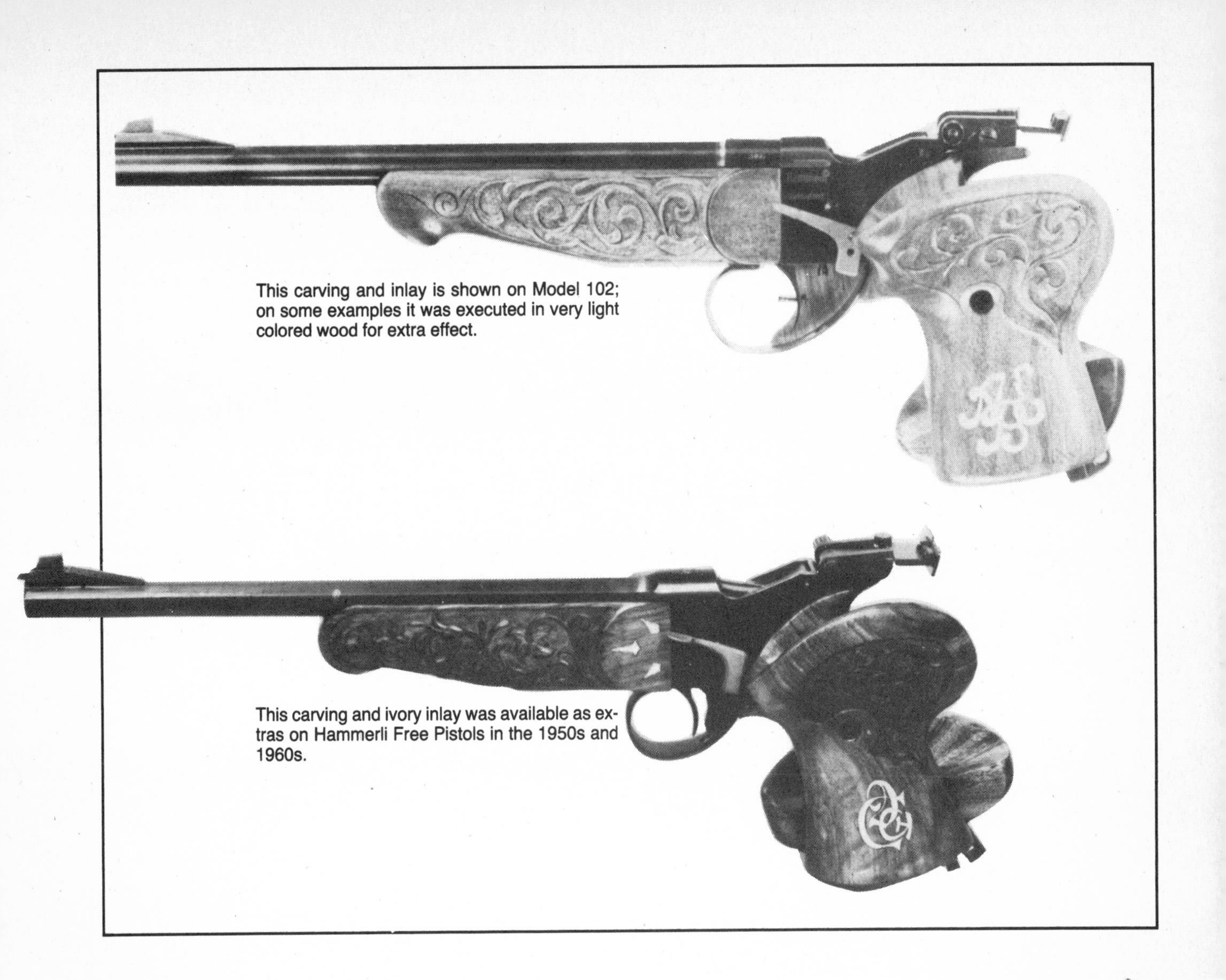

This carving and inlay is shown on Model 102; on some examples it was executed in very light colored wood for extra effect.

This carving and ivory inlay was available as extras on Hammerli Free Pistols in the 1950s and 1960s.

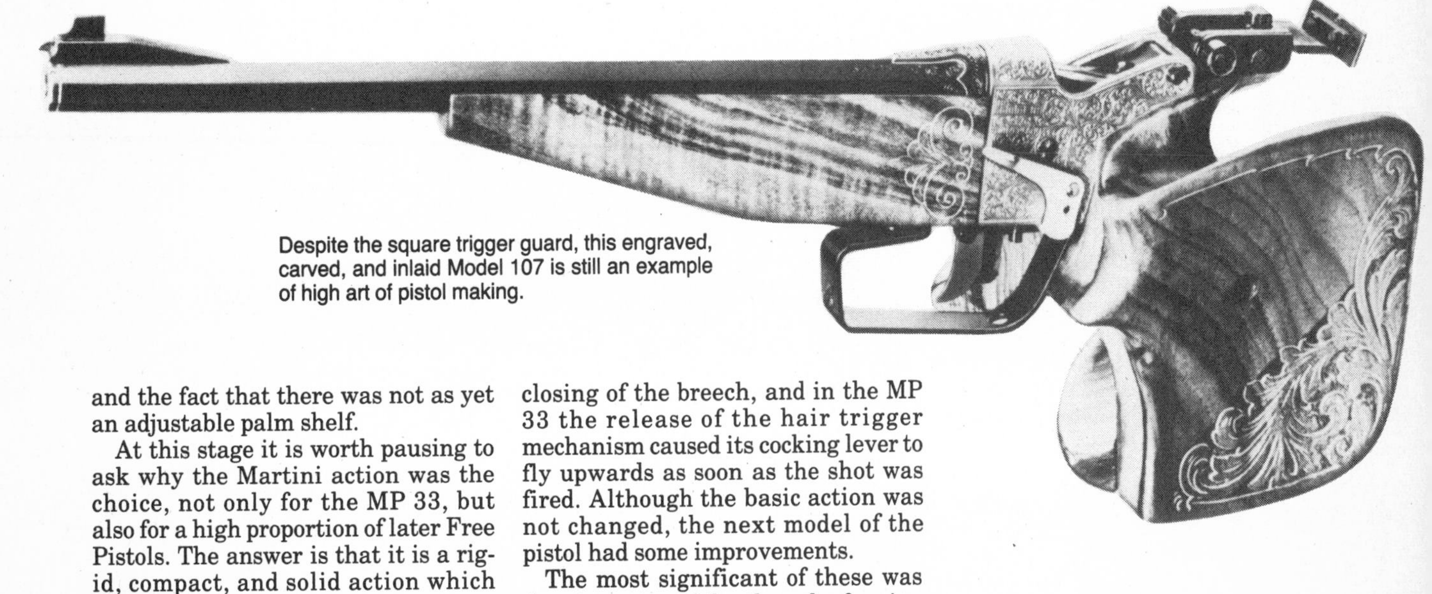

Despite the square trigger guard, this engraved, carved, and inlaid Model 107 is still an example of high art of pistol making.

and the fact that there was not as yet an adjustable palm shelf.

At this stage it is worth pausing to ask why the Martini action was the choice, not only for the MP 33, but also for a high proportion of later Free Pistols. The answer is that it is a rigid, compact, and solid action which put the line of bore low in the shooter's hand. It also provided extremely fast ignition, a vital feature in any long-barreled weapon. The hammer was internal. The action cocked on the closing of the breech, and in the MP 33 the release of the hair trigger mechanism caused its cocking lever to fly upwards as soon as the shot was fired. Although the basic action was not changed, the next model of the pistol had some improvements.

The most significant of these was the alteration of the three-leaf spring of the hair trigger mechanism to a five-leaf version, which appeared during the summer of 1950, nearly 30 years after the first appearance of the

MP 33s. Another point of note is that those pistols intended for the Swiss home market were chambered for the 22 *Extra Long* cartridge, rather than the more usual 22 Long Rifle round. This was made at the Swiss Federal Ammunition Factory at Thun, and was designated No. 7. Originally the predecessor of this round had been loaded with blackpowder.

The central feature of the Hammerli was, of course, the barrel which was rifled with four grooves, a complete turn being completed in 450mm. As the longer cartridge was not available outside Switzerland, export models of the pistol were chambered for the normal 22 Long Rifle. This, coupled with the fact that the entire prewar production was only some 200 pistols, including export models, makes a Match Pistol chambered for the 22 Extra Long cartridge an extremely desirable addition to any collection.

In 1947 the Hammerli family sold the business, and a further 100 examples of the MP 33 were produced in the summer of that year. These were modified slightly, and had a better grip; but were of the same basic design. Hammerli now dominated not only the sales market, but also the prize lists, taking the honors at the 1948 (London) Olympics, and the 1949 World Championships (both individual and team).

By the beginning of the 1950s, most manufacturers were designing new products, and Hammerli was no exception. The Model 100 appeared in summer, 1950, with serial numbers running from 1001. A more attractive shape was given to the forend, and the grip itself was set at a steeper angle. More important was the substitution of the new five-fold trigger. The mechanism was unchanged apart from minor modifications. The net result was that the new model's trigger pressure could be adjusted down to an incredible 5 grams. I have never been able to cope with such an ultra-light trigger, but I am no Free Pistol shot. *(Author Ward has, however, represented England in other forms of international pistol competition. Editor)*

The reader can judge for himself just how light such a trigger was when I say there was a considerable school of thought which wished the pistol to fire itself by the mere act of raising it to the vertical position. That is, the weight of the trigger's finger lever discharged the hair trigger mechanism. Having achieved this milestone, the shooter would then increase the pull weight just enough to be able to get the pistol to the vertical position without a discharge.

Although a discharge when the pistol was touching the bench did not forfeit points, it can be appreciated how important consistency of the action was when dealing with these very light pulls. Shooting with such pulls was clearly a highly specialized skill, but it was effective, as is witnessed by the steady rise in overall scores at this period. Although substantial numbers of shooters wanted the lightest possible trigger weight, they did not command a majority. Today tastes have changed, and many top shooters want comparatively heavy pulls – compared to those we have been considering.

The new Model 100 was capable of a consistent setting at 5 grams as opposed to the MP 33's 8 grams. In addition to this alteration to the hair trigger, the system for cocking the pistol itself was altered. The new pistols were made completely at Lenzburg. The frames were milled entirely out of a block of steel, as opposed to the earlier pattern which had two milled plates, onto which the grips were fixed. Although the Model 100 was, like all Free Pistols, liable to inconsistent trigger pressures if dirt got into the hair trigger mechanism, when properly treated they are capable of very accurate shooting. Considerable numbers are still in service today, 36 years after the model's first appearance.

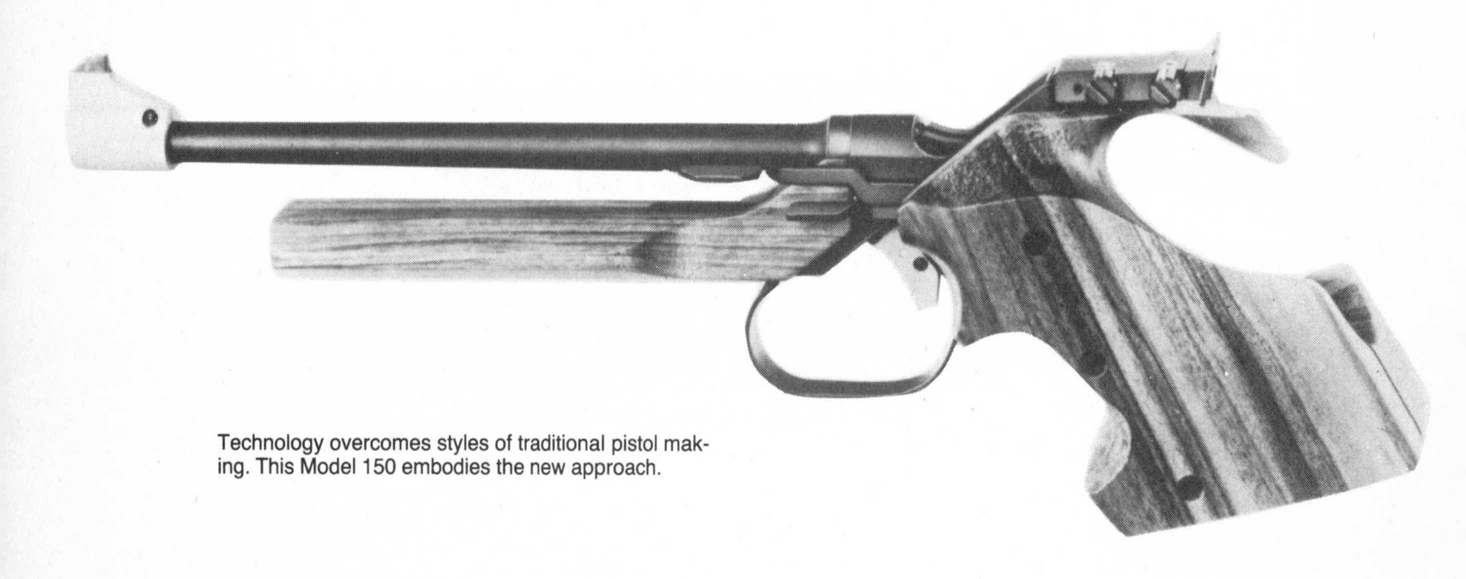

Technology overcomes styles of traditional pistol making. This Model 150 embodies the new approach.

Because the output of Free Pistols had been so small, decoration had been very much a matter for the individual purchaser. With the increase of production it became convenient to set aside pistols for decoration during production. Expense was also raising its ugly head. Some shooters were beginning to use weights to increase the weight, or alter the balance of the pistols. Hammerli decided to follow this trend, and introduced round-barreled pistols, thus being able to produce savings on the cost of the appearance, whilst maintaining the same standard for the remainder of all models. The weight was increased at the breech end and reduced by tapering towards the muzzle.

The outcome was a trio of new models, the 101, 102, and 103, which appeared in 1956. The 101 had a sandblasted barrel with a blued frame. The 102, showed a round, blued barrel with a high gloss polish. The 103 was the *modele de luxe* with highly polished octagonal blued barrel, and specially selected walnut grips. The inscription was now altered to "Hammerli Switzerland." Although the grips were modified, there were only marginal alterations to the pistol itself.

In addition to the fine finish, this model could still be obtained with a high degree of engraving, carving or inlaid ivory, according to the customer's individual requirements. I illustrate examples of this from the company's literature.

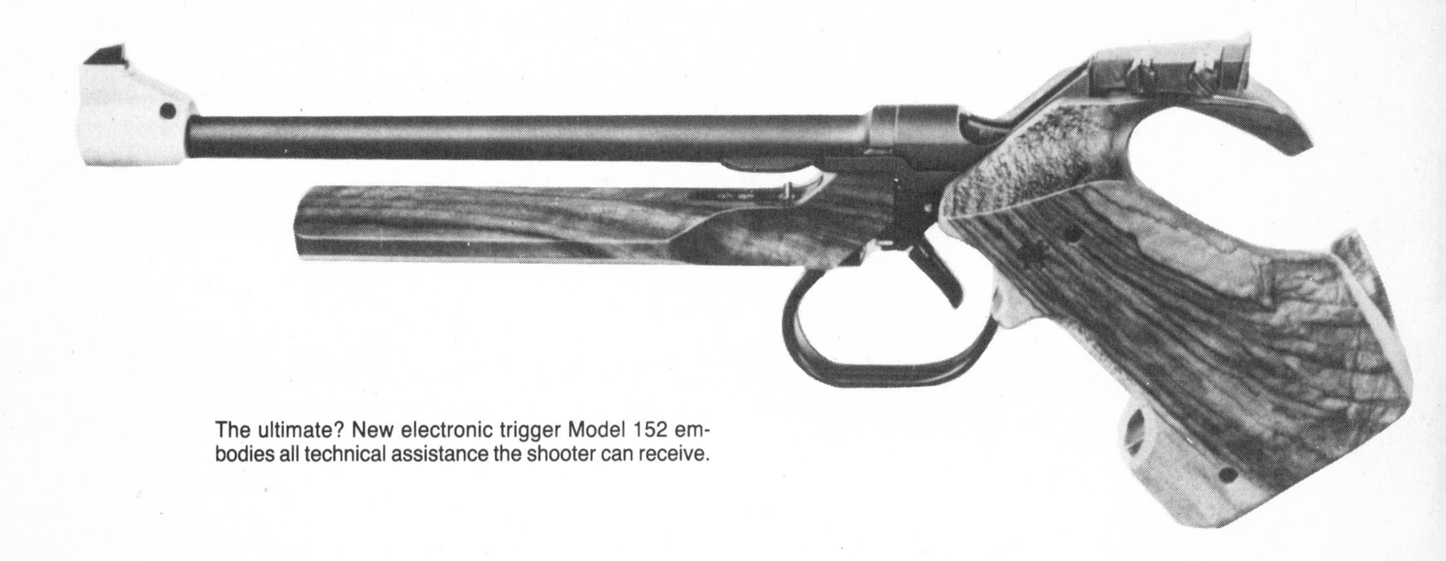

The ultimate? New electronic trigger Model 152 embodies all technical assistance the shooter can receive.

By 1962, 4600 post-war Match Pistols had been produced, and such was their high repute that an example of the Model 103 was added to the permanent collection of the Museum of Modern Art in New York, together with other outstanding examples of modern industrial design.

The next model to appear was the 104 in 1962. In light of the fact that the principal recent successes had been achieved with octagonal barreled pistols, the new model was supplied with a thinner round barrel, but with weight, balance, and center of gravity the same as the octagonal barreled pistol. In the *de luxe* version (Model 105) the octagonal barrel was retained. Numbers in the 104/5 series began at 30,000.

Some modifications, though effective, and complying with the traditional rules when introduced, are now prohibited. An example of this was the mirror sight. With this the shooter looked not at foresight and target, but at their reflections in a mirror, and arranged the backsight accordingly. The effect was to put the images into the same plane onto which the shooter could focus readily. This eliminated the time-old difficulty by which the firer had to have a sharp sight picture, keeping the target out of focus, and yet maintaining a consistent relationship between pistol and target. It cured one of the oldest difficulties in shooting, but on the other hand, managing the shot required determination by the shooter, as the increase of the length of the sight line appeared to increase the impression of wobble. Only between 100 and 200 were sold before the device was banned as being "optical." They are therefore another of Hammerli's rarities.

Competition honors continued to fall to Hammerli users in 1964, with all three Olympic Medals coming as tribute to Swiss workmanship. The top score was Maikkanen of Finland's 560, with Green (U.S.) following with 557 in second place for the Silver Medal.

Lest too much stress be placed on the purchase of new models, it is worth remembering that in the same year Ludwig Hemauer set a new Swiss National record of 572, *using a modified MP 33*. Despite this, readers will not be surprised to know that modifications continued to be made, and Models 106 and 107 emerged in late 1965, continuing to be marketed until the winter of 1971/72. There was no external difference between these and their immediate predecessors, save for another alteration to the five fold hair trigger mechanism. The change was achieved by incorporating a more powerful spring and adding an adjustment screw. The effect was to enable the shooter to select his trigger pressure anywhere between five and 100 grams. Other changes were the movement of the trigger latch a little to the right, (i.e. closer to the trigger finger) and the abandonment of the trigger feeling screw. The final pistol in this series was numbered 33,788.

Whilst top places continued to be won with Hammerli pistols, the proportion of successes was not as high as it had been. The basic design was nearly 30 years old, and did not offer scope for further improvement. How far the changes were due to the pistol being beaten technically, and how far the victories were attributable to the intensity of training followed by the Eastern bloc countries must be a matter of speculation. Wherever the truth lies, it was no doubt a realistic look at the results which induced Hammerli to decide upon a complete redesign of the pistol. (It must not be forgotten that Hammerli had its supporters in Russia, as it now has in China. Umarov, World Champion in Moscow in 1958, and Silver medalist in the Melbourne and Rome Olympics, always used a Hammerli.)

The decision to create a new model was correct, for the lead which Hammerli had held over its rivals had been whittled away by Russian victories with their TOZ-35 and the MC-55. A completely new design was decided upon, to become the Model 150.

The project was placed in the hands of Edwin Rohr (himself the 1955 World 300-meter Free Rifle record holder). Rohr concluded that the Martini action should be maintained, particularly for the good relationship of the trigger to the center of gravity. In addition, the cartridge was struck by a straight-moving firing pin, rather than the circular movement created by a pivoted hammer. Thus a shorter action could be incorporated. It also reduced vibration to a minimum.

Just how much of a change the new pistol was from the traditional design is immediately apparent. The barrel was made fully floating by separating it from the forend. The latter runs out beneath the barrel and provides the means of balancing the weapon, either by removing or adding weights inside it. At the same time the width is such that, short of intentionally inverting it, the pistol sights will never come in contact with the shooting bench. The line of the bore is as low as possible. The foresight is fixed to the tapered round barrel on a split aluminum base which encircles the barrel, and acts as a protector for the muzzle. The sights are of normal design. Each pistol has a bench test group, and the largest acceptable measurement is 20mm, i.e. approximately ¾-inch, at 50 meters. Although the prototypes were assembled in 1969, the first Model 150 pistols did not emerge until the 1972 Olympics in Munich. The serial numbers began with 15-0001. In 1974 Skanaker of Sweden broke Torsten Ullman's long established Swedish record using one of the new pistols, obtaining a score of 571 points.

The principal contrast between the Model 150 and its predecessors is a victory of utility over beauty. Though this may be a source of regret to the collector, it is the logical outcome of the pursuit of ultimate accuracy, which is a costly business. In some instances, I believe that engraving has been added to models of this series as a special order. One more striking example of the exercise of art on a Free Pistol was on Skanaker's Model 152, which was decorated with colorful traditional Scandinavian designs. Those readers who have access to *Les Cahiers du Pistolier et du Carabinier*, October 1981, issue can see it on the front cover in all its glory, decorated with flowers and insects on a pale blue background. Perhaps it's more what one would expect to encounter on Nordic antique furniture than a firearm, but nonetheless delightful.

Bolt-action Pardini Free Pistol is a forthright current attempt to deliver Hammerli benefits with a very different action. (Photo courtesy Pardini)

After the introduction of the Model 150, there was but one obvious further development to be followed. (I have no doubt that Hammerli has an ample supply of the less obvious ones up its sleeve!) Some years previously High Standard produced a pistol where the actual discharge of the firing mechanism was achieved electrically. In 1978 Hammerli introduced Model 152 with an electronic trigger. This model has technical advantages over even the best of the mechanical triggers, although at this level of competition, a great deal depends on the individual user. This was shown by the results of the 1984 Los Angeles Olympics. There, the Gold medal went to China's Xu Haifeng at 566 points using a Hammerli 150; the Silver to Skanaker with 565 points using a 152; and the Bronze to China's Wang Fu who scored 564 using a 150.

This has brought the story of the Hammerli Free Pistol up to date. What improvements will follow, I cannot tell. Though I suspect that these will not come easily, I have no doubt whatsoever that this remarkable firm will continue to be a leader of the world in the firearms sphere as it has in the 30-odd years for which I have known it and its products.

There are other famous marques which I have not discussed, in particular those from behind the Iron Curtain, which make a subject in themselves. In addition, many famous firms, such as Walther, Pardini and others, have come into or re-entered the Free Pistol field. Apart from the availability of space, I must take refuge in the fact that these are either single developments or only short series. Meanwhile Hammerlis will occupy even the most energetic collector, both physically and financially, should he decide to obtain examples of all its Free Pistols.

I must thank Mr. F. Hediger, the Sales Manager of Hammerli Ltd. for his kindness in supplying me with many of the illustrations, and for reading my manuscript. In addition he has made available to me his own article on the history of Hammerli, of which I have made free use. ●

Except where otherwise stated, all photographs are courtesy of Mr. Hediger of Hammerli, to whom the author expresses his gratitude.

Target Shooting

IT'S A SPORT YOU CAN SHARE WITH YOUR FAMILY– YOUR WHOLE FAMILY

I've been shooting for years — really enjoy it. But as the kids got older, there seemed to be less time for me to get off on my own and shoot.

Then I thought, why go alone? Why not get the family involved? When I asked, they were really excited about learning to shoot. More excited that I wanted to teach them.

We started off right, with the basics of safety and how a handgun works. And we started with the right gun — a new .22 caliber semiautomatic from Smith & Wesson. The Model 422.

The Model 422 proved to be perfect for teaching — and for learning. It's lightweight, compact, easy to handle, and surprisingly economical.

Now we all enjoy shooting. Sometimes we make an afternoon of it, complete with a picnic. It's a great way to spend time together.

I'm glad I asked.

S&W MODEL 422 - .22 CALIBER SEMIAUTOMATIC PISTOL
Available in 4½" or 6" barrel length with or without adjustable rear sight.
See the Model 422 at your Smith & Wesson dealer.

CCI
SPEER
RCBS
OUTERS
WEAVER
WE PUT THE EXPERIENCE OF A LIFETIME INTO EVERYTHING WE MAKE.
We take pride in being hunters and shooters just like yourself. Which explains why we put such a high premium on quality performance and good solid value.
Over the years we've also developed quite a reputation for technological innovation.
We're constantly working on new and better products. Not for the sake of some business plan. For the sake of millions of shooters who love the sport as much as we do.
RCBS
RELOADING STARTER KIT
FOR RIFLES AND PISTOLS
DIES AND SHELL HOLDER NOT INCLUDED
CCI
BLAZER
357 MAGNUM AMMUNITION
WEAVER
MOUNT
PRIMERS
SPEER
BULLETS
MINI MAG
OUTERS
NITRO SOLVENT
GUN OIL
New! The next generation of Weaver rifle scopes and binoculars. Look for them at your local gun dealer.
© 1988 Omark Sporting Equipment Division of Blount, Inc.
Your Shooting Partner.
CCI, Speer, RCBS, Outers & Weaver

At a time like this, the last thing you need to worry about is your rifle.
HK-91A2 Caliber .308 with Leupold 3x9 Scope
That's why more
and more sportsmen are turning to the new look in
hunting rifles...the HK-91.
Rugged. Reliable. And extremely accurate. The HK-91 is built
to perform under conditions where traditional bolt-action rifles fail.
The HK-91 has the advanced technological features that serious sportsmen demand. It exceeds the most stringent NATO accuracy standards right out of the box.
Because of Heckler and Koch's military proven delayed roller-locked bolt system, the HK-91 has very low recoil for a high powered rifle. It's easier to stay on target in case you need a second or third shot.
The barrel and receiver are manufactured with specially-coated, corrosion resistant steel. The stock and forearm are made of high strength polymers which give new depth to the word tough. In the field, the HK-91 will stand up to the kind of abuse that would ruin your wooden stocked hunting rifle.
And HK's quick detachable scope mounting system insures that you're zeroed in every time you snap your scope in place.
The choice is clear. You can hunt with a rifle designed in the last century. Or you can own the most uncompromising semi-automatic hunting rifle in the world.
HK
In a world of compromise, some don't.
H&K firearms are designed to be as safe as possible at all times. But the safe handling and responsible use of a firearm are your responsibility. Read the owner's manual carefully before using your gun. Keep all firearms in a safe place at all times. And consult your local police department for information on firearms instruction and gun ownership in your area.

John Amber and Bill Ruger were on the front page of *The New York Times,* shown at the Colt/Christie's sale, 1981, ready to bid.

on the BLOCK AGAIN

by R. L. WILSON

LONDON, ENGLAND, 1766: James Christie launches the first in a series of auctions destined to lead toward organization of an international enterprise recognized today as one of the premier auction houses in the world—Christie, Manson & Woods International Inc. — or, Christie's, as it is popularly known. Its major competitor and long-time London-based rival, Sotheby's, also now an international operation, dates back to 1745.

In the first years of sales, James Christie handled jewels of Mme. du Barry, Sir Robert Walpole's extraordinary collection of Old Master paintings (purchased for Catherine the Great of Russia), various other pictures and objects of art, plus a selection of firearms. Nearly two dozen guns were in the very first sale of the firm, and Christie's has the longest running tradition of auction sales in the arms and armor field in the world — dating back over 220 years.

Arms collecting, a centuries-old pursuit, has long looked to auctions as a route toward the breaking up of collections, the dispersal of individual or small groups of pieces, and the building of new collections. The hundreds of such sales held by Christie's and Sotheby's over the years has also created a substantial body of reference catalogs, important in establishing

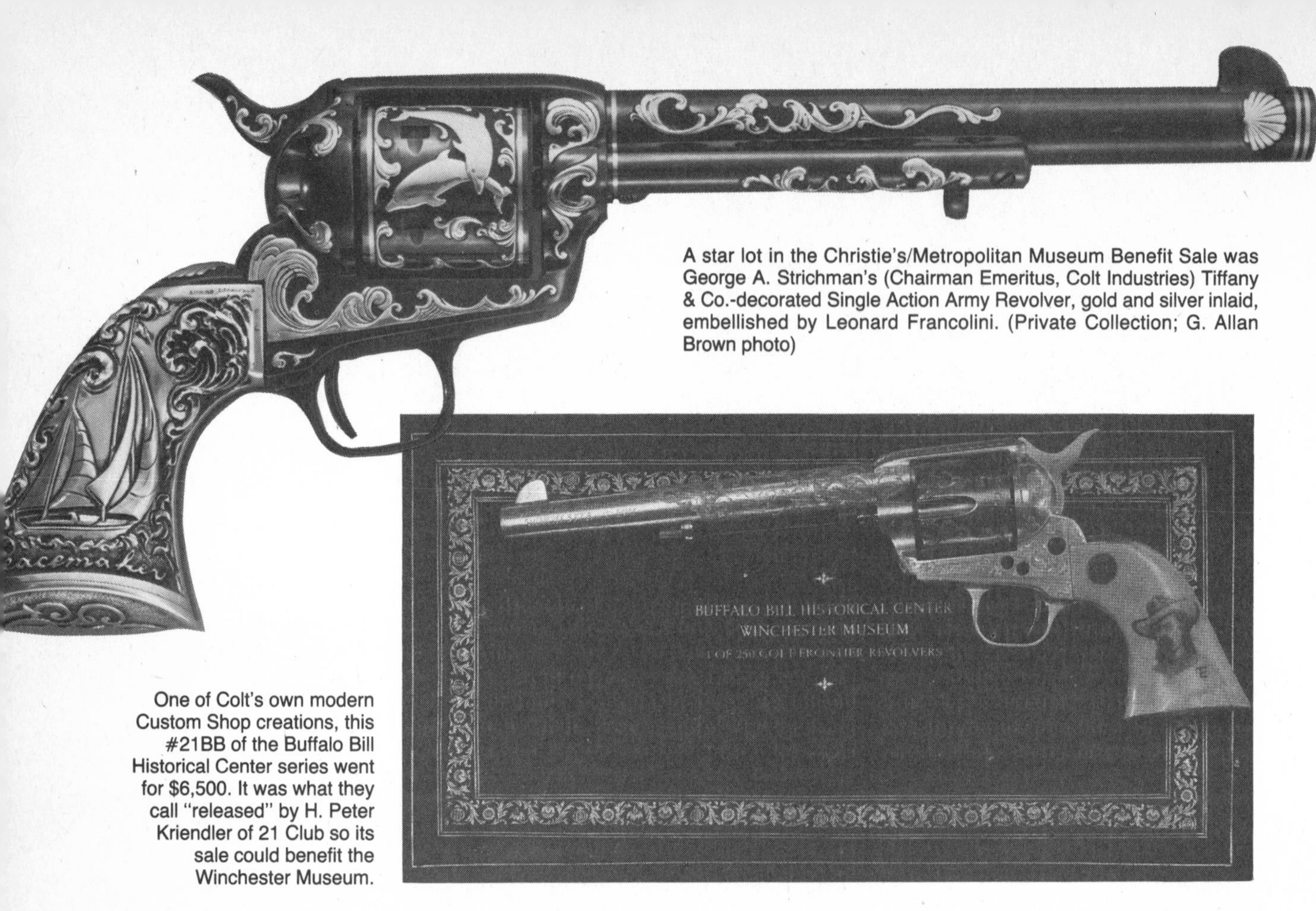

A star lot in the Christie's/Metropolitan Museum Benefit Sale was George A. Strichman's (Chairman Emeritus, Colt Industries) Tiffany & Co.-decorated Single Action Army Revolver, gold and silver inlaid, embellished by Leonard Francolini. (Private Collection; G. Allan Brown photo)

One of Colt's own modern Custom Shop creations, this #21BB of the Buffalo Bill Historical Center series went for $6,500. It was what they call "released" by H. Peter Kriendler of 21 Club so its sale could benefit the Winchester Museum.

pedigrees or "provenance," especially important in modern times, where skulduggery is an increasing problem in many areas of collecting and by no means limited to firearms.

In America, arms and armor sales, serving the collector rather than merely the dispersal of property, were given a dramatic start in connection with the Columbian Exposition in Chicago, where the Zschille Collection was displayed, then subsequently sold by Christie's in New York in 1897. The 862 items of arms and armor were first displayed by the renowned jewelry firm (itself with a strong tradition in firearms) Tiffany & Co., and many of the pieces sold are today in the Metropolitan Museum of Art, the Philadelphia Museum of Art, and other key collections. In a fascinating article in the July/August, 1981, *Man at Arms* magazine, the late Merrill Lindsay documented the "Great New York Arms Auctions," from the Zschille on up to the celebrated Colt/Christie's sale of October 7th, 1981. Lindsay noted that the great era of such sales came between the end of World War I and the beginning of World War II, with the better known buyers great American collectors, the likes of William Randolph Hearst, Clarence Mackay, Rutherford Stuyvesant, William G. Renwick, Carl Otto von Kienbusch, and Dr. Bashford Dean (first curator and founder of the Metropolitan Museum's Arms and Armor Department).

The Anderson Gallery and the American Art Association were the leading auction firms in arms and armor in America in that era. The latter was later known as Parke-Bernet, which still later merged with Sotheby's. The Metropolitan Museum was also a frequent bidder, with Dean and his successor Stephen V. Grancsay in keen pursuit of rarities. Private donations and auction purchases were of great import in building the extraordinary collection of The Metropolitan's Arms and Armor Department, without doubt the great collection of the North American continent, and ranking among the half-dozen best in the world.

However, due to the Sullivan Law of 1911, the auction houses in New York City, the financial hub of America and of considerable significance in the arms industry since the first importations to what was once termed New Amsterdam, auctions of contemporary, metallic cartridge arms in New York were non-existent, and after World War II New York sales rarely included even antique arms. Parke-Bernet had an occasional arms and armor sale post-WWII, but (after merging with Sotheby's in 1964) held only a few arms sales at their Los Angeles office, with mixed results.

Highlights of Sotheby-Parke-Bernet's Los Angeles auctions were the collections of Gerald Fox, W. Buhl Ford III, Archer Jackson and William G. Renwick (1970s to 1982). The Renwick Collection was decidedly a coup for Sotheby's, and was of such depth, size and quality that approximately 2 years were required to dispose of the thousands of lots (see *Gun Digest*, 1976, "William Goodwin Renwick . . . One of the World's Great Arms Collectors," James E. Serven).

However, in 1982, Sotheby's closed the doors of its Los Angeles gallery, and had virtually given up arms sales in New York City. Rita Rief, auctions columnist for *The New York Times*, told this writer in the early fall of 1981 that the firm had determined New York city sales of firearms were not within the law, and thus decided to shy away from them. An occasional arms sale was held by Phillips, in New York, c. 1980-81 (cataloged by decorative arts specialist David LeBeau), but these were strictly antique arms and armor, and were few in number. The field was ripe for a major New York sale: that event was the Colt/Christie's Auction of Rare and Historic Firearms, October 7th, 1981.

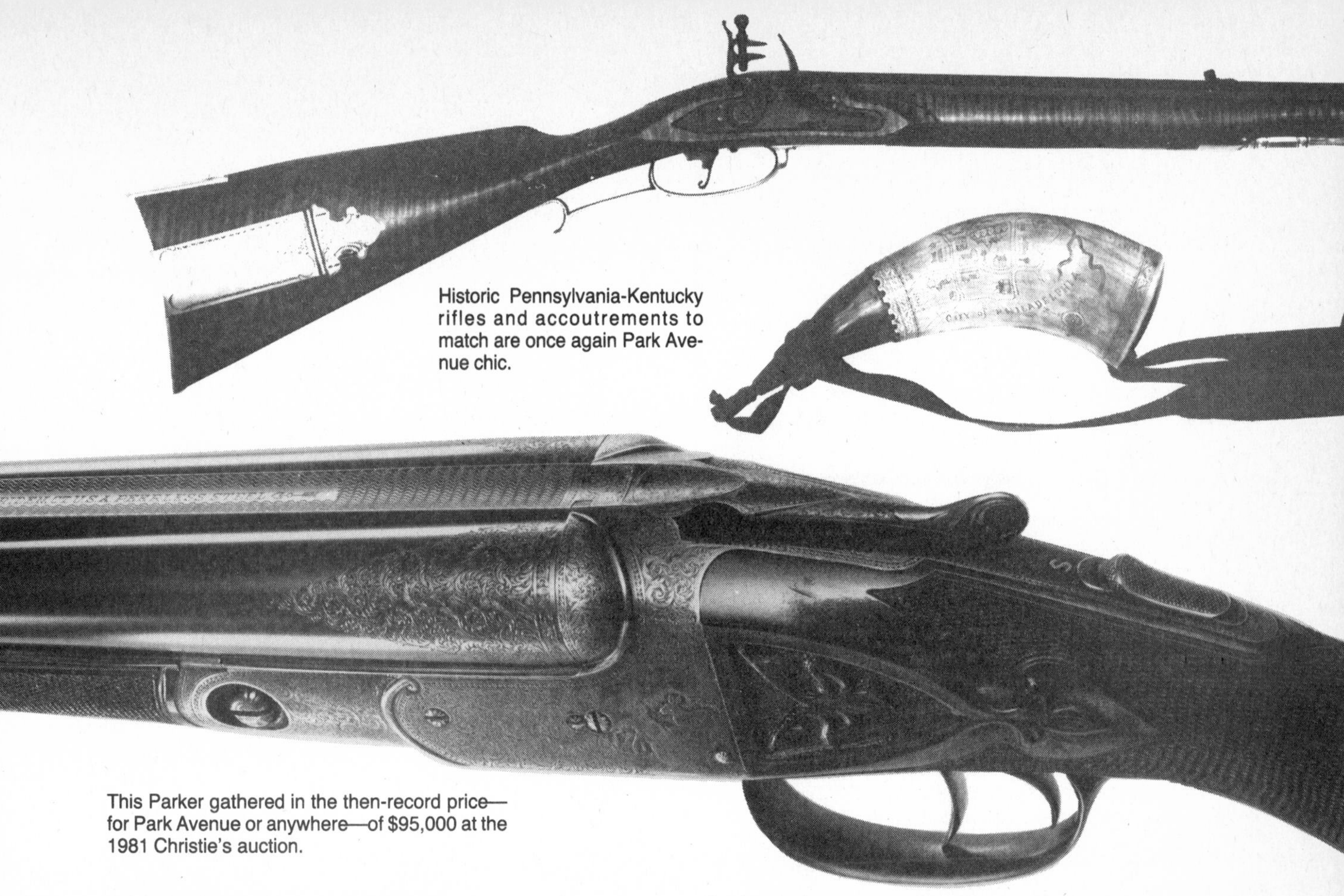

Historic Pennsylvania-Kentucky rifles and accoutrements to match are once again Park Avenue chic.

This Parker gathered in the then-record price—for Park Avenue or anywhere—of $95,000 at the 1981 Christie's auction.

The sponsors were the Colt Firearms Division (a first for Colt) and Christie's, with a total of 115 lots, presenting a cross section of antique and modern firearms and related weaponry, selected for collector and museum appeal, and offering a collection brought together from over 25 consignors, and featuring such marques as Colt, Winchester, Ruger, Purdey, Holland & Holland, Parker, Hawken, and Boutet, and the celebrated Kentucky rifle maker John Armstrong. Thanks to the legal work of New York attorney (and former chairman of Amnesty International) Mark K. Benenson, New York City authorities cooperated fully with the project, and sales of cartridge arms were made using the array of firearms licenses held by Continental Arms Corporation, a respected Fifth Avenue firm owned by Harvard graduate (class of 1930) Joseph Tonkin.

The concept of the sale was independently the conception of then-Colt President C.E. Warner and your reporter. President of Colt at the time of the sale, Gary W. French, noted in a promotional letter featured in much of the advertising:

> We take pride in supporting the venerable firm of Christie's in developing this premier event. The goal is to present to the discriminating collector and firearms enthusiast a rich selection of Colt and other-make firearms, catalogued with integrity and presented in the style and dignity these historical, mechnical, and artistic pieces of craftsmanship and engineering skills so richly warrant.

The event set over 20 records, among them:

1. Record auction price for a modern shotgun or rifle, 28-gauge Parker Al Special, $104,500 (broken by Safari Club International, 1985).
2. Record auction total single day sale in arms and armor, approximately $1,000,000. (Broken later by both Christie's and Sotheby's sales; new record by the latter, and is over $4,000,000).
3. Record auction price for a Kentucky rifle, $55,000.
4. Record auction price for an American blunderbuss, $8,250.
5. Record attendance at a collector's firearms auction (in excess of 400 present).

Furthermore, the attendant promotion made this event the most publicized in the history of arms collecting up to that time. *The New York Times* ran no less than five articles on the sale, the major story on the front page (Metropolitan section) and featuring several pictures, one showing John T. Amber and Bill Ruger in their front row seats, bidding paddles at the ready. The auction catalog was a sell-out—over 6000 copies printed, the biggest run in Christie's history of *any* auction, and one of the few catalogs to turn a profit itself. Further, the catalog Foreword, by Graham Hood, Director of Collections, Colonial Williamsburg, presented a glowing statement on the merit of arms:

> Weapons were an integral part of the station and culture of emperors, kings, noblemen, and gentry [and] the finest accomplishments of craftsmen in this genre are worthy of extended scrutiny and admiration . . . Even so conspicuous a liberal as Thomas Jefferson saw no inconsistency between his passion for architecture, landscape, music, painting, and sculpture and his interest in weapons — "one loves to possess arms" he wrote to George Washington, himself (perhaps more predictably) an enthusiast for such objects . . . Great collections of antique and modern decorated weapons were put together in the nineteenth century, of course, and continue to be in the twentieth. The art of the gunsmith and the engrav-

Text continues page 38

an AUCTION GUIDE

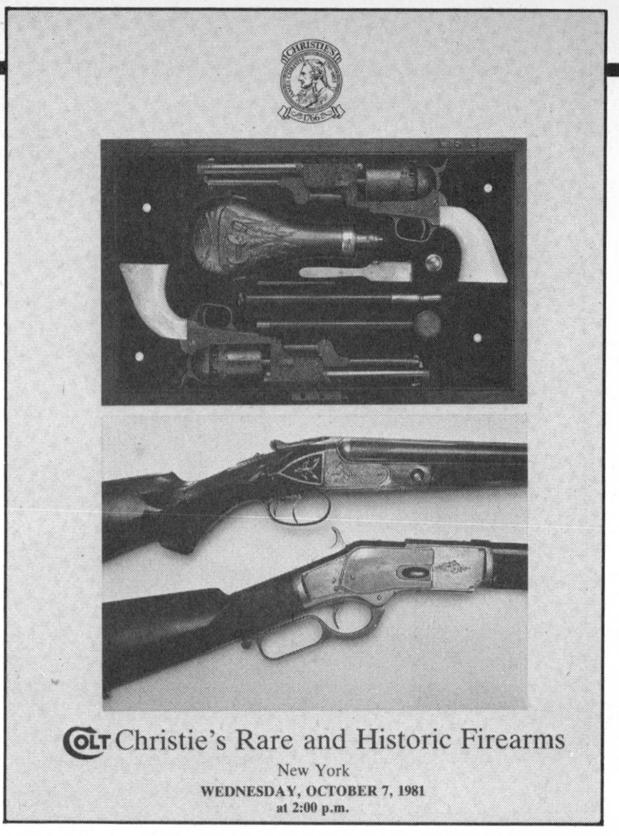

Cover of the catalog which returned arms and armor sales to New York City—the most publicized event in the history of arms collecting, with advertising and/or articles in *The New York Times, The New Yorker, Smithsonian, The American Rifleman, Connoisseur,* AP and UPI wire services, radio, television, and much of the guns and shooting press.

Firearms (and, rarely, armor) auctions are held on a largely irregular basis at sites around the United States; generally speaking the most publicized of these are held in New York City and by Little John's Antique Arms of Orange, California. For tips on bidding and other advice, some houses have brochures which can be helpful. Further, the firm's own experts are available to discuss not only objects for sale, but general background on the ins and outs of the auction business. Occasionally these experts will attend major arms shows, such as the Sahara Hotel Show, Las Vegas. Companies which have specialists on staff or have a history of arms sales are principally as follows (note that some offer subscription service for their catalogs; write for details):

Auction Houses in New York

Christie's
Attn: Paul Carella
219 E. 67th Street
New York, N.Y. 10021
(212) 606-0540/0541

The firm also has active London sales, with David Williams and Peter Hawkins specializing in the antique, and Christopher Brunker and Christopher Austyn the vintage and modern. Address: 85 Old Brompton Road, London SW7 3LD ENGLAND. Direct dial: (011441) 581-7611. Christie's is a noted fine arts and antique auction house.

Sotheby's
Attn: Florian Eitle
1334 York Avenue (at 72nd Street)
New York, N.Y. 10021
(212) 606-7000

Consultant to the firm is Nicholas McCullough. London sales are at: 34-35 New Bond St., and Bloomfield Place (off New Bond Street) London W1A 2AA ENGLAND. Direct dial: (011411) 493-8080. Noted fine arts and antiques auction house.

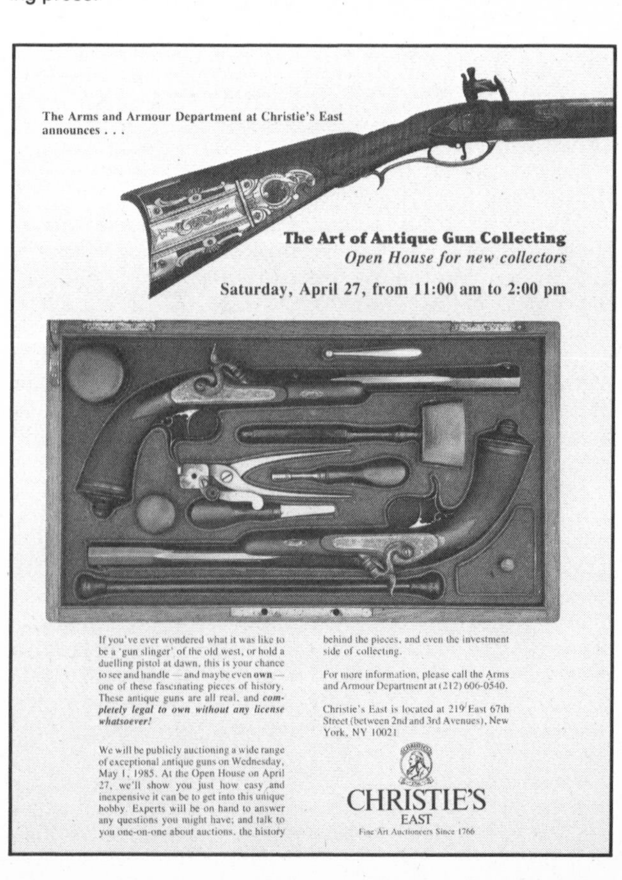

To promote gun collecting in New York, this brochure was prepared by Gregory Goodman, then consultant to Christie's for arms and armor sales, in 1985. It makes the point that antiques are legal without license or permit, considerations of history and art aside.

Phillips
406 East 79th Street
New York, N.Y. 10021

Not currently handling arms and armor sales in the U.S.; contact the London office: Phillips Blenstock House, 7 Blenheim Street, New Bond Street, London W1Y OAS ENGLAND. Direct dial: (011441) 629-6602. Noted auction house for art and antiques. Founded 1796 by James Christie's chief clerk, Harry Phillips.

William Doyle Galleries, Inc.
175 East 87th Street
New York, N.Y. 10028
(212) 427-2730

Will handle arms and armor; is a general auctioneer, known particularly for handling estates. Also, a noted house for fine arts and antiques.

Auction Houses Outside New York

Auction houses handling arms and armor, outside of New York City:

Richard A. Bourne Co., Inc.
P.O. Box 141
Hyannis Port, Mass. 02647
(617) 775-0797

The Bourne Company has produced several arms auctions since the late 1960s and holds sales at their galleries on Corporation Street, Hyannis.

Tom Keilman & Sons Auctioneers
15630 Old Highway 81
Round Rock, Texas 78664
(512) 251-2477/4236

Tom Keilman has held several arms sales, also of Western Americana, and is a general auctioneer as well. Located near Austin.

Little John's Antique Arms
No. 32 Town & Country Center
777 South Main Street
Orange, California 92668
Attn: John Gangel
(714) 972-4926

Specialists in firearms and related objects, and Western Americana; and has held several important sales. Also auctioneers in American and European antiques, art, Indian artifacts, and jewelry.

Guy, Winslow & Cass
61 Fourth Street
Stamford, Connecticut 06905

Specializing in mail order auctions, or arms and related items; the client submitting bids from published catalog descriptions (many objects illustrated), in writing, to firm.

Butterfield & Butterfield
1244 Sutter Street
San Francisco, California 94109
(415) 673-1362

General auction house, which also handles arms and armor. A major presence on the West Coast. Their consultant for arms sales is collector/dealer Greg Martin.

Kelley's Auction Service
P.O. Box 125
Woburn, Massachusetts 01801
(617) 272-9167

Specialists in estate auctions, and includes arms and armor as speciality.

James D. Julia, Inc.
RFD #1, Box 830
Fairfield, Maine 04937
(207) 453-9725

In 1987 set a record for a Tiffany & Co. mounted Winchester Model 1886 Rifle. William "Pete" Harvey does their expertising.

Richard W. Oliver
Route 1, Plaza 1
Kennebunk, Maine 04043
(207) 985-4242

Sold Bat Masterson material at a 1987 sale, plus variety of firearms.

Robert W. Skinner Inc.
Route 117
Bolton, Mass. 01740
(617) 779-5528

Held a major sword sale, 1987. As are Oliver and Julia, Skinner is a general art and antiques auction house.

O'Gallerie, Inc.
537 S.E. Ash Street
Portland, Oregon 97214
(503) 238-0202

General auction house; also handling arms and armor.

Cartridge auction house:
Tillinghast Auctioneers
Box 19-C
Hancock, New Hampshire 03449
Attn: James C. Tillinghast
(603) 525-6615

Specialist in antique ammunition; illustrated catalog published for each sale.

Auction Houses Outside U.S.

Auction houses not represented in the United States, but which do publish regular catalogs mailed on subscription to American buyers:

Weller & Dufty Ltd.
141 Bromsgrove St.
Birmingham, W. Midlands B5 6RQ
ENGLAND
(021) 692-1414/5

Specialists in arms and armor sales, and militaria; established 1835.

Wallis & Wallis
West Street Auction Galleries
Lewes, Sussex BN7 2NJ
ENGLAND
(027) 347-3137

Specialists in arms and armor sales, and militaria.

A highly recommended general guide to the world of auctions is *The Auction Companion*, Daniel J. and Katharine Kyes Leab, New York: Harper & Row, Publishers, 1981.

Continued from page 35

> er did not die out, as the objects in this catalogue show. The traditional symbol of the presentation piece survived and continued to call forth outstanding qualities of craftsmanship . . . Fine weapons, and the accessories connected with them, are frequently beautiful and important and deserve an integral place in any collection that attempts to reveal, through objects, the culture of any earlier age.

The significance of the Colt/Christie's sale was capsulized by expert Peter Hawkins in Christie's 1982 *Review of the Season*:

> The arms sale held in association with Colt Industries . . . at our Park Avenue premises was an historic occasion in many ways. It was our first gun sale in New York, the first by any company in the city for many years, probably the most distinguished public auction of American firearms ever held, and without doubt the most highly acclaimed and widely publicized.
>
> Since the idea was first suggested two years in advance, the combined efforts of Colt's, firearms historian Larry Wilson, and Christie's own experts had created widespread interest (and a measure of controversy) in the gun-collecting world. The sale brought together an unprecedented array of collectors' pieces, among them many guns previously owned by famous people — Ernest Hemingway, Charles Lindbergh, Mrs. Teddy Roosevelt and Kit Carson.
>
> Anwar Sadat was assassinated in Egypt on Tuesday, October 6, but the next day in gun-conscious New York our saleroom was filled to overflowing. As well as establishing a record for catalog sales . . . over 20 new auction records were set . . . To these records must be added the auction's most significant achievement: its contribution towards the growing public awareness of firearms as works of art . . . In the words of [an editorial writer of the Sunday *New York Times*, October 11th]: "Guns for once brought pleasure and commerce to New York City last week . . . the care with which they were handled demonstrated their meaning and value . . . the auction at Christie's was not so much a display of arms but art."

Auctions of both antique *and* modern arms had made their triumphal return to New York in style, right on Park Avenue at one of the most prestigious sales rooms in the world. To quote Rita Reif of *The New York Times*: "Gun collectors, dealers, manufacturers and onlookers gathered yesterday afternoon at Christie's, Park Avenue and 59th Street, to bid at and watch what the auction house described as the first major auction of rifles, revolvers, shotguns and pistols in this country." She went on to describe the event in a detailed, well illustrated article totaling over 2,000 words.

With this renewed interest and vitality in the field in New York, the atmosphere for auction sales is increasingly electric. There is actually a demand not only for sales of antiques, but for modern sporting arms. The availability of pieces encourages collecting, since a happy circumstance of auctions is the opportunity for buyers to handle and examine the pieces up for sale. An auction also presents the opportunity for buyers to meet the experts. An Open House for arms' collectors was held at Christie's, April 28th, 1985, where an array of authorities from several specialities in collecting were on hand, all of which encouraged active pursuit of the "fine art of arms collecting."

Adding to the impetus for sales is the ever-increasing discovery of new collectors and the re-emerging enthusiasm of old-timers, some of whom had drifted away from the field. The distinguished old Armor and Arms Club of New York is presently undergoing a revival, part of the swell of renewed and fresh interest in the field. Still another encouragement to collecting in the field is the willingness of celebrity collectors to proclaim their interest in arms. Among these stalwarts: Michael V. Korda, best selling author and the Editor-in-Chief of the major publishing house Simon & Schuster. Korda's article on firearms, including the collecting thereof, in *Penthouse* magazine (fall 1986), was accompanied by exquisite color pictures of decorated Colt firearms from another celebrity enthusiast — George A. Strichman, Chairman Emeritus, Colt Industries. The article and pictures represent a breakthrough for that 4,000,000-plus circulation monthly magazine, which had previously refused to accept advertisements on firearms.

Business tycoon William E. Simon, former Secretary of the Treasury and President of the U.S. Olympic Com-

"My wish is that these things of art which have been the joy of my life shall not be consigned to the cold tomb of a Museum and subject to the careless glance of the casual passerby, but rather that they will be disbursed under the auctioneer's hammer so that the pleasure which the acquisition of each has given me may be given again in each case to inheritors of my own taste."

From the will of
Baron Edmond de Goncourt

mittee, has publicly stated he is an arms' collector, and in October of 1985 was the featured speaker at a press luncheon at the exclusive "21" Club, marking publication of the writer's *Colt: An Americna Legend* (first book on firearms published by the art book publishing house Abbeville Press, of New York). Mel Tormé speaks out frequently and with convincing passion on his gun collecting interests, as does Barry Gray, host of the longest running talk show in America (he originated the format), on WMCA radio, New York City. Jerry Lewis, Buddy Hackett, Charlie Callas, Marty Kove, Arnold Schwarzenegger, John Milius, Sylvester Stallone, Ted Nugent, Johnny Cash, Hank Williams Jr., Gene Autry, Monte Hale, Roy Rogers and stock car racer Richard Petty number among others of the famous more than willing to proclaim their interest and love of guns. The revelations of these arms enthusiasts are part of the process of returning arms' collecting and a healthy interest in arms and armor to a position of fashion and status.

What does all this add up to for the collector in Oregon, or in Florida, or in any other part of America? The simple truth is that the reestablishment of arms and armor auctions in New York City has earned (and continues to escalate) understanding and respect for the unique artistic, historical, mechanical and romantic appeal of these inanimate objects. And is earning a recognition and respect for those who appreciate, collect, study, and write about them. The field is rightfully earning that special niche it so richly deserves as a noble and legitimate hobby.

The new wave of arms and armor auctions, especially in New York City, is reshaping the entire field of arms collecting, as well, by expanding and revitalizing the market, spreading the word to the uninitiated, and lending distinction and pride to an all-too-often previously ignored and unappreciated specialty in collecting. Auctions offer a new platform for splitting up major collections, they create new literature — indeed reference works — in the field, and serve to remind the public that arms and armor collecting is an exciting and rewarding interest. ●

Singer, composer, author, showman and gun collector Mel Tormé, with the cased Colt "Sears Roebuck" revolver presented to him on the occasion of his benefit performance for the Christie's-Metropolitan Museum of Art-Arms and Armor Department Benefit Auction, October, 1985. (Photo: Christie's New York)

Invitation to the Mel Tormé benefit performance, on behalf of the Christie's/Metropolitan Museum Benefit Auction. Note sponsorship—Sturm, Ruger & Co., and the Colt Firearms Division—and the very uptown tone—no T-shirts need apply.

PROBABLY, I could blame Chet Brown for it, although it was bound to happen sooner or later. Bob Brister, *Field & Stream*'s Shooting Editor, had been telling me for a couple of years that synthetic stocks were the way to go on a rifle that was hunted with, rather than looked at, and I said thanks, no, rifle stocks are made of wood.

But there was Chet Brown at the 1979 NRA convention with a left-hand 270 Remington that he had modified and glued into a fiberglass stock. It was an ugly rifle—seriously ugly. The barrel had been turned down and the screw holes for the iron sights crudely filled. There was enough space between the barrel and the forend for a generous-sized serpent to slither through. Chet had retained the pot-metal Remington floorplate and trigger guard, and the paint that Remington paints them with had been gouged off in spots. The stock was finished in a bilious cocoa brown color. Ugly? It could induce catatonia in an admirer of fine rifles.

Remember, though, that this was 1979, and synthetic-stocked rifles were a rarity. Moreover, left-handed bolt actions were even scarcer, and this inanimate hideosity was so exotic that I asked Chet how much. Seven hundred dollars, he said, and with the ritual swap of FFLs, it had a home.

When I got the rifle home, I put it on a postal scale and discovered the first of its virtues: it weighed 7 pounds with scope, or about a pound lighter than my lightest wood-stocked 270. Next, I snuck it to the range on a day when no one was there and shot it. The rifle would put three shots in ¾-inch as a matter of course.

So obviously I took it hunting as soon as I could, right? Wrong. It sat in the gun locker for 4 years, because rifles had *wood* stocks. Finally, in 1983, I swallowed hard and determined that this was the year of the Ugly Gun. It went to the tundra of northern Quebec where it was rained on constantly and did not shoot a caribou. Next, it traveled to South Carolina where it endured a toad-strangling downpour and did account for several whitetails. From there, it was off to Montana, where it terminated the career of a mule deer buck, and got snowed and sleeted on in the process.

All this took place in about 5 weeks, and during that time, the Ugly Gun

I Sold All My

by DAVID E. PETZAL

This Paul Jaeger 270 built on a Texas Magnum action went. It was accurate, unfussy, but needed to be re-zeroed every time a cloud passed over the sun. This day, in Wyoming, it was right on the money.

had endured about every form of weather save tropical heat, plus 8200 miles of travel by all conceivable means. And it did not budge. No matter what you subjected it to, it continued to send all its bullets to exactly the same spot.

Now we must digress, and reflect upon the nature of walnut. It is a miracle of nature. No two pieces are alike. There are few things so fascinating as to cut into a *Juglans regia* blank and see what wonders lie within. But there is another side to walnut, and no one has put it better than Norm Nelson in his eminently sensible book, *Mule Deer*. (Nelson, while dreadfully misinformed about some things, is dead right about others.)

Some gun gurus preach that barrels should be tightly bedded . . . Only a Druid would put that much faith in wood stability. A tree trunk is a giant wick so permeable that the tree sucks water 200-plus feet high through that "solid" wood. No wonder Forest Service researchers say wood cannot be truly waterproofed.

I have learned this lesson the hard way. Here are a few of the more painful examples:

In the mid-1970s, I was looking at stock blanks for a planned 30-06. Standing in the corner of the gunsmith's shop was a blindingly beautiful piece of fiddleback walnut, dark reddish brown with strong, perfectly even fiddleback graining from one end to another. I said that was the one I wanted, and the gunsmith said no, sorry, it was already promised.

So I created such a scene that he relented, and the finished stock was a knockout. But truly, there is no free lunch. First, the barrel channel contracted to such a degree that it squeezed the barrel up out of the wood. I had the forearm re-inletted, and thought my problems were over. No way. The stock then expanded longitudinally, which I've never seen before or since, and with such violence that the action screws were forced out of square with the receiver. At this point, I realized that this stock was unsalvageable and gave it to a knifemaker, who chopped it up for handle scales.

In 1972, I got from that same shop a very fancy 7mm Weatherby which, for about 5 years, was my Main Rifle. It was highly accurate and dead sta-

Lovely Wood

It really is simple: In this Remington-actioned 280, stocked many years ago by Jim Carmichel, everything is hollow, and all the metal that can be Swiss-cheesed is, and it has killed a whole bunch of game, but it weighs 8 pounds.

While this Ultra-Light 280 has no history yet, it has many, many virtues, starting with zero-holding and light weight.

This one, too. A 300 Weatherby Magnum stocked by Winston Churchill, and one of his very few stocking jobs, it was never hunted with and I sold it to buy plastic.

ble, despite its highly figured wood. In 1978, it went to Africa, and came back looking like 10 miles of bad road. I had the maker refinish and reblue it, and once again the gun was gorgeous. But no longer was it the reliable tack-driver it had been. I suspect that when the stock finish was sanded off, the wood managed to soak up enough moisture to destabilize it. Nothing could cure the problem, and the rifle is now retired.

Fancy wood, you say. A complex grain structure is asking for trouble. Well, here's another. In 1975, I got a 338, built by a top maker. For the stock, he used a dead-straight piece of French walnut, with no figure at all, the ideal stuff with which to make a working rifle. It had a heavy barrel, and was very, very accurate for 10 years. Then while checking it out prior to a hunting trip, I watched in horror as it began stringing shots vertically, and I mean *really* stringing them.

I assumed I had thrown the powder charges carelessly, and pulled the loads. But the scale showed all the charges were identical. It had to be the rifle. Sure enough. In the left side of the barrel channel, just a few inches behind the forearm tip, were three small knots. For 10 years they had lain dormant, and now, for some reason known only to nature, they had begun to swell, pressing hard against the barrel and causing it to settle erratically from shot to shot. I sanded them flat, re-sanded the wood, and was relieved to find the rifle went back to its old level of accuracy . . . for a while. After a few months, the knots blossomed forth again, and this time, I had the whole forearm hogged out and the barrel glass-bedded. I think this has done the trick.

Wood can do other interesting things. One of the rifles I presently own is a 270 of eye-bugging beauty. It has one problem: you can't depress the bolt release far enough to remove the bolt. The wood under the release has swelled, blocking the release button. So off to the gunsmith we go.

By now, you may be wondering if I store my rifles in a hothouse. Nope, they're in a heated room, and in the summer, there's a dehumidifier on 24-hour duty. It's just the nature of wood.

Then there is the matter of weight, to which I've so far given short shrift because I consider it less important than stability. For many years, the ideal weight for a big-game rifle of the 30-06/270 class was 8 pounds, with scope. That is still a fine weight for a big-game rifle; you can carry it all day, and there is enough wood and metal to hold steadily. However, with the advent of the synthetic stock, that figure has gone out the window. Melvin Forbes, who developed Ultra Light rifles and heads Ultra Light Arms, can build you a 270 that weighs 5 pounds, 12 ounces, with scope, and is a full-sized arm with a 22-inch barrel.

". . . perhaps I'll stop missing them."

Extreme light weight is of no value in some circumstances (sitting in a stand) and of extreme value in others (climbing up a mountain). It carries with it two handicaps in all circumstances. First, it makes a rifle harder to hold steady, and second, it increases recoil. I've found that I don't shoot quite as well with synthetic-stocked rifles as I do with standard-weight guns because they wave around in the breeze more, and if you're huffing and puffing, they will vibrate like timpani. However, I can think of only one critter I missed that I *might* have gotten with a heavier rifle.

Ten years ago, if you had tried to sell me a 6½-pound 300 Winchester Magnum or a 6¾-pound 338 or an 8-pound 375 H&H, I would have pummeled you about the head and shoulders. However, I now have all three such rifles, and manage to shoot them without nosebleeds, vertigo, or weeping fits. Yes, they kick—how could they not—but it is not punishing enough to be objectionable.

This is because the stocks are designed to direct the backward shove into the shoulder, not the head, and because synthetic stocks, I am convinced, give with recoil, and slow down the shove, much as a gas-operated action slows down recoil.

And so I have discovered, over the years, that if you want to take a rifle out in the real world where the weather is lousy and the climbs are long and steep, there is no substitute for man-made fibers and exotic glues. With that understood, finally I could take stock of several other facts. I wanted to go back to Africa and no one was going to send me, so I would have to raise the money myself. Also, unlike several of my more fortunate colleagues who live in palatial homes, my own humble hovel has limited space in which to store guns, which meant that if I was to acquire an arsenal of new rifles, the old rifles would have to be unloaded. It was, in short, time to sell my wood, my lovely, lovely wood.

Most of my wood-stocked rifles had been acquired back when you did not need the income of a cocaine dealer to buy from a first-rate gunsmith; hence they had increased in value and it made economic sense to sell them. Indeed, the prices being asked by present-day gunmakers of the first magnitude preclude my buying anything more from them. ("Swivel studs? Why yes, I have some nice ones that I can put on for $925 extra . . . ")

So I sold most of my wood-stocked rifles. The ones I kept were those I had either hunted with a great deal and held too many memories to part with or were so ravishing only a brutish beast could say goodbye to them. (If you were married to Rachel Ward, would you care if she could cook?)

As it now stands, I have five wood-stocked rifles that I still hunt with, and 10 synthetic-stocked guns that go into the woods. The rifles with stocks made from chemicals do not acquire character and patina; they just get battered. But they work to perfection. And that is why I sold my wood.

Epilog

I got to Africa.

At the SHOT Show in January, 1984, Chet Brown asked if he could get the Ugly Gun back and re-do it. He did. It is now quite a handsome rifle and is, if anything, more accurate than it was in its first incarnation. The gun has accounted for a lot of game, but everywhere I take it, precipitation is sure to visit.

The medical term "phantom limb" describes the fact that amputees can often "feel" their missing arm or leg. I have experienced "phantom rifle"; I can still "feel" those wood-stocked rifles I sold. With time, I hope, the feeling will pass. ●

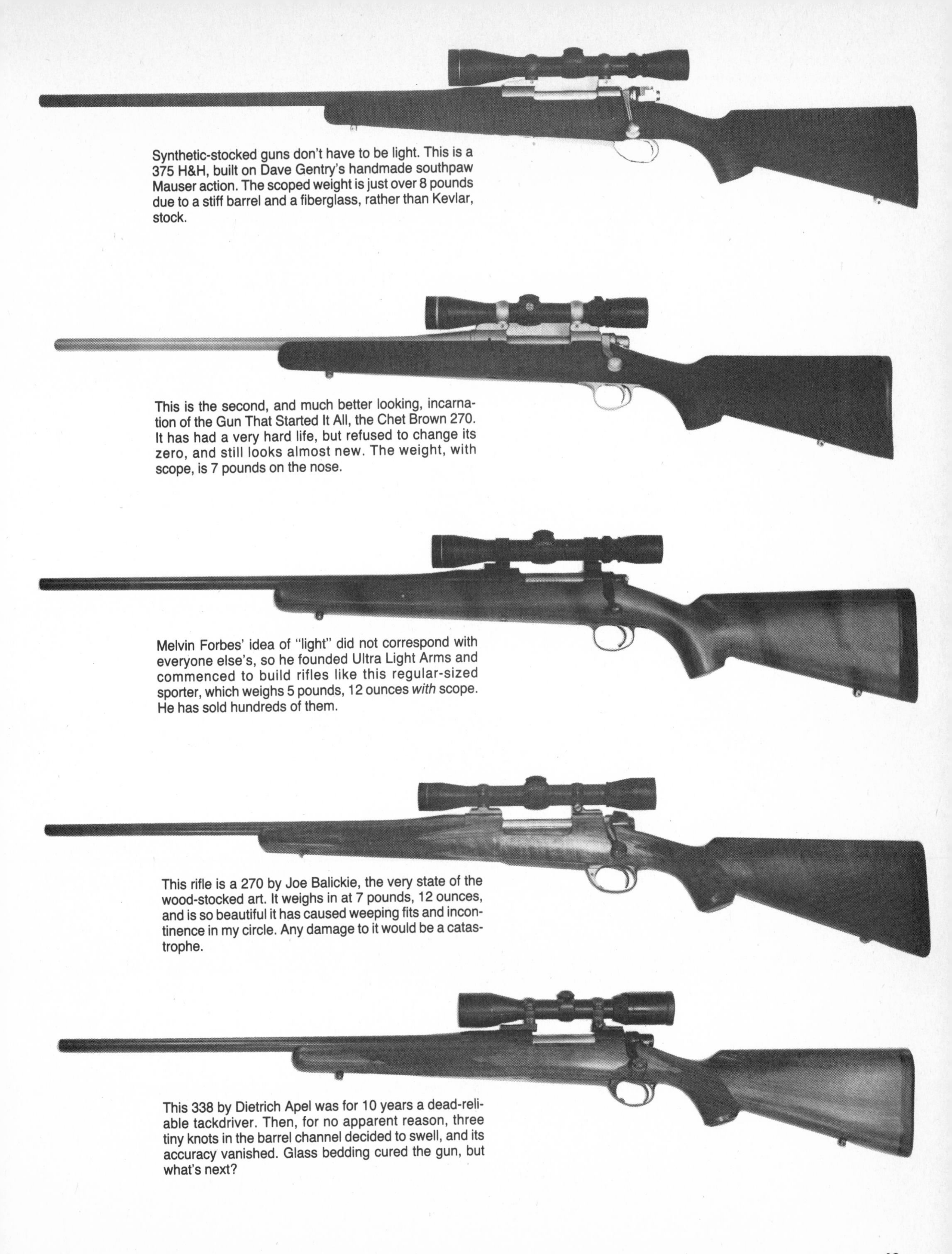

Synthetic-stocked guns don't have to be light. This is a 375 H&H, built on Dave Gentry's handmade southpaw Mauser action. The scoped weight is just over 8 pounds due to a stiff barrel and a fiberglass, rather than Kevlar, stock.

This is the second, and much better looking, incarnation of the Gun That Started It All, the Chet Brown 270. It has had a very hard life, but refused to change its zero, and still looks almost new. The weight, with scope, is 7 pounds on the nose.

Melvin Forbes' idea of "light" did not correspond with everyone else's, so he founded Ultra Light Arms and commenced to build rifles like this regular-sized sporter, which weighs 5 pounds, 12 ounces *with* scope. He has sold hundreds of them.

This rifle is a 270 by Joe Balickie, the very state of the wood-stocked art. It weighs in at 7 pounds, 12 ounces, and is so beautiful it has caused weeping fits and incontinence in my circle. Any damage to it would be a catastrophe.

This 338 by Dietrich Apel was for 10 years a dead-reliable tackdriver. Then, for no apparent reason, three tiny knots in the barrel channel decided to swell, and its accuracy vanished. Glass bedding cured the gun, but what's next?

On the 1,000,000th pistol, the falcon on the ivory grip is red, not black. Gold inlay highlights the engraving and roll markings. (Photo: Sturm, Ruger)

40 Years in

Today, William Batterman Ruger runs his company largely as he did when it was smaller, pays close attention to details and makes the final decisions. (Photo: Sturm, Ruger)

RUGER'S 22 automatic pistol has proven to be one of the most popular handguns ever made for a number of good reasons: There are enough models so they seldom need to be modified to suit the needs of the buyer; the guns function perfectly out of the box and shoot reliably with a wide variety of ammunition; and they last forever and a day. Independent laboratory tests have shown that they can shoot 41,000 rounds or more without *any* parts breakage or measurable wear!

The frosting on this cake is the low price tag. When first introduced in 1949, the Ruger pistol sold for $37.50; the Mark I target pistol had a $57.50 price tag when it came out a year later. Prices have climbed with everything else during decades of inflation, but Ruger 22s have always cost less than similar guns.

When the first Ruger ads appeared in 1949, many thought the name was an attempt to cash in on the "Luger" pistol's fame. Another popular theory among those who hung out in gun shops to debate such things was that a misprint with an "R" substituted for

An early Standard (RST4) pistol which has the Ruger falcon emblem on its left grip. First price: $37.50 (Photo: Sturm, Ruger)

Production

The Ruger 22 pistol has never been slowed up.

by DUNCAN LONG

an "L" had appeared. The Ruger did offer a somewhat similar profile to the German pistol which undoubtedly bolstered the first theory while a careful reading of the company's name at the bottom of the ads dispelled the second.

In fact, neither theory was correct.

The designer, William Batterman Ruger, was born with his name and any similarity between the Ruger and Luger (or it and other pistols like the Lahti P-40 and Nambu) was simply because the inventor's choice of good design features for his handgun.

While Sturm, Ruger & Company has grown at a rate unheard of in the gun industry, Ruger's own story isn't one of overnight success. The inventor was born in 1916 and was raised in Brooklyn, NY. Two early influences which helped shape young Ruger's future in firearms were undoubtedly a father who took the boy on short hunting trips and a grandfather who owned a farm where the youngster often spent summers shooting a 22 rifle and enjoying the outdoors.

In high school, William Ruger became the captain of his school's competition shooting team and, during these same years, haunted the New York City Library where he read all the available books about firearms. Another haunt of Ruger's was a machine shop near his home where he had the chance to see metal lathes, drills, and planers in action turning steel into machine parts.

By the time he'd left high school, the young man was already working on several new firearms designs of his own and had built up a small gun collection. His prep school at Salisbury, Connecticut, banned student ownership of firearms, but Ruger managed to keep one prized rifle hidden in an abandoned shack near the campus and often sneaked out into the woods to enjoy short shooting sessions.

Ruger returned to Brooklyn during school holidays and often was to be found in local machine shops in the area. He even managed to persuade a proprietor of one of these shops to allow him to use some power tools to create a firearm. The experimental firearm Ruger made was designed around a Krag rifle. The rifle was modified so its barrel cycled forward upon firing to reload and, in effect, Ruger's design turned the weapon from a bolt-action gun into a semi-auto rifle. The design worked well and Ruger, thinking it a new invention, applied for a patent. Unfortunately, a patent search revealed the idea had been registered nearly a decade before by a German inventor.

Ruger graduated from prep school and enrolled in the University of North Carolina. Not all his time was spent studying. He worked during spare time to convert a Savage 99 lever-action rifle into a semi-auto firearm and later described his successful conversion in an article he wrote for the *American Rifleman*.

After leaving the University, Ruger tried unsuccessfully to get a job with a number of firearms manufacturers including Savage and Colt. He spent some time working for $20 a week in Greensboro, North Carolina, in a small machine shop which manufactured knitting equipment, but finally landed a job with the U.S. Army at the Springfield Armory as a gun designer. One very disillusioned Ruger quit this blind alley in the bureaucra-

Right view of early Standard. Unlike current production pistols, early guns shared serial numbers between various models of the Ruger. (Photo: Sturm, Ruger)

Left view of Mark I Target Model (T678) introduced in 1950 and made until 1981. (Photo: Sturm, Ruger)

The magic words "Government Model" must make the MK-678-G now in production special to the designer-entrepreneur-capitalist. (Photo: Sturm, Ruger)

cy less than a year later.

Back in North Carolina, Ruger was soon making parts for a light machinegun of his own which he'd designed to conform to a memorandum released by the U.S. War Department. That led to a job with Auto Ordnance, manufacturer of the Thompson submachine gun. In 1941, he found himself working for that company in a machine shop in Bridgeport, Connecticut. He worked hard to produce a 30-caliber prototype weapon which was put through several military tests and proved to have a lot of promise, but the U.S. military had lost interest in purchasing new gun designs and Auto Ordance decided to table development of the machinegun.

Ruger left Auto Ordnance in 1946 and opened up a small business of his own, manufacturing quality carpenter's tools to sell to craftsmen. Boom times that he hoped would follow the war and produce a market for the tools didn't materialize and the business failed.

At this point, Ruger struck up a friendship with a neighbor named Alexander M. Sturm. Sturm was a painter and writer with a colorful past including time spent during WWII in the OSS and marriage to the granddaughter of President Theodore Roosevelt.

Both Sturm and Ruger collected guns. Soon after Ruger mentioned that he'd created a few guns of his own including a new pistol prototype, the two were planning a business to manufacture the 22 pistol Ruger had designed. Sturm, Ruger & Company became a reality a short time later.

The company's start-up sum of $50,000 (most of which was Sturm's) was not much to float a gun manufacturing business even with '40s' dollars. However, they didn't need to hire a lot of personnel to get into production. Ruger was able to handle the machinery design work and had a

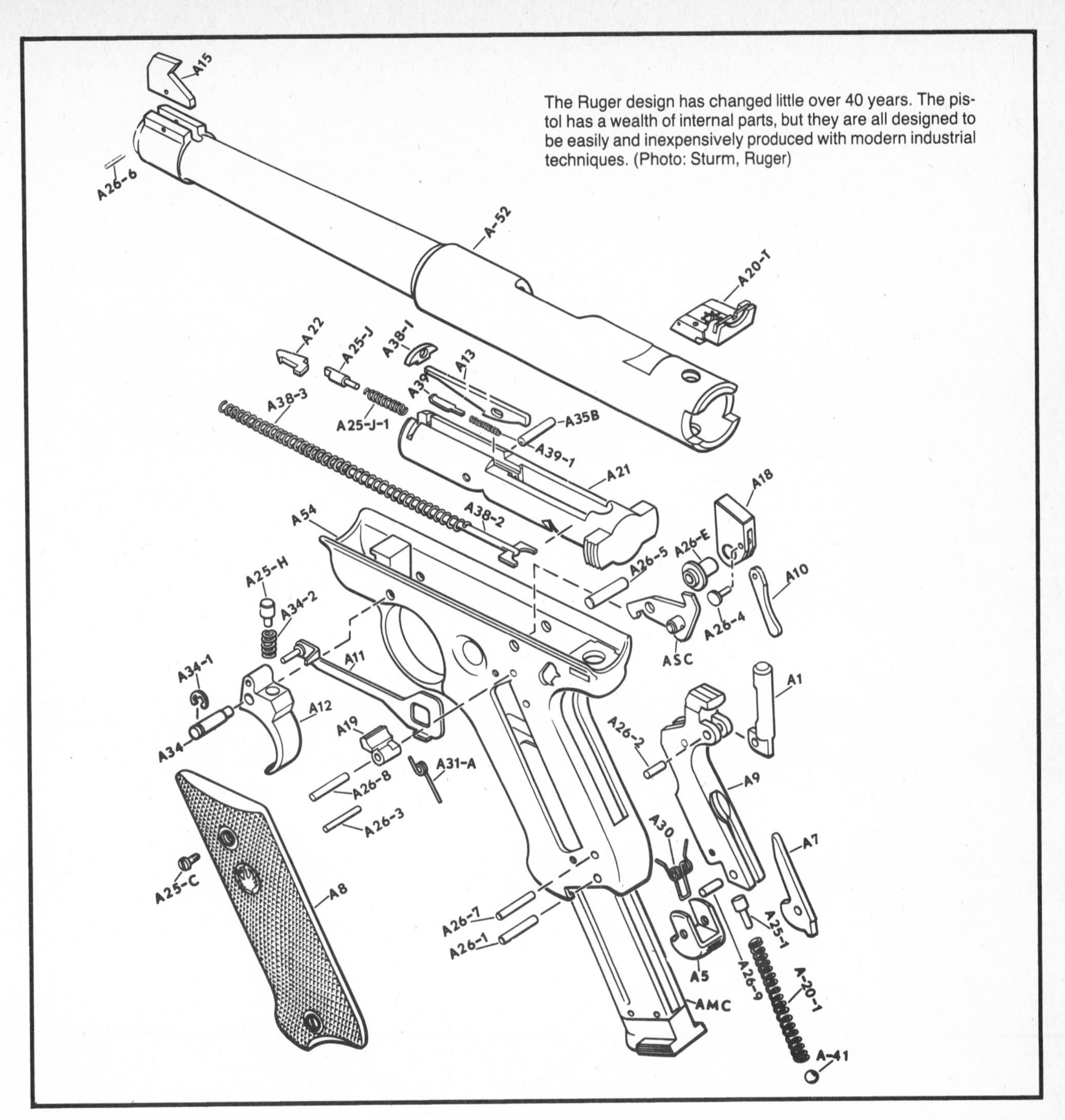

The Ruger design has changed little over 40 years. The pistol has a wealth of internal parts, but they are all designed to be easily and inexpensively produced with modern industrial techniques. (Photo: Sturm, Ruger)

wide range of knowledge of metallurgy which he'd picked up during his stint with Auto Ordnance. He could not only design a pistol, making best use of modern industrial manufacturing methods, but he could create the tools needed to produce it as well. Sturm was able to create ads for the pistols and designed the Ruger heraldic falcon.

Before meeting Sturm, Ruger had spent several years designing his pistol and getting the bugs out of it. But, as creative people say is often the case, Ruger's basic insight came in an inventive revelation. According to Ruger, one day as he was trying to come up with a solution to the gun's mechanism, "Almost as a vision, the design details and features came in loud and clear, and I was delighted. I saw the answers and they accomplished everything I wanted. I made my notes completely and correctly. There were two versions of the pistol. I could now take my choice."

Ruger chose the best solution for the gun's mechanism and started building a prototype pistol. He filed a patent application in 1946 and had the pistol perfected by 1947. The original prototype was a bit different from the final production gun. It had been adapted to use a spare Colt Woodsman magazine which the inventor had had on hand. The production prototype used to create tooling sported a pistol grip originally found on a hand drill made in Ruger's short-lived tool business, and was nearly identical to the first pistols to be sold. It had grips of thick, uncheckered wood held in place by what appear to be two rivets, and a takedown latch which is a rectangular slide release rather than the lever used on the final design.

Production started in 1949. Ruger assembled and created machine tools and fixtures to build each part of the new gun and his staff of two machin-

This view of the Mark II Standard (MK-4) shows the principal change in the new series of pistols: a bolt hold-open device. (Photo: Sturm, Ruger)

The Mark II, here with 4¾-inch barrel, replaced the original Standard pistols in 1982, but the Mark IIs are identical in shape and size to the original. (Photo: Sturm, Ruger)

ists along with 10 other men turned out runs of 1000 parts as the tools came on line. Consequently, by the time all the manufacturing equipment was made, enough stock parts were on hand to build 1000 of the pistols. The tooling work proved to be so effective the new pistols could be assembled with little or no hand fitting, something almost unheard of in the firearms industry in 1949.

Sturm, Ruger & Company's first ad appeared in the November, 1949, issue of the *American Rifleman* magazine. The ad impact was augmented by a *very* favorable review of the new firearm in the "Dope Bag" column of the magazine, testing being done under the direction of Major General J.S. Hatcher and the column edited by Al Barr. The last line of the review read, "We like this new gun a lot and at the very moderate price of $37.50 it represents real value." Orders came pouring in for the low-priced, high-quality Ruger pistol.

With the company's start-up money running low, the timing of everything was very close. Ruger paid his workers with the last of the $50,000 the same day that 100 assembled pistols were shipped out and the money paid for them was deposited in Sturm, Ruger & Company's account. While no one will ever know, it seems likely that if the review had been missing from the magazine or if the ad had appeared a month later, the business might well have gone under. However, 1100 guns were shipped out the last 2 months of 1949.

Ruger's new 22 pistol quickly became known for its ruggedness; in fact, for the next few years, the company "Parts and Service Department" consisted of a few spare parts in a cigar box since there were so few calls for replacements. More good magazine reviews as well as word-of-mouth advertising soon put the Ruger pistols into back-order even with the factory working at full capacity, a condition that was to continue until the 1970s. The Ruger ad in the March, 1950, edition of the *American Rifleman* read: "Regret—the delay filling orders for the Ruger Automatic Pistol . . . Because the demand exceeded our expectation, an interval between orders and delivery is temporarily inevitable. However, we expect to make the Ruger for a long time, and every order will be filled."

The "Standard" designation wasn't actually used by Sturm, Ruger & Company until the introduction of the Mark I series which caused a need for a name for the original gun. Two models of the Standard were produced. The original Ruger pistol with a 4¾-inch barrel had a catalog designation of the "RST4" and the 6-inch barreled-model—introduced in the autumn of 1954—became the "RST6." Twists for the barrels were 1 turn per 16 inches of barrel for early models with the more accurate 1-in-14, six-groove rifling being adopted with later pistols. The very early Standard pistols were made with a non-beveled ejection port, while those made after the introduction of the Mark I have a beveled port; early models also had narrower rear sight dovetails milled into their receivers.

Ruger often changes the specifications of his guns to upgrade their performance and/or make them easier to manufacture. Thus, many minor changes in part structure and dimensions are to be found over the years during which the Ruger 22 pistols have been produced. Several of the publicly-known changes occurred between serial numbers 2500 and 2800 when the firing pin and bolt were altered slightly and around number 2500 (possibly at the time of the other change) when the recoil spring guide, spring, and retainer started being produced as an assembly rather than loose collection of parts.

Trigger pulls on the Standard pistols have improved over time with the early guns generally having a bit more slack and over-travel than newer firearms. When the Mark Is were introduced, the target pistols' triggers and adjustable rear sights were made available as options for the Standard models. Consequently, many Standard pistols are practically Mark Is except for their lighter and/or shorter barrels.

Serial numbers of these first "Standard" pistols started with "1" (which remains in William Ruger's private collection of firearms) and were numbered consecutively as they were made until the Mark I variants were introduced. At that point, the two guns started sharing the same series of numbers so that there are gaps in numbering in each of the variants.

"Butaprene" grips are found on both styles of pistols; sharp diamond checkering is molded into the surface of the hard- rubber-like grips. Sturm, Ruger offered optional walnut grips mounted on pistols by the factory on early pistols; this practice was later discontinued because of the need to

Mark II Target Models (MK-678) simply continued a 30-plus year tradition. (Photo: Sturm, Ruger)

The Mark II Target Model replaced the Mark I Target pistols. This is the blued steel version (catalog number MK-678). (Photo: Sturm, Ruger)

produce guns at a faster rate to keep up with demand. Walnut grips were then offered as replacement parts with the customer putting them on his gun himself.

The change in medallion placement from the left grip to right on both the Standard and Mark I models came about when the original forming dies for the two pistol frame halves wore out in 1971. At that time the small cutout at the bottom of the pistol grip was moved to the left of the pistol frame and the follower button changed to that side and the medallion was moved to the right. The new frame style was designated as the "A-100" or "New Model."

Mark I and Standard pistols made in 1976 also have "Made in the 200th Year of American Liberty" stamped on them in honor of the U.S. Bicentennial. Ruger pistols made after 1977 have roll marking on the barrels which read: "BEFORE USING GUN—READ WARNINGS IN INSTRUCTION MANUAL AVAILABLE FREE FROM STURM, RUGER & COMPANY, INC., SOUTHPORT, CT., U.S.A."

After the Ruger pistol was first introduced in 1949, shooters quickly discovered that it was ideal for target use since the sights remained stationary (rather than shaking loose with extended shooting) and that the guns were capable of good accuracy with the standard Ruger barrels. Taking advantage of these facts, Jack Boudreau (who worked for Sturm, Ruger) modified a stock pistol slightly by adding Micro sights and an adjustable trigger and started shooting it very successfully in competition. In addition to getting favorable publicity for the company's pistol through high scores in shooting contests, Boudreau's customized gun became a test vehicle for a target version of the pistol which Ruger had in mind. Thus, a year after the introduction of the first Ruger pistol, a target version with a 6⅞-inch barrel and an adjustable rear Micro sight was marketed as the "Mark I" in 1950 and, at that point, the original model of the Ruger pistol became the "Standard."

As years passed, target shooters were to prove the potential accuracy of the relatively inexpensive Mark Is. Many modified guns took high places at contests like the National Civilian 22 Championships at Camp Perry a number of times with James Clark winning in 1953 with an out-of-the-box Ruger pistol, unmodified—except for some black friction tape wrapped around the grips for a better hold.

Although the Mark I was advertised in December, 1950, actual deliveries of the pistol weren't made until early in 1951. The Mark I series continued to be made until the end of 1981 and had a catalog listing of T678. The frame of the Mark I is identical to that of the Standard except for a modified trigger with stops to lower the amount of over-travel and slack. The receiver tube is also identical but has a heavier, 6⅞-inch tapered barrel (with a 1-in-14 twist) and target sights (the rear sight being adjustable-click and the front having a greater undercut for more light contrast). An effective muzzlebrake designed for use with Mark I was introduced by Ruger in 1955 and made available as an extra-cost accessory. Unfortunately the useful device has since been discontinued by the company.

Ruger took a much-needed vacation from his business in the fall of 1951. When the inventor returned from his extended hunting trip several weeks later, he found that Sturm was seriously ill in the hospital. Within 10 days, Alex Sturm was dead at the age of 29. And to commemorate Sturm's role, Ruger changed the company's heraldic falcon trademark—which had been designed by Sturm—from red to black on the 22 pistols. The change of color has remained in effect with all pistols made by Sturm, Ruger & Company since then except for a very few commemorative pistols.

Early versions of both the Standard and Mark I guns have a red falcon on their left grip panel; post-1951 guns have the black emblem. Guns made from 1951 until 1971 have the emblem on the left grip while post-1971 Rugers have it on the right grip. Strangely enough, the falcon emblem was originally a black bird on a silver background; sometime during production—and without any fanfare—the emblem was reversed to a silver bird on black, a change which suggests that the method of producing the grips or materials used in making them may have occurred at this time.

The now-rare Mark I Short Barrel (catalog number T514) was introduced in 1952; the gun had a 5¼-inch, tapered barrel and adjustable Micro sights. The front sight of this version wasn't as sharply undercut as the other Mark I models making it less abusive on holsters. Though the pistol

This is a late production Mark I Bull Barrel (T512), introduced in 1964. As its name suggests, it has a non-tapering, 5½-inch barrel. (Photo: Sturm, Ruger)

On the Mark I Bull Barrel (T512), only the barrel and front sight differed from the standard Mark I and the rear sight and trigger were identical. (Photo: Sturm, Ruger)

The Mark II Bull Barrel (MK512) was introduced in 1982 as part of the new series. It replaced the Mark I bull-barrel pistols. (Photo: Sturm, Ruger)

Like the other Mark II series pistols, the MK512 with 5½-inch bull barrel has the new bolt hold-open lever located over the left grip plate. (Photo: Sturm, Ruger)

This blued steel Mark II Bull Barrel with a 10-inch bull barrel was released as the "MK-10" in 1984. (Photo: Sturm, Ruger) was hailed by gun writers as the perfect addition to the Ruger lineup, the demand did not hold up and the model was discontinued in 1953. The year 1953 also marked the first patent, U.S. 2655839, on the Standard/Mark I pistols, with the patent search and application which Ruger had submitted in 1946 having been finally completed by the U.S. Patent Office.

As years passed, new firearms designs continued to roll out of the Sturm, Ruger & Company plant with Ruger closely overseeing the work of teams of designers. Every few years saw the introduction of completely new models of firearms from the company with variations of one or another previous models coming out yearly. Such rapid development and marketing of firearms in large volume has been unheard of in the history of firearms and Bill Ruger became a legend in his own time.

To the chagrin of marketing analysts everywhere, Ruger has not paid for "marketing studies." In the late 1970s, Ruger told an interviewer, "When manufacturers go around making surveys and asking people what they want, what they're really saying is that they don't understand the business they're in. Our business is more than a business, it is like some sports—it has a heart. I mean, guns aren't just something you make like tools or chairs or some other utility objects. Guns are valued possessions and provoke all sorts of emotional responses in people. If the manufacturer doesn't know what makes a really appealing gun, then he isn't going to have much success. I can't say I know all about it—I wish I could—but I do love guns, and that's been a big help."

In 1957, following military tests which showed Ruger's 22 pistol to be both accurate and durable, the U.S. Army and U.S. Air Force started purchasing thousands for use in training troops; Ruger roll-stamped a "US" on the Mark I pistols which it sold to the military. Some of these pistols were modified by military armorers for use by the U.S. Army Marksmanship Unit's pistol teams at Ft. Benning, Georgia.

The Mark I Bull Barrel (catalog number T512) was introduced in 1964. As its name suggests, it had a non-tapering, 5½-inch barrel. Only the barrel and front sight differed from the standard Mark I with rear sight and trigger being identical. And then the lineup of 22 pistols remained unchanged through the rest of the 1960s and most of the 1970s. The company announced the manufacture of their 1,000,000th Standard automatic pistol during the company's 30th anniversary in 1979. After displaying it at several gun shows, the gun was presented to the International Shooter Development Fund which auctioned off the firearm with the proceeds from the auction—$27,200—going to the U.S. Shooting Team.

That blued-steel, 1,000,000th pistol is covered with intricate floral engraving—right down to its grip screws—executed by Ray Viramontez. The gun also sports ivory grips provided by Bob Purdy and hand-carved by Ron Lang. The falcon emblem on the grip plate is of the original red color rather than the standard black. Gold inlay highlights areas of the engraving as well as roll markings which include William Ruger's signature and the "1000000" serial number. The pistol was encased in a velvet-lined, glass-topped walnut box and was purchased with a sealed bid by Austin M. Wortley, Jr.

With a pistol as successful as the Ruger, a manufacturer would have been perfectly justified in continuing to crank them out as they were. But Bill Ruger chose to introduce a product-improved model of the gun which he'd apparently had waiting in the wings for some time. Thus, in 1982, the Mark II series of the pistol was introduced to the shooting public.

The basic improvements in design of the Mark II variation of the pistol were the addition of a bolt-stop (activated by the magazine after the last shot was fired); a new, 10-round "M-10" magazine (with a Ruger falcon added to its base); an improved trigger shape (with a different internal pivot retainer); a modified safety (that could be activated before the pistol was loaded); cut-out scallops on the rear of the receiver tube (to allow easier grasping of the bolt ears during cocking); and a larger magazine release latch. All of the Mark II series pistols have Delrin plastic grips with a silver-falcon-on-black-background emblem on the right grip. Except for the Government model, all have barrel twists of 1-in-14.

The original Standard and Mark I pistols are readily distinguished from the later Mark IIs by the lack of a bolt hold open lever over the left grip plate. (It should be noted that on the Standard/Mark I guns, it is possible to lock the bolt open by engaging the safety after the bolt is pulled back. But for most shooters, the addition of the bolt hold open on the Mark II series was a welcome improvement over the original design.)

The last Standard/Mark I pistols made for commercial sales were run off on the last day of the year in 1981. But to mark the end of the era, a limited run of 5000 commemorative Standard pistols was made in January of 1982. These pistols bore Ruger's signature over the top of the receiver along with the caption "1 of 5000." The pistols were the first of the 22 autos to be made of stainless steel and bore the old-style red falcon emblem on the grip rather than the black medallion. Each gun was also sold in the same wooden "salt-cod" style box that the original Ruger pistols were shipped in.

It appears that stainless steel Standard pistols may have been on the Ruger drawing board for some time before actually being made. Company publicity photos showed a "stainless" Standard model which was never actually marketed. The serial number on the gun suggests that it may have been one of the 5000 run off in the commemorative series, though the roll marking of "1 of 5000" is missing from it or was removed from the photo by an artist's airbrush. At any rate, the Standard/Mark I series was discontinued before any commercially-available stainless guns were made in any other than the 5000-run group.

The Mark II Standard replaced the original Standard pistols in 1982 and is currently offered in both blued and stainless steel (which was first introduced in 1984). As with other Ruger guns, the use of stainless steel is denoted by a "K" in catalog-number prefixes of these guns. Thus, there are four models of the Mark II Standard: the MK-4 (4¾-inch barrel), MK-6 (6-inch barrel), KMK-4 (stainless steel, 4¾-inch barrel), and KMK-6 (stainless steel, 6-inch barrel). Rear and front sights and barrel taper are nearly identical in shape and size to those of the original Standard pistols.

The Mark II Target Model replaced the Mark I Target pistols. The Target Model is available in blued steel (as the MK-678) or—after 1984— stainless steel (as the KMK-678). Both versions have a tapered, 6⅞-inch barrel and the adjustable Micro-style rear sight and a sharply-angled front sight like that of the original Mark I. (The Micro sights are adjustable for windage and elevation with small screwdrivers. In 1969, the Mark I rear sight was replaced with an identical but unmarked sight devoid of the Micro brand name on it). Despite the Mark II Target Model's low price tag (about half those of other companies' target pistols), the pistols are *very* accurate;

The "1 of 5000" commemorative Standard pistol in stainless steel was made in January, 1982. These pistols bore Ruger's signature over the top of the receiver along with the caption "1 of 5000," and were Ruger's first 22 pistols in stainless. (Photo: Sturm, Ruger)

This may be the gun that never was. Sturm, Ruger never sold any stainless Standard pistols (other than the 1 of 5000 commemorative guns), but this publicity photo has captured one and its serial number: 17-00147. That is just one number above the "1 of 5000" roll-stamped pistol above, which may solve the mystery. (Photo. Sturm, Ruger)

The stainless steel Mark II Standard (KMK-6) became available to the public in 1984. Ruger's use of blued front and rear sights gives a good sight picture on these guns. (Photo: Sturm, Ruger)

The Mark II Target in stainless steel was also introduced in 1984 as the KMK-678. The pistol has a tapered, 6⅞-inch barrel and adjustable Micro-style rear sight. (Photo: Sturm, Ruger)

The stainless steel Mark II Bull Barrel (KMK-10) actually has a slightly tapered barrel to reduce its weight. (Photo: Sturm, Ruger) with quality ammunition, sub-1-inch groups at 25 yards can be enjoyed by skilled shooters.

The Mark II Bull Barrel models were also introduced in 1982 with stainless steel versions and a 10-inch bull barrel being released in 1984. In 1987, a Government Model was added to the Bull Barrel family so that there are now three barrel lengths available in blued models: 5½- (catalog number MK-512), 6⅞- (MK-678-G "Government"), and 10-inch lengths (MK-10). Stainless steel versions are currently available with 5½ or 10-inch barrels as the KMK-512 and KMK-10.

The 5½-inch bull barrels on these guns are non-tapering while the 10- and 6⅞-inch barrels have a very slight taper to cut down on weight. Except for the barrel and front sight, the Bull Barrels are identical to the Mark II Target pistols and—like the Target Pistols—all of the Bull Barrels are very accurate.

Most accurate of the group is the "Government Model" that was originally created according to U.S. Military specifications which include a 1-in-15 twist. The military has been purchasing these guns from Sturm, Ruger to replace the Mark Is and other pistols previously used for competition shooting as well as training. Once the government's guns went into production, Ruger apparently decided to take advantage of design work and favorable publicity created in obtaining the government contract to introduce a version of the gun to the public as well. Civilian models have "Government Target Model" roll marked on them while those guns actually sent to Uncle Sam read "U.S." over the serial number on the right front of the receiver.

Both the civilian and military versions of the Government pistol are targeted at the Sturm, Ruger & Company factory with a laser sighting system which assures accuracy; a test target is included with each pistol to show its potential. Military specifications call for each gun to shoot sub 1-inch groups, but most pistols are more accurate than that with many firing groups only half the required size. According to tests done by the *American Rifleman* staff using quality ammunition, the pistols are capable of groups as small as 0.18-inch at 25 yards when fired from a rest. It is also interesting to note that U.S. military tests of these pistols have found they can fire 10,000 rounds without any parts breakage or any measurable wear.

In addition to all the versions of the Ruger pistol listed above, a number of the Ruger 22s are floating around which have been created by "mix and matching" parts on stock guns as well as through custom gunsmithing work. These hybrids and mongrels create even more variations of the basic Ruger pistol and practically defy pigeonholing by collectors and historians though giving a lot of enjoyment to their owners.

Many such changes are confined to grip plate, sight, and trigger replacement/modification with many shooters carrying out such work on their own thanks to the Ruger's simple design. Other more complex changes may include replacement of the barrel, addition of barrel shrouds, nickel or teflon plating, scope mounts, etc., according to the whims and pocketbooks of the shooters and the skills and imaginations of the gunsmiths involved. Carbine versions of the pistol are also practical (though seldom if ever encountered) and a few of the Ruger pistols have even been legally converted into selective-fire "machine pistols" before the near-total Federal ban against such modifications in the U.S. after 1987.

The most notable custom work on Ruger pistols has been done by Carl J. Davis, Jim Clark, George Elliason, and John E. Giles with Tom Volquartsen currently doing some beautiful custom work. Volquartsen also gives his guns exotic names like "The Terminator," "The Predator," "The Olympic," and "The Masters" as well as more mundane labels like The Supreme and The Delux.

If the short history of Sturm, Ruger & Company is any indicator, it seems likely that William Ruger may still have a few new versions of his 22 auto pistol "up his sleeve," ready to release to the public in the near future. And there is the possibility of a 40th anniversary commemorative being released as well as a 2,000,000th pistol being probable in the early 1990s.

Ruger's company is now huge and, like many other successful businesses, has gone public; but the company is still tightly run in the same manner that it was when it was smaller with Bill Ruger paying close attention to details and making decisions as to what will be produced. Designers at Sturm, Ruger & Company, when questioned about why a firearm has been discontinued or added to the company's lineup or why stocks or lines of a firearm have been made in a certain way, often say, "Because that's the way Bill wants it."

Today, Sturm, Ruger & Company has sold well over 10 million of their various guns. And one of the company's big sellers continues to be the 22 Standard pistol which is nearly identical to that first one introduced in 1949. Ruger seems to have a fond place in his heart for the gun as well. When asked in a recent interview which was his favorite firearm, Ruger thought a moment and then answered, "Well, I'm quite fond of the No. 1 single shot rifle and the over/under shotgun. But most of all, I get sentimental over that first Standard Model 22 pistol that started things going."

As well he might. ●

Specifications of Sturm, Ruger 22 Automatic Pistols

Catalog No.	Length (inch)	Weight (Unloaded) (ozs.)	Barrel Length (inch)	Sights
RST4	8¾	36	4¾	Fixed
RST6	10	38	6	Fixed
T678	10⅞	42	6⅞	Target
T514	9¼	39	5¼	Target
T512	9½	42	5½	Target
MK-4	8 5/16	36	4¾	Fixed
MK-6	10 5/16	38	6	Fixed
KMK-4	8 5/16	36	4¾	Fixed
KMK-6	10 5/16	38	6	Fixed
MK-678	11⅛	42	6⅞	Target
KMK-678	11⅛	42	6⅞	Target
MK-512	9 13/16	42	5½	Target
MK-678-G	11⅛	46	6⅞	Target
MK-10	14¼	52	10	Target
KMK-512	9 13/16	42	5½	Target
KMK-10	14¼	52	10	Target

Early Rivals of the

Model 1911 45 Automatic

It was a well-attended race, but most of the entrants were also-rans.

by JOHN MALLOY

Having its 1905 45 pistol already in commercial production before the test trials gave Colt a decided advantage over its rivals.

PERHAPS no single automatic pistol is better known or has had more influence on automatic pistol design than the Browning-designed Colt Model 1911 45. It dominated the big-bore pistol scene of this century to such an extent that little memory is left of its early rivals. Yet these pistols, also-rans in the race against the Colt, should not be forgotten, for their influence still lives today.

Most people with an interest in firearms know that the Colt 1911 45 automatic was chosen, after some of the most extensive testing ever conducted, in a series of trials that spanned the 4-year period between 1907 and 1911. Then, in 1917, only 6 years later, the United States entered World War I. Battle experience proved the merits of the new pistol. In every instance, the 1911 gave a good account of itself when called upon. In some cases, such as its use in the hands of Corporal Alvin York, its performance became legendary.

The pistol was so good that, hardly more than a decade after the war, copies and modifications of the Colt-Browning design were being made all over the world.

It was so good that its early rivals—pistols that offered different ideas in the 1907-1917 decade—were soon all but forgotten.

The events leading up to the 1907 test trials, which gave the Colt its start to prominence, are of interest. And in those events is the story of the also-rans.

The 45-caliber Colt Single Action Army revolver had been replaced in Army hands by Colt's 1892 double-action design of 38-caliber. During the Philippine insurrection of 1899-1901 and continuing encounters with Moro tribesmen, it was found necessary to rush the obsolete Single Actions out of storage and back into service, and a quantity of 45-caliber 1878 Colt double actions were purchased. The stopping power of the old 45s proved to be far superior.

Thus, the search for a new sidearm began in the early 1900s with the consideration that it be of 45-caliber. Although semi-automatic pistols were coming into use, the cavalry firmly favored the revolver. The stage was set that any "automatic" considered must have reliability equal to that of the revolver and be of 45-caliber.

In anticipation of the tests, Frankfort Arsenal had designed two cartridges—a rimmed one for revolver use, and a rimless one for the automatic pistols.

The rimless version was very similar to a commercial round produced by Winchester Repeating Arms Co. for Colt since the spring of 1905. The WRA cartridges were made for Colt's new 45 automatic pistol, introduced in the fall of 1905. The Army round differed primarily in having a slightly longer case (.911- over .898-inch) and a slightly heavier bullet (234 over 200 grains.)

With the benefit of hindsight, it is difficult to understand why the Army, which had certainly been aware of Colt's development work, felt it needed a special round. Indeed, problems developed with the Frankfort Arsenal cartridges, and commercial ammunition (with a heavier 230-grain bullet) was used during much of the testing.

Invitations to submit pistols for testing were sent on January 31, 1906, to over 20 companies and individuals believed to be interested in developing military sidearms. The invitations included cartridge specifications (for the Frankfort cartridges) and offered to furnish a supply of ammunition to assist in preparing the pistols.

When the board convened on January 15, 1907, eight applicants had submitted nine general designs. Three were revolvers and six were automatic pistols. The revolvers are of interest themselves, but do not concern us here. The automatic pistols, at this early stage of history, represent-

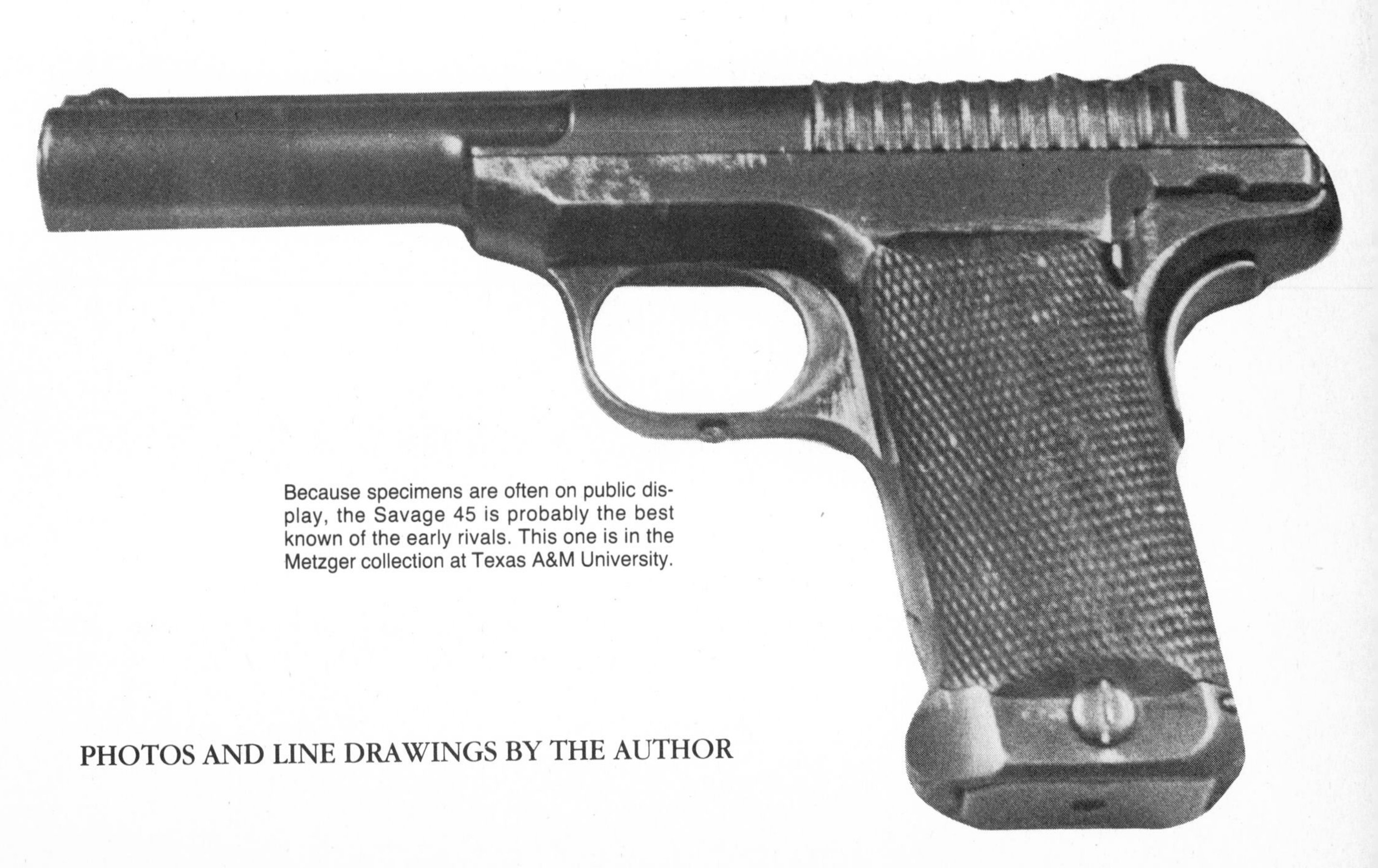

Because specimens are often on public display, the Savage 45 is probably the best known of the early rivals. This one is in the Metzger collection at Texas A&M University.

PHOTOS AND LINE DRAWINGS BY THE AUTHOR

ed a variety of concepts in competition for the first time.

The Colt was clearly the front-runner. The others were:

1. The Bergmann
2. The Knoble (actually two versions; one double action, one single action)
3. The White-Merrill
4. The Luger
5. The Savage

Three of the entries—the Bergmann, Knoble and White-Merrill pistols—were rejected early in the tests.

The fate of the Bergmann was sealed with this rather terse excerpt from the Board's report:

> "An attempt was then made to fire 20 rounds to observe the working of the pistol, but it was found that the blow of the hammer was not sufficient to discharge the cartridges, and the test was discontinued."

There is an air of mystery surrounding the unbelievably poor showing of the Bergmann 45. It seems incredible that a pistol that had obviously not been testfired with the required ammunition should arrive for these important trials without any representative, to be tested by persons unfamiliar with its operation.

Theodor Bergmann was a German inventor and industrialist, with a factory complex in Gaggenau, in southwest Germany. Largely through the efforts of his employee, Louis Schmeisser, the Bergmann pistol had become one of the first successful automatic pistols.

Always desiring a chance for military contracts, Bergmann had requested U.S. Army trials of his pistols as early as 1899. In 1903, he requested a test of his latest pistol. The caliber was 11.35mm, using a cartridge similar to the later 45 ACP. Apparently, no such test took place.

In 1905, the 9mm Bergmann pistol was adopted by Spain. Bergmann had subcontracted his pistol manufacture to the Schilling firm of Suhl. Schilling, however, was bought out by Krieghoff, which ended pistol production for Bergmann just as the Spanish contract was negotiated. Bergmann had a contract and no way to fulfill it.

To justify new expanded firearms facilities at his Gaggenau plant, Bergmann needed to obtain other contracts. He got a delay for the delivery of the Spanish pistols, and submitted a 45-caliber pistol to the U.S. Ordnance Department in June, 1906. In January, 1907, the pistol was tested at Springfield, with the dismal results mentioned.

Why did the Bergmann pistol fail so miserably? Why, with so much at stake, did Bergmann send a gun to an important test without being sure that it would function with the appropriate ammunition? Why, with company agents in both Germany and the U.S., did no Bergmann representative attend the trials to demonstrate the pistol? At this distance in time, these questions may never be answered.

Bergmann, disappointed with this failure, decided it was not economically sound to continue pistol manufacture. The Spanish contract was taken over by the Pieper firm, of Herstal, Belgium, who added their trademark "Bayard." The Bergmann-designed 9mm cartridge remains popular in Spain to this day. Denmark adopted the Bergmann-Bayard pistol in 1910; it remained the official Danish sidearm until 1946.

Theodor Bergmann retired from automatic pistol development just as that type of arm was coming into its own. One can only speculate as to what might have occurred had the Bergmann pistol made a satisfactory showing at the 1907 trials.

Faring little better than the Bergmann test pistol were the two pistols submitted by W.B. Knoble of Tacoma, Washington. The 1907 report states, ". . . several efforts to fire these weapons showed that they were so crudely

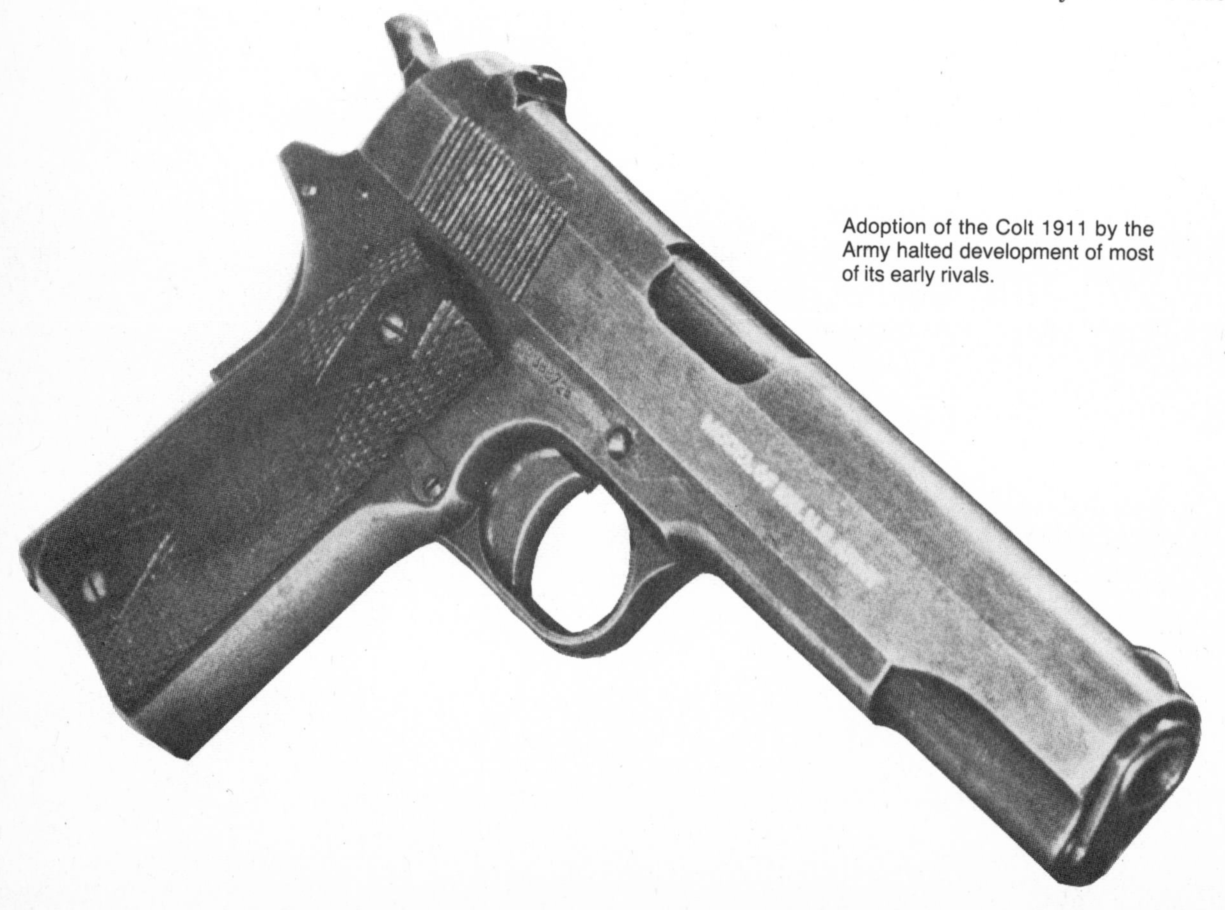

Adoption of the Colt 1911 by the Army halted development of most of its early rivals.

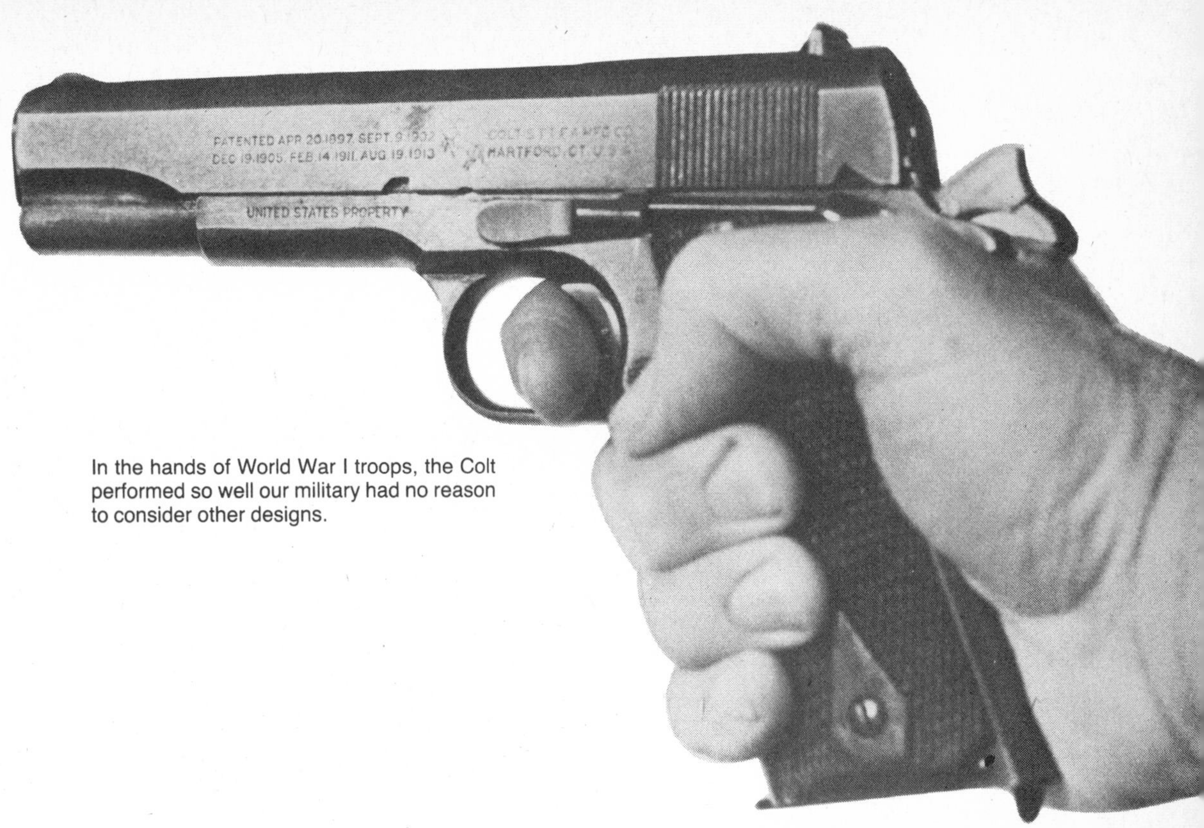

In the hands of World War I troops, the Colt performed so well our military had no reason to consider other designs.

After World War I, the superiority of the Colt was firmly established. The pistol is here carried at a 1923 training camp. The young man on the left will later become the writer's father. (Courtesy of Harold F. Malloy)

manufactured as to render any test without value . . ."

Knoble began working on automatic pistol designs about 1904 and made several prototypes. For the 1907 tests he prepared both double-action and single-action versions in 45-caliber. The double action is of special interest; it was a very early use of that feature in a semi-automatic pistol.

Knoble's plan was to have his pistols represented by von Lengerke & Detmold, New York outfitters. However, that firm dropped Knoble in order to demonstrate a planned 45 pistol by Mauser. The Mauser design, however, was never submitted. And when Mauser withdrew, so did von Lengerke & Detmold.

Knoble's pistols were tested without anyone who knew enough about them to keep the roughly-fitted prototypes functioning. The failure of his designs discouraged Knoble from further work with pistols. Although he retained his interest in firearms, his later efforts were all shoulder arms, and none gained prominence.

The White-Merrill pistol fired 211 rounds before the test was discontinued for unsatisfactory functioning.

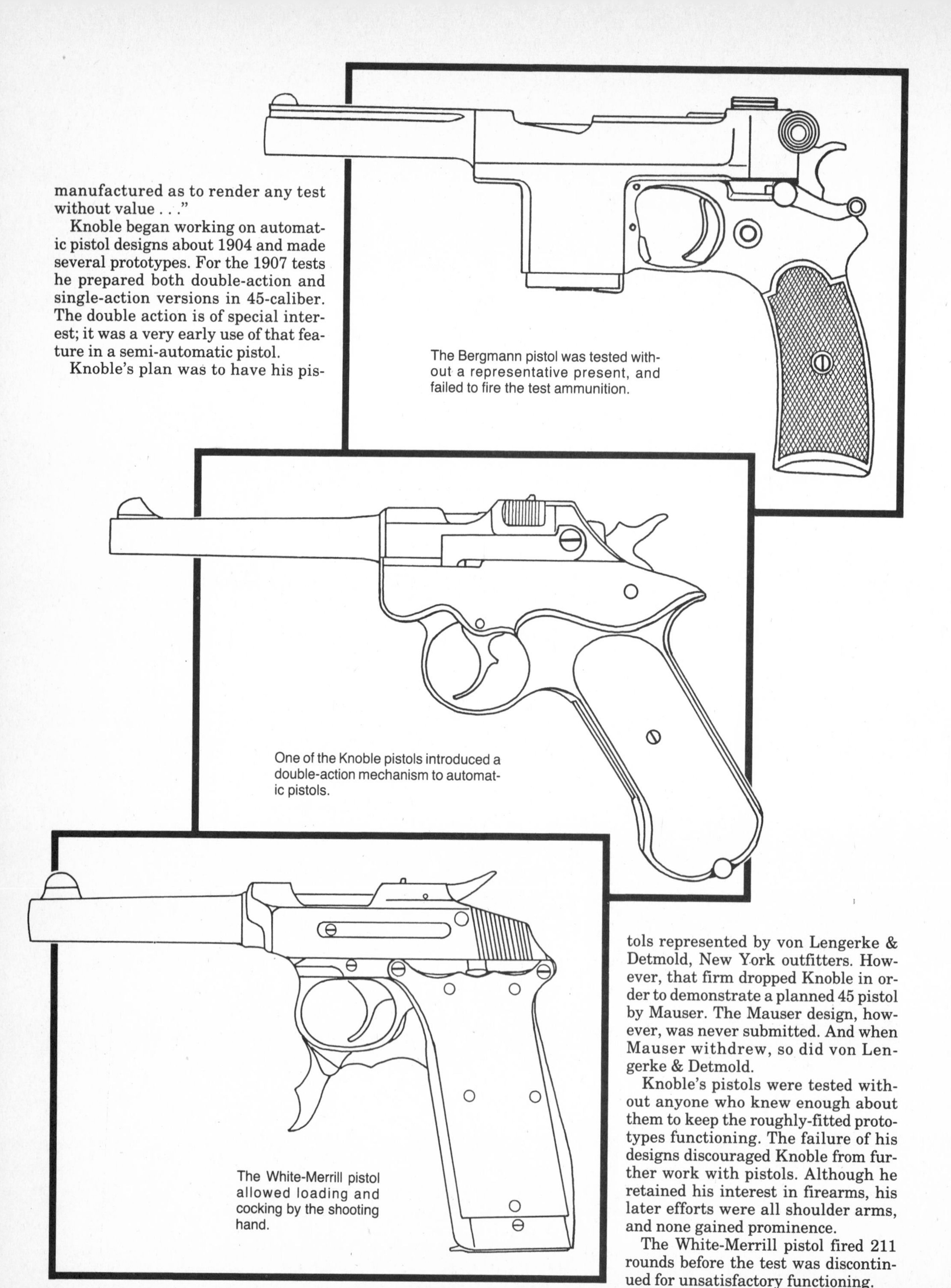

The Bergmann pistol was tested without a representative present, and failed to fire the test ammunition.

One of the Knoble pistols introduced a double-action mechanism to automatic pistols.

The White-Merrill pistol allowed loading and cocking by the shooting hand.

The feature most interesting about this arm was the special lever which allowed loading and cocking by the shooting hand. It could be loaded by means of a 10-shot stripper clip as well as with detachable magazines. The left grip was made of transparent material so that the number of rounds in the magazine could be seen. Both the front sight *and* the rear sight were fixed to the barrel, and accuracy was good. All-in-all, the pistol had much to recommend it, but at that early stage of development, it could not compete.

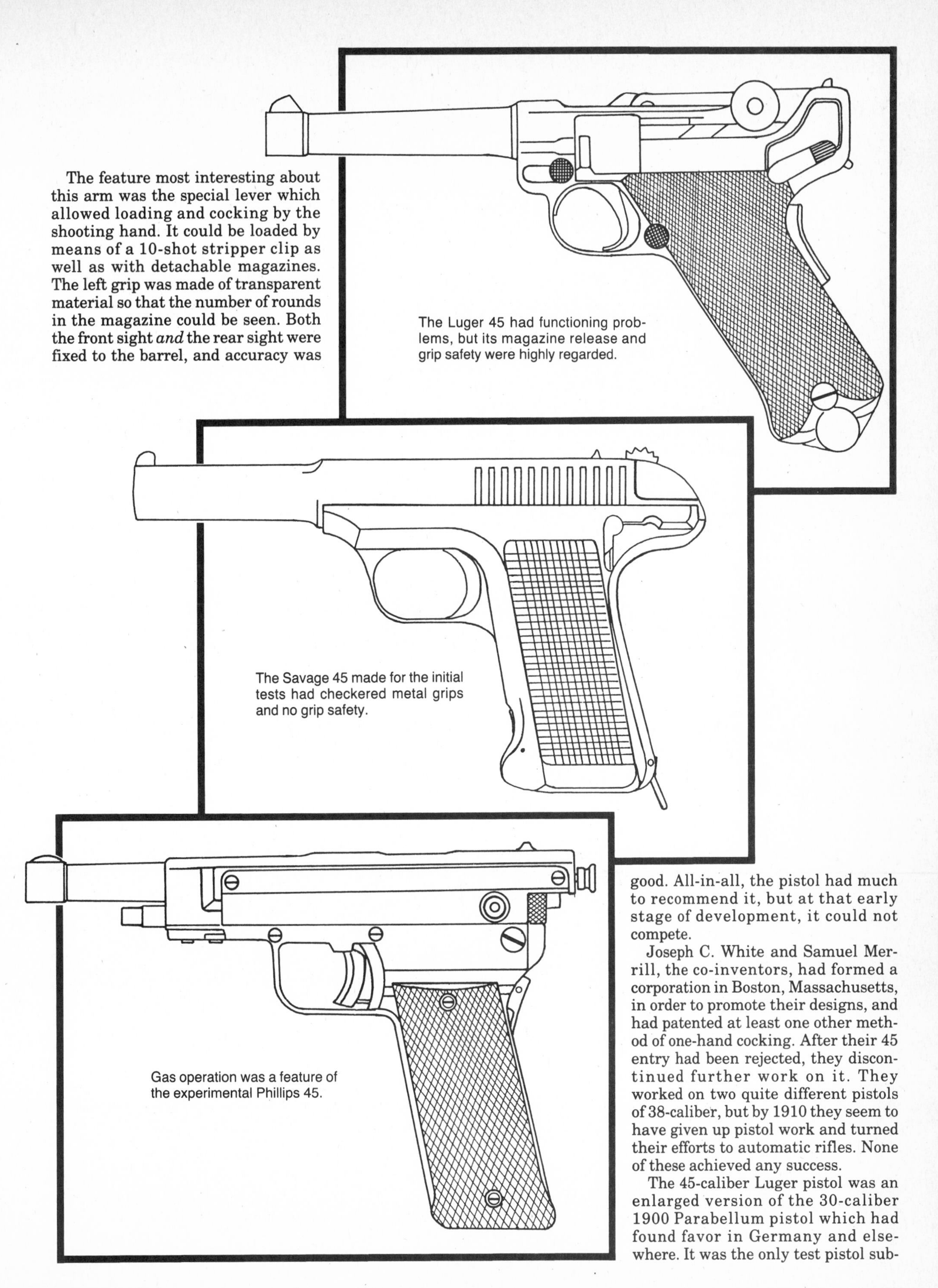

The Luger 45 had functioning problems, but its magazine release and grip safety were highly regarded.

The Savage 45 made for the initial tests had checkered metal grips and no grip safety.

Gas operation was a feature of the experimental Phillips 45.

Joseph C. White and Samuel Merrill, the co-inventors, had formed a corporation in Boston, Massachusetts, in order to promote their designs, and had patented at least one other method of one-hand cocking. After their 45 entry had been rejected, they discontinued further work on it. They worked on two quite different pistols of 38-caliber, but by 1910 they seem to have given up pistol work and turned their efforts to automatic rifles. None of these achieved any success.

The 45-caliber Luger pistol was an enlarged version of the 30-caliber 1900 Parabellum pistol which had found favor in Germany and elsewhere. It was the only test pistol submitted that had a grip safety, and one of only two that allowed ejection of the magazine by the shooting hand. These features were viewed favorably by the board and, indeed, the final victor—the Colt 1911—incorporated both of them.

The main objection to the Luger was that the toggle-joint action closed by the momentum of the moving parts, and not by positive spring action. This design required ammunition of high pressure level. Luger brought with him a supply of German-loaded cartridges, and at his request, the special ammunition, as well as that supplied by Frankfort Arsenal, was used in the tests. A total of 1022 rounds was fired. The Luger cartridges did not function appreciably better than those the Arsenal supplied, and most malfunctions related to feeding and final closing of the breechblock.

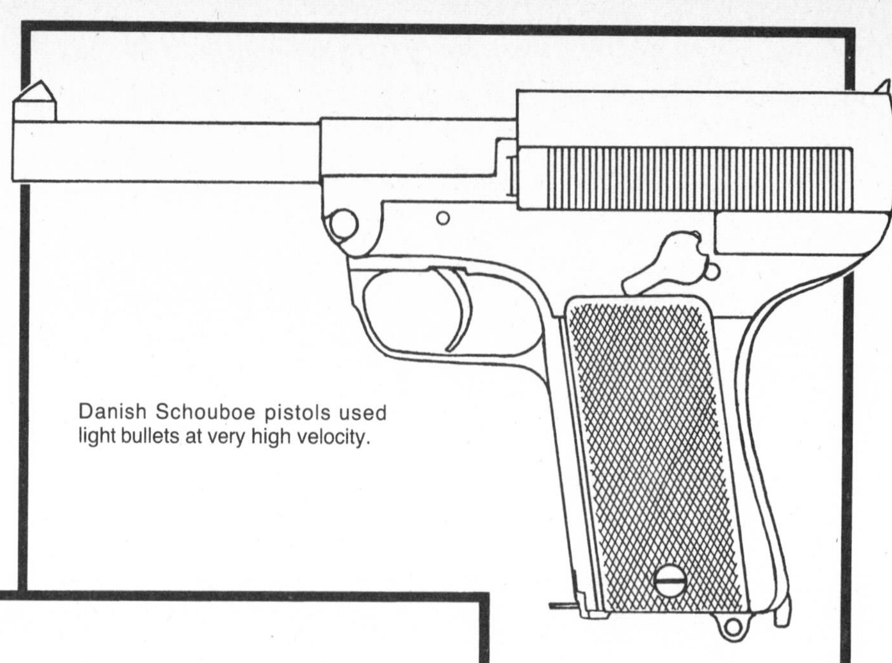

Danish Schouboe pistols used light bullets at very high velocity.

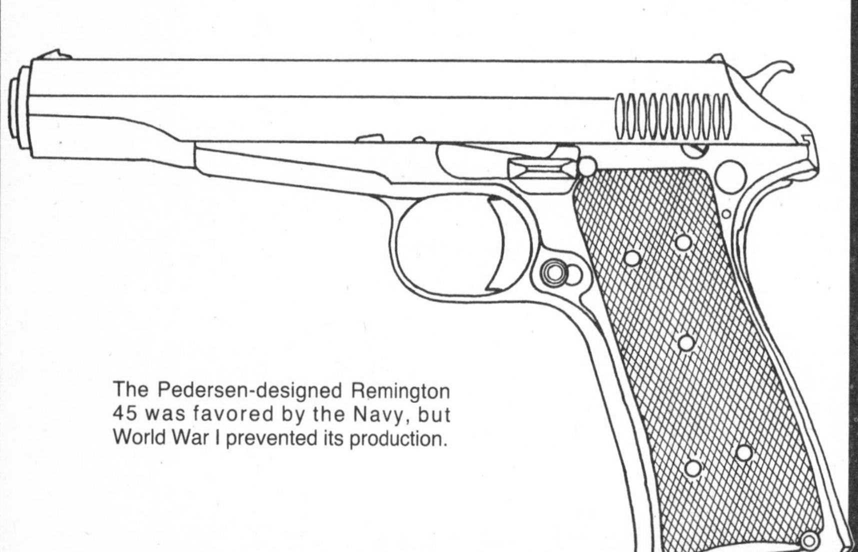

The Pedersen-designed Remington 45 was favored by the Navy, but World War I prevented its production.

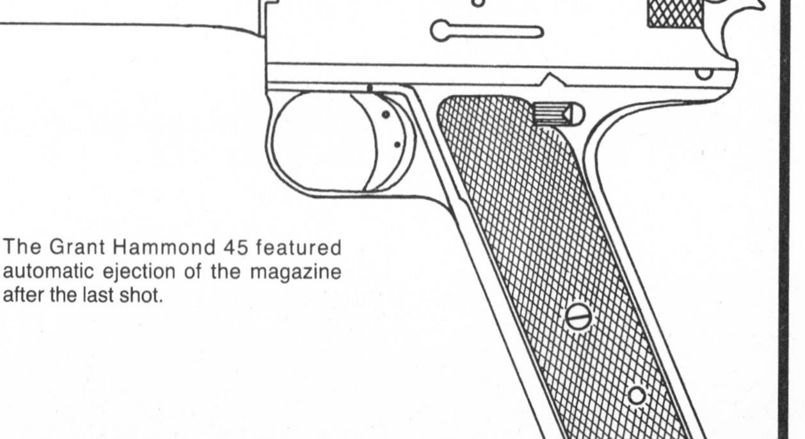

The Grant Hammond 45 featured automatic ejection of the magazine after the last shot.

The opinion of the Board was:

> The Luger automatic pistol, although it possesses manifest advantages in many particulars, is not recommended for a service test because its certainty of action, even with Luger ammunition, is not considered satisfactory . . .

However, the Luger 45 was to be given another chance. The Board authorized the purchase of 200 each of

Colt and Savage pistols for field tests. Colt readily accepted, but Savage was unwilling to tool up for such a relatively small production run. Whereupon, the contract was offered to Luger.

DWM apparently accepted the contract, then backed out shortly after acceptance. The 45 was probably enough different in size and contour so that existing machinery could not be used, and, like Savage, the firm may have been reluctant to redesign production facilities for a small contract. They may also have felt certain of the acceptance of their new 9mm pistol by the German government and wished to devote attention to preparations for its production. That pistol was indeed adopted in the following year as the P.08.

The failure of DWM to supply Lugers for the service tests gave Savage a chance to reconsider. Their pistol had been judged almost the equal of the established Colt, and lucrative future contracts might be awarded—a powerful incentive to the small company, then just 12 years old.

Savage Arms Company had been formed in 1894 by 37-year-old inventor Arthur Savage to produce his hammerless lever-action rifle. By the turn of the century, the company was looking for ways to expand its product line. About 1905, the company was approached by Elbert H. Searle of Philadelphia and his financial partner William D. Condit, of Des Moines, concerning a new automatic pistol invented by Searle. An arrangement was made whereby Savage would develop the pistol, and Searle would work with Savage for that purpose.

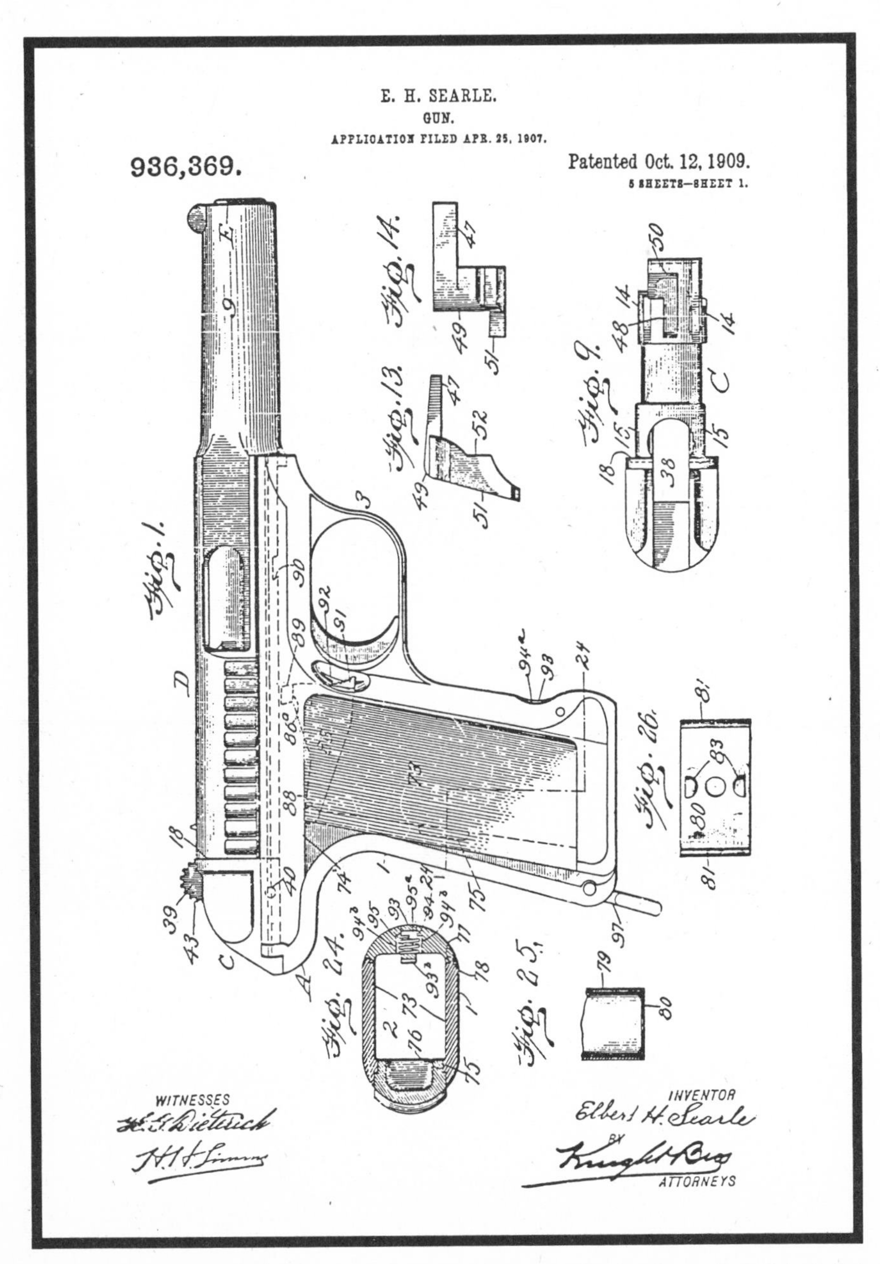

Searle's patent illustration shows a pistol that was essentially the Savage 45 of the initial tests. Note the large butt opening for the staggered-column magazine.

When the test trials were announced, Savage and Searle produced a 45-caliber specimen. The pistol had a rotating barrel which was held to the slide by a lug through a very small rotation of about 5 degrees. Rotation was supposedly resisted by the inertia of the bullet passing through the rifling.

The actual mechanics of this system have inspired considerable discussion. It seems safe to say that the barrel and slide are indeed locked at the instant of firing, but they unlock very rapidly. For all practical purposes, it was a delayed blowback system, with attendant heavier recoil than true locked-breech designs.

Containing only 34 parts, the Savage pistol was noted for its simplicity. The simple design enabled it to function well following the dust and rusting tests, and its overall functioning was actually slightly better than that of the Colt. Like the Luger, the magazine could be released by the shooting hand. The position of the latch on the lower front grip frame allowed release by the little finger of either hand. The innovative staggered magazine held eight rounds in a relatively short grip.

It has been reported that one or more of the original 1907 prototypes was lost or stolen during return to the factory after the tests. If this is so, it may have been partly responsible for the company's initial rejection of the field trial contract. Without the original test guns to examine, planning improvements would have been difficult.

Certainly, theft played a large part in the history of the Savage 45. The original shipment of 200 field trial pistols arrived at Springfield five short. Contemporary rumors credited the shortage to theft by foreign agents. Savage shipped five replacement pistols within a few weeks. However, many of the pistols developed problems with the magazines feeding improperly or unlatching prematurely. The 200 guns were shipped back to the factory for modification. This time, 72 of them were lost or stolen in transit. One can imagine Savage's frustration, but the company built more pistols, and the full number was tested in troop tests during 1910-1911.

The heavy recoil of the Savage

worked against it. One Ordnance tester was reported to have said that 500 rounds from the Savage was equivalent to 2000 rounds from the Colt. The recoil was not only uncomfortable for the shooter, it was harder on the pistol's own internal parts.

The end came during the final 6000-round endurance firing between the Savage and the improved Colt, in March, 1911. Both pistols fired 1000 rounds without problems, but the Savage's recoil began to take its toll.

The Colt, with inventor John M. Browning—then 56 years old—looking on, fired through the entire 6000 rounds without a problem.

The Savage would have outperformed most pistols, then or now, but it could not match that performance. In the final 1000 rounds, the Savage malfunctioned 31 times and five parts developed defects.

With the completion of the trials, Savage concentrated on its line of sporting rifles and the Searle-designed pocket pistols in 32 and 380 calibers. These scaled-down pistols were selling well, whereas the big 45, having lost the trials, was of relatively little interest to the general public.

There is some question as to how many Savage 45 pistols were made. Only a few prototypes were apparently made for the 1907 trials. Two-hundred had been ordered for the troop trials, but replacement of the stolen guns would have pushed that number to at least 277. It is logical that Savage, with the machinery ready to make a basically good pistol, would have made at least some for civilian sales. Various authorities have estimated the number of such additional guns at between 100 and 300.

The Savage pistol deserves a great deal of credit. Without the tough competition it offered Colt, there would not have been the need to refine the 1911 pistol to the peak of perfection it finally attained.

These trials and the subsequent adoption of the Model 1911 put an end to military efforts to develop a pistol on their own.

In the years between 1907-1909, the recoil-operated Pearce-Hawkins pistol was developed at Springfield Armory. The subsequent competition between the Savage and Colt pistols overshadowed all other weapons, and work on the Pearce-Hawkins was brought to a close.

The Phillips, also developed at Springfield Armory, was a departure from other designs in that it was gas-operated. At least one specimen was completed and tested, but it was not considered for service. The superiority of the new Colt design left little chance for such new developments.

Still, in 1912 another pistol was submitted for U.S. Army trial that had no possibility of serious consideration, but was of interest. From 1904, small quantities of the Danish Schouboe pistol had been produced in a special 11.35mm cartridge. The pistol was manufactured at the Dansk Rekylriffel Syndikat (DRS), Copenhagen, which produced Madsen machine guns. The pistol's inventor, Jens Schouboe, was Chief Engineer at DRS, and was able to keep the pistol in production in spite of its limited popularity.

Schouboe had started with a 7.65mm pistol in 1903. He wanted to make a large-bore military pistol but was faced with the limitations of his simple blowback system. He found that an extremely light bullet at high velocity would keep pressures within the limits of his design.

The 11.35mm Schouboe pistol was about the same caliber as the U.S. 45, but used a very different cartridge. The case was much shorter than that of the 45 ACP, but the big difference was in the design of the bullet. A cupronickel jacket covered a core of pine wood, protected at the base by a plug of aluminum. Weight was only about 63 grains. A heavy charge of powder pushed this light bullet at over 1600 fps. Accuracy was not particularly good, but was considered adequate for

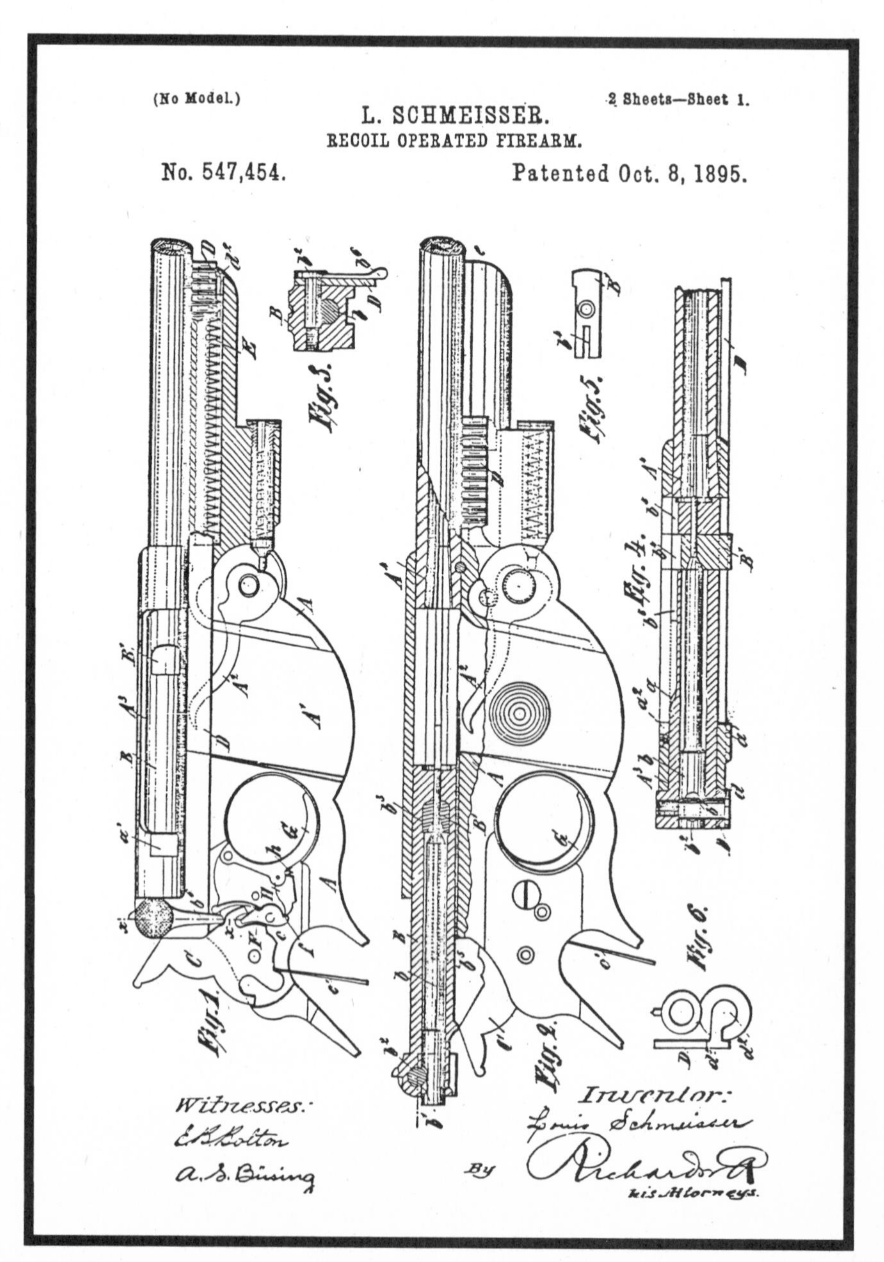

This 1895 patent, assigned to Bergmann, suggests that Louis Schmeisser was responsible for the basic Bergmann pistol design.

close-range military use. Penetration was surprisingly good.

Several variations of the 11.35mm Schouboe pistol were made, and it is not certain which one was tested by the U.S. Army at Springfield. The pistol functioned satisfactorily, but interest was focused on the high-velocity round it fired.

With the extensive testing of 1907-1911 just past, there was no chance for the Schouboe, but after its test, the Ordnance Department made up a lot of 45 ACP cartridges with wood-core bullets. Fired from the 1911 pistol, accuracy was very poor, and such experimentation stopped.

The Schouboe was never popular, even in Denmark. It was, however, the only native Danish pistol. For a time, the pistols were awarded as marksmanship prizes for Army officer cadets.

When Jens Schouboe retired from DRS in 1917, production of his pistols ended. In all probability, no more than 500 to 600 11.35mm pistols had been made.

As world war spread across Europe after 1914, there was renewed interest in military arms, and other pistols were offered for consideration.

Remington Arms Company had developed a 45-caliber pistol designed by John D. Pedersen of Jackson, Wyoming, and submitted it for U.S. Navy tests in 1917. The Remington pistol was favorably received by the Navy and contract negotiations were in progress. Then, on April 6, 1917, the United States entered the war.

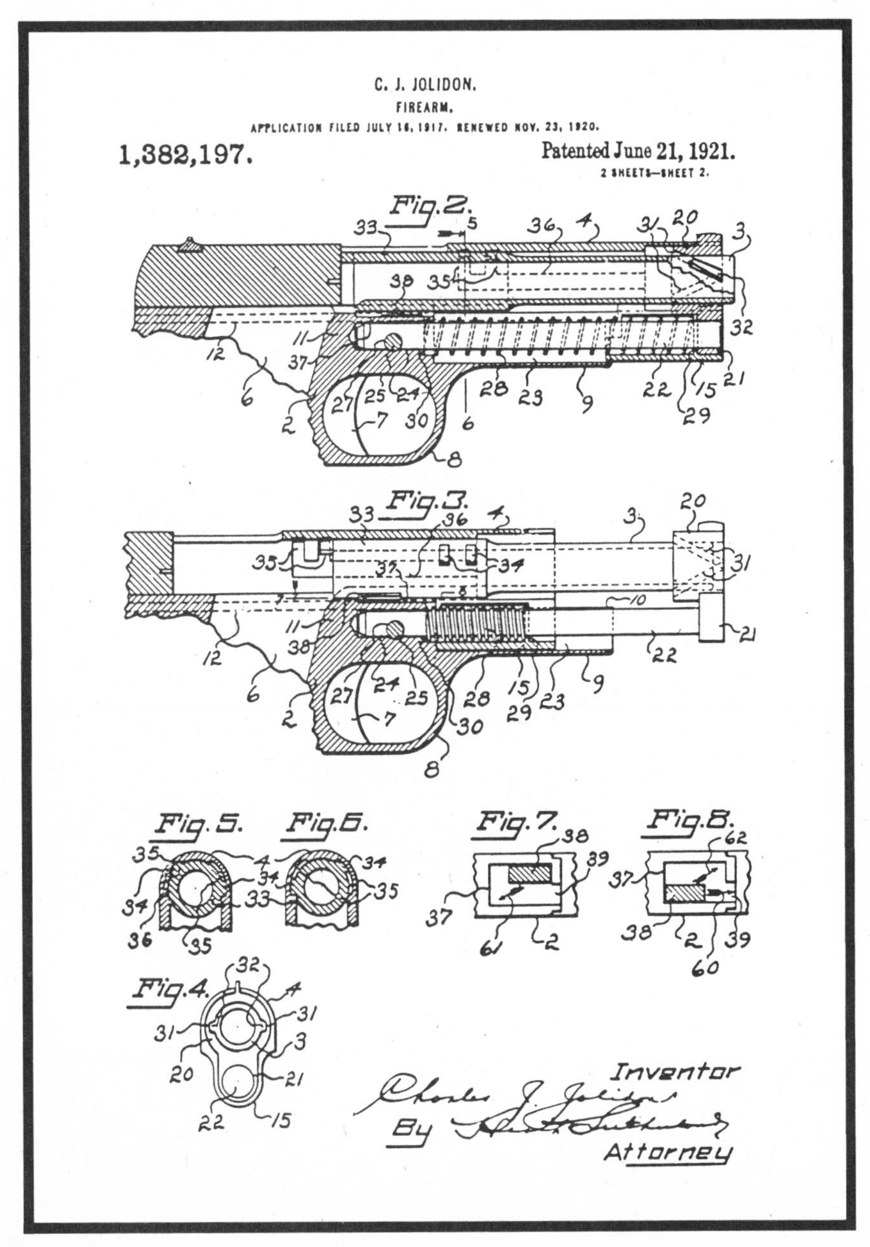

Charles Jolidon's pistol was a rotating-barrel modification of the Colt 1911. It functioned satisfactorily, but was not adopted.

The national interest lay in getting the greatest number of weapons possible into the hands of troops. Machinery to build the Colt pistol was already in operation. Instead of producing the Pedersen design, Remington was given a contract for 1911 pistols. The firm thus became one of the three manufacturers of 1911 pistols during World War I, the other manufacturers being Colt and Springfield Armory. There were 21,676 Remington 1911s made.

The Remington 45, the Pedersen design variously noted as the Model 1917 or Model 53, was never produced. The single existing specimen became resident in the Remington museum.

Pedersen gained fame as the inventor of the World War I "Pedersen Device." He continued his interest in semi-automatic arms, and developed both rifles and pistols. In the post-war years, Remington used the Pedersen design in a successful pocket pistol, the Model 51, which was offered in 32 and 380 calibers. Although the two firms had been competitors since cap-and-ball days, Remington never again challenged Colt in the field of big-bore military sidearms.

U.S. entry into the war had dashed Remington's chances of a contract for their new design, but the growing need for arms raised the hopes of other inventors during the wartime period.

In the summer of 1917, a new 45 pistol, the Grant Hammond, was submitted. Hammond, of Hartford, Connecticut, had been working on automatic pistol designs since about 1913. Around 1915, he concentrated his efforts on a relatively simple recoil-operated design which is sometimes referred to as the "Liberty" pistol.

His design seemed to studiously avoid any characteristics of the Colt 1911, and used a long exposed barrel, a hollow receiver and a cylindrical bolt. In many respects, the pistol is similar to a late White-Merrill prototype, and it is possible Hammond may have known of that earlier pistol.

The most interesting feature of the Grant Hammond pistol is the automatic ejection of the magazine after the last round has been fired. As the last round is fed, the magazine follower sets a spring-powered ejector mechanism. Then, as the action recoils from firing the last shot, the magazine catch is mechanically released and the magazine is ejected from the butt.

Aside from that novel feature,

Hammond's pistol could not offer any challenge to the Colt. It was not considered for service.

During the 1930s, Hammond became associated with High Standard Manufacturing Company. The experimental 45-caliber High Standard pistols of that period show some similarities to his 1917 pistol.

If the Colt 1911 could not be replaced, perhaps it could be improved? At least one inventor felt that if the 1911 could be simplified, it could be made faster and greater numbers could be produced.

Charles J. Jolidon, of Hartford, submitted a new design in 1917. Jolidon had had an uncertain relationship with Colt as an inventor and was familiar with the Colt pistols. His design was based on the 1911 and his trial specimen was made from a commercial 1911, but modified to use a rotating barrel.

Jolidon's design actually decreased the number of parts needed and simplified some of the machining. The specimen provided apparently performed satisfactorily in an Ordnance test, but there was never any real possibility of production. The time spent to retool for a new design would have more than offset any gains the simplification would have provided.

When the war ended, there was little reason to consider this design further. Jolidon worked on a series of blowback pocket pistols, none of which attained any success.

If there is any negative feature about the 1911, it is that it discouraged development of alternate concepts.

Automatic pistol development in the early stages at the turn of the century was closely related to the quest for military contracts. By the end of the 1907-1911 test trials, the 1911 Colt emerged as the most thoroughly-tested, most reliable and most powerful semi-automatic pistol in the service of any country.

By 1918 it had been proven in battle, was familiar to millions as a military arm, and was available commercially. There was little incentive for anyone to introduce a competing big-bore automatic.

Still, the Colt's early rivals had influences. The rejected pistols represented a variety of concepts. Many were suppressed by the Colt's superiority, but reappeared later in different forms.

The double-action feature, introduced by the 1907 Knoble, was used three decades later in some German pistols. Now, most new designs have double-action mechanisms.

The increased capacity of a detachable staggered magazine appeared with the 1907 Savage. After several decades, it reappeared with the 1935 Browning and now seems almost mandatory for any new centerfire automatic.

The push-button magazine release was introduced by the Luger, quickly adapted to the Colt, and has been almost universal for big-bore automatics. The first attempt at an ambidextrous release came with the Savage.

Different methods of loading and cocking by the shooting hand were introduced by the early White-Merrill pistols. Several European designs appeared between the wars, but were short lived. Just recently, new concepts of one-handed cocking have gained acceptance with the Heckler & Koch P9S and P7 pistols.

Gas-operated pistols—the Wildey and the Eagle—have recently appeared, recalling the Phillips pistol of Springfield Armory experiments.

With the emphasis on speed of reloading found in modern action shooting competition, we may even someday see reintroduced the magazine-ejecting feature of the 1917 Grant Hammond.

The Colt 1911 design lives on, and remains essentially unchanged. It is still considered by many to be the best pistol in the world. The also-rans are all gone, but some of their features influence modern design. ●

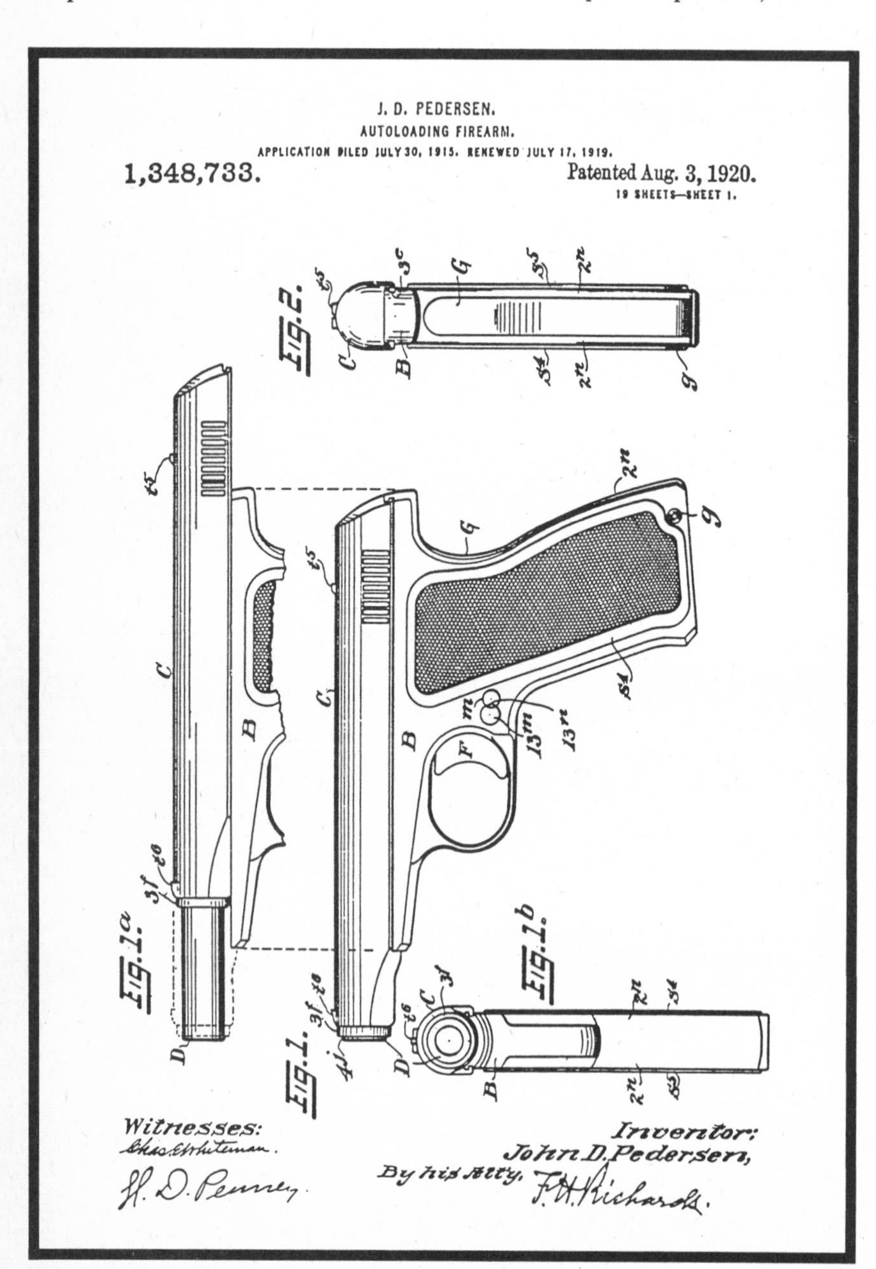

Pedersen's excellent pistol design, although not produced in 45-caliber, went on to become the popular Remington Model 51 pocket pistol.

Beretta 92F.
Quality, reliability and firepower you can depend on.

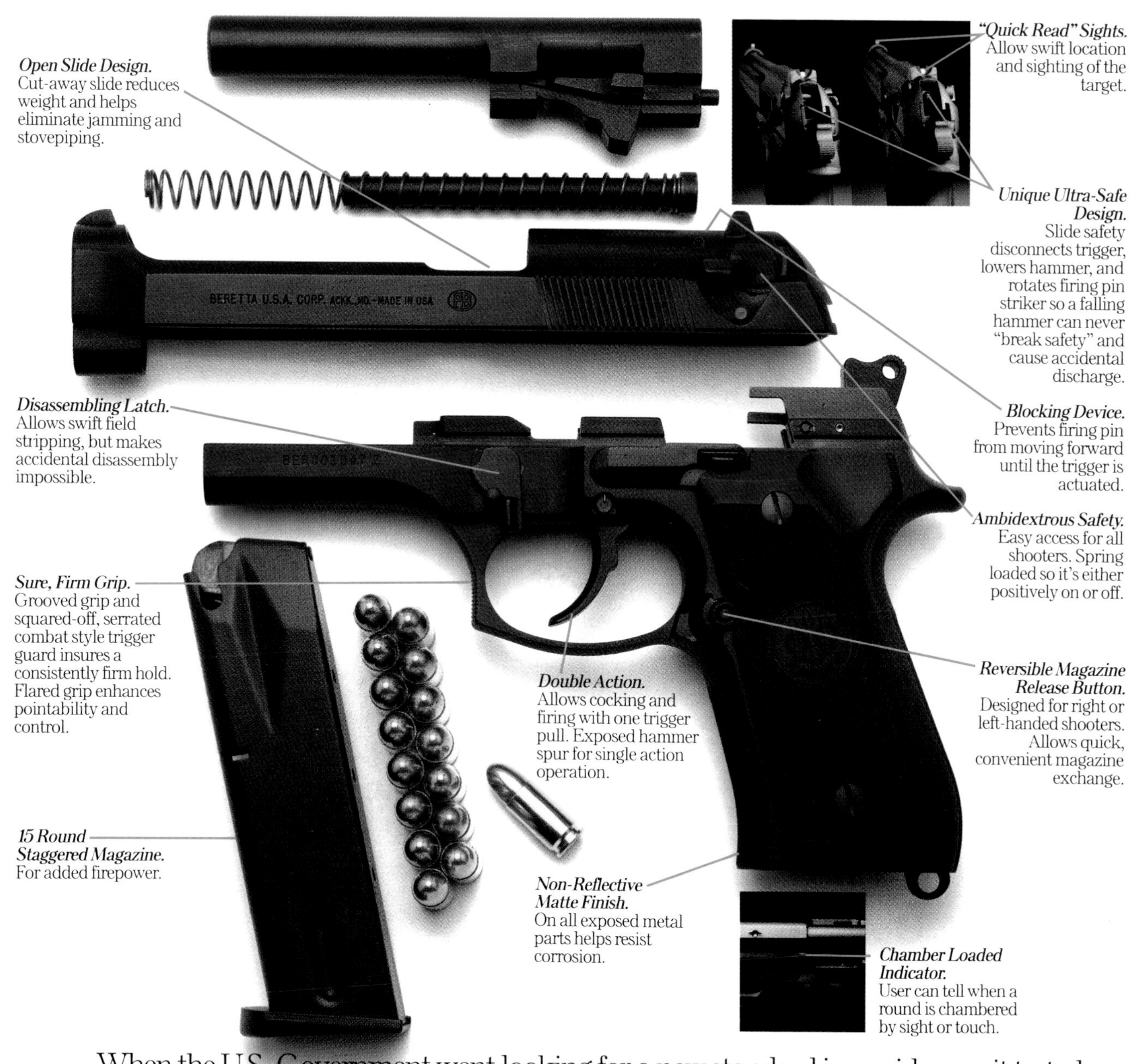

When the U.S. Government went looking for a new standard issue sidearm, it tested the best pistols in the world. The Beretta 92F 9mm Parabellum thoroughly outclassed the competition in every government performance trial.

In Accuracy. Safety. Reliability. Firepower. In grip, feel, lightness and pointability. The Military was convinced. Now America's fighting men are carrying the finest 9mm sidearm in the world.

Consistently superior quality and service have also convinced hundreds of law enforcement agencies like the North Carolina Highway Patrol and Texas Rangers to switch to Beretta. You'll be convinced too.

Check out the 92F along with the complete line of quality Beretta sporting and competition firearms at your authorized Beretta dealer today, or contact Beretta U.S.A., 17601 Beretta Drive, Accokeek, Maryland 20607, (301) 283-2191.

Beretta U.S.A.

REMEMBER WHEN OUR HEROES WERE STRAIGHT SHOOTERS?
©1987 Red Ryder Enterprises, Inc.
The Red Ryder® 50th Anniversary BB Gun: Celebrating an enduring American legend.
In this day and age, folks aren't always what they seem. But for a whole generation of American kids, Red Ryder® was the real thing: a cowboy hero who sat tall in the saddle, said what was on his mind, and swung from the heels when trouble started.
Red's fans didn't just follow his exploits at the movie house and in the comics: millions owned their very own Daisy Red Ryder BB Gun. Maybe you had one, too. And you probably know someone who's the perfect age to experience the fun of learning to shoot safely with their own Red Ryder.
Because this is the perfect beginner's BB gun. Designed for smaller hands, it's lightweight and low-velocity. But it's the special features of this anniversary edition that make it a once-in-a-lifetime gift. It's the original design you remember, with a leather saddle thong and branded walnut stock. We've inlaid a gleaming brass medallion to commemorate Red Ryder's unique place in history. And each gun has its own serial number, making it a real collector's item.
DAISY MFG. CO. 1988 1938 RED RYDER
TWO BIG EXTRAS ADD UP TO EVEN MORE FUN.
This special edition Red Ryder carries a 50 Year Warranty — by a long shot, the best airgun warranty ever. Finally, as part of Red's birthday celebration, we're adding a free Red Ryder strongbox and 5,000 Daisy Quick Silver™ BBs with every gun.
So don't let your heroes fade away. Give a Red Ryder 50th Anniversary BB Gun to someone special. Or collect one for yourself.
For ages 10 and up with adult supervision.

Daisy®
FIRST IN AIRGUNS.

NORTH AMERICAN
ARMS
All guns
represented,
are actual size.

Binoculars found this buck; a careful stalk provided the shot at only 10 paces.

Make Your Muzzleloader Work for You by Sam Fadala

THERE'S A lot more to hunting than bagging game. Everybody knows that. Hunting is a total outdoor experience. However, maybe you've noticed that your tag wrapped around the antler of a deer makes you feel better about the miles you walked, the snow you pushed , the cold felt and the total effort you put out. A special muzzleloader season, or any other hunt with a smokepole, need not be an exercise in frustration in this respect. You *can* manage your muzzleloader for freezer-filling.

The first step toward proper big game muzzleloader management is picking the right frontloader *for you*. At the very least, handle several in the gunstore. Try a shot or two with friends' favorite rifles. The dyed-in-the-buckskin boys, of course, will turn noses upward at the mere sight of a non-historical piece. Be aware of that. For these shooters, a replica of a past rifle is the only one to own. You try the non-replica muzzleloaders, too, and if one of them suits, go with it.

Many of the prettiest, best-made muzzleloaders in antique style are long-barreled and fairly heavy, which was also a tradition of the past. Packing and managing these heavier long-rifles in the field is entirely possible, but you may prefer something lighter and shorter to start with. That's why I say take a look at the non-replicas. In the early stages of black powder game-harvesting, the practical-sized non-replica rifle may be the wiser choice.

It might as well be a percussion model. Properly constructed flintlock rifles shoot with amazing reliability. However, the sparktosser does require a bit more hands-on attention than the percussion rifle. Newcomers should stick with the latter.

Ball or conical? Making the muzzleloader work for you means gaining the most accuracy from the rifle you choose. Pick ball or pick conical bullet based upon your rifle's choice. Generally speaking, twist is going to dictate which one works best in a given piece; the faster twists stabilizing conicals, the slower twists working better for patched round balls.

When you buy a 50-caliber Lyman rifle with a 1-66 rate of twist, for example, you can bet it's a ball-shooter.

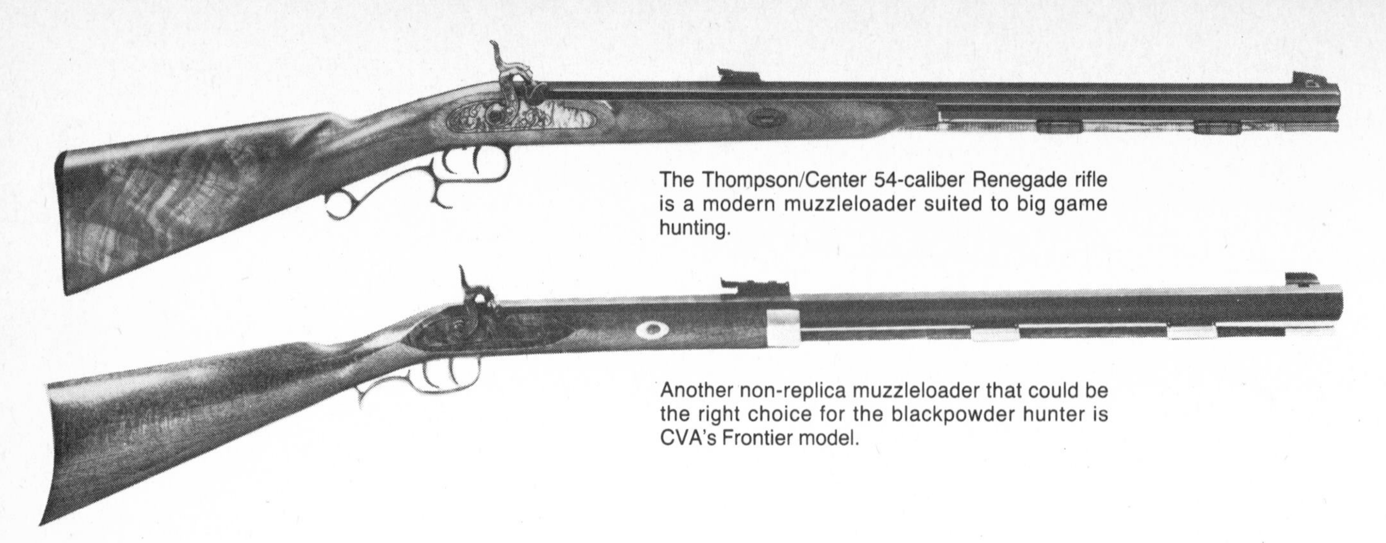

The Thompson/Center 54-caliber Renegade rifle is a modern muzzleloader suited to big game hunting.

Another non-replica muzzleloader that could be the right choice for the blackpowder hunter is CVA's Frontier model.

If you happen to purchase, on the other hand, a 50-caliber Navy Arms Mark I Hawken with the 1-36 rate of twist, consider it a conical-shooter. The latter does not sound like a very rapid rate of twist, but 1-36 is a quick twist, muzzleloader-wise.. Some quick-twist rifles do shoot patched round balls well, but generally only at lower muzzle velocities.

What about actual field performance of the two projectiles? A round-ball-shooting muzzleloader worth its salt will propel its patched pumpkin at up to 2000 fps MV, or thereabouts. The conical-tosser is going to be more in the 1500 fps MV ballpark. So the sphere starts out faster, but loses its velocity rapidly. The conical starts out slower, but retains velocity better. It's a trade-off in trajectory, and the two types of sight-in very much the same.

Harvesting big game with either sphere or conical means getting close, comparitively. You don't have to get spear-chucking close; you don't have to get bow and arrow close; but the muzzleloader is no 30-06. I consider 125 yards about as far as a hunter should shoot on deer-sized game. Seventy-five yards and closer is a lot better for larger-than-deer game, such as elk. (OK, I do have a special custom-made muzzleloader that has enough snort left at 125 yards to drop the biggest elk on the mountain. It's 54 caliber, heavy barrel, 1⅛ inches across the flats, modern gunbarrel-quality steel, 1-34 rate of twist and it handles a heavy dose of FFg that propels a 460-grain Buffalo Bullet Co. conical at up to 1800 fps MV. But that's an unusual piece, very strongly constructed, and plenty heavy.)

The ball is ruled by the wind, drifting off course in even a modest breeze. It can be deflected in the brush by a pinky-finger-sized twig. It sheds its velocity like water off a tin roof. And yet, properly placed from modest range, anything you shoot with this blob of lead keels over. Penetration of the ball is far and away greater than paper ballistics suggest possible. I've driven lead pills through mule deer rib to rib, for example, and through game bigger than deer. The ball often stops on the off-side and I have a collection of saucer-flat lead blobs, wafer-thin, that made it through a few *feet* of big game animal carcass. I remain in awe of the patched ball.

Fine accuracy with a muzzleloader is not uncommon. This target was made at 100 yards with the custom 54-caliber longrifle being displayed by Dean Zollinger. Rifle has been chronographed at 1800 fps with 460-grain Buffalo Bullet Co. bullet. That's 3300 foot pounds of energy at the muzzle.

But that doesn't mean I lack faith in the conical. Caliber for caliber, there can be no doubt that the elongated projectile carries a more authoritative message to the big game animal, provided it's fired from a rifle which allows sufficient powder charge to get that conical moving in the 1500 fps-plus class. I've chronographed a few "favorite loads" of personal shooting friends which gave the conical as low as 900 fps MV, and I'll take a ball of the same caliber starting at 2000 fps over that sort of anemia.

Load for surefire ignition if you want the muzzleloader to work for you in the big game field. The most annoying sound in all of blackpowderdom is *click*. And *psst—boom* is bad, too. Design is of first importance in ignition. Well-designed caplocks go off like clockwork. Ill-designed models don't. You'll find out which is which at the range by firing your friend's rifles; then don't buy one with an iffy ignition system. Even the best-designed frontloader won't fire on cue if you don't do your part, so keep the route from nipple vent to breech clear through proper after-shooting cleanup.

Before loading for big game, run a cleaning patch downbore to get rid of any preserving grease or oil. Run a pipe cleaner through the nipple and as far into the system as possible to soak up any oil there. Place a cap on the unloaded rifle and point the muzzle at a leaf, or bit of paper—anything that the force from the percussion cap can blow out of the way—and pull the trigger. When the hammer drops on the cap, the energy from the detonation should blast any small object away from the muzzle. If that does not occur, remove the nipple. Clean your rifle. Do not load up for big game until you're sure the route from percussion cap to powder charge is clear.

There are a few more wrinkles. Try various ball sizes. Often, but not always, a ball which closely fits bore dimensions gives best results. Use a .495-inch ball, for example, if your 50-caliber rifle will accept it with a patch of .010-inch or more. Use strong patch material. The patch is not a true gasket which seals hot gasses behind the ball; however, it's vital to the load for more reasons.

The patch transfers the rotation imparted by the rifling to the ball. It prevents any possible leading of the bore. It holds lubrication in its fibers. It helps in wedging the ball down upon the powder charge where it belongs, rather than allowing the projectile to ride upbore, creating a gap that might, upon firing, cause a walnut (lump) in the barrel or worse. It takes up the windage in the bore. A tight patch offers more inertia through friction which in turn aids obturation (bullet upset) in the bore to gain a better gas seal, so indirectly patches aid in keeping gases behind the ball, though they are not true gaskets. The patch also helps to keep the powder charge compressed, and compressed black powder burns more uniformly from one shot to the next as compared with loosely packed powder.

The patch does a lot of work, and it's worth safeguarding from the ravages of the burning powder charge. This is easily accomplished if you have hornets—real hornets, the buzzing insects that sting. Gather up a nest or two (after the hornets have left) and you have a large supply of patch backing. A couple thin sheets of hornet nest leaf pushed down on top of the powder charge make a good barrier between the powder charge and the projectile patch. The stuff will go up in smoke if you touch a match to it, but down in the bore, it's like asbestos. One of my rifles burns 120 grains of FFg, but hornet nest buffer keeps the patch nearly new.

If you must use the flinter, here's how to make that style work better for you. Again insure that the channel from the flame to powder charge is clear and the bore oil-free; a pipe

Stalk for the blackpowder shot. Get close. This hunter is about ready to bag a *javelina* at close range; here he's working for his muzzleloader, sure enough.

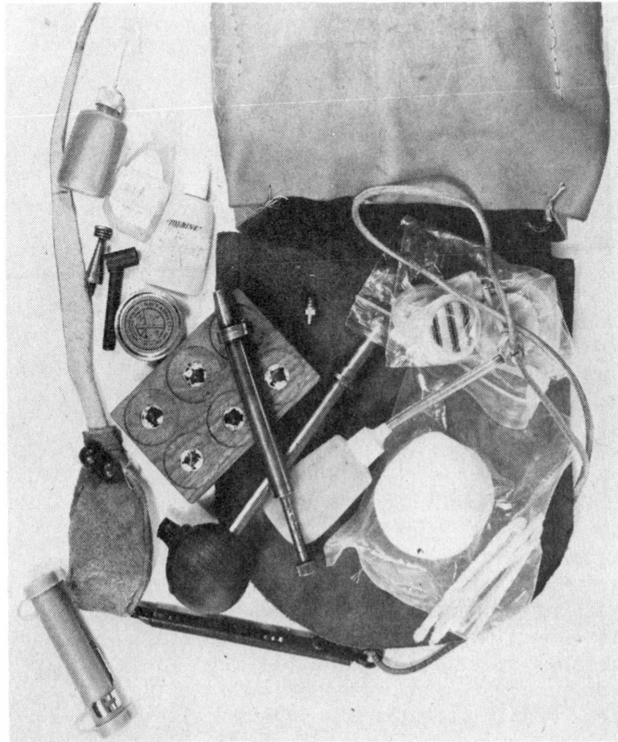

At lower left is a Butler Creek readyload unit which Fadala pockets; the other paraphernalia rides in his rifle bag, constitutes a complete field repair and reloading kit.

cleaner does the former, cleaning patches the latter. Next, block the touchhole with a vent pick or pipe cleaner and snap the frizzen forward to keep the block in place as you load the powder charge. Then seat the projectile firmly, with the touchhole block still in place. After the missile is fully seated, carefully remove the touchhole obstruction. Don't try to drag powder granules from the main charge in the breech into the touchhole. That's just what you want to *avoid*.

Fill the pan one-half to two-thirds full of FFFFg pan powder, all of it to the *outside* of the pan away from the touchhole. I carry my flinter angled so that the pan powder remains to the outside of the pan. The idea is to have a clear touchhole which will act as a route for the flash coming off of the pan powder. The flash darts across the pan, through the clear touchhole and into the main charge in the breech. If the touchhole is packed with powder, that powder has to burn out of the way before the flame can reach the breech, creating a *fuse* that slows ignition.

There is still more to making the muzzleloader work for you. Your zero should be correct. Start at about 13 yards. Get the holes to center in the bull's eye at that range. Then move out to 75 yards and put the projectile on the money again, if further sight adjustment is indeed necessary. This will provide a trajectory of right-on at 75, an inch or so low at 100 and about 6 inches low at 125 yards. Even the smallish pronghorn buck will give you a dead-center hold out to 125 yards with the muzzleloader so sighted.

You have to learn to carry the piece black powder style. Along with other obvious benefits of the cartridge age came the sling. I haven't a modern big game rifle without one. I haven't a muzzleloader with one. You learn, however, that the fine balance of the better longrifles allows a relatively easy carry, and the midsection is free for hand-carrying. You'll learn to shift the rifle from one elbow crook to the other, one hand to the other.

Boom! The ball is on the way. The next move is to reload. As a standard practice, the big game hunter should restoke his charcoal burner immediately after firing in the field, no matter how telling the shot is. And this means a speedloader, homemade or commercial. Black powder shops have the latter in various forms. My own Butler Creek speedloader holds powder on one end, ball on the other, with a plastic patch to facilitate that quick second shot. The speedloader also

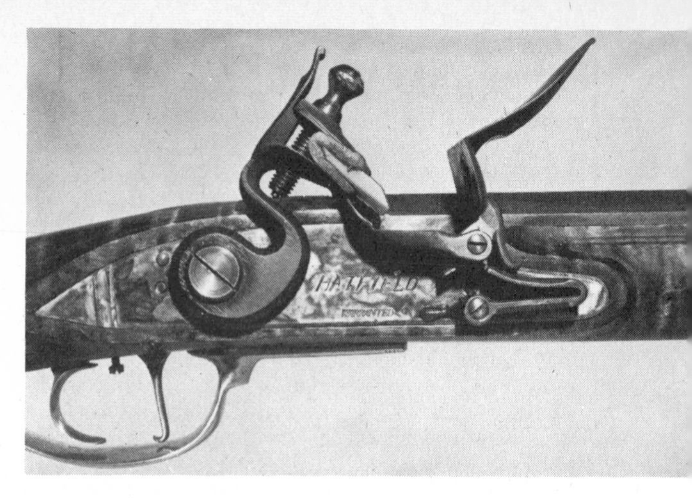

The well-designed flintlock, such as this Siler lock on a Hatfield muzzleloader, will "go off" with reliability when properly loaded.

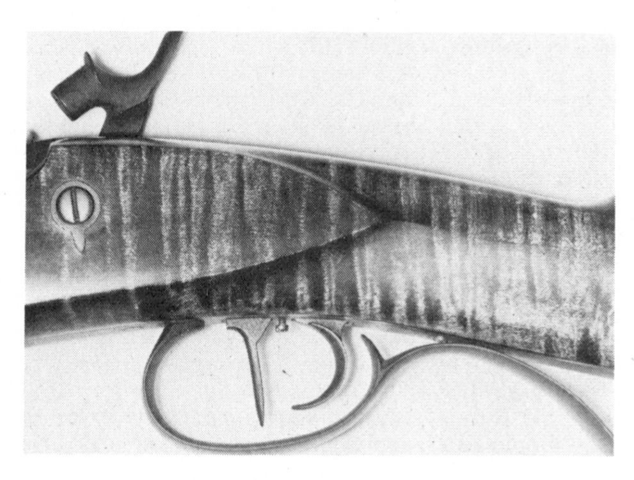

Part of making the muzzleloader work for you is learning how to use such special features as double-set triggers.

The author with his 36-caliber Hatfield flintlock rifle and a start on a bag of squirrels. Small game hunting can offer a lot of transfer of knowledge and blackpowder gun-handling to the big game field.

holds a fresh cap at the ready. It only takes seconds to dump the powder charge, flick the plastic patch down-muzzle, ball on top, ramrod ball and patch firmly on the powder charge and recap. I seat the plastic patch first, then the ball. Running both home at once in my favorite front-loader won't work.

Naturally, the muzzle is held away from the face. No matter how fast the hands move, any spark downbore is burned out before the fresh charge of powder hits it. I've never had a flare-up, but safety is the first consideration of all shooting, so the muzzle is held away from the face during the reloading operation just as it's held away from the face and fingers during the original loading stage.

I carry two speedloaders ready to go, generally in a pocket of my hunting shirt. But all the rest of my muzzleloader paraphernalia is cached in a shooting bag—popular name, "possibles bag," though the latter was entirely a different container originally. Part of making the muzzleloader work for you is carrying the right black powder gear in the hunting field. My bag, a leather Uncle Mike's model, handsome through simplicity, has all of the necessary accoutrements to maintain the muzzleloader in the field, barring an unlikely broken part.

The bag contains a small flask of powder. The flask eliminates the need for a powder horn. It holds enough powder for several extra shots, which will be enough for a day's work. A little ball bag, homemade in this case, holds extra projectiles. The short starter goes in the shooting bag, too. So does an extra nipple, some cleaning patches, extra shooting patches, pre-cut to size and pre-lubed, solvent (use a plastic eye wash bottle to hold your solvent), an in-line capper, filled with percussion caps, of course, an adjustable powder measure, a screw, a worm and a jag, all of which attach to the rifle's ramrod. Also a little bag of hornet nest. A nipple wrench is there, too. So is a vent pick. Pipe cleaners. One clean rag. All fit neatly into the leather shooting bag that rests at your side.

The right flintlock load puts FFFFg blackpowder along the outside of the pan only, not up against the touchhole. This permits the flash to dart across the pan and through the touchhole to the main powder charge.

The 54-caliber 460-grain Buffalo Bullet Company missile is a lot of bullet.

If your patches are not eaten up, as this patch was not, there is no need to use a buffer.

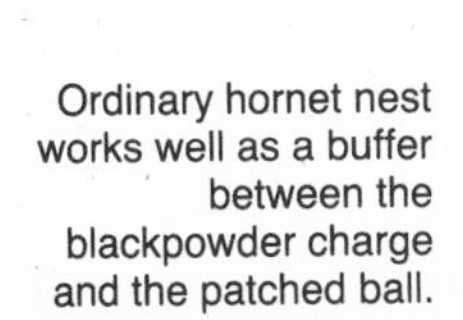

Ordinary hornet nest works well as a buffer between the blackpowder charge and the patched ball.

Part of making the muzzleloader work for you is working for the muzzleloader. You do that by hunting black powder style. If you're in whitetail coverts, pay special attention to the wind and hope for quiet ground cover, damp earth or snow that will allow a quiet approach. Maintain field position so you can get a black powder shot. For example, busting onto the edge of a meadow in hopes of getting a shot 300 yards across that field is no way to make a muzzleloader work for you. Skirt the edge, wind in your face, slowly, so that if you do get a shot, it will be within range. In the open lands, the single most effective technique I've come across to make frontloaders effective has been to take the high ground, glassing from that vantage point. A good stalk can be mounted, one which will put your black powder close for one perfect shot, once you have quarry in view.

Practice helps generate smooth field handling, too. I like to use a 32 or 36-caliber muzzleloader for small game hunting and tin can-rolling. The 32 can be cheaper to shoot than a 22 rimfire. Only 10 grains of FFFg gives about 22 Long Rifle muzzle velocity to the 45-grain .310-inch ball. That's 700 shots for a pound of powder.

Turning from the modern big game rifle to a sootburner does upgrade the challenge. Let no one tell you that you can do with a frontloader what you can do with a cartridge rifle, especially in open country hunting. That challenge comes, however, with an enjoyment-back guarantee. It's a real thrill to put a tag on a black powder buck or bull. Misfires, hangfires and inaccurate low-power loads are not the enjoyable part, so learn to make the muzzleloader work for you. ●

Double Rifles Had Glamour

The day is past, but the stories will be with us a long time for these reasons. . . .

by HOWARD E. FRENCH

On closing with heavy game, many double shooters kept extra shells in their left hand for a quick reload.

MOST PEOPLE think of double rifles as colossal-sized things, the old blackpowder rifle heaving a lead slug about the size of a shot-putter's ball while the Nitro Express rifles had banana-sized bullets spinning away under a heavy charge of Cordite.

Like most gun stories there is a bit of truth in that tale, but only a bit of truth. Not all double rifles were designed to deliver smashing power to the animal, with equal power to your shoulder. There were other double rifles. Now these weren't sissy doubles, just regular rifles used for shooting deer-sized and even smaller game. In England, people were used to the double shotgun—side-by-side of course. What could be more natural than to have a double rifle of milder recoil than an 8-bore throwing a 2-ounce bullet or 577 Nitro Express tossing a 750-grain slug, for shooting local deer and elk-sized game?

Several English firms even made double rifles in 22 rimfire! I suspect that most of these guns were made to prove that the companies could make such a small bore rifle, but they were made. Between bombs from Zeppelins in WWI and bombs, rockets and other goodies in WWII, some records of the famous English firearms firms have been destroyed. Despite this fact it is generally considered that about half a dozen 22 rimfires were made.

I have fired such a rifle, and it was incredible. A tiny, tiny double that shot beautifully and, when you opened it, the ejectors tossed the empties side by side, not a small feat for such small cases. Since so few were ever made, they really do not enter into the lore of the double, except as a tiny footnote. But there were lots of smaller bore rifles that started out with the old blackpowder arms that were used for smaller game, some of them fired what were called rook and kangaroo cartridges and were touted for use on seals, rabbits and for small bucks.

Actually some of the bigger blackpowder calibers, like the common 450 x 3¼, were often used to shoot deer-sized game. It sounds ridiculous to talk about a 45-caliber cartridge with a case 3¼ inches long being used on relatively small game, but the Express version was made for deer-sized animals. You couldn't compare the U.S. 45-70, loaded with a 500-grain bullet backed up by 70 grains of blackpowder with the 450 Black Powder Express round. The 450 3¼ cartridge, even with 120 grains of blackpowder, was loaded with light hollow-nosed bullets for roe deer, whose weight is about like that of a goat, as well as for the much larger stags. The 450 bullet, in either the lightweight hollow or solid slug, did its work on both animals. Express loads included bullets as light as 270-grain hollowpoints. In the U.S., a 45-caliber rifle cartridge loaded with a 300-grain bullet was known as an Express round.

Actually the very term "Express," so often used in connection with double rifles, started out as a muzzle-loading rifle. Purdey and Co. brought out an Express Train rifle chambered in 70-bore—the 70 means that 70 balls that fit the bore would make 1 pound (in bore dimension about like a 40-caliber)—that used a 200-grain belted bullet backed by 110 grains of blackpowder. Since the powder charge was over half the weight of the bullet, this was a fairly flat shooting rifle for a blackpowder muzzle-loading arm. Naturally the name "Express" came from the non-stop trains, the most rapid form of travel before motor cars and aircraft came into use.

At any rate the "Express" term was used for many double rifles using light hollow-nosed bullets. These bullets usually opened up on impact, just like the soft lead ball of Purdey's original muzzle-loading Express rifle did.

The Honorable T.F. Freemantle, V.D., who wrote the *Book of the Rifle*, had this to say about Express rifles: "There was much in the old days of the old express rifles failure on big game—even sambur, etc.—from the failure of gunmakers to realize that the bullet which would break up inside a Scotch stag might not get inside a much heavier animal, but though it would break up, might produce only superficial injury." In other words the express loading often failed just like a modern shooter using a varmint rifle on deer. Sometimes the small-bore varmint bullet kills adequately, and sometimes the bullet explodes on the surface of the animal without badly injuring the deer.

Breech-loading blackpowder arms were made as large as 4-bore and could toss a round ball weighing as much as 4 ounces. The largest Nitro Express rifle was the 600 Nitro which had a massive bullet of 900 grains, weighing about 2 ounces, about the same as the old blackpowder 8-bore rifle round ball projectile. Now those were guns!

Despite the oft-told tales of the double rifle resembling a double shotgun and how well the shooter could handle a double rifle, you didn't toss one of these big bore brutes to your shoulder and lightly toss off a round. The really big guns, blackpowder or nitro, required a certain sense of propriety on your part. One expert shot, trying to get the best possible group, fired an 8-bore double rifle prone and broke his collar bone.

A companion of an Austrian explorer in Africa had this to say of Count Teleki's firing of an 8-bore elephant rifle: "Taking up a position at the edge of a projecting bit of ground, the Count awaited the animal, and fired at the temples (this was an elephant) at a distance of some 30 paces with the 8-bore rifle. The shot was followed by a short, sharp trumpeting from the wounded beast, and at the same moment the Count, who was in a bad position, was flung to the ground by the recoil of the weapon, seeing as he fell that the elephant was about to charge him. Fortunately, Bedue caught the gun as the Count went down, and handed it to his master as he sprang to his feet again. There was scarcely time to cock the second barrel, but this time the shot took home, and the elephant came down with such a crash that his left tusk was broken to pieces."

As you can see, the bigger rifles required that you lock them into your shoulder, hold them tightly, and be ready for the recoil before squeezing the trigger. I have often fired a double 8-bore rifle sitting, but made certain that my feet were supported because the rifle could roll me over, just like the Count. Offhand, I usually took a step or two backwards, and I stand over 6-foot 3 inches and weigh well over 200 pounds.

Another oft-told story is that the double rifles used just one weight and shape of bullet, and if you used anything else, you couldn't hit a barn from the inside. For some reason the people who made double rifles didn't realize that. I have owned blackpowder big-bore double rifles that came with two moulds casting bullets of different weights and shapes, both a round ball and a considerably heavier conical bullet. At the ranges that

The Holland & Holland Best, the Royal Hammerless, shared top spot with very few other labels.

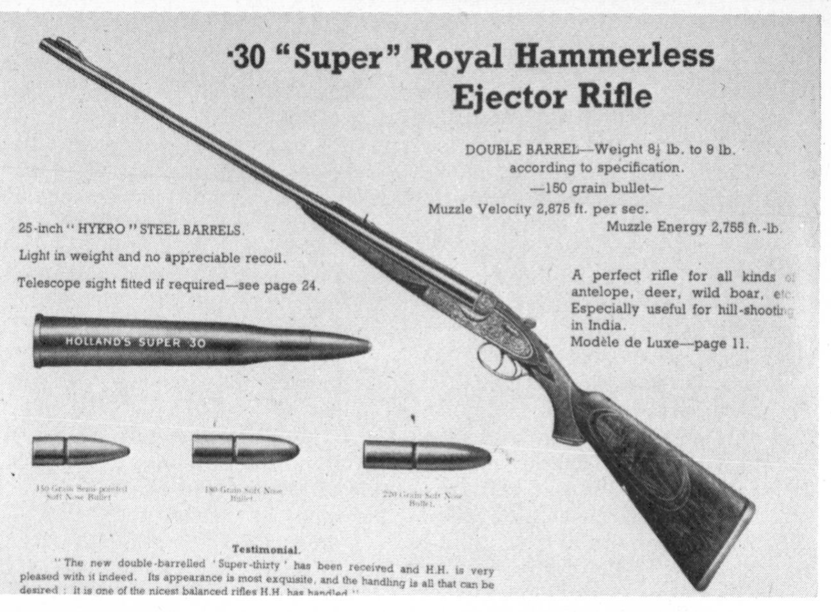

·30 "Super" Royal Hammerless Ejector Rifle

DOUBLE BARREL—Weight 8¼ lb. to 9 lb. according to specification.
—150 grain bullet—
Muzzle Velocity 2,875 ft. per sec.
Muzzle Energy 2,755 ft.-lb.

25-inch "HYKRO" STEEL BARRELS.

Light in weight and no appreciable recoil.

Telescope sight fitted if required—see page 24.

A perfect rifle for all kinds of antelope, deer, wild boar, etc. Especially useful for hill-shooting in India.
Modèle de Luxe—page 11.

HOLLAND'S SUPER 30

150 Grain Semi-pointed Soft Nose Bullet

180 Grain Soft Nose Bullet

220 Grain Soft Nose Bullet.

Testimonial.

"The new double-barrelled 'Super-thirty' has been received and H.H. is very pleased with it indeed. Its appearance is most exquisite, and the handling is all that can be desired : it is one of the nicest balanced rifles H.H. has handled."

All were not "bests," though. Army & Navy stores had serviceable rifles made for their label, sold them throughout the British Empire. This hammer rifle is for the 450 Nitro load.

Three rights and three lefts at full game ranges could get you this group from an Express rifle—plenty good enough.

Gun here is in recoil already. Tuning and zeroing doubles requires rest shooting that duplicates field positions.

they were usually fired, say 50 yards or less, these 8-bore bullets regulated perfectly. The blackpowder 450 x 3¼, a very popular round, came with bullets loaded ahead of 120 grains of blackpowder with 270-grain hollow-point and 325-grain solid bullets for a specifically regulated rifle or 310-grain hollow-nosed or 365-grain solid bullets for another differently regulated rifle.

Consequently when Rigby brought out the first "Special" or Cordite loaded 450x3¼, it was regulated for 480- and 350-grain bullets, just like the older blackpowder rounds with a choice of bullet weights for different animals. The Rigby "Special" deserves a bit of an accolade, for it was the first powerful smokeless powder big bore ever made. Rigby announced this rifle in 1898. Other rifle makers quickly adopted this caliber, and some called theirs the "High Velocity" or "High Power" or just "Cordite Express" to distinguish them from the older, blackpowder arms. Holland & Holland had a bottlenecked 450 cartridge that gave the same velocity with lower breech pressures than the straight-cased 450x3¼ cartridge. This cartridge also used various bullet weights—480-, 420- and 370-grain bullets.

Holland & Holland also offered the justly famous 375 H&H Magnum. Holland & Holland had this to say about the 375-Bore Magnum High Velocity Rifle: "It has a great advantage over any rifle of similar bore, that one can shoot the light 235-grain copper-pointed bullet against thin skinned animals at long ranges, the 270-grain soft-nose bullet for thicker-skinned game at medium ranges, and the 300-grain solid nickel or soft-nose buff-headed bullet for dangerous game at close quarters, using the same sight for each kind of bullet."

Now, Holland & Holland were talking about the flanged cases made for a double rifle, although the same thing could be said about their 375 Belted Magnum in a bolt-action repeater. In addition, the 30 "Super" double rifle, the flanged version of the famous Holland & Holland "Super-Thirty," or as we call it the 300 H&H Magnum, also used 150-, 180- and 220-grain bullets, shooting to the same sights.

Since writing this I thought I should try using different weight bullets in my own double 450 x 3¼ Nitro rifle. Proved for the full 70 grains of Cordite and a 480-grain bullet, there was no mention on the barrel or the proofmarks of using lighter weight bullets. Disregarding this, I used a Speer 400-grain bullet, a Hornady 350-grain slug and a Lyman cast 377-grain bullet. Each bullet clocked through my Oehler chronograph at over 2,000 feet per second (fps), with the Lyman cast bullet having the highest velocity—2135 fps.

I was shooting at 35 yards with a bullseye of 3¼ inches. Firing a right barrel, followed up with a left barrel, the two different pairs of jacketed bullets hit the bullseye while the cast bullets were high and to the right, in the 8 and 7 rings. The smallest group was 1¼ inches between barrels and the largest group was 2½ inches. Both bullets from each barrel shot side-by-side and did not cross at this range. For test loads I couldn't complain! I shot a lion with a 375 H&H bolt rifle at about that same range and these jacketed bullets from the double rifle would have killed that lion just as well.

Westley Richards offered a plethora of calibers. Their small bores included 22 High-Power, 250 High-Power, 30 Sherwood, 32-40 Winchester, 242 High Velocity, 256, 270, 7mm, 280, 30 U.S.A., as well as the bigger, more potent, African calibers. These older catalogs may confuse some people—the 280 probably refers to the 280 flanged round as it is unlikely that it was the Ross, a rimless cartridge. The 30 U.S.A. might well have been the 30-40 Krag, rather than the 30-03 or 30-06 Springfield cartridge.

If you didn't find the caliber you wanted, English firms would build just about any caliber you wanted. The Maharaja of Rewa wanted a special cartridge, and guns to go with it, consisting of the 600 Express round necked to 577-caliber. He got it. Even today, if you have the money, you can have a caliber built for you, even with your own name on the cartridge case.

Today, special double rifles are still being made. I have seen double 4-bore rifles, in the process of being made, in hammerless versions. When they are offered for sale, I am not sure that your Visa or Master Charge will have the limit to buy one. Since British big bore cartridges have become collectors' items, modern doubles are being made for current cartridges, rimless as well as flanged.

When people speak of how double rifles group they always mention "regulating." The barrels of double rifles are not parallel, the bores are angled from rear to front. If the barrels were aligned side-by-side, the right barrel would shoot to the right and the left barrel to the left. To align the barrels of a double rifle they are fastened at the breech while the muzzles are held in a device that allows the barrels to be moved by wedges or by re-soldering until the bullets from both barrels shoot properly. Only then are the muzzles permanently affixed. The regulating of a double is simple in theory but difficult in practice. Probably most double rifles were regulated to shoot in the tropics, using Cordite, where temperatures could run as high as 120 degrees.

The person doing the regulating does not use a bench where you sit and align your rifle over sand bags, like American shooters do. He has a special device that allows him to fire standing upright, but supported by the regulating rest. If the muzzles of a double rifle were on a conventional American rest they would not shoot properly, the gun must be held like it would be by the shooter, shooting off-hand.

I have loaded for many double rifles, and I will be the first to admit that they are not always the easiest rifle to get both barrels to shoot close enough together for hunting. The bullets start off apart—the distance between the barrels—but the recoil of the rifle affects the shooting as the barrels turn left or right, depending on which barrel is fired. The well regulated double shoots closely enough with both barrels to hit an animal at normal ranges.

I once sold a double 470 to a friend of mine, an excellent shot. At 200 yards, the rifle shot beautifully even though he was using some ancient Cordite cartridges in the old 10-round box. He then got some brand new ammo and the rifle wouldn't shoot well at all. The bullets from one barrel crossed the bullets from the other barrel. This happened when ICI—Imperial Chemical Industries—stopped making Cordite-loaded Kynoch ammunition. The brand new loads were loaded by a firm in another country using its own brand of propellant, which definitely wasn't Cordite.

The change in powder made the difference with this 470 rifle. And, I suspect, makes the difference today when people try to reload these English calibers with American powder. Cordite powder looked like strands of spa-

The British had powerful Nitro Express cartridges for double and single shot rifles. Left to right, here are: 600, 577 Rewa, 577, 500, 476, 475 No. 2, 475, 470, 450 No. 2, 500/450 and 450.

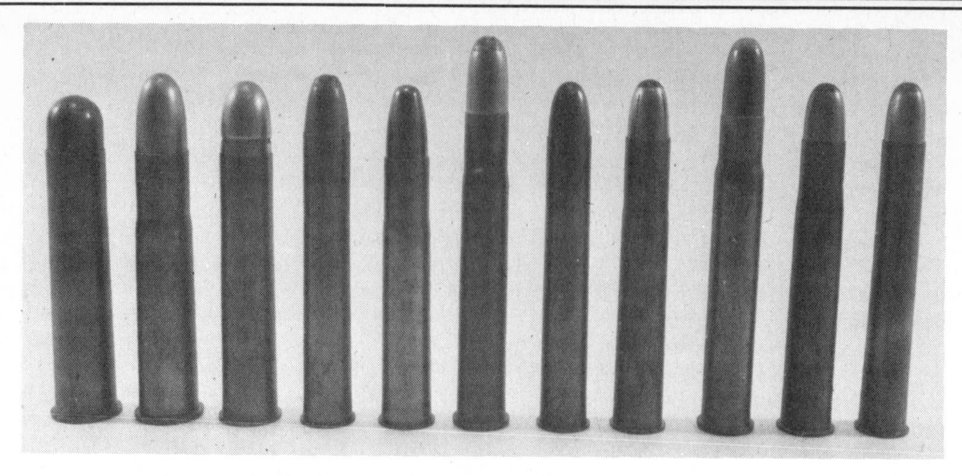

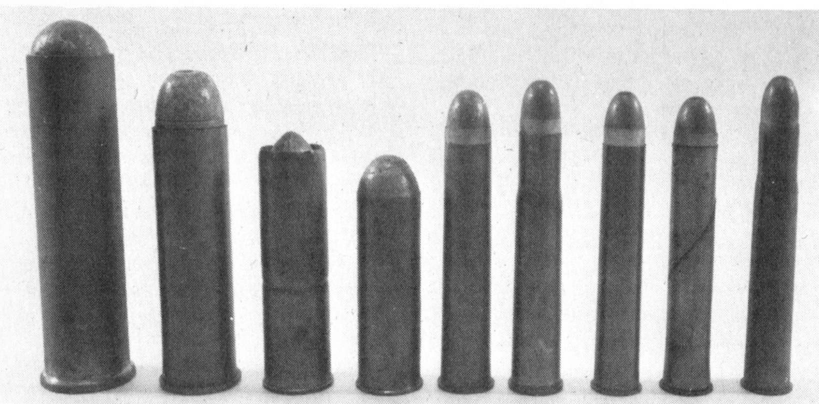

Blackpowder big-bore cartridges ran from the 4-bore, left, as well as 8-bore, 10-bore, 12-bore, 577, 577/500, 500, 500 in Eley-Boxer case and the 500/450.

Jeffery's expanding bullets had slits in the bullet jacket. Many hunters called these "dum-dum" loads.

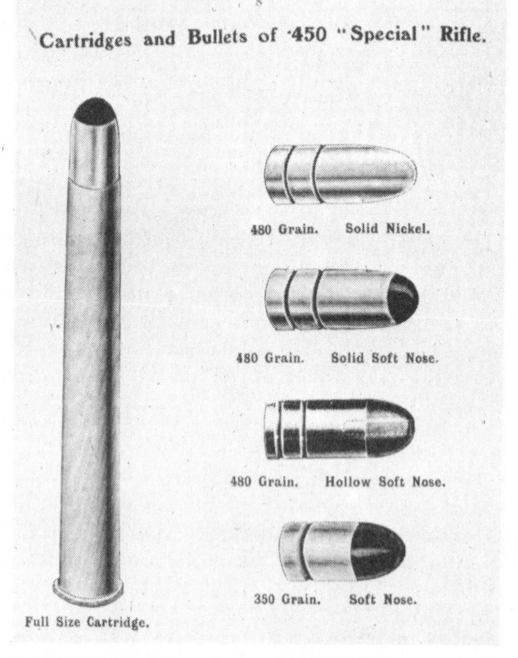

8

Cartridges and Bullets of ·450 "Special" Rifle.

480 Grain. Solid Nickel.

480 Grain. Solid Soft Nose.

480 Grain. Hollow Soft Nose.

350 Grain. Soft Nose.

Full Size Cartridge.

Rigby's Cordite rifle was originally loaded with two different bullet weights, 480 and 350 grains.

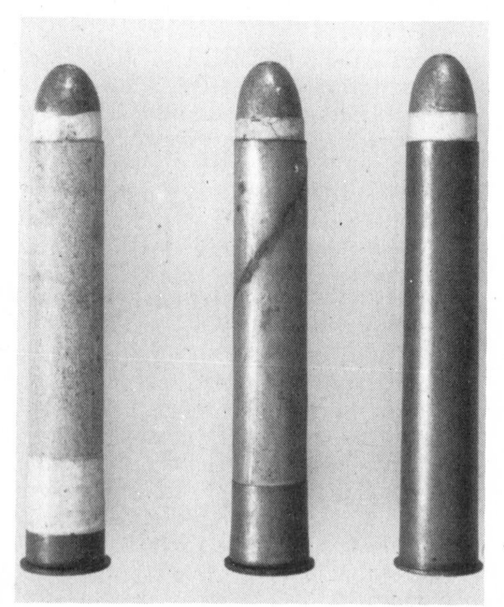

All three are 500 Eley-Boxer: one with a paper cover, the Eley-Boxer coiled brass round and the drawn brass case.

ghetti. In bottlenecked cases it had to be loaded into a cartridge case first, before the shoulder was formed on the case. It worked well in both the Arctic and in tropical regions, however, sometimes too well in the tropics as with high temperatures the breech pressure and muzzle velocity were both higher. Because of this, special loads were made up for tropical countries, with the powder supply cut just a tad. Usually the ammunition boxes for double rifles were marked as tropical loads, while cartridges for bolt-actioned rifles used full-powered loads regardless of where they were going to be used.

Now, like any reloader, I have had a bolt-action rifle shoot much better with one brand of American powder than with another brand. Imagine what you are trying to accomplish using Du Pont, Winchester, Hodgdon or other powders and trying to create the same muzzle velocity as well as the internal pressures building up in the barrel as did Cordite loads.

So, if you are going to load for a double rifle, I wish you lots of luck. It can be done, but sometimes it takes a lot of work. Despite the huge calibers, whether for elephant or not, the double rifle is not nearly as strong as a Mauser. When a firm made both double rifles and bolt-actioned repeaters, in the same caliber, the loads for flanged cartridges for the doubles were always of less intensity than the rimless or belted cartridges for bolt guns.

I have seen several double rifles made from American shotguns, usually for lower pressure cartridges. One friend made a self-opening ejector double rifle. He hadn't planned on it, but the first round blew the gun open and sailed the empty cartridge case off into the air! So, if you are going to load for one of these doubles, even an original English or European rifle, be on the cautious side.

Incidentally, you might happen on an American double rifle. Both Colt and Winchester made doubles that are exceedingly scarce. One American gunsmith, Fred Adolph of Genoa, New York, also made double rifles.

Double rifles used various devices to make them stronger, for instance, the doll's head, a device mounted on the barrel assembly that fitted into the receiver. Supposedly it looked like a "doll's" head and was tapered so that it helped lock the barrels into the action. Sometimes there was a notch in the doll's head that a bolt latched into to prevent the doll's head from moving which helped to reinforce the system. Greener's double rifles had his treble-bolted locking system which included a tang with a center hole that again entered the receiver and was locked into place by a sliding bolt. In Germany, the Kersten system, with twin side bolts, was used to lock the barrels solidly to the action. Whatever you say, the top-break or under-lever double rifle was never intended for the sort of loads one can fire in bolt-action rifles. In blackpowder arms, this didn't make much difference; however, in smokeless powder double rifles the loads must be kept on the safe side. Obviously the rifles made today, for modern cartridges, have been beefed up to account for the added pressures.

What made the double the *sine qua non* of the international big game shooter? Basically, it was because you had two rifles in one. Two barrels, two locks, usually two triggers, and you were pretty certain that when you pulled one of the triggers the gun would go off. If a cartridge had a bad primer, or even if one of the springs on one lock failed, the double rifle man could always touch off the second barrel while the shooter using a bolt-action or single shot rifle might get an unpleasant look at more fangs, tusks and other unpleasant features of a dangerous animal than he ever thought existed.

In muzzle-loading arms this was particularly true as a cap might not go off, the nipple might be clogged or even your powder might be wet. The early muzzle-loading double rifles always used fine grain blackpowder. The shooter wanted to see a bit of powder in the nipple of the gun, just to make sure that it would go off!

With breechloaders came other problems. The original cases were often of the Eley-Boxer type where the whole case was formed of brass sheeting wrapped around lacquered paper. The head was iron, and there were holes in the brass, just so you could see if there was anything underneath it! In damp weather they swelled up and either wouldn't go into the chamber, or, once in and fired, wouldn't eject!

Even if it was a drawn brass case, like our modern loads, these old-time loads were not made nearly as well as our current loads. And I am not speaking about just blackpowder loads. Karamojo Bell, using smokeless powder ammo, had many ammunition failures. Double rifles don't push the shell into the chamber like a Mauser rifle does; the cartridge must slide in smoothly.

One hunter, Victor Cavendish, had this problem with factory ammo. He had just wounded an old elephant bull when: "Cavendish's shikari told him the elephant was going to charge, and he made haste to reload his empty barrel. He opened the breech, ejected the empty case, and put in another cartridge, but he could not get the cartridge home in the chamber; he tried force, but failed—then he tried with all his might to draw it out, but in vain, and now the elephant bore down on him while he struggled with the cartridge which jammed his rifle open. There was nothing for it but to fly . . ."

So, even with factory ammunition, it pays to check each round in your chamber before going hunting. I certainly do this not only with reloads but also with factory shells, whether in a double gun or a bolt-action rifle. Incidentally, Cavendish survived although the elephant knocked him down, knelt on him, and tried to thrust its tusks through him. Miraculously, he was not badly hurt.

Despite problems with ammunition, which could tie up any gun, most big game hunters preferred the double rifle before World War II. Not only because they had virtually two rifles in one, but for other features. The second shot could be fired very rapidly, just as the rifle came down from recoil. They could also be reloaded very quietly, unlike a Mauser, Mannlicher or Lee Metford/Enfield rifle where you had to open the bolt, then ease it shut once more. Many hunters liked the under-lever hammer rifles as they opened almost without sound, and, if you held the hammers back under thumb pressure, could be cocked noiselessly. Whether the rifle was top or under lever, many hunters would also carry one barrel loaded with solid ammo and the other with soft-nose bullets. Thus they were set for virtually any game from antelope to elephant. The advantage of silent loading when stalking dangerous game is an obvious plus, and I suspect that it has many times proved a lifesaver when following up a vengeful wounded beast.

The double rifle has always been costly. To begin with the manufacturer was building, in effect, two different guns. Two barrels, two locks and the incredible effort of aligning the

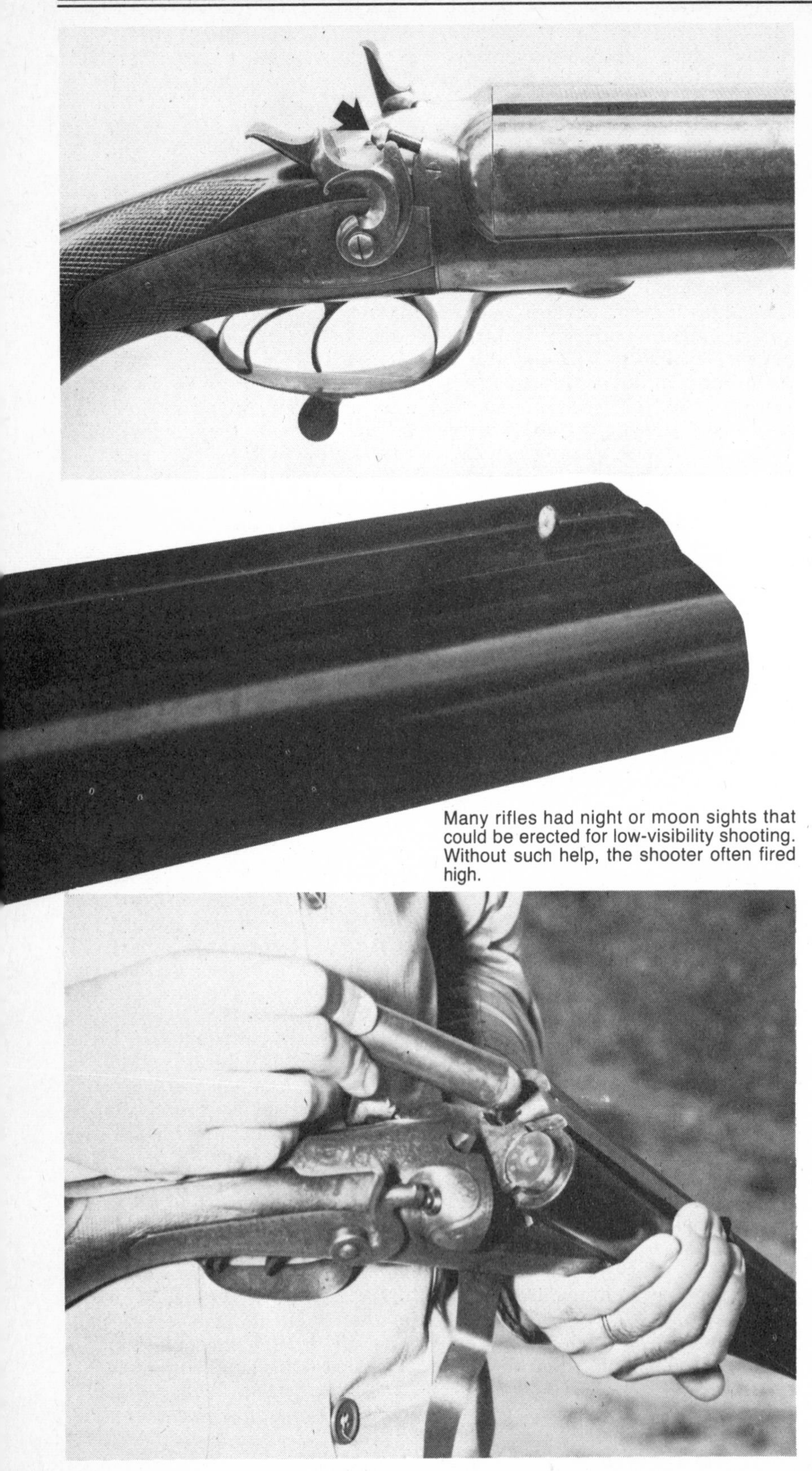
This early double rifle hammer had a flange to pull the firing pin away from the fired cartridge. This cured sticking in early guns with non-rebounding hammers.

Many rifles had night or moon sights that could be erected for low-visibility shooting. Without such help, the shooter often fired high.

Cartridges for the 8-bore rifle were massive things; even so, some shooters ran out of ammunition before bringing a big animal to bag.

two barrels to shoot accurately. Ammunition was relatively inexpensive in those days, but still the regulator might shoot up many, many rounds before he was satisfied with the accuracy of the gun. This sort of thing also escalated prices.

A shooter could ask for a less expensive gun, say a hammer gun after top-lever hammerless guns came into vogue, not ask for ejectors, fancy engraving, or an oak case that was covered in leather for the arm. However, any double was always an expensive arm to build properly, since all double rifles had to shoot well or they couldn't be sold. You might get upset if you missed a duck, but if your double rifle failed on a charging lion, anybody who knew anything about the incident would talk about the rifle and its failures, whether due to the gun or its ammunition.

When we speak of double rifles, particularly the more potent ones, we have to go back well over a century and take our hats off to Sir Samuel White Baker. Baker didn't like the usual "relatively" small-bore rifles, the 16-bore with a charge of 1½ drams of blackpowder, so he ordered a rifle from Gibbs shooting a 3-ounce round ball or a 4-ounce conical slug. He used a charge of 16 drams, 1 full ounce of blackpowder, to propel the bullet.

In contrast, others using double rifles used a much milder load. One hunter who shot a great deal in Burma was positive that his load was tremendously powerful. He was using a 10-bore double rifle and his powder charge was the bullet mould, filled with powder. Like other gun cranks, I have accumulated many items, and one is a 10-bore mould from Manton in Calcutta, India, for a muzzle-loading rifle. I promptly filled the mould with a fine grain blackpowder charge; it weighed just 3½ drams—about like a heavy 12-gauge shot load. The bullets fired with such a charge sometimes expanded on the surface skin, particularly with Asiatic buffalo or gaur, and then dropped to the ground!

Sir Samuel Baker wrote many books about exploration and hunting and gradually sportsmen followed his example and took to the heavier calibers. Baker used everything from one rifle that fired a ½-pound explosive shell to smaller calibers. For dangerous game he liked the 8-bore rifle as well as a 577 double firing a solid lead bullet.

Despite the big double rifles' massive calibers, blackpowder or smokeless, the animal didn't always tumble to the ground when hit by the bullets. E.S. Grogan had this to say about a rhino hunt:

> At 7:30 I found fresh rhinoceros spoor which I followed under a blazing sun til 12:30; the country had been very difficult, and I was just beginning to despair when I heard a snort, and looking up, saw the rhino trotting around the corner of an ant-hill, behind which he had been sleeping. On seeing me he stopped, snorting, blowing, and stamping, looking extremely nasty. I was carrying my 303, and turned around for my 4-bore, found that all my boys had bolted up a small thorn tree, from the branch of which they were hanging like a cluster of bees. They had thrown down the gun, and I was compelled to stoop down and grope about for it in the undergrowth; and I felt very uncomfortable, as in my position I offered a magnificent target. However, at last I found the gun, and, firing past his cheek, hit him full on the edge of the shoulder; instantly there arose a very hell of sound, squealing, stamping, and crashing of bushes and grass; the smoke hung like a pall around me, and I thought he was charging. Having nowhere to run to, I stayed where I was, and suddenly his huge mass dashed past the edge of the smoke-cloud, and I saw him disappear at a tremendous pace into the grass. We followed hard, but though he bled freely and lay down several times, we did not come up to him again till 3 p.m., when we found him standing at 10 yards in a bushy nullah far up in the hills. I fired the 4-bore at his shoulder, knocking him down, but he rose again, and tried to climb the far bank; so I fired the second barrel hurriedly; the cartridge split at the back, and I was knocked over a tree 2 yards behind. That stopped him, and three solid bullets from the 303 finished him.

Ewart S. Grogan, after being knocked down by the 4-bore, finally had this to say about rifles:

> As to the vexed question of the respective merits of large-bore rifles and the modern small-bores, I unhesitatingly throw my lot with the latter, the advantages of which are many and various such as—1. Greater accuracy and ease in handling. 2. Flatter trajectory and consequent minimizing of the results of judging distance wrongly. 3. Small weight of cartridges. 4. Great number of shots that can be fired without effect on the nerves owing to lack of recoil. 5. Variety of effects to be obtained by the use of various bullets. 6. Penetration (so essential with elephant). . ."Our battery consisted of a double 4-bore burning 14 drams of powder, a double 10-bore Paradox, a double 500 magnum, two double 303 express rifles, and an ordinary sporting pattern magazine 303 . . . After nearly losing a rhinoceros and quite losing three good elephant with the 4-bore, I gave it up in disgust, and took to the 303 even for heavy game, with the satisfactory result that I killed 33 elephant and only lost three afterwards.

Today no one is going to shoot as many animals as Grogan did. He was the first man to walk from South Africa to Cairo and hunted throughout the entire trip, but his thoughts on double rifles are most interesting. Today almost any double rifle is a collector's piece, yet the bigger the caliber, the higher the price. Perhaps modern collectors are missing a bet when they turn down a blackpowder arm that could still be suitable for hunting or also let some smaller Nitro rifle, like the 303, slip away when it could also be a showpiece or used in the field.

I find any double rifle to be a most interesting arm whether it is a muzzleloader, blackpowder or Nitro rifle. Often the shipping marks pasted on the outside of the gun case tell of the travels of these old rifles, and who can resist the conjured up notions of adventure that they invoke. Perhaps this is why I have found that even people who evinced no previous interest in firearms became enthralled by any of my old doubles. They have glamour. ●

Black Powder Cartridge Performance

Cartridge	Bullet Weight (grs.)	Conical	Round	Velocity (fps)	Energy (ft. lbs.)
4-bore	1,250		x	1460	5912
4-bore	1,882	x		1330	7387
8-bore	862		x	1654	5232
8-bore	1,257	x		1500	6273
10-bore	670		x	1600	3829
12-bore	547		x	1384	2324
577	570	x		1725	3761
500	340	x		1925	2795
450	270	x		1975	2336
400	230	x		1850	1747

Bullet weights for cartridges measured in "bore" reflect the fact some chambers used paper cases and the bore was the size of the inside of the paper case. Smaller calibers have weights for Express-style hollow bullets.

Nitro Express Cartridge Performance

Caliber	Bullet Weight (grs.)	Muzzle Velocity (fps)	Muzzle Energy (ft. lbs.)
400	400	2125	4006
450	480	2150	4920
500	570	2150	5844
577	750	1950	6994
600	900	1950	7590

There were variations on these cartridges. Some were loaded at different velocities for different makers and there were also different cartridge case lengths that used different loads.

CUSTOM

(Opposite page from left to right)
MIKE YEE
Krieghoff 32 Skeet set has English walnut and Angelo Bee engraving (Bilal photo)

PAUL R. NICKELS
Complete redo of Model 721 Remington now has Grizel trigger guard, Jantz safety and a 338 barrel.

GEORGE BEITZINGER
FN Model 98 in 300 Winchester has California English walnut stock, some Talley metalwork, fine checkering.

CHARLES E. GRACE
A Crandall KP33 action with integral scope mounts makes this 284. Stock is English walnut.

DAVID COSTA
This Winchester 52B has a 22-inch barrel, Claro stock, lots of nice touches. Owner: Roy A. Johnson.

(From left to right)
DAVID GENTRY
Left-hand Gentry Mauser is a 375 H&H, in fiberglass with nickeled action and stainless steel barrel—weighs 8 pounds plus.

DARWIN HENSLEY
Gibbs-Farquharson with Ross Billingsley metalwork and Jenkins case coloring in New Zealand English walnut is a 7x57.

ROBERT M. WINTER
California English walnut contains a Fred Wells barreled action rebored to 416 Hoffman, making, in all, a classic heavy rifle.

RICHARD R. BINGER (Stott's Creek Armory, Inc.)
Remodeled military Sharps-Borchardt holds 30-inch Darr 32-40 barrel. Stock is crotch-grain black walnut and all details traditional.

JERE EGGLESTON
Reworked Oberndorf Mauser has French walnut, Talley metal and Haynes engraving.

DENNIS ERHARDT
Browning BBR 300 Magnum in classically shaped and trimmed French walnut.

DAVID COSTA
A 308 in a pre- '64 Model 70 holds a Douglas barrel, claro walnut stock, first cabin metal accessories. Owner: Roy A. Johnson.

JAMES TUCKER
This simple and classic 98 Mauser in 280 Remington is stocked in English walnut.

DON KLEIN
G33-40 stocked in French walnut has Mark Lee metalwork, Biesen and Fisher trimmings, and a matched-pair twin.

DARWIN HENSLEY
G33-40 with Jim Wisner metalwork in 280 Remington has Jenkins case colors and California English walnut stock.

MAURICE OTTMAR
Mauser VZ33 action in 270 Winchester is stocked in New Zealand walnut and embellished by Tommy Kaye.

GEORGE BEITZINGER
Pre-'64 Model 70 30-06 has recontoured barrel, refined action, classic style in California English walnut.

R. H. DEVEREAUX
Model 70 Featherweight 243, barrel lightened, is held in exhibition grade birdseye maple, has forearm tip and grip cap in burl walnut.

JAMES A. TERTIN
Gander Mountain's gunsmith shows here a 30-06 with Obermeyer barrel in a Model 98 Oberndorf action stocked in Bastogne walnut.

KLAUS HIPTMAYER
Ruger No. 1 has the full treatment: stock, quarter-rib, flipup iron sights, claw mounts and Heidemarie engraving in gold and steel.

COREY O. HUEBNER
Pre-'64 Model 70 30-06 has Shilen barrel turned to featherweight, New Zealand walnut stock, weighs 7½ pounds.

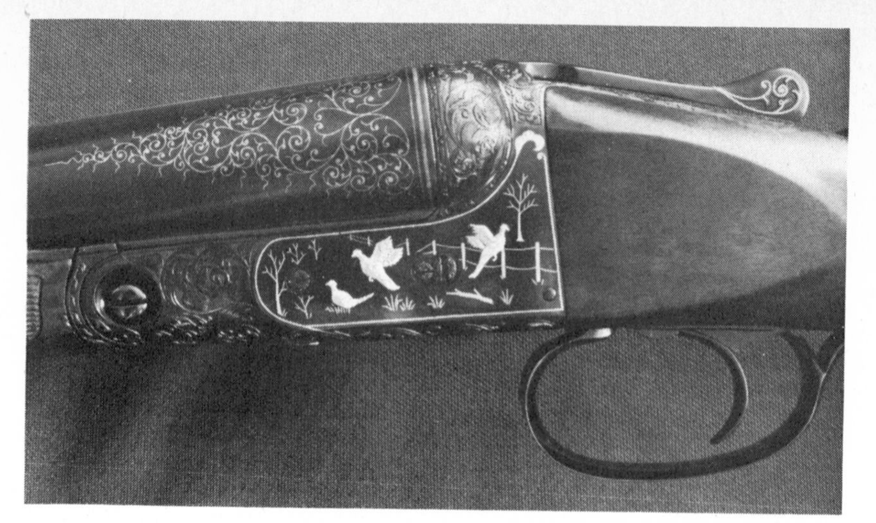

JEROME C. GLIMM

The Art of The Engraver

SAM WELCH

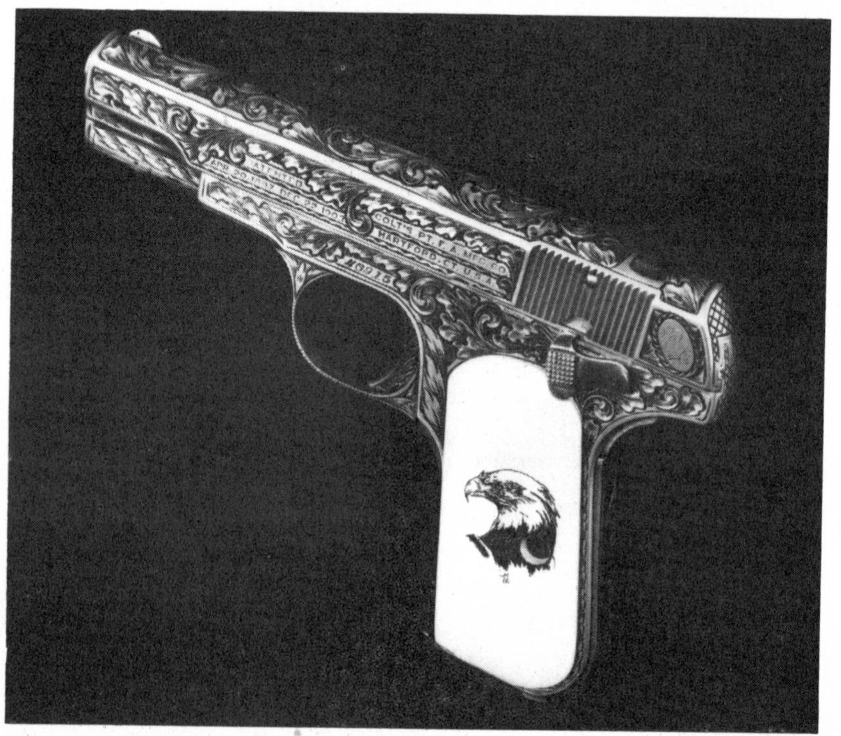

BEN SHOSTLE

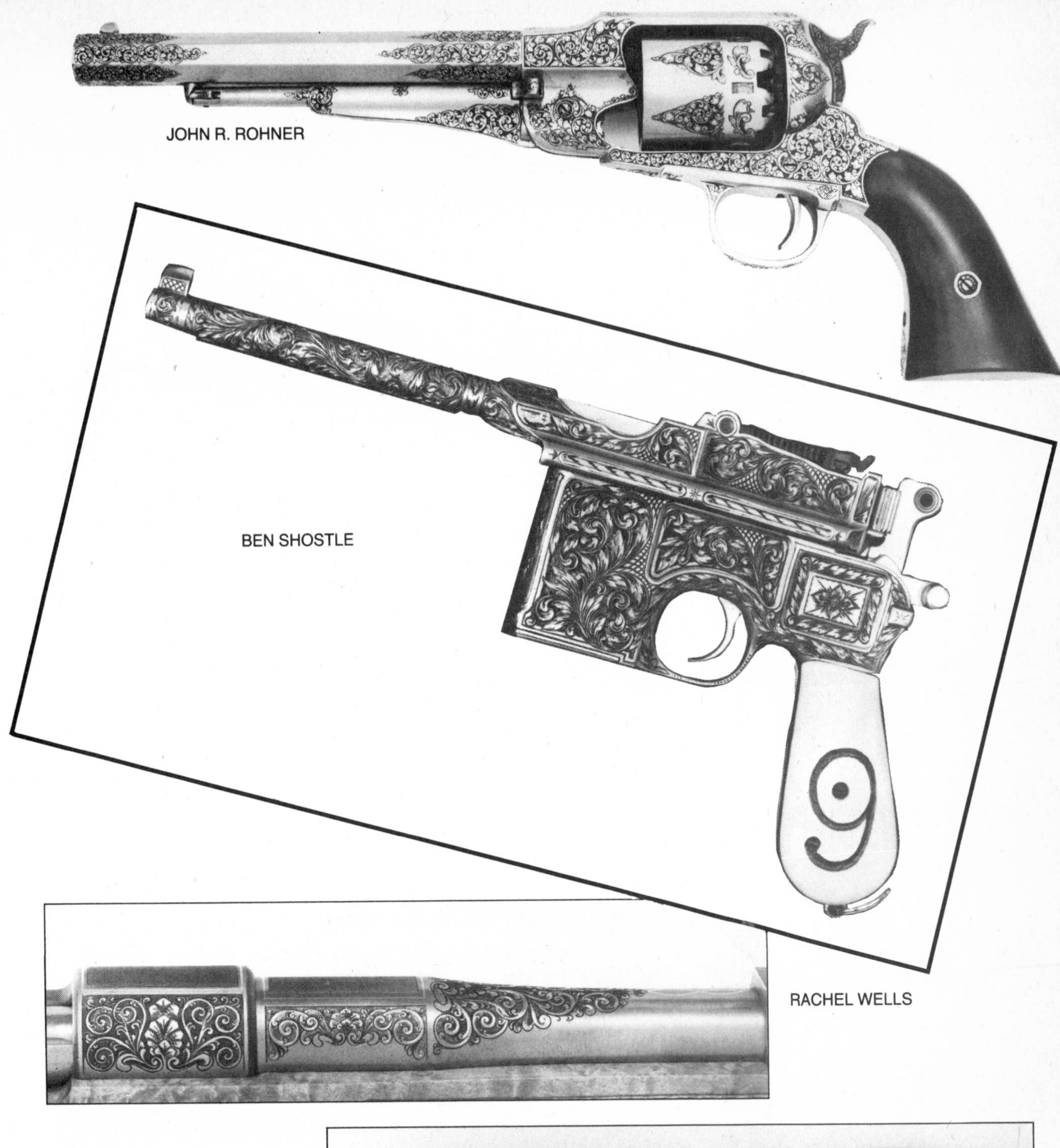

JOHN R. ROHNER

BEN SHOSTLE

RACHEL WELLS

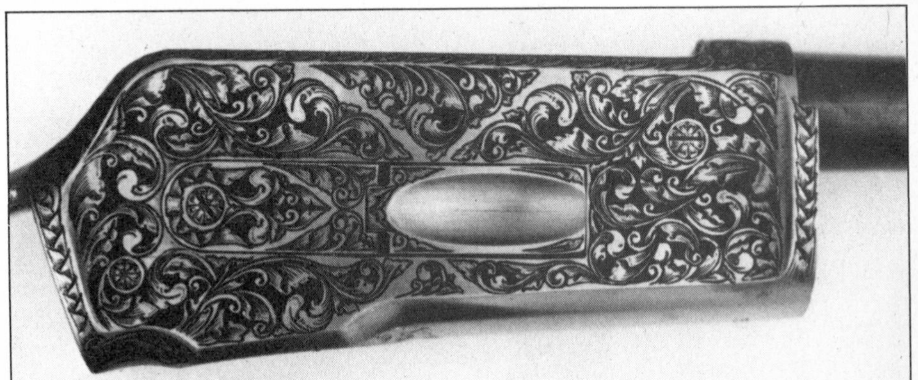

JOHN KUDLAS

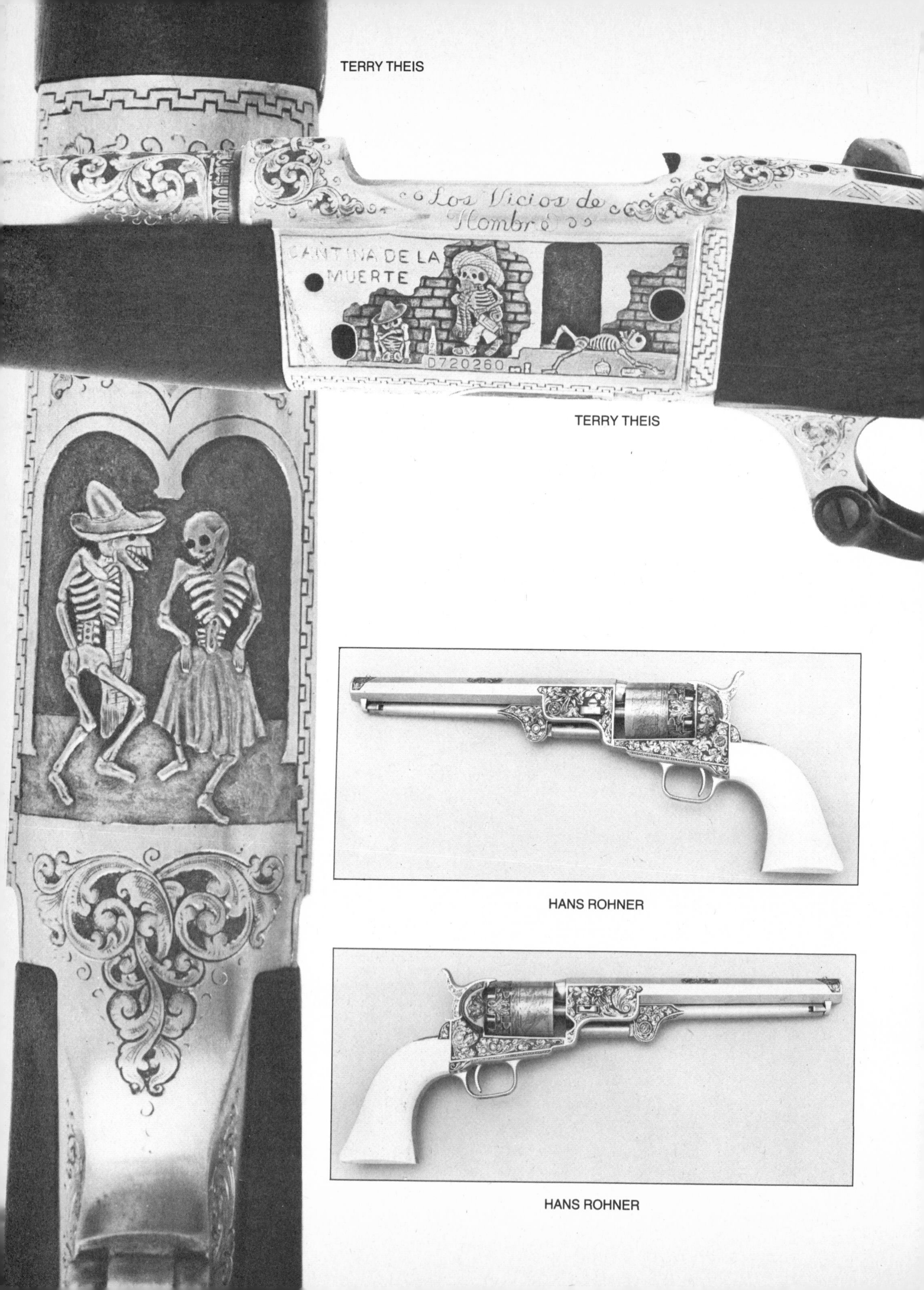

TERRY THEIS

TERRY THEIS

HANS ROHNER

HANS ROHNER

BEN SHOSTLE

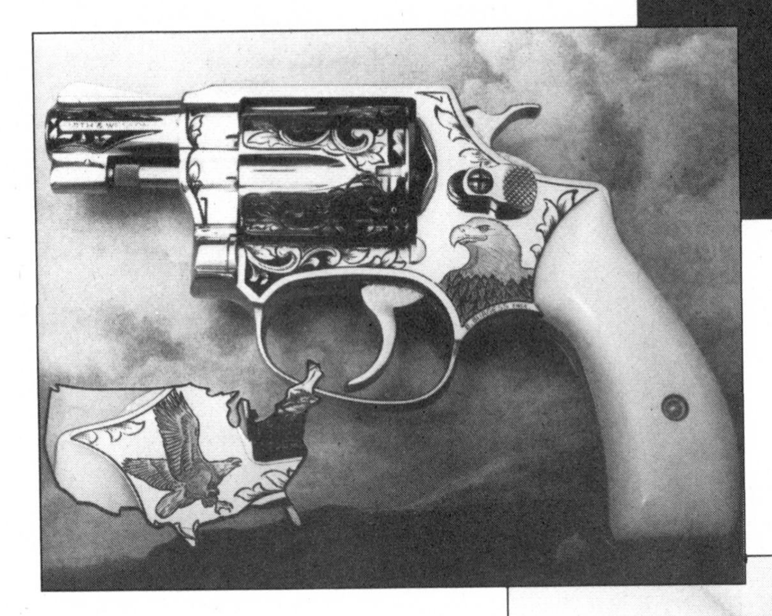

BRYON BURGESS

BILLY BATES

HEIDEMARIE HIPTMAYER

SECURITY GUNS

by CLAY HARVEY

WHAT THEY CALL battle rifles are becoming quite popular. This publication began a separate listing of them in its catalog section just a few years ago; several national magazines devote considerable space to discussions of their merit or close scrutiny of their personas; a plethora of weighty and learned tomes sit dustless on booksellers' shelves.

Why? What is it about these homely, graceless, pragmatic machines that attracts new gun buffs daily?

Well, they shoot quite well; many are artfully made; most are as reliable as an ax, tough as a hammer, and easily stripped to their fundamentals. Although they were late coming to the hunting fields, they are extraordinarily useful as game-taking instruments, regardless of what you may think or what you might read to the contrary. If they get dunked in the drink, it's but the matter of a moment to dry their innards, snap them together, and hie off after the moose you spooked when you fell out of the canoe.

Further, there are multitudes of centerfire plinkers out there who love the serious push of a big-bore rifle at their shoulders, or the spiteful bark of the little 5.56 NATO (223 to us civilians). The 22 rimfires simply bore them! And nothing is as much fun to pop tin cans with as a gun that churns out bullets real fast.

Young Allan Reeves with Ruger stainless steel Mini-14. He can shoot it.

Then there are the ex-GIs who cut their teeth on M-16s in Vietnam along with TV-indoctrinated youngsters who like the looks of battle rifles, or such paramilitary carbines as the venerable and respected UZI, or the businesslike profile of the police riot shotgun. And so what? I dote on the Colt single-action 45. Why? Because I grew up on a diet of Western flicks at the local cinema. Nowadays, Rambo is in style.

The point: Ignore resistance from the self-anointed "old guard," those who fancy their tastes as superior to everyone else's, who find only blackpowder single shots, or lever-action Winchesters, or turnbolts of the O'Connor mode to be acceptable armament. The assault rifle is here to stay—until something better comes along, at which time the current avant-garde will become the reactionaries, defending to the death their old-fashioned M-16s, and denouncing to all comers the new-fangled guns, whatever they are at the time.

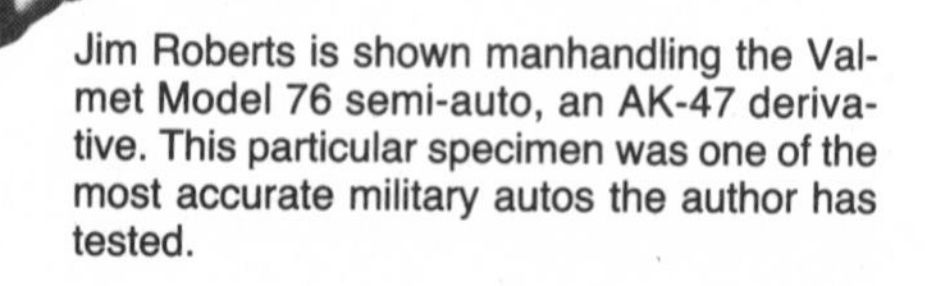

Jim Roberts is shown manhandling the Valmet Model 76 semi-auto, an AK-47 derivative. This particular specimen was one of the most accurate military autos the author has tested.

The foregoing is not offered as a defense against the army of battle-rifle detractors. I simply thought it prudent to mention why it was decided to instigate this new annual report: many *Gun Digest* readers like these guns and want to keep abreast of the latest developments.

Since the relaxation of the ban on imported military surplus arms, veritable phalanxes have been marching into this country. One of the primary purveyors of such merchandise, **Century International Arms,** puts out a catalog pregnant with possibilities. Although most are not available in "new" condition, these guns are offered through normal retail outlets and have never been sold to civilian purchasers, so I suppose that constitutes newness of sorts.

Besides, some of these military castoffs are indeed *new,* never having been fired. An example is the excellent Chinese SKS, offered by Century as "Condition New." Comrade Simonov's baby is as dependable, sturdy, and functional as ever. I tested one fairly extensively, chambered, of course, to the short Russian 7.62x39. Groups ran around 4 inches at 100 yards with good handloads featuring Hornady's 123-grain softpoint and Hodgdon's BL-C(2) propellant. Factory ammo did, ahem, less well.

Also peddled in like-new condition is the FN Model 49, one of the few semi-autos available in 8x57 Mauser. Then there are M-1 Garands, M-1 Carbines, Egyptian Rashids, Hakim 7.92 semi-autos (closely akin to the legendary Swedish Ljungman Model 42, but built in the land of the pyramids). There are, of course, multitudes of bolt-action battle rifles, from the various Mosin-Nagant permutations through Spanish Mausers and Lee-Enfields up to the fine Model 1938 Swede.

For the aficionado of modern assault weapons, Century is the sole importer of the French FAMAS-GIAT, a high-tech 223-chambered bullpup carbine that offers left or right ejection, a rubber-covered adjustable cheekpiece, well-protected battle sights that adjust not only for point of impact, but for light conditions as well. Much armored plastic is in evidence, particularly in the carrying handle and stock, and the GIAT wears an integral bipod. Even newer is the FAMAS air rifle, a visual clone of the GIAT.

The ubiquitous AK-47 is alive and well and showing up from all points of the globe. New this year at **Mitchell Arms Inc.** is the 308 version of their Yugoslavian-built semi-auto AK. Available is a wood-stocked version, a folding-stock (paratrooper) iteration, and something called the RPK Model. Such features as day-night sights, teakwood, and fitted rubber buttplates distinguish these AK permutations from those of other purveyors.

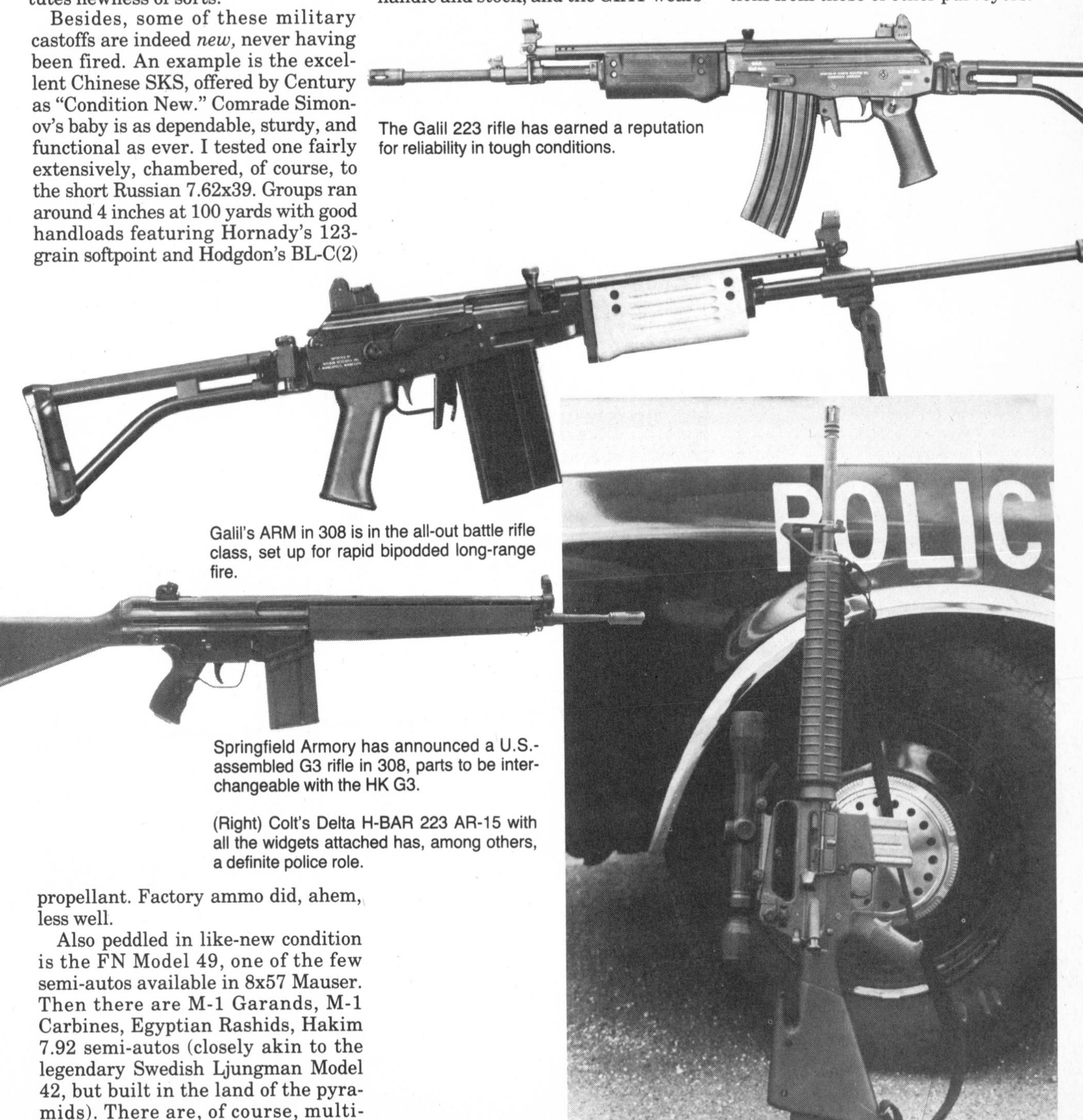

The Galil 223 rifle has earned a reputation for reliability in tough conditions.

Galil's ARM in 308 is in the all-out battle rifle class, set up for rapid bipodded long-range fire.

Springfield Armory has announced a U.S.-assembled G3 rifle in 308, parts to be interchangeable with the HK G3.

(Right) Colt's Delta H-BAR 223 AR-15 with all the widgets attached has, among others, a definite police role.

The standard UZI semi-automatic carbine in 9mm or 45 ACP has folding stock and other features seen on TV screens daily.

HK's MP-5 comes in a wide variety of profiles with a considerable kit of accoutrements, is a favorite in semi-auto version here.

According to a Mitchell Arms press release, the Spectre pistol and carbine have been approved by the BATF. These are modifications of the full-auto Spectre, and retain the single- or double-action first-shot feature, four-column magazine, and special heat-dissipating barrel. Mitchell Arms claims *no* heat build-up during rapid fire in any caliber you want so long as it's 9mm.

STOEGER has taken over the Finnish **VALMET** line, which is good news; increased availability should result. The bad news is that at this time only the 223 and 308 chamberings are cataloged—no 7.62x39. More's the pity; for several purposes, the short Russian cartridge is the best of the trio.

Stoeger shipped me off a sample of the Model 76 carbine, reamed to 223, when I returned from the SHOT Show in Las Vegas. Wow, is it well made! Wow, does it have a fine trigger! Wow, will it shoot!

How well? With the Federal 40-grain Blitz factory hollowpoint, four five-shot strings from the bench at 100 yards averaged 2 inches on the button. Switching to the 55-grain Federal hollowpoint boattail, four groups went 2.64 inches for the aggregate. Samson's fine 55-grain hollowpoint boattail stayed just under 2½ inches. Forty-four percent of my groups printed inside 2 inches, and that's for all ammo tried, with military-issue aperture sights. Accurate?

I was so impressed with the Model 76 that I called Stoeger and requested a Valmet Hunter in 308. Why the Hunter model? Because it is offered with a five-round magazine, making it much easier to carry at its balance point. If it groups like the 223, it'll never see South Hackensack again.

Incidentally, my sample M76 is the wooden-buttstock issue. There is an obligatory folding stock version, which some folks like, and which does indeed make the carbine more compact to stow, but that metal rod poking out the caboose is not exactly an aid to good shooting, nor is it the thing to snuggle your cheek against on a cold winter's morning. But to many it simply *looks* right, and that's enough. I shan't deride it, just bypass it.

NORINCO brings in the AKS, a currently-built Chinese semi-auto AK-47, and sells it complete with bayonet, cleansing apparatus, three magazines, and sundry gadgets. Chambering is 7.62x39.

I tested one recently. Quality of fabrication was acceptable, but did not bring tears of appreciation to my eyes. It worked just fine, would group on a ½-gallon bucket at 100 yards, and had a light, rolling, mushy trigger pull. Sights were 1947 state of the Soviet art. Since the importer didn't get me pricing info, I can offer little guidance to the prospective purchaser except this: If you can find one for sale at a *noticeably* cheaper price than such items as the Valmet, Mitchell, or the

The Auto-Ordnance semi-automatic Model 1927 has the great Tommy-gun profile, and this one shot very well out to 100 yards.

As Ed White illustrates, the security arm should be tested as a typical sporter if its true accuracy is to be determined. This Springfield Armory M1A averaged 1.75 inches for four five-shot strings with Federal 168-grain Match ammo.

Israeli Galil, consider it.

And speaking of the **GALIL** . . . imported by **ACTION ARMS LTD.**, of Philadelphia, the deluxe Model ARM is available in quantity, and is one nice piece of work. The Galil carbines, like the Valmet, are a cut above most AK-47 variants in both workmanship and accuracy. Further, they offer excellent trigger pulls, better in fact than those found on most bolt-action sporting rifles. There is considerable take-up, or slack, but once that is passed, the second stage is superb—light, crisp, controllable.

The ARM boasts a folding bipod with integral wire cutters, vented wood handguard, and a carrying handle. The standard AR comes in either 308 or 223, wears a plastic forend. Both versions have a folding, tubular buttstock, flip-up tritium night sights as well as the normal military peep, a thumb-operated safety on the left side of the gun in addition to the typical AK paddle at the right side of the receiver, and optional magazine capacities as high as 50 rounds. Also optional is a scope mount that requires no gunsmithing. Nice ordnance, these Galil carbines, and virtually ambidextrous.

Will they shoot? Well, my test rifles arrived in the 11th hour, but limited testing so far has turned up no groups larger than 4 inches from the AR model, and the ARM is nigh as precise. Best load in the AR is the Israeli-fabricated Samson 55-grain hollowpoint boattail. Both guns are chambered to 223, as you may have guessed.

ACTION ARMS also imports the famed **UZI** carbines and pistol. Labeled "new" in the catalog is a Mini Carbine, smaller (except in barrel length) and lighter (by 1.2 pounds) than the standard UZI. As with the elder version, both 9mm and 45 ACP chamberings are produced. The standard gun is now cataloged in 41 Action Express. Each version has a folding stock, but each goes about it in a different way.

I testfired a Mini 9mm, and a Standard 45. Both worked well, with only the 45 requiring occasional manual assistance in getting the first round from the magazine to the chamber. Accuracy was acceptable, if not competition quality.

I handed the Mini Carbine to my shooting crony Andy Riedell, along with a box of 115-grain FMJ ammo. He went over to the 25-yard range, fooled around a while, then brought me back a handful of 10-shot groups he'd fired offhand. None of them exceeded 2.9 inches.

I shot neither UZI from a rest, but blasted away a truckload of ammunition at tin cans, dirt clods, and milk jugs. I found that if I paid attention to what I was doing and squeezed the trigger carefully, I usually hit what I was aiming at. Clear out to the 100 yard bank, targets 4 to 6 inches in diameter were not safe. Not particularly scientific, I realize, but that's what UZIs are *for*.

All kinds of appurtenances are made for the UZIs. There are conversion units, even one in 22 rimfire. A traditional wood buttstock is proffered, high-capacity magazines, magazine loading tools, sight adjustment tools, magazine pouches, soft and hard carrying cases. No dearth of goodies here, folks.

Although not so finely made as the UZI—and not nearly as expensive—the **MARLIN** Camp Gun serves much the same purpose for civilian gunners. To wit: The protection of home and turf, high-volume plinking, the taking of small critters for provender or simple eradication. Marlin turns out the Camp Gun in both 9mm Luger and the 45 auto, so it has the same advantages as others of its ilk,

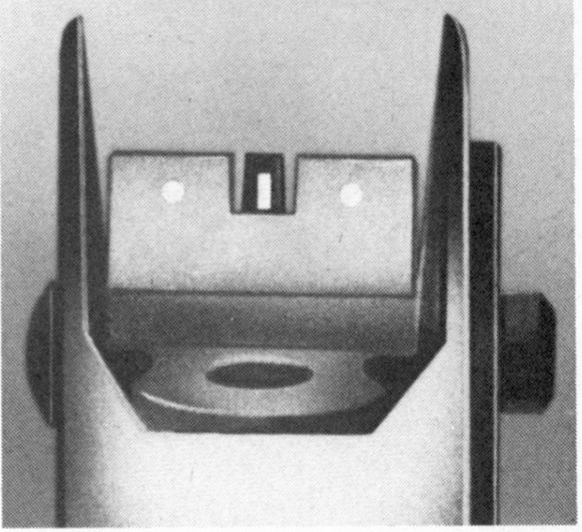

Some battle rifles like the ARM-AR have a fold-down peep sight (foreground) and a pop-up tritium night sight as shown.

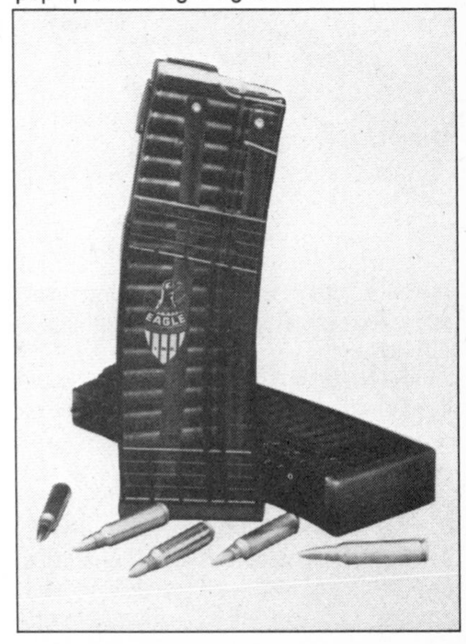

Eagle International offers this 35-round mag for the Ruger Mini-14. There is a "constant-force" spring system to provide both easy loading and reliable feeding. The exterior is strong transparent black polymer.

Cindy Lucas can shoot the big Heckler & Koch M91 easily from the sit, but it's a bit front-heavy for good offhand gunning for a lady.

Marcus Amato illustrates the practicality of some security arms here, with this Iver Johnson 30 Carbine. Even a youngster can handle it.

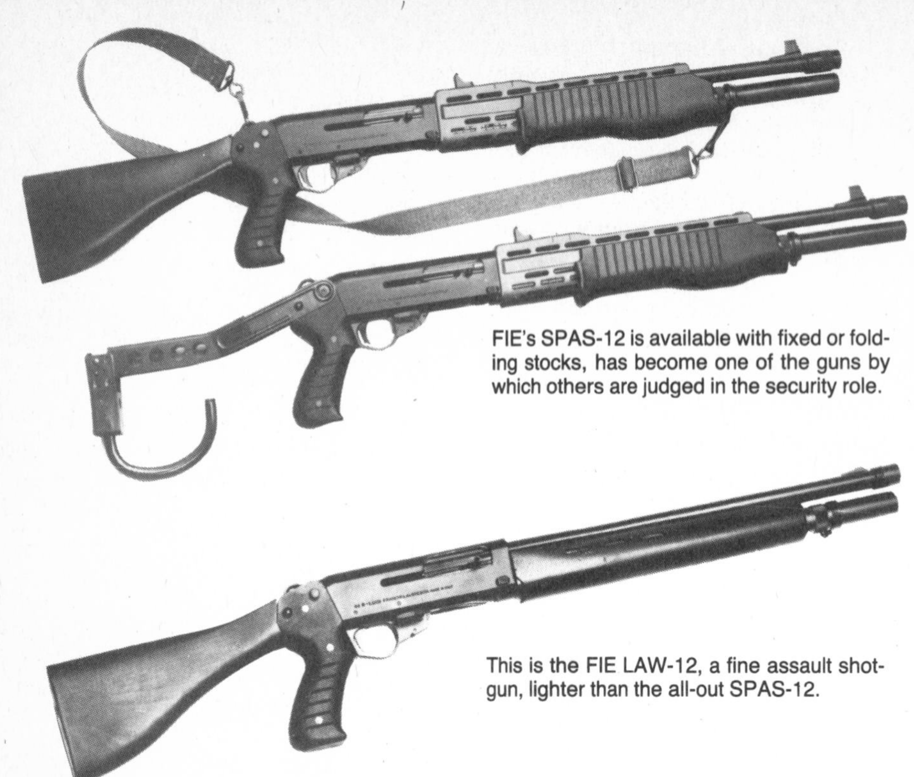

FIE's SPAS-12 is available with fixed or folding stocks, has become one of the guns by which others are judged in the security role.

This is the FIE LAW-12, a fine assault shotgun, lighter than the all-out SPAS-12.

namely inexpensive ammo, moderate bark, handy size, and a businesslike appearance.

The little carbines sell for under 300 bucks, have more-or-less conventional looks, are cloaked in old-fashioned wood and steel, and weigh only 6¼ pounds according to Marlin. The stock is a bit long in the arms, especially for younger shooters, but this helps allay the rearward shove (which is mild enough to begin with). Adjustable iron sights are provided, and mounting a scope is child's play.

I've sampled Marlins in both chamberings; accuracy was more than sufficient for any task I might expect of a carbine in this power range. In my 9mm, Speer-CCI's 115-grain Blazer hollowpoint ammo grouped 1.33 inches at 25 yards, and a handload featuring the 100-grain Speer JHP and Winchester 231 powder was just off the pace at 1.64 inches. The 45 was in the same bailiwick. Thus, I'd expect either of them to stay on a coyote's chest cavity out to perhaps 100 yards.

For defensive use, both guns get an A-plus for handling qualities and reliability. The 9mm would be my choice, since it can be had with an optional 20-shot magazine. Only a seven-rounder is sold with the 45.

Another handy American-built carbine is the **Ruger Mini-14,** sold in several models, all barrel-marked 223 Remington. There are stainless-steel versions, folding-stock renditions, guns with integral scope mounting systems. A "sporting" edition is dubbed the Ranch Rifle, and comes with scope rings and a shotgun-style buttplate.

Better is the new Mini Thirty, which rose Phoenix-like from the ashes of the defunct XGI. Reamed to 7.62x39—although with a strange .308-inch bore diameter in lieu of the proper .311-inch—the Mini Thirty is the only member of the Ruger paramilitary clan that I've been able to get to group. With select handloads, my test rifle prints a hair under 2½ inches for three five-shot strings at 100 yards. Pretty good! (Factory ammo would barely stay inside 5 inches at the same range, which is par for all 7.62 Short fodder I have tested, regardless of the rifle.)

COLT INDUSTRIES continues to manufacture the AR-15, in its various guises. Newest is the Delta H-BAR, a fast-twist, scoped, police sniper carbine with all kinds of widgets attached. Caliber is 223 in all versions, although at one time there was a 9mm number. It is not mentioned in my current catalog, so I'm uncertain of its availability at this time.

With good ammo, most AR-15s will group as well or better than many of their foreign competitors. I have heard of unmodified Colts that would print 1½-inch clusters at the 100-meter mark, but I've never encountered one. My experience with them has provided groups running in the 2½- to 3-inch range, with their favored loads.

Another American military arm, the **SPRINGFIELD ARMORY** M1A (aka the M-14), is going great guns for the Geneseo, Illinois firm. Produced in standard, Super Match, and "Bush" models, the rifles are sold only in 308 Winchester (7.62 NATO) chambering. My test rifle averaged 1.75 inches for four strings at 100 yards with Federal 168-grain Match ammunition, and with issue iron sights. One particularly memorable five-shot group was fired from 150 yards, standing, and miked 4.50 inches. A fluke, most likely. Alas, my M1A strained something down deep inside. It will now fire with the safety engaged, but will be restored to its former healthy state forthwith.

Springfield also offers the Italian-made Beretta BM-59, the M1 Garand

Bob O'Connor is shown testfiring the Benelli Super-90. This gun can be unloaded in less than 3 seconds by an average gunner, under 2 in the hands of an expert. Rifle sights are an aid to the hunter. Capacity is eight rounds.

in various permutations, and the SAR-48, a duplicate of the famed Belgian FAL/LAR. Many accessories are cataloged for the differing models; too many to cover here.

The bona fide LAR is imported by **Gun South.** It is offered in 308 only. There's a match style, the LAR "Para" (two versions), and the LAR heavy barrel, in addition to the standard rifle. For 223 fans, there is the FNC light carbine. The importer has provided neither guns nor photos, despite repeated requests. So I have no more info to report.

AUTO-ORDNANCE, on the other hand, sent along a sample of their Thompson Model M1 45 semi-auto, the infamous Tommy gun. It's a big, heavy (11¼ pounds unloaded), wickedly handsome brute. A 20-round magazine was provided, along with a sling. Available is the classic 50-shot drum as well.

My trial gun had a non-adjustable aperture sight. I was a bit apprehensive at this, but my concern proved unwarranted. The burly rifle was sighted perfectly for 100 yards, at which range it repeatedly grouped five shots into less than 8 inches with the only load tried for accuracy, the Samson 185-grain match. Functioning was perfect; nary a miscue of any sort. The Thompson just kept stuttering away.

The same went for the **HECKLER & KOCH** Model 91. Its action was stiff out of the box, but after 20 or so rounds had been sent up its pipe, things smoothed out beautifully. The H&K wasn't as accurate as my Springfield M1A, grouping at best barely under 3 inches, but it broke no parts.

No fleaweight article, the H&K seems awkward at first, what with a great deal of its weight hanging way out front. And the cocking-lever location is a puzzlement, dang near out even with the muzzle. But the more you get to know the M91, the more you like it.

As factory set, the iron sights were on the money. They're marked for 100, 200, and 300 meters, with the close-range item being a shallow V-notch instead of an aperture as is the case of the other two distances. Trigger pull in military issue guise is quite acceptable, though not up to those units provided on such AK derivatives as the Galil and the Valmet. A match trigger is available, and drops in easily.

All Heckler & Koch firearms are first-rate in the workmanship department, as one expects of Teutonic handiwork. My Model 91 was no exception; quality was first cabin.

One more centerfire, this one a turn-bolt sniper rig based on a medium Sako action. It boasts a match-grade fluted barrel and a unique steel bedding system, wears a folding Du Pont Zytel stock reinforced with 43 percent glass fiber. There is an integrated bipod, attached to the floating forend rather than the barrel. Thus, there is no point-of-impact shift as there can be when a bipod is appended directly to a barrel. The rifle has a muzzlebrake, a 10-shot capacity, and is sold by **GRENDEL INC.**, of Rockledge, Florida. The model designations are SRT-20F, 20L, and 24. I have no idea what the differences are between the numbers, and my press release only adds to the confusion.

The little FIE-imported **Franchi** "PARA" takedown 22 rimfire carbine is just the ticket for a beginner who likes the military look. It has a tubular metal buttstock, is easy to break down, comes in a nifty hard carrying case. Sights are adjustable, if rudimentary, and a scope is as readily added as on most rimfires. My test rifle has a pretty good trigger and exceptional accuracy for a self-loading 22. Good little gun.

If you perused the catalog section of last year's *Gun Digest*, you're likely to have noted that there are several companies whose wares are missing from my report. Not my fault. None of them has provided me with any information at all, so I'll merely list them here and be done with it. Maybe next year they will be on hand. They are: Barrett, maker of the Light Fifty; Beretta, producer of the AR-70; the Bushmaster AR; the Commando 45; Federal's XC-900; Iver Johnson's M1 Carbine look-alike; the Poly-Tech AKS-762; Steyr's AUG; the Weaver Arms Nighthawk. So far as I know, that's all.

Now let's look at a few shotguns.

FIE of Hialeah, Florida, brings in one of the best battle shotguns produced today, the Franchi SPAS-12. Newer to this country is the less complex (and less expensive) SAS-12 pump, and the LAW-12 semi-auto (same price as the SPAS). All function faultlessly; and my sample LAW has an excellent trigger to boot. The guns have two separate safeties, nine-shot capacity, full pistol-grip stock. A folding buttstock is standard on the SPAS-12, available on the others.

The SPAS, which will function both as a semi-automatic *and* a pump, is fairly heavy at 9.6 pounds. The other two are cataloged at 6.7 pounds. Pattern density is quite good with the open-choked LAW, and centers close to where I look. Slugs are not easy to place, due to the lack of a rear sight and the high comb. Thus, I lean to buckshot in my LAW for home defense.

From **Heckler & Koch** I borrowed a **Benelli Super-90**, billed as the fastest shotgun in the world. In the hands of a wizard like John Satterwhite, it doubtless lives up to its billing. If memory serves, John busted as many as nine clay targets, simultaneously tossed in the air, before any of them hit the ground. The elapsed time is about 1¾ seconds, I believe. Fast enough for you?

Although its construction is synthetic, the stock design on the Super-90 is conventional, even a bit lengthy in pull measurement. As a matter of fact, if it weren't for the black stock and the extended magazine tube, the Benelli would look right at home amongst a clutch of normal field grade autoloaders. To the eyes of a traditionalist, the standard Super-90 is likely the least offensive of the true paramilitary shotguns.

Other makers offer guns for the security/police/military/home-defense market. Most are simply dull-finished versions of standard pump guns, with perhaps an extended magazine tube. **WINCHESTER (USRAC)**, for instance, peddles a couple of particularly interesting models, the Stainless Marine Defender and the Stainless Police Defender. Both, as you may have surmised, are partially comprised of stainless steel. Iron sights are standard on this duo. **MOSSBERG** may well be the leading producer of security shotguns. Their line is complete, and includes some pretty impressive equipment.

Among folks who already own some of the guns we've been discussing, there's a burgeoning interest in aftermarket accessories. **B-SQUARE** makes scope mounts, for example, for virtually every firearm on the market, and many don't require drilling and tapping.

EAGLE INTERNATIONAL offers a line of specialty items for the Ruger Mini-14, including a see-through 35-round magazine. Also cataloged are a Mini-14 Quick-Detachable scope mount, a rear sight replacement, a ventilated barrel shroud, 360-degree barrel swivel, and more. Eagle makes 10-shot mags for the Remington series of sporting pumps and autos, as well as gadgets for the Ruger 10/22. The AR-7 is represented with scope mounts, Zephyr sighting systems, a flash hider, and a telescoping buttstock. ●

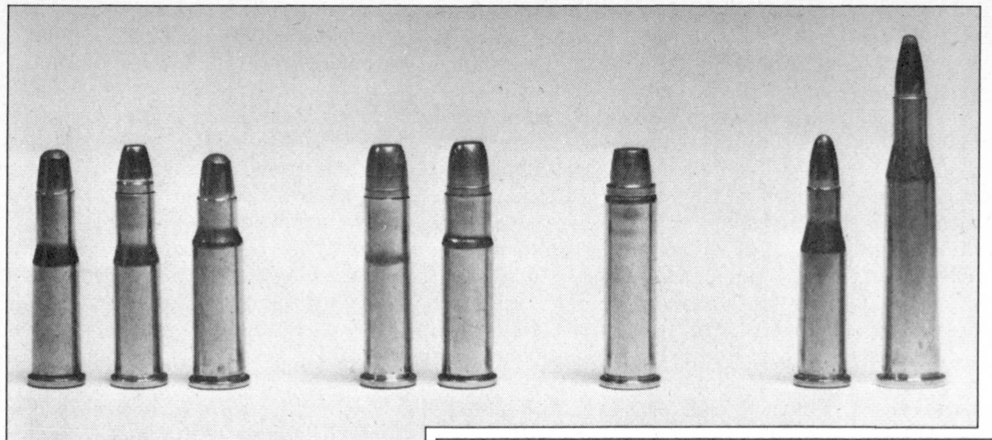

The basic ingredients of little rifle fun, from left: 25-20 with 60-gr. Hornady; 25-20 with cast bullet; 256 Winchester with 60-gr. Hornady; 32-20 and 30-357 wildcat with cast bullets; the 357 Magnum; the 218 Bee and the 219 Zipper.

The author with his most-used rifles, from left: Marlin 357; Winchester Model 65; Winchester Model 64 in 219 Zipper; Winchester 92s in 25-20 and 32-20. He holds a Browning 92 in 357.

SMALL GAME CENTERFIRES:

They're on the way back; the New Southwest loves 'em.

by HOLT BODINSON

YEARS AGO, we used to chuckle a little, out here in Arizona, when reading Henry Stebbins' fine articles on "urban" rifles in early editions of *Gun Digest*. Living as we did in the wide open ranges, nothing seemed more remote than the need for soft-speaking little rifles which wouldn't disturb Farmer Grey's Guernseys or broadcast one's presence to cranky land owners.

But times have changed and it's getting downright civilized, urbanized, and crowded out here in the Southwest and those little "soft-speaking" rifles of yore are making a big comeback. We're breaking out our once retired 25-20 and 32-20 lever actions, cleaning up old bullet moulds, and scrounging around town for those beautiful, miniature brass cases. I'm watching the return of the little Winchester.

In my memory, it wasn't the Model '73 Winchester which tamed the West, it was the little Model '92. Every ranch I ever worked on had at least one '92 Winchester in daily use and usually more. The '92 was and still is one of the world's greatest utility guns. It's a user's rifle. It's personal. Wrapping your fingers around that slim receiver, you can carry it effortlessly for hours afield. Filling its tubular magazine with those short, pistol-sized cartridges, you can shoot from sunup to sundown. Fifty shells for it will fit in your jeans pockets. When shot, it speaks softly and is easy on your shoulder, but it's deadly. And it's plumb stingy on powder and lead, especially in the 25-20 and 32-20 chamberings.

Little rifles produce dead turkeys as if they were built for the job.

Packed in saddle scabbard, parked behind the back door, hung in a pickup truck, this miniature version of the 1886 Winchester has taken more small game and varmints than one could count and more big game out here than any of us would dare admit. Yes, it handles like a rifle should handle. And when John Moses Browning sat down to design the great and equally handy Model '94, he shrewdly copied the Model '92s dimensions to a few eighths of an inch. Surprised? Compare them side-to-side sometime.

Down south of the border, the vaqueros of Mexico and South America took to the Model '92 as readily as we did. It's no small wonder that Brazil's large arms manufacturer, Rossi, today turns out thousands of Model '92 copies in 357, 44-40 and 44 Magnum. Way down under on the Australian frontier, the '92 Winchester had a tremendous following. My friend and hunting companion, Australian-born engraver Lynton McKenzie, tells of finding scores of shot-out Model '92 barrels in a relative's workshop—impressive evidence of the years of hard, daily use those little rifles gave their owners during the heydays of Australian market hunting.

Slightly over one million original '92 Winchesters were produced and almost 600,000 of those were in caliber 44-40. Yet, it seems to me that the 25-20 and 32-20 rifles and carbines were the most popular numbers here in my part of the West. And they were used on everything—rabbits, coyotes, mountain lions, javelina, deer, antelope, elk, bear and even a few mean hombres. One of the folks who raised me in Wyoming kept his family in antelope and venison throughout the Depression with an octagonal-barreled 25-20.

Some years later, I watched this same rancher with his little '92 drop a large bull elk with one 86-grain softpoint to the chest cavity. Another acquaintance felt his 32-20 saddle-ring carbine was just perfect for dropping mountain lions out of trees. A namesake of mine still carries a '92 rebarreled to 256 Winchester Magnum loaded with 90-grain cast bullets to bring home the venison whenever his name comes up in our annual deer draw. Ballistically speaking, the 25-20 and the 32-20 are not what you would call big game cartridges. But they work. None of these ranch folk ever felt undergunned.

But where the '92 Winchester and its modern copies really shine is as small game rifles. Stebbins was right. What this country needs are more small game rifles. Not noisy, high-speed varmint rifles that belch fire and flatten everything in sight, but soft-speaking, handy little iron-sighted guns capable of taking and preserving for the table the myriad small game animals that are found in every state of the union. These are the rifles that pull you out to the field between big game seasons, rifles that shoot quiet interesting pistol-sized cartridges—a pure joy to handload and fascinating to shoot. I believe such rifles put some of the sport back in sport hunting, and they are coming back to the old Southwest. If you want to give them a try, and you should, here are a few thoughts on the subject.

The Rifles

At one time in this country, every major arms manufacturer produced ideal small game rifles in 25-20 and 32-20 and some nice rimfires, too. Today, those are collector's items, with prices to reflect that sad fact. Nevertheless, it is still possible to find some reasonable buys if you don't insist on mint condition. Bores may be pitted, but if the pitting isn't severe and the action's tight, they'll still shoot, perhaps very well indeed. You can find, most frequently: the Winchester Model 1892 and Marlin Model 1894 lever actions; the Remington Model 25 and Marlin Model 27 pumps; the Savage Model 23 and Winchester Model 43 bolt actions; and the Savage Model 219 and Winchester high and low wall single shots.

Of course, you could use a modern rifle. We don't have the same variety of models and calibers, but modern reproductions of the '92 Winchester by Rossi and Browning, and Marlin's revival of their 1894 carbine are excellent values. In 357 Magnum, which I consider the maximum load that could still be thought of as a small game caliber, they represent a lot of shooting. And Marlin now offers its cute Model 1894 lever gun in—praise them—25-20 and 32-20.

The Cartridges

As an all-round candidate for the best small game cartridge, the 25-20 has a lot going for it. This modern-looking little bottlenecked cartridge offers excellent loading flexibility, accuracy and flat trajectory. The superb 60-grain high-speed factory load at approximately 2100 fps is no more, in favor of an 86-grain softpoint load jogging along at 1460 fps. When the 86-grain factory bullets could be purchased, we had no trouble loading them to 1700 fps. Lately we've had to reorganize our handloads around the excellent 60-grain 25-caliber softpoint bullet from Hornady and various cast bullets.

An almost universally accurate and mild jacketed load is the 60-grain Hornady pushed by 8.5 grains of H110 for approximately 1640 fps. Increas-

possible.

Next to the 25-20, probably the most classic small game cartridge of yore was the 32-20. Because it was chambered in the Model '73 Winchester and blackpowder Colts, the factories currently offer only a feeble 100-grain jacketed or lead bullet coasting along at 1210 fps. The old factory high-velocity loads used to give a 115-grain jacketed bullet 1600 fps, and 80-grain jacketed hollowpoint 2050 fps, so today the 32-20 is pretty much a handloading prop-

(Top, right and above) Quick to shoulder, quick to reload, the 92 can produce two clean jackrabbit kills in just three or four heartbeats.

ing the load to 12.0-13.0 grains of WW680 will give you approximately 2300 fps, superb accuracy, and explosive performance with this same bullet. However, the Hornady bullet is uncannelured as it comes from the factory. To use it safely in a tubular magazine, you must add a cannelure using one of the inexpensive hand tools readily available from C-H or Corbin.

The long-necked 25-20 case was made for cast bullets. For a quiet plinking load, place a No. 2 buckshot (0.27-inch diameter) on a 25-caliber gascheck, run them together through a .257-inch bullet sizing die, seat the resulting gaschecked round ball over 1.5 to 3.0 grains of Bullseye, smear some bullet lube over its nose, and enjoy. For normal cast bullet loads, shop for a gascheck bullet that resembles Lyman's old #257312 mould. Lyman's current mould #257420 is excellent. Both NEI and Old West Bullet Moulds produce similar designs. I currently use Old West's 82-grain gascheck design over 8.0 grains of IMR 4227 which gives me 1520 fps and 1-inch 50-yard groups in a Model '92 rifle.

Finally, don't full-length resize your brass until you have to; 25-20 brass is thin and expensive, and you might as well make it last as long as osition if you want any degree of performance.

There are two peculiarities about the 32-20 that should be taken into consideration if you want to work with it. First, it is a true 32-caliber. It takes a .310-.313-inch diameter jacketed or cast bullet. While cast bullet diameters can be tailored to fit with a proper sizing die, the most common jacketed bullets available today are the 100- and 110-grain .308-inch diameter round- or flat-nosed missiles available from component suppliers such as Speer. These bullets have thin jackets and shoot well enough; Speer's 110-grain double-cannelured flat-nosed Varminter hollowpoint is probably the best of the lot. However, a newly released bullet which should breathe new life back into the 32-20 is Hornady's .312-inch diameter 85-grain cannelured JHP designed for the 32 H & R Magnum pistol cartridge.

The other aspect of the 32-20 which warrants mentioning is that its brass case is unusually thin-walled by modern standards and does not hold up well under repeated reloadings. I think the 32-20 is, in the end, a great cast bullet cartridge and a mediocre jacketed number.

A good standard load for either 100-110-grain jacketed bullets or Lyman's #311316 gaschecked 115-grain cast bullet is 12.0-14.0 grains of IMR 4227. Great plinking loads can be worked up with #0 or #00 buckshot, either sized with a gascheck or shot as is over 1.5-3.0 grains of Bullseye.

In addition to the current crop of

Here's another set of desert jacks, done up in one go by author and his 218 Bee.

Browning, Rossi and Marlin lever guns, many thousands of original '92 Winchesters were converted to 357 Magnum during the 1950s and '60s. Because of the availability of an unbelievable array of reloading components and because of its inherent flexibility and accuracy, the 357 is the finest, modern small game rifle cartridge we have—period. It's the type of cartridge that will digest everything from round balls to 200-grain jacketed bullets without complaint and with considerable authority from a rifle-length barrel.

Reloading data on the 357 is readily available and needn't be repeated, but here are a few additional observations on the cartridge. Rifles in this caliber seem to prefer bullets in the 140-160-grain region. The Speer 140-grain JHP, the Sierra 158-grain JHP, and Lyman's #358156 155-grain gaschecked cast bullet have always been top performers with 2400 and WW296 powders. For a very quiet and deadly short-range load, try 1.5 grains of Bullseye under a 148-grain hollow base 38 Special wadcutter with the hollow base facing forward—I don't know why, but they're consistently more accurate that way. You will never go wrong with a 357.

Both the 256 Winchester Magnum and a 30-357 wildcat are based on the 357 Magnum case and since they will normally feed just fine in the modern Model '92 reproductions chambered for 357, a number of us are beginning to rebarrel our 357s. The 256 and 30-357 may very well be the 25-20s and 32-20s of the 1980s. They have a lot to offer in terms of performance and availability of cheap, strong brass. Why the factories and the shooting public haven't caught on to them is somewhat of a mystery. Marlin tried years ago to market its Model 62 lever action in 256 and 30 Carbine. They didn't sell then, but have you priced a used Model 62 in 256 recently? Or better yet, a Ruger Hawkeye in the same caliber?

While the 25-20 and 32-20 are solid citizens, the 256 and 30-357 are hotrodders. From my 18-inch barreled 256 carbine, I get 2750-2800 fps using 16.0-17.0 grains of WW680 behind Hornady's 60-grain softpoint. My shooting compadre, Frank Kelly, shoots a 30-357 and from his 24-inch barreled Model '92 obtains 2700 fps using WW296 behind 110-grain jacketed slugs and 2400 fps from 130-grain Hornady's using Re7 powder. Both cartridges are equally at home with mild cast bullet loads.

I hesitated to include the 218 Bee and 219 Zipper in a list of small game cartridges since both calibers have established their reputations as "varmint" loads. However, they are traditional and superb lever-action cartridges, and were originally introduced in lever-action Winchesters.

Both the Winchester Model 64 and the Marlin Model 336 were factory issued in 219 Zipper, and any current 30-30 can readily be rebarreled for this case today. The 218 Bee was chambered by Winchester in their neat, little Model 65 which was nothing more than a late-coming deluxe version of the '92 Winchester. The 218 case is based on the 25-20 and 32-20 family of cases so Model '92s in those calibers can easily be rebarreled to 218 with the addition of a bushed firing pin.

I must admit to having a specially warm spot in my heart for the 218 Bee in the Model 65 Winchester. With it, I probably did the best shooting of my life late one afternoon in the Arizona desert. Climbing out of a wash, I jumped four large antelope jackrabbits which simultaneously proceeded to beat it for the next county. A few seconds and four shots later from my little Bee, I was picking up four fine jacks which lay on a line, the nearest about 30 yards and the farthest 120 yards from where I stood. If they'd been a 7x7 bull elk, I couldn't have

(Top) This original equipment is more usual, typical of Model '92 rear sights, and quite adequate, properly employed. (Above) Winchester's original bolt-mounted peep sight delights author on his Model 65 218 Bee.

A 219 Zipper isn't as easy to feed as once, but either Marlin or Winchester will do, anyway.

The 218 Bee won't die, it seems, not dead, anyway, and there are plenty around.

Getting a 357 lever gun is lots easier than it used to be and the writer thinks it's never a bad choice for little rifle jobs.

been more proud. With my little Winchesters, I've made running double shots on jacks, but never a quadruple since that day. In any case, the 218 Bee will give you anywhere from 2700-2900 fps using 45-grain Sierra 224 Hornet bullets with WW296 or Re7 powder from a 24-inch Model '92.

I keep a Model 64 Winchester in 219 Zipper around the house for specialized varmint work, but the full-sized 30-30 cartridge is too big to fit into my concept of a small game load. The factories stopped making Zipper brass years ago, and a set of forming dies to rework 30-30 brass into 219s will now cost an arm and a leg. Just recently, however, Norma has begun importing 22 Savage Hi-Power brass again which is just the ticket for forming Zipper cases. Maybe I'll break that Zipper out next week and . . .

The Sights

The open rear leaf and front blade sights as furnished on original and reproduction small game rifles range from excellent to atrocious. As a general rule of thumb, you will find guns with 24-inch or longer barrels and long sight radiuses are much easier to hit with than their 18- to 20-inch carbine equivalents.

If you wish to preserve open rear sights, I would suggest you try increasing the distance between your eye and the rear sight. This can be readily accomplished by fitting an adjustable single leaf compact sight as made by Lyman or Marble or Williams or by reversing the typical factory supplied sight so that the long leaf spring base of the rear leaf is pointing toward the muzzle. Yes, it looks odd and unconventional, but it works. You'll have to try front sight variations until you find something that suits your eye and personal sight picture. I like small, flat-faced gold beads. Many of my friends like white or ivory beads.

Some of the old lever rifles carry contemporary Lyman or Marble tang sights. They're fast and really very useful as game sights, although I've never quite figured out where to put my thumb comfortably when using them.

Receiver or peep sights are probably the best small game sights available to us. Use them. I see nothing wrong in drilling and tapping an original '92 Winchester for a Williams or Lyman receiver sight, for example. Model '92s were made right up to the year 1941, and receiver sights of modern design had been available for decades by that time.

If you need a scope, use one, but try iron sights first. You may surprise yourself. Unfortunately, scopes just seem to clutter up the inherently fine, sleek lines of a small game rifle. They ruin its balance and fine carrying qualities as well.

Accuracy and Accurizing

Lever-action rifles have unjustly been accused of being inherently inaccurate. Well, they're not. Finicky, maybe, but not inaccurate. The sad reputation they have had to endure for all too many years seems to stem from the early gun writers who were under the impression that accuracy was only measured through 10-shot groups fired from a rest at the range in a relatively short period of time.

My small game-calibered '92s and '94s will average 1-inch at 50 yards and 2 to 2½ inches at 100 yards using iron sights. Yours will, too, if you spend as much time as the bolt gunners do in working up loads and shooting three-shot "sporting rifle" groups while letting the barrel cool between shots.

If you want to tread on the heels of the bolt guns, try accurizing your lever-action rifle according to the excellent instructions contained in the article entitled "Lever Action Rifles" by Helbig and Cain, which appeared in the 1965 edition of *Gun Digest*. The authors just about cover every secret we know for squeezing out the utmost accuracy from lever guns. Then add a scope to your rig, stroll on down to the range, and lay a few side bets with your shooting partners. My point is simply that most lever-action rifles will shoot better than their owners can under field conditions. Don't ever sell this unique American design short.

So, if your hunting has lost its edge and your scope-sighted super whizz bang hits everything with dull monotony, put a little fun back in life. Pick up a nice, sleek little small game rifle, stuff your pockets full of beautiful, petite cartridges, and head for the back door. You will never regret it. Never. ●

You can count the reasons for owning a Colt 10mm Auto on both hands.

After a year of redesigning and extensive testing, Colt has modified the slide and receiver system of the world renowned Government Model to accommodate the powerful new 10mm auto round. The Colt Delta Elite™ is an impressive semi-auto pistol, chambered for an equally impressive cartridge.

The 10mm auto is a hot cartridge, pure and simple. The 170 grain hollow point round leaves the muzzle at an awesome 1300 ft/sec, almost 150 ft/sec faster than the conventional 9mm. Muzzle energy is almost twice that of the 45 ACP. Impressive ballistics, in anyone's book.

Combine these statistics with the fact that this round is chambered in a pistol with a mechanism second to none, and you've got yourself a lot of pistol.

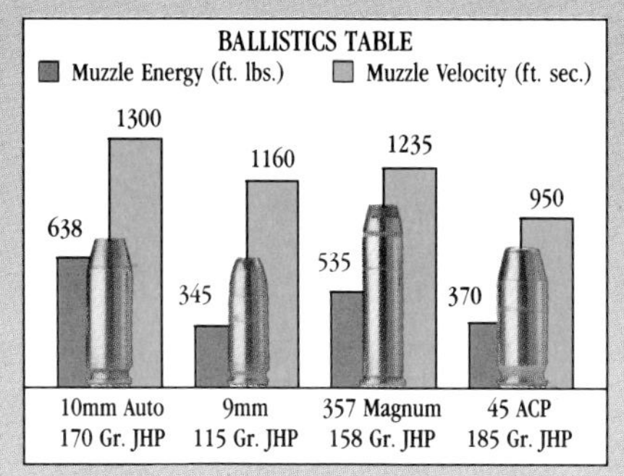

Ballistics are nominal and have been obtained from test barrels. Individual firearms may vary from these specifications.

Whether in the field, on the range or with law enforcement agencies, this is one pistol that will deliver, when it counts.

Ten reasons to own the new Colt Delta Elite. Boil it down further and you get dependability, speed and power. Those ingredients spell Colt, and shooters have been relying on this name for quite some time.

Hartford, CT 06101

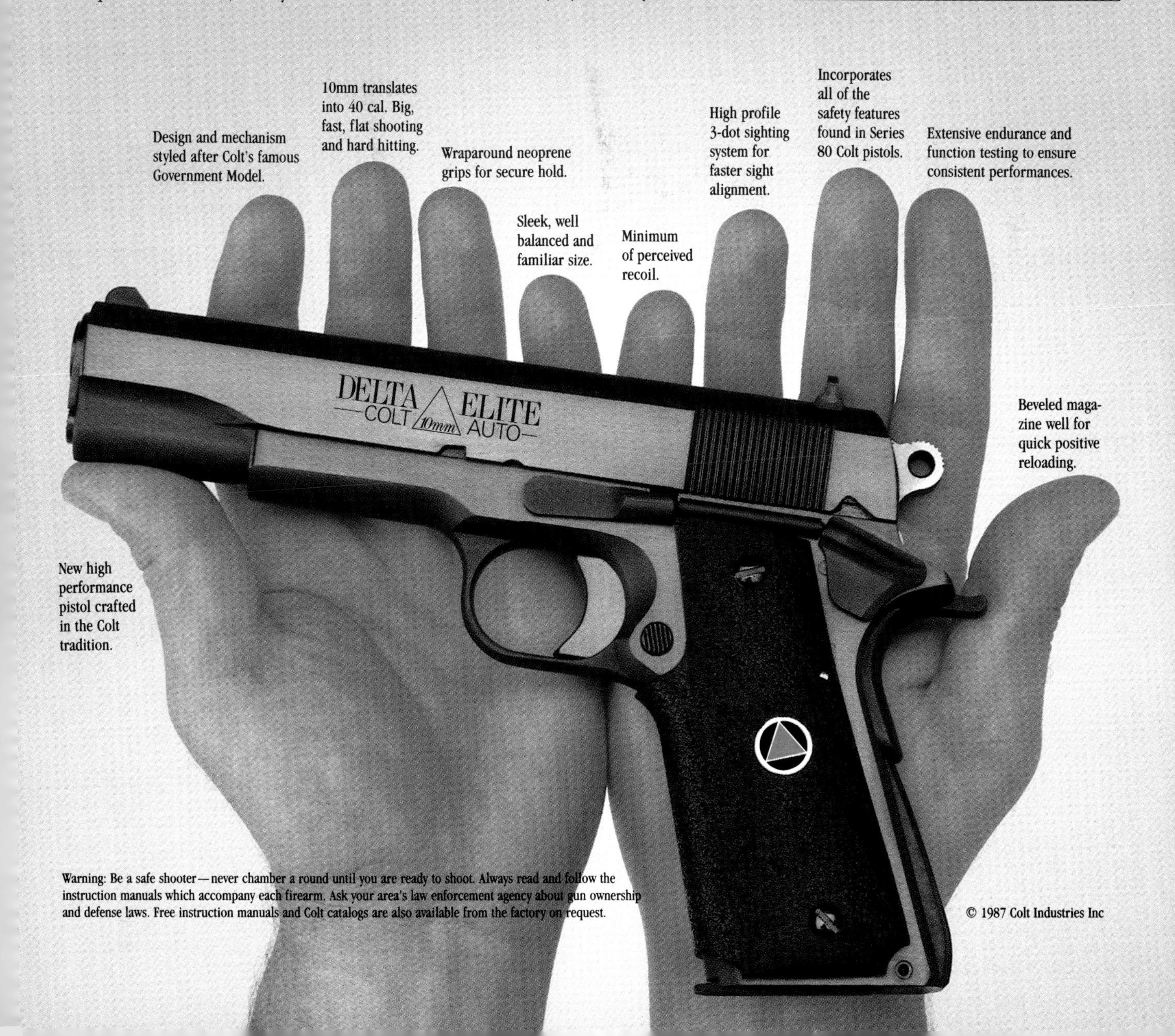

Warning: Be a safe shooter—never chamber a round until you are ready to shoot. Always read and follow the instruction manuals which accompany each firearm. Ask your area's law enforcement agency about gun ownership and defense laws. Free instruction manuals and Colt catalogs are also available from the factory on request.

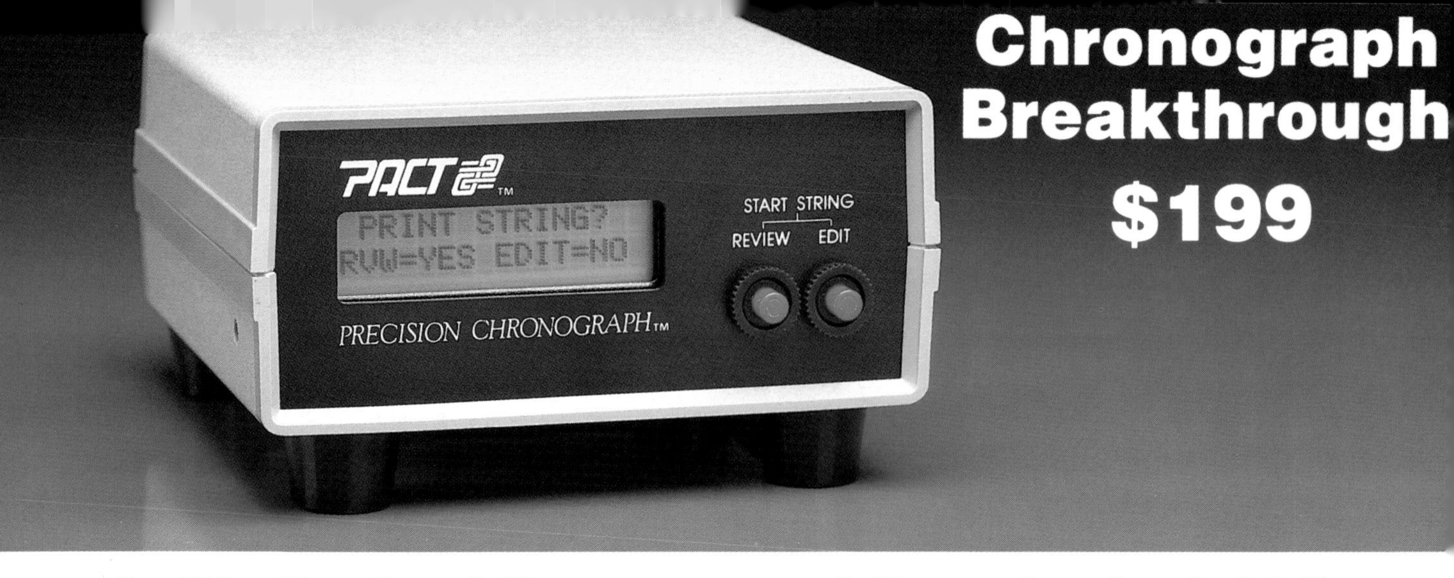

"...it's the best I've seen, and the price is right."

Rick Jamison, *Shooting Times*

Tough Choices

Until PACT introduced the PC two years ago, shooters looking for a chronograph were torn between two tough choices. To go with a full feature skyscreen based machine at a premium price, or settle for one of the low end "break screen" or "down range box" units at a more reasonable price, but lacking the ease of use and superior performance of a microprocessor based skyscreen chronograph.

Each time you fire

Each time you fire a round over the PCs' optical skyscreens, your shot number, velocity and current average velocity are displayed simultaneously, on our state of the art, easy to read, **32 character display.** All of this is done automatically, no button pushing required, so you are free to concentrate on your shooting instead of having to constantly fuss with your chronograph. In addition the shot number and its velocity are automatically **stored in memory** for your later review.

After you complete a string

When you complete a string simply press the review key to display a **complete** statistical summary of the string. This summary consists of your highest and lowest shot velocities and their corresponding shot numbers, the Extreme Spread and average velocity of your string. The Standard Deviation and Mean Absolute Deviation (a PACT exclusive and the best measure of ammunitation consistency yet developed) are calculated and displayed automatically. In addition both of these numbers are also displayed as a percent of your average (coefficient of variation or CV). We have found that this method of describing the average variation of your ammo is much more useful to the shooter who's trying to develop better, more consistant loads, than simply handing him, the "SD" of a given string. Take a look at Handloader #128 for more information.

After completing the statistical summary your PC will allow you to **review each shot** (up to 300) of your string.

- uses standard 9 volt alkaline battery (included, of course)
- easy access battery compartment
- adjustable screen separation
- Edit button allows you to remove any unwanted shot from a string, either after the shot is fired or during review.
- 4 mhz counter for better digital accuracy
- retractable tilt stand for easy viewing
- each chronograph is electronically "calibrated" to insure accuracy

PACT Skyscreens

The PACT PC uses inexpensive optical skyscreens to detect the bullet. Why didn't we set it up so that you can shoot over the box or use expensive skyscreens containing elaborate lenses to "enhance" performance? Because we think it's stupid to launch bullets over things that cost lots of money. Now we realize that **you never miss,** but rarely a day goes by that we don't get an order for a replacement skyscreen housing ($2.50).

Order Today

TOLL FREE...800 PACT INC
(in Texas 214-641-0049)

By Phone: We are happy to answer your questions and take your order. We accept Visa, MC and COD orders.*

PACT PC (with skyscreens) $199
Print Driver (installed in PC) . . . $ 25
Battery Powered Printer $125
Extra Printer Paper (6 rolls) $12
Skyscreen Bracket
(optional but nice) . . . . $ 24
Extra Skyscreens . . . . $15 ea $25 pr
Skyscreen Housings$2.50 each 4 for $9

*Shipping & Insurance $4.50 UPS ground/$10 UPS 2nd day air. Extra shipping for bracket (separate package) $3 ground/$6 2nd day air. Bank service charge for VISA/MC. COD fee $2. Write or call for foreign rates. Texas residents add appropriate sales tax.

Brochure Available covering the PACT product line of shooting timers and chronographs, $1.00.

P. O. Box 531525
Grand Prairie, TX 75053

Glint Guard™ pat. pend.

Over the years chronographs have earned a well deserved reputation for **flaky performance** when oeprated on bright sunny days. Some manufacturers deal with the problem by requiring you to put diffuser screens over their skyscreens. While this approach works, it makes set up more difficult and is prone to blow over in the wind. In addition if you fire too closely to them you may find that it has started raining bits of diffuser screen.

The PACT PC's Glint Guard™ circuitry allows us to dispense with this silliness. Glint Guard™ **internally** compensates for changes in light conditions in much the same manner as the automatic exposure feature in a modern camera.

Pact Print Driver & Printer

By having us install our optional Print Driver and purchasing our battery powered printer you will find your self in possession of the **ultimate chronograph system.** When you complete your string just press the review key. The PC will ask you if you would like to print the string. Tell it "yes" and you will be provided with a print out consisting of the string number, complete statistical summary, and the velocity of each individual shot. Keep in mind that once the Print Driver is installed you can add the printer at any time.

30 Day Money Back Guarantee

We designed the PC, we build it, and we sell it factory direct to you. We take full responsibility for your satisfaction. If you are not 100% satisfied with any PACT product, return it to us undamaged (no fair driving over it) within 30 days, and we will refund your money. That's our promise and you can depend on it.

Lifetime Warranty

The PACT PC features a **real simple repair policy.** If it breaks due to a defective part or faulty workmanship **we'll fix it free.** If you break it (people really have driven over them) we'll fix it for cost. No hassles and no questions asked.

The 56mm Light Source.

Introducing the Redfield 3x12 Ultimate Illuminator™

We're proud to introduce the finest precision sighting instrument Redfield has ever produced for hunters. The first American-made rifle scope with a 30mm one-piece outer tube and a 56mm adjustable objective. It's simply the finest rifle scope you can buy today... designed to give you the ultimate source in light-gathering ability.

Built for dusk and dawn hunting.

The Ultimate Illuminator™ gives you more usable light just before dawn and just after dusk. The light you need to pierce those dark shadows to see contrasts between field and game. The light you need to count points and determine a true aiming point. The light that **adds 15 minutes** — morning and evening to your hunting day.

This light source is achieved through a unique lens system, invented and designed by Redfield. Plus, we use a special coated glass that's designed exclusively for our Illuminator scopes ... to brighten the image and give excellent resolution.

56mm adjustable objective for maximum light-gathering ability.

Precision and accuracy.

You'll find all of our quality commitments backed by our Written Lifetime Warranty. Quarter-minute positive click adjustments. One-piece tube design for fog-proof and waterproof dependability. A superior lens system alignment for exceptional accuracy and magnum-proof stability. Plus, the Ultimate Illuminator features a European #4 reticle.

Includes 30mm rings & presentation box.

Packed in a handsome oak presentation box, the Redfield Ultimate Illuminator comes complete with lens covers and a set of our 30mm steel rotary-dovetail rings.

If you want the ultimate in rifle scopes, see your Redfield dealer. He's your source for the 56mm light source — the 3 x 12 Ultimate Illuminator.

Get our 1988 full-color catalog.
Send $1.00 to: Redfield, Dept. GD078
5800 E. Jewell Avenue,
Denver, CO 80224.

Quality Sports Optics for the Great Outdoors

New Toys For The Big Boys.

Action Arms has an armload of new products to tempt every shooter. If you think of Action Arms as just the world-famous UZI, you're in for a pleasant surprise. There also are GALIL rifles, SAMSON and UZI ammo, and more than a handful of new products.

.357 Magnum energy in 9mm sized pistols—the all-new .41 Action Express delivers. Unlike any other pistol cartridge, this new round sends a .41 caliber, 170 gr. bullet downrange at 1200 feet/second. That's 590 foot pounds at the muzzle, and it operates within normal 9mm pressures.

.41 Action Express drop-in conversion kits for popular 9mm pistols. Since the rim of the .41 Action Express is the same dimension as the 9mm, conversion is as easy as changing the barrel and magazine. Easy-to-install kits for the Browning Hi-Power, 9mm Colt Government Model & Commander and the new 9mm AT-88 are available.

The New AT-88: the AT-84 has been improved. Now, the advantage of either double action or cocked and locked carry in one pistol is combined with the new .41 Action Express chambering. An ambidextrous safety and firing pin block have also been added to this legendary design. The popular 9mm version is also available.

Two new Action Sights are the latest technology in red dot aiming. With a 1″ diameter tube and a 45 degree angle offset battery pack, the compact PRO 45 sight can be mounted with battery to the right or left. The new PRO 5 is the smallest and lightest Action Sight ever offered. Choice of right or left hand model suits any holstering need.

The new Micro Dot Scopes add true red dot aiming with quality optics. Take standard duplex crosshairs and add a tiny, intensity-adjustable red dot to the center and you have the next generation of hunting scopes: Micro Dot scopes. Hunters will appreciate the extra ½ hour at dawn and dusk—right when hunting can be most productive.

Action Scope Mounts, Accessories and Memorabilia listing has also expanded. Now there are rugged, no-gunsmith mounts for most popular hand guns and many long guns. The collection of accessories and memorabilia is so large that a special catalog had to be printed to show it all. Write for it today and also receive the full-line catalog.

action arms ltd.

P.O. Box 9573, Philadelphia, PA 19124

My Grandaddy's Shotgun

Not only loaded with memories, this first Browning over/under the author ever saw does gun business with birds every year

by CHARLES E. PETTY

TO APPRECIATE the significance of that day's event you have to understand that my grandfather was, in today's terminology, laid back. I can't recall ever seeing him lose his temper or show much excitement about anything except quail hunting, at least until that phone call one fall morning. Memory is dim as to the date, but I think it was 1947. If so, I was eight.

My grandmother called him to the phone and his only words were, "I'll be right there."

He grabbed his coat and hat and was out the door in a shot. When he returned half an hour later, the box he carried could only be a gun—and what a gun it was! A brand new, dainty little Browning Superposed 20 gauge. Reverence best describes the way he unpacked and assembled it. By current values it wasn't anything overly special, but then, in the aftermath of World War II, it must have been one of the first guns to come out of Liege.

In those days a new American gun was rare enough, but one from Belgium must have been unheard of. He had placed the order at the local hardware store as soon as the war was over and had been waiting ever since. Nobody knew anything about it for he did not confide his secrets; especially to 8-year-old-grandsons.

Some of my earliest memories are of waiting for him to return home from a quail hunt. Those were the days before I was old enough to go along and my training was limited to the classroom of the back porch where he would clean guns and birds. I had spent many an impatient Saturday afternoon waiting for his car to turn the corner onto our street. His arrival would light up the sleepy house and fill it with the exciting smells I came

"... like the magic book for this man and boy ..."

to associate with hunting—the oil and solvent for the ritual gun cleaning and the marvelous odor of fired paper shotgun shells. I suspect that's an unknown smell to a whole generation of hunters and that's too bad. Sure, the new plastic shells are better and if there was just some way to make them smell right, they'd be perfect.

The new Browning was Grandaddy's solution to a problem I suspect all hunters would wish for. Wartime shortages of shotgun shells and hunters had allowed the quail population in the North Carolina foothills where he lived to grow unchecked and, even though he had hunted, the strict rationing of ammunition had severely hampered things. He was one of only a few hunters out there doing his best. He understood, and taught me, the basic principles of game management by explaining why it was necessary to thin the coveys that were so numerous.

I didn't know it at the time, but I was getting the lessons that have formed the foundation of a lifetime of hunting and shooting. They dealt with the requisite behavior of sportsmen and instilled an abiding concern for the farmers on whose land we hunted and provided respect for the bobwhite that borders on fanaticism. And, oh, yes, a love of bird dogs came with it all.

Until I began to hunt with him, Mike, the pointer who lived in a lot at the back of the house, was a pet. I never could understand why Grandaddy wouldn't let me bring him in the house or play with him as I did my beagle puppy. The first time I saw Mike find and point a covey of quail, I knew. There *was* something special there. The passage of nearly 40 years has brought that dog legendary characteristics that are probably composites of all the good gun dogs I've known since, but I really can't remember him ever busting a covey or failing to retreive the birds that fell before Grandaddy's Browning. Maybe he did, but any such memory is so thoroughly repressed as to be nonexistent.

The morning the Browning came, Grandaddy paced around the den as if walking through a corn field, stopping occasionally to pop the gun to his shoulder and swing on a covey rising before him. It was certainly unusual behavior for such a stolid gentleman, but I swear I could see them, too. A quick lunch interrupted the fantasy hunt but then he began to gather a few things for an afternoon of shooting. Maybe the arrival of the Browning was the cause, but as he was putting clay targets and a few boxes of shells in the car he said, "Get your jacket."

That was the first time I was allowed to go along. He and some friends had rigged an informal Skeet field in a farmer's backyard and the first target off the trap disappeared in a puff of smoke, as did most of them that day, and I became convinced that Grandaddy was a super shotgun shooter. Then, with him standing behind me, I got to shoot. I'm sure my eyes were closed, and I know I didn't hit anything, but that mattered little. I had shot THE gun for my first shot ever.

Over the following weeks, anticipation built around the house, for hunting season was near. It was doubly exciting for me for, after some wheedling on my part, it was agreed I could accompany my grandfather on opening day. When Grandaddy had agreed to suffer my presence, he carefully explained my duties: To follow at a safe distance and keep my mouth shut. Not easy for a fidgety kid, but not that tough to learn when he later made me sit in the car for yelling and flushing a covey of birds.

Quail season opened on Thanksgiving and as it approached the pace of activities around the house quickened. Hunting clothes and boots came down out of the attic and he and Mike worked out in the backyard or took scouting trips to the country. Thanksgiving morning dawned crisp and clear. I know, for I hadn't slept much and was up and dressed long before anyone else in the house. When we finally got underway, it seemed to take forever to get there, and the pleasantries Grandaddy exchanged with the farmer seemed an utter waste of time. Finally we began to walk toward the ruins of an old farmhouse and Mike began to behave, as Grandaddy later explained, "birdy." His nose went down and his tail up and minutes later he froze into a point that I now know was picture perfect. Moments later a dozen bobwhites erupted from the honeysuckle patch around the old home place, and the Browning fired its first serious shots. Mike dutifully brought back three birds.

The regularity and seeming ease with which Grandaddy shot quail gave him and the gun heroic proportions that were further magnified when, a few years later, I got to try it myself. He surely had nerves of steel to stand there and calmly pick out one bird from the covey erupting around his feet and someone told me that he was one of the few hunters who had the ability to wait for two birds to cross in their flight and get both with one shot. I can't begin to guess how many I missed by shooting blindly into the brown mass. When I finally did manage to bring one down, Grandaddy thought—out loud—it must have run into a tree.

By the time I was old enough to be anything other than an occasional hunter, a bad hip had nearly ended Grandaddy's hunting days and Mike's death was a blow from which I think he never recovered. A succession of dogs came and went, but it seemed no other dog would do. It seemed if he couldn't hunt with the best, he chose not to hunt at all. Somehow, I think the end of his hunting days marked the end of his life as well, for his health deteriorated rapidly after that and, as I neared my 16th birthday, he passed away.

Years later I read Robert Ruark's magic book. *The Old Man and the Boy* and finally realized what a truly priceless gift my grandfather had given me. Those lessons have served me well and I regret more than I can tell that I never had a chance, or took the time, to thank him.

Now I feel that I am able to pay that debt. I have a son of my own, you see, and we hunt together. Trips with him never fail to revive memories of other hunts and other times and I wonder if he has ever noticed how, sometimes, my eyes seem to bother me as we walk up behind another Mike and I slide the safety off that beautiful, dainty little Browning 20. ●

HANDGUNS TODAY: SIXGUNS AND OTHERS

by HAL SWIGGETT

ON THESE NEXT few pages you will find a few new guns, a few older guns, a couple of *different* guns for this section and two brand new little cuties from companies best-known for big guns. It's been fun putting it together. Here it is—from A to W:

Anschutz

The Exemplar, Anschutz's entry into bolt-action pistols, was announced last year in 22 Long Rifle. Built on their Match 64 action, the five-shot, left-hand bolt pistol has proved to be very popular.

Now there is another. Based on their Match 54 action there is now a centerfire 22 Hornet Exemplar. Barrel length is 10 inches, same as the Long Rifle version. Both have the bolt on the left side so the hand does not have to be changed to extract the empty and put a fresh cartridge in the chamber. Both versions are European walnut stocked with stippled grip and forend rather than checkering. The magazine capacity is four rounds, one less than the rimfire version.

A rather lengthy talk with Dieter Anschutz still leaves us without a 22 WMR edition. Mr. Anschutz is against the idea. I'm for it and will keep trying.

Charter Arms

"AMERICAN MADE and Proud of It!"

So reads the top of the inside front cover of Charter Arms catalog. Several other firearms companies could make that same claim, but I sure can't criticize Charter for doing so.

Two of Charter's other claims are: reduction of critical moving parts providing longer trouble-free operation and the introduction of new alloys on non-critical parts for significant weight reduction while retaining the all-steel frame for durability. The 2-inch five-shot 38 on my desk has an ejector rod shroud; it is the newest production with black satin (it looks like Parkerizing) finish and their newest "Select-A-Grip" (laminated wood in almost the color of your choice) and it weighs in at 17 ounces on my postal

Swiggett's Predator was in 223 Remington and he used all brands of ammo. The pistol had a favorite but all shot better than most folks think a pistol will perform.

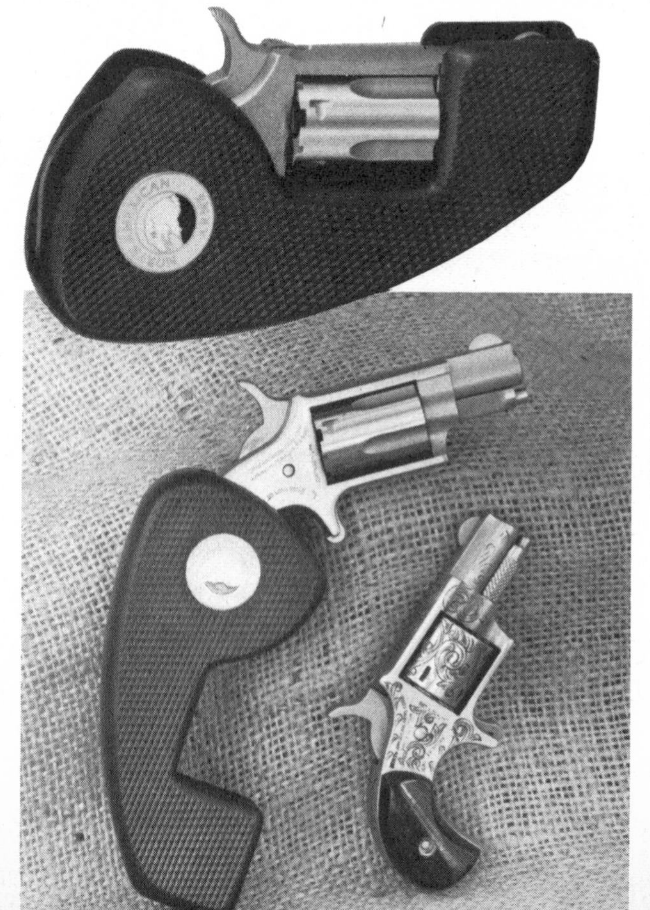

North American Arms' new Holster Grip for their mini revolver covers the trigger; then it unfolds for shooting. The engraved 22 Short NAA mini belongs to Hal's wife.

scale. Stamping on the barrel labels it as "Off Duty."

There is another 38 2-incher called Police Undercover at 17½ ounces in blue or 20 ounces in stainless that chambers six rounds of +P ammo and is capable of taking all you might want to put through it. A 4-inch version, both blue and stainless, is offered as Police Bulldog.

Also on my desk at this moment is a stainless 2-inch "Off Duty" 22 Long Rifle. It wears a darker version of the same grip, is six-shot with counterbored chambers and tops out the scale at 17½ ounces. This one, however, lacks the ejector rod shroud. (I'm not sure if that is good or bad. Skeeter Skelton found good purpose for this lack of shroud. The cylinder release latch gave his thumb a hard time so he removed it and opened the cylinder via the ejection rod. This is mentioned only as a passing point of interest and passing on the thought of a knowledgeable shooter.)

Charter has made a career out of good triggers. The 38 "Off Duty" in hand lets off crisply at a fraction under 4 pounds single action and between 11 and 12 pounds pulling through. The 22 is about 4 ounces heavier both ways and equally crisp. I was able to shoot consistent 15-yard groups, a cylinder full each time, of 1½ to 2 inches. Fixed sights and only 2 inches of barrel, but I'm not complaining.

Colt

The King Cobra, for 1988, is now available in three finishes *and* three barrel lengths. Matte stainless steel, the original finish, can now be had in 2½-, 4-, or 6-inch. Blue King Cobras are available in 4-, and 6-inch. "Ultimate" bright stainless steel, the finish first introduced in the Python line, King Cobras are being offered in 4- and 6-inch lengths.

Anschutz 22 Hornet Exemplar with four-shot magazine and 10-inch barrel drilled, tapped and grooved for any scope mounting.

Off Duty in 22 Long Rifle does without ejector rod shroud.

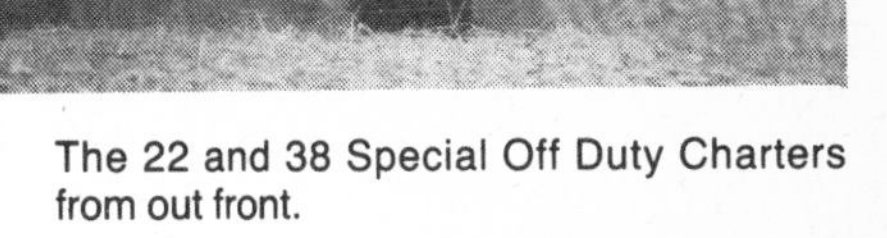

The 22 and 38 Special Off Duty Charters from out front.

And the Charter Police Undercover is a six-shot with +P capacity.

And Charter's Off Duty 38 Special is still a five-shot.

The Colt Custom Shop's latest offering is a distinctive "mini" collection: five Colt Sheriff's Model Single Action Army revolvers displayed in a custom-crafted, etched glass-topped oak gun case, that is suitable for hanging. These single actions are arranged in a circle, around a gold antiqued-finish sheriff's badge against a deep green, French-fit velvet background. Only 200 sets will be made.

Competition Arms

Competition Arms, based in Tucson, Arizona, manufactures the Competitor single shot, interchangeable barrel, pistol reviewed on these pages in the 1988 edition. Sig Himmelmann, long known for building very good single-action revolvers, had to get one back in his line and has. It is made from 17-4PH 416 Series stainless steel, wears 10½ inches of barrel and, for the moment, will be chambered only for 357 Remington Maximum (Super Mag) and 375 Super Mag. These are silhouette-shooting calibers so Sig's new six-gun will come in at 1 or 2 ounces short of the IHMSA 4-pound limit.

I visited Sig's plant on the way back from a Coues deer hunt and saw the beginnings of this new revolver. All the way home it stayed in the back of my mind and eventually a name for it hit me. I called Tucson as soon as I got home, asked Sig to get a piece of paper and pencil and put down an "S" then an "i," a "g," another "s," then a "G," "u," and "n." Put it all together and you have "SigsGun." When the new single action showed up in Las Vegas for the SHOT Show it had, stamped into the side of the barrel, "SigsGun."

Competition Arms is also the sole United States distributor of Erma handguns. This includes their Model 777, 773 and 772 Match revolvers in 357 Magnum, 32 S&W Long and 22 Long Rifle. The 357 comes in 4- and 5½-inch barrel lengths. The 32 and 22 are 6 inches only. These are match revolvers with micrometer rear sights and interchangeable front and rear blades. Grips are adjustable match types on the two smaller chamberings. The 357 may be ordered with checkered walnut or a blank match grip.

Freedom Arms

"The 454 Casull, The World's Most Powerful Revolver" is a statement that has gone undisputed. It could also say "The Best-Built Single Action In The World." That, too, would go undisputed.

The Casull single action has been priced out of reach of a lot of folks who really wanted one. Freedom honchos realized that and have tried to do something about it. There is now a "Field Grade" 454 Casull. It is exactly the same inside except that maybe the trigger hasn't received as much attention as does the Premier Grade. I have one of each and can't tell any difference in the triggers. Both are excellent.

The "Field Grade" comes in 4¾-, 7½- and 10-inch barrels. The finish is matte (only stainless steel is used in *all* of Freedom's single actions) for re-

Ruger Super Redhawk stainless steel 44 Magnum with 9½-inch barrel and Bausch & Lomb 4x silver scope.

(Left) The first animal killed with a Super Redhawk. Swiggett used Remington 240-grain factory loads.

Freedom Arms 454 Casull Field Grade 4 ¾-inch revolver.

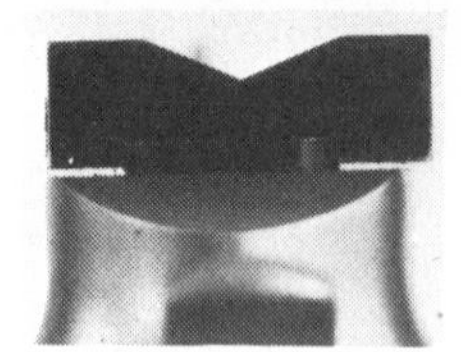

Express sights are optional . . .

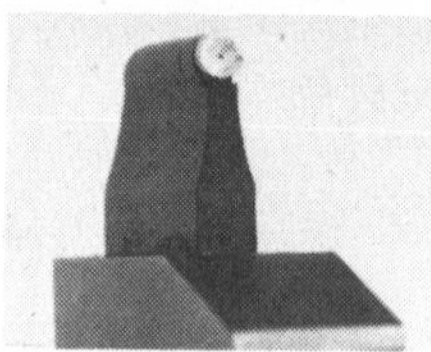

and Swiggett likes the shallow V with this bead up front.

Barrel stamping tells the story.

Cylinder walls are thick on the 454 Casull. That's the serial number.

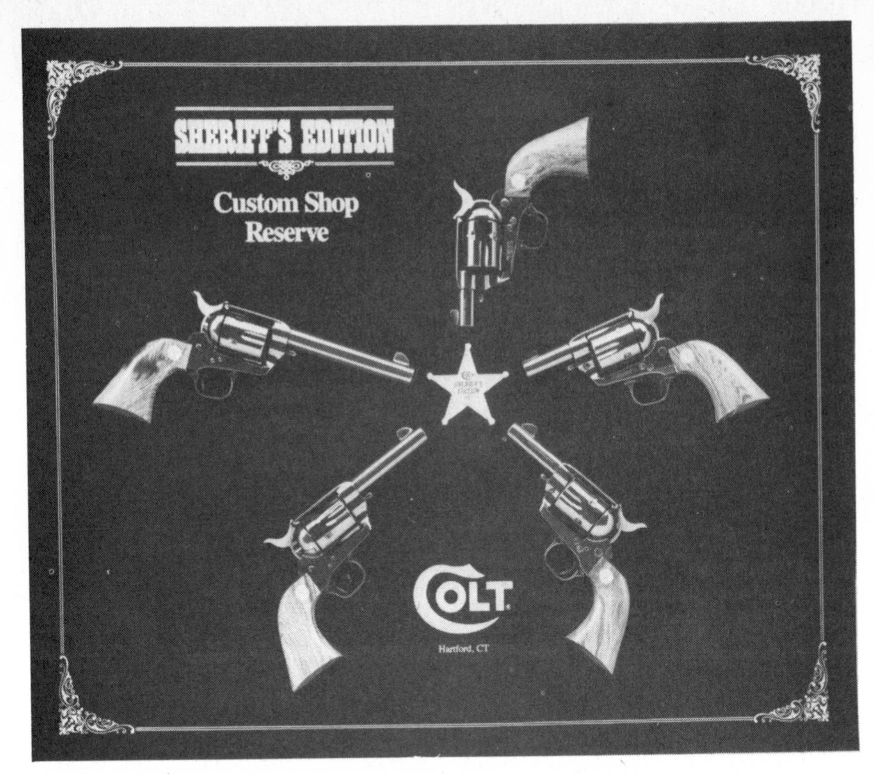

Colt Sheriff's Model Reserve Edition, a distinctive "mini" collection of five Colt Sheriff's Model SAA revolvers displayed in an etched glass-topped oak gun case that's suitable for wall mounting.

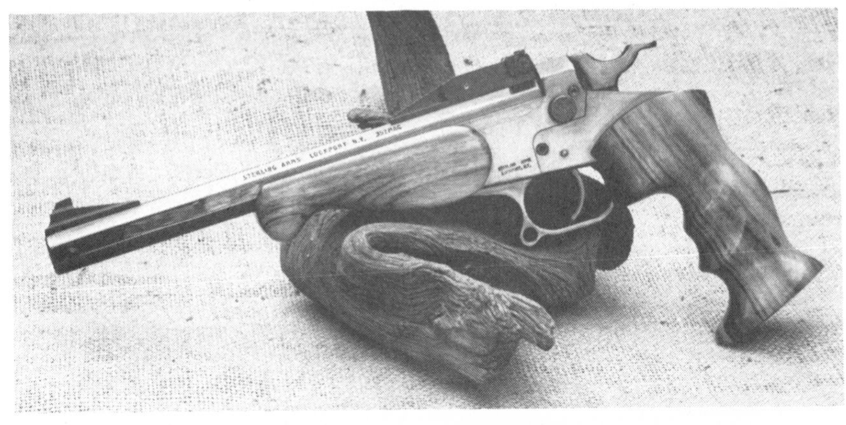

This is the early X-Caliber. Ithaca is to bring it back, they say.

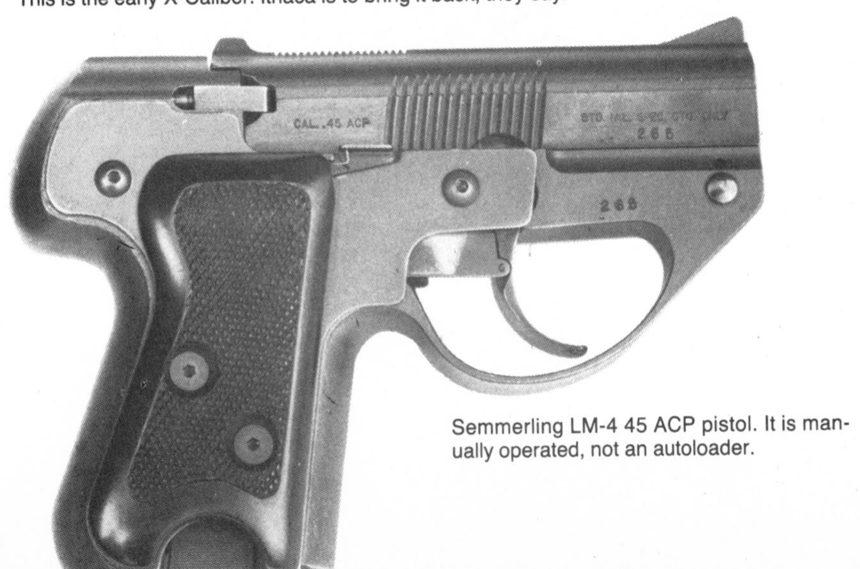

Semmerling LM-4 45 ACP pistol. It is manually operated, not an autoloader.

duced glare. Pachmayr grips are standard on the "Field Grade." I'll let you know later if I think this is a blessing. Properly-loaded 454 Casull ammunition speaks with authority. From both ends. The checkering moulded into Pachmayr's neoprene grip *can/might* gouge a bit of flesh here and there. I find smooth wood grips best for heavy-recoiling handguns. Since I have, for years, worn a light leather glove for shooting (since I found Chimere gloves I use nothing else), this really isn't a problem for me but I can see where it might be.

Freedom offers some optional sighting equipment. I had my 4¾-incher rigged with a bead front and their version of "express" rear. I find this to be fastest of all for game shooting.

The "Field Grade" is less expensive than the Premier by about one-third. Not inexpensive yet but a whole bunch closer.

Also new from Freedom is SSK Industries T'SOB three-ring scope mount designed for the 454 Casull. Not a made-to-fit, but designed by J.D. Jones specifically for this gun.

Herrett's Stocks

Long-known for their handgun stocks (the late Steve Herrett spent a lot of time years ago convincing me they are in fact stocks, not grips), Herrett's Stocks now catalogs a stock for Remington's XP-100 bolt-action single shot pistol. The stock is designed for hunters and IHMSA Unlimited shooters. It is of more conventional design rather than the space-age look of the factory hold-on-to part. The stock is made from two pieces of American walnut with the butt section joined by a doweled tongue and groove joint which, according to Herrett, is stronger than a one-piece stock. Because of the different configuration a Timney trigger comes with the stock which is designed to fit the 7mm BR or Varmint Special barreled actions. The system can be user-installed.

Ithaca

First announced on these pages in *Gun Digest*'s 36th Anniversary 1982 Edition, the X-Caliber single-shot, interchangeable barrel, break-open pistol is back. It was a good pistol then, but often new guns have a tough time getting established. Ithaca now markets the X-Caliber under their banner. Pistols shown in Las Vegas were prototypes. I was not allowed to photograph one because, and their man in

Smith & Wesson's new Classic Hunter comes only in blue and with a 6-inch barrel.

This four-position front sight was designed for the silhouette game and Swiggett thinks it is out of character on a hunting handgun.

charge was just being truthful, they did not know if the finished gun would look like the one on the wall.

The Ithaca X-Caliber will be offered in two versions: the Model 20 will be highly polished with Goncalo Alves wood and removable target sights. The Model 30 will have a sandblasted frame and barrel treated to prevent glare, Deerslayer adjustable sights plus grooved for scope mounting and American walnut wood which is satin-finished. Also, a nylon sling is included with the Model 30.

Both 10- and 15-inch barrels will be available for each model. Calibers are 22 Long Rifle, 223 Remington, 35 Remington, 357 Magnum, 357 Remington Maximum and 44 Magnum.

Kimber

Last year Kimber introduced their Predator, a single shot bolt-action pistol based on their Model 84 mini-Mauser action. Barrel length at 15¾ inches and chambered for five cartridges. Very few got in shooters' hands. Very few. I'm told by Greg Warne (he should know, he runs the company) they are now readily available, but 6mm TCU and 6x45mm have been dropped, meaning you can order the Kimber Predator in 221 Fireball, 223 Remington or 7mm TCU and get it. I tested a 223 that first time around, and with a 5x Burris scope found it to shoot at least as good as the best of rifles. Three-quarter-inch groups were common at 100 yards.

North American Arms

The little Utah-made North American Arms (NAA) mini revolvers are a mighty popular item. I will never forget, many years ago, showing my 22 WMR to a U.S. Marshal and mentioning the possibility it could, in his business, come in handy some time. He looked at it momentarily, pulled his hand out of his jacket pocket, and said, "That one's just like mine," as he displayed his mini 22 WMR in the palm of his hand.

NAA is showing nothing new in revolvers, but they do offer an unusual patented Holster Grip. Closed, the little mini rides comfortably in the plastic Holster Grip and safely so, because the trigger is completely enclosed making it virtually impossible for the gun to be fired. The Holster Grip is made with a clip on the back for slipping over a belt. Open, the holster becomes a full-sized grip allowing a more positive hold than the mini grip which comes close to getting lost in some hands.

Unfortunately it fits only 22 Short and Long Rifle mini NAA revolvers. My 22 WMR will have to continue in its so far never publicized and not easily seen hideout.

Rossi

My wife has a Rossi M851 stainless steel 4-inch 38 Special that is a glorious sight with its ventilated rib, full-length ejector rod shroud, red front sight insert and fully adjustable rear sight. It stays by her bedside, instantly within reach, and got there because I reviewed it for these pages several years ago. She liked its looks. She shot it and liked that too. I had to buy it. It hasn't been fired a lot, about 50 rounds a month, but it has proven dependable. A lot of other guns are available for her use, but she sticks to her Rossi M851.

Now there is a 357 Magnum Rossi. The M971 is available in blue only and with a single barrel length—4 inches. It's a six-shot with a full-length ejector rod shroud, striated, matte finished sight rib, serrated ramp front and fully adjustable rear sights, target-type trigger, wide, checkered hammer spur and combat/target grips of dense-grained Brazilian hardwood. Weighing in at 36 ounces the M971 is imported by Interarms as are all Rossi firearms.

Ruger

Bigger *is* better! Not always maybe, but in Ruger's case where the Super Redhawk is concerned, it's a positive statement. It looks bigger than a Redhawk. It feels bigger than a Redhawk. According to Ruger's figures it weighs, with a 7½-inch barrel, only a single ounce more.

When it first came in, it looked ugly to these aging eyes. The longer I looked at it the uglier it got. Maybe it's the way the frame extends out a full 1¾ inches beyond that of the Redhawk. A few days later, the at-that-time only silver Bausch & Lomb 4x scope in existence arrived and was instantly mounted with Ruger's integral Scope Mounting System. It no longer looked ugly. Quite the contrary. Obviously the Super Redhawk was designed for scope mounting.

Produced only in stainless steel and 44 Magnum, I'm shooting the 9½-inch barrel version (the Super Redhawk is offered with 7½- or 9½-inch barrel). The barrel is massive, measuring 13/16-inch at the muzzle. Trigger pull is clean at 64 ounces, 4 pounds, single action. Double-action pull wasn't weighed because this is a "huntin' " gun. To prove it the hammer has been lowered for better scope clearance.

The grip is new Ruger. It's the same as on the GP-100. To be sure I removed the rubber/wood grip from both then replaced them on the other gun. The cylinder is massive plus the bolt cuts are between chambers. This big Ruger Super Blackhawk is built to shoot, and shoot, and shoot.

Weight of the Super Blackhawk I'm shooting, with Ruger's scope rings and the 4x B&L scope on the 9½-inch barrel, is an even 70 ounces, that's 4.375 pounds. There are lightweight rifles weighing only a little over a pound more. So what! I'm a handgunner. I like to take on big things. So does the Super Redhawk. We'll get along just fine.

Now for something so new from

Ruger it hasn't been photographed yet. It is a 38 Special five-shot baby GP-100. Mechanically, it is virtually the same as the GP. Barrel lengths will be 2+ inches and 4 inches. There will be a six-shot 32 H&R Magnum, a 22 Long Rifle and, with a bit of urging from this gun writer, a 22 WMR, I hope. Ruger hinted at the possible chambering of Federal's new 9mm.

This new small frame Mini GP (for lack of a better name) will be built to withstand a constant feeding of +P 38 Special loads.

Semmerling

This interesting repeater has found a new home at American Derringer. It is a specialized design, of course, but useful.

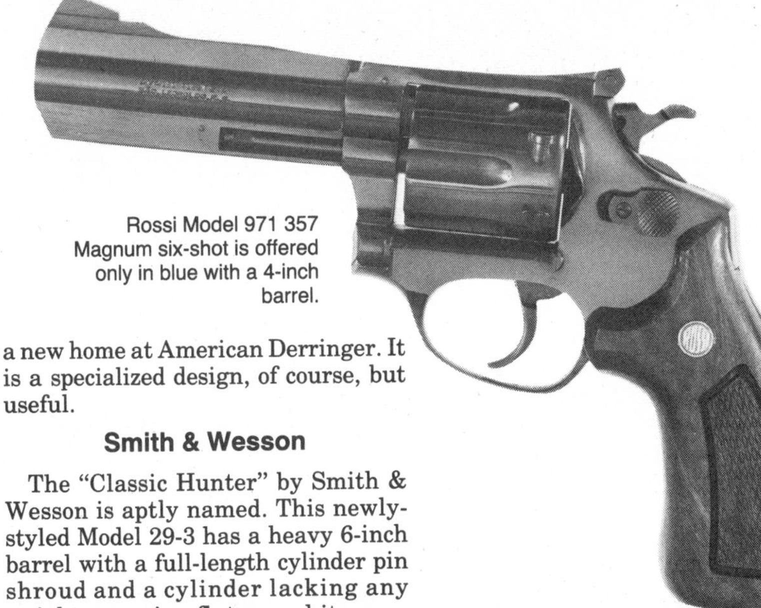

Rossi Model 971 357 Magnum six-shot is offered only in blue with a 4-inch barrel.

Smith & Wesson

The "Classic Hunter" by Smith & Wesson is aptly named. This newly-styled Model 29-3 has a heavy 6-inch barrel with a full-length cylinder pin shroud and a cylinder lacking any weight-removing flutes, and it wears a soft finger-grooved rubber grip. Other than that it is a Model 29. It's that "-3" that makes the difference.

Weighing in at an even 50 ounces, it looks like a hunting handgun, it feels like a hunting handgun, it has the sights of a hunting handgun though up front the arrangement is a bit superfluous. The Hogue finger-grooved rubber grip fits my hand perfectly so it may be a mite small for some shooters. Should you desire a standard grip, the Hogue stirrup is easily removed. Trigger pull is somewhat unusual for a modern factory handgun in that it is a consistent 64 ounces, 4 pounds, and crisp as breaking glass. There is absolutely nothing a gunsmith could do to improve this one.

Now the cylinder: There are no cylinder flutes. This makes for a much more handsome look plus adding valued weight. I like it a lot too, but I want to point out that it *is not one whit stronger than the fluted version.*

SSK

J.D. Jones calls his SSK-produced cartridge-firing behemoths Hand Cannons. Here's the reason: his current brain child is a 12.9x50.8mm JDJ—50-caliber to folks like you and me. It's built on a Remington XP-100 action. The case is Weatherby's 460 Magnum with the case head rebated to standard-size belted dimensions. It could be, according to J.D., put in a M700 Remington should anyone be interested. The case, obviously, is shortened.

What does he shoot in it? I don't know the powder or charge, but the bullet weighs 600 (six hundred) grains and initial loads zip along right smartly at about 1700 fps. I love *big-bore* guns. I watched him shoot it. I photographed him shooting it. Somehow, I left there without shooting it myself, which is how I planned it.

Taurus

I have used a Taurus 6-inch blue adjustable-sighted 357 Magnum revolver off and on for several years. It has been a good, dependable revolver. A friend, long respected by this gun writer, took on a project some many months back that interested me. He wanted to find out just how durable a Taurus double-action revolver really might be. He still doesn't know, but

The Astra 45 Colt double-action revolver is a favorite wheelgun in a favorite caliber.

Dan Wesson's no-name-yet small frame 38 Special double action—interchangeable barrel, five-shot cylinder, 2-inch barrel.

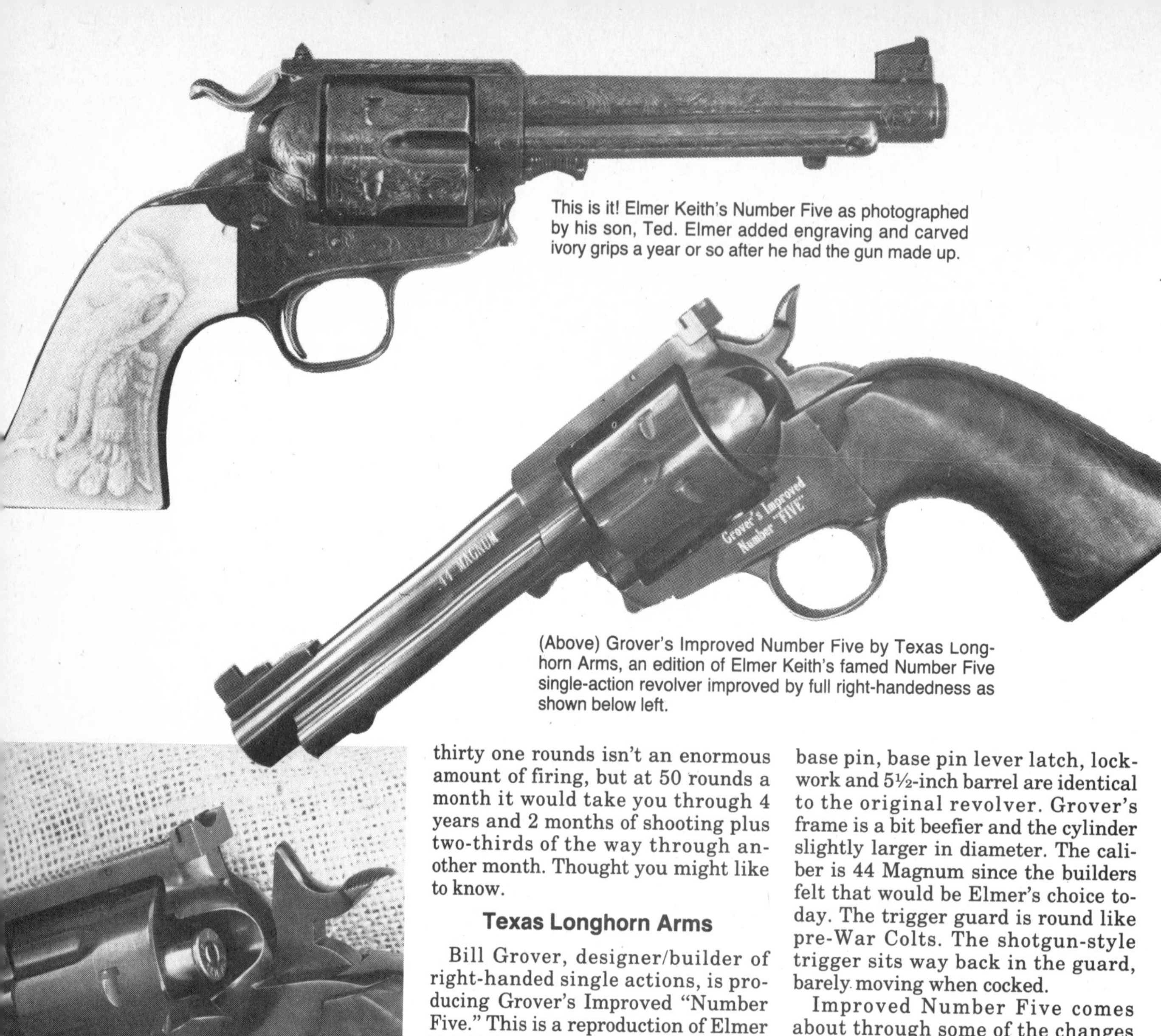

This is it! Elmer Keith's Number Five as photographed by his son, Ted. Elmer added engraving and carved ivory grips a year or so after he had the gun made up.

(Above) Grover's Improved Number Five by Texas Longhorn Arms, an edition of Elmer Keith's famed Number Five single-action revolver improved by full right-handedness as shown below left.

he tried. He obtained a Model 66 357 Magnum, had a gunsmithing friend strip it down and take a good look at everything inside, then started loaning it to friends who promised to keep track of how many times they fired it and with what.

After it had been through a good many hands, he retrieved the gun, took it back to the 'smith who looked it over before a shot was fired, for another look at the insides. The only thing detectable was a better trigger because of polishing through use. Everything else was still in the original condition. Oh yes: 2531 rounds had been fired including everything from 38 wadcutters to full 357 Magnum loads. Two thousand five hundred and thirty one rounds isn't an enormous amount of firing, but at 50 rounds a month it would take you through 4 years and 2 months of shooting plus two-thirds of the way through another month. Thought you might like to know.

Texas Longhorn Arms

Bill Grover, designer/builder of right-handed single actions, is producing Grover's Improved "Number Five." This is a reproduction of Elmer Keith's famed Number Five and made from photographs and precise measurements of Elmer's original single action. The gripstraps, grip contour, base pin, base pin lever latch, lockwork and 5½-inch barrel are identical to the original revolver. Grover's frame is a bit beefier and the cylinder slightly larger in diameter. The caliber is 44 Magnum since the builders felt that would be Elmer's choice today. The trigger guard is round like pre-War Colts. The shotgun-style trigger sits way back in the guard, barely moving when cocked.

Improved Number Five comes about through some of the changes listed above but primarily because of Grover's Improved Single Action making it possible for a right-hander to shoot, empty, reload and shoot

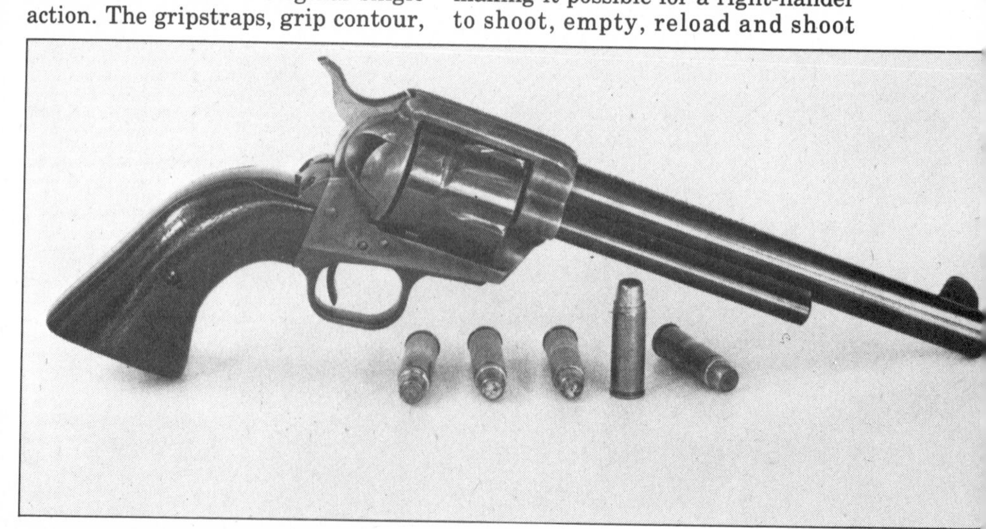

This looks like a Colt Single Action Army, but the frame, backstrap, trigger guard and loading gate came from the shop of United States Frame Specialists. The rest is Colt.

again without changing hands. The loading gate is on the *left* side rather than where Colt put it.

Number K1, photographed here, will be fully engraved by Jim Riggs, fitted with ivory grips as was the original and sold at auction with the entire proceeds, meaning every cent paid for the gun, going to the Elmer Keith Museum Foundation. This group, headed by Elmer's wife, Lorraine, and son, Ted, is working toward a museum in Boise, Idaho to house and exhibit Elmer's collection of guns and hunting trophies.

To find out more about Grover's Improved "Number Five" you will find the company name listed towards the back of this Digest. To find out more about the Elmer Keith Museum Foundation write to them at 4340 Shamrock, Boise, Idaho 83704.

Thompson/Center

Thompson/Center's list of calibers for their Contender interchangeable-barrel pistol changes from year to year. Their catalog No. 15 lists 18 chamberings with one, the 45 Colt, also digesting 3-inch 410 shotshells. T/Cs Hot Shot capsules are no longer listed.

New to the line for 1988 is the 7x30 Waters. Hunters looking for a long-range cartridge that will handle whitetail/antelope-sized animals won't go wrong with this one, especially in a Super "14" barrel.

United States Frame Specialists

If you are a fan of the Colt Single Action Army 45 revolver and have not been able to find one in good condition at a reasonable price, this might be the answer to your concern. Jeff Peskie heads up the company and their specialty is the manufacture of Colt SAA frames, backstraps, trigger guards and loading gates. The barrel, trigger assembly, grip, everything but the frame, backstrap, trigger guard and loading gate come from Colt. The frame is serial numbered in the same place as Colt revolvers. Fitting Colt parts will require the hands and knowledge of a competent gunsmith. These parts will not "drop in place" nor should they be expected to. The bit of fitting required is not beyond the capabilities of any working gunsmith. Kitchen table or backyard 'smiths might be left wanting—that's why the word competent was inserted.

Dan Wesson

Long famous for big, burly, accurate double-action revolvers, Dan Wesson brought a new toy to the Las Vegas SHOT Show. I refer to it as a "toy" because it is unlike anything offered by the Monson, Massachusetts-based company before. I'm confident it has, or will have soon, a model number, but here it will be called the Dan Wesson Small Frame Five-Shot 38 Special. Serial number of the only one of its type in existence, the one shown in Las Vegas and the one in my hands at this moment, is XSF-2.

XSF-2 is typical Dan Wesson in that it is of interchangeable-barrel design. Both a 2-inch and 4-inch barrel were shown. The short version looks like most other conventional small frame D/A revolvers except that the cylinder latch is up front a la DW and the sight groove through the topstrap is wider than usual.

Weight with the 4-inch barrel is 28½ ounces and overall length is about 8¾ inches. Height is barely short of 4⅝ inches. Weight with the 2-inch barrel is 24½ ounces and the height drops to about 4⅜ inches because of the rear sight situation.

The hammer spur is slightly curved and deeply grooved making single-action shooting easy. Trigger pull is excellent but then this is a prototype. As this is written nothing has been said about availability, but past experience with Dan Wesson tells me it won't be long or they wouldn't have shown it. As to other calibers I don't know. It would be a natural for 357 Magnum, 44 Special and yes, 32 Magnum.

Dan Wesson's big-framed 45 Colt revolvers are off and running. They have been selling faster than they come out of the plant so I haven't been able to get my hands on one. This big, ancient but very good cartridge is a favorite of mine so sooner or later I'll get my hands on a DW 45 Colt and prove what I think I already know: it too will be a good one. ●

J.D. Jones, Hand Cannon impresario, admits his 12.9x50.8mm JDJ XP-100 conversion kicks hard and so it does.

(Right) The 375 JDJ with 220-grain Hornady bullet, left, and 12.9x50.8mm with 600-grain bullet.

HANDGUNS TODAY: AUTOLOADERS

by J. B. WOOD

The Victory Arms MC5 will be imported from England by Magnum Research. Since the prototype shown here last year, there have been a few changes.

STARTING with a development we reported last year here, it seems that now **Victory Arms** of England has an import arrangement with **Magnum Research** for Davis Smith's excellent pistol, now called the Victory MC5. From the prototype shown here last year to the production version, there have been a few design changes, both mechanical and cosmetic, but the pistol remains all steel, with a double-action trigger system and a double-row magazine. A quick-change barrel system allows conversion to four chamberings—9mm Parabellum, 38 Super, 41 Action Express, and 45 Auto. Fully loaded, the MC5 holds 11 rounds in 45 Auto, 13 rounds in 41AE, and 18 rounds in 9mmP and 38 Super. I haven't fired the pistol yet, but it feels fine in the hand.

Magnum Research is already well-known, of course, for the 357 Magnum and 44 Magnum Desert Eagles, now offered in several new finishes, including camouflage. I recently examined a Desert Eagle equipped with a fine walnut grip by Herrett. The shape was subtly different from the regular grip, and exactly right.

The Grizzly Winchester Magnum from **LAR Manufacturing** has always been convertible from 45WM to 357 Magnum and 45 Auto, and now there are two new options. Conversion units are available in 10mm Auto, and in the new bottlenecked round, the 357/45WM. Suggested retail price of the conversion units is around $150. The performance figures of the 357/45WM are impressive on paper, and I'm looking forward to trying out this conversion on my own Grizzly pistol.

Until recently, I hadn't fired the **Coonan** 357 Magnum pistol, but now that I've had a Coonan Model B around for a few weeks, I have done both. I am impressed with its flawless performance, its fine workmanship, and its trigger pull which compares well with the one on my Hämmerli. One of the things that surprised me about the Coonan was its compactness. It's not a small pistol, but it's very solid and flat. Everything seems to be made just a little stronger than necessary, and it handled all the factory loads I tried in it with no problems.

Smith & Wesson has added the competition-styled Model 745 to the regular lineup. Other additions include the availability of 20-round accessory magazines for the Models 459, 469, 659, and 669, and an adjustable-sight version of the Model 645. I've been shooting a standard-sight version of the Model 645 in recent months, and its performance has been perfect. I'm particularly impressed by the feel and balance of this pistol, and the one I have is extremely accurate. From all indications, the transition of the company to the new ownership has gone smoothly, and I believe we can be assured of the same quality we have always expected from Smith & Wesson.

The **Colt** 10mm Delta Elite, new last year, has now begun to appear in gun shops, and has been tested by several firearms writers, including this one. The pistol surprised me in two ways—it was more accurate than I expected, and the felt recoil was relatively light. I would compare the recoil to a warm-loaded 38 Super. When you consider that the performance of the 10mm Auto round is close to the 41 Magnum level, that's not bad. In addition to the original Norma load, the 10mm Auto cartridge is now also being made by Hornady-Frontier and PMC. One other Colt note—they have mated the regular 380 frame with the Mustang slide and barrel, to create the Mustang Plus II. More grip, more capacity.

The other new high-performance load of nearly the same diameter as the 10mm, the 41 Action Express, has a growing list of firearms chambered for it. A most recent edition is the classic Government Model pistol from **Auto-Ordnance**, and they are also offering a conversion unit in 41AE. One of the advantages of this round is that its rebated rim allows easy conversion of almost any 9mm Parabellum pistol, since the breech face recess doesn't have to be altered. Also new from Auto-Ordnance is a compact version of their 45 pistol, the ZG-51. It has a 3½-inch barrel, is 7¼ inches in overall length, and weighs 36 ounces.

While we're in the category of government-pattern pistols, it should be noted that **Olympic Arms** of Olympia, Washington, is now offering the Safari Arms Enforcer in blue or stainless steel, and all of the original accessories familiar to shooters who liked the unique MS-Safari Arms pistols. The full-sized Matchmaster is also available from Olympic, and slides are offered in 5-, 6-, and 7-inch lengths, along with matching barrels. Another offering from Olympic is a selection of replacement barrels in 41 Action Express for the old GM 1911 and its copies, the Browning Hi-Power, and the TZ and CZ75.

As you might imagine, **Beretta USA**, and the factory in Italy, are concentrating on filling that order from the biggest of customers, the U.S. Government. At this time, more than 100,000 Model 92F pistols (called the M-9 by our military forces) have been delivered, and 6000 per month are being shipped to U.S. Ordnance centers. For those who came in late, the total contract is for 320,000 guns. It is probably because of this activity that the 380 Model 86, the 22LR Model 87, and the 22 Target Model 89 have not yet been seen here in quantity. As a Beretta footnote, the Model 92F was adopted in January, 1988, as the sidearm of the Maryland State Police.

I've been told that **Heckler & Koch** is discontinuing the P9S in 9mm chambering, with the 45 version to be dropped soon after. This will leave the P7M8 and P7M13 as their principal handguns, along with the new 380, the P7K3. This smaller version has the same squeeze-cocking action as the full 9s, and it will also have the option of converting to 22LR, though not in the same manner as the old HK4 that it replaced. The P7-series of pistols is excellent, and these guns are being used increasingly in law enforcement. Still, I'm sorry to see the departure of the P9S. A 45 Auto version is my "downstairs gun." On the other hand, my bedside gun is a P7. As you can see, I have great respect for Heckler & Koch.

A new version of the FIE TZ75 pistol, with a manual safety that allows cocked-and-locked carrying.

The commemorative 125th Anniversary version of the Hammerli Model 208.

J.B. Wood firing the 357 Magnum Coonan Model B pistol.

In the year just past, the **SIGArms** people seem to have concentrated on their sporting and military rifles, and there's no new handgun or variation to report. Of course, with the P220, P225, P226, and P230, there's little

George Kellgren with a cutaway model of his new Grendel P-10 pistol. The 10-round magazine is integral.

room for improvement. Make it right the first time, and you won't have to modify it. When the basic P220 and P230 pistols were first announced, back in 1975, one of the options listed was chambering for 22 Long Rifle. Since then, I've asked about this on several occasions. So far, the SIG people have decided to stay with the centerfires—but I still think that having 22 counterpart pistols would be great.

At the **AMT** booth at the SHOT Show last January, Harry Sanford handed me a shorter version of the 22 Magnum Automag II. While I was admiring that one, he showed me a true pocket model, with an even shorter barrel and a short grip. Both of these will be available soon. I made no exact measurements, but the "medium" gun had a barrel length of about 4 inches. As intriguing as these were, they were overshadowed by the news that Harry is adapting the unique gas-locking system of the Automag II to function with a long-cased centerfire cartridge—the 30 Carbine! No exact time-frame was mentioned, but it will probably be available by 1989.

When I heard that Taurus had a new 380 pistol, I figured that it would be a lot like the Beretta Model 84. Well, there is a resemblance, but the Taurus 380 Model 58 has its own differences. Actually, it's more like a reduced-size version of the 9mm Parabellum Taurus pistols. Available in blue or satin nickel, it has a 13-round magazine, is 7.2 inches long, and weighs 30 ounces. The grip panels are of smooth-finished Brazilian walnut. The front sight is integral with the slide, and the rear sight is dovetail-mounted.

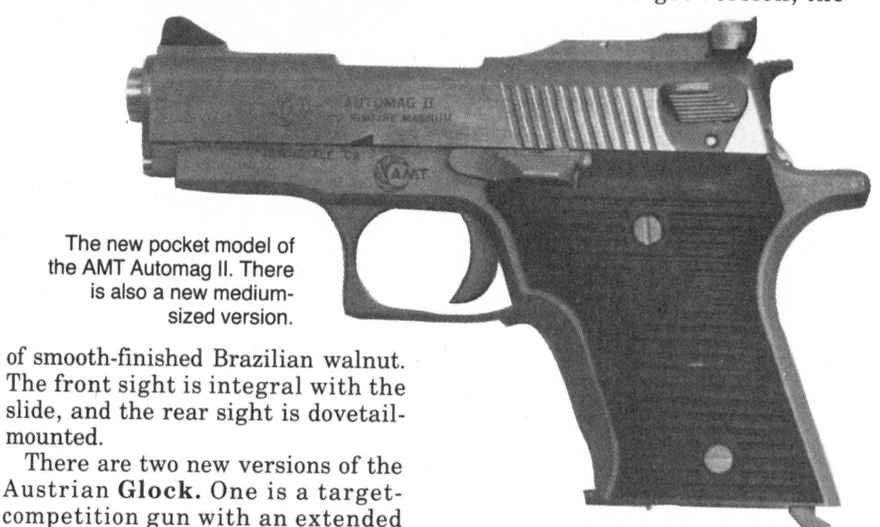

The new pocket model of the AMT Automag II. There is also a new medium-sized version.

There are two new versions of the Austrian **Glock.** One is a target-competition gun with an extended slide and adjustable rear sight, and it should be welcomed by sport shooters. And, there is a new compact version, the Glock 19, with a shorter grip, slide and barrel than the standard Glock 17. The smaller gun will be popular in law enforcement circles, especially in applications where concealment is necessary. The standard Glock 17 has already been adopted by a number of police agencies.

There is good news from **Sile Distributors:** The **Benelli** is back! The original B76, one of my favorite 9mm pistols, is again available. Along with it, Sile is offering a target model, the B76S, with target grips, an extended slide and barrel, and fully adjustable sights. The same pistols are available in 30 Luger chambering as the B80 and B80S. The B77 in 32 Auto chambering is now a regular item. And, there is a new target version, the

Rhonda Brazeau of Jennings-Bryco is holding the prototype of the new Model 48. It will be made in 22 LR, 32 Auto, and 380 Auto.

MP3S, in 32 S&W Long WC, the popular International Target load. Quite an assortment of Benelli pistols, and their availability will be welcomed by shooters who appreciate their superb ergonomics, accuracy, and high quality.

Last year, the word on the double-action version of the **Browning** Hi-Power was that it would be made in limited quantity. Now, Browning Arms has announced that the DA Hi-Power is being dropped from the line. This includes all three sizes of the pistol. The standard gun was the only one seen in the U.S., and that one not in any great numbers. According to the people at Browning, an entirely new double-action pistol is in the works. It may have some of the good features of the venerable Hi-Power, but it will not be as much like it as the DA version just dropped.

This is the AT-84P from Action Arms, the compact version, to be made in 9mm Luger and 41 Action Express.

Glock is now offering a long-slide version, and a compact model, the Glock 19, along with the standard Glock 17.

No startling news from **Ruger** this year. The 9mm P-85 still has not reached my part of the country (the Midwest) in any appreciable quantity. I have examined the pistol at the SHOT Show, but still haven't fired one. At **Detonics** in Bellevue, Washington, they're still making the little Mark I and Mark VI guns, along with the Servicemaster and the elegant Scoremaster. Detonics is under new management, and some accessory items are to be discontinued. Among these are the 451 Magnum Conversion Kit and the stainless retrofit barrels.

After a brief eclipse, **Iver Johnson** is alive and well, as a division of **AMAC**—American Military Arms Corporation. For the time being, their auto pistol line will consist of the ERMA-designed TP22 and TP25 double actions in 22LR and 25 Auto. The prototype of a Baby 25 I examined was neatly done, but not yet on stream, and for the moment, the Woodsman-like 22 Trailsman is not available.

Action Arms, the Uzi people, are now delivering their AT-84, the Swiss-made version of the Czech 75. Available in standard and compact models, the latter called the AT-84P, these high-quality pistols are offered in both 9mm Parabellum and 41 Action Express. A dovetail-mounted "overhang" rear sight with a cross-milled back face is standard on both guns. As with the original CZ75, the AT-84 provides either double-action or cocked-and-locked carry. The AT-84 pistols that I have handled show superb workmanship, as you might expect from guns made in Switzerland.

The Italian versions of the CZ75 are also excellent, as offered by **FIE** and **Excam.** Excam has the compact version, in blue or satin chrome, as well as the standard size gun, as the TA-90. A new model from FIE has the frame-mounted sear-block safety of the original Czech pistol, rather than the firing pin block of the standard TZ75, allowing cocked-and-locked carry for those who prefer that mode. This feature will also be welcomed by those who use the TZ75 in competition shooting. Both safety options will be available, and FIE also offers the pistols in blue or satin chrome.

In recent weeks I tested the new small 9mm Parabellum pistol from **Armscorp of America**, the SD9. A hammerless gun with a DA-only trigger system, the SD9 was designed by Dr. Nehemia Sirkis—reportedly no longer with the company. The pistol is now made by Sardius Industries in Israel. Small, flat, and light, the SD9 has a total capacity of eight rounds, and it is surprisingly pleasant to shoot. Its dimensions are actually less than many 380 pistols, and applications for personal defense and law enforcement back-up are obvious. It is also attractively priced.

Another great little pistol, also double-action-only, is a tiny 380 Auto designed by George Kellgren, of KG99 fame. Just 5 by 4 inches in size and weighing 15 ounces, the **Grendel** P-10 has an integral top-loading magazine, using a stripper-clip (or, as they call it, a "speed loader"). Total capacity is 11 rounds. And, the closed-bottom grip allows the attachment of their "MMH Target Designator," which is a mount that accepts a mini-flashlight.

The Desert Eagle from Magnum Research now has an optional 14-inch barrel, set up for scoped hunting.

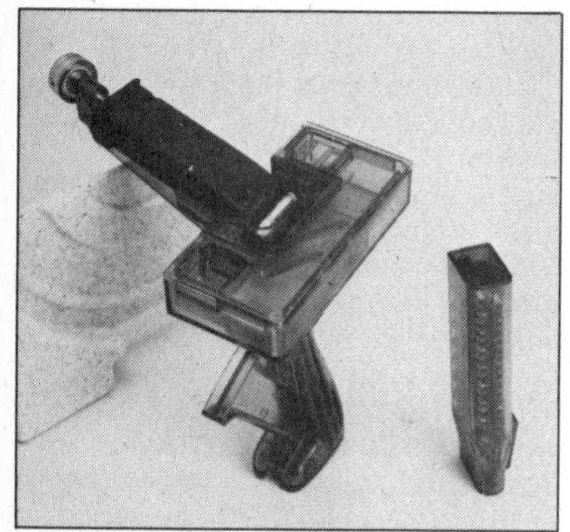

The new X-Press loader from Ram-Line will fill a 15-round 9mm magazine in 10 seconds if the optional tube is used.

For several years now, **Jennings Arms** has been making a neat little 22LR pocket pistol. Now, they are expanding the line to include a 25 Auto (Model 25), and a slightly larger pistol, the Model 38, that will be offered in 22LR, 32 Auto, and 380 Auto. The latter pistol will have dimensions of 5.3 by 3.7 inches, and a weight of 15 ounces. These guns will be marketed under the **Bryco** name, to avoid confusion with the well-known Jennings J-22 pistol. I have also handled a handsome prototype of a larger pistol, the Bryco 48, which is slated for production by mid-1988. It has very nice lines, and feels good in the hand. It will also be offered in 22LR, 32 Auto, and 380.

ERMA-Werke of West Germany is presently represented in the U.S. in only two places. Their Model EP552 and Model EP555 are made by IJ/AMAC as the TP22 and TP25. The ERMA Model EP752 is Excam's RX-22, and that firm also handles their toggle-action pistols in 22LR and 380 Auto. The neat little stainless steel double-action 380, briefly imported by Charter Arms, no longer has a U.S. agent. Someone over here should pick it up, along with the ERMA Model ESP85, a serious target pistol that is convertible from 22LR to 32 S&W Long WC.

Speaking of target pistols always brings **Hämmerli** to mind. In 1988, this grand old Swiss firm celebrated its 125th anniversary. In honor of the event, they are making a 1,000-piece limited commemorative edition of the famed Model 208 pistol. The metal and wood are appropriately engraved and carved, and the left side of the slide has "125 Jahre Hämmerli" and "1863-1988" in gold. The pistol comes in a special suede-lined walnut case. The price is probably substantial, but the buyer will not only have a fine 22 target pistol, but also an instant collector piece that is sure to appreciate in value over the years.

Norinco of China, represented in the U.S. by **China Sports, Inc.**, has a new group of 22 target pistols, three models that cover the range from casual to serious target. Their Type 54 pistol—a Tokarev with an added manual safety—is seen here now in good quantity. The last time I talked with them, the importation of their Type 59 pistol, their version of the Makarov, had still not been approved. The size and features of this pistol easily meet the import criteria, so I can't imagine why it hasn't received an okay. I like the Makarov, and I'm looking forward to trying the Type 59.

A Canadian company, **Para-Ordnance** of Scarborough, Ontario, has an interesting new accessory for owners of government-pattern guns. It's a replacement frame and large-capacity double-row magazine that takes the M1911 and its copies from eight rounds to 14 rounds in 45 Auto. The frame is made of high-strength alloy, and the assembled pistol weighs the same with a 14-round full load as the original with eight rounds. And, except for a very slight increase in grip width, the dimensions are the same, as is the grip angle. For those who are interested in more information, the full address is: Para-Ordnance, 3411 McNicoll Avenue, Scarborough, Ontario M1V 2V6, Canada.

Also for Government-pattern pistols is the new Alpha-Mag 45 magazine from **Eagle International**. Available in stainless steel or blued stainless, the Eagle Alpha-Mag holds nine rounds of 45 Auto. It has a shaped base that gives a comfortable finger rest and also acts as a cushion, and the base has a spring-powered plunger at the rear that helps to expel the empty magazine. I have tried the Alpha-Mag, and it feeds perfectly in all three of my Government-pattern pistols. There are 20-round models also planned for the Beretta 92F and SIG/Sauer P226, and 11-round models for the 10mm Colt Delta Elite and the Springfield Omega.

One of the neatest new gadgets of the year for 9mm shooters is the X-Press Loader from **Ram-Line**. You just lock a double-row 9mm magazine in place, drop a few rounds into the opening (or use the optional 20-round tube), and squeeze the handle-lever. It will load the average 15-round magazine in about 10 seconds, if the tube is used. I tried it with magazines for the Star Model 28, Browning HP, SIG/Sauer P226, and Beretta 92F, and it worked perfectly with all of them. Accessory kits are available to use the loader with 45 GM or Glock 17 magazines. For those who shoot a lot, this outfit will be a thumb-saver.

To end this year's report, some random notes: **Arminex, Ltd.** is moving from Arizona to Las Vegas, Nevada. If the Trifire pistol is made again, it will likely be double action, smaller, and 9mm. **Steel City Arms** is also leaving Pittsburgh for Las Vegas, and they have already obtained a location there for manufacture of the Double Deuce. The **Raven Arms** 25 Auto has a new safety lever that is easier to operate. The **Davis Arms** 32 Auto will soon be offered in 380 Auto. And, I was there when the first of the **Göncz** Hi-Tech pistols came off the line in California. ●

Repli-Guns:

BLASTS FROM THE PAST

by RICK HACKER

THE DIFFERENCE between men and boys can be measured by the price of their toys. In very few hobbies is this more evident than in firearms, especially with replica 19th century cartridge guns that we use for plinking and hunting today.

Are these frontier-era lever actions and six-shooters simply a romantic throwback to our childhood days of playing "cowboys and Indians," or are they a practical method of experiencing the glory years of a "Wild West" that none of us ever knew? A little of each, I think. After all, in an age of lightweight semi-automatic pistols capable of holding 16 shots, no intelligent adult buys a 3½-pound revolver that only holds six cartridges and must be manually cocked for each shot, unless he *prefers* such a gun. The same observation holds true for lever-action and single shot rifles that are clones of Victorian designs that have managed to stay alive and well in a world of fiberglass stocks and stainless steel parts. Make no mistake about the power of nostalgia: There is a dedicated coterie of romantics who gravitate toward such historic firearms, and their numbers are strong enough to keep whole industries flourishing in Italy, Japan, West Germany and the U.S.

It is ironic that these replica "romance guns" of the American frontier owe their very existence to the hard, cold reality of modern economics. It wasn't so very long ago that original Winchester 73s and Colt Single Action Armies were relatively inexpensive and for the most part were simply looked upon as old guns by most shooters, antique gun collectors notwithstanding. In fact, during my growing-up years in Phoenix during the 1950s, I can remember a certain pawn shop on South Central that always featured an assortment of used Winchester 73s and 92s selling for far less than a new 94 carbine. Even Colt SAAs carried price tags of $50 or less. Of course, in those days, everything was "pre-64" and "first generation."

By the late 1960s and early '70s, the law of supply and demand finally caught up with the Colt, Winchester, Remington and Sharps originals. Even with Colt's reintroduction of their Model P six-gun, the high cost of manufacturing this hand-fitted design, coupled with the inflationary spiral of the originals, eventually caused price tags to soar out of reach of most admirers. The Guns That Won The West had lost the War of Wallets.

An interesting phenomenon followed, overseas. With the 19th century

patents long expired, entrepreneurs were tooling up to manufacture replicas of some of America's most famous frontier firearms. Original guns were used for patterns and many parts were interchangeable with the originals. One of the few deviations were screw threads, which were metric. Today, bearing international names such as Uberti, Jaeger and Miroku, replicas of 19th century lever actions and six-guns come close to outnumbering the originals in some models. And these are more affordable as well as more practical to shoot.

For example, a superb copy of the Henry repeating rifle, as manufactured for Cimarron Arms, Dixie Gun Works, EMF and Navy Arms can be acquired for less than $600, as opposed to an original Henry which will easily cost at least five times that amount. What's more, you can shoot the replica (which is chambered for the 44-40), and that is more than you can say for the original Henry, chambered for a 44 rimfire round not made for over 50 years. The same holds true for Winchester Model 66s, also originally chambered for the 44 rimfire, whereas the modern counterpart can be chambered for a variety of centerfire cartridges, including 44-40, 38 Special and even 22 Long Rifle.

Thus, shootability, availability, and affordability are the replica's chief attractions, although costs have been gradually rising during the past few years. In fact, in a few instances, the price of a replica is approaching that of an original, as in the case of Browning's limited run of 10,000 B86 lever actions, a replica of the much coveted Winchester 1886. Still, for the most part, you can purchase a replica firearm for far less than you would pay for its 19th century ancestor, and you do not have to worry about hurting its collector value by shooting it.

How do the replicas stand up against the originals as shooters? I have owned and hunted with many originals of guns that are now being reproduced and can thus offer first-hand comparisons on many models. In the case of the Winchester 73, the modern guns handle exactly like the originals. None of the 73s could ever boast a butter-smooth action; their toggle link system made that impossible. But they are fast shooting and even though the slow-moving factory loaded 44-40 round has rather limited range and power, it is deadly accurate out to 100 yards when shot from a perfect bore . . . something that every new replica rifle possesses.

Because of their better condition, it can be said that most replicas actually shoot better than the originals can now. And because we are no longer using corrosive ammunition, the replica gun you buy today will probably last you a lot longer than its grandaddy lasted your grandaddy.

Replicas also make it practical to experience what it must have been like to shoot a rare gun. The Remington Model 1890 six-gun is a good example. It is estimated that approximately 2000 of these single actions were made between 1891 and 1894, causing it to be a much sought-after collector's item today. But with the Cimarron and EMF replica Model 1890 revolver, you can not only own one in its original 44-40 chambering, but two more in 45 Colt and 357 magnum as well!

Frontier replicas also enable the historian to actually feel what it was like to fire a particular firearm. In the case of the Henry rifle, a gun for which no currently made ammunition exists, I was able to test out Oliver Winchester's

Hacker used his 40-90 Sharps replica to drop this Montana antelope at 225 yards.

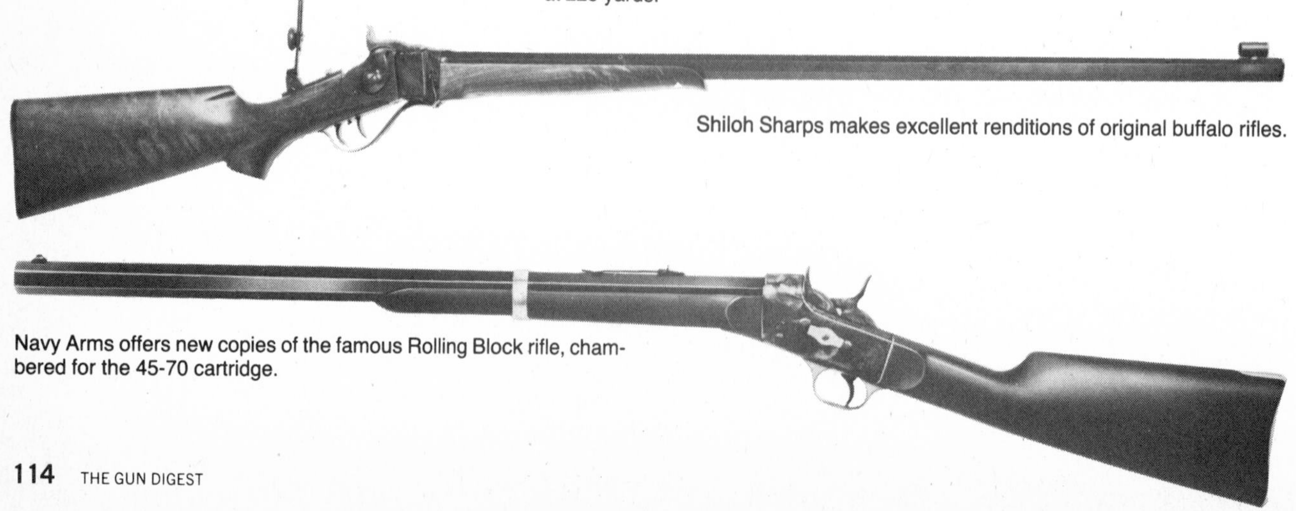

Shiloh Sharps makes excellent renditions of original buffalo rifles.

Navy Arms offers new copies of the famous Rolling Block rifle, chambered for the 45-70 cartridge.

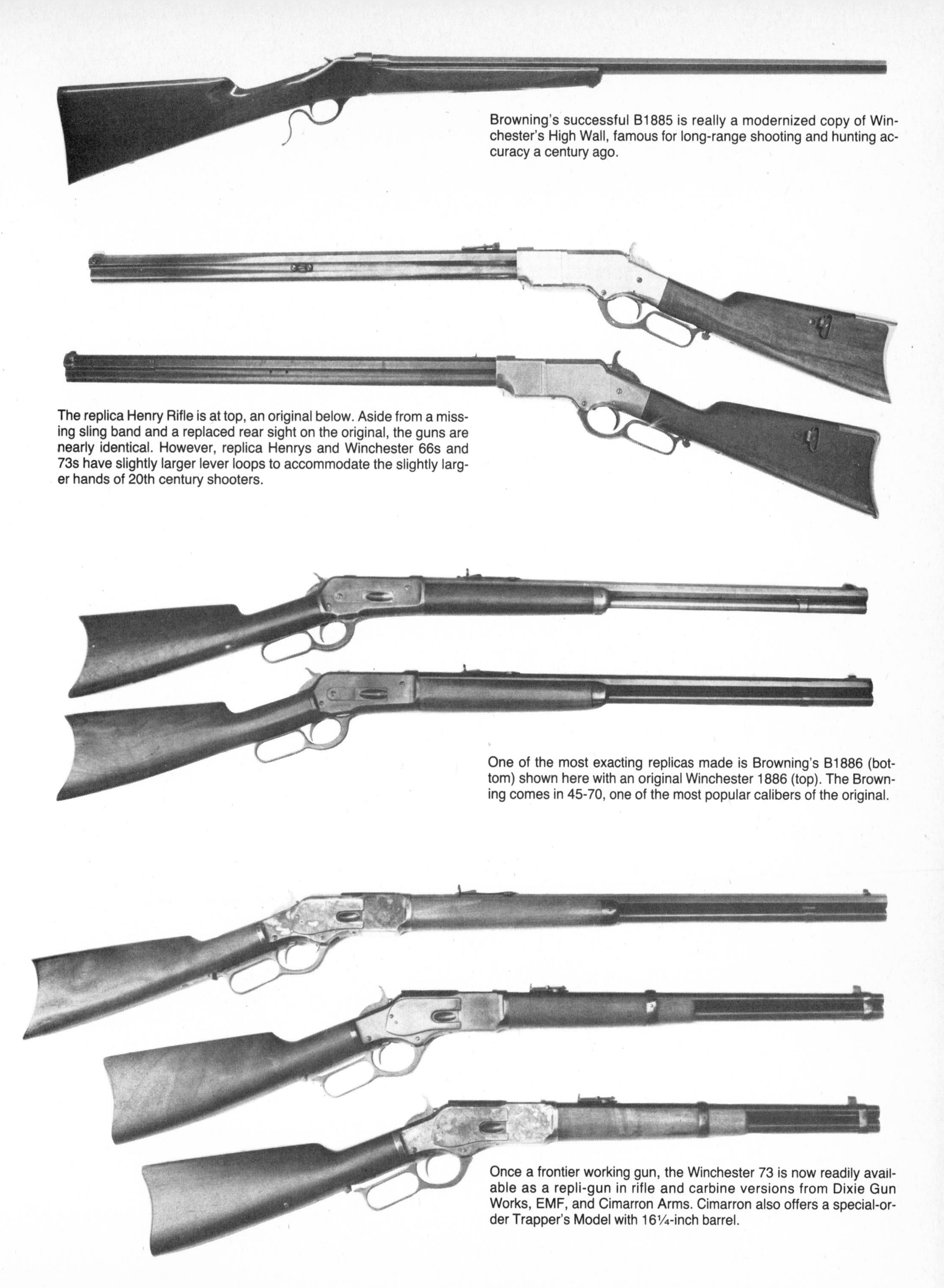

Browning's successful B1885 is really a modernized copy of Winchester's High Wall, famous for long-range shooting and hunting accuracy a century ago.

The replica Henry Rifle is at top, an original below. Aside from a missing sling band and a replaced rear sight on the original, the guns are nearly identical. However, replica Henrys and Winchester 66s and 73s have slightly larger lever loops to accommodate the slightly larger hands of 20th century shooters.

One of the most exacting replicas made is Browning's B1886 (bottom) shown here with an original Winchester 1886 (top). The Browning comes in 45-70, one of the most popular calibers of the original.

Once a frontier working gun, the Winchester 73 is now readily available as a repli-gun in rifle and carbine versions from Dixie Gun Works, EMF, and Cimarron Arms. Cimarron also offers a special-order Trapper's Model with 16¼-inch barrel.

claim of "one shot every 2 seconds" by rapidly firing my Cimarron Arms replica in 44-40. In so doing, I discovered that the loading tab of the Henry moves toward the breech with every shell that is ejected and when there are about five shots remaining, the tab hangs up on the fingers of the supporting hand, thereby causing the rifle to fail to feed the next cartridge! The hand must change position to allow the tab to continue its breechward movement or the Henry ceases to be a repeater. How many lives were lost because of this design flaw is a question history books don't answer, but it certainly must have been one of the compelling reasons that King's patented loading gate was used on the receiver of every tubular magazine Winchester lever action made since the Henry.

Repli-guns also give us choices our forefathers never had. For instance, there is no record of the factory ever producing a short-barreled Henry "Trapper," but Navy Arms now offers and both EMF and Cimarron now import a version with a 3-inch barrel.

Although replicas are invariably copies of guns that have earned a fair amount of respect in collector's circle, almost all of the currently-made copies are purchased by shooters. It's the most practical method most of us have for experiencing the shootability of historic guns that we admire but could not otherwise afford. For example, I have long been an admirer of Theodore Roosevelt and have a rather extensive collection of TR memorabilia, but I had never hunted with one of his favorite rifles, the Winchester Model 95. Thus, when Browning introduced their limited run B95, I immediately bought one chambered for the 30-06. Many of the original Winchester 1895s often developed headspace problems in this caliber, and thus are not always safe to shoot. But Browning's newly manufactured gun does not have this problem. And even though their B95 is not chambered for the big 405 Roosevelt took to Africa, the '06 has helped me experience what it must have been like on the hunting fields with Teddy in the autumn of 1909. Because it was a limited run of only 11,000 guns, many people consider the B95 to be a collectible, but in the true spirit of most replicas, I have taken mine hunting to the point where it is beginning to look like an original!

Of course, there are some people who purchase replica firearms simply as wall hangers, rather than as shooters, being content to merely gaze at the historic lines of these romance guns hanging over the fireplace. Somehow, I can't help but feel these individuals are not getting the full benefit of gun ownership. They are not doing justice to the gun or to themselves. After all, reproduction guns, unlike "commemorative" firearms, are made to be *shot*. And in many cases, such as with the Shiloh Sharps, the replica guns actually have better fitting parts than the originals. In fact, it is not uncommon for the owner of an original 19th century cartridge gun to purchase a similarly-styled replica simply so that he can shoot it, thus saving a collectible example from additional wear and tear that would certainly affect its future value. This is certainly the case with numerous owners of the famed Colt Single Action Army, as the replicas shoot exactly like the originals, even to the point of being high and off-center at 25 yards!

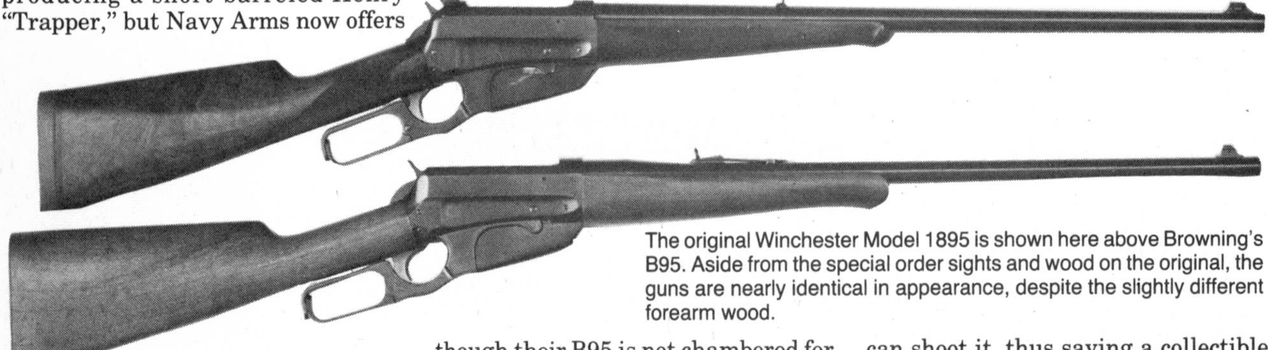

The original Winchester Model 1895 is shown here above Browning's B95. Aside from the special order sights and wood on the original, the guns are nearly identical in appearance, despite the slightly different forearm wood.

one. And one of the unsolved mysteries of yesteryear was why Winchester never chambered their popular Model 1873 for the ubiquitous 45 Colt cartridge. EMF has taken up where the original company left off and now imports a replica '73 chambered for the 45, something that never existed on the old frontier but certainly should have. Likewise, all Model 66 and 73 replica lever actions are available in 38 Special, a fairly accurate pairing of gun and cartridge that was impossible to have in the old West, as the 38 Special was not introduced until 1902.

Short-barreled Trapper Models of any of the lever-guns have always been scarce and command a premium price in the originals, but 16¼-inch Trapper Models are imported frequently by Cimarron Arms in their Model 1866 and 1873 lever-action replicas. Snubnosed single actions have always been a special-order scarcity, but Cimarron has just introduced a unique 4-inch replica Colt Sheriff's Model in its regular lineup

Hacker believes the real value of repli-guns is as shooters, a view not shared by this Texas boar, which author dropped with his B95.

Other repli-guns have amassed followings all their own and are coveted by shooters simply because of their inherent accuracy or ease of handling. This is certainly the case with Browning's Model 1885, a single shot tack-driver copied directly from the old Winchester High-Wall . . . which was also a single shot tack-driver a few generations ago. And Rossi's Puma and Browning's B92 are both fairly exact copies of the old Winchester 92 carbine, a lightweight saddle gun famed for its easy portability and silky-smooth action.

It is sort of a shame most of the replica firearms are manufactured in foreign countries. One wonders why Winchester never re-issued their famed '73, '86 or '92 lever actions the way Colt brought back their cap and ball pistols a few years back. But then, as I recall, those Colt revolvers were rather expensive when compared to the imports. *(Editor: Actually, they were made in Italy.)* Even today, reproduction Single Action Armies from Italy are extremely well made and cost about half the price of a new Colt SAA special-ordered from the factory—the old Model P is no longer in the standard Colt line and is only available from Colt's Custom Shop.

Perhaps the American firearms industry was too close to the source to really appreciate what it had. With the proliferation of replica guns during the past two decades, however, this is no longer the case and the U.S. is clearly the biggest purchaser of these clone guns. Not only are we reliving history, we are remanufacturing it. It seems only fitting that the replica guns of America's past are enabling us to appreciate and enjoy that heritage in the present. ●

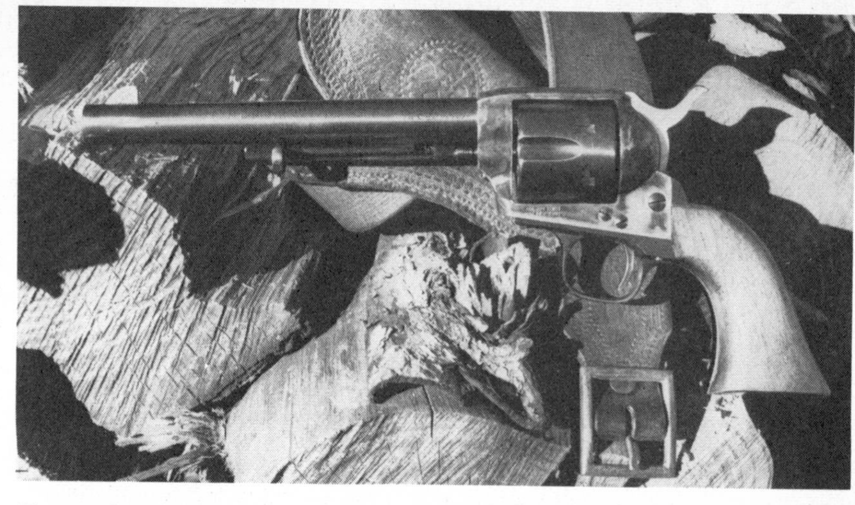

Cimarron Arms has recently "out-replicaed" the replicas by introducing a Single Action Army that even has the original Colt patent dates stamped on the gun.

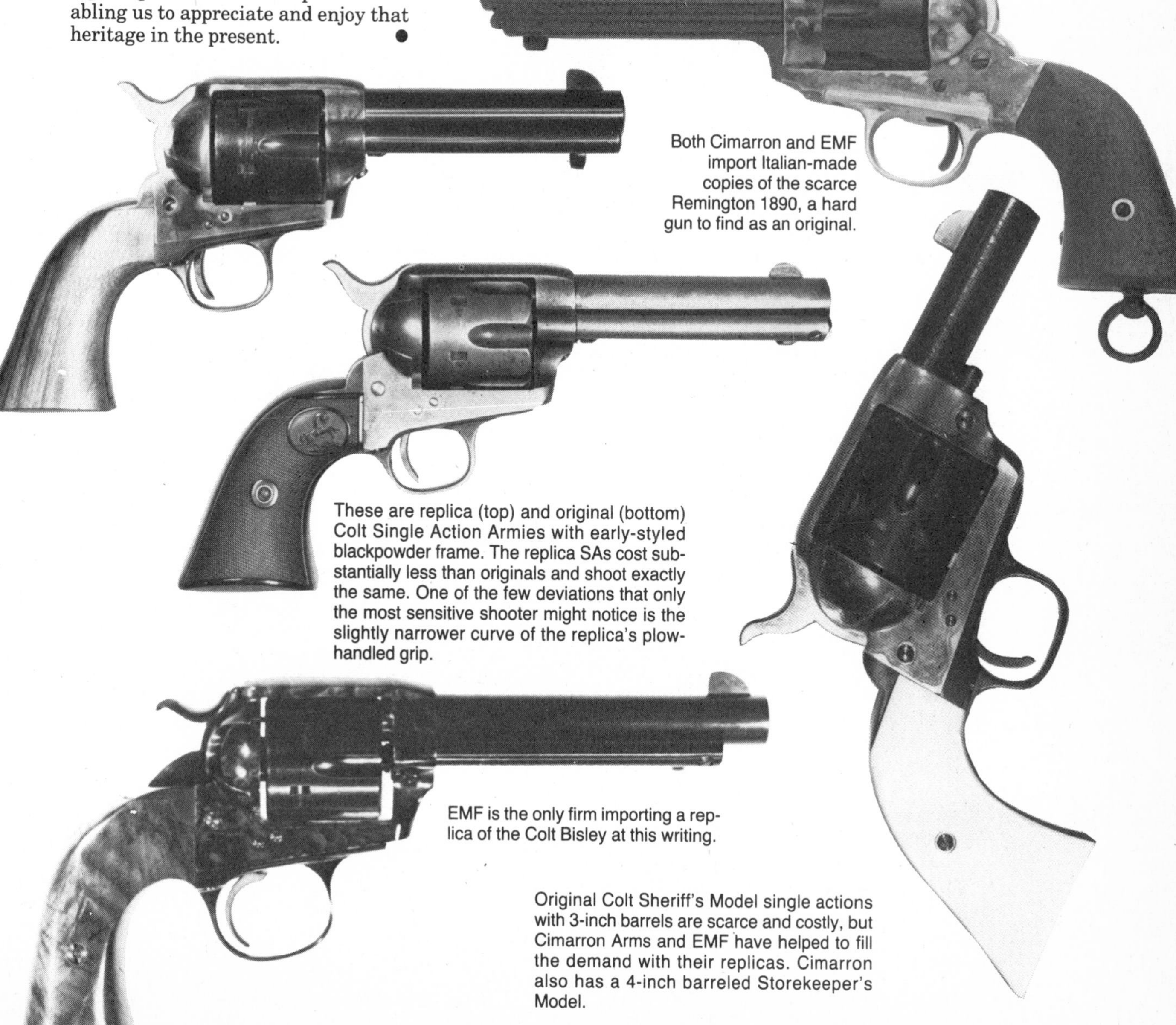

Both Cimarron and EMF import Italian-made copies of the scarce Remington 1890, a hard gun to find as an original.

These are replica (top) and original (bottom) Colt Single Action Armies with early-styled blackpowder frame. The replica SAs cost substantially less than originals and shoot exactly the same. One of the few deviations that only the most sensitive shooter might notice is the slightly narrower curve of the replica's plow-handled grip.

EMF is the only firm importing a replica of the Colt Bisley at this writing.

Original Colt Sheriff's Model single actions with 3-inch barrels are scarce and costly, but Cimarron Arms and EMF have helped to fill the demand with their replicas. Cimarron also has a 4-inch barreled Storekeeper's Model.

THE GUNS OF EUROPE

by RAYMOND CARANTA

TRADITIONALLY, the most exotic guns of American origin have been, for the European gun enthusiast, single-action revolvers, lever- and pump-action repeaters, the Colt Government Model automatic pistol and the movie-celebrated Tommy Gun. On this side of the ocean, we suppose that their European mates probably are the German bolt-action precision rifle, British side-by-side express rifles, German *drillinge*—combined rifle-shotguns—British side-by-side shotguns, selective double-action pistols and stamped sheet-metal submachine guns or assault rifles.

Now, things have changed and first-class (or even cheap) guns are permanently traded from either side of the pond in accordance with the public favor, the U.S. dollar rate and domestic laws. However, there are European products which still remain little known, some because they only meet local requirements and others because they are not produced along international economical standards.

Those which were tentatively exported to the United States did not catch the fancy of enough customers, while others do not meet the American import regulations or are made by people who simply do not care to export them, enjoying enough sales in their home country. In any event, it is the unknown-in-the-U.S. we discuss here.

Adjemian Sniper Rifles: Built on Mauser 98k service rifle actions as many others on the international market, they are chambered in 243 Winchester, 22-250, 300 Savage, 270 Winchester, 7x64, 9.3x62, 6.5x57, 308 Winchester, 300 Winchester Magnum, 308 Norma Magnum and 7mm Remington Magnum. They feature floating heavy barrels with flash hiders from 20 to 26 inches long, fully adjustable trigger pull, bipod and sights, as required. The maker, Alain Adjemian (48, rue Roger Brun—13005 Marseilles—France) is a Marseilles custom gunsmith appreciated by local long-range target shooters.

Astra 7000, Stainless Cub and Stainless Falcon automatic pistols: The Spanish Astra Company, whose products meet the American import regulations and are regularly distributed in the United States by Interarms, has made since 1972 a single-action 22 Long Rifle eight-shot automatic pistol model 7000 which is a favorite pocket gun of this writer.

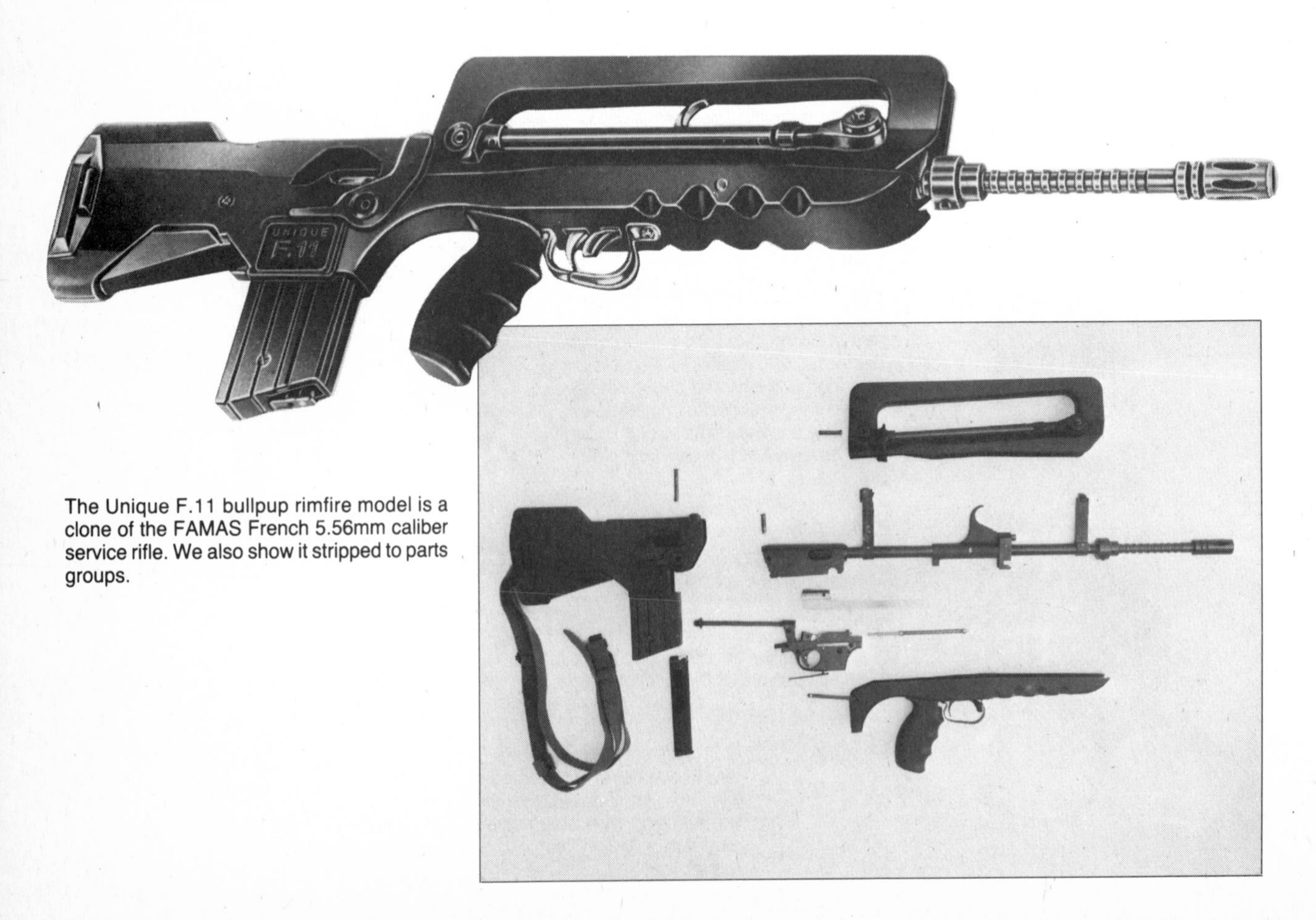

The Unique F.11 bullpup rimfire model is a clone of the FAMAS French 5.56mm caliber service rifle. We also show it stripped to parts groups.

As a matter of fact, this tiny pistol (4.92 inches overall length, 14.6 ounces empty weight) is highly accurate for its size and enables scores of about 250/300 against the ISU "Sport pistol" target at 25 meters, *off-hand*, and is characterized by a very positive feeding and strong percussion.

Astra also manufactures—since 1986—stainless steel versions of the small "Cub" 25 ACP hammer vest-pocket pistol (similar to FIE's "The Best" as made in the United States in carbon steel) and of the old single-action "Falcon" brazing-lamp style Spanish police service pistol chambered in 32 ACP and 380 ACP.

Bretton: The SGM Company (21, rue Clément Forissier—42100 Saint-Etienne—France) has made since 1938 several versions of an extremely lightweight 12-gauge over/under shotgun called the "Baby Bretton" from the name of the inventor.

This shotgun features a light alloy action opened by actuating a side key which enables pulling forward the barrel block and ejecting the empties. The 12-gauge weighs well under 5 pounds and is available with single or dual triggers.

Recently, convertible guns have been marketed in 12-, 16- and 20-gauge with interchangeable barrels and choke fittings, together with a more conventional break-open over/under, the "Basculant," chambered in the same calibers, but weighing 7 ounces more and an automatic delayed-blowback action 12-gauge "Alpha" model weighing 5.4 pounds.

Claude Bouchet: Trying to improve in the field of side-by-side express rifles is not easy in Europe, a century after the birth of the best English makes of breechloaders. That is, however, what a French gun buff, Mr.

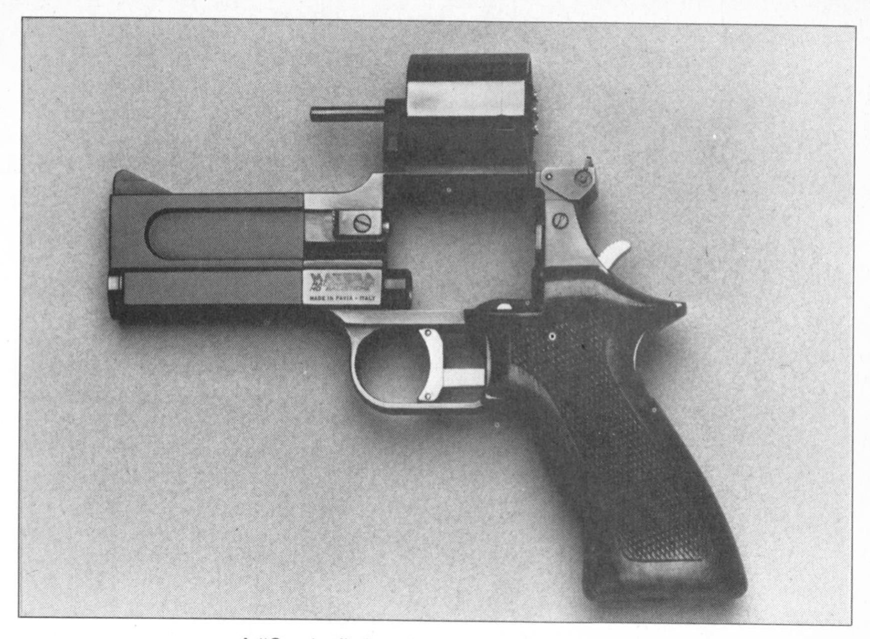

A "Combat" short-barrel six-shot 357 Magnum Mateba revolver, the Model MTR 6, opened for loading. Yes, the barrel is just above the trigger guard. And yes, next year we'll show more.

The Astra Model 7000 vest pocket automatic pistol chambered in 22 Long Rifle cannot be imported into the United States, but it can shoot very well as this 25-meter offhand target shows.

A Special Note

In place of the Shows of Europe, the estimable Raymond Caranta, editor of *Guillaume Tell*, a French gun annual, will now give us each year "The Guns of Europe," concentrating on those we are unlikely to see over here. I'm looking forward to it.

-Ken Warner

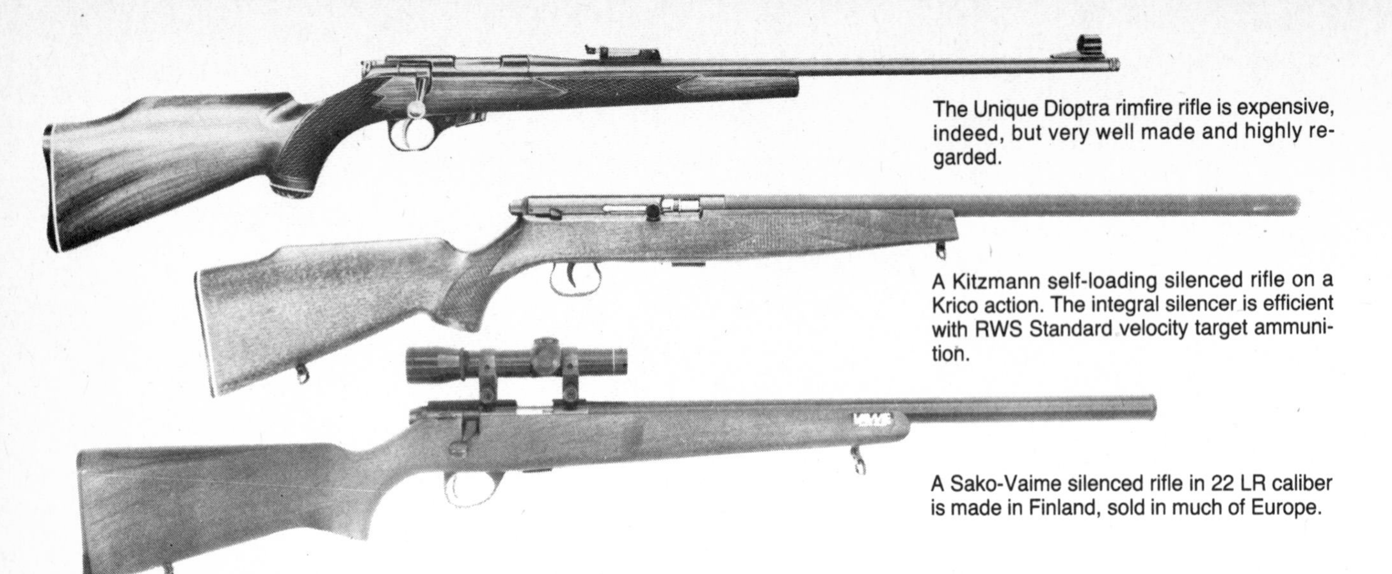

The Unique Dioptra rimfire rifle is expensive, indeed, but very well made and highly regarded.

A Kitzmann self-loading silenced rifle on a Krico action. The integral silencer is efficient with RWS Standard velocity target ammunition.

A Sako-Vaime silenced rifle in 22 LR caliber is made in Finland, sold in much of Europe.

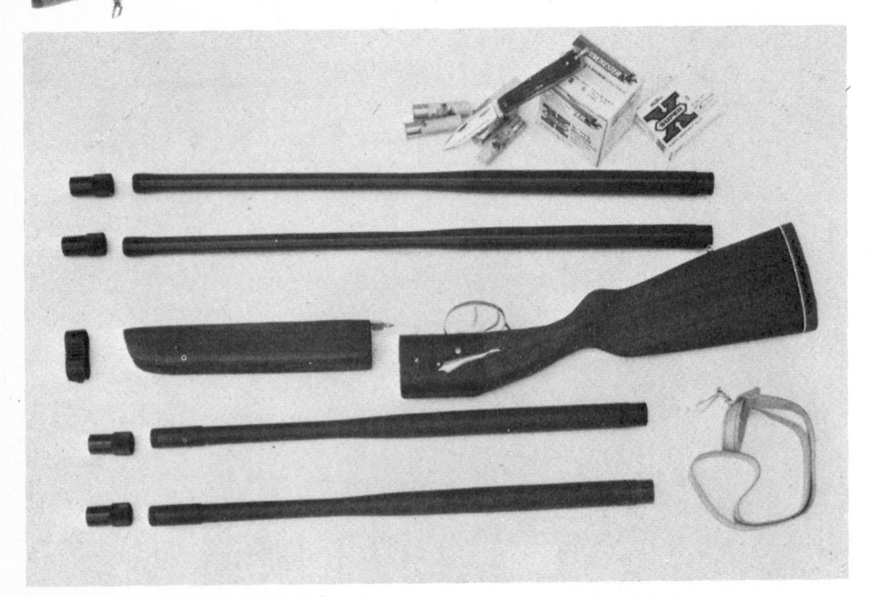

(Above and not upside down) The French Bretton over/under shotgun weighs only 4.8 pounds in 12-gauge. It now features interchangeable barrels and choke tubes in 12- and 20-gauge. (Below) The side lever unlatches the receiver and the barrels are pushed forward to load/unload.

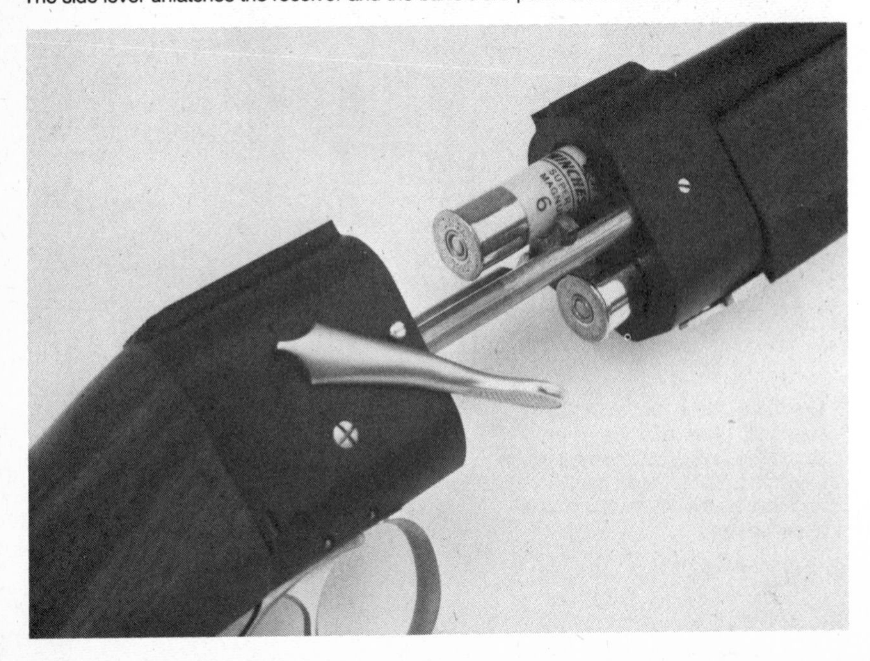

Claude Bouchet (32340 Flamarens-France) disposing of enough time and applicable facilities, tried recently to do. He displayed, at the latest SICAT exhibition in Paris, an entirely hand-made express rifle chambered in 460 Weatherby Magnum, featuring 26-inch barrels and weighing 20 pounds.

The original detachable sidelocks were designed by Bouchet himself, the trigger pull is adjustable, *the barrels cut from a single block* of 120-hectobar (1700 psi) 30 NCD 16 self-tempering steel, while the frame is machined from 90-hectobar (1280 psi) 35 NCD 16 high-frequency treated steel. The hammer fall is adjustable, barrel play can be compensated, the ejectors are selective (they group the empties 10 feet behind in a handkerchief), the barrel locking is of the Purdey type and the sidelocks are internally gold-plated.

It took 2500 hours, we were told, to make this original. Engraving and gold inlaying are made by M. Petiot, a Saint-Etienne master.

The Bouchet rifle had shot 300 rounds of devastating 460 Weatherby Magnum stuff when we testfired it at 100 meters where it shot dead-center. At that range, six shots (three rights, three lefts) held within 3½x5½ inches—five of them were in 1¾x3½ inches. At 50 meters, off-hand, our friend Jean-Pierre Briole placed two rounds 2½ inches apart, just 1½ inches under the 10-ring of the ISU "Free pistol" target. Not bad for a 20-pound express rifle developing 290 foot-pounds of recoil energy.

Feretti: Feretti is a former French navy officer who recently developed a six-shot conversion unit readily fitted to 38 Special or 357 Magnum K- and L-frame Smith & Wesson revolvers, Colt Pythons and Troopers and to French MR 73 Manurhins, enabling

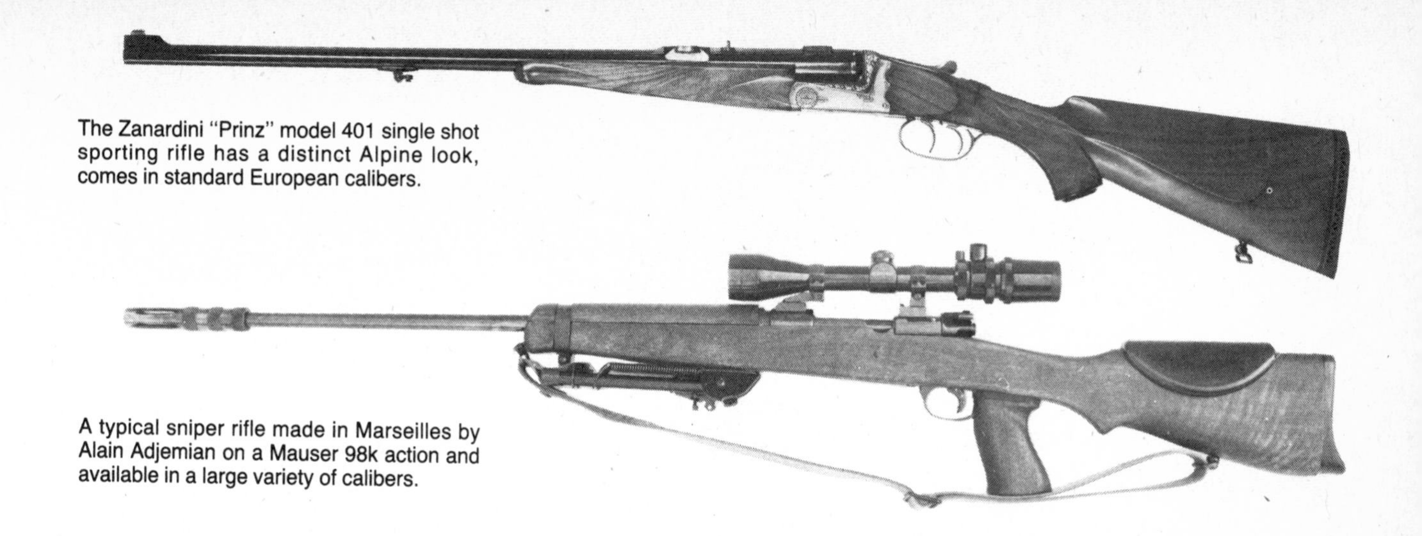

The Zanardini "Prinz" model 401 single shot sporting rifle has a distinct Alpine look, comes in standard European calibers.

A typical sniper rifle made in Marseilles by Alain Adjemian on a Mauser 98k action and available in a large variety of calibers.

their owners to shoot 22 Long Rifle rimfire ammunition.

According to our own experience, these conversions are reliable and accurate at the regular 25-meter range. The Feretti conversion units are exported by Daniel Dekaize (32, rue de Bruxelles, B1300 Wavre—Belgium).

Georges Granger: This is, by far, the most famous French custom gunmaker who is creating a few top-quality side-by-side (he also makes some over/unders on very special requests) shotguns in his Saint-Etienne shop for first-class old world celebrities such as the president of the French Republic or the king of Morocco. Many of these handmade products are diplomatic gifts and you may wait from 2 to 5 years if you want a Granger gun, as there are only five people in the shop, working from the bar, all of them being "Best French Worker," a title awarded every year by the French Government to a single craftsman after a particularly severe selection. (Bill Dowtin—Dowtin Imports, Inc., Rt. 4 Box 930A, Flagstaff, AZ 86001/602-779-1898—reports he can furnish Granger shotguns here in the U.S.)

Kitzmann: A German custom gunsmith making silenced rimfire rifles on Krico or BRNO actions whose bolt-action model was covered in *Gun Digest* some years ago. These highly efficient guns are not exported to the United States further to the American law, but they are still in production.

Mateba: This Italian company from Pavia markets small batches of unconventional top-quality revolvers chambered either in 38 Special or 357 Magnum with capacities varying

The Feretti 22 rimfire conversion unit is reliable and accurate, is made to fit several Colt and Smith & Wesson 38 and 357 revolvers.

from six to 12 shots. The address is MA-TE-BA, Via Villa Serafina 4, I 27100 Pavia, Italy.

Unique: The target automatic pistols made by this excellent French manufacturer have regularly been imported in the United States for quite a long time. Nowadays, Unique's X51 self-loading rifle is one of the most expensive in the world, but it is still popular in Europe. And now, an F.11 bullpup model is currently made by Unique using the same basic action for training with the French FA-Mas (or "Clairon") 5.56mm service rifle.

Vaime: This is a Finnish company fast becoming famous for the silenced guns they are building, mostly on Tikka and Sako actions. This is another product prohibited on the U.S. sporting market which can freely be purchased in several European countries (Vaime Oy Vaimennini Metalli—Sulantie 3—SF 04300—Hyrilä —Finland).

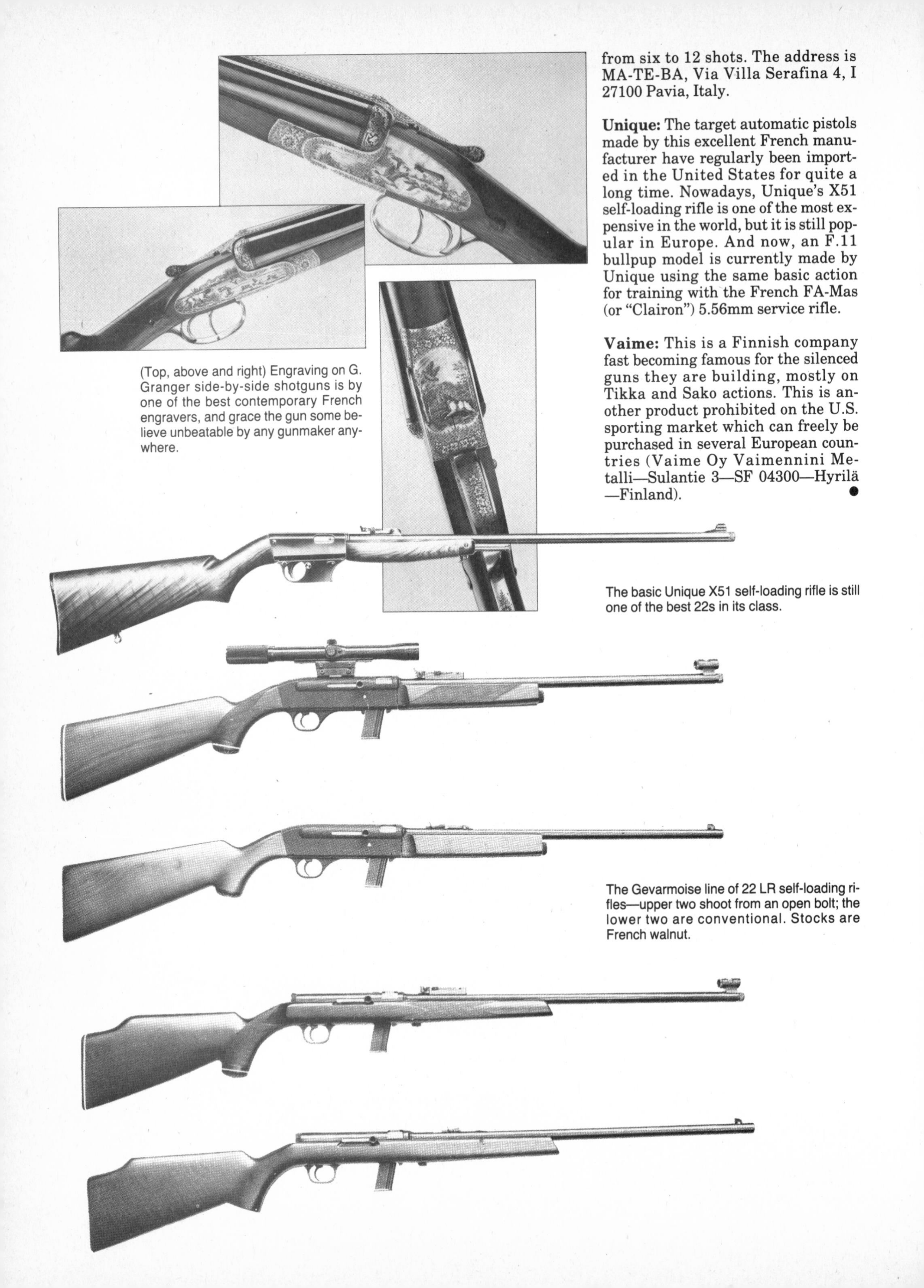

(Top, above and right) Engraving on G. Granger side-by-side shotguns is by one of the best contemporary French engravers, and grace the gun some believe unbeatable by any gunmaker anywhere.

The basic Unique X51 self-loading rifle is still one of the best 22s in its class.

The Gevarmoise line of 22 LR self-loading rifles—upper two shoot from an open bolt; the lower two are conventional. Stocks are French walnut.

Claude Bouchet, designer of the handmade 20-pound 460 Weatherby double express rifle he holds.

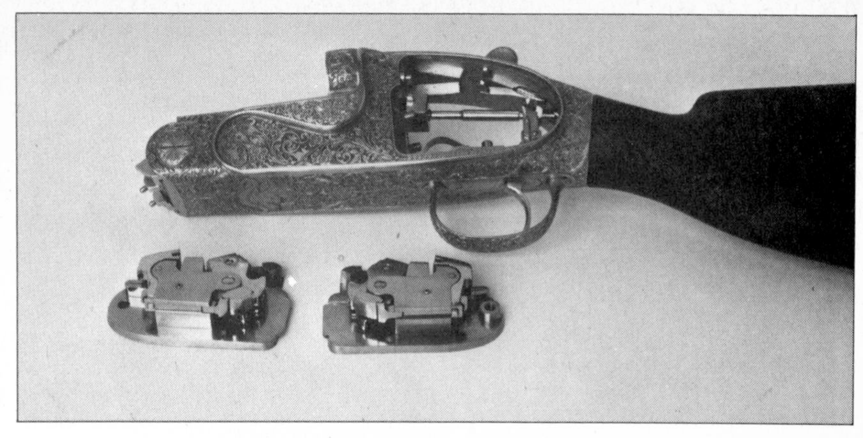

The massive receiver is as unconventional as the whole project. The interior is conventionally gold-plated.

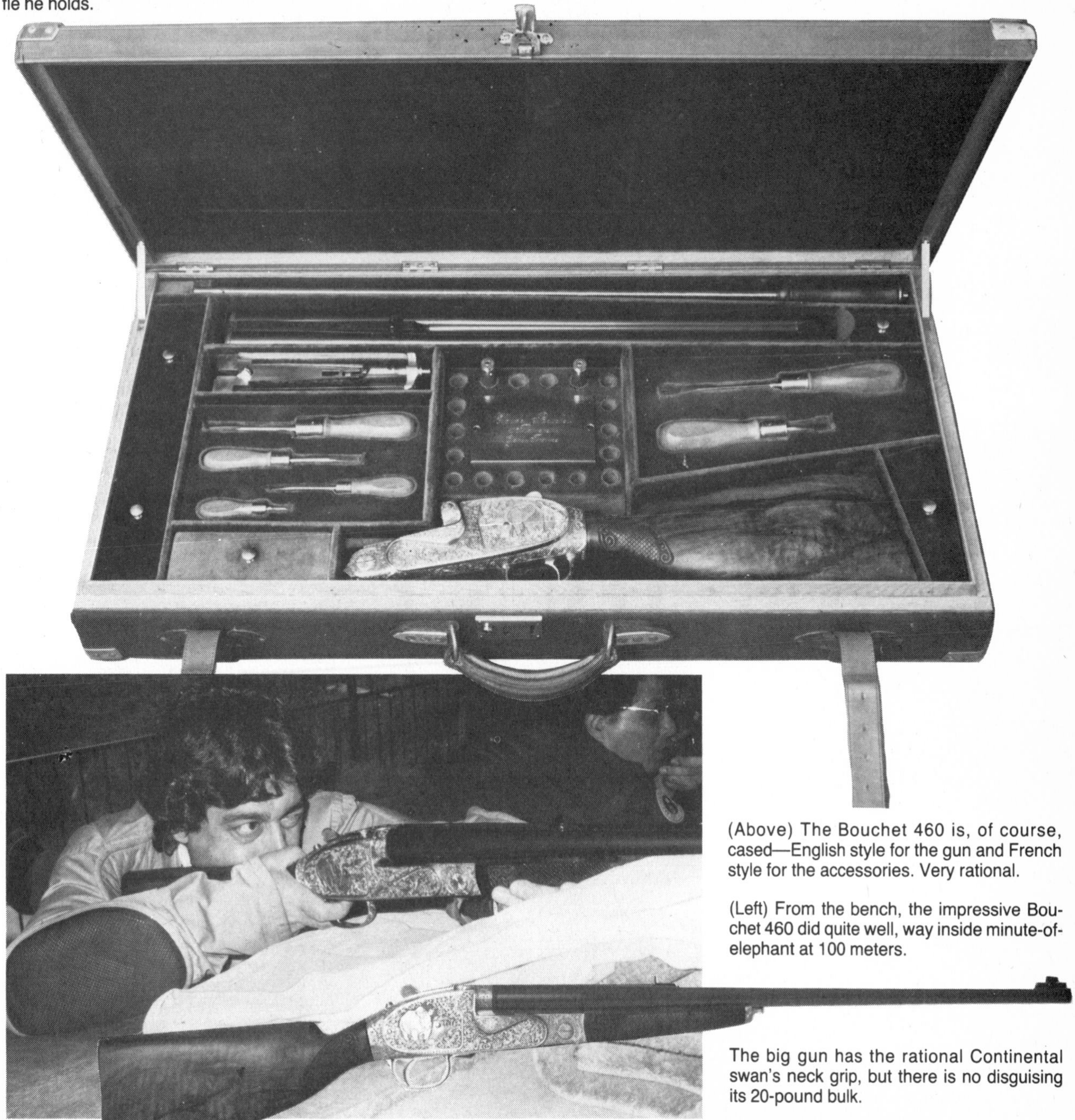

(Above) The Bouchet 460 is, of course, cased—English style for the gun and French style for the accessories. Very rational.

(Left) From the bench, the impressive Bouchet 460 did quite well, way inside minute-of-elephant at 100 meters.

The big gun has the rational Continental swan's neck grip, but there is no disguising its 20-pound bulk.

Ken Harbicht had to do these three grizzlies with a 32 Special—one shot each. They were in his yard. (Ken Harbicht photo)

OF POWER AND PLACEMENT

There is much to consider, and not all of it appears on ballistic charts.

by H. V. STENT

SITTING bugling on a Rocky Mountain, elk-calling virtuoso Randy di Biasio seduced a fine bull to within 40 yards and clobbered him with a 300 Magnum. The elk walked away and Randy had to shoot it twice more to put it down. Yet in that same Kootenay area of British Columbia, Irvine Thorne dropped a still bigger bull at 300 yards with one shot from a 30-30.

Moose are more massive than elk, and veteran hunter Bob Hagel has seen them repeatedly fail to fall to even heavily handloaded 375s. Now I don't know Hagel personally, to my regret, but I do know two moose-hunting guides who, when clients failed to anchor moose with a 30-06, 300, or whatever, regularly put the animals down with a 243 and a 25-35, respectively. And Pete Novak, northern homesteader, once killed three moose in swift succession with four shots from his Marlin 30-30 carbine; they dropped so promptly that each time another appeared he thought it was the same one getting up again.

For grizzlies, most of us might feel undergunned without a magnum; indeed, Dan Sanders took three 375 slugs to put one down, a fourth to kill it. Yet grizzly guide Jim Stanton, of Knight Inlet, B.C., carried only a 30-30 for years. John Turner shot what turned out to be the Boone & Crockett record grizzly for 1965 with that same widespread caliber. For a change, it was a 32 Winchester Special that Ken Harbicht took out when his farmyard was invaded by three grizzlies near Fort Nelson, B.C. He had one cartridge for it. With that he dropped the mother bear, then had to borrow two shells to finish the two almost-full-grown cubs.

For shooting lesser game—deer, black bear, cougar, mountain goats—guide and predator-hunter Irvine Thorne still asks for nothing stronger than the battered little 32-20 he has carried for over 40 years.

How come? Are little rifles just as effective on large game as big ones? The answer would seem to be: "Yes, if they're aimed right." It's easy to say a 22 rimfire will kill anything in North America at close range; Thorne has actually killed two grizzlies with the little 22, one pill apiece. Despite the reams written about high-velocity shock, big bullet knockdown, muzzle energy in foot pounds, penetration, the old saw still holds: "It's not what you hit 'em with, but where you hit 'em, that counts."

Shock and knockdown seem to be sometimes things, a cactus patch of disputes among experts. Energies listed in ballistics tables are just mathematical computations of the sort that prove bees can't fly; a cartridge with slathers of foot-pounds on paper may do no better on game than one with half as much.

One recent fall Ken Warner, editor of GUN DIGEST, saw three small-to-medium mule deer killed—one shot each—with three widely-differing weapons; a 308, a 270, and a 30-30 handgun, which is less powerful than a 30-30 rifle. He noted no difference in effect or in size of entrance or exit holes. Nor could the late Jack O'Connor, hunting in Africa, see that his powerful 7mm Magnum had any appreciable advantage over his wife's mild 7x57.

Aren't the powerful high-velocity rifles much superior in penetration on bigger game? That issue, too, is about as clear-cut as a mass of mud on a foggy night. Bullet construction is a big factor; an expanding bullet may penetrate a foot when a solid of the same caliber, weight, and velocity will drive through 60 or 70 inches. And expansion can be controlled by construction to almost any level between those two. It's not a bad idea, indeed, for any hunter to try out different makes of cartridges in his rifle for penetration in wood, wet paper, whatever, so he can pick a quick-expanding type for deer-sized game and get something tougher for bigger targets.

Any bullet's penetration depends not only on its construction and sectional density, but also on what it hits—soft flesh, firm meat, flimsy bones, heavy ones. So it's hard to make valid comparisons between high intensity loads and lesser ones. Firing the same bullet at different velocities indicates that the 300 Magnum actually penetrates little further than the 308 or 30-06, and they not much more than the 300 Savage. Hunters' tales of how a rear-end raking shot from a maggie will drive clear through to the boiler room while lower velocity loads no more than pierce the skin would seem to be more wishful thinking than fact.

The chief advantage of high-velocity cartridges is their flatter trajectory. A 30-30 sighted to 150 yards drops 2 feet at 300 yards, 5 feet at 400. With a 30-06 sighted to 200 yards, the corresponding drops are only 9 and 27 inches, a magnum's about 7 and 21 inches. Obviously, the shorter drops are much easier to allow for, and hunters of plains and mountain game may well prefer the magnums or similarly flat-shooting 243, 6mm, 270, or 25-06 cartridges.

But long-range shooting is a can of worms best not opened by most of us. When distances stretch much beyond 200 yards, it is only too easy to make errors of 100 yards or more in judging them. When 300 yards looks like 400 or 500, a real 400 "must be 600 at least!" Even with flat-shooting rifles, such estimating errors can throw bullets from 1 to 3 *feet* too high or too low, and one will miss or wound-lose a good game animal. Only very experienced hunters who are also top marksmen are justified in trying shots over 250 yards, and they don't make clean kills always by any means.

A doctor of my acquaintance is a whiz on targets with his 270 and a mountain hunter of long experience. Yet in a recent hunting season, he wounded and lost two elk on attempted long shots before bagging one, and very lucky he was to get a third chance. Another excellent target shot, with a fine scoped 25-06, missed a big mule deer buck, standing, three times at only 80 yards. Terrible? The vast majority of us who don't practice between hunts can and do miss deer, even moose, at half that range, often enough. What business have we trying for ¼-mile kills?

Resident hunters, such as the guides, trappers, backwoods farmers I've mentioned, just don't try long shots unless conditions are perfect, but they're hell on wheels at the quick offhand shooting which so often is all a hunter gets.

"My old Betsy just flips up pointed right where I'm looking and I shoot as soon as she hits my shoulder," averred Howard Clarke, the guide who relied on a 25-35 to drop moose his clients wounded. It's slow and small, but he knew where to shoot and how to hit it. Placement is much more important

If more than a single shot is needed, not a lot of lever time is needed between shots.

Even mule deer are more often shot close than far, and up close a light rifle is as sure as the next.

Some old-timers, who get close and shoot well, have for decades killed goats cleanly with 32-20s. (Steve Cannings photo)

Black bears don't require big gun punch, are killed in traps with 22 rimfires quite easily. (British Columbia Govt. photo)

The range at which you can make a pattern like this is your quick and sure-kill range; don't shoot farther.

than power.

What is good bullet placement?

A bullet in brain or spine will drop an animal instantly, but they're mighty small marks to hit. Also a brain shot may spoil an antlered trophy. The spine is a bigger mark, or at least a longer one, and many hunters, both horn-hoarders and meat-misers, try for it with neck shots. Some seem to do well with them. But a shot just anywhere in the neck won't do; I've seen deer neck-shot with a 30-06 amble off as if unhurt. You've got to know the spine's exact location and be precise to hit it.

A heart shot is a sure kill, but the recipient can run 100 yards or more before realizing it's dead, and can be lost in thick brush without tracking snow.

Biggest vital areas, and hence the surest to hit, are lungs and shoulders. Hit in either, an animal will often drop, and if not, rarely go very far. I like that lung shot; no meat spoiled, no barrier of big bones. Canadian conservation officers regularly kill nuisance black bears *(And I have seen proper authority in Florida kill big nuisance feral hogs dead with 22s: Editor.)* with lung shots using rimfire 22s. The shoulder shot is good, but can ruin good roasts, and more than one shoulder must be hit to surely immobilize an animal. For either lung or shoulder shots the animal must present itself broadside, and in my experience it usually does, sooner or later. But

This not-very-big Ontario moose went 650 pounds—about the weight of four deer—which is why dudes should shoot 30-06-class rifles on moose. (Ont. Dept. of Lands & Forests photo)

when the quarry isn't so obliging . . . ?

If the deer or whatever is facing you full on, a center chest shot is usually effective. If it's quartering toward you, try for the shoulder. Quartering away from you, reach for the lungs. If it rudely offers only its rump, running away, you'd better turn your back, too; a miss or a gut-shot mess are the likeliest results of shooting. On a facing-away animal standing still or moving slowly, aim high for the spine. You'll either over-shoot, a clean miss, or your bullet will break spine or pelvic bones and bring the animal down.

To get game as surely as the Thornes and the Novaks do, always aim, like them, for one of the vital spots, never just "at" the whole animal. And never shoot farther than you are reasonably sure—say, 80 percent—you can hit your chosen mark.

It's important for every hunter to know just how far that is for him. The man experienced in both hunting and target shooting will have a fair idea. Casual Joe Ordinary, who never practices between hunts—which may be years apart—has only the vaguest notion. He—or you—can find out in one afternoon without the boredom of formal target shooting, however.

With some 9- or 10-inch plates—china's great to bust, but paper or foil is a lot cheaper and easier to pick up—or anything else about the size of the lung-heart area of a nice little two-prong buck, like plastic jugs, small cartons, whatever, go out into the countryside where it is safe to shoot. Take a 22, the big-game rifle, and ammo. Set up these marks at varying distances from 30 to 100 yards and shoot at them offhand: Up rifle, quick aim, shoot, rifle down. If you score two successive hits at the closest, go to the next, and so on. Switch to the bigger rifle when the distance gets too great for the 22's drop.

Keep it up until you've found the greatest distance at which you can hit a 9- or 10-inch mark pretty consistently. Even if that's less than 100 yards, and it may be much less, when you go hunting pass up all longer shots if you want to be sure of meat to eat or horns for a hat rack.

You may hate like hell to *not* try for a buck or bull that's beyond your limit, but it's neither profitable nor ethical to shoot at ranges where you're more likely to miss or wound than to kill. Wait for a better chance. Or get yourself one of the biggest thrills in hunting by stalking closer. You may be able to extend your range limit—you can find out how far—by using the steadier sitting position, or employing a tree or rock as a rest, but then don't shoot at that range offhand.

Lots of hunters, you know, limit themselves to such arms as bows and arrows, shotguns, muzzleloaders, or pistols. They get game and take a lot of pride and pleasure doing so.

If you've been conditioned to believe that short-range shooting may be all right in the woods but can't be done in western mountain country, meet Bob Jameson: A well-known Rocky Mountain guide who has also hunted a good deal in Africa, Bob is crowded with clients from all over the United States. And he insists on their restricting their shots to not over 120 yards. Why?

"Because hardly any of them can hit game any further," Bob says bluntly.

"Can they get shots closer than that?" I marvelled.

"Of course," he smiled. "When I go

This big guy, the grizzly bear, is possible for light rifles, and power does not replace placement, but something—perhaps lots—in reserve is a good idea.

Elk are not deer—this one is about three-deer-sized—and good placement with more power shortens up the blood trail.

To drop this one right where he is—which would be more convenient than other places close by—would take *both* power and placement. (British Columbia Govt. photo)

after an elk for myself, I often shoot them under 50 yards. Other game, too."

So if you find a paper plate hard to hit at 100 yards and hopeless much beyond, not to worry; you can still get game. The mountain hunter has as much real need for ¼-mile rifle as a bull has for a brassiere. Those handy, ubiquitous—some would say iniquitous—little lever carbines of 30-30 and similar calibers are far-shooting enough for the vast majority and seem to compare surprisingly well with their bigger brothers in power and penetration. That's what Jameson uses for his elk. For those who prefer a bolt-action, or a hammerless lever Savage, the 243, 6mm, 250-3000 also have adequate power, mild recoil, good penetration, and flat trajectory as well.

Do I then claim that there's no advantage at all in using rifles more powerful than these? In spite of this evidence in their favor, I'm still a little leery about game bigger than deer. Either light rifles or powerful ones kill well enough when vital areas are hit. Neither will drop game with a bullet that misses, just grazes, or merely breaks a leg. But in areas between these two extremes—solid body hits that still miss the vitals—I'm inclined to believe that the bigger guns have an edge. How much of an edge is as uncertain as the price of Arab oil.

For whitetail and black bear, rifles of the 30-30 and 243-250 classes are fine; they've five or six times as many foot pounds of energy as the 32-20 that Irvine uses so successfully. In my experience mule deer are shot at as close range as whitetail and not perceptibly harder to kill. But for moose, elk, and grizzly, despite how well 30-30s, 243s, and such have done, I myself would be a little happier with a heavier caliber.

Sure, veteran woodsman and gun-experimenter Thor Strimbold had recorded over 20 one-shot moose kills with the good old 30-30. But he does not now recommend anything less than a 308 on the big shovelhorns for inexperienced hunters. In the same class are the 303 British, popular in Canada, and the 300 Savage; the farthest moose kill I've ever heard of, 400-450 yards, was made with a 300 Savage. My own choice might be a 7x57.

Still, bullet placement is the potent thing, and I'd be a little prouder if I felt sure enough of my shooting to rely on a milder gun. To me, killing clean with a light rifle is just about the highest pinnacle a big-game hunter can reach. ●

BUSHNELL
DIVISION OF BAUSCH & LOMB

The Adventure Continues...

Barnett's new XT SERIES

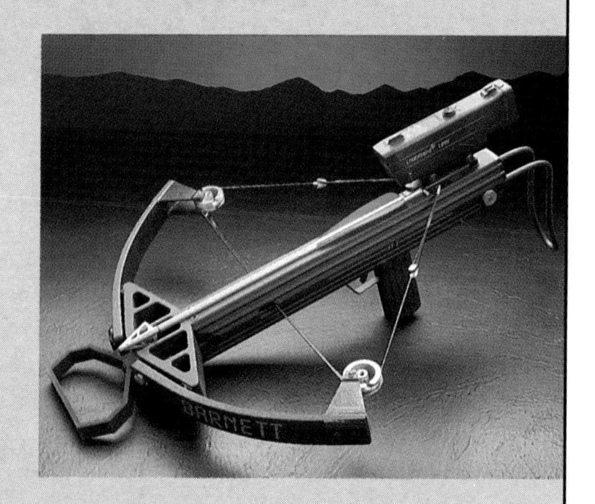

UPPER LEFT: XT-1 Recurve, UPPER RIGHT: XT-2 Compound, BOTTOM LEFT: XT-3 Pistol. (Available with broadhead).

Barnett International, the world's largest crossbow manufacturer, premieres the new XT Series including the XT-1 Recurve, XT-2 Compound, and XT-3 Pistol. These uniquely designed, paramilitary style crossbows deliver a smooth performance, are the most compact crossbows on the market and are available at very attractive prices.

The XT Series is constructed with the high aircraft quality aluminum, features Barnett's new, exclusive Veloci-speed glass prod (which improves performance and accuracy while reducing string drag), and has a hard anodized finish for maximum protection...and are manufactured in the U.S.A.

The XT-1 Recurve is the only recurve crossbow on the market with a crisp, extended trigger mechanism - which commands maximum accuracy. The XT-1 has a compact design while delivering performance-plus like the Barnett Wildcat XL, the world's best selling crossbow.

The Barnett XT Series - fun and excitement for shooting enthusiasts who demand quality, high performance, and attractive prices. The adventure awaits you...visit your local Barnett dealer today.

Barnett International Inc.

P.O. BOX 934 • DEPT. GD • ODESSA, FL 33556 • (813) 920-2241

FOR A FREE COLOR CATALOG ON BARNETT'S EXCITING PRODUCTS WRITE OR CALL TODAY.

The Lassen Community College campus is new and modern in every respect, creating a stimulating academic atmosphere.

Stock work is one of the essentials each student must master before completing the Lassen gunsmithing program.

THE ACADEMIC SMITH

Some schools offer the right stuff

IT IS inevitable that gun enthusiasts end up doing at least minor gun work, working on their own guns. For some, the hobby may be extended to helping out a friend or two and in time can become a secondary source of income. There is a constant demand for light gun work, and such things as installing scope sights, replacing iron sights, stock work, minor repair, and such are well within the capability of anyone possessed of above average mechanical ability.

Over a period of time, some amateurs become quite skilled in at least limited areas of gun work. A certain number of these individuals become so involved in the hobby they consider turning the avocation into a vocation to become full-time career gunsmiths. That's when the more sensible take stock of their own shortcomings and deficiencies, realize that they need additional training and so ask the question: Just how does one become a professional gunsmith?

Our purpose here is to point out some of the paths one can follow towards that goal and to address a few of the problems involved.

Traditionally, there have only been about three viable routes open to the would-be gunsmith. However, there is at present a more recent fourth possibility that came into being in the late 1940s, largely as the result of the GI Bill enacted during World War II, that being the gunsmithing school. We will have more to say below about that.

At one time practically all gunsmiths began their careers working as apprentices in established shops or firms under the guidance of one or

by FRANK C. BARNES

more of the masters of the art. This system worked well in the past and is just as effective today in turning out first-class gunsmiths, and still very much in vogue in Europe. Apprentice gunsmiths, however, receive little or no monetary compensation and it requires years of dedication before the novice is ready to go it alone. It is still one of the best paths to follow, but opportunities are extremely limited and current economic conditions make this approach a near impossibility for the average person. It may work well in place of high school in Europe, of course.

A truly all-round gunsmith is first and foremost a good machinist, and that's the second path a number of excellent gunsmiths have followed. First they learn to be machinists, usually by attending a trade school. Individuals who opt for this route usually have considerable gun knowledge to begin with, or if they don't, they acquire it as they go along through studying all the literature available on the subject. In any event, this is going to require a certain amount of trial and error, plus a large dose of common sense. It works for some, but there is one serious pitfall we will note a little further on.

A third way to become a gunsmith of sorts is entirely through self-study, practicing on old guns and sort of learning by doing. This method usually results in a rather narrow field of expertise, although a few individuals have established themselves by concentrating in one highly specialized area such as stockmaking or accurizing particular models. This approach will work, but requires considerable discipline and a willingness to steer clear of those areas where knowledge and skill are lacking. Also, both this and the previous choice leave the would-be gunsmith open to errors during the learning process, so that if he begins working on other people's guns too soon, he may gain a reputation as a gun butcher.

A good professional gunsmith must be more than just a machinist; he should also be knowledgeable regarding welding, heat-treating, bluing, gun mechanics, cartridge design, ballistics, handloading and other subjects necessary to run a business and work with the public. Just being interested in guns is not enough, because in today's world gunsmithing is a highly competitive business and the more one knows the better the chances of survival.

So the question arises: How does one acquire this highly technical knowledge and its application to the gunsmithing field?

We are brought to the fourth and most recent possibility, the gunsmithing school of which there are a number of types using different approaches. Some are limited, some quite broad. There are at least 14 listed in the directory at the back of this issue of GUN DIGEST. Some are correspondence schools; some are trade schools; several are regular 2-year colleges offering professional degrees in gunsmithing. This latter group provides the most complete and comprehensive programs, so I intend to cover it in some detail. It is not possible to present the curriculum for all of the seven or so colleges listed; however, by detailing the one the author is most familiar with, the reader can get a pretty good idea of what these programs consist of and what the economics might be.

Insofar as I have been able to ascertain, the academic approach to gunsmith training was initiated largely by P.O. Ackley in 1946 and 1947 at Trinidad Jr. College (now Trinidad State Community College) located in Trinidad, Colorado. This particular program was organized to teach the student all of the basic elements of gunsmithing at a truly professional level. The program was and still is very successful, although P.O. Ackley has not been associated with it for some years. The author has had personal experience with a few of the gunsmiths turned out at Trinidad (Franklin Fry of Yuma, Arizona, for one) and they have all been excellent.

A second gunsmithing program was started at Lassen Community College located at Susanville in northeastern California during 1947. This was not initially a full-fledged gunsmithing program, but rather a community service effort for hobbyists interested in

These gunsmithing students are lined up so program head Bob Dunlap can inspect and grade their efforts.

the conversion of surplus military rifles to sporting arms. However, the number of classes and students gradually expanded into a full program with emphasis shifting away from military conversions to gun repair. In 1972 the program, which had been conducted first in a Quonset hut and later in the basement of the local high school, was moved permanently to its present location on the main campus of Lassen College. Over the next several years the program was again expanded to a full 2-year course of study leading to a Gunsmithing Technician's Certificate. Finally, in 1976, a third year of advanced studies was added for those students desiring the more prestigious Professional Gunsmithing Degree.

The man known as the "father of Lassen gunsmithing" was John Wise, who took over in 1957 and taught, developed and expanded the program for the next 25 years. Robert Dunlap, hired as an instructor in 1972, is the present head of the program. For many years Lassen College has had a waiting list for gunsmithing students. Maximum enrollment was limited to 90 students. Present plans call for a further expansion of the working space and equipment to accommodate up to 125 students.

During 1983, the gunsmithing school started discussions with the Education and Training Division of the National Rifle Association to bring the unique short-term summer NRA gunsmithing classes to Lassen. During the summer of 1984 and 1985 a full schedule of some 19 different 1- and 2-week courses were offered. This summer program has also been quite successful, with students coming from all over the U.S. and Canada.

The gunsmithing school at Lassen is the one the author is personally familiar with. I know the school, the program, the staff and have taught in the NRA summer program. A summary of that program should give the reader at least an overview of what one can expect from a typical college curriculum. The enrollment factors, time element and cost will not be vastly different between schools.

As to the location, Susanville, California, is a small community of about 7,250 population nestled in a valley along the northeast slope of the Sierra Nevada Mountains; the college is just 2 miles northeast of town. Susanville is 85 miles north of Reno, Nevada. Lassen is one of the few California community colleges offering residence halls or dormitories.

The "corner of the garage" or hobby gunsmith simply cannot turn out the quality work demanded in today's market. Only the master craftsman, the true professional, can perform competently in this field. The student who holds a professional degree from an accredited college has a considerable advantage over the self-made gunsmith. Graduates of Lassen College may complete either technical or professional degrees. Technicians are considered as semiskilled, and usually end up working in a sporting goods store or related business, generally involved in repair work, installation or perhaps assisting a more experienced gunsmith. Those holding the 3-year professional degree are often employed by industry in the U.S. or other parts of the world. After a certain period of industrial work, many open up on their own.

Master gunsmiths are not made in only 3 years of college, of course. Additional on-the-job training in industry or under a master craftsman is necessary to round off the rough edges.

Students and instructors work together very closely. Here Dunlap checks to see if a student is measuring up.

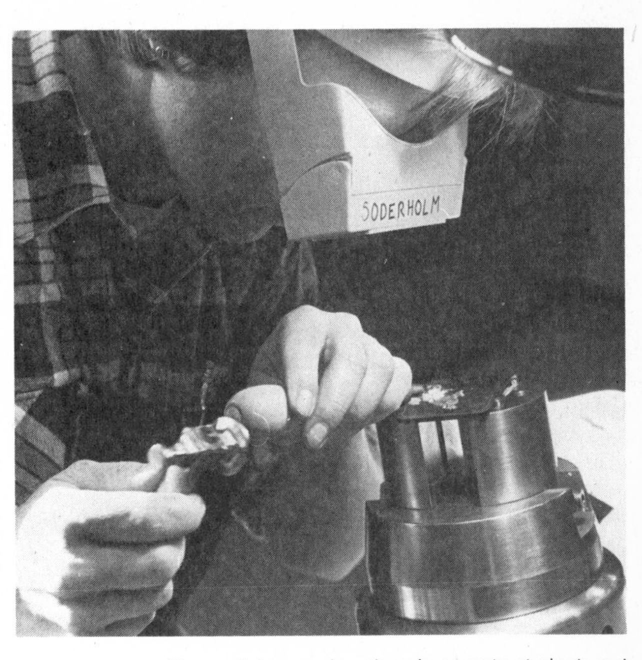

The metal engraving class is open to students not majoring in gunsmithing who simply want to learn metal engraving.

The gunsmithing program at Lassen College has a large shop area dedicated entirely to the program and includes individual work benches, lathes, drill presses, milling machines, grinders, power tools and the various accessories required for gun work. There are separate rooms for lectures, welding, lead casting, bluing and engraving. Students must provide their own hand tools and guns to work on, but reloading tools, chronograph equipment and bullet casting furnaces and moulds are available. The gunsmithing department also maintains a large library of gunsmithing books, references and periodicals.

Admission to the program requires a high school diploma, and any person 18 years of age or older can enter by

A good gunsmith must also be a good machinist, and gunsmithing schools are equipped to teach and the course of study is long enough to learn.

making out an application and sending a transcript of all high school or other college work to the Registrar. Applicants may find that there is a waiting period, since the classes are usually full and this should be considered in planning. On entering the program, all students must take courses in basic machine shop techniques. The remainder of the program will include such subjects as revolver tuning, bluing, sight installation, recoil pad installation, military rifle conversion, gun design, reloading, blackpowder firearms, stock making, soldering, brazing, welding, and other course work. When finished, the student will have worked on at least 150 guns and disassembled 35 more. The total program also includes education in business methods, record keeping, understanding security systems, reporting thefts and losses and working with public agencies.

The time involved can be either 2 or 3 years, although some students extend this to an extra fourth year after completing the professional program. The cost depends on whether or not you are a resident of California. Residents pay a tuition fee of $5 per credit and most courses provide three credits, although some are one or two. There is a maximum for residents of $55 per semester. Out of state students must pay $74 per credit and it is my understanding that this may be raised to $87 per credit in the near future. However, there are scholarships, loans, grants and work-study programs available to deserving students, and prospective non-resident students should inquire about these. Lassen College is also approved for veterans' training under public law 89-358 as well as the California state program.

In addition to the tuition costs, the student in the gunsmithing program can expect to pay out about $800 for tools and supplies for the first semester and about $600 for each semester after that. Last is the matter of living expenses. Here the student has three options: Stay in a residence hall on campus, including meals, for $2,550 per school year (1986); the same without meals for $1,000 per year; or simply live off campus and provide his own food and living. The residence hall includes an attractive recreational lounge and laundry facilities.

I don't think that attending any of the other four college gunsmithing schools would be much, if any, less expensive than Lassen College and possibly more so. The matter of resident or non-resident will weigh heavily in financial balance regardless of which college you attend. However, looking on the brighter side of the financial burden, since the student will be trained as a machinist, it would be possible to earn back the entire cash investment with 12 to 18 months work at that trade.

So there it is. If you are interested in becoming a professional gunsmith, there are several options open. While the college gunsmithing school may be the best way to go, it is certainly not for everyone. Time and money are always serious considerations. The correspondence or trade school offers an alternative to those who for one reason or another can't afford the time or the money for 2 or 3 years of college. Also there are individuals who are not interested in becoming professional gunsmiths, but who do want to develop skill or expertise in specific areas of gunsmithing. It is all a matter of individual aspirations, needs and goals, and what one intends to do with the training once it is acquired. The colleges do have an advantage in the educational and training resources available to them, because they are financed by state and federal funding along with grants and endowments. They also offer a variety of other courses that can open additional or supportive job opportunities.

Before embarking on a gunsmithing career one should understand that this is a very competitive business and any given section of the country will only support so many gunsmiths. The attrition rate among new gunsmiths opening up their own shops is quite high. Like any other business it requires capital and the ability to survive the first year or so without making a profit, or even losing money. However, the gunsmith who is also a first class machinist can often finance his way by working at that trade either full or part-time. I know at least one gunsmith who has a large gunshop and store who did this. To this day, he still works from time to time as a machinist. He says this helps finance his hunting trips in Alaska and Canada, and that is itself a commentary on gunsmithing for a living. ●

My Mountain MAGNUM...

is probably both smaller and better than the average mountain magnum.

by PETE NELSON

I BARELY glimpsed the rack as the whitetail blasted into heavy cover, but I knew this was a big buck. The Leupold's dot-reticle flashed past his shoulder as the 44 carbine bellowed. Then, I saw nothing, but heard irregular footfalls slashing through the hillside thicket, then silence.

It was 3 o'clock and raining. The Selkirk Mountains of northeast Washington had no tracking snow, and it was getting dark. Glancing at the little Marlin lever gun, I asked, "Why did I try a tough shot like that with *this* peashooter?"

Brush was profuse, and my thoughts gloomy until I followed the spoor to an alder clump and wedged therein lay an enormous six-by-five-point buck, quite dead. I patted the slab-sided carbine with sudden and fervent affection. "Quite the machine," I murmured.

The 44 Magnum kills deer efficient-

Skip ballistic hair-splitting, author advises. On most mountains you see deer close or not at all. At 50 yards, this big Washington whitetail found the 44 Magnum Marlin carbine plenty of gun.

Who said western mountains are more open than whitetail country back east? Scene here is on the Idaho side of the Bitterroot range and 100 yards would be a very long shot.

ly, because the impact velocity at moderate ranges suits the bullet construction. Some of the heavier rifle bullets won't kill as quickly, nor leave as good a blood trail, because you can't make them go fast enough to expand on a relatively small animal like a deer.

Carry a handy little rifle, put that slug ahead of the diaphragm, and you've got venison. That motto became central to my mountain deer hunting, eventually.

I didn't start out that smart, but I remember the day during the prior season I started to get less dumb. Carrying the oft-prescribed 3000 fps rifle up a hillside of brambles and boulders, I sat down to reconsider my definition of a mountain rifle.

I recalled my experiences hunting three species of deer in the mountains —the blacktail, the mule deer, and the whitetail. I had also known the whitetail from years of footsore, often fruitless pursuit as one of the wariest game animals in the northern mountains. He is the consummate free-market theorist and believes everyone, especially deer, should look out for himself. Most assiduously, he does just that, often in daunting and inhospitable terrain. In the mountains, that almost always means uphill and in the brush.

To keep from slipping down the gravelly hillside, I hooked an arm around a sapling. I pondered the concept of the so-called mountain rifle. In no direction could I see more than 60 yards. I could see other mountains miles distant, but the best I could see on the very mountain where I stood was 60 yards. Brush and the mountain's natural convexity allowed nothing more.

With that thought, I figured I was on to something, so I hoisted a throbbing foot atop a stump and furrowed my brow in contemplation of the difficulties of mountain hunting. *Mountains, I realized, have much more convex topography than concave . . . or so it appears to the rifleman afoot.*

Riflemen appreciate concavities, which allow spotting distant game and theoretically make possible long-range gunning. But once you're on a mountain, most of the terrain is convex. Where it isn't, the concavity often holds moisture. Consequently, thicker vegetation may hide the game despite the topography.

When I realized that, I finally recognized the one similarity of northern-tier mountain deer hunting to the hunting in the Midwest. In neither case is it possible to snipe the mature buck at long range except under unusual circumstances. Indeed, he must be flushed, ambushed, or plain snookered on his own turf.

From thence forward, I learned tactics and foreswore ballistics. To prove the point, I screwed an idle Leupold 1.5-5x variable with a dot-reticle onto the small but sturdy Marlin lever-action, caliber 44 Magnum. Then I beheld the hottest "mountain rifle" ever to touch my palm.

In epilogue to claiming the six-by-five pointer, the little carbine burned down two more whitetails with the total expenditure of two more cartridges. One of those bucks was practicing free-market economics at full speed through the jack pine and detritus of an old clearcut, a long shot at 65 yards. He met his 44-caliber fate in mid-bound and dropped like an anvil. The other buck I bushwhacked from a blind at 20 feet; no follow-up shot was needed.

I won't say a 44 carbine is ideal for the mountains, but it's *enough* for whitetails in the mountains 90 percent of the time. Am I serious? Well . . . of the last 11 bucks taken by hunters in our party, all save two were killed inside 60 yards. One of those two was the buck taken by the 44 carbine on the run in the clearcut at 65 yards. The only longer kill was a buck stopped at 220 yards by a single shot from a 35 Whelen. During the same period of time, two deer were missed, one at 60 yards and one at 250 yards. Accordingly, of the last 13 shooting opportunities, 11 were within the capability of a 44 Magnum carbine, or easy meat, indeed, for a scope-sighted 30-30 WCF.

Now plenty more bucks have been seen but not fired upon, being too far, too fast or both. A flag darting through timber 200 yards away is nothing to shoot at, regardless of rifle or caliber. Our deer camps have hosted respectable marksmen, but none has ever shot beyond 250 yards in that country.

Here it is important to emphasize I am talking *only* about northern-tier mountain deer hunting. I have never pulled on a pair of boots in the Southwest or Deep South, but I know that the sun's angle has to be more favorable the farther south you go in this country. Therefore, you may not need as big a scope.

In the gloomy, shadowy northern mountains, a whitetail or mulie buck is often an obscure target even under 100 yards. His color matches the November brush. On rare days when the sun shines, it plunks down behind a mountain near our camp at 2 PM. At northern latitudes in the moutains poor light is the rule.

The deer missed at 250 yards was an *extreme* range shot. Unless you know whitetails, you can't believe how hard it is to even *see* one at that range, much less get a good shot off. It was a dark, gray day, and I made the mistake of leaving my Leupold variable (mounted to a 7mm Weatherby Mark V) on the low power setting. When the buck popped out at 250 yards, I could tell it was a huge deer, but I couldn't see antlers against the brush. By the time I spun the scope up to 8x, the chance for leisurely aiming was gone, and my shot went high.

That deer, ballistically speaking, was well within the capabilities of a host of cartridges—300 Savage, 243 Winchester, 257 Roberts, 7x57, not to mention the 30-06 family and various belted cartridges. Here, on a rare, extreme-range shot in the mountains, I believe the choice of cartridge (so long as it approximates or exceeds 243 ballistics) is utterly inconsequential. And for run-of-mill shooting in 90 percent of decent buck opportunities, a lowly *revolver* cartridge, the 44 Magnum, suffices.

Most of my serious hunting is done in November, when the light is weak indeed. The furthest south I have hunted is around Gillette, Wyoming. That is hill country hunting, not true mountain hunting. The brilliant sunshine of early October and open country make it possible to pot mule deer on the far side of 250 yards, although that is done much, much less often than claimed. No long shot ever lost a yard in the re-telling. I am sure that no more than one in 10 mule deer is killed beyond 250 yards even in that open country.

Unfortunately, discussion of mountain rifles often gets sidetracked on minutiae such as whether the 270 or the 30-06 is better. Having used both the 257 Roberts and the 35 Whelen to kill a couple of dozen deer in three states, I find that even these diverse cartridges have no ballistic differences of any consequence in single-purpose deer rifles, at least where I hunt. The 257 loaded with 100-grain Sierras kills like lightning at 250 yards, and a handloader can set up either rifle for no-holdover sighting at that extreme distance.

Hair-splitting discussions about cartridges, rifle dimensions, and types of actions should take a back seat to the fact that the critical piece of equipment for northern-tier mountain hunting is the *scope*. You may not believe that you can't see antlers (large antlers!) with a quality scope on 2½x at 250 yards, but unfortunately, such is often the case, especially when there is no snow.

I once used a good 2½x scope to scan a deer's head at 35 yards as it ambled past my stand. It was 7 AM, well into legal shooting hours. I saw no antlers and thought the deer was a doe. Then the deer caught wind of some scent I had placed near the foot of the stand and hooked back. At 10 yards I saw he was a forkhorn. I had an unpunched tag burning a hole in my pocket late in the season, so getting a second chance at this buck was convenient, to say the least.

I got venison that day and learned something about low-power scopes: I don't like them. To find antlers on gloomy days against a backdrop of gray brush, you need a decent-sized objective lens and sufficient magnification. The 1.5-5x variable carried by my 44 carbine is adequate only because of the gun's short range. In fact, the 1.5x setting is virtually useless at finding antlers against brush at any distance. And 5x is marginal at even 75 yards under some conditions.

The contrast provided by a snow backdrop potentially could make even a cheap scope look good . . . except that when it snows in the mountains, cheap scopes fog internally. I abhor TV-shaped lenses, because I think they cannot be made as watertight as round lenses. Discussing optical clarity or field of view is pure frivolity unless you know first of all that you are comparing *watertight* scopes.

After all, if a bird dog had the best nose in South Dakota but was too lame to walk, you wouldn't buy him. So don't even listen to a sales talk about "clarity" of this scope or that unless the salesman is willing to demonstrate watertight integrity by putting the scope into a pan of water. If a little stream of bubbles issues forth from any part of the submerged scope, guess what? It's a piece of junk.

Northwesterners like myself tend to be phobic about fogged scopes, because we hunt in wet conditions without fail. But I happen to know it rains in every state of the union. As I write this, the Sun Bowl is being contested in a Christmas Day snowstorm in El Paso.

I hunted mulies in Wyoming 5 years in a row without seeing a drop of rain or a fleck of snow. The sixth year, it rained *and* snowed. Things were as soggy and miserable as any day in a Pacific Northwest rain forest; more so, actually, because of the gumbo-mud that almost sucked my boots off. Because I had a quality, waterproof scope, I had great hunting once I got to high, rocky ground. No fogging.

Any mountain hunter needs to be ready for bad weather. Generally, autumn weather in the mountains is less pleasant than in nearby lowlands . . . and wetter. The light is definitely poorer, especially farther north. So your scope needs not only to be waterproof but also to have sufficient light-gathering and magnification to spot antlers and then to place the bullet well. A 6x is about right, although a 4x with a decent-size objective lens might get by. The 8x is nice at times, and the quality 2.5-8x or 3-9x variables are ideal for my mountain deer hunting. Don't try to save weight by using too small a scope. If you mount a large, variable scope on a light, hard-kicking gun, you may opt for steel scope mounts. I use aluminum with no trouble and certainly no purist qualms for the 44 carbine and for my Remington 760 in 30-06. My glass-stocked 7mm Weatherby wears steel.

Flip-over, see-through, and other gimmick mounts are answers to a question that has not been asked, as someone has said. Get a good scope, mount 'er solid, and avoid gimmicks. A Montana hunting guide once characterized the sure-to-lose client as the one who shows up with a $700 rifle and a $50 scope. A few days of horseback hunting in the mountains reduces the scope to so much optical trash, unable to hold zero and probably fogged up in the bargain. If the hunter is lucky, he discovers the problem before spotting game and is able to borrow a rifle from the guide.

Whatever you attach below the scope is your choice. Within certain limits, it doesn't matter. For instance, the choice of action is largely irrelevant. If you shoot at a whitetail or mulie in heavy cover and miss, he's *gone*, man. These deer know how to dodge *cougars*; they have speed to burn. If you miss with number one, you'll see a gray blur rocket out of sight, and you'll not catch it with the crosshairs, not on my brushy mountain convexities.

So a Remington Model 7, for instance, is just as "fast" as any lever gun or auto, in that all are apt to be operated by mortal man, whose brain can barely comprehend the streaking whitetail. The first shot is everything. Use a single shot if you want. There's no penalty.

Friends, let us dispense with hair-splitting about cartridges, foot-poundage, trajectory, or even a few ounces of rifle weight. Don't risk a calculator melt-down figuring ballistics for a 300-yard opportunity that will never come. Instead, take whatever rifle you are comfortable with, and then mount the best doggoned waterproof scope you can buy. Avoid gimmick scope mounts. Choose bullets with care, and avoid the highest sectional-density bullets, which may not expand fast enough to give quick kills. Then you'll be ready for real-world, sub-250-yard deer hunting in the Northern mountains, and to understand my joy in a revolver cartridge, my mountain magnum. ●

MY BIG LITTLE MAGNUM....

this revolver cartridge is great in rifles.

by PAUL A. MATTHEWS

The author's big little sporter version of the Marlin 1894 equipped with a Lyman 66LA receiver sight. It is light, handy and a natural pointer.

WITH THE words "44 Magnum" you conjure up visions of Ruger, and Smith & Wesson and other revolvers. Indeed, for every 44 Magnum round fired in a rifle, there are probably thousands, if not tens of thousands, of similar cartridges fired from handguns. And for every 44 Magnum rifle you see in the woods, you will see half a dozen or more sidearms chambered for the same cartridge.

Why the difference, one can only speculate. It may be pure psychological—that the handgun is so much louder and raises so much more ruckus that its expression of power is greater than that of the rifle. Or it may be that the 38-inch twist in the rifle barrels just doesn't add up to the accuracy expected from a rifle. Possibly it's the challenge of getting close enough to the game to take it with a handgun, or perhaps it is a combination of all three.

Whatever the reason, the 44 Magnum as a rifle cartridge has been sadly overlooked, and yet it is this writer's opinion that this big little cartridge is one of the finest of woods-walking rifle cartridges. Within its range it is a deadly killer, and practically every rifle ever chambered for the cartridge is short, light and handy. Without any exception they all deliver anywhere from 300 to 400 fps greater muzzle velocity than the same cartridge from a revolver.

If we go back before the 44 Magnum ever existed, we find that its grandfather, the 44-40, was an exceedingly popular *rifle* cartridge. Indeed, my own grandfather, gone from the scene for over 50 years now, had one of the old Colt Lightning pump-action rifles chambered for this venerable cartridge. And I well remember the opening day of buck season in 1947 when my kid brother, a mere 14-year-old lad, used the old pump gun to take the finest eight-point buck I've seen in over 60 years.

The old-timers with their Winchester 73s and 92s, their sleek Marlin lever guns and the racy Remington pumps, all considered the 44-40 with its 200-grain bullet an all-time favorite woods cartridge. Many have claimed that the 44-40 killed more game than the 30-30, and this is highly probable as game was more plentiful at the introduction of the 44-40 than at the birthdate of the 30-30.

So as a rifle cartridge, the potential for the 44 Magnum was well established when that cartridge descended upon us as the most powerful handgun cartridge. Yet, for some reason, it really didn't take—in the rifle.

My first acquaintance with the new Marlin 1894 carbine was secondhand. A friend, an officer in the New York State Department of Conservation, purchased one of the first. It was to be his working rifle, used to dispatch crippled deer and to take care of packs of dogs running deer in the winter and spring. At first use, Bob liked the little rifle—it was light, handy, accurate and ammunition didn't weigh a lot nor did it take up much room.

But after the first box or two of factory jacketed ammo was finished and Bob went to reloads with cast bullets, his happiness with the rifle faded. A heavy shooter depends on reloading and cast bullets, and if a rifle won't perform with these, it is of little value. Bob dumped the carbine within a month.

During this same time frame, my brother also purchased a Marlin 1894 carbine as a beginner's rifle for his oldest son who was about to embark on his first deer hunt. They put a Weaver mount on that wonderful flattop receiver, mounted a Tasco scope, and went to work with factory ammo. The little rifle performed like a champ. Year after year my brother and/or one or two of his sons brought home the meat with this big little magnum. Using the factory 240-grain soft-nose bullet, it punched a hole in one side of a deer and out the other. And on more than one occasion, it left a blood trail of sufficient size so that the deer could be tracked on dry leaves—something that cannot always be said for smaller bores with far greater horsepower.

I noted the performance of this little rifle and decided I had to have one for myself. That was when I discovered that although Marlin cataloged only the carbine, they also produced a sporter model with a fairly heavy 22-inch barrel and a full-size buttstock—in short, a man's rifle. I loved that rifle, and during the first 2 years I had it, I fed it almost 7000 rounds of ammunition, most of them cast bullets. I carried it for many of my walks in the woods, and on occasion, I carried it deer hunting as my iron-sighted foul weather rifle. The Lyman 66LA receiver sight and the large bead front sight make an excellent combination for this function.

At the time I selected the Marlin, there was considerable debate in my mind whether it would be the Marlin or the Ruger semi-automatic carbine. The latter had had a lot of good things said about it and had even been used in Africa on some of the smaller game like wart hogs. However, I wanted a deer-hunting, woods-walking rifle, and in Pennsylvania the semi-automatic is illegal for such purposes. Thus, the Marlin got the nod.

Let's take a look at the Marlin 1894 without all the Madison Avenue hoopla. We've already said that as a woods rifle, it is light, short and handy. But more than that, the Marlins have for years carried a solid, flattop receiver with side ejection. They were doing this before the first Winchester 30-30 ever saw the light of day, a feature that excludes dirt from the action and provides for a low-mounted scope. And if this isn't enough, their breech-locking mechanism has been rated as one of the strongest of the exposed hammer lever guns. On top of that, the Marlins of today use a two-piece firing pin, the rear portion of which is lifted into place only when the lever is fully returned to battery position and the breechblock is fully locked. No premature firing of the cartridge here.

It is when we come to the barrel of the new Marlin 1894s that we run into controversy—barrels with Micro-Groove rifling. And in the 1894 44 Magnum, this problem is compounded with a slow 38-inch twist. Now there is nothing really wrong with the Micro-Groove concept. It is an extremely accurate form of rifling, especially with jacketed bullets. And even in the Marlin 22 rimfires, accuracy is exceptional with lead alloy bullets, albeit at the lower velocity brackets.

The 38-inch twist is another carryover from the blackpowder days of the 44-40—a carryover we could have done without. In fact, not all of the old rifles had such a slow twist. My old *Ideal Handbook No. 35* indicates that the Remington 44-40 rifle had a 20-inch twist which is more in keeping with the barrels on 44 Magnum revolvers. Why Marlin ever opted for the slow twist for a modern cartridge using fairly heavy bullets is beyond me.

And if barrel problems were not enough, the bullet manufacturers for some reason insist on a .429-inch or .4295-inch diameter instead of a full .430-inch to match the groove diameter of most 44 Magnum barrels. Yes, I know that many of the boxes are labeled .430-inch, but the micrometers tell a different story.

Despite these three compromising factors—Micro-Groove rifling, slow twist and undersize bullets—the Marlin 1894 chambered for the 44 Magnum still gives a good account of itself and has a lot to offer to the rifleman who doesn't mind a bit of experimentation in order to achieve the perform-

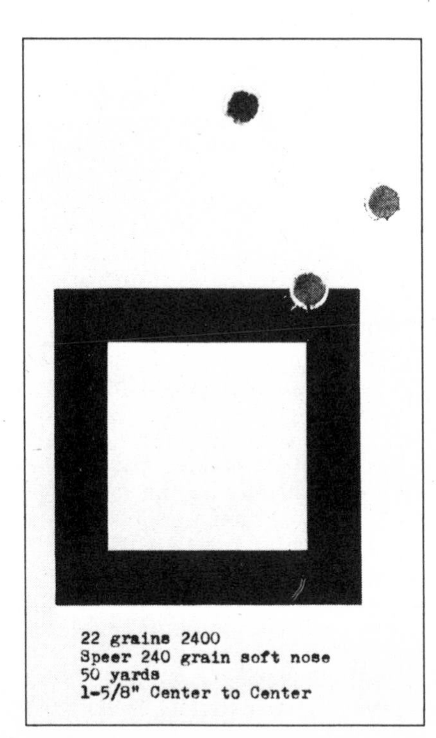

This 1⅝-inch three-shot group at 50 yards is typical of jacketed bullet accuracy from Mathews' Marlin 1894 44 Magnum. This is not bolt-gun accuracy, but it is plenty good enough for its type of hunting.

This 2-inch group was fired at the same sight settings as the other groups shown and with iron sights at 50 yards. At 5 grains each, a pound of powder will load 1400 cartridges.

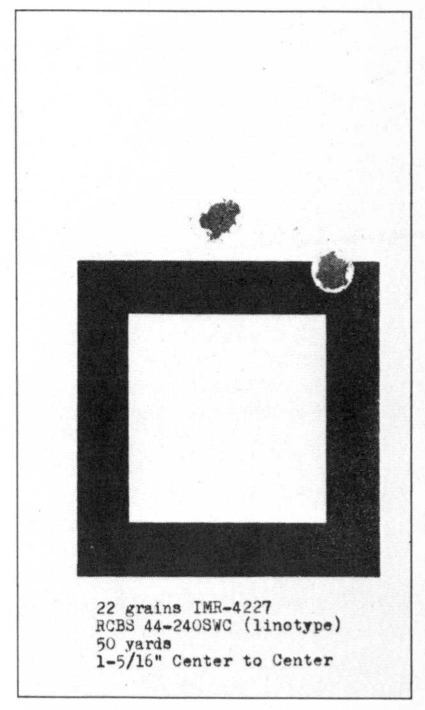

Another iron sight group at the same sight setting as the others—cast bullets in 1$\frac{5}{16}$-inch from a Micro-Groove barrel. It may require experimentation, but cast bullets will work from the Micro-Groove.

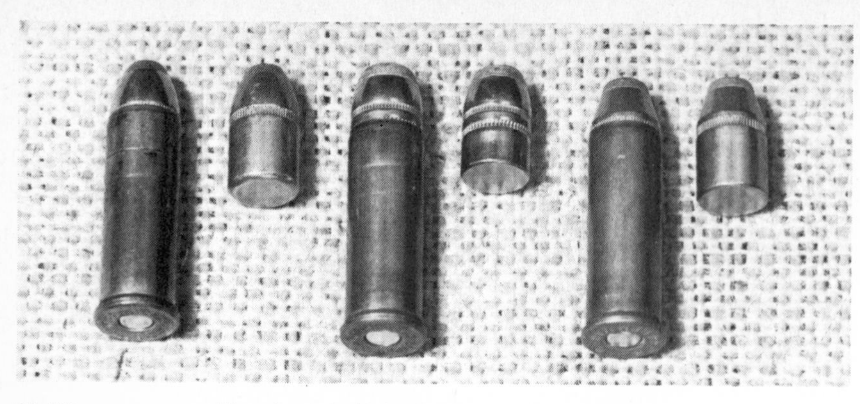

Big little magnum cartridges loaded with jacketed bullets for deer: left to right, Hornady 265-gr., 240-gr. Speer, 240-gr. Sierra bullet. The Speer bullet has a second cannelure and permits a forward seated position.

These cast bullets work well in the 1894 Marlin rifles: From left—the RCBS 44-240SWC, Lyman 429251, Lyman 429251 with a flattened nose, Lee 429-240-2R and the Lyman 429352. Author bumps a flat on the 429251 by clamping a steel plate over the press die hole and setting the bullet in the shellholder.

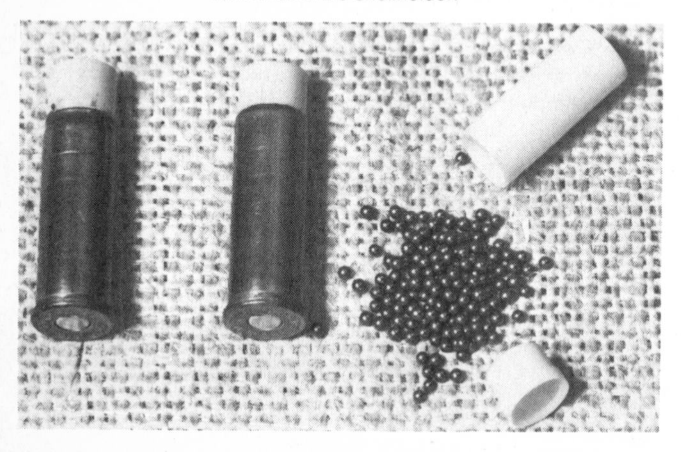

44 Magnum cartridges loaded with a Speer shot capsule and No. 9 shot, excellent for frogs, snakes or pests.

ance he wants.

As far as jacketed bullets are concerned, even those that are a half or full thousandth undersize do remarkably well, though I strongly prefer a full .430-inch diameter. The important thing I have found is to seat the bullets out as far as possible, even if it requires rolling a new cannelure for crimping. In fact, I do this to all of my 240-grain jacketed bullets to give an overall length of 1.680 inches. I use an RCBS cannelure tool which works very nicely.

With Speer 240-grain jacketed bullets seated out to the foregoing overall length and loaded with 22 grains of 2400 fired with a CCI Magnum pistol primer, I get close to 1½-inch groups at 50 yards using the Lyman 66LA receiver sight and bead front. While this kind of accuracy is not of the bolt gun variety, it is plenty good enough for any job within the range at which a 44 Magnum ought to be used. Muzzle velocity with this load is listed in most manuals as being between 1700 and 1800 fps from an 18-inch barrel. From my 22-inch barrel, it chronographs an average of 1680 fps on the Oehler 33 Chronotach with Skyscreen III.

All of the deer that my brother and his sons have taken with the little 44 have been dispatched with the 240-grain bullet. And as I said, it was usually a case of in-one-side-and-out-the-other, with the exception of one or two raking shots.

Although I am strongly opposed to fixing something that isn't broken, I have a strong inclination toward the Hornady 265-grain bullet for deer. This bullet was really designed for the excellent 444 Marlin cartridge having a muzzle velocity of about 2100 fps. As such, it is more ruggedly constructed than any of the 240-grain bullets and may not always give dependable expansion from the smaller 44 Magnum case. On the other hand, the heavier bullet definitely gives better penetration for those shots where the bullet has to fight its way through from behind the ribs into the lung and heart cavity.

I use 22 grains of Winchester-Western 296 behind this heavy bullet for a cataloged velocity of 1600 fps from an 18-inch barrel. My own 22-inch barrel gives 1541 fps. The use of H110 powder with either the 240-grain bullet or the 265-grain bullet could increase the velocity from 50 to 100 fps.

Now I realize that in today's world of 22-30-35 ZipKillers, the foregoing velocities with their attendant energy figures seem rather anemic—and maybe they are. Yet few men hesitate for a moment at taking a 44 Magnum revolver at a velocity of 200 to 300 fps LESS and going out after deer or even larger game. Nor do a host of black-powder enthusiasts hesitate for one moment in picking up a 45-caliber front-stuffer with a .440-inch ball weighing only 130 grains and going after deer. And with considerable success, I might add.

What all this adds up to is that the handgunner and frontstuffer, realizing their limitations, make the effort to get in close and put the bullet where it belongs. That exercise requires considerable skill and woods knowledge, and gives far more satisfaction than blazing away with a magazine load of excess firepower at don't-care ranges to get crippled-and-lost results!

However, with the exception of cast bullets, there is nothing that can be done with the 44 Magnum cartridge from a revolver that cannot be done a whole lot better from a rifle. This is not to cast a shadow on the handgun—far be it from that. What I am saying is that *if the 44 Magnum is a great handgun hunting cartridge, it is an even better rifle cartridge*. In fact, within its proper working range from a rifle, it is one of the finest woods-hunting cartridges to come down the pike since the advent of the 30-30.

Now, just what is the working range of the 44 Magnum? I have seen it regularly listed for deer and black bear as being 125 yards. Personally, I would cut that right in half with 75 yards being the extreme maximum range under the best of ideal conditions, and 50 yards as the average maximum range under normal woods hunting conditions.

Sure, the 44 Maggie will kill farther than 50 yards, or 75 or 100, *provided the bullet is placed exactly right.* But let's face it, with this short, stubby bullet of low sectional density, poor ballistic coefficient and steep trajectory, to say nothing of unpredictable shooting conditions, how many of us, even with a rifle, can make a precision shot at the extended ranges? Be a true hunter. Get in close and do the job right. Take some pride in your ability as a woodsman, hunter and rifleman.

The Marlin 1894 carbine is by far the most popular rifle on the market chambered for the 44 Magnum. With its 20-inch barrel, it is only 37½ inches overall and weighs an even 6 pounds. My sporter version of the same model is just 2 inches longer and ⅞ of a pound heavier. Equipped with the Lyman 66LA receiver sight, either of these little rifles makes a top-quality woods walker.

Previously, we made a few disparaging remarks about the use of cast bullets in the Micro-Groove barrel, and while these remarks are true and accurate, they do not represent the entire story. Micro-Groove barrels *will* accommodate cast bullets, but not with the same flexibility as conventional rifling. And to complicate the problems here, we have to deal with a too-slow twist.

I have run several thousand cast bullets through my Marlin, most of them from the RCBS No. 44-240SWC mould. When using the 44 Magnum case, I usually backed these bullets with 11 grains of Blue Dot. With 44 Special cases, I used 10.3 grains of Blue Dot.

One of the best ways to treat cast bullets in these Micro-Groove barrels is to save the high velocity loadings for the jacketed bullets, and cut your cast bullet velocity to about 1000 fps with a load of 5 grains of Bullseye. This makes a good, accurate 50-yard load with plenty of bullet weight and diameter to do any job from tin cans to turkeys. More than that, it is a nice quiet load that doesn't attract too much attention.

If you are insistent upon a fairly heavy cast bullet load, then I can only suggest the RCBS gas check bullet cast of linotype and loaded with about 22 grains of IMR-4227. This powder burns cooler than the double-base Hercules powders, a characteristic that helps prevent barrel leading.

It should be mentioned right here that despite the fact I strongly favor as soft a cast bullet as possible, in my 44 Marlin straight linotype or heat-treated lead bullets give the best results. There are two reaons for this, the first being that the very shallow Micro-Groove rifling gets a better grip on the hard bullets. The second reason is a bit more subtle, and has to do with the loading dies.

Due to the shorter barrel length on most handguns, and the gas escapage between the cylinder and barrel on revolvers, it becomes necessary with handgun ammunition to ignite the powder as completely as possible while the bullet is still seated in the case. In order to do this, the case mouth expansion plug on most 44 dies is a good .005-inch smaller than the bullet, whereas the same plug in a rifle die is only about .001- or .002-inch smaller. The smaller plug in the pistol die greatly increases the amount of bullet pull, or the pressure needed to move the bullet from the mouth of the case. However, one of the by-products of this increased bullet pull is deformation of soft cast bullets when they are seated in the case. That is, soft bullets are squeezed down a few thousandths in diameter, and this promotes gas cutting, barrel leading and poor accuracy in a rifle where we already have problems with exceptionally shallow grooves.

Being a straight case, the 44 Magnum offers one advantage not available from any bottleneck case, and that is the use of cases shorter than the norm. While there might be some degree of lost accuracy in using cases of 44 Special length in a 44 Magnum chamber, the little Marlin 1894 handles either cartridge equally well through the magazine and chambering mechanism.

This is really a big asset when dealing with a cartridge case that has to be belled on the mouth to accept a bullet, and then heavily crimped to help ignition and to prevent bullet setback in the magazine. With all this working of the brass, it isn't too long before cases begin to show a small crack on the lip of the case.

When this happens to a 44 Magnum case, I merely put it in my Lyman trimmer and trim the case back to 1.152 inches, the length of a 44 Special. Following this, I deprime the case and, holding it with a pair of tweezers (one leg of the tweezers through the flash hole), I stick the mouth of the case in a jar of light oil and then immerse the *mouth of the case* in molten bullet metal for about 5 seconds. After this, it is dumped in a bucket of cold water to complete the annealing process.

Cases treated in this fashion seem to last longer than in their original form. And I suppose that if a man wanted to get the maximum life from his cases, he could shorten them a second time to 44 Russian or any other suitable length that would clean up the mouth of the case.

Years ago shot loadings were available for many different cartridges. And while a charge of shot from a rifle barrel usually makes a donut pattern, it still comes in quite handy at the 5- to 10-yard ranges in dispatching a snake or gathering a mess of frogs. This is particularly true when you live in the boondocks and find a snake of dubious character curled upon the basement floor. The shot easily dispatches the snake without any damage to the rest of the premises.

Speer has offered empty 44 shot capsules for years. I usually fill them with No. 9 shot and back them with a light charge of Bullseye or Unique. While this is no "Game Getter" load, it certainly is handy and increases the versatility of an already versatile rifle and cartridge.

As a true woodsloafer cartridge/rifle combination, the Marlin 1894 chambered for the 44 Magnum has no peer. With a pocketful of assorted cartridges and loadings, one can take to the woods with the knowledge that *with one sight setting* he can take anything from frogs to deer provided he does his part in the stalking and shooting departments. This isn't to say that every load will shoot to the same point of impact, but with the heavy jacketed loads sighted in at 50 yards, the others are so close at the ranges at which they should be used that the difference is insignificant.

Today we have no justification for looking back in nostalgic longing at the old-timers who carried the 73s, 92s and 94s chambered for the 44-40. We have no justifiable reason to covet those precious moments of times gone by when some old-timer threw his 44-40 to his shoulder and sent a 200-grain soft lead slug on its way toward a deer 30 or 40 yards away. Today we have our own 44 Magnum—the Big Little Magnum—chambered in the Marlin 1894 carbine. With it we can do anything our grandsires did. All we have to do is to stir up the ambition and desire to get on our two feet and to work in close. The Big Little Magnum will do the rest. ●

SHOOTING AND HITTING

by ROGER BARLOW

LET US START with a simple fact, not always understood or even admitted, that we *hit* and we *miss* with our shotguns for exactly the same reason—*we shoot where we look.*

You seem doubtful! Well, consider this basic truth—we *point* where we look. Not just in the general direction of North, a tree, or a house. We point *exactly* to whatever we look at whether using our arm, a stick or a gun. Want to prove it to your own satisfaction? Take up a scoped rifle and mount it while looking steadily with your head up at some smallish object. Then lower your cheek to the stock and see for yourself that the crosshairs or post will be right on or surprisingly close to the object your eyes were on.

Just so can we hit with a shotgun merely by mounting it as we are looking at our target without taking precise aim along the rib or barrel. Place a clay target against a safe backstop and try it. We can even hit such a target when shooting from the hip, the gun held waist-high, our eyes intently focused on the claybird as the trigger is pulled.

So much for demolishing stationary objects without aiming. But it is almost as easy to hit a moving target if it is flying directly away from you. Try it with a trap throwing a low bird that doesn't rise appreciably. Then try it shooting from the hip! If I can do it, you can do it. There's a picture to prove it. And I think we've proven we *point where we look* and that we *shoot where we look.*

However, the situation is quite different when we come to coping with targets or game moving directly across our line of vision or at an angle. This is when most of us miss. These are the shots I invariably foozled for years after I was deadly on going-away quail.

So, if we shoot where we look, why don't we hit the crossing birds we are looking at? Of course, we all know that if our gun is pointing directly at a moving target that is crossing in front of us we will miss behind for two reasons. First because the crossing target will move an appreciable distance between the time we decide to slap the trigger and when our finger actually does so and because it takes more time yet for the lock mechanism to bestir itself enough to strike the primer and for it to ignite the powder to start the shot charge on its way up the barrel. Secondly, the moving target will also cover some additional distance while the shot pellets are traveling the 25 to 50 yards from barrel to bird. So we miss behind. By anything from inches to yards.

So does a child trying to squirt a running playmate when he points the nozzle of his hose directly at his target. But because he can *see* the stream of water arcing to pass behind his quarry, he instantly becomes aware of the need to point his hose well in front of his screaming sister and to maintain this lead to keep the stream of water where he wants it—on his squeaking sibling.

A shotgunner must also have the muzzle of his gun pointing well ahead of his crossing target and, like the boy bedeviling his sister, he must keep that muzzle moving to maintain that relationship with the target.

Shooting where he looks, author busts clays.

All very simple and straightforward. Right?

Yes. Yes, but with a BUT.

Yes, it is as simple and straightforward as it seems to be *but,* with our guns pointing where we look, we look at the wrong place all too often. And to compound our problem, we do so without realizing that we do so, and unaware of the consequences of doing so.

Let us first consider this matter of keeping a gun moving in relationship to our moving target or game and thus providing that vital lead. There are basically two ways of doing this—the "established lead" and the "swing through" techniques. Oldest and most widely utilized is the "established lead" approach. We mount the gun, leisurely or rapidly, aligning the muzzle in the plane of the target, then swing on ahead of it a certain distance and *maintain* that distance until after the trigger is slapped and the gun has fired.

If a devotee of the "swing through" system, the shooter usually starts to mount his gun with the muzzle well behind his target so that he has to swing very rapidly to catch up with it . . . slapping the trigger as the muzzle passes the bird, clay or feathered, and continuing the swing well after shooting. The rapid swing of the muzzle past the target provides, almost miraculously it seems, the required lead—a very stylish, impressive and satisfying technique, indeed.

That really appears to be all there is to hitting crossing or angling targets with a shotgun, except that in real life it is harder to do than we expected and all too easy to miss. Even experienced shooters miss more often than they care to admit. Now what causes us to miss these shots when we really know how to provide the necessary lead? When we really *know how* to score hits?

Books have been written on this

subject, and I think I read them all when I was trying to deal with my inability to connect with crossing birds, especially ducks. Not one of those books ever discussed what I myself discovered to be the root cause of the problem even when we seem to be doing everything right. Books and shooting coaches tell us that we are missing (in most cases) because we have stopped or slowed our swing. Hells bells, I *knew* that! What I didn't know, and what no one told me, was *why* I was not maintaining my swing, no matter how hard I tried. Indeed, the harder I tried the more I missed. So I gave up on ducks and stuck to quail, which everyone thinks are harder to hit than ducks, but aren't.

Now, I'm a professional motion picture cameraman with an interest in optics and the mechanics of "seeing," so when I seriously approached the matter of why we miss despite knowing perfectly well how to hit, it didn't take very long for logic and common sense to guide me to an understanding of this intriguing question.

It was interesting to consider that most of us miss all too often regardless of which of the two techniques we follow to provide that necessary lead on crossing targets. Even when we usually start off by doing everything right—by swinging on ahead to establish the lead or swinging through to do so—we still fail to hit all the birds we should hit. I was certain that whatever was going wrong was doing so near the end of the cycle, perhaps just as we were too engrossed in the act of firing to realize what was happening.

Here, what I knew about "seeing" provided fresh clues to the problem and its solution. I finally realized that I missed ducks damn near all the time because, even though I did swing ahead of one to establish the required lead, I was still really looking *at the duck* with such intensity my eyes were telling my muscles to get the gun alignment back onto the target itself, and doing so just as I was making the decision to shoot. Therefore I was almost always missing behind even when I had just seen *4 feet of daylight between the duck and my gun.*

All this was happening because it is very difficult, almost impossible, to continue to look at an invisible point in space 3 to 6 feet ahead of a duck, goose, pheasant or clay target. My targets, the only objects to actually be seen against the sky, quite naturally pulled my eyes, and the gun they controlled, away from that invisible point in space and instead locked in on the target itself. I wasn't looking where I was supposed to be looking or where I *thought* I was looking as I pulled the trigger. Therefore, I shot where I really was looking and thus missed behind my targets.

Didn't someone say, "Knowledge shall set you free?" Just *knowing* why it was so difficult to maintain a lead, or to not slow one's swing, did not actually solve this. The knowledge did set me on the right track because now, for the first time, I *knew* what the problem really was. It had *never* been that I "poked" at birds or didn't sustain my lead or swung too slowly—those were the *results* of the problem. The *problem* was strictly my inability to keep my eyes locked-in on a point in space ahead of the target together with my failure to realize this was where the trouble originated.

Now how does one shoot at a bird or clay target without looking at it? Oddly enough, just understanding what I had been doing wrong made all the difference in the world. Now that I knew my eyes had been directing my muscles to re-align the gun with the target, I could get my brain into the act to circumvent this unwanted action. Even the eyes reacted to these new instructions as best they could. They still wanted to look at the target rather than at that misbegotten invisible point in space, but now it was possible to keep them focused there. Not easy but possible. By imagining the duck had a 3-foot bill I found it much easier to keep my attention riveted on that imagined bill-tip than on an empty space ahead of the bird. I almost fell down laughing and missed the shot the first time I imagined a beak on a pheasant as long as his tail feathers. What a crazy bird! The next ringneck wasn't that lucky.

Now that my brain has, in effect, been programed to decide where the eyes are to look, and to continue looking, it is no longer necessary to resort to such subterfuges as long bills and beaks in order to maintain an established lead.

It wasn't quite as easy to prevent my eyes from forcing a slowing of my swing when using the "swing through" system. But then the problem wasn't quite as serious, for the momentum of the gun prevents a complete alignment with the target no matter what the eyes want. Nevertheless, even a slight slowing of the swing can result in misses. However, by delaying the mounting of your gun, and the start of your swing, you will have to swing harder and faster to catch up with your target and thereby reduce the effect of any involuntary slowing of your swing. Just knowing why there is sometimes this tendency to slow your gun as it passes the target is enough to effect a cure.

Because our eyes have such incredible control over how we shoot, for better or for worse, keep an eye on your eyes!

Oh, I almost forgot. I used to count myself lucky if I bagged one duck out of 10 shots. The last time I was in the marshes I got eight out of 10 opportunities. Just by remembering to look where I was supposed to look. If I can do it, *you* can do it. ●

You Could Try This:

A while ago the writer and gunsmith Walton Lam carried out some shooting tests with a scope-sighted Valmet 12 gauge O/U that have a direct bearing on the conclusions reached at an earlier date on the matter of maintaining an established lead on crossing birds seen against the sky.

Giving no magnification, the 1x Weaver scope allowed for the normal use of the shotgun with both eyes open and there was no difficulty in picking up and tracking the targets.

Both shooters experienced less than the usual problems in sustaining the desired lead. This was quite obviously related to having something out there *in front* of the birds that our eyes could see and focus upon rather than merely an invisible, imaginary point in space. With the black post right there in the sky, 3 or 4 feet ahead of the target, there was just no tendency at all for our eyes to shift back to the targets and thereby realign the gun with them after we had established the required lead.

Such a scoped shotgun, using a large dot reticle that would be seen in the sky apparently just ahead of the target, would surely be a most valuable instructional tool for any shooting coach not stubbornly wedded to conventional ideas on how to help shooters overcome the problems with which I had such difficulty for so long. One would not have to continue using such a scoped shotgun to derive important and continuing benefits from some experience with it.

—Roger Barlow

Some TRUTH About The Western Plains

It's not big booms and far shoots that put horns on the wall and meat in the skillet.

by JOHN BARSNESS

IN CASE YOU hadn't heard, the West is indeed rifle country, because any time you mention mule deer and pronghorn hunting anywhere in the U.S.A., folks volunteer opinions on just what's needed to make those long shots out there in the sage and rimrocks. Hunters have been known to agonize for months over whether a varmint-weight 6mm or a single shot 25-06 would be ideal for antelope—and then whether to mount a straight 6x or a big variable, or opt for a 7mm Magnum in case a 300-pound mule deer stands up 300 yards out, or if Powder X or Bullet Y will get another 25 yards of sure-hit range. Many embroiled in these dialogues have never seen the western shore of the Mississippi River, let alone the Missouri Breaks.

I've gotten into my share of these talks, but after a couple of decades of hunting and a few seasons guiding out here, the remark I remember more than any was uttered one afternoon at the makeshift shooting range on the Murphy Ranch, which covers several sections in the Hawk Creek drainage of south-central Montana. Mike Murphy outfits for big mule deer and pronghorn out there, and I guided for him that fall. Mike and I were helping three or four hunters sight in their rifles on the day before pronghorn season, the arms ranging from a shiny Sako in 243 topped by a 3-12x Swarovski, to a 7mm Magnum Browning semi-auto wearing a 3-9x Leupold. Not everybody was familiar with his rifle so there was some difficulty getting 'em all "lined out," as they say in cowboy country. After 1½ hours and several boxes of ammo, Mike leaned over to me and whispered, "Whatever happened to the plain ol' 270 with a 4x Weaver?"

Over the years Mike's found that clients carrying beat-up 270s and 30-06s with 4x scopes not only get sighted-in right away, but tend to kill game with one shot. Not that there aren't good shots who use truly fine equipment, quite capable of dropping pronghorn at 400 yards, but as Mike points out, "We don't take many 400-yard shots. We don't have to."

On sighting-in day he's not so much checking the scopes—though that's important—but seeing how his hunters handle their rifles, if they're familiar with bolts, safeties, sights and trajectory. He'd much rather guide somebody who can shoot quickly and accurately at 250 yards, rather than a dude who squirms around for 30 seconds trying to get the crosshairs to sit precisely above a buck at 400, because the quick guy is more likely to make clean kills. The hunters with beat-up 270s do this, and aren't afraid of scraping the stock while crawling through prickly pear.

Another thing he looks for is shiny new pants.

"They gotta put their knees or their butt on the gound *some*time," he says. "Or lean up against a dusty pickup truck. The guys with shiny pants won't do it."

There are several points to be made out of all of this, aside from the fact that though *you* may be shocked that some Western game is shot from over the hood of a pickup, there are many natives out here who wouldn't do it another way. It's legal as long as you don't shoot from a public road, and most plains outfitters pickup-hunt the customers who just aren't up to much walking. Even so, a lot of game is missed from the hood of a Chevy, mostly because any buck the hunter shoots at will be aware of said Chevy. Thus, you usually get one quick shot, often at a moving animal.

But for most of us the ideal is to spot distant game, either from the vehicle or a lonely ridge, then make the final stalk on foot. Here's where we hear of most 400-yard shots.

"There was just no way to get closer," the hunter claims, or: "They were gettin' nervous and we had to shoot from where we were."

The honest truth is that Western game is indeed *wild,* and though used to distant pickup trucks running around the hills, deer and pronghorn get nervous when people walk around with rifles. The best way to get close is

Even here in the big and wide open the shot may be well under 250 yards.

You can see mule deer forever in the ponderosa pine breaks of the West, but you don't have to shoot that far. This buck fell to a 100-yard shot.

One: You won't be standing around impatiently while the guide carefully searches every cranny of a rimrock, looking for *your* buck.

Two: You may see game your guide doesn't.

Three: With two pairs of binoculars working, there's more chance of seeing a buck before he sees you. Then there's another good chance of working into position for a *sure* 250-yard shot rather than a *maybe* 450-yarder, or a "try" at a moving animal.

It doesn't take much to buy good binoculars. Anything discounted to $150 will be adequate, and anything more should be glorious. Most guides and serious hunters are very happy with high-grade Bushnells and Nikons, or any sort of Bausch & Lomb or brand-name German glass. I haven't seen any of the Pentaxes or Leupolds out in the field yet (except for the Leupold spotting scopes, which are excellent) but suspect they work just as well. For most hunting, the standard 7x and 8x sizes are best—not because we can't hold higher powers steady, but because they're so heavy they of-

to see them *first,* before they become aware of our bipedal stance, gleaming rifle and hungry look. This is where too many first-time—and yes, long-time—plains hunters take long shots, mostly because they've spent too much money on scopes and not enough on binoculars.

I've seen it time after time. Somebody shows up with the ultimate in shooting equipment and a dinky little pair of discount-store compact binoculars just good enough to tell the difference between a Hereford and a mule deer in broad daylight at 300 yards. The guy with the Sako and Swarovski, for instance, had about $600 tied up in his scope—and a pair of 6x Korean pocket binocs. The hunter with the 7mm BAR didn't have *any* glasses.

Now it's true that most guides will have *good* glasses (and a spotting scope; if they don't you should be suspicious), but *you* should also have a pair, for a number of reasons:

Another 100-yard deer from the high plains—outfitter Mike Murphy shows the author's muley buck, taken with a 257 Roberts.

ten get left in the pickup. I have a pair of 10x50 Bushnells that work for searching distant basins from a pickup, but the 7x35 Nikons feel much better on 5-mile hikes.

Here is how it works: Last November on the Murphy Ranch, I had no one to guide for a couple of days, so my wife and I went out one afternoon, hiking up a mile-long coulee near the ranch house. We sat down on the end of a ridge overlooking several meadows between the piney ridges, and though it was only 25 degrees, the sun came out and we felt pretty good. Eileen used the 10x50s and I used the 7x35s, and just about the time the sun dropped over the western ridge, I saw a herd of deer ease into a meadow 1000 yards away. Through the good glasses I didn't even need the spotting scope to see that one had antlers.

We glassed the coulee below us and picked out a route through the creek bottom that would bring us up behind a stand of ponderosas next to the deer. By the time we'd half-run down the creek to the pines the light was fading, but the deer were still there as we eased through the powdery snow under the trees. The buck stood in the rear, all of 100 yards away, and Eileen could see his high 5x6 rack perfectly through her 4x scope. She leaned against a ponderosa and put a 150-grain Nosler through the buck's shoulders since we didn't want to search the dark timber for a lung-shot deer. He went down where he stood.

Without the good binoculars we *may* have spotted the deer as we walked the rim of the coulee, but they probably would have become aware of us about the same time, leaving us with one of those 400-yard shots. Eileen doesn't take those. In the past three hunting seasons, she's killed seven animals, including pronghorn, whitetail, mule deer and elk, with one shot each from her Browning A-Bolt 270, all at under 200 yards, because she uses her binoculars as much as her rifle.

The whole point of this is that, if you're like most of us and can only afford X dollars for optics, you're a lot better off with a $100 scope and $200 binoculars than vice versa, and even better off with the same scope and even better binoculars. Odd, but many of the hunters who show up out here with beat-up 270s carry $300 binoculars.

Part of the problem, of course, comes after using the binoculars and during the stalk. Too many hunters out on the plains forget or tend to ignore the wind—until the first time a mule deer runs out of a distant, downwind canyon. Too many hunters skyline themselves, either by clumsy walking or wearing a white 10-gallon hat on a pronghorn hunt. Of course you or I would never do any of this, but over the past few years I've come to the conclusion that the best training for a plains big game hunt is *not* shooting woodchucks at 350 yards across a meadow with a bipod-equipped 22-250, but hunting the same woodchucks (or rockchucks, or prairie dogs) with a 22 rimfire or low-velocity centerfire.

Part of the reason Eileen is so deadly comes from the summer she was assigned to keep the "gophers" (Richardson's ground squirrels) out of our country garden. She became pretty adept at shooting them out to 100 yards with Federal Spitfires, but she got even better at sneaking up behind any available cover, using anything from barbed-wire fences to old hay bales for a rest, then getting the crosshairs on a gopher and shooting *quickly* before he dropped back down his tunnel.

Try the same thing on hay-meadow woodchucks with a 22 Hornet, and you'll gain the same skills. They help when a big pronghorn is chasing does around a hillside 500 yards away, with nothing but sagebrush along the coulee between, or a 5x5 mule deer stands up from beneath a ponderosa 250 yards away and the hillside's too steep for anything but a *quick* shot from sitting.

There remain several things about plains hunting that even this practice doesn't prepare for. One is wind. Yes, the wind can blow across woodchuck pastures, but there are two big differences between that wind and sagebrush wind. Sage wind blows almost constantly in some areas, an erratic force that you may guess needs a 6-inch allowance out there at 250 yards—but have you ever tried to hold a rifle still when 30-mile gusts are trying to move your elbows sideways? More than any effect on the bullet, the wind around Big Timber, Montana, and Cody, Wyoming, will move you *and* your rifle.

Along with occasionally not being able to shoot from absolutely steady positions, wind is the big reason that there's still much value in the traditional plains *rifle*—something heavier than the mountain rifle we've grown so fond of lately—with a longer barrel to move the balance forward and the velocity up. A rifle like this, weighing 8½ or 9 pounds, stands up to a buffeting wind better than some glass-stocked wisp, and settles down much quicker in the sitting position often necessary to shoot over grass or sage. Since you're not going to carry it over any 2000-foot ridges, or even any 500-foot ridges, it won't break your knees.

My personal plains rifle is an old Remington 722 that belonged to my grandmother, caliber 257 Roberts, now wearing a piece of dense French walnut with a high, thick comb and

It doesn't hurt to have as much scope as you can afford, but it helps even more to have good accessory optics, like binoculars and spotting scope.

elegant point-pattern checkering, done by stockmaker Corey Huebner of Missoula, Montana. It weighs just about 9 pounds, and together with the 24-inch barrel it works just fine, using the 100 Nosler Partition at 3250 or the 120 at 2900. The 3-9x Weaver is always set at 6x, and at that setting it just about brackets a pronghorn's chest betwen the tip of one crosshair post and the crosshair intersection at 200 yards, or a big mule deer at 250, so I always have a good idea of just how far away they are.

The list of calibers and rifles suitable for the plains could include anything from the 243 on up, as long as it comes with a good trigger and a spitzer bullet started at 2800 fps or more. Even "whitetail" calibers like the 308 and 7mm-08 only drop 3-4 inches below point of aim at 300 yards when sighted 3 inches high at 100, when loaded with 150- and 140-grain spitzers started at that velocity. A 150-grain at 3200 from a 7mm Magnum will only get you 50 yards more.

Anything much lighter than the still-near-perfect 270 and 130-grain bullets makes Noslers, or some other controlled-expansion bullet, a near necessity. I've seen too many other bullets come apart on mule deer, and once a 100-grain comes apart there isn't much left to do the job. You may say that you'll never try a tricky angle, but it takes a bullet some time to get out to 300 yards and odd things can happen. This past fall I shot a buck pronghorn at just exactly that range. He was following some does across a sage flat, chasing them away from another buck, and I decided that if he stopped I'd take him. He did, whirling to the left to face the following buck, and I shot quickly from a rest over a tall sage. The hold behind his shoulder looked perfect, and he went down, and stayed down. Eileen said, however, that just as I'd shot he'd started to turn after his does; evidently I'd missed it during the recoil.

A lot of Western shooting problems can be solved here, but not all.

A packframe, some walking and glassing, and this pronghorn fell at 75 yards. At that range it doesn't matter much what you're shooting, though this one was taken with a Ruger '06. (Eileen Clarke photo)

On examination the 100-grain Nosler from the 257 had taken him in the left hip socket, traveled through the abdominal cavity, then through the right lung, stopping against the ribs on that side. It was still a one-shot kill, but I doubt if it would have been with most other bullets. This was on a pronghorn that didn't dress over 85 pounds. Eileen's mule deer weighed 185; I tend to think 120-150 grains of bullet work better on game that size, even with Noslers.

Actually, there is very little difference in practical trajectory or killing power in any of the '06-cased rounds, from the 25-06 up to the original, when using standard-weight "deer" bullets loaded to sane maximums. All will get around 3000 fps or a bit more, using those 120-150-grain bullets. What this comes down to is that though it is a lot of fun and games to pick the perfect plains rifle, selecting caliber, scope, and model, and then working up the ultimate load over a few days at the benchrest, if you have a 4x-scoped 6mm or 308 or 270 or 7mm Magnum or *whatever*—as long as it puts three shots inside 2 inches at 100 yards, it'll do the job. I'd rate weight and a decent trigger as far more important factors.

What we are confronting is Aldo Leopold's "one-bullet tradition," the American frontier ideal of one bullet for one animal, the notion that we should be *hunters* as well as *riflemen*. It is reassuring to have a rifle capable of taking game at 400 yards, and the skill to use it, but just because the country's open and we can see game that far away, doesn't mean we *have* to try those shots.

The 400-yard capability is more useful as a margin of error under actual field conditions. For those, wear some old jeans and maybe some soccer knee pads underneath, along with leather gloves, to keep the prickly pear out. Stay under the skyline, behind the sagebrush and downwind, and use those binoculars. Stalk so close you're sure and , if you have a chance, roll up your down vest to use as a rest under the forend. You won't get to brag up as many 400-yard shots, but you'll have more antlers on the wall. ●

Any Animal, Any Weather, Almost Anywhere: The 35 Whelen

AS I GLASSED it, there where the ore railroad to Atikokan crossed a wide marsh, the distant Ontario moose disconcertingly stared right back at me. No cover here to stalk alerted game downwind. Nothing for it but to flop prone with hasty sling, quickly calculate that seven telegraph poles between us meant—let's see—315 yards plus a bit more offside to the moose.

The cartridge I was relying on to both hit and kill *big,* big game over three football fields away was that senior citizen wildcat the 35 Whelen. This moose in 1965 was my first chance with the Whelen at game larger than deer and also by far the longest shot I'd faced with it.

That long ago and far away hunt all came back to me when Ken Warner told me in late 1987 that Remington was finally adopting this golden oldie, complete with baptismal certificate by way of chambering factory rifles for it. I was bemused that I'd been using the Whelen cartridge over half of both its lifespan and mine, too.

Germination of my big 35 began in 1952 with a pre-WWII '03. Ancient bore pitting was a wonderful excuse for reboring. The big bullet concept always had a few diehard bards, the most vocal being the late Elmer Keith. I had to find out for myself.

True, the Whelen's potency wasn't urgent for my native northern Minnesota whitetails. But hope springs eternal that big bullet mass at moderate velocity gets through brush better. That neither can be proved or disproved by "scientific method" nor

by NORM NELSON

Under 8 pounds, Nelson's venerable 35 Whelen '03 is an any-game mountain rifle with useful range and lots of power. He likes carving.

shooting tests with nice rows of brittle, same-size, hardwood dowels. A timber hunter, I think lighter bullets at higher velocities definitely have their place, but that place is not typical forest cover where hard-hunted game holes up.

The Whelen's extra power looked promising for moose and elk. In a properly throated bolt action, a 250-grain 35 spitzer can be loaded to 2500 fps muzzle velocity and mine chronographs a bit more. Thanks to both its weight and good .446 ballistic coefficient, that produces about 12 percent more energy *at 200 yards* than a composite average of 270, 280, and 30-06 big game loads.

My 24-inch tube puts the Speer 250 spitzer about 3 inches high at 100 yards, right on at 200, and a bit over a foot low at 300. Very similar to the '06 180-grain trajectory, that's flat enough for most big game hunting today. Hornady's 200-grain 35 spire point, a deadly deer bullet, shoots flatter; but its sectional density is less promising for deep penetration.

With the gun back from Parker Ackley's reboring, the fun began. I glass-bedded the action into a Herter walnut sporter stock, free-floating the barrel. The bigger bore reduced weight at outset. To cut it more, I installed an aluminum trigger guard and magazine, then made an aluminum buttplate. Dressed for sub-zero, who needs a recoil pad?

Knowing all too well what my northern Minnesota November rains, sticky snow and frigid temperatures can do to any scope optics, I wanted auxiliary sights. Gunsmith Ed Ollila installed a Pachmayr swing-off side mount for a new Bear Cub 2¾x with a special-order 6-minute Lee dot. Next I mounted self-customized open iron sights high enough for the Monte Carlo's comb line.

Then came a good Dayton-Traister trigger and knurled bolt handle. Careful lapping honed the action and silenced the Buehler safety. For a genuine blue (not black), I rust-blued the rifle.

The forearm was whittled down to a whisper for surer glove-grasp and to save weight. Unlike many of today's "classic" stocks, the Monte Carlo cheekpiece is exactly high enough to align my eye in the scope's optical axis without rubbernecking. The comb tapers *down*; toward the front, meaning that on recoil the comb slides down *away* from the cheekbone instead of levering up to replicate a bad sinus attack. Since the Whelen generates more power than an '06 at the back end as well as the front,

Late in the day with 70 pounds of big, antlered head and a couple of quarters on your back, an all-uphill pack-out often happens when you carry an 8-pound 35 Whelen.

Nelson's 35 allows loading 250-grain bullets out far enough for maximum powder capacity and performance. Speer spitzer at left is his all-round favorite; the round-nose 250s may be preferred by some for timber use.

Nelson and his long-suffering Springfield 35 Whelen are planning to catch up with late season deer across the lake. It's this kind of weather he has in mind for all-weather hunting rifles.

Second Whelen in the Nelson tribe was this rechambered Remington 760, buttstocked in Fajen French walnut. A 35 Whelen pump makes a fine timber rifle, but gives up some velocity to deeper bullet seating.

that's important in a light rifle.

When Ken Warner saw my leaf pattern and wildlife stock carving back about 1978 or so, he sighed and said atrocities are inevitable when a Swede gets hold of a jackknife. This Swede thinks even amateur, even atrocious, carving beats any checkering for fast, sure gun handling with wet, slippery gloves in a snowstorm.

Here come the judge. I wound up with a lightweight (under 8 pounds, sling and ammo aboard) hunting-accurate (1.5-2-inch, three-shot groups), *all-weather* weapon system, stocked for fast handling with minimal felt-recoil. It's a system that delivers all the ballistic ferocity needed for anything that moves where I hunt.

Tailored for the Siberian climate of Lutefisk Land and Ontario's moose bush, my big-bore '03's floated barrel, back-up sights, sure-grip stock and modest weight also make it ideal, rain or snow, in the Pacific Northwest where I moved two decades ago. There it makes a fine, any-game mountain rifle, thanks to the big 35's performance. Washington's Selkirk Range where I hunt deer is shared by a fair number of grizzlies. I pack the Whelen in the Selkirks rather than one of my smaller caliber rifles.

In 35 years, only two modifications were needed. First, when I began hunting mountain country, the original low-power scope logically gave way to a Bushnell 1.5-4.5x Scopechief VI. Second, original '03 strikers are relatively mushy. After almost losing a fine buck when the rifle misfired in 15-below weather, I fitted a new Blitz-Schnell striker spring. This noticeably speeds up lock time and should have been installed at this sporter's birth.

For combination deer-elk-moose-bear hunting, I have found the big 35 fills the gap between the general family of 27-30 calibers and the hard-kicking, heavy-to-haul big magnums—my Weatherby 340 is almost 2 pounds heavier. So the 35 Whelen is here to stay on my rack and I wish Remington well.

Oh, the first moose I started talking about? Sure, I got it. With the Whelen, you don't lose those sort of arguments. Sure, it required some holdover, but not very much, as I learned by overshooting it a couple times. Don't underrate what a big bullet can do out yonder. At well over 300 yards, both moose shoulders were demolished with lots of bone splinter secondary damage, upper lungs puree'd and spine shattered. I guess that's what Elmer Keith meant. ●

One Good Gun

Why just one? Richard Bass has had . . .

TWO GOOD 22s

IT'S FUNNY HOW images from childhood stick with us. I still have this vivid memory of an old Remington ad in *Boy's Life* . . . two boys hiking along a dry wash with their Remington bolt-action 22s coming upon an old miner trapped against a rock face by a huge (it looked gigantic in the picture) coiled, ready to strike, rattlesnake. One of the boys takes careful aim and dispatches the rattler with a perfect shot through the head much to the relief of the grateful miner. Now that's a good deed worthy of a real Boy Scout! It's the stuff heroes and daydreams are made of.

I longed for one of those Remington 22s, one with a tubular magazine like the Marlin 39A my father had and with which I was introduced to the sport of shooting. To my youthful way of looking at things, the only way a 22 looked right was with a tubular magazine. Besides, you could load up and shoot forever before reloading.

For a year or two, I had been acutely aware that on my 13th birthday a favorite uncle was going to present me with a 22 of my own. As that day approached, the anticipation and suspense were almost unbearable, and time went into slow motion. I had visions of myself hiking along like those boys in the seductive Remington ads with a good, accurate 22 in my hands, loaded with 15 Long Rifles, ready to make that heroic shot when called upon. As often happens with fantasies, I was primed for disappointment.

When the big day finally arrived, I opened the box—the shape was right! This was definitely a rifle-type box—to find not the rifle of my dreams but a Marlin Model 1100 single shot. It was not only not a Remington, but it had no tubular magazine. My disappointment was almost overwhelming, but this was a gift from a man I admired and respected, one who hunted big game with a Winchester Model 70 270 and who had driven over 600 miles to deliver it to me. The feelings I dis-

The Marlin Model 100 single shot shows no ill effects of 25-plus years of hard use, but has been set aside for the adult-sized, scope-sighted Remington Model 512.

Remington advertisements in *Boys Life*, like this one from a 1957 issue, depicted heroic deeds that could be performed with rifles. Such ads effectively seduced the author and, he suspects, many other youths as well.

played could only be and were those of thanks and appreciation.

I never performed any heroic deeds with it, but I grew to love that little Marlin and to shoot it well. I could hold my own, tin can for tin can, against my best friend and his Remington 511, the clip version of my fantasy rifle. My Marlin has accounted for hundreds of thumbtacks pressed into cardboard boxes at 50 feet or so and untold numbers of rabbits and squirrels . . . a faithful companion long after I outgrew its youth-sized stock.

I never got around to mounting a scope on it. The open sights had always seemed adequate for my purposes, and besides, a scoped rifle never seemed to me to carry very well. Over the years I somewhat forgot about the tube-fed Remington, and my dreams of being a dead-eye hero faded into reality.

Not long ago I celebrated, if anyone really does celebrate their 39th birthday, the occasion of the 26 years of ownership of my first and only 22 rifle. Perhaps it would be more accurately described as friendship. I hadn't shot it much for several years and began thinking that maybe it was about time I acquired an adult-sized 22, something along the lines of a Kimber or an Anschutz or maybe even an out-of-production Browning T-bolt. The new Ruger 77/22 was also a strong contender.

I did manage to find several of these premium 22s at a local gun show, but their prices were also premium. Just as I was about to leave disappointed, I found myself staring at an old but somehow familiar rifle lying on a table near the door. The tag on the trigger guard said, simply, "$80." I knew what I would find when I looked for the brand and model number stamped into the barrel—Remington, The Sportsmaster, Model 512.

There were minor scratches and dents in the stock, the bolt handle was loose and the bluing was somewhat worn, but the intact color case-hardening on the bolt showed the gun had actually been shot very little. I removed the bolt and held the rifle up to the light to check the bore. It looked a little dirty but no rust was apparent. I slid the *tubular magazine* out to check for dents and found none. I could feel my pulse picking up. This was the gun of my long forgotten fantasy!

Suddenly the Kimbers and the Anschutzs and the Brownings and Rugers, as beautiful as they were, were no longer of any interest to me. I could, at long last, have the 22 I had always wanted. I didn't know what it was worth. I don't think I really cared. The bolt handle was loose. Some of the scratches might be difficult to remove. The exact condition of the bore was difficult to determine without a thorough cleaning. Would he consider taking $70 for it? He would, and I walked out of there feeling like a kid.

I tightened up the bolt handle, and a thorough cleaning inside and out did in fact reveal that the rifle had been shot very little. I was eager to check out the accuracy of my latest acquisition, so I grabbed a couple of boxes of the only 22 ammo I had on hand, some Winchester Wildcat and Super X solid points, and a couple of sandbags and headed for a favorite patch of woods where I usually hunted squirrels in the fall.

The old Remington performed flawlessly, grouping the Super Xs easily into ½-inch and 1¼-inch at 25 and 50 yards respectively over the hood of my truck; the Wildcats went into groups only slightly larger, so I went squirrel hunting.

Two shots at 35-40 yards bagged an equal number of squirrels, both head shots. No heroics, just careful shooting with a good rifle. My hike back to the truck, as the sun was setting in a rosy glow, was one of the more pleasant I had taken in a long time. I had rediscovered my lost love.

This past year, I refinished the stock with True-Oil from Birchwood Casey and had the metal reblued at a local gunshop. In concession to eyes that aren't able to focus in two planes at once as well as they used to, the receiver was drilled and tapped, and a Bushnell Banner 22 1-inch diameter scope (which I consider to be the near perfect hunting glass for a 22 rifle) was mounted in Weaver rings and bases. The total cost of the rifle and improvements came to just a little under $200. With the addition of the scope, it will shoot 10 Super Xs into less than ¾-inch at 50 yards for as long as this shooter can sit still at the bench.

That's two good guns in 40 years—not bad. ●

Number 47 is a 54 and shoots fine, but mainly she's . . .

A JOY TO MY EYES

ON FEET quiet as owl wings, we went down the steep slope into black timber, the bull elk calling below. Daylight was dying and we hurried. Downhill was still rough going at 10,000 feet, but my breathing was under control as we slipped up to a tangle of blowdown.

"He's walkin' our way," my partner said. "Get ready."

I got ready—the tip of the walking stick was ground down into the damp earth for a good steady, and the rifle's forearm was crimped between the leather handle of the stick and my fingers. The clean sights lined up on him and I clicked the set trigger and touched the hair and a cloud of smoke spread in the cool sundown. Number 47 had another harvest.

Born of my desire to have a muzzleloader like an original, but specialized for my personal needs, Number 47 makes my eyes happy when I look at her. My gunmaker refused to make what I had decided on—a half-stock plains rifle, 58-caliber, rugged, heavy in the wrist with a beefy forearm. Dennis Mulford said he didn't want to build a half-stock rifle. He admired their history and utility and all that, but he liked the Lancaster School and the full-stock long rifle.

I almost turned to a different gunmaker—surely no Lancaster would fill the bill. I did not want a barrel to pole vault with. A yardstick of barrel was too much and the typical 45-caliber was much too small for my big game. I wanted a 58-caliber ball, and I wanted percussion, too.

Eventually, the phone rang: "I think the problem is solved. I was in a museum. Saw a rifle there which might interest you. It's plain. No scrollwork. No patch box. A little engraving. And that's it."

The museum rifle had begun life as a Lancaster, but somebody had lopped perhaps 10 inches of barrel away, and

Fadala poses with Dennis Mulford's Number 47, his most favorite front-stuffer.

Nicole Fadala has accompanied her father on hunts since she was 4 years old and here poses with an antelope and Number 47.

by SAM FADALA

the bore had been freshed out to 54, maybe larger. Dennis couldn't tell. The flintlock ignition system had been replaced with a drum and nipple, so she was now a caplock.

"I couldn't do no better," to quote the mountain man. I agreed. Mulford and I "shook on it" over the phone, and Number 47 went from imagination and drawing paper to reality. Being the 47th rifle of Mulford's professional career, that was her name.

The barrel came out 34 inches long. I asked for 32, but 34 balanced better. She was 54-caliber, not 58. We learned the 58s generate about 1800 fps, usually, with normal powder charges, and in order to get a heavy barrel wall in 58, a full 1⅛ inches across the flats might be wise. That would add lots of bulk to the finished product. With reasonable powder charges, the 54-caliber ball could be started off at about 2000 feet per second (fps) muzzle velocity and the barrel could be an inch across the flats.

(Left) Profile of Number 47 on a Colorado elk hunt where it killed a five-point bull elk at 70 paces—lighting brings out riflesmith Mulford's high styling.

Right-hand side of Number 47's lock. This is a drum and nipple system, used to convert flintlocks into percussion systems, with a clean-out screw like a museum gun.

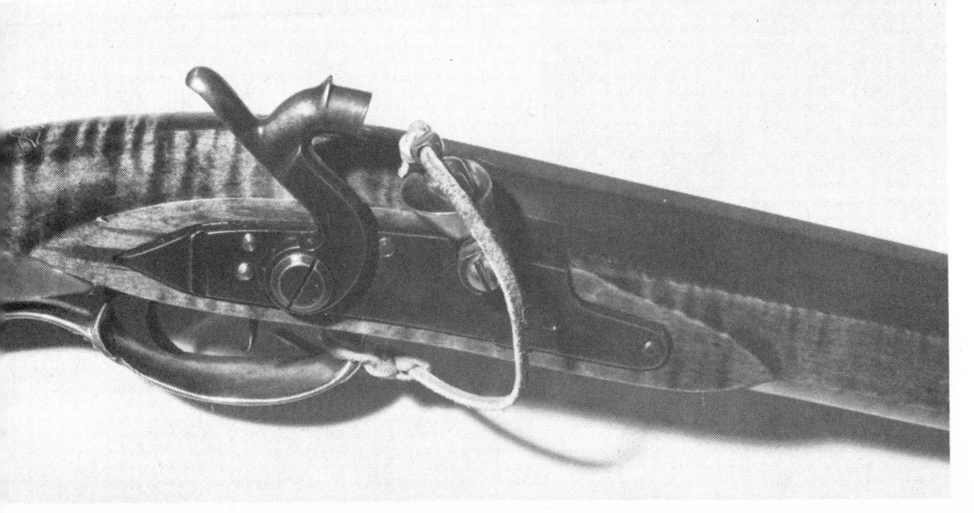

Number 47 is carried with a safety device in place to prevent hammer from striking the capped nipple. Such little touches are important with a gun you use a lot.

Dennis embedded a silver plate in the buttstock and she wore a little fine wire inlay, but all in all, Number 47 was plain. The gunmaker started the oil finish, but my fingers continued the work for a couple of years and now the wood glows with a rich luster. The wrist was strong, but not thick, and the rifle comes to shoulder slickly, the sights clean and easy to align.The multiple lever trigger is safe with the hair set at only 6 ounces.

Richard Hoch's fine barrel has a 1:79 twist. Patched balls chew a clover leaf with three shots from 50 yards rested, no matter the load from 40 grains of FFFg to 120 grains of FFg blackpowder. What I love most about Number 47 is that first shot. She fires high and to the left of sight-in with an oily bore, so I run a clean patch downbore after seating the load and that first ball cuts the bullseye every time I do my part.

I carried Number 47 in my own and other states and within a few seasons had harvested some nice antelope bucks in the 14-inch to 15-inch class, a few mule deer bucks, elk, and a free-roaming bison in Nebraska. That one good first shot really paid off because Mr. Bison was coming down a little cut occupied by me at the time, while my brother behind me was armed only with a motorized Nikon 35mm camera. The photographs show it all. Number 47 came through again, putting the ball right on target and the bull down flat.

Sighted my way, the rifle's .535-inch round ball, for that's the size she likes best, drops about 6 inches at 125 yards, and for deer-sized game there is enough energy left in the 230-grain lead pill at 125 yards for a clean kill. Of course, there is ample accuracy for a 125-yard shot, too. I fixed up a shooting bag for Number 47 with the .013-inch pre-cut and pre-lubed Irish linen patches and all the other necessaries for the hunt, and she is ever-ready to do her work.

I hunt with three *classes* of big game rifle—high velocity types with stretched-string trajectories; middle-of-the-road rifles, for me, most often, a 30-30, sometimes a 303 Savage; and my primitive rifles, where Number 47 shines.

From blackpowder close Number 47 will put away any big game on the continent. She has never misfired in the field. She has never let me down. And she really does make my eyes happy. It takes quite a rifle to give enjoyment and fulfillment just sitting there. That's Number 47—one really good gun. ●

RIFLE REVIEW

by **LAYNE SIMPSON**

AS NEW developments in rifles go, I have lots of good news from very few places. For starters, there is a new 22 rimfire from an old company whose name has long been dear to the hearts of generation after generation of kids who have experienced the joy of rushing breathlessly to the tree on Christmas morning and ripping colorful paper from a long slim box. One of our oldest and most popular wildcats has finally been taken under wing by the folks who made honest cartridges of other such classics as the 25-06, 22-250, and 257 Roberts. And while I'm on the subject of old classic cartridges, our littlest 25 and 32 have found another home up North Haven way, in a rifle still made the way we like to say they all used to be made.

A best-selling centerfire rifle during 1987 is available with a short action in 1988, and the world's best selling centerfire is now available with a laminated wood stock. It has been a long time since we've had a combination gun with good quality at a fair price, but I expect that will change during 1988. A new bolt-action 223 appears to be on its way, but it's anybody's guess as to when production rifles will find their way to dealers' shelves across this great land.

In addition to finding out about these exciting new developments plus many more in this year's Rifle Review, you'll find the answers to such age-old questions as: Is it possible to push a 140-grain, 7mm bullet to 3500 fps from an 8-pound hunting rifle and enjoy ½-minute-of-angle accuracy to boot? What action do I use when building an elk crumpler in 30-378 or 338-378? Is 65 pounds too heavy for a sheep rifle? Does anybody besides Hart and Shilen make benchrest quality rifle barrels? Read about it:

Daisy

It had to eventually happen, but I'm surprised it was later rather than sooner. I mean, after all, just think of the many thousands of us who once made life miserable for English sparrows and tin cans with our first Daisies. What if a 22 rimfire version of our favorite rifle had been available to wish for beneath the Christmas tree? Had such a rifle been available, Daisy might now be the largest producer of rimfire rifles in the world.

As I write this, Daisy has not announced firm prices for its new line of 22s, but they should range from $60 to about $110, depending on the model. Three rifles will be available, all with synthetic stocks–single shot, bolt action, and autoloader. The latter is a 10-shooter with a rather familiar looking rotary magazine. Of takedown design, the two types of barrel assemblies are rifled and smoothbore, the latter for use with 22 LR shot cartridges. Adjustable for weight of pull, the trigger assembly can be removed from the rifle and stowed separately, out of reach from inexperienced hands. On the right side of the buttstock is a knurled thumbscrew for adjusting length of pull from 12½ to 14½ inches so the rifle will grow in length, just as young arms do. Daisy will sell lots of these rifles.

Happiness is a peaceful Swedish meadow, a ULA Model 28 in 358 Norma Magnum, and a peaceful Swedish moose.

Jarrett Rifles, Inc.

Except among certain competitive shooters and bullet manufacturers who need something to check the accuracy of their products in, there isn't a great deal of demand for what we who occasionally shoot in benchrest competition call Unlimited class rail guns. Which is probably why only a couple of shops make them.

My new rail gun was built by Jarrett Rifles, Inc., and is of the switch-barrel, switch-bolt breed. In other words, in addition to having several barrels of various calibers for the gun, I also have three bolts for cartridges with 222, 308, and PPC rim diame-

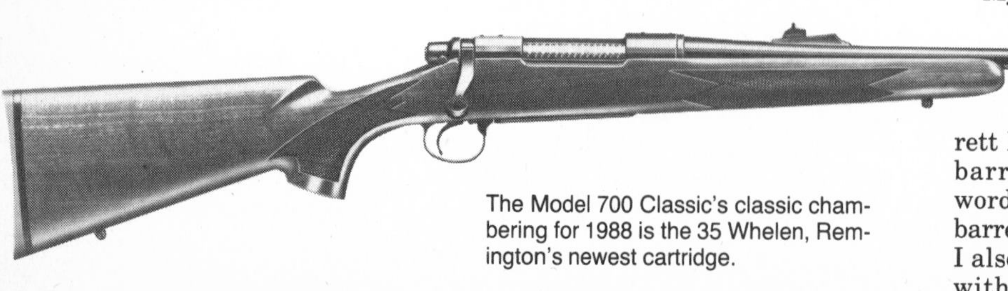

The Model 700 Classic's classic chambering for 1988 is the 35 Whelen, Remington's newest cartridge.

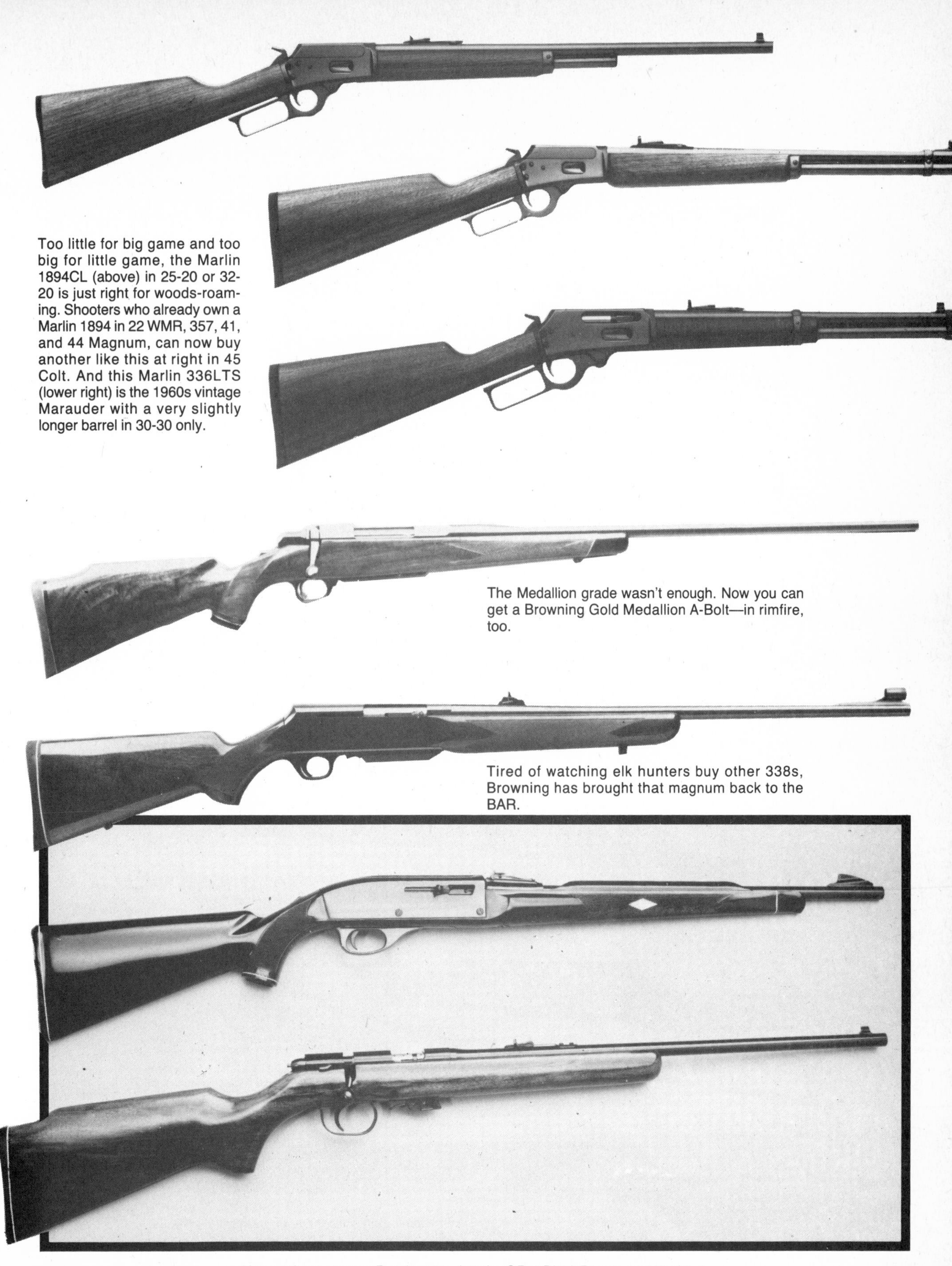

Too little for big game and too big for little game, the Marlin 1894CL (above) in 25-20 or 32-20 is just right for woods-roaming. Shooters who already own a Marlin 1894 in 22 WMR, 357, 41, and 44 Magnum, can now buy another like this at right in 45 Colt. And this Marlin 336LTS (lower right) is the 1960s vintage Marauder with a very slightly longer barrel in 30-30 only.

The Medallion grade wasn't enough. Now you can get a Browning Gold Medallion A-Bolt—in rimfire, too.

Tired of watching elk hunters buy other 338s, Browning has brought that magnum back to the BAR.

Nope—these are not Remingtons, but the GR-8 Black Beauty and the Model 122 Hamilton & Hunter from FIE.

ters. For serious paper punching, my rail gun usually wears a Bausch & Lomb 36x scope and a Hart barrel in 6mm PPC or a Wiseman barrel in 6mm BR.

When I'm out for a day of fun, my rail gun often wears its Hart barrel in 270 Winchester. I call it the world's most accurate 65-pound sheep rifle. Not long back I fed the big gun IMR-4064 and a full box of 130-grain Nosler Ballistic Tips in doses of five between barrel cleanings. The first five, five-shot groups averaged .296-inch with the smallest and largest measuring .245- and .351-inch, respectively. An additional 15 five-shot groups increased the 100-shot average to .311-inch. Not bad for an old 270 and bullets made for shooting big game and not paper.

The chaps at Jarrett also specialize in building precision big game and varmint rifles. I recently shot one with Weatherby Mark V action, fiberglass stock, and Hart barrel in 338-378. It was the standard 338 on a full-length 378 case, not the shorter KT version. While I was there, the rifle's owner, NASCAR driver Dale Earnhardt dropped by to pick it up. At any rate, the rifle burned well over 100 grains of IMR-7828 per trigger squeeze in kicking a Nosler 210-grain Partition out the muzzle at 3400 fps. The 250-grain Sierra poked along at 3200 fps. Five three-shot groups averaged slightly less than .600-inch at 100 yards. I'm sure the Jarrett muzzlebrake had a lot to do with my ability to hold such a machine so close.

Unable to resist the temptation of owning such an accurate big game rifle, I placed my order for one built around a fine-tuned Model 700 action, to be used for shooting whitetails at long range across vast southeastern clear cuts and cultivated fields. Jarrett attached a 24-inch stainless steel barrel made by Gary Schneider and pillar bedded the barreled action in a McMillan 'glass stock. The rifle is chambered for a wildcat I call the 7mm STW, formed by simply necking down the 8mm Remington Magnum case. Hugh Henriksen ground the chamber reamer and RCBS has reloading dies in stock. During last hunting season, the rifle wore a 2½-10x Schmidt & Bender. This season it will wear a new Redfield 3-12x Ultimate Illuminator. Read Bob Bell's report and you will understand why I switched.

A maximum charge of IMR-7828 in the 7mm STW pushes a 140-grain bullet along at just over 3500 fps. A 160-grain bullet exits the muzzle at 3300 fps when booted in the rump by 5010, H-870, or AA-8700. When I zero a 140-grain spitzer 3 inches high at 100 yards, it lands about 5 inches low at 400, measured by actual shooting out to that distance and not by reading exterior ballistics charts. With all bullet weights from 140-grains and up, the rifle delivers over a ton of kinetic energy at 500 yards, too far to shoot at big game but nice to have around anyhow. Best of all, the Jarrett rifle consistently shoots into .600 MOA from benchrest with no small number of groups measuring less than ½-inch. Anytime I have need for more bullet weight, I simply screw out the 7mm STW barrel and screw in the 340 Weatherby Magnum barrel. It's a switch-barrel gun, too.

Kimber

Back in 1987, Uncle Sam contracted Kimber to build a large number of target rifles around the Model 82 ac-

Available in 30-06 only, this Model 700 ADL is called the "LS" because of its laminated wood stock.

Short action fans have a Model 700 Mountain Rifle too, in 243, 308, or 7mm-08 Remington.

The Model 700 BDL is the first standard production Remington rifle in 338 Winchester Magnum.

From Remington's firepower department comes the quick-handling Model 7400 carbine with 18½-inch barrel in 30-06.

J.D. Jones will have his SSK barrels for the TC rifle soon. This one Brian Alberts is holding is 45-70.

Model 43 and Sako L-46 represented the last hurrahs for the 25-20 Winchester repeater and 32-20 Winchester cartridges. Of the 62,617 Model 43s made from 1949 until 1957, most were in 22 Hornet and 218 Bee with very few sold in 25 and 32 calibers. Even fewer shooters were ever aware of the Sako rifle in calibers other than 22 Hornet, 218 Bee, and 222 Remington, mainly because most of the 25-20s and 32-20s ended up in Australia. I'm saying all of this to say that it has been almost 30 years since a fellow could walk into a gun shop and buy a new rifle in 25-20 or 32-20. Now we can.

Called the Model 1894CL, the cute little lever-action Marlin has a two-thirds magazine for holding six cartridges and a 22-inch barrel with six lands and grooves. With the exception of a few Model 336s in 45-70, I believe the 1894CL is the first rifle offered by Marlin since World War II without a Micro-Groove barrel. Obviously, the 1894CL is too little for big game, too big for little game, and not accurate enough or flat-shooting enough for long-range varminting. Then what's it good for? If you have to ask, you've obviously never spent the day doing nothing but woods-roaming with a handy little 25-20 and its Williams Fool-Proof sight.

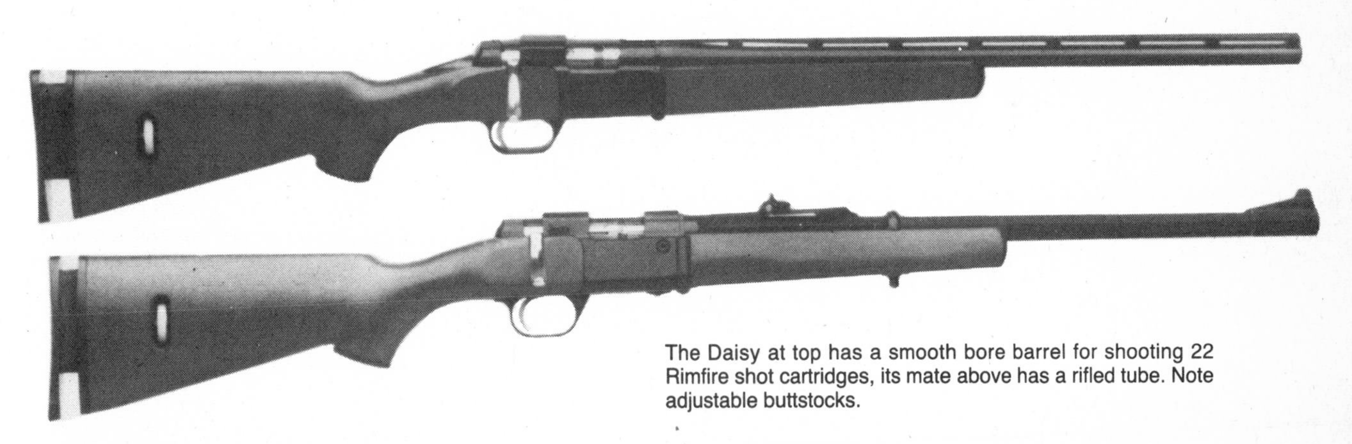

The Daisy at top has a smooth bore barrel for shooting 22 Rimfire shot cartridges, its mate above has a rifled tube. Note adjustable buttstocks.

tion for the U.S. Army. According to the folks out in Clackamas, the Army's accuracy requirements are so stringent that only Eley Tenex will shoot accurately enough to meet the requirement. Typically, the rifles are said to average less than .300-inch for 10 shots at 50 yards fired indoors.

The new Model GT (Government Target) in its civilian form is said to be identical to its GI mate. The 25-inch air-gauged barrel is of medium heavy contour with the standard 1-16-inch twist. The receiver, a single shot with solid bottom for increased rigidity, is drilled and tapped for scope mounting. Available at additional cost is a fully adjustable receiver sight designed and built by Kimber as per government specifications. The front sight is a globe-type with 10 inserts, seven with various apertures and three with posts of various widths. The Model 82GT stock has a deep forearm with accessory rail inletted into its bottom surface.

A number of chamberings appear to have been dropped from the Kimber Model 84's list of options. They include the 17 Mach IV, 5.6x50mm, 222 Remington Magnum, 257 Kimber (one of my favorites), and the 7mm T/CU. The latter wildcat is still available in the Kimber Predator, a single shot handgun built around the Model 84 action. According to the latest catalog, the Model 84 rifle is now available only in 17 Remington, 221 Fire Ball, 222, and 223.

Marlin

For many years the Winchester

Many years ago during my callow youth, I spent an entire summer of my innocent life helping a farmer clear bottomland for enough money to buy a Marlin Model 39M. Back in those days the handy little carbine was known by Marlin, my chums and me as the Mountie. Sadly enough, Marlin no longer calls its short rifle something so romantic-sounding as Mountie, nor is the long rifle called the Golden 39A anymore. Truth is, though, the "new" Model 39TDS is the old Mountie with square finger loop, hammer-block safety, and 16½-inch barrel. Like all Model 39s, it takes down with a twist of the ever-familiar knob on the side of its receiver. Unlike other 39s, the ejector doesn't fall out and hide in the leaves when the Model 39TCS is taken down. As a bonus, the 39TDS comes with a Cordura tote case that floats when it falls overboard.

Remember the Model 336 Marauder with 16¼-inch barrel in 30-30 and 35 Remington offered by Marlin back in the 1960s? It's back for 1988 but has an additional ¼-inch of barrel, is not available in 35 Remington, and is now called the Model 336LTS. The Model 70HC is called that because its detachable, banana-type magazine holds 25 22 Long Rifle cartridges. The barrel is 18 inches short.

The Marlin Model 94 family of carbines chambered for pistol cartridges keeps growing. In addition to the 357, 41, and 44 Magnum, we can now buy one in 45 Colt. The poor 356 Winchester cartridge must be suffering from an acute case of the yoyo syndrome by now. Last year Marlin offered a Model 336 so chambered and the competition dropped it; this year the competition does and Marlin doesn't. Darn good cartridge born about three decades after its time.

Remington

The best news from Ilion, in my book, is Remington's domestication of James Howe's old 35 Whelen wildcat. In addition to its two new factory loadings, the 35 Whelen was available in the Model 700 Classic and is available in the Model 7600 pump gun. I'll be mighty disappointed not to see it in the Model 700 BDL or perhaps the Model 700RS next year. Now that we have the rifle and ammunition, it would be nice to see Remington bring back the fine 250-grain pointed Core-Lokt bullet. It was one of the best ever available for shooting elk, moose, and such with the 35 Whelen, 350 Remington Magnum and 358 Norma Magnum.

Pump gun fans who turn green with envy every time a bolt gun in 280 Remington walks by can now buy a Model 7600 chambered for just that cartridge. Also new from the Remington firepower department is the Model 7400 carbine with 18½-inch barrel in 30-06. Years ago I gathered up an armful of Remington 742s in various chamberings with 18½- and 22-inch barrels. Without exception, the carbines with their short, stiff barrels shot consistently more accurately than their long-barrel mates. The snubnose rifles are much handier in thick timber or from a tree stand, too. All of which makes me wonder why the Remington autoloading carbine was ever discontinued.

Happiness can be a 35-pound 270 you wouldn't want slung over your shoulder as you stand looking up from the bottom of a sheep mountain even if it shoots right good.

Those who dote on statistics might be interested in knowing that during 1987 Remington sold more big game rifles in 280 than any other chambering. Another statistic: The Model 700 Mountain Rifle outsold all other Model 700 variants by a wide margin and more Mountain Rifles were sold in 280 than in 270 and 30-06 combined. This says a lot when we consider how popular the two older cartridges are. It probably also explains why other rifle makers are finally getting around to taking this most excellent cartridge seriously. New for '88 is the Model 700 Mountain Rifle with short action and 22-inch barrel in 7mm-08. Since it's available in one of my favorite calibers, I almost forgot to mention the 243 and 308.

Despite what you might think, I didn't name the new Model 700ADL/LS. It's called that because of its laminated wood stock. I handled one and liked the natural color of its stock. For now, 30-06 is the only caliber here, but once the pipeline is filled, other calibers will surely follow. I, for one, would like to see a Model 700 Mountain Rifle with its slim, trim stock carved from laminated wood. And now you can buy 21 Model 700s in 21 calibers. The 338 Winchester Magnum is Remington's new addition for '88.

Ruger

In January of '88, I examined what appeared to be a prototype rifle built by Ruger. With the exception of its Model 77/22 style of safety lever, the handsome little rifle was a shortened version of the Model 77 action. Its caliber was 223, and I was told the rifle might be called the Model 77 Mark II. Nobody would say if or when the rifle would be added to the Ruger line. Rumor has it, though, that we shouldn't hold our breath unless we can make it without air until about late 1989 or possibly 1990. Based on what I saw, I'd say the wait will be well worth it.

Savage

My modest battery of using guns has grown to the point where I am seldom tempted to add a new one but I will definitely make room for the new Savage Model 389 over/under. With its 222 Remington barrel hanging beneath a 12-gauge tube, the 389 is just the ticket for surprising a shy old gobbler who decides to hang up just beyond range of 2 ounces of 6s. The even more versatile 308/12-gauge version might be even more handy to have around. Its top barrel could be loaded with fine shot for wingshooting or buckshot or a slug load for four-legged game. In the meantime, its bottom barrel would push a 150-grain spitzer to over 2800 fps for deer and such or the same bullet could be loaded to about 2500 fps for gobblers.

The 389's rifle barrel can be regulated by its new owner to compensate for different points of impact of various loads by means of its adjustable hanger brackets. The 25¾-inch smooth bore barrel, with its interchangeable choke tubes, is presently chambered for the 3-inch shell. This would also be a good place to see Federal's new 3½-inch chambering since the 389 appears to be gun enough to handle the approximate 25 percent increase in chamber pressures generated by the new load. Marocchi makes the gun for Savage.

The Savage 110K, introduced last year with laminated wood stock of many colors, now has a new mate with natural hue, and a new model designation. For 1988 it's called the 110B. Also new from Savage is the Model 110F with synthetic stock of Du Pont Rynite, black in color. Its chamberings are 270, 30-06 and 7mm Remington Magnum.

(While this issue of GUN DIGEST *was in preparation, Savage filed for Chapter XI status. At least six plans for its reorganization were in work, so exactly what Savage will be marketing in 1988 is problematical. Editor)*

SSK Industries

SSK Industries has become a household name among we T/C Contender shooters who march to a different drummer (name of Jones). Whatever cartridge your heart desires, in calibers from 17 to 577, SSK will carve a custom barrel from one of Ed Shilen's blanks—so long as the cartridge generates chamber pressures compatible with the Contender handgun or Contender Carbine.

Now SSK is offering custom barrels for the TCR '83 and '87 single shot rifles in any of the JDJ family of wildcats as well as cartridges of domestic heritage, from 17 Remington to the old 45- and 50-caliber buffalo cartridges. Some of the popular chamberings are 17 Remington, 220 Swift, 6mm-284, 257 Weatherby Magnum, 6.5-06, 264 Winchester Magnum, 7mm Remington Magnum, 338-06, 375 H&H Magnum, 45-70, 405 Winchester, 45-100 Sharps, 45-120 Sharps, 50-70, 50-140 Winchester, 416 Taylor, and 416 Rigby. Indeed, the late news is SSK will have TCR barrels in such wondrous chamberings as 470 Nitro and other old-time rimmed elephant-busters.

In preparation for a bear hunt in '88, I've placed my order for a TCR '87 barrel in 45-70 caliber with SSK Arrestor muzzlebrake. The barrel will be 18 inches long which is about 1½ inches shorter than the TCR measures from buttpad to front of its receiver. When taken down, "Layne's Bear Buster" as it will be called, will stow neatly in my duffle bag. Next year I'll tell you how it shoots.

Thompson Center

The TCR '87 family of single shot rifles continues to grow. A new chambering for '88 is the marvelous 7mm-08, a cartridge that has yet to fail me on close to two dozen head of big game. As it now stands, the TCR can be had with five different barrels, 23-inch Light Sporter (nine calibers), 25⅞-inch Medium Sporter (five calibers), 12-gauge, 3-inch Magnum with screw-in choke, 12-gauge slug barrel with open sights, and 10-gauge with screw-in choke. Three different forearms are now available, as are two different buttstocks, one with 7/16-inch more drop at the heel for use with the smooth bore barrels.

Ultra Light Arms

Last year in his Testfire report on a 5.8-pound ULA Model 28 in 338 Winchester Magnum, Bob Bell compared its recoil to that of the 270 and 30-06. Probably about the time Bob was writing that piece, I was wringing out his 338's twin in 358 Norma Magnum in preparation for a moose hunt in Sweden. I let four other chaps shoot the 358 from benchrest with handloads pushing the 250-grain Speer along at 2800 fps. I also asked them to shoot my Model 20 in 7x57 Mauser. The 358 Magnum had one of Bob Kleinguenther's muzzlebrakes attached to its muzzle; the 7mm had no brake.

Three shooters opined that the 358 was more comfortable to shoot, the fourth shooter thought recoil from the two was about the same. All of which is a way of saying that when it comes to flyweight rifles and gobs of kinetic energy, Bob was exactly right; we can have our cake and eat it, too.

Of course, this also gives me a good reason for saying that the Model 28

The Marlin 39TDS is the old Mountie with 16½-inch barrel and an ejector that doesn't fall out when the rifle is taken down. Dream stuff for the young 'uns.

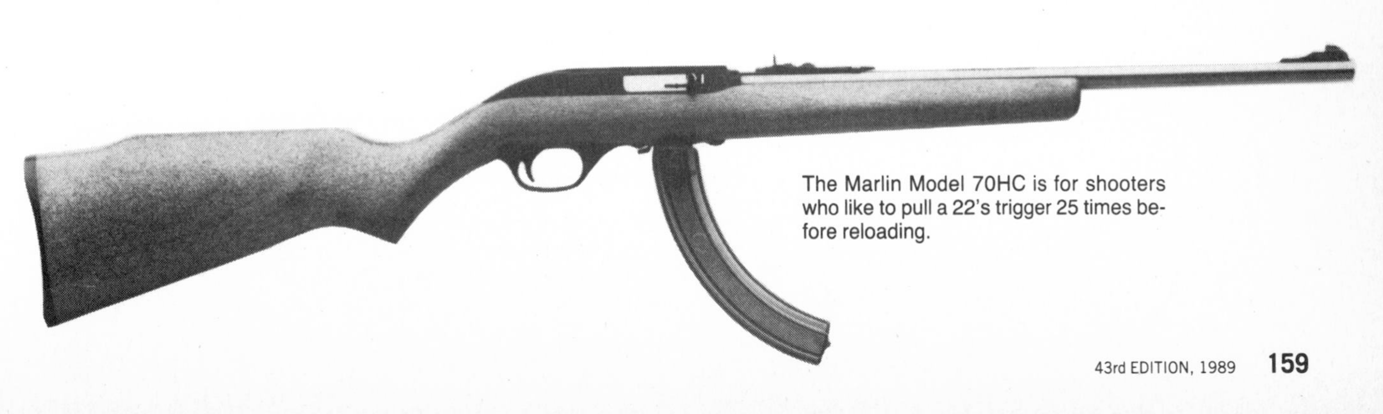

The Marlin Model 70HC is for shooters who like to pull a 22's trigger 25 times before reloading.

And I'm not talking about 40-pound rifles to be used for punching holes in a paper target over ½-mile away. Evidently, the development of new muzzlebrakes that reduce recoil of such big boomers to a manageable level has caused no small number of big game hunters to become intrigued by the possibility of delivering a big dose of punch to yon side of a wide canyon. Most hunting rifles I've seen built in these two chamberings had Weatherby Mark V actions, but one had a single shot action of the turnbolt variety. Made entirely of stainless steel, it was built by Allan Hall, the fellow who has long made popular Hall benchrest actions. A brochure is available by sending a stamped and self-addressed envelope to **Hall Manufacturing,** 1801 Yellow Leaf Road, Clanton, AL 35045.

A relatively new barrel maker who is rapidly gaining the respect and attention of many benchrest shooters is Gary Schneider, which is saying a lot when we consider how picky your average stool shooter is. Schneider barrels are button rifled and available in most calibers from 22 Long Rifle to 375. Elsewhere in this report I tell about one of his beautifully made barrels chambered for the 7mm STW wildcat. A price list is available by sending a stamped and self-addressed envelope to **Schneider Rifle Barrels, Inc.,** 12202 N. 62nd Place, Scottsdale, AZ 85245.

Have you tried any of the new targets from **Red Star Target Company**? I've been using four different models when wringing out various firearms at benchrest and have yet to find a thing to complain about. One of the rifle targets, called "Alpha and Omega," has one primary and four secondary aiming points of blaze orange. Measuring 17x22 inches overall, the entire face is divided into 1-inch squares. The "Fine Tuner" target is 8½x11 with one aiming point and ½-inch squares. The "Shabbiless" target is just the ticket for handguns with iron sights. But this turkey hunter's pick of the bunch is the "Shotgun Special." It measures a generous 34x35½ overall and has a 30-inch circle divided into four segments and with a 2-inch aiming point. Down at the bottom, two charts tell us how many lead or steel pellets of various sizes are supposed to land inside the circle when using Full, Modified, and Improved Cylinder chokes. A catalog is available by writing to Bill Turk at Red Star Target Company, 4519 Brisebois Dr. N.W., Calgary, Alberta T2L 2G3. ●

My Jarrett custom rifle in 7mm STW will average well under a minute of angle, shoots almost as flat as a moonbeam, and kills deer at distances that will take your breath away—happy distances, I call them.

spoke twice and two Swedish bull moose munched on their last water lily. Both were shot at about 200 yards. Neither traveled over 40 yards before piling up. Which makes me glad to see Norma reintroduce the 358 Magnum factory loads to American shooters in 1989. Or at least they say they intend to.

USRAC

While 1987 was an unusually big year for U.S. Repeating Arms, new chamberings in existing models seem to be the entire story in '88. The 223, 22-250, and 280 Remington are now available in the Model 70 Featherweight and the Model 70 Sporter now comes in 270 Weatherby Magnum. The 300 Weatherby Magnum, introduced in the Model 70 for the first time last year is now available in the Winlite version.

If you remember, the Model 94 Big Bore was called that because of its beefed up side panels and 375 Winchester chambering. Then came the Model 94AE (Angle Eject) with its Monte Carlo buttstock and heavy barrel in 307 and 356 calibers. Now the 375 is gone and the 356 back after being dropped during 1987. In the meantime, the 307 never went anywhere. What we now have is an Angle Eject version of the original Big Bore in 307 and 356, except the front sight is dovetailed to the barrel in lieu of sitting atop a ramp. In fact, all Model 94s now have this type of sight. Since it has no gold or silver bead for contrast, it seems obvious that USRAC officials figure that nobody uses iron sights anymore.

(USRAC has new ownership, so the circumstance is unsettled for 1988. Editor)

Things and Stuff

I am amazed at the number of custom rifles being built in a couple of wildcats with ravenous appetites for powder called 30-378 and 338-378.

THE LEADING EDGE OF BALLISTICS TECHNOLOGY

World's Best BRI Sabot Bullet

State-of-the-art ballistics in a better than ever package. BRI's patented high tech .50 caliber sabot bullet loaded in Fiocchi's finest hull. For pinpoint accuracy, extended range, and penetration, BRI Sabot 500's set the standard by which all others are judged. At the second annual Shotgun Slug World Championships, BRI Sabot 500's placed one, two, three at bench-rest. For maximum range, power and accuracy, serious hunters and target shooters choose the BRI Sabot 500.

BRI ammunition is available in 12GA. and 20GA. sporting, 12GA. and 20GA. 3″ magnum, and police 12GA. alloy models.

BRI Gualandi Slug

Gualandi slug is now available in America exclusively through BRI. BRI ammunition is available in sporting 12GA., 16GA., 20GA., .410GA.

Hunting success is only acquired with the best gun and ammo— Mossberg's Trophy Slugster and BRI.

BRI

Ballistic Research Industries

2825 Rodeo Gulch Road #8 ■ Soquel, CA 95073

(408) 476-7981

Distributed by O.F. Mossberg & Sons, Inc.

Mossberg Model 500 Trophy Slugster™

When teamed with BRI's flat shooting Sabot loads, you have a system designed for "X ring" groups at **100 yards!**

To achieve optimum accuracy the TROPHY SLUGSTER features a scope mounting base which is permanently fixed to the barrel. . . instead of the receiver. By doing this we ensure that the scope will remain aligned with the bore at all times.

The MODEL 50048 features a 24″ **rifled** barrel which imparts an additional stabilizing spin to the slug for improved down range accuracy.

For areas where hunting with rifled shotgun barrels is prohibited, the MODEL 50049 offers shooters the same TROPHY SLUGSTER features, but with a 24″ smooth bore barrel.

Whichever TROPHY SLUGSTER you choose, they have been developed to match the superb accuracy capabilities of the BRI Sabot Slug.

Scanning through thick brush produces results with Steiner's 7 x 50G Military-Marine. The "penetrating light power" actually illuminates the shade under trees. Also shown is Steiner's new Super-Comfort Strap. (No. 607C).

Penetrating Light Power

Somewhere in the darkness stands the greatest trophy of your life. In perfect position, for 30 seconds. But your eyes don't see him in the early dawn foliage, well-camouflaged and totally invisible. Will he escape you? You scan again with your Steiner Military-Marine binocular. The penetrating light power of the Steiner literally illuminates the shade under the trees like no other binocular. Fortunately, you don't have to focus, because the Steiner is sharp without focusing.

There, you see him: crystal-clear, razor sharp. You have a few seconds, enough to prepare for your best shot ever, thanks to the brightest, clearest, sharpest binocular—The Steiner. The great experience will live forever and so will the Steiner—designed for the toughest combat conditions. Isn't the military binocular of over 40 nations including the U.S. Army good enough for you?

Steiner... The right gear for the right man.

The 7 x 50C Steiner Commander RS2000 with built-in compass and rangefinder. Compass is HD-stabilized℠ for accurate, steady bearings. Electronic compass illumination for easy night bearings.

U.S.—Pioneer Marketing & Research
216 Haddon Avenue
Westmont, N.J. 08108
(609) 854-2424 • (800) 257-7742

Canada—Steiner Optik Canada, I
500 Ouellette Avenue
Windsor, Ont. N9A 1B3
(519) 258-7263

Controlled rapid fire: .357 Magnum shoots 10 rounds on target in less than 2.5 seconds.

Five powerful reasons to shoot the Desert Eagle.

The only handgun that is controllable and comfortable in Magnum calibers.

1. Firepower. The Desert Eagle unleashes unparalleled stopping power. The .357 Magnum packs 10 shots at a clip; the .41 and .44 Magnum each carry 9 shots. You'll never be second best when you shoot the Desert Eagle.

2. Low Recoil. Gas operation means the Desert Eagle is easy on your hand. You'll never have to download your ammo to practice again. You'll get the total effect of Magnum ammunition along with light recoil, quick recovery, and the fastest possible second shot in a Magnum caliber. The new, adjustable, two-stage trigger makes the gun even smoother to shoot.

Finishes include: (left to right) bright nickel, standard black, satin nickel, polished & blued. Six other finishes also available.

3. Accuracy & Reliability. The Desert Eagle shoots straight right out of the box, with effective accuracy to 200 meters (300 meters with the 14'' barrel).

4. Versatility. Use the Desert Eagle for hunting, self-defense, pins, silhouettes, or target practice. Depending on your needs, you can shoot with a 6'', 10'' or 14'' barrel. And you can shift calibers in seconds with a simple conversion kit -- no tools necessary.

5. Striking Looks. The gun looks awesome. With all the choices in frames, finishes, triggers, barrels, sights, and appointments, there are 2376 possible ways to have your Desert Eagle. You can customize it entirely to suit your own shooting needs.

Don't wait any longer. See your local dealer and ask about the Desert Eagle. Because now you have every reason to expect comfort and control in a Magnum caliber handgun.

Manufactured & Developed by

ISRAEL MILITARY INDUSTRIES

Invented, Patented & Marketed by

MAGNUM RESEARCH, INC.
P.O. Box 32221
Minneapolis, Minnesota 55432
(612) 574-1868

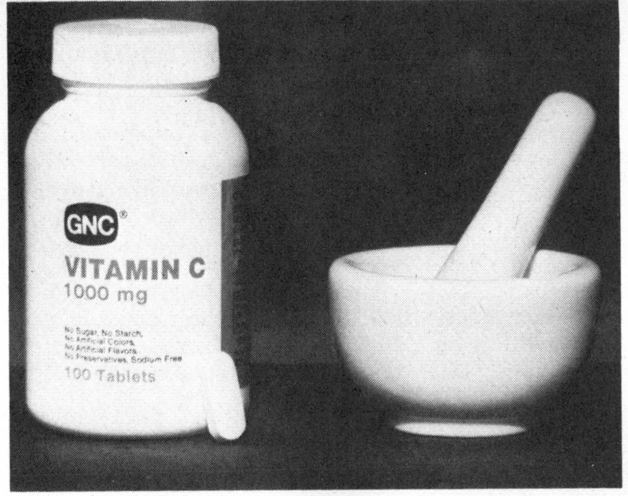

Vitamin C is one of the preferred fuel ingredients of "Gold Powder," according to patent specification. The ascorbic acid tablets from the drugstore contain binders, so it took a ceramic mortar and pestle to crush one for a shooting test.

Saltpeter is a preferred oxidizer in "Golden Powder," as it is in blackpowder, according to patent specification. Its medicinal use, shown on the back of the can, is as a diuretic.

BLACKPOWDER

Could have been

WHITE OR YELLOW . . . OR PINK!

by EDWARD M. YARD

ONE DAY I snoozed and was dreaming at the range just after shooting my favorite Thompson/Center 50-caliber Hawken with blackpowder. My hands were dirty and smelled of sulfur. Soon an unfamiliar fellow stepped to the firing line.

He took aim, standing, at his target. **"Pwrumpthat"** went his piece and a hefty bush of dust rose at once behind the 100-yard carriers. From the muzzle came a faint blue streak that turned white in a few feet and evaporated slowly as it drifted away. The only odor seemed to me like that of club soda. There wasn't a spark visible. He loaded some pale stuff and fired again, **"prumphspat,"** with the same effects.

I asked what he was shooting.

"Poodairh Brewjair," he answered.

On my inquiry, he said he was visiting from an island in the south Indian Ocean where this powder had been used for over 100 years.

"Why haven't we heard of this powder?" I questioned.

"Yew nivairh esk, " he replied.

He continued shooting for more than a dozen shots, but did not once clean his bore. His powder was tinted, not white, and light. He charged less than I would have expected to use of my own blackpowder.

Every muzzleloader shooter might have this dream sometime. It isn't entirely fantasy. When I awoke to realize that he was not there, some things I had read about came back to mind. The name of his powder seemed familiar. Aha, *deja vu*.

It is well known in the history of blackpowder development that improvements were sought. A cleaner, flashless, smokeless, and even noiseless concoction would have been welcome. Airguns were tried in quest for these virtues. And some powders were invented that might have found acceptance had smokeless powders not come along at the same time.

One of these, *Poudre Brugere,* was, of course, what had come forth in my dream. I had indeed read about it in *Chemistry of Powder and Explosives* by Tenney L. Davis. It is reported to have been more powerful than blackpowder and to have produced less smoke. It would have been pink or yellow in color. Had it been discovered somewhat earlier than it was, it might have supplanted the original gunpowder or become an alternative.

It is an example of the principle of mixing an oxidizing salt with a combustible material. Potassium nitrate, the same as in blackpowder, is the oxidizer in Poudre Brugere, but ammonium picrate, rather than charcoal, is the fuel. Saltpeter, with the chemical name of potassium nitrate and the chemical formula KNO_3, is white. The color of a powder made with it depends on what is mixed with it, here a yellow crystal or sometimes red. Another mixture of the same time, mentioned by Davis, is Raschig's white blasting powder which uses sodium cresol sulfonate as the combustible. That compound was not found in several reference manuals. Most sodium salts and cresols are white or colorless, as it is described.

Cocoa powder is seldom heard of. It was a brown-colored form, as its name implies, of blackpowder developed for artillery use. It contained partially burned rye straw charcoal, which had colloidal properties that allowed it to be formed into prismatic perforated grains that were slow and progressive burning.

The color of blackpowder derives from the charcoal used as fuel. It is not black. Dark gray, for powder made with wood charcoal, is closer. It becomes black when tumbled with graphite to glaze the surface. That was the practice at the time it got its name to distinguish it from smokeless.

When a chemical compound, nitrocellulose, that was itself a complete explosive came along, all attention turned to it. Its development was not easy. Numerous other compounds soon appeared. Many of them found wide and continued use. Nitrocellulose, wet or dry, is a powerful detonating explosive, but when colloided it is a widely useful propellant. All of its products of combustion are gases. It can work without additives, except for the solvents used to form a colloid, as a propellant.

With a material as versatile and adaptable as nitrocellulose is, and so easily manufactured from common materials, it is easy to understand why it has dominated its field and captured the major market share. And what areas of interest remained have been filled by the hundreds of other modern materials.

However, in the last days of the sway of old gunpowder, some innovations saw use. Ammonium nitrate was used in military powders. Sodium nitrate was found to have advantages and was used for blasting. Both of these were hygroscopic and had other minor disadvantages. Chlorate powders were also used and were white, or nearly so, as charcoal was replaced by starch, dextrin, or other fuels.

Guns changed, too. Breech-loading repeaters using metallic cartridges, or metallic-headed shotshells, supplanted muzzleloaders. Because the same power came from a much more compact charge that produced so little fouling that generally hundreds of shots were possible before a gun had to be cleaned, the smokeless powders, made largely of nitrocellulose, swept the field. For all practical shooting today, smokeless powders are all that is used.

For fun and hobby shooting, traditional hunting and historical re-enactment, muzzleloaders and blackpowder have been coming back. And development that waned before the turn of the century waxes again. We now have noncorrosive caps. New bullets, patches, sabots and greases abound. Blackpowder has challengers. Pyrodex, which has been around a bit over 10 years, is about the same in color as blackpowder. What is in it is the maker's—Hodgdon Powder Co.—proprietary secret. It is patented, but there is a lot of leeway in the disclosure specifications. It is said to be very much like blackpowder in its composition, but modified to make it less sensitive to ignition. This could account for its very similar performance and its hue.

A newer rival which has received some publicity, although not yet in production, is called "Golden Powder." The name derives from its color, which it acquires during manufacture. It is covered by a patent. While this takes in alternative materials, all of the preferred ones are white. A basic composition, according to the patent specification, is potassium nitrate mixed with ascorbic acid, which is Vitamin C, the common cold remedy. When mixed in water and heated for drying, the materials turn yellow. If overheated it turns red and dangerous change may then occur. Thus the drying is controlled so that it just turns golden.

Golden Powder certainly isn't black. In fact it could be as white as sugar or salt. The patent specifies that the powdered materials may be mixed dry. This eliminates heating for drying, so the two white powders stay untinted. Apparently manufacture will be done by mixing pumped water solutions and slurries, probably with some cellulosic fibers as binders, and subsequent drying at a closely controlled temperature leading to a coloring in keeping with its trade name.

Manufacturing has not yet started. There is no reliable prediction when it will. There have been demonstrations at trade shows. One writer traveled to headquarters in Las Vegas, Nevada, and was allowed to shoot a batch of it. But there isn't any data for it. Until manufacture starts with a standard production composition and unless quality control limits are set for various grades, there can be no performance figures. Even laboratory samples of Golden Powder are not

This is how the mixture of dry powdered saltpeter and a crushed vitamin C tablet look. About the amount used for a trial shot is seen as a white pile in the bottom center of this view to the right of the ball and crusher. The jar only looks full because of the dusty mixture sticking to its walls.

available.

It has been reported to be non-corrosive. The inventor, Mr. Earl Kurtz, aka "Skip," told the writer on the phone that shooting it is like giving the gun a steam bath! He also insisted during that conversation that CO_2, not CO, was the other (than water as steam) main product of combustion. That was surprising, as the author knew of no fully oxidized powder compositions and had not yet seen the patent issued to Mr. Kurtz. Both of these statements are undoubtedly true.

Later, after reading the patent, some high school chemistry references showed that the formula for ascorbic acid, Vitamin C, is $C_6H_8O_6$ and for potassium nitrate it is KNO_3. If these are mixed and they burn in the ratio of four molecular weights of the nitrate to one molecular weight of Vitamin C, the products of the reaction will be: $2K_2O + 2N_2 + 6CO_2 + 4H_2O$. Considerable heat will be released as this is a combustion process. These products will exist in that form only while hot, above the boiling temperature of water, the H_2O. Once things cool and that water (steam) begins to condense, other reactions will occur. While hot, the gases will be 66 percent of the weight and solids 34 percent.

So long as the barrel remains cool enough for some of the water vapor to condense on its bore surface, a powerful cleaning solution of potassium carbonate will form. As there is no inherent dirt in this composition or its products, an initially clean gun bore should stay that way and be protected from corrosion because the residue is alkaline. A somewhat dirty bore, but free of rust and pitting, should become clean after firing several shots with the mixture being discussed. Even though actual chemical results may vary a bit from these ideal predictions, the effects seem sure to be quite marvelous compared to what we are used to experiencing.

Results of firing 14 grains of mixed dry saltpeter and a crushed vitamin C tablet were a flattened lead ball and minimally compressed crusher, pictured here. The two blackened tufts at the right are paper patch wads pushed through the bore.

Since samples are not available, the writer did venture into an experiment to be detailed here. One small portion, less than one single ordinary powder charge, was made for trial. This description is not intended to provide information about the home preparation of propellant powder, an activity the reader is cautioned to avoid for his own and his family's safety. Even the mixing of a quantity less than enough for one rifle load poses a danger.

Common 1000 milligram Vitamin C tablets contain 15.4 grains of ascorbic acid. Each weighs about 19.6 grains and the difference is the weight of binders and excipients (which the dictionary defines as binders, also) and surface glazing. These extras may be inert dilutants or slightly deterrent in effect. Calculation indicated that 31 grains of potassium nitrate should be mixed with that amount of Vitamin C (15.4 grains) to form the theoretically balanced composition. That makes 46.4 grains weight of a gunpowder mixture.

The Vitamin C tablet was crushed and pulverized in a small ceramic mortar. Then the already powdered potassium nitrate was stirred in with care until the two materials were as completely mixed as seemed possible. The result was a white stuff that resembled powdered sugar. It flowed, but not freely. The slight coherence could be the result of the binders in the tablet. Some of this was placed on a slip of paper which was lighted with a match. When the flame reached it, it burned slowly and unevenly, with none of the swiftness with which blackpowder goes.

Fourteen grains weight filled the breech plug cavity of a Thompson/Center Hawken, so that amount was fired in the pressure gun with a 129-grain round ball with a loose paper towel patch. It shot out the ball with more of a hiss than a bang. The crusher miked .498-inch, squeezed .002-inch from .500 starting, which the tarage table lists as 3300 LUP. However, putting it in the yoke and taking it out can compress one this much, so the pressure will be considered indeterminate. The base of the patch was black. A lot of black stuff wiped out of the bore. Apparently temperature never got up to the real burning point. The fact that a vitamin pill stirred to a mixture with some diuretic medicine shot a bullet out of a rifle barrel shows that this is more than just a pipe dream. This kitchen sink experiment must not be taken in any way to imply how Golden Powder, when available, will perform. The few reports on lab samples are good.

There are many other possible compositions that might prove to be practical substitutes for blackpowder. The patent granted Mr. Kurtz mentions some alternates. So does the patent to Dan Pawlak under which Pydrodex is manufactured. *The Chemistry of Powder and Explosives,* by Davis, *Military Explosives,* Departments Of The Army And The Air Force, *Energetics of Propellant Chemistry,* by Siegel and Schieler, and the *Encyclopedia Britannica* are a few of the publications in which a great many materials are mentioned. Few of these have been fully explored or subjected to development for use as small arms propellants. When it is remembered that it took 500 years to bring blackpowder to its present performance level, and that smokeless powders have been evolving for 100, it is realistic to believe that similar efforts spent on

This pressure gun was used to testfire several propellants that are not black. The lead cylinders seen at the bottom center show by their compression in the breech what pressure was generated by each trial shot.

some of the alternate compositions would produce useful gunpowders.

The small size of the sport and recreational market for blackpowder limits the effort to find alternates. Had there been no difficulty in shipping blackpowder, Pyrodex might not have come along. There were other considerations, too, as is also certainly true for Golden Powder. There just isn't enough money in it to support the necessary R&D, or even to launch a new product like Golden Powder. And then there is tradition. Many of the people shooting muzzleloaders are motivated by a desire to relive the past. What would shooting a flintlock be without the smell and the smoke and the image of Davy Crockett?

There is an alternative that the writer has not seen mentioned. That is the potassium chlorate powders. They are dangerous to manufacture and handle, but they will work. A mixture of starch with $KClO_3$ and an accelerator, according to the Tanner patent, makes a useful propellant. The writer has run bomb calorimeter tests of it and fired it in a few guns over a period of 25 years. The two basic ingredients are white but the accelerator used in the writer's mixture is green, so it has a pale lime hue.

To see how it would do in a T/C Hawken rifle, a breech plug full of it, about 15 grains weight, was put in the pressure gun and a 129-grain round lead ball with loose paper patch was fired through a 45 caliber Hawken barrel. The Remington No. 11 cap ignited it without hesitation. The snap of the cap was obscured by a mild report as the ball buried itself in the maple log backstop. Examination of the breech and bore showed that it burned cleanly with a powdery residue, as some of the products are solids. The barrel was cleaned easily with water. After a few dry patches, wiping with WD-40 and then spraying the bore with it, there was no corrosion. Chlorate primers were notorious for causing corrosion, so this was watched for. There were no after-effects.

The ball penetrated the log about $1^5/_{16}$ inches. By wood chronograph, this figures about 600 fps. The 15-grain charge registered .025-inch compression of the lead crusher for a reading of 5700 LUP. With a more normal load and a tight greased cloth patch, something in the range of blackpowder velocity and an acceptable, but possibly high, pressure might be expected. This mixture is talcum powder-fine and dusty for handling and for loading. This fineness undoubtedly causes higher pressures than grains would.

Chlorate mixtures are sensitive to impact and friction, hence their use in primers. Without development they do not, or may not, represent a safe alternative to blackpowder. Corning and deterrent coating might do for them what similar processing did for original gunpowder. How much of a factor in their use corrosion might be is not known. Limited use in testing and shooting by the writer did not encounter any difficulty of this sort. The guns were all cleaned promptly, finishing by dispersing any water with WD-40.

The writer tried mixing potassium nitrate with Pillsbury's Best Enriched All Purpose Flour. This burned slowly and unevenly in the open. However the "All Purpose" did not include ignition by a cap in a gun, not even with an igniter charge of FFFFg blackpowder. There must be a lot of other readily available fuels to try, but gunpowder development is not on the agenda right now.

That brief description of Poudre Brugere in Davis is intriguing. Its hard grains were stable, and it wasn't hygroscopic. Its products of combustion would have given it ballistic advantages, possibly. This may account in some way for the comment that it was more powerful than blackpowder. There is nothing that would indicate it would be corrosive. Unfortunately it isn't something you could have your druggist mix up for you. It requires the same equipment to manufacture Poudre Brugere that blackpowder does. That means incorporating in a heavy wheel mill, pressing, breaking, screening, drying, etc. The risks of manufacturing are unknown. There is no report of its sensitivity to impact, ignition or other properties. It will probably have to remain a pastel propellant of memory.

We certainly hope that Golden Powder will overcome the difficulties of getting into production. A clean-burning, nearly smokeless, practically self-cleaning powder would be a dream come ture. Good things are worth waiting for.

The original gunpowder that has only recently been called blackpowder, need not necessarily have had that dark a color. Had earlier investigators and developers stumbled or started down any of these other tracks with alternative fuels, it might even have been white! ●

BUDGET SCOUT RIFLES

by JIM THOMPSON

POLITELY put, a few of us are a bit larger about the middle than we ought to be. Every year, a few of the soldiers of the saga of the great American outdoors leave the hunting field with blankets over their faces. It seems to be a lot easier for many of us to drop, say, $1,000-$2,000 on a lighter rifle than to spend a few hours a week and a lot less money developing the physical stamina to endure over the long, arduous haul, carrying a heavier, cheaper rifle. Those were my thoughts when, one day, I contemplated a spare tire not in my trunk, a rifle not in my regular arsenal, and a flyer from B-Square in Fort Worth, Texas.

I've started running regularly. I lift weights daily. There are *no* three-digit numbers in my blood pressure figures. But I'm 40 as this is written, about 185 pounds at 5 feet 8 inches. To me, that's *fat*. Living in Arizona summers, one never learns to like 115-degree heat, and most of us don't venture outdoors much. But this past summer, fully armed and with plenty of water and survival items, this former jock hiked in the desert and the Superstition Mountains, where the Lost Dutchman supposedly hides its wealth.

The rifle's main function in that environment, and for my narrow mission, is an exercise device. You may never see the Superstitions, but the rifle may still interest you.

I've purchased, built, and had built hundreds of rifles over the last 20 or so years . . . target units, military match rifles, big-bore game rifles, varminters, lightweight sporters, mostly semi-automatics and Mauser-style bolt rifles. Virtually all cost too much for desert use. My M-ls have too much setup time in them, too much money, too much match preparation and elbow grease, and are too pretty to be trekking 20-50 miles through rough, thorny cactus desert, where they'd either get torn up or sop up a desert storm and stay wet for a whole day. I only own one jazzy sporter, and it's way too delicate with a skinny barrel and enormous scope, and, besides I stupidly had the stock carved. Hell, I don't even keep it in my rifle rack. I've been haphazardly collecting—some say just accumulating—military Mausers for those two decades and some new products can give these old war-horses new desert life.

The classic advantages of the Model 98 Mauser and its three-lug locking system are well known. Less well-known are the service advantages of this rifle and its contemporaries. First, most any 98 or similar Mauser

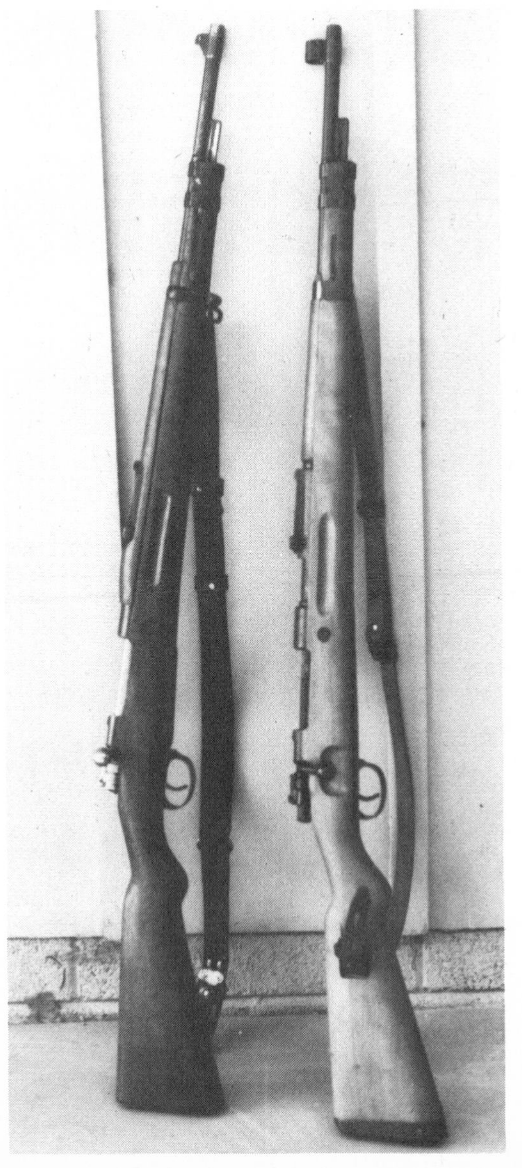

Some surplus Mausers have served in several wars, with several different armies. The Spanish M.44 (dark stock) and Czech-built Israeli 308 have cosmopolitan backgrounds and are both fully capable and 100 percent reliable after over 43 years of service.

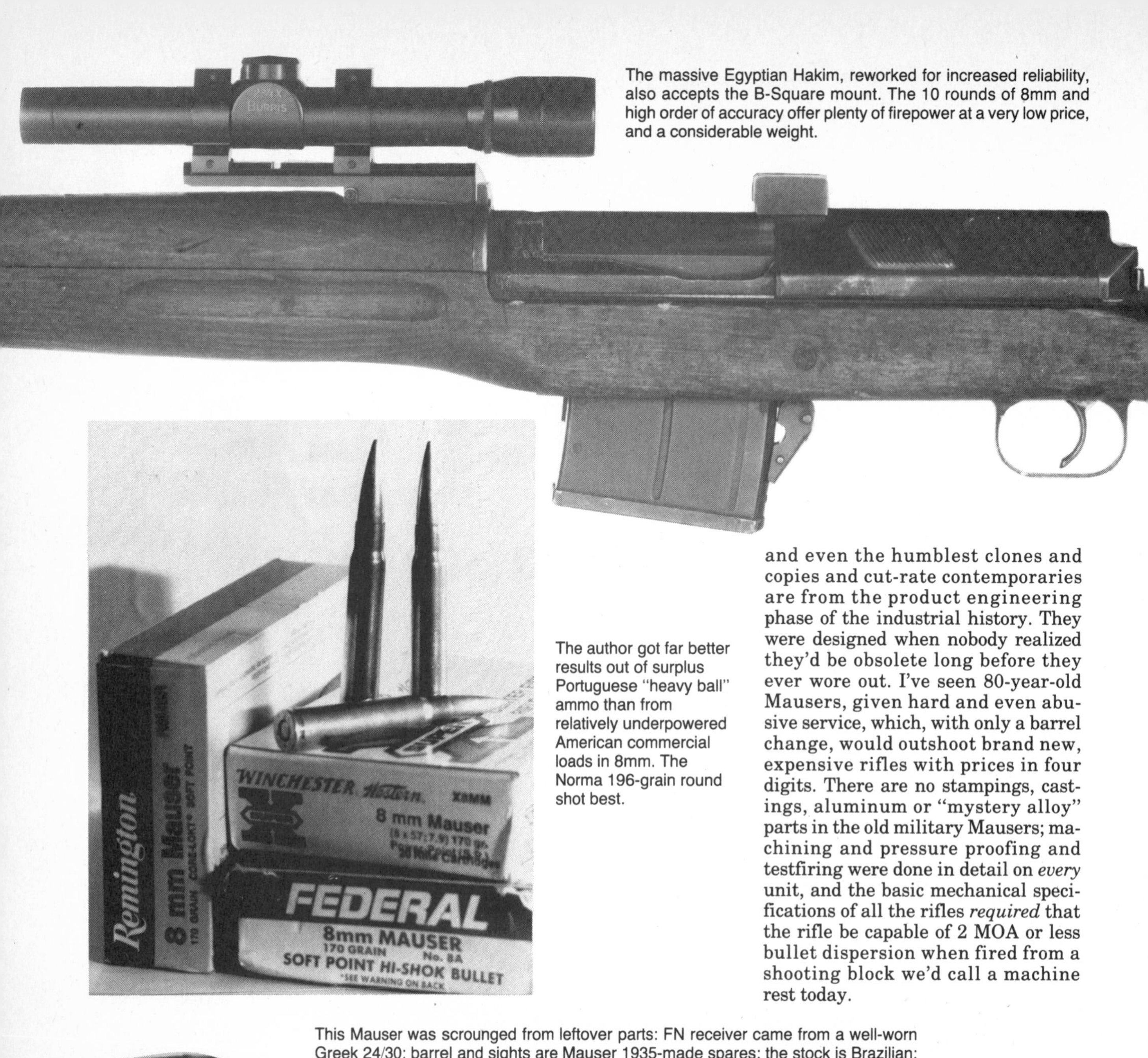

The massive Egyptian Hakim, reworked for increased reliability, also accepts the B-Square mount. The 10 rounds of 8mm and high order of accuracy offer plenty of firepower at a very low price, and a considerable weight.

The author got far better results out of surplus Portuguese "heavy ball" ammo than from relatively underpowered American commercial loads in 8mm. The Norma 196-grain round shot best.

and even the humblest clones and copies and cut-rate contemporaries are from the product engineering phase of the industrial history. They were designed when nobody realized they'd be obsolete long before they ever wore out. I've seen 80-year-old Mausers, given hard and even abusive service, which, with only a barrel change, would outshoot brand new, expensive rifles with prices in four digits. There are no stampings, castings, aluminum or "mystery alloy" parts in the old military Mausers; machining and pressure proofing and testfiring were done in detail on *every* unit, and the basic mechanical specifications of all the rifles *required* that the rifle be capable of 2 MOA or less bullet dispersion when fired from a shooting block we'd call a machine rest today.

This Mauser was scrounged from leftover parts: FN receiver came from a well-worn Greek 24/30; barrel and sights are Mauser 1935-made spares; the stock is Brazilian; fittings and furniture are Turkish, Argentine, and Polish variants. Author hard-epoxy bedded the action, barrel, even inside the handguard, to assure solid fit. David Fiden, shown here, got the rifle to group at about 2 inches at 200 yards with Portuguese heavy ball, but found it way more fun to ring the 50-yard ram's gong with open sights, whereupon several shooters with expensive silhouette rifles departed the range.

That's before glass bedding, before scopes became common, before bullet-hosing devices became state-of-the-art, back when standard military rifle barrels of 24 inches were controversial because they were probably too short. Today's *best* rifles shoot better than a stock 98 Mauser. However, a garden-variety 98 in military livery in excellent condition is mechanically capable of outshooting most of today's "off-the-rack" rifles without so much as a custom trigger.

Bear in mind, I said mechanically capable. The standard sights of the old rifles seldom allow delivery of their accuracy. The rear is too big and non-discriminatory, too hard to judge, and too far from the eye, so that even with perfect vision, precision shooting is a matter of luck and experience. The new long-eye-relief mounts for pistol-style scopes offered by B-Square and S&K solve this problem by using the rear sight base to mount any standard pistol scope with a 1-inch tube. What results is a rifle which looks much like the German sniper rifles of World War II, which wore ZF 41/1 or ZF 42 long-eye-relief scopes.

Just how accuracy in the real world can be improved on this route can be measured by two rifles set up for this article, a DWM-built Model 1908 7mm Brazilian Mauser long rifle and a La Coruna Model 44 Spanish Air Force 98kstyle medium length rifle in 8mm. The bore in the Brazilian, which was a mixed number rifle made up from parts but otherwise quite nice cosmetically, didn't look very good; edges of the lands were soft and looked worn. The Spanish rifle's bore looked good, but it was shooting way to the left, owing to some fluke of bedding or, I thought, a "tweaked" barrel. I adjusted the front sight, checked the headspace (it was perfect, even by commercial standards), and experimented further with some fresh Portuguese ammo and some Norma commercial. Both rifles grouped on the paper at 100 yards after considerable fiddling and diddling, the Brazilian at a fairly sane 3½ inches with that Norma ammo, the Spaniard at about 5 inches with the Portuguese heavy ball and the Norma 196-grain round. About then, my Tasco and Simmons scopes and B-Square mounts showed up. I first ogled a minty Israeli Mauser in 308 that had shown a remarkable alacrity at ringing the 300-yard gong where I shoot at Rio Salado here in Mesa, but instead opted to mount the glass on the reasonably credible Brazilian and the errant Spaniard.

Now, out of fresh 7mm and reduced to about 60 rounds of 1933 headstamped FN in that loading, after some difficulty in adjusting the scope mount to something near zero, I felt as if shooting groups with the ancient Brazilian would be a waste of time, but I reluctantly proceeded anyway, and blew the "x" out of the standard NRA target . . . five holes from absolutely ancient military ammo could be covered by a quarter! I found out that a lot of German Mauser barrels, especially of the 29-inch length, were honed after rifling to soften corners of the lands to facilitate cleaning and obviate erratic wear, similar to the Metford principle, and in fact was told by several collectors that my barrel was virtually mint internally.

The Spanish rifle remained the relative bad boy so far, even after scope mounting, but now I know the cause

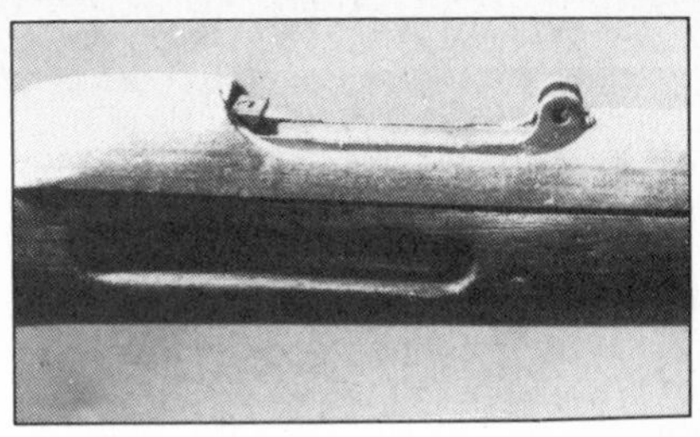

The Mauser sight base provides B-Square's mount with tie-downs.

The new mount base is "teeter-tottered" into rigidity with a set screw.

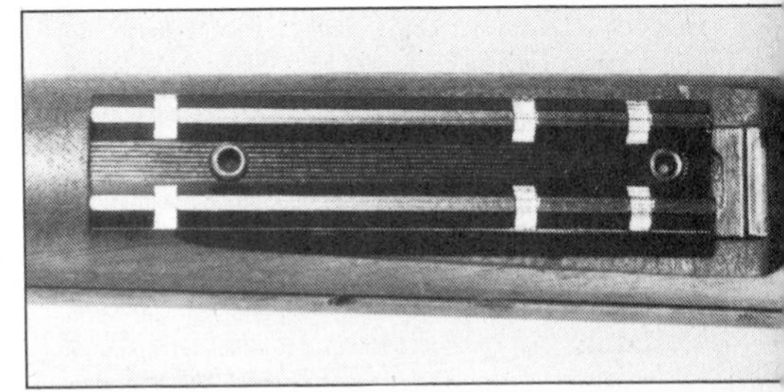

Grooving provides some variation in ring spacing.

With intermediate eye relief scope in place, budget scout rifles resemble WWI Gew.98 sniper rifles.

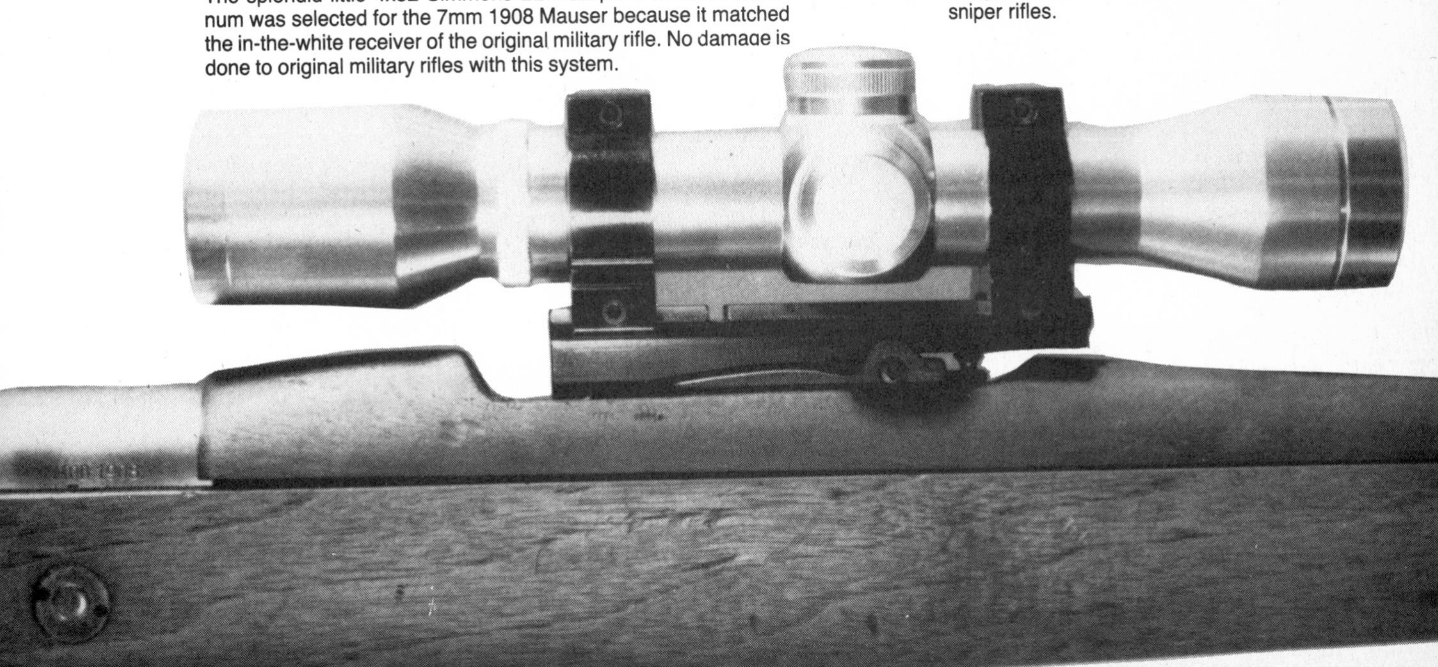

The splendid little 4x32 Simmons LER scope in brushed aluminum was selected for the 7mm 1908 Mauser because it matched the in-the-white receiver of the original military rifle. No damage is done to original military rifles with this system.

and will fix it; the 3-5-inch groups were caused by some Spanish flyboy's fixation with sandpaper and cleanliness, for the stock had been severely sanded, inside and out. The stock is so loose it may not require routing before I epoxy bed the rifle.

These conversions allow good shooting with the advantages of a fully-protected barrel, complete with handguard. The bayonet lug remains intact. The heavy stocks subdue recoil, although the poor butt design tends to localize pain. With the long eye relief mount and scope in place, the shooter retains access to charger clip loading, need not have the bolt handle or receiver modified, and so saves a lot of time and money in preparation and in the field. In my case, the weight of the militaries is fine; however, little Indonesian and other 17½-inch barreled carbines are in the country to provide lighter alternatives. The muzzle blast from some of these little cuties, though, is like a nuclear facial for the uninitiated, and the recoil is truly profound.

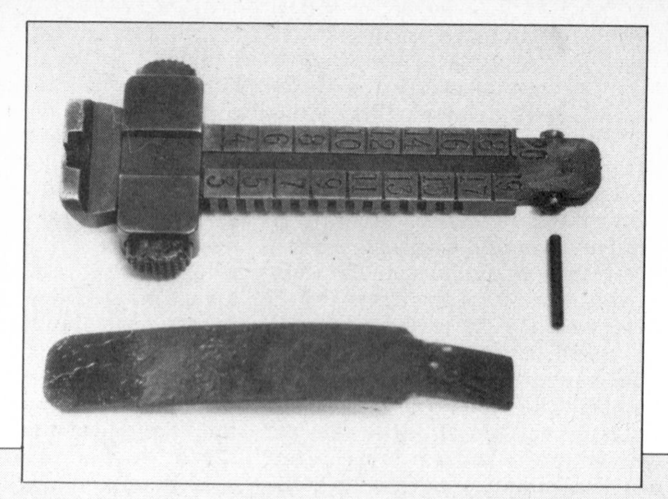

(Right and below) If these parts are stored and labeled, the budget scouter can become an all-original collector relic quite simply.

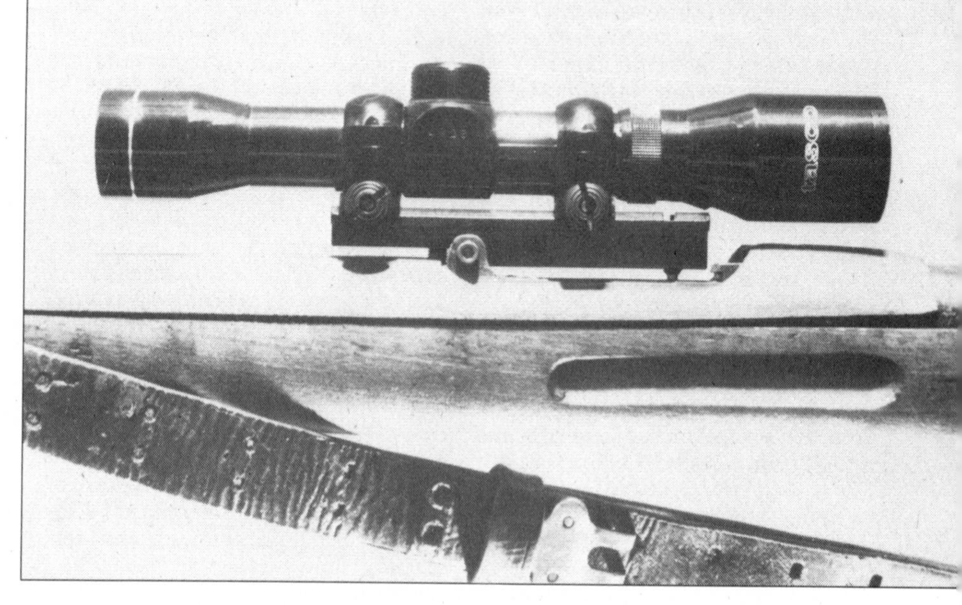

I am currently setting up a Peruvian Model 1935 FN-built 30-06 rifle for this "conversion," as it accepts B-Square's standard 98 mount base. Someone has already fitted this stock with a recoil pad, which is why I got the rifle for $85 in traded-off toys. The mounts easily switch from gun to gun with a couple of Allen wrenches, so there's a tendency emerging to test all my Mausers with scopes.

Most any 98 Mauser that's been checked for completeness, headspace, and condition is plenty safe and will shoot well, properly set up. Only the Chinese copies are questionable after the basic mechanical checks, and most of those in this country are not in a fit condition to spend much time on, anyway. I've gotten excellent accuracy from Argentine and Spanish-built rifles, Czech VZ's, German and Polish rifles, Yugoslavian and FN-built, and the Iranian-built variants, for whatever reason, usually shoot even better than the Czech rifles from which they were patterned.

Mounting the B-Square LER mount on a Mauser shouldn't take you more than 5 minutes *the first time.* I won't detail everything here, but I'll fill you in on some tricks not in the instructions that I picked up in a few weeks of experimenting.

First, when you remove the rear sight, use the sight leaf as a lever . . . lift it 20-35 degrees and press down like crazy until you feel it move down. Then draw the sight leaf aft and out. If you try to depress the spring with a tool and use another tool on the sight, it's going to take all day, drive you crazy, and fail. Just use your strong hand and 100 percent power. On the longer sights, I used the blunt handle of a small screwdriver to press down just behind the hinge point. Driving out the pin is real easy.

Do the scope mounting and base setup *exactly* as B-Square instructions tell you, letting one set-screw reach the end of its travel before inserting the other. Slight tweaky releases of one or the other after the scope is mounted *can* be used for tiny windage shifts, but never count on that. Secure screws with plumber-style teflon tape. Lok-Tite and similar products will work, but require removing and completely readjusting the set-screws, and will dry before you're done, making small adjustments annoying.

The scope base forms a kind of teeter-totter. Using a small spirit level on the internal receiver flats, across the magazine opening, and another atop the scope base, will save you a lot of time and work setting up the scope and sighting-in. Recourse to a gunsmith should be unnecessary, for you should be able to rig one of these mounts and the scope and have it rough sighted in less time than it will take you to drive to a gunsmith, perhaps in less time than the phone call required to set up other kinds of scope conversions.

The LER scope mounts are usable even with heavily modified rifles, provided the military barrel and sight base are retained. I never appreciated the feature until this application came about, but many people now find they prefer pistol-type scopes because they can scan either side of the scope, well away from the narrow acceptance angle of the optic, without the aggravation and readjustment necessary with a conventional unit.

I did not want to invest a lot of money in this project. Fully equipped, I have a total of less than $200 in any one of my hiking rifles. The Spaniard carries a Tasco 4x28 unit, secured

The author's M-1s were considered for the mountain scout role, but their value and the effort it had taken to make them into match rifles made the old Mauser turnbolts preferable.

Combined Tabular Data, Various Surplus Rifles Suitable For Use As Mountain Scout Hiking Rifles

Designation	Caliber(s)	Weight Std./lbs.	Scope Mount available*	Overall Length (In.)
Short 98 Mausers	7mm, 7.65mm, 308 Win., 8mm, 30-06	8-8.75	Several	appx. 43.6
Long Rifle (Gew.98 and similar) M.98 Mausers	as above	8.8-9.7	Several	appx. 49.2
"Carbine" M.98 Mausers (G.33/40 size w/17-18½" bbls.)	7mm, 8mm, 308, 7.65	7.3-8	Short sight base requires some trimming of B-Square mount	37-40
Swedish 94 Carbine	6.5x55mm	7.5	May be adapted f/'98 mount or B-Square Swedish	37.6
Swedish Model 38	6.5x55mm	8.5	B-Square	44.1
Swedish 96 Long Rifle	6.5x55mm	9.1	B-Square, others, some Swedish sniper equip't available	49.6
British #4 Mk.1 and similar	303 British (some 308 conversions *may* become available before 1990)	8.8	Several	
Egyptian Hakim	8mm Mauser	10.5	B-Square	49

*No-gunsmithing mounts such as B-square or S&K.

with Tasco rings, and the Brazilian has a Simmons 4x32 Model 1088. The Tasco is lighter and black, but its eye relief is rather more critical than the Simmons at about 15½ inches, with very little tolerance, for fore or aft movement of the head. The Simmons, which cost me $24 more, is too shiny, but brighter and far less critical in terms of eye relief, which means pickup is inherently faster. Both use tapered crosshairs, and have the uncluttered views I like.

If you have a collector's eye, or just a nostalgic bent, these new mounts enable you to make a military rifle into something practical and fun without spending a fortune. It's a rifle you can actually take into a hostile arena without the constant worry that you may do damage to something which costs as much as a pretty good used car.

I've just finished setting up a semi-auto Hakim with one of these rigs. That's a fairly obscure, 10-shot Egyptian semi-automatic that's accurate, ugly, and, since I reworked a few things, accurate and reliable. I may just enter some high-power matches with it, since it shoots almost as well as my fancy-pants M-1s. My total cost: $187.30. ●

Shotgun Review

by LARRY S. STERETT

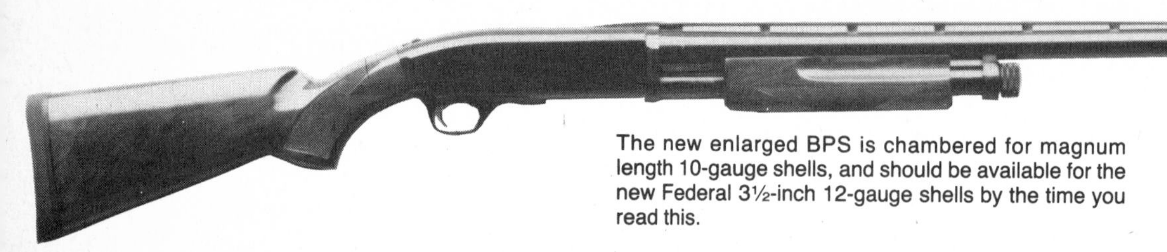

The new enlarged BPS is chambered for magnum length 10-gauge shells, and should be available for the new Federal 3½-inch 12-gauge shells by the time you read this.

A WELL-KNOWN radio news commentator of yesteryear used to start out his program with, "Ah, there's good news tonight." And so it is in 1988 for shotgunners.

Remington has announced the original Parker side-by-side (they purchased the Parker Gun Co. over 50 years ago) in a 20-gauge version. The New England Firearms Co. is producing what used to be the Harrington & Richardson single shot, break-action Topper shotgun under the name of "Pardner," one of the most economical American-made single shots on the market. Ithaca Gun is back with the "bread-n-butter" bottom-ejecting Model 37 upgraded to the Model 87.

And, there is still more good news. More 28-gauge and 16-gauge shotguns are starting to appear, in addition to more 10-gauge guns, including the Browning BPS in 10-gauge. Yes, a pump-action 10-gauge, and Browning is also producing a 20-gauge Model 12, identical to the old Winchester Model 12, but bearing the Browning name. Daisy has entered the rimfire rifle field, and included a 22 rimfire bolt-action shotgun.

Mossberg has a new pump-action shotgun available for Federal's new 12-gauge steel shotshell measuring 3½ inches long, and Browning will have two such shotguns—the BPS and the Citori. (This length of 12-gauge shotshell is not entirely new, having been manufactured in Belgium over 20 years ago, and used by this shooter nearly that long, but the shell by Federal loaded with steel shot is new.)

The bad news is that Winchester Division of Olin Corporation has decided to get out of the gun business, and in November of 1987 announced the sale of their interest in the O.K. Firearms Co., Ltd. of Tochigi City, Japan, to a group of Japanese investors. This Winchester/O.K. firm has been producing the Winchester brand of over/under and side-by-side shotguns in Japan since 1961, and the sale of such shotguns will continue for the next 2 to 3 years, ending around 1990. Thereafter, such shotguns will have no connection with the Olin Corporation, whose Winchester Division will continue to manufacture ammunition. The over/unders will be made and sold as Classic Doubles.

American Arms

The entire line has been trimmed, and the Royal, Bristol, Silver, and Excelsior over/under models dropped, along with Skeet and trap FS 200 models. The AYA Model 2 side-by-side is no longer cataloged, but there is a York Deluxe side-by-side in 12- and 20-gauge with Multi-choke barrels in a choice of 26 or 28 inches, and an English (straight grip) stock. The 12-gauge Waterfowl Special over/under is still available, as are the 10- and 12-gauge Waterfowl and Turkey Special models.

New are 10-gauge over/under Waterfowl Special and Turkey Special guns with non-reflective matte finish on exterior metal surfaces, and walnut stock and beavertail forearm. The Waterfowl Special has 32-inch barrels choked Full/Full and sling swivels and a camouflage sling for ease of carrying is provided, while the Turkey Special has 26-inch barrels with screw-in choke tubes. Both guns have double triggers, extractors, and a

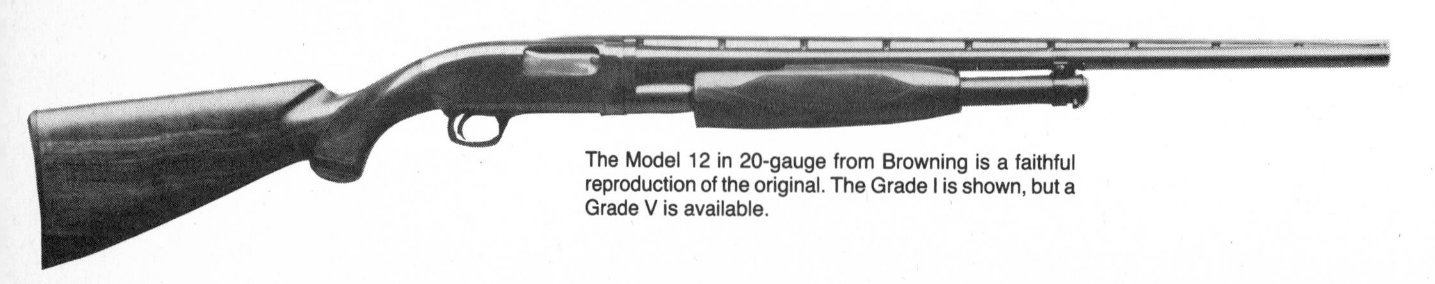

The Model 12 in 20-gauge from Browning is a faithful reproduction of the original. The Grade I is shown, but a Grade V is available.

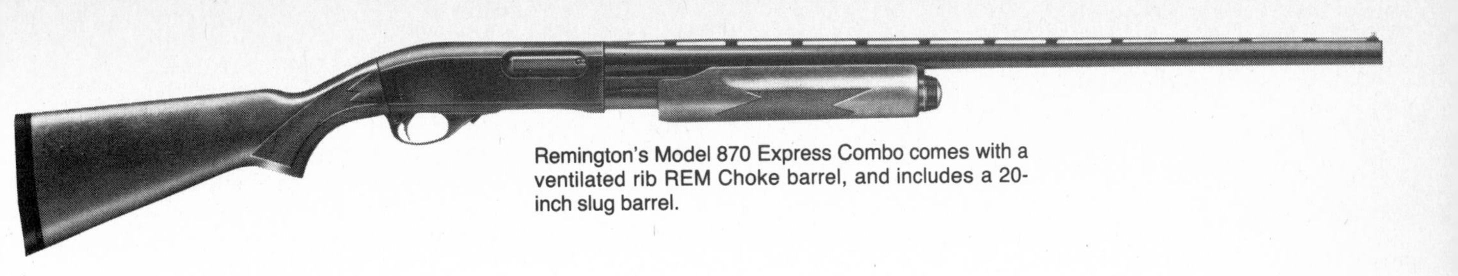

Remington's Model 870 Express Combo comes with a ventilated rib REM Choke barrel, and includes a 20-inch slug barrel.

The Parker AHE Grade is back, built by Remington again. First guns are to be 20-gauge, and very expensive.

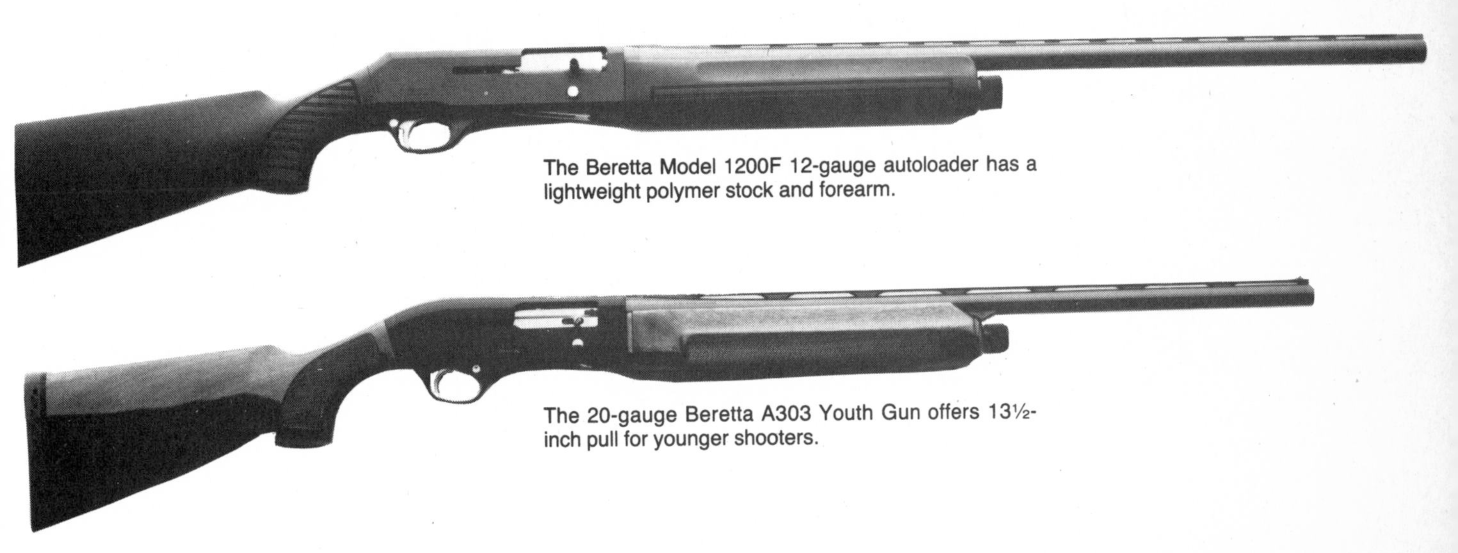

The Beretta Model 1200F 12-gauge autoloader has a lightweight polymer stock and forearm.

The 20-gauge Beretta A303 Youth Gun offers 13½-inch pull for younger shooters.

weight of approximately 9⅞ pounds, depending on the wood density. Also new is the Silver I chambered in 28-gauge and 410-bore, with 26-inch chrome-lined barrels choked Imp. Cyl./Mod.

Armsport

Every year this Miami firm manages to come up with some new models. This year there's a new side-by-side in 28-gauge with 26-inch barrels choked Modified and Full, an over/under slug gun in 12-gauge with 20-inch barrels, extractors, and double triggers, and the single barrel is now available in 410 with a 26-inch Full choke barrel. In addition, the single trigger (selective or non-selective) over/under is available in 12- or 20-gauge with 28- or 26-inch barrels, respectively, and three interchangeable choke tubes, and a choice of extractors or automatic ejectors. Armsport also has snap caps available in 10-, 12-, and 20-gauge, plus 410 and several rifle and handgun calibers.

Beretta U.S.A.

Designed for Americans, the new Onyx series from Beretta features matte black finished barrels and receivers on field grade guns. This shows off some hand engraving on the receiver, and the P. Beretta signature and Beretta logo filled with gold. Models in the series include the 687 Golden Onyx and 686 Onyx over/unders and the 626 Onyx side-by-side. All models are available in 12- and 20-gauge, chambered for 3-inch shells. Barrel lengths are 26 inches on the 626, and 26 or 28 inches on the over/unders. Other new models are the EELL in trap and Skeet versions, including the trap grade in Combo or Over-Single with barrel lengths of 30, 32 or 34 inches, and the four-barrel Skeet set with 28-inch barrels in 12, 20, 28 and 410. The EELL models feature hand checkered and finished walnut stocks and forearms, and individually signed receiver sideplates hand-engraved with scenes of flighting game birds.

Last year Beretta introduced the Sporting Clays over/unders called the Sporters, in Models 686, 687, and 682. This year there's another model available—the 12-gauge autoloading A303 Sporting with 28-inch Mobilchoke barrel. The A303 is also available in a 20-gauge version as the Youth Gun.

Under 6½ pounds, the A303 Youth has a shortened length of pull at 13½ inches.

Browning

The big news from Browning is a big bore—the pump-action BPS is now available chambered for 10-gauge 3½-inch shells. With a 30-inch Invector barrel, and a weight of 9½ pounds, the big BPS will handle all 10-gauge shotshells, including the steel loads. By the time you read this it may also be available chambered for the new Federal 12-gauge steel shot load of the same length.

In the Citori over/under field gun line a new Lightning model is now available in Grades I, III, and VI in 12-, 20- and 28-gauge and 410-bore with a choice of 26- or 28-inch Invector barrels. This new version has the older, classic-rounded pistol grip and Lightning-style forearm. The Citori will also be available in 12-gauge chambered for the new Federal Super Magnum shotshell with the 3½-inch length.

The second big item from Browning is the pump-action Model 12 in 20-gauge. Made in Japan the new Model 12 is a faithful reproduction of the original Winchester in 20-gauge with 26-inch barrel, and Grades I and V finishes. When Winchester decided to discontinue the famous Model 12, Browning apparently decided there was still a market for it, and it is a gem.

The final new shotgun in the Browning line is the B-80 Plus Hunting in 12- or 20-gauge. Invector barrel lengths range from 26 to 30 inches, depending on the gauge, and the B-80 Plus will handle both magnum (3-inch) and regular length shells. Weight of the 20-gauge B-80 Plus with alloy receiver and 26-inch barrel is 5⅞ pounds, depending on the density of the walnut pistol grip stock.

China Sports

Chinese-manufactured shotguns have been available in the U.S. for several years on an off-and-on basis. Currently there are three models available through this California firm, starting with the single shot HD12-101H, and including the over/under HL12-203 and pump-action HL12-102, which resembles the Winchester Model 12. All three models are available only in 12-gauge at present.

Classic Doubles

Winchester over/under and side-by-side shotguns are no more, or will not be shortly, but the same shotguns are available under the Classic Doubles name. The mechanisms of the Model 101 and 23 will remain substantially the same, but there will be some improvements, such as a higher grade of American walnut in the stocks and forearms, extra engraving and sculpturing of the receiver will be provided, and all single-selective triggers will be adjustable. Otherwise, the quality is the same, only the name has changed.

Daisy

If this seems an unlikely firm for shotguns, it isn't, and the shotguns are definitely small bore. The first is the Critter Gitter, a single shot bolt-action smoothbore air pistol that uses small plastic shotshells loaded with a choice of sizes 1, 4, or 8 shot. CO_2 powered and intended for farmers and others interested in reducing the local rat population, the pistol is useful within 25 feet, and will be sold through rural grain dealers, sporting goods stores and fishing tackle shops.

The second new shotgun from Daisy is a 22 rimfire labeled the Model 2221. Available as a single shot or bolt-action 10-shot repeater, the Model 2221 features a 19-inch smooth bore barrel chambered for 22 rimfire shot cartridges. With a simple tool the smooth bore barrel can be replaced with a rifled barrel having rifle sights. One feature of the new rimfire line will be an adjustable buttstock to provide a length of pull from 11½ to 14½ inches, making it suitable for youth or adult use.

F.I.E.

This Miami-based firm has shotguns for everyone, from the SPAS-12, LAW-12, and SAS-12 for police and military use, through single shot, autoloaders, and over/unders. The latest over/under is the Maroccini "Priti" from Brescia, Italy. Available in a choice of 12- or 20-gauge with 26- or 28-inch chrome-lined, fixed-choke barrels chambered for 3-inch shells, the Priti has all the features of the Sturdy over/under line, plus epoxy wood finish, scroll engraving and a rubber recoil pad. Double triggers are standard, as are ventilated side ribs and top rib, and European walnut stock and forearm. For shooters wanting a single trigger, the Deluxe Sturdy (OU-12DL) is available in 12-gauge only with a single selective trigger and 28-inch barrels having screw-in choke tubes; five choke tubes are provided with each gun. F.I.E. also has the Franchi Alcione over/under shotguns, but the Priti is one of the best values on the market today, with a retail price of under $400.

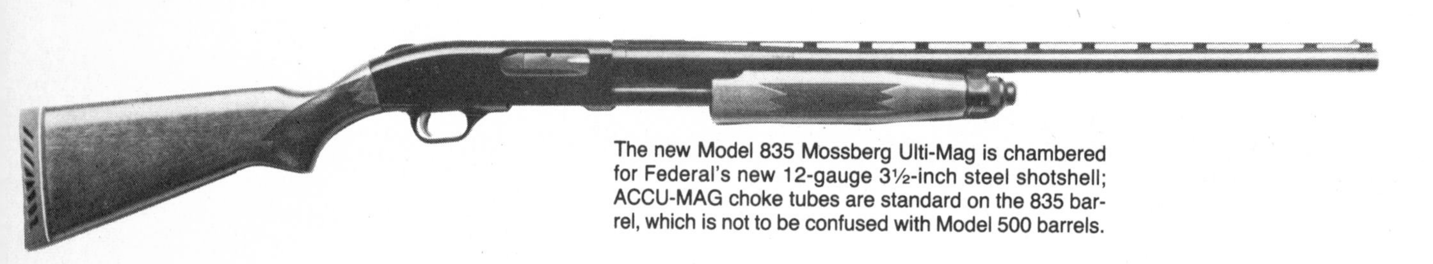

The new Model 835 Mossberg Ulti-Mag is chambered for Federal's new 12-gauge 3½-inch steel shotshell; ACCU-MAG choke tubes are standard on the 835 barrel, which is not to be confused with Model 500 barrels.

Hatfield

From out of Missouri comes a new English-style boxlock side-by-side. Tabbed the Uplander, and available only in 20-gauge with 26-inch barrels chambered for 3-inch shells, the new shotgun features a straight grip stock and splinter forearm of select XXX-fancy grade walnut with hand-cut checkering. A single, non-selective trigger and automatic ejectors are standard features, and locking is via double underlugs. Five grades of the Upland are available, and each comes with a fitted leather-bound luggage-style carrying case, complete with snap caps. Grade 1 has a color case-hardened frame, while the Grade 2 Pigeon has some hand-cut relief engraving; Grade 3 Super Pigeon has total coverage relief engraving; the Grade 4 Golden Quail has scroll engraving and six 24 karat gold inlays of quail; and the Grade 5 Woodcock has additional engraving, some stock carving

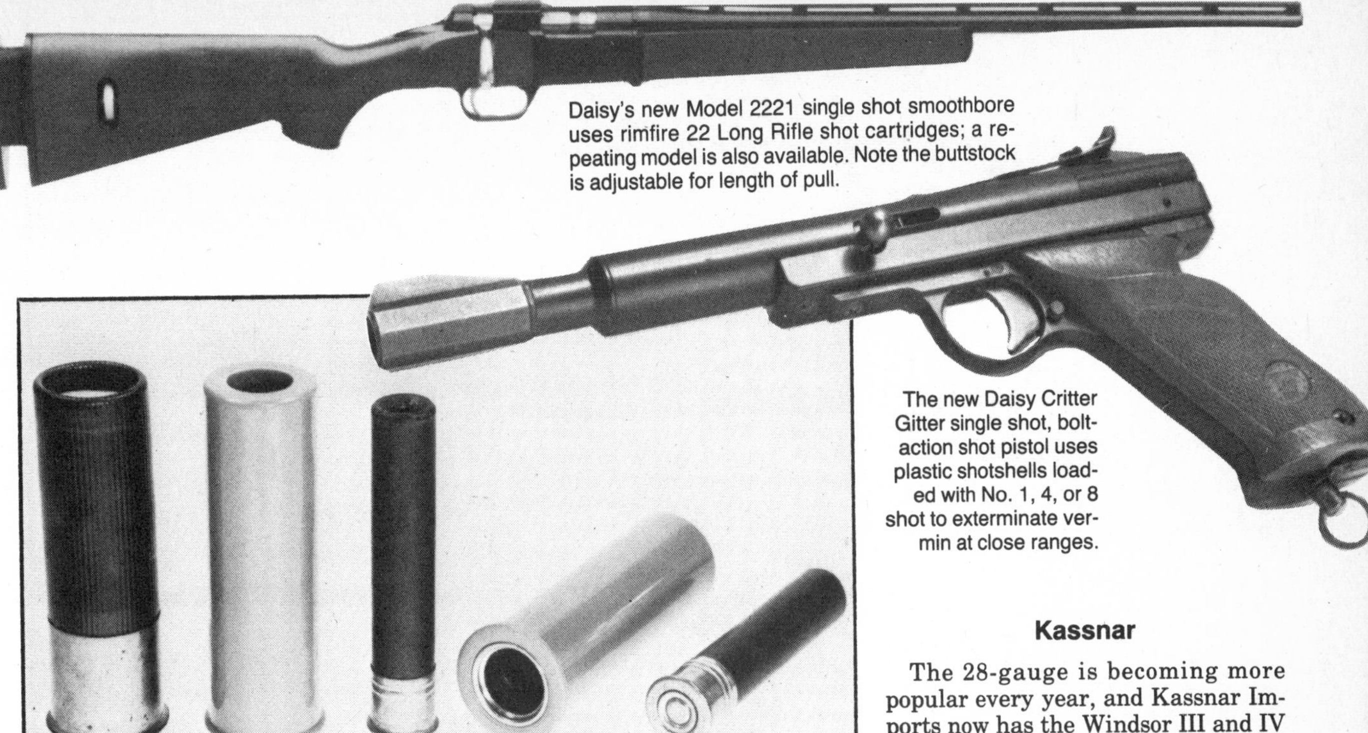

Daisy's new Model 2221 single shot smoothbore uses rimfire 22 Long Rifle shot cartridges; a repeating model is also available. Note the buttstock is adjustable for length of pull.

The new Daisy Critter Gitter single shot, bolt-action shot pistol uses plastic shotshells loaded with No. 1, 4, or 8 shot to exterminate vermin at close ranges.

For $6 each, Jesse Ramos offers his 12-gauge/410 converter—it is a convenient way to shoot 2½-inch 410s in any 12 bore.

and seven 24 karat gold inlays, including woodcocks, a squirrel, gold bands, and Diana, Goddess of the Hunt. The Hatfield is an upland game gun in the best American tradition.

Heckler & Koch

New is a field version of the Benelli M1 Super 90. Available in 12-gauge only, the new model is labeled the Montefeltro Super 90. It comes with a 28-inch ventilated rib barrel chambered for 3-inch shells, and three interchangeable choke tubes. The stock and forearm are of walnut with a high gloss finish, and a special kit is included to permit a change in drop measurements of the buttstock. In addition to the regular version for right-handed shooters, there is also a left-hand model, a Skeet version, and a 19¾-inch long slug barrel with rifle sights is available as an accessory.

Ithaca Gun

From out of the ashes, so to speak, has risen an even better bottom ejecting pump gun—the Model 87, which celebrates and commemorates the 50th anniversary of the Model 37. Available in 12- and 20-gauge in Supreme Vent Rib, Deluxe Vent Rib and Ultralight versions—the latter two with choke tubes—the field grade Model 87 is available in a 12-gauge in a Camo Vent Rib version for turkey hunters. Barrel lengths range from 25 inches to 30 inches, depending on the version, all barrels are chambered for 3-inch shells, except for the Ultralight. The barrels are still Rotoforged and the stock and forearm are of American walnut.

Other Model 87 versions include the 12-gauge M&P and DS Police Special with 20-inch barrels, and the Handgrip version in 12- or 20-gauge with a barrel length of 18½ inches. The Deerslayer is available in 12- or 20-gauge versions as a single barrel or Deluxe Combo with two barrels, and barrel lengths of 20, 25, and 28 inches are available. An Ultralight 20-gauge with 20-inch barrel is available. Newest of the Deerslayer designs is the solid-frame model Deerslayer II in 12-gauge only with an integral 25-inch rifled barrel. The Deerslayer II has an uncheckered stock and forearm.

At the top of the Ithaca Gun line is the Custom Trap Single Barrel, available in 12-gauge only in the 5E and Dollar Grade versions with a choice of 32- or 34-inch barrel. The Dollar Grade has AA Fancy walnut for the stock and forearm, and relief green gold inlays, while the 5E has A fancy walnut, less engraving and fewer gold inlays.

Kassnar

The 28-gauge is becoming more popular every year, and Kassnar Imports now has the Windsor III and IV over/under models available in this gauge with a choice of 25-, 26-, or 28-inch barrels, plus the Monarch with 28-inch barrels, and the Flyweight Monarch with 25-inch barrels. The Monarch has a blued steel receiver and extractors, while the Windsor model shotguns have coin-finished receivers with additional engraving.

A new Royal line of side-by-sides offers 12-, 16-, 20- and 28-gauge, plus 410, and double triggers and 3-inch chambers on all models but the 16-gauge. They all have straight grip walnut stocks and splinter forends. Barrel lengths are 25 inches on the 28-gauge, 26 inches on the 410 and one upland version of the 12-gauge gun. Interchangeable choke tubes have been added to the Windsor I side-by-sides in 12- and 20-gauge with 27-inch barrels.

Krieghoff International

Krieghoff and K-80 over/under shotguns have been available for many years, but the firm is not one to rest on its laurels. New is a K-80 two-barrel Skeet set with lightened barrels for tube use only. The new gun, with or without tubes, weighs the same and gives the shooter an identical gun feel and sight picture in all four gauges. Also new is the K-80 Sporting over/under with 28-inch barrels having screw-in choke tubes, a K-80 tapered-step trap rib, and a field-style pistol grip stock.

The regular K-80 Trap is now available with a 34-inch fixed Full choke barrel or screw-in choke tubes in an

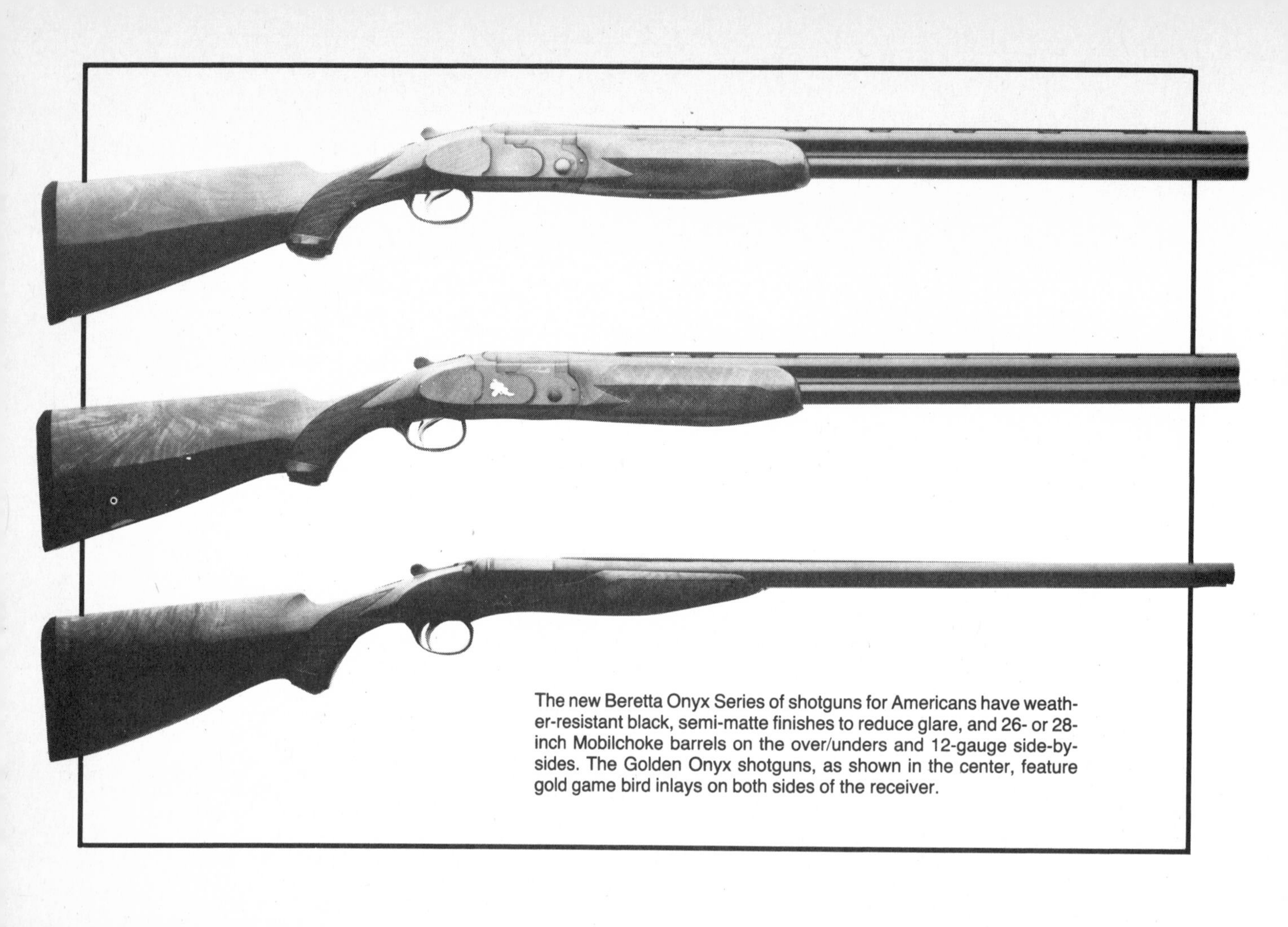

The new Beretta Onyx Series of shotguns for Americans have weather-resistant black, semi-matte finishes to reduce glare, and 26- or 28-inch Mobilchoke barrels on the over/unders and 12-gauge side-by-sides. The Golden Onyx shotguns, as shown in the center, feature gold game bird inlays on both sides of the receiver.

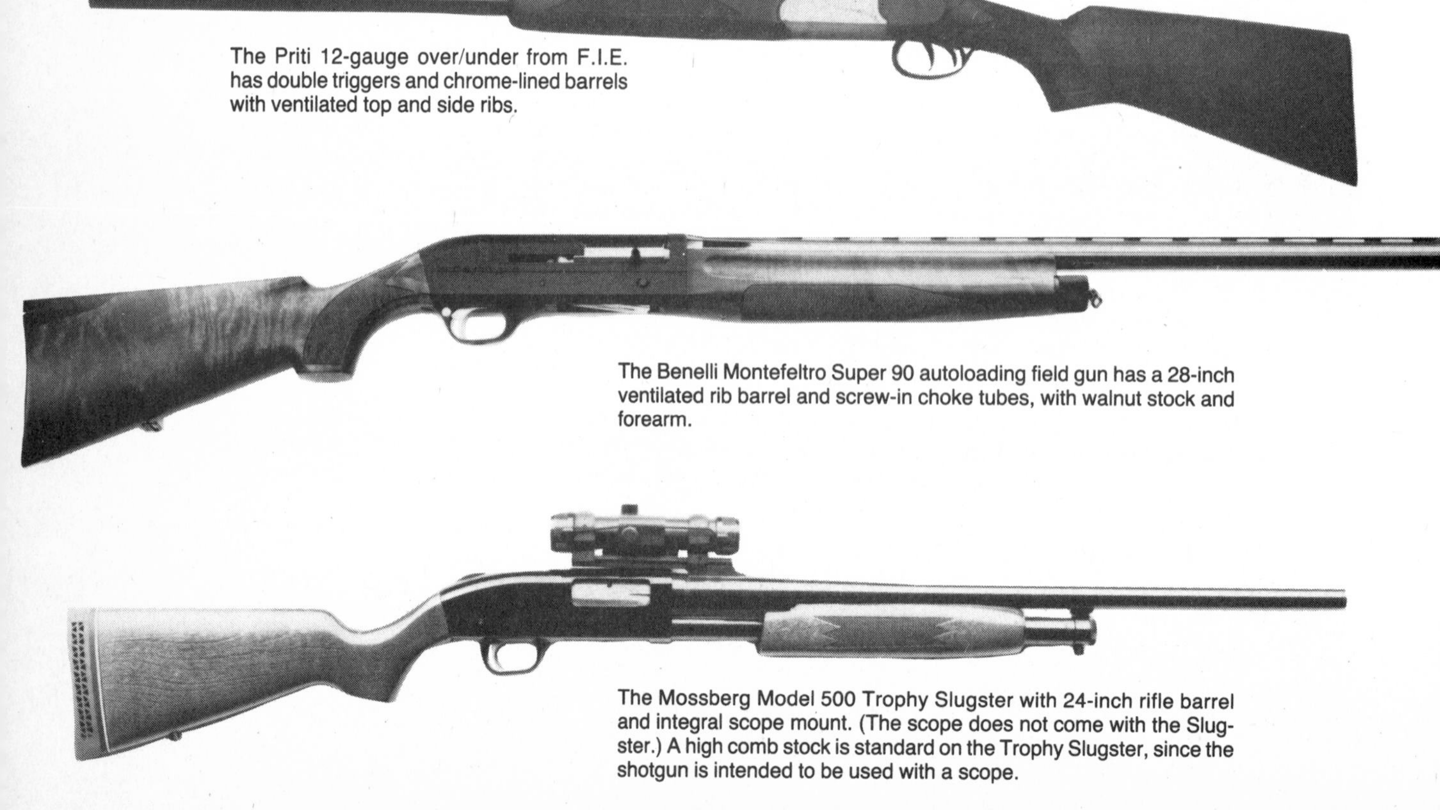

The Priti 12-gauge over/under from F.I.E. has double triggers and chrome-lined barrels with ventilated top and side ribs.

The Benelli Montefeltro Super 90 autoloading field gun has a 28-inch ventilated rib barrel and screw-in choke tubes, with walnut stock and forearm.

The Mossberg Model 500 Trophy Slugster with 24-inch rifle barrel and integral scope mount. (The scope does not come with the Slugster.) A high comb stock is standard on the Trophy Slugster, since the shotgun is intended to be used with a scope.

over-single version, and choke tubes are now available for K-80 over/under 30- and 32-inch trap barrels, plus 28-inch sporting grade barrels. Extended 2-inch and 4-inch Full choke tubes are available to fit most K-80 barrels accepting regular Krieghoff choke tubes, should a shooter want the feel and swing of a long barrel. Scheduled in time for the 1988 hunting season is a new Model Plus Krieghoff Drilling in 12-gauge, with the 16- and 20-gauge models in a scaled-down action. Several rifle calibers are available for the under barrel, and a set of interchangeable side-by-side shotgun barrels is planned for the latter part of 1988.

Mossberg

The Model 500 Accu-Steel is available with synthetic, hardwood, or camo stock and forearm, and the Model 712 autoloader in 12-gauge is now scheduled to be available by the time you read this; it has been a couple of years, or more, late in arriving, and some of the barrel combinations planned have been dropped in favor of a 28-inch barrel with Accu-II or Accu-Steel choke tubes; a 24-inch Slugster barrel with rifle sights is available as an accessory. The 28-inch barrel has a wide ventilated rib with white Bradley-type front bead and a middle bead to aid alignment. The 712 incorporates an innovative gas regulating system to permit interchangeable use of all standard length and 3-inch 12-gauge loads. The anticipated 712 Junior has been dropped.

The regular Slugster is still available with its smooth bore barrel, but there is a new Model 500 Trophy Slugster with a 24-inch rifled barrel and integral scope mount base (no open sights), and a high comb buttstock. A smooth bore version is also available.

The really big news from Mossberg is the Model 835 Ulti-Mag, a pump-action shotgun chambered for 12-gauge shells measuring 3½ inches long to be produced by Federal Cartridge Corporation. Shells of this length in 12-gauge are not new, as this writer has been using them for nearly 20 years in a single shot, and side-by-side shotguns with this chambering were available in Belgium at least this long ago. A pump action in this 12-gauge chambering is new. The actual shells used by this writer were manufactured in Belgium and used conventional paper cases and a roll crimp, but such shells have not been available with plastic cases or factory loaded with steel shot, as are the new Federal shells.

The 835 will have a 28-inch back-bored barrel with ventilated rib and interchangeable ACCU-MAG choke tubes; the 835 barrel is not to be interchanged with barrels on other Mossberg shotguns. The 835 action is similar to, but not identical with, the Model 500 action, although it will handle regular length and magnum length shells in addition to the new 3½-inch Federal shells. The new Federal shells contain 23 percent more steel pellets than the 3-inch 12-gauge magnum shells.

New England Firearms

When Harrington & Richardson went down the tube, the assets of the company were sold to a number of already established firms, except for the single shot gun. A newly formed firm—New England Firearms Co.—purchased the equipment for manufacturing this shotgun and took over the plant at Industrial Rowe. The result is the H&R Topper is enjoying a new lease on life as the "Pardner." Available in 12-gauge with a 28-inch barrel, and 20-gauge and 410-bore with 26-inch barrels, the Pardner is chambered for 3-inch shells. The 10-gauge single shot is also back, complete with 32-inch Full choke barrel and a weight of approximately 10 pounds. For those shooters wanting a two-barrel combination gun, there's the Handi-Gun with a 22-inch 20-gauge barrel chambered for 3-inch shells, and an interchangeable rifle barrel in a choice of 22 Hornet or 30-30 Winchester; the rifle barrels are drilled and tapped for scope mounts. All the New England shotguns have American hardwood stock with a walnut finish. The Pardner has a color-case-hardened receiver with blued barrel, the 10-gauge has a blued receiver and barrel, and the Handi-Gun has an electroless nickel matte finish.

Perazzi

Perazzi shotguns are well-known at the trap and Skeet ranges, but seen to lesser degree in the game fields. New is the MX4, which has the outward appearance of the MX3 Special, but with a new detachable trigger assembly with adjustable (four position) trigger to improve stock fit. Also new is the Grand American 88 Special which is available as an over/under or as a single over barrel; it has the detachable, adjustable trigger assembly and a tapered high ramp top rib. The MX4 has ventilated side ribs between the barrels, while the Grand American 88 Special has no side ribs. In the hunting gun lineup, there's the new MX12 and MX12C, with fixed choke and choke tubes, respectively. The trigger mechanism is selective and utilizes coil springs, unlike the target guns which utilize flat V springs. Barrel lengths on the hunting guns range from 26 to 27⅝ inches, while the new target guns have barrel lengths from 29½ to 34 inches, depending on the model.

Precision Sports

The Parker-Hale line from Precision is coming on strong, and the Model 640A (American) and 645A (American) side-by-sides are now available in 28-gauge and 410-bore with 27-inch barrels choked Improved Cylinder/Modified or Modified/Full. In addition, the 645A and 645E are available in two-barrel (Bi-Gauge) sets of 20- and 28-gauge with 26-inch Imp. Cyl./Mod. barrels, or 28-gauge and 410-bore with 27-inch Imp. Cyl./Mod. barrels. For shooters wanting an English-style are reasonably priced.

Remington

Last year Remington's big thing was the introduction of the Model 11-87 autoloader, but this year it is the re-introduction of the original Parker side-by-side. Built at the Parker Gun Works Division of Remington Arms Company in Ilion, New York, the new Parker will be available in the 20-gauge AHE grade. Remington purchased the original Parker Gun Company over 50 years ago and built Parker shotguns until about the time of World War II, so their ads say, in effect, the real Parker is back.

The new AHE will feature all the classic elegance of the original, but with a completely new single selective trigger and improved automatic ejectors. The barrel length will be 28 inches with any choke combination the customer desires, and a ventilated top rib will be standard. The stock of extra-select walnut will be available with a straight grip or pistol grip, and a choice of splinter or beavertail forend; checkering designs and engraving on the receiver may vary slightly from shotgun to shotgun. As Remington describes it, "It isn't just a shotgun. It's a Parker."

Other additions to the shotgun line from Ilion include the 11-87 Premier with a 26-inch fixed Skeet choke barrel, and the Monte Carlo and standard comb trap guns with fixed Full choke

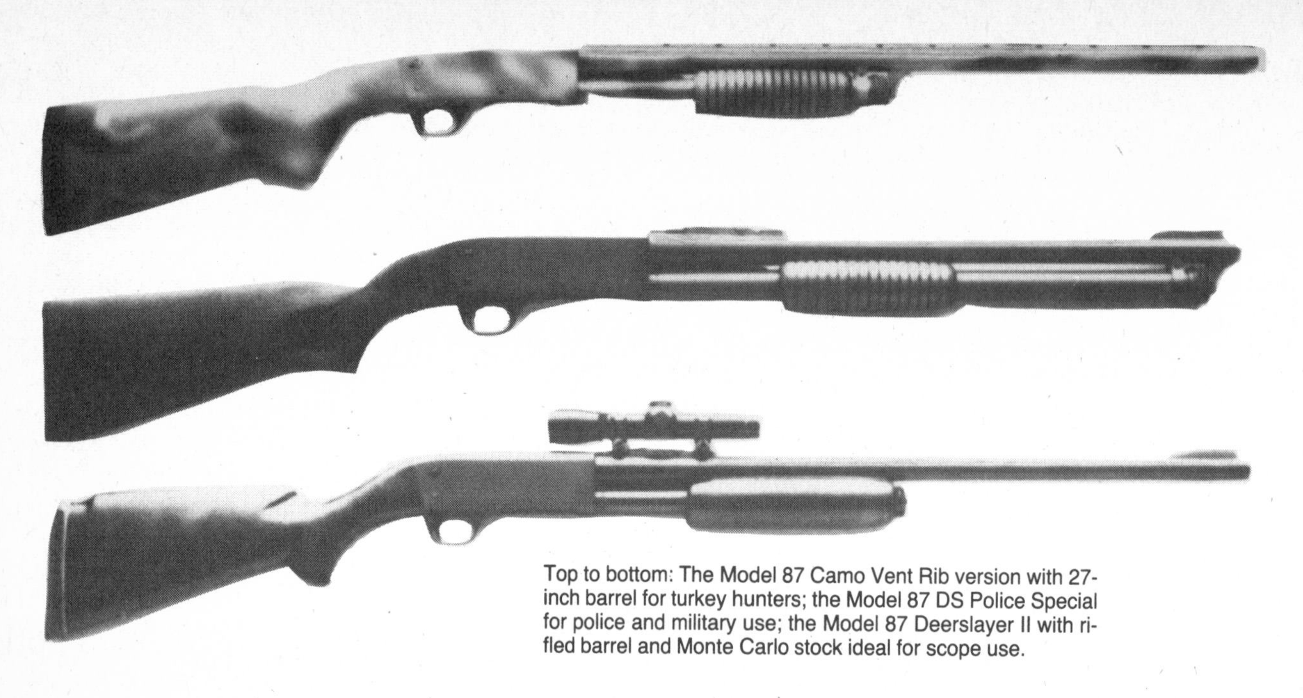

Top to bottom: The Model 87 Camo Vent Rib version with 27-inch barrel for turkey hunters; the Model 87 DS Police Special for police and military use; the Model 87 Deerslayer II with rifled barrel and Monte Carlo stock ideal for scope use.

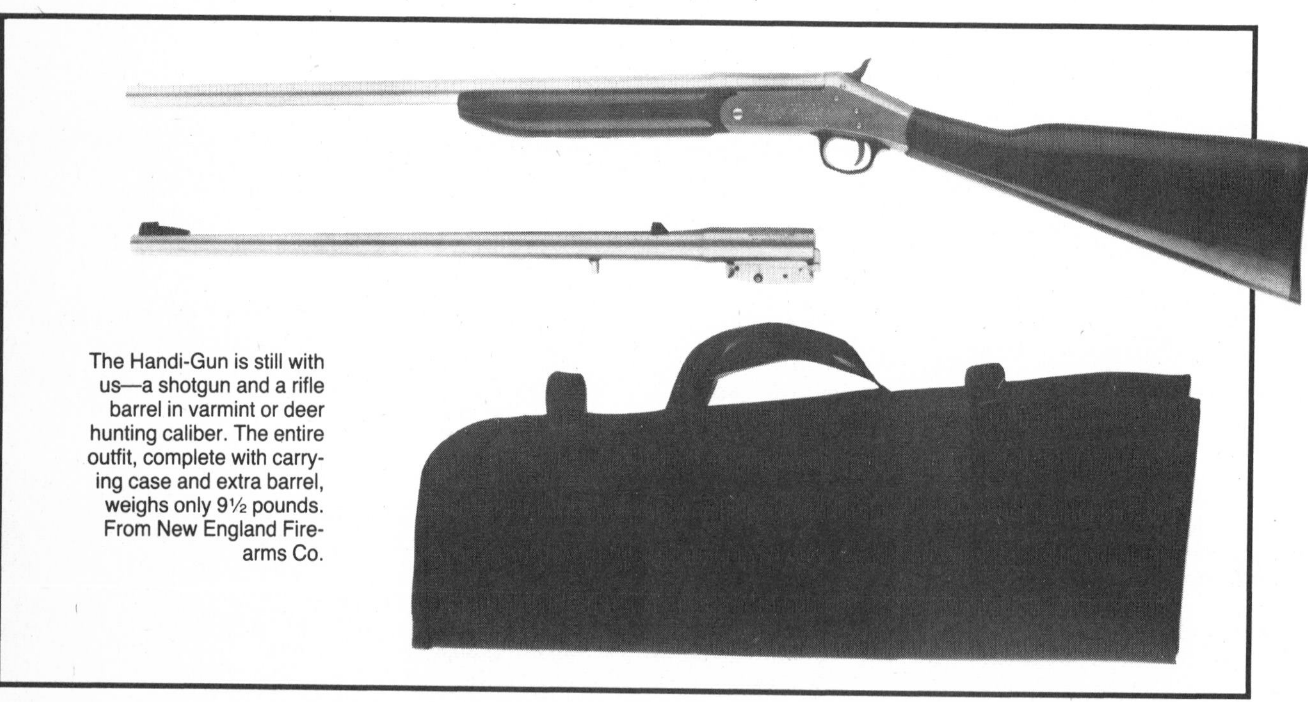

The Handi-Gun is still with us—a shotgun and a rifle barrel in varmint or deer hunting caliber. The entire outfit, complete with carrying case and extra barrel, weighs only 9½ pounds. From New England Firearms Co.

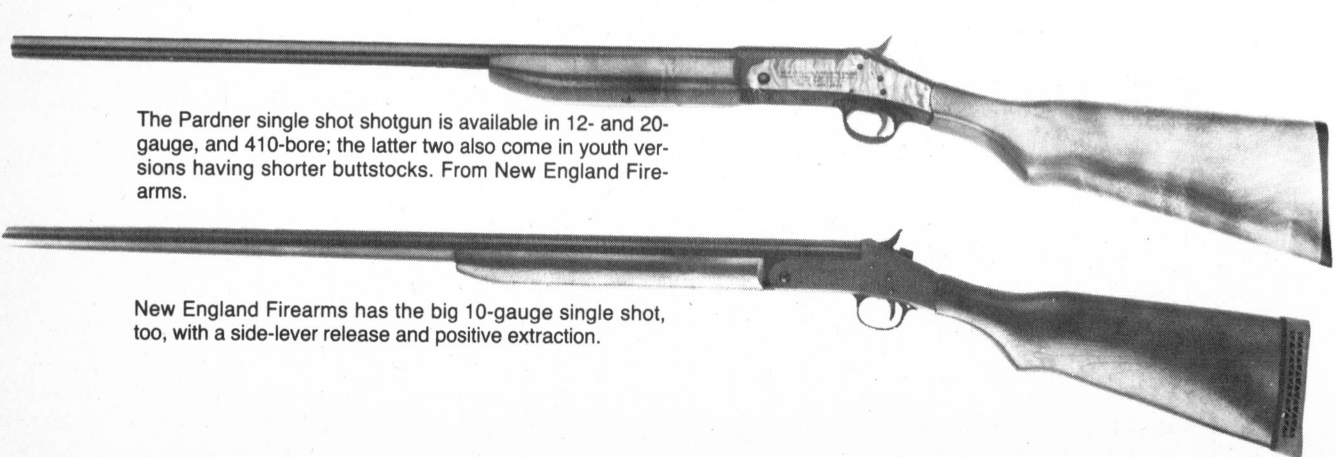

The Pardner single shot shotgun is available in 12- and 20-gauge, and 410-bore; the latter two also come in youth versions having shorter buttstocks. From New England Firearms.

New England Firearms has the big 10-gauge single shot, too, with a side-lever release and positive extraction.

30-inch barrels; the Model 870 pump gun in the TC Trap grade with standard or Monte Carlo stock will also be available now with a fixed choke 30-inch barrel, in addition to the REM-Choke version. The only other addition to the shotgun line is the Model 870 Express Combo featuring a 28-inch ventilated rib REM-choke barrel, with Modified tube, and a 20-inch Improved Cylinder barrel with rifle sights.

Savage

There are to be no more Savage 410s, the double gun line is shortened, and the pump gun line likewise. The over/under combination gun will combine 20-gauge with 22 LR, 22 WMR, 222 Remington or 30-30 as in the past, and the Camper model is still offered. We are told the very sensible Waterfowler 311 double, with barrels for steel shot in Modified and Modified, is on hold. That's the way things get when a firm goes through Chapter XI for reorganization.

SKB

The SKB line has returned and is growing. Not counting barrel lengths and gauges, there are 33 different model variations available, including the auto-loading Model 1300 in field and slug versions, the 1900 autoloader in field, trap and slug versions, and the Model 3000 autoloader in field and trap versions. The Models 200 and 400 side-by-sides are available in field versions with a choice of pistol grip or English-style (straight grip) stock, and with or without engraved sideplates in 12- or 20-gauge. SKB offers a *lot* of double guns.

Their autoloaders are gas operated, and feature Inter Choke barrels of 26-, 28-, or 30-inch lengths depending on the grade, and all have the SKB Universal Magazine Cut-Off System to permit emptying the chamber without unloading the magazine.

Also new for this year is the SKB Single Barrel Trap Gun in 12-gauge only. Similar to the old SKB Century Single, but with a lighter ventilated rib barrel in 32- or 34-inch length with Inter Choke tubes, it will be available with a choice of standard or Monte Carlo stock.

Sturm, Ruger

The 12-gauge Ruger Red Label stainless steel over/under is now available in 26- or 28-inch barrel lengths having screw-in interchangeable choke tubes. Four tubes—Full, Modified, Improved Cylinder, and Skeet choke—are provided with each shotgun, making it suitable for use on upland game, waterfowl or sporting clays. Weight of the latest Red Label is approximately 7½ pounds. Ruger also has a new American Tourister deluxe carrying case to fit the Red Label over/under shotguns.

U.S. Repeating Arms

Concentrating mainly on their rifle line this year, USRA has still upgraded their Model 1300 pump gun line. The XTR Vent Rib Winchoke version is now available with a 12-gauge 28-inch Winchoke barrel and in the Featherweight version with a 22-inch barrel in both 12- and 20-gauge. The M1300 Waterfowl Vent Rib is available with a 28-inch Winchoke barrel in the WIN-TUF grade with laminated stock and matte metal finish on external or internal parts. The 12-gauge Deer Gun is available with choice of laminated or walnut stock and forearm and a 22-inch rifled barrel for slug use. The Ranger Deer Gun still has a smooth bore barrel for rifled slug use. The regular M1300 Turkey Gun is still available, but there is a new Collector's Edition Model 1300 Turkey Gun featuring a 22-inch ventilated rib Winchoke barrel, green WIN-CAM laminated stock and forearm, gold plated trigger and gold-filled roll-engraved wild turkey scenes on the receiver.

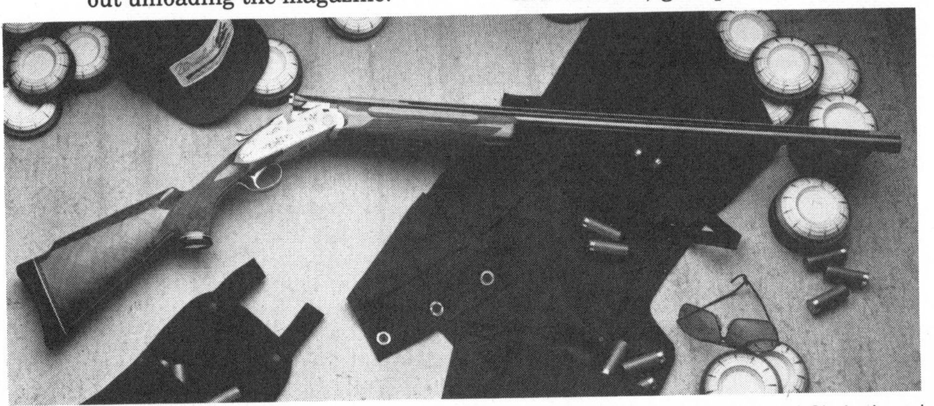

The new Athena Single Barrel Trap Gun from Weatherby has a 34-inch Multi-Choke barrel and the well-known Weatherby fit and finish.

Valmet/Stoeger Industries

Distribution of the Valmet line is now from the Stoeger firm in South Hackensack, NJ, and the shotguns are much the same as last year, including the field grade 412S, the shotgun/rifle combination gun, and the 412 ST in both standard grade and premium grade Skeet and trap guns. Except for the 20-gauge Skeet guns, all the Valmet over/under shotguns are chambered only for 12-gauge shells—standard length in the target guns and 3-inch in the field guns.

Weatherby

This South Gate firm has some new goodies for clay target shooters, starting with a new Athena Single Barrel Trap gun in 12-gauge. Featuring a Monte Carlo stock, the new Single will be available with a choice of 32- or 34-inch barrel with integral Multi-Choke system. For doubles, a separate 30- or 32-inch over/under barrel assembly can be fitted to the same action to produce a Combo. Skeet shooters have not been forgotten, and for them there is a new Athena Master Skeet Tube Set. The complete package includes a 28-inch barreled 12-gauge Athena choked Skeet-Skeet, with pairs of full-length Briley tubes in 20, 28 and 410, along with integral extractors and the tools necessary for insertion and removal of the tubes, all fitted in an aluminum carrying case. For field shooters the Athena and Orion over/under line has been expanded to include 28-gauge and 410 versions with a choice of 26- and 29-inch fixed choke barrels.

Winchester/Olin

Although the firm has sold its portion of the manufacturing facilities in Japan, it still has new shotguns available, including four new Sporting Clays over/unders in 12-gauge. These Sporting Clays feature a choice of 28- or 30-inch barrels with six Winchoke tubes. Also new is the Diamond Grade Trap Over-Single Combo, which combines a 34-inch over-single barrel with 30-inch over/under barrels alone, without having to purchase the Combo, which is good news for trap shooters. The upland game hunter has not been forgotten—the Lightweight Winchoke over/under is now available in 28-gauge with 27-inch barrels and four Winchoke tubes, and the Model 23 Custom side-by-side in 12-gauge can be had with 27-inch barrels and six Winchoke tubes. ●

HAND LOADING UPDATE

by **DEAN A. GRENNELL**

A major event is a basic loading manual like Speer's No. 11, just out.

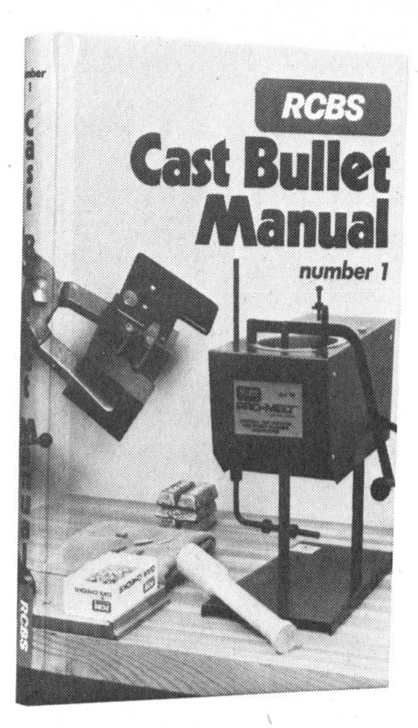

Another company heard from: RCBS now offers this manual on cast bullets.

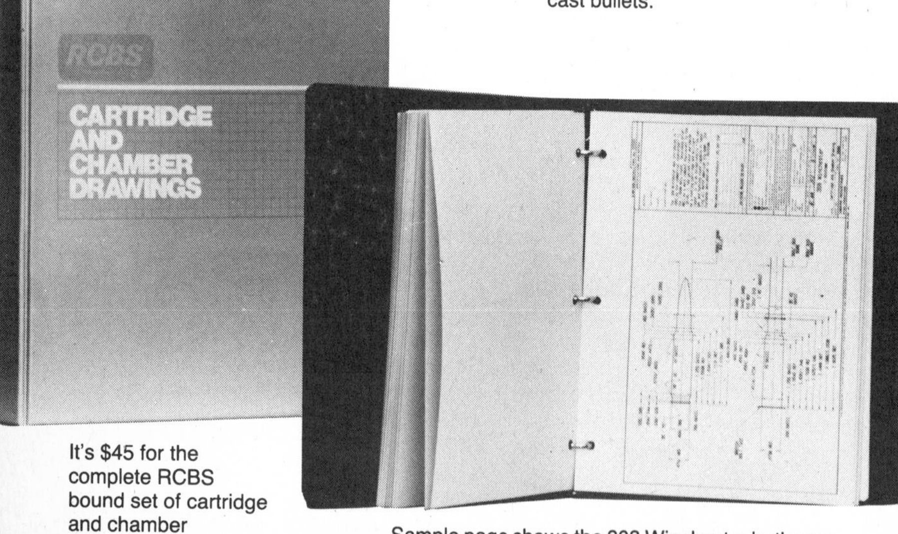

It's $45 for the complete RCBS bound set of cartridge and chamber drawings.

Sample page shows the 308 Winchester both as a loaded cartridge and as a rifle chamber.

THE 12 MONTHS since the previous report have seen some new items, not a raging torrent, perhaps, but an average year's crop for all that. Let's have a look:

In my humble opinion, a new handbook or manual of load data is an item of reloading equipment, just the same as a press or set of dies. The past year saw the publication of the 11th **Speer Manual**, a significant event. The 10th Speer Manual came out late in 1979, and they've made occasional reprintings as needed, sometimes deleting potentially troublesome blocks of data here and there, but—to the best of my knowledge—never adding anything. I was still operating with the first printing, and that led to a few minor confusions when I'd allude to a given load and a number of readers would write to ask why that load wasn't in *their* copy. Now, for at least a little while, we'll all be looking at the same book.

This book is a fat rascal, running to 621 pages at a suggested retail of $12 a copy, making it one of the best bargains your typical reloader is apt to encounter in browsing through the shops. One of the more nettlesome aspects of doing a book on reloading is that you take great pains to get every last bit of detail up to date, pack it off to the roaring presses and then spend some number of weeks before the first copy comes back, watching the appearance of all manner of new things that render it somewhat obsolete. Writing for magazines, as I've done for the past three decades and a bit, gives you the chance to update things every month or two, but it's still a rat race.

So it comes to pass that SM #11 is sharply up to date in some areas and less so in others. How were the troops in Lewiston to know that this would be the year that Remington would legitimize the 35 Whelen? That round has not been covered since the 8th edition, but, all of a sudden, it's a force in the marketplace. There is, for example, no coverage on new cartridges such as the 10mm Bren Ten Auto or 41 Action Express, but of all unlikely things, they seem to have gotten an in-house 10-inch Wildey to use in generating new data for the 45 Winchester Magnum, replacing the dope for the 10-inch T/C Contender in SM #10.

Enough comment on the things that aren't covered; let's talk about some of the things that are. For but one example, in the handgun section, they've included generous scads of data on the 32-20 WCF in the 10-inch T/C Contender barrel. In the area of handgun reloading, that has got to be one of the outstanding sleepers of the past many years and the SM #11 makes a striving effort to provide total coverage. Nine years ago, if you'd gone about offering to bet that the next Speer Manual would carry 240 different loads for the 32-20 WCF, you could have obtained some pretty attractive odds.

Earlier in the year, Speer's corporate sidekicks published the **RCBS Cast Bullet Handbook,** listing a great many different loads for bullets from the moulds they make. If you expect such loads to be wimpish affairs, down around 1150 fps, think again. Some of them get up over 2000 fps, even for use in handguns. Suggested retail price for this one is $8 per copy and well worth it to anyone interested in the use of cast bullets.

Last year, the new presses on the market consisted of moderately priced, entry-level designs such as **Lyman's** Acculine and the **RCBS** Shooting Partner. No further examples of a similar nature seem to have come along since that time, but we do have a substantially upscale loading press from a maker not previously active in that field.

This one's from **Dave Corbin,** of White City, Oregon. Corbin's a man whose previous activities have principally been devoted to the rarified field of bullet swaging. He calls this new outfit the Mity-Mite Series II and, not surprisingly, it's possible to use it for swaging bullets and quite effectively, too. Unlike the original Mity-Mite C-press and Corbin's O-frame modification of it, or his CSP-1 press, you can use the Mity-Mite II for conventional reloading as well as for bulletmaking.

The switchover is accomplished by changing a hardened steel crossbar from one pair of holes to another, thereby modifying the linkage, leverage and distance of ram-travel upward or downward, as the case may be. With the crossbar in the upper pair of holes, you have great hairy gobs of leverage that enable you to swage fairly hard alloys of lead into bullets as large as .458-inch in diameter. Move the crossbar to the lower pair of holes and you pick up enough additional ram-travel to make easy work of reloading the largest conventional rifle cartridges such as the 375 H&H Magnum, with more than ample leverage to handle the stresses involved. Basic design of the press is an O-frame, and the upper crossbar can be removed and replaced with auxiliary crossbars drilled and tapped for accessories other than the usual 7/8-14 dies.

The Mity-Mite II comes with a holder for the external punch in the Corbin system of bullet swaging dies. To use it for reloading, you need an optional shellholder adapter, currently $8 extra. I was pleased to note the adapter has an angled hole pointed toward the rear, so as to direct spent primers into a suitably positioned

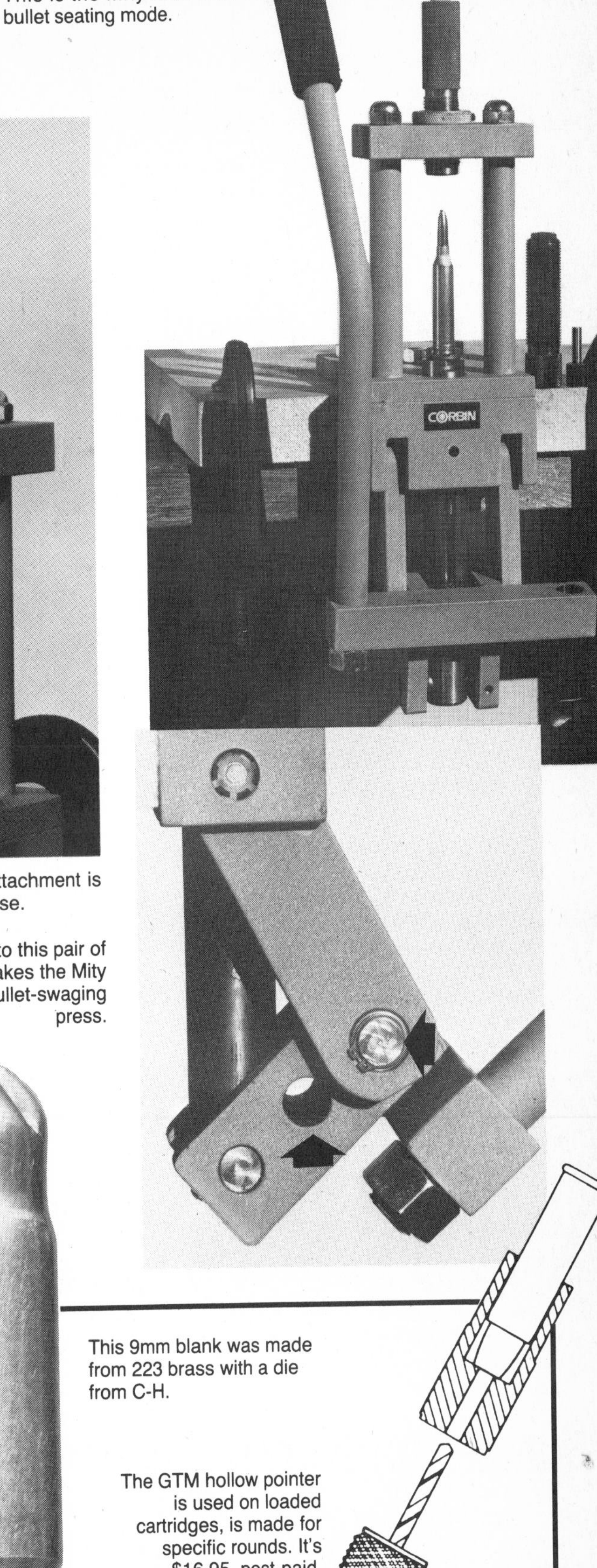

This is the Mity Mite II in bullet seating mode.

Mity Mite II priming attachment is adjustable, quite precise.

Moving pin to this pair of holes makes the Mity Mite II a bullet-swaging press.

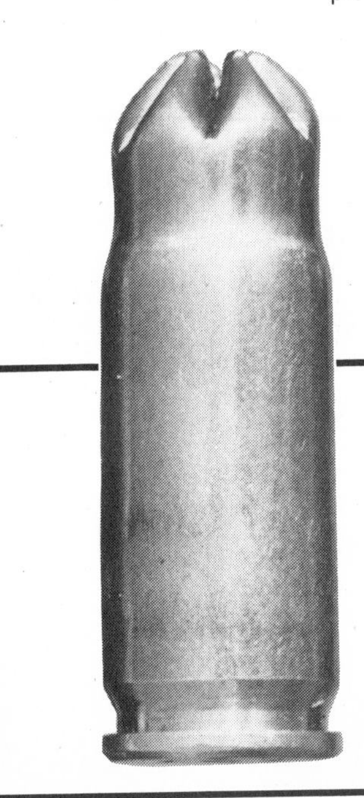

This 9mm blank was made from 223 brass with a die from C-H.

The GTM hollow pointer is used on loaded cartridges, is made for specific rounds. It's $16.95, post-paid.

RCBS Partner press is shown here on a Grennell homemade stand for which blueprints are not available.

The upgraded 4x4 stacks up into a tall piece of gear, fully accoutred.

container. Color me prejudiced if you like, but there are few traits I find more distasteful in a loading press than that of leaving the operator ankle-deep in spent primers.

Hornady Manufacturing Company has come up with what they're calling their "New Dimension" reloading die sets, designed to eliminate a number of problems all too common to reloading dies and, as an added plus, to bring the cost of a set downward substantially.

On the resizing die, there is a new expander spindle held in a new collar and collar locking system to assure precise concentricity of the assembly, including that of the decapping pin. At the same time, it positions an expanding plug that's elliptical, top to bottom. What that does is reduce friction as the resized bottleneck case is drawn back down over the plug, thus minimizing case-stretch and the need for frequent case trimming.

At its lower end, the expander spindle is tapered in the area around the decapping pin, so as to guide it smoothly into the case neck, rather than snagging, perhaps to ruin the

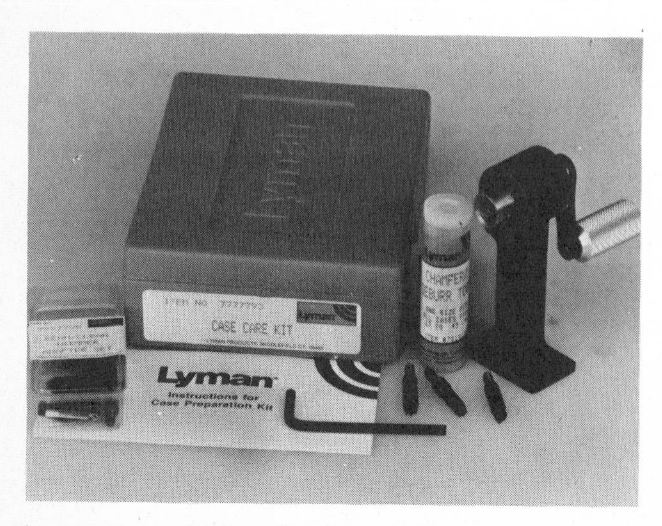

Lyman packages this Case Care Kit for reloaders who care.

For 10mm reloading gear, see Lyman: Dies are carbide types. There is a new mould, too.

Alpine Magnum Plus press certainly looks like serious gear.

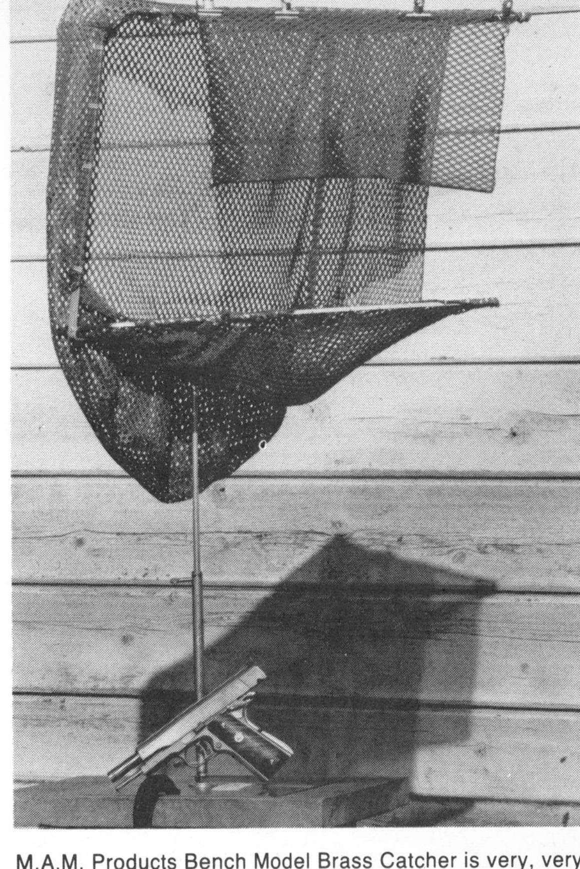

M.A.M. Products Bench Model Brass Catcher is very, very handy, but needs to be tied down.

case beyond hope of salvage. The decap pin itself is of hardened steel, guaranteed not to break in the first 2 years of normal use. The maker claims it will not break, even if a case of Berdan-primed persuasion strays into the chain of production. That doesn't imply you can convert Berdan cases for use of Boxer primers, of course. For but one thing, the primer pocket diameter doesn't match.

It does, however, offer a hopeful shortcut around the 17th law of universal hostility, as promulgated by an associate of mine named Wiley Clapp which states: "The number of Berdan-primed cases encountered on any given reloading session will exceed your supply of spare decapping pins by at least one."

Moving on to the bullet-seating die of the New Dimension set, it features a free-floating sleeve that holds the bullet in perfect alignment with the case neck as they move on up into the die to seat the bullet. It does the same thing you'd like to do by hand, if only you could reach up into the die that far.

Add what Hornady calls the Sure-Loc rings, readily securable in adjustment by means of an .095-inch hex wrench and you have what I tend to regard as a decided improvement upon the existing systems. Resizing dies for straight-walled cases have a cemented ring coated with titanium nitride to ease the frictional effort of resizing, prevent scratching of the case wall and eliminate any need for lubrication of the case before resizing as well as any need to remove the lube after sizing.

Redding will be making the Saeco lube/sizer again—apple-green instead of black.

RCBS has redesigned their manually advanced 4x4 progressive press to the new Auto 4x4. Similar to the original in many details, it now advances the shell plate automatically in a counterclockwise direction. Actuation of the RCBS Uniflow powder measure likewise is automatic, as is the feeding and seating of the primer.

Once the Auto 4x4 has been put through the start-up routine, the operator needs only to insert a case at station one, position a bullet at station four and operate the handle. The loaded round is ejected automatically.

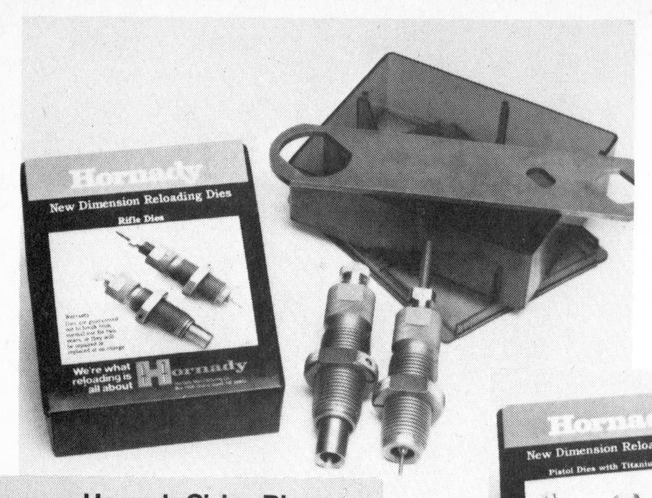

Hornady's New Dimension dies are in step with the industry move to better die technique.

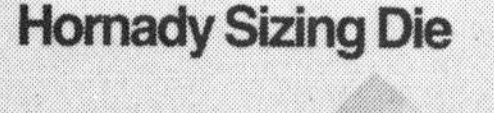

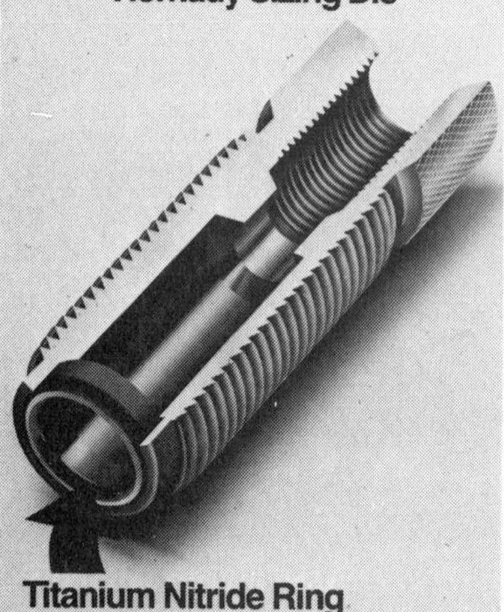

The shell plates carry the same identifying numbers as current RCBS shellholders and are available for all but numbers 5, 8, 13, 14, 22, 29 and 31. Those seven holders handle some fairly exotic cartridges and hence do not sell in large numbers.

A personal aside: The RCBS rotary case trimmer power conversion may have been in last year's catalog. If you've not tried this, I suggest you do so. Inexpensive, it's just a double-ended hex shaft that goes into an electric hand drill and a hex-socket screw that replaces the regular crank on the RCBS case trimmer. The hex shaft is ball-ended at either end, eliminating the need for precise angular alignment. It gets case trimming down to a speedy zip-zap operation, rather than the usual patience-trying ordeal. In recent times, I've gotten enmeshed in several projects that involved wholesale amounts of case trimming, and I was intensely grateful for the RCBS power conversion.

The outside neck turner attachment for the RCBS case trimmer has had virtually all of the random bugs eradicated from its design and it's reported about ready to go into full-scale production. That's a gizmo for which I've been waiting, twitching with ill-concealed impatience. Within the week just past, I would have given one of just about anything of which I had at least two to have the use of the outside neck turner for just a bit. With any kind of luck, it will be along before much longer.

Another useful item of reference material from RCBS is their book of cartridge and chamber dimension drawings, at $45 for the complete book. The drawings also are available individually for just about any standard cartridge.

While not exactly a hot new item, I think it warrants mention that the firm of **Ponsness-Warren** remains in business, producing the 800 Convertible and Du-O-Matic 375C shotshell reloaders as well as the Metal-Matic P-200 and Metallic M-II presses for metallics. Many reloaders seem to have the impression that P-W has gone out of operation, but they're still up there in Rathdrum, Idaho, producing and shipping their useful line of loading presses and I, for one, am grateful for that.

A year or two ago, the **Saeco** operation was bought up by **Redding** and moved to that firm's headquarters in Cortland, New York. Preserved fairly well intact were the Saeco line of bullet moulds, and the earlier Saeco lead hardness tester was retrieved and restored to the line, to the delighted relief of bullet casters in many unlikely places.

Now the word comes down that Redding-Saeco is restoring the Saeco lube/sizer for cast bullets to their line and that is the finest kind of good news. At some point back in the '60s, I bought a used Saeco lube/sizer and have long since come to regard it as one of my all-time great investments.

Sizing dies for the Saeco lube/sizer are available in 45 diameters from .224- to .460-inch and top punches are available in a wide variety of patterns for the various bullet nasal profiles. If you've access to a lathe, it's a simple project to make your own top punches, as they use a $^{5}/_{16}$-24 thread. At one time, former Saeco honcho Johnny Adams came up with a conversion kit that enabled the Saeco lube/sizer to handle top punches from such makers as Lyman, RCBS and—not sure about this—possibly Star, as well. Apparently, this has not as yet become available out of Cortland.

The new Redding-Saeco catalog—free on request—shows no less than 11 cast bullet mould designs that are either new or restyled for 1988. They now have no fewer than five different designs in caliber 40 for the 10mm Auto, including a pair of 170-grainers, two 200-grain and one 190-grain. There are also two new caliber 41 designs, semi-wadcutters at 170 and 200 grains which will be of interest to the growing number of fans for the 41 Action Express.

Another new Saeco design is the #058, a 210-grain bevel-based semi-wadcutter with a broad flat area out front to assure getting the attention of a slippery-surfaced bowling pin in that rather demanding area of competition. Apart from the bevel base, it resembles the old #452423 Lyman SWC, except for being lighter in weight.

For 44 fans who fancy a nice heavy round-nose design to take the place of Lyman's discontinued #429251, originally designed for the 44 S&W Russian, there is the Saeco #442, restyled for 1988, at a listed weight of 246 grains.

C-H Tool & Die now has a two die set for reloading the caliber 50 Browning machine gun cartridge, at $275 per set, and also can furnish the primers for reloading it, at $14 per 100. Another new item is their blank crimp die; $59 for most calibers, $79 in 45 ACP. For but one example, you make the 9mm Luger blank from 223 Remington brass, cut to a suitable length. The crimped portion approximately duplicates the dimensions of a regular loaded round, helping it to feed from the magazine. Blank ammo for a lot of the centerfire calibers has been hard to find and expensive if you're able to find it. Tony Sailer at C-H can supply all the fine details on these dies to interested parties. Other new items from C-H include a taper-crimp die for the 7.62x39mm—invaluable when reloading for Ruger's new Mini-30 carbine—and a battery-powered device called the C-H Quickie that makes quick and sweat-free work of filling primer feed tubes.

Incidentally, C-H can furnish carbide dies for certain of the bottleneck rifle cartridges, such as the 223 Remington but, before you rush for your checkbook, Sailer wants you to know that the brass cases have to be cleaned free of dust and gritty particles, following which they need to be lightly lubricated. It's not the same as using a carbide die on straight-sided cases. The only advantage of the carbide die is that it lasts several times as long as one of hardened steel.

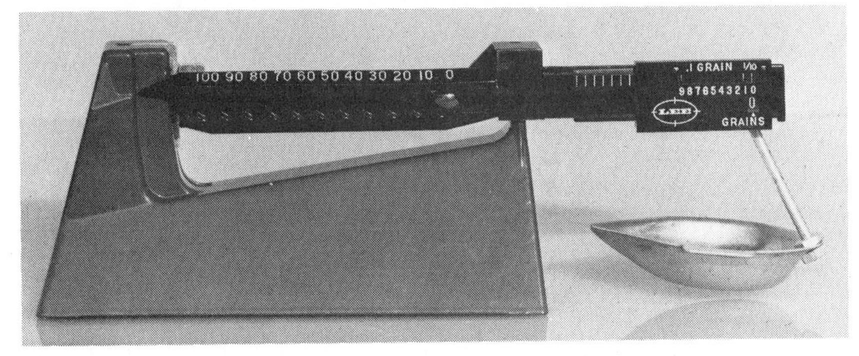

Lee Safety powder scale, here with red base, is available in colors to match most brands of loading tools.

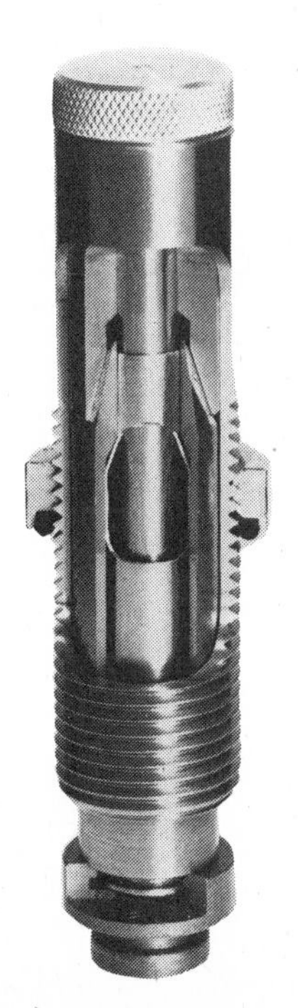

Lee collet resizing die came as near as any other to starting a run on new die techniques.

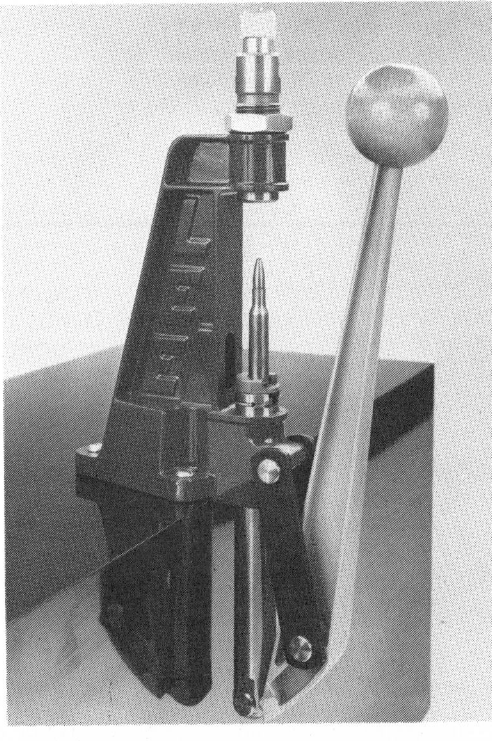

Lee's Anniversary press—$9.95 when purchased with a set of their dies—recalls the original $9.95 Lee Loader as it is meant to do.

Trammco, Inc., (Box 1258, Bellflower, CA 90706) makes and markets a novel, innovative and highly effective system for electroplating cast bullets with copper to a depth of .001- to .002-inch. The plated bullets require no further lubrication and can be driven to approximately the same velocities as conventional jacketed bullets. Gary Trammel, the firm's proprietor, can furnish full details on request.

Alpine Reloading Room, (2401 Government Way, Coeur d'Alene, ID 83814) makes and markets what we might term a large, economy-size reloading press they call the Magnum Plus. It has an eight-station turret head and a ram stroke of more than 7 inches and can be used for reloading all manner of large cartridges, up to and including some of the 37mm sizes, as well as for more conventional calibers. The turret can be custom-produced to take die sets larger than the usual ⅞-14 thread size. The Magnum Plus weighs over 200 pounds and costs over $500, but it can do things beyond the capabilities of any other loading presses readily available on the market.

Necromancer Industries, Inc., (14 Communications Way, West Newton, PA 15089) makes and markets a computer-controlled bullet casting machine with a production capability somewhere in the neighborhood of 500 bullets per hour, the exact rate being dependent upon the weight and design being cast. The price is over $700.

Lee Precision is celebrating its 30th anniversary and has a neat little loading press they sell for $9.95—provided you purchase a set of loading dies with it. That's to commemorate

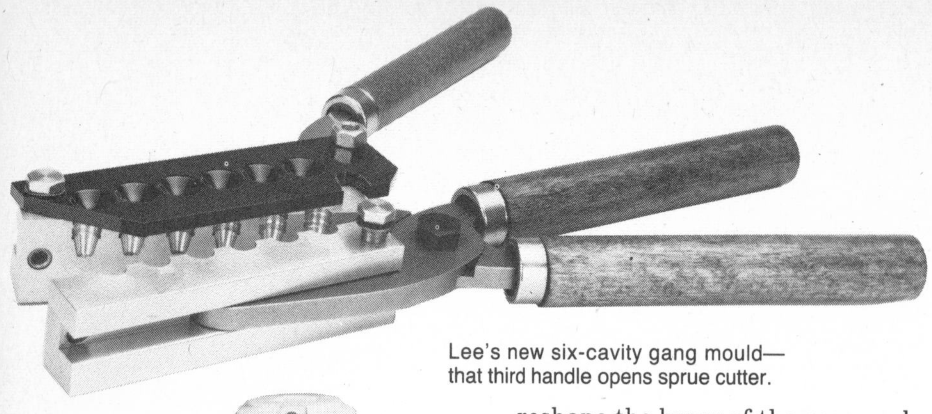

Lee's new six-cavity gang mould—that third handle opens sprue cutter.

With sprayable Liquid Alox, one more messy step can be skipped, Lee says.

the original price tag of the little Lee Loader kits of their early days.

Several new items have been added to the Lee line of bulletmaking equipment. They now have a commercial quality six-cavity bullet mould—$50 for the blocks and $15 for the handles—plus five new designs of what they call their Tumble-Lube bullets. These do not require sizing and are designed for use with Lee's new Liquid Alox lube. All you do is cast the bullets, put them in the bottom of a container such as a rinsed milk carton with the top cut off, pour a small amount of Liquid Alox over the bullets and swirl them about for a minute or so to deposit a uniform coating. Set them aside for about a day to let the coating harden and they're ready to load and shoot. I've used some of these in the 200-grain semi-wadcutter design for the 45 ACP and accuracy has been highly encouraging.

Another interesting new concept is the Lee Collet Die for bottleneck cases. The leverage of the loading press is applied to the tapered collet to reshape the brass of the case neck against the central mandrel that also positions the decapping pin. No case resizing lube is required and it's delightfully quick and simple to use. It does not resize full-length, so you need to use cases previously fired in the same gun.

The Collet Die is sold as a set with the Lee Dead-Length bullet seating die; an exclusive design in which the bullet seater abutts against the shellholder to remove all press play and seat each bullet exactly the same as all the rest. I've been using a set of these in 6mm PPC USA in my single shot Sako rifle and 100-yard groups under ½-MOA are quite commonplace with the setup: commonplace but not in the least boring!

Also new is the Lee Safety Powder Scale at $30, with a 110-grain capacity that's more than ample to weigh just about any powder charge apt to be dispensed. You can have the scale in the usual Lee red or, at your option, in green, orange or blue to match other makes of reloading equipment. I suspect Dick Lee had his tongue in his cheek when he came up with that idea.

Fairly new to the field is the **PACT** chronograph, priced below $200 for the basic model. Suggested spacing of the skyscreens is 24 inches and it works quite well. Making the screen-holding rig delightfully compact and light in weight. The computer box operates on one self-contained 9-volt alkaline battery and the panel readout is in liquid crystal display (LCD), rather than in the light-emitting diodes (LED) used by some chronograph makers. The LCD reduces current drain substantially and extends battery life proportionally.

If you choose to live a bit higher on the hog, the PACT is available with an infrared printer that records all the pertinent data on a roll of heat-sensitive paper tape. You get the PACT, with two skyscreens, for $199; the steel skyscreen bracket is another $24 and well worth it. Having a print driver installed in the PC box adds $25 and the printer itself is $125; six spare rolls of printer paper are $12.

It's a bitter fact of life about chronographs that they lie in harm's path and sometimes within the bullet's trajectory. Extra skyscreens for the PACT are $15 each, $25 per pair. It's rather likely the stray slug may only shatter the plastic photocell housing, leaving the cell still usable. In that event, extra skyscreen housings are only $2.50 each or four for $9.

Operation of the PACT is delightfully simple and straightforward. Turn on the on/off switch and press both red buttons to put it in chronograph mode. Fire as many shots as you wish over the screens. After each shot, you get a reading on the panel showing the velocity of the last shot plus a running figure for the average velocity, including the last shot. When you finish the string, press the Review button and it will read off the velocities in numbered sequence. If you wish to delete a reading, just press the Edit button.

If it's equipped with the print driver, pressing the Review button makes it ask if you wish to print the string and pressing the Review button again signifies yes and starts up the printer—provided you have it switched on and properly positioned.

M.A.M. Products (153-B Cross Slope Court, Englishtown, NJ 07726) makes and markets several different models of what they call the Brass Catcher. These are ingenious devices of netting with metal framework and, when properly positioned, they can and will catch nearly every flying empty case that comes hurtling out of autoloading firearms.

In my book, that makes it a handloading accessory for the good and simple reason that you have to recover the empty case before you can load it again. Rather often, I find myself working with cases that are expensive in the first place and enhanced in value by a lot of handwork before firing. In such an instance, something such as the Brass Catcher truly is a pearl beyond price.

The instructions that accompany the Brass Catcher emphasize the desirability of securing the unit to a solid surface with a C-clamp and I'll certainly second that particular motion. On one occasion, I forgot to take a C-clamp along and a sharp gust of wind decanted the Shell Catcher and its copious load of caught shells into a patch of grassy gravel that complicated retrieval of the cases considerably. This really is an excellent and useful rig, provided you actually follow the instructions. ●

SCOPES AND MOUNTS

by BOB BELL

Not brass, not steel, not aluminum, but graphite ...

Redfield's new 3-12x Ultimate Illuminator has a 56mm three-lens objective to provide excellent light transmission at any power, mates well with Remington 7mm Magnum for open country or mountain shooting.

MUCH AS I hate to admit it, fishing and shooting now have something in common, at least from the equipment angle. For some years now, graphite has been an important ingredient in advanced fishing rods, and a few months ago it appeared in shooting equipment—a new scope tube, to be precise. **Bushnell** is the company that has come through with this innovation.

There was a time when many scope tubes were made of brass. Some advantages of this metal are self-apparent. However, steel was obviously superior from an overall standpoint, as was hardened aluminum, and these two metals have dominated the scope field for generations. Both are still popular and doubtless will continue to be in the foreseeable future. But that doesn't mean no one has been experimenting with other materials, and work has progressed far enough that in January, 1988, Bushnell announced the first graphite-tube riflescope. It's called the Armorlite.

The Armorlite is a 3-9x variable—what else?—and the optics are essentially the same as other top-of-the-line Bushnells. That is, lenses are multicoated, the interior is dry nitrogen-purged, internal adjustments are ¼-minutes, etc. But the tube is a one-piece spinoff from space technology called Graphlon-VI. This is a graphite composite that is said to be stronger than steel and 10 percent lighter than aluminum. More important than the weight saving is the fact that the new material has a thermal coefficient of near zero. This should eliminate any problems that might result from con-

This is the new 8x56mm aus Jena, imported from West Germany by Bill Mecca of Europtic, Ltd. A brilliant scope, it doubtless will work well for any long-range hunting.

Swarovski Optik is now the U.S. distributor for the high-grade Kahles line formerly handled by Del-Sports. A new entry is the 7x56mm.

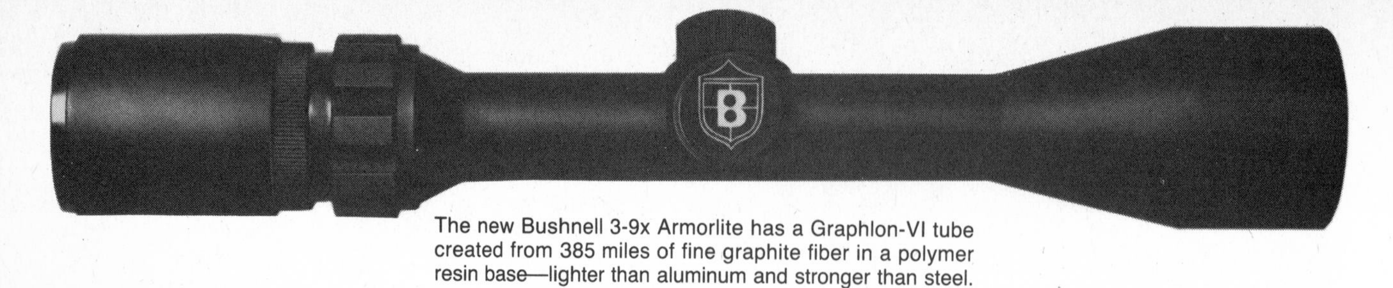

The new Bushnell 3-9x Armorlite has a Graphlon-VI tube created from 385 miles of fine graphite fiber in a polymer resin base—lighter than aluminum and stronger than steel.

traction due to cold or expansion due to heat; not that such changes are a big thing with today's steel or aluminum tubes, but minor fluctuations in point of impact have been noted with metal tubes. Bushnell designers also tell me that the graphite tube distributes external forces throughout this fibrous body material rather than transmitting them to the internal optics. Considering the beating that every scope must take when a high-intensity cartridge is fired, that, too, seems to be an advance.

In manufacture, some 385 miles of extremely fine graphite fiber is wound both circumferentially and at a lengthways angle, to increase strength. It is then set in a polymer resin base to make a strong light tube that's impervious to any normal temperature change. That is, it has been tested to −10 Fahrenheit with no problem; at the high end, the resin starts to soften as temperature approaches 400 degrees Fahrenheit.

We've no idea when other models will be available with Graphlon-VI tubes, or if other makers will follow suit. At the moment, this is a Bushnell exclusive.

Also new from Bushnell this year is a 3-9x56 in the Banner line. The big number is the objective lens diameter in millimeters, of course. Such a scope gives very high light transmission, so will be popular with long-range deer shooters in the South, who usually get their chances in near-dark conditions, and with other specialists.

Bausch & Lomb has a couple of new handgun scopes this year, a 2x in either black or silver finish, and a 4x in silver, to match the popular stainless steel outfits. All have 28mm objectives. They, too, have multicoated optics, internal ¼-minute clicks (though I'm not sure why such small adjustments are necessary here), arm-length eye relief, and wide range diopter settings to sharpen things up for either near- or farsighted shooters. They're also put together to withstand heavy recoil.

I mentioned B&L's 6-24x last year, but only in passing. Should tell you I put one on a heavy barrel M700 22-250, and it proved to be an impressive combination. While getting zeroed with the 55-grain Sierra spitzer and 36 grains 4064, one group went less than ¼-inch at 100 yards, several at 200 averaged under an inch, and one 300-yard group went just over an inch. Impacts were plus 1½ inches, plus 2, and minus 3, which is awfully flat. That evening Bob Wise and I went out to his farm and collected five chucks, all head shots. None were at exceptionally long range, but it was still a good beginning with the new scope. The optics are excellent, clear and sharp at all powers, the fine crosswires make precise aiming easy at any distance, and the wide power choice makes it easy to get the magnification best suited to the range and prevailing conditions of mirage. Like the straight 24x and 36x models, this 6-24x has a 40mm objective and ⅛-minute clicks. Numerous subsequent hunts proved that, as a rig for sit-still varmints, it's truly a top quality scope.

Aimpoint has been offering electronic sighting systems for over a decade now, battery-powered "red dot" reticles for handguns, rifles, shotguns, even bows. Currently, two series, the 1000 and 2000, are available, the latter in two lengths. The longest is only 6⅞ inches, the heaviest under 8 ounces. Basic units are 1x, with 3x boosters available for rifle use.

B-Square's newest no-gunsmithing handgun mount is for Smith & Wesson's K, L and N frame wheelguns with adjustable sights. It does not require drilling or tapping, has no clamps or straps. A standard dovetail base accepts mount rings of many makers or the electronic units popular with many handgunners, and the B-Square people say it will remain solidly in place with the heaviest 44

New Weaver scopes available from Omark include this K4 and K6.

Weaver V3, a new power spread for this line, is a small but efficient scope for big game at close to medium range.

Zeiss Diavari-C 1½x4½x18mm—Bell's favorite size of big game variable. When a critter is too far away for a 4½x, it's farther than he wants to shoot.

Magnum loads.

Other B-Square mounts are made for far more handguns and rifles than we have space to list. A few are Ruger's Mini-14, the Ranch model and the Mini-Thirty as well as the M77, Thompson/Center's TCR 83, Winchester's 94AE and other lever actions, HK sporting rifles, the Colt 45 ACP, Browning's Buck Mark, even assorted airguns. If you want to scope an unusual gun, give 'em a call.

Beeman's unusual SS (Short Scope) models now are made in Skylite versions. These have waterproof sky windows which permit ambient light to illuminate the reticle and make a conspicuous aiming point even on dreary days, without the use of batteries. Normally, the reticle appears black, but four filters are available to present a white, red, yellow or green appearance—whatever will be most useful under varying light conditions or target color. The Skylite scope is made in either 3x or 4x.

Buehler has bridge, dovetail and special scope bases to fit most anything, and rings—including 26, 26½, 27 and 30mm—to go with the bases. A recent addition is the M83 designed for handgun calibers up through the 357 Magnum. It installs without drilling or tapping on many popular models—Smith & Wesson, Ruger, Colt, and Dan Wesson, for instance. Both blue and silver versions available for most.

Burris has been involved with Jeff Cooper's Scout Rifle for several years, and in 1988 added a 1½x Scout scope to its extensive line. Eye relief of 10-14 inches permits mounting ahead of the magazine opening, which makes for easy loading and carrying. You have to pay for this in some way—there's no free lunch in optics—so field is reduced to 22 feet. That might seem small, but it works well because the scope's forward position makes it easy to shoot with both eyes open. There's little difference between the image seen by the unaided eye and the scoped one, so the unit is fast to use. It also goes well with most shotgun slug barrels.

A semi-finished mount base has been designed to easily install this scope. The two front attaching holes match the Remington rear sight hole spacing, which means only the rear hole has to be drilled and tapped in the barrel—no big job for any gunsmith or competent amateur.

For handgunners, Burris has added a pair of new, long eye relief models, a 1x with a 27-foot field and a 2½-7x with a field of 12-7½ feet. Both are suitable for use on magnums. The variable obviously has lots of application for varmint shooters and is available with or without parallax adjustment, in blue or silver finish.

There's also a new Burris mount for Ruger's Mark I and II 22 autoloader. It installs without drilling or tapping, the long base being locked to the gun by a ring that encircles the barrel just forward of the frame. The base accepts 1-inch 22 rings.

Conetrol mounts have long been known for their sleekness—primarily a result of their projectionless rings. Recently their bases have been slicked up too, by fluting all top corners. This also saves a bit of weight, but the most noticeable improvement is in appearance. The fluting is a nice "finished" detail.

Conetrol rings have been available for a year or so in 30mm diameter, to accommodate the large-objective scopes which are increasing in number and popularity. They are made in 5mm (.196-inch) height, which should handle most any scope.

EAW (Ernst Apel of Würzburg, West Germany) manufactures an extensive line of scope mounts, one or another undoubtedly being suitable for installing almost any scope on almost any rifle. Some match integral rails on the scope tube, others utilize a front ring that encircles the enlarged objective section of the tube, while still others have more conventional rings. You can even get European style claw mounts if money is no object. But the most likely choice for Americans doubtless will be the EAW Pivot Mount, which functions similarly to the well-known Redfield Jr. However, the rear unit has a spring-loaded pivot pin lock which permits

Swarovski 4x32mm and 6x36mm are two of the American Lightweight (AL) models available here. Tubes are aluminum alloy.

quick removal of the scope without tools. The maker says the scope replaces without a significant loss of zero. We've never tested this mount, but others have reported excellent results with it. Appearance is typically Germanic, which is to say it's complicated and not the "purtiest" thing I've ever seen, but in the real world that's less important than its efficiency.

Europtik, Ltd. (Dunmore, Pa.) a year or so ago started importing a line of German scopes called *aus Jena* (from Jena). Sort of a strange name, but there's no doubt that the city of Jena has long been recognized as one of the world's leading optical centers. The scopes (and a line of binoculars) are produced by **Jenoptik JENA,** GmbH, and importer Bill Mecca has no qualms about comparing them to Zeiss, which indicates the level he's aiming for.

Currently, five **aus Jena** scopes are available, the ZF4x32-M, ZF6x42-M, ZF8x56-M, VZF1.5-6x42mm, and VZF3-12x56mm. The straight powers have 26mm tubes (also available with integral rail mounts), the variables 30mm. Lenses are multicoated and standard reticle is a constantly centered three-post plex (eight other reticle styles are available). Internal adjustments are valued at 1 cm per 100 yards, which is about 1/3-minute.

We've had the opportunity to test the 8x56mm, though not in hunting season. It gave an excellent image, with the quality being particularly noted when light conditions were bad. That's typical of a good scope of this power and objective size. The twilight factor is 21+, which is as good as these ratings get. At 14 inches it's obviously no compact, but the hardened aluminum tube keeps weight down to 17 ounces, which is not unreasonable for a "stand" scope.

Hakko Shoji, of Tokyo, has several full lines of scopes, including conventional big game and rimfire models. But perhaps most interesting are their Ultra-Compacts, in either low fixed powers or 1½-4x16 variables, which a gunsmith can install on the bolt of a top-ejecting M94, say, or an AR-15 if that's of interest. They're offered with separate mounting rings or integral ATG (Adjust to Groove) units. These will clamp to most any grooved receiver of 1/4-inch to 5/8-inch width. A 1x18mm, with or without battery illumination for the reticle, is also interesting and should be useful on a rifled slug or other brush gun. Field is about 65 feet and eye relief 4-12 inches. Numerous reticles are available.

Hertel & Reuss is another West German firm producing high quality scopes, several models deriving from those they made for Weatherby years ago as his Imperial line. They also offer the Nickel models. Latest introductions in the U.S. are the 4x32, 6x40, 2-7x32 and 3-9x40, but they're only part of the Hertel & Reuss line. Some have what might be called mechanical internal adjustments, while others have the now-familiar optical adjustments which give a constantly centered reticle. Models with objectives of 42mm and larger have multicoating.

Tasco 6-24x makes a good crow outfit on 40XB-BR 222. Wide power range adapts well to mirage—which is more of a problem on prairie dogs in July than on crows in February.

New 7x56mm Kahles, available from Swarovski Optik, will handle big game at long range or varmints to a couple hundred yards.

J.B. Holden Co.'s Ironsighter mount line keeps expanding to accommodate most any rifle or handgun introduction. Countless hunters like the idea of having either the scope or iron sights available with a tip of the head. These See-Thru mounts are now available for most Rugers, including the M77/22, the Ranch Rifle, the Mini Thirty, and the Redhawk. There's also a new hinged design to make it easy to mount a 1-inch scope on any grooved receiver. Adaptors for 3/4- and 7/8-inch scopes included.

Leupold is once again offering their 1-4x in the Vari-X II line, in a special run limited edition. This is my idea of a big game scope, but obviously I'm in the minority as the vast majority of hunters opt for 3-9x. It's nice to know that there are enough on my side to justify occasional production. At bottom power it has a 70-foot field which makes it a good choice on a dangerous game rifle; if you're not annoyed by marauding lions or whatever, it'll also do the job on elk in the black timber or whitetails in the slashings.

Leupold's 8x36mm is now made with an adjustable objective, which permits fine tuning to eliminate parallax at any range. This can be helpful when you bed down near a prairie dog town for some hours of shooting. The one we've been using has the popular Duplex reticle, but it's also offered with a 0.7-minute dot. I'm hoping to use this glass on my 7mm Remington Magnum for some South Carolina whitetails. The shooting usually comes just before dark and at long range, so this 8x36 should be ideal. As with all Leupolds, the optics are outstanding.

Also available for the first time is Leupold's 6x42 with the standard Duplex reticle where formerly, it offered only a heavier version for low light situations.

Four new mounts complete this year's new scope products from Leupold—ring mounts for the Ruger M77 rifle and handgun mounts for the Dan Wesson and the Python (in either blue or silver for the Colt).

Millett now manufactures scope rings and bases for countless rifles and handguns, plus the Remington 1100 and 870 smoothbores. For some examples, there are Angle-Loc rings featuring windage adjustments for Weaver-style bases; rings to fit the machined-in Ruger M77 dovetails, also with windage; two-piece sculpted bases for most Remington and Weatherby rifles; and units for the Savage 110, Winchester 94AE, Marlin 336, etc. The shotgun models clamp onto the vent rib, thus can be installed or removed quickly. No drilling or tapping.

Millet rings of course are available with iron sights as integral parts of the top halves—a look-over instead of look-under approach.

Nikon riflescopes have been on the market for only 3 years or so, but their quality has impressed lots of shooters and now some new models are available. Six, to be precise: 4x40, 1½-4½x20, 2-7x32, 3-9x40, 4-12x40 and, for handgunners, a 2x20.

Lenses are completely multicoated, internal tube surfaces are blackened to eliminate glare or reflection, adjustments are ¼-minute clicks, and of course they are shock-, fog-, and weatherproof. Black or silver finish.

Adjustable objective has been added to Leupold's 8x36mm to permit fine focusing at any range. Pennsylvania hunter uses it for pinpoint accuracy from his deer stand.

Zeiss Diavari-C 3-9x will handle most any big game shooting chore.

Thompson/Center's short tube 4x can be had with integral rail mount or, as here, plain tube for conventional rings. Electra Dot reticle makes aiming easy even in the gloom.

Redfield's big news this year is a big scope, the Ultimate Illuminator. This is a 3-12x variable built on a 30mm tube with a 56mm objective unit that's adjustable for range. As with the earlier illuminators, this one features a triplet lens objective, for a brilliant image—as bright as you're likely to get under any ambient light conditions. Even at 12x exit pupil is almost 5mm, and only rarely does the human eye pupil open wider than that. If forced to shoot well after sundown, power can be reduced to 8x, which gives an exit pupil of 7mm—the largest the eye can absorb—and with this lens system you doubtless can aim precisely at game when it would be difficult or impossible to see at all with the naked eye. Maybe that explains one Redfield designer's statement that this is the best scope they've ever made.

It is big, though: 15½ inches and 23 ounces, which means it's not really appropriate on a M7600 Remington carbine. But I wouldn't faint if I saw such a combination in the Pennsylvania deer slashings. The legion of hunters whose profoundest philosophy is "if it's bigger, it's better" has close to the ultimate here.

Reticle is the European No. 4—a duplex minus the top vertical post. Adjustments are ¼-minute clicks, which proved accurate in our tests, and the alloy tube is one-piece, which Redfield says is 400 percent stronger than screwed-together designs. The lack of joints also reduces the possibility of leakage and eventual fogging.

The Ultimate Illuminator comes in a handsome hardwood box complete with a high set of 30mm steel rings to fit the Redfield rotary dovetail base, plus lens covers. An impressive package, everything considered. We put No. 0036 on a 7mm Magnum to do some shooting, but only at inanimate targets as it was January and no big game seasons were open in Pennsylvania. In the high mounts the objective bell clears the M700's sporter barrel by a strong ⅛-inch, which is about ideal. This outfit might not work on the heavier Varmint 700 or a bull barrel custom job—something to consider if selecting a sighting arrangement for a tree-stand deer rifle, say.

The unusual 3-12x power spread (a 4-1 rather than Redfield's conventional 3-1 ratio) results in a field of 27-10½ feet, down a bit at the low power end from the 33-11 feet of the Tradi-

Low power Schmidt & Bender variable has 30mm tube for extra strength. Not a bad idea on a 338 that kicks out a 250-grain Nosler at 2750 fps.

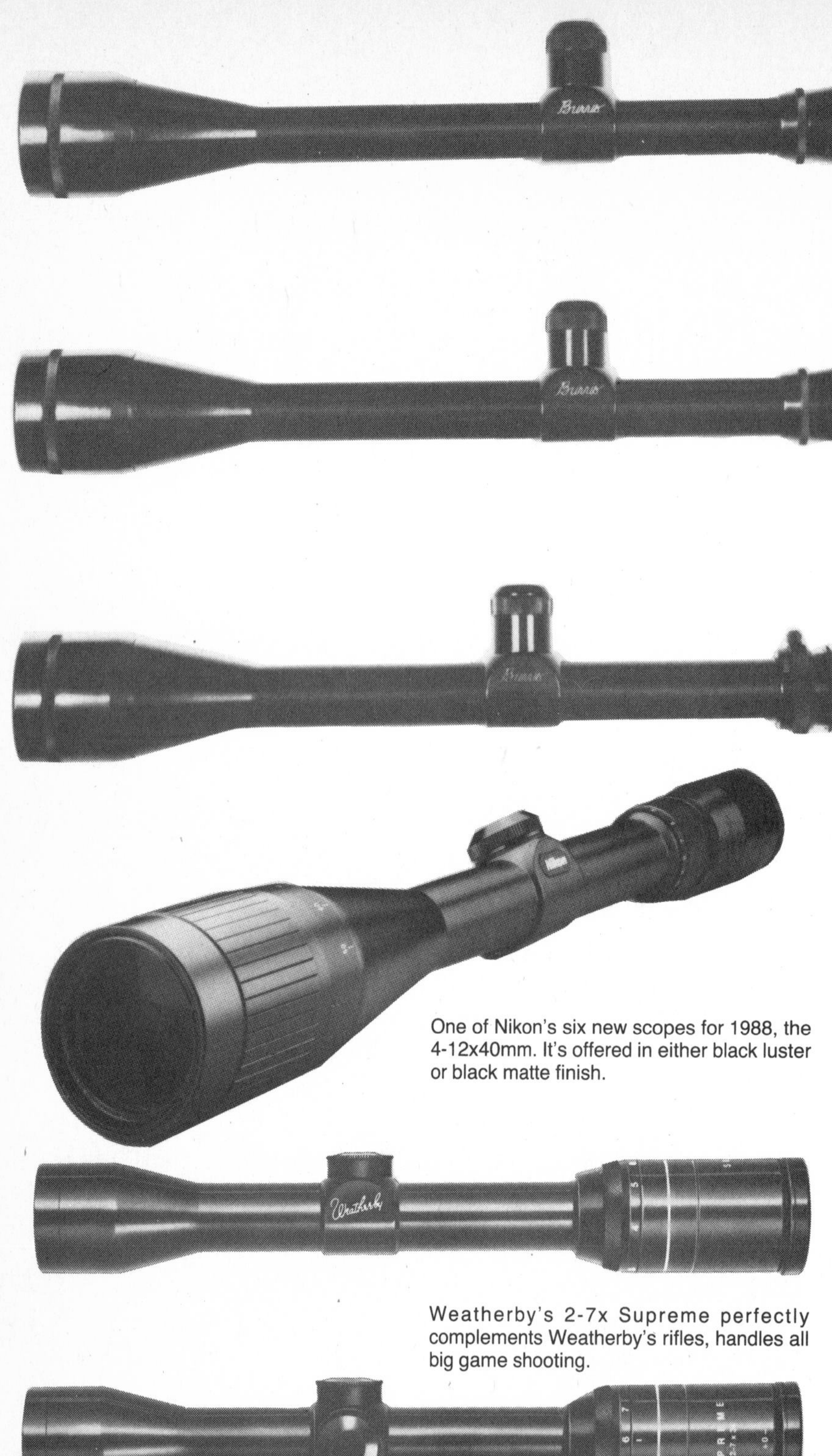

Some of the long Burris scope line—silhouette models in 10x, 12x and 6-18x. All have excellent optics and adjustments.

One of Nikon's six new scopes for 1988, the 4-12x40mm. It's offered in either black luster or black matte finish.

Weatherby's 2-7x Supreme perfectly complements Weatherby's rifles, handles all big game shooting.

tional 3-9x Illuminator. At the top end, it's surprisingly close, considering the extra 3x supplied.

Also new in 1988 are 2½x and 4x handgun scopes with brushed aluminum finish and a 2-6x pistol scope with 10-18-inch eye relief. Its field goes 25-7½ feet. Redfield handgun scopes now have ¼-minute clicks.

In the mount line, Compact rings and bases of the Jr. design are new and 25 percent lighter than standard size. Also, 30mm rings are now available for the Midline bases.

S&K Insta Mounts permit scope installation on many rifles, including a lot of military models, without drilling or tapping—in fact, usually without either major alteration of any kind or the assistance of a gunsmith. Bases are available with or without S&K steel or Weaver-type rings, and for the Aimpoint, Tascorama and Quick Point units.

Some time back I got a Ruger Mini-14 as a fun gun and to keep beside the bed just in case. It's a neat little rig. The iron sights—an adjustable aperture and blade front—doubtless would have handled a lot of the shooting this outfit is intended for, but I prefer a scope. At first I thought in terms of a straight 2½x or 1½-4½x variable, and I'm sure either would have worked fine. But I had a Leupold 4x Compact, and its small size, to say nothing of its excellent optics, seemed the perfect complement. It is, too.

Schmidt & Bender scopes are available from Jaeger, Inc., usually with a choice of steel or hardened aluminum tubes, with or without mounting rails. We've mentioned how well the little 1¼-4x works on a 338, but have mostly ignored the bigger models. As the majority of hunters prefer higher power scopes, it seems appropriate to mention that S&B also offers 1½-6x42, 2½-10x56, 1½-6x42 Sniper and 4x25 Sniper variables. In straight powers they have a 1½x15 with a 90-foot field, which should be ideal for dangerous game, and 4x36, 6x42, 8x56 and 12x42 models. That should be enough options for anyone. These are expensive scopes, retailing for $365 to $850, but they're top quality, with multicoating that results in light transmission of over 90 percent. They're tested for temperatures from −40 degrees to +122 degrees Fahrenheit, so should perform well in any hunting situation.

Simmons has three scope lines—Gold, Silver and Bronze Medals—which blanket the field; nevertheless, some new ones have been added. One is a Silver Medal 3-9x40mm wide angle. Its field is 42-14 feet, tube is one-piece, and the objective system is multicoated. The adjustment system can be set to zero after sighting-in, which is a nice touch. There are also new handgun scopes in 1x20mm, black or aluminum finish, dot and crosswire reticle; and a 7x32mm with enlarged objective and Truplex reticle. Two new shotgun scopes are offered in 1½x20mm (50-foot field, 6.8 inches, 7 ounces) and 2½x20mm (29-foot field, 7.1 inches, 7.2 ounces). There's a one-piece ordnance aluminum mount to get these onto either the 870 or 1100 Remington utilizing the trigger assembly pins. Rings are integral with the sideplate.

New Bausch & Lomb handgun scopes are tough enough for use on magnums, come in 2x or 4x, black or silver.

Swarovski Optik is now the U.S. distributor of the Kahles scope line, as well as its own, which ought to give a prospective buyer something to think

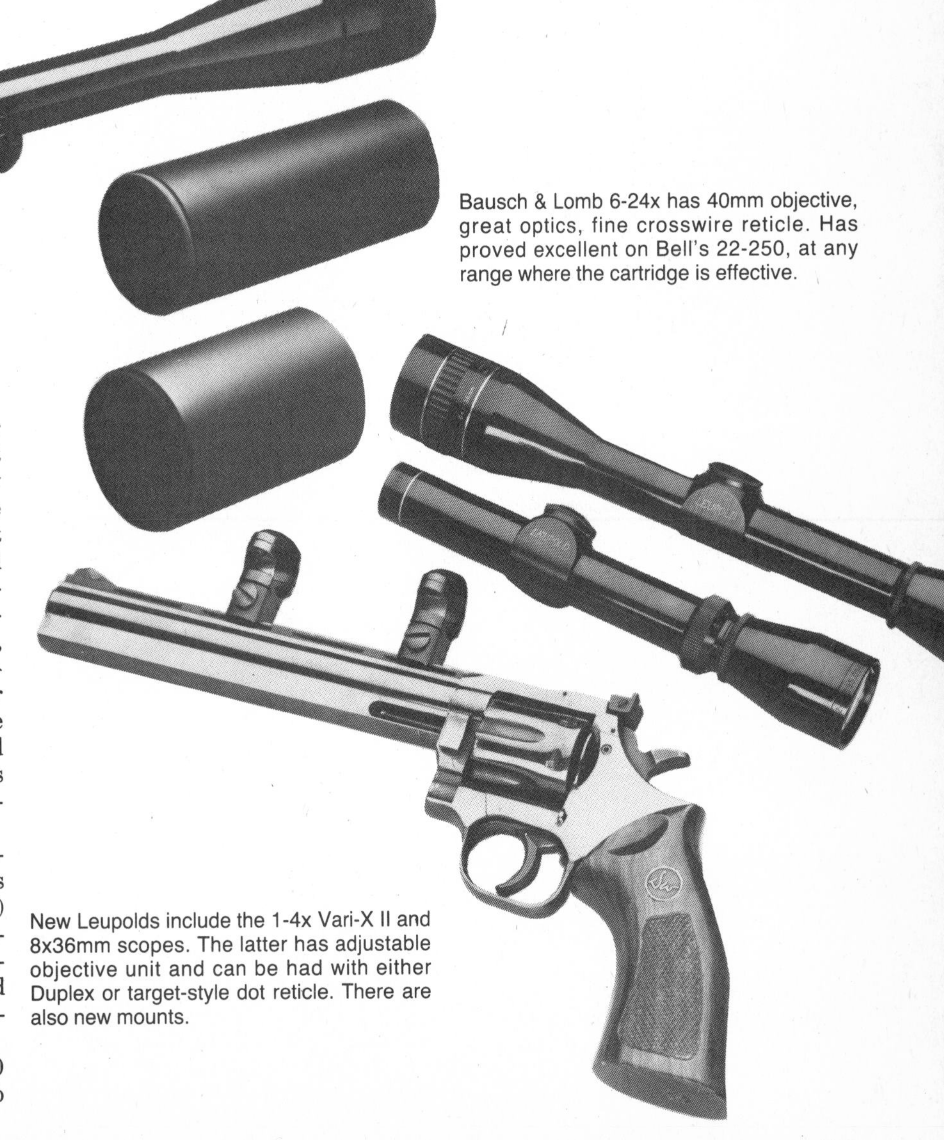

Bausch & Lomb 6-24x has 40mm objective, great optics, fine crosswire reticle. Has proved excellent on Bell's 22-250, at any range where the cartridge is effective.

New Leupolds include the 1-4x Vari-X II and 8x36mm scopes. The latter has adjustable objective unit and can be had with either Duplex or target-style dot reticle. There are also new mounts.

about. We've used several of each over the years, and it would be hard to get a more impressive pair. A brand new model in the Kahles line is the 7x56mm, which gives an 8mm exit pupil for rapid sight alignment and high twilight factor. Basic tube diameter is 26mm, though the outside diameter of the objective unit is 62mm, which means high mounts will be required on most rifles. Eight other Kahles scopes are currently available here, four more straight powers and four variables. Two unusual sizes here are a 2¼-9x42mm and a 3-12x56.

The Swarovski line continues to include both fixed and variable powers in the AL (American Lightweight) sporting versions, plus the 1½x14 Cobra and 6x ZFM for military or paramilitary use. The Cobra can be used on any firearm having standard 1-inch NATO mounting.

Tasco currently markets over 100 riflescopes and 18 handgun models, so

B-Square's newest mount holds scopes or sights like the Tasco Pro-point on Smith & Wesson's K, L and N frames.

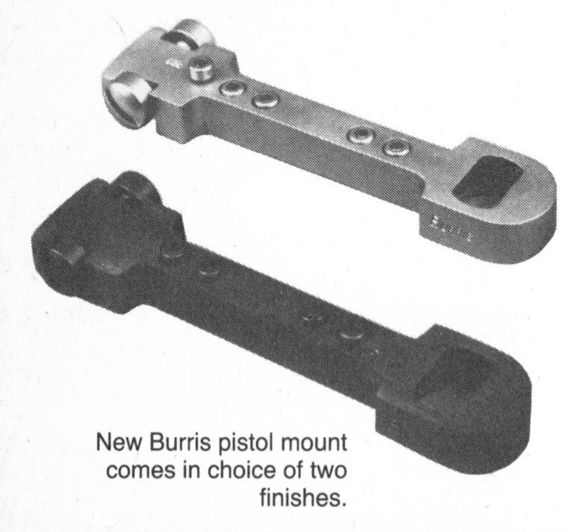

New Burris pistol mount comes in choice of two finishes.

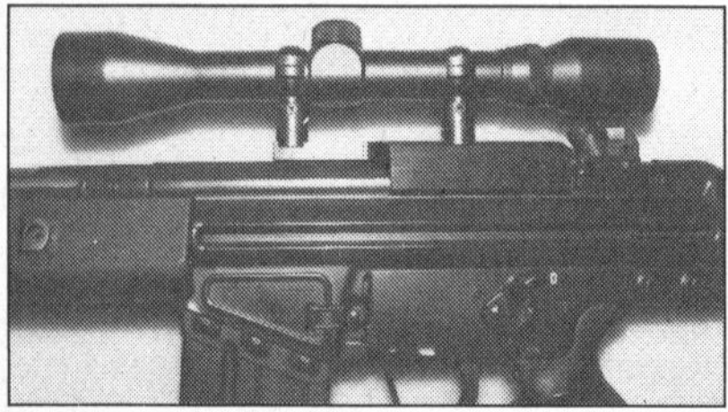

S&K Insta Mounts can be installed on hunting or military rifles. Here, riser blocks get scope at the right height on an HK.

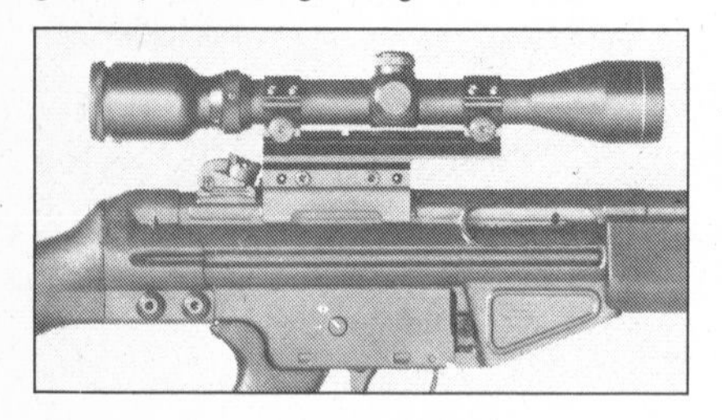

B-Square mounts are available for most everything, including HKs.

Millet puts iron sights on top of scope rings for emergency use.

you'll have to study their catalogs for details. They've just added a rubber covering for added protection and built-in mounting rings. Some models have rubber-covered windage and elevation caps which do not have to be removed for adjustment.

The new 30mm Pro-Class handgun scopes have a reticle etched on a lens—tapered crosshairs which lead the eye to a center dot. Some models have a choice of an illuminated reticle, and different units have 22, 30 or 40mm objectives. A 6x40mm doubles the power of any Tasco pistol scope previously offered.

Thompson/Center has been offering their Lobo and Recoil Proof handgun scopes for a long time now, in powers from 1½x to 4x, as most shooters probably know. The RP line also includes riflescopes of 4x and 3-9x in conventional size, plus a short-tube 4x model with either rail or conventinal ring mounting. The riflescopes feature a battery operated Electra Dot reticle. In use, both the center dot and the inner portions of the horizontal and vertical "crosswires" are illuminated for precise aiming in poor light.

Weatherby scopes have never been as attention getting as his rifles (how could they be?), but the several lines offered over the years have all been fine performers. For some years now the Supremes have done the job. There are only four centerfire models—1.7-5x20, 2-7x34, 3-9x44 and 4x44—but they'll certainly handle any kind of hunting except long-range varmints. There's also the Mark XXII 4x50 for rimfires, particularly the neat autoloader of the same model number. We wrote about it last year so we won't go into detail again, except to say that it, and the Supreme line, are worthy of mounting on the Weatherby rifles.

Weaver scopes, as explained here last year, have returned to the market, courtesy of Omark Industries. In addition to the K4 and V9 and two rimfire models covered previously, five more centerfire models are ready to go—the K2.5, K6, 1-3x V3, 2-10x V10, and the 15x KT15. Their fields of application are obvious, and one or the other will handle any kind of sighting chores a hunter is likely to face. The original K4 (well, actually it went through a series of upgradings during the almost four decades it was on the market) was said to be the most popular big game scope ever produced. The new one seems even better, so it should gain a following. We haven't used the V10 so we can't comment on its unusual 5-1 power ratio, but it obviously has a lot of possibilities—as does the KT15 for the long-range varmint specialist.

Weaver/Omark also has an extensive mount line, not only the "ugly little" detachable design that worked better than seemed possible, but also Imperial 1-inch rings and two-piece bases which work on the rotary dovetail system.

Williams Gun Sight Co. must make a mount for every sporting rifle around, in any height, over center or offset, with look-under rings or look-over iron sights. They're also made for a bunch of handguns and muzzleloaders—even bows. And of course the Williams Twilight scopes are still said to be "the highest quality in the medium priced field," and maybe they are. Current lineup includes 2½x, 4x, 1½-5x, 2-6x and 3-9x.

Zeiss has an unsurpassed—maybe unequaled—reputation in optics. Currently, two riflescope lines are available here, the Z and C types. There are five Z models, three straight powers and two variables, and six Cs, three of each type. Each line covers almost all hunting situations. In quality they're equal, but there are some basic differences. The Zs are essentially European style, the Cs American. The straight power Zs are built on 26mm tubes, the variables on 30mm. They are also offered with integral mounting rails. Internal adjustments are valued at 1cm per 100 meters (about ⅓-MOA). The most notable difference between the lines, probably, is that the Zs have the reticle in the first (forward) focal plane, which means the reticle seems to grow larger as power is increased, while the C line's reticles are in the second focal plane, so the reticle is coarse at bottom power and grows finer as the magnification is increased.

The Cs are built on 1-inch tubes and use conventional ring mounts. The click value is ¼-minute except in the 1½x12 and 1½-4½x18, where it's ⅓-minute. In general, the Cs are shorter and lighter than equivalent power Zs. The C models are offered with Z-Plex or crosswire reticle, while the straight power Zs have a choice of at least half a dozen; variable Zs have the standard Diavari reticle—three tapered posts. Both Zs and Cs have multicoated lenses.

So . . . anyone who wants a Zeiss has considerable choice. I've been using a Diatal-C 4x32 for some years. It would be hard to find a better all-round big game scope. ●

IT'S A STEEL

PARKER REPRODUCTION
WINCHESTER
WINCHESTER
SUPER-X
SUPER-X MAGNUM STEEL SHOT SHOTGUN SHELLS
STEEL SHOT
PARKER REPRODUCTIONS
by Winchester
The Parker Reproduction, called by many gun writers "the Best Shotgun for the money"; may be the answer to your steel shot problem. Superior construction, good old-fashioned quality, chromed lined bores and barrels that are brazed together rather than soldered, coupled with a $2,970 price tag, makes the Parker Reproduction DHE the best value for your dollar in 1988.
Steel a few minutes and call 1-800-647-2898 for the name of your nearest Parker Reproduction dealer and enjoy a lifetime of shooting pleasure and reliability.

BASIC TRAINING for the BIG GAME.

The Dan Wesson HUNTER's PAC is meant to be used. Some shooters practice on silhouette targets, others cut paper and yet others sharpen their skills by varmint hunting.

Consider the prairie dog, a fairly small target at say 50 or 75 yards. Seen through a variable 1.5 to 4 power scope, a superb sight picture is presented. Those of us who enjoy practicing on varmints think of this as a challenging target...a chance to refresh some basic training in preparation for bigger game.

Now let's consider the bigger game— say a whitetail— a larger target, but a skittish challenge at maybe 100 yards. However, after practicing on varmints, you will feel confident, when the cross hairs of your scoped **Dan Wesson** rest on the "kill zone".

Whether hunting or target shooting,winning performance doesn't just happen, it starts with a **Dan Wesson**, some basic training and continues with practice.

The **Hunter's Pac** features the ultimate in versatility and accuracy, available in most magnum calibers, each "**PAC**" includes an 8" vent heavy revolver, and an 8" vent shroud with either a fixed 2 power or variable 1.5 to 4 power scope already mounted.

The complete gun and accessories come in a locking attache case designed for secure, convenient travel.

Visit your local dealer or write **Dan Wesson** for more information on the **HUNTER'S PAC** and other quality handguns we offer.

Dan Wesson...the name means accuracy.

To receive a Dan Wesson patch and a copy of our latest catalog, send $1.50 to:

Dan Wesson Arms
293 Main Street
Monson, MA 01057 U.S.A.
413/267-4081

YOU ASKED FOR IT,
TAURUS HAS IT.
TAURUS PT 58 S .380 ACP
KHA01649
TAURUS PT 58 S .380 ACP
At Last, An Affordable, Quality 380 CAL
The new Taurus Model 58, 380 CAL is now available at your local gun shop.
We have taken the proven design of the world famous PT92 and produced a compact 13 shot 380 CAL pistol that meets the highest standards of accuracy and dependability.
A Taurus is an ideal choice if you're a first-time handgun buyer and perfect for the experienced shooter.
Shooting a Taurus handgun gives you the opportunity to use a product that has been built from high-quality materials to the latest specifications.
Taurus offers a comprehensive selection of styles and calibers; .22 LR, 32 Long, 38 Special, 357 Magnum, 9MM and 380.
EXCLUSIVE LIFETIME REPAIR POLICY
Taurus will repair your Taurus handgun free of charge for the lifetime of the weapon. No other handgun manufacturer makes this offer! See your dealer and ask to see the top-value Taurus line.
TAURUS
USA
International standards of craftsmanship and reliability
TAURUS INTERNATIONAL, 4563 S.W. 71st AVENUE, MIAMI, FL 33155

LARRY SMITH's LITTLE GUNS . . .

. . . he makes them one at a time.

by DAVID PHILLIPS

Photos by the Author

IMAGINE TINY guns with the complex inner workings, the engraving, even the threads on the screws all scaled down in the exact proportions of the full-sized original guns crafted by hand out of the same materials as the originals. And each one able to fire tiny handmade cap and ball ammunition.

The miniatures—the ones we're talking about—are made by Larry Smith and his wife Joan in their shop in west central Florida and are good enough to earn them a living. Watching the husband and wife team work on those beautiful little guns, you can see the pride of the craftsmen of old in their hand-made creations.

Larry Smith's interest in making miniature guns goes back to his childhood. It's an interesting story:

"I was interested in old, antique Colt revolvers, the Paterson, Walker, Dragoon models. When I was a kid there were a lot of cowboy and Indian movies. The frontier wasn't all that far removed. There were still old-timers who talked about, 'Oh, my grandfather was this and that.' They could

For this Ehlers 4th Model Paterson pocket pistol (Baby Paterson) the dime in box lid shows scale. This miniature has full working parts, engraved cylinder—even the lock on this box and the key are scaled-down exact duplicates.

This 1836 Colt Paterson holster model (the "Texas" Model) is cased with spare cylinder and accessories—case and all would fit in a pocket.

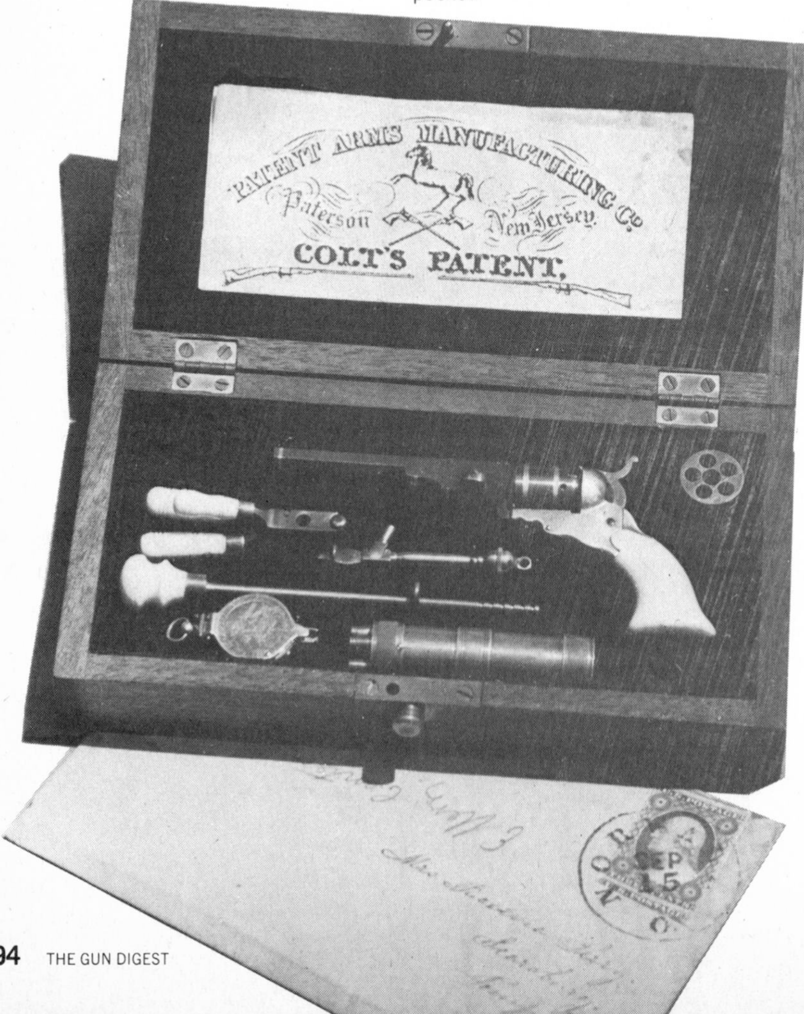

still remember back to the days of the frontier or had heard stories of it so it was still pretty prevalent in people's minds and it just fascinated me; all of that and the Civil War. So when I saw a beautiful color picture in one of the early sporting magazines of early Colt revolvers I thought this particular Paterson model was such an interesting, streamlined looking gun that I went 'Gee, I'd like to make a little tiny one of it—a model.' So that's what I proceeded to do."

That first model, done at the age of 12 or 13, was made out of lead. "I used a ballpoint pen for the barrel and drilled the cylinder out of a piece of brass with a hand drill," he recalls.

Nowadays he has reached a level of sophistication in his construction of miniatures where he is making museum quality pieces, some of which sell for close to $1,000. Largely self-taught, Larry has trained his wife Joan in the various skills required to make the miniatures and she shares the work with him. There is much preliminary work involved in fabricating the miniatures and Larry chooses with care which guns he will be producing.

"I do the ones I'm interested in," he says. "But a gun has to meet certain criteria: Is there sufficient interest in the gun that people will buy it? Will it lend itself nicely to miniaturization? The reason I picked this Remington model (Remington New Model Pocket Revolver) is you can see the trigger—it doesn't have a trigger guard so it's easier to fire than one with a trigger guard. I also consider how well a gun will look if it's engraved and the aesthetic qualities of a gun: is it interesting and streamlined looking?"

Once he has chosen a particular model for miniaturization and determined the reproduction scale he wants, Larry will break down the original gun and do accurate drawings of its parts to the scale he has chosen. Not all the guns he makes are of museum quality. He makes a slightly modified version of the Paterson Colt with a fixed trigger (the original has a retracting trigger) and a simplified action.

"My objective in building this was just to make a little revolver of the Colt pattern that could be fired like the big Colt and that would shoot really well so people could have fun with them," says Larry. "I wanted to make a gun that I could sell at a reasonable price."

The Paterson Colt he makes sells for about $200 with case and accessories. He and Joan can make four or five of these in a week. On the other hand, they make a John Ehlers 4th Model Paterson Pocket Pistol (the "baby Paterson") which is a museum quality miniature.

"All the internal parts are exact," says Larry. "I even had to make a special die to run the threads on this barrel here—these little threads where the barrel screws into the frame—there wasn't any die that I could buy that was the right size thread for that because I scaled it right down from the original. This one is fully operational: if you pull the hammer back, the trigger pops down, the cylinder revolves and it has many tiny little parts inside, exactly like the original. I've gone to such great lengths as to put the cylinder engraving on—I engraved that by hand—and the little cones on the back are exactly like the original Paterson."

It took Larry about a month and a half to build the first two of these including all the engineering, drawings and accessories. This one sells for $850 to $1,000.

As you can imagine, the preliminary work involved in one of these exact, scaled, museum quality, complex models is far greater than for the less expensive, simplified miniatures. The drawings take anywhere from a day for the simple derringers to 4 or 5 days for a complex revolver such as the baby Paterson. In addition to scale drawings, Larry often uses sheet metal templates in order to ensure that contours and other parts of the gun are accurate and true to the original.

After the initial breakdown and drawings are done, Larry gets his steel together, figures out what thicknesses he needs and begins fabrication. He cuts off lengths of steel with a power hacksaw and faces the ends with his milling machine. To bore the barrels and cylinder pins he either uses a drill fixture in the drill press or the lathe or milling machine. These guns are being built to fire actual ammunition and the work has to be very exact. The metal pieces are milled and lathed and drilled. The grips are hand-made from ivory, pearl or walnut. Even the cases and most of the ammunition is made in the shop.

One of the reasons Larry's miniatures are such faithful copies of the original guns is that he is largely using the same methods of manufacture as were used when the originals were made. True, his machinery is powered by electricity and the machines of the mid-1800s were not, but the equipment and the methods are otherwise very similar.

"The final fitting and polishing that we do—that's exactly how they had to do it in those days: by hand," Larry explains. "They took pride in their work. The big companies like Colt, Smith & Wesson and Remington were pretty well automated as far as automated machines were concerned. But still the guns, in their final stages, were hand fitted and hand polished."

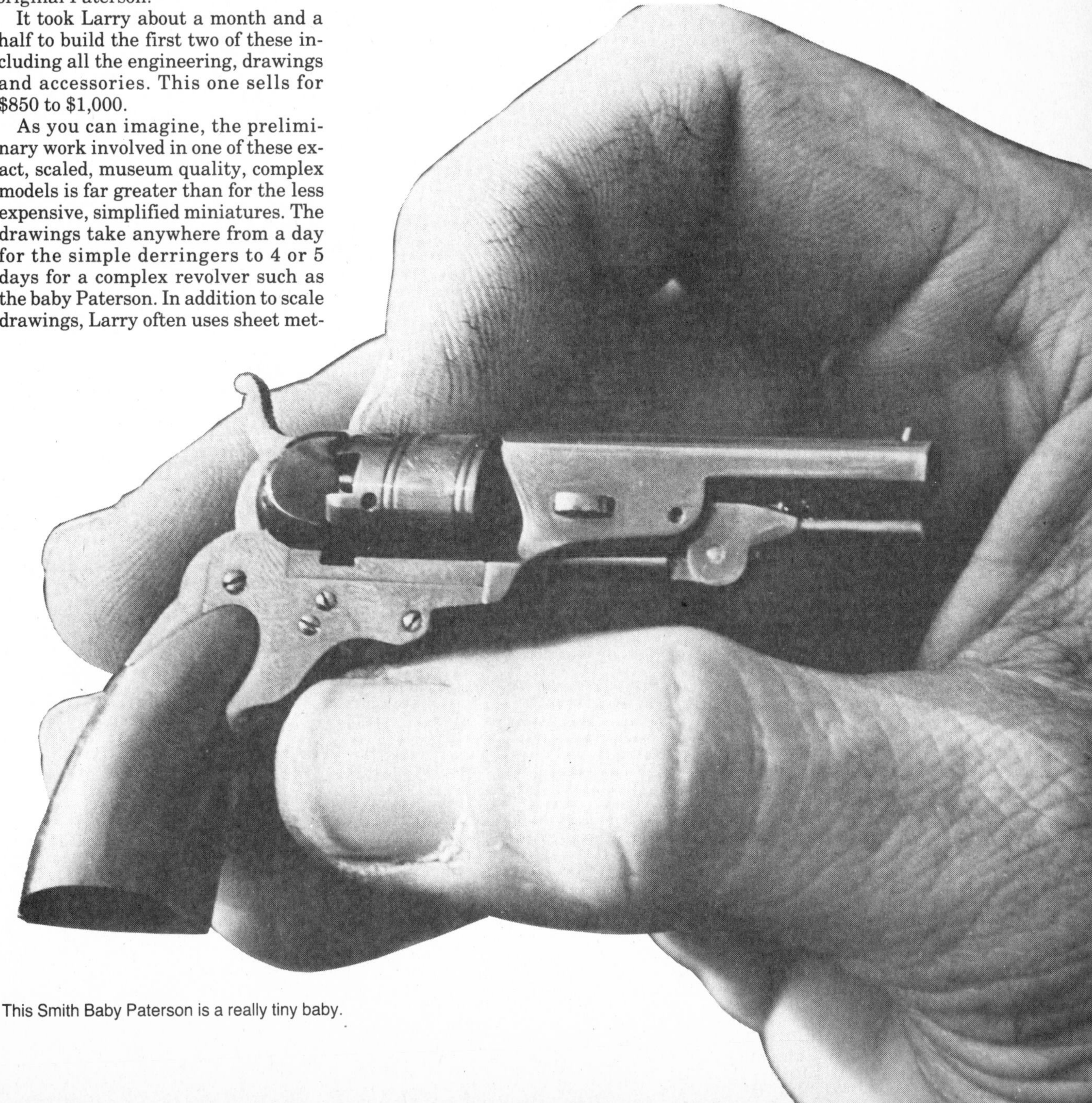

This Smith Baby Paterson is a really tiny baby.

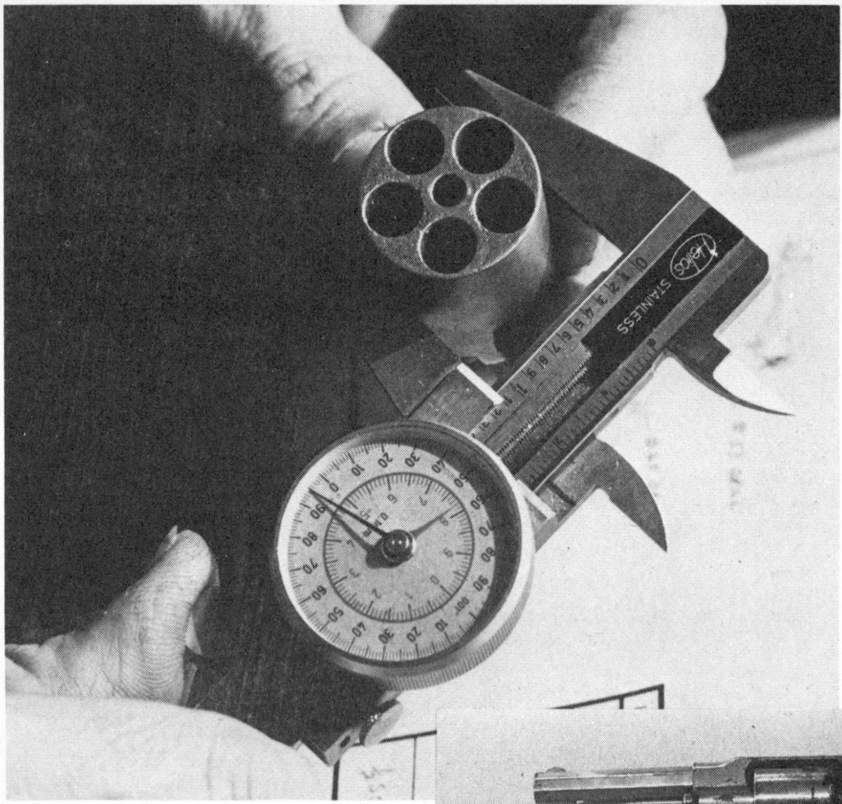

Larry Smith measures the cylinder of a Remington pocket revolver for a drawing. He takes off all dimensions from guns.

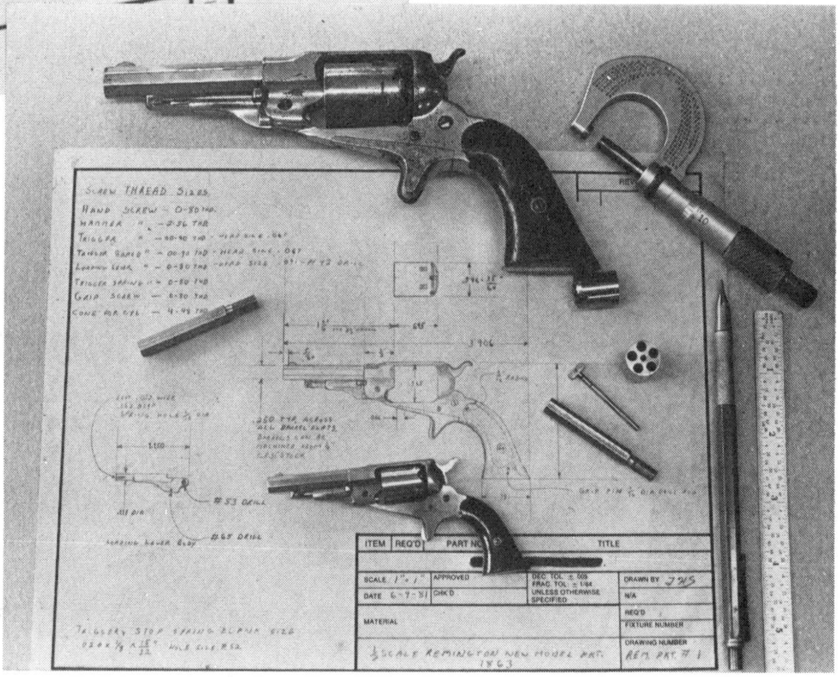

The work starts on metal only after the work on paper is finished.

In the Smith shop, Joan does most of the final polishing. Larry taught himself how to engrave and he does all the engraving by hand.

He explains the process: "Joan will polish it down to 320 grit, then I'll engrave it if it's going to be engraved, then she'll polish it down to 600 grit and then take it and give it a light buff. We're careful not to round off the corners, keeping it nice and square."

Even the springs are made from soft spring stock and then heated to harden them. Where the metal is blued, it is done by the old method of heating it to a certain temperature and plunging it in oil, a tricky process since it involves maintaining the steel at an exact temperature.

Just about everything that goes into the miniatures is made by Larry and Joan. They carve the grips from ivory or pearl or walnut; they make the boxes and even the locks and keys on the museum quality miniatures are hand made to scale—exact replicas of those on the original boxes; they finish and line the boxes; the labels are scaled down from the original labels; they make just about all their own ammunition and caps and the boxes for them; any writing or engraving on the original is scaled down and engraved on the miniature; they make leather holsters for some of the holster models. About the only things they don't make are the little brass hinges on the boxes and some of the standard screws. The attention to detail is fantastic. The standards of manufacture are very high. Each gun is test fired before the final polish and stamped as having passed inspection before it leaves the shop.

All together Larry and Joan have made about 800 miniatures since 1972, including five rifles. Customers order the guns at gun shows and specify barrel length, type of grip and any other particular details they want on their model. The Smiths always have more orders than they can possibly keep up with but they don't drop their quality or cut corners and their prices stay surprisingly low. It makes one suspect that they're in it for love rather than money and Larry confirms that they really do enjoy their work.

Larry is particularly interested in

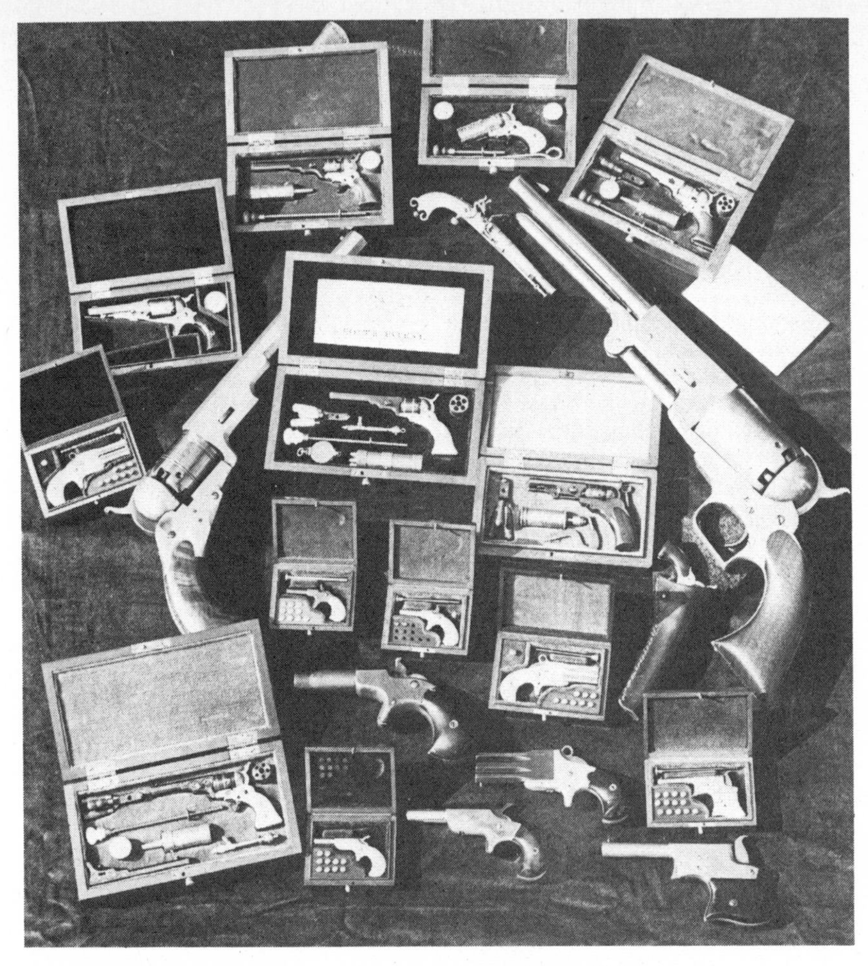

The big ones here are replicas, too, but they're original size. All the rest are Smith's teeny-tinies.

Joan Smith polishes a lot of little guns, works here on the grip of an 1836 Colt Paterson holster model. It has ivory grips and silver inlay.

the guns of the 1830s through the 1890s starting with the percussion period and going through into the cartridge gun period. He is versed not only in the history of the guns themselves but also in the history of the period in which they were used. He has a knack of tying the history in with the guns. As he demonstrates how the Colt Paterson fires—he confesses that when the grasshopper population gets too great he has seriously reduced their numbers with the miniature cap and ball '36 Colt—Larry recalls various anecdotes from history connected with the weapon: "This is from the Indian War period, late 1830s and early '40s. They were used here in the Seminole War and Samuel Colt came down here personally to sell them to the troops because he wasn't able to secure a government contract at that time . . . The troopers saw the merits in them and bought them with their own money.

"One of the first battles where the Colt Paterson pistol really made its mark," he goes on, "was when 15 Texas Rangers under Jack Hays were ambushed by 84 Indians and the troopers were armed with two of these pistols apiece. When they swooped down on them and the troopers fired their first shot, the Indians thought they had them but the Texas Rangers managed to shoot quite a number of them and chased the rest off."

Somehow seeing the guns seems to add reality to the stories. You can almost see the men with the guns that their lives depended upon.

Larry Smith is very knowledgeable in the history of this period and an expert on the guns that were in use. He can tell you who made which guns, who used them, their drawbacks and advantages and virtually anything you might want to know about them. He has a fairly complete collection of original guns from this period, quite in addition to the miniatures he has made. But above all, Larry is a master craftsman, a perfectionist who takes great pride in his work. The products that come out of the Smiths' shop are his joy to behold. Each gun in its case with all the accessories is like a little jewel, the engraving and silver inlay work perfect. And each one has its own history.

Perhaps characteristic of the man is that one of his hobbies is building scaled down steam locomotives which the kids in his neighborhood come and ride around the track laid in his garden. The trains are as beautifully made as his guns. A craftsman is a craftsman, and Larry displays his skill in everything he makes. ●

BLACK POWDER REVIEW

by DOC CARLSON

THIS YEAR, as always, I could only skim the cream at the SHOT Show. I made it a point to see all the muzzle-loading-oriented displays and booths. This doesn't really do much to cut the wear on shoe leather, however. One still has to walk every one of the miles of aisles. All in all it's a tough job, spending 3 days looking at firearms-related products and playing with all the new things, but then someone has to do it.

I noticed fewer "gee whiz" new products this year, and more no-nonsense stuff and more quality in both accessories and firearms. The industry has grown up, I think, and the maturity bodes well for the shooter.

There is also a definite shift toward the hunter, the person whose main interest in muzzle-loading is taking game in the special seasons many states offer. Tradition is secondary to many of these folks and totally out of the picture for others. They are interested in firearms and accessories that do the job with the least amount of hassle. They want something that works with minimal study and tinkering on their part. So a growing segment of the blackpowder industry serves these people.

One of the new breed of non-traditional rifles introduced this year is the Knight MK-85 Hunter made by **Modern Muzzle Loaders, Inc.** This is a rifle with the modern hunter in mind, and looks a lot more like a Remington 700 than a Hawken. The tip-off is the ramrod installed in ramrod ferrules soldered to the barrel. There are three versions—the Hunter model with a 24-inch barrel and classic walnut stock; the Stalker model with 22-inch barrel and laminated camo stock; and the Predator model with a black synthetic stock and 20-inch barrel. The stock style is the same on all, classic European, including the schnabel. The weight and balance is comparable to any modern sporter, and the modern rifle shooter will be right at home.

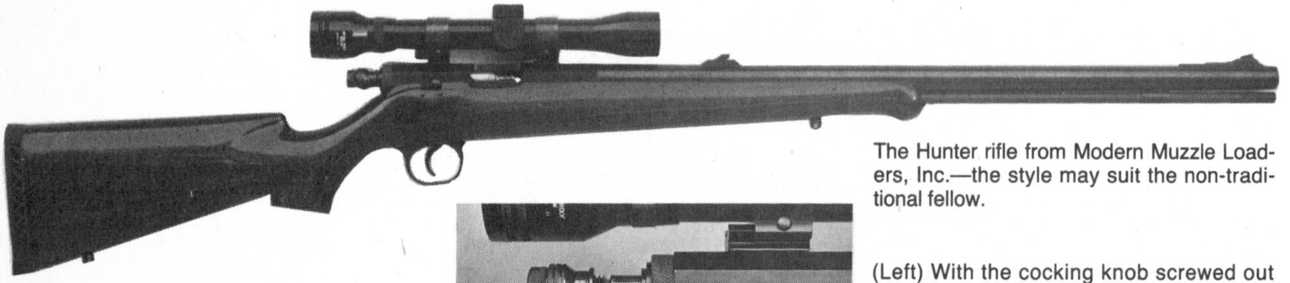

The MK-85 action is on the in-line principle, which offers two very real advantages: One, it makes scope mounting easy and has no outside ignition system to foul the scope optics, while its sighting plane is uncluttered with hammer ears and the like. Second, there is the surety of ignition. The nipple is screwed directly into the breech plug and communicates directly with the powder charge in the barrel. Ignition is instantaneous. Cleaning is easier also.

The MK-85 has coil springs so spring breakage is a thing of the past for all practical purposes. As an added bonus, the cocking knob can be screwed out a bit, drawing the striker back far enough that it won't contact the nipple. This is handy for dry-firing without battering the nipple and also works as a second safety. The primary safety is located to be easily slipped on or off with the thumb of the right hand as the rifle comes up. The Timney® featherweight trigger system that is used gives a clean, crisp pull and let off, something the modern type hunter will find very familiar.

The octagonal "receiver" portion is drilled and tapped for scope mounts, and the round barrel sports a Williams-type rear sight, fully adjustable for windage and elevation, mated with a ramp front bead. The sighting equipment is good and gives a clear sight picture.

The barrels are Bauska eight-groove muzzle-loading types with 1-in-32 twist, for the correct spin for slug-type bullets. Maxi, Buffalo and Badger bullets should shoot well in

The Hunter rifle from Modern Muzzle Loaders, Inc.—the style may suit the non-traditional fellow.

(Left) With the cocking knob screwed out slightly, the rifle can be dry-fired without nipple damage.

The Modern Muzzle Loader design is clean and uncluttered, provides positive ignition.

this rifle; patched round balls will probably give something less than target accuracy. The two calibers are 50 and 54.

All in all, I was impressed with the workmanship and handling of this new rifle. It mounts and points well and naturally. Traditionalists will have little good to say about it, I'm sure, but it will find a ready market among centerfire shooters branching out into blackpowder seasons.

Price is in the ball park—the Hunter model is to be $459.95 and the Predator and Stalker $20 more.

The **Mountain States Muzzleloading** folks were on hand with a very complete line of ramrods and the accessories to fit them. Fred Lambert, the guiding light behind Mountain States, spent 25 years working for Du Pont which accounts for his success in coming up with a synthetic ramrod that looks right, being brown wood color, and is darn near unbreakable. I say darn near because I realize that some folks take that as a challenge. The rod can be bent in a full circle with no ill effects and returns to straight. It is still stout enough for the job at hand, not having a limp or flexible feel at all. It is a welcome addition to cleaning gear, if not to replace the wood rod under the barrel.

Called the "Super Rod," these indestructible spare ramrods have a brass tip on one end that carries a jag of the correct size to clean each caliber effectively. The jag has a long tapered area for holding the cleaning patch and is concave on the end for ease of seating a round ball. The base of the jag is pinned in place on the rod so that there is little chance of it pulling off. The jag screws off and under it is a screw tip that is useful as a ball or patch puller. The opposite end of the rod is left blank so that it can be cut to length, if the owner wishes. They also make a rod with the opposite end carrying a threaded brass tip to take various swabs and jags of other sizes than the caliber the rod is intended for. Rods are made for calibers from 40 to 58. Should cover about everything.

Most of the old-timers used a much looser fitting ball patch combination than we do today. If you doubt this, when was the last time you saw a short starter among original accoutrements in a museum? The answer is never or almost never. They didn't use short starters much—didn't need them. They merely "wiped" the ball patch combination down the barrel with the ramrod. Much better for hunting anyway. Also note the small ramrods that most of the original guns carried—much too light for shoving the tight ball-patch combos we load with today. At any rate something other than the wooden rod is needed nowadays oftentimes and this synthetic rod of Mountain States fills the bill well.

Of interest also is the line of accessories that the Mountain States folks have available to fit either their rod or any other with standard thread fittings. The cotton swab is just the ticket for cleaning the bore, and the assortment of brushes they have available will get down in the corners of the rifling to get out the last vestige of fouling. Their brushes are made with the wire center core looped around the threaded base so that there is little chance of pulling the brush off the base as can happen with some of the swaged-on brushes. The swaged brushes are intended for use in breechloaders and really are not up to the heavy pull of reversing direction in a dead end muzzle-loading

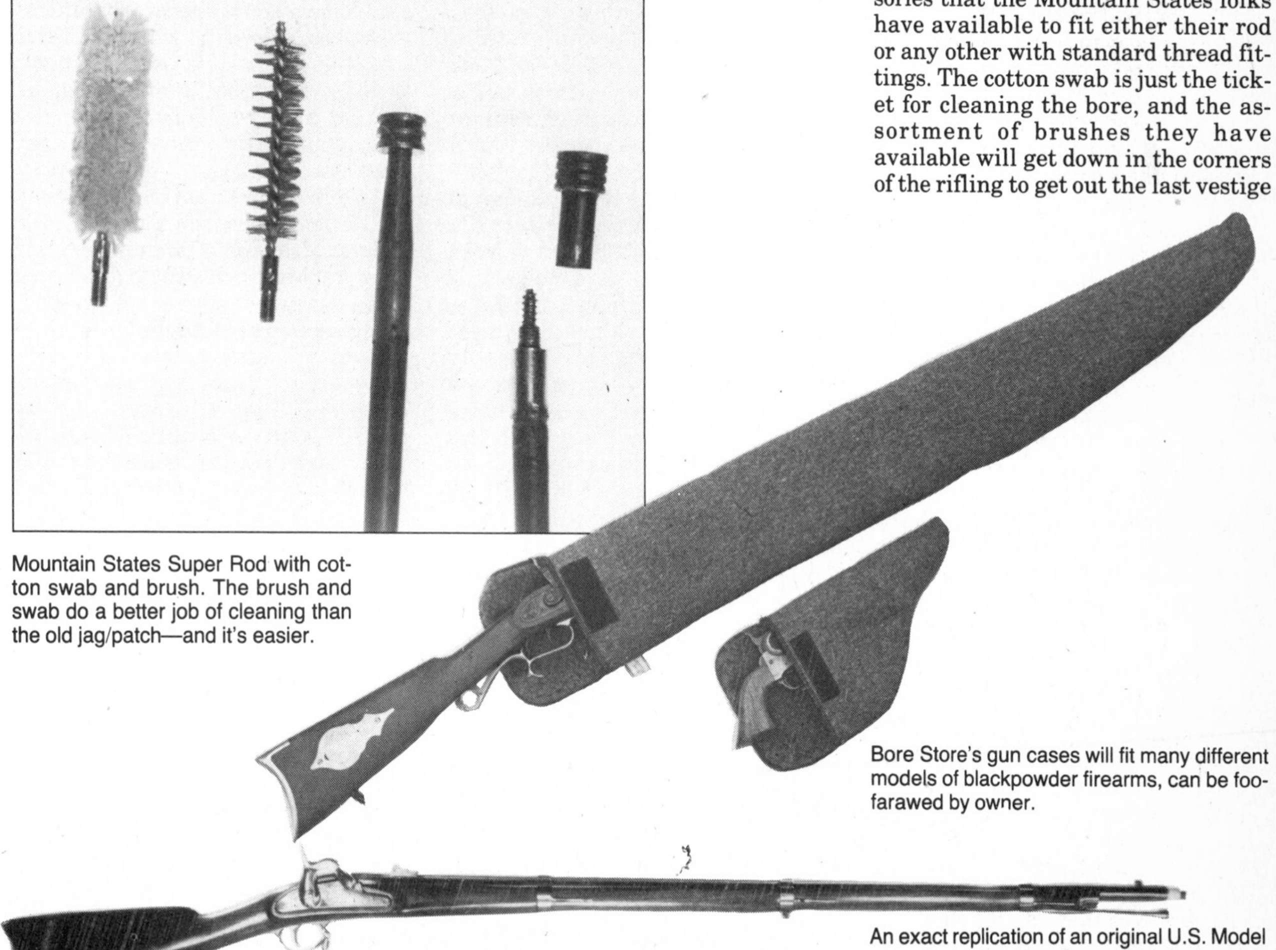

Mountain States Super Rod with cotton swab and brush. The brush and swab do a better job of cleaning than the old jag/patch—and it's easier.

Bore Store's gun cases will fit many different models of blackpowder firearms, can be foofarawed by owner.

An exact replication of an original U.S. Model 1861 Springfield has been commissioned in Japan by Dixie Gun Works. The new Miniball rifle has a one-piece walnut stock, and all the correct markings. Price will be $450.

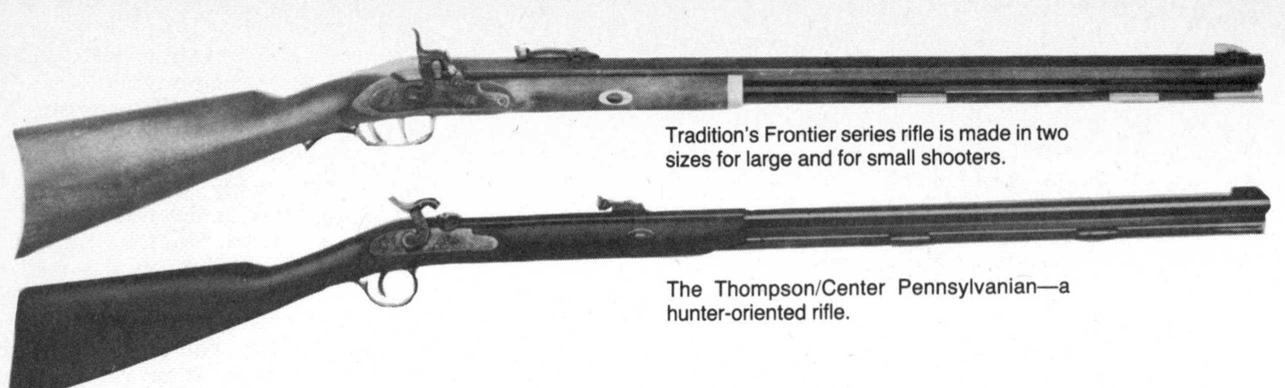

Tradition's Frontier series rifle is made in two sizes for large and for small shooters.

The Thompson/Center Pennsylvanian—a hunter-oriented rifle.

bore. You haven't lived until you pull one of these off in the bottom of the bore of your favorite rifle. It will really test your ingenuity as well as your command of the vulgar tongue to get it out, short of pulling the breech plug. Great way to spend an afternoon in the squirrel woods! Anyway, they make some nice brushes and swabs. They have also added to their line a small brass brush that looks for all the world like a small whisk broom. It screws into the end of a ramrod, is pushed down in contact with the breech and twirled. The bristles do a good job of loosening the fouling at this hard to reach place.

For those looking for a ramrod to replace the rod that came with their gun, **Blue and Gray Products, Inc.** is making a synthetic rod with both ends in place that will replace the original rod in many of the guns on the market. The rods are pretty much a copy of whatever rod came with the gun except the material is a tough, non-abrasive synthetic material that resists breakage much better than the original wood rod. Ends supplied are the same thread size as the original rod also, so all the accessories that you now have will fit. Blue and Gray makes stuff from powder can spouts through shotgun wads and quick loaders to one of the slickest nipple sealers I have had the pleasure to see. It is merely a small piece of plastic tubing of a correct size to slip over a number 11 cap. It slides over the cap and down over ther cap/nipple joint, effectively sealing out dampness. The piece of tubing is short so that it doesn't extend above the top of the cap and interfere with the hammer blow and, upon firing, the heat expands the tubing so that it comes off easily. Very ingenious and very effective.

Euroarms of America was showing a couple of new-old rifles that will be good news to traditional shooters. Euroarms bought the production tooling for several rifles from Antonio Zoli in Italy. Zoli is probably best known for the Zouave 58-caliber Civil War rifle. There have been thousands of that popular model sold to everyone from hunters to reenactors. At any rate, the first two guns coming out of the purchase of this tooling are the 1803 Harpers Ferry rifle and the 1841 Mississippi Rifle. Both are good-looking guns. The 1803 is in flintlock, of course, and is the rifle that the Lewis and Clark expedition carried up the Missouri on the Voyage of Exploration in 1804-06. The reproduction rifle has the brass furniture of the original and follows its line and design very well. The 1803 was the first rifle that the newly minted U.S. government ordered. They were made at the Harpers Ferry Armory and, being made there by individual gunsmiths, the dimension varied considerably. Later the model was standardized so there were fewer variations in barrel contours and such.

The 1803's half-stock style is slim and light in comparison with military rifles of the day. The forward ramrod pipe shows the typical funnel shape that was an identifying feature of this rifle, and the distinctive brass patch box, along with brass buttplate and trigger guard, further set it off. Overall, the rifle shows a good balance and feel that will be equally at home in the hunting field or target range. Its good looks and authentic styling will make it fit in at any buckskinner rendezvous.

Now for the best part—Zoli built the 1803 for some time. They were sold by Navy Arms Company and were known as a pretty good rifle with one fault. Zoli was already making the Zouave Civil War musket in 58 Minie when the 1803 was added to the line. So, it was logical to change the original 54-caliber to 58 and use the same basic barrel that the Zouave used. The result was a gun that looked right but never really was popular with the traditionalist. The original 1803 was a round-ball rifle, and it rankled the buckskinner types to shoot Minie balls in the gun. It didn't handle .575-inch round ball very well either.

Anyway, at the SHOT Show, while looking over the prototype rifle, I mentioned all this to discover the Italian builder of these rifles was not aware the original guns were 54s, and was very receptive to changing the caliber back. So it appears that this rifle will be made in 54 with 7 lands and grooves and a slow twist. In other words, a round-ball gun. This should be good news to the buckskin crowd and especially the Lewis and Clarkers.

As a practical hunting rifle, along traditional lines, the gun should be popular also. The 1803's military parentage shows up in a rugged lock with large enough hammer and frizzen to be a good sparker for reliable ignition. I have, personally, always liked the style of the 1803 and have carried one on several hunting excursions. Now that the caliber will be changed it "just doesn't get any better than this," as they say. Price will be $380 which will keep it within reach of most.

The Mississippi Rifle that Euroarms is bringing back is also a very nice-looking military type rifle. This is a copy of the 1841 model that was very popular with the troops of the time and was the first general issue percussion long arm to be made at government armories. It was called the Yager Rifle, from *jaeger*, German for hunter or huntsman, indicative of the degree of accuracy attributed to the rifle. The rifles were issued about 1847 to the First Mississippi Regiment commanded by a young officer named Jefferson Davis who went on to bigger and better things as the President of the Confederate States of America. Because of its identification with this famous regiment of rifles, the name Mississippi Rifle was coined.

The original pattern guns were made at the Harpers Ferry Arsenal and production-run guns were also made there. Later, in 1845, contractors were employed, including Remington. The Zouave Remington of Civil War fame was an outgrowth of this contract, the Zouave being part-way between the Mississippi and the 1861

Springfield rifles. The original caliber of this rifle was also 54 round ball with many of them being bored out to take the 58 Minie bullet after 1855. There is some chance that this rifle may be made in the original 54-caliber or may be offered in both calibers as an option.

The 1841 is shorter than the standard U.S. musket used during the Civil War which gives it a nice feel and balance. The brass hardware sets off the European walnut stock and makes a very nice-looking rifle that will rival the venerable Remington Zouave copies that are so much in evidence. The price on the Mississippi Rifle will be $380, somewhat different from the $11 that Remington and Lawrence, Kendall and Robbins companies charged the U.S. government for the guns when they made them on contract back in 1845.

Connecticut Valley Arms now offers a Siber-pattern pistol, copied from a fine target gun built by the famous Swiss gunsmith. The original is in a European museum and copies of this gun have been highly sought after by those that are involved in International Muzzleloading Competition. Now CVA has brought the gun to the market at a price of $315, considerably under what earlier copies have been commanding.

The gun is well balanced with a bag-type grip, a half-stocked pistol in 45-caliber. The 10½-inch octagon barrel is rifled with 12 lands and grooves with a 1 in 22-inch twist, well set up for target shooting. The single set trigger is adjustable for let-off and the rear sight is screw adjustable for elevation. The CVA folks tell me that fancy wood will be used in all the production guns.

There has been a definite increase in the interest in shotguns in the muzzle-loading field of late, and CVA seems to be one of the leaders of the pack with a 410 called the Brittany II, a side-by-side double with 24-inch round, Cylinder-bore barrels, fired by percussion locks hooked up to double triggers. The barrels are supplied with a hook breech system for easy take down and cleaning. The Brittany II is set up with about a 13-inch pull and weighs in at 6½ pounds with an overall length of 38 inches. At a price of $167.95 for the completed gun or $120.95 for the kit, it will be a hit for the beginning shooter.

CVA has at least two shotguns available in kit form. This allows the gun to be fitted to the shooter as the gun is finished, and the fit of a shotgun is more critical to hitting than with a rifle so I expect kit guns will be very popular. I don't believe even the first-time kit builder will have problems, and the pull, drop and pitch of the gun can be adjusted as the assembler goes along.

Thompson/Center has the "Pennsylvania Hunter," a no-frills rifle designed for the hunter. The half round-half octagon blued barrel is 31 inches long and cut with rifling .010-inch deep, 1 turn in 66 inches for use with patched round ball. It is for the hunter who either prefers or is required by law to use round ball for hunting. It is made in 50-caliber in either flint or percussion ignition. The shotgun-style stock features a flat buttplate of a hard rubber-like material; there's a large trigger guard of blued steel, big enough for use with gloves, and a single, hunting-style trigger. Overall length is 48 inches and the gun weighs in at around 7½ pounds. The breech system is the typical Thompson/Center hooked system easily taken down. I liked the look and handling qualities of the new gun. It's to be priced at $265 for percussion and $280 for flint versions.

October Country, makers of nice quality hunting bags and the like, has added several bags to their line with the shotgunner in mind. These are all made of top quality oil-tanned leather that is very supple yet is rugged and holds its shape very well. All seams are double stitched where needed for strength. The bags are designed to handle the weight that shotgunners often carry in the field to keep their guns supplied with shot and powder. Shotguns require more "foo-fa-rah" than the average rifle to keep them running in the field. The pouches and shot bags from October Country fill this need.

The first of these bags is called the English Fowler bag. This large bag measures 8 inches by 10 inches and has two inside compartments for wads. The bag is large enough to carry all sorts of gear—probably more than you'll need. We all do that, it seems. Its strap is a full 2 inches wide, a real plus when carrying much weight for an extended period of time, and has a shot pouch or "snake" attached with an Irish-type spout for dispensing shot, and it will hold a couple of pounds of shot.

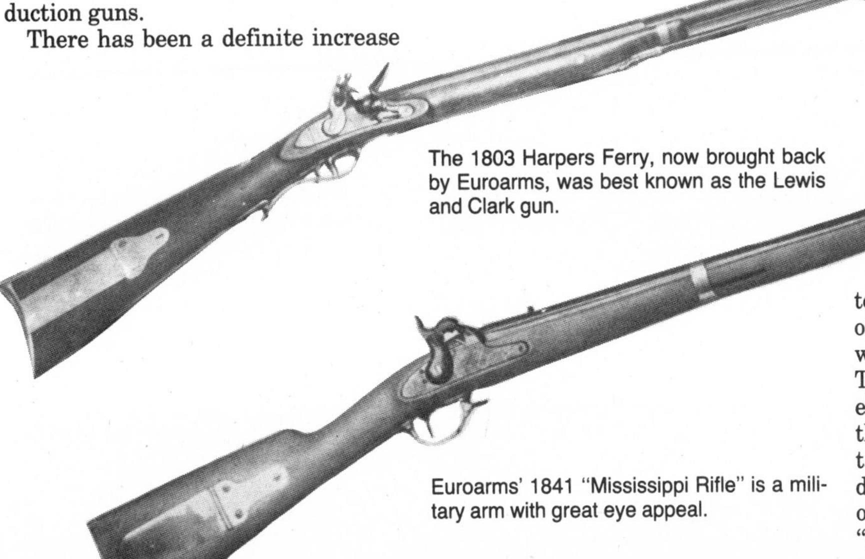

The 1803 Harpers Ferry, now brought back by Euroarms, was best known as the Lewis and Clark gun.

Euroarms' 1841 "Mississippi Rifle" is a military arm with great eye appeal.

The other new product from the October Country outfit is a rebirth of the old "shot snake" that was popular with shotgun hunters of yesteryear. This is a wide strap that holds an elongated shot flask or pouch—hence the name "snake." The long shot container coils around the body and helps distribute the weight of the 3 pounds of shot that the pouch holds. The "snake" ends in an Irish-type dispenser head—the type that features a dipper-type dispenser.

Both shotgun accessories are well

made and will last long enough to hand down to at least one generation of grandchildren. The English Fowler bag is priced at $92.25 with the shot pouch attached and $70.25 without it. The Shot Snake is priced at $39.50.

There has always been a shortage of gun cases for muzzle-loading arms. The long length of most of the rifles and shotguns of this ilk preclude the use of many of the modern cases—besides they just don't look right with a muzzle-loading arm. The alternative was to get into either custom made ones or fairly high priced leather cases. There has been little in the way of reasonably priced protective muzzle-loading gun cases until now. An outfit with the unlikely name of **Bore Stores Inc.** is making a very reasonably priced gun case for all types of guns, including the longer muzzleloaders. They are synthetic, but they will probably pass muster at most of the traditionalists' gatherings, if "duded up" a bit, and are certainly the answer to a hunter's prayer for a cheap, well-made protective gun case. With reasonable handling, these cases will protect your favorite muzzleloader, or modern gun for that matter, against rust, dings and scratches. The cases are closed with a flap that is secured with Velcro. Just fine for most purposes—the traditionalist may want to replace that with a tie. They are made in several lengths and sizes for rifles and pistols both and priced under 10 bucks. **Traditions, Inc.** has expanded their line into the hunter market. A new rifle that I noticed was their Hunter model. This is basically the old tried-and-true brass-mounted Hawken-type rifle with some hunting ideas added. It's rifled with a 1 in 66-inch twist for patched round ball shooting; buttplate, trigger guard and ramrod ferrules are all blackened so that no shine or reflection is likely. It has standard double-set triggers typical of the breed. It is available in either 50- or 54-caliber and should find ready acceptance in the hunting field priced at $259.

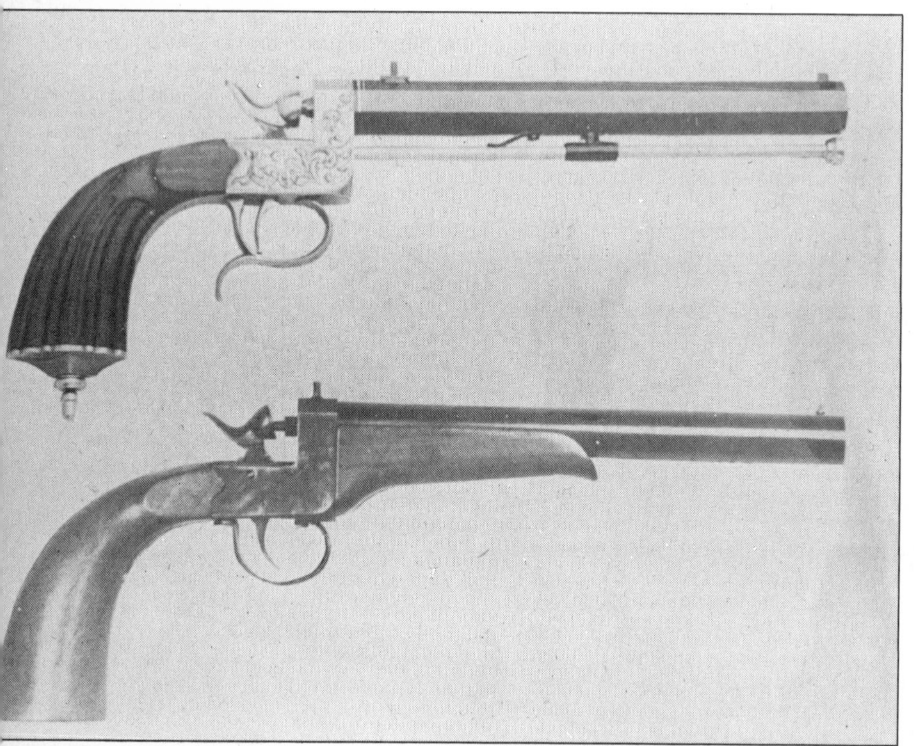

The Zimmer or Parlor pistols from Trail Guns Armory/Pedersoli come in two versions—the deluxe, above, and standard, below.

There is also the Frontier series of rifle which is basically the standard half-stock-plain-Jane rifle that has been their stock in trade for some time, but they now offer both a rifle and carbine model of this simple rugged little hunting rifle. The Standard version is available in flint or percussion ignition and in 50 or 45 calibers. The barrel length is 29 inches and the triggers are double-set double-throw—the gun is very similar to the Hunter except it has brass hardware, a flatter buttplate, beechwood stock, and only one barrel key. The carbine Frontier rifle sports a 25½-inch barrel and is available in percussion only. The entire gun is scaled down so that it fits the smaller statured shooter very well. The two guns are identical, in percussion at least, except for size, and might be a nice pair for a husband and wife or father and son or daughter. The smaller gun would be "just like Dad's." Sort of a nice idea, I thought.

What do you do when the weather is bad and you have the urge to do a bit of shooting to keep your eye sharp? Well, one answer is to do as they did in the 1800s and pick up your Zimmer pistol. Called "Parlor Guns," these little rifles and pistols had small bores and used the force from a percussion cap to propel a lead ball with surprising accuracy to 10 yards or so. They were very popular in Europe and to a lesser extent in the U.S. during the 19th century. Now it's possible to have one of these guns without going to the trouble and expense of finding an original. **Pedersoli/Trail Guns Armory** have brought a small Zimmer to the market. The guns are also available in 36-caliber so that the same "feeling" gun can be used in the field.

The Zimmer pistol is a 4.3mm caliber (about .17) and weighs in at about 1½ pounds. The barrel length is 8$^{1}/_{16}$ inches and the overall length is 12$^{19}/_{32}$ inches. The small pistol fits the hand well and points nicely. It would be just the thing to while away a rainy afternoon or to shoot in the backyard on a sunny one. The only charge used is a percussion cap which drives the small lead sphere with surprising force. Accuracy is good enough to make it interesting.

The little gun is made in two versions, a plain model with case-hardened frame and plain wood stock and forend and a deluxe version with fluted buttstock and engraved frame. The deluxe version has no forend and a ramrod is attached under the barrel. To fire, the lead ball is seated down the barrel and a cap is put onto the nipple. That's all. About as simple as it's possible to get. A full afternoon's shooting session costs about what a six-pack of your favorite libation would cost.

I'll probably have one of these for both target practice and to entertain the neighborhood sparrow population—I doubt that the bullet will do more than make them very nervous, but it'll be fun to see if they can be hit. Should be a pretty good outfit to handle our Nebraska grasshoppers. I always wanted to get one of record size to hang on the living room wall. ●

Don Robinson, stockmaker of Halifax amid the hand tools of his trade.

The Man Who Sculptures Airguns

by DAVID WAYLAND

IT WAS A pleasant and slightly overcast English morning when the station wagon pulled up in front of my hotel in York. Ann and Don Robinson introduced themselves and we proceeded through the green Yorkshire countryside to their home in a quiet suburb in Halifax, about 45 minutes away.

We stopped for a bit at the John Boddy Timber Co., while Don picked out a few blanks for stocks and I browsed through a veritable supermarket of rare woods. There was a wide choice of woods not ordinarily found in the States: apple, elm, sweet chestnut, sycamore plus many varieties of walnut and tropical woods. The lumber prices seemed reasonable to me until I made the conversion to dollars.

The Robinson shop occupies a one-car garage and spills over into a built-on shed. It is, of course, one *British* car

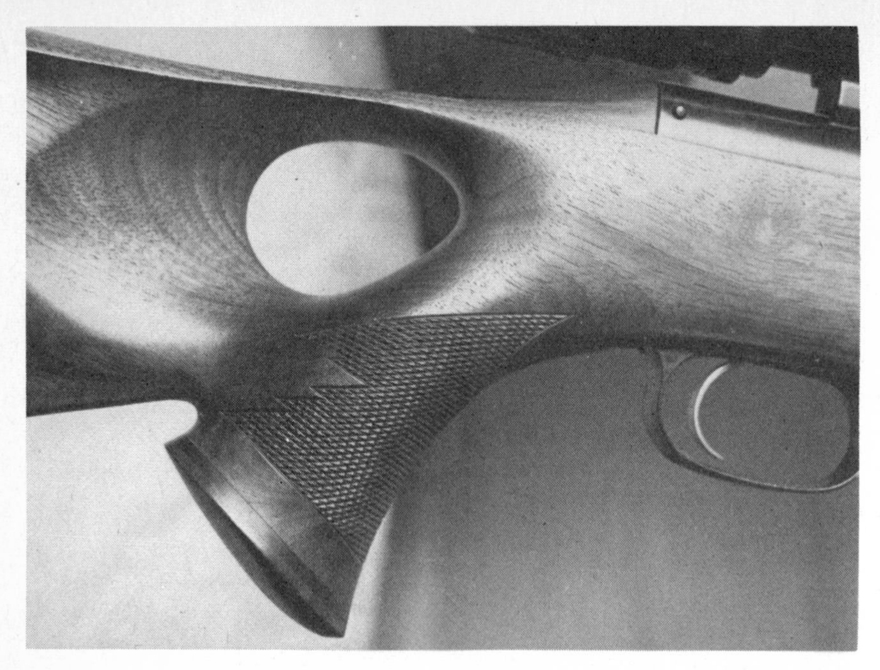

A rakish checkering pattern adorns this sleek thumbhole stock for a Weihrauch sporter. Note the gracefully curved custom trigger.

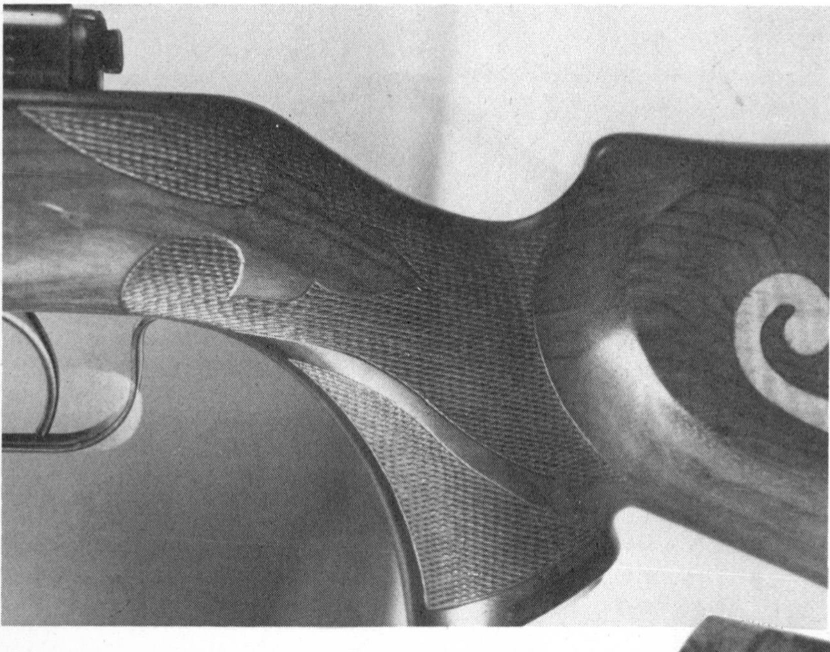

A close-up of a Bubinga stock with inlays for an FWB 124 sporter. The extra weight of a tropical wood stock helps steady the air rifle in competitive field shoots now popular in the UK.

in dimension. Every corner was filled with stock blanks, tools and unidentified boxes. Robinson works almost entirely with hand tools so there were no pantograph carving machines or pneumatic sanders that fill the shops of his Stateside counterparts.

The U.K. shooter bears the burden of an overly protective and unsympathetic government. In a population of about 50 million there are only about 180,000 firearms certificates. Without this precious document the only way to enjoy the shooting sports is with airguns. Airgun shooters must hew to the officially permitted 12 foot pounds power limit for an air rifle, so a 177-caliber airgun cannot exceed approximately 800 fps in muzzle velocity. Given that limit, the shooter is free to exploit his airgun's potential as far as his pocket will stretch. And that brings some shooters to Robinson.

Don Robinson had always been interested in guns, but got his first real exposure to their inner workings during service as an armorer in the RAF. There he became intimately involved with FN automatic rifles, Sterling submachine guns, Bren guns, Stens, and Browning auto pistols. After his service, he worked as an inspector for an engineering firm and began stockmaking part time. He has now been a full-time stockmaker for 7 years.

During my visit, the phone rang repeatedly with calls from customers and potential customers. It was obvious Robinson works the customer's side of the street. He will modify the customer's present stock more often than make a new stock from scratch. He will slim and reshape it to improve the aesthetics and handling qualities. This means adding rare wood gripcaps and forend tips, rubber buttplates, inlays, checkering, stippling,

Extra fine hand checkering covers this set of grips for a mint pre-war Colt Woodsman.

adding a scope height cheekpiece, even converting a conventional stock to a thumbhole design.

The results are uninhibited and delightfully intricate. His friendly, outgoing personality is matched by the enthusiastically flamboyant styles and decoration of his stocks.

Some inlays he makes himself, others such as veneer *fleur-de-lis* or rampant eagles are purchased from offshore suppliers. Stippling is commonly seen on match-grade airguns and can provide attractive and practical noslip areas for gripping, but Robinson takes the idea at least one step further and uses stippling techniques to

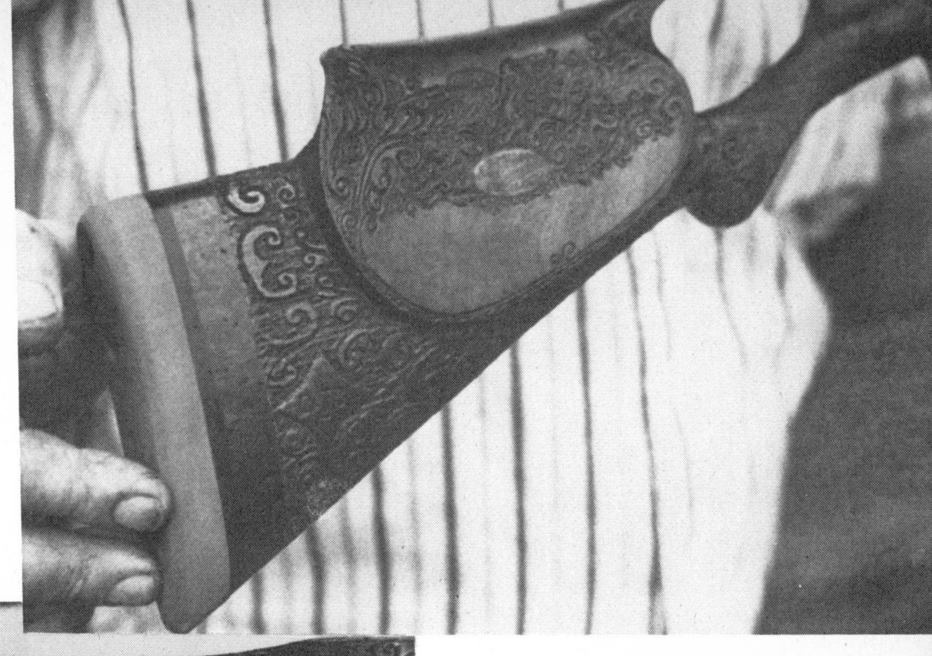

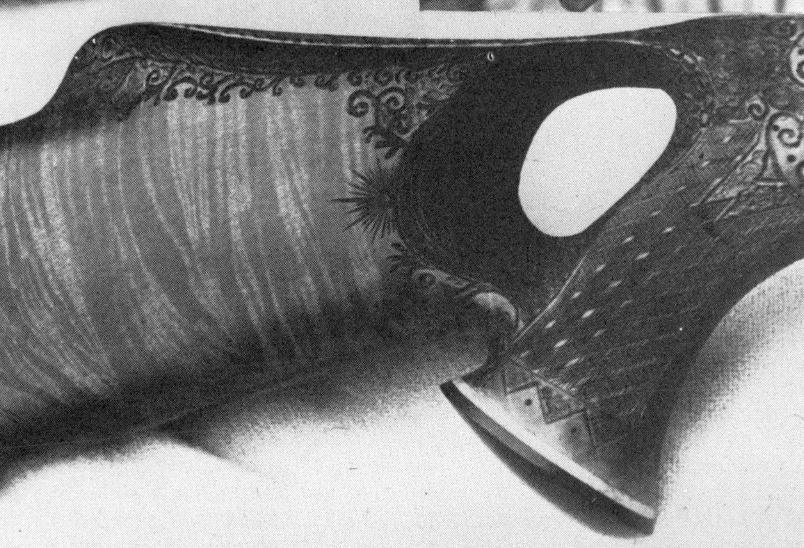

Ornate stippling decorates the buttstock of this air rifle. The stock has been converted to a thumbhole pattern and is surprisingly comfortable and sturdy.

A typical Robinson treatment of a handsomely figured piece of walnut. Ebony cap has ivorywood spacer set off by skipline checkering and stippling.

Free-form skipline checkering, inlays and overlays on a BSA stock. British airgunners are partial to more flamboyant styles than conservative firearms shooters.

create floral curves and patterns to delight the eye. Traditionalist firearms buffs will find this style unconventional, but most British airgun shooters have never owned a firearm and unless they are or become wealthy landowners may never own a firearm. They are less influenced by established gunmakers and more willing to accept more ornate styles.

Trying to find a category for Don Robinson's work is impossible. He may be a man out of his time, a throwback to the Pennsylvania custom gunmakers of the early 19th century. His work shows a joyful enthusiasm for decoration that is not in the least stifled by the stuffy conventions of Birmingham or London.

Robinson supports his business with regular "adverts" in airgun magazines. A prolific writer, he contributes articles on stockmaking, and over the years has developed an enthusiastic following. In response to inquiries, he mails out a packet of Xeroxed sheets giving prices and many shots of past work. This literature conveys the free-wheeling spirit of a talented maverick.

A typical low-end job might consist of slimming down the wrist of a stock, installing a rubber buttpad, a bit of stippling, and a refinish. At the other end of the spectrum, a customer might go for a stock made from scratch of exhibition grade Bubinga with *fleur-de-lis* checkering, ivorywood inlays, ebony gripcap and buttplate, plus a customized trigger and refinishing job on the metal.

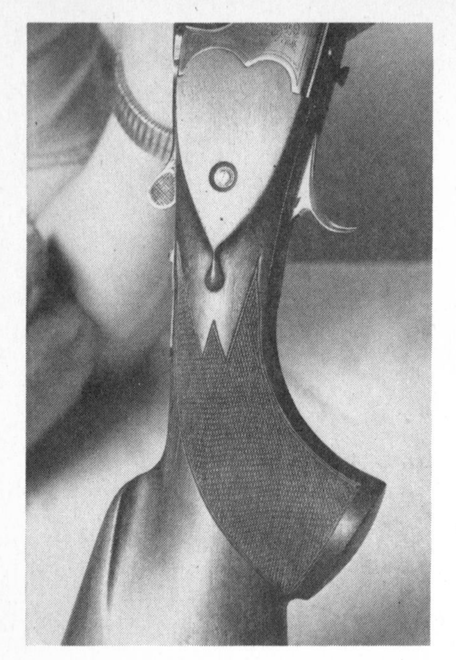

A traditional checkering pattern on a traditional shotgun stock. Robinson matches the style to the shooter's tastes.

One of the interesting custom features Robinson often adds to a stock is a Wundhammer swell made of lignum vitae or rosewood added to the existing stock. He claims the harder wood resists wear on the checkering and is favored by many airgun shooters.

In most cases, an air rifle is shot and handled a good deal more than the average firearm. It isn't uncommon for an enthusiastic airgunner to fire many hundreds of shots in a session. The low cost of ammunition and the close proximity of places to shoot are the main attractions of airgunning the world over.

Robinson's prices are reasonable by any standard. Modifications to factory stocks are the best buys: £7 for slimming a forend; £5 to reshape the grip; £7 to reshape the cheekpiece. Fitting an add-on high cheekpiece runs from £21 to £40 depending on wood. Grip-caps run £3 to £6; silver oval inlays are £8; forearm tips range from £12 to £20 depending on wood and whether the stock is a split-forend barrel cocker or a solid side lever. For a deluxe stock made of rosewood, prices start at £400. Don does a variety of metal work as well—bluing, browning, tuning, sight mounting, and trigger work.

It is encouraging to see a free spirit happily plying the custom gunstock trade amid the chilling regulations of an anti-gun government. Don Robinson is an outstanding example of the craftsman-entrepreneur at work. And he's fun, too. ●

TESTFIRE GD REPORT

TESTFIRE an AIR-GUN FIT for an EDITOR

by **J.I. GALAN**

THERE IS no doubt ultra-fancy guns tend to place their owners in one heck of a quandary. That has been my view for many years and is one of the reasons—besides an unwillingness to sell mama and the kids into slavery—I don't own such expensive shooting works of art. Most lavishly decorated guns are terrific performers crying out to be used on the one hand, while on the other hand,their exquisite elegance and finish almost demand that they be handled little—if at all.

The Editor-in-Chief deftly sidestepped all that, at least temporarily, by asking *me* if I'd be willing to shoot a brand-new custom air rifle by British gunmaker Don Robinson. Not needing any extensive prompting in matters of airguns, particularly after being told how truly gorgeous the gun in question was, I quickly succumbed to the temptation and several days later the heavily insured package arrived at my doorstep.

Being told over the telephone that a gun is a "one-of-a-kind presentation grade" or "beautifully stocked" rifle did not really prepare me for what I found inside that thick carton. Although the term "work of art" most certainly applies, it by no means can describe in its entirety the superlative workmanship exhibited by this air rifle. In fact, my apprehension index must have shot up dramatically—suppose something happened to that gun while in my possession? That was the first impression.

Robinson chose the Weihrauch

The deeply curved non-factory trigger has a gold-tone finish. The factory trigger guard has been gold-plated.

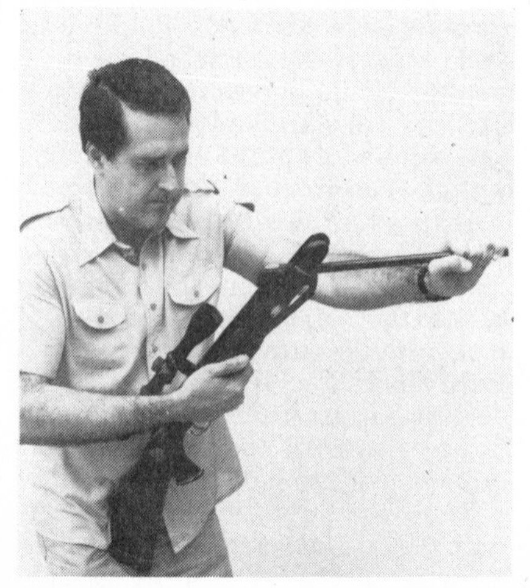

The short 16-inch barrel combined with a stout mainspring make this air rifle a bit hard to cock.

HW80K as the basis for his lavish treatment. The HW80K is the carbine version of the standard HW80. As a barrel-cocking spring-piston rifle, the HW80 has a solid reputation for its ample power, accuracy and overall quality and is one of the most popular magnum air rifles around. The carbine version shares that distinction.

This custom HW80K measures 41½ inches overall, with a 16-inch barrel. That relatively short barrel translates into a rather stout cocking effort certain to put muscles into anyone using it on a regular basis. The Robinson creation manages to tip the scales at around 8½ pounds. For my tests, I installed a Tasco 4x40 telesight and with telesight mounted, the rifle weighed 8¾ pounds; not exactly what I would care to lug around afield, but then, I don't think that anyone in his right mind would do that with such a fancy gun.

The stock of the HW80K is a vivid billboard for Don Robinson's skill, all the stops pulled. The rifle is unique in almost every way. The thumbhole style provides a massive, yet sleek and curved, pistol grip with French skip-line checkering and a black cap with white-line spacer. The forearm has the same checkering, a buy with a black tip and white-line spacer of its own. The stock above the trigger area is stippled, as is the front surface of the pistol grip. All of this contrasts rather sharply with superbly executed scrollwork of the butt and other areas of the stock. Not only is the surface of the stock gorgeous in every way, but so is the grain of the wood.

The teardrop-shaped cheekpiece ensures a "head up" position from the shooter due to its straight-line design. A black cap with white-line spacer located at the rear of the compression cylinder adds a gentle taper to the stock as it meets the blued steel of the action. Bringing up the rear there is a thick, ventilated rubber recoil pad with white-line spacer.

Metal surfaces also exhibit some distinctive touches. The trigger guard, for example, has been gold-plated, while the original Weihrauch trigger blade has been replaced by a deeply curved steel blade with a golden finish. Some narrow areas atop the rear of the cylinder and barrel have been stippled and refinished in gold tone also. Incidentally, the world-renown Rekord trigger unit of Weihrauch air rifles is still very much in evidence, despite the non-factory trigger blade. The button that disengages the automatic trigger safety is also non-factory, with a broad knurled surface.

Despite my initial apprehension about scratching the gun in any way, I was itching to put it through its paces and the results were most impressive. My electronic chronograph disclosed an average muzzle velocity of 732 fps for this 22-caliber air rifle with H&N Match (wadcutter) pellets weighing approximately 14 grains apiece. Those figures mean that the rifle on test produced an average muzzle energy of 16.6 foot pounds with the above H&N pellets. Gingerly resting the rifle on sandbags and firing at 25 yards, most five-round groups were small enough to be completely covered by a dime, with all pellet holes actually touching. Surprisingly, RWS Hobby pellets, being much lighter than H&N Match, produced average muzzle velocities of just 707 fps, while Beeman Silver Sting pointed pellets achieved an average muzzle velocity of 728 fps, with terrific penetration besides. The firing behavior of such a powerful air rifle is quite pleasant, by the way, with only a subdued "thunk" for a discharge report, even with the short barrel. It is obvious that the power plant has been tuned, judging by the absence of harsh recoil and vibration.

The time soon arrived when this super-refined HW80K had to return to the remote halls of editorial Valhalla. After experiencing what such a beautiful air rifle can do, it is clear that it would be a shame not to take it out once in a while and fire at least a couple dozen rounds with it. It can simply occupy a prominent place among other shooting works of art, of course. Either way, this superbly crafted gun is certain to please its owner, even if it creates a bit of a pleasant dilemma. ●

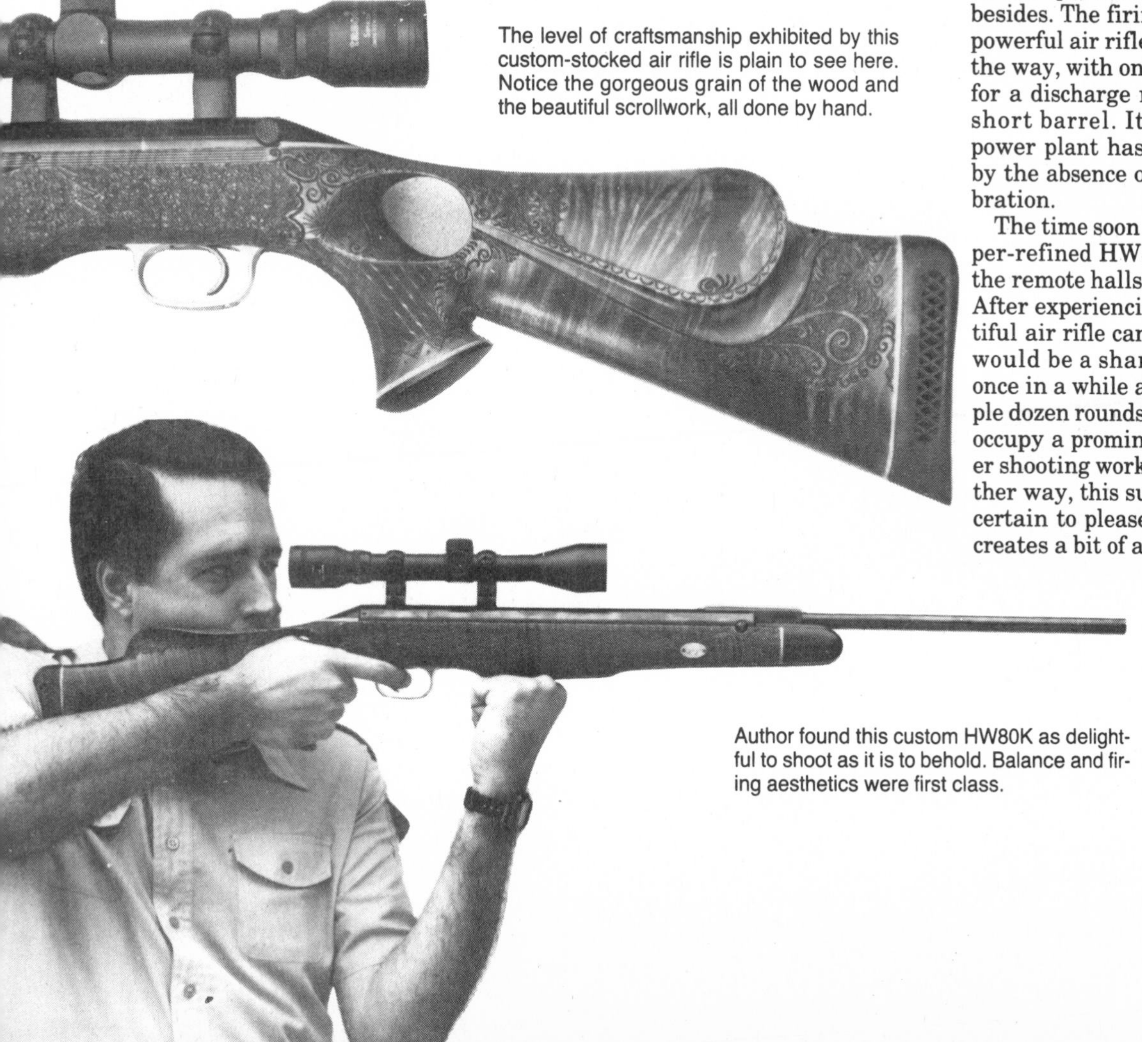

The level of craftsmanship exhibited by this custom-stocked air rifle is plain to see here. Notice the gorgeous grain of the wood and the beautiful scrollwork, all done by hand.

Author found this custom HW80K as delightful to shoot as it is to behold. Balance and firing aesthetics were first class.

TAURUS 92 and 99

STAY THE COURSE

by JIM THOMPSON

THE GENERALITIES of the Taurus story are well-known . . . purchase of plant facilities from Smith & Wesson and Beretta, who had operated factories in Brazil to service the Latin American market, ownership by Bangor Punta, once the blanket organization which also owned S&W. Less well-known is the fact that Taurus has been in business since 1939, makes a much larger variety of firearms than they market here in the U.S., and makes use of an industrial base in Brazil far better developed than most North Americans realize. Their revolvers and semi-automatic pistols, after more than 20 years of marketing in the U.S., are beginning to get serious notice, and the PT.92 and PT.99 automatics are the flagships of the line.

The latest PT.92 and PT.99 pistols offer satin chrome/nickel as a finish option, employ very nice Brazilian walnut grips in oil finish, offer the American-style left-side magazine release, and a recurved "combat" trigger guard style. The PT.99 offers an adjustable sight, and this sight has changed to a more robust configuration than earlier editions. The sight is micrometer click adjustable for both windage and elevation, and my specimen used the familiar "white dot" alignment system.

I put about 600 rounds of Fiocchi, Geco, Federal, Winchester Silvertips, and Norma round-nose through the PT.99, and this time around, experienced no malfunctions of any kind. Beretta, Taurus, and aftermarket magazines were used without distinction. I noticed that spring tension on the more recent Taurus magazines has been slightly increased over older models, and the lower tension of older models may have accounted for some of the "rock-'n'-roll" jams where rounds got jolted around atop the follower.

Firing a full 15-round magazine every time, on no occasion did the

Stripped, the Taurus PT.99 displays its precision and its ancestry. New magazines are cut to work with all models and variants of Taurus and Beretta magazine catches—top, lower left, and butt.

"spread" thus created at 25 yards exceed 5 inches from any position; from rest, it sometimes came close to 3½ inches. This won't win precision matches, but it's better than many—if not most—service-style 9mm pistols. Most barrel play on the Taurus was horizontal, reflected in a horizontal dispersion of shots resembling an egg on its side. Match barrels are now available for this pistol and its Beretta predecessor which could (in this pistol's case if properly fitted by a smith) diminish group size to its vertical maximum of about 2½ inches.

The secret to this durable aircraft aluminum frame is the manner in which edges and corners are "melted," maintaining tension and fit without introducing excessive tension and friction in the slide-frame fit. When I was researching and measuring back

While only blue Taurus PT.99s and 92s have been made so far—this is a blue PT.99—nickel finish will be offered soon.

The ejection "port" of Taurus big-bore automatics comprises over half the slide's length, so many otherwise annoying problems are eliminated before they start.

Recoil recovery and rapidity of fire with the Taurus are excellent.

in 1985 for a carbon steel copy of the unit, it wasn't my intention to claim greater wear resistance, though that might have been a side effect of the material change. I was looking for greater weight and mass for match shooters, and intended to offer a longer, compensated, nose-heavy match barrel and conversion kit to 38 Super at the same time to make a quality IPSC-style package. The Sao Paulo factory of Taurus executes the subtle operations on the PT.99 frame about as well as anybody in the world, and milled internals are about as precise as you'll see on any comparable pistol.

At a list price about $300 less than the Beretta, PT.92 and PT.99 are certainly alternatives worth thinking about for the *pistolero* in the market for a large-magazine 9mm. ●

Old Friends

My interaction with these Beretta offspring is long-standing. As a consumer, gun writer, and would-be manufacturer of a carbon-steel Beretta-cum-Taurus frame, I've spent a lot of time analyzing these pistols, from different points of view. They and the Berettas from which they were modeled have gone through several generations of change since the '70s, and both now feature passive firing pin safeties in which the chambered cartridge cannot be discharged save with the trigger fully back. Manual safeties on both the Italian original and the Brazilian pistol are now ambidextrous, though the Taurus retains its original position just above and behind the grip.

Earlier Beretta-based Taurus automatics retained the left rear magazine release and safety of the early M92s.

What everyone always asks when it's discovered the Beretta and the Taurus are being tested side-by-side is inevitable: "Which one's better?" The Taurus is tighter fitted in slide-frame junctures, the underbarrel Walther-style lock on the Taurus is typically more secure than on Berettas, and the "melting" of edges to minimize danger of cracking on the alloy frame on the Brazilian pistol is at least as well executed as on the Italian original. This is the third simultaneous test I've done of the two brands, and the Taurus pistols have always scored higher for accuracy, though they jam once in a while—I've had seven jams in a total of over 4000 rounds, all failures to feed with short bulleted jacketed hollowpoints which may have acquired odd angles of attack from recoil. I've yet to have my first jam with a Beretta in about the same amount of firing. The Taurus is set up like a sporting pistol; tolerances in the Beretta are military "service" style. Of course, a whole new generation of pistolsmiths has arisen, which can modify either pistol to "match" accuracy. And trigger jobs on either pistol are common and quite straightforward. Double actions on either are a trifle too stiff for most people, though single action on my most recent PT.99 broke at just over 4 pounds, right where I like it.

TESTFIRE

GD TESTFIRE REPORT

BROWNING'S HEAVY BUCK MARK VARMINT

by **HAL SWIGGETT**

BROWNING autoloading 22 Long Rifle pistols are made to be shot — and shot—and shot. This writer assumed that and proceeded to put his assumption to test. You think I'm kidding? The pistol journeyed from South Texas to outward from Kalispell, Montana, with a 5x Burris scope atop and *no* sighting in. There was, however, an ample supply of Federal Spitfire hollowpoint ammo. Why the super-speed stuff? Columbia ground squirrels, my friend. Starting at about 25 yards fair-sized rocks were the first targets. Once on them distances increased as rock size diminished until cartridge boxes could be hit on the 100-yard berm, and we were ready.

Columbia ground squirrels are more or less half the size of a full-grown prairie dog. Not very big targets. Accuracy of the Federal Spitfire sort of amazed the near-half-dozen shooters making every effort to shoot it faster than Federal could load it. We lost the war but came mighty close to winning that particular battle—I guarantee.

Back home most every brand of 22s available went through the pistol with nary a hangup and with at least the accuracy we have come to expect from long, heavy pistol barrels. Some of the 50-yard groups would have made a match target rifle hustle its bustle to stay in sight. One 10-shot group of Remington high velocity—not Match, regular garden-variety high velocity—printed a group so tight the 10 shots could not be counted. Most would stay under a half-dollar for five shots. Many could be covered with a quarter. I'm not favoring any brand because the Varmint Browning shot all well. The Remington 10-shot group was singled out because it was exceptional.

Browning Buck Mark Varmint with Simmons 1.5x4 scope or later 5x Burris shot well. Trigger pull was crisp at 42 ounces.

The gun is ideally suited to small game—that is, cottontail, squirrel and the like—except for a few quirks. Quirks like, with scope and mounts, 60 ounces of weight. This comes about realistically. The barrel measures .900-inch in diameter with no taper and is 9 7/8 inches long. The slide, unlike most autoloaders, is designed with a solid sight base along the top which never moves. With the scope mounted there is little to get a hold on to chamber that first round when the pistol is carried on a vehicle seat with the slide closed, as I carry it and without a cartridge in the chamber. Any carry with the slide closed and the magazine inserted would be the same.

I've found it best to carry it in my hands while walking through pastures. There are shoulder holsters available but I prefer this one in my hands. Obviously, when I'm walking in woods or pasture, there *is* a cartridge in the chamber in case a jackrabbit or squirrel attacks.

Several cottontails, only three squirrels of the eating variety, and 19 quail have fallen to the Browning plus more jackrabbits than I've tried to catalog. Head-shooting Texas quail is prime sport *if* you have a pistol sufficiently accurate for the job. This Browning Buck Mark Varmint qualified easily.

Swiggett's grandson Darryl found this Montana fence post a mighty good rest during the Columbia ground squirrel shoot.

Though I've mentioned Federal Spitfires for varmint squirreling I stick to solids in normal high velocity for eatin' game. The super speeds are great on jackrabbits.

If you're looking for a holster pistol, easy to carry and keep handy *all* the time, better pass this 3¾-pounder by. If an extremely accurate pistol is the only concern, this Varmint edition will satisfy the most discriminating. May I suggest, should you go this route, the installation of at least a 4x *good* scope. Higher magnifications of 5x, 6x and even 7x aren't out of order. The Browning Buck Mark Varmint is that good and besides, it wasn't built for a pocket pistol. ●

Ammunition, Ballistics and Components

Federal's recently announced 9mm Federal cartridge is now undergoing design changes to prevent chambering in 38 S&W revolvers.

by EDWARD A. MATUNAS

This buck is proof that the 140-grain 7mm bullet works well on deer-sized game. Rifle is Remington 700 BDL with Kevlar stock; chamber is for 280 Remington.

An old-time favorite wildcat—the 35 Whelen—has been returned by Remington in 200- and 250-grain loadings.

The new Remington 45 Auto shot cartridges will function the slide of a 1911 type semi-auto and are ideal for small pests at short ranges.

As THINGS go in the life of a gun writer, 1987 passed pleasantly. An especially bountiful harvest was taken of deer, both nearby and far away. Too, the folks at the manufacturing end of the business have come up with enough new stuff to keep me busy for another year or so. This observation applies once again and exceptionally so to Remington. A-Square's super fine game ammo is proving a real delight on the test range.

Here's the nitty-gritty of what's new and of noteworthy importance in ammunition, components and ballistics:

Remington

Continued ammunition development gives the impression that Remington is trying to insure that its customers can get all their ammo requirements from a single source. One example is their new 45 Automatic shot cartridge. It is loaded with approximately 650 No. 12 pellets. The front of the case is crimped in the familiar pie-fold of the World War II grenade launching cartridges and some of the R. Kiesel-type line-throwing rounds. The new round fed from auto pistol magazines and cycled a slide flawlessly. Patterns at 15 feet were adequate for small pests and rodents.

Handgunners using the 7mm BR will be pleased to hear it is now available in a 140-grain factory loading. With the same bullet used to load the 7mm-08 Remington and the 280 Remington, the new load turns better than 1000 foot pounds at 200 yards when fired from a 15-inch barrel.

Destined to catch a lot of attention is factory-loaded ammunition for the 35 Whelen. Available are 200-grain pointed softpoint and 250-grain

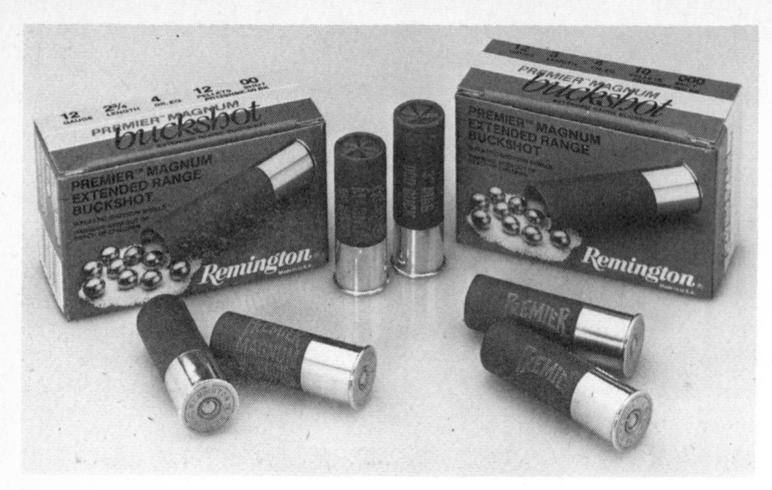

Premium grade buckshot loads are available from Remington in 10-gauge 000 and 12-gauge 00 sizes.

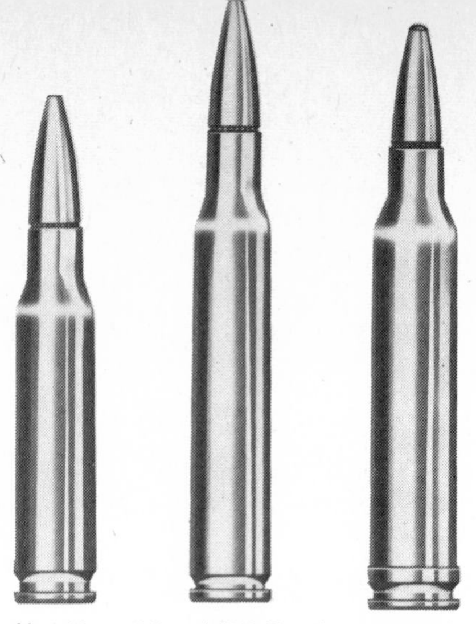

New 7mm-08 and 280 Remington rounds use 120-grain bullets and a new 7mm Remington Magnum load uses a 140-grain bullet.

semi-round-nose bullets. (Both a bolt- and a pump-action Remington rifle are chambered for the Whelen). The 35 Whelen came to be in 1922 when James Howe (of Griffin and Howe fame) necked down Col. Whelen's 40-caliber wildcat to 35-caliber so as to give it a better shoulder.

The 35 Whelen is a very useful, all-round big game cartridge, equally suitable for deer and moose or elk, and with a recoil level well below that of most popular magnums. Both bullet weights will provide more than a ton and a half of muzzle energy. Reloaders should be able to improve downrange factory load performance by using bullets with sharper profiles.

Remington offers the 308 Winchester in a new weight, a 168-grain boattail hollowpoint bullet. It is intended for match shooting, law enforcement, and, perhaps, long-range hunting. And there is a new 120-grain hollowpoint bullet in both 7mm-08 Remington and 280 Remington. Intended to slay varmints, both loads provide high muzzle velocities. The same 140-grain 7mm bullet discussed above also appears in a new 7mm Remington Magnum loading. The worth of this 140-grain softpoint was proven at a recent get-together. Remington supplied three dozen 280 Remington Mountain rifles with a box of 140-grain pointed softpoint ammo to go with each. Most of us took two deer, as well as a number of javelina. Even a few boar were killed. Ammo performance could not be faulted.

There is a new pistol load, an 88-grain hollowpoint 9mm Luger with a sizzling 1500 fps muzzle velocity and an impressive 462 foot pounds of muzzle energy. Such a very light bullet will lose velocity and energy rapidly, but at short ranges should be devastating. There is also now a 115-grain FMC (full metal case) 9mm load.

A 357 Magnum 180-grain SJHP (semi-jacketed hollowpoint) is designed to bring high retained terminal ballistics for metallic silhouette shooters. The scalloped nose should help insure plenty of expansion. This load has the highest retained 100-yard energy of all 10 Remington offerings in this caliber.

There is a 41 Remington Magnum load with a 170-grain SJHP bullet.

New Remington Rifle Cartridge Loads For 1988

Caliber	Bullet Weight (grs.)	Velocity in fps (range in yards)					Energy in fpe (range in yards)					Trajectory in inches (range in yards)				
		-0-	100	200	300	400	-0-	100	200	300	400	-0-	100	200	300	400
7mm BR Rem.[1]	140 PSP	2215	2012	1821	1643	NA	1525	1259	1031	839	NA	−0.9	+3.0	−1.8	−17.1	NA
7mm-08 Rem.	120 HP	3000	2725	2467	2223	1992	2398	1979	1621	1316	1058	−1.5	+2.0	+0.2	− 7.3	−21.0
280 Rem.	120 HP	3150	2866	2599	2348	2110	2643	2188	1800	1468	1186	−1.5	+2.0	+0.6	− 6.0	−18.9
7mm Rem. Mag.	140 PSP	3175	2923	2684	2458	2243	3133	2655	2240	1878	1564	−1.5	+2.6	+2.0	− 3.4	−14.3
308 Win.	168 BTHP	2680	2493	2314	2143	1979	2678	2318	1998	1713	1460	−0.9	+2.6	+0.4	− 8.3	−24.9
35 Whelen	200 PSP	2675	2378	2100	1841	1606	3177	2510	1957	1506	1145	−0.9	+2.6	0.0	−10.6	−31.5
35 Whelen	250 SP	2400	2066	1761	1492	1269	3197	2369	1722	1235	893	−0.9	+2.6	+1.6	−18.0	−49.8
44 Rem. Mag.[2]	210 SJHP	1920	1477	1155	982	NA	1719	1017	622	450	NA	−0.9	0.0	−15.4	NA	NA

[1]From 15″ test barrel. [2]From 20″ test barrel. All others from 24″ test barrels

New Remington Handgun Cartridge Loads For 1988

Caliber	Bullet Weight (grs.)	Velocity in fps (range in yards)			Energy in fpe (range in yards)			Mid-Range Trajectory	
		-0-	50	100	-0-	50	100	50 yds.	100 yds.
9mm Luger	88 HP	1500	1191	1012	440	277	200	0.6″	3.1″
9mm Luger	115 FMC	1135	1041	973	329	277	242	0.9″	4.0″
357 Mag.[1]	180 SJHP	1145	1053	985	524	443	388	0.9″	3.9″
31 Rem. Mag.	170 SJHP	1420	1166	1014	761	513	388	0.7″	3.2″
44 Rem. Mag.[2]	210 SJHP	1495	1312	1167	1042	803	634	0.6″	2.5″

[1]Velocity from 8⅜″ vented test barrel. [2]Velocity from 6½″ vented test barrel. All others from 4″ test barrel.

When sighted-in at 100 yards the 50-yard point of impact is only 3.2 inches high. This is a flat-shooting load, indeed.

There are a number of new Remington steel shot loads using No. 3s and even a steel shot duplex loading of No. 1 and No. 3 shot. I'm going to stick out my neck a bit and suggest that No. 3 steel shot may well prove to be the most universal steel shot size for ducks ranging in size from tiny teal to the outsized white-winged scoters. And the new steel 1x3s will probably be the best bet for combining the taking of ducks and geese with a single load. All Remington needs now are some B-size steel pellets for geese and some 1⅜-ounce 12-gauge steel shot loads.

New 10-gauge steel shot loads include 1¾-ounce loadings in BB and Nos. 1, 2, and 3 pellet sizes at a muzzle velocity of 1260 fps. Once again the No. 3 steel pellets seem to offer a good combination of pattern density and pellet energy at most duck hunting ranges. The larger No. 2 steel pellets will, of course, be the best selection for long-range duck shooting.

In lead shot, two new Duplex loads are available. For turkey hunters, the new 2x4 and 4x6 shot combinations may have appeal. And where lead shot is still legal for waterfowl, the 2x4 loading should prove ideal for a goose/duck shell. These new loads are available in both 12-gauge common lengths. The longer shell is loaded with 1⅞ ounces of shot while the standard length shell holds 1½ ounces.

With 90 percent of today's turkey hunters using No. 6 or No. 4 pellets (according to a Remington survey) the new 4x6 load should enable hunters to combine the best features of both shot sizes. I can hear the comments already: "I hit 'em with a 2x4 (or 4x6)."

And the answer: "Say what?"

Remington's 1988 Component Bullets

Caliber	Weight in grains	Style
17	25	HP Power-Lokt
22	50	HP Power-Lokt
22	55	HP Power-Lokt
6mm	80	HP Power-Lokt
6mm	100	Pointed SP Core-Lokt
25	87	HP Power-Lokt
25	120	Pointed SP Core-Lokt
27	130	Pointed SP Core-Lokt
27	130	Bronze Point
7mm	150	Pointed SP Core-Lokt
7mm	175	Pointed SP Core-Lokt
30	150	Bronze Point
30	150	Pointed SP Core-Lokt
30	180	Bronze Point
30	180	Pointed SP Core-Lokt
25	50	Full Metal Case
9mm	115	Jacketed HP
9mm	124	Full Metal Case
38/357	95	Semi-jacketed HP
38/357	125	Semi-jacketed HP
38/357	158	Semi-jacketed HP
38/357	148	Lead Wadcutter HB
38/357	158	Lead semi-wadcutter
41	210	Soft Point
41	210	Lead
44	180	Semi-jacketed HP
44	240	Soft Point
44	240	Semi-jacketed HP
45	185	Jacketed HP
45	230	Full Metal Case

Specifications For Remington's New 12-Gauge Nickel Lokt Buckshot

Shell Length (inch)	Pellet Count	Buckshot Size	Velocity fps (@ 3 feet)
3	10	000	1225
3	15	00	1210
3	24	1	1040
3	41	4	1210
2¾	12	00	1290
2¾	34	4	1250

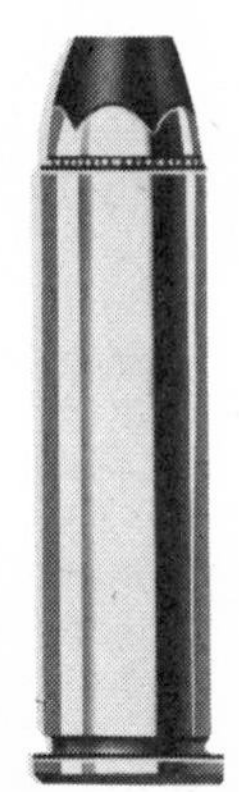

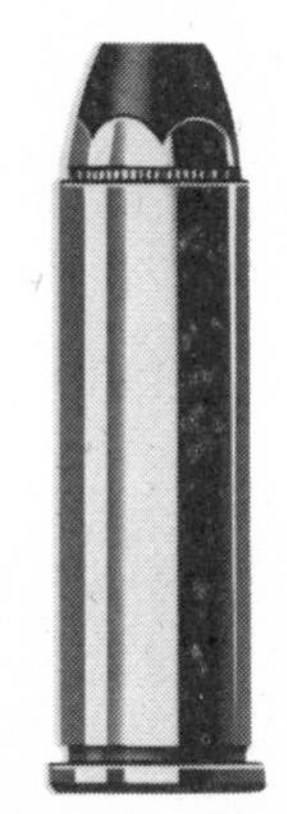

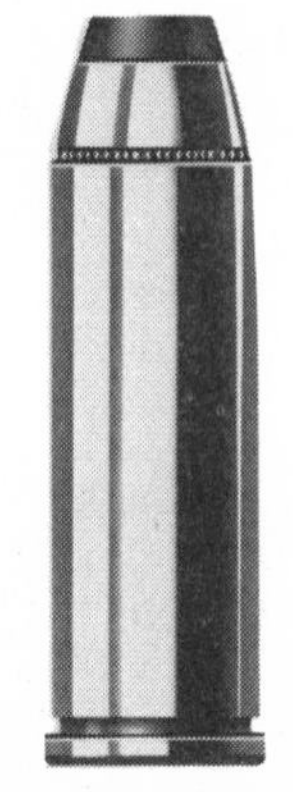

(From left to right) New 357, 41 and 44 Magnum loads from Remington include 180-grain HP, 170-grain HP and 210-grain HP, respectively.

The news I enjoyed most from Remington was that they are back in the bullet business. Not every bullet used in Remington factory ammo is available, but most of the really popular numbers are. Specifics of the 30 available bullets are shown in the close by tabulation. I'm just tickled silly with the renewed availability of my favorite Core-Lokt bullets.

Winchester

The big news from Olin this year is a premium line of ammunition called Supreme. For the present, the new line of cartridges consists of eight loads, one each in 22-250 Remington, 243 Winchester, 270 Winchester, 30-30 Winchester, 308 Winchester, 300

Winchester Magnum and two loads for the 30-06 Springfield.

Increased accuracy, higher downrange velocity and energy, and better bullet mushroom are the features of the new line, according to spokesman John Falk. Both the 22-250 Remington and the 243 Winchester loads are loaded with Hornady bullets; a 52-grain hollowpoint boattail and a 100-grain softpoint boattail, respectively.

The remaining loads all use improved Silvertip bullets. The 30-30 has a 150-grain flat base version while the remaining cartridges (270, 308, 30-06, and 300 Winchester Magnum) all use a newly designed sharp-nosed, boattail version of the famous aluminum-capped Winchester bullet.

The 270's 140-grain bullet was probably chosen to satisfy those who favor either the 130- or 150-grain bullets with but a single projectile. Muzzle velocity is suggested at 2960 fps for a 24-inch barrel. I hope so, as the 270 often is short-changed compared to advertised ballistics.

Both the 308 and the 30-06 will have a 180-grain spitzer boattail Silvertip and the 30-06 will have a 165-grain version of the same style bullet. The 300 Winchester Magnum is to be loaded with a 190-grain bullet.

At press time, Winchester supplied ballistics for the 22-250 Remington

Winchester's new Supreme line of centerfire cartridges features, primarily, Silvertip bullets, most with boattails, does good downrange job. Yes, that is a rifle bullet about to demolish the glass of water. It has in fact, already begun.

Winchester Supreme Centerfire Rifle Line Exterior Ballistics

Cartridge	Wgt. (grs.)	Bullet Manufacturer	Type	Velocity (fps) Muzzle	100	200	300	Energy (fpe) Muzzle	100	200	300	Trajectory (yards) 100	200	250	300
22-250 Rem. (control)	52	Hornady	HPBT	3750	3268	2835	2442	1624	1233	928	689	2.0	1.7	0	− 3.0
243 Win. (control)	100	Hornady	BTSP	2960	2712	2477	2254	1946	1633	1363	1128	1.9	0	−3.0	− 7.6
270 Win.	140	Winchester	STBT	2970	2762	2563	2373	2743	2372	2043	1752	1.8	0	− 2.8	− 7.1
30-30 Win.	150	Winchester	ST	2390	2018	1684	1398	1902	1356	944	651	1.7	−4.3	−11.6	−22.7
30-06 Spring.	165	Winchester	STBT	2800	2597	2402	2216	2873	2471	2114	1799	2.1	0	− 3.3	− 8.2
	180	Winchester	STBT	2700	2503	2314	2133	2914	2504	2140	1819	2.3	0	− 3.5	− 8.8
308 Win.	180	Winchester	STBT	2610	2424	2245	2074	2723	2348	2015	1719	2.5	0	− 3.8	− 9.4

and the 243 Winchester which were from control lots of ammo. Production ammo figures might be different. Also supplied were ballistics for the 270 Winchester, 30-30 Winchester, 308 Winchester and 30-06 Springfield. Specifications for the 300 Winchester Magnum loading were not available. The nearby table shows the Winchester-supplied data which was based on 24-inch test barrels.

Also new from Winchester are a 64-grain 223 Remington load designed for light big game (deer and antelope) along with FMC and softpoint loads for the 7.62x39 Russian. Some new and decidedly upland type steel shot loadings in 12- and 20-gauge, with shot sizes 5 and 7, and a new 2-ounce 12-gauge 3-inch Magnum loading are also now loaded.

Federal (and Norma too!)

Federal has developed a 9mm Luger variation cartridge, differing in that it had a good-sized rim to enable it to be used in a revolver. (Ruger's?) However, it was quickly discovered that the round would chamber in 38 S&W revolvers, a definite no-no. At this writing, the new 9mm is undergoing a design change to prevent such inadvertent usage, and perhaps by the time you read this, both ammo and a revolver will be available. Federal intends ballistics for this round to surpass all 38 Special +P or 9mm Luger levels. For 9mm Luger fans, there is a new match grade loading with a 124-grain truncated cone FMC bullet at a muzzle velocity of 1120 fps.

Federal is also now selling steel shot loads in 16-gauge. Shot sizes will be 2 and 4. However, 16-gauge users often have older shotguns which are not suitable for use with steel shot. Be certain your shotgun is OK for steel before using this new ammo.

Other new steel shot loads include 10-gauge and 12-gauge shells with BBB-size pellets and 12-gauge loads with T and No. 3 shot sizes. A 20-gauge steel shot load using No. 3 pellets is also available.

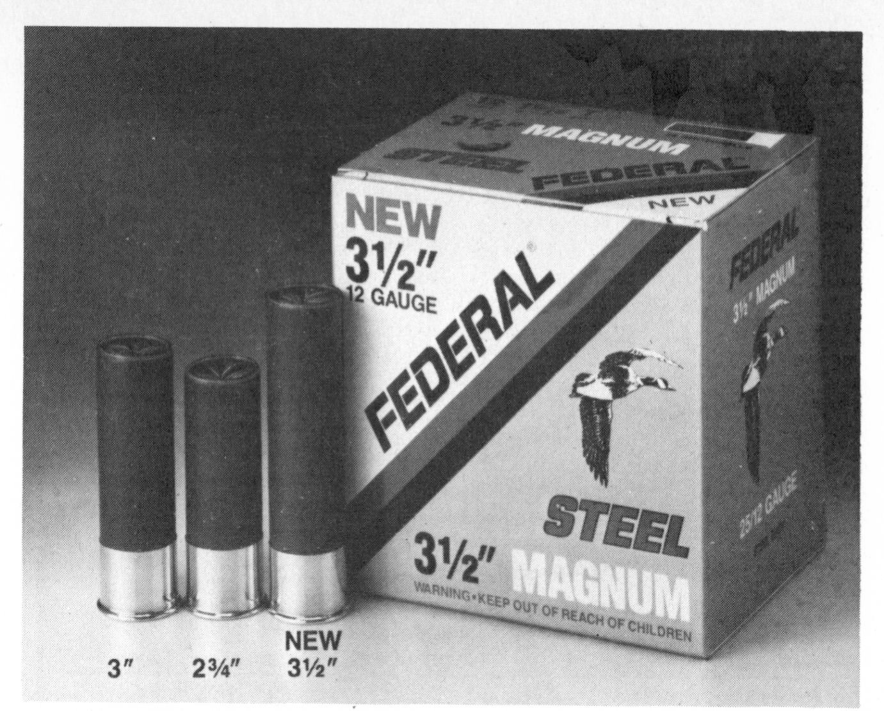

The all-new Federal 12-gauge 3½-inch shell will give steel shot loads some much needed punch.

The Norma line of ammunition, including the hard-to-get calibers, is now being distributed by Federal. That should make the Norma rounds a lot easier to find.

Really new is a 12-gauge ultimate steel shot loading employing a 3½-inch (no mistake—that's three-and-a-half) case. Initially, the new length shell will be loaded with F, T, BB, and No. 2 steel pellets with a muzzle velocity of 1300 fps. Shot charge weight is 1⁹⁄₁₆ ounces. These new steel loads will, therefore, have a higher velocity and a heavier pellet charge weight than most of the ubiquitous 1½-ounce 12-gauge 2¾-inch magnum lead loads that have proven to be so effective for waterfowl. Mossberg states it will offer shotguns for the new shell. Let's hope some of the other highly popular waterfowl shotguns are modified for the new round.

The availability of Norma ammo in recent years has, at best, been spotty. And that's too bad because Norma loads some otherwise impossible-to-get ammo, i.e. 6.5 Jap, 6.5 Carcano, 7.7 Jap, etc. But wait! Federal Cartridge Company has taken on the exclusive U.S. distribution of the Norma ammunition line. Thus, for the first time, we have a serious shot (pun intended) at getting Norma. Federal will also be distributing Norma brass, but not powder or bullets.

New under the Norma brand will be a 6.5 x 52mm Carcano loading using a 139-grain softpoint and a 7.65 x 53mm Argentine round with a 180-grain bullet. A second bullet weight for the 7.62x54R Russian will also be available. It's 150 grains.

Federal has expanded its very popular low-priced brand known as American Eagle. Rounds for the 223 Remington, 6.5x50 Japanese, 6.5x55 Swedish, 30 Carbine, 308 Winchester, 30-06 Springfield, 7.62x39 Soviet, 7.62x54R Russian, 25 Auto, 32 Auto, 380 Auto, 9mm Luger, 38 Special, 357 Magnum, 44 Magnum and 45 Auto are now loaded. It's not hard to see some Norma influence in the expanded lineup.

Three new calibers have been added to Federal's Premium line—6mm Remington, 7x57mm Mauser and 280 Remington. The 6mm loading is a 100-grain Nosler Partition bullet. This, in my opinion, is the only suitable bullet for light big game hunting with 6mm cartridges. Now, if Federal would do the same for the far more popular 243, that caliber would have a perfect factory light big game load, too.

Just 4 years shy of its 100th birthday, the 7mm Mauser has more than amply stood the test of time. And Federal has given it a unique potential for performance by loading it in their Premium line using the superb 140-grain Nosler Partition bullet. And the 280 also gets a Partition bullet—one of 150 grains weight. Of the 23 big game loads in Federal's Premium line, 12 are loaded with the excellent Nosler Partition bullet.

There is a Federal Sporting Clays target load that has no protective shotcup. As in days past, the shot column will rub on the bore and a fair number of pellets will deform. The deformed pellets will scatter more quickly from the pattern and thereby give a larger pattern at shorter ranges for those very tough, close-in shots.

A Premium loading of 00 Buck and 4 Buck in 10-gauge and 4 Buck in 12-gauge are also new, as is a less expensive target load in 12-gauge called Top Gun. The manner in which Federal reduced cost (by about $20 per case) was to use a less expensive case. If you're a non-reloader these new loads should have a lot of appeal. And there is a Premium 28-gauge hunting load using ¾-ounce of 6, 7½ or 8 extra hard shot.

Rimfire fans may find the new 22 Long CB load ideal for use when noise must be held to a minimum. Muzzle velocity will be about 700 fps from most rimfire barrels. Why Federal has put the Hi-Power brand on this load escapes me.

Federal has been selling a 308 Winchester Match load to police departments, military groups and others on a special order basis. This same load will now become part of the standard product line. It incorporates the very accurate Sierra 168-grain Match King and the Federal 210 Match primer. Muzzle velocity is 2600 fps.

A-Square

A-Square continues to make available a large number of the hard-to-find big-bore rounds such as the 9.3 x 62, 9.3 x 74R, 375 Nitro Express 2½-inch, 375 Weatherby, 416 Rigby, 404 Jeffrey, 450 Short A-Square, 500/465 Nitro Express, 505 Gibbs, and the 500 A-Square. All in all, there are approximately 100 different loads in some 38 calibers available. These start with the comparatively diminutive 7x57mm Mauser (with a Monolithic® solid of 175 grains) and progress on up to the 577 Nitro Express (with 750-grain bullet in full steel jacket, Dead Tough® softpoint and Lion Load® softpoint style bullets).

Importantly, A-Square also makes bullets and cases available as components to reloaders. Many owners of the larger bore "African" caliber firearms will find A-Square ammunition and components a quality answer to their ammo requirements. During recent months, I had the opportunity to range test three additional A-Square loads in the 300 H&H Magnum, 338 Winchester Magnum and the 375 H&H Magnum. Tested were Monolithic 220-grain solids, 250-grain Lion Loads, and 300-grain Dead Tough loads. Accuracy was superb and velocities very uniform.

Of particular interest is the fact that the A-Square Monolithic solids are true solids, a single homogeneous alloy rather than the lead core/metal jacket type which we often erroneously call "solids." Persons with sufficient experience on truly big African game are well aware of the bullet failures that occur with all types of so-called "solid" bullets (see the accompanying photos). The Monolithic solids cannot fail due to ruptured jackets, riveted bullet noses or jacket core separations. The homogeneous, very hard Monolithic solid will continue to penetrate, on a straight path, so long as there is sufficient bullet energy left to allow it to do so.

Arthur B. Alphin, founder of A-Square and bullet designer, has proved on more than just a few occasions that his ammunition has what it takes to anchor really big game. Some African game departments use A-Square ammo. If you're going to take on any of the big ones, take a long, hard look at A-Square's ammo line. It may well prove to be exactly what's needed. New for 1988 are some eight cartridge loadings, three bullets and three unprimed cartridge cases.

New A-Square Ammo And Components For 1988

Ammo

Caliber	Bullet Weight (grs.)	Type
375 Nitro Express 2½	270	Soft Point
375 Flanged	300	Monolithic Solid
375 Flanged	300	Dead Tough SP
375 Flanged	300	Lion Load SP
450/400	400	Monolithic Solid
450/400	400	Soft Point
505 Gibbs	525	Monolithic Solid
505 Gibbs	525	Soft Point

Bullets

Diameter	Weight (grs.)	Type
.409"	400	Monolithic Solid
.488"	500	Monolithic Solid
.505"	525	Monolithic Solid

Unprimed Cases

375 Nitro Express 2½"
375 Flanged
450/400

Omark

Aggressive as always, Omark once again has broadened an already wide product range. Blazer ammunition now includes a 124-grain TMJ (totally metal jacket) 9mm Luger loading. It is especially designed for European pistols which do not function as crisply as intended with lighter weight bullets. The Blazer ammo line now also includes a new bulk packaging for 45 Automatic 230-grain ammo as well as the mentioned 9mm load. The packaging is a plastic replica of the old GI ammo cans, though not nearly as large, and holds 100 rounds of 45 Automatic or 150 rounds of 9mm Luger. The plastic ammo containers are reusable and are handy for tackle storage.

Big game, really big game, responds well to A-Square ammo which comes in a wide range of calibers and three bullet types. This buffalo was taken by Art Alphin, of A-Square, using his own ammo and rifle.

Three new handgun bullets have been added to the Speer lineup. A 41-caliber TMJ 210-grain projectile and a 38-caliber TMJ 125-grain bullet are completely encased in copper via an electroplating process and offer advantages to the silhouette shooter.

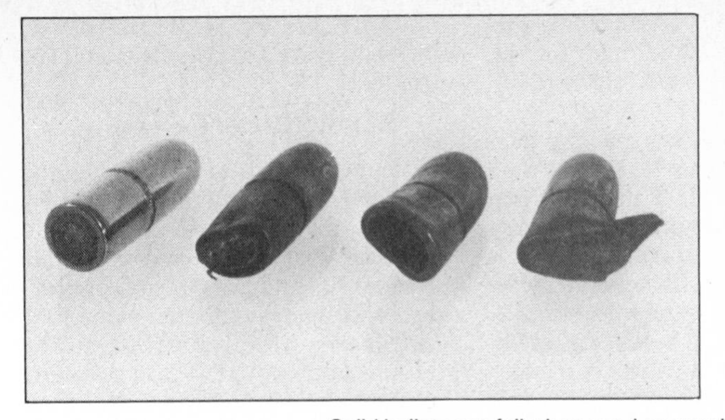

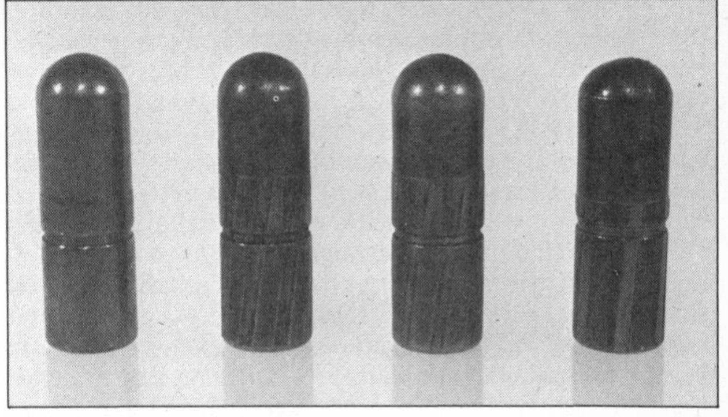

Solid bullets can fail when used on very heavy African game, and at left is how solid bullet failures look (alongside an unfired bullet). All three fired bullets were shot from a 458 Magnum and recovered from elephant. At right are one unfired and three A-Square Monolithic Solids, also recovered from elephant.

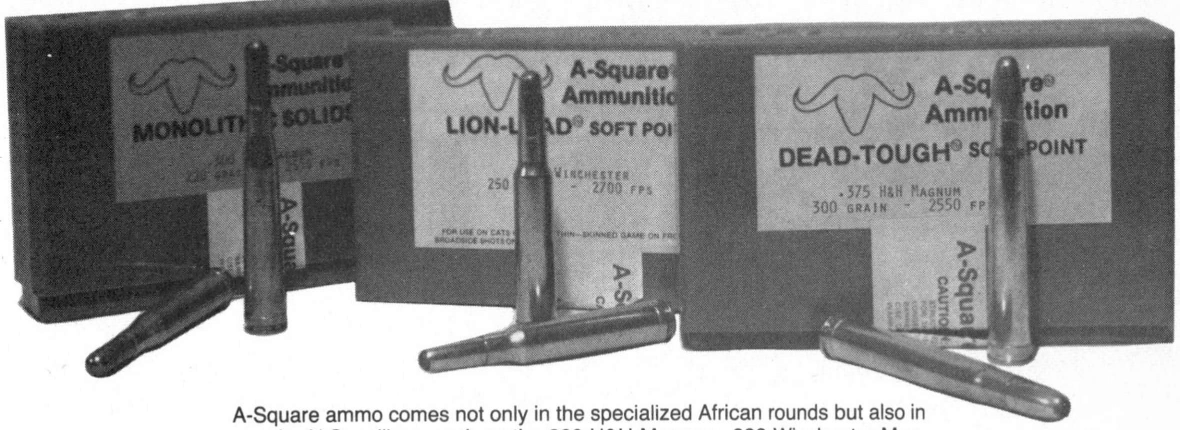

A-Square ammo comes not only in the specialized African rounds but also in popular U.S. calibers such as the 300 H&H Magnum, 338 Winchester Magnum and the 375 H&H Magnum.

The third new bullet is a heavily constructed 9mm 124-grain protected softpoint, notched bullet. Omark cautions that this bullet expands at velocities over 1250 fps. That means it's best suited to the 38 Super pistols or to 9mm Luger carbines which allow this velocity to be reached or exceeded because of increased barrel length.

Speer 30-caliber 165-grain spitzer bullets have undergone redesigning. The shank area of the bullet jacket has been notably thickened and internal flutes have been added to the nose area. Purpose of the changes is to improve weight retention at high velocity and to improve low speed expansion. Sounds like it should work.

For those of you caught up in reloading the 50-caliber BMG (Browning Machine Gun) cartridge for use in heavy bolt-action rifles, CCI is now offering a primer specifically for the job—their #35. I suspect not many of you will care, but those who do will be overjoyed with easy (well, relatively so) access to primers.

Finally, there is a new 22LR match round designed for use in handguns. Velocity from a 6-inch barrel is quoted at 940 fps with the 40-grain lead bullet, packed 50 to a box.

Thompson/Center

The T/C Maxi-Ball muzzleloading bullet enjoys a superb reputation as a target projectile. Its accuracy has become almost legendary. I've managed numerous three-shot groups at 50 yards which measured between 3/8- and 3/4-inch, center to center. But when used on game, this same bullet has over-penetrated, without expansion, every time, regardless of which caliber version was used (45, 50 or 54). This occurred even with maximum powder charges.

To correct the problem T/C is making available a Maxi-Hunter bullet. Like its target shooting cousin, the Maxi-Hunter must be lubricated by the shooter. Both T/C bullet lubricant or Crisco® work just fine.

Accuracy tests showed that in some T/C rifles the Maxi-Hunter was up to producing useful hunting accuracy. One Hawken 50-caliber barrel refused to shoot noteworthy groups with the Maxi-Hunter. I suspect an eroded "chamber" area to be the culprit. Group sizes, for three shots at 50 yards, averaged approximately 2 inches for three 50-caliber and two 54-caliber test rifles.

Gelatin block tests showed flawless expansion for both 50- and 54-caliber versions of the new Hunter bullet. The 45-caliber variation was not tested. Preliminary tests on whitetails suggest that the new Maxi-Hunter bullets are effective. Expansion was uniform and final bullet diameters ranged between 3/4- and 1-inch. All gelatin testing, as well as deer hunting, were done with maximum powder charges of FFg (100 grains/50-caliber, 120 grains/54-caliber).

Nosler

Nosler continues to expand its line of Ballistic Tip bullets. These use a very sharp polycarbonate tip to insure freedom from recoil damage in the magazine and the flattest possible trajectory. Currently, these protected point, positive expanding bullets are available in 25-, 26-, 27-, 28- and 30-caliber. New this year are a 140-grain .277-inch bullet and a 125-grain .308-inch bullet. All Ballistic Tip bullets feature Nosler's solid base boattail construction.

The new 30-caliber 125-grain Ballistic Tips might prove to be exactly the right bullets for antelope or other game that does not exceed a weight of

100 pounds on the hoof. I'll put this thought to the test on some Montana antelope this coming season. Will report on the results in the next issue.

If you haven't yet tried Ballistic Tip bullets, they are indeed the answer to battered bullet noses as a result of recoil while the round is in the magazine. Battered bullet noses simply are not as accurate nor do they retain their original ballistic coefficient. The very sharp nose profile and boattail base of the ballistic tip bullets provide the very highest possible downrange energy and flattest trajectory.

PMC

The folks at Pan Metal Corporation continue to widen their ammunition product line. Especially interesting is their new Ultramag handgun ammo. The Ultramag features a tubular bullet made of bronze. It's just what it sounds like, a heavy tube with a hole from front to rear. The nose of the tube has a bit of a taper, perhaps to give the bullet some eye appeal. The tubular bullet is seated on top of a nylon wad which effectively seals gases.

Velocity level is very impressive. In a 2½-inch barrel revolver using the Ultramag 38 Special +P load, with its 66-grain tubular bullet, we recorded an average velocity of 1371 fps with a velocity standard deviation of 39 fps. That's mighty impressive. This load has 275 foot pounds of energy from our 2½-inch barrel—again mighty impressive. Velocities of 1500+ fps and energies of 330+ foot pounds are certainly feasible with longer barrel lengths. There is also a 44 Special Ultramag tubular bullet loading.

Accuracy at short ranges (7 yards) was difficult to ascertain as it was sometimes impossible to decide which holes in the target were from the nylon wads and which were from the bullets. At 25 yards, however, the nylon wads no longer struck the target. Based on our limited test samples we can say accuracy appeared satisfactory for most purposes. Point of impact (due to very low recoil) is 6 inches below that of standard loadings at 25 yards.

PMC's new for 1988 list also includes: 33-grain truncated cone, ultra velocity 22LR as well as a 40-grain Long Rifle Match loading; 357 Magnum 158-grain lead semi-wadcutter gaschecked load; and 200-grain FMJ target loading for the 45 Automatic. If you have been looking for a reliable source of 10mm handgun ammo for your Colt Delta, PMC has it—both 170-grain JHP and 200-grain TCFMJ are available.

New in the rifle ammo line are a 100-grain 257 Weatherby, 130-grain and 140-grain 270 Weatherby, as well as 140- and 160-grain 7mm Weatherby loads. A match grade loading of the 223 Remington will also be made.

Finally, if you've been hankering to build a really big bolt-action rifle, PMC is now loading a 660-grain FMJ bullet in the 50-caliber Browning Machine Gun case. From 22 rimfire to 50 BMG sure covers one big heap of territory!

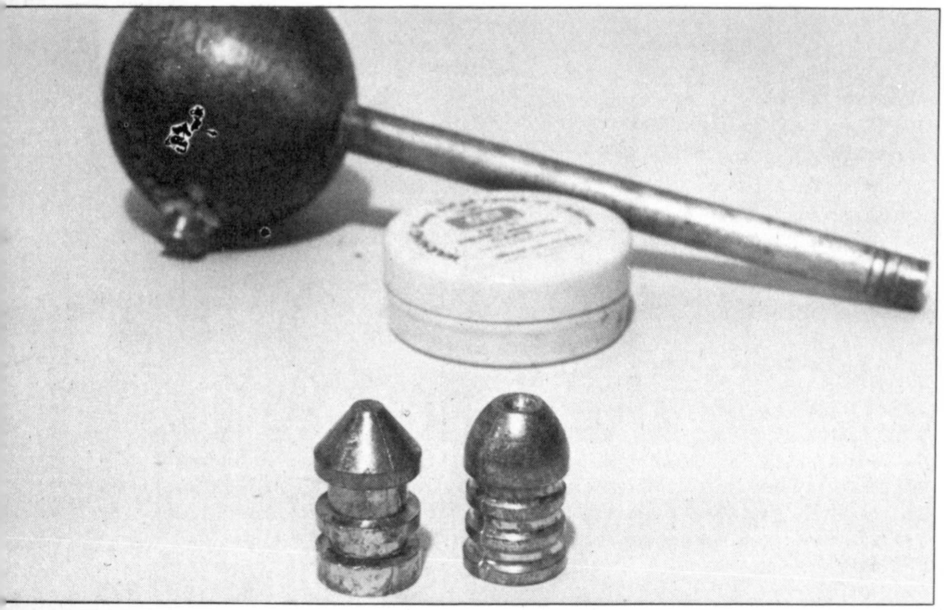

Thompson/Center's highly accurate target style muzzle-loading bullet, the T/C Maxi-Ball (on the left) now has competition. The T/C Maxi-Hunter bullet (on the right) expands well in big game size animals and supplies adequate hunting accuracy in many 45-, 60-, and 54-caliber rifles.

Buffalo Bullet Company

Not every soft lead muzzle-loading bullet, despite beliefs to the contrary, will expand on big game. Even on 200-pound deer I have experienced far too many in and out bullet penetrations, with no evidence of even a hint of expansion. So this past season the Matunas family put the Buffalo brand muzzle-loading bullets to the test. Buffalo Bullets are pure lead projectiles designed especially for the hunting muzzle-loading enthusiast.

Accuracy with all three style 54-caliber bullets (425-grain HPHB, 435-grain RNHB, and 460-grain RNSB) and two 50-caliber bullets (385-grain HPHB and 410-grain HPSB) was great. And expansion performance on deer was excellent. My 15-year-old son, Glen, killed the biggest buck of the year with one shot using the 50-caliber hollowpoint/hollow base Buffalo bullet, fired from a T/C Renegade, using 99 grains of FFg. His dad and his brother also took nice deer with other style Buffalo bullets. Perhaps the round-nose, hollow base bullet in 54-caliber will prove to be the best expander. A bit more game shooting needs to be done to support our findings which were based on extensive gelatin block testing and four deer.

Sierra

As you have probably come to expect, Sierra continues to add new bullets to its already very broad line. For the 7mm fans, and there are a bunch of you, there are a new 100-grain hollowpoint for varminting and a new 160-grain hollowpoint boattail. And the 10mm pistoleros have a 150-grain jacketed hollowpoint and 180-grain jacketed hollowpoint, both with the superb Power Jacket® design. That brings the Sierra line to over 130 bullets.

In the area of improvements, the 30-caliber 150- and 170-grain 30-30 style bullets now have the six nose notches of the Power Jacket design Sierra has pioneered in handgun bullets. Better expansion is almost assured.

Also, the justly famous 180-grain hollowpoint boattail 30-caliber bullet has had its bearing surface increased. This has been done by modifying the bullet's boattail. Sierra claims a notable increase in accuracy.

Special tip: If you own one of the new Sako 6mm PPC rifles, try some Hodgdon H322 (newly manufactured) along with Federal small rifle match primers and Sierra's 70-grain 6mm hollowpoint boattail benchrest style bullets. Bet you will be pleased with the resulting ½ MOA accuracy!

Hornady

Hornady has a new loaded round for 44 Magnum hunters, specifically designed for game smaller than deer. It uses a 180-grain jacketed hollowpoint and the manufacturer claims a muzzle velocity of 1600 fps. Sounds like an ideal woodchuck loading.

Specifically for handgun hunters are several new bullets: 80-grain 6mm spire point and 130-grain .308-inch spire point. These are manufactured with expansion at handgun velocities kept as an important criterion. Internal bullet nose notches and thinner jackets get the job done.

Non-Toxic Components

NTC is now into the fourth edition of its steel shot reloading data and it includes a total of 108 different loadings for 2¾-inch 12-gauge, 3-inch 12-gauge and 3½-inch 10-gauge. Cases covered include Winchester AA, Peters Blue Magic, Remington Premier Target, Remington RXP, Remington Unibody, Federal Gold Medal, Activ, Federal Paper, Federal Plastic, Winchester Plastic (steel shot), Dan Arms, and a bunch of others. If you are going to load steel shot, this data is a must. It is based on the exclusive use of NTC wads and steel shot. For more info write to NTC at P.O. Box 4202, Portland, OR 97208 or call 503-226-7710.

NTC wads now include three different 12-gauge and one 10-gauge style. All the reloader need do now is find a better way to slit the wads. The factory solution just isn't what it could.

This huge 10-pointer was felled by the author's 15-year-old son Glen with a single 50-caliber hollowpoint/hollow base Buffalo bullet and a T/C Renegade percussion rifle.

Buffalo Bullets give the muzzleloader the convenience of prelubrication and the accuracy of a swaged bullet.

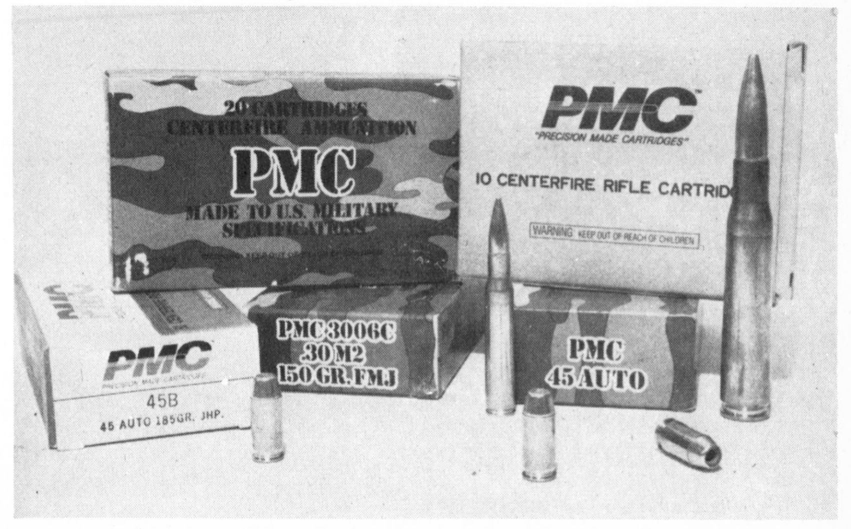

The PMC line of ammo now includes even the 50 BMG round (extreme right).

The PMC bullet used in the Ultramag loads is a bronze tube which is pushed by a plastic obturating wad. The bullet is fast—very fast—and creates a cookie cutter-like channel.

Sako

Sako ammunition is imported by Stoeger and is available to dealers through the importer. During late 1987, two variations of Sako ammo became what is undoubtedly the most accurate centerfire factory ammunition produced. This high level of accuracy was obtained with Sako ammo in 22 PPC (with 52-grain bullet) and 6mm PPC (with 70-grain bullet) cartridges. Consistent 10-shot groups of ½-inch or less (at 100 yards) were obtained with the 22-caliber round and groups averaging $^{6}/_{10}$-inch were obtained with the 6mm PPC rounds. This at a velocity of 3400 fps for the 22 and 3140 fps for the 6mm. Not every handload tried in the test rifles would do as well. That's mighty fine and, heretofore, unheard of accuracy with factory cartridges. If you want a super accurate target or varmint gun for which you can purchase superbly accurate factory ammo, consider one of the new Sako single shot rifles chambered for either of the PPC cartridges, along with a good supply of Sako ammunition. The combination really works better than any other.

Accurate Arms

Accurate Arms Company believes that reloaders are going to assemble a bunch of 7.62 x 39 Russian rounds. At least enough to justify its newest powder number—1680. According to Rich

Sierra's new 100-grain 7mm bullet should prove superb for varminting.

Sierra has a 7mm diameter 160-grain hollowpoint for those who prefer this configuration for large game.

And 10mm fans now have two Sierra bullets from which to choose, a 180-grain hollowpoint and a 150-grain variation.

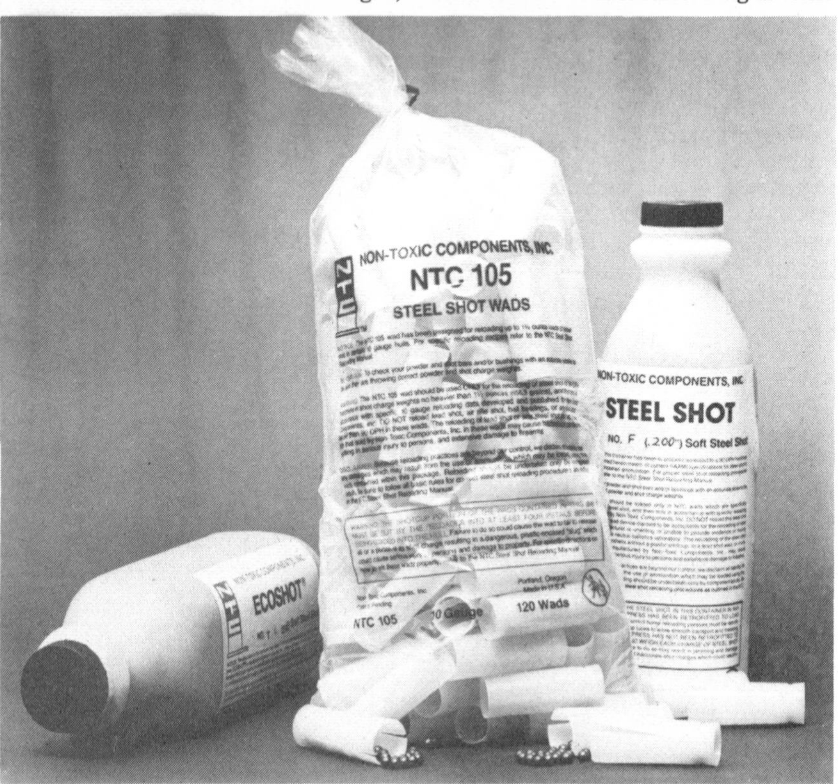

NTC continues to offer reloading components for steel shot, including a number of wads in 10- and 12-gauge, as well as a wide range of steel shot sizes.

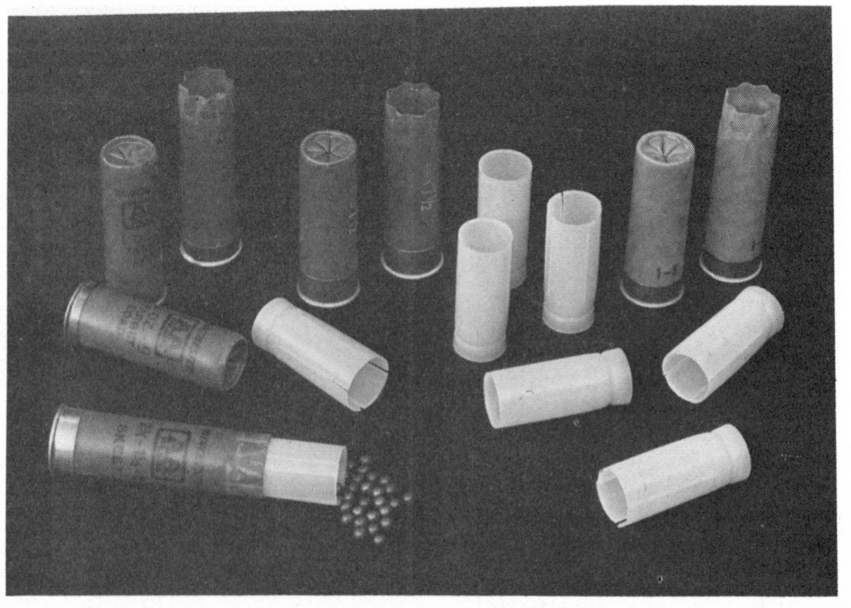

The NTC 12 TW wad is new and is designed for loading steel shot in tapered wall hulls such as the Winchester AA and Remington Premier.

Basch at Accurate, 1680 is the optimum propellant for this assault rifle cartridge. It has been used in both commercial and military loadings.

This 1680 should also work well in the Hornet, 30M1 Carbine and the 357 Remington Maximum. Accurate can supply data for 1680. Write to Sporting Lines Manager, Accurate Arms Co., Box 167, McEwen TN, 37101. The new powder is available in 1- and 8-pound containers.

BELL

Brass Extrusion Laboratories Ltd. (BELL) offers the handloader and ammo user some real odd-balls, not otherwise easy to come by. Ammo and/or brass in such oddities as 600 Nitro Express, 45 RCBS 3¼-inch, 43 Remington Spanish, 11mm Beaumont M71/78, 405 Winchester and 280 Ross are just some of the goodies available.

BELL has added brass in the 401 Herters Magnum and 401 Winchester calibers. Also new are cases suitable for forming to 6mm PPC. These are basic as 7.62x39 cases with small rifle primer pockets and *no* flash holes drilled. They are available in both rimless and rimmed (for single shot actions) versions.

If you own one of those old Griffin and Howe sporters chambered for the 2-R Lovell, BELL can help. They have a 25-20 single shot case that can be easily reformed. For more info write to Jim Bell Jr., at 800 Maple Lane, Bensenville, IL 60106 or call 312-595-2792.

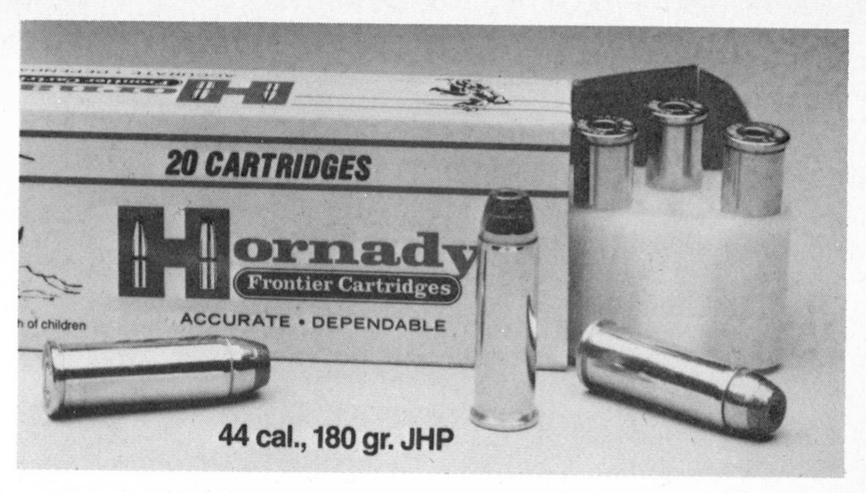

Hornady's new 180-grain JHP loading for the 44 Magnum.

Hercules

Hercules has announced three new

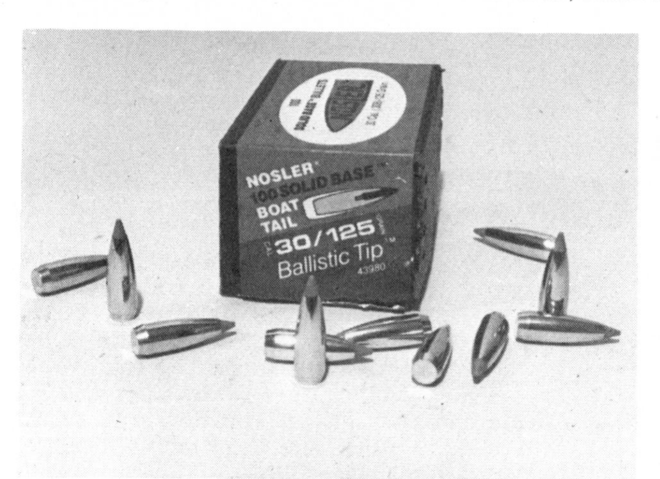

Nosler's new 30-caliber 125-grain Ballistic Tip should be perfect for antelope.

Rubright custom-made bullets—a plain-Jane package for extremely fancy accuracy.

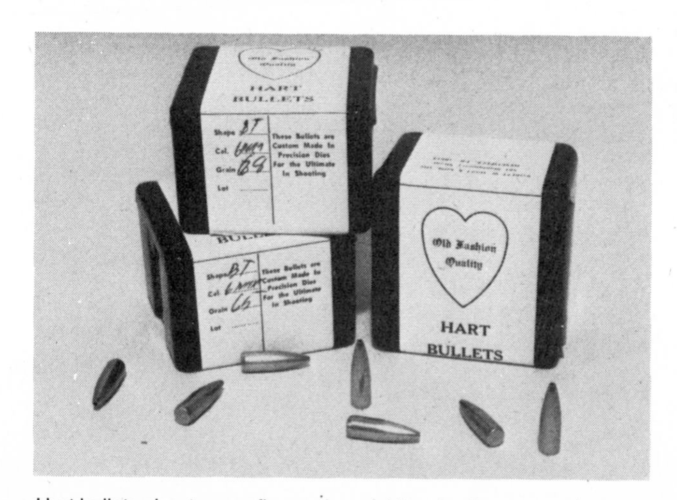

Hart bullets shoot super fine and are fairly priced.

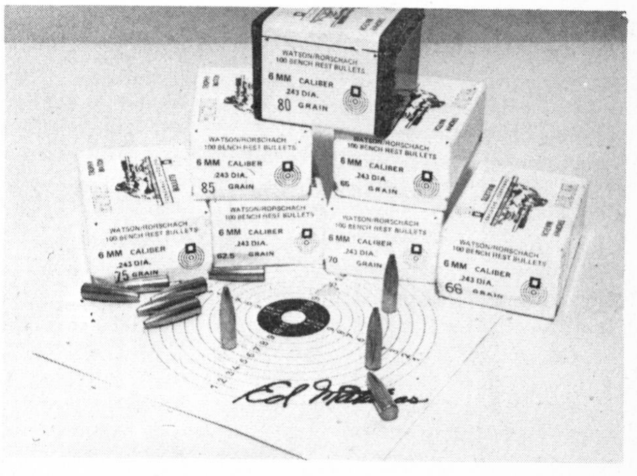

Watson bullets are tops in quality and come in a wide range of weights.

rifle powders. The first, Reloder 15, is said to be for medium capacity cartridges and an outstanding performer in the 22-250. Reloder 19 is suggested as suitable for large capacity and magnum cases, especially with lighter bullets. The third, Reloder 22, is claimed to provide the highest possible velocity with heavy bullets in calibers such as 7mm Remington Magnum, 300 Winchester Magnum and 338 Winchester Magnum.

No test samples or data were available at press time.

The news from Hercules are three new powder speeds to be called Reloder 15, 19, and 22—imported from Nobel.

Those Great Custom Bullets

Sometimes we get so caught up in doing things the same way that we miss some real opportunities. For example: Did you know that you can purchase some really superb 22 and 6mm benchrest bullets direct from the custom makers at a price nearly identical to what you pay for mass produced bullets? No, I'm not talking about bullets from someone who has a swage and decides he should be in the bullet business. The bullets I'm referring to are the ones used by the serious benchrest competitors to win matches and set world records.

During the past year I had the time and the right rifles (a pair of Sakos chambered for the 22 PPC and 6mm PPC cartridges) to take a hard look at a great number of the custom bullets. Some were simply outstanding.

Rubright Bullets come to the shooter in a no frills zip lock plastic bag of the plain-Jane variety. But the bullets are anything but ordinary. I tested 62.5-grain (7 ogive) flat base, 65-grain (8 ogive) flat base and boattail, as well as 68-grain (7 ogive) flat and boattail base 6mm bullets. Each was of the hollowpoint configuration and each was superbly accurate.

I also shot 1000 Berger Bullets in the 6mm diameter including 200 each of 62, 65, 68 and 80 grains, flat bases all. These bullets, in my 6mm PPC, never gave a 10-shot group larger than ¼-inch and most groups were considerably smaller. The Berger bullets come 100 to a reusable plastic box. The maker prefers interested parties to call rather than to write (see nearby tabulation). These were truly among the very finest bullets I have ever used.

The Watson Trophy Match bullets are proudly identified by the maker as being manufactured on Rorschach bullet dies. These also are superbly accurate. To date I've fired these in 62.5-, 65-, 68-, 70-, 75-, 80- and 85-grain weights. My PPC loved every one except the longer 85-grain bullet. Not the bullet's fault, mind you. Results with the 65-, 68-, and 70-grain weights were as expected with the 6mm PPC; simply tiny one-hole groups—very tiny, indeed.

And no less impressive were three different Hart bullets and a Bruno bullet I tried.

It would seem that the best way to decide upon which bullet will be best in your rifle with your load and loading techniques, would be to give each a try. Believe me, it will be hard to choose.

For those interested in such things, I used Hodgdon H322 (newly manufactured), Federal small rifle match primers and fully prepared Sako cases for the testing. And at this writing, I remember but a single group that wasn't a one-holer. At about $10 per hundred I can't think of any way to beat the price or accuracy. If sub-minute of angle groups are your goal, then give at least a few of these bullets a try. I'm betting you will be hooked forever.

Custom 22 and 6mm Benchrest Bullet Sources

Berger Bullets
Call (602) 846-5791

Bruno Bullets
10 Fifth St.
Kelayres, PA 18231
(717) 929-1791

Robert W. Hart & Son Inc.
401 Montgomery St.
Nescopeck, PA 18635

Rubright Bullets
1008 S. Quince Road
Walnutport, PA 18088

Ed Watson, Trophy Match Bullets
2404 Wade Hampton Blvd.
Greenville, SC 29615
(803) 244-7948

Conclusion

Well, these are the highlights of the best items reviewed for inclusion in this effort. Some items were not mentioned due to their uncertain longevity. And a few were probably overlooked due to manufacturers' oversights in bringing them to our attention. But those included should give even the most timid shooter plenty to think about and perhaps, happily, to have a go-around with.

Good shooting. ●

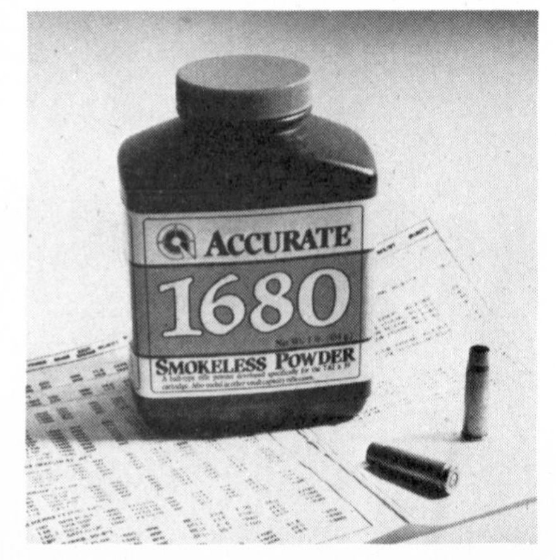

Accurate Arms 1680 powder is especially for the 7.62x39 Russian.

AVERAGE CENTERFIRE RIFLE CARTRIDGE BALLISTICS AND PRICES

Caliber	Bullet Wgt. Grs.	VELOCITY (fps) Muzzle	100 yds.	200 yds.	300 yds.	400 yds.	ENERGY (ft. lbs.) Muzzle	100 yds.	200 yds.	300 yds.	400 yds.	TRAJ. (in.) 100 yds.	200 yds.	300 yds.	400 yds.	Approx. Price per box
17 Rem.	25	4040	3284	2644	2086	1606	906	599	388	242	143	+2.0	+ 1.7	− 3.7	−17.4	**NA**
22 Hornet	45	2690	2042	1502	1128	948	723	417	225	127	90	+1.0	−5.3	+27.6	—	**$21.99***
218 Bee	46	2760	2102	1550	1155	961	778	451	245	136	94	+1.0	−5.2	−26.3	—	**36.85***
222 Rem.	50	3140	2602	2123	1700	1350	1094	752	500	321	202	+2.0	− 0.4	−10.6	−33.1	**9.38**
222 Rem.	55	3020	2562	2147	1773	1451	1114	801	563	384	257	+2.0	+ 0.4	−10.5	−31.8	**9.38**
222 Rem. Mag.	55	3240	2748	2305	1906	1556	1282	922	649	444	296	+2.0	+ 0.2	− 8.2	−26.3	**NA**
223 Rem.	40	3650	3010	2450	1950	1530	1185	805	535	340	205	+2.0	+ 1.0	− 5.9	−22.0	**11.04**
223 Rem.	55	3240	2747	2305	1906	1556	1282	922	649	444	296	+2.0	+ 0.2	− 8.2	−26.3	**10.29**
224 Wea. Mag.[2]	55	3650	3192	2780	2403	2056	1627	1244	943	705	516	+2.0	+ 2.0	− 2.4	−12.2	**NA**
22-250 Rem.	40	4000	3320	2720	2200	1740	1420	980	660	430	265	+2.0	+ 1.8	− 3.2	−15.5	**11.46**
22-250 Rem.	55	3680	3137	2656	2222	1832	1654	1201	861	603	410	+2.0	+ 1.3	− 4.3	−17.1	**10.71**
220 Swift	50	4110	3610	3135	2680	NA	1875	1450	1090	800	NA	+2.0	+ 2.8	+	− 6.9	**21.43**
22 Savage Hi-Power	71	2790	2295	1885	1560	NA	1225	830	560	383	NA	+2.0	+ 0.8	−12.6	—	**22.71**
243 Win.	80	3350	2955	2593	2259	1951	1993	1551	1194	906	676	+2.0	+ 0.9	− 5.4	−18.6	**12.86**
243 Win.	85	3320	3070	2830	2600	2380	2080	1770	1510	1280	1070	+2.0	+ 1.2	− 4.5	−14.2	**14.28+**
243 Win.	100	2960	2697	2449	2215	1993	1945	1615	1332	1089	882	+2.0	+ 0.2	− 7.5	−22.2	**12.86+**
6mm Rem.	80	3470	3064	2694	2352	2036	2139	1667	1289	982	736	+2.0	+ 1.1	− 4.5	−16.5	**12.86**
6mm Rem.	100	3100	2829	2573	2332	2104	2133	1777	1470	1207	983	+2.0	+ 0.6	− 6.1	−19.2	**12.86**
240 Wea. Mag.[2]	87	3500	3202	2924	2663	2416	2366	1980	1651	1370	1127	+2.0	+ 2.2	− 1.8	−10.6	**NA**
240 Wea. Mag.[2]	100	3395	3106	2835	2581	2339	2559	2142	1785	1478	1215	+2.0	+ 1.6	− 3.0	−12.8	**NA**
25-20 Win.	86	1460	1194	1030	931	858	407	272	203	165	141	+	− 8.2	−23.5	—	**24.98***
25-35 Win.	117	2230	1866	1545	1282	1097	1292	904	620	427	313	+2.0	− 5.3	−27.4	—	**16.17**
250-3000 Savage	100	2820	2504	2210	1936	1684	1765	1392	1084	832	630	+2.0	− 0.6	−10.4	−29.5	**13.70**
257 Roberts	100	3000	2633	2295	1982	1697	1998	1539	1169	872	639	+2.0	− 0.4	− 9.4	−27.2	**15.13**
257 Roberts	117	2650	2291	1961	1663	1404	1824	1363	999	718	512	+2.0	− 1.0	−15.0	—	**14.36**
25-06 Rem.	87	3440	2995	2591	2222	1884	2286	1733	1297	954	686	+2.0	+ 1.1	− 5.1	−18.4	**13.94**
25-06 Rem.	90	3440	3043	2680	2340	2034	2364	1850	1435	1098	827	+2.0	+ 1.2	− 4.2	−16.6	**13.94**
25-06 Rem.	100	3230	2893	2580	2287	2014	2316	1858	1478	1161	901	+2.0	+ 0.8	− 5.7	−18.9	**13.95**
25-06 Rem.	120	2990	2730	2484	2252	2032	2382	1985	1644	1351	1100	+2.0	+	− 7.5	−22.0	**13.94**
257 Wea. Mag.[2]	87	3825	3456	3118	2805	2513	2826	2308	1878	1520	1220	+2.0	+ 2.7	− 0.3	− 7.7	**NA**
257 Wea. Mag.[2]	100	3555	3237	2941	2665	2404	2806	2326	1920	1556	1283	+2.0	+ 2.1	− 1.8	−10.5	**NA**
257 Wea. Mag.[2]	117	3300	2882	2502	2152	1830	2829	2158	1626	1203	870	+2.0	+ 1.2	− 5.1	−18.9	**NA**
6.5x50 Jap.	139	2360	2185	2035	1900	NA	1720	1475	1243	1083	NA	+2.0	− 1.6	−13.4	NA	**22.71**
6.5x50 Jap.	156	2065	1870	1690	1530	NA	1480	1215	990	810	NA	+2.0	− 4.6	−23.3	NA	**22.71**
6.5x52 Carcano	156	2430	2210	2000	1800	NA	2045	1690	1385	1125	NA	+2.0	− 2.0	−14.7	NA	**22.71**
6.5x55 Swedish	140	2855	2665	2500	2350	NA	2350	2210	1930	1677	NA	+2.0	0.6	− 6.7	NA	**22.71**
6.5x55 Swedish	156	2645	2415	2205	2010	NA	2425	2015	1701	1414	NA	+2.0	− 1.0	−12.1	NA	**22.71**
6.5 Rem. Mag.	120	3210	2905	2621	2353	2102	2745	2248	1830	1475	1177	+2.0	+ 0.7	− 5.6	−19.3	**NA**
264 Win.	140	3030	2782	2548	2326	2114	2854	2406	2018	1682	1389	+2.0	+ 0.4	− 6.6	−18.4	**18.93**
270 Win.	100	3430	3021	2649	2305	1988	2612	2027	1557	1179	877	+2.0	− 1.0	− 4.9	−17.5	**13.95**
270 Win.	130	3060	2776	2510	2259	2022	2702	2225	1818	1472	1180	+2.0	− 0.4	− 6.8	−20.8	**13.94**
270 Win.	150	2850	2585	2336	2100	1879	2705	2226	1817	1468	1175	+2.0	− 0.4	− 9.2	−25.8	**13.94**
270 Wea.Mag.[2]	100	3760	3380	3033	2712	2412	3139	2537	2042	1633	1292	+2.0	− 2.4	− 0.9	− 8.9	**NA**
270 Wea.Mag.[2]	130	3375	3100	2842	2598	2366	3287	2773	2330	1948	1616	+2.0	+ 1.9	− 2.4	−11.6	**NA**
270 Wea.Mag.[2]	150	3245	3019	2803	2598	2402	3507	3034	2617	2248	1922	+2.0	+ 1.8	− 3.0	−12.8	**NA**
7x30 Waters	120	2700	2300	1930	1600	1330	1940	1405	990	685	470	+2.0	2.0	−11.0	−20.0	**13.94**
7mm-08 Rem.	140	2860	2625	2402	2189	1988	2542	2142	1793	1490	1228	+2.0	0.2	− 8.4	−23.9	**NA**
7mm Mauser	140	2660	2435	2221	2018	1827	2199	1843	1533	1266	1037	+2.0	1.0	−11.1	−29.7	**14.18**
7mm Mauser	150	2755	2540	2330	2135	NA	2530	2150	1810	1515	NA	+2.0	+	− 8.4	NA	**14.18**
7mm Mauser	175	2440	2137	1857	1603	1382	2313	1774	1340	998	742	+2.0	− 2.7	−17.6	—	**14.18**
7x57R	150	2690	2475	2285	2080	NA	2410	2040	1830	1515	NA	+2.0	+	− 8.4	NA	**23.81**
280 Rem.	140	3000	2758	2528	2309	2102	2797	2363	1986	1657	1373	—	—	—	—	**19.07+**
280 Rem.	150	2970	2699	2444	2203	1975	2937	2426	1989	1616	1299	+2.0	+ 0.2	− 7.5	−22.4	**19.91**
280 Rem.	165	2820	2510	2220	1950	1701	2913	2308	1805	1393	1060	+2.0	0.6	−10.3	−29.3	**19.91**
7x64 Brenneke	150	2890	2600	2330	2115	NA	2780	2250	1810	1490	NA	+2.0	+ 0.6	− 8.4	NA	**23.81**
284 Win.	150	2860	2595	2344	2108	1886	2724	2243	1830	1480	1185	+2.0	− 0.2	− 8.8	−25.2	**18.28**
7mm Rem. Mag.	150	3110	2830	2568	2320	2085	3221	2667	2196	1792	1448	+2.0	+ 0.6	− 6.1	−19.3	**17.26**
7mm Rem. Mag.	160	2950	2730	2520	2320	2120	3090	2650	2250	1910	1600	+2.0	+ 0.4	− 7.1	−21.6	**19.07+**
7mm Rem. Mag.	175	2860	2645	2440	2244	2057	3178	2718	2313	1956	1644	+2.0	+	− 7.9	−22.7	**17.26**
7mm Wea. Mag.[2]	139	3400	3138	2892	2659	2437	3567	3039	2580	2181	1832	+2.0	+ 2.1	− 2.1	−11.1	**NA**
7mm Wea. Mag.[2]	160	3200	3004	2816	2637	2464	3637	3205	2817	2469	2156	+2.0	+ 1.7	− 3.0	−12.6	**NA**
30 Carbine[1]	110	1990	1567	1236	1035	923	967	600	373	262	208	+1.0	−11.5	—	—	**8.93**
30 Rem.	170	2120	1822	1555	1328	1153	1696	1253	913	666	502	+2.0	5.7	−27.8	—	**NA**
30-30 Win.	55	3400	2693	2085	1570	1187	1412	886	521	301	172	+2.0	+	−10.2	−35.0	**NA**
30-30 Win.	125	2570	2090	1660	1320	1080	1830	1210	770	480	320	+2.0	− 2.4	−19.4	—	**10.95**
30-30 Win.	150	2390	1973	1605	1303	1095	1902	1296	858	565	399	+2.0	− 4.2	−25.6	—	**10.95**
30-30 Win.	170	2200	1895	1619	1381	1191	1827	1355	989	720	535	+2.0	− 4.8	−25.1	—	**10.95**
300 Savage	150	2630	2311	2015	1743	1500	2303	1779	1352	1012	749	+2.0	− 1.6	−13.9	−36.6	**14.10**
300 Savage	180	2350	2137	1935	1745	1570	2207	1825	1496	1217	985	+2.0	− 2.6	−19.7	—	**14.10**
303 Savage	190	1890	1612	1372	1183	1055	1507	1096	794	591	469	+2.0	− 8.8	−38.1	—	**18.74**
30-40 Krag	180	2430	2213	2207	1813	1632	2360	1957	1610	1314	1064	+2.0	− 2.2	−15.0	−38.5	**14.68**
307 Win.	150	2760	2321	1924	1575	1289	2538	1795	1233	826	554	+2.0	− 1.4	−15.4	—	**14.10**
308 Win.	55	3770	3215	2726	2286	1888	1735	1262	907	638	435	+2.0	+ 1.4	− 4.2	−15.8	**NA**
308 Win.	150	2820	2533	2263	2009	1774	2648	2137	1705	1344	1048	+2.0	− 0.6	10.0	−28.1	**13.94**
308 Win.	165	2700	2520	2330	2160	1990	2670	2310	1990	1700	1450	+2.0	+	− 8.4	−24.3	**13.94**
308 Win.	180	2620	2393	2178	1974	1782	2743	2288	1896	1557	1269	2.0	− 1.2	−11.7	−31.3	**13.94**
30-06 Spring.	55	4080	3485	2965	2502	2083	2033	1483	1074	764	530	+2.0	+ 1.9	− 2.1	−11.7	**NA**
30-06 Spring.	150	2910	2617	2342	2083	1843	2820	2281	1827	1445	1131	+2.0	− 0.2	− 8.5	−24.6	**13.94**
30-06 Spring.	165	2800	2534	2283	2047	1825	2872	2352	1909	1534	1220	+2.0	− 0.6	− 9.9	−27.5	**14.54**
30-06 Spring.	180	2700	2469	2250	2042	1846	2913	2436	2023	1666	1362	+2.0	− 0.8	−10.5	−28.6	**13.94**
30-06 Spring.	220	2410	2130	1870	1632	1422	2837	2216	1708	1301	758	+2.0	− 2.7	−20.5	NA	**13.94**
7.5x55 Swiss	180	2650	2460	2250	2060	NA	2800	2380	2020	1690	NA	+2.0	− 0.2	− 9.2	NA	**23.81**
7.62x54R Russ.	180	2575	2360	2165	1975	NA	2650	2270	1875	1560	NA	+2.0	− 0.6	−10.4	NA	**24.06**
308 Norma Mag.	180	3020	2780	2580	2385	NA	3645	3095	2670	2270	NA	+2.0	+ 1.4	− 5.9	NA	**28.76**
300 H&H Mag.	180	2880	2640	2412	2196	1990	3315	2785	2325	1927	1583	+2.0	− 0.2	− 8.3	−23.7	**19.12**
300 Win. Mag.	150	3290	2951	2636	2342	2068	3605	2900	2314	1827	1424	+2.0	+ 0.9	− 5.3	−17.8	**18.18**
300 Win. Mag.	180	2960	2745	2540	2344	2157	3501	3011	2578	2196	1859	+2.0	+	− 7.3	−20.9	**18.17**
300 Win. Mag.	200	2830	2680	2530	2380	2240	3560	3180	2830	2520	2230	+2.0	+ 0.6	− 6.2	−19.1	**20.02+**
300 Win. Mag.	220	2680	2448	2228	2020	1823	3508	2927	2424	1993	1623	+2.0	− 1.0	−11.0	−29.5	**19.12**
300 Wea. Mag.[2]	110	3900	3441	3028	2652	2305	3714	2891	2239	1717	1297	+2.0	+ 2.6	− 0.6	− 9.2	**NA**
300 Wea. Mag.[2]	150	3600	3297	3015	2751	2502	4316	3621	3028	2520	1709	+2.0	+ 2.3	− 1.2	− 9.2	**NA**
300 Wea. Mag.[2]	180	3300	3077	2865	2663	2470	4352	3784	3280	2834	2438	+2.0	− 2.6	− 3.0	−12.4	**NA**
300 Wea. Mag.[2]	220	2905	2498	2126	1787	1490	4122	3047	2207	1560	1085	+2.0	− 0.1	− 9.9	−22.3	**NA**
7.7x58 Jap.	130	2950	2635	2340	2065	NA	2513	2005	1581	1230	NA	+2.0	+ 0.2	− 7.9	NA	**24.07**
7.7x58 Jap.	180	2495	2290	2100	1920	NA	2485	2100	1765	1475	NA	+2.0	+ 1.2	−12.2	NA	**24.07**
7.65x53 Argen.	150	2660	2390	2120	1870	NA	2355	1895	1573	1224	NA	+2.0	− 0.2	− 9.1	NA	**22.71**
303 British	180	2460	2124	1817	1542	1311	2418	1803	1319	950	687	+2.0	− 2.8	−21.3	—	**17.77**
8mm Rem. Mag.	185	3080	2761	2464	2186	1927	3896	3131	2494	1963	1525	+2.0	+ 0.4	− 7.0	−21.7	**NA**
8mm Rem. Mag.	220	2830	2581	2346	2123	1913	3912	3254	2688	2201	1787	+2.0	− 0.4	− 9.1	−25.5	**NA**
8mm Mauser	170	2360	1969	1622	1333	1123	2102	1463	993	651	476	+2.0	− 4.1	−24.9	—	**14.36**

CAUTION: PRICES CHANGE. CHECK AT GUNSHOP.

AVERAGE CENTERFIRE RIFLE CARTRIDGE BALLISTICS AND PRICES

Caliber	Bullet Wgt. Grs.	VELOCITY (fps) Muzzle	100 yds.	200 yds.	300 yds.	400 yds.	ENERGY (ft. lbs.) Muzzle	100 yds.	200 yds.	300 yds.	400 yds.	TRAJ. (in.) 100 yds.	200 yds.	300 yds.	400 yds.	Approx. Price per box
8x57 JS Mauser	165	2855	2525	2225	1955	NA	2985	2335	1733	1338	NA	+2.0	+	− 8.0	NA	**22.71**
8x57 JS Mauser	196	2525	2195	1895	1625	NA	2780	2100	1560	1150	NA	+2.0	− 2.0	−15.7	NA	**22.71**
32-20 Win.	100	1210	1021	913	834	769	325	231	185	154	131	+	−32.3	—	—	**17.84**
32 Win. Spl.	170	2250	1921	1626	1372	1175	1911	1393	998	710	521	+2.0	− 4.7	−24.7	—	**11.62**
338 Win. Mag.	200	2960	2658	2375	2110	1862	3890	3137	2505	1977	1539	+2.0	+	− 8.2	−24.3	**21.91**
338 Win. Mag.	210	2830	2590	2370	2150	1940	3735	3130	2610	2155	1760	+2.0	− 0.2	− 8.7	−24.7	**24.21**
338 Win. Mag.	225	2780	2572	2374	2184	2003	3862	3306	2816	2384	2005	+2.0	− 1.4	−11.1	−27.8	**21.91**
338 Win. Mag.	250	2660	2456	2261	2075	1898	3927	3348	2837	2389	1999	+2.0	− 0.8	−10.5	−28.2	**24.42**+
340 Wea. Mag.[2]	200	3260	3011	2775	2552	2339	4719	4025	3420	2892	2429	+2.0	+ 1.6	− 3.3	−13.5	**NA**
340 Wea. Mag.[2]	210	3250	2991	2746	2515	2295	4924	4170	3516	2948	2455	+2.0	+ 1.7	− 3.3	−13.8	**NA**
340 Wea. Mag.[2]	250	3000	2806	2621	2443	2272	4995	4371	3812	3311	2864	+2.0	+ 1.0	− 5.0	−16.8	**NA**
351 Win. S.L.	180	1850	1556	1310	1128	1012	1368	968	686	508	409	+	−13.6	—	—	**40.41**
35 Rem.	150	2300	1874	1506	1218	1039	1762	1169	755	494	359	+2.0	− 5.1	−27.8	—	**12.86**
35 Rem.	200	2080	1698	1376	1140	1001	1921	1280	841	577	445	+2.0	− 5.3	−32.1	—	**12.86**
356 Win.	200	2460	2114	1797	1517	1284	2688	1985	1434	1022	732	+2.0	− 3.0	−18.9	—	**21.87**
358 Win.	200	2490	2171	1876	1610	1379	2753	2093	1563	1151	844	+2.0	− 2.6	−17.5	—	**23.02**
357 Magnum	180	1550	1160	980	860	770	960	535	383	295	235	+	−23.4	—	—	**20.41**
350 Rem. Mag.	200	2710	2410	2130	1870	1631	3261	2579	2014	1553	1181	+2.0	− 1.2	−12.1	−32.9	**NA**
9.3x57 Mauser	286	2065	1820	1580	1400	NA	2715	2100	1622	1274	NA	+2.0	− 2.8	−25.9	—	**27.54**
9.3x62 Mauser	286	2360	2090	1830	1580	NA	3545	2770	2177	1622	NA	+2.0	− 2.0	−23.2	—	**27.54**
375 Win.	200	2200	1841	1526	1268	1089	2150	1506	1034	714	527	+2.0	− 5.2	−27.4	—	**18.82**
375 Win.	250	1900	1647	1424	1239	1103	2005	1506	1126	852	676	+2.0	− 7.9	−34.8	—	**18.82**
375 H&H Mag.	270	2690	2420	2166	1928	1707	4337	3510	2812	2228	1747	+2.0	− 1.0	−11.5	−31.4	**22.74**
375 H&H Mag.	300	2530	2171	1843	1551	1307	4263	3139	2262	1602	1138	+2.0	− 2.6	−17.1	—	**23.95**
378 Wea. Mag.[2]	270	3180	2976	2781	2594	2415	6062	5308	4635	4034	3495	+2.0	+ 1.6	− 3.4	−13.2	**NA**
378 Wea. Mag.[2]	300	2925	2576	2252	1952	1680	5698	4419	3379	2538	1881	+2.0	+	− 8.7	−26.9	**NA**
38-40 Win.	180	1160	999	901	827	764	538	399	324	273	233	+	−23.4	—	—	**30.12***
38-55 Win.	255	1320	1190	1091	1018	963	987	802	674	587	525	+	−18.1	—	—	**17.51**
44-40 Win.	200	1190	1006	900	822	756	629	449	360	300	254	+	−33.3	—	—	**28.06***
44 Rem. Mag.	240	1760	1380	1114	970	878	1650	1015	661	501	411	+	−17.6	—	—	**10.85**
444 Marlin	240	2350	1815	1377	1087	941	2942	1755	1010	630	472	+2.0	− 5.8	−32.7	—	**NA**
444 Marlin	265	2120	1733	1405	1160	1012	2644	1768	1162	791	603	+2.0	− 6.8	−33.4	—	**NA**
45-70 Gov.	300	1880	1650	1425	1235	1105	2355	1815	1355	1015	810	+	−12.8	—	—	**16.67**
45-70 Gov.	405	1330	1168	1055	977	918	1590	1227	1001	858	758	+	−24.6	—	—	**16.68**
458 Win. Mag.	500	2040	1823	1623	1442	1237	4620	3689	2924	1839	1469	+2.0	− 5.6	−26.4	—	**29.21**
458 Win. Mag.	510	2040	1770	1527	1319	1157	4712	3547	2540	1970	1239	+2.0	− 6.4	−27.3	—	**29.21**
460 Wea. Mag.[2]	500	2700	2404	2128	1869	1635	8092	6416	5026	3878	2969	+2.0	− 0.6	−10.7	−31.3	**NA**

From 24″ barrel except as noted (1 = 20″ bbl.; 2 = 26″ bbl.). Energies and velocities based on most commonly used bullet profile. Variations can and will occur with different bullet profiles and/or different lots of ammunition as well as individual barrels. Trajectory based on scope reticle 1.5″ above center of bore line. + indicates bullet strikes point of aim.

NOTES: * = 50 cartridges to a box pricing (all others 20 cartridges to a box pricing)
NA = Information not available from the manufacturer.
— = Trajectory falls more than 40 inches below line of sight.
+ = Premium priced ammunition.

Please note that the actual ballistics obtained in your gun can vary considerably from the advertised ballistics. Also, ballistics can vary from lot to lot, even within the same brand. All prices were correct at the time this table was prepared. All prices are subject to change without notice.

CENTERFIRE HANDGUN CARTRIDGES—BALLISTICS AND PRICES

Caliber	Bullet Gr.	Bullet Style	Velocity (fps) Muzzle	Velocity (fps) 50 yds.	Energy (ft. lbs.) Muzzle	Energy (ft. lbs.) 50 yds.	Barrel Length In Inches	Approx. price/box
22 Rem. Jet	40	JSP	2100	1790	390	285	8⅜	**$ NA**
221 Rem. Fireball	50	JSP	2650	2380	780	630	10½	**NA**
25 Auto	45	LE	815	729	66	53	2	**14.72**
25 Auto	50	FMC	760	707	64	56	2	**13.78**
30 Luger	93	FMC	1220	1110	305	253	4½	**24.74**
30 Carbine	110	JHP, FMC	1740	1552	740	588	10	**8.93***
32 S&W	85, 88	LRN	680	645	90	81	3	**13.12**
32 S&W Long	98	LRN, LWC	705	670	115	98	4	**13.85**
32 H&R Mag.	85	JHP	1100	1020	230	195	4½	**17.30**
32 H&R Mag.	95	LSWC	1030	940	225	190	4½	**15.30**
32 Short Colt	80	LRN	745	665	100	79	4	**13.02**
32 Long Colt	82	LRN	755	715	100	93	4	**13.61**
32 Auto	60	STHP	970	895	125	107	4	**18.12**
32 Auto	71	FMC	905	855	129	115	4	**15.60**
380 Auto	85, 88	JHP	1000	921	189	160	3¾	**15.92**
380 Auto	95	FMC	955	865	190	160	3¾	**15.92**
38 Auto	130	FMC	1040	980	310	275	4½	**16.85**
38 Super Auto + P	115	JHP	1300	1147	431	336	5	**NA**
38 Super Auto + P	125	STHP	1240	1130	427	354	5	**20.65**
38 Super Auto + P	130	FMC	1215	1099	426	348	5	**16.85**
9mm Luger	115	JHP	1160	1060	345	285	4	**19.34**
9mm Luger	115	STHP	1225	1095	383	306	4	**22.43**
9mm Luger	123, 124	FMC	1110	1030	339	292	4	**19.34**
38 S&W	146	LRN	685	650	150	135	4	**14.60**
38 Short Colt	125	LRN	730	685	150	130	4	**NA**
38 Special	148	LWC	710	634	166	132	4V	**15.27**
38 Special	110	STHP	945	894	218	195	4V	**21.55**
38 Special	158	LRN, LSWC	753	721	200	182	4V	**15.27**
38 Special	95	JHP	1175	1044	291	230	4V	**21.55**
38 Special + P	110	JHP	995	926	242	210	4V	**18.59**
38 Special + P	125	JSP, JHP	945	898	248	224	4V	**18.59**
38 Special + P	158	LSWC, LHP	890	855	278	257	4V	**16.26**
357 Magnum	110	JHP	1295	1094	410	292	4V	**20.41**
357 Magnum	125	JHP, JSP	1450	1240	583	427	4V	**20.41**
357 Magnum	145	STHP	1290	1155	535	428	4V	**22.20**
357 Magnum	158	JSP, LSWC, JHP	1235	1104	535	428	4V	**20.41**
357 Magnum	180	JHP	1090	980	475	385	4V	**20.41**
357 MAXIMUM	158	JHP	1825	1588	1168	885	10½	**NA**
357 MAXIMUM	180	JHP	1555	1328	966	705	10½	**NA**
10mm Auto	165	JHP	1400	NA	719	NA	NA	**NA**
10mm Auto	200	FMC	1200	NA	635	NA	NA	**NA**
41 Rem. Mag.	175	STHP	1250	1120	607	488	4V	**31.13**
41 Rem. Mag.	210	LSWC	965	898	434	376	4V	**22.90**
41 Rem. Mag.	210	JHP, JSP	1300	1162	788	630	4V	**10.92***
44 Special	200	LSWC HP, STHP	900	830	360	305	6½	**20.58**
44 Special	246	LRN	755	725	310	285	6½	**20.59**
44 Rem. Mag.	180	JHP	1610	1365	1036	745	4V	**11.04***
44 Rem. Mag.	210	STHP	1250	1106	729	570	4V	**12.58**
44 Rem. Mag.	220	FMC	1390	1260	945	775	6½V	**28.56**
44 Rem. Mag.	240	LSWC	1000	947	533	477	6½V	**22.45**
44 Rem. Mag.	240	LSWC/GC	1350	1186	971	749	4V	**26.42**
44 Rem. Mag.	240	JHP, JSP	1180	1081	741	623	4V	**10.85***
45 Auto	185	JWC	770	707	244	205	5	**22.40**
45 Auto	185	JHP	940	890	363	325	5	**22.40**
45 Auto	230	FMC	810	776	335	308	5	**21.57**
45 Auto Rim.	230	LRN	810	770	335	305	5½	**NA**
45 Win. Mag.	230	FMC	140	1232	1001	775	5	**25.85**
45 Colt	225	JHP, LHP	900	860	405	369	5½	**20.90**
45 Colt	250, 255	LRN	860	820	420	380	5½	**8.49***

Notes: Blanks are available in 32 S&W, 38 S&W and 38 Special. V after barrel length indicates test barrel was vented and produced results approximating a revolver with its cylinder to barrel gap.

Abbreviations: JSP (jacketed soft point); LE (lead expanding); FMC (full metal case); JHP (jacketed vertip hollow point); LHP (lead hollow point); LSWCHP (lead semi-wadcutter); STHP (silvertip hollow point); LHP (lead hollow point); LSWCHP (lead semi-wadcutter hollow point); LSWC/GC (lead semi-wadcutter with gas check); JWC (jacketed wadcutter)

*20 rounds per box; all others 50 rounds per box

You're always a WINNER when you read AMERICAN HANDGUNNER and GUNS MAGAZINE

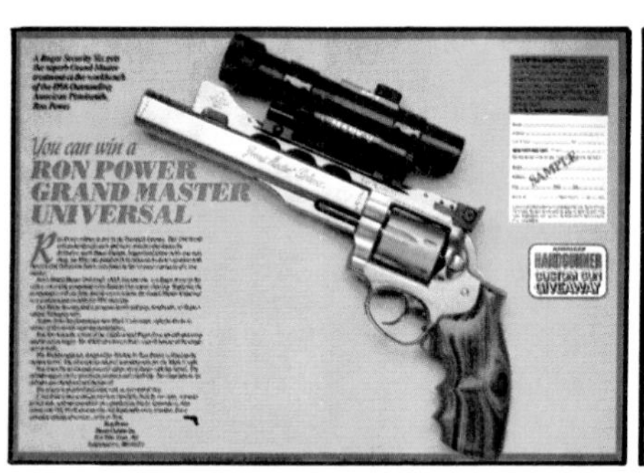

GUNS MAGAZINE GIVES YOU A CHANCE TO WIN EVERY MONTH.

GUNS Magazine's "Gun of the Month" giveaway puts a new gun in a lucky reader's hand every month.

So even if you don't win the Century .45-70 revolver pictured on the other side, you will get a chance to win again and again if you read GUNS regularly.

SAVE 63% OFF THE SINGLE COPY PRICE.

(39% off the regular subscription price.)

Through this special offer, you can subscribe to GUNS Magazine for a full year for only $9.95 . . . It's the lowest one year rate available. Plus every issue gives you features like these:

- **Classic Guns** – who makes them, where to find them.
- **Custom Guns** – handguns, rifles, and shotguns.
- **Test reports**, handloading, and MUCH MORE!

WINNING COVERAGE FOR AMERICA'S HANDGUNNERS.

You'll read about custom handguns in every issue of AMERICAN HANDGUNNER, and you'll get a chance to win one through the "Custom Gun Giveaway." But every issue gives you much more . . . That's probably why more "handgunners" rely on it for handgun news than any other handgun magazine.

SAVE 45% OFF THE SINGLE COPY PRICE.

(44% off the regular subscription price.)

Through this special offer, you can subscribe to AMERICAN HANDGUNNER for a full year for only $9.75 . . . It's the lowest one year rate around. Plus every issue gives you features like these and MORE:

- **Test reports** – old guns, new guns and rare guns.
- **Pistolsmithing** – how to modify and get the most out of your gun.
- **Match coverage** – Bianchi Cup, Masters, Steel Challenge.

GUN GIVEAWAY

ENTRY CERTIFICATE

NO POSTAGE NECESSARY IF MAILED IN THE UNITED STATES

BUSINESS REPLY MAIL

FIRST CLASS PERMIT NO. 10677 SAN DIEGO CA

POSTAGE WILL BE PAID BY ADDRESSEE

PRIZE COMMITTEE
Suite 200
591 Camino de la Reina
San Diego, CA 92108 -9986

GUN GIVEAWAY ENTRY DEADLINE:

July 4, 1989

Win a Century .45-70 revolver.

SEND FOR YOUR FREE ISSUE OF GUNS MAGAZINE!

If you shoot, hunt or just collect guns, you'll enjoy it more when you read GUNS Magazine every month. See for yourself – send for your FREE copy today!

SEND FOR YOUR FREE ISSUE OF AMERICAN HANDGUNNER!

Send for your FREE copy today and discover for yourself why it's America's first and best handgun magazine.

RIMFIRE AMMUNITION—BALLISTICS AND PRICES

Cartridge Type	Bullet Wt. Grs.	Bullet Type	Velocity (fsp) 22½" Barrel Muzzle	50 yds.	100 Yds.	Energy (ft. lbs.) 22½" Barrel Muzzle	50 Yds.	100 Yds.	Velocity (fps) 6" Barrel Muzzle	50 Yds.	Energy (ft. lbs.) 6" Barrel Muzzle	50 Yds.	Approx. Price Per Box 50 Rds.	100 Rds.
22 CB Short (CCI & Win.)	29	solid	727	667	610	34	29	24	706	—	32	—	NA	$3.83
22 CB Long (CCI only)	29	solid	727	667	610	34	29	24	706	—	32	—	NA	3.83
22 Short Match (CCI only)	29	solid	830	752	695	44	36	31	786	—	39	—	NA	3.83
22 Short Std. Vel. (Rem. only)	29	solid	1045	—	810	70	—	42	865	—	48	—	1.80	NA
22 Short H. Vel. (Fed., Rem., Win.)	29	solid	1095	—	903	77	—	53	—	—	—	—	1.80	NA
22 Short H. Vel. (CCI only)	29	solid	1132	1104	920	83	65	55	1065	—	73	—	NA	2.94
22 Short H. Vel. HP (Rem. only)	27	HP	1120	—	904	75	—	49	—	—	—	—	1.91	NA
22 Short H. Vel. HP (CCI only)	27	HP	1164	1013	920	81	62	51	1077	—	69	—	NA	3.13
22 Long Std. Vel. (CCI only)	29	solid	1180	1038	946	90	69	58	1031	—	68	—	NA	2.79
22 Long H. Vel. (Fed., Rem.)	29	solid	1240	—	962	99	—	60	—	—	—	—	1.91	NA
22 LR Pistol Match (Win. only)	40	solid	—	—	—	—	—	—	1060	950	100	80	5.10	NA
22 LR Match (Rifle) (CCI only)	40	solid	1138	1047	975	116	97	84	1027	925	93	76	4.28	2.79
22 LR Std. Vel.	40	solid	1138	1046	975	115	97	84	1027	925	93	76	1.72	3.59
22 LR H. Vel.	40	solid	1255	1110	1017	140	109	92	1060	—	100	—	1.72	3.59
22 LR H. Vel. HP	36-38	HP	1280	1126	1010	131	101	82	1089	—	95	—	1.99	4.15
22 LR-Hyper Vel. (Fed., Rem., Win.,(2))	33-34	HP	1500	1240	1075	165	110	85	—	—	—	—	1.99	NA
22 LR-Hyper Vel.	36	solid	1410	1187	1056	159	113	89	—	—	—	—	1.75	NA
22 Stinger (CCI only)	32	HP	1640	1277	1132	191	115	91	1395	1060	138	80	3.52	NA
22 Win. Mag. Rimfire	40	FMC or HP	1910	1490	1326	324	197	156	1428	—	181	—	6.07	NA
22 LR Shot (CCI, Fed., Win.)	—	#11 or #12 shot	1047	—	—	—	—	—	950	—	—	—	4.58	NA
22 Win. Mag. Rimfire Shot (CCI only)	—	#11 shot	1126	—	—	—	—	—	1000	—	—	—	4.24	NA
22 Win. Mag. Rimfire	50	JHP	1650	—	1280	300	—	180	—	—	—	—	Unk	NA

Please Note: The actual ballistics obtained from your gun can vary considerably from the advertised ballistics. Also, ballistics can vary from lot to lot even with the same brand. All prices were correct at the time this chart was prepared. All prices are subject to change without notice.

(1) per 250 rounds. (2) also packaged 250 rounds per box.

SHOTSHELL LOADS AND PRICES

Winchester-Western, Remington-Peters, Federal

Dram Equivalent	Shot Ozs.	Load Style	Shot Sizes	Brands	Average Price Per Box	Nominal Velocity (fps)
10 Gauge 3½" Magnum						
4½	2¼	Premium(1)	BB, 2, 4, 6	Fed., Win.	$26.47	1205
4¼	2	H.V.	BB, 2, 4, 5, 6	Fed.	24.87	1210
Max	1¾	Slug, rifled	Slug	Fed.	6.06	1280
Max	54 pellets	Buck, Premium(1)	4 (Buck)	Fed., Win.	6.03	1100
Max	18 pellets	Buck, Premium(1)	00 Buck	Fed., Win.	6.03	1100
Max	1¾	Steel shot	BB, 2	Win.	22.39	1260
4¼	1⅝	Steel shot	BB, 2	Fed.	22.38	1285
12 Gauge 3" Magnum						
4	1⅞	DuPlex Premium	BBx4-2x6	Rem.	NA	1210
4	1⅞	Premium(1)	BB, 2, 4, 6	Fed., Rem., Win.	16.27	1210
4	1⅝	Premium(1)	2, 4, 5, 6	Fed., Rem., Win.	15.46	1280
4	1⅞	H.V.	BB, 2, 4	Fed., Rem.	15.56	1210
4	1⅝	H.V.	2, 4, 6	Fed., Rem.	14.39	1280
4	Variable	Buck, Premium(1)	000, 00, 1, 4	Fed., Rem., Win.	3.05	1210 to 1225
3½	1¼	DuPlex Premium	BBx2-BBx4-2x6	Rem.	NA	1375
3½	1⅜	Steel Shot	BB, 1, 2, 4	Fed.	15.65	1245
3½	1¼	Steel Shot	F, T, BBB, BB 1, 2, 4	Rem., Win.	14.38	1375
4	2	Premium(1)	BB, 2, 4, 6	Fed.	18.27	1175
Max	1	Slug, rifled	Slug	Rem.	4.77	1760
12 Gauge 2¾" Hunting & Target						
3¾	1½	DuPlex Premium	BBx4-2x6	Rem.	NA	1260
3¾	1½	Premium(1), Mag.	BB, 2, 4, 5, 6	Fed., Rem., Win.	14.57	1260
3¾	1½	H.V., Mag.	BB, 2, 4, 5, 6	Fed., Rem.	12.94	—
3¾	1¼	H.V., Premium(1)	2, 4, 6, 7½	Fed., Rem.	11.50	1330
3¾	1¼	H.V., Promo	BB, 2, 4, 5, 6 7½, 8, 9	Fed., Rem., Win.	8.78	1330
3¼	1¼	Std. Vel., Premium(1)	7½, 8	Fed., Rem.	10.07	1220
3¼	1⅛	Std. Vel., Premium(1)	7½, 8	Fed., Rem.	9.73	1255
3¼	1¼	Std. Vel.	6, 7½, 8, 9	Fed., Rem., Win.	8.89	1220
3¼	1⅛	Std. Vel.	4, 5, 6, 7½, 8, 9	Fed., Rem., Win.	8.12	1255
3¼	1	Std. Vel., Promo	6, 7½, 8	Fed., Rem., Win.	5.87	1290
Max.	1¼	Slug, rifled, Mag.	Slug	Fed.	4.28	1490
Max.	1	Slug, rifled	Slug	Fed., Rem., Win.	3.46	1560
Max.	1	Slug, rifled, hi-vel.	Slug	Rem.	NA	1680
4	Variable	Buck, Mag., Premium(1)	00, 1, 4 (Buck)	Fed., Rem., Win.	8.28	1075 to 1290
3¾	Variable	Buck, Premium(1)	000, 00, 0, 1, 4 (Buck)	Fed., Rem., Win.	7.58	1250 to 1325
3¾	1⅜	H.V.	2, 4, 6	Fed.	12.14	1295
3¼	1¼	Pigeon	6, 7½, 8	Fed., Win.	9.09	1220
3	1⅛	Trap & Skeet	7½, 8, 9	Fed., Rem., Win.	8.18	1200
2¾	1⅛	Trap & Skeet	7½, 8, 8½, 9	Fed., Rem., Win.	8.18	1145
2¾	1	Trap & Skeet	7½, 8, 8½	Fed., Rem., Win.	8.01	1180
3¾	1¼	Steel Shot	BB, 1, 2, 4, 6	Fed., Win.	14.38	1275
3¾	1⅛	Steel Shot	1, 2, 4, 6	Fed., Rem., Win.	13.19	1365
3¾	1⅛	DuPlex Premium	BBx2-BBx4, 2x6	Rem.	NA	1365
16 Gauge 2¾"						
3¼	1¼	H.V., Mag., Premium(1)	2, 4, 6	Fed., Win.	12.76	1260
3¼	1⅛	H.V., Promo.	4, 5, 6, 7½, 9	Fed., Rem., Win.	8.62	1295
2¾	1⅛	Std. Vel.	4, 6, 7½, 8, 9	Fed., Rem., Win.	8.12	1185
2½	1	Std. Vel., Promo.	6, 7½, 8	Fed., Win.	5.87	1165
Max.	⅘	Slug, rifled	Slug	Fed., Rem., Win.	3.46	1570
Max.	12 pellets	Buck	1 (Buck)	Fed., Rem., Win.	3.05	1225
20 Gauge 3" Magnum						
3	1¼	Premium(1)	2, 4, 6	Fed., Rem., Win.	12.91	1185
3	1¼	H.V.	2, 4, 6, 7½	Fed., Rem.	12.01	1185
Max.	18 pellets	Buck	2 (Buck)	Fed.	3.72	1200
Max.	1	Steel Shot	2, 4, 6	Fed., Rem., Win.	12.60	1330
20 Gauge 2¾" Hunting & Target						
2¾	1⅛	Premium(1), Mag.	4, 6, 7½	Fed., Rem., Win.	11.42	1175
2¾	1⅛	H.V., Mag.	4, 6, 7½	Fed., Rem.	10.67	1175
2¾	1	H.V., Premium(1)	4, 6	Fed., Rem.	9.97	1220
2¾	1	H.V., Promo.	4, 5, 6, 7½, 8, 9	Fed., Rem., Win.	8.30	1220
2½	1	Std. Vel., Premium(1)	7½, 8	Fed., Rem.	8.79	1165
2½	1	Std. Vel.	4, 5, 6, 7½, 8, 9	Fed., Rem., Win.	7.61	1165
2¼	⅞	Promo	6, 7½, 8	Fed., Rem., Win.	5.87	1210
Max.	¾	Slug, rifled	Slug	Fed., Rem., Win.	3.21	1570
Max.	20 pellets	Buck	3 (Buck)	Fed., Rem., Win.	3.03	1200
2½	⅞	Skeet	8, 9	Fed., Rem., Win.	7.66	1200
2¾	¾	Steel Shot	4, 6	Fed., Win.	11.90	1425
28 Gauge 2¾" Hunting & Target						
2¼	¾	H.V., Premium(1)	6, 7½	Fed., Rem., Win.	10.13	1295
2	¾	Skeet	9	Fed., Rem., Win.	9.06	1200
410 Bore Hunting & Target						
Max.	11/16	3" H.V.	4, 5, 6, 7½, 8	Fed., Rem., Win.	8.66	1135
Max.	½	2½" H.V.	4, 6, 7½	Fed., Rem., Win.	7.36	1135
Max.	½	2½" Target	9	Fed., Rem., Win.	7.50	1200
Max.	⅕	Slug, rifled	Slug	Fed., Rem., Win.	3.05	1815

(1) Premium shells usually incorporate high antimony extra hard shot and a granulated polyethelene buffer to increase pattern density at long ranges. In general, prices are per 25-round box. Rifled slugs and buckshot prices are per 5-round pack. Premium buckshot prices per 10-round pack. Not every brand is available in every shot size. Price of Skeet and trap loads may vary widely.

LINSEED RUBBING OIL

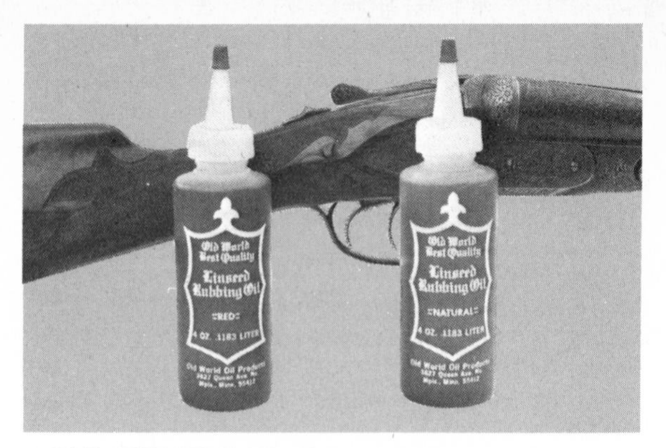

OLD WORLD Oil Products has been offering best-quality linseed oil for over a decade. Long recognized as *the* professional gun stock finish, linseed oil brings out the full character and quality of a walnut gun stock.

This superior linseed oil is available in red or amber shades. Serves perfectly for the expert refinishing of old gun lumber or the complete and total enhancement of a brand new gun stock.

This particular product is also ideal when it comes to the care of original, oil-finished stocks.

Each bottle of this excellent linseed oil comes complete with instructions. Simply send $5.00 for your postpaid 4 oz. bottle of red or amber OLD WORLD Linseed Oil.

OLD WORLD OIL PRODUCTS

STOCK BEDDING COMPOUND

Introduced by Brownells as an update of their well known Acraglas® Stock Bedding Compound, Acraglas Gel® Stock Bedding Compound has a smooth consistency that will not drip, run or leach out from between wood and metal after being put into the gunstock. Acraglas Gel® is formulated with nylon derivatives for greater "thin strength," shock resistance and stability over normal temperature extremes. Shrinkage is less than 1/10 of 1%. Blends with atomized metals. Easy to use, 1-to-1 mix.

Acraglas Gel® 2-Gun 4-oz. Kit sells for $9.25. Larger 16 oz. Shop Kit is $25.70. Kits contain two-part special formula, bedding epoxy, stock-matching dye, mixing sticks and dish, release agent and detailed instructions.

BROWNELLS, INC.

PROFESSIONAL HUNTER BULLETS

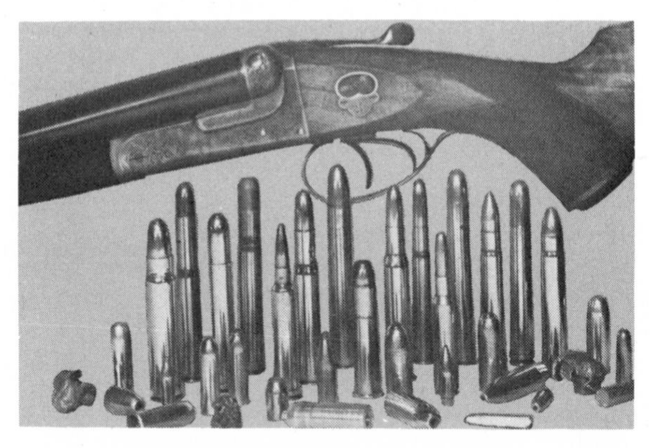

Bill McBride, of Professional Hunter Supplies, has been making, testing and supplying bullets for heavy, dangerous game in Africa. These bullets have been, and are being used by government agencies for elephant and cape buffalo control. The bullets are also used by various professional hunters doing safari work in Zimbabwe, Zambia and Tanzania. Bullets incorporating ideas from field research are today used on dangerous game.

Professional Hunter Supplies offers various Solids and Soft Nose bullets in calibers from 7mm through 600 N.E. including 12 bore.

Individual customer specifications may be special ordered. Prices start at $22.50 per 25 bullets. Write for free brochure.

PROFESSIONAL HUNTER SUPPLIES

See manufacturers' addresses following this section.

POWERED ENGRAVING TOOL

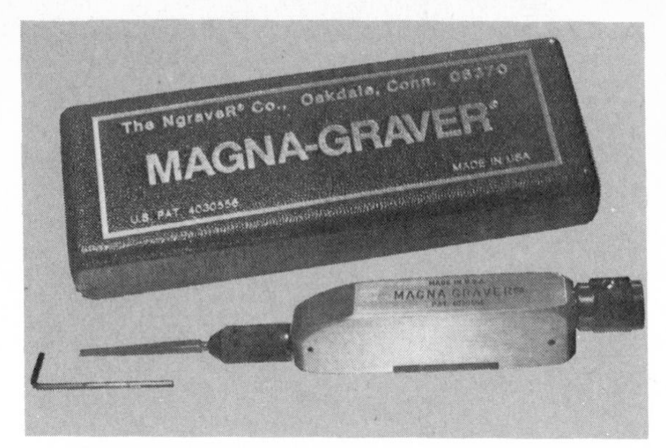

The ability to engrave in metal was brought to the masses by The NgraveR® Company with the introduction 10 years ago of their flex-shaft powered impact tool. The latest version, the MagnaGraver®, has new needle bearings, heavier output shaft, and improved spring assembly. The result is a long-lasting tool with 50% greater impact. Satisfied owners in 50 States and most foreign countries attest to the MagnaGraver® being the lowest cost and most versatile engraving handpiece available. Weighs 5 oz., with gold anodize and black oxide finish, comes in a fitted metal case. Operates from any standard flex-shaft machine. With wrench and instructions, the MagnaGraver® retails for $185. The standard M/100 impact tool is $170.

THE NGRAVER® COMPANY

LEARN GUN REPAIR

Learn gun repair. Modern School has been teaching gun repair the home study way since 1946 to over 45,000 students. All courses are Nationally Accredited and Approved for GI benefits. Courses are complete and include all lessons (including how to get your FFL) Tool Kit, Powley Calculator and Powley Computer, Gun Digest, Gun Parts Catalogue, Mainspring Vise, School Binders, Brownell's Catalogue, Pull & Drop Gauge, Trigger Pull Gauge, Two Parchment Diplomas ready for framing, Free Consultation Service. Get into a career where you can enjoy what you are doing. Learn to start your own business and make money in your spare time too. No previous experience is needed. Write or call for free information. No obligation. No salesman will call.

MODERN GUN REPAIR SCHOOL

ADJUSTABLE PEEP SIGHT DISC

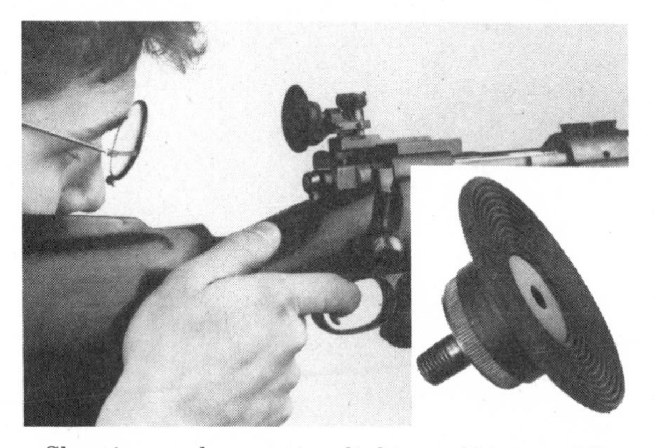

Shooting under varying light conditions, with a peep sight, can be highly frustrating.

Fortunately, the people at the Merit Corporation have come up with a solution—an adjustable peep sight disk.

As lighting conditions vary, shooters can now instantly adjust the aperture diameter of the Merit Iris Rifle Disc to maintain a clear sight picture.

The Iris aperture is adjustable from .022 to .125 inches diameter opening and has an internal click spring to maintain its setting.

The Master Disc includes a 1½-inch diameter replaceable light shield and is available in a lens disc model that will hold a prescription ground lens.

Contact Merit for a free brochure.

MERIT CORPORATION

CHECKERING TOOLS

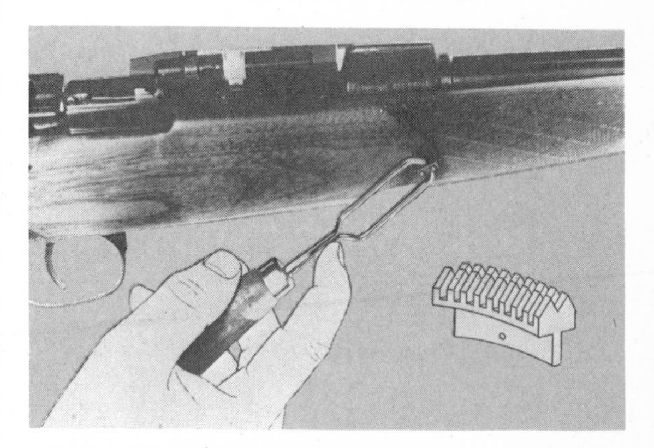

FULL-VIEW checkering tools have been on the market since 1949. The tool features a split shank (which allows the gunsmith to fully view his work at all times), and an adjustable head which lets him checker at any desired angle. FULL-VIEW cutters are made of the highest quality tool steel and come in sizes 16, 18, 20, 22, 24, 26, and 32 lines per inch. The teeth are self-cleaning and cut equally well backwards and forwards. FULL-VIEW checkering tools include holders; spacing, single line, superfine, skip-line, and border cutters; and short corner tools. A special checkering kit sells for $20 (plus $2.00 for shipping). Send for a *free* descriptive folder that comes complete with prices and hints for better checkering.

W.E. BROWNELL CHECKERING TOOLS

See manufacturers' addresses following this section.

SHOOTER'S MARKETPLACE

CUSTOM GUN CASES

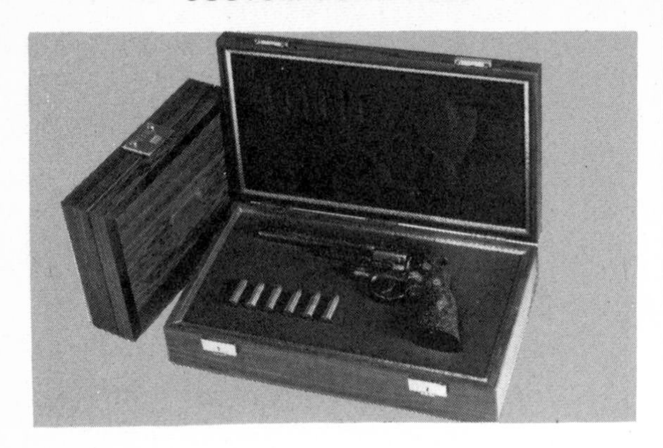

Quality-Built cases for many different size weapons. "Old fashioned craftsmanship." Durable, abrasive resistant finish, with the beauty of a textured Rosewood woodgrain. Fittings all polished brass. Unique "*REVERSIBLE* MEMORY PADS," in luxurious Black and vibrant Red, *automatically mold themselves* to custom fit your favorite weapons. A gasket helps seal out dust and moisture.

High quality key locks, standard; combination locks, optional. Brass presentation plate included for your engraving. Nine sizes from 5½"x8"x2½" to 13½"x35½"x3½". Priced from $53.00 to $186.00. Visa and Mastercard accepted.

For free information write the manufacturer or call toll free.

WAMCO, INC.

RELOADER'S SUPPLY CATALOG

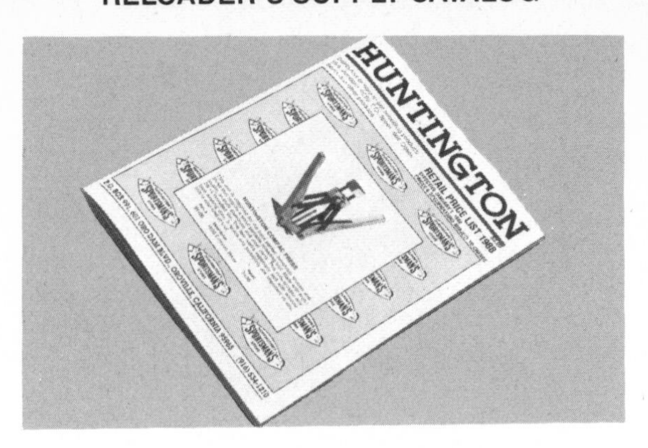

HUNTINGTON DIE SPECIALTIES is this nation's *foremost* supplier of hard-to-get reloading products plus standard RCBS, CCI, Speer, Bell cases, Sierra bullets and other products. They also manufacture the well-known Huntington Compac Press.

If you're a serious handloader who's looking for something unusual, a beginner who's looking for a place to start, or a dealer who's trying to fill a customer's needs, the Huntington catalog is a must. It's the sort of reloader's "tool" that quickly becomes part of the bench.

Both the Retail and Dealer's Catalogs normally sell for $3.00 each. If you'll mention you saw it in *Shooter's Marketplace,* it's yours for the asking.

HUNTINGTON DIE SPECIALTIES

IMPROVED 60mm SPOTTING SCOPE

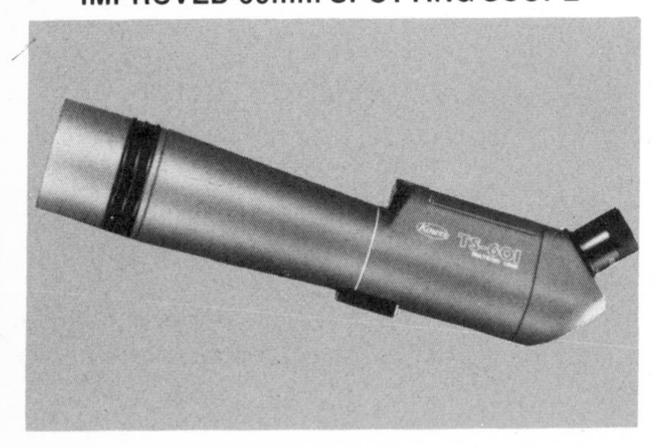

INNOVATION in 60mm Conventional Spotting Scope!

The TS-601 is equipped with a multi-coated lens that lets the shooter see a clear, brighter and sharper target than any other conventional 60mm spotting scope.

Bayonet mounting is included for simple eyepiece changing.

Also optional photo capability. Available in 20x Wide, 25x, 25x Long Eye Relief, 40x, 20x-60x zoom.

Manufacturer's suggested retail: $479.90 for TS-601 with 25x eyepiece. Straight type also available.

For more information on the TS-601 Spotting Scope, and other Kowa Optimed products, write or call the manufacturer direct.

KOWA OPTIMED, INC.

HANDGUNNERS CATALOG

Whether you're a Competition Shooter, Handgun Hunter, or Handgun Enthusiast, WILSON'S carries what you need.

An excellent line of quality handgun accessories, and service, is readily available.

WILSON'S is a complete handgun accessory company. They currently stock such brand names as Wilson Combat, Safariland, Bo-Mar, Bianchi, Pachmayr, Hogue, Leupold, Davis, RIG, Wolff, Clark and Uncle Mike's.

Most orders are shipped within 24 hours and their fill rate is 95+%.

Send $3.00 for their latest full-color catalog, which will be credited toward your first order from Wilson's Gun Shop.

WILSON'S GUN SHOP, INC.

See manufacturers' addresses following this section.

REVOLVER SPEEDLOADER

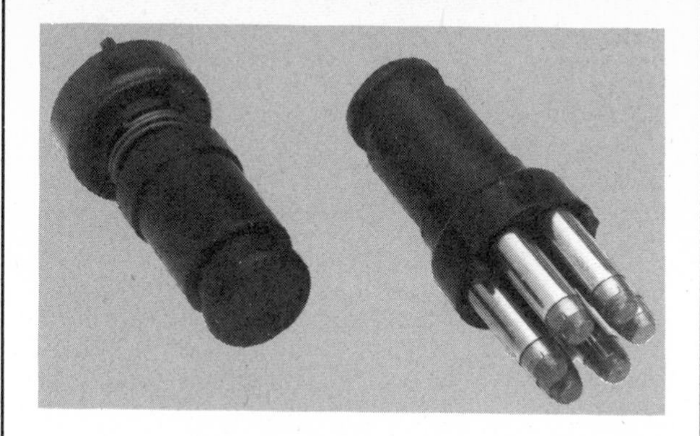

Previously imported from Austria in limited quantities, the immensely popular Jet Loader™ proved difficult to find. Now in the United States, the all new Safariland Super Comp III Speedloader improves upon the European design.

Advances in composition, spring design and action improve the Comp III while retaining popular Jet Loader™ features. Comp III is the only speedloader to utilize the positive loading force of spring pressure. Lack of gravity feed makes the Comp III the fastest loader made. "Zero to six in milliseconds." Safariland has, for immediate delivery, the all new Super Comp III for K frames, an all new Split Six single carrier, and a duty style tandem carrier. For further info contact Safariland.

SAFARILAND LTD., INC.

UNIQUE HANDGUN REST

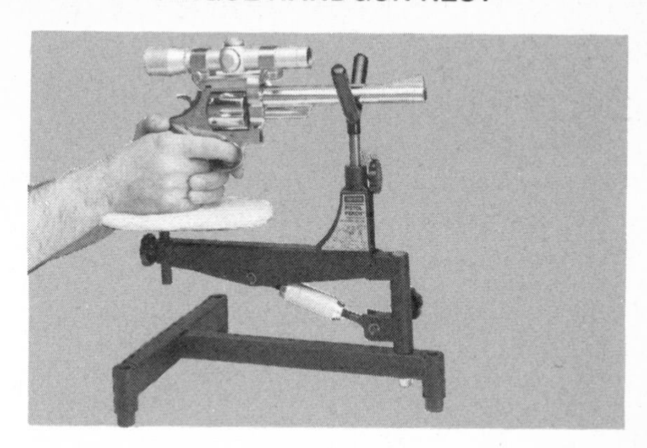

The Outers PISTOL PERCH™ handgun rest replaces bulky, sandbags. This traveling bench rest adds support, yet adjusts vertically and pivots horizontally for a variety of shooting positions. The three-point stance helps stabilize the rest on uneven surfaces. Constructed of durable, though light, square tubular steel and finished with non-glare heat sealed paint. OUTERS also manufactures a PISTOL PERCH™ accessory for use with the VARMINTER™ rifle rest. It attaches to the rifle rest and utilizes the shooting features of the rest (the same as the PISTOL PERCH™), providing an option for the VARMINTER™ owner.

Suggested retail: PISTOL PERCH™ $79.95; VARMINTER™ PISTOL PERCH accessory $29.95.

OUTERS LABS/OMARK INDUSTRIES

AK 47-STYLE AIR RIFLE

The AK47 lookalike air rifle in 177 caliber, is used by the Chinese for training. Features folding stock that locks in both opened and closed position, side lever cocking with built-in safety which does not allow the gun to be fired unless cocking lever is down in locked position.

Barrel length is 15″ with military adjustable front sight and military style tangent rear sight, side sling swivels, wood forend and pistol grip and brown plastic stock panels, just like the original.

New manufacture. A versatile airgun for the hunter, collector and the target shooter. Manufacturer's suggested retail price: $79.95 MODEL NO. AKS 177.

For more info, write direct.

NAVY ARMS COMPANY

REAMERS & GAUGES

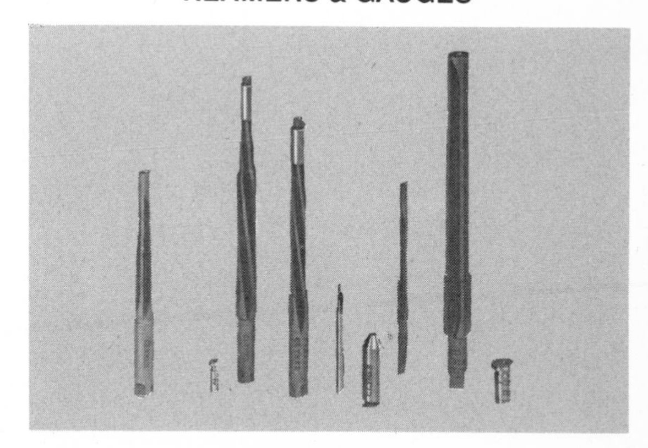

The leader in the field of chambering reamers and headspace gauges for the gunsmith and serious shooter/hobbyist, Clymer Manufacturing Co. continues to expand its line of tooling available from stock. Reamers and Gauges are available in all popular rifle, pistol, and shotgun calibers. Many other cutting tools are also offered to facilitate alteration of factory-standard firearms to meet an individual shooter's requirements.

Clymer Manufacturing will help the wildcatter in designing a new cartridge and gladly provide technical assistance in design and manufacture of specialized tooling not normally carried in stock. A 36-page Clymer catalog is available for $2.00. Call Clymer direct.

CLYMER MANUFACTURING CO.

See manufacturers' addresses following this section.

SHOTGUN SLUG

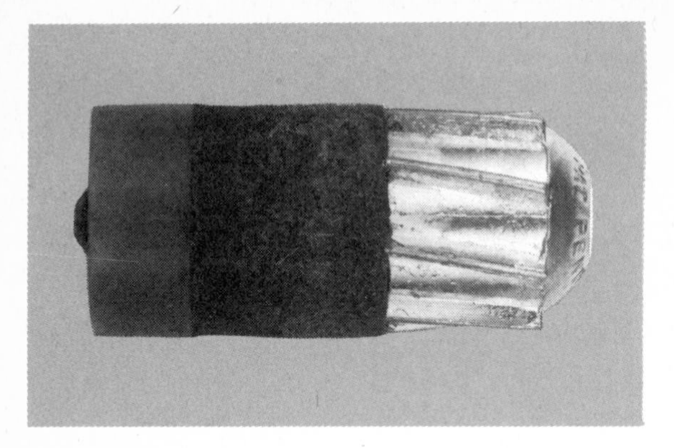

The VITT/BOOS 12 Gauge Aerodynamic Shotgun Slug has a sectional density of .155 and a ballistic co-efficient of .125, far surpassing any 12-gauge slug on the market today. The muzzle velocity of 1490 fps and muzzle energy of 2835 fpe exceeds that of the 300-grain 375 H&H. Even at 100 yards the velocity of 1260 fps and energy of 2024 fpe still surpasses the 375 H&H. At 200 yards the slug still retains a velocity of 950 fps and energy of 1153 fpe. The assembly consists of four parts: A Solid Lead slug, a Felt Wad, an overpowder wad and a Gas Check all permanently attached by a screw. Total weight is 1.32 oz. or 580 grains. Used only by handloaders for the past 20 years, it is now available as loaded ammo. For more info, send a S.A.S.E.

VITT/BOOS AERODYNAMIC SLUG

SOVIET PISTOL BOOK

Soviet Russian Postwar Military Pistols and Cartridges 1945-1986, a thoroughly researched and well documented study of these little known handguns by arms historian Fred A. Datig. Traces Russian pistol use from 1900, experiments of the 1930s and '40s leading to the Makarov's adoption.

Covers the Makarov, elusive Stechkin "APS," and the recently adopted 5.45mm PSM in great detail. Also Soviet clandestine pistols, contemporary Soviet pistol ammunition.

152 8½ x 11″ pages, over 100 illustrations, hard bound.....$29.95, plus $3 postage and handling. Buy together with their *System Mauser* (Mauser "broomhandles," 272 pages, fully illustrated, $24.95), they'll pay postage and handling on both.

HANDGUN PRESS

SEE THROUGH SCOPE COVERS

STORM KING® scopecovers by Anderson Manufacturing, Inc., allow the hunter to sight through the scope, or even take a shot without removing the cover.

This extra edge is ideal for those split-second shots at fast moving game.

STORM KING® provides great protection for expensive scopes and flips to the side to reveal clean, clear optics.

The scopecovers come with clear or haze-colored lenses and are offered in 21 different sizes to provide a custom fit for nearly all scopes (trace both ends of scope for this service). Manufacturer's suggested retail price is $12.95 per set, $13.95 for haze. Write for more information.

STORM KING/ANDERSON MFG.

BULLET COLLATER

The R.D.P. Bullet collater will feed all bullets base down at the rate of up to six thousand rounds an hour. It is adaptable to THE TOOL by R.D.P. May be retrofitted to Ammo Load, Camdex, and any lubrisizing or swaging machine by advising R.D.P.—at the time of order—which of the above presses, lubrisizer or swaging machine the collator is to be used on.

The collater will feed cast and lubed or jacketed bullets.

Complete with light sensor shut off, exclusive alloy steel ring, solid steel base plate and stand and a high quality belt drive, the unit sells for $730.00.

One unit can be converted to run all calibers and adapted to all machines. For info call or write.

R.D.P. TOOL CO., INC.

See manufacturers' addresses following this section.

NEW GRUNT DEER CALL

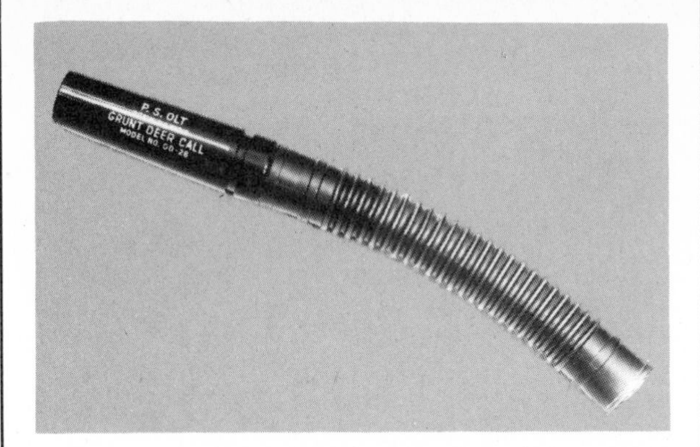

The P.S. Olt Company, Pekin, Illinois, is now manufacturing a new grunt deer call. The new deer call produces the grunting sounds made by rutting bucks tending does in the estrus. These sounds cause jealousy in other bucks in the area, and bring them in to fight. The new model will be called the GD-26 Grunt Deer call. The GD-26 is molded in moistureproof and durable ABS Cycolac, and uses a long-lasting Mylar reed for years of troublefree performance. It is furnished with a grunt tube, but can be blown without the tube for variations in sound. Easy to blow with good volume. The Olt GD-26 Grunt will be furnished in hangup packaging. The 1988 List Price: $12.95.

Write for more information.

P.S. OLT COMPANY

GUNSMITHING LATHE

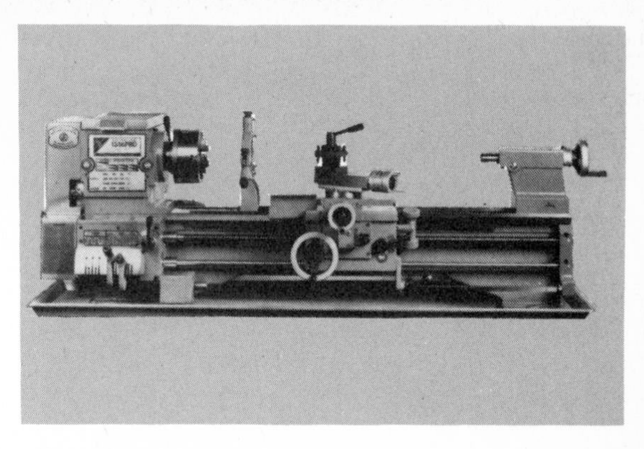

Blue Ridge's most popular full size gunsmithing lathe is the Jet 13x36 PBD. Features, quality and affordability make it the choice of the trade. With the 36″ center distance and 1½″ spindle bore all chambering, choke work, crowning and contouring on barrels can be performed with ease.

Blue Ridge also complements the lathe with a full line accessory selection including 4-jaw chucks, stands, and tools.

Send for your free copy of the complete Blue Ridge catalog or call toll free. Mention Gun Digest for a special package price. Blue Ridge offers a complete selection of lathes, mills and machine shop supplies for the professional gunsmith as well as the advanced hobbyist.

BLUE RIDGE MACHINERY & TOOLS

UNIQUE SANDBAG REST

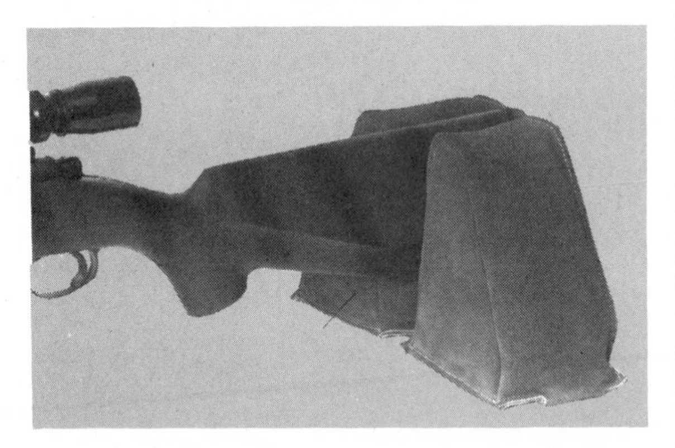

Ultra Light Arms (ULA) just announced their new recoil eliminating Bench Wizard sandbag system for benchrest shooting.

1. Absorbs up to 90% of your gun's recoil while shooting from a Bench Rest.
2. The extra mass of these 10-pound, sand-filled bags provides maximum stability for precision shooting.
3. Point of bullet strike remains unchanged when shooting from the shoulder after sighting-in with the Bench Wizard.
4. Soft leather construction of the bags will not scratch or mar your gun.

The Bench Wizard works. Aids accuracy, and reduces recoil. Suggested retail price: $49.95.

ULTRA LIGHT ARMS, INC.

PROFESSIONAL BORE SOLVENT

ACCUBORE is a new brushless solvent specially formulated for professional use. Its powerful formula removes copper, powder and lead residue in minutes. You can now spend more time shooting and less time cleaning.

This solvent uses a gentle chemical action to remove guilding metal from the bore of high performance guns. Copper fouling can now be wiped out of the bore with soft cotton patches. Enhances accuracy in guns that show symptoms of being shot out.

ACCUBORE has a unique color indicator that tells you when your gun is fouled with copper. Accuracy begins with a clean bore...

Manufacturer's suggested retail price: $5.95 per 4.0 oz. bottle. Write For More Info!

RTI RESEARCH, LTD.

See manufacturers' addresses following this section.

COMBO CLEANING KIT

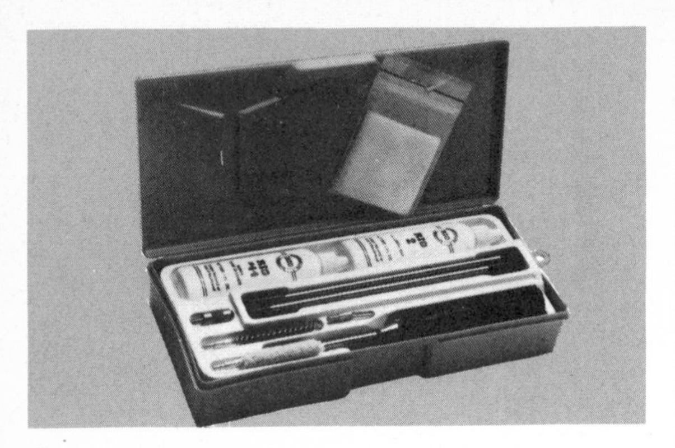

Rig Cleaning Kits are complete!

Each kit has specific tools for cleaning a single caliber (25, 270 or 30 cal.). Each kit contains a bronze brush, steel patch puller, cotton swab, and cotton patches.

Additionally, each kit has a bottle of #44 bore cleaner, #2 Rig rust preventive, and a shotgun brush adapter. Each rod has a Delrin handle with a 4″ stainless steel rod, a brass bore guide, plus four 7½″ stainless steel extensions.

The rod is centerless ground to remove any imperfections. This rod has been designed to fit all rifles and handguns from 25 caliber up, and will fit all shotguns. Price: $29.95.

Write for free catalog.

RIG PRODUCTS

CUSTOM ENGRAVING

Ben Shostle can create your heirloom. From the most classic elegance to a lovely, simple monogram. His distinct style is internationally recognized and available to those who want quality engraving. Ben is currently Vice President of The Firearms Engravers Guild of America, and holds the coveted "Professional" status in the Guild.

While all styles are available, he is best known for his deep sculptured gold, magnificent work. Shostle's work and that of other known artists, engravers and scrimshanders, is available for sale and viewing at their showroom. The Gun Room is open daily except Sunday and Monday.

Appointments with The Gun Room are available by calling in advance. A brochure is $1.00.

THE GUN ROOM

BIG BORE HANDGUN HUNTING BULLETS

	.44 CALIBER (.429)		
	240 JHP	260 JFP	300 JFP
Unfired bullet			
Medium velocity			
High velocity			

Freedom Arms, a leader in handgun hunting, introduces its expanded line of bullets. Designed for modern high velocity hunting loads, they provide accuracy, penetration and retained weight.

These bullets feature an exclusive hard alloy core and a .032-inch heavy jacket. This reinforced construction insures bullet integrity under high pressure loads, improving accuracy. Provides optimum penetration and retained weight on big game animals. Close weight tolerances are maintained.

Available in 44 (.429) and 45 (.452) calibers in 240 Jacketed Hollow Point, 260 and 300 grain Jacketed Flat Point. A dual cannelure on 44 caliber bullets provides flexibility in loading.

Contact your dealer or Freedom Arms.

FREEDOM ARMS

BALLISTICS SOFTWARE/IBM PC

COMPUTER SHOOTER® CRIMELAB is now being used by the militarty to train combat arms personnel in ballistics. Law enforcement agencies also appreciate the greatly reduced time spent at the firing range with evidence firearms and the handy calculation utilities.

Easy to use, yet extremely powerful, the program includes graphic displays of path, angle, drop, energy, sound lag, time, velocity, and drift for any downrange interval.

COMPUTER SHOOTER® SPORTSMAN is designed for the hunter or target shooter.

Manufacturer's suggested retail prices: CRIME LAB—$500.00, SPORTSMAN—$69.00. Call for more information.

BALLISTICS RESEARCH GROUP, KAYUSOFT INTL.

See manufacturers' addresses following this section.

SHOOTING GLASSES APERTURE

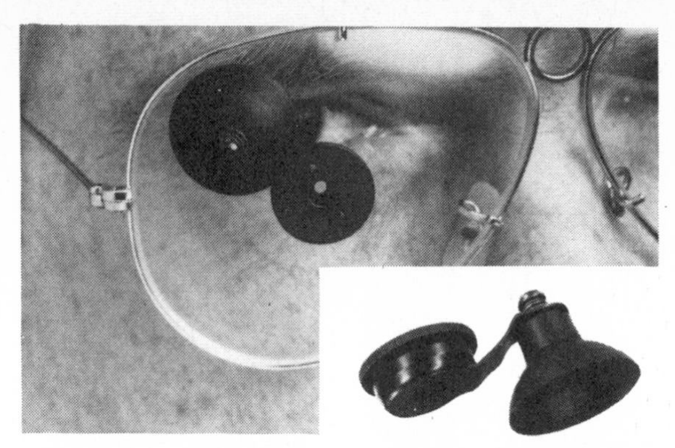

Pistol shooters can now see their sights and target clearly with the Merit Optical Attachment and its instantly adjustable diameter aperture.

An aperture (pinhole) will increase your eyes' depth of field (range of focus) dramatically.

The optical attachment is instantly adjustable from .022 to .156 inches which allows the shooter to make adjustments for different light conditions on the range.

Additionally, using an aperture distinctly improves the shooter's concentration by actually helping the shooter maintain a consistent position of the head.

Contact Merit for a FREE brochure with more details.

MERIT CORPORATION

DERRINGERS

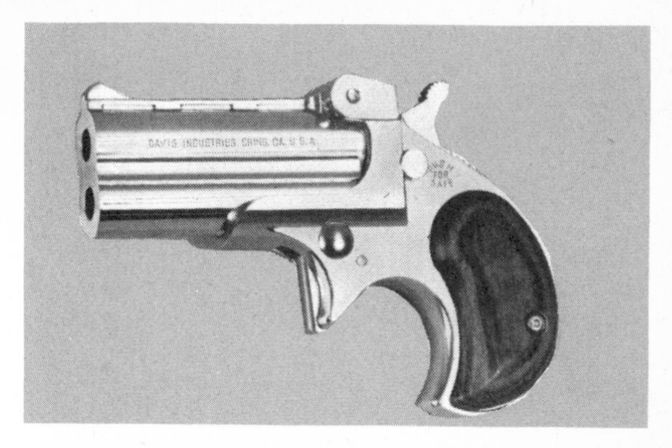

Davis Industries offers its derringers in four calibers: 22 Long Rifle, 22 WMR, 25 Auto, and 32 Auto. All four calibers come with your choice of chrome or black teflon finish.

Davis derringers are 100% made in the U.S.A. and backed by the industry's finest guarantee: If anything goes wrong with your Davis derringer, Davis will fix it or replace the firearm FREE for the life of the original purchaser.

Davis uses a special high-strength non-ferrous alloy cast frame, precision machined and fitted with quality steel internal parts and laminated wood grips. Metal surfaces are hand-polished and *every derringer is test-fired.* The suggested retail price is $64.90.

DAVIS INDUSTRIES

NO-GUNSMITHING SCOPE MOUNT

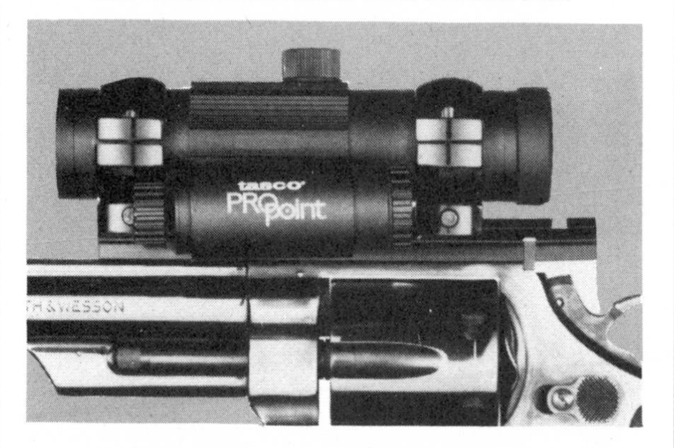

Computer designed and engineered to stay on 44 magnums and also to fit 22s, B-Square's new mount fits all Smith & Wesson K, L, and N frame guns with adjustable sights. B-Square's technically superior mount does not require drilling, tapping, clamps, or straps. It is guaranteed to stay on round after round of your heaviest loads.

B-SQUARE's mount has a standard mounting dovetail so any Weaver-type ring or Aimpoint, Tascorama, etc., can be attached. Manufacturer's suggested list price is only *$49.95* in blue finish or *$59.95* in stainless finish. One mount fits *all* S&W guns.

It's available at dealers and distributors everywhere, or contact B-SQUARE for more information.

B-SQUARE CO.

CORDURA BASKETWEAVE HOLSTER

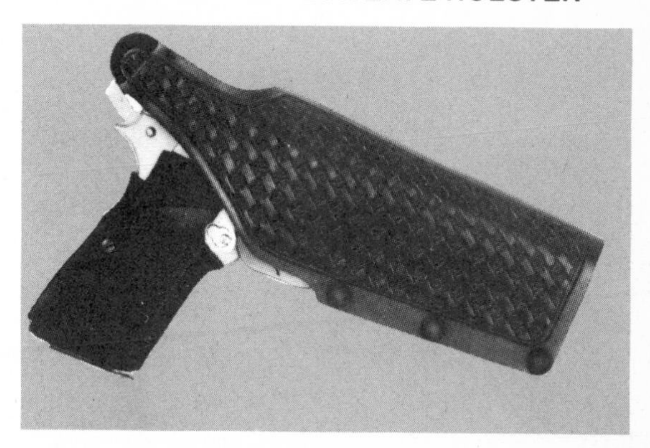

The patented Pachmayr® basketweave-design holster looks like leather, but has none of the disadvantages of leather or cordura® nylon.

This Contour-Fit™ holster is manufactured from an inert synthetic material which is impervious to moisture, solvents, fuels, heat or cold.

It won't shrink, mildew, sweat, unravel, tear, or break. Each model is made to fit the handgun for which it was designed—no sloppy loose fitting "generic" sizes. Your handgun is carried comfortably in a very secure, protective, lightweight, easy-to-draw, thumb-break holster.

Models available for Browning Hi-Power, Colt Gov't. 45, S&W "K" and "L" frames. For more information, write Pachmayr directly.

PACHMAYR, LTD.

See manufacturers' addresses following this section.

NEW SCOPE COVER

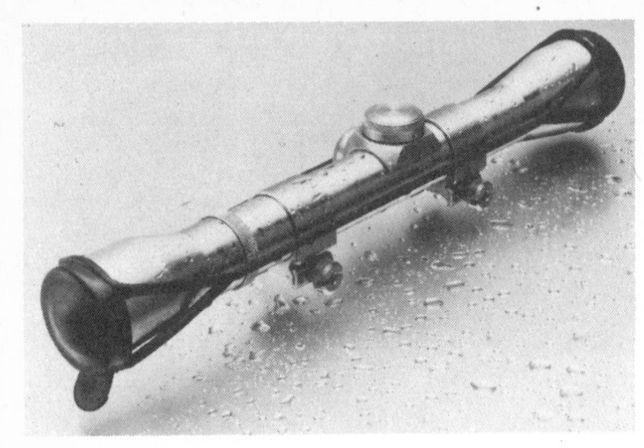

The BIKINI™ Scope Cover is designed for the sportsman who wants simple, single-piece scope protection. One size fits all popular models and makes of telescopic sights.

The BIKINI™ Scope Cover is a quick clearing one-piece scope cover made of two water-tight rubber cups, joined by stretch-band retainers. To clear the cover from your scope, simply lift on the tab that projects from the rear cup and the cover clears quickly and quietly.

If you're a hunter or shooter you're sure to appreciate the BIKINI™ Cover's simplicity and effectiveness. Manufactured by the makers of the well known Butler Creek "flip-open" scope and camera lens covers! Write for more info.

BUTLER CREEK CORP.

HIGH-MELT BULLET LUBE

Rooster Labs now offers a choice of hardnesses in high-melt cannelure lubricants. ZAMBINI is the hard tough version.

It comes in 2″ x 6″ sticks for the commercial reloader, and 1″ x 4″ hollow and solid sticks. Lube-sizer must be warmed.

HVR is soft but firm, and applies more easily. 1″ x 4″ sticks only.

Meant for high velocity pistol and rifle, both lubes melt at 220°F, neither will melt and kill the powder.

Rooster Red lubes now enable the individual to make professional quality bullets. 2″ x 6″ sticks cost $4.00. 1″ x 4″ suggested retail $3.00, $135.00 per bulk pack of 100 sticks. Write Rooster Laboratories direct for more information.

ROOSTER LABORATORIES

SEMI-AUTO AMMO

To answer the growing demand for semi-automatic ammunition by law enforcement agencies, 3-D Ammunition and Bullets has added a good selection of quality, low-cost semi-automatic calibers to its Impact line.

This includes 45 ACP's in a 200-grain hollowpoint, 230-grain lead and plated round-nose and 230-grain full metal jacket; 380 automatics in a 90-grain jacketed hollowpoint and 95-grain full metal jacket; 10mm automatics in a 150- or 180-grain jacketed hollowpoint; 9mm's in a 115-grain jacketed hollowpoint, 115- or 124-grain full metal jacket, and 125-grain lead or plated round-nose.

For more information, contact 3-D for a FREE BROCHURE.

3-D AMMUNITION & BULLETS

RESTORING LETTERING

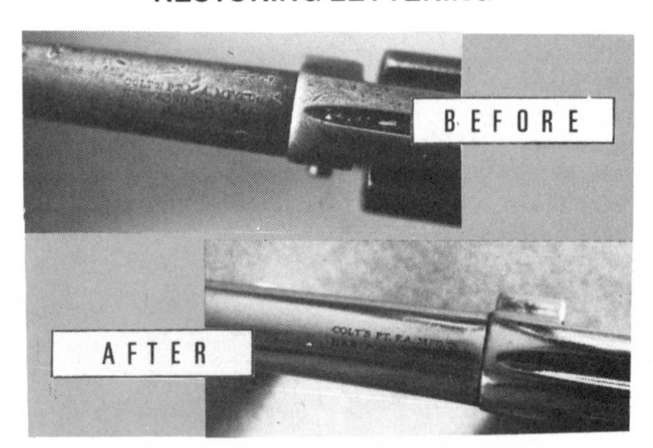

A video tape demonstration by Ed Pranger shows how to restore lettering on firearms. He calls his system "Indirect Photo-Engraving." It can also be used to mark new work; lettering, logos, etc.

No dangerous chemicals or expensive equipment are required.

The necessary typesetting and photography is usually an outside service. The balance of the work can be conveniently completed at your home or in the shop.

The only other expense is for an ingredient costing around $75.00 (and the contents of the box will do 25 or more guns). A 3-M product.

Price for the V.H.S. tape is $50.00 postpaid. Wash. state add $3.75 tax.

ED PRANGER

See manufacturers' addresses following this section.

SCREWDRIVER SET

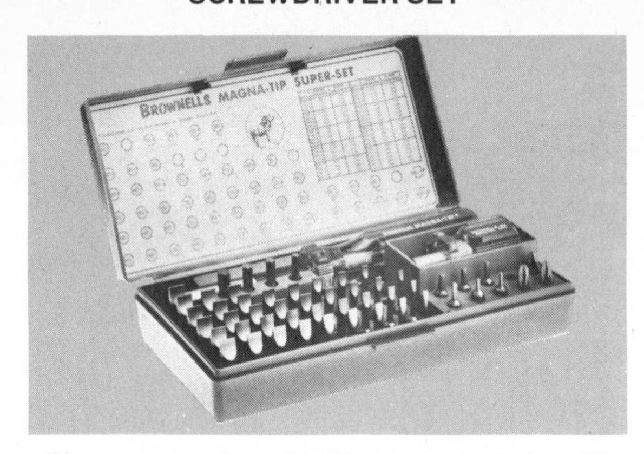

Throw away that ill fitting screwdriver. The Brownells Magna-Tip® Super-Set gives you 39 custom, true hollow ground, graduated screwdriver bits that fit 99.9% of all gun screw slots. This unique system has nine different blade widths ranging from .120″ to .360″, each with three to six blade thicknesses from narrowest/thinnest through widest/thickest. The complete *52 Bit Master Super-Set Plus* from Brownells includes 39 Custom Gunsmith bits and 10 Allen and three Phillips bits *plus* two handles, tray and case. Suggested retail price: $63.75. The Brownells *"Pro" Super-Set Plus* of 39 Custom Gunsmith Bits, two handles, tray and case is immediately available for a suggested retail price of only $52.77

BROWNELLS, INC.

PELLET FIRING CONVERSIONS

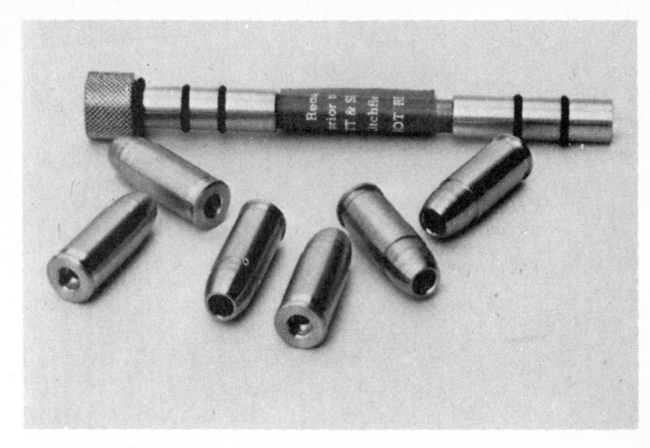

Jett & Co.'s Convert-a-Pell kit enables the shooter to convert his favorite handgun to shoot inexpensive pellets. Available for any caliber from 380 through 45LC, each Convert-a-Pell kit contains a barrel adaptor tube (to convert one's firearm bore to .177 caliber) and six brass "cartridges."

No special tools, no disassembly, and no reloading expertise required.

Will not harm bore, action, or component parts of any handgun. A 22 centerfire version of the Convert-a-Pell kit, a complete line of accessories, and a version of the kit for 243 through 303 British are also available. You can practice year round, indoors or out, when shooting with Convert-a-Pell. Manufacturer's suggested retail: Rifled Kit, $39.95.

JETT & CO., INC.

RIFLED SHOTGUN BARRELS

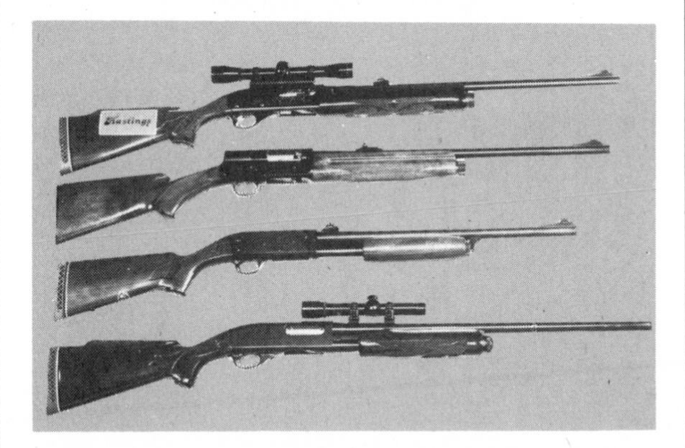

The Hastings Paradox Rifled Slug Barrel, for the shotgun hunter who insists on the accuracy only a rifled bore can provide, is the only off-the-shelf rifled shotgun barrel designed to be an exact replacement on popular makes of shotguns.

Each barrel is produced with a high finish, exacting tolerances and precise contours, and is available in 20″ or 24″ lengths with either rifle sights or special scope mounts installed.

Hastings Paradox slug barrels are available at fine gunshops, or directly from Hastings. Hastings also manufactures the Choke-Tube II system, integral choke barrels and specialized trap and Skeet barrels, and offers a full range of smithing services. Write or call for more info.

HASTINGS BARRELS

CUSTOM PRE-FINISH STOCK

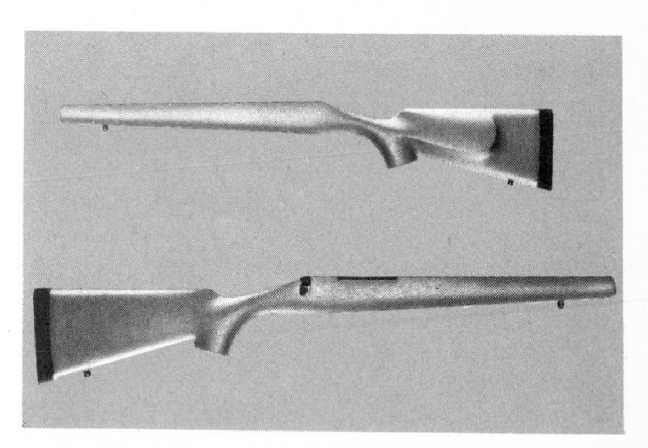

The Custom Pre-Finish stock is a Classic style hunting stock made for most factory barreled actions. Made in a dark gray, textured finish, the Custom Pre-Finish has a standard length of pull and a standard pad.

Weight is a light 1½ pounds.

Inletting is precisely fitted using a duplicate factory action. Add 10-15 minutes to bolt together the rifle with the epoxy compound included, and maximum performance is combined with the stability of synthetics. The Custom Pre-Finish stock is guaranteed for *all* calibers, and highly recommended for Magnum.

Write the manufacturer direct for more information.

BROWN PRECISION, INC.

See manufacturers' addresses following this section.

MAGNUM AIR PISTOL

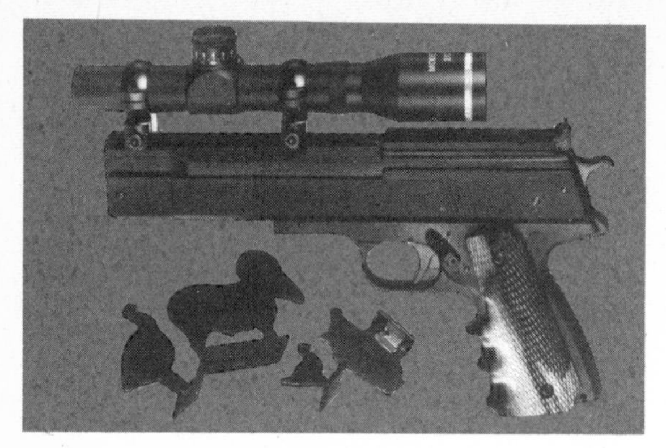

Not everyone can afford a Mercedes, but almost every shooter can stretch some to have the best in adult airguns. You Can Afford the Beeman P1—the magnum adult air pistol which stands at the top of sporting air pistols. (Shown with optional Beeman 25 scope.)

While they may cost a bit more, Beeman's proven quality and backing are well worth it. Beeman Precision offers an amazing range of both airguns *and* firearms.

Beeman's Adult Airgun/Firearms Catalog, which normally sells for $2.00, is free for the asking when you mention you saw this offer in *Shooter's Marketplace.* Write or call for more info on this or other Beeman Products.

BEEMAN PRECISION ARMS, INC.

AUXILIARY CARTRIDGES/BULLETS

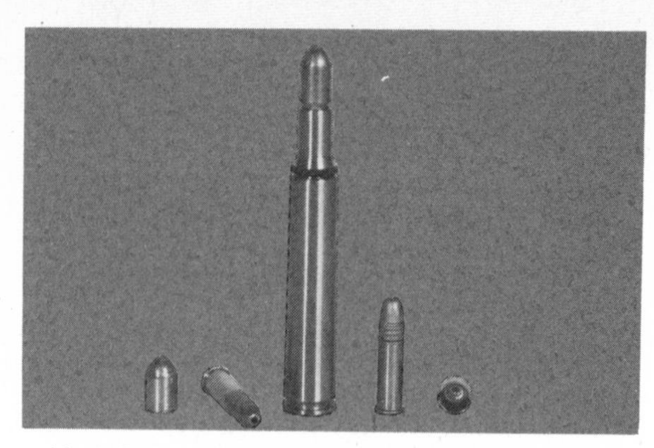

Alex, Inc., is offering new auxiliary cartridges that use 22 LR hollow point ammunition to power bore-sized, swaged lead bullets. These enable owners of rifles such as the 270 and 7mm to have the benefit of an accurate; low-powered target and small game load without reloading.

These auxiliary cartridges have an approximate velocity of 800 fps and give 1-inch, five shot groups at 25 yards.

Available in the following calibers: 250 Sav., 257 Roberts, 25-06 Rem., 270 Win., 280 Rem., 7mm Rem. Mag., 308 Win., 30-06, and 300 Win. Mag.

Price: Auxiliary Cartridge & 100 Alex Bullets—$25.00 p.p.

Extra Alex Bullets $5.00 per 100 p.p.

ALEX, INC.

SEE-THROUGH SCOPE MOUNTS

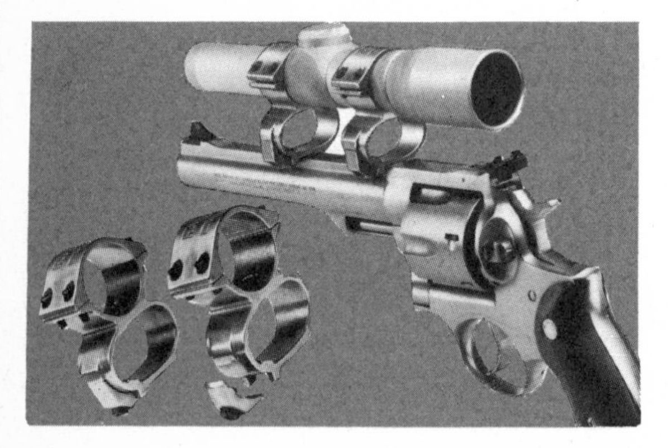

For long guns and handguns. Shown above is the Ruger Redhawk KRH-44 with integral bases, with "no-gunsmithing" Holden Model 732ss steel see-thru mounts. Convert your gun to a double-duty "Ironsighter!" This 2-way sighting system will make you a better hunter. Use your scope—or tilt your head to use your Ironsighters. Also available for: •centerfire rifles •22 cal. rimfire handguns •shotguns-slug barreled •muzzleloaders. New Wide Ironsighters are available in High Profile and Low Profile models. They're made from the highest tensile strength aluminum alloy available—for maximum rigidity and accuracy! Send for your FREE Ironsighter catalog with complete details on the original "See-Thru" scope mounts.

J.B. HOLDEN CO.

SHOTGUN AMMO CARRIER

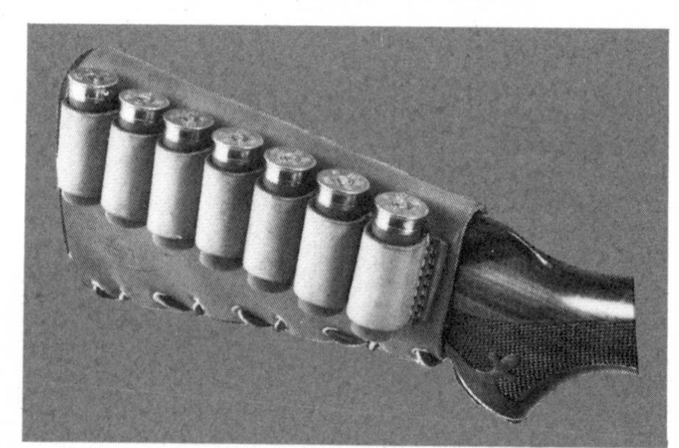

Milt Sparks Leather, long known for practical holsters, offers an all leather shotgun ammo carrier which will not slip forward under recoil. The Cold Comfort Shotgun Cheekpiece laces on to your shotgun's buttstock, providing seven extra rounds which will always be with your gun. No more fumbling in boxes or pockets. Lacing eyelets are padded by a leather gusset, and there are no rivets to scratch the stock. Available in 12 gauge only.

The #C/C Cold Comfort Shotgun Cheek Piece is available direct from the manufacturer for $35.00 in natural tan, $40.00 in black or dark cordovan, plus $2.00 postage and handling per unit.

A catalog of Milt Sparks's full line of holsters is available for $2.00.

MILT SPARKS LEATHER

See manufacturers' addresses following this section.

PROTECTIVE GUN OIL

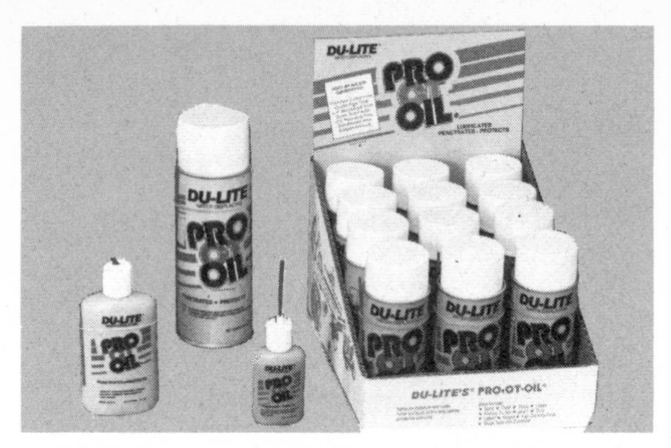

Du-Lite Pro-Ct-Oil is a unique oil product that penetrates, removes moisture, and leaves a long lasting, lubricating, rust preventative film.

Du-Lite has manufactured bluing supplies and protective oils for gunsmiths and gun manufacturers since 1939, and Pro-Ct-Oil is the same oil used by major gun makers like Sturm, Ruger & Co., U.S. Repeating Arms, Thompson/Center Arms, and Charter Arms.

Now available to the public, Pro-Ct-Oil is ideal for protection and lubrication of firearms, fishing and boating equipment, tools, and assemblies.

Pro-Ct-Oil is packaged in 1¼ oz. and 4 oz. squeeze bottles, and in 4 oz. and 12 oz. aerosol cans.

Call or write for full information.

DU-LITE CORPORATION

SEMI-AUTOMATIC PISTOL

The Davis Industries 32 Auto, when matched with the right ammunition, out-performs 380 Automatics using FMJ loads as a backup or personal defense posture.

Davis uses a high-strength non-ferrous alloy frame and slide, fitted with a steel insert breechblock and steel barrel and firing mechanism. The solid steel striker has a circular "collar" to protect the sear—a much stronger design than most guns of this type. Sights are integral with the slide and provide a large, clear sight picture.

The Davis P-32 is available in chrome, black teflon, or satin nickel.

Suggested list: $87.50.

Write or call direct for more info.

DAVIS INDUSTRIES

LASER SIGHT

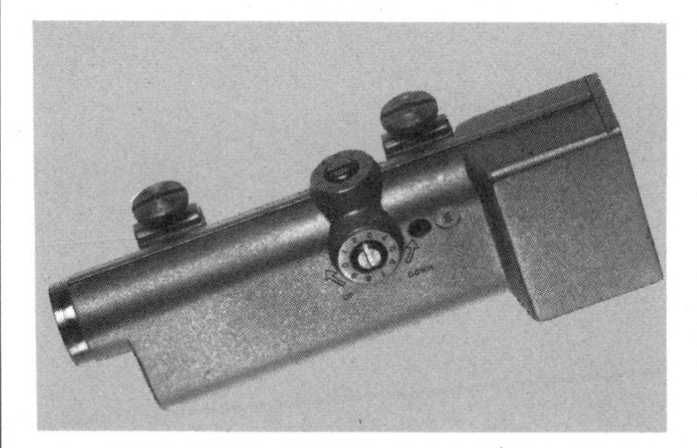

The Laserscope™, Model FA-6 is rugged, lightweight and reliable. Its advanced design allows instant, sure-shot accuracy with all guns, pistols, revolvers, and bows for all law enforcement agencies, hunters, and sports games. Also available is the powerful Laserscope™, Model FA-9 for use on rifles, and the Model FA-9P for use on submachine guns.

Laser Devices designs, engineers, and manufactures the complete Laserscope™ in-house, including the HeNe laser tubes. A full range of mounts and accessories are available.

You can train around the clock with the patented, re-usable ACCUR-AIM™ Laser Target or special Daytime Glasses, for training *with* or *without* live ammunition.

LASER DEVICES, INC.

LIGHTWEIGHT FOLDING SAW

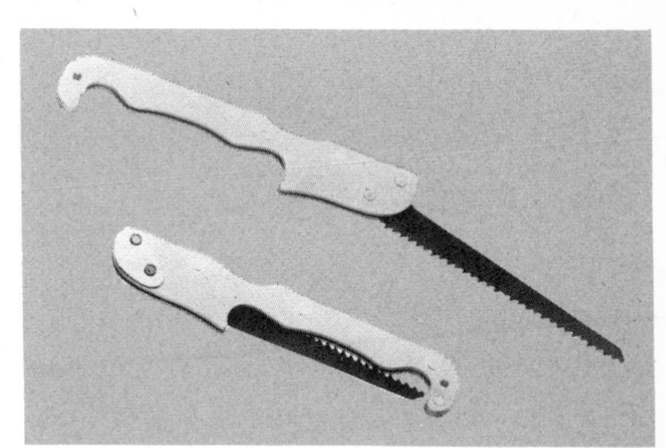

Only 2¾ ounces and 7″ long in the closed position, this lightweight folding saw was developed to fit the needs of the hunter,camper, or backpacker who may need a high quality, efficient saw but doesn't want to carry around bulky equipment.

In the positive lock open position, the 5″ carbon steel blade will easily handle any wilderness task—from field dressing big game to sawing small trees. In the closed position, it is convenient and easy to carry. The high-strength anodized aluminum handle and stainless locking mechanism means years of carefree use. Even miles from camp, you're always prepared with a Wilderness Folding Saw.

Mfg. suggested retail price $29.95. Cordura nylon case available at $4.50.

WILDERNESS TRADING COMPANY, LTD.

See manufacturers' addresses following this section.

.410 BUCKSHOT

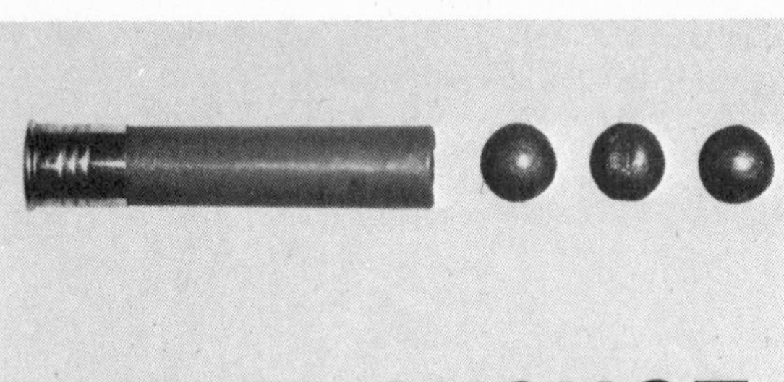

American Derringer Corp. has recently begun delivery of its new .410 Buckshot. It is loaded with three pellets of 000 Buckshot (.357″ Diameter). Muzzle velocity is 1300 fps; total muzzle energy is 930 foot pounds, or 310 fpe per pellet. This Buckshot load greatly increases the stopping power and effectiveness of the .410 Shotgun. .410 Buckshot can be used in any modern shotgun or pistol chambered for either 2½″ .410, 3″ .410, 45 Colt/.410 2″ (American Derringer Model 1 Pistol), or 45 Colt/.410 3″ (American Derringer Model 4 Snake Pistol or Model 6 Survival Pistol). The ammunition is loaded by Winchester exclusively for American Derringer. Suggested retail is $4.95. Write for the name of your nearest dealer.

AMERICAN DERRINGER

COLD WEATHER BOOT

Servus Rubber Company's Northerner line has introduced a high-tech boot designed for comfort in low temperature work or sport conditions. The Polartek™ boot will withstand the coldest conditions with a three zone insulation package of a soft removable lined innerboot to retain body heat, a 400-gram Thinsulate® thermal barrier and a thick, Ensolite® sole cold shield. This waterproof boot has a new ozone resistant cleat sole rubber bottom and a stain proof, puncture resistant Condesa® ballistic polypropylene fabric and leather trimmed top. The Polartek™ boot is well suited for hunting or fishing, especially when the wearer is stationary in a very cold environment. Available in Black or Golden Brown in sizes 6-14. Contact Servus for info.

SERVUS RUBBER COMPANY, INC.

RED-DOT OPTICAL SIGHT

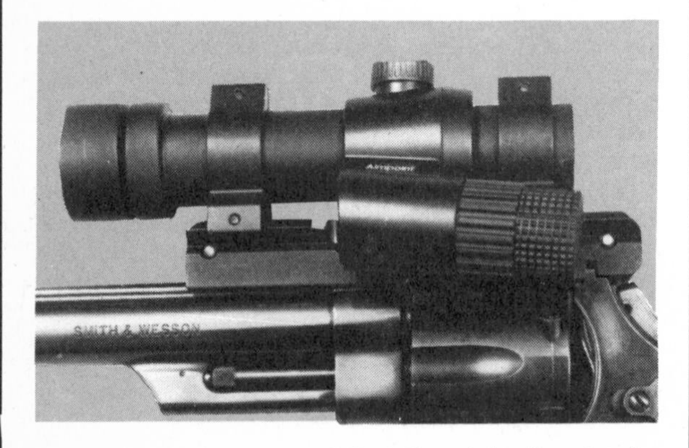

Aimpoint, the original Red-Dot sight for pistols, rifles, shotguns and bows has been serving shooters and hunters for over a decade. Indeed, Aimpoint's Red-Dot sight is one of the most advanced multipurpose electronic sighting systems made; and, the results in the field, and in competition, speak well of this unique product.

Easy to use?

You bet. Just put the red dot on the target and pull the trigger. No parallax, no focusing and no need to center the dot. It's one of the fastest "on-target" optical sights ever made. Easily mounts to any firearms using standard Weaver or Aimpoint mounting systems. For more information, write direct or call Aimpoint.

AIMPOINT

CARBELITE RIFLE/SHOTGUN STOCKS

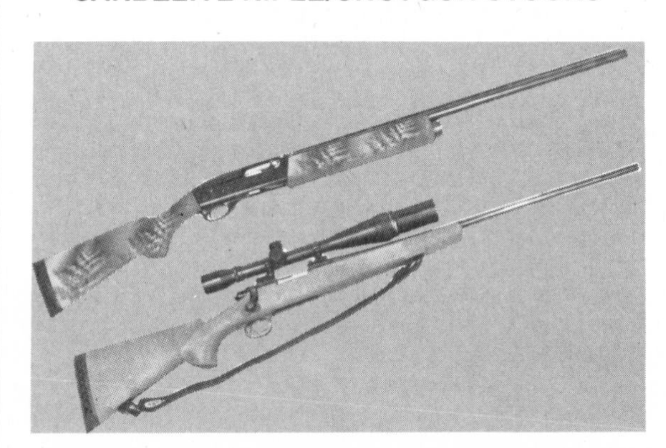

A high-tech manufacturing process combining Kevlar, continuous fiber bands, and lateral reinforcement of woven panels of fiberglass make the Bell & Carlson Carbelite stocks one of the strongest stocks available. Durable baked-on finishes in black, gray, green camo or brown camo make this lightweight stock impervious to moisture, heat, and cold. A lifetime warranty comes with each stock.

A unique "retrofit" feature eliminates custom fitting for many popular rifle actions and the Remington 870 & 1100 Model Shotguns. Includes a fitted recoil pad and fine-line checkering.

Suggested retail on rifle stocks is only $119.95 and for shotguns (buttstock & forearm) $97.50 For more info on all Bell & Carlson stocks, write or call.

BELL & CARLSON

See manufacturers' addresses following this section.

AMMUNITION CARRIERS

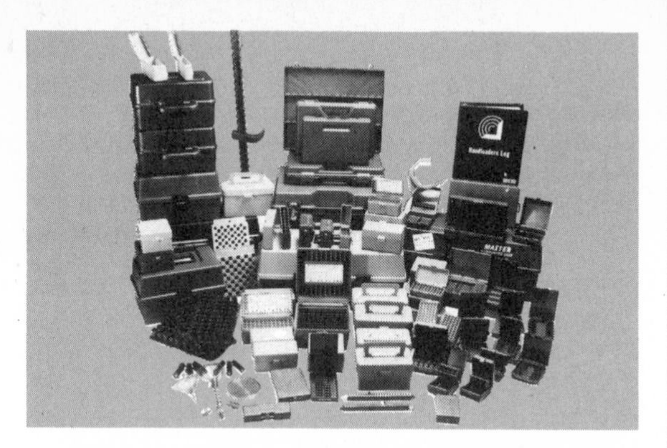

MTM's offering of CASEGARD® ammunition carriers is the most extensive on the market. There are units of various capacities for handgun, rifle, shotgun and small bore ammunition—twenty two models in more than fifty configurations. Hunters, competition shooters and casual plinkers around the world rely upon CASEGARD®, and every product is backed up by MTM's 3-year Guarantee.

MTM offers an excellent variety of unique products for both the hunter and shooter, as well as the reloader.

Their CASEGARD® Line of ammo carriers have proved their value in the field for years.

Write or call for MTM Molded Products Company direct for a FREE catalog.

MTM MOLDED PRODUCTS CO.

FIREARMS CATALOG

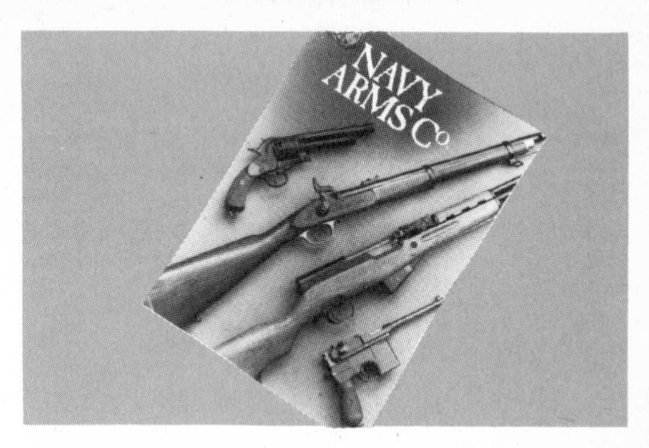

Navy Arms was created in 1958 to market newly manufactured cap and ball revolvers.

Since those days in the 1950s, Navy Arms has produced an ever expanding line of black powder firearms.

The "YANK" and "REB" revolvers became registered trade marks of the firm denoting the first two Navy-styled guns to be produced by the company some 30 years ago.

To bridge the gap from the 19th to the 20th century, NAVY ARMS offers an excellent line of military surplus firearms from sources located all over the world.

For more detailed information, send $2.00 for a complete Navy Arms catalog.

NAVY ARMS COMPANY

GUN PARTS CATALOG

The Gun Parts Corporation is continuing in the fine NUMRICH ARMS tradition by offering a brand new, updated (450+ Pages) 14th Ed. catalog.

You'll find complete listing and pricing of the more than 250 million gun parts they currently have in stock.

This is a standard reference for gunsmiths, shooters, collectors and military organizations worldwide.

It consists of machine guns, military, U.S., foreign, commercial and antique gun parts—all of which they stock. This catalog contains hundreds of schematic drawings.

To order, simply send $4.95. (Foreign surface mail orders: $8.95—Write for Airmail quote.)

THE GUN PARTS CORPORATION

HOME GUNSMITHING LATHE

The name "Unimat" has been around the gun trade for over 30 years. Great for firing pins, bushings, pistol barrels, bolts, or any small part requiring precision machining. The Unimat 3 has 8 spindle speeds, a cast iron bed, precision headstock bearings and fully adjustable gibs. It is a miniature universal machine tool for longitudinal turning, facing, external and internal taper turning, drilling, milling, dividing, sawing, grinding, polishing, combing, grooving, coving, and wood turning.

Send for FREE color brochure and complete Blue Ridge catalog or call toll free. Mention Gun Digest for special package price. Blue Ridge offers a complete selection of lathes, mills and machine shop supplies for the gunsmith.

BLUE RIDGE MACHINERY & TOOLS

See manufacturers' addresses following this section.

SHOOTING ACCESSORIES

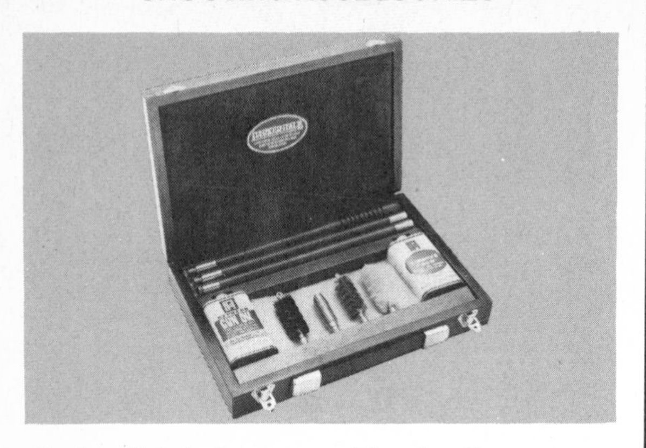

Parker-Hale's famous quality shooting accessories are once again available in the U.S., imported from England by Precision Sports, a Division of Cortland Line Company.

British-made throughout, the following Parker-Hale accessories provide the knowledgeable shooter with a standard of excellence equal to his choice of fine guns.

- Presentation Cleaning Sets
- Snap Caps
- Rosewood Shotgun Rods
- Steel Rifle Rods
- Phosphor Bronze Brushes
- Jags, Loops, and Mops
- Youngs "303" Cleaner
- Express Oil
- Rangoon Oil
- 009 Nitro Solvent
- Black Powder Solvent
- Comet Super Blue

PARKER-HALE/PRECISION SPORTS

SLUG SHOTGUN SIGHTS

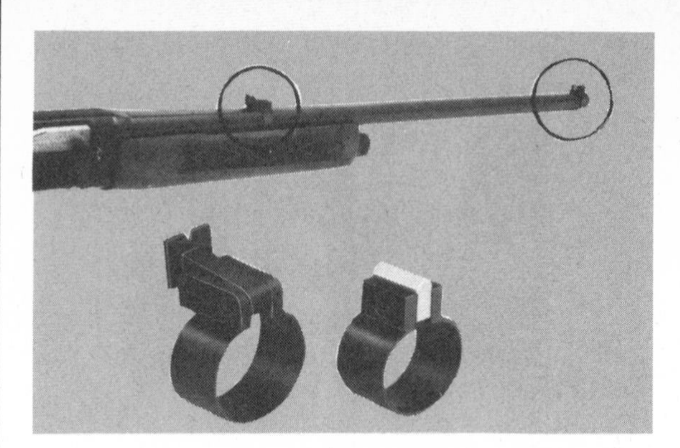

Slug Sights are a simple, rugged, and easy to attach set of sights for non-ribbed single-barreled shotguns, such as pumps, auto-loaders, bolts and single shots.

These Sights will provide for the precise sighting necessary for the accurate use of slugs in shotguns, without drilling, tapping, or interfering with the gun's action.

Made of a tough non-marring black nylon, **Slug Sights** actually stretch and lock to the shotgun's barrel. The Sights are low profile with Blaze Orange front sight blades, and are fully adjustable for elevation and windage.

Only $9.95, **Slug Sights** are available in 12, 16, and 20 gauges. Write or Call For More Info!

INNOVISION ENTERPRISES

TARGET SYSTEM

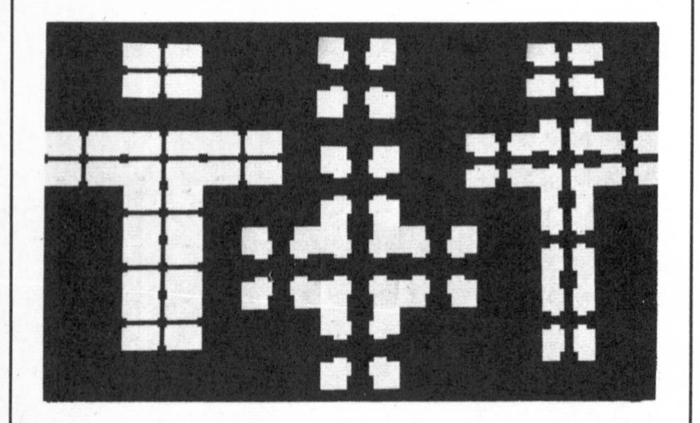

The new -X-Spand Target System is designed to help the shooter perform various exterior ballistics tests at close, medium or long ranges. Ideal for rimfires on up, reloads or factory ammo. Expand the target size and test the extreme ranges that high power rifles are capable of attaining. Calibrate precision ballistics for shotgun patterns, and exact load data. Two target sizes with three distinct, compatible patterns: the Very Fine, Fine and Coarse pattern targets. Two complete systems, Standard or Metric design. 75 targets, 25 of each target pattern: Special $23.00 (Canadian dollars). *Very Fine Pattern,* 12x18" targets effective to 200 yds. *Fine Pattern,* effective to 500 yds. *Coarse Pattern,* 18x18" targets for ranges beyond 500 yds. Write for info.

MAKI INDUSTRIES

NEW SHOOTING BENCH

Joe Hall's Shooting Products just announced the addition of complete plans for a portable/adjustable shooter's bench. This unique product is vertically and angularly adjustable to 8 different positions and is adaptable to all shooters and terrain.

Joe Hall's shooting experts, have designed a bench which enables the rifle and handgun shooter to practice and repeat "off-hand" shooting positions both on the range and in the field. The bench, when folded, carries like a suitcase and measures about 48" x 18" x 6" deep.

Plans include all dimensions and complete list of materials.

Plans are available at $9.95 plus $2.50 shipping and handling.

JOE HALL'S SHOOTING PRODUCTS, INC.

See manufacturers' addresses following this section.

MANUFACTURERS' ADDRESSES

AIMPOINT
Attn.: Dept. GD-89
203 Elden St.
Herndon, VA 22070 (703-471-6828)

ALEX, INC.
Dept. SM'89
P.O. Box 3034
Bozeman, MT 59715

AMERICAN DERRINGER CORP.
Dept. GD-89
P.O. Box 8983
Waco, TX 76714 (817-799-9111)

BALLISTICS RESEARCH GROUP
KayuSoft International
Star Rt.
Spray, OR 97874 (503-462-3934)

BEEMAN PRECISION ARMS, INC.
Attn.: Dept. SM'89
3440 Airway Dr.
Santa Rosa, CA 95403-2040 (707-578-7900)

BELL & CARLSON
Dept. GD-89 509 N. 5th St.
Atwood, KS 67730 (913-626-3204)

BLUE RIDGE MACHINERY AND TOOLS, INC.
Dept. GD-89
P.O. Box 536
Hurricane, WV 25526
(1-800-872-6500 ; in WV 304-562-3538)

BROWN PRECISION INC.
P.O. Box 270GD
Los Molinos, CA 96055 (916-384-2506)
(*Order line* 1-800-543-2506)

W.E. BROWNELL CHECKERING TOOLS
Dept. GD-89
3356 Moraga Pl.
San Diego, CA 92117

BROWNELLS, INC.
Dept. GD-89
222 West Liberty
Montezuma, IA 50171

B-SQUARE CO.
Dept. GDSM
P.O. Box 11281
Fort Worth, TX 76110 (817-923-0964)

BUTLER CREEK CORPORATION
Dept. GDSM 290 Arden Dr.
Belgrade, MT 59714 (406-388-1356)

CLYMER MANUFACTURING CO., INC.
Dept. GD-89
1645 West Hamlin Rd.
Rochester Hills, MI 48063 (313-853-5555)

DAVIS INDUSTRIES, INC.
Dept. S.M.
15150 Sierra Bonita Lane
Chino, CA 91710 (714-597-4726)

DU-LITE CORPORATION
Dept. GD-89 171 River Rd.
Middletown, CT 06457 (203-347-2505)

FREEDOM ARMS
P.O. Box 1776
Freedom, WY 83120

THE GUN PARTS CORP.
Successors to Numrich Arms Corp.
P.O. Box SMP
West Hurley, NY 12491 (914-679-2417)

THE GUN ROOM
Ben Shostle, Engraver
Dept. GDSM
1121 Burlington
Muncie, IN 47302 (317-282-9073)

HANDGUN PRESS
Box 406X
Glenview, IL 60025

JOE HALL'S SHOOTING PRODUCTS INC.
443 Wells Road
Doylestown, PA 18901

HASTINGS BARRELS
Dept. SM'89
Box 224
Clay Center, KS 67432 (913-632-2184)

J.B. HOLDEN CO.
Attn.: Jerry B. - S.M.
P.O. Box 320
Plymouth, MI 48170

HUNTINGTON DIE SPECIALTIES
Attn.: Buzz Huntington
P.O. Box 991
Oroville, CA 95965 (916-534-1210)

INNOVISION ENTERPRISES
Dept. GDSM
728 Skinner Drive
Kalamazoo, MI 49001 (616-382-1681)

JETT & CO., INC.
R.R. #3 Box 167B
Litchfield, IL 62056 (217-324-3779)

KOWA OPTIMED, INC.
Attn.: Dept. SM'89
20001 S. Vermont Ave.
Torrance, CA 90502 (213-327-1913)

LASER DEVICES, INC.
Dept. GDSM
#5 Hangar Way
Watsonville, CA 95076 (408-722-8300)

MAKI INDUSTRIES
26 - 10th St., S.E. Dept. GD-89
Medicine Hat, AB T1A 1P7
CANADA (403-526-7997)

MERIT CORPORATION
Attn.: C.M. Grant
Dept. SM'89 Box 9044
Schenectady, NY 12309 (518-346-1420)

MODERN GUN REPAIR SCHOOL
Dept. GBK89
2538 N. 8th Street
Phoenix, AZ 85006 (602-990-8346)

MTM MOLDED PRODUCTS CO.
P.O. Box 14117
Dayton, OH 45414 (513-890-7461)

NAVY ARMS COMPANY
689 Bergen Blvd.
Ridgefield, NJ 07657 (201-945-2500)

THE NGRAVER® COMPANY
Dept. GD-89
879 Raymond Hill Rd.
Oakdale, CT 06370

OLD WORLD OIL PRODUCTS
Dept. GD-89
3827 Queen Ave. North
Minneapolis, MN 55412 (612-522-5037)

P.S. OLT CO.
GD-89
P.O. Box 550
Pekin, IL 61554

OUTERS LABORATORIES
Attn.: John Wiggert, S.M.
P.O. Box 39
Onalaska, WI 54650 (608-783-1515)

PACHMAYR, LTD.
1875 S. Mountain Ave.
Monrovia, CA 91016

PARKER-HALE/PRECISION SPORTS DIV.
Mr. Greg Pogson
Dept. GD-89
P.O. Box 708-5588
Cortland, NY 13045-5588

ED PRANGER
1414 7th Street
Anacortes, WA 98221 (206-293-3488)

PROFESSIONAL HUNTER SUPPLIES
Dept. GD-89
444½ Main St., P.O. Box 608
Ferndale, CA 95536

R.D.P. TOOL COMPANY, INC.
Dept. SM'89
49162 McCoy Ave.
East Liverpool, OH 43920 (216-385-5129)

RIG PRODUCTS
Attn.: GDSM
87 Coney Island Dr.
Sparks, NV 89431-6317 (702-331-5666)

ROOSTER LABORATORIES
Attn.: Dept. SM'89
P.O. Box 412514
Kansas City, MO 64141 (816-474-1622)

RTI RESEARCH LTD.
Dept. SM'89
P.O. Box 48300
Bentall Three Tower
Vancouver, B.C. V7X 1A1
CANADA (604-588-5141)

SAFARILAND LTD., INC.
1941 So. Walker Ave.
Monrovia, CA 91016 (818-357-7902)

SERVUS RUBBER COMPANY, INC.
1136 2nd St.
Box 36
Rock Island, IL 61201-0036
(1-800-222-2668; In IL 1-800-225-2668)

MILT SPARKS LEATHER
Dept. DB
P.O. Box 187
Idaho City, ID 83631 (208-392-6695)

STORM KING
ANDERSON MANUFACTURING COMPANY
P.O. Box 536
Kent, WA 98032

3-D AMMUNITION AND BULLETS
112 Plum St. - P.O. Box J
Doniphan, NE 68832 (402-845-2285)

ULTRA LIGHT ARMS, INC.
Attn.: M. Forbes, Dept. GD-89
Box 1270
Granville, WV 26534 (304-599-5687)

VITT/BOOS AERODYNAMIC SLUG
Attn.: Raymond Boos
2178 Nichols Ave.
Stratford, CT 06497

WAMCO, INC.
Dept. GD-89
Mingo Loop, P.O. Box 337
Oquossoc, ME 04964 (1-800-227-1415)

WILDERNESS TRADING COMPANY, LTD.
Dept. D.
P.O. Box 13230
Shawnee Mission, KS 66212
(1-800-872-4866)

WILSON'S GUN SHOP, INC.
Rt. 3, Box 211-D
P.O. Box 578
Berryville, AR 72616 (501-545-3618)

GUNDEX®

A listing of all the guns in the catalog, by name and model, alphabetically and numerically.

A

B

C

D

E

F

G

H

I

J

K

L

S

T

U

V

W

Z

Includes models suitable for several forms of competition and other sporting purposes.

AMT 45 ACP HARDBALLER LONG SLIDE
Caliber: 45 ACP.
Barrel: 7″.
Length: 10½″ over-all.
Stocks: Wrap-around rubber.
Sights: Fully adjustable rear sight.
Features: Slide and barrel are 2″ longer than the standard 45, giving less recoil, added velocity, longer sight radius. Has extended combat safety, serrated matte rib, loaded chamber indicator, wide adjustable trigger. From AMT.
Price: **$499.00**

AMT Long Slide

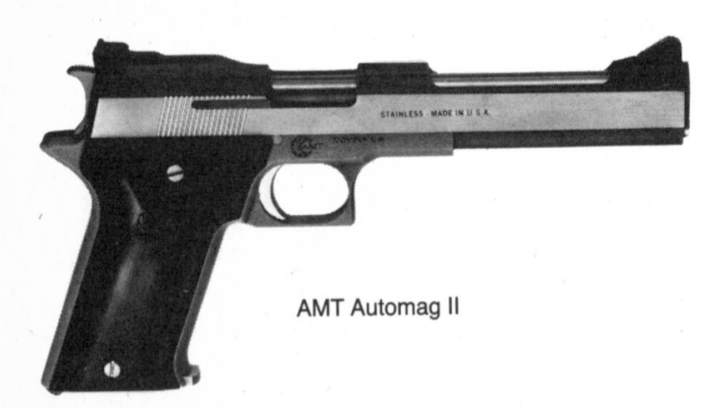

AMT Automag II

AMT AUTOMAG II AUTO PISTOL
Caliber: 22 WMR, 10-shot magazine.
Barrel: 3⅜″, 4½″, 6″.
Weight: About 23 oz. **Length:** 9⅜″ over-all.
Stocks: Smooth black composition.
Sights: Blade front, Millett adjustable rear.
Features: Made of stainless steel. Gas-assisted action. Exposed hammer. Slide flats have brushed finish, rest is sandblast. Squared triggerguard. Introduced 1986. From AMT.
Price: **$329.00**

AMT LIGHTNING AUTO PISTOL
Caliber: 22 LR, 10-shot magazine.
Barrel: Tapered or Bull—6½″, 8½″, 10″; Bull—5″.
Weight: 45 oz. (6½″ barrel). **Length:** 10¾″ over-all (6½″ barrel).
Stocks: Checkered wrap-around rubber.
Sights: Blade front, Millett adjustable rear.
Features: Made of stainless steel. Uses Clark trigger with adjustable stops; receiver grooved for scope mounting; trigger guard spur for two-hand hold; interchangeable barrels. Introduced 1984. From AMT.
Price: 5″ bull, 6½″ tapered or bull **$289.00**
Price: 8½″, tapered or bull **$289.00**
Price: 10″, tapered or bull **$289.00**

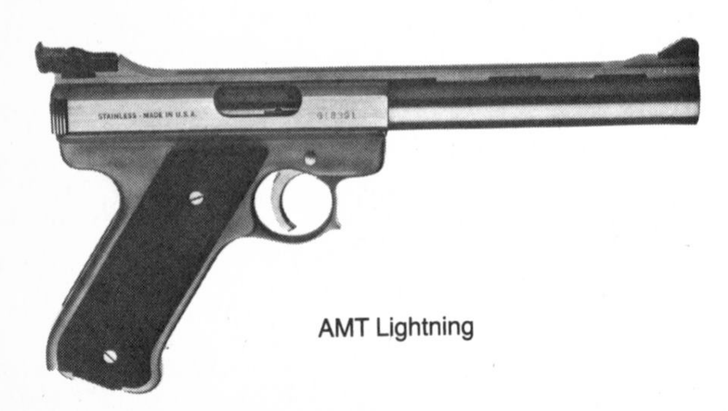

AMT Lightning

AMT "BACKUP" AUTO PISTOL
Caliber: 22 LR, 8-shot magazine; 380 ACP, 5-shot magazine
Barrel: 2½″.
Weight: 18 oz. **Length:** 4.25″ over-all.
Stocks: Checkered Lexon.
Sights: Fixed, open, recessed.
Features: Concealed hammer, blowback operation; manual and grip safeties. All stainless steel construction. Smallest domestically-produced pistol in 380. From AMT.
Price: 22 LR or 380 ACP **$237.00**

AMT Backup

AMT 45 ACP HARDBALLER
Caliber: 45 ACP.
Barrel: 5″.
Weight: 39 oz. **Length:** 8½″ over-all.
Stocks: Wrap-around rubber.
Sights: Adjustable.
Features: Extended combat safety, serrated matte slide rib, loaded chamber indicator, long grip safety, beveled magazine well, adjustable target trigger. All stainless steel. From AMT
Price: **$465.00**
Price: Government model (as above except no rib, fixed sights) **$403.00**

ACTION ARMS AT-84 DA PISTOL
Caliber: 9mm Para., 15 shots; 41 Action Express, 10 shots.
Barrel: 4.72″.
Weight: 35.3 oz. **Length:** 8.1″ over-all.
Stocks: Checkered walnut.
Sights: Blade front, rear drift-adjustable for windage.
Features: Double action; polished blue finish. Introduced 1987. Imported from Switzerland by Action Arms Ltd.
Price: **$525.00**
Price: Model 84P (3.66″ bbl., 7.24″ o.a.l., weighs 32.1 ozs., and has 13/8-shot magazine) **$525.00**

AMERICAN ARMS TT9MM AUTO PISTOL
Caliber: 9mm Para., 9-shot magazine.
Barrel: 4.5″.
Weight: 32 oz. **Length:** 8″ over-all.
Stocks: Grooved plastic
Sights: Fixed.
Features: Single-action mechanism. Blue finish. Imported from Yugoslavia by American Arms, Inc. Introduced 1988.
Price: **$288.00**

CAUTION: PRICES CHANGE. CHECK AT GUNSHOP.

AMERICAN ARMS EP380 AUTO PISTOL
Caliber: 380 ACP, 7-shot magazine.
Barrel: 3½".
Weight: 25 oz. **Length:** 6½" over-all.
Stocks: Checkered wood.
Sights: Fixed.
Features: Double action. Made of stainless steel. Slide-mounted safety. Imported from West Germany by American Arms, Inc. Introduced 1988.
Price: **$540.00**

AMERICAN ARMS PK22 D/A AUTO PISTOL
Caliber: 22 LR, 8-shot magazine.
Barrel: 3.3".
Weight: 22 oz. **Length:** 6.3" over-all.
Stocks: Checkered plastic.
Sights: Fixed.
Features: Double action. Polished blue finish. Slide-mounted safety. Made in the U.S. by American Arms, Inc.
Price: **$199.00**

ASTRA A-90 DOUBLE-ACTION AUTO PISTOL
Caliber: 9mm Para. (15-shot), 45 ACP (9-shot).
Barrel: 3.75".
Weight: 40 oz. **Length:** 7" over-all.
Stocks: Checkered black plastic.
Sights: Square blade front, square notch rear drift-adjustable for windage.
Features: Double or single action; loaded chamber indicator; combat-style trigger guard; optional right-side slide release (for left-handed shooters); automatic internal safety; decocking lever. Introduced 1985. Imported from Spain by Interarms.
Price: Blue.......... **$450.00**

ASTRA CONSTABLE AUTO PISTOL
Caliber: 22 LR, 10-shot; 380 ACP, 7-shot.
Barrel: 3½".
Weight: 26 oz.
Stocks: Moulded plastic.
Sights: Adj. rear.
Features: Double action, quick no-tool takedown, non-glare rib on slide. 380 available in blue, stainless steel, or chrome finish. Engraved guns also available—contact the importer. Imported from Spain by Interarms.
Price: Blue, 22 .... **$325.00**
Price: Chrome, 22 .... **$330.00**
Price: Blue, 380 .... **$305.00**

AUTO-ORDNANCE 1911A1 AUTOMATIC PISTOL
Caliber: 9mm Para., 38 Super, 9-shot; 41 Action Express, 8-shot; 45 ACP, 7-shot magazine.
Barrel: 5".
Weight: 39 oz. **Length:** 8½" over-all.
Stocks: Checkered plastic with medallion.
Sights: Blade front, rear adj. for windage.
Features: Same specs as 1911A1 military guns—parts interchangeable. Frame and slide blued; each radius has non-glare finish. Made in U.S. by Auto-Ordnance Corp.
Price: 45 cal.......... **$344.95**
Price: 9mm, 38 Super, 41 A.E. **$381.95**

Consult our Directory pages for the location of firms mentioned.

BEEMAN MINI P-08 AUTO PISTOL
Caliber: 380 ACP (5-shot).
Barrel: 3.5".
Weight: 22½ oz. **Length:** 7⅜" over-all.
Stocks: Checkered hardwood.
Sights: Fixed.
Features: Toggle action similar to original "Luger" pistol. Slide stays open after last shot. Has magazine and sear disconnect safety systems. Imported from West Germany by Beeman.
Price: **$389.50**

AMERICAN ARMS ZC380 AUTO PISTOL
Caliber: 380 ACP, 8-shot magazine.
Barrel: 3.75".
Weight: 26 oz. **Length:** 6.5" over-all.
Stocks: Checkered plastic.
Sights: Fixed.
Features: Single-action mechanism. Polished blue finish. Imported from Yugoslavia by American Arms, Inc. Introduced 1988.
Price: **$288.00**

Astra A-90 Pistol

Astra A-60 Double Action Pistol
Similar to the Constable except in 380 only, with 13-shot magazine, slide-mounted ambidextrous safety. Available in blued steel only. Introduced 1980.
Price: **$400.00**

AUSTRALIAN AUTOMATIC ARMS SAP PISTOL
Caliber: 223, 20- or 30-shot magazine.
Barrel: 10.5".
Weight: 5.9 lbs. **Length:** 20.5" over-all.
Stocks: Checkered composition.
Sights: Protected post front, revolving aperture rear adjustable for windage.
Features: Gas operated with short-stroke mobile cylinder. Hammer forged barrel with chrome chamber and bore. Imported from Australia by Kendall International.
Price: **$750.00**

Auto-Ordnance 1911A1

BEEMAN MODEL P-08 AUTO PISTOL

Caliber: 22 LR, 8-shot magazine.
Barrel: 4".
Weight: 25 oz. **Length:** 7¾" over-all.
Stocks: Checkered hardwood.
Sights: Fixed.
Features: Has toggle action similar to original "Luger" pistol. Slide stays open after last shot. Imported from West Germany by Beeman.
Price: **$389.50**

Beeman P-08

BERNARDELLI PO18 DA PISTOL

Caliber: 9mm Para., 16-shot magazine.
Barrel: 4.8".
Weight: 36.3 ozs. **Length:** 6.2" over-all.
Stocks: Checkered, contoured plastic standard; walnut optional.
Sights: Low profile combat sights.
Features: Manual thumb safety, half-cock, magazine safties, auto-locking firing pin block safety; ambidextrous magazine release. Introduced 1987. From Mandall Shooting Supplies.
Price: With plastic grips **$595.00**

Bernardelli PO 18

BERNARDELLI MODEL 60 AUTO PISTOL

Caliber: 22 LR, 10-shot; 32 ACP, 9-shot; 380 ACP, 7-shot.
Barrel: 3½".
Weight: 26½ oz. **Length:** 6½" over-all.
Stocks: Checkered plastic with thumbrest.
Sights: Ramp front, white outline rear adj. for w. & e.
Features: Hammer block slide safety; loaded chamber indicator; dual recoil buffer springs; serrated trigger; inertia-type firing pin. Imported from Italy by Mandall Shooting Supplies.
Price: **$289.95**

Beretta Model 87

BERETTA MODEL 84/85 DA PISTOLS

Caliber: 380 ACP, 13-shot magazine; 22 LR, 7-shot (M87).
Barrel: 3.82".
Weight: About 23 oz. (M84/85), 20.8 oz. (M87). **Length:** 6.8" over-all.
Stocks: Glossy black plastic (wood optional at extra cost).
Sights: Fixed front, drift-adjustable rear.
Features: Double action, quick take-down, convenient magazine release. Introduced 1977. Imported from Italy by Beretta USA.
Price: Model 84 (380 ACP) **$456.00**
Price: Model 84 wood grips **$484.00**
Price: Model 84 nickel finish **$512.00**
Price: Model 85 nickel finish **$406.00**
Price: Model 85 plastic grips **$378.00**
Price: Model 85 wood grips **$392.00**
Price: Model 87, 22 LR, 7-shot magazine **$412.00**
Price: Model 87 Long Barrel, 22 LR, single action **$427.00**
Price: Model 89 Sport Wood, single action, 22 LR................ **$525.00**

Beretta Model 950 BS-4

BERETTA MODEL 950 BS AUTO PISTOL

Caliber: 22 Short, 6-shot; 25 ACP, 8-shot.
Barrel: 2.5".
Weight: 9.9 oz. (22 Short, 10.2 oz.) **Length:** 4.5" over-all.
Stocks: Checkered black plastic.
Sights: Fixed.
Features: Single action. Thumb safety; tip-up barrel for direct loading/unloading, cleaning. From Beretta U.S.A.
Price: Blue, 25 .... **$152.00**
Price: Blue, 22 .... **$152.00**
Price: EL model (gold etching) **$217.00**

Beretta Model 21

Beretta Model 21 Pistol

Similar to the Model 950 BS. Chambered for 22 LR and 25 ACP. Both double action. 2.5" barrel, 4.9" over-all length. 7-round magazine on 22 cal.; 8-round magazine on 25 cal; 22 cal. available in nickel finish. Both have walnut grips. Introduced in 1985.
Price: 22 cal **$215.00**
Price: 22 cal, nickel finish.. **$238.00**
Price: 25 cal **$215.00**
Price: EL model, 22 or 25.. **$250.00**

CAUTION: PRICES CHANGE. CHECK AT GUNSHOP.

BERETTA MODEL 92F PISTOL

Caliber: 9mm Parabellum, 15-shot magazine.
Barrel: 4.9″.
Weight: 34 oz. **Length:** 8.5″ over-all.
Stocks: Checkered black plastic; wood optional at extra cost.
Sights: Blade front, rear adj. for w.
Features: Double-action. Extractor acts as chamber loaded indicator, squared trigger guard, grooved front and back straps, inertia firing pin. Matte finish. Introduced 1977. Imported from Italy by Beretta USA.
Price: With plastic grips **$596.00**
Price: With wood grips **$616.00**

Beretta Model 92F

BRNO CZ 83 DOUBLE ACTION PISTOL

Caliber: 32, 15-shot; 380, 13-shot.
Barrel: 3.7″.
Weight: 26.5 oz. **Length:** 6.7″ over-all.
Stocks: Checkered black plastic.
Sights: Blade front, rear adj. for w.
Features: Double-action; ambidextrous magazine release and safety. Polished or matte blue. Imported from Czechoslovakia by Saki International.
Price: **$425.00**

BROWNING BUCK MARK 22 PISTOL

Caliber: 22 LR, 10-shot magazine.
Barrel: 5½″.
Weight: 32 oz. **Length:** 9½″ over-all.
Stocks: Black moulded composite with skip-line checkering.
Sights: Ramp front, rear adj. for w. and e.
Features: All steel, matte blue finish, gold-colored trigger. Buck Mark Plus has laminated wood grips. Made in U.S. Introduced 1985. From Browning.
Price: Buck Mark **$189.75**
Price: Buck Mark Plus.......... **$227.75**

Browning Buck Mark Silhouette

Same as the Buck Mark except has 9⅞″ heavy barrel with .900″ diameter; hooded front sight with interchangeable posts, Millett Gold Cup 360 SIL rear on a special top sighting plane. Grips and fore-end are black multi-laminated wood. Introduced 1987.
Price: **$309.95**

Browning Buck Mark Varmint

Browning Hi-Power

BRNO CZ 75 AUTO PISTOL

Caliber: 9mm Para., 15-shot magazine.
Barrel: 4.7″.
Weight: 35 oz. **Length:** 8″ over-all.
Stocks: Checkered wood.
Sights: Blade front, rear adj. for w.
Features: Double action; blued finish. Imported from Czechoslovakia by Saki International.
Price: **$599.00**

BRNO CZ-85 Auto Pistol

Same gun as the CZ-75 except has ambidextrous slide release and safety levers, is available in 9mm Para. and 7.65, contoured composition grips, matte finish on top of slide. Introduced 1986.
Price: **$655.00**

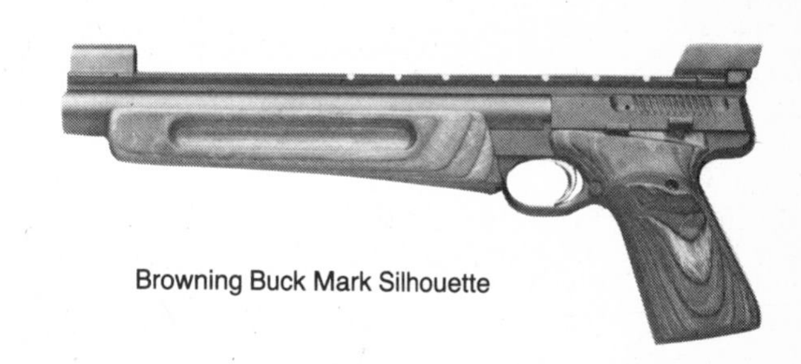

Browning Buck Mark Silhouette

Browning Buck Mark Varmint

Same as the Buck Mark except has 9⅞″ heavy barrel with .900″ diameter and full-length scope base (no open sights); black multi-laminated wood grips, with optional fore-end. Over-all length is 14″, weight is 48 oz. Introduced 1987.
Price: **$279.95**

Consult our Directory pages for the location of firms mentioned.

BROWNING HI-POWER 9mm AUTOMATIC PISTOL

Caliber: 9mm Parabellum, 13-shot magazine.
Barrel: 4²¹⁄₃₂″.
Weight: 32 oz. **Length:** 7¾″ over-all.
Stocks: Walnut, hand checkered, or black Polyamide.
Sights: ⅛″ blade front; rear screw-adj. for w. and e. Also available with fixed rear (drift-adj. for w.).
Features: External hammer with half-cock and thumb safeties. A blow on the hammer cannot discharge a cartridge; cannot be fired with magazine removed. Fixed rear sight model available. Ambidextrous safety available only with matte finish, moulded grips. Imported from Belgium by Browning.
Price: Fixed sight model, walnut grips **$449.95**
Price: 9mm with rear sight adj. for w. and e., walnut grips **$491.95**
Price: Standard matte black finish, fixed sight, moulded grips, ambidextrous safety **$414.95**

CAUTION: PRICES CHANGE. CHECK AT GUNSHOP.

Browning BDA-380

BRYCO MODEL 25 AUTO PISTOL
Caliber: 25 ACP, 6-shot magazine.
Barrel: 2.5″.
Weight: 11 oz. **Length:** 5″ over-all.
Stocks: Polished resin-impregnated wood.
Sights: Fixed.
Features: Safety locks sear and slide. Choice of satin nickel, bright chrome or black Teflon finishes. Introduced 1988. From Jennings Firearms.
Price: **$89.95**

BUSHMASTER AUTO PISTOL
Caliber: 223, 30-shot magazine.
Barrel: 11½″ (1-10″ twist).
Weight: 5¼ lbs. **Length:** 20½″ over-all.
Stocks: Synthetic rotating grip swivel assembly.
Sights: Post front, adjustable open "Y" rear
Features: Steel alloy upper receiver with welded barrel assembly, AK-47-type gas system, aluminum lower receiver, one-piece welded steel alloy bolt carrier assembly. From Bushmaster Firearms.
Price: **$339.95**
Price: With matte electroless nickel finish **$379.95**

Calico Model 100-P

COLT GOV'T MODEL MK IV/SERIES 80
Caliber: 9mm, 38 Super, 45 ACP, 7-shot.
Barrel: 5″.
Weight: 38 oz. **Length:** 8½″ over-all.
Stocks: Checkered walnut.
Sights: Ramp front, fixed square notch rear.
Features: Grip and thumb safeties and internal firing pin safety, grooved trigger. Accurizor barrel and bushing.
Price: Blue, 45 ACP. **$565.95**
Price: Bright stainless, 45 ACP **$659.95**
Price: 9mm, blue only **$569.95**
Price: 38 Super, blue. **$569.95**
Price: Stainless steel, 45 ACP. **$599.95**

Colt 10mm Delta Elite
Similar to the Government Model except chambered for 10mm auto cartridge. Has three-dot high profile front and rear combat sights, rubber combat stocks with Delta medallion, internal firing pin safety, and new recoil spring/buffer system. Blue only. Introduced 1987.
Price: **$626.95**

BROWNING BDA-380 DA AUTO PISTOL
Caliber: 380 ACP, 13-shot magazine.
Barrel: $3\frac{13}{16}$″.
Weight: 23 oz. **Length:** 6¾″ over-all.
Stocks: Smooth walnut with inset Browning medallion.
Sights: Blade front, rear drift-adj. for w.
Features: Combination safety and de-cocking lever will automatically lower a cocked hammer to half-cock and can be operated by right or left-hand shooters. Inertia firing pin. Introduced 1978. Imported from Italy by Browning.
Price: Blue. **$429.95**
Price: Nickel **$452.95**

BRYCO MODEL 38 AUTO PISTOLS
Caliber: 22 LR, 6-shot magazine.
Barrel: 2.8″.
Weight: 15 oz. **Length:** 5.3″ over-all.
Stocks: Polished resin-impregnated wood.
Sights: Fixed.
Features: Safety locks sear and slide. Choice of satin nickel, bright chrome or black Teflon finishes. Introduced 1988. From Jennings Firearms.
Price: 22 LR, 32 ACP **$99.95**
Price: 380 ACP. **$129.95**

BRYCO MODEL 48 AUTO PISTOLS
Caliber: 22 LR, 32 ACP, 380 ACP, 6-shot magazine.
Barrel: 4″.
Weight: 19 oz. **Length:** 6.7″ over-all.
Stocks: Polished resin-impregnated wood.
Sights: Fixed.
Features: Safety locks sear and slide. Choice of satin nickel, bright chrome or black Teflon finishes. Announced 1988. From Jennings Firearms.
Price: 22 LR, 32 ACP **$99.95**
Price: 380 ACP. **$129.95**

CALICO MODEL 100-P AUTO PISTOL
Caliber: 22 LR, 100-shot magazine.
Barrel: 6″.
Weight: 3.7 lbs. (loaded). **Length:** 17″ over-all.
Stocks: Moulded composition.
Sights: Adjustable post front, notch rear.
Features: Aluminum alloy frame; flash suppressor; pistol grip compartment; ambidextrous safety. Uses same helical-feed magazine as M-100 Carbine. Introduced 1986. Made in U.S. From Calico.
Price: **$249.95**

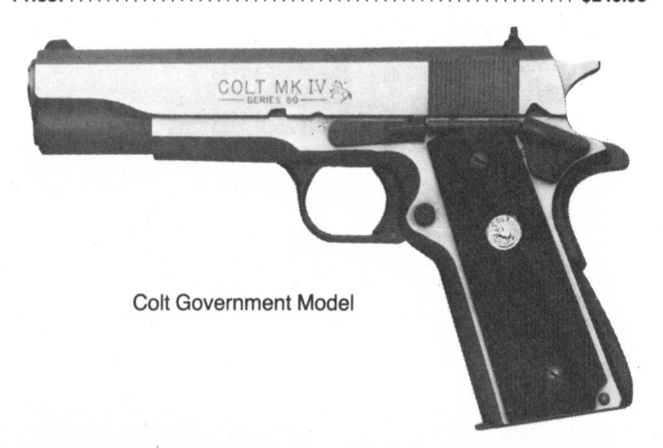

Colt Government Model

COLT OFFICERS ACP MK IV/SERIES 80
Caliber: 45 ACP, 6-shot magazine.
Barrel: 3½″.
Weight: 34 oz. **Length:** 7¼″ over-all.
Stocks: Checkered walnut.
Sights: Ramp blade front with white dot, square notch rear with two white dots.
Features: Trigger safety lock (thumb safety), grip safety, firing pin safety; grooved trigger; flat mainspring housing. Also available with lightweight alloy frame and in stainless steel. Introduced 1985.
Price: Matte finish **$549.95**
Price: Blue. **$565.95**
Price: L.W., matte finish **$565.95**
Price: Stainless **$599.95**
Price: Bright stainless **$659.95**

Colt Combat Elite MK IV/Series 80

Similar to the Government Model except in 45 ACP only, has stainless frame with ordnance steel slide and internal parts. High profile front, rear sights with three-dot system, extended grip safety, beveled magazine well, rubber combat stocks. Introduced 1986.

Price: **$689.95**

Colt Combat Elite

COLT COMBAT COMMANDER AUTO PISTOL

Caliber: 45 ACP, 7-shot; 38 Super Auto, 9mm Luger, 9-shot.
Barrel: 4¼".
Weight: 36 oz. **Length:** 7¾" over-all.
Stocks: Checkered walnut.
Sights: Fixed, glare-proofed blade front, square notch rear.
Features: Grooved trigger and hammer spur; arched housing; grip and thumb safeties.
Price: Blue, 9mm **$569.95**
Price: Blue, 45 .... **$565.95**
Price: Blue, 38 Super **$569.95**

Colt Lightweight Commander Mark IV/Series 80

Same as Commander except high strength aluminum alloy frame, wood panel grips, weight 27½ oz. 45 ACP only.

Price: Blue........ **$565.95**

Colt 380 Government

COLT 380 GOVERNMENT MODEL

Caliber: 380 ACP, 7-shot magazine.
Barrel: 3¼".
Weight: 21¾ oz. **Length:** 6" over-all.
Stocks: Checkered composition.
Sights: Ramp front, square notch rear, fixed.
Features: Scaled down version of the 1911A1 Colt G.M. Has thumb and internal firing pin safeties. Introduced 1983.
Price: Blue........ **$365.95**
Price: Nickel **$406.95**
Price: Coltguard **$386.95**

Colt Mustang Plus II

Similar to the 380 Government Model except has the shorter barrel and slide of the Mustang. Blue finish only. Introduced 1988.

Price: **$365.95**

Colt Mustang 380, Mustang Pocket Lite

Similar to the standard 380 Government Model. Mustang has steel frame (18.5 oz.), Pocket Lite has aluminum alloy (12.5 oz.). Both are ½" shorter than 380 GM, have 2¾" barrel. Introduced 1987.

Price: Mustang 380, blue **$365.95**
Price: As above, nickel **$406.95**
Price: As above, Coltguard **$386.95**
Price: Mustang Pocket Lite, blue........ **$369.95**

Coonan 357 Magnum

COONAN 357 MAGNUM PISTOL

Caliber: 357 Mag., 7-shot magazine.
Barrel: 5".
Weight: 42 oz.
Length: 8.3" over-all.
Stocks: Smooth walnut.
Sights: Open, adjustable.
Features: Unique barrel hood improves accuracy and reliability. Many parts interchange with Colt autos. Has grip, hammer, half-cock safeties. From Coonan Arms.
Price: Model B (linkless barrel, interchangeable ramp front sight, new rear sight)........ **$650.00**

Davis P-32

DAVIS P-32 AUTO PISTOL

Caliber: 32 ACP, 6-shot magazine.
Barrel: 2.8".
Weight: 22 oz. **Length:** 5.4" over-all.
Stocks: Laminated wood.
Sights: Fixed.
Features: Choice of black Teflon or chrome finish. Announced 1986. Made in U.S. by Davis Industries.
Price: **$87.50**

DETONICS "SERVICEMASTER" AUTO PISTOL
Caliber: 45 ACP, 7-shot magazine.
Barrel: 4¼".
Weight: 32 oz. **Length:** 7⅞" over-all.
Stocks: Pachmayr rubber.
Sights: Fixed combat.
Features: Stainless steel construction; thumb and grip safeties; extended grip safety. Polished slide flats, rest matte.
Price: **$975.00**

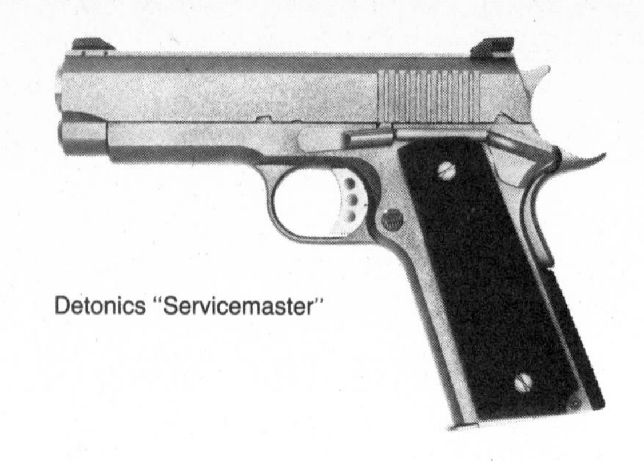
Detonics "Servicemaster"

DETONICS "COMBAT MASTER" MK VI, MK I
Caliber: 45 ACP, 6-shot magazine.
Barrel: 3½".
Weight: 29 oz. **Length:** 6¾" over-all, 4½" high.
Stocks: Checkered walnut.
Sights: Combat type, fixed and adj. sights avail.
Features: Has a self-adjusting cone barrel centering system, beveled magazine inlet, "full clip" indicator in base of magazine; standard 7-shot (or more) clip can be used in the 45. Throated barrel and polished feed ramp. Introduced 1977. From Detonics.
Price: MK I, matte finish, fixed sights **$725.00**
Price: MK VI, polished stainless, adj. sights **$795.00**

Desert Eagle 357

DESERT EAGLE MAGNUM PISTOL
Caliber: 357 Mag., 9-shot; 41 Mag., 44 Mag., 8-shot.
Barrel: 6", 10", 14", interchangeable.
Weight: 357 Mag.—52 oz. (alloy), 62 oz. (steel); 41 Mag., 44 Mag.—56 oz. (alloy), 66.9 oz. (stainless).
Length: 10¼" over-all. (6" bbl.).
Stocks: Wrap-around soft rubber.
Sights: Blade on ramp front, combat style rear. Adjustable available.
Features: Rotating three-lug bolt; ambidextrous safety; combat-style triggerguard; adjustable trigger optional. Military epoxy finish. Satin, bright nickel, hard chrome, polished and blued finishes available. Imported from Israel by Magnum Research Inc.
Price: 357, 6" bbl., standard pistol **$589.00**
Price: As above, alloy frame **$589.00**
Price: As above, stainless steel frame **$629.00**
Price: 41 Mag., 6", standard pistol **$699.00**
Price: 41 Mag., alloy frame **$699.00**
Price: 41 Mag., stainless steel frame **$739.00**
Price: 44 Mag., 6", standard pistol **$717.00**
Price: As above, alloy frame **$717.00**
Price: As above, stainless steel frame **$750.00**

ENCOM MK IV ASSAULT PISTOL
Caliber: 45 ACP, 30-shot magazine.
Barrel: 4.5"; 6", 8", 10" optional.
Weight: 6 lbs. **Length:** 12.6" over-all (4.5" barrel).
Stocks: Black composition.
Sights: Fixed.
Features: Semi-auto fire only. Side-loading magazine. Interchangeable barrels. Optional retractable stock available with 18½" barrel. Made in the U.S. by Encom America, Inc. Introduced 1988.
Price: **$279.95**

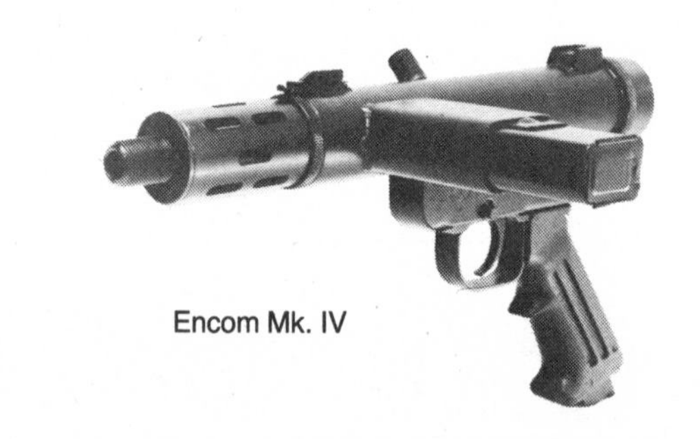
Encom Mk. IV

ENCOM MP-9, MP-45 ASSAULT PISTOLS
Caliber: 9mm, 45 ACP, 10, 30, 40 or 50-shot magazine.
Barrel: Interchangeable 4½", 6", 8", 10", 18", 18½".
Weight: 6 lbs. (4½" bbl.). **Length:** 11.8" over-all (4½" bbl.).
Stocks: Retractable wire stock.
Sights: Post front, fixed Patridge rear.
Features: Blowback operation, fires from closed breech with floating firing pin; right or left-hand models available. Made in U.S. From Encom America, Inc.
Price: 9mm or 45 ACP, standard pistol **$275.00**
Price: As above, Mini Pistol (3½" bbl.) **$250.00**
Price: Carbine (18½" bbl., retractable wire stock) **$390.00**

Erma ESP 85A

ERMA SPORTING PISTOL MODEL ESP 85A
Caliber: 22 LR, 8-shot, 32 S&W Long, 5-shot.
Barrel: 6".
Weight: 41 oz. **Length:** 10" over-all.
Stocks: Checkered walnut with thumbrest and adjustable left- or right-hand shelf.
Sights: Interchangeable blade front, micro. rear adjustable for windage and elevation.
Features: Interchangeable caliber conversion kit; adjustable trigger, trigger stop. Comes with lockable carrying case. Imported from West Germany by Competition Arms, Inc. Introduced 1988.
Price: .... **NA**

FALCON PORTSIDER AUTO PISTOL
Caliber: 45 ACP, 7-shot magazine.
Barrel: 5".
Weight: 38 oz. **Length:** 8½" over-all.
Stocks: Checkered walnut.
Sights: Fixed combat.
Features: Made of 17-4 stainless steel. Enlarged left-hand ejection port, extended ejector, long trigger, combat hammer, extended safety, wide grip safety. Introduced 1986. From Falcon Firearms.
Price: **$580.00**

RELOADING
BALLISTICS
HANDLOADING

©1988 Winchester/Olin Corporation, East Alton, IL 62024

But love field trips.

Winchester has done your homework for you. About a decade's worth. Developing a new line of ammunition that matches the performance of the best handloads.

We call it Supreme®. And there's a hand-loading, benchrest-shooting bunch of writers out there that wouldn't dispute the name. Not after testing it against their own pet loads.

Supreme starts with the bullet handloaders wish they could start with. Winchester's Silvertip® Boattail. Designed with sophisticated aero-ballistics computer programs, the bullet has the best combination yet of accuracy, downrange energy and knockdown power.

With our Silvertips, and a couple of great Hornadys®, we're manufacturing Supreme cartridges to handload specs, slowing down production, quadrupling quality control, and hand-inspecting every round.

Such perfection doesn't come cheap. Nor in any great quantity. Nor in any but the most popular cartridges for now. But if you do get your hands on a box, you won't need to handload to find the perfect round. You'll just have to find the perfect trophy to use it on.

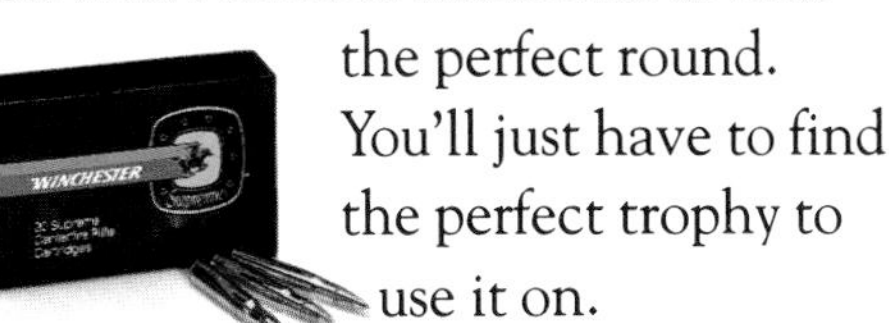

F.I.E. "THE BEST" A27B PISTOL

Caliber: 25 ACP, 6-shot magazine.
Barrel: 2½".
Weight: 13 oz. **Length:** 4⅜" over-all.
Stocks: Checkered walnut.
Sights: Fixed.
Features: All steel construction. Has thumb and magazine safeties, exposed hammer. Blue finish only. Introduced 1978. Made in U.S. by F.I.E. Corp.
Price: **$154.95**

F.I.E. "TZ-75" DA AUTO PISTOL

Caliber: 9mm Parabellum, 15-shot magazine; 41 Action Express, 11-shot magazine.
Barrel: 4.72".
Weight: 35.33 oz. **Length:** 8.25" over-all.
Stocks: Smooth European walnut. Checkered rubber optional.
Sights: Undercut blade front, open rear adjustable for windage.
Features: Double action trigger system; squared-off trigger guard; rotating slide-mounted safety. Introduced 1983. Imported from Italy by F.I.E. Corp.
Price: **$424.95**
Price: Satin chrome with red outline sights **$444.95**

F.I.E. "TITAN 25" PISTOL

Caliber: 25 ACP, 6-shot magazine.
Barrel: 2 7/16".
Weight: 12 oz. **Length:** 4⅝" over-all.
Stocks: Smooth walnut.
Sights: Fixed.
Features: External hammer; fast simple takedown. Made in U.S.A. by F.I.E. Corp.
Price: Blue **$74.95**
Price: Dyna-Chrome **$84.95**
Price: 24K gold with bright blue frame, smooth walnut grips **$99.95**

F.I.E. "TITAN II" PISTOLS

Caliber: 32 ACP, 380 ACP, 6-shot magazine; 22 LR, 10-shot magazine.
Barrel: 3⅞".
Weight: 25¾ oz. **Length:** 6¾" over-all.
Stocks: Checkered nylon, thumbrest-type; walnut optional.
Sights: Adjustable.
Features: Magazine disconnector, firing pin block. Standard slide safety. Available in blue or chrome. Introduced 1978. Imported from Italy by F.I.E. Corp.
Price: 32 or 380, blue **$209.95**
Price: 32 or 380, chrome **$224.95**
Price: 22 LR, blue **$154.95**

FEATHER MINI-AT AUTO PISTOL

Caliber: 22 LR, 20-shot magazine.
Barrel: 6".
Weight: 30 oz. **Length:** 15¼" over-all.
Stocks: Moulded composition.
Sights: Protected blade front, adjustable notch rear.
Features: Matte black finish. From Feather Enterprises. Introduced 1987.
Price: **$219.95**

Glock 19

F.I.E. "SUPER TITAN II" PISTOLS

Caliber: 32 ACP, 12-shot; 380 ACP, 11-shot.
Barrel: 3⅞".
Weight: 28 oz. **Length:** 6¾" over-all.
Stocks: Smooth, polished walnut.
Sights: Adjustable.
Features: Blue finish only. Introduced 1981. Imported from Italy by F.I.E. Corp.
Price: 32 or 380 .... **$249.95**

F.I.E. "TZ-75"

F.I.E. "Titan 25"

F.I.E. Titan II

GLOCK 17 AUTO PISTOL

Caliber: 9mm Para., 17-shot magazine.
Barrel: 4.48".
Weight: 21.8 oz. (without magazine). **Length:** 7.40" over-all.
Stocks: Black polymer.
Sights: Dot on front blade, white outline rear adj. for w. and e.
Features: Polymer frame, steel slide; double-action trigger with "Safe Action" system; mechanical firing pin safety, drop safety; simple take-down without tools; locked breech, recoil operated action. Adopted by Austrian armed forces 1983. NATO approved 1984. Imported from Austria by Glock, Inc.
Price: With extra magazine, magazine loader, cleaning kit **$511.60**
Price: Model 17L (6" barrel) **$740.53**

Glock 19 Auto Pistol

Similar to the Glock 17 except has a 4" barrel, giving an over-all length of 6.9" and weight of 21.2 oz. Magazine capacity is 15 rounds. Introduced 1988.
Price: **$511.60**

GONCZ HIGH-TECH LONG PISTOL

Caliber: 9mm Para., 30 Mauser, 38 Super, 18- and 32-shot magazine; 45 ACP, 10- and 20-shot magazine.
Barrel: 4″, 9.5″.
Weight: 3 lbs., 10 oz. (with 4″ barrel). **Length:** 10½″ over-all (with 4″ barrel).
Stocks: Alloy grooved pistol grip.
Sights: Front adjustable for elevation, rear adjustable for windage.
Features: Fires from closed bolt; floating firing pin; safety locks the firing pin. All metal construction. Barrel threaded for accessories. Matte black oxide and anodized finish. Designed by Lajos J. Goncz. Introduced 1985. From Goncz Co.
Price: With 9½″ barrel **$350.00**
Price: With 4″ barrel **$340.00**

Goncz High-Tech Pistol

Grendel P-10

GRENDEL P-10 AUTO PISTOL

Caliber: 380 ACP, 10-shot magazine.
Barrel: 3″.
Weight: 15 oz. **Length:** 5.3″ over-all.
Stocks: Checkered polycarbonate metal composite.
Sights: Fixed.
Features: Double action only with a low inertia safety hammer system. Magazine loads from the top. Matte black, electroless nickel or green finish. Introduced 1987. From Grendel, Inc.
Price: Black finish **$150.00**
Price: Green finish **$155.00**
Price: Electroless nickel **$165.00**

HAMMERLI MODEL 212 HUNTER'S PISTOL

Caliber: 22 LR
Barrel: 4.9″.
Weight: 31 oz. **Length:** 8.5″ over-all.
Stocks: Checkered walnut.
Sights: White dot front adjustable for elevation, rear adjustable for windage.
Features: Semi-automatic based on the Model 208, intended for field use. Uses target trigger system which is fully adjustable. Comes with tool kit. Imported from Switzerland by Osborne's Supplies. Introduced 1984.
Price: About **$1,471.00**

Hammerli 212

Heckler & Koch P7-M8

HECKLER & KOCH P7M8 AUTO PISTOL

Caliber: 9mm Parabellum, 8-shot magazine.
Barrel: 4.13″.
Weight: 29 oz. **Length:** 6.73″ over-all.
Stocks: Stippled black plastic.
Sights: Fixed, combat-type.
Features: Unique "squeeze cocker" in front strap cocks the action. Gas-retarded action. Squared combat-type trigger guard. Blue finish. Compact size. Imported from West Germany by Heckler & Koch, Inc.
Price: P7M8 .... **$881.00**
Price: P7M13 (13-shot capacity, matte black finish, ambidextrous magazine release, forged steel frame) **$1,099.00**

Heckler & Koch P7K3 Auto Pistol

Similar to the P7M8 and P7M13 except chambered for 380 ACP, 8-shot magazine. Uses an oil-filled buffer to decrease recoil. Introduced 1988.
Price: **$881.00**
Price: 22 LR conversion unit **$428.00**

HECKLER & KOCH VP 70Z DOUBLE ACTION AUTO

Caliber: 9mm Para., 18-shot magazine.
Barrel: 4½″.
Weight: 32½ oz. **Length:** 8″ over-all.
Stocks: Black stippled plastic.
Sights: Ramp front, channeled slide rear.
Features: Recoil operated, double action. Only 4 moving parts. Double column magazine. Imported from West Germany by Heckler & Koch, Inc. Limited availability.
Price: **$399.00**
Price: Extra magazine **$27.00**

HECKLER & KOCH P9S DOUBLE ACTION AUTO

Caliber: 45 ACP, 7-shot magazine.
Barrel: 4″.
Weight: 31 oz. **Length:** 7.6″ over-all.
Stocks: Checkered black plastic.
Sights: Open combat type.
Features: Double action; polygonal rifling; delayed roller-locked action with stationary barrel. Loaded chamber and cocking indicators; cocking/decocking lever. **Limited quantity available.** Imported from West Germany by Heckler & Koch, Inc.
Price: P-9S Combat Model, 45 ACP **$1,299.00**
Price: P9S Target Model, 45 ACP **$1,382.00**

CAUTION: PRICES CHANGE. CHECK AT GUNSHOP.

Helwan "Brigadier"

Holmes MP-83

INTRATEC TEC-9 AUTO PISTOL
Caliber: 9mm Para., 36-shot magazine.
Barrel: 5″.
Weight: 50 oz. **Length:** 12½″ over-all.
Stock: Moulded composition.
Sights: Fixed.
Features: Semi-auto, fires from closed bolt; firing pin block safety; matte blue finish. Comes wih 1″ black nylon sling. From Intratec.
Price: **$247.95**
Price: TEC-9S (as above, except stainless) **$306.95**

Intratec TEC-9M Pistol
Similar to the TEC-9 except smaller. Has 3″ barrel, weighs 44 oz.; 20-shot magazine.
Price: **$226.95**
Price: TEC-9MS (as above, stainless) **$286.95**

INTRATEC SCORPION AUTO PISTOL
Caliber: 22 LR, 30-shot magazine.
Barrel: 4″.
Weight: 30 oz. **Length:** 11³⁄₁₆″ over-all.
Stocks: Moulded composition.
Sights: Protected post front, rear adjustable for windage and elevation.
Features: Ambidextrous cocking knobs and safety. Matte black finish. Accepts any 10/22-type magazine. Announced 1988. Made in U.S. by Intratec.
Price: **$154.95**

IVER JOHNSON ENFORCER MODEL 3000 AUTO
Caliber: 30 M1 Carbine, 15- or 30-shot magazine.
Barrel: 9½″.
Weight: 4 lbs. **Length:** 17″ over-all.
Stocks: American walnut with metal handguard.
Sights: Gold bead ramp front. Peep rear.
Features: Accepts 15 or 30-shot magazines. From Iver Johnson.
Price: Blue finish **$333.20**

HELWAN "BRIGADIER" AUTO PISTOL
Caliber: 9mm Parabellum, 8-shot magazine.
Barrel: 4.5″.
Weight: 32 oz. **Length:** 8″ over-all.
Stocks: Grooved plastic.
Sights: Blade front, rear adjustable for windage.
Features: Polished blue finish. Single action design. Cross-bolt safety. Imported by Interarms.
Price: **$249.00**

HOLMES MP-83 ASSAULT PISTOL
Caliber: 9mm, 16- or 32-shot; 10mm, 12- or 25-shot; 45, 10- or 20-shot.
Barrel: 6″.
Weight: 3½ lbs. **Length:** 14½″ over-all.
Stocks: Walnut grip and fore-end.
Sights: Post front, open adj. rear.
Features: All steel construction, blue finish. Deluxe package includes gun, foam-lined travel case, Zytel stock, black metal vent, barrel shroud, extra magazine and sling. From Holmes Firearms.
Price: **$500.00**
Price: Deluxe **$525.00**
Price: Caliber conversion kit **$220.00**

Holmes MP-22 Assault Pistol
Similar to the MP-83 except chambered for 22LR, 32-shot capacity. Weighs 2½ lbs., has bolt-notch safety.
Price: **$450.00**
Price: Deluxe **$525.00**

Intratec TEC-9

Intratec Scorpion

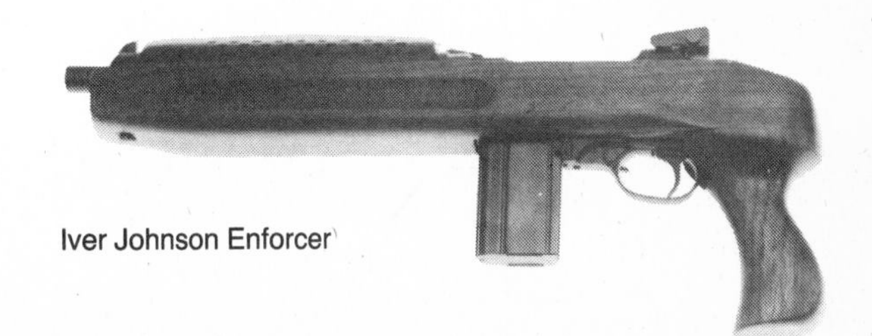
Iver Johnson Enforcer

Iver Johnson TP22

IVER JOHNSON TP22, TP25 AUTO PISTOL

Caliber: 22 LR, 25 ACP, 7-shot magazine.
Barrel: 2.85″.
Weight: 14½ oz. **Length:** 5.39″ over-all.
Stocks: Black checkered plastic.
Sights: Fixed.
Features: Double action; 7-shot magazine. Introduced 1981. Made in U.S. From Iver Johnson's.
Price: Either caliber, blue **$191.65**
Price: As above, nickel **$206.12**

JENNINGS J-22 AUTO PISTOL

Caliber: 22 LR, 6-shot magazine.
Barrel: 2½″.
Weight: 13 oz. **Length:** 4 15/16″ over-all.
Stocks: Walnut on chrome or nickel models; checkered black Cycolac on Teflon model.
Sights: Fixed.
Features: Choice of bright chrome, satin nickel or black Teflon finish. Introduced 1981. From Jennings Firearms.
Price: About **$69.95**

Jennings J-22 Pistol

KORRIPHILA HSP 701 DA AUTO PISTOL

Caliber: 9mm Para., 38 W.C., 38 Super, 45 ACP, 9-shot magazine in 9mm, 7-shot in 45.
Barrel: 4″ (Type I), 5″ (Type II, III).
Weight: 35 oz.
Stocks: Checkered walnut.
Sights: Ramp or target front, adj. rear.
Features: Delayed roller lock action with Budichowsky system. Double/single or single action only. Very limited production. Imported from West Germany by Osborne's. Introduced 1986.
Price: About.. **$3,400.00**

Korriphila HSP 701

Korth Auto Pistol

KORTH SEMI-AUTOMATIC PISTOL

Caliber: 9mm Parabellum, 13-shot magazine.
Barrel: 4½″.
Weight: 35 oz. **Length:** 10½″ over-all.
Stocks: Checkered walnut.
Sights: Combat-adjustable
Features: Double action; 13-shot staggered magazine; forged machined frame and slide. Matte and polished finish. Introduced 1985. Imported from West Germany by Osborne's.
Price: About.. **$3,715.00**

L.A.R. Grizzly Mk. I

L.A.R. GRIZZLY WIN MAG MK I PISTOL

Caliber: 357 Mag., 357/45, 10mm, 45 Win. Mag., 45 ACP, 7-shot magazine.
Barrel: 5.4″, 6.5″.
Weight: 51 oz. **Length:** 10½″ over-all.
Stocks: Checkered rubber, non-slip combat-type.
Sights: Ramped blade front, fully adjustable rear.
Features: Uses basic Browning/Colt 1911-A1 design; interchangeable calibers; beveled magazine well; combat-type flat, checkered rubber mainspring housing; lowered and back-chamfered ejection port; polished feed ramp; throated barrel; solid barrel bushings. Available in satin hard chrome, matte blue, Parkerized finishes. Announced 1983. From L.A.R. Mfg. Inc.
Price: 45 Win. Mag.. **$675.00**
Price: 357 Mag. **$699.00**
Price: Conversion units (357 Mag.) **$149.00**
Price: As above, 45 ACP **$132.00**

L.A.R. Grizzly Win Mag 8″ & 10″

Similar to the standard Grizzly Win Mag except has lengthened slide and either 8″ or 10″ barrel. Available in 45 Win. Mag., 45 ACP, 357/45 Grizzly Win. Mag., 10mm or 357 Magnum. Introduced 1987.

Price: 8″, 45 ACP, 45 Win. Mag., 357/45 Grizzly Win. Mag........ **$1,250.00**
Price: As above, 10″.. **$1,313.00**
Price: 8″, 357 Magnum **$1,275.00**
Price: As above, 10″.. **$1,337.00**

CAUTION: PRICES CHANGE. CHECK AT GUNSHOP.

Llama Large Frame Auto

Llama Small Frame Auto

OMEGA AUTO PISTOL
Caliber: 38 Super (9-shot), 10mm, 45 ACP (7-shot).
Barrel: 5″, 6″.
Weight: 45.3 oz. (6″ barrel).
Stocks: Pachmayr checkered rubber.
Sights: Blade front, fully adjustable rear.
Features: Convertible between calibers; ported barrels. Based on 1911-A1 but with improved barrel lock-up. Introduced 1987. From Springfield Armory.
Price: Single caliber, 38 Super, 10mm or 45 ACP **$849.00**

PACHMAYR DOMINATOR PISTOL
Caliber: 22 Hornet, 223, 7mm-06, 308, 35 Rem., 45 Rem., 44 Mag., single shot.
Barrel: 10½″ (44 Mag.), 14″ all other calibers.
Weight: 4 lbs. (14″ barrel). **Length:** 16″ over-all (14″ barrel).
Stocks: Pachmayr Signature system.
Sights: None furnished; drilled and tapped for scope mounting.
Features: Bolt-action pistol on 1911A1 frame. Comes as complete gun. Introduced 1988. From Pachmayr.
Price: Either barrel. **$524.50**

Partisan Avenger

LLAMA LARGE FRAME AUTO PISTOL
Caliber: 38 Super, 45 ACP.
Barrel: 5″
Weight: 40 oz. **Length:** 8½″ over-all.
Stocks: Checkered walnut.
Sights: Fixed.
Features: Grip and manual safeties, ventilated rib. Imported from Spain by Stoeger Industries.
Price: Blue. **$352.00**
Price: Satin chrome, 45 ACP only. **$471.00**

LLAMA COMPACT FRAME AUTO PISTOL
Caliber: 9mm Para., 9-shot, 45 ACP, 7-shot.
Barrel: 4 5/16″.
Weight: 37 oz.
Stocks: Smooth walnut.
Sights: Blade front, rear adjustable for windage.
Features: Scaled-down version of the Large Frame gun. Locked breech mechanism; manual and grip safeties. Introduced 1985. Imported from Spain by Stoeger Industries.
Price: Blue only **$352.00**

LLAMA SMALL FRAME AUTO PISTOLS
Caliber: 22 LR, 32, 380.
Barrel: 3 11/16″.
Weight: 23 oz. **Length:** 6½″ over-all.
Stocks: Checkered plastic, thumb rest.
Sights: Fixed front, adj. notch rear.
Features: Ventilated rib, manual and grip safeties. Model XV is 22 LR, Model IIIA is 380. Both models have loaded indicator; IIIA is locked breech. Imported from Spain by Stoeger Industries.
Price: Blue, 22 LR,. **$290.00**
Price: Blue, 32, 380. . . . . **$299.00**
Price: Satin chrome, 22 LR or 380 . . . . **$377.00**

LLAMA M-82 DA AUTO PISTOL
Caliber: 9mm Para., 15-shot magazine.
Barrel: 4¼″.
Weight: 39 oz. **Length:** 8″ over-all.
Stocks: Matte black polymer.
Sights: Blade front, rear drift adjustable for windage. High visibility three-dot system.
Features: Double-action mechanism; ambidextrous safety. Introduced 1987. Imported from Spain by Stoeger Industries.
Price: **$751.00**

Omega Auto

PARTISAN AVENGER AUTO PISTOL
Caliber: 45 ACP, 30-shot magazine.
Barrel: 6¼″.
Weight: 5 lbs., 7 oz. **Length:** 11″ over-all.
Stocks: Smooth composition.
Sights: Protected blade front, fixed rear.
Features: Semi-auto only. Fires from a closed bolt. Uses standard M-3 "Grease Gun" magazine. Introduced 1988. Made in U.S. From Patriot Dist. Co.
Price: **$445.00**

RANGER 1911A1 45 AUTO PISTOL

Caliber: 45 ACP, 7-shot magazine.
Barrel: 5″.
Weight: 38 oz. **Length:** 8½″ over-all.
Stocks: Checkered walnut.
Sights: Glare-proof front, square-notch rear drift-adj. for windage.
Features: Made in U.S. from 4140 steel and other high-strength alloys. Barrel machined from a forged billet. Introduced 1988. From Federal Ordnance, Inc.
Price: Standard model **$427.95**
Price: With extended slide release and safety **$436.95**
Price: With ambidextrous slide release and safety **$446.95**

Ranger 1911A1

RAVEN MP-25 AUTO PISTOL

Caliber: 25 ACP, 6-shot magazine.
Barrel: 2⁷⁄₁₆″.
Weight: 15 oz. **Length:** 4¾″ over-all.
Stocks: Smooth walnut or ivory-colored plastic.
Sights: Ramped front, fixed rear.
Features: Available in blue, nickel or chrome finish. Made in U.S. Available from Raven Arms.
Price: **$69.95**

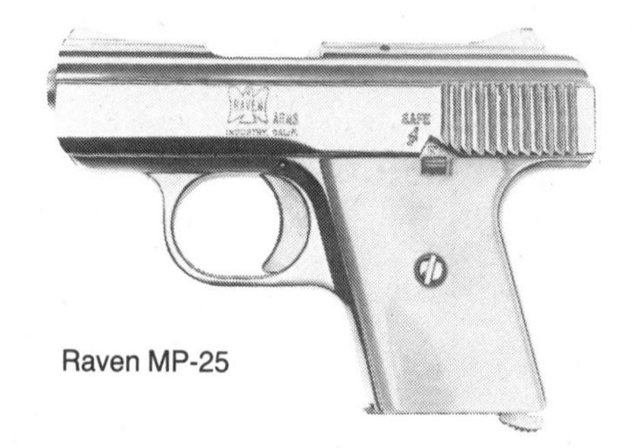

Raven MP-25

RUGER P-85 AUTOMATIC PISTOL

Caliber: 9mm Para., 15-shot magazine.
Barrel: 4.50″.
Weight: 32 oz. **Length:** 7.84″ over-all.
Stocks: Grooved "Xenoy" composition.
Sights: Square post front, square notch rear adj. for windage, both with white dot inserts.
Features: Double action with ambidextrous slide-mounted safety which blocks firing pin and disengages firing mechnaism. Slide is 4140 chrome-moly steel, frame is a lightweight aluminum alloy, both finished matte black. Ambidextrous magazine release. Introduced 1986.
Price: **$295.00**
Price: P-85 C (comes with plastic case, extra magazine) **$325.00**

Ruger P-85

Ruger Mark II Stainless

RUGER MARK II STANDARD AUTO PISTOL

Caliber: 22 LR, 10-shot magazine.
Barrel: 4¾″ or 6″.
Weight: 36 oz. (4¾″ bbl.). **Length:** 8⁵⁄₁₆″ (4¾″ bbl.).
Stocks: Checkered hard rubber.
Sights: Fixed, wide blade front, square notch rear adj. for w.
Features: Updated design of the original Standard Auto. Has new bolt hold-open device, 10-shot magazine, magazine catch, safety, trigger and new receiver contours. Introduced 1982.
Price: Blued (MK 4, MK 6) **$199.80**
Price: In stainless steel (KMK 4, KMK 6) **$266.40**

SAFARI ARMS MATCHMASTER PISTOL

Caliber: 45 ACP, 6-shot magazine.
Barrel: 5″.
Weight: 40 oz. **Length:** 8.7″ overall.
Stocks: Checkered plastic.
Sights: Combat adjustable.
Features: Beavertail grip safety, ambidextrous extended safety, extended slide release, combat hammer, threaded barrel bushing; throated, ported, tuned. Finishes: blue, Parkerize, matte. Also available in a lightweight version (30 oz.) and stainless steel. Available from Olympic Arms, Inc.
Price: **$595.00**

Safari Arms Enforcer Pistol

Shortened version of the Matchmaster. Has 3.8″ barrel, over-all length of 7.7″, and weighs 40 oz. (standard weight), 27 oz. in lightweight version. Other features are the same. From Olympic Arms, Inc.
Price: **$595.00**

SEECAMP LWS 32 STAINLESS DA AUTO

Caliber: 32 ACP Win. Silvertip, 6-shot.
Barrel: 2″, integral with frame.
Weight: 25 cal. 12 oz., 32 cal. 10.5 oz. **Length:** 4⅛″ over-all.
Stocks: Black plastic.
Sights: Smooth, no-snag, contoured slide and barrel top.
Features: Aircraft quality 17-4 PH stainless steel. Inertia operated firing pin. Hammer fired double action only. Hammer automatically follows slide down to safety rest position after each shot—no manual safety needed. Magazine safety disconnector. Polished stainless. Introduced 1980. From L.W. Seecamp.
Price: **$290.00**

SCARAB SKORPION AUTO PISTOL

Caliber: 9mm Parabellum, 32-shot magazine.
Barrel: 4.63".
Weight: 3.5 lbs. **Length:** 12.25" over-all.
Stocks: Stained polymer.
Sights: Fixed, open.
Features: Semi-auto fire only. Ambidextrous cocking knobs. Comes with one magazine, front hangar and leather hand strap, imitation sound suppressor, padded carrying case, flash hider, leather shoulder strap, 22 LR sub-caliber conversion. Made in U.S. Announced 1988. From Armitage International, Ltd.
Price: **$279.50**

Scarab Skorpion

SIG P-210-2 AUTO PISTOL

Caliber: 7.65mm or 9mm Para., 8-shot magazine.
Barrel: 4¾".
Weight: 31¾ oz. (9mm) **Length:** 8½" over-all.
Stocks: Checkered black composition.
Sights: Blade front, rear adjustable for windage.
Features: Lanyard loop; matte finish. Conversion unit for 22 LR available. Imported from Switzerland by Osborne's, SIGARMS and Mandall Shooting Supplies.
Price: P-210-2 Service Pistol (SIGARMS, Mandall) .. **$1,485.00** to **$1,895.00**
Price: P-210-2 (Osborne's), about........ **$1,400.00**
Price: 22 Cal. Conversion unit (Osborne's), about........ **$825.00**

SIG P-210-6

SIG P-210-6 AUTO PISTOL

Caliber: 9mm Para., 8-shot magazine.
Barrel: 4¾".
Weight: 36.2 oz. **Length:** 8½" over-all.
Stocks: Checkered black plastic; walnut optional.
Sights: Blade front, micro. adj. rear for w. & e.
Features: Adjustable trigger stop; target trigger; ribbed front stap; sandblasted finish. Conversion unit for 22 LR consists of barrel, recoil spring, slide and magazine. Imported from Switzerland by Osborne's and SIGARMS, Inc.
Price: P-210-6 (SIGARMS)........ **$1,754.00**
Price: 22 Cal. Conversion unit (Osborne's) **$1,035.00**
Price: As above, from SIGARMS **$719.00**
Price: P-210-6 (Osborne's)........ **$1,800.00**

SIG-Sauer P-220

SIG-SAUER P-220 "EUROPEAN" AUTO PISTOL

Caliber: 9mm, 38 Super; 45 ACP. (9-shot in 9mm and 38 Super, 7 in 45).
Barrel: 4⅜".
Weight: 28¼ oz. (9mm). **Length:** 7¾" over-all.
Stocks: Checkered black plastic.
Sights: Blade front, drift adj. rear for w.
Features: Double action. De-cocking lever permits lowering hammer onto locked firing pin. Squared combat-type trigger guard. Slide stays open after last shot. Imported from West Germany by SIGARMS, Inc.
Price: "European" **$632.50**
Price: "American" (side-button magazine release, 45 ACP only) **$687.50**

SIG-SAUER P-225 DA AUTO PISTOL

Caliber: 9mm Parabellum, 8-shot magazine.
Barrel: 3.8".
Weight: 26 oz. **Length:** 7³⁄₃₂" over-all.
Stocks: Checkered black plastic.
Sights: Blade front, rear adjustable for windage.
Features: Double action. De-cocking lever permits lowering hammer onto locked firing pin. Squared combat-type trigger guard. Shortened, lightened version of P-220. Imported from West Germany by SIGARMS, Inc.
Price: **$715.00**

SIG-SAUER P-226 DA Auto Pistol

Similar to the P-220 pistol except has 15-shot magazine, 4.4" barrel, and weighs 26½ oz. 9mm only.Imported from West Germany by SIGARMS, Inc.
Price: Blue........ **$742.50**
Price: Electroless nickel **$819.50**
Price: K-Kote (Polymer) finish **$764.50**

SIG-Sauer P226

SIG-SAUER P-230 DA AUTO PISTOL

Caliber: 32 ACP, 8-shot; 380 ACP, 7-shot.
Barrel: 3¾".
Weight: 16 oz. **Length:** 6½" over-all.
Stocks: Checkered black plastic.
Sights: Blade front, rear adj. for w.
Features: Double action. Same basic action design as P-220. Blowback operation, stationary barrel. Introduced 1977. Imported from West Germany by SIGARMS, Inc.
Price: **$495.50**
Price: In stainless steel (P-230 SL)........ **$577.50**

SMITH & WESSON MODEL 422 AUTO
Caliber: 22 LR, 10-shot magazine.
Barrel: 4½", 6".
Weight: 22 oz. (4½", bbl.) **Length:** 7½" over-all (4½" bbl.).
Stocks: Checkered plastic (Field), checkered walnut (Target).
Sights: Field — serrated ramp front, fixed rear; Target — Patrige front, adjustable rear.
Features: Aluminum frame, steel slide, brushed blue finish; internal hammer. Introduced 1987.
Price: 4½", 6", fixed sight. **$198.00**
Price: As above, adjustable sight **$234.50**

Smith & Wesson 422

SMITH & WESSON MODEL 439 DOUBLE ACTION
Caliber: 9mm Luger, 8-shot magazine.
Barrel: 4".
Weight: 30 oz. **Length:** 7⅝" over-all.
Stocks: Checkered walnut.
Sights: Serrated ramp front, square notch rear is fully adj. for w. & e. Also available with fixed sights.
Features: Rear sight has protective shields on both sides of the sight blade. Frame is aluminum alloy. Firing pin lock in addition to the regular rotating safety. Magazine disconnector. Comes with two magazines. Ambidextrous safety standard. Introduced 1980.
Price: Blue, from **$472.00**
Price: Adjustable sight, from **$498.50**
Price: Model 639 (stainless), from **$523.50**

Smith & Wesson Model 659

SMITH & WESSON MODEL 459 DOUBLE ACTION
Caliber: 9mm Luger, 14-shot magazine.
Barrel: 4".
Weight: 30 oz. **Length:** 7⅝" over-all.
Stocks: Checkered high-impact nylon.
Sights: ⅛" square serrated ramp front, square notch rear is fully adj. for w. & e. Also available with fixed sights.
Features: Alloy frame. Rear sight has protective shields on both sides of blade. Firing pin lock in addition to the regular safety. Magazine disconnector. Comes with two magazines. Ambidextrous safety standard. Introduced 1980.
Price: Blue, from **$501.50**
Price: Adjustable sight, from **$528.00**
Price: Model 659 (stainless), from **$553.00**

Smith & Wesson Model 469

Smith & Wesson Model 469 Mini-Gun
Basically a cut-down version of the Model 459 pistol. Gun has a 3½" barrel, 12-round magazine, over-all length of 6$^{13}/_{16}$", and weighs 26 oz. Also accepts the 14-shot Model 459 magazine. Cross-hatch knurling on the recurved-front trigger guard and backstrap; magazine has a curved finger extension; bobbed hammer; sandblast blue finish with pebble-grain grips. Ambidextrous safety standard. Introduced 1983.
Price: **$478.50**
Price: Stainless Model 669. .... **$522.50**

Consult our Directory pages for the location of firms mentioned.

Smith & Wesson Model 645

SMITH & WESSON MODEL 645 DOUBLE ACTION
Caliber: 45 ACP, 8-shot magazine.
Barrel: 5".
Weight: 37.5 ozs. **Length:** 8⅝" over-all.
Stocks: Checkered high-impact nylon.
Sights: Red ramp front, rear drift-adjustable for windage, or fully adjustable.
Features: Double action. Made of stainless steel. Has manual hammer-drop, magazine disconnect and firing pin safeties. Cross-hatch knurling on the recurved front trigger guard and backstrap; bevelled magazine well. Introduced 1985.
Price: Fixed sight.. **$622.00**
Price: Adjustable sight **$649.00**

CAUTION: PRICES CHANGE. CHECK AT GUNSHOP.

Spectre D/A

SPECTRE DOUBLE ACTION AUTO PISTOL

Caliber: 9mm Para., 30-shot magazine.
Barrel: 8″.
Weight: 2.2 lbs. **Length:** 13.7″ over-all.
Stocks: Black composition grip.
Sights: Post front, flip rear.
Features: Double action mechanism fires from closed bolt. Introduced 1987. Imported by Mitchell Arms, Inc.
Price: **$670.00**

SPORTARMS TOKAREV MODEL 213

Caliber: 9mm Parabellum, 8-shot magazine.
Barrel: 4.5″.
Weight: 31 oz. **Length:** 7.6″ over-all.
Stocks: Grooved plastic.
Sights: Fixed.
Features: Blue finish, hard chrome optional. 9mm version of the famous Russian Tokarev pistol. Made in China by Norinco; imported by Sportarms of Florida. Introduced 1988.
Price: Blue, about **$259.75**
Price: Hard chrome, about **$329.75**

Springfield Armory 1911-A1

SPRINGFIELD ARMORY 1911-A1 AUTO PISTOL

Caliber: 9mm or 45 ACP, 8-shot magazine.
Barrel: 5″.
Weight: 2¼ lbs. **Length:** 8½″ over-all.
Stocks: NA.
Sights: Blade front, rear drift-adjustable for windage.
Features: All forged parts, including frame, barrel, slide. All new production. Custom slide and parts available. Introduced 1985. From Springfield Armory.
Price: Complete pistol, Parkerized **$362.00**
Price: Complete pistol, blued **$383.00**
Price: 45 to 9mm conversion kit, Parkerized...................... **$169.00**
Price: As above, blued **$177.00**

Springfield Armory 1911-A1 Defender

Similar to the standard 1911-A1 except has fixed combat-style sights, bevelled magazine well, extended thumb safety, bobbed hammer, walnut stocks, serrated front strap, and comes with two stainless steel magazines. Available in 45 ACP only, choice of blue or Parkerized finish. Introduced 1988.
Price: Blue.. **$454.00**
Price: Parkerized **$434.00**

Springfield Armory 1911-A1 Combat Commander

Similar to the standard 1911-A1 except slide and barrel are ½″ shorter. Comes with bobbed hammer and walnut stocks. Available in 45 ACP only; choice of blue or Parkerized finish. Introduced 1988.
Price: Blue.. **$467.00**
Price: Parkerized **$447.00**

Springfield Combat Commander

STAR MODEL 30M & 30PK DOUBLE-ACTION PISTOLS

Caliber: 9mm Para., 15-shot magazine.
Barrel: 4.33″ (Model M); 3.86″ (Model PK).
Weight: 40 oz. (M); 30 oz. (PK). **Length:** 8″ over-all (M); 7.6″ (PK).
Stocks: Checkered black plastic.
Sights: Square blade front, square notch rear click-adjustable for windage and elevation.
Features: Double or single action; grooved front and backstraps and trigger guard face; ambidextrous safety cams firing pin forward; removable backstrap houses the firing mechanism. Model M has steel frame; Model PK is alloy. Introduced 1984. Imported from Spain by Interarms.
Price: Model M or PK **$510.00**

Star Model 30 PK

STAR BM, BKM AUTO PISTOLS

Caliber: 9mm Para., 8-shot magazine.
Barrel: 3.9″.
Weight: 25 oz.
Stocks: Checkered walnut.
Sights: Fixed.
Features: Blue or chrome finish. Magazine and manual safeties, external hammer. Imported from Spain by Interarms.
Price: Blue, BM and BKM....................................... **$360.00**
Price: Chrome, BM only **$375.00**

STAR MODEL PD AUTO PISTOL
Caliber: 45 ACP, 6-shot magazine.
Barrel: 3.94″.
Weight: 28 oz. **Length:** 7 7/16″ over-all.
Stocks: Checkered walnut.
Sights: Ramp front, fully adjustable rear.
Features: Rear sight milled into slide; thumb safety; grooved non-slip front strap; nylon recoil buffer; inertia firing pin; no grip or magazine safeties. Imported from Spain by Interarms.
Price: Blue. **$395.00**

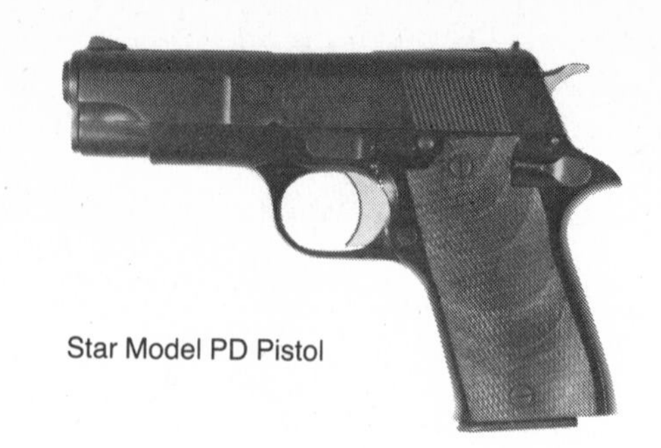
Star Model PD Pistol

STEEL CITY "DOUBLE DEUCE" PISTOL
Caliber: 22 LR, 7-shot; 25 ACP, 6-shot.
Barrel: 2½″.
Weight: 18 oz. **Length:** 5½″ over-all.
Stocks: Rosewood.
Sights: Fixed.
Features: Double-action; stainless steel construction with matte finish; ambidextrous slide-mounted safety. From Steel City Arms, Inc.
Price: 22 or 25 cal **$289.95**

Steel City Double Deuce

STEEL CITY "WAR EAGLE" PISTOL
Caliber: 9mm Para., 15-shot magazine.
Barrel: 4″, 6″.
Weight: NA. **Length:** NA.
Stocks: Rosewood.
Sights: Fixed and adjustable.
Features: Double action; matte-finished stainless steel; ambidextrous safety. Announced 1986.
Price: **$550.00**

TANARMI TA90 DA AUTO PISTOL
Caliber: 9mm Parabellum, 15-shot magazine.
Barrel: 4.75″.
Weight: 35 oz. **Length:** 8.25″ over-all.
Stocks: Checkered neoprene rubber.
Sights: Blade front, white outline rear.
Features: Improved version of the Czech CZ75. Chrome plated barrel and trigger, extended slide release lever. Available in matte blue or matte chrome. Imported from Italy by Excam.
Price: Matte blue **$415.00**
Price: Matte chrome **$430.00**

Tanarmi Baby TA90 Auto Pistol
Similar to the standard TA90 except has ¾″ shorter barrel/slide, ½″ shorter grip. Barrel length 4″, weight is 30 oz., 12-shot magazine.
Price: Matte blue **$430.00**
Price: Matte chrome **$450.00**

Tanarmi TA90

TARGA GT380XE PISTOL
Caliber: 380 ACP, 11-shot magazine.
Barrel: 3.88″.
Weight: 28 oz. **Length:** 7.38″ over-all.
Stocks: Smooth hardwood.
Sights: Adj. for windage.
Features: Blue finish. Ordnance steel. Magazine disconnector, firing pin and thumb safeties. Introduced 1980. Imported by Excam.
Price: 380 cal., blue. **$235.00**

Targa GT380XE

TARGA MODEL GT27 AUTO PISTOL
Caliber: 25 ACP, 6-shot magazine.
Barrel: 2 7/16″.
Weight: 12 oz. **Length:** 4⅝″ over-all.
Stocks: Smooth walnut.
Sights: Fixed.
Features: Safety lever take-down; external hammer with half-cock. Assembled in U.S. by Excam, Inc.
Price: Blue. **$75.00**
Price: Chrome. **$80.00**

CAUTION: PRICES CHANGE. CHECK AT GUNSHOP.

Targa GT26 Auto Pistol
Similar to the GT27 except has steel frame, push-button magazine release and magazine disconnect safety. Contoured smooth walnut grips. Satin blue finish. Imported from Italy by Excam, assembled in U.S.A.
Price: **$115.00**

Targa GT26

TARGA MODELS GT22, GT32, GT380 AUTO PISTOLS
Caliber: 22 LR, 10-shot; 32 ACP or 380 ACP, 6-shot magazine.
Barrel: 4⅞".
Weight: 26 oz. **Length:** 7⅜" over-all.
Stocks: Walnut.
Sights: Fixed blade front; rear drift-adj. for w.
Features: Chrome or blue finish; magazine, thumb, and firing pin safeties; external hammer; safety lever take-down. Imported from Italy by Excam, Inc.
Price: 22 cal., blue **$200.00**
Price: 22 cal., nickel **$215.00**
Price: 32 cal., blue **$200.00**
Price: 32 cal., chrome **$215.00**
Price: 380 cal., blue **$212.00**
Price: 380 cal., chrome **$220.00**
Price: 380 cal., chrome, engraved **$245.00**
Price: 380 cal., blue, engraved **$235.00**

Targa GT380

TARGA GT22T TARGET AUTO
Caliber: 22LR, 12-shot.
Barrel: 6".
Weight: 30 oz. **Length:** 9" over-all.
Stocks: Checkered walnut, with thumbrest.
Sights: Blade on ramp front, rear adjustable for windage.
Features: Blue finish. Finger-rest magaznine. Imported by Excam.
Price: **$200.00**

TAURUS MODEL PT-92AF AUTO PISTOL
Caliber: 9mm Para., 15-shot magazine.
Barrel: 4.92".
Weight: 34 oz. **Length:** 8.54" over-all.
Stocks: Brazilian walnut.
Sights: Fixed notch rear. Three-dot sight system.
Features: Double action, exposed hammer, chamber loaded indicator. Inertia firing pin. Blue finish. Imported by Taurus International.
Price: **$381.51**
Price: Satin nickel finish **$393.38**

Taurus PT-99AF Auto Pistol
Similar to the PT-92 except has fully adjustable rear sight, smooth Brazilian walnut stocks and is available in polished blue or stain nickel. Introduced 1983.
Price: Polished blue **$408.74**
Price: Satin nickel **$422.23**

Taurus PT99AF

TAURUS MODEL PT58 AUTO PISTOL
Caliber: 380 ACP, 13-shot magazine.
Barrel: 4.01".
Weight: 30 oz.
Stocks: Brazilian walnut.
Sights: Integral blade on slide front, notch rear. Three-dot system.
Features: Double action with exposed hammer; inertia firing pin. Introduced 1988. Imported by Taurus International.
Price: Blue **$359.90**
Price: Satin nickel **$366.45**

UZI® PISTOL
Caliber: 9mm Parabellum, 45 ACP.
Barrel: 4.5".
Weight: 3.8 lbs. **Length:** 9.45" over-all.
Stocks: Black plastic.
Sights: Post front with white dot, open rear click adjustable for windage and elevation, two white dots..
Features: Semi-auto blow-back action; fires from closed bolt; floating firing pin. Comes in a moulded plastic case with 20-round magazine; 25 and 32-round magazines available. Imported from Israel by Action Arms. Introduced 1984.
Price: **$579.00**

UZI Pistol

CAUTION: PRICES CHANGE. CHECK AT GUNSHOP.

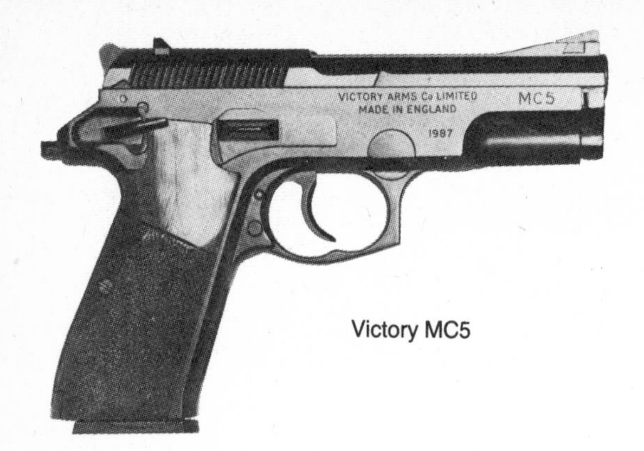

Victory MC5

VICTORY MC5 AUTO PISTOL
Caliber: 9mm Para., 38 Super (17-shot magazine), 41 Action Express (12-shot), 45 ACP (10-shot).
Barrel: 4", 6", 7½", interchangeable.
Weight: 45 oz. **Length:** 8½" over-all (4⅜" barrel).
Stocks: High-impact plastic.
Sights: Patridge three-dot system; ramped non-snag front, rear adjustable for windage with different heights available.
Features: Double-action auto; chamber loaded indicator; exposed hammer; ambidextrous safety, magazine catch, slide release; open-top slide. Introduced 1988. Imported from England by Magnum Research, Inc.
Price: MC5 . . . . **$459.00**
Price: Extra barrels **$100.00**
Price: Extra magazines **$25.00**

WALTHER PP AUTO PISTOL
Caliber: 22 LR, 8-shot; 32 ACP, 380 ACP, 7-shot.
Barrel: 3.86".
Weight: 23½ oz. **Length:** 6.7" over-all.
Stocks: Checkered plastic.
Sights: Fixed, white markings.
Features: Double action; manual safety blocks firing pin and drops hammer; chamber loaded indicator on 32 and 380; extra finger rest magazine provided. Imported from Germany by Interarms.
Price: 22 LR **$815.00**
Price: 32 . . . . **$795.00**
Price: 380 . . . . **$815.00**
Price: Engraved models . . . . **On Request**

Walther PP Auto Pistol

Walther American PPK Auto Pistol
Similar to Walther PPK/S except weighs 21 oz., has 6-shot capacity. Made in the U.S. Introduced 1986.
Price: Stainless, 380 ACP only **$515.00**
Price: Blue, 380 ACP only **$515.00**

Walther American PPK/S Auto Pistol
Similar to Walther PP except made entirely in the United States. Has 3.27" barrel with 6.1" length over-all. Introduced 1980.
Price: 380 ACP only **$515.00**
Price: As above, stainless **$515.00**

WALTHER P-38 AUTO PISTOL
Caliber: 22 LR, 9mm Para., 8-shot.
Barrel: 4 15/16" (9mm), 5 1/16" (22 LR).
Weight: 28 oz. **Length:** 8½" over-all.
Stocks: Checkered plastic.
Sights: Fixed.
Features: Double action; safety blocks firing pin and drops hammer; chamber loaded indicator. Matte finish standard, polished blue, engraving and/or plating available. Imported from Germany by Interarms.
Price: 22 LR **$995.00**
Price: 9mm **$895.00**
Price: Steel frame **$1,225.00**
Price: Engraved models . . . . **On Request**

Walther P-38 Auto Pistol

Walther P-5 Auto Pistol
Latest Walther design that uses the basic P-38 double-action mechanism. Caliber 9mm Para., barrel length 3½"; weight 28 oz., over-all length 7".
Price: **$999.00**

WALTHER P-88 AUTO PISTOL
Caliber: 9mm Para., 15-shot magazine.
Barrel: 4".,
Weight: 31½ oz. **Length:** 7⅜" over-all.
Stocks: Checkered black composition.
Sights: Blade front, rear adj. for w. and e.
Features: Double action with ambidextrous decocking lever and magazine release; alloy frame; loaded chamber indicator; matte finish. Imported from Germany by Interarms.
Price: **$1,165.00**

WALTHER MODEL TPH AUTO PISTOL
Caliber: 22 LR, 6-shot magazine.
Barrel: 2¼".
Weight: 14 oz. **Length:** 5⅜" over-all
Stocks: Checkered black composition.
Sights: Blade front, rear drift-adjustable for windage.
Features: Made of stainless steel. Scaled-down version of the Walther PP/PPK series. Made in U.S. Introduced 1987. From Interarms.
Price: **$350.00**

Walther TPH

Wildey Auto

WILDEY AUTOMATIC PISTOL
Caliber: 9mm Win. Mag., 45 Win. Mag., 475 Wildey Mag., 357 Peterbuilt.
Barrel: 5", 6", 7", 8" (45 Win. Mag.); 8", 10" (475 Wildey Mag.). Interchangeable.
Weight: 64 oz. (5" barrel). **Length:** 11" over-all (7" barrel).
Stocks: Checkered hardwood.
Sights: Ramp front, fully adjustable rear.
Features: Gas-operated action. Made of stainless steel. Has three-lug rotary bolt. Double action. Made in U.S. by Wildey, Inc.
Price: **$895.00**

WILKINSON "LINDA" PISTOL
Caliber: 9mm Para., 31-shot magazine.
Barrel: $8\frac{5}{16}$".
Weight: 4 lbs., 13 oz. **Length:** $12\frac{1}{4}$" over-all.
Stocks: Checkered black plastic pistol grip, maple fore-end.
Sights: Protected blade front, aperture rear.
Features: Fires from closed bolt. Semi-auto only. Straight blowback action. Cross-bolt safety. Removable barrel. From Wilkinson Arms.
Price: **$324.93**

Wilkinson "Sherry"

WILKINSON "SHERRY" AUTO PISTOL
Caliber: 22 LR, 8-shot magazine.
Barrel: $2\frac{1}{8}$".
Weight: $9\frac{1}{4}$ oz. **Length:** $4\frac{3}{8}$" over-all.
Stocks: Checkered black plastic.
Sights: Fixed, groove.
Features: Cross-bolt safety locks the sear into the hammer. Available in all blue finish or blue slide and trigger with gold frame. Introduced 1985.
Price: **$149.95**

COMPETITION HANDGUNS

Models specifically designed for classic competitive shooting sports.

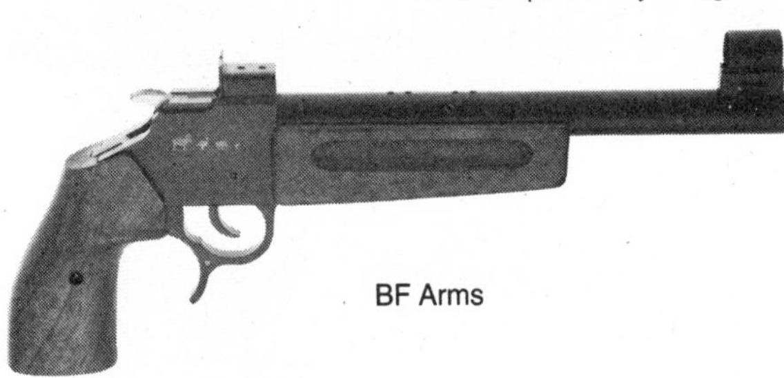
BF Arms

B F ARMS SINGLE SHOT PISTOL
Caliber: 7mm Super Mag., 7mm/375 Super Mag., 32-20, 30 Herrett, 357 Mag., 357 Max.
Barrel: 10".
Weight: 46 oz.
Stocks: Ambidextrous, oil-finished walnut with fore-end.
Sights: Hooded front, fully adjustable match rear.
Features: Falling block short-stroke action. Wilson air-gauged match-grade barrel. Flat black oxide finish. Drilled and tapped for standard scope mounts. Made in U.S. by B F Arms. Introduced 1988.
Price: Silhouette, with sights **$285.00**
Price: Hunter, no sights **$259.50**

Beeman/Unique 69

BEEMAN/UNIQUE D.E.S. 69 TARGET PISTOL
Caliber: 22 LR, 5-shot magazine.
Barrel: 5.91".
Weight: 35.3 oz. **Length:** 10.5" over-all.
Stocks: French walnut target-style with thumbrest and adjustable shelf; hand-checkered panels.
Sights: Ramp front, micro. adj. rear mounted on frame; 8.66" sight radius.
Features: Meets U.I.T. standards. Comes with 260-gram barrel weight; 100, 150, 350 gram weights available. Fully adjustable match trigger; dry firing safety device. Imported from France by Beeman.
Price: Right-hand **$1,065.00**
Price: Left-hand **$1,060.00**

Beeman/Unique 2000-U

BEEMAN/UNIQUE MODEL 2000-U MATCH PISTOL
Caliber: 22 Short, 5-shot magazine.
Barrel: 5.9".
Weight: 43 oz. **Length:** 11.3" over-all.
Stocks: Anatomically shaped, adjustable, stippled French walnut.
Sights: Blade front, fully adjustable rear; 9.7" sight radius.
Features: Light alloy frame, steel slide and shock absorber; five barrel vents reduce recoil, three of which can be blocked; trigger adjustable for position and pull weight. Comes with 340-gram weight housing, 160-gram available. Imported from France by Beeman. Introduced 1984.
Price: Right-hand **$1,198.00**
Price: Left-hand **$1,260.00**

Bernardelli Model 69

Chipmunk Silhouette

BERNARDELLI MODEL 69 TARGET PISTOL

Caliber: 22 LR, 10-shot magazine.
Barrel: 5.9″.
Weight: 38 oz. **Length:** 9″ over-all.
Stocks: Wrap around, hand-checkered walnut with thumbrest.
Sights: Fully adjustable and interchangeable target-type.
Features: Conforms to U.I.T. regulations. Has 7.1″ sight radius, .27″ wide grooved trigger with 40-45 oz. pull. Manual thumb safety and magazine safety. Introduced 1987. From Mandall Shooting Supplies.
Price: **$289.95**

CHIPMUNK SILHOUETTE PISTOL

Caliber: 22 LR.
Barrel: 14⅞″.
Weight: About 2 lbs. **Length:** 20″ over-all.
Stock: American walnut rear grip.
Sights: Post on ramp front, peep rear.
Features: Meets IHMSA 22-cal. unlimited category for competition. Introduced 1985.
Price: **$149.95**

COLT GOLD CUP NAT'L MATCH MK IV/Series 80

Caliber: 45 ACP, 7-shot magazine.
Barrel: 5″, with new design bushing.
Weight: 39 oz. **Length:** 8½″.
Stocks: Blue—Checkered walnut, gold plated medallion; stainless has black walnut.
Sights: Ramp-style front, Colt-Elliason rear adj. for w. and e., sight radius 6¾″.
Features: Arched or flat housing; wide, grooved trigger with adj. stop; ribbed-top slide, hand fitted, with improved ejection port.
Price: Blue.......... **$729.95**
Price: Stainless.......... **$783.95**
Price: Bright stainless.......... **$835.95**

Colt Gold Cup Series 80

COMPETITOR SINGLE SHOT PISTOL

Caliber: 22 LR, 223, 7mm TCU, 7mm Int., 30 Herrett, 357 Maximum, 41 Mag., 44 Mag., 454 Casull, 375 Super Mag. Others on special order.
Barrel: 10.5″, 14″.
Weight: NA **Length:** NA
Stocks: Smooth walnut with thumb rest.
Sights: Ramp front, open adjustable rear.
Features: Interchangeable barrels of blue ordnance or bright stainless steel; ventilated barrel shroud; receiver has integral scope mount. Introduced 1987. From Competition Arms, Inc.
Price: With 10.5″ bbl.......... **$562.50**
Price: With 14″ bbl.......... **$578.50**
Price: Extra barrels, 10.5″, standard calibers.......... **$93.75**
Price: Special calibers, add.......... **$62.50**

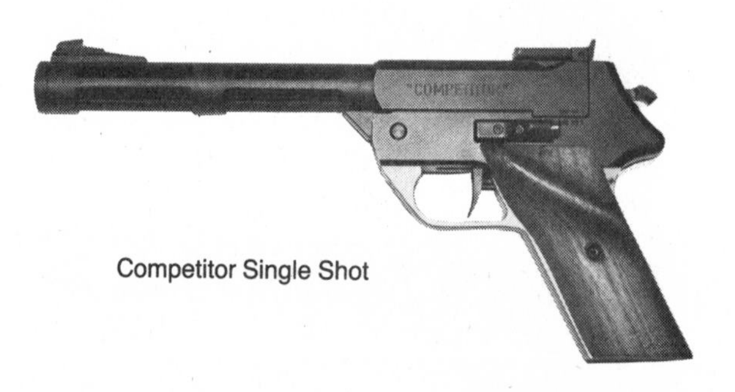

Competitor Single Shot

DETONICS SCOREMASTER TARGET PISTOL

Caliber: 45 ACP, 451 Detonics Magnum, 7-shot magazine.
Barrel: 5″ heavy match barrel with recessed muzzle; 6″ optional.
Weight: 42 oz. **Length:** 8⅜″ over-all.
Stocks: Pachmayr checkered with matching mainspring housing.
Sights: Blade front, Low-Base Bomar rear.
Features: Stainless steel; self-centering barrel system; patented Detonics recoil system; combat tuned; ambidextrous safety; extended grip safety; National Match tolerances; extended magazine release. Comes with two spare magazines, three interchangeable front sights, and carrying case. Introduced 1983. From Detonics.
Price: 45 ACP or 451 Mag., 6″ barrel.......... **$1,150.00**
Price: As above, 5″ barrel.......... **$1,110.00**

Detonics Janus Scoremaster Pistol

Similar to the standard Scoremaster except in 45 ACP only and comes with extra 5.6″ compensated barrel and is easily convertible. With longer barrel, the front sight is mounted on the specialist compensator. Over-all length with 5.6″ barrel is 10″, weight is 46 oz. Adjustable Millett rear sight, hand-serrated custom front. Has 8-shot magazine. Made of stainless steel with polished slide flats. Introduced 1988.
Price: **$1,650.00**

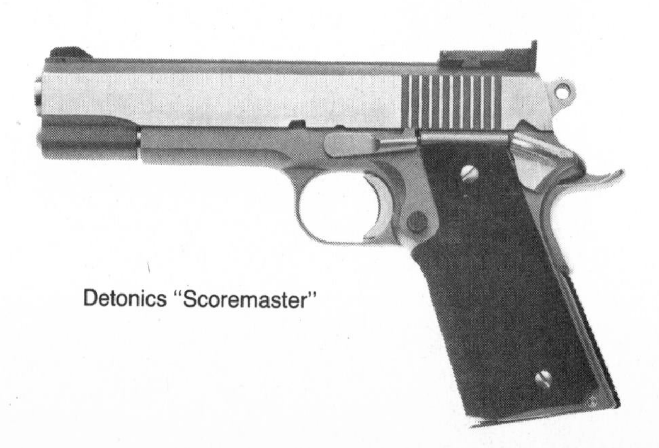

Detonics "Scoremaster"

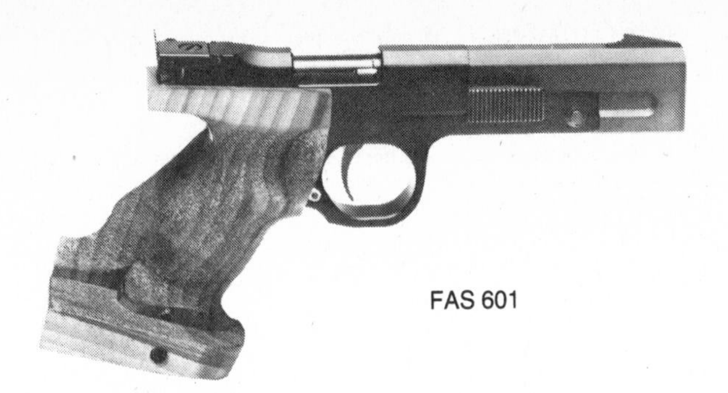
FAS 601

FAS 602 MATCH PISTOL

Caliber: 22 LR, 5-shot.
Barrel: 5.6″.
Weight: 37 oz. **Length:** 11″ over-all.
Stocks: Walnut wrap-around; sizes small, medium or large, or adjustable.
Sights: Match. Blade front, open notch rear fully adj. for w. and e. Sight radius is 8.66″.
Features: Line of sight is only 11/32″ above centerline of bore; magazine is inserted from top; adjustable and removable trigger mechanism; single lever takedown. Full 5 year warranty. Imported from Italy by Mandall and Osborne's.
Price: From Osborne's, about $895.00
Price: From Mandall $1,095.00

FAS 601 Match Pistol

Similar to SP 602 except has different match stocks with adj. palm, shelf, 22 Short only for rapid fire shooting; weighs 40 oz., 5.6″ bbl.; has gas ports through top of barrel and slide to reduce recoil; slightly different trigger and sear mechanisms.
Price: From Osborne's, 601, 603, about $1,050.00
Price: From Mandall $1,095.00

HAMMERLI MODEL 150 FREE PISTOL

Caliber: 22 LR, single shot.
Barrel: 11.3″.
Weight: 43 ozs. **Length:** 15.35″ over-all.
Stocks: Walnut with adjustable palm shelf.
Sights: Sight radius of 14.6″. Micro rear sight adj. for w. and e.
Features: Single shot Martini action. Cocking lever on left side of action with vertical operation. Set trigger adjustable for length and angle. Trigger pull weight adjustable between 5 and 100 grams. Guaranteed accuracy of .78″, 10 shots from machine rest. Imported from Switzerland by Osborne's, Mandall Shooting Supplies and Beeman.
Price: About (Mandall) $1,699.50
Price: With electric trigger (Model 152), about (Mandall) $1,799.50
Price: Model 150 (Osborne's) $1,850.00
Price: Model 152 (Osborne's) $1,980.00
Price: Model 150 (Beeman, right hand) $1,980,00
Price: Model 152 (Beeman, right hand) $2,105.00

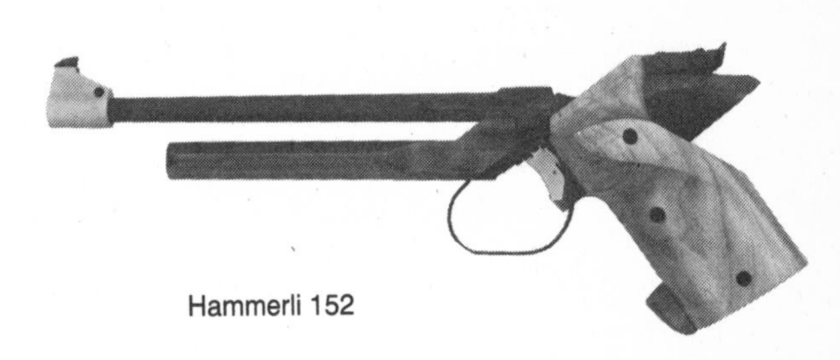
Hammerli 152

Hammerli 208

HAMMERLI STANDARD, MODELS 208, 211, 215

Caliber: 22 LR.
Barrel: 5.9″, 6-groove.
Weight: 37.6 oz. (45 oz. with extra heavy barrel weight). **Length:** 10″.
Stocks: Walnut. Adj. palm rest (208), 211 has thumbrest grip.
Sights: Match sights, fully adj. for w. and e. (click adj.). Interchangeable front and rear blades.
Features: Semi-automatic, recoil operated. 8-shot clip. Slide stop. Fully adj. trigger (2¼ lbs. and 3 lbs.). Extra barrel weight available. Imported from Switzerland by Osborne's, Mandall Shooting Supplies, Beeman.
Price: Model 208, approx. (Mandall) $1,399.50
Price: Model 211, approx. (Mandall) $1,295.00
Price: Model 215, approx. (Mandall) $1,295.00
Price: Model 208 (Osborne's), about $1,555.00
Price: Model 211 (Osborne's), about $1,515.00
Price: Model 215 (Osborne's), about $1,226.00
Price: Model 208 (Beeman) $1,580.00
Price: Model 211 (Beeman) $1,413.00
Price: Model 215 (Beeman) $1,175.00

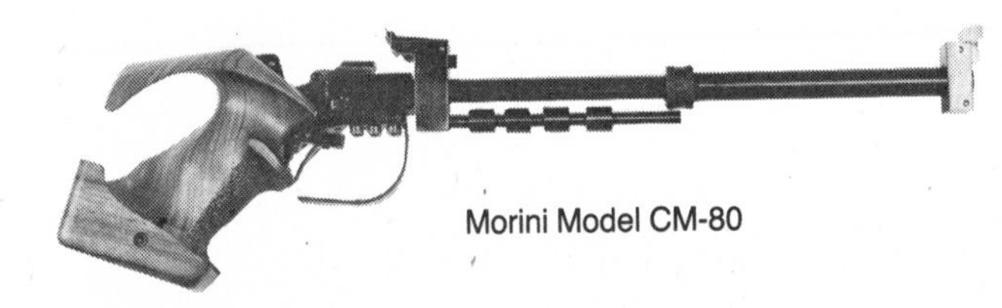
Morini Model CM-80

MORINI MODEL CM-80 SUPER COMPETITION

Caliber: 22 Long Rifle, single shot.
Barrel: 10″, free floating.
Weight: 30 oz., with weights. **Length:** 21.25″ over-all.
Stocks: Walnut, adjustable or wrap-around in three sizes.
Sights: Match; square notch rear adjustable for w. and e.; up to 15.6″ radius.
Features: Adjustable grip/frame angle, adjustable barrel alignment, adjustable trigger weight (5 to 120 grams), adjustable sight radius. Comes with 20-shot test target (50 meters) and case. Introduced 1985. Imported from Italy by Osborne's.
Price: Standard $1,100.00
Price: Deluxe $1,400.00

HAMMERLI MODEL 232 RAPID FIRE PISTOL

Caliber: 22 Short, 6-shot.
Barrel: 5″, with six exhaust ports.
Weight: 44 oz. **Length:** 10.4″ over-all.
Stocks: Stippled walnut; wraparound on Model 232-2, adjustable on 232-1.
Sights: Interchangeable front and rear blades, fully adjustable micrometer rear.
Features: Recoil operated semi-automatic; nearly recoilless design; trigger adjustable from 8.4 to 10.6 oz. with three lengths offered. Wraparound grips available in small, medium and large sizes. Imported from Switzerland by Osborne's, Beeman, Mandall. Introduced 1984.
Price: Model 232-1, (Osborne's), about $1,285.00
Price: Model 232-2, (Osborne's), about $1,330.00
Price: Model 232-1 (Beeman) $1,300.00
Price: Model 232-2 (Beeman) $1,490.00

Pardini Fiocchi Standard

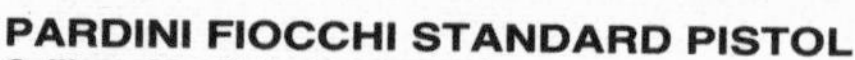

PARDINI FIOCCHI STANDARD PISTOL
Caliber: 22 LR, 5-shot magazine.
Barrel: 4.9″.
Weight: 37 ozs. **Length:** 11.7″ over-all.
Stocks: Match-type stippled walnut.
Sights: Match-type undercut blade front, fully adjustable open rear.
Features: Match trigger. Matte blue finish. Comes with locking case. Imported from Italy by Fiocchi of America.
Price: **$868.75**

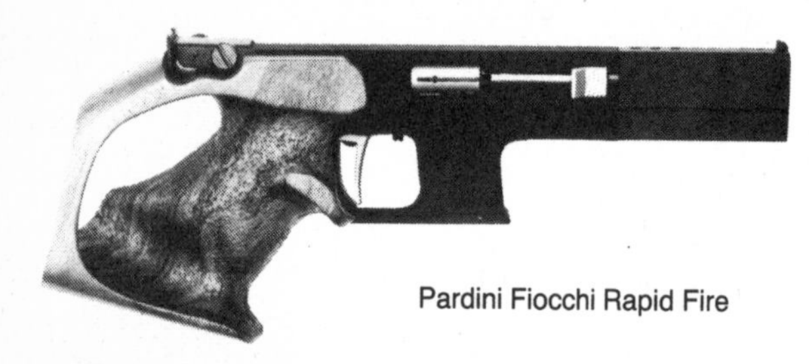

Pardini Fiocchi Rapid Fire

PARDINI FIOCCHI RAPID FIRE MATCH
Caliber: 22 Short, 5-shot magazine.
Barrel: 5.1″.
Weight: 34.5 ozs. **Length:** 11.7″ over-all.
Stocks: Stippled walnut, match-type.
Sights: Post front, fully adjustable rear.
Features: Alloy bolt. Has 14.9″ sight radius. Imported from Italy by Fiocchi of America.
Price: **$893.75**

PARDINI FIOCCHI 32 MATCH PISTOL
Caliber: 32 S&W Long, 5-shot magazine.
Barrel: 4.9″.
Weight: 38.7 ozs. **Length:** 11.7″ over-all.
Stocks: Stippled walnut match-type with adjustable palm shelf.
Sights: Match. Undercut blade front, fully adjustable open rear.
Features: Match trigger. Recoil compensation system. Imported from Italy by Fiocchi of Amercica.
Price: **$906.25**

Pardini Fiocchi Free Pistol

PARDINI FIOCCHI FREE PISTOL
Caliber: 22 LR, single shot.
Barrel: 4.9″.
Weight: 37 ozs. **Length:** 11.7″ over-all.
Stocks: Walnut, special hand-fitting free-pistol design.
Sights: Post front, fully adjustable open rear.
Features: Rotating bolt-action design. Has 8.6″ sight radius. Imported from Italy by Fiocchi of America.
Price: **$962.50**

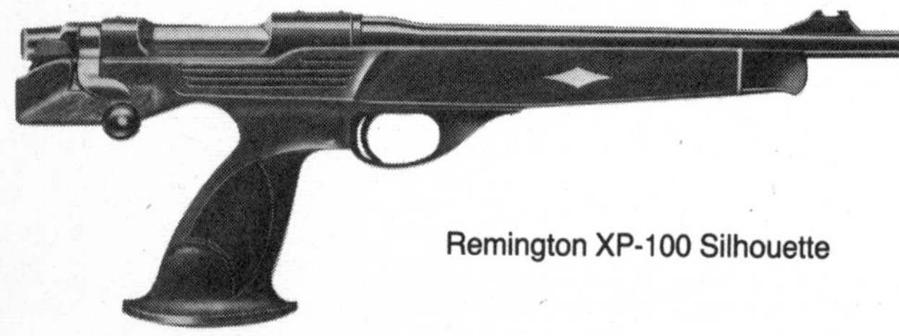

Remington XP-100 Silhouette

REMINGTON XP-100 SILHOUETTE PISTOL
Caliber: 7mm BR Remington, 35 Remington, single shot.
Barrel: 14¾″.
Weight: 4⅛ lbs. **Length:** 21¼″ over-all.
Stock: Brown nylon, one piece, checkered grip.
Sights: None furnished. Drilled and tapped for scope mounts.
Features: Universal grip fits right or left hand; match-type grooved trigger, two-position thumb safety.
Price: 7mm BR Rem **$380.00**
Price: 35 Rem **$393.00**

Ruger Government Target

RUGER MARK II TARGET MODEL AUTO PISTOL
Caliber: 22 LR, 10-shot magazine.
Barrel: 6⅞″.
Weight: 42 oz. **Length:** 11⅛″ over-all.
Stocks: Checkered hard rubber.
Sights: .125″ blade front, micro click rear, adjustable for w. and e. Sight radius 9⅜″. Introduced 1982.
Price: Blued (MK-678) **$249.75**
Price: Stainless (KMK-678) **$316.35**

Ruger Mark II Bull Barrel
Same gun as the Target Model except has 5½″ or 10″ heavy barrel (10″ meets all IHMSA regulations). Weight with 5½″ barrel is 42 oz., with 10″ barrel, 52 oz.
Price: Blued (MK-512, MK-10) **$249.75**
Price: Stainless (KMK-512, KMK-10) **$316.35**

Ruger Mark II Government Target Model
Same gun as the Mark II Target Model except has higher sights and is roll marked "Government Target Model" on the right side of the receiver below the rear sight. Identical in all respects to the military model used for training U.S. armed forces except for markings. Comes with factory test target. Introduced 1987.
Price: Blued (MK678G) **$288.60**

CAUTION: PRICES CHANGE. CHECK AT GUNSHOP.

SAKO TRIACE MATCH PISTOL
Caliber: 22 Short, 22 Long Rifle, 32 S&W Long, 6-shot magazine.
Barrel: 5.9".
Weight: 44.3 oz. to 48.3 oz. (depending on caliber). **Length:** 11.0" over-all.
Stocks: Fully adjustable walnut.
Sights: Blade front, micrometer adjustable rear.
Features: Semi-auto match pistol comes in three calibers. Trigger is adjustable for sear engagement, weight of pull, free travel and position. Comes with carrying case, tool/cleaning kit, two magazines. Imported from Finland. Available from Osborne's
Price: Three-caliber system, about **$2,800.00**

Smith & Wesson 29 Silhouette

SMITH & WESSON MODEL 29 SILHOUETTE
Caliber: 44 Magnum, 6-shot.
Barrel: 10⅝".
Weight: 58 oz. **Length:** 16³⁄₁₆" over-all.
Stocks: Over-size target-type, checkered Goncalo Alves.
Sights: Four-position front to match the four distances of silhouette targets; micro-click rear adjustable for windage and elevation.
Features: Designed specifically for silhouette shooting. Front sight has click stops for the four pre-set ranges. Introduced 1983.
Price: **$510.00**

Smith & Wesson Model 41

SMITH & WESSON 22 AUTO PISTOL MODEL 41
Caliber: 22 LR, 10-shot clip.
Barrel: 7".
Weight: 43½ oz. **Length:** 12" over-all.
Stocks: Checkered walnut with thumbrest, usable with either hand.
Sights: Front, ⅛" Patridge undercut; micro click rear adj. for w. and e.
Features: ⅜" wide, grooved trigger with adj. stop.
Price: S&W Bright Blue....................................... **$536.00**

SMITH & WESSON 38 MASTER MODEL 52 AUTO
Caliber: 38 Special (for mid-range W.C. with flush-seated bullet only), 5-shot magazine.
Barrel: 5".
Weight: 40.5 oz. with empty magazine. **Length:** 8⅝" over-all.
Stocks: Checkered walnut.
Sights: ⅛" Patridge front, S&W micro click rear adj. for w. and e.
Features: Top sighting surfaces matte finished. Locked breech, moving barrel system; checked for 10-ring groups at 50 yards. Coin-adj. sight screws. Dry firing permissible if manual safety on.
Price: S&W Bright Blue....................................... **$694.00**

SMITH & WESSON MODEL 745 AUTO
Caliber: 45 ACP, 8-shot magazine.
Barrel: 5".
Weight: 38.75 oz. **Length:** 8⅝" over-all.
Stocks: Checkered walnut.
Sights: Serrated ramp front, square notch high visibility rear adj. for w.
Features: Stainless steel frame, blued slide, hammer, trigger, sights. Comes with two magazines. Introduced 1987.
Price: **$699.00**

SMITH & WESSON 22 MATCH HEAVY BARREL M-41
Caliber: 22 LR, 10-shot clip.
Barrel: 5½" heavy.
Weight: 44½ oz. **Length:** 9" over-all.
Stocks: Checkered walnut with modified thumbrest, usable with either hand.
Sights: ⅛" Patridge on ramp base. S&W micro click rear adj. for w. and e.
Features: ⅜" wide, grooved trigger; adj. trigger stop.
Price: S&W Bright Blue, satin matted top area.................... **$536.00**

Smith & Wesson Model 52

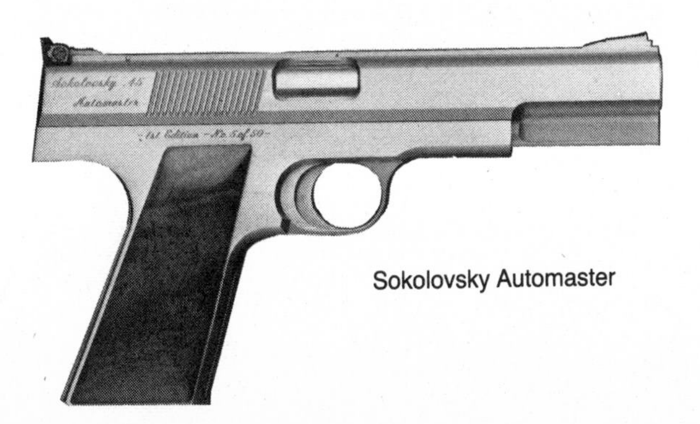

Sokolovsky Automaster

SOKOLOVSKY 45 AUTOMASTER
Caliber: 45 ACP, 6-shot magazine.
Barrel: 6".
Weight: 3.6 lbs. **Length:** 9½" over-all.
Stocks: Smooth walnut.
Sights: Ramp front, Millett fully adjustable rear.
Features: Intended for target shooting, not combat. Semi-custom built with precise tolerances. Has special "safety trigger" next to regular trigger. Most parts made of stainless steel. Introduced 1985. From Sokolovsky Corp.
Price: **$4,500.00**

CAUTION: PRICES CHANGE. CHECK AT GUNSHOP.

TAURUS MODEL 86 MASTER REVOLVER

Caliber: 38 Spec., 6-shot.
Barrel: 6″ only.
Weight: 34 oz. **Length:** 11¼″ over-all.
Stocks: Over-size target-type, checkered Brazilian walnut.
Sights: Patridge front, micro. click rear adj. for w. and e.
Features: Blue finish with non-reflective finish on barrel. Imported from Brazil by Taurus International.
Price: $257.38
Price: Model 96 Scout Master, same except in 22 cal. $257.38

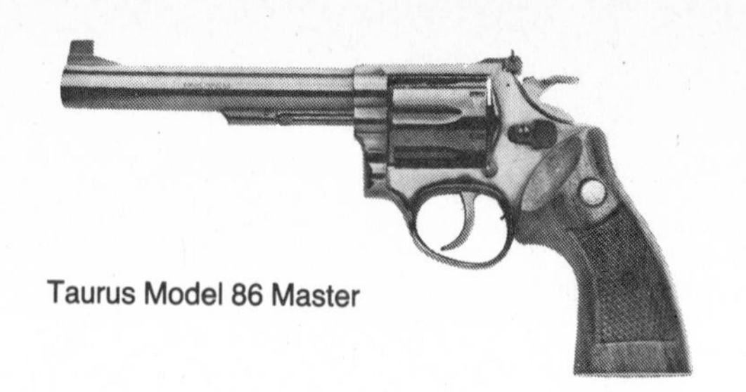
Taurus Model 86 Master

Thompson/Center Super 14 Contender

THOMPSON/CENTER SUPER 14 CONTENDER

Caliber: 22 LR, 222 Rem., 223 Rem., 6mm TCU, 7mm TCU, 7 x 30 Waters, 30-30 Win., 35 Rem., 357 Rem. Maximum, 44 Mag., single shot.
Barrel: 14″.
Weight: 45 oz. **Length:** 17¼″ over-all.
Stocks: T/C "Competitor Grip" (walnut and rubber).
Sights: Fully adjustable target-type.
Features: Break-open action with auto safety. Interchangeable barrels for both rimfire and centerfire calibers. Introduced 1978.
Price: $345.00
Price: With Armour Alloy II finish $415.00
Price: Extra barrels, blued $155.00
Price: As Above, Armour Alloy $195.00

UBERTI "PHANTOM" SA SILHOUETTE

Caliber: 357 Mag., 44 Mag.
Barrel: 10½″.
Weight: NA. **Length:** NA.
Stocks: Walnut target-style.
Sights: Blade on ramp front, fully adj. rear.
Features: Hooked trigger guard. Introduced 1986. Imported by Benson Firearms, Uberti USA.
Price: $539.00

WALTHER FREE PISTOL

Caliber: 22 LR, single shot.
Barrel: 11.7″.
Weight: 48 ozs. **Length:** 17.2″ over-all.
Stocks: Walnut, special hand-fitting design.
Sights: Fully adjustable match sights.
Features: Special electronic trigger. Matte finish blue. Introduced 1980. Imported from Germany by Interarms.
Price: $1,750.00

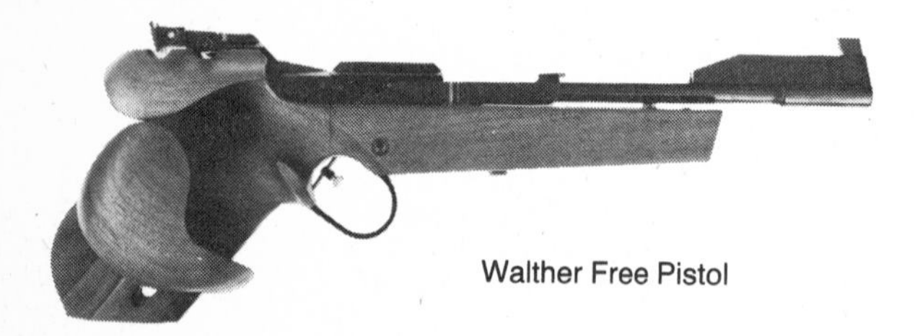
Walther Free Pistol

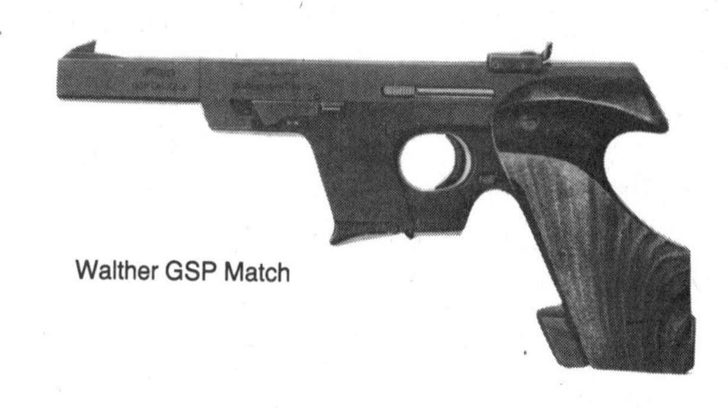
Walther GSP Match

WALTHER GSP MATCH PISTOL

Caliber: 22 LR, 32 S&W wadcutter (GSP-C), 5-shot.
Barrel: 5¾″.
Weight: 44.8 oz. (22 LR), 49.4 oz. (32). **Length:** 11.8″ over-all.
Stocks: Walnut, special hand-fitting design.
Sights: Fixed front, rear adj. for w. & e.
Features: Available with either 2.2 lb. (1000 gm) or 3 lb. (1360 gm) trigger. Spare mag., bbl. weight, tools supplied in Match Pistol Kit. Imported from Germany by Interarms.
Price: GSP $1,300.00
Price: GSP-C $1,500.00
Price: 22 LR conversion unit for GSP-C $800.00
Price: 22 Short conversion unit for GSP-C $825.00
Price: 32 S&W conversion unit for GSP-C $975.00

Walther OSP Rapid-Fire Pistol

Similar to Model GSP except 22 Short only, stock has adj. free-style hand rest.
Price: $1,475.00

DAN WESSON MODEL 40 SILHOUETTE

Caliber: 357 Maximum, 6-shot.
Barrel: 6″, 8″, 10″.
Weight: 64 oz. (8″ bbl.) **Length:** 14.3″ over-all (8″ bbl.).
Stocks: Smooth walnut, target-style.
Sights: ⅛″ serrated front, fully adj. rear.
Features: Meets criteria for IHMSA competition with 8″ slotted barrel. Blue or stainless steel.
Price: Blue, 6″ $508.32
Price: Blue, 8″ $525.19
Price: Blue, 10″ $543.41
Price: Stainless, 6″ $568.97
Price: Stainless, 8″ slotted $595.13
Price: Stainless, 10″ $609.03

Dan Wesson Model 40

WICHITA SILHOUETTE PISTOL

Caliber: 22-250, 7mm IHMSA, 308. Other calibers available on special order. Single shot.
Barrel: 14-15/16".
Weight: 4½ lbs. **Length:** 21⅜" over-all.
Stocks: American walnut with oil finish. Glass bedded.
Sights: Wichita Multi-Range sight system.
Features: Comes with left-hand action with right-hand grip. Fluted bolt, flat bolt handle. Action drilled and tapped for Burris scope mounts. Non-glare satin blue finish. Wichita adjustable trigger. Introduced 1979. From Wichita Arms.
Price: Center grip stock **$900.00**
Price: As above except with Rear Position Stock and target-type Lightpull trigger **$975.00**

Wichita Silhouette

WICHITA MK-40 SILHOUETTE PISTOL

Caliber: 22-250, 7mm IHMSA, 308 Win. F.L. Other calibers available on special order. Single shot.
Barrel: 13", non-glare blue; .700" dia. muzzle.
Weight: 4½ lbs. **Length:** 19⅜" over-all.
Stocks: American walnut with oil finish.
Sights: Wichita Multi-Range sighting system.
Features: Aluminum receiver with steel insert locking lugs, measures 1.360" O.D.; three locking lug bolts, three gas ports; flat bolt handle; completely adjustable Wichita trigger. Introduced 1981. From Wichita Arms.
Price: **$800.00**

WICHITA CLASSIC PISTOL

Caliber: Any, up to and including 308 Win.
Barrel: 11¼", octagon.
Weight: About 5 lbs.
Stocks: Exhibition grade American black walnut. Checkered 20 lpi. Other woods available on special order.
Sights: Micro open sights standard. Receiver drilled and tapped for scope mount.
Features: Receiver and barrel octagonally shaped, finished in non-glare blue. Bolt has three locking lugs and three gas escape ports. Completely adjustable Wichita trigger. Introduced 1980. From Wichita Arms.
Price: **$2,950.00**
Price: Engraved, in walnut presentation case **$4,850.00**

WICHITA HUNTER, INTERNATIONAL PISTOL

Caliber: 22 LR, 22 Mag., 7mm INT-R, 7x30 Waters, 30-30 Win., 32 H&R Mag., 357 Mag., 357 Super Mag., single shot.
Barrel: 10½".
Weight: International — 3 lbs., 13 oz.; Hunter — 3 lbs., 14 oz.
Stocks: Walnut grip and fore-end.
Sights: International — target front, adjustable rear; Hunter has scope mount only.
Features: Made of 17-4PH stainless steel. Break-open action. Grip dimensions same as Colt 45 auto. Safety supplied only on Hunter model. Extra barrels are factory fitted. Introduced 1983. Available from Wichita Arms.
Price: International **$484.95**
Price: Hunter.. **$484.95**
Price: Extra barrels **$265.00**

Wichita Silhouette/Hunter

HANDGUNS—DOUBLE ACTION REVOLVERS, SERVICE & SPORT

Includes models suitable for hunting and competitive courses for fire, both police and international.

Armscor 38

ARMSCOR 38 REVOLVER

Caliber: 38 Spec.
Barrel: 4".
Weight: 32 oz.
Stocks: Checkered Philippine mahogany.
Sights: Ramp front, rear adj. for windage.
Features: Ventilated rib; polished blue finish. Introduced 1986. Imported from the Philippines by Pacific International Merchandising Corp.
Price: **$139.95**

ASTRA 357 MAGNUM REVOLVER

Caliber: 357 Magnum, 6-shot.
Barrel: 4", 6", 8½".
Weight: 40 oz. (6" bbl.) **Length:** 11¼" (6" bbl.).
Stocks: Checkered walnut.
Sights: Fixed front, rear adj. for w. and e.
Features: Swing-out cylinder with countersunk chambers, floating firing pin. Target-type hammer and trigger. Imported from Spain by Interarms.
Price: 4", 6" **$295.00**
Price: 8½" **$305.00**

Astra Model 44, 45 Double Action Revolver

Similar to the 357 Mag. except chambered for 44 Mag. or 45 Colt. Barrel length of 6" only, giving over-all length of 11⅜". Weight is 2¾ lbs. Introduced 1980.
Price: 44 Mag., 6", stainless.. **$425.00**

CAUTION: PRICES CHANGE. CHECK AT GUNSHOP.

CHARTER ARMS POLICE BULLDOG

Caliber: 32 H&R Mag., 38 Special, 6-shot.
Barrel: 4″, 4″ straight taper bull.
Weight: 21 oz. **Length:** 9″ over-all.
Stocks: Hand checkered American walnut; square butt.
Sights: Patridge-type ramp front, notched rear (adjustable on 32 Mag.).
Features: Spring loaded unbreakable beryllium copper firing pin; steel frame; accepts +P ammunition; full length ejection of fired cases.
Price: Blue, 32 Mag. **$208.00**
Price: Blue, 38 Spec.. .... **$201.00**
Price: Stainless steel, 38 Spec. only **$263.00**

Charter Arms Police Bulldog

CHARTER ARMS BULLDOG

Caliber: 44 Special, 5-shot.
Barrel: 2½″, 3″.
Weight: 19 oz. **Length:** 7¾″ over-all.
Stocks: Checkered walnut, Bulldog.
Sights: Patridge-type front, square-notch rear.
Features: Wide trigger and hammer; beryllium copper firing pin.
Price: Service Blue 3″ **$211.00**
Price: Stainless steel. **$267.00**
Price: Service blue, 2½″ **$211.00**
Price: Stainless steel, 2½″ **$270.00**
Price: Stainless steel, 3″, neoprene grips **$267.00**

Charter Arms Stainless Bulldog

Charter Arms Bulldog Tracker

Similar to the standard Bulldog except chambered for 357 Mag., has adjustable rear sight, 2½″, 4″ or 6″ bull barrel, ramp front sight, square butt checkered walnut grips on 4″ and 6″; Bulldog-style grips on 2½″. Available in blue finish only.
Price: **$214.00**

CHARTER ARMS TARGET BULLDOG

Caliber: 357 Mag. or 44 Spec., 5-shot.
Barrel: 4″.
Weight: 21 oz. **Length:** 9″ over-all.
Stocks: Square butt.
Sights: Blade front, rear adj. for w. and e.
Features: Shrouded barrel and ejector rod. All-steel frame. Introduced 1986.
Price: 357 Mag. **$232.00**
Price: 44 Spec. **$240.00**

CHARTER ARMS BULLDOG PUG

Caliber: 44 Special, 5-shot.
Barrel: 2½″.
Weight: 19 oz. **Length:** 7¼″ over-all.
Stocks: Bulldog walnut or neoprene.
Sights: Ramp front, notch rear.
Features: Shrouded ejector rod; wide trigger and hammer spur. Introduced 1986.
Price: **$234.00**

CHARTER ARMS UNDERCOVER REVOLVER

Caliber: 38 Special, 5-shot; 32 S & W Long, 6-shot.
Barrel: 2″, 3″.
Weight: 16 oz. (2″) **Length:** 6¼″ (2″).
Stocks: Checkered walnut.
Sights: Patridge-type ramp front, notched rear.
Features: Wide trigger and hammer spur. Steel frame. Police Undercover, 2″ bbl. (for 38 Spec. +P loads) carry same prices as regular 38 Spec. guns.
Price: Polished Blue **$195.00**
Price: 32 S & W Long, blue, 2″ **$195.00**
Price: Stainless, 38 Spec., 2″. **$252.00**

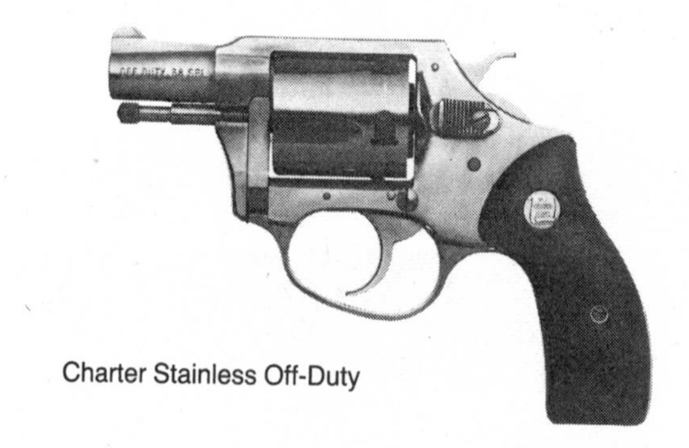

Charter Stainless Off-Duty

Charter Arms Off-Duty Revolver

Similar to the Undercover except 38 Special only, 2″ barrel, Mat-Black non-glare finish. This all-steel gun comes with Red-Dot front sight and choice of smooth or checkered walnut or neoprene grips. Also available in stainless steel. Introduced 1984.
Price: Mat-Black finish **$164.00**
Price: Stainless steel. **$219.00**

Charter Arms Pathfinder

Same as Undercover but in 22 LR or 22 Mag., and has 2″, 3″ or 6″ bbl. Fitted with adjustable rear sight, ramp front. Weight 18½ oz.
Price: 22 LR, blue, 3″ **$204.00**
Price: 22 LR, square butt, 6″ **$237.00**
Price: Stainless, 22 LR, 3″ **$257.00**
Price: 2″, either caliber, blue only **$204.00**

Charter Arms Police Undercover

Similar to the standard Undercover except 2″ barrel only, chambered for the 32 H&R Magnum and 38 Spec. (6-shot). Patridge-type front with fixed square notch rear. Blue finish or stainless steel; checkered walnut grips. Also available with Pocket Hammer and with steel frame. Introduced 1984.
Price: Standard hammer, 32 Mag., blue **$198.00**
Price: Pocket Hammer, 32 Mag., blue **$202.00**
Price: Standard hammer, 38 Spec., blue. **$195.00**
Price: Pocket Hammer, 38 Spec., blue **$198.00**
Price: Standard hammer, 38 Spec., stainless. **$252.00**
Price: Pocket Hammer, 38 Spec., stainless **$256.00**

CAUTION: PRICES CHANGE. CHECK AT GUNSHOP.

COLT KING COBRA REVOLVER

Caliber: 357 Magnum, 6-shot.
Barrel: 2½", 4", 6" (STS); 4", 6" (BSTS); 4", 6" (blue).
Weight: 42 oz. (4" bbl.). **Length:** 9" over-all (4" bbl.).
Stocks: Checkered rubber.
Sights: Red insert ramp front, adj. white outline rear.
Features: Stainless steel; full length contoured ejector rod housing, barrel rib; matte finish. Introduced 1986.
Price: STS, 2½", 4", 6" **$414.95**
Price: BSTS 4", 6" **$449.95**
Price: Blue, 4", 6" **$389.95**

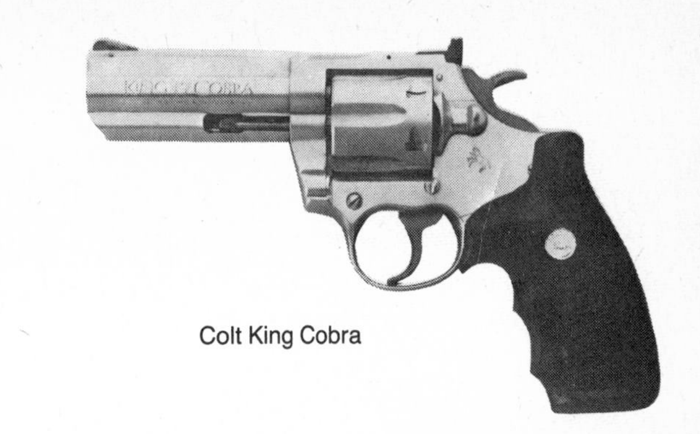

Colt King Cobra

COLT PYTHON REVOLVER

Caliber: 357 Magnum (handles all 38 Spec.), 6-shot.
Barrel: 2½", 4", 6" or 8", with ventilated rib.
Weight: 38 oz. (4" bbl.). **Length:** 9¼" (4" bbl.).
Stocks: Checkered walnut, target type.
Sights: ⅛" ramp front, adj. notch rear.
Features: Ventilated rib; grooved, crisp trigger; swing-out cylinder; target hammer.
Price: Blue, 2½", 4", 6", 8" **$729.95**
Price: Stainless, 2½", 4", 6" **$835.95**
Price: Bright stainless, 2½", 4", 6" **$859.95**

Colt Python 357

ERMA SPORTING REVOLVER

Caliber: 22 LR, 32 S&W Long, 357 Mag.
Barrel: 4", 5½", 6".
Weight: 44 to 48 oz. **Length:** 9½" overall (4" barrel).
Stocks: Stippled walnut service-type and adjustable match grip.
Sights: Interchangeable blade front, micro. adjustable rear for windage and elevation.
Features: Polished blue finish. Comes with both grip styles. Adjustable trigger. Imported from West Germany by Competition Arms, Inc. Introduced 1988.
Price: .... **NA**

Erma Sporting

F.I.E. "TITAN TIGER" REVOLVER

Caliber: 38 Special.
Barrel: 2" or 4".
Weight: 27 oz. **Length:** 6¼" over-all. (2" bbl.)
Stocks: Checkered plastic, Bulldog style. Walnut optional.
Sights: Fixed.
Features: Thumb-release swing-out cylinder, one stroke ejection. Made in U.S.A. by F.I.E. Corp.
Price: Blue **$169.95**

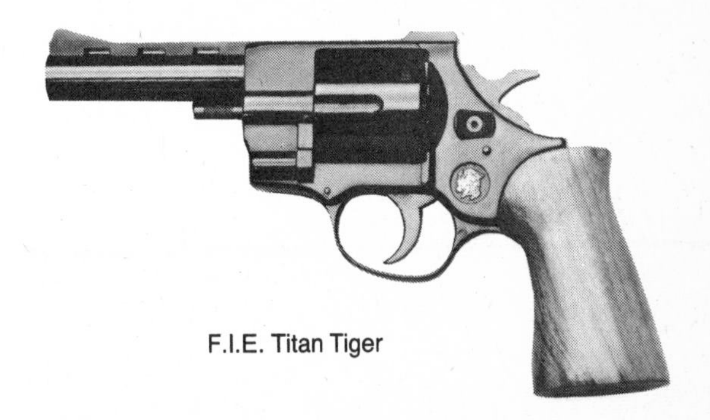

F.I.E. Titan Tiger

F.I.E. "ARMINIUS REVOLVERS"

Caliber: 38 Special, 357 Magnum, 32 S&W, 22 Magnum, 22 LR.
Barrel: 2", 3", 4", 6".
Weight: 35 oz. (6" bbl.). **Length:** 11" over-all (6" bbl.).
Stocks: Checkered plastic; walnut optional.
Sights: Ramp front, fixed rear on standard models, w. & e. adj. on target models.
Features: Thumb-release, swing-out cylinder. Ventilated rib, solid frame, swing-out cylinder. Interchangeable 22 Mag. cylinder available with 22 cal. versions. Imported from West Germany by F.I.E. Corp.
Price: .... **$154.95** to **$239.95**

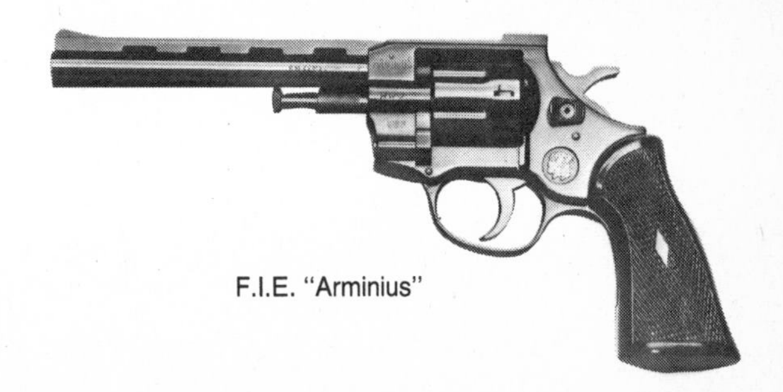

F.I.E. "Arminius"

KORTH REVOLVER

Caliber: 22 LR, 22 Mag., 357 Mag., 9mm Parabellum.
Barrel: 3", 4", 6".
Weight: 33 to 38 oz. **Length:** 8" to 11" over-all.
Stocks: Checkered walnut, sport or combat.
Sights: Blade front, rear adjustable for windage and elevation.
Features: Four interchangeable cylinders available. Major parts machined from hammer-forged steel; cylinder gap of .002". High polish blue finish. Presentation models have gold trim. Imported from Germany by Osborne's, Beeman.
Price: Polished (Osborne's), about **$2,045.00**
Price: From Beeman .... **$1,936.00** to **$2,800.00**

LLAMA COMANCHE III REVOLVERS

Caliber: 357 Mag.
Barrel: 4″, 6″.
Weight: 28 oz. **Length:** 9¼″ (4″ bbl.).
Stocks: Checkered walnut.
Sights: Fixed blade front, rear adj. for w. & e.
Features: Ventilated rib, wide spur hammer. Satin chrome finish available. Imported from Spain by Stoeger Industries.
Price: Blue finish **$301.00**
Price: Satin chrome **$357.00**

Llama Super Comanche IV, V Revolver

Similar to the Comanche except: large frame, 357 (Comanche V) or 44 Mag. (Comanche IV), 4″, 6″ or 8½″ barrel only (357 Mag), 6″, 8½″ (44 Mag.); 6-shot cylinder; smooth, extra wide trigger; wide spur hammer; over-size walnut, target-style grips. Weight is 3 lbs., 2 ozs. Blue finish only.
Price: 44 Mag. **$393.00**
Price: 357 Mag. **$414.00**

NEW ENGLAND FIREARMS DA REVOLVERS

Caliber: 22 LR (9-shot), 32 H&R Mag. (5-shot).
Barrel: 2½″ or 4″.
Weight: 25 oz. (22 LR, 2½″). **Length:** 7″ over-all (2½″ bbl.).
Stocks: American walnut.
Sights: Fixed on 2½″ models, fully adjustable on 4″.
Features: Choice of blue or nickel finish. Introduced 1988. From New England Firearms Co.
Price: .... **NA**

ROSSI MODEL 971 REVOLVER

Caliber: 357 Mag., 6-shot.
Barrel: 4″, heavy.
Weight: 36 oz. **Length:** 9″ over-all.
Stocks: Checkered Brazillian hardwood.
Sights: Blade front, fully adjustable rear.
Features: Full length ejector rod shroud; matted sight rib; target-type trigger, wide-checkered hammer spur. Introduced 1988. Imported from Brazil by Interarms.
Price: .... **$249.00.**

ROSSI MODEL 88 STAINLESS REVOLVER

Caliber: 32 S&W, 38 Spec., 5-shot.
Barrel: 2″, 3″.
Weight: 22 oz. **Length:** 7.5″ over-all.
Stocks: Checkered wood, service-style.
Sights: Ramp front, square notch rear drift adjustable for windage.
Features: All metal parts except springs are of 440 stainless steel; matte finish; small frame for concealability. Introduced 1983. Imported from Brazil by Interarms.
Price: 3″ barrel **$210.00**
Price: M88/2 (2″ barrel) **$210.00**

ROSSI MODEL 511 SPORTSMAN'S 22 REVOLVER

Caliber: 22 LR, 6-shot.
Barrel: 4″.
Weight: 30 oz. **Length:** 9″ over-all.
Stocks: Checkered wood.
Sights: Orange-insert ramp front, fully adj. square notch rear.
Features: All stainless steel. Shrouded ejector rod; heavy barrel; integral sight rib. Introduced 1986. Imported from Brazil by Interarms.
Price: **$235.00**

ROSSI MODEL 951 REVOLVER

Caliber: 38 Special, 6-shot.
Barrel: 3″, 4″, vent. rib.
Weight: 30 oz. **Length:** 9″ over-all.
Stocks: Checkered hardwood, combat-style.
Sights: Colored insert front, fully adjustable rear.
Features: Polished blue finish, shrouded ejector rod. Medium-size frame. Introduced 1985. Imported from Brazil by Interarms.
Price: M951, blue **$235.00**
Price: M851 (as above, stainless) **$249.00**

Llama Super Comanche

ROSSI MODEL 68 REVOLVER

Caliber: 38 Spec.
Barrel: 2″, 3″.
Weight: 22 oz.
Stocks: Checkered wood.
Sights: Ramp front, low profile adj. rear.
Features: All-steel frame, Thumb latch operated swing-out cylinder. Introduced 1978. Imported from Brazil by Interarms.
Price: 38, blue, 3″ **$183.00**
Price: M68/2 (2″ barrel) **$183.00**
Price: 3″, nickel **$193.00**

Rossi Model 971

Rossi Model 88 Stainless

Rossi Model 85 Stainless

CAUTION: PRICES CHANGE. CHECK AT GUNSHOP.

RUGER GP-100 REVOLVERS

Caliber: 357 Magnum, 6-shot.
Barrel: 4″ (heavy), 6″, and 6″ heavy.
Weight: About 40 oz. **Length:** 9.3″ over-all (4″ bbl.).
Stocks: Ruger Cushioned Grip (live rubber with Goncalo Alves inserts).
Sights: Interchangeable front blade, fully adj. rear.
Features: Uses all new action and frame incorporating improvements and features of both the Security-Six and Redhawk revolvers. Full length ejector shroud. Satin blue and stainless. Introduced 1986.
Price: GP-141 (4″ heavy bbl.) **$360.40**
Price: GP-160 (6″ bbl.) **$360.40**
Price: GP-161 (6″ heavy bbl.) **$360.40**
Price: KGP-141 (stainless, 4″ heavy bbl.) **$392.20**
Price: KGP-160 (stainless, 6″ bbl.) **$392.20**
Price: KGP-161 (stainless, 6″ heavy bbl.) **$392.20**

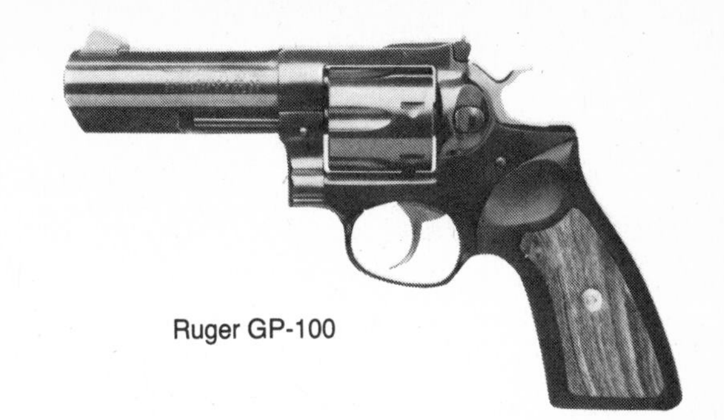

Ruger GP-100

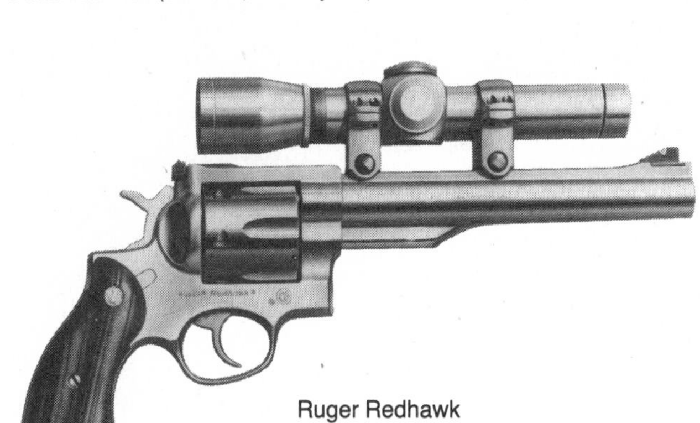

Ruger Redhawk

Ruger Super Redhawk

Smith & Wesson 38 M&P Heavy Barrel Model 10

Same as regular M&P except: 4″ heavy ribbed bbl. with ramp front sight, square rear, square butt, wgt. 33½ oz.
Price: Blued **$305.00**
Price: Nickeled **$315.00**

SMITH & WESSON Model 13 H.B. M&P

Caliber: 357 and 38 Special, 6-shot.
Barrel: 3″ or 4″.
Weight: 34 oz. **Length:** 9 5/16″ over-all (4″ bbl.).
Stocks: Checkered walnut, service.
Sights: ⅛″ serrated ramp front, fixed square notch rear.
Features: Heavy barrel, K-frame, square butt (4″), round butt (3″).
Price: Blue **$310.00**
Price: Model 65, as above in stainless steel **$337.00**

SMITH & WESSON MODEL 15 COMBAT MASTERPIECE

Caliber: 38 Special, 6-shot.
Barrel: 2″, 4″, 6″, 8⅜″.
Weight: 32 oz. **Length:** 9 5/16″ (4″ bbl.).
Stocks: Checkered walnut. Grooved tangs.
Sights: Front, Baughman Quick Draw on ramp, micro click rear, adjustable for w. and e.
Price: Blued, 2″, 4″, 6″ **$330.50**
Price: Blue, 8⅜″ **$341.50**

RUGER REDHAWK

Caliber: 41 Mag., 44 Rem. Mag., 6-shot.
Barrel: 5½″, 7½″.
Weight: About 54 oz. (7½″ bbl.). **Length:** 13″ over-all (7½″ barrel).
Stocks: Square butt Goncalo Alves.
Sights: Interchangeable Patridge-type front, rear adj. for w. & e.
Features: Stainless steel, brushed satin finish, or blued ordnance steel. Has a 9½″ sight radius. Introduced 1979.
Price: Blued, 41 Mag., 44 Mag., 5½″, 7½″ **$397.00**
Price: Blued, 41 Mag., 44 Mag., 7½″, with scope mount, rings **$430.00**
Price: Stainless, 41 Mag., 44 Mag., 5½″, 7½″ **$447.50**
Price: Stainless, 41 Mag., 44 Mag., 7½″, with scope mount, rings ... **$482.50**

Ruger Super Redhawk Revolver

Similar to the standard Redhawk except has a heavy extended frame with the Ruger Integral Scope Mounting System on the wide top strap. The wide hammer spur has been lowered for better scope clearance. Incorporates the mechanical design features and improvements of the GP-100. Choice of 7½″ or 9½″ barrrel, both with ramp front sight base with Redhawk-style interchangeable insert sight blades, adjustable rear sight. Comes with Ruger "Cushioned Grip" panels of live rubber and Goncalo Alves wood. Satin polished stainless steel, 44 Magnum only. Introduced 1987.
Price: KSRH-7 (7½″), KSRH-9 (9½″) **$510.00**

SMITH & WESSON M&P Model 10 REVOLVER

Caliber: 38 Special, 6-shot.
Barrel: 2″, 4″.
Weight: 30½ oz. **Length:** 9¼″ over-all.
Stocks: Checkered walnut, Service. Round or square butt.
Sights: Fixed, ramp front, square notch rear.
Price: Blued **$305.00**
Price: Nickeled, 4″ only **$315.50**

S&W Model 10-H.B.

S&W Model 13

SMITH & WESSON MODEL 17 K-22 MASTERPIECE
Caliber: 22 LR, 6-shot.
Barrel: 4″, 6″, 8⅜″.
Weight: 39 oz. (6″ bbl.). **Length:** 11⅛″ over-all.
Stocks: Checkered walnut, service.
Sights: Patridge front with 6″, 8⅜″, serrated on 4″, S&W micro. click rear adjustable for windage and elevation.
Features: Grooved tang, polished blue finish.
Price: 4″, 6″ bbl. **$347.50**
Price: 8⅜″ bbl. **$391.00**

S&W Model 19

SMITH & WESSON 357 COMBAT MAGNUM Model 19
Caliber: 357 Magnum and 38 Special, 6-shot.
Barrel: 2½″, 4″, 6″.
Weight: 36 oz. **Length:** 9 9/16″ (4″ bbl.).
Stocks: Checkered Goncalo Alves, target. Grooved tangs.
Sights: Front, ⅛″ Baughman Quick Draw on 2½″ or 4″ bbl., Patridge on 6″ bbl., micro click rear adjustable for w. and e.
Features: Also available in nickel finish.
Price: S&W Bright Blue, adj. sights, from **$319.50**

S&W Model 25

SMITH & WESSON MODEL 25 REVOLVER
Caliber: 45 Colt, 6-shot.
Barrel: 4″, 6″, 8⅜″.
Weight: About 46 oz. **Length:** 11⅜″ over-all (6″ bbl.).
Stocks: Checkered Goncalo Alves, target-type.
Sights: S&W red ramp front, S&W micrometer click rear with white outline.
Features: Available in Bright Blue or nickel finish; target trigger, target hammer. Contact S&W for complete price list.
Price: 4″, 6″, blue **$408.00**
Price: 8⅜″, blue or nickel **$415.50**

SMITH & WESSON 357 MAGNUM M-27 REVOLVER
Caliber: 357 Magnum and 38 Special, 6-shot.
Barrel: 4″, 6″, 8⅜″.
Weight: 45½ oz. (6″ bbl.). **Length:** 11 5/16″ (6″ bbl.).
Stocks: Checkered walnut, Magna. Grooved tangs and trigger.
Sights: Serrated ramp front, micro click rear, adjustable for w. and e.
Price: S&W Bright Blue, 4″.......... **$429.50**
Price: As above, 6″ **$403.00**
Price: 8⅜″ bbl., sq. butt, target hammer, trigger, stocks.......... **$410.00**

S&W Model 29

SMITH & WESSON 44 MAGNUM Model 29 REVOLVER
Caliber: 44 Magnum, 44 Special or 44 Russian, 6-shot.
Barrel: 4″, 6″, 8⅜″, 10⅝″.
Weight: 47 oz. (6″ bbl.), 44 oz. (4″ bbl.). **Length:** 11⅜″ overall (6″ bbl.).
Stocks: Oversize target type, checkered Goncalo Alves. Tangs and target trigger grooved, checkered target hammer.
Sights: ⅛″ red ramp front, micro click rear, adjustable for w. and e.
Features: Includes presentation case.
Price: S&W Bright Blue or nickel, 4″, 6″.......... **$458.50**
Price: 8⅜″ bbl., blue **$468.50**
Price: 10⅝″, blue only (AF) **$510.00**
Price: Model 629 (stainless steel), 4″, 6″ **$485.00**
Price: Model 629, 8⅜″ barrel.......... **$501.50**

S&W "Classic Hunter"

SMITH & WESSON MODEL 29 "CLASSIC HUNTER"
Caliber: 44 Magnum, 6-shot.
Barrel: 6″ heavy with full-length lug.
Weight: 52 oz.
Stocks: Hogue soft neoprene.
Sights: Click adjustable front, rear adjustable for windage and elevation.
Features: Non-fluted cylinder; blue finish. Introduced 1988.
Price: .... **$474.50.**

S&W Model 31

SMITH & WESSON 32 REGULATION POLICE Model 31
Caliber: 32 S&W Long, 6-shot.
Barrel: 2″, 3″.
Weight: 18¾ oz. (3″ bbl.). **Length:** 7½″ (3″ bbl.).
Stocks: Checkered walnut, Magna.
Sights: Fixed, 1/10″ serrated ramp front, square notch rear.
Features: Blued.
Price:.......... **$337.00**

CAUTION: PRICES CHANGE. CHECK AT GUNSHOP.

SMITH & WESSON 1953 Model 34, 22/32 KIT GUN
Caliber: 22 LR, 6-shot.
Barrel: 2″, 4″.
Weight: 24 oz. (4″ bbl.). **Length:** 8⅜″ (4″ bbl. and round butt).
Stocks: Checkered walnut, round or square butt.
Sights: Front, serrated ramp, micro. click rear, adjustable for w. & e.
Price: Blued $338.50
Price: Model 63, as above in stainless, 4″.......... $371.50

SMITH & WESSON 38 CHIEFS SPECIAL & AIRWEIGHT
Caliber: 38 Special, 5-shot.
Barrel: 2″, 3″.
Weight: 19½ oz. (2″ bbl.); 13½ oz. (AIRWEIGHT). **Length:** 6½″ (2″ bbl. and round butt).
Stocks: Checkered walnut, round or square butt.
Sights: Fixed, serrated ramp front, square notch rear.
Price: Blued, standard Model 36.......... $312.00
Price: As above, nickel.......... $322.50
Price: Blued, Airweight Model 37 .... $331.00
Price: As above, nickel.......... $344.00

Smith & Wesson Bodyguard Model 49, 649 Revolvers
Same as Model 38 except steel construction, weight 20½ oz.
Price: Blued, Model 49 .... $331.50
Price: Stainless Model 649.......... $377.50

SMITH & WESSON 41 MAGNUM Model 57 REVOLVER
Caliber: 41 Magnum, 6-shot.
Barrel: 4″, 6″ or 8⅜″.
Weight: 48 oz. (6″ bbl.). **Length:** 11⅜″ (6″ bbl.).
Stocks: Oversize target type checkered Goncalo Alves.
Sights: ⅛″ red ramp front, micro. click rear, adj. for w. and e.
Price: S&W Bright Blue or nickel 4″, 6″.......... $406.50
Price: 8⅜″ bbl. $421.00
Price: Stainless, Model 657, 4″, 6″ $433.00
Price: As above, 8⅜″.......... $448.00

SMITH & WESSON MODEL 64 STAINLESS M&P
Caliber: 38 Special, 6-shot.
Barrel: 2″, 4″.
Weight: 34 oz. **Length:** 9⁵⁄₁₆″ over-all.
Stocks: Checkered walnut, service style.
Sights: Fixed, ⅛″ serrated ramp front, square notch rear.
Features: Satin finished stainless steel, square butt.
Price:.......... $331.50

SMITH & WESSON MODEL 66 STAINLESS COMBAT MAGNUM
Caliber: 357 Magnum and 38 Special, 6-shot.
Barrel: 2½″, 4″, 6″.
Weight: 36 oz. **Length:** 9⁹⁄₁₆″ over-all.
Stocks: Checkered Goncalo Alves target.
Sights: Front, Baughman Quick Draw on ramp, micro click rear adj. for windage and elevation.
Features: Satin finish stainless steel.
Price: From.......... $363.00

SMITH & WESSON MODEL 586 DISTINGUISHED COMBAT MAGNUM
Caliber: 357 Magnum.
Barrel: 4″, 6″, 8⅜″, full shroud.
Weight: 46 oz. (6″), 41 oz. (4″).
Stocks: Goncalo Alves target-type with speed loader cutaway.
Sights: Baughman red ramp front, four-position click-adj. front, S&W micrometer click rear (or fixed).
Features: Uses new L-frame, but takes all K-frame grips. Full length ejector rod shroud. Smooth combat-type trigger, semi-target type hammer. Trigger stop on 6″ models. Also available in stainless as Model 686. Introduced 1981.
Price: Model 586, blue, 4″ $367.00
Price: Model 586, nickel, from.......... $378.00
Price: Model 686, stainless, from $394.00
Price: Model 581, fixed sight, blue, 4″ $335.50
Price: Model 681, fixed sight, stainless $362.00
Price: Model 586, 6″, adj. front sight, blue.......... $407.00
Price: As above, 8⅜″.......... $423.50
Price: Model 686, 6″, adj. front sight.......... $430.50
Price: As above, 8⅜″.......... $447.00

SMITH & WESSON BODYGUARD MODEL 38
Caliber: 38 Special, 5-shot.
Barrel: 2″.
Weight: 14½ oz. **Length:** 6⁵⁄₁₆″ over-all.
Stocks: Checkered walnut.
Sights: Fixed serrated ramp front, square notch rear.
Features: Alloy frame; internal hammer.
Price: Blued $350.50
Price: Nickeled.......... $363.00

Smith & Wesson Model 60 Chiefs Special Stainless
Same as Model 36 except: 2″ bbl. and round butt only.
Price: Stainless steel.......... $357.00

S&W Model 649

S&W Model 57

SMITH & WESSON MODEL 67 K-38 STAINLESS COMBAT MASTERPIECE
Caliber: 38 Special, 6-shot.
Barrel: 4″.
Weight: 32 oz. (loaded). **Length:** 9⁵⁄₁₆″ over-all.
Stocks: Checkered walnut, service style.
Sights: Front, Baughman Quick Draw on ramp, micro click rear adj. for windage and elevation.
Features: Stainless steel. Square butt frame with grooved tangs.
Price:.......... $360.00

S&W Model 686

SPORTARMS MODEL HS38S REVOLVER

Caliber: 38 Special, 6 shot.
Barrel: 3", 4".
Weight: 31.3 oz. **Length:** 8" overall (3" barrel).
Stocks: Checkered hardwood; round butt on 3" model, target-style on 4".
Sights: Blade front, adjustable rear.
Features: Polished blue finish; ventilated rib on 4" barrel. Made in West Germany by Herbert Schmidt; imported by Sportarms of Florida.
Price: About **$150.00**

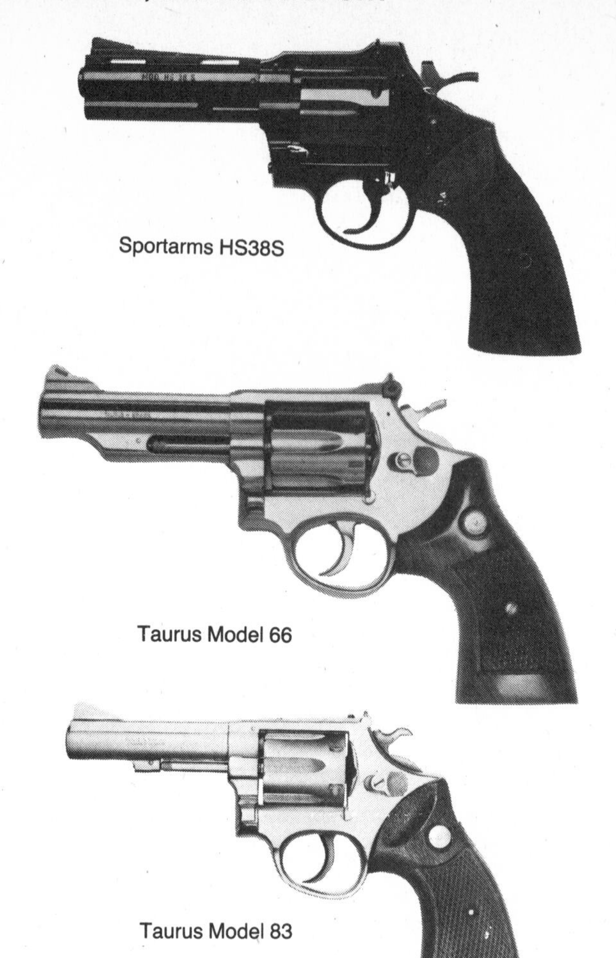

Sportarms HS38S

Taurus Model 66

Taurus Model 83

TAURUS MODEL 66 REVOLVER

Caliber: 357 Magnum, 6-shot.
Barrel: 3", 4", 6".
Weight: 35 oz.
Stocks: Checkered walnut, target-type. Standard stocks on 3".
Sights: Serrated ramp front, micro click rear adjustable for w. and e. Red ramp front with white outline rear on stainless models only.
Features: Wide target-type hammer spur, floating firing pin, heavy barrel with shrouded ejector rod. Introduced 1978. From Taurus International.
Price: Blue... **$233.45**
Price: Satin nickel **$243.92**
Price: Stainless steel... **$296.41**
Price: Model 65 (similar to M66 except has a fixed rear sight and ramp front), blue, 3" or 4" only **$216.47**
Price: Model 65, satin nickel, 3" or 4" only... **$227.60**

TAURUS MODEL 73 SPORT REVOLVER

Caliber: 32 S&W Long, 6-shot.
Barrel: 3", heavy.
Weight: 22 oz. **Length:** 8¼" over-all.
Stocks: Oversize target-type, checkered Brazilian walnut.
Sights: Ramp front, notch rear.
Features: Imported from Brazil by Taurus International.
Price: Blue... **$193.92**
Price: Satin nickel **$211.10**

TAURUS MODEL 80 STANDARD REVOLVER

Caliber: 38 Spec., 6-shot.
Barrel: 3" or 4".
Weight: 31 oz. (4" bbl.). **Length:** 9¼" over-all (4" bbl.).
Stocks: Checkered Brazilian walnut.
Sights: Serrated ramp front, square notch rear.
Features: Imported from Brazil by Taurus International.
Price: Blue... **$187.90**
Price: Satin nickel **$199.39**

Taurus Model 82

TAURUS MODEL 82 HEAVY BARREL REVOLVER

Caliber: 38 Spec., 6-shot.
Barrel: 3" or 4", heavy.
Weight: 33 oz. (4" bbl.). **Length:** 9¼" over-all (4" bbl.).
Stocks: Checkered Brazilian walnut.
Sights: Serrated ramp front, square notch rear.
Features: Imported from Brazil by Taurus International.
Price: Blue, about **$187.90**
Price: Satin nickel, about **$199.39**

TAURUS MODEL 83 REVOLVER

Caliber: 38 Spec., 6-shot.
Barrel: 4" only, heavy.
Weight: 34½ oz.
Stocks: Over-size checkered walnut.
Sights: Ramp front, micro. click rear adj. for w. & e.
Features: Blue or nickel finish. Introduced 1977. Imported from Brazil by Taurus International.
Price: Blue... **$197.82**
Price: Satin nickel **$208.15**

TAURUS MODEL 85 REVOLVER

Caliber: 38 Spec., 5-shot.
Barrel: 2", 3".
Weight: 21 oz.
Stocks: Checkered walnut.
Sights: Ramp front, square notch rear.
Features: Blue, satin nickel finish or stainless steel. Introduced 1980. Imported from Brazil by Taurus International.
Price: Blue... **$199.88**
Price: Satin nickel, 3" only **$214.43**
Price: Stainless steel... **$253.09**

Taurus Model 85

TAURUS MODEL 669 REVOLVER
Caliber: 357 Mag., 6 shot.
Barrel: 4″, 6″.
Weight: 37 oz. (4″ bbl.)
Stocks: Checkered walnut, target type.
Sights: Serrated ramp front, micro. click rear adjustable for windage and elevation.
Features: Wide target-type hammer, floating firing pin, full length barrel shroud. Introduced 1988. Imported by Taurus International.
Price: Blue **$241.85**
Price: Stainless **$304.80**

Taurus Model 669

UBERTI "INSPECTOR" REVOLVER
Caliber: 32 S&W Long, 38 Spec., 6-shot.
Barrel: 3″, 4″, 6″.
Weight: 24 oz. (3″ bbl.). **Length:** 8″ over-all (3″ bbl.).
Stocks: Checkered walnut.
Sights: Blade on ramp front, fixed or adj. rear.
Features: Blue or chrome finish. Introduced 1986. Imported from Italy by Benson Firearms, Uberti USA.
Price: Blue, fixed sights **$429.00**
Price: Blue, adj. sights, 4″, 6″ only **$465.00**
Price: Chrome, fixed sights **$459.00**
Price: Chrome, adj. sights, 4″, 6″ only **$499.00**

Uberti Inspector

DAN WESSON MODEL 41V & MODEL 44V
Caliber: 41 Mag., 44 Mag., 6-shot.
Barrel: 4″, 6″, 8″, 10″; interchangeable.
Weight: 48 oz. (4″). **Length:** 12″ over-all (6″ bbl.).
Stocks: Smooth.
Sights: ⅛″ serrated front, white outline rear adjustable for windage and elevation.
Features: Available in blue or stainless steel. Smooth, wide trigger with adjustable over-travel; wide hammer spur. Available in Pistol Pac set also.
Price: 41 Mag., 4″, vent. **$412.80**
Price: As above except in stainless **$461.98**
Price: 44 Mag., 4″, blue **$431.45**
Price: As above except in stainless **$507.30**

Dan Wesson 44 Magnum

Dan Wesson 9-2, 15-2 & 32M Revolvers
Same as Models 8-2 and 14-2 except they have adjustable sight. Model 9-2 chambered for 38 Special, Model 15-2 for 357 Magnum. Model 32M is chambered for 32 H&R Mag. Same specs and prices as for 15-2 guns. Available in blue or stainless. Contact Dan Wesson for complete price list.
Price: Model 9-2 or 15-2, 2½″, blue **$337.64**
Price: As above except in stainless **$366.07**

Dan Wesson Model 32M

DAN WESSON MODEL 22 REVOLVER
Caliber: 22 LR, 22 WMR, 6-shot.
Barrel: 2½″, 4″ 6″, 8″, 10″; interchangeable.
Weight: 36 oz. (2½″), 44 oz. (6″). **Length:** 9¼″ over-all (4″ barrel).
Stocks: Checkered; undercover, service or over-size target.
Sights: ⅛″ serrated, interchangeable front, white outline rear adjustable for windage and elevation.
Features: Built on the same frame as the Dan Wesson 357; smooth, wide trigger with over-travel adjustment, wide spur hammer, with short double-action travel. Available in Brite blue or stainless steel. Contact Dan Wesson for complete price list.
Price: 2½″ bbl., blue **$337.64**
Price: As above, stainless **$366.07**
Price: With 4″, vent. rib, blue **$369.97**
Price: As above, stainless **$398.41**
Price: Stainless Pistol Pac, 22 LR **$689.01**

DAN WESSON MODEL 8-2 & MODEL 14-2
Caliber: 38 Special (Model 8-2); 357 (14-2), both 6-shot.
Barrel: 2½″, 4″, 6″, 8″; interchangeable.
Weight: 30 oz. (2½″). **Length:** 9¼″ over-all (4″ bbl.)
Stocks: Checkered, interchangeable.
Sights: ⅛″ serrated front, fixed rear.
Features: Interchangeable barrels and grips; smooth, wide trigger; wide hammer spur with short double action travel. Available in stainless or Brite blue. Contact Dan Wesson for complete price list.
Price: Model 8-2, 2½″, blue **$267.15**
Price: As above except in stainless **$311.38**
Price: Model 714-2 Pistol Pac, stainless **$516.68**

Both classic six-shooters and modern adaptations for hunting and sport.

CENTURY MODEL 100 SINGLE ACTION

Caliber: 30-30, 375 Win., 444 Marlin, 45-70, 50-70.
Barrel: 6½", 8" (standard), 10", 12". Other lengths to order.
Weight: 6 lbs. (loaded). **Length:** 15" over-all (8" bbl.).
Stocks: Smooth walnut.
Sights: Ramp front, Millett adj. square notch rear.
Features: Highly polished high tensile strength manganese bronze frame, blue cylinder and barrel; coil spring trigger mechanism. Calibers other than 45-70 start at $1,500.00. Introduced 1975. Made in U.S. From Century Gun Dist., Inc.
Price: 8" barrel, 45-70 .... **$780.00**
Price: 10" barrel, 45-70 .... **$810.00**
Price: 12" barrel, 45-70 .... **$840.00**

Century Model 100

CIMARRON U.S. CAVALRY MODEL SINGLE ACTION

Caliber: 45 Colt
Barrel: 7½"
Weight: 42 oz. **Length:** 13½" overall
Stocks: Walnut.
Sights: Fixed.
Features: Has "A.P. Casey" markings; "U.S." plus patent dates on frame, serial number on backstrap, trigger guard, frame and cylinder, "APC" cartouche on left grip; color case-hardened frame and hammer, rest charcoal blue. Exact copy of the original. Imported by Cimarron Arms.
Price: **$459.00**

Cimarron U.S. Cavalry

Cimarron Artillery Model Single Action

Similar to the U.S. Cavalry model except has 5½" barrel, weighs 39 oz., and is 11½" over-all.
Price: **$459.00**

CIMARRON SHERIFF MODEL SINGLE ACTION

Caliber: 22 LR, 22 WMR, 38 Spec., 357 Mag., 44 WCF, 45 Colt.
Barrel: 4".
Weight: 38 oz. **Length:** 10" over-all.
Stocks: Walnut.
Sights: Fixed.
Features: Patent dates on frame; serial number on backstrap, trigger guard, frame and cylinder. Modern or old-style blue. Uses blackpowder frame. Imported by Cimarron Arms.
Price: **$389.00**

COLT SINGLE ACTION ARMY REVOLVER

Caliber: 45 Colt, 6-shot.
Barrel: 3", 4¾", 5½", 7½", 10".
Weight: 37 oz. (5½" bbl.). **Length:** 10⅞" over-all (5½" bbl).
Stocks: Black composite rubber with eagle and shield crest.
Sights: Fixed. Grooved top strap, blade front.
Features: Blue with color case-hardened frame or all nickel with walnut stocks. Available in limited quantities through the Colt Custom Shop only.
Price: From **$1,045.00**

CIMARRON "OLD MODEL" SINGLE ACTION

Caliber: 22 LR, 22 WMR, 38 WCF, 357 Mag., 44 WCF, 45 Colt.
Barrel: 3", 4", 4¾", 5½", 7½".
Weight: 39 oz. **Length:** 10" over-all (4" barrel).
Stocks: Walnut.
Sights: Blade front, fixed or adjustable rear.
Features: Uses "old model" blackpowder frame with "Bullseye" ejector. Imported by Cimarron Arms.
Price: Standard model **$389.00**
Price: "A" engraving (30 percent coverage) **$589.00**
Price: "B" engraving (50 percent coverage) **$699.00**
Price: "C" engraving (100 percent coverage) **$1,099.00**

Cimarron Sheriff Model

Dakota Bisley

DAKOTA BISLEY MODEL SINGLE ACTION

Caliber: 22 LR, 22 WMR., 32-20, 32 H&R Mag., 357, 30 Carbine, 38-40, 44 Spec., 44-40, 45 Colt, 45 ACP.
Barrel: 4⅝", 5½", 7½".
Weight: 37 oz. **Length:** 10½" over-all with 5½" barrel.
Stocks: Smooth walnut.
Sights: Blade front, fixed groove rear.
Features: Colt-type firing pin in hammer; color case-hardened frame, blue barrel, cylinder, steel backstrap and trigger guard. Also avail. in nickel, factory engraved. Imported by E.M.F.
Price: All calibers, bbl. lengths **$540.00**
Price: Combo models—22 LR/22 WMR, 32-20/32 H&R, 357/9mm, 44-40/44 Spec., 45 Colt/45 ACP **$600.00**
Price: Nickel, all cals. **$640.00**
Price: Engraved, all cals., lengths **$700.00**

DAKOTA SINGLE ACTION REVOLVERS

Caliber: 22 LR, 22 WMR., 357 Mag., 30 Carbine, 32-20, 32 H&R Mag., 38-40, 44-40, 44 Spec., 45 Colt, 45 ACP.
Barrel: 3½", 4⅝", 5½", 7½", 12", 16¼".
Weight: 45 oz. **Length:** 13" over-all (7½" bbl.).
Stocks: Smooth walnut.
Sights: Blade front, fixed rear.
Features: Colt-type hammer with firing pin, color case-hardened frame, blue barrel and cylinder, brass grip frame and trigger guard. Available in blue or nickel plated, plain or engraved. Imported by E.M.F.
Price: 22 LR, 30 Car., 357, 44-40, 45 Colt, 4⅝", 5½", 7½" **$480.00**
Price: 22 LR/22 WMR, 45 Colt/ 45 ACP, 32-20/32 H&R, 357/9mm, 44-40/44 Spec., 5½", 7½" **$580.00**
Price: 357, 44-40, 45, 12" **$520.00**
Price: 357, 44-40, 45, 3½" **$520.00**

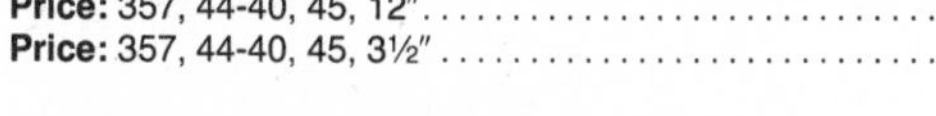

Dakota Single Action

DAKOTA 1875 OUTLAW REVOLVER

Caliber: 357, 44-40, 45 Colt.
Barrel: 7½".
Weight: 46 oz. **Length:** 13½" over-all.
Stocks: Smooth walnut.
Sights: Blade front, fixed groove rear.
Features: Authentic copy of 1875 Remington with firing pin in hammer; color case-hardened frame, blue cylinder, barrel, steel backstrap and brass trigger guard. Also available in nickel, factory engraved. Imported by E.M.F.
Price: All calibers **$485.00**
Price: Nickel **$520.00**
Price: Engraved **$600.00**

Dakota 1890 Police

Dakota 1890 Police Revolver

Similar to the 1875 Outlaw except has 5½" barrel, weighs 40 oz., with 12½" over-all length. Has lanyard ring in butt. Calibers 357, 44-40, 45 Colt. Imported by E.M.F.
Price: All calibers **$500.00**
Price: Nickel **$540.00**
Price: Engraved **$600.00**

F.I.E. "TEXAS RANGER" REVOLVER

Caliber: 22 LR, 22 WMR.
Barrel: 4¾", 6½", 9".
Weight: 31 oz. (4¾" bbl.). **Length:** 10" over-all.
Stocks: American walnut.
Sights: Blade front, notch rear.
Features: Single-action, blue/black finish. Introduced 1983. Made in the U.S. by F.I.E.
Price: 22 LR, 4¾" **$104.95**
Price: As above, convertible (22 LR/22 WMR) **$124.95**
Price: 22 LR, 6½" **$104.95**
Price: As above, convertible (22 LR/22 WMR) **$124.95**
Price: 22 LR, 9" **$104.95**
Price: As above, convertible (22 LR/22 WMR) **$124.95**

F.I.E. "Texas Ranger"

F.I.E. "Little Ranger" Revolver

Similar to the "Texas Ranger" except has 3¼" barrel, birdshead grips. Introduced 1986. Made in U.S. by F.I.E.
Price: 22 LR **$104.95**
Price: 22 LR/22 WMR convertible **$124.95**

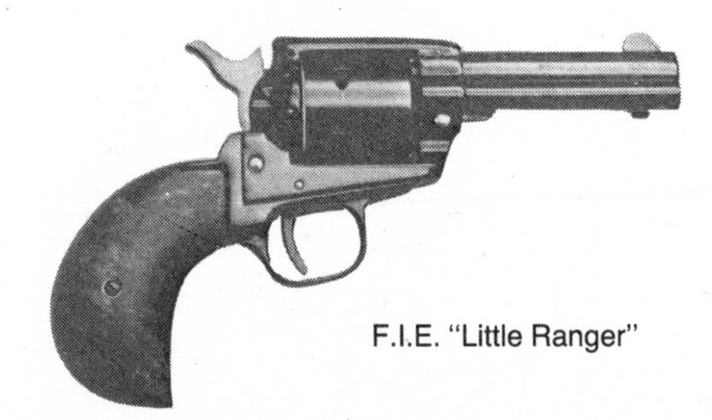

F.I.E. "Little Ranger"

F.I.E. "Buffalo Scout"

F.I.E. "BUFFALO SCOUT" REVOLVER

Caliber: 22 LR/22 WMR.
Barrel: 4¾".
Weight: 32 oz. **Length:** 10" over-all.
Stocks: Black checkered nylon, walnut optional.
Sights: Blade front, fixed rear.
Features: Slide spring ejector. Blue, chrome, gold or blue with gold backstrap and trigger guard models available. Imported from Italy by F.I.E.
Price: Blued, 22 LR **$89.95**
Price: Blue, 22 convertible **$110.95**
Price: Chrome, 22 LR **$104.95**
Price: Chrome, convertible **$126.95**
Price: "Yellow Rose," gold, 22 convertible **$149.95**

F.I.E. "Yellow Rose" Limited Edition Revolver

Same gun as the "Buffalo Scout" revolver except is completely 24 karat gold plated and has ivory polymer grips scrimshawed with a map of Texas, the Texas state flag and a single yellow rose highlighted with green leaves. Comes in a French fitted presentation case of American walnut, lined and fitted with contrasting velvet. Polished brass-plated hinge and lock. From F.I.E. Introduced 1987.
Price: **$349.95**

F.I.E. "HOMBRE" SINGLE ACTION REVOLVER

Caliber: 357 Mag., 44 Mag., 45 Colt.
Barrel: 6″ or 7½″.
Weight: 45 oz. (6″ bbl.).
Stocks: Smooth walnut with medallion.
Sights: Blade front, grooved topstrap (fixed) rear.
Features: Color case hardened frame. Bright blue finish. Super-smooth action. Introduced 1979. Imported from West Germany by F.I.E. Corp.
Price: **$249.95**
Price: 24K gold plated **$429.95**

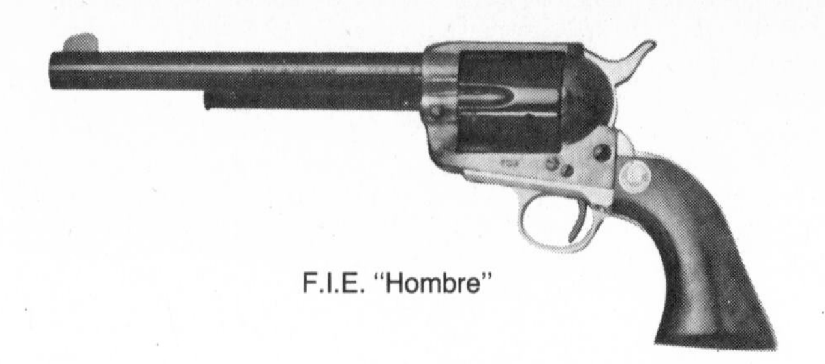
F.I.E. "Hombre"

FREEDOM ARMS 454 CASULL

Caliber: 44 Mag., 45 Colt, 454 Casull, 5-shot.
Barrel: 4¾″, 6″, 7½″, 10″.
Weight: 50 oz. **Length:** 14″ over-all (7½″ bbl.).
Stocks: Impregnated hardwood.
Sights: Blade front, notch or adjustable rear.
Features: All stainless steel construction; sliding bar safety system. Lifetime warranty. Made in U.S.A.
Price: Fixed sight **$995.00**
Price: Adjustable sight **$1,085.00**
Price: Field Grade, adjustable sight, (matte stainless finish, Pachmayr Presentation grips, 4¾″, 7½″, 10″) **$795.00**
Price: Field Grade, fixed sight, 4¾″ only **$725.00**

Freedom 454 Field Grade

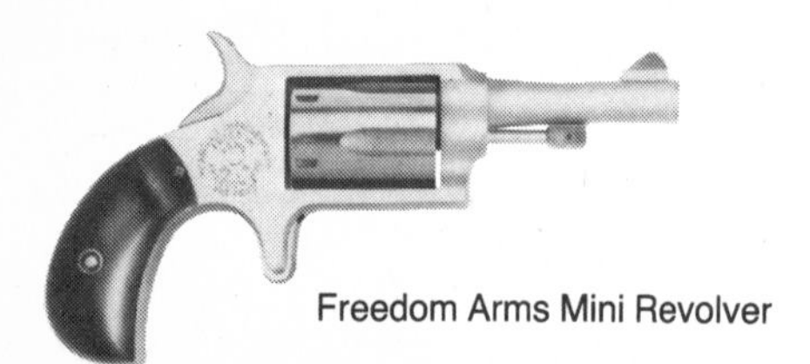
Freedom Arms Mini Revolver

FREEDOM ARMS MINI REVOLVER

Caliber: 22 Short, Long, Long Rifle, 5-shot; 22 WMR., 4-shot.
Barrel: 1″.
Weight: 4 oz. **Length:** 4″ over-all.
Stocks: Impregnated hardwood.
Sights: Blade front, notch rear.
Features: Made of stainless steel, simple take down; half-cock safety; floating firing pin; cartridge rims recessed in cylinder. Comes in gun rug. Lifetime warranty. Also available in percussion — see black powder section. From Freedom Arms.
Price: 22 LR, 1″ barrel **$139.20**
Price: 22 WMR, 1″ barrel **$160.45**

Freedom Arms Boot Gun

Similar to the Mini Revolver except 22 WMR only, has 3″ barrel, weighs 5 oz. and is 5⅞″ over-all. Has over-size grips, floating firing pin. Made of stainless steel. Lifetime warranty. Comes in rectangular gun rug. Introduced 1982. From Freedom Arms.
Price: 22 WMR **$199.95**

MITCHELL SINGLE ACTION ARMY REVOLVERS

Caliber: 22 LR, 357 Mag., 44 Mag., 45 Colt, 6-shot.
Barrel: 4¾″, 5½″, 6″, 6½″, 7½″, 10″ 12″, 18″.
Weight: NA. **Length:** NA
Stocks: One-piece walnut.
Sights: Serrated ramp front, fixed or adjustable rear.
Features: Color case-hardened frame, brass backstrap, balance blued; hammer block safety. Stainless steel and dual cylinder models available. Imported by Mitchell Arms.
Price: Fixed sight, 22 LR, 4¾″, 5½″, 7½″ **$259.95**
Price: As above, 357,45 .... **$264.95**
Price: As above, 44 Mag. **$269.95**
Price: Adjustable sight, 22 LR, 4¾″, 5½″, 7½″ **$265.00**
Price: As above, 357, 45 .... **$279.95**
Price: As above, 44 Mag. **$284.95**
Price: Stainless steel, 22 LR, 4¾″, 5½″, 7½″ **$299.00**
Price: As above, 357 Mag. **$319.95**
Price: 44 Mag./44-40, dual cylinder, 4¾″, 6″, 7½″ **$319.95**
Price: 22 LR/22 Mag., dual cylinder, 4¾″, 5½″, 7½″ **$275.00**
Price: Silhouette Model, 44 Mag., 10″, 12″, 18″ **$299.95**

Mitchell Single Action

Consult our Directory pages for the location of firms mentioned.

North American Mini

NORTH AMERICAN MINI-REVOLVERS

Caliber: 22 S, 22 LR, 22 WMR., 5-shot.
Barrel: 1⅛″, 1⅝″, 2½″.
Weight: 4 to 6.6 oz. **Length:** 3⅝″ to 6⅛″ over-all.
Stocks: Laminated wood.
Sights: Blade front, notch fixed rear.
Features: All stainless steel construction. Polished satin and matte finish. From North American Arms.
Price: 22 Short, 1⅛″ bbl. **$135.00**
Price: 22 LR, 1⅛″ bbl. **$136.00**
Price: 22 LR, 1⅝″ bbl. **$137.00**
Price: 22 WMR, 1⅝″ bbl. **$156.00**
Price: 22 WMR, 2½″ bbl. **$171.00**

PHELPS HERITAGE I, EAGLE I REVOLVERS
Caliber: 444 Marlin, 45-70, 6-shot.
Barrel: 8″ or 12″.
Weight: 5½ lbs. **Length:** 19½″ over-all (12″ bbl.).
Stocks: Smooth walnut.
Sights: Ramp front, adjustable rear.
Features: Single action; polished blue finish; safety bar. From E. Phelps Mfg. Co.
Price: Heritage I (45-70), Eagle I (444 Marlin) 8″ barrel, about **$680.00**
Price: As above, 12″ barrel, about **$700.00**

Ruger N.M. Blackhawk

Ruger N.M. Bisley Blackhawk

Ruger Small Frame New Model Bisley
Similar to the New Model Single-Six except frame is styled after the classic Bisley "flat-top." Most mechanical parts are unchanged. Hammer is lower and smoothly curved with a deeply checkered spur. Trigger is strongly curved with a wide smooth surface. Longer grip frame designed with a hand-filling shape, and the trigger guard is a large oval. Dovetail rear sight drift-adjustable for windage; front sight base accepts intechangeable square blades of various heights and styles. Available with an unfluted cylinder and roll engraving, or with a fluted cylinder and no engraving. Weight about 41 oz. Chambered for 22 LR and 32 H&R Mag., 6½″ barrel only. Introduced 1985.
Price: **$286.38**

RUGER NEW MODEL SUPER SINGLE-SIX CONVERTIBLE REVOLVER
Caliber: 22 LR, 6-shot; 22 WMR in extra cylinder.
Barrel: 4⅝″, 5½″, 6½″, or 9½″ (6-groove).
Weight: 34½ oz. (6½″ bbl.). **Length:** 11¹³⁄₁₆″ over-all (6½″ bbl.).
Stocks: Smooth American walnut.
Sights: Improved Patridge front on ramp, fully adj. rear protected by integral frame ribs.
Features: New Ruger "interlocked" mechanism, transfer bar ignition, gate-controlled loading, hardened chrome-moly steel frame, wide trigger, music wire springs throughout, independent firing pin.
Price: 4⅝″, 5½″, 6½″, 9½″ barrel **$245.03**
Price: 5½″, 6½″ bbl. only, stainless steel........................ **$308.58**

SPORTARMS MODEL HS21S SINGLE ACTION
Caliber: 22 LR or 22LR/22 WMR combo, 6 shot.
Barrel: 5½″.
Weight: 33.5 oz. **Length:** 11″ over-all.
Stocks: Smooth hardwood.
Sights: Blade front, rear drift adjustable for windage.
Features: Available in blue or chrome with imitation stag or wood stocks. Made in West Germany by Herbert Schmidt; imported by Sportarms of Florida.
Price: 22 LR, blue, "stag" grips, about........................... **$80.00**
Price: 22LR/22 WMR Combo, chrome, wood stocks, about **$120.00**

RUGER NEW MODEL SUPER BLACKHAWK
Caliber: 44 Magnum, 6-shot. Also fires 44 Spec.
Barrel: 7½″ (6-groove, 20″ twist), 10½″.
Weight: 48 oz. (7½″ bbl.) 51 oz. (10½″ bbl.). **Length:** 13⅜″ over-all (7½″ bbl.).
Stocks: Genuine American walnut.
Sights: ⅛″ ramp front, micro click rear adj. for w. and e.
Features: New Ruger interlocked mechanism, non-fluted cylinder, steel grip and cylinder frame, square back trigger guard, wide serrated trigger and wide spur hammer.
Price: Blue (S-47N, S-411N) **$330.23**
Price: Stainless (KS-47N, KS-411N) **$360.75**

RUGER NEW MODEL BLACKHAWK REVOLVER
Caliber: 30 Carbine, 357 Mag./38 Spec., 41 Mag., 44 Mag., 45 Colt, 6-shot.
Barrel: 4⅝″ or 6½″, either caliber, 5½″ (44 Mag. only), 7½″ (30 Carbine, 45 Colt only).
Weight: 42 oz. (6½″ bbl.). **Length:** 12¼″ over-all (6½″ bbl.).
Stocks: American walnut.
Sights: ⅛″ ramp front, micro click rear adj. for w. and e.
Features: New Ruger interlocked mechanism, independent firing pin, hardened chrome-moly steel frame, music wire springs throughout.
Price: Blue, 30 Carbine (7½″ bbl.), BN31 .... **$275.00**
Price: Blue, 357 Mag. (4⅝″, 6½″) BN34, BN36 .... **$286.10**
Price: Blue, 357/9mm (4⅝″, 6½″) BN34X, BN36X................. **$299.70**
Price: Blue, 44 Mag. (5½″) S45N **$330.23**
Price: Blue, 41 Mag., 44 Mag., 45 Colt (4⅝″, 6½″) BN41, BN42, BN44, BN45.. **$286.10**
Price: Stainless, 357 Mag. (4⅝″, 6½″) KBN34, KBN36............. **$352.43**

Ruger New Model Bisley
Similar to standard New Model Blackhawk except the hammer is lower with a smoothly curved, deeply checkered wide spur. The trigger is strongly curved with a wide smooth surface. Longer grip frame has a hand-filling shape. Adjustable rear sight, ramp-style front. Available with an unfluted cylinder and roll engraving, or with a fluted cylinder and no engraving. Fixed or adjustable sights. Chambered for 357, 41, 44 Mags. and 45 Colt; 7½″ barrel; over-all length of 13″. Introduced 1985.
Price: **$340.77**

Ruger Bisley Single-Six

Ruger New Model Single-Six Revolver
Similar to the Super Single-Six revolver except chambered for 32 H&R Magnum (also handles 32 S&W and 32 S&W Long). Weight is about 34 oz. with 6½″ barrel. Barrel lengths: 4⅝″, 5½″, 6½″, 9½″. Introduced 1985.
Price: **$235.32**

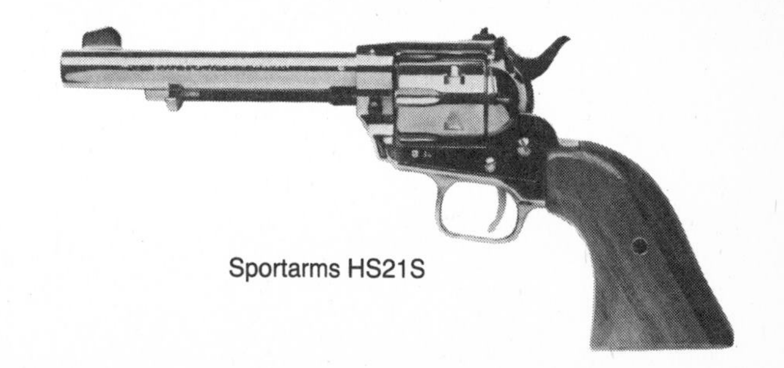
Sportarms HS21S

Super Six Golden Bison

SUPER SIX GOLDEN BISON 45-70 REVOLVER
Caliber: 45-70, 6-shot.
Barrel: 8″, 10½″, octagonal.
Weight: 5 lbs., 12 oz. (8″ bbl.) **Length:** 15″ over-all (8″ bbl.).
Stocks: Smooth walnut.
Sights: Blaze orange blade front on ramp, Millett fully adjustable rear.
Features: Cylinder frame and grip frame of high tensile Manganese bronze; hammer of Manganese bronze with a hardened steel pad for firing pin contact; all coil springs; full-cock, cross-bolt interlocking safety and traveling safeties. Choice of antique brown or blue/black finish. Lifetime warranty. Comes in a fitted black walnut presentation case. Made in the U.S. by Super Six Limited.
Price: Golden Bison (8″ bbl.) **$1,895.00**
Price: Golden Bison Bull (10½ bbl.) **$1,995.00**

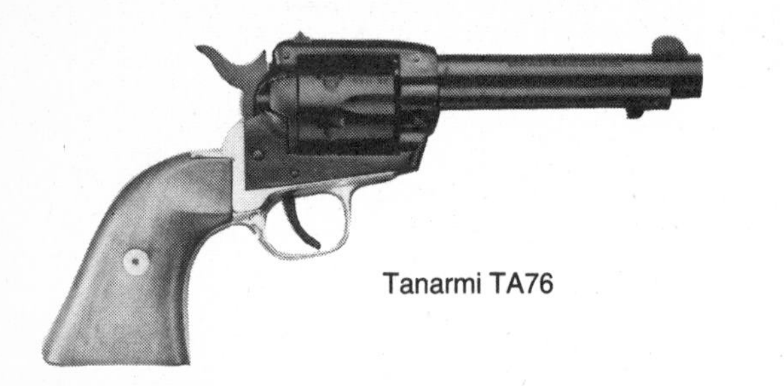

Tanarmi TA76

TANARMI S.A. REVOLVER MODEL TA76
Caliber: 22 LR, 22 WMR, 6-shot.
Barrel: 4¾″, 6″ or 9″.
Weight: 32 oz. **Length:** 10″ over-all.
Stocks: Walnut.
Sights: Blade front, rear adj. for w. & e.
Features: Manual hammer block safety. Imported from Italy by Excam.
Price: 22 LR, blue 4¾″ **$95.00**
Price: Combo, blue, 4¾″....................................... **$105.00**
Price: 22 LR, chrome, 4¾″..................................... **$99.00**
Price: Combo, chrome, 4¾″.................................... **$121.00**
Price: Combo, blue, 6″ **$115.00**
Price: Combo, blue, 9″ **$115.00**

TEXAS LONGHORN GROVER'S IMPROVED NO. FIVE
Caliber: 44 Magnum, 6-shot.
Barrel: 5½″.
Weight: 44 oz. **Length:** NA.
Stocks: Fancy AAA walnut.
Sights: Square blade front on ramp, fully adjustable rear.
Features: Music wire coil spring action with double locking bolt; polished blue finish. Hand-made in limited 1,200-gun production. Grip contour, straps, over-sized base pin, lever latch and lockwork identical copies of Elmer Keith design. Lifetime warranty to original owner. Introduced 1988.
Price:... **$985.00**

Texas Longhorn Grover's No. 5

TEXAS LONGHORN RIGHT-HAND SINGLE ACTION
Caliber: All centerfire pistol calibers.
Barrel: 4¾″.
Weight: NA. **Length:** NA.
Stocks: One-piece fancy walnut, or any fancy AAA wood.
Sights: Blade front, grooved top-strap rear.
Features: Loading gate and ejector housing on left side of gun. Cylinder rotates to the left. All steel construction; color case-hardened frame; high polish blue; music wire coil springs. Lifetime guarantee to original owner. Introduced 1984. From Texas Longhorn Arms.
Price: South Texas Army Limited Edition — hand-made, only 1,000 to be produced; "One of One Thousand" engraved on barrel............ **$1,500.00**

Texas Longhorn Sesquicentennial Model Revolver
Similar to the South Texas Army Model except has ¾-coverage Nimschke-style engraving, antique golden nickel plate finish, one-piece elephant ivory grips. Comes with hand-made solid walnut presentation case, factory letter to owner. Limited edition of 150 units. Introduced 1986.
Price: **$2,500.00**

Texas Longhorn Arms Texas Border Special
Similar to the South Texas Army Limited Edition except has 3½″ barrel, birds-head style grip. Same special features. Introduced 1984.
Price: **$1,500.00**

Texas Longhorn Arms Cased Set
Set contains one each of the Texas Longhorn Right-Hand Single Actions, all in the same caliber, same serial numbers (100, 200, 300, 400, 500, 600, 700, 800, 900). Ten sets to be made (#1000 donated to NRA museum). Comes inhand-tooled leather case. All other specs same as Limited Edition guns. Introduced 1984.
Price: **$5,750.00**
Price: With ¾-coverage "C-style" engraving.................... **$7,650.00**

Texas Longhorn Arms West Texas Flat Top Target
Similar to the South Texas Army Limited Edition except choice of barrel length from 7½″ through 15″; flat-top style frame; ⅛″ contoured ramp front sight, old model steel micro-click rear adjustable for w. and e. Same special features. Introduced 1984.
Price: **$1,500.00**

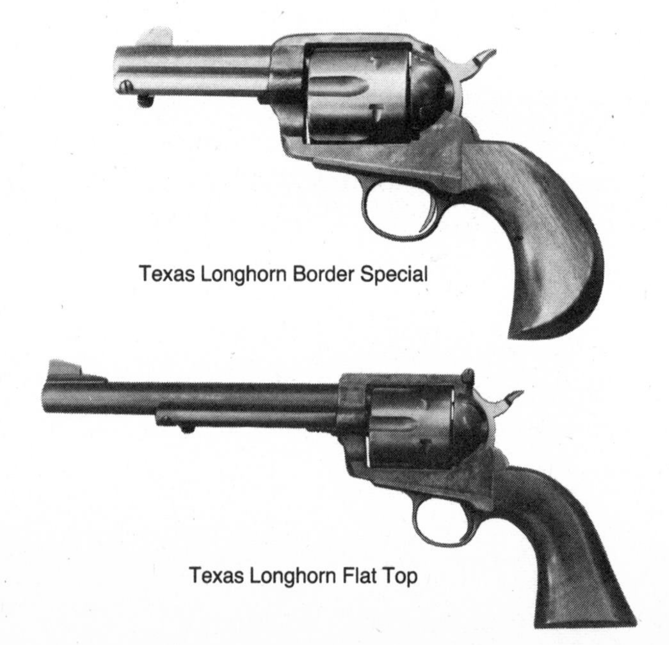

Texas Longhorn Border Special

Texas Longhorn Flat Top

CAUTION: PRICES CHANGE. CHECK AT GUNSHOP.

UBERTI 1873 CATTLEMAN SINGLE ACTIONS

Caliber: 22 LR, 22 WMR, 32-20, 38 Spec., 38-40, 357 Mag., 44 Spec., 44-40, 45 Colt, 6-shot.
Barrel: 4¾", 5½", 7½"; 44-40, 45 Colt also with 3".
Weight: 38 oz. (5½" bbl.). **Length:** 10¾" over-all (5½" bbl.).
Stocks: One-piece smooth walnut.
Sights: Blade front, groove rear; fully adjustable rear.
Features: Steel or brass backstrap, trigger guard; color case-hardened frame, blued barrel, cylinder. Imported from Italy by Benson Firearms, Uberti USA.
Price: Steel backstrap, trigger guard, fixed sights **$375.00**
Price: As above, adj. sight **$399.00**
Price: Brass backstrap, trigger guard, fixed sights.......... **$345.00**
Price: As above, adj. sight **$375.00**

Uberti Cattleman

Uberti 1873 Buckhorn Single Action

A slightly larger version of the Cattleman revolver. Available in 44 Magnum or 44 Magnum/44-40 convertible, otherwise has same specs.
Price: Steel backstrap, trigger guard, fixed sights **$385.00**
Price: As above, brass **$355.00**
Price: Convertible (two cylinders) add **$40.00**

Uberti 1873 Buntline Single Action

Available in 357 Mag., 44-40 or 45 Colt (Cattleman frame), 44 Mag./44-40 convertible (Buckhorn frame) with 18" barrel. Weight is 3.6 lbs. with an over-all length of 23". Same sight and frame options as Cattleman and Buckhorn.
Price: Steel backstrap, trigger guard, fixed sight **$409.00**
Price: As above, adj sight.......... **$435.00**
Price: Brass backstrap, trigger guard, fixed sight.......... **$379.00**
Price: As above, adj. sight **$409.00**
Price: Convertible, add **$65.00**
Price: Shoulder stock **$135.00**

UBERTI 1875 SA ARMY "OUTLAW" REVOLVER

Caliber: 357 Mag., 44-40, 45 Colt, 6-shot.
Barrel: 7½".
Weight: 44 oz. **Length:** 13¾" over-all.
Stocks: Smooth walnut.
Sights: Blade front, notch rear.
Features: Replica of the 1875 Remington S.A. Army revolver. Brass trigger guard, color case-hardened frame, rest blued. Imported by Benson Firearms, Uberti USA.
Price: **$355.00**
Price: Nickel plated **$395.00**

UBERTI 1873 STALLION SINGLE ACTION

Caliber: 22 LR/22 WMR convertible.
Barrel: 4¾", 5½", 6½", round.
Weight: 36 oz. **Length:** 10¾" over-all.
Stocks: One-piece walnut.
Sights: Blade front, groove rear or ramp front, adjustable rear.
Features: Smaller version of the Cattleman with same frame options. Imported from Italy by Benson Firearms, Uberti USA.
Price: Steel backstrap, trigger guard, fixed sights **$375.00**
Price: As above, adj. sight **$399.00**
Price: Brass, fixed sights **$345.00**
Price: As above, adj. sight **$375.00**
Price: Stainless, fixed sight **$425.00**
Price: As above, adj. sight **$450.00**

UBERTI 1890 ARMY "OUTLAW" REVOLVER

Caliber: 357 Mag., 44-40, 45 Colt, 6 shot.
Barrel: 5½".
Weight: 37 oz. **Length:** 12½" over-all.
Stocks: American walnut.
Sights: Blade front, groove rear.
Features: Replica of the 1890 Remington single-action. Brass trigger guard, rest is blued. Imported by Benson Firearms, Uberti USA.
Price: **$369.00**
Price: Nickel plated **$409.00**

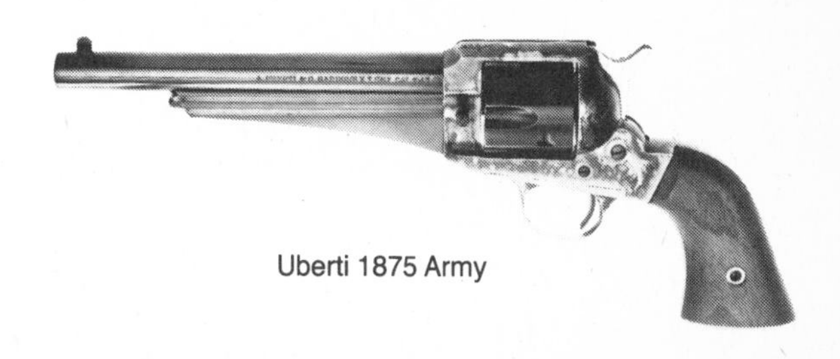

Uberti 1875 Army

Uberti 1873 Stallion

HANDGUNS—MISCELLANEOUS

Specially adapted single-shot and multi-barrel arms.

American Derringer Semmerling

AMERICAN DERRINGER SEMMERLING LM-4

Caliber: 9mm Para., 7-shot magazine; 45 ACP, 5-shot magazine.
Barrel: 3.625".
Weight: 24 oz. **Length:** 5.2" over-all.
Stocks: Checkered plastic on blued guns, rosewood on stainless guns.
Sights: Open, fixed.
Features: Manually-operated repeater. Height is 3.7", width is 1". Comes with manual, leather carrying case, spare stock screws, wrench. From American Derringer Corp.
Price: Blued.......... **$1,250.00**
Price: Stainless steel **$1,500.00**

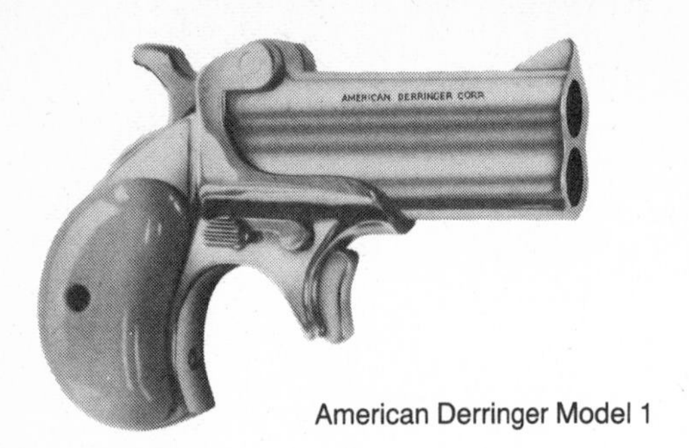

American Derringer Model 1

AMERICAN DERRINGER MODEL 1

Caliber: 22 LR, 22 WMR, 22 Hornet, 223 Rem., 30 Luger, 30-30 Win., 32 ACP, 38 Super, 380 ACP, 38 Spec., 9x18, 9mm Para., 357 Mag., 357 Maximum, 10 mm, 41 Mag., 38-40, 44-40 Win., 44 Spec., 44 American, 44 Mag., 45 Colt, 45 ACP, 410-ga. (2½").
Barrel: 3".
Weight: 15½ oz. (38 Spec.). **Length:** 4.82" over-all.
Stocks: Rosewood, Zebra wood.
Sights: Blade front.
Features: Made of stainless steel with high-polish or satin finish. Two shot capacity. Manual hammer block safety. Introduced 1980. Available in almost any pistol caliber. Contact the factory for complete list of available calibers and prices. From American Derringer Corp.
Price: 22 LR or WMR **$218.00**
Price: 22 Hornet, 223 Rem. **$369.00**
Price: 38 Spec. **$187.50**
Price: 357 Maximum **$250.00**
Price: 357 Mag. **$225.00**
Price: 9x18, 9mm, 380, 38 Super **$172.50**
Price: 10 mm **$218.00**
Price: 44 Spec, 44 American **$275.00**
Price: 38-40, 44-40 Win., 45 Colt, 45 Auto Rim **$275.00**
Price: 30-30, 41, 44 Mags., 45 Win. Mag. **$369.00**
Price: 45-70, single shot **$312.00**
Price: 45 Colt, 410, 2½" **$312.00**
Price: 45 ACP, 10mm Auto **$218.00**

AMERICAN DERRINGER MODEL 3

Caliber: 38 Special.
Barrel: 2.5".
Weight: 8.5 oz. **Length:** 4.9" over-all.
Stocks: Rosewood.
Sights: Blade front.
Features: Made of stainless steel. Single shot with manual hammer block safety. Introduced 1985. From American Derringer Corp.
Price: **$115.00**

American Derringer Model 4

Similar to the Model 1 except has 4.1" barrel, over-all length of 6", and weighs 16½ oz.; chambered for 3" 410-ga. shotshells or 45 Colt. Can be had with 45-70 upper barrel and 3" 410-ga. or 45 Colt bottom barrel. Made of stainless steel. Manual hammer block safety. Introduced 1985.
Price: 3" 410/45 Colt (either barrel) **$350.00**
Price: 3" 410/45 Colt or 45-70 (Alaskan Survival model) **$369.00**

American Derringer Model 7

Similar to Model 1 except made of high strength aircraft aluminum. Weighs 7½ oz., 4.82" o.a.l., rosewood stocks. Available in 22 LR, 32 S&W Long, 32 H&R Mag., 380 ACP, 38 S&W, 38 Spec., 44 Spec. Introduced 1986.
Price: 22 LR or 38 Spec. **$187.50**
Price: 38 S&W, 380 ACP, 32 S&W Long **$157.50**
Price: 32 H&R Mag. **$172.50**
Price: 44 Spec. **$500.00**

American Derringer Model 6

Similar to the Model 1 except has 6" barrels chambered for 3" 410 shotshells or 45 Colt, rosewood stocks, 8.2" o.a.l. and weighs 21 oz. Shoots either round for each barrel. Manual hammer block safety. Introduced 1986.
Price: High polish or satin finish **$369.00**
Price: Gray matte finish **$350.00**

American Derringer Texas Commemorative

A Model 1 Derringer with solid brass frame, stainless steel barrel and stag grips. Available in 38 Special, 44-40 Win., 44 American or 45 Colt. Introduced 1987.
Price: **$285.00**

ANSCHUTZ EXEMPLAR BOLT ACTION PISTOL

Caliber: 22 LR, 5-shot; 22 WMR, 22 Hornet, 5-shot.
Barrel: 10", 14".
Weight: 3½ lbs. **Length:** 17" over-all.
Stock: European walnut with stippled grip and fore-end.
Sights: Hooded front on ramp, open notch rear adjustable for w. and e.
Features: Uses Match 64 action with left-hand bolt; Anshultz #5091 two-stage trigger set at 9.85 oz. Receiver grooved for scope mounting; open sights easily removed. Introduced 1987. Imported from West Germany by PSI.
Price: 22 LR **$375.00**
Price: 22 LR, left-hand **$405.00**
Price: 22 LR, 14" barrel **$419.50**
Price: 22 Hornet **$758.00**

Anschutz Exemplar

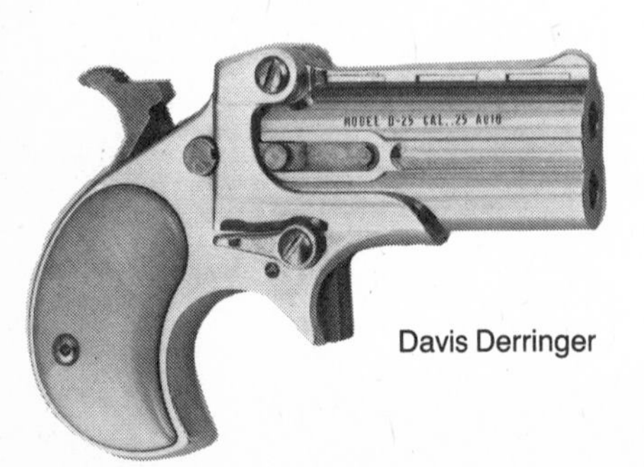

Davis Derringer

Consult our Directory pages for the location of firms mentioned.

DAVIS DERRINGERS

Caliber: 22 LR, 22 WMR, 25 ACP, 32 ACP.
Barrel: 2.4".
Weight: 9.5 oz. **Length:** 4" over-all.
Stocks: Laminated wood.
Sights: Blade front, fixed notch rear.
Features: Choice of black Teflon or chrome finish; spur trigger. Introduced 1986. Made in U.S. by Davis Industries.
Price: **$64.90**

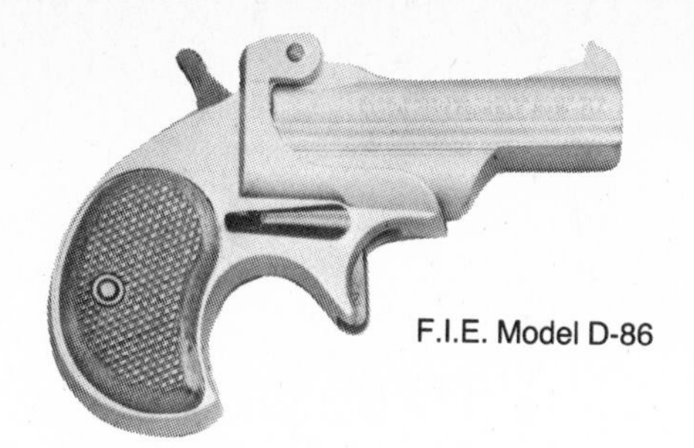

F.I.E. Model D-86

F.I.E. D-86 DERRINGER

Caliber: 38 Special.
Barrel: 3″.
Weight: 14 oz.
Stocks: Checkered black nylon, walnut optional.
Sights: Fixed.
Features: Dyna-Chrome or blue finish. Spur trigger. Tip-up barrel; extractors. Made in U.S. by F.I.E. Corp.
Price: With nylon grips **$94.95**
Price: With walnut grips **$114.95**

FEATHER GUARDIAN ANGEL PISTOL

Caliber: 9mm Parabellum.
Barrel: 2″.
Weight: 17 oz. **Length:** 5½″ over-all.
Stocks: Black composition.
Sights: Fixed.
Features: Uses a pre-loaded two-shot drop-in "magazine." Stainless steel construction; matte finish. From Feather Enterprises. Announced 1988.
Price: **$169.95**

Feather Guardian Angel

INTRATEC TEC COMPANION DERRINGER

Caliber: 32 H&R Mag., 38 Spec., 357 Mag., 2 shot.
Barrel: 3″.
Weight: 13 oz. **Length:** 4⅝″ over-all.
Stock: Moulded composition.
Sights: Blade front, fixed rear.
Features: Double action; swing-out barrels; one-stroke ejector; automatic selector; trigger/hammer block safety; matte black finish. From Intratec.
Price: **$114.95**

Intratec TEC-38

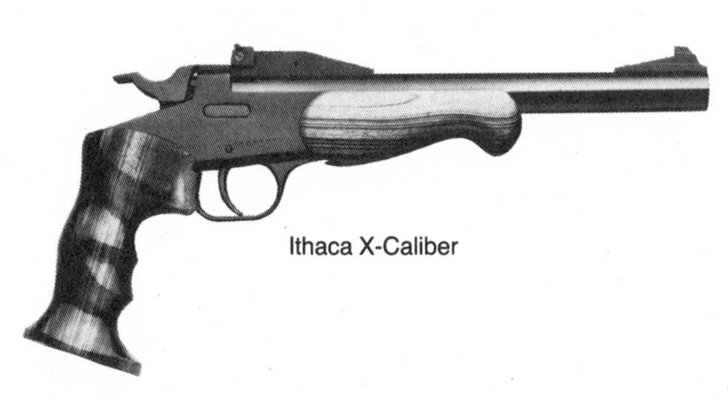

Ithaca X-Caliber

ITHACA X-CALIBER SINGLE SHOT

Caliber: 22 LR, 223 Rem., 35 Rem., 357 Mag., 357 Max., 44 Mag.
Barrel: 10″, 15″.
Weight: 3¼ lbs. **Length:** 15″ over-all (10″ barrel).
Stocks: Goncalo Alves grip and fore-end on Model 20; American walnut on Model 30.
Sights: Blade on ramp front; Model 20 has adjustable, removeable target-type rear. Model 30 has step-adjustable Deerslayer and is grooved for scope mounting.
Features: Dual firing pin for RF/CF use. Model 20 has polished blue finish, Model 30 has matte teflon finish and comes with sling.
Price: Model 20, Model 30, 10″ or 15″ **$256.00**

Kimber Predator

KIMBER PREDATOR PISTOL

Caliber: 221 Fireball, 223 Rem., 6mm TCU, 6 x45, 7mm TCU; single shot.
Barrel: 15¾″.
Weight: About 5½ lbs. **Length:** NA
Stock: AA claro walnut (Hunter); French walnut (Supergrade).
Sights: None furnished. Accepts Kimber scope mount system.
Features: Uses the Kimber Model 84 mini-Mauser action. Supergrade has ebony fore-end tip, 22 l.p.i. checkering. Introduced 1987.
Price: Hunter.. **$995.00**
Price: Supergrade **$1,195.00**

LJUTIC LJ II PISTOL

Caliber: 22 WMR.
Barrel: 2¾″.
Stocks: Checkered walnut.
Sights: Fixed.
Features: Double action; ventilated rib; side-by-side barrels; positive on/off safety. Introduced 1981. From Ljutic Industries.
Price: **$1,199.00**

MANDALL/CABANAS PISTOL

Caliber: 177, pellet or round ball; single shot.
Barrel: 9″.
Weight: 51 oz. **Length:** 19″ over-all.
Stock: Smooth wood with thumb rest.
Sights: Blade front on ramp, open adjustable rear.
Features: Fires round ball or pellets with 22 blank cartridge. Automatic saftety; muzzle brake. Imported from Mexico by Mandall Shooting Supplies.
Price: **$125.00**

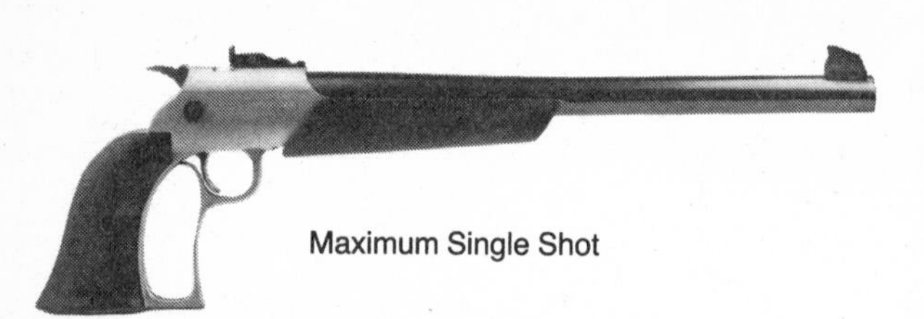
Maximum Single Shot

MAXIMUM SINGLE SHOT PISTOL

Caliber: 22 Hornet, 22 BR, 223 Rem., 22-250, 6mm BR, 6mm-223, 243, 250 Savage, 6.5mm-35, 7mm TCU, 7mm BR, 7mm-35, 7mm INT-R, 7mm-08, 7mm Rocket, 7mm Super Mag., 30 Herrett, 308 Win., 32-20, 357 Mag., 357 Maximum, 358 Win., 44 Mag.
Barrel: 8¾", 10½", 14".
Weight: 61 oz. (10½" bbl.), 67 oz. (14" bbl.). **Length:** 15", 18½" over-all (with 10½" and 14" bbl., respectively).
Stocks: Smooth walnut stocks and fore-end.
Sights: Ramp front, fully adjustable open rear.
Features: Falling block action; drilled and tapped for M.O.A. scope mounts; integral grip frame/receiver; adjustable trigger; Douglas barrel (interchangeable); Armoloy finish. Introduced 1983. Made in U.S. by M.O.A. Corp.
Price: 8¾", 10", 14" **$499.00**
Price: Extra barrels **$129.00**
Price: Scope mount **$39.00**

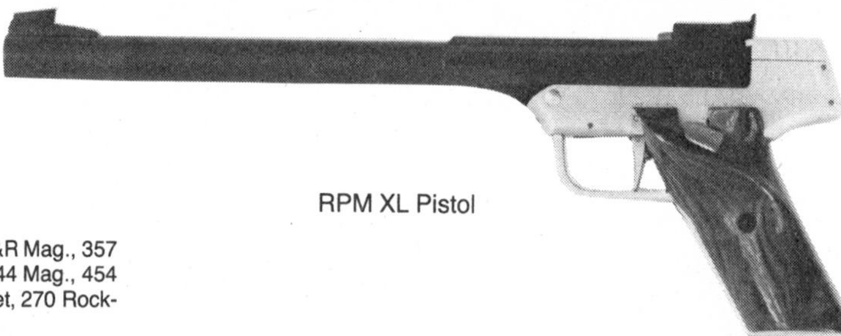
RPM XL Pistol

RPM XL SINGLE SHOT PISTOL

Caliber: 22 LR, 22 WMR, 225 Win., 25 Rocket, 6.5 Rocket, 32 H&R Mag., 357 Max., 357 Mag., 30-30 Win., 30 Herrett, 357 Herrett, 41 Mag., 44 Mag., 454 Casull, 375 Win., 7mm UR, 7mm Merrill, 30 Merrill, 7mm Rocket, 270 Rocket, 270 Max., 45-70.
Barrel: 8" slab, 10", 10¾", 12", 14" bull; 450" wide vent. rib, matted to prevent glare.
Weight: About 60 oz. **Length:** 12¼" over-all (10¾" bbl.).
Stocks: Smooth walnut with thumb and heel rest.
Sights: Front .125" blade (.100" blade optional); Millett or ISGW rear adj. for w. and e.
Features: Polished blue finish, hard chrome optional. Barrel is drilled and tapped for scope mounting. Cooking indicator visible from rear of gun. Has spring-loaded barrel lock, positive hammer block thumb safety. Trigger adjustable for weight of pull and over-travel. For complete price list contact RPM.
Price: Regular ¾" frame, right-hand action **$585.00**
Price: As above, left-hand action **$610.00**
Price: Wide ⅞" frame, right-hand action only **$635.00**
Price: Extra barrel, 8"-10¾" **$180.00**
Price: Extra barrel, 12"-14" **$250.00**

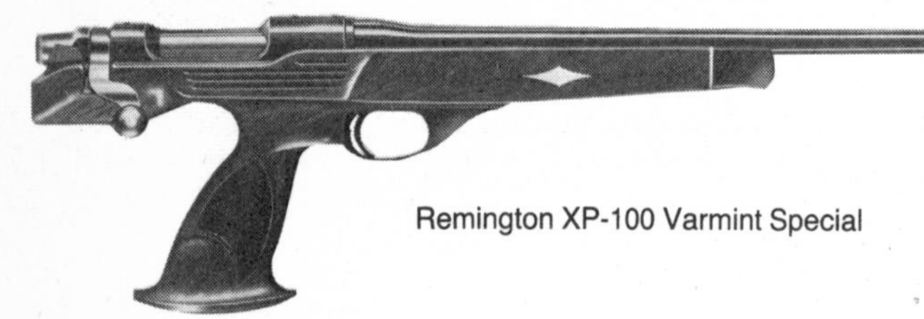
Remington XP-100 Varmint Special

REMINGTON XP-100 "VARMINT SPECIAL"

Caliber: 223 Rem., single shot.
Barrel: 10½", ventilated rib.
Weight: 60 oz. **Length:** 16¾".
Stock: Brown nylon one-piece, checkered grip with white spacers.
Sights: Tapped for scope mount.
Features: Fits left or right hand, is shaped to fit fingers and heel of hand. Grooved trigger. Rotating thumb safety, cavity in fore-end permits insertion of up to five 38 cal., 130-gr.metal jacketed bullets to adjust weight and balance. Included is a black vinyl, zippered case.
Price: Including case, about **$373.00**

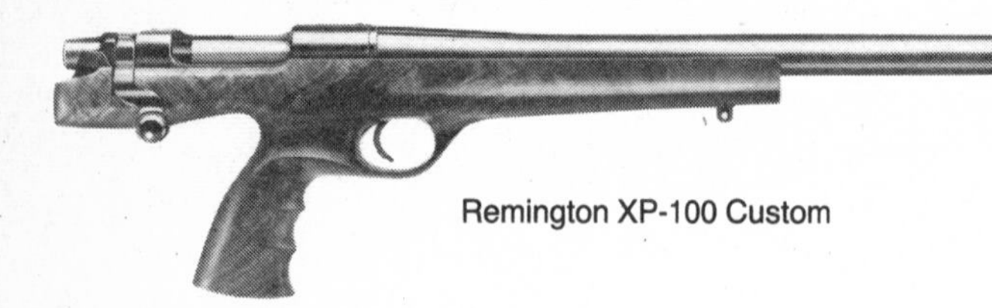
Remington XP-100 Custom

Remington XP-100 Custom Long Range Pistol

Similar to the XP-100 "Varmint Special" except chambered for 223 Rem. (heavy barrel), 7mm-08 Rem. and 35 Rem.; comes with sights—interchangeable blade on ramp front, fully adjustable Bo-Mar rear. Custom Shop 14½" barrel, Custom Shop English walnut stock in right- or left-hand configuration. Action tuned in Custom Shop. Weight is under 4½ lbs. Introduced 1986.
Price: **$907.00**

Texas Longhorn "Jezebel"

TEXAS LONGHORN "THE JEZEBEL" PISTOL

Caliber: 22 Short, Long, Long Rifle, single shot.
Barrel: 6".
Weight: 15 oz. **Length:** 8" over-all.
Stocks: One-piece fancy walnut grip (right or left hand), walnut fore-end.
Sights: Bead front, fixed rear.
Features: Hand-made gun. Top-break action; all stainless steel; automatic hammer block safety; music wire coil springs. Barrel is half round, half octagon. Announced 1986. From Texas Longhorn Arms.
Price: About **$250.00**

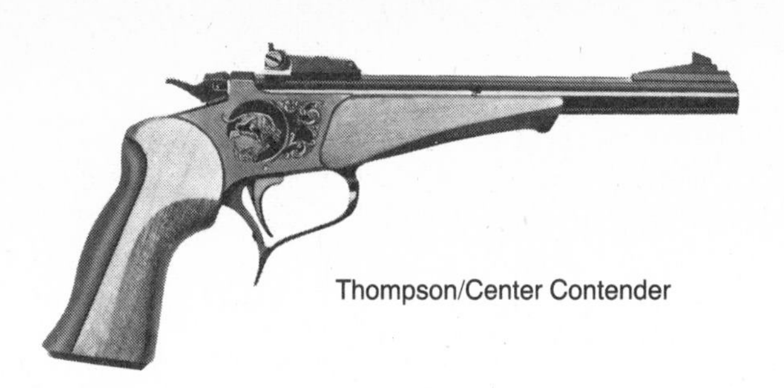
Thompson/Center Contender

THOMPSON/CENTER ARMS CONTENDER

Caliber: 7mm TCU, 30-30 Win., 22 S, L, LR, 22 WMR, 22 Hornet, 223 Rem., 30 Carbine, 9mm Para., 7 x 30 Waters, 32 H&R Mag., 32-20 Win., 357 Mag., 357 Rem. Max., 44 Mag., 45/410, single shot.
Barrel: 10″, tapered octagon, bull barrel and vent. rib.
Weight: 43 oz. (10″ bbl.). **Length:** 13¼″ (10″ bbl.).
Stocks: T/C "Competitor Grip." Right or left hand.
Sights: Under-cut blade ramp front, rear adj. for w. & e.
Features: Break-open action with auto-safety. Single-action only. Interchangeable bbls., both caliber (rim & centerfire), and length. Drilled and tapped for scope. Engraved frame. See T/C catalog for exact barrel/caliber availability.
Price: Blued (rimfire cals.) **$335.00**
Price: Blued (centerfire cals.) **$335.00**
Price: With Armour Alloy II finish **$405.00**
Price: With internal choke **$410.00**
Price: As above, vent. rib **$425.00**
Price: Extra bbls. (standard octagon) **$145.00**
Price: Bushnell Phantom scope base **$13.50**
Price: 45/410, vent. rib, internal choke bbl. **$165.00**

UBERTI ROLLING BLOCK TARGET PISTOL

Caliber: 22 LR, 22 WMR., 22 Hornet, 357 Mag., single shot.
Barrel: 9⅞″, half-round, half-octagon.
Weight: 44 oz. **Length:** 14″ over-all.
Stocks: Walnut grip and fore-end.
Sights: Blade front, fully adj. rear.
Features: Replica of the 1871 rolling block target pistol. Brass trigger guard, color case-hardened frame, blue barrel. Imported by Benson Firearms, Uberti USA.
Price: **$305.00**

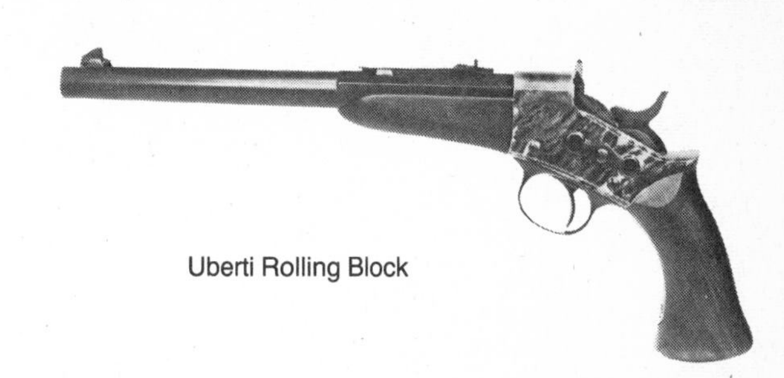
Uberti Rolling Block

ULTRA LIGHT ARMS MODEL 20 REB HUNTER'S PISTOL

Caliber: 22-250 thru 308 Win. standard. Most silhouette calibers and others on request. 5-shot magazine.
Barrel: 14″, Douglas No. 3.
Weight: 4 lbs.
Stock: Composite Kevlar, graphite reinforced. Du Pont Imron paint in green, brown , black and camo.
Sights: None furnished. Scope mount included.
Features: Timney adjustable trigger; two position, three-function safety; benchrest quality action; matte or bright stock and metal finish; right or left-hand action. Shipped in hard case. Introduced 1987. From Ultra Light Arms.
Price: **$1,300.00**

Ultra Light Model 20

CENTERFIRE RIFLES—MILITARY STYLE AUTOLOADERS

Suitable for, and adaptable to, certain kinds of competitions as well as sporting purposes, such as hunting.

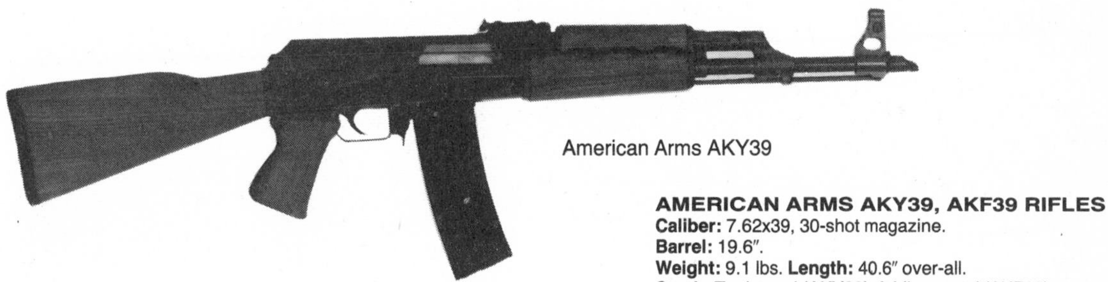
American Arms AKY39

AMAC LONG RANGE RIFLE

Caliber: 50 BMG.
Barrel: 33″, fully fluted, free floating.
Weight: 30 lbs. **Length:** 55.5″ over-all.
Stock: Composition. Adjustable drop and comb.
Sights: Comes with Leupold Ultra M1 20x scope.
Features: Bolt-action long range rifle. Comes with Automatic Ranging Scope Base. Adjustable trigger. Rifle breaks down for transport, storage. From Iver Johnson.
Price: **$8,500.00**

AMERICAN ARMS AKY39, AKF39 RIFLES

Caliber: 7.62x39, 30-shot magazine.
Barrel: 19.6″.
Weight: 9.1 lbs. **Length:** 40.6″ over-all.
Stock: Teakwood (AKY39), folding metal (AKF39).
Sights: Hooded post front, open adjustable rear. Flip-up Tritium night sights front and rear.
Features: Matte blue finish on metal, oil-finished wood. Imported from Yugoslavia by American Arms, Inc.
Price: Wood stock (AKY30) **$595.00**
Price: Folding metal stock (AKF39) **$625.00**

AUTO-ORDNANCE MODEL 27 A-1 THOMPSON

Caliber: 45 ACP, 30-shot magazine.
Barrel: 16″.
Weight: 11½ lbs. **Length:** About 42″ over-all (Deluxe).
Stock: Walnut stock and vertical fore-end.
Sights: Blade front, open rear adj. for w.
Features: Recreation of Thompson Model 1927. Semi-auto only. Deluxe model has finned barrel, adj. rear sight and compensator; Standard model has plain barrel and military sight. From Auto-Ordnance Corp.
Price: Deluxe **$716.00**
Price: Standard (horizontal fore-end) **$716.00**
Price: 1927A5 Pistol (M27A1 without stock; wgt. 7 lbs.) **$622.50**
Price: Lightweight model **$631.50**

AUSTRALIAN AUTOMATIC ARMS SAR RIFLE

Caliber: 223, 5- or 20-shot magazine.
Barrel: 16.25″.
Weight: 7.5 lbs. **Length:** 35.8″ over-all.
Stock: Fixed composition.
Sights: Protected post front, revolving aperture read adjustable for windage.
Features: Gas operated with short-stroke mobile cylinder. Hammer forged barrel with chrome chamber and bore. Imported from Australia by Kendall International.
Price: **$775.00**

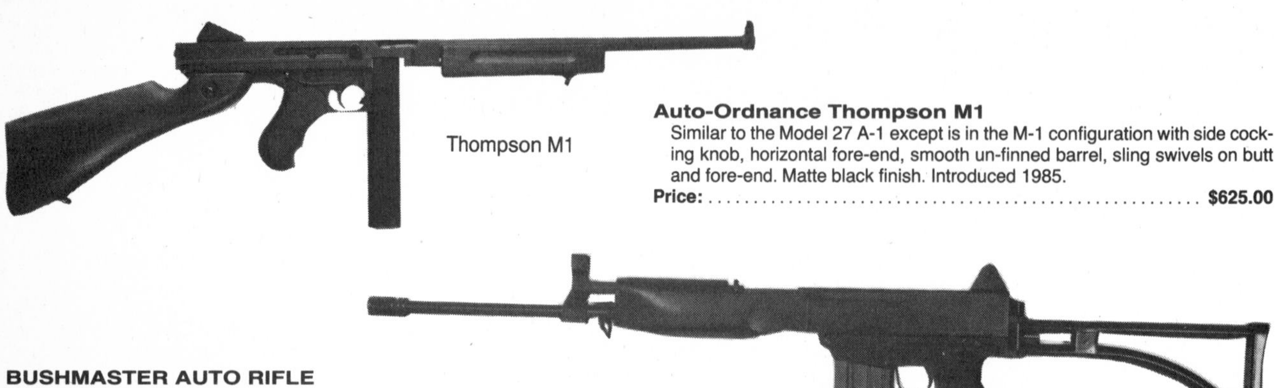

Thompson M1

Auto-Ordnance Thompson M1

Similar to the Model 27 A-1 except is in the M-1 configuration with side cocking knob, horizontal fore-end, smooth un-finned barrel, sling swivels on butt and fore-end. Matte black finish. Introduced 1985.
Price: **$625.00**

BUSHMASTER AUTO RIFLE

Caliber: 223, 30-shot magazine
Barrel: 18½″.
Weight: 6¼ lbs. **Length:** 37.5″ over-all.
Stock: Rock maple.
Sights: Protected post front adj. for elevation, protected quick-flip rear peep adj. for windage; short and long range.
Features: Steel alloy upper receiver with welded barrel assembly; AK-47-type gas system, aluminum lower receiver; silent sling and swivels; bayonet lug; one-piece welded steel alloy bolt carrier assembly. From Bushmaster Firearms.
Price: With maple stock **$384.95**
Price: With nylon-coated folding stock **$394.95**
Price: Matte electroless finish, maple stock **$394.95**
Price: As above, folding stock **$394.95**

Bushmaster Auto Rifle

BERETTA AR70 SPORTER RIFLE

Caliber: 223, 8- and 30-shot magazines.
Barrel: 17.2″.
Weight: 8.3 lbs. **Length:** 38″ over-all.
Stock: Black high-impact plastic.
Sights: Blade front, diopter rear adjustable for windage and elevation.
Features: Matte black epoxy finish; easy take-down. Comes with both magazines, cleaning kit, carrying strap. Imported from Italy by Beretta U.S.A. Corp. Introduced 1984.
Price: **$800.00**

Barrett Light-Fifty

BARRETT LIGHT-FIFTY MODEL 82A-1

Caliber: 50 BMG, 11-shot detachable box magazine.
Barrel: 33″.
Weight: 35 lbs. **Length:** 63″ over-all.
Stock: Uni-body construction.
Sights: None furnished.
Features: Semi-automatic, recoil operated with recoiling barrel. Three-lug locking bolt; six-port harmonica-type muzzle brake. Bipod legs and M-60 mount standard. Fires same 50-cal. ammunition as the M2HB machine gun. Introduced 1985. From Barrett Firearms.
Price: Parkerized **$5,995.00**

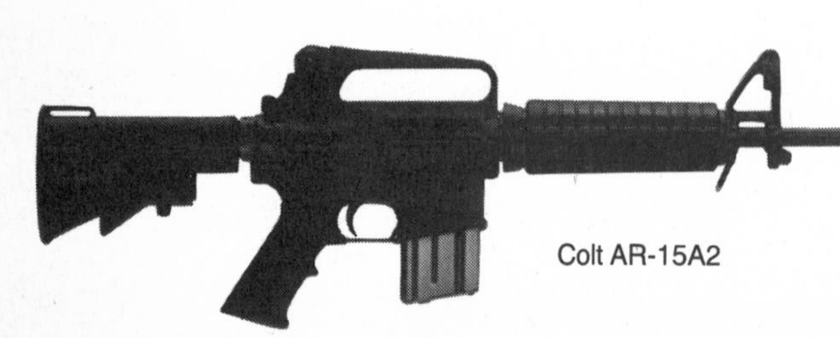

Colt AR-15A2

COLT AR-15A2 CARBINE

Caliber: 223 Rem.
Barrel: 16″.
Weight: 5.8 lbs. **Length:** 35″ over-all (extended).
Stock: Telescoping aluminum.
Sights: Post front, adjustable for elevation, flip-type rear for short, long range, windage.
Features: 5-round detachable box magazine, flash suppressor, sling swivels. Forward bolt assist included. Introduced 1985.
Price: Limited availability **$769.95**

Colt AR-15A2 Delta H-BAR

Colt AR-15A2-Delta H-BAR
Similar to the AR-15A2 Carbine except has standard stock, is refined and inspected by the Colt Custom Shop. Comes with a 3-9x rubber armored scope and removeable cheek piece, adjustable scope mount, black leather military-style sling, cleaning kit, and hard carrying case. Pistol grip has Delta medallion. Introduced 1987.
Price: **$1,359.95**

Colt AR-15A2 H-BAR
Similar to the AR-15A2 Delta H-BAR except has heavy barrel, 800-meter M-16A2 rear sight adjustable for windage and elevation, case deflector for left-hand shooters, target-style nylon sling. Introduced 1986.
Price: **$869.95**

Daewoo AR110C Auto Carbine
Similar to the MAX-1 except has a folding buttstock giving over-all length of 38.9" (extended), 28.7" (folded). Weight is 7.5 lbs.; barrel length is 18.3". Has hooded post front sight, adjustable peep rear. Uses AR-15/M-16 magazines. Introduced 1985. Imported from Korea by Pacific International.
Price: **$399.95**

COMMANDO ARMS CARBINE
Caliber: 45 ACP.
Barrel: 16½".
Weight: 8 lbs. **Length:** 37" over-all.
Stock: Walnut buttstock.
Sights: Blade front, peep rear.
Features: Semi-auto only. Cocking handle on left side. Choice of magazines—5, 20, 30 or 90 shot. From Gibbs Guns.
Price: Mark 9 or Mark 45, blue **$259.00**
Price: Nickel plated **$304.00**

Daewoo AR100

DAEWOO AR100 AUTO RIFLE
Caliber: 5.56mm (223), 30-round magazine.
Barrel: 17".
Weight: 6.5 lbs. **Length:** 38.4" over-all (butt extended).
Stock: Retractable.
Sights: Post front, adjustable peep rear.
Features: Machine-forged receiver; gas-operated action; uses AR-15/M-16 magazines. Introduced 1985. Imported from Korea by Pacific International.
Price: **$429.95**

FN-LAR Competition

FN-LAR COMPETITION AUTO
Caliber: 308 Win., 20-shot magazine.
Barrel: 21" (24" with flash hider).
Weight: 9 lbs., 7 oz. **Length:** 44½" over-all.
Stock: Black composition butt, fore-end and pistol grip.
Sights: Post front, aperture rear adj. for elevation, 200 to 600 meters.
Features: Has sling swivels, carrying handle, rubber recoil pad. Consecutively numbered pairs available at additional cost. Imported by Gun South, Inc.
Price: **$3,179.00**

FN-LAR Heavy Barrel 308 Match
Similar to FN-LAR competition except has wooden stock and fore-end, heavy barrel, folding metal bidpod. Imported by Gun South, Inc.
Price: With wooden, stock. **$4,175.00**
Price: With synthetic stock **$3,776.00**

FN-LAR Paratrooper 308 Match 50-64
Similar to FN-LAR competition except with folding skeleton stock, shorter barrel, modified rear sight. Imported by Gun South, Inc.
Price: **$3,239.00**

FN 308 Model 50-63
Similar to the FN-LAR except has 18" barrel, skeleton-type folding buttstock, folding cocking handle. Introduced 1982. Imported from Belgium by Gun South, Inc.
Price: **$3,239.00**

FNC AUTO RIFLE
Caliber: 223 Rem.
Barrel: 18".
Weight: 9.61 lbs.
Stock: Synthetic stock.
Sights: Post front; flip-over aperture rear adj. for elevation.
Features: Updated version of FN-FAL in shortened carbine form. Has 30-shot box magazine, synthetic pistol grip, fore-end. Introduced 1981. Imported by Gun South, Inc.
Price: Standard model. **$2,204.00**
Price: Paratrooper, with folding stock **$2,322.00**

FNC Auto Rifle

Federal XC-900/XC-450

FEDERAL XC-900/XC-450 AUTO CARBINES

Caliber: 9mm Para., 32-shot magazine; 45 ACP.
Barrel: 16.5″ (with flash hider).
Weight: 8 lbs. **Length:** 34½″ over-all.
Stock: Detachable tube steel; adjustable stock optional.
Sights: Hooded post front, peep rear adjustable for w. and e.
Features: Quick takedown for transport, storage. All heli-arc welded steel construction. Made in U.S. by Federal Engineering Corp.
Price: Phosphate finish, either cal. **$513.50**
Price: As above, with adj. stock **$561.54**
Price: With teflon finish, nylon covered fore-end, hard-chrome bolt . **$610.94**
Price: As above, with adj. stock **$656.44**

FEATHER AT-9 AUTO CARBINE

Caliber: 9mm Parabellum, 32-shot magazine.
Barrel: 16″.
Weight: 5 lbs. **Length:** 33½″ overall (stock extended).
Stock: Telescoping wire, composition pistol grip.
Sights: Hooded post front, adjustable aperture rear.
Features: Semi-auto only. Matte black finish. From Feather Enterpirses. Announced 1988.
Price: **$499.95**

Galil Auto Rifle

GALIL 308 AR SEMI-AUTO RIFLE

Caliber: 308 Win., 25-shot magazine.
Barrel: 18.5″.
Weight: 9.6 lbs. **Length:** 39″ over-all (stock extended).
Stock: Tube-type metal folding stock.
Sights: Post-type front, flip-type "L" rear.
Features: Gas operated, rotating bolt. Cocking handle, safety and magazine catch can be operated from either side. Introduced 1982. Imported from Israel by Action Arms Ltd.
Price: **$849.00**
Price: As above in 223 (16.1″ bbl., 36.5″ o.a.l., 35-shot magazine)... **$795.00**

Galil Model ARM Semi-Auto Rifle

Similar to the standard AR models except comes with folding bipod with integral wire cutter, vented hardwood handguard and carrying handle. Other specs are the same. Introduced 1987.
Price: 223 .... **$875.00**
Price: 308 .... **$940.00**

Goncz Carbine

GONCZ HIGH-TECH CARBINE

Caliber: 9mm Para., 30 Mauser, 38 Super, 18- and 32-shot magazine; 45 ACP, 10- and 20-shot magazine.
Barrel: 16.1″.
Weight: 4 lbs., 2 oz. **Length:** 31″ over-all.
Stock: Grooved alloy pistol grip, black high-impact plastic butt. Walnut optional at extra cost.
Sights: Front adjustable for e., rear adjustable for w.
Features: Fires from closed bolt; floating firing pin; safety locks the firing pin; all metal construction; barrel threaded for accessories. Matte black oxide and anodized finish. Designed by Lajos J. Goncz. Introduced 1985. From Goncz Co.
Price: **$385.00**
Price: With halogen light **$500.00**
Price: With laser sight system **$1,495.00**

Heckler & Koch HK-91

HECKLER & KOCH HK-91 AUTO RIFLE

Caliber: 308 Win., 5- or 20-shot magazine.
Barrel: 17.71″.
Weight: 9½ lbs. **Length:** 40¼″ over-all.
Stock: Black high-impact plastic.
Sights: Post front, aperture rear adj. for w. and e.
Features: Delayed roller-lock action. Sporting version of West German service rifle. Takes special H&K clamp scope mount. Imported from West Germany by Heckler & Koch, Inc.
Price: HK-91 A-2 with plastic stock **$932.00**
Price: HK-91 A-3 with retractable metal stock **$1,098.00**
Price: HK-91 scope mount with 1″ rings **$346.00**

Heckler & Koch HK-93 Auto Rifle

Similar to HK-91 except in 223 cal., 16.13″ barrel, over-all length of 35½″, weighs 7¾ lbs. Same stock, fore-end.
Price: HK-93 A-2 with plastic stock **$932.00**
Price: HK-93 A-3 with retractable metal stock **$1,098.00**

CAUTION: PRICES CHANGE. CHECK AT GUNSHOP.

Heckler & Koch HK-94

HECKLER & KOCH HK-94 AUTO CARBINE

Caliber: 9mm Parabellum, 15-shot magazine.
Barrel: 16".
Weight: 6½ lbs. (fixed stock). **Length:** 34¾" over-all.
Stock: High-impact plastic butt and fore-end or retractable metal stock.
Sights: Hooded post front, aperture rear adjustable for windage and elevation.
Features: Delayed roller-locked action; accepts H&K quick-detachable scope mount. Introduced 1983. Imported from West Germany by Heckler & Koch, Inc.
Price: HK-94-A2 (fixed stock) **$932.00**
Price: HK-94-A3 (retractable metal stock) **$1,098.00**
Price: 30-shot magazine....................................... **$33.75**
Price: Clamp to hold two magazines **$25.00**

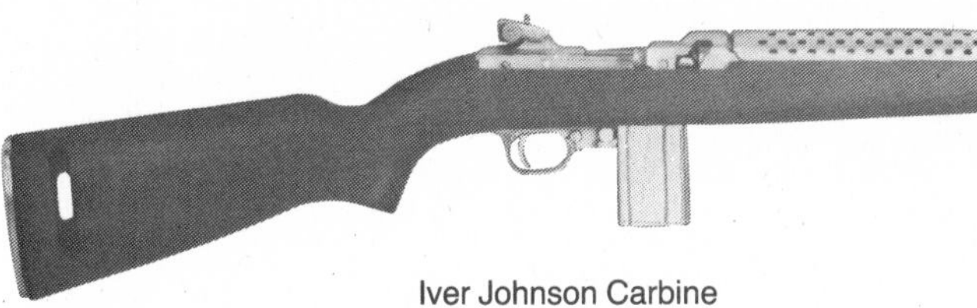

Iver Johnson Carbine

IVER JOHNSON PM30HB CARBINE

Caliber: 30 U.S. Carbine.
Barrel: 18" four-groove.
Weight: 6½ lbs. **Length:** 35½" over-all.
Stock: Glossy-finished hardwood or walnut.
Sights: Click adj. peep rear.
Features: Gas operated semi-auto carbine. 15-shot detachable magazine. Made in U.S.A.
Price: Blue finish, hardwood stock **$265.00**
Price: Blue finish, walnut stock **$291.50**
Price: Paratrooper.. **$291.50**

MAS 223 Auto

MAS 223 SEMI-AUTO RIFLE

Caliber: 223, 25-shot magazine.
Barrel: 19.2".
Weight: About 8 lbs. **Length:** 29.8" over-all.
Stock: Rubber-covered adjustable check piece converts to left- or right-hand shooters.
Sights: Adjustable blade front with luminescent spot for night use, aperture adj. rear.
Features: Converts to left- or right-hand ejection. Armored plastic guards vital parts, including sights. Civilian version of the French FAMAS assault rifle. Introduced 1986. Imported from France by Century Arms.
Price: With spare parts kit, bipod, sling, spare magazine, about ... **$1,295.00**

Mitchell AK-47

MITCHELL AK-47 SEMI-AUTO RIFLE

Caliber: 223, 308, 7.62x39, 30-shot magazine.
Barrel: 19.6".
Weight: 9.1 lbs. **Length:** 40.6" over-all with wood stock.
Stock: Teak.
Sights: Hooded post front, open adj. rear.
Features: Gas operated semi-automatic. Last-round bolt hold-open. Imported from Yugoslavia by Mitchell Arms.
Price: Wood stock **$675.00**
Price: With folding metal stock **$698.00**

Mitchell Heavy Barrel AK-47

Same gun as the standard AK-47 except has heavy finned barrel, heavy fore-end, fully adjustable day or night sights. Available with or without folding, detachable bipod.
Price: **$995.00**

Mitchell M-76

MITCHELL M-76 COUNTER-SNIPER RIFLE

Caliber: 7.9 mm.
Barrel: 21.8". Muzzle brake, flash hider.
Weight: 10.9 lbs. **Length:** 44.6" over-all.
Stock: Teak.
Features: Uses AK-47 action. Optional scope, night sight, mounts available. Imported from Yugoslavia by Mitchell Arms.
Price: **$1,525.00**

MITCHELL M-59 SEMI-AUTO RIFLE
Caliber: 7.62x39, 10-shot magazine.
Barrel: 18″.
Weight: 9 lbs. **Length:** 44″ over-all.
Stock: Walnut.
Sights: Hooded post front, open adj. rear.
Features: Gas-operated likeness of the SKS rifle. Imported from Yugoslavia by Mitchell Arms.
Price: **$666.00**

NORINCO OFFICER'S NINE CARBINE
Caliber: 9mm Parabellum, 25-round magazine.
Barrel: 16.1″.
Weight: 8.4 lbs. **Length:** 24.4″ over-all (stock folded).
Stock: Folding metal.
Sights: Post-type front, flip-type rear.
Features: Blue finish. Similar to the famous Israeli submachine gun. Imported from China by Pacific International. Introduced 1988.
Price: **$459.95**

Poly Tech AK47/S

POLY TECH AK-47/S AUTO RIFLE
Caliber: 7.62x39, 30-shot magazine; optional 5-, 20- 40-shot box magazines, 75-round drum magazine available.
Barrel: 16⅜″.
Weight: 8.2 lbs. **Length:** 34⅜″ over-all.
Stock: Oil-finished Chiu wood.
Sights: Protected post front, leaf rear graduated to 800 meters.
Features: Semi-auto version of the original AK-47. Receiver is machined from bar stock. Chrome lined barrel, chromed gas piston; phosphated bolt and bolt carrier. Spring-loaded firing pin. Comes with three 30-shot magazines, cleaning kit, web sling, oil bottle and an original AK-47-pattern bayonet. Imported from China by Poly Technologies, Inc.
Price: **$579.95**

Poly Tech AKS-762 Folding Stock Rifle
Similar to the AKS-762 Wood Stock rifle except has side-folding skeleton stock. Semi-auto version of the Chinese Type 56-2 assault rifle. No bayonet mount.
Price: **$449.95**

Poly Tech M-14/S

POLY TECH M-14/S AUTO RIFLE
Caliber: 7.62mm NATO, 20-shot box magazine.
Barrel: 22″ (without flash hider).
Weight: 9.2 lbs. **Length:** 43 3/10″ over-all.
Stock: Oil-finished Chinese walnut, fiberglass handguard (walnut optional).
Sights: Square blade front, click adjustable aperture rear.
Features: Semi-auto only. Receiver is machined from chrome-moly steel. Chrome lined barrel, chromed gas piston. Parkerized finish. Announced 1988. Imported from China by Poly Technologies, Inc.
Price: **$709.95**

POLY TECH AKS-762 AUTO RIFLE
Caliber: 7.62x39, 30-shot magazine; optional 5-, 20- and 40-shot, 75-round drum magazines available.
Barrel: 16⅜″.
Weight: About 8.4 lbs. **Length:** 34⅜″ over-all.
Stock: Oil-finished Chiu wood.
Sights: Hooded post front, leaf rear graduated to 800 meters.
Features: Semi-auto version of the Chinese Type 56 (AKM) rifle. Chrome-lined barrel, chromed gas piston, phospated bolt and bolt carrier, rest blued. Spring-loaded firing pin. Comes with detachable Type 56 spike bayonet, sling, cleaning kit, oil bottle. Imported from China by Poly Technologies, Inc.
Price: Wood or folding metal stock **$419.95**

Ruger Mini Thirty

RUGER MINI-14/5R RANCH RIFLE
Caliber: 223 Rem., 5-shot detachable box magazine.
Barrel: 18½″.
Weight: 6.4 lbs. **Length:** 37¼″ over-all.
Stock: American hardwood, steel reinforced.
Sights: Ramp front, fully adj. rear.
Features: Fixed piston gas-operated, positive primary extraction. New buffer system, redesigned ejector system. Ruger S100RH scope rings included. 20-shot magazines available from Ruger dealers, 30-shot magazine available only to police departments and government agencies.
Price: Mini-14/5R, blued **$437.00**
Price: Mini-14/5RF, blued, folding stock **$515.00**
Price: K Mini-14/5R, stainless **$478.50**
Price: K Mini-14/5RF, stainless, folding stock.......... **$541.00**

Ruger Mini Thirty Rifle
Similar to the Mini-14 Ranch Rifle except modified to chamber the 7.62x39 Russian service round. Weight is about 7 lbs., 3 oz. Has 6-groove barrel with 1-10″ twist, Ruger Integral Scope Mount bases and folding peep rear sight. Detachable 5-shot staggered box magazine. Blued finish. Introduced 1987.
Price: **$437.00**

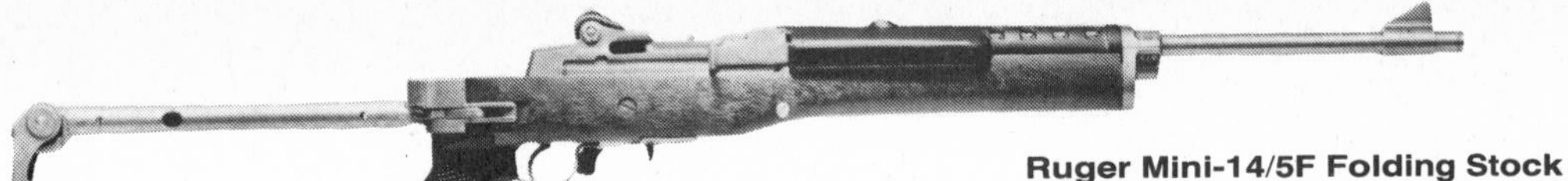

Ruger Mini-14/5F

Ruger Mini-14/5F Folding Stock

Same as the Ranch Rifle except available with folding stock, checkered high impact plastic vertical pistol grip. Over-all length with stock open is 37¾", length closed is 27½". Weight is about 7¾ lbs.

Price: Blued ordnance steel, standard stock, Mini-14/5 .... **$437.00**
Price: Stainless, K-Mini 14/5 .... **$447.00**
Price: Blued, folding stock, Mini-14/5 F **$483.50**
Price: Stainless, folding stock, K-Mini-14/5 F **$514.50**

Spectre Carbine

SPECTRE AUTO CARBINE

Caliber: 9mm Para., 30-shot magazine.
Barrel: 16.5".
Weight: 5.3 lbs. **Length:** 35.5" over-all (stock extended).
Stock: Folding metal.
Sights: Post front, two-position flip rear.
Features: Double- or single-action fire; 50-shot magazine available. Introduced 1987. Imported by Mitchell Arms, Inc.
Price: **$680.00**

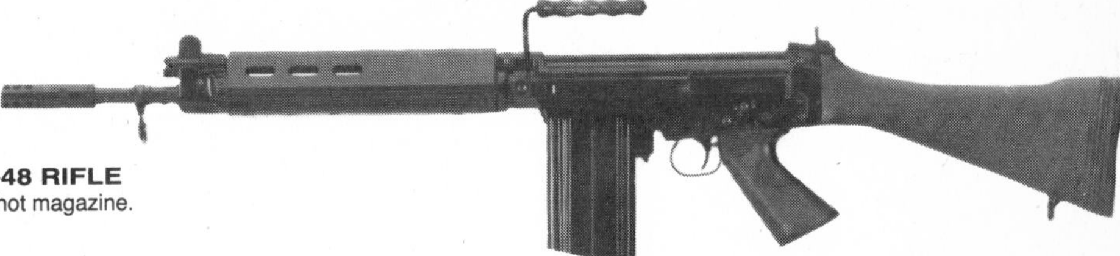

Springfield Armory SAR-48 Bush

SPRINGFIELD ARMORY SAR-48 RIFLE

Caliber: 7.62mm NATO (308 Win.), 20-shot magazine.
Barrel: 21".
Weight: 9.9 lbs. **Length:** 43.3" over-all.
Stock: Fiberglass.
Sights: Adjustable front, adjustable peep rear.
Features: New production. Introduced 1985. From Springfield Armory.
Price: Standard model **$899.00**
Price: "Bush" rifle, 18" barrel **$899.00**
Price: Heavy Barrel rifle **$899.00**
Price: Model 22, 22 LR trainer **$760.00**
Price: Para model, folding stock **$969.00**

Springfield Armory M1A

SPRINGFIELD ARMORY M1A RIFLE

Caliber: 7.62mm NATO (308), 243 Win., 5-, 10- or 20-shot box magazine.
Barrel: $25\frac{1}{16}$" with flash suppressor, 22" without suppressor.
Weight: 8¾ lbs. **Length:** 44¼" over-all.
Stock: American walnut or birch with walnut colored heat-resistant fiberglass handguard. Matching walnut handguard available.
Sights: Military, square blade front, full click-adjustable aperture rear.
Features: Commercial equivalent of the U.S. M-14 service rifle with no provision for automatic firing. From Springfield Armory. Military accessories available including 3-9x56 ART scope and mount.
Price: Standard M1A rifle, about **$782.00**
Price: Match Grade, about **$998.00**
Price: Super Match (heavy premium barrel), about **$1,231.00**
Price: M1A-A1 Assault Rifle, walnut stock, about **$859.00**
Price: As above, folding stock, about **$874.00**

Springfield Armory BM-59 Alpine

SPRINGFIELD ARMORY BM-59

Caliber: 7.62mm NATO (308 Win.), 20-shot box magazine.
Barrel: 17.5".
Weight: 9¼ lbs. **Length:** 38.5" over-all.
Stock: Walnut, with trapped rubber butt pad.
Sights: Military square blade front, click adj. peep rear.
Features: Full military-dress Italian service rifle. Available in selective fire or semi-auto only. Refined version of the M-1 Garand. Accessories available include: folding alpine stock, muzzle brake/flash suppressor/grenade launcher combo, bipod, winter trigger, grenade launcher sights, bayonet, oiler. Extremely limited quantities. Introduced 1981.
Price: Standard Italian model, about **$1,248.00**
Price: Alpine model, about **$1,435.00**
Price: Alpine Paratrooper model, about **$1,624.00**
Price: Nigerian Mark IV model, about **$1,365.00**

Springfield Armory M1

SPRINGFIELD ARMORY M1 GARAND RIFLE

Caliber: 308, 30-06, 8-shot clip.
Barrel: 24".
Weight: 9½ lbs. **Length:** 43½" over-all.
Stock: Walnut, military.
Sights: Military square blade front, click adjustable peep rear.
Features: Commercially-made M-1 Garand duplicates the original service rifle. Introduced 1979. From Springfield Armory.
Price: Standard, about **$761.00**
Price: National Match, about **$897.00**
Price: Ultra Match, about.......... **$1,033.00**
Price: M1-D Sniper, no scope or mount, about.......... **$1,033.00**
Price: M1-T26 "Tanker," walnut stock, about.......... **$797.00**
Price: As above, folding stock, about.......... **$774.00**
Price: Standard M-1 Garand with Beretta-made receiver, about... **$1,510.00**

STEYR A.U.G. AUTOLOADING RIFLE

Caliber: 223 Rem.
Barrel: 20".
Weight: 8½ lbs. **Length:** 31" over-all.
Stock: Synthetic, green. One-piece moulding houses receiver group, hammer mechanism and magazine.
Sights: 1.5x scope only; scope and mount form the carrying handle.
Features: Semi-automatic, gas-operated action; can be converted to suit right or left-handed shooters, including ejection port. Transparent 30- or 40-shot magazines. Folding vertical front grip. Introduced 1983. Imported from Austria by Gun South, Inc.
Price: Right or left-hand model.......... **$1,362.00**

Steyr A.U.G. Rifle

UZI® CARBINE

Caliber: 9mm Parabellum, 41 Action Express, 45 ACP.
Barrel: 16.1".
Weight: 8.4 lbs. **Length:** 24.4" (stock folded).
Stock: Folding metal stock. Wood stock available as an accessory.
Sights: Post-type front, "L" flip-type rear adj. for 100 meters and 200 meters. Both click-adjustable for w. and e.
Features: Adapted to meet BATF regulations, this semi-auto has the same qualities as the famous submachine gun. Made by Israel Military Industries. Comes in moulded carrying case with sling, magazine, sight adjustment key. Exclusively imported from Israel by Action Arms Ltd. 9mm introduced 1980; 45 ACP introduced 1985; 41 A.E. introduced 1987.
Price:.......... **$698.00**

UZI Carbine

UZI® Mini Carbine
Similar to the UZI Carbine except shorter receiver dimensions and has a forward-folding metal stock. Available in 9mm Para. or 45 ACP; 19.75" barrel; over-all length of 35.75" (26.1" folded); weight is 7.2 lbs. Introduced 1987.
Price:.......... **$698.00**

Valmet M-76

Valmet M78 Semi-Auto
Similar to M76 except chambered only for 308 Win., has 24¼" heavy barrel, weighs 11 lbs., 43¼" over-all; 20-shot magazine; bipod; machined receiver. Length of pull on wood stock dimensioned for American shooters. Rear sight adjustable for w. and e., open-aperture front sight; folding carrying handle. Imported from Finland by Valmet.
Price:.......... **$999.00**

VALMET M-76 STANDARD RIFLE

Caliber: 223, 15 or 30-shot magazine, or 308, 20-shot magazine.
Barrel: 16¾".
Weight: About 8½ lbs. **Length:** 37¾" over-all.
Stock: Wood, synthetic or folding metal type; composition fore-end.
Sights: Hooded adjustable post front, peep rear with luminous night sight.
Features: Semi-automatic only. Has sling swivels, flash suppressor. Bayonet, cleaning kit, 30-shot magazine, scope adaptor cover optional. Imported from Finland by Valmet.
Price: Wood stock.......... **$699.00**
Price: Folding stock.......... **$825.00**
Price: Synthetic stock.......... **$795.00**

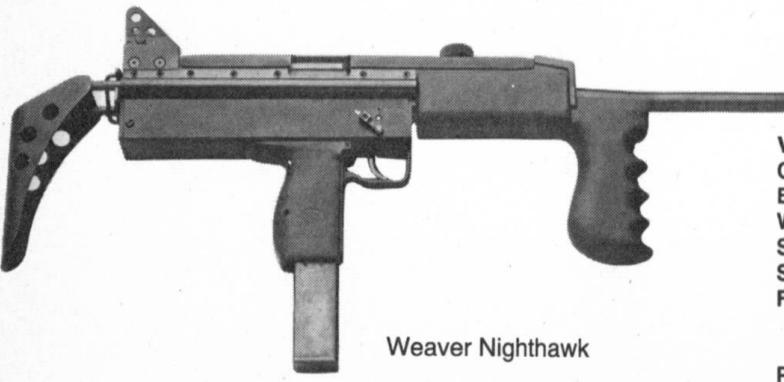
Weaver Nighthawk

WEAVER ARMS NIGHTHAWK

Caliber: 9mm Para., 25-shot magazine.
Barrel: 16.1".
Weight: 7 lbs. **Length:** 26½" (stock retracted).
Stock: Retractable metal frame.
Sights: Hooded blade front, adjustable peep V rear.
Features: Semi-auto fire only; fires from a closed bolt. Has 21" sight radius. Black nylon pistol grip and finger-groove front grip. Matte black finish. Introduced 1983. From Weaver Arms Corp.
Price:.......... **$525.00**

Includes models for hunting, adaptable to and suitable for certain competition.

Browning High Power Rifle

BROWNING HIGH-POWER AUTO RIFLE

Caliber: 243, 270, 280, 30-06, 308.
Barrel: 22″ round tapered.
Weight: 7⅜ lbs. **Length:** 43″ over-all.
Stock: French walnut p.g. stock (13⅝″×2″×1⅝″) and fore-end, hand checkered.
Sights: Adj. folding-leaf rear, gold bead on hooded ramp front, or no sights.
Features: Detachable 4-round magazine. Receiver tapped for scope mounts. Trigger pull 3½ lbs. Imported from Belgium by Browning.
Price: Grade I, with sights **$574.95**
Price: Grade I, no sights.................................... **$559.95**

Browning Big Game BAR

Similar to the standard BAR except has silver-gray receiver with engraved and gold inlaid whitetail deer on the right side, a mule deer on the left; a gold-edged scroll banner frames "One of Six Hundred" on the left side, the numerical edition number replaces "One" on the right. Chambered only in 30-06. Fancy, highly figured walnut stock and fore-end. Introduced 1983.
Price: **$3,550.00**

Browning Magnum Auto Rifle

Same as the standard caliber model, except weighs 8⅜ lbs., 45″ over-all, 24″ bbl., 3-round mag. Cals. 7mm Mag., 300 Win. Mag., 338 Win. Mag.
Price: Grade I, with sights **$634.95**
Price: Grade I, no sights.................................... **$619.95**

Heckler & Koch HK630

HECKLER & KOCH HK770 AUTO RIFLE

Caliber: 308 Win., 3-shot magazine.
Barrel: 19.6″.
Weight: 7½ lbs. **Length:** 42.8″ over-all.
Stock: European walnut. Checkered p.g. and fore-end.
Sights: Vertically adjustable blade front, open, fold-down, rear adj. for w.
Features: Has the delayed roller-locked system and polygonal rifling. Magazine catch located at front of trigger guard. Receiver top is dovetailed to accept clamp-type scope mount. Imported from West Germany by Heckler & Koch, Inc. Limited availability.
Price: **$797.00**
Price: HK630,223 Rem.................................... **$784.00**
Price: HK940, 30-06 .... **$917.00**

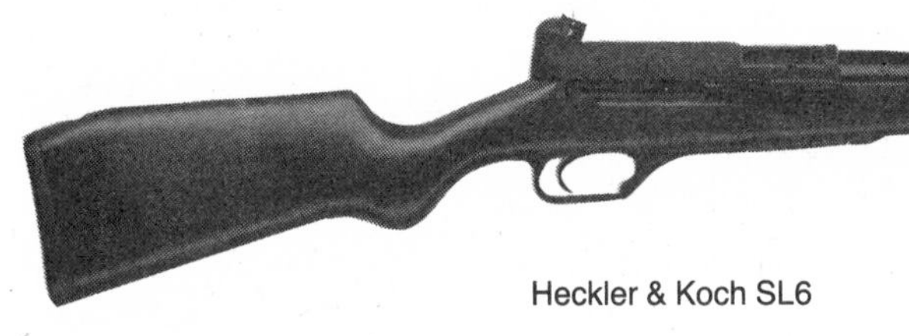

Heckler & Koch SL6

HECKLER & KOCH SL7 AUTO RIFLE

Caliber: 308 Win., 3-shot magazine.
Barrel: 17″.
Weight: 8 lbs. **Length:** 39¾″ over-all.
Stock: European walnut, oil finished.
Sights: Hooded post front, adjustable aperture rear.
Features: Delayed roller-locked action; polygon rifling; receiver is dovetailed for H&K quick-detachable scope mount. Introduced 1983. Imported from West Germany by Heckler & Koch, Inc. Limited availability.
Price: **$797.00**
Price: Model SL6 (as above except in 223 Rem.) **$784.00**

Marlin Model 45

MARLIN MODEL 9 CAMP CARBINE

Caliber: 9mm Parabellum, 12-shot magazine (20-shot available).
Barrel: 16½″, Micro-Groove® rifling.
Weight: 6¾ lbs. **Length:** 35½″ over-all.
Stock: Walnut-finished hardwood; rubber butt pad; Mar-Shield® finish.
Sights: Ramp front with bead with Wide-Scan™ hood, adjustable open rear.
Features: Manual bolt hold-open; Garand-type safety, magazine safety; loaded chamber indicator; receiver drilled, tapped for scope mounting. Introduced 1985.
Price: **$294.95**

Marlin Model 45 Carbine

Similar to the Model 9 except chambered for 45 ACP, 7-shot magazine. Introduced 1986.
Price: **$294.95**

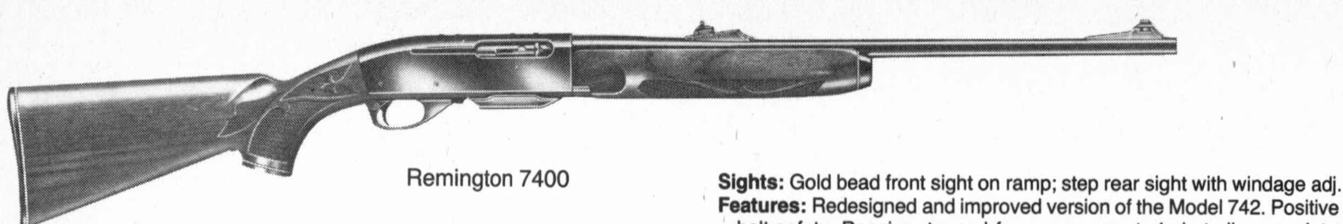

Remington 7400

REMINGTON MODEL 7400 AUTO RIFLE

Caliber: 243 Win., 270 Win., 280 Rem., 308 Win. and 30-06, 4-shot magazine.
Barrel: 22" round tapered.
Weight: 7½ lbs. **Length:** 42" over-all.
Stock: Walnut, deluxe cut checkered p.g. and fore-end.
Sights: Gold bead front sight on ramp; step rear sight with windage adj.
Features: Redesigned and improved version of the Model 742. Positive cross-bolt safety. Receiver tapped for scope mount. 4-shot clip mag. Introduced 1981.
Price: About **$440.00**
Price: Carbine (18½" bbl., 30-06 only) **$440.00**
Price: D Grade, about **$2,291.00**
Price: F Grade, about **$4,720.00**
Price: F Grade with gold inlays, about **$7,079.00**

Valmet Hunter

VALMET HUNTER AUTO RIFLE

Caliber: 223, 15-, 30-shot magazines; 243, 9-shot magazine; 308, 5- 9- and 20-shot magazines.
Barrel: 20½".
Weight: 8 lbs. **Length:** 42" over-all.
Stock: American walnut butt and fore-end. Checkered palm-swell p.g. and fore-end.
Sights: Blade front, open flip-type rear.
Features: Uses semi-auto Kalashnikov-type gas-operated action with rotating bolt. Stock is adjustable for length via spacers. Optional cleaning kit, sling, ejection buffer, scope mount. Introduced 1986. Imported from Finland by Valmet.
Price: **$795.00**

CENTERFIRE RIFLES—LEVER, SLIDE & MISC.

Both classic arms and recent designs in American-style repeaters for sport and field shooting.

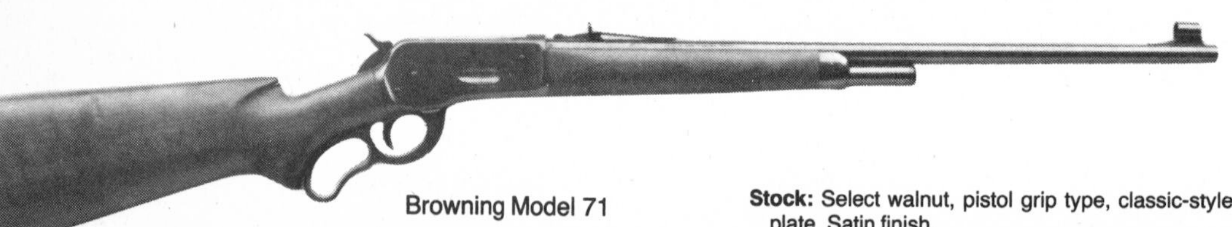

Browning Model 71

BROWNING MODEL 71 LEVER ACTION RIFLE

Caliber: 348 Win., 4-shot magazine.
Barrel: 20" (Carbine), 24" (Rifle).
Weight: 8 lbs., 2 oz. (Rifle). **Length:** 45" over-all (Rifle).
Stock: Select walnut, pistol grip type, classic-style fore-end. Flat metal butt-plate. Satin finish.
Sights: Hooded front, open buckhorn rear.
Features: Reproduction of the Winchester Model 71 with half-length magazine tube, uncheckered wood; blue finish. High Grade model has extra quality wood with high gloss finish and fine checkering. Barrel and magazine are blued, receiver and lever are grayed and have scroll engraving with gold plated big game. Production limited to 3,000 Rifles, 3,000 Carbines. Introduced 1987. Imported from Japan by Browning.
Price: Grade I, Rifle or Carbine **$599.95**
Price: High Grade, Rifle or Carbine **$979.95**

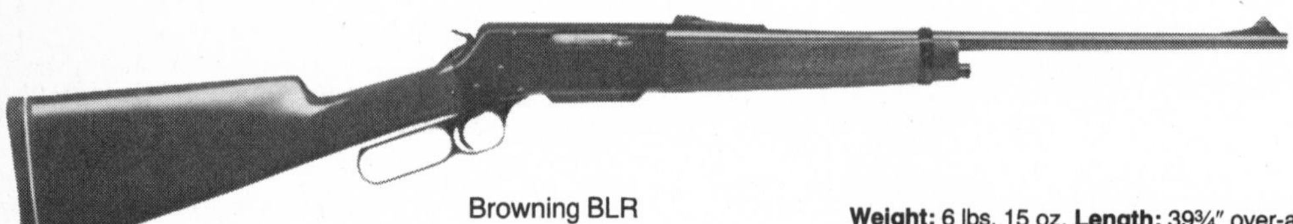

Browning BLR

BROWNING BLR MODEL 81 LEVER ACTION RIFLE

Caliber: 222, 223, 22-250, 243, 257 Roberts, 7mm-08, 308 Win. or 358 Win., 4-shot detachable magazine.
Barrel: 20" round tapered.
Weight: 6 lbs. 15 oz. **Length:** 39¾" over-all.
Stock: Checkered straight grip and fore-end, oil finished walnut. Gold bead on hooded ramp front; low profile square notch adj. rear, or no sights.
Sights: Gold bead on hooded ramp front; low profile square notch adj. rear.
Features: Wide, grooved trigger; half-cock hammer safety. Receiver tapped for scope mount. Recoil pad installed. Imported from Japan by Browning.
Price: With sights **$472.50**
Price: No sights **$457.50**

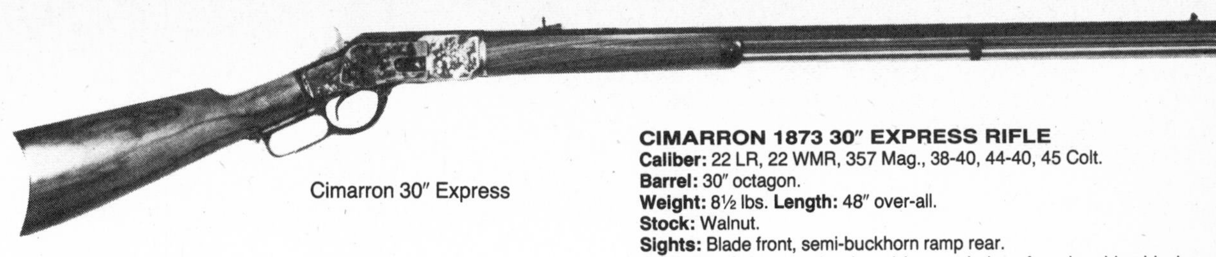

Cimarron 30″ Express

CIMARRON 1873 30″ EXPRESS RIFLE
Caliber: 22 LR, 22 WMR, 357 Mag., 38-40, 44-40, 45 Colt.
Barrel: 30″ octagon.
Weight: 8½ lbs. **Length:** 48″ over-all.
Stock: Walnut.
Sights: Blade front, semi-buckhorn ramp rear.
Features: Color case-hardened frame; choice of modern blue-black or charcoal blue for other parts. Barrel marked "Kings Improvement." From Cimarron Arms.
Price: **$695.00**

Cimarron 1873 "Button" Half-Magazine
Similar to the 1873 Express except has 24″ barrel with half-magazine.
Price: **$695.00**

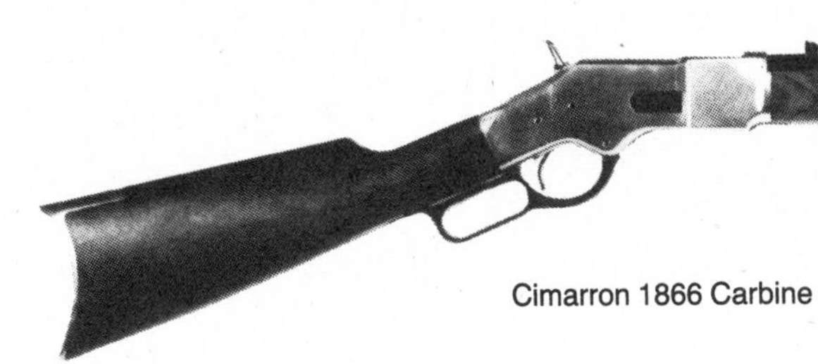

Cimarron 1866 Carbine

CIMARRON 1866 HALF-MAGAZINE CARBINE
Caliber: 22 LR, 22 WMR, 38 Spec., 38-40, 44-40.
Barrel: 24″.
Weight: 7½ lbs. **Length:** 43″ over-all.
Stock: Walnut.
Sights: Blade front, original-type folding rear.
Features: Half-magazine style (button). Choice of modern blue-black or old-style charcoal blue. From Cimarron Arms.
Price: **$595.00**

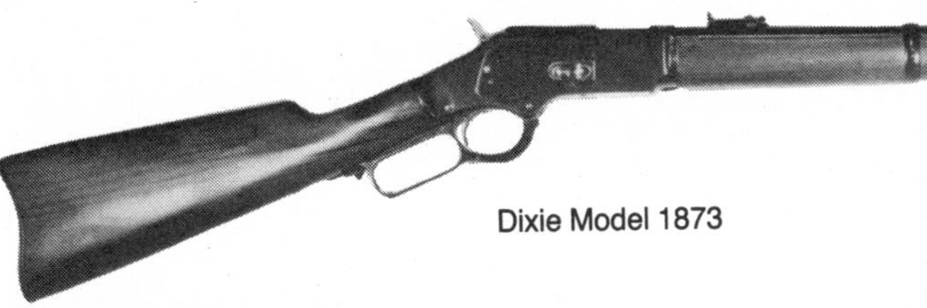

Dixie Model 1873

DIXIE ENGRAVED MODEL 1873 RIFLE
Caliber: 44-40, 11-shot magazine.
Barrel: 20″, round.
Weight: 7¾ lbs. **Length:** 39″ over-all.
Stock: Walnut.
Sights: Blade front, adj. rear.
Features: Engraved and case hardened frame. Duplicate of Winchester 1873. Made in Italy. From Dixie Gun Works.
Price: **$595.00**
Price: Plain, blued carbine **$495.00**

E.M.F. HENRY CARBINE
Caliber: 44-40 or 44 rimfire.
Barrel: 21″.
Weight: About 9 lbs. **Length:** About 39″ over-all.
Stock: Oil stained American walnut.
Sights: Blade front, rear adj. for e.
Features: Reproduction of the original Henry carbine with brass frame and buttplate, rest blued. From E.M.F.
Price: Standard **$1,380.00**
Price: Engraved **$1,598.00**

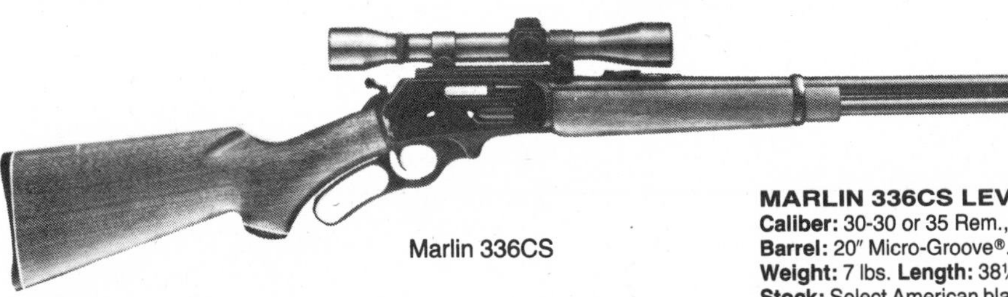

Marlin 336CS

MARLIN 336CS LEVER ACTION CARBINE
Caliber: 30-30 or 35 Rem., 6-shot tubular magazine.
Barrel: 20″ Micro-Groove®.
Weight: 7 lbs. **Length:** 38½″ over-all.
Stock: Select American black walnut, capped p.g. with white line spacers. Mar-Shield® finish.
Sights: Ramp front with Wide-Scan™ hood, semi-buckhorn folding rear adj. for w. & e.
Features: Hammer-block safety. Receiver tapped for scope mount, offset hammer spur; top of receiver sand blasted to prevent glare.
Price: Less scope **$325.95**

Marlin 30AS Lever Action Carbine
Same as the Marlin 336CS except has walnut-finished hardwood p.g. stock, 30-30 only, 6-shot. Hammer-block safety.
Price: **$320.95**

Marlin 336LTS

Marlin 336LTS Lever Action Carbine
Similar to the 336CS except has 16¼″ barrel, weighs 6½ lbs., and over-all length of 34⅜″. Rubber rifle butt pad. Introduced 1988.
Price: **$325.95**

Marlin 1894S

MARLIN 1894S LEVER ACTION CARBINE
Caliber: 41 Magnum, 44 Special, 44 Magnum, 45 Colt, 10-shot tubular magazine
Barrel: 20″ Micro-Groove®.
Weight: 6 lbs. **Length:** 37½″ over-all.
Stock: American black walnut, straight grip and fore-end. Mar-Shield® finish. Rubber rifle butt pad.
Sights: Wide-Scan™ hooded ramp front, semi-buckhorn folding rear adj. for w. & e.
Features: Hammer-block safety. Receiver tapped for scope mount, offset hammer spur, solid top receiver sand blasted to prevent glare.
Price: **$357.95**

Marlin Model 1894CL Rifle
Similar to the 1894S except chambered for 25-20 Win. and 32-20 Win. Has 6-shot magazine, 22″ barrel with standard rifling, over-all length of 38¾″, weight of 6¼ lbs. Introduced 1988.
Price: **$383.95**

Marlin Model 1894CS Carbine
Similar to the standard Model 1894S except chambered for 38 Special/357 Magnum with 9-shot magazine, 18½″ barrel, hammer-block safety, brass bead front sight. Introduced 1983.
Price: **$357.95**

Marlin 1894CL

Marlin Model 1894CL Classic
Similar to the 1894CS except chambered for 25-20 and 32-20 Win. Has 6-shot magazine, 22″ barrel with 6-groove rifling, brass bead front sight, adjustable semi-buckhorn folding rear. Hammer block safety. Weighs 6¼ lbs., over-all length of 38¾″. Introduced 1988.
Price: **$383.95**

MARLIN 444SS LEVER ACTION SPORTER
Caliber: 444 Marlin, 5-shot tubular magazine.
Barrel: 22″ Micro-Groove®.
Weight: 7½ lbs. **Length:** 40½″ over-all.
Stock: American black walnut, capped p.g. with white line spacers, rubber rifle butt pad. Mar-Shield® finish; swivel studs.
Sights: Hooded ramp front, folding semi-buckhorn rear adj. for w. & e.
Features: Hammer-block safety. Receiver tapped for scope mount; offset hammer spur.
Price: **$385.95**

MARLIN 1895SS LEVER ACTION RIFLE
Caliber: 45-70, 4-shot tubular magazine.
Barrel: 22″ round.
Weight: 7½ lbs. **Length:** 40½″ over-all.
Stock: American black walnut, full pistol grip. Mar-Shield® finish; rubber butt-pad; q.d. swivel studs.
Sights: Bead front with Wide-Scan™ hood, semi-buckhorn folding rear adj. for w. & e.
Features: Hammer-block safety. Solid receiver tapped for scope mounts or receiver sights; offset hammer spur.
Price: **$385.95**

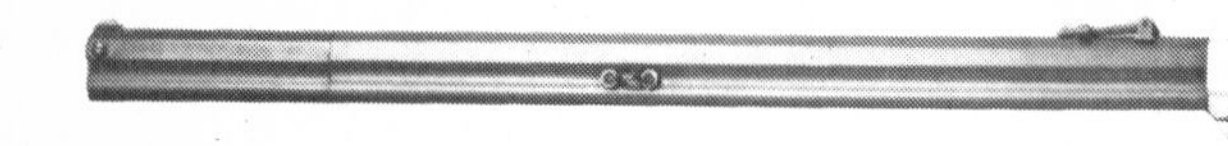

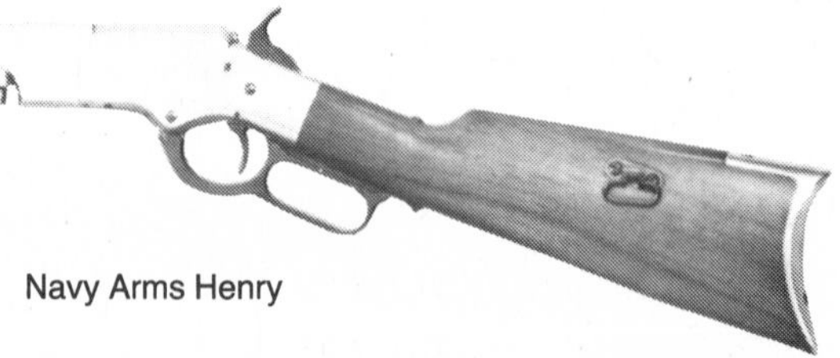

Navy Arms Henry

NAVY ARMS HENRY CARBINE
Caliber: 44-40 or 44 rimfire.
Barrel: 24″.
Weight: About 8¼ lbs. **Length:** 39″ over-all.
Stock: Oil-stained American walnut.
Sights: Blade front, rear adj. for e.
Features: Reproduction of the original Henry carbine with brass frame and buttplate, rest blued. Will be produced in limited edition of 1,000 standard models, plus 50 engraved guns. Made in U.S. by Navy Arms.
Price: Standard **$769.00**
Price: Engraved **$1,849.00**
Price: Iron Frame rifle (similar to Carbine except has blued frame) . **$933.00**
Price: Military Rifle (similar to Carbine except has sling swivels, different rear sight) **$769.00**
Price: Trapper model (16½″ bbl., 7¼ lbs., 34½″ o.a.l.) **$769.00**

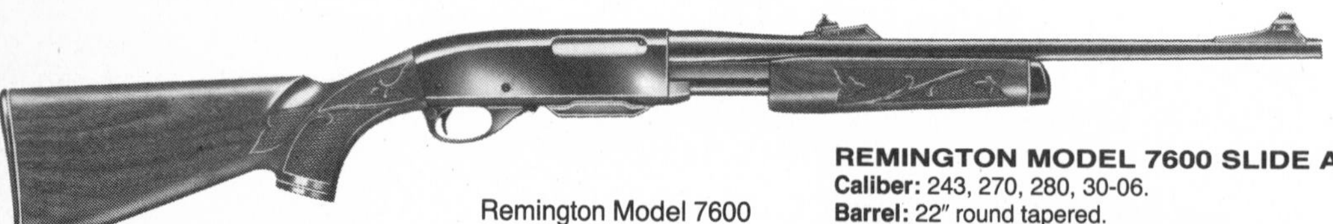

Remington Model 7600

REMINGTON MODEL 7600 SLIDE ACTION
Caliber: 243, 270, 280, 30-06.
Barrel: 22″ round tapered.
Weight: 7½ lbs. **Length:** 42″ over-all.
Stock: Cut-checkered walnut p.g. and fore-end, Monte Carlo with full cheekpiece.
Sights: Gold bead front sight on matted ramp, open step adj. sporting rear.
Features: Redesigned and improved version of the Model 760. Detachable 4-shot clip. Cross-bolt safety. Receiver tapped for scope mount. Also available in high grade versions. Introduced 1981.
Price: About **$400.00**
Price: Carbine (18½″ bbl., 30-06 only) **$400.00**

Consult our Directory pages for the location of firms mentioned.

Rossi Carbine

ROSSI SADDLE-RING CARBINE M92 SRC
Caliber: 38 Spec./357 Mag., 44 Spec./44-40, 44 Mag., 10-shot magazine.
Barrel: 20″.
Weight: 5¾ lbs. **Length:** 37″ over-all.
Stock: Walnut.
Sights: Blade front, buckhorn rear.
Features: Recreation of the famous lever-action carbine. Handles 38 and 357 interchangeably. Has high-relief puma medallion inlaid in the receiver. Introduced 1978. Imported by Interarms.
Price: **$282.00**
Price: Blue, engraved **$327.00**
Price: 44 Spec./44 Mag. (Model 65) **$297.00**

Rossi Puma M92 SRS Short Carbine
Similar to the standard M92 except has 16″ barrel, over-all length of 33″, in 38/357 only. Puma medallion on side of receiver. Introduced 1986.
Price: **$282.00**

Savage Model 99C

SAVAGE 99C LEVER ACTION RIFLE
Caliber: 243 or 308 Win., detachable 4-shot magazine.
Barrel: 22″, chrome-moly steel.
Weight: 8 lbs. **Length:** 41¾″ over-all.
Stock: Walnut with checkered p.g. and fore-end, Monte Carlo comb.
Sights: Hooded ramp front, adjustable ramp rear sight. Tapped for scope mounts.
Features: Grooved trigger, top tang slide safety locks trigger and lever. Brown rubber butt pad, q.d. swivel studs, push-button magazine release.
Price: **$459.00**

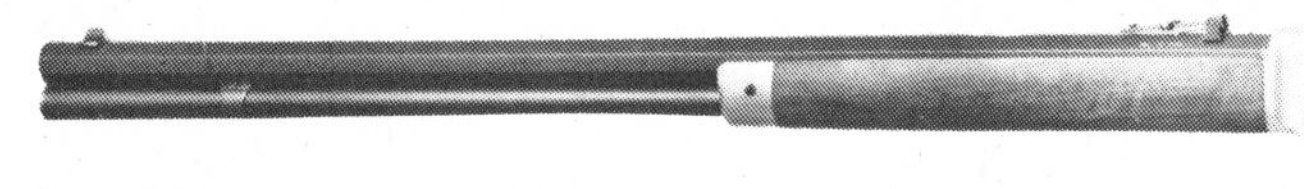

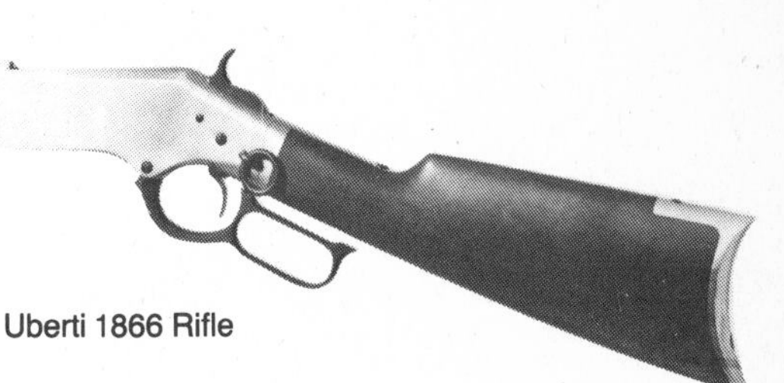

Uberti 1866 Rifle

UBERTI MODEL 1866 SPORTING RIFLE
Caliber: 22 LR, 22 WMR, 38 Spec., 44-40.
Barrel: 24¼″, octagonal.
Weight: 8.1 lbs. **Length:** 43¼″ over-all.
Stock: Walnut.
Sights: Blade front adj. for w., rear adj. for e.
Features: Frame, buttplate, fore-end cap of polished brass, balance charcoal blued. Imported by Benson Firearms, Uberti USA.
Price: **$759.00**
Price: Yellowboy Carine (19″ round bbl.) **$629.00**
Price: Yellowboy "Indian" Carbine (engraved receiver, "nails" in wood) **$709.00**
Price: 1866 "Red Cloud Commemorative" Carbine **$709.00**
Price: 1866 "Trapper's Model" Carbine (16″ bbl.) **$629.00**

UBERTI HENRY RIFLE
Caliber: 44-40.
Barrel: 24¼″, half octagon.
Weight: 9.2 lbs. **Length:** 43¾″ over-all.
Stock: American Walnut.
Sights: Blade front, rear adj. for e.
Features: Frame, elevator, magazine follower, buttplate are brass, balance blue (also available in polished steel). Imported by Benson Firearms, Uberti USA.
Price: **$845.00**
Price: Henry Carbine (22¼″ bbl.) **$845.00**

UBERTI 1875 ARMY TARGET REVOLVING CARBINE
Caliber: 357 Mag., 44-40, 45 Colt, 6 shot.
Barrel: 18″.
Weight: 4.9 lbs. **Length:** 37″ over-all.
Stock: Walnut.
Sights: Ramp front, rear adj. for elevation.
Features: Polished brass trigger guard and buttplate, color case-hardened frame. Carbine version of the 1875 revolver. Imported by Benson Firearms, Uberti USA.
Price: Blue barrel, cylinder **$529.00**
Price: Nickeled barrel, cylinder **$645.00**

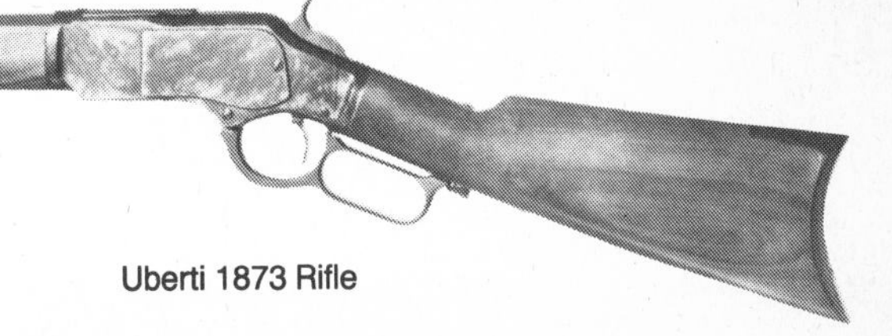

Uberti 1873 Rifle

UBERTI 1873 SPORTING RIFLE
Caliber: 22 LR, 22 WMR, 38 Spec., 357 Mag., 44-40, 45 Colt.
Barrel: 24¼″, octagonal.
Weight: 8.1 lbs. **Length:** 43¼″ over-all.
Stock: Walnut.
Sights: Blade front adj. for w., open rear adj. for e.
Features: Color case-hardened frame, blued barrel, hammer, lever, buttplate, brass elevator. Imported by Benson Firearms, Uberti USA.
Price: **$830.00**
Price: 1873 Carbine (19″ round bbl.) **$769.00**
Price: 1873 Carbine, nickel plated **$889.00**
Price: 1873 "Trapper's Model" Carbine (16″ bbl.) **$769.00**

UBERTI 1873 CATTLEMAN REVOLVING CARBINE

Caliber: 22 LR/22 WMR, 38 Spec., 357 Mag., 44-40, 45 Colt, 6-shot.
Barrel: 18".
Weight: 4.4 lbs. **Length:** 34" over-all.
Stock: Walnut.
Sights: Blade front, groove rear, or adjustable target.
Features: Carbine version of the single-action revolver. Brass buttplate, color case-hardened frame, blued cylinder and barrel. Imported by Benson Firearms, Uberti USA.
Price: Fixed Sight **$459.00**
Price: Target sight **$495.00**
Price: 22 convertible (two cyls.) fixed sight **$489.00**
Price: As above, target sights **$529.00**

WINCHESTER MODEL 94 SIDE EJECT RIFLE

Caliber: 30-30, (12" twist), 6-shot tubular magazine.
Barrel: 16", 20".
Weight: 6½ lbs. **Length:** 37¾" over-all.
Stock: Straight grip walnut stock and fore-end.
Sights: Hooded blade front, semi-buckhorn rear. Drilled and tapped for receiver sight and scope mount.
Features: Solid frame, forged steel receiver; side ejection, exposed rebounding hammer with automatic trigger-activated safety transfer bar. Introduced 1984.
Price: 30-30, about **$299.00**
Price: With 1.5-4.5x Bushnell scope, mounts **$342.00**
Price: Trapper model (16" bbl., 30-30), about **$274.00**
Price: As above, 45 Colt, 44 Mag./44 Spec., about **$296.00**
Price: With Win-Tuff laminated hardwood stock **$299.00**
Price: Long Barrel Rifle (24" bbl., long fore-end) **$286.00**

Uberti 1873 Buckhorn 44-Cal. Revolving Carbine

Similar to 1873 Cattleman Carbine except slightly larger proportions. Available in 44 Mag. or 44 Mag./44-40 convertible.
Price: Fixed sights **$469.00**
Price: Target sights **$509.00**
Price: Convertible (two cylinders), fixed sights **$515.00**
Price: Convertible, target sights **$549.00**

WINCHESTER MODEL 94 BIG BORE SIDE EJECT

Caliber: 307 Win., 356 Win., 6-shot magazine.
Barrel: 20".
Weight: 7 lbs. **Length:** 38⅝" over-all.
Stock: Monte Carlo-style American walnut. Satin finish.
Sights: Hooded ramp front, semi-buckhorn rear adjustable for w. & e.
Features: All external metal parts have Winchester's deep blue high polish finish. Rifling twist 1 in 12". Rubber recoil pad fitted to buttstock. Introduced 1983. Made under license by U.S. Repeating Arms Co.
Price: About **$299.00**

Winchester Ranger Side Eject Carbine

Same as Model 94 Side Eject except has 5-shot magazine, American hardwood stock and fore-end, no front sight hood. Introduced 1985.
Price: About **$244.00**
Price: With 4x32 Bushnell scope, mounts, about **$278.00**

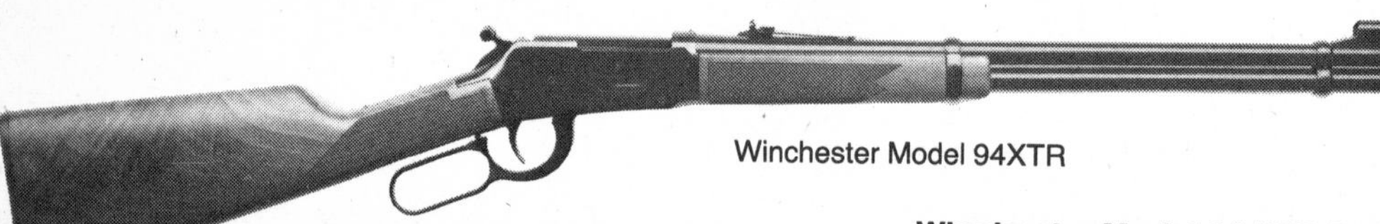

Winchester Model 94XTR

Winchester Model 94XTR Side Eject, 7x30 Waters

Same as Model 94 Side Eject except has 24" barrel, chambered for 7x30 Waters, 7-shot magazine, over-all length of 41¾" and weight is 7 lbs. Barrel twist is 1-12". Rubber butt pad instead of plastic. Introduced 1984.
Price: About **$312.00**

Winchester Model 94 XTR Deluxe Rifle

Similar to the Winchester Model 94 Side Eject except has better walnut butt and fore-end with special XTR cut checkering, solid rubber butt pad, satin finish. Roll-engraved barrel legend. High polish blue finish. Introduced 1988.
Price: **$426.00**

CENTERFIRE RIFLES—BOLT ACTIONS

Includes models for a wide variety of sporting and competitive purposes and uses.

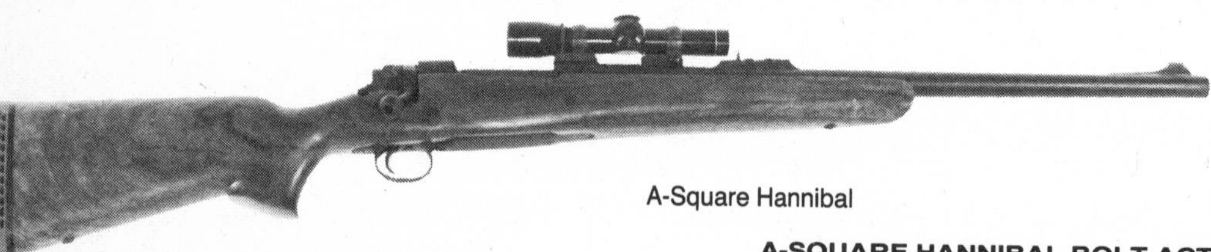

A-Square Hannibal

A-SQUARE CAESAR BOLT ACTION RIFLE

Caliber: Group I—270, 30-06, 9.3x62; Group II—7mm Rem. Mag., 300 Win. Mag., 338 Win. Mag., 416 Taylor, 458 Win. Mag.; Group III—300 H&H, 300 Wea., 8mm Rem. Mag., 340 Wea., 9.3x64, 375 H&H, 375 Wea., 416 Hoffman, 450 Ackley.
Barrel: 20" to 26" (no-cost customer option).
Weight: 8½ to 11 lbs.
Stock: Claro walnut with hand-rubbed oil finish; classic style with A-Square Coil-Chek® features for reduced recoil; flush detachable swivels. Customer choice of length of pull.
Sights: Choice of three-leaf express, forward or normal-mount scope, or combination (at extra cost).
Features: Matte non-reflective blue, double cross-bolts, steel and fiberglass reinforcement of wood from tang to fore-end tip; Mauser-style claw extractor; expanded magazine capacity. Right or left hand. Introduced 1984. Made in U.S. by A-Square Co., Inc.
Price: Group I calibers **$1,575.00**
Price: Group II calibers **$1,650.00**
Price: Group III calibers **$1,650.00**

A-SQUARE HANNIBAL BOLT ACTION RIFLE

Caliber: Group I—270, 30-06, 9.3x62; Group II—7mm Rem. Mag., 300 Win. Mag., 338 Win. Mag., 416 Taylor, 458 Win. Mag.; Group III—300 H&H, 300 Wea., 8mm Rem. Mag., 340 Wea., 9.3x64, 375 H&H, 375 Wea., 416 Hoffman, 450 Ackley; Group IV—338 A-Square, 378 Wea., 416 Rigby, 404 Jeffrey, 460 Short A-Square, 460 Wea., 500 A-Square.
Barrel: 20" to 26" (no-cost customer option).
Weight: 8½ to 11 lbs.
Stock: Claro walnut with hand-rubbed oil finish; classic style with A-Square Coil-Chek® features for reduced recoil; flush detachable swivels. Customer choice of length of pull.
Sights: Choice of three-leaf express, forward or normal-mount scope, or combination (at extra cost).
Features: Matte non-reflective blue, double cross-bolts, steel and fiberglass reinforcement of wood from tang to fore-end tip; Mauser-style claw extractor; expanded magazine capacity. Right hand only. Introduced 1983. Made in U.S. by A-Square Co., Inc.
Price: Group I calibers **$1,410.00**
Price: Group II calibers **$1,480.00**
Price: Group III calibers **$1,540.00**
Price: Group IV calibers **$1,600.00**

Anschutz Classic 1700

ANSCHUTZ BAVARIAN BOLT ACTION RIFLE
Caliber: 22 Hornet, 222 Rem., detachable clip.
Barrel: 24".
Weight: 7¼ lbs. **Length:** 43" over-all.
Stock: European walnut with Bavarian check rest. Checkered p.g. and fore-end.
Sights: Hooded ramp front, folding leaf rear.
Features: Uses the improved 1700 Match 54 action with adjustable trigger. Drilled and tapped for scope mounting. Introduced 1988. Imported from Germany by Precision Sales International.
Price: **$1,099.00**

ANSCHUTZ CLASSIC 1700 RIFLES
Caliber: 22 Hornet (1432D), 5-shot clip; 222 Rem. (1532D), 2-shot clip.
Barrel: 23½", 13/16" dia. heavy.
Weight: 7¾ lbs. **Length:** 42½" over-all.
Stock: Select European walnut with checkered pistol grip and fore-end.
Sights: None furnished, drilled and tapped for scope mounting.
Features: Adjustable single stage trigger. Receiver drilled and tapped for scope mounting. Introduced 1988. Imported from Germany by PSI.
Price: 22 Hornet **$1,099.00**
Price: 222 Rem. **$1,099.00**

Anschutz Custom 1700 Rifles
Similar to the Classic models except have roll-over Monte Carlo cheekpiece, slim fore-end with Schnabel tip, Wundhammer palm swell on pistol grip, rosewood grip cap with white diamond insert. Skip-line checkering on grip and fore-end. Introduced 1988. Imported from Germany by PSI.
Price: 22 Hornet **$1,099.00**
Price: 222 Rem. **$1,099.00**

Beeman/HW 60J

BEEMAN/HW 60J BOLT ACTION RIFLE
Caliber: 222 Rem.
Barrel: 22.8".
Weight: 6.5 lbs. **Length:** 41.7" over-all.
Stock: Walnut with cheekpiece; cut checkered p.g. and fore-end.
Sights: Hooded blade on ramp front, open rear.
Features: Polished blue finish; oil-finished wood. Imported from West Germany by Beeman. Introduced 1988.
Price: **$688.00**

ARMSPORT 2801 BOLT ACTION RIFLE
Caliber: 243, 308, 30-06, 7mm Rem. Mag., 300 Win. Mag.
Barrel: 24".
Weight: 8 lbs.
Stock: European walnut with Monte Carlo comb.
Sights: Ramp front, open adj. rear.
Features: Blue metal finish, glossy wood. Introduced 1986. Imported from Italy by Armsport.
Price: **$575.00**

Beeman/Krico Model 420

Beeman/Krico Model 620/720 Bolt Action Rifle
Similar to the Model 600/700 except has 20.75" barrel, weighs 6.8 lbs., and has full-length Mannlicher-style stock with metal Schnabel fore-end tip; double set trigger with optional match trigger available. Receiver drilled and tapped for scope mounting. Imported from West Germany by Beeman.
Price: Model 620 (243 Win.) **$1,830.00**
Price: Model 720 (270 Win.) **$1,820.00**
Price: Model 720 (30-06) **$1,845.00**

BEEMAN/KRICO MODEL 400 BOLT ACTION RIFLE
Caliber: 22 Hornet, 5-shot magazine.
Barrel: 23.5".
Weight: 6.8 lbs. **Length:** 43" over-all.
Stock: Select European walnut, curved European comb with cheekpiece; solid rubber butt pad; cut checkered grip and fore-end.
Sights: Blade front on ramp, open rear adjustable for windage.
Features: Detachable box magazine; action has rear locking lugs, twin extractors. Available with single or optional match and double set trigger. Receiver grooved for scope mounts. Made in West Germany. Imported by Beeman.
Price: **$1,225.00**
Price: Model 420 (as above except 19.5" bbl., full-length Mannlicher-style stock, double set trigger) **$1,425.00**

Beeman/Krico Model 640 Varmint

BEEMAN/KRICO MODEL 640 VARMINT RIFLE
Caliber: 222 Rem., 4-shot magazine.
Barrel: 23.75".
Weight: 9.6 lbs. **Length:** 43½" over-all.
Stock: Select European walnut with high Monte Carlo comb, Wundhammer palm swell, rosewood fore-end tip; cut checkered grip and fore-end.
Sights: None furnished. Drilled and tapped for scope mounting.
Features: Free-floating heavy bull barrel; double set trigger with optional match trigger available. Imported from West Germany by Beeman.
Price: **$1,697.00**

BEEMAN/KRICO MODEL 700L DELUXE RIFLE
Caliber: 17 Rem., 222, 223, 22-250, 243, 308, 7x57, 7x64, 270, 30-06, 9.3x62, 8x68S, 7mm Rem. Mag., 300 Win. Mag., 9.3x64.
Barrel: 24" (26" in magnum calibers).
Weight: 7.5 lbs. **Length:** 44" over-all (24" barrel).
Stock: Traditional European style, select fancy walnut with rosewood Schnable fore-end, Bavarian cheekpiece, 28 lpi checkering.
Sights: Hooded front ramp, rear adjustable for windage.
Features: Butterknife bolt handle; gold plated single-set trigger; front sling swivel attached to barrel with ring; silent safety. Introduced 1983. Made in West Germany. Imported by Beeman.
Price: Model 700, magnum calibers **$1,953.00**

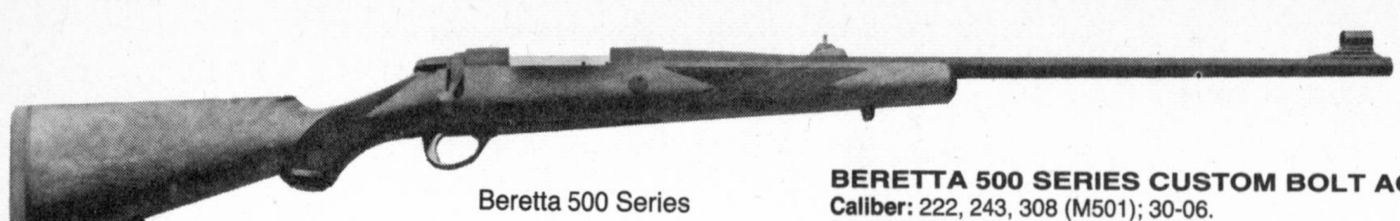
Beretta 500 Series

BERETTA 500 SERIES CUSTOM BOLT ACTION RIFLES
Caliber: 222, 243, 308 (M501); 30-06.
Barrel: 23," to 24".
Weight: 6.8 to 8.4 lbs. **Length:** NA
Stock: Close-grained walnut with oil finish, hand checkering.
Sights: None furnished; drilled and tapped for scope mounting.
Features: Model 500 — short action; 501 — medium action. All models have rubber butt pad. Imported from Italy by Beretta U.S.A. Corp. Introduced 1984.
Price: Model 500 and 501 .... **$725.00**

BRNO ZKB 680 FOX BOLT ACTION RIFLE
Caliber: 22 Hornet, 222 Rem., 5-shot magazine.
Barrel: 23½".
Weight: 5 lbs., 12 oz. **Length:** 42½" over-all.
Stock: Turkish walnut, with Monte Carlo.
Sights: Hooded front, open adj. rear.
Features: Detachable box magazine; adj. double set triggers. Imported from Czechoslovakia by Saki International.
Price: **$499.00**

BRNO ZKK 600, 601, 602 BOLT ACTION RIFLES
Caliber: 30-06, 270, 7x57, 7x64 (M600); 223, 243, 308 (M601); 8x68S, 375 H&H, 458 Win. Mag. (M602), 5-shot magazine.
Barrel: 23½" (M600, 601), 25" (M602).
Weight: 6 lbs., 3 oz. to 9 lbs., 4 oz. **Length:** 43" over-all (M601).
Stock: Walnut.
Sights: Hooded ramp front, open folding leaf adj. rear.
Features: Adjustable set trigger (standard trigger included); easy-release floorplate; sling swivels. Imported from Czechoslovakia by Saki International.
Price: ZKK 600 Standard **$599.00**
Price: As above, Monte Carlo stock **$649.00**
Price: ZKK 601 Standard **$549.00**
Price: As above, Monte Carlo stock **$599.00**
Price: ZKK 602, Monte Carlo stock............................. **$749.00**
Price: As above, standard stock **$689.00**

Browning Short Action A-Bolt
Similar to the standard A-Bolt except has short action for 22-250, 243, 257 Roberts, 7mm-08, 308 chamberings. Available in Hunter or Medallion grades. Weighs 6½ lbs. Other specs essentially the same. Introduced 1985.
Price: Medallion, no sights.................................... **$502.95**
Price: Hunter, no sights **$432.95**
Price: Hunter, with sights **$487.95**

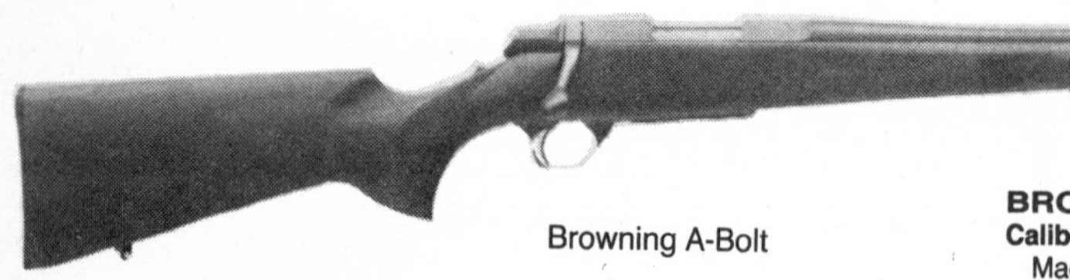
Browning A-Bolt

BROWNING A-BOLT RIFLE
Caliber: 25-06, 270, 30-06, 280, 7mm Rem. Mag., 300 Win. Mag., 338 Win. Mag., 375 H&H Mag.
Barrel: 22" medium sporter weight with recessed muzzle; 26" on mag. cals.
Weight: 6½ to 7½ lbs. **Length:** 44¾" over-all. (Magnum and standard), 41¾" (short action).
Stock: Classic style American walnut; recoil pad standard on magnum calibers.
Features: Short-throw (60°) fluted bolt, three locking lugs, plunger-type ejector; adjustable trigger is grooved and gold plated. Hinged floorplate, detachable box magazine (4 rounds std. cals., 3 for magnums). Slide tang safety. Medallion has glossy stock finish, rosewood grip and fore-end caps, high polish blue. Introduced 1985. Imported from Japan by Browning.
Price: Medallion, no sights.................................... **$502.95**
Price: Hunter, no sights **$432.95**
Price: Hunter, with sights **$487.95**
Price: Medallion, 375 H & H Mag., with sights **$587.95**

Browning A-Bolt "Stainless Stalker"
Similar to the Hunter model A-Bolt except receiver is made of stainless steel; the rest of the exposed metal surfaces are finished with a durable matte silver-gray. Graphite-fiberglass composite textured stock. No sights are furnished. Available in 270, 30-06, 7mm Rem. Mag. Introduced 1987.
Price: **$551.95**
Price: Composite Stalker (as above with checkered stock) **$432.95**

Browning A-Bolt Left Hand
Same as the Medallion model A-Bolt except has left-hand action and is available only in 270, 30-06, 7mm Rem. Mag. Introduced 1987.
Price: **$524.95**

Browning Micro Medallion

Browning A-Bolt Micro Medallion
Similar to the standard A-Bolt except is a scaled-down version. Comes with 20" barrel, shortened length of pull (13⁵⁄₁₆"); three-shot magazine capacity; weighs 6 lbs., 1 oz. Available in 243, 308, 7mm-08, 257 Roberts, 22-250. Introduced 1988.
Price: No sights **$502.95**

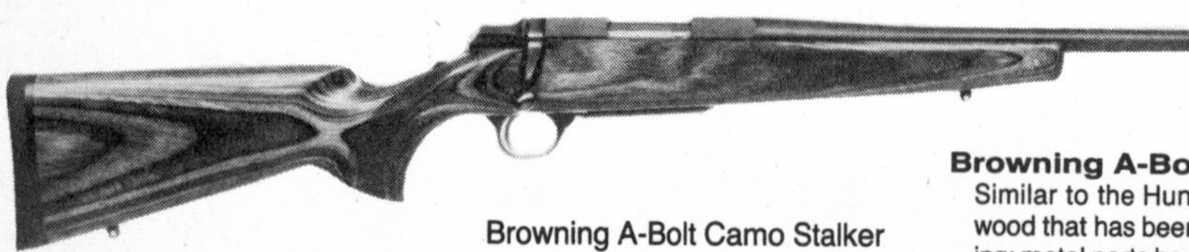
Browning A-Bolt Camo Stalker

Browning A-Bolt "Camo Stalker"
Similar to the Hunter model A-Bolt except the stock is of multi-laminated wood that has been stained varying shades of black and green; cut checkering; metal parts have a matte, non-glare finish. No sights are furnished. Available in 270, 30-06, 7mm Rem. Mag. Introduced 1987.
Price: **$459.95**

CAUTION: PRICES CHANGE. CHECK AT GUNSHOP.

Browning A-Bolt Pronghorn Antelope Issue
Same specifications as standard A-Bolt except available only in 243 Win. and has detailed engraving on the receiver flats, floorplate, trigger guard and at the rear of the barrel. Each side of the receiver has a different pronghorn study in 24 karat gold plating. Stock is a high grade of walnut with skipline checkering and a pearl border and high gloss finish. Brass spacers separate the rosewood caps and recoil pad. Limited edition of 500 rifles. Introduced 1987.
Price: **$1,240.00**

Browning A-Bolt Gold Medallion
Similar to the standard A-Bolt except has select walnut stock with brass spacers between rubber recoil pad and between the rosewood grip cap and fore-end tip; gold-filled barrel inscription; palm-swell pistol grip, Monte Carlo comb, 22 lpi checkering with double borders; engraved receiver flats. In 270, 30-06, 7mm Rem. Mag. only. Introduced 1988.
Price: **$624.95**

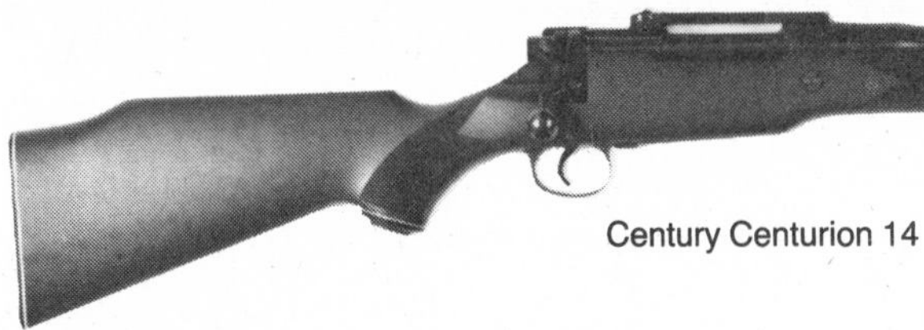

Century Centurion 14

CENTURY CENTURION 14 SPORTER
Caliber: 303 British, 7mm Rem. Mag., 300 Win. Mag., 5-shot magazine.
Barrel: 24″.
Weight: NA. **Length:** 43.3″ over-all.
Stock: Walnut-finished European hardwood. Checkered p.g. and fore-end. Monte Carlo comb.
Sights: None furnished.
Features: Uses modified Pattern 14 Enfield action. Drilled and tapped for scope mounting. Blue finish. From Century International Arms.
Price: 303, about **$225.95**
Price: Magnum calibers, about **$251.95**

Century Swedish

CENTURY SWEDISH SPORTER #38
Caliber: 6.5 x 55 Swede, 5-shot magazine.
Barrel: 24″.
Weight: NA. **Length:** 44.1″ over-all.
Stock: Walnut-finished European hardwood with checkered p.g. and fore-end; Monte Carlo comb.
Sights: Blade front, adjustable rear.
Features: Uses M38 Swedish Mauser action; comes with Holden Ironsighter see-through scope mount. Introduced 1987. From Century International Arms.
Price: About **$212.95**

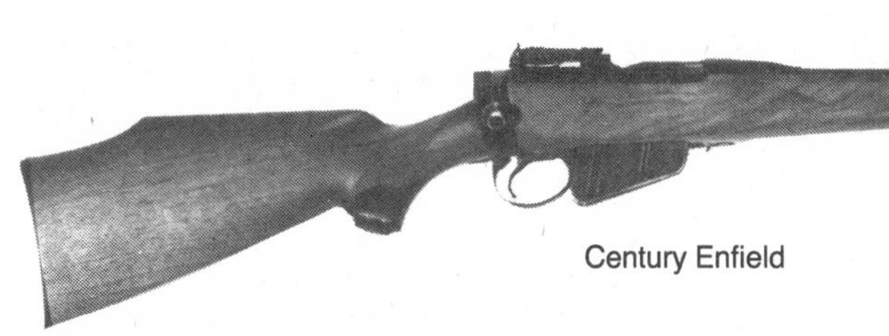

Century Enfield

CENTURY ENFIELD SPORTER #4
Caliber: 303 British, 10-shot magazine.
Barrel: 25.2″.
Weight: NA. **Length:** 44.5″ over-all.
Stock: Beechwood with checkered p.g. and fore-end, Monte Carlo comb.
Sights: Blade front, adjustable aperture rear.
Features: Uses Lee-Enfield action; blue finish. Introduced 1987. From Century International Arms.
Price: **$185.95**
Price: Jungle Sporter (20½″ bbl.) **$207.95**

CHAMPLIN RIFLE
Caliber: All std. chamberings, including 458 Win. and 460 Wea. Many wildcats on request.
Barrel: Any length up to 26″ for octagon. Choice of round, straight taper octagon, or octagon with integral quarter rib, front sight ramp and sling swivel stud.
Weight: About 8 lbs. **Length:** 45″ over-all.
Stock: Hand inletted, shaped and finished. Checkered to customer specs. Select French, Circassian or claro walnut. Steel p.g. cap, trap buttplate or recoil pad.
Sights: Bead on ramp front, 3-leaf folding rear.
Features: Right-hand Champlin action, tang safety or optional shroud safety, Canjar adj. trigger, hinged floorplate.
Price: From **$5,400.00**

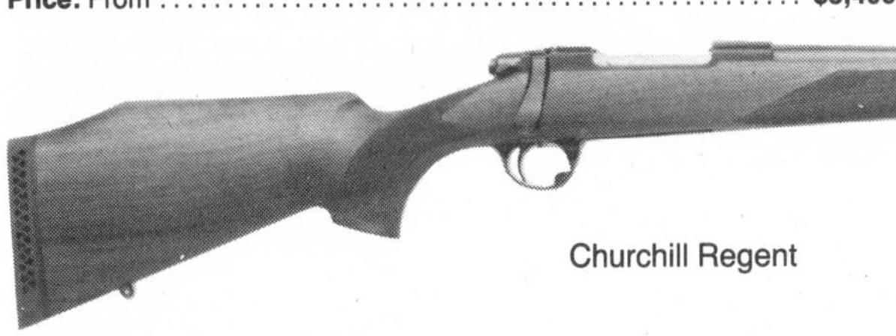

Churchill Regent

CHURCHILL BOLT ACTION RIFLE
Caliber: 243, 25-06, 270, 308, 30-06 (4-shot magazine), 7mm Rem. Mag., 300 Win. Mag. (3-shot).
Barrel: 22″ (7mm Rem. Mag. has 24″).
Weight: 7½ lbs. **Length:** 42½″ over-all with 22″ barrel.
Stock: European walnut, checkered p.g. and fore-end. Regent grade has Monte Carlo, Highlander has classic design.
Sights: Gold bead on ramp front, fully adj. rear.
Features: Positive safety locks trigger; oil-finished wood; swivel posts; recoil pad. Imported by Kassnar Imports, Inc. Introduced 1986.
Price: Highlander, without sights, either cal. **$350.00**
Price: As above, with sights **$380.00**
Price: Regent, without sights **$549.00**
Price: As above, with sights **$579.00**

Churchill Highlander Bolt Action Rifle
Similar to the Regent except has a classic-style stock of standard-grade European walnut. Highlander Combo includes rifle without iron sights, q.d. swivels, cobra-style sling, rings, bases, and 3-9x32 scope.
Price: Highlander with sights **$379.00**
Price: Highlander Combo **$409.00**
Price: Highlander without sights **$349.00**

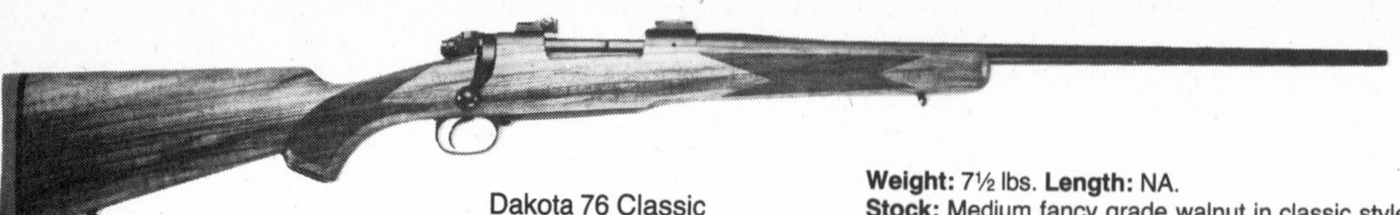

Dakota 76 Classic

DAKOTA 76 CLASSIC BOLT ACTION RIFLE

Caliber: 257 Roberts, 270, 280, 30-06, 7mm Rem. Mag., 338 Win. Mag., 300 Win. Mag., 375 H&H, 458 Win. Mag.
Barrel: 23″.
Weight: 7½ lbs. **Length:** NA.
Stock: Medium fancy grade walnut in classic style. Checkered p.g. and fore-end; solid butt pad.
Sights: None furnished; drilled and tapped for scope mounts.
Features: Has many features of the original Model 70 Winchester. One-piece rail trigger guard assembly; steel grip cap. Adjustable trigger. Many options available. Introduced 1988. From Dakota Arms, Inc.
Price: From **$1,750.00**

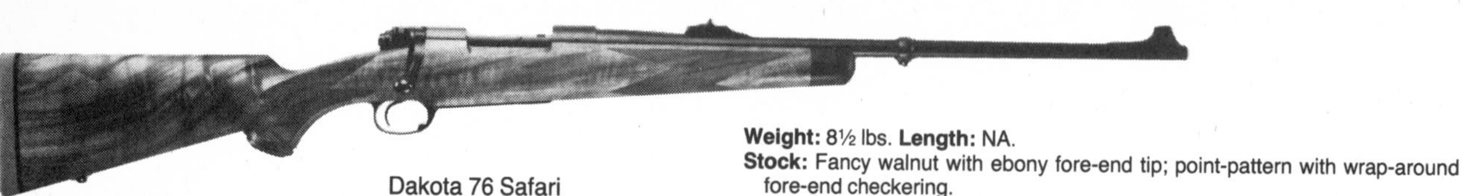

Dakota 76 Safari

DAKOTA 76 SAFARI BOLT ACTION RIFLE

Caliber: 338 Win. Mag., 300 Win. Mag., 375 H&H, 458 Win. Mag.
Barrel: 23″.
Weight: 8½ lbs. **Length:** NA.
Stock: Fancy walnut with ebony fore-end tip; point-pattern with wrap-around fore-end checkering.
Sights: Ramp front, standing leaf rear.
Features: Has many features of the original Model 70 Winchester. Barrel band front swivel, inletted rear. Cheekpiece with shadow line. Steel grip cap. Introduced 1988. From Dakota Arms, Inc.
Price: From **$2,750.00**

Du Biel Modern Classic

Du BIEL ARMS BOLT ACTION RIFLES

Caliber: Standard calibers 22-250 thru 458 Win. Mag. Selected wildcat calibers available.
Barrel: Selected weights and lengths. Douglas Premium.
Weight: About 7½ lbs.
Stock: Five styles. Walnut, maple, laminates. Hand checkered.
Sights: None furnished. Receiver has integral milled bases.
Features: Basically a custom-made rifle. Left or right-hand models available. Five-lug locking mechanism; 36-degree bolt rotation; adjustable Canjar trigger; oil or epoxy stock finish; Presentation recoil pad; jeweled and chromed bolt body; sling swivel studs; lever latch or button floorplate release. All steel action and parts. Introduced 1978. From Du Biel Arms.
Price: Rollover Model, left or right-hand .... **$ 2,500.00**
Price: Thumbhole, left or right hand **$2,500.00**
Price: Classic, left or right hand **$2,500.00**
Price: Modern Classic, left or right hand........................ **$2,500.00**
Price: Thumbhole Mannlicher, left or right hand **$2,500.00**

Francotte Rifle

AUGUSTE FRANCOTTE BOLT ACTION RIFLES

Caliber: 243, 270, 7x64, 30-06, 308, 300 Win. Mag., 338, 7mm Rem. Mag., 375 H&H, 416 Rigby, 458 Win. Mag.
Barrel: 23½″ standard; other lengths on request.
Weight: 7.61 lbs. (medium cals.), 11.1 lbs. (magnum cals.).
Stock: Fancy European walnut. To customer specs.
Sights: To customer specs.
Features: Basically a custom gun, Francotte offers many options. Imported from Belgium by Armes de Chasse.
Price: .... **NA**

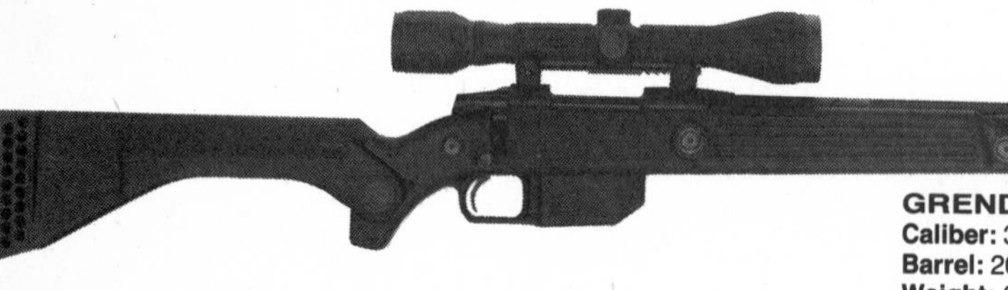

Grendel SRT

GRENDEL SRT COMPACT RIFLE

Caliber: 308 Win., 9-shot magazine.
Barrel: 20″ (Models 20F [fluted], 20L [not fluted]), 24″ (Model 24, not fluted).
Weight: 6.7 lbs. (Model 20F). **Length:** 40.8″ over-all (Model 20F), open; folds to 30″ length.
Stock: Folding Du Pont Zytel reinforced with glass fiber.
Sights: None furnished. Integral scope bases.
Features: Uses Sako A-2 action. Muzzle brake. Fore-end has a rod for sling swivel and will accept M-16 clip-on bipod. Uses Sako scope mount. Introduced 1987. From Greendel, Inc.
Price: SRT-20F (fluted barrel) **$510.00**
Price: SRT-20L (non-fluted)................................... **$480.00**
Price: SRT-24 (non-fluted).................................... **$480.00**

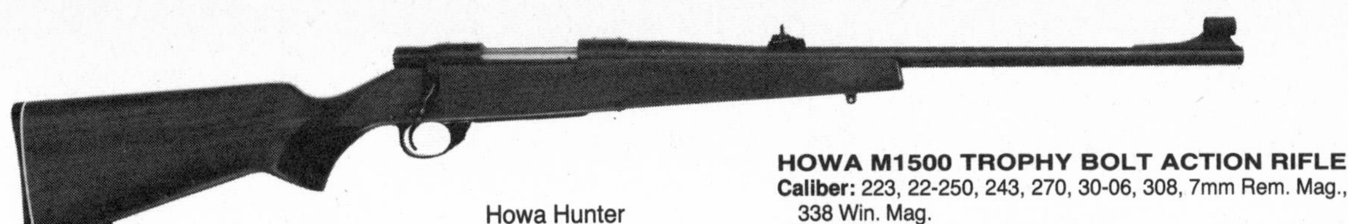

Howa Hunter

Howa Model 1500 Hunter Rifle

Similar to the Grade II except has checkered hardwood stock without recoil pad; available in 223, 243, 270, 30-06, 7mm Rem. Mag., with sights. Introduced 1987.

Price: $440.00

HOWA M1500 TROPHY BOLT ACTION RIFLE

Caliber: 223, 22-250, 243, 270, 30-06, 308, 7mm Rem. Mag., 300 Win. Mag., 338 Win. Mag.

Barrel: 22″ (24″ in magnum calibers.).

Weight: 7½-7¾ lbs. **Length:** 42″ over-all (42½″ for 270, 30-06, 7mm).

Stock: American walnut with Monte Carlo comb and cheekpiece; 18 l.p.i. checkering on p.g. and fore-end.

Sights: Hooded ramp gold bead front, open round-notch rear adj. for w. & e. Drilled and tapped for scope mounts.

Features: Trigger guard and magazine box are a single unit with a hinged floorplate. Comes with q.d. swivel studs. Composition non-slip buttplate with white spacer. Magnum models have rubber recoil pad. Introduced 1979. Imported from Japan by Interarms.

Price: $465.00

Howa Lightning

Howa Model 1500

Similar to the standard 1500 except has a 22″ heavy barrel and fully adjustable trigger. Chambered for 22-250 and 223. Weighs 9 lbs. 5 oz. Skipline checkering, q.d. swivels. Introduced 1982.

Price: Parkerized, oil finished stock $515.00

Howa Lightning Rifle

Similar to the Howa Trophy model except comes with lightweight Carbolite stock; weighs 7 lbs. Available in 270, 30-06, 7mm Rem. Mag. Introduced 1988.

Price: 270, 30-06 .... $465.00

Price: 7mm Rem. Mag. $480.00

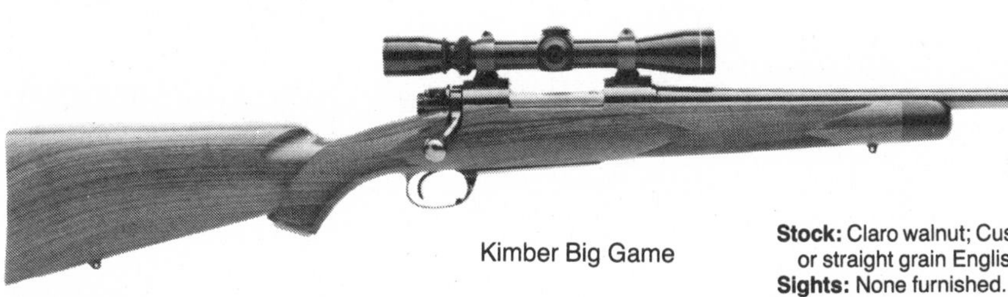

Kimber Big Game

KIMBER BIG GAME RIFLE

Caliber: 270, 280, 7mm Rem. Mag., 30-06, 300 Win. Mag., 338 Win. Mag., 375 H&H.

Barrel: 22″ (24″ for magnum).

Weight: About 7¾ lbs. **Length:** 42″ over-all (22″ bbl.).

Stock: Claro walnut; Custom Classic and Super America have AAA fancy claro or straight grain English walnut.

Sights: None furnished.

Features: Three styles available—Classic, Custom Classic, Super America. Mauser-style extractor; Model 70-type override trigger design, ejector, three-position safety; Mauser-style bolt stop; Featherweight M70 barrel profile (except 338, 375). Introduced 1988.

Price: Classic $985.00

Price: Custom Classic $1,230.00

Price: Super America $1,385.00

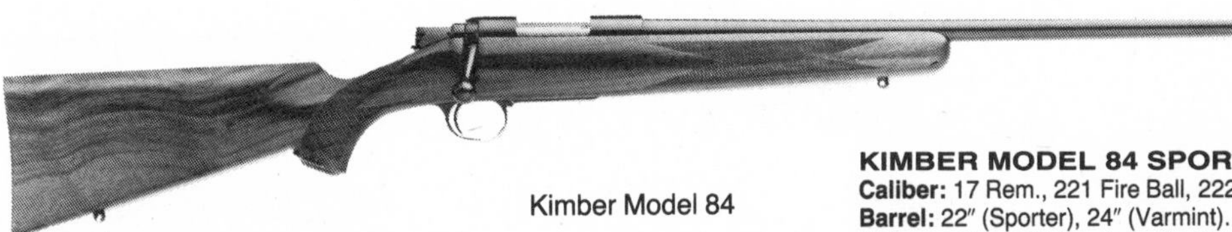

Kimber Model 84

Kimber Model 82, 84 Super America

Super-grade version of the Models 82 and 84. Has a Classic stock only of specially selected, high-grade, California claro walnut, with Continental beaded cheekpiece and ebony fore-end tip; borderless, full-coverage 20 lpi checkering; Niedner-type checkered steel buttplate. Options include barrel quarter-rib with a folding leaf sight, skeleton grip cap, checkered bolt knob. Available in 22 Long Rifle, 22 Magnum, 22 Hornet, 17 Rem., 221 Rem., 222 Rem., 223 Rem.

Price: Model 82, 22 Long Rifle, less 4x scope $1,150.00

Price: Model 82, 22 Hornet, less scope $1,195.00

Price: Model 84, 223 Rem. $1,285.00

KIMBER MODEL 84 SPORTER

Caliber: 17 Rem., 221 Fire Ball, 222 Rem., 223 Rem., 5-shot magazine.

Barrel: 22″ (Sporter), 24″ (Varmint).

Weight: About 6¼ lbs. **Length:** 40½″ over-all (Sporter).

Stock: Two styles available. "Classic" is Claro walnut with plain, straight comb; "Custom Classic" is of fancy select grade Claro walnut, ebony fore-end tip, Niedner-style buttplate. All have 18 lpi hand cut, borderless checkering, steel grip cap, checkered steel buttplate.

Sights: Hooded ramp front with bead, folding leaf rear (optional).

Features: All new Mauser-type head locking bolt action; steel trigger guard and hinged floorplate; Mauser-type extractor; fully adjustable trigger; chrome-moly barrel. Three-position safety (new in '87.) Round-top receiver drilled and tapped for scope mounting. Varmint gun prices same as others. Introduced 1984. Contact Kimber for full details.

Price: Classic stock, no sights $885.00

Price: Continental (222, 223 only) $985.00

Price: Custom Classic stock, no sights $1,130.00

Price: Kimber scope mounts, from $48.00

Price: Open sights fitted (optional) $55.00

KIMBER MODEL 82 SPORTER

Caliber: 22 Hornet, 3-shot flush-fitting magazine; 218 Bee, 25-20, single shot.
Barrel: 22½", 6 grooves; 1-in-14" twist; 24" heavy.
Weight: About 6¼ lbs. **Length:** 42" over-all.
Stock: Three styles available. "Classic" is Claro walnut with plain, straight comb; "Custom Classic" is of fancy select grade Claro walnut, ebony fore-end tip, Niedner-style butt-plate. All have 18 lpi hand cut, borderless checkering, steel grip cap, checkered steel buttplate.
Sights: Hooded ramp front with bead, folding leaf rear (optional).
Features: All steel construction; twin rear horizontally opposed locking lugs; fully adjustable trigger; rocker-type safety. Receiver grooved for Kimber scope mounts. Available in true left-hand version in selected models. Introduced 1982. Contact Kimber for full details.
Price: Classic stock, no sights (left hand also avail.) **$795.00**
Price: Continental **$895.00**
Price: Custom Classic, no sights (left hand also avail.) **$1,040.00**
Price: Kimber scope mounts, from **$48.00**
Price: Open sights fitted (optional) **$55.00**

MARK X AMERICAN FIELD SERIES

Caliber: 22-250, 243, 25-06, 270, 7x57, 7mm Rem. Mag., 308 Win., 30-06, 300 Win. Mag.
Barrel: 24".
Weight: 7 lbs. **Length:** 45" over-all.
Stock: Genuine walnut stock, hand checkered with 1" sling swivels.
Sights: Ramp front with removable hood, open rear sight adjustable for windage and elevation.
Features: Mauser-system action. One piece trigger guard with hinged floor plate, drilled and tapped for scope mounts and receiver sight, hammer-forged chrome vanadium steel barrel. Imported from Yugoslavia by Interarms.
Price: With adj. trigger, sights **$550.00**
Price: 7mm Rem. Mag., 300 Win. Mag **$565.00**

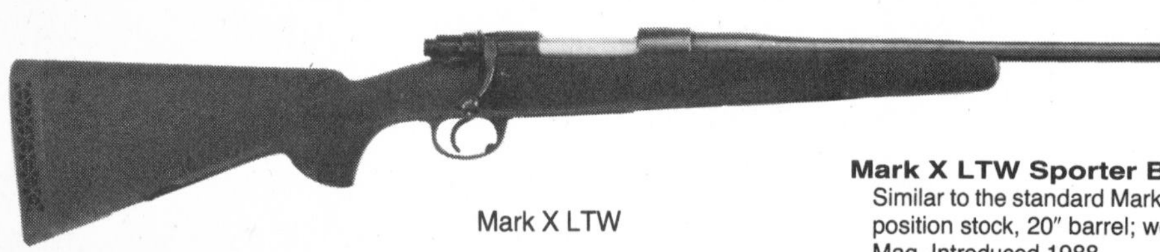

Mark X LTW

Mark X Viscount Rifle

Same gun and features as the Mark X Sporting Rifle except has stock of European hardwood. Imported from Yugoslavia by Interarms. Reintroduced 1987.
Price: **$440.00**
Price: 7mm Rem. Mag., 300 Win. Mag **$455.00**

Mark X LTW Sporter Bolt Action Rifle

Similar to the standard Mark X except comes with lightweight Carbolite composition stock, 20" barrel; weighs 7 lbs. Available in 270, 30-06, 7mm Rem. Mag. Introduced 1988.
Price: 270, 30-06 . . . . **$465.00**
Price: 7mm Rem. Mag. **$480.00**

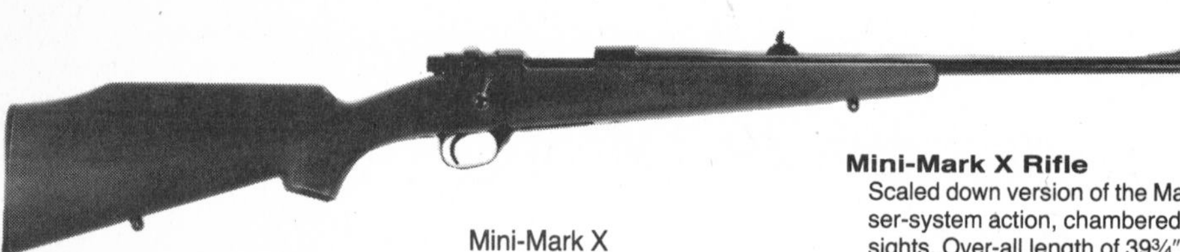

Mini-Mark X

Mini-Mark X Rifle

Scaled down version of the Mark X Sporting Rifle. Uses miniature M98 Mauser-system action, chambered for 223 Rem.; 20" barrel with open adjustable sights. Over-all length of 39¾", weight 6.35 lbs. Drilled and tapped for scope mounting. Checkered hardwood stock. Adjustable trigger. Introduced 1987. Imported from Yugoslavia by Interarms.
Price: **$460.00**

MAUSER 225 BOLT ACTION RIFLE

Caliber: 243, 25-06, 270, 7x57, 308, 30-06, 4-shot magazine (standard); 257 Wea., 270 Wea., 7mm Rem. Mag., 300 Win. Mag., 300 Wea., 308 Norma Mag., 375 H&H, 3-shot magazine (magnum).
Barrel: 24" (standard), 26" (magnum).
Weight: About 8 lbs. **Length:** 44½" over-all (24" bbl.).
Stock: Oil finished, hand checkered European walnut with Monte Carlo. Recoil pad and swivel studs standard.
Sights: None furnished. Drilled and tapped for scope mounts. Open sights, rings, bases avail. from KDF.
Features: Three-lug, front-locking action with ultra-fast lock time. Imported from West Germany by KDF, Inc.
Price: Standard calibers **$1,075.00**
Price: Magnum calibers. **$1,125.00**

Parker-Hale 81 Classic

Parker-Hale Model 1100 Lightweight Rifle

Similar to the Model 81 Classic except has slim barrel profile, hollow bolt handle, alloy trigger guard/floorplate. The Monte Carlo stock has a Schnabel fore-end, hand-cut checkering, swivel studs, palm swell pistol grip. Comes with hooded ramp front sight, open Williams rear adjustable for windage and elevation. Same calibers as Model 81. Over-all length is 43", weight 6½ lbs., with 22" barrel. Imported from England by Precision Sports, Inc. Introduced 1984.
Price: **$559.95**
Price: Optional set trigger **$84.95**

PARKER-HALE MODEL 81 CLASSIC RIFLE

Caliber: 22-250, 243, 6mm Rem., 270, 6.5x55, 7x57, 7x64, 308, 30-06, 300 Win. Mag., 7mm Rem. Mag., 4-shot magazine.
Barrel: 24".
Weight: About 7¾ lbs. **Length:** 44½" over-all.
Stock: European walnut in classic style with oil finish, hand-cut checkering; palm swell pistol grip, rosewood grip cap.
Sights: Drilled and tapped for open sights and scope mounting. Scope bases included.
Features: Uses Mauser-style action; one-piece steel, Oberndorf-style trigger guard with hinged floorplate; rubber butt pad; quick-detachable sling swivels. Imported from England by Precision Sports, Inc. Introduced 1984.
Price: **$799.95**
Price: Optional set trigger **$84.95**

 CAUTION: PRICES CHANGE. CHECK AT GUNSHOP.

Parker-Hale 1200 Super

PARKER-HALE MODEL 1200 SUPER BOLT ACTION

Caliber: 22-250, 243, 6mm, 25-06, 270, 6.5x55, 7x57, 7x64, 308, 30-06, 8mm, 7mm Rem. Mag., 300 Win. Mag.
Barrel: 24".
Weight: About 7½ lbs. **Length:** 44½" over-all.
Stock: European walnut, rosewood grip and fore-end tips, hand-cut checkering; roll-over cheekpiece; palm swell pistol grip; ventilated recoil pad; wrap-around checkering.
Sights: Hooded post front, open rear.
Features: Uses Mauser-style action with claw extractor; gold plated adjustable trigger; silent side safety locks trigger, sear and bolt; aluminum trigger guard. Imported from England by Precision Sports, Inc. Introduced 1984.
Price: **$659.95**
Price: Optional set trigger **$84.95**

Parker-Hale Model 81 African Rifle

Similar to the Model 81 Classic except chambered only for 300 H&H, 308 Norma Mag., 375 H&H and 9.3x62. Has adjustable trigger, barrel band front swivel, African express rear sight, engraved receiver. Classic-style stock has a solid butt pad, checkered p.g. and fore-end. Introduced 1986.
Price: **$999.95**

Parker-Hale Model 1200 Super Clip Rifle

Same as the Model 1200 Super except has a detachable steel box magazine and steel trigger guard. Imported from England by Precision Sports, Inc. Introduced 1984.
Price: **$699.95**
Price: Optional set trigger **$84.95**

PARKER-HALE MODEL 2100 MIDLAND RIFLE

Caliber: 22-250, 243, 6mm, 270, 6.5x55, 7x57, 7x64, 308, 30-06.
Barrel: 22".
Weight: About 7 lbs. **Length:** 43" over-all.
Stock: European walnut, cut-checkered pistol grip and fore-end; sling swivels.
Sights: Hooded post front, flip-up open rear.
Features: Mauser-type action has twin front locking lugs, rear safety lug, and claw extractor; hinged floorplate; adjustable single stage trigger; silent side safety. Imported from England by Precision Sports, Inc. Introduced 1984.
Price: **$369.95**

Parker-Hale Model 1100M African Magnum

Similar to the Model 1000 Standard except has 24" barrel, 46" over-all length, weighs 9½ lbs., and is chambered for 375 H&H Magnum, 404 Jeffery and 458 Win. Magnum. Has hooded post front sight, shallow V-notch rear, 180° flag safety (low 45° scope safety available). Specially lengthened steel magazine has hinged floorplate; heavily reinforced, glass bedded and weighted stock has a ventilated rubber recoil pad. Imported from England by Precision Sports, Inc. Introduced 1984.
Price: **$899.95**

Parker-Hale Model 1000 Standard Rifle

Similar to the Model 1200 Super except has standard walnut Monte Carlo stock with satin finish, no rosewood grip/fore-end caps; fitted with checkered buttplate, standard sling swivels. Imported from England by Precision Sports, Inc. Introduced 1984.
Price: **$499.95**
Price: Optional set trigger **$84.95**

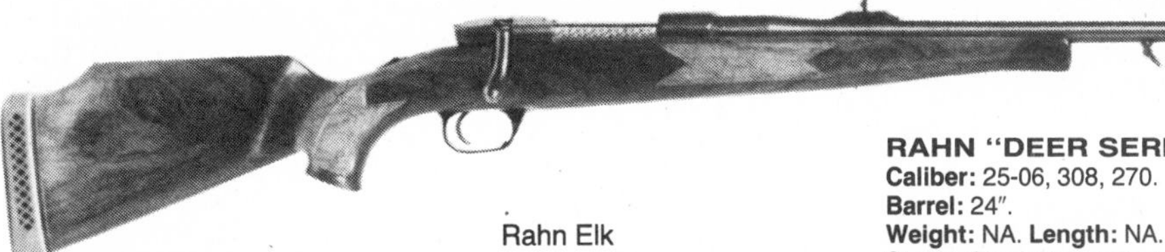

Rahn Elk

RAHN "DEER SERIES" BOLT ACTION RIFLE

Caliber: 25-06, 308, 270.
Barrel: 24".
Weight: NA. **Length:** NA.
Stock: Circassian walnut with rosewood fore-end and grip caps, Monte Carlo cheekpiece, semi-Schnabel fore-end; hand checkered.
Sights: Bead front, open adjustable rear. Drilled and tapped for scope mount.
Features: Free floating barrel; rubber recoil pad; one-piece trigger guard with hinged, engraved floorplate; 22 rimfire conversion insert available. Introduced 1986. From Rahn Gun Works, Inc.
Price: **$800.00**
Price: With custom stock made to customer specs **$850.00**

Rahn "Elk Series" Rifle

Similar to the "Deer Series" except chambered for 6mmx56, 30-06, 7mm Rem. Mag. and has elk head engraving on floorplate. Introduced 1986.
Price: **$850.00**
Price: With stock made to customer specs **$900.00**

Rahn "Safari Series" Rifle

Similar to the "Deer Series" except chambered for 308 Norma Mag., 300 Win. Mag., 8x68S, 9x64. Choice of Cape buffalo, rhino or elephant engraving. Gold oval nameplate with three initials. Introduced 1986.
Price: **$950.00**
Price: With stock made to customer specs **$1,000.00**

Rahn "Himalayan Series" Rifle

Similar to the "Deer Series" except chambered for 5.6x57 or 6.5x68S, short stock of walnut or fiberglass, and floorplate engravings of a yak with scroll border. Introduced 1986.
Price: **$850.00**
Price: With walnut stock made to customer specs **$900.00**

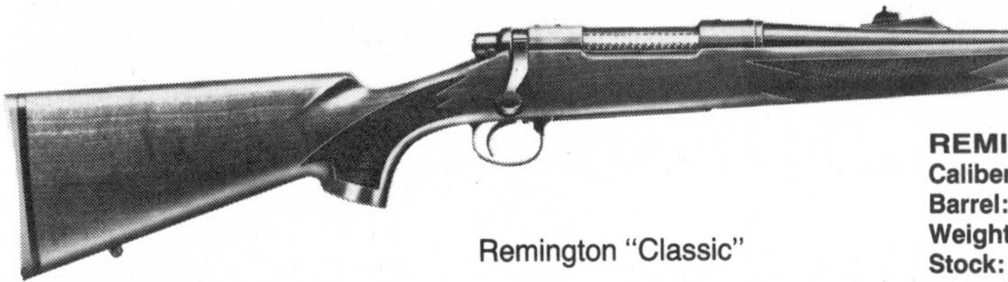

Remington "Classic"

REMINGTON 700 "CLASSIC" RIFLE

Caliber: 35 Whelen only, 4-shot magazine.
Barrel: 24".
Weight: About 7¾ lbs. **Length:** 44½" over-all.
Stock: American walnut, 20 l.p.i. checkering on p.g. and fore-end. Classic styling. Satin finish.
Sights: Hooded ramp front, step-adjustable rear. Receiver drilled and tapped for scope mounting.
Features: A "classic" version of the M700ADL with straight comb stock. Fitted with rubber recoil pad. Sling swivel studs installed. Limited production in 1987 only.
Price: About **$440.00**

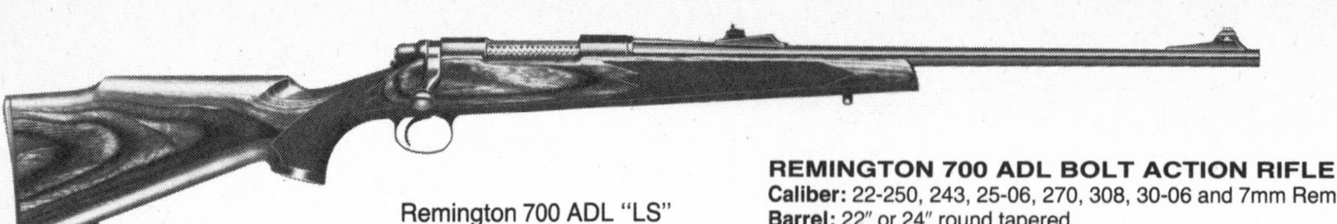

Remington 700 ADL "LS"

REMINGTON 700 ADL BOLT ACTION RIFLE

Caliber: 22-250, 243, 25-06, 270, 308, 30-06 and 7mm Rem. Mag.
Barrel: 22″ or 24″ round tapered.
Weight: 7 lbs. **Length:** 41½″ to 43½″ over-all.
Stock: Walnut. RKW finished p.g. stock with impressed checkering, Monte Carlo.
Sights: Gold bead ramp front; removable, step-adj. rear with windage screw.
Features: Side safety, receiver tapped for scope mounts.
Price: About **$380.00**
Price: 7mm Rem. Mag., about........ **$400.00**
Price: Model 700 ADL/LS (laminated stock, 30-06 only)........ **$440.00**

Remington Model 700 Gun Kit

Same as the Model 700 ADL except comes with a completely inletted walnut stock furnished in rough-shaped condition. Long or short 700 ADL action, blind magazine, factory sights, swivel studs, butt plate. Directions and three checkering templates are included. Available in 243, 308, 270, 30-06, 7mm Rem. Mag.
Price:........ **$333.00**
Price: 7mm Rem. Mag........ **$353.00**

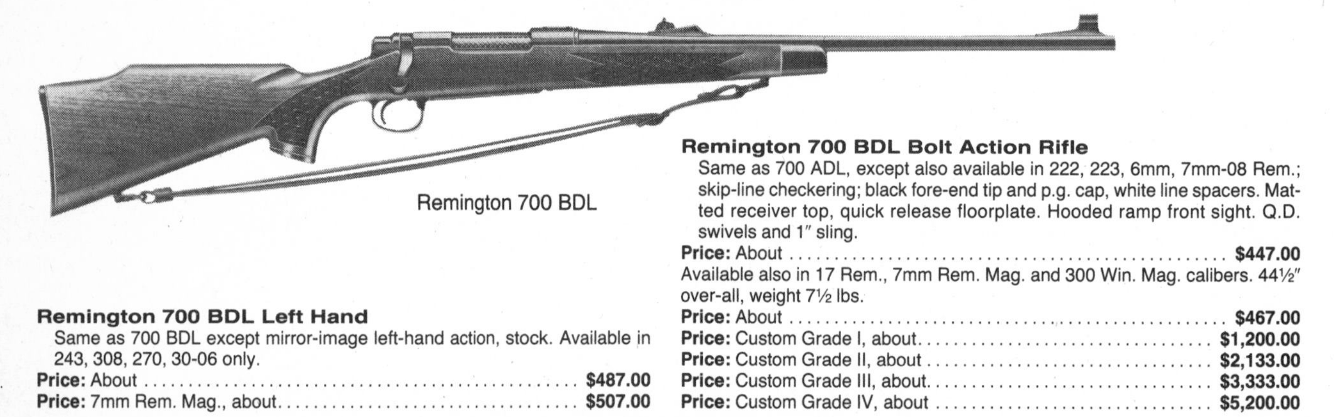

Remington 700 BDL

Remington 700 BDL Bolt Action Rifle

Same as 700 ADL, except also available in 222, 223, 6mm, 7mm-08 Rem.; skip-line checkering; black fore-end tip and p.g. cap, white line spacers. Matted receiver top, quick release floorplate. Hooded ramp front sight. Q.D. swivels and 1″ sling.
Price: About **$447.00**
Available also in 17 Rem., 7mm Rem. Mag. and 300 Win. Mag. calibers. 44½″ over-all, weight 7½ lbs.
Price: About **$467.00**
Price: Custom Grade I, about........ **$1,200.00**
Price: Custom Grade II, about **$2,133.00**
Price: Custom Grade III, about........ **$3,333.00**
Price: Custom Grade IV, about **$5,200.00**

Remington 700 BDL Left Hand

Same as 700 BDL except mirror-image left-hand action, stock. Available in 243, 308, 270, 30-06 only.
Price: About **$487.00**
Price: 7mm Rem. Mag., about........ **$507.00**

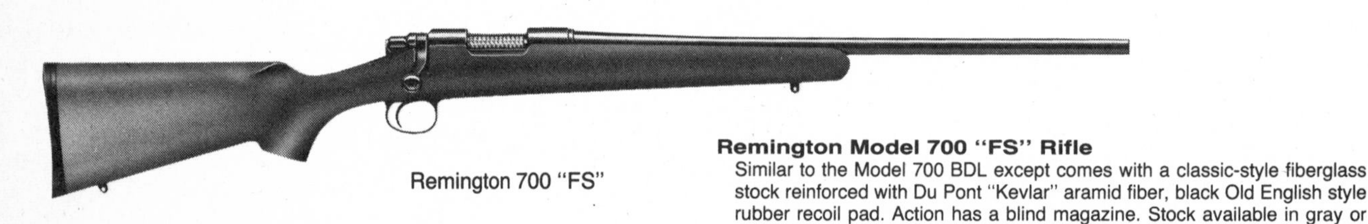

Remington 700 "FS"

Remington Model 700 "FS" Rifle

Similar to the Model 700 BDL except comes with a classic-style fiberglass stock reinforced with Du Pont "Kevlar" aramid fiber, black Old English style rubber recoil pad. Action has a blind magazine. Stock available in gray or camouflage. Right-hand actions available in 243, 308, 7mm Rem. Mag.; left-hand in 270, 30-06, 7mm Rem. Mag. Weight is 6⅝ lbs. (long action), 6½ lbs. (short action). Introduced 1987.
Price:........ **$613.00**
Price: 7mm Rem. Mag........ **$633.00**

Remington 700 BDL Varmint Special

Same as 700 BDL, except 24″ heavy bbl., 43½″ over-all, wgt. 9 lbs. Cals. 222, 223, 22-250, 243, 6mm Rem., 7mm-08 Rem. and 308. No sights.
Price: About **$476.00**

Remington Model 700 "Mountain Rifle"

Similar to the 700 BDL except weighs 6¾ lbs., has a 22″ tapered barrel. Redesigned pistol grip, straight comb, contoured cheekpiece, satin stock finish, fine checkering, hinged floorplate and magazine follower, 2-position thumb safety. Chambered for 243, 270 Win., 7mm-08, 280 Rem., 30-06, 308, 4-shot magazine. Over-all length is 42½″. Introduced 1986.
Price: About **$447.00**

Remington 700 Safari

Similar to the 700 BDL except 8mm Rem. Mag., 375 H&H or 458 Win. Magnum calibers only with heavy barrel. Hand checkered, oil finished stock in classic or Monte Carlo style with recoil pad installed. Delivery time is about 5 months.
Price: About **$827.00**

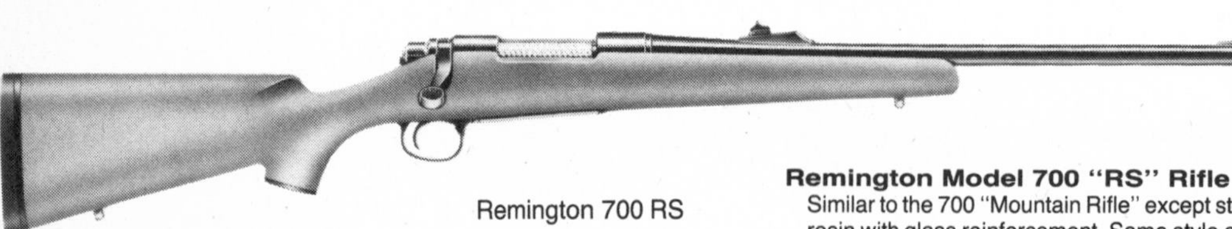

Remington 700 RS

Remington Model 700 "RS" Rifle

Similar to the 700 "Mountain Rifle" except stock is of a Du Pont thermoplastic resin with glass reinforcement. Same style as the "Mountain Rifle," available in gray or camo with lightly textured finish (cheekpiece left smooth). Solid butt pad, grip cap with Remington logo. Right-hand, long action only with hinged floorplate in 270, 280 Rem., 30-06, 22″ barrel, weight 6¾ lbs. Introduced 1987.
Price:........ **$547.00**

Remington Model 700 Custom "KS" Mountain Rifle

Similar to the 700 "Mountain Rifle" except has Kevlar reinforced resin synthetic stock. Available in both left- and right-hand versions. Chambered for 270 Win., 280 Rem., 30-06, 7mm Rem. Mag., 300 Win. Mag., 338 Win. Mag., 8mm Rem. Mag., 375 H&H, all with 24″ barrel only. Weight is 6 lbs., 6 oz. Introduced 1986.
Price: About **$867.00**

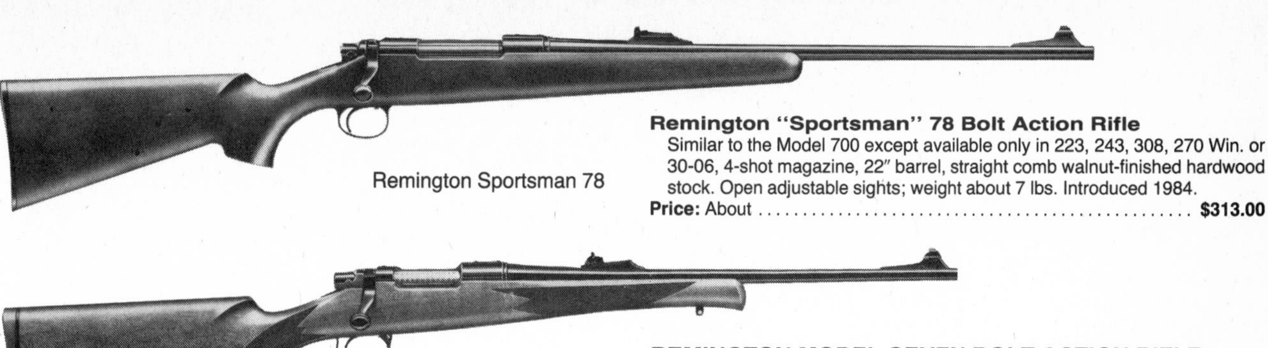

Remington Sportsman 78

Remington "Sportsman" 78 Bolt Action Rifle

Similar to the Model 700 except available only in 223, 243, 308, 270 Win. or 30-06, 4-shot magazine, 22″ barrel, straight comb walnut-finished hardwood stock. Open adjustable sights; weight about 7 lbs. Introduced 1984.

Price: About **$313.00**

Remington Model Seven

REMINGTON MODEL SEVEN BOLT ACTION RIFLE

Caliber: 223 Rem. (5-shot), 243, 7mm-08, 6mm, 308 (4-shot).
Barrel: 18½″.
Weight: 6¼ lbs. **Length:** 37½″ over-all.
Stock: Walnut, with modified Schnabel fore-end. Cut checkering.
Sights: Ramp front, adjustable open rear.
Features: New short action design; silent side safety; free-floated barrel except for single pressure point at fore-end tip. Introduced 1983.
Price: About **$440.00**

Remington Model Seven "FS" Rifle

Similar to the standard Model Seven except has a fiberglass stock reinforced with Du Pont Kevlar aramid fiber. Classic style in gray or camo, rubber butt pad. Weight is 5½ lbs. Calibers 243, 7mm-08, 308. Introduced 1987.

Price: **$600.00**

Remington Model Seven Custom "KS"

Similar to the standard Model Seven except has a stock of lightweight Kevlar aramid fiber and chambered only for 35 Rem. and 350 Rem. Mag. Barrel length is 20″, weight 5¾ lbs. Same stock features, design as the "FS" rifle. Comes with iron sights and is drilled and tapped for scope mounting. Special order through Remington Custom Shop. Introduced 1987.

Price: **$867.00**

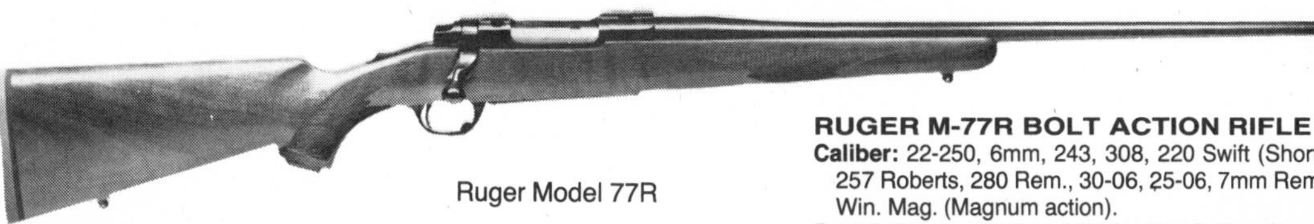

Ruger Model 77R

RUGER M-77R BOLT ACTION RIFLE

Caliber: 22-250, 6mm, 243, 308, 220 Swift (Short Stroke action); 270, 7x57, 257 Roberts, 280 Rem., 30-06, 25-06, 7mm Rem. Mag., 300 Win. Mag., 338 Win. Mag. (Magnum action).
Barrel: 22″ round tapered (24″ in 220 Swift and magnum action calibers).
Weight: 6¾ lbs. **Length:** 42″ over-all (22″ barrel).
Stock: Hand checkered American walnut, p.g. cap, sling swivel studs and recoil pad.
Sights: None supplied; comes with scope rings.
Features: Integral scope mount bases, diagonal bedding system, hinged floor plate, adj. trigger, tang safety.
Price: With Ruger steel scope rings, no sights (M-77R) **$460.00**

Ruger M-77RS Magnum Rifle

Similar to Ruger 77 except magnum-size action. Calibers 270, 7x57, 30-06, 243, 308, 25-06, 7mm Rem. Mag., 300 Win. Mag., 338 Win. Mag., with 24″ barrel. Weight about 7 lbs. Integral-base receiver, Ruger 1″ rings and open sights.

Price: **$518.00**

Ruger M-77RS Tropical Rifle

Similar to the Model 77RS Magnum except chambered only for 458 Win. Mag., 24″ barrel, steel trigger guard and floorplate. Weight about 8¾ lbs. Comes with open sights and Ruger 1″ scope rings.

Price: **$600.00**

Ruger International 77

Ruger International M-77RSI Rifle

Same as the standard Model 77 except has 18½″ barrel, full-length Mannlicher-style stock, with steel fore-end cap, loop-type sling swivel. Integral base receiver, open sights, Ruger 1″ steel rings. Improved front sight. Available in 22-250, 250-3000, 243, 308, 270, 30-06. Weighs 7 lbs. Length over-all is 38⅜″.

Price: **$524.00**

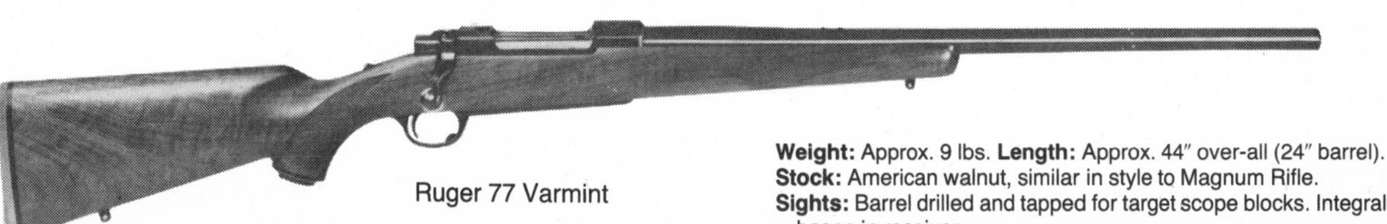

Ruger 77 Varmint

RUGER M-77V VARMINT

Caliber: 22-250, 220 Swift, 243, 25-06, 308.
Barrel: 24″ heavy straight tapered, 24″ in 220 swift.
Weight: Approx. 9 lbs. **Length:** Approx. 44″ over-all (24″ barrel).
Stock: American walnut, similar in style to Magnum Rifle.
Sights: Barrel drilled and tapped for target scope blocks. Integral scope mount bases in receiver.
Features: Ruger diagonal bedding system. Ruger steel 1″ scope rings supplied. Fully adj. trigger. Barreled actions available in any of the standard calibers and barrel lengths.
Price: **$482.00**

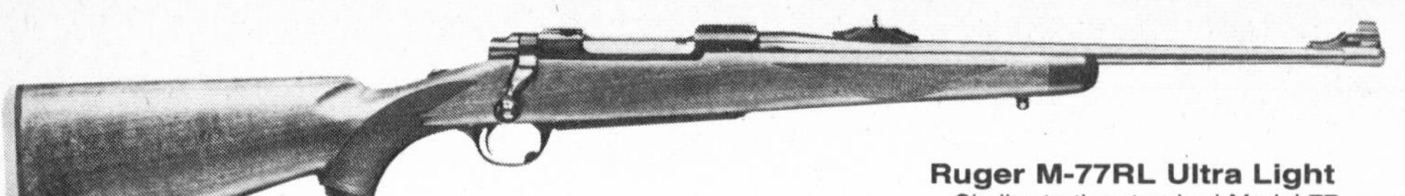
Ruger Ultra Light

Ruger M-77RL Ultra Light
Similar to the standard Model 77 except weighs only 6 lbs., chambered for 243, 270, 30-06, 257, 22-250, 250-3000 and 308; barrel tapped for target scope blocks; has 20″ Ultra Light barrel. Over-all length 40″. Ruger's steel 1″ scope rings supplied. Introduced 1983.
Price: **$498.00**

Ruger M-77RLS Ultra Light Carbine
Similar to the Model 77RL Ultra Light except has 18½″ barrel, Ruger Integral Scope Mounting System, iron sights, and hinged floorplate. Available in 270, 30-06 (Magnum action); 243, 308 (Short Stroke action). Weight is 6 lbs., over-all length 38⅞″. Introduced 1987.
Price: M-77RLS **$498.00**

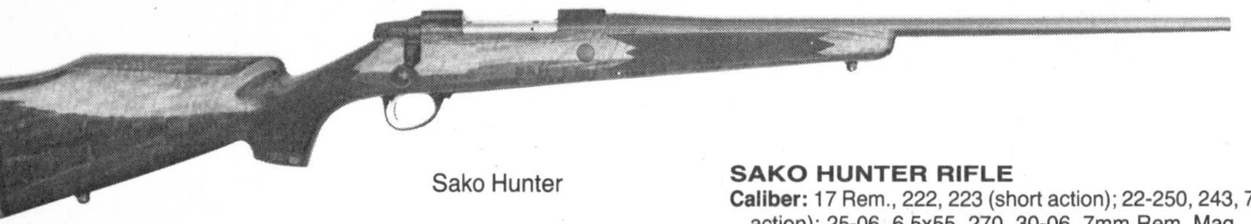
Sako Hunter

SAKO HUNTER RIFLE
Caliber: 17 Rem., 222, 223 (short action); 22-250, 243, 7mm-08, 308 (medium action); 25-06, 6.5x55, 270, 30-06, 7mm Rem. Mag., 7x64, 300 Win. Mag., 338 Win. Mag., 9.3x62, 375 H&H Mag., 300 Wea. Mag. (long action).
Barrel: 22″ to 24″ depending on caliber.
Weight: 5¾ lbs. (short); 6¼ lbs. (med.); 7¼ lbs. (long).
Stock: Hand-checkered European walnut.
Sights: None furnished. Scope mounts included.
Features: Adj. trigger, hinged floorplate. Imported from Finland by Stoeger.
Price: 17 Rem. **$850.00**
Price: 222, 223, 22-250, 243, 308, 7mm-08 .... **$820.00**
Price: Long action cals. (except magnums) **$840.00**
Price: Magnum cals. **$850.00**
Price: 375 H&H **$860.00**
Price: 300 Wea. **$870.00**

Sako Fiberclass Sporter
Similar to the Hunter except has a black fiberglass stock in the classic style, with wrinkle finish, rubber butt pad. Barrel length is 23″, weight 7 lbs., 2 oz. Comes with scope mounts. Introduced 1985.
Price: 17 Rem. **$1,160.00**
Price: Short, medium, long action, std. cals. **$1,130.00**
Price: Magnum cals. **$1,160.00**

Sako Safari Grade Bolt Action
Similar to the Hunter except available in long action, calibers 300 Win. Mag., 338 Win. Mag. or 375 H&H Mag. only. Stocked in French walnut, checkered 20 l.p.i., solid rubber butt pad; grip cap and fore-end tip; quarter-rib "express" rear sight, hooded ramp front. Front sling swivel band-mounted on barrel.
Price: **$2,115.00**

Sako Hunter Left-Hand Rifle
Same gun as the Sako Hunter except has left-hand action, stock with dull finish. Available in long action and magnum calibers only. Introduced 1987.
Price: Standard calibers **$950.00**
Price: Magnum calibers **$960.00**
Price: 375 H&H **$970.00**

Sako Hunter LS

Sako Hunter LS Rifle
Same gun as the Sako Hunter except has laminated stock with dull finish. Chambered for same calibers. Introduced 1987.
Price: Short and medium action **$925.00**
Price: Long action **$940.00**
Price: Magnum cals. **$945.00**

Sako Carbine

Sako Carbine
Same 18½″ barreled action and calibers as Sako Carbine but with conventional oil-finished stock of the Hunter model. Introduced 1986.
Price: 22-250, 243, 7mm-08, 308 Win. **$820.00**
Price: 25-06, 6.5x55, 270, 7x64, 30-06 .... **$840.00**
Price: 7mm Rem. Mag., 300 Win., 338 Win., 375 H&H. **$850.00**
Price: As Fiberclass with black fiberglass stock, 25-06, 270, 30-06 **$1,130.00**
Price: As above, 7mm Rem. Mag., 308 Mag., 338 Win., 375 H&H . **$1,160.00**

Sako Heavy Barrel
Same as std. Super Sporter except has beavertail fore-end; available in 222, 223 (short action), 22 PPC, 6mm PPC (single shot), 22-250, 243, 308 (medium action). Weight from 8¼ to 8½ lbs. 5-shot magazine capacity.
Price: 222, 223 (short action) **$1,035.00**
Price: 22-250, 243, 308 (medium action) **$1,035.00**
Price: 22 PPC, 6mm PPC (single shot) **$925.00**

Sako Mannlicher-Style Carbine
Same as the Carbine except has full "Mannlicher" style stock, 18½″ barrel, weighs 7½ lbs., chambered for 222 Rem., 243, 25-06, 270, 308 and 30-06, 7mm Rem. Mag., 300 Win. Mag., 338 Win. Mag., 375 H&H. Introduced 1977. From Stoeger.
Price: **$885.00**
Price: Magnum cals. **$915.00**
Price: 375 H&H **$935.00**

CAUTION: PRICES CHANGE. CHECK AT GUNSHOP.

Sako Deluxe Sporter

Sako Super Deluxe Sporter

Similar to Deluxe Sporter except has select European walnut with high gloss finish and deep cut oak leaf carving. Metal has super high polish, deep blue finish.

Price: **$2,115.00**

Sako Deluxe Sporter

Same action as Hunter except has select wood, rosewood p.g. cap and fore-end tip. Fine checkering on top surfaces of integral dovetail bases, bolt sleeve, bolt handle root and bolt knob. Vent. recoil pad, skip-line checkering, mirror finish bluing.

Price: **$1,065.00**
Price: 7mm Rem. Mag., 300 Win. Mag., 338 Mag., 375 H&H...... **$1,090.00**

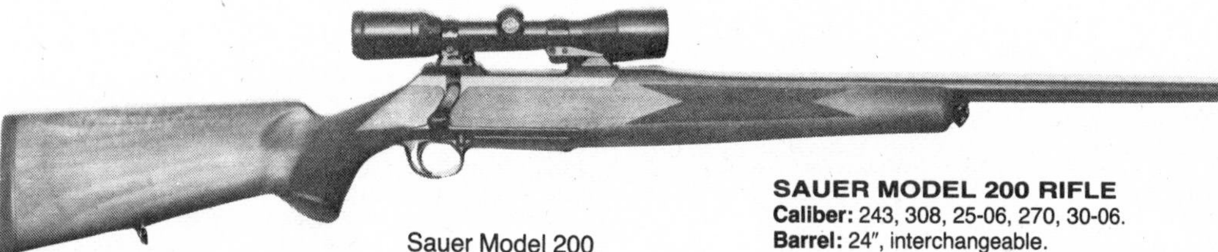

Sauer Model 200

SAUER 90 RIFLE

Caliber: 22-250, 243, 308 (Short, Stutzen) 25-06, 270, 30-06, (Medium, Stutzen); 7mm Rem. Mag., 300 Win., 300 Wea., 375 H&H (Magnum); 458 Win. Mag. (Safari).
Barrel: 20″ (Stutzen), 24″, 26″.
Weight: 7 lbs., 6 oz. (Junior). **Length:** 42½″ over-all.
Stock: European walnut with oil finish, recoil pad.
Sights: Post front on ramp, open rear adj. for w.
Features: Detachable 3-4 round box magazine; rear bolt locking lugs; 65° bolt throw; front sling swivel on barrel band. Introduced 1986. Imported from West Germany by Sigarms.
Price: About.. **$1,175.00**
Price: Safari, about... **$1,675.00**

SAUER MODEL 200 RIFLE

Caliber: 243, 308, 25-06, 270, 30-06.
Barrel: 24″, interchangeable.
Weight: 6⅔ lbs. (Alloy) to 7¾ lbs. (Steel). **Length:** 44″ over-all.
Stock: European walnut with recoil pad; checkered p.g. and fore-end.
Sights: None furnished. Drilled and tapped for iron sights and scope mount.
Features: Easily interchangeable barrels, buttstock and fore-end; removable box magazine; steel and alloy versions; left-hand models available. Introduced 1986. Imported from West Germany by Sigarms.
Price: Standard Grade, about **$875.00**
Price: LUX Grade, about.................................... **$1,075.00**
Price: Carbon fiber, about.................................. **$1,200.00**
Price: Magnum (special order, 7mm Rem. Mag., 300 Win. Mag. **$815.00**

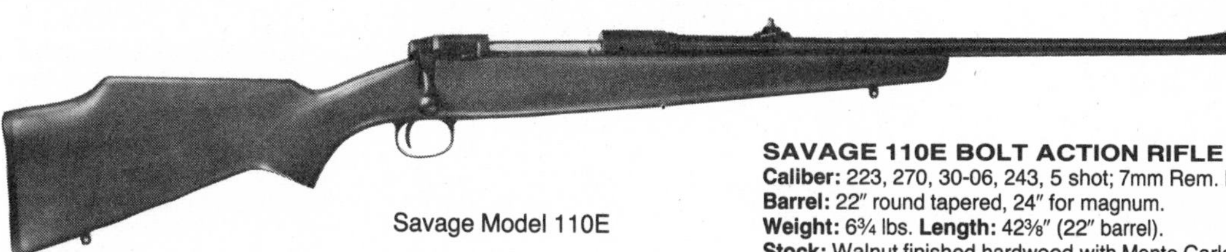

Savage Model 110E

Savage Model 110F Bolt Action Rifle

Similar to the Model 110E except chambered only for 270, 30-06, 7mm Rem. Mag., and has a black Du Pont Rynite® stock with black butt pad. Introduced 1988.

Price: **$329.00**

SAVAGE 110E BOLT ACTION RIFLE

Caliber: 223, 270, 30-06, 243, 5 shot; 7mm Rem. Mag., 4 shot.
Barrel: 22″ round tapered, 24″ for magnum.
Weight: 6¾ lbs. **Length:** 42⅜″ (22″ barrel).
Stock: Walnut finished hardwood with Monte Carlo; hard rubber buttplate.
Sights: Ramp front, step adj. rear.
Features: Top tang safety, receiver tapped for scope mount. Full floating barrel; adjustable trigger.
Price: **$259.00**
Price: Without sights **$249.00**

Savage Model 110B Bolt Action Rifle

Similar to the Model 110E except has brown laminated Monte Carlo stock with brown butt pad. Weighs 6¾ lbs. Introduced 1988.

Price: **$329.00**

Steyr-Mannlicher Professional

STEYR-MANNLICHER MODEL M

Caliber: 7x64, 7x57, 25-06, 270, 30-06. Left-hand action cals.—7x64, 25-06, 270, 30-06. Optional cals.—6.5x57, 8x57JS, 9.3x62, 6.5x55, 7.5x55.
Barrel: 20″ (full-stock); 23.6″ (half-stock).
Weight: 6.8 lbs. to 7.5 lbs. **Length:** 39″ (full-stock); 43″ (half-stock).
Stock: Hand checkered walnut. Full Mannlicher or std. half stock with M.C. and rubber recoil pad.
Sights: Ramp front, open U-notch rear.
Features: Choice of interchangeable single or double set triggers. Detachable 5-shot rotary magazine. Drilled and tapped for scope mounting. Available as "Professional" model with Parkerized finish and synthetic stock (right hand action only). Imported by Gun South, Inc.
Price: Full-stock (carbine).................................. **$1,939.00**
Price: Half-stock (rifle)..................................... **$1,812.00**
Price: For left-hand action (full stock) add about **$173.00**
Price: Professional model (full stock) **$1,532.00**

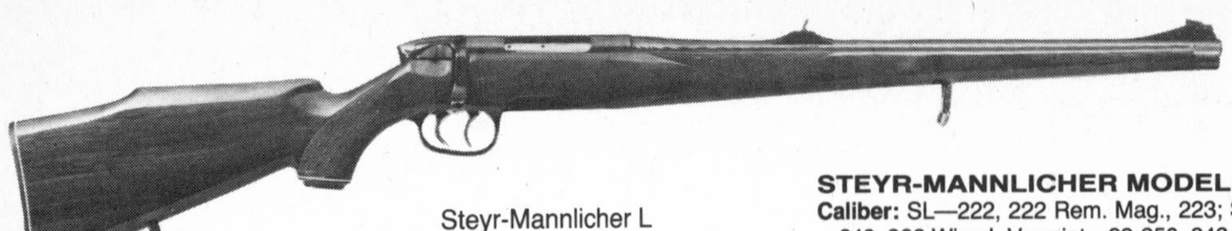

Steyr-Mannlicher L

Steyr-Mannlicher "Luxus"

Similar to Steyr-Mannlicher Models L and M except has single set trigger and detachable 3-shot steel magazine. Same calibers as L and M. Oil finish or high gloss lacquer on stock.

Price: Full-stock $2,495.00
Price: Half-stock $2,364.00

STEYR-MANNLICHER MODELS S & S/T

Caliber: Model S—300 Win. Mag., 338 Win. Mag., 7mm Rem. Mag., 300 H&H Mag., 375 H&H Mag. (6.5x68, 8x68S, 9.3x64 optional); S/T—375 H&H Mag., 458 Win. Mag. (9.3x64 optional).
Barrel: 25.6"
Weight: 8.4 lbs. (Model S). **Length:** 45" over-all.
Stock: Half-stock with M.C. and rubber recoil pad. Hand checkered walnut. Available with optional spare magazine inletted in butt.
Sights: Ramp front, U-notch rear.
Features: Choice of interchangeable single or double set triggers, detachable 4-shot magazine. Drilled and tapped for scope mounts. Imported by Gun South, Inc.

Price: Model S.. $1,952.00
Price: Model S/T 375 H&H, 458 Win. Mag. $2,176.00

STEYR-MANNLICHER MODELS SL & L

Caliber: SL—222, 222 Rem. Mag., 223; SL Varmint—222; L—22-250, 6mm, 243, 308 Win.; L Varmint—22-250, 243, 308 Win.
Barrel: 20" (full-stock); 23.6" (half-stock).
Weight: 6 lbs. (full-stock). **Length:** 38¼" (full-stock).
Stock: Hand checkered walnut. Full Mannlicher or standard half-stock with Monte Carlo.
Sights: Ramp front, open U-notch rear.
Features: Choice of interchangeable single or double set triggers. Five-shot detachable "Makrolon" rotary magazine, 6 rear locking lugs. Drilled and tapped for scope mounts. Imported by Gun South, Inc.

Price: Full-Stock $1,939.00
Price: Half-stock $1,812.00

Steyr-Mannlicher Varmint, Models SL and L

Similar to standard SL and L except chambered only for 222 Rem. (SL), 22-250, 243, 308. Has 26" heavy barrel, no sights (drilled and tapped for scope mounts). Choice of single or double set triggers. Five-shot detachable magazine.

Price: $1,939.00

Ultra Light Model 20

Ultra Light Arms Model 20S Rifle

Similar to the Model 20 except uses short action chambered for 17 Rem., 222 Rem., 223 Rem., 22 Hornet. Has 22" Douglas Premium No. 1 contour barrel, weighs 4¾ lbs., 41" over-all length.

Price: $1,800.00
Price: Model 20S Left Hand (left-hand action and stock) $1,900.00

Ultra Light Arms Model 28 Rifle

Similar to the Model 20 except in 264, 7mm Rem. Mag., 300 Win. Mag., 338 Win. Mag. Uses 24" Douglas Premium No. 2 contour barrel. Weighs 5½ lbs., 45" over-all length. KDF or U.L.A. recoil arrestor built in. Any custom feature available on any U.L.A. product can be incorporated.

Price: Right hand $2,350.00
Price: Left hand.. $2,450.00

ULTRA LIGHT ARMS MODEL 20 RIFLE

Caliber: 17 Rem., 22 Hornet, 222 Rem., 222 Rem. Mag., 223 Rem., 22-250, 6mm Rem., 243, 250-3000, 257 Roberts, 257 Ackley, 7x57, 7x57 Ackley, 7mm-08, 284 Win., 300 Savage, 358 Win.
Barrel: 22" or 24" Douglas Premium No. 1 contour.
Weight: 4½ lbs. **Length:** 41½" over-all.
Stock: Composite Kevlar, graphite reinforced. Du Pont Imron paint colors — green, black, brown and camo options. Choice of length of pull.
Sights: None furnished. Scope mount included.
Features: Timney adj. trigger; two-position three-function safety. Benchrest quality action. Matte or bright stock and metal finish. 3" magazine length. Shipped in a hard case. From Ultra Light Arms, Inc.

Price: Right hand $1,800.00
Price: Model 20 Left Hand (left-hand action and stock)........... $1,900.00
Price: Model 24 (25-06, 270, 7mm Express Rem., 30-06, 3⅜" magazine length).. $1,875.00
Price: Model 24 Left Hand (left-hand action and stock)........... $1,975.00

VOERE 2155, 2165 BOLT ACTION RIFLE

Caliber: 22-250, 270, 308, 243, 30-06, 7x64, 5.6x57, 6.5x57, 6.5x55, 8x57 JRS, 7mm Rem. Mag., 300 Win. Mag., 8x68S, 9.3x62, 9.3x64, 6.5x68.
Stock: European walnut, hog-back style; checkered pistol grip and fore-end.
Sights: Ramp front, open adjustable rear.
Features: Mauser-type action with 5-shot detachable box magazine; double set or single trigger; drilled and tapped for scope mounting. Imported from Austria by L. Joseph Rahn. Introduced 1984.

Price: M2165, standard calibers, single trigger.................. $885.00
Price: As above, double set triggers.......................... $925.00
Price: M2165, magnum calibers, single trigger.................. $915.00
Price: As above, double set triggers.......................... $955.00
Price: M2165, full-stock, single trigger........................ $925.00
Price: As above, double set triggers.......................... $985.00
Price: M2155 (as above, no jeweling, military safety, single trigger). $700.00
Price: As above, double triggers.............................. $750.00

Voere Model 2165

Consult our Directory pages for the location of firms mentioned.

CAUTION: PRICES CHANGE. CHECK AT GUNSHOP.

Weatherby Mark V

WEATHERBY EUROMARK BOLT ACTION RIFLE

Caliber: All Weatherby calibers except 224, 22-250.
Barrel: 24″ or 26″ round tapered.
Weight: 6½ to 10½ lbs. **Length:** 44¼″ over-all (24″ bbl.).
Stock: Walnut, Monte Carlo with extended tail, fine-line hand checkering, satin oil finish, ebony fore-end tip and grip cap with maple diamond, solid butt pad.
Sights: Optional (extra).
Features: Cocking indicator; adj. trigger; hinged floor plate; thumb safety; q.d. sling swivels. Introduced 1986.
Price: With 24″ barrel (240, 257, 270, 7mm, 30-06, 300), right- or left-hand **$1,040.00**
Price: 26″ No. 2 Contour barrel, right- or left-hand (300 only)...... **$1,060.00**
Price: 340 W.M., 26″, right- or left-hand **$1,060.00**
Price: 378 W.M., 26″, right or left-hand.......... **$1,214.00**
Price: 460 W.M., 26″, right or left-hand.......... **$1,354.00**

WEATHERBY MARK V BOLT ACTION RIFLE

Caliber: All Weatherby cals., plus 22-250 and 30-06
Barrel: 24″ or 26″ round tapered.
Weight: 6½-10½ lbs. **Length:** 43¼″-46½″ over-all.
Stock: Walnut, Monte Carlo with cheekpiece, high luster finish, checkered p.g. and fore-end, recoil pad.
Sights: Optional (extra).
Features: Cocking indicator, adj. trigger, hinged floorplate, thumb safety, quick detachable sling swivels.
Price: Cals. 224 and 22-250, std. bbl., right-hand only **$971.00**
Price: With 26″ semi-target bbl., right-hand only **$987.00**
Price: Cals. 240, 257, 270, 7mm, 30-06 and 300 (24″bbl.) right- or left-hand **$991.00**
Price: With 26″ No. 2 contour bbl., right-hand or 300 W.M. left only **$1,011.00**
Price: Cal. 340 (26″ bbl.), right- or left-hand.......... **$1,011.00**
Price: Cal. 378 (26″ bbl.), right- or left-hand.......... **$1,165.00**
Price: Cal. 460 (26″ bbl.), right- or left-hand.......... **$1,305.00**

Weatherby Mark V Rifle Left Hand

Available in all Weatherby calibers, plus 30-06 with 24″ barrel. Left hand 26″ barrel available in 300 and 340 calibers. Not available in 224 WM and 22-250 Varmintmaster.

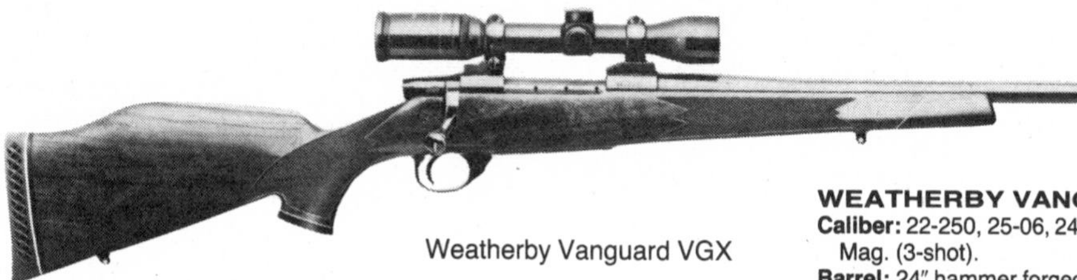

Weatherby Vanguard VGX

Weatherby Vanguard Fiberguard Rifle

Uses the Vanguard barreled action and a forest green or black wrinkle-finished fiberglass stock. All metal is matte blue. Has a 20″ barrel, weighs 6½ lbs., measures 40″ in 223, 243, and 308; 40½″ in 270, 7mm Rem. Mag., 30-06. Accepts same scope mount bases as Mark V action. Introduced 1985.
Price: Right-hand only.......... **$560.00**

WEATHERBY VANGUARD VGX, VGS RIFLES

Caliber: 22-250, 25-06, 243, 270, and 30-06 (5-shot); 7mm Rem. and 300 Win. Mag. (3-shot).
Barrel: 24″ hammer forged.
Weight: 7⅞ lbs. **Length:** 44½″ over-all.
Stock: American walnut, p.g. cap and fore-end tip, hand inletted and checkered. 13½″ pull.
Sights: Optional, available at extra cost.
Features: Side safety, adj. trigger, hinged floorplate, receiver tapped for scope mounts. Imported from Japan by Weatherby.
Price: VGS **$467.00**
Price: VGX—deluxe wood, different checkering, ventilated recoil pad **$600.00**

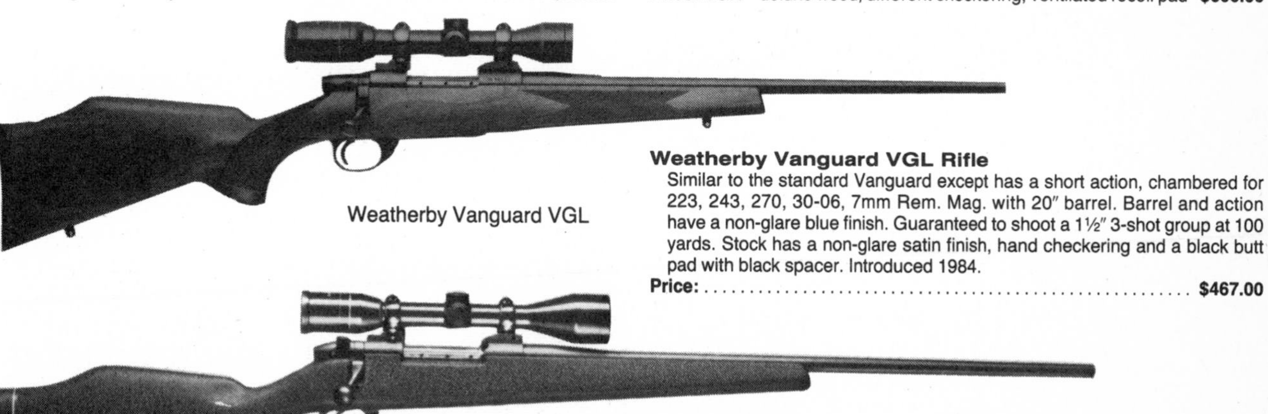

Weatherby Vanguard VGL

Weatherby Fibermark

Weatherby Vanguard VGL Rifle

Similar to the standard Vanguard except has a short action, chambered for 223, 243, 270, 30-06, 7mm Rem. Mag. with 20″ barrel. Barrel and action have a non-glare blue finish. Guaranteed to shoot a 1½″ 3-shot group at 100 yards. Stock has a non-glare satin finish, hand checkering and a black butt pad with black spacer. Introduced 1984.
Price:.......... **$467.00**

Weatherby Fibermark Rifle

Same as the standard Mark V except the stock is of fiberglass; finished with a non-glare black wrinkle finish and black recoil pad; receiver and floorplate have low luster blue finish; fluted bolt has a satin finish. Available in left- or right-hand, 24″ or 26″ barrel, 240 Weatherby Mag. through 340 Weatherby Mag. calibers. Introduced 1983.
Price: 240 W.M. through 300 W.M., 24″ bbl. **$1,123.00**
Price: 240 W.M. through 340 W.M., 26″ bbl., right-hand or 300, 340 W.M. left-hand only **$1,143.00**

Weatherby Lazer Mark V Rifle

Same as standard Mark V except stock has extensive laser carving under cheekpiece on butt, p.g. and fore-end. Introduced 1981.
Price: 22-250, 224 Wea., 24″ bbl., right-hand only.......... **$1,085.00**
Price: As above, 26″ bbl., right-hand only **$1,100.00**
Price: 240 Wea. thru 300 Wea., 24″ bbl., right- or left-hand **$1,105.00**
Price: As above, 26″ bbl., right-hand or 300 W.M. left-hand.......... **$1,125.00**
Price: 340 Wea., right- or left-hand **$1,127.00**
Price: 378 Wea., right- or left-hand **$1,281.00**
Price: 460 Wea., right- or left-hand **$1,421.00**

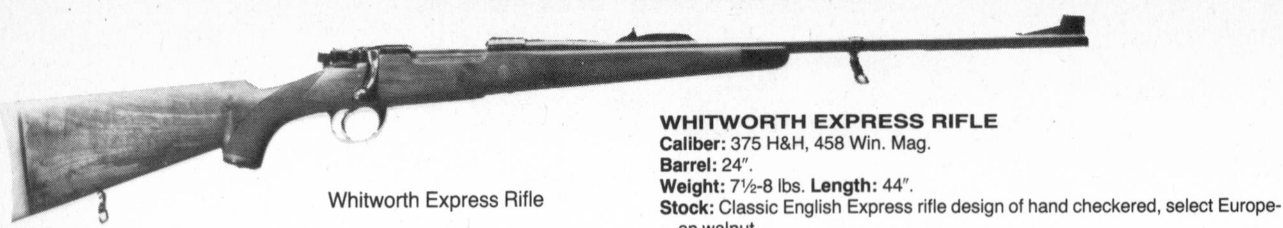
Whitworth Express Rifle

WHITWORTH EXPRESS RIFLE

Caliber: 375 H&H, 458 Win. Mag.
Barrel: 24″.
Weight: 7½-8 lbs. **Length:** 44″.
Stock: Classic English Express rifle design of hand checkered, select European walnut.
Sights: Three leaf open sight calibrated for 100, 200, 300 yards on ¼-rib, ramp front with removable hood.
Features: Solid rubber recoil pad, barrel-mounted sling swivel, adjustable trigger, hinged floor plate, solid steel recoil cross bolt.
Price: 375, 458, with express sights. **$690.00**

Wichita Varmint Rifle

WICHITA CLASSIC RIFLE

Caliber: 17 Rem. thru 308 Win., including 22 and 6mm PPC.
Barrel: 21⅛″.
Weight: 8 lbs. **Length:** 41″ over-all.
Stock: AAA Fancy American walnut. Hand-rubbed and checkered (20 l.p.i.). Hand-inletted, glass bedded, steel grip cap. Pachmayr rubber recoil pad.
Sights: None. Drilled and tapped for scope mounting.
Features: Available as single shot or repeater. Octagonal barrel and Wichita action, right or left-hand. Checkered bolt handle. Bolt is hand-fitted, lapped and jewelled. Adjustable Canjar trigger is set at 2 lbs. Side thumb safety. Firing pin fall is 3/16″. Non-glare blue finish. From Wichita Arms.
Price: Single shot **$2,950.00**
Price: With blind box magazine **$3,200.00**

WICHITA VARMINT RIFLE

Caliber: 17 Rem. thru 308 Win., including 22 and 6mm PPC.
Barrel: 20⅛″.
Weight: 9lbs. **Length:** 40⅛″ over-all.
Stock: AAA Fancy American walnut. Hand-rubbed finish, hand-checkered, 20 l.p.i. pattern. Hand-inletted, glass bedded, steel grip cap, Pachmayr rubber recoil pad.
Sights: None. Drilled and tapped for scope mounts.
Features: Right or left-hand Wichita action with three locking lugs. Available as a single shot or repeater with 3-shot magazine. Checkered bolt handle. Bolt is hand fitted, lapped and jeweled. Side thumb safety. Firing pin fall is 3/16″. Non-glare blue finish. From Wichita Arms.
Price: Single shot **$1,975.00**
Price: With blind box magazine **$2,225.00**

Winchester 70 Lightweight

WINCHESTER MODEL 70 LIGHTWEIGHT RIFLE

Caliber: 270, 30-06 (standard action); 22-250, 223, 243, 308 (short action), both 5-shot magazine, except 6-shot in 223.
Barrel: 22″.
Weight: 6¼ lbs. **Length:** 40½″ over-all (std.), 40″ (short).
Stock: American walnut with satin finish, deep-cut checkering.
Sights: None furnished. Drilled and tapped for scope mounting.
Features: Three position safety; stainless steel magazine follower; hinged floorplate; sling swivel studs. Introduced 1984.
Price: With sights, about. **$399.00**
Price: With Win-Tuff laminated stock **$409.00**
Price: With Win-Cam green-shaded laminated stock, 270, 30-06 only **$476.00**

Winchester 70 XTR Express

WINCHESTER 70 XTR SPORTER

Caliber: 22-250, 223, 243, 270, 270 Wea., 30-06, 264 Win. Mag., 7mm Rem. Mag., 300 Win. Mag., 300 Wea. Mag., 338 Win. Mag., 3-shot magazine.
Barrel: 24″.
Weight: 7¾ lbs. **Length:** 44½″ over-all.
Stock: American walnut with Monte Carlo cheekpiece. XTR checkering and satin finish.
Sights: None furnished; optional hooded ramp front, adjustable folding leaf rear.
Features: Three-position safety, detachable sling swivels, stainless steel magazine follower, rubber butt pad, epoxy bedded receiver recoil lug. Made under license by U.S. Repeating Arms Co.
Price: With sights, about. **$465.00**
Price: Without sights, about **$451.00**
Price: 300 Wea. Mag., without sights, about. **$468.00**

WINCHESTER 70 XTR SUPER EXPRESS MAGNUM

Caliber: 375 H&H Mag., 458 Win. Mag., 3-shot magazine.
Barrel: 24″ (375), 22″ (458).
Weight: 8½ lbs.
Stock: American walnut with Monte Carlo cheekpiece. XTR wrap-around checkering and finish.
Sights: Hooded ramp front, open rear.
Features: Two steel crossbolts in stock for added strength. Front sling swivel mounted on barrel. Contoured rubber butt pad. Made under license by U.S. Repeating Arms Co.
Price: About **$793.00**

Winchester Model 70 Winlite Rifle

Similar to the Model 70 XTR Sporter except has McMillan black fiberglass stock. No sights are furnished but receiver is drilled and tapped for scope mounting. Available in 270, 280, 30-06 (22″ barrel, 4-shot magazine), 7mm Rem. Mag., 300 Wea., 300 Win. Mag., 338 Win. Mag. (24″ barrel, 3-shot magazine). Weight is 6¼-6½ lbs. for 270, 30-06, 6¾-7 lbs. for 7mm Mag., 338. Introduced 1986.
Price: About **$636.00**
Price: 300 Weatherby, about **$654.00**

Winchester 70 Featherweight

Winchester Model 70 XTR Featherweight
Available with standard action in 270 Win., 280 Rem., 30-06, short action in 22-250, 223, 243, 308; 22″ tapered Featherweight barrel; classic-style American walnut stock with Schnabel fore-end, wrap-around XTR checkering fashioned after early Model 70 custom rifle patterns. Red rubber butt pad with black spacer; sling swivel studs. Weighs 6¾ lbs. (standard action), 6½ lbs. (short action). Introduced 1984.
Price: About **$465.00**

Winchester Ranger

Winchester Ranger Rifle
Similar to Model 70 XTR Sporter except chambered only for 243, 270, 30-06, with 22″ barrel. American hardwood stock, no checkering, composition butt plate. Metal has matte blue finish. Introduced 1985.
Price: About **$336.00**
Price: Ranger Youth, 243 only, scaled-down stock **$345.00**

CENTERFIRE RIFLES—SINGLE SHOTS

Classic and modern designs for sporting and competitive use.

Browning Model 1885

BROWNING MODEL 1885 SINGLE SHOT RIFLE
Caliber: 223, 22-250, 30-06, 270, 7mm Rem. Mag., 45-70.
Barrel: 28″.
Weight: About 8½ lbs. **Length:** 43½″ over-all.
Stock: Walnut with straight grip, Schnabel fore-end.
Sights: None furnished; drilled and tapped for scope mounting.
Features: Replica of J.M. Browning's high-wall falling-block rifle. Octagon barrel with recessed muzzle. Imported from Japan by Browning. Introduced 1985.
Price: **$671.95**

Ljutic Space Rifle

LJUTIC RECOILESS SPACE RIFLE
Caliber: 22-250, 30-30, 30-06, 308, single-shot.
Barrel: 24″.
Weight: 8¾ lbs. **Length:** 44″ over-all.
Stock: Walnut stock, fore-end and grip.
Sights: Iron sights or scope mounts.
Features: Revolutionary design has anti-recoil mechanism. Twist-bolt action uses six moving parts. Scope and mounts extra. Introduced 1981. From Ljutic Industries.
Price: **$3,695.00**

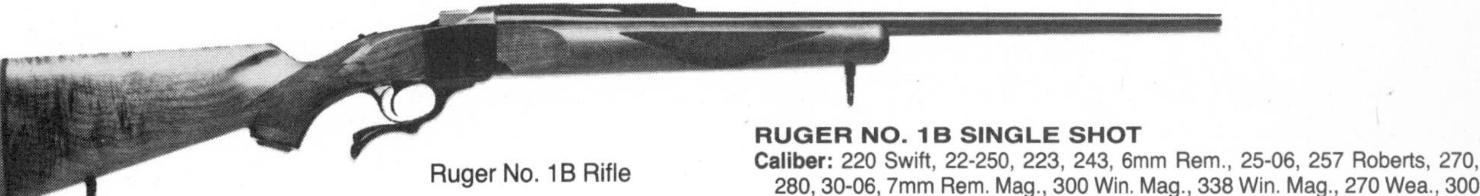

Ruger No. 1B Rifle

RUGER NO. 1B SINGLE SHOT
Caliber: 220 Swift, 22-250, 223, 243, 6mm Rem., 25-06, 257 Roberts, 270, 280, 30-06, 7mm Rem. Mag., 300 Win. Mag., 338 Win. Mag., 270 Wea., 300 Wea.
Barrel: 26″ round tapered with quarter-rib; with Ruger 1″ rings.
Weight: 8 lbs. **Length:** 43⅜″ over-all.
Stock: Walnut, two-piece, checkered p.g. and semi-beavertail fore-end.
Sights: None, 1″ scope rings supplied for integral mounts.
Features: Under lever, hammerless falling block design has auto ejector, top tang safety.
Price: **$575.00**
Price: Barreled action **$389.50**

Ruger No. 1S Medium Sporter
Similar to the No. 1B Standard Rifle except has Alexander Henry-style fore-end, adjustable folding leaf rear sight on quarter-rib, ramp front sight base and dovetail-type gold bead front sight. Calibers 7mm Rem. Mag., 338 Win. Mag., 300 Win. Mag. with 26″ barrel, 45-70 with 22″ barrel. Weight about 7½ lbs. in 45-70.
Price: No. 1S **$575.00**
Price: Barreled action **$389.50**

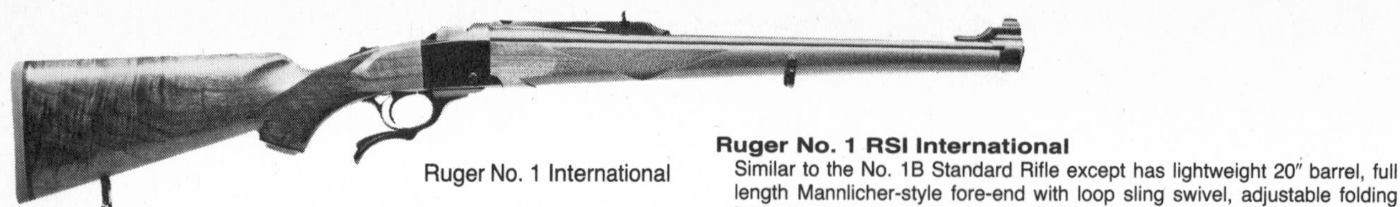

Ruger No. 1 International

Ruger No. 1 RSI International
Similar to the No. 1B Standard Rifle except has lightweight 20" barrel, full length Mannlicher-style fore-end with loop sling swivel, adjustable folding leaf rear sight on quarter rib, ramp front with gold bead. Calibers 243, 30-06, 270 and 7x57. Weight is about 7¼ lbs.
Price: No. 1RSI **$595.00**
Price: Barreled action **$389.50**

Ruger No. 1A Light Sporter
Similar to the No. 1B Standard Rifle except has lightweight 22" barrel, Alexander Henry-style fore-end, adjustable folding leaf rear sight on quarter-rib, dovetailed ramp front with gold bead. Calihers 243, 30-06, 270 and 7x57. Weight about 7¼ lbs.
Price: No. 1A **$575.00**
Price: Barreled action **$389.50**

Ruger No. 1H Tropical Rifle
Similar to the No. 1B Standard Rifle except has Alexander Henry fore-end, adjustable folding leaf rear sight on quarter-rib, ramp front with dovetail gold bead front, 24" heavy barrel. Calibers 375 H&H (weight about 8¼ lbs.) and 458 Win. Mag. (weight about 9 lbs.).
Price: No. 1H **$575.00**
Price: Barreled action **$389.50**

Ruger No. 1V Special Varminter
Similar to the No. 1B Standard Rifle except has 24" heavy barrel. Semi-beavertail fore-end, barrel tapped for target scope block, with 1" Ruger scope rings. Calibers 22-250, 220 Swift, 223, 25-06, 6mm. Weight about 9 lbs.
Price: No. 1V **$575.00**
Price: Barreled action **$389.50**

NAVY ARMS ROLLING BLOCK RIFLE
Caliber: 45-70.
Barrel: 30".
Stock: Walnut finished.
Sights: Fixed front, adj. rear.
Features: Reproduction of classic rolling block action. Available in Buffalo Rifle (octagonal bbl.) and Creedmoor (half-round, half-octagonal bbl.) models. From Navy Arms.
Price: 26", 30" full octagon barrel **$489.00**
Price: Creedmoor Model, 30" full octagon **$521.00**
Price: 30", half-round **$489.00**
Price: 26", half-round **$489.00**
Price: Half-round Creedmoor **$521.00**

C. SHARPS ARMS NEW MODEL 1875 RIFLE
Caliber: 22 LR Stevens, 32-40 & 38-55 Ballard, 40-90 3¼", 40-90 2⅝", 40-70 2 1/10", 40-70 2¼", 40-70 2½", 40-50 1 11/16" 40-50 1⅞", 45-90 2 4/10" 45-70 2 1/10".
Barrel: 24", 26", 30" (standard); 32", 34" optional.
Weight: 8-12 lbs.
Stock: Walnut, straight grip, shotgun butt with checkered steel buttplate.
Sights: Silver blade front, Rocky Mountain buckhorn rear.
Features: Recreation of the 1875 Sharps rifle. Production guns will have case colored receiver. Available in Custom Sporting and Target versions upon request. Announced 1986. From C. Sharps Arms Co.
Price: 1875 Carbine (24" tapered round bbl.) **$575.00**
Price: 1875 Saddle Rifle (26" tapered oct. bbl.) **$650.00**
Price: 1875 Sporting Rifle (30" tapered oct. bbl.) **$650.00**

Consult our directory pages for the location of firms mentioned.

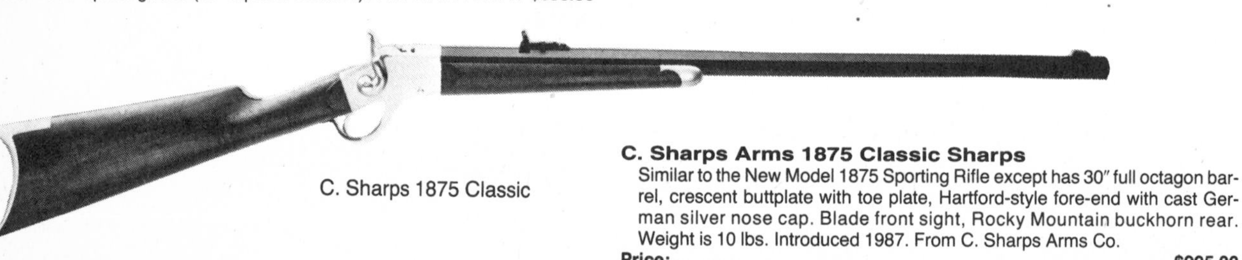

C. Sharps 1875 Classic

C. Sharps Arms 1875 Classic Sharps
Similar to the New Model 1875 Sporting Rifle except has 30" full octagon barrel, crescent buttplate with toe plate, Hartford-style fore-end with cast German silver nose cap. Blade front sight, Rocky Mountain buckhorn rear. Weight is 10 lbs. Introduced 1987. From C. Sharps Arms Co.
Price: **$995.00**

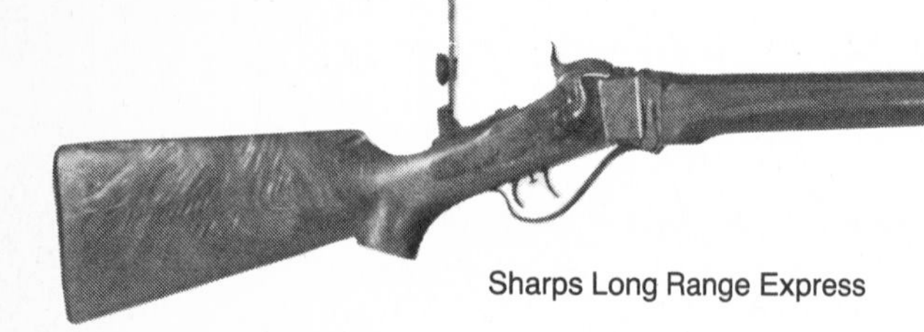

Sharps Long Range Express

SHILOH SHARPS 1874 LONG RANGE EXPRESS
Caliber: 40-50 BN, 40-70 BN, 40-90 BN, 45-70 ST, 45-90 ST, 45-110 ST, 50-70 ST, 50-90 ST, 50-110 ST, 32-40, 38-55, 40-70 ST, 40-90 ST.
Barrel: 34" tapered octagon.
Weight: 10½ lbs. **Length:** 51" over-all.
Stock: Oil-finished semi-fancy walnut with pistol grip, shotgun-style butt, traditional cheek rest and accent line. Schnabel fore-end.
Sights: Globe front, sporting tang rear.
Features: Recreation of the Model 1874 Sharps rifle. Double set triggers. Made in U.S. by Shiloh Rifle Mfg. Co.
Price: **$795.00**
Price: Sporting Rifle No. 1 (similar to above except with 30" bbl., blade front, buckhorn rear sight) **$775.00**
Price: Sporting Rifle No. 3 (similar to No. 1 except straight-grip stock, standard wood) **$675.00**

Shiloh Sharps "The Jaeger"
Similar to the Montana Roughrider except has half-octagon 26" lightweight barrel, calibers 30-40, 30-30, 307 Win., 45-70. Standard supreme black walnut.
Price: **$750.00**

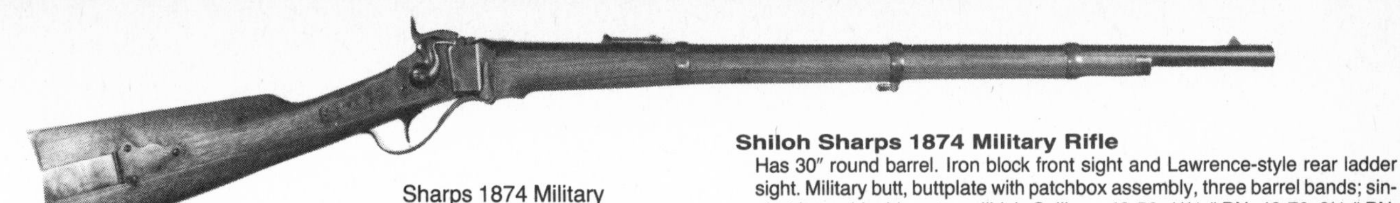

Sharps 1874 Military

Shiloh Sharps 1874 Military Rifle
Has 30″ round barrel. Iron block front sight and Lawrence-style rear ladder sight. Military butt, buttplate with patchbox assembly, three barrel bands; single trigger (double set availble). Calibers 40-50x$1\frac{11}{16}$″ BN, 40-70x$2\frac{1}{10}$″ BN, 40-90 BN, 45-70x$2\frac{1}{10}$″ ST, 50-70 ST.
Price: **$800.00**

Shiloh Sharps 1874 Montana Roughrider
Similar to the No. 1 Sporting Rifle except available with half-octagon or full octagon barrel in 24″, 26″, 28″, 30″, 34″ lengths; standard supreme or semi-fancy wood, shotgun, pistol grip or military-style butt. Weight about $8\frac{1}{2}$ lbs. Calibers 30-40, 30-30, 40-50x$1\frac{11}{16}$ BN, 40-70x$2\frac{1}{10}$ BN, 45-70x$2\frac{1}{10}$ ST. Globe front and tang sight optional.
Price: Standard supreme **$725.00**
Price: Semi-fancy **$775.00**

Shiloh Sharps 1874 Business Rifle
Similar to No. 3 Rifle except has 28″ heavy round barrel, military-style buttstock and steel buttplate. Weight about $9\frac{1}{2}$ lbs. Calibers 40-50 BN, 40-70 BN, 40-90 BN, 45-70 ST, 45-90 ST, 50-70 ST, 50-100 ST, 32-40, 38-55, 40-70 ST, 40-90 ST.
Price: **$650.00**
Price: 1874 Carbine (similar to above except 24″ round bbl., single trigger—double set avail.). **$650.00**
Price: 1874 Saddle Rifle (similar to Carbine except has 26″ octagon barrel, semi-fancy shotgun butt) **$750.00**

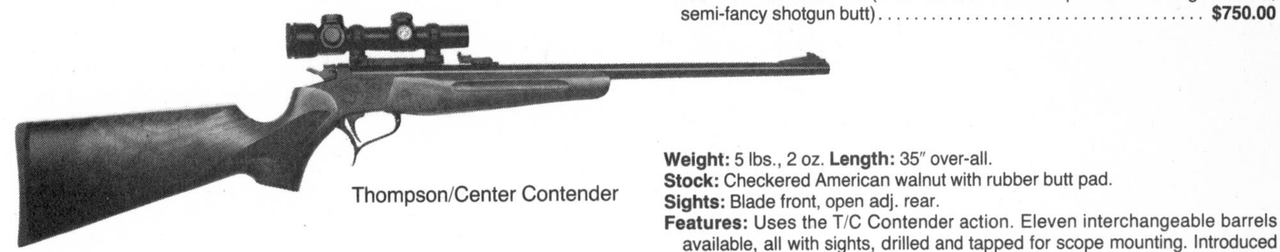

Thompson/Center Contender

THOMPSON/CENTER CONTENDER CARBINE
Caliber: 22 LR, 22 Hornet, 223 Rem., 7mm T.C.U., 7x30 Waters, 30-30 Win., 357 Rem. Maximum, 35 Rem., 44 Mag., 410, single shot.
Barrel: 21″.
Weight: 5 lbs., 2 oz. **Length:** 35″ over-all.
Stock: Checkered American walnut with rubber butt pad.
Sights: Blade front, open adj. rear.
Features: Uses the T/C Contender action. Eleven interchangeable barrels available, all with sights, drilled and tapped for scope mounting. Introduced 1985. Offered as a complete Carbine only.
Price: Rifle calibers **$370.00**
Price: Extra barrels, rifle calibers, each **$160.00**
Price: 410 shotgun **$390.00**
Price: Extra 410 barrel **$180.00**

Thompson/Center TCR Hunter

UBERTI ROLLING BLOCK BABY CARBINE
Caliber: 22 LR, 22 WMR, 22 Hornet, 357 Mag., single shot.
Barrel: 22″.
Weight: 4.8 lbs. **Length:** $35\frac{1}{2}$″ over-all.
Stock: Walnut stock and fore-end.
Sights: Blade front, fully adj. open rear.
Features: Resembles Remington New Model No. 4 carbine. Brass trigger guard and buttplate; color case-hardened frame, blued barrel. Imported by Benson Firearms, Uberti USA.
Price: **$360.00**

THOMPSON/CENTER TCR '87 SINGLE SHOT RIFLE
Caliber: 22 Hornet, 222 Rem., 223 Rem., 22-250, 243 Win., 270, 308, 7mm-08, 30-06, 32-40 Win., 12 ga. slug.
Barrel: 23″ (standard), $25\frac{7}{8}$″ (heavy).
Weight: About $6\frac{3}{4}$ lbs. **Length:** $39\frac{1}{2}$″ over-all.
Stock: American black walnut, checkered p.g. and fore-end.
Sights: None furnished.
Features: Break-open design with interchangeable barrels. Single-stage trigger. Cross-bolt safety. Made in U.S. by T/C. Introduced 1983.
Price: With Medium Sporter barrel (223, 22-250, 7mm-08, 308, 32-40 Win.) **$395.00**
Price: With Light Sporter barrel (22 Hornet, 222, 223, 22-250, 243, 270, 308, 30-06) **$395.00**
Price: 12 ga. slug barrel **$165.00**
Price: Extra Medium or Light Sporter barrel **$165.00**

DRILLINGS, COMBINATION GUNS, DOUBLE RIFLES

Designs for sporting and utility purposes worldwide.

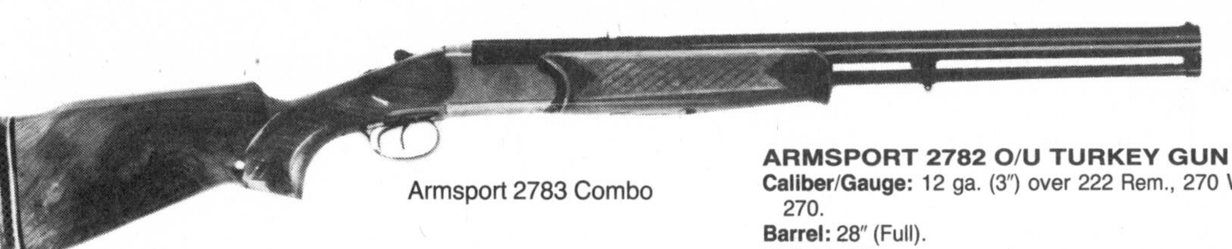

Armsport 2783 Combo

ARMSPORT 2782 O/U TURKEY GUN
Caliber/Gauge: 12 ga. (3″) over 222 Rem., 270 Win.; 20 ga. over 222, 243, 270.
Barrel: 28″ (Full).
Weight: 8 lbs.
Stock: European walnut.
Sights: Blade front, leaf rear.
Features: Ventilated top and middle ribs; flip-up rear sight; silvered receiver. Introduced 1986. Imported from Italy by Armsport.
Price: 12/222 .... **$750.00**
Price: All other listed calibers **$1,350.00**

BRNO SUPER EXPRESS O/U DOUBLE RIFLE

Caliber: 7x65R, 9.3x74R, 375 H&H, 458 Win. Mag.
Barrel: 23½."
Weight: 8½ to 9 lbs. **Length:** 40" over-all.
Stock: European walnut with raised cheekpiece, skip-line checkering.
Sights: Bead on ramp front, quarter-rib with open rear.
Features: Sidelock action with engraved sideplates; double set triggers; selective automatic ejectors; rubber recoil pad. Barrels regulated for 100 meters. Imported from Czechoslovakia by BRNO U.S.A., Inc.
Price: **$3,900.00**

BRNO ZH SERIES 300 COMBINATION GUN

Caliber/Gauge: 5.6x52R/12 ga., 5.6x50R Mag./12, 7x57R/12, 7x57R/16.
Barrel: 23½" (Full).
Weight: 7.9 lbs. **Length:** 40½" over-all.
Stock: Walnut.
Sights: Bead on blade front, folding leaf rear.
Features: Boxlock action; 8-barrel set for combination calibers and o/u shotgun barrels in 12 ga. (Field, Trap, Skeet) and 16 ga. (Field). Imported from Czechoslovakia by BRNO U.S.A., Inc.
Price: **$3,500.00**

BERETTA EXPRESS S689, SSO DOUBLE RIFLES

Caliber: 30-06, 9.3x74R, 375 H&H, 458 Win. Mag., 458 H&H.
Barrel: 23", 25.5".
Weight: 7.7lbs.
Stock: European walnut, hand-checkered grip and fore-end.
Sights: Blade front on ramp, open V-notch rear.
Features: Boxlock action (689), sidelock action (SSO) with silvered, engraved receiver; ejectors; double triggers; recoil pad. Imported from Italy by Beretta U.S.A. Corp. Introduced 1984.
Price: S689, 30-06, 9.3x74R.................... **$3,640.00** to **$49,000.00**
Price: SSO, 375 H&H, 458 Win. Mag............ **$11,900.00** to **$14,250.00**

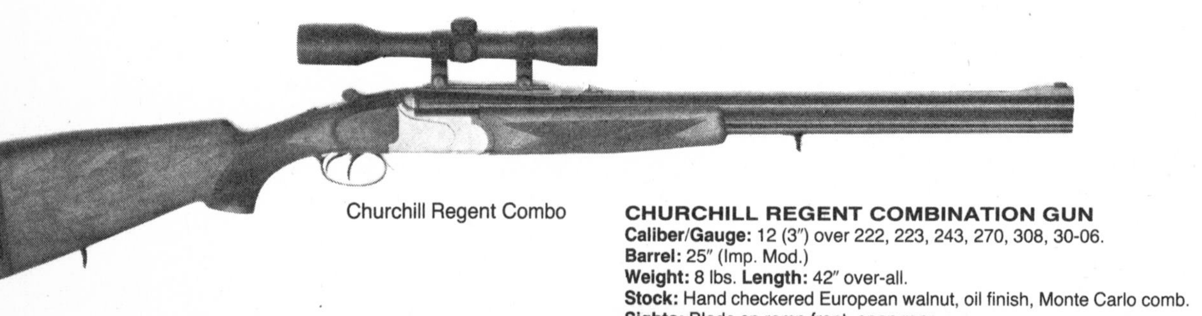

Churchill Regent Combo

CHURCHILL REGENT COMBINATION GUN

Caliber/Gauge: 12 (3") over 222, 223, 243, 270, 308, 30-06.
Barrel: 25" (Imp. Mod.)
Weight: 8 lbs. **Length:** 42" over-all.
Stock: Hand checkered European walnut, oil finish, Monte Carlo comb.
Sights: Blade on ramp front, open rear.
Features: Silvered, engraved receiver; double triggers; dovetail scope mount. Imported by Kassnar Imports, Inc. Introduced 1985.
Price: **$739.00**

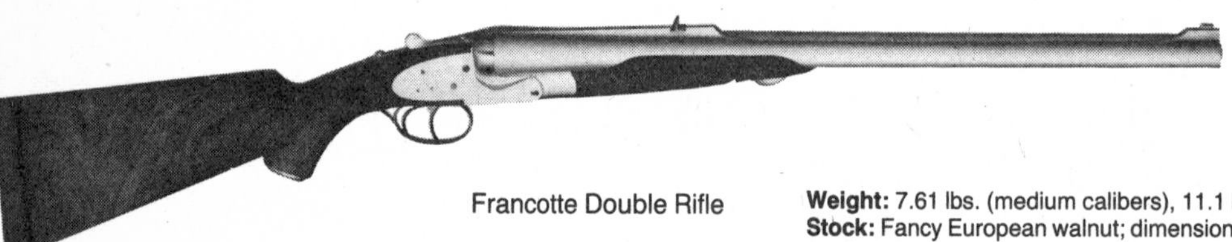

Francotte Double Rifle

AUGUSTE FRANCOTTE DOUBLE RIFLES

Caliber: 243, 7x57R, 7x65R, 8x57JRS, 270, 30-06, 308, 338, 300 Win. Mag., 9.3x74R, 375 H&H, 416 Rigby, 458 Win. Mag.; others on request.
Barrel: 23½" standard; other lengths on request.
Weight: 7.61 lbs. (medium calibers), 11.1 lbs. (mag. calibers).
Stock: Fancy European walnut; dimensions to customer specs. Straight or pistol grip style.
Sights: Bead on ramp front, leaf rear on quarter-rib; to customer specs.
Features: Chopper lump barrels; special extractor for rimmed cartridges; back-action sidelocks; double trigger with hinged front trigger. Automatic or free safety. Wide range of options available. Imported from Belgium by Armes de Chasse.
Price: .... **NA**

Heym 88B Safari

HEYM MODEL 88B SAFARI DOUBLE RIFLE

Caliber: 375 H&H, 458 Win. Mag., 470 Nitro Express.
Action: Boxlock with interceptor sear. Automatic ejectors with disengagement sear.
Barrel: 25".
Weight: About 10 lbs.
Stock: Best quality Circassian walnut; classic design with cheekpiece; oil finish, hand-checkering; Presentation butt pad; steel grip cap.
Sights: Large silver bead on ramp front, quarter-rib with three-leaf express rear.
Features: Double triggers; engraved, silvered frame. Introduced 1985. Imported from West Germany by Paul Jaeger, Inc.
Price: 375 and 458.. **$9,800.00**
Price: 470 Nitro Express.................................... **$9,800.00**
Price: Trap door grip cap.................................... **$350.00**
Price: Best quality leather case.............................. **$550.00**

Consult our Directory pages for the location of firms mentioned.

CAUTION: PRICES CHANGE. CHECK AT GUNSHOP.

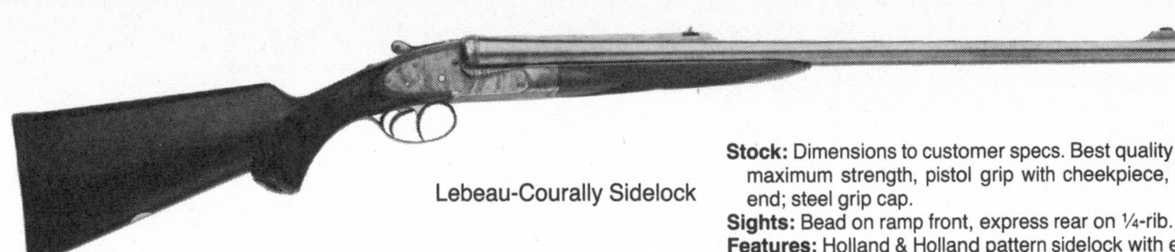

Lebeau-Courally Sidelock

LEBEAU-COURALLY SIDELOCK DOUBLE RIFLE

Caliber: 8x57 JRS, 9.3x74R, 375 H&H, 458 Win.
Barrel: 23½" to 26".
Weight: 7 lbs., 8 oz. to 9 lbs., 8 oz.
Stock: Dimensions to customer specs. Best quality French walnut selected for maximum strength, pistol grip with cheekpiece, splinter or beavertail fore-end; steel grip cap.
Sights: Bead on ramp front, express rear on ¼-rib.
Features: Holland & Holland pattern sidelock with ejectors, chopper lump barrels; reinforced action with classic pattern; choice of numerous engraving patterns; can be furnished with scope in fitted claw mounts. Imported from Belgium by Wm. Larkin Moore.
Price: From **$25,000.00**
Price: Box-lock, from **$12,800.00**

MANDALL/ZANARDINI DOUBLE RIFLE

Caliber: 470 Nitro Express.
Barrel: 24".
Weight: 9¼ lbs. **Length:** 42¼" over-all.
Stock: Walnut with cheekpiece; rubber butt pad. Checkered p.g. and fore-end.
Sights: Bead on ramp front, folding two-leaf rear.
Features: Color case-hardened and engraved boxlock action with double triggers. Imported from Italy by Mandall Shooting Supplies.
Price: **$8,995.00**

Mandall/Zanardini

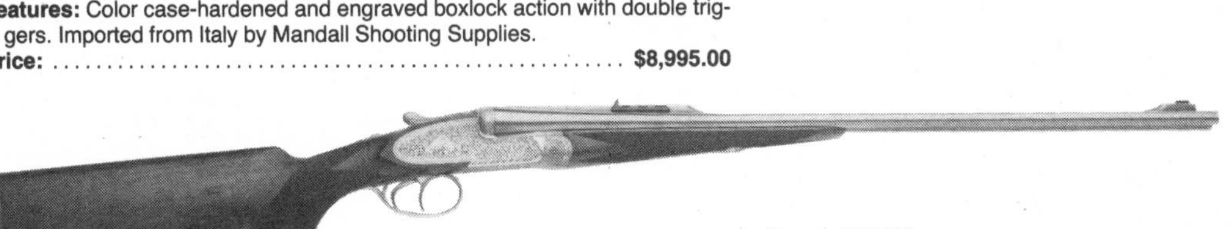

Perugini-Visini "Selous"

PERUGINI-VISINI MODEL "SELOUS" SIDELOCK DOUBLE RIFLE

Caliber: 30-06, 7mm Rem. Mag., 7x65R, 9.3x74R, 270 Win., 300 H&H, 338 Win., 375 H&H, 458 Win. Mag., 470 Nitro.
Barrel: 22"-26".
Weight: 7¼ to 10½ lbs., depending upon caliber. **Length:** 41" over-all (24" bbl.).
Stock: Oil-finished walnut, checkered grip and fore-end; cheekpiece.
Sights: Bead on ramp front, express rear on ¼-rib.
Features: True sidelock action with ejectors; sideplates are hand detachable; comes with leather trunk case. Introduced 1983. Imported from Italy by Wm. Larkin Moore.
Price: **$21,800.00**

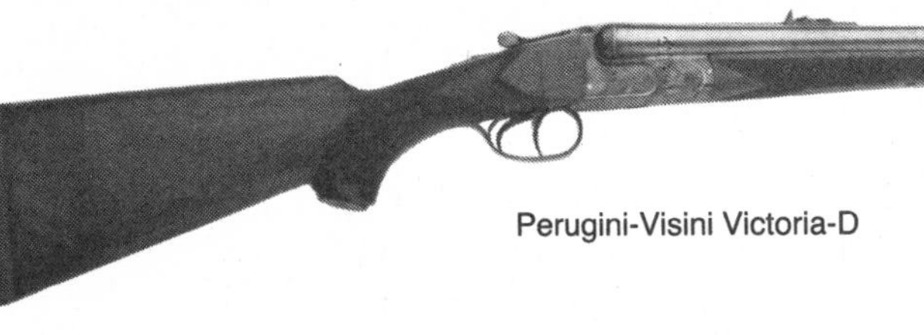

Perugini-Visini Victoria-D

Perugini-Visini Victoria Double Rifles

A boxlock double rifle which shares many of the same features of the Selous model. Calibers 7x65R, 30-06, 9.3x74R, 375 H&H Mag., 458 Win. Mag., 470; double triggers; automatic ejectors. Many options available, including an extra 20-ga. barrel set.
Price: Victoria-M (7x65R, 30-06, 9.3x74R), from about **$6,800.00**
Price: Victoria-D (375, 458, 470), from about **$12,500.00**

Savage Model 24-C

SAVAGE MODEL 24-C O/U

Caliber/Gauge: 22 S, L, LR over 20 ga.
Action: Take-down, low rebounding visible hammer. Single trigger, barrel selector spur on hammer.
Barrel: 20" separated barrels; Cyl. choke.
Weight: 5¾ lbs. **Length:** 36½" over-all (taken down 20").
Stock: Walnut finished hardwood.
Sights: Ramp front, rear open adj. for e. Grooved for tip-off scope mount.
Features: Trap door butt holds one shotshell and ten 22 cartridges, comes with special carrying case. Measures 7"x22" when in case.
Price: **$199.00**

Savage Model 24-V

Similar to Model 24-C except 222 Rem., 223 Rem. or 30-30 and 3" 20 ga.; 24" barrel; stronger receiver; color case-hardened frame; folding leaf rear sight; receiver tapped for scope.
Price: **$249.00**

SAVAGE MODEL 24 O/U COMBINATION GUN

Caliber/Gauge: 22 LR or 22 WMR over 20 ga. (3").
Barrel: 24"; separated with floating front mount.
Weight: 6½ lbs. **Length:** 40" over-all.
Stock: Walnut-finished hardwood with Monte Carlo.
Sights: Ramp front, adjustable sporting rear. Grooved for tip-off mount.
Features: Barrel selector in hammer; bottom opening lever.
Price: **$179.00**

SAVAGE MODEL 389 O/U COMBINATION

Caliber/Gauge: 12 ga. over 222 or 308.
Barrel: 25¾" separated barrels with floating front mount for windage, elevation adjustment. Has choke tubes.
Weight: NA. **Length:** NA.
Stock: Oil-finished walnut with recoil pad, cut-checkered grip and fore-end.
Sights: Blade front, folding leaf rear. Vent. rib milled for scope mount.
Features: Matte finish, extractors, double triggers, q.d. swivel studs. Introduced 1988.
Price: **$759.00**

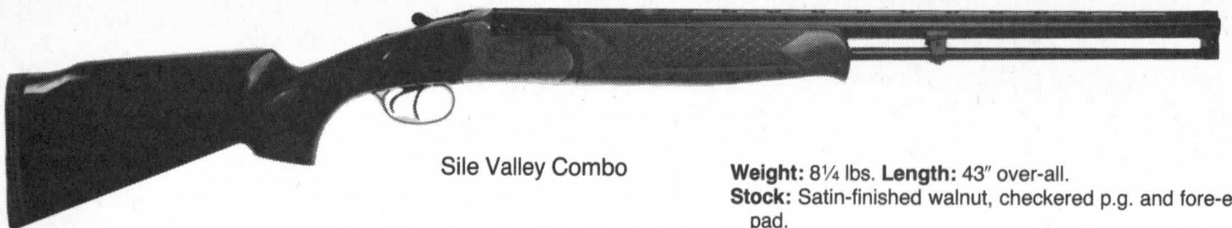

Sile Valley Combo

SILE VALLEY COMBO GUN
Caliber/Gauge: 12 ga. over 222 Rem. or 308 Win., 3″ chamber.
Barrel: 23½″ (Cyl.).
Weight: 8¼ lbs. **Length:** 43″ over-all.
Stock: Satin-finished walnut, checkered p.g. and fore-end; checkpiece; recoil pad.
Sights: Ramp front, folding rear. Accepts claw-type scope mount.
Features: Automatic safety; double triggers; engraved and silvered receiver. Imported by Sile.
Price: **$679.95**

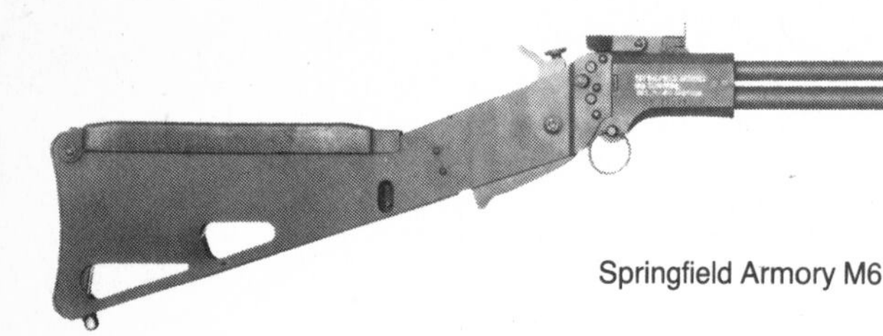

Springfield Armory M6

SPRINGFIELD ARMORY M6 SCOUT SURVIVAL RIFLE
Caliber: 22 LR, 22 WMR, 22 Hornet over 410 shotgun.
Barrel: 18″.
Weight: 4 lbs. **Length:** 31½″ over-all.
Stock: Steel, folding, with magazine for 15 22 LR, four 410 cartridges.
Sights: Blade front, military aperture for 22; V-notch for 410.
Features: All metal construction. Designed for quick disassembly and minimum maintenance. Folds for compact storage. Introduced 1982. Made in U.S. by Springfield Armory.
Price: About **$122.00**

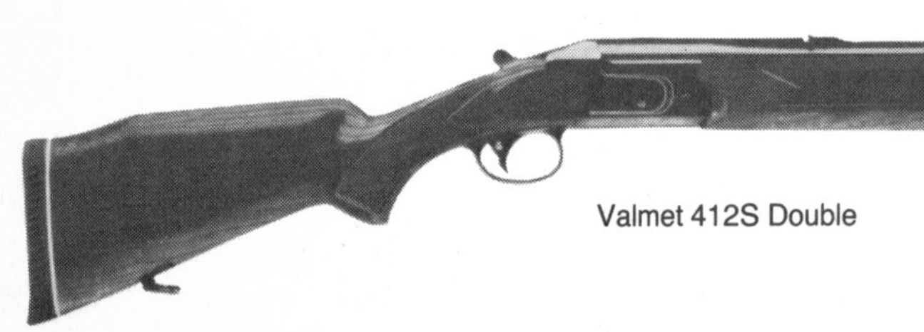

Valmet 412S Double

VALMET 412S COMBINATION GUN
Caliber/Gauge: 12 over 222, 308, 30-06, 9.3x74R.
Barrel: 24″ (Imp. Mod.).
Weight: 7⅝ lbs.
Stock: American walnut, with recoil pad. Monte Carlo style. Standard measurements 14″x1⅗″x2″x2⅗″.
Sights: Blade front, flip-up-type open rear.
Features: Barrel selector on trigger. Hand checkered stock and fore-end. Barrels are screw-adjustable to change bullet point of impact. Barrels are interchangeable. Introduced 1980. Imported from Finland by Valmet.
Price: **$1,099.00**
Price: Extra barrels, from **$524.00**

VALMET 412S DOUBLE RIFLE
Caliber: 30-06, 9.3x74R.
Barrel: 24″.
Weight: 8⅝ lbs.
Stock: American walnut with Monte Carlo style.
Sights: Ramp front, adjustable open rear.
Features: Barrel selector mounted in trigger. Cocking indicators in tang. Recoil pad. Valmet scope mounts available. Interchangeable barrels. Introduced 1980. Imported from Finland by Valmet.
Price: Extractors, 30-06.......... **$1,205.00**
Price: With ejectors, 9.3x74R.......... **$1,315.00**

A. ZOLI RIFLE-SHOTGUN O/U COMBO
Caliber/Gauge: 12 ga. over 222, 308 or 30-06.
Barrel: Combo—24″, shotgun—28″ (Mod. & Full).
Weight: About 8 lbs. **Length:** 41″ over-all (24″ bbl.)
Stock: European walnut.
Sights: Blade front, flip-up rear.
Features: Available with German claw scope mounts on rifle/shotgun barrels. Comes with set of 12/12 (Mod. & Full) barrels. Imported from Italy by Mandall Shooting Supplies.
Price: With two barrel sets **$1,695.00**

RIMFIRE RIFLES—AUTOLOADERS

Designs for hunting, utility and sporting purposes, including training for competition.

AMT Lightning 25/22

AMT LIGHTNING 25/22 RIFLE
Caliber: 22 LR, 25-shot magazine.
Barrel: 18″, tapered or bull.
Weight: 6 lbs. **Length:** 26½″ (folded), 37″ (open).
Stock: Folding stainless steel.
Sights: Ramp front, rear adjustable for windage.
Features: Made of stainless steel with matte finish. Receiver dovetailed for scope mounting. Extended magazine release. Standard or "bull" barrel. Introduced 1984. From AMT.
Price: **$269.95**

AMT Lightning Small-Game Hunting Rifle
Same as the Lightning 25/22 except has conventional stock of black fiberglass-filled nylon, checkered at the grip and fore-end, and fitted with Uncle Mike's swivel studs. Removable recoil pad provides storage for ammo, cleaning rod and survival knife. No iron sights—comes with 4x, 1″ scope and mounts. Has a 22″ target weight barrel, weighs 6¾ lbs., over-all length of 40½″. Introduced 1987. From AMT.
Price: With scope.......... **$269.95**

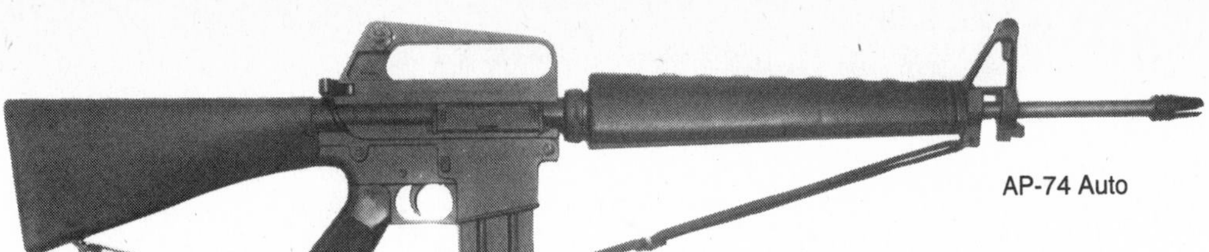
AP-74 Auto

AP-74 AUTO RIFLE

Caliber: 22 LR, 32 ACP, 15-shot magazine.
Barrel: 20″, including flash reducer.
Weight: 6½ lbs. **Length:** 38½″ over-all.
Stock: Black plastic.
Sights: Ramp front, adj. peep rear.
Features: Pivotal take-down, easy disassembly. AR-15 look-alike. Sling and sling swivels included. Imported by EMF.
Price: 22 LR **$295.00**
Price: 32 ACP **$320.00**

Anschutz Model 525

ANSCHUTZ DELUXE MODEL 525 AUTO

Caliber: 22 LR, 10-shot clip.
Barrel: 24″.
Weight: 6½ lbs. **Length:** 43″ over-all.
Stock: European hardwood; checkered pistol grip, Monte Carlo comb, beavertail fore-end.
Sights: Hooded ramp front, folding leaf rear.
Features: Rotary safety, empty shell deflector, single stage trigger. Receiver grooved for scope mounting. Introduced 1982. Imported from Germany by PSI.
Price: **$409.00**

ARMSCOR MODEL 20P AUTO RIFLE

Caliber: 22 LR, 15-shot magazine.
Barrel: 20¾″.
Weight: 5.5 lbs. **Length:** 39¾″ overall.
Stock: Walnut-finished mahogany.
Sights: Bead front, rear adjustable for e.
Features: Receiver grooved for scope mounting. Blued finish. Introduced 1987. Imported from the Philippines by Armscor.
Price: About **$95.95**
Price: Model 2000 (as above except has checkered stock, fully adj. sight), about **$98.95**

ARMSCOR AK22 AUTO RIFLE

Caliber: 22 LR, 15-shot magazine.
Barrel: 18½″.
Weight: 7 lbs. **Length:** 36″ over-all.
Stock: Plain mahogany.
Sights: Post front, open rear adjustable for w. and e.
Features: Resembles the AK-47. Matte black finish. Introduced 1987. Imported from the Philippines by Armscor.
Price: About **$171.95**

ARMSCOR MODEL 1600 AUTO RIFLE

Caliber: 22 LR, 15-shot magazine.
Barrel: 18″.
Weight: 5¼ lbs. **Length:** 38½″ over-all.
Stock: Black ebony wood.
Sights: Post front, aperture rear.
Features: Resembles Colt AR-15. Matte black finish. Introduced 1987. Imported from the Philippines by Armscor.
Price: About **$121.95**
Price: M1600R (as above except has retractable buttstock, ventilated fore-end), about **$137.95**

Auto-Ordnance 1927A-3

AUTO ORDNANCE MODEL 1927A-3

Caliber: 22 LR, 10, 30 or 50-shot magazine.
Barrel: 16″, finned.
Weight: About 7 lbs.
Stock: Walnut stock and fore-end.
Sights: Blade front, open rear adjustable for windage and elevation.
Features: Recreation of the Thompson Model 1927, only in 22 Long Rifle. Alloy receiver, finned barrel.
Price: **$487.50**

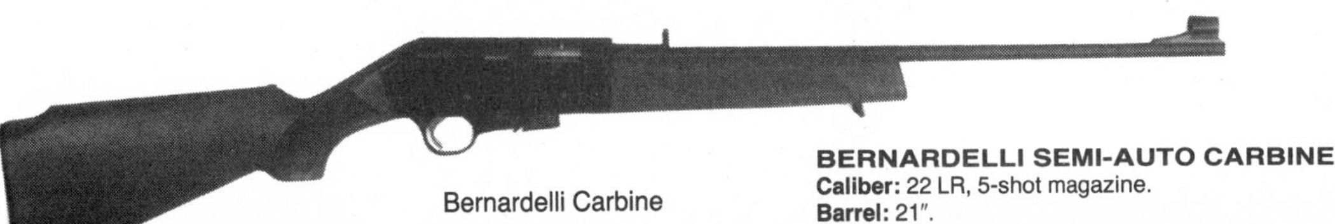
Bernardelli Carbine

BERNARDELLI SEMI-AUTO CARBINE

Caliber: 22 LR, 5-shot magazine.
Barrel: 21″.
Weight: 5 lbs., 3 oz. **Length:** 40″ over-all.
Stock: European hardwood.
Sights: Hooded post front, open adjustable rear.
Features: Blued barrel, painted receiver. Imported from Italy by Mandall Shooting Supplies.
Price: **$299.50**

CAUTION: PRICES CHANGE. CHECK AT GUNSHOP.

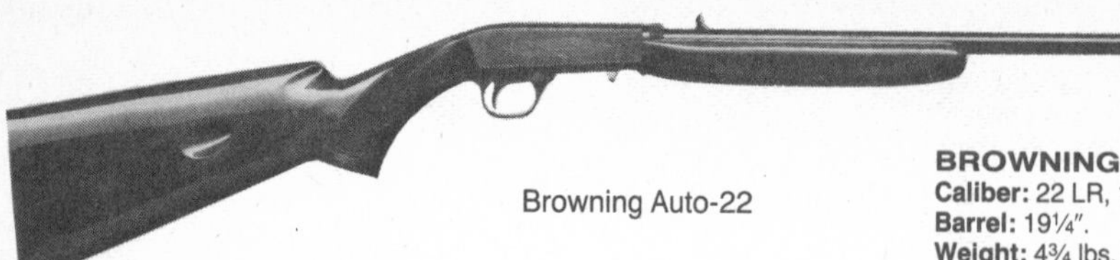

Browning Auto-22

BROWNING AUTO-22 RIFLE
Caliber: 22 LR, 11-shot.
Barrel: 19¼".
Weight: 4¾ lbs. **Length:** 37" over-all.
Stock: Checkered select walnut with p.g. and semibeavertail fore-end.
Sights: Gold bead front, folding leaf rear.
Features: Engraved receiver with polished blue finish; cross-bolt safety; tubular magazine in buttstock; easy take down for carrying or storage. Imported from Japan by Browning.
Price: Grade I **$328.50**

Browning Auto-22 Grade VI
Same as the Grade I Auto-22 except available with either grayed or blued receiver with extensive engraving with gold-plated animals: right side pictures a fox and squirrel in a woodland scene; left side shows a beagle chasing a rabbit. On top is a portrait of the beagle. Stock and fore-end are of high grade walnut with a double-bordered cut checkering design. Introduced 1987.
Price: Grade VI, blue or gray receiver. **$674.95**

CALICO MODEL 100 CARBINE
Caliber: 22 LR, 100-shot magazine.
Barrel: 16".
Weight: 5.7 lbs. (loaded). **Length:** 35.8" over-all (stock extended).
Stock: Folding steel.
Sights: Post front adjustable for e., notch rear adjustable for w.
Features: Uses alloy frame and helical-feed magazine; ambidextrous safety; removable barrel assembly; pistol grip compartment; flash suppressor; bolt stop. Made in U.S. From Calico.
Price: **$299.95**

Calico Model 100

Calico Model 100S Sporter
Similar to the Model 100 except has hand-rubbed wood buttstock and fore-end. Weight is 4¾ lbs. Introduced 1987.
Price: **$318.95**

Charter AR-7 Explorer

CHARTER AR-7 EXPLORER CARBINE
Caliber: 22 LR, 8-shot clip.
Barrel: 16" alloy (steel-lined).
Weight: 2½ lbs. **Length:** 34½"/16½" stowed.
Stock: Moulded black Cycloac, snap-on rubber butt pad.
Sights: Square blade front, aperture rear adj. for e.
Features: Take-down design stores bbl. and action in hollow stock. Light enough to float.
Price: Black, Silvertone or camouflage finish **$115.00**

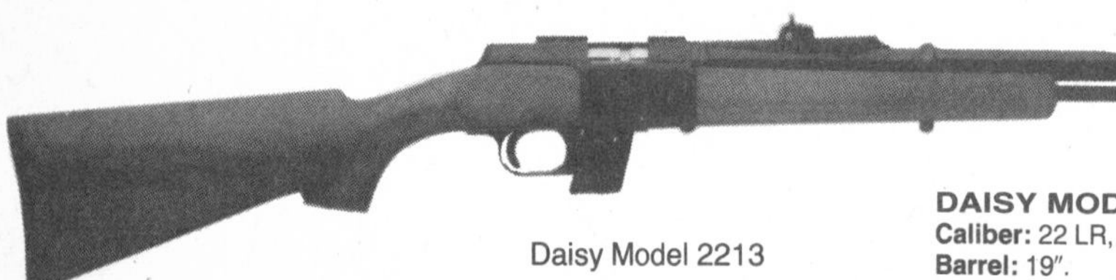

Daisy Model 2213

DAISY MODEL 2213 AUTO RIFLE
Caliber: 22 LR, 7-shot clip.
Barrel: 19".
Weight: 6.5 lbs. **Length:** 34.75" over-all.
Stock: Walnut.
Sights: Blade on ramp front, fully adjustable, removable notch rear.
Features: Removable trigger assembly; adjustable trigger; receiver dovetailed for scope mounting. Introduced 1988.
Price: About **$110.00**

Daisy Model 2203 Auto Rifle
Similar to the Model 2213 except has a moulded copolymer stock that is adjustable for length of pull. Introduced 1988.
Price: About **$80.00**

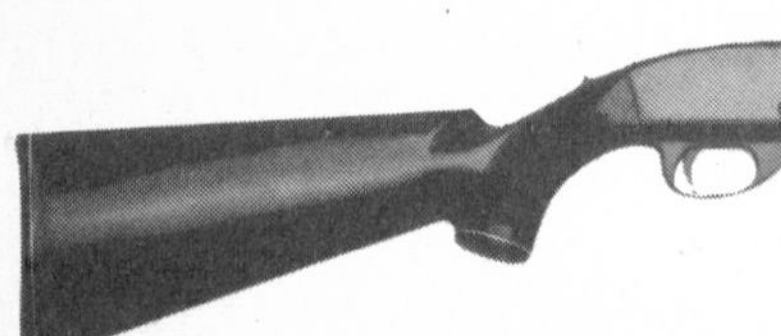

F.I.E. Black Beauty

F.I.E. GR-8 BLACK BEAUTY AUTO RIFLE
Caliber: 22 LR, 14-shot tubular magazine.
Barrel: 19⅝".
Weight: 4 lbs. **Length:** 38½" over-all.
Stock: Moulded black nylon, checkered pistol grip and fore-end.
Sights: Blade on ramp front, adjustable open rear.
Features: Made mostly of moulded nylon; tube magazine housed in buttstock; top tang safety; receiver grooved for tip-off scope mounts. Imported from Brazil by F.I.E. Introduced 1984.
Price: **$109.95**

F.I.E./FRANCHI PARA CARBINE
Caliber: 22 LR, 11-shot magazine.
Barrel: 19".
Weight: 4 lbs., 12 oz. **Length:** 39¼" over-all.
Stock: Metal skeleton buttstock, walnut p.g. and fore-end.
Sights: Hooded front, open adj. rear.
Features: Take-down rifle comes in its own fitted carrying case. Receiver grooved for scope mounting. Tube magazine feeds through buttplate. Limited production. Introduced 1986. Imported from Italy by F.I.E. Corp.
Price: **$234.95**

CAUTION: PRICES CHANGE. CHECK AT GUNSHOP.

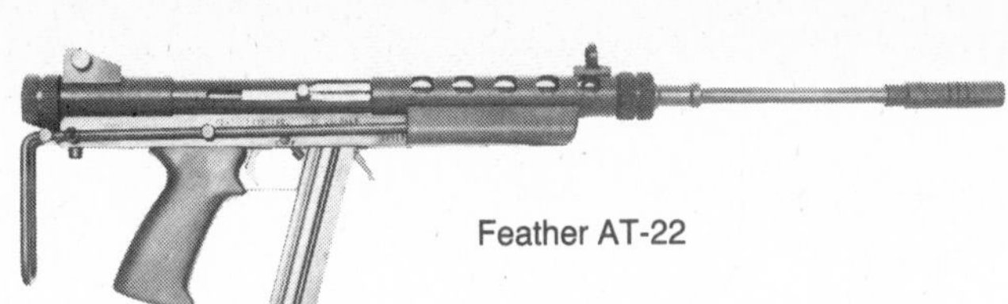

Feather AT-22

FEATHER AT-22 AUTO CARBINE

Caliber: 22 LR, 20-shot magazine.
Barrel: 17″.
Weight: 3.25 lbs. **Length:** 34.75″ over-all (stock extended).
Stock: Telescoping wire; composition pistol grip.
Sights: Protected post front, adjustable aperture rear.
Features: Removable barrel. Length when folded is 26″. Matte black finish. Scope, mount, sling, barrel shroud shown are optional. From Feather Enterpirses. Introduced 1986.
Price: **$239.95**

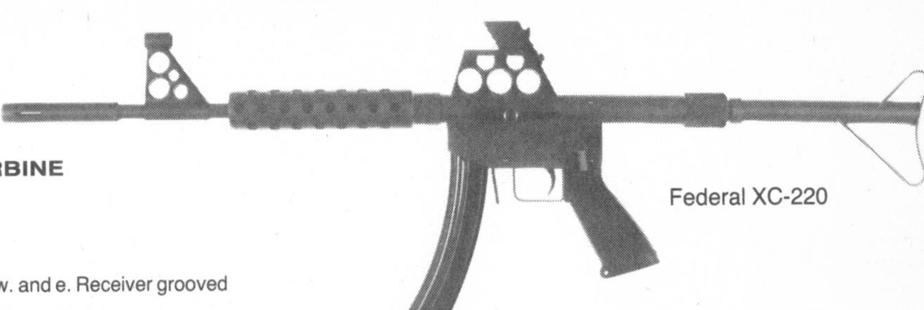

Federal XC-220

FEDERAL MODEL XC-220 AUTO CARBINE

Caliber: 22 LR, 28-shot magazine.
Barrel: 16.5″ (with flash hider).
Weight: 7½ lbs. **Length:** 34½″ over-all.
Stock: Detachable tube steel.
Sights: Hooded post front, peep rear adjustable for w. and e. Receiver grooved for scope mounting.
Features: Parkerized finish; all heli-arc welded steel construction; quick takedown. From Federal Engineering Corp.
Price: **$341.25**

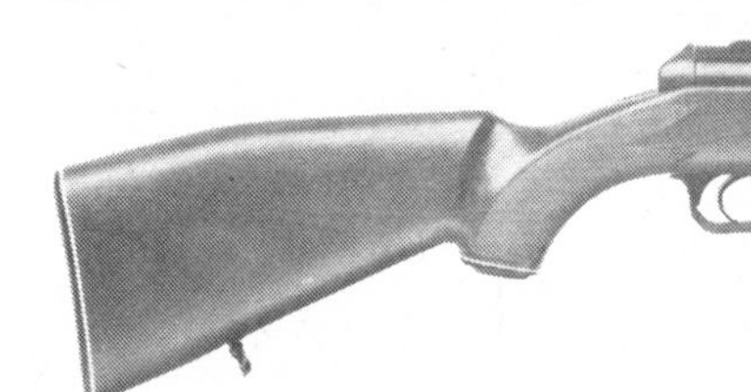

Heckler & Koch 300

HECKLER & KOCH MODEL 300 AUTO RIFLE

Caliber: 22 WMR, 5-shot box mag.
Barrel: 19¾″.
Weight: 5¾ lbs. **Length:** 39½″ over-all.
Stock: European walnut, Monte Carlo with cheek rest; checkered p.g. and Schnabel fore-end.
Sights: Post front adj. for elevation, V-notch rear adj. for windage.
Features: Polygonal rifling, comes with sling swivels; straight blow-back inertia bolt action; single-stage trigger (3½-lb. pull). Clamp scope mount with 1″ rings available at extra cost. Limited quantity available. Imported from West Germany by Heckler & Koch, Inc.
Price: HK300 .... **$598.00**

Illinois Arms 180

ILLINOIS ARMS CO. MODEL 180 AUTO

Caliber: 22 LR, 22 Short Magnum; 165-round magazine.
Barrel: 18″.
Weight: 9 lbs. **Length:** 37″ over-all.
Stock: Fiber-reinforced composition standard; walnut and retractable optional.
Sights: Protected post front, adjustable rear; receiver grooved for scope mounting or laser sight.
Features: Finned barrel; top-mounted 165-round magazine; matte blue-black finish. Parts interchage with the American 180. Made in U.S. Introduced 1988. From Illinois Arms Co.
Price: **$798.00**
Price: With walnut stock **$918.00**
Price: Optional retractable stock **$105.00**

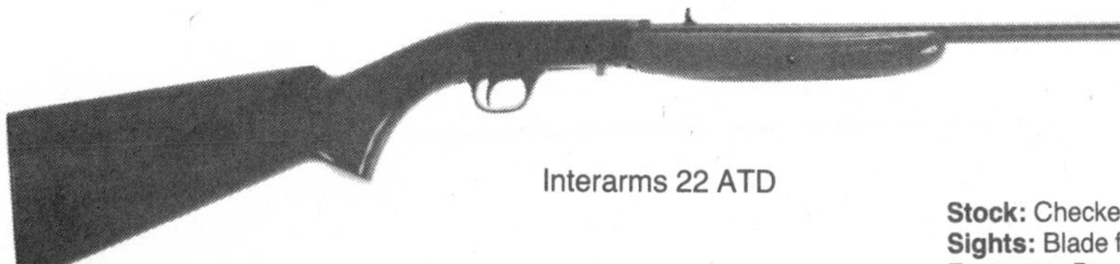

Interarms 22 ATD

INTERARMS MODEL 22 ATD RIFLE

Caliber: 22 LR, 11-shot magazine.
Barrel: 19.4″.
Weight: 4.6 lbs. **Length:** 36.6.″ over-all.
Stock: Checkered hardwood.
Sights: Blade front, open adjustable rear.
Features: Browning-design takedown action for storage, transport. Cross-bolt safety. Tube magazine loads through buttplate. Blue finish with engraved receiver. Introduced 1987. Imported from China by Interarms.
Price: **$179.00**
Price: With camouflage case. **$195.00**

Iver Johnson 3112

IVER JOHNSON MODEL 3112 RIFLE

Caliber: 22 Long Rifle (15-shot magazine).
Barrel: 18″.
Weight: 5.8 lbs. **Length:** 38″ over-all.
Stock: Walnut-finished hardwood.
Sights: Blade front, peep rear adjustable for w. and e.
Features: Resembles the U.S. 30-cal. M-1 Carbine. Introduced 1985. From Iver Johnson.
Price: **$166.50**

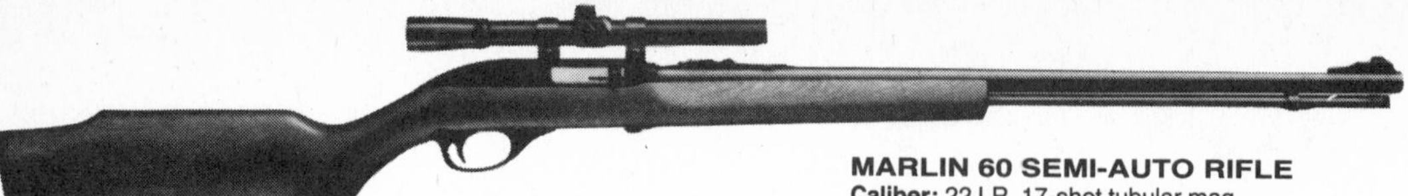
Marlin Model 60

MARLIN 60 SEMI-AUTO RIFLE
Caliber: 22 LR, 17-shot tubular mag.
Barrel: 22″ round tapered.
Weight: About 5½ lbs. **Length:** 40½″ over-all.
Stock: Walnut finished Monte Carlo, full pistol grip; Mar-Shield® finish.
Sights: Ramp front, open adj. rear.
Features: Matted receiver is grooved for tip-off mounts. Manual bolt hold-open; automatic last-shot bolt hold-open.
Price: $124.95

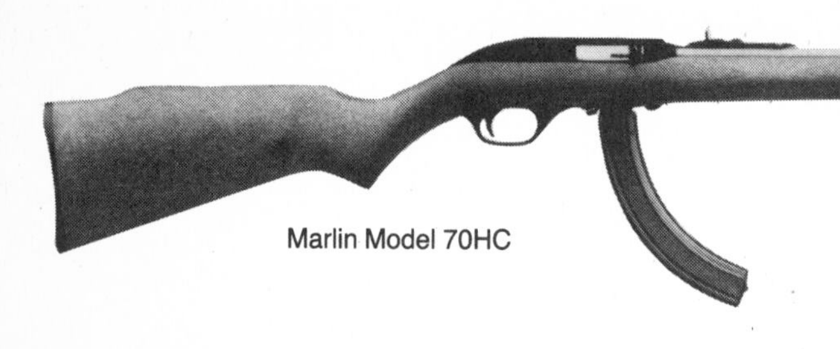
Marlin Model 70HC

MARLIN MODEL 70HC AUTO
Caliber: 22 LR, 25-shot clip magazine.
Barrel: 18″ (16-groove rifling).
Weight: 5 lbs. **Length:** 36½″ over-all.
Stock: Walnut-finished hardwood with Monte Carlo, full p.g. Mar-Shield® finish.
Sights: Ramp front, adj. open rear. Receiver grooved for scope mount.
Features: Receiver top has serrated, non-glare finish; cross-bolt safety; manual bolt hold-open.
Price: $130.95

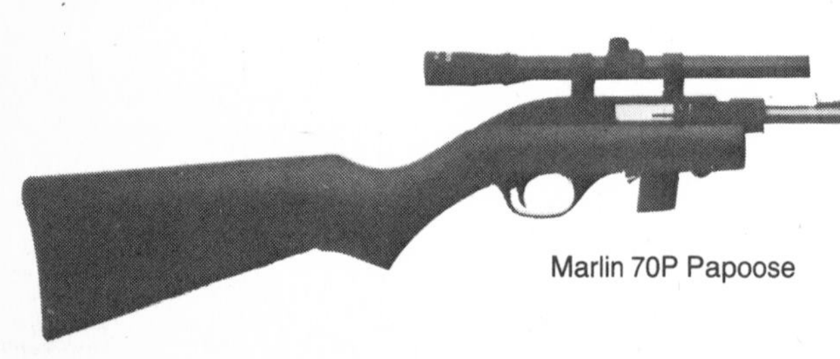
Marlin 70P Papoose

Marlin Model 70P Papoose
Similar to the Model 70 except is a take-down model with easily removable barrel—no tools needed. Has 16¼″ Micro-Groove® barrel, walnut-finished hardwood stock, ramp front, adjustable open rear sights, cross-bolt safety. Take-down feature allows removal of barrel without tools. Over-all length is 35¼″, weight is 3¾ lbs. Receiver grooved for scope mounting. Comes with 4x scope, mounts and zippered case. Introduced 1986.
Price: With scope........ $153.95

MARLIN MODEL 995 SEMI-AUTO RIFLE
Caliber: 22 LR, 7-shot clip magazine
Barrel: 18″ Micro-Groove®.
Weight: 5 lbs. **Length:** 36¾″ over-all.
Stock: American black walnut, Monte Carlo-style, with full pistol grip. Checkered p.g. and fore-end; white buttplate spacer; Mar-Shield® finish.
Sights: Ramp bead front with Wide-Scan™ hood; adjustable folding semi-buckhorn rear.
Features: Receiver grooved for tip-off scope mount; bolt hold-open device; cross-bolt safety. Introduced 1979.
Price: $156.95

MARLIN MODEL 75C SEMI-AUTO RIFLE
Caliber: 22 LR, 13-shot tubular magazine.
Barrel: 18″.
Weight: 5 lbs. **Length:** 36½″ over-all.
Stock: Walnut-finished hardwood; Monte Carlo with full p.g.
Sights: Ramp front, adj. open rear.
Features: Manual bolt hold-open; automatic last-shot bolt hold-open; cross-bolt safety; receiver grooved for scope mounting.
Price: $124.95

Mitchell AK-22

MITCHELL AK-22 SEMI-AUTO RIFLE
Caliber: 22 LR, 29-shot magazine; 22 WMR, 10-shot magazine.
Barrel: 16½″.
Weight: 3.1 lbs. **Length:** 38″ over-all.
Stock: European walnut.
Sights: Post front, open adj. rear.
Features: Replica of the AK-47 assult rifle. Wide magazine to maintain appearance. Imported from Italy by Mitchell Arms.
Price: 22 LR $275.00
Price: 22 WMR........ $285.00

Mitchell Galil/22

MITCHELL GALIL/22 AUTO RIFLE
Caliber: 22 LR, 29-shot magazine; 22 WMR, 10-shot magazine.
Barrel: 16.5″.
Weight: 5.7 lbs. **Length:** 36″ over-all.
Stock: European walnut butt, grip, fore-end.
Sights: Post front adjustable for elevation, rear adjustable for windage.
Features: Replica of the Israeli Galil rifle. Introduced 1987. Imported by Mitchell Arms, Inc.
Price: 22 LR $259.95
Price: 22 WMR........ $274.95

CAUTION: PRICES CHANGE. CHECK AT GUNSHOP.

Mitchell M-16/22

MITCHELL MAS/22 AUTO RIFLE
Caliber: 22 LR, 29-shot magazine; 22 WMR, 10-shot magazine.
Barrel: 16.5″.
Weight: 4.7 lbs. **Length:** 28.5″ over-all.
Stock: Walnut butt, grip and fore-end.
Sights: Adjustable post front, flip-type aperture rear.
Features: Bullpup design resembles French armed forces rifle. Top cocking lever, flash hider. Introduced 1987. Imported by Mitchell Arms, Inc.
Price: 22 LR $259.95
Price: 22 WMR.. $274.95

MITCHELL M-16/22 RIFLE
Caliber: 22 LR.
Barrel: 18.5″.
Weight: 6.1 lbs. **Length:** 39″ over-all.
Stock: Black composition.
Sights: Adjustable post front, adjustable aperture rear.
Features: Replica of the AR-15 rifle. Full width magazine. Comes with military-type sling. Introduced 1987. Imported by Mitchell Arms, Inc.
Price: 22 LR $259.95
Price: 22 WMR, 32 ACP.. $274.95

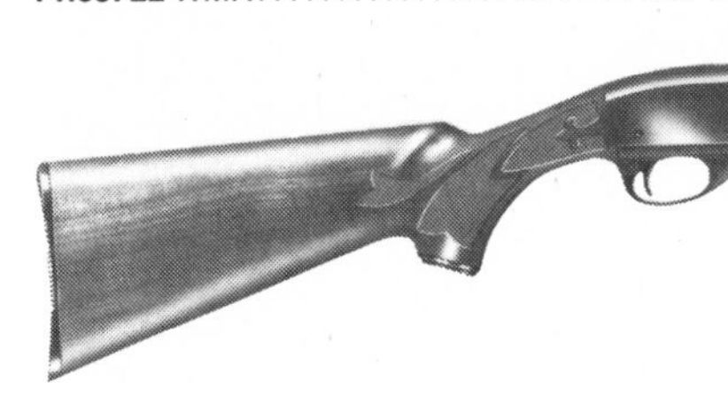

Remington 552 BDL

REMINGTON 552BDL AUTOLOADING RIFLE
Caliber: 22 S (20), L (17) or LR (15) tubular mag.
Barrel: 21″ round tapered.
Weight: About 5¾ lbs. **Length:** 40″ over-all.
Stock: Full-size, walnut. Checkered grip and fore-end.
Sights: Bead front, open rear adj. for w. & e.
Features: Positive cross-bolt safety, receiver grooved for tip-off mount.
Price: About $192.00

Ruger 10/22 RB

RUGER 10/22 AUTOLOADING CARBINE
Caliber: 22 LR, 10-shot rotary mag.
Barrel: 18½″ round tapered.
Weight: 5 lbs. **Length:** 37¼″ over-all.
Stock: American hardwood with p.g. and bbl. band.
Sights: Gold bead front, folding leaf rear adj. for e.
Features: Detachable rotary magazine fits flush into stock, cross-bolt safety, receiver tapped and grooved for scope blocks or tip-off mount. Scope base adapter furnished with each rifle.
Price: Model 10/22 RB (birch stock)............................ $176.00
Price: Model 10/22 R (American walnut stock)................... $196.00

Ruger 10/22 Auto Sporter
Same as 10/22 Carbine except walnut stock with hand checkered p.g. and fore-end; straight buttplate, no bbl. band, has sling swivels.
Price: Model 10/22 DSP $222.00

VOERE MODEL 2115 AUTO RIFLE
Caliber: 22 LR, 8 or 15-shot magazine.
Barrel: 18.1″.
Weight: 5.75 lbs. **Length:** 37.7″ over-all.
Stock: Walnut-finished beechwood with cheekpiece; checkered pistol grip and fore-end.
Sights: Post front with hooded ramp, leaf rear.
Features: Clip-fed autoloader with single stage trigger, wing-type safety. Imported from Austria by L. Joseph Rahn. Introduced 1984.
Price: Model 2115 .... $325.00
Price: Model 2114S (as above except no cheekpiece, checkering or white line spacers at grip, buttplate) $330.00

TRADEWINDS MODEL 260-A AUTO RIFLE
Caliber: 22 LR, 5-shot (10-shot mag. avail.).
Barrel: 22½″.
Weight: 5¾ lbs. **Length:** 41½″.
Stock: Walnut, with hand checkered p.g. and fore-end.
Sights: Ramp front with hood, 3-leaf folding rear, receiver grooved for scope mount.
Features: Double extractors, sliding safety. Imported by Tradewinds.
Price: $250.00

Weatherby Mark XXII

WEATHERBY MARK XXII AUTO RIFLE, CLIP MODEL
Caliber: 22 LR only, 5- or 10-shot clip.
Barrel: 24″ round contoured.
Weight: 6 lbs. **Length:** 42¼″ over-all.
Stock: Walnut, Monte Carlo comb and cheekpiece, rosewood p.g. cap and fore-end tip. Skip-line checkering.
Sights: Gold bead ramp front, 3-leaf folding rear.
Features: Thumb operated tang safety. Single shot or semi-automatic side lever selector. Receiver grooved for tip-off scope mount. Single pin release for quick takedown.
Price: $454.00

Weatherby Mark XXII Tubular Model
Same as Mark XXII Clip Model except 15-shot tubular magazine.
Price: $454.00

CAUTION: PRICES CHANGE. CHECK AT GUNSHOP.

RIMFIRE RIFLES—LEVER & SLIDE ACTIONS

Classic and modern models for sport and utility, including training.

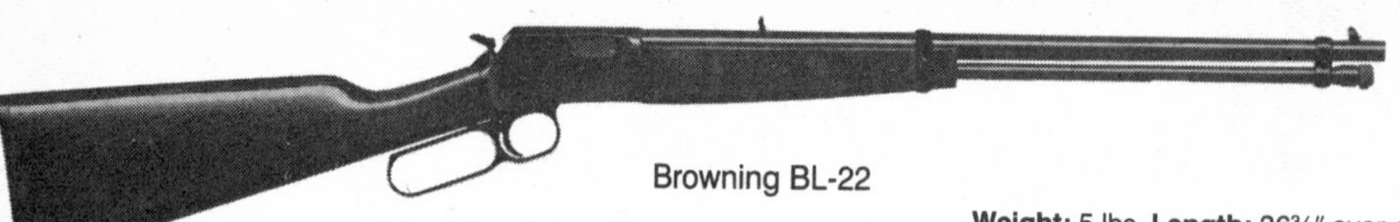

Browning BL-22

BROWNING BL-22 LEVER ACTION RIFLE
Caliber: 22 S(22), L(17) or LR(15). Tubular mag.
Barrel: 20″ round tapered.
Weight: 5 lbs. **Length:** 36¾″ over-all.
Stock: Walnut, 2-piece straight grip Western style.
Sights: Bead post front, folding-leaf rear.
Features: Short throw lever, half-cock safety, receiver grooved for tip-off scope mounts. Imported from Japan by Browning.
Price: Grade I **$286.95**
Price: Grade II (engraved receiver, checkered grip and fore-end) . . . **$326.95**

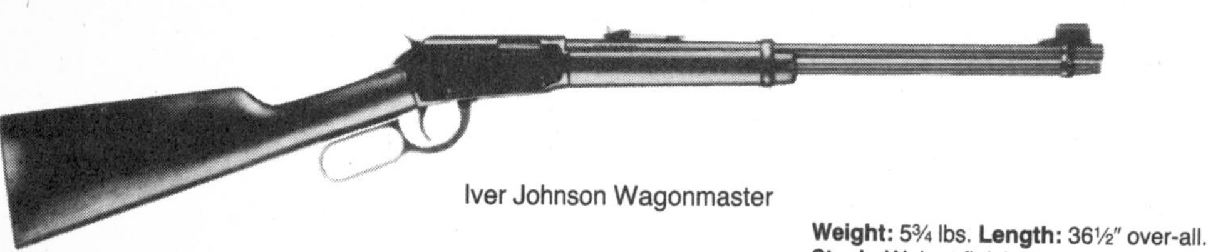

Iver Johnson Wagonmaster

IVER JOHNSON WAGONMASTER RIFLE
Caliber: 22 Long Rifle (21 Short, 17 Long, 15 Long Rifle), 22 WMR (12-shot magazine).
Barrel: 19″.
Weight: 5¾ lbs. **Length:** 36½″ over-all.
Stock: Walnut-finished hardwood.
Sights: Hooded ramp front, open adjustable rear.
Features: Polished blue finish. Receiver grooved for scope mounting. Introduced 1985. From Iver Johnson.
Price: 22 Long Rifle **$166.50**
Price: 22 WMR **$187.50**

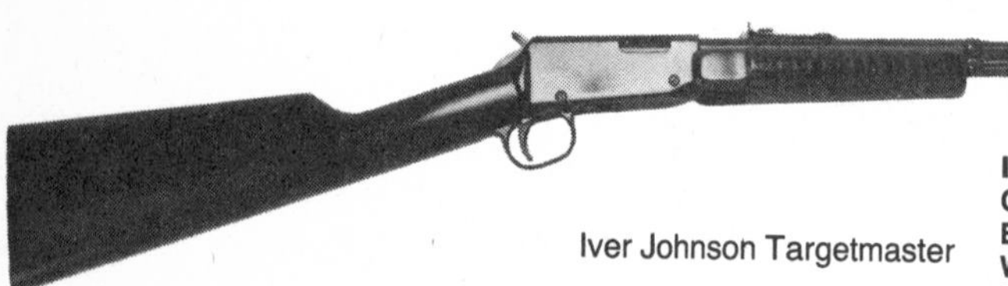

Iver Johnson Targetmaster

IVER JOHNSON TARGETMASTER RIFLE
Caliber: 22 Long Rifle (19 Short, 15 Long, 12 Long Rifle).
Barrel: 18″.
Weight: 5¾ lbs. **Length:** 36½″ over-all.
Stock: Walnut-finished hardwood.
Sights: Hooded ramp front, open adjustable rear.
Features: Polished blue finish. Receiver grooved for scope mounting. Introduced 1985. From Iver Johnson.
Price: Standard or Youth Model **$166.50**

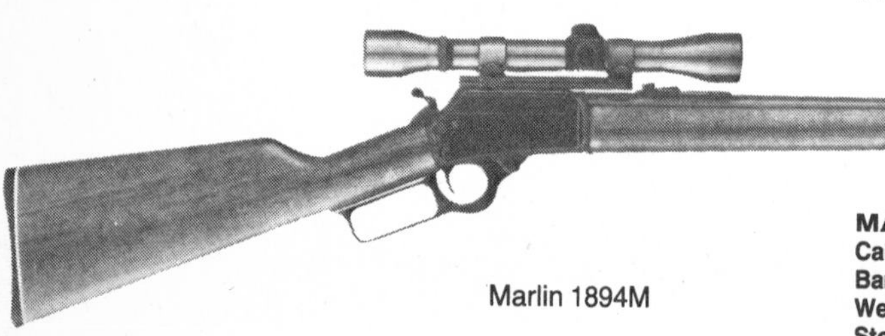

Marlin 1894M

MARLIN MODEL 1894M CARBINE
Caliber: 22 WMR, 10-shot magazine.
Barrel: 20″ Micro-Groove®.
Weight: 6¼ lbs. **Length:** 37½″ over-all.
Stock: Straight grip stock of American black walnut, Mar-Shield® finish.
Sights: Ramp front with brass bead, adjustable semi-buckhorn folding rear.
Features: Has hammer block safety. Side-ejecting solid-top receiver tapped for scope mount or receiver sight; squared finger lever, reversible offset hammer spur for scope use. Scope shown is optional. Introduced 1983.
Price: **$357.95**

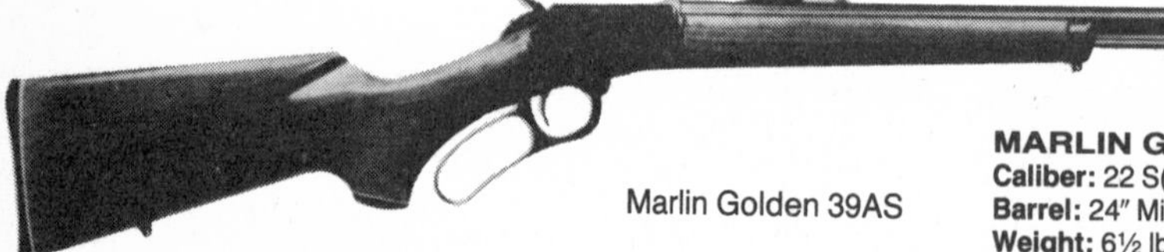

Marlin Golden 39AS

MARLIN GOLDEN 39AS LEVER ACTION RIFLE
Caliber: 22 S(26), L(21), LR(19), tubular magazine.
Barrel: 24″ Micro-Groove®.
Weight: 6½ lbs. **Length:** 40″ over-all.
Stock: American black walnut with white line spacers at p.g. cap and buttplate; Mar-Shield® finish. Swivel studs.
Sights: Bead ramp front with detachable Wide-Scan™ hood, folding rear semi-buckhorn adj. for w. and e.
Features: Hammer-block safety; rebounding hammer. Take-down action, receiver tapped for scope mount (supplied), offset hammer spur; gold plated steel trigger.
Price: **$318.95**

Consult our Directory pages for the location of firms mentioned.

CAUTION: PRICES CHANGE. CHECK AT GUNSHOP.

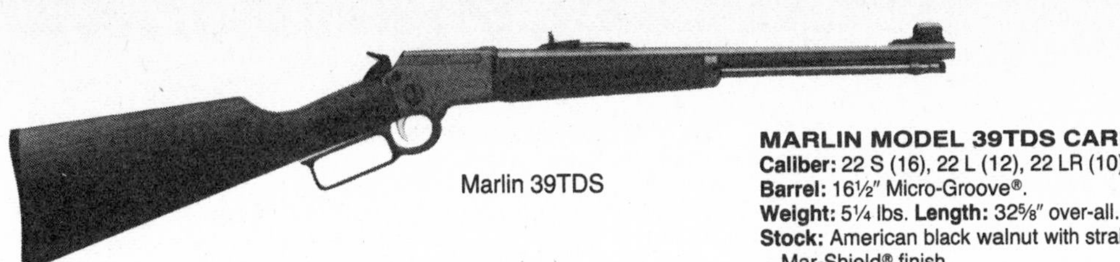
Marlin 39TDS

MARLIN MODEL 39TDS CARBINE

Caliber: 22 S (16), 22 L (12), 22 LR (10).
Barrel: 16½" Micro-Groove®.
Weight: 5¼ lbs. **Length:** 32⅝" over-all.
Stock: American black walnut with straight grip; short fore-end with blued tip. Mar-Shield® finish.
Sights: Ramp front with Wide-Scan™ hood, adjustable semi-buckhorn rear.
Features: Take-down style, comes with carrying case. Hammer-block safety, rebounding hammer; blued metal, gold-plated steel trigger. Introduced 1988.
Price: With case **$355.95**

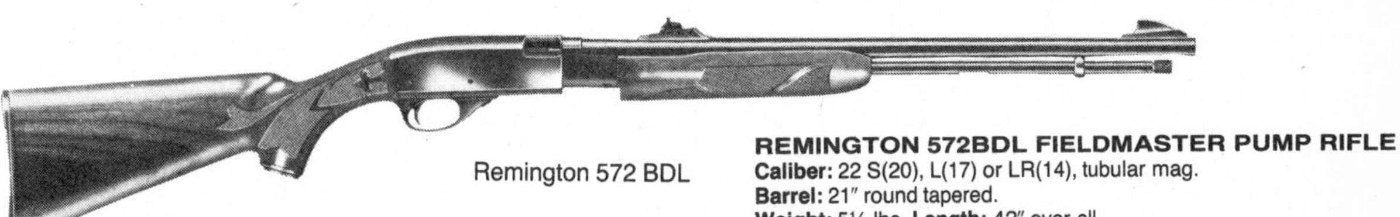
Remington 572 BDL

REMINGTON 572BDL FIELDMASTER PUMP RIFLE

Caliber: 22 S(20), L(17) or LR(14), tubular mag.
Barrel: 21" round tapered.
Weight: 5½ lbs. **Length:** 42" over-all.
Stock: Walnut with checkered p.g. and slide handle.
Sights: Blade ramp front; sliding ramp rear adj. for w. & e.
Features: Cross-bolt safety, removing inner mag. tube converts rifle to single shot; receiver grooved for tip-off scope mount.
Price: About **$203.00**

Rossi 62 SA

ROSSI 62 SA PUMP RIFLE

Caliber: 22 S, L or LR, 22 WMR.
Barrel: 23", round or octagon.
Weight: 5¾ lbs. **Length:** 39¼" over-all.
Stock: Walnut, straight grip, grooved fore-end.
Sights: Fixed front, adj. rear.
Features: Capacity 20 Short, 16 Long or 14 Long Rifle. Quick takedown. Imported from Brazil by Interarms.
Price: Blue.. **$192.00**
Price: Nickel **$207.00**
Price: Blue, with octagon barrel.. **$217.00**
Price: 22 WMR, as Model 59.. **$237.00**

Rossi 62 SAC Carbine

Same as standard model except has 16¼" barrel. Magazine holds slightly fewer cartridges.
Price: Blue.. **$192.00**
Price: Nickel **$207.00**

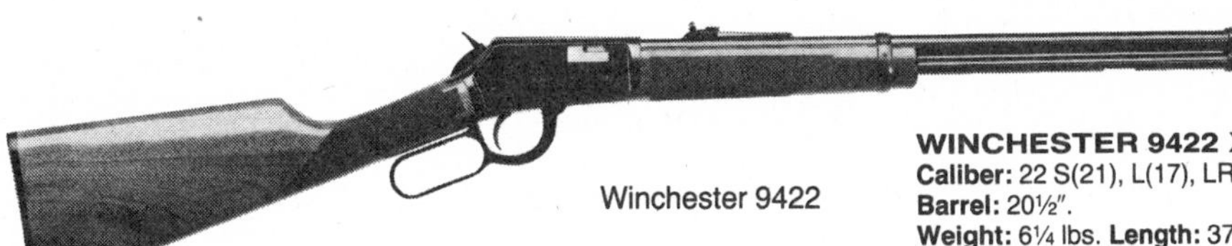
Winchester 9422

WINCHESTER 9422 XTR LEVER ACTION RIFLE

Caliber: 22 S(21), L(17), LR (15), tubular mag.
Barrel: 20½".
Weight: 6¼ lbs. **Length:** 37⅛" over-all.
Stock: American walnut, 2-piece, straight grip (no p.g.).
Sights: Hooded ramp front, adj. semi-buckhorn rear.
Features: Side ejection, receiver grooved for scope mounting, takedown action. Has XTR wood and metal finish. Made under license by U.S. Repeating Arms Co.
Price: About **$324.00**
Price: With Win-Tuff laminated stock, about.................... **$331.00**

Winchester 9422M XTR Lever Action Rifle

Same as the 9422 except chambered for 22 WMR cartridge, has 11-round mag. capacity.
Price: About **$324.00**
Price: With Win-Cam stock, about **$331.00**
Price: With Win-Tuff laminated stock, about.................... **$331.00**

Winchester 9422 Pistol Grip

Winchester 9422 XTR Pistol Grip

Similar to 9422 XTR except has uncheckered, satin-finished walnut stock with fluted comb, crescent steel buttplate, curved finger lever, and capped pistol grip. Over-all length is 39⅛", barrel length 22½", weight is 6½ lbs. In 22 Short, Long, Long Rifle and 22 WMR. Introduced 1985.
Price: About **$324.00**

CAUTION: PRICES CHANGE. CHECK AT GUNSHOP.

Includes models for a variety of sports, utility and competitive shooting.

Anschutz 1416/1516

ANSCHUTZ DELUXE 1416/1516 RIFLES

Caliber: 22 LR (1416D), 5-shot clip; 22 WMR (1516D), 4-shot clip.
Barrel: 22½″.
Weight: 6 lbs. **Length:** 41″ over-all.
Stock: European walnut; Monte Carlo with cheekpiece, Schnabel fore-end, checkered pistol grip and fore-end.
Sights: Hooded ramp front, folding leaf rear.
Features: Uses Model 1403 target rifle action. Adjustable single stage trigger. Receiver grooved for scope mounting. Imported from Germany by PSI.
Price: 1416D, 22 LR **$552.00**
Price: 1516D, 22 WMR **$572.80**
Price: 1416D Classic left-hand **$630.00**

Anschutz 1418D/1518D Deluxe Rifles

Similar to the 1416D/1516D rifles except has full-length Mannlicher-style stock, shorter 19¾″ barrel. Weighs 5½ lbs. Stock has buffalo horn Schnabel tip. Double set trigger available on special order. Model 1418D chambered for 22 LR, 1518D for 22 WMR Imported from Germany by PSI.
Price: 1418D **$750.00**
Price: 1518D **$788.00**

Anschutz 1422/1522

ANSCHUTZ 1422D/1522D CLASSIC RIFLES

Caliber: 22 LR (1422D), 5-shot clip; 22 WMR (1522D), 4-shot clip.
Barrel: 24″.
Weight: 7¼ lbs. **Length:** 43″ over-all.
Stock: Select European walnut; checkered pistol grip and fore-end.
Sights: Hooded ramp front, folding leaf rear.
Features: Uses Match 54 action. Adjustable single stage trigger. Receiver drilled and tapped for scope mounting. Introduced 1982. Imported from Germany by PSI.
Price: 1422D, 22LR **$873.00**
Price: 1522D, 22 WMR **$898.00**

Anschutz 1422D/1522D Custom Rifles

Similar to the Classic models except have roll-over Monte Carlo cheekpiece, slim fore-end with Schnabel tip, Wundhammer palm swell on pistol grip, rosewood grip cap with white diamond insert. Skip-line checkering on grip and fore-end. Introduced 1982. Imported from Germany by PSI.
Price: 1422D **$939.00**
Price: 1522D **$967.00**

Anschutz Bavarian

ANSCHUTZ BAVARIAN BOLT ACTION RIFLE

Caliber: 22 LR, 22 WMR, 5-shot clip.
Barrel: 24″.
Weight: 7¼ lbs. **Length:** 43″ over-all.
Stock: European walnut with Bavarian cheek rest. Checkered p.g. and fore-end.
Sights: Hooded ramp front, folding leaf rear.
Features: Uses the improved 1700 Match 54 action with adjustable 5096 trigger. Drilled and tapped for scope mounting. Introduced in 1988. Imported from Germany by Precision Sales International.
Price: **$967.00**

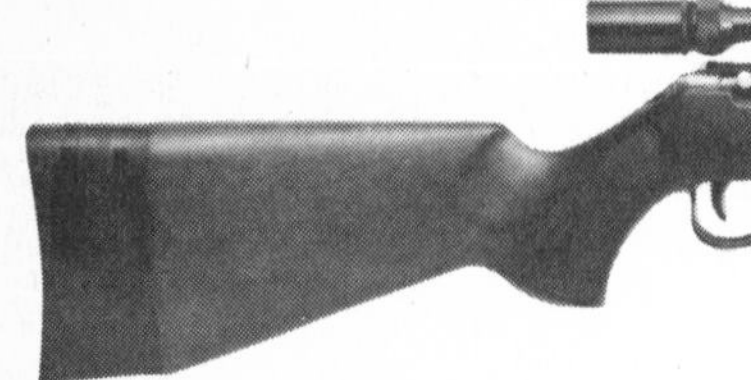
Anschutz Achiever

ANSCHUTZ ACHIEVER BOLT ACTION RIFLE

Caliber: 22 LR, 5-shot clip.
Barrel: 19½″.
Weight: 5 lbs. **Length:** 35½″ to 36⅔″ over-all.
Stock: Walnut-finished hardwood with adjustable buttplate, vented fore-end, stippled pistol grip. Length of pull adjustable from 11⅞″ to 13″.
Sights: Hooded front, open rear adjustable for w. and e.
Features: Uses Mark 2000-type action with adjustable two-stage trigger. Reciever grooved for scope mounting. Designed for training in junior rifle clubs and for starting young shooters. Introduced 1987. Imported from West Germany by PSI.
Price: **$319.50**
Price: Sight Set #1 .... **$54.00**

ARMSCOR MODEL 14P BOLT ACTION RIFLE

Caliber: 22 LR, 5-shot magazine.
Barrel: 23″.
Weight: 6 lbs. **Length:** 41.5″ over-all.
Stock: Walnut-finished mahogany.
Sights: Bead front, rear adjustable for e.
Features: Receiver grooved for scope mounting. Blued finish. Introduced 1987. Imported from the Philippines by Armscor.
Price: About **$99.95**

Armscor Model 1500 Rifle

Similar to the Model 14P except chambered for 22 WMR. Has 21.5″ barrel, double lug bolt, checkered stock, weighs 6.5 lbs. Introduced 1987.
Price: About **$156.95**

CAUTION: PRICES CHANGE. CHECK AT GUNSHOP.

Beeman/HW 60J-ST

BEEMAN/HW 60J-ST BOLT ACTION RIFLE

Caliber: 22 LR.
Barrel: 22.8″.
Weight: 6.5 lbs. **Length:** 41.7″ over-all.
Stock: Walnut with cheekpiece, cut checkered p.g. and fore-end.
Sights: Hooded blade on ramp front, open rear.
Features: Polished blue finish; oil-finished walnut. Imported from West Germany by Beeman. Introduced 1988.
Price: **$488.00**

Beeman/Krico 320

BEEMAN/KRICO MODEL 320 BOLT ACTION RIFLE

Caliber: 22 LR, 5-shot magazine.
Barrel: 19.5″.
Weight: 6 lbs. **Length:** 38½″ over-all.
Stock: Select European walnut; full-length Mannlicher-style with curved European comb and cheekpiece; cut checkered grip and fore-end.
Sights: Blade front on ramp, open rear adjustable for windage.
Features: Single or double set trigger; blued steel fore-end cap; detachable box magazine. Imported from West Germany by Beeman.
Price: **$1,100.00**

BRNO ZKM 452 BOLT ACTION RIFLE

Caliber: 22 LR, 5- or 10-shot magazine.
Barrel: 25″.
Weight: 6 lbs., 10 oz. **Length:** 43½″ over-all.
Stock: Beechwood.
Sights: Hooded bead front, open rear adj. for e.
Features: Blue finish; oiled stock with checkered p.g. Imported from Czechoslovakia by BRNO U.S.A., Inc.
Price: **$399.00**

Browning A-Bolt 22

BROWNING A-BOLT 22 BOLT ACTION RIFLE

Caliber: 22 LR, 5- and 15-shot magazines standard.
Barrel: 22″.
Weight: 5 lbs., 9 oz. **Length:** 40¼″ over-all.
Stock: Walnut with cut checkering, rosewood grip cap and fore-end tip.
Sights: Offered with or without open sights. Open sight model has ramp front and adjustable folding leaf rear.
Features: Short 60-degree bolt throw. Top tang safety. Grooved for 22 scope mount. Drilled and tapped for full-size scope mounts. Detachable magazines. Gold-colored trigger preset at about 4 lbs. Imported from Japan by Browning. Introduced 1986.
Price: A-Bolt 22, no sights **$319.95**
Price: A-Bolt 22, with open sights **$329.95**

Browning A-Bolt Gold Medallion

Similar to the standard A-Bolt except stock is of high-grade walnut with brass spacers between stock and rubber recoil pad and between the rosewood grip cap and fore-end. Medallion-style engraving covers the receiver flats, and the words "Gold Medallion" are engraved and gold filled on the right side of the barrel. High gloss stock finish. Introduced 1988.
Price: **$423.95**

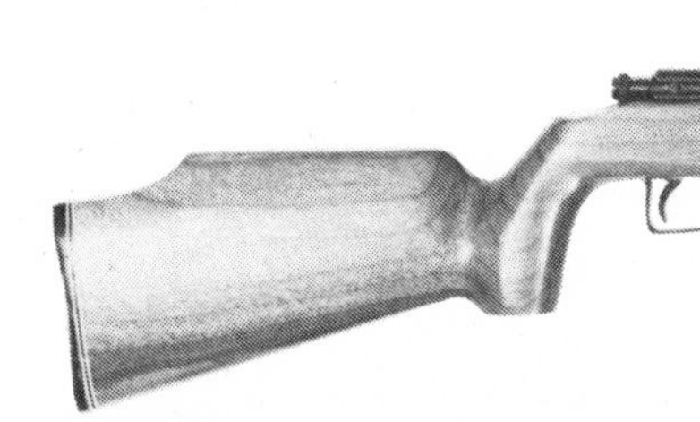

Cabanas Master

CABANAS MASTER BOLT ACTION RIFLE

Caliber: 177, round ball or pellet; single shot.
Barrel: 19½″.
Weight: 8 lbs. **Length:** 45½″ over-all.
Stock: Walnut target-type with Monte Carlo.
Sights: Blade front, fully adjustable rear.
Features: Fires round ball or pellet with 22-cal. blank cartridge. Bolt action. Imported from Mexico by Mandall Shooting Supplies. Introduced 1984.
Price: **$150.00**
Price: Varmint model (21½″ barrel, 4½ lbs., 41″ o.a.l. varmint-type stock) **$109.95**

Cabanas Leyre Bolt Action Rifle

Similar to Master model except 44″ over-all, has sport/target stock.
Price: **$134.95**
Price: Model R83 (17″ barrel, hardwood stock, 40″ o.a.l.) **$79.95**
Price: Mini 82 Youth (16½″ barrel, 33″ o.a.l., 3½ lbs.) **$69.95**
Price: Pony Youth (16″ barrel, 34″ o.a.l., 3.2 lbs.) **$79.95**
Price: Safari **$99.95**

CABANAS LASER RIFLE

Caliber: 177.
Barrel: 19″.
Weight: 6 lbs., 12 oz. **Length:** 42″ over-all.
Stock: Target-type thumbhole.
Sights: Blade front, open fully adjustable rear.
Features: Fires round ball or pellets with 22 blank cartridge. Imported from Mexico by Mandall Shooting Supplies.
Price: **$159.95**

Cabanas Espronceda IV Bolt Action Rifle

Similar to the Leyre model except has full sporter stock, 18¾ barrel, 40″ over-all length, weighs 5½ lbs.
Price: **$119.95**

Century Weekender

CENTURY WEEKENDER SPORTER RIFLE

Caliber: 22 LR, 5-shot magazine.
Barrel: 23.5″.
Weight: NA. **Length:** 42″ over-all.
Stock: European hardwood.
Sights: Hooded blade front, open adjustable rear.
Features: Blue finish; sling swivels. Introduced 1987. Imported by Century International Arms.
Price: **$86.95**

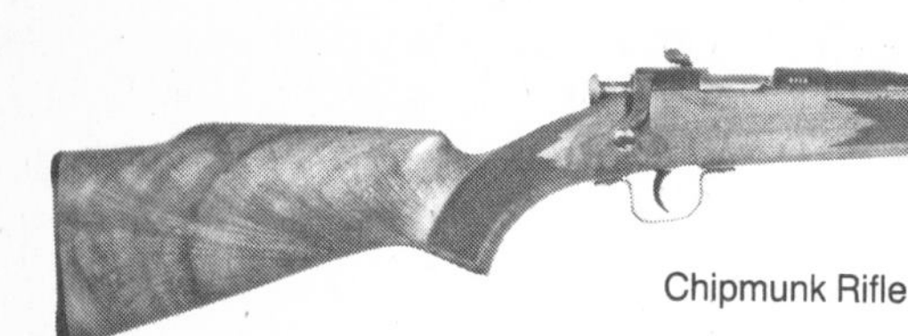

Chipmunk Rifle

CHIPMUNK SINGLE SHOT RIFLE

Caliber: 22, S, L, LR, single shot.
Barrel: 16⅛″.
Weight: About 2½ lbs. **Length:** 30″ over-all.
Stock: American walnut, or camouflage.
Sights: Post on ramp front, peep rear adj. for windage and elevation.
Features: Drilled and tapped for scope mounting using special Chipmunk base ($9.95). Made in U.S.A. Introduced 1982. From Chipmunk Mfg.
Price: **$129.95**
Price: Deluxe Model with hand checkered fancy stock **$179.95**

Daisy Legacy 2202

DAISY LEGACY 2202 BOLT ACTION REPEATER

Caliber: 22 LR, 10-shot rotary magazine.
Barrel: 19″. Octagonal barrel shroud.
Weight: 6.5 lbs. **Length:** 34.75″ to 36.75″ (variable).
Stock: Moulded lightweight copolymer.
Sights: Blade on ramp front, fully adjustable removeable rear.
Features: Adjustable buttstock length; removeable bolt and trigger assembly; adjustable trigger pull; barrel interchanges with smoothbore unit. Receiver dovetailed for scope mounting. Introduced 1988. Made in U.S. by Daisy.
Price: About **$75.00**

Daisy Legacy 2212 Bolt Action Repeater

Same as the Model 2202 except has walnut stock, fixed length of pull.
Price: About **$99.00**

Daisy Legacy 2222

Daisy Legacy 2222 Bolt Action Repeater

Same as the Model 2202 except comes with a smoothbore barrel with ventilated rib, bead front sight. Barrel interchanges with rifled unit.
Price: About **$90.00**

Daisy Legacy 2232 Bolt Action Repeater Combo

Same gun as the Model 2202 except comes with both rifled and smoothbore barrels, floatable nylon Cordura carrying case, takedown tool and cleaning kit.
Price: About **$125.00**
Price: As above with walnut stock, about **$149.00**

Daisy Legacy 2201

DAISY LEGACY 2201 BOLT ACTION SINGLE SHOT

Caliber: 22 LR.
Barrel: 19″. Octagonal barrel shroud.
Weight: 6.5 lbs. **Length:** 34.75″ to 36.75″ (variable)
Stock: Moulded copolymer.
Sights: Blade on ramp front, fully adjustable removeable notch rear.
Features: Adjustable buttstock length; removeable bolt and trigger assembly; adjustable trigger pull; barrel interchanges with smoothbore unit. Receiver dovetailed for scope mounting. Introduced 1988. Made in U.S. by Daisy.
Price: About **$65.00**

Daisy Legacy 2221 Single Shot Smoothbore

Similar to the Model 2201 except has smoothbore barrel with ventilated rib and bead front sight. Designed for shooting 22 RF shotshells. Weighs 6 lbs.
Price: About **$80.00**

Daisy Legacy 2231 Bolt Action Combo

Same as the Model 2201 except comes with both rifled and smoothbore barrels, waterproof, floatable nylon Cordura carrying case, takedown tool and cleaning kit.
Price: About **$110.00**

Daisy Legacy 2211 Bolt Action Single Shot

Same gun as the Model 2201 except comes with walnut stock, fixed length of pull.
Price: About **$94.95**

CAUTION: PRICES CHANGE. CHECK AT GUNSHOP.

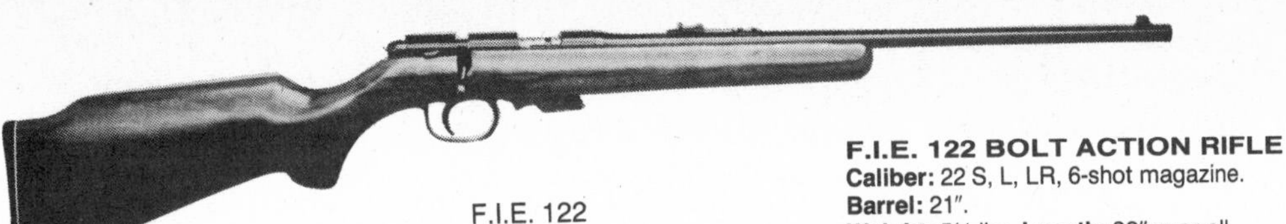

F.I.E. 122

F.I.E. 122 BOLT ACTION RIFLE
Caliber: 22 S, L, LR, 6-shot magazine.
Barrel: 21″.
Weight: 5½ lbs. **Length:** 39″ over-all.
Stock: Walnut-finished hardwood.
Sights: Blade front, open rear adj. for w. & e.
Features: Sliding wing-type safety lever, double extractors, red cocking indicator, receiver grooved for scope mounts. Imported from Brazil by F.I.E. Introduced 1986.
Price: **$109.95**

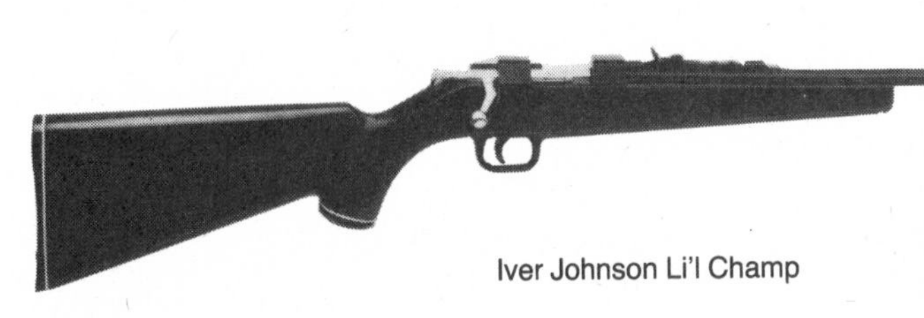

Iver Johnson Li'l Champ

IVER JOHNSON LI'L CHAMP RIFLE
Caliber: 22 S, L, LR, single shot.
Barrel: 16¼″.
Weight: 3 lbs., 2 oz. **Length:** 32½″ over-all.
Stock: Moulded composition.
Sights: Blade on ramp front, adj. rear.
Features: Sized for junior shooters. Nickel-plated bolt. Made in U.S.A. Introduced 1986. From Iver Johnson.
Price: **$91.50**

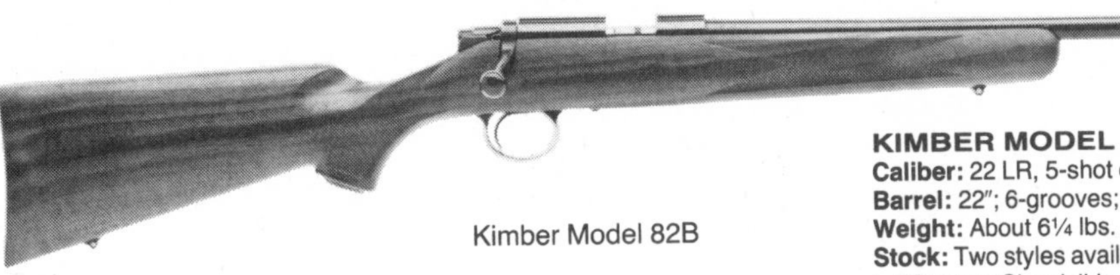

Kimber Model 82B

KIMBER MODEL 82B BOLT ACTION RIFLE
Caliber: 22 LR, 5-shot detachable magazine.
Barrel: 22″; 6-grooves; 1-in 16″ twist; 24″ varmint.
Weight: About 6¼ lbs. **Length:** 40½″ over-all (Sporter).
Stock: Two styles available. "Classic" is Claro walnut with plain, straight comb; "Custom Classic" is of fancy select grade Claro walnut, ebony fore-end tip, Niedner-style buttplate; "Continental" has a full-length Mannlicher-style stock with steel nose cap and barrel band. All have 18 lpi hand cut, borderless checkering, steel grip cap, checkered steel buttplate. Fully inletted swivel studs.
Sights: Hooded ramp front with bead, folding leaf rear (optional).
Features: High quality, adult-sized, bolt action rifle. Barrel screwed into receiver; rocker-type silent safety; twin rear locking lugs. All steel construction. Fully adjustable trigger; receiver grooved for Kimber scope mounts. High polish blue. Barreled actions available. Also available in true left-hand version in selected models. Made in U.S.A. Introduced 1979. Contact Kimber for full details.
Price: 22 LR Classic stock, no sights, plain or heavy bbl. (left hand avail.) **$750.00**
Price: Continental **$850.00**
Price: As above, Custom Classic, plain or heavy bbl. (left hand avail.) **$995.00**
Price: Kimber scope mounts, from **$48.00**
Price: Optional open sights fitted.. **$55.00**

Kimber Model 82, 84 Super America
Super-grade version of the Models 82 and 84. Has the Classic stock only of specially selected, high-grade, California claro walnut, with Continental beaded cheekpiece and ebony fore-end tip; borderless, full-coverage 20 lpi checkering; Niedner-type checkered steel buttplate. Options include barrel quarter-rib with a folding leaf sight, skeleton grip cap, checkered bolt knob. Available in 22 Long Rifle, 17 Rem., 22 Hornet, 221 Fireball, 222 Rem., 223 Rem.
Price: Model 82 22 Long Rifle, less scope........................ **$1,150.00**
Price: Model 82 22 Hornet, less scope........................ **$1,195.00**
Price: Model 84, 223 .... **$1,285.00**

Marlin 782

MARLIN 780 BOLT ACTION RIFLE
Caliber: 22 S, L, or LR; 7-shot clip magazine.
Barrel: 22″ Micro-Groove.
Weight: 5½ lbs. **Length:** 41″.
Stock: Monte Carlo American black walnut with checkered p.g. and fore-end. White line spacer at buttplate. Mar-Shield® finish.
Sights: Wide-Scan™ ramp front, folding semi-buckhorn rear adj. for w. & e.
Features: Receiver anti-glare serrated and grooved for tip-off scope mount.
Price: **$161.95**

Marlin 781 Bolt Action Rifle
Same as the Marlin 780 except tubular magazine holds 25 Shorts, 19 Longs or 17 Long Rifle cartridges. Weight 6 lbs.
Price: **$168.95**

Marlin 782 Bolt Action Rifle
Same as the Marlin 780 except 22 WMR cal. only, weight about 6 lbs. Comes with swivel studs.
Price: **$178.95**

Marlin 783 Bolt Action Rifle
Same as Marlin 782 except Tubular magazine holds 12 rounds of 22 WMR ammunition.
Price: **$185.95**

Marlin 25 Bolt Action Repeater
Similar to Marlin 780, except walnut finished p.g. stock, adjustable open rear sight, ramp front.
Price: **$125.95**

CAUTION: PRICES CHANGE. CHECK AT GUNSHOP.

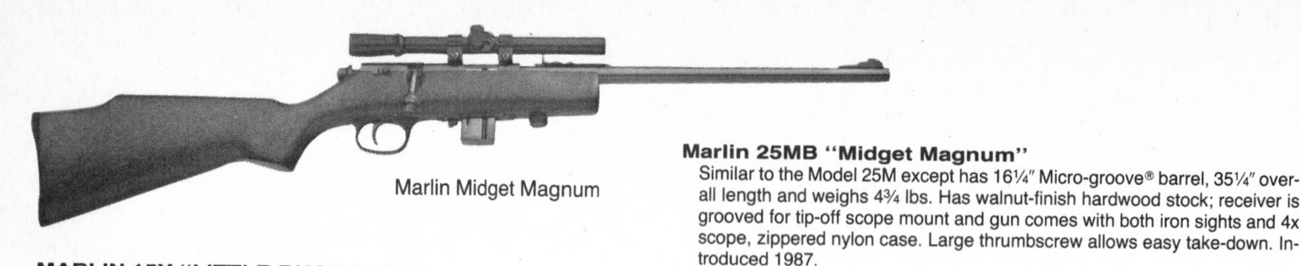

Marlin Midget Magnum

MARLIN 15Y "LITTLE BUCKAROO"
Caliber: 22, S, L, LR, single shot.
Barrel: 16¼" Micro-Groove®.
Weight: 4¼ lbs. **Length:** 33¼" over-all.
Stock: One-piece walnut-finished hardwood with Monte Carlo; Mar-Shield® finish.
Sights: Ramp front, adjustable open rear.
Features: Beginner's rifle with thumb safety, easy-load feed throat, red cocking indicator. Receiver grooved for scope mounting. Introduced 1984.
Price: $120.95

Marlin 25MB "Midget Magnum"
Similar to the Model 25M except has 16¼" Micro-groove® barrel, 35¼" over-all length and weighs 4¾ lbs. Has walnut-finish hardwood stock; receiver is grooved for tip-off scope mount and gun comes with both iron sights and 4x scope, zippered nylon case. Large thrumbscrew allows easy take-down. Introduced 1987.
Price: $172.95

Marlin Model 25M Bolt Action Rifle
Similar to the Model 25 except chambered for 22 WMR. Has 7-shot clip magazine, 22" Micro-Groove® barrel, walnut-finished hardwood stock. Introduced 1983.
Price: $141.95

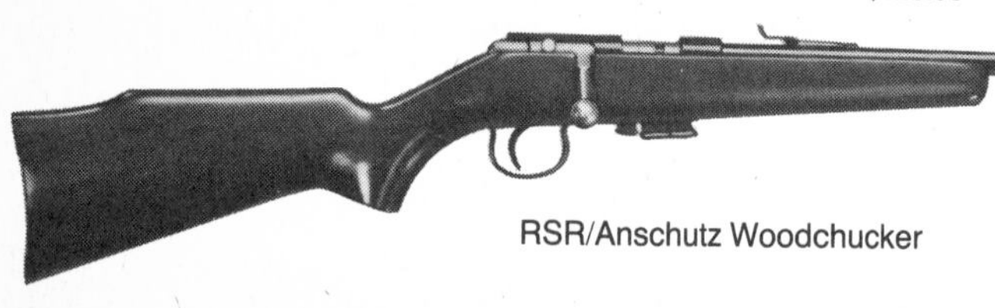

RSR/Anschutz Woodchucker

RSR/ANSCHUTZ WOODCHUCKER RIFLE
Caliber: 22 LR, 5-shot clip.
Barrel: 16¼".
Weight: 3 lbs., 10 oz. **Length:** 32¼" over-all.
Stock: Hardwood; 12" length of pull.
Sights: Bead front, U-notch rear with step elevator.
Features: Dual opposing extractors; receiver grooved for scope mounting. Made in Germany by Anschutz; imported by RSR Wholesale Guns, Inc.
Price: $175.95

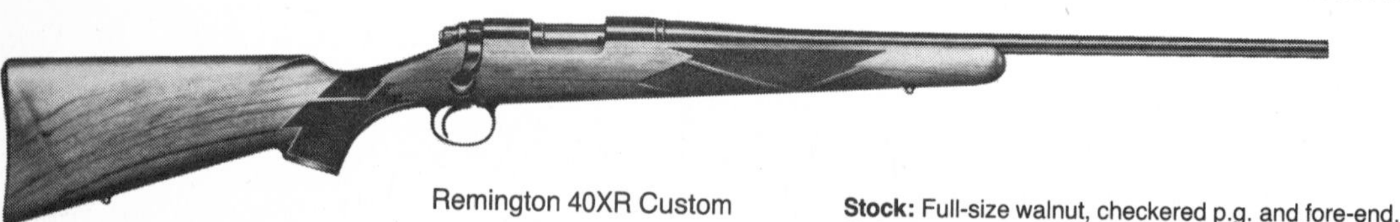

Remington 40XR Custom

REMINGTON 40XR RIMFIRE CUSTOM SPORTER
Caliber: 22 LR.
Barrel: 24".
Weight: 10 lbs. **Length:** 42½" over-all.
Stock: Full-size walnut, checkered p.g. and fore-end.
Sights: None furnished; drilled and tapped for scope mounting.
Features: Custom Shop gun. Duplicates Model 700 centerfire rifle.
Price: Grade I $1,200.00
Price: Grade II.. $2,133.00
Price: Grade III $3,333.00
Price: Grade IV... $5,200.00

Remington Model 541-T

REMINGTON MODEL 581-S "SPORTSMAN" RIFLE
Caliber: 22 S, L or LR. 5-shot clip mag.
Barrel: 24" round.
Weight: 4¾ lbs. **Length:** 42⅜" over-all.
Stock: Walnut finished hardwood, Monte Carlo with p.g.
Sights: Bead post front, screw adj. open rear.
Features: Sliding side safety, wide trigger, receiver grooved for tip-off scope mounts. Comes with single-shot adapter. Reintroduced 1986.
Price: About $184.00

REMINGTON MODEL 541-T
Caliber: 22 S, L, LR, 5-shot clip.
Barrel: 24".
Weight: 5⅞ lbs. **Length:** 42½" over-all.
Stock: Walnut, cut-checkered p.g. and fore-end. Satin finish.
Sights: None. Drilled and tapped for scope mounts.
Features: Clip repeater. Thumb safety. Re-introduced 1986.
Price: About $333.00

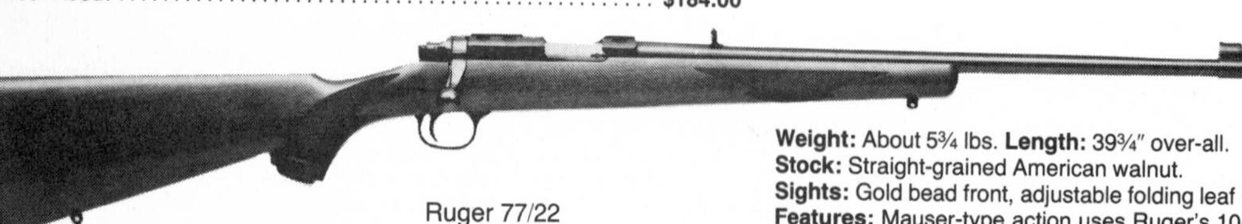

Ruger 77/22

RUGER 77/22 RIMFIRE BOLT ACTION RIFLE
Caliber: 22 Long Rifle, 10-shot magazine.
Barrel: 20".
Weight: About 5¾ lbs. **Length:** 39¾" over-all.
Stock: Straight-grained American walnut.
Sights: Gold bead front, adjustable folding leaf rear, or no sights.
Features: Mauser-type action uses Ruger's 10-shot rotary magazine; 3-position safety; simplified bolt stop; patented bolt locking system. Uses the dual-screw barrel attachment system of the 10/22 rifle. Integral scope mounting system with 1" Ruger rings. Introduced 1983.
Price: 77/22 R (plain barrel, no sights, with Ruger 1" rings) $364.50
Price: 77/22 S (gold bead front sight, folding leaf rear) $364.50
Price: 77/22 RS (scope rings and open sights) $384.50

CAUTION: PRICES CHANGE. CHECK AT GUNSHOP.

Varner Favorite

VARNER FAVORITE SINGLE SHOT RIFLE

Caliber: 22 LR.
Barrel: 21½"; half round, half octagon.
Weight: 5 lbs.
Stock: American walnut.
Sights: Blade front, open step-adjustable rear and peep.
Features: Recreation of the Stevens Favorite rifle with takedown barrel. Target grade barrel. Made in U.S. Introduced 1988. From Varner Sporting Arms, Inc.
Price: Field Grade **$249.00**
Price: Sporter Grade (finely figured walnut) **$369.00**
Price: Presentation Grade (AAA Fancy walnut, checkered grip and fore-end, includes hard custom takedown case) **$495.00**

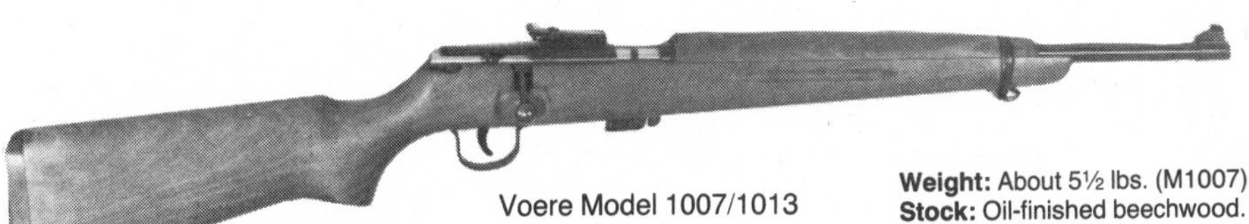

Voere Model 1007/1013

VOERE MODEL 1007/1013 BOLT ACTION RIFLE

Caliber: 22 LR (M1007 Biathlon), 22 WMR (M1013).
Barrel: 18".
Weight: About 5½ lbs. (M1007)
Stock: Oil-finished beechwood.
Sights: Hooded front, open adjustable rear.
Features: Single-stage trigger (M1013 available with double set). Military-look stock; sling swivels. Convertible to single shot. Imported from Austria by L. Joseph Rahn. Introduced 1984.
Price: 1007 Biathlon **$310.00**
Price: 1013, 22 WMR **$350.00**

COMPETITION RIFLES—CENTERFIRE & RIMFIRE

Includes models for classic American and ISU target competition and other sporting and competitive shooting.

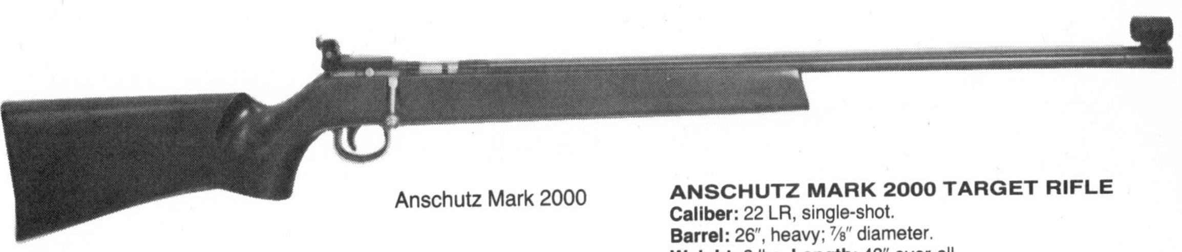

Anschutz Mark 2000

ANSCHUTZ MODEL 64-MS, 64-MS LEFT

Caliber: 22 LR, single shot.
Barrel: 21¾", medium heavy; ⅞" diameter.
Weight: 8 lbs. 1 oz. **Length:** 39½" over-all.
Stock: Walnut finished hardwood, silhouette-type.
Sights: None furnished. Receiver drilled and tapped for scope mounting.
Features: Designed for metallic silhouette competition. Stock has stippled checkering, contoured thumb groove with Wundhammer swell. Two-stage #5091 trigger. Slide safety locks sear and bolt. Introduced 1980. Imported from West Germany by PSI.
Price: Model 64-MS **$663.00**
Price: Model 64-MS Left **$733.00**
Price: 64-MS FWT (same as 64-MS except weighs about 6¼ lbs.... **$596.00**

ANSCHUTZ MARK 2000 TARGET RIFLE

Caliber: 22 LR, single-shot.
Barrel: 26", heavy; ⅞" diameter.
Weight: 8 lbs. **Length:** 43" over-all.
Stock: Walnut finished hardwood.
Sights: Globe front (insert-type), micro-click peep rear.
Features: Has 3-lb. single-stage trigger; stock has thumb groove, Wundhammer swell, full length slide rail. Imported from West Germany by PSI.
Price: Without sights **$399.50**
Price: Sight set #2 .... **$43.50**

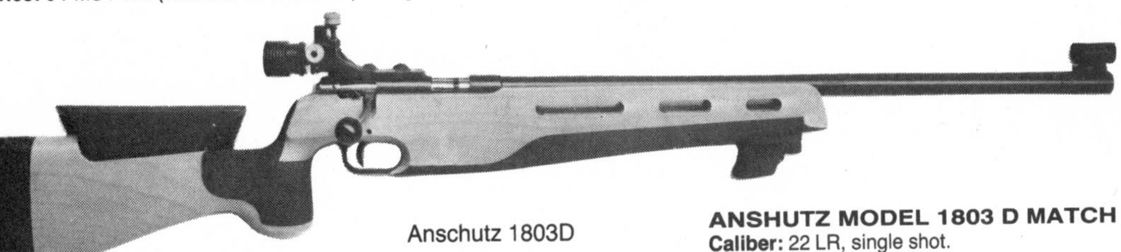

Anschutz 1803D

ANSHUTZ MODEL 1803 D MATCH RIFLE

Caliber: 22 LR, single shot.
Barrel: 25½", ¾" diameter.
Weight: 8.6 lbs. **Length:** 43¾" over-all.
Stock: Walnut-finished hardwood with adjustable cheekpiece; stippled grip and fore-end.
Sights: None furnished.
Features: Uses Anshultz Match 64 action and #5091 two-stage trigger. A medium weight rifle for intermediate and advanced Junior Match competition. Introduced 1987. Imported from West Germany by PSI.
Price: Right-hand **$739.00**
Price: Left-hand **$842.50**

ANSCHUTZ MODEL 1403D MATCH RIFLE

Caliber: 22 LR only, single shot.
Barrel: 26"; 11/16" dia.
Weight: 7¾ lbs. **Length:** 44" over-all.
Stock: Walnut finished hardwood, cheekpiece, checkered p.g., beavertail fore-end, adj. buttplate.
Sights: None furnished.
Features: Sliding side safety, adj. #5053 single stage trigger, receiver grooved for Anschutz sights. Imported from West Germany by PSI.
Price: Without sights $667.50
Price: M1403D left hand $724.50

ANSCHUTZ 1808ED SUPER RUNNING TARGET

Caliber: 22 LR, single shot.
Barrel: 23½"; ⅞" diameter.
Weight: 9¼ lbs. **Length:** 42" over-all.
Stock: European hardwood. Heavy beavertail fore-end, adjustable cheekpiece, buttplate, stippled pistol grip and fore-end.
Sights: None furnished. Receiver grooved for scope mounting.
Features: Uses Super Match 54 action. Adjustable trigger from 14 oz. to 3.5 lbs. Removable sectioned barrel weights. **Special Order Only.** Introduced 1982. Imported from Germany by PSI.
Price: Right hand $1,235.00
Price: Left hand, 1808EDL $1,359.00

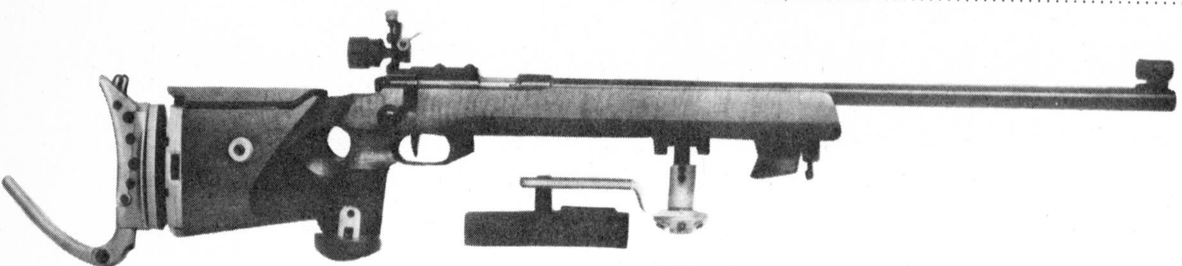

Anschutz Model 1913

Anschutz 1913 Super Match Rifle

Same as the Model 1911 except European walnut International-type stock with adj. cheekpiece, adj. aluminum hook buttplate, adjustable hand stop, weight 15½ lbs., 46" over-all. Imported from West Germany by PSI.
Price: Right hand, no sights $2,067.00
Price: M1913-L (left-hand action and stock) $2,237.00

ANSCHUTZ 1911 MATCH RIFLE

Caliber: 22 LR, single shot.
Barrel: 27¼" round (1" dia.).
Weight: 11 lbs. **Length:** 46" over-all.
Stock: Walnut-finished European hardwood; American prone style with Monte Carlo, cast-off cheekpiece, checkered p.g., beavertail fore-end with swivel rail and adj. swivel, adj. rubber buttplate.
Sights: None. Receiver grooved for Anschutz sights (extra). Scope blocks.
Features: Two-stage #5018 trigger adjustable from 2.1 to 8.6 oz. Extremely fast lock time. Imported from West Germany by PSI.
Price: Right hand, no sights $1,444.00
Price: M1911-L (true left-hand action and stock) $1,570.00

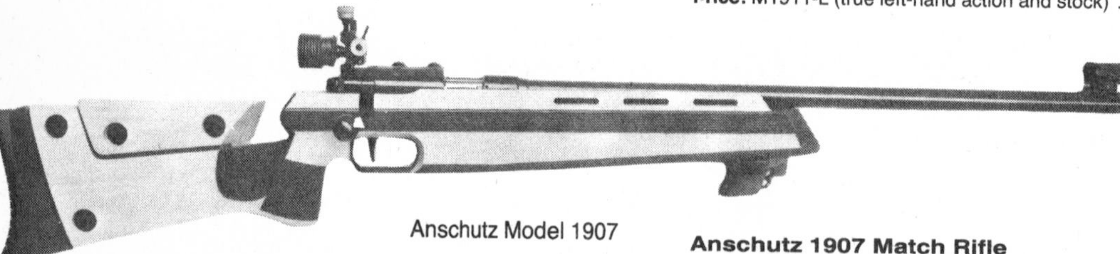

Anschutz Model 1907

Anschutz 1907 Match Rifle

Same action as Model 1913 but with ⅞" diameter 26" barrel. Length is 44½" over-all, weight 10 lbs. Blond wood finish with vented fore-end. Designed for ISU requirements, suitable for NRA matches.
Price: Right hand, no sights $1,232.00
Price: M1907-L (true left-hand action and stock) $1,340.00

Anschutz Model 1910 Super Match II

Similar to the Super Match 1913 rifle except has a stock of European hardwood with tapered fore-end and deep receiver area. Hand and palm rests not included. Uses Match 54 action. Adjustable hook buttplate and cheekpiece. Sights not included. Introduced 1982. Imported from Germany by PSI.
Price: Right hand $1,844.00
Price: Left hand $2,000.00

Anschutz Model 54.18 MS Silhouette Rifle

Same basic features as Anschutz 1913 Super Match but with special metallic silhoutte European hardwood stock and two-stage trigger. Has 22" barrel; receiver drilled and tapped.
Price: $1,129.00
Price: Model 54.18 MSL (true left-hand version of above) $1,228.00

ANSCHUTZ 1827B BIATHLON RIFLE

Caliber: 22 LR, 5-shot magazine.
Barrel: 21½".
Weight: 9 lbs. with sights. **Length:** 42½" over-all.
Stock: Walnut-finished hardwood; cheekpiece, stippled pistol grip and fore-end.
Sights: Globe front specially designed for Biathlon shooting, micrometer rear with hinged snow cap.
Features: Uses Match 54 action and adjustable trigger; adjustable wooden buttplate, Biathlon butthook, adjustable hand-stop rail. **Special Order Only.** Introduced 1982. Imported from Germany by PSI.
Price: Right hand $1,598.00
Price: Left hand $1,801.00

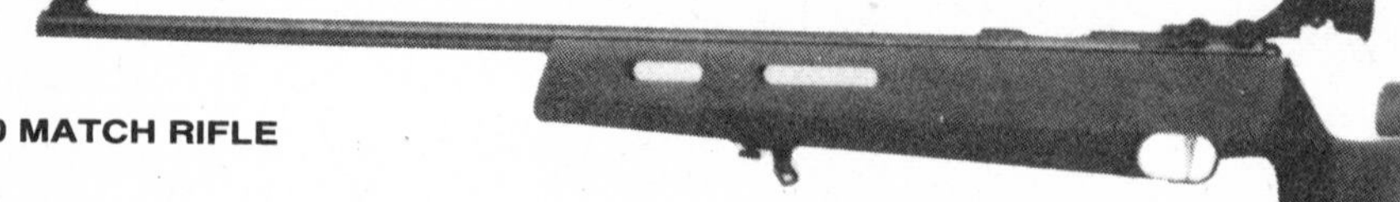

Beeman/HW 660

BEEMAN/HW 660 MATCH RIFLE

Caliber: 22 LR.
Barrel: 26".
Weight: 10.7 lbs. **Length:** 45.3" over-all.
Stock: Match-type walnut with adjustable cheekpiece and buttplate.
Sights: Globe front, match aperture rear.
Features: Adjustable match trigger; stippled p.g. and fore-end; fore-end accessory rail. Imported from West Germany by Beeman. Introduced 1988.
Price: $725.00

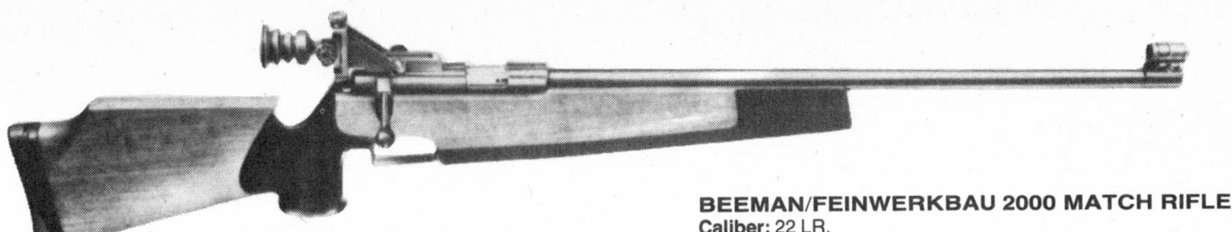

Beeman/FWB 2000

BEEMAN/FEINWERKBAU 2600 TARGET RIFLE

Caliber: 22 LR, single shot.
Barrel: 26.3″.
Weight: 10.6 lbs. **Length:** 43.7″ over-all.
Stock: Laminated hardwood and hard rubber.
Sights: Globe front with interchangeable inserts; micrometer match aperture rear.
Features: Identical smallbore companion to the Beeman/FWB 600 air rifle. Free floating barrel. Match trigger has fingertip weight adjustment dial. Introduced 1986. Imported from West Germany by Beeman.
Price: Right hand **$1,375.00**
Price: Left hand... **$1,550.00**

BEEMAN/FEINWERKBAU 2000 MATCH RIFLE

Caliber: 22 LR.
Barrel: 26¼″; 22″ for Mini-Match.
Weight: 9 lbs. 12 oz. **Length:** 43¾″ over-all (26¼″ bbl.).
Stock: Standard match. Walnut with stippled p.g. and fore-end; walnut-stained birch for the Mini-Match.
Sights: Globe front with interchangeable inserts; micrometer match aperture rear.
Features: Meets ISU standard rifle specifications. Shortest lock time of any small bore rifle. Electronic or mechanical trigger, fully adjustable for weight, release point, length, lateral position, etc. Available in Standard and Mini-Match models. Introduced 1979. Imported from West Germany by Beeman.
Price: Model 2000.............................. **$1,285.00** to **$1,850.00**
Price: Mini-Match .... **$1,225.00** to **$1,675.00**

Beeman/Krico 340

BEEMAN/KRICO 340 SILHOUETTE RIFLE

Caliber: 22 Long Rifle, 5-shot clip.
Barrel: 21″, match quality.
Weight: 7.5 lbs. **Length:** 39.5″ over-all.
Stock: European walnut match-style designed for off-hand shooting. Suitable for right- or left-hand shooters. Stippled grip and fore-end.
Sights: None furnished. Receiver grooved for tip-off mounts.
Features: Free-floated heavy barrel; fully adjustable two-stage match trigger or double set trigger. Meets NRA official MS rules. Introduced 1983. Imported by Beeman.
Price: **$1,186.00**

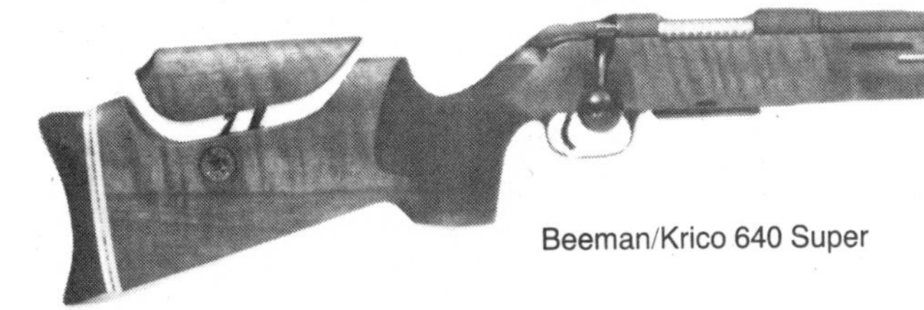

Beeman/Krico 640 Super

FINNISH LION STANDARD TARGET RIFLE

Caliber: 22 LR, single shot.
Barrel: 27⅝″.
Weight: 10½ lbs. **Length:** 44 9⁄16″ over-all.
Stock: French walnut, target style.
Sights: None furnished. Globe front, International micrometer rear available.
Features: Optional accessories: palm rest, hook buttplate, fore-end stop and swivel assembly, buttplate extension, 5 front sight aperture inserts, 3 rear sight apertures, Allen wrench. Adjustable trigger. Imported from Finland by Mandall Shooting Supplies.
Price: **$550.00**

BEEMAN/WEIHRAUCH HW60 TARGET RIFLE

Caliber: 22 LR, single shot.
Barrel: 26.8″.
Weight: 10.8 lbs. **Length:** 45.7″ over-all.
Stock: Walnut with adjustable buttplate. Stippled p.g. and fore-end. Rail with adjustable swivel.
Sights: Hooded ramp front, match-type aperture rear.
Features: Adj. match trigger with push-button safety. Left-hand version also available. Introduced 1981. Imported from West Germany by Beeman.
Price: Right hand... **$698.00**
Price: Left hand **$739.00**

BEEMAN/KRICO 640 SUPER SNIPER

Caliber: 308.
Barrel: 26″. Specially designed match bull barrel, matte blue finish, with muzzle brake/flash hider.
Weight: 9.6 lbs. **Length:** 44¾″ over-all.
Stock: Select walnut with oil finish. Spring-loaded, adj. cheekpiece, adjustable recoil pad.
Sights: None furnished. Drilled and tapped for scope mounts.
Features: Match trigger with 10mm wide shoe; single standard or double set trigger available. All metal has matte blue finish. Bolt knob has 1¼″ diameter. Scope mounts available for special night-sight devices. Imported from West Germany by Beeman.
Price: Without scope, mount................................ **$2,363.00**

HECKLER & KOCH PSG-1 MARKSMAN RIFLE

Caliber: 308, 5- and 20-shot magazines.
Barrel: 25.6″, heavy.
Weight: 17.8 lbs. **Length:** 47.5″ over-all.
Stock: Matte black high impact plastic, adj. for length, pivoting butt cap, vertically-adj. cheekpiece; target-type pistol grip with adj. palm shelf.
Sights: Hendsoldt 6x42 scope.
Features: Uses HK-91 action with low-noise bolt closing device; special fore-end with T-way rail for sling swivel or tripod. Gun comes in special foam-fitted metal transport case with tripod, two 20-shot and two-5-shot magazines, cleaning rod. Imported from West Germany by Heckler & Koch, Inc. Introduced 1986.
Price: **$8,599.00**

Parker-Hale M87

PARKER-HALE M87 TARGET RIFLE
Caliber: 308 Win., 243, 6.5x55, 30-06, 300 Win. Mag. (other calibers on request), 5-shot detachable box magazine.
Barrel: 26" heavy.
Weight: About 10 lbs. **Length:** 45" over-all.
Stock: Walnut target-style, adjustable for length of pull; solid buttpad; accessory rail with hand-stop. Deeply stippled grip and fore-end.
Sights: None furnished. Receiver dovetailed for Parker-Hale "Roll-Off" scope mounts.
Features: Mauser-style action with large bolt knob. Parkerized finish. Introduced 1987. Imported from England by Precision Sports.
Price: **$1,175.00**

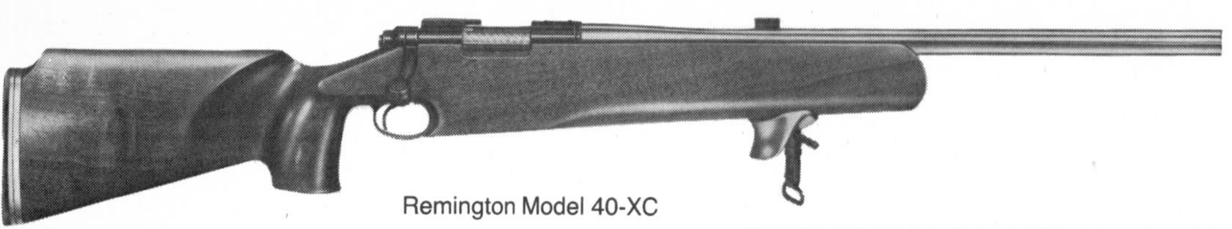

Remington Model 40-XC

REMINGTON MODEL 40XB-BR
Caliber: 22 BR Rem., 222 Rem., 223, 6mmx47, 6mm BR Rem., 7.62 NATO (308 Win.).
Barrel: 20" (light varmint class), 26" (heavy varmint class).
Weight: Light varmint class, 7¼ lbs.; heavy varmint class, 12 lbs. **Length:** 38" (20" bbl.), 44" (26" bbl.).
Stock: Select walnut.
Sights: None. Supplied with scope blocks.
Features: Unblued stainless steel barrel, trigger adj. from 1½ lbs. to 3½ lbs. Special 2/2-oz. trigger at extra cost. Scope and mounts extra.
Price: About... **$1,000.00**
Price: Extra for 2-oz. trigger, about............................. **$133.00**

REMINGTON 40-XC NAT'L MATCH COURSE RIFLE
Caliber: 7.62 NATO, 5-shot.
Barrel: 23¼", stainless steel.
Weight: 10 lbs. without sights. **Length:** 42½" over-all.
Stock: Walnut, position-style, with palm swell.
Sights: None furnished.
Features: Designed to meet the needs of competitive shooters firing the national match courses. Position-style stock, top loading clip slot magazine, anti-bind bolt and receiver, bright stainless steel barrel. Meets all I.S.U. Army Rifle specifications. Adjustable buttplate, adjustable trigger.
Price: About.. **$1,000.00**
Price: Model 40-XC KS (Kevlar stock) **$1,133.00**

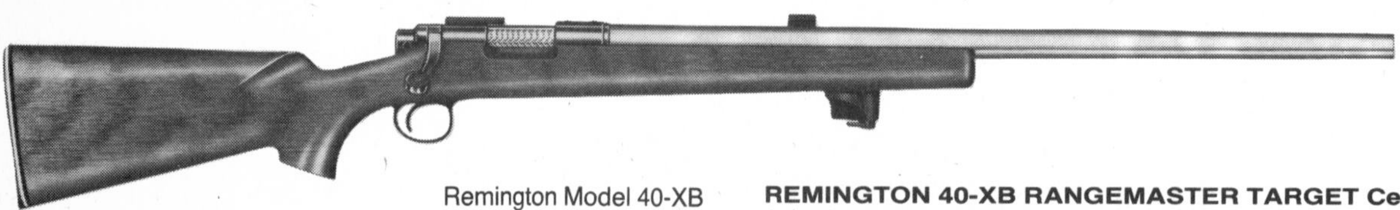

Remington Model 40-XB

Remington 40-XB KS Varmint Special
Similar to the standard Model 40-XB except has Du Pont Kevlar aramid fiber stock with straight comb, cheekpiece, palm-swell grip, black recoil pad. Swivel studs easily removable. Stock color is satin black with light texture. Single shot or repeater. Chamberings include 220 Swift. Introduced 1987. Custom Shop order.
Price: Single shot.. **$1,067.00**
Price: Repeater... **$1,147.00**
Price: Extra for 2-oz. trigger.................................. **$133.00**

REMINGTON 40-XB RANGEMASTER TARGET Centerfire
Caliber: 222 Rem., 22-250, 6mm Rem., 243, 25-06, 7mm Rem. Mag., 30-338 (30-7mm Rem. Mag.), 300 Win. Mag., 7.62 NATO (308 Win.), 30-06, single shot.
Barrel: 27¼" round (Stand. dia.—¾", Hvy. dia.—⅞").
Weight: Std.—9¼ lbs., Hvy.—11¼ lbs. **Length:** 47" over-all.
Stock: American walnut with high comb and beavertail fore-end stop. Rubber non-slip buttplate.
Sights: None. Scope blocks installed.
Features: Adjustable trigger pull. Receiver drilled and tapped for sights.
Price: Standard s.s., stainless steel barrel, about **$933.00**
Price: Repeating model, about................................ **$1,013.00**
Price: Extra for 2-oz. trigger, about............................. **$133.00**

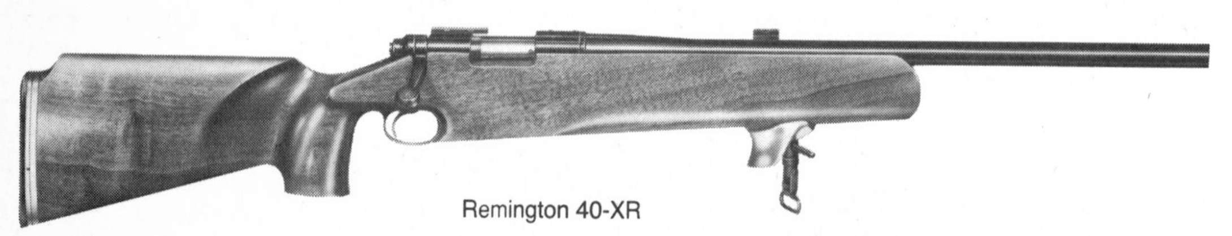

Remington 40-XR

REMINGTON 40-XR RIMFIRE POSITION RIFLE
Caliber: 22 LR, single-shot.
Barrel: 24", heavy target.
Weight: 10 lbs. **Length:** 43" over-all.
Stock: Position-style with front swivel block on fore-end guide rail.
Sights: Drilled and tapped. Furnished with scope blocks.
Features: Meets all I.S.U. specifications. Deep fore-end, buttplate vertically adjustable, wide adjustable trigger.
Price: About **$933.00**
Price: Model 40-XR KS (Kevlar stock) **$1,067.00**

Consult our Directory pages for the location of firms mentioned.

Springfield M1A Match

SPRINGFIELD ARMORY M1A SUPER MATCH

Caliber: 308 Win.
Barrel: 22", heavy Douglas Premium, or Hart stainless steel.
Weight: About 10 lbs. **Length:** 44½" overall.
Stock: Heavy walnut competition stock with longer pistol grip, contoured area behind the rear sight, thicker butt and fore-end, glass bedded.
Sights: National Match front and rear.
Features: Has new figure-eight style operating rod guide, new stock design. Introduced 1987. From Springfield Armory, Inc.
Price: About.......... **$1,231.00**

SPRINGFIELD ARMORY M-21 SNIPER RIFLE

Caliber: 308 Win.
Barrel: 22", Douglas heavy, air-gauged.
Weight: 15.25 lbs. (with bipod, scope mount). **Length:** 44¼" over-all.
Stock: Heavy walnut with adjustable comb, ventilated recoil pad. Glass bedded.
Sights: National Match front and rear.
Features: Refinement of the standard M1-A rifle. Has specially knurled shoulder for new figure-eight operating rod guide. New style folding and removable bipod. Guaranteed to deliver MOA accuracy. Comes with six 20-round magazines, leather military sling, cleaning kit. Introduced 1987. From Springfield Armory.
Price: **$2,320.00**

SPRINGFIELD ARMORY MODEL 700 BASR

Caliber: 308 Win., 5-shot magazine.
Barrel: 26" heavy Douglas Premium, 1-11" twist.
Weight: 13.5 lbs. (with bipod, scope, mount). **Length:** 46.25" over-all.
Stock: Synthetic fiber with rubber recoil pad.
Sights: None furnished.
Features: Comes with leather military sling and Parker-Hale folding, adjustable bipod, Guaranteed to deliver MOA accuracy with Federal Match ammunition. Introduced 1987. From Springfield Armory.
Price: **$1,994.00**
Price: Model 24, with stainless barrel.......... **$2,288.00**
Price: As above with adjustable stock.......... **$2,496.00**

STEYR-MANNLICHER MATCH UIT RIFLE

Caliber: 243 Win. or 308 Win., 10-shot magazine.
Barrel: 25.5".
Weight: 10.9 lbs. **Length:** 44.48" over-all.
Stock: Walnut with stippled grip and fore-end. Special UIT Match design.
Sights: Walther globe front, Walther peep rear.
Features: Double-pull trigger adjustable for let-off point, slack, weight of first-stage pull, release force and length; buttplate adjustable for height and length. Meets UIT specifications. Introduced 1984. Imported from Austria by Gun South, Inc.
Price: **$2,350.00**

Steyr SSG Marksman

STEYR-MANNLICHER SSG MARKSMAN

Caliber: 308 Win.
Barrel: 25.6".
Weight: 8.6 lbs. **Length:** 44.5" over-all.
Stock: Choice of ABS "Cycolac" synthetic half-stock or walnut. Removable spacers in butt adjusts length of pull from 12¾" to 14".
Sights: Hooded blade front, folding leaf rear.
Features: Parkerized finish. Choice of interchangeable single or double set triggers. Detachable 5-shot rotary magazine (10-shot optional). Drilled and tapped for scope mounts. Imported from Austria by Gun South, Inc.
Price: Synthetic half-stock.......... **$1,592.00**
Price: Walnut half-stock.......... **$1,995.00**
Price: SSG PII (large bolt knob, heavy bbl., no sights, fore-end rail). **$1,995.00**

Steyr-Mannlicher SSG Match
Same as Model SSG Marksman except has heavy barrel, match bolt, Walther target peep sights and adj. rail in fore-end to adj. sling travel. Weight is 11 lbs.
Price: Synthetic half-stock.......... **$1,875.00**
Price: Walnut half-stock.......... **$2,125.00**

Tanner Free Rifle

TANNER 300 METER FREE RIFLE

Caliber: 308 Win., 7.5 Swiss, single shot.
Barrel: 28.7".
Weight: 15 lbs. **Length:** 45.3" over-all.
Stock: Seasoned walnut, thumb-hole style, with accessory rail, palm rest, adjustable hook butt.
Sights: Globe front with interchangeable inserts, Tanner-design micrometer-diopter rear with adjustable aperture.
Features: Three-lug revolving-lock bolt design; adjustable set trigger; short firing pin travel; supplied with 300-meter test target. Imported from Switzerland by Osborne's Supplies. Introduced 1984.
Price: About.......... **$3,900.00**

CAUTION: PRICES CHANGE. CHECK AT GUNSHOP.

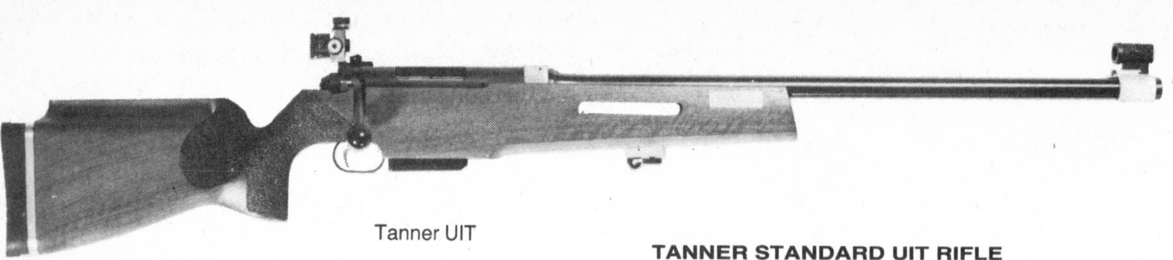

Tanner UIT

TANNER 50 METER FREE RIFLE
Caliber: 22 LR, single shot.
Barrel: 27.7".
Weight: 13.9 lbs. **Length:** 43.4" over-all.
Stock: Seasoned nutwood with palm rest, accessory rail, adjustable hook butt-plate.
Sights: Globe front with interchangeable inserts, Tanner micrometer-diopter rear with adjustable aperture.
Features: Bolt action with externally adjustable set trigger. Supplied with 50-meter test target. Imported from Switzerland by Osborne's Supplies. Introduced 1984.
Price: About. **$2,950.00**

TANNER STANDARD UIT RIFLE
Caliber: 308, 7.5mm Swiss, 10-shot.
Barrel: 25.8".
Weight: 10.5 lbs. **Length:** 40.6" over-all.
Stock: Match style of seasoned nutwood with accessory rail; coarsely stippled pistol grip; high cheekpiece; vented fore-end.
Sights: Globe front with interchangeable inserts, Tanner micrometer-diopter rear with adjustable aperture.
Features: Two locking lug revolving bolt encloses case head. Trigger adjustable from ½ to 6½ lbs.; match trigger optional. Comes with 300-meter test target. Imported from Switzerland by Osborne's. Introduced 1984.
Price: About. **$3,700.00**

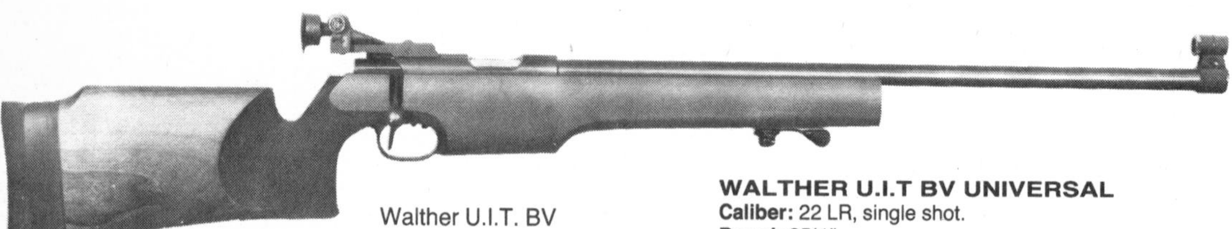

Walther U.I.T. BV

Walther GX-1 Match Rifle
Same general specs as U.I.T. except has 25½" barrel, over-all length of 44½", weight of 15½ lbs. Stock is designed to provide every conceivable adjustment for individual preference and anatomical compatibility. Left-hand stock available on special order. Imported from Germany by Interarms.
Price: **$2,100.00**

WALTHER U.I.T BV UNIVERSAL
Caliber: 22 LR, single shot.
Barrel: 25½".
Weight: 10 lbs., 3 oz. **Length:** 44¾" over-all.
Stock: Walnut, adj. for length and drop; fore-end guide rail for sling or palm rest.
Sights: Globe-type front, fully adj. aperture rear.
Features: Conforms to both NRA and U.I.T. requirements. Fully adj. trigger. Left-hand stock available on special order. Imported from Germany by Interarms.
Price: **$1,625.00**

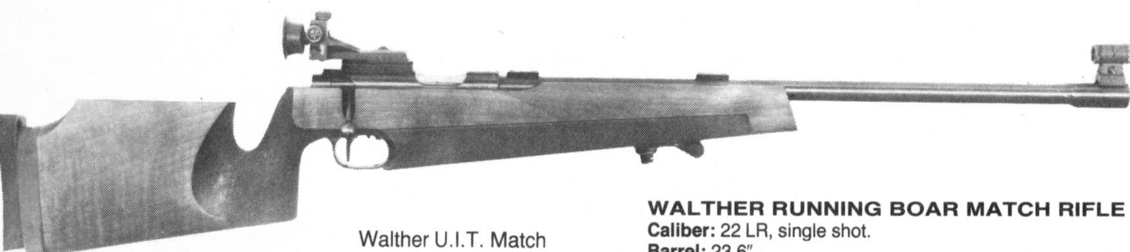

Walther U.I.T. Match

Walther U.I.T. Match
Same specifications and features as standard U.I.T. Super rifle but has scope mount bases. Fore-end has new tapered profile, fully stippled. Imported from Germany by Interarms.
Price: **$1,500.00**

WALTHER RUNNING BOAR MATCH RIFLE
Caliber: 22 LR, single shot.
Barrel: 23.6".
Weight: 8 lbs. 5 oz. **Length:** 42" over-all.
Stock: Walnut thumb-hole type. Fore-end and p.g. stippled.
Features: Especially designed for running boar competition. Receiver grooved to accept dovetail scope mounts. Adjustable cheekpiece and butt plate. 1.1 lb. trigger pull. Left-hand stock available on special order. Imported from Germany by Interarms.
Price: **$1,200.00**

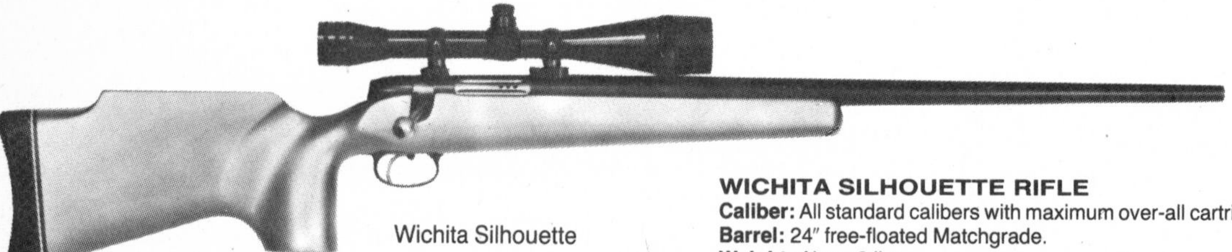

Wichita Silhouette

WICHITA SILHOUETTE RIFLE
Caliber: All standard calibers with maximum over-all cartridge length of 2.800".
Barrel: 24" free-floated Matchgrade.
Weight: About 9 lbs.
Stock: Metallic gray fiberthane with ventilated rubber recoil pad.
Sights: None furnished. Drilled and tapped for scope mounts.
Features: Legal for all NRA competitions. Single shot action. Fluted bolt, 2-oz. Canjar trigger; glass-bedded stock. Introduced 1983. From Wichita Arms.
Price: **$2,150.00**
Price: Left-hand **$2,400.00**

CAUTION: PRICES CHANGE. CHECK AT GUNSHOP.

Includes a wide variety of sporting guns and guns suitable for various competitions.

ARMSPORT 2751 GAS AUTO SHOTGUN

Gauge: 12, 3″ chamber.
Barrel: 28″ (Mod.), 30″ (Full).
Weight: 7 lbs.
Stock: European walnut.
Features: Gas-operated action; blued receiver with light engraving. Introduced 1986. Imported from Italy by Armsport.
Price: With fixed choks $575.00
Price: Blue, choke tubes, 28″ bbl. $650.00
Price: With silvered receiver $675.00

BENELLI M1 SUPER 90 FIELD AUTO SHOTGUN

Gauge: 12, 3″ chamber.
Barrel: 28″ (choke tubes).
Weight: 7 lbs., 4 oz.
Stock: High impact polymer.
Sights: Metal bead front.
Features: Sporting version of the military & police gun. Uses the rotating Montefeltro bolt system. Ventilated rib; blue finish. Imported from Italy by Heckler & Koch
Price: $655.00

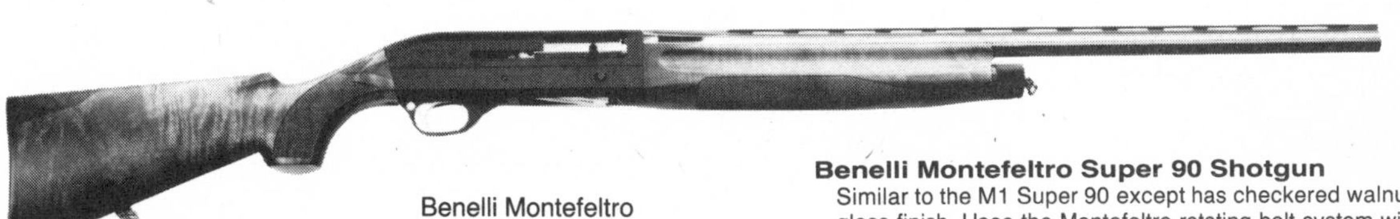

Benelli Montefeltro

Benelli Montefeltro Super 90 Shotgun

Similar to the M1 Super 90 except has checkered walnut stock with high-gloss finish. Uses the Montefeltro rotating bolt system with a simple inertia recoil design. Has 28″ barrel with Imp., Mod., full choke tubes. Weight is 6 lbs., 14 oz. Finish is matte black. Introduced 1987.
Price: Right hand $664.00
Price: Left hand $724.00

BERETTA A-303 AUTO SHOTGUN

Gauge: 12 or 20, 2¾″ or 3″ chamber.
Barrel: 12-ga.—22″ (Slug), 26″ (Imp. Cyl., Skeet or Mobilchoke), 28″ (Mod. or Mobilchoke); 30 ″ (Full or Mobilchoke) 32″ (Full or Mobilchoke); 20-ga—22″ (Cyl./Slug) 24″ (Youth); 26″ (Mobilchoke or Skeet); 28″ (Mobilchoke); 30″ (Mobilchoke).
Weight: About 6½ lbs., 20 gauge; about 7½ lbs., 12 gauge.
Stock: American walnut; hand-checkered grip and fore-end.
Features: Gas-operated action, alloy receiver, magazine cut-off, push-button safety. Mobilchoke models come with three interchangeable flush-mounted screw-in choke tubes. Imported from Italy by Beretta U.S.A. Introduced 1983.
Price: 12 or 20 ga., standard chokes $506.00
Price: Mobilchoke, 12 ga. or 20 ga. $574.000
Price: 12 ga. trap with Monte Carlo stock $660.00
Price: 12 ga. trap with standard trap stock $606.00
Price: 12 or 20 ga. skeet $606.00
Price: Slug, 12 or 20 ga. $554.00
Price: A303 Youth Gun, 20 ga., 3″ chamber, 24″ barrel, Mobilchoke $574.00
Price: A303 Sporting clays $660.00

BERETTA 1200F and FP

Gauge: 12 ga., 2¾″ chamber.
Barrel: 28″ (Mod., Model 1200F); 20″ (Cyl., Model 1200 FP).
Weight: 7.3 lbs.
Stock: Special strengthened technopolymer, matte black finish
Features: Resists abrasion and adverse effects of water, salt and other damaging materials associated with tough field conditions. Imported from Italy by Beretta U.S.A. Introduced 1988.
Price: 1200 F or 1200 FP $440.00

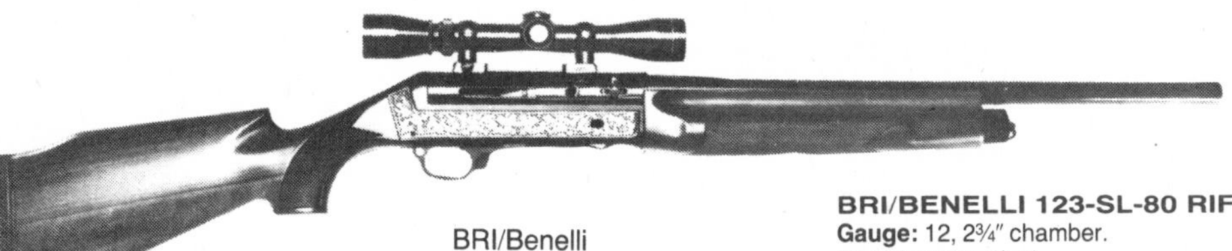

BRI/Benelli

BRI/BENELLI 123-SL-80 RIFLED SHOTGUN

Gauge: 12, 2¾″ chamber.
Barrel: 24⅛″, rifled.
Weight: 9 lbs. **Length:** 45½″ over-all.
Stock: European walnut with checkered p.g. and fore-end.
Sights: None furnished. Drilled and tapped for scope mounting.
Features: Rifled bore. Quick interchangeable barrels; cross-bolt safety; engraved receiver; recoil pad. From Ballistic Research Industries.
Price: $895.00

Browning Sweet Sixteen

BROWNING AUTO-5 LIGHT 12 and 20, SWEET 16

Gauge: 12, 16, 20; 5-shot; 3-shot plug furnished; 2¾″ or 3″ chamber.
Action: Recoil operated autoloader; takedown.
Barrel: 26″, 28″, 30″ Invector (choke tube) barrel; also available with Light 20 ga. 28″ (Mod.) or 26″ (Imp. Cyl.) barrel.
Weight: 12, 16 ga. 7¼ lbs., 20 ga. 6⅜ lbs.
Stock: French walnut, hand checkered half-p.g. and fore-end. 14¼″ × 1⅝″ × 2½″.
Features: Receiver hand engraved with scroll designs and border. Double extractors, extra bbls. interchangeable without factory fitting; mag. cut-off; cross-bolt safety. Buck Special no longer inventoried, but can be ordered as a Buck Special extra barrel, plus an action only. Imported from Japan by Browning.
Price: Light 12, 20, Sweet 16, vent. rib., Invector $664.95
Price: Extra Invector barrel $230.95
Price: Extra fixed-choke barrel (Light 20 only) $194.95
Price: 12, 16, 20 Buck Special barrel $234.00

Browning Auto-5 Gold Classic
Same as the standard Auto-5 Light 12 with 28″ (Mod.) barrel. Has engraved hunting and wildlife scenes with gold animals and portrait. Only 500 will be made, each numbered "1 of Five Hundred," etc. with "Browning Gold Classic." Select, figured walnut, special checkering with carved border, and the semi-pistol grip stock. Introduced 1984.
Price: Auto-5 Gold Classic **$6,500.00**

Browning Auto-5 Magnum 20
Same as Magnum 12 except 26″ or 28″ barrel with Invector choke tubes. With ventilated rib, 7½ lbs.
Price: Invector only **$685.95**
Price: Extra Invector barrel. **$230.95**

Browning Auto-5 Magnum 12
Same as standard Auto-5 except chambered for 3″ magnum shells (also handles 2¾″ magnum and 2¾″ HV loads). 28″ Mod., Full; 30″ and 32″ (Full) bbls. Comes with Invector choke tubes. 14″x1⅝″x2½″ stock. Recoil pad. Wgt. 8¾ lbs.
Price: With Invector choke tubes. **$685.95**
Price: Extra Invector barrel. **$230.95**

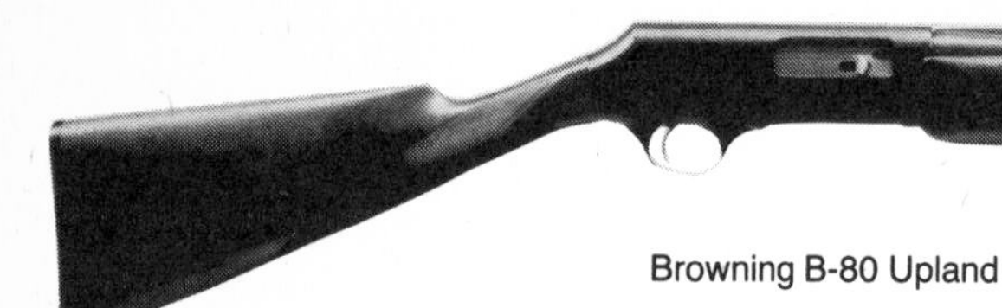

Browning B-80 Upland

BROWNING B-80 PLUS AUTO SHOTGUN
Gauge: 12 or 20, 2¾," & 3″ chamber
Barrel: 24″ (Slug), 26″ (Imp. Cyl., Cyl., Skeet, Full, Mod.), 28″ (Full, Mod.) 30″ (Full), 32″ (Full). Invector barrels in 22″, 26″, 28″, 30″, 12 or 20 ga.
Weight: 12 ga. about 7 lbs., 20 ga. about 5¾ lbs.
Stock: 14¼″ × 1⅝″ × 2½″. Hand checkered French walnut. Solid black recoil pad.
Features: Shoots all popular factory 2¾″ and 3″ loads without adjustment. Vent. rib barrels have non-reflective rib; alloy receiver; cross-bolt safety; interchangeable barrels. Buck Special no longer inventoried, but can be ordered as a Buck Special extra barrel and action only. Introduced 1981. Imported from Belgium by Browning.
Price: Invector, vent. rib, 12 or 20 ga.. **$588.95**
Price: Extra Invector barrels. **$207.95**
Price: Extra fixed-choke barrels, 20 ga. only. **$131.25**
Price: Extra Buck Special barrel **$207.95**

Browning B-80 Upland Special Auto Shotgun
Same as standard B-80 except has 22″ Invector barrel. Straight grip stock with 14″ length of pull; 12 and 20 gauge. Introduced 1986.
Price: **$589.95**

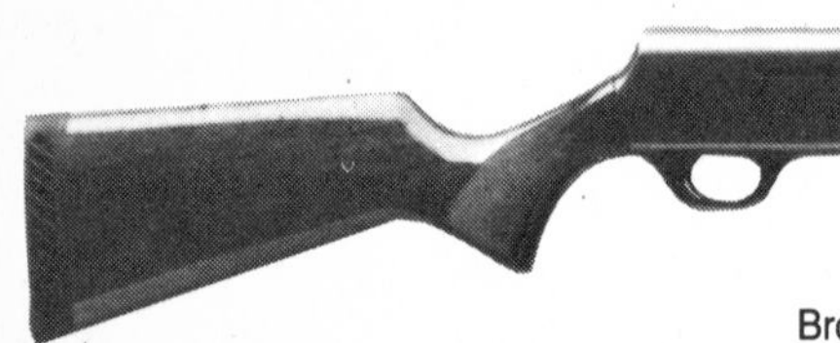

Browning A-500

BROWNING A-500 AUTO SHOTGUN
Gauge: 12 only, 3″ chamber.
Barrel: 24″ Buck Special, 26″, 28″, 30″ with Invector choke tubes.
Weight: 7 lbs., 7 oz. (30″ barrel). **Length:** 49½″ over-all (30″ bbl.).
Stock: 14¼″ x 1½″ x 2½″; select walnut with gloss finish; checkered p.g. and fore-end; black vent. recoil pad.
Sights: Metal bead front.
Features: Uses a short-recoil action with four-lug rotary bolt and composite and coil spring buffering system. Shoots all loads without adjustment. Has a magazine cut-off, Invector chokes. Introduced 1987. Imported from Belgium by Browning.
Price: **$559.95**
Price: Extra Invector and Back Special barrels. **$199.95**

COSMI AUTOMATIC SHOTGUN
Gauge: 12 or 20, 2¾″ or 3″ chamber.
Barrel: 22″ to 34″. Choke (including choke tubes) and length to customer specs. Boehler steel.
Weight: About 6¼ lbs. (20 ga.).
Stock: Length and style to customer specs. Hand-checkered exhibition grade circassian walnut standard.
Features: Hand-made, essentially a custom gun. Recoil-operated auto with tip-up barrel. Made completely of stainless steel (lower receiver polished); magazine tube in buttstock holds 7 rounds. Double ejectors, double safety system. Comes with fitted leather case. Imported from Italy by Incor Inc.
Price: From **$7,100.00**

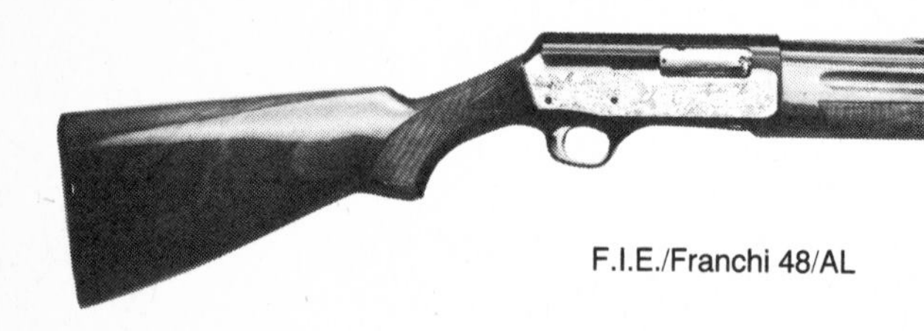

F.I.E./Franchi 48/AL

F.I.E./FRANCHI 48/AL AUTO SHOTGUN
Gauge: 12 or 20, 5-shot, 2¾″ or 3″ chamber.
Action: Recoil-operated automatic.
Barrel: 24″ (Imp. Cyl. or Cyl.); 26″ (Imp. Cyl. or Mod); 28″ (Skeet, Mod. or Full); 30″, 32″ (Full). Interchangeable barrels.
Weight: 12 ga. 6¼ lbs., 20 ga. 5 lbs. 2 oz.
Stock: Epoxy-finished walnut, with cut-checkered pistol grip and fore-end.
Features: Chrome-lined bbl., easy takedown, 3-round plug provided. Ventilated rib barrel. Imported from Italy by F.I.E.
Price: Vent. rib 12, 20 . . . . **$454.95**
Price: Hunter model (engraved) **$489.95**
Price: 12 ga. Magnum. **$489.95**
Price: Extra barrel **$179.95**

F.I.E./Franchi Slug Gun
Same as Standard automatic except 22″ Cylinder bored plain barrel, adj. rifle-type sights.
Price: 12 or 20 ga., standard **$454.95**
Price: As above, Hunter grade **$489.95**
Price: Extra barrel **$179.95**

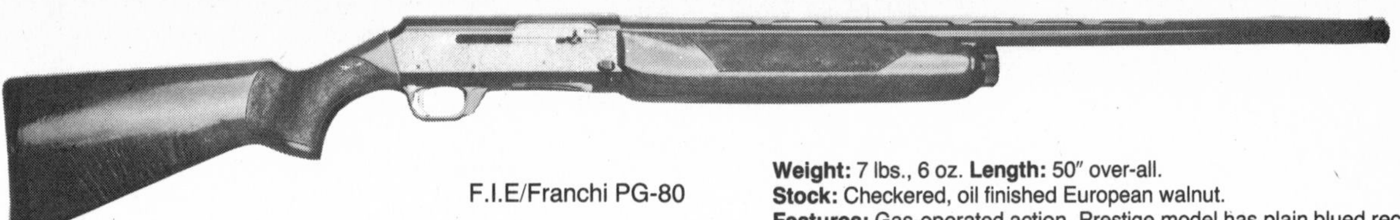

F.I.E/Franchi PG-80

F.I.E./FRANCHI PRESTIGE, ELITE SHOTGUNS
Gauge: 12, 2¾″, or 3″ chamber.
Barrel: 24″ (Slug), 26″ (Imp. Cyl.), 26″, 28″ (Mod.), 28″ (Full), 30″, 32″ (3″ Full).
Weight: 7 lbs., 6 oz. **Length:** 50″ over-all.
Stock: Checkered, oil finished European walnut.
Features: Gas-operated action. Prestige model has plain blued receiver, Elite has engraved receiver. Both models have 7mm-wide vent. rib. Gas piston is stainless steel. Introduced 1985. Imported from Italy by F.I.E. Corp.
Price: Prestige **$489.95**
Price: Elite **$539.95**
Price: Extra barrels **$179.95**

Mossberg 5500 MK II

MOSSBERG MODEL 5500 MKII AUTO SHOTGUN
Gauge: 12, 2¾″ chamber.
Barrel: 28″ (ACCU-CHOKE Full, Mod., Imp. Cyl. tubes).
Weight: 7½ lbs. **Length:** 48″ over-all.
Stock: 14″x1½″x2½″. Walnut-stained hardwood with checkered grip, fore-end; recoil pad.
Sights: White front bead, brass mid-bead.
Features: Twin extractors, ambidextrous thumb safety; interchangeable barrels accept choke tubes for steel shot. Extra 3″ chamber ACCU-CHOKE barrels available. Announced 1988.
Price: About **$294.95**

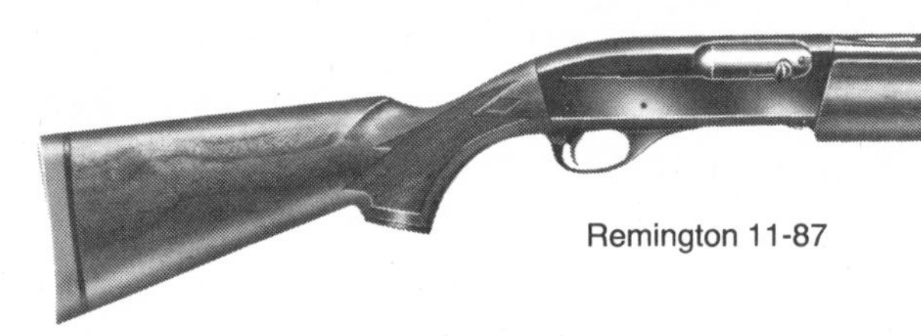

Remington 11-87

REMINGTON MODEL 11-87 PREMIER SHOTGUN
Gauge: 12 ga., 3″ chamber.
Barrel: 26″, 28″, 30″ REM Choke tubes.
Weight: About 8¼ lbs. **Length:** 46″ over-all (26″ bbl.).
Stock: Walnut with satin finish; cut checkering; solid brown butt pad; no white spacers.
Sights: Bradley-type white-faced front, metal bead middle.
Features: Pressure compensating gas system allows shooting 2¾″ or 3″ loads interchangeably with no adjustments. Stainless magazine tube; redesigned feed latch, barrel support ring on operating bars; pinned fore-end. Introduced 1987.
Price: **$527.00**
Price: Left hand **$573.00**

Remington Model 11-87 Special Purpose Deer Gun
Similar to the 11-87 Special Purpose Magnum except has 21″ barrel with rifle sights and fixed Imp. Cyl. slug choke. Gas system set to handle all 2¾″ and 3″ slug, buckshot, high velocity field and magnum loads. Not designed to function with light 2¾″ field loads. Introduced 1987.
Price: **$499.00**

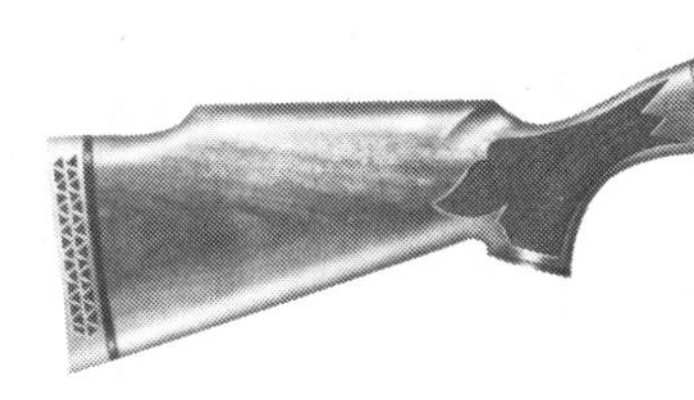

Remington 11-87 Trap

Remington Model 11-87 Premier Trap
Similar to 11-87 Premier except trap dimension stock with straight or Monte Carlo comb; select walnut with satin finish and Tournament-grade cut checkering; 30″ barrel with Trap Full or REM Chokes (Trap Full, Trap Extra Full, Trap Super Full). Gas system set for 2¾″ shells only. Introduced 1987.
Price: With straight stock, REM choke **$580.00**
Price: As above, Trap Full choke **$567.00**
Price: With Monte Carlo stock **$593.00**
Price: As above, Trap Full choke **$580.00**

Remington Model 11-87 Premier Skeet
Similar to 11-87 Premier except Skeet dimension stock with cut checkering, satin finish, two-piece buttplate; 26″ barrel with Skeet or REM Chokes (Skeet, Imp. Skeet). Gas system set for 2¾ shells only. Introduced 1987.
Price: **$573.00**
Price: With Skeet choke **$560.00**

Remington Model 11-87 Special Purpose Magnum
Similar to the 11-87 Premier except has dull stock finish, Parkerized exposed metal surfaces. Bolt and carrier have dull blackened coloring. Comes with 26″ or 30″ barrel with Rem Chokes, padded Cordura nylon sling and q.d. swivels. Introduced 1987.
Price: **$525.00**

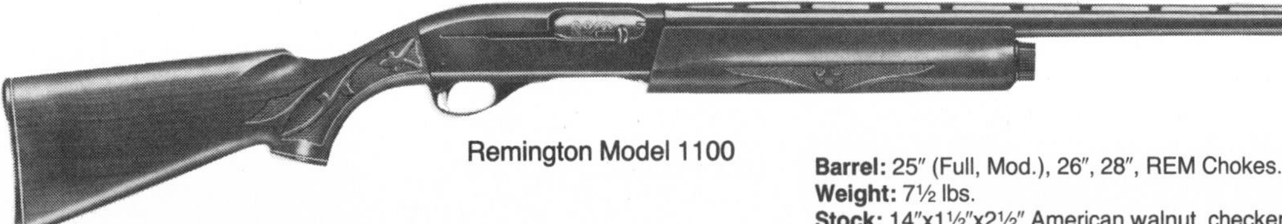

Remington Model 1100

REMINGTON MODEL 1100 AUTO
Gauge: 20, 28, 410.
Barrel: 25″ (Full, Mod.), 26″, 28″, REM Chokes.
Weight: 7½ lbs.
Stock: 14″x1½″x2½″ American walnut, checkered p.g. and fore-end.
Features: Quickly interchangeable barrels. Matted receiver top with scroll work on both sides of receiver. Cross-bolt safety.
Price: With REM chokes about **$533.00**

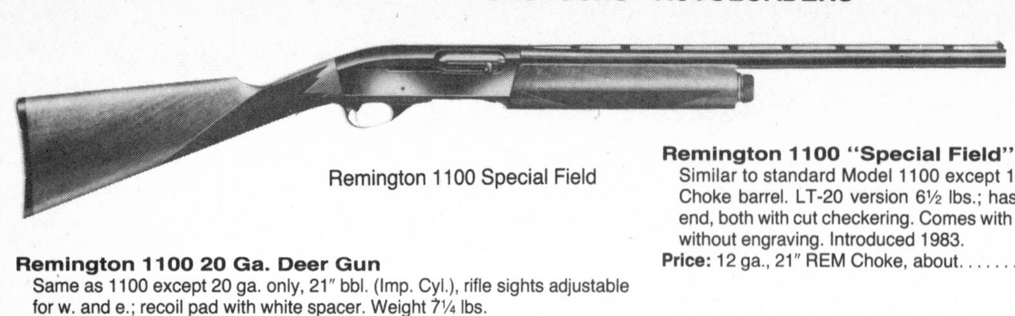

Remington 1100 Special Field

Remington 1100 20 Ga. Deer Gun
Same as 1100 except 20 ga. only, 21″ bbl. (Imp. Cyl.), rifle sights adjustable for w. and e.; recoil pad with white spacer. Weight 7¼ lbs.
Price: About $480.00

Remington 1100D Tournament Auto
Same as 1100 Standard except vent. rib, better wood, more extensive engraving.
Price: About.. $2,291.00

Remington 1100F Premier Auto
Same as 1100D except select wood, better engraving.
Price: About.. $4,720.00
Price: With gold inlay, about.................................. $7,079.00

SKB MODEL 1300 AUTO SHOTGUN
Gauge: 12, 2¾″ or 3″, 20, 3″.
Barrel: 22″ (Slug), 26″, 28″ (Inter Choke tubes).
Weight: 6½ to 7¼ lbs. **Length:** 48¼″ over-all (28″ barrel).
Stock: 14½″x1½″x2½″. Walnut, with hand checkered grip and fore-end.
Sights: Metal bead front.
Features: Gas operated with Universal Automatic System. Blued receiver. Magazine cut-off system. Introduced 1988. Imported from Japan by Ernie Simmons Ent.
Price: Field $495.00
Price: 1300 Slug... $499.00

TRADEWINDS H-170 AUTO SHOTGUN
Gauge: 12 only, 2¾″ chamber.
Action: Recoil-operated automatic.
Barrel: 26″, 28″ (Mod.) and 28″ (Full), chrome lined.
Weight: 7 lbs.
Stock: Select European walnut stock, p.g. and fore-end hand checkered.
Features: Light alloy receiver, 5-shot tubular magazine, ventilated rib. Imported from Italy by Tradewinds.
Price:.. $395.00

Remington 1100 "Special Field"
Similar to standard Model 1100 except 12 ga. only, comes with 21″ REM Choke barrel. LT-20 version 6½ lbs.; has straight-grip stock, shorter fore-end, both with cut checkering. Comes with vent rib only; matte finish receiver without engraving. Introduced 1983.
Price: 12 ga., 21″ REM Choke, about........................... $520.00

Remington 1100 LT-20 and Small Gauge
Same as 1100 except 20 and 28 ga. 2¾″ (5-shot). 45½″ over-all. Available in 25″ bbl. (Full, Mod., or Imp. Cyl.) only.
Price: With vent rib, about $525.00
Price: 3″ Magnum $533.00

Remington 1100 Tournament Skeet
Same as the 1100 except 26″ bbl., special Skeet boring, vent. rib (high rib on LT-20), ivory bead front and metal bead middle sights. 14″×1½″×2½″ stock. 20, 28, 410 ga. Wgt. 7½ lbs., cut checkering, walnut, new receiver scroll.
Price: Tournament Skeet (28, 410), about $589.00
Price: Tournament Skeet (20), about............................ $589.00

SKB Model 1900 Auto Shotgun
Similar to the Model 1300 except has engraved bright-finish receiver, grip cap, gold plated trigger. Introduced 1988.
Price: Field $550.00
Price: Slug gun (22″ barrel, rifle sights) $550.00
Price: Deluxe Trap (2¾″ chamber, 30″ barrel with Inter Choke tubes, Monte Carlo stock) $575.00

SKB Model 1900 Trap
Similar to the Model 1900 Field except in 12 gauge only (2¾″ chamber), 30″ barrel with Inter Choke tubes and 9.5mm wide rib. Introduced 1988.
Price:.. $575.00

SKB Model 3000 Auto Shotgun
Similar to the Model 1900 except has more elaborate engraving, initial plate in buttstock.
Price: Field $585.00
Price: Trap $595.00

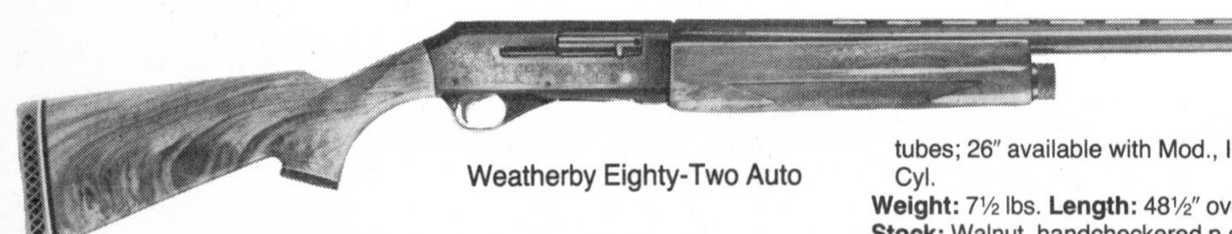

Weatherby Eighty-Two Auto

WEATHERBY EIGHTY-TWO AUTO
Gauge: 12 only, 2¾″ and 3″ chamber.
Barrel: 22″ Slug (with sights), 26″, 28″, 30″ with IMC (Integral Multi-Choke) tubes; 26″ available with Mod., Imp. Cyl., Skeet, others with Full, Mod., Imp. Cyl.
Weight: 7½ lbs. **Length:** 48½″ over-all (28″ bbl.).
Stock: Walnut, handcheckered p.g. and fore-end, rubber recoil pad.
Features: Gas-operated autoloader with "Floating Piston." Cross-bolt safety, fluted bolt, gold plated trigger. Each gun comes with three flush fitting IMC choke tubes. Imported from Japan by Weatherby. Introduced 1982.
Price:.. $555.00
Price: Extra interchangeable barrel $229.00
Price: Extra IMC choke tubes $16.00

Winchester Ranger

WINCHESTER RANGER AUTO SHOTGUN
Gauge: 12 and 20, 2¾″ chamber.
Barrel: 28″ vent. rib with Winchoke tubes (Imp. Cyl., Mod., Full), or 28″ plain barrel (Mod.)
Weight: 7 to 7¼ lbs. **Length:** 48⅝″ over-all.
Stock: Walnut-finished hardwood, finger-grooved fore-end with deep cut checkering.
Sights: Metal bead front.
Features: Cross-bolt safety, front-locking rotating bolt, black serrated buttplate, gas-operated action. Made under license by U.S. Repeating Arms. Co.
Price: Vent. rib with Winchoke, about........................... $291.00
Price: Deer barrel combo, about................................ $331.00
Price: Deer gun, about $288.00

Includes a wide variety of sporting guns and guns suitable for competitive shooting.

ARMSPORT 2755 PUMP SHOTGUN

Gauge: 12, 3" chamber.
Barrel: 28" (Mod.), 30" (Full).
Weight: 7 lbs.
Stock: European walnut.
Features: Ventilated rib; rubber recoil pad; polished blue finish. Introduced 1986. Imported from Italy by Armsport.
Price: Fixed chokes $395.00
Price: 28", 30", choke tubes $465.00
Price: Police model with 20" (Imp. Cyl.), black receiver $375.00

ARMSCOR MODEL 30 PUMP SHOTGUN

Gauge: 12, 5-shot magazine.
Barrel: 28" (Mod.), 30" (Full).
Weight: 7.3 lbs. **Length:** 47" over-all. (28").
Stock: Plain mahogany.
Sights: Metal bead front.
Features: Double action bars; blue finish; grooved fore-end. Introduced 1987. Imported from the Philippines by Armscor.
Price: About $199.95

Browning Model 12

BROWNING MODEL 12 PUMP SHOTGUN

Gauge: 20, 2¾" chamber.
Barrel: 26" (Mod.).
Weight: 7 lbs., 1 oz. **Length:** 45" over-all.
Stock: 14"x2½"x1½". Select walnut with cut checkering, semi-gloss finish; Grade V has high-grade walnut.
Features: Reproduction of the Winchester Model 12. Has high post floating rib with grooved sighting plane; cross-bolt safety in trigger guard; polished blue finish. Limited to 8,500 Grade I and 4,000 Grade V guns. Introduced 1988. Imported from Japan by Browning.
Price: Grade I $699.95
Price: Grade V $1,100.00

BRI "SPECIAL" RIFLED PUMP SHOTGUN

Gauge: 12, 3" chamber.
Barrel: 24" (Cyl.) rifled.
Weight: 7½ lbs. **Length:** 44" over-all.
Stock: Walnut with high straight comb. Rubber recoil pad.
Sights: None. Comes with scope mount on barrel.
Features: Uses Mossberg Model 500 Trophy Slugster action; double slide bars, twin extractors, dual shell latches; top receiver safety. From Ballistic Research Industries. Introduced 1988.
Price: About $645.00

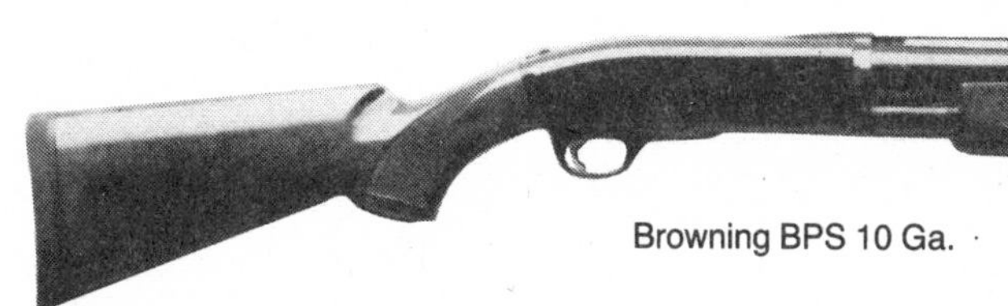

Browning BPS 10 Ga.

BROWNING BPS PUMP SHOTGUN

Gauge: 10, 3½" chamber; 12 or 20 gauge, 3" chamber (2¾" in target guns), 5-shot magazine.
Barrel: 10 ga.—24" Buck Special, 28", 30", 32" Invector; 22", 24", 26", 28", 30", 32" (Imp. Cyl., Mod. or Full). Also available with Invector choke tubes, 12 or 20 ga.; Upland Special has 22" barrel with Invector tubes.
Weight: 7 lbs. 8 oz. (28" barrel). **Length:** 48¾" over-all (28" barrel).
Stock: 14¼"x1½"x2½". Select walnut, semi-beavertail fore-end, full p.g. stock.
Features: Bottom feeding and ejection, receiver top safety, high post vent. rib. Double action bars eliminate binding. Vent. rib barrels only. Introduced 1977. Imported from Japan by Browning.
Price: Grade I Hunting, Upland Special, Invector $433.50
Price: Extra Invector barrel $185.95
Price: Buck Special barrel with rifle sights $191.95
Price: Grade I Hunting, 10 ga. $508.50
Price: Extra 10 ga. Invector barrel $218.95
Price: Extra Buck Special barrel $224.95

Browning BPS Pump Shotgun (Ladies and Youth Model)

Same as BPS Upland Special except 20 ga. only, 22" Invector barrel, stock has pistol grip with recoil pad. Length of pull is 13¼". Introduced 1986.
Price: $433.50

Browning BPS "Stalker" Pump Shotgun

Same gun as the standard BPS except all exposed metal parts have a matte blued finish and the stock has a durable black finish with a black recoil pad. Available in 12 ga. with 3" chamber, 22", 28", 30" barrel with Invector choke system. Introduced 1987.
Price: $433.50

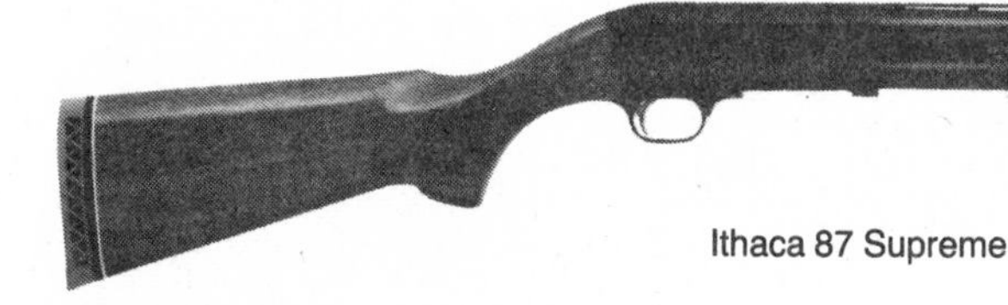

Ithaca 87 Supreme

ITHACA MODEL 87 SUPREME PUMP SHOTGUN

Gauge: 12, 20, 3" chamber, 5-shot magazine.
Barrel: 26" (Imp. Cyl., Mod., Full), 28" (Mod.), 30" (Full). Vent. rib.
Weight: 6¾ to 7 lbs.
Stock: 14"x1½"x2¼". Full fancy-grade walnut, checkered p.g. and slide handle.
Sights: Raybar front.
Features: Bottom ejection, cross-bolt safety. Polished and blued engraved receiver. Reintroduced 1988. From Ithaca Acquisition Corp.
Price: $831.00
Price: M87 Camo Vent (28", Mod. choke tube, camouflage finish) $472.00

ITHACA MODEL 87 DEERSLAYER SHOTGUN

Gauge: 12, 20, 3" chamber.
Barrel: 20", 25" (Special Bore).
Weight: 6 to 6¾ lbs.
Stock: 14"x1½"x2¼". American walnut. Checkered p.g. and slide handle.
Sights: Raybar blade front on ramp, rear adjustable for windage and elevation, and grooved for scope mounting.
Features: Bored for slug shooting. Bottom ejection, cross-bolt safety. Reintroduced 1988. From Ithaca Acquisition Corp.
Price: $377.00
Price: Ultralight Deerslayer (20 ga. only, 2¾", 5 lbs.) $412.00
Price: Deluxe Combo (12 and 20 ga. barrels) $472.00

Ithaca Deerslayer II Rifled Shotgun

Similar to the Deerslayer except has rifled 25" barrel and uncheckered American walnut stock and fore-end. Monte Carlo comb. Solid frame construction. Introduced 1988.
Price: $472.00

Ithaca Model 87 Ultralight Pump Shotgun
Similar to the Model 87 Supreme except the receiver is made of aircraft-quality aluminum. Available in 12 ga., 2¾" chamber or 20 ga., 2¾" chamber, 25" (Mod.) with choke tube. Weight is 5 lbs. (20 ga.), 6 lbs. (12 ga.). Reintroduced 1988.
Price: $430.00

Ithaca Model 87 Deluxe Pump Shotgun
Similar to the Model 87 Supreme Vent Rib except comes with choke tubes in 25", 26", 28" (Mod.), 30" (Full). Standard-grade walnut.
Price: $395.00

Mossberg Model 835

MOSSBERG MODEL 835 ULTI-MAG PUMP
Gauge: 12, 3½" chamber.
Barrel: 28", ACCU-MAG choke tubes.
Weight: 7¾ lbs. **Length:** 48½" over-all.
Stock: 14"x1½"x2½". Walnut-stained hardwood or camo synthetic; both have recoil pad.
Sights: White bead front, brass mid-bead.
Features: Backbored barrel to reduce recoil, improve patterns. Ambidextrous thumb safety, twin extractors, dual slide bars. Announced 1988.
Price: About $399.95

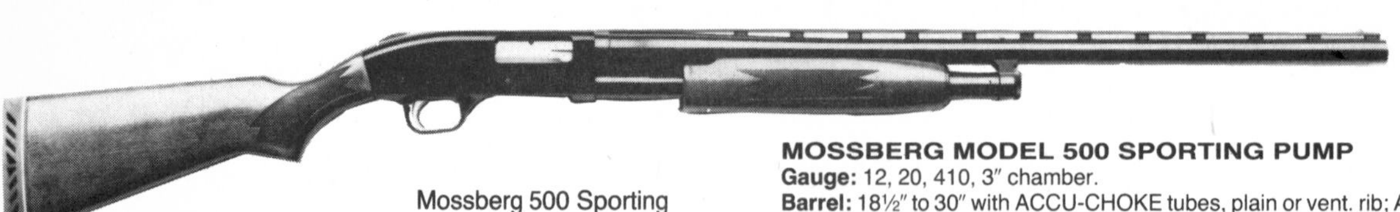

Mossberg 500 Sporting

MOSSBERG MODEL 500 SPORTING PUMP
Gauge: 12, 20, 410, 3" chamber.
Barrel: 18½" to 30" with ACCU-CHOKE tubes, plain or vent. rib; ACCU-STEEL tubes for steel shot.
Weight: 6¼ lbs. (410), 7¼ lbs. (12). **Length:** 48" over-all (28" barrel).
Stock: 14"x1½"x2½". Walnut-stained hardwood. Checkered grip and fore-end.
Sights: White bead front, brass mid-bead.
Features: Ambidextrous thumb safety, twin extractors, disconnecting safety, dual action bars. From Mossberg.
Price: From about $247.95
Price: Sporting Combos (field barrel and Slugster barrel), from $278.95

MOSSBERG MODEL 500 TROPHY SLUGSTER
Gauge: 12, 3" chamber.
Barrel: 24", smooth or rifled bore. Plain (no rib).
Weight: 7¼ lbs. **Length:** 44" overall.
Stock: 14" pull, 1⅜" drop at heel. Walnut-stained hardwood; high comb design with recoil pad and q.d. swivel studs.
Features: Ambidextrous thumb safety, twin extractors, dual slide bars. Comes with scope mount. Introduced 1988.
Price: Smoothbore, about.......... $289.95
Price: Rifled bore, about.......... $307.95

Mossberg Model 500 Camo Pump
Same as the Model 500 Sporting Pump except entire gun is covered with special camouflage finish. Available with synthetic field or Speedfeed stock. Receiver drilled and tapped for scope mounting. Comes with q.d. swivel studs, swivels, camouflage sling. In 12 ga. only.
Price: From about $289.95
Price: Camo Combo (as above with extra Slugster barrel), from about $334.95

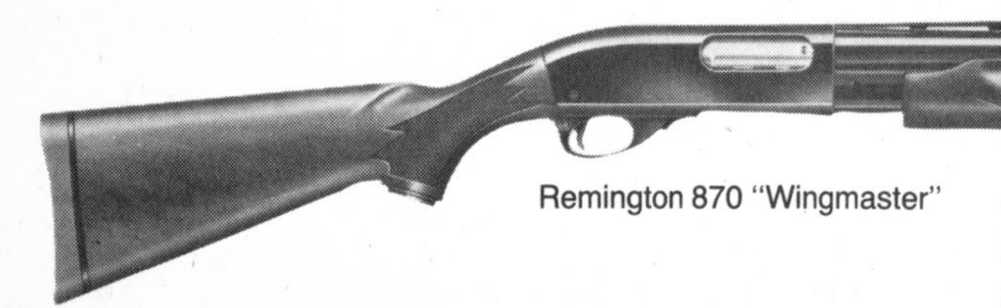

Remington 870 "Wingmaster"

REMINGTON MODEL 870 WINGMASTER
Gauge: 12, 3" chamber.
Barrel: 26", 28", 30" (REM Chokes).
Weight: 7¼ lbs. **Length:** 46½" over-all (26" bbl.).
Stock: 14"x2½"x1". American walnut with satin finish, cut checkered p.g. and fore-end. Rubber butt pad.
Sights: Ivory bead front, metal mid-bead.
Features: Double action bars; cross-bolt safety; blue finish. Available in right- or left-hand style. Introduced 1986.
Price: $429.00
Price: Left hand $472.00
Price: Brushmaster Deer Gun (rifle sights, 20" bbl., fixed choke) $381.00
Price: Deer Gun, left hand $423.00
Price: 20 ga., vent. rib, 26", 28" (REM Choke) $427.00
Price: As above, Youth Gun (21" REM Choke, 13" stock) $417.00

Remington Model 870 Brushmaster Deluxe
Carbine version of the M870 with 20" bbl. (Imp. Cyl.) for rifled slugs. 40½" over-all, wgt. 6½ lbs. Recoil pad. Adj. rear, ramp front sights, 12 or 20 ga. Deluxe.
Price: Brushmaster 12 ga., about $381.00
Price: As above, 20 ga.......... $365.00

Remington Model 870 Express
Similar to the 870 Wingmaster except has a walnut-toned, hardwood stock with solid, black recoil pad and pressed checkering on grip and fore-end. Outside metal surfaces have a black oxide finish. Comes only with 28" vent rib barrel with a Mod. REM Choke tube. Introduced 1987.
Price: $223.00
Price: Express Combo (with extra 20" Deer barrel) $320.00

Remington Model 11-87 Special Purpose Magnum
Similar to the 11-87 Premier except has dull stock finish, Parkerized exposed metal surfaces. Bolt and carrier have dull blackened coloring. Comes with 26" or 30" barrel with Rem Chokes, padded Cordura nylon sling and q.d. swivels. Introduced 1987.
Price: $525.00

Remington 870 High Grades
Same as 870 except better walnut, hand checkering. Engraved receiver and bbl. Vent. rib. Stock dimensions to order.
Price: 870D, about $2,291.00
Price: 870F, about $4,720.00
Price: 870F with gold inlay, about $7,079.00

Remington 870 Small Gauges
Exact copies of the large ga. Model 870, except that guns are offered in 28 and 410 ga. 25" barrel (Full, Mod., Imp. Cyl.). D and F grade prices same as large ga. M870 prices.
Price: With vent. rib barrel, about $427.00

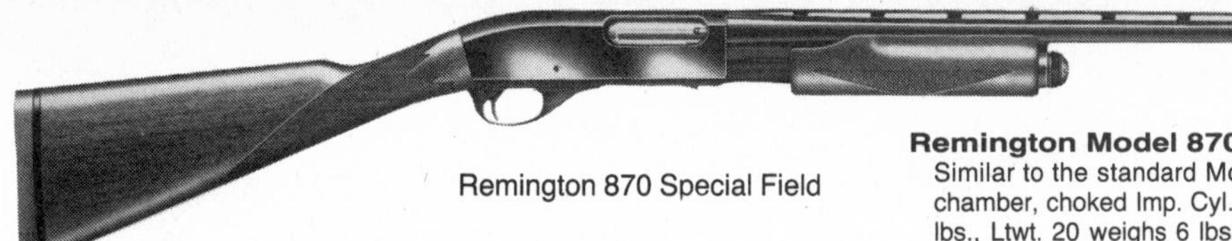
Remington 870 Special Field

Remington Model 870 "Special Field"
Similar to the standard Model 870 except comes with 21″ barrel only, 3″ chamber, choked Imp. Cyl., Mod., Full and REM Choke; 12 ga. weighs 6¾ lbs., Ltwt. 20 weighs 6 lbs.; has straight-grip stock, shorter fore-end, both with cut checkering. Vent. rib barrel only. Introduced 1984.
Price: 12 or 20 ga., REM Choke, about **$429.00**

Remington 870 "Special Purpose" Magnum
Similar to the Model 870 except chambered only for 12-ga., 3″ shells, vent. rib. 26″ or 30″ REM Choke barrel. All exposed metal surfaces are finished in dull, non-reflective black. Wood has an oil finish. Comes with padded Cordura 2″ wide sling, quick-detachable swivels. Chrome-lined bores. Dark recoil pad. Introduced 1985.
Price: About **$420.00**

Remington 870 TC Trap
Same as the M870 except 12 ga. only, 30″ fixed Full or REM Choke, vent. rib bbl., ivory front and white metal middle beads. Special sear, hammer and trigger assy. 14⅜″×1½″×1⅞″ stock with recoil pad. Hand fitted action and parts. Wgt. 8 lbs.
Price: Model 870TC Trap, REM choke, about **$547.00**
Price: As above, fixed choke **$533.00**
Price: TC Trap with Monte Carlo stock, about **$560.00**
Price: As above, fixed choke **$547.00**

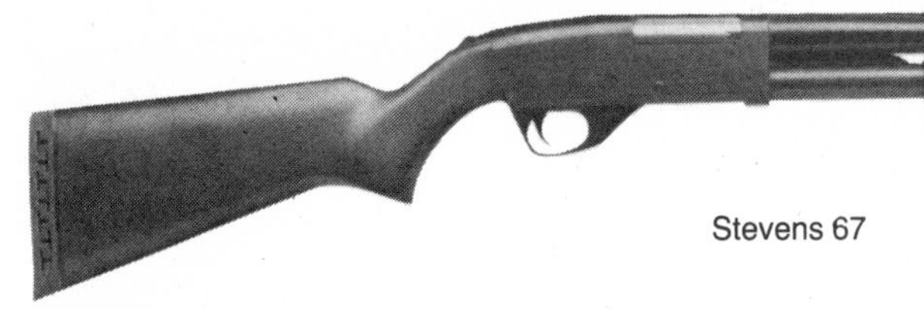
Stevens 67

STEVENS MODEL 67 PUMP SHOTGUN
Gauge: 12, 20 (2¾″ & 3″).
Barrel: 28″ (Mod.).
Weight: 7 lbs. **Length:** 47½″ over-all (28″ bbl.).
Stock: Walnut-finished hardwood; grooved slide handle. 14″x1½″x2½″.
Sights: Metal bead front.
Features: Grooved slide handle, top tang safety, steel receiver. From Savage Arms. Introduced 1981.
Price: Model 67L Lobo **$159.00**
Price: Model 67 Slug Gun (21″ barrel, rifle sights) **$184.00**
Price: Model 67-VRT (as above with vent. rib) **$199.00**

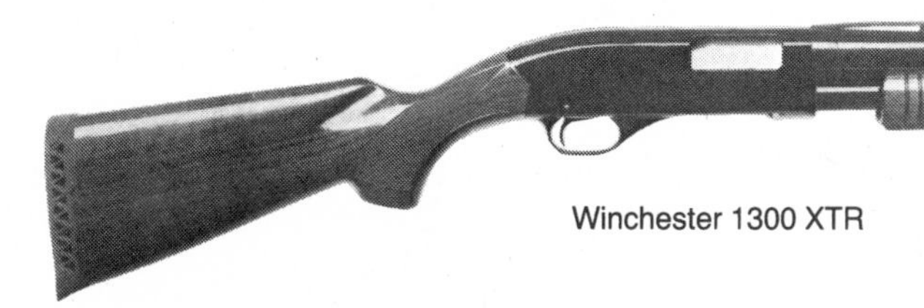
Winchester 1300 XTR

WINCHESTER MODEL 1300XTR FEATHERWEIGHT PUMP
Gauge: 12 and 20, 3″ chamber, 5-shot capacity.
Barrel: 22″, vent. rib, with Full, Mod., Imp. Cyl. Winchoke tubes.
Weight: 6⅜ lbs. **Length:** 42⅝″ over-all.
Stock: American walnut, with deep cut checkering on pistol grip, traditional ribbed fore-end; high luster finish.
Sights: Metal bead front.
Features: Twin action slide bars; front-locking rotating bolt; roll-engraved receiver; blued, highly polished metal; cross-bolt safety with red indicator. Introduced 1984.
Price: About **$324.00**

Winchester Model 1300 Rifled Deer Gun
Same as the Model 1300 except has rifled 22″ barrel, Win-Tuff laminated stock or walnut, rifle-type sights. Introduced 1988.
Price: Walnut stock **$367.00**
Price: Laminated stock **$378.00**

Winchester Model 1300 Turkey
Similar to the standard Model 1300 Featherweight except 12 ga. only, 30″ barrel with Mod., Full and Extra Full Winchoke tubes, matte finish wood and metal, and comes with recoil pad, Cordura sling and swivels.
Price: About **$338.00**
Price: With Win-Cam green-shaded laminated stock, about **$349.00**
Price: National Wild Turkey Federation edition.................... **$368.00**

Winchester 1300 Waterfowl Pump
Similar to the 1300 Featherweight except in 3″ 12 ga. only, 30″ vent. rib barrel with Winchoke system; stock and fore-end of walnut with low-luster finish. All metal surfaces have special non-glare matte finish. Introduced 1985.
Price: About **$338.00**
Price: With laminated stock **$349.00**
Price: Combo Pac with extra 22″ barrel.......................... **$425.00**

WINCHESTER RANGER PUMP GUN
Gauge: 12 or 20, 3″ chamber, 4-shot magazine.
Barrel: 28″ vent rib with Full, Mod., Imp. Cyl. Winchoke tubes.
Weight: 7 to 7¼ lbs. **Length:** 48⅝″ to 50⅝″ over-all.
Stock: Walnut finished hardwood with ribbed fore-end.
Sights: Metal bead front.
Features: Cross-bolt safety, black rubber butt pad, twin action slide bars, front-locking rotating bolt. Made under license by U.S. Repeating Arms Co.
Price: Vent. rib barrel, Winchoke, about **$255.00**

Winchester Ranger Pump Gun Combination
Similar to the standard Ranger except comes with two barrels: 22″ (Cyl.) deer barrel with rifle-type sights and an interchangeable 28″ vent. rib Winchoke barrel with Full, Mod. and Imp. Cyl. choke tubes. Available in 12 and 20 gauge 3″ only, with recoil pad. Introduced 1983.
Price: With two barrels, about **$300.00**

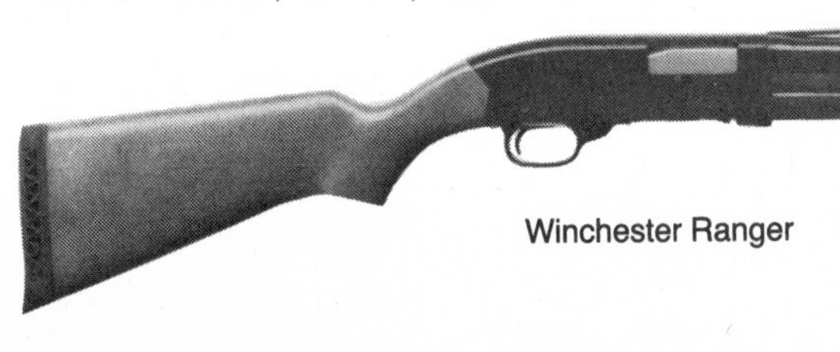
Winchester Ranger

Winchester Ranger Youth Pump Gun
Similar to the standard Ranger except chambered only for 3″ 20 ga., 22″ vent. rib barrel with Winchoke tubes (Full, Mod., Imp. Cyl.) or 22″ plain barrel with fixed Mod. choke. Weighs 6½ lbs., measures 41⅝″ o.a.l. Stock has 13″ pull length and gun comes with discount certificate for full-size stock. Introduced 1983. Made under license by U.S. Repeating Arms Co.
Price: Vent. rib barrel, Winchoke, about **$268.00**
Price: Plain barrel, Mod. choke, about........................... **$230.00**

Includes a variety of game guns and guns for competitive shooting.

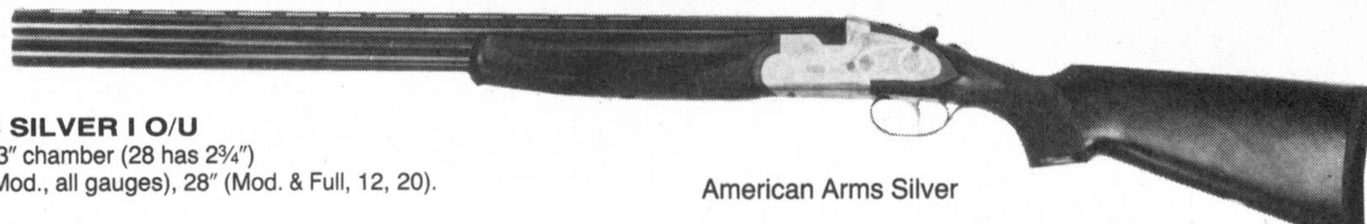

American Arms Silver

AMERICAN ARMS SILVER I O/U

Gauge: 12, 20, 28, 410, 3″ chamber (28 has 2¾″)
Barrel: 26″ (Imp. Cyl. & Mod., all gauges), 28″ (Mod. & Full, 12, 20).
Weight: About 6¾ lbs.
Stock: 14⅛″x1⅜″x2⅜″. Checkered walnut.
Sights: Metal bead front.
Features: Boxlock action with scroll engraving, silver finish. Chrome-lined barrels. Manual safety. Rubber recoil pad. Introduced 1987. Imported by American Arms, Inc.
Price: 12 or 20 gauge **$459.00**
Price: 28 or 410 .... **$585.00**

American Arms Silver II Shotgun

Similar to the Silver I except in 12 or 20 gauge only with 26″ (12 and 20) or 28″ (12 ga. only), choke tubes, automatic selective ejectors, single selective trigger. Weight is 6 lbs., 15 oz. for 12 gauge, 6 lbs., 10 oz. in 20 gauge.
Price: **$620.00**

American Arms Bristol

AMERICAN ARMS BRISTOL O/U SHOTGUN

Gauge: 12 or 20, 3″ chamber.
Barrel: 26″ (12 and 20), 28″ (12 only). Choke tubes.
Weight: 7 lbs., 1 oz. (12 ga.), 6 lbs., 12 oz. (20 ga.).
Stock: 14⅛″x1⅜″x2⅜″. Hand checkered walnut with oil finish.
Sights: Metal bead front.
Features: Boxlock action with dummy sideplates and silver finish, scroll engraving; single selective, gold-colored trigger; chrome-lined bores; manual safety; automatic selective ejectors. Imported from Italy by American Arms, Inc. Introduced 1987.
Price: **$850.00**

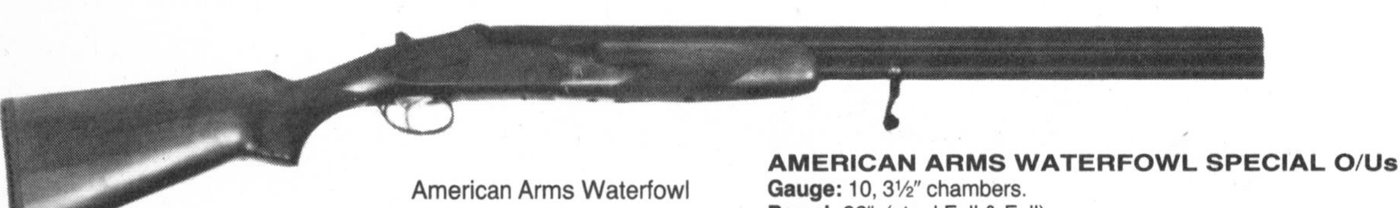

American Arms Waterfowl

AMERICAN ARMS WATERFOWL SPECIAL O/Us

Gauge: 10, 3½″ chambers.
Barrel: 32″: (steel Full & Full).
Weight: 9 lbs., 15 oz.
Stock: 14½″x1⅜″x2⅜″. Checkered walnut with dull finish.
Sights: Metal bead front.
Features: Boxlock action with non-reflective sideplates and barrels; chrome-lined barrels; double triggers; extractors; sling swivels. Comes with camouflage sling. Introduced 1988. Imported by American Arms, Inc.
Price: **$875.00**
Price: 12-ga. Waterfowl Special (as above except in 12 ga., 3½″ chamber, 28″ with choke tubes, selective ejectors, single selective trigger) **$650.00**

American Arms Turkey Special

Similar to the Waterfowl Special 10-gauge gun except has 26″ barrels with choke tubes. Double triggers, extractors.
Price: **$940.00**

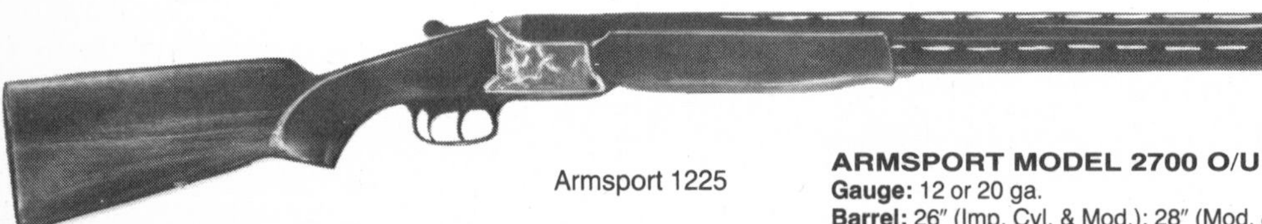

Armsport 1225

ARMSPORT MODEL 2700 O/U

Gauge: 12 or 20 ga.
Barrel: 26″ (Imp. Cyl. & Mod.); 28″ (Mod. & Full); vent, rib.
Weight: 8 lbs.
Stock: European walnut, hand checkered p.g. and fore-end.
Features: Single selective trigger, automatic ejectors, engraved receiver. Imported by Armsport.
Price: M2733/2735 (Boss-type action, 12, 20, extractors) **$590.00**
Price: M2741/2743 (as above with ejectors) **$650.00**
Price: M2730/2731 (as above with single trigger, screw-in chokes) . **$775.00**
Price: M2705 (410 ga., 26″ Imp. & Mod., double triggers) **$595.00**
Price: M2720 (as above with single trigger) **$650.00**

ARMSPORT MODEL 2700 O/U GOOSE GUN

Gauge: 10 ga., 3½″ chambers.
Barrel: 27″ (Imp. & Mod.), 32″ (Full & Full).
Weight: About 9.8 lbs.
Stock: European walnut.
Features: Boss-type action; double triggers; extractors. Introduced 1986. Imported from Italy by Armsport.
Price: **$950.00**

ARMSPORT 1225/1226 O/U FOLDING SHOTGUN

Gauge: 12, 20, 3″ chambers.
Barrel: 26″ (Imp. & Mod.), 28″ (Mod. & Full).
Weight: 6 lbs.
Stock: European walnut.
Features: Top-break folding action; double triggers; extractors; silvered receiver with light engraving. Introduced 1986. Imported from Italy by Armsport.
Price: **$375.00**

ARMSPORT 2900 TRI-BARREL SHOTGUN

Gauge: 12, 3″ chambers.
Barrel: 28″ (Imp. Cyl. & Mod. & Full).
Weight: 7¾ lbs.
Stock: European walnut.
Features: Top-tang barrel selector: double triggers; silvered, engraved frame. Introduced 1986. Imported from Italy by Armsport.
Price: **$1,850.00**

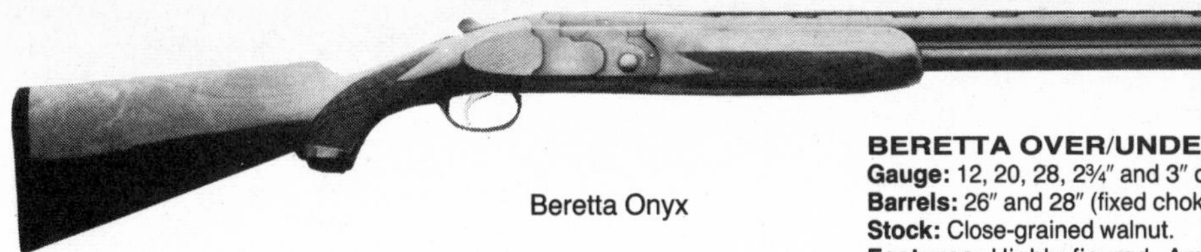

Beretta Onyx

BERETTA MODEL SO5, SO6 SHOTGUNS

Gauge: 12, 2¾" chambers
Barrel: To customer's specs.
Stock: To customer's specs.
Features: SO5—Trap, Skeet and Sporting Clays models available in standard SO5 and SO5 EELL; SO6— SO6 and SO6 EELL are field models made to customer specifications. SO6 has a case-hardened receiver with contour hand engraving. SO6 EELL has hand-engraved receiver in a fine floral or "fine English" pattern, with bas-relief chisel work and gold inlays. SO6 and SO6 EELL are available, at no extra charge, with sidelocks removable by hand. Imported from Italy by Beretta U.S.A.
Price: SO5 Trap, Skeet, Sporting **$14,250.00**
Price: SO5 EELL Trap, Skeet, Sporting **$21,750.00**
Price: SO6 Field, Custom Specs **$16,125.00**
Price: SO6 EELL Field, Custom Specs **$24,975.00**

BERETTA OVER/UNDER FIELD SHOTGUNS

Gauge: 12, 20, 28, 2¾" and 3" chambers.
Barrels: 26" and 28" (fixed chokes or Mobilchoke tubes).
Stock: Close-grained walnut.
Features: Highly-figured, American walnut stocks and fore-ends, and a unique, weather-resistant finish on barrels. Available in two grades: Golden Onyx has individual game game scenes of flushing pheasant and rising ducks on the receiver; the 686 Onyx bears a gold P. Beretta signature on each side of the receiver. Imported from Italy by Beretta U.S.A.
Price: 686 Onyx **$1,035.00**
Price: 686 two bbl. Set **$1,600.00**
Price: 686 Field **$925.00**
Price: 687L Field **$1,300.00**
Price: 687 Golden Onyx **$1,665.00**
Price: 687 EL .... **$2,450.00** to **$2,520.00**
Price: 687 EELL .... **$3,500.00** to **$3,640.00**

Beretta 682 Sporting

BERETTA SPORTING CLAYS SHOTGUNS

Gauge: 12 and 20, 2¾" chambers
Barrel: 28", Mobilchoke.
Stock: Close-grained walnut.
Sights: Luminous front sight and center bead.
Features: Equipped with Beretta Mobilchoke flush-mounted screw-in choke tube system. Models vary according to grade, from field-grade Beretta 686 Sporting with its floral engraving pattern, to competition-grade Beretta 682 Sporting with its brushed satin finish and adjustable length of pull, to the 687 Sporting with intricately hand-engraved game scenes, fine line, deep-cut checkering. Imported from Italy by Beretta U.S.A. Corp.
Price: 686 Sporting **$1,680.00**
Price: 682 Sporting **$2,100.00**
Price: 687 Sporting **$2,240.00**
Price: 687 Sporting (20-gauge) **$2,240.00**

BERETTA SERIES 682 OVER/UNDERS

Gauge: 12, 2¾" chambers.
Barrel: Skeet—26" and 28"; trap—30" and 32", Imp. Mod. & Full and Mobilchoke; trap mono shotguns—32" and 34" Mobilchoke; trap top single guns—32" and 34" Full and Mobilchoke; trap combo sets—from 30" o/u, 32" unsingle to 32" o/u, 34" top single.
Stock: Close-grained walnut, hand checkered.
Sights: Luminous front sight and center bead.
Features: Trap Monte Carlo stock has deluxe trap recoil pad. Various grades available; contact Beretta U.S.A. for details. Imported from Italy by Beretta U.S.A. Corp.
Price: 682 Skeet **$2,030.00**
Price: 682 Trap **$2,030.00**
Price: 682 Trap Mono Shotguns **$1,890.00**
Price: 682 Trap Top Single Shotguns .... **$1,960.00** to **$2,030.00**
Price: 682 Trap Combo Sets .... **$2,520.00** to **$2,800.00**

BRNO 500 OVER/UNDER SHOTGUN

Gauge: 12, 2¾" chambers.
Barrel: 27½" (Full & Mod.).
Weight: 7 lbs. **Length:** 44½" over-all.
Stock: Walnut, with raised cheekpiece.
Features: Boxlock action with ejectors; double triggers; acid-etched engraving. Imported from Czechoslovakia by Saki International.
Price: **$899.00**

BABY BRETTON OVER/UNDER SHOTGUN

Gauge: 12 or 20, 2¾" chambers.
Barrel: 27½" (Cyl., Imp. Cyl., Mod., Full choke tubes).
Weight: About 5 lbs.
Stock: Walnut, checkered pistol grip and fore-end, oil finish.
Features: Receiver slides open on two guide rods, is locked by a large thumb lever on the right side. Extractors only. Light alloy barrels. Imported from France by Mandall Shooting Supplies.
Price: **$895.00**
Price: Deluxe (silvered, engraved receiver, double triggers, 12, 16, 20 ga.) **$1,295.00**

BRNO Super

BRNO SUPER OVER/UNDER SHOTGUN

Gauge: 12, 2¾" or 3" chambers.
Barrel: 27½" (Full & Mod.).
Weight: 7 lbs., 4 oz. (Field). **Length:** 44" over-all.
Stock: Walnut, with raised cheekpiece.
Features: Sidelock action with double safety interceptor sears; double triggers on Field model; automatic selective ejectors; engraved sideplates. Trap and Skeet models available. Imported from Czechoslovakia by Saki International.
Price: **$899.00**

BRNO CZ 581 OVER/UNDER SHOTGUN

Gauge: 12, 2¾" or 3" chambers.
Barrel: 28" (Full & Mod.).
Weight: 7 lbs., 6 oz. **Length:** 45½" over-all.
Stock: Turkish walnut with raised cheekpiece.
Features: Boxlock action; automatic selective ejectors; automatic safety; sling swivels; vent. rib; double triggers. Imported from Czechoslovakia by Saki International.
Price: **$649.00**

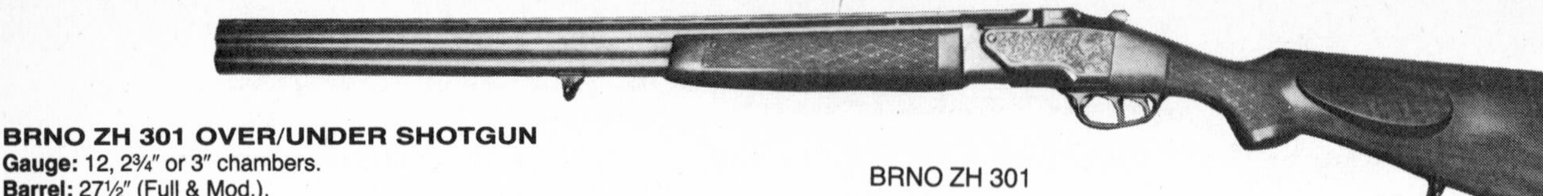
BRNO ZH 301

BRNO ZH 301 OVER/UNDER SHOTGUN

Gauge: 12, 2¾" or 3" chambers.
Barrel: 27½" (Full & Mod.).
Weight: 7 lbs. **Length:** 44½" over-all.
Stock: Walnut.
Features: Boxlock action with acid-etch engraving; double triggers. Imported from Czechoslovakia by Saki International.
Price: $599.00

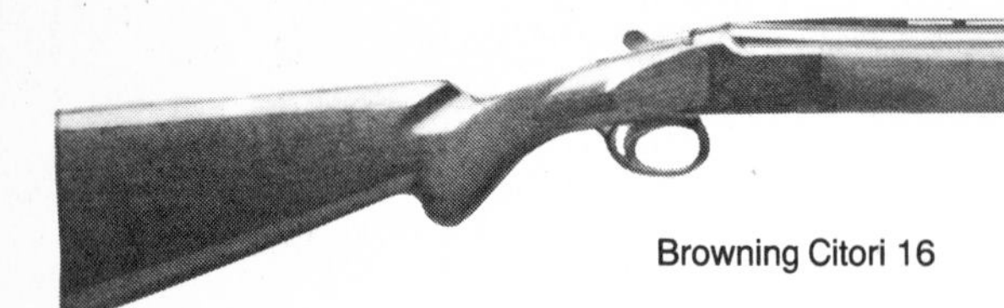
Browning Citori 16

BROWNING CITORI O/U SHOTGUN

Gauge: 12, 16, 20, 28 and 410.
Barrel: 26", 28" (Mod. & Full, Imp. Cyl. & Mod.), in 28 and 410. Also offered with Invector choke tubes.
Weight: 6 lbs. 8 oz. (26" 410) to 7 lbs. 13 oz. (30" 12-ga.).
Length: 43" over-all (26" bbl.).
Stock: Dense walnut, hand checkered, full p.g., beavertail fore-end. Field-type recoil pad on 12 ga. field guns and trap and Skeet models.
Sights: Medium raised beads, German nickel silver.
Features: Barrel selector integral with safety, auto ejectors, three-piece takedown. Imported from Japan by Browning.
Price: Grade I Hunting, Invector $948.00
Price: Grade III, Invector, 12 and 20 .... $1,282.00
Price: Grade VI, Invector, 12 and 20 .... $1,880.00
Price: Grade I, 28 and 410, fixed chokes $937.00
Price: Grade III, 28 and 410, fixed chokes $1,410.00
Price: Grade VI, 28 and 410, high post rib, fixed chokes $1,990.00
Price: Grade I Lightning, Invector, 12, 16 20 .... $958.00
Price: Grade III Lightning, Invector, 12, 16, 20 .... $1,292.00
Price: Grade VI Lightning, Invector, 12, 16, 20 .... $1,890.00

Browning Citori O/U Skeet Models

Similar to standard Citori except 26", 28" (Skeet & Skeet) only; stock dimensions of 14⅜"×1½"×2", fitted with Skeet-style recoil pad; conventional target rib and high post target rib.
Price: Grade I Invector (high post rib) $1,048.00
Price: Grade I, 12 & 20 (high post rib) $1,014.00
Price: Grade I, 28 & 410 (high post rib) $1,060.00
Price: Grade III, 12 and 20 (high post rib) $1,410.00
Price: Grade VI, 12 and 20 (high post rib) $1,990.00
Price: Four barrel Skeet set—12, 20, 28, 410 barrels, with case, Grade I only $3,397.00
Price: Grade III, four-barrel set (high post rib) $3,728.00
Price: Grade VI, four-barrel set (high post rib) $4,237.00
Price: Grade I, three-barrel set $2,365.00
Price: Grade III, three-barrel set $2,625.00
Price: Grade VI, three-barrel set $3,255.00

Browning Citori O/U Trap Models

Similar to standard Citori except 12 gauge only; 30", 32" (Full & Full, Imp. Mod. & Full, Mod. & Full), 34" single barrel in Combo Set (Full, Imp. Mod., Mod.), or Invector model; Monte Carlo cheekpiece (14⅜"×1⅜"×1⅜"×2"); fitted with trap-style recoil pad; conventional target rib and high post target rib.
Price: Grade I, Invector high post target rib $1,060.00
Price: Grade III, Invector, high post target rib $1,410.00
Price: Grade VI, Invector, high post target rib $1,990.00

Consult our Directory pages for the location of firms mentioned.

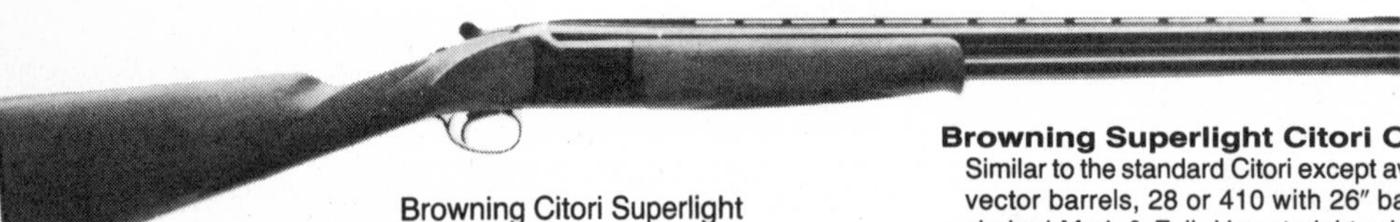
Browning Citori Superlight

Browning Superlight Citori Over/Under

Similar to the standard Citori except available in 12, 20 with 24", 26" or 28" Invector barrels, 28 or 410 with 26" barrels choked Imp. Cyl. & Mod. or 28" choked Mod. & Full. Has straight grip stock, Schnabel fore-end tip. Superlight 12 weighs 6 lbs., 9 oz. (26" barrels); Superlight 20, 5 lbs., 12 oz. (26" barrels). Introduced 1982.
Price: Grade I only, 28 or 410 .... $937.00
Price: Grade III, Invector, 12 or 20 .... $1,282.00
Price: Grade III, 28 or 410 .... $1,410.00
Price: Grade VI, Invector, 12 or 20 .... $1,880.00
Price: Grade VI, 28 or 410 .... $1,990.00
Price: Grade I Invector, 12 or 20 .... $974.00
Price: Grade I Invector, Upland Special (24" bbls.), 12 or 20 .... $974.00

Browning Limited Edition Waterfowl Superposed

Same specs as the Superposed Gold Classic. Available in 12 ga. only, 28" (Mod. & Full). Limited to 500 guns, the edition number of each gun is inscribed in gold on the bottom of the receiver with "Black Duck" and its scientific name. Sides of receiver have two gold inlayed black ducks, bottom has two, and one on the trigger guard. Receiver is completely engraved and grayed. Stock and fore-end are highly figured dark French walnut with 24 lpi checkering, hand-oiled finish, checkered butt. Comes with form-fitted, velvet-lined, black walnut case. Introduced 1983.
Price: $8,000.00
Price: Similar treatment as above except for the Pintail Duck Issue $7,700.00

BROWNING OVER/UNDER GOLD CLASSIC

Gauge: 20, 2¾" chambers.
Barrel: 26" (Imp. Cyl. & Mod.).
Weight: 6⅜ lbs.
Stock: 14¼"x1⅝"x2½". Select walnut with straight grip, schnabel fore-end.
Features: Receiver has upland setting of bird dogs, pheasant and quail in inlaid gold on satin gray finish. Stock has fine checkering and decorative carving with oil finish. Introduced 1984. Made in Belgium.
Price: $6,000.00

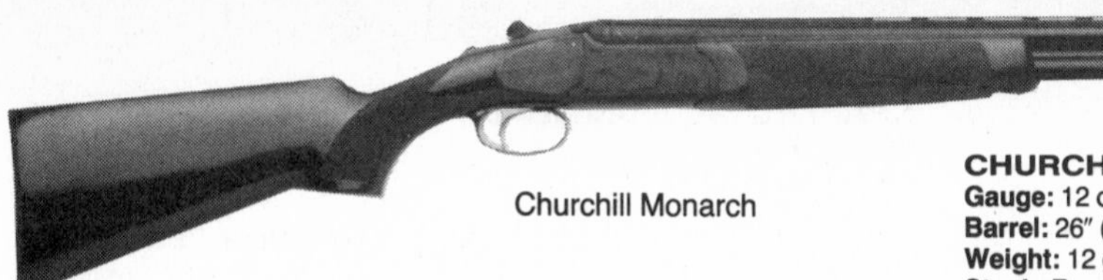

Churchill Monarch

CHURCHILL MONARCH OVER/UNDER SHOTGUNS

Gauge: 12 or 20, 3″ chambers.
Barrel: 26″ (Imp. Cyl. & Mod.), 28″ (Mod. & Full). Chrome lined.
Weight: 12 ga.—7½ lbs., 20 ga.—6½ lbs.
Stock: European walnut with checkered p.g. and fore-end.
Features: Single selective trigger; blued, engraved receiver; vent. rib. Introduced 1986. Imported by Kassnar Imports, Inc.
Price: .... **$419.00** to **$449.00**

Churchill Regent Over/Under Shotguns

Similar to the Windsor Grade except better wood with oil finish, better engraving; available only in 12 or 20 gauge (3″ chambers), 27″ barrels, with ICT interchangeable choke tubes (Imp. Cyl., Mod., Full). Regent VII has dummy sideplates. Introduced 1984.
Price: Regent VII, 12 or 20 ga. **$889.00**

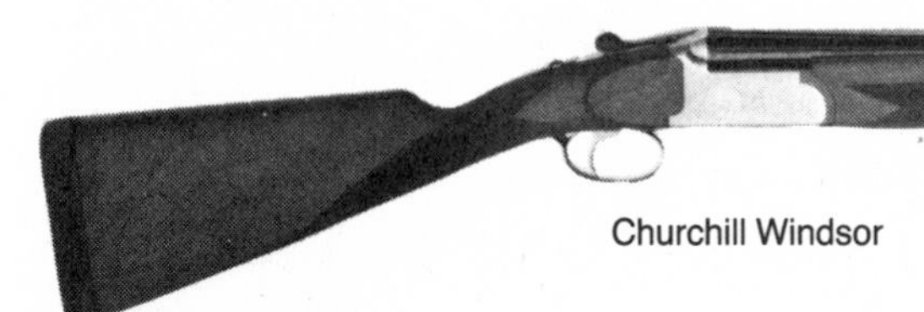

Churchill Windsor

CHURCHILL WINDSOR OVER/UNDER SHOTGUNS

Gauge: 12, 20, 28, 410, 3″ chambers.
Barrel: 26″ (Skeet & Skeet, Imp. Cyl. & Mod.), 28″ (Mod. & Full), 30″ (Mod. & Full, Full & Full), 12 ga.; 26″ (Skeet & Skeet, Imp. Cyl. & Mod.), 28″ (Mod. & Full) 20 ga.; 25″, 26″ (Imp. Cyl. & Mod), 28″ (Mod. & Full), 28 ga.; 24″ , 26″ (Full & Full), 410 ga.; or 27″, 30″ ICT choke tubes.
Stock: European walnut, checkered pistol grip, oil finish.
Features: Boxlock action with silvered, engraved finish; single selective trigger; automatic ejectors on Windsor IV, extractors only on Windsor III. Also available in Flyweight version with 23″, 25″ barrels, fixed or ICT chokes, straight-grip stock. Imported from Italy by Kassnar. Introduced 1984.
Price: Windsor III .... **$549.00** to **$649.00**
Price: Windsor IV .... **$619.00** to **$719.00**

Churchill Regent Trap & Skeet

Trap has ventilated side rib, Monte Carlo stock, Churchill recoil pad. Oil finished wood, fine checkering, chrome bores. Weight is 8 lbs. Regent Skeet available in 12 or 20 ga., 26″ (Skeet & Skeet); oil finished stock measures 14½″x1½″x2⅜″. Both guns have silvered and engraved receivers. Introduced 1984.
Price: Regent Trap (30″ Imp. Mod. & Full) **$869.00**
Price: Regent Skeet, 12 or 20 ga. **$809.00**

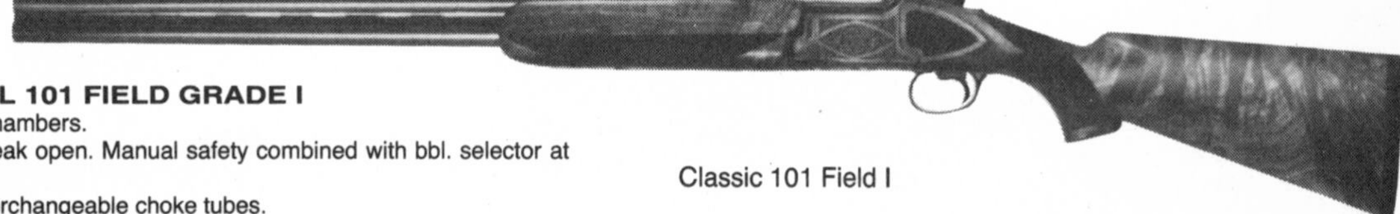

Classic 101 Field I

CLASSIC MODEL 101 FIELD GRADE I

Gauge: 12 or 20, 3″ chambers.
Action: Top lever, break open. Manual safety combined with bbl. selector at top of receiver tang.
Barrel: 25½″, 28″, interchangeable choke tubes.
Weight: 12 ga. 7 lbs. **Length:** 44⅞″ over-all.
Stock: 14½″ x 1½″ x 2½″. Checkered walnut p.g. and fore-end; fluted comb. Straight English or standard.
Features: Single selective adjustable trigger, auto ejectors. Hand engraved blued receiver. Suitable for steel shot. Chrome lined bores and chambers. Comes with hard gun case. Manufactured in and imported from Japan by Classic Doubles.
Price: **$2,335.00**

Classic Model 101 Waterfowler

Same as Model 101 Field Grade except in 12 ga. only, 3″ chambers, 30″ barrels. Comes with four choke tubes: Mod., Imp. Mod., Full, Extra-Full. Nonglare wood finish, matte blued receiver with hand etching and engraving. Introduced 1981. Manufactured in and imported from Japan by Classic Doubles.
Price: **$1,865.00**

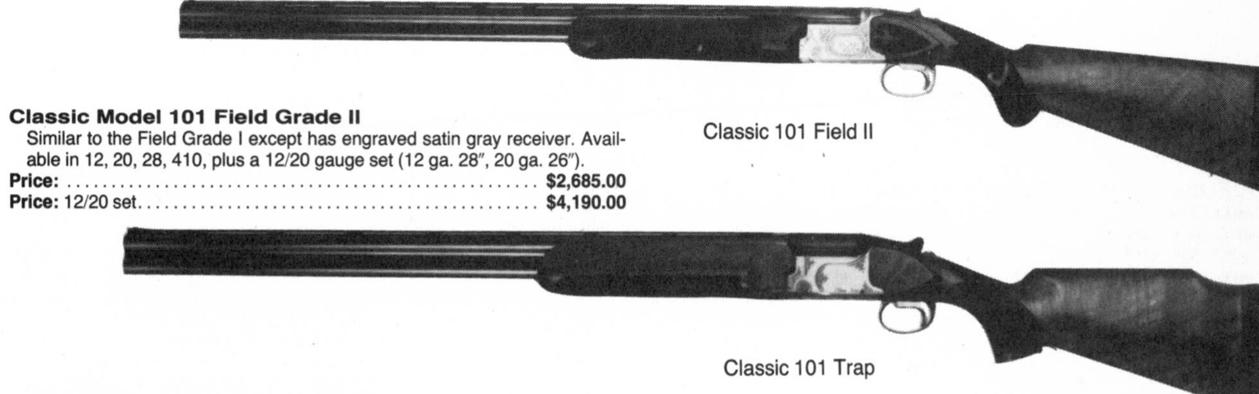

Classic 101 Field II

Classic Model 101 Field Grade II

Similar to the Field Grade I except has engraved satin gray receiver. Available in 12, 20, 28, 410, plus a 12/20 gauge set (12 ga. 28″, 20 ga. 26″).
Price: **$2,685.00**
Price: 12/20 set **$4,190.00**

Classic 101 Trap

Classic Model 101 Trap and Skeet

Similar to the Model 101 Field Grades except designed for target competition. Barrels have high, tapered vent. rib; barrel vents for Skeet guns, barrel ports for trap guns; Skeet models have mechnical trigger, trap have inertia trigger. Stocks pre-drilled for recoil reducer, and are quick detachable. Standard or Monte Carlo stock. Trap available as o/u, single barrel or Combo.
Price: Trap, from **$2,535.00**
Price: Skeet, 12 and 20 .... **$2,335.00**
Price: Skeet, 410 .... **$5,840.00**

Classic Model 101 Sporter O/U

Similar to the Field Grade II except designed for Sporting Clays and has different balance than a field gun. Available in 12 ga. only with 28″ or 30″ barrels with six choke tubes. Top of frame and top lever have matte finish. Frame has silvered finish, light engraving.
Price: **$2,425.00**
Price: Combo includes both barrel sets **$3,610.00**

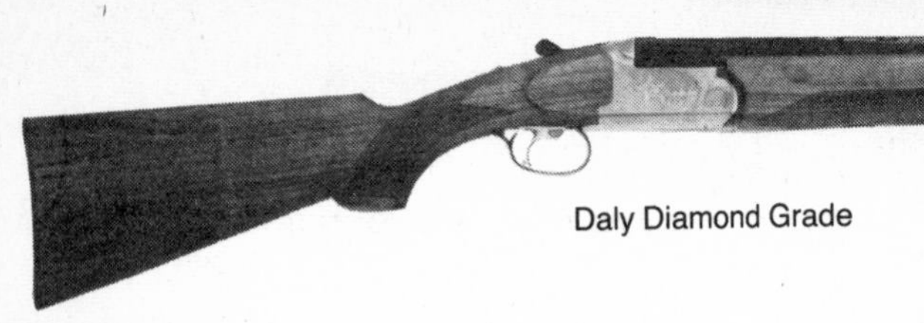

Daly Diamond Grade

CHARLES DALY DIAMOND TRAP OVER/UNDER

Gauge: 12.
Barrel: 30″ (Imp. Mod. & Full).
Weight: 7lbs.
Stock: Select extra-fancy European walnut, oil finish. Monte Carlo comb.
Features: Boxlock action with single selective competition trigger; silvered and engraved receiver; selective automatic ejectors; 22 lpi checkering on grip and fore-end. Imported from Italy by Outdoor Sports Headquarters. Introduced 1984.
Price: **$1,050.00**

Charles Daly Diamond Skeet Over/Under

Similar to the standard Diamond Trap except has oil-finished Skeet stock, competition vent. rib, target trigger. Available in 12 gauge only, 26″ (Skeet & Skeet).
Price: **$1,000.00**

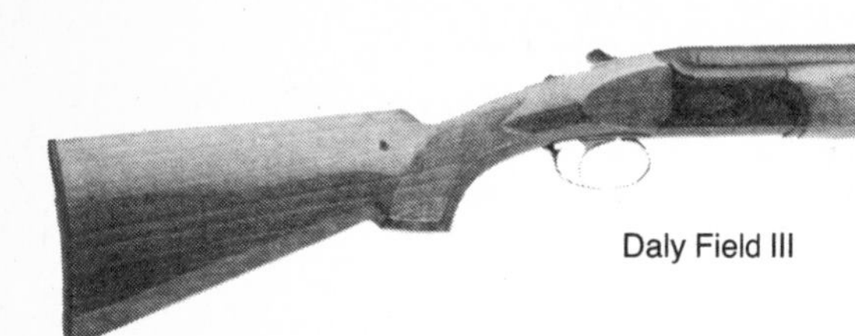

Daly Field III

CHARLES DALY FIELD III OVER/UNDER

Gauge: 12 or 20.
Barrel: 26″ (Imp. Cyl. & Mod.), 28″, 30″ (Full & Mod.); vent. rib.
Weight: About 6¾ lbs.
Stock: Select European walnut, checkered pistol grip and fore-end.
Features: Single selective trigger; extractors only; blued and engraved frame; chrome lined bores. Imported from Italy by Outdoor Sports Headquarters. Introduced 1984.
Price: **$450.00**

Charles Daly Superior II Over/Under

Similar to the Field III model except single selective trigger; auto ejectors, better wood, silvered receiver, more and better engraving. Same barrel lengths and chokes.
Price: **$875.00**

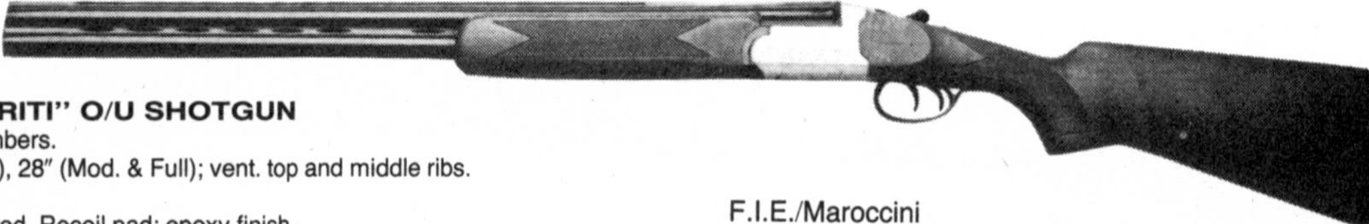

F.I.E./Maroccini

F.I.E./MAROCCINI "PRITI" O/U SHOTGUN

Gauge: 12 or 20 ga., 3″ chambers.
Barrel: 26″ (Imp. Cyl. & Mod.), 28″ (Mod. & Full); vent. top and middle ribs.
Weight: 7¾ lbs.
Stock: Walnut, hand checkered. Recoil pad; epoxy finish.
Features: Auto safety; extractors; double triggers; engraved antique silver receiver. Imported from Italy by F.I.E.
Price: **$399.95**

KRIEGHOFF K-80 O/U TRAP SHOTGUN

Gauge: 12, 2¾″ chambers.
Barrel: 30″, 32″ (Imp. Mod. & Full).
Weight: About 8½ lbs.
Stock: Four stock dimensions available; all have palm-swell grips. Checkered walnut.
Features: Satin nickel receiver. Selective mechnical trigger, adjustable for position. Ventilated step rib. Introduced 1980. Imported from West Germany by Krieghoff International, Inc.
Price: Standard grade **$4,480.00**
Price: K-80 Unsingle (32″, 34″, Full), Standard **$5,350.00**
Price: K-80 Top Single (34″, Full), Standard **$4,745.00**
Price: K-80 Combo (two-barrel set), Standard **$6,880.00**

KRIEGHOFF K-80 SKEET SHOTGUN

Gauge: 12, 2¾″ chambers.
Barrel: 28″ (Skeet & Skeet or optional Tula chokes).
Weight: About 7¾ lbs.
Stock: American Skeet or straight Skeet stocks, with palm-swell grips. Walnut.
Features: Satin gray receiver finish. Selective mechanical trigger adjustable for position. Standard 5/16″ vent. rib. Introduced 1980. Imported from West Germany by Krieghoff International, Inc.
Price: Standard, Skeet chokes **$4,390.00**
Price: As above, Tula chokes **$4,550.00**
Price: Lightweight model (weighs 7 lbs.), Standard **$4,250.00**
Price: Two-Barrel Set (tube concept), 12 ga., standard **$6,200.00**

Krieghoff K-80 International Skeet

Similar to the Standard Skeet except has ½″ ventilated Broadway-style rib, special Tula chokes with gas release holes at muzzle. International Skeet stock. Comes in fitted aluminum case.
Price: Standard grade **$4,725.00**

F.I.E./FRANCHI "ALCIONE S" OVER/UNDER

Gauge: 12 ga. only, 3″ chambers.
Barrel: 26″ (Imp. Cyl. & Mod.), 28″ (Mod. & Full).
Weight: 6 lbs. 13 oz.
Stock: French walnut with cut checkered pistol grip and fore-end. Recoil pad; epoxy finish.
Features: Top tang safety, automatic ejectors, single selective trigger. Chrome plated bores. Decorative scroll on silvered receiver. Introduced 1982. Imported from Italy by F.I.E. Corp.
Price: Diamond Grade **$724.95**

KRIEGHOFF K-80 PIGEON SHOTGUN

Gauge: 12, 2¾″ chambers.
Barrel: 28″, 30″ standard, 29″ optional (Imp. Mod. & Special Full).
Weight: About 8 lbs.
Stock: Four stock dimensions available. Checkered walnut.
Features: Choice of steel or Dural receiver, both with satin gray finish, engraving. Selective mechanical trigger adjustable for position. Ventilated step rib. Free-floating barrels. Comes with hard case. Introduced 1980. Imported from West Germany by Krieghoff International.
Price: Standard grade **$4,480.00**

Krieghoff K-80 Sporting Clays Over/Under

Similar to the Pigeon model gun except has a Schnabel fore-end tip and comes with screw-in choke tubes. Introduced 1988.
Price: Standard grade **$4,930.00**

Krieghoff K-80 Four-Barrel Skeet Set

Similar to the Standard Skeet except comes with barrels for 12, 20, 28, 410 in 28″ length with Tula choke system. Comes with fitted leather case with canvas cover.
Price: Standard grade **$8,980.00**

CAUTION: PRICES CHANGE. CHECK AT GUNSHOP.

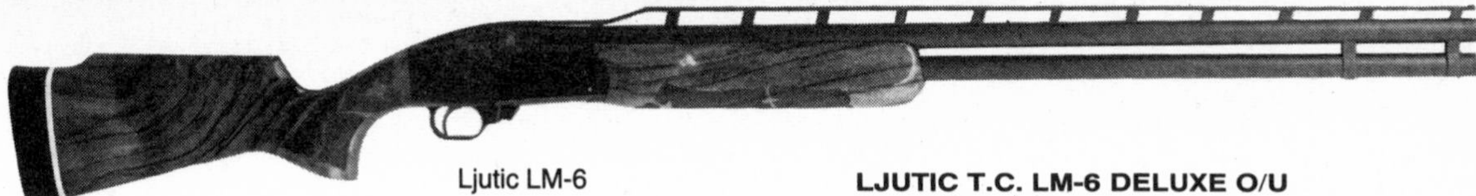
Ljutic LM-6

Ljutic Four Barrel Skeet Set
LM-6 over/under 12-ga. frame with matched set of four 28″ barrels in 12, 20, 28 and 410. Ljutic Paternator chokes and barrel are integral. Stock is to customer specs, of fine American or French walnut with EX (or Extra) Fancy checkering.
Price: Four barrel set **$26,995.00**

MERKEL OVER/UNDER SHOTGUNS
Gauge: 12, 16, 20, 28, 410, 2¾″, 3″ chambers.
Barrel: 26″, 26¾″, 28″ (standard chokes).
Weight: 6 to 7 lbs.
Stock: European walnut. Straight English or pistol grip.
Features: Models 200E and 201E are boxlocks, 203E and 303E are sidelocks. All have auto. ejectors, articulated front triggers. Auto. safety, selective and non-selective triggers optional. Imported from East Germany by Armes de Chasse.
Price: 200E, about **$2,400.00**
Price: 201E, about **$3,100.00**
Price: 203E (sidelock), about **$6,400.00**
Price: 303E (sidelock), about **$10,200.00**

LJUTIC T.C. LM-6 DELUXE O/U
Gauge: 12 ga.
Barrel: 28″ to 34″, choked to customer specs for live birds, trap, International Trap.
Weight: To customers specs.
Stock: To customer specs. Oil finish, hand checkered.
Features: Custom-made gun. Hollow-milled rib, pull or release trigger, push-button opener in front of trigger guard. From Ljutic Industries.
Price: Super Deluxe LM-6 o/u **$9,984.00**
Price: Over/under Combo (interchangeable single barrel, two trigger guards, one for single trigger, one for doubles) **$14,995.00**
Price: Extra over-under barrel sets, 29″–32″ **$4,995.00**

Consult our Directory pages for the location of firms mentioned.

Navy Bird Hunter

NAVY ARMS MODEL 410 O/U SHOTGUN
Gauge: 410, 3″ chambers.
Barrel: 26″ (Full & Full, Skeet & Skeet).
Weight: 6¼ lbs.
Stock: European walnut; checkered p.g. and fore-end.
Features: Chrome-lined barrels, hard chrome finished receiver with engraving, vent. rib. Single trigger. Imported from Italy by Navy Arms. Introduced 1986.
Price: **$299.00**

NAVY ARMS MODEL 83/93 BIRD HUNTER O/U
Gauge: 12, 20, 3″ chambers.
Barrel: 28″ (Imp. Cyl. & Mod., Mod. & Full).
Weight: About 7½ lbs.
Stock: European walnut, checkered grip and fore-end.
Sights: Metal bead front.
Features: Boxlock action with double triggers; extractors only; silvered, engraved receiver; vented top and middle ribs. Imported from Italy by Navy Arms. Introduced 1984.
Price: Model 83 (extractors) **$482.00**
Price: Model 93 (ejectors) **$559.00**

Navy Arms Model 95/96
Same as the 83/93 Bird Hunter except comes with five interchangeable choke tubes. Model 96 has gold-plated single trigger and ejectors.
Price: Model 95 (extractors) **$598.00**
Price: Model 96 (ejectors) **$715.00**

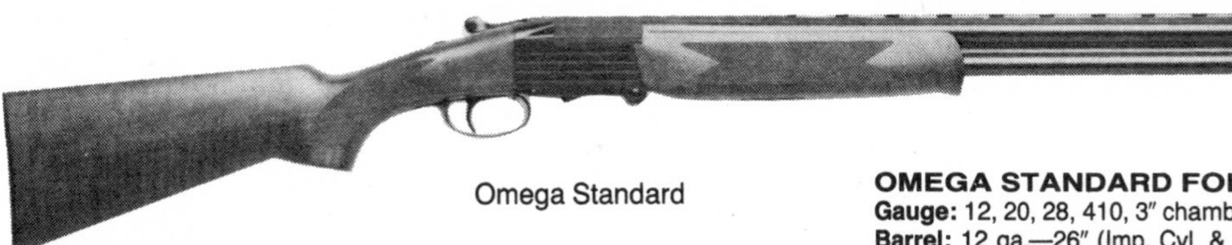
Omega Standard

Omega Deluxe Over/Under
Similar to the Standard model except does not fold. In 12 ga. only, 26″ (Imp. Cyl. & Mod), 28″ (Mod. & Full), 3″ chambers. Weight about 7¼ lbs. Single non-selective trigger. Introduced 1988.
Price: **$369.00**

OMEGA STANDARD FOLDING O/U SHOTGUN
Gauge: 12, 20, 28, 410, 3″ chambers.
Barrel: 12 ga.—26″ (Imp. Cyl. & Mod.), 28″ (Mod. & Full); 20 ga.—26″ (Imp. Cyl. & Mod.), 28″ (Mod. & Full); 28 ga.—26″ (Imp. Cyl. & Mod., Mod. & Full); 410—26″ (Full & Full).
Weight: About 6-7½ lbs.
Stock: Checkered European walnut.
Features: Single trigger; automatic safety; vent rib. Imported from Italy by Kassnar Imports, Inc. Introduced 1986.
Price: **$319.00**

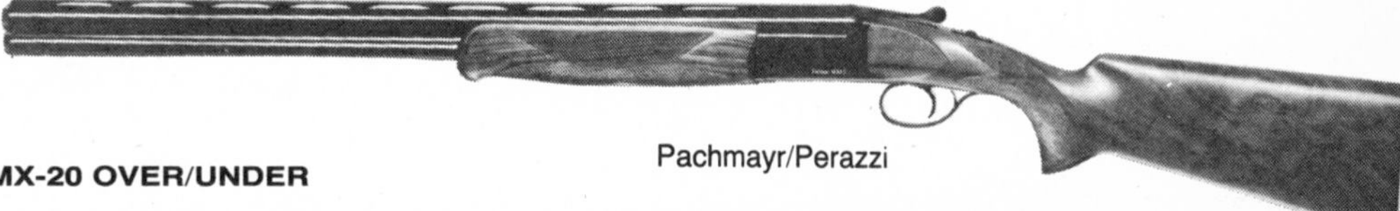
Pachmayr/Perazzi

PACHMAYR/PERAZZI MX-20 OVER/UNDER
Gauge: 20, 3″ chambers.
Barrel: 26″ (Cyl., Imp. Cyl., Mod., Imp. Mod., Full choke tubes). Fixed chokes available.
Weight: 6 lbs., 8 oz.
Stock: 14½″x1⅜″x2¼″x1½″; select European walnut with 26 l.p.i. checkering, checkered butt.
Sights: Nickel silver front bead.
Features: Boxlock action, uses special 20-gauge frame. Carved schnabel-type fore-end. Single selective trigger, automatic selective ejectors, manual safety. Comes with lockable fitted case. Introduced 1986. From Pachmayr, Ltd.
Price: **$3,995.00**

PERAZZI MX8/MX8 SPECIAL TRAP, SKEET

Gauge: 12, 2¾" chambers.
Barrel: Trap–29½" (Imp. Mod. & Extra Full), 31½" (Full & Extra Full). Choke tubes optional. Skeet–27⅝" (Skeet & Skeet).
Weight: About 8½ lbs. (Trap); 7 lbs., 15 oz. (Skeet).
Stock: Interchangeable and custom made to customer specs.
Features: Has detachable and interchangeable trigger group with flat V springs. Flat 7/16" ventilated rib. Many options available. Imported from Italy by Perazzi U.S.A., Inc.
Price: From **$4,700.00**
Price: MX8 Special (adj. four-position trigger), from **$4,900.00**
Price: MX8 Special Single (32" or 34" single barrel, step rib), from . **$4,600.00**
Price: MX8 Special Combo (o/u and single barrel sets), from **$7,100.00**

Perazzi Grand American 88 Special

Similar to the MX8 except has tapered 7/16" x 5/16" high ramped rib. Choked Imp. Mod. & Full, 29½" barrels.
Price: From **$7,100.00**
Price: Special Single (32" or 34" single barrel), from **$4,650.00**

PERAZZI MIRAGE SPECIAL SPORTING O/U

Gauge: 12, 2¾" chambers.
Barrel: 27⅝", 28⅜" (Imp. Mod. & Extra Full).
Weight: 7 lbs., 12 oz.
Stock: To customer specs; interchangeable.
Features: Has adjustable four-position trigger; flat 7/16" x 5/16" vent. rib. Many options available. Imported from Italy by Perazzi U.S.A., Inc.
Price: **$4,900.00**

Perazzi Mirage Special Four Gauge Skeet

Similar to the Mirage Sporting model except has Skeet dimensions, interchangeable, adjustable four-position trigger assembly. Comes with four barrel sets in 12, 20, 28, 410, flat 5/16" x 5/16" rib.
Price: From **$11,400.00**
Price: MX3 Special Set, from **$10,200.00**

PERAZZI MX12 HUNTING OVER/UNDER

Gauge: 12, 2¾" chambers.
Barrel: 26", 27⅝" (Mod. & Full). choke tubes available (MX12C).
Weight: 7 lbs., 4 oz.
Stock: To customer specs; interchangeable.
Features: Single selective trigger; coil springs used in action; schnabel fore-end tip. Imported from Italy by Perazzi U.S.A., Inc.
Price: From **$4,550.00**
Price: MX12C (with choke tubes), from **$4,850.00**

Perazzi MX3 Special Single, Over/Under

Similar to the MX8 Special except has an adjustable four-position trigger, high 7/16" x 5/16" rib, weighs 8½ lbs. Choked Mod. & Full.
Price: From **$4,400.00**
Price: MX3 Special Single (32" or 34" single barrel), from **$3,550.00**
Price: MX3 Special Combo (o/u and single barrel sets), from **$5,400.00**

Perazzi MX4 Over/Under

Similar to the MX3 Special and has same locking system as the MX8, but with detachable, four-position trigger assembly for improved stock fit. Bottom barrel fires first. Has flat 7/16" x 7/16" rib; 29½" barrels only. Skeet version choked Skeet & Skeet, 27⅝" barrels, weighs 7 lbs., 15 oz. MX4C has choke tubes.
Price: .... **NA**

Perazzi Mirage Special Skeet Over/Under

Similar to the MX8 Skeet except has adjustable four-position trigger, Skeet stock dimensions.
Price: From **$4,900.00**

Perazzi MX1, MX1B Sporting Over/Under

Similar to the MX8 except has ramped, tapered rib, interchangeable trigger assembly with leaf hammer springs, 27⅝" barrels choked Imp. Mod. & Extra Full. Weight is 7 lbs., 12 oz.
Price: From **$4,800.00**
Price: MX1B (as above except has flat conventional rib), from **$4,800.00**

PERAZZI TM1 SPECIAL SINGLE TRAP

Gauge: 12, 2¾" chambers.
Barrel: 32" or 34" (Extra Full).
Weight: 8 lbs., 6 oz.
Stock: To customer specs; interchangeable.
Features: Tapered and stepped high rib; adjustable four-position trigger. Also available with choke tubes. Imported from Italy by Perazzi U.S.A., Inc.
Price: From **$3,700.00**
Price: TMX Special Single (as above except special high rib), from **$3,700.00**

Perazzi MX20 Hunting Over/Under

Similar to the MX12 except 20-ga. frame size. Available in 20, 28, 410 with 2¾" or 3" chambers, 26" only, and choked Mod. & Full. Weight is 6 lbs., 6 oz.
Price: From **$8,000.00**
Price: MX20C (as above, 20 ga. only, choke tubes), from **$8,300.00**

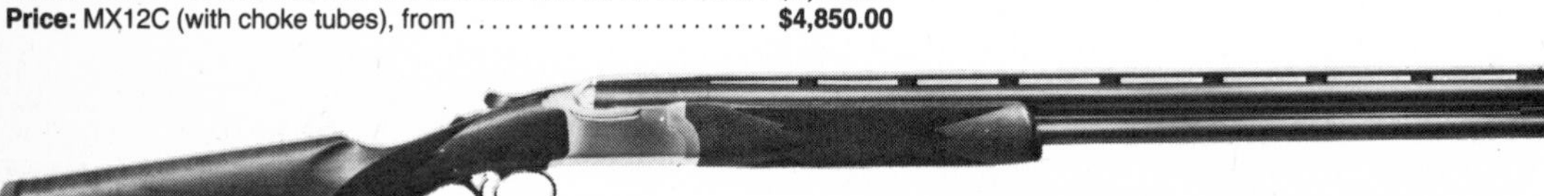

Ruger 12 Ga. Red Label

ROTTWEIL 72 AMERICAN SKEET

Gauge: 12, 2¾" chambers.
Barrel: 26¾" (Skeet & Skeet).
Weight: About 7½ lbs.
Stock: 14½" × 1⅜" × 1⅜" × ¼". Select French walnut with satin oil finish; hand checkered grip and fore-end; double ventilated recoil pad.
Sights: Plastic front in metal sleeve, center bead.
Features: Interchangeable trigger groups with coil springs; interchangeable buttstocks; special .433" ventilated rib; matte finish silvered receiver with light engraving. Introduced 1978. Imported from West Germany by Dynamit Nobel.
Price: **$2,395.00**

RUGER "RED LABEL" O/U SHOTGUN

Gauge: 20 and 12, 3" chambers.
Barrel: 20 ga.—26", 28" (Skeet & Skeet, Imp. Cyl. & Mod.), 28" (Imp. Cyl. & Mod., Full & Mod.); 12 ga.—26", 28" (Skeet & Skeet, Imp. Cyl. & Mod., Full & Mod.); 12 ga.—26", 28" (Skeet, Imp. Cyl., Mod., Full Screw-In choke tubes).
Weight: About 7 lbs. (20 ga.), 7½ lbs. (12 ga.). **Length:** 43" over-all (26" barrels).
Stock: 14"x1½"x2½". Straight gain American walnut. Checkered p.g. and fore-end, rubber recoil pad.
Features: Automatic safety/barrel selector, stainless steel trigger. Patented barrel side spacers may be removed if desired. 20 ga. available in blued steel only, 12 ga. available only with stainless receiver. 20 ga. introduced 1977; 12 ga. introduced 1982.
Price: 20 ga., blued **$798.00**
Price: 12 ga., stainless receiver **$798.00**
Price: As above, screw-In choke tubes **$987.50**

 CAUTION: PRICES CHANGE. CHECK AT GUNSHOP.

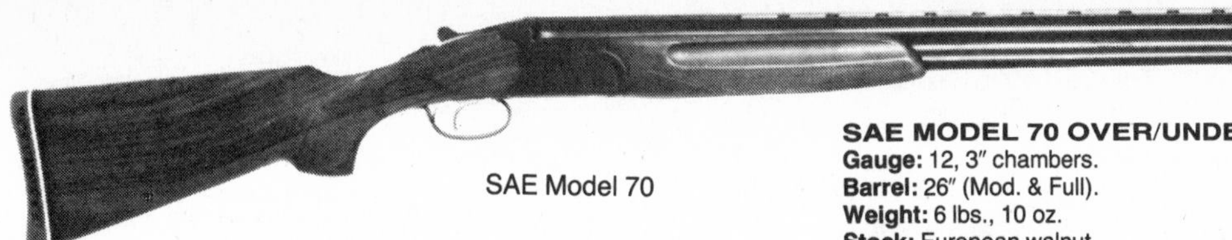
SAE Model 70

SAE MODEL 70 OVER/UNDER SHOTGUN

Gauge: 12, 3″ chambers.
Barrel: 26″ (Mod. & Full).
Weight: 6 lbs., 10 oz.
Stock: European walnut.
Features: Boxlock action with single mechanical trigger, automatic selective ejectors, automatic safety. Blued, engraved receiver. Introduced 1987. Imported from Spain by Spain America Ent.
Price: $475.80
Price: Model 70 Multichoke (12 ga. only, 27″, choke tubes, silvered receiver) $525.70

SAE Model 66C Over/Under

Similar to the Model 70 except has dummy sideplates, extensive engraving and gold inlays, oil-finished walnut with Monte Carlo. Available in 12 ga. only, 26″ (Skeet & Skeet), 28″ (Mod. & Full).
Price: $1,375.95

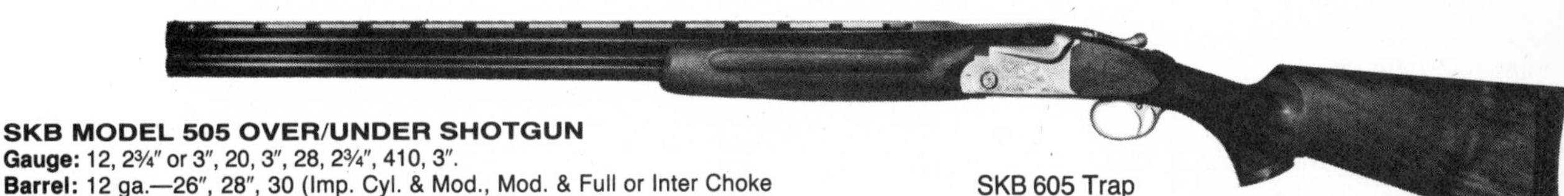
SKB 605 Trap

SKB MODEL 505 OVER/UNDER SHOTGUN

Gauge: 12, 2¾″ or 3″, 20, 3″, 28, 2¾″, 410, 3″.
Barrel: 12 ga.—26″, 28″, 30 (Imp. Cyl. & Mod., Mod. & Full or Inter Choke tubes), 20 ga.—26″, 28″ (Imp. Cyl. & Mod., Mod. & Full or Inter Choke tubes), 28 and 410—26″, 28″ (Imp. Cyl. & Mod., Mod. & Full).
Weight: 6.6 to 7.4 lbs. **Length:** 45$^{3}/_{16}$″ over-all.
Stock: 14⅛″x1½″x2$^{3}/_{16}$″. Hand checkered walnut.
Sights: Metal bead front.
Features: Blued boxlock action; ejectors; single selective trigger. Introduced 1988. Imported from Japan by Ernie Simmons Enterprises.
Price: $795.00
Price: Two-barrel Field Set, 12 and 20, choke tubes $1,250.00
Price: As above, 28 and 410, fixed chokes $1,250.00
Price: Model 505 Trap, Skeet $825.00
Price: Model 505 Single Barrel Trap........ $825.00
Price: Skeet set, 20, 28, 410 .... $1,850.00

SKB Model 605 Over/Under Shotgun

Similar to the Model 505 except has silvered, engraved receiver.
Price: $975.00
Price: Two-barrel Field Set, 12 and 20 ga., choke tubes........ $1,450.00
Price: As above, 28 and 410, fixed chokes $1,450.00
Price: Model 605 Trap, Skeet $995.00
Price: Model 605 Single Barrel Trap........ $995.00
Price: Skeet Set, 20, 28, 410 .... $1,995.00

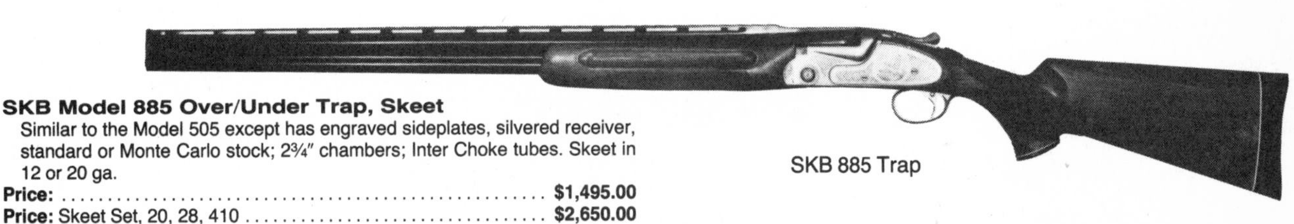
SKB 885 Trap

SKB Model 885 Over/Under Trap, Skeet

Similar to the Model 505 except has engraved sideplates, silvered receiver, standard or Monte Carlo stock; 2¾″ chambers; Inter Choke tubes. Skeet in 12 or 20 ga.
Price: $1,495.00
Price: Skeet Set, 20, 28, 410 .... $2,650.00

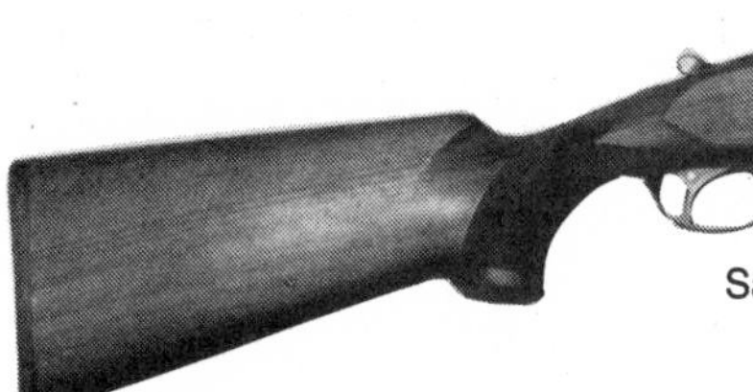
Sauer Franchi S

SAUER-FRANCHI O/U SHOTGUNS

Gauge: 12, 2¾″ chambers.
Barrel: 28″ (Imp. Cyl. & Imp. Mod., Mod. & Full, Skeet 1 & Skeet 2); 29″ (Special Trap).
Weight: 7½ lbs. **Length:** 45⅓″ over-all.
Stock: European walnut.
Features: Blued frame on Standard model, others with silvered, engraved frames; single selective trigger; selective auto. ejectors; vent. rib. Introduced in U.S. 1986. Imported from West Germany by Sigarms..
Price: Standard, about $785.00
Price: Regent, about $825.00
Price: Favorit, about $875.00
Price: Diplomat, about........ $1,520.00
Price: Sporting S, Trap, Skeet models, about $1,375.00

SAN MARCO WILDFOWLER O/U

Gauge: 10, 3½″ chambers.
Barrel: 28″, 32″ (Full & Full).
Weight: 9 lbs, 3 oz. **Length:** 50″ over-all (32″ barrel).
Stock: 14$^{1}/_{16}$″x1½″x2″. Walnut, checkered p.g. and fore-end.
Features: Boxlock action, extractors, or ejectors, non-selective double triggers. Matte finish on metal. Imported by Ballistic Products, Inc.
Price: With extractors $625.00
Price: With ejectors $725.00

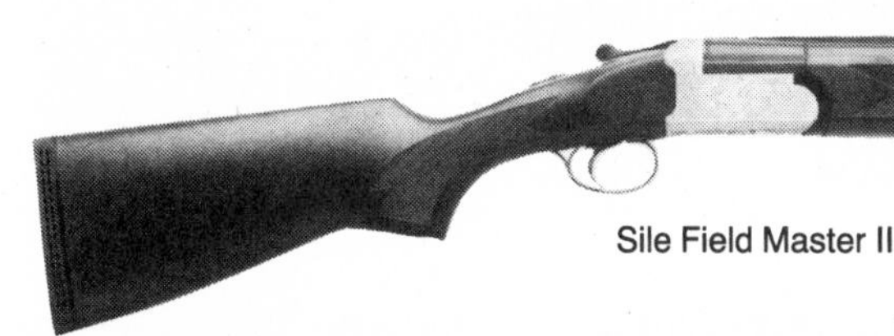
Sile Field Master II

SILE FIELD MASTER II O/U SHOTGUN

Gauge: 12, 3″ chambers.
Barrel: 28″ (Cyl., Imp. Cyl., Mod., Imp. Mod., Full choke tubes).
Weight: 7½ lbs. **Length:** 45¼″ over-all.
Stock: Satin-finished walnut, cut-checkered p.g. and fore-end.
Features: Single selective trigger; extractors; automatic safety; engraved silvered receiver. Imported by Sile.
Price: $475.95
Price: Field Hunter I (similar to above except 26″ (Imp. Cyl. & Mod.) or 28″ (Mod. & Full) $335.95
Price: Field Hunter II (as above except with choke tubes) $391.95

Sile Trap King O/U Shotgun
Similar to the Field Master II except has 2¾" chambers, 30" barrels choked Mod. & Full or Full & Full. Walnut Monte Carlo stock with palm swell and recoil pad. Weight is 8½ lbs. Automatic ejectors.
Price: $559.95

Sile Field King Super Light, Field Hunter, Slug Master O/U
Similar to the Field Master II except in 12 ga. only with 28" barrels (Mod. & Full). Weighs 6¼ lbs. Imported by Sile.
Price: $489.95
Price: Field Hunter (similar to above, with 23½" Cyl. & Cyl. barrels, ramp front sight, folding rear) $391.95
Price: Slug Master $461.95

SIMSON/SUHL MODEL 85 EJ OVER/UNDER
Gauge: 12, 2¾" chambers.
Barrel: 28" (Imp. Cyl. & Mod.).
Weight: 6¾ lbs.
Stock: European walnut; pistol grip style.
Features: Anson & Deeley modified boxlock action with double triggers, manual safety. Cold hammer forged barrels, double locking lugs. Choking and patterning for steel shot (by importer). Auto safety, vent. rib optional. Imported from East Germany by Armes de Chasse.
Price: $1,000.00

Sile Field King, Skeet King O/U Shotgun
Similar to the Field Master II except 26", 28" (Imp. Cyl. & Mod.), 28" (Mod. & Full) for Field; Skeet has 26" (Skeet & Skeet); both fixed chokes. Single non-selective trigger.
Price: $391.95

SILE SKY STALKER OVER/UNDER
Gauge: 20, 28, 410, 3" chambers.
Barrel: 26", 28" (Imp. Cyl. & Mod., Mod. & Full, Full & Full, Skeet & Skeet).
Weight: About 6¾ lbs.
Stock: Walnut-finished hardwood, checkered p.g. and fore-end.
Features: Folds in half for storage or carry. Mechanical extractors; single non-selective trigger. Imported by Sile.
Price: $239.95

STOEGER/IGA OVER/UNDER SHOTGUN
Gauge: 12, 20, 3" chambers.
Barrel: 26" (Full & Full, Imp. Cyl. & Mod.), 28" (Mod. & Full).
Weight: 6¾ to 7 lbs.
Stock: 14½"x1½"x2½". Oil finished hardwood with checkered pistol grip and fore-end.
Features: Manual safety, single trigger, extractors only, ventilated top rib. Introduced 1983. Imported from Brazil by Stoeger Industries.
Price: $380.00

Techi-Mec SPL 640

TECHNI-MEC MODEL SR 692 EM OVER/UNDER
Gauge: 12, 16, 20, 2¾" or 3" chambers.
Barrel: 26", 28", 30" (Mod., Full, Imp. Cyl., Cyl.).
Weight: 6½ lbs.
Stock: 14½"x ½"x2½". European walnut with checkered grip and fore-end.
Features: Boxlock action with dummy sideplates, fine game scene engraving: single selective trigger; automatic ejectors available. Imported from Italy by L. Joseph Rahn. Introduced 1984.
Price: $725.00
Price: Slug gun $685.00

TECHNI-MEC MODEL SPL 640 FOLDING O/U
Gauge: 12, 16, 20, 28, 2¾" chambers; 410, 3" chambers.
Barrel: 26" (Mod. & Full).
Weight: 5½ lbs.
Stock: European walnut.
Features: Gun folds in half for storage, transportation. Chrome lined barrels; ventilated rib; photo-engraved silvered receiver. Imported from Italy by L. Joseph Rahn, Mandall. Introduced 1984.
Price: Double triggers $260.00
Price: Single trigger $275.00
Price: Model SPL 642, double triggers $275.00
Price: As above, single trigger $285.00

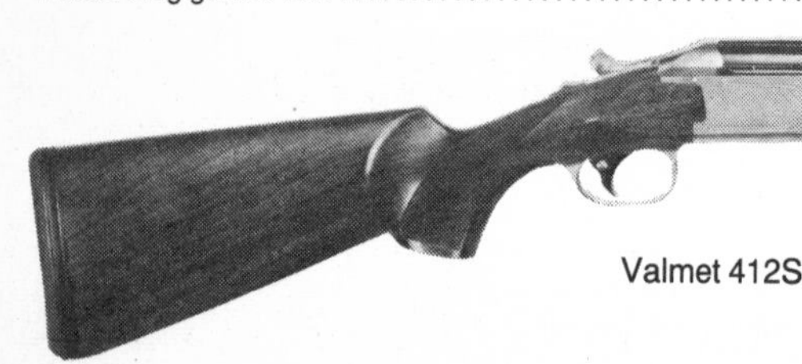
Valmet 412S

VALMET MODEL 412S FIELD GRADE OVER-UNDER
Gauge: 12, 20, 3" chambers.
Barrel: 24", 26", 28", 30" with stainless steel screw-in chokes (Imp. Cyl., Mod., Imp. Mod, Full); 20 ga. 28" only.
Weight: About 7¼ lbs.
Stock: American walnut. Standard dimensions—13⁹⁄₁₀"x1½"x2⅖". Checkered p.g. and fore-end.
Features: Free interchangeability of barrels, stocks and fore-ends into double rifle model, combination gun, etc. Barrel selector in trigger; auto. top tang safety; barrel cocking indicators. Introduced 1980. Imported from Finland by Valmet.
Price: Model 412S (ejectors) $959.00

WEATHERBY ORION O/U SHOTGUN
Gauge: 12 or 20 ga., 3" chambers; 2¾" on Trap gun.
Action: Boxlock (simulated side lock).
Barrel: Fixed choke, 12, 20 ga.—26", 28" (Skeet & Skeet); IMC Multi-Choke tubes; 12, 20, 410, Field models—26" (Skeet, Imp. Cyl., Mod.), 28" (Imp. Cyl., Mod., Full), 30" (12 ga. only. Full, Mod., Full); o/u Trap models—30", 32" (Mod., Imp. Mod., Full).
Weight: 7 lbs., 8 oz. (12 ga., 26").
Stock: American walnut, checkered p.g. and fore-end. Rubber recoil pad. Dimensions for field and Skeet models, 20 ga., 14"x1½"x2½".
Features: Selective auto ejectors, single selective mechanical trigger. Top tang safety, Greener cross-bolt. Introduced 1982. Imported from Japan by Weatherby.
Price: Skeet, fixed choke $1,011.00
Price: 12 or 20 ga. IMC Multi-Choke, Field $1,000.00
Price: IMC Multi-Choke, Trap $1,051.00
Price: Extra IMC choke tubes $16.00

Valmet 412 ST Trap and Skeet
Target versions of the 412S gun with hand-honed actions, mechanical single triggers, elongated forcing cones and stainless steel choke tubes. Target safety is locked in "Fire" position (removal of a screw converts it to automatic safety); automatic ejectors; cocking indicators. Walnut stocks with double palm swells are quickly interchangeable. Trap guns have high stepped rib, 30", 32" O-U and 32", 34" single barrels; Skeet guns in 12, 20 ga. with 28" barrels.

Grade II guns have semi-fancy wood, matte nickel finished receiver with matte blue locking bolt and lever, gold trigger, pre-drilled stock for insertion of a recoil reducer, more checkering at stock wrist. Introduced 1987.
Price: Grade I $1,149.00
Price: Grade II $1,449.00

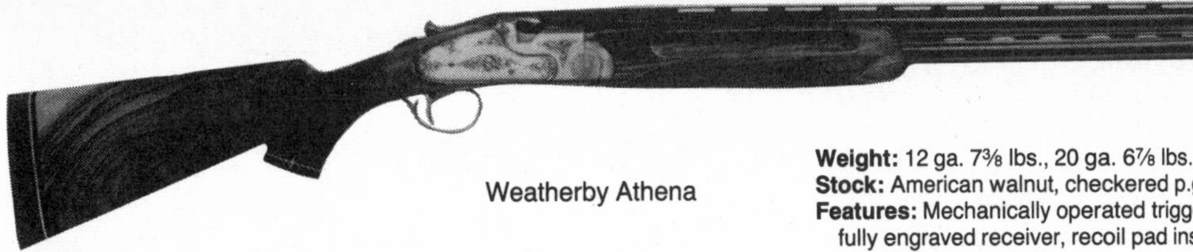

Weatherby Athena

WEATHERBY ATHENA O/U SHOTGUN

Gauge: 12, 20, 28, 410, 3″ chambers; 2¾″ on Trap gun.
Action: Boxlock (simulated side lock) top lever break-open. Selective auto ejectors, single selective trigger (selector inside trigger guard).
Barrel: Fixed choke, 12, 20 ga.—26″, 28″ (Skeet & Skeet); IMC Multi-Choke tubes 12, 20, 410, Field models—26″ (Skeet, Imp. Cyl., Mod.), 28″ (Imp. Cyl., Mod., Full), 30″ (12 ga. only. Full, Mod., Full); o/u Trap models—30″, 32″ (Mod., Imp. Mod., Full).
Weight: 12 ga. 7⅜ lbs., 20 ga. 6⅞ lbs.
Stock: American walnut, checkered p.g. and fore-end (14¼″×1½″×2½″).
Features: Mechanically operated trigger. Top tang safety, Greener cross-bolt, fully engraved receiver, recoil pad installed. IMC models furnished with three interchangeable flush-fitting choke tubes. Imported from Japan by Weatherby. Introduced 1982.
Price: Skeet, fixed choke. **$1,601.00**
Price: 12 or 20 ga., IMC Multi-Choke, Field. **$1,590.95**
Price: IMC Multi-Choke Trap **$1,611.00**
Price: Extra IMC Choke tubes **$16.00**
Price: Master Skeet Tube Set (12-ga. gun with six Briley tubes in 20, 28, 410) **$3,200.00**

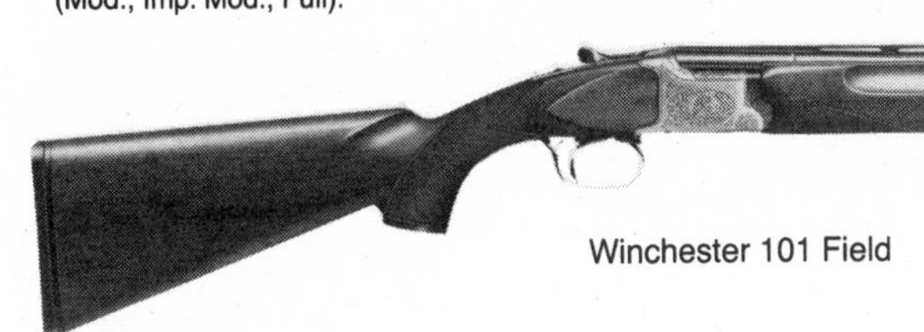

Winchester 101 Field

WINCHESTER 101 WINCHOKE O/U FIELD GUN

Gauge: 12, or 20, 3″ chambers.
Action: Top lever, break open. Manual safety combined with bbl. selector at top of receiver tang.
Barrel: 27″, Winchoke interchangeable choke tubes.
Weight: 12 ga. 7 lbs. Others 6½ lbs. **Length:** 44¾″ over-all.
Stock: 14″×1½″×2½″. Checkered walnut p.g. and fore-end; fluted comb.
Features: Single selective trigger, auto ejectors. Hand engraved satin gray receiver. Comes with hard gun case. Manufactured in and imported from Japan by Winchester Group, Olin Corp.
Price: **$1,495.00**
Price: Two Barrel Set (12 and 20) **$2,330.00**

Winchester Model 101 Waterfowl Winchoke

Same as Model 101 Field Grade except in 12 ga. only, 3″ chambers, 30″ barrels. Comes with four Winchoke tubes: Mod., Imp. Mod., Full, Extra-Full. Blued receiver with hand etching and engraving. Introduced 1981. Manufactured in and imported from Japan by Winchester Group, Olin Corp.
Price: **$1,595.00**

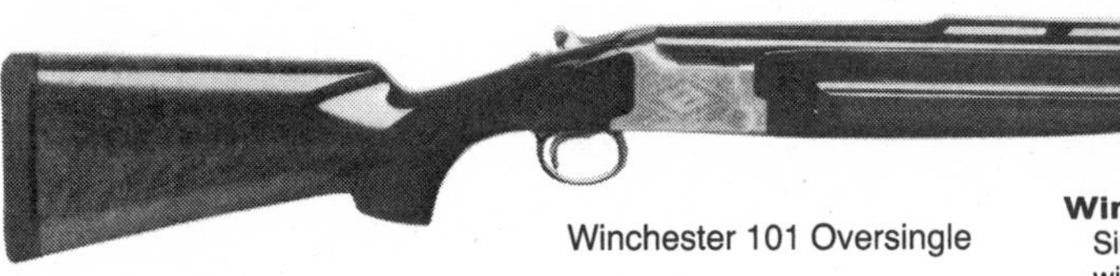

Winchester 101 Oversingle

Winchester Model 101 Pigeon Grade

Similar to the Model 101 Field except comes in two styles: Lightweight-Winchoke (12 or 20 ga., six choke tubes for 12 ga., four for 20, 28 ga., 27″, 28″), Featherweight (12 or 20 ga., Imp. Cyl. & Mod., 25½″), all with 3″ chambers. Vent. rib barrel with middle bead, fancy American walnut. Featherweight has English-style stock. Hard case included. Introduced 1983. Manufactured in and imported from Japan by Winchester Group, Olin Corp.
Price: Featherweight **$1,580.00**
Price: Lightweight-Winchoke **$1,915.00**

Winchester 101 Diamond Grade Target Guns

Similar to the Model 101 except designed for trap and Skeet competition, with tapered and elevated rib, anatomically contoured trigger and internationally-dimensioned stock. Receiver has deep-etched diamond-pattern engraving. Skeet guns available in 12, 20, 28 and 410 with ventilated muzzles to reduce recoil. Trap guns in 12 ga. only; over/under, combination and single-barrel configurations in a variety of barrel lengths with Winchoke system. Straight or Monte Carlo stocks available. Introduced 1982. Manufactured in and imported from Japan by Winchester Group, Olin Corp.
Price: Trap, o/u, standard and Monte Carlo, 30″, 32″. **$1,860.00**
Price: Trap, o/u-single bbl. combo sets, Unsingle. **$2,940.00**
Price: Skeet, 12 and 20. . . . . **$1,915.00**
Price: Skeet, 28 and 410. . . . . **$1,915.00**
Price: Four barrel Skeet set (12, 20, 28, 410) **$5,095.00**
Price: Trap Oversingle, 34″, Monte Carlo or std. stock **$2,145.00**
Price: As above, combo **$3,495.00**

Winchester American Flyer

Consult our Directory pages for the location of firms mentioned.

Winchester American Flyer Live Bird Gun, Combo Set

Similar to the Model 101 except 12 ga. only (2¾″ chambers), 28″ barrels with under barrel fitted with internal Winchoke system and four tubes; over barrel choked Extra Full. Combination Set includes an extra set of 29½″ barrels with same choke specs. Back-bored barrels, matte finish on top of receiver, competition vent. rib. Full fancy American walnut reverse-tapered stock. Comes with luggage-type case. Blued receiver with gold wire border inlays, gold pigeon inlay. Introduced 1987.
Price: 28″ or 29½″ **$2,870.00**
Price: Combination Set, 28″, 29½″ **$3,590.00**

Winchester Quail Special O/U Small Frame

Similar to the Model 101 except built with small frame for 28 and 410 gauge (3″ chambers). 28 gauge has internal Winchoke system and four tubes with 25½″ barrels; 410 has 25½″ barrels choked Full & Mod. Silvered, engraved receiver. Introduced 1987.
Price: **$2,200.00**

Zanoletti 2000 Field

PIETRO ZANOLETTI MODEL 2000 FIELD O/U
Gauge: 12 only.
Barrel: 28″ (Mod. & Full).
Weight: 7 lbs.
Stock: European walnut, checkered grip and fore-end.
Sights: Gold bead front.
Features: Boxlock action with auto ejectors, double triggers; engraved receiver. Imported from Italy by Mandall Shooting Supplies. Introduced 1984.
Price: **$695.00**

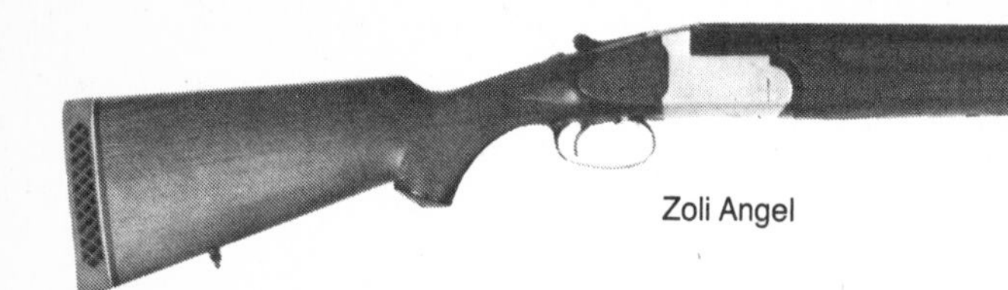

Zoli Angel

A. ZOLI MODEL ANGEL FIELD GRADE O/U
Gauge: 12, 20.
Barrel: 26″, 28″, 30″ (Mod. & Full).
Weight: About 7½ lbs.
Stock: Straight grained walnut with checkered grip and fore-end.
Sights: Gold bead front.
Features: Boxlock action with single selective trigger, auto ejectors; extra-wide vent. top rib. Imported from Italy by Mandall Shooting Supplies.
Price: **$895.00**
Price: Condor model **$895.00**

A. ZOLI DELFINO S.P. O/U
Gauge: 12 or 20, 3″ chambers.
Barrel: 28″ (Mod. & Full); vent. rib.
Weight: 5½ lbs.
Stock: Walnut. Hand checkered p.g. and fore-end; cheekpiece.
Features: Color case hardened receiver with light engraving; chrome lined barrels; automatic sliding safety; double triggers; ejectors. From Mandall Shooting Supplies.
Price: **$895.00**

SHOTGUNS—SIDE-BY-SIDES

Variety of models for utility and sporting use, including some competitive shooting.

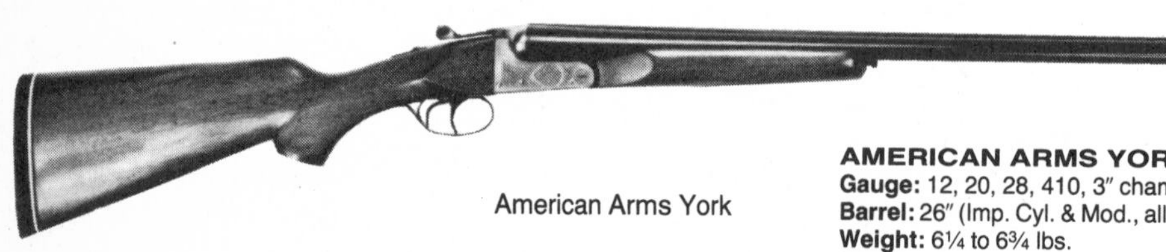

American Arms York

AMERICAN ARMS YORK DOUBLE SHOTGUN
Gauge: 12, 20, 28, 410, 3″ chambers (except 28, 2¾″).
Barrel: 26″ (Imp. Cyl. & Mod., all gauges), 28″ (Mod. & Full, 12 and 20 gauges).
Weight: 6¼ to 6¾ lbs.
Stock: 14⅛″x1⅜″x2⅜″. Hand-checkered walnut with gloss finish.
Sights: Metal bead front.
Features: Boxlock action with English-style scroll engraving, silvered finish. Double triggers, extractors. Independent floating firing pins. Manual safety. Five year warranty. Introduced 1987. Imported from Spain by American Arms, Inc.
Price: 12 or 20 gauge **$499.00**
Price: 28 or 410 .... **$530.00**

American Arms Derby Side-by-Side
Similar to the York model except has sidelock action with English-style engraving on the silvered sideplates. Straight-grip walnut stock with splinter fore-end, hand rubbed oil finish. Double or single non-selective trigger, automatic selective ejectors. Same chokes, rib, barrel lengths as the York. Has 5-year warranty. From American Arms, Inc.
Price: 12 and 20, double trigger **$830.00**
Price: As above, single trigger **$875.00**
Price: 28 and 410, double trigger **$875.00**
Price: As above, single trigger **$900.00**
Price: Two-barrel set, 20/28 ga., double triggers **$1,095.00**
Price: As above, single trigger **$1,125.00**

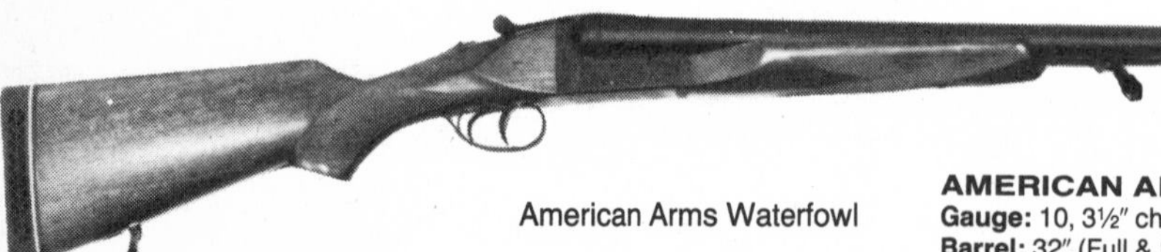

American Arms Waterfowl

AMERICAN ARMS WATERFOWL SPECIAL
Gauge: 10, 3½″ chambers.
Barrel: 32″ (Full & Full). Flat rib.
Weight: 10 lbs., 13 oz.
Stock: 14$\frac{5}{16}$″x1⅜″x2⅜″. Hand checkered walnut with beavertail fore-end, full pistol grip, dull finish, rubber recoil pad.
Features: Boxlock action with double triggers. All metal has Parkerized finish. Comes with camouflaged sling, sling swivels, 5-year warranty. Introduced 1987. Imported from Italy by American Arms, Inc.
Price: **$645.00**

American Arms Turkey Special Side-by-Side
Similar to the Waterfowl Special except in 12 ga. with 3″ chambers, 26″ barrels with choke tubes. Comes with camouflage sling, swivels, 5-year warranty. From American Arms, Inc.
Price: **$550.00**
Price: As above, 10 ga. **$695.00**

Arizaga Model 31

ARIZAGA MODEL 31 DOUBLE SHOTGUN
Gauge: 12, 16, 20, 28, 410
Barrel: 26″, 28″ (standard chokes).
Weight: 6 lbs., 9 oz. **Length:** 45″ over-all.
Stock: Straight English style or pistol grip.
Features: Boxlock action with double triggers; blued, engraved receiver. Imported by Mandall Shooting Supplies.
Price: **$399.95**

BGJ 10 Gauge

BGJ 10 GAUGE MAGNUM SHOTGUN
Gauge: 10 ga. (3½″ chambers).
Action: Boxlock.
Barrel: 32″ (Full).
Weight: 11 lbs.
Stock: 14½″x1½″x2⅝″. European walnut, checkered at p.g. and fore-end.
Features: Double triggers; color hardened action, rest blued. Front and center metal beads on matted rib; ventilated rubber recoil pad. Fore-end release has positive Purdey-type mechanism. Imported from Spain by Mandall Shooting Supplies.
Price: **$599.95**

BERNARDELLI SERIES S. UBERTO DOUBLES
Gauge: 12, 16, 20, 28, 2¾″ or 3″ chambers.
Barrel: 25⅝″, 26¾″, 28″, 29⅛″ (Mod. & Full).
Weight: 6 to 6½ lbs.
Stock: 14³⁄₁₆″x2⅜″x1⁹⁄₁₆″ standard dimensions. Select walnut with hand checkering.
Features: Anson & Deeley boxlock action with Purdey locks, choice of extractors or ejectors. Uberto 1 has color case-hardened receiver, Uberto 2 and F.S. silvered and differ in amount and quality of engraving. Custom options available. Prices vary with importer and are shown respectively. Imported from Italy by Armes De Chasse and Mandall Shooting Supplies.
Price: S. Uberto 1 .... **$1,297.20** to **$1,217.96**
Price: As above with ejectors .... **$1,428.00** to **$1,373.52**
Price: S. Uberto 2 .... **$1,356.00** to **$1,275.58**
Price: As above with ejectors .... **$1,486.80** to **$1,430.16**
Price: S. Uberto F.S. .... **$1,560.00** to **$1,492.46**
Price: As above with ejectors .... **$1,690.80** to **$1,647.00**

Bernardelli Series Roma Shotguns
Similar to the Series S. Uberto Models except with dummy sideplates to simulate sidelock action. In 12, 20, 28 gauge, 25½″, 26¾″, 28″, 29″ barrels. Straight English or pistol grip stock. Chrome-lined barrels, boxlock action, double triggers, ejectors, automatic safety. Checkered butt. Special choke combinations, barrel lengths optional.
Price: Roma 3, about **$1,400.00**
Price: Roma 4, about **$1,600.00**
Price: Roma 6, about **$2,000.00**

ARMSPORT 1050 SIDE-BY-SIDE SHOTGUNS
Gauge: 12, 20, 410, 3″ chambers.
Barrel: 12 ga.—28″ (Mod. & Full), 20 ga., 410—26″ (Imp. Cyl. & Mod.).
Weight: 5¾-6 lbs.
Stock: European walnut
Features: Double triggers; extractors; silvered, engraved receiver. Introduced 1986. Imported from Italy by Armsport.
Price: 12, 20 ga. **$595.00**
Price: 28, 410 .... **$595.00**

Bernardelli System Holland H. Side-by-Side
True sidelock action. Available in 12 gauge only, reinforced breech, three round Purdey locks, automatic ejectors, folding right trigger. Model VB Liscio has color case-hardened receiver and sideplates with light engraving. VB and VB Tipo Lusso are silvered and engraved.
Price: VB Liscio .... **$6,840.00** to **$6,716.00**
Price: VB .... **$7,680.00** to **$7,782.00**
Price: VB Tipo Lusso .... **$9,240.00** to **$9,107.00**

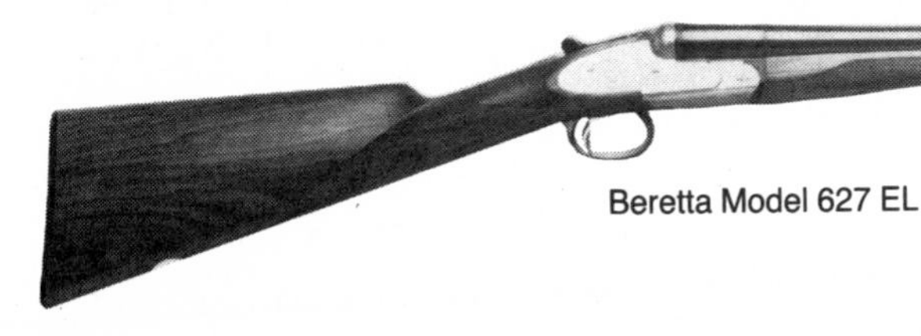
Beretta Model 627 EL

BERETTA SIDE-BY-SIDE FIELD SHOTGUNS
Gauge: 12 and 20, 2¾″ and 3″ chambers.
Barrels: 26″ and 28″ (fixed and Mobilchoke tubes).
Stocks: Close-grained American walnut.
Features: Front and center beads on a raised ventilated rib. Has P. Beretta signature on each side of the receiver, while a gold gauge marking is inscribed atop the rib. Imported from Italy by Beretta U.S.A.
Price: 626 Field **$995.00**
Price: 626 Onyx **$1,265.00**
Price: 627 EL **$1,995.00**
Price: 627 EELL (pistol grip or straight English stock) **$3,500.00**

BRNO ZP 149

BRNO ZP149, ZP349 SIDE-BY-SIDE
Gauge: 12, 2¾″ or 3″ chambers.
Barrel: 28½″ (Full & Mod.).
Weight: 7 lbs., 3 oz. **Length:** 45″ over-all.
Stock: Turkish or Yugoslavian walnut with raised cheekpiece.
Features: Sidelock action with double triggers, auto ejectors, barrel indicators, auto safety. Imported from Czechoslovakia by Saki International.
Price: ZP 149, standard **$589.00**
Price: As above, engraved **$609.00**
Price: ZP 349, extractors, standard **$629.00**
Price: As above, engraved **$649.00**

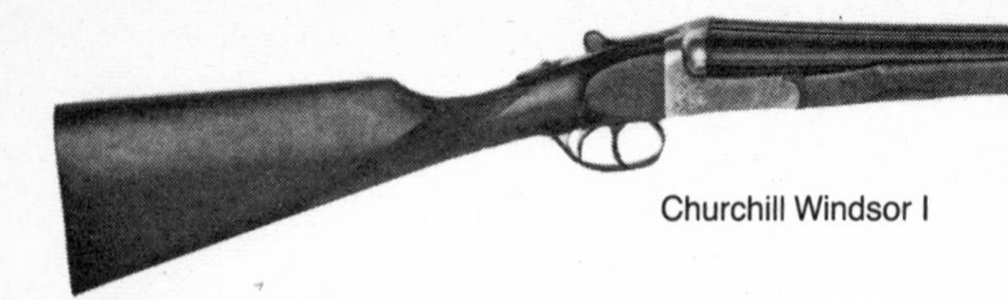

Churchill Windsor I

CHURCHILL ROYAL SIDE-BY-SIDE SHOTGUN

Gauge: 12 (3″), 16 (2¾″), 20, 28, 410 (3″).
Barrel: 12 ga.—26″ (Imp. Cyl. & Mod.), 28″ (Mod. & Full); 16 ga.—28″ (Mod. & Full); 20 ga.–28″ (Imp. Cyl. & Mod., Mod. & Full); 410—26″ (Full & Full).
Weight: 5¾ to 6½ lbs.
Stock: Straight-grip style of checkered European walnut.
Features: Color case-hardened boxlock action with double triggers, extractors; chromed barrels with concave rib. Introduced 1988. Imported by Kassnar.
Price: .... **$559.00** to **$589.00**

CHURCHILL WINDSOR SIDE-BY-SIDE SHOTGUNS

Gauge: 10 (3½″), 12, 16, 20, 28, 410 (2¾″ 16 ga., 3″ others).
Barrel: 24″ (Mod. & Full), 410 and 20 ga.; 26″ (Imp. Cyl. & Mod., Mod. & Full); 28″ (Mod. & Full, Skeet & Skeet—28 ga.); 30″ (Full & Full, Mod. & Full); 32″ (Full & Full—10 ga.).
Weight: About 7½ lbs. (12 ga.).
Stock: Hand checkered European walnut with rubber butt pad.
Features: Anson & Deeley boxlock action with silvered and engraved finish; automatic top tang safety; double triggers; beavertail fore-end. Windsor I with extractors only. Also available in Flyweight versions, 23″, 25″, fixed or ICT chokes, straight stock. Imported from Spain by Kassnar. Introduced 1984.
Price: Windsor I, 10 ga. .... **$679.00** to **$969.00**
Price: Windsor I, 12 through 410 ga. .... **$559.00** to **$629.00**

Classic Model 201

CLASSIC MODEL 201 DOUBLE

Gauge: 12, 20, 28/410.
Barrel: 26″ (Imp. Cyl. & Mod); choke tubes available on 12 ga. model only; 28″ (Imp. Cyl. & Mod., Mod. & Full) for 28/410 set.
Weight: About 7 lbs. **Length:** 43¼″ over-all (26″ barrel).
Stock: 14½″ x 1½″ x 2¼″. Fancy grade American walnut. Straight English on 20 ga. only.
Features: Automatic selective ejectors; elongated forcing cones; top automatic tang safety. Suitable for steel shot. Blued frame. Imported from Japan by Classic Doubles.
Price: 12 ga. **$2,685.00**
Price: 20 ga. **$2,830.00**
Price: 28/410 set. **$4,500.00**

CRUCELEGUI HERMANOS MODEL 150 DOUBLE

Gauge: 12, 16 or 20, 2¾″ chambers.
Action: Greener triple crossbolt.
Barrel: 20″, 26″, 28″, 30″, 32″ (Cyl. & Cyl., Full & Full, Mod. & Full, Mod. & Imp. Cyl., Imp. Cyl. & Full, Mod. & Mod.).
Weight: 5 to 7¼ lbs.
Stock: Hand checkered walnut, beavertail fore-end.
Features: Exposed hammers; double triggers; color case-hardened receiver; sling swivels; chrome lined bores. Imported from Spain by Mandall Shooting Supplies.
Price: **$399.95**
Price: Model 225 (hammerless version) **$399.95**

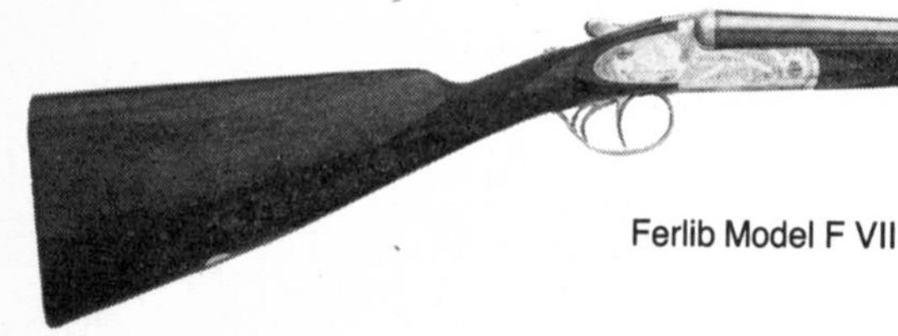

Ferlib Model F VII

FERLIB MODEL F VII DOUBLE SHOTGUN

Gauge: 12, 20, 28, 410.
Barrel: 25″ to 28″.
Weight: 5½ lbs. (20 ga.).
Stock: Oil-finished walnut, checkered straight grip and fore-end.
Features: Boxlock action with fine scroll engraved, silvered receiver. Double triggers standard. Introduced 1983. Imported from Italy by Wm. Larkin Moore.
Price: 12 or 20 ga. **$4,750.00**
Price: 28 or 410 ga. **$5,488.00**
Price: Extra for single trigger **$375.00**

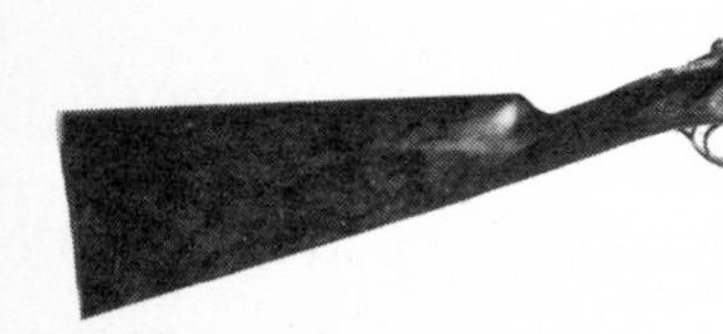

Francotte Double

AUGUSTE FRANCOTTE SIDE-BY-SIDE SHOTGUNS

Gauge: 12, 16, 20, 28, 410.
Barrel: 26″ thru 30″. To customer specs.
Weight: 6.61 lbs. (12 ga.).
Stock: To customer specs. English, pistol grip, half-pistol grip; European walnut.
Features: Chopper lump barrels; BAR action sidelocks or boxlock. Full selection of options available from the maker. Imported from Belgium by Armes de Chasse.
Price: .... **NA**

Garbi Model 51B

GARBI MODEL 51B SIDE-BY-SIDE

Gauge: 12, 16, 20, 2¾″ chambers.
Barrel: 28″ (Mod. & Full).
Weight: 5½ to 6½ lbs.
Stock: Walnut, to customer specs.
Features: Boxlock action; hand-engraved receiver; hand-checkered stock and fore-end; double triggers; extractors. Introduced 1980. Imported from Spain by L. Joseph Rahn, Inc.
Price: Model 51B, 12, 16, 20 ga., ejectors **$1,100.00**

CAUTION: PRICES CHANGE. CHECK AT GUNSHOP.

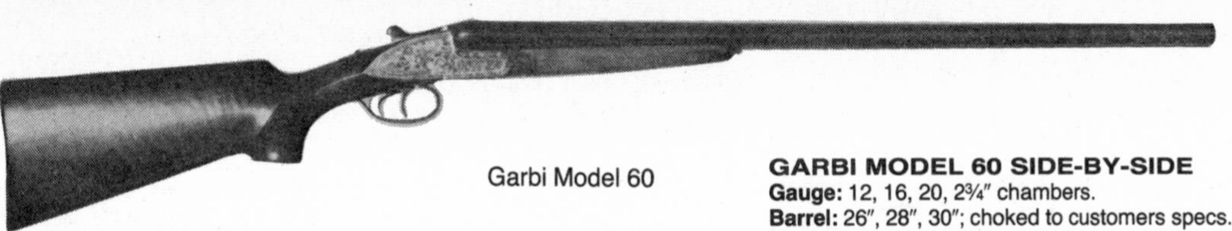

Garbi Model 60

GARBI MODEL 60 SIDE-BY-SIDE
Gauge: 12, 16, 20, 2¾" chambers.
Barrel: 26", 28", 30"; choked to customers specs.
Weight: 5½ to 6½ lbs.
Stock: Select walnut. Dimensions to customer specs.
Features: Sidelock action. Scroll engraving on receiver. Hand checkered stock. Double triggers. Extractors. Imported from Spain by L. Joseph Rahn, Inc.
Price: Model 60A, 12 ga. only **$1,000.00**
Price: With demi-bloc barrels and ejectors, 12, 16, 20 ga. **$1,440.00**

Garbi Model 62
Similar to Model 60 except choked Mod. & Full, plain receiver with engraved border, demi-bloc barrels, gas exhaust valves, jointed triggers, extractors. Imported from Spain by L. Joseph Rahn.
Price: Model 62A, 12 ga., only.................................. **$987.00**
Price: Model 62B, 12, 16, 20 ga., ejectors...................... **$1,400.00**

Garbi Model 71

GARBI MODEL 71 DOUBLE
Gauge: 12, 16, 20, 28.
Barrel: 26", 28" choked to customer specs.
Weight: 5 lbs., 15 oz. (20 ga.).
Stock: 14½"x2¼"x1½". European walnut. Straight grip, checkered butt, classic fore-end.
Features: Sidelock action, automatic ejectors, double triggers standard. Color case-hardened action, coin finish optional. Five other models are available. Imported from Spain by L. Joseph Rahn and Wm. Larkin Moore.
Price: Model 71 .... **$2,200.00** to **$2,600.00**

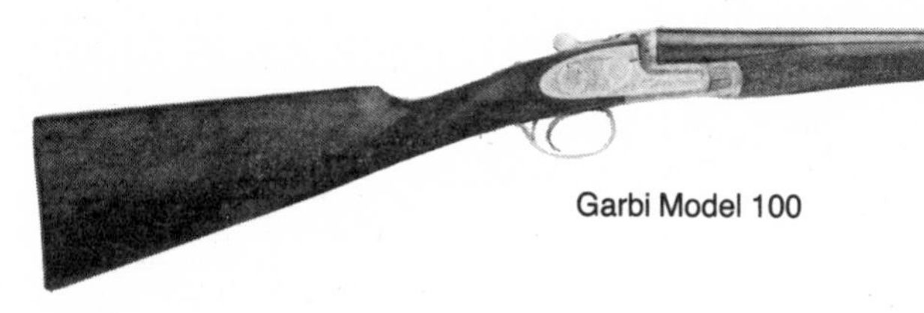

Garbi Model 100

GARBI MODEL 100 DOUBLE
Gauge: 12, 16, 20, 28.
Barrel: 26", 28", choked to customer specs.
Weight: 5½ to 7½ lbs.
Stock: 14½"x2¼"x1½". European walnut. Straight grip, checkered butt, classic fore-end.
Features: Sidelock action, automatic ejectors, double triggers standard. Color case-hardened action, coin finish optional. Single trigger; beavertail fore-end, etc. optional. Five other models are available. Imported from Spain by Wm. Larkin Moore and L. Joseph Rahn.
Price: From.................................... **$2,450.00** to **$3,000.00**

Garbi Model 101 Side-by-Side
Similar to the Garbi Model 100 except is available with optional level, file-cut, Churchill or ventilated top rib, and in a 12-ga. pigeon or wildfowl gun. Has Continental-style floral and scroll engraving, select walnut stock. Better over-all quality than the Model 100. Imported from Spain by L. Joseph Rahn and Wm. Larkin Moore.
Price: .... **$3,700.00** to **$4,500.00**

Garbi Model 103A, B Side-by-Side
Similar to the Garbi Model 100 except has Purdey-type fine scroll and rosette engraving. Better over-all quality than the Model 101. Model 103B has nickel-chrome steel barrels, H&H-type easy opening mechanism; other mechanical details remain the same. Imported from Spain by Wm. Larkin Moore and L. Joseph Rahn, Inc.
Price: Model 103A, from .... **$3,700.00** to **$4,500.00**
Price: Model 103B, from .... **$5,244.00** to **$6,000.00**

GARBI MODEL 102 SHOTGUN
Gauge: 12, 16, 20.
Barrel: 12 ga.—25" to 30", 16 & 20 ga.—25" to 28". Chokes as specified.
Weight: 20 ga.—5 lbs., 15 oz. to 6 lbs., 4 oz.
Stock: 14½"×2¼"×1½"; select walnut.
Features: Holland pattern sidelock ejector with chopper lump barrels, Holland-type large scroll engraving. Double triggers (hinged front) std., non-selective single trigger available. Many options available. Imported from Spain by L. Joseph Rahn and Wm. Larkin Moore.
Price: From.................................... **$3,700.00** to **$4,500.00**

Garbi Model 200

Garbi Model 200 Side-by-Side
Similar to the Garbi Model 100 except has barrels of nickel-chrome steel, heavy-duty locks, magnum proofed. Very fine continental-style floral and scroll engraving, well figured walnut stock. Other mechanical features remain the same. Imported from Spain by L. Joseph Rahn and Wm. Larkin Moore.
Price: .... **$5,300.00** to **$6,250.00**

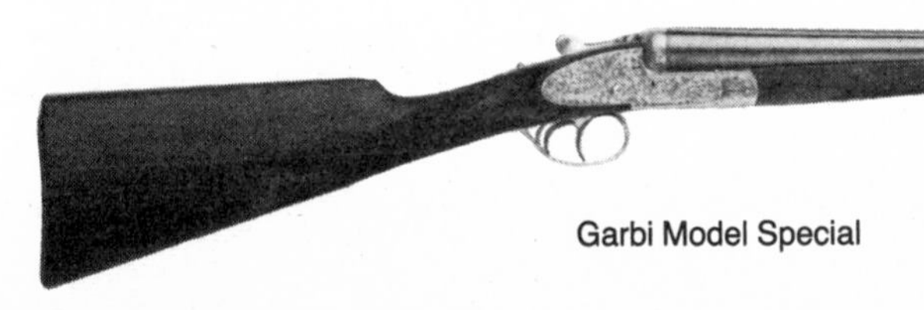

Garbi Model Special

Garbi Model Special Side-by-Side
Similar to the Garbi Model 100 except has best quality wood and metal work. Special game scene engraving with or without gold inlays, fancy figured walnut stock. Imported from Spain by Wm. Larkin Moore.
Price: From **$6,250.00**

HATFIELD UPLANDER SHOTGUN

Gauge: 20, 3″ chambers.
Barrel: 26″ (Imp. Cyl. & Mod.).
Weight: 5¾ lbs.
Stock: Straight English style, special select XXX fancy walnut. Hand rubber oil finish. Splinter fore-end.
Features: Double locking under lug boxlock action; color case-hardened frame; single non-selective trigger. Introduced 1988. From Hatfield.
Price: Grade 1 .... **$995.00**
Price: Grade 2.......... **$1,495.00**
Price: Grade 3.......... **$2,495.00**
Price: Grade 4.......... **$3,995.00**
Price: Grade 5.......... **$5,595.00**

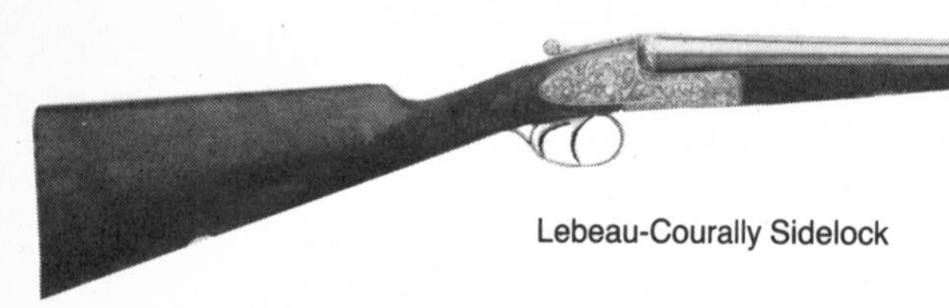
Lebeau-Courally Sidelock

MERCURY MODEL G1032 DOUBLE BARREL SHOTGUN

Gauge: 10, 3½″ chambers.
Action: Triple-lock Anson & Deeley type.
Barrel: 32″ (Full & Full).
Weight: 10⅛ lbs.
Stock: 14″x1⅝″x2¼″ walnut, checkered p.g. stock and beavertail fore-end, recoil pad.
Features: Double triggers, front hinged, auto safety, extractors; safety gas ports, engraved frame. Imported from Spain by Tradewinds.
Price: **$480.00**

OMEGA FOLDING SIDE-BY-SIDE SHOTGUNS

Gauge: 20, 28, 410, 3″ chambers.
Barrel: 20 ga.—26″ (Imp. Cyl. & Mod.); 28 ga.—26″ (Mod. & Full); 410—26″ (Full & Full).
Weight: 5½ lbs.
Stock: Standard has checkered beechwood, Deluxe has walnut; Standard has semi-pistol grip.
Features: Blued barrels and receiver; top tang safety. Imported from Italy by Kassnar. Introduced 1984.
Price: Standard .... **$229.00** to **$269.00**
Price: Deluxe **$250.00**

Parker-Hale 645E

PERUGINI-VISINI CLASSIC DOUBLE SHOTGUN

Gauge: 12, 20, 2¾″ or 3″.
Barrel: NA.
Weight: NA. **Length:** NA.
Stock: Straight English type of high grade European briar walnut; oil finish.
Features: H&H-type hand-detachable sidelocks internally gold plated; single or double triggers; automatic ejectors. Many options available. Imported from Italy by Wm. Larkin Moore.
Price: From about.......... **$12,000.00**

Perugini-Visini Liberty Double Shotgun

A boxlock gun that shares many of the same features of the Classic model. Available in 12, 20, 28, 410, 2¾″ or 3″ chambers. Many options available and can be had as a matched pair.
Price: From about.......... **$5,900.00**

LEBEAU-COURALLY BOXLOCK SHOTGUN

Gauge: 12, 16, 20, 28.
Barrel: 26″ to 30″, choked to customer specs.
Weight: 6 lbs., 6 oz. to 8 lbs., 4 oz. (12 ga.)
Stock: Dimensions to customer specs. Select French walnut with hand rubbed oil finish, straight grip (p.g. optional), splinter fore-end (beavertail optional).
Features: Anson & Deeley boxlock with ejectors, Purdey-type fastener; choice of rounded action, with or without sideplates; choice of level rib, file cut or smooth; choice of numerous engraving patterns. Imported from Belguim by Wm. Larkin Moore.
Price: **$11,300.00**

LEBEAU-COURALLY SIDELOCK SHOTGUN

Gauge: 12, 16, 20 (standard), 28 (optional).
Barrel: 26″ to 30″, choked to customer specs.
Weight: 6 lbs., 6 oz. to 8 lbs., 4 oz. (12 ga.)
Stock: Dimensions to customer specs. Best quality French walnut with hand rubbed oil finish, straight grip stock and checkered butt (std.), classic splinter fore-end.
Features: Holland & Holland pattern sidelock ejector double with chopper lump barrels; choice of classic or rounded action; concave or level rib, file cut or smooth; choice of numerous engraving patterns. Can be furnished with H&H type self-opening mechanism. Imported from Belguim by Wm. Larkin Moore.
Price: From **$22,700.00**
Price: Boxlock, from.......... **$11,300.00**

MERKEL SIDE-BY-SIDE SHOTGUNS

Gauge: 12, 16, 20, 2¾″ or 3″ chambers
Barrel: 26″, 26¾″, 28″ (standard chokes).
Weight: 6 to 7 lbs.
Stock: European walnut. Straight English or pistol grip.
Features: Models 47E, 147E, 122 are boxlocks; others are sidelocks. All have double triggers, double lugs and Greener cross-bolt locking and automatic ejectors. Choking and patterning for steel shot (by importer). Upgraded wood, engraving, etc. optional. Imported from East Germany by Armes de Chasse.
Price: Model 47E, about.......... **$950.00**
Price: Model 147E, about **$1,500.00**
Price: Model 47S, about **$2,600.00**
Price: Model 147S, about **$3,300.00**
Price: Model 247S, about **$3,300.00**
Price: Model 347S, about **$3,700.00**
Price: Model 447S, about **$4,200.00**

PARKER-HALE MODEL "600" SERIES DOUBLES

Gauge: 12, 16, 20, 2¾″ chambers; 28, 410, 3″ chambers.
Barrel: 25″, 26″, 27″, 28″ (Imp. Cyl. & Mod., Mod. & Full).
Weight: 12 ga., 6¾-7 lbs.; 20 ga., 5¾-6 lbs.
Stock: 14½″×1½″×2½″. Hand checkered walnut with oil finish. "E" (English) models have straight grip, splinter fore-end, checkered butt. "A" (American) models have p.g. stock, beaver-tail fore-end, buttplate.
Features: Boxlock action; silvered, engraved action; auto safety; ejectors or extractors. E-models have double triggers, concave rib (XXV models have Churchill-type rib); A-models have single, non-selective trigger, raised matted rib. Made in Spain by Ugartechea. Imported by Precision Sports. Introduced 1986.
Price: 640E (12, 16, 20; 26″, 28″), extractors **$529.95**
Price: 640E (28, 410; 27″ only), extractors **$599.95**
Price: 640A (12, 16, 20; 26″, 28″), extractors **$629.95**
Price: 640A (28, 410, 27″ only), extractors **$699.95**
Price: 645E (12, 16, 20; 26″, 28″), with ejectors **$679.95**
Price: 645E (28, 410; 27″), with ejectors **$749.95**
Price: 645A (12, 16, 20; 26″, 28″) with ejectors.......... **$779.95**
Price: 645A (28, 410, 27″ only), ejectors **$849.95**
Price: 645E-XXV (12, 16, 20; 25″), with ejectors **$699.95**
Price: 645E-XXV (28, 410, 27″), with ejectors **$779.95**
Price: 645E Bi-Gauge (20/28 or 28/410), ejectors **$1,199.95**
Price: 645A Bi-Gauge (20/28 or 28/410), ejectors **$1,295.95**
Price: 670E (12, 16, 20, 26″, 28″) sidelock, with ejectors **$2,900.00**
Price: 670E (28, 410; 27″) sidelock, with ejectors.......... **$3,100.00**
Price: 680E-XXV (12, 16, 20; 25″) sidelock, ejectors, case-color action.......... **$2,700.00**
Price: 680E-XXV (28, 410; 25″) sidelock, ejectors, case-color action **$2,900.00**

CAUTION: PRICES CHANGE. CHECK AT GUNSHOP.

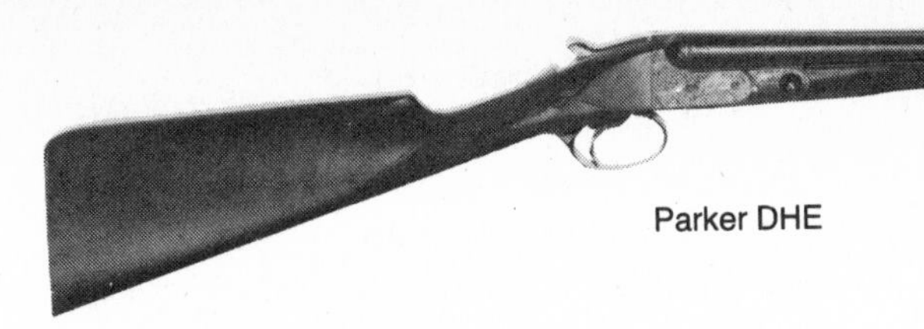
Parker DHE

PARKER DHE SIDE-BY-SIDE SHOTGUN

Gauge: 12, 20, 28, 2¾″ or 3″ chambers.
Barrel: 26″ (Imp. Cyl. & Mod., 2¾″ chambers), Skeet & Skeet available, 28″ (Mod. & Full, 3″ chambers only).
Weight: About 6¾ lbs. (12 ga.), 6½ lbs. (20 ga.), 5½ lbs. (28 ga.), 5 lbs. (410).
Stock: Fancy American walnut, checkered grip and fore-end. Straight stock or pistol grip, splinter or beavertail fore-end; 28 l.p.i. checkering.
Features: Reproduction of the original Parker—most parts interchangeable with original. Double or single selective trigger; checkered skeleton buttplate; selective ejectors; bores hard chromed, excluding choke area. Two-barrel sets available. Hand engraved scroll and scenes on case-hardened frame. Fitted leather trunk included. Limited production. Introduced 1984. Made by Winchester in Japan. Imported by Parker Div. of Reagent Chemical.
Price: D Grade, one barrel set **$2,970.00**
Price: B Grade **$3,970.00**
Price: A-1 Special **$8,740.00**

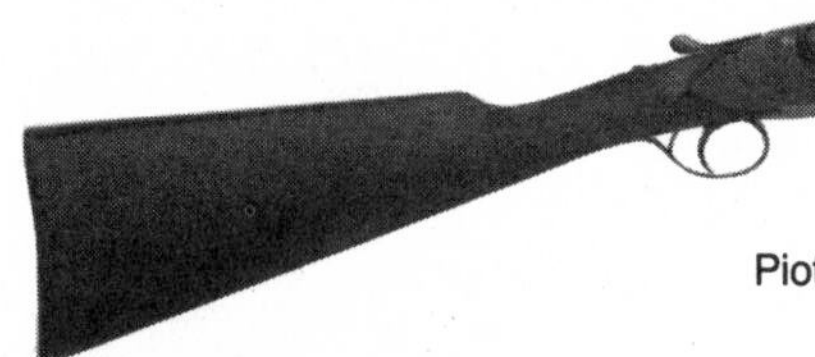
Piotti Model Piuma

PIOTTI MODEL PIUMA SIDE-BY-SIDE

Gauge: 12, 16, 20, 28, 410.
Barrel: 25″ to 30″ (12 ga.), 25″ to 28″ (16, 20, 28, 410).
Weight: 5½ to 6¼ lbs. (20 ga.).
Stock: Dimensions to customer specs. Straight grip stock with checkered butt, classic splinter fore-end, hand rubbed oil finish are standard; pistol grip, beavertail fore-end, satin luster finish optional.
Features: Anson & Deeley boxlock ejector double with chopper lump barrels. Level, file-cut rib, light scroll and rosette engraving, scalloped frame. Double triggers with hinged front standard, single non-selective optional. Coin finish standard, color case-hardened optional. Imported from Italy by Wm. Larkin Moore.
Price: **$5,700.00**

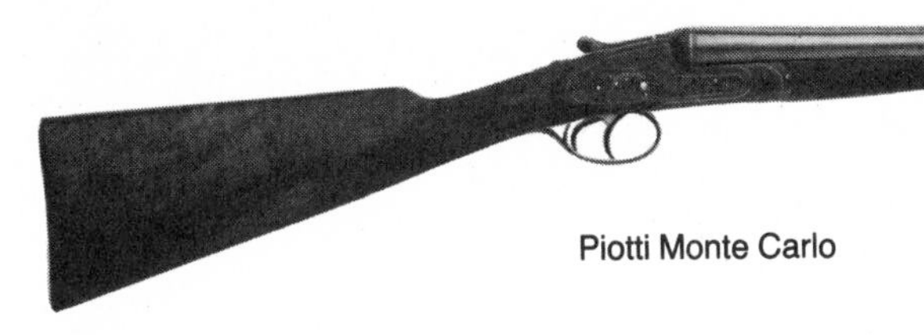
Piotti Monte Carlo

PIOTTI KING NO. 1 SIDE-BY-SIDE

Gauge: 12, 16, 20, 28, 410.
Barrel: 25″ to 30″ (12 ga.), 25″ to 28″. (16, 20, 28 410). To customer specs. Chokes as specified.
Weight: 6½ lbs. to 8 lbs. (12 ga., to customer specs.)
Stock: Dimensions to customer specs. Finely figured walnut; straight grip with checkered butt with classic splinter fore-end and hand-rubbed oil finish standard. Pistol grip, beavertail fore-end, satin luster finish optional.
Features: Holland & Holland pattern sidelock action, auto ejectors. Double trigger with front trigger hinged standard; non-selective single trigger optional. Coin finish standard; color case-hardened optional. Top rib: level, file cut standard; concave, ventilated optional. Very fine, full coverage scroll engraving with small floral bouquets, gold crown in top lever, name in gold, and gold crest in fore-end. Imported from Italy by Wm. Larkin Moore.
Price: **$12,500.00**

Piotti Model Monte Carlo Side-by-Side

Similar to the Piotti King No. 1 except has Purdey-style scroll and rosette engraving, no gold inlays, over-all workmanship not as finely detailed. Other mechanical specifications remain the same. Imported from Italy by Wm. Larkin Moore.
Price: **$10,200.00**

Piotti Model King Extra Side-by-Side

Similar to the Piotti King No. 1 except highest quality wood and metal work. Choice of either bulino game scene engraving or game scene engraving with gold inlays. Engraved and signed by a master engraver. Exhibition grade wood. Other mechanical specifications remain the same. Imported from Italy by Wm. Larkin Moore.
Price: **$18,000.00**

Piotti Model Lunik Side-by-Side

Similar to the Piotti King No. 1 except better over-all quality. Has Renaissance-style large scroll engraving in relief, gold crown in top lever, gold name, and gold crest in fore-end. Best quality Holland & Holland-pattern sidelock ejector double with chopper lump (demi-bloc) barrels. Other mechanical specifications remain the same. Imported from Italy by Wm. Larkin Moore.
Price: **$13,400.00**

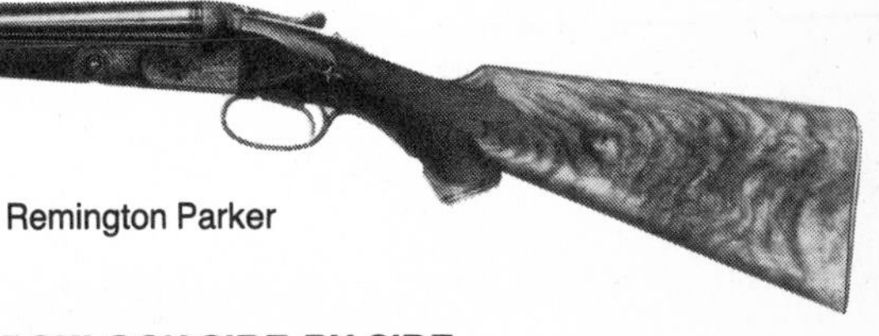
Remington Parker

REMINGTON PARKER AHE SIDE-BY-SIDE

Gauge: 20, 2¾″ chambers.
Barrel: 28″ (any combination of Skeet, Imp. Cyl., Mod., Full chokes).
Weight: About 6½ lbs.
Stock: Circassian or American walnut; straight or pistol grip; beavertail or splinter fore-end; rubber recoil pad, Parker buttplate or engraved skeleton steel buttplate. Checkered 28 lpi.
Features: Custom-made gun. Single selective trigger, automatic ejectors; scroll-engraved color case-hardened receiver. Automatic ejectors. Limited production. Reintroduced 1988. From Remington.
Price: From **$11,700.00**

RIZZINI BOXLOCK SIDE-BY-SIDE

Gauge: 12, 20, 28, 410.
Barrel: 25″ to 30″ (12 ga.), 25″ to 28″ (20, 28, 410).
Weight: 5½ to 6¼ lbs. (20 ga.).
Stock: Dimensions to customer specs. Straight grip stock with checkered butt, classic splinter fore-end, hand rubbed oil finish are standard; pistol grip, beavertail fore-end, satin luster finish optional.
Features: Anson & Deeley boxlock ejector double with chopper lump barrels. Level, file-cut rib, light scroll and rosette engraving, scalloped frame. Double triggers with hinged front standard, single non-selective optional. Coin finish standard, color case-hardened optional. Imported from Italy by Wm. Larkin Moore.
Price: 12, 20 ga., from **$9,700.00**
Price: 28, 410 ga., from **$12,400.00**

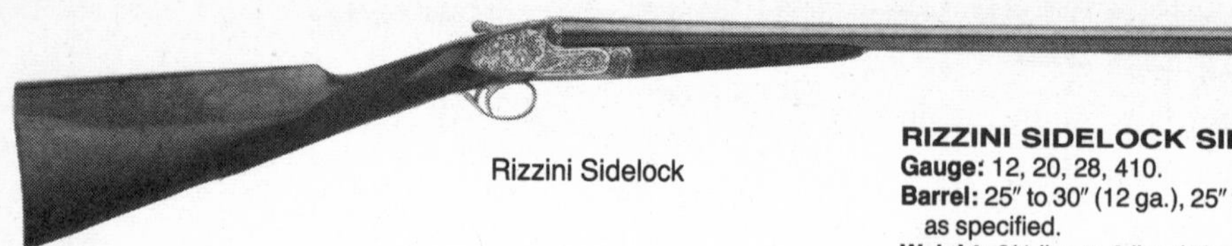

Rizzini Sidelock

RIZZINI SIDELOCK SIDE-BY-SIDE
Gauge: 12, 20, 28, 410.
Barrel: 25" to 30" (12 ga.), 25" to 28" (20, 28, 410). To customer specs. Chokes as specified.
Weight: 6½ lbs. to 8 lbs. (12 ga., to customer specs.)
Stock: Dimensions to customer specs. Finely figured walnut; straight grip with checkered butt with classic splinter fore-end and hand-rubbed oil finish standard. Pistol grip, beavertail fore-end, satin luster finish optional.
Features: Holland & Holland pattern sidelock action, auto ejectors. Double trigger with front trigger hinged standard; non-selective single trigger optional. Coin finish standard; color case-hardened optional. Top rib level, file cut standard; concave, ventilated optional. Very fine, full coverage scroll engraving with small floral bouquets, gold crown in top lever, name in gold, and gold crest in fore-end. Imported from Italy by Wm. Larkin Moore.
Price: 12, 20 ga., from **$17,500.00**
Price: 28, 410 ga., from **$21,600.00**

ROSSI "SQUIRE" DOUBLE BARREL
Gauge: 12, 20, 410, 3" chambers.
Barrel: 12—28" (Mod. & Full); 20 ga.—26" (Imp. Cyl. & Mod.), 28" (Mod. & Full); 410—26" (Full & Full).
Weight: About 7½ lbs.
Stock: Walnut-finished hardwood.
Features: Double triggers, raised matted rib, beavertail fore-end. Massive twin underlugs mesh with synchronized sliding bolts. Introduced 1978. Imported by Interarms.
Price: 12 or 20 ga. **$352.00**
Price: 410 .... **$357.00**

Rossi Overland

ROSSI OVERLAND DOUBLE BARREL
Gauge: 12, 20, 410, 3" chambers
Action: Sidelock with external hammers; Greener crossbolt.
Barrel: 12 ga., 20" (Imp. Cyl. & Mod.), 28" (Mod. & Full), 20 ga., 20", 26" (Imp. Cyl. & Mod.), 410 ga., 26" (Full & Full).
Weight: 6½ to 7 lbs.
Stock: Walnut p.g. with beavertail fore-end.
Features: Solid raised matted rib. Exposed hammers. Imported by Interarms.
Price: 12 or 20 .... **$332.00**
Price: 410 .... **$337.00**

S.A.B. RENATO GAMBA DOUBLE SHOTGUNS
Gauge: 12, 20, 28.
Barrel: 26¾", 28" (standard chokes).
Weight: 6¾ to 7 lbs.
Stock: European walnut. Straight English or pistol grip.
Features: Boxlock action, double triggers, chrome-lined barrels. Ejectors and automatic safety optional. Imported by Armes de Chasse.
Price: Principessa (boxlock), about **$1,500.00**
Price: Oxford (boxlock), about **$1,800.00**
Price: London (sidelock), about **$5,000.00**

SAE Model 209E Double
Similar to the Model 340X except has coin-finish engraved receiver, available in 12, 20, 410 (2¾"). Fancy, oil-finished walnut.
Price: **$884.00**

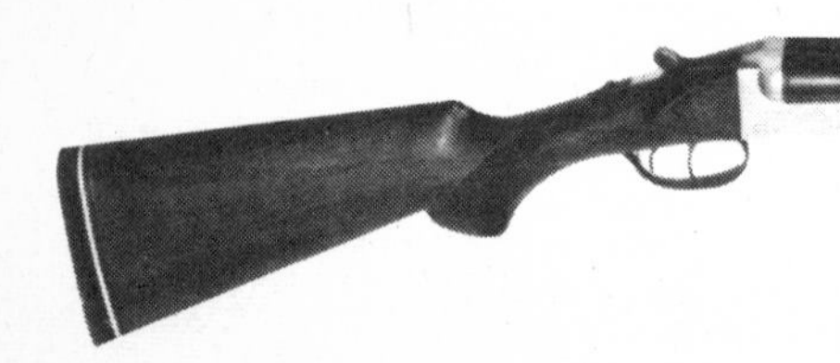

SAE 210S

SAE MODEL 210S DOUBLE
Gauge: 12, 20, 410, 3" chambers.
Barrel: 26" (Mod. & Full), 28" (Mod. & Imp. Cyl.).
Weight: 7 lbs.
Stock: European walnut with p.g., splinter fore-end.
Features: Boxlock action with double triggers, automatic safety, extractors. Introduced 1987. Imported from Spain America Ent.
Price: **$427.70**

SAE Model 340X Double
Similar to the Model 210S except is true sidelock. Available in 12 or 20 ga. (2¾"), 26" (Mod. & Full), 28" (Mod. & Imp. Cyl.). Color case-hardened receiver with engraving. Weight is 6.9 lbs. Selective ejectors, double triggers.
Price: **$648.70**

SKB Model 200

SKB MODEL 200 DOUBLE SHOTGUN
Gauge: 12, 20, 3" chambers.
Barrel: 25", 26" (Inter Choke tubes).
Weight: 6 lbs., 10 oz. (12 ga.). **Length:** 42⅛" over-all (26" barrels).
Stock: 14" x 1½" x 2⅝". Walnut with checkered grip and fore-end, recoil pad.
Sights: Metal bead front.
Features: Engraved boxlock action with silvered finish. Gold-plated trigger. Introduced 1988. Imported from Japan by Ernie Simmons Enterprises.
Price: **$895.00**
Price: Model 200E with straight English-style stock **$895.00**

SKB Model 400 Double Shotgun
Similar to the Model 200 except has engraved and silvered sideplates. Standard or straight English-style stock.
Price: **$1,195.00**

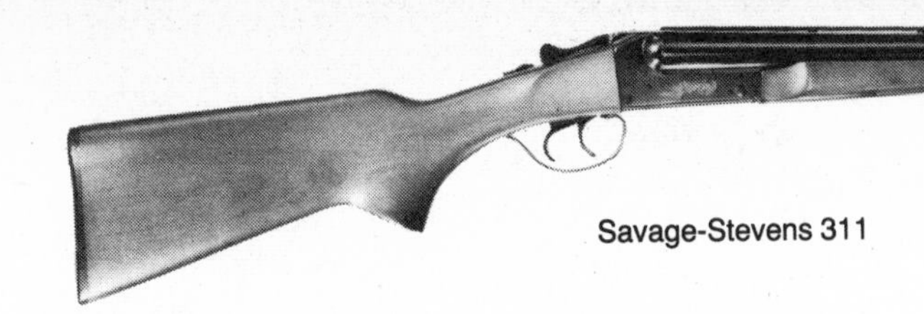
Savage-Stevens 311

SAVAGE-STEVENS MODEL 311 DOUBLE

Gauge: 12, 20, 3" chambers.
Action: Top lever, hammerless; double triggers, auto. top tang safety.
Barrel: 28" (Mod. & Full).
Weight: 7 lbs. **Length:** 43¾" over-all.
Stock: 14" x 1½" x 2½". Walnut finish, p.g., fluted comb.
Features: Automatic top tang safety. Extractors; double triggers.
Price: $249.00

Savage Model 311 "Waterfowler" Double

Similar to the Model 311 except in 12 ga. only (3" chambers) with 28" barrels choked for Full steel shot pattern; has low gloss finish. Introduced 1988.
Price: $339.00

W&C Scott Bowood DeLuxe Game Gun

Similar to the Chatsworth Grande Luxe except less ornate metal and wood work; checkered 24 l.p.i. at fore-end and pistol grip. Imported from England by L. Joseph Rahn.
Price: 12 or 16 ga. $8,000.00
Price: 20 or 28 ga. $8,400.00

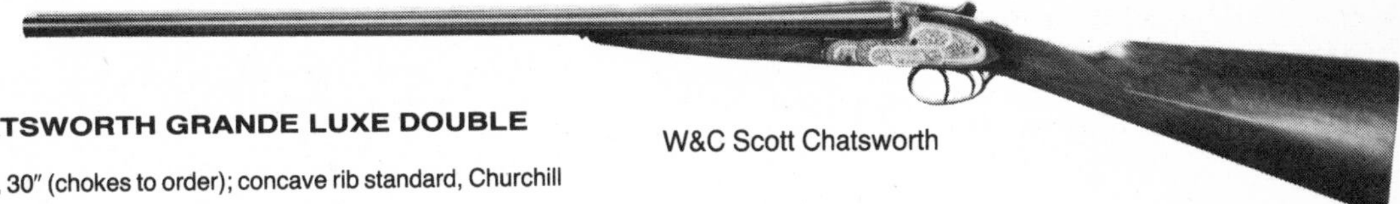
W&C Scott Chatsworth

W&C SCOTT CHATSWORTH GRANDE LUXE DOUBLE

Gauge: 12, 16, 20, 28.
Barrel: 25", 26", 27", 28", 30" (chokes to order); concave rib standard, Churchill or flat rib optional.
Weight: About 6½ lbs. (12 ga.).
Stock: 14¾"x1½"x2¼", or made to customer specs. French walnut with 32 l.p.i. checkering.
Features: Entirely hand fitted; boxlock action (sideplates optional); English scroll engraving; gold name plate shield in stock. Imported from England by L. Joseph Rahn.
Price: 12 or 16 ga. $9,000.00
Price: 20 or 28 ga. $9,500.00

W&C Scott Kinmount Game Gun

Similar to the Bowood DeLuxe Game Gun except less ornate engraving and wood work; checkered 20 l.p.i.; other details essentially the same. Imported from England by L. Joseph Rahn.
Price: 12 or 16 ga. $7,000.00
Price: 20 or 28 ga. $7,300.00

IGA Side-by-Side

STOEGER/IGA SIDE-BY-SIDE SHOTGUN

Gauge: 12, 20, 28, 2¾" chambers; 410, 3"chambers.
Barrel: 26" (Full & Full, 410 only, Imp. Cyl. & Mod.), 28" (Mod. & Full).
Weight: 6¾ to 7 lbs.
Stock: 14½"x1½"x2½". Oil-finished hardwood. Checkered pistol grip and fore-end.
Features: Automatic safety, extractors only, solid matted barrel rib. Double triggers only. Introduced 1983. Imported from Brazil by Stoeger Industries.
Price: $265.00
Price: Coach Gun, 12 or 20 ga., 20" bbls. $260.00

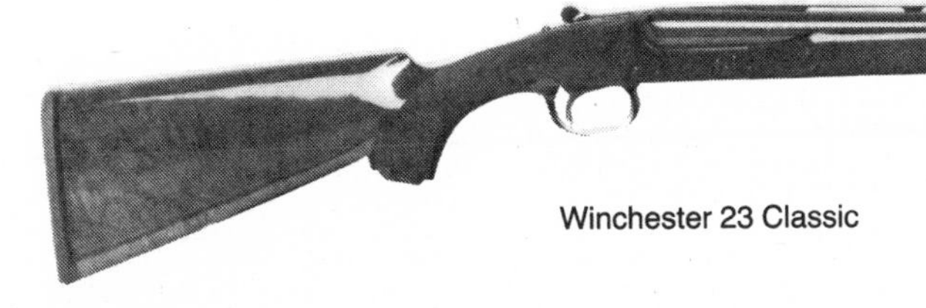
Winchester 23 Classic

WINCHESTER MODEL 23 CLASSIC SHOTGUN

Gauge: 12, 20, 28, 410.
Barrel: 26" (Imp. Cyl. & Mod., except 410 Mod. & Full).
Weight: 5⅞ to 7 lbs. **Length:** 43¼" over-all.
Stock: 14½"x1½"x2⅜". Fancy grade American walnut with pistol grip.
Features: Blued receiver with scroll engraving; gold inlay on bottom: pheasant on 12, 20, quail on 28, 410. Ebony inlay in fore-end, gold initial plate in stock. Single selective trigger, automatic safety, selective ejectors. Introduced 1986. Imported from Japan by Winchester Group, Olin Corp.
Price: 12 and 20 gauge $1,975.00
Price: 28 and 410 gauge $2,080.00

Consult our Directory pages for the location of firms mentioned.

Winchester Model 23 Light Duck

Same basic features as the standard Model 23 Pigeon Grade except has plain, blued frame, 28" barrels choked Full and Full; 20 ga.; 3" chambers. Comes with hard case. Matching serial numbers to previously issued Heavy Duck. Introduced 1983.
Price: $1,095.00
Price: Golden Quail (12 ga., 25½", Imp. Cyl. & Mod.) $2,000.00
Price: Golden Quail 410 .... $2,190.00
Price: Custom Two Barrel Set (20, 28 ga. bbls., full fancy walnut, leather luggage-style case) $4,735.00

Winchester Custom Model 23 Shotgun

Same as the Model 23 Classic except has plain blued receiver with no engraving, internal Winchoke system with six tubes (Extra Full, Full, Mod., Imp. Mod., Imp. Cyl., Skeet). Chrome-lined bores and chambers suitable for steel shot. Comes with luggage-style case. Introduced 1987.
Price: $1,715.00

SHOTGUNS—BOLT ACTIONS & SINGLE SHOTS

Variety of designs for utility and sporting purposes, as well as for competitive shooting.

American Arms Single

AMERICAN ARMS SINGLE BARREL SHOTGUN

Gauge: 12, 20, 410, 3″ chamber.
Barrel: 26″ (Full, 410 ga.), 28″ (Mod., Full).
Weight: About 6½ lbs.
Stock: Walnut-finished hardwood with checkered grip, fore-end.
Sights: Bead front.
Features: Manual thumb safety; chrome-lined barrel. Imported from Italy by American Arms, Inc. Introduced 1988.
Price: $108.00

American Arms Waterfowl Special
Similar to the Single Barrel model except chambered for 10 ga. 3½″, has 30″ (Full) barrel. Matte finish.
Price: $160.00

American Arms Camper

American Arms Camper Special
Similar to the Single Barrel except has 21″ barrel (Mod.), over-all length of 27″, pistol grip instead of buttstock. Gun folds for storage, carry. Matte finish.
Price: $108.00

American Arms Turkey Special
Similar to the Single Barrel except chambered for 10 ga. 3½″, has 26″ barrel with choke tube. Matte finish.
Price: $189.00

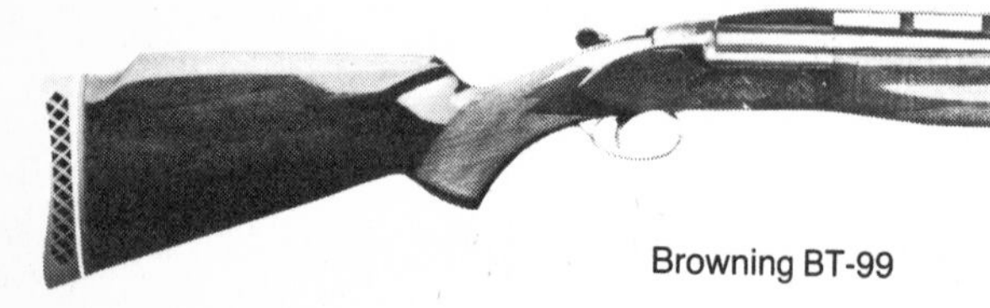

Browning BT-99

BROWNING BT-99 COMPETITION TRAP SPECIAL

Gauge: 12 gauge only 2¾″ chamber.
Action: Top lever break-open, hammerless.
Barrel: 32″ or 34″ with 11/32″ wide high post floating vent. rib. Comes with Invector choke tubes or fixed Full, Imp. Mod.
Weight: 8 lbs. (32″ bbl.).
Stock: French walnut; hand checkered, full pistol grip, full beavertail fore-end; recoil pad. Trap dimensions with M.C. 14⅜″×1⅜″×1⅜″×2″.
Sights: Ivory front and middle beads.
Features: Gold-plated trigger with 3½-lb. pull, deluxe trap-style recoil pad, auto ejector, no safety. Available with either Monte Carlo or standard stock. Imported from Japan by Browning.
Price: Grade I Invector.................................... $1,005.00
Price: As above, non-Invector.............................. $981.00

F.I.E. "S.S.S." SINGLE BARREL

Gauge: 12, 20, 410, 3″ chamber.
Action: Button-break on trigger guard.
Barrel: 18½″ (Cyl.).
Weight: 6½ lbs.
Stock: Walnut finished hardwood, full beavertail fore-end.
Features: Exposed hammer. Automatic ejector. Imported from Brazil by F.I.E. Corp.
Price: $129.95

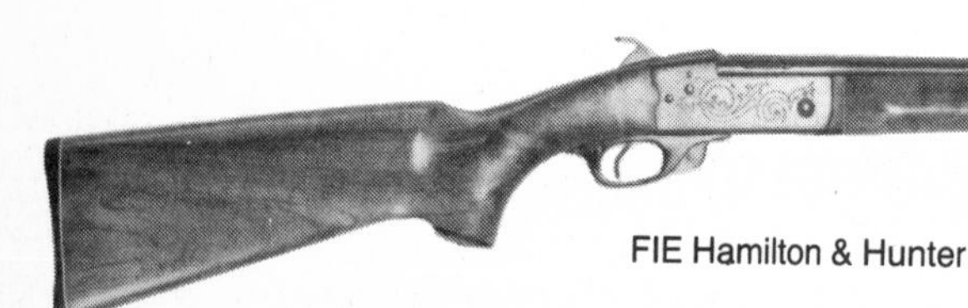

FIE Hamilton & Hunter

F.I.E. "HAMILTON & HUNTER" SINGLE BARREL

Gauge: 12, 20, 410, 3″ chamber.
Barrel: 12, 20 ga. 28″ (Full); 410 ga. (Full).
Weight: 6½ lbs.
Stock: Walnut stained hardwood, beavertail fore-end.
Sights: Metal bead front.
Features: Trigger guard button is pushed to open action. Exposed hammer, auto ejector, three-piece takedown. Imported from Brazil by F.I.E. Corp.
Price: $98.95
Price: Youth model $98.95

Ithaca Custom Trap

ITHACA 5E CUSTOM TRAP SINGLE BARREL

Gauge: 12, 2¾″ chamber.
Barrel: 32″, 34″ (Full).
Weight: 8½ lbs.
Stock: 14⅜″ x 1⅜″ x 1⅜″. AA Fancy American walnut.
Sights: White bead front, brass middle bead.
Features: Frame, top lever, trigger guard extensively engraved and gold inlaid. Reintroduced 1988. From Ithaca Acquisition Corp.
Price: $7,176.00
Price: 5E Dollar Trap...................................... $10,000.00

CAUTION: PRICES CHANGE. CHECK AT GUNSHOP.

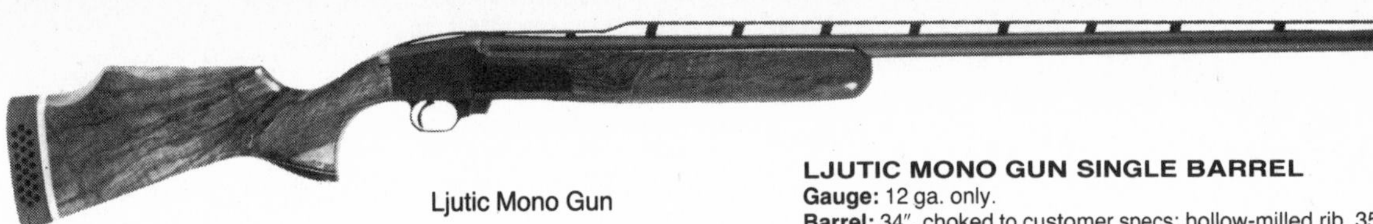

Ljutic Mono Gun

LJUTIC MONO GUN SINGLE BARREL
Gauge: 12 ga. only.
Barrel: 34", choked to customer specs; hollow-milled rib, 35½" sight plane.
Weight: Approx. 9 lbs.
Stock: To customer specs. Oil finish, hand checkered.
Features: Totally custom made. Pull or release trigger; removable trigger guard contains trigger and hammer mechanism; Ljutic pushbutton opener on front of trigger guard. From Ljutic Industries.
Price: **$3,695.00**
Price: With standard, medium or Olympic rib, custom 32"-34" bbls. **$3,795.00**
Price: As above with screw-in choke barrel **$3,995.00**

KRIEGHOFF KS-5 TRAP GUN
Gauge: 12, 2¾" chamber.
Barrel: 32", 34"; Full choke or choke tubes.
Weight: About 8½ lbs.
Stock: 14⅜" x 1⅞" x 1⅜" x 1⅜" or 14⅜" x 2" x 1½" x 1½". Walnut.
Features: Ventilated tapered step rib. Adjustable trigger or release trigger. Receiver finished with electroless nickel. Available with adjustable comb stock. Introduced 1988. Imported from West Germany by Krieghoff International, Inc.
Price: Fixed choke, cased **$2,395.00**

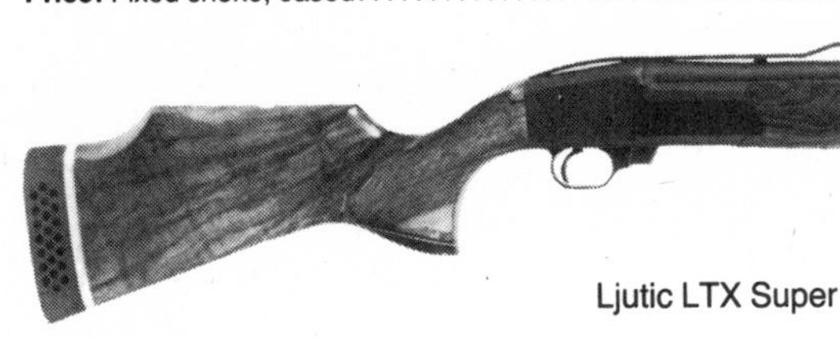

Ljutic LTX Super

Ljutic LTX Super Deluxe Mono Gun
Super Deluxe version of the standard Mono Gun with high quality wood, extra-fancy checkering pattern in 24 l.p.i., double recessed choking. Available in two weights: 8¼ lbs. or 8¾ lbs. Extra light 33" barrel; medium-height rib. Introduced 1984. From Ljutic Industries.
Price: **$4,995.00**
Price: With three screw-in choke tubes **$5,595.00**

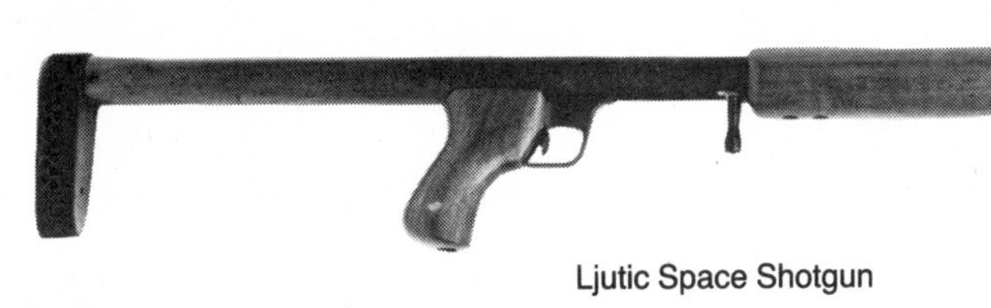

Ljutic Space Shotgun

LJUTIC RECOILLESS SPACE GUN SHOTGUN
Gauge: 12 only, 2¾" chamber.
Barrel: 30" (Full). Screw-in or fixed-choke barrel.
Weight: 8½ lbs.
Stock: 14½" to 15" pull length; universal comb; medium or large p.g.
Sights: Vent. rib.
Features: Pull trigger standard, release trigger available; anti-recoil mechanism. Revolutionary new design. Introduced 1981. From Ljutic Industries.
Price: From **$3,695.00**

Marlin Model 55

MARLIN MODEL 55 GOOSE GUN BOLT ACTION
Gauge: 12 only, 2¾" or 3" chamber.
Action: Bolt action, thumb safety, detachable 2-shot clip. Red cocking indicator.
Barrel: 36" (Full).
Weight: 8 lbs. **Length:** 56¾" over-all.
Stock: Walnut-finished hardwood, p.g., ventilated recoil pad. Swivel studs. Mar-Shield® finish.
Features: Brass bead front sight, U-groove rear sight.
Price: **$213.95**

NAVY ARMS MODEL 105 FOLDING SHOTGUN
Gauge: 12, 20, 410, 3" chamber.
Barrel: 28" (Full); 26" (Full) in 410 ga.
Stock: Walnut-stained hardwood. Checkered p.g. and fore-end. Metal bead front.
Features: Folding, hammerless, top-lever action with cross-bar action. Chrome-lined barrel, blued receiver. Deluxe has vent. rib, engraved hard-chrome receiver. Introduced 1987. From Navy Arms.
Price: Model 105S Standard **$144.50**
Price: Model 105L Deluxe **$158.00**

NEW ENGLAND FIREARMS "PARDNER" SHOTGUN
Gauge: 12, 20, 410, 3" chamber.
Barrel: 12 ga.—28" (Full, Mod.); 20 ga.—26" (Full, Mod.); 410—26" (Full).
Weight: About 5½ lbs. **Length:** 43" over-all (28" barrel).
Stock: Walnut-finished hardwood; 13¾" pull length (12½" youth).
Features: Transfer-bar ignition; side lever action release. Color case-hardened receiver, blued barrel. Introduced 1987. From New England Firearms Co.
Price: .... **NA**

NEW ENGLAND FIREARMS "HANDI-GUN"
Caliber/Gauge: 22 Hornet or 30-30; 20 ga., 3" chamber.
Barrel: 22", interchangeable.
Weight: 6½ lbs. **Length:** 37" over-all.
Stock: American hardwood.
Sights: Rifle—ramp front, open adjustable rear; shotgun barrel has front bead.
Features: Break-open single shot with interchangeable barrels. Matte electroless nickel finish. Introduced 1987. From New England Firearms Co.
Price: Two-barrel system, with carrying case .... **NA**

New England Firearms 10 Gauge Shotgun
Similar ot the 12 ga. "Pardner" except chambered for 3½" 10 ga. shell, has 32" (Full) barrel, giving 47" o.a.l. Introduced 1987.
Price: .... **NA**

CAUTION: PRICES CHANGE. CHECK AT GUNSHOP.

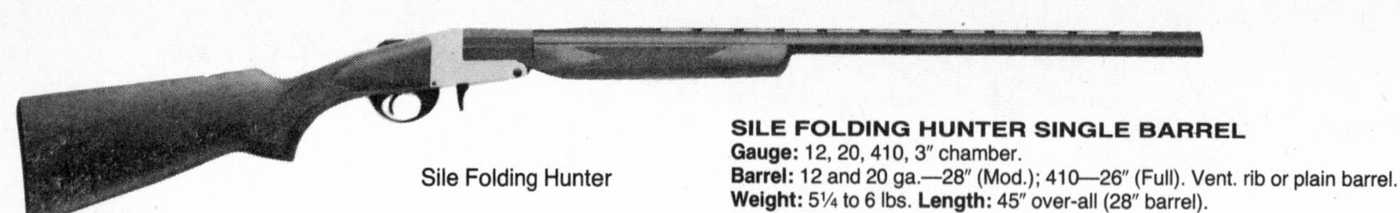

Sile Folding Hunter

SILE FOLDING HUNTER SINGLE BARREL

Gauge: 12, 20, 410, 3″ chamber.
Barrel: 12 and 20 ga.—28″ (Mod.); 410—26″ (Full). Vent. rib or plain barrel.
Weight: 5¼ to 6 lbs. **Length:** 45″ over-all (28″ barrel).
Stock: Walnut, checkered p.g. and fore-end.
Features: Folds in half for storage or carry. Manual safety. Engraved, chromed receiver. Imported by Sile.
Price: Vent. Rib **$139.95**
Price: Plain barrel **$125.95**

Sile Protector

Sile Protector Single Barrel Shotgun
Similar to the Folding Hunter except has grooved walnut pistol grip (no butt-stock), fore-end; 19¾″ barrel; weighs 4.1 lbs., 27″ over-all. In 12, 20, 410 ga. Extractor only. Folds for carry or storage. From Sile.
Price: **$111.95**

WEATHERBY ATHENA SINGLE BARREL TRAP

Gauge: 12, 2¾″ chamber.
Barrel: 32″, 34″ (Full, Mod., Imp. Mod. Multi-Choke tubes).
Weight: About 8½ lbs. **Length:** 49½″ over-all with 32″ barrel.
Stock: 14⅜″ x 1⅜″ x 2⅛″ x 1¾″. American walnut with checkered p.g. and fore-end.
Sights: White front, brass middle bead.
Features: Engraved, silvered sideplate receiver; ventilated rubber recoil pad. Can be ordered with an extra over-under barrel set. Introduced 1988. Imported from Japan by Weatherby.
Price: **$1,611.00**
Price: Combo **$2,100.00**

STOEGER/IGA SINGLE BARREL SHOTGUN

Gauge: 12, 2¾″, 20, 410, 3″.
Barrel: 12, 20 ga.—26″, 28″ (Imp. Cyl., Mod., Full), 410—28″ (Imp. Cyl., Mod., Full).
Weight: 5¼ lbs.
Stock: 14″ x 1½″ x 2½″. Brazilian hardwood.
Sights: Metal bead front.
Features: Exposed hammer with half-cock safety; extractor; blue finish. Introduced 1987. Imported from Brazil by Stoeger Industries.
Price: **$95.00**

SHOTGUNS—MILITARY & POLICE

Designs for utility, suitable for and adaptable to competitions and other sporting purposes.

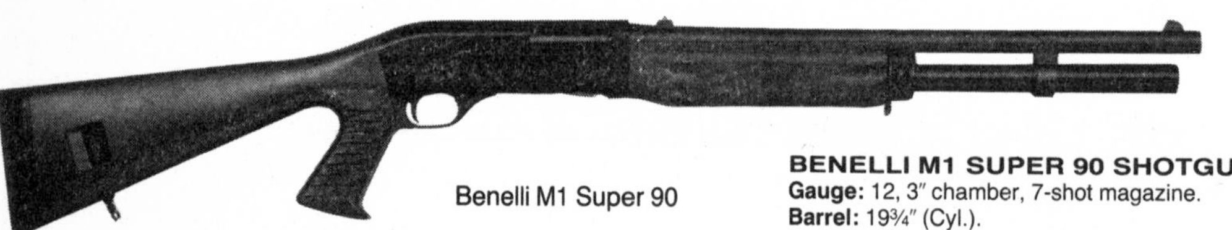

Benelli M1 Super 90

BENELLI M1 SUPER 90 SHOTGUN

Gauge: 12, 3″ chamber, 7-shot magazine.
Barrel: 19¾″ (Cyl.).
Weight: 7 lbs., 4 oz. **Length:** 39¾″ over-all.
Stock: High-impact polymer with sling loop in side of butt; rubberized pistol grip on optional SWAT stock.
Sights: Post front, buckhorn rear adj. for w.
Features: Alloy receiver with rotating locking lug bolt; matte finish; automatic shell release lever. Comes with carrier for speed loading and magazine reducer plug. Optional vent. rib and interchangeable barrels available. Introduced 1986. Imported by Heckler & Koch, Inc.
Price: **$613.00**
Price: With pistol grip stock **$649.50**

ARMSCOR MODEL 30R RIOT GUN

Gauge: 12, 6- or 8-shot capacity.
Barrel: 20″ (Cyl.).
Weight: 6¾ lbs. **Length:** 39″ over-all.
Stock: Plain mahogany.
Sights: Metal bead front.
Features: Double action bars; blue finish; grooved fore-end. Introduced 1987. Imported from the Philippines by Armscor.
Price: About **$202.95**

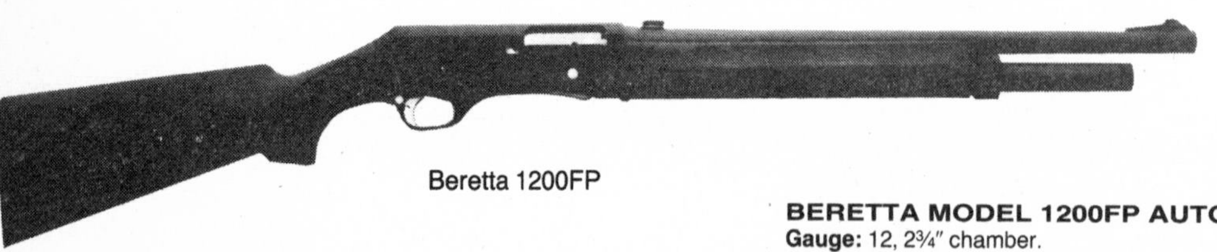

Beretta 1200FP

BERETTA MODEL 1200FP AUTO SHOTGUN

Gauge: 12, 2¾″ chamber.
Barrel: 20″ (Cyl.).
Weight: 7.3 lbs. **Length:** NA
Stock: Special strengthened technopolymer, matte black finish.
Sights: Fixed rifle type.
Features: Has 6-shot magazine. Introduced 1988. Imported from Italy by Beretta U.S.A.
Price: **$440.00**

Consult our Directory pages for the location of firms mentioned.

CAUTION: PRICES CHANGE. CHECK AT GUNSHOP.

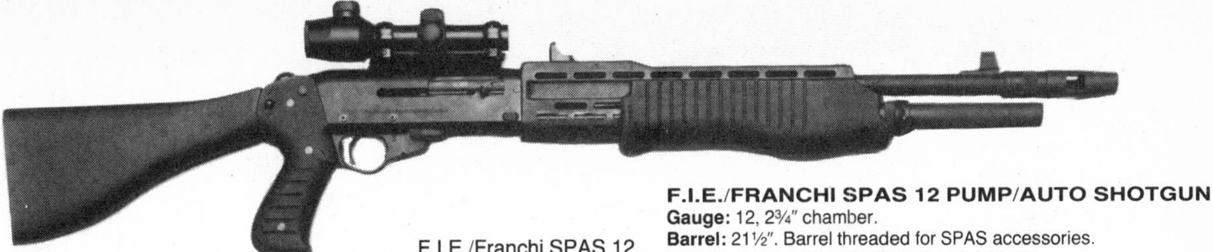

F.I.E./Franchi SPAS 12

F.I.E./FRANCHI SPAS 12 PUMP/AUTO SHOTGUN

Gauge: 12, 2¾" chamber.
Barrel: 21½". Barrel threaded for SPAS accessories.
Weight: 9.6 lbs. **Length:** 31¾" (stock folded).
Stock: Folding metal or optional fixed composition.
Sights: Blade front, aperture rear.
Features: Functions as pump and/or gas-operated auto. Has 8-shot magazine. Parkerized alloy receiver, chrome lined bore, resin pistol grip and pump handle. Made in Italy by Franchi. Introduced 1983. Imported by F.I.E. Corp.
Price: $599.95
Price: Mod. or Full choke tube $39.95
Price: Optional fixed stock $74.95

F.I.E/Franchi LAW 12 Auto Shotgun

A semi-automatic-only lightweight variation of the SPAS 12 pump/auto. Has a 21½" barrel, 8-shot magazine, matte black finish. Over-all length is 41½", weight about 7½ lbs. Stock and pistol grip of nylon resin is detachable. Accessories include shot diverter tube, Full or Modified choke tubes, scope mount, olive drab sling, take-down tool, carry handle. Introduced 1987. Imported from Italy by F.I.E.
Price: $559.95

F.I.E./Franchi SAS 12

F.I.E./Franchi SAS 12 Pump Shotgun

A slide-action-only, lightweight variation of the SPAS 12 pump/auto shotgun, with the same specifications as the LAW 12. Introduced 1987. Imported from Italy by F.I.E.
Price: $359.95

Holmes Model 88

HOLMES MODEL 88 PUMP SHOTGUN

Gauge: 12, 2¾" chamber, 5- or 10-shot magazine.
Barrel: 18¼" (Cyl.); 20" (choke tubes).
Weight: 9 lbs. **Length:** 38¼" over-all (18¼" barrel).
Stock: Synthetic.
Sights: Post front, fixed rear.
Features: Double action bars; matte blue finish. Announced 1988. From Holmes Firearms.
Price: With one magazine $495.00
Price: Extra magazines, each $40.00

ITHACA MODEL 87 M&P DSPS SHOTGUNS

Gauge: 12, 3" chamber, 5 or 8-shot magazine.
Barrel: 20" (Cyl.).
Weight: 7 lbs.
Stock: Walnut.
Sights: Bead front on 5-shot, rifle sights on 8-shot.
Features: Parkerized finish; bottom ejection; cross-bolt safety. Reintroduced 1988. From Ithaca Acquisition Corp.
Price: M&P, 5-shot $338.00
Price: DSPS, 8-shot $338.00

Ithaca Model 87 Hand Grip Shotgun

Similar to the Model 87 M&P except has black polymer pistol grip and slide handle with nylon sling. In 12 or 20 gauge, 18½" barrel (Cyl.), 5-shot magazine. Reintroduced 1988.
Price: $355.00

Mossberg 500

MOSSBERG MODEL 500 SECURITY SHOTGUNS

Gauge: 12, 2¾" chamber.
Barrel: 18½", 20" (Cyl.).
Weight: 7 lbs.
Stock: Walnut-finished hardwood; synthetic field or Speedfeed.
Sights: Metal bead front.
Features: Available in 6- or 8-shot models. Top-mounted safety, double action slide bars, swivel studs, rubber recoil pad. Blue, Parkerized or electroless nickel finishes. Price list not complete—contact Mossberg for full list.
Price: From about $251.95
Price: Mini Combo (as above except also comes with a handguard and pistol grip kit), from about $258.95
Price: Maxi Combo (as above except also comes with an extra field barrel), from about $279.95

Mossberg Model 500 Mariner Pump

Similar to the Model 500 Security except all metal parts finished with MARINECOAT, a Teflon and metal coating to resist rust and corrosion. Choice of synthetic field or Speedfeed stocks or pistol grip.
Price: From about $349.95
Price: Mini Combo (as above except includes handguard and pistol grip kit), about $389.95

Mossberg 590

Mossberg Bullpup

Mossberg Model 590 Military Shotgun

Similar to the Model 500 Security except has 20″ barrel only, 9-shot magazine. Available with wood stock, synthetic field, Speedfeed stock. Introduced 1987.

Price: Wood stock, blue **$328.95**
Price: Speedfeed stock, Parkerized **$402.95**
Price: Synthetic stock, Parkerized **$369.95**

MOSSBERG 500 BULLPUP

Gauge: 12, 2¾″ chamber; 6- or 8-shot.
Barrel: 18½″, 20″ (Cyl.).
Weight: 9½ lbs. (6 shot). **Length:** 28½″ over-all (18½″ bbl.).
Stock: Bullpup design of high-impact plastics.
Sights: Fixed, mounted in carrying handle.
Features: Uses the M500 pump shotgun action. Cross-bolt and grip safeties. Introduced 1986.
Price: 6 shot **$394.95**
Price: 8 shot **$409.95**

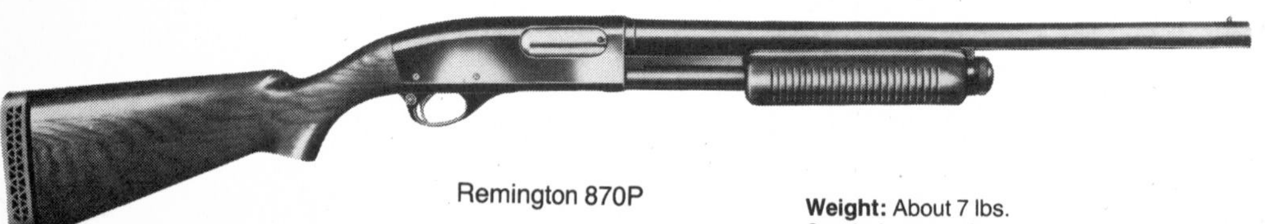

Remington 870P

REMINGTON MODEL 870P POLICE SHOTGUN

Gauge: 12, 3″ chamber.
Barrel: 18″, 20″ (Police Cyl.), 20″ (Imp. Cyl.).
Weight: About 7 lbs.
Stock: Lacquer-finished hardwood or folding stock.
Sights: Meal bead front or rifle sights.
Features: Solid steel receiver, double-action slide bars.
Price: Wood stock, 18″ or 20″, bead sight, about **$312.00**
Price: Wood stock, 20″, rifle sights, about **$333.00**

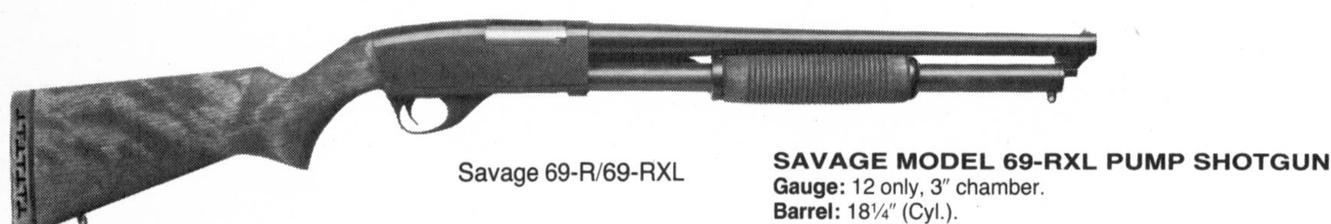

Savage 69-R/69-RXL

Savage Model 69-RXG Pump Shotgun

Similar to the Model 69-RXL except has pistol grip and grooved slide handle of DuPont Rynite® composition. Introduced 1988.

Price: **$189.00**

SAVAGE MODEL 69-RXL PUMP SHOTGUN

Gauge: 12 only, 3″ chamber.
Barrel: 18¼″ (Cyl.).
Weight: 6½ lbs. **Length:** 38″ over-all.
Stock: Walnut-finished hardwood.
Sights: Bead front.
Features: Top tang safety, 7-shot magazine. Stock has fluted comb and full pistol grip, ventilated rubber pad. QD swivel studs. Introduced 1982.
Price: **$179.00**

STEVENS MODEL 311-R GUARD GUN DOUBLE

Gauge: 12 ga., 3″ chambers.
Barrel: 18¼″ (Cyl. & Cyl.).
Weight: 6¾ lbs. **Length:** 34″ over-all.
Stock: Walnut-finished hardwood.
Sights: Bead front.
Features: Top tang safety, double triggers, color case-hardened frame, blue barrels. Ventilated rubber recoil pad. Introduced 1982.
Price: **$249.00**

USAS-12 AUTO SHOTGUN

Gauge: 12, 2¾″; 10- or 20-shot drum magazine.
Barrel: 18¼″ (Cyl.).
Weight: 10 lbs. **Length:** 38″ over-all.
Stock: Composition butt, pistol grip, fore-end.
Sights: Fixed.
Features: Gas-operated action; Parkerized finish. From Gilbert Equipment Co.
Price: **$700.00**

Winchester Defender

WINCHESTER DEFENDER PUMP GUN

Gauge: 12, 3″ chamber, 5 or 8-shot capacity.
Barrel: 18″ (Cyl.).
Weight: 6¾ lbs. **Length:** 38⅝″ over-all.
Stock: Walnut finished hardwood stock and ribbed fore-end.
Sights: Metal bead front.
Features: Cross-bolt safety, front-locking rotating bolt, twin action slide bars. Black rubber butt pad. Made under license by U.S. Repeating Arms Co.
Price: 8-shot, about **$233.00**
Price: 5-shot, about **$224.00**
Price: As above with rifle sights, about **$240.00**
Price: Defender Combo (with p.g. and extra 28″ bbl.) **$261.00**
Price: As above with extra vent. rib bbl. **$280.00**

Winchester Pistol Grip Pump Security Shotguns

Same as regular Security Series but with pistol grip and fore-end of high-impact resistant ABS plastic with non-glare black finish. Introduced 1984.

Price: Pistol Grip Defender, about **$233.00**

Winchester "Stainless Marine" Pump Gun

Same as the Defender except has bright chrome finish, stainless-steel barrel, rifle-type sights only. Has special fore-end cap for easy cleaning and inspection.

Price: About **$387.00**

The following pages catalog the black powder arms currently available to U.S. shooters. These range from quite precise replicas of historically significant arms to toally new designs created expressly to give the black powder shooter the benefits of modern technology.

Most of the replicas are imported, and many are available from more than one source. Thus, examples of a given model such as the 1860 Army revolver or Zouave rifle purchased from different importers may vary in price, finish and fitting. Most of them bear proof marks, indicating that they have been test fired in the proof house of their country of origin.

A list of the importers and the retail price range are included with the description for each model. Many local dealers handle more than one importer's products, giving the prospective buyer an opportunity to make his own judgment in selecting a black powder gun. Most importers have catalogs available free or at nominal cost, and some are well worth having for the useful information on black powder shooting they provide in addition to their detailed descriptions and specifications of the guns.

A number of special accessories are also available for the black powder shooter. These include replica powder flasks, bullet moulds, cappers and tools, as well as more modern devices to facilitate black powder cleaning and maintenance. Ornate presentation cases and even detachable shoulder stocks are also available for some black powder pistols from their importers. Again, dealers or the importers will have catalogs.

The black powder guns are arranged in four sections: Single Shot Pistols, Revolvers, Muskets & Rifles, and Shotguns. The guns within each section are arranged roughly by date of the original, with the oldest first. Thus the 1836 Paterson replica leads off the revolver section, and flintlocks precede percussion arms in the other sections.

BLACK POWDER SINGLE SHOT PISTOLS—FLINT & PERCUSSION

Scottish Black Watch

Dixie Charleville

Dixie Queen Anne

Lyman Plains Pistol

BLACK WATCH SCOTCH PISTOL

Caliber: 577 (.550″ round ball).
Barrel: 7″, smoothbore.
Weight: 1½ lbs. **Length:** 12″ over-all.
Stock: Brass.
Sights: None.
Features: Faithful reproduction of this military flintlock. From Dixie.
Price: $135.00

CHARLEVILLE FLINTLOCK PISTOL

Caliber: 69 (.680″ round ball).
Barrel: 7½″.
Weight: 48 oz. **Length:** 13½″ over-all.
Stock: Walnut.
Sights: None.
Features: Brass frame, polished steel barrel, iron belt hook, brass buttcap and backstrap. Replica of original 1777 pistol. Imported by Dixie.
Price: $140.00

DIXIE QUEEN ANNE FLINTLOCK PISTOL

Caliber: 50 (.490″ round ball).
Barrel: 7½″, smoothbore.
Stock: Walnut.
Sights: None.
Features: Browned steel barrel, fluted brass trigger guard, brass mask on butt. Lockplate left in the white. Made by Pedersoli in Italy. Introduced 1983. Imported by Dixie Gun Works.
Price: $131.00
Price: Kit $115.00

LYMAN PLAINS PISTOL

Caliber: 50 or 54.
Barrel: 8″, 1-in-30″ twist, both calibers.
Weight: 50 oz. **Length:** 15″ over-all.
Stock: Walnut half-stock.
Sights: Blade front, square notch rear adj. for windage.
Features: Polished brass trigger guard and ramrod tip, color case-hardened coil spring lock, spring-loaded trigger, stainless steel nipple, blackened iron furniture. Hooked patent breech, detachable belt hook. Introduced 1981. From Lyman Products.
Price: Finished $159.95
Price: Kit $129.00

DIXIE PENNSYLVANIA PISTOL

Caliber: 44 (.430″ round ball).
Barrel: 10″ (⅞″ octagon).
Weight: 2½ lbs.
Stock: Walnut-stained hardwood.
Sights: Blade front, open rear drift-adj. for windage; brass.
Features: Available in flint only. Brass trigger guard, thimbles, nosecap, wedgeplates; high-luster blue barrel. Imported from Italy by Dixie Gun Works.
Price: Finished $119.95
Price: Kit $88.75

BLACK POWDER SINGLE SHOT PISTOLS—FLINT & PERCUSSION

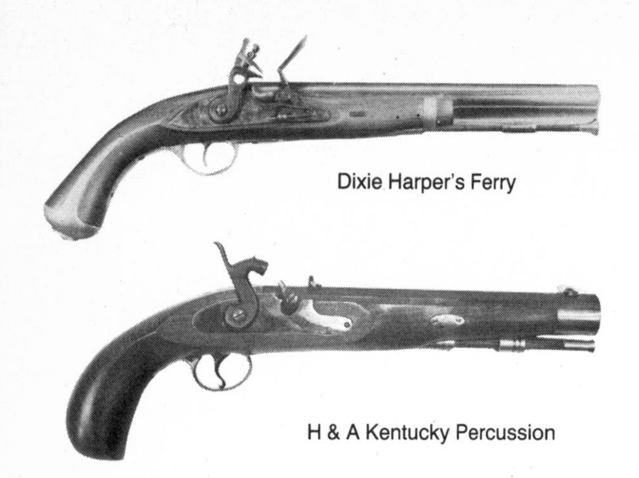

Dixie Harper's Ferry

H & A Kentucky Percussion

Kentucky Percussion Pistol
Similar to flint version but percussion lock. Imported by The Armoury, Navy Arms, CVA, Armsport, Hopkins & Allen, Muzzle Loaders, Inc., Traditions.
Price: .... **$97.50** to **$139.00**
Price: In kit form (Traditions, Armoury).......... **$35.95** to **$102.00**
Price: Single cased set (Navy Arms) **$230.00**
Price: Double cased set (Navy Arms) **$360.00**

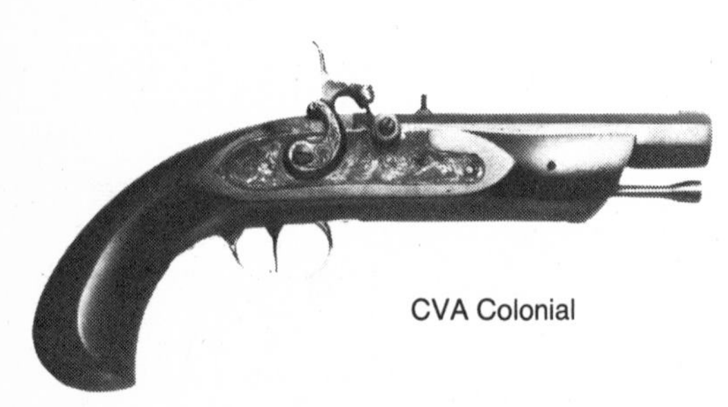

CVA Colonial

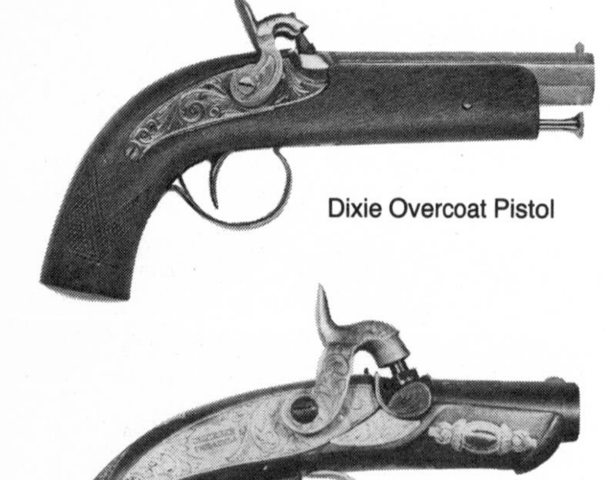

Dixie Overcoat Pistol

Dixie Lincoln Derringer

PHILADELPHIA DERRINGER PERCUSSION PISTOL
Caliber: 45.
Barrel: 3⅛″.
Weight: 16 oz. **Length:** 7″ over-all.
Stock: Select hardwood.
Sights: Fixed.
Features: Engraved wedge holder and bbl. Imported by CVA.
Price: **$74.95**
Price: Kit form.......... **$41.95**

HARPER'S FERRY 1806 PISTOL
Caliber: 58 (.570″ round ball).
Barrel: 10″.
Weight: 40 oz. **Length:** 16″ over-all.
Stock: Walnut.
Sights: Fixed.
Features: Case-hardened lock, brass mounted browned bbl. Replica of the first U.S. Gov't.-made flintlock pistol. Imported by Navy Arms, Dixie, EMF.
Price: .... **$$165.00** to **270.00**
Price: Kit (Dixie) **$135.00**

KENTUCKY FLINTLOCK PISTOL
Caliber: 44, 45.
Barrel: 10⅛″.
Weight: 32 oz. **Length:** 15½″ over-all.
Stock: Walnut.
Sights: Fixed.
Features: Specifications, including caliber, weight and length may vary with importer. Case-hardened lock, blued bbl.; available also as brass bbl. flint Model 1821. Imported by Armsport, Navy Arms (44 only), The Armoury, EMF.
Price: .... **$40.95** to **$207.00**
Price: In kit form, from.......... **$90.00** to **$112.00**
Price: Single cased set (Navy Arms) **$235.00**
Price: Double cased set (Navy Arms) **$389.00**

CVA COLONIAL PISTOL
Caliber: 45.
Barrel: 6¾″, octagonal, rifled.
Length: 12¾″ over-all.
Stock: Selected hardwood.
Features: Case-hardened lock, brass furniture, fixed sights. Steel ramrod. Available in percussion only. Imported by CVA.
Price: Finished **$86.95**
Price: Kit **$57.95**

DIXIE OVERCOAT PISTOL
Caliber: 39.
Barrel: 4″ smoothbore.
Weight: 13 oz. **Length:** 8″ over-all.
Stock: Walnut-finished hardwood. Checkered p.g.
Sights: Bead front.
Features: Shoots .380″ balls. Breech plug and engraved lock are burnished steel finish; barrel and trigger guard blued.
Price: Engraved model **$34.50**

DIXIE W. PARKER FLINTLOCK PISTOL
Caliber: 45.
Barrel: 11″, rifled.
Weight: 40 oz. **Length:** 16½″ over-all.
Stock: Walnut.
Sights: Blade front, notch rear.
Features: Browned barrel, silver plated trigger guard, finger rest, polished and engraved lock. Double set triggers. Imported by Dixie Gun Works.
Price: **$270.00**

DIXIE LINCOLN DERRINGER
Caliber: 41.
Barrel: 2″, 8 lands, 8 grooves.
Weight: 7 oz. **Length:** 5½″ over-all.
Stock: Walnut finish, checkered.
Sights: Fixed.
Features: Authentic copy of the "Lincoln Derringer." Shoots .400″ patched ball. German silver furniture includes trigger guard with pineapple finial, wedge plates, nose, wrist, side and teardrop inlays. All furniture, lockplate, hammer, and breech plug engraved. Imported from Italy by Dixie Gun Works.
Price: With wooden case **$285.95**
Price: Kit (not engraved).......... **$89.95**

CAUTION: PRICES CHANGE. CHECK AT GUNSHOP.

Dixie Philadelphia

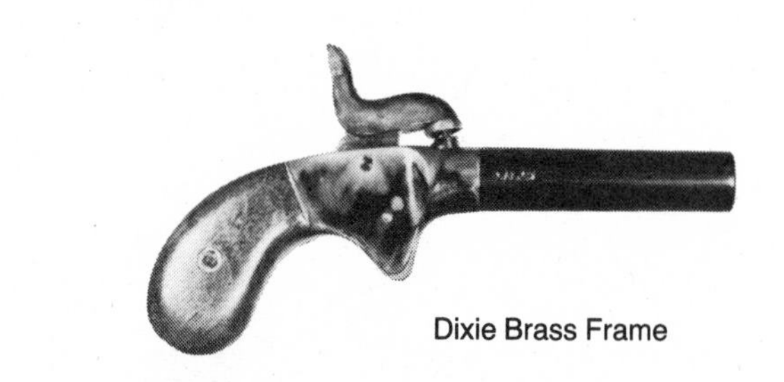
Dixie Brass Frame

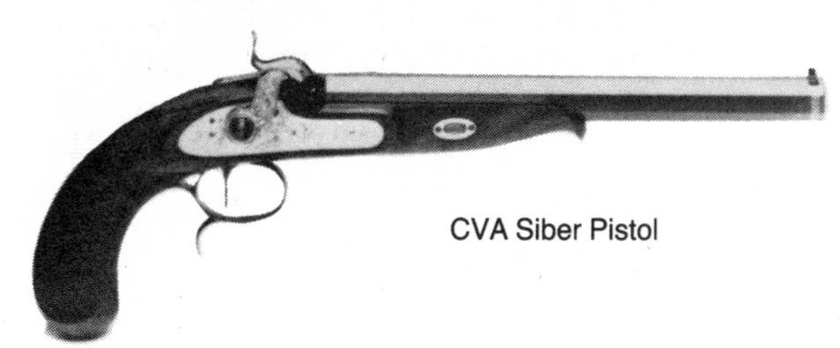
CVA Siber Pistol

FRENCH-STYLE DUELING PISTOL
Caliber: 44.
Barrel: 10″.
Weight: 35 ozs. **Length:** 15¾″ over-all.
Stock: Carved walnut.
Sights: Fixed.
Features: Comes with velvet-lined case and accessories. Imported by Mandall Shooting Supplies.
Price: **$295.00**

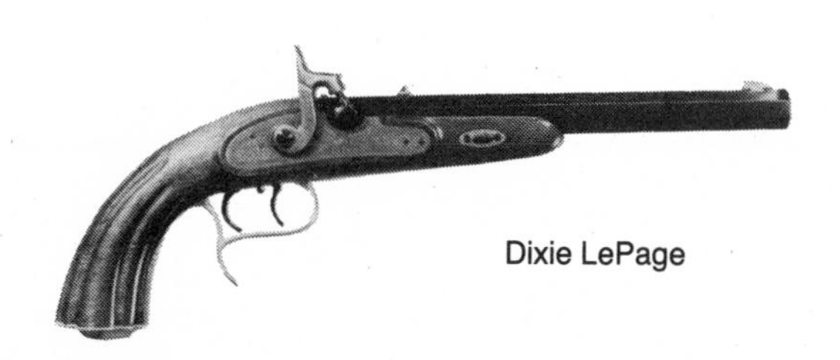
Dixie LePage

NAVY ARMS LE PAGE DUELING PISTOL
Caliber: 45.
Barrel: 9″, octagon, rifled.
Weight: 34 oz. **Length:** 15″ over-all.
Stock: European walnut.
Sights: Adjustable rear.
Features: Single set trigger. Polished metal finish. From Navy Arms.
Price: Percussion **$312.00**
Price: Single cased set, percussion **$560.00**
Price: Double cased set, percussion **$900.00**
Price: Flintlock, rifled **$340.00**
Price: Flintlock, smoothbore **$340.00**
Price: Flintlock, single cased set **$659.00**
Price: Flintlock, double cased set **$1,100.00**

DIXIE PHILADELPHIA DERRINGER
Caliber: 41.
Barrel: 3½″, octagon.
Weight: 8 oz. **Length:** 5½″ over-all.
Stock: Walnut, checkered p.g.
Sights: Fixed.
Features: Barrel and lock are blued; brass furniture. From Dixie Gun Works.
Price: **$45.00**

DIXIE BRASS FRAME DERRINGER
Caliber: 41.
Barrel: 2½″.
Weight: 7 oz. **Length:** 5½″ over-all.
Stocks: Walnut.
Features: Brass frame, color case-hardened hammer and trigger. Shoots .395″ round ball. Engraved model available. From Dixie Gun Works.
Price: Plain model **$49.95**
Price: Engraved model **$74.95**
Price: Kit form, plain model **$42.50**

DIXIE ABILENE DERRINGER
Caliber: 41.
Barrel: 2½″, 6-groove rifling.
Weight: 8 oz. **Length:** 6½″ over-all.
Stock: Walnut.
Features: All steel version of Dixie's brass-framed derringers. Blued barrel, color case-hardened frame and hammer. Shoots .395″ patched ball. Comes with wood presentation case.
Price: **$69.95**
Price: Kit form **$51.95**

CVA SIBER PISTOL
Caliber: 45.
Barrel: 10½″.
Weight: 34 oz. **Length:** 15½″ over-all.
Stock: High-grade French walnut, checkered grip.
Sights: Barleycorn front, micro adjustable rear.
Features: Reproduction of pistol made by Swiss watchmaker Jean Siber in the 1800s. Precise lock and set trigger give fast lock time. Has engraving, blackened stainless barrel, trigger guard. Imported by CVA.
Price: **$314.95**

MOORE & PATRICK FLINT DUELING PISTOL
Caliber: 45.
Barrel: 10″, rifled.
Weight: 32 oz. **Length:** 14½″ over-all.
Stock: European walnut, checkered.
Sights: Fixed.
Features: Engraved, silvered lock plate, blue barrel. German silver furniture. Imported from Italy by Hopkins & Allen, Dixie.
Price: **$285.00**

DIXIE LE PAGE PERCUSSION DUELING PISTOL
Caliber: 45.
Barrel: 10″, rifled.
Weight: 40 oz. **Length:** 16″ over-all.
Stock: Walnut, fluted butt.
Sights: Blade front, notch rear.
Features: Double set triggers. Blued barrel; trigger guard and butt cap are polished silver. Imported by Dixie Gun Works.
Price: **$225.00**

DIXIE SCREW BARREL PISTOL
Caliber: .445″.
Barrel: 2½″.
Weight: 8 oz. **Length:** 6½″ over-all.
Stock: Walnut.
Features: Trigger folds down when hammer is cocked. Close copy of the originals once made in Belgium. Uses No. 11 percussion caps.
Price: **$89.00**
Price: Kit **$53.00**

BLACK POWDER SINGLE SHOT PISTOLS—FLINT & PERCUSSION

ELGIN CUTLASS PISTOL
Caliber: 44 (.440").
Barrel: 4¼".
Weight: 21 oz. **Length:** 12" over-all.
Stock: Walnut.
Sights: None.
Features: Replica of the pistol used by the U.S. Navy as a boarding weapon. Smoothbore barrel. Available as a kit or finished. Made in U.S. by Navy Arms.
Price: Kit $78.50
Price: Finished $104.95

NAVY ARMS SNAKE EYES
Caliber: 36.
Barrel: 2⅝", double barrel.
Weight: 24 ozs. **Length:** 6¾" over-all.
Stocks: Composition pearl.
Sights: None.
Features: Solid brass barrels and receiver. Also comes in kit form, 90% complete with only 14 pieces. From Navy Arms.
Price: Complete $74.95
Price: Kit $54.00

ETHAN ALLEN PEPPERBOX
Caliber: 36.
Barrel: 3⅛", four smoothbore barrels.
Weight: 38 oz. **Length:** 9" over-all.
Stock: Walnut.
Sights: None.
Features: Steel barrels, brass receiver. Also comes in kit form, 90% completed. From Navy Arms.
Price: Complete $79.95
Price: Kit $59.25

NEW ORLEANS ACE
Caliber: 44.
Barrel: 3½", rifled or smoothbore.
Weight: 16 oz. **Length:** 9" over-all.
Stock: Walnut.
Sights: None.
Features: Solid brass frame (receiver). Available complete or in kit form. Kit is 90% complete, no drilling or tapping, fully inletted. From Navy Arms.
Price: Complete (smoothbore) $58.50
Price: Kit (smoothbore) $43.25

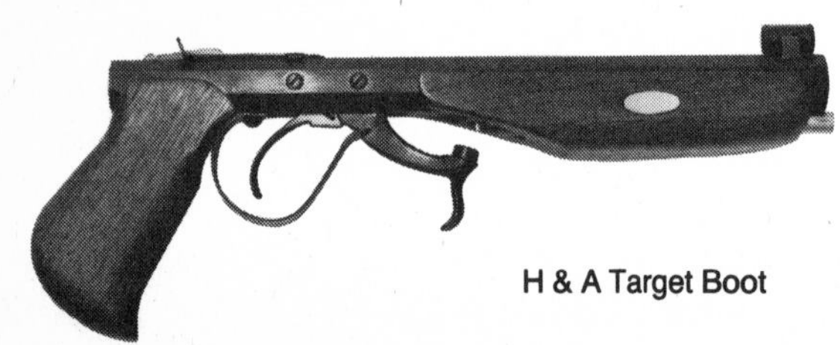

H & A Target Boot

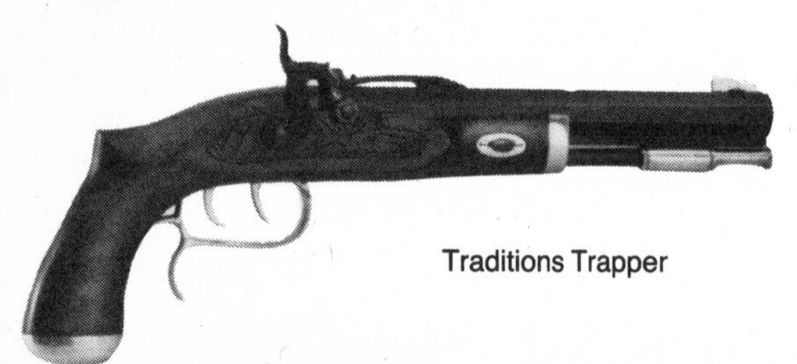

Traditions Trapper

Dixie Tornado Pistol

Elgin Cutlass Pistol

NAVY ARMS DUCKFOOT
Caliber: 36.
Barrel: 2⅞", three barrels.
Weight: 32 oz. **Length:** 10½" over-all.
Stock: Walnut.
Sights: None.
Features: Steel barrels and receiver, brass frame. Also comes in kit form, 90% completed, no drilling or tapping. From Navy Arms.
Price: Complete $69.95
Price: Kit $48.95

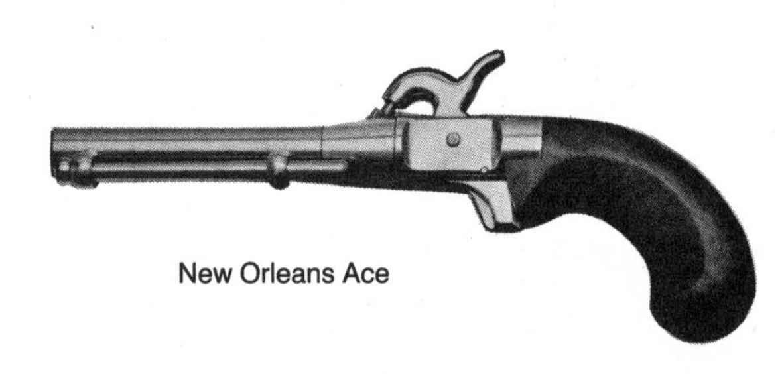

New Orleans Ace

HOPKINS & ALLEN BOOT PISTOL
Caliber: 45.
Barrel: 6".
Weight: 42 oz. **Length:** 13" over-all.
Stock: Walnut.
Sights: Silver blade front, rear adj. for e.
Features: Under-hammer design. From Hopkins & Allen.
Price: Kit form $78.65
Price: Target version with wood fore-end, ramrod, hood front sight, elevator rear $98.80

CVA VEST POCKET DERRINGER
Caliber: 44.
Barrel: 2½", brass.
Weight: 7 oz.
Stock: Two-piece walnut.
Features: All brass frame with brass ramrod. A muzzle-loading version of the Colt No. 3 derringer.
Price: Finished $43.95
Price: Kit $37.95

TRADITIONS TRAPPER PISTOL
Caliber: 45, 50.
Barrel: 10¾", ⅞" flats.
Weight: 1¾ lbs. **Length:** 16⅝" over-all.
Stock: Beech.
Sights: Blade front, adjustable rear.
Features: Double set triggers; brass butt cap, trigger guard, wedge plate, fore-end tip, thimble. From Traditions Inc.
Price: $108.00
Price: Kit $85.00

DIXIE TORNADO TARGET PISTOL
Caliber: 44 (.430" round ball).
Barrel: 10", octagonal, 1-in-22" twist.
Stock: Walnut, target-style. Left unfinished for custom fitting. Walnut fore-end.
Sights: Blade on ramp front, micro-type open rear adjustable for windage and elevation.
Features: Grip frame style of 1860 Colt revolver. Improved model of the Tingle and B.W. Southgate pistol. Trigger adjustable for pull. Frame, barrel, hammer and sights in the white, brass trigger guard. Comes with solid brass, walnut-handled cleaning rod with jag and nylon muzzle protector. Introduced 1983. From Dixie Gun Works.
Price: $151.95

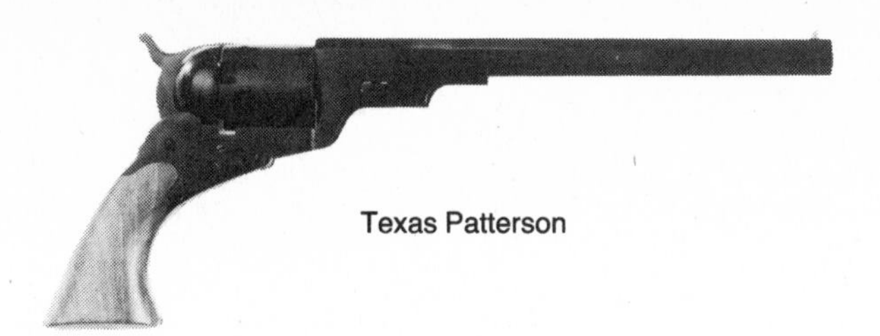
Texas Patterson

TEXAS PATERSON 1836 REVOLVER

Caliber: 36 (.376″ round ball).
Barrel: 7½″.
Weight: 42 oz.
Stocks: One-piece walnut.
Sights: Fixed.
Features: Copy of Sam Colt's first commercially-made revolving pistol. Has no loading lever but comes with loading tool. From Dixie Gun Works, Navy Arms.
Price: .... **$310.00** to **$320.00**

WALKER 1847 PERCUSSION REVOLVER

Caliber: 44, 6-shot.
Barrel: 9″.
Weight: 84 oz. **Length:** 15½″ over-all.
Stocks: Walnut.
Sights: Fixed.
Features: Case-hardened frame, loading lever and hammer; iron backstrap; brass trigger guard; engraved cylinder. Imported by CVA, Muzzleloaders, Inc., Navy Arms, Dixie, Armsport, Benson Firearms.
Price: About .... **$185.00** to **$295.00**
Price: Single cased set (Navy Arms) **$350.00**
Price: Preassembled kit (CVA) **$166.95**

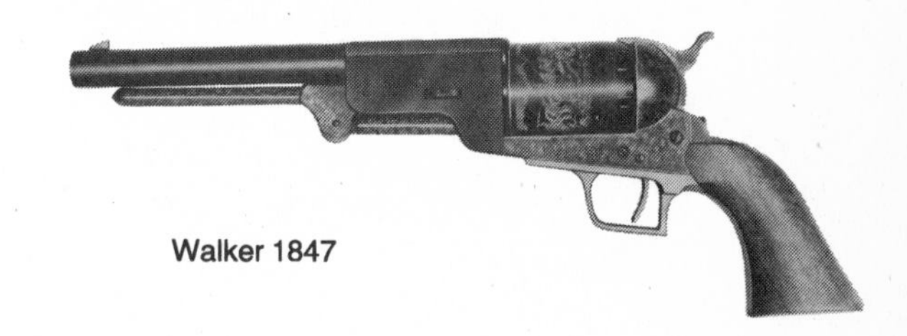
Walker 1847

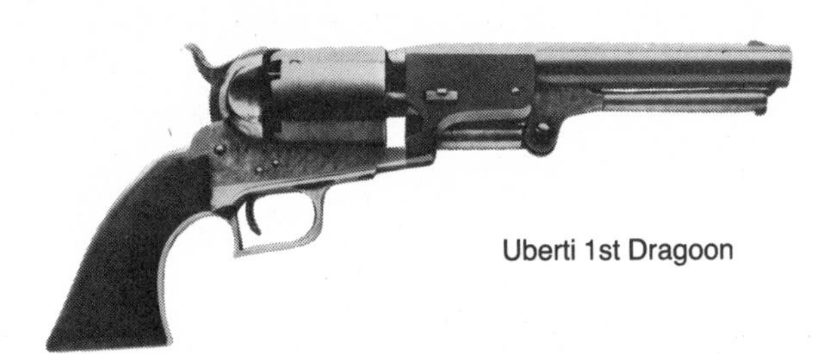
Uberti 1st Dragoon

UBERTI 1st MODEL DRAGOON

Caliber: 44.
Barrel: 7½″, part round, part octagon.
Weight: 64 oz.
Stocks: One piece walnut.
Sights: German silver blade front, hammer notch rear.
Features: First model has oval bolt cuts in cylinder, square-back flared trigger guard, V-type mainspring, short trigger. Ranger and Indian scene roll-engraved on cylinder. Color case-hardened frame, loading lever, plunger and hammer; blue barrel, cylinder, trigger and wedge. Available with old-time charcoal blue or standard blue-black finish. Polished brass backstrap and trigger guard. From Benson Firearms, Uberti USA.
Price: **$240.00**

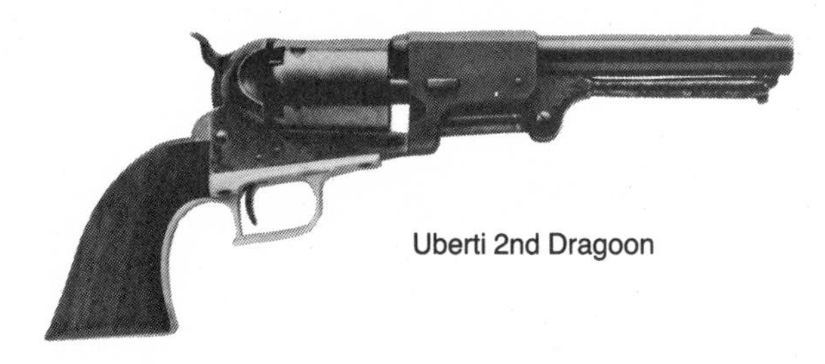
Uberti 2nd Dragoon

Uberti 2nd Model Dragoon Revolver

Similar to the 1st Model except this model is distinguished by its rectangular bolt cuts in the cylinder.
Price: **$240.00**
Price: As Confederate Tucker & Sherrard, with 3rd Model loading lever and special cylinder engraving.......... **$240.00**

Uberti 3rd Model Dragoon Revolver

Similar to the 2nd Model except for oval trigger guard, long trigger, modifications to the loading lever and latch. Imported by Benson Firearms, Uberti USA.
Price: Military (frame cut for shoulder stock, steel backstrap) **$269.00**
Price: Civilian (brass backstrap, trigger guard).......... **$240.00**
Price: Western (silver-plated backstrap, trigger guard).......... **$269.00**
Price: Shoulder stock **$139.00**

Dixie Third Dragoon

DIXIE THIRD MODEL DRAGOON

Caliber: 44 (.454″ round ball).
Barrel: 7⅜″.
Weight: 4 lbs., 2½ oz.
Stocks: One-piece walnut.
Sights: Brass pin front, hammer notch rear, or adjustable folding leaf rear.
Features: Cylinder engraved with Indian fight scene. This is the only Dragoon replica with folding leaf sight. Brass backstrap and trigger guard; color case-hardened steel frame, blue-black barrel. Imported by Dixie Gun Works.
Price: **$185.00**

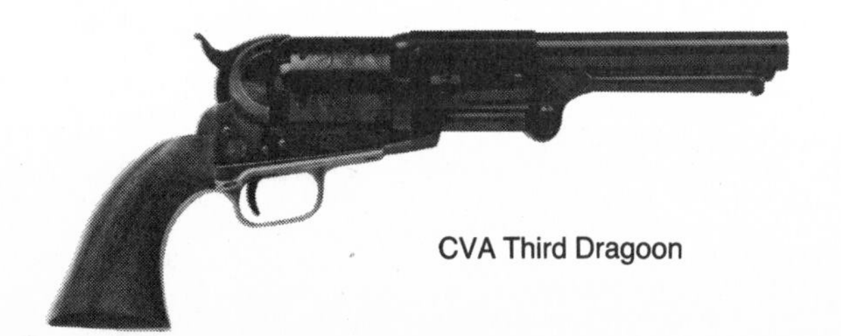
CVA Third Dragoon

CVA Third Model Colt Dragoon

Similar to the Dixie Third Dragoon except has 7½″ barrel, weighs 4 lbs., 6 ozs., blade front sight. Over-all length of 14″. 44 caliber, 6-shot.
Price: **$182.95**

Dixie 1848

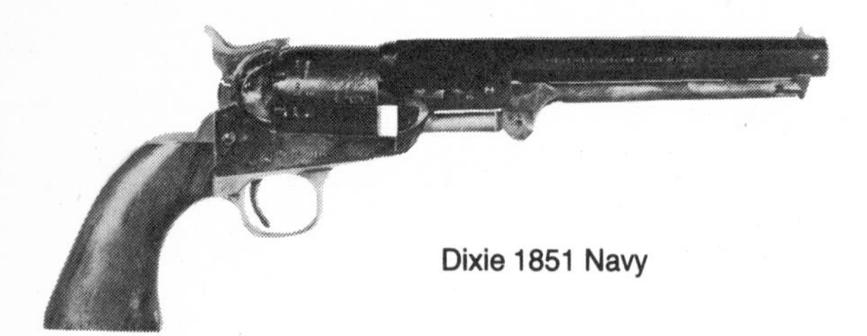

Dixie 1851 Navy

Uberti 1851 Squareback

1851 SHERIFF MODEL PERCUSSION REVOLVER

Caliber: 36, 44, 6-shot.
Barrel: 5".
Weight: 40 oz. **Length:** 10½" over-all.
Stocks: Walnut.
Sights: Fixed.
Features: Brass backstrap and trigger guard; engraved navy scene; case-hardened frame, hammer, loading lever. Imported by E.M.F, Sile.
Price: Steel frame **$170.00**
Price: Brass frame.................................. **$90.95** to **$125.00**
Price: Kit, brass or steel frame .... **$114.00** to **$160.00**

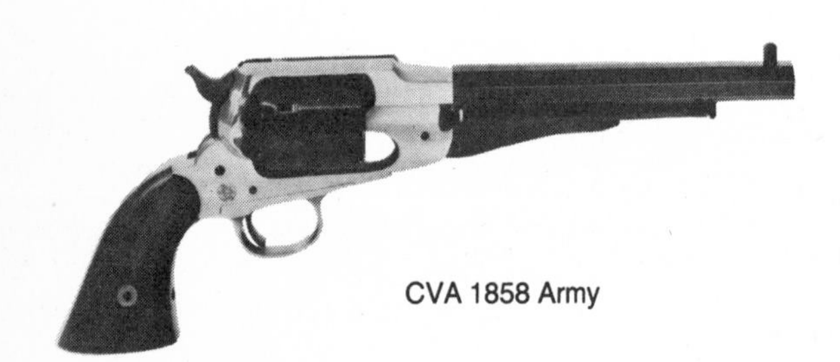

CVA 1858 Army

Uberti 1861 Navy Percussion Revolver

Similar to 1851 Navy except has round 7½" barrel, rounded trigger guard, German silver blade front sight, "creeping" loading lever. Available with fluted or round cylinder. Imported by Benson Firearms, Uberti USA.
Price: Steel backstrap, trigger guard, cut for stock **$245.00**
Price: Brass backstrap, trigger guard............................ **$229.00**
Price: Silver plated backstrap, trigger guard..................... **$249.00**
Price: Stainless steel.. **$305.00**

CVA 1858 Remington Target

Similar to the New Model 1858 Remington except has ramped blade front sight, adjustable rear.
Price:... **$182.95**

1848 BABY DRAGOON, 1849 POCKET, WELLS FARGO REVOLVERS

Caliber: 31.
Barrel: 3", 4", 5"; 7 groove, RH twist.
Weight: About 21 oz.
Stocks: Varnished walnut.
Sights: Brass pin front, hammer notch rear.
Features: No loading lever on Baby Dragoon or Wells Fargo models. Unfluted cylinder with stagecoach holdup scene; cupped cylinder pin; no grease grooves; one safety pin on cylinder and slot in hammer face; straight (flat) mainspring. From Benson Firearms, Dixie, Uberti USA.
Price: 6" barrel, with loading lever (Dixie) **$150.00**
Price: Brass backstrap, trigger guard (Benson, Uberti USA)........ **$229.00**
Price: As above, silver plated (Benson, Uberti USA)............... **$240.00**

NAVY MODEL 1851 PERCUSSION REVOLVER

Caliber: 36, 44, 6-shot.
Barrel: 7½".
Weight: 44 oz. **Length:** 13" over-all.
Stocks: Walnut finish.
Sights: Post front, hammer notch rear.
Features: Brass backstrap and trigger guard; some have 1st Model squareback trigger guard, engraved cylinder with navy battle scene; case-hardened frame, hammer, loading lever. Imported by The Armoury, Navy Arms, Benson Firearms, Muzzleloaders Inc., E.M.F., Dixie, Euroarms of America, Armsport, Hopkins & Allen, CVA., Sile, Uberti USA.
Price: Brass frame.................................. **$90.00** to **$229.00**
Price: Steel frame .... **$125.00** to **$229.00**
Price: Stainless (Benson, Uberti USA)........................... **$295.00**
Price: Sillver-plated backstrap, trigger guard (Benson, Uberti USA). **$249.00**
Price: Kit form..................................... **$87.95** to **$119.95**
Price: Engraved model (Dixie)................................... **$135.00**
Price: Single cased set, steel frame (Navy Arms) **$250.00**
Price: Double cased set, steel frame (Navy Arms) **$414.00**
Price: London Model with iron backstrap (Benson, Uberti USA)..... **$245.00**

ARMY 1851 PERCUSSION REVOLVER

Caliber: 44, 6-shot.
Barrel: 7½".
Weight: 45 oz. **Length:** 13" over-all.
Stocks: Walnut finish.
Sights: Fixed.
Features: 44 caliber version of the 1851 Navy. Imported by The Armoury, E.M.F.
Price:... **$95.00** to **$140.00**

1851 NAVY-SHERIFF

Same as 1851 Sheriff model except has 4" barrel. Imported by Benson, CVA, (5½" bbl.),E.M.F., Euroarms of America, Uberti USA.
Price:... **$80.00** to **$229.00**
Price: Kit (CVA) **$91.95**
Price: Engraved, brass and nickel plated (CVA), with flask **$200.00**
Price: Stainless steel (Benson, Uberti USA)...................... **$295.00**

NEW MODEL 1858 ARMY PERCUSSION REVOLVER

Caliber: 36 or 44, 6-shot.
Barrel: 6½" or 8".
Weight: 40 oz. **Length:** 13½" over-all.
Stocks: Walnut.
Sights: Blade front, groove-in-frame rear.
Features: Replica of Remington Model 1858. Also available from some importers as Army Model Belt Revolver in 36 cal., shortened and lightened version of the 44. Target Model (Benson, Uberti USA, Navy) has fully adj. target rear sight, target front, 36 or 44. Imported by CVA (as 1858 Remington Army), Dixie, Navy Arms, Hopkins & Allen, The Armoury, E.M.F., Euroarms of America (engraved, stainless and plain), Armsport, Benson Firearms, Muzzle Loaders, Inc., Uberti USA.
Price: Steel frame .... **$135.00** to **$229.00**
Price: Steel frame kit (Euroarms) **$143.00**
Price: Single cased set (Navy Arms) **$277.00**
Price: Double cased set (Navy Arms) **$467.00**
Price: Nickel finish (E.M.F.) **$152.75**
Price: Stainless steel Model 1858 (Euroarms, Uberti, Sile, Navy Arms, Benson) .... **$140.00** to **$299.00**
Price: Target Model 1858 (Euroarms, Uberti, Sile, Navy, E.M.F., Benson) .... **$95.95** to **$239.00**
Price: Brass frame, finished (CVA, Navy Arms, Sile)...... **$97.95** to **$134.95**
Price: As above, kit (CVA, Dixie, Navy Arms)........... **$94.75** to **$132.00**

Navy 1858 Remington-Style

NAVY ARMS 1858 REMINGTON-STYLE REVOLVER
Caliber: 44.
Barrel: 8″.
Weight: 2 lbs., 13 ozs.
Stocks: Smooth walnut.
Sights: Dovetailed blade front.
Features: First exact reproduction—correct in size and weight to the original, with progressive rifling; highly polished with blue finish, silver-plated trigger guard. From Navy Arms.
Price: Deluxe model **$315.00**

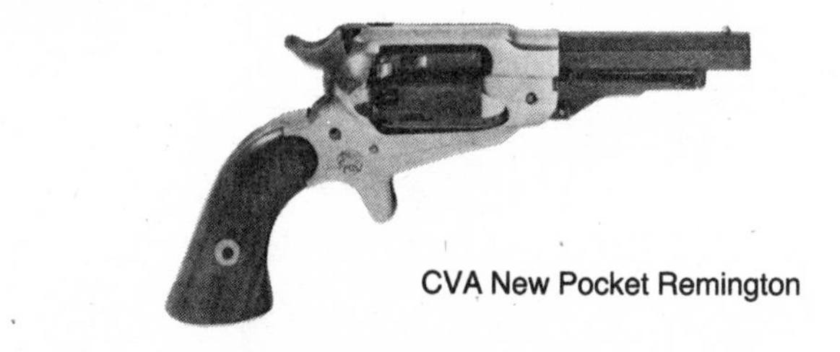
CVA New Pocket Remington

CVA NEW MODEL POCKET REMINGTON
Caliber: 31.
Barrel: 4″, octagonal.
Weight: 15½ oz. **Length:** 7½″ over-all.
Stocks: Two-piece walnut.
Sights: Post front, grooved top-strap rear.
Features: Spur trigger, brass frame with blued barrel and cylinder. Available finished or in kit form. Introduced 1984.
Price: Finished **$91.95**
Price: Kit **$76.95**

Dixie 1860 Army

1860 ARMY PERCUSSION REVOLVER
Caliber: 44, 6-shot.
Barrel: 8″.
Weight: 40 oz. **Length:** 13⅝″ over-all.
Stocks: Walnut.
Sights: Fixed.
Features: Engraved navy scene on cylinder; brass trigger guard; case-hardened frame, loading lever and hammer. Some importers supply pistol cut for shoulder detachable shoulder stock, have accessory stock available. Imported by E.M.F., CVA, Navy Arms, The Armoury, Dixie (half-fluted cylinder, not roll engraved), Euroarms of America (brass or steel model), Armsport, Hopkins & Allen, Benson Firearms, Muzzleloaders, Inc., Sile, Uberti USA.
Price: About .... **$132.95** to **235.00**
Price: Single cased set (Navy Arms,) **$274.00**
Price: Double cased set (Navy Arms) **$460.00**
Price: 1861 Navy: Same as Army except 36 cal., 7½″ bbl., wt. 41 oz., cut for shoulder stock; round cylinder (fluted avail.), from E.M.F., CVA (brass frame) .... **$229.00** to **$249.00**
Price: Steel frame kit (E.M.F., Euroarms) **$140.00**
Price: Stainless steel (Benson, Uberti USA) **$305.00**

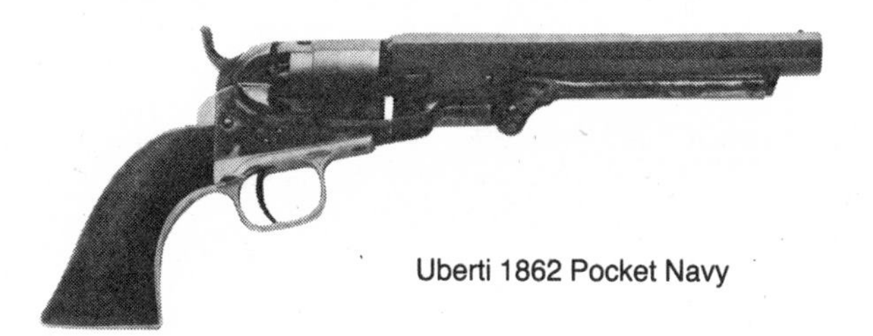
Uberti 1862 Pocket Navy

GRISWOLD & GUNNISON PERCUSSION REVOLVER
Caliber: 36 or 44, 6-shot.
Barrel: 7½″.
Weight: 44 oz. (36 cal.). **Length:** 13″ over-all.
Stocks: Walnut.
Sights: Fixed.
Features: Replica of famous Confederate pistol. Brass frame, backstrap and trigger guard; case-hardened loading lever; rebated cylinder (44 cal. only). Rounded Dragoon-type barrel. Imported by Navy Arms, (as Reb Model 1860), Benson, E.M.F., Uberti USA.
Price: About **$229.00**
Price: Kit (E.M.F.) **$73.50**
Price: Single cased set (Navy Arms) **$230.00**
Price: Double cased set (Navy Arms) **$370.00**
Price: Reb 1860 (Navy Arms) **$119.50**

1862 POCKET POLICE PERCUSSION REVOLVER
Caliber: 36, 5-shot.
Barrel: 4½″, 5½″, 6½″, 7½″.
Weight: 26 oz. **Length:** 12″ over-all (6½″ bbl.).
Stocks: Walnut.
Sights: Fixed.
Features: Round tapered barrel; half-fluted and rebated cylinder; case-hardened frame, loading lever and hammer; silver or brass trigger guard and backstrap. Imported by CVA, Navy Arms (5½″ only), Benson Firearms, Uberti USA.
Price: About **$229.00**
Price: Single cased set with accessories (Navy Arms) **$300.00**
Price: Stainless steel (Benson, Uberti USA) 4½″, 5½″ **$289.00**
Price: Kit (CVA) **$81.95**
Price: With silver-plated backstrap, trigger guard (Benson, Uberti USA) **$245.00**

UBERTI 1862 POCKET NAVY PERCUSSION REVOLVER
Caliber: 36, 5-shot.
Barrel: 4½″, 5½″, 6½″, octagonal, 7-groove, LH twist.
Weight: 27 oz. (5½″ barrel). **Length:** 10½″ over-all (5½″ bbl.).
Stocks: One piece varnished walnut.
Sights: Brass pin front, hammer notch rear.
Features: Rebated cylinder, hinged loading lever, brass or silver-plated backstrap and trigger guard, color cased frame, hammer, loading lever, plunger and latch, rest blued. Has original-type markings. From Benson Firearms, Inc., Uberti USA..
Price: With brass backstrap, trigger guard **$229.00**
Price: With silver-plated backstrap, trigger guard **$245.00**
Price: Stainless steel (4½″, 5½″ only) **$289.00**

ROGERS & SPENCER PERCUSSION REVOLVER
Caliber: 44.
Barrel: 7½″.
Weight: 47 oz. **Length:** 13¾″ over-all.
Stocks: Walnut.
Sights: Cone front, integral groove in frame for rear.
Features: Accurate reproduction of a Civil War design. Solid frame; extra large nipple cut-out on rear of cylinder; loading lever and cylinder easily removed for cleaning. From Euroarms of America (standard blue, engraved, burnished, target models), Muzzle Loaders, Inc., Navy Arms.
Price: .... **$120.00** to **$240.00**
Price: Nickel plated **$120.00**
Price: Engraved (Euroarms) **$236.00**
Price: Kit version **$95.00**
Price: Target version **$234.00**
Price: Brushed satin chrome (Navy Arms) **$259.00**
Price: Burnished London Gray (Euroarms) **$239.00**

LE MAT CAVALRY MODEL REVOLVER

Caliber: 44/65.
Barrel: 6¾" (revolver); 4⅞" (single shot).
Weight: NA.
Stocks: Hand-checkered walnut.
Sights: Post front, hammer-notch rear.
Features: Exact reproduction with all-steel construction; 44-cal. 9-shot cylinder, 65-cal. single barrel; color case-hardened hammer with selector; spur trigger guard; ring at butt; lever-type barrel release. From Navy Arms.
Price: Cavalry model (lanyard ring, spur trigger guard)............. **$500.00**
Price: Army model (round trigger guard, pin-type barrel release) **$500.00**
Price: Naval-style (thumb selector on hammer) **$500.00**

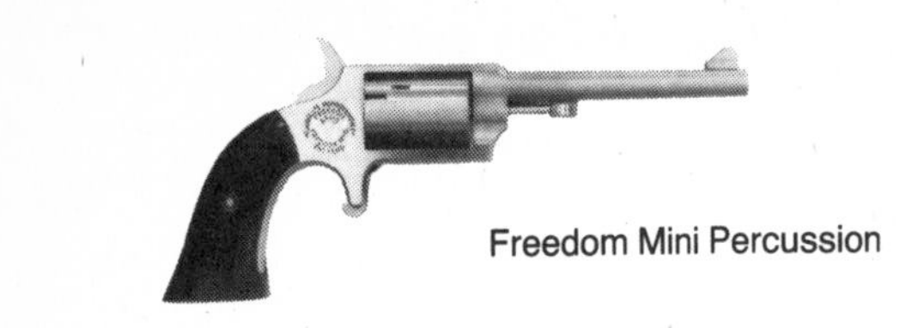

Freedom Mini Percussion

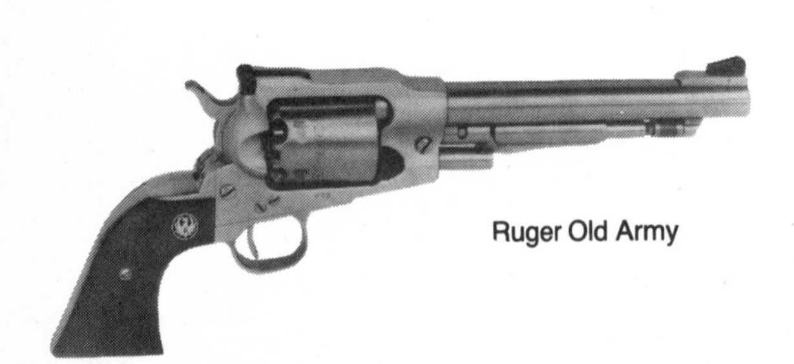

Ruger Old Army

RUGER 44 OLD ARMY PERCUSSION REVOLVER

Caliber: 44, 6-shot. Uses .457" dia. lead bullets.
Barrel: 7½" (6-groove, 16" twist).
Weight: 46 oz. **Length:** 13¾" over-all.
Stocks: Smooth walnut.
Sights: Ramp front, rear adj. for w. and e.
Features: Stainless steel standard size nipples, chrome-moly steel cylinder and frame, same lockwork as in original Super Blackhawk. Also available in stainless steel in very limited quantities. Made in USA. From Sturm, Ruger & Co.
Price: Stainless steel (Model KBP-7) **$356.31**
Price: Blued steel (Model BP-7) **$279.17**

SPILLER & BURR REVOLVER

Caliber: 36 (.375" round ball).
Barrel: 7", octagon.
Weight: 2½ lbs. **Length:** 12½" over-all.
Stocks: Two-piece walnut.
Sights: Fixed.
Features: Reproduction of the C.S.A. revolver. Brass frame and trigger guard. Also available as a kit. From Dixie, Navy Arms.
Price: .... **$125.00** to **$142.00**
Price: Kit form **$65.00**
Price: Single cased set (Navy Arms) **$252.00**
Price: Double cased set (Navy Arms) **$417.00**

Le Mat Cavalry Model

DIXIE "WYATT EARP" REVOLVER

Caliber: 44.
Barrel: 12" octagon.
Weight: 46 oz. **Length:** 18" over-all.
Stocks: Two piece walnut.
Sights: Fixed.
Features: Highly polished brass frame, backstrap and trigger guard; blued barrel and cylinder; case-hardened hammer, trigger and loading lever. Navy-size shoulder stock ($45.00) will fit with minor fitting. From Dixie Gun Works.
Price: **$130.00**

FREEDOM ARMS PERCUSSION MINI REVOLVER

Caliber: 22, 5-shot.
Barrel: 1", 1¾", 3".
Weight: 4¾ oz. (1" bbl.).
Stocks: Simulated ebony.
Sights: Fixed.
Features: Percussion version of the 22 RF gun. All stainless steel; spur trigger. Gun comes with leather carrying pouch, bullet seating tool, powder measure, 20 29-gr. bullets. Introduced 1983. From Freedom Arms.
Price: 1" barrel **$184.50**

BLACK POWDER MUSKETS & RIFLES

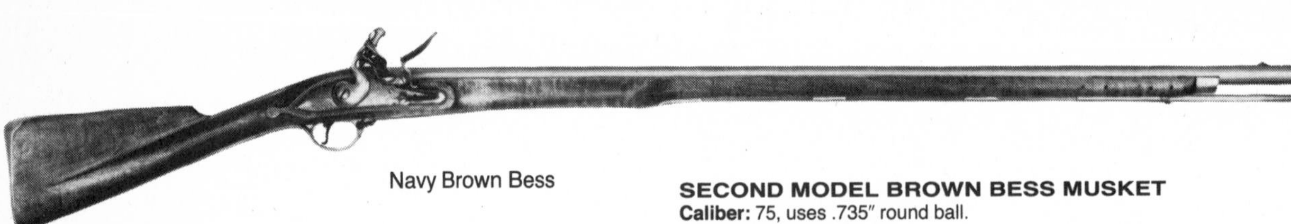

Navy Brown Bess

NAVY ARMS CHARLEVILLE MUSKET

Caliber: 69.
Barrel: 44⅝".
Weight: 8¾ lbs. **Length:** 59⅜" over-all.
Stock: Walnut.
Sights: Blade front.
Features: Replica of Revolutionary War 1763 musket. Bright metal, walnut stock. From Navy Arms.
Price: Finished **$550.00**
Price: Kit **$450.00**

SECOND MODEL BROWN BESS MUSKET

Caliber: 75, uses .735" round ball.
Barrel: 42", smoothbore.
Weight: 9½ lbs. **Length:** 59" over-all.
Stock: Walnut (Navy); walnut-stained hardwood (Dixie).
Sights: Fixed.
Features: Polished barrel and lock with brass trigger guard and buttplate. Bayonet and scabbard available. From Navy Arms, Dixie, E.M.F.
Price: Finished .... **$399.00** to **$750.00**
Price: Kit (Dixie, Navy) .... **$375.00** to **$430.00**

CAUTION: PRICES CHANGE. CHECK AT GUNSHOP.

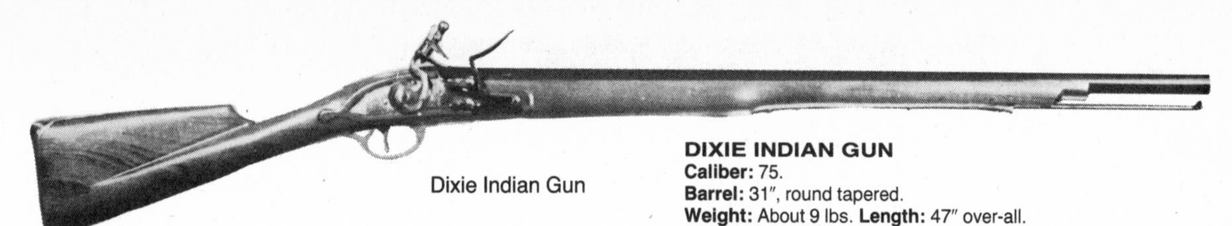
Dixie Indian Gun

DIXIE INDIAN GUN
Caliber: 75.
Barrel: 31", round tapered.
Weight: About 9 lbs. **Length:** 47" over-all.
Stock: Hardwood.
Sights: Blade front.
Features: Modified Brown Bess musket; brass furniture, browned lock and barrel. Lock is marked "GRICE 1762" with crown over "GR." Serpent-style sideplate. Introduced 1983.
Price: Complete **$375.00**
Price: As above, in kit form **$360.00**

Dixie Tennessee Rifle

DIXIE TENNESSEE MOUNTAIN RIFLE
Caliber: 32 or 50.
Barrel: 41½", 6-groove rifling, brown finish.
Length: 56" over-all.
Stock: Walnut, oil finish; Kentucky-style.
Sights: Silver blade front, open buckhorn rear.
Features: Recreation of the original mountain rifles. Early Schultz lock, interchangeable flint or percussion with vent plug or drum and nipple. Tumbler has fly. Double-set triggers. All metal parts browned. From Dixie.
Price: Flint or percussion, finished rifle, 50 cal. **$335.00**
Price: Kit, 50 cal **$275.00**
Price: Left-hand model, flint or perc. **$335.00**
Price: Left-hand kit, flint or perc., 50 cal. **$275.00**
Price: Squirrel Rifle (as above except in 32 cal. with 13/16" barrel), flint or percussion **$335.00**
Price: Kit, 32 cal., flint or percussion **$275.00**

KENTUCKY FLINTLOCK RIFLE
Caliber: 44, 45 or 50.
Barrel: 35".
Weight: 7 lbs. **Length:** 50" over-all.
Stock: Walnut stained, brass fittings.
Sights: Fixed.
Features: Available in Carbine model also, 28" bbl. Some variations in detail, finish. Kits also available from some importers. Imported by Navy Arms, The Armoury, CVA (45-cal. only), Armsport, Muzzleloaders, Inc.
Price: About . . . . **$217.95** to **324.00**
Price: Kit form (CVA, percussion) . . . . **$127.95** to **$148.95**
Price: Deluxe model, flint or percussion, 50-cal. (Navy Arms) **$275.00**

Kentucky Percussion Rifle
Similar to flintlock except percussion lock. Finish and features vary with importer. Imported by Navy Arms (45 cal.), The Armoury, CVA, Armsport (rifle-shotgun combo), Muzzle Loaders, Inc.
Price: About **$299.00**
Price: Armsport combo **$235.00**
Price: 50 cal. (Navy Arms) **$299.00**
Price: Kit, 45 cal. (CVA) **$134.95**

KENTUCKIAN RIFLE & CARBINE
Caliber: 44.
Barrel: 35" (Rifle), 27½" (Carbine).
Weight: 7 lbs. (Rifle), 5½ lbs. (Carbine). **Length:** 51" (Rifle) over-all, Carbine 43".
Stock: Walnut stain.
Sights: Brass blade front, steel V-ramp rear.
Features: Octagon bbl., case-hardened and engraved lock plate. Brass furniture. Imported by Dixie, Armsport.
Price: Rifle or carbine, flint **$225.00**
Price: As above, percussion **$210.00**

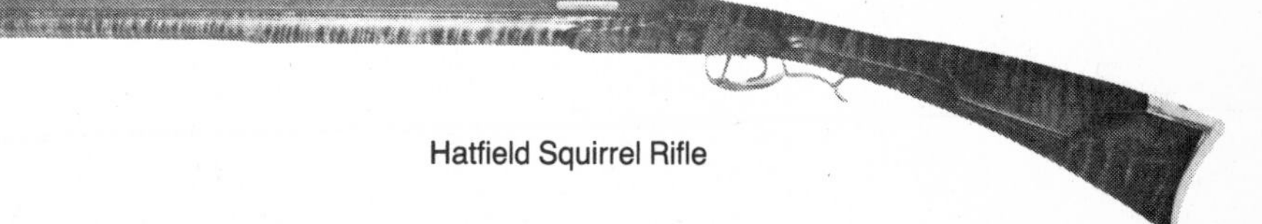
Hatfield Squirrel Rifle

HATFIELD SQUIRREL RIFLE
Caliber: 36, 45, 50.
Barrel: 39½", octagon, 32" on half-stock.
Weight: 8 lbs. (32 cal.).
Stock: American fancy maple fullstock.
Sights: Silver blade front, buckhorn rear.
Features: Recreation of the traditional squirrel rifle. Available in flint or percussion with brass trigger guard and buttplate. From Hatfield Rifle Works. Introduced 1983.
Price: Full stock, flint or percussion Grade I **$399.95**
Price: As above, Grade II **$465.95**
Price: As above, Grade III **$565.95**

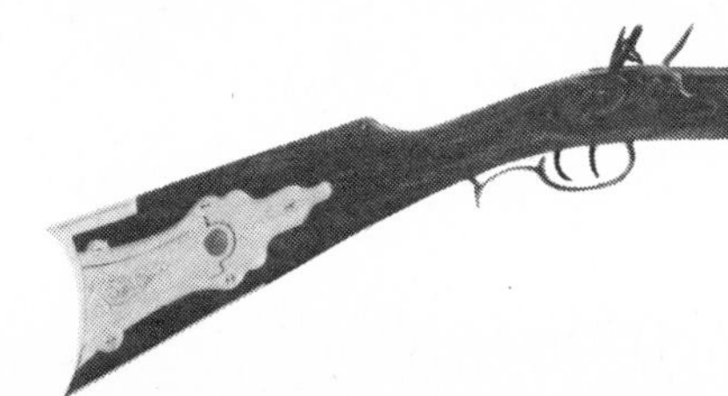
CVA Pennsylvania

CVA PENNSYLVANIA LONG RIFLE
Caliber: 50.
Barrel: 40", octagonal; 7/8" flats.
Weight: 8 lbs., 3 oz. **Length:** 55¾" over-all.
Stock: Select walnut.
Sights: Brass blade front, fixed semi-buckhorn rear.
Features: Color case-hardened lock plate, brass buttplate, toe plate, patchbox, trigger guard, thimbles, nosecap; blued barrel, double-set triggers; authentic V-type mainspring. Introduced 1983. From CVA.
Price: Finished, percussion **$331.95**
Price: Finished, flintlock **$322.95**

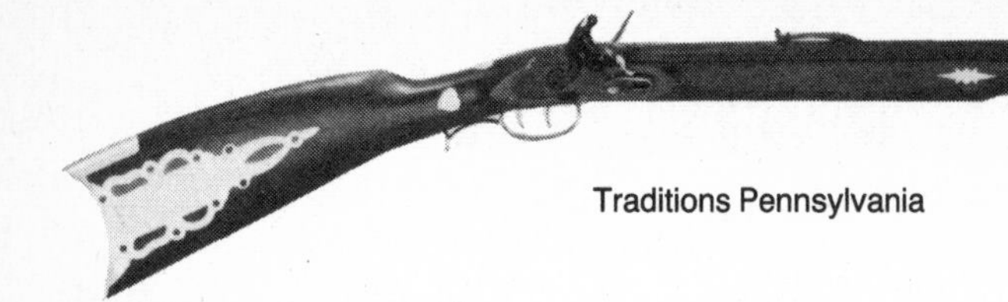

Traditions Pennsylvania

TRADITIONS PENNSYLVANIA RIFLE

Caliber: 45, 50.
Barrel: 41⅜", ⅞" flats.
Weight: 9 lbs. **Length:** 56⅝" over-all.
Stock: Walnut.
Sights: Blade front, adjustable rear.
Features: Brass patch box and ornamentation. Double set tirggers. From Traditions Inc.
Price: Flintlock **$300.00**
Price: Percussion **$290.00**
Price: Shenandoah rifle, flint **$196.00**
Price: As above, percussion **$186.00**

THOMPSON/CENTER PENNSYLVANIA HUNTER RIFLE

Caliber: 50.
Barrel: 31", half octagon, half round.
Weight: About 7½ lbs. **Length:** 48" over-all.
Stock: Black walnut.
Sights: Open, adjustable.
Features: Rifled 1:66" for round ball shooting. Available in flintlock or percussion.
Price: Percussion **$265.00**
Price: Flintlock **$280.00**

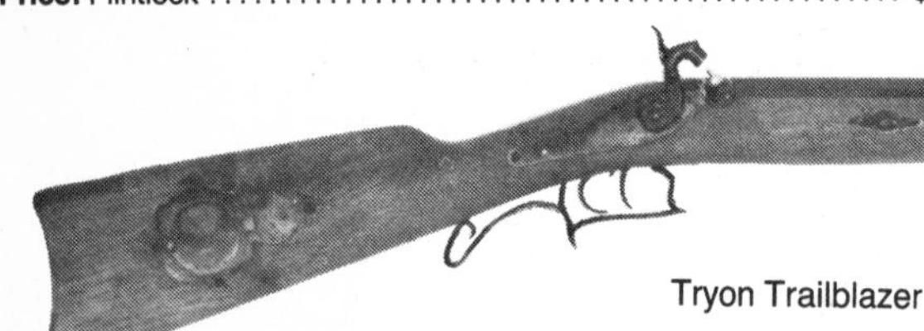

Tryon Trailblazer

TRYON TRAILBLAZER RIFLE

Caliber: 50.
Barrel: 32", 1" flats.
Weight: 9 lbs. **Length:** 48" over-all.
Stock: European walnut with cheekpiece.
Sights: Blade front, semi-buckhorn rear.
Features: Reproduction of a rifle made by George Tyron about 1820. Double-set triggers, back action lock, hooked breech with long tang. From Armsport.
Price: **$445.00**

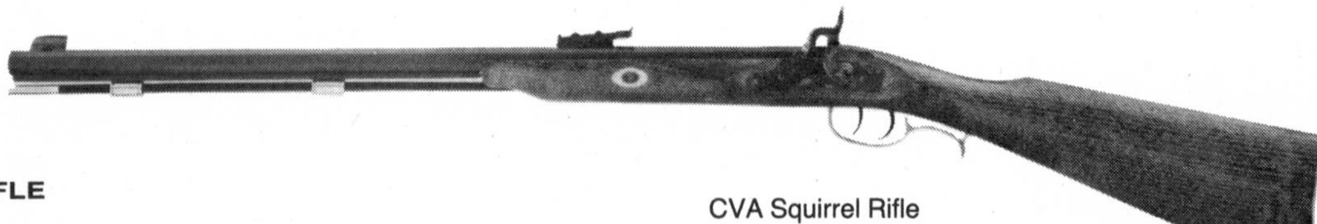

CVA Squirrel Rifle

CVA SQUIRREL RIFLE

Caliber: 32.
Barrel: 25", octagonal; 11/16" flats.
Weight: 5 lbs., 12 oz. **Length:** 40¾" over-all.
Stock: Hardwood.
Sights: Beaded blade front, fully adjustable hunting-style rear.
Features: Available in right- or left-hand versions. Color case-hardened lock plate, brass buttplate, trigger guard, wedge plates, thimbles; double set triggers; hooked breech; authentic V-type mainspring. Introduced 1983. From CVA.
Price: Finished, percussion, right-hand **$182.95**
Price: Finished, left-hand **$191.95**
Price: Kit, percussion, right-hand **$126.95**
Price: As above, left hand **$134.95**
Price: As above, right hand with 32 or 45 cal. barrel **$142.95**

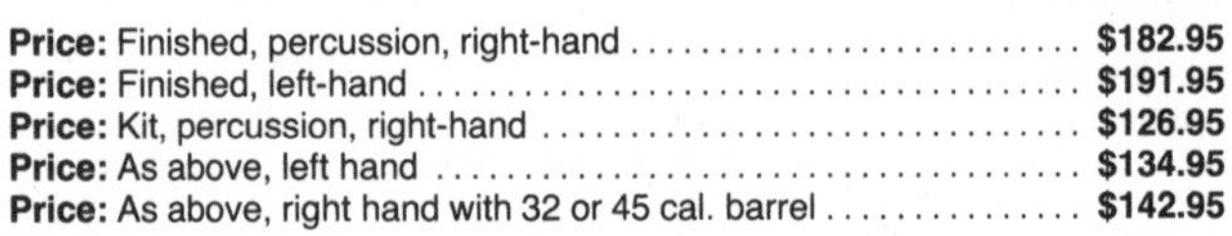

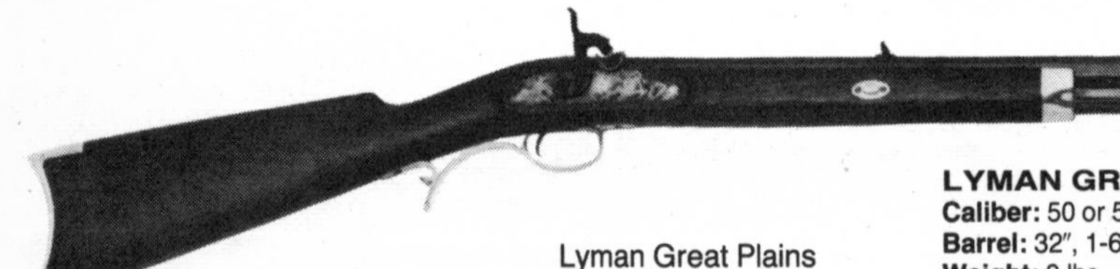

Lyman Great Plains

LYMAN GREAT PLAINS RIFLE

Caliber: 50 or 54 cal.
Barrel: 32", 1-66" twist.
Weight: 9 lbs.
Stock: Walnut.
Sights: Steel blade front, buckhorn rear adj. for w. & e. and fixed notch primitive sight included.
Features: Blued steel furniture. Stainless steel nipple. Coil spring lock, Hawken-style trigger guard and double set triggers. Round thimbles recessed and sweated into rib. Steel wedge plates and toe plate. Introduced 1979. From Lyman.
Price: Percussion **$314.95**
Price: Flintlock **$334.95**
Price: Percussion kit **$244.95**

Consult our Directory pages for the location of firms mentioned.

CHENEY PLAINS RIFLE

Caliber: 50, 54.
Barrel: 30"; 1" flats; 1-in-70" twist.
Weight: 8½ to 9 lbs. **Length:** 47¼" over-all.
Stock: Full- or half-stock; birdseye northern maple.
Sights: Blade front, drift-adjustable buckhorn rear.
Features: Hot browned steel, polished brass or browned furniture, hand-rubbed oil on wood; single set trigger; custom fit cleaning jag supplied. From Cheney Firearms Co.
Price: Percussion or flintlock **$449.00**

PENNSYLVANIA FULL STOCK RIFLE

Caliber: 45 or 50.
Barrel: 32" rifled, 15/16" dia.
Weight: 8½ lbs.
Stock: Walnut.
Sights: Fixed.
Features: Available in flint or percussion. Blued lock and barrel, brass furniture. Offered complete or in kit form. From The Armoury.
Price: Flint **$250.00**
Price: Percussion **$225.00**

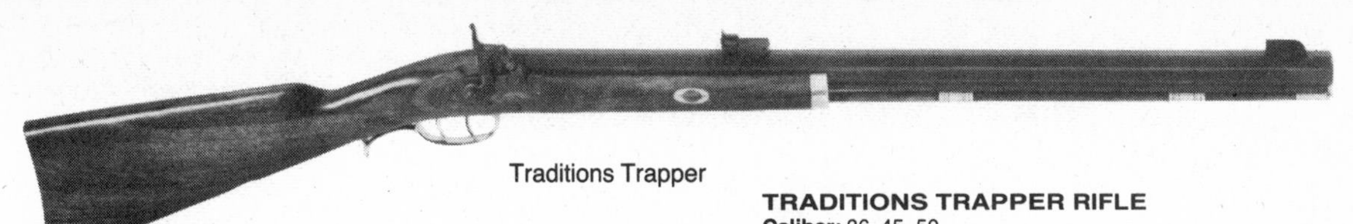

Traditions Trapper

CVA KENTUCKY RIFLE

Caliber: 45 (.451″ bore).
Barrel: 33½″, rifled, octagon (7/8″ flats).
Length: 48″ over-all.
Stock: Select hardwood.
Sights: Brass Kentucky blade-type front, fixed open rear.
Features: Available in either flint or percussion. Stainless steel nipple included. From CVA.
Price: Percussion **$229.95**
Price: Percussion kit **$134.95**

TRADITIONS TRAPPER RIFLE

Caliber: 36, 45, 50.
Barrel: 25″; 7/8″ flats.
Weight: 5 lbs. **Length:** 40½″ over-all.
Stock: Beech.
Sights: Beaded blade front, adjustable rear.
Features: Metal ramrod, brass furniture. From Traditions Inc.
Price: **$178.00**
Price: Frontier Scout (similar to above except shorter length of pull, weighs 4¾ lbs., 27″ bbl., 45 or 50 cal.) **$156.00**

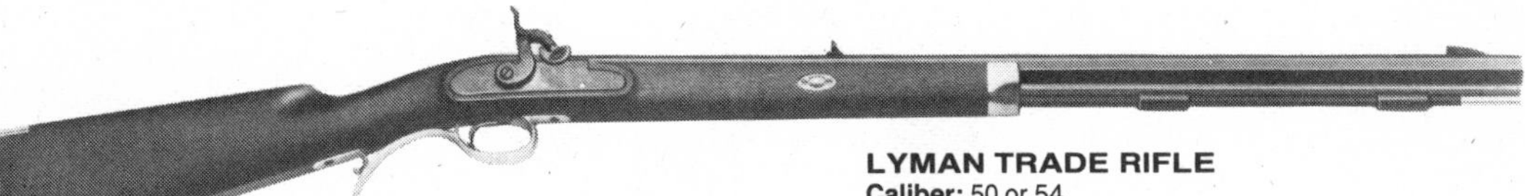

Lyman Trade Rifle

LYMAN TRADE RIFLE

Caliber: 50 or 54.
Barrel: 28″ octagon, 1-48″ twist.
Weight: 8¾ lbs. **Length:** 45″ over-all.
Stock: European walnut.
Sights: Blade front, open rear adj. for w. or optional fixed sights.
Features: Fast twist rifling for conical bullets. Polished brass furniture with blue steel parts, stainless steel nipple. Hook breech, single trigger, coil spring percussion lock. Steel barrel rib and ramrod ferrules. Introduced 1980. From Lyman.
Price: Percussion **$229.95**
Price: Kit, percussion **$179.95**
Price: Flintlock **$254.95**

Navy Country Boy

NAVY ARMS COUNTRY BOY RIFLE

Caliber: 32, 36, 45, 50.
Barrel: 26″.
Weight: 6 lbs.
Stock: Walnut.
Sights: Blade front, adjustable rear.
Features: Octagonal rifled barrel; blue finish; hooked breech; Mule Ear lock for fast ignition. From Navy Arms.
Price: **$250.00**
Price: Kit **$192.00**

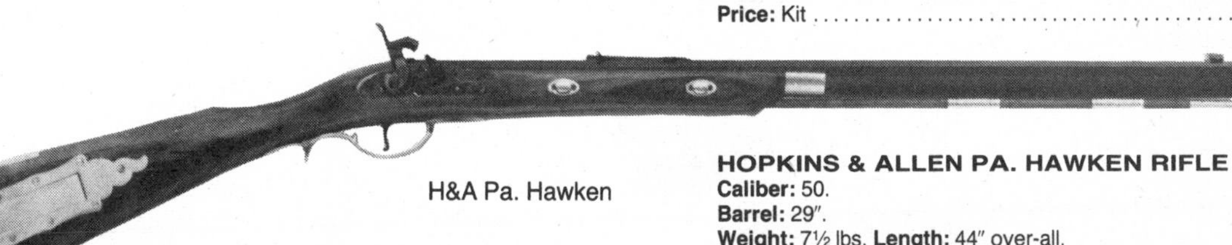

H&A Pa. Hawken

HOPKINS & ALLEN PA. HAWKEN RIFLE

Caliber: 50.
Barrel: 29″.
Weight: 7½ lbs. **Length:** 44″ over-all.
Stock: Walnut.
Sights: Blade front, open rear adjustable for elevation.
Features: Single trigger, dual barrel wedges. Convertible ignition system. Brass patch box.
Price: With percussion lock **$250.00**
Price: Conversion kit (percussion to flint) **$45.95**

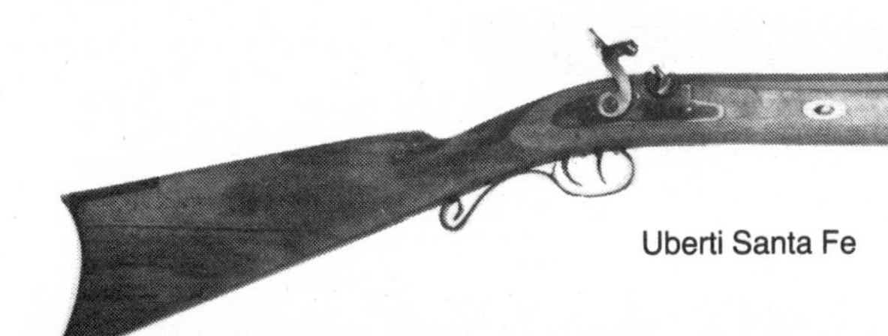

Uberti Santa Fe

UBERTI SANTA FE HAWKEN RIFLE

Caliber: 50 or 54.
Barrel: 32″, octagonal.
Weight: 9.8 lbs. **Length:** 50″ over-all.
Stock: Walnut, with beavertail cheekpiece.
Sights: German silver blade front, buckhorn rear.
Features: Browned finish, color case-hardened lock, double triggers, German silver ferrule, wedge plates. Imported by Benson Firearms, Uberti USA.
Price: **$385.00**
Price: Kit **$339.00**

Dixie Delux Cub

DIXIE DELUX CUB RIFLE
Caliber: 40.
Barrel: 28″.
Weight: 6½ lbs.
Stock: Walnut.
Sights: Fixed.
Features: Short rifle for small game and beginning shooters. Brass patchbox and furniture. Flint or percussion.
Price: Finished **$250.00**
Price: Kit **$205.00**

HOPKINS & ALLEN BRUSH RIFLE
Caliber: 36 or 45.
Barrel: 25″, octagon, 15/16″ flats.
Weight: 7 lbs.
Stock: Hardwood.
Sights: Silver blade front, notch rear.
Features: Convertible ignition system. Brass furniture. Introduced 1983.
Price: Percussion **$227.90**
Price: Pre-assembled kit, percussion **$159.90**
Price: Kit, percussion **$119.45**

TRYON RIFLE
Caliber: 50, 54.
Barrel: 34″, octagon; 1-63″ twist.
Weight: 9 lbs. **Length:** 49″ over-all.
Stock: European walnut with steel furniture.
Sights: Blade front, fixed rear.
Features: Reproduction of an American plains rifle with double set triggers and back-action lock. Imported from Italy by Dixie.
Price: **$299.00**
Price: Kit **$249.00**

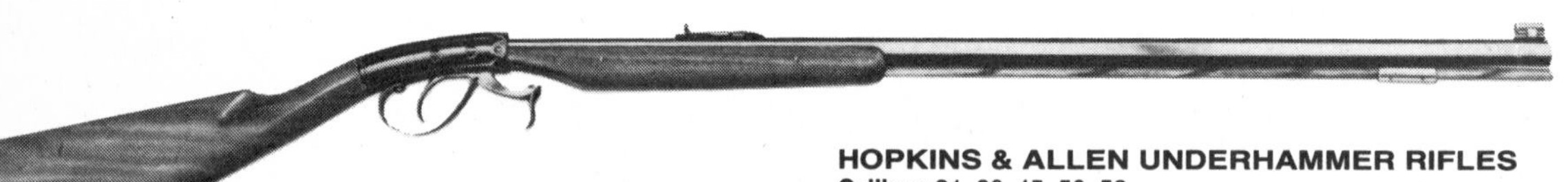

H&A Heritage

HOPKINS & ALLEN UNDERHAMMER RIFLES
Caliber: 31, 36, 45, 50, 58.
Barrel: 20″, 25″ 32″, 42″, octagonal.
Weight: 6½ lbs. **Length:** 37″ over-all.
Stock: American walnut.
Features: Blued barrel and receiver, black buttplate. All models available with straight or pistol grip stock. Offered as kits, pre-assembled kits ("white" barrel, unfinished stock), or factory finished. Prices shown are for factory finished guns.
Price: Buggy, cals. 31, 36, 45, 20″ or 25″ bbl. × 15/16″ **$247.75**
Price: Heritage, 36, 45, 50-cal., 32″ bbl. × 15/16″ **$261.65**
Price: Deerstalker, 58-cal., 28″ bbl. × 1⅛″ **$270.25**
Price: Target, 45-cal, 42″ bbl. × 1⅛″ **$284.10**

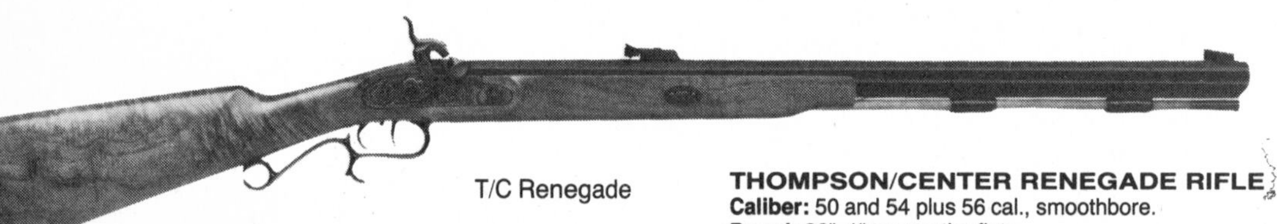

T/C Renegade

THOMPSON/CENTER RENEGADE RIFLE
Caliber: 50 and 54 plus 56 cal., smoothbore.
Barrel: 26″, 1″ across the flats.
Weight: 8 lbs.
Stock: American walnut.
Sights: Open hunting (Partridge) style, fully adjustable for w. and e.
Features: Coil spring lock, double set triggers, blued steel trim.
Price: Percussion model **$275.00**
Price: Flintlock model, 50 cal. only **$285.00**
Price: Percussion kit **$200.00**
Price: Flintlock kit **$210.00**
Price: Left-hand precussion, 50 or 54 cal **$285.00**

Thompson/Center Renegade Hunter
Similar to standard Renegade except has single trigger in a large-bow shotgun-style trigger guard, no brass trim. Available im 50 caliber only. Color case-hardened lock, rest blued. Introduced 1987. From Thompson/Center.
Price: **$255.00**

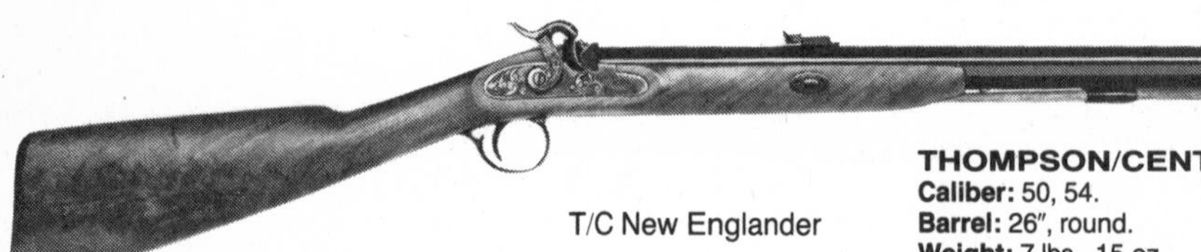

T/C New Englander

THOMPSON/CENTER NEW ENGLANDER RIFLE
Caliber: 50, 54.
Barrel: 26″, round.
Weight: 7 lbs., 15 oz.
Stock: American walnut.
Sights: Open, adjustable.
Features: Color case-hardened percussion lock with engraving, rest blued. Also accepts 12-ga. shotgun barrel. Introduced 1987. From Thompson/Center.
Price: Right or left-hand model **$225.00**
Price: Accessory 12 ga. barrel, right hand **$97.50**
Price: As above, left hand **$105.00**

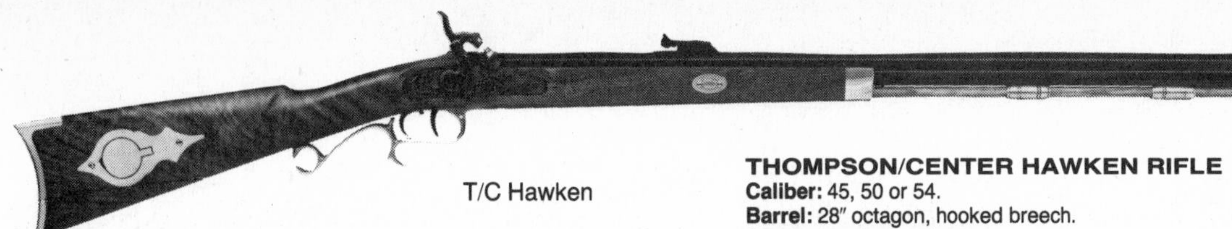

T/C Hawken

THOMPSON/CENTER HAWKEN RIFLE

Caliber: 45, 50 or 54.
Barrel: 28" octagon, hooked breech.
Stock: American walnut.
Sights: Blade front, rear adj. for w. & e.
Features: Solid brass furniture, double set triggers, button rifled barrel, coiltype main spring. From Thompson/Center Arms.
Price: Percussion Model (45, 50 or 54 cal.) **$325.00**
Price: Flintlock model (50 cal.) **$340.00**
Price: Percussion kit **$230.00**
Price: Flintlock kit **$245.00**

THOMPSON/CENTER CHEROKEE RIFLE

Caliber: 32, 45.
Barrel: 24", 13/16" across flats.
Weight: About 6 lbs.
Stock: American walnut.
Sights: Open hunting style; round notch rear fully adjustable for w. and e.
Features: Single trigger only. Interchangeable barrels. Brass buttplate, trigger guard, fore-end escutcheons and lock plate screw bushing. Introduced 1984.
Price: 32, 45 caliber **$265.00**
Price: Interchangeable 32, 45-cal. barrel **$115.00**
Price: Kit, percussion, 32, 45 .... **$200.00**
Price: Kit barrels **$80.00**

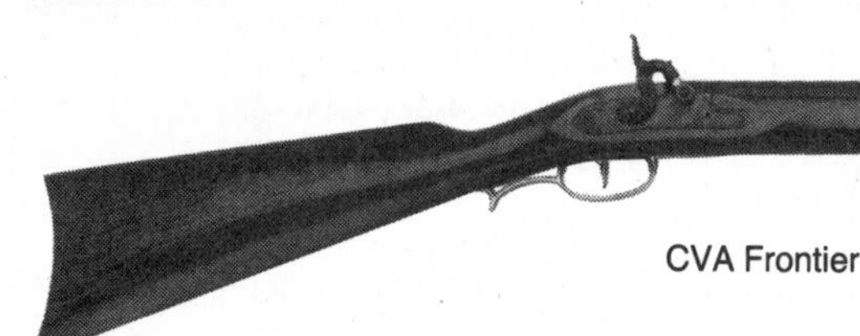

CVA Frontier

CVA FRONTIER RIFLE

Caliber: 50.
Barrel: 24" octagon; 15/16" flats.
Weight: 6½ lbs. **Length:** 40" over-all.
Stock: Select hardwood.
Sights: Brass blade front, fixed open rear.
Features: Color case-hardened lockplate, screw-adjustable sear engagement, V-type mainspring. Early style brass trigger with tension spring. Brass buttplate, trigger guard, wedge plate, nose cap, thimble. From CVA.
Price: **$167.95**
Price: Kit **$119.95**

CVA MOUNTAIN RIFLE

Caliber: 50, 54.
Barrel: 32" octagon, 15/16" flats.
Weight: 9 lbs. **Length:** 48" over-all.
Stock: European walnut with cheekpiece.
Sights: German silver blade front, adjustable open rear.
Features: Color case-hardened and engraved lockplate; bridle, fly, screw-adjustable sear engagement. Double set triggers. Pewter nose cap, trigger guard, buttplate. From CVA.
Price: Either caliber **$307.95**

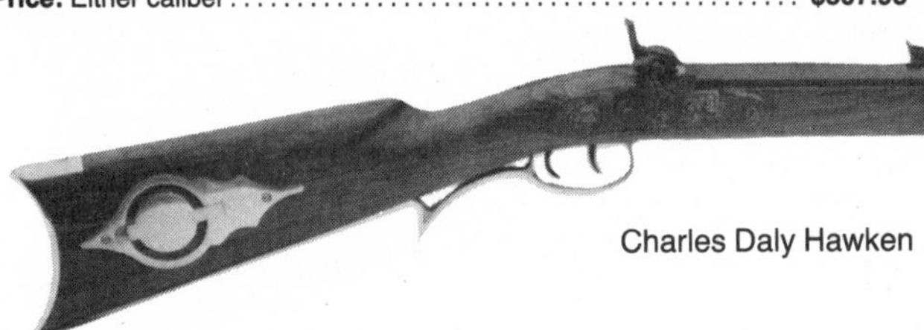

Charles Daly Hawken

CHARLES DALY HAWKEN RIFLE

Caliber: 45, 50, 54.
Barrel: 28" octagonal, 7/8" flats.
Weight: 7½ lbs. **Length:** 45½" over-all.
Stock: European hardwood.
Sights: Blade front, open fully adjustable rear.
Features: Color case-hardened lock uses coil springs; trigger guard, buttplate, fore-end cap, ferrules and ramrod fittings are polished brass. Left-hand model available in 50-cal. only. Imported by Outdoor Sports Headquarters. Introduced 1984.
Price: Right-hand, percussion **$259.95**
Price: Left-hand, percussion (50-cal. only) **$289.00**
Price: Right-hand, flintlock **$299.00**
Price: Left-hand, flintlock (50-cal. only) **$319.00**
Price: Wilderness Hawken (50 cal. only) **$189.95**

ARMOURY R140 HAWKIN RIFLE

Caliber: 45, 50 or 54,.
Barrel: 29"
Weight: 8¾ to 9 lbs. **Length:** 45¾" over-all.
Stock: Walnut, with cheekpiece.
Sights: Dovetail front, fully adjustable rear.
Features: Octagon barrel, removable breech plug; double set triggers; blued barrel, brass stock fittings, color case-hardened percussion lock. From Armsport, The Armoury.
Price: .... **$225.00** to **$280.00**

CVA HAWKEN RIFLE

Caliber: 50.
Barrel: 28", octagon; 1" across flats; 1-66" twist.
Weight: 8 lbs. **Length:** 44" over-all.
Stock: Select walnut.
Sights: Beaded blade front, fully adj. open rear.
Features: Fully adj. double set triggers; brass patch box, wedge plates, nosecap, thimbles; trigger guard and buttplate; blued barrel; color case-hardened, engraved lockplate. Percussion only. Hooked breech, chrome bore. Introduced 1981.
Price: Finished rifle percussion **$322.95**
Price: Presentation Grade (checkered walnut stock, engraved lock plate) **$585.95**
Price: St. Louis Hawken (as above, except does not have chrome bore; hardwood stock) finished **$199.95**
Price: As above, kit **$151.95**
Price: As above, combo kit (50, 54-cal. bbls.) **$167.95**

CVA Missouri Ranger Rifle

Similar to the St. Louis Hawken except has blackened nose cap, trigger guard, thimbles and wedge plates and black rubber buttplate. Has brass blade front sight, fixed semi-buckhorn rear; adjustable double set trigger. Weight 7 lbs., 8 oz. From CVA.
Price: Finished, right-hand **$174.95**
Price: Finished, left-hand **$182.95**
Price: Kit (right-hand only) **$129.95**

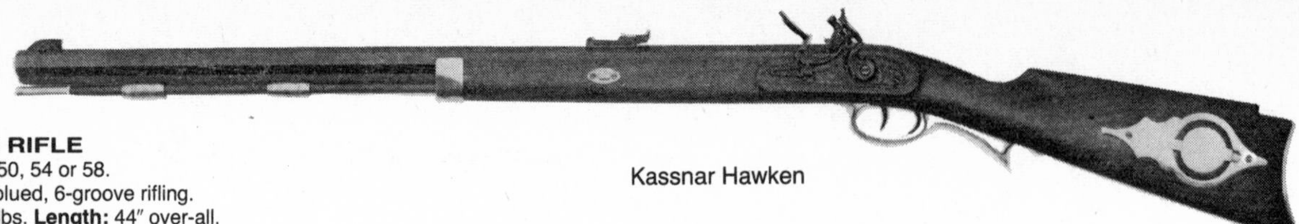

Kassnar Hawken

HAWKEN RIFLE

Caliber: 45, 50, 54 or 58.
Barrel: 28", blued, 6-groove rifling.
Weight: 8¾ lbs. **Length:** 44" over-all.
Stock: Walnut with cheekpiece.
Sights: Blade front, fully adj. rear.
Features: Coil mainspring, double set triggers, polished brass furniture. Introduced 1977. From Kassnar (flint or percussion, right- or left-hand), Muzzle Loaders, Inc., Armsport, Hopkins & Allen, 50-cal. only, Traditions, Sile.
Price: .... **$245.00** to **$275.00**
Price: True left-hand rifle, percussion (Kassnar) **$279.00**
Price: As above, flintlock (Kassnar) **$309.00**
Price: Right-hand percussion, Carbine (Kassnar) **$249.00**
Price: St. Louis Hawken with steel furniture (Muzzle Loaders, Inc.) . **$193.00**
Price: Hawken Deluxe rifle or carbine with hard chrome bore (Sile) . **$219.95**
Price: Hawken Hunter, as above except has black-finished furniture (Sile) **$244.95**
Price: Hawken Deluxe Prefinished Kit (Sile) **$195.00**

ITHACA-NAVY HAWKEN RIFLE

Caliber: 50 and 54.
Barrel: 32" octagonal, 1-inch dia.
Weight: About 9 lbs.
Stock: Walnut.
Sights: Blade front, rear adj. for w.
Features: Hooked breech, 1⅞" throw percussion lock. Attached twin thimbles and under-rib. German silver barrel key inlays, Hawken-style toe and buttplates, lock bolt inlays, barrel wedges, entry thimble, trigger guard, ramrod and cleaning jag, nipple and nipple wrench. Introduced 1977. From Navy Arms
Price: Complete, percussion **$480.00**
Price: Kit, percussion **$374.00**

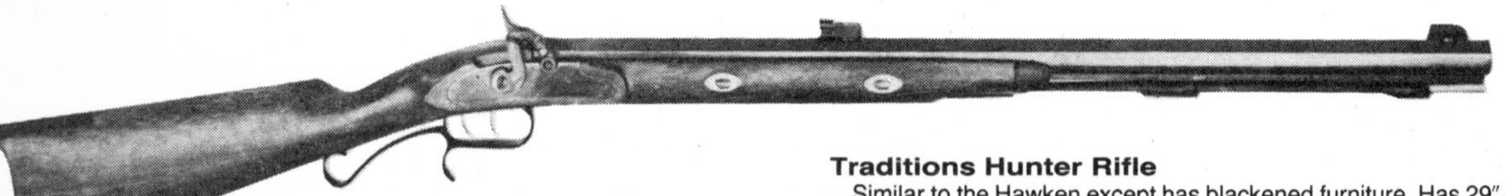

Traditions Hunter

Traditions Hunter Rifle

Similar to the Hawken except has blackened furniture. Has 29" barrel with 1" flats.
Price: Percussion only, 50 or 54 cal. **$259.00**
Price: Hawken Woodsman (similar to above, brass furniture, 50 cal. only, beech stock) **$200.00**
Price: Frontier (beech stock, 45 cal., flintlock) **$185.00**
Price: As above, 50 cal. percussion only **$175.00**
Price: Frontier Carbine (25⅛" bbl., 45, 50 cal., percussion) **$175.00**

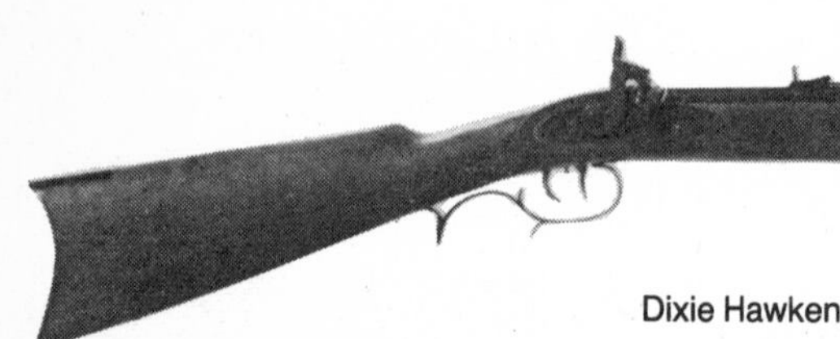

Dixie Hawken

DIXIE HAWKEN RIFLE

Caliber: 45, 50, 54.
Barrel: 30".
Weight: 8 lbs. **Length:** 46½" over-all.
Stock: Walnut
Sights: Blade front, adjustable rear.
Features: Blued barrel, double set triggers, steel crescent buttplate. Imported by Dixie.
Price: Finished **$225.00**
Price: Kit **$185.00**

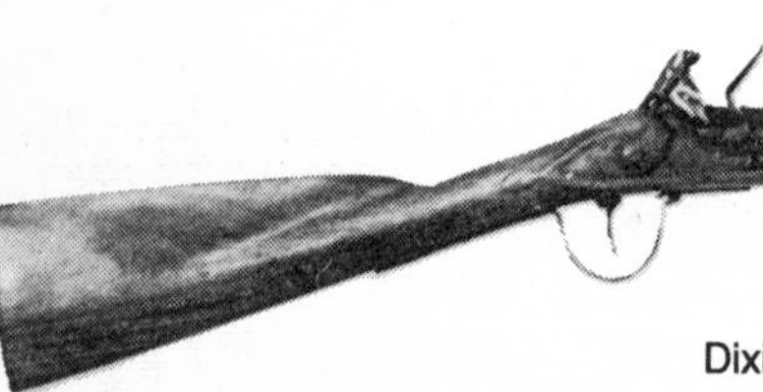

Dixie Trade Gun

DIXIE NORTHWEST TRADE GUN

Caliber/Gauge: 20 (.600" round ball or 1 oz.#6 shot).
Barrel: 36", smoothbore.
Weight: 7½ lbs. **Length:** 53½" over-all.
Stock: Walnut, 13½" pull.
Sights: Brass blade front only.
Features: Flintlock. Brass buttplate, serpentine sideplate; browned barrel, Wheeler flint lock, trigger guard; hickory ramrod with brass tip. From Dixie Gun Works.
Price: Finished **$495.00**
Price: Kit **$350.00**

Dixie Wesson Rifle

DIXIE PERCUSSION WESSON RIFLE

Caliber: 50.
Barrel: 28"; 1⅛" octagon, with false muzzle.
Length: 45" over-all.
Sights: Hand checkered walnut.
Stock: Blade front, rear adj. for e.
Features: Adjustable double set triggers, color case-hardened frame. Comes with loading rod and loading accessories. From Dixie Gun Works.
Price: With false muzzle **$395.00**

CAUTION: PRICES CHANGE. CHECK AT GUNSHOP.

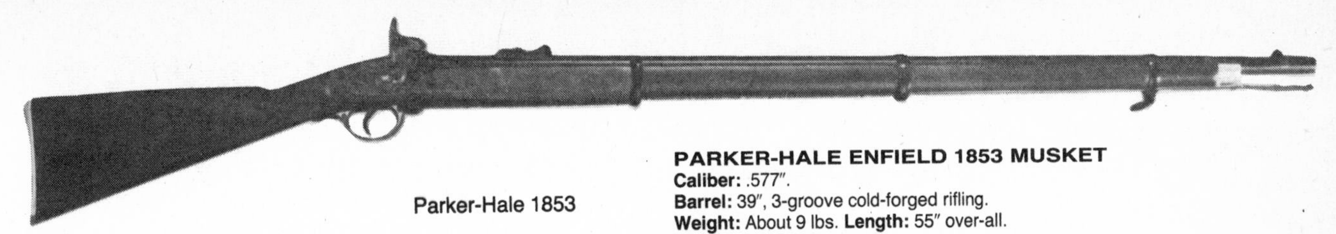

Parker-Hale 1853

PARKER-HALE ENFIELD 1853 MUSKET
Caliber: .577".
Barrel: 39", 3-groove cold-forged rifling.
Weight: About 9 lbs. **Length:** 55" over-all.
Stock: Seasoned walnut.
Sights: Fixed front, rear step adj. for elevation.
Features: Three band musket made to original specs from original gauges. Solid brass stock furniture, color hardened lockplate, hammer; blued barrel, trigger. Imported from England by Navy Arms.
Price: **$475.00**

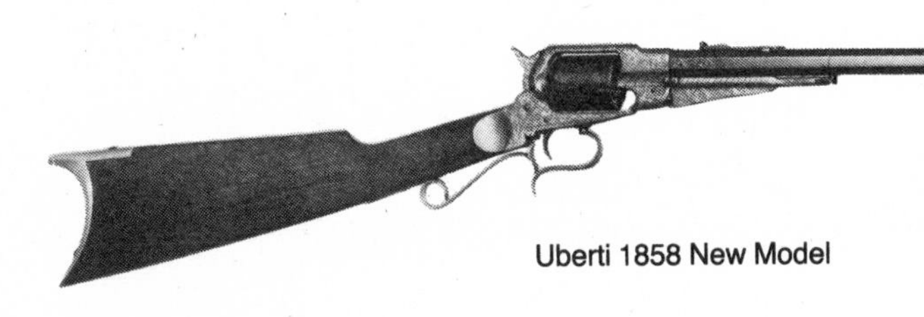

Uberti 1858 New Model

UBERTI 1858 NEW ARMY REVOLVING CARBINE
Caliber: 44.
Barrel: 18".
Weight: 4.6 lbs. **Length:** 37" over-all.
Stock: Walnut.
Sights: Ramp front, rear adjustable for e.
Features: Carbine version of the 1858 New Army revolver. Brass trigger guard and buttplate; blued, tapered octagonal barrel. Imported from Italy by Benson Firearms, Uberti USA.
Price: **$385.00**

London Armory 3-Band Enfield

LONDON ARMORY 3-BAND 1853 ENFIELD
Caliber: 58 (.577" Minie, .575" round ball, .580" maxi ball).
Barrel: 39".
Weight: 9½ lbs. **Length:** 54" over-all.
Stock: European walnut.
Sights: Inverted "V" front, traditional Enfield folding ladder rear.
Features: Recreation of the famed London Armory Company Pattern 1862 Enfield Musket. One-piece walnut stock, brass buttplate, trigger guard and nosecap. Lockplate marked "London Armoury Co." and with a British crown. Blued Baddeley barrel bands. From Dixie, Euroarms of America, Navy Arms, Muzzle Loaders, Inc.
Price: About .... **$395.00** to **$427.00**
Price: Assembled kit (Euroarms)............................... **$380.00**

LONDON ARMORY 2-BAND ENFIELD 1858
Caliber: .577" Minie, .575" round ball.
Barrel: 33".
Weight: 10 lbs. **Length:** 49" over-all.
Stock: Walnut.
Sights: Folding leaf rear adjustable for elevation.
Features: Blued barrel, color case-hardened lock and hammer, polished brass buttplate, trigger guard, nose cap. From Navy Arms, Euroarms of America, Dixie.
Price: .... **$325.00** to **$450.00**
Price: Assembled kit (Euroarms)............................... **$365.00**

LONDON ARMORY ENFIELD MUSKETOON
Caliber: 58, Minie ball.
Barrel: 24", round.
Weight: 7-7½ lbs. **Length:** 40½" over-all.
Stock: Walnut, with sling swivels.
Sights: Blade front, graduated military-leaf rear.
Features: Brass trigger guard, nose cap, buttplate; blued barrel, bands, lockplate, swivels. Imported by Euroarms of America.
Price: Kit (fully assembled).................................... **$322.00**

PARKER-HALE ENFIELD PATTERN 1858 NAVAL RIFLE
Caliber: 577".
Barrel: 33".
Weight: 8½ lbs. **Length:** 48½" over-all.
Stock: European walnut.
Sights: Blade front, step adj. rear.
Features: Two-band Enfield percussion rifle with heavy barrel. 5-groove progressive depth rifling, solid brass furniture. All parts made exactly to original patterns. Imported from England by Navy Arms.
Price: **$500.00**

Parker-Hale 1861

PARKER-HALE ENFIELD 1861 MUSKETOON
Caliber: 58.
Barrel: 24".
Weight: 7 lbs. **Length:** 40½" over-all.
Stock: Walnut.
Sights: Fixed front, adj. rear.
Features: Percussion muzzleloader, made to original 1861 English patterns. Imported from England by Navy Arms.
Price: **$400.00**

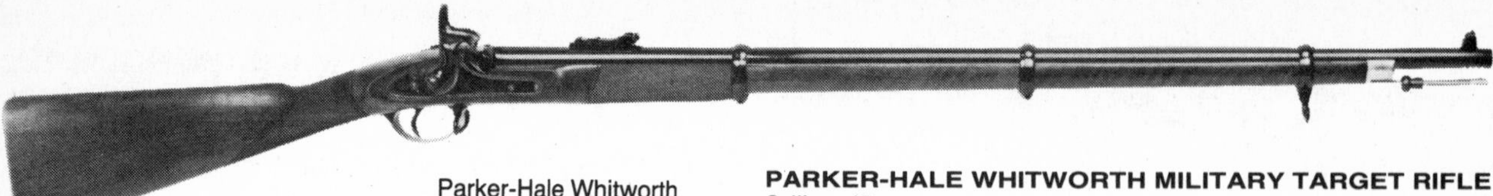

Parker-Hale Whitworth

PARKER-HALE VOLUNTEER RIFLE
Caliber: 451″.
Barrel: 32″.
Weight: 9½ lbs. **Length:** 49″ over-all.
Stock: Walnut, checkered wrist and fore-end.
Sights: Globe front, adjustable ladder-type rear.
Features: Recreation of the type of gun issued to volunteer regiments during the 1860s. Rigby-pattern rifling, patent breech, detented lock. Stock is glass bedded for accuracy. Comes with comprehensive accessory/shooting kit. From Navy Arms.
Price: **$725.00**

PARKER-HALE WHITWORTH MILITARY TARGET RIFLE
Caliber: 45.
Barrel: 36″.
Weight: 9¼ lbs. **Length:** 52½″ over-all.
Stock: Walnut. Checkered at wrist and fore-end.
Sights: Hooded post front, open step-adjustable rear.
Features: Faithful reproduction of the Whitworth rifle, only bored for 45-cal. Trigger has a detented lock, capable of being adjusted very finely without risk of the sear nose catching on the half-cock bent and damaging both parts. Introduced 1978. Imported from England by Navy Arms.
Price: **$750.00**

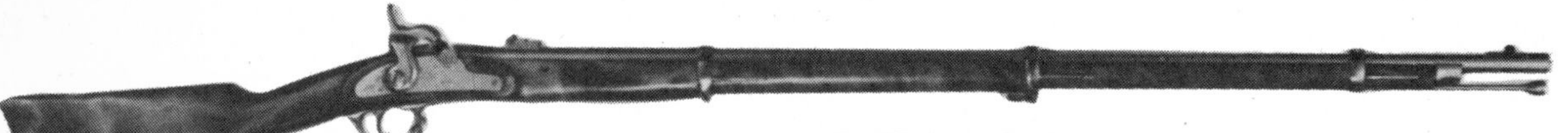

Dixie Springfield

COOK & BROTHER CONFEDERATE CARBINE
Caliber: 58.
Barrel: 24″.
Weight: 7½ lbs. **Length:** 40½″ over-all.
Stock: Select walnut.
Features: Recreation of the 1861 New Orleans-made artillery carbine. Color case-hardened lock, browned barrel. Buttplate, trigger guard, barrel bands, sling swivels and nosecap of polished brass. From Euroarms of America.
Price: **$365.00**

DIXIE 1863 SPRINGFIELD MUSKET
Caliber: 58 (.570″ patched ball or .575″ Minie).
Barrel: 50″, rifled.
Stock: Walnut stained.
Sights: Blade front, adjustable ladder-type rear.
Features: Bright-finish lock, barrel, furniture. Reproduction of the last of the regulation muzzleloaders. Imported from Japan by Dixie Gun Works.
Price: Finished **$475.00**
Price: Kit **$330.00**

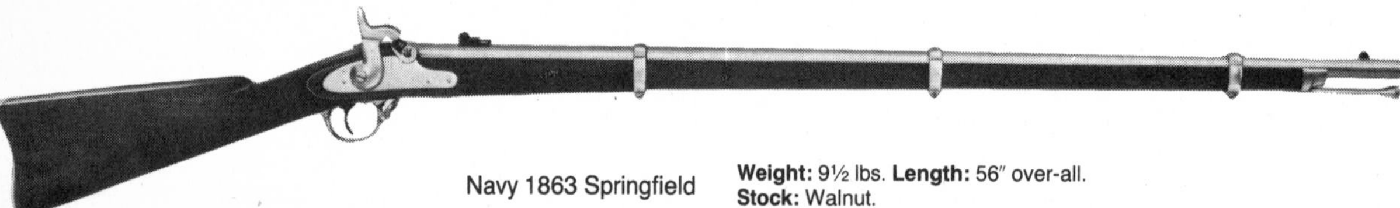

Navy 1863 Springfield

NAVY ARMS 1863 SPRINGFIELD
Caliber: 58, uses .575″ mini-ball.
Barrel: 40″, rifled.
Weight: 9½ lbs. **Length:** 56″ over-all.
Stock: Walnut.
Sights: Open rear adj. for elevation.
Features: Full-size 3-band musket. Polished bright metal, including lock. From Navy Arms.
Price: Finished rifle **$500.00**
Price: Kit **$400.00**

Dixie Zouave

Mississippi Model 1841 Percussion Rifle
Similar to Zouave rifle but patterned after U.S. Model 1841. Imported by Dixie.
Price: **$430.00**

ZOUAVE PERCUSSION RIFLE
Caliber: 58, 59.
Barrel: 32½″.
Weight: 9½ lbs. **Length:** 48½″ over-all.
Stock: Walnut finish, brass patch box and buttplate.
Sights: Fixed front, rear adj. for e.
Features: Color case-hardened lock plate, blued barrel. from Dixie, Euroarms (M1863).
Price: About **$275.00**
Price: Kit (Euroarms)... **$263.00**

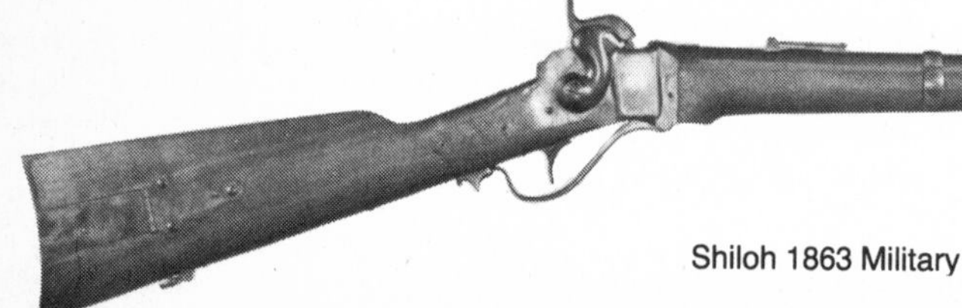

Shiloh 1863 Military

SHILOH SHARPS 1863 MILITARY RIFLE
Caliber: 54.
Barrel: 30″, round.
Weight: 8 lbs., 12 oz.
Stock: Military-style butt, steel buttplate and patch box. Standard-grade walnut.
Sights: Iron block front, Lawrence-style ladder rear.
Features: Recreation of the 1863 percussion rifle. Made in U.S. by Shiloh Rifle Mfg. Co.
Price: **$800.00**
Price: 1863 Military Carbine (as above except has 22″ round bbl. band on military-style fore-end, saddle bar and ring)........................ **$650.00**

Shiloh 1863 Sporting

Shiloh Sharps Model 1863 Sporting Rifle
Similar to the Military Carbine except has 30″ octagon barrel, blade front and sporting rear sights, shotgun butt available, steel buttplate, schnabel fore-end. Standard-grade wood (semi-fancy available).
Price: **$695.00**

Shiloh Sharps 1862 Confederate Robinson
Recreation of the 54-cal. 1862 Confederate Robinson carbine with 21½″ round barrel; iron block front, fixed V-notch rear sights; brass buttplate and barrel band; sling swivel on buttstock. Weight is about 7½ lbs.
Price: **$750.00**

Santfl Schuetzen

Rigby-style Target

SANFTL SCHUETZEN PERCUSSION TARGET RIFLE
Caliber: 45 (.445″ round ball).
Barrel: 29″, ⅞″ octagon.
Weight: 9 lbs. **Length:** 43″ over-all.
Stock: Walnut, schuetzen-style.
Sights: Open tunnel front post, peep rear adjustable for windage & elevation.
Features: True back-action lock with "backward" hammer; screw-in breech plug; buttplate, trigger guard and stock inlays are polished brass. Imported from Italy by Dixie Gun Works.
Price: **$595.00**

RIGBY-STYLE TARGET RIFLE
Caliber: .451.
Barrel: 32½″.
Weight: 7¾ lbs.
Stock: Walnut; hand-checkered pistol grip, fore-end.
Sights: Target front with micrometer adjustment; adjustable Vernier peep rear.
Features: Comes cased with loading accessories—bullet starter, bullet sizer, special ramrod. Introduced 1985. From Navy Arms.
Price: **$550.00**

CVA EXPRESS RIFLE
Caliber: 50 (.490″ ball).
Barrel: 28″, round.
Weight: 9 lbs.
Stock: Walnut-stained hardwood.
Sights: Bead and post front, adjustable rear.
Features: Double rifle with twin percussion locks and triggers. Hooked breech. Introduced 1985. From CVA.
Price: Finished **$362.95**
Price: Kit **$301.95**
Price: Presentation Express (hand-checkered stock, engraved and polished locks, hammers, tang) **$742.95**

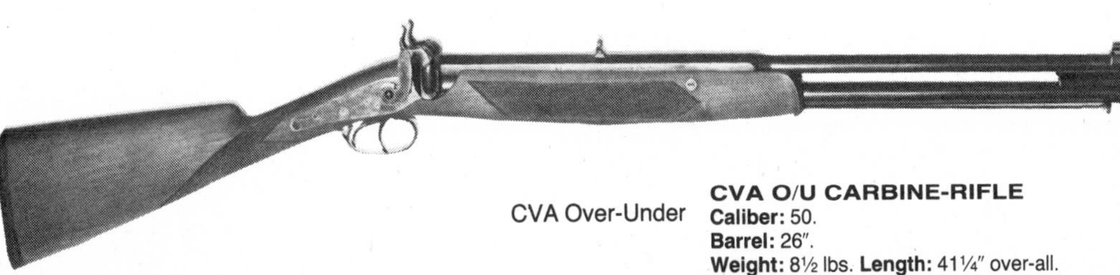

CVA Over-Under

CVA O/U CARBINE-RIFLE
Caliber: 50.
Barrel: 26″.
Weight: 8½ lbs. **Length:** 41¼″ over-all.
Stock: Checkered walnut.
Sights: Blade front with gold bead, folding rear adjustable for w. and e.
Features: Two-shot over/under with two hammers, two triggers. Polished blue finish. From CVA.
Price: **$441.95**

KODIAK DOUBLE RIFLE
Caliber: 54x54, 58x58, 50x50 and 58-cal./12 ga. optional.
Barrel: 28″, 5 grooves, 1-in-48″ twist.
Weight: 9½ lbs. **Length:** 43¼″ over-all.
Stock: Czechoslovakian walnut, hand checkered.
Sights: Adjustable bead front, adjustable open rear.
Features: Hooked breech allows interchangeability of barrels. Comes with sling and swivels, adjustable powder measure, bullet mould and bullet starter. Engraved lockplates, top tang and trigger guard. Locks and top tang polished, rest blued. Introduced 1976. Imported from Italy by Trail Guns Armory, Inc.
Price: 50, 54, 58 cal. SxS **$549.50**
Price: 50 cal. x 12 ga., 58x12 .... **$549.50**
Price: Spare barrels, all calibers **$294.25**
Price: Spare barrels, 12 ga. x 12 ga. **$195.00**

Consult our Directory pages for the location of firms mentioned.

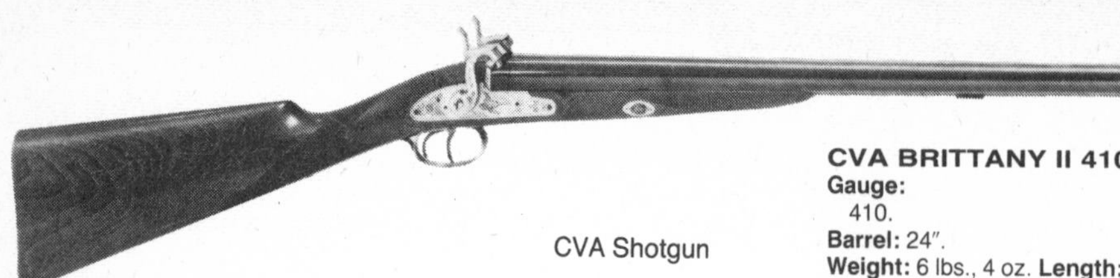

CVA Shotgun

CVA TRAPPER PERCUSSION
Gauge: 12.
Barrel: 28". Choke tubes (Mod., Imp., Full).
Weight: NA. **Length:** 46" over-all.
Stock: English-style straight grip of walnut-finished hardwood.
Sights: Brass bead front.
Features: Single blued barrel; color case-hardened lockplate and hammer; screw adjustable sear engagements, V-type mainspring; brass wedge plates; black trigger guard and tang. From CVA.
Price: Finished **$227.95**
Price: Kit **$189.95**

CVA BRITTANY II 410 PERCUSSION SHOTGUN
Gauge:
410.
Barrel: 24".
Weight: 6 lbs., 4 oz. **Length:** 38" over-all.
Stock: Hardwood with pistol grip, M.C. comb.
Sights: Brass bead front.
Features: Color case-hardened lockplates; double triggers (front is hinged); brass wedge plates; stainless nipple. Introduced 1986. From CVA.
Price: Finished **$167.95**
Price: Kit **$120.95**

HOPKINS & ALLEN PERCUSSION SHOTGUN
Gauge: 12.
Barrel: 28".
Weight: 6 lbs.
Stock: Walnut. Checkered wrist and fore-end.
Features: Hooked breech design for easy take down. Engraved lockplates. Imported by Hopkins & Allen.
Price: **$260.00**

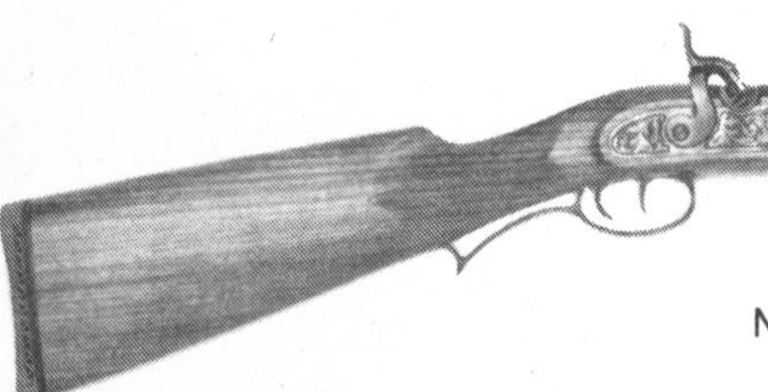

Navy Hunter

NAVY ARMS HUNTER SHOTGUN
Gauge: 20.
Barrel: 28½", interchangeable choke tubes (Full, Mod.).
Stock: Walnut, Hawken-style, checkered p.g. and fore-end.
Sights: Bead front.
Features: Chrome-lined barrel; rubber butt pad; color case-hardened lock; double set triggers; blued furniture. Comes with two flush-mounting choke tubes. Introduced 1986. From Navy Arms.
Price: **$315.00**

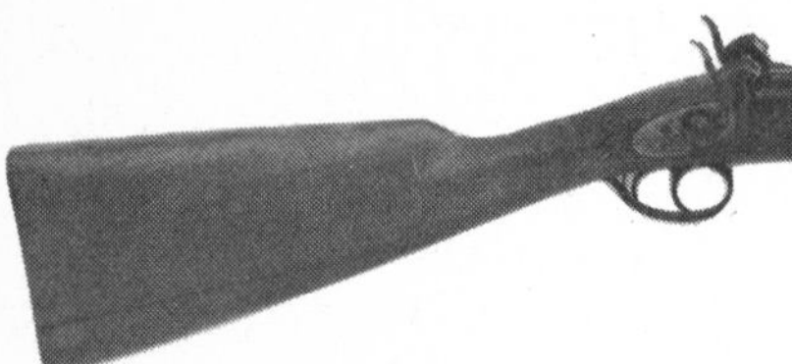

Navy T&T Shotgun

NAVY ARMS T&T SHOTGUN
Gauge: 12.
Barrel: 28" (Full & Full).
Weight: 7½ lbs.
Stock: Walnut.
Sights: Bead front.
Features: Color case-hardened locks, blued steel furniture. From Navy Arms.
Price: **$432.00**

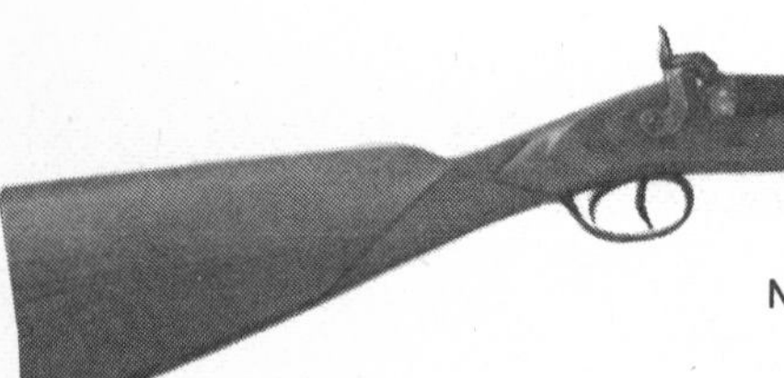

Navy Fowler

NAVY ARMS FOWLER SHOTGUN
Gauge: 12.
Barrel: 28".
Weight: 7 lbs., 12 oz. **Length:** 45" over-all.
Stock: Walnut.
Features: Color case-hardened lockplates and hammers; checkered stock. Imported by Navy Arms.
Price: Fowler model, 12 ga. only **$332.00**
Price: Fowler kit, 12 ga. only **$249.00**

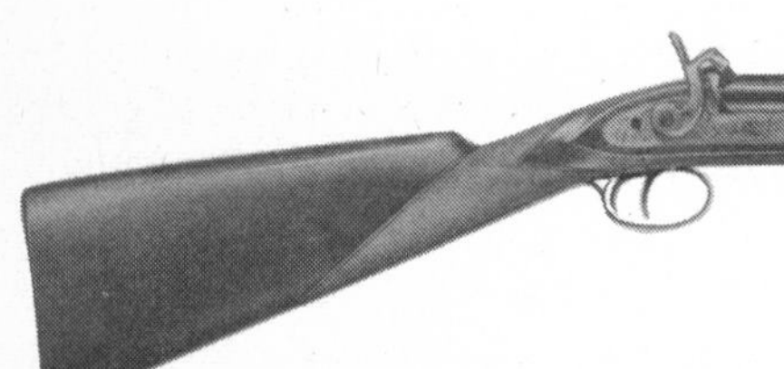

Dixie Double Barrel

DIXIE MAGNUM PERCUSSION SHOTGUN
Gauge: 10, 12.
Barrel: 30" (Imp. Cyl. & Mod.) in 10 ga.; 28" in 12 ga.
Weight: 6¼ lbs. **Length:** 45" over-all.
Stock: Hand checkered walnut, 14" pull.
Features: Double triggers, light hand engraving. Case-hardened locks in 12 ga.; polished steel in 10 ga. with sling swivels. From Dixie.
Price: Upland **$325.00**
Price: 12 ga. kit **$305.00**
Price: 10 ga. **$365.00**
Price: 10 ga. kit **$305.00**

CAUTION: PRICES CHANGE. CHECK AT GUNSHOP.

BLACK POWDER SHOTGUNS

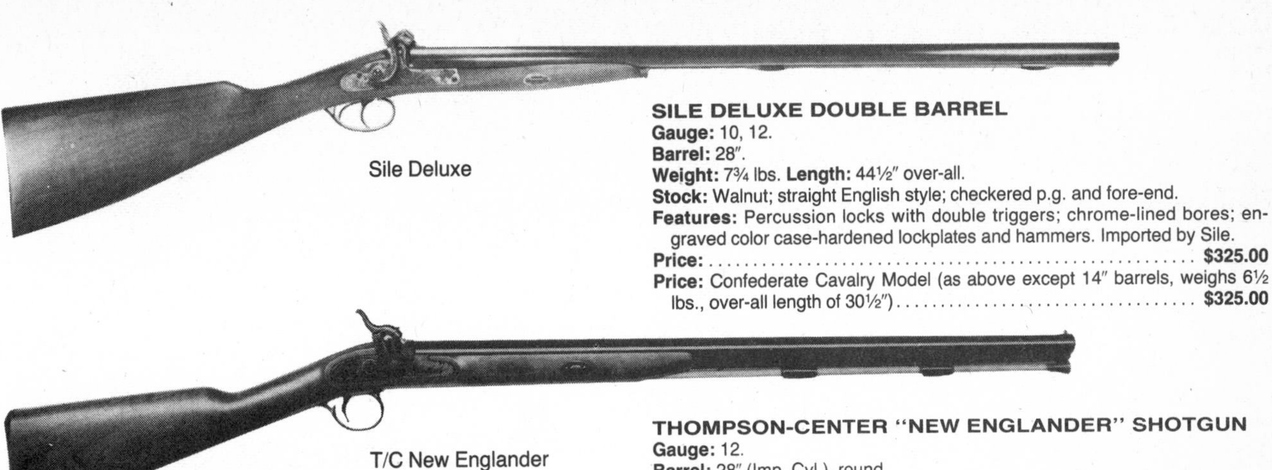

Sile Deluxe

T/C New Englander

SILE DELUXE DOUBLE BARREL

Gauge: 10, 12.
Barrel: 28″.
Weight: 7¾ lbs. **Length:** 44½″ over-all.
Stock: Walnut; straight English style; checkered p.g. and fore-end.
Features: Percussion locks with double triggers; chrome-lined bores; engraved color case-hardened lockplates and hammers. Imported by Sile.
Price: $325.00
Price: Confederate Cavalry Model (as above except 14″ barrels, weighs 6½ lbs., over-all length of 30½″) $325.00

THOMPSON-CENTER "NEW ENGLANDER" SHOTGUN

Gauge: 12.
Barrel: 28″ (Imp. Cyl.), round.
Weight: 5 lbs., 2 oz.
Stock: Select American black walnut with straight grip.
Features: Percussion lock is color case-hardened, rest blued. Also accepts 26″ round 50- and 54-cal. rifle barrel. Introduced 1986.
Price: Right hand $210.00
Price: Left hand $225.00
Price: Accessory rifle barrel, right hand, 50 or 54 .... $97.50
Price: As above, left hand $105.00

TRAIL GUNS KODIAK 10 GAUGE DOUBLE

Gauge: 10.
Barrel: 20″, 30¾″ (Cyl. bore).
Weight: About 9 lbs. **Length:** 47⅛″ over-all.
Stock: Walnut, with cheek rest. Checkered wrist and fore-end.
Features: Chrome-plated bores; engraved lockplates, brass bead front and middle sights; sling swivels. Introduced 1980. Imported form Italy by Trail Guns Armory.
Price: $350.00

AIR GUNS—HANDGUNS

AIR MATCH MODEL 600 PISTOL

Caliber: 177, single shot.
Barrel: 8.8″.
Weight: 32 oz. **Length:** 13.19″ over-all.
Power: Single stroke pneumatic.
Stocks: Match-style with adjustable palm shelf.
Sights: Interchangeable post front, fully adjustable match rear with interchangeable blades.
Features: Velocity of 420 fps. Adjustable trigger with dry-fire option. Available with three different grip styles, barrel weight, sight extension. Add $5.00 for left-hand models. Introduced 1984. Imported from Italy by Great Lakes Airguns.
Price: With adjustable or fixed grip $529.50

Air Match 600

AIR SHOT BSA SCORPION PISTOL

Caliber: 177 or 22, single shot.
Barrel: 7⅞″, rifled steel.
Weight: 54 oz. **Length:** 15 ¾″ over-all.
Power: Spring-piston, single-stroke pneumatic.
Stocks: Contoured moulded plastic with thumb-rest, checkering.
Sights: Hooded adjustable front post or bead, fully adjustable match rear.
Features: Velocity of 510 fps (177), 380 fps (22). Adjustable trigger; automatic safety; receiver grooved for scope mounting. Imported from England by Air-Shot Corp.
Price: $94.95

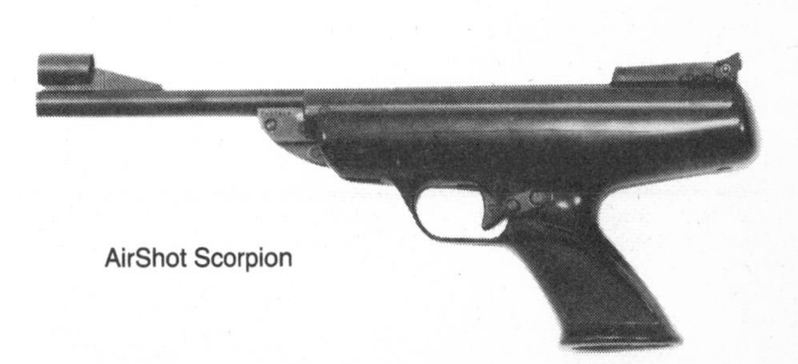

AirShot Scorpion

BEEMAN P1 MAGNUM AIR PISTOL

Caliber: 177, 20, 22, single shot.
Barrel: 8.4″.
Weight: 2.5 lbs. **Length:** 11″ over-all.
Power: Top lever cocking; spring piston.
Stocks: Checkered walnut.
Sights: Blade front, square notch rear with click micrometer adjustments for w. and e. Grooved for scope mounting.
Features: Dual power for 177 and 20 cal: low setting gives 350-400 fps; high setting 500-600 fps. Rearward expanding mainspring simulates firearm recoil. All Colt 45 auto grips fit gun. Dry firing feature for practice. Optional wooden shoulder stock. Introduced 1985. Imported by Beeman.
Price: 177, 22 cal. $288.00
Price: 20 cal. $295.00

Beeman P1 Magnum

BEEMAN/FEINWERKBAU MODEL 2 CO_2 PISTOL

Caliber: 177, single shot.
Barrel: 8.9″ or 10.1″.
Weight: 2.5 lbs. **Length:** 16.1″ or 14.8″ over-all.
Power: Special CO_2 cylinder.
Stocks: Stippled walnut with adjustable palm shelf.
Sights: Blade front with interchangeable inserts; open micro. click rear with adjustable notch width.
Features: Power adjustable from 360 fps to 525 fps. Fully adjustable trigger; three weights for balance and weight adjustments. Short-barrel Mini-2 model also available. Introduced 1983. Imported by Beeman.
Price: Right-hand **$780.00**
Price: Left-hand **$840.00**
Price: Mini-2, right hand **$790.00**
Price: Mini-2, left hand **$860.00**

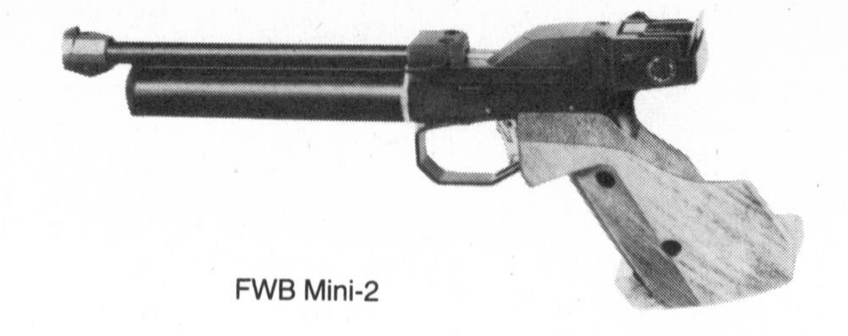
FWB Mini-2

BEEMAN/WEBLEY HURRICANE PISTOL

Caliber: 177 or 22, single shot.
Barrel: 8″, rifled.
Weight: 2.4 lbs. **Length:** 11½″ over-all.
Power: Spring piston.
Stocks: Thumbrest, checkered high-impact synthetic.
Sights: Hooded front; micro-click rear adj. for w. and e.
Features: Velocity of 470 fps (177-cal.). Single stroke cocking, adjustable trigger pull, manual safety. Rearward recoil like a firearm pistol. Steel piston and cylinder. Scope base included; 1.5x scope **$49.95** up extra. Shoulder stock available. Introduced 1977. Imported from England by Beeman.
Price: **$149.95**

Beeman/Webley Hurricane

BEEMAN/WEBLEY TEMPEST AIR PISTOL

Caliber: 177 or 22, single shot.
Barrel: 6.75″, rifled ordnance steel.
Weight: 32 oz. **Length:** 9″ over-all.
Power: Spring piston.
Stocks: Checkered black epoxy with thumbrest.
Sights: Post front; rear has sliding leaf adjustable for w. and e.
Features: Adjustable trigger pull, manual safety. Velocity 470 fps (177 cal.). Steel piston in steel liner for maximum performance and durability. Unique rearward spring simulates firearm recoil. Shoulder stock available. Introduced 1979. Imported from England by Beeman.
Price: **$129.95**

Beeman/Webley Tempest

BEEMAN/FEINWERKBAU FWB-65 MKII AIR PISTOL

Caliber: 177, single shot.
Barrel: 6.1″ or 7.5″, removeable bbl. wgt. avail.
Weight: 42 oz. **Length:** 13.3″ or 14.1″ over-all.
Power: Spring, sidelever cocking.
Stocks: Walnut, stippled thumbrest; adjustable or fixed.
Sights: Front, interchangeable post element system, open rear, click adj. for w. & e. and for sighting notch width. Scope mount avail.
Features: New shorter barrel for better balance and control. Cocking effort 9 lbs. 2-stage trigger, 4 adjustments. Quiet firing, 525 fps. Programs instantly for recoil or recoilless operation. Permanently lubricated. Steel piston ring. Special switch converts trigger from 17.6 oz. pull to 42 oz. let-off. Imported by Beeman.
Price: Right-hand .... **$775.00** to **$795.00**
Price: Left-hand, 6.1″ barrel **$825.00**
Price: Model 65 Mk.I (7.5″ bbl.) .... **$725.00** to **$779.00**

FWB 65 Mk. II

Beeman/Weihrauch HW-70

BEEMAN/WEIHRAUCH HW-70 AIR PISTOL

Caliber: 177; single shot.
Barrel: 6¼″, rifled.
Weight: 38 oz. **Length:** 12¾″ over-all.
Power: Spring, barrel cocking.
Stocks: Plastic, with thumbrest.
Sights: Hooded post front, square notch rear adj. for w. and e.
Features: Adj. trigger. 24-lb. cocking effort, 410 fps MV; automatic barrel safety. Imported by Beeman.
Price: From Beeman **$147.50**

Benjamin 242/247

Crosman 357

Crosman Model 3357 Spot Marker

Same specs as 8″ Model 357 but shoots 50-cal. paint balls. Has break-open action for quick loading 6-shot clip of paint balls. CO_2 power allows repeater firing; hammer block safety; adjustable rear sight, blade front.

Price: About **$89.00**

CROSMAN MODEL 1322 AIR PISTOL

Caliber: 22, single shot.
Barrel: 8″, button rifled.
Weight: 37 oz. **Length:** 13⅝″.
Power: Hand pumped.
Sights: Blade front, rear adj. for w. and e.
Features: Moulded plastic grip, hand size pump forearm. Cross-bolt safety. Also available in 177/BB cal. as **Model 1377**.
Price: About **$50.00**
Price: 1377, about **$50.00**

CROSMAN/BLASER CONVERSION KIT

Caliber: 177, single shot.
Barrel: 5½″, rifled steel.
Weight: 16 oz.
Power: CO_2 Powerlet.
Sights: Blade front, open adj. rear.
Features: Velocity about 400 fps. Converts Colt 45 auto (Series 70 and earlier) into an airgun—replaces slide and magazine and gives same weight and balance, trigger pull, sights as the Colt. About 60 shots per Powerlet.
Price: About **$130.00**

CROSMAN/SKANAKER MATCH AIR PISTOL

Caliber: 177.
Barrel: 9.94″.
Weight: 37 oz. **Length:** 16.38″ over-all.
Power: Refillable CO_2 cylinders.
Stocks: Stippled hardwood adjustable for thickness; adjustable palm shelf.
Sights: Three-way adjustable post front, open rear with three interchangeable leaves.
Features: Velocity of 550 fps. Angled, adjustable match trigger can be aligned to fit the natural position of the trigger finger. Barrel is hinged near the muzzle for loading. Introduced 1987.
Price: About **$600.00**

BEEMAN/FEINWERKBAU MODEL 90 PISTOL

Caliber: 177, single shot.
Barrel: 7.5″, 12-groove rifling.
Weight: 3.0 lbs. **Length:** 16.4″ over-all.
Power: Spring piston, single stroke sidelever cocking.
Stocks: Stippled walnut with adjustable palm shelf.
Sights: Interchangeable blade front, fully adjustable open notch rear.
Features: Velocity of 475 to 525 fps. Has new adjustable electronic trigger. Recoilless action, metal piston ring and dual mainsprings. Cocking effort is 12 lbs. Introduced 1983. Imported by Beeman.
Price: .... **$880.00** to **$955.00**

BENJAMIN 242/247 SINGLE SHOT PISTOLS

Caliber: 177 and 22.
Weight: 32 oz. **Length:** 11¾″ over-all.
Power: Hand pumped.
Stocks: Walnut pump handle, optional walnut grips.
Sights: Blade front, open adjustable rear.
Features: Bolt action; fingertip safety; adjustable power.
Price: Model 242 (22 cal.) **$86.95**
Price: Model 247 (177 cal.) **$86.95**

CROSMAN MODEL 357 AIR PISTOL

Caliber: 177, 6- or 10-shot.
Barrel: 4″ (Model 357 Four), 6″ (Model 357 Six), 8″ (Model 357 Eight); rifled steel.
Weight: 32 oz. (6″) **Length:** 11⅜″ over-all.
Power: CO_2 Powerlet.
Stocks: Checkered wood-grain plastic.
Sights: Ramp front, fully adjustable rear.
Features: Average 430 fps (Model 357 Six). Break-open barrel for easy loading. Single or double action. Vent rib barrel. Wide, smooth trigger. Two speed loaders come with each gun.
Price: 4″ or 6″, about **$55.00**
Price: 8″, about **$60.00**
Price: Model 1357 (as above, except shoots BBs, 6-shot clip), about **$55.00**

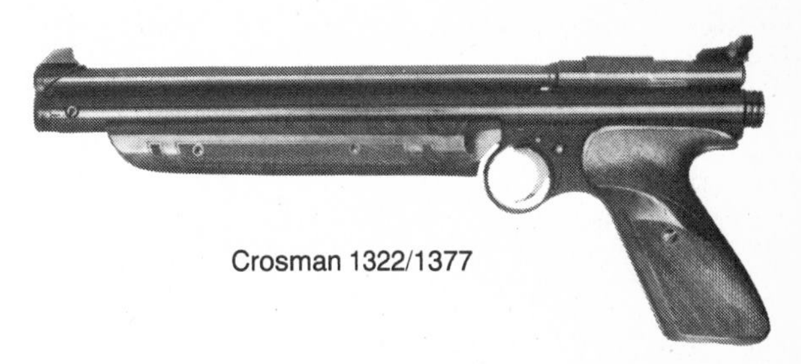

Crosman 1322/1377

Crosman/Blaser

CROSMAN 338 AUTO PISTOL

Caliber: BB, 20-shot magazine.
Barrel: 5″, steel.
Weight: 24 oz. **Length:** 8½″ over-all.
Power: CO_2 Powerlet.
Stocks: Checkered plastic.
Sights: Patridge front, adjustable rear.
Features: Velocity about 370 fps. Replica of the Walther P-38 pistol. Semi-automatic repeater; thumb-operated lever safety. Introduced 1986.
Price: About **$42.00**

DAISY POWER LINE MODEL 44 REVOLVER
Caliber: 177 pellets, 6-shot.
Barrel: 6″, rifled steel; interchangeable 4″ and 8″.
Weight: 2.7 lbs.
Power: CO_2.
Stocks: Moulded plastic with checkering.
Sights: Blade on ramp front, fully adjustable notch rear.
Features: Velocity up to 400 fps. Replica of 44 Magnum revolver. Has swing-out cylinder and interchangeable barrels. Introduced 1987. From Daisy.
Price: **$56.00**

Power Line 44

Daisy Power Line 92

DAISY POWER LINE MODEL 92 PISTOL
Caliber: 177 pellets, 10-shot magazine.
Barrel: Rifled steel.
Weight: 2.15 lbs. **Length:** 8.5″ over-all.
Power: CO_2.
Stocks: Cast checkered metal.
Sights: Blade front, adjustable V-slot rear.
Features: Semi-automatic action; 400 fps. Replica of the official 9mm sidearm of the United States armed forces.
Price: About **$57.00**

Daisy Model 188

DAISY MODEL 188 BB PISTOL
Caliber: BB.
Barrel: 9.9″, steel smoothbore.
Weight: 1.67 lbs. **Length:** 11.7″ over-all.
Stocks: Die-cast metal; checkered with thumbrest.
Sights: Blade and ramp front, open fixed rear.
Features: 24-shot repeater. Spring action with under-barrel cocking lever. Grip and receiver of die-cast metal. Introduced 1979.
Price: About **$21.00**

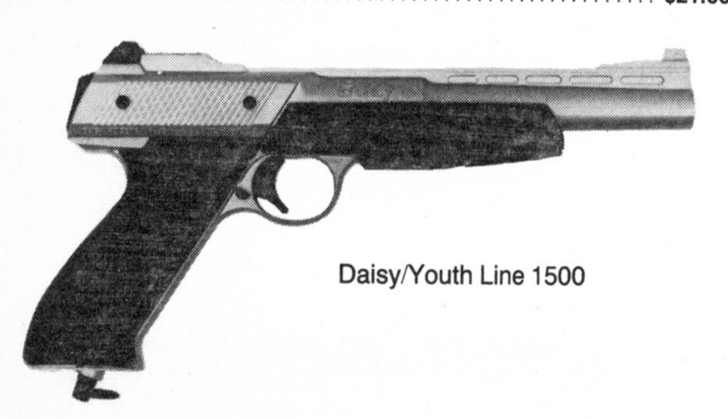
Daisy/Youth Line 1500

DAISY/YOUTH LINE MODEL 1500 PISTOL
Caliber: BB, 60-shot reservoir.
Barrel: 1.5″, smooth bore.
Weight: 22 oz. **Length:** 11.1″ over-all.
Power: Daisy CO_2 cylinder
Stocks: Moulded wood-grain plastic with checkering.
Sights: Blade on ramp front, fully adjustable notch rear.
Features: Velocity of 340 fps. Gravity feed magazine. Cross-bolt safety.
Price: About **$32.00**

Power Line 777

DAISY/POWER LINE MATCH 777 PELLET PISTOL
Caliber: 177, single shot.
Barrel: 9.61″ rifled steel by Lothar Walther.
Weight: 32 oz. **Length:** 13½″ over-all.
Power: Sidelever, single pump pneumatic.
Stocks: Smooth hardwood, fully contoured with palm and thumb rest.
Sights: Blade and ramp front, match-grade open rear with adj. width notch, micro. click adjustments.
Features: Adjustable trigger; manual cross-bolt safety. MV of 385 fps. Comes with cleaning kit, adjustment tool and pellets. From Daisy.
Price: About **$199.50**

DAISY/POWER LINE 717 PELLET PISTOL
Caliber: 177, single shot.
Barrel: 9.61″.
Weight: 2.8 lbs. **Length:** 13½″ over-all.
Stocks: Moulded wood-grain plastic, with thumbrest.
Sights: Blade and ramp front, micro, adjustable notch rear.
Features: Single pump pneumatic pistol. Rifled steel barrel. Cross-bolt trigger block. Muzzle velocity 385 fps. From Daisy. Introduced 1979.
Price: About **$56.00**

Daisy/Power Line 747 Pistol
Similar to the 717 pistol except has a 12-groove rifled steel barrel by Lothar Walther. Velocity of 360 fps. Manual cross-bolt safety.
Price: About **$85.00**

DAISY/POWER LINE CO_2 1200 PISTOL
Caliber: BB, 177.
Barrel: 10½″, smooth.
Weight: 1.6 lbs. **Length:** 11.1″ over-all.
Power: Daisy CO_2 cylinder.
Stocks: Contoured, checkered moulded wood-grain plastic.
Sights: Blade ramp front, fully adj. square notch rear.
Features: 60-shot BB reservoir, gravity feed. Cross-bolt safety. Velocity of 420-450 fps for more than 100 shots. From Daisy.
Price: About **$32.00**

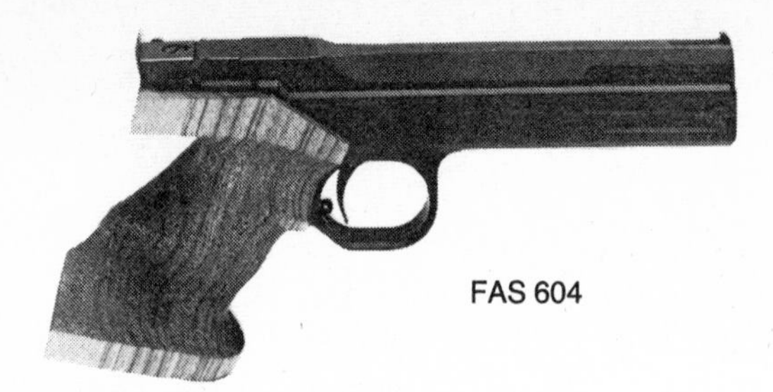
FAS 604

FAS MODEL 604 AIR PISTOL

Caliber: 177, single shot.
Barrel: 7.4", 10-groove rifled steel.
Weight: 2.3 lbs. **Length:** 11.3" over-all.
Power: Single stroke pneumatic.
Stocks: Anatomically shaped stippled walnut; small, medium, large sizes.
Sights: Adjustable.
Features: Top of receiver is cocking arm, requires 13 lbs. effort. Adjustable trigger may be dry-fired without fully cocking pistol. Imported from Italy by Osborne's. Introduced 1984.
Price: **$395.00**

FAS MODEL AP 604 AIR PISTOL

Caliber: 177, single shot.
Barrel: 7.5", 10-groove rifled steel.
Weight: 2.3 lbs. **Length:** 11.3" over-all.
Power: Single stroke pneumatic.
Stocks: Anatomically shaped stippled hardwood.
Sights: Post front, fully adjustable rear.
Features: Velocity of 370 fps. Top of receiver is cocking arm, requires 13 lbs. effort. Adjustable trigger may be dry-fired without fully cocking pistol. Imported from Italy by Great Lakes Airguns.
Price: **$479.50**

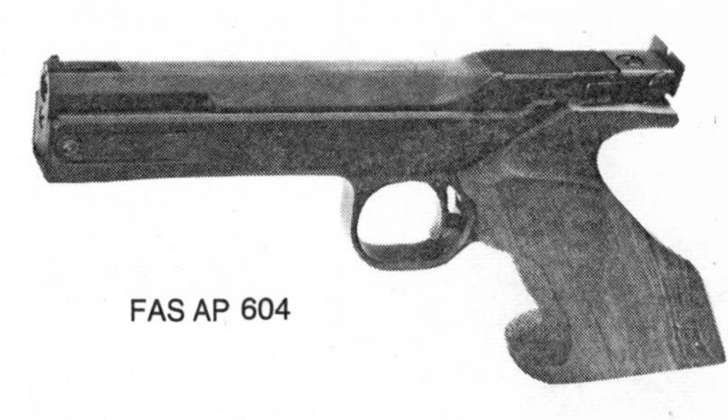
FAS AP 604

"GAT" AIR PISTOL

Caliber: 177, single shot.
Barrel: 7½" cocked, 9½" extended.
Weight: 22 oz.
Power: Spring piston.
Stocks: Composition.
Sights: Fixed.
Features: Shoots pellets or darts. Matte black finish. Imported by Stone Enterprises, Inc.
Price: **$19.95**

Marksman Model 17

MARKSMAN 17 AIR PISTOL

Caliber: 177, single shot.
Barrel: 7.5".
Weight: 46 oz. **Length:** 14.5" over-all.
Power: Spring air, barrel-cocking.
Stocks: Checkered composition with right-hand thumb rest.
Sights: Tunnel front, fully adj. rear.
Features: Velocity of 330-360 fps. Introduced 1986. Imported from Spain by Marksman Products.
Price: **$86.95**

MARKSMAN PLAINSMAN 1049 CO_2 PISTOL

Caliber: BB, 100-shot repeater.
Barrel: 5⅞", smooth.
Weight: 28 oz. **Length:** 9½" over-all.
Stocks: Simulated walnut with thumbrest.
Power: 8.5 or 12.5 gram CO_2 cylinders.
Features: Velocity of 400 fps. Three-position power switch. Auto. ammunition feed. Positive safety.
Price: **$37.50**

MARKSMAN #1010 REPEATER PISTOL

Caliber: 177, 20-shot repeater.
Barrel: 2½", smoothbore.
Weight: 24 oz. **Length:** 8¼" over-all.
Power: Spring.
Features: Thumb safety. Black finish. Uses BBs, darts or pellets. Repeats with BBs only.
Price: Matte black finish **$20.50**
Price: Model 1010X (as above except nickel plated) **$28.00**

Marksman 1010

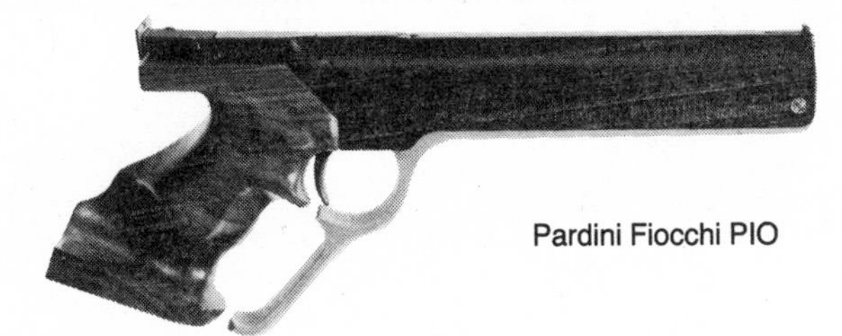
Pardini Fiocchi PIO

PARDINI FIOCCHI PIO MATCH AIR PISTOL

Caliber: 177.
Barrel: 7.7".
Weight: 37 ozs. **Length:** 14" over-all.
Power: Single stroke pneumatic.
Stocks: Stippled walnut with palm shelf.
Sights: Post front, fully adjustable open rear.
Features: Muzzle velocity of 425 fps. Cocking lever forms trigger guard. Imported from Italy by Fiocchi of America.
Price: **$375.00**

RWS/DIANA MODEL 6M MATCH AIR PISTOL

Caliber: 177, single shot.
Barrel: 7".
Weight: 3 lbs. **Length:** 16" over-all.
Power: Spring air, barrel cocking.
Stocks: Walnut-finished hardwood with thumbrest.
Sights: Adjustable front, micro. click open rear.
Features: Velocity of 410 fps. Recoilless double piston system, moveable barrel shroud to protect front sight during cocking. Imported from West Germany by Dynamit Nobel-RWS, Inc.
Price: Right hand **$335.00**
Price: Left hand **$350.00**

RWS/DIANA MODEL 5G AIR PISTOL
Caliber: 177, single shot.
Barrel: 7″.
Weight: 2¾ lbs. **Length:** 16″ over-all.
Power: Spring air, barrel cocking.
Stocks: Plastic, thumbrest design.
Sights: Tunnel front, micro click open rear.
Features: Velocity of 410 fps. Two-stage trigger with automatic safety. Imported from West Germany by Dynamit Nobel-RWS, Inc.
Price: **$150.00**

RWS Model 5G

RWS/Diana MODEL 5GS Air Pistol
Same as the Model 5G except comes with 1.5x15 pistol scope with ramp-style mount, muzzle brake/weight. No open sights supplied. Introduced 1983.
Price: **$210.00**

RWS Model 10

RWS/Diana Model 10 Match Air Pistol
Refined version of the Model 6M. Has special adjustable match trigger, oil finished and stippled match grips, barrel weight. Also available in left-hand version, and with fitted case.
Price: Model 10 .... **$595.00**
Price: Model 10, left-hand **$640.00**
Price: Model 10, with case **$625.00**
Price: Model 10, left-hand, with case **$670.00**

Record Champion

RECORD "JUMBO" DELUXE AIR PISTOL
Caliber: 177, single shot.
Barrel: 6″, rifled.
Weight: 1.9 lbs. **Length:** 7.25″ over-all.
Power: Spring air, lever cocking.
Stocks: Smooth walnut.
Sights: Post front, fully adjustable open rear.
Features: Velocity of 322 fps. Thumb safety. Grip magazine compartment for extra pellet storage. Introduced 1983. Imported from West Germany by Great Lakes Aiguns.
Price: **$79.95**

RECORD CHAMPION AIR PISTOL
Caliber: 177, 12-shot repeater.
Barrel: 7.6″, rifled.
Weight: 2.8 lbs. **Length:** 10.2″ over-all.
Power: Spring air, sidelever cocking.
Stocks: Smooth hardwood. Contoured target style available.
Sights: Post front, fully adjustable rear.
Features: Velocity of 420 fps. Magazine loads into bottom of grip. Ambidextrous grips. Introduced 1987. Imported from West Germany by Great Lakes Airguns.
Price: **$136.54**

Sharp "U-FP"

Sheridan Model HB

SHARP MODEL "U-FP" CO_2 PISTOL
Caliber: 177, single shot.
Barrel: 8″, rifled steel.
Weight: 2.4 lbs. **Length:** 11.6″ over-all.
Power: 12 gram CO_2 cylinder.
Stocks: Smooth hardwood. Walnut target stocks available.
Sights: Post front, fully adjustable target rear.
Features: Variable power adjustment up to 545 fps. Adjustable trigger. Also available with adjustable field sight. Imported from Japan by Great Lakes Airguns.
Price: With target sights **$199.50**
Price: With field sights **$179.50**

SHERIDAN MODEL HB PNEUMATIC PISTOL
Caliber: 5mm, single shot.
Barrel: 9⅜″, rifled.
Weight: 36 oz.. **Length:** 12″ over-all.
Power: Underlever pneumatic pump.
Stocks: Checkered simulated walnut; fore-end is walnut.
Sights: Blade front, fully adjustable rear.
Features: "Controller-Power" feature allows velocity and range control by varying the number of pumps—3 to 10. Maximum velocity of 400 fps. Introduced 1982. From Sheridan Products.
Price: **$86.95**

WALTHER CP CO_2 AIR PISTOL
Caliber: 177, single shot.
Barrel: 9″.
Weight: 40 oz. **Length:** 14¾″ over-all.
Power: CO_2.
Stocks: Full target type stippled wood with adjustable hand-shelf.
Sights: Target post front, fully adjustable target rear.
Features: Velocity of 520 fps. CO_2 powered; target-quality trigger; comes with adaptor for charging with standard CO_2 air tanks, case, and accessories. Introduced 1983. Imported from West Germany by Interarms.
Price: **$825.00**
Price: Junior Model (modified grip, shorter gas cylinder) **$825.00**

CAUTION: PRICES CHANGE. CHECK AT GUNSHOP.

Gas Auto Mag

COMMAND POST GAS AUTO MAG PISTOL
Caliber: 25-cal. plastic shot.
Barrel: NA
Weight: 2 lbs. **Length:** 10" over-all.
Power: Liquid charge Flon-12 gas system.
Stocks: Checkered black plastic.
Sights: Ramp front, adjustable rear.
Features: Nickel finish. Replica of the Auto Mag pistol. Available from The Command Post, Inc.
Price: **$79.98**

Model 645

COMMAND POST MODEL 645 PISTOL
Caliber: 25-cal. plastic shot.
Barrel: NA
Weight: 12 oz. **Length:** 9" over-all.
Power: Spring-air, slide cocking.
Stocks: Checkered black plastic.
Sights: Ramp front, notch rear.
Features: Replica of the Model 645 auto pistol. Stainless finish.
Price: **$29.98**

COMMAND POST M-11 GAS PISTOL
Caliber: 25-cal. plastic shot.
Barrel: NA
Weight: 3 lbs. **Length:** 15" over-all.
Power: Direct gas power.
Stocks: Moulded plastic.
Sights: Post front, aperture rear.
Features: Full-size replica of the MAC-11. Removeable fake suppressor. Front hand strap. Semiauto fire. Available from The Command Post, Inc.
Price: **$64.98**

M-11 Gas Pistol

Airsoft 04

COMMAND POST AIRSOFT 04
Caliber: 25-cal. plastic pellets.
Barrel: Smoothbore.
Weight: 1.1 lbs. **Length:** 10.5" over-all.
Power: Spring.
Stocks: Woodgrain moulded grip with checkering.
Sights: Blade and ramp front, notched rear.
Features: Fully detailed replica of a classic 44 Magnum, six-shot revolver with swing-out cylinder for easy loading.
Price: About **$33.00**

Consult our Directory pages for the location of firms mentioned.

COMMAND POST AIRSOFT 09
Caliber: 25-cal. plastic shot.
Barrel: Smoothbore.
Weight: 12 oz. **Length:** 9.5" over-all.
Power: Slide action, spring air.
Stocks: Moulded grip with checkering.
Sights: Blade front, notched rear.
Features: Detailed replica of the official 9mm sidearm recently adopted by the U.S. Armed Forces, the Beretta 9mm. Takes seven-shot clip, ejects spent shells.
Price: About **$24.98**

Airsoft 09

COMMAND POST AIRSOFT 13
Caliber: 25-cal. plastic shot.
Barrel: Smoothbore.
Weight: 2.6 lbs. **Length:** 15.5" over-all.
Power: Bolt action, spring air.
Stocks: Moulded grip and receiver.
Sights: Post front, notched rear.
Features: Replica of the world-famous Israeli semi-automatic assault pistol; loads with 22-shot clip.
Price: About **$39.98**

Airsoft 57

COMMAND POST AIRSOFT 57 REVOLVER
Caliber: 25 (6mm) plastic pellets; 6-shot.
Barrel: Smoothbore.
Weight: NA. **Length:** 10½″ over-all.
Stocks: Moulded woodgrain with checkering.
Sights: Blade and ramp front, notch rear.
Features: Fires spring-activated 25-cal. plastic pellets loaded into plastic cartridges. Cylinder swings out for loading. Introduced 1985.
Price: About $24.98

COMMAND POST AIRSOFT 45
Caliber: 25-cal. plastic shot.
Barrel: Smoothbore.
Weight: 12 oz. **Length:** 8.5″ over-all.
Power: Slide cocking, spring air.
Stocks: Moulded grip with checkering.
Sights: Ramp front, notched rear.
Features: Detailed replica of the 45 auto pistol. Holds seven-shot clip, ejects spent shells.
Price: About $24.98

COMMAND POST AIRSOFT 59 PISTOL
Caliber: 25 (6mm) plastic pellets; 10-shot clip.
Barrel: Smoothbore.
Weight: NA. **Length:** 9″ over-all.
Stocks: Moulded with checkering.
Sights: Blade and ramp front, notch rear.
Features: Fires 25-cal. plastic pellets loaded into plastic cartridges. Clip fed, semi-auto action ejects spent shells. Introduced 1985.
Price: About $24.98

COMMAND POST TRACER SCORPION
Caliber: 25-cal. plastic glow shot.
Barrel: NA.
Weight: 2½ lbs. **Length:** 24″ over-all (stock extended).
Power: Spring piston, bolt action.
Stock: Moulded woodgrain composition; folding wire butt.
Sights: Post front, notch rear.
Features: Shoots "glow BBs" for tracer effect. Available from The Command Post, Inc.
Price: $89.98

Tracer Scorpion

AIR GUNS—LONG GUNS

Air Arms Firepower

AIR ARMS FIREPOWER AIR RIFLE
Caliber: 22, 35-shot Auto-Load system.
Barrel: 14¾″, Walther with 12 grooves.
Weight: 7 lbs., 8 oz. **Length:** 40½″ over-all.
Power: Spring-air, sidelever.
Stock: Synthetic, military-style.
Sights: Blade on ramp front, adjustable aperture rear.
Features: Velocity of 700+ fps. Adjustable trigger; removeable sights; receiver grooved for scope mounting. High polish blue finish; sling swivels. Introduced 1987. Imported from England by Great Lakes Airguns.
Price: $277.00

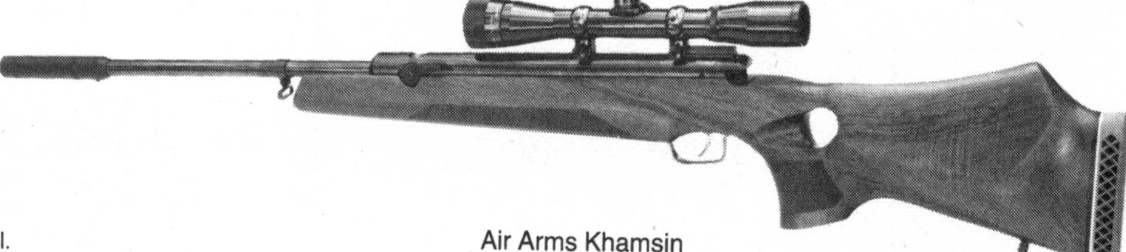
Air Arms Khamsin

AIR ARMS MODEL KHAMSIN
Caliber: 177, 22; single shot.
Barrel: 15″, rifled.
Weight: 8 lbs., 2 oz. **Length:** 39¾″ over-all.
Power: Spring-air, side-lever cocking.
Stock: Oil-finished French walnut thumbhole-style, with cut checkering on p.g. and fore-end. Ventilated rubber buttplate and sling swivels.
Sights: None furnished. Comes with scope anti-slip block.
Features: Velocity up to 852 fps (177 cal.). Polished brass trigger and trigger guard. Introduced 1987. Imported from England by Great Lakes Airguns.
Price: Either caliber $486.58
Price: With AutoLoad 34-pellet magazine $527.93

Air Arms Model Bora
Similar to the Mistral model except has 11″ barrel, weighs 7.7 lbs. and has 35.8″ over-all length. Velocity up to 872 fps (177 cal.). Imported from England by Great Lakes Airguns.
Price: 177 or 22 .... $277.00
Price: With AutoLoad 34-pellet magazine $294.21

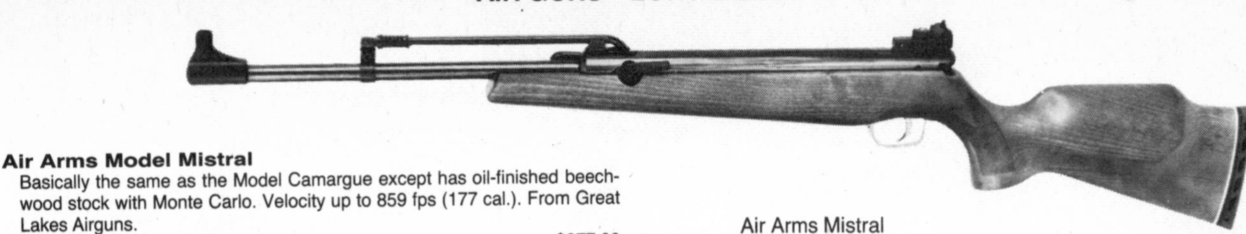

Air Arms Mistral

Air Arms Model Mistral
Basically the same as the Model Camargue except has oil-finished beechwood stock with Monte Carlo. Velocity up to 859 fps (177 cal.). From Great Lakes Airguns.
Price: Either 177 or 22 caliber **$277.00**
Price: With AutoLoad 34-pellet magazine **$294.21**

Air Arms Model Camargue
Basically the same as the Khamsin model except has a Tyrolean-style stock, post front sight with protective ears, micrometer-adjustable aperture rear. Velocity up to 871 fps (177 cal.). From Great Lakes Airguns.
Price: Either caliber **$363.91**
Price: With AutoLoad 34-pellet magazine **$433.26**

BSA Airsporter-S

AIR SHOT BSA AIRSPORTER-S RIFLES
Caliber: 177 or 22, single shot.
Barrel: 14.3" (Carbine), 19.5" (Rifle).
Weight: 7.4 lbs. (Carbine), 8 lbs. (Rifle) **Length:** 39.5" over-all (Carbine).
Power: Spring-piston, single-stroke pneumatic; under lever cocking.
Stock: Walnut-stained hardwood with Monte Carlo comb, checkered p.g., fore-end; vent. recoil pad.
Sights: Hooded adjustable front bead/blade, fully adjustable match rear.
Features: Velocity of 825 fps (177), 600 fps (22). "Maxigrip" scope mounting system; two-stage adjustable match trigger. Fixed heavy barrel with loading plug. Imported from England by AirShot Corp.
Price: **$246.95**

Air Shot BSA Airsporter Stutzen
Similar to the Airsporter-S except has full-length Mannlicher-style stock with Monte Carlo comb, cheekpiece, 14" barrel, over-all length of 39", weight of 7.8 lbs., low-profile rear sight.
Price: **$286.95**

BSA Mercury

AIR SHOT BSA MERCURY AIR RIFLE
Caliber: 177 or 22, single shot.
Barrel: 18.5", rifled steel.
Weight: 7 lbs. **Length:** 43.5" over-all.
Power: Spring-piston, single-stroke pneumatic, barrel cocking.
Stock: Walnut-stained hardwood with Monte Carlo comb, checkered p.g., vent. recoil pad.
Sights: Hooded adjustable front, fully adjustable rear.
Features: Velocity of 700 fps (177), 550 fps (22). Two-stage adjustable trigger. Receiver grooved for scope mounting. Imported from England by AirShot Corp.
Price: **$156.95**

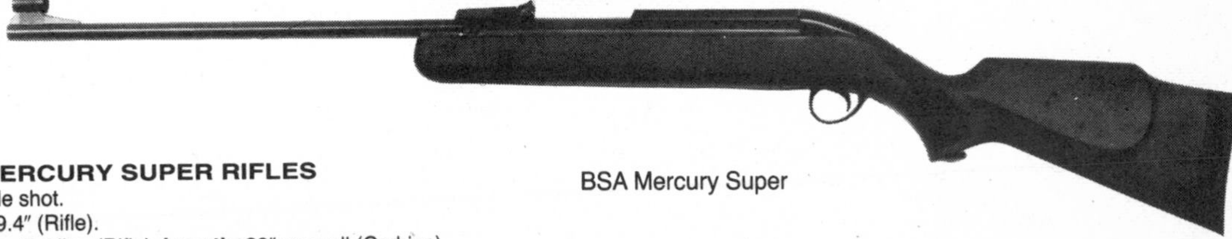

BSA Mercury Super

AIR SHOT BSA MERCURY SUPER RIFLES
Caliber: 177 or 22, single shot.
Barrel: 14" (Carbine), 19.4" (Rifle).
Weight: 6.8 lbs. (Carbine, 7.4 lbs. (Rifle). **Length:** 39" over-all (Carbine).
Power: Spring-piston, single-stroke pneumatic, barrel cocking.
Stock: Walnut-stained hardwood with Monte Carlo comb, checkered p.g. and fore-end, vent. recoil pad.
Sights: Hooded adjustable front bead/blade, fully adjustable match rear.
Features: Velocity of 850 fps (177), 625 fps (22). "Maxigrip" scope mounting system with arrestor block. Two-stage adjustable match trigger. Imported from England by AirShot Corp.
Price: **$194.95**

BSA Meteor Super

AIR SHOT BSA METEOR SUPER AIR RIFLE
Caliber: 177 or 22, single shot.
Barrel: 18.5", rifled steel.
Weight: 6 lbs. **Length:** 42" over-all.
Power: Spring-piston, single-stroke pneumatic, barrel cocking.
Stock: Walnut-stained hardwood with Monte Carlo comb, vent. recoil pad.
Sights: Hooded adjustable front, fully adjustable rear.
Features: Velocity of 800 fps (177), 585 fps (22). Adjustable trigger. Receiver grooved for scope mounting. Imported from England by AirShot Corp.
Price: **$115.95**

Air Shot Meteor Air Rifle
Similar to the Meteor Super except has straight-comb stock. Comes with extra aperture rear sight.
Price: **$97.95**

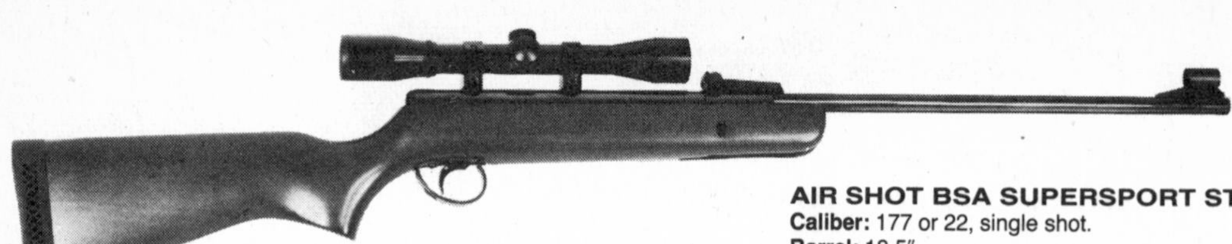

BSA Supersport Standard

AIR SHOT BSA SUPERSPORT STANDARD RIFLE
Caliber: 177 or 22, single shot.
Barrel: 18.5″.
Weight: 6 lbs., 6 oz. **Length:** 42″ over-all.
Power: Spring-piston, single-stroke pneumatic.
Stock: Walnut-stained hardwood with ventilated rubber recoil pad.
Sights: Hooded adjustable front bead/blade, fully adjustable match rear.
Features: Velocity of 950 fps (177), 700 fps (22). Single-stage adjustable trigger, silent safety. Receiver grooved for scope mounting. Imported from England by AirShot Corp.
Price: **$179.95**

Air Shot BSA Supersport Custom
Similar to the Standard except has checkered Monte Carlo stock, "Maxigrip" scope mounting system with arrestor block.
Price: **$286.95**

Air Shot Survival

AIR SHOT SURVIVAL CARBINE
Caliber: 177, 25-shot feed tube.
Barrel: 12″, rifled steel.
Weight: 5 lbs., 10 oz. **Length:** 32″ over-all.
Power: Spring-piston, single-stroke pneumatic.
Stock: Moulded composition, folding skeleton butt.
Sights: Hooded ramp front, fully adjustable match rear.
Features: Velocity of 625 fps. Automatic safety. Receiver grooved for scope mounting. Comes with web sling. Imported from Brazil by AirShot Corp.
Price: **$71.95**

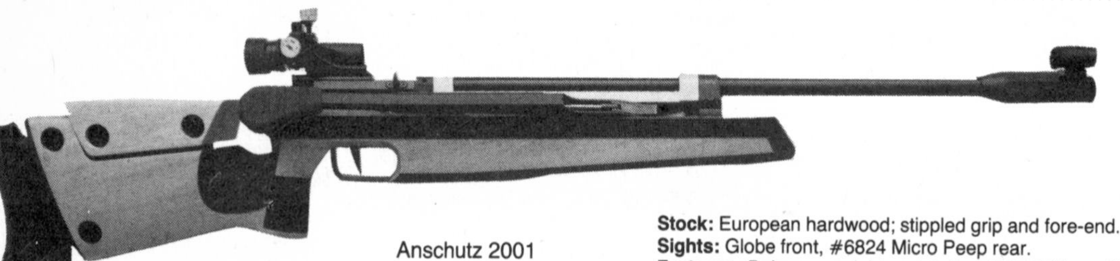

Anschutz 2001

ANSCHUTZ 2001 MATCH AIR RIFLE
Caliber: 177, single shot.
Barrel: 26″.
Weight: 10½ lbs. **Length:** 44½″ over-all.
Stock: European hardwood; stippled grip and fore-end.
Sights: Globe front, #6824 Micro Peep rear.
Features: Balance, weight match the 1907 ISU smallbore rifle. Uses #5019 match trigger. Recoil and vibration free. Fully adjustable cheekpiece and buttplate. Introduced 1988. Imported from Germany by Precision Sales International.
Price: Right hand **$1,290.00**
Price: Left hand.......... **$1,355.00**

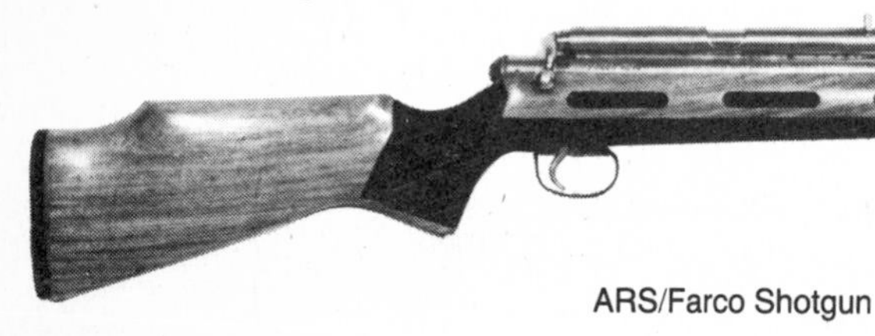

ARS/Farco Shotgun

ARS/FARCO CO_2 AIR SHOTGUN
Caliber: 51 (28 gauge).
Barrel: 30″.
Weight: 7 lbs. **Length:** 48½″ over-all.
Power: 10-oz. refillable CO_2 tank.
Stock: Hardwood.
Sights: Bead front, fixed dovetail rear.
Features: Gives over 100 ft. lbs. energy for taking small game. Imported by Air Rifle Specialists.
Price: **$400.00**

Beeman/FWB 124

BEEMAN/FEINWERKBAU 124/127 MAGNUM
Caliber: 177 (FWB-124); 22 (FWB-127); single shot.
Barrel: 18.3″, 12-groove rifling.
Weight: 6.8 lbs. **Length:** 43½″ over-all.
Power: Spring piston air; single stroke barrel cocking.
Stock: Walnut finished hardwood.
Sights: Tunnel front; click-adj. rear for w., slide-adj. for e.
Features: Velocity 680-820 fps, cocking effort of 18 lbs. Forged steel receiver; nylon non-drying piston and breech seals. Auto. safety, adj. trigger. Hand-checkered p.g. and fore-end, high comb cheekpiece, and buttplate with white spacer. Imported by Beeman.
Price: Deluxe model, right hand **$399.98**
Price: As above, left hand **$439.98**

CAUTION: PRICES CHANGE. CHECK AT GUNSHOP.

BEEMAN/FEINWERKBAU 300-S SERIES MATCH RIFLE

Caliber: 177, single shot.
Barrel: 19.9", fixed solid with receiver.
Weight: Approx. 10 lbs. with optional bbl. sleeve. **Length:** 42.8" over-all.
Power: Single stroke sidelever, spring piston.
Stock: Match model—walnut, deep fore-end, adj. buttplate.
Sights: Globe front with interchangeable inserts. Click micro. adj. match aperture rear. Front and rear sights move as a single unit.
Features: Recoilless, vibration free. Five-way adjustable match trigger. Grooved for scope mounts. Permanent lubrication, steel piston ring. Cocking effort 9 lbs. Optional 10 oz. bbl. sleeve. Available from Beeman.
Price: Right-hand **$859.00**
Price: Left-hand **$930.00**

BEEMAN BETA AIR RIFLE

Caliber: 177 or 22.
Barrel: 18.8".
Weight: 8.4 lbs. **Length:** 44.5" over-all.
Power: Spring-piston, barrel cocking.
Stock: Stained beech; Monte Carlo comb and cheekpiece; cut-checkered p.g.; rubber butt pad.
Sights: Blade on ramp front, open adjustable rear.
Features: Anti-vibration mechanism. Imported by Beeman.
Price: .... **NA**

FWB 300-S Universal

BEEMAN/FEINWERKBAU 300-S "UNIVERSAL" MATCH

Caliber: 177, single shot.
Barrel: 19.9".
Weight: 10.2 lbs. (without barrel sleeve). **Length:** 43.3" over-all.
Power: Spring piston, single stroke sidelever.
Stock: Walnut, stippled p.g. and fore-end. Detachable cheekpieces (one std., high for scope use.) Adjustable buttplate, accessory rail. Buttplate and grip cap spacers included.
Sights: Two globe fronts with interchangeable inserts. Rear is match aperture with rubber eyecup and sight viser. Front and rear sights move as a single unit.
Features: Recoilless, vibration free. Grooved for scope mounts. Steel piston ring. Cocking effort about 9½ lbs. Barrel sleeve optional. Left-hand model available. Introduced 1978. Imported by Beeman.
Price: Right-hand **$998.00**
Price: Left-hand **$1,075.00**

BEEMAN/FEINWERKBAU 300-S MINI-MATCH

Caliber: 177, single shot.
Barrel: 17⅛".
Weight: 8.8 lbs. **Length:** 40" over-all.
Power: Spring piston, single stroke sidelever cocking.
Stock: Walnut. Stippled grip, adjustable buttplate. Scaled-down for youthful or slightly built shooters.
Sights: Globe front with interchangeable inserts, micro. adjustable rear. Front and rear sights move as a single unit.
Features: Recoilless, vibration free. Grooved for scope mounts. Steel piston ring. Cocking effort about 9½ lbs. Barrel sleeve optional. Left-hand model available. Introduced 1978. Imported by Beeman.
Price: Right-hand **$870.00**
Price: Left-hand **$879.00**

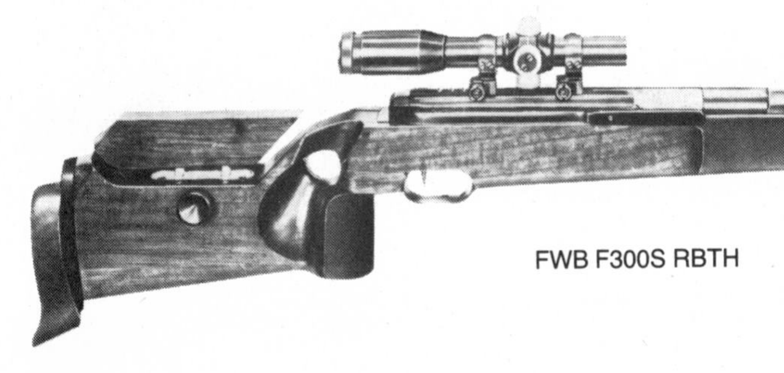
FWB F300S RBTH

BEEMAN/FEINWERKBAU F300-S RUNNING BOAR (TH)

Caliber: 177, single shot.
Barrel: 19.9", rifled.
Weight: 10.9 lbs. **Length:** 43" over-all.
Power: Single stroke sidelever, spring piston.
Stock: Walnut with adjustable buttplate, grip cap and comb. Designed for fixed and moving target use.
Sights: None furnished; grooved for optional scope.
Features: Recoilless, vibration free. Permanent lubrication and seals. Barrel stabilizer weight included. Crisp single-stage trigger. Available from Beeman.
Price: Right-hand **$910.00**
Price: Left-hand **$998.00**

BEEMAN/FEINWERKBAU MODEL 601 AIR RIFLE

Caliber: 177, single shot.
Barrel: 16.6".
Weight: 10.8 lbs. **Length:** 43" over-all.
Power: Single stroke pneumatic.
Stock: Special laminated hardwoods and hard rubber for stability.
Sights: Tunnel front with interchangeable inserts, click micrometer match aperture rear.
Features: Recoilless action; double supported barrel; special, short rifled area frees pellet from barrel faster so shooter's motion has minimum effect on accuracy. Fully adjustable match trigger. Trigger and sights blocked when loading latch is open. Imported by Beeman. Introduced 1984.
Price: Right-hand **$1,175.00**
Price: Left-hand **$1,295.00**

Beeman/FWB 601 Running Target

Similar to the standard Model 600. Has 16.9" barrel (33.7" with barrel sleeve); special match trigger, short loading gate which allows scope mounting. No sights—built for scope use only. Introduced 1987.
Price: Right hand **$1,125.00**
Price: Left hand **$1,255.00**
Price: Running target scope mounts **$139.95**

BEEMAN/FWB C60 CO_2 RIFLE

Caliber: 177.
Barrel: 16.9". With barrel sleeve, 25.4".
Weight: 10 lbs. **Length:** 42.6" over-all.
Stock: Laminated hardwood and hard rubber.
Sights: Tunnel front with interchangeable inserts, quick release micro. click match aperture rear.
Features: Similar features, performance as Beeman/FWB 600. Virtually no cocking effort. Right or left hand. Running target version available. Introduced 1987. Imported from Germany by Beeman.
Price: Right-hand **$1,085.00**
Price: Left-hand **$1,185.00**

BEEMAN/HARPER AIRCANE

Caliber: 22 and 25, single shot.
Barrel: 31½", rifled.
Weight: 1 lb. **Length:** 34" over-all.
Features: Walking cane also acts as an airgun. Solid walnut handle with polished brass ferrule. Available in various hand-carved models. Intricate deep engraving on the ferrule. Uses rechargeable air "cartridges" loaded with pellets. Kit includes separate pump, extra cartridges and fitted case. Introduced 1987. Imported by Beeman.
Price: Basic set **$495.95**
Price: Goose, Labrador, Spaniel sets **$555.00**

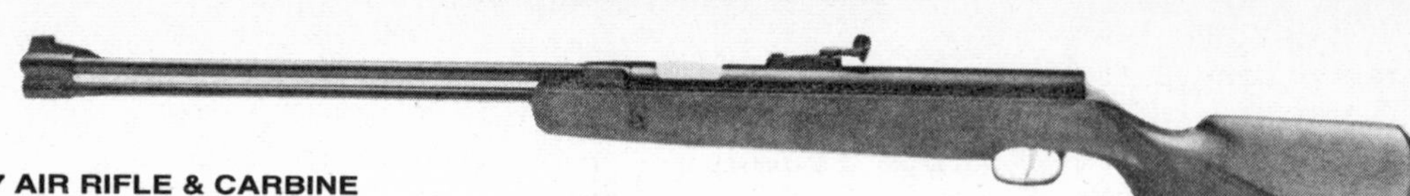

Beeman HW77

BEEMAN/HW77 AIR RIFLE & CARBINE

Caliber: 177 or 22, single shot.
Barrel: 14.5″ or 18.5″, 12-groove rifling.
Weight: 8.9 lbs. **Length:** 39.7″ or 43.7″ over-all.
Power: Spring-piston; underlever cocking.
Stock: Walnut-stained beech; rubber buttplate, cut checkering on grip; cheekpiece.
Sights: Blade front, open adjustable rear.
Features: Velocity 830 fps. Fixed-barrel with fully opening, direct loading breech. Extended underlever gives good cocking leverage. Adjustable trigger. Grooved for scope mounting. Carbine has 14.5″ barrel, weighs 8.7 lbs., and is 39.7″ over-all. Imported by Beeman.
Price: Right-hand **$399.98**
Price: Left-hand **$439.98**

Beeman Carbine C1

BEEMAN CARBINE MODEL C1

Caliber: 177, single shot.
Barrel: 14″, 12-groove rifling.
Weight: 6¼ lbs. **Length:** 38″ over-all.
Power: Spring-piston, barrel cocking.
Stock: Walnut-stained beechwood with rubber butt pad.
Sights: Blade front, rear click-adjustable for windage and elevation.
Features: Velocity 830 fps. Adjustable trigger. Receiver grooved for scope mounting. Imported by Beeman.
Price: **$199.95**

Beeman/Webley Omega

BEEMAN/WEBLEY OMEGA AIR RIFLE

Caliber: 177.
Barrel: 19¼″, rifled.
Weight: 7.8 lbs. **Length:** 43½″ over-all.
Power: Spring-piston air; barrel cocking.
Stock: Walnut-stained beech with cut-checkered grip; cheekpiece; rubber butt-pad.
Features: Special quick-snap barrel latch; self-lubricating piston seal; receiver grooved for scope mounting. Introduced 1985. Imported from England by Beeman.
Price: **$349.50**

BEEMAN HW 35L/35EB SPORTER RIFLES

Caliber: 177 (35L), 177 or 22 (35EB), single shot.
Barrel: 19½″.
Weight: 8 lbs. **Length:** 43½″ over-all (35L).
Power: Spring, barrel cocking.
Stock: Walnut finish with high comb, full pistol grip.
Sights: Globe front with five inserts, target micrometer rear with rubber eyecup.
Features: Fully adjustable trigger, manual safety. Thumb-release barrel latch. Model 35L has Bavarian cheekpiece stock, 35EB has walnut, American-style stock with cheekpiece, sling swivels, white spacers. Imported by Beeman.
Price: Model 35L **$317.50**
Price: Model 35EB **$337.50**

BEEMAN/HW 55 TARGET RIFLES

Model:	**55SM**	**55MM**	**55T**
Caliber:	177	177	177
Barrel:	18½″	18½″	18½″
Length:	43½″	43½″	43½″
Wgt. lbs.:	7.8	7.8	7.8
Rear sight:	All aperture		
Front sight:	All with globe and 4 interchangeable inserts.		
Power:	All spring (barrel cocking). 660-700 fps.		
Price:	**$389.50**	**$489.50**	**$539.50**

Features: Trigger fully adj. and removable. Micrometer rear sight adj. for w. and e. in all. Pistol grip high comb stock with beavertail fore-end, walnut finish stock on 55SM. Walnut stock on 55MM, Tyrolean stock on 55T. Imported by Beeman.

BEEMAN/WEBLEY VULCAN II DELUXE

Caliber: 177 or 22, single shot.
Barrel: 17″, rifled.
Weight: 7.6 lbs. **Length:** 43.7″ over-all.
Power: Spring-piston air, barrel cocking.
Stock: Walnut. Cut checkering, rubber butt pad, cheekpiece. Standard version has walnut-stained beech.
Sights: Hooded front, micrometer rear.
Features: Velocity of 830 fps (177), 675 fps (22). Single stage adjustable trigger; receiver grooved for scope mounting. Self-lubricating piston seal. Introduced 1983. Imported by Beeman.
Price: Standard **$199.95**
Price: Deluxe **$269.95**

BEEMAN R1 LASER AIR RIFLE

Caliber: 177, 20, 22, 25, single shot.
Barrel: 16.1″ or 19.6″.
Weight: 8.4 lbs. **Length:** 41.7″ over-all (16.1″ barrel).
Power: Spring-piston, barrel cocking.
Stock: Laminated wood with Monte Carlo comb and cheekpiece; checkered p.g. and fore-end; rubber butt pad.
Sights: Tunnel front with interchangeable inserts, open adjustable rear.
Features: Velocity up to 1,050 fps (177). Receiver grooved for scope mounting. Imported by Beeman.
Price: 177 or 22 cal. **$750.00**
Price: 20 cal. **$760.00**
Price: 25 cal. .... **NA**

Beeman R7 Air Rifle

Similar to the R8 model except has lighter ambidextrous stock, match grade trigger block; velocity of 680-700 fps; barrel length 17″; weight 5.8 lbs. Milled steel safety. Imported by Beeman.
Price: **$219.98**

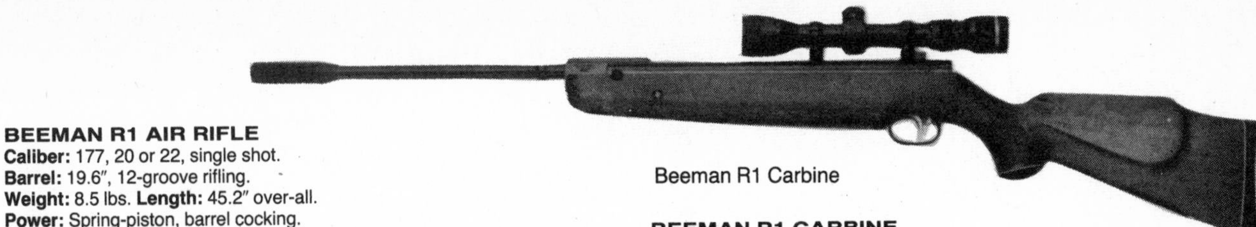

Beeman R1 Carbine

BEEMAN R1 AIR RIFLE

Caliber: 177, 20 or 22, single shot.
Barrel: 19.6″, 12-groove rifling.
Weight: 8.5 lbs. **Length:** 45.2″ over-all.
Power: Spring-piston, barrel cocking.
Stock: Walnut-stained beech; cut checkered pistol grip; Monte Carlo comb and cheekpiece; rubber buttpad.
Sights: Tunnel front with interchangeable inserts, open rear click adjustable for windage and elevation. Grooved for scope mounting.
Features: Velocity of 940-1050 fps (177), 860 fps (20), 800 fps (22). Non-drying nylon piston and breech seals. Adjustable metal trigger. Milled steel safety. Right- or left-hand stock. Custom and Super Laser versions available. Imported by Beeman.
Price: Right-hand **$379.95**
Price: Left-hand **$419.95**

BEEMAN R1 CARBINE

Caliber: 177, 20, 22, 25, single shot.
Barrel: 16.1″.
Weight: 8.6 lbs. **Length:** 41.7″ over-all.
Power: Spring-piston, barrel cocking.
Stock: Stained beech; Monte Carlo comb and checkpiece; cut-checkered p.g.; rubber butt pad.
Sights: Tunnel front with interchangeable inserts, open adjustable rear; receiver grooved for scope mounting.
Features: Velocity up to 1,000 fps (177). Non-drying nylon piston and breech seals. Adjustable metal trigger. Right- or left-hand stock. Imported by Beeman.
Price: 177 or 22, right hand **$379.95**
Price: 20 cal., right hand...................................... **$389.95**
Price: 25 cal., right hand...................................... **$384.95**

Beeman R10 Deluxe

BEEMAN R10 AIR RIFLES

Caliber: 177, 20, 22, single shot.
Barrel: 16.1″ and 19.7″; 12-groove rifling.
Weight: 7.9 lbs. **Length:** 46″ over-all.
Power: Spring-piston, barrel cocking.
Stock: Standard—walnut finished hardwood with M.C. comb, rubber buttplate; Deluxe has white spacers at grip cap, buttplate, checkered grip, cheekpiece, rubber buttplate.
Sights: Tunnel front with interchangeable inserts, open rear click adj. for w. and e. Receiver grooved for scope mounting.
Features: Over 1000 fps. in 177 cal. only; 26 lb. cocking effort; milled steel safety and body tube. Right- and left-hand models, Custom and Super Laser versions available. Introduced 1986. Imported by Beeman.
Price: .... **$299.98** to **$409.98**

BEEMAN R8 AIR RIFLE

Caliber: 177, single shot.
Barrel: 18.3″.
Weight: 7.2 lbs. **Length:** 43.1″ over-all.
Power: Barrel cocking, spring-piston.
Stock: Walnut with Monte Carlo cheekpiece; checkered pistol grip.
Sights: Globe front, fully adjustable rear; interchangeable inserts.
Features: Velocity of 735 fps. Similar to the R1. Nylon piston and breech seals. Adjustable match-grade, two-stage, grooved metal trigger. Milled steel safety. Rubber buttpad. Imported by Beeman.
Price: **$299.98**

Benjamin 342/347

BENJAMIN 342/347 AIR RIFLES

Caliber: 22 or 177, pellets or BB; single shot.
Barrel: 23″, rifled.
Weight: 6 lbs. **Length:** 35″ over-all.
Power: Hand pumped.
Features: Bolt action, walnut Monte Carlo stock and pump handle. Ramp-type front sight, adj. stepped leaf type rear. Push-pull safety.
Price: M342, 22 .... **$104.05**
Price: M347, 177 .... **$104.05**

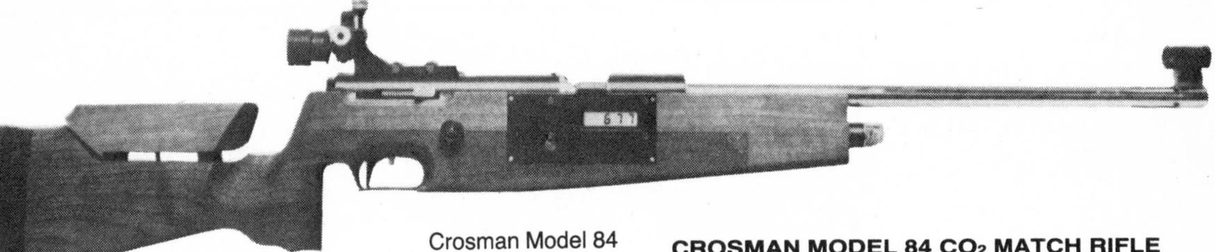

Crosman Model 84

CROSMAN MODEL 66 POWERMASTER

Caliber: 177 (single shot) or BB
Barrel: 20″, rifled, solid steel.
Weight: 3 lbs., 14 oz. **Length:** 38½″ over-all.
Stock: Wood-grained plastic; checkered p.g. and fore-end.
Sights: Ramp front, fully adjustable open rear.
Features: Velocity about 675 fps. bolt action, cross-bolt safety. Introduced 1983.
Price: About **$42.00**
Price: Model 664X (as above, with 4x scope)..................... **$45.00**

CROSMAN MODEL 84 CO_2 MATCH RIFLE

Caliber: 177, single shot.
Barrel: 21″. Barrel has a chrome shroud to give extra sight radius.
Weight: 9 lbs., 9 oz. **Length:** 45.5″ over-all.
Power: Refillable CO_2 cylinders.
Stock: Walnut; Olympic match design with stippled pistol grip and fore-end, adjustable buttplate and comb.
Sights: Match sights—globe front, micrometer adjustable rear.
Features: A CO_2 pressure regulated rifle with adjustable velocity up to 720 fps. Each CO_2 cylinder has more than enough power to complete a 60-shot Olympic match course. Electric trigger adjustable from ½-oz. to 3 lbs. Each gun can be custom fitted to the shooter. Made in U.S.A. Introduced 1984.
Price: About.. **$1,379.00**

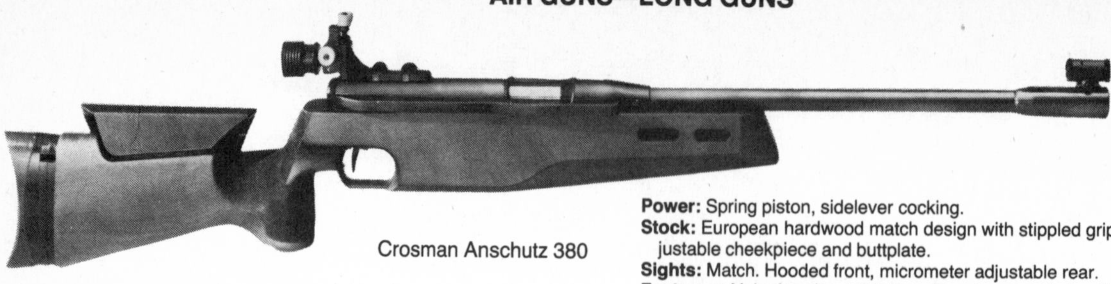

Crosman Anschutz 380

CROSMAN ANSCHUTZ MODEL 380 AIR RIFLE
Caliber: 177, single shot.
Barrel: 20¼".
Weight: 10.8 lbs. **Length:** 42⅛" over-all.
Power: Spring piston, sidelever cocking.
Stock: European hardwood match design with stippled grip and fore-end. Adjustable cheekpiece and buttplate.
Sights: Match. Hooded front, micrometer adjustable rear.
Features: Velocity about 600 fps. Recoiless and vibration free; two-stage match trigger adjustable from 2.1-oz. to 8.6-oz. pull. Available in left-hand model. Imported from West Germany by Crosman.
Price: Right-hand, about **$950.00**
Price: Left-hand, about **$987.00**

Crosman A*I*R* 17

CROSMAN A*I*R* 17
Caliber: BB and 177, 200-shot reservoir.
Barrel: 19½", steel.
Weight: 3 lbs., 1 oz. **Length:** 36¾" over-all.
Power: Pneumatic.
Stock: Black textured ABS plastic.
Features: Velocity of 450 fps (BB), 400 fps (pellet). Single-pump replica of the M-16 rifle. Comes with four-shot pellet clip. Storage compartment in stock. Introduced 1986.
Price: About **$39.00**

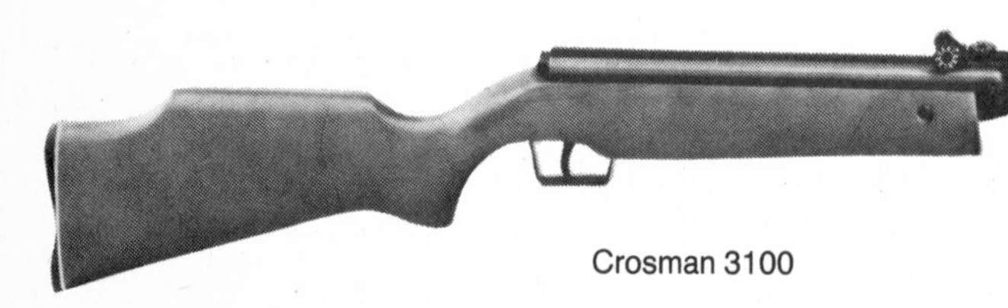

Crosman 3100

CROSMAN MODEL 3100 RIFLE
Caliber: 177, single shot.
Barrel: 16 7/16".
Weight: 6 lbs. **Length:** 39¾" over-all.
Power: Spring-air, barrel cocking.
Stock: Hardwood with Monte Carlo.
Sights: Hooded front with three apertures, micro. adj. rear.
Features: Velocity of 600 fps. Single-stroke cocking; adjustable trigger; thumb safety; rubber buttplate. Introduced 1986. Imported by Crosman.
Price: About **$59.00**

Crosman Z-77

CROSMAN Z-77 CARBINE
Caliber: BB, 20-shot magazine.
Barrel: 7", steel.
Weight: 35 oz. **Length:** 16½" over-all (closed), 25" (open).
Power: CO_2 Powerlet.
Stock: Folding shoulder stock.
Sights: Post front, open rear.
Features: Velocity about 400 fps. Replica of the UZI. Semi-automatic action. Gives about 80 shots per Powerlet. Comes with sling. Introduced 1987.
Price: About **$49.00**

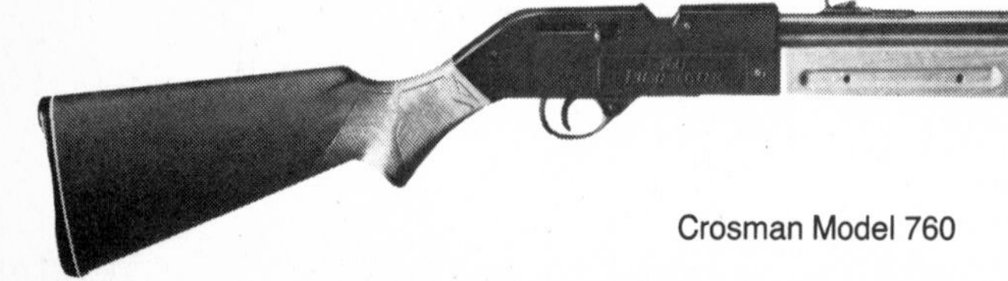

Crosman Model 760

CROSMAN MODEL 781 SINGLE PUMP
Caliber: 177, BB, 4-shot pellet clip, 195-shot BB magazine.
Barrel: 19½".
Weight: 2 lbs., 14 oz. **Length:** 34¾" over-all.
Power: Pneumatic, single pump.
Stock: Wood-grained plastic; checkered p.g. and fore-end.
Sights: Blade front, open adjustable rear.
Features: Velocity of 350-400 fps (pellets). Uses only one pump. Hidden BB reservoir holds 195 shots; pellets loaded via 4-shot clip. Introduced 1984.
Price: About **$29.00**

CROSMAN MODEL 760 PUMPMASTER
Caliber: 177 pellets or BB, 200-shot.
Barrel: 19½", steel.
Weight: 3 lbs., 1 oz. **Length:** 36" over-all.
Power: Pneumatic, hand pump.
Features: Short stroke, power determined by number of strokes. Walnut finished plastic checkered stock and fore-end. Post front sight and adjustable rear sight. Cross-bolt safety. Introduced 1983.
Price: About **$30.00**

CAUTION: PRICES CHANGE. CHECK AT GUNSHOP.

CROSMAN MODEL 2200 MAGNUM AIR RIFLE

Caliber: 22, single shot.
Barrel: 19″, rifled steel.
Weight: 4 lbs., 12 oz. **Length:** 39″ over-all.
Stock: Full-size, wood-grained plastic with checkered p.g. and fore-end.
Sights: Ramp front, open step-adjustable rear.
Features: Variable pump power—3 pumps give 395 fps, 6 pumps 530 fps, 10 pumps 620 fps (average). Full-size adult air rifle. Has white line spacers at pistol grip and buttplate. Introduced 1978.
Price: About **$54.00**

CROSMAN MODEL 2100 CLASSIC AIR RIFLE

Caliber: 177 pellets or BBs, 200-shot BB magazine.
Barrel: 21″, rifled.
Weight: 4 lbs., 13 oz. **Length:** 39¾″ over-all.
Power: Pump-up, pneumatic.
Stock: Wood-grained checkered ABS plastic.
Features: Three pumps give about 450 fps, 10 pumps about 795 fps. Crossbolt safety; concealed reservoir holds over 180 BBs.
Price: About **$54.00**

CROSMAN MODEL 6300 CHALLENGER AIR RIFLE

Caliber: 177, single shot.
Power: Spring-air, barrel-cocking.
Stock: Stained hardwood.
Sights: Hooded front, micrometer adjustable rear.
Features: Velocity of 690 to 720 fps. Adjustable trigger; automatic safety; comes with mount base for peep sight or scope. Introduced 1985.
Price: About **$126.00**

CROSMAN MODEL 788 BB SCOUT RIFLE

Caliber: BB only.
Barrel: 14″, steel.
Weight: 2 lbs. 7 oz. **Length:** 31½″ over-all.
Stock: Wood-grained ABS plastic.
Sights: Blade on ramp front, open adj. rear.
Features: Variable pump power—3 pumps give MV of 330 fps, 6 pumps 437 fps, 10 pumps 500 fps (BBs, average). Steel barrel, cross-bolt safety. Introduced 1978.
Price: About **$26.00**

CROSMAN MODEL 6100 CHALLENGER RIFLE

Caliber: 177, single shot.
Weight: 7 lbs., 12 oz. **Length:** 46″ over-all.
Power: Spring air, barrel cocking.
Stock: Stained hardwood with checkered pistol grip, rubber recoil pad.
Sights: Hooded front, micro.-adj. rear.
Features: Average velocity 820 fps. Automatic safety, two-stage adjustable trigger. Receiver grooved for scope mounting. Introduced 1982. Imported from West Germany by Crosman Air Guns.
Price: About **$200.00**

Crosman Model 6500 Challenger Air Rifle

Similar to the Model 6300 except has tunnel front sight with interchangeable bead for post or aperture inserts; positive barrel locking mechanism; automatic safety; rubber butt pad. Introduced 1985.
Price: About **$140.00**

Daisy Model 95

DAISY YOUTHLINE RIFLES

Model:	**95**	**111**	**105**
Caliber:	BB	BB	BB
Barrel:	18″	18″	13½″
Length:	35.2″	34.3″	29.8″
Power:	Spring	Spring	Spring
Capacity:	700	650	400
Price: About	**$30.00**	**$26.00**	**$20.00**

Features: Model 95 stock and fore-end are wood; 105 and 111 have plastic stocks.

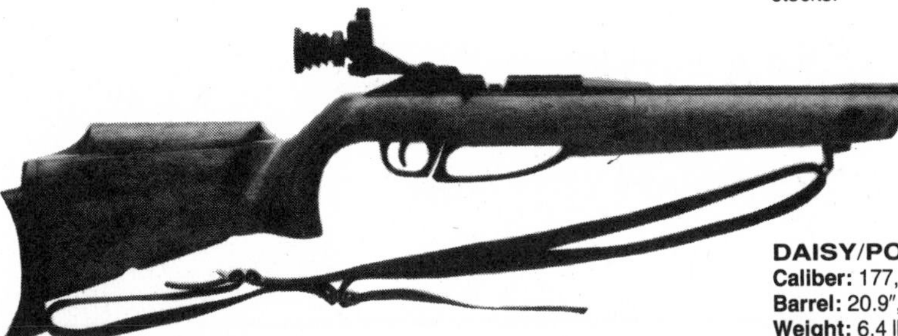

Daisy 753

DAISY/POWER LINE MODEL 753 TARGET RIFLE

Caliber: 177, single shot.
Barrel: 20.9″, Lothar Walther.
Weight: 6.4 lbs. **Length:** 39.75″ over-all.
Power: Recoilless pneumatic, single pump.
Stock: Walnut with adjustable cheekpiece and buttplate.
Sights: Globe front with interchangeable inserts, diopter rear with micro. click adjustments.
Features: Includes front sight reticle assortment, web shooting sling.
Price: About **$235.00**

Daisy Model 840

DAISY MODEL 840

Caliber: 177 pellet (single-shot) or BB (350-shot).
Barrel: 19″, smoothbore, steel.
Weight: 2.7 lbs. **Length:** 36.8″ over-all.
Stock: Moulded wood-grain stock and fore-end.
Sights: Ramp front, open, adj. rear.
Features: Single pump pneumatic rifle. Muzzle velocity 335 fps (BB), 300 fps (pellet). Steel buttplate; straight pull bolt action; cross-bolt safety. Fore-end forms pump lever. Introduced 1978.
Price: About **$33.00**

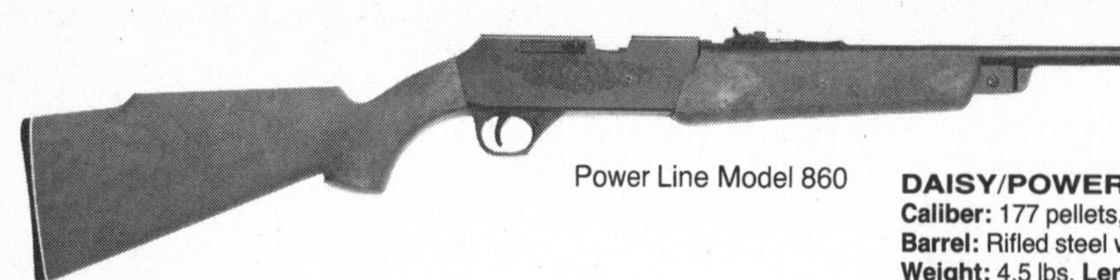

Power Line Model 860

DAISY/POWER LINE 856 PUMP-UP AIR GUN
Caliber: 177 (pellets), BB, 100-shot BB magazine.
Barrel: Rifled steel with shroud.
Weight: 2¾ lbs. **Length:** 37.4″ over-all.
Power: Pneumatic pump-up.
Stock: Moulded wood-grain plastic.
Sights: Ramp and blade front, open rear adjustable for e.
Features: Velocity from 315 fps (two pumps) to 650 fps (10 pumps). Finger grooved fore-end. Cross-bolt trigger-block safety. Introduced 1985. From Daisy.
Price: About **$37.00**

DAISY/POWER LINE 900 PELLET REPEATER
Caliber: 177 pellets, 5-shot clip.
Barrel: Rifled steel.
Weight: 4.3 lbs. **Length:** 38.4″ over-all.
Power: Spring air.
Stock: Full-length moulded stock with checkering, cheekpiece, white spacers.
Sights: Blade and ramp front, V-slot rear fully adjustable for w. & e.
Features: Easy loading, automatic indexing five-shot clip. Heavy die-cast metal receiver, dovetail mount for scope, heavy die-cast pump lever. Single pump for 545 fps muzzle velocity.
Price: About **$67.00**

DAISY/POWER LINE 880 PUMP-UP AIR GUN
Caliber: 177 pellets, BB.
Barrel: Rifled steel with shroud.
Weight: 4.5 lbs. **Length:** 37¾″ over-all.
Power: Pneumatic pump-up.
Stock: Wood-grain moulded plastic with Monte Carlo cheekpiece.
Sights: Ramp front, open rear adj. for e.
Features: Crafted by Daisy. Variable power (velocity and range) increase with pump strokes. 10 strokes for maximum power. 100-shot BB magazine. Cross-bolt trigger safety. Positive cocking valve.
Price: About **$51.00**

DAISY/POWER LINE 860 PUMP-UP AIR GUN
Caliber: 177 (pellets), BB, 100-shot BB magazine.
Barrel: Rifled steel with shroud.
Weight: 4.18 lbs. **Length:** 37.4″ over-all.
Power: Pneumatic pump-up.
Stock: Moulded wood-grain with Monte Carlo cheekpiece.
Sights: Ramp and blade front, open rear adjustable for e.
Features: Velocity from 315 fps (two pumps) to 650 fps (10 pumps). Shoots BBs or pellets.Heavy die-cast metal receiver. Cross-bolt trigger-block safety. Introduced 1984. From Daisy.
Price: About **$45.00**

Daisy/Power Line Model 814
Similar to the Model 914 except has a detachable wire stock and pistol grip. Weight is 2.8 lbs.
Price: About **$44.00**

Daisy Model 914

DAISY/POWER LINE MODEL 914
Caliber: BB or 177.
Barrel: 19″, smoothbore.
Weight: 6 lbs. **Length:** 38.2″ over-all.
Power: Single-stroke pneumatic.
Stock: Moulded plastic.
Sights: Ramp front, peep rear.
Features: Velocity of 335 fps. Resembles a famous sporter rifle.
Price: About **$42.50**

DAISY/POWER LINE MODEL 922
Caliber: 22, 5-shot clip.
Barrel: Rifled steel with shroud.
Weight: 4.5 lbs. **Length:** 37¾″ over-all.
Stock: Moulded wood-grained plastic with checkered p.g. and fore-end, Monte Carlo cheekpiece.
Sights: Ramp front, fully adj. open rear.
Features: Muzzle velocity from 270 fps (two pumps) to 530 fps (10 pumps). Straight pull bolt action. Separate buttplate and grip cap with white spacers. Introduced 1978.

Power Line Model 922

Price: About **$61.00**
Price: Models 970/920 (as above with hardwood stock and fore-end), about... **$100.00**

Daisy Model 953

DAISY/POWER LINE 953
Caliber: 177 pellets.
Barrel: 20.9″; 12-groove rifling, high-grade solid steel by Lothar Walther(TM), precision crowned; bore sized for precision match pellets.
Weight: 5.08 lbs. **Length:** 38.9″ over-all.
Power: Single-pump pneumatic.
Stock: Full-length, select American hardwood, stained and finished; black buttplate with white spacers.
Sights: Globe front with four aperture inserts; precision micrometer adjustable rear peep sight mounted on a standard ⅜″ dovetail receiver mount.
Features: Single-shot
Price: About **$149.50**

Daisy Red Ryder

DAISY 1938 RED RYDER COMMEMORATIVE
Caliber: BB, 650-shot repeating action.
Barrel: Smoothbore steel with shroud.
Weight: 2.2 lbs. **Length:** 35.4″ over-all.
Stock: Wood stock burned with Red Ryder lariat signature.
Sights: Post front, adjustable V-slot rear.
Features: Wood fore-end. Saddle ring with leather thong. Lever cocking. Gravity feed. Controlled velocity. Commemorates one of Daisy's most popular guns, the Red Ryder of the 1940s and 1950s.
Price: About **$41.00**

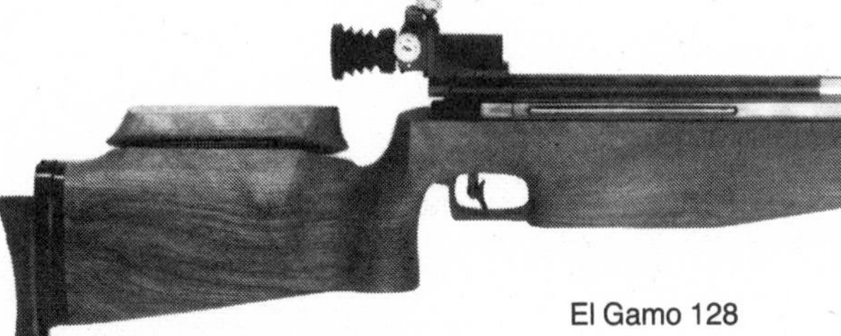
El Gamo 128

EL GAMO MODEL 128 MATCH RIFLE
Caliber: 177, single shot.
Barrel: 17.5″; Lothar Walther with 12 lands and grooves; sized for match pellets.
Weight: 10.6 lbs. **Length:** 43.3″ over-all.
Power: Recoilless pneumatic, single pump.
Stock: Match-style hardwood with sling rail and adjustable rubber buttplate.
Sights: Anschutz front and rear; globe front, diopter rear.
Features: Adjustable trigger. Imported from Spain by Daisy.
Price: About **$800.00**

EL GAMO 126 SUPER MATCH TARGET RIFLE
Caliber: 177, single shot.
Barrel: Match grade, precision rifled.
Weight: 10.6 lbs. **Length:** 43.8″ over-all.
Power: Single pump pneumatic.
Stock: Match-style, hardwood, with stippled grip and fore-end.
Sights: Hooded front with interchangeable elements, fully adjustable match rear.
Features: Velocity of 590 fps. Adjustable trigger; easy loading pellet port; adjustable buttpad. Introduced 1984. Imported from Spain by Daisy.
Price: About **$329.50**

FX-2 Air Rifle
Similar to the FX-1 except weighs 5.8 lbs., 41″ over-all; front sight is hooded post on ramp, rear sight has two-way click adjustments. Adjustable trigger. Imported by Beeman.
Price: **$79.50**

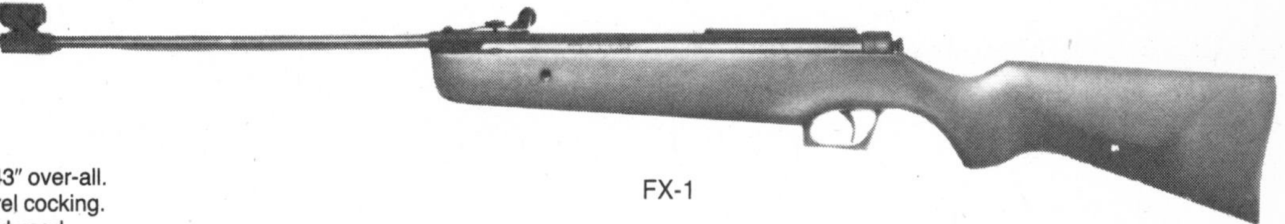
FX-1

FX-1 AIR RIFLE
Caliber: 177, single shot.
Barrel: 18″, rifled.
Weight: 6.6 lbs. **Length:** 43″ over-all.
Power: Spring-piston, barrel cocking.
Stock: Walnut-stained hardwood.
Sights: Tunnel front with interchangeable inserts; rear with rotating disc to give four sighting notches.
Features: Velocity 680 fps. Match-type adjustable trigger. Receiver grooved for scope mounting. Imported by Beeman.
Price: **$99.50**

Consult our Directory pages for the location of firms mentioned.

FAMAS Air Rifle

FAMAS SEMI-AUTO AIR RIFLE
Caliber: 177, 10-shot magazine.
Barrel: 19.2″.
Weight: About 8 lbs. **Length:** 29.8″ over-all.
Power: 12 gram CO_2.
Stock: Synthetic bullpup design.
Sights: Adjustable front, aperture rear.
Features: Velocity of 425 fps. Duplicates size, weight and feel of the centerfire MAS French military rifle in caliber 223. Introduced 1988. Imported from France by Century International Arms.
Price: **$395.00**

"GAT" AIR RIFLE
Caliber: 177, single shot.
Barrel: 17¼″ cocked, 23¼″ extended.
Weight: 3 lbs.
Power: Spring piston.
Stock: Composition.
Sights: Fixed.
Features: Velocity about 450 fps. Shoots pellets, darts, corks. Imported by Stone Enterprises, Inc.
Price: **$39.95**

MARKSMAN 29 AIR RIFLE
Caliber: 177 or 22, single shot.
Barrel: 18.5″.
Weight: 6 lbs. **Length:** 41.5″ over-all.
Power: Spring air, barrel cocking.
Stock: Stained hardwood.
Sights: Blade front, open adj. rear.
Features: Velocity of 790-830 fps (177), 610-640 fps (22). Introduced 1986. Imported from England by Marksman Products.
Price: Either caliber **$183.95**

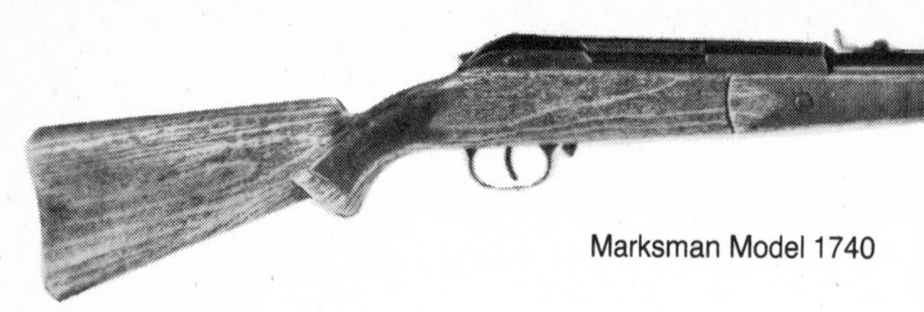
Marksman Model 1740

MARKSMAN 70 AIR RIFLE

Caliber: 177 or 22, single shot.
Barrel: 19.75″.
Weight: 8 lbs. **Length:** 45.5″ over-all.
Power: Spring air, barrel cocking.
Stock: Stained hardwood with M.C. cheekpiece, rubber butt-pad, cut checkered p.g.
Sights: Hooded front, open fully adj. rear.
Features: Velocity of 910-940 fps (177), 740-780 fps (22); two-stage adj. trigger. Introduced 1986. Imported from West Germany by Marksman Products.
Price: 177 or 22 .... **$258.95**

MARKSMAN 1740 AIR RIFLE

Caliber: 177 or 100-shot BB repeater.
Barrel: 15½″, smoothbore.
Weight: 5 lbs., 1 oz. **Length:** 36½″ over-all.
Power: Spring, barrel cocking.
Stock: Moulded high-impact ABS plastic.
Sights: Ramp front, open rear adj. for e.
Features: Automatic safety; fixed front, adj. rear sight; shoots 177 cal. BB's, pellets and darts. Velocity about 475-500 fps.
Price: **$40.00**
Price: Model 1780 (shoots only pellets) **$45.00**

Marksman 55 Air Rifle

Similar to the Model 70 except has uncheckered hardwood stock, no cheekpiece, plastic butt-plate. Over-all length is 45.25″, weight is 7½ lbs. Available in 177 caliber only.
Price: **$217.00**

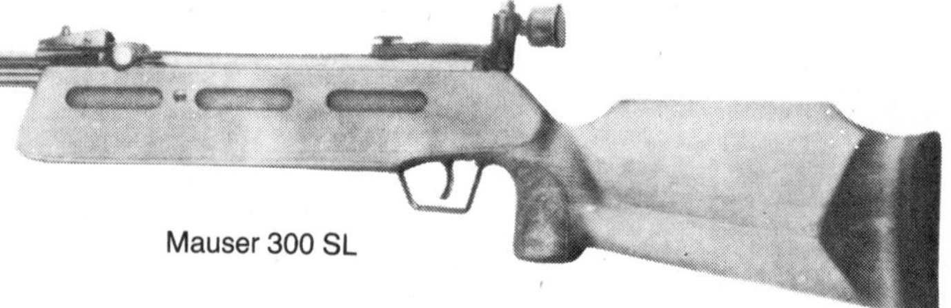
Mauser 300 SL

MAUSER MODEL 300 SL AIR RIFLE

Caliber: 177, single shot.
Barrel: 18.9″.
Weight: 8 lbs., 8 oz. **Length:** 43.7″ over-all.
Power: Spring air, under-lever cocking.
Stock: Match style, hardwood, with stippled p.g., rubber buttpad.
Sights: Tunnel front, match aperture rear.
Features: Velocity of 550-600 fps. Dovetail mount for diopter or scope. Automatic safety. Imported from West Germany by Marksman Products.
Price: **$291.95**

RWS/DIANA MODEL 24 AIR RIFLE

Caliber: 177, 22; single shot.
Barrel: 17″, rifled.
Weight: 6 lbs. **Length:** 42″ over-all.
Power: Spring air, barrel cocking.
Stock: Beech.
Sights: Hooded front, adjustable rear.
Features: Velocity of 700 fps (177). Easy cocking effort; blue finish. Imported from West Germany by Dynamit Nobel-RWS, Inc.
Price: **$140.00**
Price: Model 34 (as above, except 19″ bbl., 7½ lbs., adj. trigger, synthetic seals) **$210.00**

RWS/DIANA MODEL 52 AIR RIFLE

Caliber: 177, 22; single shot.
Barrel: 17″, rifled.
Weight: 8½ lbs. **Length:** 43″ over-all.
Power: Spring air, side-lever cocking.
Stock: Beech.
Sights: Ramp front, adjustable rear.
Features: Velocity of 1100 fps (177). Blue finish. Solid rubber buttpad. Imported from West Germany by Dynamit Nobel-RWS, Inc.
Price: **$325.00**

RWS/DIANA MODEL 75T 01 MATCH AIR RIFLE

Caliber: 177, single shot.
Barrel: 19″.
Weight: 11 lbs. **Length:** 43.7″ over-all.
Power: Spring air, side-lever cocking.
Stock: Oil finished walnut with stippled grip, adjustable buttplate, accessory rail. Conforms to I.S.U. rules.
Sights: Globe front with 5 inserts, fully adjustable match peep rear.
Features: Velocity of 574 fps. Fully adjustable trigger. Model 75 HV has stippled fore-end, adjustable cheekpiece. Uses double opposing piston system for recoilless operation. Imported from West Germany by Dynamit Nobel-RWS, Inc.
Price: Model 75T 01 .... **$770.00**
Price: Model 75 HVT 01 .... **$860.00**
Price: Model 75T 01 left-hand **$800.00**
Price: Model 75 HVT 01 left-hand **$900.00**
Price: Model 75 UT 01 (adj. cheekpiece, buttplate, M82 sight) **$920.00**

RWS/DIANA MODEL 36 AIR RIFLE

Caliber: 177, 22; single shot.
Barrel: 19″, rifled.
Weight: 8 lbs. **Length:** 45″ over-all.
Power: Spring air, barrel cocking.
Stock: Beech.
Sights: Hood front (interchangeable inserts avail.), adjustable rear.
Features: Velocity of 1000 fps (177-cal.). Comes with scope mount; two-stage adjustable trigger. Imported from West Germany by Dynamit Nobel-RWS, Inc.
Price: **$250.00**
Price: Model 38 (as above, walnut stock) **$280.00**

RWS/DIANA MODEL 45 AIR RIFLE

Caliber: 177, single shot.
Weight: 7¾ lbs. **Length:** 46″ over-all.
Power: Spring air, barrel cocking.
Stock: Walnut-finished hardwood with rubber recoil pad.
Sights: Globe front with interchangeable inserts, micro. click open rear with four-way blade.
Features: Velocity of 820 fps. Dovetail base for either micrometer peep sight or scope mounting. Automatic safety. Imported from West Germany by Dynamit Nobel-RWS, Inc.
Price: 177 .... **$225.00**

RWS/Diana Model 75KT 01 Running Boar Air Rifle

Similar to the Model 75 Match except has adjustable cheekpiece and buttplate, different stock, sandblasted barrel sleeve, detachable barrel weight, elevated-grip cocking lever, and a 240mm scope mount. Introduced 1983.
Price: **$880.00**

SAE MODEL 92 AIR RIFLE

Caliber: 177, single shot.
Barrel: NA.
Weight: 7.2 lbs. **Length:** NA.
Power: Spring-air, side-lever cocking.
Stock: European hardwood.
Sights: Tunnel front, open rear adj. for w. and e.
Features: Velocity of 650 fps. Adjustable trigger. Cocking effort of 19 lbs. Imported from Spain by Spain America Ent.
Price: **$185.00**
Price: Model 47 (as above, with vertical p.g.) **$185.00**

SAE Jet 900

SAE MODEL JET 900 AIR RIFLE

Caliber: 177, single shot.
Barrel: NA.
Weight: 7.5 lbs. **Length:** 46" over-all.
Power: Spring-air, barrel cocking.
Stock: Hardwood.
Sights: Hooded post front, open fully adjustable rear.
Features: Velocity of 900 FPS. Two-stage adjustable trigger, automatic safety. Imported from Spain by Spain America Ent.
Price: **$225.00**

SAE MODEL 73 AIR RIFLE

Caliber: 177, single shot.
Barrel: 21".
Weight: 6.7 lbs. **Length:** 43" over-all.
Power: Spring-air, barrel cocking.
Stock: Hardwood.
Sights: Tunnel front, open rear adj. for w. and e.
Features: Velocity of 650 fps. cocking effort about 8 lbs. Imported from Spain by Spain America Ent.
Price: **$150.00**
Price: Model 61C (as above, 16" bbl.) **$135.00**
Price: Model 15 (as above, 17" bbl.) **$105.00**
Price: Model Norica Young (M61C with colored, painted wood) **$125.00**

SAE Commando

SAE COMMANDO AIR CARBINE

Caliber: 177, single shot.
Barrel: 16".
Weight: 5.1 lbs. **Length:** 27" over-all.
Power: Spring-air, barrel cocking.
Stock: Retractable steel, camouflage painted fore-end.
Sights: Hooded post front, open rear adj. for w. and e.
Features: Velocity of 500 fps. Blue finish. Imported from Spain by Spain America Ent.
Price: **$135.00**

Sheridan CO_2

SHERIDAN BLUE AND SILVER STREAK RIFLES

Caliber: 5mm (20 cal.), single shot.
Barrel: 18½", rifled.
Weight: 5 lbs. **Length:** 37" over-all.
Power: Hand pumped (swinging fore-end).
Features: Rustproof barrel and piston tube. Takedown. Thumb safety. Mannlicher-type walnut stock.
Price: Blue Streak **$109.85**
Price: Silver Streak **$113.95**

SHERIDAN CO_2 AIR RIFLES

Caliber: 5mm (20 cal.), single shot.
Barrel: 18½", rifled.
Weight: 6 lbs. **Length:** 37" over-all.
Power: Standard 12 gram CO_2 cylinder.
Stock: Walnut sporter.
Sights: Open, adj. for w. and e. Optional Sheridan-Williams 5D-SH receiver sight or Weaver D4 scope.
Features: Bolt action single-shot, CO_2 powered. Velocity approx. 514 fps, manual thumb safety. Blue or Silver finish.
Price: CO_2 Blue Streak **$96.20**
Price: CO_2 Silver Streak **$100.55**
Price: CO_2 Blue Streak with receiver sight **$114.40**
Price: CO_2 Blue Streak with scope **$131.90**

Sterling HR-83

THEOBEN SIROCCO CLASSIC AIR RIFLE

Caliber: 177 or 22.
Barrel: 15½", Anschutz.
Weight: 7¾ lbs. **Length:** 44" over-all.
Power: Gas-ram piston. Variable power.
Stock: Hand-checkered walnut.
Sights: None supplied. Comes with scope mount.
Features: Velocity 1,100 fps (177), 900 fps (22). Adjustable recoil pad, barrel weight. Choked or unchoked barrel. Imported from England by Air Rifle Specialists.
Price: **$860.00**
Price: Grand Prix model (as above except thumbhole stock) **$940.00**

STERLING HR-81/HR-83 AIR RIFLE

Caliber: 177 or 22, single shot.
Barrel: 18½".
Weight: 8½ lbs. **Length:** 42½" over-all.
Power: Spring air (barrel cocking).
Stock: Stained hardwood, with cheekpiece, checkered pistol grip.
Sights: Tunnel-type front with four interchangeable elements, open adjustable V-type rear.
Features: Velocity of 700 fps (177), 600 fps (22). Bolt action with easily accessible loading port; adjustable single-stage match trigger; rubber recoil pad. Integral scope mount rails. Scope and mount optional. Introduced 1983. Made in U.S.A. by Benjamin Air Rifle Co.
Price: HR 81-7 (177 cal., standard walnut stock) **$259.44**
Price: HR 81-2 (as above, 22 cal.) **$269.67**
Price: HR 83-7 (177 cal., deluxe walnut stock) **$368.23**
Price: HR 83-2 (as above, 22 cal.) **$372.74**
Price: For 4x40 wide angle scope, add **$82.35**

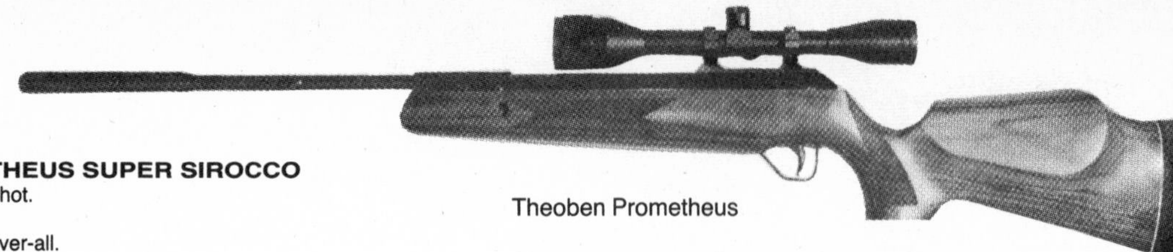
Theoben Prometheus

THEOBEN-PROMETHEUS SUPER SIROCCO
Caliber: 177 or 22; single shot.
Barrel: 15¾".
Weight: NA. **Length:** 44" over-all.
Power: Gas-ram piston.
Stock: English walnut, checkered p.g. and fore-end.
Sights: None furnished; scope base and rings provided.
Features: Velocity 950-1200 fps. One-stroke cocking mechanism with captive gas-ram piston. Designed to shoot Prometheus and Titan Black pellets. Imported from England by Fisher Enterprises.
Price: Deluxe Super Sirocco **$870.00**
Price: Grand Prix **$925.00**
Price: Eliminator (thumbhole stock) **$1,475.00**

Theoben Sirocco Eliminator Air Rifle
Similar to the Sirocco Grand Prix except more powerful. Gives 1,400 fps in 177 cal., 1,100 fps in 22. Walnut thumbhole stock, adjustable recoil pad, scope mount. Variable power. Barrel weight, leather cobra sling, swivels. Choked barrel only.
Price: **$1,450.00**

WALTHER LGR UNIVERSAL MATCH AIR RIFLE
Caliber: 177, single shot.
Barrel: 25.5".
Weight: 13 lbs. **Length:** 44¾" over-all.
Power: Spring air, barrel cocking.
Stock: Walnut match design with stippled grip and fore-end, adjustable cheekpiece, rubber butt pad.
Features: Has the same weight and contours as the Walther U.I.T. rimfire target rifle. Comes complete with sights, accessories and muzzle weight. Imported from West Germany by Interarms.
Price: **$1,100.00**

Walther LGR Running Boar Air Rifle
Same basic specifications as standard LGR except has a high comb thumbhole stock. Has adjustable cheekpiece and buttplate, no sights. Introduced 1977.
Price: **$975.00**

AIR GUNS—AIR SOFT LONG GUNS

COMMAND POST UZI PUMP
Caliber: 25-cal. plastic shot.
Barrel: NA.
Weight: 4 lbs. **Length:** 25" over-all (stock extended).
Power: Spring-air, pump action.
Stock: Black plastic.
Sights: Post front, aperture rear.
Features: Full-size replica of the Uzi submachine gun. Available from The Command Post, Inc.
Price: **$109.98**

Uzi Pump

COMMAND POST M-60 A1
Caliber: 25-cal. plastic shot.
Barrel: NA.
Weight: 14 lbs. **Length:** 42" over-all.
Power: Gas powered.
Stock: Moulded plastic.
Sights: Tangent rear, high-post front.
Features: Full-size, full-auto replica of the U.S. M-60 machinegun. Available from The Command Post, Inc.
Price: **$1,398.98**

MP5 A-3

COMMAND POST MP5-A3 CARBINE
Caliber: 25 (6mm) plastic BB, 42-shot magazine.
Barrel: Smoothbore.
Weight: 2 lbs., 14 oz. **Length:** 25" over-all (stock extended).
Power: Air piston; bolt action.
Stock: Metal and plastic.
Sights: Protected post front, aperture rear.
Features: Accuracy range of 50-70 feet. Telescoping stock version of the famous German submachine gun. Comes with 100 BBs. Available from The Command Post, Inc.
Price: **$89.98**
Price: Model G-3A4 .... **$169.98**

COMMAND POST AIRSOFT 12
Caliber: 25-cal. plastic shot.
Barrel: Smoothbore.
Weight: 3.25 lbs. **Length:** 18.5" over-all.
Power: Pump or bolt action, spring air.
Stock: Moulded grip.
Sights: Blade front, notched rear.
Features: Detailed replica of a famous American-made semi-automatic firearm; takes 30-shot clip.
Price: About **$62.00**

Command Post Grease Gun

COMMAND POST GREASE GUN
Caliber: 25 (6mm) plastic BB, 30-shot magazine.
Barrel: Smoothbore.
Weight: 4 lbs. **Length:** 22½" over-all (stock folded).
Power: Air piston; bolt action.
Stock: Moulded plastic; telescoping wire butt.
Sights: Blade front, aperature rear.
Features: Accuracy range of 25-35 feet. Realistic copy of the WWII submachine gun. Cartridges are automatically ejected and fed upon cocking. Available from The Command Post, Inc.
Price: **$159.98**

Airsoft 15

COMMAND POST AIRSOFT 15
Caliber: 25-cal. plastic shot.
Barrel: Smoothbore.
Weight: 2.5 lbs. **Length:** 15.5" over-all.
Power: Pump action, spring air.
Stock: Moulded receiver and grip.
Sights: Post front, 4-way adjustable rear.
Features: Detailed replica of the famous German-made police weapon. 12-shot banana clip, automatically ejects spent shells.
Price: About **$62.00**

Airsoft 14

COMMAND POST AIRSOFT 14
Caliber: 25-cal. plastic shot.
Barrel: Smoothbore.
Weight: 2.9 lbs. **Length:** 26" over-all.
Power: Pump or bolt action, spring air
Stock: Hardwood stock with moulded pistol and pump grips.
Sights: Blade front, adjustable rear peep sight.
Features: Fully-detailed replica of a famous semi-automatic rifle; takes 10-shot clip.
Price: About **$49.98**

Command Post XM-177E2

COMMAND POST XM-177E2 CARBINE
Caliber: 25 (6mm) plastic BB, 13-shot.
Barrel: Smoothbore.
Weight: 4 lbs. **Length:** 32½" over-all.
Power: Air piston; bolt action or semi-auto with blowback assist.
Stock: Moulded plastic; collapsible.
Sights: Post front, aperture rear.
Features: Accuracy range of 40-50 feet. Exact replica of the popular assault rifle. Comes with 40 BBs, two blowback assist cartridges, 60 blowback caps, takedown wrenches, blowback cartridge tools, sling. Available from The Command Post, Inc.
Price: **$98.98**
Price: As above except M-16 replica **$98.98**

Airsoft 870

COMMAND POST AIRSOFT 870
Caliber: 25-cal. plastic shot.
Barrel: Smoothbore.
Weight: 3.6 lbs. **Length:** 40" over-all.
Power: Slide action, spring air.
Stock: Moulded, with checkering.
Sights: Bead front.
Features: Detailed replica of Remington 870 Wingmaster; authentic working action, five-shot magazine, ejects spent shells.
Price: About **$66.00**

007 PUMP ACTION PAINT BALL PISTOL

Caliber: 68, 16-shot magazine.
Barrel: 4½".
Weight: 2 lbs., 10 oz. **Length:** 10¼" over-all.
Power: 12-gram CO_2.
Stocks: Checkered plastic.
Sights: Blade front, notch rear.
Features: Velocity of 205 fps, muzzle energy of 4.5 ft. lbs. Gives 20+ shots per CO_2. Rapid loading. Introduced 1987. From The Command Post, Inc.
Price: $119.98

007 Sport Paint Ball Pistol

Similar to the 007 Pump except has 25-shot magazine, 6" barrel, wire stock, combat pump handle. Custom built by The Command Post, Inc.
Price: $179.98

007 Tournament Paint Ball Pistol

Similar to the 007 Pump except has 25-shot gravity magazine, 2" barrel extension. Custom built by The Command Post, Inc.
Price: $199.98

3357 D/A PAINT BALL REVOLVER

Caliber: 50, 6-shot cylinder.
Barrel: 6".
Weight: 2 lbs., 12 oz. **Length:** 12½" over-all.
Power: 12-gram CO_2.
Stocks: Checkered plastic.
Sights: Ramped blade front, adjustable notch rear.
Features: Velocity of 230 fps, muzzle energy of 2.1 ft. lbs. Gives 30-70 shots per CO_2; metal construction; single or double action. Introduced 1987. From The Command Post, Inc.
Price: $89.98

Model 85

PURSUIT RAPID FIRE PAINT PISTOL

Caliber: 68 (paint balls), 10-shot magazine.
Barrel: 6½".
Weight: 36 oz. **Length:** 9" over-all.
Power: 12-gram CO_2.
Stocks: Smooth wood with thumbrest.
Sights: Bead front, adjustable rear.
Features: Shoots 68-cal. paint balls; uses gravity-feed magazine. Comes with Rapid Fire Pump Kit. From Pursuit Marketing, Inc.
Price: $135.00

PURSUIT PMI I PAINT PISTOL

Caliber: 68 (paint balls), 10-shot magazine.
Barrel: 10¼".
Weight: 36 oz. **Length:** 14⅜" over-all.
Power: 12-gram CO_2.
Stocks: Checkered, with thumbrest.
Sights: Bead front, open rear.
Features: Rapid-fire, pump-action long-barrel pistol uses factory centerfire bolt. Uses gravity or direct-feed magazine. Introduced 1988. From Pursuit Marketing, Inc.
Price: $169.00

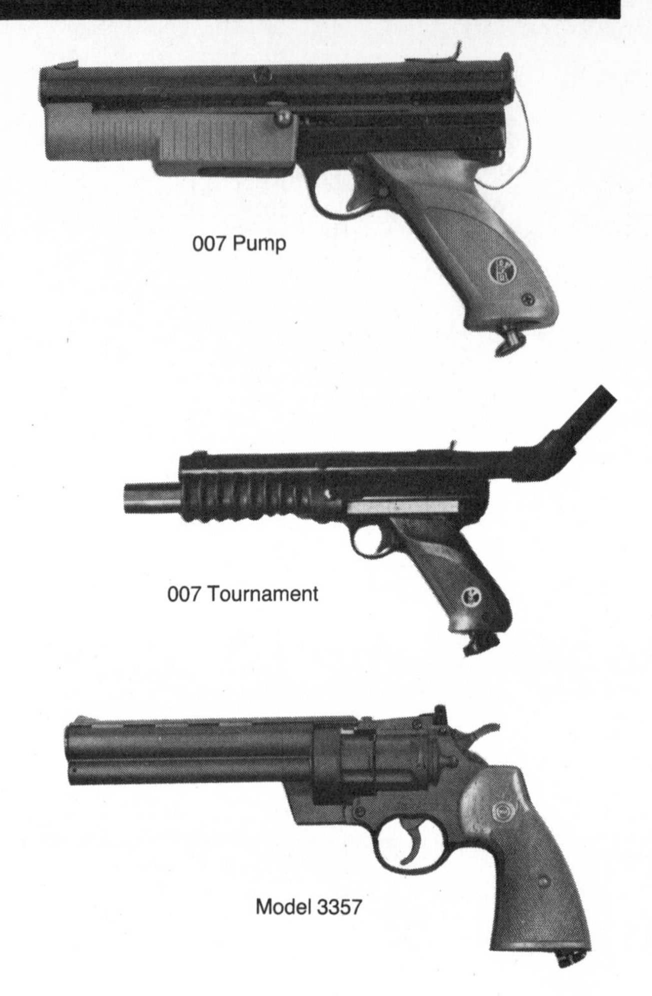

007 Pump

007 Tournament

Model 3357

MODEL 85 PAINT BALL MACHINE PISTOL

Caliber: 9.5 mm, 24-shot removeable magazine.
Barrel: 5", rifled.
Weight: 25 oz. **Length:** 9⅜" over-all.
Stocks: Resin.
Sights: Blade front, notch rear.
Features: Velocity of 440 fps, muzzle energy of 3.4 ft. lbs. Stainless steel impregnated in fiber-filled resin construction. Has a cyclic rate of 1,200 rounds per minute; fires from open bolt; reloadable cartridges. Not a firearm by B.A.T.F. standards. Introduced 1987. Made in Canada. From Para-Ordnance, Inc.
Price: $299.95

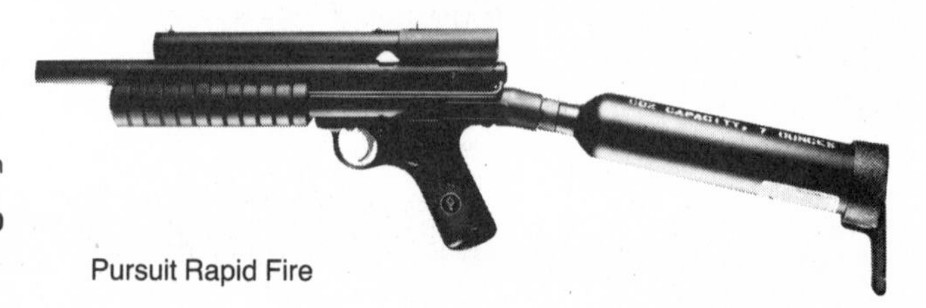

Pursuit Rapid Fire

Pursuit PMI II Paint Pistol

Similar to the PMI I pistol except comes only with 7-oz. Constant Air system, new factory 6-inch aluminum pump handle. Weight, including air tank, is 3¾ lbs. Introduced 1988.
Price: $280.00
Price: Pursuit 68 Magnum (as above with direct feed loading) $325.00

AIR GUNS—PAINT BALL HANDGUNS

SPLATMASTER® 102 MARKING PISTOL

Caliber: 68 (paint balls), 12-shot magazine.
Barrel: 5¾″.
Weight: 1.8 lbs. **Length:** 12¼″ over-all.
Power: 12.5 gram CO_2 cylinder.
Stocks: Checkered fiber reinforced plastic.
Sights: Open, fixed.
Features: Velocity at about 260 fps. Shoots 68-cal. paint-balls. Made of fiber reinforced plastic with an aluminum valve system. Moulded in a camouflage pattern. Gives about 30 shots per CO_2 cylinder. Introduced 1987. From National Survival Game, Inc.
Price: **$89.95**

Splatmaster

Uzi Mk. I

UZI MKI PUMP ACTION PAINT BALL GUN

Caliber: 68, 38-shot magazine.
Barrel: 7″.
Weight: 2 lbs., 8 oz. **Length:** 16″ over-all.
Power: 12-gram CO_2.
Stocks: Grooved plastic.
Sights: Blade front, notch rear.
Features: Velocity of 210 fps, muzzle energy of 4.7 ft. lbs. Gives 30+ shots per CO_2; rapid-load magazine. Introduced 1987. Imported from Canada by The Command Post, Inc.
Price: **$119.98**

AIR GUNS—PAINT BALL LONG GUNS

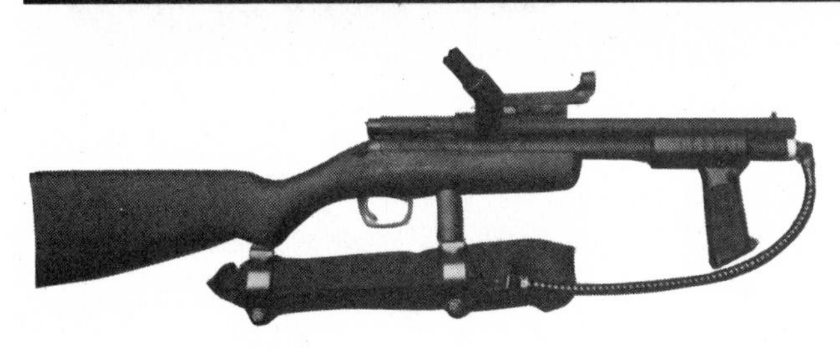

Black Widow

BLACK WIDOW PAINT BALL GUN

Caliber: 68, 25-shot magazine.
Barrel: NA.
Weight: 12 lbs. **Length:** 34″ over-all.
Power: 7-oz. bulk CO_2.
Stock: Black-painted wood.
Sights: Optic Point sighting device.
Features: Combat-grip pump. Matte finish on entire gun. From The Command Post, Inc.
Price: **$429.98**

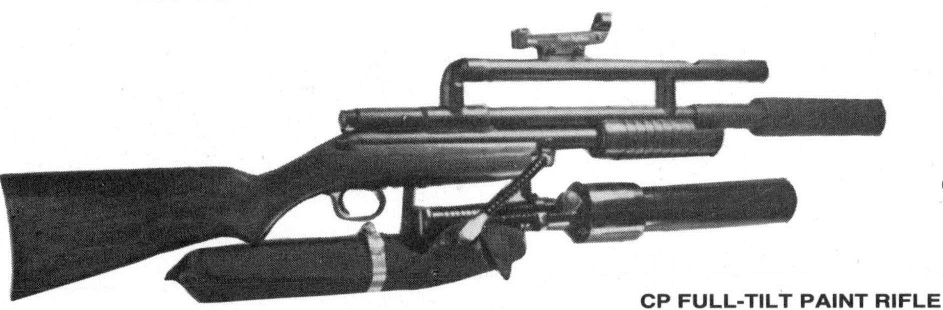

CP Full-Tilt

CP FULL-TILT PAINT RIFLE

Caliber: 68, 20-shot Posi-Feed magazine.
Barrel: NA.
Weight: 12 lbs. **Length:** 29″ over-all.
Power: 10-oz. bulk CO_2.
Stock: Wood
Sights: Optic Point sighting device.
Features: Noise suppressor, combat pump. "M-79" paint Grenade Launcher installed. Spring-fed magazine. Custom built by The Command Post, Inc.
Price: **$798.78**

Consult our Directory pages for the location of firms mentioned.

CUSTOM GRAVITY-FEED PAINT RIFLE

Caliber: 68, 25-shot magazine.
Barrel: NA.
Weight: 7 lbs. **Length:** 28″ over-all.
Power: 12-gram CO_2.
Stock: Wood.
Sights: Optic Point sighting device.
Features: Gravity feed; over-size Delron pump. Custom built by The Command Post, Inc.
Price: **$259.98**

NINJA PAINT BALL GUN

Caliber: 68, 20-shot magazine.
Barrel: 11″.
Weight: 9 lbs. **Length:** 28″ over-all.
Power: 10-oz. bulk CO_2 system.
Stock: Moulded composition.
Sights: 1.5x scope.
Features: Velocity about 225 fps. Gives up to 500 shots per charge. Converts to pistol. Gravity-feed magazine. Available from The Command Post, Inc.
Price: **$379.98**

007 Assault

007 ASSAULT PUMP PAINT BALL GUN

Caliber: 68, 15-shot magazine.
Barrel: 16″.
Weight: 6 lbs., 5 oz. **Length:** 35″ over-all (stock extended).
Power: 12-gram CO_2 or 10-oz. bulk CO_2 tank.
Stock: Folding, plastic and hard rubber over steel.
Sights: Adjustable Optic Point Site.
Features: Velocity of 240 fps, muzzle energy of 6.1 ft. lbs. Convertible power source—20 shots per CO_2 or 500+ shots from remotely mounted bulk tank. Steel construction. Introduced 1987. Custom built by The Command Post, Inc.
Price: **$359.98**

PMI CUSTOM PAINT BALL GUN

Caliber: 68, 20-shot magazine.
Barrel: NA.
Weight: 6 lbs. **Length:** 26″ over-all.
Power: 10-oz. bulk CO_2.
Stock: Moulded black plastic.
Sights: Post front, notch rear.
Features: Velocity about 290 fps. Easily converted to 12-gram CO_2. Custom built by The Command Post, Inc.
Price: **$289.98**

PMI Custom

Pursuit Rifle

PURSUIT PAINT RIFLE

Caliber: 68 (paint balls), 15-shot magazine.
Barrel: 12″.
Weight: 5 lbs. **Length:** 31″ over-all.
Power: 12-gram CO_2.
Stock: Smooth maple.
Sights: Bead front.
Features: Shoots 68-cal. paint balls; gravity-feed magazine. Comes with Rapid Fire Pump Kit. From Pursuit Marketing, Inc.
Price: **$170.00**

SAMURAI PAINT BALL GUN

Caliber: 68, 20-shot gravity magazine.
Barrel: NA.
Weight: 9½ lbs. **Length:** 26″ over-all.
Power: 10-oz. bulk CO_2.
Stock: Moulded black plastic.
Sights: Post front, notch rear.
Features: Fast pump action. Easily converts to 12-gram CO_2. Custom built by The Command Post, Inc.
Price: **$299.98**

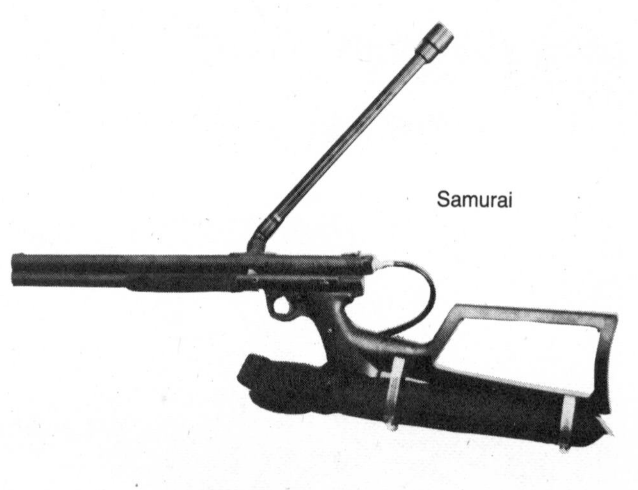

Samurai

SNIPER PUMP MK II PAINT BALL GUN

Caliber: 68, 25-shot magazine.
Barrel: NA.
Weight: 6 lbs. **Length:** 26″ over-all.
Power: 12-gram CO_2 or 7-oz. bulk CO_2 tank.
Stock: Wire.
Sights: 1.5x scope.
Features: Velocity of about 240 fps. Up to 350 shots per tank. Custom built by The Command Post. Inc.
Price: **$299.98**

Sniper Mk. II

Tippmann SMG-60

TIPPMANN SMG-60 AUTOMATIC

Caliber: 60 (paint balls), 15-shot magazine.
Barrel: 11″.
Weight: 5 lbs. **Length:** 29″ over-all.
Power: CO_2 cylinder.
Stock: 8-oz. CO_2 cylinder forms stock.
Sights: Fixed.
Features: Velocity of 290-300 fps. Selective-fire paint-ball gun (semi- or full-auto). Full-auto rate of fire is 600 r.p.m. Open bolt, blowback action. Introduced 1987. From Tippmann Arms Co.
Price: **$349.00**

CAUTION: PRICES CHANGE. CHECK AT GUNSHOP.

Chokes & Brakes

Briley Screw-In Chokes

Installation of these choke tubes requires that all traces of the original choking be removed, the barrel threaded internally with square threads and then the tubes are custom fitted to the specific barrel diameter. The tubes are thin and, therefore, made of stainless steel. Cost of installation for single-barrel guns (pumps, autos) runs **$75.00;** un-single target guns run **$150.00;** over-unders and side-by-sides cost **$150.00** per barrel. Steel shot, add **$10.00.** Prices include one choke tube and a wrench for disassembly. Extra tubes are **$40.00** each.

Cellini Stabilizer System

Designed for handgun, rifle and shotgun applications, the Cellini Stabilizer System is available as a removable factory-installed accessory. Over-all length is 2½", weight is 3.5 ounces, and the unit must be installed by the maker. It is said to reduce muzzle jump to nearly zero, even for automatic weapons. Cost starts at **$89.00**. Contact Cellini for full details.

Cutts Compensator

The Cutts compensator is one of the oldest variable choke devices available. Manufactured by Lyman Gunsight Corporation, it is available with a steel body. A series of vents allows gas to escape upward and downward. For the 12-ga. Comp body, six fixed-choke tubes are available: the Spreader—popular with skeet shooters; Improved Cylinder; Modified; Full; Superfull, and Magnum Full. Full, Modified and Spreader tubes are available for 12, or 20, and an Adjustable Tube, giving Full through Improved Cylinder chokes, is offered in 12, or 20 gauges. Cutts Compensator, complete with wrench, adaptor and any single tube **$68.80;** with adjustable tube **$89.80.** All single choke tubes **$18.95** each. No factory installation available.

Emsco Choke

E.M. Schacht of Waseca, Minn., offers the Emsco, a small diameter choke which features a precision curve rather than a taper behind the 1½" choking area. 9 settings are available in this 5 oz. attachment. Its removable recoil sleeve can be furnished in dural if desired. Choice of three sight heights. For 12, 16 or 20 gauge. Price installed, **$32.50, plus postage.** Not installed, **$24.50.**

Gentry Quiet Muzzle Brake

Developed by gunmaker David Gentry, the "Quiet Muzzle Brake" is said to reduce recoil by 65 to 80 percent with no loss of accuracy or velocity. There is no increase in noise level because the noise and gasses are directed away from the shooter. The barrel is threaded for installation and the unit is blued to match the barrel finish. Price, installed, is **$150.00.**

KDF Recoil Arrestor

This threaded muzzle brake has 24 pressure ports that direct combustion gases in all directions to reduce felt recoil up to a claimed 80% without affecting accuracy or ballistics. It is said to reduce felt recoil of a 30-06 to that of a 243. Price is about **$150.00** installed. From KDF Inc.

Lyman CHOKE

The Lyman CHOKE is similar to the Cutts Comp in that it comes with fixed-choke tubes or an adjustable tube, with or without recoil chamber. The adjustable tube version sells for **$39.95** with recoil chamber, in 12 or 20 gauge. Lyman also offers Single-Choke tubes at **$18.95.** This device may be used with or without a recoil-reduction chamber; cost of the latter is **$8.95** extra. Available in 12 or 20 gauge only. No factory installation offered.

Mag-Na-Port

Electrical Discharge Machining works on any firearm except those having non-conductive shrouded barrels. EDM is a metal erosion technique using carbon electrodes that control the area to be processed. The Mag-na-port venting process utilizes small trapezoidal openings to direct powder gases upward and outward to reduce recoil.

No effect is had on bluing or nickeling outside the Magna-port area so no refinishing is needed. Cost for the Mag-na-port treatment is **$59.00** for revolvers, **$80.00** for auto pistols, **$75.00** for rifles, plus transportation both ways, and **$2.50** for handling.

Poly-Choke

Marble Arms Corp., manufacturer of the Poly-Choke adjustable shotgun choke, now offers two models in 12, 16, 20, and 28 gauge—the Ventilated and Standard style chokes. Each provides nine choke settings including Xtra-Full and Slug. The Ventilated model reduces 20% of a shotgun's recoil, the company claims, and is priced at **$71.00.** The Standard Model is **$63.00.** Postage not included. Contact Marble Arms for more data.

Reed-Choke

Reed-Choke is a system of interchangeable choke tubes that can be installed in any single or double-barreled shotgun, including over-unders. The existing chokes are bored out, the muzzles over-bored and threaded for the tubes. A choice of three Reed-Choke tubes are supplied—Skeet, Imp. Cyl., Mod., Imp. Mod., or Full. Flush fitting, no notches exposed. Designed for thin-walled barrels. Made from 174 stainless steel. Cost of the installation is **$179.95** for single-barrel guns, **$229.95** for doubles. Extra tubes cost **$40** each. Postage and handling charges are **$8.50.**

Pro-Port

A compound ellipsoid muzzle venting process similar to Mag-na-porting, only exclusively applied to shotguns. Like Mag-na-porting, this system reduces felt recoil, muzzle jump, and shooter fatigue. Very helpful for Trap doubles shooters. Pro-Port is a patented process and installation is available in both the U.S. and Canada. Cost for the Pro-Port process is **$110.00** for over-unders (both barrels); **$80.00** for only the bottom barrel; and **$69.00** for single barrel shotguns. Prices do not include shipping and handling.

Techni-Port

The Techni-Port recoil compensation system is intended for revolvers, single-shot pistols and rifles. This is a machined process which involves back-boring the muzzle (with a 30° internal crown) and cutting an oval port on each side of the barrel. The process is said to reduce muzzle jump up to 60% and felt recoil up to 50%, with no reduction in velocity or accuracy. Cost of the Techni-Port process is **$99.95**, plus **$6.00** for return freight and insurance. Available from Delta Vectors, Inc.

Walker Choke Tubes

This interchangeable choke tube system uses an adaptor fitted to the barrel without swaging. Therefore, it can be fitted to any single-barreled gun. The choke tubes use the conical-parallel system as used on all factory-choked barrels. These tubes can be used in Winchester, Mossberg, Smith & Wesson, Weatherby, or similar barrels made for the standard screw-in choke system. Available for 10 gauge, 12, 16 and 20. Factory installation (single barrel) with choice of Standard Walker Choke tube is **$95.00, $190.00** for double barrels with two choke tubes. A full range of constriction is available. Contact Walker Arms for more data.

Walker Full Thread Choke Tubes

An interchangeable choke tube system using fully threaded inserts. Designed specifically for over-under or side-by-side shotgun barrels, but can be installed in single barrels, and is nearly invisible. No swaging, adaptor or change in barrel exterior dimensions. Available in 12 or 20 gauge. Factory installation cost: **$100.00,** single barrel with one choke tube; **$200.00** for double barrels with two choke tubes. Contact Walker Arms Co. for more data.

Sporting Leaf and Open Sights

BURRIS SPORTING REAR SIGHT
Made of spring steel, supplied with multi-step elevator for coarse adjustments and notch plate with lock screw for finer adjustments. Price **14.49**

LYMAN No. 16
Middle sight for barrel dovetail slot mounting. Folds flat when scope or peep sight is used. Sight notch plate adjustable for e. White triangle for quick aiming. 3 heights: A—.400" to .500", B—.345" to .445", C—.500" to .600". Price **$10.95**

MARBLE FALSE BASE #72, #73, #74
New screw-on base for most rifles replaces factory base. 3/8" dovetail slot permits installation of any folding rear sight. Can be had in sweat-on models also. Price **$5.50**

MARBLE CONTOUR RAMP #14R
For late model Rem. 725, 740, 760, 742 rear sight mounting. 9/16" between mounting screws. Accepts all sporting rear sights. Price . . . **$12.25**

MARBLE FOLDING LEAF
Flat-top or semi-buckhorn style. Folds down when scope or peep sights are used. Reversible plate gives choice of "U" or "V" notch. Adjustable for elevation. Price **$10.95**
Also available with both w. and e. adjustment **$12.75**

MARBLE SPORTING REAR
With white enamel diamond, gives choice of two "U" and two "V" notches of different sizes. Adjustment in height by means of double step elevator and sliding notch piece. For all rifles; screw or dovetail installation.
Price: . . . . . . **$11.25-$12.75**

Marble #20.

MARBLE #20 UNIVERSAL
New screw or sweat-on base. Both have .100" elevation adjustment. In five base sizes. Three styles of U-notch, square notch, peep. Adjustable for w. and e.
Price: Screw-on **$18.50**
Price: Sweat-on **$17.00**

MILLETT RIFLE SIGHT
Open, fully adjustable rear sight fits standard 3/8" dovetail cut in barrel. Choice of white outline or target rear blades, .360". Front with white or orange bar, .343", .400", .430", .460", .500", .540".
Price: Rear sight **$47.29**
Price: Front sight **$10.49**

MILLETT SCOPE-SITE
Open, adjustable or fixed rear sights dovetail into a base integral with the top scope-mount ring. Blaze orange front ramp sight is integral with the front ring half. Rear sights have white outline aperture. Provides fast, short radius, Patridge-type open sights on top of the scope. Can be used with all Millett rings.
Price: Scope-Site ring set, adjustable **$69.95**
Price: As above, fixed **$39.95**
Price: Convertible Top Cap set, adjustable **$56.95**
Price: As above, fixed **$26.95**

WICHITA MULTI RANGE SIGHT SYSTEM
Designed for silhouette shooting. System allows you to adjust the rear sight to four repeatable range settings, once it is pre-set. Sight clicks to any of the settings by turning a serrated wheel. Front sight is adjustable for weather and light conditions with one adjustment. Specify gun when ordering.
Price: Rear sight **$77.00**
Price: Front sight **$44.00**

WILLIAMS DOVETAIL OPEN SIGHT
Open rear sight with w. and e. adjustment. Furnished with "U" notch or choice of blades. Slips into dovetail and locks with gib lock. Heights from .281" to .531". Price with blade **$13.00**
Price: Less Blade **$8.55**

WILLIAMS GUIDE OPEN SIGHT
Open rear sight with w. and e. adjustment. Bases to fit most military and commercial barrels. Choice of square "U" or "V" notch blade, 3/16", 1/4", 5/16", or 3/8" high. Price with blade **$15.70**
Price: Extra blades, each **$4.45**
Price: Less blade **$11.25**

Micrometer Receiver Sights

BEEMAN/WEIHRAUCH MATCH APERTURE SIGHT
Micrometer 1/4-minute click adjustment knobs with settings indicated on scales. Price **$79.95**

BEEMAN/FEINWERKBAU MATCH APERTURE SIGHTS
Locks into one of four eye-relief positions. Micrometer 1/4-minute click adjustments; may be set to zero at any range. Extra windage scale visible beside eyeshade. Primarily for use at 5 to 20 meters. Price **$159.95**

BEEMAN SPORT APERTURE SIGHT
Positive click micrometer adjustments. Standard units with flush surface screwdriver adjustments. Deluxe version has target knobs.
Price: Standard **$34.98**
Price: Deluxe **$39.98**

FREELAND TUBE SIGHT
Uses Unertl 1" micrometer mounts. For 22-cal. target rifles, inc. 52 Win., 37, 40X Rem. and BSA Martini. Price **$150.00**

LYMAN No. 57
1/4-min. clicks. Stayset knobs. Quick release slide, adjustable zero scales. Made for almost all modern rifles. Price **$54.95**

LYMAN No. 66
Fits close to the rear of flat-sided receivers, furnished with Stayset knobs. Quick release slide, 1/4-min. adj. For most lever or slide action or flat-sided automatic rifles. Price **$54.95**

LYMAN No. 66U
Light-weight, designed for most modern shotguns with a flat-sided, round-top receiver. 1/4-minute clicks. Requires drilling, taping. Not for Browning A-5, Rem. M11. Price **$54.95**

MILLETT ASSAULT RIFLE SIGHTS
Fully adjustable, heat-treated nickel steel peep aperture receiver sights for AR-15, Mini-14. AR-15 rear sight has w. & e. adjustments; non-glare replacement ramp-style front also available. Mini-14 sight has fine w. & e. adjustments; replaces original.
Price: Rear sight for above three guns **$45.95**
Price: Front and rear combo for AR-15 . . . . . . **$55.95**
Price: Front sight for AR-15 . . . . . . **$10.95**
Price: Front and rear combo for Mini-14 . . . . . . **$60.95**
Price: Front sight for Mini-14 . . . . . . **$15.95**

WILLIAMS FP
Internal click adjustments. Positive locks. For virtually all rifles, T/C Contender, Heckler & Koch HK-91, Ruger Mini-14, plus Win., Rem. and Ithaca shotguns. Price, from **$45.50**
With Twilight Aperture **$46.90**
With Target Knobs **$54.05**
With Target Knobs & Twilight Aperture **$55.45**
With Square Notched Blade **$47.90**
With Target Knobs & Square Notched Blade **$56.55**
FP-GR (for dovetail-grooved receivers, 22s and air guns) **$45.50**

WILLIAMS 5-D SIGHT
Low cost sight for shotguns, 22's and the more popular big game rifles. Adjustment for w. and e. Fits most guns without drilling or tapping. Also for Br. SMLE. Price **$25.80**
With Twilight Aperture **$27.20**
With Shotgun Aperture **$25.80**

WILLIAMS GUIDE
Receiver sight for .30 M1 Car., M1903A3 Springfield, Savage 24's, Savage-Anschutz rifles and Wby. XXII. Utilizes military dovetail; no drilling. Double-dovetail W. adj., sliding dovetail adj. for e. Price **$24.50**
With Twilight Aperture **$25.90**
With Open Sight Blade **$22.50**

Front Sights

LYMAN HUNTING SIGHTS
Made with gold or white beads 1/16" to 3/32" wide and in varying heights for most military and commercial rifles. Dovetail bases. Price . . . **$7.50**

MARBLE STANDARD
Ivory, red, or gold bead. For all American made rifles, 1/16" wide bead with semi-flat face which does not reflect light. Specify type of rifle when ordering. Price **$6.75**

MARBLE-SHEARD "GOLD"
Shows up well even in darkest timber. Shows same color on different colored objects; sturdily built. Medium bead. Various models for different makes of rifles so specify type of rifle when ordering. Price **$8.50**

MARBLE CONTOURED
Same contour and shape as Marble-Sheard but uses standard 1/16" or 3/32" bead, ivory, red or gold. Specify rifle type. Price **$7.75**

MARBLE PATRIDGE
Gold-faced Patridge front sight is available in .250" or .34" widths and heights from .260" to .538". Price **$8.50**

POLY-CHOKE
Rifle front sights available in six heights and two widths. Model A designed to be inserted into the barrel dovetail; Model B is for use with standard .350 ramp; both have standard 3/8" dovetails. Gold or ivory color 1/16" bead. Price **$4.95**

Globe Target Front Sights

FREELAND SUPERIOR
Furnished with six 1" plastic apertures. Available in 4½"-6½" lengths. Made for any target rifle. Price **$46.00**
Price: With 6 metal insert apertures **$49.00**
Price: Front base **$12.50**

FREELAND TWIN SET
Two Freeland Superior Front Sights, long or short, allow switching from 50 yd. to 100 yd. ranges and back again without changing rear sight adjustment. Sight adjustment compensation is built into the set; just interchange and you're "on" at either range. Set includes 6 plastic apertures. Price **$67.00**

FREELAND MILITARY
Short model for use with high-powered rifles where sight must not extend beyond muzzle. Screw-on base; six plastic apertures. Price .. **$46.00**
Price: With 6 metal apertures **$49.00**
Price: Front base **$12.50**

LYMAN No. 17A TARGET
Includes 7 interchangeable inserts; 4 apertures, one transparent amber and two posts .50" and .100" in width. Price **$22.95**

Ramp Sights

LYMAN SCREW-ON RAMP
Used with 8-40 screws but may also be brazed on. Heights from .10" to .350". Ramp without sight **$13.50**

MARBLE FRONT RAMPS
Available in either screw-on or sweat-on style. 5 heights; 3/16", 5/16", 3/8", 7/16", 9/16". Standard 3/8" dovetail slot. Price **$13.75**
Hoods for above ramps **$3.00**

WILLIAMS SHORTY RAMP
Companion to "Streamlined" ramp, about ½" shorter. Screw-on or sweat-on. It is furnished in 1/8", 3/16", 9/32", and 3/8" heights without hood only.
Price: **$9.95**

WILLIAMS STREAMLINED RAMP
Hooded style in screw-on or sweat-on models. Furnished in 9/16", 7/16", 3/8", 5/16", 3/16" heights. Price with hood **$17.80**
Price: Without hood................................. **$14.70**

Handgun Sights

BO-MAR DE LUXE BMCS
Gives 3/8" w. and e. adjustment at 50 yards on Colt Gov't 45, sight radius under 7". For GM and Commander models only. Uses existing dovetail slot. Has shield-type rear blade. Price **$54.75**

BO-MAR LOW PROFILE RIB & ACCURACY TUNER
Streamlined rib with front and rear sights; 7⅛" sight radius. Brings sight line closer to the bore than standard or extended sight and ramp. Weighs 5 oz. Made for Colt Gov't 45, Super 38, and Gold Cup 45 and 38. Price **$89.00**

BO-MAR COMBAT RIB
For S&W Model 19 revolver with 4" barrel. Sight radius 5¾"; weight 5½ oz. Price **$79.00**

BO-MAR FAST DRAW RIB
Streamlined full length rib with integral Bo-Mar micrometer sight and serrated fast draw sight. For Browning 9mm, S&W 39, Colt Commander 45, Super Auto and 9mm. Price **$79.00**

BO-MAR WINGED RIB
For S&W 4" and 6" length barrels—K-38, M10, HB 14 and 19. Weight for the 6" model is about 7¼ oz. Price.......................... **$89.00**

BO-MAR COVER-UP RIB
Adj. rear sight, winged front guards. Fits right over revolver's original front sight. For S&W 4" M-10HB, M-13, M-58, M-64 & 65, Ruger 4" models SDA-34, SDA-84, SS-34, SS-84, GF-34, GF-84. Price........... **$85.00**

C-MORE SIGHTS
Replacement front sight blades offered in two types and five styles. Made of DuPont Acetal, they come in a set of five high-contrast colors: blue, green, pink, red and yellow. Easy to install. Patridge style for Colt Python (all barrels), Ruger Super Blackhawk (7½"), Ruger Blackhawk (4⅝"); Ramp style for Python (all barrels), Blackhawk (4⅝"), Super Blackhawk (7½" and 10½"). From Mag-num Sales Ltd., Inc. Price, per set........... **$14.95**

MMC MODEL 84 SIGHT SYSTEM
Available with either service or target leaf for Colt 1911 type pistols, as well as Browning's P-35. Sleek, sculptured styling, blends smoothly with the lines of the pistol. High visibility white outline or 2-dot rear sight blades (3-dot system) give instant-aim sighting for low-light conditions.
Price: Rear sight **$50.70**
Price: Front sight (depending on style), from **$10.40**

MMC COMBAT FIXED REAR SIGHT (Colt 1911-Type Pistols)
This veteran MMC sight is well known to those who prefer a true combat sight for "carry" guns. Steel construction for long service. Choose from a wide variety of front sights.
Price: Combat Fixed Rear, plain **$17.55**
Price: As above, white outline **$22.50**
Price: Combat Front Sight for above, six styles, from.......... **$4.90**

MMC M/85 ADJUSTABLE REAR SIGHT
Designed to be compatiable with the Ruger P-85 front sight. Fully adjustable for windage and elevation.
Price: M/85 Adjustable Rear Sight, plain **$49.95**
Price: As above, white outline **$54.95**

MMC M/85.

MMC STANDARD ADJUSTABLE REAR SIGHT
Available for Colt 1911 type, Ruger Standard Auto, and now for S&W 469, and 659 pistols. No front sight change is necessary, as this sight will work with the original factory front sight.
Price: Standard Adjustable Rear Sight, plain leaf **$43.90**
Price: Standard Adjustable Rear Sight, white outline **$48.70**

MMC MINI-SIGHT
Miniature size for carrying, fully adjustable, for maximum accuracy with your pocket auto. MMC's Mini-Sight will work with the factory front sight. No machining is necessary, easy installation. Available for Walther PP, PPK, and PPK/S pistols. Will also fit fixed sight Browning High Power (P-35).
Price: Mini-Sight, plain **$55.65**
Price: Mini-Sight, white bar............................ **$60.45**

MILLETT SERIES 100 ADJUSTABLE SIGHTS
Replacement sights for revolvers and auto pistols. Positive click adjustments for windage and elevation. Designed for accuracy and ruggedness. Made to fit S&W, Colt, Beretta, SIG Sauer P220, P225, P226, Ruger P-85, Ruger GP-100 (and others), Glock 17, CZ-75, TZ-75, Dan Wesson, Browning, AMT Hardballer. Rear blades are available in white outline or positive black target. All steel construction and easy to install.
Price:.................................... **$41.95** to **$67.29**

MILLETT MARK SERIES PISTOL SIGHTS
Mark I and Mark II replacement combat sights for government-type auto pistols, including H&K P7. Mark I is high profile, Mark II low profile. Both have horizontal light deflectors.
Price: Mark I, front and rear **$29.39**
Price: Mark II, front and rear........................... **$41.95**
Price: For H&K P7 .... **$41.95**

MILLETT REVOLVER FRONT SIGHTS
All-steel replacement front sights with either white or orange bar. Easy to install. For Ruger GP-100, Redhawk, Security-Six, Police-Six, Speed-Six, Colt Trooper, Diamondback, King Cobra, Peacemaker, Python, Dan Wesson 22 and 15-2. Price .... **$11.59 to $13.59**

MILLETT DUAL-CRIMP FRONT SIGHT
Replacement front sight for automatic pistols. Dual-Crimp uses an all-steel two-point hollow rivet system. Available in nine heights and four styles. Has a skirted base that covers the front sight pad. Easily installed with the Millett Installation Tool Set. Available in Blaze Orange Bar, White Bar, Serrated Ramp, Plain Post. Price.............................. **$13.59**

MILLETT STAKE-ON FRONT SIGHT
Replacement front sight for automatic pistols. Stake-On sights have skirted base that covers the front sight pad. Easily installed with the Millett Installation Tool Set. Available in seven heights and four styles—Blaze Orange Bar, White Bar, Serrated Ramp, Plain Post. Price **$13.59**

OMEGA OUTLINE SIGHT BLADES
Replacement rear sight blades for Colt and Ruger single action guns and the Interarms Virginian Dragoon. Standard Outline available in gold or white notch outline on blue metal. From Omega Sales. Price **$7.95**

OMEGA MAVERICK SIGHT BLADES
Replacement "peep-sight" blades for Colt, Ruger SAs, Virginian Dragoon. Three models available—No. 1, Plain, No. 2, Single Bar, No. 3 Double Bar Rangefinder. From Omega Sales. Price, each............... **$ 6.95**

TRIJICON SELF-LUMINOUS SIGHTS
Three-dot sighting system uses self-luminous inserts in the sight blade and leaf. Tritium "lamps" are mounted in a metal cylinder and protected by a polished crystal sapphire. For most popular handguns, fixed or adjustable sights, and some rifles. From Armson, Inc.
Price:.................................... **$25.95** to **$189.90**

THOMPSON/CENTER "ULTIMATE" SIGHTS
Replacement front and rear sights for the T/C Contender. Front sight has four interchangeable blades (.060″, .080″, .100″, .120″), rear sight has four notch widths of the same measurements for a possible 16 combinations. Rear sight can be used with existing soldered front sights.
Price: Front sight..................................... **$25.00**
Price: Rear sight **$65.00**

WICHITA SIGHT SYSTEMS
For 45 auto pistols. Target and Combat styles available. Designed by Ron Power. All-steel construction, click adjustable. Each sight has two traverse pins, a large hinge pin and two elevation return springs. Sight blade is serrated and mounted on an angle to deflect light. Patridge front for target, ramp front for combat. Both are legal for ISPC and NRA competitons.
Rear sight, target or combat **$54.50**
Front sight, patridge or ramp **$9.85**

WICHITA GRAND MASTER DELUXE RIBS
Ventilated rib has wings machined into it for better sight acquisition. Made of stainless steel, sights blued. Uses Wichita Multi-Range rear sight, adjustable front sight. Made for revolvers with 6″ barrel.
Price: Model 301 (adj. sight K-frames with custom bbl. of 1.000″-1.032″ dia., L and N frames with 1.062″-1.100″ bbl.) **$143.00**
Price: Model 302 (fixed-sight K-frames; M10, 65, 13 with 1.000″ bbl. N-frame with 1.062″ bbl.)................................ **$143.00**
Price: Model 303 (Model 29, 629 with factory bbl., adj. sight K, L, N frames) **$143.00**

WICHITA DOUBLE MASTER RIB
Ventilated rib has wings machined on either side of fixed front post sight for better acquisition and is relieved for Mag-na-ports. Milled to accept Weaver See-Thru-style rings. Made of blued steel. Has Wichita Multi-Range rear sight system. Made for Model 29/629 with factory barrel, and all adjustable-sight K, L and N frames.
Price: Model 403..................................... **$128.95**

Shotgun Sights

ACCURA-SITE
For shooting shotgun slugs. Three models to fit most shotguns—"A" for vent. rib barrels, "B" for solid ribs, "C" for plain barrels. Rear sight has windage and elevation provisions. Easily removed and replaced. Includes front and rear sights. Price......................... **$25.95** to **$27.95**

Slug Sights

LYMAN
Three sights of over-sized ivory beads. No. 10 Front (press fit) for double barrel or ribbed single barrel guns . . . **$3.50**; No. 10D Front (screw fit) for non-ribbed single barrel guns (comes with wrench) . . . **$4.50**; No. 11 Middle (press fit) for double and ribbed single barrel guns .... **$3.50**.

MMC M&P COMBAT SHOTGUN SIGHT SET
A durable, protected ghost ring aperture, combat sight made of steel. Fully adjustable for windage and elevation.
Price: M&P Sight Set (front and rear)......................... **$69.95**
Price: As above, installed **$79.95**

MARBLE
FOR DOUBLE BARREL SHOTGUNS (PRESS FIT)
Marble 214—Ivory front bead, 11/64″ . . . **$3.55; 215**—same with .080″ rear bead and reamers . . . **$11.70. Marble 220**—Bi-color (gold and ivory) front bead, 11/64″ and .080″ rear bead, with reamers . . . **$13.50; Marble 221**—front bead only . . . **$5.15. Marble 223**—Ivory rear .080″ . . . **$3.35. Marble 224**—Front sight reamer for 214-221 beads . . . **$2.55; Marble 226**—Rear sight reamer for 223. Price.................................. **$2.55**

MARBLE
FOR SINGLE OR DB SHOTGUNS (SCREW-ON FIT)
Marble 217—Ivory front bead 11/64″ . . . **$3.90**; Marble 216 . . . **$8.00; Marble 218**—Bi-color front, 11/64″ . . . **$5.60; Marble 219** . . . **$9.80; Marble 223T**—Ivory rear .080″ Price **$5.30**
Marble Bradley type sights 223BT—1/8″, 5/64″ and 11/64″ long. Gold, Ivory or Red bead... **$3.15**

MILLETT SHURSHOT SHOTGUN SIGHT
A sight system for shotguns with a ventilated rib. Rear sight attaches to the rib, front sight replaces the front bead. Front has an orange face, rear has two orange bars. For 870, 1100, or other models.
Price: Front and rear **$15.95**
Price: Adjustable front and rear.......................... **$21.95**

POLY-CHOKE
Replacement front sights in four styles—Xpert, Poly Bead, Xpert Mid Rib sights, and Bev-L-Block. Xpert Front available in 3x56, 6x48 thread, 3/32″ or 5/32″ shank length, gold, ivory (**$4.35**); or Sun Spot orange bead (**$4.35**); Poly Bead is standard replacement 1/8″ bead, 6x48 (**$2.20**); Xpert Mid Rib in tapered carrier (ivory only) or 3x56 threaded shank (gold only), **$3.35**; Hi and Lo Blok sights with 6x48 thread, gold or ivory (**$3.35**) or Sun Spot Orange (**$4.35**). From Marble Arms.

SLUG SIGHTS
Made of non-marring black nylon, front and rear sights stretch over and lock onto the barrel. Sights are low profile with blaze orange front blade. Adjustable for windage and elevation. For plain-barrel (non-ribbed) guns in 12, 16 and 20 gauge. From Innovision Ent.
Price:.. **$9.95**

WILLIAMS GUIDE BEAD SIGHT
Fits all shotguns, 1/8″ ivory, red or gold bead. Screws into existing sight hole. Various thread sizes and shank lengths. Price.............. **$4.50**

WILLIAMS SHOTGUN RAMP
Designed to elevate the front bead for slug shooting or for guns that shoot high. Diameters to fit most 12, 16, 20 ga. guns. Fastens by screw-clamp, no drilling required. Price, with Williams gold bead **$11.20**
Price: Without bead **$8.20**
Price: With Guide Bead **$12.70**

Sight Attachments

FREELAND LENS ADAPTER
Fits 1 1/8″ O.D. presciption ground lens to all standard tube and receiver sights for shooting without glasses. Price without lens **$66.50**
Clear lens ground to prescription **$24.00**
Yellow or green prescription lens **$24.00**

MERIT IRIS SHUTTER DISC
Eleven clicks gives 12 different apertures. No. 3 Disc (**$50.00**) and Master, primarily target types, 0.22″ to .125″; No. 4, 1/2″ dia. hunting type, .025″ to .155″. Available for all popular sights. The Master Disc, with flexible rubber light shield, is particularly adapted to extension, scope height, and tang sights. All Merit Deluxe models have internal click springs; are hand fitted to minimum tolerance.
Master Deluxe **$60.00**
No. 4 Hunting Disc **$40.00**

MERIT LENS DISC
Similar to Merit Iris Shutter (Model 3 or Master) but incorporates provision for mounting prescription lens integrally. Lens may be obtained locally from your optician. Sight disc is 7/16″ wide (Mod. 3), or 3/4″ wide (Master). Model 3 Deluxe. Price.................................... **$63.00**
Master Deluxe **$74.00**

MERIT OPTICAL ATTACHMENT
For revolver and pistol shooters, instantly attached by rubber suction cup to regular or shooting glasses. Any aperture .020″ to .156″. Price, Deluxe (swings aside).. **$60.00**

WILLIAMS APERTURES
Standard thread, fits most sights. Regular series 3/8″ to 1/2″ O.D., .050″ to .125″ hole. "Twilight" series has white reflector ring. .093″ to .125″ inner hole. Price, regular series . . . **$3.85.** Twilight series **$5.25**
Wide open 5/16″ aperture for shotguns fits 5-D and Foolproof sights. Price **$6.80**

SCOPES & MOUNTS
HUNTING, TARGET ■ & VARMINT ■ SCOPES

Maker and Model	Magn.	Field at 100 Yds (feet)	Relative Bright-ness	Eye Relief (in.)	Length (in.)	Tube Diam. (in.)	W&E Adjust-ments	Weight (ozs.)	Price	Other Data
Action Arms										
Pro V[1]	0	—	—	—	5⅛	1	Int.	5.5	$195.00	Variable intensity LED red aiming dot. Average battery life up to 500 hours. Waterproof, nitrogen filled aluminum tube. Fits most standard 1" rings. [1]Also available in Pro V 45° for left or right-side positioning of battery pack. Same price.
Inter Aims										
Mark V	0	—	—	—	5	1	Int.	6	189.00	Mark V for rifles, handguns, shotguns. Projects red dot aiming point. Dot size 1½" @ 100 yds. Pro V intended for handguns. Dot size less than 1½" @ 100 yds. Both waterproof. Battery life 50-10,000 hours. Imported by ADCO Int'l.
Pro V	0	—	—		4.5	1	Int.	3.9	229.00	
Aimpoint										
AP 1000[1]	0	—	—	—	6	—	Int.	7.8	159.95	Illuminates red dot in field of view. No parallax (dot does not need to be centered). Unlimited field of view and eye relief. On/off, adj. intensity. Dot covers 3" @ 100 yds. Mounts avail. for all sights and scopes. [1]Clamps to Weaver-type bases. Available in blue (AP1000-B) or stainless (AP1000-S) finish. 3x scope attachment (for rifles only), $94.95. [2]Requires 1" rings. Black or stainless finish. 3x scope attachment (for rifles only). $99.95. From Aimport. Made in Sweden.
Series 2000 Short[2]	0	—	—	—	5	1	Int.	5.3	209.95	
Series 2000 Long[2]	0	—	—	—	7.25	1	Int.	6	229.95	
Armson										
O.E.G.	0	—	—	—	5⅛	1	Int.	4.3	151.90	Shows red dot aiming point. No batteries needed. Standard model fits 1" ring mounts (not incl.). Other models available for many popular shotguns, para-military rifles and carbines. Also available is a smaller model for rimfire rifles, with dovetail mount.
Armsport										
415	4	19	13.7	3.5	11.5	¾	Int.	6	22.00	[1]Duplex reticle. Crosshair reticle, $90. 4x20, $79, 4x32, $82 (Duplex). [2]Parallax adjustment. [3]For black powder rifles. Polished brass tube with mounts. 4x32 W.A., 4x40 W.A., 6x40 W.A. also avail. Contact Armsport for full details.
3720	3-7	22.5-9.5	43.5-8.1	2.4	11	¾	Int.	8.4	56.00	
2½x32	2.5	32	163.8	3.7	12	1	Int.	9.3	86.00	
4x40[1]	4	29	100	3.5	12.5	1	Int.	9	97.00	
6x32	6	17.8	28	3.2	12	1	Int.	9	86.00	
1.5-4.5x32	1.5-4.5	55.1-20.4	707.6-64	4-3.1	11.8	1	Int.	14.1	124.00	
2-7x32	2-7	50-19	81-22	3.1-2.9	12.2	1	Int.	13.8	124.00	
3-9x40	3-9	35.8-12.7	176.9-19.4	3.1-2.9	12.8	1	Int.	15.2	131.00	
4-12x40 WA[2]	4-12	31-11	36-10.9	2.9-2.8	14.7	1	Int.	16.4	245.00	
4x15 BP-1[3]	4	19	13	3.5	32	¾	Int.	44	110.00	
Bausch & Lomb										
2x Handgun	2	22.5	—	10-24	8.4	1	Int.	6.7	269.95	All except Target scopes have ¼-minute click adjustments; Target scopes have ⅛-minute adjustments with standard turrets and expanded turret knobs. Target scopes come with sunshades, screw-onlens caps. Contact Bushnell for details.
4x Handgun	4	25	—	10-20	8.4	1	Int.	7.0	289.95	
4x Balfor Compact	4	25	—	3.3	10.0	1	Int.	10.0	319.95	
1.5-6x	1.5-6	75-18	294-18.4	3.3	10.6	1	Int.	10.5	399.95	
2-8x Balvar Compact	2-8	51-13	—	3.5	10.0	1	Int.	11.5	419.95	
3-9x40	3-9	36-12	—	3.2	13.0	1	Int.	16.2	409.95	
2.5-10x Balvar	2.5-10	43.5-11	—	3.3	13.8	1	Int.	13	459.95	
6-24x Varmint	6-24	18-4.5	66.1-4.2	3.1	16.6	1	Int.	20.1	509.95	
■ 6x-24x Target	6-24	18-4.5	—	3.3	16.9	1	Int.	20.1	599.95	
■ 24x Target	24	4.7	—	3.2	15.2	1	Int.	15.7	599.95	
■ 36x Target	36	3.5	—	3.2	15.2	1	Int.	15.7	599.95	
Beeman										
Blue Ring 20[1]	1.5	14	150	11-16	8.3	¾	Int.	3.6	49.95	All scopes have 5-pt. reticle, all glass, fully coated lenses. [1]Pistol scope; cast mounts included. [2]Pistol scope; silhouette knobs. [3]Rubber armor coating; built-in double adj. mount, parallax-free setting. [4]Objective focus, built-in double-adj. mount; matte finish. [5]Objective focus. [6]Has 8 lenses; objective focus; milled mounts included. [7]Includes cast mounts. [8]Objective focus; silhouette knobs; matte finish. [9]Has 9 lenses; objective focus. [10]Also in "L" models with reticle lighted by ambient light or tiny add-on illuminator. Lighted models slightly higher priced. Imported by Beeman.
Blue Ribbon 25[2]	2	19	150	10-24	9 1/16	1	Int.	7.4	129.95	
SS-1[3]	2.5	30	61	3.25	5½	1	Int.	7	179.95	
SS-2[4,10]	3	34.5	74	3.5	6.8	1.38	Int.	13.6	225.00	
Blue Ribbon 50R[5]	2.5	33	245	3.5	12	1	Int.	11.8	169.98	
Blue Ring 35R[6]	3	25	67	2.5	11¼	¾	Int.	5.1	69.98	
30A[7]	4	21	21	2	10.2	¾	Int.	4.5	36.95	
Blue Ribbon 66R[8]	2-7	62-16	384-31	3	11.4	1	Int.	14.9	239.95	
Blue Ring 45R[9]	3-7	26-12	67-9	2.5	10⅝	¾	Int.	6	99.95	
Blue Ring 49R[5]	4	30	64	3	11.8	1	Int.	11.3	69.95	
MS-1	4	23	30	3.5	7.5	1	Int.	8	199.95	
SS-3[4]	1.5-4	44.6-24.6	172-24	3	5.75	⅞	Int.	8.5	250.00	
Blue Ribbon 67R[8]	3-9	435-15	265-29	3	14.4	1	Int.	15.2	349.00	
Blue Ribbon 68R[8]	4-12	30.5-11	150-13.5	3	14.4	1	Int.	15.2	379.95	
Blue Ribbon 54R[5]	4	29	96	3.5	12	1	Int.	12.3	169.98	
SS-2[4,10]	4	24.6	41	5	7	1.38	Int.	13.7	250.00	
29	4	21	21	2	10.2	¾	Int.	4.5	19.95	
Burris										
Fullfield										All scopes avail. in Plex reticle except Micro which has fine cross hair only. Steel-on-steel click adjustments. [1]Dot reticle $13 extra. [2]Post crosshair reticle $13 extra. [3]Matte satin finish $11 extra. [4]Available with parallax adjustment $28 extra (standard on 10x, 12x, 4-12x, 6-18x). [5]Silver Safari finish $20 extra. [6]Target knobs $20 extra. [7]Sunshade avail. [8]Avail. with Fine Plex reticle. LER = Long Eye Relief; IER = Intermediate Eye Relief; XER = Extra Eye Relief. From Burris.
1½x	1.6	62	—	3¼	10¼	1	Int.	9.0	178.95	
2½x	2.5	55	—	3¼	10¼	1	Int.	9.0	188.95	
4x[1,2,3]	3.75	36	—	3¼	11¼	1	Int.	11.5	198.95	
6x[1,3]	5.8	23	—	3¼	13	1	Int.	12.0	214.95	
10x[1,4,6,7,8]	9.8	12	—	3¼	15	1	Int.	15	262.95	
12x[1,4,6,7,8]	11.8	10.5	—	3¼	15	1	Int.	15	269.95	
1¾-5x[1,2]	1.7-4.6	66-25	—	3¼	10⅞	1	Int.	13	238.95	
2-7x[1,2,3]	2.5-6.8	47-18	—	3¼	12	1	Int.	14	263.95	
3-9x[1,2,3]	3.3-8.7	38-15	—	3¼	12⅝	1	Int.	15	278.95	
4-12x[1,4,8]	4.4-11.8	27-10	—	3¼	15	1	Int.	18	326.95	
6-18x[1,4,6,7,8]	6.5-17.6	16-7	—	3¼	15.8	1	Int.	18.5	338.95	
Mini Scopes										
4x[4,5]	3.6	24	—	3¾-5	8¼	1	Int.	7.8	156.95	

HUNTING, TARGET ■ & VARMINT ■ SCOPES

Maker and Model	Magn.	Field at 100 Yds (feet)	Relative Bright-ness	Eye Relief (in.)	Length (in.)	Tube Diam. (in.)	W&E Adjust-ments	Weight (ozs.)	Price	Other Data
Burris (cont'd.)										
6x[1,4]	5.5	17	—	3¾-5	9	1	Int.	8.2	**171.95**	
2-7x	2.5-6.9	32-14	—	3¾-5	12	1	Int.	10.5	**212.95**	
3-9x[5]	3.6-8.8	25-11	—	3¾-5	12⅝	1	Int.	11.5	**218.95**	
4-12x[4]	4.5-11.6	19-8	—	3¾-4	15	1	Int.	15	**289.95**	
Handgun										
1½-4x LER[1,5]	1.6-3.8	16-11	—	11-25	10¼	1	Int.	11	**253.95**	
2½-7x LER[4,5]	2.7-6.7	12-7.5	—	11-28	12	1	Int.	12.5	**262.95**	
1x LER[1]	1.1	27	—	10-24	8¾	1	Int.	6.8	**149.95**	
2xLER[4,5,6]	1.7	21	—	10-24	8¾	1	Int.	6.8	**155.95**	
3x LER[4,6]	2.7	17	—	10-20	8⅞	1	Int.	6.8	**168.95**	
4x LER[1,4,5,6]	3.7	11	—	10-22	9⅝	1	Int.	9.0	**175.95**	
5x LER[1,4,6]	4.5	8.7	—	12-22	10⅞	1	Int.	9.2	**189.95**	
7x IER[1,4,5,6]	6.5	6.5	—	10-16	11¼	1	Int.	10	**203.95**	
10x IER[1,4,6]	9.5	4	—	8-12	13½	1	Int.	14	**252.95**	
2x Micro	1.7	15	—	7-24	9⅛	1	Int.	4	**142.95**	
3x Micro	2.7	17	—	8-22	9⅛	1	Int.	4	**142.95**	
Scout Scope										
1½x XER[3]	1.5	22	—	7-18	9	1	Int.	7.3	**157.95**	
2¾x XER[3]	2.7	15	—	7-14	9⅜	1	Int.	7.5	**162.95**	
Bushnell										
Armorlite 3-9x40	3-9	39-13	—	3.3	12	1	Int.	12.5	**349.95**	All ScopeChief, Banner and Custom models come with Multi-X reticle, with or without BDC (bullet drop compensator) that eliminates hold-over. Prismatic Rangefinder (PRF) on some models. Contact Bushnell for data on full line. Prices include BDC—deduct $5 if not wanted. Add $30 for PRF. BDC feature available in all Banner models, except 2.5x. [1]4-times zoom ratio. [4]Has battery powered lighted reticle. Contact Bushnell for complete details.
Scope Chief VI	4	29	96	3½	12	1	Int.	9.3	**153.95**	
Scope Chief VI	3-9	35-12.6	267-30	3.3	12.6	1	Int.	14.3	**241.95**	
Scope Chief VI	3-9	39-13	241-26.5	3.3	12.1	1	Int.	13	**301.95**	
Scope Chief VI	2½-8	45-14	247-96	3.3	11.2	1	Int.	12.1	**215.95**	
Scope Chief VI	1½-4½	73.7-24.5	267-30	3.5-3.5	9.6	1	Int.	9.5	**211.95**	
Scope Chief VI	4-12	29-10	150-17	3.2	13.5	1	Int.	17	**297.95**	
Sportview Rangemaster 3-9x	3-9	38-12	—	3.5	11.75	1	Int.	10	**111.95**	
■ Sportview Rangemaster 4-12x	4-12	27-9	—	3.2	13.5	1	Int.	14	**128.95**	
Sportview Standard 4x	4	28	—	4	11.75	1	Int.	9.5	**60.95**	
Sportview Standard 3-9x	3-9	38-12	—	3.5	11.75	1	Int.	10	**81.95**	
Banner 22 Rimfire 4x	4	28	—	3	11.9	1	Int.	8	**59.95**	
Banner 22 Rimfire 3-7x	3-7	29-13	—	2.5	10	¾	Int.	6.5	**67.95**	
Banner 3-9x56	3-9	39-12.5	—	3.5	14.4	1	Int.	18.4	**247.95**	
Banner Lite-Site 1.5-6x	1.5-6	60-15	—	3.2	9.8	1	Int.	12.4	**269.95**	
Banner Lite-Site 3-9x	3-9	36-12	—	3.3	13.6	1	Int.	14	**269.95**	
Banner Trophy WA 1.75-5x	1.75-5	68.5-24.5	—	3.2	10.4	1	Int.	10.2	**134.95**	
Banner Trophy WA 4x	4	34.2	—	3.4	12.4	1	Int.	11.9	**121.95**	
Banner Trophy WA 3-9x	3-9	39-13	—	3.3	11.8	1	Int.	12.9	**139.95**	
Banner Shotgun 2.5x	2.5	45	—	3.5	10.9	1	Int.	8	**79.95**	
Banner Standard 4x	4	29	—	3.5	12	1	Int.	10	**115.95**	
Banner Standard 6x	6	19.5	—	3	13.5	1	Int.	11.5	**143.95**	
Banner Standard 3-9x	3-9	43-14	—	3	12.1	1	Int.	14	**135.95**	
Banner Standard 4-12x	4-12	29-10	—	3.2	13.5	1	Int.	15.5	**209.95**	
Charles Daly										
4x32	4	28	—	3.25	11.75	1	Int.	9.5	**65.00**	[1]For shotgun use. [2]Pistol scopes. From Outdoor Sports Headquarters.
4x40 WA	4	36	—	3.25	13	1	Int.	11.5	**95.00**	
6x40 WA	6	23	—	3	12.75	1	Int.	15	**100.00**	
2.5x32	2.5	47	—	3	12.25	1	Int.	10	**75.00**	
2-7x32 WA	2-7	56-17	—	3	11.5	1	Int.	12	**119.00**	
3-9x40	3-9	35-14	—	3	12.5	1	Int.	11.25	**77.00**	
3-9x40 WA	3-9	36-13	—	3	12.75	1	Int.	12.5	**115.00**	
4-16x40	4-16	25-7	—	3	14.25	1	Int.	16.75	**130.00**	
1-3.5x20[1]	1-3.5	91-31	—	3.5	9.75	1	Int.	16.25	**158.00**	
2x20[2]	2	16	—	16-25	8.75	1	Int.	6.5	**105.00**	
4x28[2]	4	6.5	—	16-25	9.3	1	Int.	8	**105.00**	
aus Jena										
ZF4x32-M	4	32	—	3.5	10.8	26mm	Int.	10	**320.00**	Fixed power scopes have 26mm alloy tubes, variables, 30mm alloy; rings avail. from importer. Also avail. with rail mount. Multi-coated lenses. Waterproof and fogproof. ⅓-min. clicks. Choice of nine reticles. Imported from W. Germany by Europtik, Ltd.
ZF6x42-M	6	22	—	3.5	12.6	26mm	Int.	13	**355.00**	
ZF8x56-M	8	17	—	3.5	14	26mm	Int.	17	**415.00**	
YZF1.5-6x42-M	1.5-6	67.8-22	—	3.5	12.6	30mm	Int.	14	**535.00**	
VZF3-12x56-M	3-12	30-11	—	3.5	15	30mm	Int.	18	**595.00**	
Kahles										
2.5 x 20[1]	2.5	61	—	3.25	9.6	1	Int.	12.7	**450.00**	[1]Steel only. [2]Lightweight model weighs 11 oz. [3]Aluminum only. [4]Lightweight model weighs 16 oz. [5]Lightweight model weighs 12.7 oz. [6]Lightweight model weighs 16 oz. [7]Lightweight model weighs 15.5 oz. [8]Lightweight model weighs 18 oz. Lightweight models priced slightly higher. Imported by Swarovski America, Ltd.
4 x 32[2]	4	33	—	3.25	11.3	1	Int.	15	**465.00**	
7 x 56[3]	7	20	—	3.25	14.4	1	Int.	16	**610.00**	
8 x 56[4]	8	17.1	—	3.25	14.4	1	Int.	23	**595.00**	
1.4-4.5 x 20[5]	1.1-4.5	79-29.5	—	3.25	10.5	30mm	Int.	15	**560.00**	
1.5-6 x 42[6]	1.5-6	61-21	—	3.25	12.6	30mm	Int.	20	**625.00**	
2.2-9 x 42[7]	2.2-9	39.5-15	—	3.25	13.3	30mm	Int.	20.4	**765.00**	
3-12 x 56[8]	3-12	30-11	—	3.25	15.25	30mm	Int.	25	**835.00**	
K-ZF84 (6x42)	6	23	—	3.25	15.5	1	Int.	17.5	**860.00**	
Kilham										
Hutson Handgunner II	1.7	8	—	—	5½	⅞	Int.	5.1	**119.95**	Unlimited eye relief; internal click adjustments; crosshair reticle. Fits Thompson/Center rail mounts, for S&W K, N, Ruger Blackhawk, Super, Super Single-Six, Contender
Hutson Handgunner	3	8	—	10-12	6	⅞	Int.	5.3	**119.95**	

CAUTION: PRICES CHANGE. CHECK AT GUNSHOP.

HUNTING, TARGET ■ & VARMINT ■ SCOPES

Maker and Model	Magn.	Field at 100 Yds (feet)	Relative Brightness	Eye Relief (in.)	Length (in.)	Tube Diam. (in.)	W&E Adjustments	Weight (ozs.)	Price	Other Data
Laserscope										
FA-6	—	—	—	—	6.2	—	Int.	11	**399.00**	Projects high intensity beam of laser light onto target as an aiming point. Adj. for w. & e. FA-6 uses two 9V, others use eight AA batteries. Come with rings, switch, fastener. From Laser Devices, Inc.
FA-9	—	—	—	—	12	—	Int.	16	**449.00**	
FA-9P	—	—	—	—	9	—	Int.	14	**449.00**	
Lasersight										
LS45	0	—	—	—	7.5	—	Int.	8.5	**459.95**	Projects a highly visible beam of concentrated laser light onto the target. Adjustable for w. & e. Visible up to 500 yds. at night. For handguns, rifles, shotguns. Uses two standard 9V batteries. From Imatronic Lasersight.
Leatherwood										
ART II	3.0-8.8	31-12	—	3.5	13.9	1	Int.	42	**750.00**	Compensates for bullet drop via external circular cam. Matte gray finish. Designed specifically for the M1A/M-14 rifle. Quick Detachable model for rifles with Weaver-type bases. From North American Specialties.
Leupold										
M8-2X EER[1]	1.8	22.0	—	12-24	8.1	1	Int.	6.8	**184.80**	Constantly centered reticles, choice of Duplex, tapered CPC, Leupold Dot, Crosshair and Dot. CPC and Dot reticles extra. [1]2x and 4x scope have from 12"-24" of eye relief and are suitable for handguns, top ejection arms and muzzleloaders. [2]3x9 Compact, 6x Compact, 12x, 3x9, 3.5x10 and 6.5x20 come with Adjustable Objective. [3]Target scopes have 1-min divisions with ¼ min clicks, and Adjustable Objectives. 50-ft. Focus Adaptor available for indoor target ranges, **$44.80.** Sunshade available for all Adjustable Objective scopes, **$13.05.** [4]Also available in matte finish for about **$20.00** extra. [5]Dot or Duplex; focused at 300 yds. with A.O. **$368.40.**
M8-2X EER Silver[1]	1.8	22.0	—	12-24	8.1	1	Int.	6.8	**202.70**	
M8-4X EER[1]	3.5	9.5	—	12-24	8.4	1	Int.	7.6	**225.65**	
M8-4X EER Silver[1]	3.5	9.5	—	12-24	8.4	1	Int.	8.5	**243.50**	
M8-2.5X Compact	2.3	42	—	4.3	8.5	1	Int.	7.4	**203.50**	
M8-4X Compact	3.6	26.5	—	4.1	10.3	1	Int.	8.5	**232.40**	
2-7x Compact	2.5-6.6	41.7-16.5	—	3.8-3.0	9.9	1	Int.	8.5	**293.15**	
6x Compact & A.O.	5.7	16	—	3.9	10.7	1	Int.	8.5	**276.95**	
3-9x Compact & A.O.	3.2-8.5	34.5-13.5	—	3.8-3.1	11	1	Int.	9.5	**355.90**	
M8-4X[4]	3.6	28	—	4.4	11.4	1	Int.	8.8	**253.40**	
M8-6X	5.9	18.0	—	4.3	11.4	1	Int.	9.9	**248.15**	
M8-8X[2]	7.8	14.5	—	4.0	12.5	1	Int.	13.0	**330.90**	
M8-8x36[5]	7.7	14	—	3.7	11.8	1	Int.	10	**330.90**	
M8-12X[2]	11.6	9.2	—	4.2	13.0	1	Int.	13.5	**335.30**	
6.5 x 20 Target AO	6.5-19.2	14.8-5.7	—	5.3-3.7	14.2	1	Int.	16	**542.95**	
M8-12X Target[3]	11.6	9.2	—	4.2	13.0	1	Int.	14.5	**408.85**	
M8-24X[3]	24.0	4.7	—	3.2	13.6	1	Int.	14.5	**542.95**	
M8-36X[3]	36.0	3.2	—	3.4	13.9	1	Int.	15.5	**542.95**	
Vari-X-II 1X4	1.5-3.9	70.5-29.5	—	5.5	9.1	1	Int.	8.5	**250.80**	
Vari-X-II 2X7	2.5-6.6	44.0-19.0	—	4.1-3.7	10.7	1	Int.	10.4	**301.90**	
Vari-X-II 3X9[1,4]	3.5-9.0	32.0-13.5	—	4.1-3.7	12.3	1	Int.	14.5	**324.30**	
Vari-X-III 1.5X5	1.5-4.6	66.0-24.0	—	4.7-3.5	9.4	1	Int.	9.3	**344.20**	
Vari-X-III 2.5X8[4]	2.7-7.9	38.0-14.0	—	4.2-3.4	11.3	1	Int.	11.0	**388.20**	
Vari-X-III 3.5X10	3.4-9.9	29.5-10.5	—	4.6-3.6	12.4	1	Int.	13.0	**406.10**	
Vari-X-III 3.5X10[2]	3.4-9.9	29.5-10.5	—	4.6-3.6	12.4	1	Int.	14.4	**443.60**	
Vari-X-III 6.5X20[2]	6.5-19.2	14.8- 5.7	—	5.3-3.7	14.2	1	Int.	16	**481.00**	
Mirador										
RXW 4x40[1]	4	37	—	3.8	12.4	1	Int.	12	**161.95**	[1]Wide Angle scope. Multi-coated objective lens. Nitrogen filled; waterproof; shockproof. From Mirador Optical Corp.
RXW 1.5-5x20[1]	1.5-5	46-17.4	—	4.3	11.1	1	Int.	10	**170.95**	
RXW 3-9x40	3-9	43-14.5	—	3.1	12.9	1	Int.	13.4	**224.95**	
Nikon										
4x40	4	26	—	3.4	11.6	1	Int.	13.5	**234.00**	Multi-coated lenses; ¼-minute windage and elevation adjustments; nitrogen filled; waterproof. From Nikon Inc.
1.5-4.5x20	1.5-4.5	67.5-22.5	—	3.7	10	1	Int.	11.8	**300.00**	
2-7x32	2-7	43-12	—	4.1	11.4	1	Int.	12.3	**343.00**	
3-9x40	3-9	34.5-11.5	—	3.5-3.4	12.3	1	Int.	16	**377.00**	
Pentax										
4x	4	35	—	3¼	11.6	1	Int.	12.2	**220.00**	Multi-coated lenses, fog-proof, water-proof, nitrogen filled. Penta-Plex reticle. Click ¼-m.o.a. adjustments. Matte finish **$5.00** extra. Imported by Pentax Corp.
6x	6	20	—	3¼	13.4	1	Int.	13.5	**250.00**	
2-7x	2-7	42.5-17	—	3-3¼	12	1	Int.	14	**300.00**	
3-9x	3-9	33-13.5	—	3-3¼	13	1	Int.	15	**320.00**	
3-9x Mini	3-9	26.5-10.5	—	3¾	10.4	1	Int.	13	**270.00**	
RWS										
100S	4	—	—	8	10½	¾		7	**47.00**	Air gun scopes. All have Dyna-Plex reticle. Imported from Japan by Dynamit Nobel of America.
150S	3-7	—	—	8	10½	¾		8	**60.00**	
200S	4	—	—	8	11¾	⅞		11½	**70.00**	
250S	3-7	—	—	8	11¾	⅞		12	**80.00**	
300	4	—	—	8	12¾	1		11	**110.00**	
350	4	—	—	8	10	1		10	**95.00**	
400	2-7	—	—	8	12¾	1		12	**150.00**	
800	1.5	—	—	28	8¾	1		6	**100.00**	
CS-10	2.5	—	—	8	5¾	1		7	**100.00**	
Redfield										
Ultimate Illuminator 3-12x[6]	2.9-11.7	27-10.5	—	3-3½	15.4	30mm	Int.	23	**714.95**	*Accutrac feature avail. on these scopes at extra cost. Traditionals have round lenses. 4-Plex reticle is standard. [1]"Magnum Proof." Specially designed for magnum and auto pistols. Uses "Double Dovetail" mounts. Also in brushed aluminum finish, 2½x **$211.95,** 4x **$222.95.** [2]With matte finish **$468.95.** [3]Also available with matte finish at exta cost. [4]All Golden Five Star scopes come with Butler Creek flip-up lens covers. [5]Black anodized finish. [6]56mm adj. objective; European #4 reticle; comes with 30mm steel rings with Rotary Dovetail System, hardwood box. ¼-min. click adj.
Illuminator Trad. 3-9x	2.9-8.7	33-11	—	3½	12¾	1	Int.	17	**414.95**	
Illuminator Widefield 3-9x*[2]	2.9-8.7	38-13	—	3½	12¾	1	Int.	17	**459.95**	
Tracker 4x[3]	3.9	28.9	—	3½	11.02	1	Int.	9.8	**134.95**	
Tracker 2-7x[3]	2.3-6.9	36.6-12.2	—	3½	12.20	1	Int.	11.6	**172.95**	
Tracker 3-9x[3]	3.0-9.0	34.4-11.3	—	3½	14.96	1	Int.	13.4	**192.95**	
Traditional 4x¾"	4	24½	27	3½	9⅜	¾	Int.	—	**125.95**	
Traditional 2½x	2½	43	64	3½	10¼	1	Int.	8½	**161.95**	
Golden Five Star 4x[4]	4	28.5	58	3.75	11.3	1	Int.	9.75	**187.95**	
Golden Five Star 6x[4]	6	18	40	3.75	12.2	1	Int.	11.5	**206.95**	
Golden Five Star 2-7x[4]	2.4-7.4	42-14	207-23	3-3.75	11.25	1	Int.	12	**244.95**	
Golden Five Star 3-9x[4]	3.0-9.1	34-11	163-18	3-3.75	12.50	1	Int.	13	**262.95**	
Golden Five Star 4-12xA.O.*[4]	3.9-11.4	27-9	112-14	3-3.75	13.8	1	Int.	16	**337.95**	

Maker and Model	Magn.	Field at 100 Yds (feet)	Relative Brightness	Eye Relief (in.)	Length (in.)	Tube Diam. (in.)	W&E Adjustments	Weight (ozs.)	Price	Other Data
Redfield, (cont'd.)										
Golden Five Star 6-18xA.O.*[4]	6.1-18.1	18.6	50-6	3-3.75	14.3	1	Int.	18	357.95	
Compact Scopes										
Golden Five Star Compact 4x	3.8	28	—	3.5	9.75	1	Int.	8.8	184.95	
Golden Five Star Compact 6x	6.3	17.6	—	3.5	10.70	1	Int.	9.5	204.95	
Golden Five Star Compact 2-7x	2.4-7.1	40-16	—	3-3.5	9.75	1	Int.	9.8	241.95	
Golden Five Star Compact 3-9x	3.3-9.1	32-11.25	—	3-3.5	10.7	1	Int.	10.5	258.95	
Golden Five Star Compact 4-12x	4.1-12.4	22.4-8.3	—	3-3.5	12	1	Int.	13	326.95	
Pistol Scopes										
2½xMP[1]	2.5	9	64	14-19	9.8	1	Int.	10.5	192.95	
4xMP[1]	3.6	9	—	12-22	9-11/16	1	Int.	11.1	205.95	
Golden Five Star 1-4x	1.3-4.0	80-26	—	3-3.75	9.50	1	Int.	10.25	234.95	
2-6x[5]	2-5.5	25-7	—	10-18	10.4	1	Int.	11	250.95	
Widefield Low Profile Compact										
Widefield 4xLP Compact	3.7	33	—	3.5	9.35	1	Int.	10	227.95	
Widefield 3-9x LP Compact	3.3-9	37.0-13.7	—	3-3.5	10.20	1	Int.	13	291.95	
Low Profile Scopes										
Widefield 2¾xLP	2¾	55½	69	3½	10½	1	Int.	8	214.95	
Widefield 4xLP	3.6	37½	84	3½	11½	1	Int.	10	239.95	
Widefield 6xLP	5.5	23	—	3½	12¾	1	Int.	11	261.95	
Widefield 1¾x5xLP	1¾-5	70-27	136-21	3½	10¾	1	Int.	11½	294.95	
Widefield 2x7xLP*	2-7	49-19	144-21	3½	11¾	1	Int.	13	304.95	
Widefield 3x-9xLP*	3-9	39-15	112-18	3½	12½	1	Int.	14	335.95	
Schmidt & Bender										
Vari-M 1¼-4x20[1]	1¼-4	96-16	—	3¼	10.4	30mm	Int.	12.3	525.00	[1]All steel. [2]Black chrome finish. [3]For silhouette and varmint shooting. Choice of nine reticles. 30-year warranty. All have ⅓-min. click adjustments, centered reticles, nitrogen filling. Most models avail. in aluminum with mounting rail. Imported from West Germany by Paul Jaeger, Inc.
Vari-M 1½-6x42	1½-6	60-19.5	—	3¼	12.2	30mm	Int.	17.5	550.00	
Vari-M 2½-10x56	2½-10	37.5-12	—	3¼	14.6	30mm	Int.	21.9	675.00	
All Steel 1½x15[2]	1½	90	—	3¼	10	1	Int.	11.8	399.00	
All Steel 4x36[2]	4	30	—	3¼	11.4	1	Int.	14	429.00	
All Steel 6x42[2]	6	21	—	3¼	13.2	1	Int.	17.3	429.00	
All Steel 8x56[2]	8	16.5	—	3¼	14.8	1	Int.	21.9	499.00	
■ All Steel 12x42[3]	12	16.5	—	3¼	13	1	Int.	17.9	429.00	
Shepherd										
3940-E	3-9	43.5-15	178-20	3.3	13	1	Int.	17	444.00	[1]Also avail. as 310-MOA, 310-1, 310-E (**$376.00**) with ultra fine crosshair. [2]Also avail. as Model 27-4 for rimfires (**$345.00**). Reticle patterns set for shooter's choice of ballistics. Dual reticle system with instant range finder, bullet drop compensator. Waterproof, nitrogen filled, shock-proof. From Shepherd Scope Ltd.
310-2[1]	3-10	35.3-11.6	178-16	3-3.75	12.8	1	Int.	18	376.00	
27-2[2]	2.5-7.5	42-14	164-18	2.5-3	11.6	1	Int.	16.3	349.00	
Simmons										
1002 Rimfire[1]	4	23	—	3	11.5	¾	Int.	6	9.95	[1]With ring mount. [2]With ring mount. [3]With rings. [4]3-9x32; also avail. 3-9x40 as #1038. [5]Avail. in brushed aluminum finish as #1052. [6]Avail. with silhouette knobs as #1085, in brushed aluminum as #1088. [7]½-min. dot or Truplex; Truplex reticle also avail. with dot. Sunshade, screw-in lens covers. Parallax adj.; Silhouette knobs; graduated drums. [8]"Simcoat" multi-coating on all lenses, 44mm obj. lens, high-gloss finish, parallax adj., polarized and yellow screw-in filters, ¼-min. click adj., leather lens covers incl. M1045—Presidential Ranger Gold Medal also avail. in 4-12x (**$348.75**), 6.5-20x (**$390.00**). M1044 has 44mm obj., Simcoat. M1086 Silver Medal pistol scope. Also in 2-6x, 2x20, 4x32. M1013 Silver Series "Quad." Also avail. 3-12x, 4-16x, 6-24x. Truplex reticle in all models. All scopes sealed, fog-proof, with constantly centered reticles. Imported from Japan by Simmons Outdoor Corp. **Partial listing.** Contact Simmons for complete details. Prices are approximate.
1004 Rimfire[2]	3-7	22.5-9.5	—	3	11	¾	Int.	8.4	31.50	
1007 Rimfire[3]	4	25	—	3	10	1	Int.	9	84.75	
1005 Waterproof	2½	46	—	3	11.5	1	Int.	9.3	72.00	
1013	1-4	63.1-15.7	—	3.5	9.8	1	Int.	8.8	119.25	
1025 W.A.	6	24.5	—	3	12.4	1	Int.	12	111.25	
1026 W.A.	1½-4½	86-28.9	—	3-3¼	10.6	1	Int.	13.2	123.75	
1027 W.A.	2-7	54.6-18.3	—	3-3¼	12	1	Int.	12.8	123.75	
1044 WA	3-10	36.2-10.5	—	3.9-3.3	13.1	1	Int.	16.3	198.75	
1036 Mono Tube[4]	3-9	42-14	—	3-3¼	13.3	1	Int.	13	191.25	
1040 Mono Tube	2-7	54-18	—	3-3¼	13.1	1	Int.	12.9	187.50	
1045	3-9	42-14	—	4-3.3	13.0	1	Int.	16.3	348.75	
1050 Compact[5]	4	22	—	3	9	1	Int.	9.1	150.00	
1054 Compact	3-9	40-14	—	3-3¼	10.5	1	Int.	10.5	195.00	
1074	6½-20	18-6	—	3	15	1	Int.	16	247.50	
1075	6½-10	22-12	—	3	15	1	Int.	16	247.50	
1076[7]	15	8	—	3	15	1	Int.	16	195.00	
1078[7]	24	6	—	3	15	1	Int.	16	202.50	
1073 Sil. Airgun	2-7	54.6-18.3	—	3-3¼	12.1	1	Int.	15.7	165.00	
1080 Handgun	2	18	—	10-20	7.1	1	Int.	8.1	105.00	
1084 Handgun[6]	4	9	—	10-20	8.7	1	Int.	9.5	150.00	
1086 Handgun	1-3	37.2-12.1	—	13-27	10.7	1	Int.	10.5	240.00	
1087 Handgun	2-6	16-6	—	13-27	11	1	Int.	10.8	281.25	
1090 Shotgun	1.5	49.9	—	5	6.8	1	Int.	7.0	117.00	
21005 Shotgun	2.5	29	—	4.6	7.1	1	Int.	7.1	52.50	
Gold Medal Series										
1067[8]	3-9	42-14	216-54	3.3	13	1	Int.	16.2	330.00	
1068[8]	4-12	31-11	121-14	3.9-3.2	14.2	1	Int.	19.1	337.00	
Swarovski Habicht										
Nova 1.5x20	1.5	61	—	3¼	9.6	1	Int.	12.7	470.00	All models offered in either steel or lightweight alloy tubes except 1.5x20, ZFM 6x42 and Cobras. Weights shown are for lightweight versions. Choice of nine constantly centered reticles. Eyepiece recoil mechanism and rubber ring shield to protect face. Cobra and ZFM also available in NATO Stanag 2324 mounts. Imported by Swarovski America Ltd.
Nova 4x32	4	33	—	3¼	11.3	1	Int.	15	500.00	
Nova 6x42	6	23	—	3¼	12.6	1	Int.	17.9	540.00	
Nova 8x56	8	17	—	3¼	14.4	1	Int.	23	635.00	
Nova 1.5 6x42	1.5-6	61-21	—	3¼	12.6	1	Int.	16	685.00	
Nova 2.2-9x42	2.2-9	39.5-15	—	3¼	13.3	1	Int.	15.5	835.00	
Nova 3-12x56	3-12	30-11	—	3¼	15.25	1	Int.	18	910.00	

CAUTION: PRICES CHANGE. CHECK AT GUNSHOP.

HUNTING, TARGET ■ & VARMINT ■ SCOPES

Maker and Model	Magn.	Field at 100 Yds (feet)	Relative Bright-ness	Eye Relief (in.)	Length (in.)	Tube Diam. (in.)	W&E Adjust-ments	Weight (ozs.)	Price	Other Data
Swarovski, (cont'd.)										
ZFM 6x42	6	23	—	3¼	12.5	1	Int.	18	**710.00**	
Cobra 1.5-14	1.5	50	—	3.9	7.87	1	Int.	10	**550.00**	
A-Line Scopes										
4x32A	4	30	—	3.2	11.5	1	Int.	10.8	**450.00**	
6x36A	6	21	—	3.2	11.9	1	Int.	11.5	**500.00**	
3-9x36A	3-9	39-13.5	—	3.3	11.9	1	Int.	13	**655.00**	
Swift										All Swift Mark I scopes, with the exception of the 4x15, have Quadraplex reticles and are fog-proof and waterproof. The 4x15 has crosshair reticle and is non-waterproof.
600 4x15	4	16.2	—	2.4	11	¾	Int.	4.7	**14.00**	
650 4x32	4	29	—	3½	12	1	Int.	9	**53.50**	
653 4x40 WA	4	35½	—	3¾	12¼	1	Int.	12	**63.00**	
654 3-9x32	3-9	35¾-12¾	—	3	12¾	1	Int.	13¾	**64.00**	
656 3-9x40 WA	3-9	42½-13½	—	2¾	12¾	1	Int.	14	**78.00**	
657 6x40	6	18	—	3¾	13	1	Int.	10	**72.00**	
Tasco										[1]Water, fog & shockproof; fully coated optics; ¼-min. click stops; haze filter caps; lifetime warranty. [2]30/30 range finding reticle. [3]World Class Wide Angle; Supercon multi-coated optics; Opti-Centered[R] 30/30 rangefinding reticle; lifetime warranty. [4]Shock-absorbing 30mm tubes; 44 and 52mm objective lenses; Opti-Centered[R] 30/30 rangefinding reticle. [5]Selective Bi-reticle display—converts from 30/30 to lighted post reticle. [6]Illuminated Opti-Centered Post Reticle. [7]⅓ greater zoom range. [8]Trajectory compensating scopes, Opti-Centered stadia reticle. [9]Anodized finish. [10]True one-power scope. [11]Coated optics; cross hair reticle; ring mounts included to fit most 22, 10mm receivers. [12]Fits Remington 870, 1100.
WA 1x20 Wide Angle[1,3]	1	97	400.0	3	9¾	1	Int.	9.5	**199.95**	
WA 1-3.5x20 Wide Angle[1,3,10]	1-3½	115-31	400.0-32.4	3½	9¾	1	Int.	10.2	**219.95**	
WA 4x40 Wide Angle[1,3]	4	36	100.0	3¼	13	1	Int.	11.5	**129.85**	
WA 3-9x40 Wide Angle[1,3]	3-9	43½-15	176.8-19.3	3⅛	12¾	1	Int.	12.5	**159.85**	
WA 2.5x32 Wide Angle[1,3]	2½	47	163.8	3	12⅛	1	Int.	10	**159.95**	
WA 2-7x32 Wide Angle[1,3]	2-7	56-17	256.0-20.2	3¼	11½	1	Int.	12	**159.95**	
WA 1.75-5x20 Wide Angle[1,3]	1¾-5	72-24	129.9-16.0	3	10⅝	1	Int.	9.8	**199.95**	
EU 4x44[1,2,4]	4	29	121.0	3	12⅜	30mm	Int.	16	**299.95**	
EU 6x44[1,2,4]	6	20	53.2	3	12⅜	30mm	Int.	16	**299.95**	
EU 39x44[1,2,4]	3-9	37½-14	213.1-23.0	3	12⅛	30mm	Int.	18.5	**319.95**	
EUI 39x44 (SBD)[1,4,5]	3-9	37½-13	213.1-23.0	3¼	12⅝	30mm	Int.	18.5	**599.95**	
EU 3-12x52[1,2,4]	3-12	33-8½	299.2-18.4	3	12¼	30mm	Int.	18.5	**349.95**	
IR 3-9x40 WA[1,3,6]	3-9	40-15	176.8-19.3	3	12¾	1	Int.	14.8	**399.95**	
W 3-12x40 MAG-IV[1,2,7]	3-12	33-11	176.8-10.8	3	12⅛	1	Int.	12	**129.95**	
W 4-16x40 MAG-IV[1,2,7]	4-16	25½-7	100.0-6.2	3	14¼	1	Int.	16.75	**169.95**	
TR 3-12x32[1,2]	3-12	34-9	112.3-6.7	3	12¾	1	Int.	12	**179.95**	
TR 4-16x40[1,2]	4-16	25½-7	100.0-6.2	3	14¼	1	Int.	16.75	**249.95**	
W 4x32[1,2,9]	4	28	64.0	3	11¾	1	Int.	9.5	**59.95**	
SW 4x32[1,2,9]	4	24½	256.0	4	9⅞	1	Int.	9.1	**119.95**	
W 3-9x32[1,2,9]	3-9	35-14	112.3-12.2	3¼	12¾	1	Int.	12.3	**79.95**	
P1x22	1	65-24	—	8-28	7¾	1	Int.	8	**199.95**	
P2x22	2	26-18	—	10-24	7¾	1	Int.	7.6	**199.95**	
P4x30	4	7-6	—	12-24	9¾	1	Int.	12.1	**259.95**	
P6x40	6	5-5½	—	12-23	11	1	Int.	14.2	**349.95**	
RF 4x15[11]	4	21	13.6	2½	11	¾	Int.	4	**14.95**	
RF 4x20DS[11]	4	20	25.0	2½	10½	¾	Int.	3.8	**23.95**	
SG 2.5x32 with Shotgun Mount[1,12]	2½	42	163.8	3¼	11¾	1	Int.	15.7	**129.95**	
Thompson/Center										[1]May be used on light to medium recoil guns, including muzzleloaders. Coated lenses, nitrogen filled, lifetime warranty. [2]For heavy recoil guns. Nitrogen filled. Duplex reticle only. Target turrets avail. on 1½x, 3x models. Electra Dot illuminated reticle available in RP 2½x ($40 extra) and RP 3x ($45 extra).[3] Rifle scopes have Electra Dot reticle. [4]Rail model for grooved receivers also available—**$195.00.** With Electra Dot reticle. Silver finish 3x RP Electra Dot **$205.00.**
Lobo 1½ x[1]	1.5	16	127	11-20	7¾	⅞	Int.	5	**115.00**	
Lobo 3x[1]	3	9	49	11-20	9	⅞	Int.	6.3	**120.00**	
RP 1½ x[2]	1.5	28	177	11-20	7½	1	Int.	5.1	**150.00**	
RP 2½x[2]	2.5	15	64	11-20	8½	1	Int.	6.5	**150.00**	
RP 3x[2]	3	13	44	11-20	8¾	1	Int.	5.4	**150.00**	
RP 4x[2]	4	10	71	12-20	9¼	1	Int.	10.4	**170.00**	
TC 4x Rifle[3]	4	29	64	3.3	12⅞	1	Int.	12.3	**200.00**	
TC 3/9V Rifle[3]	3-9	35.3-13.2	177-19	3.3	12⅞	1	Int.	15.5	**275.00**	
Short Tube 8630[4]	4	29	20	3	7¾	1	Int.	10.1	**190.00**	
Trijicon Spectrum										[1]Self-luminous low-light reticle glows in poor light; allows choice of red, amber or green via a selector ring on objective end. [2]Advanced Combat Optical Gunsight for AR-15, M-16, with integral mount. [3]Reticle glows only red in poor light. From Armson, Inc.
4x40[1]	4	38	—	3.0	12.2	1	Int.	15.0	**289.00**	
6x56[1]	6	24	—	3.0	14.1	1	Int.	20.3	**389.00**	
1-3x20[1]	1-3	94-33	—	3.7-4.9	9.6	1	Int.	13.2	**354.00**	
3-9x40[1]	3-9	35-14	—	3.3-3.0	13.1	1	Int.	16.0	**364.00**	
3-9x56[1]	3-9	35-14	—	3.3-3.0	14.2	1	Int.	21.5	**464.00**	
ACOG[2]	4	37	—	1.5	5.8	—	Int.	9.7	**595.00**	
4x32 Red[3]	4	29	—	3.3	11.6	1	Int.	10.2	**198.00**	
Unertl										[1]Dural ¼ MOA click mounts. Hard coated lenses. Non-rotating objective lens focusing. [2]¼ MOA click mounts. [3]With target mounts. [4]With calibrated head. [5]Same as 1" Target but without objective lens focusing. [6]Price with ¼ MOA click mounts. [7]With new Posa mounts. [8]Range focus until near rear of tube. Price is with Posa mounts. Magnum clamp. With standard mounts and clamp ring **$332.00.**
■ 1" Target	6,8,10	16-10	17.6-6.25	2	21½	¾	Ext.	21	**181.00**	
■ 1¼" Target[1]	8,10,12,14	12-16	15.2-5	2	25	¾	Ext.	21	**244.00**	
■ 1½" Target	8,10,12,14 16,18,20	11.5-3.2	—	2¼	25½	¾	Ext.	31	**275.00**	
■ 2" Target[2]	8,10,12, 14,16,18, 24,30,36	8	22.6-2.5	2¼	26¼	1	Ext.	44	**375.00**	
■ Varmint, 1¼∞[3]	6,8,10,12	1-7	28-7.1	2½	19½	⅞	Ext.	26	**242.00**	
■ Ultra Varmint, 2"[4]	8,10 12,15	12.6-7	39.7-11	2½	24	1	Ext.	34	**351.00**	
Unertl										
■ Small Game[5]	4,6	25-17	19.4-8.4	2¼	18	¾	Ext.	16	**138.00**	
■ Vulture[6]	8 10	11.2 10.9	29 18½	3-4 —	15⅝ 16⅛	1	Ext.	15½	**270.00**	
■ Programmer 200[7]	8,10,12 14,16,18, 20,24,30,36	11.3-4	39-1.9	—	26½	1	Ext.	45	**465.00**	
■ BV-20[8]	20	8	4.4	4.4	17⅞	1	Ext.	21¼	**332.00**	

HUNTING, TARGET ■ & VARMINT ■ SCOPES

Maker and Model	Magn.	Field at 100 Yds (feet)	Relative Bright-ness	Eye Relief (in.)	Length (in.)	Tube Diam. (in.)	W&E Adjust-ments	Weight (ozs.)	Price	Other Data
Weatherby										
Mark XXII	4	25	50	2.5-3.5	11¾	⅞	Int.	9.25	105.00	Lumiplex reticle in all models. Blue-black, non-glare finish.
Supreme 1¾-5x20	1.7-5	66.6-21.4	—	3.4	10.7	1	Int.	11	260.00	
Supreme 2-7x34	2.1-6.8	59-16	—	3.4	11¼	1	Int.	10.4	270.00	
Supreme 4x44	3.9	32	—	3	12½	1	Int.	11.6	270.00	
Supreme 3-9x44	3.1-8.9	36-13	—	3.5	12.7	1	Int.	11.6	320.00	
Weaver										
K2.5	2.5	35	—	3.7	10.2	1	Int.	8.5	144.44	Micro-Trac adjustment system with ¼-min. clicks on K2.5, K4, V3, V9, V10, RK4, RV7; ⅛-min. clicks on K6, KT15. All have Dual-X reticle. One-piece aluminum tube, gloss finish, nitrogen filled, multi-coated lenses, waterproof. From Weaver.
K4	4	30	—	3.3	11.8	1	Int.	10.8	177.78	
K6	6	20	—	3.6	13	1	Int.	11.2	188.89	
V3	1-3	95-35	—	3.9-3.7	9.5	1	Int.	9.5	200.00	
V9	2.9-8.7	37-13	—	3.5-3.4	13	1	Int.	11.2	222.22	
V10	1.9-9.3	46-11	—	3.3	12.6	1	Int.	12.8	277.78	
KT15	14.6	7.5	—	3.2	15.8	1	Int.	16.1	266.67	
RK4	3.8	25	—	3	10.8	⅞	Int.	7.7	122.22	
RV7	2.2-6.5	43-15	—	2.9-2.6	11.5	⅞	Int.	8.5	151.11	
Williams										
Twilight Crosshair	1½-5	57¾-21	177-16	3½	10¾	1	Int.	10	186.50	
Twilight Crosshair	2½	32	64	3¾	11¼	1	Int.	8½	132.00	TNT models
Twilight Crosshair	4	29	64	3½	11¾	1	Int.	9½	138.00	
Twilight Crosshair	2-6	45-17	256-28	3	11½	1	Int.	11½	186.50	
Twilight Crosshair	3-9	36-13	161-18	3	12¾	1	Int.	13½	196.00	
Pistol Scopes										
Twilight 1.5x	1.5	19	177	18-25	8.2	1	Int.	6.4	136.50	
Twilight 2x	2	17.5	100	18-25	8.5	1	Int.	6.4	138.50	
Zeiss										
Diatal C 4x32	4	30	—	3.5	10.6	1	Int.	11.3	525.00	All scopes have ¼-minute click-stop adjustments. Choice of Z-Plex or fine crosshair reticles. Rubber armored objective bell, rubber eyepiece ring. Lenses have T-Star coating for highest light transmission. Z-Series scopes offered in non-rail tubes with duplex reticles only. Imported from West Germany by Zeiss Optical, Inc.
Diatal C 6x32	6	20	—	3.5	10.6	1	Int.	11.3	565.00	
Diatal C 10x36	10	12	—	3.5	12.7	1	Int.	14.1	675.00	
Diatal ZA 4x32	4	34.5	—	3.5	10.8	1.02 (26mm)	Int.	10.6	525.00	
Diatal ZA 6x42	6	22.9	—	3.5	12.7	1.02 (26mm)	Int.	13.4	620.00	
Diatal ZA 8x56	8	18	—	3.5	13.8	1.02 (26mm)	Int.	17.6	710.00	
Diavari C 1.5-4.5	1.5-4.5	72-27	—	3.5	11.8	1	Int.	13.4	790.00	
Diavari C 3-9x36	3-9	36-13	—	3.5	11.2	1	Int.	15.2	915.00	
Diavari ZA 1.5-6	1.5-6	65.5-22.9	—	3.5	12.4	1.18 (30mm)	Int.	18.5	870.00	
Diavari ZA 2.5-10	2.5-10	41-13.7	—	3.5	14.4	1.18 (30mm)	Int.	22.8	1,030.00	

■ Signifies target and/or varmint scope. Hunting scopes in general are furnished with a choice of reticle—crosshairs, post with crosshairs, tapered or blunt post, or dot crosshairs, etc. The great majority of target and varmint scopes have medium or fine crosshairs but post or dot reticles may be ordered. W—Windage E—Elevation MOA—Minute of angle or 1" (approx.) at 100 yards, etc.

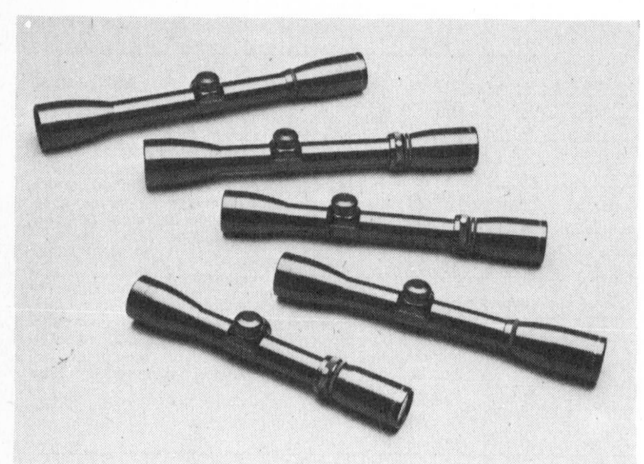

Pentax 4x, 2-7x, 3-9x, 6x, 3-9x Mini.

Interaims Mark V.

Burris Scout 2¾x.

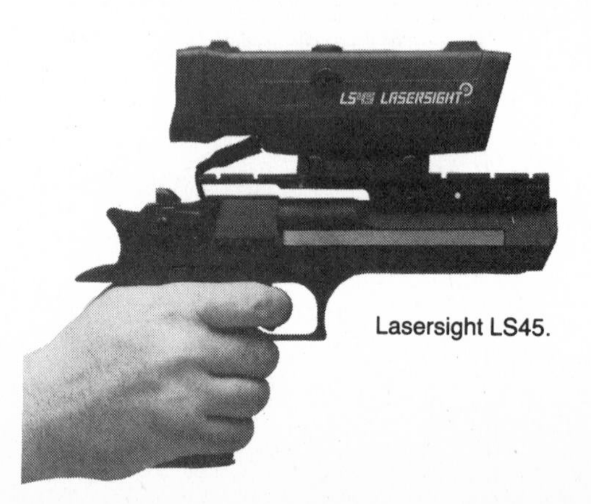

Lasersight LS45.

CAUTION: PRICES CHANGE. CHECK AT GUNSHOP.

SCOPE MOUNTS

Maker, Model, Type	Adjust.	Scopes	Price	Suitable for
Action Arms	No	1" split rings.	**$32.00**	For UZI, Ruger Mk. II, Mini-14, Win. 94, AR-15, Rem. 870, Ithaca 37, and many other popular rifles, handguns. From Action Arms.
Aimpoint	No	1"	**34.95-79.95**	For many popular revolvers, auto pistols, shotguns, military-style rifles/carbines, sporting rifles. Most require no gunsmithing. Contact Aimpoint for details.
Aimtech	No	One piece base	**59.95**	Mounts scopes, electronics, lasers using a Weaver-type base. For S&W K, L and N frames. No gunsmithing, sight removal. Attaches to side of frame. In satin black or "stainless" finish. From L&S Technologies, Inc.
A.R.M.S.				
Swan G-3	No	Weaver-type	**145.00**	[1]See through mount. [2]Also FNC—$89.00. From A.R.M.S., Inc.
M16A1A2/AR-15[1]	No	Weaver-type rail	**37.90**	
FN FAL LAR	No	Weaver-type rail	**95.00**	
FN FAL LAR Para.[2]	No	—	**120.00**	
Beretta AR-70	No	—	**59.00**	
Armson				
AR-15[1]	No	O.E.G.	**28.95**	[1]Fastens with one nut. [2]Models 181, 182, 183, 184, etc. [3]Claw mount. [4]Claw mount, bolt cover still easily removable. From Armson, Inc.
Mini-14[2]	No	O.E.G.	**39.95**	
H&K[3]	No	O.E.G.	**54.95**	
UZI[4]	No	O.E.G.	**54.95**	
Armsport				
100 Series[1]	No	1" rings. Low, med., high	**10.50**	[1]Weaver-type rings. [2]Weaver-type base; most popular rifles. Made in U.S. From Armsport.
104 22-cal.	No	1".	**10.50**	
201 See-Thru	No	1"	**13.50**	
1-Piece Base[2]	No		**5.00**	
2-Piece Base[2]	No		**2.50**	
B-Square				
Pistols				[1]Clamp-on, blue finish. Stainless finish **$59.95.** [2]For Bushnell Phantom only. [3]Blue finish; stainless finish **$59.95.** [4]Clamp-on, for Bushnell Phantom only, blue; stainless finish **$49.95.** [5]Requires drilling & tapping. [6]No gunsmithing, no sight removal; blue; stainless finish **$59.95.** [7]Weaver-style rings. Rings not included with Weaver-type bases. Partial listing of mounts shown here. Contact B-Square for more data. B-Square makes mounts for the following military rifles: AK47/AKS, Egyptian Hakim, French MAS 1936, M91 Argentine Mauser, Model 98 Brazilian and German Mausers, Model 93 Spanish Mauser (long and short), Model 1916 Mauser, Model 38 and 96 Swedish Mausers, Model 91 Russian (round and octagon receivers), Chinese SKS 56, SMLE No. 1, Mk. III, 1903 Springfield, U.S. 30-Cal. Carbine. All use long eye relief scopes, all priced at **$39.95.** Those following replace gun's rear sight: AK47/AKS, P14/1917 Enfield, FN49, M1 Garand, M1-A/M14 (no sight removal), SMLE No. 1, MK III/No. 4 & 5, MK I, 1903/1903-A3 Springfield, Beretta AR 70 (no sight removal), Japanese 7.7 Arisaka.
Beretta/Taurus 92/99	—	1"	**69.95**	
Browning Buck Mark	No	1"	**29.95**	
Colt 45 Auto	E only	1"	**69.95**	
Colt Python[1]	E	1"	**49.95**	
Daisy 717/722 Champion[2]	No	1"	**19.95**	
Daisy 44 Mono-Mount	—	1"	**9.95**	
Dan Wesson Clamp-On[3,7]	E	1"	**49.95**	
Hi-Standard Victor	W&E	1"	**49.95**	
Ruger 22 Auto Mono-Mount[4]	No	1"	**39.95**	
Ruger Single-Six[5]	No	1"	**39.95**	
S&W K, L, N frame	No	1"	**49.95**	
T-C Contender	W&E	1"	**49.95**	
Rifles				
Mini-14[6]	W&E	1"	**49.95**	
M-94 Side Mount	W&E	1"	**49.95**	
Ruger 77	W&E	1"	**49.95**	
Ruger Ranch/Mini-30	W&E	1"	**49.95**	
SMLE Side Mount	W&E	1"	**49.95**	
Rem. Model Seven, 600, 660, etc.[7]	No	1" One piece base	**9.95**	
Military				
M1-A	W&E	1"	**59.95**	
AR-15/16	W&E	1"	**49.95**	
FN-LAR/FAL[7]	E only	1"	**99.50**	
HK-91/93/94[7]	E only	1"	**69.95**	
Shotguns				
Benelli Super 90	No	1"	**49.95**	
Browning A-5	No	1"	**49.95**	
Franchi 48/AL	No	1"	**49.95**	
Franchi Elite, Prestige, SPAS	No	1"	**49.95**	
Ithaca 37, Mag 10	No	1"	**39.95**	
Mossberg 500, 712, 5500	No	1"	**39.95**	
Rem. 870/1100	No	1"	**39.95**	
Remington 870, 1100 (and L.H.)	No	1"	**39.95**	
S&W 1000P	No	1"	**39.95**	
Beeman				
Double Adjustable	W&E	1"	**29.98**	All grooved receivers and scope bases on all known air rifles and 22-cal. rimfire rifles (½" to ⅝"—6mm to 15mm). [1]Centerfire rifles. Scope detaches easily, returns to zero.[2] Designed specifically for Krico rifles.
Deluxe Ring Mounts	No	1"	**28.98**	
Professional Mounts	W&E	1"	**98.95**	
Professional Pivot[1]	W	1"	**269.50**	
Buehler[2]	W	1"	**59.98**	
Buehler				
One Piece (T)[1]	W only	1" split rings, 3 heights. 1" split rings, engraved 26mm split rings, 2 heights 30mm split rings, 1 height	**Complete—71.50** **Rings only—98.75** **Rings only—52.00** **Rings only—62.50**	[1]Most popular models. [2]Sako dovetail receivers. [3]15 models. [4]No drilling & tapping. [5]Aircraft alloy, dyed blue or to match stainless; for Colt Diamondback, Python, Trooper, Ruger Blackhawk, Single-Six, Security-Six, S&W K-frame, Dan Wesson.
One Piece Micro Dial (T)[1]	W&E	1" split rings.	**Complete—91.50**	
Two Piece (T)[1]	W only	1" split rings.	**Complete—71.50**	
Two Piece Dovetail (T)[2]	W only	1" split rings.	**Complete—88.00**	
One Piece Pistol (T)[3]	W only	1" split rings.	**Complete—71.50**	
One Piece Pistol Stainless (T)[1]	W only	1" stainless rings.	**Complete—93.00**	
One Piece Ruger Mini-14 (T)[4]	W only	1" split rings.	**Complete—88.00**	
One Piece Pistol M83 Blue[4,5]	W only	1" split rings.	**Complete—81.50**	
One Piece Pistol M83 Silver[4,5]	W only	1" stainless rings.	**Complete—95.00**	

CAUTION: PRICES CHANGE. CHECK AT GUNSHOP.

SCOPE MOUNTS

Maker, Model, Type	Adjust.	Scopes	Price	Suitable for
Burris				
Supreme One Piece (T)[1]	W only	1" split rings, 3 heights.	**1 piece-base—23.95**	[1]Most popular rifles. Universal, rings, mounts fit Burris. Universal, Redfield, Leupold and Browning bases. Comparable prices. [2]Browning Standard 22 Auto rifle. [3]Grooved receivers. [4]Universal dovetail; accept Burris, Universal, Redfield, Leupold rings. For Dan Wesson, S&W, Virginian, Ruger Blackhawk, Win. 94. [5]Medium standard front, extension rear, per pair. Low standard front, extension rear, per pair. [6]Mini scopes, scopes with 2" bell, for M77R. Selected rings and bases available with matte Safari finish.
Trumount Two Piece (T)	W only	1" split rings, 3 heights.	**2 piece base—21.95**	
Browning Auto Mount[2]	No	3/4", 1" split rings.	**18.49**	
Rings Mounts[3]	No	3/4", 1" split rings.	**1" rings—18.95**	
L.E.R. Mount Bases[4]	No	1" split rings.	**21.95**	
Extension Rings[5]	No	1" scopes.	**37.95**	
Ruger Ring Mount[6]	W only	1" split rings.	**42.95**	
Std. 1" Rings	—	Low, medium, high heights	**30.95**	
Zee Rings	—	Fit Weaver bases; medium and high heights	**25.95**	
Bushnell				
Detachable (T) mounts only[1]	W only	1" split rings, uses Weaver base.	**Rings—16.95**	[1]Most popular rifles. Includes windage adj.
22 mount	No	1" only.	**Rings— 7.95**	
Clearview				
Universal Rings (T)[1]	No	1" split rings.	**19.95**	[1]All popular rifles including Sav. 99. Uses Weaver bases. [2]Allows use of open sights. [3]For 22 rimfire rifles, with grooved receivers or bases. [4]Fits 13 models. Broadest view area of the type. [5]Side mount for both M94 and M94-375 Big Bore.
Mod 101, & 336[2]	No	1" split rings.	**19.95**	
Broad-View[4]	No	1"	**19.95**	
Model 22[3]	No	3/4", 7/8", 1"	**11.95**	
94 Winchester [5]	No	1"	**19.95**	
Conetrol				
Huntur[1]	W only	1", 26mm, 26.5mm solid or split rings, 3 heights.	**59.91**	[1]All popular rifles, including metric-drilled foreign guns. Price shown for base, two rings. Matte finish. [2]Gunnur grade has mirror-finished rings, satin-finish base. Price shown for base, two rings. [3]Custum grade has mirror-finished rings and mirror-finished, streamlined base. Price shown for base, 2 rings. [4]Win. 94, Krag, older split-bridge Mannlicher-Schoenauer, Mini-14, M-1 Garand, etc. Prices same as above. [5]For all popular guns with integral mounting provision, including Sako, BSA, Ithacagun, Ruger, H&K and many others. Also for grooved-receiver rimfires and air rifles. Prices same as above. [6]For XP-100, T/C Contender, Colt SAA, Ruger Blackhawk, S&W. [7]Sculptured 2-piece bases as found on fine custom rifles. Price shown is for base alone. Also available unfinished—**$74.91**. [8]Replaces Ruger rib, positions scope farther back. [9]30mm rings made in projectionless style, medium height only. Three-ring mount available for T/.C Contender pistol, in Conetrol's three grades.
Gunnur[2]	W only	1", 26mm, 26.5mm solid or split rings, 3 heights.	**74.91**	
Custum[3]	W only	1", 26mm, 26.5mm solid or split rings, 3 heights.	**89.91**	
One Piece Side Mount Base[4]	W only	1", 26mm, 26.5mm solid or split rings, 3 heights.		
Daptar Bases[5]	W only	1", 26mm, 26.5mm solid or split rings, 3 heights.		
Pistol Bases, 2 or 3-ring[6]	W only	1" scopes.		
Fluted Bases[7]	W only	Standard Conetrol rings	**99.99**	
Ruger No. 1 Base[8]	W only	1", 26mm, 26.5mm solid or split rings.	**NA**	
30mm Rings[9]	W only	30mm	**49.98-69.96**	
EAW				
Quick Detachable Top Mount[1]	W&E	1"/26mm	**175.00-185.00**	[1]Also 30mm rings to fit Redfield or Leupold-type bases, low and high, **$75.** Most popular rifles. Elevation adjusted with variable-height sub-bases for rear ring. Imported by Del Sports, Inc., Paul Jaeger, Inc.
	W&E	1"/26mm with front extension ring.	**175.00-199.00**	
	W&E	30mm	**175.00-199.00**	
	W&E	30mm with front extension ring.	**175.00-199.00**	
Griffin & Howe				
Standard Double Lever (S).	No	1" or 26mm split rings.	**180.00**	All popular models (Garand **$215**). All rings **$75**. Top ejection rings available.
Holden				
Wide Ironsighter®	No	1" Split rings.	**23.95**	[1]Most popular rifles including Ruger Mini-14, H&R M700, and muzzleloaders. Rings have oval holes to permit use of iron sights. [2]For 1" dia. scopes. [3]For 3/4" or 7/8" dia. scopes. [4]For 1" dia. extended eye relief scopes. [5]702—Browning A-Bolt; 709—Marlin 39A. [6]732—Ruger 77/22 R&RS, No. 1 Ranch Rifle; 777 fits Ruger 77R, RS. Both 732, 777 fit Ruger integral bases.
Ironsighter Center Fire[1]	No	1" Split rings.	**23.95**	
Ironsighter S-94	No	1" split rings	**29.95**	
Ironsighter 22 cal. rimfire				
Model #500[2]	No	1" Split rings.	**12.95**	
Model #600[3]	No	7/8" Split rings also fits 3/4".	**12.95**	
Series #700[5]	No	1", split rings	**23.95**	
Model 732, 777[6]	No	1", split rings	**54.95**	
Ironsighter Handguns[4]	No	1" Split rings.	**29.95**	
Jaeger				
QD, with windage (S)	W only	1", 3 heights.	**250.00**	All popular models. From Paul Jaeger, Inc.
Kimber				
Standard[1]	No	1", split rings	**48.00**	[1]High rings; low rings—**$45.00**; both only for Kimber rifles. [2]For Kimber rifles only. Also avail. for Mauser (FN,98) Rem. 700, 721, 722, 725, Win. M70, Mark X. [3]Vertically split rings; for Kimber and other popular CF rifles.
Double Lever[2]	No	1", split rings	**82.50**	
Non-Detachable[3]	No	1", split rings	**48.00**	
Kris Mounts				
Side-Saddle[1]	No	1", 26mm split rings.	**11.98**	[1]One-piece mount for Win. 94. [2]Most popular rifles and Ruger. [3]Blackhawk revolver. Mounts have oval hole to permit use of iron sights.
Two Piece (T)[2]	No	1", 26mm split rings.	**7.98**	
One Piece (T)[3]	No	1", 26mm split rings.	**11.98**	
KWIK MOUNT				
Shotgun Mount	No	1"	**39.95**	Wrap-around design; no gunsmithing required. Models for Browning A-5 12 ga., Rem. 870/1100, S&W 916, Savage 67 12 ga., Mossberg 500, Ithaca 37 & 51 12 ga., S&W 1000/3000, Win. 1400. From KenPatable Ent.
Kwik-Site				
KS-See-Thru[1]	No	1"	**21.95**	[1]Most rifles. Allows use of iron sights. [2]22-cal. rifles with grooved receivers. Allows use of iron sights. [3]Model 94, 94 Big Bore. No drilling or tapping. Also in non-adjustable model **$30.95.** [4]Most rifles. One-piece solid construction. Use on Weaver bases. 32mm obj. lens or larger. [5]Non-see-through model; for grooved receivers. [6]Allows Mag Lite or C or D, Mini Mag Lites to be mounted atop See-Thru mounts. [7]Fits any Redfield, Tasco, Weaver or universal-style dovetail base. Bright blue, black matte or satin finish. Standard, high heights.
KS-22 See-Thru[2]	No	1"'	**18.95**	
KS-W94[3]	Yes	1"	**39.95**	
KSM Bench Rest[4]	No	1"	**30.95**	
KS-WEV	No	1"	**21.95**	
KS-WEV-HIGH	No	1"	**21.95**	
KS-T22 1"[5]	No	1"	**18.95**	
KS-FLM Flashlite[6]	No	Mini or C cell flashlight	**49.95**	
KS-T88[7]	No	1", 30mm	**9.75**	
Laserscope	No	Laserscope	**37.95 to 69.95**	Mounts Laserscope above or below barrel. For most popular military-type rifles, UZI, H&K submachine guns, Desert Eagle pistols. From Laser Devices, Inc.

CAUTION: PRICES CHANGE. CHECK AT GUNSHOP.

SCOPE MOUNTS

Maker, Model, Type	Adjust.	Scopes	Price	Suitable for
Lasersight	No	LS45 only	34.95 to 149.00	For the LS45 Lasersight. Allows LS45 to be mounted alongside any 1" scope. Universal adapter attaches to any full-length Weaver-type base. For most popular military-type rifles, Mossberg. Rem. Shotguns, Python, Desert Eagle, S&W N frame, Colt 45ACP. From Imatronic Lasersight.
Leupold				
STD Bases[1]	W only	One- or two-piece bases	21.50	[1]Rev. front and rear combinations. [2]Avail. polished, matte finish. [3]Base and two rings; Ruger, S&W, T/C; add $5.00 for silver finish. [4]Rem. 700, Win. 70-type actions. [5]For Ruger No. 1, 77/22; interchangeable with Ruger units. [6]For dovetailed rimfire rifles. [6]Sako; medium, low. [8]Must be drilled, tapped for each action. [9]Unfinished bottom, top completed; sold singly.
STD Rings[2]		1" Super low, low, medium, high	31.10	
STD Handgun mounts[3]	No		54.80	
Dual Dovetail Bases[1,4]	No		21.50	
Dual Dovetail Rings		1", Super low, low	31.10	
Ring Mounts[5,6,7]	No	1"	78.70	
Gunmaker Base[8]	W only	1"	14.20	
Gunmaker Ring Blanks[9]		1"	20.50	
Leatherwood				
Bridge Bases[1]	No	ART II	15.00	[1]Many popular bolt actions. From North American Specialties.
M1A/M-14 Q.D.	No	ART II	100.00	
AR-15/M-16 Base	No	ART II	18.00	
FN-FAL Base	No	ART II	95.00	
FN Para. Base	No	ART II	105.00	
Steyr SSG Base	No	ART II	55.00	
Marlin				
One Piece QD (T)	No	1" split rings.	14.95	Most Marlin lever actions.
Millett				
Black Onyx Smooth		1" Low, medium, high	26.95	Rem. 40X, 700, 722, 725, Ruger 77 (round top) Weatherby, etc. FN Mauser, FN Brownings, Colt 57, Interarms MkX, Parker-Hale, Sako (round receiver), many others. [1]Fits Win. M70, 70XTR, 670, Browning BBR, BAR, BLR, A-Bolt, Rem. 7400/7600, Four, Six, Marlin 336, Win. 94 A.E., Sav. 110. [2]To fit Weaver-type bases. Also for Colt, Dan Wesson, Ruger handguns—**$39.95-$87.45.** Avail. for Scope-Site (fixed, $39.95, or adjustable, $69.95, Onyx Smooth, $26.95, Chaparral Engraved, $39.95. Universal Bases also for Browning BAR, BLR, A-Bolt, Rem. 7400, 7600, Marlin 336, Win. 94 AE, Savage 110. [3]Engraved. Smooth **$26.95.** [4]For Rem. 870, 1100; smooth. [5]Two and three-ring sets for Colt Python, Trooper, Diamondback, Peacekeeper, Dan Wesson, Ruger Redhawk, Super Redhawk.
Chaparral Engraved		Engraved	39.95	
Universal Two Piece Bases				
700 Series	W only	Two-piece bases	20.95	
FN Series	W only	Two-piece bases	20.95	
70 Series[1]	W only	1", two-piece bases	20.95	
Angle-Loc[2] Rings	W only	1", low, medium, high	39.95	
Ruger 77 Rings[3]	—	1"	39.95	
Shotgun Rings[4]	—	1"	26.95	
Handgun Bases, Rings[5]	—	1"	29.95-44.85	
Redfield				
JR-SR(T)[1]	W only	¾", 1", 26mm, 30mm	**JR—19.95-50.95 SR—25.95-39.95**	[1]Low, med. & high, split rings. Reversible extension front rings for 1". 2-piece bases for Sako. Colt Sauer bases $39.85. [2]Split rings for grooved 22's. See-thru mounts $16.15. [3]Used with MP scopes for: S&W K or N frame. XP-100, Colt J or I frame. T/C Contender, Colt autos, black powder rifles. [4]One- and two-piece aluminum base; three ring heights. [5]For compact scopes on Browning A-Bolt long action, Remington 700, Winchester 70A.
Ring (T)[2]	No	¾" and 1".		
Double Dovetail MP[3]	No	1", split rings.	58.95	
Midline Base & Rings[4]	No	1".	11.95	
Widefield See-Thru Mounts[4]	No	1".	19.95	
Compact[5]	W only	1".	49.95	
S&K				
Insta-Mount (T) base only[1]	W only	Use S&K rings only.	**20.00-73.00**	[1]1903, A3, M1 Carbine, Lee Enfield #1, MK. III, #4, #5, M1917, M98 Mauser, FN Auto, AR-15, AR-180, M-14, M-1, Ger. K-43, Mini-14, M1-A, Krag, AKM, AK-47, Win. 94. [2]Most popular rifles already drilled and tapped, Horizontally and vertically split rings, matte or high gloss.
Conventional rings and bases[2]	W only	1" split rings.	**50.00**	
SKulptured Bases, Rings[2]	W only	1", 26mm, 30mm	**From 50.00**	
SSK Industries				
T'SOB	No	1".	**45.00-145.00**	Custom installation using from two to four rings (included). For T/C Contender, most 22 auto pistols. Ruger and other S.A. revolvers, Ruger, Dan Wesson, S&W, Colt D.A. revolvers. Black or white finish.
Sako				
QD Dovetail	W only	1" only.	99.95	Sako, or any rifle using Sako action, 3 heights available, Stoeger, importer.
Simmons				
1401	No	1"	8.50	Weaver-type bases. #1401 (low) also in high style (#1403). #1406, 1408 for grooved receiver 22s. Bases avail. for most popular rifles; one- and two-piece styles. Most popular rifles; 1-piece bridge mount. Ring sets—$39.00. [1]For 22 RF rifles.
1406	No	1"	8.50	
1408	No	1"	17.50	
Tasco				
791 and 793 series[1]	No	1", regular or high.	11.95	[1]Many popular rifles. [2]For 22s with grooved receivers. [3]Most popular rifles. [4]"Quick Peep" 1" ring mount; fits all 22-cal. rifles with grooved receivers. [5]For Ruger Mini-14; also in brushed aluminum. [6]Side mount for Win. 94. [7]Side mount rings and base for Win. 94 in 30-30, 375 Win. [8]Avail. for most rifles. Steel or aluminum rings.
797[2]	No	Split rings.	11.95	
799[4]	No	1" only	11.95	
885 BK[7]	No	1" only	23.95	
895[6]	No	1" only	5.95	
896[5]	No	1" only	39.95	
800L Series (with base)[3]	No	1" only. Rings and base.	15.95	
World Class[8]				
Steel Bases	Yes	1", 26mm, 30mm	29.95	
Steel Rings	Yes	1", 26mm	39.95	
Steel 30mm Rings	Yes	30mm	79.95	
Thompson/Center				
Contender 9746[1]	No	T/C Lobo	13.50	[1]All Contenders except vent. rib. [2]T/C rail mount scopes; all Contenders except vent. rib. [3]All S&W K and Combat Masterpiece, Hi-Way Patrolman, Outdoorsman, 22 Jet, 45 Target 1955. Requires drilling, tapping. [4]Blackhawk, Super Blackhawk, Super Sin-
Contender 9741[2]	No	2½, 4 RP	13.50	
Contender 7410	No	Bushnell Phantom 1.3, 2.5x	13.50	
S&W 9747[3]	No	Lobo or RP	13.50	

SCOPE MOUNTS

Maker, Model, Type	Adjust.	Scopes	Price	Suitable for
Thompson/Center (cont'd.)				
Ruger 9748[4]	No	Lobo or RP	13.50	gle-Six. Requires drilling, tapping. [5]45 or 50 cal.; replaces rear sight. [6]Rail mount scopes; 54-cal. Hawken, 50, 54, 56-cal. Renegade. Replaces rear sight. [7]Cherokee 32 or 45 cal., Seneca 36 or 45 cal. Replaces rear sight. Carbine mount #9743 for Short Tube scope #8640, $10.50.
Hawken 9749[5]	No	Lobo or RP	13.50	
Hawken/Renegade 9754[6]	No	Lobo or RP	13.50	
Cherokee/Seneca[7]	No	Lobo or RP	13.50	
New Englander 9757	No	Lobo or RP	13.50	
Unertl				
Posa (T)[1]	Yes	¾", 1" scopes.	Per set 70.00	[1]Unertl target or varmint scopes. [2]Any with regular dovetail scope bases.
¼ Click (T)[2]	Yes	¾", 1" target scopes.	Per set 100.00	
Weaver				
Detachable Mounts				[1]Nearly all modern rifles. Low, med., high. 1" extension $27.1" med. stainless steel $35.33.[2] Nearly all modern rifles, shotguns. [3]Most modern big-bore rifles; std., high. [4]22s with ⅜" grooved receivers. [5]Nearly all modern rifles. 1" See-Thru extension $27. [6]Most modern big bore rifles. [7]No drilling, tapping. For Colt Python, Trooper, 357, Officer's Model, Ruger Blackhawk & Super, Mini-14, Security-Six, 22 auto pistols, Redhawk, Blackhawk SRM 357, S&W current K, L with adj. sights. [8]For Rem. 870/1100, Mossberg 500. No gunsmithing. [9]For some popular sporting rifles. [10]Dovetail design mount for Rem. 700, Win. 70, FN Mauser, low, med., high rings; std., extension bases. From Weaver
Top Mount[1]	No	1"	23.11	
		⅞"	22.22	
Side Mount[2]	No	1"	24.44	
		1" Long	28.89	
Pivot Mount[3]	No	1"	31.33	
Tip-Off Mount[4]	No	⅞"	17.78	
		1"	22.67	
See-Thru Mount				
Tip-Off[4]	No	⅞"	16.67	
		1"	23.11	
Detachable[5]	No	1"	23.11	
Integral[6]	No	1"	17.22	
Mount Base System[7]				
Blue Finish	No	1"	60.11	
Stainless Finish	No	1"	84.11	
Shotgun Mount System[8]	No	1"	60.11	
Rifle Mount System[9]	No	1"	26.67	
Imperial Mount Systems[10]				
Bases, pair	Yes	1"	22.33	
Rings, pair	No	1"	32.22	
Wideview				
WSM-22	No	1".	14.95	Models for many popular rifles—$18.95. Low ring, high ring and grooved receiver types—$7.95. From Wideview Scope Mount Corp.
WSM-94	No	1".	20.95	
WSM-94AE	No	1".	22.95	
Williams				
Offset (S)[1]	No	⅞", 1", 26mm solid, split or extension rings.	59.30	[1]Most rifles, Br. S.M.L.E. (round rec) $3.85 extra. [2]Same. [3]Most rifles including Win. 94 Big Bore. [4]Many modern rifles. [5]Most popular rifles.
QC (T)[2]	No	Same.	43.90	
QC (S)[3]	No	Same.	48.55	
Sight-Thru[4]	No	1", ⅞" sleeves $3.20.	21.00	
Streamline[5]	No	1" (bases form rings).	21.00	

(S)—Side Mount (T)Top Mount 22mm—.866" 25.4mm = 1"1.024" 26.5mm = 1.045" 30mm = 1.81"

Aimtech S&W mount.

SSK T'SOB mount.

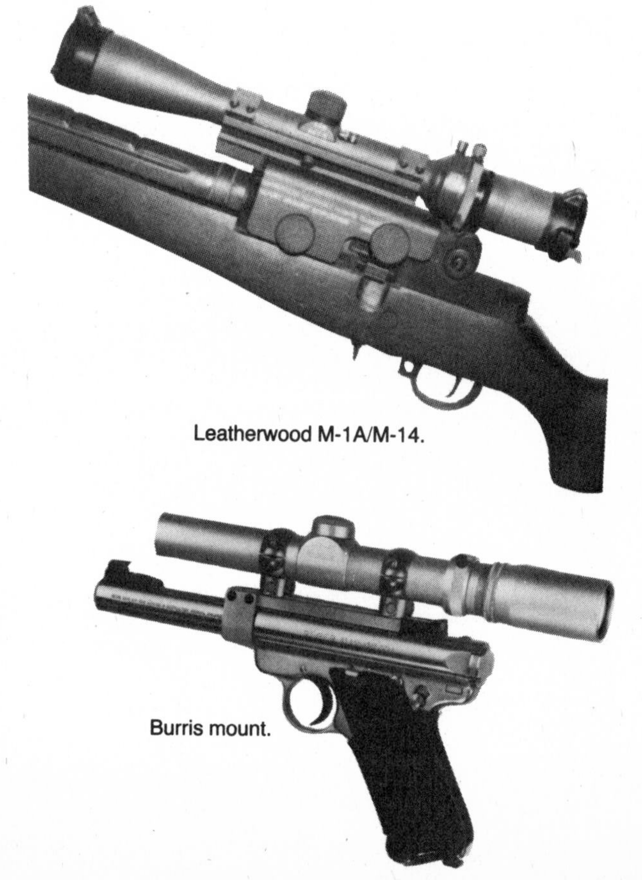

Leatherwood M-1A/M-14.

Burris mount.

CAUTION: PRICES CHANGE. CHECK AT GUNSHOP.

SPOTTING SCOPES

Weatherby Sightmaster

Mirador TTB Draw-Tube

Mirador SIB Scopes

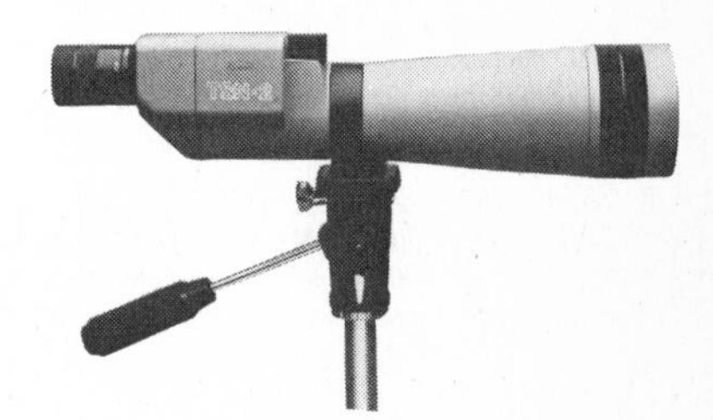

Kowa TSN-2

BAUSCH & LOMB DISCOVERER—15x to 60x zoom, 60mm objective. Constant focus throughout range. Field at 1000 yds. 40 ft (60x), 156 ft. (15x). Comes with lens caps. Length 17½", wgt. 47¼ oz.

Price: ... **$379.95**

BUSHNELL SPACEMASTER II—70mm objective. Field at 1000 yds., 158' to 37'. Relative brightness, 5.76. Wgt., 50 oz. Length closed, 13"; prism focusing.

Price: Without eyepiece ... **$259.95**
15x, 20x, 40x and 60x eyepieces, each ... **$55.95**
22x wide angle eyepiece ... **$69.95**

BUSHNELL ZOOM SPACEMASTER II—15x-45x zoom. 70mm objective. Field at 1000 yards 130'-65'. Relative brightness 9-1.7. Wgt. 53 oz., length 14". Shooter's stand tripod, carrying case.

Price: ... **$439.95**

BUSHNELL COMPETITOR—40mm objective, 20x. Prismatic. Field at 1000 yards 140'. Minimum focus 33'. Length 10", weight 14.5 oz.

Price: With tripod ... **$113.95**

BUSHNELL TROPHY—15x-45x zoom. Rubber armored, prismatic. 60mm objective. Field at 1000 yards 110' to 65'. Minimum focus 20'. Length with caps 11.6", weight 36 oz.

Price: With tripod and carrying case ... **$399.95**
Interchangeable eyepieces—15x, 20x, 22x, 25x, 60x, each ... **$53.95**
15-36x zoom eyepiece ... **$135.95**

KOWA TSN-1-45°—Off-set-type. 77mm objective, 25x, fixed and zoom eyepieces; field at 1000 yds. 94'; relative brightness 9.6; length 15.4"; wgt. 48.8 oz. Lens shade and caps. Straight-type (TSN-2) also available with similar specs and prices.

Price: ... **$539.95**
Price: 20x-60x zoom eyepiece ... **$179.95**
Price: 20x eyepiece (wide angle) ... **$134.95**
Price: 25x, 40x eyepiece ... **$84.95, $99.95**
Price: 25x LER eyepiece ... **$134.95**

KOWA TS-6—Compact straight-type. 60mm objective, 25x fixed power eyepiece; field at 1000 yards 93'; relative brightness 5.8; length 12.5"; weight 25 oz. Lens shade and caps included. Off-set type also available (TS-7).

Price: ... **$355.90**
Price: 25x eyepiece ... **$58.95**
Price: 20x eyepiece (wide angle) ... **$71.95**
Price: 40x eyepiece ... **$35.95**
Price: 25x LER eyepiece ... **$119.95**

KOWA TS-601—45° off-set type. 60mm multi-coated objective, 25x fixed and zoom eyepieces; field at 1000 yards 93'; relative brightness 5.8; length 14.8"; weight 37 oz. Comes with lens shade and caps. Straight-type also available (TS-602).

Price: ... **$473.90**
Price: 25x eyepiece ... **$83.95**
Price: 20x eyepiece (wide angle) ... **$97.95**
Price: 40x eyepiece ... **$87.95**
Price: 20x-60x zoom eyepiece ... **$179.95**
Price: 25x LER eyepiece ... **$134.95**

KOWA TS-9C—Straight-type. 50mm objective, 20x compact model; fixed power eyepieces; objective focusing down to 17 ft.; field at 1000 yds. 157'; relative brightness 6.3; length 9.65"; wgt. 22.9 oz. Lens caps.

Price: ... **$140.95**
Price: 15x, 20x eyepieces, each ... **$25.95**
Price: 11x-33x zoom eyepiece ... **$79.95**
Price: As above, rubber armored (TS-9R) ... **$154.95**

LEUPOLD 20x50 COMPACT—50mm objective, 20x. Field at 100 yards 11.5 ft.; eye relief 1"; length 9.4"; weight 17.5 oz. Comes with Cordura nylon case.

Price: ... **$450.00**
Price: Armored model ... **$476.80**
Price: Tripod ... **$68.05**

LEUPOLD 25x50 COMPACT—50mm objective, 25x. Field at 100 yds. 8.3 ft.; eye relief 1"; length over-all 9.4"; weight 17.5 oz. Comes with Cordura nylon case.

Price: ... **$476.80**
Price: Armored model ... **$503.55**
Price: Armored, with reticle ... **$530.55**
Price: Tripod ... **$68.05**

LEUPOLD 20x60 SPOTTING SCOPE—60mm objective, 20x. Field at 100 yards 11.5 ft., eye relief 1"; length 12.9", weight 21 oz. Comes with Cordura nylon case.

Price: ... **$476.80**
Price: Tripod ... **$68.05**

LEUPOLD 30x60 SPOTTING SCOPE—60mm objective, 30x. Field at 100 yds. 6.4 ft.; eye relief 1"; length over-all 12.9"; weight 21 oz. Comes with Cordura case.

Price: ... **$503.55**
Price: Armored model ... **$530.55**
Price: Tripod ... **$68.05**

MIRADOR TTB SERIES—Draw tube armored spotting scopes. Available with 75mm or 80mm objective. Zoom model (28x-62x, 80mm) is 11⅞" (closed), weighs 50 ozs. Field at 1000 yds. 70-42 ft. Comes with lens covers.

Price: 28-62x80mm ... **$782.95**
Price: 32x80mm ... **$665.95**
Price: 26-58x75mm ... **$692.95**
Price: 30x75mm ... **$575.95**

MIRADOR SSD SPOTTING SCOPES—60mm objective, 15x, 20x, 22x, 25x, 40x, 60x, 20-60x; field at 1000 yds. 37 ft.; length 10¼"; weight 33 ozs.

Price: 15x, 20x, 25x, 40x, 60x ... **$422.95**
Price: 22x Wide Angle ... **$431.95**
Price: 20-60x Zoom ... **$539.95**
Price: As above, with tripod, case ... **$719.95**

MIRADOR SIA SPOTTING SCOPES—Similar to the SSD scopes except with 45° eyepiece. Length of 12¼", weight 39 ozs.

Price: 15x, 20x, 25x, 40x, 60x ... **$530.95**
Price: 22x Wide Angle ... **$539.95**
Price: 20-60x Zoom ... **$647.95**

MIRADOR SSA SPOTTING SCOPES—Lightweight, slender version of the SSD series with 50mm objective. Length 11⅛", weight 28 ozs.

Price: 12x, 16x, 20x, 32, 48x ... **$305.95**
Price: 18x Wide Angle ... **$314.95**
Price: 16-48x Zoom ... **$422.95**

MIRADOR SSR SPOTTING SCOPES—50mm objective. Similar to SSD except rubber armored in black or camouflage. Length 11⅛", weight 31 ozs.

Price: Black, 12x, 16x, 20x, 32x, 48x **$359.95**
Price: Black, 18x Wide Angle **$368.95**
Price: Black, 16-48x Zoom **$476.95**
Price: Camouflage, 12x, 16x, 20x, 32x, 48x **$368.95**
Price: Camouflage, 18x Wide Angle **$377.95**
Price: Camouflage, 16-48x Zoom **$485.95**

MIRADOR SSF FIELD SCOPES—Fixed or variable power, choice of 50mm, 60mm, 75mm objective lens. Length 9¾", weight 20 ozs. (15-32x50).

Price: 20x50mm **$215.95**
Price: 25x60mm **$269.95**
Price: 30x75mm **$323.95**
Price: 15-32x50mm Zoom **$341.95**
Price: 18-40x60mm Zoom **$395.95**
Price: 22-47x75mm Zoom **$449.95**

MIRADOR SRA MULTI ANGLE SCOPES—Similar to SSF Series except eyepiece head rotates for viewing from any angle.

Price: 20x50mm **$350.95**
Price: 25x60mm **$395.95**
Price: 30x75mm **$440.95**
Price: 15-32z50mm Zoom **$476.95**
Price: 18-40x60mm Zoom **$521.95**
Price: 22-47x75mm Zoom **$566.95**

MIRADOR SIB SPOTTING SCOPES—Short-tube, 45° scopes with porro-prism design. 50mm and 60mm objective. Length 10¼", weight 18.5 ozs. (15-32x50mm); field at 1000 yds. 129-81 ft.

Price: 20x50mm **$287.95**
Price: 25x60mm **$332.95**
Price: 15-32x50mm Zoom **$413.95**
Price: 18-40x60mm Zoom **$485.95**

PENTAX MODEL 300—Catadioptric 20x spotting scope has 68mm objective, interchangeable 24x, 33x eyepieces. Field of view 45 ft. at 1000 feet. Length over-all is 5.9", weight is 26.5 oz. Comes with table top tripod, hood and case.

Price: **$390.00**
Price: With Rubber Armor (300R) **$490.00**
Price: 24x, 33x eyepiece **$56.00**

PENTAX MODEL 500—Similar to the Model 300 except is 25x, has field of view of 31 ft. at 1000 ft. Interchangeable 40x, 55x eyepieces. Over-all length of 7.8", weight 31.7 oz. Comes with table top tripod, hood and case.

Price: **$450.00**
Price: With Rubber Armor (500R) **$550.00**
Price: 40x, 55x eyepiece **$56.00**

REDFIELD 30x CAT SPOTTER—60mm objective, 30x. Field of view 9.5 ft. at 100 yds. Uses catadioptric lens system. Length over-all is 7.5", weight is 11.5 oz. Eye relief 0.5". Also comes in camo armor coating.

Price: **$452.95**
Price: With Armor Camouflage **$466.95**

REDFIELD REGAL II & III—Regal II has 60mm objective, interchangeable 25x and 18x-40x zoom eyepieces. Regal III has 50mm objective, interchangeable 20x and 15x-32x zoom eyepieces, and is shorter and lighter. Field at 1000 yds.—Regal II, 125 ft. @ 25x; Regal III, 157 ft. @ 20x. Both have dual rotation of eyepiece and scope body. With aluminum carrying case, tripod.

Price: Regal II **$659.95**
Price: Regal III **$621.95**

REDFIELD REGAL IV & V—Conventional straight thru viewing. Regal IV has 60mm objective and interchangeable 25x and 20x-60x zoom eyepieces. Regal V has 50mm objective and 20x and 16x-48x zoom eyepieces and is shorter and lighter. Field at 1000 yds.—Regal IV, 94 ft. @ 25x; Regal V, 118 ft. @ 20x. Both come with tripod and aluminum carrying case.

Price: Regal IV **$678.95**
Price: As above with black rubber Armorcoat **$697.95**
Price: Regal V **$621.95**

REDFIELD REGAL VI—60mm objective, 25x fixed and 20x-60x interchangeable eyepieces. Has 45° angled eyepiece, front-mounted focus ring, 180° tube rotation. Field at 1000 yds., 94 ft. @ 25x; length, 12¼"; weight, 40 oz. Comes with tripod, aluminum carrying case.

Price: Regal VI **$734.95**

SIMMONS 1209 COMPACT—50mm objective, 25x. Camouflage finish. Length is 9", weight 30 oz. Comes with tripod.

Price: **$115.50**

SIMMONS 1210—50mm objective, 25x standard, 16, 20, 40, 48, 16-36x zoom eyepieces available. Field at 1000 yds. 22 ft. Length 12.2", weight 32 oz. Comes with tripod, 3x finder scope with crosshair.

Price: About **$187.00**
Price: Fixed eyepieces **$57.00**
Price: Zoom eyepiece **$150.00**

SIMMONS 1215—50mm objective, 25x standard, 16, 20, 40, 48, 16-36x zoom eyepieces available. Field at 1000 yds. 22 ft. Length 12.2", weight 48 oz. Comes with tripod, 3x finder scope with crosshair. Green camo rubber.

Price: About **$292.00**
Price: Fixed eyepieces **$57.00**
Price: Zoom eyepiece **$150.00**

SIMMONS 1220—60mm objective, 25x standard, 16, 20, 40, 48, 16-36x zoom eyepieces available. Field at 1000 yds. 22 ft. Length 13.8", weight 44 oz. with tripod (included). Has 3x finder scope with crosshairs.

Price: About **$345.00**
Price: Fixed eyepieces **$57.00**
Price: Zoom eyepiece **$150.00**

SIMMONS 1299 15-60x ZOOM—60mm objective, 15-60x zoom. Field at 1000 yds. 156-40 ft. Slide-out sunshade. Has 3x finder scope. Photo adaptable and comes with a photo adapter tube for T-mount cameras. Black finish. Tripod not included.

Price: **$375.00**

SWAROVSKI HABICHT HAWK 30x75S TELESCOPE—75mm objective, 30x. Field at 1,000 yds. 90ft. Minimum, focusing distance 90 ft. Length: closed 13 in., extended 20½". Weight: 47 oz. Precise recognition of smallest details even at dusk. Leather or rubber covered, with caps and carrying case.

Price: **$685.00**

Same as above with short range supplement. Minimum focusing distance 24 to 30 ft. **$870.00**

SWAROVSKI 25-40x75 TELESCOPE—75mm objective, variable power from 25x to 40x with a field of 98 ft. (25x) and 72 ft. (40x). Minimum focusing distance 66 ft. Length closed is 11.3", extended 15.6"; weight 46.8 oz. Rubber covered.

Price: Standard **$980.00**

SWIFT TELEMASTER M841—60mm objective. 15x to 60x variable power. Field at 1000 yards 160 feet (15x) to 40 feet (60x). Wgt. 3.4 lbs. 17.6" over-all.

Price: **$385.00**

SWIFT M700 SCOUT—9x-30x, 30mm spotting scope. Length 15½", weighs 2.1 lbs. Field of 204 ft. (9x), 60 ft. (30x).

Price: **$140.00**

SWIFT SEARCHER M839—60mm objective, 20x, 40x. Field at 1000 yds. 118 ft. (30x), 59 ft. (40x). Length 12.6", weight 3 lbs. Rotating eyepiece head for straight or 45-degree viewing.

Price: **$380.00**
Price: 30x, 50x eyepieces, each **$45.00**
Price: Tripod **$36.00**

TASCO 17ET SPOTTING SCOPE—60mm objective lens, 20-60x zoom with black metal tripod, micro-adjustable elevation control.

Price: **$199.95**

TASCO 20E SPOTTING SCOPE—50mm objective lens, 15-45x zoom. Field at 1,000 yds. 95-42 ft.; includes tripod with pan-head lever.

Price: **$119.95**

TASCO 25TPC WORLD CLASS CAMO RUBBER COVERED—60mm objective lens, 25x, BAK-4 prism. Accepts available 15x, 20x, 40x, 60x, & 20-60x eyepieces and photo-adaptor tube. Field at 1,000 yds. 105'. Matching olive drab tripod, Weight 38.3 oz., length 11⅞".

Price: **$849.95**

TASCO 25TPCZ WORLD CLASS CAMO ARMORED ZOOM—Same as above, but with 20-60x eyepiece. Field at 1,000 yds. 97 ft. @ 20x.

Price: **$1,049.95**

TASCO 34TZ RUBBER COVERED—50mm objective lens, 15-40x zoom. Field at 1,000 yards 136 ft. With tripod, weight 29.9 oz., length 13¾".

Price: **$329.95**

TASCO 9000T WORLD CLASS SPOTTING SCOPE—60mm objective lens, 15-60x zoom. Field at 1,000 yds. 160 ft. @ 15x. Fully multi-coated optics, includes camera adaptor and camera case.

Price: **$459.95**
Price: 9002T (same as 9000T but includes a tripod with pan-head lever) **$519.95**

UNERTL "FORTY-FIVE"—54mm objective. 20x (single fixed power). Field at 100 yds. 10'10"; eye relief 1"; focusing range infinity to 33 ft. Wgt. about 32 oz.; over-all length 15¾". With lens covers.

Price: With multi-layer lens coating **$348.00**
Price: With mono-layer magnesium coating **$270.00**

UNERTL RIGHT ANGLE—63.5mm objective, 24x. Field at 100 yds., 7 ft. Relative brightness, 6.96. Eye relief, ½". Wgt., 41 oz. Length closed, 19". Push-pull and screw-focus eyepiece. 16x and 32x eyepieces **$50.00** each.

Price: **$306.00**

UNERTL STRAIGHT PRISMATIC—Same as Unertl Right Angle except: straight eyepiece and wgt. of 40 oz.

Price: **$262.00**

UNERTL 20x STRAIGHT PRISMATIC—54mm objective. 20x. Field at 100 yds., 8.5 ft. Relative brightness, 6.1. Eye relief, ½". Wgt. 36 oz. Length closed, 13½". Complete with lens covers.

Price: **$220.00**

UNERTL TEAM SCOPE—100mm objective. 15x, 24x, 32x eyepieces. Field at 100 yds. 13 to 7.5 ft. Relative brightness, 39.06 to 9.79. Eye relief, 2" to 1½". Weight 13 lbs. 29⅞" overall. Metal tripod, yoke and wood carrying case furnished (total weight, 80 lbs.)

Price: **$1,200.00**

WEATHERBY—60mm objective, 20x-60x zoom

Price: Scope only **$329.95**
Price: Scope and tripod **$397.00**
Price: Tripod for above **$76.00**

PERIODICAL PUBLICATIONS

Airgun World
10 Sheet St., Windsor, Berks., SL4 1BG, England.£13.20 (£18.00 overseas) for 12 issues. Monthly magazine catering exclusively to the airgun enthusiast.

Alaska Magazine
Alaska Northwest Pub. Co., Box 4-EEE, Anchorage, AK 99509. $21.00 yr. Hunting, Fishing and Life on the Last Frontier articles of Alaska and western Canada.

American Airgunner (Q)
Gary J. Cobb, P.O. Box 711, Comanche, TX 76442. $15 yr. Anything and everything about airguns.

American Field†
222 W. Adams St., Chicago, IL 60606. $25.00 yr. Field dogs and trials, occasional gun and hunting articles.

American Firearms Industry
Nat'l. Assn. of Federally Licensed Firearms Dealers, 2801 E. Oakland Park Blvd., Ft. Lauderdale, FL 33306. $25 yr. For firearms retailers, distributors and manufacturers. (Also **AFI Outdoor Videos.**)

American Handgunner*
591 Camino de la Reina, San Diego, CA 92108. $14.75 yr. Articles for handgun enthusiasts, collectors and hunters.

American Hunter (M)
Natl. Rifle Assn., 1600 Rhode Island Ave. N.W., Washington, DC 20036. $20.00 yr. Wide scope of hunting articles.

American Rifleman (M)
National Rifle Assn., 1600 Rhode Island Ave., N.W., Wash., DC 20036. Publications Div., 470 Spring Park Pl., Suite 1000, Herndon, VA 22070. $20.00 yr. Firearms articles of all kinds.

The American Shotgunner
P.O. Box 3351, Reno, NV 89505. $24.00 yr. Official publ. of the American Assn. of Shotgunning. Shooting, reloading, hunting, investment collecting, new used gun classifieds.

American Survival Guide
McMullen Publishing, Inc., 2145 West La Palma Ave., Anaheim, CA 92801. 12 issues $21.98.

American West*
Amer. West Management Corp., 7000 E. Tanque Verde Rd., Suite #30, Tucson, AZ 85715. $15.00 yr.

Angler & Hunter
Ontario's Wildlife Magazine, P.O. Box 1541, Peterborough, Ont. K9J 7H7, Canada. $17.50 yr. Canada; all others $21.50 yr. for 10 issues.

ARMI
New Fashion Media, Avenue Louise 60, B1050 Brussels, Belgium. Belg. Franc 3000 for 11 issues. Arms, shooting, ammunition; French text.

Arms Collecting (Q)
Museum Restoration Service P.O. Drawer 390, Bloomfield, Ont., Canada K0K 1G0 and P.O. Box 70, Alexandria Bay, NY 13607. $12.50 yr. $35.00 3 yrs. $60.00 5 yrs.

Arms & Outdoor Digest
Nat'l. Assn. of Federally Licensed Firearms Dealers, 2801 E. Oakland Pk. Blvd., Ft. Lauderdale, FL 33306. $10.00 yr. For firearms and outdoor retailers.

Australian Shooters' Journal
Sporting Shooter's Assn. of Australia, P.O. Box 2066, Kent Town SA 5067, Australia. $30.00 yr. locally; $40.00 yr. overseas surface mail only. Hunting and shooting articles.

The Backwoodsman Magazine
Rte. 8, Box 579, Livingston, TX 77351. $12.00 for 6 issues pr. yr.; sample copy $2.25. Subject incl. muzzle-loading, woodslore, trapping, homesteading, black powder cartridge guns, 19th century how-to.

The Black Powder Report
The Buckskin Press, Inc., P.O. Box 969, Bozeman, MT 59771. $18.00 yr. Shooting, hunting, gun-building and restoration articles; entire section for BP cartridge rifles.

The Blade Magazine*
P.O. Box 22007, Chattanooga, TN 37422. $15.99 yr. Add $13 f. foreign subscription. A magazine for all enthusiasts of the edged blade.

Combat Handguns*
Harris Publications, Inc., 1115 Broadway, New York, NY 10010. Single copy $2.75 U.S.A.; $2.95 Canada.

Deer Unlimited*
P.O. Box 509, Clemson, SC 29631. $12.00 yr.

Deutsches Waffen Journal
Journal-Verlag Schwend GmbH, Postfach 100340, D7170 Schwäbisch Hall, Germany. DM85.00 yr. plus DM16.80 for postage. Antique and modern arms. German text.

Ducks Unlimited, Inc. (M)
1 Waterfowl Way, Long Grove, IL 60047

The Field
Associated Magazines Ltd., Carmelite House, London EC4Y OJA, England. £30.00 sterling U.S. (approx. $50.00) yr. Hunting and shooting articles, and all country sports.

Field & Stream
Times Mirror Magazines, 1515 Broadway, New York, NY 10036. $11.94 yr. Articles on firearms plus hunting and fishing.

Fur-Fish-Game
A.R. Harding Pub. Co., 2878 E. Main St., Columbus, OH 43209. $11.00 yr. "Gun Rack" column by Don Zutz.

Gray's Sporting Journal
Gray's Sporting Journal Inc., 205 Willow St., So. Hamilton, MA 01982. $26.50 per yr. f. 4 consecutive issues. Hunting and fishing journals.

Gun Owner (Q)
Gun Owners Inc., 1125 Front St., Suite 300, Sacramento, CA 95814. With membership $20 yr.; single copy $3. An outdoors magazine for sportsmen everywhere.

The Gun Report
World Wide Gun Report, Inc., Box 111, Aledo, IL 61231. $27.00 yr. For the antique and semi-modern gun collector; dealers.

The Gunrunner
Div. of Kexco Publ. Co. Ltd., Box 565, Lethbridge, Alb., Canada T1J 3Z4. $20.00 yr. Monthly newspaper, listing everything from antiques to artillery.

Gun List
Box 7387, Columbia, MO 65205. $12.00 yr. (12 issues); $22.00 2 yrs.

Gun Show Calender (Q)
700 E. State St., Iola, WI 54990. $11.95 yr. Gun shows listed chronologically by date, and alphabetically by state.

Gun Week†
Second Amendment Foundation, P.O. Box 488, Station C, Buffalo, NY 14209. $24.00 yr. U.S. and possessions; $29.00 yr. other countries. Tabloid paper on guns, hunting, shooting and collecting.

Gun World
Gallant Publishing Co., 34249 Camino Capistrano, Capistrano Beach, CA 92624. $17.00 yr. For the hunting, reloading and shooting enthusiast.

Guns & Ammo
Petersen Pub. Co., 8490 Sunset Blvd., Los Angeles, CA 90069. $17.94 yr. Guns, shooting, and technical articles.

Guns
Guns Magazine, P.O. Box 85201, San Diego, CA 92138. $14.95 yr. In-depth articles on a wide range of guns, shooting equipment and related accessories for gun collectors, hunters and shooters.

Guns Review
Ravenhill Pub. Co. Ltd., Box 35, Standard House, Bonhill St., London EC 2A 4DA, England. £15.60 sterling (approx. U.S. $26) USA & Canada yr. For collectors and shooters.

Handgun Quarterly (Q)
PJS Publications, News Plaza, P.O. Box 1790, Peoria, IL 61656. Cover price $3.95; subscriptions $13.95 f. 4 issues. Various recreational uses of handguns; hunting, silhouette, practical pistol and target shooting.

Handloader*
Wolfe Pub. Co. Inc., 6471 Airpark Dr., Prescott, AZ 86301 $16.00 yr. The journal of ammunition reloading.

Hunt Magazine*
TimberLine-B, Inc., P.O. Box 58069, Renton, WA 98058. $8.97 yr.; Canadian & foreign countries add U.S. $8 f. postage. Geared to the serious hunter, with action hunting articles.

The IMAS Journal (M)
International Military Arms Society, 3021 Benjamin Dr., Wichita, KS 67204. Military gun collecting articles.

The Insider Gun News
The Gunpress Publishing Co., 3091 Abingdon St., Arlington, VA 22206. Editor John D. Aquilino. $50.00 yr. (12 issues). Newsletter by former NRA communications director.

INSIGHTS*
NRA, 1600 Rhode Island Ave. N.W., Washington, DC 20036. Editor Brenda K. Dalessandro. $8.00 yr, which includes NRA junior membership, $9.00 for adult subscriptions (12 issues). Plenty of details for the young hunter and target shooter.

International Shooting Sport*/UIT Journal
International Shooting Union (UIT), Bavariaring 21, D-8000 Munich 2, Fed. Rep. of Germany. Europe: (Deutsche Mark) DM39.00 yr., p.p.; outside Europe: DM45.00. For the International target shooter.

The Journal of the Arms & Armour Society (M)
ARE North (Secy.), Dept. of Metalwork, Victoria and Albert Museum, London, England. $20.00 yr. Articles for the historian and collector.

Journal of the Historical Breechloading Smallarms Assn.
Publ. annually, Imperial War Museum, Lambeth Road, London SE1 6HZ, England. $8.00 yr. Articles for the collector plus mailings of lecture transcripts, short articles on specific arms, reprints, newsletters, etc.; a surcharge is made f. airmail.

Kaliber
Uitgeverij Magnum, Marktstraat 237, 6431 LR Hoensbroek, Netherlands. 6 issues f20.00/Bfr.400. Magazine for the sportshooter.

Knife World
Knife World Publications, P.O. Box 3395, Knoxville, TN 37927. $10.00 yr., $17.00 2 yrs. Published monthly f. knife enthusiasts and collectors. Articles on custom and factory knives; other knife related interests.

Law and Order
Law and Order Magazine, 1000 Skokie Blvd., Wilmette, IL 60091. $15.00 yr. Articles on weapons for law enforcement, etc.

Man At Arms*
P.O. Box 460, Lincoln, RI 02865. $20.00 yr, plus $7.00 for foreign subscribers. The magazine of arms collecting-investing, with excellent brief articles for the collector of antique arms and militaria.

MAN/MAGNUM
S.A. Man (1982) (Pty) Ltd., P.O. Box 35204, Northway, Durban 4065, Rep. of South Africa. SA Rand 36.00 f. 12 issues. Africa's only publication on hunting, shooting, firearms, bushcraft, knives, etc.

The Marlin Collector (M)
R.W. Paterson, 407 Lincoln Bldg., 44 Main St., Champaign, IL 61820.

Muzzle Blasts (M)
National Muzzle Loading Rifle Assn., P.O. Box 67, Friendship, IN 47021. $19.75 yr. For the black powder shooter.

Muzzleloader Magazine*
Rebel Publishing Co., Inc., Route 5, Box 347-M, Texarkana, TX 75501. $12.00 U.S., $15.00 U.S. for foreign subscribers a yr. The publication for black powder shooters.

National Defense (M)*
American Defense Preparedness Assn., Rosslyn Center, Suite 900, 1700 North Moore St., Arlington, VA 22209. $25.00 yr. Articles on military-related topics, including weapons, materials technology, management.

National Knife Magazine (M)
Natl. Knife Coll. Assn., 7201 Shallowford Rd., Chattanooga, TN 37421. Membership $15 yr, $40.00 International yr.

National Rifle Assn. Journal (British) (Q)
Natl. Rifle Assn. (BR.), Bisley Camp, Brookwood, Woking, Surrey, England. GU24, OPB. $25.00 inc. air postage.

National Wildlife*
Natl. Wildlife Fed., 1412 16th St. N.W., Washington, DC 20036. $15.00 yr. (6 issues); *International Wildlife,* 6 issues, $15.00 yr. Both, $20.00 yr., plus membership benefits. Write to this addr., attn.: Membership Services Dept., for the proper information.

New Zealand Wildlife (Q)
New Zealand Deerstalkers Assoc. Inc., P.O. Box 6514, Wellington, N.Z. $30.00 (N.Z.). Hunting, shooting and firearms/game research articles.

North American Hunter* (M)
7901 Flying Cloud Dr., P.O. Box 35557, Minneapolis, MN 55435. $18.00 yr. (6 issues). Articles on North American game hunting.

Outdoor Life
Times Mirror Magazines, 380 Madison Ave., New York, NY 10017. Special 1-yr. subscription, $9.97. Extensive coverage of hunting and shooting. Shooting column by Jim Carmichel.

Petersen's HUNTING Magazine
Petersen Publishing Co., P.O. Box 3353, Los Angeles, CA 90074. $11.97 yr.; foreign countries $24.94 yr. Hunting articles for all game; test reports.

Point Blank
Citizens Committee for the Right to Keep and Bear Arms (sent to contributors), Liberty Park, 12500 NE 10th Pl., Bellevue, WA 98005

The Police Marksman*
6000 E. Shirley Lane, Montgomery, AL 36117. $16.95 yr. For law enforcement personnel.

Police Times (M)
Membership Records, 1100 NE 125th St., No. Miami, FL 33161

Popular Mechanics
Hearst Corp., 224 W. 57th St., New York, NY 10019. $13.97 yr. Firearms, camping, outdoors oriented articles.

Precision Shooting
Precision Shooting, Inc., 37 Burnham St., East Hartford, CT 06108. $18.00 yr. Journal of the International Benchrest Shooters, National Benchrest Shooting Assn., and target shooting in general.

Rifle*
Wolfe Publishing Co. Inc., 6471 Airpark Dr., Prescott, AZ 86301. $16.00 yr. The sporting firearms journal.

Rod & Rifle Magazine
Lithographic Serv. Ltd., P.O. Box 38-138, Petone, New Zealand. $30.00 yr. (6 issues) Hunting and shooting articles.

Safari* (M)
Safari Magazine, 4800 W. Gates Pass Rd., Tucson, AZ 85745. $20 (6 times). The journal of big game hunting, published by Safari Club International.

Schweizer Waffen-Magazin
Orell Füssli Zeitschriften, Postfach CH-8036 Zürich, Switzerland. SF 114.50 (approx. U.S. $73.90 air mail) f. 10 issues. Modern and antqiue arms. German text.

Second Amendment Reporter
Second Amendment Fdn., James Madison Bldg., 12500 NE 10th Pl., Bellevue, WA 98005. $15.00 yr. (non-contributors).

Shooting Industry
Publisher's Dev. Corp., 591 Camino de la Reina, Suite 200, San Diego, CA 92108. $50.00 yr. To the trade $25.00.

Shooting Magazine
10 Sheet St., Windsor, Berks. SL4 1BG England. £14.40, or £19.50 overseas for 12 issues. Monthly journal catering mainly to clay pigeon shooters, with informed articles on rough and game shooting.

Shooting Sports News
Creative Communications, Inc., 122 Lafayette Ave., Laurel, MD 20707. Information, news and comments on the shooting industry, prepared for dealers of firearms and accessories. (Trade paper)

The Shooting Times & Country Magazine (England)†
10 Sheet St., Windsor, Berkshire SL4 1BG, England. £51 (approx. $91.00) yr. (52 issues). Game shooting, wild fowling, hunting, game fishing and firearms articles.

Shooting Times
PJS Publications, News Plaza. P.O. Box 1790, Peoria, IL 61656. $15.97 yr. Guns, shooting, reloading; articles on every gun activity.

The Shotgun News‡
Snell Publishing Co., Box 669, Hastings, NE 68901. $15.00 yr.; all other countries $100.00 yr. Sample copy $3.00. Gun ads of all kinds.

Shotgun Sports
P.O. Box 340, Lake Havasu City, AZ 86403. $24.00 yr.

Shotgun West
1253 7th St. #101, Santa Monica, CA 90401. $8.50 yr. Trap, Skeet and international shooting, scores; articles, schedules.

The Sixgunner (M)
Handgun Hunters International, P.O. Box 357, MAG. Bloomingdale, OH 43910

The Skeet Shooting Review
National Skeet Shooting Assn., P.O. Box 680007, San Antonio, TX 78268. $15.00 yr. (Assn. membership of $20.00 includes mag.) Competition results, personality profiles of top Skeet shooters, how-to articles, technical, reloading information.

Soldier of Fortune
Subscription Dept., P.O. Box 348, Mt. Morris, IL 61054. $26.00 yr.; $33.00 foreign.

Sporting Goods Business
Gralla Pub., 1515 Broadway, New York, NY 10036. Trade journal.

The Sporting Goods Dealer
1212 No. Lindbergh Blvd., St. Louis, MO 63132. $50.00 yr. The sporting goods trade journal.

Sporting Gun
Bretton Court, Bretton, Peterborough PE3 8DZ, England £19.00 (approx. U.S. $32.00) (airmail £29.00) yr. For the game and clay enthusiasts.

Sports Afield
The Hearst Corp., 250 W. 55th St., New York, NY 10019. $13.97 yr. Grits Gresham on firearms, ammunition and Thomas McIntyre, Lionel Atwill, Gerald Almy on hunting.

Sports Merchandiser
A WRC Smith Publication, 1760 Peachtree Rd. NW, Atlanta, GA 30357. Trade Journal.

The Squirrel Hunter
P.O. Box 254, Hoskinston, KY 40844. $12.00 yr. Articles about squirrel hunting.

TACARMI
Via E. De Amicis, 25;20123 Milano, Italy. $60.00 yr. approx. Antique and modern guns. (Italian text.)

Then And Now*
P.O. Box 842, Mount Vernon, WA 98273. $15.00 for 6 issues. Magazine for black powder activities; test reports.

Trap & Field
1000 Waterway Blvd., Indianapolis, IN 46202. $20.00 yr. Official publ. Amateur Trapshooting Assn. Scores, averages, trapshooting articles.

Turkey Call* (M)
Natl. Wild Turkey Federation, Inc., P.O. Box 530, Edgefield, SC 29824. $15.00 w. membership (6 issues p. yr.)

The U.S. Handgunner* (M)
U.S. Revolver Assn., 96 West Union St., Ashland, MA 01721. $6.00 yr. General handgun and competition articles. Bi-monthly sent to members.

VDB-Aktuel (Q)
GFI Verlag, Theodor-Heuss Ring 62, 5000 Köln 1, West Germany. For hunters, target shooters and outdoor people. (German text.)

Waterfowler's World*
P.O. Box 38306, Germantown, TN 38183. $14.00 yr.

Wild Sheep (M) (Q)
Foundation For North American Wild Sheep, 720 Allen Ave., Cody, WY 82414. Official journal of the foundation.

Wisconsin Sportsman*
Wisconsin Sportsman, Inc., P.O. Box 2266, Oshkosh, WI 54903. $9.95. Hunting, hiking, outdoors articles.

---

*Published bi-monthly † Published weekly ‡ Published three times per month. All others are published monthly.
M = Membership requirements; write for details. Q = Published Quarterly.

The Arms Library for

COLLECTOR • HUNTER • SHOOTER • OUTDOORSMAN

A selection of books—old, new and forthcoming—for everyone in the arms field, with a brief description by . . . JOE RILING

IMPORTANT NOTICE TO BOOK BUYERS

Books listed here may be bought from Ray Riling Arms Books Co., 6844 Gorsten St. P.O. Box 18925, Philadelphia, PA 19119, phone 215/438-2456. Joe Riling, the proprietor, is the researcher and compiler of "The Arms Library" and a seller of gun books for over 30 years.

The Riling stock includes books classic and modern, many hard-to-find items, adn many not obtainable elsewhere. These pages list a portion of the current stock. They offer prompt, complete service, with delay shipments occuring only on out-of-print or out-of stock books.

NOTICE FOR ALL CUSTOMERS: Remittance in U.S. funds must accompany all orders. For U.S. add $1.75 per book for postage and insurance. Minimum order $10.00. For UPS add 50% to mailing costs.

All foreign countries add $3 per book for postage and handling. All foreign orders are shipped at the buyer's risk unless an additional $5 for insurance is included.

Payments in excess of order or for "Backorders" are credited or fully refunded at request. Books "As-Ordered" are not returnable except by permission and a handling charge on these of $2.00 per book is deducted from refund or credit. Only Pennsylvania customers must include current sales tax.

A full variety of arms books also available from Rutgers Book Center, 127 Raritan Ave., Highland Park, NJ 08904.

***New Book**

ballistics and handloading

***ABC's of Reloading, 4th Edition,** by Dean A. Grennell, DBI Books, Inc., Northbrook, IL, 1988. 288 pp., illus. Paper covers. $14.95.

An all-new book with everything from a discussion of the basics up through and including advanced techniques and procedures.

American Ammunition and Ballistics, by Edward A. Matunas, Winchester Press, Piscataway, NJ, 1979. 288 pp., illus. $18.95.

A complete reference book covering all presently made and much discontinued American rimfire, centerfire, and shotshell ammunition.

The Art of Bullet Casting from Handloader & Rifle Magazines 1966-1981, compiled by Dave Wolfe, Wolfe Publishing Co., Prescott, AZ, 1981. 258 pp., illus. Paper covers. $12.95. Deluxe hardbound. $19.50.

Articles from "Handloader" and "Rifle" magazines by authors such as Jim Carmichel, John Wootters, and the late George Nonte.

Ballistic Science for the Law Enforcement Officer, by Charles G. Wilber, Ph.D., Charles C. Thomas, Springfield, IL, 1977. 309 pp., illus. $56.00.

A scientific study of the ballistics of civilian firearms.

Basic Handloading, by George C. Nonte, Jr., Outdoor Life Books, New York, NY, 1982. 192 pp., illus. Paper covers. $4.50.

How to produce high-quality ammunition using the safest, most efficient methods known.

The Bullet's Flight, by Franklin Mann, Wolfe Publishing Co., Inc., Prescott, AZ, 1980. 391 pp., illus. $22.00.

The ballistics of small arms. A reproduction of Harry Pope's personal copy of this classic with his marginal notes.

Cartridges of the World, 5th Edition, by Frank Barnes, DBI Books, Inc., Northbrook, IL, 1985. 416 pp., illus. Paper covers. $16.95.

Completely updated encyclopedic work on cartridges.

Cast Bullets, by Col. E. H. Harrison, A publication of the National Rifle Association of America, Washington, DC, 1979. 144 pp., illus. Paper covers. $12.95.

An authoritative guide to bullet casting techniques and ballistics.

Computer for Handloaders, by Homer Powley. A slide rule plus 12 page instruction book for use in finding charge, most efficient powder and velocity for any modern centerfire rifle. $7.95.

Discover Swaging, by David R. Corbin, Stackpole Books, Harrisburg, PA, 1979. 283 pp., illus. $18.95.

A guide to custom bullet design and performance.

Extended Ballistics for the Advanced Rifleman, by Art Blatt, Pachmayr, Inc., Los Angeles, CA, 1986. 379 pp. Spiral bound. $12.95.

Enhanced data on all factory centerfire rifle loads from Federal, Hornady, Norma, Remington, Weatherby, and Winchester.

The Gun Digest Black Powder Loading Manual, by Sam Fadala, DBI Books, Inc., Northbrook, IL, 1982. 244 pp., illus. Paper covers. $13.95.

Covers 450 loads for 86 of the most popular black powder rifles, handguns and shotguns.

Gun Digest Book of Handgun Reloading, by Dean A. Grennell and Wiley Clapp, DBI Books, Inc., Northbrook, IL, 1987. 256 pp., illus. Paper covers. $12.95.

Detailed discussions of all aspects of reloading for handguns, from basic to complex. New loading data.

Handbook for Shooters and Reloaders, by P.O. Ackley, Salt Lake City, UT, 1970, *Vol. I,* 567 pp., illus. $12.50. *Vol. II,* a new printing with specific new material. 495 pp., illus. $12.50.

Handbook of Metallic Cartridge Reloading, by Edward Matunas, Winchester Press, Piscataway, NJ, 1981. 272 pp., illus. $18.95.

Up-do-date, comprehensive loading tables prepared by four major powder manufacturers.

The Handbook of Shotshell Reloading, by Kenneth W. Couger, SKR Industries, San Angelo, TX, 1984. 248 pp., illus. Paper covers. $17.95.

All the present-day methods and techniques and up-to-date advice on reloading equipment and components.

Handloader's Digest, 11th Edition, edited by Ken Warner, DBI Books, Inc., Northbrook, IL. 1987. 352 pp. illus. paper covers. $15.95.

The big book on handloading with dozens of "how-to" features, covering everything from tools and material to techniques and tips. Complete catalog section.

Handloader's Guide, by Stanley W. Trzoniec, Stoeger Publishing Co., So., Hackensack, NJ, 1985. 256 pp., illus. Paper covers. $11.95.

The complete step-by-step fully illustrated guide to handloading ammunition.

Handloader's Manual of Cartridge Conversions, by John J. Donnelly, Stoeger Publishing Co., So. Hackensack, NJ, 1986. Unpaginated. Paper covers, $24.95; cloth, $34.95.

From 14 Jones to 70-150 Winchester in English and American cartridges, and from 4.85 U.K. to 15.2x28R Gevelot in metric cartridges. Over 900 cartriges described in detail.

Handloading, by Bill Davis, Jr., NRA Books, Wash., D.C., 1980. 400 pp., illus. Paper covers. $15.95.

A complete update and expansion of the NRA Handloader's Guide.

Hodgdon Powder Data Manual No. 25, Hodgdon Powder Co., Inc., Shawnee Mission, KS, 1986. 544 pp., illus. $16.95.

For the first time includes data for Hercules, Winchester, and DuPont powders.

Handloading for Hunters, by Don Zutz, Winchester Press, Piscataway, NJ, 1977. 288 pp., illus. Paper covers. $12.95.

Precise mixes and loads for different types of game and for various hunting situations with rifle and shotgun.

The Home Guide to Cartridge Conversions, by Maj. George C. Nonte Jr., The Gun Room Press, Highland Park, NJ, 1976. 404 pp., illus. $19.95.

Revised and updated version of Nonte's definitive work on the alteration of cartridge cases for use in guns for which they were not intended.

Hornady Handbook of Cartridge Reloading, Hornady Mfg. Co., Grand Island, NE, 1981. 650 pp., illus. $15.95.

New edition of this famous reloading handbook. Latest loads, ballistic information, etc.

Lyman Cast Bullet Handbook, 3rd Edition, edited by C. Kenneth Ramage, Lyman Publications, Middlefield, CT, 1980. 416 pp., illus. Paper covers. $17.95.

Information on more than 5,000 tested cast bullet loads and 19 pages of trajectory and wind drift tables for cast bullets.

Lyman Black Powder Handbook, ed. by C. Kenneth Ramage, Lyman Products for Shooters, Middlefield, CT, 1975. 239 pp., illus. Paper covers $13.95.
The most comprehensive load information ever published for the modern black powder shooter.
Lyman Pistol & Revolver Handbook, edited by C. Kenneth Ramage, Lyman Publications, Middlefield, CT, 1978. 280 pp., illus. Paper covers. $13.95.
An extensive reference of load and trajectory data for the handgun.
Lyman Reloading Handbook No. 46, edited by C. Kenneth Ramage, Lyman Publications, Middlefield, CT, 1982. 300 pp., illus. $17.95.
A large and comprehensive book on reloading. Extensive list of loads for jacketed and cast bullets.
Lyman Shotshell Handbook, 3rd Edition, edited by C. Kenneth Ramage, Lyman Publications, Middlefield, CT, 1984. 312 pp., illus. Paper covers. $17.95.
Has 2,000 loads, including slugs and buckshot, plus feature articles and a full color I.D. section.
Manual of Pistol and Revolver Cartridges, Volume 1, Centerfire and Metric Calibers, by Hans A. Erlmeier and Jakob H. Brandt, Journal-Verlag, Weisbaden, Germany, 1967. 271 pp., illus. $34.95.
Specifications for each cartridge cataloged; tells bullet and case type with important case dimensions.
***Manual of Pistol and Revolver Cartridges, Volume 2, Centerfire U.S. and British Calibers,** by Hans A. Erlmeier and Jakob H. Brandt, Journal-Verlag, Weisbaden, Germany, 1981. 270 pp., illus. $34.95
Catalog system allows cartridges to be traced either by caliber or alphabetically.
***Metallic Cartridge Redloading, 2nd Edition,** by Edward A. Matunas, DBI Books, Inc., Northbrook, IL., 1988. 320 pp., illus. Paper covers. $15.95
A true reloading manual with a wealth of invaluable technical data provided by a recognized expert.
Military Ballistics, by C.L. Farrar and D.W. Leeming, Pergamon Press, Oxford, England, 1983. 200 pp., illus. Paper covers. $35.00.
Principles of ballistics, illustrated by reference of military applications.
***The Military Cartridges Caliber 7.62x51mm NATO, Their Development and Variants,** by Jakob H. Brandt et al, Journal-Verlag, Schwabish Hall, W. Germany, N.D. 314 pp., illus. $65.00
This encyclopedia reference book is the complete work on the 7.62mm cartridge. Text is in both German and English. Lengths and weights as well as markings, powders and more are listed for over 350 variants.
Modern Handloading, by Maj. Geo. C. Nonte, Winchester Press, Piscataway, NJ, 1972. 416 pp., illus. $15.00.
Covers all aspects of metallic and shotshell ammunition loading, plus more loads than any book in print.
Nosler Reloading Manual Number Two, Nosler Bullets, Inc., Bend, OR, 1981. 308 pp., illus. $13.95.
Thorough coverage of powder data, specifically tailored to the well known Nosler partition and solid base bullets.
Pet Loads, by Ken Waters, Wolfe Publishing Co., Prescott, AZ, 3rd edition, 1986. 2 volumes of 636 pp. Limp fabricoid covers. $27.50.
Ken Water's favorite loads that have appeared in "Handloader" magazine.
Practical Handgun Ballistics, by Mason Williams, Charles C. Thomas, Publisher, Springfield, IL, 1980. 215 pp., illus. $35.00.
Factual information on the practical aspects of ammunition performance in revolvers and pistols.
Precision Handloading, by John Withers, Stoeger Publishing Co., So. Hackensack, NJ, 1985. 224 pp., illus. Paper covers. $11.95.
An entirely new approach to handloading ammunition.
Rediscover Swaging, by David R. Corbin, Corbin Manufacturing and Supply, Inc., Phoenix, OR, 1983. 240 pp., illus. $18.50.
A new textbook on the subject of bullet swaging.
Reloader's Guide, 3rd Edition, by R.A. Steindler, Stoeger Publishing Co., So. Hackensack, NJ, 1984. 224 pp., illus. Paper covers. $9.95.
Complete, fully illustrated step-by-step guide to handloading ammunition.
Reloading for Shotgunners, 2nd Edition, edited by Robert S.L. Anderson, DBI Books, Inc., Northbrook, IL, 1985. 256 pp., illus. Paper covers. $12.95.
The very latest in reloading information for the shotgunner.
Sierra Bullets Reloading Manual, Second Edition, by Robert Hayden et al, The Leisure Group, Inc., Santa Fe Springs, CA, 1978. 700 pp., illus. Looseleaf binder. $18.95.
Includes all material in the original manual and its supplement updated, plus a new section on loads for competitive shooting.
Sierra Bullets Updated Supplement Reloading Manual, by Robert Hayden, et al, The Leisure Group, Inc., Santa Fe Springs, CA, 1985. Loose-leaf pages in binder. $21.95.
An updated supplement of loose-leaf pages to create a 2nd edition handgun manual for the most comprehensive reloading material ever assembled.
Sixgun Cartridges and Loads, by Elmer Keith, The Gun Room Press, Highland Park, NJ, 1986. 151 pp., illus. $19.95.
A manual covering the selection, uses and loading of the most suitable and popular revolver cartridges. Originally published in 1936. Reprint.
***Speer Reloading Manual Number 11,** edited by members of the Speer research staff, Omark Industries, Lewiston, ID, 1987. 621 pp., illus. $13.00
Reloading manual for rifles and pistols.
Why Not Load Your Own? by Col. T. Whelen, A. S. Barnes, New York, 1957, 4th ed., rev. 237 pp., illus, $10.95.
A basic reference on handloading, describing each step, materials and equipment. Loads for popular cartridges are given.
Yours Truly, Harvey Donaldson, by Harvey Donaldson, Wolfe Publ. Co., Inc., Prescott, AZ, 1980. 288 pp., illus. $19.50.
Reprint of the famous columns by Harvey Donaldson which appeared in "Handloader" from May 1966 through December 1972.

Air Rifles, by D.E. Hiller, Hiller Airguns, Chorley, England, 1986. 282 pp., illus. Paper covers. $22.50.
World's only collector's guide for air rifles with valuations and auction prices in Sterling and U.S. dollars.
The American Cartridge, by Charles R. Suydam, Borden Publishing Co., Alhambra, CA, 1986. 184 pp., illus. $12.50.
An illustrated study of the rimfire cartridge in the United States.
American Percussion Revolvers, by Frank M. Sellers and Samuel E. Smith, Museum Restoration Service, Ottawa, Canada, 1971. 231 pp., illus. $29.95.
The ultimate reference book on American percussion revolvers.
"... And Now Stainless", by Dave Ecker with Bob Zwirz, Charter Arms Corp., Bridgeport, CT, 1981. 165 pp., illus. $15.00.
The Charter Arms story. Covers all models to date.
***ARMAX, The Journal of the Winchester Arms Museum, Volume 1, Number 1, Spring/Summer, 1987; Volume 1, Number 2, Fall/Winter 1987,** by Herbert G. Houze, The Buffalo Bill Historical Center, Cody, WY, 1987. 96 pp. ea., illus. Paper covers. $20.00 each.
The 1861 inventory of the arms and miscellaneous material in the office of Colonel Samuel Colt is covered in these first issues.
Arms & Accoutrements of the Mounted Police 1873-1973, by Roger F. Phillips and Donald J. Klancher, Museum Restoration Service, Ont., Canada, 1982. 224 pp., illus. $49.95.
A definitive history of the revolvers, rifles, machine guns, cannons, ammunition, swords, etc. used by the NWMP, the RNWMP and the RCMP during the first 100 years of the Force.
Arms Makers of Eastern Pennsylvania: The Colonial Years to 1790, by James B. Whisker and Roy F. Chandler, Acorn Press, Bedford, PA, 1984. Unpaginated. $10.00.
Definitive work on Eastern Pennsylvania gunmakers.
Arms Makers of Maryland, by Daniel D. Hartzler, George Shumway, York, PA, 1975. 200 pp., illus. $40.00.
A thorough study of the gunsmiths of Maryland who worked during the late 18th and early 19th centuries.
***Axis Pistols, Volume 2,** by Jan C. Still, Jan C. Still, Douglas AK, 1987. 354 pp., illus. $46.00.
The pistols of Germany and her allies in two World Wars.
Basic Documents on U.S. Marital Arms, commentary by Col. B. R. Lewis, reissue by Ray Riling, Phila., PA., 1956 and 1960. *Rifle Musket Model 1855.* The first issue rifle of musket caliber, a muzzle loader equipped with the Maynard Primer, 32 pp. $2.50. *Rifle Musket Model 1863.* The Typical Union muzzle-loader of the Civil War, 26 pp. $1.75. *Breech-Loading Rifle Musket Model 1866.* The first of our 50 caliber breechloading rifles, 12 pp. $1.75. *Remington Navy Rifle Model 1870.* A commercial type breech-loader made at Springfield, 16 pp. $1.75 *Lee Straight Pull Navy Rifle Model 1895.* A magazine cartridge arm of 6mm caliber. 23 pp. $3.00. *Breech-Loading Arms* (five models)-27 pp. $2.75. *Ward-Burton Rifle Musket 1871*-16 pp. $2.50. *U.S. Magazine Rifle and Carbine (cal. 30) Model 1892*(the Krag Rifle) 36 pp. $3.00.
***The Belton Systems, 1758 and 1784-86: America's First Repeating Firearms,** by Robert Held, Andrew Mowbray, Inc., Lincoln, RI, 1986. 93 pp., illus. Limited, numbered edition. Stiff paper covers. $40.00.
This monograph examines the first repeating firearms to be made in America, their history, their functions, their position in relation to analogous arms in America and Europe.
Beretta Automatic Pistols, by J.B. Wood, Stackpole Books, Harrisburg, PA, 1985. 192 pp., illus. $19.95.
Only English-language book devoted entirely to the Beretta line. Includes all important models.
Beretta: The World's Oldest Industrial Dynasty, by Marco Morin and Robert Held, Acquafresca Deditrice, Chiasso, Switzerland, 1983. 282 pp., illus. $44.95.
The evolution of the Beretta company with complete coverage of the guns produced. A bilingual book: Italian and English.
Blue Book of Gun Values, 8th Editon, compiled by S.P. Fjestad, Investment Rarities, Inc., Minneapolis, MN, 1986. 621 pp., illus. Paper covers. $14.95.
Uses percentage grading system to accurately determine each gun's value based on its unique condition.
***Breech-Loading Carbines of the United States Civil War Period,** by Brig. Gen. John Pitman, Armory Publications, Tacoma, WA, 1987. 94 pp., illus. $29.95.
The first in a series of previously unpublished manuscripts originated by the late Brigadier General John Putnam. Exploded drawings showing parts actual size follow each sectioned illustration.
The Bren Gun Saga, by Thomas B. Dugelby, Collector Grade Publications, Toronto, Canada, 1986. 300 pp., illus. $50.00.
Contains information on all models of Bren guns used by all nations.
The British Falling Block Rifle from 1865, by Jonathon Kirton, Armory Publications, Tacoma, WA, 1985. 247 pp., illus. $39.95.
Covers inventors and producers of British falling-block breechloaders.
British Military Longarms 1715-1865, by D.W. Bailey, Arms & Armour Press, London, England, 1986. 160 pp., illus. $19.95.
166 different guns photographed in full-length views plus detailed close-ups of locks, markings and structural variations.
British Military Pistols 1603-1888, by R.E. Brooker, Jr., The Gun Room Press, Highland Park, NJ, 1983. 139 pp., illus. $49.95.
Covers flintlock and percussion pistols plus cartridge revolvers up to the smokeless powder period.
***The British Service Lee,** by Ian Skennerton, Ian Skennerton, Margate, Australia, 1987. 410 pp., illus. $45.00.
Lee-Metford and Lee-Enfield rifles and carbines, 1880-1980.

The Broomhandle Pistol 1896-1936, by Wayne R. Erickson and Charles E. Pate, E & P Enterprises, San Antonio, TX, 1985. 300 pp., illus. $49.95.
A new updated publication on the Mauser Broomhandle pistol. Detailed historical and text information, plus a collector's value guide.
The Browning Connection, by Richard Rattenbury, Buffalo Bill Historical Center, Cody, WY, 1982. 71 pp., illus. Paper covers. $10.00.
Patent prototypes in the Winchester Museum.
Browning .22 Caliber Rifles 1914-1984, by Homer C. Tyler, Homer C. Tyler, Jefferson City, MO, 1985. 304 pp., illus. $39.95.
Serial numbers and annual production figures, grades, special orders and variations, etc.
The Burnside Breech Loading Carbines, by Edward A. Hull, Andrew Mowbray, Inc., Lincoln, RI, 1986. 95 pp., illus. $16.00.
No. 1 in the "Man at Arms Monograph Series". A model-by-model historical/technical examination of one of the most widely used cavalry weapons of the American Civil War based upon important and previously unpublished research.
California Gunsmiths 1846-1900, by Lawrence P. Sheldon, Far Far West Publ., Fair Oaks, CA, 1977. 289 pp., illus. $29.65.
A study of early California gunsmiths and the firearms they made.
Carbines of the Civil War, by John D. McAulay, Pioneer Press, Union City, TN, 1981. 123 pp., illus. Paper covers. $7.95.
A guide for the student and collector of the colorful arms used by the Federal cavalry.
Cartology Savalog, by Gerald Bernstein, Gerald Bernstein, St. Louis, MO, 1976. 177 pp., illus. Paper covers. $8.95.
An infinite variations catalog of small arms ammunition stamps.
***The Cartridge Collectors Notebook, From the Library of Charles H. Yust, Jr.,** edited by Stephen L. Fuller, Military Arms Research Service, San Jose, CA. 1987. 122 pp., illus. Paper covers. $14.95.
A compilation of articles published in "The American Rifleman" and "Gun Digest" from 1957-1975, supplemented by numerous notes and drawings from the author's personal files.
The Cartridge Guide, by Ian V. Hogg, Stackpole Books, Harrisburg, PA, 1982. 160 pp., illus. $24.95.
The small arms ammunition identification manual.
Cartridges of the World, 5th Edition, by Frank Barnes, edited by Ken Warner, DBI Books, Inc., Northbrook, IL, 1985. 416 pp., illus. Paper covers. $16.95.
Complete and authoritative data on rifle and pistol cartridges, shotshells, loads and ammunition components. The "bible" for collectors and reloaders.
A Catalog Collection of 20th Century Winchester Repeating Arms Co., compiled by Roger Rule, Alliance Books, Inc., Northridge, CA, 1985. 396 pp., illus. $29.95.
Reflects the full line of Winchester products from 1901-1931 with emphasis on Winchester firearms.
***Civil War Breechloading Rifles,** by John D. McAulay, Andrew Mowbray, Inc., Lincoln, RI, 1987. 128 pp., illus. Paper covers. $12.00.
A survey of the innovative infantry arms of the American Civil War.
Civil War Carbines, by A.F. Lustyik. World Wide Gun Report, Inc., Aledo, Ill, 1962. 63 pp., illus. Paper covers. $3.50.
Accurate, interesting summary of most carbines of the Civil War period, in booklet form, with numerous good illus.
***A Collector's Guide to Colt's .38 Automatic Pistols,** by Douglas G. Sheldon, Douglas Sheldon, Willernie, MN, 1987. 185 pp., illus. Paper covers. $19.95.
The production history of the .38 caliber Colt automatic pistols.
A Collector's Guide to Tokarev Pistols, by John Remling, Collector's Services, East Stroudsburg, PA, 1985. 81 pp., illus. $12.95.
Covers all models and variations of this firearm.
***Colonial Frontier Guns,** by T.M. Hamilton, Pioneer Press, Union City, TN, 1988. 176 pp., illus. Paper covers. $13.95.
A complete study of early flint muskets of this country.
Colt, An American Legend, by R.L. Wilson, Abbeville Press, New York, NY, 1985. 310 pp., illus. $55.00.
Every model Colt ever produced is shown in magnificent color.
The Colt-Burgess Magazine Rifle, by Samuel L. Maxwell Sr., Samuel L. Maxwell, Bellvue, WA, 1985. 176 pp. illus. $35.00.
Serial numbers, engraved arms, newly discovered experimental models, etc.
***Colt Cavalry, Artillery and Militia Revolvers 1873-1903,** by Keith Cochran, Cochran Publishing Co., Rapid City, SD, 1988. 288 pp., illus. $45.00.
A history and text book of the Colt Cavalry Model revolver with a complete analysis, nearly every variation and mark illustrated.
Colt Engraving, by R.L. Wilson, The Gun Room Press, Highland Park, NJ, 1982. 560 pp., illus. $69.95.
New and completely revised edition of the author's original work on finely engraved Colt firearms.
Colt Firearms from 1836, by James E. Serven, new 8th edition, Stackpole Books, Harrisburg, PA, 1979. 398 pp., illus. Deluxe ed. $49.95.
Excellent survey of the Colt company and its products. Updated with new SAA production chart and commemorative list.
The Colt Heritage, by R.L. Wilson, Simon & Schuster, 1979. 358 pp., illus. $75.00.
The official history of Colt firearms 1836 to the present.
Colt Peacemaker Encyclopedia, by Keith Cochran, Keith Cochran, Rapid City, SD, 1986. 434 pp., illus. $59.95.
A must book for the Peacemaker collector.
Colt Peacemaker Ready-Reference Handbook, by Keith Cochran, Cochran Publishing Co., Rapid City, ND, 1985. 76 pp., illus. Paper covers. $12.95.
A must book for the SAA collector.
***Colt Peacemaker Yearly Variations,** by Keith Cochran, Keith Cochran, Rapid City, SD, 1987. 96 pp., illus. $17.95.
A definitive, precise listing for each year the Peacemaker was manufactured from 1873-1940.
Colt Pistols 1836-1976, by R.L. Wilson in association with R.E. Hable, Jackson Arms, Dallas, TX, 1976. 380 pp., illus. $125.00.
A magnificently illustrated book in full-color featuring Colt firearms from the famous Hable collection.
***Colt Revolvers and the U.S. Navy 1865-1889,** by C. Kenneth Moore, Dorrance and Co., Bryn Mawr, PA, 1987. 140 pp., illus. $29.95.
The Navy's use of all Colt handguns and other revolvers during this era of great change.
The Colt Rifle 1884-1902, by Ted Tivey, Ted Tivey, N.S.W., Australia, 1984. 119 pp., illus. $30.00.
Covers the production era of the Colt slide action "Lightning" models made for the sporting world.
Colt's Dates of Manufacture 1837-1978, by R.L. Wilson, published by Maurie Albert,Coburg, Australia; N.A. distributor I.D.S.A. Books, Hamilton, OH, 1983. 61 pp. $10.00.
An invaluable pocket guide to the dates of manufacture of Colt firearms up to 1978.
Colt's SAA Post War Models, George Garton, revised edition, Gun Room Press, Highland Park, NJ, 1987. 166 pp., illus. $29.95.
The complete facts on Colt's famous post war single action army revolver using factory records to cover types, calibers, production numbers and many variations of this popular firearm.
Colt's Variations of the Old Model Pocket Pistol, 1848 to 1872, by P.L. Shumaker. Borden Publishing, Co., Alhambra, CA, 1966, a reprint of the 1957 edition. 150 pp., illus. $13.95.
A useful tool for the Colt specialist and a welcome return of a popular source of information that had been long out-of-print.
The Colt Whitneyville-Walker Pistol, by Lt. Col. Robert D. Whittington, Brownlee Books, Hooks, TX, 1984. 96 pp., illus. Limited edition. $20.00.
A study of the pistol and associated characters 1846-1851.
***Confederate Revolvers,** by William A. Gary, Taylor Publishing Co., Dallas, TX, 1987. 174 pp., illus. $45.00.
Comprehensive work on the rarest of Confederate weapons.
Contemporary Makers of Muzzleloading Firearms, by Robert Weil, Screenland Press, Burbank, CA, 1981. 300 pp., illus. $39.95.
Illustrates the work of over 30 different contemporary makers.
Dance & Brothers: Texas Gunmakers of the Confederacy, by Gary Wiggins, Moss Publications, Orange, VA, 1986. 151 pp., illus. $29.95.
Presents a thorough and detailed study of the legendary Texas gunmakers, Dance & Brothers.
The Deringer in America, Volume 1, The Percussion Period, by R.L. Wilson and L.D. Eberhart, Andrew Mowbray Inc., Lincoln, RI, 1985. 271 pp., illus. $48.00.
A long awaited book on the American percussion deringer.
Development of the Henry Cartridge and Self-Contained Cartridges for the Toggle-Link Winchesters, by R. Bruce McDowell, A.M.B., Metuchen, NJ, 1984. 69 pp., illus. Paper covers. $10.00.
From powder and ball to the self-contained metallic cartridge.
Early Indian Trade Guns: 1625-1775, by T.M. Hamilton, Museum of the Great Plains, Lawton, OK, 1968. 34 pp., illus. Paper covers. $7.95.
Detailed descriptions of subject arms, compiled from early records and from the study of remnants found in Indian country.
Eley Brothers Cartridge Catalog and Price List 1910-11, reprinted by Armory Publications, Tacoma, WA, 1984, 92 pp., illus. Paper covers. $18.95.
Fascimile reprint gives specifications for every cartridge manufactured by Eley Brothers during this period. Lots of ballistic data.
English Gunmakers, by DeWitt Bailey and Douglas A. Nie, ARCO Publishing Co., New York, NY, 1978. 127 pp., illus. $24.95.
The Birmingham and Provincial gun trade in the 18th & 19th centuries.
English Pistols: The Armories of H.M. Tower of London Collection, by Howard L. Blackmore, Arms and Armour Press, London, England, 1985. 64 pp., illus. $17.95.
All the pistols described and pictured are from this famed collection.
European Firearms in Swedish Castles, by Kaa Wennberg, Bohuslaningens Boktryckeri AB, Uddevalla, Sweden, 1986. 156 pp., illus. $45.00.
The famous collection of Count Keller, the Ettersburg Castle collection, and others. English text.
Evolution of the Winchester, by R. Bruce McDowell, Armory Publications, Tacoma, WA, 1986. 200 pp., illus. $37.50.
Historic lever-action, tubular-magazine firearms.
Fifteen Years in the Hawken Lode, by John D. Baird, The Gun Room Press, Highland Park, NJ, 1976. 120 pp., illus. $17.95.
A collection of thoughts and observations gained from many years of intensive study of the guns from the shop of the Hawken brothers.
Firearms in Colonial America: The Impact on History and Technology 1492-1792, by M.L. Brown, Smithsonian Institution Press, Wash., D.C., 1980. 449 pp., illus. $55.00.
An in-depth coverage of the history and technology of firearms in Colonial North America.
Firearms of the American West, 1803-1865, by Louis A. Garavaglia and Charles G. Worman, University of New Mexico Press, Albuquerque, NM, 1985. 300 pp. illus. $35.00.
An encyclopedic study tracing the development and uses of firearms on the frontier during this period.
Firearms of the American West, 1866-1894, by Louis A. Garavaglia, and Charles G. Wormer, University of New Mexico Press, Albuquerque, NM, 1985. 448 pp., illus. $40.00.
The second volume in this study examines guns as an integral part of the frontier experience in a society where peace officers and judges were few.
Firepower from Abroad: The Confederate Enfield and the LeMat Revolver, by Wiley Sword, Andrew Mowbray, Inc., Lincoln, RI, 1986. 119 pp., illus. $16.00.
No. 2 in the "Man at Arms Monograph Series." With new data on a variety of Confederate smallarms.

Flayderman's Guide to Antique American Firearms and Their Values, 4th Edition, by Norm Flayderman, DBI Books, Inc., Northbrook, IL, 1987. 624 pp., illus. Paper covers. $22.95.
Updated fourth edition of this bible of the antique gun field.
Frank and George Freund and the Sharps Rifle, by Gerald O. Kelver, Gerald O. Kelver, Brighton, CO, 1986. 60 pp., illus. Paper covers. $8.00.
Pioneer gunmakers of Wyoming Territory and Colorado.
The .45-70 Springfield, by Albert J. Frasca and Robert H. Hall, Springfield Publishing Co., Northridge, CA, 1980. 380 pp., illus. $49.50.
A carefully researched book on the trapdoor Springfield, including all experimental and very rare models.
The 45/70 Trapdoor Springfield Dixie Collection, compiled by Walter Crutcher and Paul Oglesby, Pioneer Press, Union City, TN, 1975. 600 pp., illus. Paper covers. $9.95.
An illustrated listing of the 45-70 Springfields in the Dixie Gun Works Collection. Little known details and technical information is given, plus current values.
French Military Weapons, 1717-1938, Major James E. Hicks, N. Flayderman & Co., Publishers, New Milford, CT, 1973. 281 pp., illus. $22.50.
Firearms, swords, bayonets, ammunition, artillery, ordnance equipment of the French army.
Game Guns and Rifles, by Richard Akehurst, Arms and Armour Press, London, England, 1985. 176 pp., illus. $24.95.
Reprint of a classic account on sporting arms.
***The German Assault Rifle 1935-1945,** by Peter R. Senich, Paladin Press, Boulder, CO, 1987. 328 pp., illus. $39.95.
A complete review of machine carbines, machine pistols and assault rifles employed by Hitler's Wehrmacht during WWII.
Great British Gunmakers 1540-1740, by W. Keith Neal and D.H.L. Back, Historical Firearms, London, England, 1984. 479 pp., illus. $135.00.
A limited, numbered edition covering a total of 159 English gunmakers.
***Great Century of Guns,** by Branko Bogdanovic and Ivan Valencak, W.H. Smith Publishers, Inc., N.Y., NY, 1986. 286 pp., illus. $24.95.
Not only describes the most famous and widespread firearms, but also gives an insight into the society in which these arms were created.
Gun Collector's Digest, 4th Edition, edited by Joseph J. Schroeder, DBI Books, Inc., Northbrook, IL, 1985. 224 pp., illus. Paper covers. $12.95.
The latest edition of this sought-after series.
Gun Digest Book of Modern Gun Values, 6th Edition, by Jack Lewis, ed. by Harold A. Murtz, DBI Books, Inc., Northbrook, IL, 1987. 448 pp., illus. Paper covers. $15.95.
Updated and expanded edition of the book that's become the standard for valuing modern firearms.
Gunmakers of London 1350-1850, by Howard L. Blackmore, George Shumway Publisher, York, PA, 1986. 222 pp., illus. $85.00.
A listing of all the known workmen of gun making in the first 500 years, plus a history of the guilds, cutlers, armourers, founders, blacksmiths, etc. 260 gunmarks are illustrated.
The Gunsmiths and Gunmakers of Eastern Pennsylvania, by James B. Whisker and Roy Chandler, Old Bedford Village Press, Bedford, PA, 1982. 130 pp., illus. Limited, numbered edition. Paper covers. $17.50.
Locates over 2,000 gunsmiths practicing before 1900, with references and documentation.
The Gunsmiths and Gunmakers of Western Pennsylvania, by James B. Whisker and Vaughn E. Whisker, Old Bedford Village Press, Bedford, PA, 1982. 103 pp., illus. Limited, numbered and signed edition. Paper covers. $17.50.
Lists over 650 names of gunsmiths practicing before 1900.
Gunsmiths of Ohio—18th & 19th Centuries: Vol. I, Biographical Data, by Donald A. Hutslar, George Shumway, York, PA, 1973. 444 pp., illus. $35.00.
An important source book, full of information about the old-time gunsmiths of Ohio.
Handbook of the Pedersen Self-Loading Rifles Model P.A., a facsimile reprint of this Vickers-Armstrongs Ltd. manual, ca. 1930s by Robert T. Sweeney, San Francisco, CA, 1985. 32 pp., illus. Paper covers. $9.50.
Reprint of an original operator's manual for the British version of a semiautomatic military arm that was a major contender of the Garand rifle.
The Hawken Rifle: Its Place in History, by Charles E. Hanson, Jr., The Fur Press, Chadron, NE, 1979. 104 pp., illus. Paper covers. $6.00.
A definitive work on this famous rifle.
Hawken Rifles, The Mountain Man's Choice, by John D. Baird, The Gun Room Press, Highland Park, NJ, 1976. 95 pp., illus. $17.95.
Covers the rifles developed for the Western fur trade. Numerous specimens are described and shown in photographs.
Historic Pistols: The American Martial Flintlock 1760-1845, by Samuel E. Smith and Edwin W. Bitter, The Gun Room Press, Highland Park, NJ, 1986. 353 pp., illus. $64.50.
Cover over 70 makers and 163 models of American martial arms.
Historical Hartford Hardware, by William W. Dalrymple, Colt Collector Press, Rapid City, SD, 1976. 42 pp., illus. Paper covers. $5.50.
Historically associated Colt revolvers.
A History of Browning Guns from 1831, J.M. and M.S. Browning, reprinted by Eastman's Firearms, Inc., Fitzgerald, GA, 1986. 62 pp., illus. Paper covers. $14.95.
Reprint of a pamphlet published in 1942 by the Browning Arms Co.
A History of the John M. Browning Semi-Automatic .22 Caliber Rifle, by Homer C. Tyler, Jefferson City, MO, 1982. 58 pp., illus. Paper covers. $10.00.
All models and variations are shown. Includes engraved guns.
History of Winchester Firearms 1866-1980, by Duncan Barnes, et al,Winchester Press, Piscataway, NJ, 1985. 256 pp., illus. $18.95.
A most complete and authoritative account of Winchester firearms.

How to Buy and Sell Used Guns, by John Traister, Stoeger Publishing Co., So. Hackensack, NJ, 1984. 192 pp., illus. Paper covers. $9.95.
A new guide to buying and selling guns.
The Illustrated Encyclopedia of Ammunition, by Ian V. Hogg, Chartwell Books, Inc., Secaucus, NJ, 1985. 253 pp., illus. $15.95.
A complete and updated illustrated survey of ammunition for small arms, mortar and artillery weapons.
***Illustrations of United States Military Arms 1776-1903 and Their Inspector's Marks,** compiled by Turner Kirkland, Pioneer Press, Union City, TN, 1988. 37 pp., illus. Paper covers. $4.95.
Reprinted from the 1949 Bannerman catalog. Valuable information for both the advanced and beginning collector.
Jane's Directory of Military Small Arms Ammunition, Jane's Publishing Co., Ltd., London, England, 1985. 124 pp., illus. $24.95.
Guide to all currently available military small arms cartridges.
Japanese Handguns, by Frederick E. Leithe, Borden Publishing Co., Alhambra, CA, 1985. 160 pp., illus. $19.95.
All identification guide to all models and variations of Japanese handguns.
The Kentucky Rifle: A True American Heritage in Picture, by The Kentucky Rifle Association, The Forte Group of Creative Companies, Inc., Alexandria, VA, second edition, 1985. 110 pp., illus. $27.50.
This classic essay reveals both the beauty and the decorative nature of the Kentucky by providing detailed photographs of some of the most significant examples of American rifles, pistols, and accoutrements.
Kentucky Rifles and Pistols 1756-1850, compiled by members of the Kentucky Rifle Association, Wash., DC, Golden Age Arms Co., Delaware, OH, 1976. 275 pp., illus. $35.00.
Profusely illustrated with more than 300 examples of rifles and pistols never before published.
Know Your Broomhandle Mausers, by R.J. Berger, Blacksmith Corp., Southport, CT, 1985. 96 pp., illus. Paper covers. $6.95.
An interesting story on the big Mauser pistol and its variations.
Know Your Ruger Single Action Revolvers 1953-1963, by John C. Dougan, edited by John T. Amber, Blacksmith Corp., Southport, CT, 1981. 199 pp., illus. $35.00.
A definitive reference work for the Ruger revolvers produced in the period 1953-1963.
The Krag Rifle Story, by Franklin B. Mallory and Ludwig Olson, Springfield Research Service, Silver Spring, MD, 1979. 224 pp., illus. $20.00.
Covers both U.S. and European Krags. Gives a detailed description of U.S. Krag rifles and carbines and extensive data on sights, bayonets, serial numbers, etc.
Krag Rifles, by William S. Brophy, The Gun Room Press, Highland Park, NJ, 1980. 200 pp., illus. $29.95.
The first comprehensive work detailing the evolution and various models, both military and civilian.
Lever Action Magazine Rifles Derived from the Patents of Andrew Burgess, by Samuel L. Maxwell Sr., Samuel L. Maxwell, Bellevue, WA, 1976. 368 pp., illus. $29.95.
The complete story of a group of lever action magazine rifles collectively referred to as the Burgess/Morse, the Kennedy or the Whitney.
Longrifles of Pennsylvania, Volume 1, Jefferson, Clarion & Elk Counties, by Russel H. Harringer, George Shumway Publisher, York, PA, 1984. 200 pp., illus. $40.00.
First in series that will treat in great detail the longrifles and gunsmiths of Pennsylvania.
The Luger Book, by John Walter, Arms & Armour Press, London, England, 1987. 288 pp., illus. $45.00.
The encyclopedia of the Borchardt and the Borchardt-Luger handguns, 1885-1985.
Mauser Bolt Rifles, by Ludwig Olson, F. Brownell & Son, Inc., Montezuma, IA, 1976. 364 pp., illus. $39.95.
The most complete, detailed, authoritative and comprehensive work ever done on Mauser bolt rifles.
Military Pistols of Japan, by Fred L. Honeycutt, Jr., Julin Books, Lake Park, FL. 1982. 167 pp., illus. $24.00.
Covers every aspect of military pistol production in Japan through WWII.
Military Rifles of Japan, by Fred L. Honeycutt, Jr. and F. Pratt Anthony, Julin Books, Lake Park, FL, 2nd edition, 1983. 206 pp., illus. $29.00.
Limited, signed and numbered edition. Includes the early Murata period, markings, etc.
***M1 Carbine,** by Larry Ruth, Gunroom Press, Highland Park, NJ, 1987. 291 pp., illus. Cloth $24.95; Paper $17.95.
The origin, development, manufacture and use of this famous carbine of WWII.
***Military Holsters of World War 2,** by Eugene J. Bender, Taylor Publishing Co., Dallas, TX 1984. 205 pp., illus. $35.00.
Covers 24 nations which produced holsters for their military weapons.
Modern Guns, Fred Adolph Catalog, reprinted by Armory Publications, Tacoma, WA, 1983. 67 pp., illus. Paper covers. $10.95.
Reprint of a scarce American gun catalog of the early 1900s.
Modern Guns Identification and Values, revised 6th Edition, edited by Russell Quertermous and Steve Quertermous, Collector Books, Paducah, KY, 1985. 432 pp., illus. Paper covers. $12.95.
A guide to the current values of modern revolvers, pistols, rifles, and shotguns.
More Single Shot Rifles, by James C. Grant, The Gun Room Press, Highland Park, NJ, 1976. 324 pp., illus. $25.00.
Details the guns made by Frank Wesson, Milt Farrow, Holden, Borchardt, Stevens, Remington, Winchester, Ballard and Peabody-Martini.
Simeon North: First Official Pistol Maker of the United States, by S. North and R. North, The Gun Room Press, Highland Park, NJ, 1972. 207 pp., illus. $9.95.
Reprint of the rare first edition.

The Northwest Gun, by Charles E. Hanson, Jr., Nebraska State Historical Society, Lincoln, NB, 1976. 85 pp., illus., paper covers. $6.00.
Number 2 in the Society's "Publications in Anthropology." Historical survey of rifles which figured in the fur trade and settlement of the Northwest.
Official Price Guide to Collector Handguns, 4th Edition, 1987, Random House, Westminster, MD, 1987. 308 pp., illus. Paper covers. $14.95.
Updated and revised edition of this important price guide to collector handguns.
The P-08 Parabellum Luger Automatic Pistol, edited by J. David McFarland, Desert Publications, Cornville, AZ, 1982. 20 pp., illus. Paper covers. $6.00.
Covers every facet of the Luger, plus a listing of all known Luger models.
The P-38 Pistol: The Contract Pistols 1940-45, Volume Two, by Warren H. Buxton, Ucross Books, Los Alamos, NM, 1984. 247 pp., illus. $45.50.
The production of the pistol in Germany and its occupied areas during the war by firms other than Walther.
Paterson Colt Pistol Variations, by R.L. Wilson and R. Phillips, Jackson Arms Co., Dallas, TX, 1979. 250 pp., illus. $35.00.
A tremendous book about the different models and barrel lengths in the Paterson Colt story.
Pennsylvania Longrifles of Note, by George Shumway, George Shumway, Publisher, York, PA, 1977. 63 pp., illus. Paper covers. $6.95.
Illustrates and describes samples of guns from a number of Pennsylvania rifle-making schools.
The Pinfire System, by Gene P. Smith and Chris C. Curtis, The Pinfire System, San Francisco, CA, 1983. 216 pp., illus. $50.00.
The first attempt to record the invention, development and use of pinfire cartridge arms and ammunition.
***Pollard's History of Firearms,** edited by Claude Blair, Macmillan Publishing Co., N.Y., NY, 1983. 559 pp., illus. $40.00.
The most comprehensive survey of the origins and development of world firearms from the Middle Ages to the present day.
The Radom Pistol, by Robert J. Berger, Robert J. Berger, Milford, CT, 1981. 99 pp., illus. Paper covers. $12.50.
The complete story of the VIS (Radom) pistol.
The Rare and Valuable Antique Arms, by James E. Serven, Pioneer Press, Union City, TN, 1976. 106 pp., illus. Paper covers. $4.95.
A guide to the collector in deciding which direction his collecting should go, investment value, historic interest, mechanical ingenuity, high art or personal preference.
Reloading Tools, Sights and Telescopes for Single Shot Rifles, by Gerald O. Kelver, Brighton, CO, 1982. 163 pp., illus. Paper covers. $10.00.
A listing of most of the famous makers of reloading tools, sights and telescopes with a brief description of the products they manufactured.
Rifles in Colonial America, Vol. I, by George Shumway, George Shumway, Publisher, York, PA, 1980. 353 pp., illus. $49.50.
An extensive photographic study of American longrifles made in the late Colonial, Revolutionary, and post-Revolutionary periods.
Rifles in Colonial America, Vol. II, by George Shumway, George Shumway, Publisher, York, PA, 1980. 302 pp., illus. $49.50.
Final volume of this study of the early evolution of the rifle in America.
***The Rimfire Cartridge in the United States and Canada 1857-1984,** by John L. Barber, Armory Publications, Tacoma, WA, 1987. 221 pp., illus. $39.95.
An illustrated history of its manufacturers and their patents.
The Ross Rifle Story, by R. Phillips, F. Dupuis, J. Chadwick, John A. Chadwick, Nova Scotia, Canada, 1984. 475 pp., illus. $49.50.
This book explores the myths and folklore surrounding Ross and his rifle and tries to set the record straight.
Ruger Rimfire Handguns 1949-1982, by J.C. Munnell, G.D.G.S. Inc., McKeesport, PA, 1982. 189 pp., illus. Paper covers. $13.50.
Updated edition with additional material on the semi-automatic pistols and the New Model revolvers.
Samuel Colt's New Model Pocket Pistols; The Story of the 1855 Root Model Revolver, by S. Gerald Keogh, S.G. Keogh, Ogden, UT, 1974. 31 pp., illus., paper covers. $5.00.
Collector's reference on various types of the titled arms, with descriptions, illustrations, and historical data.
Scottish Arms Makers, by Charles E. Whitelaw, Arms and Armour Press, London, England, 1982. 363 pp., illus. $29.95.
An important and basic addition to weapons reference literature.
Serial Numbers on U.S. Martial Arms, by Franklin B. Mallory, Springfield Research Service, Silver Spring, MD, 1983. 103 pp., illus. Paper covers. $10.00.
A valuble aid to collectors of U.S. martial arms.
Serial Numbers on U.S. Martial Arms, Volume 2 compiled by Springfield Research Service, Silver Spring, MD, 1986. 209 pp., illus. Paper covers. $15.00.
Contains information on about 33,800 individual U.S. military weapons, rifles and handguns.
Sharps Firearms, by Frank Seller, Frank M. Seller, Denver, CO, 1982. 358 pp., illus. $39.95.
Traces the development of Sharps firearms with full range of guns made including all martial variations.
***Simonov SKS-45 Type Carbines,** by Wyant LaMont and Stephen Fuller, Pantera Groups, Burbank, CA, 1988. 218 pp., illus. $21.95.
Covers the history of the development of the rifle, numerous combat photographs and detailed directions for maintenance and repair.
Southern Derringers of the Mississippi Valley, by Turner Kirkland. Pioneer Press, Tenn., 1971. 80 pp., illus., paper covers. $2.00.
A guide for the collector, and a much-needed study.
***Soviet Russian Postwar Military Pistols and Cartridges,** by Fred A. Datig, Handgun Press, Glenview, IL, 1988. 152 pp., illus. $29.95.
Thoroughly researched, this definitive sourcebook covers the development and adoption of the Makarov, Stechkin and the new PSM pistols. Also included is coverage on Russian clandestine weapons and pistol cartridges.
The Springfield 1903 Rifles, by Lt. Col. William S. Brophy, USAR, Ret., Stackpole Books Inc., Harrisburg, PA, 1985. 608 pp., illus. $49.95.
The illustrated, documented story of the design, development, and production of all the models, appendages, and accessories.
Springfield Shoulder Arms 1795-1865, by Claud E. Fuller, S. & S. Firearms, Glendale, NY, 1986. 76 pp., illus. Paper covers. $15.00.
Exact reprint of the scarce 1930 edition of one of the most definitive works on Springfield flintlock and percussion muskets ever published.
Still More Single Shot Rifles, by James J. Grant, Pioneer Press, Union City, TN, 1979. 211 pp., illus. $17.50.
A sequel to the author's classic works on single shot rifles.
***System Mauser: A Pictorial History of the 1896 Self-Loading Pistol,** by John W. Breathed, Jr. and Joseph J. Schroeder, Jr., Handgun Press, Glenview, IL, 1987. 273 pp., illus. $24.95.
The definitive work on this famous German handgun.
The 36 Calibers of the Colt Single Action Army, by David M. Brown. Publ. by the author at Albuquerque, NM, new reprint 1971. 222 pp., well-illus. $65.00.
Edited by Bev Mann of "Guns" Magazine. This is an unusual approach to the many details of the Colt S.A. Army revolver. Halftone and line drawings of the same models make this of especial interest.
The Thompson Submachine Gun 1986 Supplement, by Roger A. Cox, Roger A. Cox, Atlanta, GA, 1986. 38 pp., illus. Paper covers. $11.95.
Additional history and information on the distribution of the Thompson.
Thoughts on the Kentucky Rifle in its Golden Age, by Joe Kindig, George Shumway, Publisher, York, PA, 1984. 561 pp., illus. $75.00.
A new printing of the classic work on Kentucky rifles.
The Trapdoor Springfield, by M.D. Waite and B.D. Ernst, The Gun Room Press, Highland Park, NJ, 1983. 250 pp., illus. $29.95.
The first comprehensive book on the famous standard military rifle of the 1873-92 period.
Underhammer Guns, by H.C. Logan. Stackpole Books, Harrisburg, PA, 1965. 250 pp., illus. $10.00.
A full account of an unusual form of firearm dating back to flintlock days. Both American and foreign specimens are included.
***UK and Commonwealth FALS,** by R. Blake Stevens, Collector Grade Publications, Toronto, Canada, 1987. 260 pp., illus. Paper covers. $30.00.
The complete story of the L1A1 in the UK, Australia and India.
U.S. Enfield, by Ian Skennerton, Ian Skennerton, Margate, Australia, 1983. 190 pp., illus. $21.50.
Covers both the British pattern and the U.S. Model 1917 rifles.
United States Martial Flintlocks, by Robert M. Reilly, Andrew Mowbray, Inc., Lincoln, RI, 1986. 236 pp., illus. $39.50.
A comprehensive illustrated history of the flintlock in America from the Revolution to the demise of the system.
U.S. Military Small Arms 1816-1865, by Robert M. Reilly, The Gun Room Press, Highland Park, NJ, 1983. 270 pp., illus. $35.00.
Covers every known type of primary and secondary martial firearms used by Federal forces.
Walther P-38 Pistol, by Maj. George Nonte, Desert Publications, Cornville, AZ, 1982. 100 pp., illus. Paper covers. $7.50.
Complete volume on one of the most famous handguns to come out of WWII. All models covered.
Walther Models PP and PPK, 1929-1945, by James L. Rankin, assisted by Gary Green, James L. Rankin, Coral Gables, FL, 1974. 142 pp., illus. $25.00.
Complete coverage on the subject as to finish, proof marks and Nazi Party inscriptions.
Walther Volume II, Engraved, Presentation and Standard Models, by James L. Rankin, J.L. Rankin, Coral Gables, FL, 1977. 112 pp., illus. $25.00.
The new Walther book on embellished versions and standard models. Has 88 photographs, including many color plates.
Walther, Volume III, 1908-1980, by James L. Rankin, Coral Gables, FL, 1981. 226 pp., illus. $30.00.
Covers all models of Walther handguns from 1908 to date, includes holsters, grips and magazines.
***Weapons of the American Civil War,** by Ian Hogg, Outlet Books, Inc., Secaucus, NJ, 1987. 176 pp., illus. $9.98.
Civil War weaponry and it effectiveness upon the battlefield. Weapons of all caliber are fully described and examined within their historic context.
The Whitney Firearms, by Claud Fuller. Standard Publications, Huntington, W. Va., 1946. 334 pp., many plates and drawings. $40.00.
An authoritative history of all Whitney arms and their maker. Highly recommended. An exclusive with Ray Riling Arms Books Co.
The William M. Locke Collection, compiled by Robert B. Berryman, et al, The Antique Armory, Inc., East Point, GA, 1973. 541 pp., illus. $45.00.
A magnificently produced book illustrated with hundreds of photographs of guns from one of the finest collection of American firearms ever assembled.
The Winchester Book, Silver Anniversary Edition, by George Madis, David Madis Gun Book Distributor, Dallas, TX, 1986. 650 pp., illus. $44.50.
A new, revised 25th anniversary edition of this classic book on Winchester firearms. Complete serial ranges have been added.
Winchester Commemoratives, by Tom Trolard, Commemorative Investment Press, Plano, TX, 1986. 183 pp., illus. $49.95
The complete pictoral collection of all the Winchester commemoratives.
Winchester Dates of Manufacture 1849-1984, by George Madis, Art and Reference House, Brownsboro, TX, 1984. 59 pp. $5.95.
A most useful work, compiled from records of the Winchester factory.
The Winchester Handbook, by George Madis, Art & Reference House, Lancaster, TX, 1982. 287 pp., illus. $19.95.
The complete line of Winchester guns, with dates of manufacture, serial numbers, etc.

COLLECTORS (cont.)

Winchester: The Golden Age of American Gunmaking and the Winchester 1 of 1000, by R.L. Wilson, Winchester Arms Museum, Cody, WY, 1983. 144 pp., illus. $45.00.

The author traces the evolution of the firm; against this background he then examines the Winchester Model 1873 and 1876, 1 of 100 and 1000 series rifles.

Winchester's 30-30, Model 94, by Sam Fadala, Stackpole Books, Inc., Harrisburg, PA, 1986. 223 pp., illus. $24.95.

The story of the rifle America loves.

Allied Military Fighting Knives and the Men Who Made Them Famous, by Robert A. Buerlein, American Historical Foundation, Richmond, VA, 1985. 183 pp., illus. $34.95.

The background, development and variations of the allied military fighting knives are chronicled and the tales of the men who used them are told.

American Knives; The First History and Collector's Guide, by Harold L. Peterson, The Gun Room Press, Highland Park, NJ, 1980. 178 pp., illus. $17.95.

A reprint of this 1958 classic. Covers all types of American knives.

American Primitive Knives 1770-1870, by G.B. Minnes, Museum Restoration Service, Ottawa, Canada, 1983. 112 pp., illus. $14.95.

Origins of the knives, outstanding specimens, structural details, etc.

The Ames Sword Co., 1829-1935, by John D. Hamilton, Mowbray Co., Providence, RI, 1983. 255 pp., illus. $45.00.

The story of the most prolific American sword makers over the longest period of time.

The American Sword, 1775-1945, by Harold L. Peterson, Ray Riling Arms Books, Co., Phila., PA, 1980. 286 pp. plus 60 pp. of illus. $35.00.

1977 reprint of a survey of swords worn by U.S. uniformed forces, plus the rare "American Silver Mounted Swords, (1700-1815)."

The Art of Blacksmithing, by Alex W. Bealer, Funk & Wagnalls, New York, NY, revised edition, 1976. 438 pp., illus. $21.95.

Required reading for anyone who makes knives or is seriously interested in the history of cutlery.

The Bayonet An Evolution and History, by R.D.C. Evans and Frederick J. Stephens, Militaria Collector Inc., Northridge, CA, 1985. 200 pp., illus. Paper covers. $19.95.

Traces the story of the bayonet through the centuries from its simple beginnings in 17th century France up to the present age.

***Bayonets from Janzen's Notebook,** by Jerry L. Janzen, Published by the author, Tulsa, OK, 1987. 252 pp., illus. Paper covers. $20.00.

Covers 800 bayonets from 49 countries.

Blacksmithing for the Home Craftsman, by Joe Pehoski, Joe Pehoski, Washington, TX, 1973. 44 pp., illus. Paper covers. $5.00.

This informative book is chock-full of drawings and explains how to make your own forge.

Blades and Barrels, by H. Gordon Frost, Wallon Press, El Paso, TX, 1972. 298 pp., illus. $19.95.

The first full scale study about man's attempts to combine an edged weapon with a firearm.

Commando Dagger, by Leroy Thompson, Paladin Press, Boulder, CO, 1984. 176 pp., illus. $25.00.

The complete illustrated history of the Fairbairn-Sykes fighting knife.

***The Complete Bladesmith: Forging Your Way to Perfection,** by Jim Hrisoulas, Paladin Press, Boulder, CO, 1987. 192 pp., illus. $25.00.

Novice as well as experienced bladesmith will benefit from this definitive guide to smithing world-class blades.

Custom Knife...II, by John Davis Bates, Jr., and James Henry Schippers, Jr., Custom Knife Press, Memphis, TN, 1974. 112 pp., illus. $20.00.

The book of pocket knives and folding hunters. A guide to the 20th century makers' art.

Custom Knifemaking, by Tim McCreight, Stackpole Books, Inc., Harrisburg, PA., 1985. 224 pp., illus. $14.95.

Ten projects from a master craftsman.

For Knife Lovers Only, by Harry K. McEvoy, Knife World Publ., Knoxville, TN, 1979, 67 pp., illus. Paper covers. $4.95.

A fascinating and unusual approach to the story of knives.

The German Bayonet, by John Walter, Arms and Armour Press, London, England, 1982. 128 pp., illus. $24.95.

A comprehensive history of the regulation patterns 1871-1945.

***Gun Digest Book of Knives, 3rd Edition,** by Jack Lewis and Roger Combs, DBI Books, Inc., Northbrook, IL, 1988. 256 pp., illus. Paper covers. $12.95.

All new edition covers practically every aspect of the knife world.

How to Make Knives, by Richard W. Barney & Robert W. Loveless, Beinfield Publ., Inc., No. Hollywood, CA, 1977. 178 pp., illus. $15.00.

A book filled with drawings, illustrations, diagrams, and 500 how-to-do-it photos.

The Japanese Sword, by Kanzan Sato, Kodansha International Ltd. and Shibundo, Tokyo, Japan, 1983. 210 pp., illus. $19.95.

The history and appreciation of the Japanese sword, with a detailed examination of over a dozen of Japan's most revered blades.

Japanese Swordsmanship, by Gordon Warner and Don. F. Draeger, Weatherhill, New York, NY, 1984. 296 pp., illus. $29.95.

Technique and practice of Japanese swordsmanship.

Kentucky Knife Traders Manual No. 6, by R.B. Ritchie, Hindman, KY, 1980. 217 pp., illus. Paper covers. $10.00.

Guide for dealers, collectors and traders listing pocket knives and razor values.

Knife Throwing a Practical Guide, by Harry K. McEvoy, Charles E. Tuttle Co., Rutland, VT, 1973. 108 pp., illus. Paper covers. $3.95.

If you want to learn to throw a knife this is the "bible".

***Knives '89, 9th Edition,** edited by Ken Warner, DBI Books, Inc., Northbrook, IL, 1988. 256 pp., illus. Paper covers. $13.95.

Covers trends and technology for both custom and factory knives.

Levine's Guide to Knives And Their Values, by Bernard Levine, DBI Books, Inc., Northbrook, IL, 1985. 480 pp., illus. Paper covers. $19.95.

An important guide to today's knife values and collecting them.

Light But Efficient, by Albert N. Hardin, Jr. and Robert W. Hedden, Albert N. Hardin, Jr., Pennsauken, NJ, 1973. 103 pp., illus. $8.95.

A study of the M1880 Hunting and M1890 intrenching knives and scabbards.

***Military Swords of Japan 1868-1945,** by Richard Fuller and Ron Gregory, Arms and Armour Press, London, England, 1986. 127 pp., illus. $24.95.

A wide-ranging survey of the swords and dirks worn by the armed forces of Japan until the end of the WWII.

The Modern Blacksmith, by Alexander G. Weygers, Van Nostrand Reinhold Co., NY, 1977. 96 pp., illus. $10.95.

Shows how to forge objects out of steel. Use of basic techniques and tools.

Naval Swords, by P.G.W. Annis, Stackpole Books, Harrisburg, PA, 1970. 80 pp., illus. $12.50.

British and American naval edged weapons 1660-1815.

Practical Blacksmithing, edited by J. Richardson, Outlet Books, NY, 1978. four volumes in one, illus. $9.98.

A reprint of the extremely rare, bible of the blacksmith. Covers every aspect of working with iron and steel, from ancient uses to modern.

Rice's Trowel Bayonet, reprinted by Ray Riling Arms Books, Co., Phila., PA, 1968. 8 pp., illus. Paper covers. $3.00.

A facsimile reprint of a rare circular originally published by the U.S. Government in 1875 for the information of U.S. Troops.

The Samurai Sword, by John M. Yumoto, Charles E. Tuttle Co., Rutland, VT, 1958. 191 pp., illus. $12.50.

A must for anyone interested in Japanese blades, and the first book on this subject written in English.

The Samurai Sword: An American Perspective, by Gary Murtha, H.S.M. Publications, Independence, MO, 1980. 126 pp., illus. $30.00.

The origin and development of the sword and its historical background.

The Samurai Sword: An American Perspective, Vol. 2, Sword Fittings, by Gary Murtha, R&M Enterprises, Kansas City, MO, 1984. 156 pp., illus. $30.00.

Identification of signatures, family crests, and designs that are encountered on Japanese sword fittings.

Scottish Swords from the Battlefield at Culloden, by Lord Archibald Campbell, The Mowbray Co., Providence, RI, 1973. 63 pp., illus. $12.00.

A modern reprint of an exceedingly rare 1894 privately printed edition.

Secrets of the Samurai, by Oscar Ratti and Adele Westbrook, Charles E. Tuttle Co. Rutland, VT, 1983. 483 pp., illus. $35.00.

A survey of the martial arts of feudal Japan.

Survival/Fighting Knives, by Leroy Thompson, Paladin Press, Boulder, CO, 1986. 104 pp., illus. Paper covers. $14.00.

Covers utility blades, hollow-handled survival knives—both commercial and custom-made—survival kits, folders, combat and street-fighting knives, and knife specs and evaluations.

The Sword in the Age of Chivalry, by R. Ewar Oakeshott, Arms & Armour Press, London, England, 1982. 160 pp., illus. $32.50.

A classic work—the result of 25 years of research by an authority whose work is acknowledged by scholars all over the world.

Sword of the Samurai, by George R. Parulski, Jr., Paladin Press, Boulder, CO, 1985. 144 pp. illus. $21.95.

The classical art of Japanese swordsmanship.

***Swords from Public Collections in the Commonwealth of Pennsylvania,** edited by Bruce S. Bazelon, Andrew Mowbray Inc., Lincoln, RI, 1987. 127 pp., illus. Paper covers. $12.00.

Contains new information regarding swordmakers of the Philadelphia area.

Tomahawks Illustrated, by Robert Kuck, Robert Kuck, New Knoxville, OH, 1977. 112 pp., illus. Paper covers. $10.00.

A pictorial record to provide a reference in selecting and evaluating tomahawks.

World Bayonets 1800 to the Present, by Anthony Carter, Arms & Armour Press, London, England, 1987. 72 pp., illus. $14.95.

Pictures and describes 258 different bayonets and features the latest price guide.

Advanced Muzzleloader's Guide, by Toby Bridges, Stoeger Publishing Co., So. Hackensack, NJ, 1985. 256 pp., illus. Paper covers. $11.95.

The complete guide to muzzle-loading rifles, pistols and shotguns—flintlock and percussion.

***Air Gun Digest, 2nd Edition,** by J.I. Galan, DBI Books, Inc., Northbrook, IL, 1988. 256 pp., illus. Paper covers. $12.95.

Everything from A to Z on air gun history, trends and technology.

The AK47 Story, by Edward Ezell, Stackpole Books, Harrisburg, PA, 1988. 256 pp., illus. Paper covers. $12.95.

Evolution of the Kalashnikov weapons.

American Gunsmiths, by Frank M. Sellers, The Gun Room Press, Highland Park, NJ, 1983. 349 pp. $39.95.
A comprehensive listing of the American gun maker, patentee, gunsmith and entrepreneur.
American Tools of Intrigue, by John Minnery & Jose Ramos, Desert Publications, Cornville, AZ, 1981. 128 pp., illus. Paper covers. $10.00.
Clandestine weapons which the Allies supplied to resistance fighters.
Archer's Digest, 4th Edition, edited by Roger Combs, DBI Books, Inc., Northbrook, IL, 1986. 256 pp., illus. Paper covers. $12.95.
Authoritative information on all facets of the archer's sport.
Assault Pistols, Rifles and Submachine Guns, by Duncan Long, Paladin Press, Boulder, CO, 1986. 152 pp., illus. Paper covers. $19.95.
A detailed guide to modern military, police and civilian combat weapons, both foreign and domestic.
Be an Expert Shot with Rifle or Shotgun, by Clair Rees, Winchester Press, Piscataway, NJ, 1984. 192 pp., illus. $19.95.
The illustrated self-coaching method that turns shooters into fine marksmen.
***Beginner's Guide to Guns and Shooting, Revised Edition,** by Clair F. Rees, DBI Books, Inc., 1988. 224 pp., illus. Paper covers. $12.95.
Indispensable to the beginner, and an enlightened review for the seasoned sportsman.
Benchrest Actions and Triggers, by Stuart Otteson, Wolfe Publishing Co., Inc., Prescott, AZ, 1983. 61 pp., illus. Paper covers. $9.50.
A combined reprinting of the author's "Custom Benchrest Actions" articles which appeared in "Rifle" Magazine.
Buckskins and Black Powder, by Ken Grissom, Winchester Press, Piscataway, NJ, 1983. 224 pp., illus. $15.95.
A mountain man's guide to muzzleloading.
Carbine; The Story of David Marshall "Carbine" Williams, by Ross E. Beard, Jr., The Sandlapper Store, Inc., Lexington, SC, 1977. 315 pp., illus. Deluxe limited edition, numbered and signed by the author and "Carbine." $25.00.
The story of the man who invented the M1 Carbine and holds 52 other firearms patents.
Colonial Riflemen in the American Revolution, by Joe D. Huddleston, George Shumway Publisher, York, PA, 1978. 70 pp., illus. $18.00.
This study traces the use of the longrifle in the Revolution for the purpose of evaluating what effects it had on the outcome.
Competitive Shooting, by A.A. Yuryev, introduction by Gary L. Anderson, NRA Books, The National Rifle Assoc. of America, Wash., DC, 1985. 399 pp., illus. $29.95.
A unique encyclopedia of competitive rifle and pistol shooting.
The Complete Black Powder Handbook, by Sam Fadala, DBI Books, Inc. Northbrook, IL, 1979. 288 pp., illus. Paper covers. $12.95.
Everything you want to know about black powder firearms and their shooting.
Complete Book of Shooting: Rifles, Shotguns, Handguns, by Jack O'Connor, Stackpole Books, Harrisburg, PA, 1983. 392 pp., illus. $24.95.
A thorough guide to each area of the sport, appealing to those with a new or ongoing interest in shooting.
The Complete Book of Target Shooting, by Wes Blair, Stackpole Books, Harrisburg, PA, 1984. 416 pp., illus. $24.95.
The encyclopedia of up-to-date shooting information.
The Complete Book of Thompson Patents, compiled by Don Thomas, The Gun Room Press, Highland Park, NJ, 1981. 482 pp., illus. Paper covers. $15.95.
From John Blish's breech closure patented in 1915 to Charles W. Robin's automatic sear release of 1947. Includes all other firearm patents granted to the developers of the famed "Tommy Gun."
The Complete Book of Trick & Fancy Shooting, by Ernie Lind, The Citadel Press, Secaucus, NJ, 1977. 159 pp., illus. Paper covers. $6.00.
Step-by-step instructions for acquiring the whole range of shooting skills with rifle, pistol and shotgun.
The Complete Encyclopedia of Arms and Weapons, by Leonid Tarassuk and Claude Blair, Charles Scribner's Sons, New York, N.Y., 1983. 560 pp., illus. $41.50.
Describes armor, crossbows, swords, daggers, cannon, pistols, rifles, bayonets, etc. Comprehensive and arranged alphabetically.
The Complete Guide to Game Care and Cookery, by Sam Fadala, DBI Books, Inc., Northbrook, IL, 1981. 288 pp., illus. Paper covers. $12.95.
A step-by-step journey beginning with meat-hunting philosophy and tactics through what to do with the game once you've brought it down. Includes many recipes.
Crossbows, Edited by Roger Combs, DBI Books, Inc., Northbrook, IL, 1986. 192 pp., illus. Paper covers. $10.95.
Complete, up-to-date coverage of the hottest bow going—and the most controversial.
Dead Aim, by Lee Echols, Acme Printing Co., San Diego, CA, a reprint, 1972. 116 pp., illus. $9.95.
Nostalgic antics of hell-raising pistol shooters of the 1930's.
The Encyclopedia of Infantry Weapons of World War II, by Ian V. Hogg, Harper & Row, New York, NY, 1977. 192 pp., illus. $15.95.
A fully comprehensive and illustrated reference work including every major type of weapon used by every army in the world during World War II.
Encyclopedia of Modern Firearms, Vol. 1, compiled and publ. by Bob Brownell, Montezuma, IA, 1959. 1057 pp. plus index, illus. $50.00. Dist. by Bob Brownell, Montezuma, IA 50171.
Massive accumulation of basic information of nearly all modern arms pertaining to "parts and assembly." Replete with arms photographs, exploded drawings, manufacturers' lists of parts, etc.
Experts on Guns & Shooting, by G.T. Teasdale-Buckell, Ashford Press, Southampton, England, 1986. 590 pp., illus. $49.95.
Reprint of the scarce 1900 edition. Covers the great names of today's English gunmakers.
The FP-45 Liberator Pistol, 1942-1945, by R.W. Koch, Research, Arcadia, CA, 1976. 116 pp., illus. $15.00.
A definitive work on this unique clandestine weapon.
***Firearms for Survival,** by Duncan Long, Paladin Press, Boulder, CO, 1988. 144 pp., illus. Paper covers. $16.95.
First complete work on survival firearms for self-defense, hunting, and all-out combat.
Flayderman's Guide to Antique American Firearms and Their Values, 4th Edition, by Norm Flayderman, DBI Books, Inc., Northbrook, IL, 1987. 624 pp., illus. Paper covers. $22.95.
Updated fourth edition of this bible of the antique gun field.
The German Sniper, 1914-1945, by Peter R. Senich, Paladin Press, Boulder, CO, 1982. 468 pp., illus. $49.95.
The development and application of Germany's sniping weapons systems and tactics traced from WW I through WW II.
Good Guns, by Stephen Bodio, Nick Lyons Books, New York, NY, 1986. 128 pp., illus. $14.95.
A celebration of fine sporting guns.
Great Sporting Posters, by Sid Latham, Stackpole Books, Harrisburg, PA, 1980. 48 pp., illus. Paper covers. $19.95.
Twenty-three full-color reproductions of beautiful hunting and fishing poster art, mostly of the early 1900s.
***Gun Digest. 1989, 43rd Edition,** edited by Ken Warner, DBI Books, Inc., Northbrook, IL, 1988. 480 pp., illus. Paper covers. $17.95.
The latest edition of the "World's Greatest Gun Book."
The Gun Digest Book of Assault Weapons, edited by Jack Lewis, DBI Books, Inc., Northbrook, IL, 1986. 256 pp., illus. Paper covers. $12.95.
An in-depth look at the history and uses, test reports.
Gun Digest Book of Holsters and Other Gun Leather, edited by Roger Combs, DBI Books, Inc., Northbrook, IL, 1983. 256 pp., illus. $11.95.
An in-depth look at all facets of leather goods in conjunction with guns. Covers design, manufacture, uses, etc.
***Gun Digest Book of Metallic Silhouette Shooting, 2nd Edition,** by Elgin Gates, DBI Books, Inc., Northbrook, IL, 1979. 256 pp., illus. Paper covers. $11.95.
Examines all aspects of this fast growing sport including history, rules and meets.
Gun Digest Book of Modern Gun Values, 6th Edition, by Jack Lewis, ed. by Harold A. Murtz, DBI Books, Inc., Northbrook, IL, 1987. 448 pp., illus. Paper covers. $15.95.
Updated and expanded edition of the book that's become the standard for valuing modern firearms.
Gun Digest Book of Sporting Dogs, by Carl P. Wood, DBI Books, Inc., Northbrook, IL, 1985. 256 pp., illus. Paper covers. $11.95.
Investigates various training philosophies, problem dogs, training for versatility, kenneling, etc. Covers most all hunting/sporting dogs.
Gun Digest Treasury, 6th Edition, edited by Ken Warner, DBI Books, Inc., Northbrook, IL, 1987. 320 pp., illus. Paper covers. $14.95.
The best articles from the first 40 years of "Gun Digest" are compiled here in one book. Complete indexes for all "Gun Digest," "Guns Illustrated," "Gun Digest Hunting Annual" and "Handloader's Digest" through 1987 editions.
Gunfounding & Gunfounders, by A.N. Kennard, Arms & Armour Press, London, England, 1987. 128 pp., illus. $35.00.
A directory of cannon founders from earliest times to 1850.
***Guns Illustrated 1989, 21st Edition,** edited by Harold A. Murtz, DBI Books, Inc., Northbrook, IL, 1988. 320 pp., illus. Paper covers. $15.95.
The lastest edition of this much acclaimed annual.
Guns, Loads, and Hunting Tips, by Bob Hagel, Wolfe Publishing Co., Prescott, AZ, 1986. 509 pp., illus. $19.95.
A large hardcover book literally packed with shooting, hunting and handloading wisdom.
***Guns and Shooting Yearbook 1988,** by Outdoor Life Magazine editors, Stackpole Books, Harrisburg, PA, 1988. 192 pp., illus. $19.95.
***Guns of the Elite,** by George Markham, Arms and Armour Press, Poole, England, 1987. 184 pp., illus. $24.95.
Special Forces firearms, 1940 to the present.
Gunshot Wounds, by Vincent J.M. DiMaio, M.D., Elsevier Science Publishing Co., New York, NY. 1985. 331 pp. illus. $65.00.
Practical aspects of firearms, ballistics, and forensic techniques.
Gun Talk, edited by Dave Moreton, Winchester Press, Piscataway, NJ, 1973. 256 pp., illus. $9.95.
A treasury of original writing by the top gun writers and editors in America. Practical advice about every aspect of the shooting sports.
The Gun That Made the Twenties Roar, by Wm. J. Helmer, rev. and enlarged by George C. Nonte, Jr., The Gun Room Press, Highland Park, NJ, 1977. Over 300 pp., illus. $17.95.
Historical account of John T. Thompson and his invention, the infamous "Tommy Gun."
The Gunfighter, Man or Myth? by Joseph G. Rosa, Oklahoma Press, Norman, OK, 1969. 229 pp., illus. (including weapons). Paper covers. $9.95.
A well-documented work on gunfights and gunfighters of the West and elsewhere. Great treat for all gunfighter buffs.
The Gunfighters, by Dale T. Schoenberger, The Caxton Printers, Ltd., Caldwell, ID, 1971. 207 pp., illus. $18.95.
Startling expose of our foremost Western folk heroes.
Guns of the American West, by Joseph G. Rosa, Crown Publishers, New York, NY, 1985. 192 pp., illus. $24.95.
More than 300 photos, line drawings and engravings complement this lively account of the taming of the West.
Guns & Shooting: A Selected Bibliography, by Ray Riling, Ray Riling Arms Books Co., Phila., PA, 1982. 434 pp., illus. Limited, numbered edition. $75.00.
A limited edition of this superb bibliographical work, the only modern listing of books devoted to guns and shooting.
Hatcher's Notebook, by Maj. Gen. J. S. Hatcher. Stackpole Books, Harrisburg, Pa., 1952. 2nd ed. with four new chapters, 1957. 629 pp., illus. $24.95.
A dependable source of information for gunsmiths, ballisticians, historians, hunters, and collectors.

GENERAL (cont.)

"Hell, I Was There!", by Elmer Keith, Peterson Publishing Co., Los Angeles, CA, 1979. 308 pp., illus. $19.50.
Adventures of a Montana cowboy who gained world fame as a big game hunter.

Hit the White Part, by Massad Ayoob, Concord, NH, 1982. 107 pp., illus. Paper covers. $7.95.
Second Chance, the art of bowling pin shooting.

How to Make Practical Pistol Leather, by J. David McFarland, Desert Publications, Cornville, AZ. 1982. 68 pp., illus. Paper covers. $8.00.
A guide for designing and making holsters and accessories for law enforcement, security, survival and sporting use.

Instructions to Young Sportsmen, by Lt. Col. Peter Hawker, Ashford Press, Southampton, England, 1986. 507 pp., illus. $39.95.
Facsimile reprint of the classic 7th edition published in 1833.

***Jane's Infantry Weapons 1987-1988, 13th Edition,** edited by Ian Hogg, Jane's Publishing Co., London, England, 1987. 1000 pp., illus. $150.00.
The authoritative guide to major infantry equipment in service worldwide.

Kill or Get Killed, by Col. Rex Applegate, new rev. and enlarged ed. Paladin Press, Boulder, CO, 1976. 421 pp., illus. $19.95.
For police and military forces. Last word on mob control.

The Last Book: Confessions of a Gun Editor, by Jack O'Connor, Amwell Press, Clinton, NJ, 1984. 247 pp., illus. $30.00.
Jack's last book. Semi-autobiographical.

The Law Enforcement Book of Weapons, Ammunition and Training Procedures, Handguns, Rifles and Shotguns, by Mason Williams, Charles C. Thomas, Publisher, Springfield, IL, 1977. 496 pp., illus. $85.00.
Data on firearms, firearm training, and ballistics.

Lyman Muzzleloader's Handbook, 2nd Edition, edited by C. Kenneth Ramage, Lyman Publications, Middlefield, CT, 1982. 248 pp., illus. Paper covers. $11.95.
Hunting with rifles and shotguns, plus muzzle loading products.

The Manufacture of Gunflints, by Sydney B.J. Skertchly, facsimile reprint with new introduction by Seymour de Lotbiniere, Museum Restoration Service, Ontario, Canada, 1984. 90 pp., illus. $24.50.
Limited edition reprinting of the very scarce London edition of 1879.

Master Tips, by J. Winokur, Potshot Press, Pacific Palisades, CA, 1985. 96 pp., illus. Paper covers. $11.95.
Basics of practical shooting.

Meditations on Hunting, by Jose Ortega y Gasset, Charles Scribner's Sons, New York, NY, 1985. 132 pp. Paper covers. $7.95.
Anticipates with profound accuracy the direction and basic formations of discipline which does not yet exist, a true ecology of men. A new printing of this 1942 classic.

Military Small Arms of the 20th Century, 5th Edition, by Ian V. Hogg and John Weeks, DBI Books, Inc., Northbrook, IL, 1985. 304 pp., illus. Paper covers. $16.95.
Fully revised and updated edition of the standard reference in its field.

Modern Airweapon Shooting, by Bob Churchill & Granville Davis, David & Charles, London, England, 1981. 196 pp., illus. $21.00.
A comprehensive, illustrated study of all the relevant topics, from beginnings to world championship shooting.

Modern Law Enforcement Weapons and Tactics, by Wiley M. Clapp, DBI Books, Inc. Northbrook, IL, 1987. 256 pp., illus. Paper covers. $13.95.
An in-depth look at weapons, equipment and tactics used by law enforcement agencies of today.

Modern Rifles, Shotguns and Pistols, by Ian V. Hogg, Exeter Books, New York, NY, 1985. 112 pp., illus. $7.98.
Describes the most interesting recent developments in the design and manufacture of each of these types of weapons.

Modern Small Arms, by Major Frederick Myatt, Crescent Books, New York, NY, 1978. 240 pp., illus. $12.98.
An illustrated encyclopedia of famous military firearms from 1873 to the present day.

No Second Place Winner, by Wm. H. Jordan, publ. by the author, Shreveport, LA (Box 4072), 1962. 114 pp., illus. $12.50.
Guns and gear of the peace officer, ably discussed by a U.S. Border Patrolman for over 30 years, and a first-class shooter with handgun, rifle, etc.

Olson's Encyclopedia of Small Arms, by John Olson, Winchester Press, Piscataway, NJ, 1985. 336 pp., illus. $22.95.
The most complete, authoritative, and up-to-date reference available for shooters, ballisticians, gun collectors, and everyone interested in firearms.

Olympic Shooting, by Colonel Jim Crossman, NRA, Washington, DC, 1978. 136 pp., illus. $12.95.
The complete, authoritative history of U.S. participation in the Olympic shooting events from 1896 until the present.

Outdoor Life's Guns and Shooting Yearbook, 1987, edited by Jim Carmichel, Stackpole Books, Harrisburg, PA, 1987. 190 pp., illus. $19.95.
The 3rd "Yearbook" offering the gun enthusiast not only valuable reference information but also excellent gun and shooting articles.

***Outdoor Life Gun Data Book,** by F. Philip Rice, Outdoor Life Books, N.Y., NY, 1987. 412 pp., illus. $27.95.
All the facts and figures that hunters, marksmen, handloaders and other gun enthusiasts need to know.

E.C. Prudhomme, Master Gun Engraver, A Retrospective Exhibition: 1946-1973, intro. by John T. Amber, The R.W. Norton Art Gallery, Shreveport, LA, 1973. 32 pp., illus., paper covers. $5.00.
Examples of master gun engraving by Jack Prudhomme.

The Quiet Killers II: Silencer Update, by J. David Truby, Paladin Press, Boulder, CO, 1979. 92 pp., illus. Paper covers. $8.00.
A unique and up-to-date addition to your silencer bookshelf.

***A Rifleman Went to War,** by H.W. McBride, Lancer Militaria, Mt. Ida, AR, 1987. 398 pp., illus. $19.95.
The classic account of practical marksmanship on the battlefields of WWI.

***Shooter's Bible, 1989, No. 80,** edited by William Jarrett, Stoeger Publishing Co., So. Hackensack, NJ, 1988. 576 pp. illus. Paper covers. $14.95.
A standard firearms reference book for decades.

The Shooter's Workbench, by John A. Mosher, Winchester Press, Piscataway, NJ, 1977. 256 pp., illus. $22.50.
Accessories the shooting sportsman can build for the range or shop, for transport and the field, and for the handloading bench.

Shooting, by Edward A. Matunas, Stackpole Books, Harrisburg, PA, 1986. 416 pp., illus. $31.95.
How to become an expert marksman with rifle, shotgun, handgun, muzzleloader and bow.

Small Arms Today, by Edward Ezell, Stackpole Books, Harrisburg, PA, 1984. 224 pp., illus. Paper covers. $16.95.
Latest reports on the world's weapons and ammunition.

Small Arms of the World, 12th Edition, by W.H.B. Smith, revised by Edward C. Ezell, Stackpole Books, Harrisburg, PA, 1983. 1,024 pp., illus. $49.95.
An encyclopedia of global weapons—over 3,500 entries.

The SPIW: Deadliest Weapon that Never Was, by R. Blake Stevens, and Edward C. Ezell, Collector Grade Publications, Inc., Toronto, Canada, 1985. 138 pp., illus. $29.95.
The complete saga of the fantastic flechette-firing Special Purpose Individual Weapon.

Sporting Arms of the World, by Ray Bearse, Outdoor Life/Harper & Row, N.Y., 1977. 500 pp., illus. $15.95.
A mammoth, up-to-the-minute guide to the sporting world's favorite rifles, shotguns, handguns.

Steindler's New Firearms Dictionary, by R.A. Steindler, Stackpole Books, Inc., Harrisburg, PA, 1985. 320 pp., illus. $24.95.
Completely revised and updated edition of this standard work.

The Street Smart Gun Book, by John Farnam, Police Bookshelf, Concord, NH, 1986. 45 pp., illus. Paper covers. $11.95.
Weapon selection, defensive shooting techniques, and gunfight-winning tactics from one of the world's leading authorities.

Stress Fire, Vol. 1: Stress Fighting for Police, by Massad Ayoob, Police Bookshelf, Concord, NH, 1984. 149 pp., illus. Paper covers. $9.95.
Gunfighting for police, advanced tactics and techniques.

***Survival Guns,** by Mel Tappan, the Janus Press, Rouge River, OR, 1987. 458 pp., illus. Paper covers. $14.95.
A guide to the selection, modification and use of firearms and related devices for defense, food gathering, predator and pest control under conditions of long term survival.

Thompson Guns 1921-1945, Anubis Press, Houston, TX, 1980. 215 pp., illus. Paper covers. $10.00.
Facsimile reprinting of five complete manuals on the Thompson submachine gun.

The Trapper's Handbook, by Rick Jamison, DBI Books, Inc., Northbrook, IL, 1983. 224 pp., illus. Paper covers. $12.95.
Gives the ins and outs of successful trapping from making scent to marketing the pelts. Tips and solutions to trapping problems.

A Treasury of Outdoor Life, edited by William E. Rae, Stackpole Books, Harrisburg, PA, 1983. 520 pp., illus. $24.95.
The greatest hunting, fishing, and survival stories from America's favorite sportsman's magazine.

Triggernometry, by Eugene Cunningham. Caxton Printers Lt., Caldwell, ID, 1970. 441 pp., illus. $14.95.
A classic study of famous outlaws and lawmen of the West—their stature as human beings, their exploits and skills in handling firearms. A reprint.

***Vietnam Weapons Handbook,** by David Rosser-Owen, Patrick Stephens, Wellingborough, England, 1986. 136 pp., illus. Paper covers. $9.95.
Covers every weapon used by both sides.

Weapons of the American Revolution, and Accoutrements, by Warren Moore. A & W Books, NY, 1974. 225 pp., fine illus. $25.00.
Revolutionary era shoulder arms, pistols, edged weapons, and equipment are described and shown in fine drawings and photographs, some in color.

The Winchester Era, by David Madis, Art & Reference House, Brownsville, TX, 1984. 100 pp., illus. $14.95.
Story of the Winchester company, management, employees, etc.

You Can't Miss, by John Shaw and Michael Bane, John Shaw, Memphis, TN, 1983. 152 pp., illus. Paper covers. $9.95.
The secrets of a successful combat shooter; tells how to better your defensive shooting skills.

The Art of Engraving, by James B. Meek, F. Brownell & Son, Montezuma, IA, 1973. 196 pp., illus. $29.95.
A complete, authoritative, imaginative and detailed study in training for gun engraving. The first book of its kind—and a great one.

Artistry in Arms, The R.W. Norton Gallery, Shreveport, LA., 1970. 42 pp., illus. Paper, $5.00.
The art of gunsmithing and engraving.

Building the Kentucky Pistol, by James R. Johnston, Golden Age Arms Co., Worthington, OH, 1974. 36 pp., illus. Paper covers. $4.00.
A step-by-step guide for building the Kentucky pistol. Illus. with full page line drawings.

Building the Kentucky Rifle, by J.R. Johnston. Golden Age Arms Co., Worthington, OH, 1972. 44 pp., illus. Paper covers. $5.00.
How to go about it, with text and drawings.

Checkering and Carving of Gun Stocks, by Monte Kennedy. Stackpole Books, Harrisburg, PA, 1962. 175 pp., illus. $27.95.
Rev., enlarged clothbound ed. of a much sought-after, dependable work.

Clyde Baker's Modern Gunsmithing, revised by John E. Traister, Stackpole Books, Harrisburg, PA, 1981. 530 pp., illus. $24.95.
A revision of the classic work on gunsmithing.

***The Colt .45 Automatic Shop Manual,** by Jerry Kuhnhausen, VSP Publishers, McCall, ID, 1987. 200 pp., illus. Paper covers. $19.95.
Covers repairing, accurizing, trigger/sear work, action tuning, springs, bushings, rebarreling, and custom .45 modification.

The Complete Rehabilitation of the Flintlock Rifle and Other Works, by T.B. Tyron. Limbo Library, Taos, NM, 1972. 112 pp., illus. Paper covers. $6.95.
A series of articles which first appeared in various issues of the "American Rifleman" in the 1930s.

Contemporary American Stockmakers, by Ron Toews, The Dove Press, Enid, OK, 1979. 216 pp., illus. $80.00.
The only reference book on its subject. Over 200 detailed photographs of fine rifle stocking.

The Craft of the Gunsmith, by G.W. Spearing, Blandford Press, Dorset, England, 1987. 144 pp., illus. $14.95.
A world master gunsmith reveals his secrets of building, repairing and renewing a gun, quite literally, lock, stock and barrel.

Do-It-Yourself Gunsmithing, by Jim Carmichel, Outdoor Life-Harper & Row, New York, NY, 1977. 371 pp., illus. $16.95.
The author proves that home gunsmithing is relatively easy and highly satisfying.

Firearms Assembly 3: The NRA Guide to Rifle and Shotguns, NRA Books, Wash., D.C., 1980. 264 pp., illus. Paper covers. $11.50.
Text and illustrations explaining the takedown of 125 rifles and shotguns, domestic and foreign.

Firearms Assembly 4: The NRA Guide to Pistols and Revolvers, NRA Books, Wash., D.C., 1980. 253 pp., illus. Paper covers. $11.50.
Text and illustrations explaining the takedown of 124 pistol and revolver models, domestic and foreign.

Firearms Blueing and Browning, by R.H. Angier. Stackpole Books, Harrisburg, PA, 151 pp., illus. $12.95.
A useful, concise text on chemical coloring methods for the gunsmith and mechanic.

First Book of Gunsmithing, by John E. Traister, Stackpole Books, Harrisburg, PA, 1981. 192 pp., illus. $18.95.
Beginner's guide to gun care, repair and modification.

Gun Care and Repair, by Monte Burch, Winchester Press, Piscataway, NJ, 1978. 256 pp., illus. $15.95.
Everything the gun owner needs to know about home gunsmithing and firearms maintenance.

The Gun Digest Book of Firearms Assembly/Disassembly Part I: Automatic Pistols, by J.B. Wood, DBI Books, Inc., Northbrook, IL, 1979. 320 pp., illus. Paper covers. $12.95.
A thoroughly professional presentation on the art of pistol disassembly and reassembly. Covers most modern guns, popular older models, and some of the most complex pistols ever produced.

The Gun Digest Book of Firearms Assembly/Disassembly Part II: Revolvers, by J. B. Wood, DBI Books, Inc., Northbrook, IL, 1979. 320 pp., illus. Paper covers. $12.95.
How to properly dismantle and reassemble both the revolvers of today and of the past.

The Gun Digest Book of Firearms Assembly/Disassembly Part III: Rimfire Rifles, by J. B. Wood, DBI Books, Inc., Northbrook, IL, 1980. 288 pp., illus. Paper covers. $12.95.
A most comprehensive, uniform, and professional presentation available for disassembling and reassembling most rimfire rifles.

The Gun Digest Book of Firearms Assembly/Disassembly Part IV: Centerfire Rifles, by J. B. Wood, DBI Books, Inc., Northbrook, IL, 1980. 288 pp., illus. Paper covers. $12.95.
A professional presentation on the disassembly and reassembly of centerfire rifles.

The Gun Digest Book of Firearms Assembly/Disassembly, Part V: Shotguns, by J.B. Wood, DBI Books, Inc., Northbrook, IL, 1980. 288 pp., illus. Paper covers. $12.95.
A professional presentation on the complete disassembly and assembly of 26 of the most popular shotguns, new and old.

The Gun Digest Book of Firearms Assembly/Disassembly Part VI: Law Enforcement Weapons, by J.B. Wood, DBI Books, Inc., Northbrook, IL, 1981. 288 pp., illus. Paper covers. $12.95.
Step-by-step instructions on how to completely dismantle and reassemble the most commonly used firearms found in law enforcement arsenals.

Gun Digest Book of Gun Care, Cleaning and Refinishing, Book One: Handguns, by J.B. Wood, DBI Books, Inc., Northbrook, IL, 1984. 160 pp., illus. Paper covers. $9.95.
The how, when and why of proper maintenance: revolvers, autoloaders, blackpowder handguns.

Gun Digest Book of Gun Care, Cleaning and Refinishing, Book Two: Long Guns, by J.B. Wood, DBI Books, Inc., Northbrook, IL, 1984. 160 pp., illus. Paper covers. $9.95.
The care and maintenance of long guns with meticulous detail and step-by-step, illustrated, clearly written text.

The Gun Digest Book of Pistolsmithing, by Jack Mitchell, DBI Books, Inc., Northbrook, IL, 1980. 288 pp., illus. Paper covers. $12.95.
An expert's guide to the operation of each of the handgun actions with all the major functions of pistolsmithing explained.

Gun Digest Book of Riflesmithing, by Jack Mitchell, DBI Books, Inc., Northbrook, IL, 1982. 256 pp., illus. Paper covers. $12.95.
The art and science of rifle gunsmithing. Covers tools, techniques, designs, finishing wood and metal, custom alterations.

Gun Digest Book of Shotgun Gunsmithing, by Ralph Walker, DBI Books, Inc., Northbrook, IL, 1983. 256 pp., illus. Paper covers. $12.95.
The principles and practices of repairing, individualizing and accurizing modern shotguns by one of the world's premier shotgun gunsmiths.

Gun Owner's Book of Care, Repair & Improvement, by Roy Dunlap, Outdoor Life-Harper & Row, NY, 1977. 336 pp., illus. $12.95.
A basic guide to repair and maintenance of guns, written for the average firearms owner.

Guns and Gunmaking Tools of Southern Appalachia, by John Rice Irwin, Schiffer Publishing Ltd., 1983. 118 pp., illus. Paper covers. $9.95.
The story of the Kentucky rifle.

Gunsmith Kinks, by F.R. (Bob) Brownell. F. Brownell & Son, Montezuma, IA, 1st ed., 1969. 496 pp., well illus. $12.95.
A widely useful accumulation of shop kinks, short cuts, techniques and pertinent comments by practicing gunsmiths from all over the world.

Gunsmith Kinks 2, by Bob Brownell, F. Brownell & Son, Publishers, Montezuma, IA, 1983. 496 pp., illus. $14.95.
An incredible collection of gunsmithing knowledge, shop kinks, new and old techniques, short-cuts and general know-how straight from those who do them best—the gunsmiths.

Gunsmithing, by Roy F. Dunlap. Stackpole Books, Harrisburg, PA, 714 pp., illus. $27.95.
Comprehensive work on conventional techniques, incl. recent advances in the field. Valuable to rifle owners, shooters, and practicing gunsmiths.

Gunsmithing at Home, by John E. Traister, Stoeger Publishing Co., So. Hackensack, NJ, 1985. 256 pp., illus. Paper covers. $11.95.
Over 25 chapters of explicit information on every aspect of gunsmithing.

***Gunsmithing With Simple Hand Tools,** by Andrew Dubino, Stackpole Books, Harrisburg, PA, 1987. 205 pp., illus. $19.95.
How to repair, improve, and add a touch of class to the guns you own.

The Gunsmith's Manual, by J.P. Stelle and Wm.B. Harrison, The Gun Room Press, Highland Park, NJ, 1982. 376 pp., illus. $15.00.
For the gunsmith in all branches of the trade.

Gunstock Finishing and Care, by A. Donald Newell, Stackpole Books, Harrisburg, PA, 1982. 512 pp., illus. $22.95.
The most complete resource imaginable for finishing and refinishing gun wood.

Home Gun Care & Repair, by P.O. Ackley, Stackpole Books, Harrisburg, PA, 1969. 191 pp., illus. Paper covers. $6.95.
Basic reference for safe tinkering, fixing, and converting rifles, shotguns, handguns.

Home Gunsmithing Digest, 3rd Edition, by Tommy L. Bish, DBI Books, Inc., Northbrook, IL, 1984. 256 pp., illus. Paper covers. $12.95.
The know-how supplied by an expert.

How to Build Your Own Wheellock Rifle or Pistol, by George Lauber, The John Olson Co., Paramus, NJ, 1976. Paper covers. $12.50.
Complete instructions on building these arms.

How to Build Your Own Flintlock Rifle or Pistol, by George Lauber, The John Olson Co., Paramus, NJ, 1976. Paper covers. $12.50.
The second in Mr. Lauber's three-volume series on the art and science of building muzzle-loading black powder firearms.

How to Build Your Own Percussion Rifle or Pistol, by George Lauber, The John Olson Co., Paramus, NJ, 1976. Paper covers, $12.50.
The third and final volume of Lauber's set of books on the building of muzzle-loaders.

Learn Gunsmithing, by John Traister, Winchester Press, Piscataway, NJ, 1980. 202 pp., illus. $16.95.
The troubleshooting method of gunsmithing for the home gunsmith and professional alike.

The Modern Kentucky Rifle, How to Build Your Own, by R.H. McCrory. McCrory, Wantagh, NY, 1961. 68 pp., illus., paper bound. $6.00.
A workshop manual on how to fabricate a flintlock rifle. Also some information on pistols and percussion locks.

The NRA Gunsmithing Guide—Updated, by Ken Raynor and Brad Fenton, National Rifle Association, Wash., DC, 1984. 336 pp., illus. Paper covers. $15.95.
Material includes chapters and articles on all facets of the gunsmithing art.

Pistolsmithing, by George C. Nonte, Jr., Stackpole Books, Harrisburg, PA, 1974. 560 pp., illus. $27.95.
A single source reference to handgun maintenance, repair, and modification at home, unequaled in value.

Recreating the American Longrifle, by William Buchele, et al, George Shumway, Publisher, York, PA, 1983. 175 pp., illus. Paper covers. $20.00; Cloth $27.50.
Includes full-scale plans for building a Kentucky rifle.

Respectfully Yours H.M. Pope, compiled and edited by G.O. Kelver, Brighton, CO, 1976. 266 pp., illus. $16.50.
A compilation of letters from the files of the famous barrelmaker, Harry M. Pope.

***The S&W Revolver: A Shop Manual,** by Jerry Kuhnhausen, VSP Publishers, McCall, ID, 1987. 152 pp., illus. Paper covers. $19.95.
Covers accurizing, trigger jobs, action tuning, rebarreling, barrel setback, forcing cone angles, polishing and rebluing.

Survival Gunsmithing, by J.B. Wood, Desert Publicatios, Cornville, AZ, 1986. 92 pp., illus. Paper covers. $9.95.
A guide to repair and maintenance of many of the most popular rifles, shotguns and handguns.

The Trade Gun Sketchbook, by Charles E. Hanson, The Fur Press, Chadron, NB, 1979. 48 pp., illus. Paper covers. $4.00.
Complete full-size plans to build seven different trade guns from the Revolution to the Indian Wars and a two-thirds size for your son.

The Trade Rifle Sketchbook, by Charles E. Hanson, The Fur Press, Chadron, NB, 1979. 48 pp., illus. Paper covers. $4.00.
Includes full scale plans for ten rifles made for Indian and mountain men; from 1790 to 1860, plus plans for building three pistols.

American Pistol and Revolver Design and Performance, by L. R. Wallack, Winchester Press, Piscataway, NJ, 1978. 224 pp., illus. $19.95.
How different types and models of pistols and revolvers work, from trigger pull to bullet impact.
American Police Handgun Training, by Charles R. Skillen and Mason Williams, Charles C. Thomas, Springfield, IL, 1980. 216 pp., illus. $32.50.
Deals comprehensively with all phases of current handgun training procedures in America.
Askins on Pistols and Revolvers, by Col. Charles Askins, NRA Books, Wash., D.C., 1980. 144 pp., illus. Paper covers. $14.95.
A book full of practical advice, shooting tips, technical analysis and stories of guns in action.
Automatics, Fast Firepower, Tactical Superiority, by Duncan Long, Paladin Press, Boulder, CO, 1986. 136 pp., illus. Paper covers. $14.95.
The plus and minuses of dozens of automatic pistols are presented. Field stripping procedures for various pistol models are given.
Blue Steel and Gun Leather, by John Bianchi, Beinfeld Publishing, Inc., No. Hollywood, CA, 1978. 200 pp., illus. $12.95.
A complete and comprehensive review of holster uses plus an examination of available products on today's market.
Browning Hi-Power Pistols, Desert Publications, Cornville, AZ, 1982. 20 pp., illus. Paper covers. $6.00.
Covers all facets of the various military and civilian models of this gun.
The Browning High Power Automatic Pistol, by R. Blake Stevens, Collector Grade Publications, Toronto,Canada, 1984. 271 pp., illus. $39.95.
Exhaustive new treatise on this famous automatic pistol.
Colt Automatic Pistols, by Donald B. Bady, Borden Publ. Co., Alhambra, CA, 1974. 368 pp., illus. $19.95.
The rev. and enlarged ed. of a key work on a fascinating subject. Complete information on every automatic marked with Colt's name.
The Colt .45 Auto Pistol, compiled from U.S. War Dept. Technical Manuals, and reprinted by Desert Publications, Cornville, AZ, 1978. 80 pp., illus. Paper covers. $7.50.
Covers every facet of this famous pistol from mechanical training, manual of arms, disassembly, repair and replacement of parts.
***Combat Guns,** edited by Chris Bishop and Ian Drury, Chartwell Books, Inc., Secaucus, NJ, 1987. 286 pp., illus. $22.95.
An illustrated encyclopedia of 20th century firearms.
Combat Handguns, edited by Edward C. Ezell, Stackpole Books, Harrisburg, PA, 1980. 288 pp., illus. $19.95.
George Nonte's last great work, edited by Edward C. Ezell. A comprehensive reference volume offering full coverage of automatic handguns vs. revolvers, custom handguns, combat autoloaders and revolvers—domestic and foreign, and combat testing.
Combat Shooting for Police, by Paul B. Weston. Charles C. Thomas, Springfield, IL, 1967. A reprint. 194 pp., illus. $35.50.
First publ. in 1960 this popular self-teaching manual gives basic concepts of defensive fire in every position.
The Complete Book of Combat Handgunning, by Chuck Taylor, Desert Publications, Cornville, AZ, 1982. 168 pp., illus. Paper covers. $16.95.
Covers virtually every aspect of combat handgunning.
Consumer's Guide to Handguns, by Aaron S. Zelman and Lt. Michael L. Neuens, Stackpole Books, Harrisburg, PA, 1986. 208 pp., illus. Paper covers. $16.95.
Tough, unbiased test reports show you which guns are reliable and your best values.
The Defensive Use of the Handgun for the Novice, by Mason Williams, Charles C. Thomas, Publisher, Springfield, IL, 1980. 226 pp., illus. $35.00.
This book was developed for the home owner, housewife, elderly couple, and the woman who lives alone. Basic instruction for purchasing, loading and firing pistols and revolvers.
Fast and Fancy Revolver Shooting, by Ed. McGivern, Anniversary Edition, Winchester Press, Piscataway, NJ, 1984. 484 pp., illus. $15.95.
A fascinating volume, packed with handgun lore and solid information by the acknowledged dean of revolver shooters.
Flattops & Super Blackhawks, by H.W. Ross, Jr., H.W. Ross, Jr., Bridgeville, PA, 1979. 93 pp., illus. Paper covers. $9.95.
An expanded version of the author's book "Ruger Blackhawks" with an extra chapter on Super Blackhawks and the Mag-Na-Ports with serial numbers and approximate production dates.
***Great Combat Handguns,** by Leroy Thompson and Rene Smeets, Blandford Press, Poole, England, 1987. 224 pp., illus. $29.95.
A guide to using, collecting and training with handguns.
The Gun Digest Book of Combat Handgunnery, by Jack Lewis and Jack Mitchell, DBI Books, Inc., Northbrook, IL, 1983. 288 pp., illus. Paper covers. $12.95.
From the basics to competition, training and exercises.
Gun Digest Book of Firearms Assembly/Disassembly Part I: Automatic Pistols, by J.B. Wood, DBI Books, Inc., Northbrook, IL, 1979. 320 pp., illus. Paper covers. $12.95.
A thoroughly professional presentation on the art of pistol disassembly and reassembly. Covers most modern guns, popular older models, and some of the most complex pistols ever produced.
Gun Digest Book of Firearms Assembly/Disassembly Part II: Revolvers, by J.B. Wood, DBI Books, Inc., Northbrook, IL, 1979. 320 pp., illus. Paper covers. $12.95.
How to properly dismantle and reassemble both the revolvers of today and of the past.
Gun Digest Book of Gun Care, Cleaning and Refinishing, Book One: Handguns, by J.B. Wood, DBI Books, Inc., Northbrook, IL, 1984. 160 pp., illus. Paper covers. $9.95.
The how, when and why of proper maintenance: revolvers, autoloaders, blackpowder handguns.
Gun Digest Book of Handgun Reloading, by Dean A. Grennell and Wiley M. Clapp, DBI Books, Inc., Northbrook, IL, 1987. 256 pp., illus. Paper covers. $12.95.
Detailed discussions of all aspects of reloading for handguns, from basic to complex. New loading data.
***Gun Digest Book of Metallic Silhouette Shooting, 2nd Edition,** by Elgin Gates, DBI Books, Inc., Northbrook, IL, 1988. 256 pp., illus. Paper covers. $12.95.
All about the rapidly growing sport. With a history and rules of the International Handgun Metallic Silhouette Association.
The Gun Digest Book of 9mm Handguns, by Dean A. Grennell and Wiley Clapp, DBI Books, Inc., Northbrook, IL, 1986. 256 pp., illus. Paper covers. $12.95
The definitive book on the 9mm pistol.
The Gun Digest Book of Pistolsmithing, by Jack Mitchell, DBI Books, Inc., Northbrook, IL, 1980. 288 pp., illus. Paper covers. $12.95.
An expert's guide to the operation of each of the handgun actions with all the major functions of pistolsmithing explained.
Hallock's .45 Auto Handbook, by Ken Hallock, The Mihan Co., Oklahoma City, OK, 1981. 178 pp., illus. Paper covers. $11.95.
For gunsmiths, dealers, collectors and serious hobbyists.
Handgun Digest, 1st Edition, by Dean A. Grennell, DBI Books, Inc., Northbrook, IL, 1987. 256 pp., illus. Paper covers. $12.95.
Full coverage of all aspects of handguns and handgunning from a highly readable, knowledgable author.
***Handguns '89,** by Wiley Clapp, DBI Books, Inc., Northbrook, IL, 1988. 224 pp., illus. Paper covers. $12.95.
A new annual giving a complete overview of handguns.
Handguns for Self Defence, by Gerry Gore, Macmillan South Africa, Johannesburg, South Africa, 1981. 164 pp., illus. Paper covers. $15.00.
Choosing the gun, basic skills, the draws, stopping power, etc.
Handguns of the World, by Edward C. Ezell, Stackpole Books, Harrisburg, PA., 1981. 704 pp., illus. $39.95.
Encyclopedia for identification and historical reference that will be appreciated by gun enthusiasts, collectors, hobbyists or professionals.
High Standard Automatic Pistols 1932-1950, by Charles E. Petty, American Ordnance Publ., Charlotte, NC, 1976. 124 pp., illus. $20.00.
A definitive source of information for the collector of High Standard pistols.
The Illustrated Encyclopedia of Pistols and Revolvers, by Major Frederick Myatt, Crescent Books, New York, NY, 1980. 208 pp., illus. $14.95.
An illustrated history of handguns from the 16th century to the present day.
Know Your 45 Auto Pistols—Models 1911 & A1, by E.J. Hoffschmidt, Blacksmith Corp., Southport, CT, 1974. 58 pp., illus. Paper covers. $6.95.
A concise history of the gun with a wide variety of types and copies.
Know Your Walther P.38 Pistols, by E.J. Hoffschmidt, Blacksmith Corp., Southport, CT, 1974. 77 pp., illus. Paper covers. $6.95.
Covers the Walther models Armee, M.P., H.P., P.38—history and variations.
Know Your Walther PP & PPK Pistols, by E.J. Hoffschmidt, Blacksmith Corp., Southport, CT, 1975. 87 pp., illus. Paper covers. $6.95.
A concise history of the guns with a guide to the variety and types.
The Luger Pistol (Pistole Parabellum), by F.A. Datig. Borden Publ. Co., Alhambra, CA, 1962. 328 pp., well illus. $19.95.
An enlarged, rev. ed. of an important reference on the arm, its history and development from 1893 to 1945.
Luger Variations, by Harry E. Jones, Harry E. Jones, Torrance, CA, 1975. 328 pp., 160 full page illus., many in color. $35.00.
A rev. ed. of the book known as "The Luger Collector's Bible."
Lugers at Random, by Charles Kenyon, Jr., Handgun Press, Glenview, IL, 1st ed., 1970. 416 pp., profusely illus. $29.95.
An impressive large side-opening book carrying throughout alternate facing-pages of descriptive text and clear photographs. A new boon to the Luger collector and/or shooter.
The M1911A1 Automatic Pistol: Proud American Legend, edited by the American Historical Foundation, Richmond, VA, 1985. 240 pp., illus. Paper covers. $8.95.
Contains reprints of rare government manuals, combat photographs and original works by the foundation staff.
Mauser Pocket Pistols 1910-1946, by Roy G. Pender, Collectors Press, Houston, TX, 1971. 307 pp. $25.00.
Comprehensive work covering over 100 variations, including factory boxes and manuals. Over 300 photos. Limited, numbered ed.
The Mauser Self-Loading Pistol, by Belford & Dunlap, Borden Publ. Co., Alhambra, CA. Over 200 pp., 300 illus., large format. $18.95.
The long-awaited book on the "Broom Handles," covering their inception in 1894 to the end of production. Complete and in detail: pocket pistols, Chinese and Spanish copies, etc.
Modern American Centerfire Handguns, by Stanley W. T. Trzoniec, Winchester Press, Piscataway, NJ, 1981. 260 pp., illus. $24.95.
The most comprehensive reference on handguns in print.
The New Handbook of Handgunning, by Paul B. Weston, Charles C. Thomas, Publisher, Springfield, IL, 1980. 102 pp., illus. $22.50.
A step-by-step, how-to manual of handgun shooting.
The Pistol Book, by John Walter, Arms & Armour Press, London, England, 1983. 176 pp., illus. $19.95.
A concise and copiously illustrated guide to the handguns available today.
The Pistol Guide, by George C. Nonte, Stoeger Publ. Co., So. Hackensack, NJ, 1980. 256 pp., illus. Paper covers. $10.95.
A unique and detailed examination of a very specialized type of gun: the autoloading pistol.

HANDGUNS (cont.)

Pistol & Revolver Guide, 3rd Ed., by George C. Nonte, Stoeger Publ. Co., So. Hackensack, NJ, 1975. 224 pp., illus. Paper covers. $6.95.
The standard reference work on military and sporting handguns.
Police Handgun Manual, by Bill Clede, Stackpole Books, Inc., Harrisburg, PA, 1985. 128 pp., illus. $13.95.
How to get street-smart survival habits.
Quick or Dead, by William L. Cassidy, Paladin Press, Boulder, CO, 1978. 178 pp., illus. $12.95.
Close-quarter combat firing, with particular reference to prominent twentieth-century British and American methods of instruction.
Report of Board on Tests of Revolvers and Automatic Pistols. From the *Annual Report* of the Chief of Ordnance, 1907. Reprinted by J.C. Tillinghast, Marlow, NH, 1969. 34 pp., 7 plates, paper covers. $5.00.
A comparison of handguns, including Luger, Savage, Colt, Webley-Fosbery and other makes.
Revolvers, by Ian V. Hogg, Arms & Armour Press, London, England, 1984. 72 pp., illus. $14.95.
An illustrated guide with prices based on recent auction records.
Revolver Guide, by George C. Nonte, Jr., Stoeger Publishing Co., So. Hackensack, NJ, 1980. 288 pp., illus. Paper covers. $10.95.
Fully illustrated guide to selecting, shooting, caring for and collecting revolvers of all types.
Ruger Automatic Pistols and Single Action Revolvers, Book 3, by Hugo A. Lueders, Blacksmith Corp., Southport, CT, 1983. 95 pp., illus. Paper covers. $17.50.
A key reference for every Ruger enthusiast, collector and dealer.
Shoot a Handgun, by Dave Arnold, PVA Books, Canyon County, CA, 1983. 144 pp., illus. Paper covers. $8.95.
A complete manual of simplified handgun instruction.
Shoot to Win, by John Shaw, Blacksmith Corp, Southport, CT, 1985. 160 pp., illus. Paper covers. $9.95.
The lessons taught here are of interest and value to all handgun shooters.
Sixgun Cartridges and Loads, by Elmer Keith, reprint edition by The Gun Room Press, Highland Park, NJ, 1984. 151 pp., illus. $19.95.
A manual covering the selection, use and loading of the most suitable and popular revolver cartridges.
Skeeter Skelton's Handgun Tales, by Skeeter Skelton, PJS Publications, Peoria, IL, 1984. 114 pp., illus. $12.50.
Skelton's favorite holsters and handguns, etc.
Target Pistol Shooting, by K.B. Hinchliffe, David and Charles, London, 1981. 235 pp., illus. $28.00.
A complete guide to target shooting designed to give the novice and expert guidance on the correct techniques for holding, aiming, and firing pistols.
The Walther P-38 Pistol, by Maj. Geo. C. Nonte, Paladin Press, Boulder, CO, 1975. 90 pp., illus. Paper covers. $7.50.
Covers all facets of the gun—development, history, variations, technical data, practical use, rebuilding, repair and conversion.
The Women's Guide to Handguns, by Jim Carmichel, Stoeger Publishing Co., So. Hackensack, NJ, 1984. 190 pp., illus. Paper covers. $8.95.
For women interested in learning how to select, buy, store, carry, care for and use a handgun.

NORTH AMERICA

***Advanced Deer Hunting,** by John Weiss, Stackpole Books, Harrisburg, PA, 1988. 352 pp., illus. $28.95.
New strategies based on the latest studies of whitetail behavior.
Advanced Wild Turkey Hunting & World Records, by Dave Harbour, Winchester Press, Piscataway, NJ, 1983. 264 pp., illus. $19.95.
The definitive book, written by an authority who has studied turkeys and turkey calling for over 40 years.
After Your Deer is Down, by Josef Fischl and Leonard Lee Rue, III, Winchester Press, Piscataway, NJ, 1981. 160 pp., illus. Paper covers. $10.95.
The care and handling of big game, with a bonus of venison recipes.
Alaska Game Trails with a Master Guide, by Charles J. Keim, Alaska Northwest Publishing Co., Anchorage, AK, 1984. 310 pp., illus. Paper covers. $6.95.
High adventure tales of fair chase with Alaska's first master guide, Hal Waugh.
***Alaska Wilderness Hunter,** by Harold Schetzle, Great Northwest Publishing and Distributing Co., Anchorage, AK, 1987. 224 pp., illus. $19.95.
A superb collection of Alaska hunting adventures by master guide Harold Schetzle.
All About Deer in America, edited by Robert Elman, Winchester Press, Piscataway, NJ, 1976. 256 pp., illus. $15.95.
Twenty of America's great hunters share the secrets of their hunting success.
All About Small-Game Hunting in America, edited by Russell Tinsley, Winchester Press, Piscataway, NJ, 1976. 308 pp., illus. $16.95.
Collected advice by the finest small-game experts in the country.
All About Varmint Hunting, by Nick Sisley, The Stone Wall Press, Inc., Wash., DC, 1982. 182 pp., illus. Paper covers. $8.95.
The most comprehensive up-to-date book on hunting common varmints found throughout North America.
All About Wildfowling in America, by Jerome Knap, Winchester Press, Piscataway, NJ, 1977. 256 pp., illus. $13.95.
More than a dozen top writers provide new and controversial ideas on how and where to hunt waterfowl successfully.
All-American Deer Hunter's Guide, edited by Jim Zumbo and Robert Elman, Winchester Press, Piscataway, NJ, 1983. 320 pp., illus. $29.95.
The most comprehensive, book yet published on American deer hunting.
All Season Hunting, by Bob Gilsvik, Winchester Press, Piscataway, NJ, 1976. 256 pp., illus. $14.95.
A guide to early-season, late-season and winter hunting in America.
Art and Science of Whitetail Hunting, by Kent Horner, Stackpole Books, Harrisburg, PA, 1986. 192 pp., illus. Paper covers. $11.95.
How to interpret the facts and find deer.
Bear Hunting, by Jerry Meyer, Stackpole Books, Harrisburg, PA, 1983. 224 pp., illus. $16.95.
First complete guide on the how-to's of bear hunting. Information on every type of bear found in the U.S. and Canada.
Bear in Their World, by Erwin Bauer, an Outdoor Life Book, New York, NY, 1985. 254 pp., illus. $32.95.
Covers all North American bears, including grizzlies, browns, blacks, and polars.
The Best of Babcock, by Havilah Babcock, selected and with an introduction by Hugh Grey, The Gunnerman Press, Auburn Hills, MI, 1985. 262 pp., illus. $19.95.
A treasury of memorable pieces, 21 of which have never before appeared in book form.
The Best of Nash Buckingham, by Nash Buckingham, selected, edited and annotated by George Bird Evans, Winchester Press, Piscataway, NJ, 1973. 320 pp., illus. $17.95.
Thirty pieces that represent the very cream of Nash's output on his whole range of outdoor interests—upland shooting, duck hunting, even fishing.
The Best of Jack O'Connor, by Jack O'Connor, Amwell Press, Clinton, NJ, 1984. 192 pp., illus. $27.50.
A collection of Jack O'Connor's finest writings.
The Best of Sheep Hunting, compiled by John Batten, Amwell Press, Clinton, NJ, 1986. 250 pp., illus. $37.50.
An anthology of the finest stories on international sheep hunting ever compiled.
***Big Game, Big Country,** by Dr. Chauncey Guy Suits, Great Northwest Publishing and Distributing Co., Anchorage, AK, 1987. 224 pp., illus. $19.95.
Chronicals more than a decade of high-quality wilderness hunting by one of this country's more distinguished big game hunters.
Big Game of North America, Ecology and Management, by Wildlife Management Institute, Stackpole Books, Harrisburg, PA, 1983. 512 pp., illus. $34.95.
An outstanding reference for professionals and students of wildlife management.
Big Game Record of British Columbia, compiled by the Trophy Wildlife Records Club of British Columbia, Nanoose, British Columbia, 1983. 216 pp., illus. $35.00.
The official record book for native big game trophies taken in British Columbia.
Bird Hunting with Dalrymple, by Byron W. Dalrymple, Stackpole Books, Harrisburg, PA, 1986. 256 pp., illus. $24.95.
The rewards of shotgunning across North America.
The Bobwhite Quail Book, Compiled by Lamar Underwood, Amwell Press, Clinton, NJ, 1981. 442 pp., illus. $25.00.
An anthology of the finest stories on Bobwhite quail ever assembled under one cover.
Bobwhite Quail Hunting, by Charley Dickey, printed for Stoeger Publ. Co., So. Hackensack, NJ, 1974. 112 pp., illus., paper covers. $3.95.
Habits and habitats, techniques, gear, guns and dogs.
The Book of the Wild Turkey, by Lovett E. Williams, Jr., Winchester Press, Piscataway, NJ, 1981. 204 pp., illus. $21.95.
A definitive reference work on the wild turkey for hunter, game manager, conservationist, or amateur naturalist.
***The Book Shop Moose Book,** by James MacNeil, Highway Book Shop, Cobalt, Ontario, Canada, 1986. 112 pp., illus. Paper covers. $6.50.
A most useful guide for the prospective moose hunter.
Boone and Crockett Club's 19th Big Game Awards, 1983-85, edited by Wm. H. Nesbitt. Boone and Crockett Club, Dumfries, VA, 1986. $25.00.
Data on over 1,400 trophies (in 30 categories) that were accepted during 1983-85, giving rank in category, final score, selected measurement, locality taken and name(s) of hunter and owner.
***The Bottoms,** by David Hagerbaumer and Dwight Schuh, Amwell Press, Clinton, NJ, 1988. 128 pp., illus. $37.50.
The Bottoms comprise a geographic area in the Midwest, along the Mississippi River. It tells the story that lives in dreams, if not the memory, of every serious waterfowler.
Bowhunter's Digest, 2nd Edition, by Chuck Adams, DBI Books, Inc., Northbrook, IL, 1981. 288 pp., illus. Paper covers. $12.95.
All-new edition covers all the necessary equipment and how to use it, plus the fine points to improve your skills.
***Bowhunting for Mule Deer,** by Dwight Schuh, Stoneydale Press Publishing Co., Stevensville, MT, 1987. 178 pp., illus. $14.95.
A detailed quide for hunting open-country bucks.
***Brown Feathers,** by Steven J. Julak, Stackpole Books, Harrisburg, PA, 1988. 224 pp., illus. $16.95.
Waterfowling tales and upland dreams.
Bugling for Elk, by Dwight Schuh, Stoneydale Press Publishing Co., Stevensville, MT, 1983. 162 pp., illus. $14.95.
A complete guide to early season elk hunting.
Campfires and Game Trails: Hunting North American Big Game, by Craig Boddington, Winchester Press, Piscataway, NJ, 1985. 295 pp., illus. $19.95.
How to hunt North America's big game species.

HUNTING (cont.)

The Complete Book of Hunting, by Robert Elman, Abbeville Press, New York, NY, 1982. 320 pp., illus. $29.95.

A compendium of the world's game birds and animals, handloading, international hunting, etc.

The Complete Book of the Wild Turkey, by Roger M. Latham, Stackpole Books, Harrisburg, Pa., 1978. 228 pp., illus. $14.95.

A new revised edition of the classic on American wild turkey hunting.

The Complete Guide to Bird Dog Training, by John R. Falk, Winchester Press, Piscataway, NJ, 1976. 256 pp., illus. $16.95.

How to choose, raise, train, and care for a bird dog.

The Complete Guide to Bowhunting Deer, by Chuck Adams, DBI Books, Inc., Northbrook, IL, 1984. 256 pp., illus. Paper covers. $12.95.

Plenty on equipment, bows, sights, quivers, arrows, clothes, lures and scents, stands and blinds, etc.

The Complete Guide to Game Care and Cookery, by Sam Fadala, DBI Books, Inc., Northbrook, IL., 1981. 288 pp., illus. Paper covers. $12.95.

How to dress, preserve and prepare all kinds of game animals and birds.

The Complete Smoothbore Hunter, by Brook Elliot, Winchester Press, Piscataway, NJ, 1986. 240 pp., illus. $16.95.

Expert advice and information on guns and gunning for all varities of game.

The Complete Turkey Hunt, by William Morris Daskal, El-Bar Enterprises Publishers, New York, NY, 1982. 129 pp., illus. Paper covers. $7.95.

Covers every aspect of turkeys and turkey hunting, by an expert.

***Complete Turkey Hunting,** by John Phillips, Stackpole Books, Harrisburg, PA, 1988. 320 pp., illus. $24.95.

The definitive work on hunting America's largest game bird.

Confessions of an Outdoor Maladroit, by Joel M. Vance, Amwell Press, Clinton, NJ, 1983. $20.00.

Anthology of some of the wildest, irreverent, and zany hunting tales ever.

***The Corey Ford Sporting Treasury,** by Corey Ford, Willow Creek Press, Wautoma, WI, 1987. 351 pp. $25.00

Minutes of the "Lower Forty" and other treasured Corey Ford stories return to print.

Covey Rises and Other Pleasures, by David H. Henderson, Amwell Press, Clinton, NJ, 1983. 155 pp., illus. $17.50.

A collection of essays and stories concerned with field sports.

Coveys and Singles: The Handbook of Quail Hunting, by Robert Gooch, A.S. Barnes, San Diego, CA, 1981. 196 pp., illus. $11.95.

The story of the quail in North America.

Deer and Deer Hunting: The Serious Hunter's Guide, by Dr. Rob Wegner, Stackpole Books, Harrisburg, PA, 1984. 384 pp., illus. $29.95.

In-depth information from the editor of "Deer & Deer Hunting" magazine. Major bibliography of English language books on deer and deer hunting from 1838-1984.

***Deer and Deer Hunting Book 2,** by Robert Wegner, Stackpole Books, Harrisburg, PA, 1987. 400 pp., illus. $29.95.

Strategies and tactics for the advanced hunter.

The Deer Book, edited by Lamar Underwood, Amwell Press, Clinton, NJ, 1982. 480 pp., illus. $25.00.

An anthology of the finest stories on North American deer ever assembled under one cover.

Deer Hunting, by R. Smith, Stackpole Books, Harrisburg, PA, 1978. 224 pp., illus. Paper covers. $10.95.

A professional guide leads the hunt for North America's most popular big game animal.

Deer Hunter's Guide to Guns, Ammunition, and Equipment, by Edward A. Matunas, an Outdoor Life Book, distributed by Stackpole Books, Harrisburg, PA, 1983. 352 pp., illus. $24.95.

Where-to-hunt for North American deer. An authoritative guide that will help every deer hunter get maximum enjoyment and satisfaction from his sport.

***Deer Hunter's Yearbook 1988,** by Outdoor Life Magazine editors, Stackpole Books, Harrisburg, PA, 1988. 192 pp., illus. $19.95.

A collection of articles from "Outdoor Life" Magazine on hunting deer.

Deer in Their World, by Erwin Bauer, Stackpole Books, Harrisburg, PA, 1984. 256 pp., illus. $29.95.

A showcase of more than 250 natural habitat deer photographs. Substantial natural history of North American deer.

The Desert Bighorn its Life History, Ecology, and Management, edited by Gale Monson and Lowel Sumner, University of Arizona Press, Tucson, AZ, 1985. 370 pp., illus. Paper covers. $14.95.

There is nothing else around that can tell you anywhere near as much about desert sheep.

Dove Hunting, by Charley Dickey, Galahad Books, NY, 1976. 112 pp., illus. $6.00.

This indispensable guide for hunters deals with equipment, techniques, types of dove shooting, hunting dogs, etc.

Drummer in the Woods, by Burton L. Spiller, Stackpole Books, Harrisburg, PA, 1980. 240 pp., illus. $19.95.

Twenty-one wonderful stories on grouse shooting by "the Poet Laureate of Grouse."

The Duck Hunter's Book, edited by Lamar Underwood, Amwell Press, Clinton, NJ, 1983. 650 pp., illus. $25.00.

Anthology of the finest duck hunting stories ever written.

The Duck Hunter's Handbook, by Bob Hinman, revised, expanded, updated edition, Winchester Press, Piscataway, NJ, 1985. 288 pp., illus. $15.95.

The duck hunting book that has it all.

The Duck-Huntingest Gentlemen, by Keith C. Russell et al, Winchester Press, Piscataway, NJ, 1980. 284 pp., illus. $17.95.

A collection of stories on waterfowl hunting.

Ducks of the Mississippi Flyway, ed. by John McKane, North Star Press, St. Cloud, MN, 1969. 54 pp., illus. Paper covers. $6.95.

A duck hunter's reference. Full color paintings of some 30 species, plus descriptive text.

Early American Waterfowling, 1700's-1930, by Stephen Miller, Winchester Press, Piscataway, NJ, 1986. 256 pp., illus. $27.95.

Two centuries of literature and art devoted to the nation's favorite hunting sport.

The Education of Pretty Boy, by Havilah Babock, The Gunnerman Press, Auburn Hills, MI, 1985. 160 pp., illus. $19.95.

Babcock's only novel, a heartwarming story of an orphan boy and a gunshy setter.

Elk and Elk Hunting, by Hart Wixom, Stackpole Books, Harrisburg, PA, 1986. 288 pp., illus. $29.95.

Your practical guide to fundamentals and fine points of elk hunting.

Elk Hunting in the Northern Rockies, by Ed. Wolff, Stoneydale Press, Stevensville, MT, 1984. 162 pp., illus. $14.95.

Helpful information about hunting the premier elk country of the northern Rocky Mountain states—Wyoming, Montana and Idaho.

Expert Advice on Gun Dog Training, by David Michael Duffy, revised, expanded, updated edition, Winchester Press, Piscataway, NJ, 1985. 288 pp., illus. $15.95.

America's top professional trainers reveal how you can use their methods.

Fair Chase, by Jim Rikhoff, Amwell Press, Clinton, NJ, 1984. 323 pp.,illus. $25.00.

A collection of hunting experiences from the Arctic to Africa, Mongolia to Montana, taken from over 25 years of writing.

***Field Dressing Small Game and Fowl,** by James Churchill, Stackpole Books, Harrisburg, PA, 1987. 112 pp., illus. Paper covers. $10.95.

The illustrated guide to dressing 20 birds and animals.

***Field Judging Trophy Animals,** by William Shuster, Stackpole Books, Harrisburg, PA, 1987. 132 pp., illus. Paper covers. $8.95.

Expert advice and practical suggestions.

***Fireside Waterfowler,** edited by David E. Wesley and William G. Leitch, A Ducks Unlimited Book, Stackpole Books, Harrisburg, PA, 1987. 357 pp., illus. $29.95.

Fundamentals of duck and goose hunting.

***Fireworks in the Peafield Corner,** by Archibald Rutledge, Amwell Press, Clinton, NJ, 1986. 357 pp., illus. In slipcase. $30.00

A treasury of the best of the sage of Hampton plantation, Archibald Rutledge, the first poet laureate of South Carolina.

For Whom the Ducks Toll, by Keith C. Russell, et al, Winchester Press, Piscataway, NJ, 1984. 288 pp., illus. Slipcased, limited and signed edition. $30.00. Trade edition. $16.95.

A select gathering of memorable waterfowling tales by the author and 68 of his closest friends.

The Formidable Game, by John H. Batten, Amwell Press, Clinton, NJ, 1983. 264 pp., illus. $175.00.

Deluxe, limited, signed and numbered edition. Big game hunting in India, Africa and North America by a world famous hunter.

Fur Trapping in North America, by Steven Geary, Winchester Press, Piscataway, NJ, 1985. 160 pp., illus. Paper covers. $10.95.

A comprehensive guide to techniques and equipment, together with fascinating facts about fur bearers.

A Gallery of Waterfowl and Upland Birds, by Gene Hill, with illustrations by David Maass, Pedersen Prints, Los Angeles, CA, 1978. 132 pp., illus. $44.95.

Gene Hill at his best. Liberally illustrated with fifty-one full-color reproductions of David Maass' finest paintings.

Game in the Desert Revisited, by Jack O'Connor, Amwell Press, Clinton, NJ, 1984. 306 pp., illus. $27.50.

Reprint of a Derrydale Press classic on hunting in the Southwest.

Getting the Most out of Modern Waterfowling, by John O. Cartier, St. Martin's Press, NY, 1974. 396 pp., illus. $17.95.

The most comprehensive, up-to-date book on waterfowling imaginable.

Georgia's Greatest Whitetails, by Duncan Dobie, Bucksnort Publishing, Marietta, GA, 1986. 476 pp., illus. $24.00.

Georgia's greatest whitetails, featuring all of the spine-tingling stories behind these record-breaking bucks, 42 in all.

Goose Hunting, by Charles L. Cadieux, A Stonewall Press Book, distributed by Winchester Press, Piscataway, NJ, 1979. 197 pp., illus. $16.95.

Personal stories of goose hunting from Quebec to Mexico.

The Gordon MacQuarrie Trilogy, by Gordon MacQuarrie, compiled and edited by Zack Taylor, Willow Creek Press, Oshkosh, WI, 1985. A three book, slip-cased set. $45.00.

Three-volume set comprising: **Stories of the Old Duck Hunters and Other Drivel, More Stories of the Old Duck Hunters, Last Stories of the Old Duck Hunters.**

The Grand Spring Hunt for America's Wild Turkey Gobbler, by Bart Jacob with Ben Conger, Winchester Press, Piscataway, NJ, 1985. 176 pp., illus. $15.95.

The turkey book for novice and expert alike.

Grizzly Country, by Andy Russell. A.A. Knopf, NYC, 1973, 302 pp., illus. $15.95.

Many-sided view of the grizzly bear and his world, by a noted guide, hunter and naturalist.

Grizzlies Don't Come Easy, by Ralph Young, Winchester Press, Piscataway, NJ, 1981. 200 pp., illus. $15.95.

The life story of a great woodsman who guided famous hunters such as O'Connor, Keith, Fitz, Page and others.

The Grizzly Book/The Bear Book, two volume set edited by Jack Samson, Amwell Press, Clinton, NJ, 1982. 304 pp.; 250 pp., illus. Slipcase. $37.50.

A delightful pair of anthologies. Stories by men such as O'Connor, Keith, Fitz, Page, and many others.

***Grouse and Grouse Hunting,** by Frank Woolner, Nick Lyons Books, N.Y.,NY, 1987. 192 pp., illus. $18.95.

An authoritative and affectionate portrait of one of America's greatest game birds.

Grouse Hunter's Guide, by Dennis Walrod, Stackpole Books, Harrisburg, PA, 1985. 192 pp., illus. $16.95.

Solid facts, observations, and insights on how to hunt the ruffed grouse.

HUNTING (cont.)

Gun Digest Book of the Hunting Rifle, by Jack Lewis, DBI Books, Inc., Northbrook, IL, 1983. 256 pp., illus. Paper covers. $12.95.
A thorough and knowledgeable account of today's hunting rifles.

Gun Digest Book of Sporting Dogs, by Carl P. Wood, DBI Books, Inc., Northbrook, IL, 1985. 256 pp., illus. Paper covers. $11.95.
Investigates various training philosophies, problem dogs, training for versatility, kenneling, etc. Covers most all hunting/sporting dogs.

Hal Swiggett on North American Deer, by Hal Swiggett, Jolex, Inc., Oakland, NJ, 1980. 272 pp., illus. Paper covers. $8.95.
Where and how to hunt all species of North American deer.

***Horned and Antlered Game,** by Erwin Bauer, Stackpole Books, Harrisburg, PA, 1987. 256 pp., illus. $32.95.
This book features spectacular color photographs and text brimming with animal lore.

Horns in the High Country, by Andy Russell, Alfred A. Knopf, NY, 1973. 259 pp., illus. Paper covers. $12.95.
A many-sided view of wild sheep and their natural world.

How to Get Your Deer, by John O. Cartier, Stackpole Books, Harrisburg, PA, 1986. 320 pp., illus. $24.95.
An authoritative guide to deer hunting that shows you how to match wits with your quarry and win.

How to Hunt, by Dave Bowring, Winchester Press, Piscataway, NJ, 1982. 208 pp., illus. Paper covers. $10.95; Cloth. $15.00.
A basic guide to hunting big game, small game, upland birds, and waterfowl.

Hunt Elk, by Jim Zumbo, Winchester Press, Piscataway, NJ, 1985. 256 pp., illus. $17.95.
A complete guide by one of America's foremost hunting writers.

The Hunter's Book of the Pronghorn Antelope, by Bert Popowski and Wilf E. Pyle, Winchester Press, Piscataway, NJ, 1982. 376 pp., illus. $17.95.
A comprehensive, copiously illustrated volume and a valuable guide for anyone interested in the pronghorn antelope.

A Hunter's Fireside Book, by Gene Hill, Winchester Press, Piscataway, NJ, 1972. 192 pp., illus. $14.95.
An outdoor book that will appeal to every person who spends time in the field—or who wishes he could.

The Hunter's Rifle, by Col. Charles Askins, The National Rifle Association, Wash., D.C., 1984. 176 pp., illus. Paper covers. $17.95.
A book on the hunting rifle and cartridges for killing big game.

The Hunter's Shooting Guide, by Jack O'Connor, Outdoor Life Books, New York, NY, 1982. 176 pp., illus. Paper covers. $5.95.
A classic covering rifles, cartridges, shooting techniques for shotguns/rifles/handguns.

The Hunter's World, by Charles F. Waterman, Winchester Press, Piscataway, NJ, 1983. 250 pp., illus. $29.95.
A classic. One of the most beautiful hunting books ever produced.

Hunting the American Wild Turkey, by Dave Harbour, Stackpole Books, Harrisburg, PA, 1975. 256 pp., illus. $14.95.
The techniques and tactics of hunting North America's largest, and most popular, woodland game bird.

Hunting America's Game Animals and Birds, by Robert Elman and George Peper, Winchester Press, Piscataway, NJ, 1975. 368 pp., illus. $16.95.
A how-to, where-to, when-to guide—by 40 top experts—covering the continent's big, small, upland game and waterfowl.

Hunting America's Mule Deer, by Jim Zumbo, Winchester Press, Piscataway, NJ, 1981. 272 pp., illus. $17.95.
The best ways to hunt mule deer. The how, when, and where to hunt all seven sub-species.

Hunting Dog Know-How, by D.M. Duffey, Winchester Press, Piscataway, NJ, 1983. 208 pp., illus. Paper covers. $9.95.
Covers selection, breeds, and training of hunting dogs, problems in hunting and field trials.

Hunting Ducks and Geese, by Steven Smith, Stackpole Books, Harrisburg, PA, 1984. 160 pp., illus. $14.95.
Hard facts, good bets, and serious advice from a duck hunter you can trust.

Hunting Fringeland Deer, by David Richey, Stackpole Books, Harrisburg, PA, 1987. 208 pp., illus. $24.95.
Tactics for trail watching, stillhunting and driving whitetails in farmlands, edge country and populated areas.

***Hunting in the Southlands,** edited by Lamar Underwood, Amwell Press, Clinton, NJ, 1987. 565 pp., illus. $35.00.
An anthology of the best stories of southern hunts including dove, turkey, waterfowl, deer, quail and more.

***Hunting North America's Big Game,** by Bob Hagel, Stackpole Books, Harrisburg, PA, 1987. 220 pp., illus. $27.95.
Complete and reliable coverage on how to approach, track, and shoot game in different terrains.

***Hunting on Horseback,** by Jim Ottman, Paladin Press, Boulder, CO, 1987. 151 pp., illus. $16.95.
Advice on how to get into shape for a horseback hunt, in addition to providing tips about weapons, ammunition, equipment, setting up a base camp and packing with a horse.

***Hunting on Three Continents with Jack O'Connor,** by Jack O'Connor with an introduction by John Batten, Safari Press, Long Beach, CA, 1987. 303 pp., illus. $35.00.
A collection of the author's best material written for Petersen's "Hunting" Magazine during the years 1973-1977.

Hunting Predators for Hides and Profits, by Wilf E. Pyle, Stoeger Publishing Co., So. Hackensack, NJ, 1985. 224 pp., illus. Paper covers. $11.95.
The author takes the hunter through every step of the hunting/marketing process.

Hunting Rabbits and Hares, by Richard P. Smith, Stackpole Books, Harrisburg, PA, 1986. 160 pp., illus. Paper covers. $12.95.
The complete guide to North America's favorite small game.

Hunting the Rocky Mountain Goat, by Duncan Gilchrist, Duncan Gilchrist, Hamilton, MT, 1983. 175 pp., illus. Paper covers. $10.95.
Hunting techniques for mountain goats and other alpine game. Tips on rifles for the high country.

Hunting and Stalking Deer Throughout the World, by Kenneth G. Whitehead, Batsford Books, London, 1982. 336 pp., illus. $35.00.
Comprehensive coverage of deer hunting areas on a country-by-country basis, dealing with every species in any given country.

Hunting the Southwest, by Jack Samson, The Amwell Press, Clinton, NJ, 1985. 172 pp., illus. In slipcase $27.50.
The most up-to-date look at one of the most difficult and diverse hunting areas in the world today.

Hunting Trophy Deer, by John Wootters, Winchester Press, Piscataway, NJ, 1983. 265 pp., illus. $15.95.
All the advice you need to succeed at bagging trophy deer.

***Hunting Upland Gamebirds.** by Steve Smith, Stackpole Books, Harrisburg, PA, 1987. 176 pp., illus. $16.95.
What the wingshooter needs to know about the birds, the game, and the new clay games.

Hunting Wild Turkeys in the Everglades, by Frank P. Harben, Harben Publishing Co., Safety Harbor, FL, 1983. 341 pp., illus. Paper covers. $8.95.
Describes techniques, ways and means of hunting this wary bird.

Hunting the Woodlands for Small and Big Game, by Luther A. Anderson, A. S. Barnes & Co., New York, NY, 1980. 256 pp., illus. $12.00.
A comprehensive guide to hunting in the United States. Chapters on firearms, game itself, marksmanship, clothing and equipment.

I Don't Want to Shoot an Elephant, by Havilah Babcock, The Gunnerman Press, Auburn Hills, MI, 1985. 184 pp., illus. $19.95.
Eighteen delightful stories that will enthrall the upland gunner for many pleasurable hours

In Search of the Wild Turkey, by Bob Gooch, Greatlakes Living Press, Ltd., Waukegan, IL, 1978. 182 pp., illus. $9.95.
A state-by-state guide to wild turkey hot spots, with tips on gear and methods for bagging your bird.

Jaybirds Go to Hell on Friday, by Havilah Babcock, The Gunnerman Press, Auburn Hills, MI, 1985. 149 pp. illus. $19.95.
Sixteen jewels that re-establish the lost art of good old-fashioned yarn telling.

A Listening Walk ... and Other Stories, by Gene Hill, Winchester Press, Piscataway, NJ, 1985. 208 pp., illus. $15.95.
Vintage Hill. Over 60 stories.

Lords of the Pinnacles: Wild Goats of the World, by Raul Valdez, Wild Sheep and Goat International, Mesilla, NM, 1985. 212 pp., illus. $59.95.
Limited, numbered and signed edition. The first comprehensive survey of the life histories, internal anatomy, and hunting of the wild goats of the world.

Making Game: An Essay on Woodcock, by Guy De La Valdene, Willow Creek Press, Oshkosh, WI, 1985. 202 pp. illus. $20.00.
The most delightful book on woodcock yet published.

Marsh Tales, by William N. Smith, Tidewater Publishers, Centreville, MD, 1985. 228 pp., illus. $15.95.
Market hunting, duck trapping, and gunning.

Matching the Gun to the Game, by Clair Rees, Winchester Press, Piscataway, NJ, 1982. 272 pp., illus. $17.95.
Covers selection and use of handguns, black-powder firearms for hunting, matching rifle type to the hunter, calibers for multiple use, tailoring factory loads to the game.

Measuring and Scoring North American Big Game Trophies, by Wm. H. Nesbitt and Philip L. Wright, The Boone and Crockett Club, Alexandria, VA, 1986. 176 pp., illus. $15.00.
The Boone and Crockett Club official scoring system, with tips for field evaluation of trophies.

Meat on the Table: Modern Small-Game Hunting, by Galen Geer, Paladin Press, Boulder CO, 1985. 216 pp., illus. $16.95.
All you need to know to put meat on your table from this comprehensive course in modern small-game hunting.

Mixed Bag, by Jim Rikhoff, National Rifle Association of America, Wash., DC, 1981. 284 pp., illus. Paper covers. $9.95.
Reminiscences of a master raconteur.

Modern Pheasant Hunting, by Steve Grooms, Stackpole Books, Harrisburg, PA, 1982. 224 pp., illus. Paper covers. $8.95.
New look at pheasants and hunters from an experienced hunter who respects this splendid gamebird.

Modern Waterfowl Guns and Gunning, by Don Zutz, Stoeger Publishing Co., So. Hackensack, NJ, 1985. 224 pp., illus. Paper covers. $11.95.
Up-to-date information on the fast-changing world of waterfowl guns and loads.

More and Better Pheasant Hunting, by Steve Smith, Winchester Press, Piscataway, NJ, 1986. 192 pp., illus. $15.95.
Complete, fully illustrated, expert coverage of the bird itself, the dogs, the hunt, the guns, and the best places to hunt.

More Grouse Feathers, by Burton L. Spiller. Crown Publ., NY, 1972. 238 pp., illus. $15.00.
Facsimile of the original Derrydale Press issue of 1938. Guns and dogs, the habits and shooting of grouse, woodcock, ducks, etc. Illus by Lynn Bogue Hunt.

More Than a Trophy, by Dennis Walrod, Stackpole Books, Harrisburg, PA, 1983. 256 pp., illus. Paper covers. $12.95.
Field dressing, skinning, quartering, and butchering to make the most of your valuable whitetail, blacktail or mule deer.

More Stories of the Old Duck Hunter, by Gordon MacQuarrie, Willow Creek Press, Oshkosh, WI, 1983. 200 pp., illus. $15.00.
Collection of 18 treasured stories of The Old Duck Hunters originally published in major magazines of the 1930s and '40s.

Mostly Tailfeathers, by Gene Hill, Winchester Press, Piscataway, NJ, 1975. 192 pp., illus. $14.95.
An interesting, general book about bird hunting.

HUNTING (cont.)

***Mostly Huntin'**, by Bill Jordan, Everett Publishing Co., Bossier City, LA, 1987. 254 pp., illus. $20.50.
Jordan's hunting adventures in North America, Africa, Australia, South America and Mexico.
Movin' Along with Charley Dickey, by Charlie Dickey, Winchester Press, Piscataway, NJ, 1985. 224 pp., illus. $14.95.
More wisdom, wild tales, and wacky wit from the Sage of Tallahassee.
Mule Deer, by Norm Nelson, Stackpole Books, Harrisburg, PA, 1987. 192 pp., illus. $16.95.
How to bring home North America's big deer of the West.
Murry Burnham's Hunting Secrets, by Murry Burnham with Russell Tinsley, Winchester Press, Piscataway, NJ, 1984. 244 pp., illus. $17.95.
One of the great hunters of our time gives the reasons for his success in the field.
The Muzzleloading Hunter, by Rick Hacker, Winchester Press, Piscataway, NJ, 1981. 283 pp., illus. $19.95.
A comprehensive guide for the black powder sportsman.
My Health is Better in November, by Havilah Babcock, University of S. Carolina Press, Columbia, SC, 1985. 284 pp., illus. $19.95.
Adventures in the field set in the plantation country and backwater streams of South Carolina.
My Lost Wilderness: Tales of an Alaskan Woodsman, by Ralph Young, Winchester Press, Piscataway, NJ, 1983. 193 pp., illus. $15.95.
True tales of an Alaskan hunter, guide, fisherman, prospector, and backwoodsman.
New England Grouse Shooting, by William Harnden Foster, Willow Creek Press, Oshkosh, WI, 1983. 213 pp., illus. $45.00.
A new release of a classic book on grouse shooting.
***North American Big Game Animals,** by Bryon W. Dalrymple and Erwin Bauer, Outdoor Life Books/Stackpole Books, Harrisburg, PA, 1985. 258 pp., illus. $29.95.
Complete illustrated natural histories. Habitat, movements, breeding, birth and development, signs, and hunting.
North American Elk: Ecology and Management, edited by Jack Ward Thomas and Dale E. Toweill, Stackpole Books, Harrisburg, PA, 1982. 576 pp., illus. $39.95.
The definitive, exhaustive, classic work on the North American Elk.
The North American Waterfowler, by Paul S. Bernsen, Superior Publ. Co., Seattle, WA, 1972. 206 pp., Paper covers. $4.95.
The complete inside and outside story of duck and goose shooting. Big and colorful, illus. by Les Kouba.
Of Bears and Man, by Mike Cramond, University of Oklahoma Press, Norman, OK, 1986. 433 pp., illus. $29.95.
The author's lifetime association with bears of North America. Interviews with survivors of bear attacks.
Of Bench and Bears; Alaska's Bear Hunting Judge, by Richard C. Folta, Great Northwest Publishing and Distributing Co., Anchorage, AK, 1986. 224 pp., illus. $20.00.
Alaska's bear hunting judge who personally bagged some 200 bears during his half century of Alaskan hunting.
On Bears and Bear Hunting, by Duncan Gilchrist, Amwell Press, Clinton, NJ, 1984. 260 pp., illus. $27.50.
The author's experiences as a bear guide and taker of over 150 bears of all species make this a definitive work on bears.
On Target for Successful Turkey Hunting, by Wayne Fears, Target Communications, Mequon, WI, 1983. 92 pp., illus. Paper covers. $5.95.
Professional turkey hunting advice.
The Old Pro Turkey Hunter, by Gene Nunnery, Gene Nunnery, Meridian, MS, 1980. 144 pp., illus. $12.95.
True facts and old tales of turkey hunters.
1001 Hunting Tips, by Robert Elman, Winchester Press, Piscataway, NJ, 1983. 544 pp., illus. $22.50.
New edition, updated and expanded. A complete course in big and small game hunting, wildfowling and hunting upland birds.
***The Only Good Bear is a Dead Bear,** by Jeanette Hortick Prodgers, Falcon Press, Helena, MT, 1986. 204 pp. Paper covers. $7,95.
A collection of the West's best bear stories.
Opening Shots and Parting Lines: The Best of Dickey's Wit, Wisdom, and Wild Tales for Sportsmen, by Charley Dickey, Winchester Press, Piscataway, NJ, 1983. 208 pp., illus. $14.95.
Selected by the writer who has entertained millions of readers in America's top sporting publications—49 of his best pieces.
The Orvis Book of Upland Bird Shooting, by Geoffrey Norman, Winchester Press, Piscataway, NJ, 1985. 155 pp., illus. $15.95.
A marvelously full and helpful look at the compelling world of upland bird shooting.
The Outdoor Life Bear Book, edited by Chet Fish, an Outdoor Life book, distributed by Stackpole Books, Harrisburg, PA, 1983. 352 pp., illus. $26.95.
All-time best personal accounts of terrifying attacks, exciting hunts, and intriguing natural history.
The Outdoor Life Deer Hunter's Encyclopedia, by John Madson, et al, Stackpole Books, Inc., Harrisburg, PA, 1985. 800 pp. illus. $49.95.
The largest, most comprehensive volume of its kind ever published.
Outdoor Life Deer Hunters Yearbook, 1987, by contributors to Outdoor Life magazine, Stackpole Books, Harrisburg, PA, 1987. 192 pp., illus. $19.95.
The 5th annual collection of deer and deer hunting stories drawn from "Outdoor Life," "Hunting Guns," and "Deer and Big Game."
Outdoor Yarns & Outright Lies, by Gene Hill and Steve Smith, Stackpole Books, Inc. Harrisburg, PA, 1984. 168 pp.,illus. $16.95.
Fifty or so stories by two good sports.
The Outlaw Gunner, by Harry M. Walsh, Tidewater Publishers, Cambridge, MD, 1973. 178 pp., illus. $12.50.
A colorful story of market gunning in both its legal and illegal phases.
Picking Your Shots, by Steve Smith, Stackpole Books, Harrisburg, PA, 1986. 160 pp., illus. $16.95.
Stories of dogs and birds, and guns and days afield.
Pinnell and Talifson: Last of the Great Brown Bear Men, by Marvin H. Clark, Jr., Great Northwest Publishing and Distributing Co., Spokane, WA, 1980. 224 pp., illus. $20.00.
The story of these famous Alaskan guides and some of the record bears taken by them.
Popular Sporting Rifle Cartridges, by Clay Harvey, DBI Books, Inc., Northbrook, IL, 1984. 320 pp., illus. Paper covers. $13.95.
Provides the hunter/shooter with extensive information on most of the cartridges introduced during this century.
The Practical Hunter's Dog Book, Updated and Expanded, by John R. Falk, Winchester Press, Piscataway, NJ, 1984. 336 pp., illus. Paper covers. $11.95.
Everything you need to know from selecting a puppy to basic and advanced training, health care and breeding.
The Practical Hunter's Handbook, by Anthony J. Acerrano, Winchester Press, Piscataway, NJ, 1978. 224 pp., illus. Paper covers. $12.95.
How the time-pressed hunter can take advantage of every edge his hunting situation affords him.
Predator Caller's Companion, by Gerry Blair, Winchester Press, Piscataway, NJ, 1981. 280 pp., illus. $18.95.
Predator calling techniques and equipment for the hunter and trapper.
***Predators of North America,** by Erwin Bauer, Stackpole Books, Harrisburg, PA, 1988. 256 pp., illus. $34.95.
Pronghorn, North America's Unique Antelope, by Charles L. Cadieux, Stackpole Books, Harrisburg, PA, 1986. 256 pp., illus. $24.95.
The practical guide for hunters.
Quail Hunting in America. by Tom Huggler, Stackpole Books, Harrisburg, PA, 1987. 288 pp. illus. $19.95.
Tactics for finding and taking bobwhite, valleys, Gambel's Mountain, scaled-blue, and Mearn's quail by season and habitat.
Ralf Coykendall's Duck Decoys and How to Rig Them, revised by Ralf Coykendall, Jr., Winchester Press, Piscataway, NJ, 1983. 128 pp., illus. Slipcased. $21.95.
For every discriminating book collector and sportsman, a superb new edition of a long out-of-print classic.
Ranch Life and the Hunting Trail, by Theodore Roosevelt, Readex Microprint Corp., Dearborn, MI. 1966 186 pp. With drawings by Frederic Remington. $22.50.
A facsimile reprint of the original 1899 Century Co., edition. One of the most fascinating books of the West of that day.
Recollections of a Longshore Gunner, by "BB," The Boydell Press, Suffolk, England, 1979. 86 pp., illus. $11.50.
Wildfowling adventures after geese on the Scottish coast.
Records of Alaska Big Game, edited by Norman B. Grant, Alaska Big Game Trophy Club, Anchorage, Alaska, 1971, 111 pp., illus. $95.00.
Contains the recorded and tabulated trophies of Alaskan big game, including the name of the hunter, date and place of hunt, and measurement.
Records of Exotics, Volume 2, 1978 Edition, compiled by Thompson B. Temple, Thompson B. Temple, Ingram, TX, 1978. 243 pp., illus. $15.00.
Lists almost 1,000 of the top exotic trophies bagged in the U.S. Gives complete information on how to score.
***Records of North American Whitetailed Deer,** by the editors of the Boone and Crockett Club, Dumfries, VA, 1987. 256 pp., illus. Flexible covers. $15.00.
Contains data on 1,293 whitetail trophies over the all-time record book minimum, listed and ranked by state or province and divided into typical and non-typical categories.
Ridge Runners & Swamp Rats, by Charles F. Waterman, Amwell Press, Clinton, NJ, 1983. 347 pp. illus. $25.00.
Tales of hunting and fishing.
Ringneck! Pheasants & Pheasant Hunting, by Ted Janes, Crown Publ., NY, 1975. 120 pp., illus. $8.95.
A thorough study of one of our more popular game birds.
Sheep and Sheep Hunting, by Jack O'Connor, Winchester Press, Piscataway, NJ, Memorial Edition, 1985. 576 pp., illus. Paper covers. $19.95.
A definitive book on the wild sheep.
Charles Sheldon Trilogy, by Charles Sheldon, Amwell Press, Clinton, NJ, 1983. 3 volumes in slipcase. **The Wilderness of the Upper Yukon,** 363 pp., illus.; **The Wilderness of the North Pacific Coast Islands,** 246 pp., illus.; **The Wilderness of Denali,** 412 pp., illus. Deluxe edition. $205.00.
Custom-bound reprinting of Sheldon's classics, each signed and numbered by the author's son, William G. Sheldon.
Spring Turkey Hunting, by John M. McDaniel, Stackpole Books, Harrisburg, PA, 1986. 224 pp., illus. $21.95.
The serious hunter's guide.
Squirrels and Squirrel Hunting, by Bob Gooch. Tidewater Publ., Cambridge, MD, 1973. 148 pp., illus. $8.95.
A complete book for the squirrel hunter, beginner or old hand. Details methods of hunting, squirrel habitat, management, proper clothing, care of the kill, cleaning and cooking.
***The Still-Hunter,** by Theodore S. Van Dyke, reprinted by the Gunnerman Press, Auburn Hills, MI, 1988. 390 pp., illus. $21.95.
Covers each aspect of this fine sport in such complete detail that both the novice and the experienced hunter will profit from its reading.
Strayed Shots and Frayed Lines, edited by John E. Howard, Amwell Press, Clinton, NJ, 1982. 425 pp., illus. $25.00.
Anthology of some of the finest, funniest stories on hunting and fishing ever assembled.
***Successful Big Game Hunting,** by Duncan Gilchrist, Stoneydale Publishing Co., Stevensville, MT, 1987. 176 pp., illus. $14.95.
Secrets of a big game hunter-guide.
Successful Deer Hunting, by Sam Fadala, DBI Books, Inc., Northbrook, IL, 1983. 288 pp., illus. Paper covers. $12.95.
Here's all the dope you'll need—where, why, when and how—to have a successful deer hunt.

HUNTING (cont.)

Successful Goose Hunting, by Charles L. Cadieux, Stone Wall Press, Inc., Wash., D.C., 1986. 240 pp., illus. $24.95.
A complete book on modern goose hunting by a lifetime waterfowler and professional wildlifer.
Successful Turkey Hunting, by J. Wayne Fears, Target Communications, Mequon, WI, 1983. 92 pp., illus. Paper covers. $5.95.
How to be more successful and get more enjoyment from turkey hunting.
Successful Waterfowling, by Zack Taylor, Crown, Publ., NY, 1974. 276 pp., illus. Paper covers. $15.95.
The definitive guide to new ways of hunting ducks and geese.
***Taking Big Bucks,** by Ed Wolff, Stoneydale Press, Stevensville, MT, 1987. 169 pp., illus. $14.95.
Solving the whitetail riddle.
Tales of Quails 'n Such, by Havilah Babcock, University of S. Carolina Press, Columbia, SC, 1985. 237 pp. $19.95.
A group of hunting stories, told in informal style, on field experiences in the South in quest of small game.
Through the Brazilian Wilderness, by Theodore Roosevelt, Greenwood Press, Westport, CT, 1982. Reprinting of the original 1914 work. 370 pp., illus. $22.50.
An account of a zoogeographic reconnaissance through the Brazilian hinterland.
***Timberdoodle,** by Frank Woolner, Nick Lyons Books, N.Y., NY, 1987. 168 pp., illus. $18.95.
The classic guide to woodcock and woodcock hunting.
Topflight; A Speed Index to Waterfowl, by J.A. Ruthven & Wm. Zimmerman, Moebius Prtg. Co., Milwaukee, WI, 1968. 112 pp. $8.95.
Rapid reference for specie identification. Marginal color band of book directs reader to proper section. 263 full color illustrations of body and feather configurations.
Track of the Kodiak, by Marvin H. Clark, Great Northwest Publishing and Distributing Co., Anchorage, AK, 1984. 224 pp., illus. $20.00.
A full perspective on Kodiak Island bear hunting.
Tranquillity, by Col. H.P. Sheldon, Willow Creek Press, Oshkosh, WI, 1986. In slipcase with its acclaimed companion volumes. **Tranquillity Revisited** and **Tranquillity Regained.** The 3 volume set. $45.00.
A reprint of this 1936 Derrydale Press classic set.
The Trophy Hunter, by Col. Allison, Stackpole Books, Harrisburg, PA, 1981. 240 pp., illus. $24.95.
Action-packed tales of hunting big game trophies around the world—1860 to today.
Trophy Hunter in Asia, by Elgin T. Gates, Charger Productions Inc., Capistrano Beach, CA, 1982. 272 pp., illus. $19.95.
Fascinating high adventure with one of America's top trophy hunters.
***Trophy Rams of the Brooks Range Plus Secrets of a Sheep and Mountain Goat Guide,** by Duncan Gilchrist, Pictorial Histories Publishing Co., Missoula, MT, 1984. 176 pp., illus. $19.95.
Covers hunting a remote corner of the Brooks Range for virgin herds of dall rams.
The Turkey Hunter's Book, by John M. McDaniel, Amwell Press, Clinton, NJ, 1980. 147 pp., illus. Paper covers. $9.95.
One of the most original turkey hunting books to be published in many years.
Turkey Hunter's Digest, by Dwain Bland, DBI Books, Inc., Northbrook, IL, 1986. 256 pp., illus. Paper covers. $12.95.
Describes and pictures all varieties of turkey. Offers complete coverage on calls, calling techniques, appropriate guns, bows, cameras and other equipment.
Turkey Hunting, Spring and Fall, by Doug Camp, Outdoor Skills Bookshelf, Nashville, TN, 1983. 165 pp., illus. Paper covers. $12.95.
Practical turkey hunting, calling, dressing and cooking, by a professional turkey hunting guide.
Turkey Hunter's Guide, by Byron W. Dalrymple, et al, a publication of The National Rifle Association, Washington, DC, 1979. 96 pp., illus. Paper covers. $9.95.
Expert advice on turkey hunting hotspots, guns, guides, and calls.
Unrepentant Sinner, by Colonel Charles Askins, Paladin Press, Boulder CO, 1985. 320 pp., illus. $17.95.
As one of the world's greatest big-game hunters, Askins recalls his adventures.
The Upland Gunner's Book, edited by George Bird Evans, The Amwell Press, Clinton, NJ, 1986. 286 pp., illus. In slipcase. $27.50.
An anthology of the finest stories ever written on upland game hunting.
Victorian Shooting Days, by Derek Johnson, The Boydell Press, Suffolk, England, 1981. 11 pp., illus. $16.95.
Describes the weapons used by these sportsmen, and results of the author's researches on East Anglian gunsmiths
The Waterfowl Gunner's Book, edited by F. Phillips Williamson, The Amwell Press, Clinton, NJ, 1986. 282 pp., illus. In slipcase. $27.50.
An anthology of the finest duck hunting stories ever gathered under one cover.
The Whispering Wings of Autumn, by Gene Hill and Steve Smith, Amwell Press, Clinton, NJ, 1982. 192 pp., illus. $17.50.
A collection of both fact and fiction on two of North America's most famous game birds, the Ruffed Grouse and the Woodcock.
White-Tailed Deer: Ecology and Management, by Lowell K. Halls, Stackpole Books, Harrisburg, PA, 1984. 864 pp., illus. $39.95.
The definive work on the world's most popular big-game animal.
The Whitetail Deer Hunter's Handbook, by John Weiss, Winchester Press, Piscataway, NJ, 1979. 256 pp., illus. Paper covers. $12.95.
Wherever you live, whatever your level of experience, this handbook will make you a better deer hunter.
Whitetail Hunting, by Jim Dawson, Stackpole Books, Harrisburg, PA, 1982. 224 pp., illus. $14.95.
New angles on hunting whitetail deer.
***The Wild Bears,** by George Laycock, Outdoor Life Books, N.Y., NY, 1987. 272 pp., illus. $31.95.
The story of the grizzly, brown and black bears, their conflicts with man, and their chances of survival in the future.
Wild Sheep and Wild Sheep Hunters of the Old World, by Raul Valdez, Wild Sheep & Goat International, Mesilla,NM, 1983. 207 pp., illus. Limited, signed and numbered edition. $65.00.
A definitive work on Old World sheep hunting.
The Wild Sheep of the World, by Raul Valdez, Wild Sheep and Goat International, Mesilla, NM, 1983. 150 pp., illus. $45.00.
The first comprehensive survey of the world's wild sheep written by a zoologist.
The Wild Turkey Book, edited and with special commentary by J. Wayne Fears, Amwell Press, Clinton, NJ, 1982. 303 pp., illus. $22.50.
An anthology of the finest stories on wild turkey ever assembled under one cover.

AFRICA/ASIA

The Adventures of an Elephant Hunter, by James Sutherland, Trophy Room Books, Encino, CA, 1985. 324 pp., illus. $75.00.
Facsimile reprint of a very scarce book on elephant hunting.
***The African Elephant and its Hunters,** by Dennis D. Lyell, Trophy Room Books, Agoura, Ca, 1987. 200 pp., illus. $75.00.
Limited, numbered facsimile edition of this scarce 1924 book.
***African Game Trails,** by Theodore Roosevelt, Galago Publishing Ltd., Alberton, RSA, 1986. 504 pp., illus. $40.00.
The account of Roosevelt's 1908 safari to Africa with his son Kermit.
African Hunter, by Baron Bror von Blixen-Finecke, St. Martin's Press, New York, NY, 1986. 284 pp., illus. $14.95.
Reprint of the scarce 1938 edition. An African hunting classic.
African Hunting and Adventure, by William Charles Baldwin, Books of Zimbabwe, Bulawayo, 1981. 451 pp., illus. $75.00.
Facsimile reprint of the scarce 1863 London edition. African hunting and adventure from Natal to the Zambesi.
***African Nature Notes and Reminiscences,** by F. Courteney Selous, Galago Publishing Ltd., Alberton, RSA, 1986. 356 pp., illus. $40.00.
Reprint of the very scarce 1910 edition and the hardest to find of all of this author's works.
African Rifles & Cartridges, by John Taylor. The Gun Room Press, Highland Park, NJ, 1977. 431 pp., illus. $21.95.
Experiences and opinions of a professional ivory hunter in Africa describing his knowledge of numerous arms and cartridges for big game. A reprint.
***The African Safari,** by P. Jay Fetner, St. Martin's Press, Inc., N.Y., NY, 1987. 700 pp., illus. $60.00.
A lavish, superbly illustrated, definitive work that brings together the practical elements of planning a safari with a proper appreciation for the animals and their environment.
African Section Special Field Edition SCI 4th Edition Record Book of Trophy Animals, edited by C.J. McElroy, Safari Club International, Tucson, AZ, 1984. 302 pp., illus. Paper covers. $20.00.
Tabulations of outstanding big game trophies.
***After Big Game in Central Africa,** by Eduoard Foa, Safari Press, Long Beach, CA, 1987. 330 pp., illus. In slipcase. $60.00.
Foa was a collector for theParis Natural History Museum and hunting in what is, today, Tanzania and Zambia.
Bell of Africa, by Walter (Karamojo) D. M. Bell, Neville Spearman, Suffolk, England, 1983. 236 pp., illus. $35.00.
Autobiography of the greatest elephant hunter of them all.
Big Game and Big Game Rifles, by John Taylor, Trophy Room Books, Encino, CA, 1986. 215 pp. illus. Limited, numbered reprint edition. $60.00.
Facsimile reprint of the much sought after 1948 edition.
Big Game Hunting Around the World, by Bert Klineburger and Vernon W. Hurst, Exposition Press, Jericho, NY, 1969. 376 pp., illus. $30.00.
The first book that takes you on a safari all over the world.
Big Game Hunting in North-Eastern Rhodesia, by Owen Letcher, St. Martin's Press, New York, NY, 1986. 272 pp., illus. $15.95.
A classic reprint and one of the very few books to concentrate on this fascinating area, a region that today is still very much safari country.
The Book of the Lion, by Sir Alfred E. Pease, St. Martin's Press, New York, NY, 1986. 305 pp., illus. $15.95.
Reprint of the finest book ever published on the subject. The author describes all aspects of lion history and lion hunting, drawing heavily on his own experiences in British East Africa.
***A Breath From the Veldt,** by J.G. Millais, Galago Publishers, Ltd., Alberton, RSA, 1986. 236 pp., illus. $45.00.
Reprint of a classic on African hunting by an artist/writer.
***Chronicles of a Second African Trip,** by George Eastman, The Friends of the University of Rochester Libraries, Rochester, NY, 1987. 89 pp., illus. In slipcase. $35.00.
Eastman's exciting story of his pursuit of elephant and white rhino. Beautifully illustrated with photographs by Martin Johnson.
Death in the Dark Continent, by Peter Capstick, St. Martin's Press, New York, NY, 1983. 238 pp., illus. $15.95.
A book that brings to life all the suspense, fear and exhileration of stalking ferocious killers under primitive, savage conditions, with the ever present threat of death.
Death in the Long Grass, by Peter Hathaway Capstick, St. Martin's Press, New York, NY, 1977. 297 pp., illus. $15.95.
A big game hunter's adventures in the African bush.
Death in the Silent Places, by Peter Capstick, St. Martin's Press, New York, NY, 1981. 243 pp., illus. $15.95.
The author recalls the extraordinary careers of legendary hunters such as Corbett, Karamojo Bell, Stigand and others.
Dusty Days and Distant Drums, by William R. Rindome, Game Fields Press, Lake Oswego, OR, 1984. 258 pp., illus. $37.50.
An African hunting chronicle.

HUNTING (cont.)

Elephant, by Commander David Enderby Blunt, The Holland Press, London, England, 1985. 260 pp., illus. $35.00.
A study of this phenomenal beast by a world-leading authority.
The Elephant Hunters of the Lado, by Major W. Robert Foran, Amwell Press, Clinton, NJ, 1981. 311 pp., illus. Limited, numbered, and signed edition, in slipcase. $175.00.
From a previously unpublished manuscript by a famous "white hunter."
Elephant Hunting in East Equatorial Africa, by Arthur H. Neumann, Books of Zimbabwe, Bulawayo, 1982. 455 pp., illus. $85.00.
Facsimile reprint of the scarce 1898 London edition. An account of three years ivory hunting under Mount Kenya.
***Elephants of Africa,** by Dr. Anthony Hall-Martin, New Holland Publishers, London, England, 1987. 120 pp., illus. $75.00.
A superbly illustrated overview of the African elephant with reproductions of paintings by the internationally acclaimed wildlife artist Paul Bosman.
First Wheel, by Bunny Allen, Amwell Press, Clinton, NJ, 1984. Limited, signed and numbered edition in the NSFL "African Hunting Heritage Series." 292 pp., illus. $100.00.
A white hunter's diary, 1927-47.
***From Mt. Kenya to the Cape,** by Craig Boddington, Safari Press, Long Beach, CA, 1987. 274 pp., illus. $45.00.
Ten years of African hunting adventures.
Green Hills of Africa, by Ernest Hemingway. Charles Scribner's Sons, NY, 1963. 285 pp., illus. Paper covers. $9.95.
A famous narrative of African big-game hunting, first published in 1935.
***Horn of the Hunter,** by Robert Ruark, Safari Press, Long Beach, CA, 1987. 315 pp., illus. $35.00.
Ruark's most sought-after title on African hunting, here in reprint.
***Horned Death,** by John Burger, Safari Press, Long Beach, CA, 1987. 342 pp., illus. In slipcase. $60.00.
Reprint of the experiences of the famous John Burger who shot over 1,000 African buffalo during a lifetime of control hunting throughout Africa.
***The Hunter is Death,** by T.V. Bulpin, Safari Press, Long Beach, CA, 1987. 348 pp., illus. $30.00.
This is the life story of George Rushby, professional ivory hunter who killed the man-eating lions of the Njombe district.
***A Hunter's Life in South Africa,** by R. Gordon Cumming, Galago Publishers, Ltd., Alberton, RSA. 373 pp., illus. $45.00.
One of the most flamboyant of the better known African hunters and his adventures.
A Hunter's Wanderings in Africa, by F. C. Selous, Books of Zimbabwe, Bulawayo, 1981. 455 pp., illus. $85.00.
A facsimile reprint of the 1881 London edition. A narrative of nine years spent among the game of the interior of South Africa.
Hunting the African Buffalo, edited by Jim Rickhoff, Amwell Press, Clinton, NJ, 1985. 575 pp., illus. $225.00.
Deluxe, limited, signed and numbered edition of the most definitive work on hunting the African Cape buffalo that has ever been compiled.
Hunting the African Elephant, compiled by Jim Rickhoff, Amwell Press, Clinton, NJ, 1986. 625 pp., illus. $225.00.
An anthology of classics by famous authors and hunters such as Bell, O'Connor, Keith, Dyer, Selous, and others.
Hunting the Elephant in Africa, by Captain C.H. Stigand, St. Martin's Press, New York, NY, 1986. 379 pp., illus. $14.95.
A reprint of the scarce 1913 edition; vintage Africana at its best.
***Hunting in Many Lands,** ed. by Theodore Roosevelt and George Bird Grinnel, The Boone and Crockett Club, Dumfries, VA, 1987. 447 pp., illus. $40.00.
Limited edition reprint of this 1895 classic work on hunting in Africa, India, Mongolia, etc.
***Jim Corbett's India,** selected by R.E. Hawkins, Oxford University Press, Oxford, NY, 1986. 250 pp., illus. Paper covers. $9.95.
Stories from "Maneaters of Kumaon," "My India," "Jungle Lore" and other books by Jim Corbett.
Karamojo Safari, by W.D.M. Bell, Neville Spearman, Suffold, England, 1984. 288 pp., illus. $35.00.
The true story of Bell's life in Karamojo.
***Lake Ngami,** by Charles Anderson, New Holland Press, London, England, 1987. 576 pp., illus. $35.00.
Originally published in 1856. Describes two expeditions into what is now Botswana, depicting every detail of landscape and wildlife.
***Maneaters and Marauders,** by John Taylor, Trophy Room Books, Agoura, CA, 1987. 200 pp., illus. Limited, numbered edition. $60.00.
The adventures of one of the most experienced professional African hunters.
The Man-Eaters of Tsavo, by Lt. Col. J.H. Patterson, St. Martin's Press, New York, NY, 1986. 346 pp., illus. $14.95.
A reprint of the scarce original book on the man-eating lions of Tsavo.
Memories of an African Hunter, by Denis D. Lyell, St. Martin's Press, New York, NY, 1986. 288 pp., illus. $15.95.
A reprint of one of the truly great writers on African hunting. A gripping and highly readable account of Lyell's many years in the African bush.
Mongolia Hunter, by Patrick J. Steward, Shikar Publishing Co., Santa Fe, NM, 1987. 247 pp., illus. $75.00.
The history and customs of Mongolia, the complete story of hunting in that stark land since the days of Genghis Khan.
***Persia: Safari on the Summits,** by Richardo Medem Sanjuan, Trophy Room Press, Aguoura, CA, 1987. 200 pp., illus. Limited, numbered edition. $90.00.
Finest book on Persian hunting written by a Western world author.
***Peter Capstick's Africa: A Return to the Long Grass,** by Peter Hathaway Capstick, St. Martin's Press, N.Y., NY, 1987. 213 pp., illus. $29.95.
A first-person adventure in which the author returns to the long grass for his own dangerous and very personal excursion.
***Portraits of the Game and Wild Animals of Southern Africa,** by William Cornwallis Harris, Galago Publishers, Ltd., Alberton, RSA, 1987. 144 pp., illus. $35.00.
Reprint of the rarest and most expensive of all books on African wildlife. 32 full color reproductions of the author's drawings of African game animals.
The Recollections of an Elephant Hunter 1864-1875, by William Finaughty, Books of Zimbabwe, Bulawayo, Zimbabwe, 1980. 244 pp., illus. $85.00.
Reprint of the scarce 1916 privately published edition. The early game hunting exploits of William Finaughty in Matabeleland and Nashonaland.
Safari: The Last Adventure, by Peter Capstick, St. Martin's Press, New York, NY, 1984. 291 pp., illus. $15.95.
A modern comprehensive guide to the African Safari.
Tales of the Big Game Hunters, selected and introduced by Kenneth Kemp, The Sportman's Press, London, 1986. 209 pp., illus. $35.00.
Writings by some of the best known hunters and explorers, among them: Frederick Courteney Selous, R.G. Cumming, Sir Samuel Baker, and elephant hunters Neumann and Sutherland.
Tanzania Safari, by Brian Herne, Amwell Press, Clifton, NJ, 1982. 259 pp., illus. Limited, signed and numbered edition. Slipcase. $125.00.
The story of Tanzania and hunting safaris, professional hunters, and a little history, too.
Travel and Adventure in South-East Africa, by Frederick Courteney Selous, Hippocrene Books, Inc., New York, NY, 1985. 503 pp., illus. Paper covers. $11.95.
Reprint of the scarce 1893 edition. Covers the 11 year period from the point where the author's "A Hunter's Wanderings" left off.
Uganda Safaris, by Brian Herne, Winchester Press, Piscataway, NJ, 1979. 236 pp., illus. $12.95.
The chronicle of a professional hunter's adventures in Africa.
The Wanderings of an Elephant Hunter, by W.D.M. Bell, Neville Spearman, Suffolk, England, 1981. 187 pp., illus. $35.00.
The greatest of elephant books by perhaps the greatest elephant hunter of all times, "Karamojo" Bell.
A White Hunters Life, by Angus MacLagan, an African Heritage Book, published by Amwell Press, Clinton, NJ, 1983. 283 pp., illus. Limited, signed, and numbered deluxe edition, in slipcase. $100.00.
True to life, a sometimes harsh yet intriguing story.
Wild Ivory, by Horace S. Mazet, Nautulus Books, No. Plainfield, NJ, 1971. 280 pp., illus. $30.00.
The true story of the last of the old elephant hunters.
***Wild Sports of Southern Africa,** by William Cornwallis Harris, New Holland Press, London, England, 1987. 376 pp., illus. $35.00.
Originally published in 1863, describes the author's travels in Southern Africa.
***With a Rifle in Mongolia,** by Count Hoyos-Sprizenstein, Safari Press, Long Beach, CA, 1987. 144 pp., illus. In slipcase. $85.00.
First English edition of the author's 1911 expedition to Mongolia and China.

The Accurate Rifle, by Warren Page, Winchester Press, Piscataway, NJ, 1973. 256 pp., illus. Paper covers. $9.95.
A masterly discussion. A must for the competitive shooter hoping to win, and highly useful to the practical hunter.
The AK-47 Assault Rifle, Desert Publications, Cornville, AZ, 1981. 150 pp., illus. Paper covers. $7.50.
Complete and practical technical information on the only weapon in history to be produced in an estimated 30,000,000 units.
The AR-15/M16, A Practical Guide, by Duncan Long, Paladin Press, Boulder, CO, 1985. 168 pp., illus. Paper covers. $16.95.
The definitive book on the rifle that has been the inspiration for so many modern assault rifles.
American Rifle Design and Performance, by L.R. Wallack, Winchester Press, Piscataway, NJ, 1977. 288 pp., illus. $20.00.
An authoritative, comprehensive guide to how and why every kind of sporting rifle works.
Big Game Rifles and Cartridges, by Elmer Keith, reprint edition by The Gun Room Press, Highland Park, NJ, 1984. 161 pp., illus. $19.95.
Reprint of Elmer Keith's first book, a most original and accurate work on big game rifles and cartridges.
The Black Rifle, M16 Retrospective, R. Blake Stevens and Edward C. Ezell, Collector Grade Publications, Toronto, Canada, 1987. 400 pp., illus. $47.50.
The complete story of the M16 rifle and its development.
The Bolt Action: A Design Analysis, by Stuart Otteson, edited by Ken Warner, Winchester Press, Piscataway, NJ, 1976. 320 pp., illus. $35.00.
Precise and in-depth descriptions, illustrations and comparisons of 16 bolt actions.
The Bolt Action, Volume 2, by Stuart Otteson, Wolfe Publishing Co., Inc. Prescott, AZ, 1985. 289 pp., illus. $22.50.
Covers 17 bolt actions from Newton to Ruger.
Bolt Action Rifles, revised edition, by Frank de Haas, DBI Books, Inc., Northbrook, IL, 1984. 448 pp., illus. Paper covers. $14.95.
A revised edition of the most definitive work on all major bolt-action rifle designs. Detailed coverage of over 110 turnbolt actions, including how they function, take-down and assembly, strengths and weaknesses, dimensional specifications.
The Book of the Garand, by Maj.-Gen. J.S. Hatcher, The Gun Room Press, Highland Park, NJ, 1977. 292 pp., illus. $15.00.
A new printing of the standard reference work on the U.S. Army M1 rifle.

RIFLES (cont.)

***The Breech-Loading Single-Shot Rifle,** by Major Ned H. Roberts and Kenneth L. Waters, Wolfe Publishing Co., Prescott, AZ, 1987. 333 pp., illus. $28.50.

A comprehensive history of the evolution of Scheutzen and single shot rifles.

The Commerical Mauser '98 Sporting Rifle, by Lester Womack, Womack Associates, Publishers, Prescott, AZ, 1980. 69 pp., illus. $25.00.

The first work on the sporting rifles made by the original Mauser plant in Oberndorf.

Custom Muzzleloading Rifles, by Toby Bridges, Stackpole Books, Harrisburg, PA. 1986. 224 pp., illus. Paper covers. $16.95.

An illustrated guide to building or buying a handcrafted muzzleloader.

F.N.-F.A.L. Auto Rifles, Desert Publications, Cornville, AZ, 1981. 130 pp., illus. Paper covers. $7.50.

A definitive study of one of the free world's finest combat rifles.

The Fighting Rifle, by Chuck Taylor, Paladin Press, Boulder, CO, 1983. 184 pp., illus. Paper covers. $16.95.

The difference between assault and battle rifles and auto and light machine guns.

The First Winchester, by John E. Parsons, Winchester Press, Piscataway, NJ, 1977. 207 pp., illus. $35.00.

The story of the 1866 repeating rifle.

A Forgotten Heritage; The Story of a People and the Early American Rifle, by Harry P. Davis, The Gun Room Press, Highland Park, NJ, 1976. 199 pp., illus. $9.95.

Reprint of a very scarce history, originally published in 1941, the Kentucky rifle and the people who used it.

The Golden Age of Single-Shot Rifles, by Edsall James, Pioneer Press, Union City, TN, 1975. 33 pp., illus. Paper covers. $2.75.

A detailed look at all of the fine, high quality sporting single-shot rifles that were once the favorite of target shooters.

The Great Rifle Controversy, by Edward Ezell, Stackpole Books, Harrisburg, PA, 1984. 352 pp., illus. $29.95.

Search for the ultimate infantry weapon from WW II through Vietnam and beyond.

The Gun Digest Book of Firearms Assembly/Disassembly Part III: Rimfire Rifles, by J.B. Wood, DBI Books, Inc., Northbrook, IL, 1980. 288 pp., illus. Paper covers. $12.95.

A most comprehensive, uniform, and professional presentation available for disassembling and reassembling most rimfire rifles.

The Gun Digest Book of Firearms Assembly/Disassembly Part IV: Centerfire Rifles, by J.B. Wood, DBI Books, Inc., Northbrook, IL, 1980. 288 pp., illus. Paper covers. $12.95.

A professional presentation on the disassembly and reassembly of centerfire rifles.

Gun Digest Book of Gun Care, Cleaning and Refinishing, Book Two: Long Guns, by J.B. Wood, DBI Books, Inc., Northbrook, IL, 1984. 160 pp., illus. Paper covers. $9.95.

The care and maintenance of long guns with meticulous detail and step-by-step, illustrated, clearly written text.

Gun Digest Book of the Hunting Rifle, by Jack Lewis, DBI Books, Inc., Northbrook, IL, 1983. 256 pp., illus. Paper covers. $11.95.

Covers all aspects of the hunting rifle—design, development, different types, uses, and more.

Gun Digest Book of Riflesmithing, by Jack Mitchell, DBI Books, Inc., Northbrook, IL, 1982. 256 pp., illus. Paper covers. $11.95.

Covers major and minor gunsmithing operations for rifles—locking systems, triggers, safeties, rifling, crowning, scope mounting, and more.

Jim Carmichel's Book of the Rifle, by Jim Carmichel, an Outdoor Life Book, New York, NY, 1985. 564 pp., illus. $34.95.

The most important book of the author's career, and the most comprehensive ever published on the subject.

Keith's Rifles for Large Game, by Elmer Keith, The Gun Room Press, Highland Park, NJ, 1986. 406 pp., illus. $39.95.

Covers all aspects of selecting, equipping, use and care of high power rifles for hunting big game, especially African.

Know Your M1 Garand, by E. J. Hoffschmidt, Blacksmith Corp., Southport, CT, 1975, 84 pp., illus. Paper covers. $6.95.

Facts about America's most famous infantry weapon. Covers test and experimental models, Japanese and Italian copies, National Match models.

Managing & Mastering the Set Triggered Rifle, by Frank de Haas, Frank de Haas, Orange City, IA, 1986. 56 pp., illus. Paper covers. $5.95.

A manual on how to get the most out of a set-triggered rifle for the sport of target shooting and hunting, and doing it safely.

Manufacture of the Model 1903 Springfield Service Rifle, by Fred H. Colvin and Ethan Viall, et al. Wolfe Publishing Co., Inc., Prescott, AZ, 1985. 450 pp., illus. $29.95.

In three parts. Part 1 is a reprint of Colvin and Viall's 1917 work **U.S. Rifles and Machine Guns**; Part 2 is G.P.O. 1911 **Instructions to Bidders ... Model 1903**; Part 3 is a reprint of two articles on the Springfield from 1928 issues of "Army Ordnance" magazine.

The M-14 Rifle, facsimile reprint of FM 23-8, Desert Publications, Cornville, AZ, 50 pp., illus. Paper $5.95.

In this well illustrated and informative reprint, the M-14 and M-14E2 are covered thoroughly.

M1 Carbine Owner's Manual, M1, M2 & M3 .30 Caliber Carbines, Firepower Publications, Cornville, AZ, 1984. 102 pp., illus. Paper covers. $9.95.

The complete book for the owner of an M1 carbine.

The Mini-14, by Duncan Long, Paladin Press, Boulder, CO, 1987. 120 pp., illus. Paper covers. $10.00.

History of the Mini-14, the factory-produced models, specifications, accessories, suppliers, and much more.

Modern Military Bullpup Rifles, by T.B. Dugelby, Collector Grade Publications, Toronto, Canada, 1984. 97 pp., illus. $20.00.

The EM-2 concept comes to age.

The Modern Rifle, by Jim Carmichel, Winchester Press, Piscataway, NJ, 1975. 320 pp., illus. $15.95.

The most comprehensive, thorough, up-to-date book ever published on today's rifled sporting arms.

***Mr. Single Shot's Book of Rifle Plans,** by Frank de Haas, Frank de Haas, Orange City, IA, 1987. 84 pp., illus. Paper covers. $22.95.

With detailed instructions and drawings on how to build four unique breech-loading single-shot rifles.

North American FALs, by R. Blake Stevens, Collector Grade Publications, Toronto, Canada, 1979. 166 pp., illus. Paper covers. $20.00.

NATO's search for a standard rifle.

100 Years of Shooters and Gunmakers of Single Shot Rifles, by Gerald O. Kelver, Brighton, CO, 1975. 212 pp., illus. Paper covers. $10.00.

The Schuetzen rifle, targets and shooters, primers, match rifles, original loadings and much more. With chapters on famous gunsmiths like Harry Pope, Morgan L. Rood and others.

The Pennsylvania Rifle, by Samuel E. Dyke, Sutter House, Lititz, PA, 1975. 61 pp., illus. Paper covers. $5.00.

History and development, from the hunting rifle of the Germans who settled the area. Contains a full listing of all known Lancaster, PA, gunsmiths from 1729 through 1815.

The Revolving Rifles, by Edsall James, Pioneer Press, Union City, TN, 1975. 23 pp., illus. Paper covers. $2.50.

Valuable information on revolving cylinder rifles, from the earliest matchlock forms to the latest models of Colt and Remington.

The Rifle Book, by Jack O'Connor, Random House, NY, 1978. 337 pp., illus. Paper covers. $13.95.

The complete book of small game, varmint and big game rifles.

Rifle Guide, by Robert A. Steindler, Stoeger Publishing Co., South Hackensack, NJ, 1978. 304 pp., illus. Paper covers. $9.95.

Complete, fully illustrated guide to selecting, shooting, caring for, and collecting rifles of all types.

Rifle and Marksmanship, by Judge H.A. Gildersleeve, reprinted by W.S. Curtis, Buckinghamshire, England, 1986. 131 pp., illus. $25.00.

Reprint of a book first published in 1878 in New York, catering to the shooter of early breech-loaders and late muzzle-loaders.

Rifle Shooting as a Sport, by Bernd Klingner, A.S. Barnes and Co., Inc., San Diego, CA, 1980. 186 pp., illus. Paper covers. $15.00.

Basic principles, positions and techniques by an international expert.

The Rifleman's Rifle: Winchester's Model 70, 1936-63, by Roger C. Rule, Alliance Books, Inc., Northridge, CA, 1982. 368 pp., illus. $59.95.

The most complete reference book on the Model 70, with much fresh information on the Model 54 and the new Model 70s.

Ned H. Roberts and the Schuetzen Rifle, edited by Gerald O. Kelver, Brighton, CO, 1982. 99 pp., illus. $10.00.

A compilation of the writings of Major Ned H. Roberts which appeared in various gun magazines.

The Ruger No. 1, by J.D. Clayton, edited by John T. Amber, Blacksmith Corp., Southport, CT, 1983. 200 pp., illus. $39.50.

Covers this famous rifle from original conception to current production.

Schuetzen Rifles, History and Loading, by Gerald O. Kelver, Gerald O. Kelver, Publisher, Brighton, CO, 1972. Illus. $10.00.

Reference work on these rifles, their bullets, loading, telescopic sights, accuracy, etc. A limited, numbered ed.

The Sporting Rifle and its Projectiles, by Lieut. James O Forsyth, The Buckskin Press, Big Timber, MT, 1978. 132 pp., illus. $25.00.

Facsimile reprint of the 1863 edition, one of the most authoritative books ever written on the muzzle-loading round ball sporting rifle.

The Springfield Rifle M1903, M1903A1, M1903A3, M1903A4, Desert Publications, Cornville, AZ, 1982. 100 pp., illus. Paper covers. $6.95.

Covers every aspect of disassembly and assembly, inspection, repair and maintenance.

***The Sturm, Ruger 10/22 Rifle and .44 Magnum Carbine,** by Duncan Long, Paladin Press, Boulder, CO, 1988. 108 pp., illus. Paper covers. $10.00.

An in-depth look at both weapons detailing the elegant simplicity of the Ruger design. Offers specifications, troubleshooting procedures and ammunition recommendations.

Henry Wilkinson's Observations on Muskets, Rifles and Projectiles, a facsimile reprint of the scarce 1852 London edition. Reprinted by W.S. Curtis, Bucks, England, 1983. 63 pp., illus. Paper covers. $12.95.

Includes the author's scarce work "Treatise on Elastic Concave Wadding."

***The American Shotgun,** by David F. Butler, edited by C. Kenneth Ramage, Lyman Publications, Middlefield, CT, 1973. 243 pp., illus. Paper covers. $14.95.

A comprehensive history of the American smoothbore's evolution from Colonial times to the present day.

American Shotgun Design and Performance, by L.R. Wallack, Winchester Press, Piscataway, NJ, 1977. 184 pp., illus. $16.95.

An expert lucidly recounts the history and development of American shotguns and explains how they work.

The Art of Shooting, by Charles Lancaster, Ashford Press, Southampton, England, 1986. 212 pp., illus. $34.95.

Reprint of a classic and reliable work on the use of the shotgun.

The Best Shotguns Ever Made in America, by Michael McIntosh, Charles Scribner's Sons, New York, NY, 1981. 185 pp., illus. $17.95.

Seven vintage doubles to shoot and treasure.

The British Shotgun, Volume 1, 1850-1870, by I.M. Crudington and D.J. Baker, Barrie & Jenkins, London, England, 1979. 256 pp., illus. $29.95.

An attempt to trace, as accurately as is now possible, the evolution of the shotgun during its formative years in Great Britain.

SHOTGUNS (cont.)

Churchill's Game Shooting, edited by Macdonald Hastings, Arms & Armour Press, London, England, 1979. 252 pp., illus. Paper covers. $15.00.
The standard textbook on the successful use of the shotgun.
***Clay Target Shooting,** by Paul Bentley, A&C Black, London, England, 1987. 144 pp., illus. $25.00.
Practical book on clay target shooting written by a very successful internatinal competitor, providing valuable professional advice and instruction for shooters of all disciplines.
Combat Shotgun Training, by Charles R. Skillen, Charles C. Thomas, Publisher, Springfield, IL. 1982. 201 pp., illus. $40.00.
Complete, authoritative information on the use of the shotgun in law enforcement.
The Double Shotgun, by Don Zutz, Winchester Press, Piscataway, NJ, 1985. 304 pp., illus. $19.95.
Revised, updated, expanded edition of the history and development of the world's classic sporting firearms.
Game Gun, by Richard S. Grozik, Willow Creek Press, Oshkosh, WI, 1986. 150 pp., illus. $39.00.
Transports you to the workshops of the finest gunmakers in England, Europe, Canada, and the U.S. through picture and text.
The Golden Age of Shotgunning, by Bob Hinman, Wolfe Publishing Co., Inc., Prescott, AZ, 1982. $17.95.
A valuable history of the late 1800s detailing that fabulous period of development in shotguns, shotshells and shotgunning.
The Gun Digest Book of Firearms Assembly/Disassembly, Part V: Shotguns, by J.B. Wood, DBI Books, Inc., Northbrook, IL, 1980. 288 pp., illus. Paper covers. $12.95.
A professional presentation on the complete disassembly and assembly of 26 of the most popular shotguns, new and old.
Gun Digest Book of Gun Care, Cleaning and Refinishing, Book Two: Long Guns, by J.B. Wood, DBI Books, Inc., Northbrook IL, 1984. 160 pp., illus. Paper covers. $9.95.
The care and maintenance of long guns with meticulous detail and step-by-step, illustrated, clearly written text.
Gun Digest Book of Shotgun Gunsmithing, by Ralph Walker, DBI Books, Inc., Northbrook, IL, 1983. 256 pp., illus. Paper covers. $12.95.
The principles and practices of repairing, individualizing and accurizing modern shotguns by one of the world's premier shotgun gunsmiths.
Gun Digest Book of Trap and Skeet Shooting, by Art Blatt, DBI Books, Inc., Northbrook, IL, 1984. 288 pp., illus. Paper covers. $12.95.
Valuable information for both beginner and seasoned shooter.
Hartman on Skeet, by Barney Hartman, Stackpole Books, Harrisburg, PA, 1973. 143 pp., illus. $10.00.
A definitive book on Skeet shooting by a pro.
The History of W. & C. Scott Gunmakers, by J.A. Crawford and P.G. Whatley, second edition, Rowland Ward's at Holland & Holland, Ltd., London, England, 1986. 92 pp., illus. $22.50.
The guns, gunmaking operations, tables of serial numbers for W. & C. Scott and Webley & Scott guns and rifles from 1865-1980.
How to be a Winner Shooting Skeet & Trap, by Tom Morton, Tom Morton, Knoxville, MD, 1974. 144 pp., illus. Paper covers. $10.95.
The author explains why championship shooting is more than a physical process.
L.C. Smith Shotguns, by Lt. Col. William S. Brophy, The Gun Room Press, Highland Park, NJ, 1979. 244 pp., illus. $29.95.
The first work on this very important American gun and manufacturing company.
***Lefever: Guns of Lasting Fame,** by Robert W. (Bob) Elliot and Jim Cobb, Robert W. (Bob) Elliot, Lindale, TX, 1986. 174 pp., illus. $29.95.
Hundreds of photographs, patent drawings and production figures are given on this famous maker's shotguns.
A Manual of Clayshooting, by Chris Cradock, Hippocrene Books, Inc., New York, NY, 1983. 192 pp., illus. $29.95.
Covers everything from building a range to buying a shotgun, with lots of illustrations and diagrams.
Matt Eastman's Guide to Browning Sporting Firearms' Serial Numbers, 1924 to Present, together with, **Matt Eastman's Guide to Browning Sporting Firearms 1924-1985,** compiled by Matt Eastman, Fitzgerald, GA, 1986. 32; 11 pp. The two booklets. Paper covers. $15.95.
Covers all the Belgian and Japanese guns from 1924 to present.
The Modern Shotgun, by Major Sir Charles Burrard, Ashford Press, Southampton, England, 1986 reprint of this 3-volume set. The set, $125.00.
Reprinting of the most classic and informative work on the shotgun.
The Mysteries of Shotgun Patterns, by George G. Oberfell and Charles E. Thompson, Oklahoma State University Press, Stillwater, OK, 1982. 164 pp., illus. Paper covers. $25.00.
Shotgun ballistics for the hunter in non-technical language, with information on improving effectiveness in the field.
The Orvis Wing-Shooting Handbook, by Bruce Bowlen, Nick Lyons Books, New York, NY, 1985. 83 pp., illus. Paper covers. $8.95.
Proven techniques for better shotgunning.
Parker, America's Finest Shotgun, by Peter H. Johnson, Stackpole Books, Inc., Harrisburg, PA, 1985. 272 pp., illus. $17.95.
A look at one of the rarest and finest shotguns in history.
The Parker Gun, by Larry L. Baer, The Gun Room Press, Highland Park, NJ, 1983. 240 pp., illus. $29.95.
The only comprehensive work on the subject of America's most famous shotgun.
Plans and Specifications of the L.C. Smith Shotgun, by Lt. Col. William S. Brophy, USAR Ret., F. Brownell & Son, Montezuma, IA, 1982. 247 pp., illus. $19.95.
The only collection ever assembled of all the drawings and engineering specifications on the incomparable and very collectable L.C. Smith shotgun.
Police Shotgun Manual, by Bill Clede, Stackpole Books, Harrisburg, PA, 1986. 128 pp., illus. $13.95.
How to survive against all odds. Latest shotgun techniques for tough situations.
The Police Shotgun Manual, by Robert H. Robinson, Charles C. Thomas, Springfield, IL 1973. 153 pp., illus. $29.95.
A complete study and analysis of the most versatile and effective weapon in the police arsenal.
Purdey's, the Guns and the Family, by Richard Beaumont, David and Charles, Pombret, VT, 1984. 248 pp., illus. $34.95.
Records the history of the Purdey family from 1814 to today, how the guns were and are built and daily functioning of the factory.
Recreating the Double Barrel Muzzle-Loading Shotgun, by William R. Brockway, George Shumway Publisher, York, PA, 1985. 198 pp., illus. Paper covers, $20.00; Cloth, $27.50.
Treats the making of double guns of classic type.
Reloading for Shotgunners, 2nd Edition, edited by Robert S.L. Anderson, DBI Books, Inc., Northbrook, IL, 1985. 256 pp., illus. Paper covers. $12.95.
The very latest in reloading information for the shotgunner.
75 Years with the Shotgun, by C.T. (Buck) Buckman, Valley Publ., Fresno, CA, 1974. 141 pp., illus. $10.00.
An expert hunter and trapshooter shares experiences of a lifetime.
Score Better at Trap, by Fred Missildine, Winchester Press, Piscataway, NJ, 1976. 159 pp., illus. $22.50.
An essential book for all trap shooters.
The Shooting Field: One Hundred and Fifty Years with Holland and Holland, by Peter King, Blacksmith Corp., Southport, CT, 1985. 176 pp., illus. $39.95.
History of this famous firm and its guns.
The Shotgun, by Macdonald Hastings, David & Charles, London, England, 1983. 240 pp., illus. $34.95.
The story of the shotgun's development since Lt. Col. Peter Hawker made gunning a gentleman's recreation up to the present day.
The Shotgun Book, by Jack O'Connor, Alfred A. Knopf, New York, NY, 2nd rev. ed., 1981. 341 pp., illus. Paper covers. $13.95.
An indispensable book for every shotgunner containing authoritative information on every phase of the shotgun.
The Shotgun in Combat, by Tony Lesce, Desert Publications, Cornville, AZ, 1979. 148 pp., illus. Paper covers. $10.00.
A history of the shotgun and its use in combat.
Shotgun Digest, 3rd Edition, edited by Jack Lewis, DBI Books, Inc., Northbrook, IL 1986. 256 pp., illus. Paper covers. $12.95.
A new look at shotguns.
The Shotgun: History and Development, by Geoffrey Boothroyd, A & C Black Publisher, Ltd. London, England, 1986. 256 pp., illus. $29.95.
From the days of the flintlock, through the percussion era to the early pin-fire breechloaders, and the later hammer centerfire breechloaders.
Shotgunners Guide, by Monte Burch, Winchester Press, Piscataway, NJ, 1980. 208 pp., illus. $18.95.
A basic book for the young and old who want to try shotgunning or who want to improve their skill.
Shotgunning: The Art and the Science, by Bob Brister, Winchester Press, Piscataway, NJ, 1976. 321 pp., illus. $17.95.
Hundreds of specific tips and truly novel techniques to improve the field and target shooting of every shotgunner.
Shotguns and Gunsmiths, The Vintage Years, by Geoffrey Boothroyd, A & C Black, London, England, 1986. 240 pp., illus. $32.50.
The guns made by Boswell, Purdey, Lang, Scott, Grant, Greener, and Westley Richards.
The Sporting Shotgun: A User's Handbook, by Robin Marshall-Ball, Stonewall Press, Wash., DC, 1982. 176 pp., illus. $23.95.
An important international reference on shotgunning in North America and Europe, including Britain.
Sure-Hit Shotgun Ways, by Francis E. Sell, Stackpole Books, Harrisburg, PA, 1967. 160 pp., illus. $25.00.
On guns, ballistics and quick skill methods.
Skeet Shooting with D. Lee Braun, edited by R. Campbell, Grosset & Dunlap, NY, 1967. 160 pp., illus. Paper covers $5.95.
Thorough instructions on the fine points of Skeet shooting.
Trapshooting with D. Lee Braun and the Remington Pros., ed. by R. Campbell. Remington Arms Co., Bridgeport, CT. 1969. 157 pp., well illus., Paper covers. $5.95.
America's masters of the scattergun give the secrets of professional marksmanship.
U.S. Shotguns, All Types, reprint of TM9-285, Desert Publications, Cornville, AZ, 1987. 257 pp., illus. Paper covers. $9.95.
Covers operation, assembly and disassembly of 9 shotguns used by the U.S. armed forces.
The Winchester Model Twelve, by George Madis, David Madis, Dallas, TX, 1984. 176 pp., illus.$19.95.
A definitive work on this famous American shotgun.
Winchester Shotguns and Shotshells, by Ronald W. Stadt, Armory Publications, Tacoma, WA, 1984. 200 pp., illus. $29.50.
From the hammer double to the Model 59.
Wing & Shot, by R.G. Wehle, Country Press, Scottsville, NY, 1967. 190 pp., illus. $24.95.
Step-by-step account on how to train a fine shooting dog.
The World's Fighting Shotguns, by Thomas F. Swearengen, T. B. N. Enterprises, Alexandria, VA 1979. 500 pp., illus. $34.95.
The complete military and police reference work from the shotgun's inception to date, with up-to-date developments.

ARMS ASSOCIATIONS IN AMERICA AND ABROAD

UNITED STATES

ALABAMA

Alabama Gun Collectors Assn.
Secretary, P.O. Box 6080, Tuscaloosa, AL 35405

ALASKA

Alaska Gun Collectors Assn.
P.O. Box 101522, Anchorage, AK 99510

ARIZONA

Arizona Arms Assn.
Lois Fobes, Secy., P.O. Box 17061, Tucson, AZ 85731

CALIFORNIA

California Waterfowl Assn.
3840 Rosin Ct., #100, Sacramento, CA 95834
Greater Calif. Arms & Collectors Assn.
Donald L. Bullock, 8291 Carburton St., Long Beach, CA 90808
Los Angeles Gun & Ctg. Collectors Assn.
F.H. Ruffra, 20810 Amie Ave., Apt. #9, Torrance, CA 90503

COLORADO

Colorado Gun Collectors Assn.
L.E. (Bud) Greenwald, 2553 So. Quitman St., Denver, CO 80219

CONNECTICUT

Ye Conn. Gun Guild, Inc.
Dick Fraser, P.O. Box 425, Windsor, CT 06095

FLORIDA

Florida Gun Collectors Assn., Inc.
John D. Hammer, 5700 Mariner Dr., 304-W, Tampa, FL 33609
Tampa Bay Arms Collectors' Assn.
John Tuvell, 2461 — 67th Ave. S., St. Petersburg, FL 33712
Unified Sportsmen of Florida
P.O. Box 6565, Tallahassee, FL 32314

GEORGIA

Georgia Arms Collectors
Michael Simmons, P.O. Box 277, Alpharetta, GA 30239

ILLINOIS

American Coon Hunters Assn.
Floyd E. Butler, Box 30, Ingraham, IL 62434
Illinois State Rifle Assn.
520 N. Michigan Ave., Room 615, Chicago, IL 60611
Illinois Gun Collectors Assn.
T.J. Curl, Jr., P.O. Box 971, Kankakee, IL 60901
Mississippi Valley Gun & Cartridge Coll. Assn.
Lawrence Maynard, R.R. 2, Aledo, IL 61231
Sauk Trail Gun Collectors
Gordell M. Matson, P.O. Box 1113, Milan, IL 61264
Wabash Valley Gun Collectors Assn., Inc.
Eberhard R. Gerbsch, 416 South St., Danville, IL 61832

INDIANA

Indiana Sportsmen's Council-Legislative
Maurice Latimer, P.O. Box 93, Bloomington, IN 47402
Indiana State Rifle & Pistol Assn.
Thos. Glancy, P.O. Box 552, Chesterton, IN 46304
Southern Indiana Gun Collectors Assn., Inc.
Harold M. McClary, 509 N. 3rd St., Boonville, IN 47601

IOWA

Central States Gun Collectors Assn.
Avery Giles, 1104 S. 1st Ave., Marshtown, IA 50158

KANSAS

Kansas Cartridge Coll. Assn.
Bob Linder, Box 84, Plainville, KS 67663

KENTUCKY

Kentuckiana Arms Coll. Assn.
Tony Wilson, Pres., Box 1776, Louisville, KY 40201
Kentucky Gun Collectors Assn., Inc.
Ruth Johnson, Box 64, Owensboro, KY 42302

LOUISIANA

Washitaw River Renegades
Sandra Rushing, P.O. Box 256, Main St., Grayson, LA 71435

MARYLAND

Baltimore Antique Arms Assn.
Stanley I. Kellert, E-30, 2600 Insulator Dr., Baltimore, MD 21230

MASSACHUSETTS

Bay Colony Weapons Collectors, Inc.
Ronald B. Santurjian, 47 Homer Rd., Belmont, MA 02178
Massachusetts Arms Collectors
John J. Callan, Jr., P.O. Box 1001, Worcester, MA 01613

MICHIGAN

Royal Oak Historical Arms Collectors, Inc.
Nancy Stein, 25487 Hereford, Huntington Woods, MI 48070

MISSISSIPPI

Mississippi Gun Collectors Assn.
Jack E. Swinney, P.O. Box 16323, Hattiesburg, MS 39404

MISSOURI

Mineral Belt Gun Coll. Assn.
D.F. Saunders, 1110 Cleveland Ave., Monett, MO 65708
Missouri Valley Arms Collectors Assn., Inc.
L.P. Brammer II, Membership Secy., P.O. Box 33033, Kansas City, MO 64114

MONTANA

Montana Arms Collectors Assn.
Lewis E. Yearout, 308 Riverview Dr. East, Great Falls, MT 59404
The Winchester Arms Coll. Assn.
Richard Berg, P.O. Box 6754, Great Falls, MT 59406

NEW HAMPSHIRE

New Hampshire Arms Collectors, Inc.
Frank H. Galeucia, Rte. 28, Box 44, Windham, NH 03087

NEW JERSEY

Englishtown Benchrest Shooters Assn.
Michael Toth, 64 Cooke Ave., Carteret, NJ 07008
Experimental Ballistics Associates
Ed Yard, 110 Kensington, Trenton, NJ 08618
Jersey Shore Antique Arms Collectors
Joe Sisia, P.O. Box 100, Bayville, NJ 08721
New Jersey Arms Collectors Club, Inc.
Angus Laidlaw, 230 Valley Rd., Montclair, NJ 07042

NEW YORK

Empire State Arms Coll. Assn.
P.O. Box 2328, Rochester, NY 14623
Iroquois Arms Collectors Assn.
Kenneth Keller, club secy., (Susann Keller, show secy.) 214 - 70th St., Niagara Falls, NY 14304
Mid-State Arms Coll. & Shooters Club
Jack Ackerman, 24 S. Mountain Terr. Binghamton, NY 13903

NORTH CAROLINA

Carolina Gun Collectors Assn.
Jerry Ledford, 3231 - 7th St. Dr. NE, Hickory, NC 28601

OHIO

Central Ohio Gun and Indian Relic Coll. Assn.
Coyt Stookey, 134 E. Ohio Ave., Washington C.H., OH 43160
Ohio Gun Collectors, Assn.
P.O. Box 24 F, Cincinnati, OH 45224
The Stark Gun Collectors, Inc.
William I. Gann, 5666 Waynesburg Dr., Waynesburg, OH 44688

OKLAHOMA

Indian Territory Gun Collector's Assn.
P.O. Box 4491, Tulsa, OK 74159

OREGON

Oregon Cartridge Coll. Assn.
Terry A. White, 9480 S. Gribble Rd., Canby, OR 97013
Oregon Arms Coll. Assn., Inc.
Ted Dowd, P.O. Box 25103, Portland, OR 97225

PENNSYLVANIA

Presque Isle Gun Coll. Assn.
James Welch, 156 E. 37 St., Erie, PA 16504

SOUTH CAROLINA

Belton Gun Club, Inc.
J.K. Phillips, Route 1, Belton, SC 29627
South Carolina Shooting Assn.
P.O. Box 210133, Columbia, SC 29221

SOUTH DAKOTA

Dakota Territory Gun Coll. Assn., Inc.
Curt Carter, Castlewood, SD 57223

TENNESSEE

Smoky Mountain Gun Coll. Assn., Inc.
Hugh W. Yabro, Pres., P.O. Box 23225, Knoxville, TN 37933
Tennessee Gun Collectors Assn., Inc.
M.H. Parks, 3556 Pleasant Valley Rd., Nashville, TN 37204

TEXAS

Houston Gun Collectors Assn., Inc.
P.O. Box 741429, Houston, TX 77274
Texas Cartridge Coll. Assn., Inc.
Dick Salzer, 2600 S. Gessner, #504
Houston, TX 77063
Texas State Rifle Assn.
P.O. Drawer 710549, Dallas, TX 75371

WASHINGTON

Washington Arms Collectors, Inc.
J. Dennis Cook, P.O. Box 7335, Tacoma, WA 98407

WISCONSIN

Great Lakes Arms Coll. Assn., Inc.
Edward C. Warnke, 2913 Woodridge Lane, Waukesha, WI 53186
Wisconsin Gun Collectors Assn., Inc.
Lulita Zellmer, P.O. Box 181, Sussex, WI 53089

WYOMING

Wyoming Gun Collectors
Bob Funk, Box 1805, Riverton, WY 82501

NATIONAL ORGANIZATIONS

Amateur Trapshooting Assn.
601 W. National Rd., Vandalia, OH 45377
American Association of Shotgunning
P.O. Box 3351, Reno, NV 89505
American Custom Gunmakers Guild
c/o Jan's Secretariat, 220 Division St., Northfield, MN 55057
American Defense Preparedness Assn.
Rosslyn Center, Suite 900, 1700 N. Moore St., Arlington, VA 22209
American Pistolsmiths Guild
J.D. Jones, Pres., Rt. 1, Della Dr., Bloomingdale, OH 43910
American Police Pistol & Rifle Assn.
1100 N.E. 125th St., No. Miami, FL 33161
American Single Shot Rifle Assn.
L.B. Thompson, 987 Jefferson Ave., Salem, OH 44460
American Society of Arms Collectors, Inc.
George E. Weatherly, P.O. Box 460, DeSoto, TX 75115
Association of Firearm and Toolmark Examiners
Eugenia A. Bell, Secy., 7857 Esterel Dr., LaJolla, CA 92037; membership sec'y.: Andrew B. Hart, 80 Mountain View Ave., Rensselaer, NY 12144
Boone & Crockett Club
241 South Fraley Blvd., Dumfries, VA 22026
British Empire Military Collectors Assn.
Tim Palmer, Rt. 2 Box 207A, Moses Lake, WA 98837/509-765-5038
Browning Collectors Assn.
Mrs. Judy A. Rogers, 4928 Merrick Ave., Grand Island, NE 68801
The Cast Bullet Assn., Inc.
Ralland J. Fortier, Membership Director, 4103 Foxcraft Dr., Traverse City, MI 49684
Citizen Committee for the Right to Keep and Bear Arms
Natl. Hq.: Liberty Park, 12500 N.E. Tenth Pl., Bellevue, WA 98005
Colt Collectors Assn.
P.O. Box 11464, St. Paul, MN 55111
Deer Unlimited of America, Inc.
P.O. Box 509, Clemson, SC 29631
Ducks Unlimited, Inc.
One Waterfowl Way, Long Grove, IL 60047
Experimental Ballistics Associates
Ed Yard, 110 Kensington, Trenton, NJ 08618
Firearms Engravers Guild of America
Robert Evans, Secy., 332 Vine St., Oregon City, OR 97045
Foundation For North American Wild Sheep
720 Allen Ave., Cody, WY 82414
Garand Collectors Assn.
P.O. Box 181, Richmond, KY 40475
Handgun Hunters International
J.D. Jones, Dir., P.O. Box 357 MAG, Bloomingdale, OH 43910
Harrington & Richardson Gun Coll. Assn.
George L. Cardet, 525 N.W. 27th Ave., Suite 201, Miami, FL 33125
International Benchrest Shooters
Joan Borden, RD 1, Box 244A, Tunkhannock, PA 18657
International Cartridge Coll. Assn., Inc.
Victor v. B. Engel, 1211 Walnut St., Williamsport, PA 17701
International Military Arms Society
Robert Jensen, 3021 Benjamin Dr., Wichita, KS 67204
The Mannlicher Collectors Assn.
Rev. Don L. Henry, Secy., P.O. Box 7144, Salem, OR 97303
Marlin Firearms Coll. Assn., Ltd.
Dick Paterson, Secy., 407 Lincoln Bldg., 44 Main St., Champaign, IL 61820
Miniature Arms Collectors/Makers Society Ltd.
Joseph J. Macewicz, Exec. Secy., 104 White Sand Lane, Racine, WI 53402
National Assn. of Federally Licd. Firearms Dealers
Andrew Molchan, 2801 E. Oakland Park Blvd., Ft. Lauderdale, FL 33306
National Automatic Pistol Collectors Assn.
Tom Knox, P.O. Box 15738, Tower Grove Station, St. Louis, MO 63163
National Bench Rest Shooters Assn., Inc.
Pat Baggett, 2027 Buffalo, Levelland, TX 79336
National Muzzle Loading Rifle Assn.
Box 67, Friendship, IN 47021
National Reloading Mfrs. Assn.
4905 S.W. Griffith Dr., Suite 101, Beaverton, OR 97005
National Rifle Assn. of America
1600 Rhode Island Ave., N.W., Washington, DC 20036
National Shooting Sports Fdtn., Inc.
Robert T. Delfay, Exec. Director, 555 Danbury Rd., Wilton, CT 06897/203-762-1320
National Skeet Shooting Assn.
Mike Hampton, Exec. Director, P.O. Box 680007, San Antonio, TX 78268-0007
National Varmint Hunters Assn. (NVHA)
P.O. Box 17962, San Antonio, TX 78217
National Wild Turkey Federation, Inc.
P.O. Box 530, Edgefield, SC 29824
North American Airgunners Assn.
R.J. Ledbetter, Dir., Box 12935, Winston-Salem, NC 27117
North American Hunting Club
P.O. Box 35557, Minneapolis, MN 55435
North-South Skirmish Assn., Inc.
T.E. Johnson, Jr., 9700 Royerton Dr., Richmond, VA 23228
Remington Society of America
Gordon Stanley, 380 S. Tustin Ave., Orange, CA 92666
Ruger Collector's Assn., Inc.
P.O. Box 1778, Chino Valley, AZ 86323
Safari Club International
Holt Bodinson, 4800 W. Gates Pass Rd., Tucson, AZ 85745/602-620-1220
Sako Collectors Assn., Inc.
Karen Reed, 1725 Woodhill Ln., Bedford, TX 76021
Second Amendment Foundation
James Madison Building, 12500 N.E. 10th Pl., Bellevue, WA 98005
Smith & Wesson Coll. Assn.
William Orr, P.O. Box 458, Rossville, GA 37041
The Society of American Bayonet Collectors
P.O. Box 44021, Baton Rouge, LA 70804
Southern California Schuetzen Society
Dean Lillard, 34657 Ave. E., Yucaipa, CA 92399
Sporting Arms & Ammunition Manufacturers Institute (SAAMI)
555 Danbury Rd., Wilton, CT 06897
The Thompson/Center Assn.
Joe Wright, Pres., Box 792, Northboro, MA 01532
U.S. Revolver Assn.
Chick Shuter, 96 West Union St., Ashland, MA 01721
The Webley & Scott Collectors Assn.
R. Guy Sizer, 1261 Marywood Lane, Apt. 230, Richmond, VA 23220
Winchester Arms Collectors Assoc.
Richard Berg, Secy., P.O. Box 6754, Great Falls, MT 59406
World Fast Draw Assn.
Dick Plum, 16421 McFadden, Apt. 350, Tustin, CA 92680

AUSTRALIA

Sporting Shooters' Assn. of Australia Inc.
P.O. Box 2066, Kent Town SA 5067, Australia

CANADA

ALBERTA

Canadian Historical Arms Society
P.O. Box 901, Edmonton, Alb., Canada T5J 2L8
National Firearms Assn.
Natl. HQ: P.O. Box 1779, Edmonton, Alta. T5J 2P1, Canada

BRITISH COLUMBIA

Historial Arms Collectors Society of B.C.
P.O. Box 86166, North Vancouver, B.C., V7L 4J8, Canada

MANITOBA

The Association of Automatic Firearms Collectors and Shooters
131 Nemy Cresent, Winnipeg, MB R2Y 0K6, Canada

ONTARIO

The Ontario Handgun Assn.
1711 McCowan Rd., Suite 205, Scarborough, Ont., M1S 2Y3, Canada
Tri-County Antique Arms Fair
P.O. Box 122, RR #1, North Lancaster, Ont., K0C 1Z0, Canada

EUROPE

ENGLAND

Arms and Armour Society of London
A.R.E. North. Dept. of Metalwork, Victoria & Albert Museum, South Kensington, London SW7 2RL
Historial Breechloading Smallarms Assn.
D.J. Penn, M.A., Imperial War Museum, Lambeth Rd., London SE 1 6HZ, England. Journal and newsletter are $8 a yr. seamail; surcharge for airmail
National Rifle Assn.
(Great Britain)
Bisley Camp, Brookwood, Woking, Surrey, GU24 OPB, England/048-67-2213

FRANCE

Syndicat National de l'Arquebuserie du Commerce de l'Arme Historique
B.P. No. 3, 78110 Le Vesinet, France

GERMANY (WEST)

Deutscher Schützenbund
Lahnstrasse 120 6200 Wiesbaden-Klarenthal, West Germany

NEW ZEALAND

New Zealand Deerstalkers Assn.
Mr. Shelby Grant, P.O. Box 6514, Wellington, New Zealand

SOUTH AFRICA

Historical Firearms Soc. of South Africa
P.O. Box 145, 7725 Newlands, Republic of South Africa
South African Reloaders Assn.
Box 27128, Sunnyside, Pretoria 0132, South Africa

Directory of the Arms Trade

INDEX TO THE DIRECTORY

AMMUNITION (Commercial)

Activ Industries, Inc., P.O. Box F, 100 Zigor Rd., Kearneysville, WV 25430/304-725-0451 (shotshells only)
Alberts Corp., 519 East 19th St., Paterson, NJ 07514/201-684-1676
Brass Extrusion Laboratories, Ltd., 800 W. Maple Lane, Bensenville, IL 60106/312-595-2792
Cascade Cartridge Inc., (See Omark)
Dynamit Nobel-RWS Inc., 105 Stonehurst Court, Northvale, NJ 07647/201-767-1995(RWS)
Eley-Kynoch, ICI-America, Wilmington, DE 19897/302-575-3000
Elite Ammunition, P.O. Box 3251, Hinsdale, IL 60522/312-366-9006
Estate Cartridge Inc., P.O. Box 3702, Conroe, TX 77305 (shotshell)
Federal Cartridge Co., 900 Ehlen Dr., Anoka, MN 55303/612-422-2840
Fisher Enterprises, 655 Main St. #305, Edmonds, WA 98020/206-776-4365 (Prometheus airgun pellets)
Freedom Arms Co., P.O. Box 1776, Freedom, WY 83120/307-883-2468
Frontier Cartridge Division-Hornady Mfg. Co., Box 1848, Grand Island, NE 68801/308-382-1390
Hansen Cartridge Co., 244 Old Post Rd., Southport, CT 06490/203-259-5424
ICI-America, Wilmington, DE 19897/302-575-3000(Eley-Kynoch)
Liquid Assets, Inc., P.O. Box 4005, Key West, FL 33040 (P.E.A.C.E.)
Mitchell Arms, Inc., 3411 Lake Center Dr., Santa Ana, CA 92704/714-957-5711
Omark Industries, P.O. Box 856, Lewiston, ID 83501/208-746-2351
P.P.C. Corp., 625 E. 24th St., Paterson, NJ 07514
Palcher Ammunition, Techstar Engineering, Inc., 2239 S. Huron Ave., Santa Ana, CA 92705/714-556-7384
Precision Prods. of Wash., Inc., N. 311 Walnut Rd., Spokane, WA 99206/509-928-0604 (Exammo)
Prometheus/Titan Black (See Fisher Enterprises)
RWS (See Dynamit Nobel)
Remington Arms Co., 1077 Market St., Wilmington, DE 19898
Southern Ammunition Co, Inc., Rte. 1, Box 6B, Latta, SC 29565/803-752-7751
3-D Inv., Inc., Box J, Main St., Doniphan, NE 68832/402-845-2285
United States Ammunition Co. (USAC), Inc., 45500 - 15th St. East, Tacoma, WA 98424/206-922-7589
Weatherby's, 2781 E. Firestone Blvd., South Gate, CA 90280
Winchester, 427 N. Shamrock St., East Alton, IL 62024/618-258-2000

AMMUNITION (Custom)

A Square Co., Inc., Rt. 4, Simmons Rd., Madison, IN 47250/812-273-3633
Accuracy Systems Inc., 15205 N. Cave Creek Rd., Phoenix, AZ 85032/602-971-1991
Allred Bullet Co., 932 Evergreen Dr., Logan, UT 84321/801-752-6983
Beal's Bullets, 170 W. Marshall Rd., Lansdowne, PA 19050/215-259-1220 (Auto Mag Specialists)
Black Mountain Bullets, Rte. 3, Box 297, Warrenton, VA 22186/703-347-1199
Brass Extrusion Labs. Ltd., (B.E.L.L.) 800 W. Maple Lane, Bensenville, IL 60106/312-595-2792
Russell Campbell Custom Loaded Ammo, 219 Leisure Dr., San Antonio, TX 78201/512-735-1183
Cartridges Unlimited, Rt. 1, Box 50, South Kent, CT 06785/203-927-3053 (British Express; metric; U.S.)
Cor-Bon Bullet Co., P.O. Box 10126, Detroit, MI 48210/313-894-2373
Cumberland Arms, Rt. 1, Box 1150, Shafer Rd., Blantons Chapel, Manchester, TN 37355
Custom Tackle & Ammo, P.O. Box 1886, Farmington, NM 87499/505-632-3539
Elko Arms, 28 rue Ecole Moderne, 7400 Soignies, Belgium/32-67.33.29.34
E.W. Ellis Sport Shop, RFD 1, Box 315, Corinth, NY 12822
Ellwood Epps Northern Ltd., 210 Worthington St. W., North Bay, Ont. PIB 3B4, Canada
Estate Cartridge Inc., P.O. Box 3702, Conroe, TX 77305/409-539-9144 (shotshell)
Jack First Distributors, Inc., 44633 Sierra Hwy., Lancaster, CA 93534/805-945-6981
Ramon B. Gonzalez, P.O. Box 370, Monticello, NY 12701/914-794-4515
"Gramps" Antique Cartridges, Ellwood Epps, Box 341, Washago, Ont. L0K 2B0 Canada/705-689-5348
Hardin Specialty Distributors, P.O. Box 338, Radcliff, KY 40160/502-351-6649
R.H. Keeler, 817 "N" St., Port Angeles, WA 98362/206-457-4702
K.K. Arms Co., Star Route Box 671, Kerrville, TX 78028/512-257-4718
KTW Inc., 710 Foster Park Rd., Lorain, OH 44053/216-233-6919
Lindsley Arms Cartridge Co., Inc., P.O. Box 757, 20 Crescent St., Henniker, NH 03242/603-428-3127 (inq. S.A.S.E.)
Lomont Precision Bullets, 4236 West 700 South, Poneto, IN 46781/219-694-

6792 (custom cast bullets only)
McConnellstown Reloading & Cast Bullets, Inc., R.D. 3, Box 40, Huntingdon, PA 16652/814-627-5402
Mack's Sport Shop, Box 1155, Kodiak, AK 99615/907-486-4276
MagSafe Ammo, P.O. Box 5692, Olympia, WA 98503/206-456-4623
North American Arms, 1800 North 300 West, Spanish Fork, UT 84660/801-798-7401
Numrich Arms Corp., 203 Broadway, W. Hurley, NY 12491
Patriot Mfg. & Sales, Banyan Plaza, Suite 334, Box 9000, Sebring, FL 33870/813-655-1798
Precision Ammo Co., P.O. Box 63, Garnerville, NY 10923/914-947-2720
Precision Prods. of Wash., Inc., N. 311 Walnut Rd., Spokane, WA 99206/509-928-0604 (Exammo)
Anthony F. Sailer-Ammunition (AFSCO), 731 W. Third St., Owen, WI 54460/715-229-2516
Sanders Cust. Gun Serv., 2358 Tyler Lane, Louisville, KY 40205
George W. Spence, 115 Locust St., Steele, MO 63877/314-695-4926 (boxer-primed cartridges)
The 3-D Company, Box J, Main St., Doniphan, NE 68832/402-845-2285 (reloaded police ammo)
R. A. Wardrop, P.O. Box 245, Mechanicsburg, PA 17055/717-766-9663
Zero Ammunition Co., Inc., P.O. Box 1188, Cullman, AL 35056/205-739-1606

AMMUNITION (Foreign)

Action Arms Ltd., P. O. Box 9573, Philadelphia, PA 19124/215-744-0100
Beeman Inc., 3440-GD Airway Dr., Santa Rosa, CA 95403/707-578-7900
Dan/Arms, RD 6, Box 674F, Ruppsville, Allentown, PA 18106/215-391-1966
Dynamit Nobel-RWS, Inc., 105 Stonehurst Court, Northvale, NJ 07647/210-767-1995(RWS, Geco, Rottweil)
Fiocchi of America, Inc., Rt. 2, Box 90-8, Ozark, MO 65721/417-725-4118
Gun South, Inc., P.O. Box 129, 108 Morrow Ave. Trussville, AL 35173/205-655-8299
Hansen Cartridge Co., 244 Old Post Rd., Southport, CT 06490/203-259-5424
Hirtenberger Patronen-, Zundhutchen- & Metallwarenfabrik, A.G., Leobersdorfer Str. 33, A2552 Hirtenberg, Austria
Hunters Specialty, Inc., 130 Orchard Dr., Pittsburgh, PA 15235/412-795-8885 (Hirtenberger)
Paul Jaeger, Inc., P.O. Box 449, 1 Madison Ave., Grand Junction, TN 38039/901-764-6909 (RWS centerfire ammo)
Kendall International Arms, 418 Fithian Ave., Paris, KY 40361/606-987-6946 (Lapua)
Lapua (See Kendall International)
PMC Ammunition, 4890 So. Alameda, Vernon, CA 90058/213-587-7100
RWS (Rheinische-Westfälische Sprengstoff) See Dynamit Nobel; Paul Jaeger, Inc.
Sports Emporium, 1414 Willow Ave., Philadelphia, PA 19126 (Danarms shotshells)

AMMUNITION COMPONENTS—BULLETS, POWDER, PRIMERS

A Square Co., Inc., Rt. 4, Simmons Rd., Madison, IN 47250/812-273-3633 (cust. bull.; brass)
Accurate Arms Co., Inc., (Propellents Div.), Rt. 1, Box 167, McEwen, TN, 37101/615-729-4207/4208 (powders)
Acme Custom Bullets, 5708 Evers Rd., San Antonio, TX 78238/512-680-4828
Alaska Bullet Works, P.O. Box 54, Douglas, AK 99824/907-789-1576 (Alaska copper-bond cust. bull.; Kodiak bonded core bullets)
Alberts Corp., 519 E. 19th St., Paterson, NJ 07514/201-684-1676 (swaged bullets)
Allred Bullet Co., 932 Evergreen Dr., Logan, UT 84321/801-752-6983 (custom bullets)
American Bullets, P.O. Box 15313, Atlanta, GA 30333/404-482-4253
American Products Co., 14729 Spring Valley Rd., Morrison, IL 61270/815-772-3336 (12-ga. shot wad)
Ammo-O-Mart Ltd., P.O. Box 125, Hawkesbury, Ont., Canada K6A 2R8/613-632-9300 (Nobel powder)
Ballistic Prods., Inc., Box 408, 2105 Daniels St., Long Lake, MN 55356/612-473-1550 (shotgun powders, primers)
Ballistic Research Industries (BRI), 2825 S. Rodeo Gulch Rd. #8, Soquel, CA 95073/408-476-7981 (Sabo shotgun slug; Gualandislug)
Barnes Bullets, Inc., P.O. Box 215, American Fork, UT 84003/801-756-4222
Bell's Gun & Sport Shop, 3309-19 Mannheim Rd., Franklin Pk., IL 60131/312-678-1900
Berger Bullets, 4234 N. 63rd Ave., Phoenix, AZ 85033/602-846-5791 (cust. 22, 6mm benchrest bull.)
Bergman and Williams, 2450 Losee Rd., Suite F, No. Las Vegas, NV 89030/702-642-1091 (copper tube 308 cust. bull.; lead wire i. all sizes)
Bitterroot Bullet Co., Box 412, Lewiston, ID 83501/208-743-5635 (Broch.:USA, Can. & Mexico $1 plus legal size env., intl. $2; lit. pkg.: USA, Can. & Mexico $7.50, intl. $10.50
Black Mountain Bullets, Rte. 3, Box 297, Warrenton, VA 22186/703-347-1199 (custom Fluid King match bullets)
B.E.L.L., Brass Extrusion Laboratories, Ltd., 800 W. Maple Lane, Bensenville, IL 60106 312/595-2792
Bruno Bullets, 10 Fifth St. Kelayres, PA 18231/717-929-1791 (22, 6mm benchrest bull.)
Buffalo Rock Shooters Supply, R. Rt. 1, Ottawa, IL 61350/815-433-2471
Bullet Swaging Supply, Inc., P.O. Box 1056, 303 McMillan Rd., West Monroe, LA 71219/318-387-7257
CCI, (See: Omark Industries)
CheVron Bullets, R.R. 1, Ottawa, IL 61350/815-433-2471
Colorado Sutlers Arsenal, Box 991, Granby, CO 80446/303-887-2813
Competition Bullets Inc., 9996-29 Ave., Edmonton, Alb. T6N 1A2, Canada/403-463-2817
Cooper-Woodward, 8073 Canyon Ferry Rd., Helena, MT 59601/406-475-3321
Corbin Mfg. & Supply, Inc., 600 Industrial Circle, P.O. Box 2659, White City, OR 97503/503-826-5211 (bullets)
Cor-Bon Custom Bullets, P.O. Box 10126, Detroit, MI 48210/313-894-2373 (375, 44, 45 solid brass partition bull.)
DuPont, (See IMR Powder Co.)
Dynamit Nobel-RWS Inc., 105 Stonehurst Court, Northvale, NJ 07647/201-767-1995 (RWS percussion caps)
Eagle Bullet Works, P.O. Box 2104, White City, OR 97503/503-826-7143 (Div-Cor 375, 224, 257 cust. bull.)
Excaliber Wax, Inc., P.O. Box 432, Kenton, OH 43326/419-673-0512 (wax bullets)
Federal Cartridge Co., 900 Ehlen Dr., Anoka, MN 55303/612-422-2840 (primers)
Fisher Enterprises, 655 Main St. #305, Edmonds, WA 98020/206-776-4365
Forty Five Ranch Enterprises, 119 S. Main, Miami, OK 74354/918-542-9307
Fowler Bullets, 3731 McKelvey St., Charlotte, NC 28215/704-568-7661 (benchrest bullets)
Glaser Safety Slug, P.O. Box 8223, Foster City, CA 94404/415-345-7677
GOEX, Inc., Belin Plant, 1002 Springbrook Ave., Moosic, PA 18507/717-457-6724 (blackpowder)
Golden Powder International Sales, Inc., 8444 Wilshire Blvd., Suite 201, Beverly Hills, CA 90211/213-653-1301 (Golden Powder/blackpowder)
Green Bay Bullets, P.O. Box 10446, 1486 Servais St., Green Bay, WI 54307-54304/414-497-2949 (cast lead bullets)
Grills-Hanna Bulletsmith Co., Lt., Box 655, Black Diamond, Alb. TOL OHO Canada/403-652-4393 (38, 9mm, 12-ga.)
Grizzly Bullets, 2137 Hwy. 200, Trout Creek, MT 59874/406-847-2627 (cust.)
GTM Co., George T. Mahaney, 15915B E. Main St., La Puente, CA 91744 (all brass shotshells)
Gun City, 212 West Main Ave., Bismarck, ND 58501/701-223-2304
Hansen Custom Bullets, 3221 Shelley St., Mohegan, NY 10547
Hardin Specialty Distr., P. O. Box 338, Radcliff, KY 40160/502-351-6649 (empty, primed cases)
Harrison Bullet Works, 6437 E. Hobart St., Mesa, AZ 85205/602-985-7844 (cust. swaged .41 Mag. bullets)
Robert W. Hart & Son, Inc. 401 Montgomery St., Nescopeck, PA 18635/717-752-3655
Hercules Inc., Hercules Plaza, Wilmington, DE 19894 (smokeless powder)
Hodgdon Powder Co. Inc., P.O. Box 2932, Shawnee Mission, KS 66201/913-362-9455 (smokeless, Pyrodex and black powder)
Hoffman New Ideas, Inc., 821 Northmoor Rd., Lake Forest, IL 60045/312-234-4075 (practice sub.vel. bullets)
Hornady Mfg. Co., P.O. Drawer 1848, Grand Island, NE 68802/308-382-1390
Hunters Specialty, Inc., 130 Orchard Dr., Pittsburgh, PA 15235/412-795-8885 (Hirtenberger bullets)
Huntington's, 601 Oro Dam Blvd., Oroville, CA 95965/916-534-1210
IMR Powder Co., Rt. 5 Box 247E, Plattsburgh, NY 12901/518-561-9530
Jaro Manuf., P.O. Box 6125, 206 E. Shaw, Pasadena, TX 77506/713-472-0417 (bullets)
Ka Pu Kapili, P.O. Box 745, Honokaa, HI 96272 (Hawaiian Special cust. bullets)
Kendall International Arms, 418 Fithian Ave., Paris, KY 40361/606-987-6946 (Lapua bull.)
Kodiak Custom Bullets, 8261 Henry Circle, Anchorage, AK 99507/907-349-2282
L.L.F. Die Shop, 1281 Highway 99 North, Eugene, OR 97402/503-688-5753
Lage Uniwad Co., 1814 21st St., Eldora, IA 50627/515-858-2634
Lapua (See Kendall International Arms)
Ljutic Ind., Inc., Box 2117,Yakima, WA 98907/509-248-0476 (Mono-wads)
Lomont Precision Bullets, 4236 West 700 South, Poneto, IN 46781/219-694-6792 (custom cast bullets)
Paul E. Low Jr., R.R. 1, Dunlap, IL 61525/309-685-1392 (jacketed 44- & 45-cal. bullets)
Lyman Products Corp., Rte. 147, Middlefield, CT 06455
McConnellstown Reloading & Cast Bullets, Inc., R.D. 3, Box 40, Huntingdon, PA 16652/814-627-5402
Mack's Sport Shop, Box 1155, Kodiak, AK 99615/907-486-4276 (cust. bull.)
Magnus Bullet Co., Inc., P.O. Box 2225, Birmingham, AL 35201/205-785-3357
Marshall Enterprises, 792 Canyon Rd., Redwood City, CA 94062/415-356-1230
Metallic Casting & Copper Corp. (MCC), 214 E. Third St., Mt. Vernon, NY 10550/914-1311 (cast bullets)
Michael's Antiques, Box 591, Waldoboro, ME 04572 (Balle Blondeau)
Miller Trading Co., 20 S. Front St., Wilmington, NC 28401/919-762-7107 (bullets)
Non-Toxic Components, Inc., P.O. Box 4202, Portland, OR 97208/503-226-7110 (steel shot kits)
NORMA (See Federal Cartridge Co.)
Nosler Bullets Inc., 107 S.W. Columbia, Bend, OR 97702/503-382-5108
Old Western Scrounger, 12924 Hwy A-12, Montague, CA 96064/916-459-5445
Omark Industries, P.O. Box 856, Lewiston, ID 83501/208-746-2351
Oro-Tech Industries, Inc., 1701 W. Charleston Blvd., Suite 510, Las Vegas, NV 89102/702-382-8109 (Golden Powder)
PMC Ammunition, 4890 So. Alameda, Vernon, CA 90058/213-587-7100
Patriotic Manufacturing & Sales, Banyan Plaza, Suite 334, Box 9000, Sebring,

FL 33870/813-655-1798 (cust. bullets)
Pepperbox Gun Shop, P.O. Box 922, East Moline, IL 61244/309-796-0616 (257, 224 rifle cal. custom swaged bullets)
Polywad, Inc., P.O. Box 7916, Macon, GA 31209 (Spred-Rs for shotshells)
Pyrodex, See: Hodgdon Powder Co., Inc. (black powder substitute)
Robert Pomeroy, Morison Ave., East Corinth, ME 04427/207-285-7721 (formed cases, bullets)
Power Plus Enterprises, Inc., P.O. Box 6070, Columbus, GA 31907/404-561-1717 (12-ga. shotguns slugs; 308, 45 ACP, 357 cust. bull.)
Precision Ammo Co., P.O. Drawer 86, Valley Cottage, NY 10989/914-947-2710
Precision Swaged Bullets, Rte. 1, Box 93H, Ronan, MT 59864/406-676-5135 (silhouette; out-of-prods. Sharps)
Professional Hunter Supplies, P.O. Box 608; 444½ Main St., Ferndale, CA 95536/707-786-9460 (408, 375, 308, 510 cust. bull.)
Prometheus/Titan Black (See Fisher Enterprises)
Reardon Products, P.O. Box 126, Morrison, IL 61270/815-772-3155 (dry-lube powder)
Redwood Bullet Works, 3559 Bay Rd., Redwood City, CA 94063/415-367-6741 (cust. bullets)
Remington-Peters, 1007 Market St., Wilmington, DE 19898
Rubright Bullets, 1008 S. Quince Rd., Walnutport, PA 18088/215-767-1239 (cust. 22 & 6mm benchrest bullets)
S&S Precision Bullets, 22963 La Cadena, Laguna Hills, CA 92653/714-768-6836 (linotype cast bull.)
Sansom Bullets, 2506 Rolling Hills, Dr., Greenville, TX 75401 (custom)
Sierra Bullets Inc., 10532 So. Painter Ave., Santa Fe Springs, CA 90670
Southern Ammunition Co., Inc., Rt. 1, Box 6B, Latta, SC 29565/803-752-7751
Speer Products, Box 856, Lewiston, ID 83501
Sport Flite, P.O. Box 1082, Bloomfield Hills, MI 48308/313-647-3747 (zinc bases, gas checks)
Supreme Products Co., 1830 S. California Ave., Monrovia, CA 91016/800-423-7159/818-357-5395 (rubber bullets)
Swift Bullet Co., RR. 1, Box 140A, Quinter, KS 67752/913-754-3959 (375 big game, 224 cust.)
Tallon Bullets, 1194 Tidewood Dr., Bethel Park, PA 15102/412-471-4494 (dual. diam. 308 cust.)
Taracorp Industries, 16th & Cleveland Blvd., Granite City, IL 62040/618-451-4400 (Lawrence Brand lead shot)
Thunderbird Cartridge Co., P.O. Box 302, Phoenix, AZ 85001/602-237-3823 (powder)
Traft Gunshop, P.O. Box 1078, Buena Vista, CO 81211/303-395-6034 (cust. bull.)
Trophy Bonded Bullets, P.O. Box 262348, Houston, TX 77207/713-645-4499 (big game 458, 308, 375 bonded cust. bullets only)
Vitt/Boos, 2178 Nichols Ave., Stratford, CT 06497/203-375-6859 (Aerodynamic shotgun slug, 12-ga. only)
Ed Watson, Trophy Match Bullets, 2404 Wade Hampton Blvd., Greenville, SC 29615/803-244-7948 (22, 6mm cust. benchrest bull.)
Winchester/Olin, 427 N. Shamrock St., East Alton, IL 62024/618-258-2000
Worthy Products, Inc., Box 88 Main St., Chippewa Bay, NY 13623/315-324-5450 (slug loads)
Zero Bullet Co. Inc., P.O. Box 1188, Cullman, AL 35056/205-739-1606

ANTIQUE ARMS DEALERS

AD Hominem, R.R. 3, Orillia, Ont., L3V 6H3, Canada/705-689-5303
Antique Arms Co., David F. Saunders, 1110 Cleveland, Monett, MO 65708/417-235-6501
Antique Gun Parts, Inc., 1118 S. Braddock Ave., Pittsburgh, PA 15218/412-241-1811
Beeman Precision Arms, Inc., 3440-GD Airway Dr., Santa Rosa, CA 95403/707-578-7900 (airguns only)
Wm. Boggs, 1243 Grandview Ave., Columbus, OH 43212
Can Am Enterprises, 350 Jones Rd., Fruitland, ON L0R 1L0, Canada/416-643-4357 (catalog $2)
Century Intl. Arms, Inc., 5 Federal St., St. Albans, VT 05478/802-527-1252
Chas. Clements, Handicrafts Unltd., 1741 Dallas St., Aurora, CO 80010/303-364-0403
David Condon, Inc., P.O. Box 312, 14502-G Lee Rd., Chantilly, VA 22021/703-631-7748
Continental Kite & Key Co. (CONKKO), P.O. Box 40, Broomall, PA 19008/215-356-0711
John Corry, 628 Martin Lane, Deerfield, IL 60015/312-541-6250 (English guns)
Dixie Gun Works, Inc., P.O. Box 130, Gun Powder Lane, Union City, TN 38261/901-885-0561
Peter Dyson Ltd., 29-31 Church St., Honley, Huddersfield, W. Yorksh. HD7 2AH, England/0484-661062 (acc. f. ant. gun coll.; custom-and machine-made)
Ed's Gun House, Box 62, Rte. 1, Minnesota City, MN 55959/507-689-2925
Ellwood Epps Northern Ltd., 210 Worthington St. W., North Bay, Ont. PIB 3B4 Canada
William Fagan, Box 26100, Fraser, MI 48026/313-465-4637
Jack First Distributors, Inc., 44633 Sierra Hwy., Lancaster, CA 93534/805-945-6981
N. Flayderman & Co., P.O. Box 2446, Ft. Lauderdale, FL 33303/305-761-8855
The Flintlock Muzzle Loading Gun Shop, 1238 "G" So. Beach Blvd., Anaheim, CA 92804/714-821-6655
Chet Fulmer, P.O. Box 792, Rt. 2, Buffalo Lake, Detroit Lakes, MN 56501/218-847-7712
Robert S. Frielich, 396 Broome St., New York, NY 10013/212-254-3045
Garcia National Gun Traders, Inc., 225 S.W. 22nd Ave., Miami, FL 33135
Herb Glass, P.O. Box 25, Bullville, NY 10915/914-361-3021
James Goergen, Rte. 2, Box 182BB, Austin, MN 55912/507-433-9280
Griffin's Guns & Antiques, R.R. 4, Peterboro, Ont., Canada K9J 6X5/705-745-7022
Guncraft Sports, Inc., 125 E. Tyrone Rd., Oak Ridge, TN 37830/615-483-4024
Hansen & Company, 244 Old Post Rd., Southport, CT 06490/203-259-6222
Kelley's Harold Kelley, Box 125, Woburn, MA 01801/617-935-3389
Krider's Gun Shop, 114 W. Eagle Rd., Havertown, PA 19083/215-789-7828
Lever Arms Serv. Ltd., 2131 Burrard St. Vancouver, B.C., Canada V6J 3H8/604-736-0004
Liberty Antique Gunworks, 19 Key St., P.O. Box 183GD, Eastport, ME 04631/207-853-2327
Log Cabin Sport Shop, 8010 Lafayette Rd., Lodi, OH 44254/216-948-1082
Lone Pine Trading Post, Jct. Highways 61 and 248, Minnesota City, MN 55959/507-689-2925
Arthur McKee, 121 Eaton's Neck Rd., Northport, L.I., NY 11768/516-757-8850 (Rem. double shotguns)
Michael's Antiques, Box 591, Waldoboro, ME 04572
Charles W. Moore, R.D. #1, Box 276, Schenevus, NY 12155/607-278-5721
Museum of Historical Arms, 1038 Alton Rd., Miami Beach, FL 33139/305-672-7480 (ctlg $5)
Muzzleloaders Etc. Inc., 9901 Lyndale Ave. So., Bloomington, MN 55420/612-884-1161
New Orleans Arms Co., 5001 Treasure St., New Orleans, LA 70186/504-944-3371
Old Western Scrounger, 12924 Hwy A-12, Montague, CA 96064/916-459-5445 (write for list; $2)
Pioneer Guns, 5228 Montgomery, (Cincinnati) Norwood, OH 45212/513-631-4871
Pony Express Sport Shop, Inc., 16606 Schoenborn St., Sepulveda, CA 91343/818-895-1231
Martin B. Retting, Inc., 11029 Washington, Culver City, CA 90232/213-837-2412
Rutgers Gun & Boat Center, 127 Raritan Ave. Highland Park, NJ 08904/201-545-4344
San Francisco Gun Exch., 124 Second St., San Francisco, CA 94105/415-982-6097
Charles Semmer, 7885 Cyd Dr., Denver, CO 80221/303-429-6947
Don L. Shrum's Cape Outfitters, Rt. 2 Box 437-C, Cape Girardeau, MO 63701/314-335-4103
S&S Firearms, 74-11 Myrtle Ave., Glendale, NY 11385/718-497-1100
Steves House of Guns, Rte. 1, Minnesota City, MN 55959/507-689-2573
Stott's Creek Armory Inc., R 1 Box 70, Morgantown, IN 46160/317-878-5489
James Wayne, 308 Leisure Lane, Victoria, TX 77904/512-578-1258
Ward & Van Valkenburg, 114-32nd Ave. N., Fargo, ND 58102
M.C. Wiest, 125 E. Tyrone Rd., Oak Ridge, TN 37830/615-483-4024
Lewis Yearout, 308 Riverview Dr. E., Great Falls, MT 59404

APPRAISERS, GUNS, ETC.

Ad Hominem, R.R. 3, Orillia, ON L3V 6H3, Canada/705-689-5303
Antique Gun Parts, Inc., 1118 So. Braddock Ave., Pittsburgh, PA 15218/412-241-1811
Ahlman's, Rt. 1, Box 20, Morristown, MN 55052/507-685-4244
The Armoury Inc., Route 202, New Preston, CT 06777/203-868-0001
Beeman Precision Arms, Inc., 3440-GD Airway Dr., Santa Rosa, CA 95403/707-578-7900 (airguns only)
Christie's-East, 219 E. 67th St., New York, NY 10021/212-606-0400
E. Christopher Firearms Co., Inc., Route 128 & Ferry St., Miamitown, OH 45041/513-353-1321
Chas. Clements, Handicrafts Unltd., 1741 Dallas St., Aurora, CO 80010/303-364-0403
David Condon, Inc., P.O. Box 312, 14502-G Lee Rd., Chantilly, VA 22021/703-631-7748
John Corry, 628 Martin Lane, Deerfield, IL 60015/312-541-6250 (English guns)
Custom Tackle & Ammo, P.O. Box 1886, Farmington, NM 87499/505-632-3539
D.O.C. Specialists (Doc & Bud Ulrich), 2209 So. Central Ave., Cicero, IL 60650/312-652-3606
Ed's Gun House, Ed Kukowski, Route 1, Box 62, Minnesota City, MN 55952/507-689-2925
Ellwood Epps (Orillia) Ltd., R.R. 3, Hwy. 11 No., Orillia, Ont. L3V 6H3, Canada/705-699-5333
N. Flayderman & Co., Inc., P.O. Box 2446, Ft. Lauderdale, FL 33303/305-761-8855
Richard Geer, P.O. Box 1303, St. Charles, IL 60174/312-377-4625
James Goergen Rte. 2, Box 182BB, Austin, MN 55912/507-433-9280
"Gramps" Antique Cartridges, Ellwood Epps, Box 341, Washago, Ont. L0K 2B0 Canada/705-689-5348
Leon E. "Bud" Greenwald, 2553 S. Quitman St., Denver, CO 80219/303-935-3850
Griffin & Howe, 36 West 44th St., Suite 1011, New York, NY 10036/212-921-0980
Griffin & Howe, 33 Claremont Rd., Bernardsville, NJ 07924/201-766-2287
Guncraft Sports, Inc., 125 E. Tyrone Rd., Oak Ridge, TN 37830/615-483-4024
Hansen and Company, 244-246 Old Post Rd., Southport, CT 06490/203-259-6222

Lew Horton Sports Shop, 450 Waverly St., Framingham, MA 01772/617-485-3060
Kelley's, Harold Kelley, Box 125, Woburn, MA 01801/617-935-3389
Kenneth Kogan, P.O. Box 130, Lafayette Hills, PA 19444/215-233-4509
Liberty Antique Gunworks, 19 Key St., P.O. Box 183GD, Eastport, ME 04631/207-853-2327
Lone Pine Trading Post, Jct. Highways 248 & 61, Minnesota City, MN 55959/507-689-2925
Elwyn H. Martin, 937 So. Sheridan Blvd., Lakewood, CO 80226/303-922-2184
Miller Trading Co., 20 So. Front St., Wilmington, NC 28401/919-762-7107
The Museum of Historical Arms, Inc., 1038 Alton Rd., Miami Beach, FL 33139/305-672-7480
New England Arms Co., Lawrence Lane, Kittery Point, ME 03905/207-439-0593
Orvis Co. Inc., 10 River Rd., Manchester, VT 05254/802-362-3622
PM Airservices Ltd., P.O. Box 1573, Costa Mesa, CA 92628/714-968-2689
Pioneer Guns, 5228 Montgomery Rd., Norwood, OH 45212/513-631-4871
Pony Express Sport Shop, Inc., 16606 Schoenborn St., Sepulveda, CA 91343/818-895-1231
John Richards, Rte. 2, Box 325, Bedford, KY 40006/502-255-7222
Steel City Arms, Inc., P.O. Box 81926, Pittsburgh, PA 15217/412-461-3100
Dale A. Storey, DGS, Inc., 305 N. Jefferson, Casper, WY 82601/307-237-2414
James C. Tillinghast, P.O. Box 405GD, Hancock, NH 03449/603-525-66151
M. C. Wiest, 125 E. Tyrone Rd., Oak Ridge, TN 37830/615-483-4024
Lewis Yearout, 308 Riverview Dr. East, Great Falls, MT 59404/406-761-0589

AUCTIONEERS, GUNS, ETC.

Alberts Corp., 519 East 19th St., Paterson, NJ 07514/201-684-1676
Richard A. Bourne & Co. Inc., Box 141, Hyannis Port, MA 02647/617-775-0797
Christie's-East, 219 E. 67th St., New York, NY 10021/212-606-0400
Tom Keilman, 12316 Indian Mount, Austin, TX 78758
Kelley's, Harold Kelley, Box 125, Woburn, MA 01801/617-935-3389
"Little John's" Antique Arms, 777 S. Main St., Orange, CA 92668
Wayne Mock, Inc., Box 37, Tamworth, NH 03886/603-323-8749
Parke-Bernet (see Sotheby's)
Sotheby's, 1334 York Ave. at 72nd St., New York, NY 10021
James C. Tillinghast, Box 405GD, Hancock, NH 03449/603-525-6615

BOOKS (ARMS), Publishers and Dealers

Armory Publications, P.O. Box 44372, Tacoma, WA 98444/206-531-4632
Arms & Armour Press, Cassell TLC, Artillery House, Artillery Row, London SW1P 1RT England
Beeman Precision Arms Inc., 3440GD Airway Dr., Santa Rosa, CA 95403/707-578-7900 (airguns only)
Blacksmith Corp., P.O. Box 424, Southport, CT 06490/203-367-4041
Blacktail Mountain Books, 42 First Ave. West, Kalispell, MT 59901/406-257-5573
DBI Books, Inc., 4092 Commercial Ave., Northbrook IL 60062/312-272-6310
Dove Press, P.O. Box 3882, Enid, OK 73702/405-234-4347
Fortress Publications Inc., P.O. Box 9241, Stoney Creek, Ont. L8G 3X9, Canada/416-662-3505
Guncraft Books, Div. of Ridge Guncraft Sports, Inc., 125 E. Tyrone Rd., Oak Ridge, TN 37830/615-483-4024
The Gun Room Press, 127 Raritan Ave., Highland Park, NJ 08904/201-545-4344
Gunnerman Books, P.O. Box 4292, Auburn Hills, MI 48057/313-879-2779
Handgun Press, Box 406, Glenview, IL 60025/312-724-8816
Kopp Publishing Co., Box 224E, Hwy 13 South, Rte. 1, Lexington, MO 64067/816-259-2636
Lyman, Route 147, Middlefield, CT 06455
The Outdoorsman's Bookstore, Llangorse, Brecon, County Powys LD3 7UE, England
Paladin Press, P.O. Box 1307, Boulder, CO 80306/303-443-7250
Petersen Publishing Co., 84990 Sunset Blvd., Los Angeles, CA 99069
Gerald Pettinger Arms Books, Route 2, Russell, IA 50238/515-535-2239
Ray Riling Arms Books Co., 6844 Gorsten St., P.O. Box 18925, Philadelphia, PA 19119/215-438-2456
Rutgers Book Center, Mark Aziz, 127 Raritan Ave., Highland Park, NJ 08904/201-545-4344
Stackpole Books, Cameron & Kelker Sts., Telegraph Press Bldg., Harrisburg, PA 17105
Stoeger Publishing Co., 55 Ruta Court, South Hackensack, NJ 07606
Tara Press, P.O. Box 17211, Tucson, AZ 85731/602-296-5333
Ken Trotman Ltd., 135 Ditton Walk, Unit 11, Cambridge CB5 8QD, England
Paul Wahl Corp., P.O. Box 500, Bogota, NJ 07603-0500/201-261-9245
Winchester Press, 220 Old New Brunswick Rd., Piscataway, NJ 08854/201-981-0820
Wolfe Publishing Co., Inc., 6471 Air Park Dr., Prescott, AZ 86301/602-445-7810

BULLET & CASE LUBRICANTS

C-H Tool & Die Corp., 106 N. Harding St., Owen, WI 54460/715-229-2146
Clenzoil Corp., P.O. Box 1226, Sta. C, Canton, OH 44708/216-833-9758
Cooper-Woodward, 8073 Canyon Ferry Rd., Helena, MT 59601/406-475-3321 (Perfect Lube)
Corbin Mfg. & Supply Inc., 600 Industrial Circle, P.O. Box 2659, White City, OR 97503/503-826-5211
Dillon Precision Prods., Inc., 7442 E. Butherus Dr., Scottsdale, AZ 85260/602-948-8009
Green Bay Bullets, 1486 Servais St., Green Bay, WI 54304/414-497-2949 (EZE-Size case lube)
Javelina Products, P.O. Box 337, San Bernardino, CA 92402/714-882-5847 (Alox beeswax)
Jet-Aer Corp., 100 Sixth Ave., Paterson, NJ 07524
LeClear Industries, 1126 Donald Ave., P.O. Box 484, Royal Oak, MI 48068/313-588-1025
Lee Precision, Inc., 4275 Hwy. U, Hartford, WI 53027/414-673-3075
M&M Engineering, 10642 Arminta St., Sun Valley, CA 91352/818-842-8376 (case lubes)
Lyman Products Corp., Rte. 147, Middlefield, CT. 06455 (Size-Ezy)
Micro-Lube, P.O. Box 117, Mesilla Park, NM 88047/505-524-4215
M&N Bullet Lube, P.O. Box 495, 151 N.E. Jefferson St., Madras, OR 97741/503-475-2992
Northeast Industrial, Inc., P.O. Box 249, 405 N. Canyon Blvd., Canyon City, OR 97820/503-575-2513 (Ten X-Lube; NEI mold prep)
Pacific Tool Co., P.O. Box 2048, Ordnance Plant Rd., Grand Island, NE 68801/308-384-2308
Ponsness-Warren, P.O. Box 8, Rathdrum, ID 83858/208-687-2231 (case lubes)
Radix Research & Marketing, Box 247, Woodland Park, CO 80866/303-687-3182 (Magnum Dri-Lube)
Redding Inc., 1089 Starr Rd., Cortland, NY 13045/607-753-3331
Rooster Laboratories, P.O. Box 412514, Kansas City, MO 64141/816-474-9711
SAECO (See Redding)
Sandia Die & Cartridge Co., Route 5, Box 5400, Albuquerque, NM 87123/505-298-5729
Shooters Accessory Supply (SAS) (See Corbin Mfg. & Supply)
Tamarack Prods., Inc., P.O. Box 625, Wauconda, IL 60084/312-526-9333 (Bullet lube)

BULLET SWAGE DIES AND TOOLS

Bullet Swaging Supply, Inc., P.O. Box 1056, 303 McMillan Rd., West Monroe, LA 71291/318-387-7257
C-H Tool & Die Corp., 106 N. Harding St., Owen, WI 54460/715-229-2146
Mrs. Lester Coats, 416 Simpson Ave., North Bend, OR 97459/503-756-6995 (lead wire core cutter)
Corbin Mfg. & Supply Inc., 600 Industrial Circle, P.O. Box 2659, White City, OR 97503/503-826-5211
Hollywood Loading Tools (See M&M Engineering)
Huntington Die Specialties, 601 Oro Dam Blvd., Oroville, CA 95965/916-534-1210
L.L.F. Die Shop, 1281 Highway 99 North, Eugene, OR 97402/503-688-5753
M&M Engineering, 10642 Arminta St., Sun Valley, CA 91352/818-842-8376
Rorschach Precision Products, P.O. Box 151613, Irving, TX 75015/214-790-3487
SAS Dies, (See Corbin Mfg. & Supply)
Seneca Run Iron Works Inc., dba "Swagease", P.O. Box 3032, Greeley, CO 80633/303-352-1452 (muzzle-loading round ball)
Sport Flite Mfg., Inc., 2520 Industrial Row, Troy, MI 48084/313-280-0648

CARTRIDGES FOR COLLECTORS

AD Hominem, R.R. 3, Orillia, Ont., Canada L3V 6H3/705-689-5303
Ammo-Mart Ltd., P.O. Box 125, Hawkesbury, ON, K6A 2R8 Canada/613-632-9300
Ida I. Burgess, Sam's Gun Shop, 25 Squam Rd., Rockport, MA 01966/617-546-6839
Cameron's, 16690 W. 11th Ave., Golden CO 80401/303-279-7365
Cartridges Unlimited, R. 1, Box 50, South Kent, CT 06785/203-927-3053
Creative Cartridge Co., 56 Morgan Rd., Canton, CT 06019/203-693-2529
Chas. E. Duffy, Williams Lane, West Hurley, NY 12419/914-679-2997
Tom M. Dunn, 1342 So. Poplar, Casper, WY 82601/307-237-3207
Ellwood Epps (Orillia) Ltd., Hwy. 11 North, Orillia, Ont. L3V 6H3, Canada/705-689-5333
Excaliber Wax, Inc., P.O. Box 432, Kenton, OH 43326/419-673-0512
Jack First Distributors, Inc., 44633 Sierra Hwy., Lancaster, CA 93534/805-945-6981
GTM Co., Geo. T. Mahaney, 15915B East Main St., La Puente, CA 91744/818-768-5806
Richard Geer, P.O. Box 1303, St. Charles, IL 60174/312-377-4625
Glaser Safety Slug, Inc., P.O. Box 8223, Foster City, CA 94404/415-345-7677
"Gramps" Antique Cartridges, Ellwood Epps, Box 341, Washago, Ont., Canada L0K 2B0
Griffin's Guns & Antiques, R.R. #4, Peterboro, Ont. K9J 6X5, Canada/705-745-7022
Gun Parts Corp., Box 2, West Hurley, NY 12491/914-679-2417
Hansen and Company, 244-246 Old Post Rd., Southport, CT 06490/203-259-6222
Idaho Ammunition Service, 410 21st Ave., Lewiston, ID 83501
Kelley's, Harold Kelley, Box 125, Woburn, MA 01801/617-935-3389
Metallic Casting & Copper Corp. (MCC), 214 E. Third St., Mt. Vernon, NY

10550/914-664-1311
Old Western Scrounger, 12924 Hwy. A-12, Montague, CA 96064/916-459-5445
Jesse Ramos, P.O. Box 7105, La Puente, CA 91744/818-369-6384
San Francisco Gun Exchange, Inc., 124 Second St., San Francisco, CA 94105/415-982-6097
James C. Tillinghast, Box 405GD, Hancock, NH 03449/603-525-6615 (list $1)
Ward & VanValkenburg, 114-32nd Ave. No., Fargo, ND 58102/701-232-2351
Lewis Yearout, 308 Riverview Dr. E., Great Falls, MT 59404

CASES, CABINETS AND RACKS—GUN

API Outdoors Inc., 602 Kimbrough Dr., Tallulah, LA 71282/318-574-4903 (racks)
Alco Carrying Cases, 601 W. 26th St., New York, NY 10001/212-675-5820 (aluminum)
Bob Allen Co., 214 S.W. Jackson, Des Moines, IA 50315/515-283-2191/800-247-8048 (carrying)
The American Import Co., 1453 Mission St., San Francisco, CA 94103/415-863-1506
Armes de Chasse, P.O. Box 827, Chadsford, PA 19317/215-388-1146
Art Jewel Ltd., Eagle Business Ctr., 460 Randy Rd., Carol Stream, IL 60188/312-260-0040 (cases)
Beeman Precision Arms, Inc., 3440-GDD Airway Dr., Santa Rosa, CA 95403/707-578-7900
Bore Stores, Rt. 66, Box 430, Yellville, AR 72687 (synthetic cases)
Boyt Co., Div. of Welsh Sportg. Gds., P.O. Drawer 668, Iowa Falls, IA 50126/515-648-4626
Browning, Rt. 4, Box 624-B, Arnold, MO 63010
China IM/EX, P.O. Box 27573, San Francisco, CA 94127/415-661-2212 (soft-type cases)
Chipmunk Mfg. Co., 114 E. Jackson, P.O. Box 1104, Medford, OR 97501/503-664-5585 (cases)
Dara-Nes Inc., see: Nesci
Dart Mfg. Co., 4012 Bronze Way, Dallas, TX 75237/214-333-4221
Detroit-Armor Corp., 2233 No. Palmer Dr., Schaumburg, IL 60103/312-397-4070 (Saf-Gard steel gun safe)
Doskocil Mfg. Co., Inc., P.O. Box 1246, Arlington, TX 75010/817-467-5116 (Gun Guard carrying)
Ellwood Epps (Orillia) Ltd., R.R. 3, Hwy, 11 North, Orillia, Ont. L3V 6H3, Canada/705-689-5333 (custom gun cases)
Flambeau Plastics Corp., 801 Lynn, Baraboo, WI 53913
Fort Knox Security Products, 1051 N. Industrial Park Rd., Orem, UT 84057/801-224-7233 (safes)
Gun Parts Corp., Box 2, West Hurley, NY 12491/914-679-2417 (cases)
Hansen and Hansen, 244 Old Post Rd., Southport, CT 06490/203-259-7337
Marvin Huey Gun Cases, P.O. Box 22456, Kansas City, MO 64113/816-444-1637 (handbuilt leather cases)
Jumbo Sports Prods., P.O. Box 280-Airport Rd., Frederick, MD 21701
Kalispel Metal Prods. (KMP), P.O. Box 267, Cusick, WA 99119/509-445-1121 (aluminum boxes)
Kane Products Inc., 5572 Brecksville Rd., Cleveland, OH 44131/216-524-9962
Kolpin Mfg., Inc., Box 231, Berlin, WI 54923/414-361-0400
Marble Arms Corp., 420 Industrial Park, Gladstone, MI 49837/906-428-3710
Bill McGuire, 1600 No. Eastmont Ave., East Wenatchee, WA 98801
Nesci Enterprises, Inc., P.O. Box 119, Summit St., East Hampton, CT 06424/203-267-2588 (firearms security chests)
Paul-Reed, Inc., P.O. Box 227, Charlevoix, MI 49720
Penguin Industries, Inc., Airport Industrial Mall, Coatesville, PA 19320/215-384-6000
Proofmark, Ltd., P.O. Box 183, Alton, IL 62002/618-463-0120 (Italian Emmebi leather cases)
Protecto Plastics, Div. of Penguin Ind., Airport Industrial Mall, Coatesville, PA 19320/215-384-6000 (carrying cases)
Quality Arms, Inc., P.O. Box 19477, Houston, TX 77224/713-870-8377
Rahn Gun Works, Inc., 470 Market S.W., Box 33, Grand Rapids, MI 49503/616-235-6469 (leather trunk cases)
Red Head Brand Corp., 4949 Joseph Hardin Dr., Dallas, TX 75236/214-333-4141
Saf-T-Case Mfg. Co., 6327 Town Hill, Dallas, TX 75214
San Angelo Co., 1841 Industrial Ave., San Angelo, TX 76904/915-655-7126
Schulz Industries, 16247 Minnesota Ave., Paramount, CA 90723/213-439-5903 (carrying cases)
Security Gun Chest, (See Tread Corp.)
Sweet Home Inc., Subs, of Will-Burt Co., P.O. Box 250, Sweet Home, OR 97386/503-367-5185 (gun safes)
Tread Corp., P.O. Box 13207, Roanoke, VA 24032/703-982-6881 (security gun chest)
WAMCO, Inc., Mingo Loop, P.O. Box 337, Oquossoc, ME 04964-0337/800-227-1415 (wooden display cases)
Weather Shield Sports Equipm. Inc., Rte. #3, Petoskey Rd., Charlevoix, MI 49720
Wilson Case Co., 906 Juniata Ave., Juniata, NE 68955/402-751-2145 (cases)

CHOKE DEVICES, RECOIL ABSORBERS & RECOIL PADS

Action Products Inc., 22 N. Mulberry St., Hagerstown, MD 21740/800-228-7763 (rec. shock eliminator)
Arms Ingenuity Co., Box 1; 51 Canal St., Weatogue, CT 06089/203-658-5624 (Jet-Away)
Armsport, Inc., 3590 N.W. 49th St., Miami, FL 33142/305-635-7850 (choke devices)
Baer Custom Guns, 1725 Minesite Rd., Allentown, PA 18103/215-398-2362 (compensator syst. f. 45 autos)
Briley Mfg. Co., 1085-B Gessner, Houston, TX 77055/713-932-6995 (choke tubes)
C&H Research, 115 Sunnyside Dr., Lewis, KS 67552/316-324-5445 (Mercury recoil suppressor)
Vito Cellini, Francesca Inc., 3115 Old Ranch Rd., San Antonio, TX 78217/512-826-2584 (recoil reducer; muzzle brake)
Clinton River Gun Serv. Inc., 30016 S. River Rd., Mt. Clemens, MI 48045 (Reed Choke)
Reggie Cubriel, 15610 Purple Sage, San Antonio, TX 78255/512-695-3364 (leather recoil pads)
Delta Vectors, Inc., 7119 W. 79th St., Overland Park, KS 66204/913-642-0307 (Techni-Port recoil compensation)
Edwards Recoil Reducer, 269 Herbert St., Alton, IL 62002/618-462-3257
Emsco Variable Shotgun Chokes, 101 Second Ave., S.E., Waseca, MN 56093/507-835-1779
Fabian Bros. Sptg. Goods, Inc., 1510 Morena Blvd., Suite "I," San Diego, CA 92110/619-223-3955 (DTA Muzzle Mizer rec. abs.; MIL/brake)
Freshour Mfg., 1914-15th Ave. North, Texas City, TX 77590/713-945-7726 (muzzle brakes)
David Gentry Custom Gunmaker, 314 N. Hoffman, P.O. Box 1440, Belgrade, MT 59714/406-388-4867 (muzzle brakes)
Griggs Products, P.O. Box 789; 270 So. Main St., Suite 103, Bountiful, UT 84010/801-295-9696 (recoil director)
Gun Parts Corp., Box 2, West Hurley, NY 12491/914-679-2417
William E. Harper, The Great 870 Co., P.O. Box 6309, El Monte, CA 91734/213-579-3077
I.N.C., Inc., 1133 Kresky #4, Centralia, WA 98531/206-330-2042 (Sorbothane Kick-Eez recoil pad)
KDF, Inc., 2485 Hwy. 46 N., Seguin, TX 78155/512-379-8141 (muzzle brake)
La Paloma Marketing, 4210 E. La Paloma Dr., Tucson, AZ 85718/602-881-4750 (Action rec. shock eliminator)
Lyman Products Corp., Rte. 147, Middlefield, CT. 06455 (Cutts Comp.)
Mag-na-port International, Inc., 41302 Executive Drive, Mt. Clemens, MI 48045/313-469-6727 (muzzle-brake system)
Mag-Na-Port of Canada, 1861 Burrows Ave., Winnipeg, Manitoba R2X 2V6, Canada
Marble Arms Corp., 420 Industrial Park, Box 111, Gladstone, MI 49837/906-428-3710 (Poly-Choke)
Pachmayr Ltd., 1875 So. Mountain Ave., Monrovia, CA 91016/818-423-9704 (recoil pads)
P.A.S.T. Corp., 210 Park Ave., P.O. Box 7372, Columbia, MO 65205/314-449-7278 (recoil reducer shield)
Poly-Choke (See Marble Arms)
Pro-Port Ltd., 41302 Executive Dr., Mt. Clemens, MI 48045/313-469-7323
Protektor Model, 7 Ash St., Galeton, PA 16922/814-435-2442 (shoulder recoil pad)
Reed Choke (See Clinton River Gun Svc.)
Shogun Mfg. Inc., 304 So. Main St., P.O. Box 306, Kirksville, MO 63501/816-627-0500
Supreme Products Co., 1830 S. California Ave., Monrovia, CA 91016/800-423-7159/818-357-5395 (recoil pads)
Upper Missouri Trading Co., 304 Harold St., Crofton, NE 68730/402-388-4844
Walker Arms Co., Inc., Rte. 2, Box 73, Highway 80 West, Selma, AL 36701/205-872-6231

CHRONOGRAPHS AND PRESSURE TOOLS

Competition Electronics, Inc., 2542 Point O' Woods Dr., Rockford, IL 61111/815-877-3322
Custom Chronograph Inc., 5305 Reese Hill Rd., Sumas, WA 98295/206-988-7801
D&H Precision Tooling, 7522 Barnard Mill Rd., Ringwood, IL 60072/815-653-9611 (Pressure Testing Receiver)
H-S Precision, Inc., 112 N. Summit St., Prescott, AZ 86302/602-445-0607 (press. barrels)
Paul Jaeger, Inc., P.O. Box 449, 1 Madison Ave., Grand Junction, TN 38039
Oehler Research, Inc., P.O. Box 9135, Austin, TX 78766/512-327-6900
P.A.C.T. Inc., P.O. Box 531525, Grand Prairie, TX 75053/214-641-0049 (Precision chronogr.)
Quartz-Lok, 13137 N. 21st Lane, Phoenix, AZ 85029/602-863-2729
Tepeco, P.O. Box 342, Friendswood, TX 77546/713-482-2702 (Tepeco Speed-Meter)

CLEANING & REFINISHING SUPPLIES

American Gas & Chemical Co., Ltd., 220 Pegasus Ave., Northvale, NJ 07647/201-767-7300 (TSI gun lube)
Anderson Mfg. Co., P.O. Box 536, 6813 S. 220th St., Kent, WA 98032/206-872-7602 (stock finishes)
Armite Labs., 1845 Randolph St., Los Angeles, CA 90001/213-587-7744 (pen oiler)
Beeman Precision Arms, Inc., 3440-GD Airway Dr., Santa Rosa, CA 95403/707-578-7900 (airguns only)
Belltown, Ltd., RR2, Box 69, Kent, CT 06757/203-354-5750 (gun cleaning cloth kit)
Birchwood-Casey, 7900 Fuller Rd., Eden Prairie, MN 55344/612-927-7933
Blacksmith Corp., P.O. Box 424, Southport, CT 06490/800-531-2665 (Arctic Friction Free gun clg. equip.)
Blue and Gray Prods., Inc., R.D. #6, Box 362, Wellsboro, PA 16901/717-724-1383
Break-Free Corp., P.O. Box 25020, Santa Ana, CA 92799/714-953-1900 (lubricants)

Jim Brobst, 299 Poplar St., Hamburg, PA 19526/215-562-2103 (J-B Bore Cleaning Compound)
Brownells, Inc., 222 W. Liberty, Montezuma, IA 50171/515-623-5401
Browning Arms, Rt. 4, Box 624-B, Arnold, MO 63010
Chopie Mfg. Inc., 700 Copeland Ave., La Crosse, WI 54601/608-784-0926 (Black-Solve gun cleaner)
Clenzoil Corp., Box 1226, Sta. C, Canton, OH 44708/216-833-9758
Crouse's Country Cover, P.O. Box 160, Storrs, CT 06268/203-429-3710 (Masking Gun Oil)
J. Dewey Mfg. Co., 186 Skyview Dr., Southbury, CT 06488/203-264-3064 (one-piece gun clg. rod)
Dri-Slide, Inc., 411 N. Darling, Fremont, MI 49412/616-924-3950
The Dutchman's Firearms Inc., 4143 Taylor Blvd., Louisville, KY 40215/502-366-0555
Forster Products, 82 E. Lanark Ave., Lanark, IL 61046/815-493-6360
Fountain Prods., 492 Prospect Ave., W. Springfield, MA 01089/413-781-4551
Forty-Five Ranch Enterpr., 119 S. Main St., Miami, OK 74354/918-542-9307
Gun Parts Corp. (Successors to Numrich Arms Parts Div.), Box 2, West Hurley, NY 12491/914-679-2417 (gun blue)
Heller & Levin Associates, Inc., 88 Marlborough Court, Rockville Center, NY 11570/516-764-9349
Frank C. Hoppe Division, Penguin Ind., Inc., Airport Industrial Mall, Coatesville, PA 19320/215-384-6000
Hydrosorbent Products, Box 675D, Rye, NE 10580 (silica gel dehumidifier)
J-B Bore Cleaner, 299 Poplar St., Hamburg, PA 19526/215-562-2103
Ken Jantz Supply, 222 E. Main, Davis, OK 73030/405-369-2316
Jet-Aer Corp., 100 Sixth Ave., Paterson, NJ 07524 (blues & oils)
Kellog's Professional Prods., Inc., 325 Pearl St., Sandusky, OH 44870/419-625-6551
K.W. Kleinendorst, R.D. #1, Box 113B, Hop Bottom, PA 18824/717-289-4687 (rifle clg. cables)
Terry K. Kopp, Highway 13 South, Lexington, MO 64067/816-259-2636 (stock rubbing compound; rust preventative grease)
LPS Chemical Prods., Holt Lloyd Corp., 4647 Hugh Howell Rd., Box 3050, Tucker, GA 30084/404-934-7800
Mark Lee, P.O. Box 20379, Minneapolis, MN 55420/612-431-1727 (rust blue solution)
LEM Gun Specialties, P.O. Box 87031, College Park, GA 30337 (Lewis Lead Remover)
Lynx Line Gun Prods. Div., Protective Coatings, Inc., 773 Harkness Dr., Adrian, MI 49221/517-263-7800
MJL Industries, Inc., P.O. Box 122, McHenry, IL 60050/815-344-1040 (Rust Free)
Marble Arms Co., 420 Industrial Park, Gladstone, MI 49837/906-428-3710
Mike Marsh, Croft Cottage, Main St., Elton, Derbyshire DE4 2BY, ENGLAND/062-988-669 (gun accessories)
Micro Sight Co., 242 Harbor Blvd., Belmont, CA 94002/415-591-0769 (bedding compound)
Mount Labs, Inc. (See: LaPaloma Marketing, Inc.)
Nesci Enterprises, Inc., P.O. Box 119, Summit St., East Hampton, CT 06424/203-267-2588
Old World Oil Products, 3827 Queen Ave. No., Minneapolis, MN 55412/612-522-5037 (gun stock finish)
Omark Industries, P.O. Box 856, Lewiston, ID 83501/208-746-2351
Original Mink Oil, Inc., P.O. Box 20191, 11021 N.E. Beech St., Portland, OR 97220/503-255-2814
Outers Laboratories, Div. of Omark Industries, Route 2, Onalaska, WI 54650/608-781-5800
Ox-Yoke Originals, Inc., 34 W. Main St., Milo, ME 04463/800-231-8313 (dry lubrication patches)
Parker-Hale/Precision Sports, P.O. Box 708, Cortland, NY 13045
Bob Pease Accuracy, P.O. Box 787, Zipp Rd., New Braunfels, TX 78131/512-625-1342
A. E. Pennebaker Co., Inc., P.O. Box 1386, Greenville, SC 29602/803-235-8016 (Pyro Dux)
Precision Sports, P.O. Box 708, 3736 Kellogg Rd., Cortland, NY 13045/607-756-2851 (Parker-Hale)
R&S Industries Corp., 1312 Washington Ave., St. Louis, MO 63103/314-241-8464 (Miracle All Purpose polishing cloth)
RTI Research Ltd., P.O. Box 48300, Bental Three Tower, Vancouver, B.C. V7X 1A1, Canada/604-588-5141 (Accubore chemical bore cleaner)
Reardon Prod., P.O. Box 126, Morrison, IL 61270/815-772-3155 (Dry-Lube)
Rice Protective Gun Coatings, 235-30th St., West Palm Beach, FL 33407/305-848-7771
Richards Classic Oil Finish, John Richards, Rt. 2, Box 325, Bedford, KY 40006/502-255-7222 (gunstock oils, wax)
Rig Products, 87 Coney Island Dr., Sparks, NV 89431/703-331-5666
Rusteprufe Labs., Rte. 5, Sparta, WI 54656/608-269-4144
Rust Guardit, see: Schwab Industries
Schwab Industries, Inc., P.O. Box 1269, Sequim, WA 98382/206-683-2944
Tyler Scott, Inc., 8170 Corporate Park Dr., Cincinnati, OH 45242, Suite 141/513-489-2202 (ML black solvent; patch lube)
Seacliff Inc., 2210 Santa Anita, So. El Monte, CA 91733/818-350-0515 (portable parts washer)
Secoa Technologies, Inc., 3915 U.S. Hwy. 98 So., Lakeland, FL 33801/813-665-1734 (Teflon coatings)
Shooter's Choice (See Venco Industries)
TDP Industries, Inc., 603 Airport Blvd., Doylestown, PA 18901/215-345-8687
Taylor & Robbins, Box 164, Rixford, PA 16745 (Throat Saver)
Texas Platers Supply Co., 2453 W. Five Mile Parkway, Dallas, TX 75233
Totally Dependable Products; See: TDP
Treso Inc., P.O. Box 4640, Pagosa Springs, CO 81157/303-731-2295 (mfg. Durango Gun Rod)
C. S. Van Gorden, 1815 Main St., Bloomer, WI 54724/715-568-2612 (Van's Instant Blue)
United States Products Co., 518 Melwood Ave., Pittsburgh, PA 15213/412-621-2130 (Gold Medallion bore cleaner/conditioner)
Venco Industries, Inc., 16770 Hilltop Park Pl., Chagrin Falls, OH 44022/216-543-8808 (Shooter's Choice bore cleaner & conditioner)
WD-40 Co., P.O. Box 80607, San Diego, CA 92138-9021/619-275-1400
J. C. Whitney & Co., 1917 Archer Ave., Chicago, IL 60680 (gunstock finish)
Williams Gun Sight, 7389 Lapeer Rd., Davison, MI 48423 (finish kit)
Wisconsin Platers Supply Co., (See Texas Platers Supply Co.)
Zip Aerosol Prods., See Rig

CUSTOM GUNSMITHS

Accuracy Gun Shop, Lance Martini, 3651 University Ave., San Diego, CA 92104/619-282-8500
Accuracy Systems Inc., 15203 N. Cave Creek Rd., Phoenix, AZ 85032/602-971-1991
Accuracy Unlimited, 16036 N. 49 Ave., Glendale, AZ 85306/602-978-9089
Ahlman's Inc., R.R. 1, Box 20, Morristown, MN 55052/507-685-4244
Don Allen Inc., HC55, Box 326, Sturgis, SD 57785/605-347-5227
American Custom Gunmakers Guild, c/o Jan Melchert, Exec. Scy., 220 Division St., Northfield, MN 55057/507-645-8811
Amrine's Gun Shop, 937 Luna Ave., Ojai, CA 93023
Ann Arbor Rod and Gun Co., 1946 Packard Rd., Ann Arbor, MI 48104/313-769-7866
Armament Gunsmithing Co., Inc., 525 Route 22, Hillside, NJ 07205/201-686-0960
Arms Services Corp., 330 Lockhouse Rd., Westfield, MA 01085/413-562-4196
Armurier Hiptmayer, P.O. Box 136, Eastman, Que. JOE 1P0, Canada/514-297-2492
Ed von Atzigen, The Custom Shop, 890 Cochrane Crescent, Peterborough, Ont., K9H 5N3 Canada/705-742-6693
Richard W. Baber, Alpine Gun Mill, 1507 W. Colorado Ave., Colorado Springs, CO 80904/303-634-4867
Bain & Davis Sptg. Gds., 307 E. Valley Blvd., San Gabriel, CA 91776/213-283-7449
Baer Custom Guns, 1725 Minesite Rd., Allentown, PA 18103/215-398-2362 (rifles)
Joe J. Balickie, Rte. 2, Box 56-G, Apex, NC 27502/919-362-5185
Barnes Custom Shop, dba Barnes Bullets Inc., P.O. Box 215, American Fork, UT 84003
Barta's Gunsmithing, 10231 US Hwy., #10, Cato, WI 54206/414-732-4472
Donald Bartlett, 31829-32nd Pl. S.W., Federal Way, WA 98023/206-927-0726
R. J. Beal, Jr., 170 W. Marshall Rd., Lansdowne, PA 19050/215-259-1220
Behlert Precision, RD 2 Box 63, Route 611 North, Pipersville, PA 18947/215-766-8681 (custom)
George Beitzinger, 116-20 Atlantic Ave., Richmond Hill, NY 11419/718-847-7661
Bell's Custom Shop, 3309 Mannheim Rd., Franklin Park, IL 60131/312-678-1900 (handguns)
Dennis M. Bellm Gunsmithing, Inc., 2376 So. Redwood Rd., Salt Lake City, UT 84119/801-974-0697
Bennett Gun Works, 561 Delaware Ave., Delmar, NY 12054/518-439-1862
Bergmann & Williams, 2450 Losee Rd., Suite F, No. Las Vegas, NV 89030/702-642-1091
Gordon Bess, 708 Royal Gorge Blvd., Canon City, CO 81212/303-275-1073
Al Biesen, 5021 Rosewood, Spokane, WA 99208/509-328-9340
Roger Biesen, W. 2039 Sinto Ave., Spokane, WA 99201
Stephen L. Billeb, Box 1176, Big Piney, WY 83113/307-276-5627
E.C. Bishop & Son Inc., 119 Main St., P.O. Box 7, Warsaw, MO 65355/816-438-5121
Duane Bolden, 1295 Lassen Dr., Hanford, CA 93230/209-582-6937 (rust bluing)
Charles Boswell (Gunmakers), Div. of Saxon Arms Ltd., 615 Jasmine Ave. No., Unit J,Tarpon Springs, FL 34689/813-938-4882
Kent Bowerly, Metolious Meadows Dr., H.C.R. Box 1903, Camp Sherman, OR 97730/503-595-6028
Larry D. Brace, 771 Blackfoot Ave., Eugene, OR 97404/503-688-1278
Brazos Arms Co., 7314 Skybright Lane, Houston, TX 77095/713-463-0826 (gunsmithing)
A. Briganti, 475 Rt. 32, Highland Mills, NY 10930/914-692-4409
Brown Precision Inc., P.O. Box 270GD, 7786 Molinos Ave., Los Molinos, CA 96055/800-543-2506/916-384-2506 (rifles)
Brown's Gun Shop, Ed Brown, Rte. 2 Box 2922, Perry, MO 63462/314-565-3261
David Budin, Main St., Margaretville, NY 12455/914-568-4103
Ida I. Burgess, Sam's Gun Shop, 25 Squam Rd., Rockport, MA 01966/617-546-6839 (bluing repairs)
Leo Bustani, P.O. Box 8125, W. Palm Beach, FL 33407/305-622-2710
Cache La Poudre Rifleworks, 140 No. College Ave., Ft. Collins, CO 80524/303-482-6913 (cust. ML)
Cameron's Guns, 16690 W. 11th Ave., Golden, CO 80401
Lou Camilli, 4700 Oahu Dr. N.E., Albuquerque, NM 87111/505-293-5259 (ML)
Dick Campbell, 20000 Silver Ranch Rd., Conifer, CO 80433/303-697-9150
Ralph L. Carter, Carter's Gun Shop, 225 G St., Penrose, CO 81240/303-372-6240
Larry T. Caudill, 1025A Palomas Dr. S.E., Albuquerque, NM 87108/505-255-2515
Shane Caywood, P.O. Box 321, Minocqua, WI 54548/715-356-5414
R. MacDonald Champlin, P.O. Box 693, Manchester, NH 03105/603-483-8559 (ML rifles and pistols)
F. Bob Chow's Gun Shop, Inc., 3185 Mission St., San Francisco, CA 94110/415-282-8358
E. Christopher Firearms Co., Inc., Route 128 & Ferry St., Miamitown, OH 45041/513-353-1321
Classic Arms Corp., P.O. Box 8, Palo Alto, CA 94302/415-321-7243
Clinton River Gun Serv. Inc., 30016 S. River Rd., Mt. Clemens, MI 48045/313-468-1090
Charles H. Coffin, 3719 Scarlet Ave., Odessa, TX 79762/915-366-4729

Jim Coffin, 250 Country Club Lane, Albany, OR 97321/503-928-4391
David Costa, 94 Orient Ave., Arlington, MA 02174/617-643-9571
C. Ed Cox, 166 W. Wylie Ave., Washington, PA 15301/412-228-2932
Crocker, 1510 - 42nd St., Los Alamos, NM 87544 (rifles)
J. Lynn Crook, Rt. 6, Box 295-A, Lebanon, TN 37087/615-449-1930
Cumberland Arms, Rt. 1, Box 1150, Shafer Rd., Blantons Chapel, Manchester, TN 37355
Cumberland Knife & Gun Works, 5661 Bragg Blvd., Fayetteville, NC 28303/919-867-0009 (ML)
Custom Gun Guild, 2646 Church Dr. Doraville, GA 30340/404-455-0346
D&D Gun Shop, 363 Elmwood, Troy, MI 48083/313-583-1512
Dakota Arms, Inc., HC 55 Box 326, Sturgis, SD 57785/605-347-4686
Homer L. Dangler, Box 254, Addison, MI 49220/517-547-6745 (Kentucky rifles; brochure $3)
Sterling Davenport, 9611 E. Walnut Tree Dr., Tucson, AZ 85715/602-749-5590
Davis Co., 2793 Del Monte St., West Sacramento, CA 95691/916-372-6789
Ed Delorge, 2231 Hwy. 308, Thibodaux, LA 70301/504-447-1633
Jack Dever, 8520 N.W. 90, Oklahoma City, OK 73132/405-721-6393
R. H. Devereaux, D. D. Custom Rifles, 5240 Mule Deer Dr., Colorado Springs, CO 80919/719-548-8468
Dilliott Gunsmithing, Inc., Rt. 3, Box 340, Scarlett Rd., Dandridge, TN 37725/615-397-9204
Dominic DiStefano, 4303 Friar Lane, Colorado Springs, CO 80907
William Dixon, Buckhorn Gun Works, Rt. 4 Box 1230, Rapid City, SD 57702/605-787-6289
C. P. Donnelly-Siskiyou Gun Works, 405 Kubli Rd., Grants Pass, OR 97527/503-846-6604
Dowtin Gunworks (DGW), Rt. 4 Box 930A, Flagstaff, AZ 86001/602-779-1898
Charles E. Duffy, Williams Lane, West Hurley, NY 12491/914-679-2997
Duncan's Gunworks Inc., 1619 Grand Ave., San Marcos, CA 92069/619-727-0515
Jere Eggleston, P.O. Box 50238, Columbia, SC 29250/803-799-3402
Elko Arms, Dr. L. Kortz, 28 rue Ecole Moderne, B-7400 Soignies, H.T., Belgium
Bob Emmons, 238 Robson Rd., Grafton, OH 44044/216-458-5890
Englishtown Sporting Goods, Inc., David J. Maxham, 38 Main St., Englishtown, NJ 07726/201-446-7717
Dennis Erhardt, P.O. Box 502, Canyon Creek, MT 59633/406-368-2298
Ken Eyster, Heritage Gunsmiths Inc., 6441 Bishop Rd., Centerburg, OH 43011/614-625-6131
Andy Fautheree, P.O. Box 4607, Pagosa Springs, CO 81157/303-731-5003 (cust ML; send SASE)
Ted Fellowes, Beaver Lodge, 9245-16th Ave., S.W., Seattle, WA 98106/206-763-1698 (muzzleloaders)
Ferris Firearms, 1827 W. Hildebrand, San Antonio, TX 78201/512-734-0304
Fiberpro Inc., Robert Culbertson, 3636 California St., San Diego, CA 92101/619-295-7703 (rifles)
Jack First Distributors Inc., 44633 Sierra Highway, Lancaster, CA 93534/805-945-6981
Marshall F. Fish, Rt. 22 North, Box 2439, Westport, NY 12993/518-962-4897
Jerry A. Fisher, 1244-4th Ave. West, Kalispell, MT 59901/406-755-7093
Flaig's Inc., 2200 Evergreen Rd., Millvale, PA 15209/412-821-1717
Flint Creek Arms Co., P.O. Box 205, 136 Spring St., Philipsburg, MT 59858 (bluing, repairs)
Flynn's Cust. Guns, P.O. Box 7461, Alexandria, LA 71306/318-445-7130
James W. Fogle, RR 2, Box 258, Herrin, IL 62948/618-988-1795
Larry L. Forster, Box 212, 220-1st St. N.E., Gwinner, ND 58040/701-678-2475
Pete Forthofer's Gunsmithing, 711 Spokane Ave., Whitefish, MT 59937/406-862-2674
Fountain Products, 492 Prospect Ave., West Springfield, MA 01089/413-781-4651
Frank's Custom Rifles, 7521 E. Fairmount Pl., Tucson, AZ 85715/602-885-3901
Freeland's Scope Stands, 3737—14th Ave., Rock Island, IL 61201/309-788-7449
Fredrick Gun Shop, 10 Elson Drive, Riverside, RI 02915/401-433-2805
Frontier Shop & Gallery, Depot 1st & Main, Riverton, WY 82501/307-856-4498
Fuller Gunshop, Cooper Landing, AK 99572
Karl J. Furr, 76 East 350 No., Orem, UT 84057/801-225-2603
Gander Mountain, Inc., P.O. Box 128, Wilmot, WI 53192/414-862-2344
Garcia Natl. Gun Traders, Inc., 225 S.W. 22nd Ave., Miami, FL 33135
Gator Guns & Repair, 6255 Spur Hwy., Kenai, AK 99611/907-283-7947
David Gentry Custom Gunmaker, P.O. Box 1440, Belgrade, MT 59714/406-388-4867 (cust. Montana Mtn. Rifle)
Edwin Gillman, 33 Valley View Dr., Hanover, PA 17331/717-632-1662
Gilman-Mayfield, 1552 N. 1st, Fresno, CA 93703/209-237-2500
Dale Goens, Box 224, Cedar Crest, NM 87008
A. R. Goode, 4125 N.E. 28th Terr., Ocala, FL 32670/904-622-9575
Goodling's Gunsmithing, R.D. #1, Box 1097, Spring Grove, PA 17362/717-225-3350
Gordie's Gun Shop, Gordon Mulholland, 1401 Fulton St., Streator, IL 61364/815-672-7202
Charles E. Grace, 10144 Elk Lake Rd., Williamsburg, MI 49690/616-264-9483
Roger M. Green & J. Earl Bridges, P.O. Box 984, 435 East Birch, Glenrock, WY 82637/307-436-9804
Griffin & Howe, 36 W. 44th St., Suite 1011, New York, NY 10036/212-921-0980
Griffin & Howe, 33 Claremont Rd., Bernardsville, NJ 07924/201-766-2287
Guncraft, Inc., 117 W. Pipeline, Hurst, TX 76053/817-282-1464
Guncraft Sports, Inc., 125 E. Tyrone Rd., Oak Ridge, TN 37830/615-483-4024
Gunsite Gunsmithy, Box 451, Paulden, AZ 86334/602-636-4104
The Gun Works, Joe Williams, 236 Main St., Springfield, OR 97477/503-741-4118 (ML)
H-S Precision, Inc., 112 N. Summit, Prescott, AZ 86302/602-445-0607
Hagn Rifles & Actions, Martin Hagn, Box 444, Cranbrook, B.C. VIC 4H9, Canada/604-489-4861 (s.s. actions & rifles)
Fritz Hallberg, Silver Shields Inc., 7544 Lemhi #9; P.O. Box 7601, Boise, ID 83707/208-323-8991
Charles E. Hammans, P.O. Box 788, 2022 McCracken, Stuttgart, AR 72160/501-673-1388
Hammond Custom Guns, 619 S. Pandora, Gilbert, AZ 85234/602-892-3437
Dick Hanson, Hanson's Gun Center, 521 So. Circle Dr., Colorado Springs, CO 80910/303-634-4220
Harkrader's Cust. Gun Shop, 825 Radford St., Christiansburg, VA 24073
Rob't W. Hart & Son Inc., 401 Montgomery St., Nescopeck, PA 18635/717-752-3655 (actions, stocks)
Hartmann & Weiss KG, Rahlstedter Bahnhofstr. 47, 2000 Hamburg 73, W. Germany/040-677-55-85
Hubert J. Hecht, Waffen-Hecht, P.O. Box 2635, Fair Oaks, CA 95628/916-966-1020
Stephen Heilmann, P.O. Box 657, Grass Valley, CA 95945/916-272-8758
Iver Henriksen, 1211 So. 2nd St. W, Missoula, MT 59801 (Rifles)
Darwin Hensley, P.O. Box 179, Brightwood, OR 97011/503-622-5411
Heppler's Gun Shop, 6000 B Soquel Ave., Santa Cruz, CA 95062/408-475-1235
Klaus Hiptmayer, P.O. Box 136, Eastman, PQ JOE 1PO, Canada/514-297-2492
Wm. Hobaugh, The Rifle Shop, Box M, Philipsburg, MT 59858/406-859-3515
Duane A. Hobbie Gunsmithing, 2412 Pattie Ave., Wichita, KS 67216/316-264-8266
Richard Hodgson, 9081 Tahoe Lane, Boulder, CO 80301
Hoenig and Rodman, 6521 Morton Dr., Boise, ID 83705/208-375-1116
Peter Hofer, F. Lang-Str. 13, A-9170 Ferlach, Austria/0-42-27-3683 (cust.)
Dick Holland, 422 N.E. 6th St., Newport, OR 97365/503-265-7556
Hollis Gun Shop, 917 Rex St., Carlsbad, NM 88220/505-835-3782
Bill Holmes, Rt. 2, Box 242, Fayetteville, AR 72701/501-521-8958
Alan K. Horst, P.O. Box 68, 402 E. St., Albion, WA 99102/509-332-7109 (cust.)
Corey O. Huebner, 3604 S. 3rd W., Missoula, MT 59801/406-721-9647
Steven Dodd Hughes, P.O. Box 11455, Eugene, OR 97440/503-485-8869 (ML; ctlg. $3)
Al Hunkeler, Buckskin Machine Works, 3235 So. 358th St., Auburn, WA 98001/206-927-5412 (ML)
Hyper-Single Precision SS Rifles, 520 E. Beaver, Jenks, OK 74037/918-299-2391
Campbell H. Irwin, Hartland Blvd. (Rt. 20), East Hartland, CT 06027/203-653-3901
Jackalope Gun Shop, 1048 S. 5th St., Douglas, WY 82633/307-358-3854
Paul Jaeger, Inc. P.O. Box 449, 1 Madison Ave., Grand Junction, TN 38039/901-764-6909
R. L. Jamison, Jr., Route 4, Box 200, Moses Lake, WA 98837/509-762-2659
Jarrett Rifles, Inc., Rt. 1 Box 411, Jackson, SC 29831/803-471-3616 (rifles)
Jenkins Enterprises, Inc., 12317 Locksley Lane, Auburn, CA 95603/916-823-9652
Jerry's Gun Shop, 9220 Ogden Ave., Brookfield, IL 60513/312-485-5200
Jim's Gun Shop, James R. Spradlin, 113 Arthur, Pueblo, CO 81004/719-543-9462
Neal G. Johnson, Gunsmithing Inc., 111 Marvin Dr., Hampton, VA 23666/804-838-8091
Peter S. Johnson, The Orvis Co., Inc., 10 River Rd., Manchester, VT 05254/802-362-3622
L. E. Jurras & Assoc., Box 680, Washington, IN 47501/812-254-7698
Ken's Gun Specialties, K. Hunnell, Rt. 1 Box 147, Lakeview, AR 72642/501-431-5606
Kesselring Gun Shop, 400 Pacific Hiway No., Burlington, WA 98233/206-724-3113
Benjamin Kilham, Kilham & Co., Main St., Box 37, Lyme, NH 03768/603-795-4112
Don Klein Custom Guns, Rt. 2, P.O. Box 277, Camp Douglas, WI 54618/608-427-6948
K. W. Kleinendorst, R.D. #1, Box 113B, Hop Bottom, PA 18824/717-289-4687
Terry K. Kopp, Highway 13 South, Lexington, MO 64067/816-259-2636
J. Korzinek, R.D. #2, Box 73, Canton, PA 17724/717-673-8512 (riflesmith) (broch. $2)
Krider's Gun Shop, 114 W. Eagle Rd., Havertown, PA 19083/215-789-7828
Lee Kuhns, 652 Northeast Palson Rd., Paulsbo, WA 98370/206-692-5790
Sam Lair, 520 E. Beaver, Jenks, OK 74037/918-299-2391 (single shots)
Maynard Lambert, Kamas, UT 84036
Ron Lampert, Rt. 1, Box 177, Guthrie, MN 56461/218-854-7345
Harry Lawson Co., 3328 N. Richey Blvd., Tucson, AZ 85716/602-326-1117
John G. Lawson, (The Sight Shop), 1802 E. Columbia, Tacoma, WA 98404/206-474-5465
Mark Lee, P.O. Box 20379, Minneapolis, MN 55420/612-431-1727
Frank LeFever & Sons, Inc., R.D. #1, Box 31, Lee Center, NY 13363/315-337-6722
Liberty Antique Gunworks, 19 Key St., P.O. Box 183GD, Eastport, ME 04631/207-853-2327
Lilja Precision Rifle Barrels, Inc., 245 Compass Creek Rd., P.O. Box 372, Plains, MT 59859/406-826-3084
Al Lind, 7821—76th Ave. S.W., Tacoma, WA 98498/206-584-6363
Ljutic Ind., Box 2117, Yakima, WA 98904 (shotguns)
James W. Lofland, 2275 Larkin Rd., Boothwyn, PA 19061/215-485-0391 (SS rifles)
London Guns Ltd., P.O. Box 3750, Santa Barbara, CA 93130/805-683-4141
Longbranch Gun Bluing Co., 2455 Jacaranda Lane, Los Osos, CA 93402/805-528-1792
McCann's Muzzle-Gun Works, Tom McCann, 200 Federal City Rd., Pennington, NJ 08534/609-737-1707 (ML)
McCormick's Gun Bluing, 609 N.E. 104th Ave., Vancouver, WA 98664/206-256-0579
Dennis McDonald, 8359 Brady St., Peosta, IA 52068/319-556-7940
Stan McFarland, 2221 Idella Ct., Grand Junction, CO 81506/303-243-4704 (cust. rifles)
Bill McGuire, 1600 N. Eastmont Ave., East Wenatchee, WA 98801
MPI Stocks, 7011 N. Reno Ave., Portland, OR 97203/503-289-8025 (rifles)
Darrell Madis, 2453 Five-Mile Pkwy. Dallas, TX 75233/214-330-7168

Mag-na-port International, Inc., 41302 Executive Dr., Mt. Clemens, MI 48045/313-469-6727
Nick Makinson, R.R. #3, Komoka, Ont. N0L 1R0 Canada/519-471-5462 (English guns; repairs & renovations)
Monte Mandarino, 136 Fifth Ave. West, Kalispell, MT 59901/406-257-6208 (Penn. rifles)
Lowell Manley Shooting Supplies, 3684 Pine St., Deckerville, MI 48427/313-376-3665
Marquart Precision Co., P.O. Box 1740, Prescott, AZ 86302/602-445-5646
Elwyn H. Martin, Martin's Gun Shop, 937 S. Sheridan Blvd., Lakewood, CO 80226/303-922-2184
Maryland Gun Works, Ltd., TEC Bldg., 10097 Tyler Pl. #8, Ijamsville, MD 21754/301-831-8456
Mashburn Arms & Sporting Goods Co., Inc., 1218 N. Pennsylvania, Oklahoma City, OK 73107/405-236-5151
Seely Masker, Custom Rifles, 261 Washington Ave., Pleasantville, NY 10570/914-769-2627
Geo. E. Matthews & Son Inc., 10224 S. Paramount Blvd., Downey, CA 90241
Maurer Arms, 2154-16th St., Akron, OH 44314/216-745-6864 (muzzleloaders)
John E. Maxson, 3507 Red Oak Lane, Plainview, TX 79072/806-293-9042 (high grade rifles)
R. M. Mercer, 216 S. Whitewater Ave., Jefferson, WI 53549/414-674-3839
Miller Arms, Inc., Dean E. Miller, P.O. Box 260, St. Onge, SD 57779/605-578-1790
Miller Gun Works, S. A. Miller, P.O. Box 1053, 1440 Peltier Dr., Point Roberts, WA 98281/206-945-7014
Tom Miller, c/o Huntington's Sportsman's Store, 601 Oro Dam Blvd., Oroville, CA 95965/916-534-1210
Earl Milliron, 1249 N.E. 166th Ave., Portland, OR 97230/503-252-3725
Hugh B. Mills, Jr., 3615 Canterbury Rd., New Bern, NC 28560/919-637-4631
Monell Custom Guns, Red Mill Road, RD #2, Box 96, Pine Bush, NY 12566/914-744-3021
Wm. Larkin Moore & Co., 31360 Via Colinas, Suite 109, Westlake Village, CA 91361/818-889-4160
J. W. Morrison Custom Rifles, 4015 W. Sharon, Phoenix, AZ 85029/602-978-3754
Mitch Moschetti, P.O. Box 27065, Cromwell, CT 06416/203-632-2308
Mountain Bear Rifle Works, Inc., Wm. Scott Bickett, 100-B Ruritan Rd., Sterling, VA 22170/703-430-0420
Larry Mrock, R.F.D. 3, Box 207, Woodhill-Hooksett Rd., Bow, NH 03301/603-224-4096 (broch. $3)
William Neighbor, Bill's Gun Repair, 1007 Burlington St., Mendota, IL 61342/815-539-5786
Bruce A. Nettestad, R.R. 1, Box 140, Pelican Rapids, MN 56572/218-863-4301
New England Arms Co., Lawrence Lane, Kittery Point, ME 03905/207-439-0593
Newman Gunshop, 119 Miller Rd., Agency, IA 52530/515-937-5775 (ML)
Paul R. Nickels, P.O. Box 71043, Las Vegas, NV 89170/702-798-7533
Ted Nicklas, 5504 Hegel Rd., Goodrich, MI 48438/313-797-4493
William J. Nittler, 290 More Dr., Boulder Creek, CA 95006/408-338-3376 or 408-438-7331 (shotgun bbls. & actions;repairs)
Jim Norman, Custom Gunstocks, 14281 Cane Rd., Valley Center, CA92082/619-749-6252
Nu-Line Guns, 1053 Caulks Hill Rd., Harvester, MO 63303/314-441-4500
Eric Olson, 12721 E. 11th Ave., Spokane, WA 99216
Vic Olson, 5002 Countryside Dr., Imperial, MO 63052/314-296-8086
Oregon Trail Riflesmiths, Inc., P.O. Box 51, Mackay, ID 83251/208-588-2527
The Orvis Co., Inc., Peter S. Johnson, Rt. 7A, Manchester, VT 05254/802-362-3622
Maurice Ottmar, Box 657, 113 East Fir, Coulee City, WA 99115/509-632-5717
Pachmayr Ltd., 1875 So. Mountain Ave., Monrovia, CA 91016/818-357-7771
Jay A. Pagel, 1407 4th St. NW, Grand Rapids, MN 55744/218-326-3003 (cust. gunmaking & refinishing)
Pasadena Gun Center, 206 E. Shaw, Pasadena, TX 77506/713-472-0417
Paterson Gunsmithing, 438 Main St., Paterson, NJ 07502/201-345-4100
John Pell, 410 College Ave., Trinidad, CO 81082/719-846-9406
Penrod Precision, 126 E. Main St., P.O. Box 307, No. Manchester, IN 46962/219-981-8385
A. W. Peterson Gun Shop, 1693 Old Hwy. 441, Mt. Dora, FL 32757 (ML)
Eugene T. Plante, Gene's Custom Guns, 3890 Hill Ave., White Bear Lake, MN 55110/612-429-5105
Professional Gunsmiths of America, Hwy 13 South, Box 224E, Lexington, MO 64067/816-259-2636
Rifle Shop, Box M, Philipsburg, MT 59858
J. J. Roberts, 166 Manassas Dr., Manassas Park, VA 22111/703-330-0448
Wm. A. Roberts Jr., Rte. 4, Box 75, Athens, AL 35611/205-232-7027 (ML)
Don Robinson, Pennsylvania Hse., 36 Fairfaix Crescent, Southowram, Halifax, W. Yorkshire HX3 9SQ, England (airifle stocks)
Rocky Mountain Rifle Works, Ltd., 1707 14th St., Boulder, CO 80302/303-443-9189
Bob Rogers Guns, P.O. Box 305, 344 S. Walnut St., Franklin Grove, IL 61031/815-456-2685
Royal Arms, 1210 Bert Acosta, El Cajon, CA 92020/619-448-5466
R.P.S. Gunshop, 11 So. Haskell, Central Point, OR 97502/503-664-5010
Russell's Rifle Shop, Route 5, Box 92, Georgetown, TX 78626/512-778-5338
SSK Industries, Rt. 1, Della Dr., Bloomingdale, OH 43910/614-264-0176
Sanders Custom Gun Serv., 2358 Tyler Lane, Louisville, KY 40205
Sandy's Custom Gunshop, Rte. #1, Box 4, Rockport, IL 62370/217-437-4241
Roy V. Schaefer, 965 W. Hilliard Lane, Eugene, OR 97404/503-688-4333
Schumaker's Gun Shop, Rte. 4, Box 500, Colville, WA 99114/509-684-4848
Schwartz Custom Guns, 9621 Coleman Rd., Haslett, MI 48840/517-339-8939
David W. Schwartz Custom Guns, 2505 Waller St., Eau Claire, WI 54701/715-832-1735
Thad Scott Fine Guns Inc., P.O. Box 412, Indianola, MS 38751/601-887-5929
Butch Searcy Co., 15 RD3804, Farmington, NM 87401/505-327-3419
Shane's Gunsmithing, P.O. Box 321, Hwy. 51 So., Minocqua, WI 54548/715-356-7675
Shaw's, Finest in Guns, 9447 W. Lilac Rd., Escondido, CA 92026/619-728-7070
E. R. Shaw Inc., Small Arms Mfg. Co., Thoms Run Rd. & Prestley, Bridgeville, PA 15017/412-221-4343
Shell Shack, 113 E. Main, Laurel, MT 59044/406-628-8986 (ML)
Dan A. Sherk, 9701-17th St. Dawson Creek, B.C. V1G 4H7 Canada/604-782-5630
Shilen Rifles, Inc., 205 Metro Park Blvd., Ennis, TX 75119/214-875-5318
Shiloh Rifle Mfg. Co., Inc., P.O. Box 279; 20 Centennial Dr., Big Timber, MT 59011/406-932-4454
Harold H. Shockley, 204 E. Farmington Rd., Hanna City, IL 61536/309-565-4524 (hot bluing & plating)
Shootin' Shack, 1065 Silverbeach Rd. #1, Riviera Beach, FL 33403/305-842-0990 ('smithing services)
Shootist Supply, John Cook, 622 5th Ave., Belle Fourche, SD 57717/605-892-2811
Simmons Gun Spec., 700 So. Rogers Rd., Olathe, KS 66062/913-782-3131
John R. Skinner, c/o Orvis Co., 10 River Rd., Manchester, VT 05254
Steve Sklany, 566 Birch Grove Dr., Kalispell, MT 59901/406-755-4527 (Ferguson rifle)
Jerome F. Slezak, 1290 Marlowe, Lakewood (Cleveland), OH 44107/216-221-1668
Art Smith, 4124 Thrushwood Lane, Minnetonka, MN 55345/612-935-7829
John Smith, 912 Lincoln, Carpentersville, IL 60110
Jordan T. Smith, c/o Orvis Co., 10 River Rd., Manchester, VT 05254
Snapp's Gunshop, 6911 E. Washington Rd., Clare, MI 48617/517-386-9226
Fred D. Speiser, 2229 Dearborn, Missoula, MT 59801/406-549-8133
Spencer Reblue Service, 1820 Tupelo Trail, Holt, MI 48842/517-694-7474 (electroless nickel plating)
Sportsmen's Equip. Co., 915 W. Washington, San Diego, CA 92103/619-296-1501
Sportsmen's Exchange & Western Gun Traders, Inc., P.O. Box 111, 560 S. "C" St., Oxnard, CA 93030/805-483-1917
Ken Starnes, Rt. 1, Box 269, Scroggins, TX 75480/214-365-2312
Steelman's Gun Shop, 10465 Beers Rd., Swartz Creek, MI 48473/313-753-4884
Keith Stegall, Box 696, Gunnison, CO 81230
Date Storey, 1764 S. Wilson, Casper, WY 82601/307-237-2414
Stott's Creek Armory Inc., R 1 Box 70, Morgantown, IN 46160/317-878-5489 (antique only)
Victor W. Strawbridge, 6 Pineview Dr., Dover Point, Dover, NH 03820/603-742-0013
W. C. Strutz, Rifle Barrels, Inc., P.O. Box 611, Eagle River. WI 54521/715-479-4766
Suter's House of Guns, 332 N. Tejon, Colorado Springs, CO 80902/303-635-1475
A. D. Swenson's 45 Shop, P.O. Box 606, Fallbrook, CA 92028
Talmage Enterprises, 451 Phantom Creek Lane, P.O. Box 512, Meadview, AZ 86444/602-564-2380
Target Airgun Supply, P.O. Box 428, South Gate, CA 90280/213-569-3417
Taylor & Robbins, Box 164, Rixford, PA 16745
James A. Tertin, c/o Gander Mountain, P.O. Box 128 - Hwy. W, Wilmot, WI 53192/414-862-2344
Larry R. Thompson, Larry's Gun Shop, 521 E. Lake Ave., Watsonville, CA 95076/408-724-5328
Daniel Titus, 872 Penn St., Bryn Mawr, PA 19010/215-525-8829
Tom's Gunshop, Tom Gillman, 4435 Central, Hot Springs, AR 71913/501-624-3856
Trader Perry's Discount Guns & Repair, 649 Mercedes Ave., Manteca, CA 95336/209-823-7363
David Trevallion, R. 1, Box 39, Kittery Point, ME 03905/207-439-6822
Trinko's Gun Serv., 1406 E. Main, Watertown, WI 53094
James C. Tucker, 205 Trinity St., Woodland, CA 95695/916-662-3109
Dennis A. "Doc" & Bud Ulrich, D.O.C. Specialists, Inc., 2209 S. Central Ave., Cicero, IL 60650/312-652-3606
Upper Missouri Trading Co., Inc., Box 181, Crofton, MO 68730
Milton Van Epps, Rt. 69-A, Parish, NY 13131/313-625-7251
Gil Van Horn, P.O. Box 207, Llano, CA 93544
John Vest, P.O. Box 1552, Susanville, CA 96130/916-257-7228
Vic's Gun Refinishing, 6 Pineview Dr., Dover, NH 03820/603-742-0013
Walker Arms Co., Inc., Rt. 2, Box 73, Hiwy 80 West, Selma, AL 36701/205-872-6231
R. D. Wallace, Star Rt. 1 Box 76, Grandin, MO 63943/314-593-4773
R. A. Wardrop, Box 245, 409 E. Marble St., Mechanicsburg, PA 17055
Weatherby's, 2781 Firestone Blvd., South Gate, CA 90280/213-569-7186
Weaver Arms Co., P.O. Box 8, Dexter, MO 63841/314-568-3800 (ambidextrous bolt action)
Cecil Weems, P.O. Box 657, Mineral Wells, TX 76067/817-325-1462
Wells Sport Store, Fred Wells, 110 N. Summit St., Prescott, AZ 86301/602-445-3655
R. A. Wells Ltd., 3452 N. 1st Ave., Racine, WI 53402/414-639-5223
Robert G. West, 3973 Pam St., Eugene, OR 97402/503-689-6610
Terry Werth, 1203 Woodlawn Rd., Lincoln, IL 62656/217-732-1300
Western Gunstocks Mfg. Co., 550 Valencia School Rd., Aptos, CA 95003
Duane Wiebe, P.O. Box 497, Lotus, CA 95651/916-626-6240
David W. Wills, 2776 Brevard Ave., Montgomery, AL 36109/205-272-8446
Williams Gun Sight Co., 7389 Lapeer Rd., Davison, MI 48423
Williamson-Pate Gunsmith Service, 117 W. Pipeline, Hurst, TX 76053/817-282-1464
Wilson's Gun Shop, P.O. Box 578, Rt. 3, Box 211-D, Berryville, AR 72616/501-545-3616
Robert M. Winter, R.R. 2, Box 484, Menno, SD 57045/605-387-5322
Wisner's Gun Shop, Inc., P.O. Box 58; Hiway 6, Adna, WA 98552/206-748-8942
Lester Womack, 512 Westwood Dr., Prescott, AZ 86301/602-778-9624
Mike Yee, 29927-56 Pl. S., Auburn, WA 98001/206-839-3991
Russ Zeeryp, 1601 Foard Dr., Lynn Ross Manor, Morristown, TN 37814

CUSTOM METALSMITHS

Alley Supply Co., P.O. Box 848, Gardnerville, NV 89410/702-782-3800
Armament Gunsmithing Co., Inc., 525 Route 22, Hillside, NJ 07205/201-686-0960
Baer Custom Guns, 1725 Minesite Rd., Allentown, PA 18103/215-398-2362
Barta's Gunsmithing, 10231 US Hwy 10, Cato, WI 54206/414-732-4472
George Beitzinger, 116-20 Atlantic Ave., Richmond Hill, NY 11419/718-847-7661
Al Biesen & Assoc., West 2039 Sinto Ave., Spokane, WA 99201/509-328-6818
Ross Billingsley & Brownell, Box 25, Dayton, WY 82836/307-655-9344
E.C. Bishop & Son Inc., 119 Main St., P.O. Box 7, Warsaw, MO 65355/816-438-5121
Gregg Boeke, Rte. 2, Box 149, Cresco, IA 52136/319-547-3746
Larry D. Brace, 771 Blackfoot Ave., Eugene, OR 97404/503,688-1278
A. Briganti, 475 Rt. 32, Highland Mills, NY 10930/914-692-4409
Leo Bustani, P.O. 8125, W. Palm Beach, FL 33407/305-622-2710
C&G Precision, 10152 Trinidad, El Paso, TX 79925/915-592-5496
Ralph L. Carter, 225 G St., Penrose, CO 81240/303-372-6240
Clinton River Gun Serv. Inc., 30016 S. River Rd., Mt. Clemens, MI 48045/313-468-1090
Dave Cook, 5831-26th Lane, Brampton, MI 49837/906-428-1235
David Costa, 94 Orient Ave., Arlington, MA 02174/617-643-9571
Crandall Tool & Machine Co., 1545 N. Mitchell St., Cadillac, MI 49601/616-775-5562
Gordon D. Crocker, 1510 - 42nd St., Los Alamos, NM 87544/505-667-9117
Daniel Cullity Restorations, 209 Old County Rd., East Sandwich, MA 02537/508-888-1147
Custom Gun Guild, Frank Wood, 2646 Church Dr., Doraville, GA 30340/404-455-0346
D&D Gun Shop, 363 Elmwood, Troy, MI 48083/313-583-1512
D&H Precision Tooling, 7522 Barnard Mill Rd., Ringwood, IL 60072/815-653-9611
Jack Dever, 8520 N.W. 90th, Oklahoma City, OK 73132/405-721-6393
Dilliott Gunsmithing, Inc., Rte. 3 Box 340, Scarlett Rd., Dandridge, TN 37725/615-397-9204
Dominic DiStefano, 4303 Friar Lane, Colorado Springs, CO 80907/303-599-3366
Ken Eyster Heritage Gunsmiths Inc., 6441 Bishop Rd., Centerburg, OH 43011/614-625-43031
Flaig's Inc., 2200 Evergreen Rd., Millvale, PA 15209/412-821-1717
Fountain Prods., 492 Prospect Ave., W. Springfield, MA 01089/413-781-4651
Frank's Custom Rifles, 7521 E. Fairmount Pl., Tucson, AZ 85715/602-885-3901
Fredrick Gun Shop, 10 Elson Dr., Riverside, RI 02915/401-433-2805 (engine turning)
Geo. M. Fullmer, 2499 Mavis St., Oakland, CA 94601/415-533-4193 (precise chambering—300 cals.)
K. Genecco Gun Works, 10512 Lower Sacramento Rd., Stockton, CA 95210/209-951-0706
David Gentry Custom Gunmaker, P.O. Box 1440, Belgrade, MT 59714/406-388-4867
Roger M. Green & J. Earl Bridges, P.O. Box 984, 435 East Birch, Glenrock, WY 82637/307-436-9804
Griffin & Howe, 36 West 44th St., Suite 1011, New York, NY 10036/212-921-0980
Griffin & Howe, 33 Claremont Rd., Bernardsville, NJ 07924/201-766-2287
Hagn Rifles & Actions, Martin Hagn, Box 444, Carnbrook, B.C. VIC 4H9, Canada/604-489-4861
Hammond Custom Guns, 619 S. Pandora, Gilbert, AZ 85234/602-892-3437
Harkrader's Custom Gun Shop, 825 Radford St., Christiansburg, VA 24073
Robert W. Hart & Son, Inc., 401 Montgomery St., Nescopeck, PA 18635/717-752-3655
Hubert J. Hecht, Waffen-Hecht, P.O. Box 2635, Fair Oaks, CA 95628/916-966-1020
Stephen Heilmann, P.O. Box 657, Grass Valley, CA 95945/916-272-8758
Heppler's Gun Shop, 6000 B Soquel Ave., Santa Cruz, CA 95062/408-475-1235
Klaus Hiptmayer, P.O. Box 136, R.R. 112 #750, Eastman, Que. J0E1P0, Canada/514-297-2492
Wm. H. Hobaugh, Box M, Philipsburg, MT 59858/406-859-3515
Hollis Gun Shop, 917 Rex St., Carlsbad, NM 88220/505-885-3782
Paul Jaeger, Inc., P.O. Box 449, 1 Madison St., Grand Junction, TN 38039/901-764-6909
R. L. Jamison, Jr., Rt. 4, Box 200, Moses Lake, WA 98837/509-762-2659
Ken Jantz, 222 E. Main, Davis, OK 73030/405-369-2316
Jenkins Enterprises, Inc., 12317 Locksley Lane, Auburn, CA 95603/916-823-9652
Neil A. Jones, RD #1, Box 483A, Saegertown, PA 16433/814-763-2769
L. E. Jurras & Assoc., Box 680, Washington, IN 47501/812-254-7698
Kennons Custom Rifles, 5408 Biffle Rd., Stone Mountain, GA 30088/404-469-9339
Benjamin Kilham, Kilham & Co., Main St., Box 37, Lyme, NH 03768/603-795-4112
Terry K. Kopp, Highway 13 South, Lexington, MO 64067/816-259-2636
Ron Lampert, Rt. 1, Box 177, Guthrie, MN 56461/218-854-7345
Mark Lee, P.O. Box 20379, Minneapolis, MN 55420/612-431-1727
Lilja Precision Rifle Barrels, Inc., 245 Compass Creek Rd., P.O. Box 372, Plains, MT 59859/406-826-3084
Stan McFarland, 2221 Idealla Ct., Grand Junction, CO 81505/303-243-4704
McIntyre Tools & Guns, P.O. Box 491, State Rd. #1144, Troy, NC 27371/919-572-2603
Miller Arms, Inc., P.O. Box 260, St. Onge, SD 57779/605-578-1790
J. W. Morrison Custom Rifles, 4015 W. Sharon, Phoenix, AZ 85029/602-978-3754
Mullis Guncraft, 3518 Lawyers Road East, Monroe, NC 28110/704-283-8789
Bruce A. Nettestad, Rt. 1, Box 140, Pelican Rapids, MN 56572/218-863-4301
Vic Olson, 5002 Countryside Dr., Imperial, MO 63052/314-296-8086
Pasadena Gun Center, 206 E. Shaw, Pasadena, TX 77506/713-472-0417
James Pearson, The Straight Shooter Gun Shop, 8132 County LS Rt. 2, Newton, WI 53063/414-726-4676
Penrod Precision, 126 E. Main St., P.O. Box 307, No. Manchester, IN 46962/219-982-8385
Precise Chambering Co., 2499 Mavis St., Oakland, CA 94601/415-533-4193
Precise Metalsmithing Enterprises, James L. Wisner, 146 Curtis Hill Rd., Chehalis, WA 98532/206-748-3743
Bob Rogers Gunsmithing, P.O. Box 305; 344 S. Walnut St., Franklin Grove, IL 61031/815-456-2685
Butch Searcy Co., 15 RD 3804, Farmington, NM 87401/505-327-3419
Harold H. Shockley, 203 E. Farmington Rd., Hanna City, IL 61536/309-565-4524
Snapp's Gunshop, 6911 E. Washington Rd., Clare, MI 48617/517-386-9226
Dale A. Storey, DGS, Inc., 305 N. Jefferson, Casper, WY 82601/307-237-2414
Dave Talley, P.O. Box 821, Glenrock, WY 82637/307-436-8724
J. W. Van Patten, P.O. Box 145, Foster Hill, Milford, PA 18337/717-296-7069
Vic's Gun Refinishing, 6 Pineview Dr., Dover, NH 03820/603-742-0013
Herman Waldron, Box 475, Pomeroy, WA 99347/509-843-1404
R. D. Wallace, Star Rt. 1 Box 76, Grandin, MO 63943/314-593-4773
Fred Wells, Wells Sport Store, 110 N. Summit St., Prescott, AZ 86301/602-445-3655
Terry Werth, 1203 Woodlawn Rd., Lincoln, IL 62656/217-732-3870
Robert G. West, 3973 Pam St., Eugene, OR 97402/503-689-6610
John Westrom, Precise Firearm Finishing, 25 N.W. 44th Ave., Des Moines, IA 50313/515-288-8680

DECOYS

Advance Scouts, Inc. 2741 Patton Rd., Roseville, MN 55113/612-639-1326 (goose getters)
Carry-Lite, Inc., 5203 W. Clinton Ave., Milwaukee, WI 53223/414-355-3520
Deer Me Products Co., Box 34, 1208 Park St., Anoka, MN 55303/612-421-8971 (Anchors)
Flambeau Prods. Corp., 15981 Valplast Rd., Middlefield, OH 44062/216-632-1631
Kenneth J. Klingler, P.O. Box 141; Thistle Hill, Cabot, VT 05647/802-426-3811
Penn's Woods Products, Inc., 19 W. Pittsburgh St., Delmont, PA 15626/412-468-8311
Royal Arms, 1210 Bert Acosta, El Cajon, CA 92020/619-448-5466 (wooden, duck)
Ron E. Skaggs, P.O. Box 34; 114 Miles Ct., Princeton, IL 61356/815-875-8207

ENGRAVERS, ENGRAVING TOOLS

John J. Adams, P.O. Box 167, Corinth, VT 05039/802-439-5904
Gary Allard, Creek Side Metal & Woodcrafters, Fishers Hill, VA 22626/703-465-3903
Robert L. Barnard, Rt. 2 Box 327, Fordyce, AR 71742/501-352-5861
Billy R. Bates, 2905 Lynnwood Circle S.W., Decatur, AL 35603/205-355-3690
Sid Bell Originals Inc., R.D. 2, Box 219, Tully, NY 13159/607-842-6431
Jim Bina, P.O. Box 6532, Evanston, IL 60204/312-475-6377
Weldon Bledsoe, 6812 Park Place Dr., Fort Worth, TX 76118/817-589-1704
C. Roger Bleile, 5040 Ralph Ave., Cincinnati, OH 45238/513-251-0249
Rudolph V. Bochenski, 1410 Harlem Rd., Cheektowaga, NY 14206/716-896-3619
Erich Boessler, Gun Engraving Intl., Am Vogeltal 3, 8732 Munnerstadt, W. Germany/9733-9443
Ralph P. Bone, 718 N. Atlanta, Owasso, OK 74055/918-272-9745
Henry "Hank" Bonham, 218 Franklin Ave., Seaside Heights, NJ 08751/201-793-8309
Dan Bratcher, 311 Belle Air Pl., Carthage, MO 64836/417-358-1518
Frank Brgoch, 1580 So. 1500 East, Bountiful, UT 84010/801-295-1885
Dennis B. Brooker, 502 Hwy 92, Prole, IA 50229/515-961-8200
Brownells, Inc., 222 W. Liberty, Montezuma, IA 50171/515-623-5401 (engraving tools)
Byron Burgess, 710 Bella Vista Dr., Morro Bay, CA 93442/805-772-3974
E. Christopher Firearms Co., Inc., Route 128 & Ferry St., Miamitown, OH 45041/513-353-1321
Winston Churchill, Twenty Mile Stream Rd., RFD Box 29B, Proctorsville, VT 05153/802-226-7772
Clark Engravings, P.O. Box 80746, San Marino, CA 91108/818-287-1652
Frank Clark, 3714-27th St., Lubbock, TX 79410/806-799-1187
Crocker Engraving, 1510 - 42nd St., Los Alamos, NM 87544
Daniel Cullity, 209 Old County Rd., East Sandwich, MA 02537/508-888-1147
Custom Gun Guild, 2646 Church Dr., Doraville, GA 30340/404-455-0346
Ed Delorge, 2231 Hwy. 308, Thibodaux, LA 70301/504-447-1633
James R. DeMunck, P.O. Box 16523, Rochester, NY 14616/716-225-0626 (SASE)
W. R. Dilling Engravers, Rod Dilling, 105 N. Ridgewood Dr., Sebring, FL 33870/813-385-0647
Mark Drain, S.E. 3211 Kamilche Point Rd., Shelton, WA 98584/206-426-5452
Michael W. Dubber, 5325 W. Mill Rd., Evansville, IN 47712/812-963-6156
Robert Evans, 332 Vine St., Oregon City, OR 97045/503-656-5693
Ken Eyster, Heritage Gunsmiths Inc., 6441 Bishop Rd., Centerburg, OH 43011/614-625-6131
John Fanzoi, P.O. Box 25, Ferlach, Austria 9170
Jacqueline Favre, 3111 So. Valley View Blvd., Suite B-214, Las Vegas, NV 89102/702-876-6278

Armi FERLIB, 46 Via Costa, 25063 Gardone V.T. (Brescia), Italy
Firearms Engravers Guild of America, Robert Evans, Secy., 332 Vine St., Oregon City, OR 97045/503-656-5693
Jeff W. Flannery Engraving Co., 11034 Riddles Run Rd., Union, KY 41091/606-384-3127 (color ctlg. $5)
James W. Fogle. RR 2, Box 258, Herrin, IL 62948/618-988-1795
Fountain Prods., 492 Prospect Ave., W. Springfield, MA 01089/413-781-4651
Henry Frank, Box 984, Whitefish, MT 59937/406-862-2681
Leonard Francolini, 56 Morgan Rd., Canton, CT 06019/203-693-2529
GRS Corp., P.O. Box 748, 900 Overland St., Emporia, KS 66801/316-343-1084 (Gravermeister tool)
Jerome C. Glimm, 19 S. Maryland, Conrad, MT 59425/406-278-3574
Howard V. Grant, Hiawatha 153, Woodruff, WI 54568/715-356-7146
Griffin & Howe, 36 West 44th St., Suite 1011, New York, NY 10036/212-921-0980
Griffin & Howe, 33 Claremont Rd., Bernardsville, NJ 07924/201-766-2287
Gurney Engraving Method, #513-620 View St., Victoria, B.C. V8W 1J6 Canada/604-383-5243
John K. Gwilliam, 218 E. Geneva Dr., Tempe, AZ 85282/602-894-1739
Bryson J. Gwinnell, P.O. Box 998, Southwick, MA 01077
Hand Engravers Supply Co., 4348 Newberry Ct., Dayton, OH 45432/513-426-6762
Paul A. Harris Hand Engraving, 10630 Janet Lee, San Antonio, TX 78230/512-341-5121
Jack O. Harwood, 1191 S. Pendlebury Lane, Blackfoot, ID 83221/208-785-5368
Frank E. Hendricks, Master Engravers, Inc., Star Rt. 1A, Box 334, Dripping Springs, TX 78620/512-858-7828
Heidemarie Hiptmayer, R.R. 112, #750, P.O. Box 136, Eastman, Que. J0E 1PO, Canada/514-297-2492
Alan K. Horst, P.O. Box 68, 402 E. St., Albion, WA 99102/509-332-7109
Ken Hurst, P.O. Box 116, Estill, SC 29918/803-625-3070
Ralph W. Ingle, Master Engraver, #4 Missing Link, Rossville, GA 30741/404-866-5589 (color broch. $5)
Paul Jaeger, Inc., P.O. Box 449, 1 Madison Ave., Grand Junction, TN 38039/901-764-6909
Ken Jantz Supply, 222 E. Main, Davis, OK 73030/405-369-2316 (tools)
Bill Johns, 1113 Nightingale, McAllen, TX 78501/512-682-2971
Steven Kamyk, 9 Grandview Dr., Westfield, MA 01085/413-568-0457
T. J. Kaye, Rt. 2 Box 139A, Yoakum, TX 77995
Lance Kelly, 1824 Royal Palm Dr., Edgewater, FL 32032/904-423-4933
Jim Kelso, Rt. 1, Box 5300, Worcester, VT 05682/802-229-4254
E. J. Koevenig Engraving Service, P.O. Box 55, Rabbit Gulch, Hill City, SD 57745/605-574-2239
John Kudlas, 622-14th St. S.E., Rochester, MN 55904/507-288-5579
Nelson H. Largent, Silver Shield's Inc., 7614 Lemhi #1, Boise, ID 83709/208-323-8991
Leonard Leibowitz, 1202 Palto Alto St., Pittsburgh, PA 15212/412-231-5388 (etcher)
Franz Letschnig, Master-Engraver, 620 Cathcart, Rm. 422, Montreal, Queb. H3B 1M1, Canada/514-875-4989
Steve Lindsay, R.R.2 Cedar Hills, Kearney, NE 68847/308-236-7885
London Guns Ltd., P.O. Box 3750, Santa Barbara, CA 93130/805-683-4141
Dennis McDonald, 8359 Brady St., Peosta, IA 52068/319-556-7940
Lynton S.M. McKenzie, 6940 N. Alvernon Way, Tucson, AZ 85718/602-299-5090
Wm. H. Mains, 3111 S. Valley View Blvd., Suite B-214, Las Vegas, NV 89102/702-876-6278
Robert E. Maki, School of Firearms Engraving, P.O. Box 947, Northbrook, IL 60065/312-724-8238
Laura Mandarino, 136 5th Ave. West, Kalispell, MT 59901/406-257-6208
George Marek, P.O. Box 213, Westfield, MA 01086/413-568-9816
Frank Mele, Longdale Rd., Mahopac, NY 10541/914-225-8872
S. A. Miller, Miller Gun Works, P.O. Box 1053, 1440 Peltier Dr., Point Roberts, WA 98281/206-945-7014
Frank Mittermeier, 3577 E. Tremont Ave., New York, NY 10465/212-828-3843 (tool)
Mitch Moschetti, P.O. Box 27065, Denver, CO 80227/303-936-1184
Gary K. Nelson, 975 Terrace Dr., Oakdale, CA 95361/209-847-4590
NgraveR Co., 879 Raymond Hill Rd., Oakdale, CT 06370/203-848-8031 (tool)
New Orleans Arms Co., P.O. Box 26087, New Orleans, LA 70186/504-944-3371
New Orleans Jewelers Supply, 206 Chartres St., New Orleans, LA 70130/504-523-3839 (engr. tool)
Oker's Engraving, 365 Bell Rd., Bellford Mtn. Hts., P.O. Box 126, Shawnee, CO 80475/303-838-6042
Pachmayr Ltd., 1875 So. Mountain Ave., Monrovia, CA 91016/818-357-7771
C. R. Pedersen & Son, 2717 S. Pere Marquette, Ludington, MI 49431/616-843-2061
E. Larry Peters, c/o Kimber, 9039 SE Janssen Rd., Clackamas, OR 97015/503-656-6016
Scott Pilkington, P.O. Box 125, Dunlap, TN 37237/615-592-3786
Paul R. Piquette, 80 Bradford Dr., Feeding Hills, MA 01030/413-786-5811
Eugene T. Plante, Gene's Custom Guns, 3890 Hill Ave., P.O. Box 10534, White Bear Lake, MN 55110/612-429-5105
Jeremy W. Potts, 1680 So. Granby, Aurora, CO 80012/303-752-2528
Wayne E. Potts, 912 Poplar St., Denver, CO 80220/303-355-5462
Ed Pranger, 1414-7th St., Anacortes, WA 98221/206-293-3488
Proofmark, Ltd., P.O. Box 183, Alton, IL 62002/618-463-0120 (Italian Bottega Incisioni)
E. C. Prudhomme, #426 Lane Building, 610 Marshall St., Shreveport, LA 71101/318-425-8421
Leonard Puccinelli Design, P.O. Box 3494, Fairfield, CA 94533/707-422-3122
Martin Rabeno, Spook Hollow Trading Co., Box 37F, RD #1, Ellenville, NY 12428/914-647-4567
Jim Riggs, 206 Azalea, Boerne, TX 78006/512-249-8567 (handguns)
J. J. Roberts, 166 Manassas Dr., Manassas Park, VA 22111/703-330-0448
John R. and Hans Rohner, 710 Sunshine Canyon, Boulder, CO 80302/303-444-3841
Bob Rosser, 142 Ramsey Dr., Albertville, AL 35950/205-878-5388
Joe Rundell, 6198 Frances Rd., Clio, MI 48420/313-687-0559
Robert P. Runge, 94 Grove St., Ilion, NY 13357/315-894-3036
Shaw's "Finest In Guns," 9447 W. Lilac Rd., Escondido, CA 92026/619-728-7070
George Sherwood, Box 735, Winchester, OR 97495/503-672-3159
Ben Shostle, The Gun Room, 1201 Burlington Dr., Muncie, IN 47302/317-282-9073
W. P. Sinclair, 46 Westbury Rd., Edington, Wiltshire BA13 4PG, England
Ron Skaggs, P.O. Box 34, 114 Miles Ct., Princeton, IL 61356/815-875-8207
Mark A. Smith, 200 N. 9th, Sinclair, WY 82334/307-324-7929
Ron Smith, 3601 West 7th St., Ft. Worth, TX 76107/817-732-4623
Terry Theis, P.O. Box 252, Harper, TX 78631/512-864-4384
George W. Thiewes, 1846 Allen Lane, St. Charles, IL 60174/312-584-1383
Denise Thirion, Box 408, Graton, CA 95444/707-829-1876
Robert B. Valade, 931-3rd. Ave., Seaside, OR 97138/503-738-7672
John Vest, P.O. Box 1552, Susanville, CA 96130/916-257-7228
Ray Viramontez, 4348 Newberry Ct., Dayton, OH 45432/513-426-6762
Vernon G. Wagoner, 2325 E. Encanto, Mesa, AZ 85203/602-835-1307
R. D. Wallace, Star Rt. 1 Box 76, Grandin, MO 63943
Terry Wallace, 385 San Marino, Vallejo, CA 94590
Floyd E. Warren, 1273 State Rt. 305 N.E., Cortland, OH 44410/216-638-4219
Kenneth W. Warren, Mountain States Engraving, P.O. Box 4631, Scottsdale, AZ 85261/602-991-5035
Rachel Wells, 110 N. Summit St., Prescott, AZ 86301/602-445-3655
Sam Welch, CVSR Box 2110, Moab, UT 84532/801-259-7620
Claus Willig, Siedlerweg 17, 8720 Schweinfurt, West Germany/09721-41446
Bernie Wolfe, 900 Tony Lama, El Paso, TX 79915 (engraving, plating, scrimshawing)
Mel Wood, P.O. Box 1255, Sierra Vista, AZ 85636/602-455-5541

GAME CALLS

Burnham Bros., Box 669, 912 Main St., Marble Falls, TX 78654/512-693-3112
Joe Hall's Shooting Products, Inc., 443 Wells Rd., Doylestown, PA 18901/215-345-6354
Lohman Mfg. Co., P.O. Box 220, Neosho, MO 64850/417-451-4438
Mallardtone Game Calls, 2901 16th St., Moline, IL 61265/309-762-8089
Phil. S. Olt Co., Box 550, Pekin, IL 61554/309-348-3633
Quaker Boy Inc., 6426 West Quaker St., Orchard Parks, NY 14127/716-662-3979
Penn's Woods Products, Inc., 19 W. Pittsburgh St., Delmont, PA 15626
Pete Rickard, Inc., Box 209B, Cobleskill, NY 12043/518-234-2731
Scotch Game Call Co., Inc., 6619 Oak Orchard Rd., Elba, NY 14058/716-757-9958
Johnny Stewart Game Calls, Inc., Box 7954, 5100 Fort Ave., Waco, TX 76714/817-772-3261
Tink's Safariland Hunting Corp., P.O. Box NN, McLean, VA 22101/703-356-0622

GUN PARTS, U.S. AND FOREIGN

Armes de Chasse, P.O. Box 827, Chadds Ford, PA 19317/215-388-1146
Armsport, Inc., 3590 N.W. 49th St., Miami, FL 33142/305-635-7850
Badger Shooter's Supply, 106 So. Harding, Owen, WI 54460/715-229-2101
Behlert Custom Guns, Inc., RD 2, Box 36C, Route 611 North, Pipersville, PA 18947/215-766-8681 (handgun parts)
Can Am Enterprises, 350 Jones Rd., Fruitland, ON L0R 1L0, Canada/416-643-4357 (catalog $2)
Caspian Arms, 14 No. Main St., Hardwick, VT 05843/802-472-6454
Cherokee Gun Accessories, 4127 Bay St. Suite 226, Fremont, CA 94538/415-471-5770
D&E Magazines Mfg., P.O. Box 4876-D, Sylmar, CA 91342
Charles E. Duffy, Williams Lane, West Hurley, NY 12491
Essex Arms, Box 345, Island Pond, VT 05846/802-723-4313 (.45 1911A1 frames & slides)
Falcon Firearms Mfg. Corp., P.O. Box 3748, Granada Hills, CA 91344/818-885-0900 (barrels; magazines)
Federal Ordnance Inc., 1443 Potrero Ave., So. El Monte, CA 91733/213-350-4161
Jack First Distributors Inc., 44633 Sierra Highway, Lancaster, CA 93534/805-945-6981
Gun Parts Corp., Box 2, West Hurley, NY 12491/914-679-2417
Gun-Tec, P.O. Box 8125, W. Palm Beach, FL 33407 (Win. mag. tubing; Win. 92 conversion parts; SASE f. reply)
Hansen and Hansen, 244 Old Post Rd., Southport, CT 06490/203-259-7337
Hastings, Box 224, 822-6th St., Clay Center, KS 67432/913-632-3169
Heller & Levin Associates, Inc., 88 Marlborough Court, Rockville Center, NY 11570/516-764-9349
Liberty Antique Gunworks, 19 Key St., P.O. Box 183GD, Eastport, ME 04631/207-853-2327 (S&W only; ctlg. $5)
Walter H. Lodewick, 2816 N.E. Halsey, Portland, OR 97232/503-284-2554 (Winchester parts)
Arthur McKee, 121 Eaton's Neck Rd., Northport, L.I., NY 11768/516-757-8850 (micrometer rec. sights)
John V. Martz, 8060 Lakeview Lane, Lincoln, CA 95648/916-645-2250 (parts for Luger and P-38s)
Olympic Arms Inc. dba SGW, 624 Old Pacific Hwy. S.E., Olympia, WA 98503/206-456-3471
Pacific Intl. Merch. Corp., 2215 "J" St., Sacramento, CA 95816/916-446-2737 (Vega 45 Colt mag.)
Pre-64 Winchester Parts Co., P.O. Box 8125, West Palm Beach, FL 33407 (send stamped env. w. requ. list)
Quality Parts Co., 101 Hanover St., Portland, ME 04101/800-556-SWAT

Martin B. Retting, Inc., 11029 Washington Blvd., Culver City, CA 90232/213-837-2412
Royal Ordnance Works Ltd., P.O. Box 3245, Wilson, NC 27893/919-237-0515
Sarco, Inc., 323 Union St., Stirling, NJ 07980/201-647-3800
Sherwood Intl. Export Corp., 18714 Parthenia St., Northridge, CA 91324
Clifford L. Smires, R.D. 1, Box 100, Columbus, NJ 08022/609-298-3158 (Mauser rifle parts)
Springfield Sporters Inc., R.D. 1, Penn Run, PA 15765/412-254-2626
Triple-K Mfg. Co., 2222 Commercial St. San Diego, CA 92113/619-232-2066 (magazines, gun parts)
U.S.F.S. (United States Frame Specialists), P.O. Box 7762, Milwaukee, WI 53207/414-643-6387 (SA frames; back straps)

GUNS (U.S.-made)

AMAC (See Iver Johnson)
AMT (Arcadia Machine & Tool), 536 N. Vincent Ave., Covina, CA 91722/818-915-7803
Accuracy Systems, Inc., 15205 N. Cave Creek Rd., Phoenix, AZ 85032/602-971-1991
American Arms, Inc., P.O. Box 27163, Salt Lake City, UT 84127/801-971-5006
American Derringer Corp., 127 N. Lacy Dr., Waco, TX 76705/817-799-9111
American Industries, 8700 Brookpark Rd., Cleveland, OH 44129/216-398-8300
Arminex Ltd., 10231 N. Scottsdale Rd., #B13, Scottsdale, AZ 85253/602-998-6616
Armitage International, Ltd., 1635-A Blue Ridge Blvd., Seneca, SC 29678/803-882-5900 (Scarab Skorpion 9mm pistol)
Armes de Chasse, 3000 Valley Forge Circle, King of Prussia, PA 19406/215-783-6133
A Square Co., Inc., Rt. 4, Simmons, Rd., Madison, IN 47250/812-273-3633
Auto-Ordnance Corp., Williams Lane, West Hurley, NY 12491/914-679-7225
BF Arms, 1123 So. Locust, Grand Island, NE 68801/308-382-1121 (single shot pistol)
BJT, 445 Putman Ave., Hamden, CT 06517 (stainless double derringer)
Barrett Firearms Mfg., Inc., P.O. Box 1077, Murfreesboro, TN 37133/615-896-2938 (Light Fifty)
Beretta U.S.A., 17601 Beretta Dr., Accokeek, MD 20607/301-283-2191
Browning (Gen. Offices), Rt. 1, Morgan, UT 84050/801-876-2711
Browning (Parts & Service), Rt. 4, Box 624-B, Arnold, MO 63010/314-287-6800
Bryco Arms (Distributed by Jennings Firearms)
Bushmaster Firearms Co., 999 Roosevelt Trail, Bldg. #3, Windham, ME 04062 (police handgun)
Calico (California Instrument Co.), 405 E. 19th St., Bakersfield, CA 93305/805-323-1327
Caspian Arms, 14 No. Main St., Hardwick, VT 05843/802-472-6454
Century Gun Dist., Inc., 1467 Jason Rd., Greenfield, IN 46140/317-462-4524 (Century Model 100 SA rev.)
Champlin Firearms, Inc., Box 3191, Enid, OK 73702/405-237-7388
Charter Arms Corp., 430 Sniffens Ln., Stratford, CT 06497/203-377-8080
Chipmunk Manufacturing Inc., 114 E. Jackson, P.O. Box 1104, Medford, OR 97501/503-664-5585 (22 S.S. rifle)
Colt Firearms, P.O. Box 1868, Hartford, CT 06101/203-236-6311
Commando Arms (See Gibbs Guns, Inc.)
Competition Arms, Inc., 1010 S. Plumer, Tucson, AZ 85719/602-792-1075
Coonan Arms, Inc., 830 Hampden Ave., St. Paul, MN 55114/612-646-6672 (357 Mag. Autom.)
Dakota Arms, Inc., HC 55 Box 326, Sturgis, SD 57785/605-347-4686 (B.A. rifles)
Davis Industries, 15150 Sierra Bonita Lane, Chino, CA 91710/714-591-4726 (derringers; 32 auto pistol)
Detonics Mfg. Corp., 13456 S.E. 27th Pl., Bellevue, WA 98005/206-747-2100 (auto pistol)
DuBiel Arms Co., 1724 Baker Rd., Sherman, TX 75090/214-893-7313
E.M.F. Co. Inc., 1900 East Warner Ave. 1-D, Santa Ana, CA 92705/714-261-6611
Encom America, Inc., P.O. Box 5314, Atlanta, GA 30307/404-525-2801
Excalibur (See Arminex)
Excam, Inc., 4480 East 11th Ave., Hialeah, FL 33013/305-681-4661
F.I.E. Corp. (See Firearms Import & Export Corp.)
Falcon Firearms Mfg. Corp., P.O. Box 3748, Granada Hills, CA 91344/818-885-0900 (handguns)
Falling Block Works, P.O. Box 3087, Fairfax, VA 22038/703-476-0043
Feather Enterprises, 2500 Central Ave., Boulder, CO 80301/303-442-7021
Federal Eng. Corp., 2335 So. Michigan Ave., Chicago, IL 60616/312-842-1063
Firearms Imp. & Exp. Corp., P.O. Box 4866, Hialeah Lakes, Hialeah, FL 33014/305-685-5966 (FIE)
Freedom Arms Co., P.O. Box 1776, Freedom, WY 83120 (mini revolver, Casull rev.)
Freedom Arms Marketing (See: L.A.R. Mfg. Co.)
Frontier Shop & Gallery, Depot 1st & Main, Riverton, WY 82501/307-856-4498
Gibbs Guns, Inc., Rt. 2, Greenback, TN 37742/615-856-2813 (Commando Arms)
Gilbert Equipment Co., Inc., P.O. Box 9846, Mobile, AL 36609
Göncz Co., 11526 Burbank Blvd., #18, No. Hollywood, CA 91601/818-505-0408
Grendel, Inc., P.O. Box 908, Rockledge, FL 32955/305-636-1211
Hatfield Rifle Works, 2020 Calhoun, St. Joseph, MO 64501/816-279-8688 (squirrel rifle)
Holmes Firearms Corp., Rte. 6, Box 242, Fayetteville, AR 72703
Hopkins & Allen Arms, 3 Ethel Ave., P.O. Box 217, Hawthorne, NJ 07507/201-427-1165 (ML)
Lew Horton Dist. Co. Inc., 175 Boston Rd., Southboro, MA 01772/617-485-3060
Hyper-Single Precision SS Rifles, 520 E. Beaver, Jenks, OK 74037
Illinois Arms Co., Inc., 1401 Ardmore, Itasca, IL 60143/312-773-0303
Interarms Ltd., 10 Prince St., Alexandria, VA 22323/703-548-1400
Intratec, 12405 S.W. 130th St., Miami, FL 33186/305-232-1821
Ithaca Gun, 123 Lake St., Ithaca, NY 14850/607-273-0200
Jennings Firearms Inc., 3680 Research Way, Carson City, NV 89706/702-588-6884
Jennings-Hawken, 326½-4th St. N.W., Winter Haven, FL 33880 (ML)
Iver Johnson, 2202 Redmond Rd., Jacksonville, AR 72076/501-982-9491
KK Arms Co., Karl Kash, Star Route, Box 671, Kerrville, TX 78028/512-257-4718 (handgun)
Kimber of Oregon, Inc., 9039 S.E. Jannsen Rd., Clackamas, OR 97015/503-656-1704
Kimel Industries, Box 335, Matthews, NC 28105/704-821-7663
L.A.R. Manufacturing Co., 4133 West Farm Rd., West Jordan, UT 84084/801-255-7106 (Grizzly Win Mag pistol)
Law Enforcement Ordnance Corp., Box 649, Middletown, PA 17057/717-944-5500 (Striker-12 shotgun)
Ljutic Ind., Inc., P.O. Box 2117, 732 N 16th Ave., Yakima, WA 98907/509-248-0476 (Mono-Gun)
Loven-Pierson, Inc., 4 W. Main, P.O. Box 377, Apalachin, NY 13732/607-625-2303 (ML)
Magnum Sales, Div. of Mag-na-port, 41302 Executive Drive, Mt. Clemens, MI 48045/313-469-7534 (Ltd. editions & customized guns for handgun hunting)
Marlin Firearms Co., 100 Kenna Drive, New Haven, CT 06473
Merrill Pistol (See RPM)
Michigan Arms Corp., 363 Elmwood, Troy, MI 48083/313-583-1518 (ML)
M.O.A. Corp., 7996 Brookville-Salem Rd., Brookville, OH 45309/513-833-5559 (Maximum pistol)
O.F. Mossberg & Sons, Inc., 7 Grasso St., No. Haven, CT 06473
Navy Arms Co., 689 Bergen Blvd., Ridgefield, NJ 07657
New England Firearms Co., Inc., Industrial Rowe, Gardner, MA 01440/617-632-9393
North American Arms, 1800 North 300 West, Spanish Fork, UT 84660/801-798-7401
Olympic Arms Inc. dba SGW, 624 Old Pacific Hwy. S.E., Olympia, WA 98503/206-456-3471 (Safari Arms)
Oregon Trail Riflesmiths, Inc., P.O. Box 51, Mackay, ID 83251/208-588-2527 (ML)
Pachmayr, Ltd., 1875 So. Mountain Ave., Monrovia, CA 91016/818-357-7771
Patriot Distribution Co., 2872 So. Wentworth Ave., Milwaukee, WI 53207/414-769-0760 (Partisan Adventure assault pistol)
Pennsylvania Arms Co., Box 128, Duryea, PA 18642/717-457-4014
E. F. Phelps Mfg., Inc., 700 W. Franklin St., Evansville, IN 47710/812-423-2599 (Heritage I in 45-70)
Phillips & Bailey, Inc., 815A Yorkshire St., Houston, TX 77022/713-699-4288 (357/9 Ultra, rev. conv.)
Precision Small Parts, 155 Carlton Rd., Charlottesville, VA 22901
RPM (R&R Sporting Arms, Inc.), 150 Viking Ave., Brea, CA 92621/714-990-2444 (XL pistol; formerly Merrill)
Rahn Gun Works, Inc., 470 Market SW, Box 33, Grand Rapids, MI 49503/616-235-0634
Raven Arms, 1300 Bixby Dr., Industry, CA 91745/818-961-2511 (P-25 pistols)
Remington Arms Co., 1007 Market St., Wilmington, DE 19898
Ruger (See Sturm, Ruger & Co.)
Savage Industries, Inc., Springdale Rd., Westfield, MA 01085/413-562-2361
L.W. Seecamp Co., Inc., P.O. Box 255, New Haven, CT 06502/203-877-3429
C. Sharps Arms Co., Inc., P.O. Box 885, Big Timber, MT 59011/406-932-4353
Shiloh Rifle Mfg. Co., Inc., P.O. Box 279; 201 Centennial Dr., Big Timber, MT 59011/406-932-4454
Smith & Wesson, Inc., 2100 Roosevelt Ave., Springfield, MA 01101
Sokolovsky Corp., P.O. Box 70113, Sunnyvale, CA 94086/408-245-9268 (45 Automaster pistol)
Springfield Armory, Inc., 420 W. Main St., Geneseo, IL 61254/309-944-5631
SSK Industries, Rt. 1, Della Dr., Bloomingdale, OH 43910/614-264-0176
Steel City Arms, Inc., P.O. Box 81926, Pittsburgh, PA 15217/412-461-3100 (d.a. "Double Deuce" pistol)
Sturm, Ruger & Co., Inc., Lacey Place, Southport, CT 06490/203-259-7843
Super Six Limited, P.O. Box 266, Elkhorn, WI 53121/414-723-5058
Texas Longhorn Arms, Inc., P. O. Box 703, Richmond, TX 77469/713-341-0775 (S.A. sixgun)
Thompson/Center Arms, Farmington Rd., P.O. Box 5002, Rochester, NH 03867/603-332-2394
Tippmann Arms Co., 4402 New Haven Ave., Ft. Wayne, IN 46803/219-422-6448
Trail Guns Armoury, 1422 E. Main St., League City, TX 77573/713-332-5833 (muzzleloaders)
Trapper Gun, Inc., 18717 E. 14 Mile Rd., Fraser, MI 48026/313-792-0133 (handguns)
The Ultimate Game Inc., P.O. Box 1856, Ormond Beach, FL 32075/904-677-4358
Ultra Light Arms Co., P.O. Box 1270; 214 Price St., Granville, WV 26534/304-599-5687
United States Frame Specialists, Inc. (U.S.F.S.), P.O. Box 7762, Milwaukee, WI 53207/414-643-6387
U.S. Repeating Arms Co., P.O. Box 30-300, New Haven, CT 06511/203-789-5000
Varner Sporting Arms, Inc., 100-F N. Cobb Pkwy., Marietta, GA 30062/404-422-5468
Weatherby's, 2781 E. Firestone Blvd., South Gate, CA 90280
Weaver Arms Corp., 6265 Greenwich Dr., Suite 201, San Diego, CA 92122/619-452-2551
Dan Wesson Arms, 293 Main St., Monson, MA 01057/413-267-4081
Wichita Arms, 444 Ellis, Wichita, KS 67211/316-265-0661
Wildey Inc., P.O. Box 475, Brookfield, CT 06804/203-355-9000
Wilkinson Arms, 26884 Pearl Rd., Parma, ID 83660/208-722-6771
Winchester, (See U.S. Repeating Arms)
Wyoming Armory, Inc., Forest Pl., Bedford, WY 83112/307-883-2151

GUNS (Foreign)

Action Arms, P.O. Box 9573, Philadelphia, PA 19124/215-744-0100
American Arms, Inc., 715 E. Armour Rd., N. Kansas City, MO 64116/816-474-3161
Anschutz (See PSI)
Armes de Chasse, P.O. Box 827, Chadds Ford, PA 19317/215-388-1146 (Merkel, Mauser pistols)
Armscor Precision, 1175 Chess Dr., Suite 204, Foster City, CA 94404/415-349-3592
Arms Corp. of the Philippines (See: Armscor Precision)
Armsport, Inc., 3590 N.W. 49th St., Miami, FL 33142/305-635-7850
Bauska Mfg. Corp., P.O. Box 2270, 1694 Whalebone Dr., Kalispell, MT 59901/406-752-8082
Beeman Precision Arms, Inc., 3440-GD Airway Dr., Santa Rosa, CA 95403/707-578-7900 (FWB, Weihrauch, Unique, Cork, Hammerli firearms)
Benelli Armi, S.p.A. (See: Sile Distributors—handguns; Heckler & Koch—Shotguns)
Benson Firearms Ltd., P.O. Box 30137, Seattle, WA 98103/800-521-0714 (A. Uberti replicas)
Beretta U.S.A., 17601 Beretta Dr., Accokeek, MD 20607/301-283-2191
Charles Boswell (Gunmakers), Div. of Saxon Arms Ltd., 615 Jasmine Ave. N., Unit J, Tarpon Springs, FL 34689/813-938-4882
Bretton, 21 Rue Clement Forissier, 42-St. Etienne, France
Britarms/Berdan (Gunmakers Ltd.), See: Action Arms
BRNO (See Saki International)
Browning (Gen. Offices), Rt. 1, Morgan, UT 84050/801-876-2711
Browning, (parts & service), Rt. 4, Box 624-B, Arnold, MO 63010/314-287-6800
Century Intl. Arms Inc., 5 Federal St., St. Albans, VT 05478/802-527-1252
Ets. Chapuis, 23, rue de Montorcier, BP15, 42380 St. Bonnet-le-Chateau, France
Cimarron Arms, 9439 Katy Freeway, Houston, TX 77024 (Uberti)
Classic Doubles Int., 1001 Craig Rd., Suite 353, St. Louis, MO 63146/314-997-7281 (shotguns)
Conco Arms, P.O. Box 159, Emmaus, PA 18049/215-967-5477 (Larona)
Connecticut Valley Arms Co., 5988 Peachtree Corners East, Norcross, GA 30071/404-449-4687 (CVA)
Diana Import, 842 Vallejo St., San Francisco, CA 94133
Charles Daly (See Outdoor Sports HQ)
Dikar s. Coop. (See Connecticut Valley Arms Co.)
Dixie Gun Works, Inc., Hwy 51, South, Union City, TN 38261/901-885-0561 ("Kentucky" rifles)
Dowtin Imports, Inc., Rt. 4 Box 930A, Flagstaff, AZ 86001/602-779-1898 (G. Granger sidelock shotgun)
Dynamit Nobel-RWS Inc., 105 Stonehurst Court, Northvale, NJ 07647/201-767-1995 (Rottweil)
Peter Dyson Ltd., 29-31 Church St., Honley, Huddersfield, Yorkshire HD7 2AH, England (accessories f. antique gun collectors)
E.M.F. Co. Inc. (Early & Modern Firearms), 1900 E. Warner Ave. 1-D, Santa Ana, CA 92705/714-261-6611
Elko Arms, 28 rue Ecole Moderne, 7400 Soignes, Belgium
Euroarms of America, Inc., P.O. Box 3277, 1501 Lenoir Dr., Winchester, VA 22601/703-662-1863 (ML)
Excam Inc., 4480 E. 11 Ave., P.O. Box 3483, Hialeah, FL 33013/305-681-4661
Exel Arms of America, 14 Main St., Gardner, MA 01440/617-632-5008
F.I.E. Corp. (See Firearms Import & Export Corp.)
J. Fanzoj, P.O. Box 25, Ferlach, Austria 9170
Armi FERLIB di Libero Ferraglio, 46 Via Costa, 25063 Gardone V.T. (Brescia), Italy
Fiocchi of America, Inc., Rt. 2, Box 90-8, Ozark, MO 65721/417-725-4118
Firearms Imp. & Exp. Corp., (F.I.E.), P.O. Box 4866, Hialeah Lakes, Hialeah, FL 33014/305-685-5966
Auguste Francotte & Cie, S.A., rue de Trois Juin 109, 4400 Herstal-Liege, Belgium
Frankonia Jagd, Hofmann & Co., Postfach 6780, D-8700 Wurzburg 1, West Germany
Freeland's Scope Stands, Inc., 3737 14th Ave., Rock Island, IL 61201/309-788-7449
Frigon Guns, 627 W. Crawford, Clay Center, KS 67432/913-632-5607 (cust.-made)
Renato Gamba, S.p.A., Gardone V.T. (Brescia), Italy (See Steyr Daimler Puch of America Corp.)
Armas Garbi, Urki #12, Eibar (Guipuzcoa) Spain (shotguns, See W. L. Moore)
Glock, Inc., 5000 Highlands Pkwy. #190, Smyrna, GA 30080/404-432-1202
George Granger, 66 Cours Fauriel, 42 St. Etienne, France
Griffin & Howe, 36 West 44th St., Suite 1011, New York, NY 10036/212-921-0980 (Purdey, Holland & Holland)
Griffin & Howe, 33 Claremont Rd., Bernardsville, NJ 07924/201-766-2287
Gun South, P.O. Box 129, 108 Morrow Ave., Trussville, AL 35173/205-655-8299 (Steyr, FN, Mannlicher)
Hallowell & Co., 340 West Putnam Ave., Greenwich, CT 06830/203-869-2190 (Agents for John Rigby & Co.)
Heckler & Koch Inc., 14601 Lee Rd., Chantilly, VA 22021/703-631-2800
Heym, Friedr. Wilh., see: Paul Jaeger, Inc.; G.E. Nygren Associates, Inc.
Incor, Inc., P.O. Box 132, Addison, TX 75001/214-931-3500 (Cosmi auto shotg.)
Interarmco, See Interarms (Walther)
Interarms Ltd., 10 Prince St., Alexandria, VA 22313/703-548-1400
Interport Inc., P.O. Box 1796, St. George, UT 84770/801-628-5792
Paul Jaeger Inc., P.O. Box 449, 1 Madison Ave., Grand Junction, TN 38039/901-764-6909 (Heym)
John Jovino Co., 5 Centre Market Pl., New York, NY 10013/212-925-4881 (Terminator)
KDF, Inc., 2485 Hwy 46 No., Seguin, TX 78155/512-379-8141 (Mauser rifles)
Kassnar Imports, P.O. Box 6097, Harrisburg, PA 17112/717-652-6101
Kendall International, 418 Fithian Ave., Paris. KY 40361/606-987-6946
Keng's Firearms Specialty, 6030 Hwy 85, #222, Riverdale, GA 30274
Kimel Industries, Box 335, Matthews, NC 28105/704-821-7663
Robert Kleinguenther Firearms, P.O. Box 2020, Seguin, TX 78155/512-372-5050
Llama (See Stoeger)
MRE Dist. Inc., 19 So. Bayles Ave., Pt. Washington, NY 11050/516-883-9226
Magnum Research, Inc., P.O. Box 3221, Minneapolis, MN 55432/612-574-1868 (Israeli Galil)
Mandall Shtg. Suppl., 3616 N. Scottsdale Rd., Scottsdale, AZ 85252/602-945-2553
Mannlicher (See Steyr Daimler Puch of Amer.)
Mauser-Werke Oberndorf, P. O. Box 1349, 7238 Oberndorf/Neckar, West Germany
Mendi s. coop. (See Connecticut Valley Arms Co.)
Merkuria, FTC, Argentinska 38, 17000 Prague 7, Czechoslovakia (BRNO)
Mitchell Arms, Inc., 3411 Lake Center Dr., Santa Ana, CA 92704/714-957-5711
Mitchell Arms Corp., 116 East 16th St., Costa Mesa, CA 92627/714-548-7701 (Uberti pistols)
Wm. Larkin Moore & Co., 31360 Via Colinas, Suite 109, Westlake Village, CA 91361/818-889-4160 (Garbi, Ferlib, Piotti, Perugini Visini)
Navy Arms Co., 689 Bergen Blvd., Ridgefield, NJ 07657
G.E. Nygren Associates, Inc., P.O. Box 6188, Fort Wayne, IN 46896/219-747-9148 (Heym)
Osborne's, P.O. Box 408, Cheboygan, MI 49721/616-625-9626 (Hammerli; Tanner rifles; Korth)
Outdoor Sports Headquarters, Inc., 967 Watertower Lane, Dayton, OH 45449/513-865-5855 (Charles Daly shotguns)
PM Air Services Ltd., P.O. Box 1573, Costa Mesa, CA 92626/714-968-2689
PTK International, Inc., 2814 New Spring Rd., Suite 340, Atlanta, GA 30339/404-438-9699 (mil. auto rifles)
Pachmayr Gun Works, 1875 So. Mountain Ave., Monrovia, CA 91016/818-357-7771
Pacific Intl. Merch. Corp., 2215 "J" St., Sacramento, CA 95816/916-446-2737
Para-Ordnance Mfg. Inc., 3411 McNicoll Ave., Scarborough, ON M1V 2V6, Canada/416-297-7895
Parker Reproductions, 124 River Rd., Middlesex, NJ 08846/201-469-0100
Parker-Hale, Bisleyworks, Golden Hillock Rd., Sparbrook, Birmingham B11 2PZ, England
Perazzi U.S.A. Inc., 206 S. George St., Rome, NY 13440/315-337-8566
Poly Technologies, Inc. (See PTK International, Inc.)
Precision Sales Intl. Inc., PSI, P.O. Box 1776, Westfield, MA 01086/413-562-5055 (Anschutz)
Precision Sports, P.O. Box 708, Kellogg Rd., Cortland, NY 13045/607-756-2851 (Parker-Hale)
Proofmark, Ltd., P.O. Box 183, Alton, IL 62002/618-463-0120 (Bettinsoli shotguns)
Quality Arms, Inc., Box 19477, Houston, TX 77224/713-870-8377 (Bernardelli; Ferlib; Bretton shotguns)
Quantetics Corp., Imp.-Exp. Div., 582 Somerset St. W., Ottawa, Ont. K1R 5K2 Canada/613-237-0242 (Unique pistols-Can. only)
Rahn Gun Works, Inc., 470 Market SW, Box 33, Grand Rapids, MI 49503/616-235-0634
Ravizza Carlo Caccia Pesca, s.r.l., Via Melegnano 6, 20122 Milano, Italy
Rottweil, (See Dynamit Nobel)
S.A.E., Inc. (See: Spain America Enterprises)
Saki International, 19800 Center Ridge Rd., Rocky River, OH 44116/216-331-3533
Samco Enterprises, Inc., 6995 N.W. 43rd St., Miami, FL 33166/305-593-9782
Sauer (See Sigarms)
Savage Industries, Inc., Springdale Rd., Westfield, MA 01085/413-562-2361
Thad Scott, P.O. Box 412; Hwy 82 West, Indianola, MS 38751/601-887-5929 (Perugini Visini; Bertuzzi; Mario Beschi shotguns)
Don L. Shrum's Cape Outfitters, Rt. 2 Box 437-C, Cape Girardeau, MO 63701/314-335-4103
Sigarms Inc., 470 Spring Park Pl., Unit 900, Herndon, VA 22070/703-481-6660
Sile Distributors, 7 Centre Market Pl., New York, NY 10013/212-925-4111
Ernie Simmons Enterprises, 719 Highland Ave., Lancaster, PA 17603/717-392-0021 (SKB shotguns)
Franz Sodia Jagdgewehrfabrik, Schulhausgasse 14, 9170 Ferlach, (Karnten) Austria
Southern Gun & Tackle Distributors, 13490 N.W. 45th Ave., Opa-Locka (Miami), FL 33054/305-685-8451
Spain America Enterprises Inc., 8581 N.W. 54th St., Miami, FL 33166/305-593-5173
Sportarms of Florida, 5555 N.W. 36 Ave., Miami, FL 33142/305-635-2411
Springfield Armory, 420 W. Main St., Geneseo, IL 61254/309-944-5631 (Bernardelli)
Steyr-Daimler-Puch, Gun South, Inc., Box 6607, 7605 Eastwood Mall, Birmingham, AL 35210/800-821-3021 (rifles)
Stoeger Industries, 55 Ruta Ct., S. Hackensack, NJ 07606/201-440-2700
Taurus International Mfg. Inc., P.O. Box 558567, Ludlam Br., Miami, FL 33155/305-662-2529
Tradewinds, Inc., P.O. Box 1191, Tacoma, WA 98401
Uberti USA, Inc., 41 Church St., New Milford, CT 06776/203-355-8827
Ignacio Ugartechea, Apartado 21, Eibar, Spain
Valmet Sporting Arms Div., 55 Ruta Ct., S. Hackensack, NJ 07606 (sporting types)
Verney-Carron, B.P. 72, 54 Boulevard Thiers, 42002 St. Etienne Cedex, France
Perugini Visini & Co. s.r.l., Via Camprelle, 126, 25080 Nuvolera (Bs.), Italy
Waffen-Frankonia, see: Frankonia Jagd
Weatherby's, 2781 Firestone Blvd., So. Gate, CA 90280/213-569-7186
Weaver Arms Corp., 6265 Greenwich Dr., Suite 201, San Diego, CA 92122/619-452-2551
Whittington Arms, Box 489, Hooks, TX 75561
Winchester, Olin Corp., 120 Long Ridge Rd., Stamford, CT 06904
Zavodi Crvena Zastava (See Interarms)

GUNS (Air)

Air Rifle Specialists, 311 East Water St., Elmira, NY 14901/607-734-7340
Beeman Precision Arms, Inc., 3440-GD Airway Dr., Santa Rosa, CA 95403/707-578-7900 (Feinwerkbau, Weihrauch, Webley)
Benjamin Air Rifle Co., 2600 Chicory Rd., Racine, WI 53403/414-554-7900
Brass Eagle Inc., 3876 Midhurst Lane, Mississauga, Ont. L4Z 1C7, Canada/416-848-4844 (paint ball guns)
The Command Post, Inc., P.O. Box 1500, Crestview, FL 32536/904-682-2492 (airsoft, air and paintball marking guns)
Crosman Airguns, a Coleman Co., Routes 5 and 20, E. Bloomfield, NY 14443/716-657-6161
Daisy Mfg. Co., P.O. Box 220, Rogers, AR 72756/501-636-1200
Dynamit Nobel-RWS Inc., 105 Stonehurst Ct., Northvale, NJ 07647/201-767-1995 (Dianawerk)
Fiocchi of America, Inc., Rt. 2 Box 90-8, Ozark, MO 65721/417-725-4118
Fisher Enterprises, 655 Main St. #305, Edmonds, WA 98020/206-776-4365
Great Lakes Airguns, 6175 So. Park Ave., Hamburg, NY 14075/716-648-6666
Gil Hebard Guns, Box 1, Knoxville, IL 61448
Interarms, 10 Prince, Alexandria, VA 22313 (Walther)
Kendall International, 418 Fithian Ave., Paris, KY 40361/606-987-6946 (Italian Airmatch)
Mandall Shooting Supplies, Inc., 3616 N. Scottsdale Rd., Scottsdale, AZ 85252/602-945-2553 (Cabanas line)
Marksman Products, 5622 Engineer Dr., Huntington Beach, CA 92649/714-898-7535
McMurray & Son, 109 E. Arbor Vitae St., Inglewood, CA 90301/213-412-0558 (custom airguns)
National Survival Game, Inc., Box 1439, Main St., New London, NH 03257/603-735-5151
Phoenix Arms Co., Phoenix House, Churchdale Rd., Eastbourne, East Sussex BN22 8PX, England (Jackal)
Power Line (See Daisy Mfg. Co.)
Pursuit Marketing, Inc. (PMI), 1966 Raymond Dr., Northbrook, IL 60062
Sheridan Products, Inc., 2600 Chicory Rd., Racine, WI 53403/414-554-7900
Stone Enterprises Ltd., Rt. 609, P.O. Box 335, Wicomico Church, VA 22579/804-580-5114
Target Airgun Supply, P.O. Box 428, South Gate, CA 90280/213-569-3417
Tippman Pneumatics, Inc., 4402 New Haven Ave., Fort Wayne, IN 46803/219-422-6448

GUNS & GUN PARTS, REPLICA AND ANTIQUE

Antique Arms Co., David E. Saunders, 1110 Cleveland, Monett, MO 65708/417-235-6501
Antique Gun Parts, Inc., 1118 S. Braddock Ave., Pittsburgh, PA 15218/412-241-1811 (ML)
Armsport, Inc., 3590 N.W. 49th St., Miami, FL 33142
Beeman Precision Arms, Inc., 3440-GDD Airway Dr., Santa Rosa, CA 95403/707-578-7900
Benson Firearms Ltd., P.O. Box 30137, Seattle, WA 98103/800-521-0714, Ext. 631
Cache La Poudre Rifleworks, 140 No. College Ave., Fort Collins, CO 80524/303-482-6913
Leonard Day & Sons, Inc., One Cottage St., P.O. Box 723, East Hampton, MA 01027/413-527-7990
Dixie Gun Works, Inc., Hwy 51, South, Union City, TN 38261/901-885-0561
Andy Fautheree, P.O. Box 4607, Pagosa Springs, CO 81157/303-731-5003
Federal Ordnance Inc., 1443 Portrero Ave., So. El Monte, CA 91733/213-350-4161
Jack First Distributors, Inc., 44633 Sierra Hwy., Lancaster, CA 93534/805-945-6981
Fred Goodwin, Goodwin's Gun Shop, Silver Ridge, Sherman Mills, ME 04776/207-365-4451 (Winchester rings & studs)
Gun Parts Corp., Box 2, West Hurley, NY 12491/914-679-2417
Hansen and Company, 244 Old Post Rd., Southport, CT 06490/203-259-6222
Hopkins & Allen Arms, 3 Ethel Ave., P.O. Box 217, Hawthorne, NJ 07507/201-427-1165
Terry K. Kopp, Highway 13 South, Lexington, MO 64067/816-259-2636 (restoration & pts. 1890 & 1906 Winch.)
The House of Muskets, Inc., P.O. Box 4640, Pagosa Springs, CO 81157/303-731-2295 (ML supplies; catalog $3)
Liberty Antique Gunworks, 19 Key St., P.O. Box 183GD, Eastport, ME 04631/207-853-2327 (S&W only; ctlg. $5)
Log Cabin Sport Shop, 8010 Lafayette Rd., Lodi, OH 44254/216-948-1082 (ctlg. $30)
Edw. E. Lucas, 32 Garfield Ave., East Brunswick, NJ 08816/201-251-5526 (45/70 Springfield parts; some Sharps, Spencer parts)
Lyman Products Corp., Middlefield, CT 06455
Tommy Munsch Gunsmithing, Rt. 2, Box 248, Little Falls, MN 56345/612-632-6695 (Winchester obsolete parts only; list $1.50; oth. inq. SASE)
Precise Metalsmithing Ent., James L. Wisner, 146 Curtis Hill Rd., Chehalis, WA 98532/206-748-3743 (pre '68-M70 Winchester)
Ram Line, Inc., 15611 W. 6th Ave., Golden, CO 80401/303-279-0886
S&S Firearms, 88-21 Aubrey Ave., Glendale, NY 11385/718-497-1100
Sarco, Inc., 323 Union St., Stirling, NJ 07980/201-647-3800
Shiloh Rifle Mfg. Co., Inc., P.O. Box 279; 201 Centennial Dr., Big Timber, MT 59011/406-932-4454
South Bend Replicas, Inc., 61650 Oak Rd., South Bend, IN 46614/219-289-4500 (ctlg. $6)
C. H. Stoppler, 1426 Walton Ave., New York, NY 10452 (miniature guns)
Stott's Creek Armory Inc., R 1 Box 70, Morgantown, IN 46160/317-878-5489
Uberti USA, Inc., 41 Church St., New Milford, CT 06776/203-355-8827
Upper Missouri Trading Co., 304 Harold St., Crofton, NE 68730/402-388-4844
Weisz Antique Gun Parts, P.O. Box 311, Arlington, VA 22210/703-243-9161
W. H. Wescombe, P.O. Box 488, Glencoe, CA 95232 (Rem. R.B. parts)

GUNS, SURPLUS—PARTS AND AMMUNITION

M. Braun, 32, rue Notre-Dame, 2440 Luxembourg, Luxemburg
Can Am Enterprises, 350 Jones Rd., Fruitland, Ont. LOR ILO, Canada/416-643-4357 (Enfield rifles; catalog $2)
Century Intl. Arms, Inc., 5 Federal St., St. Albans, VT 05478/802-527-1252
Federal Ordnance, Inc., 1443 Potrero Ave., So. El Monte, CA 91733/818-350-4161
Garcia National Gun Traders, 225 S.W. 22nd, Miami, FL 33135
Gun Parts Corp. Box 2, West Hurley, NY 12491/914-679-2417
Hansen and Company, 244 Old Post Rd., Southport, CT 06490/203-259-6222
Lever Arms Service Ltd., 2131 Burrard St., Vancouver, B.C., Canada V6J 3H8/604-736-0004
Paragon Sales & Services, Inc., P.O. Box 2022, Joliet, IL 60434 (ammunition)
Raida Intertraders S.A., Raida House, 1-G Ave. de la Couronne, B1050 Brussels, Belgium (surplus guns)
Sarco, Inc., 323 Union St., Stirling, NJ 07980/201-647-3800 (military surpl. ammo)
Sherwood Intl. Export Corp., 18714 Parthenia St., Northridge, CA 91324/818-349-7600
Southern Ammunition Co., Inc., Rte. 1, Box 6B, Latta, SC 29565/803-752-7751
Southern Armory, P.O. Box 879, Hillsville, VA 24343/703-236-7835 (modern military parts)
Springfield Sporters, Inc., R.D. 1, Penn Run, PA 15765/412-254-2626

GUNSMITHS, CUSTOM (see Custom Gunsmiths)

GUNSMITHS, HANDGUN (see Pistolsmiths)

GUNSMITH SCHOOLS

Colorado School of Trades, 1575 Hoyt, Lakewood, CO 80215/303-233-4697
Lassen Community College, P.O. Box 3000, Hiway 139, Susanville, CA 96130/916-257-6181
Robert E. Maki, School of Engraving, P.O. Box 947, Northbrook, IL 60065/312-724-8238 (firearms engraving ONLY)
Modern Gun Repair School, 2538 No. 8th St., Phoenix, AZ 85006/602-990-8346 (home study)
Montgomery Technical College, P.O. Box 787, Troy, NC 27371/919-572-3691 (also 1-yr. engraving school)
Murray State College, Gunsmithing Program, 100 Faculty Dr., Tishomingo, OK 73460/405-371-2371
North American Correspondence Schools, The Gun Pro School, Oak & Pawnee St., Scranton, PA 18515/717-342-7701
Penn. Gunsmith School, 812 Ohio River Blvd., Avalon, Pittsburgh, PA 15202/412-766-1812
Piedmont Technical College, P.O. Box 1197, Roxboro, NC 27573/919-599-1181
Pine Technical Institute, 1100 Fourth St., Pine City, MN 55063/612-629-6764
Professional Gunsmiths of America, 13 Highway Route 1, Box 224E, Lexington, MO 64067/816-259-2636
Shenandoah School of Gunsmithing, P.O. Box 300, Bentonville, VA 22610/703-743-5494
Southeastern Community College—North Campus, 1015 Gear Ave.; P.O. Drawer F, West Burlington, IA 52655/319-752-2731
Trinidad State Junior College, 600 Prospect, Trinidad, CO 81082/719-846-5631
Yavapai College, 1100 East Sheldon St., Prescott, AZ 86301/602-445-7300

GUNSMITH SUPPLIES, TOOLS, SERVICES

Don Allen, Inc., HC55, Box 326, Sturgis, SD 57785/605-347-5227 (stock duplicating machine)
Alley Supply Co., Carson Valley Industrial Park, P.O. Box 848, Gardnerville, NV 89410/702-782-3800 (JET line lathes, mills, etc.; Sweany Site-A-Line Optical bore collimator)
Anderson Mfg. Co., P.O. Box 536, 6813 S. 220th St., Kent, WA 98032/206-872-7602 (tang safe)
Armite Labs., 1845 Randolph St., Los Angeles, CA 90001/213-587-7744 (pen oiler)
B-Square Co., Box 11281, Ft. Worth, TX 76110/800-433-2909
Jim Baiar, 490 Halfmoon Rd., Columbia Falls, MT 59912 (hex screws)
Baron Technology, 62 Spring Hill Rd., Trumbull, CT 06611/203-452-0515 (chemical etching, plating)
Behlert Custom Guns, Inc., RD 2 Box 36C, Route 611 North, Pipersville, PA 18947/215-766-8680
Dennis M. Bellm Gunsmithing, Inc., dba P.O. Ackley Rifle Barrels, 2376 S. Redwood Rd., Salt Lake City, UT 84119/801-974-0697 (rifles only)
Al Biesen, W. 2039 Sinto Ave., Spokane, WA 99201 (grip caps, buttplates)
Roger Biesen, 5021 W. Rosewood, Spokane, WA 99208/509-328-9340
Blue Ridge Machinery and Tools, Inc., P.O. Box 536-GD, 2806 Putnam Ave., Hurricane, WV 25526/304-562-3538/800-872-6500 (gunsmithing lathe, mills & shop suppl.)
Briganti Custom Gun-Smithing, P.O. Box 56, 475-Route 32, Highland Mills, NY 10930/914-692-4409 (cold rust bluing, hand polishing, metal work)
Brownells, Inc., 222 W. Liberty, Montezuma, IA 50171/515-623-5401
W.E. Brownell Checkering Tools, 3356 Moraga Place, San Diego, CA 92117/619-276-6146

Buehler Scope Mounts, 17 Orinda Way, Orinda, CA 94563/415-254-3201
Burgess Vibrocrafters, Inc. (BVI), Rte. 83, Grayslake, IL 60030
M.H. Canjar, 500 E. 45th, Denver, CO 80216/303-295-2638 (triggers, etc.)
Chapman Mfg. Co., P.O. Box 250, Rte. 17 at Saw Mill Rd., Durham, CT 06422/203-349-9228
Chicago Wheel & Mfg. Co., 1101 W. Monroe St., Chicago, IL 60607/312-226-8155 (Handee grinders)
Chopie Mfg., Inc., 700 Copeland Ave., LaCrosse, WI 54603/608-784-0926
Classic Arms Corp., P.O. Box 8, Palo Alto, CA 94302/415-321-7243 (floorplates, grip caps)
Clymer Mfg. Co., Inc., 1645 W. Hamlin Rd., Rochester Hills, MI 48309/313-541-5533 (reamers)
Dave Cook, 720 Hancock Ave., Hancock, MI 49930 (metalsmithing only)
Crouse's Country Cover, P.O. Box 160, Storrs, CT 06268/203-429-3720 (Masking Gun Oil)
Dayton-Traister Co., 4778 N. Monkey Hill Rd., Oak Harbor, WA 98277/206-675-3421 (triggers; safeties)
Dem-Bart Hand Checkering Tools, Inc., 6807 Hiway #2, Snohomish, WA 98290/206-568-7356
Dremel Mfg. Co., 4915-21st St., Racine, WI 53406 (grinders)
Chas. E. Duffy, Williams Lane, West Hurley, NY 12491
The Dutchman's Firearms Inc., 4143 Taylor Blvd., Louisville, KY 40215/502-366-0555
Peter Dyson Ltd., 29-31 Church St., Honley, Huddersfield, West Yorksh. HD7 2AH, England/0484-661062 (accessories f. antique gun coll.)
Edmund Scientific Co., 101 E. Gloucester Pike, Barrington, NJ 08007/609-547-3488
Jack First Distributors, Inc., 44633 Sierra Hwy., Lancaster, CA 93534/805-945-6981
Jerry Fisher, 1244 4th Ave. West, Kalispell, MT 59901/406-755-7093
Forster Products, Inc., 82 E. Lanark Ave., Lanark, IL 61046/815-493-6360
G. R. S. Corp., P.O. Box 748, 900 Overlander St., Emporia, KS 66801/316-343-1084 (Gravermeister; Grave Max tools)
Garrett Accur-Lt. D.F.S. Co., P.O. Box 8675, Ft. Collins, CO 80524/303-224-3067
Gilmore Pattern Works, P.O. Box 50084, Tulsa, OK 74150/918-245-9627 (Wagner safe-T-planer)
Grace Metal Prod., 115 Ames St., Elk Rapids, MI 49629/616-264-8133 (screw drivers, drifts)
Gunline Tools, 2970 Saturn St., Brea, CA 92621/714-993-5100
Gun Parts Corp., Box 2, West Hurley, NY 12491/914-679-2417
Gun-Tec, P.O. Box 8125, W. Palm Beach, Fl 33407 (files; SASE f. reply)
Half Moon Rifle Shop, 490 Halfmoon Rd., Columbia Falls, MT 59912/406-892-4409 (hex screws)
Henriksen Tool Co., Inc., P.O. Box 668, Phoenix, OR 97535/503-535-2309 (reamers)
Huey Gun Cases (Marvin Huey), P.O. Box 22456, Kansas City, MO 64113/816-444-1637 (high grade English ebony tools)
Ken Jantz Supply, 222 E. Main, Davis, OK 73030/405-369-2316
JGS Precision Tool Mfg., 1141 S. Sumner Rd., Coos Bay, OR 97420/503-267-4331
Jeffredo Gunsight Co., 1629 Via Monserate, Fallbrook, CA 92028 (trap buttplate)
Jim's Gun Shop, James R. Spradlin, 113 Arthur, Pueblo, CO 81004/719-543-9462 ("Belgian Blue" rust blues; stock fillers)
Kasenit Co., Inc., P.O. Box 726, 3 King St., Mahwah, NJ 07430/201-529-3663 (surface hardening compound)
Terry K. Kopp, Highway 13 South, Lexington, MO 64067/816-259-2636 (stock rubbing compound; rust preventive grease)
J. Korzinek, RD#2, Box 73, Canton, PA 17724/717-673-8512 (stainl. steel bluing; broch. $2)
John G. Lawson, (The Sight Shop) 1802 E. Columbia Ave., Tacoma, WA 98404/206-474-5465
Lea Mfg. Co., 237 E. Aurora St., Waterbury, CT 06720/203-753-5116
Mark Lee Supplies, P.O. Box 20379, Minneapolis, MN 55420/612-431-1727
Liberty Antique Gunworks, 19 Key St., P.O. Box 183GD, Eastport, ME 04631/207-853-2327 (spl. S&W tools)
Lock's Phila. Gun Exch., 6700 Rowland Ave., Philadelphia, PA 19149/215-332-6225
Longbranch Gun Bluing Co., 2455 Jacaranda Lane, Los Osos, CA 93402/805-528-1792
McIntyre Tools, P.O. Box 491/State Road #1144, Troy, NC 27371/919-572-2603 (shotgun bbl. facing tool)
McMillan Rifle Barrels, U.S. International, P.O Box 3427, Bryan, TX 77805/409-846-3990 (services)
Mike Marsh, Croft Cottage, Main St., Elton, Derbyshire DE4 2BY, England/062-988-6699 (gun accessories)
Meier Works, Steve Hines, Box 328, 2102-2nd Ave., Canyon, TX 79015/806-655-7806 (European accessories)
Michaels of Oregon Co., P.O. Box 13010, Portland, OR 97213/503-255-6890
Miller Single Trigger Mfg. Co., R.D. 1, Box 99, Millersburg, PA 17061/717-692-3704 (selective or non-selective f. shotguns)
Miniature Machine Co. (MMC), 210 E. Poplar St., Deming, NM 88030/505-546-2151 (screwdriver grinding fixtures)
Frank Mittermeier, 3577 E. Tremont, New York, NY 10465/212-828-3843
N&J Sales Co., Lime Kiln Rd., Northford, CT 06472/203-484-0247 (screwdrivers)
Palmgren Steel Prods., Chicago Tool & Engineering Co., 8383 South Chicago Ave., Chicago, IL 60617/312-721-9675 (vises, etc.)
Panavise Prods., Inc., 2850 E. 29th St., Long Beach, CA 90806/213-595-7621
Pilkington Gun Co., P.O. Box 1296, Muskogee, OK 74402/918-683-9418 (Q.D. scope mt.)
Redman's Rifling & Reboring, Route 3, Box 330A, Omak, WA 98841/509-826-5512 (22 RF liners)
Roto/Carve, 6509 Indian Hills Rd., Minneapolis, MN 55435/612-944-5150 (tool)
A.G. Russell Co., 1705 Hiway 71 North, Springdale, AR 72764/501-751-7341 (Arkansas oilstones)
Schaffner Mfg. Co., Emsworth, Pittsburgh, PA 15202 (polishing kits)
Seacliff International Inc., 2210 Santa Anita, So. El Monte, CA 91733/818-350-0515 (portable parts washer)
Shaw's, 9447 W. Lilac Rd., Escondido, CA 92026/619-728-7070
L.S. Starrett Co., 121 Crescent St., Athol, MA 01331/617-249-3551
Texas Platers Supply Co., 2453 W. Five Mile Parkway, Dallas, TX 75233 (plating kit)
Timney Mfg. Inc., 3065 W. Fairmount Ave., Phoenix, AZ 85017/602-274-2999 (triggers)
Stan de Treville, Box 33021, San Diego, CA 92103/619-298-3393 (checkering patterns)
Twin City Steel Treating Co., Inc. 1114 S. 3rd, Minneapolis, MN 55415/612-332-4849 (heat treating)
Walker Arms Co., Inc., Rt. 2, Box 73, Hwy. 80 W, Selma, AL 36701/205-872-6231 (tools)
Weaver Arms Co., P.O. Box 8, Dexter, MO 63841/314-568-3800 (action wrenches & transfer punches)
Will-Burt Co., 169 So. Main, Orrville, OH 44667 (vises)
Williams Gun Sight Co., 7389 Lapeer Rd., Davison, MI 48423
Wilson Arms Co., 63 Leetes Island Rd., Branford, CT 06405/203-488-7297
W.C. Wolff Co., P.O. Box 232, Ardmore, PA 19003/215-896-7500 (springs)

HANDGUN ACCESSORIES

Ajax Custom Grips, Inc., Div. of A. Jack Rosenberg & Sons, 12229 Cox Lane, Dallas, TX 75244/214-241-6302
Bob Allen Companies, 214 S.W. Jackson St., Des Moines, IA 50302/515-283-2191
American Gas & Chemical Co., Ltd., 220 Pegasus Ave., Northvale, NJ 07647/201-767-7300 (clg. lube)
Armson, Inc., P.O. Box 2130, Farmington Hills, MI 48018/313-478-2577
Armsport, Inc., 3590 N.W. 49th St., Miami, FL 33142/305-635-7850
Baramie Corp., 6250 E. 7 Mile Rd., Detroit, MI 48234 (Hip-Grip)
Bar-Sto Precision Machine, 73377 Sullivan Rd., Twentynine Palms, CA 92277/619-367-2747
Behlert Precision, RD 2 Box 63, Route 611 North, Pipersville, PA 18947/215-766-8681
Brauer Bros. Mfg. Co., 2020 Delmar Blvd., St. Louis, MO 63103/314-231-2864
Centaur Systems, Inc., 15127 NE 24th, Suite 114, Redmond, WA 98052/206-392-8472 (Quadra-Lok bbls.)
Central Specialties Co., 200 Lexington Dr., Buffalo Grove, IL 60089/312-537-3300 (trigger locks only)
D&E Magazines Mfg., P.O. Box 4876-D, Sylmar, CA 91342 (clips)
Detonics Firearms Industries, 13456 SE 27th Pl., Bellevue, WA 98005/206-747-2100
Doskocil Mfg. Co., Inc, P.O. Box 1246, Arlington, TX 75010/817-467-5116 (Gun Guard cases)
Essex Arms, Box 345, Island Pond, VT 05846/802-723-4313 (45 Auto frames)
Frielich Police Equipment, 396 Broome St., New York, NY 10013/212-254-3045 (cases)
R. S. Frielich, 211 East 21st St., New York, NY 10010/212-777-4477 (cases)
Glock, Inc., 5000 Highlands Parkway #190, Smyrna, GA 30080/404-432-1202
Gun Parts Corp., Box 2, West Hurley, NY 12491/914-679-2417
Gil Hebard Guns, 125-129 Public Square, Knoxville, IL 61448
K&K Ammo Wrist Band, R.D. #1, Box 448-CA18, Lewistown, PA 17044/717-242-2329
King's Gun Works, 1837 W. Glenoaks Blvd., Glendale, CA 91201/818-956-6010
Terry K. Kopp, Highway 13 South, Lexington, MO 64067/816-259-2636
Lee's Red Ramps, 7252 E. Ave. U-3, Littlerock, CA 93543/805-944-4487 (ramp insert kits; spring kits)
Lee Precision Inc., 4275 Hwy. U, Hartford, WI 53027 (pistol rest holders)
Liberty Antique Gunworks, 19 Key St., P.O. Box 183GD, Eastport, ME 04631/207-853-2327 (shims f. S&W revs.)
Kent Lomont, 4236 West 700 South, Poneto, IN 46781 (Auto Mag only)
Lone Star Gunleather, 1301 Brushy Bend Dr., Round Rock, TX 78681/512-255-1805
Los Gatos Grip & Specialty Co., P.O. Box 1850, Los Gatos, CA 95030 (custom-made)
MTM Molded Prods. Co., 3370 Obco Ct., Dayton, OH 45414/513-890-7461
Millett Industries, 16131 Gothard St., Huntington Beach, CA 92647/714-842-5575
No-Sho Mfg. Co., 10727 Glenfield Ct., Houston, TX 77096/713-723-5332
Jim Noble Co., 1305 Columbia St., Vancouver, WA 98660/206-695-1309
Omega Sales, Inc., P.O. Box 1066, Mt. Clemens, MI 48403/313-469-6727
Harry Owen (See Sport Specialties)
Pachmayr Ltd., 1875 So. Mountain Ave., Monrovia, CA 91016/818-357-7771 (cases)
Pacific Intl. Mchdsg. Corp., 2215 "J" St., Sacramento, CA 95818/916-446-2737 (Vega 45 Colt comb. mag.)
Poly-Choke Div., Marble Arms Corp., 420 Industrial Park, Gladstone, MI 49837/906-428-3710 (handgun ribs)
Ranch Products, P.O. Box 145, Malinta, OH 43535 (third-moon clips)
Ransom Intl. Corp., 1040 Sandretto Dr., Suite J, Prescott, AZ 86302/602-778-7899
SSK Industries, Rt. 1, Della Dr., Bloomingdale, OH 43910/614-264-0176
Safariland Ltd., Inc., 1941 S. Walker, Monrovia, CA 91016/818-357-7902
Sile Distributors, 7 Centre Market Pl., New York, NY 10013
Robert Sonderman, 735 W. Kenton, Charleston, IL 61920/217-345-5429 (solid walnut fitted handgun cases; other woods)
Sport Specialties, (Harry Owen), Box 5337, Hacienda Hts., CA 91745/213-968-5806 (.22 rimfire adapters; .22 insert bbls. f. T/C Contender, autom. pistols)
Sportsmen's Equipment Co., 415 W. Washington, San Diego, CA 92103/619-296-1501

Turkey Creek Enterprises, Rt. 1, Box 10, Red Oak, CA 74563/918-754-2884 (wood handgun cases)
Melvin Tyler Mfg.-Dist., 1326 W. Britton, Oklahoma City, OK 73114/405-842-8044 (grip adaptor)
Wardell Precision Handguns Ltd., Box 4132 New River Stage 1, New River, AZ 85029/602-465-7258
Whitney Sales, P.O. Box 875, Reseda, CA 91335/818-345-4212
Wilson's Gun Shop, P.O. Box 578, Rt. 3, Box 211-D, Berryville, AR 72616/501-545-3616

HANDGUN GRIPS

Ajax Custom Grips, Inc., Div. of A. Jack Rosenberg & Sons, 12229 Cox Lane, Dallas, TX 75244/214-241-6302
Altamont Mfg. Co., 510 N. Commercial St., P.O. Box 309, Thomasboro, IL 61878/217-643-3125
Art Jewel Enterprises Ltd., Eagle Business Ctr., 460 Randy Rd., Carol Stream, IL 60188/312-260-0040 (Eagle grips)
Barami Corp., 6250 East 7 Mile Rd., Detroit, MI 48234/313-891-2536
Bear Hug Grips, Inc., P.O. Box 25944, Colorado Springs, CO 80936/303-598-5675 (cust.)
Beeman Precision Arms, Inc., 3440-GD Airway Dr., Santa Rosa, CA 95403/707-578-7900 (airguns only)
Behlert Precision, RD 2 Box 63, Route 611 North, Pipersville, PA 18947/215-766-8681
Boone's Custom Ivory Grips, Inc., 562 Coyote Rd., Brinnon, WA 98320/206-796-4330
Fab-U-Grip, An-Lin Enterprises, Inc., P.O. Box 550, Vineland, NJ 08360/609-652-1089
Fitz Pistol Grip Co., P.O. Box 171, Douglas City, CA 96024/916-778-3136
Gun Parts Corp., Box 2, West Hurley, NY 12491/914-679-2417
Herrett's , Box 741, Twin Falls, ID 83303/208-733-1498
Hogue Combat Grips, P.O. Box 2038, Atascadero, CA 93423/805-466-6266 (Monogrip)
Paul Jones Munitions Systems, (See Fitz Co.)
Russ Maloni (See Russwood)
Monogrip, (See Hogue)
Monte Kristo Pistol Grip Co., Box 171, Douglas City, CA 96024/916-778-3136
Mustang Custom Pistol Grips, see: Supreme Products Co.
Pachmayr Ltd., 1875 So. Mountain Ave., Monrovia, CA 91016/818-357-7771
Robert H. Newell, 55 Coyote, Los Alamos, NM 87544/505-662-7135 (custom stocks)
Olympic Arms Inc. dba SGW, 624 Old Pacific Hwy. S.E., Olympia, WA 98503/206-456-3471
A. Jack Rosenberg & Sons, 12229 Cox Lane, Dallas, TX 75234/214-241-6302 (Ajax)
Royal Ordnance Works Ltd., P.O. Box 3254, Wilson, NC 27893/919-237-0515
Russwood Custom Pistol Grips, P.O. Box 460, East Aurora, NY 14052/716-842-6012 (cust. exotic woods)
Jean St. Henri, 6525 Dume Dr., Malibu, CA 90265/213-457-7211 (custom)
Sile Dist., 7 Centre Market Pl., New York, NY 10013/212-925-4111
Sports Inc., P.O. Box 683, Park Ridge, IL 60068/312-825-8952 (Franzite)
Supreme Products Co., 1830 S. California Ave., Monrovia, CA 91016/800-423-7159/818-357-5359
R. D. Wallace, Star Rte. 1 Box 76, Grandin, MO 63943/314-593-4773 (cust. only)
Wayland Prec. Wood Prods., Box 1142, Mill Valley, CA 94942/415-381-3543
Wilson's Gun Shop, P.O. Box 578, Rt. 3, Box 211-D, Berryville, AR 72616/501-545-3616

HEARING PROTECTORS

AO Safety Prods., Div. of American Optical Corp., 14 Mechanic St., Southbridge, MA 01550/617-765-9711 (ear valves, ear muffs)
Bausch & Lomb, 635 St. Paul St., Rochester, NY 14602
Bilsom Interntl., Inc., 11800 Sunrise Valley Dr., Reston, VA 22091/703-620-3950 (ear plugs, muffs)
David Clark Co., Inc., 360 Franklin St., P.O. Box 15054, Worcester, MA 01615/617-756-6216
Gun Parts Corp., Box 2, West Hurley, NY 12491/914-679-2417
Marble Arms Corp., 420 Industrial Park, Box 111, Gladstone, MI 49837/906-428-3710
North Consumer Prods. Div., 16624 Edwards Rd., P.O. Box 7500, Cerritos, CA 90702/213-926-0545 (Lee Sonic ear valves)
Safety Direct, 23 Snider Way, Sparks, NV 89431/702-354-4451 (Silencio)
Smith & Wesson, 2100 Roosevelt Ave., Springfield, MA 01101
Willson Safety Prods. Div., P.O. Box 622, Reading, PA 19603 (Ray-O-Vac)

HOLSTERS & LEATHER GOODS

Alessi Holsters, Inc., 2465 Niagara Falls Blvd., Tonawanda, NY 14150/716-691-5615
Bob Allen Companies, 214 S.W. Jackson, Des Moines, IA 50315/515-283-2191
American Enterprises, 649 Herbert, El Cajon, CA 92020/619-588-1222
American Sales & Mfg. Co., P.O. Box 677, Laredo, TX 78040/512-723-6893
Andy Arratoonian, The Cottage, Sharow, Ripon HG4 5BP, England (0765-5858)
Rick M. Bachman (see Old West Reproductions)
Bang-Bang Boutique, 720 N. Flagler Dr., Fort Lauderdale, FL 33304/305-463-7910
Barami Corp., 6250 East 7 Mile Rd., Detroit, MI 48234/313-891-2536
Beeman Precision Arms, Inc., 3440-GD Airway Dr., Santa Rosa, CA 95403/707-578-7900 (airguns only)
Behlert Precision, RD 2 Box 63, Route 611 North, Pipersville, PA 18947/215-766-8681
Bianchi International Inc., 100 Calle Cortez, Temecula, CA 92390/714-676-5621
Ted Blocker's Custom Holsters, 409 West Bonita Ave. San Dimas, CA 91773/714-599-4415
Border Guns & Leather, Box 1423, Deming, NM 88031 (Old West cust.)
Boyt Co., Div. of Welsh Sptg., P.O. Box 220, Iowa Falls, IA 51026/515-648-4626
Brauer Bros. Mfg. Co., 2020 Delmar, St. Louis, MO 63103/314-231-2864
Browning, Rt. 4, Box 624-B, Arnold, MO 63010
J.M. Bucheimer Co., P.O. Box 280, Airport Rd., Frederick, MD 21701/301-662-5101
Buffalo Leather Goods, Inc., 100 E. Church St., El Dorado, AR 71730
Cathey Enterprises, Inc., 3423 Milam Dr., P.O. Box 2202, Brownwood, TX 76804/915-643-2553
Cattle Baron Leather Co., Dept. GD9, P.O. Box 100724, San Antonio, TX 78201/512-697-8900 (ctlg. $3)
Chace Leather Prods., Longhorn Div., 507 Alden St., Fall River, MA 02722/617-678-7556
Cherokee Gun Accessories, 4127 Bay St., Suite 226, Fremont, CA 94538/415-471-5770
China IM/EX, P.O. Box 27573, San Francisco, CA 94127/415-661-2212
Chas. Clements, Handicrafts Unltd., 1741 Dallas St., Aurora, CO 80010/303-364-0403
Dart Manufacturing Co., 4012 Bronze Way, Dallas, TX 75237/214-333-4221
Davis Leather Co., G. Wm. Davis, 3930 Valley Blvd., Unit F, Walnut, CA 91789/714-598-5620
DeSantis Holster & Leather Co., 140 Denton Ave., New Hyde Park, NY 11040/516-354-8000
El Paso Saddlery, P.O. Box 27194, El Paso, TX 79926/915-544-2233
Ellwood Epps Northern Ltd., 210 Worthington St. W., North Bay, Ont. P1B 3B4, Canada (custom made)
GALCO Gun Leather, 4311 W. Van Buren, Phoenix, AZ 85043/602-233-0596
Glock, Inc., 5000 Highlands Pkwy. #190, Smyrna, GA 30080/404-432-1202 (holsters)
Gould & Goodrich Leather Inc., E. McNeil St.; P.O. Box 1479, Lillington, NC 27546/919-893-2071 (licensed mfgr. of S&W leather products)
Gun Parts Corp., Box 2, West Hurley, NY 12491/914-679-2417
High North Products, P.O. Box 2, Antigo, WI 54409/715-623-5117 (1-oz. Mongoose gun sling)
Ernie Hill Speed Leather, 3128 S. Extension Rd., Mesa, AZ 85202/602-831-1919
Holster Outpost, 649 Herbert St., El Cajon, CA 92020/619-588-1222
Horseshoe Leather Prods., (See Andy Arratoonian)
Hoyt Holster Co., Inc., P.O. Box 69, Coupeville, WA 98239/206-678-6640
Don Hume, Box 351, Miami, OK 74355/918-542-6604
Hunter Corp., 3300 W. 71st Ave., Westminster, CO 80030/303-427-4626
John's Custom Leather, 525 S. Liberty St., Blairsville, PA 15717/412-459-6802
Jumbo Sports Prods., P.O. Box 280, Airport Rd., Frederick, MD 21701
Kane Products, Inc., 5572 Brecksville Rd., Cleveland, OH 44131/216-524-9962 (GunChaps)
Kirkpatrick Leather Co., P.O. Box 3150, Laredo, TX 78044/512-723-6631
Kolpin Mfg. Inc., P.O. Box 231, Berlin, WI 54923/414-361-0400
George Lawrence Co., 1435 N.W. Northrup, Portland, OR 97209/503-228-8244
Lone Star Gunleather, 1301 Brushy Bend Dr., Round Rock, TX 78681/512-255-1805
Michael's of Oregon, Co., P.O. Box 13010, Portland, OR 97213/503-255-6890 (Uncle Mike's)
No-Sho Mfg. Co., 10727 Glenfield Ct., Houston, TX 77096/713-723-5332
Jim Noble Co., 1305 Columbia St., Vancouver, WA 98660/206-695-1309 (Supreme quick-draw shoulder holster, etc.)
Kenneth L. Null-Custom Concealment Holsters, R.D. #5, Box 197, Hanover, PA 17331 (See Seventrees)
Old West Reproductions, R. M. Bachman, 1840 Stag Lane, Kalispell, MT 59901/406-755-6902 (ctlg. $3)
Orient-Western, P.O. Box 27573, San Francisco, CA 94127
Pony Express Sport Shop Inc., 1606 Schoenborn St., Sepulveda, CA 91343/818-895-1231
Red Head Brand Corp., 4949 Joseph Hardin Dr., Dallas, TX 75236/214-333-4141
Rogers Holsters Co., Inc., 1736 St. Johns Bluff Rd., Jacksonville, FL 32216/904-641-9434
Roy's Custom Leather Goods, Hwy, 1325 & Rawhide Rd., P.O. Box G, Magnolia, AR 71753/501-234-1566
Safariland Leather Products, 1941 So. Walker Ave., Monrovia, CA 91016/818-357-7902
Safety Speed Holster, Inc., 910 So. Vail, Montebello, CA 90640/213-723-4140
Schulz Industries, 16247 Minnesota Ave., Paramount, CA 90723/213-439-5903
Sile Distr., 7 Centre Market Pl., New York NY 10013/212-925-4111
Smith & Wesson Leather (See Gould & Goodrich)
Milt Sparks, Box 187, Idaho City, ID 83631/208-392-6695 (broch. $2)
Strong Holster Co., 105 Maplewood Ave., Gloucester, MA 01931/617-281-3300
Torel, Inc., 1053 N. South St., P.O. Box 592, Yoakum, TX 77995/512-293-2341 (gun slings)
Triple-K Mfg. Co., 2222 Commercial St., San Diego, CA 92113/619-232-2066
Uncle Mike's (See Michaels of Oregon)
Viking Leathercraft, Inc., 2248-2 Main St., Chula Vista, CA 92011/619-429-8050
Walt Whinnery, 1947 Meadow Creek Dr., Louisville, KY 40218/502-458-4361
Wild Bill Cleaver, Rt. 4, Box 462, Vashon, WA 98070 (antique holstermaker)
Wildlife Leather Inc., P.O. Box 339, Merrick, NY 11566/516-378-8588 (lea. gds. w. outdoor themes)
Zeus International, P.O. Box 953, Tarpon Springs, FL 33589/813-863-5029 (all leather shotshell belt)

HUNTING AND CAMP GEAR, CLOTHING, ETC.

API Outdoors Inc., 602 Kimbrough Dr., Tallulah, LA 71282/318-574-4903
Bob Allen Co., 214 S.W. Jackson, Des Moines, IA 50315/515-283-2191/800-247-8048
Eddie Bauer, 15010 NE 36th St., Redmond, WA 98052
L. L. Bean, Freeport, ME 04032
Bear Archery, R.R. 4, 4600 Southwest 41st Blvd., Gainesville, FL 32601/904-376-2327 (Himalayan backpack)
Big Beam, Teledyne Co., 290 E. Prairie St., Crystal Lake, IL 60014 (lamp)
Browning, Rte. 1, Morgan, UT 84050
Challanger Mfg. Co., Box 550, Jamaica, NY 11431 (glow safe)
Chippewa Shoe Co., P.O. Box 2521, Ft. Worth, TX 76113/817-332-4385 (boots)
Coleman Co., Inc., 250 N. St. Francis, Wichita, KS 67201
Danner Shoe Mfg. Co., P.O. Box 22204, Portland, OR 97222/503-653-2920 (boots)
DEER-ME Prod. Co., Box 34, Anoka, MN 55303/612-421-8971 (tree steps)
Dunham Co., P.O. Box 813, Brattleboro, VT 05301/802-254-2316 (boots)
Durango Boot, see: Georgia/Northlake
Frankonia Jagd, Hofmann & Co., Postfach 6780, D-8700 Wurzburg 1, West Germany
Game-Winner, Inc., 2625 Cumberland Parkway, Suite 220, Atlanta, GA 30339/404-434-9210 (camouflage suits; orange vests)
Gander Mountain, Inc., P.O. Box 128, Hwy. "W", Wilmot, WI 53192/414-862-2344
Georgia/Northlake Boot Co., P.O. Box 10, Franklin, TN 37064/615-794-1556 (Durango)
Gun Club Sportswear, Box 477, Des Moines, IA 50302
Bob Hinman Outfitters, 1217 W. Glen, Peoria, IL 61614
Hunter's Specialties, Inc., 5285 Rockwell Dr. N.E., Cedar Rapids, IA 52402/319-395-0321
Kenko Intl. Inc., 8141 West I-70 Frontage Rd. No., Arvada, CO 80002/303-425-1200 (footwear & socks)
Langenberg Hat Co., P.O. Box 1860, Washington, MO 63090/314-239-1860
Liberty Trouser Co., 2301 First Ave. North, Birmingham, AL 35203/205-251-9143
Life Knife Inc., P.O. Box 771, Santa Monica, CA 90406/213-821-6192
Marathon Rubber Prods. Co. Inc., 510 Sherman St., Wausau, WI 54401/715-845-6255 (rain gear)
Marble Arms Corp., 420 Industrial Park, Gladstone, MI 49837
Northlake Boot Co., 1810 Columbia Ave., Franklin, TN 37064/615-794-1556
The Orvis Co., 10 River Rd., Manchester, VT 05254/802-362-3622 (fishing gear; clothing)
P.A.S.T. (Precision Action Sports Technologies), 210 Park Ave., Columbia, MO 65203/314-449-7278 (shooting shirts)
Precise International, 3 Chestnut St., Suffern, NY 10901/914-357-6200
Pyromid, Inc., 625 Ellis St., Suite 209, Mountain View, CA 94043/415-964-6991 (portable camp stove)
Ranger Mfg. Co., Inc., 1536 Crescent Dr., Augusta GA 30919/404-738-3469 (camouflage suits)
Ranger Rubber Co., 1100 E. Main St., Endicott, NY 13760/607-757-4260 (boots)
Red Ball, 100 Factory St., Nashua, NH 03060/603-881-4420 (boots)
Red Head Brand Corp., 4949 Joseph Hardin Dr., Dallas, TX 75236/214-333-4141
Refrigiwear, Inc., 71 Inip Dr., Inwood, Long Island, NY 11696
Re-Heater Inc., 96302 S. Western Ave. #5, Lomita, CA 90717 (re-usable portable heat pack)
SanLar Co., N3784 Liberty St., Sullivan, WI 53178/414-593-8086 (huntg. sweatsuits, camouflage clothing)
Servus Rubber Co., 1136 2nd St., P.O. Box 3610 Rock Island, IL 61204 (footwear)
Teledyne Co., Big Beam, 290 E. Prairie St., Crystal Lake, IL 60014
10-X Mfg. Products Group, 2828 Forest Lane, Suite 1107, Dallas, TX 75234/214-243-4016
Thermos Div., KST Co., Norwich, CT 06361 (Pop Tent)
Norm Thompson, 1805 N.W. Thurman St., Portland, OR 97209
Tink's Safariland Hunting Corp., P.O. Box NN, McLean, VA 22101/703-356-0622 (camouflage rain gear)
Utica Duxbak Corp., 1745 S. Acoma St., Denver, CO 80223/303-778-0324
Waffen-Frankonia, see: Frankonia Jagd
Walker Shoe Co., P.O. Box 1167, Asheboro, NC 27203-1167/919-625-1380 (boots)
Wolverine Boots & Shoes Div., Wolverine World Wide, 9341 Courtland Dr., Rockford, MI 49351/616-866-1561 (footwear)
Woolrich Woolen Mills, Mill St., Woolrich, PA 17779/717-769-6464

KNIVES AND KNIFEMAKER'S SUPPLIES—FACTORY and MAIL ORDER

Alcas Cutlery Corp., 1116 E. State St., Olean, NY 14760/716-372-3111 (Cutco)
Atlanta Cutlery, Box 839, Conyers, GA 30207/404-922-3700 (mail order, supplies)
L. L. Bean, 386 Main St., Freeport, ME 04032/207-865-3111 (mail order)
Benchmark Knives (See Gerber)
Boker USA, Inc., 14818 West 6th Ave., Suite #17A, Golden, CO 80401/303-279-5997
Bowen Knife Co., P.O. Box 590, Blackshear, GA 31516/912-449-4794
Browning, Rt. 1, Morgan, UT 84050/801-876-2711
Buck Knives, Inc., P.O. Box 1267; 1900 Weld Blvd., El Cajon, CA 92022/619-449-1100 or 800-854-2557
Camillus Cutlery Co., 52-54 W. Genesee St., Camillus, NY 13031/315-672-8111 (Sword Brand)
W. R. Case & Sons Cutlery Co., Owens Way, Bradford, PA 16701/814-368-4123
Cattle Baron Leather Co., P.O. Box 100724, Dept. GD9, San Antonio, TX 78201/512-697-8900 (ctlg. $3)
Charter Arms Corp., 430 Sniffens Lane, Stratford, CT 06497/203-377-8080 (Skatchet)
Chicago Cutlery Co., 5420 N. County Rd. 18, Minneapolis, MN 55428/612-533-0472
E. Christopher Firearms Co., Inc., Route 128 & Ferry St., Miamitown, OH 45041/513-353-1321 (supplies)
Chas. Clements, Handicraft Unltd., 1741 Dallas St., Aurora, CO 80010/303-364-0403 (exotic sheaths)
Collins Brothers Div. (belt-buckle knife), See Bowen Knife Co.
Colonial Knife Co., P.O. Box 3327, Providence, RI 02909/401-421-1600 (Master Brand)
Compass Industries, Inc., 104 East 25th St., New York, NY 10010/212-473-2614
Crosman Blades™, The Coleman Co., 250 N. St. Francis, Wichita, KS 67201
Custom Knifemaker's Supply (Bob Schrimsher), P.O. Box 308, Emory, TX 75440/214-473-3330
Custom Purveyors, Maureen Devlet's, P.O. Box 886, Fort Lee, NJ 07024/201-886-0196 (mail order)
Damascus-USA, P.O. Box 220, Howard, CO 81233/719-942-3527
Dixie Gun Works, Inc., P.O. Box 130, Union City, TN 38261/901-885-0700 (supplies)
Eze-Lap Diamond Prods., Box 2229, 15164 Weststate St., Westminster, CA 92683/714-847-1555 (knife sharpeners)
Gerber Legendary Blades, 14200 S.W. 72nd Ave., Portland, OR 99223/503-639-6161
Gutmann Cutlery Co., Inc., 120 S. Columbus Ave., Mt. Vernon, NY 10553/914-699-4044
H & B Forge Co., Rte. 2 Geisinger Rd., Shiloh, OH 44878/419-895-1856 (throwing knives, tomahawks)
Russell Harrington Cutlery, Inc., Subs. of Hyde Mfg. Co., 44 River St., Southbridge, MA 01550/617-765-0201 (Dexter, Green River Works)
J. A. Henckels Zwillingswerk, Inc., 9 Skyline Dr., Hawthorne, NY 10532/914-592-7370
Indian Ridge Traders (See Koval Knives)
Ken Jantz Supply, 222 E. Main, Davis, OK 73030/405-369-2316 (supplies)
Jet-Aer Corp., 100 Sixth Ave., Paterson, NJ 07524/201-278-8300
KA-BAR Cutlery Inc., 5777 Grant Ave., Cleveland, OH 44105/216-271-4000
KA-BAR Knives, Collectors Division, 434 No. 9th St., Olean, NY 14760/716-372-5611
Kershaw Knives/Kai Cutlery USA Ltd., Stafford Bus. Pk., 25300 SW Parkway, Wilsonville, OR 97070/503-636-0111
Knifeco, P.O. Box 5271, Hialeah Lakes, FL 33014/305-635-2411
Knife and Gun Finishing Supplies, P.O. Box 13522, Arlington, TX 76013/817-274-1282
Koval Knives/IRT, P.O. Box 26155, Columbus, OH 43226/614-888-6486 (supplies)
Lamson & Goodnow Mfg. Co., 45 Conway St., Shelburne Falls, MA 03170/413-625-6331
Lansky Sharpeners, P.O. Box 800, Buffalo, NY 14221/716-634-6333 (sharpening devices)
Life Knife Inc., P.O. Box 771, Santa Monica, CA 90406/ 213-821-6192
Linder Solingen Knives, 4401 Sentry Dr., Tucker, GA 30084/404-939-6915
Al Mar Knives, Inc., P.O. Box 1626, 5755 SW Jean Rd., Suite 101, Lake Oswego, OR 97034/503-635-9229
Matthews Cutlery, 4401 Sentry Dr., Tucker, GA 30084/404-939-6915 (mail order)
R. Murphy Co., Inc., 13 Groton-Harvard Rd., P.O. Box 376, Ayer, MA 01432/617-772-3481 (StaySharp)
Nordic Knives, 1643-C Copenhagen Dr., Solvang, CA 93463 (mail order)
Normark Corp., 1710 E. 78th St., Minneapolis, MN 55423/612-869-3291
Ontario Knife, Queen Cutlery Co., P.O. Box 500, Franklinville, NY 14737/716-676-5527 (Old Hickory)
Parker Cutlery, 6928 Lee Highway, Chattanooga, TN 37415/615-894-1782
Plaza Cutlery Inc., 3333 Bristol, #161, South Coast Plaza, Costa Mesa, CA 92626/714-549-3932 (mail order)
Precise International, 3 Chestnut St., Suffern, NY 10901/914-357-6200
Queen Cutlery Co., 507 Chestnut St., Titusville, PA 16354/800-222-5233
R & C Knives and Such, P.O. Box 1047, Manteca, CA 95336/209-239-3722 (mail order; ctlg. $2)
Randall-Made Knives, Box 1988, Orlando, FL 32802/305-855-8075 (ctlg. $1)
Rigid Knives, P.O. Box 816, Hwy. 290E, Lake Hamilton, AR 71951/501-525-1377
A. G. Russell Co., 1705 Hiwy. 471 No., Springdale, AR 72764/501-751-7341
Bob Sanders, 2358 Tyler Lane, Louisville, KY 40205/502-454-3338 (Swedish Bahco steel)
San Diego Knives, P.O. Box 326, Lakeside, CA 92040/619-561-5900
Schrade Cutlery Corp., 1776 Broadway, New York, NY 10019/212-757-1814
Sheffield Knifemakers Supply, P.O. Box 141, Deland, FL 32720/904-775-6453
Smith & Wesson, 2100 Roosevelt Ave., Springfield, MA 01101/413-781-8300
Jesse W. Smith Saddlery, N. 307 Haven St., Spokane, WA 99202/509-534-3229 (sheathmakers)
Swiss Army Knives, Inc., P.O. Box 846, Shelton, CT 06484/203-929-6391
Tekna, 1075 Old County Rd., Belmont, CA 94002/415-592-4070
Thompson/Center, P.O. Box 2426, Rochester, NH 03867/603-332-2394
Tru-Balance Knife Co., 2155 Tremont Blvd., N.W., Grand Rapids, MI 49504/616-453-3679
Utica Cutlery Co., 820 Noyes St., Utica, NY 13503/315-733-4663 (Kutmaster)
Valor Corp., 5555 N.W. 36th Ave., Miami, FL 33142/305-633-0127
Wenoka Cutlery, P.O. Box 8238, West Palm Beach, FL 33407/305-845-6155
Western Cutlery Co., 1800 Pike Rd., Longmont, CO 80501/303-772-5900
Walt Whinnery, Walts Cust. Leather, 1947 Meadow Creek Dr., Louisville, KY 40218/502-458-4361 (sheathmaker)
Wyoming Knife Co., 101 Commerce Dr., Ft. Collins, CO 80524/303-224-3454

LABELS, BOXES, CARTRIDGE HOLDERS

Corbin Mfg. & Supply, Inc., P.O. Box 2659, White City, OR 97503/503-826-5211
Del Rey Products, P.O. Box 91561, Los Angeles, CA 90009/213-823-0494
E-Z Loader, Del Rey Products, P.O. Box 91561, Los Angeles, CA 90009
Hunter Co., Inc., 3300 W. 71st Ave., Westminster, Co 80030/303-472-4626
Peterson Label Co., P.O. Box 186, 23 Sullivan Dr., Redding Ridge, CT 06876/203-938-2349 (cartridge box labels; Targ-Dots)

LOAD TESTING and PRODUCT TESTING, (CHRONOGRAPHING, BALLISTIC STUDIES)

Accuracy Systems Inc., 15205 N. Cave Creek Rd., Phoenix, AZ 85032/602-971-1991
Ballistic Research, Tom Armbrust, 1108 W. May Ave., McHenry, IL 60050/815-385-0037 (ballistic studies, pressure & velocity)
Ballistics Research Group, Kayusoft Intl., Star Route, Spray, OR 97874/503-462-3934 (computer software "Computer Shooter")
W.W. Blackwell, 9826 Sagedale, Houston, TX 77089/ 713-484-0935 (computer program f. internal ball. f. rifle cartridges; "Load from a Disk")
Corbin Applied Technology, P.O. Box 2171, White City, OR 97503/503-826-5211
D&H Precision Tooling, 7522 Barnard Mill Rd., Ringwood IL 60072/815-653-9611 (Pressure testing equipment)
H-S Precision, Inc., 112 N. Summit, Prescott, AZ 86302/602-445-0607
Hutton Rifle Ranch, P.O. Box 45236, Boise, ID 83711/208-384-5461 (ballistic studies)
Kent Lomont, 4236 West 700 South, Poneto, IN 45781/219-694-6792 (handguns, handgun ammunition)
Plum City Ballistics Range, Norman E. Johnson, Rte. 1, Box 29A, Plum City, WI 54761/715-647-2539
Quartz-Lok, 13137 N. 21st Lane, Phoenix, AZ 85029/602-863-2729
Russell's Rifle Shop, Rte. 5, Box 92, Georgetown, TX 78626/512-778-5338 (load testing and chronographing to 300 yds.)
John M. Tovey, 4710 - 104th Lane NE, Circle Pines, MN 55014/612-786-7268
H. P. White Laboratory, Inc., 3114 Scarboro Rd., Street, MD 21154/301-838-6550

MISCELLANEOUS

Action, Left-Hand, David Gentry Custom Gunmaker, 314 N. Hoffman, P.O. Box 1440, Belgrade, MT 59714/406-388-4867
Action, Mauser-style only, Crandall Tool & Machine Co., 1545 N. Mitchell St., Cadillac, MI 49601/616-775-5562
Action, Single Shot, Miller Arms, Inc., P.O. Box 260, St. Onge, SD 57779 (deHaas-Miller)
Activator, B.M.F. Activator, Inc., P.O. Box 262364, Houston, TX 77207/713-477-8442
Adapters for Subcalibers, Harry Owen, P.O. Box 5337, Hacienda Hts., CA 91745/818-968-5806
Airgun Accessories, Beeman Precision Arms, Inc., 3440-GD Airway Dr., Santa Rosa, CA 95403/707-578-7900 (Beeman Pell seat, Pell Size, etc.)
Air Gun Combat Game Supplies, The Ultimate Game Inc., P.O. Box 1856, Ormond Beach, FL 32075/904-677-4358 (washable pellets, marking pistols/rifles)
Archery, Bear, R.R. 4, 4600 Southwest 41st Blvd., Gainesville, FL 32601/904-376-2327
Arms Restoration, Jenkins Enterprises, Inc., 12317 Locksley Lane, Auburn, CA 95603/916-823-9652
Assault Rifle Accessories, Cherokee Gun Accessories, 4127 Bay St. Suite 226, Fremont, CA 94538/415-471-5770
Assault Rifle Accessories, Feather Enterprises, 2500 Central Ave., Boulder, CO 80301/303-442-7021
Assault Rifle Accessories, Ram-Line, Inc., 15611 W. 6th Ave., Golden, CO 80401/303-279-0886 (folding stock)
Bedding Kit, Fenwal, Inc., Resins Systems Div., 50 Main St., Ashland, MA 01721 (Tru-Set)
Belt Buckles, Herrett's Stocks, Inc., Box 741, Twin Falls, ID 83303/208-733-1498 (laser engr. hardwood)
Belt Buckles, Pilgrim Pewter Inc., R.D. 2, Tully, NY 13159/607-842-6431
Benchrest & Accuracy Shooters Equipment, Bob Pease Accuracy, P.O. Box 787, Zipp Road, New Braunfels, TX 78130/512-625-1342
Benchrest Rifles & Accessories, Robert W. Hart & Son Inc., 401 Montgomery St., Nescopeck, PA 18635/717-752-3655
Bore Collimator, Alley Supply Co., P.O. Box 848, Gardnerville, NV 89410/702-782-3800 (Sweany Site-A-Line optical collimator)
Bull-Pup Conversion Kits, Bull-Pup Industries Inc., P.O. Box 187, Pioneertown, CA 92268/619-228-1949
Cannons, South Bend Replicas Ind., 61650 Oak Rd., S. Bend, IN 44614/219-289-4500 (ctlg. $6)
Cartridge Adapters, Sport Specialties, Harry Owen, Box 5337, Hacienda Hts., CA 91745/213-968-5806 (ctlg. $3)
Case Gauge, Plum City Ballistics Range, Rte. 1, Box 29A, Plum City, WI 54761/715-647-2539
Cased, high-grade English tools, Marvin Huey Gun Cases, P.O. Box 22456, Kansas City, MO 64113/816-444-1637 (ebony, horn, ivory handles)
Cherry Converter, Amimex Inc., 2660 John Montgomery Dr., Suite #3, San Jose, CA 95148/408-923-1720 (shotguns)
Clips, D&E Magazines Mfg., P.O. Box 4876-D, Sylmar, CA 91342 (handgun and rifle)
Computer & PSI Calculator, Hutton Rifle Ranch, P.O. Box 45236, Boise, ID 83711/208-384-5461
Computer Systems, Corbin Applied Technology, P.O. Box 2171, White City, OR 97503/503-826-5211 (software, books f. ballistic research)
Convert-A-Pell, Jett & Co., Inc., RR#3 Box 167-B, Litchfield, IL 62056/217-324-3779
Crossbows, Barnett International, 1967 Gunn Highway, Odessa, FL 33552/813-920-2241
Damascus Steel, Damascus-USA, P.O. Box 220, Howard, CO 81233/719-942-3527
Deer Drag, D&H Prods. Co., Inc., 465 Denny Rd., Valencia, PA 16059/412-898-2840
Dehumidifiers, Buenger Enterprises, P.O. Box 5286, Oxnard, CA 93030/805-985-0541
Dehumidifiers, Hydrosorbent Products, Box 675D, Rye NY 10580 (silica gel dehumidifier)
Dryer, Thermo-Electric, Golden-Rod, Buenger Enterprises, Box 5286, Oxnard, CA 93030/805-985-0541
E-Z Loader, Del Rey Prod., P.O. Box 91561, Los Angeles, CA 90009/213-823-04494 (f. 22-cal. rifles)
Ear-Valve, North Consumer Prods. Div., 16624 Edwards Rd., Cerritos, CA 90702/213-926-0545 (Lee-Sonic)
Embossed Leather Belts, Wallets, Wildlife Leather, Inc., P.O. Box 339, Merrick, NY 11566/516-378-8588 (outdoor themes)
Farrsight, Farr Studio, 1231 Robinhood Rd., Greenville, TN 37743/615-638-8825 (sighting aids for handgunners—clip on aperture)
Firearms Training, Ballistics Research Group, Kayusoft Intl., Star Route, Spray, Or 97874/503-462-3934 (computer software "Computer Shooter")
Game Hoist, Cam Gear Ind., P.O. Box 1002, Kalispell, MT 59901 (Sportsmaster 500 pocket hoist)
Game Scent, Buck Stop Lure Co., Inc., 3600 Grow Rd., Box 636, Stanton, MI 48888/517-762-5091
Game Scent, Pete Rickard, Inc., Rte. 1, Box 209B, Cobleskill, NY 12043/518-234-2731 (Indian Buck lure)
Game Scent, Tink's Safariland Hunting Corp., P.O. Box NN, McLean, VA 22101/703-356-0622 (buck lure)
Gas Pistol, Penguin Ind., Inc., Airport Industrial Mall, Coatesville, PA 19320/215-384-6000
Grip Caps, Classic Arms Corp., P.O. Box 8, Palo Alto, CA 94301/415-321-7243
Gun Bedding Kit, Fenwal, Inc., Resins System Div., 50 Main St., Ashland, MA 01721/617-881-2000
Gun Covers, E. Christopher Firearms Co., Inc., Route 128 & Ferry St., Miamitown, OH 45041/513-353-1321 (Gunnysox)
Gun Jewelry, Sid Bell Originals, R.D. 2, Box 219, Tully, NY 13159/607-842-6431 (jewelry for sportsmen)
Gun Jewelry, Pilgrim Pewter Inc., R.D. 2, Box 219, Tully, NY 13159/607-842-6431
Gun Jewelry, Sports Style Assoc., 148 Hendricks Ave., Lynbrook, NY 11563
Gun photographer, Mustafa Bilal, 5429 Russell Ave. NW, Suite 202, Seattle, WA 98107/206-782-4164
Gun photographer, John Hanusin, 3306 Commercial, Northbrook, IL 60062/312-564-2706
Gun photographer, Intl. Photographic Assoc., Inc., 4500 E. Speedway, Suite 90, Tucson, AZ 85712/602-326-2941
Gun photographer, Charles Semmer, 7885 Cyd Dr., Denver, CO 80221/303-429-6947
Gun photographer, Weyer Photo Services, Ltd., 333-14th St., Toledo, OH 43624/419-241-5454
Gun photographer, Steve White, 1920 Raymond Dr., Northbrook, IL 60062/312-564-2720
Gun Safety, Gun Alert Covers, Master Products, Inc., P.O. Box 8474, Van Nuys, CA 91409/818-365-0864
Gun Sling, La Paloma Marketing, 4210 E. LaPaloma Dr., Tucson, AZ 85718/602-881-4750 (Pro-sling system)
Gun Slings, Torel, Inc., 1053 N. South St., Yoakum, TX 77995
Gun Vise, Pflumm Gun Mfg. Co., 6139 Melrose Lane, Shawnee, KS 66203/913-268-3105
Hand Exerciser, Action Products, Inc., 22 No. Mulberry St., Hagerstown, MD 21740/301-797-1414
Horsepac, Yellowstone Wilderness Supply, P.O. 129, West Yellowstone, MT 59758/406-646-7613
Horsepacking Equipment/Saddle Trees, Ralide West, P.O. Box 998, 299 Firehole Ave., West Yellowstone, WY 59758/406-646-7612
Hugger Hooks Co., 3900 Easley Way, Golden, CO 80403/303-279-6160
Insect Repellent, Armor, Div. of Buck Stop, Inc., 3015 Grow Rd., Stanton, MI 48888
Insert Chambers, GTM Co., Geo. T. Mahaney, 15915B E. Main St., La Puente, CA 91744 (shotguns only)
Insert Barrels and Cartridge Adapters, Sport Specialties, Harry Owen, Box 5337, Hacienda Hts., CA 91745/213-968-5806 (ctlg. $3)
Knife Sharpeners, Lansky Sharpeners, P.O. Box 800, Buffalo, NY 14221/716-634-6333
Laser Aim, Laser Aim, Inc., 100 S. Main St., Box 581, Little Rock, AR 72203
Laser Aim, Laser Devices, Inc., #5 Hangar Way, Watsonville, CA 95076/408-722-8300
Locks, Gun, Bor-Lok Prods., 105 5th St., Arbuckle, CA 95912
Locks, Gun, Master Lock Co., 2600 N. 32nd St., Milwaukee, WI 53245
Lugheads, Floorplate Overlays, Sid Bell Originals, Inc., RD 2, Box 219, Tully, NY 13159/607-842-6431
Lug Recess Insert, P.P.C. Corp., 625 E. 24th St. Paterson, NJ 07514
Magazines, San Diego Knives, P.O. Box 326, Lakeside, CA 92040/619-561-5900 (auto pist., rifles)
Magazines, Mitchell Arms Inc., 3411 Lake Center Dr., Santa Ana, CA 92704/714-957-5711 (stainless steel)
Magazines, Ram-Line, Inc., 15611 W. 6th Ave., Golden, CO 80401/303-279-0886
Miniature Cannons, Karl J. Furr, 76 East, 350 North, Orem, UT 84057/801-225-2603 (replicas; Gatling guns)
Miniature Guns, Tom Konrad, P.O. Box 118, Shandon, OH 45063/513-738-1379

Monte Carlo Pad, Hoppe Division, Penguin Ind., Airport Industrial Mall, Coatesville, PA 19320/215-384-6000
Old Gun Industry Art, Hansen and Company, 244 Old Post Rd., Southport, CT 06490/203-259-6222
Police Batons & Accessories, Armament Systems and Procedures, Inc., P.O. Box 1794, Appleton, WI 54913/414-731-7075
Powderhorns, Frontier, 2910 San Bernardo, Laredo, TX 78040/512-723-5409
Powderhorns, Tennessee Valley Mfg., P.O. Box 1125, Corinth, MS 38834
Practice Ammunition, Hoffman New Ideas Inc., 821 Northmoor Rd., Lake Forest, IL 60045/312-234-4075
Practice Wax Bullets, Brazos Arms Co., 7314 Skybright Lane, Houston, TX 77095/713-463-0826
Ram Line, Inc., 15611 W. 6th Ave., Golden, CO 80401/303-279-0886 (accessories)
Ransom Handgun Rests, Ransom Intl. Corp., P.O. Box 3845, Prescott, AZ 86302/602-778-7899
Reloader's Record Book, Reloaders Paper Supply, Don Doerkson, P.O. Box 556, Hines, OR 97738/503-573-7060
Rifle Magazines, Butler Creek Corp., 290 Arden Dr., Belgrade, MT 59714/406-388-1356 (30-rd. Mini-14)
Rifle Magazines, Condor Mfg. Inc., 415 & 418 W. Magnolia Ave., Glendale, CA 91204/818-240-1745 (25-rd. 22-cal.)
Rifle Magazines, Miller Gun Works, P.O. Box 1053, 1440 Peltier Dr., Point Roberts, WA 98281/206-945-7014 (30-cal. M1 15&30-round)
Rifle Slings, Bianchi International, 100 Calle Cortez, Temecula, CA 92390/714-676-5621
Rifle Slings, Butler Creek Corp., 290 Arden Dr., Belgrade, MT 59714/406-388-1356
Rifle Slings, Chace Leather Prods., Longhorn Div., 507 Alden St., Fall River, MA 02722/617-678-7556
Rifle Slings, High North Products, P.O. Box 2, Antigo, WI 54409/715-623-5117 (1-oz. Mongoose gun sling)
Rifle Slings, John's Cust. Leather, 525 S. Liberty St., Blairsville, PA 15717/412-459-6802
Rifle Slings, Kirkpatrick Leather Co., P.O. Box 3150, Laredo, TX 78044/512-723-6631
Rifle Slings, Schulz Industr., 16247 Minnesota Ave., Paramount, CA 90723/213-439-5903
RIG, NRA Scoring Plug, Rig Products, 87 Coney Island Dr., Sparks, NV 89431/702-331-5666
Rubber Cheekpiece, W. H. Lodewick, 2816 N.E. Halsey, Portland, OR 97232/503-284-2554
Rust Prevention, Rusteprufe Laboratories, Rte. 5, Sparta, WI 54656/608-269-4144
Saddle Rings, Studs, Fred Goodwin, Sherman Mills, ME 04776
Safeties, William E. Harper, The Great 870 Co., P.O. Box 6309. El Monte, CA 91734/213-579-3077 (f. Rem. 870P)
Safeties, Williams Gun Sight Co., 7389 Lapeer Rd., Davison, MI 48423
Safety Slug, Glaser Safety Slug, P.O. Box 8223, Foster City, CA 94404/415-345-7677
Sav-Bore, Saunders Sptg. Gds., 338 Somerset St., N. Plainfield, NJ 07060
Scrimshaw, Henry "Hank" Bonham, 218 Franklin Ave., Seaside Heights, NJ 08751/201-793-8309
Scrimshaw, Boone Trading Co., 562 Coyote Rd., Brinnon, WA 98320/206-796-4330
Scrimshaw, G. Marek, P.O. Box 213, Westfield, MA 01086/413-568-9816
Sharpening Stones, A. G. Russell Co., 1705 Hiway 71 North, Springdale, AR 72764/501-751-7341 (Arkansas Oilstones)
Shell Catcher, Condor Mfg. Inc., 415 & 418 W. Magnolia Ave., Glendale, CA 91204/818-240-1745
Shooting Coats, 10-X Products Group, 2828 Forest Lane, Suite 1107, Dallas, TX 75234/214-243-4016
Shooting Glasses, American Optical Corp., 14 Mechanic St., Southbridge, MA 01550/617-765-9711
Shooting Glasses, Bausch & Lomb, Inc., 42 East Ave., Rochester, NY 14603/800-828-5423 (Ray Ban®)
Shooting Glasses, Bilsom Intl., Inc., 11800 Sunrise Valley Dr., Reston, VA 22091/703-620-3950
Shooting Glasses, Willson Safety Prods. Division, P.O. Box 622, Reading, PA 19603
Shooting Gloves, James Churchill Glove Co., Box 298, Centralia, WA 98531 (singles only, right or left)
Shooting Range Equipment, Caswell Internatl. Corp., 1221 Marshall St. N.E., Minneapolis, MN 55413/612-379-2000
Shotgun Barrel, Pennsylvania Arms Co., Box 128, Duryea, PA 18642/717-457-4014 (rifled)
Shotgun bore, Custom Shootg. Prods., 8505 K St., Omaha, NE 68127
Shotgun Converter, Amimex Inc., 2660 John Montgomery Dr., Suite #3, San Jose, CA 95148/408-923-1720
Shotgun Ribs, Poly-Choke Div., Marble Arms Corp., 420 Industrial Park, Gladstone, MI 49837/906-428-3710
Shotgun Sight, bi-ocular, Trius Prod., Box 25, Cleves, OH 45002
Shotgun Specialist, Moneymaker Guncraft, 1420 Military Ave., Omaha, NE 68131/402-556-0226 (ventilated, free-floating ribs)
Shotshell Adapter, PC Co., 5942 Secor Rd., Toledo, OH 43623/419-472-6222 (Plummer 410 converter)
Shotshell Adapter, Jesso Ramos, P.O. Box 7105, La Puente, CA 91744/818-369-6384 (12 ga./410 converter)
Snap Caps, Edwards Recoil Reducer, 269 Herbert St., Alton, IL 62002/618-462-3257
Springs, W. C. Wolff Co., P.O. Box 232, Ardmore, PA 19003/215-896-7500
Stock Duplicating Machine, Don Allen, Inc., HC55, Box 326, Sturgis, SD 47785/605-347-5227
Supersound, Edmund Scientific Co., 101 E. Gloucester Pike, Barrington, NJ 08007/609-547-3488 (safety device)
Swivels, Michaels, P.O. Box 13010, Portland, OR 97213/503-255-6890
Swivels, Sile Dist., 7 Centre Market Pl., New York, NY 10013/212-925-4111
Swivels, Williams Gun Sight Co., 7389 Lapeer Rd., Davison, MI 48423
Tomahawks, H&B Forge Co., Rt. 2, Shiloh, OH 44878/419-896-2075
Tree Stand, Climbing, API Outdoors Inc., 602 Kimbrough Dr., Tallulah, LA 71282/318-574-4903
Tree Steps, Deer Me Products Co., Box 34, 1208 Park St., Anoka, MN 55303/612-421-8971
Trophies, V.H. Blackinton & Co., P.O. Box 1300, 221 John L. Dietsch Blvd., Attleboro Falls, MA 02763/617-699-4436
Trophies, F. H. Noble & Co., 888 Tower Rd., Mundelein, IL 60060
Walking Sticks, Life Knife Inc., P.O. Box 771, Santa Monica, CA 90406/213-821-6192
Warning Signs, Delta Ltd., P.O. Box 777, Mt. Ida, AR 71957
World Hunting Info., J/B Adventures & Safaris, Inc., 6312 S. Fiddlers Green Circle, Suite 330N, Englewood CO 80111/303-771-0977
World Hunting Info., Wayne Preston, Inc., 3444 Northhaven Rd., Dallas, TX 75229/214-358-4477

MUZZLE-LOADING GUNS, BARRELS or EQUIPMENT

Luther Adkins, Box 281, Shelbyville, IN 46176/317-392-3795 (breech plugs)
Allen Firearms Co., 2879 All Trades Rd., Santa Fe, NM 87501/505-471-6090
Anderson Mfg. Co., P.O. Box 536, Kent, WA 98032/206-872-7602 (Flame-N-Go fusil; Accra-Shot)
Antique Gun Parts, Inc., 1118 S. Braddock Ave., Pittsburgh, PA 15218/412-241-1811 (parts)
Armoury, Inc., Rte. 202, New Preston, CT 06777
Armsport, Inc., 3590 N.W. 49th St., Miami, FL 33142/305-635-7850
B-Square Co., P.O. Box 11281, Ft. Worth, TX 76109/817-923-0964
Bauska Mfg. Corp., P.O. Box 2270, 1694 Whalebone Dr., Kalispell, MT 59901/406-752-8082
Beaver Lodge, 9245 16th Ave. S.W., Seattle, WA 98106/206-763-1698 (cust. ML)
Beeman Precision Arms, Inc., 3440-GDD Airway Dr., Santa Rosa, CA 95403/707-578-7900
Benson Firearms Ltd., P.O. Box 30137, Seattle, WA 98103/800-521-0714 (A. Uberti replicas)
Blackhawk East, Box 2274, Loves Park, IL 61131 (blackpowder)
Blackhawk Mtn., Box 210, Conifer, CO 80433 (blackpowder)
Blackhawk West, Box 285, Hiawatha, KS 66434 (blackpowder)
Blue and Gray Prods., Inc. RD #6, Box 362, Wellsboro, PA 16901/717-724-1383 (equipment)
Butler Creek Corp., 290 Arden Dr., Belgrade, MT 59714/406-388-1356 (poly & maxi patch)
Cache La Poudre Rifleworks, 140 N. College, Ft. Collins, CO 80524/303-482-6913 (custom muzzleloaders)
R. MacDonald Champlin, P.O. Box 693, Manchester, NH 03105/603-483-8557 (custom muzzleloaders)
Cheney Firearms Co., P.O. Box 321, Woods Cross, UT 84087 (rifles)
Chopie Mfg. Inc., 700 Copeland Ave., LaCrosse, WI 54601/608-784-0926 (nipple wrenches)
Connecticut Valley Arms Co. (CVA), 5988 Peachtree East, Norcross, GA 30071/404-449-4687 (kits also)
Cumberland Knife & Gun Works, 5661 Bragg Blvd., Fayetteville, NC 28303/919-867-0009
Earl T. Cureton, Rte. 2, Box 388, Willoughby Rd., Bulls Gap, TN 37711/615-235-2854 (powder horns)
Homer L. Dangler, Box 254, Addison, MI 49220/517-547-6745
Leonard Day & Sons, Inc., One Cottage St., P.O. Box 723, East Hampton, MA 01027/413-527-7990
Denver Arms, Ltd., P.O. Box 4640, Pagosa Springs, CO 81157/303-731-2295 (S.A.S.E.)
Dixie Gun Works, Inc., P.O. Box 130, Union City, TN 38261
Peter Dyson Ltd., 29-31 Church St., Honley, Huddersfield, W. Yorksh. HD7 2AH, England/0484-661062 (acc. f. ML shooter replicas)
EMF Co., Inc., 1900 E. Warner Ave. 1-D, Santa Ana, CA 92705/714-261-6611
Euroarms of America, Inc., P.O. Box 3277, 1501 Lenoir Dr., Winchester, VA 22601/703-662-1863
F.P.F. Co., P.O. Box 211, Van Wert, OH 45891 (black powder accessories)
Andy Fautheree, P.O. Box 4607, Pagosa Springs, CO 81157/303-731-5003 (cust. ML guns; must send SASE)
Ted Fellowes, Beaver Lodge, 9245 16th Ave. S.W., Seattle, WA 98106/206-763-1698 (cust. ML)
Marshall F. Fish, Rt. 22 N., Box 2439, Westport, NY 12993/518-962-4897 (antique ML repairs)
The Flintlock Muzzle Loading Gun Shop, 1238 "G" So. Beach Blvd., Anaheim, CA 92804/714-821-6655
Forster Prods., 82 E. Lanark Ave., Lanark, IL 61046/815-493-6360
Frontier, 2910 San Bernardo, Laredo, TX 78040/512-723-5409 (powderhorns)
Getz Barrel Co., Box 88, Beavertown, PA 17813/717-658-7263 (barrels)
GOEX, Inc., Belin Plant, Moosic, PA 18507/717-457-6724 (black powder)
A. R. Goode, 4125 N.E. 28th Terr., Ocala, FL 32670/904-622-9575 (ML rifle barrels)
Guncraft Inc., 117 W. Pipeline, Hurst, TX 76053/817-282-1464
Gun Parts Corp., Box 2, West Hurley, NY 12491/914-679-2417
The Gun Works, 236 Main St., Springfield, OR 97477/503-741-4118 (supplies)
Hatfield Rifle Works, 2020 Calhoun, St. Joseph, MO 64501/816-279-8688 (squirrel rifle)
Hopkins & Allen, 3 Ethel Ave., P.O. Box 217, Hawthorne, NJ 07507/201-427-1165
The House of Muskets, Inc., P.O. Box 4640, Pagosa Springs, CO 81157/303-731-2295 (ML bbls. & supplies; catalog $3)
Steven Dodd Hughes, P.O. Box 11455, Eugene, OR 97440/503-485-8869 (cust. guns; ctlg. $3)
Al Hunkeler, Buckskin Machine Works, 3235 So. 358th St., Auburn, WA 98001/206-927-5412 (ML guns)

Jennings-Hawken, 326½-4th St. N.W., Winter Haven, FL 33880
Jerry's Gun Shop, 9220 Odgen Ave., Brookfield, IL 60513/312-485-5200
Wm. Large Gun & Mach. Shop, R.R. #1, Box 189B, Ironton, OH 45638/614-532-5298
Leding Loader, R.R. #1, Box 645, Ozark, AR 72949 (conical ldg. acc. f. ML)
Lever Arms Serv. Ltd., 2131 Burrard St., Vancouver, BC V6J 3H8/604-736-0004, Canada
Log Cabin Sport Shop, 8010 Lafayette Rd., Lodi, OH 44254/216-948-1082 (ctlg. $3)
Loven-Pierson Inc., 4 W. Main, P.O. Box 377, Apalachin, NY 13732/607-625-2303
Lyman Products Corp., Rte. 147, Middlefield, CT 06455
McCann's Muzzle-Gun Works, 200 Federal City Rd., Pennington, NJ 08534/609-737-1707
McKeown's Sporting Arms, R.R. 4, Pekin, IL 61554/309-347-3559 (E-Z load rev. stand)
Maurer Arms, 2154-16th St., Akron, OH 44314/216-745-6864 (cust. muzzle-loaders)
Michigan Arms Corp., 363 Elmwood, Troy, MI 48083/313-583-1518
Modern Muzzleloading, Inc., Highway 136 East, P.O. Box 130, Lancaster, MO 63548/816-457-2125
Mountain State Muzzleloading Supplies, Inc., Box 154-1, Rt. #2 Williamstown, WV 26187/304-375-7842
Muzzleload Magnum Products (MMP), Rt. 6 Box 384, Harrison, AR 72601/501-741-5019
Muzzleloaders Etc., Inc., Jim Westberg, 9901 Lyndale Ave. S., Bloomington, MN 55420/612-884-1161
Muzzle Loaders, Inc., 9566 Old Keene Mill Rd., Burke, VA 22015/703-866-0990
Navy Arms Co., 689 Bergen Blvd., Ridgefield, NJ 07657/201-945-2500
Newman Gunshop, 119 Miller Rd., Agency, IA 52530/515-937-5775 (custom ML rifles)
October Country, P.O. Box 969, Hayden Lake, ID 83835
Oregon Trail Riflesmiths, Inc., P.O. Box 51, Mackay, ID 83251/208-588-2527
Ox-Yoke Originals Inc., 34 W. Main St., Milo, ME 04463/800-231-8313 (dry lubr. patches)
A. W. Peterson Gun Shop, 1693 Old Hwy. 441 N., Mt. Dora, FL 32757
Phyl-Mac, 609 N.E. 104th Ave., Vancouver, WA 98664/206-256-0579
R.V.I., P.O. Box 1439 Stn. A, Vancouver, B.C. V6C 1AO, Canada/604-524-3214 (high grade BP acc.)
Richland Arms, 321 W. Adrian St., Blissfield, MI 49228
H. M. Schoeller, 569 So. Braddock Ave., Pittsburgh, PA 15221
Tyler Scott, Inc., 8170 Corporate Park Dr., Suite 141, Cincinnati, OH 45242/513-489-2209 (Shooter's choice black solvent; patch lube)
C. Sharps Arms Co., Inc., P.O. Box 885, Big Timber, MT 59011/406-932-4353
Sile Distributors, 7 Centre Market Pl., New York, NY 10013/213-925-4111
C. E. Siler Locks, 7 Acton Woods Rd., Candler, NC 28715/704-667-9991 (flint locks)
South Bend Replicas, Inc., 61650 Oak Rd., South Bend, IN 46614/219-289-4500 (ctlg. $6)
The Swampfire Shop, 1693 Old Hwy. 441 N., Mt. Dora, FL 32757/904-383-0595
Tennessee Valley Mfg., P.O. Box 1125, Corinth, MS 38834 (powderhorns)
Ten-Ring Precision, Inc., 1449 Blue Crest Lane, San Antonio, TX 78232/512-494-3063
Traditions, Inc., 452 Main St.; P.O. Box 235, Deep River, CT 06417/203-526-9555 (guns, kits, accessories)
Trail Guns Armory, 1422 E. Main, League City, TX 77573/713-332-5833
Uberti USA, Inc., 41 Church St., New Milford, CT 06776/203-355-8827
Upper Missouri Trading Co., 304 Harold St., Crofton, NE 68730/402-388-4844
Warren Muzzle Loading, Hwy. 21, Ozone, AR 72854 (black powder accessories)
Fred Wells, Wells Sport Store, 110 N. Summit St., Prescott, AZ 86301/602-445-3655
W. H. Wescomb, P.O. Box 488, Glencoe, CA 95232/209-293-7010 (parts)
Williamson-Pate Gunsmith Serv., 117 W. Pipeline, Hurst, TX 76053/817-282-1464
Winchester Sutler, HC 38 Box 1000, Winchester, VA 22601/703-888-3595 (haversacks)
Winter & Associates, 239 Hillary Dr., Verona, PA 15147/412-795-4124 (Olde Pennsylvania ML accessories)

PISTOLSMITHS

Accuracy Gun Shop, Lance Martini, 3651 University Ave., San Diego, CA 92104/619-282-8500
Accuracy Systems, Inc., 15205 N. Cave Creek Rd., Phoenix, AZ 85032/602-971-1991
Accuracy Unlimited, 16036 N. 49 Ave., Glendale, AZ 85306/602-978-9089
Ahlman's Inc., R.R. #1 Box 20, Morristown, MN 55052/507-685-4243
Alpha Precision, Inc., Rte. 1, Box 35-1, Preston Rd., Good Hope, GA 30641/404-267-6163
American Pistolsmiths Guild, Rt. 1, Della Dr., Bloomingdale, OH 43910/614-264-0176
Ann Arbor Rod and Gun Co., 1946 Packard Rd., Ann Arbor, MI 48104/313-769-7866
Armament Gunsmithing Co., Inc., 525 Route 22, Hillside, NJ 07205/201-686-0960
Armson, Inc., P.O. Box 2130, Farmington Hills, MI 48018/313-478-2577
Richard W. Baber, Alpine Gun Mill, 1507 W. Colorado Ave., Colorado Springs, CO 80904/303-634-4867
Baer Custom Guns, 1725 Minesite Rd., Allentown, PA 18103/215-398-2362 (accurizing 45 autos and Comp II Syst.; cust. XP100s, P.P.C. rev.)
Bain & Davis Sptg. Gds., 307 E. Valley Blvd., San Gabriel, CA 91776/213-573-4241
Bar-Sto Precision Machine, 73377 Sullivan Rd., Twentynine Palms, CA 92277/619-367-2747(S.S. bbls. f. 45 ACP)
Barta's Gunsmithing, 10231 US Hwy. #10, Cato, WI 54206/414-732-4472
R. J. Beal, Jr., 170 W. Marshall Rd., Lansdowne, PA 19050/215-259-1220 (conversions, SASE f. inquiry)
Behlert Precision, RD 2 Box 63, Route 611 North, Pipersville, PA 18947/215-766-8681 (short actions)
Bell's Custom Shop, 3309 Mannheim Rd., Franklin Park, IL 60131/312-678-1900
Bowen Classic Arms Corp., P.O. Box 67, Louisville, TN 37777/615-984-3583
C. T. Brian, 2723 W. Hunt St., Decatur, IL 62526/217-429-2290
Brown's Gun Shop, Ed Brown, Rte. 2 Box 2922, Perry, MO 63462/314-565-3261
Leo Bustani, P.O. Box 8125, W. Palm Beach, FL 33407/305-622-2710
F. Bob Chow, Gun Shop, Inc., 3185 Mission, San Francisco, CA 94110/415-282-8358
Dick Campbell, 20000 Silver Ranch Rd., Conifer, CO 80433/303-697-9150 (PPC guns; custom)
Cellini's, Francesca Inc., 3115 Old Ranch Rd., San Antonio, TX 78217/512-826-2584
The Competitive Pistol Shop, John Henderson, 5233 Palmer Dr., Ft. Worth, TX 76117/817-834-8479
D&D Gun Shop, 363 Elmwood, Troy, MI 48083/313-583-1512
Davis Co., 2793 Del Monte St., West Sacramento, CA 95691/916-372-6789
Leonard Day & Sons, Inc., One Cottage St., P.O. Box 723, East Hampton, MA 01027/413-527-7990
Dilliott Gunsmithing, Inc., Rte. 3, Box 340, Dandridge, TN 37725
Dominic DiStefano, 4303 Friar Lane, Colorado Springs, CO 80907/303-599-3366 (accurizing)
Duncan's Gunworks Inc., 1619 Grand Ave., San Marcos, CA 92069/619-727-0515
Dan Dwyer, 915 W. Washington, San Diego, CA 92103/619-296-1501
Englishtown Sptg. Gds. Co., Inc., David J. Maxham, 38 Main St., Englishtown, NJ 07726/201-446-7717
Ferris Firearms, 1827 W. Hildebrand, San Antonio, TX 78201/512-734-0304
Jack First Distributors, Inc., 44633 Sierra Hwy., Lancaster, CA 93534/805-945-6981
Fountain Prods., 492 Prospect Ave., W. Springfield, MA 01089/413-781-4651
Frielich Police Equipment, 396 Broome St., New York, NY 10013/212-254-3045
Gilman-Mayfield, 1552 N. 1st., Fresno, CA 93703/209-237-2500
Keith Hamilton, P.O. Box 871, Gridley, CA 95948/916-846-2361
Gil Hebard Guns, Box 1, Knoxville, IL 61448
Richard Heinie, 821 E. Adams, Havana, IL 62644/309-543-4535
James W. Hoag, 8523 Canoga Ave., Suite C, Canoga Park, CA 91304/818-998-1510
Campbell H. Irwin, Hartland Blvd. (Rt. 20), East Hartland, CT 06027/203-653-3901
Paul Jaeger, Inc., P.O. Box 449, 1 Madison Ave., Grand Junction, TN 38039/901-764-6909
J. D. Jones, Rt. 1, Della Dr., Bloomingdale, OH 43910/614-264-0176
Reeves C. Jungkind, 5805 N. Lamar Blvd., Austin, TX 78752/512-442-1094
L. E. Jurras & Assoc., P.O. Box 680, Washington, IN 47501/812-254-7698
Ken's Gun Specialties, Rt. 1, Box 147, Lakeview, AR 72642/501-431-5606
Benjamin Kilham, Kilham & Co., Main St., Box 37, Lyme, NH 03768/603-795-4112
Terry K. Kopp, Highway 13 South, Lexington, MO 64067/816-259-2636 (rebblg., conversions)
LaFrance Specialties, P.O. Box 178211, San Diego, CA 92117/619-293-3373
Nelson H. Largent, Silver Shield's Inc., 7614 #1 Lemhi, Boise, ID 83709
William R. Laughridge, Cylinder & Slide Shop, 515 E. Military Ave., Fremont, NE 68025/402-721-4277
John G. Lawson, The Sight Shop, 1802 E. Columbia Ave., Tacoma, WA 98404/206-474-5465
Kent Lomont, 4236 West South, Poneto, IN 46781/219-694-6792 (Auto Mag only)
George F. Long, 1500 Rougue River Hwy., Ste. F, Grants Pass, OR 97527/503-476-7552
Mac's .45 Shop, Box 2028, Seal Beach, CA 90740/213-438-5046
Mag-na-port International, Inc., 41302 Executive Drive, Mt. Clemens, MI 48045/313-469-6727
Robert A. McGrew, 3315 Michigan Ave., Colorado Springs, CO 80910/303-636-1940
Philip Bruce Mahony, 1-223 White Hollow Rd., Lime Rock, CT 06039/203-435-9341
Rudolf Marent, 9711 Tiltree, Houston, TX 77075/713-946-7028 (Hammerli)
Elwyn H. Martin, Martin's Gun Shop, 937 So. Sheridan Blvd., Lakewood, CO 80226/303-922-2184
John V. Martz, 8060 Lakeview Lane, Lincoln, CA 95648/916-645-2250 (cust. German Lugers & P-38s)
Alan C. Marvel, 3922 Madonna Rd., Jarretsville, MD 21084/301-557-7270
Maryland Gun Works, Ltd., TEC Bldg., 10097 Tyler Pl. #8, Ijamsville, MD 21754/301-831-8456
Mullis Guncraft, 3518 Lawyers Road East, Monroe, NC 28110/704-283-8789
William Neighbor, Bill's Gun Repair, 1007 Burlington St., Mendota, IL 61342/815-539-5786
Nu-Line Guns, 1053 Caulks Hill Rd., Harvester, MO 63303/314-441-4501
Nygord Precision Products, P.O. Box 8394, La Crescenta, CA 91214/818-352-3027
Pachmayr Ltd., 1875 So. Mountain Ave., Monrovia, CA 91016/818-357-7771
Frank J. Paris, 13945 Minock Dr., Redford, MI 48239/313-255-0888
Paterson Gunsmithing, 438 Main St., Paterson, NJ 07502/201-345-4100
Phillips & Bailey, Inc., 815A Yorkshire St., Houston, TX 77022/713-699-4288
J. Michael Plaxco, Rt. 1, Box 203, Roland, AR 72135/501-868-9787
Power Custom, Inc., P.O. Box 1604, Independence, MO 64055/816-833-3102
Precision Specialties, 131 Hendom Dr., Feeding Hills, MA 01030/413-786-3365

RPS Gunshop,11 So. Haskell St., Central Point, OR 97502/503-664-5010
Roberts Custom Guns (Dayton Traister Co.), 4778 N. Monkey Hill Rd., Oak Harbor, WA 98277/206-675-3421
Bob Rogers Gunsmithing, P.O. Box 305; 344 S. Walnut St., Franklin Grove, IL 61031/815-456-2685 (custom)
SSK Industries (See: J. D. Jones)
L. W. Seecamp Co., Inc., Box 255, New Haven, CT 06502/203-877-3429
Harold H. Shockley, 204 E. Farmington Rd., Hanna City, IL 61536/309-565-4524
Hank Shows, dba The Best, 1078 Alice Ave., Ukiah, CA 95482/707-462-9060
Spokhandguns Inc., Vern D. Ewer, P.O. Box 370, 1206 Fig St., Benton City, WA 99320/509-588-5255
Sportsmens Equipmt. Co., 915 W. Washington, San Diego, CA 92103/619-296-1501 (specialty limiting trigger motion in autos)
James R. Steger, 1131 Dorsey Pl., Plainfield, NJ 07062
Irving O. Stone, Jr., 73377 Sullivan Rd., Twentynine Palms, CA 92277/619-367-2747
Victor W. Strawbridge, 6 Pineview Dr., Dover Pt., Dover, NH 03820
A. D. Swenson's 45 Shop, P.O. Box 606, Fallbrook, CA 92028
Randall Thompson, 654 Lela Pl., Grand Junction, CO 81504/303-434-4971
"300" Gunsmith Service, 4655 Washington St., Denver, CO 80216/303-295-2437
Timney Mfg. Co., 3065 W. Fairmount Ave., Phoenix, AZ 85017/602-274-2999
Trapper Gun, 18717 East 14 Mile Rd., Fraser, MI 48026/313-792-0134
Dennis A. "Doc" & Bud Ulrich, D.O.C. Specialists, 2209 So. Central Ave., Cicero, IL 60650/312-652-3606
Vic's Gun Refinishing, 6 Pineview Dr., Dover, NH 03820/603-742-0013
Walters Industries, 6226 Park Lane, Dallas, TX 75225/214-691-5150
Wardell Precision Handguns Ltd., Box 4132 New River Stage 1, New River, AZ 85029/602-465-7258
Wilson's Gun Shop, P.O. Box 578, Rt. 3, Box 211-D, Berryville, AR 72616/501-545-3616
Wisner's Gun Shop Inc., P.O. Box 58; Hiway 6, Adna, WA 98552/206-748-8942

REBORING AND RERIFLING

P.O. Ackley (See Dennis M. Bellm Gunsmithing, Inc.)
Amimex Inc., 3174 Stimson Way, San Jose, CA 95135/408-274-7816
Barnes Custom Shop, dba Barnes Bullets Inc., P.O. Box 215, American Fork, UT 84003
Bauska Mfg. Corp., P.O. Box 2270, 1694 Whalebone Dr., Kalispell, MT 59901/406-752-8082
Dennis M. Bellm Gunsmithing Inc., 2376 So. Redwood Rd., Salt Lake City, UT 84119/801-974-0697 (price list $3; rifle only)
A. R. Goode, 4125 N.E. 28th Terr., Ocala, FL 32760/904-622-9575
H-S Precision, Inc., 112 N. Summit, Prescott, AZ 86302/602-445-0607
Terry K. Kopp, Highway 13 South, Lexington, MO 64067/816-259-2636 (Invis-A-Line bbl.; relining)
LaBounty Precision Reboring, P.O. Box 186, 7968 Silver Lk. Rd., Maple Falls, WA 98266/206-599-2047
Matco, Inc., 126 E. Main St., No. Manchester, IN 46962/219-982-8282
Nu-Line Guns, 1053 Caulks Hill Rd., Harvester, MO 63303/314-441-4500
Redman's Reboring & Rerifling, Route 3, Box 330A, Omak, WA 98841/509-826-5512
Ridgetop Sporting Goods, P.O. Box 306; 42907 Hilligoss Ln. East, Eatonville, WA 98328/206-832-6422
Siegrist Gun Shop, 8752 Turtle Rd., Whittemore, MI 48770/517-873-3929
Snapp's Gunshop, 6911 E. Washington Rd., Clare, MI 48617
J. W. Van Patten, P.O. Box 145, Foster Hill, Milford, PA 18337/717-296-7069
Robt. G. West, 3973 Pam St., Eugene, OR 97402/503-689-6610 (barrel relining)

RELOADING TOOLS AND ACCESSORIES

Activ Industries, Inc., P.O. Box F, 100 Zigor Rd., Kearneysville, WV 25430/304-725-0451 (plastic hulls, wads)
Advance Car Mover Co., Inc., Rowell Div., P.O. Box 1181, 112 N. Outagamie St., Appleton, WI 54912/414-734-1878 (bottom pour lead casting ladles)
American Products Co., 14729 Spring Valley Rd., Morrison, IL 61270/815-772-3336 (12-ga. shot wad)
Ammo Load Inc., 1560 E. Edinger, Suite G, Santa Ana, CA 92705/714-558-8858
Arcadia Machine & Tool (AMT), 536 No. Vincent Ave. Covina, CA 91722/818-915-7803 (Autoscale)
Ballistic Products, Inc., P.O. Box 408, 2105 Daniels St., Long Lake, MN 55356/612-473-1550 (f. shotguns)
Benson Ballistics, Box 3796, Mission Viejo, CA 92690
Colorado Sutlers Arsenal, Box 991, Granby, CO 80446/303-887-2813
B-Square Eng. Co., Box 11281, Ft. Worth, TX 76110/800-433-2909
Ballistic Prods., P.O. Box 488, 2105 Shaughnessy Circle, Long Lake, MN 55356/612-473-1550
Ballistic Research Industries (BRI), 2825 S. Rodeo Gulch Rd. #8, Soquel, CA 95073/408-476-7981 (shotgun slugs)
Belding & Mull, Inc., P.O. Box 428, 100 N. 4th St., Philipsburg, PA 16866/814-342-0607
Berdon Machine Co., P.O. Box 9457, Yakima, WA 98909/509-453-0374 (metallic press)
Bonanza (See: Forster Products)
C-H Tool & Die Corp., 106 N. Harding St., Owen, WI 54460/715-229-2146
Camdex, Inc., 2330 Alger, Troy, MI 48083/313-528-2300
Carbide Die & Mfg. Co., Inc., P.O. Box 226, Covina, CA 91723/213-337-2518
Carter Gun Works, 2211 Jefferson Pk. Ave., Charlottesville, VA 22903
Cascade Cartridge, Inc., (See: Omark)
Cascade Shooters, 63990 Deschutes Mkt. Rd., Bend, OR 97701/503-382-1257 (bull. seating depth gauge)
Chevron Case Master, R.R. 1, Ottawa, IL 61350
Mrs. Lester Coats, 416 Simpson Ave., No. Bend, OR 97459/503-756-6995 (lead wire core cutter)
Colorado Shooter's Supply, P.O. Box 132, Fruita, CO 81521/303-858-9191 (Hoch cust. bull. moulds)
Colorado Sutlers Arsenal, Box 991, Granby, CO 80446/303-887-2813
Container Development Corp., 424 Montgomery St., Watertown, WI 53094
Continental Kite & Key Co., (CONKKO) P.O. Box 40, Broomall, PA 19008/215-356-0711 (primer pocket cleaner)
Cooper-Woodward, 8073 Canyon Ferry Rd., Helena, MT 59601/406-475-3321 (Perfect Lube)
Corbin Mfg. & Supply Inc., 600 Industrial Circle, P.O. Box 2659, White City, OR 97503/503-826-5211
Custom Products, RD #1, Box 483A, Saegertown, PA 16443/814-763-2769 (decapping tool, dies, etc.)
J. Dewey Mfg. Co., 186 Skyview Dr., Southbury, CT 06488/203-264-3064
Dillon Precision Prods., Inc., 7442 E. Butherus Dr., Scottsdale, AZ 85260/602-948-8009
Efemes Enterprises, Box 691, Colchester, VT 05446 (Berdan decapper)
Fitz, Box 171, Douglas City, CA 96024 (Fitz Flipper)
Flambeau Prods. Corp., 15981 Valplast Rd., Middlefield, OH 44062/216-632-1631
Forster Products Inc., 82 E. Lanark Ave., Lanark IL 61046/815-493-6360
Francis Tool Co., P.O. Box 7861, Eugene, OR 97401/503-345-7457 (powder measure)
Freechec' (See: Paco)
Geo. M. Fullmer, 2499 Mavis St., Oakland, CA 94601/415-533-4193 (seating die)
Hanned Precision, P.O. Box 2888, Sacramento, CA 95812/916-381-0986 (22-SGB tool)
Hart Products, Rob W. Hart & Son Inc., 401 Montgomery St., Nescopeck, PA 18635/717-752-3655
Hensley & Gibbs, P.O. Box 10, Murphy, OR 97533 (bullet moulds)
Richard Hoch, The Gun Shop, 62778 Spring Creek Rd., Montrose, CO 81401/303-249-3625 (custom Schuetzen bullet moulds)
Hoffman New Ideas Inc., 821 Northmoor Rd., Lake Forest, IL 60045/312-234-4075 (spl. gallery load press)
Hollywood Loading Tools (See M & M Engineering)
Hornady Mfg. Co., P.O. Drawer 1848, Grand Island, NE 68802/308-382-1390
Hulme see: Marshall Enterprises (Star case feeder)
Huntington, 601 Oro Dam Blvd., Oroville, CA 95965/916-534-1210 (Compact Press)
JACO Precision Co., 11803 Indian Head Dr., Austin, TX 78753/512-836-44180 (JACO precision neck turner)
Javelina Products, Box 337, San Bernardino, CA 92402 (Alox beeswax)
Neil Jones, RD #1, Box 483A, Saegertown, PA 16433/814-763-2769 (decapping tool, dies)
Paul Jones Munitions Systems (See Fitz Co.)
King & Co., Edw. R. King, Box 1242, Bloomington, IL 61701
Lage Uniwad Co., 1814 21st St., Eldora, IA 50627/515-858-2364 (Universal Shotshell Wad)
Leding Loader, R.R. #1, Box 645, Ozark, AR 72949 (conical loadg. acc. f. ML)
Lee Custom Engineering, Inc. (See Mequon Reloading Corp.)
Lee Precision, Inc., 4275 Hwy. U, Hartford, WI 53027/414-673-3075
L. L. F. Die Shop, 1281 Highway 99 N., Eugene, OR 97402/503-688-5753
Ljutic Industries Inc., P.O. Box 2117, 732 N. 16th Ave., Yakima, WA 98907/509-248-0476 (plastic wads)
Lock's Phila. Gun Exch., 6700 Rowland, Philadelphia, PA 19149/215-332-6225
Lyman Products Corp., Rte. 147, Middlefield, CT 06455
McKillen & Heyer Inc., 37603 Arlington Dr., Box 627, Willoughby, OH 44094/216-942-2491 (case gauge)
Paul McLean, 2670 Lakeshore Blvd., W., Toronto, Ont. M8V 1G8 Canada/416-259-3060 (Universal Cartridge Holder)
MEC, Inc. (See Mayville Eng. Co.)
M&M Engineering, 10642 Arminta St., Sun Valley, CA 91352/818-842-8376
MMP, R.R. 6 Box 384, Harrison, AR 72601/501-741-5019 (Tri-Cut trimmer; Power powder trickler)
MTM Molded Products Co., 3370 Obco Ct., P.O. Box 14117, Dayton, OH 45414/513-890-7461
Magma Eng. Co., P.O. Box 161, Queen Creek, AZ 85242/602-987-9008
Marquart Precision Co., P.O. Box 1740, Prescott, AZ 86302/602-445-5646 (precision case-neck turning tool)
Marshall Enterprises, 792 Canyon Rd., Redwood City, CA 94062/415-365-1230 (Hulme autom. case feeder f. Star rel.)
Mayville Eng. Co., 715 South St., Mayville, WI 53050/414-387-4500 (shotshell loader)
Mequon Reloading Corp., P.O. Box 253, Mequon, WI 53092/414-673-3060
Metallic Casting & Copper Corp. (MCC), 214 E. Third St., Mt. Vernon, NY 10550/914-664-1311
Midway Arms Inc., 7450 Old Highway 40 West, Columbia, MO 65201/314-445-9521 (cartridge boxes)
Mo's Competitor Supplies, P.A.S., 34 Delamar Dr., Brookfield, CT 06804 (neck turning tool)
Multi-Scale Charge Ltd., 55 Maitland St. Suite 310, Toronto, Ont. M4Y 1C9, Canada/416-276-6292
Necromancer Industries, Inc., 14 Communications Way, West Newton, PA 15089/412-872-8722 (Compucaster automated bull. casting machine)
Non-Toxic Components, Inc., P.O. Box 4202, Portland, OR 97208/503-226-7110
Normington Co., Box 6, Rathdrum, ID 83858 (powder baffles)
Northeast Industrial Inc., N.E.I., P.O. Box 249, 405 N. Canyon Blvd., Canyon City, OR 97820/503-575-2513 (bullet mould)
Ohaus Scale, (See RCBS)
Old Western Scrounger, 12924 Hwy. A-12, Montague, CA 96064/916-459-5445 (Press f. 50-cal. B.M.G round)
Omark Industries, Box 856, Lewiston, ID 83501/208-746-2351

P&P Tool Co., 125 W. Market St., Morrison, IL 61270/815-772-7618 (12-ga. shot wad)
Pacific Tool Co., P.O. Box 2048, Ordnance Plant Rd., Grand Island, NE 68801/308-384-2308
Paco, Box 17211, Tucson, AZ 85731 (Freechec' tool for gas checks)
Pak-Tool, Roberts Products, 25238 S. E. 32nd, Issaquah, WA 98027/206-392-8172
Pflumm Gun Mfg., 6139 Melrose Ln., Shawnee, KS 66203/913-268-3105 (Drawer Vise)
Pitzer Tool Co., RR #3, Box 50, Winterset, IA 50273/515-462-4268 (bullet lubricator & sizer)
Plum City Ballistics Range, Norman E. Johnson, Rte. 1, Box 29A, Plum City, WI 54761/715-647-2539
Ponsness-Warren, P.O. Box 8, Rathdrum, ID 83858/208-687-2231
Marian Powley, 27131 183 Ave., Eldridge, IA 52748/319-285-9214
Quinetics Corp., P.O. Box 29007, San Antonio, TX 78229/516-684-8561 (kinetic bullet puller)
RCBS (See Omark Industries)
R.D.P. Tool Co. Inc., 49162 McCoy Ave., East Liverpool, OH 43920/216-385-5129 (progressive loader)
Ransom Intl. Corp., P.O. Box 3845, 1040 Sandretto Dr., Suite J, Prescott, AZ 86302/602-778-7899 (Grandmaster progr. loader)
Redding Inc., 1089 Starr Rd., Cortland, NY 13045/607-753-3331
Reloaders Paper Supply, Don Doerksen, P.O. Box 556, Hines, OR 97738/503-573-7060 (reloader's record book)
Rochester Lead Works, 76 Anderson Ave., Rochester, NY 14607/716-442-8500 (leadwire)
Rorschach Precision Prods., P.O. Box 151613, Irving, TX 75015/214-790-3487 (carboloy bull. dies)
SAECO (See Redding)
SSK Industries, Rt. 1, Della Drive, Bloomingdale, OH 43910/614-264-0176
Sandia Die & Cartridge Co., Rte. 5, Box 5400, Albuquerque, NM 87123/505-298-5729
Vernon C. Seeley, Box 6, Osage, WY 82723/307-465-2264 (Osage arbor press)
Shannon Associates, P.O. Box 32737, Oklahoma City, OK 73123
Shooters Accessory Supply, (See Corbin Mfg. & Supply)
Jerry Simmons, 715 Middlebury St., Goshen, IN 46526/219-533-8546 (Pope de- & recapper)
J. A. Somers Co., P.O. Box 49751, Los Angeles, CA 90049 (Jasco)
Sport Flite Mfg., Inc., P.O. Box 1082, Bloomfield Hills, MI 48303/313-647-3747 (swaging dies)
Star Machine Works, 418 10th Ave., San Diego, CA 92101/619-232- 3216
Stuart Products, Inc., P.O. Box 1587, Easley, SC 29641/803-859-9360 (sight vise)
Trammco, Inc., P.O. Box 1258, Bellflower, CA 90706/213-428-5250 (Electra-Jacket bullet plater)
Trico Plastics, 590 S. Vincent Ave., Azusa, CA 91702
Tru Square Metal Products, 640 First St. S.W., P.O. Box 585, Auburn, WA 98002/206-833-2310 (Thumler's tumbler case polishers; Ultra Vibe 18)
Vibra-Tek Co., 1844 Arroya Rd., Colorado Springs, CO 80906/303-634-8611 (brass polisher; Brite Rouge)
Weatherby, Inc., 2781 Firestone Blvd., South Gate, CA 90280/213-569-7186
Weaver Arms Ltd., P.O. Box 3316, Escondido, CA 92025/619-746-2440 (progr. loader)
Webster Scale Mfg. Co., P.O. Box 188, Sebring, FL 33870/813-385-6362
Whitetail Design & Engineering Ltd., 9421 E. Mannsiding Rd., Clare, MI 48617/517-386-3932 (Match Prep primer pocket tool)
Whits Shooting Stuff, P.O. Box 1340, Cody, WY 82414
L. E. Wilson, Inc. P.O. Box 324, 404 Pioneer Ave., Cashmere, WA 98815/509-782-1328

RESTS—BENCH, PORTABLE, ETC.

Armor Metal Products, P.O. Box 4609, Helena, MT 59604/406-442-5560 (portable shooting bench)
B-Square Co., P.O. Box 11281, Ft. Worth, TX 76109/800-433-2909
Cravener's Gun Shop, 1627 - 5th Ave., Ford City, PA 16226/412-763-8312
Decker Shooting Products, 1729 Laguna Ave., Schofield, WI 54476/715-359-5873 (rifle rests)
The Gun Case, 11035 Maplefield, El Monte, CA 91733
Joe Hall's Shooting Products, Inc., 443 Wells Rd., Doylestown, PA 18901/215-345-6354 (adj. portable)
Harris Engineering, Inc., Barlow, KY 42024/502-334-3633 (bipods)
Rob. W. Hart & Son, 401 Montgomery St., Nescopeck, PA 18635
Tony Hidalgo, 12701 S.W. 9th Pl., Davie, FL 33325/305-476-7645 (adj. shooting seat)
J. B. Holden Co., 295 W. Pearl, P.O. Box 320, Plymouth, MI 48170/313-455-4850
Hoppe's Div., Penguin Industries, Inc., Airport Industrial Mall, Coatesville, PA 19320/251-384-6000 (bench rests and bags)
Metro Straight-Shooter, 38 Livonia Ave., Brooklyn, NY 11212/800-443-7734 (shooting bench)
Protektor Model Co., 7 Ash St., Galeton, PA 16922/814-435-2442 (sandbags)
Ransom Intl. Corp., 1040 Sandretto Dr., Suite J, P.O. Box 3845, Prescott, AZ 86302/602-778-7899 (handgun rest)
San Angelo Mfg. Co., 1841 Industrial Ave., San Angelo, TX 76904/915-655-7126
Sharpshooter's Rest, Box 70, Cleveland, MO 64734/816-331-5113 (portable)
Suter's, Inc., House of Guns, 332 N. Tejon, Colorado Springs, CO 80902/303-635-1475
Turkey Creek Enterprises, Rt. 1, Box 65, Red Oak, OK 74563/918-754-2884 (portable shooting rest)
Wichita Arms, 444 Ellis, Wichita, KS 67211/316-265-06612

RIFLE BARREL MAKERS

P.O. Ackley Rifle Barrels (See Dennis M. Bellm Gunsmithing Inc.)
Amimex Inc., 3174 Stimson Way, San Jose, CA 95135/408-274-7816
Jim Baiar, 490 Halfmoon Rd., Columbia Falls, MT 59912/406-892-4409
Bauska Mfg. Corp., P.O. Box 2270, 1694 Whalebone Dr., Kalispell, MT 59901/406-752-8082
Dennis M. Bellm Gunsmithing Inc., 2376 So. Redwood Rd., Salt Lake City, UT 84119/801-974-0697; price list $3 (new rifle bbls., incl. special & obsolete)
Leo Bustani, P.O. Box 8125, West Palm Beach, FL 33407/305-622-2710 (Win.92 take-down; Trapper 357-44 mag. bbls.; SASE f. reply)
Ralph L. Carter, Carter's Gun Shop, 225 G St., Penrose, CO 81240/303-372-6240
J. A. Clerke Co., P.O. Box 627, Pearblossom, CA 93553/805-945-0714
Competition Arms, Inc., 1010 S. Plumer Ave., Tucson, AZ 85719/602-792-1075
Charles P. Donnelly & Son, Siskiyou Gun Works, 405 Kubli Rd., Grants Pass, OR 97527/503-846-6604
Douglas Barrels, Inc., 5504 Big Tyler Rd., Charleston, WV 25313/304-776-1341
David Gentry Custom Gunmaker, 314 N. Hoffman, P.O. Box 1440, Belgrade, MT 59714/406-388-4867
Getz Barrel Co., Box 88, Beavertown, PA 17813/717-658-7263
A. R. Goode, 4125 N.E. 28th Terr., Ocala, FL 32670/904-622-9575
H-S Precision, Inc., 112 N. Summit, Prescott, AZ 86302/602-445-0607
Half Moon Rifle Shop, 490 Halfmoon Rd., Columbia Falls, MT 59912/406-892-4409
Hart Rifle Barrels, Inc., RD 2, Lafayette, NY 13084/315-677-9841
Hastings, Box 224, 822-6th St., Clay Center, KS 67432/913-632-3169 (shotguns ONLY)
Jackalope Gun Shop, 1048 S. 5th St., Douglas, WY 82633/307-358-3441
Terry K. Kopp, Highway 13 South, Lexington, MO 64067/816-259-2636 (22-cal. blanks)
Krieger Barrels, Inc., N114 W18697 Clinton Dr., Germantown, WI 53022/414-255-9593
Lilja Precision Rifle Barrels, Inc., 245 Compass Creek Rd., P.O. Box 372, Plains, MT 59859/406-826-3084
Marquart Precision Co., P.O. Box 1740, Prescott, AZ 86302/602-445-5646
Matco, Inc., 126 E. Main St., No. Manchester, IN 46962/219-982-8282
McMillan Rifle Barrels U.S. International, P.O. Box 3427, Bryan, TX 77805/409-846-3990
Nu-Line Guns, 1053 Caulks Hill Rd., Harvester, MO 63303/314-441-4500
Olympic Arms Inc. dba SGW, 624 Old Pacific Hwy. S.E., Olympia, WA 98503/206-456-3471
John T. Pell Octagon Barrels, (KOGOT), 410 College Ave., Trinidad, CO 81082/719-846-9406
Pence Precision Barrels, RR #2 RD 900S, So. Whitley, IN 48787/219-839-4745
Pennsylvania Arms Co., Box 128, Duryea, PA 18642/717-457-4014 (rifled shotgun bbl. only)
Redman's Rifling & Reboring, Rt. 3, Box 330A, Omak, WA 98841/509-826-5512
Rocky Mountain Rifle Works, Ltd., 1707 14th St., Boulder, CO 80302/303-449-9189
Sanders Cust. Gun Serv., 2358 Tyler Lane, Louisville, KY 40205
Gary Schneider, 12202 N. 62d Pl., Scottsdale, AZ 85254/602-948-2525
SGW, Inc., D. A. Schuetz, 624 Old Pacific Hwy. S.E., Olympia, WA 98503/206-456-3471
E. R. Shaw, dba Small Arms Mfg. Co., Thoms Run Rd. & Prestley, Bridgeville, PA 15017/412-221-4343 (also shotgun bbls.)
Shilen Rifles, Inc., 205 Metro Park Blvd., Ennis, TX 75119/214-875-5318
Shiloh Rifle Mfg. Co., Inc., P.O. Box 279; 201 Centennial Dr., Big Timber, MT 59011/406-932-4454
W. C. Strutz, Rifle Barrels, Inc., P.O. Box 611, Eagle River, WI 54521/715-479-4766
Fred Wells, Wells Sport Store, 110 N. Summit St., Prescott, AZ 86301/602-445-3655
Bob Williams, P.O. Box 143, Boonsboro, MD 21713
Wilson Arms, 63 Leetes Island Rd., Branford, CT 06405/203-488-7297

SCOPES, MOUNTS, ACCESSORIES, OPTICAL EQUIPMENT

A.R.M.S., Inc. (Atlantic Research Marketing Systems), 230 W. Center St., West Bridgewater, MA 02379/617-584-7816 (mounts)
Action Arms Ltd., P.O. Box 9573, Philadelphia, PA 19124/215-744-0100
Adco International, 1 Wyman St., Woburn, MA 01801/617-938-8060 (InterAims Mark V sight)
Aimpoint U.S.A., 203 Elden St., Suite 302, Herndon, VA 22070/703-471-6828 (electronic sight)
Aimtech (See L&S Technologies)
Alley Suppl. Co., P.O. Box 848, Gardnerville, NV 89410/702-782-3800
American Arms, Inc., P.O. Box 27163, Salt Lake City, UT 84127/801-972-5006
The American Import Co., 1453 Mission, San Francisco, CA 94103/415-863-1506
Anderson Mfg. Co., P.O. Box 536, 6813 S. 220th St., Kent, WA 98032/206-872-7602 (lens cap)
Armsport, Inc., 3590 N.W. 49th St., Miami, FL 33122/305-635-7850
Armson, Inc., P.O. Box 2130, Farmington Hills, MI 48018/313-478-2577 (O.E.G.)
Avin Industries Lasersight, 1847 Camino Palmero, Hollywood, CA 90046/213-851-9816 (Laser aiming system)
B-Square Co., Box 11281, Ft. Worth, TX 76109/800-433-2909 (Mini-14 mount)
Bausch & Lomb Inc., 42 East Ave., Rochester, NY 14603/800-828-5423

Beeman Precision Arms, Inc., 3440-GD Airway Dr., Santa Rosa, CA 95403/707-578-7900 (airguns only)
Bennett, 561 Delaware, Delmar, NY 12054/518-439-1862 (mounting wrench)
Browning Arms, Rt. 4, Box 624-B, Arnold, MO 63010
Buehler Scope Mounts, 17 Orinda Highway, Orinda, CA 94563/415-254-3201
Burris Co. Inc., 331 E. 8th St., Box 1747, Greeley, CO 80632/303-356-1670
Bushnell, 300 N. Lone Hill Ave., San Dimas, CA 91773/714-592-8000
Butler Creek Corp., 290 Arden Dr., Belgrade, MT 59714/406-388-1356 (lens caps)
Clear View Mfg. Co., Inc., 413 So. Oakley St., Fordyce, AR 71742/501/352-8557 (SEE-THR mounts)
Colt Firearms, P.O. Box 1868, Hartford, CT 06101/203-236-6311
Compass Instr. & Optical Co., Inc., 104 E. 25th St., New York, NY 10010
Conetrol Scope Mounts, Hwy 123 South, Seguin, TX 78155
Cougar Optics, P.O. Box 115, Groton, NY 13073/607-898-5747
D&H Prods. Co., Inc., 465 Denny Rd., Valencia, PA 16059/412-898-2840 (lens covers)
Del-Sports Inc., Main St., Margaretville, NY 12455/914-586-4103 (Kahles scopes; EAW mts.)
Dickson (See American Import Co.)
Dynamit Nobel-RWS, Inc., 105 Stonehurst Court, Northvale, NJ 07647/201-767-1995
Europtik, Ltd., P.O. Box 319, Dunmore, PA 18509/717-347-6049
Flaig's, Babcock Blvd., Millvale, PA 15209
Freeland's Scope Stands, Inc., 3737 14th, Rock Island, IL 61201/309-788-7449
Griffin & Howe, Inc., 36 West 44th St., Suite 1011, New York, NY 10036/212-921-0980
Griffin & Howe, 33 Claremont Rd., Bernardsville, NJ 07924/201-766-2287
Gun Parts Corp., Box 2, West Hurley, NY 12491/914-679-2419
Heckler & Koch, Inc., 14601 Lee Rd., Chantilly, VA 22021/703-631-2800
H.J. Hermann Leather Co., Rt. 1, P.O. Box 525, Skiatook, OK 74070/918-396-1226 (lens caps)
J.B. Holden Co., 295 W. Pearl, P.O. Box 320, Plymouth, MI 48170/313-455-4850
Imatronic Lasersight, P.O. Box 520, Batavia, IL 60510/312-879-0020 (Laser Sight)
Interarms, 10 Prince St., Alexandria, VA 22313
Paul Jaeger, Inc., P.O. Box 449, 1 Madison Ave., Grand Junction, TN 38039/901-764-6909 (Schmidt & Bender; EAW mts., Noble)
Jason Empire Inc., 9200 Cody, P.O. Box 14930, Overland Park, KS 66214/913-888-0220
Kahles of America, Div. of Del-Sports, Inc., Main St., Margaretville, NY 12455/914-586-4103
Kassnar Imports, Inc., P.O. Box 6097, Harrisburg, PA 17112/717-652-6101
Kenko Intl. Inc., 8141 West I-70 Frontage Rd. No., Arvada, CO 80002/303-425-1200 (optical equipment)
KenPatable Ent. Inc., P.O. Box 19422, Louisville, KY 40219/502-239-5447
Kilham & Co., Main St., Box 37, Lyme, NY 03768/603-795-4112 (Hutson handgun scopes)
Kowa Optimed, Inc., 20001 S. Vermont Ave., Torrance, CA 90502/213-327-1913
Kris Mounts, 108 Lehigh St., Johnstown, PA 15905
Kwik Mount (See KenPatable)
Kwik-Site, 5555 Treadwell, Wayne, MI 48184/313-326-1500
L&S Technologies, Inc., P.O. Box 223, Thomasville, GA 31799 (mount system f. handguns)
Laser Devices, Inc., #5 Hangar Way, Watsonville, CA 95076/408-722-8300 (Laser Sight)
Lasersight Inc., 1847 Camino Palmero, Hollywood, CA 90046/213-851-9816 (Laser aiming system)
E. Leitz, Inc., 24 Link Dr., Rockleigh, NJ 07647/201-767-1100
Leupold & Stevens Inc., P.O. Box 688, Beaverton, OR 97075/503-646-9171
Jake Levin and Son, Inc., 9200 Cody, Overland Park, KS 66214
W.H. Lodewick, 2816 N.E. Halsey, Portland, OR 97232/503-284-2554 (scope safeties)
Lyman Products Corp., Route 147, Middlefield, CT. 06455
Mandall Shooting Supplies, 7150 E. 4th St., Scottsdale, AZ 85252
Marble Arms Co., 420 Industrial Park, Gladstone, MI 49837/906-428-3710
Marlin Firearms Co., 100 Kenna Dr., New Haven, CO 06473
Michaels of Oregon, P.O. Box 13101, Portland, OR 97213 (QD scope covers)
Military Armament Corp., P.O. Box 111, Mt. Zion Rd., Lingleville, TX 76461 (Leatherwood)
Millett Industries, 16131 Gothard St., Huntington Beach, CA 92647/714-842-5575 (mounts)
Mirador Optical Corp., P.O. Box 11614, Marina Del Rey, CA 90295/213-821-5587
Mitchell Arms, Inc., 3411 Lake Center Dr., Santa Ana, CA 92704/714-957-5711
Nikon Inc., 623 Stewart Ave., Garden City, NY 11530/516-222-0200
North American Specialties, 1370 Logan Ave., Suite B, Costa Mesa, CA 92627/714-979-4867 (Leatherwood scopes)
Olympic Arms Inc. dba SGW, 624 Old Pacific Hwy. S.E., Olympia, WA 98503/206-456-3471 (mounts)
Omark Industries (See Weaver)
Orchard Park Enterprise, P.O. Box 563, Orchard Park, NY 14127/716-662-2255 (Saddleproof mounts only)
Pachmayr Ltd., 1875 So. Mountain Ave., Monrovia, CA 91016/818-357-7771
PaycheX Industries, 520 Moore St., Albion, NY 14411/716-589-7787 (mounts)
Pentax Corp., 35 Inverness Dr. E., Englewood CO 80112/303-799-8000 (riflescopes)
Pilkington Gun Co., P.O. Box 1296, Muskogee, OK 74402/918-693-9418 (Q. D. mt.)
Pioneer Marketing & Research Inc., 216 Haddon Ave. Suite 522, Westmont, NJ 08108/609-854-2424 (German Steiner binoculars; scopes)
Ram Line, Inc., 15611 W. 6th Ave., Golden, CO 80401/303-279-0886 (see-thru mt. f. Mini-14)
Ranging, Inc., Routes 5 & 20, East Bloomfield, NY 14443/716-657-6161
Ray-O-Vac, Willson Prod. Div., P.O. Box 622, Reading, PA 19603 (shooting glasses)
Redfield Gun Sight Co., 5800 E. Jewell Ave., Denver, CO 80224/303-757-6411
S & K Mfg. Co., Box 247, Pittsfield, PA 16340/814-563-7808 (Insta-Mount)
SSK Industries, Rt. 1, Della Dr., Bloomingdale, OH 43910/614-264-0176 (bases)
Sanders Cust. Gun Serv., 2358 Tyler Lane, Louisville, KY 40205 (MSW)
Schmidt & Bender, see: Paul Jaeger, Inc.
Seattle Binocular & Scope Repair Co., P.O. Box 46094, Seattle, WA 98146
Shepherd Scope Ltd., Box 189, Waterloo, NE 68069/402-779-2424
Sherwood Intl. Export Corp., 18714 Parthenia St., Northridge, CA 91324/818-349-7600 (mounts)
Shooters Supply, 1120 Tieton Dr., Yakima, WA 98902/509-452-1181 (mount f. M14/M1A rifles)
W.H. Siebert, 22720 S.E. 56th St., Issaquah, WA 98027
Simmons Outdoor Corp., 14205 S.W. 119 Ave., Miami, FL 33186/305-252-0477
Spacetron Inc., Box 84, Broadview, IL 60155(bore lamp)
Springfield Armory, Inc., 420 W. Main St., Genesco, IL 61254/309-944-5631
Steiner binoculars (See Pioneer Marketing & Research)
Stoeger Industries, 55 Ruta Ct., S. Hackensack, NJ 07606/201-440-2700
Supreme Lens Covers, (See Butler Creek) (lens caps)
Swarovski Optik,Div. of Swarovski America Ltd., One Kenny Dr., Cranston, RI 02920/401-463-6400
Swift Instruments, Inc., 952 Dorchester Ave., Boston, MA 02125
Tasco Sales, Inc., 7600 N.W. 26th St., Miami, FL 33122/305-591-3670
Tele-Optics, 5514 W. Lawrence Ave., Chicago, IL 60630/312-283-7757 (optical equipment repair services only; binoculars)
Tele-Optics Inc., P.O. Box 176, 219 E. Higgins Rd., Gilberts, IL 60136/312-426-7444 (spotting scopes)
Thompson/Center Arms, Farmington Rd., P.O. Box 5002, Rochester, NH 03867/603-332-2394 (handgun scope)
Tradewinds, Inc., Box 1191, Tacoma, WA 98401
Trijicon rifle scopes (See Armson, Inc.)
John Unertl Optical Co., 1224 Freedom Rd., Mars, PA 16046/412-776-9700
United Binocular Co., 9043 S. Western Ave., Chicago, IL 60620
Wasp Shooting Systems, Box 241, Lakeview, AR 72642/501-431-5606 (mtg. system f. Ruger Mini-14 only)
Weatherby's, 2781 Firestone, South Gate, CA 90280/213-569-7186
Weaver, Omark Industries, Box 856, Lewiston, ID 83501/208-746-2351
Weaver Scope Repair Service, 1121 Larry Mahan Dr., Suite B, El Paso, TX 79925/915-593-1005
Wide View Scope Mount Corp., 26110 Michigan Ave., Inkster, MI 48141/313-274-1238
Williams Gun Sight Co., 7389 Lapeer Rd., Davison, MI 48423
Boyd Williams Inc., 8701-14 Mile Rd. (M-57),Cedar Springs, MI 49319 (BR)
Carl Zeiss Inc.,Consumer Prods. Div., Box 2010, 1015 Commerce St., Petersburg, VA 23803/804-861-0033

SIGHTS, METALLIC

Accur-Sites, The Jim J. Tembelis Co., Inc., P.O. Box 114, 216 Loper Ct.,Neenah, WI 54956/414-722-0039 (shotgun)
Alley Supply Co., P.O. Box 848, Gardnerville, NV 89410/702-782-3800
Armson, Inc., P.O. Box 2130, Farmington Hills, MI 48018/313-478-2577
Beeman Precision Arms, Inc., 3440-GDD Airway Dr., Santa Rosa, CA 95403/707-578-7900
Behlert Custom Sights, Inc., RD 2 Box 63, Route 611 North, Pipersviflle, PA 18947/215-766-8681
Bo-Mar Tool & Mfg. Co., Rt. 12, Box 405, Longview, TX 75605/214-759-4784
Burris Co., Inc., 331-8th St., P.O. Box 1747, Greeley, CO 80632/303-356-1670
Cherokee Gun Accessories, 4127 Bay St., Suite 226, Fremont, CA 94538/415-471-5770 (Tritium Tacsight)
J. A. Clerke Co., P.O. Box 627, Pearblossom, CA 93553/805-945-0714
Farr Studio, 1231 Robinhood Rd., Greeneville, TN 37743/615-638-8825 (sighting aids—clip-on aperture; the Farr Sight; the Concentrator)
Andy Fautheree, P.O. Box 4607, Pagosa Springs, CO 81157/303-731-5003 ("Calif. Sight" f. ML; must send SASE)
Freeland's Scope Stands, Inc., 3734-14th Ave., Rock Island, IL 61201/309-788-7449
Gun Parts Corp., Box 2, West Hurley, NY 12491/914-679-2417
Paul Jaeger, Inc., P.O. Box 449, 1 Madison Ave., Grand Junction, TN 38039/901-764-6909
James W. Lofland, 2275 Larkin Rd., Boothwyn, PA 19061/215-485-0391 (single shot replica)
Hester Bros. Wholesale Co. (HESCO), Rt. 4, Greenville Rd., Highway 109, La Grange, GA 30240/404-884-4057
Innovision Enterprises, 728 Skinner Dr., Kalamazoo, MI 49001/616-382-1681 (Slug Sights)
Lyman Products Corp., Rte. 147, Middlefield, CT 06455
MMC Co., Inc., 210 E. Poplar, Deming, NM 88030
Marble Arms Corp., 420 Industrial Park, Box 111, Gladstone, MI 49837/906-428-3710
Meprolight Night Sights (See Hester Bros.)
Merit Corp., Dept. GD, P.O. Box 9044, Schenectady, NY 12309/518-346-1420
Millett Ind., 16131 Gothard St., Huntington Beach, CA 92647/714-842-5575
Miniature Mach. Co., 210 E. Poplar, Deming, NM 88030/505-546-2151 (MMC)
Omega Sales, Inc., P.O. Box 1066, Mt. Clemens, MI 48043/313-469-6727
Poly Choke Div., Marble Arms Corp., 420 Industrial Park, Gladstone, MI 49837/906-428-3710
Redfield Gun Sight Co., 5800 E. Jewell St., Denver, CO 80224/303-757-6411
Simmons Gun Specialties, Inc., 700 S. Rodgers Rd., Olathe, KS 66062/913-782-3131
Slug Site Co., Ozark Wilds, Versailles, MO 65084/314-378-6430
Tradewinds, Inc., Box 1191, Tacoma, WA 98401
Wichita Arms, 444 Ellis, Wichita, KS 67211/316-265-0661
Williams Gun Sight Co., 7389 Lapeer Rd., Davison, MI 48423

STOCKS (Commercial and Custom)

Ahlman's Inc., R.R. 1, Box 20, Morristown, MN 55052
Don Allen Inc., HC55, Box 326, Sturgis, SD 57785/605-347-5227
Angelo & Little Custom Gun Stock Wood, N 4026 Sargent St. Spokane, WA 99212/509-926-0794 (blanks only)
Ann Arbor Rod and Gun Co., 1946 Packard Rd., Ann Arbor, MI 48104/313-769-7866
Anton Custom Gunstocks, owner Paul D. Hillmer, 7251 Hudson Heights, Hudson, IA 50643/319-988-3941
Bain & Davis Sporting Goods, Walter H. Little, 307 E. Valley Blvd., San Gabriel, CA 91776/213-283-7449 (cust.)
Joe J. Balickie, Custom Stocks, Rte. 2, Box 56-G, Apex, NC 27502/919-362-5185
Bartas Gunsmithing, 10231 U.S.H.#10, Cato, WI 54206/414-732-4472
Donald Bartlett, 31829-32nd Pl. S.W., Federal Way, WA 98023/206-927-0726
Beeman Precision Arms, Inc., 3440GD Airway Dr., Santa Rosa, CA 95403/707-578-7900 (airguns only)
Dennis M. Bellm Gunsmithing, Inc., 2376 So. Redwood Rd., Salt Lake City, UT 84119/801-974-0697
Al Biesen, West 2039 Sinto Ave., Spokane, WA 99201
Roger Biesen, 5021 W. Rosewood, Spokane, WA 99208/509-328-9340
Stephen L. Billeb, Box 1176, Big Piney, WY 83113/307-276-5627
E.C. Bishop & Son Inc., 119 Main St., Box 7, Warsaw MO 65355/816-438-5121
Gregg Boeke, Rte. 2, Box 149, Cresco, IA 52136/319-547-3746 (cust.)
John M. Boltin, P.O. Box 644, Estill, SC 29918/803-625-4111
Kent Bowerly, Metolious Meadows Dr., H.C.R. Box 1903, Camp Sherman, OR 97730/503-595-6028 (custom)
Larry D. Brace, 771 Blackfoot Ave., Eugene, OR 97404/503-688-1278
Garnet D. Brawley, P.O. Box 668, Prescott, AZ 86301/602-445-4768 (cust.)
Frank Brgoch, #1580 South 1500 East, Bountiful, UT 84010/801-295-1885
A. Briganti, 475 Rt. 32, Highland Mills, NY 10930/914-692-4409
Brown Precision Co., P.O. Box 270GD; 7786 Molinos Ave., Los Molinos, CA 96055/916-384-2506
Jack Burres, 10333 San Fernando Road, Pacoima, CA 91331/818-899-8000 (English, Claro, Bastogne Paradox walnut blanks only)
Calico Hardwoods, Inc., 1648 Airport Blvd., Windsor, CA 95492/707-546-4045 (blanks)
Lou Camilli, 4700 Oahu Dr. N.E., Albuquerque, NM 87111/505-293-5259
Dick Campbell, 20000 Silver Ranch Rd., Conifer, CO 80433/303-697-9150 (custom)
Kevin Campbell, 10152 Trinidad, El Paso, TX 79925/915-592-5496 (cust.)
Larry T. Caudill, 1025A Palomas Dr. S.E., Albuquerque, NM 87108/505-255-2515 (custom)
Shane Caywood, P.O. Box 321, Minocqua, WI 54548/715-356-5414 (cust.)
Winston Churchill, Twenty Mile Stream Rd., RFD, Box 29B, Proctorsville, VT 05153
J. A. Clerke Co., P.O. Box 627, Pearblossom, CA 93553/805-945-0714
Clinton River Gun Serv., Inc., 30016 S. River Rd., Mt. Clemens, MI 48045/313-468-1090
Charles H. Coffin, 3719 Scarlet Ave., Odessa, TX 79762/915-366-4729
Jim Coffin, 250 Country Club Lane, Albany, OR 97321/503-928-4391
David Costa, 94 Orient Ave., Arlington, MA 02174/617-643-9571 (cust.)
Reggie Cubriel, 15610 Purple Sage, San Antonio, TX 78255/512-695-3364 (cust. stockm.)
Custom Gun Guild, 2646 Church Dr., Doraville, GA 30340/404-455-0346
D&D Gun Shop, 363 Elmwood, Troy, MI 48083/313-583-1512 (cust.)
Dahl's Custom Stocks, Rt. 4, Box 558, Lake Geneva, WI 53147/414-248-2464
Homer L. Dangler, Box 254, Addison, MI 49220/517-547-6745
Sterling Davenport, 9611 E. Walnut Tree Dr., Tucson, AZ 85715/602-749-5590
Jack Dever, 8520 N.W. 90, Oklahoma City, OK 73132/405-721-6393
R.H. "Dick" Devereaux, D.D. Custom Rifles, 5240 Mule Deer Dr., Colorado Springs, CO 80919/719-548-8468
William Dixon, Buckhorn Gun Works, Rte. 4 Box 1230, Rapid City, SD 57702/605-787-6289
Dowtin Gunworks (DGW), Rt. 4 Box 930A, Flagstaff, AZ 86001/602-779-1898 (cust.)
Dowtin Imports, Inc., Rt. 4 Box 930A, Flagstaff, AZ 86001/602-779-1989 (blanks—French, Turkish, Kashmir)
Duncan's Gunworks Inc., 1619 Grand Ave., San Marcos, CA 92069/619-727-0515 (cust.)
D'Arcy A. Echols, 164 W. 580 S., Providence, UT 84332/801-753-2367 (cust.)
Jere Eggleston, P.O. Box 50238, Columbia, SC 29250/803-799-3402 (cust.)
Bob Emmons, 238 Robson Road, Grafton, OH 44044 (custom)
Englishtown Sporting Goods Co., Inc., David J. Maxham, 38 Main St., Englishtown, NJ 07726/201-446-7717 (custom)
Ken Eyster Heritage Gunsmiths Inc., 6441 Bishop Rd., Centerburg, OH 43011/614-625-6131 (cust.)
Reinhart Fajen Inc., 1000 Red Bud Dr., P.O. Box 338, Warsaw, MO 65355/816-438-5111
Ted Fellowes, Beaver Lodge, 9245 16th Ave. S.W., Seattle WA 98106/206-763-1698 (cust. ML)
Fiberlite, 601 Lockwood, Houston, TX 77011/713/924-3600 (synthetic)
Fiberpro Inc., 3636 California St., San Diego, CA 92101/619-295-7703 (blanks; fiberglass; Kevlar)
Jerry A. Fisher, 1244-4th Ave. W., Kalispell, MT 59901/406-755-7093
Flaig's Inc., 2200 Evergreen Rd., Millvale, PA 15209/412-821-1717
Flynn's Cust. Guns, P.O. Box 7461, Alexandria, LA 71301/318-455-7130
Donald E. Folks. 205 W. Lincoln St., Pontiac, IL 61764/815-844-7901 (custom trap, Skeet, livebird stocks)
Larry L. Forster, Box 212, 220 First St. N.E., Gwinner, ND 58040/701-678-2475
Fountain Prods., 492 Prospect Ave., W. Springfield, MA 01089 (cust.)
Frank's Custom Rifles, 7521 E. Fairmount Pl., Tucson, AZ 85715/602-885-3901
Freeland's Scope Stands, Inc., 3737 14th Ave., Rock Island, IL 61201/309-788-7449
Game Haven Gunstocks, 13750 Shire Rd., Wolverine, MI 49799/616-525-8238 (Kevlar riflestocks)
Garrett Accur-Lt. D.F.S. Co., P.O. Box 8675, Fort Collins, CO 80524/303-224-3067 (fiberglass)
K. Genecco Gun Works, 10512 Lower Sacramento Rd., Stockton, CA 95210/209-951-0706
Dale Goens, Box 224, Cedar Crest, NM 87008
Goodling's Gunsmithing, R.D.#1, Box 1007, Spring Grove, PA 17632/717-225-3350 (cust.)
Gordie's Gun Shop, Gordon Mulholland, 1401 Fulton St., Streator, IL 61364/815-672-7202 (cust.)
Gary Goudy, 263 Hedge Rd., Menlo Park, CA 94025/415-322-1338 (cust.)
Charles E. Grace, 10144 Elk Lake Rd., Williamsburg, MI 49690/616-264-9483
Roger M. Green & J. Earl Bridges, 435 E. Birch, P.O. Box 984, Glenrock, WY 82637/307-436-9804 (Teyssier French walnut blanks)
Greene's Machine Carving, 17200 W. 57th Ave., Golden, CO 80403 (blanks & custom)
Griffin & Howe, 36 West 44th St., Suite 1011, New York, NY 10036/212-921-0980
Griffin & Howe, 33 Claremont Rd., Bernardsville, NJ 07924/201-766-2287
Guncraft, Inc., 117 W. Pipeline, Hurst, TX 76053/817-282-1464
Gun Parts Corp., Box 2, West Hurley, NY 12491/914-679-2417 (commercial)
Harper's Custom Stocks, 928 Lombrano St., San Antonio, TX 78207/512-732-5780
Robert W. Hart & Son, Inc., 401 Montgomery St., Nescopeck, PA 18635/717-752-3655 (cust.)
Hubert J. Hecht, Waffen-Hecht, P.O. Box 2635, Fair Oaks, CA 95628/916-966-1020
Heppler's Gun Shop, 6000 B Soquel Ave., Santa Cruz, CA 95062/408-475-1235
Keith M. Heppler, 540 Banyan Circle, Walnut Creek, CA 94598/415-934-3509 (cust. rifle)
Warren Heydenberk, Box 354 RD4, Quakertown, PA 18951/215-538-2682
Klaus Hiptmayer, P.O. Box 136, Eastman, Que., J0E 1P0 Canada/514-297-2492
Hoenig & Rodman, 6521 Morton Dr., Boise, ID 83705/208-375-1116 (stock duplicating machine)
Hollis Gun Shop, 917 Rex St., Carlsbad, NM 88220
Corey O. Huebner, 3604 S. 3rd W., Missoula, MT 59801/406-721-9647 (cust.)
Paul Jaeger, Inc., P.O. Box 449, 1 Madison Ave., Grand Junction, TN 38039/901-764-6909
Robert L. Jamison, Rt. 4, Box 200, Moses Lake, WA 98837/509-762-2659 (cust. target)
Jenkins Enterprises, Inc., 12317 Locksley Lane, Auburn, CA 95603/916-823-9652 (custom)
Jim's Gun Shop, James R. Spradlin, 113 Arthur, Pueblo, CO 81004/719-543-9462 (cust.)
Johnson Wood Products, I.D. Johnson & Sons, Rte. #1, Strawberry Point, IA 52076/319-933-4930 (blanks)
Neal G. Johnson, Gunsmithing, Inc., 111 Marvin Dr., Hampton, VA 23666/804-838-8091
David Kartak, SRS Box 3042, South Beach, OR 97366/503-867-4951 (custom)
Don Klein, Rt. 2, P.O. Box 277, Camp Douglas, WI 54618/608-427-6948 (cust.)
Kenneth J. Klingler, P.O. Box 141; Thistle Hill, Cabot, VT 05647/802-426-3811 (carving only)
Richard Knippel, 825 Stoddard Ave., Modesto, CA 95350/209-529-6205 (cust.)
Harry Lawson Co., 3328 N. Richey Blvd., Tucson, AZ 85716/602-326-1117
Frank LeFever Arms & Sons, Inc., R.D.#1, Box 31, Lee Center, NY 13363/315-337-6722
Al Lind, 7821 76th Ave. S.W., Tacoma, WA 98498/206-584-6361 (cust.)
MPI Stocks, P.O. Box 03266, 7011 N. Reno Ave., Portland, OR 97203/503-289-8025 (fiberglass)
Monte Mandarino, 136 Fifth Ave. West, Kalispell, MT 59901/406-257-6208
Dennis McDonald, 8359 Brady St., Peosta, IA 52068/319-556-7940 (cust.)
Stan McFarland, 2221 Idella Ct., Grand Junction, CO 81505/303-243-4704
Bill McGuire, 1600 N. Eastmont Ave., East Wenatchee, WA 98801/509-884-6021
George E. Mathews & Son, Inc., 10224 S. Paramount Blvd., Downey, CA 90241/213-862-6719
Maurer Arms, Carl R. Maurer, 2154-16th St., Akron, OH 44314/216-745-6864
John E. Maxson, 3507 Red Oak Lane, Plainview, TX 79072/806-293-9042
Meadow Industries, P.O. Box 450, Marlton, NJ 08053/609-953-0922
R. M. Mercer, 216 S. Whitewater Ave., Jefferson, WI 53549/414-674-3839
Robt. U. Milhoan & Son, Rt. 3, Elizabeth, WV 26143
Miller Arms, Inc., D. E. Miller, P.O. Box 260, St. Onge, SD 57779/605-578-1790
Miller Gun Works, S.A. Miller, P.O. Box 1053, 1440 Peltier Dr., Point Roberts, WA 98281/206-945-7014
Earl Milliron Custom Guns & Stocks, 1249 N.E. 166th Ave., Portland, OR 97230/503-252-3725
Mitchell Arms, Inc., 3411 Lake Center Dr., Santa Ana, CA 92704/714-957-5711
Monell Custom Guns, Red Mill Road, RD#2, Box 96, Pine Bush, NY 12566/914-744-3021 (custom)
J.W. Morrison Custom Rifles, 4015 W. Sharon, Phoenix, AZ 85029
New England Arms Co., Lawrence Lane, Kittery Point, ME 03905/207-439-0593
Paul R. Nickels, P.O. Box 71043, Las Vegas, NV 89170/702-798-7533
Ted Nicklas, 5504 Hegel Rd., Goodrich, MI 48438/313-797-4493 (custom)
Jim Norman, Custom Gunstocks, 14281 Cane Rd., Valley Center, CA 92082/619-749-6252
Vic Olson, 5002 Countryside Dr., Imperial, MO 63052/314-296-8086 (custom)
Maurice Ottmar, Box 657, 113 E. Fir, Coulee City, WA 99115/509-632-5717
Pachmayr Gun Works, 1220 S. Grand Ave., Los Angeles, CA 90015 (blanks and custom jobs)
Pasadena Gun Center, 206 E. Shaw, Pasadena, TX 77506/713-472-0417
Paulsen Gunstocks, Rte. 71, Box 11, Chinook, MT 59523/406-357-3403 (blanks)
Wallace E. Reiswig, Claro Walnut Gunstock Co., 1235 Stanley Ave., Chico, CA 95928/916-342-5188 (California walnut blanks)
Don Robinson, Pennsylvania Hse., 36 Fairfax Crescent, Southowram, Halifax, W. Yorksh. HX3 9SW, England (blanks only)
Bob Rogers Gunsmithing, P.O. Box 305, 344 S. Walnut St., Franklin Grove, IL 61031/815-456-2685

Royal Arms, 1210 Bert Acosta, El Cajon, CA 92020/619-448-5466
Sanders Cust. Gun Serv., 2358 Tyler Lane, Louisville, KY 40205 (blanks)
Roy Schaefer, 965 W. Hilliard Lane, Eugene, OR 97404/503-688-4333 (commercial blanks)
Schwartz Custom Guns, 9621 Coleman Rd., Haslett, MI 48840/517-339-8939
David W. Schwartz, 2505 Waller St., Eau Claire, WI 54701/715-832-1735
Butch Searcy Co., 15 RD 3804, Farmington, NM 87401/505-327-3419 (cust.)
Shaw's, The Finest in Guns, 9447 W. Lilac Rd., Escondido, CA 92026/619-728-7070 (custom only)
Dan A. Sherk, 9701-17th St., Dawson Creek, B.C. V1G 4H7, Canada/604-782-5630 (custom)
Shogun Mfg. Co., 336 S. 300 East, Provo, UT 84601/801-377-0348 (Convert-A-Stock)
Hank Shows, The Best,1078 Alice Ave., Ukiah, CA 95482/707-462-9060
Sile Dist., 7 Centre Market Pl., New York, NY 10013/213-925-4111
Six Enterprises, 6564 Hidden Creek Dr., San Jose, CA 95120/408-268-8296 (fiberglass)
Ed Sowers, 8331 DeCelis Pl., Unit C, Sepulveda, CA 91343/818-893-1233 (custom hydro-coil gunstocks)
Fred D. Speiser, 2229 Dearborn, Missoula, MT 59801/406-549-8133
Sport Serv. Ctr., 2364 N. Neva, Chicago, IL 60635/312-889-1114 (custom)
Sportsmen's Equip. Co., 915 W. Washington, San Diego, CA 92103/714-296-1501 (carbine conversions)
Keith Stegall, Box 696, Gunnison, CO 81230
Talmage Enterprises, 451 Phantom Creek Lane, P.O. Box 512, Meadview, AZ 86444/602-564-2380
Tiger-Hunt, Michael D. Barton, P.O. Box 214, Jerome, PA 15937/814-479-2215 (curly maple stock blanks)
Trevallion Gunstocks, R.1, Box 39, Kittery Point, ME 03905/207-439-6822 (cust.)
Trinko's Gun Service, 1406 E. Main St., Watertown, WI 53094/414-261-5175
James C. Tucker, 205 Trinity St., Woodland, CA 95695/916-662-3109 (cust.)
Milton van Epps, Rt. 69-A, Parish, NY 13131/315-625-7251
Gil Van Horn, P.O. Box 207, Llano, CA 93544
John Vest, P.O. Box 1552, Susanville, CA 96130/916-257-7228 (classic rifles)
Vic's Gun Refinishing, 6 Pineview Dr., Dover, NH 03820/603-742-0013
Ed von Atzigen, The Custom Shop, 890 Cochrane Cres., Peterborough, Ont. K9H 5N3, Canada/705-742-6693 (cust.)
R. D. Wallace, Star Rt. 1, Box 76, Grandin, MO 63943/314-593-4773 (cust.)
Weatherby's, 2781 Firestone, South Gate, CA 90280/213-569-7186
Cecil Weems, P.O. Box 657, Mineral Wells, TX 76067/817-325-1462
Frank R. Wells, 7521 E. Fairmount Pl., Tucson, AZ 85715/602-885-3901
Fred Wells, 110 N. Summit St., Prescott, AZ 86301/602-445-3655
Terry Werth, 1203 Woodlawn Rd., Lincoln, IL 62656/217-732-1300 (cust.)
Robert G. West, 3973 Pam St., Eugene, OR 97402/503-689-6610
Western Gunstocks Mfg. Co., 550 Valencia School Rd., Aptos, CA 95003
Duane Wiebe, P.O. Box 497, Lotus, CA 95651
Bob Williams, P.O. Box 143, Boonsboro, MD 21713
Williamson-Pate Gunsmith Service, 117 W. Pipeline, Hurst, TX 76053/817-282-1464
Jim Windish, 2510 Dawn Dr., Alexandria, VA 22306/703-765-1994 (walnut blanks)
David W. Wills, 2776 Brevard Ave., Montgomery, AL 36109/305-272-8446
Robert M. Winter, R.R. 2, Box 484, Menno, SD 57045/605-387-5322
Wisner's Gun Shop Inc., P.O. Box 58; Hiway 6, Adna, WA 98552/206-748-8942
Mike Yee, 29927-56 Pl. S., Auburn, WA 98001/206-839-3991
Russell R. Zeeryp, 1601 Foard Dr., Lynn Ross Manor, Morristown, TN 37814
Dean A. Zollinger, Rt. 2, Box 135-A, Rexburg, ID 83440/208-356-6167

TARGETS, BULLET & CLAYBIRD TRAPS

Beeman Precision Arms, Inc., 3440-GD Airway Dr., Santa Rosa, CA 95403/707-578-7900 (airguns only)
Caswell International Corp. Inc., 1221 Marshall St. N.E., Minneapolis, MN 55413/612-379-2000 (target carriers; commercial shooting ranges)
J.G. Dapkus Co., P.O. Box 180, Cromwell, CT 06416/203-632-2308 (live bull-seye targets)
Data-Targ, (See Rocky Mountain Target Co.)
Detroit-Armor Corp., Detroit Bullet Trap Div., 2233 N. Palmer Dr., Schaumburg, IL 60103/312-397-4070 (Shooting Ranges)
The Dutchman's Firearms Inc., 4143 Taylor Blvd., Louisville, KY 40215/502-366-0555
Ellwood Epps Northern Ltd., 210 Worthington St., W., North Bay, Ont. P1B 3B4, Canada (hand traps)
Hunterjohn, P.O. Box 477, St. Louis, MO 63166 (shotgun patterning target)
Jaro Manuf., 206 E. Shaw, Pasadena, TX 77506/713-472-0417 (paper targets)
Millard F. Lerch, Box 163, 10842 Front St., Mokena, IL 60448 (bullet target)
MCM (Mathalienne de Construction Mecanique), P.O. Box 18, 17160 Matha, France (claybird traps)
MTM Molded Prods. Co., 3370 Obco Ct., Dayton, OH 45414/513-890-7461
Maki Industries, 26-10th St. S.E., Medicine Hat, AB T1A 1P7, Canada/403-526-7997 (X-Spand Target System)
Outers Laboratories, Div. of Omark Industries, Rte. 2, Onalaska, WI 54650/608-783-1515 (claybird traps)
Peterson Instant Targets, Inc., P.O. Box 755, Bethel, CT 06801/203-791-0456 (paste-ons; Targ-Dots)
Phillips Enterprises, Inc., 3600 Sunset Ave., Ocean, NJ 07712/201-493-3191 (portable target holder)
Remington Arms Co., 1007 Market St., Wilmington, DE 19898 (claybird traps)
Rocky Mountain Target Co., P.O. Box 700, Black Hawk, SD 57718/605-787-5946 (Data-Targ)
Julio Santiago, P.O. Box O, Rosemount, MN 55068/612-890-7631 (targets)
Sheridan Products, Inc., 2600 Chicory Rd., Racine, WI 54303/414/554-7900 (traps)
Trius Prod., Box 25, Cleves, OH 45002/513-914-5682 (claybird, can thrower)
U.S. Repeating Arms Co., P.O. Box 30-300, New Haven, CT 06511/203-789-5000 (claybird traps)
Winchester, Olin Corp., 120 Long Ridge Rd., Stamford, CT 06904

TAXIDERMY

Jack Atcheson & Sons, Inc., 3210 Ottawa St., Butte, MT. 59701
Dough's Taxidermy Studio, Doug Domedion, 5112 Edwards Rd., Medina, NY 14103/716-798-4022 (deer head specialist)
Jonas Bros., Inc., 1037 Broadway, Denver, CO 80203 (catlg. $2)
Kulis Freeze-Dry Taxidermy, 725 Broadway Ave., Bedford, OH 44146
Mark D. Parker, 8811 Rogers Rd., Longmont, CO 80501/303-772-0214

TRAP & SKEET SHOOTERS EQUIP.

The American Import Co., 1453 Mission St., San Francisco, CA 94103/415-863-1506 (Targetthrower; claybird traps)
Anton Custom Gunstocks, owner Paul D. Hillmer, 7251 Hudson Heights, Hudson, IA 50643/319-988-3941
Briley Mfg. Co., 1085-B Gessner, Houston, TX 77055/713-932-6995 (choke tubes)
C&H Research, 115 Sunnyside Dr., Lewis, KS 67552/316-324-5445 (Mercury recoil suppressor)
D&H Prods. Co., Inc., 465 Denny Rd., Valencia, PA 16059/412-898-2840 (snap shell)
Euroarms of America, Inc., 1501 Lenoir Dr.; P.O. Box 3277, Winchester, VA 22601/703-662-1863
Frigon Guns, 627 W. Crawford, Clay Center, KS 67432/913-632-5607
Griggs Products, P.O. Box 789; 270 S. Main St., Suite 103, Bountiful, UT 84010/801-295-9696 (recoil redirector)
Ken Eyster Heritage Gunsmiths, Inc., 6441 Bishop Rd., Centerburg, OH 43011/614-625-6131 (shotgun competition choking)
Hoppe Division, Penguin Inds. Inc., Airport Mall, Coatesville, PA 19320/215-384-6000 (Monte Carlo pad)
Hunter Co., Inc., 3300 W. 71st Ave., Westminster, CO 80030/303-427-4626
Ljutic Industries Inc., P.O. Box 2117; 732 N 16th Ave., Yakima, WA 98907/509-248-0476
MCM (Mathalienne de Construction de Mecanique), P.O. Box 18, 17160 Matha, France (claybird traps)
Meadow Industries, P.O. Box 450, Marlton, NJ 08053/609-953-0922 (stock pad, variable; muzzle rest)
Wm. J. Mittler, 290 Moore Dr., Boulder Creek, CA 95006/408-338-3376 or 408-438-7331 (shotgun choke specialist)
Moneymaker Guncraft, 1420 Military Ave., Omaha, NE 68131/402-556-0226 (free-floating, ventilated ribs)
William J. Nittler, 111 Bean Creek Rd., Scotts Valley, CA 95066/408-438-7331 (shotgun barrel repairs)
Jim Noble Co., 1305 Columbia St., Vancouver, WA 98660/206-695-1309
Outers Laboratories, Div. of Omark Industries, Route 2, Onalaska, WI 54650/608-783-1515 (trap, claybird)
Protektor Model Co., 7 Ash St., Galeton, PA 16922/814-435-2442
Remington Arms Co., P.O. Box 1939, Bridgeport, Ct. 06601 (trap, claybird)
Daniel Titus, Shooting Specialties, 872 Penn St., Bryn Mawr, PA 19010/215-525-8829 (hullbag)
Trius Products, Box 25, Cleves, OH 45002/513-941-5682 (can thrower; trap, claybird)
Winchester-Western, New Haven, CT 06504 (trap, claybird)
Zeus International, P.O. Box 953, Tarpon Springs, FL 34688/813-863-5029

TRIGGERS, RELATED EQUIP.

Brownells, Inc., 222 W. Liberty, Montezuma, IA 50171/515-623-5401
M.H. Canjar Co., 500 E. 45th Ave., Denver, CO 80216/303-295-2638 (triggers)
Central Specialties Co., 200 Lexington Dr., Buffalo Grove, IL 60089/312-537-3300 (trigger locks only)
Crown City Arms, Inc., P.O. Box 550, Cortland, NY 13045/607-753-8238
Custom Products, Neil A. Jones, RD #1, Box 483A, Saegertown, PA 16433/814-763-2769 (trigger guard)
Cycle Dynamics Inc., 74 Garden St., Feeding Hills, MA 01030/413-786-0141
Dayton-Traister Co., 4778 N. Monkey Hill Rd., Oak Harbor, WA 98277/206-675-3421 (triggers)
Electronic Trigger Systems, 4124 Thrushwood Lane, Minnetonka, MN 55345/612-935-7829
Flaig's, 2200 Evergreen Rd., Millvale, PA 15209/412-821-1717 (trigger shoes)
Gun Parts Corp., Box 2, West Hurley, NY 12491/914-679-2419
Bill Holmes, Rt. 2, Box 242, Fayetteville, AR 72701/501-521-8958 (trigger release)
Neil A. Jones, see: Custom Products
Meier Works, Steve Hines, Box 328, Canyon, TX 79015/806-655-7806 (shotgun trigger guard)
Miller Single Trigger Mfg. Co., R.D. 1, Box 99, Millersburg, PA 17061/717-692-3704 (selective or non-selective f. shotguns)
Bruce A. Nettestad, Rt. 1, Box 140, Pelican Rapids, MN 56572/218-863-4301 (trigger guards)
Pachmayr Ltd., 1875 So. Mountain Ave., Monrovia, CA 91016/818-357-7771 (trigger shoe)
Pacific Tool Co., P.O. Box 2048, Ordnance Plant Rd., Grand Island, NE 68801 (trigger shoe)
Serrifile Inc., P.O. Box 508, Littlerock, CA 93543/805-945-0713
Timney Mfg. Co., 3065 W. Fairmount Ave., Phoenix, AZ 85017/602-274-2999 (triggers)
Melvin Tyler Mfg.-Dist., 1326 W. Britton Rd., Oklahoma City, OK 73114/405-842-8044 (trigger shoe)
U.S.F.S. (United States Frame Specialists), P.O. Box 7762, Milwaukee, WI 53207/414-643-6387
Williams Gun Sight Co., 7389 Lapeer Rd., Davison, MI 48423 (trigger shoe)

Highlights of This Issue

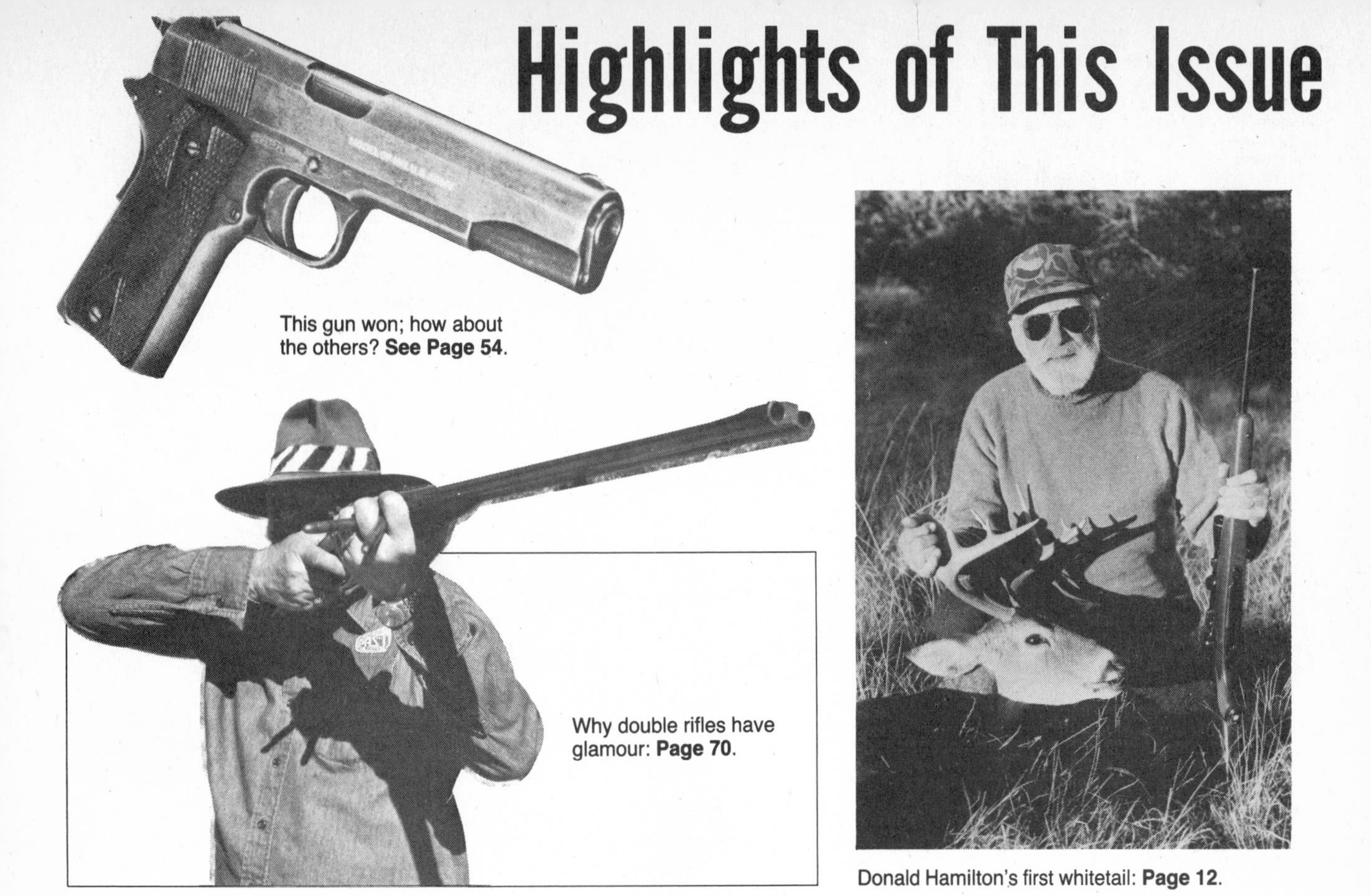

This gun won; how about the others? **See Page 54**.

Why double rifles have glamour: **Page 70**.

Donald Hamilton's first whitetail: **Page 12**.

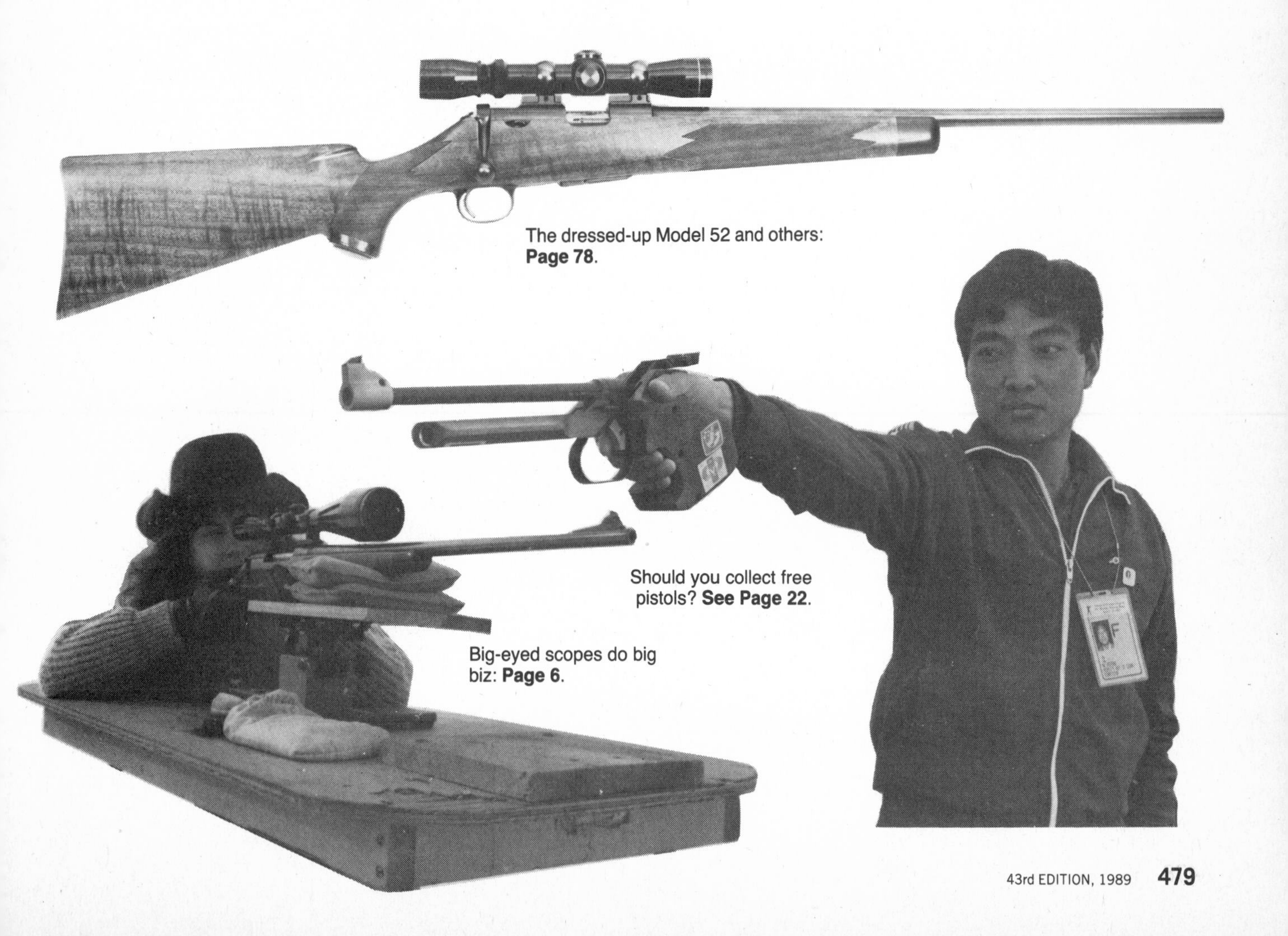

The dressed-up Model 52 and others: **Page 78**.

Should you collect free pistols? **See Page 22**.

Big-eyed scopes do big biz: **Page 6**.

Highlights of This Issue

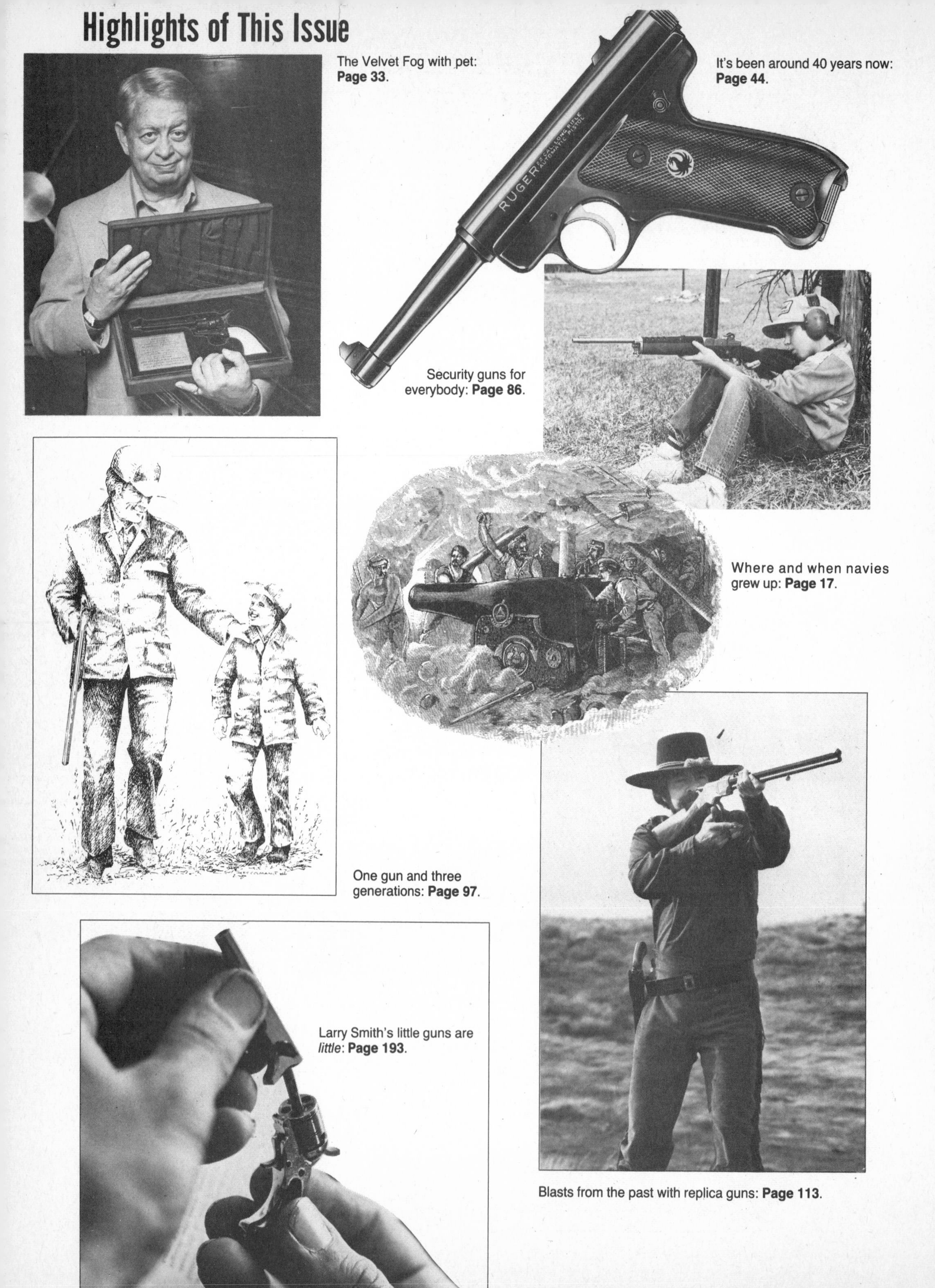

The Velvet Fog with pet: **Page 33**.

It's been around 40 years now: **Page 44**.

Security guns for everybody: **Page 86**.

Where and when navies grew up: **Page 17**.

One gun and three generations: **Page 97**.

Larry Smith's little guns are *little*: **Page 193**.

Blasts from the past with replica guns: **Page 113**.

MW00452261

ULTIMATE GARDENING

A Complete Guide to Cultivating Your Perfect Garden, from Flowers, Vegetables, and Herbs to Succulents, Shrubs, and More

From the staff of GARDENING KNOW HOW
Complied and edited by
NANCY J. HAJESKI
with LISA PURCELL, FINN MOORE,
and MAIA CORNISH-KEEFE

San Diego, California

Contents

FOREWORD

HAPPY GARDENING!

We at Gardening Know How are very pleased to introduce you to our first print publication, *Gardening Know How: Ultimate Gardening*. In this book, you'll find all our combined knowledge and expertise, a wealth of information, and resources from our team of passionate gardeners.

Collectively, we've gardened in every region of the United States and many parts of the world, too. We have expertise in a wide range of topics, from creating native gardens and wildlife habitats to small-space edible gardening, houseplants, and more.

Here at Gardening Know How, we're on a mission to turn the whole world into gardeners. We're passionate about gardening and all the benefits it provides: community connection; wildlife habitat; pollinator protection; delicious, nutritious food; beauty; and, most especially, joy! Gardeners today are even contributing to the fight against climate change through regenerative gardening and other practices. We truly believe the world is a better place with more gardeners in it.

Each year, millions of gardeners visit our website to find the information and inspiration they need to achieve the garden of their dreams. And now, you can do the same with this comprehensive guide that covers all things gardening, from A to Z. Whether you're an apartment dweller with an affection for houseplants, a novice gardener putting in your first annual flowers, or a master gardener looking to learn how to transform your veggie harvest into delicious meals, you'll find everything you need right here.

And to ensure that you'll always have access to the most up-to-date information, we've added links and QR codes throughout the book that will connect you directly to our videos, guides, and other content on our website that allow you to "Dig Deeper" on any topic within these covers.

We know how dirt feels between our fingers, how thrilling it can be to see your first seedling or blossom of the year appear and how good it tastes to bite into that fresh fruit you just picked from your very own garden. And because we're gardeners too, our goal is simple: we want to make sure you get to experience that too! We hope this book brings you many, many hours of fun-filled and productive gardening.

As always, Happy Gardening!

Peggy Doyle, CEO &
Heather Rhoades, Owner
GARDENING KNOW HOW

Gardening Know How has brought together talented individuals who bring their wealth of experience and expertise to both the website and this book. Meet the team (starting at top row, left): 1. Caroline Bloomfield, 2. Allie Kerkhoff, 3. Liz Baessler, 4. Heather Rhoades, 5. Uwe Kerkhoff, 6. Erica Dame, 7. Nikki Tilley, 8. Kyle McCann, 9. Amy Draiss, 10. Peggy Doyle, 11. Sean Collins, 12. Laura Walters.

GARDENING KNOW HOW is more than a simple website. Along with informative articles on just about every aspect of gardening, GARDENING KNOW HOW offers expert-led courses and workshops (top), inspiring "Backyard Stories" of transformed spaces and innovative ideas, (middle, lower left), Video How-To's (lower right), and so much more.

INTRODUCTION

FROM TINY SEEDS DO MIGHTY GARDENS GROW . . .

Many gardeners will admit that gardening can become an addiction. The act of putting hard, fertile little nubs in the ground and over time watching them produce flowers, fruits, vegetables, herbs, succulents, shrubs, and even trees, provides so miraculous a result that they want to replicate it over and over. Plus, this astonishment at the simple process of growing something from almost nothing really never wanes. Seasoned horticulturalists are just as pleased when their planting beds flourish as novice gardeners are proudly observing their first crop of tomatoes.

Gardens require a fair amount of work, especially in the early days, when a layout or design needs to be created, soil requires tilling and amending, and the seeds or seedlings need to go into the ground. Yet gardens give back freely, yielding flowers for display, produce and herbs for the table, shrubs and trees for shade, and a bounty of seeds so that you can start the whole process over again the following spring.

One thing that most gardeners share—besides telltale dirt under their fingernails and way too many zucchinis—is their fondness for reading books on gardening. Even the old pros like to leaf through the pages seeking tips and tricks from other gardeners or gardening writers . . . and that is where the editors of the GARDENING KNOW HOW website come in. They have plumbed their backgrounds on all aspects of gardening to help create a comprehensive, richly illustrated guide for gardeners of all levels.

GET THE DIRT ON GARDENS

In this guidebook, readers will not only discover the basics of starting a garden from scratch but also gain ideas for designs that work within an existing landscape. They will learn how to water, feed, and harvest their plants, as well as find out the steps for testing and amending soil with organic matter and for finishing off beds with mulch.

Here you will find entire chapters devoted to cultivating successful flower gardens, kitchen gardens, herb gardens, succulents, and shrubs. Each of the profile pages devoted to a specific plant includes an At a Glance box with basic statistics and growing guidelines.

In the chapter on garden problems, you will encounter the major weeds, insect and animal pests, and diseases

A garden starts with hard work—getting down on your knees and digging in the dirt to give your plants a chance to grow and thrive.

A garden in bloom is restorative to the soul, but it is not just about nurturing thriving plants. Gardens are also spaces to let our imaginations run free, spaces in which to create unique enviroments that let us express ourselves, no matter our individual styles.

that can afflict your plants, along with some effective solutions that don't always require the use of toxic chemicals. There are also chapters on embellishing your garden with structures, sheds, pathways, lighting, furniture, fire pits, cooking areas, lounging areas, and those perennial favorites, water features, which covers fountains, bubblers, ponds, reflection pools, streams, and waterfalls.

Gardeners now know the benefits of attracting pollinators to the yard, and in light of this you will be introduced to three major players—bees, butterflies, and birds, especially hummingbirds. All the amenities you need to provide are here, as well as a list and photos of the top flowers that will bring them onto your property.

Finally, the editors of GARDENING KNOW HOW turn to the indoor garden, offering helpful overviews of houseplant maintenance, pests and diseases, and even a section on how to best display and light your beauties. More than two dozen listings cover indoor plants that require high-to-medium light and those that do well in low light.

Throughout this guide you will find feature spreads on topics that include garden styles, specialty gardens, native plants, beneficial weeds and wildflowers, lawn alternatives, ornamental grasses, ground covers, garden trees, ferns, cacti, onions, roses, and orchids. Many of these features include colorful galleries that showcase examples of the plants under discussion. Look for hands-on projects to work on with children, too.

The staff at GARDENING KNOW HOW has also contributed a number of special boxes with those rare nuggets of information that gardeners love, including helpful Staff Hacks, Editor's Tips, and Editor's Picks, as well as Dig Deeper guides—with QR codes and URLs—that refer readers to similar topics on their website.

PART ONE

The Outdoor Gardener

CHAPTER ONE

LEARNING THE BASICS

There is much joy to be taken from creating a garden, yet there is a lot more to the endeavor than poking a hole in the ground and dropping in a seedling or two. Before the garden even takes shape, the gardener must evaluate a number of factors that will affect the outcome at the end of the growing season. The three main elements to consider are soil—the quality of the growing medium found at the garden site; location—the spot you choose to create your garden, which includes not only soil but also the amount of sunlight, topographic features, aspect, drainage, and level of moisture; and climate—which includes issues like rainfall, temperature, length of growing season, harshness of winters, and weather events. A better understanding of soil, location, and climate will increase your chances of achieving the garden of your dreams.

SOIL BASICS

The success or failure of a garden, any type of in-ground garden, depends on many factors—sunlight, location, climate, pests, diseases, and level of care. But arguably the most critical of these factors is soil quality.

Soil furnishes growing plants with nutrients, water, and air. It allows for healthy root systems and multiplication of bulbs, tubers, or corms. Put simply, poor soil produces poor plants. Rich, dark loam may be every gardener's wish, but few ever are blessed with it from the start. Instead, the typical plot of ground has its own blend of minerals and organic and inorganic matter that largely determines which crops, shrubs, or trees can be successfully grown there. Enrichment is the solution for creating a more forgiving plot. Although conditioning soil is a continuous process that takes patience and hard work, this labor will pay off in healthy foliage, beautiful blooms, and bountiful harvests. But first, you need to determine what type of soil you are dealing with and what its pH level is.

SOIL TYPES

Soil is categorized into six types: clay, sand, silt, peat, chalk, and loam. Each type is based on the dominating size of the particles within a soil. The first three types are those most commonly found by gardeners. See box below for descriptions of the six types.

Clay soil

Clay soil feels lumpy and sticky when wet and rock hard when dry. It lacks drainage but is full of nutrients. When enhanced, this soil will support development and growth of perennials and shrubs, such as aster, bergamot, and flowering quince; summer crop vegetables, which end up high-yielding vigorous plants in clay; and fruit trees, ornamental trees, and shrubs. (Early vegetables are difficult to grow in clay soil because of its cool, compact nature.)

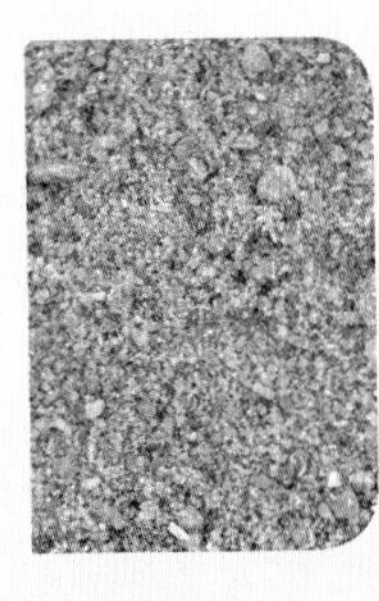

Sandy soil

Sandy soil feels gritty; it drains easily, dries out quickly, and is easy to cultivate. It warms up fast in spring, but holds fewer nutrients, which can wash away during wet spells. Add organic amendments like glacial rock dust, greensand, and kelp meal, and be sure to mulch. Sandy soil supports shrubs and bulbs like tulips and hibiscus; root crops like carrots and potatoes; and lettuce, strawberries, peppers, corn, squash, and tomatoes.

Silty soil

Silty soil is soft and somewhat "soapy." It retains moisture well and is frequently rich in nutrients. Easily cultivated, it can be compacted with little effort. Adding composted organic matter will improve drainage and structure while adding nutrients. The resulting great garden soil will support shrubs, climbers, grasses, and perennials such as New Zealand flax; moisture-loving trees such as willow, birch, dogwood, and cypress; and most vegetable and fruit crops.

Peaty soil

Peaty soil is dark, damp, and spongy due to higher levels of peat (partially decayed vegetation). This acidic soil slows down decomposition, which leads to fewer nutrients. It heats up quickly in spring and can retain water, which requires drainage. Blend peaty soil with organic matter and compost, as well as lime to reduce acidity. Peat supports shrubs like heather, witch hazel, and azalea, and vegetables such as brassicas, legumes, and root crops.

Chalky soil

Chalky soil is large grained and often stony. It drains freely and usually overlays chalk or limestone bedrock. Because the soil is alkaline, it can cause stunted growth and yellowish leaves. Using appropriate fertilizers and balancing the pH will help. Adding humus improves water retention and workability. Chalky soil supports trees, bulbs, and shrubs, such as lilac, weigela, Madonna lilies, pinks, and mock orange; and vegetables like spinach, beets, sweet corn, and cabbage.

Loamy soil

Loamy soil, a mix of sand, silt, and clay, is fine-textured, slightly damp, and tends to be acidic. Its desirable qualities include great structure, adequate drainage, moisture retention, nutrients, and easy cultivation. It warms up quickly in spring yet resists drying out in summer. Adding organic nutrients is essential to soil vitality. Loam supports climbers, perennials, shrubs, and tubers such as wisteria, dog's-tooth violets, *Rubus*, and delphinium, and most vegetable and berry crops.

Four Aspects of Garden Soil

In addition to general soil types, there are other aspects you should consider when garden soil quality needs improvement.

1. Tilth. This is the soil's physical condition and larger-scale structure. It includes whether or not the soil has aggregates (clumps) and what size they are, whether it has channels where water can enter and drain, and its level of aeration. Soil with good tilth provides a structure that supports healthy root growth.

2. Water-holding capacity. This is partially a function of the soil type, but there are other things that alter it. Ideally, soil should be well drained but hold enough water to support healthy plant growth.

3. Nutrient-holding capacity. This term refers to the soil's ability to hold onto minerals that plants use as nutrients. Clay soils, with their greater nutrient holding capacity, have the potential to be very fertile. They may need work, however, to overcome their tendency to become compacted or clumpy.

4. Percentage of organic matter. This is very important in promoting biological activity in the soil; it affects the water and nutrient-holding capacity and the tilth.

DETERMINING SOIL TYPE

There are a number of simple tests you can perform at home that will help determine your soil type. The results will guide you when it comes time to add amendments.

Water test

Pour water onto a bare spot of soil. If it drains quickly, that indicates sandy or gravelly soil. With clay soils, the water will take its time sinking in.

Squeeze test

Scoop up a handful of soil and softly compress it in your fist. If the soil is sticky and slick to the touch and remains in the same shape when you release the pressure, it is clay soil. If the soil feels spongy, it's peaty soil. Sandy soil feels gritty and easily crumbles apart. Loamy and silty soils feel smooth textured and hold their shape for a short period of time.

Squeezing a handful of soil is a simple method of determining a garden's soil type.

Settle test

Add a handful of soil to a transparent container, add water, and shake it well. Leave the soil to settle for at least 12 hours.

- *Clay and silty soils.* These produce cloudy water with a layer of particles at the bottom.
- *Sandy soils.* These leave the water mostly clear, and the particles will form a layer at the bottom of the container.
- *Peaty soils.* These show many particles floating on the surface; the water will be slightly cloudy with only a thin layer at the bottom.
- *Chalky soils.* These leave a layer of whitish, gritty fragments on the bottom, and the water will be a pale gray.
- *Loam.* This leaves the water quite clear, with layered particles at the bottom.

TESTING SOIL FOR PH AND NUTRIENTS

Two important factors of soil are its pH level and its primary nutrients.

Testing for pH

The standard pH for soils ranges between 4.0 and 8.5. Most plants prefer soil that has a pH between 6.5 and 7—the level at which nutrients and minerals tend to thrive. You can buy a pH testing kit from a local garden center or order one online. Generally speaking, in regions with soft water your garden will have acid soil; hard water areas will likely have alkaline soil.

READ MORE AT GARDENING KNOW HOW

Find out more about soil by following the URL or QR code.

- **"Anti-depressant Microbes: How Dirt Makes You Happy"** (URL = gkh.us/60021)

Some pH meters are simple gauges of pH level, while others will also digitally indicate moisture and sunlight levels.

Testing for nutrients

A soil test kit allows you to assess the primary nutrients nitrogen, phosphorus, and potassium (N-P-K), as well as pH levels. By determining its exact condition, you can fertilize more effectively and economically. Test periodically throughout the growing season.

LOCATION

Before selecting a garden plot, consider the factors that will affect your plants—things like sunlight, wind, drainage, access to water, foot traffic patterns—as well as the visual balance between the placement of lawn, shrubs, flowers, and vegetables.

Location-wise, your choices of where to plant your garden are limited by the extent of your property. And if your region has clay soil, chances are that is what you'll be dealing with. If tall trees shade the entire yard, that is your lot, literally. On the other hand, if the sun beats down upon the lawn without a lick of shade, at least you can plant several saplings and begin to add some cover. Likewise, there are other solutions to problem locations: hilly terrain can be terraced, lackluster flat terrain can be built up into berms or raised beds. Dry terrain can be irrigated for flowering plants or produce or turned into a drought-resistant xeriscape that uses hardy ground covers and alpine plants instead of grass. For every challenge your yard may present, there is some way for a clever and resourceful gardener to ameliorate it.

You must also deal with the question of size, of determining how large your garden should be. Maybe it's better to have one small garden in a sunny location and a larger shade garden situated under a row of trees. That way you've created two spots of interest. For a produce garden, placement near the kitchen is ideal, but sunlight trumps proximity to the house when it comes to the needs of most vegetables and fruit. If the sunniest spot is out near the garage, that's where the produce garden goes.

AVAILABLE LIGHT

The level of sunlight varies from season to season, sometimes even hour to hour—as the sun moves across the sky, the quality of the light changes, often softening, even in a sunny garden. Similarly, a shady garden will get dappled sunlight peeking through the tree canopy at some point.

The sunny yard

You are to be envied if your yard enjoys more than six hours of sunshine. Some of the most beautiful garden plants and many key crops require full sun. Sun-loving perennials include daisy, coreopsis, purple coneflower, lavender, sedum, daylily, bee balm, lamb's ear, artemisia, dianthus, and hibiscus. Consider them candidates for planting in an island bed. Annuals that do well in sun include petunia, ageratum, geranium, salvia, marigold, portulaca, sunflower, and zinnia. Use them to fill in the fronts of your borders. Sun-loving produce includes tomatoes, corn, green beans, cucumbers, okra, melons, sweet potatoes, pumpkins, zucchini, eggplant, and jalapeño peppers. Herbs that like to bask in full sun include basil, tarragon, dill, lavender, chives, echinacea, and stevia.

The shady yard

Do not despair if much of your yard is overhung with trees or shadowed by buildings. An ever-increasing number of attractive shade plants are available at garden centers, along with new varieties of familiar shade standbys like hosta and coral bells. You can also look into the many popular plants that thrive in semi-shade. Just determine which areas of your shady yard are sprinkled with sunlight, and you're ready to dig.

The key factors of a location's available light, topography, aspect, and drainage will determine what kinds of plants will grow there. Yet any plantings can be a good thing: home gardeners can play a part in reducing the emissions of greenhouse gases and encourage soil and plants to absorb carbon dioxide and help decrease global warming.

TOPOGRAPHY

The literal ups and downs of your landscape can make gardening . . . interesting. But a wise gardener soon learns to make the most of a rocky hillside or parched plateau. Your topography also affects the type of sunlight you receive. In temperate regions the sun does not position itself directly overhead, even at noon, so its rays tend to fall more or less perpendicular to a slope, and with some intensity. On flat ground, however, the sun's rays are dissipated across a wider area, so their strength is diluted.

Your garden's terrain can dictate the kind of garden you can create. For hillside terrain, the angle of the sun will determine which plants will thrive.

Uphill battles

Some of the world's most interesting gardens have been planted on craggy hillsides. Landscaping aids such as railroad ties, concrete retaining stones, even bricks, can create a terraced garden that invites the eye to travel upward from layer to layer. Tiered plantings of flowers, grasses, and shrubs also prevent soil erosion and, when mulched, can help retain moisture. Plants with root systems that help preserve soil in hilly conditions include ivy, vinca, creeping juniper, creeping phlox, and forsythia. Coir netting or windbreaks can also be used to keep soil in place on especially windy terraces.

Choosing plants that help keep soil erosion in check is smart and eco-friendly. Ground covers, such as creeping phlox, look gorgeous while controlling erosion.

On the level

If your lawn is flat and lacks any interesting contours, consider creating a raised berm, an island garden with an elevated center, or a dry stream bed of tumbled rocks and alpine plants that will add texture to the space. A flat lawn would make an ideal place for installing raised beds . . . or creating a Japanese-style garden with raked sand, artfully placed rocks, and simple, elegant plantings.

ASPECT

The aspect of a garden refers to which direction the plants face in terms of sunlight, exposure to rain or snow, and the like. In the Northern Hemisphere, south-facing gardens (north-facing beds in the Southern Hemisphere) attract more hours of sunshine and are therefore the best locations to plant in cooler regions. In hotter regions, north-facing gardens make more sense, reducing potentially damaging exposure to the tropic sun.

DRAINAGE

Few things are worse for plants than a waterlogged garden. If the lawn remains squishy after a rainfall in the area where you plan to excavate, you need to either pick a new location or choose one of these solutions.

- Prick, split, or spike the soil to facilitate drainage.
- Dig in a lot of compost or organic matter that will aid drainage.
- Create slopes that direct water to a surface drain or into flower beds with moisture-loving plants.
- Install land drains—underground perforated pipes that channel water away from flooding zones.
- Use absorbent bark mulch to remove water from the garden.
- Add more plants to the area, which will quickly drink up the excess water.

How much sunlight reaches a garden is a key factor in choosing plants. For the darkened base of garden trees, shade-loving flowers like impatiens will add color.

CLIMATE

Your regional climate is another key factor you need to take into consideration when planning a garden. How long or short is your growing season? How warm does it get at night during summers in your area? Tomatoes and peppers want to know! How much rainfall do you get on average each year? In milder or semi-tropical climates, many tender perennials will come back each year. In temperate climates with harsh winters, gardeners treat those same perennials as annuals that will die back in fall—although some will self-seed and maintain their spot in the garden.

The terrain that surrounds your home will also affect your garden's climate. Nearby woodlands or mountains may be able to protect your plants from wind and rain. If you live on an open grassland or a desert area, wind might become something you need to prepare for with stakes and burlap wraps for your plantings. Gardens located above lakes or rivers may benefit from the sunlight reflected off the surface of the water. Proximity to forests and large masses of water, like lakes or oceans, can affect the climate through transpiration and evaporation.

Speaking of humidity, which is the presence and percentage of water vapor in the air, this is yet another factor that affects your garden and can influence the success or failure of your plantings. Plants require moisture, which would make it seem like humidity is good for gardens. But when it's really sunny and hot out—let's call that tomato weather—and humidity increases significantly, it can bring along with it a number of unpleasant companions, like gray mold, powdery mildew, downy mildew, and late blight fungus. Fortunately, the return of hot, dry weather will often halt the incursion. Vegetables and fruits that thrive in humidity include lima beans, okra, 'Black Beauty' eggplant, and 'Blacktail Mountain' watermelon.

Smart gardeners work within the constraints of their climate. Even desert dwellers can create enchanting landscapes using plants that thrive under sunny, hot, and dry conditions.

A community garden can create a leafy green haven for city dwellers. In a garden such as this one in New York City's Greenwich Village, gardeners must factor in the effects of an urban microclimate, which may be hotter than the general Northeast climate.

MICROCLIMATES

Sometimes your surroundings can end up creating a microclimate. This is a local set of atmospheric conditions, especially ones that differ from the surrounding area. The difference may be slight or significant, and it may affect an area of only a few square yards—as with a cave or garden bed—or an area of many square miles. Microclimates can be found in most places but are most pronounced in topographically dynamic zones such as mountainous areas, islands, and coastal areas. Heavy urban areas, where brick, concrete, and asphalt all heat up in the sun then re-radiate that heat into the ambient air, can create what is referred to as an "urban heat island," or UHI. This microclimate is also driven by a lack of cooling vegetation.

Being aware of your regional climate, any microclimates, and your hardiness zone makes it easier to factor in the growing season, timing and amount of rainfall, and temperature ranges in order to ensure the plants you've chosen are right for your location.

GARDENING IN THE AGE OF CLIMATE CHANGE

Climate change is very much in the news these days. You are probably wondering if the issues brought on by these altered weather patterns are affecting your own garden. Most likely they are. Climate change is causing disruptions in nature's norms all over the world, even in your backyard.

As the world climate changes, plants will have to cope with the new normal. That may mean that plants in warming areas will flower early and fall victim to frosts. Or plants that require a certain number of chill hours to fruit, such as apple trees, may postpone flowering. The changes can also can create pollinator issues—the insects and birds that pollinate a plant's flowers might arrive at the wrong time. This can be an even greater problem for species that need to cross-pollinate. The blossoming times of the two species might no longer be in sync, and the pollinators might not be around.

You may also notice changes in the type and amount of precipitation in your area. Some areas are getting more rain than usual, while others are getting far less. In the northeastern United States, for example, gardeners are seeing more rain. And it is falling in short, hard downpours with periods of dry weather in between. This weather pattern change results in topsoil runoff and compacted garden beds.

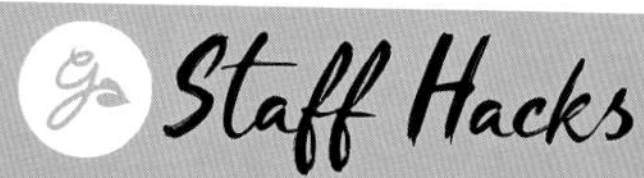

Amy Grant, GKH Writer, encourages beginner gardeners: "Dive in. Gardening isn't about perfection. Sure, you can strive for perfection, but half the fun is the journey getting there. Just know that you are going to make mistakes along the way—that's life. We all make mistakes and hopefully we learn from them."

An old-fashioned rain barrel is really an idea for a modern age. These simple objects will capture water, allowing you to irrigate your plants in drier weather without raising your utility bill or increasing the size of your carbon footprint.

Making a Difference

You can't stop climate change on your own, but you can certainly work to decrease your carbon footprint. First, you can reduce water consumption in your garden, especially during hot, dry weather. The keywords here are mulch (to hold in the moisture), rain barrels (to capture water), and drip irrigation (to get the water exactly where you need it).

You can also increase your composting efforts. Place non-meat kitchen scraps and garden detritus in the compost bin. This reduces your carbon pollution, especially the potent greenhouse gas methane. In addition, compost can be used in place of harmful chemical fertilizers to enrich your soil.

Planting trees is another smart way to address climate change through gardening. Trees absorb carbon pollution (CO2) from the atmosphere, which is to everyone's benefit. Plus, shade trees help keep your home cool in the summer, helping you to cut back on the use of energy-guzzling air conditioners.

CHAPTER TWO

GARDEN TOOLS AND ACCESSORIES

Maintaining a healthy, productive garden—preparing the soil, planting, weeding, deadheading, and harvesting—depends on a dozen or so time-tested tools. But even if you start out content with hand tools, you will soon find yourself progressing to power tools like hedge clippers, edgers, and weed-eaters. And every few seasons, you might even need to rent a piece of really big equipment, a rototiller, skid steer, or compactor, to give your garden a refresh.

Once you have collected the right implements for the type of gardening you enjoy, the next step is making sure they stay in good working condition with frequent cleaning and oiling. Otherwise you will find yourself replacing them every few seasons. In addition to tools, you'll require yard equipment, like ladders and wheelbarrows, as well as clothing and accessories specifically geared to gardeners.

100
75

HAND TOOLS

When choosing hand tools it is critical to examine how the implement is made. The way the handle is attached to a digging tool can either mean a lifetime of use or instant breakage when you hit that first rock. The least-expensive tools will likely have a tang and ferrule attachment. These are cheaply made and usually separate after a short time. Solid-socket tools have a forged connection from handle to working end. These are more expensive but will provide a lifetime of service. The most expensive option offers a seamless solid-strap attachment that isn't going anywhere.

Another consideration is comfort. The grip is crucial when picking out hand tools. A padded grip will result in fewer blisters and aching hands. Non-slip grips are useful when working in the rain, while ergonomic grips reduce hand stress from clasping too hard. Larger handles minimize strain and give a better grasp of the tool.

Always test out an implement—pantomime the motion you will be repeating with the tool to see if it is the right length, grip, and weight for you. The length of the handle should allow maximum exertion with minimal effort. Longer handles allow for a two-handed grip and better leverage. These may also be helpful to a gardener with a physical disability.

THE RIGHT TOOL FOR THE JOB

There are many different types of tools for gardening and each has a special purpose. Digging tools, like shovels and spades, can be used to cultivate, plant, or clear a plot. Long-handled shovels reduce the need to squat or kneel, but there is still no substitute for a hand trowel for up-close digging.

A hoe chops weeds and makes neat rows, while a spading fork breaks up soil clods and turns compost piles with ease. There are various types of cultivators that are useful in the vegetable garden as you get it ready for spring. Rakes come in the flexible style, useful for raking up leaves, or the hard rake option, which breaks up soil or thatches the lawn.

Most reputable garden centers can advise you about various tools and their purposes. They will also have a wide range of basic garden tools for beginners.

Effective Weeding Tools

Weeds can quickly get out of control and crowd out desirable plants. High-quality, ergonomic weeding hand tools help you keep weeds in check while reducing stress on your back, knees, and wrists. But when it comes to choosing weeders, no single tool is right for everybody. Do you fight weeds with long taproots? If you don't get the root, the bits left behind will generate a new plant. You'll need a different tool for shallow-rooted weeds or those with runners or stolons. Are weeds popping up between pavers or along sidewalks or driveways? Removing them requires different tools than you'll need for weeds that grow around vegetables or flowers. If you have trouble kneeling or bending, look for long-handled weeders. Quality weeding tools needn't be fancy, and they shouldn't break the bank. Still, quality tools may cost a little more, but they're worth it. Sturdy tools last longer, and they can be resharpened.

Japanese hand hoe

Japanese hori hori knife

Fishtail/dandelion weeder

Stirrup hoe

- **Japanese hand hoe.** Its super-sharp blades power through small weeds when you scrape the hoe across the soil; it comes in various types and sizes. The pointy end pulls out stubborn weeds, cuts through compacted soil, or digs out trenches.
- **Fishtail/dandelion weeder.** This easily plucks up dandelions, but also works well in sidewalk crevices or between pavers.
- **Japanese hori hori knife.** This continues to grow in popularity; the smooth edge is made for cutting or slicing, while the serrated edge saws through roots and sod and prunes small branches. Or use it like a trowel for digging in small areas.
- **Stirrup hoe.** This tool features a stirrup-shaped blade that's sharp on both sides. When pushed back and forth, the blade chops weeds off at the base.

HAND TOOLS

Trowel
This indispensable small shovel is used for digging planting holes, weeding, and scooping up soil. Look for models with depth measurements.

Hand rake
Also called a cultivator, this large-tined, curved fork breaks up clumped or rocky soil, mixes in amendments, or loosens weeds.

Cuttlefish hand tiller
Combining a hand rake and hand hoe, use this to till garden soil.

Spray bottle
Use for misting plants or spot spraying insecticide.

Garden tote
A sturdy, washable cloth or canvas bag with side pockets will hold hand tools and other gardening aids.

Bulb planter
The tube-shaped head removes a cylinder of soil, leaving behind a pocket for your bulb.

Scissors and shears
Gardening scissors and shears deadhead flowers and harvest tender herbs.

Plant markers
Use these to identify seedlings or herbs.

Knife
Use to cut string or twine for staking or pry out small rocks.

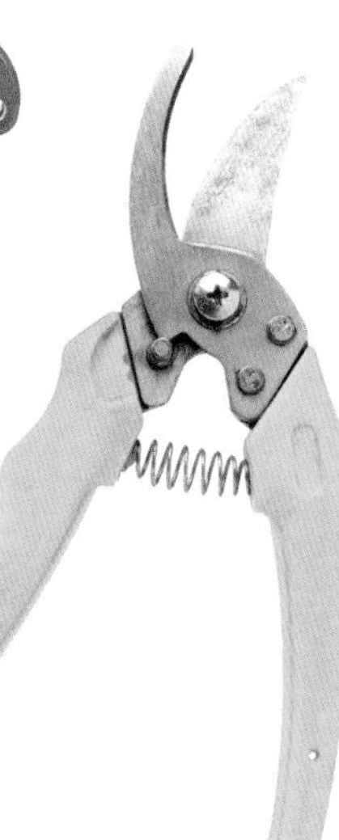

Secateurs/ pruning clippers
Spring-loaded snippers harvest flowers or herbs, prune small branches, deadhead roses, cut through roots, and divide root balls.

It is a smart idea to label your seedlings in their trays. Markers and labels are also easy DIY projects. For small seedling pots and trays, try Popsicle sticks. For larger pots or for outdoor plants, you can recycle corks, pebbles, shells, bamboo skewers, plastic containers, cans, and broken terra-cotta pots.

LARGE TOOLS

No matter how small their planting beds might be, at some point most gardeners will require larger tools. A sturdy shovel comes to mind, as well as a leaf rake and a pair of hedge trimmers. The tools listed below are only a sampling of the many garden implements available at your local garden center, but they are the most useful.

LARGE TOOLS

Shovels and spades
A long-handled garden shovel is typically bowl-shaped (concave) with a rounded, pointed, or square tip; use to dig holes, turn soil, break up roots, and dig out perennials to divide or transplant. A spade can be flat (or nearly flat) with a straight edge or have a round or pointed tip, and it is usually shorter than a shovel; use to edge lawns, segment and remove sod, dig large holes, and transport soil and mulch.

Hoe
This ancient tool is used to cultivate soil or chop weeds.

Aerator
Uses metal spikes to break up compacted thatch in lawns to improve drainage. Some are push tools that rotate, others look like spades with spikes instead of blades.

Hedge clippers
Keeps your shrubs and hedges tidy.

Garden claw
This long-handed tool with a claw of twisted metal at the bottom is used to cultivate, loosen, and aerate soil, and to weed.

Tree lopper
Trims suckers and errant branches from trees; some models have extendable handles to reach upper limbs.

Leaf rake
This rake's springy tines pick up leaves, grass clippings, and other lawn debris.

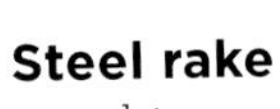

Steel rake
Use this rigid rake to smooth out soil or work in amendments.

Forks
The manure fork or pitchfork, with rounded, curved tines, is used to spread mulch or hay over beds. The spading fork has four narrow tines and is used to turn over soil and to gently lift perennials for replanting. The digging fork, with flattened tines, pries root vegetables from the soil.

Cleaning and Sharpening Tools

Nothing is more frustrating, when you plan a few hours of spring gardening, than discovering that your trusty garden pruners rusted shut over the winter or the wooden handle of your favorite trowel has split. Caring for your tools properly will extend their life and save you money down the road.

- Every spring place your tools on a tarp, and evaluate their condition. Check for rust, dull blades, and parched wood.
- Wash tools with mild detergent, and then dry them with lint-free cloth. Fine-grained steel wool is effective against rust or other stains.
- Apply machine oil to all metal surfaces, especially moving parts, and reapply it after using tools.
- With a mild bleach solution, wipe down cutting tools like saws, shears, or pruners to stop the possible spread of disease.
- Sharpen tools or shovel blades on a whetstone or with an all-purpose file, holding it at a 45-degree angle.
- Twice a season, sand wooden handles with medium-grit sand paper and rub in a protective coat of linseed oil. Never leave wooden tools outside.

POWER TOOLS

Most gardeners find that as their gardens or plantings expand, they come to rely on one or more of these power tools. Manufacturers typically offer tools with a choice of electric or battery power; some tools also run on gasoline. If possible, invest in brand names. You will get longevity and great performance and have a better chance at finding replacement parts and batteries.

Leaf blower
Makes it a breeze to clean up the yard after raking or mowing.

Lawn mower
Unless you have a really tiny lawn or no lawn, a mower is essential. Choose traditional push style, self-propelled, or, for larger properties, a riding mower.

Hedge trimmer
Clips and shapes your shrubs and hedges. Choose from electric or battery-powered.

Weed-whacker/weed-eater
This guy is your best friend when it's time to neaten up the garden, eliminate clumps of tall weeds, or trim back the plant borders and walkways. Choose from gas, electric, or battery powered.

Pressure washer
High-pressure streams of water power out the grime on porches, decks, patios, siding, brick, sidewalks, and driveways.

Edger
This handy tool provides those precise lawn edges you see in landscaping magazines.

Chainsaw
For the really tough trimming or lopping jobs; smaller versions are useful in garden settings.

Rental Equipment

Sometimes a special project requires the use of one of these big boys. Many of them are available for one- or two-day rentals; check with your local home improvement store or online.

- **Rototiller.** This levels the ground and aerates large beds in preparation for planting, especially of vegetables.
- **Skid steer loader.** Often called a Bobcat, this versatile vehicle's variety of attachments allow it to lift pallets of pavers, mulch, or plants as well as handle excavations, rotary tilling, stump removal, post hole digging, demolition, and debris removal.
- **Fence post driver.** Also known as a post pounder, post driver, post rammer, post knocker, or fence driver, it is used for driving fence posts into soil surfaces. This heavy steel pipe, closed at the top, with handles welded onto the sides, fits over the post and is repeatedly lifted and dropped; the weight of the driver does the hard work. There are also gas-powered automatic drivers.
- **Plate compacter.** This tool shrinks the pore space between particles of soil and increases density. Necessary to level the base layer when creating a paver patio, path, or driveway.
- **Brush hog.** This tough rotary mower attaches to the back of a tractor using a three-point hitch and is driven via a power take-off. Ideal for clearing dense brush, tangled weeds, and thickets.

YARD EQUIPMENT

Gardeners and non-gardeners alike need to maintain their property, and this is where these basic yard-care pieces come in. The good news is that they are sturdy additions to your home's inventory and rarely need to be replaced.

YARD ESSENTIALS

Hose
Choose from traditional plastic or expandable models; some are even retractable. Look into "hose quick" technology that replaces screw-on hose attachments with pop-off fittings. Many gardeners prefer watering wands over spray nozzles because they offer more pinpoint control.

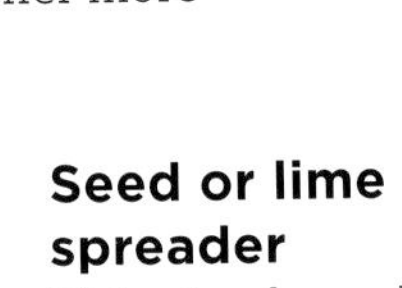

Seed or lime spreader
This simple push tool is used for broadcasting on lawns or freshly turned earth.

Wheelbarrow
The indispensable king of the yard and garden; they are invaluable for bigger jobs like shuttling plants, pots, soil, amendments, edging stones, or bricks from place to place, as well as transporting pruning scraps, leaves, and grass clippings to the compost bin. Guaranteed to save your back!

Small wagon
A child's metal wagon, like a Radio Flyer, makes a great way to transport plant flats, pots, and heavy bags of soil or amendments.

Yard cart
Similar to a wheelbarrow, but usually square shaped with two or four wheels. Some push forward, others are drawn forward with a single handle. Used to transport wood, plants, soil, amendments—anything heavy or cumbersome. Certain models are able to dump their contents.

Editor's Picks

For gardeners who have trouble bending, a wheeled "scoot," often called a creeper, is a rolling seat that allows them to sit as they garden.

Trug
This kind of flat, handled basket has been used for centuries to gather flowers or produce.

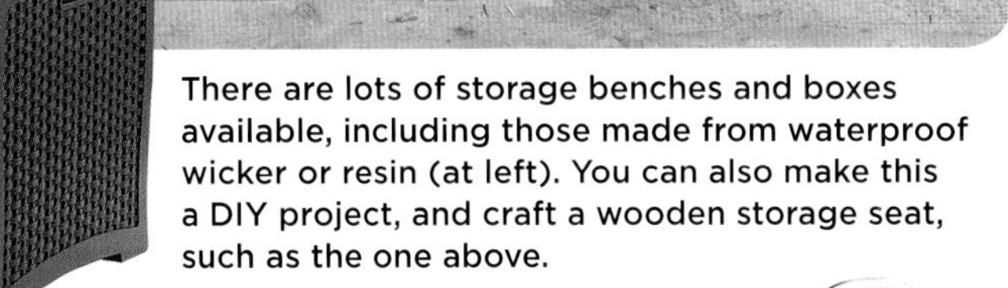

There are lots of storage benches and boxes available, including those made from waterproof wicker or resin (at left). You can also make this a DIY project, and craft a wooden storage seat, such as the one above.

Round plastic bin
This large, handled tote can hold tools, soil, gardening refuse, kitchen scraps for composting, or ice and drinks during a patio party.

Storage bench
This covered bin features seating above and stores garden, deck, or pool supplies below.

Step ladder
Useful for getting to those high-up, hard-to-reach places. Choose aluminum over wood for durability. Consider purchasing a convertible model that turns into an extension ladder and a scaffold.

Watering can
Old-fashioned, but still useful for spot watering, hydrating hangers and containers, and adding diluted fertilizer to plants that require feeding.

Compost bin
These containers, either tumbling or stationary, break down yard trimmings and kitchen scraps into rich, dark compost.

Tractor
Few people with large yards ever regret this investment. Tractors are generally used for hauling wood, fencing, or other heavy objects, but they can tow a garden cart or spreader or be fitted with a mower or auger attachment.

APPAREL AND ACCESSORIES

Gardening is good for the body, mind, and spirit, but nothing ruins a Zen moment in the garden like a painful scratch from a rose thorn or an itchy bug bite. Even though gardening is a fairly safe hobby, there are risks too. Consider the following hazards gardeners face on a regular basis.

- Sunburn and heatstroke
- Bug bites and stings
- Rashes
- Scratches and scrapes from twigs and thorns
- Accidents with pruning scissors
- Pesticide and herbicide exposure
- Carpal tunnel syndrome

Protective garden clothing and healthful aids can help you avoid the worst of sunburn, bug bites, and scratches, keeping you safer outside. There are also some disease risks that come with working in the soil, including tetanus and Legionnaires' disease. Gardeners should always make sure they are up to date on their tetanus shots. To prevent the rare but possible microbial diseases, wash your hands thoroughly after each gardening session.

HARMFUL SUNLIGHT

Considering what we now know about the cumulative dangers of sunlight, it is vital to keep covered up while gardening outdoors. But if long sleeves and long pants seem oppressive on really hot days, make sure to apply a good sunscreen to any exposed skin. Throughout the gardening year, choose fabrics that are known to block ultraviolet radiation. Unbleached cotton contains lignins, which absorb UV rays. Most fabrics with a tight weave—denim, linen, canvas, polyester, nylon, synthetic blends, and wool—also offer protection. Be aware, however, that any fabric that stretches can reduce UV blocking by up to 50 percent.

Gardening can be hard and dirty work, but it is certainly satisfying. To protect yourself outdoors, be sure to dress properly, with shirts with long sleeves (that you can roll up if it gets too hot), sturdy footgear, long trousers or overalls, and a brimmed hat.

CLOTHES AND ACCESSORIES

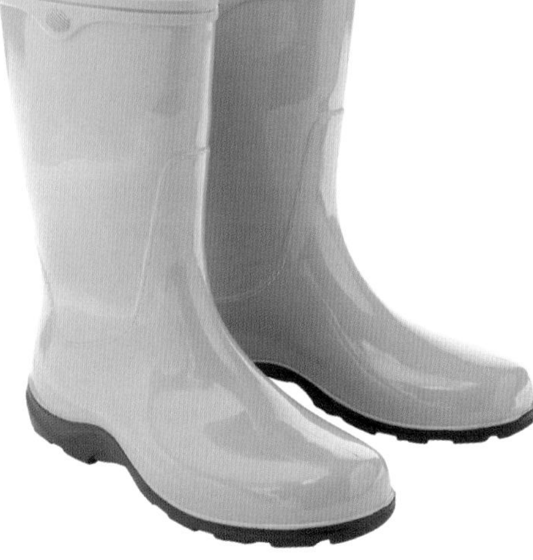

Rubber garden boots
"Wellies" are great for working in wet soil or if it's damp outside. It is also easy to hose off any dirt, mud, or other debris.

Large bandanna or hand towel
Just a swipe keeps sweat off your face, head, and arms. A bandanna can also hold back your hair while you work.

Sturdy shoes or work boots
Protect your feet and ankles from sprains and sharp objects with a pair of sturdy shoes or work boots.

Carpenter's half apron
This handy garment keeps garden and health aids at your fingertips. The more pockets, the better!

Gardening gloves
These should be thick enough to protect you from thorns and thistles but thin enough to allow you to work comfortably. Gloves also protect your hands from the sun and any chemicals you use.

Neck-cooling scarf
Use a damp scarf with expanding gel pellets inside to avoid heat exhaustion on a humid day.

Insect spray or lotion
Protect yourself from biting flies, gnats, wasps, hornets, mosquitoes, and ticks on the buggiest days.

Sunscreen
Essential for protecting you from harmful UV rays. Use a minimum SPF 30 on your face.

Plastic goggles
Be sure to cover your eyes while using any power tools in the yard.

Wide-brimmed hat
Worn as a sun shield, it should cover your scalp and shade your face.

Thermal water bottle
Be sure to keep hydrated as you garden, and remember that sports drinks can replace lost electrolytes.

Knee pads/ kneeling cushion
Protect your vulnerable knees as you garden.

Long-sleeved shirt
Protect your neck, back, and arms from the sun.

CHAPTER THREE

CREATING THE GARDEN

One benefit of creating a planting bed from scratch is that you can design it in any style you like—big or small, curved or geometric, raised or flat—whatever strikes your fancy. Before you work out a garden plan, however, take some time to look through gardening books for layouts you love, as well as the flower mixes or vegetable choices that appeal to you. That way you can look up the plants, and make sure they are right for your regional climate. The staff at garden centers is an excellent source of information on which plants will thrive in your area and whether they need a lot of sun or not. Once you have a relationship with a garden center or nursery, it will become your go-to destination whenever you need advice or recommendations.

DETERMINING THE LAYOUT

Carving a flower bed or vegetable garden out of a section of lawn or patch of weeds may seem like an intimidating task. Where do you even begin? Before starting on any sort of bed, you need to assess the landscape. Take a stroll around your property and note the available light and nearby structures, so you can choose a suitable location. Determine the whereabouts of any underground utility lines and the nearest water source—you don't want the garden dozens of feet from the end of the hose.

Location can make all the difference between vividly blooming flowers and lackluster or wilted blossoms and bumper crops of vegetables versus a few weedy specimens even the woodchucks don't want. So choose your plants wisely based on your garden's location—or chose your location based on the plants you intend to grow. Fortunately, flowers come in a choice of sun lovers, shade lovers, and those that do well in semi-shade. Most vegetables have trickier requirements when it comes to sun and heat. Many veggies, like tomatoes and peppers, require sun by day and warm nights, while others, such as some lettuce varieties, enjoy shadier conditions and cooler weather.

SKETCH IT OUT

Before you start digging up your bed, it's a good idea to make several sketches of how you would like the finished garden to look. This is important, as it allows you to play around with ideas, like the size and shape of the flower bed or whether you should add a path or seating area. It will also make it easier when choosing plants, as these should always be compatible with your hardscape—buildings, walls, fences, etc. And in a flower garden, always remember to choose plants of varying heights for visual interest. Although it is common to place low plants in front, medium plants in the middle, and taller plants in back, some variation of this order adds a nice tension to the garden. With vegetables, it is helpful to note that some species do well together, and others seem to clash. (*See* page 175 for more on companion planting.) Also be sure to place the taller plants to the north of the space, so they don't overshadow the smaller plants and block the sun.

Two configurations are popular with many gardeners and work with both flowers and vegetables: border gardens and island gardens.

Border gardens

These are situated against a backdrop, such as a house, shed, fence, hedge, or walkway. This type of bed is viewed primarily from one side. Typically, bed designs for borders feature tall plants at the back and mid-sized plants in the central area. Shorter plants, generally those measuring less than 10 inches in height, line the front of a border-style flower bed.

Island gardens

These are positioned in the yard with no backdrop. They can be square, round, rectangular, or any other shape that strikes your fancy. Unlike borders, island flower beds can be viewed from all sides—and that also means they receive sunlight from multiple directions. The layout is similar to a border, except taller plants are located in the center of the island with plants that are smaller placed toward the outer edges of the bed.

An island flower bed can be a simple circle or a more complicated shape, depending on how much space you have and your personal desires. Low-growing plants usually ring the outer edges of the island, and taller species stand in the center.

LAY OUT THE GARDEN'S SHAPE

Whether you choose a border or an island, once you have an idea of the garden shape you want, use a flexible hose, landscaping spray paint, or cooking flour to mark it out on the lawn. Then with a flat-ended shovel, dig out the grass all around the perimeter of your garden bed to establish a boundary. You are now ready to begin preparing your garden beds.

A typical border design features plants graduating in size from small to large, front to back.

Plotting out your garden starts with its location on your property and its basic shape. Once you have those factors decided, you can move on to which plants will go where.

Editor's Tip

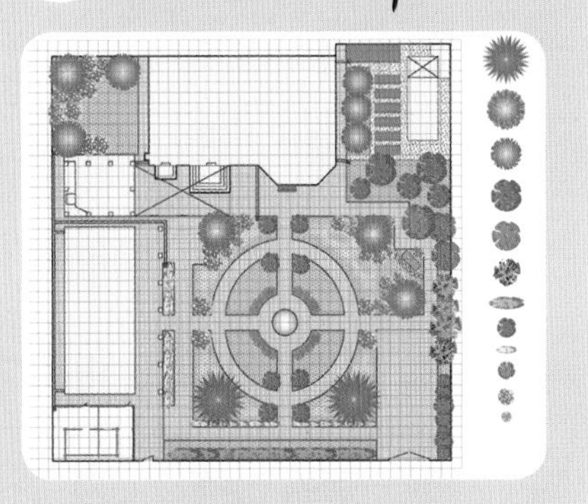

Few of us are talented-enough artists to realistically render our garden ideas. That is really no hindrance, though, in getting your ideas down on paper or on screen. You can always use the tried-and-true method of drawing out your garden on graph paper, using symbols to indicate which plants are which or using cut-out shapes to move around until you find placements that best fit. There are also many easy-to-use garden design apps that let you visualize your plan, and their cost can fit any budget, from free to pricey. You can choose from hundreds of templates that you can customize to your specifications and add elements like types of plants, trees, and shrubs, along with walls, fencing, hardscape, lighting, and furnishings.

You can also create mood boards—online or on paper—clipping garden images that appeal to you. Use these as inspiration when planning out your actual garden.

A GALLERY OF
GARDEN STYLES

From the geometric lines of a formal garden to the delightful chaos of a cottage garden, there is a style sure to appeal to everyone. The style that is right for you depends on many factors, particularly the terrain and climate of the region you live in. You might want a garden for a specific purpose, such as growing food or providing a tranquil space to recharge in. Whatever factors those requirements entail, you are really limited only by your specific taste and imagination.

CONTAINER GARDEN
Great for those with limited or unsuitable outdoor space, container gardens offer gardeners a chance to grow a variety of plants, including ornamentals.

COTTAGE GARDEN
Originating in England, this cozy and colorful style incorporates traditional materials, dense plantings, and a mixture of ornamental and edible plants.

FORMAL GARDEN
The hallmarks of this ancient style of gardening are a clear structure and geometric shapes in a symmetrical layout that lend a garden stately beauty.

HERB GARDEN
Wonderfully fragrant, herb gardens have real appeal to anyone who wants to bring fresh tastes from their backyards straight to their kitchens.

JAPANESE GARDEN
A traditional garden style that reflects Japanese aesthetics, it highlights the natural landscape, avoids excess ornamentation, and features water and rocks.

KITCHEN/POTAGER GARDEN
Cooking with your own homegrown produce has numerous benefits, from offering the freshest garden-to-table veggies to saving on grocery bills.

KNOT GARDEN
Medieval Europeans first created these fragrant gardens to organize culinary and medicinal plants. Modern gardeners love them for their intricate beauty.

ROCK GARDEN
The contrast between rugged rocks and the delicate alpine flowers traditionally used in this style adds depth to a garden and brightens a hard-to-plant area.

ROOF GARDEN
As ever-increasing numbers of city dwellers crave the serenity of a green space, gardens set on urban rooftops are gaining in popularity.

WOODLAND GARDEN
Layers of vegetation in a naturalistic setting mark this verdant garden style that feature plants that thrive on the forest floor and in the shade of taller trees.

XERISCAPE
This style of landscaping, which incorporates native plants that require little or no irrigation or other maintenance, is perfect for desert dwellers.

GARDEN BEDS

There are two basic types of garden beds: those that are on or near the same level as the lawn and raised beds, which elevate the soil above ground level and are contained by some kind of wall or border.

LEVEL BEDS

Once you know the location and shape of your garden bed, you're ready to excavate it. Depending on its location and size, starting a bed often begins with the removal of grass. There are several ways to accomplish this: dig it out, apply herbicide (make this one a last resort), or smother it with cardboard or newspaper.

After digging out a new garden bed, arrange your plant selections, still in their pots, to map out their planting positions before putting them in the ground.

Digging out the bed

If you choose to dig out the grass in your new bed, it will be easier to use a flat-ended shovel or spade. Follow these four steps:

1. After you have established a border by digging down about 4 to 5 inches (10–12.5 cm) around the bed's perimeter, you need to remove the grass. Cut the sod into small squares, and pry it from the planting area with the end of the shovel. (Excess sod can be incorporated into thin areas of your lawn and watered.)
2. Clear out any rocks or debris with a hoe or metal rake.
3. Loosen the soil with a pitchfork or spade. If it's a new garden, loosen to a depth of at least 8 to 12 inches (20–30 cm) so that roots can grow down. If it is a spring refresh, you probably won't have to dig so deep.
4. Add organic matter on a day when the soil is moist but not wet. Spread a minimum of 2 to 3 inches (5–7.5 cm) of compost or aged manure onto your soil. Some gardeners will dig the organic matter into the soil, others have a no-dig philosophy that exposes fewer weed seeds and does not disturb the soil structure. They leave the compost on the surface and let the worms do the digging in. The usual recommended ratio is 1 to 3 (2.5–7.5 cm) inches of organic amendment mixed into to 6 to 8 (15–20 cm) inches of ground soil.

No-dig flower beds

Most people prefer the no-dig approach to creating a bed. It starts with eliminating the grass as in the dig method. Although using herbicides can effectively kill grass, the ground may not be suitable for planting until much later, because most of these products are not environmentally friendly. You can, however, quickly and effectively remove grass without the use of harmful chemicals simply by using cardboard or newspaper to smother it out. You can start the no-dig bed in early spring for summer planting or build a flower bed in the autumn, as grass begins to go dormant. Fill the area with cardboard or several layers of newspaper and saturate with water. Add about 6 inches (15 cm) of compost or rich soil on top, with another layer of organic mulch (like straw) on top of this. You can plant a flowerbed right away if the grass was dug out or within the next season using the no-dig method.

Dig out grass in squared clumps that you can later use to fill in thin lawn areas.

Editor's Tip

To remove potential weeds in a new ground plot, slightly scuff the soil, then cover the space with a warming layer of clear plastic. Once the weed seedlings crop up, pull them out or remove them with a hoe. Don't disturb the soil before planting, or new weed seeds will rise to the surface.

You can build cold frames from a variety of materials. Here, plywood frames are covered with removable recycled window frames to protect a crop of leafy salad vegetables. In winter, the gardener will re-attach the window frames to cover the potted plants inside the frame, ensuring their protection from wind and dropping temperatures.

COLD FRAMES IN THE GARDEN

Often called the "poor man's greenhouse," a cold frame allows the gardener to lengthen the garden season, harden off seedlings, start seedlings earlier, and overwinter tender dormant plants. Gardening with cold frames is nothing new; they've been around for generations.

Growing plants in a cold frame

There are a number of ways to build a cold frame. They may be made out of plywood, concrete, or hay bales and covered with old windows, Plexiglas, or plastic sheeting. Whatever materials you choose, all cold frames are simple structures used to capture solar energy and create an insulated microclimate. Veggies, especially leafy green ones like arugula, kale, lettuce, spinach, and cabbage, along with broccoli, beet, green onion, and radish, do well in a cold frame environment.

If you are using cold frames to protect tender plants from winter temps, cut the plants back as much as possible before the first autumn frost. If they aren't already in pots, put them in large plastic containers, and fill them with soil. Pack the cold frame with the pots. Fill in any large air gaps between pots with leaves or mulch. Water the plants.

Thereafter, you will need to monitor the conditions inside the cold frame. Keep the soil damp inside it, but not wet. Cover the frame with a white plastic cover or the like to keep out most of the light. Too much light will encourage active growth, and it isn't the right season for that yet. The white plastic will also keep the sun from over heating the cold frame.

Seedlings can be transferred to the cold frame or started directly in it. If sowing directly into the cold frame, have it in place two weeks before seeding to warm the soil. If you start them inside and transfer them to the frame, you can start those six weeks earlier than normal. Keep an eye on the amount of sun, moisture, temps, and wind within the frame. Seedlings benefit from warmer temps and moisture, but winds, heavy rain, or too much heat can kill them.

Monitoring temperatures

Growing plants in a cold frame requires the constant monitoring of temperature, moisture, and ventilation. Most seeds germinate in soil that is around 70° F (21° C), although some crops like it a little warmer or cooler. Air temps are also important.

- Cool-season crops prefer temps around 65 to 70° F (18–21° C) during the day and 55 to 60° F (13–15.5° C) at night.
- Warm-season crops like temps 65 to 75° F (18–24° C) during the day and not lower than 60° F (15.5° C) at night.

Careful monitoring and response are important. If the frame is too warm, vent it. If the cold frame is too cold, cover the glass with straw or another padding to conserve heat. To vent the cold frame, raise the sash on the opposite side from which the wind is blowing to protect tender, young plants. Completely open the sash or remove it on warm, sunny days. Close the sash in the late afternoon once the danger of excess heat has passed and before the evening air turns chilly.

Watering in a cold frame

Water plants early in the day so the foliage has time to dry before the frame is closed. Only water the plants when they are dry. For transplanted or direct-sown plants, very little water is necessary because the cold frame retains moisture and temperatures are still cool. As temps increase and the frame is open longer, introduce more water. Allow the soil surface to dry between watering but not until the plants wilt.

To find out more about cold frames, follow these URLs.

- **"Cold Frame Construction: How to Build a Cold Frame for Gardening"** (URL = gkh.us/19795)
- **"Cold Frames and Frost: Learn About Fall Gardening in a Cold Frame"** (URL = gkh.us/124333)
- **"Keeping Plants in a Cold Frame — Using Cold Frames for Overwintering Plants"** (URL = gkh.us/124421)

A mix of leafy greens, root veggies, and flowers flourish in an attractive raised bed.

A gardener harvests radishes. Raised gardens contain looser soil than level beds, which is ideal for root crops because they provide an optimum environment for root growth.

RAISED BEDS

Are you looking for a vegetable or flower garden that eliminates a lot of the work required by other gardens? Consider growing plants in raised boxes. Because they are elevated above the level of the walkways, these beds require less bending, making them easier on your knees and back. If you live in a colder region, consider that a raised garden bed can help wet, cold soils dry out and warm up more quickly in spring. Plus, they allow you to plant earlier and produce fewer weeds. They allow you to match soil type to the plants you wish to grow: slightly acidic for hydrangeas? No problem.

A raised vegetable garden is also an excellent alternative for growing plants on difficult sites, such as hillsides. Here, depths can be adjusted easily to fit the slope of the hill. Raised beds are useful if your soil is poor or if there's some other reason you can't dig into the soil. And their tight plantings reduce the presence of weeds, and their accessibility makes invasive insects easy to remove or discourage.

Elevated gardens are easier to maintain because they are accessible from all sides. They also save on space and allow plants to grow closer together, resulting in more moisture for the crops and less weed growth. With raised beds, you have the option of creating a plot as small as you like, and then adding onto it as time, experience, and your individual needs require. Finally, you can cover your raised beds before planting with black plastic or cardboard to block light against weeds and protect them from snow, rain, and erosion.

Design a raised garden

Depending on your specific needs, raised beds can take many forms. Nearly any material that holds soil and retains its shape can be used to edge a raised garden bed. Wood, concrete blocks, bricks, stones, or logs are easily available and inexpensive. A galvanized steel container with a drainage hole or a water trough will also work well. Wood is the most common material used, but you should stay away from any lumber that has been pressure treated, as the chemicals that are used to treat the wood can leach into the soil and harm plants.

Raised garden boxes are typically laid out in a rectangular shape approximately 3 feet (1 m) in width. This width measurement allows all areas of the bed, including the center, to be easily accessible. The length of a raised vegetable garden depends on your personal choice, but the depth of the raised garden boxes should be at least 6 to 12 inches (15–30 cm) to allow for the proper root development of plants.

Positioning Raised Beds

The optimal place to locate a raised garden bed will be based on a host of factors, including:

- Available sunlight
- Soil porosity
- Soil texture
- Soil nutrient levels
- Soil pH
- Wind exposure
- Moisture availability
- Previous pest issues
- Distance from house
- Proximity to trees
- Microclimates

The Berm

There is a third option beyond flat plots or raised rectangular beds. That is the berm, a rounded mound of soil (and, sometimes, fill) built upon an otherwise level patch of land and planted with flowers and shrubs to improve the design of a property. It may or may not have some kind of retaining wall. Berms add height and visual interest to a yard and have many of the same pluses as raised beds—ease of access and less-compacted soil—but they integrate more gracefully into the landscape. They also serve as privacy screens and windbreaks and can redirect drainage. Recommended plantings include a mix of dwarf fruit trees and shrubs, arborvitae, ornamental grasses, perennial flowers, border annuals, and succulents.

Creating a berm in a section of a lawn can add visual interest to a home property, adding lovely shapes and lively colors to what might otherwise be a bland expanse of uninterrupted green.

Creating paths between the beds makes maintenance easier and looks attractive, too. You can create paths by spreading a weed barrier of plastic or other gardening fabric between each bed and covering it with a suitable mulching material, such as gravel or pebbles. The pathways should be wide enough for easy accessibility to the beds with additional room for a wheelbarrow. Generally, a width of 2 to 3 feet (0.6–1 m) is sufficient.

Don't forget to locate the plot near a water source—a spigot, pump, well, or cistern. When applying water to raised gardens, it is better to use soaker hoses which can be placed directly on the bed; sprinklers work but are more likely to spread diseases if the foliage stays excessively wet. The use of organic mulches, such as straw or hay, can also help these beds to retain moisture.

Soil for raised beds

When you are ready, fill your new beds with commercial soil. For older beds, mix the existing soil with compost or manure. As the levels of soil are built up, keep adding compost to further improve its structure and drainage. When you begin planting crops or flowers in the beds, place taller varieties to the north to prevent shading of the smaller varieties.

If you are planting in a flat bed using ground soil, you will likely need to increase the quality with amendments (*see* pages 40–41). With raised beds, one of the benefits is that the gardener fills the boxes with fresh soil, either compost they have created or amended soil purchased from a garden center.

There are several types of soil sold in garden centers, which may be confusing to gardening novices. Topsoil is considered dirt, while some potting soils and all peat mosses are "soil-less."

- *Topsoil.* This rich soil, taken from the top layers of a field, is sand or clay (ground-up rocks) mixed with organic materials such as compost. It is meant for in-the-ground planting. Topsoil is heavy and holds a lot of water, keeping plant roots moist. It is dense and packs down easily.
- *Peat moss.* This growing medium is completely soil-less. You can use straight peat moss as your potting mix, but be careful not to overwater. Peat moss all by itself can stay wet for a long time after plants are watered.
- *Potting soil.* This kind of soil is ideal for planting in containers. It provides the proper texture for plants in a small space, whether they are grown indoors or out. Potting soil is a mixture of peat moss and other organic materials like coco coir or coconut husks, vermiculite, shredded bark, and composted sawdust. It allows water to drain easily, and the roots to dry out quickly. It is mostly air so that it is light and fluffy and difficult to pack down.

The recommended combination of mediums for raised beds is 60 percent topsoil, 30 percent compost, and 10 percent potting soil, but gardeners often noodle with the percentages until they find the combination that works best for their conditions.

PREP THE AUTUMN GARDEN FOR SPRING

Whether you're prepping new beds in the fall or amending existing beds, it pays to incorporate plenty of organic matter into the soil. Work the soil when it is damp, not wet. For new beds or existing beds with no plants, amend with 2 to 3 inches (5–7.5 cm) of compost mixed well and deeply with soil. An additional 3- to 4-inch (7.5–10 cm) layer of mulch will slow down weeds. For beds with existing plants, you need to add 2 to 3 inches (5–7.5 cm) of compost to the top layer of soil. If this is difficult due to root systems, just a layer atop the surface will repel weeds and conserve moisture. Keep compost away from plant stems and trunks. As for organic matter, compost is king, but chicken or cow manure are also tops, provided you add them in the fall and allow them to age.

ASSESSING AND AMENDING SOIL

Your garden soil might have originally had a healthy structure and contained all the nutrients plants require, but over time the ground compacted and the nutrients were used up. If the soil has had organic amendments added continuously, however, it may be rich enough without additions. This is when you need a soil test (*see* page 15). Various soil-testing meters can be purchased at nurseries and other plant centers. You can also send a soil sample to your local Agricultural Extension office for analysis. It is important to know your soil's pH as well. For most plants, a healthy pH is between 6.0 and 7.0. Lower numbers indicate acidic soil, which reduces a plant's ability to access nutrients. Acid soil will benefit from an application of lime prior to fertilizing, which will help neutralize the pH.

TYPES OF AMENDMENTS

Beds that utilize ground soil often need amendments to create the optimal growing conditions. There are two types of amendments, organic and inorganic. Organic or natural amendments include a number of materials such as straw, leaves, and biosolids. Compost and peat are also used to fertilize the soil and prevent pest infestation. Beneficial fungi, bacteria, and worms gain energy from the organic matter in the soil and will soon break down these amendments. Amendments like manure and grass clippings decompose quickly and will quickly improve soil. But compost, peat, and wood chips decompose more slowly; they are used when the goal is to achieve long-lasting soil improvement.

Inorganic amendments include tire pieces, pea gravel, and sand. Over time, these can deplete the soil's naturally occurring nutrients.

IMPROVING SOIL

Sandy, clay, and silty are the soil types most often seen in home gardens (*see* page 14), and their qualities will determine what specific kinds of amendments you require.

To amend soil for growing vegetables, a gardener begins the process of preparing a soil mixture from vermicompost, biohumus, vermiculite, and perlite.

Sandy soil

Water quickly runs out of sandy soil, so it can be hard for it to retain the nutrients that plants need to thrive. Sandy soil is filled with sand—small pieces of eroded rock—so it has a gritty texture and few pockets to hold water or nutrients. Look for amendments that increase its ability to retain water and nutrients. Well-rotted manure or compost (including grass clippings, humus, and leaf mold) will provide a fast solution. You can also add vermiculite or peat, but they only increase soil's ability to hold onto water and will add little nutrient value. When amending sandy soil, watch the salt levels. Compost and manure contain high levels that can damage growing plants. If your sandy soil is already high in salt, such as in a seaside garden, use plant-based compost or sphagnum peat, amendments with the lowest salt levels.

Clay soil

Sticky, damp clay soil does hold nutrients and when amended, it has good fertility. But clay soils have very fine particles, and their tiny pore spaces leave little room for roots to find needed air or water. The best way to improve clay is to work in a large amount of organic materials like bark, sawdust, manure, leaf mold, compost, and peat moss to a depth of 1 to 2 feet (30–60 cm). Break up any clods or clumps to allow the formation of those necessary air pockets. Perlite and crushed pumice will also keep the soil loose.

Silty soil

This type of soil has real possibilities—it holds moisture and is often rich in nutrients. Its main drawback is that it can lack drainage and structure. By working in some composted organic matter, you will be adding nutrients, as well as improving drainage and structure.

Gypsum

Lime

Vermiculite

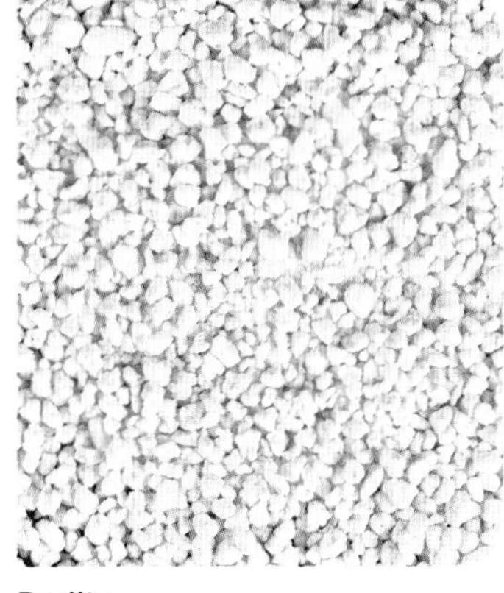

Perlite

COMPACTED SOIL SOLUTIONS

Compacted soil occurs when something collapses the air pockets in between its components. It has a variety of causes: pressure from foot traffic or heavy machinery, like cars; if the ground is worked in less-than-ideal conditions—say, the soil is too wet when you till; if the soil doesn't have enough organic material to fluff it up; working the soil when it is too dry; and working it too often.

Roots in compacted soil must work harder to grow, which means that there will be fewer roots, and the plant will take up fewer nutrients and less water. There are a number of amendments that specifically loosen compacted soil.

Gypsum

Gypsum is calcium sulfate, a mineral that excels at breaking up compacted soil, especially clay.

Lime

Lime, ground limestone, raises soil pH but also helps to loosen soil.

Vermiculite

Vermiculite, a hydrous phyllosilicate mineral, takes the form of glossy flakes in shades from dark gray to sandy brown. In garden beds or pots, it increases water and nutrient retention and aerates the soil.

Perlite

Perlite is an amorphous volcanic glass that improves aeration and modifies soil substructure, keeping it loose and well-draining.

Layering with Lasagna Gardening

There is a simple way to improve garden soil that uses waste materials you are likely to have around the house. The method, introduced by Patricia Lanza in her 1998 book *Lasagna Gardening,* promises "no digging, no tilling, no weeding."

Start in autumn by layering the grass of the designated garden plot with 5 inches (12.5 cm) of brown matter (for carbon)—shredded leaves, cardboard, and newspaper, peat, pine needles, then 3 inches (7.5 cm) of green matter (for nitrogen)—grass clippings, garden trimmings, vegetable scraps. Repeat these layers for 20 inches (50 cm), then cover with 5 inches (12.5 cm) of garden soil. Keep the entire plot moist. As these layers "cook" down, they enrich and aerate the soil and keep weeds at bay. Once planted up, mulch the garden with straw or grass clippings.

A gardener places cardboard over a plot as the first step in creating a lasagna garden.

NOURISHING THE GARDEN

There may be some confusion among gardeners about the difference between amendments, fertilizers, and products called plant food. Simply put, fertilizers improve the supply of nutrients in the soil, directly affecting plant growth. Soil amendments improve soil's physical condition (e.g., soil structure, water infiltration), indirectly affecting plant growth. Plant food is a naturally occurring form of sustenance that plants produce themselves, in part through photosynthesis. Additives calling themselves plant food are more likely a type of fertilizer.

Many gardeners believe the best time to fertilize is the spring, when plants are at their peak growing cycle—leafing out, flowering, or putting out new growth. This is also when increasing soil temperatures allow plants to uptake nutrients at the proper rate.

Use a soil test to determine the type of fertilizer you require. This indicates the nutrients and minerals lacking in your soil. Each plant's needs differ, so it is also important to know the nutrient requirements of specific varieties. There are also fertilizers geared to certain plant species, specifically formulated for rhododendrons, say, or for roses. On the other hand, all-purpose fertilizers provide the basic nutrients and minerals most plants need and are a good option in many cases.

The choice of fertilizers can be overwhelming, with so many different types for sale at garden centers. A soil test can help you determine which will work best in your garden.

MICRONUTRIENTS

Those three bold numbers featured on packages of fertilizer are known as fertilizer grade. Each number represents the percentage of three key macronutrients found in the mix: nitrogen, phosphorus, and potassium (potash), or N-P-K.

Nitrogen

Nitrogen is part of all living cells and a necessary part of all proteins, enzymes, and metabolic processes involved in the synthesis and transfer of energy. It is a constituent of chlorophyll, the green pigment responsible for photosynthesis, and helps with rapid growth and increased seed and fruit production.

Phosphorus

Phosphorus is an essential part of photosynthesis and is involved in the formation of all oils, sugars, starches, etc. It helps transform solar energy into chemical energy, aids proper plant maturation, and encourages blooming and root growth.

Potassium

Potassium is absorbed by plants in larger amounts than any other mineral element except nitrogen and, in some cases, calcium. It helps to build protein, aids photosynthesis, enhances fruit quality, and reduces diseases.

Other macronutrients

Other macronutrients include calcium—essential for cell wall structure and transport of elements; magnesium—critical for photosynthesis and activating growth enzymes; sulfur—essential for production of protein, developing enzymes and vitamins.

MICRONUTRIENTS

Micronutrients for the garden include boron—which aids production of sugar and carbohydrates; copper—important for reproductive growth; chloride—which assists plant metabolism; iron—critical for forming chlorophyll; manganese—which aids nitrogen metabolism and breaking down of carbs; molybdenum —which aids the use of nitrogen; and zinc—essential for transportation of carbs.

CHOOSING FERTILIZER

When shopping for fertilizer, consider how the capabilities of each nutrient relate to what you are growing. Higher percentages of nitrogen encourage vigorous leafy growth and rich green color and work best for foliage plants and grasses. Phosphorus ensures healthy roots and blooms, fruits, and seeds in flowering plants and vegetables. Potassium keeps plants healthy by enhancing overall growth, while regulating root and top growth. In plant-specific fertilizers, azalea mixes add extra iron for larger blooms, while bulb fertilizers offer higher percentages of root-building phosphorus.

Natural and synthetic fertilizers

Organic fertilizers contain only natural ingredients, those digested by soil microorganisms that then release the nutrients in a form available to plants. Natural fertilizers contain healthful microorganisms like biological compounds, fungi, algae, or bacteria, all of which help your plant thrive. These microorganisms need a soil temperature of at least 50° F (10° C), often higher, to work their magic, which is why it makes sense to fertilize in spring.

Natural fertilizers are available in three forms:

- *Single-ingredient options.* These include cow manure, poultry manure, seaweed, blood meal, bone meal, feather meal, cottonseed meal, alfalfa meal, leaf litter, compost, bone, wood ash, and worm castings.
- *Granular blends.* These use a mix of the animal, plant, and mineral ingredients listed above; they usually offer an N-P-K ratio of 4-5-4 or 3-3-3.
- *Liquid fertilizers.* These may have fewer macronutrients, but they also contain trace nutrients, amino acids, and vitamins. These fertilizers include liquid kelp, fish emulsion, and fish hydrosylate.

You can work both granular fertilizer and liquid fertilizer into the soil surface. Another option is to add a time-release fertilizer that allows for slow uptake and continuous feeding of plants like vegetables and ornamentals.

Synthetic, or inorganic, fertilizers contain no natural ingredients. They are water-soluble and are almost immediately taken up by plants. While this provides a quick boost of nutrients and rapid greening, the color won't last long. Gardeners must regularly reapply synthetic fertilizers to keep the results from fading. Synthetic fertilizers do little to stimulate soil life, improve soil texture, or promote long-term fertility. They can also leach into waterways. Synthetic fertilizer needs to be used cautiously—apply too much and it may burn your lawn and plants. They come in liquid, pellet, granule, and spike forms; the nutrients they contain and the percentages are listed on the label.

In order to avoid overfertilizing your garden, even with natural products, carefully follow label instructions. And be sure to test your soil every three or four years to determine if fertilizing is even necessary.

FEEDING THE KITCHEN GARDEN

Fertilizing vegetables, berries, and melons is a must if you wish to get the highest yields and best-quality produce. A soil test can determine what specific fertilizers are needed. The most common recommendations for vegetable gardens are nitrogen and phosphorus, but these aren't the only nutrients a healthy garden requires. Plants are composed primarily of carbon, hydrogen, and oxygen, nutrients absorbed from the air and water, but a fertile garden must have more than 14 additional macro- and micronutrients for healthiest growth. As with flower gardens, there are two types of fertilizer for kitchen gardens: synthetic and natural. Most produce needs a balanced fertilizer, such as a 10-10-10, but some need additional potassium. Leafy greens often only require nitrogen.

Manure tea is a simple decoction to make. Put a few shovelfuls of manure into a porous bag and then steep the bag in a tub of water until it looks like weak tea. Use the manure tea when you water to add supplemental organic nutrients. Another vegetable garden fertilizer option is to side dress your plants. This means placing a nitrogen-rich organic fertilizer beside each row of plants. As the plants are watered, the roots absorb the nutrients from the fertilizer.

Synthetic fertilizers, such as blue corn fertilizer made of the essential N-P-K nutrients, are highly popular because they can be very effective. Caution must be taken with them, however; they can be toxic, and should never be used in gardens frequented by children and pets.

Derived from raw chicken manure, chicken manure pellets offer a less messy and odoriferous way to apply natural fertilizers to your garden. They work well for vegetables, flowers, fruit trees, and native plants.

MULCHING OPTIONS

To mulch or not is a personal choice. Some traditionalist gardeners do not mulch their plants or crops. They rely on the soil to insulate plants from heat and cold and to retain enough moisture to supply water to thirsty roots. Yet, increasing numbers of gardeners are realizing the many benefits of adding mulch to a garden plot. If nothing else, mulch makes a garden more attractive and "finished" looking. The color you choose can highlight scattered solo plantings and provide a frame for group plantings.

One of mulch's most valuable properties is the ability to retain moisture in the soil. Other advantages include the following:

- Organic mulches break down over time and contribute nutrients that increase soil health. This can be very helpful in areas with poor soil.
- Mulch piled around plant crowns can reduce winter injury and also help with weed control.
- Mulch is able to protect soil from wind or rain erosion.
- Mulch creates a visual barrier that protects plants from weed eaters and lawnmowers.
- Certain evergreen mulches, such as cypress, cedar, or pinewood chips, do an excellent job of repelling ticks, fleas, and gnats.

TYPES OF MULCH

The wide variety of mulches available at garden centers can be broken down into two main groups—organic and inorganic. Organic mulch tends to cost less than synthetic mulch, but it has to be replaced more frequently due to deterioration.

Organic

Organic, or natural, mulches include such things as hardwood chips, pine straw, grass clippings, fresh or old hay, straw, oyster shells, pine needles, and crushed leaves.

A garden bed with and without mulch. Here, the rusty red of the cedar chips complements the green fronds of a Bismarck palm tree, highlighting its color.

Inorganic

Inorganic, or synthetic, mulches include pebbles, crushed rock, glass rondels, plastic, rubber mats, or chips. Pebbles, crushed rock, and glass rondels look very polished in a garden, but in summer they can heat up and might tend to dry out the soil.

The best mulch for your garden depends on your personal preference and budget. If you are interested in improving soil fertility, choose an organic mulch. Gardeners wishing to keep their gardens completely organic, however, should be careful when choosing natural mulch that contains dyes (*see* below). For gardeners with large landscaped areas who don't like to fuss too much, synthetic mulch may be the best option.

Common Types of Mulch

Red cedar chips | Pebbles | Pine bark

Glass rondels | Rubber chips | Oyster shells

IS DYED MULCH SAFE?

Gardeners love the fact that hardwood or bark chips come in a variety of

Colored Plastic Mulch

A recent arrival on the gardening scene, rolls of plastic mulch are increasingly found in farms and kitchen gardens, where "plasticulture" is used to modify microclimates and improve crops. Plastic mulch warms the soil, minimizes evaporation, limits nutrients leaching from soil, and results in earlier harvests. Perhaps the most interesting aspect is that different color mulches are impacting various crops.

- **Black.** Black, the most prevalent and least expensive plastic mulch, is said to suppress weeds better, thanks to its opacity. It also raises soil temperature up to 5 degrees at a 2-inch (5 cm) depth.
- **Red.** Plastic mulch in red works better for crops like tomatoes, which yielded 20 percent more fruit in studies, while strawberries were sweeter and had a better fragrance.
- **Blue.** This color mulch is better than black if you are planting cantaloupes, summer squash, or cucumbers.
- **Silver.** This light-colored mulch is great at keeping aphids and whiteflies away and also reduces populations of cucumber beetles.
- **Brown and green.** These two mulches are available in infrared transmitting plastic (IRT). This warms up your soil better than regular plastic mulch at the start of the growing season.

These heirloom tomato plants have been mulched with red plastic sheets. Recent studies show that this new type of mulch will aid in the ripening of the future fruit.

shades, from pale cedar, to reds, browns, and even black. These dyed mulches can be very aesthetically pleasing and make landscape plants and beds stand out, but not all dyed mulches are safe or healthy for plants.

Although most mulches are colored with harmless dyes, like iron oxide-based dyes for red or carbon-based dyes for black and dark brown, some cheaper mulches can be dyed with harmful or toxic chemicals.

Generally, if the price of colored mulch seems too good to be true, you should spend the extra money for a higher quality—and safer—mulch.

Bear in mind that it is not the dye that is of concern when it comes mulches, but rather the wood. Most natural mulches, like cedar mulch or pine bark, are made directly from trees, but many colored mulches are made from recycled wood—like old pallets, decks, packing crates, and the like. These recycled bits of treated wood can contain chromates copper arsenate (CCA). Although using CCA to treat wood was banned in 2003, this wood is sometimes still collected from demolition sites or other sources and recycled into dyed mulches. CCA-treated wood can kill beneficial soil bacteria, beneficial insects, earthworms, and even young plants. It can also be harmful to the people spreading this mulch and animals who dig in it. Dyed mulches also break down more slowly than natural mulches and can deplete nitrogen from the soil. Better alternatives are pine needles, natural double- or triple-processed mulch, cedar mulch, or pine bark. These mulches also will not fade as quickly as dyed mulches.

WATERING THE GARDEN

When it comes to watering their gardens, many people struggle over questions such as, "How often should I water my plants?" or "How much water should I give my garden at a time?" It's really not that complicated, but there are some factors that should be considered. These include the type of soil you are dealing with, the size of your garden or beds, the types of plants or crops you are growing, and what your climate or weather is like. Naturally, seasonal rainfall makes a difference in a garden's water needs. A wet autumn followed by a snowy winter will start your spring garden off with good levels of ground moisture.

WHEN TO WATER

While the general rule of thumb is about an inch or two of water each week using deep, infrequent watering as opposed to the more frequent shallow watering, this really depends on a number of factors.

- *Soil type.* This a primary consideration. Sandy soil is going to hold less water than heavier, more-absorbent clay soil. Therefore, it's going to dry out faster, while the clay-like soil will hold moisture longer (and is more susceptible to overwatering). This is why amending the soil with compost is so important. Healthier soil drains better but allows for some water retention. Applying surface mulch is also a good idea, helping to keep moisture in the soil and reducing water needs.
- *Weather conditions.* These determine when to water garden plants. If you're having a hot spell, for example, you'll have to water more often. Of course, in rainy conditions, little watering is needed. Most container plants need watering on a daily basis in hot, dry conditions—sometimes twice or even three times a day. Hanging plants also need more attention in prolonged heat.
- *Plant varieties.* These, too, dictate when and how often to water. Different plants have different watering needs. Larger plants need more water, as do newly planted ones. Vegetables, bedding plants, and many perennials have shallower root systems and also require more frequent watering, some daily—especially in temps over 85° F (30° C).
- *Time of day.* This also dictates when a garden should be watered. The most suitable time for watering is early morning, which reduces evaporation, but late afternoon or early evening are okay, too—provided you keep the foliage from getting wet, which can lead to fungal issues.

A raised-bed vegetable garden has been fitted with a drip irrigation system with hoses that run along the plants' bases. This watering system is both good for the environment and good for your budget, possibly reducing water use by 30 to 50 percent.

If you are conservation-minded, you might consider setting up a water collection barrel under your gutter downspout or employing a child's wading pool to collect rainwater. Use floating mosquito dunks to prevent these insect pests from breeding in any standing water, and make sure there are a few bricks or rocks in the pool in case any small animals tumble in while drinking.

Five Watering Mistakes

The following are some errors gardeners should be aware of.

1. Avoid watering in bright sunlight, where much of the water will evaporate.

2. Don't allow a strong overhead spray of water to pummel your tender plants; this also wastes water, which ends up on foliage instead of in the soil. Splashed-up soil can add the risk of disease to leaves.

3. Don't underwater or overwater the garden. Some dried organic bedding products, like peat, take time to rehydrate, so after the initial watering, wait a bit, then check how far the water has gone down into the soil. If only an inch or so, then water again. Overwatering is often a problem with containers that have no drainage hole. The end result is root rot. In garden plots, signs of overwatering are foliage yellowing and wilting.

4. Never water all your plants the same way. In every garden there are plants with different water needs and at different stages of development. Delicate seedlings need to be watered differently (soaker hose or hand watering) than hardy perennials (irrigation or hose watering). Thirsty fruiting plants, like tomatoes, require more water than leafy greens or succulents.

5. Failure to mulch, a practice that helps retain soil moisture, can have serious repercussions, especially with crops like potatoes, where the yield goes way down if the soil dries out.

Knowing when and how to water a garden correctly can ensure a healthy growing season with lush plants. Watering cans are a traditional method of garden irrigation, but it is labor-intensive and best reserved for small plots or container plantings.

An automatic hose timer. With this device you can set the duration of watering times. The timer will automatically shut off at the end time you've specified.

HOW MUCH WATER SHOULD I GIVE MY PLANTS?

Deep watering encourages deeper and stronger root growth. Therefore, watering gardens about 2 inches (5 cm) or so once a week is preferable. Watering more often, but less deeply, only leads to weaker root growth and evaporation.

TYPES OF WATERING SYSTEMS

Overhead sprinklers are often frowned upon, except on lawns, as these lose more water to evaporation. Soaker hoses or drip irrigation systems set between the plant rows are always a better option, with water going straight to the roots, while keeping foliage dry. Both these systems can be fitted with automatic timers that make sure your plants are getting watered on a regular basis, even while you are away from home.

Of course, there are the old standbys—hand watering with a hose, wand, or watering can. Because the latter process is more time consuming, it's best reserved for smaller garden areas, container plants, and seedling trays.

HELPFUL TOOLS

There are a number of tools and gadgets that will quickly prove their worth at watering time.

- *Automatic hose timer.* This will turn on your soaker hose a set number of times a week.
- *Variable-pattern spray nozzle using quick-connect technology.* This is a system that allows you to easily connect and disconnect hose attachments
- *Hose-splitting device.* This allows you to place a soaker hose and timer on one connector and a regular watering hose with nozzle on the other.
- *Hose-end sprayer receptacles.* These allow you to spread fertilizer or other amendments around the garden while you water.

CHAPTER FOUR

THE FLOWER GARDEN

For many of us, a flower garden represents a battle, one of rampant beauty challenged by industry . . . often ordered and tidy at its center, but a bit overgrown at the edges. Restraint should be its watchword, but abundance its motto.

Whether you have 50 square feet to play with or 500, always keep in mind that you are merely the custodial artist of this space but in no true sense the creator. That title goes to Chance, for what is a garden if not an eternal gaming wheel? This does not mean you cannot de-stress here or take pleasure in its earthy victories. A proper flower garden is a haven for everyone, even those who toil in its service. And in case you fear running out of lovelies to cultivate, reflect that there are nearly 400,000 flowering plants in the world, yet fewer than 5 percent are regularly grown.

PROPER PLANTING TECHNIQUES

Whether you purchased your flowering bedding plants in small pots from a nursery or grew them from seeds, you naturally want to give these youngsters the best start possible when you place them in the ground. But even if you've done this before, some questions might still pop up—regarding hole size, depth, spacing, light requirements, or watering. Never fear . . . the five simple steps below will guide you through the entire process, putting you well on the way to achieving a showpiece garden with abundant blooms.

STEP 1
FINDING THE RIGHT SPOT

The first thing you need to determine is whether your plants need sun, shade, or semi-shade. This info should be listed on the seed packet or plant tag. Next, place your pots on the ground in the areas where they will get the appropriate amount of sunlight or shade—sun-lovers out in the open, shade-lovers under some kind of cover, semi-shade plants in areas with partial sunlight. If the planting instructions say "full sun" that means six hours or more of direct sunlight per day, though not necessarily continuously. Semi-shade typically means four to six hours of sun per day. Shade definitions vary depending on how intense the shade really is. Dappled shade, when the sun peeks through the tree canopy, gets more light than deep shade, an area shadowed by foliage or an overhang.

STEP 2
DIG THE HOLE

Lush flower gardens start with healthy soil. Most flowering plants grow best in loose, well-drained soil with a lot of organic amendments. You don't need to dig up the whole garden to plant flowers, but do dig up enough soil so that you can add compost to improve soil structure and add nutrients. The hole should be at least as deep and wide as the root ball of the plant.

Mass planting is used to fill in garden or landscape areas with groupings of flowers. This creates drama, adds quick color, and minimizes weed growth. Plant groupings using the trench method—with a spade, dig an open trench of the appropriate depth and size, place the plants in position, then carefully backfill around the roots.

Avoid digging or handling soil when it is wet to prevent compaction, which decreases the amount of space between soil particles, which is needed for roots to grow. To test for wetness, dig a small soil sample from a 3-inch (7.5 cm) hole. Squeeze the soil into a ball, and then toss the ball onto a hard surface. If the soil holds together, it's too wet for planting. If the earth ball shatters, it is okay to plant.

STEP 3
PLANT YOUR FLOWERS

To plant seedlings you have started yourself, follow the seed packet directions on how deep to plant and how far apart to place them. With potted plants, there are usually care and planting instructions on the plastic tag. Otherwise take a quick look online. Most potted plants should be positioned so that the garden soil is the same level as the soil in the pot. Some

Step 1 is bringing your potted plants out to the garden bed and carefully planning the placement of each, keeping in mind the amount and quality of light and shade the flower bed receives.

Step 2 is digging the hole. Be sure each hole is as deep and wide as the root ball of the plant that will go in it and that each hole is spaced the recommended distance from the others.

Planting Bulbs

Bulbs are a bit trickier to plant than potted specimens are. It is absolutely critical to plant them at the depth and distance apart indicated on their labels.

- Experienced gardeners plant bulbs in groups: simply dig a trench of the appropriate size and depth, then loosen the soil 2 to 4 inches (5–10 cm) below the bulb depth.
- Place the bulbs in the trench, pointy side up, making sure to properly space them.
- Fill the trench with soil, and press firmly with your hands. Indicate the planting area with stakes and twine so you won't accidentally dig it up.

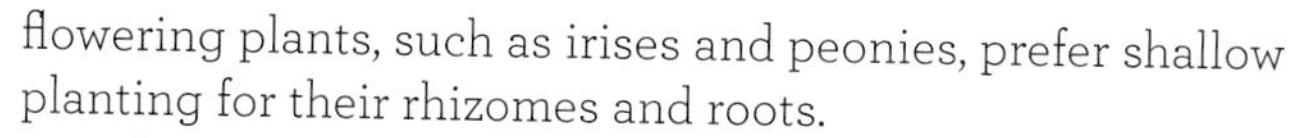

flowering plants, such as irises and peonies, prefer shallow planting for their rhizomes and roots.

To free potted plants, squeeze the container to loosen the soil. Invert the pot in your hand and the plant should fall out easily. If it doesn't, check for roots that may be growing through the bottom holes. These can be snipped off and removed. If the exposed plant is potbound, with roots circling the base, gently tease them loose before placing the plant in the hole. This allows the roots to spread out in a healthy manner rather than continuing to grow in a circle. Gently backfill the hole.

Step 3 is planting. Carefully remove each plant from its pot, gently loosening the roots, and then place it into the hole you've dug. Once the plant is in the ground, backfill the soil around it.

STEP 4
WATER DEEPLY AND ADD MULCH

Once your new flowers are in the ground, thoroughly soak the soil. Flowering plants typically require 1 to 2 inches of moisture each week to remain healthy and bloom consistently. If you don't receive enough rain during a given week, get out the hose. It's a good practice to water deeply and less frequently, rather than shallowly and more often; this stimulates the roots of the plants to grow deeper. On the other hand, don't ever let your soil become waterlogged, or your roots may rot.

Many gardeners place a thick layer of organic mulch, such as shredded bark or pine needles, around their new plants. This not only makes the garden space look attractive, the mulch helps slow down evaporation, reduces how often you need to water, and also discourages weeds.

Step 4 is watering. Your new flowering plants each need an initial inch or two of water to soak the soil. You might also want to add a layer of organic mulch at this time.

STEP 5
AFTERCARE

Harvesting flowers for arrangements actually makes some plants healthier and denser, while deadheading spent blossoms, such as on zinnias or dahlias, encourages the plants to keep blooming. Maintain the tidy look of your flower garden by removing any dead plants or browning foliage—daylilies often need withered leaves clipped off—and with occasional fresh mulch and a weekly edging of the lawn.

Step 5 is really ongoing. It is taking care of the plants as they grow, watering as necessary, deadheading spent blooms to keep the plant flowering, clipping dead leaves, or adding more mulch.

BUYING PLANTS AND SEEDS

A century ago, dedicated gardeners hunted for fresh sources of new plants beside the local farm shop or garden club swap meet. Today that is no longer the case. In early spring, commercial nurseries and big box home improvement stores are simply brimming with tempting specimens—including flowers, foliage plants, fruits and vegetables, shrubs, and succulents. Meanwhile, online plant sites offer everything from old-fashioned favorites to the trendiest exotics. Yet, in spite of all the brick-and-mortar retailers and the countless online garden shops, one of the oldest outlets for plants and seeds, the mail-order catalog, still continues to enthrall gardeners.

A selection of seed catalogs from a variety of companies. Even if many of us shop mostly online or at local stores, these are like wish books of all the plants that we covet.

MAIL-ORDER CATALOGS

One of the ways gardeners survive the "deprivations" of winter is by pouring over seed and plant catalogs and jotting down wish lists of the items they plan to order. Usually around the New Year these publications appear in the mailbox, harbingers of spring and finer weather to come.

Plant catalogs have a history that goes back 400 years, to the first-known garden catalog—bulb catalog *Florilegium amplissimum et selectissimum* by Dutch grower Emanuel Sweerts—which appeared at the 1612 Frankfurt Fair. It doubtless inspired a similar sense of excitement and expectation in those early horticulturists.

Modern catalogs typically feature popular varieties of flowers, shrubs, trees, and produce, along with information on their eventual height, spread, and bloom time. Many showcase new cultivars and may offer heirloom species that hark back to the gardens of earlier decades. Some companies feature organic selections, wildflowers, native plants, or seeds from the national seed bank. Some give back to community or global concerns. If price is an issue, a number pride themselves on keeping costs relatively low. Catalogs can also tell you which plants do best in your growing region and advise you on species considered invasives in your state, those that are disease resistant, and which ones attract pollinators. Not

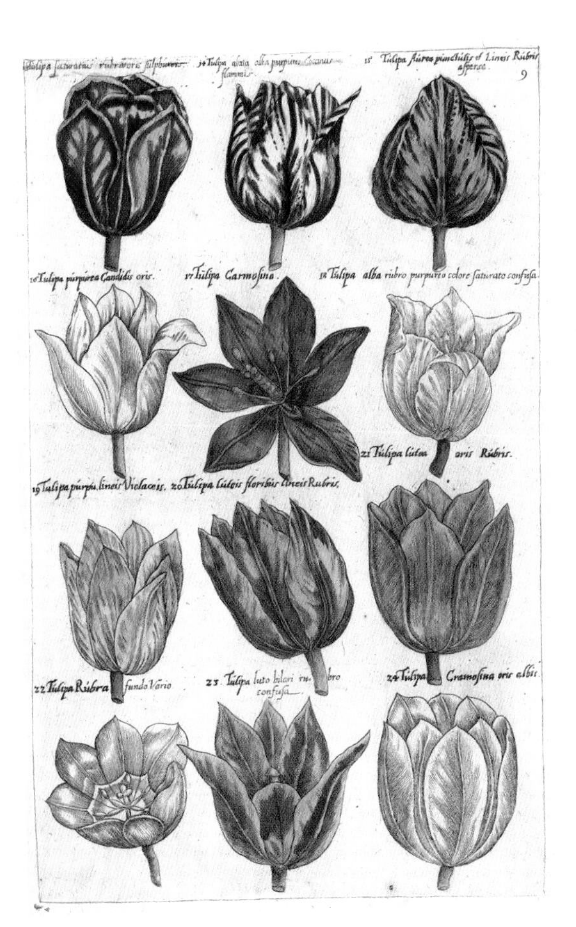

A hand-colored page of tulips from *Florilegium amplissimum et selectissimum.* Emanuel Sweerts, a Dutch gardener and florist specializing in exotics, first published the *Florilegium* in 1612, showing roughly 560 different flowers. It was essentially an unpriced sale catalog of Sweerts's plant stock.

surprisingly, most mail-order companies now also sell online and offer catalogs online. Still, the printed catalogs remain a cherished winter distraction.

Among the most popular catalogs are:

- *Baker Creek Heirloom Seeds* (rareseeds.com). Great old-time seeds with unusual edibles. Supplies poor countries with seeds.
- *Bountiful Gardens* (bountiful garden.org). Certified as an Organic Handler and based in Willits, California. Also offer books, videos, and a curated selection of favorite garden tools.
- *Brecks* (brecks.com). A long-time resource for an immense variety of tulips direct from Holland.
- *Burpee* (burpee.com). Founded in Philadelphia in 1881, one of America's largest seed companies.
- *Gurneys Seed & Nursery* (gurneys.com). A trusted garden source since 1866.
- *Jackson & Perkins* (jacksonandperkins.com). Growing award-winning roses for more than a century.
- *Seed Savers Exchange* (seedsavers.org). Conserving biodiversity with over 20,000 varieties in an underground freezer.
- *Territorial Seed Company* (territorialseed.com). Excellent varieties of heirloom seeds and hybrids.
- *White Flower Farm* (whiteflowerfarm.com). This Litchfield, Connecticut, nursery has been shipping ornamentals since 1950.

Staff Hacks

Laura Walters, GKH Junior Editor, advises: "Collect seeds after flowers fade to expand your garden for free! Larkspur seeds are especially easy to harvest. Wait until seed pods become dry. Shake plants to tell if they are ready—seed pods should sound like tiny maracas. Pop open pods to collect seeds. Sow larkspur seeds in fall for beautiful, low-maintenance blooms next summer."

ONLINE PLANT STORES

Gardeners now have the convenience of ordering garden plants and houseplants from various online sources without ever leaving home. Some favorite shops include the following.

- *Amazon*. Offers a great variety of houseplants and nursery picks
- *Antique Rose Emporium*. Extensive choice of historic rose varieties, including stunning 'Julia Child' or whimsical 'Mermaid'
- *Bloomscape*. Order a plant, pick a terra-cotta pot.
- *Bluestone Perennials*. Endless assortment, something for most aesthetic sensibilities
- *Brighter Bloomers*. Offers a selection of evergreens, flowering trees, palm trees, and perennials. Also Care Resource Center.
- *Etsy*. Different sellers offer a variety of plants and trees.
- *Fastgrowingtrees.com*. Online tree shop also sells shrubs, hedges, houseplants, and tools.
- *Great Gardens Plants*. Hundreds of plants, including vines and climbers.
- Greenery NYC. Prices start as low as $12.
- *Home Depot*. More plants here than at their brick-and-mortar locations
- *Horti*. Subscribe for a new plant delivery every month.

When a catalog says a plant is shipped "bare-root," you will receive a dormant plant with exposed roots. This plant needs to be placed in the ground as soon as possible, after a 12-hour soak; otherwise the roots need to be kept moist.

- *Lively Boot*. Lets you create a magazine-worthy landscape that is safe for your pets
- *Logee's*. Offers many rare plants and other garden needs
- *Lowe's*. Impressive online garden shop, though not all plants are available for delivery
- *Monrovia*. Allows shoppers to connect with local garden centers and avoid big box stores
- *Nature Hills*. Offering a wide range of plants, including overstocks with reduced prices
- *Plant.com*. Herbs, bonsai, and more
- *Plant's Delight Nursery*. Offers a wide array of flowering plants for sun and shade.
- *The Sill*. A popular plant retailer on Instagram
- *The Tree Center*. Trees, shrubs, and bushes galore, plus the Arrive and Thrive Guarantee

If you want to leave your home to look for seeds and plants, try a garden center or other store. Here an open-air flower market wows shoppers with walls of flower seed packets, displays of live potted cacti, and bins overflowing with flower bulbs.

SPROUTING FLOWER SEEDS INDOORS

Starting annual and perennial flowers from seeds is an easy way to add colorful blooms to your home landscape. Considering that seed packets are far less expensive than potted, well-grown nursery stock, this method is also quite cost effective. Starting flowers indoors also allows you to get a jump on the growing season. If you sow your seeds at the right time for your area, you'll have strong, vigorous seedlings ready to go into the ground once the regular growing season begins. In regions with shorter growing seasons, this is especially ideal.

You first need to consider the growth requirements of the plants—whether each flower type is cold hardy or tender to frost. This information will help you to determine the best time to start seeds. Depending upon how quickly the plant grows, flowers seeded indoors generally take about four to eight weeks before the projected outdoor transplant date, which should take place after the estimated date of your region's final frost.

Gather your soil, trays, seeds, and other tools to prepare for planting your seedlings. Look for eco-friendly and biodegradable seedling trays made of recycled pulp.

All the items needed to start seeds can be found online, at nurseries, big box stores, or discount stores. Most seedling starter kits are fairly inexpensive and often reusable. Or you can create your own starter kit by using egg cartons as flats, mixing your own seed starter medium, and planting seeds saved from the previous year's harvest.

- Flats or peat pots
- Seed starter mix or peat disks
- Water (a spray bottle works best on delicate seedlings)
- Clear lid or plastic wrap
- ID stakes

PREPARING THE TRAYS

First fill a seed flat or tray of peat pots with potting soil or other seed-starting medium. Firm up the soil, mist it until damp, and then sow the seeds at the depth indicated on the packet. Some seeds require light for best germination, while others will need to be covered with soil. (Once germination has commenced, however, the baby plants will need light to photosynthesize. Indirect, but bright light provides the best growing conditions.)

Water the seed trays again, then cover with a lid or plastic wrap and keep the flat in a warm location. The optimum germination temperature for most seeds is 70 to 75° F (21–24° C). Avoid placing flats in hot, southern windows, as the plants will become leggy and dry out. Also choose a spot away from drafts but not next to a heating vent or radiator. Certain heat-loving species that need additional warmth to germinate can be assisted with a heated seedling mat. Keep the soil moist, and remove the cover to let it breathe for a bit each day to avoid damping off. Once the seedlings are evident, move the flat to a bright location with protection from searing sun. A sunny window may provide ample sunlight for many species, but others will benefit from the use of grow lights.

TIME TO POT UP

Once the seedlings have reached an adequate size, usually 3 or 4 inches (7.5–10 cm), with vigorous foliage, you can move them into small pots. Now they are ready to be hardened off—acclimated to growing outside. This process involves placing the pots outside for several hours, increasing the time every few days. By the end of a week or so, you should be able to place the seedings in the ground without worry.

Both annual and perennial plants respond well to indoor starts. The best candidates include those with small seeds and those that grow very slowly before becoming established. Other good candidates include those that may have special germination requirements, such as a period of cold stratification—a method that replicates outdoor conditions by placing seeds in the refrigerator.

Please note that many fast-growing plants might be better suited to direct sowing, because certain species can quickly outgrow their seed containers and become root bound. Other, more delicate varieties might need to be directly sown as well, as root disturbances during transplanting could greatly reduce their vigor during the growing season.

Once your seedlings reach a certain size, transfer them to sturdier pots, and begin getting them used to the outdoor life.

10 Best Flowers to Start From Seed

The following 10 plants have proven to be reliable growers and quick bloomers when started indoors from seeds. Plus, all of them will return for a second season if you use the "pull-and-shake" method of replanting. In this method, you simply pull up the old plants, carry them to where you want flowers next year, and give them a good shake. The clever seeds then know what to do.

1. SWEET ALYSSUM
(Lobularia maritima)
This fragrant annual, a favorite of hoverflies and other beneficial insects, softens the edge of beds and walkways. For more information, *see* page 82.

2. CALENDULA
(Calendula officinalis)
This fast-growing, cheerfully golden flower, also called pot marigold, has a long history as a medicinal, skin-healing herb. For more information, *see* page 222.

3. JOHNNY JUMP-UP
(Viola tricolor)
Also known as mini-pansy or field pansy, this quick-blooming flower partners well with spring-flowering bulbs. For information about pansies, *see* Pansy, page 77.

4. CORNFLOWER
(Centaurea cyanus)
Also known as bachelor's button, this old-fashioned blue beauty is beloved of bees and has edible petals. For more information, *see* page 67.

5. NIGELLA
(Nigella damascene)
Commonly called love-in-a-mist, its charming pastel flowers, framed by lacy foliage, mature into exotic seed pods that are lovely in dried arrangements.

6. NASTURTIUM
(Tropaeolum majus)
This tasty edible flower attracts bees and other pollinators; interplants with cucumbers or tomatoes to deter pests. For more information, *see* page 231.

7. ANNUAL PHLOX
(Phlox drummondii)
This hardy annual, a favorite of butterflies, provides beautiful cut flowers for bouquets in shades from white to yellow to pink to deep red; some are bicolor.

8. PETUNIA
***(Petunia* spp.)**
This pest-resistant favorite comes in endless colors that look great in borders and containers; some are grown for fragrance. For more information, *see* page 78.

9. CALIFORNIA POPPY
(Eschscholzia californica)
These striking golden flowers can go from seed to bloom in 60 days. Plants reseed effortlessly and provide protein-rich pollen.

10. SUNFLOWER
(Helianthus annuus)
The cold-hardy seedlings often survive spring frosts and grow into towering, eternally cheerful, adults. For more information, *see* page 81.

A GALLERY OF
SPECIALTY GARDENS

Once a gardener gets the knack for growing flowers, they often become more selective. Along with this new sense of discrimination comes the desire to create something more than just a random mix of different varieties, no matter how attractive. This thoughtful curation results in what is called the themed or "statement" garden, a growing space that focuses on one singular aspect of blooming plants: their color, their scent, their connection to literature, history, or the Bible, or any number of other traits. This garden may be tucked in a corner of the backyard or given pride of place in a front yard, but the appeal of a themed garden rarely wanes. It often becomes a spark for the senses and represents an elevation of the gardener's art.

Themed gardens are nothing new—gardeners have been growing related plants since medieval monks gathered in one place species known for their medicinal powers. In 1906, famed illustrator Walter Crane put together a collection of flowers and other plants mentioned in Shakespeare's plays and sonnets that gardeners of the time could use as inspiration.

MOON GARDEN

A night garden composed of pale flowers, night bloomers, and silver or variegated foliage plants can be entrancing and haunting in equal measure. Consider night bloomers like evening primrose and moonflower; pale blooms like daisies, white iris, creeping phlox, sweet alyssum, viburnum, and mock orange; and glimmering foliage additions like dusty miller. Add sublime scents with white roses, white lilac, sweet alyssum, and white nicotiana.

GOTH GARDEN

This moody, intense space makes an interesting alternative to the glowing Moon Garden. A goth-themed garden focuses on black or deep purple flowers and foliage. Consider 'Diabolo' ninebark, 'Queen of Night' tulip, 'The Watchman' hollyhock, 'Old Black Magic' iris, and 'Sophistica Blackberry' petunia for dramatic impact. Purple sweet potato vines, 'Palace Purple' heuchera, and deep burgundy coleus add suitably hued foliage.

SHAKESPEARE GARDEN

Taking its cues from the Bard of Avon, this Elizabethan garden showcases some of the 175 plants and herbs mentioned in his collected works. A number of these gardens can be found at accessible locations like Stratford-on-Avon and in New York's Central Park. Choices include bachelor button, carnation, columbine, daffodil, daisy, fennel, holly, larkspur, lavender, mandrake, mint, narcissus, peony, poppy, rosemary, rose, strawberry, violet, willow, and yew.

STUMPERY

Like something out of a Lewis Carroll fantasy, this unique type of strolling garden (famously interpreted at Highgrove by Prince Charles of Great Britain) creates a tranquil atmosphere garden. It draws inspiration from the Victorian tradition of growing ferns among upturned tree stumps and incorporates large, uprooted, weathered stumps in a shaded glade or along a shadowy path, accompanied by feathery ferns and other understory plants.

SCENT GARDEN

Enjoy a mix of delicate or intoxicating aromas by planting a collection of scented flowers that are sure to attract bees, butterflies, moths, and hummingbirds. Make sure to incorporate a low bench for olfactory sampling. Top candidates include lily-of-the-valley, gardenia, jasmine, nicotiana, bee balm, freesia, plumeria, peony, wisteria, lavender, tuberose, mandevilla, phlox, sweet pea, honeysuckle, roses, and dianthus.

TEA GARDEN

These gardens set a mood of ease and tranquility and are small versions of pleasure gardens—parks open to the public for recreation—that occur in several cultures. In Japan, the *roji* acts as the entrance to a tea house. In addition to stepping-stone pathways, they feature native plants, moss, and grasses and a space to sit and converse. Consider growing herbs like chamomile, lemon balm, and lavender, that can actually be used to make tea.

SALSA GARDEN

This small plot contains everything you might need to create authentic Mexican dishes and spicy sauces. In a sunny spot, combine cilantro, tomatoes, tomatillos, several types of peppers including bell, poblano, and jalapeño, and sweet onions. What more is there to say . . . but Ole! (You should also consider a Pizza Garden with oregano, fresh basil, peppers, and onions as another classic ethnic alternative.)

APOTHECARY GARDEN

This garden features traditional herbs and plants that would have served as restoratives or medicines as far back as biblical times. Some are still in use today, brewed in teas or chewed to ease pain. Consider planting angelica, clary sage, rose, hops, rosemary, lemon balm, lavender, motherwort, echinacea, peppermint, and wild bergamot. Invest in a book on herbs and other medicinal plants to create your own health aids.

Dig Deeper

READ MORE AT GARDENING KNOW HOW

One way of creating a specialty garden is to choose plants that bloom in various tones of a single color. No matter what your favorite color is, you are sure to find flowers to create a monochromatic-themed garden. Just follow these URLs to find out more.

- **"Yellow Color Schemes — How to Create a Yellow Garden"** (URL = gkh.us/20817)
- **"Blue Garden Plan — Designing and Using Blue Plants in Gardens"** (URL = gkh.us/21200)
- **"Pink Plants in Gardens: Tips for Planning a Pink Garden Design"** (URL = gkh.us/175854)

CONTAINER GARDENS

Setting plants in attractive containers and placing them in artful groups around your patio or deck can create as much of a relaxing garden space as a proper bed full of blooms. These portable gardens are especially useful for people with small or paved yards, those living in rental properties where they mustn't disturb the landscaping, and apartment dwellers who want to make the most of a balcony or terrace.

A window box arrangement shows effective use of the three elements of container planting: tall flowers at the back, pretty middle flowers, and greenery spilling over the edge.

THE THREE ELEMENTS

To create balance and movement in any container, it is important to mix plants of three basic shapes—thrillers, fillers, and spillers. Just be sure that the plants you combine in one pot have similar sun and watering requirements.

Thrillers

These are the striking, tall plants at the back, the vertical elements that grab the viewer's attention. Examples include salvia, dahlia, cosmos, aster, dragon-wing or angel-wing begonia, geranium, and, in larger pots, canna.

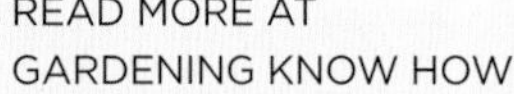

READ MORE AT GARDENING KNOW HOW

You can create your own stone-look container with hypertufa, a blend of peat moss, perlite, and quick-set concrete that is molded into pots and is far lighter than concrete. The porous material is perfect for alpine plants and succulents that require good drainage. To find out more about creating hypertufa pots, just follow this URL or scan the QR code.

- **"How to Make Hypertufa Containers for Gardens"** (URL = gkh.us/19870)

Fillers

These are the midsize plants, clumping and compact, often combined for pops of color. Effective fillers include lobelia, sweet alyssum, pansy, ageratum, begonia, petunia, coleus, dusty miller, caladium, sedum, gerbera daisy, lantana, gazania, and heuchera.

Spillers

These showy specimens tumble and cascade over the edge of the container, reducing its hard edge. Ideal candidates include sweet potato vine (purple or green), string of beads, burro's tail, calibrachoa, bacopa, ivy, nasturtium, vinca, and trailing begonia.

To maintain visual interest, make sure your plants are displayed at differing heights. Use plant stands, plinths, pavers, small benches, or wooden crates to elevate at least half your specimens. An easy way to gain height is placing a wooden plank over two upright cinder blocks. It also helps for the space to have a central feature—a cafe table and chairs, a fountain, or a small sculpture—around which the containers can be arranged.

Be aware that container plants need frequent watering and some effort to keep them from baking in the hot summer sun.

PLANTING A CONTAINER

Your first step should be deciding on pot size: for a mix of plants, the container should be at least 12 inches (30 cm) wide. Annuals need 8 inches (20 cm) of soil, while grasses and small shrubs may need several feet. Choose potting soil, which contains sterilized soil and other ingredients, or "soil-less mixes" consisting of peat moss, compost, and perlite or vermiculite. For shallow-rooted plants in tall pots, fill the bottom half with terra-cotta shards or packing peanuts to promote drainage. Add larger center plants first, and then work outward, backfilling as you go. Water well before placing in the garden.

TYPES OF POTS

There are many choices for containers, from formal stone to whimsical recycled household items.

Terra-cotta

These reddish clay pots are the garden standard. Unglazed examples lose water quickly, so they are best for shady spots. Use only glazed terra-cotta in sunny areas. In cold weather, these pots will flake, chip, and crack.

Ceramic

With their glazed sides, these pots help soil retain moisture. They come in a variety of colors and patterns, but some may require drainage holes.

Wood

Planter boxes create a classic look. Cedar weathers well in its natural state, but for other wooden containers, add several coats of outdoor paint before exposure to the elements. Wood should also be lined with plastic to avoid rot.

Stone

Nothing adds class and elegance to a garden like a graceful stone container. Stone insulates and can overwinter in cold regions without harm. Ideal for evergreens or other hardy specimens you want to keep outdoors.

Concrete

This material provides insulation, moderating temperatures and moisture loss, but it is quite heavy. Always place a concrete container in its final location before planting.

Metal

Sleek containers give a garden a modern, urban feel, while older versions are great for a cozy garden. Set up near a water source, as metal can heat up the soil and needs frequent cooling.

Plastic

These are an economical option for gardeners with lots of plants. Many plastic pots have self-watering features, such as a built-in reservoir. They also come in hanging varieties. To refresh faded containers, use special spray paints intended for plastic.

Resin

These attractive planters ape the look of stone or concrete at a fraction of the price—and the weight. Made of a mix of stone aggregate and resin or fiberglass, they are virtually frost-proof.

Recycled containers

Many gardeners enjoy reusing kitchen containers, like colorful tomato sauce cans or storage tins, to grow plants. Just make sure you add drainage holes. Spray-painted tires can be used as planters in a number of ways: flat, upright, or hanging . . . even by turning them inside out. Flea market finds like old buckets, woven baskets, porcelain trays, and even old cowboy boots are often called into service in the container garden. Let your imagination run wild!

ANNUAL FLOWERS

Annuals—flowers or foliage plants that grow for one season—are the mainstay of many gardens. Often called bedding plants, they are the colorful fillers in perennial plots, the shade plants that bloom under tree canopies, and the hardy sun-lovers that thrive during the heat of summer. Some even generate light, alluring scents. When planted in individual containers, they populate patios, porches, and decks. In window boxes, they elevate curb appeal. And even though they may not return year after year, the concentration of flower color and the range of foliage patterns that annuals bring to a garden is rarely matched by their staider perennial cousins.

THE LONG BLOOMERS

Annual garden plants germinate from seed, then blossom, and finally set seeds before dying back. Although they must be replanted each year, they are generally showier than perennials, with a long blooming period from spring to just before the first autumn frost. Most annuals require good-to-rich soil, decent drainage, and feeding every two weeks.

Plants referred to as "hardy annuals" are those that can be seeded directly into the soil in early spring. These include cornflower and calendula. Half-hardy perennials, like dahlia and tuberous begonia, get started indoors and cannot be planted until all chance of frost is over. In regions with cold winters, they must be dug up and their root systems stored in a cool, dry area.

Planting annuals among green foliage is fast and easy. Bright and cheerful annuals are perfect for adding color to almost any kind of flower bed.

Annual flowers, such as colorful petunias, lobelia, and calibrachoa, are versatile plants that look stunning in containers of all kinds. Hanging baskets, for example, are eye-popping beauties that draw the eye upward and create decorative spaces where plants normally don't grow. They also bring the garden closer to the house, patio, lanai, or deck.

To learn more about annual flowers and to get suggestions about how you can incorporate them into your own garden, follow these links.

- **"Annual Plant Cycle: What Is an Annual Plant"** (URL = gkh.us/58816)
- **"Annual Garden Design: Creating a Garden Masterpiece with Annual Plants"** (URL = gkh.us/?p=4)
- **"Fall Blooming Annuals – Fall Annuals to Plant in Your Garden"** (URL = gkh.us/168300)

African Daisy

A bedding of purple, yellow, orange, red, and white African daisies in full bloom mass together in perfect harmony.

Osteospermum, or the African daisy, is a genus of flowering plants belonging to the Calenduleae, one of the smaller tribes of the sunflower/daisy family, Asteraceae. In recent years they have become an increasingly popular plant for use in border gardens and flower arrangements. Originally native to southern and eastern Africa and the Arabian peninsula, the plant's original 70 species now include more than 40 cultivars. The flowers take the form of disk florets and ray florets, with colors that range from white to yellow and orange to pink and even bicolor.

GROWING AFRICAN DAISIES

African daisies require conditions similar to those found in Africa—heat and full sun. They also need well-drained soil and, in fact, will tolerate dry soils. Osteospermums are annuals and, like most annuals, they enjoy extra fertilizer—try feeding weekly with a general fertilizer. They are, however, one of the few annuals that will still bloom if they are planted in poor soil.

You can expect the flowers to start blooming about midsummer. If you have grown them from seed, they might not start blooming until late summer. You can expect them to grow between 1 and 3 feet (30 cm–1 m) in height.

Editor's Picks

Here are just a few of the many *Osteospermum* cultivars available in garden centers and catalogs.

- 'Margarita Pink Flare' in bright raspberry pink
- 'Margarita White Spoon' in white with a violet-blue underside
- 'Serenity Bronze' in orange bronze fading to pink
- 'Sunadora Palermo' in salmon pink
- 'Sunadora Valencia' in pale orange fading to pale yellow
- 'Zion Blue Denim' in blue-violet
- 'Zion Copper Amethyst' in golden-orange, fading to magenta pink, and fading again to dark purple at the flower center

At a Glance

SCIENTIFIC NAME: *Osteospermum* spp.

FAMILY: Calenduleae

HEIGHT: 1 to 3 feet (30 cm–1 m)

WIDTH: 12 to 24 inches (30–60 cm)

BLOOMS: Midsummer

SOIL pH: Acidic

LIGHT: Full sun

STARTING AFRICAN DAISIES FROM SEED

You can buy African daisies from a local nursery in seedling form or as mature plants, but you can also grow them from seed. They should be started indoors about six to eight weeks before the last frost in your region.

African daisies need light to germinate, so you simply need to sprinkle the seeds on top of the soil to plant them. Do not cover them. Then place your tray or flat in a cool, well-lit location. Do not use heat to germinate them—the seeds do not like it. The seedlings should appear in about two weeks. Once they are 2 to 3 inches (5–7.5 cm) high, you can transplant them into individual pots, where they will continue to grow until the last frost has passed. At this point, harden the seedlings by leaving them outdoors during the day. After a week or so, you can plant the seedlings directly in your garden, 12 to 18 inches (30–45 cm) apart for best growth. They will bloom around 80 days from seeding; the blooming period can extend up to eight weeks if old flowers are removed.

WHERE TO USE AFRICAN DAISIES

These versatile plants work well in a number of garden settings.

- Try placing them in the middle-height area of border plantings or in clumps in mixed beds. They don't work as well in wildflower meadows or other naturalized gardens.
- Use them as container plantings on patios or decks combined with sun-loving trailing plants like sweet potato vines.
- Create a color contrast by combining your African daisies with foliage plants in yellow or chartreuse or those with variegated leaves.

Ageratum

Peeking out from under the soft, whitish green foliage of dusty miller, pom-poms of ageratum offer a pop of eye-catching blue in a rock garden.

These fluffy blue plants, also known as floss flowers, add a desirable pop of color to your garden beds or containers and even do well in semi-shaded areas. Native to Central America, Mexico, and some parts of the American Southwest, this tropical or warm-weather annual now boasts more than 60 cultivars. Although a few wild varieties may reach about 30 inches (75 cm), the more compact garden plants range only from 8 to 18 inches (20–45 cm) in height. The soft, rounded flowers occur in various shades of blue, purple, pink, or white—with blue being most common. The pink and white cultivars are somewhat less popular than the blue; they tend to wither early and take on a worn, brown look.

GROWING AGERATUMS

Caring for ageratums is simple and easy, particularly for the beginning or intermediate gardener. Well-grown ageratum plants can be found in most garden centers or nurseries. They can also be started from seed indoors, 8 to 10 weeks before the final frost in your region. Set up your seeding trays or flats, and scatter the seeds on the soil. Cover them thinly with soil, or not at all, as they need sunlight to germinate. Then place them in a window with northern or eastern light. Once the seedlings reach 2 to 3 inches (5–7.5 cm) in height, transfer them to small pots. After the chance of frost is past, start hardening the seedlings by leaving them outside during the day for longer and longer periods. In a week or so, you can plant them in the ground, 8 to 15 inches (20–38 cm) apart.

Caring for ageratums includes regular watering until the plant is established. Use warm water to irrigate the plant for a bounty of blue in your garden. Ageratum flowers bloom from spring until autumn when receiving proper care; in rare cases, they sometimes return the following year. Deadhead spent blooms to encourage more flowers.

Be sure to remove ageratums from bedding flats, and plant them in a timely manner. They can dry out and wither if left in flats too long.

SCIENTIFIC NAME: *Ageratum houstonianum*

FAMILY: Asteraceae

HEIGHT: 4 to 36 inches (10 cm–1 m)

WIDTH: 6 to 18 inches (15–45 cm)

BLOOMS: Late spring to autumn

SOIL pH: Slightly acidic to slightly alkaline

LIGHT: Full sun to semi-shade

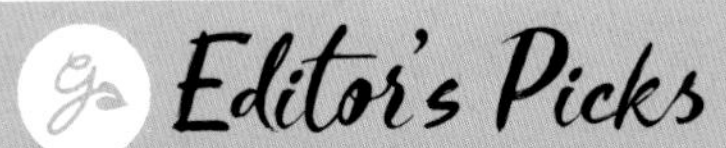

Popular varieties of ageratum offer a range of blue hues, as well as some in pink, white, or bicolor forms.

- **'Hawaii'. This variety has blooms of royal blue; it flowers early and is one of the most long lasting.**
- **'Blue Mink'. This cultivar has lovely powder blue flowers and reaches 12 inches (30 cm) in height.**
- **'Blue Danube'. This compact variety blooms in a medium-blue shade.**
- **'Pink Improved'. This cultivar features blooms with a dark pink center that fades to pale pink at the outer edges.**
- **'Southern Cross'. This tall variety of ageratum produces pale blue and white blossoms.**

USES FOR AGERATUM:

- Plant them in the front of borders or in clumps in a mixed bed or rock garden.
- Place ageratum in containers or window boxes along with red geraniums and white dusty miller for a striking mix of red, white, and blue.
- Plant under cornflowers and beside lobelia for a "blue-on-blue" theme. Use a blue-and-white Chinese porcelain planter to complete the effect.

Begonia

Its compact growing habit makes the wax begonia *(Begonia semperflorens)* a top choice for mass plantings. Landscapers love it for creating islands or other shaped flower beds.

SCIENTIFIC NAME: *Begonia semperflorens*

FAMILY: Begoniaceae

HEIGHT: 6 to 18 inches (15–45 cm)

WIDTH: 6 to 12 inches (15–30 cm)

BLOOMS: Spring to autumn

SOIL pH: Neutral to slightly acidic

LIGHT: Full sun to partial shade

Of the many types of begonia, one commonly planted in home gardens is *Begonia semperflorens.* Known as wax, bedding, or annual begonias, these small, fleshy plants with their delicate flowers are one of the world's most popular bedding choices. Their cousins, the striking foliage begonias, have their legions of fans as well.

The *Begonia* genus has more than 1,500 named species and several thousand hybrids. They are ideal plants for hybridization—crossing readily and possessing a striking variability. Originally native to tropical understories in Central and South America, Asia, and Africa, most modern begonias are hybrids that cannot produce seeds. But they propagate readily from leaf cuttings or rhizome division.

HOW TO GROW BEGONIAS

Wax begonias grow quickly and easily fill in spaces in the garden that will benefit from their attractive, compact foliage and frilly flowers. Leaves may be green or a bronze-maroon with single or double flowers in pink, white, and red. Begonias can be a focal point when planted en masse—landscapers often use them to create logos or corporate initials—and they make excellent additions to container combinations. They are not picky when it comes to location either: you can plant them in filtered sun or partial shade. Begonias are also deer resistant.

ANNUAL BEGONIA CARE

Once your begonias are planted, be sure to keep the soil moist, but not too wet. A well-draining potting mix worked into your garden soil simplifies this task. Always water begonias at the base to avoid leaf spot and the possibility of fungal diseases.

The most compact and healthy begonias result from deadheading spent blooms and pinching back new growth. Plants may also be cut back in autumn and brought into the house. Once inside, keep the soil moist, provide humidity with a pebble tray, and place in bright, filtered light. Leaf cuttings may be propagated in water to provide additional plants. Divide them in spring for more outdoor specimens.

Seven Types of Begonias

The wide variety of begonias have been classified into different types.

- **Semperflorens.** Called wax begonias because of the waxy appearance of their leaves, in temperate areas these tropical perennials are grown as annuals.
- **Cane.** These grow from straight, sometimes brittle stems and are prized for both their blooms and their foliage. The popular and beautiful angel wing and dragon wing begonias are cane-types.
- **Shrub.** Shrub begonias grow in mounding piles from multiple stems and range in size from small plants to huge specimens.
- **Rhizomatous.** Growing from thick underground rhizomes, these are known for their beautiful leaf shapes and colors; they include some commonly cultivated indoor begonias.
- **Tuberous.** Primarily grown for their showy flowers, these begonias include trailing and upright varieties. They have a short dormant period in the autumn and winter.
- **Trailing.** Trailing begonias with their pendant growth and displays of flowers are ideal for hanging baskets.
- **Rex.** These rhizomatous begonias deserve special mention for their showy and beautiful leaves, with an impressive array of shapes and colors, including green, red, purple, silver, white, and many bicolor and tricolor combinations.

Calibrachoa

Calibrachoas are lovely little petunia-like ornamental flowers that are popularly known as "million bells." They work well in hanging baskets or massed in borders.

Calibrachoa, also called million bells or trailing petunia, may be a fairly new species, but this dazzling, spreading plant is a must-have in the garden. The name "million bells" comes from its hundreds of small, bell-like flowers that resemble miniature petunias. Calibrachoa is a tender perennial that produces mounds of foliage, growing only to a foot in height, with trailing stems and flowers in solid shades of violet, blue, pink, red, magenta, yellow, bronze, and white, as well as in two tones, stripes, patterns, and stunning double blooms. The leaves are oval and feel a bit sticky. The plant's trailing habit makes it perfect for use in hanging baskets, containers, or as a small-area ground cover.

Introduced to gardeners in the early 1990s, all cultivars of calibrachoa are hybrids, with the original species native to South America. They are prolific bloomers from spring to frost, and both butterflies and hummingbirds are attracted to their one-inch blossoms. The plant is winter hardy in semitropical regions and is most commonly cultivated as an annual in cooler climates.

GROWING CALIBRACHOA PLANTS

Calibrachoa prefer moist but well-drained organically rich soil that is slightly acidic (5 to 6.5 pH). Too much acid, however, will retard growth. Although they enjoy full sun, these plants will take very light shade and may tolerate some drought. In fact, plants in semi-shade will survive longer into the summer months, especially in warmer regions.

Purchase or plant your seedlings in spring, and set out after the last frost in your region.

CARING FOR THE PLANT

Caring for calibrachoa requires minimal work. The soil should be kept fairly moist but not soggy, especially in full sun areas, as plants may succumb to the intense heat of summer. Container plants and those in hanging baskets require more watering. Because it blooms almost continuously, calibrachoa appreciates periodic diluted fertilizer applications in the garden, though you might need to more regularly fertilize containers and hanging baskets.

Deadheading is not required, as this plant is considered to be "self-cleaning," meaning the spent flowers readily drop off following the blooming period. You can pinch the stalks back to encourage a more compact growth habit.

SCIENTIFIC NAME: *Calibrachoa* spp.

FAMILY: Solanaceae

HEIGHT: 6 to 12 inches (15–30 cm)

WIDTH: 12 to 24 inches (30–60 cm)

BLOOMS: Spring to frost

SOIL pH: Acidic

LIGHT: Sun to partial shade

CALIBRACHOA PROPAGATION

These plants produce little seed, if any, and must be vegetatively propagated. Most of these hybrid cultivars are patented (trademark of the Suntory Company), which prohibits calibrachoa propagation in commercial markets. Home gardeners can, however, propagate their own plants through cuttings that are overwintered indoors.

Try to find a stem that has small buds but no flowers on it. Cut this stem off at least 6 inches (15 cm) from the tip, removing any lower leaves. Place your cuttings in an equal mix of potting soil and peat moss, and then water well. Place your cuttings in bright light, and keep them moist and warm (about 70° F, or 21° C). Roots should begin to develop within a couple of weeks.

Editor's Picks

Here is just a sampling of Calibrachoa varieties in many colors.

- 'Cabaret Hot Pink' in bright pink
- 'Cabaret Purple Glow' in purple
- 'Crackling Fire' in neon orange
- 'Million Bells® Terra Cotta' in orange streaked with red and gold
- 'MiniFamous Double Blue' in deep blue-purple
- 'Superbells® Double Chiffon' in pale lemon yellow
- 'Superbells® Pomegranate Punch' in gradients of red

Celosia

Plumed celosia flowers *(Celosia argentea)* in neon pink, deep red, and bright gold light up a flower bed with their feathery plumes. Different varieties of celosia have different heads, with the cockscomb varieties resembling convoluted coral or brains.

If you're in the mood to plant something a little different to enliven your deck or dazzle your neighbors, consider celosia plants. The generic name is derived from the Ancient Greek word *kelos,* meaning "burning," and refers to the flamelike flower heads, which come in red, white, yellow, and deep pink. Native to the Mediterranean and East Africa, the plant has 9 popular garden cultivars out of its total 60 species.

GROWING CELOSIA

This bright, eye-catching annual is easy to grow—as long as you provide it with well-drained soil and at least five hours of sunshine per day. Although classified as an annual—it doesn't tolerate cold weather and is quickly killed by frost—the plant may be grown year-round in semitropical or tropical regions.

Celosia is easily propagated by planting seeds indoors about four weeks before the last expected frost in spring or sowing them directly into the garden after all danger of frost has passed. Seeds germinate in temperatures between 65 and 70° F (18–21° C). Or you can purchase potted plants at a garden center or nursery.

CARING FOR THE PLANT

Celosia care is relatively simple. Water plants regularly, keeping in mind that the soil should be moist but never waterlogged. Although the plant is somewhat drought tolerant, flower spikes end up smaller and less dramatic in dry conditions.

Apply a weak solution of a general-purpose, water-soluble fertilizer every two to four weeks. Be careful not to overfeed celosia. If the plant appears hale and hearty or if the soil is especially rich, fertilizer might not be needed.

Deadhead regularly by pinching or clipping wilted blooms. This keeps the plants neat, encourages more blooms, and prevents rampant reseeding. Watch out for pests like spider mites or aphids. Spray as needed with insecticidal soap spray or horticultural oil. These plants tend to be sturdy, but taller plants might require staking to keep them upright.

CELOSIA IN THE GARDEN

Use celosias profusely in a flower border, mixed bed, or rock garden. Or plant specimens in one color along a path or walkway, like bright soldiers in a row. They make attractive container plants, especially mixed with chartreuse and white foliage plants, like sweet potato vine and licorice plant or if placed beside variegated coleus. When young, the edible leaves taste like spinach; the flowers can also be dried while at the height of blooming and used for indoor plant arrangements.

SCIENTIFIC NAME: *Celosia* spp.

FAMILY: Amaranthaceae

HEIGHT: 8 to 36 inches (20 cm–1 m)

WIDTH: 18 inches (45 cm)

BLOOMS: July to September

SOIL pH: Acidic to neutral

LIGHT: Full sun to semi-shade

Types of Flower Heads

There are three distinct types of celosia based on flower structure: plumed, wheat, and cockscomb.

- **Plumed cultivars.** These have multiple flower stalks and feathery blooms and grow between 8 and 24 inches (20–60 cm) tall.
- **Wheat flower stalks.** Looking like the head of a grain crop, these range from 12 to 36 inches (30 cm–1 m) tall and are the most limited in colors.
- **Cockscomb cultivars.** With coral or brain-looking blooms, these grow between 12 and 36 inches (30 cm–1 m) tall. The name comes from the red version's similarity to a rooster comb.

Cleome

Tones of pink and purple lend a garden planted with *Cleome spinosa* a delicate beauty. These tall annuals, with their aromatic leaves and fragrant spidery flower heads, are a great addition to a pollinator garden: the nectar attracts hummingbirds, bees, and butterflies, and the seeds are a food source for birds.

SCIENTIFIC NAME: *Cleome* spp.

FAMILY: Cleomaceae

HEIGHT: 1.5 to 5 feet (4–1.5 m)

WIDTH: 12 to 24 inches (30–60 cm)

BLOOMS: Summer

SOIL pH: Acidic to neutral

LIGHT: Full sun, part sun

Also known as spider flower, spider weed, spider leg, stinking clover, and Rocky Mountain bee plant, cleome is a tall, annual garden staple that stands out in the backs of borders or along any fence or wall. It is named for its tall, leggy appearance and the shape of its leaves. When young, these weedy-looking plants are not going to win any beauty contests—they only begin to bloom when well established. But to their many advocates, there are few tall annuals that create a focal point and draw the eye as well. They are also a favorite with butterflies and hummingbirds, who flock to them all summer long.

The flowers are intricate, large, and showy. They may be white, pink, lavender, or rose, or bicolored, with combinations of pink or lilac with white. They bloom in summer and often last until the first frost occurs. Deadheading spent flowers encourages longer bloom times.

Once established, these South American natives are drought tolerant, and they will hold up well during summer's heat. Because they resist the effects of drought, cleomes also make an ideal addition to the xeriscape garden, where water conservation is a big consideration.

Even though cleome is an annual, its flowers reseed so prolifically the plants are sure to return year after year. Seed pods can also be removed before bursting and used to introduce cleome to other parts of your garden or flower beds.

Planting cleome in the vegetable garden helps to attract beneficial insects and may deter some of the harmful bugs that damage crops.

HOW TO GROW CLEOME

Growing cleomes simply requires planting seeds in your chosen location. Almost any location is appropriate, as cleomes will grow and produce their "spider" flower in full sun or partial shade. The location does not need to offer any particular type of soil, but it must be well drained.

Seeds may be started inside, but a complicated schedule of lighting, temperature fluctuation, and bottom heat is required for indoor germination. This is usually not worth the effort of the regular gardener, since the plants do so well when seeded directly into the ground.

Be aware that older cleome plant cultivars are sometimes difficult to transplant and might wither away if you try transplanting them. Newer cultivars, some in dwarf varieties of the cleome plant, have no fragrance and do not produce the following year's flowers, as the seeds are sterile. Traditional varieties of cleome are useful as background plants for shorter, sun-loving flowers and as stand-alone specimens when planting cleomes in masses.

Cornflower/ Bachelor's Button

Cornflowers got their name from their habit of vigorously growing through English corn crops, patching the countryside with fields of blue. Cultivated varieties, also known as bachelor's buttons, come in a range of other hues, such as pink, lavender, and white.

Cornflowers, also known as bachelor's buttons, are an old-fashioned species many people might recall from their grandmother's garden. In fact, these pretty blue flowers have adorned European and North American gardens for centuries—and as introduced European natives, they naturalized easily in most parts of the United States.

The frilly, showy, lightly fragrant flowers have a delightful unruly habit. The blooms may be single or double and mature to about 1.5 inches (4 cm) in width. They grow on multi-branching stems that can reach 1 to 4 feet (30 cm–1.2 m) high. In addition to the traditional blue color, they are also available in shades of purple, red, white, and pink.

These versatile annuals can play many roles in the landscape—plant them in borders, cottage gardens, rock gardens, and sunny areas where they can spread and naturalize. They also do well in containers, providing they are placed in full or partial sun, and offer a lovely contrast to other species with yellow, rust, cream, or pink flowers. Or consider combining the red, white and blue varieties of cornflower for a patriotic display on the 4th of July or Memorial Day.

Cornflowers can also be used indoors; they last a long time in cut flower bouquets and even longer in dried arrangements. In past centuries, this bright flower was often worn in the lapel of courting a gentleman, hence the common name bachelor's button.

HOW TO GROW CORNFLOWERS

Growing cornflowers can be as simple as broadcasting or planting seeds outdoors in spring. Seeds may also be started earlier inside and moved to the garden when any danger of frost has passed. The seedlings need well-drained soil, which may be poor and rocky or somewhat fertile, and prefer full-sun locations. They only require watering to get them started; once established, the plant is drought resistant and will self-seed for a continuing display over the coming years.

SCIENTIFIC NAME: *Centaurea cyanus*

FAMILY: Asteraceae

HEIGHT: 1 to 4 feet (30 cm–1.2 m)

WIDTH: 12 to 18 inches (30–45 cm)

BLOOMS: Spring, summer

SOIL pH: Alkaline

LIGHT: Full or partial sun

CARING FOR THE PLANT

As young plants mature, pinch them back for denser growth and more buds. Deadheading spent blooms will prevent prolific self-seeding and control next year's spread of cornflowers. Weeding out sprigs growing in unwanted areas may also be necessary.

Perennial Bachelor's Button

In spite of its one-time popularity, this true garden classic *(Centaurea montana)* is no longer as well-known as the annual variety. It features 2-inch (5 cm), vivid, cornflower blue flowers with distinctive, fringed petals and central, black-tipped bracts. When in full bloom, the flowers exude a delicious peach fragrance. The foliage is an attractive green with a soft, silvery fuzz that keeps deer away. They make ideal plants for a cottage or cutting garden.

Cosmos

The saturated magenta and two-toned pink of *Cosmos bipinnatus* is set off by the flowers' lacy green foliage. These bright flowers look great in cottage gardens or in natural gardens that use native species to attract bees, butterflies, and other beneficial insects.

Cosmos plants, with their daisylike flowers sitting atop tall stems and their lacy foliage, are an essential addition to many summer gardens. They reach varying heights, occur in many colors, and add a frilly texture to the flower bed. Plus growing this low-maintenance plant is cinch.

The papery flowers are produced in a capitulum—a cluster of flowers on a stem—and display a ring of broad ray florets and a center of disc florets. Colors include white, golden yellow, pink, magenta, orange, yellow, red, and chocolate.

Because they can grow fairly tall, cosmos plants should be featured at the back of a descending garden or border or in the center of an island garden. Taller specimens go well with goat's beard, coneflowers, cleome, and black-eyed Susans. Shorter varieties make very colorful, airy edging plants. Taller varieties may need staking if not planted in an area protected from the wind. Cosmos groupings can even be used as screens to hide unsightly elements in the landscape, such as ground-level air conditioning units or ductwork. They are ideal as cut flowers for indoor display or in posies and bouquets, and they provide a pretty background for other flowers in an arrangement.

The variety known as *Cosmos sulphureus,* or yellow cosmos, is considered invasive in the southeast United States. Check with representatives from your local extension office to learn about any restrictions in your area.

HOW TO GROW COSMOS

The key growing tip is to plant cosmos in soil that has not been heavily amended. These flowers are native to scrublands and sunny fields in Mexico, so a hot dry climate, along with poor-to-average soil, are optimum conditions for cosmos to thrive.

The plants can be purchased from garden centers in bedding flats, but are easy to start from seeds. Scatter the seeds onto a bare, prepared area in a mostly sunny location. Once established, this annual flower self-seeds and will provide more cosmos flowers in the area for years to come.

Cosmos care includes deadheading spent blossoms. This practice forces growth lower on the flower stem and results in a stronger plant with more flowers. While some pests, like aphids, flea beetles, and thrips, feed on cosmos, they're easy to control with a strong spray of water or insecticidal soap. Aster yellows, bacterial wilt, and powdery mildew may also affect cosmos. Spacing plants far enough apart to ensure good airflow helps to avoid most diseases.

SCIENTIFIC NAME: *Cosmos bipinnatus*

FAMILY: Asteraceae

HEIGHT: 12 inches to 6 feet (30 cm–1.8 m)

WIDTH: 12 to 36 inches (30–1 m)

BLOOMS: Summer through autumn

SOIL pH: Acidic

LIGHT: Full sun

Varieties of Cosmos

More than 20 varieties of cosmos plants exist, both annual and perennial varieties. Two annual varieties are primarily grown in the United States—*Cosmos bipinnatus,* called the Mexican aster, and *C. sulphureus,* or yellow cosmos. Yellow cosmos is somewhat shorter and more compact than the commonly used Mexican aster. Another interesting variety is *C. astrosanguineus,* the chocolate cosmos, which is dark reddish brown, almost black, and has a chocolate scent.

Geranium

Lipstick red zonal geraniums *(Pelargonium* x *hortorum)* make a vivid display in a terra-cotta planter. Also called garden geraniums, they are naturals in containers and hanging baskets, and they also look lovely in a garden bed or border.

Geraniums make popular bedding plants in the garden, but they're also commonly grown indoors or outside in containers or hanging baskets. Although the majority of gardeners know them as geraniums, zonal geraniums, annual geraniums, or regal geraniums are not true members of the *Geranium* genus like cranesbill (hardy geranium), but rather members of the *Pelargonium* genus. This distinction was made in 1789; nonetheless, the common label persists to this day.

These perennial natives of southern Africa are treated as annuals in temperate regions, but they can easily be overwintered inside and replanted or propagated the following spring. The single or double flowers form large, spherical clusters in a wide variety of shades—red, purple, pink, magenta, orange, salmon, white, and bicolor. There are also shrubby evergreen varieties that are mainly cultivated for their scented leaves, which may be lobed, toothed, or incised and are sometimes variegated in color.

HOW TO GROW GERANIUMS

Depending on where you grow geraniums, their needs will be somewhat different.

Outdoors, the plants require a lot of light, so locate your geraniums in an area with at least six to eight hours of sun. Because these plants must be protected from cold, wait until the threat of frost has passed before bringing them outside. They prefer moist, well-draining soil similar to indoor potting soil, with equal amounts of soil, peat, and perlite. They also like soil that is slightly acidic. In garden beds, space plants about 10 to 18 inches (25–45 cm) apart and around the same depth as in their original pots. Mulching is also recommended to help retain moisture.

Indoors, geraniums need lots of light for blooming, but they will tolerate moderate light conditions. They prefer temperatures of around 65 to 70° F (18–21° C) during the day and 55° F (13° C) at night—positioning them near a window can provide cooler evening temps. These plants also need to be grown in well-draining potting soil.

CARE OF GERANIUMS

Whether indoors or out, geranium care is pretty basic. Indoors, watering should be done deeply but only once the soil begins to feel dry.

Outdoors, water at least weekly, although potted plants may need daily watering in hot weather. When watering outdoors, it's best to avoid overhead irrigation, as this can lead to pests or disease issues. Apply a water-soluble houseplant fertilizer or a 5-10-5 fertilizer with additional organic matter every four-to-six weeks throughout the plant's active growing season.

Indoor or potted plants may require repotting if they become overgrown, which is usually indicated by wilting between waterings. Regular deadheading of spent flowers will encourage additional blooming.

Geranium plants root easily from cuttings and can be propagated in autumn for the overwintering of outdoor plants. They can also be dug up and brought inside.

Note: Geraniums are toxic to humans, dogs, cats, and possibly other pets.

At a Glance

SCIENTIFIC NAME: *Pelargonium* spp.

FAMILY: Geraniaceae

HEIGHT: 6 to 36 inches (15 cm–1 m)

WIDTH: 10 to 24 inches (25–60 cm)

BLOOMS: Mid-spring to first frost

SOIL pH: Slightly acidic

LIGHT: Full sun, with possible noonday semi-shade

Dig Deeper

READ MORE AT GARDENING KNOW HOW

To find out more about both caring for and propagating your geraniums, follow these links.

- **"Geranium Seed Propagation: Can You Grow a Geranium From Seed"** (URL = gkh.us/134768)
- **"Geranium Winter Care: How to Save Geraniums Over the Winter"** (URL = gkh.us/477)
- **"How to Prune Geranium Plants"** (URL = gkh.us/3288)

A GALLERY OF
NATIVE PLANTS

In recent years, there has been a movement among gardeners to revisit the native plants that originally grew in their area. Most gardeners realize that many of their favorite bedding plants are imports from other parts of the world—exotics from Mexico, Central and South America, Africa, Asia, and other tropical or semitropical regions. These introduced plants tend to be more colorful and more showy than native species, which is probably why they became the go-to choice of landscapers and home gardeners for decades. Yet, with increasing frequency, garden centers and specialty nurseries are offering native plants alongside the exotics.

A plant is considered native if it has occurred naturally in a particular region, ecosystem, or habitat without human introduction. Exotic plants that evolved in other parts of the world or were cultivated by humans into forms that don't exist in nature do not support wildlife as well as native plants. They might not actually harm the environment, but they are not the plants that the bees, butterflies, and birds in your region are accustomed to seeking out for nectar and pollen gathering, egg-laying and larvae feeding, and seed gathering. They are also not plants that are well adapted to your specific soil type, soil acidity, levels of sunlight, and weather conditions. Another plus for native species is that they are hardier than the imports and are more likely to survive extremes of weather.

TOP NATIVE PLANTS:

Along with popular native plants like aster, coneflower, bee balm, and black-eyed Susan, there are a number of lesser-known natives that are gaining in popularity. Why not invite one or more of these into your garden?

READ MORE AT GARDENING KNOW HOW

To find out more about creating these natural-style gardens, just follow these links.

- **"Designing Native Gardens: Gardening with Native Plants"** (URL = gkh.us/127)
- **"Gardening with Natives – Learn About Native Plant Environments in the Garden"** (URL = gkh.us/126)

Goldenrod 'Fireworks'
(Solidago rugosa)
This beautiful late-season native wildflower adds color to late summer and autumn gardens. It's a favorite among pollinators and seed-eating birds. Many goldenrods spread aggressively, but 'Fireworks' has a tamer habit. 'Fireworks' grows to 3 feet (1 m) tall and up to 2 feet (60 cm) wide.

Ironweed
(Vernonia fasciculata)
Plant for late-season color. Purple flowers open in late summer and linger into autumn, providing late-season nectar for butterflies and other pollinators. Migrating hummingbirds, goldfinches, and sparrows also visit this wispy bloomer. Grows 4 to 7 feet (1.2–2 m) tall by 2 to 4 (60 cm–1.2 m) feet wide.

Milkweed
***(Asclepias* spp.)**
These nectar-rich plants welcome butterflies and many other pollinators (including bees), and they are host plants for monarch butterflies. Most grow 2 to 3 feet (60 cm–1 m) tall by 1 to 2 feet (30–60 cm) wide, but unlike some other "weeds" they don't take over the garden.

Natives by Location

Many of North America's common flowering plants are similar to those found in Europe, sharing the same genera but belonging to different species. The following native plants are only a sampling of those that grow in a given area.

NORTHEAST
Obedient plant (above), swamp milkweed, cinnamon fern, Solomon's seal, American witch hazel, bottle gentian, shooting star, blue-eyed grass, and shadblow

MIDWEST
Cardinal flower (above), prairie dropseed, little bluestem, tall white beardtongue, wild bergamot, blazing star, and ox-eye daisy

SOUTH
Oakleaf hydrangea (above), wild blue indigo, black tupelo, spicebush, 'Blue Shadow' fothergilla, lady fern, , Franklin tree, and woodland phlox

SOUTHWEST
Mexican evening primrose (above), Parry's penstemon, black dalea, desert spoon, blackfoot daisy, chocolate flower, Apache plume, Mexican hat plant, chuparosa, Santa Rita purple prickly pear, common bearberry, and switchgrass

WEST
Blue bonnet (above), Indian paintbrush, chicory, mountain larkspur, gentian, bluehead gilla, lupine, bluebells, skullcap, milkvetch, deerweed, trefoil, agave, arnica, sagebrush, sweetbush, cane cholla, woolly locoweed, fleabane, angelica, and pussytoes

CANADA
Pink lady's-slipper (above), Jack-in-the-pulpit, ghost pipe, eastern mountain avens, Gulf of St. Lawrence aster, lakeside daisy. Lake Louise arnica, pink tickseed, purple pitcher plant, Riddell's goldenrod, prairie crocus, and Provancher's fleabane

Variegated Solomon's seal
***(Polygonatum falcatum* 'Variegatum')**
Ideal for moist or dry shade, this plant offers season-long interest: white, fragrant blooms in spring that lure pollinators and hummingbirds. In autumn, variegated leaves shift to gold tones; flowers form dark berries. Grows 2 to 3 feet (60 cm–1 m) tall and 1 foot (30 cm) wide.

Wild blue indigo
(Baptisia australis)
This native perennial achieves shrub size as plants sink a deep taproot that searches out water to fuel top growth. Blue flower spikes appear in late spring above blue-green leaves. Snip branches for the vase. Grows 4 feet (1.2 m) tall and 2 to 3 feet (60 cm–1 m) wide.

Impatiens

Shade-loving impatiens are favorites with homeowners who want to add vibrant color to darkened areas of their garden. Every spring, garden centers offer them in a host of hues.

SCIENTIFIC NAME: *Impatiens* spp.

FAMILY: Balsaminaceae

HEIGHT: 6 to 36 inches (15–1 m)

WIDTH: 6 to 36 inches (15–1 m)

BLOOMS: Spring, summer

SOIL pH: Slightly acidic

LIGHT: Part shade to full shade

Impatiens plants fill a major gap in many gardens—that of the vibrantly hued, easy-to-grow shade plant. Shade gardens often lack colorful flowers—hostas and heucheras are beautiful foliage plants, but their flowers are nothing to rave about. Impatiens, meanwhile, come in a variety of pastel and neon shades like white, coral, pink, magenta, violet, purple, orange, red, orange-red, yellow, and bi-color and even offer double-blossoming varieties. Native to Africa, Eurasia, and New Guinea, these tender perennials are treated as annuals in temperate regions. With their mounding habit, they gloriously fill in the space allotted them. Gardeners have learned to depend on these bright and cheerful flowers to light up any dark or shady part of the yard.

PLANTING IMPATIENS

Impatiens, also known as busy Lizzie, are normally purchased as well-rooted plants from the garden center. Make sure you keep your plants well watered until you get them in the ground—they will wilt quickly if they dry out. They are ready to plant once all danger of frost has passed.

You can use these diminutive flowers as bedding or border plants or in containers. They enjoy moist, well-draining soil that is slightly acidic. If you would like to plant them in full sun, they will need to be acclimated to the harsher light. You can do this by exposing them to an increasing amount of sunlight over the course of a week or so.

You can plant impatiens flowers quite close to one another, 2 to 4 inches (5–10 cm) apart if you like. The closer they are planted together, the faster the plants will grow together to form a bank of lovely flowers.

CARING FOR IMPATIENS

Once your impatiens are in the ground, they will need at least 2 inches (5 cm) of water a week. If the temperatures rise above 85° F (30° C), they will need at least 4 inches (10 cm) per week. If the area where they are planted does not receive that much rainfall, you will need to water them yourself. Impatiens in containers need watering daily, and watering twice a day if temperatures rise above 85° F (30° C).

Impatiens do best if fertilized regularly. Use a water-soluble fertilizer every two weeks through spring and summer. You can also apply slow-release fertilizer at the beginning of the spring season, and then once again halfway through summer. Another plus of impatiens is that they do not need to be deadheaded; they self-clean their spent flowers and will bloom profusely all season long.

The flowers can also be easily propagated from seeds or cuttings.

New Guinea Impatiens

For those who love impatiens but want a plant that thrives in moderate sunlight, New Guinea impatiens, or sun impatiens, makes a good alternative. *Impatiens hawkeri* also belongs in the family Balsaminaceae and is native to Papua New Guinea and the Solomon Islands. It has been bred and hybridized to produce a line of garden plants with colors similar to its cousin, but with narrower, more bronzy leaves and a greater tolerance for light.

Lantana

Lantana bursts into bloom with a profusion of vibrant blossoms that attract butterflies.

These verbena-like flowers have long been admired for their extended bloom time. Native to the tropical Americas, the West Indies, and Mexico, they are grown as hardy perennials in warmer regions and as annuals in temperate regions. The flowers come in a multitude of colors, including red, orange, yellow, blue, white, and pink. The shades often mix within one cluster for a bicolor effect. The leaves have a sandpapery feel and give off a sharp citrus fragrance. There are over 150 varieties of this tough heat- and drought-tolerant plant with two main habits—trailing and upright.

Trailing varieties come in many colors and look great in mixed gardens, containers, or as ground covers. They also make showy "spillers" in hanging baskets. Upright lantana, which also has many color variations, can grow up to 6 feet (1.8 m) tall in certain climates and is an excellent addition to any flower bed or landscape.

HOW TO GROW LANTANA

Lantanas simply need a sunny location and well-draining soil. Because the flowers prefer slightly acidic conditions, mulch with pine needles to increase levels of acidity. Plant lantanas in spring, once the threat of cold weather and frost have ceased. They prefer warm weather, so new growth may at first be slow to appear. But once warm weather arrives, your plants will grow abundantly and bloom profusely.

Attracting Pollinators

Butterfly gardening has become increasingly popular, not only because butterflies are beautiful, but also because they assist in pollination. Butterflies have a highly evolved sense of smell and are attracted to the sweet-scented nectar of many plants. They also are drawn to plants with bright blue, purple, pink, white, yellow, and orange blooms and prefer plants with flat or dome-shaped clusters of small tubal flowers on which they can perch as they sip nectar. So do lantanas have the right attributes to attract butterflies? You bet they do!

Butterflies that commonly visit lantana for its nectar are hairstreaks, swallowtails, monarchs, checkered whites, cloudless sulfurs, red spotted purples, red admirals, painted ladies, zebra longwings, Gulf fritillaries, queens, great southern whites, and Atlas.

SCIENTIFIC NAME: *Lantana camara*

FAMILY: Verbenaceae

HEIGHT: 1 to 2 feet (30–60 cm)

WIDTH: 2 to 4 feet (60 cm–1.2 m)

BLOOMS: Late spring to frost

SOIL pH: Neutral

LIGHT: Full sun

CARING FOR LANTANA

While newly planted lantanas require frequent watering, once established, these plants require little maintenance and are even tolerant of somewhat dry conditions. A good soaking about once a week should keep them relatively happy. Lantana plants can be given a light dose of fertilizer each spring, but too much may inhibit their overall flowering. To encourage reblooming, trim the tips periodically.

COMMON PROBLEMS

Lantanas are generally healthy, but you may encounter the following issues on occasion.

- *Powdery mildew.* This may result if the plant is not given enough light. In addition, the plant may develop root rot if it is kept too wet.
- *Sooty mold.* This kind of mold causes black discoloration on the leaves and is most often attributed to insect pests, such as whiteflies.
- *Lace bugs.* Common insect pests, lace bugs will cause the foliage to turn gray or brown and then drop off.

Note: Lantana is toxic to animals.

Lobelia

Dainty lobelia spills from a woven planter. These rich cobalt flowers can stand alone, but they also work well paired with golden yellow, rich red, or silvery white companions.

SCIENTIFIC NAME: *Lobelia* spp.

FAMILY: Campanulaceae

HEIGHT: 6 to 9 inches (15–23 cm)

WIDTH: 8 to 12 inches (20–30 cm)

BLOOMS: Summer to first frost

SOIL pH: Slightly acidic to neutral

LIGHT: Full sun to partial shade

The lobelia plant is an attractive tender perennial that is grown as an annual in many temperate regions. Lobelia is an easy-to-grow, carefree plant that enjoys cool weather and will continue to produce flowers through the first frost. This summertime bloomer was originally native to nearly all the temperate and warmer regions of the world, except central and eastern Europe and western Asia. There are more than 400 species in the *Lobelia* genus, and as a member of the bellflower family, lobelia is related to Canterbury bells and balloon flowers.

The plants have a trailing habit, and although most varieties are compact, growing only 3 to 5 inches (7.5–12.5 cm) tall, others can grow up to 3 feet (1 m). Colors are also variable, with white, pink, red, and blue varieties available; however, violet-blue is probably the most commonly seen shade. These plants make great additions in borders, along creeks or ponds, as ground covers, or in containers—especially hanging baskets. The blue specimens look especially charming when mixed in containers with red geraniums or begonias, along with yellow marigolds and silvery dusty miller.

GROWING LOBELIA

Annual lobelia will grow nearly anywhere. These plants typically require an area with full sun but will tolerate partial shade, and they also prefer moist, rich soil.

Lobelia seeds can be sown directly in the garden or sprouted indoors for later transplanting. Start seeds indoors about 10 to 12 weeks prior to the last frost in your region. Spread the tiny seeds just on top of the soil and water thoroughly. Place them in a warm, well-lit area. The seedlings should pop up within a week or two, at which time you can begin thinning them out. After all danger of frost is gone and the plants are at least 2 to 3 inches (5–7.5 cm) tall, transplant them to the garden—spacing them about 4 to 6 inches (10–15 cm) apart.

CARE OF THE PLANTS

Once established, the lobelia plant requires little maintenance. Still, during hot, dry periods, lobelia will require frequent watering, especially plants kept in containers or hanging baskets. A general-purpose liquid fertilizer can be given once a month or every four to six weeks, if desired.

Lobelia should grace your garden with its beautiful double-lipped tubular blooms starting in summer and continuing on up to the first frost. Although it's not necessary, you can deadhead spent blossoms to maintain a neat appearance and encourage more blooms.

Lobelia Species

Varieties of lobelia commonly found in the home garden—in addition to *L. erinus*—include *L. cardinalis* (cardinal flower), *L. siphilitica* (blue cardinal flower), and *L. inflata* (Indian tobacco). The common name Indian tobacco (above) derived from the fact that Native Americans once smoked it to treat asthma. Also known as pukeweed, doctors once prescribed it to induce vomiting.

Marigold

French marigolds fill a raised bed. These versatile and easy-care flowers work just about anywhere, but try them in your kitchen garden between tomatoes, which have similar growing conditions. Research indicates that planting marigolds with tomato plants can protect the tomatoes from harmful root-knot nematodes in the soil.

SCIENTIFIC NAME: *Tagetes* spp.

FAMILY: Asteraceae

HEIGHT: 4 to 48 inches (10 cm–1.2 m)

WIDTH: 6 to 24 inches (15–60 cm)

BLOOMS: Summer

SOIL pH: Slightly acidic to neutral

LIGHT: Full sun

Marigolds, with their warm colors and fern-like foliage, are among the first flowers many gardeners remember growing. Originally native to southern North America, especially Mexico, marigolds offer many color choices, including lemon yellow, golden yellow, deep orange, bronze, and red and gold bicolor. The size and construction of the flowers may vary widely, from tiny single-petal flowers of the signet marigolds to the large double-petal blossoms of the African marigolds. Yet all marigolds show their membership in the Aster family with their characteristic daisy-like appearance. Some people also refer to calendulas as pot marigolds, but they are not related to the flowers we know as marigolds.

Marigold Species

There are three species of marigold, along with hybrids.

- **African (or Mexican) marigold.** This marigold, *Tagetes erecta,* has large blooms and tends to grow tall.
- **French marigold.** Popular and hardy, *T. patula* includes some dwarf varieties.
- **Signet marigold.** Also called single, golden, or lemon marigold, *T. tenuifolia* is an edible plant with long stems and looks like a daisy.
- **Triploid hybrids.** A cross between the African and French types, they are typically multi-colored.

GROWING MARIGOLDS

It's easy to grow your own marigolds indoors from seeds, providing you make sure your seedlings will be ready for spring transplanting—so start them indoors about 50 to 60 days before your final frost.

Fill a bedding tray with damp soil-less potting mix. Sprinkle the marigold seeds over the potting mix, and top the seeds with a thin layer of vermiculite. Cover the tray with plastic wrap, and place it in a warm spot, such as the top of the refrigerator. Marigold seeds do not need any light to germinate.

Check the seeds daily for germination; they typically take three to four days to germinate but might take longer in a cooler location. Once the seedlings appear, remove the plastic wrap, and move the tray to a location that gets at least five hours or more of light. Keep the potting mix damp by watering from below. Once the seedlings have two sets of true leaves, transplant them into pots where they can grow indoors under real or artificial light until the last frost has passed.

WHERE TO PLANT MARIGOLDS

These versatile flowers enjoy full sun and hot days and grow well in dry or moist soil. This hardiness is one of the reasons that they are often used as bedding plants and in containers. Once marigolds are planted, they need very little care; you only need to water them if the weather has been very dry for several weeks. In containers, however, water them daily. You can feed them water-soluble fertilizer once a month, but they seem to do just as well without fertilizer.

To greatly increase the number of blooms and extend the blooming period, deadhead spent blossoms. Dried, spent blossoms can also be kept in a cool, dry place to supply seeds for next year's display of fiery orange, red, and yellow flowers.

Morning Glory

SCIENTIFIC NAME: *Ipomoea purpurea* (syn. *Convolvulus purpureus)*

FAMILY: Convolvulaceae

HEIGHT: 6 to 10 feet (1.8–3 m)

WIDTH: 3 to 6 feet (1–1.8 m)

BLOOMS: Summer to autumn

SOIL pH: Neutral, acidic

LIGHT: Full sun

The climbing vines and vibrantly hued blooms of morning glory cover an old wooden fence and garden gate at the height of a sunny summer morning. *Ipomoea tricolor* 'Heavenly Blue' is a lovely cultivar in cornflower blue with heart-shaped leaves.

Few things delight a gardener first thing in the morning like the sight of deep blue morning glories twining around a porch railing or deck upright. Morning glories are a common sight in many landscapes, and while some varieties are described as noxious weeds, the fast-growing vining plants also make lovely additions to the garden—if kept in check. Native to Mexico and Central America, they have a light fragrance and are popular with butterflies and hummingbirds.

The plants produce attractive funnel-shaped blossoms in various shades—white, red, blue, purple, and yellow—along with attractive heart-shaped leaves. Blooming usually occurs anywhere from early summer through September, with tightly furled flowers opening in the morning and closing in the afternoon. Although most are annuals, in some warmer regions the plants may come back; they can also reseed themselves in almost any region.

Although these annual vines are in the same botanical family as sweet potatoes, they don't produce edible tubers. In fact, all morning glory species are toxic to people and pets.

GROWING MORNING GLORIES

Growing morning glories is easy. They do well in containers when provided with a trellis or when placed in a hanging planter. In the garden they prefer full sun but can tolerate very light shade. They are also known for their tolerance for poor, dry soils and are notorious for establishing themselves in any slightly disturbed area—garden edges, fence rows, and even roadsides, where the plant is often seen flourishing. Nevertheless, give your morning glories a boost with well-drained soil that is kept moist but not soggy.

WHEN TO PLANT MORNING GLORIES

These plants are easily started: simply sow seeds directly in the garden after the threat of frost has passed and the soil has warmed up. Indoors, the seeds should be started about four to six weeks before the last frost in your area. Morning glories have relatively hard seed coats, so the seeds need to be soaked in water overnight. Or you can nick them before sowing. Plant the seeds about ½ inch (1 cm) deep and space them out about 8 to 12 (20 to 30 cm). Once the plants have reached about 6 inches (15 cm) or so in height, you may want to provide some type of support for the vine to twine around.

CARE OF MORNING GLORIES

Once established, these plants require little attention. As mentioned, the soil should be kept moist, but not wet. During dry periods, it helps to water them once or twice a week. Container plants may require additional watering, especially in warmer regions. To reduce reseeding and control unwanted spreading, remove the spent blooms as they fade or collect and dispose of all the dead vines after the first killing frost in autumn.

One of the appeals of morning glories is to see the blooms cascading from a support. While the plant is still small, be sure to provide a sturdy trellis for the vines to climb. Weave the vines horizontally through s trellis or other support, and train them to grow downward through the trellis when the vine reaches the top.

Pansy

SCIENTIFIC NAME: *Viola x wittrockiana*

FAMILY: Violaceae

HEIGHT: 4 to 8 inches (10–20 cm)

WIDTH: 4 to 6 inches (10–15 cm)

BLOOMS: Spring, summer, autumn

SOIL pH: Slightly acidic

LIGHT: Full or partial sun

Bright yellow and purple pansies display deep red centers. These lively flowers have long been garden favorites, perfect in both garden beds and containers. The common name comes from the French word *pensée,* which translates to "thought" or "remembrance."

In early spring, these eternally cheerful harbingers of warmer weather are often the only bedding plants gardeners find available in nurseries. But no mind, they do their jobs by brightening up the still-drab landscapes of March and April. There are also autumn-hardy varieties that can be added to autumn displays.

Pansies are members of the viola family, originating from the small and delicate variety known as Johnny-jump up. (Consider mixing a few of these original violas in your landscape with pansies to add contrast and texture.) Our current pansies were developed in Iver, Buckinghamshire, England, in the early 1800s when Lord Gambier and his gardener William Thompson began crossing various *Viola* species. Today's pansies may be annuals, short-season perennials, or biennials, but in temperate areas with cold winters they are most often treated as annuals.

The pansy makes a great accompaniment to spring-blooming bulbs such as crocus, tulip, snowdrop, and daffodil, coming into full bloom just as the flowering bulbs are starting to fade. You might also want to experiment by combining specimens of different sizes and colors for dramatic effect in both the garden and containers. In addition to pairing well with spring bulbs, pansies also look great with sweet alyssum, blue and white lobelia, marigolds, and geraniums, as well as container spillers like calibrachoa, sweet potato plant, and licorice plant.

Today's hybrid versions of pansies are more adaptable to heat than those of the past; they also boast larger blooms that are displayed with more vigor. Most specimens prefer daytime temps of the 60° F (16° C) range and nighttime temps around 40° F (4° C). Breeders have created cultivars with the familiar pansy "face" to go with the drooping head of the pansy plant. Newer varieties prefer a full or part-sun location and are happy in hanging baskets, combination containers, and flower borders.

HOW TO GROW PANSIES

Pansies may be started from seed or purchased as seedlings from the local garden center.

Pansies are heavy feeders, so proper preparation of the soil goes a long way toward getting the most from your plants. Work in organic material, such as compost or well-rotted leaves, to a 4-inch (10 cm) depth before planting pansies. This accommodates their need for well-draining soil and provides nutrients as the organic material decomposes. Bear in mind that plants grown from seed may not bloom until the second year, as pansies are biennial.

When growing pansies in well-prepared soil, the need for fertilization will be minimal. Pansies also prefer acidic soil, so do not add limestone unless indicated by a soil test. Other pansy care is simple, just water and deadhead pansies for a longer period of blooms.

Editor's Picks

There is a seemingly endless list of pansy varieties, in just about every color combination imaginable.

- **'Black Moon' in deep black**
- **'Bingo' in shades of yellow, pink, purple, white, blue, and red**
- **'Delta' in shades of pink, white, blue, yellow, purple and red**
- **'Happy Face' in yellow, white, red, pink, purple and blue**
- **'Imperial' in shades of yellow, pink, purple, white, and blue**
- **'Super Majestic Giant' in pink, purple, white, yellow, blue and red**
- **'Ultima Silhouette' in shades of white, pink, and purple**

Petunia

Masses of magenta, lavender, and striped petunias nestle against a garden wall. This versatile and colorful plant is a summertime favorite for baskets and flower beds.

SCIENTIFIC NAME: *Petunia*

FAMILY: Solanaceae

HEIGHT: 6 to 24 inches (15–60 cm)

WIDTH: Up to 36 inches (1 m)

BLOOMS: Spring, summer, autumn

SOIL pH: Acidic

LIGHT: Full sun

These vigorous, trumpet-shaped beauties have won the hearts of many gardeners in many nations. They grow quickly, bloom abundantly, and come in such an assortment of colors and patterns that even pollinators get a bit dazed. Meanwhile, the branching, light green foliage is hairy and can be sticky to the touch.

Native to South America, the plants were observed by early Spanish explorers, who noted that they were called *petun,* meaning "worthless tobacco" in a Tupi-Guarani language. In 1823, French king Joseph Bonaparte sent explorers to Argentina, and they brought back samples of the flower. The colorful blooms were a hit with European gardeners, and the genus was eventually named *Petunia*.

CARE OF PETUNIAS

Most gardeners buy their petunias as potted plants, which are readily available at just about anyplace that sells bedding flowers.

Petunias require regular watering and as much sunlight as possible. Spreading petunias are pickiest about hydration and need at least weekly waterings. While petunias will grow in partial shade, fuller, more abundant blooms are produced in direct sun. The soil intended for planting should have plenty of well-composted organic matter worked in.

Endless Petunias

This genus has produced a huge variety of cultivars that are generally sold as hybrids. Petunias may feature single or double blooms; ruffled or smooth petals; striped, veined, and solid colors; mounding and cascading growth habits; and even a touch of fragrance.

To dig deeper, *see* "Types of Petunia Plants — What Are the Different Petunia Flowers" (URL = gkh.us/86282)

- **Grandiflora petunia.** These blooms often grow upright but may spill over the sides of your container.
- **Multiflora petunia.** This variety has smaller flowers and a more abundant bloom.
- **Milliflora petunia.** This dainty miniature petunia is compact and reblooming.
- **Spreading petunia.** This is only 6 inches (15 cm) tall but can function as a flowering ground cover and rapidly spread over a selected area.

Plan on weekly fertilization with a balanced, water-soluble fertilizer designed for flowering plants. They are heavy feeders, so petunias appreciate weekly feedings. On older varieties you will need to pinch off spent blooms, but newer petunias do not require deadheading—though it still stimulates blooming. Make sure to remove the base of the flower to stop it from going to seed. Plants that go to seed stop blooming. When purchasing young petunias, choose plants with a compact form and unopened buds. Open blooms are best removed after planting for a more abundant show in the future.

PETUNIA PROBLEMS

Pests that sometimes bother petunias include aphids, flea beetles, slugs, and snails that feed on stems and leaves. Most pests can be picked off, hosed off with a blast of water, or eliminated with a natural insecticide. Petunias are susceptible to fungal diseases, such as gray mold, especially in rainy regions. Look for varieties with a high tolerance for moisture if you live in a wet climate.

Primrose

Polyanthus primroses (*Primula* x *polyantha*) are one of the first flowers to blossom in spring. Offered in many colors, some bloom in eye-catching bicolor combinations.

Primroses bloom in early spring and are suitable for use in garden beds and borders, as well as in containers. When given the proper growing conditions in warmer regions, these vigorous plants will multiply each year, adding stunning colors to the landscape. In colder regions, they are treated as annuals.

Blooms may last throughout summer, and, in some areas, they will continue to delight during the autumn season. Most primrose flowers found in gardens are polyanthus hybrids *(Primula* x *polyantha),* which range in color from white, cream and yellow to orange, red, pink, blue, and purple.

There's a lot of diversity in primrose flowers. Some have clusters of blooms on a single stem, while other primulas have one flower per stem, with stems that create clusters of flowers that skim the rosette of leaves. They may remain evergreen in the areas where they are hardy.

GROWING PRIMROSES

Primroses are easy to nurture, as they are quite hardy and adaptable. Originally native to the Americas, they typically prefer damp, woodland-like conditions. You can find bedding primroses at most garden centers and nurseries. Look for specimens that are healthy in appearance, preferably with unopened buds. Primroses can also be grown from seeds in an equal mixture of soil, sand, and peat moss. This can be done indoors or outside, depending on the time of year and the climate in your area. Generally, seeds are sown indoors (outdoors in cold frames) during winter. Once seedlings have obtained their second or third leaves, they can be transplanted into the garden. Cuttings to propagate plants can also be taken from some varieties during summer.

English Primrose

The *Primula* genus contains at least 500 species. Along with the polyanthus primrose, the classic English primrose *(Primula vulgaris),* native to western and southern Europe, northwest Africa, and parts of southwest Asia, is often found in gardens. It blooms in a host of colors, including blue, purple, pink, red, white, orange, and yellow.

SCIENTIFIC NAME: *Primula* spp.

FAMILY: Primulaceae

HEIGHT: 6 to 20 inches (15–50 cm)

WIDTH: 8 to 20 inches (20–50 cm)

BLOOMS: Spring

SOIL pH: Acidic

LIGHT: Partial sun to shade

PRIMROSE CARE

Primroses should be planted in lightly shaded areas with well-drained soil, preferably amended with organic matter. Set primrose plants about 6 to 12 inches (15–30 cm) apart and 4 to 6 inches (10–15 cm) deep. Water thoroughly after planting and about once a week thereafter. Add a layer of mulch around the plants to help retain moisture.

Supply light applications of organic fertilizer throughout the growing season, and regularly prune dead leaves and spent blooms. To collect the seeds, wait until late summer or early autumn, then store them in a cool, dry place until the following planting season.

PROBLEMS WITH PRIMROSES

Slugs and snails are common pests affecting primrose plants. These can be controlled with non-toxic slug bait placed around the garden. Spider mites and aphids may also attack but can be eliminated by spraying with soapy water. Primrose plants without enough drainage may also be prone to crown rot and root rot. Try amending the soil with compost or relocating the plants to a well-drained site. Too much moisture may lead to fungal infections, which can be prevented by good watering habits and adequate spacing between plants.

Note: Primroses are toxic to both humans and pets.

Snapdragon

Spikes of snapdragons, with their rows of puffy blossoms, work well in the middle of a flower bed. With an impressive array of color choices, from dainty pastels to rich saturated hues, you're sure to find a mix that will work well with your other plantings.

Snapdragons are both stately and comical. They stand properly erect in the middle of gardens, but up close their bulbous blooms always invite a pinch. Native to the Mediterranean area, including Europe, Syria, and Turkey, they are also known as dog's mouth, lion's mouth, or toad's mouth.

Numerous varieties of snapdragon exist, with dwarf, intermediate, and tall flowering stems that provide something of a unique profile within the garden. Taller varieties may reach 3 feet (1 m) or remain as short as 6 inches (15 cm). The flowers are available in white, yellow, pink, red, orange, peach, purple, and violet, in fact most colors, except blue. Plant them so that they either coordinate or contrast with other early spring bloomers.

In the flower garden, these flowers provide cool seasonal color and a midsized specimen to balance tall background plants and shorter bedding plants in the front. Planting snapdragons outside in the garden is often among the first late-winter gardening tasks. This fragrant annual can handle frost, so start getting them in the ground early for the most abundant blooms and best performance.

HOW TO GROW SNAPDRAGONS

Snapdragons appreciate a full-sun location with well-draining soil. Don't forget a few well-placed snips to transform this plant into a bushy, filled-out specimen. Clip the top stem and any long side shoots to encourage more flowers and create a more attractive shape. Further care of snapdragons includes appropriate watering. After planting your snapdragons, keep them moist for the first few weeks. Once established, snapdragons require regular watering—provide approximately an inch (2.5 cm) of water per week in times of no rainfall. Water near the crown of the plant and avoid overhead watering to keep your snapdragon healthy. For mature plants, let the soil dry about an inch (2.5 cm) deep before watering.

CARING FOR SNAPDRAGONS

Tall varieties of snapdragons may require staking to remain upright. When blooms begin to fade due to summer's heat, clip the plant down by one-third to one-half and expect more blooms when temperatures begin to cool in autumn. The removal of spent blooms will also encourage the plant to continue flowering. Be sure to add mulch around the plant bases. Though most often sold as annuals, snapdragons are actually tender perennials, and some may return the following year, especially if their base is protected by a layer of mulch.

SNAPDRAGONS VS. PESTS

This plant is deer resistant and grows well in sunny, outlying areas where these pests are prone to nibble. Planting snapdragons in the vegetable garden may offer some protection from browsing deer as well.

Take advantage of the showy, often fragrant blooms by bringing cut stems indoors for arrangements, or intermingle plantings of snapdragon with heat-loving angelonia, a similarly structured plant in the summer flower bed. Add snapdragons to those bare sunny areas of your landscape after working organic materials into the soil.

At a Glance

SCIENTIFIC NAME: *Antirrhinum majus*

FAMILY: Plantaginaceae

HEIGHT: 6 to 48 inches (15 cm–1.2 m)

WIDTH: 6 to 12 inches (15–30 cm)

BLOOMS: Spring to autumn

SOIL pH: Slightly acidic to neutral

LIGHT: Full sun to partial shade

Editor's Picks

Here is just a tiny sampling of stunning snapdragon varieties.

- **'Peach Breeze' in yellow, salmon, and bright pink multicolored**
- **'Black Prince' in purplish black**
- **'Bright Butterflies' in**
- **'Encore Autumn Amethyst' in red, pink, purple, yellow, and white**
- **'Candy Showers' in orange, rose, and yellow**

Sunflower

A field of sunflowers fill a field near a weathered barn. These garden favorites are beloved of songbirds, who will flock to the copious seeds at the center of spent blooms.

Sunflowers are one of the easiest flowers you can grow in the garden. So easy, in fact, that they are frequently used to introduce young children to the joys of gardening. Many of us fondly remember planting the black and white seeds of giant sunflowers and watching in wonder as they grew to tower into the sky. Just because sunflowers are easy to grow, however, they should not be dismissed from the grown-up garden. Today, the variety of sunflowers available to home gardeners is astonishing, and, as an added bonus, sunflowers will attract songbirds birds to your yard.

SUNFLOWER VARIETIES

These American native plants now range in size from dwarf varieties, which can be as small as a foot and a half (46 cm) tall, to giant varieties, which grow to be over 12 feet (4 m) tall. Their colors vary from very pale yellows to dark, burgundy reds and all shades of yellow, red, and orange. The blooms have a wide central disk surrounded by short petals and grow on a hairy, sturdy, upright stem that can be several feet high. Sunflowers also have different petal counts. While a single layer of petals is still the most common, quite a few varieties have double and teddy bear petal layers.

SUNFLOWER CARE

If you are adding sunflowers to your garden, there are a few things to keep in mind.

- Sunflowers need sun. Make sure that the location you choose gets full sun for at least six to eight hours a day.
- It's good to know that sunflowers are not picky about soil quality. Yet they are plants and will likely do better in enriched soil.
- Sunflower seed shells contain a substance toxic to grass. So, either harvest the heads before the seeds fall out or plant your sunflowers where you don't mind any nearby grass being killed. Make sure seeds left for the birds are contained in a feeder, or they will scatter shells everywhere.
- Consider the height of the sunflower variety you have chosen. A giant 12-foot (4 m) variety might end up shading the surrounding flowers like a small tree.
- Sunflower seeds should be soaked for up to 12 hours prior to planting. Sow them 1.5 inches (46 cm) deep, and 6 to 10 inches (30–25 cm) apart.

So if you have fond memories of the tall yellow sunflowers that you planted as a child, why not give this old garden favorite another try?

At a Glance

SCIENTIFIC NAME: *Helianthus annuus*

FAMILY: Asteraceae

HEIGHT: 3 to 10 feet (1–3 m)

WIDTH: 1.5 to 3 feet (46 cm–1 m)

BLOOMS: Summer to autumn

SOIL pH: Acidic, neutral, alkaline

LIGHT: Full sun

Editor's Tip

Sunflowers are one of the easiest flowers you can grow in the garden. So easy, in fact, that they are frequently used to introduce young children to the joys of gardening. Many of us fondly remember planting the black and white seeds of giant sunflowers and watching in wonder as they grew to tower into the sky. Just because sunflowers are easy to grow, however, they should not be dismissed from the grown-up garden. Today, the variety of sunflowers available to home gardeners is astonishing, and, as an added bonus, sunflowers will attract songbirds birds to your yard.

For a fun DIY project you can enjoy with your children, scan the code or follow the link to "Flower Gardening Ideas for Kids – Making a Sunflower House with Kids." (URL = gkh.us/15296)

Sweet Alyssum

A massed planting of sweet alyssum results in low-growing clusters of fragrant white, lilac, and violet flowers. Plant them to fill in nooks and crannies on walkways and walls.

SCIENTIFIC NAME: *Lobularia maritima*

FAMILY: Brassicaceae

HEIGHT: 3 to 10 inches (7.5–25 cm)

WIDTH: 2 to 4 inches (5–10 cm)

BLOOMS: Spring, autumn

SOIL pH: Neutral to acidic

LIGHT: Full or partial sun

With its pleasant honey-like aroma, sweet alyssum—also known as sweet Alison—is a welcome addition for those gardeners who love fragrant flowers. It has other bonuses: few annual plants can match the heat and drought hardiness of sweet alyssum. This member of the mustard family was originally native to Europe, but it has naturalized in the United States and thrives in a wide range of regions. It grows somewhat aggressively and is actually listed as an invasive species in California. Although not frost-tolerant, sweet alyssum plants will self-seed and can provide years of bright color in milder climates.

Sweet alyssum flowers are useful in dry zones, and work well in alpine rock gardens, borders, planters, and hanging baskets. They also work as pollinator attractors, luring beneficial insects such as bees, butterflies, moths, hoverflies, and ladybirds, as well as hummingbirds, to your garden.

They are small plants that may reach 3 to 10 inches in height (7.5–25 cm) and produce clusters of tiny flowers in clumps. The blooms come in pink, salmon, purple, white, and yellow. They generally bloom from June to October, and cutting back spent flowers can encourage production of new blooms.

HOW TO GROW SWEET ALYSSUM

Growing sweet alyssum requires well-drained soil with moderate moisture. These plants are tolerant of many types of soils, but neutral or slightly acidic soil is best. Start from seed indoors in early spring, and transplant after the danger of frost has passed. Surface-sow the tiny seeds and keep lightly moist until germination, which will usually take around 15 to 20 days. When the seedlings have several pairs of true leaves and soil temperatures are at least 60° F (16° C), transplant them into a prepared garden bed. Before transplanting your seedlings, check the drainage in your soil by digging a hole and filling it with water. If soil doesn't drain quickly, work in compost, leaf litter, or grit, such as sand, to increase the porosity of the soil. Keep the bed weed-free to reduce competition for resources and provide even moisture.

In mild climates, you can also plant sweet alyssum flowers from seed straight into the garden. Choose a location that has full sun, although the plants can tolerate partial shade, as well. Prepare the soil prior to planting by weeding, working in organic amendments, and raking out any obstructions.

CARING FOR THE PLANTS

Sweet alyssum plants require little maintenance, although they will do poorly in boggy areas and may suffer if inadequate moisture is provided. They are not particularly prone to any pest problems, but they may develop stem rot or leaf blight where too much shade prevents the leaves and soil from drying out after rain or watering. Botrytis blight is a particularly common problem for sweet alyssum plants when they are grown in overly wet areas. Trim back the stems after blooming for an endless display of colorful, vibrant flowers.

Sweet alyssum varieties are available in colors that range from pinks, purples, and whites to even yellows, along with those with variegated petals. Here is just a sampling.

- **'Blushing Princess' in variegated lavender, deep purple, and white**
- **'Carpet of Snow' in dainty white**
- **'Easter Bonnet' in magenta-violet**
- **'Mountain Gold' in bright yellow**
- **'Navy Blue' in rich, deep aqua or dark purple**
- **'Oriental Nights' in purple-lilac**
- **'Rosie O'Day' in pure pink or white**
- **'Royal Carpet' in bright purple**
- **'Snow Crystals' in icy white**

Sweet Pea

Delicate sweet peas are favorites with gardeners who love an informal cottage garden feel. For plants with the signature scent, look for "heirloom" or "antique" varieties.

Sweet peas are justly named "sweet" because of their delightful fragrance. In recent years, breeders have put fragrance on the back burner, selectively breeding plants with outstanding flowers and a wide range of vibrant colors at the expense of fragrance. This can make it difficult to find sweet pea flowers with their original signature scent. You can still find fragrant varieties, often labeled as "old fashioned" or "heirloom," but modern varieties also have their charm. These flowers are easy to care for and provide a lovely range of pink, purple, and white flowers. They prefer long, cool summers, and they don't last past spring in areas where summers are particularly hot. Where winters are mild, try growing sweet peas during autumn and winter as well.

HOW TO GROW SWEET PEA

Sweet pea flowers come in both bush and climbing types. Both types are vines, but the bush variety doesn't grow as tall and can support itself without the aid of a trellis. If you are growing climbing sweet peas, have your trellis in place before planting the sweet pea seeds so that you don't damage the roots by trying to install it later. Avoid planting them near a wall where air can't circulate freely.

Plant sweet pea seeds in spring while there is still a chance of light frost. The seeds have a tough coat that makes it difficult for them to germinate without a little help; to improve their chances, you can soak the seeds in warm water for 24 hours to soften the seed coat, or nick the seeds with a file or sharp knife to make it easier for water to penetrate the seed. Choose a sunny or lightly shaded site and prepare the soil by working in a 2-inch (5 cm) layer of compost to improve soil fertility and drainage. Sow the seeds 1 inch (2.5 cm) deep, spacing climbing types 6 inches apart (15 cm) and bush types 1 foot (30 cm) apart. The sweet pea seeds usually emerge in about 10 days, but it can take two weeks or more.

SCIENTIFIC NAME: *Lathyrus odoratus*

FAMILY: Fabaceae

HEIGHT: 6 to 8 feet (2–2.4 m)

WIDTH: 2 to 3 feet (60 cm–1 m)

BLOOMS: Summer to autumn

SOIL pH: Alkaline

LIGHT: Full sun to partial shade

CARING FOR THE PLANTS

Pinch out the growing tips of the plants when they are about 6 inches (15 cm) tall to stimulate lateral growth and bushiness. This is a good time to mulch the plants as well. Water the soil around the plants frequently enough to keep it moist, applying the water slowly and deeply. Fertilize with half-strength liquid fertilizer twice during the growing season; too much fertilizer encourages an overabundance of foliage at the expense of actual flowers. Pick off spent flowers to encourage new blossoms.

Note: Sweet pea seeds resemble edible peas, but they are toxic if eaten. If children are helping in the garden, make sure they don't put them in their mouths.

Editor's Tip

Try growing sweet peas in a kitchen garden, where they will attract bees and other pollinators necessary for some vegetables, such as squashes, cucumber, pumpkin, eggplant, okra, and watermelon, to produce fruit. Plant them along a fence, or mix them in with pole beans.

Vinca

Annual vinca, or Madagascar periwinkle (*Catharanthus roseus*), goes by many other names, including bright eyes, Cape periwinkle, graveyard plant, old maid, pink periwinkle, and rose periwinkle. Whatever you call it, it makes a great bedding or container flower.

SCIENTIFIC NAME: *Catharanthus roseus*

FAMILY: Apocynaceae

HEIGHT: 6 to 18 inches (15–45 cm)

WIDTH: 6 to 18 inches (15–45 cm)

BLOOMS: June to frost

SOIL pH: Acidic

LIGHT: Full sun to partial shade

Vinca, also known as Madagascar periwinkle, is a spectacular plant with pretty flowers and shiny green foliage. Often used as a ground cover or trailing accent, it was previously known as *Vinca rosea*. This species does not have the hardiness of its look-alike cousin, *Vinca minor*, or common periwinkle, which is an invasive ground cover. *Vinca rosea* is a perennial in its native Madagascar and is grown as an annual in cooler regions. It will grow well if it receives a decent amount of sun, and the sandy loam soil is well draining.

The plant is characterized by its starry flowers, glossy leaves, and persistent fruits. The flowers occur in shades of white, pink, salmon, red, and rosy-purple.

GROWING VINCA FROM SEED

Annual vinca self-seeds, but the most common method of establishment is through cuttings. Vinca seeds can also be collected from the seedpods found under the fading flowers. Drop the pods into a paper bag, and place them in a warm, dry spot. Shake the bag every day until the pods are completely dry. Open them carefully, and remove the tiny black seeds. After a period of dormancy, sow the seeds under light soil and cover with newspaper, which should be removed once they germinate—at 70 to 75° F (21–24° C) in around one week. Once the chance of frost is past, place the young plants in your garden.

CARING FOR THE PLANT

The biggest issue with vinca is overwatering, so exercise caution to ensure a dry garden bed. These plants are extremely affected by heavy rains or excess irrigation and may develop root rot in such situations. In temperate zones, water the plants only until established, and then during only the hottest and driest periods. The plant grows in either partial shade or partial sun. Another key for a healthy specimen is heat.

It is effective to plant vinca in a raised bed or one amended heavily with sand or other grit. Poor soil actually produces the best and most prolific flowers, while excessively fertile soils can adversely affect the number of blooms. It is not necessary to feed the plants, except at emergence and installation. Pinch off new stems to promote a bushier plant. You can also prune back the woody stems to improve the plant's appearance and promote flowering.

In warm regions this easy-care plant rewards you with season-long drama; in temperate zones, which usually result in a shorter season, you will still have several months of beauty. Either way, vinca is a worthy addition to most landscapes.

Note: Annual vinca is toxic to humans, dogs, and cats.

Vinca minor

For many gardeners, the names "vinca" and "periwinkle" bring to mind the common periwinkle (*Vinca minor*). With its dainty blue-purple blooms that give its name to the lovely pale indigo color, *Vinca minor* is an attractive plant. It is a tough, low-maintenance, and pest-free spreader with pretty broadleaf foliage that make it useful as a ground cover. Use it with caution, however: it is considered an invasive species in parts of the United States. Check your agricultural authority before planting to learn the status of *Vinca minor* in your area.

Zinnia

Some of the easiest annuals to grow, zinnias bring an explosion of color wherever they go. The show lasts from late spring until the first autumn frost. Butterflies and hummingbirds are attracted to the cheery flowers that bloom in nearly every bright color imaginable.

SCIENTIFIC NAME: *Zinnia elegans*

FAMILY: Asteraceae

HEIGHT: 1 to 4 feet (30 cm–1.2 m)

WIDTH: 12 to 18 inches (30–45 cm)

BLOOMS: Late spring to summer

SOIL pH: Acidic

LIGHT: Full sun

Zinnia flowers *(Zinnia elegans)* are a colorful and long-lasting addition to any flower garden. They grow best in regions with high average temperatures, but they are hardy enough to grow comfortably in most climates. They can bloom in pink, orange, red, purple, yellow, white, and green, with lance-shaped leaves that are sandpapery in texture. These flowers have several varieties, and they can differ quite a bit in size, shape, and blooming season.

HOW TO GROW ZINNIA

Zinnia plants are inexpensive and easy to cultivate, particularly when growing them from seed. Seeds of zinnia flowers should usually be sown directly into a flower bed—or wherever else you plan for them to end up permanently—as developing roots do not like to be disturbed.

If you wish to start zinnia plants from seeds indoors, plant the seeds in peat pots or other biodegradable containers that can be planted directly into the garden later. Start seeds four to six weeks before the last predicted frost date in your area. Zinnias should first begin to show growth outdoors when average temperatures are above 50° F (10° C).

Properly space the seeds for growing zinnia plants, usually several inches to a couple of feet apart, depending on the expected size of the mature plant. This will allow for adequate air circulation around the plants as they grow. Powdery mildew and other diseases can attack zinnia flowers that are planted too close together.

CARE OF THE PLANTS

Once fully established, zinnias don't usually need to be watered regularly. If needed, a soaker hose is ideal for keeping foliage and petals dry while providing much-needed irrigation—be sure to water the soil at the base of the plant, not the plant itself. It is also a good idea to water zinnias early in the morning, which allows the foliage and flowers ample time to dry off before nightfall. Lack of adequate sunlight during the day can make it difficult for the plant to dry fully after watering, which can lead to rot and mildew.

Keep the soil moist, but not soggy, for young plants. Mature zinnias require less watering, as grown flowers are somewhat drought tolerant. With proper placement and correct watering, zinnia plants can provide several months of vivid and varied flowers.

Zinnia plants can benefit from deadheading and flower removal. Clipping the plant back often will encourage new growth, resulting in healthier and more abundant blooms.

READ MORE AT GARDENING KNOW HOW

Zinnias are often available at garden centers as potted plants. Still, anyone can grow these colorful flowers from seed, even gardening newbies. To learn how, follow the URL below, or scan the QR code above to watch the informative video.

- **"How to Grow Zinnia from Seed for Beginners"** (URL = gkh.us/187153)

Perennials work brilliantly for those who want to replace turfgrass lawns with pollinator-friendly meadow-like spaces. Species like coneflowers in white and purple play well against the bright golden yellow of black-eyed Susans.

PERENNIAL FLOWERS

Perennials are plants that live year after year, able to overwinter in the garden without being brought indoors. Depending on the species, some may last for a decade or more, while others (especially many flowering perennials) may only survive for two to five years. Perennial trees and shrubs, on the other hand, are known for their significant lifespans. Herbaceous examples die back to the ground after the first hard freeze but maintain a dormant root structure. Come spring, new growth pokes its head above the ground . . . and the cycle starts again. These hardy perennials can also be sown directly into the ground rather than being started indoors, but they will not bloom until the following year.

A GARDENER'S SECRET WEAPON

Many experienced gardeners will tell you that perennials are their secret weapon—producing flowers or foliage season after season, with minimal care and few pests to contend with. Although annuals generally have showier flowers and provide longer color than perennials, they need to be planted every year, while perennials keep on giving. A combination of the two types may result in the maximum period of blossoming with a revolving rainbow of colors. Plus, some perennials, like coneflowers, do not drop their faded flower heads and so provide food for birds well into the colder months.

Today, the list of available perennial flowers is mind boggling, and each year breeders debut additional cultivars. Check online local nurseries for plants suitable to your area.

READ MORE AT GARDENING KNOW HOW

To learn more about perennial flowers and to get suggestions about how you can incorporate them into your own garden, follow these links.

- **"Gardening with Perennials — How to Design a Perennial Garden"** (URL = gkh.us/?p=5)
- **"Easy Care Perennials for Every Garden"** (URL = gkh.us/180006)
- **"Landscaping with Neighbors: Planting a Friendly Neighbor Perennial Garden"** (URL = gkh.us/135697)

Fragrant pink peonies in full bloom. Perennials are the stalwarts of the garden, coming back each spring after going dormant in winter.

Aster

The blue flowers of the alpine aster *(Aster alpinus)* peek out from a crevice between granitic rocks. Also called the alpine daisy or rock aster, it works well in rock gardens, along with terrace beds, the front of borders, or along dry stone walls.

SCIENTIFIC NAME: *Aster* spp.

FAMILY: Asteraceae

HEIGHT: 1 to 6 feet (30 cm–1.8 m)

WIDTH: 1 to 4 feet (30 cm–1.2 m)

BLOOMS: Summer, autumn

SOIL pH: Neutral, acidic

LIGHT: Full sun

Aster flowers add vibrant bursts of color to the usual reds and browns of autumn, and they are surprisingly easy to care for. Asters often bloom in late summer and autumn, although some variants—such as the alpine aster—bloom in spring. There are more than 600 varieties of asters. Although most common asters have pink or purple flowers, several variants can also be found in blue or white. They may reach several feet in height, or they can be compact and mounding, as with the alpine type. Asters can be paired with other late-blooming flowers, such as coneflowers and goldenrod for a striking autumnal display.

HOW TO GROW ASTERS

Asters are some of the simplest plants to grow, as their hardy nature makes it easy for them to adjust to most environments. They may be started from seed in spring, but they are most often purchased as a potted plant; in either case, asters should be planted in full or partial sun in loamy, well-drained soil. Keep new plantings moist, and continue watering until blooms cease.

CARING FOR THE PLANT

Although asters are relatively low-maintenance, there are a few points to keep in mind when caring for them. They should be fertilized with a balanced plant food about once a month. When watering them, make sure to water the soil at the base of the plant without splashing the flowers and leaves. Getting water or fertilizer on the leaves will encourage powdery mildew and other fungal diseases.

Organic mulch can hold in moisture and supply nutrients as it breaks down. Apply a layer of mulch within a few inches of the base of the plant but leave some space between the mulch and the stem. Mulch also acts as an insulator, keeping the plant's roots from getting too hot or too cold.

COMMON PROBLEMS

As plants go, asters are quite hardy. There are, however, several common pests and diseases that can become a problem if left untreated. Some aster plant diseases, such as rust and powdery mildew, are superficial and will not affect the plants' health or ability to bloom. They can be treated with fungicide. Some other, more serious, diseases include root rot, wilt, and foot rot, all of which can result in the death of the plant. The easiest way to avoid rot is by planting asters only in well-draining soil. Dead or wilting stems should be pruned. Botrytis blight, another disease that will kill off blossoms, can usually be prevented by careful watering; blight tends to form when the leaves and flowers of the plant are soaked in water.

Pests can pose serious problems with asters. Spider mites and lace bugs are common pests, and while they won't kill the plants, they will give them an unhealthy appearance. A good way to keep insects at bay is to keep the leaves of asters dry and to plant them with good spacing. You should also take care to clear away any weeds and debris, as bugs tend to thrive in moist, overgrown areas.

Aster Varieties

The two main garden asters are the alpine aster *(Aster alpinus)* and the European Michaelmas daisy, or Italian aster *(A. amellus)*. Two popular garden asters have recently been reclassified: New England asters and New York asters *(Symphyotrichum novi-belgii,* formerly *A. novi-belgii)*. The New England aster, also known as hairy Michaelmas daisy or Michaelmas daisy, tends to be taller and grow to between 3 and 4 feet tall (1–1.2 m) tall. New York asters, also known as Michaelmas daisies, generally top off at 2 feet (60 cm).

Astilbe

SCIENTIFIC NAME: *Astilbe* spp.

FAMILY: Saxifragaceae

HEIGHT: 6 to 24 inches (15–60 cm)

WIDTH: 6 to 60 inches (15–1.5 m)

BLOOMS: Spring, summer

SOIL pH: Slightly acidic

LIGHT: Partial shade

A variety of astilbe fills a corner of a garden. Taking center stage is *Astilbe* 'Montgomery' *(A. japonica)* with its compact, dark magenta-red flowers held in dense plumes.

Likely the focal point of any shady summer flower bed, astilbe flowers can be recognized by their tall, fluffy plumes that tower above frilly, fern-like foliage. These distinctive flowers make great companions for other shade-tolerant plants, such as hosta and hellebores. There are 25 five species of *Astilbe*, as well as hundreds of hybrids between those widely varying species. Some are borne on arching stems, while others stand erect; their flowers range in color from bright whites to dark purples, though most land in a middle range of pastel pinks. In addition, both the blooming period and the potential height the flowers can grow to vary by species: astilbe flowers may reach from a few inches to a few feet in height.

Astilbe plants flourish with the right soil, food, and location, and if you plant several varieties together, you can keep these flowers blooming for months.

HOW TO GROW ASTILBE

Astilbe plants can grow happily in shade, but their flowers are more productive in an area where gentle morning or dappled sun can reach them for about an hour or two. The flowers also need correct soil and moisture to flourish: they prefer rich, organic type soil. Organic material such as compost can be used to enrich the soil, as well as adding drainage. If your shady areas have poor, lean, or rocky soil, work in some compost a few weeks before planting your astilbes there. The soil should be loosened at least 8 to 12 inches (20–30 cm) deep so that the roots have plenty of room to develop. When planting, keep the crown of the plant at the same level as the top layer of soil. Water well when planting and keep the soil consistently moist.

CARING FOR THE PLANT

To properly care for astilbe, you should water them regularly throughout their period of active growth. They will need extra water if planted in direct sunlight, as over-exposure to sunlight can cause the leaves to dry and turn brown. Occasionally enriching the soil with compost or fertilizing with an organic product or fertilizer high in phosphorus is also recommended. Astilbes prefer loose soil that drains well.

Under the right conditions and care, astilbes will display their large, feathery plumes. Spent plumes can be cut back in spring or left alone to dry; they will not bloom again, and so they do not necessarily need to be pruned. The plants can also be divided about every four years, as desired. Proper care for astilbe plants can result in delicate, long-lasting blooms throughout spring and summer.

READ MORE AT GARDENING KNOW HOW

Among the many astilbe plant varieties are those with flowers of red, white, pink, or lavender, but also different tones of foliar color. Peruse any plant catalog and you will find astilbe varieties for almost any taste. Pay attention to the planting zone, as some astilbe plants are hardier than others. To learn more about these fluffy flowers, follow the URL below, or scan the QR code above.

- **"Best Astilbe Varieties — Types of Astilbe Good for Planting in Gardens"** (URL = gkh.us/84453)

Bee Balm

The vibrant blooms of red bee balm *(Monarda didyma)* cluster in a summer garden. Bee balm is noted for its spiky flowers, which also come in shades of purple and pink. As its name implies, bees love these flowers, which also attract hummingbirds.

SCIENTIFIC NAME: *Monarda* spp.

FAMILY: Lamiaceae

HEIGHT: 2 to 4 feet (60 cm–1.2 m)

WIDTH: 2 to 3 feet (60 cm–1 m)

BLOOMS: Summer

SOIL pH: Slightly acidic

LIGHT: Full or partial sun

The bee balm plant, also known as wild bergamot or its genetic name *Monarda,* is a North American native that thrives in woodland areas. The varieties you find in garden centers will most likely be a cultivars of one of three *Monarda* species: *M. didyma, M. fistulosa,* and *M. puntata*. The flower has an open, daisy-like shape, with thin, spiky petals in shades of red, pink, purple, and white. Bee balm plants are perennial, coming back year after year to add cheerful bursts of color to your garden.

Bee balm blooms are very attractive to bees, butterflies, and hummingbirds, which makes them a prized choice for gardeners looking to draw more pollinators to their gardens. The leaves and flowers are also often used in teas and natural remedies.

HOW TO GROW BEE BALM

Bee balm plants prefer moist, rich soil. They should be planted in a sunny spot, although they will tolerate shade, particularly in hot-summer areas. Plant them in any protected spot that would benefit from a bright shot of color. Most varieties of *Monarda* are between 2 to 4 feet tall (60 cm–1.2 m), but there are also a number of dwarf varieties that grow to be less than 10 inches (25 cm) in height. Dwarf varieties are excellent for container gardens, window boxes, or smaller flower beds, where you can appreciate the shaggy, tubular blooms without fear of it becoming overgrown. Pick the blooms frequently to encourage flower production. Deadheading, or removing spent flowers, will also promote a new flush of blooms.

CARING FOR THE PLANT

Growing bee balm is fairly easy, as long as you keep the soil moist. It will also help to use a good, multipurpose fertilizer, which should be worked into the soil around the base of the plant. If you want a bushier plant, pinch off the stem tips as new growth appears in the early spring. In late autumn, cut bee balm down to just a few inches tall. In particularly cold areas, it may collapse completely to the ground during the winter only to reappear hale and hearty in the spring.

COMMON PROBLEMS

Bee balm is susceptible to powdery mildew, which appears as a gray, powdery dust on the buds and leaves in moist, cool weather. If your plants develops mildew, you can treat them with natural remedies or a fungicide spray from your local garden center. Mildew can also be prevented by planting bee balm where it will have good air circulation and avoiding watering from overhead.

If your bee balm plant refuses to flower, there are a number of likely causes. The most common problem is a lack of sunlight. Bee balm thrives best in full sun, and most varieties need six to eight hours of sunlight per day in order to bloom well. A plant that doesn't get enough sunlight is also often leggy looking, with long stems and few leaves. If your bee balm is showing both of these symptoms, try relocating it to a sunnier spot. Alternatively, look for special cultivars that are designed to thrive in the shade.

Beware of overfertilization. Bee balms are light feeders, so too much fertilizer (especially if it's rich in nitrogen) can result in lots of leafy growth and very few flowers. Overwatering, excess humidity, and age can also cause limited blooming.

Black-eyed Susan

Rudbeckia 'American Gold Rush' peeks over a garden fence. These cheerful flowers look great in cottage gardens and in native or xeriscape plantings.

The black-eyed Susan flower *(Rudbeckia hirta)* is a versatile, heat- and drought-tolerant specimen that makes a charming addition to any garden. Native to the central United States, these plants, as with many wildflowers, are simple and rewarding to grow. They bloom all summer long, providing weeks of bright color and velvety foliage with little maintenance. They are related to the daisy, as is evident in their sunburst of narrow, rounded petals; due to this similarity, they are also referred to as gloriosa daisies.

Black-eyed Susan plants may be annual, biennial, or short-lived perennials, depending on each individual variety. Their height can vary as well, ranging from dwarf varieties, which grow only a few inches high, to others that climb up to several feet. These somewhat unpredictable, vibrant wildflowers begin blooming in late spring and last throughout the summer.

The black-eyed Susan flower is also valued for its ability to attract butterflies, bees, and other pollinators to the garden. Deer, rabbits, and other wildlife may also be drawn to it, however, which they may consume or use for shelter. To keep unwanted wildlife at bay, it's a good idea to plant black-eyed Susans near lavender, rosemary, or other pest-repellent plants in your garden.

HOW TO GROW BLACK-EYED SUSAN

It doesn't take much convincing for black-eyed Susans to grow from seeds, but the seeds themselves can be a little hard to come by. You can buy the seeds yourself, or you can clip them from the heads of a dried-out plant during the fall. After being left to dry on a newspaper or paper towel for several weeks, the seeds should be ready to plant when spring comes. You can also start seeds indoors, in which case you should begin around six to eight weeks before the start of spring. Plant the seeds roughly ¼ inch (0.635 cm) deep in rich soil and keep moist. These plants can have rather delicate roots, so it's generally best to grow seedlings in peat pots rather than transplant them.

Editor's Tip

If you want to direct seed your black-eyed Susans, they can go into the prepared bed from two to four weeks before your average last frost. You can also try "winter sowing" by placing seeds in a mini-greenhouse in the autumn garden. Using a halved water jug, add soil and a top layer of vermiculite, and then seal the middle with duct tape but leave the spout open.

At a Glance

SCIENTIFIC NAME: *Rudbeckia hirta*

FAMILY: Asteraceae

HEIGHT: 2 to 3 feet (60 cm–1 m)

WIDTH: 1 to 2 feet (30–60 cm)

BLOOMS: Summer

SOIL pH: Slightly acidic

LIGHT: Full sun

CARING FOR THE PLANT

Black-eyed Susan should be deadheaded regularly. Removing the spent and dried blooms will encourage new bloom growth and help the plant stay sturdy and compact. It also can stop or slow the spread of black-eyed Susans to nearby areas, as the plant's seeds are contained in the blooms. Seeds may be allowed to dry on the stem for reseeding or collected and dried for replanting in other areas. It should be noted that seeds of this flower do not necessarily grow to the same height as the parent from which they were collected.

Bleeding Heart

Delicate rows of pinkish red bleeding heart blossoms make an attention-getting display in a shady, early springtime garden.

When the blooms of the bleeding heart plant appear in early spring, they quickly become the centerpiece of any garden. These eye-catching plants look just like their namesake, with pink heart-shaped flowers that hang in rows from arching stems. The first leaves to emerge are a soft bluish green, while the flowers may be pink and white or solid white, as is the case with the bleeding heart cultivar 'Alba'. Bleeding hearts love shade and cool temperatures, and they will continue to bloom until high summer temperatures cause them to go dormant. They are toxic to humans and animals.

This plant, which is native to Siberia, northern China, Korea, and Japan, is the sole species in the monotypic genus *Lamprocapnos*, but it is still widely referenced under its old name *Dicentra spectabilis* (now listed as a synonym).

GROWING BLEEDING HEART

It's important to keep the soil consistently moist around your bleeding heart plants. Bleeding hearts prefer highly organic, moist soil; water regularly and provide additional compost, manure, or mulch. Soil that is oversaturated with water, however, is likely to cause them to develop root rot. Ideally, bleeding hearts should be planted in well-draining and nutrient-rich soil in a cool, shady area. They can tolerate humidity well, but they are sensitive to both heat and drought.

As summer temperatures rise, your bleeding hearts will begin to yellow and enter dormancy. Do not cut back foliage as it begins to turn yellow or brown; this is the time when your plant is storing food reserves for the next year. No deadheading is needed, as bleeding hearts will self-seed for the next season if left alone.

COMMON PROBLEMS

Bleeding hearts require consistently moist soil but are vulnerable to root rot, so overwatering them or planting in poorly draining soil will often keep this plant from thriving. Fungal infections and mildew are also a concern, as is the case with most shade plants; these problems can usually be treated with a commercial fungicide.

Bleeding hearts can also be vulnerable to a number of pests; aphids, slugs, and snails are particularly frequent offenders. Aphids are a common garden pest, and a heavy infestation can quickly weaken and kill a plant. Insecticidal soaps or sprays should be effective enough to prevent damage from aphids or other insects, although neem oil or homemade pest repellent are also valid options. Snails and slugs, on the other hand, are best dealt with manually by picking up and discarding them one at a time. Alternative solutions, such as slug bait and diatomaceous earth, might also prove effective. To avoid attracting slugs and snails, keep the area around the plant free of leaves and other debris, and limit mulch to 3 inches (7.5 cm) or less.

SCIENTIFIC NAME: *Lamprocapnos spectabilis* (formerly *Dicentra spectabilis*)

FAMILY: Papaveraceae

HEIGHT: 6 inches to 3 feet (15 cm–1 m)

WIDTH: 1 to 3 feet (30 cm–1 m)

BLOOMS: Spring

SOIL pH: Slightly acidic or neutral

LIGHT: Partial to full shade

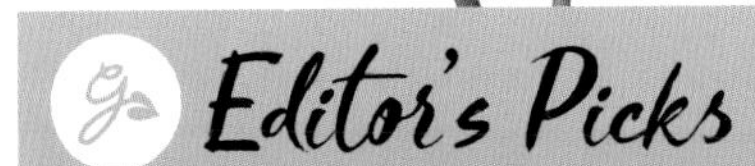

Here is just a sampling of bleeding heart varieties in shades of red, pink, and white.

- **'Amore Pink' in pale pink**
- **'Aurora' in paper white**
- **'Bacchanal' in light burgundy**
- **'Burning Hearts in neon red**
- **'Candy Hearts' in candy pink**
- **'King of Hearts' in the classic pinkish red**
- **'Pearl Drops' in white with a hint of pink running down the center**
- **'Valentine' in true red**

Chrysanthemum

An autumn garden comes alive with a variety of containers displaying chrysanthemums in orange, dark pink, yellow, and pale pink. Readily available as potted plants, mums are welcoming flowers to line a home's walkway or to place around an entrance staircase.

Chrysanthemums, also known as "hardy mums," are ubiquitous autumn flowers that come in almost every conceivable color. The many varieties and hybrids of mums can be found all over the world, although they were first cultivated in China as early as the 15th century BCE. Chrysanthemums can also come in perennial and annual forms. Annual mums *(Chrysanthemum multicaule)* have thinner, strappy leaves with less-defined teeth, while the leaves of perennial mums *(C. morifolium)* are wide and deeply notched. Chrysanthemums also have very different connotations throughout the world. In the United States, for instance, the flowers are associated with friendship, joy, and health and are used in many autumn displays; in much of western Europe, they are instead associated with death and mourning.

HOW TO GROW CHRYSANTHEMUMS

In northern regions, planting your potted chrysanthemums in spring will give them the best chance of survival, as they are more likely to last through the winter once firmly established. In warmer southern areas, mums may be planted in either spring or autumn, though autumn offers the benefit of avoiding summer heat. In all areas, chrysanthemums should be planted in well-draining soil. These plants are fairly adaptable to a wide range of soil types, but they will thrive in highly organic soils. They also prefer a sunny spot in the garden. Chrysanthemums will grow in partial shade but might get leggy when reaching for sunlight. Shade-grown mums will have weaker stems and exhibit less flowering.

CARING FOR THE PLANT

"Pinching" is one of the most important aspects of caring for chrysanthemums, because it greatly encourages late summer and autumn blooms. Begin pinching back growing mums when new growth is 4 to 6 inches (10–15 cm) long, removing the stem above the second set of leaves. This directs the growth downward and ensures your chrysanthemum flowers don't bloom too early. Continue pinching new growth on all shoots through June. The removed plant material can also be rooted as cuttings for additional mums to give to friends or to plant in other areas of the garden. Some of the newer chrysanthemum cultivars do not need pinching, but most of them will still benefit from the practice.

SCIENTIFIC NAME: *Chrysanthemum* spp.

FAMILY: Asteraceae

HEIGHT: 2 to 3 feet (60 cm–1 m)

WIDTH: 1 to 3 feet (30 cm–1 m)

BLOOMS: Autumn

SOIL pH: Slightly acidic or neutral

LIGHT: Full sun

It is also advisable to fertilize chrysanthemums in spring—ideally using a time-release fertilizer—and to plant them far enough apart that each plant gets optimum air circulation. Also, plant mums where they are somewhat protected from strong winds, such as in a bed sheltered by a wall or building. Strong winds or a pounding rain can break the stems and flatten established plants, so be advised. A heavy layer of mulch in the autumn is appropriate in areas that experience particularly cold winters.

COMMON PROBLEMS

Chrysanthemums are known to attract sap-sucking insects, such as spider mites and aphids, which can lead to an infestation. Neem oil and other natural spray insecticides are effective against these pests.

Clemats

Lush flowering clematis climbs over a garden fence. This classic blooming vine looks great planted over arbors, trellises, and other decorative support structures.

Clematis is one of the most popular and commonly grown flowering vines, and for good reason: these vividly colorful, adaptable flowers can differ wildly in size, shape, color, and spread, depending on variety, some of which can grow as tall as 30 feet! Originally of Chinese and Japanese origin, clematis can be found in shades of blue, purple, red, white, pink, and yellow, and—because many varieties have different blooming times—proper planning can result in a multicolored display of flowering vines during the entire growing season.

HOW TO GROW CLEMATIS

Clematis plants need plenty of space for adequate airflow as well as a rich, well-draining planting area. Make sure to dig a hole large enough to comfortably accommodate the plant—most varieties will need at least a hole 2-foot-deep (60 cm)—and enrich the soil with compost or fertilizer prior to planting. It may also help to cut the plant back some before planting to lessen shock as it adapts to its new environment.

Clematis vines prefer sunny locations (at least six hours of sun is needed for proper blooming), but their roots and soil need to be kept cool. An easy way to accomplish this is by planting some type of ground cover or shallow-rooted perennial plants around the clematis to provide shade. A 2-inch (5 cm) layer of mulch can also be laid down to keep the roots cool and moist.

Growing clematis vines must be supported in some fashion as well. The type of support system is usually dependent on the variety grown. For instance, poles are acceptable choices for smaller clematis vines, which can range anywhere from 2 to 5 feet (60 cm–1.5 m) in height. Arbors may be more suitable for growing larger types, which can easily climb over 10 feet (3 m) in height. Most varieties, however, do quite well growing along a trellis or fence.

CARING FOR THE PLANT

Once established, the care of clematis vines is minimal, with the exception of regular watering. They should be watered about an inch or so weekly, and more deeply during dry spells. Mulch should be replenished each spring.

Annual pruning may also be required to keep clematis plants looking their best, control the spread of far-reaching plants, and encourage healthy growth. The type of clematis vine grown dictates when and how it should be pruned. For example, early spring blooming varieties should be pruned back as soon as possible following their blooming period but before July, as they bud on the previous season's growth. Large flowering types that bloom in mid-spring should be cut back to the topmost buds in late winter or early spring.

Clematis has one quirk—the plant likes its base to be cool and its vines to be in sun. One way to accomplish this is to plant it in the shade of a tree stump that sits in a sunny patch. Or consider a small dead tree or shrub, which will quickly become a support for the vine.

At a Glance

SCIENTIFIC NAME: *Clematis* spp.

FAMILY: Ranunculaceae

HEIGHT: Herbaceous 2 to 5 feet (60 cm–1.5 m); large-flowered hybrids 8 to 30 feet (2.4–9 m)

WIDTH: 3 to 20 feet

BLOOMS: Various times

SOIL pH: Slightly acidic

LIGHT: Full or partial sun

Dig Deeper

READ MORE AT GARDENING KNOW HOW

Scan the QR code or follow the link below to learn how to keep these climbers in check.

- **"How to Prune Clematis: Tips for Pruning Clematis Vines"** (URL = gkh.us/17800)

RETHINKING THE LAWN

Landscapers say that when viewing a home's undulating landscape of flowers, shrubs, and trees, a neatly clipped green lawn provides a level spot for the eyes to rest. But the traditional sprawling urban lawn is high maintenance and requires considerable amounts of water. Many gardeners, and an increasing number of homeowners, are discovering the benefits of replacing all or some of their lawn with alternative plantings. By including plant beds within the lawn, they are making their yards more aesthetically pleasing, while providing space for flowers, herbs, shrubs, and vegetables to grow. Removing the grass also reduces time-consuming lawn care, such as mowing and raking, as well as the expense of seeding, weeding, and fertilizing. This concept has become so popular that one of the fastest-growing trends in residential landscaping is replacing the suburban lawn with non-grass options.

ELIMINATING GRASS

To add planting areas to your landscape, you need to eliminate the turfgrass that makes up your lawn. Turfgrass species, such as Kentucky bluegrass, Bermuda grass, or ryegrass, are bred to be tenacious and to spread, so unless you remove that grass and its roots, it will continue pop up in your new planting bed. Below are several ways to clear out grass.

Remove the sod

Cutting sod into pieces and prying it out will ensure grass won't grow up through your garden. Start by marking out the perimeter with string or a hose, then cut the edge with a sharp

Once a highly desired status symbol for suburbanites, more and more busy homeowners are rejecting these high-maintenance swaths of uninterrupted green.

Many homeowners are reducing lawn size and replacing grass with native ground covers, trees, shrubs, perennial flower beds, and other diverse plantings that are cheaper to maintain and far better for the environment than green turfgrass.

shovel, slice the sod into narrow strips, and dig it up. This is very taxing work, however, and it removes some of the topsoil from your plot. It's a good idea to amend the remaining soil after removing sod.

Solarize the lawn

This method takes patience and planning, but if your lawn has a lot of weedy patches, it is the way to go. Solarizing kills grass and everything growing in it by intensifying the sun's heat through sheets of plastic.

Cover the area of your planned garden with one or two layers of thick plastic and leave it in place for 6 to 12 weeks. The heat of the sun will bake any plants beneath the plastic. Sealing the edges keeps the heat in and speeds up the process. Once the grass is withered, remove the plastic, add amendments to the soil, and start planting. The dead grass will decompose right into the ground.

Smother the grass

This easy method involves denying the grass air until it dies naturally. This method requires a fair amount of time, however, as long as six months, so autumn is a good time to start the process. Almost any material can be used—old newspaper, chunks of carpeting, or pieces of cardboard. Once you've marked out your garden space, gather your materials, and then lay them over the grass. By spring, you can begin planting. If your lawn looks messy with the patchwork coverings, scatter mulch over the top.

You can also use the lasagna method of creating a healthy bed of soil above the grass (*see* page 41). A thick layer of organic matter smothers the grass over the winter while creating a rich bed of soil for planting.

Alternatives to Grass

Many types of plants can be used to replace a turf lawn, depending on whether you want to retain a low-growth profile or create a rising "meadow" effect. Some possibilities are listed below.

FESCUE AND ORNAMENTAL GRASS

Both fescue and ornamental grasses are tolerant of everyday wear and tear and thrive in a variety of locations. Tall fescues are coarse, drought tolerant, and provide a very low maintenance lawn for your home. There are numerous types of low-maintenance ornamental grasses, although sticking to a native variety will increase your chances of success. A native grass lawn requires little supplemental water once it's established and doesn't suffer from many pest or disease problems. Native grasses can be mown or left alone to create the appearance of a natural prairie.

FLOWERS, HERBS, AND VEGETABLES

Another option for your lawn consists of carefully placed flower beds, which significantly decreases your mowing. Or create a meadow that adds striking color and texture to your landscape by mixing wildflowers with prairie grasses. Or consider a vegetable garden in one large plot or in several smaller beds. What's better than trading lawn chores for produce you can harvest? Herbs can add a delightful fragrance to your yard, plus they hold up well under foot traffic. Popular choices include creeping thyme, chamomile, sweet woodruff, and pennyroyal.

GROUND COVERS

These low-growing plants spread easily in even the toughest sites, providing dense plantings that will eventually benefit the soil beneath. They add appealing texture, and some varieties offer seasonal blooms and colorful autumn foliage. Nitrogen-fixing plants, like clover (above), act as a soil conditioner. Ajuga is a creeping evergreen that works well in both sun and shade. Some varieties have purple foliage. Ivy is perfect in a shady site that doesn't take grass well. For more information, *see* pages 152–153.

XERISCAPE

If you really want to reduce water usage and end up with a low-maintenance haven, consider creating a xeriscape. This type of drought-resistant landscape is often seen in the American Southwest, but it can be adapted to almost any climate with a bit of research to find out which plants are native to your region. Its chief features are plantings of hardy perennials and herbs, like coneflower and lavender, along with ornamental grasses, succulents, cacti, and alpine plants. Pebbles or gravel are often used to create an attractive ground cover.

Columbine

Colorado blue columbines bloom in a delicate bicolor combo. *Aquilegia* comes in a dazzling array of colors and forms. Some varieties can be single colors, while other are doubles, such as purple-white, purple-yellow, and red-yellow, usually with a yellow eye.

Columbine is an easy-to-grow, spring-blooming perennial that was originally a native North American wildflower. Today, it boasts more than 70 species that flower in a variety of colors that include purple, deep burgundy, pink, yellow, white, and blue and an array of bicolor combinations. The dainty, bobbing blossoms rise on stems above the attractive, dark green foliage, which turns maroon in autumn. The bell-shaped flowers with their nectar-filled red spurs are also favorites of hummingbirds and butterflies and can be used in cut-flower arrangements, as well.

HOW TO GROW COLUMBINE

Columbines aren't too particular about soil, as long it's well-draining and not too dry. They enjoy full sun in most areas, but they don't like it very hot, especially during summer. Therefore, in warmer areas like the American South, grow them in partial shade, and give them plenty of mulch to help keep the soil moist. Mulch will also help insulate and protect these plants during winter in cooler regions.

Columbines start easily from seed and will readily multiply once established. The seeds can be directly sown in the garden anytime between early spring and mid-summer. There's no need to cover them as long as they receive plenty of light. Put pre-established plants in the ground at the same time, with the crown placed at soil level. Spacing for both seeds and plants should be anywhere from 1 to 2 feet (30–60 cm).

CARING FOR THE PLANT

After planting, water regularly until the plant is well established. After that, only weekly watering is necessary outside of extended periods of drought. You should also add a water-soluble fertilizer to the soil once a month, as regular fertilizing will help produce brighter blooms and thicker foliage.

Regular deadheading can also be performed to encourage additional blooming. If self-seeding becomes an issue, both the foliage and remaining seedpods can be cut back in the autumn. Although some gardeners prefer to not allow them to self-seed, it is often recommended, as columbine plants are generally short-lived, with an average lifespan of about three or four years. If desired, these plants can also be divided every few years.

At a Glance

SCIENTIFIC NAME: *Aquilegia* spp.

FAMILY: Ranunculaceae

HEIGHT: 1 to 3 feet (30 cm–1 m)

WIDTH: 1 to 2 feet (30–60 cm)

BLOOMS: Spring to summer

SOIL pH: Acidic to neutral

LIGHT: Full to partial sun

COMMON PROBLEMS

Although columbines are not prone to any particular diseases, pests such as leaf miners can occasionally become an issue. Treating plants with natural insecticide or neem oil is a good way to control these pests. Pruning columbine plants back to the basal foliage shortly after blooming can also help ward off insects that might harm them. You may even be lucky enough to see a second set of stem growth within a few weeks, leading to another wave of blooms.

Editor's Picks

Explore the many varieties of columbine available. Here is a small sampling of the many choices.

- **'Biedermeier' in a mix of whites, reds, purples, pinks, and bicolors**
- **'Blackcurrant Ice' in mauve and creamy yellow**
- **'Blue Dream' in baby blue**
- **'Crimson Star' in red and white**
- **'Dragonfly' in purples, whites, yellows, and bicolors**
- **'Green Apples' in pale green**
- **'Little Lanterns' in red and yellow**
- **'Sunshine' in butter yellow**

Coneflower

Echinacea purpurea 'White Swan' shows the same height and form as the better-known pink variety of coneflower. The scientific name *Echinacea* is from the Greek and means "spiny one," a reference to the spiny sea urchins that the ripe flower heads of this plant resemble.

The coneflower is one of the more popular perennial flowers found in home gardens. Originally a wildflower endemic to the American prairies, it is extremely easy to grow—especially compared to many of the more delicate and finicky perennials—and produces large, daisy-like flowers. These flowers are composed of the longer lower ray florets (often drooping), while the flower head contains individual florets that are hermaphroditic, having both male and female organs in each flower.

The purple coneflower, or *Echinacea purpurea,* is the most common variety, although many others can be found in an assortment of different sizes and colors. 'Cheyenne red', for example, displays a mix of bright red, cream, orange, and yellow flowers. 'Magnus' produces violet flowers that grow up to 7 inches across, and 'Greenline' produces flowers in an unusually vivid shade of green. Coneflowers are extremely hardy plants and can grow in most climates, though they may need some extra care during especially cold winters before they are fully established.

Coneflowers are also particularly useful plants. They have been used in herbal remedies and traditional medicine for centuries and are still sometimes used today to help fight minor infections and colds. They also attract bees and butterflies, ensuring that nearby plants are exposed to plenty of pollinators. The sturdy stalks, which may reach up to 5 feet (1.5 m) in height, rarely bend or require staking to maintain their upright appearance. Coneflowers are drought tolerant, require hardly any maintenance, and are not commonly eaten by deer.

HOW TO GROW CONEFLOWERS

Coneflowers tend to bloom best in relatively lean soil; rich or heavily amended soil may result in lush foliage but poor flowering. They should be planted in full to partial sun, leaning towards full sun in colder regions. In hotter climates, consider positioning the plant so that it receives direct morning sunlight and late afternoon shade, which will protect it from burning.

SCIENTIFIC NAME: *Echinacea* spp.

FAMILY: Asteraceae

HEIGHT: 2 to 5 feet (60 cm–1.5 m)

WIDTH: 1 to 2 feet (30–60 cm)

BLOOMS: Summer

SOIL pH: Neutral to acidic

LIGHT: Full or partial sun

CARING FOR THE PLANTS

Once planted and established, coneflowers require very little maintenance. In most cases, you won't need to water them at all, because they can usually get enough water from rainfall alone. Purple coneflowers in particular are very drought resistant and often thrive in dry summers.

Additional fertilization can be useful if your coneflowers aren't blooming properly; if flowers are small or poorly developed, try working a small amount of well-composted organic material into the soil around the plants. When the flower's late-summer blooms begin to look tired or ragged, cut the plant back by a third. This rejuvenates it and often produces a new display of beautiful blooms that can last until the first frost.

READ MORE AT GARDENING KNOW HOW

Bright coneflowers are versatile plants, with a host of varieties in many colors that have multiple uses. Learn more about these, as well as what to plant alongside them, by following the links below.

- **"Types of Coneflower — Learn About Different Kinds of Coneflower Plants"** (URL = gkh.us/127286)
- **"Coneflower Herbal Uses — Growing Echinacea Plants as Herbs"** (URL = gkh.us/127270)
- **"Companion Plants for Echinacea: Learn What to Plant with Coneflowers"** (URL = gkh.us/97347)

Coreopsis

SCIENTIFIC NAME: *Coreopsis* spp.

FAMILY: Asteraceae

HEIGHT: 2 to 4 feet (60 cm–1.2 m)

WIDTH: 1 to 2 feet (30–60 cm)

BLOOMS: Summer to autumn

SOIL pH: Neutral to acidic

LIGHT: Full sun

The bicolor blooms of *Coreopsis grandiflora* create a sea of brilliant, show-stopping color. Cheerful coreopsis is the state wildflower of Florida.

Coreopsis, also known as tickseed, pot of gold, or calliopsis, is a rare source of lasting summer color that lingers long after most other perennial flowers have faded from the garden. It is a member of the Asteraceae family, as is evident from its daisy-like blooms. Coreopsis is native to the United States, with 33 species known and listed by the Natural Resources Conservation Service of the USDA. The flower's many varieties come in a range of colors—including traditional yellow, red, pink, and white—and most feature a dark brown or maroon center that contrasts sharply with the vibrant outer petals. Individual varieties differ in height and may also be either annual or perennial.

GROWING COREOPSIS

To plant coreopsis, simply seed a prepared, full-sun area of un-amended soil in the spring. Coreopsis seeds need light to germinate, so only cover them sparingly with soil, or simply press the seeds into moist soil. Keep the seeds watered consistently until germination, which usually takes place within 21 days. Once established, coreopsis should be watered regularly; though they are relatively drought-resistant, they will bloom much more vibrantly with consistent watering. Regularly deadheading spent blooms also encourages production of more flowers, and you can cut the plant back by one-third in late summer for longer-lasting blooms. Beyond regular watering and optional pruning, coreopsis plants will usually thrive when left to their own devices. Fertilization of fully established specimens is unnecessary, and too much fertilizer may actually limit flower production.

OVERWINTERING YOUR PLANTS

Preparation for winter should begin during autumn. Cutting back coreopsis during the autumn isn't always the healthiest thing for the plant; leaving dead growth in place during winter actually provides a certain amount of vital insulation for the roots. Be sure to remove wilted blooms, however, especially if you want to prevent rampant reseeding. If you do decide to cut your coreopsis back in the autumn or winter, be sure to leave at least 2 or 3 inches (5–7.5 cm) of stems in place—cutting too severely before a difficult winter might kill the plant.

Surround the plant with plenty of mulch in autumn, regardless of your decision to cut back or not. Apply at least 2 or 3 inches (5–7.5 cm) and more if you live in a colder region. Don't fertilize the coreopsis after late summer or early autumn—this is not the time to encourage new, tender growth that can be zapped when temperatures drop. Continue to water coreopsis until the ground freezes. It may sound counterintuitive, but roots in moist soil can actually withstand freezing temperatures better than those in dry soil. The plant will now enter a dormant stage of growth, and no further winter care is necessary. When spring comes, remove the mulch once frost no longer threatens, and don't wait too long, as damp mulch can invite pests and disease. This is a good time to apply a bit of general-purpose fertilizer, topped by a thin layer of fresh mulch.

Coreopsis Species

There are six main species of coreopsis for the garden.

- ***C. auriculate.*** This dwarf variety, called lobed tickseed or mouse-ear tickseed, is bright yellow.
- ***C. lanceolate.*** This yellow species grows wild along roadsides and in meadows and fields.
- ***C. rosea.*** As the name implies, this species bears delicate pink blooms with yellow centers.
- ***C. tinctoria.*** This showy species, called dyer's coreopsis or golden tickseed, is bright yellow with maroon centers.
- ***C. verticillate.*** With thin, threadlike leaves, this is called yellow coreopsis or whorled tickseed.
- ***C. grandiflora.*** Known as large-flowered coreopsis, this species bears yellow toothed flowers with a maroon or burgundy center.

Cranesbill

Geranium magnificum, **called purple cranesbill, is one the varieties of this pretty little flower. Its long blooming season makes cranesbill a great addition to a flower bed.**

Cranesbills, or hardy geraniums, are adaptable, compact, and long-blooming, making them a favorite low-effort, high-reward flower. The plant takes its common name from the shape of the fruit capsule, which resembles the long beak of a waterbird. It is a native North American plant with myriad varieties, and it comes in colors ranging from pinks, blues, and vivid purples to subdued whites.

This is a variable genus; some varieties can be as short as 6 inches (15 cm) or as tall as 3 feet (1 m). The delicate, frilly flowers bloom profusely and propagate very easily, often reseeding and spreading abundantly with little human intervention needed. They tend to bloom in late spring and last until autumn, although some particularly hardy varieties can last until the first frost of winter.

HOW TO GROW CRANESBILL

Growing cranesbill can be as easy as planting nursery specimens and watching them blossom when conditions are somewhat damp. These flowers grow best in consistently moist soil when first planted but become somewhat drought tolerant when properly established. Growing cranesbill in fertile soil also encourages the plant to spread, if needed. Most cranesbill varieties thrive in full sun to partial sun, though many will also tolerate full shade.

When considering planting cranesbill, choose a spot with a decent amount of sunlight and a good deal of room for the flowers to sprawl, clipping the edges back if necessary to keep them within their boundaries. Some varieties may be used as ground cover, while others are commonly employed as border plants. Cranesbill should be planted so the crown of the plant is at soil level; planting the crown too deep can damage or kill the plant.

CARE OF CRANESBILL

Beyond the usual removal of spent blooms and occasional watering, cranesbill requires little to no maintenance once established; they are not particularly prone to disease, and few pests tend to target them over other plants. Mildew can become a minor risk in especially humid areas, and overwatering them can encourage root rot. For optimum flower growth and spread, make sure the soil is rich and highly organic, provide occasional light fertilization if needed, and leave them to thrive with little-to-no maintenance.

SCIENTIFIC NAME: *Geranium* spp.

FAMILY: Geraniaceae

HEIGHT: 6 to 24 inches (15–60 cm)

WIDTH: 2 to 3 feet (60 cm–1 m)

BLOOMS: Late spring

SOIL pH: Acidic to neutral

LIGHT: Full to partial sun

Keep Your Garden in Bloom

Many gardeners maintain a continuous show of flowers in their gardens through three seasons. This is accomplished by planting sequential bloomers. Try combining early bloomers like tulip or daffodil with mid-spring annuals and long-lasting perennials like cranesbill—the latter will camouflage the browning leaves of fading bulb plants. As summer approaches, add later-blooming perennials like coneflower, bee balm, and black-eyed Susan along with some bright summer annuals. Finally, as summer wanes, it's time to display the autumn benchwarmers—chrysanthemum, aster, autumn pansies, and ornamental millet.

Creeping Phlox

White and purple creeping phlox cascades over an old stone wall in the spring. The plant's dense blooming habit makes it suitable for use in borders or as a ground cover.

Creeping phlox, also called moss phlox, produces a colorful spring carpet of soft pastel hues and is one of the earliest bloomers in temperate regions. Native to the Appalachian Mountains, it is a spreading, mat-forming plant that boasts needle-like foliage and erect clusters of large, fragrant, star-shaped flowers in lavender-blue, rose-pink, violet, or white. It is also a rather low-maintenance plant; it can grow comfortably over old bricks or jagged rocks and in low-quality soil, making it a great solution for problem areas that you've had difficulty filling in. Consider planting it in between paving stones, in a container or hanger, or in the front row of a bright spring flower bed.

Creeping phlox blooms in spring and produces long, spreading stems, which become woody with age. This thicker growth ceases to produce flowers over time and should be cut back to encourage the newer, softer stems that do bloom.

HOW TO GROW CREEPING PHLOX

Planting creeping phlox is pretty simple. These hardy perennials have an easy-going nature and thrive in a variety of conditions; they are resistant to heat and light frost, and almost any soil is suitable for growing them, as long as it is in full sun to partial shade. For best results, plant starter specimens in a sunny location where the soil can be kept moist but well drained. Dig in some organic amendments to enrich the soil and water the plant until it is established. Plant creeping phlox at soil level and avoid burying the stems in the earth.

CARING FOR YOUR PLANTS

Little special care or maintenance is necessary to maintain creeping phlox. The plant benefits from an early spring application of fertilizer to encourage new growth and flowering. It should be watered weekly in areas without regular rainfall, especially during hot summer periods. In high temperatures, plants in or adjacent to rockeries might show signs of scorching due to their surroundings heating up.

The stems can be cut back after flowering to promote a second bloom. You might also consider cutting the plant back in late winter to allow for rejuvenation and to produce young, more compact stems.

Watch for mites and other pests, and be sure to deal with these infestations as soon as they are spotted using an organic insecticidal soap or spray.

SCIENTIFIC NAME: *Phlox stolonifera*

FAMILY: Polemoniaceae

HEIGHT: 6 to 12 inches (15–30 cm)

WIDTH: 9 to 18 inches (23–45 cm)

BLOOMS: Spring, summer

SOIL pH: Acidic, neutral, alkaline

LIGHT: Full or partial sun

To propagate creeping phlox, simply dig up the entire plant, preserving the root ball, and cut through the center of the plant and through the roots with a sharp soil knife or spade. Replant one half of the phlox in the original hole and plant the second half elsewhere. This process can be done every few years and can result in healthier plants and increased ground cover.

Editor's Picks

Here is just a sampling of creeping phlox varieties in shades from white to purple and bicolor or striped.

- 'Amazing Grace' in white with a magenta eye
- 'Candy Stripe' in pink with a crimson eye and white stripes
- 'Emerald Blue' in lavender-blue
- 'Fort Hill' in rose pink
- 'Purple Beauty' in bright purple with a deep violet center
- 'Scarlet Flame' in magenta-pink
- 'Violet Pinwheels' in lilac

Daisy

What brings to mind carefree summer days more than white and yellow daisies lifting their faces to the sky? These bright flowers are one of the best known of all species.

The common daisy—also known as the English daisy, lawn daisy, and *Bellis perennis*—is generally accepted as the standard example of the daisy family. Daisies are available in a variety of colors in both single and double forms. The classic white daisies, however, with contrasting bright yellow centers tend to be sturdier, and these seem to be the most common choices for lawns and gardens. *Bellis perennis* tolerates cold winters and has some resistance to frost, but it struggles in hot, dry summers. Other, more heat-resistant daisy variants may be more suitable for particularly hot climates. Daisy petals usually close at night, opening again when the sun rises.

Space Invaders

As daisies self-seed and spread very easily, you might face some difficulty containing and removing them from spaces you want kept clear. Common daisy flowers grow from a taproot that plunges straight down deep into the ground; this means that, unless the entire root is removed, the flowers will likely return. Regularly mowing, fertilizing, and aerating your lawn will help prevent daisies from growing, because they prefer patchy areas with dense or poor-quality soil. Healthy, dense grass cover will also keep daisies from getting a foothold in your lawn.

At a Glance

SCIENTIFIC NAME: *Bellis perennis*

FAMILY: Asteraceae

HEIGHT: 3 to 6 inches (7.5–15 cm)

WIDTH: 6 to 8 inches (15–20 cm)

BLOOMS: Summer

SOIL pH: Neutral

LIGHT: Full sun to partial shade

However beloved this classic flower is, the daisy has traditionally been considered an enemy of neat, carefully manicured lawns, because they can easily reseed and spread like a weed. Yet, as ideas about the function of lawns have changed over time, daisies have gained some popularity as purpose-grown ground cover. They are easy to maintain plants, environmentally friendly, and don't require the extensive investment of money and time usually required for the upkeep of a traditional turf lawn. And imagine just how pretty they will look when the flowers are all in bloom.

HOW TO GROW DAISIES

You should sow daisy seeds in spring or early fall. If you find them springing up in your garden, it is usually best to leave them where they grow; however, if you want to try transplanting a daisy, dig deep to make sure you get the entire root system. When replanting, the roots should be buried equally deeply.

Daisies are adaptable to a fair range soil types and sunlight. They can grow in poor or lean soil, and they don't particularly prefer rich soil. Moist, well-draining soil is ideal, however, and they thrive best in cool climates. The blooming of daisy flowers might slow during the hottest summer days and return in cooler temperatures of late summer or early autumn.

CARING FOR THE PLANTS

Daisies require little to no maintenance. Once established, they need only occasional watering during dry weather. You can also deadhead for aesthetic purposes, if you desire. Beyond that, daisies will essentially take care of themselves.

Delphinium

Long stalks of purple, lavender, and pink delphinium lean over a garden's retaining wall. These showy flowers work alone or as the backing plant in a mixed flower bed.

SCIENTIFIC NAME: *Delphinium* spp.

FAMILY: Ranunculaceae

HEIGHT: 2 to 6 feet (60 cm–1.8 m)

WIDTH: 1 to 3 feet (30 cm–1 m)

BLOOMS: Summer to early autumn

SOIL pH: Neutral to slightly acidic

LIGHT: Partial sun

The long stalks and tall, vibrant blooms of delphinium *(Delphinium* spp.), also known as larkspur, are sure to stand out in any garden. Delphiniums come in a range of shades; the most common variety is a deep blue, but they can also be found in lavender, pink, purple, red, white, and yellow. Groups of delphinium are usually best planted at the back of flower beds or on their own (away from smaller flowers), as each spike of flowers can easily reach up to 6 feet (1.8 cm) in height. Some shorter varieties do exist, though these can still dwarf other flowers.

HOW TO GROW DELPHINIUMS

Delphiniums may be propagated from seed or basal cuttings. If you're planning on growing delphinium seeds, they can be started indoors in late winter.

Plant delphinium in a sunny area with soil that is consistently moist, and be sure not to let them dry out. Though these are summer flowers, they do not tolerate extreme temperature changes or full-sun exposure. Gentle morning sun with afternoon shade is preferable, especially when planted in hotter zones. Mulch is also helpful in retaining moisture and keeping roots cool.

Delphiniums will perform best when planted in well-draining, neutral to slightly acidic soil. Fertilize new delphiniums regularly during the early stages of growth—primarily during spring—as well as during the flowering period. Ideally, use well-composted organic material, such as cow manure, but a basic 10-10-10 granular fertilizer will also work. Yellowing foliage or stunted growth often indicates the plant needs more fertilizer.

CARING FOR THE PLANTS

Deadheading is an important part of caring for delphiniums. Deadhead the husks of spent blooms, and cut back spent flower stalks in early summer. When all spent blooms are removed and moisture and fertilization requirements are met, you can expect a bountiful resurgence of blooms in late summer or early autumn. Often, this may be the final show for this short-lived perennial, but the striking beauty of this second showing will be worth the effort. Taller varieties may require staking, especially when planted in areas with heavy rain or wind, as their stems are hollow and can bend or break easily under this type of stress.

Delphiniums are at risk for a handful of diseases and pests; keep an eye on young plants in particular. Make sure that the soil continues to drain properly to avoid root rot, and never propagate from diseased plants.

Editor's Picks

From white to deep purple, the color range of delphiniums brings cool tones to a garden. Here are just a few of the varieties available.

- **'Aurora Blue' in rich blue**
- **'Blue Bird' in periwinkle blue with a white center**
- **'Cobalt Dreams' in rich, true blue**
- **'Faust' in very vivid blue**
- **'Guardian White' in bright white**
- **'Highlander Blueberry Pie' with tints of blue with pale pink centers**
- **'King Arthur' in royal purple with a white center**
- **'Million Dollar Blush' in delicate rose**
- **'Pagan Purples' in bold purple**
- **'Sunny Skies' in light sky blue**
- **'Royal Aspirations' in royal blue**

Foxglove

Foxglove stalks growing tall in the summer sun with flowers in full bloom add vertical drama to a flower bed. These classic flowers work well at the back of borders in cottage or woodland gardens.

Tall, stately, and vibrant, foxgloves (*Digitalis* spp.) have long been valued for their distinctive and colorful bell-shaped blossoms. Foxglove flowers grow on stems that can reach 6 feet (1.8 m) in height, depending on variety, and their clusters of gently drooping flowers can be found in shades of white, lavender, yellow, pink, red, and purple. They are rather hardy plants and can tolerate a large range of temperatures, and they thrive in full sun to partial shade, with some midday and afternoon shade for optimum performance. The hotter the summers, the more shade this plant needs—they should be planted in full shade in areas with extremely high summer temperatures.

Rusty foxgloves are the tallest variety of this specimen, often reaching 6 feet (1.8 m) in height, and may require staking. The Foxy Hybrid variety, on the other hand, reaches just 2 to 3 feet (60 cm–1 m), making them a good option for those growing foxgloves in smaller gardens. The foxglove plant is also grown commercially for distillation of the heart medication Digitalis.

HOW TO GROW FOXGLOVES

Foxglove plants grow best in rich, well-draining soil that is kept continually moist. As perennials, they can be encouraged to regrow and self-seed if you make sure to keep the soil from drying out or becoming too saturated. Foxgloves may be grown from seed and will usually produce blossoms in their second year. If spent flower heads are not removed, the plants will reseed themselves abundantly. If desired, propagating new foxgloves from these seeds is as easy as leaving the last flowers of the season to dry on the stalk; they will drop seeds for new growth. Thin the seedlings that spring up the next year to about 18 inches (45 cm) apart, allowing growing plants room to develop. Alternatively, you can deadhead and cut back spent foxgloves to prevent reseeding.

Foxgloves and Bumblebees

Foxgloves attract many pollinators, including hoverflies, hummingbirds, and, in particular, bumblebees. Along with their height, shape, and long blooming time, the purple-pink, bell-shaped flowers have large landing lips and hairs that have evolved specifically to feed this long-tongue species, which can reach the nectar waiting deep inside the flowers.

At a Glance

SCIENTIFIC NAME: *Digitalis* spp.

FAMILY: Plantaginaceae

HEIGHT: 2 to 5 feet (60 cm–1.5 m)

WIDTH: 1 to 2 feet (30–60 cm)

BLOOMS: Early summer

SOIL pH: Slightly acidic

LIGHT: Full to partial sun

CARING FOR THE PLANTS

Foxgloves thrive best in cool environments with good air circulation. Humidity is not a large concern, though it is important to avoid overwatering. They can be sensitive to diseases like rot, fungus, and mildew, all of which can be prevented with properly draining soil, good air circulation, and occasional fungicide if needed. Insects like aphids, slugs, and Japanese beetles can also be an issue, but these can usually be treated safely with insecticidal soaps or sprays.

Note: Children and pets should be kept away from foxgloves, as all parts of the plant are toxic when consumed. Many people take advantage of this fact to keep pests like deer and rabbits away from the garden, as these animals usually know to avoid foxgloves. Hummingbirds, on the other hand, are attracted to foxglove nectar.

Hellebore

Making its appearance in late winter, hellebore, also known as Lenten rose or winter rose, is one of the first flowers to bloom in the garden.

Hellebore flowers (*Helleborus* spp.) bloom in late winter to early spring, sometimes flowering even as the ground is still covered with snow. Like other early bloomers, such as crocuses and snowdrops, hellebores are a welcome sign of the approach of warmer weather. These flowers are especially fragrant and long-lasting, sometimes remaining attractive for several months. One reason for their longevity is that the outer "petals" of the hellebore are actually sepals, a type of specialized leaf. These exist to protect the true petals at the center of the flower, and they can last for months after the actual petals are spent.

Different varieties of the hellebore plant offer an impressive range of flower colors, including white, pink, black, red, blue, green, and yellow, all usually featuring white or yellow centers.

HOW TO GROW HELLEBORES

When growing from seed or division, plant the hellebore in well-draining, organic soil. They thrive in partial sun or full shade in the summer (with more shade in areas with hotter summers) but prefer full sun in the winter. One way to achieve this is by planting hellebores under deciduous trees: this will provide partial shade in the summer, and then full sun in the autumn and winter when the leaves fall from the branches.

Five Varieties of Hellebore

There are five main varieties of the rose-like genus *Helleborus.*

- ***H. argutifolius.*** Also called the Corsican hellebore, it blooms in pale green.
- ***H. foetidus.*** Also called stinking hellebore, it blooms in green edged in red.
- ***H. niger.*** Also called the Christmas rose, this white variety can bloom earlier than other hellebores.
- ***H. orientalis.*** Also called the Lenten rose, it comes in many different colors, like purple, maroon, apricot, and white.
- ***H.* x *hybridus.*** There are several hybrid hellebore flowers.

SCIENTIFIC NAME: *Helleborus* spp.

FAMILY: Ranunculaceae

HEIGHT: 1 to 2 feet (30–60 cm)

WIDTH: 1 to 3 feet 1 to 2 feet (30 cm–1 m)

BLOOMS: Late winter to early spring

SOIL pH: Neutral

LIGHT: Partial to full shade in summer; full sun in winter

Hellebore seeds should be planted in autumn, as they will need a roughly 60-day period of consistent moisture and low temperatures. Planting seeds in the autumn allows this to happen naturally in areas with cold winters. You may need to wait two to three years to see blooms on hellebores grown from seed, especially if the seeds are allowed to go dormant before germinating. Divide overgrown clumps in spring, after flowering, or in autumn.

Hellebore plants should be kept in moist soil while growing, although they can be susceptible to root rot if left to soak in poor-draining soil for too long. They should be planted in an area with good air circulation and room for growth.

CARING FOR THE PLANTS

Once established, hellebore care is minimal. Remove any older leaves that appear damaged or withered. Careful fertilization can help encourage growth; however, too much nitrogen may result in overdeveloped foliage and a shortage of blooms. Hellebore is disliked by deer and other animal pests prone to munching on plants.

Note: All parts of the hellebore plant are poisonous when ingested, so take care to keep children and pets away.

Hollyhock

Colossal stalks of the puffy blooms of an apricot gladioli in full bloom tower over other plants. These showy flowers are a staple of informal cottage gardens.

Hollyhocks (*Alcea* spp.) are popular, distinctive flowers that can easily grow up to 8 feet (2.4 m) tall. These towering plants stand high above most other flowers, adding a lovely vertical element to any garden. There are over 60 varieties of hollyhock, all of which range in color, size, and preferred environments. The common hollyhock sports vivid pink flowers; other varieties come in a host of colors. With single and double blooms, along with an array of hues, there is sure to be a hollyhock to please everyone. Below are just a few.

- 'Blacknight' has dramatic purple-black single-form flowers.
- 'Bride's Bouquet' is a delicate salmon pink and pure white
- Chater's Chestnut Brown' is a double red-brown variety.
- Chater's Salmon Queen' is pale salmon with apricot-pink highlights.
- 'Crème de Cassis' is a charming bright raspberry and white.
- 'Icicle' is a double flower in icy white.
- 'Indian Spring' comes in a range of colors, including pink, rose, and yellow.
- 'O Hara' is eye-catching scarlet red.
- 'Peaches 'n' Dreams' is a double flower in pretty pastel peach.
- 'Spring Celebrities Lilac' is a double in lavender-blue.
- 'Sunshine' is pale yellow.
- 'The Watchman' is a striking black-maroon.

Planting several varieties of this plant is a great way to foster a garden of unique, long-lasting blooms. Hollyhock is known to attract hummingbirds and butterflies and has also been used historically in herbal medicine as a moisturizer, laxative, and anti-inflammatory treatment.

HOW TO GROW HOLLYHOCKS

Hollyhocks need full sun and moist, rich, well-drained soil. If you are growing them from seeds, sow them outside about a week before the last frost. If you are planting seedlings, wait to plant them until about two to three weeks after the last frost. The seeds need to be planted only just below the surface of the soil, no more than ¼-inch (6.35 mm) deep, and they should be spaced about 2 feet (60 cm) apart to give them adequate room to spread out. You can also plant dormant bare-root hollyhocks.

Hollyhocks are short-lived perennials, which means that most varieties will only live for two to three years. Their lifespan can be extended by removing growing flowers as soon as they fade. If you live in a non-tropical region, cutting them back to the ground and mulching them will also help. Despite their limited individual lifespan, hollyhocks easily reseed; as long as conditions are maintained, new plants will continually grow from the dropped seeds of the older plants. They can also benefit from fertilizer or compost in the spring.

At a Glance

SCIENTIFIC NAME: *Alcea* spp.

FAMILY: Malvaceae

HEIGHT: 5 to 8 feet (1.5–2.4 m)

WIDTH: 1 to 2 feet (3–60 cm)

BLOOMS: Summer

SOIL pH: Acidic, neutral, or alkaline

LIGHT: Full to partial sun

CARE OF THE PLANTS

Hollyhocks are relatively self-sufficient; just make sure they get four to six hours of sun every day. Keep new plants well-watered, but once established, they are quite drought tolerant. They are, however, vulnerable to a few specific issues. Keep watch for fungal rust in particular, which will typically attack the lower leaves before spreading to upper leaves. To help keep rust to a minimum, make sure the plant has adequate air circulation, apply occasional fungicide, and water the plant from below to avoid soaking the leaves.

Dig Deeper

READ MORE AT GARDENING KNOW HOW

To learn more about treating hollyhock rust, scan the QR code or follow this link.

- **"Hollyhock Rust Treatment: How to Control Hollyhock Rust In Gardens"** (URL = gkh.us/100824)

Lupine

Lupinus polyphyllus, the garden lupine, makes a good companion plant in various gardens because it increases the soil nitrogen for certain vegetables and other plants.

SCIENTIFIC NAME: *Lupinus* spp.

FAMILY: Fabaceae

HEIGHT: 3 to 4 feet (1–1.2 m)

WIDTH: 1 to 2 feet (30–60 cm)

BLOOMS: Spring, summer

SOIL pH: Acidic to neutral

LIGHT: Full sun

Lupines (*Lupinus* spp.) are attractive and spiky, reaching up to 4 feet (1.2 cm) in height and adding color and texture to the backdrop of any flower bed. These perennial wildflowers are easy to grow and maintain, and they will return over and over once established and allowed to reseed. The lupine plant grows from a long taproot that extends deep into the earth, so they don't like to be moved or transplanted if it can be avoided. They grow wild in some areas of the United States, where they are common hosts for the larvae of several endangered species of butterflies. Wildflowers of the lupine plant generally come in hues of blues and white, although domesticated lupines can have flowers in blues, yellows, pinks, and purples.

Lupine plants also produce legumes, called lupin beans, which have been eaten in regions of Europe, Africa, the Americas, and the Middle East for thousands of years. Lupin beans are most commonly pickled or ground into flour, although they are also used in plant-based meat and dairy substitutes.

HOW TO GROW LUPINES

Growing lupines is as simple as planting seeds or cuttings into a sunny area with well-draining soil. If planting lupine from seed, scratch the seed surface or soak them overnight in lukewarm water to soften the outer coating and make it easier to penetrate. Seeds can be chilled for a week in the refrigerator prior to planting. Alternatively, you can plant lupine seeds in the autumn or early winter and let them chill in the ground until spring. Lupines produce many seeds each season that will easily grow into more flowers the following year if not removed. They thrive best in cool climates, though mulch will help keep their roots cool and retain soil moisture during especially long, hot summers.

CARE OF THE PLANTS

To encourage blooms, fertilize lupines with a plant food that is high in phosphorus. Lupine plants are also "nitrogen-fixing" plants, which means they harbor useful bacteria that can increase nitrogen levels in soil. This makes them a great addition to vegetable gardens or any area where nitrogen-loving plants will be grown. Avoid using nitrogen-rich fertilizer on lupines, however, as it may encourage excessive growth of foliage and do little to promote flowering.

Deadheading spent blooms will encourage more blooms in the future, although allowing seeds to drop from dried flowers will encourage reseeding. Flowering ground cover planted beneath lupines will help keep roots cool and will also benefit from the increased nitrogen in the soil.

Editor's Picks

Here is just a tiny sampling of lupine cultivars that you can try.

- **'Chandelier' in creamy primrose to golden yellow**
- **'The Chatelaine' in bicolor bubblegum pink and white**
- **'The Governor' in bicolor ultramarine blue and white**
- **'My Castle; in rosy carmine**
- **'The Pages' in brick red**
- **'Russell' in salmon, cream, dark purple, and magenta**

Mullein

Tall spires of sunshine yellow common mullein add a cheerful note to the summertime landscape. These wildflowers are finding a place in cultivated gardens that feature native plants that are hardy and low maintenance, as well as beautiful.

The tall spikes and distinctive yellow rosettes of common mullein are striking in any environment. These flowers can often be found growing wild in abandoned places, such as along fences and roadsides, the edges of forests, and in vacant lots. Common mullein, *Verbascum thapsus,* was historically used as an herbal treatment for coughs, congestion, chest colds, bronchitis, and inflammation. Native Americans and soldiers during the Civil War era also made teas from leaves of mullein plants to treat asthma. During the 1800s, settlers in North America used it to treat tuberculosis. Many people today still make teas and herbal infusions from dried mullein leaves and flowers for a variety of uses.

Common mullein plants are large, erect specimens with huge, furry leaves and tall stalks of yellow flower rosettes. They are a popular choice in gardens and landscaping for their hardy nature, ability to thrive in poor-quality soil, and long-lasting flowers. They reseed prolifically, however, and can be difficult to remove. Each plant can produce over 100,000 seeds, which can potentially stay dormant for decades before germination. Although common mullein is considered a weed in some regions, there are more than 450 varieties of mullein, including over 300 that can grow in the garden or natural areas without risk of abundant reseeding. These ornamental or hybrid mulleins can produce white, pink, lavender, and yellow flowers.

SCIENTIFIC NAME: *Verbascum thapsus*

FAMILY: Scrophulariaceae

HEIGHT: 2 to 10 feet (60 cm–3 m)

WIDTH: 1 to 3 feet (30 cm–1 m)

BLOOMS: Summer

SOIL pH: Slightly alkaline

LIGHT: Full sun

HOW TO GROW MULLEIN

Mullein is extremely easy to cultivate. It can be planted just about anywhere and requires little to no human intervention; once it has sprouted, just watch it grow. Common mullein plants can grow as tall as 10 feet (3 m) when flowering, and you can expect to spend a fair amount of time removing spent blooms if you don't want them to spread. Removing the flower stalk before seeds have dispersed will also help avoid abundant reseeding.

Ornamental varieties of mullein, alternatively, are much less invasive and may need a little more care. Generally, mullein plants prefer dry, slightly alkaline soil, and can be planted in any area with good soil drainage and full sun. Their towering size may mean that you need to provide some protection from the wind to help keep stalks from breaking. Many new varieties have been bred to smaller sizes, some reaching only a few feet in height. Allow plenty of space for plants to develop.

Other Mulleins

Along with common mullein, you can also think about planting one of the other *Verbascums.*

- **Moth mullein** *(V. blattaria),* with white or yellow flowers
- **Nettle-leaf mullein** *(V. chaixii),* a compact variety with a range of cultivars in various colors
- **Olympic, or Greek mullein** *(V. olympicum),* with branching stalks of bright yellow flowers
- **Purple mullein** *(V. phoeniceum),* a compact variety with dark purple or violet flowers

Oriental Poppy

Red oriental poppies, with their papery scarlet petals and deep black eye, make a bold statement in a flower garden. Along with the red, there are cultivars in a variety of hues.

Three thousand years ago, gardeners were already growing oriental poppies and their *Papaver* cousins all over the world. Oriental poppy plants *(P. orientale)* have remained a garden favorite ever since. Once planted, they require no special care and will last for many years. Their original, vibrant, red-orange color is still the most popular for growing, though modern varieties can be found in a range of colors that will fit into any garden's color scheme.

HOW TO GROW ORIENTAL POPPIES

Nurseries rarely carry potted oriental poppy plants because they are difficult to transplant; you will have more success growing them from seeds. Once sown, they do not like to be disturbed, so the easiest method is to sow the seeds directly into the ground. Select a site that gets plenty of sun—at least six hours a day—and turn over the top inch or two (2.5–5 cm) of soil. Poppies aren't particular about their soil, but they are fussy about drainage. If the soil's drainage is poor, amend it with a couple of inches of compost before planting. They should be planted in spring in areas with cold winters, or in autumn in areas with warmer winters.

To plant, simply sprinkle seeds onto the surface of the soil. Do not cover the seeds—they need light to germinate. Regularly water the area, keeping it moist but not soggy, until the seeds germinate, which should take about two weeks. When the seedlings are about one inch (2.5 cm) tall, thin them to 6 inches (15 cm) apart to give the flowers room to grow.

CARING FOR THE PLANTS

Careful placement is essential. Once planted, oriental poppies don't like to move, and they might not survive being transplanted. They can be particularly susceptible to root rot if planted in soggy or poorly draining soil. They should be fertilized, but only infrequently—roughly once a year is all they need.

Oriental poppies relish the cool temperatures of early spring and autumn. Their bright blossoms open just as most spring bulbs are finished, but they will go dormant in the summer, so it might be a good idea to plant them alongside flowers that will cover the "bald spots" they leave behind. It's also important to allow these flowers to die back during the summer, as overwatering oriental poppies in an effort to keep them alive will likely kill them for good. Instead, they should be allowed to go dormant in the heat of summer to return again when the weather cools.

SCIENTIFIC NAME: *Papaver orientale*

FAMILY: Papaveraceae

HEIGHT: 1 to 3 feet (30 cm–1 m)

WIDTH: 1 to 2 feet (30–60 cm)

BLOOMS: Spring, summer

SOIL pH: Neutral

LIGHT: Full sun

California Poppies

Do you love the papery look of poppies? Try the California poppy *(Eschscholzia californica)*. This member of the Papaveraceae is the state flower of California, where profusions of these sunny yellow-orange flowers bloom in the spring and summer along country roads and freeways throughout much of the Golden State. Plant masses of them in a native-style garden.

Peony

Peonies are large, showy, and fragrant, making them essential in a sunny flower garden. Plant elegant peony bushes in groups to add a stylish note to your borders.

Native to Asia, Europe, and western North America, the peony *(Paeonia)* is a flowering plant in the sole genus of the Paeoniaceae family. The flowers bloom for about a week between late spring and early summer. Select early, mid-season, and late-blooming varieties for a long-lasting display of graceful, growing peonies that will last all summer. They also make exquisite cut flowers, easy to store in the fridge to later create elegant bouquets and other floral arrangements.

There are thousands of cultivars of garden peonies. They are split into five main types: single bloom, double bloom, semi-double bloom, anemone, and Japanese. They come in a variety of colors, from blush to bright pink, white, peach, and red. The most common is the herbaceous garden peony, pretty spring bloomers you're likely to see in most people's gardens. There are also fernleaf, woodland, tree, and Itoh peonies, the last of which are a cross between tree and garden peonies.

HOW TO GROW PEONIES

You can buy peonies as potted plants or as tubers. Potted peonies do best when planted in autumn, but you can plant them anytime during the growing season; plant tubers in autumn only. Choose a sunny spot with enough room for your peony to grow 3 to 4 feet (1–1.2 m) both horizontally and vertically. Think carefully about the site; once it is in the ground it doesn't like to be moved.

CARING FOR THE PLANTS

Fertilize peonies for the first couple years in early spring or just after flowering. Older, established bushes need little maintenance. Just add a layer of compost, and mulch around plants in spring, making sure not to pile the mulch around the stems. If blooms diminish, feed plants with a low-nitrogen fertilizer or work bone meal into the soil under the plants once every three to five years.

Divide every peonies few years, ideally following a summer with low flower production, and then replant in autumn. To divide, use a sharp knife to split the bulbs, leaving three to five "eyes" (pink, bullet-shaped buds) on each division. Replant so that the eyes are about an inch deep (2.5 cm) and allow 3 feet (1 m) of space between each plant. Incorporate organic matter into the soil to help the newly divided plants thrive.

Peonies are not particularly vulnerable to insects, but they may be infected by fungal diseases, such as botrytis blight, which is caused by cool, wet weather, and leaf blotch. These fungal diseases may damage stems, leaves, and flowers, which could lead to the death of the entire plant. Heavily infected plants should be removed and disposed of safely to avoid risking the health of other flowers. If you suspect your peonies were killed by fungal disease, plant any future peonies in a different area in the autumn. Water peonies early in the day and maintain good airflow around each plant.

To grow bigger blooms, try disbudding by pinching off smaller side buds, leaving the main terminal flower bud. Disbudding results in fewer blooms, but each flower will be larger and healthier. Flowers may become too heavy for the stems to support, however, especially on double bloom varieties. You can stake peonies in spring before foliage produces leaves. Many garden centers sell peony-specific metal frames, although a tomato cage will do in a pinch.

SCIENTIFIC NAME: *Paeonia* spp.

FAMILY: Paeoniaceae

HEIGHT: 1 to 3 feet (30 cm–1 m)

WIDTH: 2 to 3 feet (60 cm–1 m)

BLOOMS: Late spring

SOIL pH: Neutral

LIGHT: Full sun

READ MORE AT GARDENING KNOW HOW

You can learn how to make this lovely flower last a lifetime.

- **"How to Grow a Peony That Lasts 70 Years"** (URL = gkh.us/186657)

Speedwell

The vivid electric blue blossoms of common speedwell *(Veronica officinalis)* brighten a sunny spot in an ornamental rock garden. The common variety is just one of hundreds.

Planting speedwell (*Veronica* spp.) in the garden is a great way to enjoy long-lasting blooms throughout the summer season. These easy-to-care-for perennial plants require little maintenance once established, making them an ideal choice for any busy gardener.

There are roughly 500 species of the *Veronica* genus, with the plants falling in two main categories: bushy (or mat-forming) and spiked. Bushy varieties, such as *V. officinalis* (common speedwell, by far the most well-known) grow from 1 inch to 1 foot tall and produce dense clusters of flowers. Spiked varieties form tall spires of brightly colored, butterfly-friendly flowers. Among the many varieties you will find an array of vibrant blue, pink, violent, and white blooms.

The plant has a long blooming season, from June to August; if cared for properly, speedwell flowers will bloom for six to eight weeks throughout the summer months. Speedwell perennials are deer and rabbit resistant, but butterflies and hummingbirds are attracted to their dizzying hues. They are fairly pest and disease resistant as well, with the exception of some issues like powdery mildew, spider mites, and thrips.

HOW TO GROW SPEEDWELL

Speedwell plants can tolerate a wide range of conditions; they are not particular about the acidity or quality of their soil, which can be loamy, sandy, or clay-dense, or the temperatures they are exposed to, and they will grow in full sun or partial shade. They thrive best with full sun exposure, however, and speedwell planted in well-draining soil will be less susceptible to fungal diseases and rot.

Speedwell can be sown from seed, although these plants are more commonly found in nurseries; nursery-grown speedwell can be transplanted into your garden in spring, skipping several weeks otherwise spent germinating seeds. Speedwell seeds can be started indoors or outdoors: start roughly four to six weeks before the last spring frost if starting indoors, or well after the last frost if starting outdoors.

Speedwell seeds need light and moisture to germinate; press them into the surface of the soil without fully burying them and keep the soil moist for two to three weeks.

CARING FOR THE PLANTS

Speedwell is hardy and drought resistant, but it should be watered in the summer when there is less than an inch (2.5 cm) of rainfall per week. Other than providing water and sunlight, speedwell is a very low-maintenance plant. In order to facilitate maximum blooming, it is advisable to remove faded, spent flower spikes and periodically divide the plant every few years in the early spring or autumn. The tallest speedwell specimens generally require staking, and their stems should be cut back to an inch or so above ground level in late autumn after the first frost.

At a Glance

SCIENTIFIC NAME: *Veronica* spp.

FAMILY: Plantaginaceae

HEIGHT: 1 inch to 3 feet (2.5 cm–1 m)

WIDTH: 1 to 3 feet (30 cm–1 m)

BLOOMS: Spring, summer

SOIL pH: Acidic, neutral, or alkaline

LIGHT: Full to partial sun

Editor's Picks

Of the hundreds of *Veronica* species, there are some that work especially well in home gardens.

- Alpine speedwell *(V. alpina).* Airy spikes of white, rose, pink, pale or deep blue flowers; use in rock gardens or containers.
- Gentian speedwell *(V. gentianoides).* Spikes of powder blue to white flowers; use in borders, containers, and rock gardens.
- Turkish speedwell *(V. liwanensis).* Clusters of bright blue flowers; use as ground cover or a lawn substitute, and in rock gardens.
- Mountain speedwell *(V. montana).* Tiny lilac flowers; use as ground cover, in rock gardens, borders, and containers.
- Creeping speedwell *(V. repens).* Small, pale blue or white flowers; use as a ground cover, a lawn substitute, and in rock gardens.
- Spike speedwell *(V. spicata).* Spikes of tiny flowers; use in containers or butterfly gardens.

Sweet William

SCIENTIFIC NAME: *Dianthus barbatus*

FAMILY: Caryophyllaceae

HEIGHT: 1 to 2 feet (30–60 cm)

WIDTH: 6 to 18 inches (15–45 cm)

BLOOMS: Late spring, early summer

SOIL pH: Neutral to alkaline

LIGHT: Full to partial sun

Dainty sweet William, or *Dianthus barbatus,* fills a garden with a spicy, sweet scent. These old-fashioned flowers are a mainstay of informal cottage gardens.

Native to southern Europe and parts of Asia, sweet William *(Dianthus barbatus)* is prized for its densely packed, flattened clusters of small, brightly colored flowers. The origins of its name have been lost over time, but it first appeared in 1596, when botanist John Gerard included the flower in his garden catalog. The "sweet" appellation, however, surely derives from it strong, sweet fragrance, with its spicy notes similar to cinnamon or cloves. This lovely scent attracts bees, birds, and butterflies.

The plants are relatively small, and they usually grow to between 6 and 18 inches (15–45 cm) tall. Variants of these flowers are most often found in pink, salmon, red, and white hues. The foliage is slender and sparsely spread across thick stems. Most plants in the *Dianthus* genus had very short blooming seasons until 1971, when a breeder learned how to grow varieties that did not set seed and, therefore, had a prolonged bloom period. Modern varieties will typically bloom from spring to early autumn.

HOW TO GROW SWEET WILLIAM

Plant sweet Williams in full sun. They will tolerate partial shade, but they should receive at least 6 hours of sunlight each day. These plants need fertile, well-draining soil. They are less picky about soil acidity, but neutral to slightly alkaline soil will provide the best results.

These plants can be safely transplanted if purchased as blooms from garden centers. Their seeds are also readily available and may be started indoors six to eight weeks before the danger of frost has passed. Plant them at the same level they reached in pots or planters indoors. Plant them quite far apart from each other, keeping 12 to 18 inches (30–45 cm) between the plants. Do not add mulch around them, and water them only at the base of the plant to keep the foliage dry and prevent mildew spotting.

CARING FOR THE PLANTS

These flowers are very straightforward to care for. Water the plants when dry and more often during periods of low rainfall. Apply fertilizer every six to eight weeks. You may also work a slow-release fertilizer into the soil when first planting, which will release you from the need to regularly feed the plants later on. Some varieties are self-sowing, so deadheading is extremely important to reduce unwanted plant growth and encourage additional blooming. This perennial variety in particular is short lived and should be propagated through division, tip cuttings, or even layering.

Dianthus Varieties

Dianthus flowers like sweet William belong to a family of plants that encompasses about 340 species. Two popular garden species are the carnation *(D. caryophyllus)* and the pink *(D. plumarius,* shown above). They are all characterized by the spicy fragrance their blooms emit. These plants may be found as hardy annuals, biennials, or perennials and are most often used in borders or potted displays. Carnations have a long history as cut flowers.

Trumpet Vine

Trumpet vine, also known as trumpet creeper, blankets a fence with a profusion of showy vermilion flowers. Use caution if you decide to use trumpet vine in your garden plans: this fast-growing perennial is an aggressive spreader that can choke out other plants.

Trumpet vine *(Campsis radicans)*, also known as trumpet creeper, is a fast-growing perennial vine native to the woodlands of China and North America. This plant is extremely easy to propagate, and although some gardeners consider the plant invasive, trumpet vines can be kept under control with adequate care and pruning.

Its beautiful flowers, ranging in color from yellow to orange or red, are great at attracting hummingbirds to your garden. The flowers tend to bloom throughout summer and into autumn, though the blooming period may be shorter on vines planted in shady locations. After flowering, trumpet vines produce attractive bean-like seedpods. The woody vines are usually strong enough to endure winter, while other growth will generally die back, returning again in spring. These vines can reach a whopping 25 to 40 feet (7.6–12 m) in just one season, so keeping their size under control with pruning is often necessary. If allowed to grow unreservedly, trumpet vine can readily take over an area and can be extremely difficult to get rid of once established.

HOW TO GROW TRUMPET VINE

This easily grown vine is also not very fussy about its lighting needs, thriving in both full sun and partial shade. It prefers well-draining soil, but the plant is resilient enough to adapt to soil of nearly any quality and will grow quite quickly all on its own.

Be sure to choose a suitable location prior to planting trumpet vine, as well as a sturdy support structure. It is important that you plant the vine some distance from any buildings. Planting too close to your house or an outbuilding could result in structural damage from the vine's creeping roots. They can work their way under shingles and even potentially cause damage to foundations. A trellis, fence, or large pole works well as a support structure; however, do not allow the vine to climb trees: as it grows, it can strangle and eventually kill a tree.

To control its spread, containment is another consideration. Some gardeners find it useful to plant their trumpet vines in large, containers, such as 5-gallon (19-liter) buckets with their bottoms cut away. They then sink the buckets into the ground. This helps keep the vine's spreading habit under control by limiting the range its roots can extend.

If you locate the vine in an area large enough where you can routinely prune or mow its roots, you can cultivate it without adding a support structure, and treat it more like a flowering shrub.

SCIENTIFIC NAME: *Campsis radicans*

FAMILY: Bignoniaceae

HEIGHT: 25 to 40 feet (7.6–12 m)

WIDTH: 5 to 10 feet (1.5–3 m)

BLOOMS: Summer

SOIL pH: Neutral

LIGHT: Full sun to partial shade

CARING FOR THE PLANTS

Trumpet vine is a vigorous grower and requires little care once established. Water only as needed and do not fertilize. In most cases, pruning is the only maintenance you will need to perform. This vigorous grower requires regular pruning to keep it under control. Most of the pruning should take place in early spring or in autumn, with springtime generally preferable. The plant may be severely pruned back to just a few buds. Deadheading the flower pods as they appear is another good idea, as this will help prevent the plant from reseeding in other areas of the garden.

READ MORE AT GARDENING KNOW HOW

If your trumpet vine has become invasive, scan the QR code or follow this link to find out how you can remove it.

- **"Tips to Get Rid of Trumpet Vine in the Garden "** (URL = gkh.us/2445)

Yarrow

Flat-topped clusters of yarrow rise above feathery green leaves. These flowers, native to many regions of the world, are perfect for natural-style and pollinator gardens. Members of the *Achillea* genus are used as food plants by the larvae of some Lepidoptera species

Yarrow *(Achillea millefolium)* is an herbaceous flowering perennial, native to temperate regions of the Northern Hemisphere in Asia, Europe, and North America, where it grows as a wildflower in grasslands and open forest. Its flat-topped clusters of small, creamy whitish flowers sit atop a featherlike, gray-green, leafy, and usually hairy stem, which accounts for the species name, *millefolium* (Latin for "a thousand leaves").

Once known a *herba militaris,* yarrow has been used as a medicinal herb to treat the bleeding of minor wounds and swollen or cramping muscles, as well as to reduce fever or to help with relaxation. Other common names for this species include gordaldo, nosebleed plant, old man's pepper, devil's nettle, sanguinary, milfoil, soldier's woundwort, thousand-leaf, thousand-seal, and *plumajillo* (Spanish for "little feather"). As with any medicinal herb, yarrow should not be consumed without first consulting a physician.

On the non-medicinal side, yarrow herb is an astringent and is sometimes used as an ingredient in facial washes and shampoo.

Yarrow is useful for combating soil erosion, and it is an especially useful companion plant, attracting beneficial insects and repelling some pests. It is a great plant to feature in a pollinator garden. It provides food for a variety of insects, moths, beetles, and wasps, and some species of cavity-nesting birds, such as starlings, use the plant as nesting material.

Whether you decide to grow yarrow in a flower bed or in your herb or pollinator garden, it makes a lovely addition to any environment. This plant is particularly low-maintenance, so it needs virtually no special care once fully established.

HOW TO GROW YARROW

Yarrow is most often propagated by division, so chances are you'll be buying your yarrow as a plant from a garden center or taking a cutting from a friend. Space your plants 12 to 24 inches (30–60 cm) apart if you're planting more than one plant at a time.

You can also start yarrow indoors from seed about six to eight weeks before the projected date of the last frost. Sow the seeds in moist, normal potting soil. Just barely cover the seeds with the soil, and then place the pot in a sunny and warm location. The seeds should germinate in 14 to 21 days, depending on the conditions. You can speed up the germination by covering the top of the pot with plastic wrap to keep in moisture and heat. Remove the plastic wrap once the seeds have sprouted.

Whether your yarrow plants are grown from seed or bought as full plants, it's important to plant them in full sun. They thrive in a wide variety of soils (although they do best in well-drained soil) but do not tolerate shade well. Yarrow will even grow in very poor, dry soils with low nutrient levels. Some caution should be taken when growing yarrow, as in the right conditions, it can become invasive and difficult to control.

At a Glance

SCIENTIFIC NAME: *Achillea millefolium*

FAMILY: Asteraceae

HEIGHT: 2 to 3 feet (60 cm–1 m)

WIDTH: 2 to 3 feet (60 cm–1 m)

BLOOMS: Summer, autumn

SOIL pH: Neutral

LIGHT: Full sun

CARING FOR THE PLANTS

Once you have planted your yarrow, it shouldn't need much additional care. It doesn't need to be fertilized and only needs to be watered during times of severe drought. Although it needs little maintenance, it is susceptible to a few diseases and pests. The most common diseases are botrytis mold and powdery mildew, both of which will appear as a white powdery covering on the leaves and can be treated with a fungicidal soap or spray. Yarrow plants are also occasionally affected by spittlebugs, which can be deterred with an organic insecticide.

Note: Yarrow plants can be toxic to dogs, cats, and horses.

Editor's Picks

Yarrow's tiny disk blossoms look like clusters of miniature daisies. In the wild the flowers are white, but there are many cultivars of this plant that bloom in various shades of pink, white, red, and yellow.

- **'Apple Blossom' in purplish pink**
- **'Cerise Queen' in deep pink**
- **'Gold' in bright yellow**
- **'King Edward' in pale yellow**
- **'Moonshine' in bright yellow**
- **'New Vintage Rose' in vibrant, deep pink to red**
- **'Paprika' in brick red**
- **'Strawberry Seduction,' in magenta**
- **'Summer Pastels' in mauve, orange-red, pink, purple, rose, and salmon**

FLOWERING BULBS, TUBERS, AND RHIZOMES

Spring-blooming bulbs go into the ground in autumn before the first hard frost; they require a dormant period in cold weather before they come to life. These include tulip (above), daffodil, crocus, and hyacinth.

Summer-blooming bulbs can't withstand cold winter temperatures, so plant them in late spring. In autumn, you can dig them up and store them in a cool place. Summer bloomers include gladiolus, canna, and iris.

Autumn-blooming bulbs are planted in late summer to early autumn. They usually bloom that first autumn—instant gratification!—and happily overwinter in the ground. They include autumn crocus (above), snowdrop, and sternbergia.

These perennial garden favorites contain their own source of nourishment, which helps them leaf out and flower during the growing season and survive during dormant periods. True bulbs (daffodils, tulips, hyacinths) are complete plants within a tiny package. They produce stems from the base of the bulb and survive from year to year. Corms (crocus, gladiolus) are usually short, squat stems filled with food storage tissue. Tubers (dahlias) are underground roots with fleshy, food-storing parts that resemble tubers. Rhizomes (iris, bamboo) are bulb-like power packs that grow along the soil surface.

BULB LAYERING IDEAS

If you desire those enviable masses of spring flowers often seen in magazines, choose large, medium, and small bulbs, then layer them according to planting depth. By selecting species with different bloom times, you can have diverse flower displays from spring through winter. For spring specimens, try the classic combos of grape hyacinth, daffodils, and tulips. For summer color, plant lilies and gladioli. The autumn garden can offer begonias and calla lilies. Don't forget about winter; in temperate zones, crocus can even peek through snow.

Keep an eye toward heights and colors. Plan out your layering in advance—don't just pop in bulbs willy-nilly and expect a polished garden to result. Calculate the effect you desire so your bulb garden will offer a continuous swath of color and a variety of silhouettes.

READ MORE AT GARDENING KNOW HOW

Scan the QR code above to learn the differences between these types of plants. To get tips on how to incorporate bulb flowers into your garden, just follow the links below.

- **"Types of Flower Bulbs — Learn About Different Bulb Types"** (URL = gkh.us/51354)
- **"Summer Garden Bulbs — When to Plant Bulbs for Summer Flowers"** (URL = gkh.us/144838)
- **"Year-Round Bulbs — Planning a Bulb Garden for All Seasons"** (URL = gkh.us/143863)

Amaryllis

SCIENTIFIC NAME: *Amaryllis* spp.

FAMILY: Amaryllidaceae

HEIGHT: 1 to 2 feet (30–60 cm)

WIDTH: 6 to 12 inches (15–30 cm)

BLOOMS: Spring

SOIL pH: Slightly acidic -

LIGHT: Full sun to partial shade

Amaryllis, with its festive red and white varieties, has become increasingly popular as a winter holiday gift plant, undoubtedly because its bulbs bloom very freely indoors.

Amaryllis, in the tribe Amaryllideae, is a small genus of flowering bulbs containing only two species: *A. paradisicola* and the better known *A. belladonna,* a native of the Western Cape region of South Africa. The amaryllis flower is also known as belladonna lily, Jersey lily, naked lady, amarillo, Easter lily, and March lily. Despite the "lily" in many of the common names, it is only a distant relative—the name comes from its similar flower shape and growth habit.

Amaryllis is a popular holiday gift plant, because it can be grown as an indoor potted plant that blooms in winter if kept inside and maintained properly. It can also be grown outside, as it thrives in warmer climates.

HOW TO GROW AMARYLLIS

Amaryllis bulbs are easy to grow outside, provided you live in a suitable region, and they are resistant to pests, such as deer and many rodents. Whether you plant the bulbs themselves or transplant already-grown plants, timing is important. New bulbs are typically planted in autumn, alongside many other spring bloomers. Amaryllis starters that you purchase or receive as a gift can be planted outside in spring after the threat of frost has passed. You can also move currently blooming plants outside, although you'll want to gradually acclimate them to their new environment before doing so.

When moving plants outdoors, consider sun exposure; indoor plants being moved outside will need a slow introduction to increased light levels. Amaryllis can tolerate both sun and shade fairly well, but it typically fares better somewhere in between. Too much sunlight can lead to leaf burn, but flowering may be limited in too much shade.

Amaryllis bulbs prefer well-draining soil. You can improve drainage by creating raised beds or mixing in some organic matter, like peat or compost. Amended soil will also provide amaryllis with nutrients for healthy growth. Planting outdoors is much the same as in containers: the bulb should be planted neck-deep, keeping the top third sticking up above soil level. Space plants 12 to 18 inches (30–45 cm) apart, and water well following planting until they are fully established.

Amaryllis are perfect for out-of-season forcing, or tricking a bulb into flowering indoors. You can try to stimulate the bulb by placing it on a warming mat. Next, fertilize with a diluted (by half) water soluble food every two to three weeks. Rotate the pot every few days as growth continues to keep the stalk straight.

To learn how to care for the plant after it flowers, follow the link to "Amaryllis Care After Flowering: Learn About Post Bloom Care of Amaryllis" (URL = gkh.us/86149), or scan the QR code.

CARING FOR THE PLANTS

Amaryllis usually appreciates at least one feeding upon emergence in early spring. Although not strictly necessary, additional nutritionally balanced fertilizer can be applied a time or two throughout the growing season, as needed. Amaryllis also needs to be kept moist throughout the growing season, though established plants are fairly drought tolerant. Forced winter-blooming bulbs grown indoors and then transplanted outdoors will eventually revert back to their natural spring blooming cycle. Once flowers have faded, remove the stalks.

You can expect foliage to remain through much of the summer before succumbing to autumn frosts. Adding a 2-inch (5 cm) layer of mulch around the plants will not only help conserve moisture and reduce weed growth but will also offer them added protection when cooler temperatures arrive. Given adequate care, you can expect to see beautiful blooms each year. Should plants become overcrowded, divide the clumps and separate them as needed. This can also help with reduced blooming, as can a bloom-boosting fertilizer or bone meal.

Anemone

A range of brilliant colors and forms makes *Anemone coronaria,* known as the poppy anemone, Spanish marigold, or windflower, a favorite for early spring bloom. Anemones are excellent for vibrant edgings or cut-flower beds. Don't worry about snipping a few flowers while in bloom for bouquets or floral arrangements: it won't hurt your plants.

Anemone plants have low-clumping foliage and colorful blooms. Often referred to as windflowers, these carefree plants are commonly found dotting the landscapes of many home gardens. There are several types of anemones, including both spring-flowering and autumn-blooming varieties. An interesting difference between these varieties—which can be an important factor in caring for anemones as they grow—is how each of these types grow. For instance, spring-blooming anemone plants will generally grow from rhizomes or tubers; autumn-flowering types, however, usually have fibrous roots. Most anemones have delicate, single-blossom flowers, though some varieties feature larger double blooms.

HOW TO GROW ANEMONES

You can grow anemones just about anywhere. Caution should be taken with respect to their location, however, because their spreading growth habit can become rather invasive. Therefore, when growing anemones, consider placing them in bottomless containers (such as a large bucket with the base removed) when planting them in the garden. When these containers are buried with the plant inside, they effectively restrict the plant's roots from expanding too far horizontally, while allowing them freedom to expand vertically.

Anemones can be planted in spring or autumn, depending on the type you have. They can be very difficult to grow from seed, so it is generally advisable to purchase them from a garden center or propagate via division from an already-established plant. Anemone roots can be safely dug up, divided, and replanted, or the roots can be stored inside to wait out the winter, and then replanted in the spring. If you have stored your anemone roots over the winter, be sure to soak the roots overnight before planting, and then place them in well-draining, fertile soil, preferably in a slightly shaded area. Plant anemones about 3 to 4 inches (7.5–10 cm) deep, and space them about 4 to 6 inches (7.5–15 cm) apart. The seedlings that sprout when growing anemones from seed should be left outside throughout the winter under a good layer of mulch.

CARING FOR THE PLANTS

Once established, little maintenance is necessary—simply water as needed and remove old foliage regularly by cutting it back to the ground prior to periods of new growth. Rhizomatous clumps can be divided every two to three years during spring. Tuberous types are best separated during their dormant period, usually in summer.

Note: Anemones are toxic to humans and pets if consumed in large enough quantities, as they contain an oil called protoanemonin that can cause stomach and skin irritation. Be sure to plant them in areas where they will not be accessible to unattended children or animals.

SCIENTIFIC NAME: *Anemone* spp.

FAMILY: Ranunculaceae

HEIGHT: 6 inches to 4 feet (15 cm–1.2 m)

WIDTH: 2 to 3 feet (60 cm–1 m)

BLOOMS: Spring, summer, autumn

SOIL pH: Acidic to neutral

LIGHT: Full to partial shade

Anemone Species

Here are just a few of the many *Anemone* species.

- ***A. caroliniana,*** or Carolina anemone, in white, soft rose, or purple
- ***A. coronaria,*** or poppy anemone, in white, pink, blue, purple, and red
- ***A. drummondii,*** or Drummond's anemone, in white to violet
- ***A. hortensis,*** or broad-leaved anemone, in bluish white to mauve to red-purple
- ***A. virginiana,*** or thimbleweed, in white

Bearded Iris

SCIENTIFIC NAME: *Iris* spp.

FAMILY: Iridaceae

HEIGHT: 1 to 3 feet (30 cm–1 m)

WIDTH: 1 to 2 feet (30–60 cm)

BLOOMS: Spring

SOIL pH: Neutral

LIGHT: Full sun

Striking amethyst-purple bearded irises stand against a fence in the back of a flower bed. These regally beautiful flowers are one of the world's favorite perennial bulbs.

Iris is a diverse genus, with groups within it labeled as "bearded," "beardless," and "crested." All irises share sword-like leaves and flowers with three petals that grow upright, known as standards, and three downward-growing petals known as falls. In bearded irises, the falls have a hairy texture, giving the flower the "bearded" part of its name.

Bearded iris is popular for its stunning flowers that bloom in a variety of colors. It grows from a rhizome, which is a modified underground stem that grows and spreads horizontally in the soil. The name iris comes from the Greek name for the goddess of the rainbow, which indicates how much color variety there is to be found in this perennial plant. There are hundreds of bearded iris varieties from which to choose, giving you a wide range of options for size, shape, and color. Different varieties of bearded iris can grow between under 1 foot (30 cm) tall for the miniature cultivars and up to over 3 feet (1 m) for the tallest.

HOW TO GROW IRISES

The best time to plant bearded iris rhizomes for bountiful spring blooms is in late summer or early autumn. Plant the rhizomes horizontally, with the top of each one just at the surface of the soil. It is important not to plant them too deeply; they need sunlight to grow properly. Plant your irises in areas with soil that drains well and that gets at least six hours of sunlight per day. You can add organic material, such as compost or a balanced fertilizer, when planting—be sure to avoid adding too much nitrogen, however, as this can limit flower growth.

CARING FOR THE PLANTS

Once your irises are established, you likely won't need to water them unless you have an extended drought. These self-sufficient flowers are hardy and quite drought tolerant, and they only need to be divided every few years. Regular division not only keeps the plants flowering profusely, it also helps stave off problems with iris borer and soft rot.

Bearded irises can be divided any time after flowering, but late summer is a good time to replant your divisions. Divide the plants by pulling the rhizomes up from the soil and removing newer rhizomes attached to at least a few leaves to replant elsewhere. Cut back the leaves by about two-thirds before you replant them or share them with other gardeners.

To encourage consistent, healthy blooms, simply cut off the stalks after flowers have bloomed, remove any dead leaves, and cut leaves back in the autumn.

Note: Iris plants are toxic to dogs and cats.

Editor's Picks

Here is just a tiny sampling of stunning bearded iris cultivars.

- 'Aachen Prince' in dark blue
- 'Best Bet' with pale violet-blue standards and deep violet-blue falls
- 'Champagne Elegance' with pale pink standards and apricot falls
- 'Dame de Coeur' with raspberry pink standards and tangerine falls
- 'Forever Blue' in lavender-blue
- 'Gala Madrid' with deep yellow standards and reddish purple falls
- 'Glamazon' with butterscotch standards and bold rose falls with a soft butterscotch undertone
- 'Obsidian' in all black
- 'Ocelot' with pale peach standards and deep, dark maroon falls
- 'Pink Attraction' in pale pink

Canna Lily

A stand of red-and-yellow cannas makes a stylish statement. Tall and erect, with showy, paddle-shaped leaves, these flowers are great for areas with hot summers.

Canna, the only genus of flowering plants in the family Cannaceae, consists of 10 species. Most of the canna we see in gardens today are cultivars of those species, which are native to much of South America, Central America, the West Indies, and Mexico. The canna plant is a rhizomatous perennial with tropical-like foliage and large flowers that resemble that of an iris, and although it is often called "canna lily," it is not a lily at all. Cannas are low maintenance and easy to grow, and both their flowers and foliage offer long-lasting color that attracts the eye in any garden. The flowers can be found in red, orange, pink, or yellow. Depending on the variety, foliage color varies from green to maroon, bronze, and variegated types.

HOW TO GROW CANNA

Cannas can be planted outdoors in warm climates, or they make great indoor container plants in colder areas. Plant cannas in spring after the threat of frost has passed. Groups of cannas should be planted about a foot or two (30–60 cm) apart to give the plants room to expand as they mature. Technically they don't have a top or bottom, but most canna rhizomes can be planted horizontally with the eyes facing up. Cover the rhizomes with 3 to 6 inches (7.5–15 cm) of soil, water well, and then apply a layer of mulch to retain moisture.

Typically grown as annuals in cooler regions, given the proper conditions, cannas can fill your garden with vibrant color year after year. They like plenty of sunlight, so they will thrive best if placed in full sun. They can also tolerate partial shade, though they may not produce as many flowers. Cannas like moist conditions, but they will tolerate nearly any well-draining soil that is either neutral or slightly acidic. They appreciate bog-like conditions as well: for best results, their soil should be rich in organic matter.

CARING FOR THE PLANTS

Once established, cannas need to be kept moist. They also require a monthly fertilizer that is relatively high in phosphate for continual blooming. In warm areas, cannas can usually be left planted outside through winter. In colder regions, it's usually necessary to dig up and store the rhizomes in the autumn, at which point they can also be overwintered in pots. They should be kept in a cool, dry location in the house. In spring, overwintered cannas can be replanted or simply moved back outdoors in their pots. You can also divide the plant during this time if necessary.

The waxy, water-repellent leaves of cannas are generally resistant to fungal infection and rot, though they can be susceptible to pets such as slugs and snails.

SCIENTIFIC NAME: *Canna* spp.

FAMILY: Cannaceae

HEIGHT: 1 to 10 feet (30 cm–3 m)

WIDTH: 1 to 6 feet (30 cm–1.8 m)

BLOOMS: Summer

SOIL pH: Acidic to neutral

LIGHT: Full sun

Editor's Picks

Canna cultivars include several groupings, including ones based on the spectacular foliage.

- 'Antonin Crozy' in carmine
- 'Auguste Ferrier' with green and purple variegated foliage
- 'Constitution' in pale powder pink
- 'Eureka' in pale primrose yellow
- 'Madame Butterfly' in ivory overlaid with shell pink
- 'Toucan Rose" in rosy pink
- 'Ra' in buttercup yellow
- 'Valentine' in blood red
- 'Wyoming' in brilliant orange

Calla Lily

Elegant white calla lily blooms rise above deep green foliage. Along with the classic white, these flowers come in yellow, orange, pink, rose, lavender, and dark maroon.

Although they are not technically true lilies, calla lilies (*Zantedeschia* spp.) are extraordinary flowers. Native to southern Africa north to Malawi, the genus has been introduced on all continents except Antarctica. The elegant *Zantedeschias* go by the names "calla" and "calla lily" for *Z. elliottiana* and *Z. rehmannii* and "arum lily" for *Z. aethiopica*. These beautiful plants are available in a multitude of bloom colors, including pink, white, orange, black, and red. They make an ideal addition to any flowerbed, but they also grow easily in containers indoors.

HOW TO GROW CALLA LILIES

Calla lilies are easy to grow; in fact, in some regions, they are considered an invasive species due to their hardy and fast-spreading nature. These plants do not generally require too much attention to keep them healthy, and proper soil quality and location are about the only important things to consider. Ideally, calla lilies should be planted in loose, well-drained soil. They prefer to be located in full sun or partial shade in warmer climates. They can tolerate high heat and humidity, so tropical environments will suit them well.

Calla lilies are typically planted in the spring. Wait until the threat of frost has passed, and the soil has warmed sufficiently before planting. Plant the rhizomes quite deep, about 4 inches (10 cm) for best results, and space them approximately a foot (30 cm) apart. Once planted, the area should be watered well and often. The plants should be kept moist, and they will also benefit from a monthly dose of fertilizer throughout the growing season.

CARING FOR THE PLANTS

Once established, calla lilies don't require much care beyond keeping them watered and fertilized. An adequate layer of mulch around the plants will help keep the soil moist and free of weeds.

Calla lilies require a dormant period once flowering has ceased. During this time, you should water them less frequently to allow the plant to die back. If you grow calla lilies in containers, cease watering, and move the plant to a dark area once the foliage has faded. Regular watering can resume within two to three months. Although calla lilies can remain in the ground year-round in warmer climates, they should be overwintered inside in cooler areas.

To overwinter your plants, dig up the rhizomes in autumn, usually after the first frost, and shake off any soil. Allow them to dry out for a few days before storing the rhizomes for winter. Calla lilies should be stored in peat moss and kept in a cool, dry area, preferably in the dark, until warmer temperatures return in spring.

SCIENTIFIC NAME: *Zantedeschia* spp.

FAMILY: Araceae

HEIGHT: 2 to 3 feet (60 cm–1 m)

WIDTH: 1 to 2 feet (30–60 cm)

BLOOMS: Summer

SOIL pH: Acidic

LIGHT: Full to partial sun

Note: All parts of calla lilies are toxic, so they should be planted where they will not be accessible to unsupervised children or pets.

READ MORE AT GARDENING KNOW HOW

To learn more about caring for calla lilies, as well as how you can plant them in containers, follow these links.

- **"Calla Lily Watering: How Much Water Do Calla Lilies Need** (URL = gkh.us/107325)
- **"Planting a Calla Lily in a Pot: Care of Container Grown Calla Lilies** (URL = gkh.us/110511)

Crocus

One of the first signs of spring, glossy purple crocuses break through the soil to add lively color to the bare ground, serving as heralds of the coming warmer season.

Crocuses are one of the most popular varieties of the early-spring bloomers. These white, purple, and pink flowers are native to central and eastern Europe, North Africa, the Middle East, and parts of Asia and China. They are highly adaptable flowers that have become part of the North American landscape, providing much-needed late-winter cheer and marking the beginning of spring. The bulbs of the crocus flower are technically vertically oriented "corms," though they function essentially the same as true bulbs during planting.

HOW TO GROW CROCUS

Crocuses thrive in cold to moderate winter conditions, but they will likely fail to grow in hot climates. The corms are smaller than the bulbs of other plants, so they dry out faster than large bulbs. Therefore, the best time to plant crocus is early in autumn, right after you buy them. Plant them in the open rather than the shade (unless you live in a particularly warm climate). because crocuses like plenty of sunshine.

You can plant them in flower beds or in the lawn, but make sure you don't cut or mow the grass until their leaves turn yellow and disappear. Applying weed killer to the grass where crocuses are planted will also harm them, especially if you apply them while the crocus plant leaves are still green and actively growing.

Crocuses prefer a gritty or sandy, well-drained soil. A rock garden or herb garden is a great site to plant them, and small perennial herbs that thrive in such places make good plant companions. Adding 5-10-5 fertilizer when planting crocuses will help them develop.

In a rock garden or herb garden, it is a good idea to plant crocuses under creeping phlox or mat-forming thymes. Your crocuses will grow right through these ground-hugging plants, and the ground cover plants will protect the small, delicate crocus flowers from the elements.

CARING FOR THE PLANTS

Animal pests like deer, rabbits, and squirrels can be a big problem for crocus bulbs. Squirrels and other rodents will dig up the bulbs and eat them, and deer will graze on the early foliage. You can cover the spring bulb bed with wire mesh to prevent squirrel damage, and there are a number of commercial deer repellents you can employ to prevent them from feeding on your flowers. Deer-repellent plants planted nearby might also help protect your crocuses.

SCIENTIFIC NAME: *Crocus* spp.

FAMILY: Iridaceae

HEIGHT: 2 to 6 inches (5–15 cm)

WIDTH: 1 to 3 inches (2.5–7.5 cm)

BLOOMS: Spring

SOIL pH: Neutral

LIGHT: Full to partial sun

When the flowers are spent, leave the foliage until it dies back. Every two to three years, crocus clumps should be divided in autumn when they are dormant. To divide a crocus clump, dig up the clump, and cut it into pieces with several bulbs attached and at least four healthy stems. Fertilize crocus beds with a slow-release fertilizer in autumn, according to the manufacturer's instructions.

Editor's Tips

When purchasing crocus bulbs, be sure to check when they will bloom. The spring-flowering varieties get most of the attention, but autumn crocuses are worth a look. These have bigger and bolder flowers than their cousin and flower in late summer and autumn, often during autumnal rains after the heat of summer. Autumn-blooming *Crocus sativus* is the saffron crocus, which produces the vivid red stamens used as a spice in cooking. Because they appear so similar to the poisonous *Colchicum autumnale,* which is also called autumn crocus, to be safe, only harvest the stamens from flowers you have planted yourself.

Daffodil

***Narcissus poeticus*, or the poet's daffodil, makes a happy display. One of the first spring bloomers, cheerful daffodils have long been associated with rebirth and new beginnings.**

SCIENTIFIC NAME: *Narcissus* spp.

FAMILY: Amaryllidaceae

HEIGHT: 6 to 30 inches (15–75 cm)

WIDTH: 6 to 12 inches (15–30 cm)

BLOOMS: Spring

SOIL pH: Neutral to acidic

LIGHT: Full to partial sun

Daffodils (*Narcissus* spp.) are a lovely addition to any spring garden. These ubiquitous and easy-to-care-for flowers add bright spots of sunshine that will return year after year. There are several thousand cultivars of daffodils available, with shapes, sizes, and colors of all kinds; most varieties range from classic bright yellow to white, orange, and pink.

Daffodils do more than just provide cheerful color after the winter months. They can enrich your garden and even improve the pollination of other plants. They come out of dormancy before many other plants, which means they are active and prepared to catch the water and nutrients that come with spring rains, which would otherwise be wasted. When daffodils die back in spring, they add those nutrients back to the soil where other plants can use them.

Early daffodil blooms attract early pollinators too, helping other plants, such as fruit trees, thrive. Their far-reaching roots can also prevent or minimize erosion, as well as keep unwanted grasses from competing with other plants for nutrients.

HOW TO GROW DAFFODILS

The best time to plant daffodils is as soon as they are available in early autumn. Many people choose to grow daffodils in shaped formations; for instance, planting a loose circle of about seven bulbs with three in the center, or in rows to create a square. For aesthetic reasons, you might choose to mix different cultivars within each planting group, or alternatively plant groupings of individual varieties.

Plant the daffodil bulbs with the pointy end up and the fatter, somewhat flattened end pointing down. Plant twice as deep as the bulb is tall; for example, for a 2-inch (5 cm) bulb base to tip, dig a 6-inch (15 cm)deep hole so that the bulb sits 4 inches (10 cm) below the soil level. Deep planting helps prevent frost heave and protects the bulbs from accidental damage from spades and rakes. Plant the bulbs more deeply in sandy soil and more shallowly in heavier, clay soils.

Cover the bulbs with soil, and water well. Mulch the area with pine bark, chopped leaves, or whatever you usually use to help retain moisture and protect them from pests.

In temperate climates, daffodils will bloom in mid-spring, but they will flower sooner in a region with warmer winters and later in colder regions.

Types of Daffodils

These carefree flowers come in several forms.

- **Trumpet, or long cup.** Large cups as long or longer than the petals.
- **Large cup.** Big flowers with prominent cups; can be trumpet-like, bowl-shaped, or flat with smooth or heavily ruffled edges.
- **Small cup.** Short cups less than a third of the length of the petals.
- **Double.** Multiple layers of outer petals; at center is a bouquet of petals, rather than a cup.
- **Jonquilla.** Petite flowers, with small open cups.
- **Cyclamineus.** Small, narrow cups surrounded by reflexed petals.
- **Poeticus.** Small flat cup, typically a green-ringed yellow, surrounded by large white petals; very fragrant.
- **Split corona.** Cups split into segments and are pressed back against the petals.
- **Tazetta.** Clusters of small, intensely fragrant flowers with short cups.
- **Triandrus.** Two or more downward-facing flowers per stem; often very fragrant.

Dahlia

SCIENTIFIC NAME: *Dahlia* spp.

FAMILY: Asteraceae

HEIGHT: 1 to 6 feet (30 cm–1.8 m)

WIDTH: 1 to 3 feet (30 cm–1 m)

BLOOMS: Summer, autumn

SOIL pH: Neutral to acidic

LIGHT: Full sun

Dahlias in full bloom are simply stunning. With a seemingly endless variety of shapes, sizes, and colors, these long-lasting bloomers are a worthy ornamental selection, lending vibrancy to a garden from midsummer into autumn.

Dahlias are late-blooming, widely popular plants that grow from tubers. These vividly colored and distinctive flowers are native to Mexico and Central America, though their many varieties can now be found in gardens all over the world. With thousands of named cultivars available, ornamental dahlias offer a vibrant palette of colors that is simply unmatched. Larger blooms, which have a long vase life, are also ideal for bouquets and cut flower arrangements. Growing these beautiful plants is relatively simple, but they will require some special care.

HOW TO GROW DAHLIAS

Once the last frost of spring has passed, it's safe to begin planting dahlia tubers. Find a spot where they'll receive full sun, and be sure the soil is very well draining. Tubers that sit in wet soil tend to become mushy and rot. Each healthy tuber should have at least one eye.

Before planting the tubers, set up sturdy support stakes. These will keep you from accidentally damaging the tubers later, when your growing plants will definitely need support. It is generally recommended to sink 6-foot (1.8 m) stakes to a depth of 1 foot (30 cm).

Next to the stakes, dig your planting holes 6 to 8 inches (15–20 cm) deep for tall varieties and 2 to 3 inches (5–7.5 cm) deep for shorter varieties. Make sure the tubers are spaced 18 to 24 inches (45–60 cm) apart. Place the tubers in the holes flat on their sides, and cover with soil. Mulching over the top helps keep the weeds down, which your dahlias will appreciate.

CARING FOR THE PLANTS

Dahlia experts advise that you allow only the one strongest shoot to develop from each tuber, so that your plants bloom prolifically with large flowers. When the plant is 10 to 12 inches (25–30 cm) high, gently pull the soil away from the tuber to remove the extra shoots, snipping them off right at the edge. Again cover the tuber with soil. These extra shoots can be easily rooted for new plants.

When your plants are at this height, carefully tie them loosely to the support stakes with soft yarn, nylon stockings, or soft twine. Your plants will need an inch of water every week throughout the growing season and double that if the weather is dry. It is also important to keep your dahlia bed free of weeds and prune away broken stems. By the time they get to be around 15 inches (39 cm) tall, pinch off their suckers to strengthen the plant.

Healthy dahlias usually aren't plagued by pests, but a few can pose threats. Thrips, snails, spider mites, earwigs, and grasshoppers can be treated with insecticidal soap, neem oil, or a chemical-free slug repellent. Natural predators like birds, frogs, and toads will also help control pests.

Note: Dahlias are toxic to dogs and cats.

Staff Hacks

Tonya Barnett, GKH Writer, offers advice on working with horizontal trellis netting for large dahlia beds: "Without a doubt, dahlias are gorgeous additions to landscapes and cut-flower gardens. While dwarf cultivars are available, many growers prefer taller types. Large cultivars benefit greatly from staking, as it is often required for them to remain upright. Strong stakes and/or tomato cages are most popular, but these structures may be difficult to use in larger plantings. Instead, use trellis netting to stake large, wide dahlia beds. Rather than affixing netting vertically to supports, secure netting across plants in a horizontal position. The plants grow steadily through each hole in the netting. Depending on the plants' mature height, several layers of netting may be needed in order to achieve the best results."

Daylily

SCIENTIFIC NAME: *Hemerocallis* spp.

FAMILY: Asphodelaceae

HEIGHT: 1 to 5 feet (30 cm–1.5 m)

WIDTH: 2 to 4 feet (60 cm–1.2 m)

BLOOMS: Spring, summer

SOIL pH: Acidic

LIGHT: Full sun

A bed of late-summer-flowering daylilies. Low-maintenance daylilies produce abundant flowers in striking colors. You can look for blooms to burst forth beginning in midsummer and continuing into early autumn, with new blossoms opening each day.

Gardeners have been growing daylilies (*Hemerocallis*) for centuries. From the 15 or so original species found in Asia and Central Europe, we now have approximately 35,000 hybrids from which to choose, and more are developed every year. Their beautiful flowers last only one day, yet a mature clump can produce 200 to 400 blooms over the course of a month or more. These unique flowers will be of particular joy to any gardener who simply doesn't have time for fussier plants: daylilies are so hardy and easy to care for that they have often been said to thrive on neglect!

HOW TO GROW DAYLILIES

Early spring or early autumn are the best times for planting daylilies, but you can plant them whenever the ground isn't too frozen to dig a hole. If your soil is sandy or heavy clay, amend it with plenty of organic matter. They prefer slightly acid soil, but they are adaptable enough that this shouldn't be much of a concern.

Choose a site where your growing daylilies will receive at least six hours of sun. Morning sun is best, particularly in warmer areas where the blazing afternoon sun can scorch the leaves. These hardy plants will tolerate shade, although their blooms won't be as prolific. Cut excess foliage back to 6 inches (15 cm) if foliage is overproduced in the shade.

Dig your hole twice as wide and deep as the root spread. Place the plant so the crown (the part where the roots meet the stem) is about 1 inch (2.5 cm) below ground level. Fill in the hole with your amended soil, and water well. Keep the new plants well watered for a few weeks until the roots are established. Daylilies are vigorous growers and can be divided every three or four years. Because of the vast number of varieties available, they make great specimens to trade with neighbors and friends.

CARING FOR THE PLANTS

Daylilies can essentially be planted and then left to their own devices, but there are a few things you can do to provide the best environment for these otherwise self-sustaining plants. A basic 10-10-10 fertilizer in the spring and during bloom will encourage larger and healthier flowers. Daylilies are quite drought-tolerant once established, so they can simply be watered as needed during dry periods.

Daylilies will perform best if you remove their seed pods, as leaving them on the plant will diminish the following year's bloom. In early spring, you can remove the dead leaves and weeds from the surrounding ground. A cover of mulch will also keep the weeds down, though it isn't necessary for the plant itself. Once fully grown, a daylily's leaves are so thick that they tend to shade out surrounding weeds.

Disease is rare among most varieties of daylily, and most common insect pests can be deterred with an application of all-purpose insecticidal soap or spray.

READ MORE AT GARDENING KNOW HOW

Follow these links to learn more about caring for these prolific bloomers.

- **"Daylily Tuber Winter Care — Learn About Overwintering Daylily Plants** (URL = gkh.us/130337)
- **"Are Daylilies Edible — Can I Eat Daylilies** (URL =gkh.us/160672)
- **"When to Cut Back Daylilies: Tips for Daylily Trimming in Gardens** (URL = gkh.us/130351)

Fritillaria

Crown imperial *(Fritillaria imperialis)* makes a dramatic statement with a prominent whorl of downward-facing flowers at the top of the stem, topped by a "crown" of spiky leaves. Also known as Kaiser's crown, its wild form is a vibrant orange-red, but cultivated varieties extend the palette to include a true scarlet, as well as orange and yellow.

Fritillaria is certain to catch the eye of a gardener who is searching out some unusual specimens for an ornamental garden. From unassuming to bold varieties, there are about 170 species of these summer-dormant, bulbous plants. There are two, however, that work especially well for home planting.

Fritillarias are true lilies, growing from non-tunicate bulbs, meaning they do not have the papery outer coating found on many plant bulbs. Found growing in the wild across the Northern Hemisphere, they flourish best in areas with a dry summer climate. *Fritillaria imperialis,* or crown imperial, has the showiest flowers of the species, but some say it also has a malodorous fragrance reminiscent of a skunk's scent. These fritillaria bulbs—natives of the Anatolian plateau to the Himalayan foothills—have nodding flowers, topped with a tuft of "crowning" foliage. The snakeshead lily, *Fritillaria meleagris,* has a checkered or mottled pattern on its drooping blooms. Native to the flood river plains of Europe, this species goes by many other names, including chess flower, frog-cup, guinea-hen flower, leper lily (because its shape resembles the bell lepers once carried), Lazarus bell, chequered lily, chequered daffodil, and drooping tulip.

GROWING FRITILLARIA BULBS

Wildflower fritillaria lilies are an excellent choice for the gardener who wants an out-of-the-ordinary specimen among more common spring-blooming bulbs. Delicate and exotic, fritillaria flower varieties may appear difficult to grow, but most fritillaria care is simple after the large bulbs bloom. The hardy bulbs produce best when planted in moist soil in a sunny to part shade location in the flower bed, where the growing plant might reach 4 feet (1.2 m) or higher in spring.

Use wildflower fritillaria lilies as stand-alones, in groupings, or as an addition to a traditional bulb bed. *Imperialis* and *meleagris* types are available in some local nurseries and through mail order catalogs.

Be prepared to plant bulbs as soon as they arrive. Plant larger bulbs with the base about 5 inches (12.5 cm) below the soil surface; smaller Fritillaria bulbs should be planted about 3 inches (7.5 cm) down. Plant bulbs in well-drained soil and keep it moist until the root system is established.

SCIENTIFIC NAME: *Fritillaria* spp.

FAMILY: Liliaceae

HEIGHT: 8 inches to 5 feet (20 cm–1.5 m)

WIDTH: Up to 12 inches (15 cm)

BLOOMS: Spring

SOIL pH: Mildly alkaline

LIGHT: Full sun to partial shade

FRITILLARIA CARE

Fritillaria bulbs resist deer, squirrels, and bulb-digging rodents and may help protect other bulbs that are favorites of the critters.

Wildflower fritillaria lilies, as with other lily bulbs, like cool roots. If possible, plant a low-growing ground cover to shade the bulbs of the growing plant or mulch the plant to protect it from the summer sun. Separate the plants every two years. Remove young bulblets, and replant in moist, shady conditions for more of this unusual flower every year.

Fritillaria Varieties

There are 170 species of this highly variable bulb species. Here is a tiny sampling of other *Fritillaria* species.

- ***F. acmopetala.*** The pointed-petal fritillary has pale green, bulb-shaped blooms that appear in mid-spring.
- ***F. affinis.*** In yellowish or greenish brown with dense yellow mottling to purplish black with little mottling, this variable species is known as the chocolate lily.
- ***F. persica.*** Known as the Persian lily, this variety comes in shades of ivory to dark maroon-purple.
- ***F. pudica.*** Known as the yellow fritillary, it has small, bell-shaped flowers.
- ***F. thunbergii.*** The Thunberg fritillary is a green color, checkered in dark purple.

Gladiolus

The papery white petals of a gladiolus stands out against its vibrant-colored brethren. These old-fashioned flowers are popular as the back row of a gradated flower bed, and they make wonderful blooms for bouquets and other floral arrangements

Gladiolus plants, also known as flag flowers and sword lilies, are hot-weather-loving plants that are native to Asia, Mediterranean Europe, South Africa, and tropical Africa. The genus name comes from the Latin diminutive of *gladius*, meaning "a sword," after the distinctive shape of the plant's leaves. Gladioli grow from summer-blooming bulbs that produce tall spikes covered with elegant orchid-like blooms.

The flowers can bloom from June through to the first frost of autumn with proper care. Planting new corms every few weeks will help keep these tall, multicolored flowers blooming all summer long. Gladiolus flowers also attract useful pollinators, making them great additions to vegetable patches and herb gardens.

HOW TO GROW GLADIOLI

Start planting gladiolus corms in mid-spring, well after the last frost has passed. These summer flowers cannot tolerate cold soil, and the corms might rot if planted too early. They prefer well-drained and even sandy soil, and they prefer full-sun exposure. You will want to plant these tall flowers deeper than usual to provide adequate support against strong winds and their own weight; they should also be staked for extra support if they have no other wind protection.

Gladiolus corms look like oversized crocus corms: they have a brown fiber wrapper with a small flat bottom, and sometimes they already have pointy shoots showing at the top. To plant them, dig a trench about 8 inches (20 cm) deep and long enough that you can space your corms about half a foot (15 cm) apart. Planting 10 corms or so at a time will produce a nicely sized display once they are fully established.

Fertilize the base of the trench with 5-10-10 or 5-10-5 fertilizer, making sure to mix the soil and fertilizer well so you don't burn the corms. Add a layer of unfertilized soil before placing the corms into the trench, then cover them with soil, and water well. After planting the first set, you can continue to plant new corms every two weeks. They take 70 to 100 days to grow and flower, so this staggered planting will provide vibrant flowers right on through summer.

CARING FOR THE PLANTS

Gladioli are quite hardy in hot climates, but they don't handle cold weather well. It's a good idea to dig the corms up for storage four to six weeks after the last flowers have faded. Trim back the leaves to within an inch (2.5 cm) of each corm after digging them up and shaking off as much soil as you can, and then let them dry for a week or so. Once the corms have dried, brush off any remaining soil and store them in a cool, dry, dark place until spring.

At a Glance

SCIENTIFIC NAME: *Gladiolus* spp.

FAMILY: Iridaceae

HEIGHT: 2 to 5 feet (60 cm–1.5 m)

WIDTH: 1 to 3 feet (30–1 m)

BLOOMS: Summer

SOIL pH: Acidic

LIGHT: Full sun

Editor's Picks

Gladiolus is among the top 10 bestselling florist flowers worldwide. These tall show-stoppers come in a host of colors. Here are just a few.

- 'Black Beauty' in deep maroon
- 'Blue Bird' in lavender-blue
- 'Canary Bird' in bright yellow
- 'Charm' in soft pink
- 'Glorianda' in pink to salmon
- 'Green Star' in light green
- 'Jester' with yellow ruffled petals and a deep red center
- 'Nova Lux' in yellow to orange
- 'St. Georges' in vivid red
- 'White Prosperity' in snow white

Hyacinth

Intensely fragrant, hyacinths add life to a springtime flower bed. Their waxy, densely packed florets come in a rainbow of colors, from pale pastels to saturated jewel tones.

One of the earliest spring bulbs is the hyacinth. This native of the eastern Mediterranean usually appears after crocus (but before tulips) and has old-fashioned charm combined with a sweet, distinctive scent. Its signature fragrance has historically been used in French perfume, and its bright flowers are a traditional part of Persian New Year's celebrations. It gained particular fame in the 18th century, when more than 2,000 cultivars of *Hyacinthus orientalis* were grown in the Netherlands to sate the gardening public's fascination with this spring bloomer. Its dense clusters of tiny lily-like flowers are borne along a central stalk and come in a rainbow of colors, including shades of white, pink, red, orange, yellow, blue, and violet.

HOW TO GROW HYACINTHS

Hyacinth bulbs need to be planted in autumn so the bulb experiences winter temperatures and breaks dormancy. In warmer regions where the bulbs cannot be exposed to consistently cold temperatures (around 40 to 45° F, or 4 to 7° C) for at least 12 weeks, they can be chilled in the fridge instead.

Hyacinths need well-draining soil to thrive, and one of the most common problems they face is waterlogged soil. If soil doesn't drain well, the bulbs will just sit in water and are then prey to rot. Prior to planting the bulbs, perform a drainage test by digging a trench, filling it with water, and noting how long it takes to drain. If water is still sitting in the trench a half hour later, amend the soil by mixing in leaf litter or other organic amendments, compost, or even some sand or pebbles. In heavy clay soils, consider planting in a raised bed to encourage drainage.

Editor's Tip

Potted hyacinths are a popular springtime gift. If you've received one, don't think of throwing out these lovely scented flowers after they bloom. Just remove the hyacinth bulbs from the pot, separating multiple bulbs, if necessary. You can then follow the usual planting procedure.

At a Glance

SCIENTIFIC NAME: *Hyacinthus*

FAMILY: Asparagaceae

HEIGHT: 6 to 12 inches (15–30 cm)

WIDTH: 3 to 6 inches (7.5–30 cm)

BLOOMS: Spring

SOIL pH: Neutral to acidic

LIGHT: Full to partial sun

Plant in autumn, around September to October. Choose fat, large bulbs with no signs of disease and decay. Plant them at least three to four times as deep as they are tall, with the pointed side facing up.

The flowers perform best in full sun but will still produce blooms in partial shade. Ideally, they should experience at least six hours per day of sunlight. If your soil has low nutrient levels, you can mix in a 5-5-10 slow-release plant food. Hyacinths usually need no care between planting and blooming, as the soil will naturally cool to the low temperatures needed for the 12-week chilling period before they can bloom.

CARING FOR THE PLANTS

In good soil, these sweet flowers need little maintenance. Water after planting if no rainfall is expected, and feed bulbs every spring with bulb food. When adding bulb food, scratch the fertilizer into the soil around the bulbs, and water well. Once flowers are finished blooming, cut off the flower stalks but leave the foliage to produce and store energy for the following year's growth. Once leaves are yellow and limp, you can usually just easily pull them from the soil. Slugs are occasional pests, but deer and rabbits tend to avoid this plant due to its oxalic acid content.

Note: Hyacinth bulbs are toxic to humans and animals if ingested, and they can cause mild skin irritation.

Lily

Asiatic lilies in shades of pink, from pale rose to magenta, make a stunning spring display. This type of lily is just one of the many that are popular with gardeners everywhere.

Growing lilies from bulbs is a favorite pastime of many gardeners. The flower of the lily plant (*Lilium* spp.) is a trumpet shape and comes in many colors that include pink, orange, yellow, and white. The stems of the flower range from 2 to 6 feet (60 cm–2 m). There are many types of lilies, but the general care of the plants is basically the same.

Planting Asiatic lilies (*L. asiatica*) in the landscape provides the earliest lily bloom. The secret to beautiful, long-lasting flowers is learning the right way to plant them. You'll be rewarded with colorful and bountiful blooms on this prized perennial.

HOW TO GROW ASIATIC LILIES

Scout out a sunny to partly sunny location that will give the plant at least six hours of sunlight each day. Be sure this location is away from any browsing deer; Asiatic bulbs are edible, and deer will prove that fact true if given a chance to dine.

Prepare the soil ahead of time. It should be well-draining, which may require the addition of organic material worked in several inches (about 8 cm) deep. If you already have rich, organic soil in the planting area, make sure it is loose and well-draining 6 to 8 inches (15–20 cm) deep. Bulbs of this lily should never sit in soggy soil. Work up sandy or clay soil by adding organic, well-composted materials. Peat moss, sand, or straw mixed into the beds before planting will improve drainage. Soil should drain well but hold moisture to nourish the growing lilies.

Autumn is the season to plant the bulbs, a few weeks before the winter brings freezing temperatures. This allows a good root system to develop. The bulbs must have the winter chill to produce big blooms.

Plant the bulbs three times as deep as the height of the bulb, with the flat end down, then mulch lightly to retain moisture. In spring, plant short annuals around the bulbs to shade them.

ASIATIC LILY PLANT CARE

Fertilize your plantings for optimum bloom. If you have followed the steps above, the organic matter in the soil gives your plants a good start. You can top dress with slow-release fertilizer, as well, or feed in early spring with fish emulsion, worm castings, compost tea, or a nitrogen plant food.

When buds appear, feed with a high phosphorus food or bone meal to make blooms bigger and last longer. Fertilize in limited amounts: too much fertilizer, even the organic types, can create lush green foliage but limit blooms. Proper care of your Asiatic lily bulbs goes a long way in creating a beautiful display.

SCIENTIFIC NAME: *Lilium* spp.

FAMILY: Liliaceae

HEIGHT: 18 inches to 4 feet (45 cm–1.3 m)

WIDTH: 4 to 6 inches (10–15 cm)

BLOOMS: Late spring to early summer

SOIL pH: Slightly acidic

LIGHT: Full to partial sun

Types of Lilies

Lilies comes in many shapes and sizes, with a wide range of colors and scents. Some of the other most popular types of lilies include the following.

- **Trumpet lily.** Often called the Easter lily, its huge, waxy trumpet flowers exude a heavy, sweet fragrance.
- **Tiger lily.** This is a hardy lily, with recurved and freckled flowers. It will multiply in clumps and produce more than a dozen flowers on each stem. Colors range from a golden yellow to a deep red.
- **Rubrum lily.** The rubrum lily resembles the tiger lily, although the colors range from white to deep pink, and it has a sweet scent.
- **Oriental lily.** This group of hybrids blooms in mid- to late summer, the last lilies to bloom. They have a spicy fragrance and come in pink, white, red, and bicolor. The popular 'Stargazer' (shown at left) is part of this group.
- **Martagon lily.** Also called Turk's cap lily, the martagon lily has whorled leaves and downward-facing flowers, with as many as 20 blooms on one stem. It comes in many colors and is often freckled with flecks of color. Martagons do not grow well in hot climates.

Muscari

Muscari forms dense clusters of upside-down urn-shaped florets that look like tiny bunches of grapes and emit a lovely, sweet scent. This spring bulb is also known as grape hyacinth for its resemblance to the larger flower.

SCIENTIFIC NAME: *Muscari* spp.
FAMILY: Asparagaceae
HEIGHT: 6 to 8 inches (15–20 cm)
WIDTH: 3 to 6 inches (7.5–15 cm)
BLOOMS: Spring
SOIL pH: Neutral to acidic
LIGHT: Full sun to partial shade

Muscari, or grape hyacinths, look much like little miniature hyacinths. These plants are quite a bit smaller, reaching only 6 to 8 inches (15–20 cm) in height, and they easily spread in just about any environment. This plant's common name is in reference to the small, bell-shaped clusters of cobalt blue flowers that it sports, which often resemble bunches of grapes. The botanical name *Muscari* hails from the Greek word for "musk," an allusion to the sweet, aromatic scent emitted by the flowers. Most grape hyacinth varieties are frost-resistant and readily attract pollinators like bees and butterflies. Some consider these perennial bulbs to be invasive due to their fast-spreading nature, but they can be kept under control with careful maintenance. One bulb will usually produce one to three flower stalks with 20 to 40 flowers per stalk.

HOW TO GROW MUSCARI

Muscari plants start from small, fleshy little bulbs. Keep in mind that these small bulbs can dry out much more easily than the bigger ones, so plan on planting them early in the autumn so that they get enough moisture. They grow in sun or light shade, so they're not too picky about where in the garden you plant them. They don't like extremes, however, so don't plant them where it's too wet or too dry.

If your goal is a neat, orderly garden, be careful where you plant muscari bulbs, because they can spread very quickly. If you aren't looking forward to pulling up unwanted flowers from other parts of your garden, plant them where you won't mind them spreading freely.

Plant the bulbs in autumn, placing them 3 to 4 inches (7.5–10 cm) deep and 2 inches (5 cm) apart. Massing these small flowers in groups of 10 or more will ensure a full and lively showing when they bloom. An inclusion of bone meal at planting, and again post-bloom, will improve the overall health of the plants. Water well during active growth and flowering, and reduce once the foliage begins to die back.

The leaves will show up quickly after planting the bulbs. Muscari plants send their leaves up out of the ground in autumn, but the blue flower spikes likely won't appear until mid-spring. There might be some variation in bloom color, depending on which variety you plant, but smoky blue is by far the most common hue.

CARING FOR THE PLANTS

Muscari plants require very little care after they flower. They do just fine with natural rainfall in most climates, and they don't need fertilizer. Once their leaves die off, you can cut them back; in the autumn, new leaves will grow long before the return of the first flowers of spring.

READ MORE AT GARDENING KNOW HOW

When the muscari, or grape hyacinth, blooming season comes to an end, you need to care for the bulbs to protect and preserve them so that they can bloom again the following year. Scan the QR code or check this link to find out how.

- **"Grape Hyacinth After Flowering — Learn About Muscari Care After Blooming"** (URL = gkh.us/84280)

Scilla

The diminutive bell-shaped flowers of scilla nod over their arching maroon stalks. In spring, this flower carpets the ground in shades of blue, as well as white, pink, and purple.

Scilla *(Scilla siberica),* also known as Siberian squill, sapphire star, or wood squill, is a small but tough plant that thrives in cold climates. Scilla plants can be identified by the little tufts of grasslike foliage that emerge first, before being shortly followed by slender stems supporting up to three delicate, royal blue flowers. As the common name implies, scilla is native to Siberia, as well as other parts of Russia and Eurasia.

Extremely cold-hardy, scillas never require lifting for winter storage. They can also be chilled and then forced into bloom indoors any time of year. Their cold-weather preferences also make them particularly early bloomers, often blooming through the frost of early spring. These plants are also quite adaptable, and they spread easily once established. They are commonly used in rock gardens, naturalized areas, and as an edging for flower beds and walkways, and they look stunning in large drifts.

HOW TO GROW SCILLA

In the autumn, plant scilla bulbs 5 inches (12.5 cm) deep and 2 to 4 inches (5–10 cm) apart with the pointed end facing up. Once the first grasslike leaves emerge, you can expect blooms that last for two to three weeks in early spring. Scillas aren't picky about sunlight and can thrive in anything from full sun to partial shade. They need a well-drained patch of soil to prevent root and bulb rot. Soil that is rich in organic matter is best; if you have poor-quality soil, you can improve the organic content of the soil by working in a 2-inch (5 cm) layer of compost before planting.

Scilla plants grows well under deciduous trees, where they will complete their early bloom cycle before the tree leafs out and casts full shade. You can also try planting them in lawns where they will usually complete their bloom cycle before the grass needs mowing. Try to wait until the foliage begins to die back before mowing, and if you must use a weed killer, do so in autumn rather than spring. They combine well with other early spring-blooming bulbs, such as crocus and daffodil.

CARING FOR THE PLANTS

Scillas are essentially maintenance-free when planted in a suitable location. To promote their growth, fertilize the plants when the foliage emerges with a bulb fertilizer or a granular fertilizer that is low in nitrogen and high in phosphorus. Alternatively, you can deadhead the faded flowers to reduce self-seeding and prevent overcrowding and unwanted spreading. You can leave the foliage to die back naturally, because these plants are small enough that any dying foliage is easily hidden behind other plants as they emerge in spring.

At a Glance

SCIENTIFIC NAME: *Scilla siberica*

FAMILY: Asparagaceae

HEIGHT: 3 to 8 inches (7.5–20 cm)

WIDTH: 3 to 6 inches (7.5–15 cm)

BLOOMS: Spring

SOIL pH: Acidic

LIGHT: Full sun to partial shade

Wood Hyacinths

Another scilla that is available is *Scilla campanulata.* Like its close cousin, *S. siberica,* these are spring-blooming bulbs. Commonly known as wood hyacinths or Spanish bluebells, they are also classified under the name *Hyacinthoides hispanica.* The flowers resemble the fragrant wild bluebells that carpets woodlands of the British Isles and are quite a bit larger than those of *S. siberica.* The bell-shaped flowers come in violet, lavender, pink, and white.

Siberian Iris

A cluster of blue *Iris sibirica,* known as Siberian iris or Siberian flag, flourishes in a waterside meadow. Most garden varieties are hybrids of two species, *I. sibirica* and *I. sanguinia.* They are very adaptable and hardy plants, with graceful stems and a neat growth habit that make them suitable for perennial borders and for landscaping.

Smaller than its relative the bearded iris, Siberian iris *(Iris sibirica)* offers a reliable perennial bloom that will return for many years. The easily recognizable blooms of this flower follow the typical iris configuration, with three petals on top, known as standards, and three drooping petals below, known as falls. The flowers are usually deep purple with patches of yellow or white toward the center of the plant, but some varieties have yellow, red, pink, white, or blue flowers. They also vary in height, reaching anywhere from 1 to 4 feet (30 cm–1.2 m) tall. They attract bees and butterflies, yet animal pests like deer and rabbits tend to avoid them.

GROWING SIBERIAN IRISES

This plant is native across Europe and into Central Asia, and its widespread home area might account for its adaptability to a range of planting times. To enjoy new blooms in spring, plant the bulbs in late summer or in autumn. If autumn planting time has passed, or if you live in a particularly cold climate, planting Siberian iris in spring is perfectly fine; just don't expect blooms the same year. They grow easily in containers as well, so you can plant them indoors at any time.

Siberian irises thrive best when planted in rich, fertile soil with good drainage, although they are adaptable enough to perform well in lean or poor soil. Similarly, they prefer full sun, but will comfortably tolerate up to partial shade. They can be propagated from root divisions, although their dense, fibrous roots can make this a rather difficult process.

Like many other early bloomers, Siberian irises need to undergo a chilling period during winter in order to bloom again the following spring. They may fail to produce flowers in areas with warm winters. Do not bring them inside to overwinter

CARING FOR THE PLANTS

Keep the soil consistently moist until the plants are established, about a year. Water the established plants regularly and lightly, but avoid overwatering, as Siberian irises can be vulnerable to crown rot. They should be divided every three to four years, or the rhizomatous roots can become overgrown and limit flower production. Feed them in spring with a nitrogen-rich fertilizer, and fertilize again when blooms are spent. They are generally hardier than larger irises, such as the bearded iris, and insect pests are unlikely to pose any substantial threat.

SCIENTIFIC NAME: *Iris sibirica*

FAMILY: Iridaceae

HEIGHT: 1 to 4 feet (30 cm–1.2 m)

WIDTH: 2 to 3 feet (60 cm–1 m)

BLOOMS: Spring, summer

SOIL pH: Acidic to neutral

LIGHT: Full to partial sun

Note: Like most irises, these flowers can be toxic to humans and pets.

Editor's Picks

Purple is the most well-known Siberian iris color, but there are quite a few others to choose from. This is a small sampling of cultivars.

- 'Blueberry Fair' in ruffled blue
- 'Butter and Sugar' in white and buttery yellow
- 'Caesar's Brother' in deep purple
- 'Fond Kiss' in white with a delicate pink flush
- 'Granny Jean' in mauve-pink
- 'Lavender Bounty' in lavender-pink
- 'Silver Edge' in pale blue and silver
- 'Sultan's Ruby' in deep magenta
- 'White Swirl' in ivory-white

Tulip

Tulips in a vast array of colors line the walkway of a formal garden. This flower has endured as a garden favorite for centuries, making it one of the world's best-loved blooms.

SCIENTIFIC NAME: *Tulipa* spp.

FAMILY: Liliaceae

HEIGHT: 9 to 24 inches (23–60 cm)

WIDTH: 6 to 9 inches (15–23 cm)

BLOOMS: Spring

SOIL pH: Acidic to neutral

LIGHT: Full sun

The tulip (*Tulipa* spp.) is one of the most recognizable and widespread flowers of all. Native to the arid regions of Central Asia, it can now be found all over the world, but it is often associated with the Netherlands. There, in spring, fields of this flower color the landscape, and the cultivated forms of the tulip are often called "Dutch tulips." Lovely Dutch tulips were once so popular that they sparked "tulip mania," the first recorded speculative economic bubble in history, when the prices of the bulbs soared to extraordinarily high levels in 1634 before collapsing the market in 1637.

Today, there are thousands of varieties available in just about every color. The original species have a limited color range of mostly reds and yellows, and they tend to have smaller flowers than modern cultivars and hybrids. They usually have cup-like flowers with rounded petals, with one flower and three petals per stem.

HOW TO GROW TULIPS

Tulips are quite easy to plant, and they grow very quickly. Pick a sunny spot in your garden that has good drainage, as tulips won't grow well in shade and will rot in wet soil.

Preparing the soil before planting will give your tulips a better chance of thriving. First, loosen the soil about a foot (30 cm) deep and add some compost or dried manure to the soil. You can also add some 5-10-5 or 5-10-10 granular fertilizer to help the bulbs grow. Mix the existing soil, amendments, and fertilizer together until well blended.

After you have properly prepared the site for the tulip bulbs, you can dig the individual planting holes. Be sure to dig each hole three times as deep as the tulip bulb is tall. There should be twice as much soil over the tip of the bulb as the height of the bulb, so if your tulip bulb measures 2 (5 cm) inches tall, dig your hole 6 inches (15 cm) deep so that you have 4 inches (10 cm) of soil above the bulb.

For a decent-sized display, plant the bulb in groups of 10, and space them a couple of inches (5 cm) apart. Plant the bulbs with the pointy end facing up. Cover the bulbs with soil, water them thoroughly, and then cover the area with a mulch of pine bark or shredded leaves to protect them.

READ MORE AT GARDENING KNOW HOW

These iconic garden mainstays can also bloom indoors. To find out how, scan the QR code or follow the link below.

- **"Growing Tulips Indoors: How to Force Tulip Bulbs"** (URL = gkh.us/2896)

CARING FOR THE PLANT

Tulips, unfortunately, happen to be a favorite food for many pest animals, such as deer, rabbits, and squirrels. Both the bulbs and the mature plants are at risk of being eaten, so effective pest deterrents will likely be necessary in areas with significant wildlife. Insect pests and disease are less-common concerns, though they can be susceptible to bulb rot and some fungal infections. In most cases, bulbs afflicted with fungus should be discarded, and new bulbs should be treated with fungicide before planting. Well-draining soil can also help prevent rot, mildew, and fungus from setting in.

Note: Tulips can be toxic to humans and pets.

CHAPTER FIVE

THE FOLIAGE GARDEN

Did you know that green is the most easily seen color? This calming effect makes green very soothing on the eyes. Yet, in the garden this beneficial hue is often overlooked, with the multitude of flower colors taking center stage. Yet a foliage-only garden in shades of green can have just as much impact and appeal as a traditional garden. Foliage plants of any color provide texture, pattern, shape, personality, and year-round interest.

Succulents and cacti are also chosen more for shape and texture and not necessarily for their flowers—although some do bloom in spectacular fashion. Many of these drought-resistant plants originated in the American Southwest, Mexico, and Central America, but they are popular with gardeners from cooler climates, who simply overwinter them indoors. Some are even cold-weather hardy and come springing back each year. There is a reason *Sempervivum* is called "live forever"!

DESIGNING WITH PATTERN AND TEXTURE

Once you begin incorporating foliage plants into your gardens, you'll find that they add a whole new dimension of textures, forms, and colors. Another plus is that some of them—such as dusty miller, licorice plant, artemisia, and hens and chicks—retain their general shape and texture during winter, providing architectural elements to a garden denuded of its more tender specimens.

Don't overlook all the pluses that ornamental grasses lend to a garden. Their varied textures can add a certain softness to the environment, along with interesting movement.

TEXTURE

Leaf and stem texture is an important element in the foliage garden. Texture defines contours and creates contrast. If foliage plants were limited to only one type of leaf texture, or even a few, the garden would certainly lose its appeal—think of a long, monotonous evergreen hedge. Yet, by using a wide range of textural specimens when designing with foliage plants, this is unlikely to happen. Leaf and stem textures include those that are waxy, rough, fuzzy, velvety, prickly, sticky, and smooth. For example, some foliage plants, such as lamb's ear, are covered with tiny hairs, making them soft and velvety to the touch. Other plants, like yuccas or stinging nettles, bear bristles, spines, hairs, or thorns, making them tricky to handle, but quite interesting to view.

Ornamental grasses can add instant texture to the foliage garden—and maintain that appeal throughout the year, even into winter. Some garden favorites include blue fescue, maiden grass, Japanese silver grass, and fountain grass. (For more information, *see* pages 140–141)

Ferns, with their feathery fronds, are great for adding texture to a hard-edged garden space, say, along a stone wall. The Japanese painted fern not only offers striking texture, but its silver and burgundy foliage displays an unusual color combination. (For more information, *see* pages 146–147.)

Think of the forms of your plant selections and how they play off one another. Here the rounded white-edged leaves of a variegated hosta surround the feathery leaves of taller ferns. Both work together to highlight the graceful fountain standing amidst them.

FORM

Foliage plants also come in a variety of shapes and sizes. Some have leaves that are rounded, some are serrated, and others are straight and sword-like, feathery, scalloped, or heart-shaped. There are even leaves that curl or twist into interesting shapes. Some plants reach massive heights, others remain rather short, and, of course, there is a wide array of plants in between.

Hostas are one of the most commonly used foliage plants in the garden. With their dense, rounded shapes, they are perfect as foundation, pathway, or driveway plantings, plus they come back reliably every year. When choosing other plants to showcase form, look to elephant ear, ajuga, caladium, hosta, artemisia, and various ground covers.

Consider including a strong focal point in the foliage garden. This could be as simple as one large dramatic display, like a stand of elephant ears, or a tinkling stone fountain with foliage plants arranged around it.

PATTERN

In addition to their many colors and hues, foliage plants often feature complex patterns of swirls, stripes, and speckles; some even have multicolor blotches, spatters, and splatters worthy of a modern artist. In addition, there are also patterns created by the leaf's veins, called venation, that add visual interest. There are two main types of venation.

- *Reticulate or pinnate venation.* Here, veinlets form a weblike network. This type of venation is generally present in the dicotyledonous plants, with seed embryos that produce two leaves. Rose and hibiscus leaves are good examples.
- *Parallel venation.* Here, the veins run parallel to each other. This is generally a characteristic of monocotyledonous plants, with seed embryos that produce one leaf. Examples include the leaves of lilies, irises, and grasses.
- *Dichotomous, or palmate, venation.* This refers to when the veins fan out from each other like tree branches. This pattern is seen in the leaf of the *Ginkgo biloba*.

COLOR

The number of colors available in foliage plants is astounding, ranging from deep forest green to emerald, kelly, lime, and olive green, teal, dusty blue, deep gray, pale gray, white, cream, silver, dark purple, burgundy, magenta, cherry red, scarlet, hot pink, salmon, yellow, gold, mustard, orange, ocher, bronze, caramel, and chocolate. Is it any wonder that some people beholding a variegated foliage garden for the first time can't quite believe there are no flowers on display? For the record, many foliage plants do bloom, but their flowers are usually small and fleeting. It's all about leaf and stem appeal with these beauties.

Consider species that offer a range of colors, like hostas, which vary from light and dark green to blue-green, chartreuse, and variegated shades. Other species that add color include chameleon plant, caladium, Persian shield, heuchera, and coleus.

~ ~ ~ ~ ~ ~

A garden space combining a variety of foliage plants—with an emphasis on form, texture, and color placement—can be just as beautiful and captivating as one bursting with a riot of blooms. If you are curious about the types of foliage plants available commercially, there are numerous online resources and catalogs to help, along with your friendly neighborhood plant nursery. Be sure to select plants that thrive in your particular area, or plan to winter delicate specimens indoors.

With an impressive range of shapes, sizes, textures, forms, patterns, and colors, foliage plants can be lively—and essential—additions to a home garden.

FOLIAGE PLANTS

Foliage plants are versatile additions to any garden. As noted previously, they create unique statements gardens on their own when attention is paid to arrangement, shape, texture, and color. They also provide interest and contrast in flower gardens—green and silver foliage groupings offer a cool contrast to the visual heat of tropical blooms or vivid bedding plants. Consider using them in borders, islands, berms, cottage gardens, along walkways, and especially in formal gardens, where the impact is based on creating a pleasing geometry rather than being dependent on bright colors.

CONTAINER GARDENING WITH FOLIAGE PLANTS

Foliage plants also make excellent candidates for containers, window boxes, and hanging planters. The dangling vinca vine, the English ivy, the sweet potato vine in chartreuse or deep purple, and the ghostly licorice plant: these are all examples of foliage plants that can be used to great effect as "spillers" in boxes and hangers. There are also plenty of "filler" specimens that have a clumping or mounding habit, such perennials as artemisia, heuchera, and hosta, or an upright habit, like annuals dusty miller and coleus. Coleus in particular, with its wide choice of colorful patterns, provides a perfect pop of brightness.

Foliage plants like the dramatic caladium, with its leaves that come in shades of green, white, pink, magenta, burgundy, and red, can add color and texture to a shady spot beneath garden trees.

READ MORE AT GARDENING KNOW HOW

To learn more about foliage plants and to get suggestions about how you can incorporate them into your own garden, follow these links.

- **"Leaves That Stand Out: Growing Plants with Beautiful Foliage"** (URL = gkh.us/132922)
- **"Gardening with Foliage Plants: How to Create an All Green Foliage Garden"** (URL = gkh.us/332)
- **"Plants with Blue Foliage: Learn About Plants That Have Blue Leaves"** (URL = gkh.us/92081)
- **"Add a Pop of Red to Your Garden Bed — 5 Plants with Fabulous Red Foliage"** (URL = gkh.us/172754)

Intermingling different species of foliage plants can create interesting effects. Here, the soft, neutral silver of dusty miller prevents two varieties of brightly hued coleus from competing with each other.

Artemisia

Silver mound artemisia *(Artemisia schmidtiana* 'Silver Mound') is a small, resilient plant, resistant to deer, rabbits, and many other pests, making it an excellent addition for outlying rock gardens or beds near wooded or natural areas.

With 300 species after its name, the genus *Artemisia* includes a wide range of plants: annuals, perennials, and even woody shrubs. Those cultivated for the home garden, however, are the herbaceous perennials, and one of the best choices for this is the silver mound artemisia *(Artemisia schmidtiana* 'Silver Mound'), the only member of the genus with a prostrate, spreading habit. Unlike other *Artemisias,* the silver mound plant is not invasive.

A member of the Asteraceae, this cultivar, often called silver mound wormwood, is a relatively small plant. Scattered among tall, flowering summer blooms, it serves as a long-lasting ground cover, shading out growing weeds and further reducing its care.

Fine, delicate foliage and an attractive, mounding habit are just two of the reasons gardeners like growing the silver mound artemisia. As you learn about growing and caring for the plant, you will likely find other reasons to grow a few more in the garden, including the facts that it is low maintenance and drought and pest resistant.

This attractive plant is useful as a spreading border for a flower bed, as edging in a perennial garden, and for growing along paths and walkways. The delicate foliage retains its shape and color during the hottest months of summer.

GROWING SILVER MOUND

As with many foliage plants, *Artemisias* are typically planted from nursery-grown plants. Spring is a good time to put them in the ground, as soon as the soil can be worked. The silver mound performs best when located in a full-to-partial-sun location in average soil. Planting in less than fertile soil decreases some aspects of its care. Soils that are too rich or too poor can result in splitting, dying out, or separating in the middle of the mound. This is best corrected by division of the plant. Regular division is a part of caring for silver mound, but is required less often if planted in the proper soil.

CARING FOR THE PLANT

Silver mound artemisia care, other than division every two to three years, consists of infrequent watering during periods of no rain and a midsummer trim, usually around the time the insignificant flowers appear in late June. Trimming keeps the plant tidy and helps it maintain its mounding shape and avoid splitting. You can also propagate artemisia by seed, cuttings, or division.

SCIENTIFIC NAME: *Artemisia schmidtiana* 'Silver Mound'

FAMILY: Asteraceae

HEIGHT: 12 inches (30 cm)

WIDTH: 18 inches (45 cm)

FOLIAGE COLOR: Silver-green

SOIL pH: Neutral to alkaline

LIGHT: Full sun to partial shade

COMMON PROBLEMS

As for diseases and pests, with proper care in the right growing conditions, artemisia experiences few problems. Overwatering, high humidity, damp conditions, or poor air circulation can result in mildew, rust, or root rot. The plant's strong, pungent scent repels most garden pests, such as deer that also dislike its bitter taste, but watch for insects like aphids, mites, scale, or leaf beetles.

Editor's Tips

With its elegant silver foliage, artemisia can be incorporated into your landscape in many ways.

- **Combine silver mound artemisia with pastel flowers, such as pale purple lavender.**
- **Plant it with bright blooms, like bee balm, for a bold contrast.**
- **Contrast its rounded shape with spiky plants like salvia.**
- **Use it in a moon garden with other pale foliage plants, like dusty miller.**

Caladium

Caladium in the garden The plants grow from tuberous corms known as bulbs.

These dramatic-yet-delicate plants are greatly favored for their multicolored foliage, which occurs in green, white, red, or pink or a mix of shades. Caladiums can be grown in containers or clumped together within beds and borders. There are numerous varieties found in either the fancy-leaved or the strap-leaved cultivars, all of which make a strong statement in the landscape. Native to Central America and South America, these tropical perennials are treated as annuals in temperate regions.

GROWING CALADIUMS

Planting caladium bulbs is easy, and with proper care they will last for years. Caladiums can be purchased as potted plants or dormant tubers.

Their size depends on the variety chosen. Generally, each tuber has a large bud that is surrounded by smaller ones. To make it easier for these smaller buds to grow, many gardeners find it helpful to carve out the large bud with a knife. Of course, this is up to the individual and will not adversely affect the overall growth of your caladiums.

Bulbs can be planted directly in the garden during spring or started indoors four to six weeks before the average last frost date. Soil temperature is an important consideration, as planting too early outdoors can cause tubers to rot. These plants thrive in moist, well-drained soil and are happier in partial shade. Be sure to plant caladiums about 4 to 6 inches (10–15 cm) deep, and space them 4 to 6 inches (10–15 cm) apart.

If you're starting caladiums indoors, keep them in a warm room with plenty of light until outside temperatures are warm enough to transplant. Caladium tubers should be planted with the knobs, or eye buds, facing up. This may be difficult to distinguish in some varieties, but those planted upside down will still emerge, only more slowly.

CARING FOR THE PLANTS

The most important factors in caladium care are feeding and watering. Fertilizer will help strengthen the plants in order to produce adequate tubers for the following year. Use liquid fertilizer every two weeks during the growing season or slow-release pellets.

Caladiums also need to be watered on a weekly basis, more often during dry spells. Plants grown in containers should be checked daily and watered as needed. Applying mulch around the base can help conserve and maintain moisture, even for plants in containers.

Because caladiums are considered tender perennials, in cold climates you must dig up plants in autumn and store them indoors over winter. Once their foliage yellows and begins falling over, you can carefully lift the plants from the ground. Place the plants in a warm, dry location for several weeks to dry out. Then cut off the foliage, place the tubers in a netted bag or box, and cover in dry peat moss. Store the tubers in a cool, dry location. Once spring returns, you can replant them outdoors. Caladiums in containers, however, can be overwintered indoors like any houseplant.

Note: Caladiums are toxic to humans and pets.

SCIENTIFIC NAME: *Caladium*

FAMILY: Araceae

HEIGHT: 12 to 30 inches (30–75 cm)

WIDTH: 12 to 24 inches (30–60 cm)

FOLIAGE COLOR: Variegated combinations of green, pink, red, and white

SOIL pH: Slightly acidic

LIGHT: Full to partial shade

Fancy Leaf Caladiums

Fancy leaf caladiums *(Caladium x hortulanum)* are great additions to the often all-too-green shade garden. With well over a dozen cultivars, ranging from white through pink to deep, dark red with contrasting edges and veins, fancy leaf caladium bulbs offer enough variety to satisfy the fussiest gardener.

For more information, scan the QR code or follow the link to "Tips for Growing Fancy Leaf Caladiums" (URL = gkh.us/6132)

Coleus

Several varieties of coleus, massed together, demonstrate this plant's diversity. You can use them alone or place them with other plants that complement their colors.

At a Glance

SCIENTIFIC NAME: *Coleus* spp.

FAMILY: Lamiaceae

HEIGHT: 6 to 36 inches (15 cm–1 m)

WIDTH: 6 to 36 inches (15 cm–1 m)

FOLIAGE COLOR: Purple, red, orange, pink, green, and yellow and variegated combinations and patterns

SOIL pH: Slightly acidic to neutral

LIGHT: Partial shade to full shade

Perhaps you know them as painted nettle or poor man's croton, depending on where you're located, but for many of us we simply know them as coleus plants *(Coleus blumei)*. They have some of the most stunningly colored foliage—in combinations of green, yellow, pink, red, maroon, and many more— and also have a wide variety of leaf sizes and overall shapes. This means that no matter what area you are looking to put coleus, you can find one that will be perfect. These plants are great for adding color in the garden (or home), especially in those dark, drab-looking corners.

GROWING COLEUS

Coleus is probably one of the easiest plants to grow and propagate. In fact, the plants root so easily that you can even start cuttings in a glass of water. They can also be propagated by seed indoors about 8 to 10 weeks prior to your last expected spring frost.

Coleus can be added to beds and borders for interest or grown in containers. They need fertile, well-draining soil and usually perform best in areas with partial shade, though many varieties can also tolerate sun.

When growing coleus, keep in mind that these beauties can grow rapidly. Plant coleus close together as bedding plants or tuck them into baskets and containers for a fast-growing and spectacular addition.

CARING FOR THE PLANTS

Caring for coleus is just as easy. They need to be kept moist, especially newly planted coleus. Container plants also require more frequent watering than those grown in the garden. Although it's not required, the plants can be given a boost of half-strength liquid fertilizer during their active growth in spring and summer. Their spiked flowers usually appear in summer; however, these can be removed if desired. You can also pinch the shoots of young coleus plants to produce bushier growth.

Another factor to consider when caring for coleus is overwintering, because these plants, which are considered tender annuals, are highly susceptible to cold temperatures. They must therefore be either dug up, potted, and brought indoors for overwintering or grown through cuttings to establish additional plants.

Editor's Picks

Here is just a sampling of the many varieties of coleus to choose from.

- **'Black Dragon' in dramatic dark maroon-purple**
- **'Campfire' in a solid rusty red**
- **'Dragon Heart' in chartreuse with a fuchsia center bleeding to burgundy**
- **'Fishnet Stockings' in bright electric lime with burgundy veining**
- **'Kong Red' in red with a dark burgundy center, a magenta inner stripe, and chartreuse edges**
- **'Watermelon' in medium green with a bright magenta center and burgundy bleeding through leaf veins**
- **'Wizard Jade' with a creamy white center and a sharp green border**

Dig Deeper

READ MORE AT GARDENING KNOW HOW

Find out how to increase your coleus collection and how to ensure they survive the winter by following the links below.

- **"How to Propagate Coleus from Seed or Cuttings"** (URL = gkh.us/5164)
- **"Winterizing Coleus: How to Overwinter Coleus"** (URL = gkh.us/5091)

A GALLERY OF
ORNAMENTAL GRASSES

There are more than 10,000 grass species in the world. Grasslands account for more than 20 percent of Earth's vegetation and are found mostly in temperate and tropical climates. Grasses evolved around 55 million years ago, and, in fact, a massive and ancient bed of seagrass, *Posidonia oceanica,* in the Mediterranean is thought to be the oldest living organism on Earth, possibly between 80,000 and 200,000 years old.

Ornamental grasses, those created to enhance gardens and lawn plantings, are bred to be hardy, attractive, and noninvasive . . . to a point. Many are perennial. Due to their low maintenance and adaptability to various conditions, they have become immensely popular in modern landscapes. Hardy ornamentals also add winter interest to the property, especially with their blades and seed heads sticking up through mounds of snow. All told, grasses provide texture, color, height, movement, and even sound to the garden.

TYPES OF ORNAMENTAL GRASS

Two of the most common hardy ornamental grasses are *Calamagrostis,* or feather reed grass, and *Miscanthus,* or maiden grass. Not surprisingly, both of these grasses have a wide range of cultivars available to gardeners. Rushes and cordgrass are shade-tolerant plants that grow well in areas with standing water, like beside ponds. Drought-resistant grasses, often used in xeriscaping, include blue oat grass, pampas grass, and blue fescue.

Some grasses that spread by rhizomes may become invasive, but placing them in pots will keep them contained. This also gives you the ability to move tender specimens to sheltered locations when cold or inclement weather hits. As the season progresses, you can reposition them to best effect on the deck or patio. Potential container grasses include Japanese blood grass, sedge, and foxtail grass.

BAMBOO

This tall, upright grass (*Bambusa* spp. or *Phyllostachys* spp.) springs from spreading underground rhizomes. Early on, it requires watering to form a root system; otherwise it grows quickly, often out of control (check its status in your area). The swaying stems and lacy leaves add a tropical feel to any space.

BLUE FESCUE

Festuca glauca, commonly known as blue fescue, consists of a low-growing mound of dense, bright silver-blue foliage and upright flower plumes on long stems that start out silver, then turn tan. Used in borders or edging, it reaches 12 inches (30 cm) in height and width. It is deer- and drought-resistant.

BLUE OAT GRASS

An international award winner, *Helictotrichon sempervirens/Avena candida,* with its narrow steel-blue leaves and clumping habit, is low-maintenance and semi-evergreen. This grass does great in full sun and dry soils with good drainage and when mature can reach heights of 3 to 6 feet (1–1.8 m).

FEATHER REED GRASS

For a feather reed grass, try the award-winning 'Karl Foerster' cultivar of *Calamagrostis* x *acutiflora*. This low-maintenance, pest-resistant grass variety displays feathery, upright flower plumes that can reach 6 feet (1.8 m). These plumes sway in the breeze, contributing to its elegance.

FOXTAIL BARLEY

Hordeum jubatum has arching, elegant leaves and feathery flower spikes in green, pale pink, or purple that turn tan as the grass matures. It blooms from late spring to midsummer and reaches 2 feet (60 cm) in height. Great in borders, beds, mass plantings, and meadows, it also lasts in dried arrangements.

GOLDEN SEDGE

For a prime example of this ornamental grass, try the award-winning cultivar of *Carex elata,* 'Aurea' or 'Bowles Golden'. It is resistant to deer and wet conditions, and its shiny yellow blades have fine green edges. The hairlike, iridescent foliage mixes well with flowering bulbs or perennials.

HAKONE GRASS

Hakonechloa macra originated around Mount Hakone in Japan and is known for its beautiful blades and exotic clumping habit. The plant's slender stems look like tiny bamboo stalks, and the cultivars 'All Gold' and 'Aureola' feature variegated green and gold leaves. Water at least weekly.

JAPANESE BLOOD GRASS

The green forms of *Imperata cylindrica* are invasive, but its reds are far less so. Look for sterile cultivars like low-maintenance 'Rubra', which stands upright and offers green leaves tipped with vivid red. It grows up to 4 feet (1.2 m) once established in moist, well-drained soil.

JAPANESE SEDGE

For a Japanese sedge choice, try 'Everest,' a cultivar of *Carex oshimensis* that grows up to 18 inches (45 cm) high and has beautiful narrow, dark, glossy green leaves with silver-white edges. It is vigorous and easy to grow, even in shady areas, and its color contrasts beautifully with many flowers.

MAIDEN GRASS

Miscanthus sinensis boasts cultivars in several sizes. The 3-foot (1 m) 'Little Kitten' has fine-textured, lush foliage and narrow green leaves that turn many shades of brown in the autumn. 'Gracillimus', or Chinese silver grass, with its flushed purple flower plumes can hit an impressive 6 feet (1.8 m) in height.

NEW ZEALAND FLAX

With its deep-red, purplish-bronze color, and broad, strap-like leaves, *Phormium tenax* has become increasingly popular with landscapers. It typically reaches heights of 5 feet (12.5 cm). It must be de-clumped every few years, but this provides new plants for the garden. For more information, *see* page 149,

PINK MUHLY GRASS

Muhly grass *(Muhlenbergia capillaris)* is a variety of ornamental grass with spectacular showgirl flair. Also known as pink hairgrass, sweetgrass, gulf muhlygrass, mist grass, and hairawn muhly, this stunning grass displays best in large clumps in perennial borders or native gardens.

PUMILA

Native to South America, this variety of *Cortaderia selloana* is a compact pampas grass with narrow, greenish gray leaves. From late summer to mid-winter, it bears extravagant, silky, creamy white plumes. This soil-tolerant grass can reach 6 feet (1.8 m) high and 4 feet (1.2 m) wide.

PURPLE FOUNTAIN GRASS

A dramatic *Pennisetum setaceum* variety called 'Rubrum' offers graceful movement and beautiful color—rich deep-red foliage and arching, crimson plumes. Rubrum prefers full sun or partial shade and is ignored by deer. It matures to 5 feet (1.5 m) in height and 4 feet (1.2 m) in width.

QUAKING GRASS

Briza media gets it name from its habit of trembling in the lightest breeze. It starts out green with tints of purple, and then fades to tan. Its flat pikelets resemble puffy oats with leaves that are a soft, deep green. It is drought-tolerant, looks great in naturalized areas, and is perfect in dried-flower arrangements.

SOFT RUSH GRASS

With its narrow, round, upright habit and bright green foliage, *Juncus effusus* looks wonderful planted around ponds and in meadows. A native of North America, this easy-care grass requires full sun, but it is tolerant of drought. It typically reaches 4 feet (1.2 m) in height.

SWITCH GRASS

Switch grass *(Panicum virgatum)* is a main species of the North American tallgrass prairie. Look for ornamental cultivars with a columnar form, with stiff round stems. The dense, upright blades range in color from medium-green to olive to blue-green; the cultivar 'Rehbraun' turns to rich red-purple in autumn.

ZEBRA GRASS

Zebra grass (*Miscanthus sinensis* 'Zebrinus') is a striking ornamental. It is known for the soft yellow rings around its spiky leaves. Its leaf colors include bright green, buff-silver, pinkish copper, and rich gold, depending on age. Imposing zebra grass can grow to a towering 7 feet (2.1 m) in height.

Coral Bells

In full bloom, dainty pink flowers rise above the rich brownish red of *Heuchera* 'Chocolate Ruffles.' *Heuchera,* popularly known as coral bells, adds color and interest to a woodland garden.

If you're looking for stunning color in the garden, consider planting coral bells. Not only will you fall in love with its intense variety of foliage hues, you will also receive the added bonus of lively flower color.

Coral bells *(Heuchera* spp.) is also known as alumroot. *Heuchera* is an interesting genus of perennials, comprising more than 50 species that are native to North America. These perennial plants are listed as evergreens or semi-evergreens in many climates, which means they bring year-round interest, even under a layer of frost. Their large and often heart-shaped leaves are their greatest draw, coming in several colors, like bronze, purple, and green. They vary in size in shape, too, with cultivars that are more rounded or ruffled, and the colors can be solid or variegated.

Their tiny clusters of bell-shaped blooms, which give the plant its common name, perch atop spiky stalks that rise above the foliage. Blooming in late spring to early summer, the flowers are just as impressive as the foliage. There are also late-blooming types available, and the flower color varies, too, with colors ranging from white and pink to light coral and deep red. Butterflies, bees, hummingbirds, and other pollinators find these delicate blooms attractive.

Their low-growing, mounding habit makes them a suitable addition to the edges of woodland or natural gardens, especially if planted in masses with other foliage specimens like hosta, fern, and caladium. They're also great companions for many types of perennial plants, such as the shade-loving bleeding heart, iris, and astilbe. You can also grow coral bells in containers.

GROWING CORAL BELLS

You can easily grow coral bells in the garden. These plants grow naturally in wooded areas; therefore, when planting coral bells, you'll want to mimic these growing conditions by placing them in shade or filtered sun. Give these plants moist, but well-draining soil—preferably enriched with compost or another type of organic matter, such as leaf compost or pine bark fines.

Coral bells can be propagated in spring by seed or through cuttings. Seeds, however, require at least a six-week cold period prior to planting. Division can also be done in spring or autumn.

SCIENTIFIC NAME: *Heuchera* spp.

FAMILY: Saxifragaceae

HEIGHT: 8 to 18 inches (20–45 cm)

WIDTH: 12 to 24 inches (15–30 cm)

FOLIAGE COLOR: Nearly every color, from silver to nearly black

SOIL pH: Slightly acidic, neutral

LIGHT: Partial shade

CARING FOR THE PLANT

Once established, these plants require little in the way of maintenance, other than occasional watering, though container-grown plants may require more water. You can deadhead spent blooms, if desired. Although these plants generally do not rebloom, this will improve its overall appearance. In addition, you should cut back any old, woody growth in spring.

There are few insect or disease problems that affect coral bells, but do keep an eye out for leaf scorch during hot, dry conditions with too much sun.

Editor's Picks

Here is just a small sampling of the many colorful varieties of coral bells available for the home garden.

- **'Amber Waves' in true amber that darkens through the season**
- **'Berry Smoothie' in purple and red**
- **'Canyon Belle' in green with bright red flowers**
- **'Chocolate Ruffle' in rich chocolate with a deep burgundy underside**
- **'Green Spice' in green with dark purple veining**
- **'Palace Purple' in olive to bronze-green to deep purple with a wine red underside**
- **'Plum Pudding' in deep purple with pale pink blooms**
- **'Pretty Pistachio' in chartreuse to lime green with bright pink flowers**
- **'Southern Comfort' in a peach that matures to amber**

Dusty Miller

Silvery dusty miller brings out the best in any of its companions. Its muted tones work well with the vivid colors in a flower garden or the cool greens of a foliage garden.

The dusty miller plant *(Senecio cineraria)* is an interesting landscape addition, grown for its silvery gray foliage. With its lacy leaves and subdued, neutral coloration, it makes an attractive companion for many blooms in the garden, acting as a contrast that lets the bright colors of garden flowers really shine. And care for dusty miller is minimal, once the plant is established.

GROWING DUSTY MILLER

Dusty miller, also called silver dust, is easily found in garden centers and nurseries. You can also sow seeds of this tender perennial in the ground after the last spring frosts. In about two to three weeks, the seedlings appear, and by the first year the seedlings will transform into rounded mounds that grow as tall as 1 foot (30 cm) but will often remain shorter. The plant is adaptable to many soil types, thriving in acidic clay to sandy loam soils. The soil must be well-draining to avoid root rot. Water regularly right after planting, and withhold water once roots have developed and the plant is growing.

DUSTY MILLER CARE

Although the dusty miller flowers bloom in midsummer, the small yellow blooms are small and not considered showy. The foliage, however, is long lasting and drought resistant. As with most silvery, furry plants, growing dusty miller helps the garden remain attractive through the heat of the summer. It will also tolerate frost.

Dusty miller is often grown as an annual and discarded after the first season. It is however, an herbaceous perennial and might return, depending on your region.

The growing plant can handle the heat, but it is best planted where afternoon shade is available during the hottest months of summer.

Watch to see if your plant becomes leggy, which will call for a midsummer trim. Any flowers can be removed to keep the plant compact, but be sure to leave a few flowers to bloom in late summer if you want your dusty miller to self-seed.

SCIENTIFIC NAME: *Jacobaea maritima* (also known as *Senecio cineraria)*

FAMILY: Asteraceae

HEIGHT: 12 to 24 inches (30–60 cm)

WIDTH: 12 to 24 inches (30–60 cm)

FOLIAGE COLOR: Pale silvery green

SOIL pH: Acidic

LIGHT: Full sun

How to Use Dusty Miller

With its subtle coloration, dusty miller brings out the best in its companions. Here are just a few ways you can use this foliage plant in your garden.

- Dusty miller can be used as a background plant for low-growing creeping annual plants, such as wave petunias or creeping phlox.
- It can be attractively placed among ornamental grasses.
- Use it in flower bed borders or as part of an outdoor container planting.
- Take advantage of dusty miller's drought tolerance and interplant it in a xeric garden, away from the water source. Include native shrubs and flowers, apply a pre-emergence weed preventer, or mulch, and forget about dusty miller care for the summer. During periods of extreme drought, however, even xeric gardens benefit from an occasional soaking.
- Dusty miller's silvery leaves brilliantly set off flowers in cool colors, such as purple ajuga, and it goes equally as well with flowers in hot colors like red begonia.
- Plant dusty miller with white flowers in a moon garden.

Elephant's Ear

The enormous leaves of elephant ear—in this case, *Colocasia esculenta*—make a dramatic display in a garden, proving that foliage plants can be just as eye-catching as flowers.

Elephant ear is the common name for several species in three plant genera—*Colocasia, Alocasia,* and *Xanthosoma*. The most common one is *Colocasia esculenta,* also known as taro. These fast-growing plants will achieve their full size within two months. They originated in Asia, Australia, Central America, South America, and Africa, but are now found in gardens throughout the world.

This impressive tender perennial provides a bold effect in nearly any landscape setting with its large, heart-shaped, tropical-looking foliage, which is reminiscent of the shape of actual elephant ears. The leaves can reach 3 feet (1 m) in length and 2 feet (60 cm) in width in the tropics; in colder climates, they will remain smaller but still be impressive. Although they rarely flower, the bloom is a yellowish white.

Elephant ears have a number of uses in the garden. The plants come in a variety of colors and sizes, making them good choices as background plants, ground covers, or as edging, especially around ponds, along walkways, or in patio enclosures. They are also used as accent plants in tropical-themed water or bog gardens. Their most common use, however, is as an accent or focal point in grouped plantings. Many are also well adapted to growing in containers.

GROWING ELEPHANT EARS

Growing elephant ear is easy. Most of these plants require rich, moist soil and can be grown in full sun, although they generally prefer partial shade. The tubers can be placed directly outdoors once the threat of frost or freezing temperatures has ceased in your area. Plant the tubers about 2 to 3 inches (5–7.5 cm) deep, blunt end down. You can also start elephant ears indoors, approximately eight weeks prior to the last frost date. If growing them in containers, use a rich, organic potting soil, and plant them at the same depth. Harden off elephant ears for about a week prior to placing them outdoors.

Editor's Tip

To acclimate tender young plants to life outdoors, you will need to harden them. This process of hardening, or "hardening off," allows a plant to gradually transition from a protected indoor environment to outdoor conditions of fluctuating temperatures, wind, and full sun exposure.

At a Glance

SCIENTIFIC NAME: *Colocasia, Alocasia,* and *Xanthosoma* spp.

FAMILY: Araceae

HEIGHT: 2 to 6 feet (60 cm–1.8 m)

WIDTH: 2 to 6 feet (60 cm–1.8 m)

FOLIAGE COLOR: Emerald green to black, brown, and golden chartreuse

SOIL pH: Acidic

LIGHT: Full sun to partial shade

CARING FOR ELEPHANT EARS

Once established, elephant ears require little attention. During dry spells, you may want to water plants regularly, especially those growing in containers. Although not it's absolutely necessary, you may also want to periodically apply a slow-release fertilizer to the soil.

Elephant ears cannot survive winter outdoors. Freezing temperatures will kill the foliage and damage tubers. Therefore, in areas with harsh, cold winters—like those in northernmost regions—the plants must be dug up and stored indoors.

Cut the foliage back to about a couple of inches (5 cm) after the first frost, and then carefully dig up the plants. Allow the tubers to dry out for about a day or two and then store them in peat moss or shavings. Place them in a cool, dark area, such as a basement or crawlspace. Container plants can either be moved indoors or overwintered in a basement or protected porch.

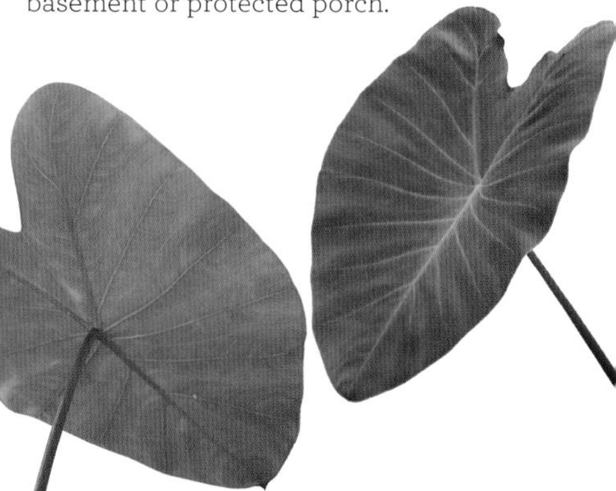

Hosta

Several varieties of lush hosta line a winding path. These low-maintenance and shade-tolerant foliage plants are perfect for filling in areas of the garden that get little sun.

Hostas, also known as plantain lilies, are a perennial favorite among gardeners, like reliable old friends you can always count on. Their clumping habit, attractive foliage, and easy care make them ideal for foundation plantings or low-maintenance gardens. Their tendency to return every year, like horticultural clockwork, makes them de rigueur for anyone with a smidgen of shade.

Originating in eastern Asia and brought to Europe in the 1700s, hostas today boast over 2,500 cultivars, with such variety in leaf shape, size, color, and texture, that an entire garden could be devoted to growing hostas alone—and still amaze the onlooker. Hosta leaves come in a selection of greens, ranging from a color so deep it's called blue to a light chartreuse to a soft creamy white, with plenty of patterns and variegations besides. The funnel-shaped blossoms form on tall scapes in shades of white, cream, pink, pale blue, lavender, or purple.

GROWING HOSTAS

Growing hostas is easy, but knowing some basics will help you encourage plants to reach their full potential. Hostas are typically sold at garden centers as potted transplants or bare-root divisions. They can be planted in early spring or as soon as the heat of summer ends in early autumn. Most types will fully mature in four to eight years.

Although hosta plants are touted as shade lovers, successfully growing them in the shade depends on color. A good rule of thumb for placement is "the lighter the foliage, the brighter the sun." Deeper, darker foliage retains its color best in moderate shade. The variegated specimens need more sunlight to keep their white and gold stripes gleaming. All hostas need some shade and few, if any, will do well in strong direct sunlight.

For optimum results, plant hostas in rich organic soil with a slightly acidic pH. Dig the planting hole about a foot (24 cm) deep and wide enough to accommodate the spread of a full-sized plant. This will make it easier for the roots to establish a foothold and begin their horizontal spread. In spite of their almost tropical look, hostas are rugged and once established, they tolerate almost any soil and will grow for years.

Drainage is also most important. Dormant season crown rot is one of the few diseases that attack these plants. When newly planted, keep the roots moist, not wet. Once established, hosta plants aren't fussy and are very tolerant of summer drought.

SCIENTIFIC NAME: *Hosta* spp.

FAMILY: Asparagaceae

HEIGHT: 6 inches to 4 feet (15 cm–1.2 m)

WIDTH: 1 foot to 6 feet (30 cm–1.8 m)

FOLIAGE COLOR: Light yellow to deep forest green to powdery blue and variegated combinations and patterns

SOIL pH: Slightly acidic

LIGHT: Shade, partial shade

CARING FOR THE PLANTS

To keep your hostas healthy, fertilize them each spring with an all-purpose garden fertilizer. Additional summer fertilizing may be helpful, but not necessary. Granular fertilizers should never sit on the leaves.

Hostas are relatively disease free. Many deer find them tasty, however, but daffodils may keep them away. Slugs are also a menace, but can be thwarted with a sprinkling of sand, coffee grounds, or liquid coffee around the plant base.

Note: Hostas are toxic to dogs, cats, and horses. Plant them accordingly.

Dig Deeper

READ MORE AT GARDENING KNOW HOW

Scan the QR code or follow this link to learn how to keep your hostas healthy.

- **"What Causes Holes in Hosta Leaves — Preventing Holes in Leaves of Hosta"** (URL = gkh.us/131163)

A GALLERY OF
GARDEN FERNS

Ferns are one of the oldest groups of plants on earth, with a fossil record dating back close to 400 million years. Yet, most of the earliest ferns have since gone extinct; the diversity of ferns seen today evolved relatively recently in geologic time, somewhere in the last 70 million years. They nonetheless remain the second-most diverse group of vascular plants, behind flowering plants. Currently, there are 21 fern families divided into 212 genera and roughly 10,500 species.

Although we are accustomed to seeing graceful ferns under woodland tree canopies, they do equally well in the shady home garden. Ferns that are tolerant of winter temperatures can be grown year-round in temperate regions. Many can also withstand summer heat, making them particularly ideal in a southern landscape. This hardiness, as well as their strong survival instinct, makes them extremely forgiving. They are excellent for naturalizing and often grow where other plants fail. As long as ferns are planted in rich, well-drained soil, receive regular mulching, and adequate water during dry periods, they will reward the gardener with their graceful textures year after year.

Few pests bother ferns other than the occasional passing slug. If your specimens become too large, divide them in early spring.

HARDY GARDEN FERNS

Ferns make excellent companions for woodland plantings like hosta, columbine, lady's mantle, heuchera, liriope, and caladium. They also look good interspersed with landscaping rocks, fallen logs, or uprooted tree stumps. Many garden ferns are deciduous—dying back in autumn and producing new shoots called croziers in spring—but others are evergreen.

Editor's Tips

Here are a few pointers for planting and maintaining ferns. Ferns take time to become established, so be patient.

- If your plot has heavy soil at planting time, break it up and lighten it with compost.
- Plant ferns so the crown is flush with the surrounding soil or slightly above to prevent crown rot. Mulch in spring to retain moisture.
- Keep ferns well watered for the first few years. Try to plant them in spring or autumn, when rain is more plentiful.
- With evergreen ferns like Christmas fern, thin the old ragged fronds in spring as the new ones appear.

AUTUMN FERN
The autumn fern *(Dryopteris erythrosora)*, is a dwarf, semi-evergreen fern that will add year-round interest to your shade garden. Its arching, frilly, papery fronds turn a coppery pink in spring, green in summer, and copper in autumn. Also known as Japanese shield fern, the plant prefers very wet soil.

BIRD'S NEST FERN
The bird's nest fern *(Asplenium nidus)* plant gets its name from the fact that the center of the plant resembles a bird's nest. They are epiphytic, meaning they grow on the surface of other plants. With their flat, wavy or crinkly fronds, their appearance can bring to mind a seaweed plant growing on dry land.

BOSTON FERN
Native to the humid swamps of Florida, Mexico, and South America, annual *Nephrolepis exaltata* is also called the sword fern. The green, deltoid-shaped leaflets arch down and are slightly serrated. Popular both indoors and out, this fern sprawls up and out to 3 feet (1 m). For more information, *see* page 354.

BRACKEN FERN
Bracken fern *(Pteridium aquilinum)* is an aggressive and widespread North American fern that thrives in dry shade gardens. The coarse, divided, triangular green fronds arise in spring and last until first frost. Plants reach 3 to 4 feet (1–1.2 m) in height and widths of 4 to 5 feet (1.2 –1.5 m).

CHRISTMAS FERN
This perennial fern, *Polystichum acrostichoides*, was so named because it stays green through the winter holidays. The lance-shaped, evergreen fronds emerge in spring and form fountain-like clusters. Planted in part-to-full shade, mature specimens may grow 2 feet (60 cm) tall and wide.

CINNAMON FERN
Osmundastrum cinnamomeum is a North American fern especially adapted to wet areas. It produces upright, stiff, yellow-green fronds in early spring, while cinnamon-colored fibers emerge from the base. It requires full to part shade and grows 2 to 3 feet (60 cm to 1 m) tall and wide.

HAY-SCENTED FERN

True to its name, *Dennstaedtia punctilobula* emits the sweet scent of new-mown hay when brushed. Lacy, narrow, triangular, yellow-green fronds emerge in spring. The fern tolerates part shade to full sun, fills in naturally beside streams and ponds, and reaches 18 to 24 inches (45–60 cm) in height.

INTERRUPTED FERN

Osmunda claytoniana, a genus with one species, produces silvery-white fiddle heads in spring, followed by vase-shaped rosettes of soft, broad, greenish yellow fronds. The fronds are "interrupted" in the middle with long, fertile leaflets that fall off by midsummer. Average height is 3 feet (1 m) tall.

JAPANESE PAINTED FERN

Athyrium niponicum pictum displays arching, triangular fronds with eye-catching green and silver foliage and dark maroon midribs. Japanese painted fern will add texture to shade gardens, look great with hostas, and will reach 12 to 18 inches (30–45 cm) in height, 18 to 24 inches (45–60 cm) in width.

KIMBERLY QUEEN FERN

Kimberly Queen fern *(Nephrolepis obliterata)* is a sword fern, so called due to the long sword-like fronds that are held high and erect and attain a height of 24 to 36 inches (60 cm–1 m). Also known as the Australian sword fern, it is suitable as an indoor or container plant, especially in hanging baskets

LADY FERN

Lady fern (*Athyrium filix-femina)* is a large, lush, upright, feathery fern that is native throughout North and South America. This highly variable species is a fast-grower, drought resistant, and thrives in damp, shady woodland regions. It can reach heights and widths up to 3 feet (1 m).

MALE FERN

Dryopteris filix-mas is a common evergreen fern of the temperate Northern Hemisphere, especially Europe, Asia, and North America. It favors the damp understory of woodlands as well as hedge-banks, rocks, and screes. Shaped like a vase, it can grow up to 5 feet (1.5 m) in height.

OSTRICH FERN

The ostrich fern *(Matteuccia struthiopteris)* is a large, vase-shaped fern with intricately textured fronds. It can reach 3 to 5 feet (1–1.5 m) in height and will spread and form dense colonies in moist soil. In spring, the emerging fiddleheads are delectable when sautéed in a bit of olive oil.

RABBIT'S FOOT FERN

Rabbit's foot fern *(Davallia fejeensis),* also called squirrel's foot fern, gets its name from the furry rhizomes that creep over the top of a plant pot. With its tropical origins, it is great for backyard, terrace, patio, and deck containers that can be moved indoors during cool weather or as houseplants.

ROYAL FERN

Also known as old world royal fern, *Osmunda regalis,* which is native to Europe, Africa and Asia, adds interesting texture and color to shady areas. It has large, twice-cut leaves that sometimes produce bead-like sori (spores) at the tips. It lends an air of elegance to sturdier companion foliage plants.

SENSITIVE FERN

Sensitive fern *(Onoclea sensibilis),* also called bead fern, has stalks with a decorative, beaded appearance. The common name comes from its sensitivity to frost. The sterile fronds are a light to brown-mottled green; the long lobes bear deep cuts that almost reach the stem. Spring fiddleheads are pale red.

SOUTHERN MAIDENHAIR

Southern maidenhair fern *(Adiantum capillus-veneri)* is a distinctive fern, with its dark stalks and gray-green, feathery foliage. Often grown indoors, it generally prefers to be in pots when grown outside and will need humus-rich, moist, well-drained soil. It can reach heights of 3 feet (1 m).

WESTERN SWORD FERN

Polystichum munitum, an evergreen fern abundant in the moist, coniferous woodlands of western North America, has also naturalized in Great Britain and Ireland. Dark green fronds grow in a tight clump spreading out radially from a round base, reaching 18 inches to 6 feet (45 cm–1.8 m) tall.

Lamb's Ear

Lamb's ear *(Stachys byzantina)* is a lovely spring foliage plant. Its velvety, silver-green tongue-shaped leaves swirl from rosettes to make a showy display, perfect for a sensory garden, where touch is an essential element.

This easy-care Mediterranean native is a low-growing, evergreen, spreading perennial with velvety, silvery gray-green foliage. Gardeners choose lamb's ear *(Stachys byzantina)* primarily for the color and texture of its elliptical leaves and often recommend it for children's and sensory gardens because of its soft, fleecy feel, the source of its name. If left to bloom in summer, it will produce spikes of pink- to purple-colored flowers.

Lamb's ear is used primarily for its foliage, but the plant's low-growing, mat-forming habit makes it ideal for use as a ground cover. Group specimens in open borders alongside other perennial plants or grow them in containers. They look especially effective behind that other shade garden favorite, 'Palace Purple' coral bells, with its brilliant purple-red foliage. In addition to their visual appeal, the plants' fuzzy leaves can be used as a "band-aid" for healing wounds and easing painful bee stings.

GROWING LAMB'S EAR

As long as you provide suitable conditions, growing lamb's ear in the garden is simple. It's hardy in most temperate regions, plus the plant's Middle Eastern origins make it superb for growing in drought-like conditions. In fact, lamb's ears are tolerant enough to grow almost anywhere, with a growth rate that is medium but steady.

Plant lamb's ear in spring, in full sun or partial shade, and in holes no deeper than their original pots. Prevent overcrowding by spacing the plants at least 1 foot (30 cm) apart. You can add a bit of compost to the holes prior to planting, if desired.

Water new plants thoroughly, but do not waterlog them. Although lamb's ear can tolerate poor soil, the soil should be well-draining, as the plant dislikes overly moist conditions, especially in shady areas.

CARING FOR THE PLANTS

Once established, lamb's ear requires little maintenance. Water only when the soil is significantly dry. Watch the foliage carefully in rainy or humid regions, as moisture can lead to rotting. Spreading mulch under the leaves can help prevent this. Trim the growth back in the spring, and prune out brown leaves as needed. To keep the plants from spreading, deadhead spent blooms. In addition to self-seeding, the plant can be propagated through division in spring or autumn.

SCIENTIFIC NAME: *Stachys byzantina*

FAMILY: Lamiaceae

HEIGHT: 9 to 18 inches (23–45 cm)

WIDTH: 12 to 18 inches (30–45 cm)

FOLIAGE COLOR: Silvery greenish gray

SOIL pH: Acidic, alkaline, neutral

LIGHT: Full to partial sun

A Sensory Garden

It's easy to create a sensory garden with plants that are edible, touchable, have a pleasant aroma, rustle in the breeze, or offer dazzling colors. These gardens are especially suited to young children, seniors, and the disabled. As individuals explore the space, they are called upon to use their other four senses in addition to sight. Appropriate sensory plants include touchably fuzzy lamb's ear and rounded allium; scented honeysuckle, chamomile, curry plant, and jasmine; edible, textural, and scented herbs like dill, mint, sage, and rosemary; and audible plants like plumed grasses or bamboo. Butterfly bushes will attract buzzing bees, which will add to the auditory experience.

New Zealand Flax

At a Glance

SCIENTIFIC NAME: *Phormium tenax*

FAMILY: Asphodelaceae

HEIGHT: 1 to 6 feet (30 cm–1.8 m)

WIDTH: 1 to 3 feet (20 cm–1 m)

FOLIAGE COLOR: Green, yellow, pink, red, purple, burgundy, and bronze

SOIL pH: Acidic

LIGHT: Full sun to partial shade

The large tufts of stiff, upright, sword-shaped leaves of New Zealand flax form a striking centerpiece in a foliage garden. This impressive evergreen comes in an array of colors.

New Zealand flax is a large, often colorful, spiky plant that creates an arresting focal point in gardens or containers. Once thought to be related to agave, the plant has since been classified in the *Phormium* genus. These plants are popular ornamentals in temperate regions; with their fan-like form and easy growth from rhizomes, they make excellent accents in containers, perennial gardens, and in coastal regions.

The plant is most known for its dramatic swordlike, keel-shaped leaves. New cultivars and hybrids are available with foliage in bright shades of yellow, pink, red, purple, burgundy, and bronze. There are even variegated flaxes to create contrast. Some varieties are small enough to use in containers, while others can reach several feet in diameter and grow to over 6 feet (1.8 m) tall, with an amazing potential height of 20 feet (6 m) in perfect conditions.

This is a rather slow-growing species that can take several years to mature. On adult plants, the flower stalks shoot up above the leaves and produce curving, tubular red or yellow blossoms that are high in nectar and favored by hummingbirds. Attractive seed pods form after the flowers bloom, but they can be deadheaded to prevent self-seeding.

Historically, all parts of the plant were once utilized: the fibrous leaves were used to make baskets and textiles, the Māori people prepared medicine from the leaves and roots, face powder was made from the pollen, and old stems were roped together as rafts.

GROWING NEW ZEALAND FLAX

New Zealand flax is a slow-growing perennial that should go into the ground in spring. The most common method of propagation is through division, and fully rooted specimens are widely available at nursery centers.

One of the plant's main requirements is well-draining soil. Boggy or heavy clay will reduce growth and contribute to rotten stems and rhizomes. New Zealand flax tolerates partial sun but will perform better in full sun. The plant attracts birds, but it is not attractive to deer. It is also useful for erosion control.

Editor's Picks

Here is a small sampling of New Zealand flax cultivars.

- **'Apricot Queen' in soft yellow edged in green with a tinge of apricot**
- **'Carousel' in green with a pink edge**
- **'Dusky Chief' in dark purple-red**
- **'Flamingo' in salmon pink with green and yellow stripes**
- **'Misty Cream' in yellow, apricot, pink, and brown**
- **'Platt's Black' in matte chocolate**
- **'Rainbow Queen' in bronze-green with thick salmon pink edges**
- **'Shiraz' in wine red**
- **'Wings of Gold' in olive green with a creamy yellow margin**

CARING FOR THE PLANTS

Hybrid plants are not as durable as the two foundation species. They require more water and some shelter from hot sunlight, which can burn leaf tips. Most species are reliably hardy to 20° F (-6° C), but all can be moved indoors in autumn to prevent damage. Use 2 inches (5 cm) of organic mulch around the root zone to conserve moisture, prevent weeds, and insulate the rhizomes.

Occasional pruning is necessary when damage has occurred to the leaves due to sun or cold or exposure in windy or exposed sites. Flax thrives in poor soils, so fertilization is not necessary, but annual top dressings of compost will add nutrients to the soil. If plants are grown in sufficient warmth, New Zealand flax has few insect or disease complaints.

Papyrus

Better known by the common names papyrus, *Cyperus papyrus* is a species of aquatic flowering plant belonging to the sedge family, Cyperaceae. With its dramatic, grassy rays springing from tall stems, it can be a true show-stopper in a bog garden.

Also known as umbrella plant, King Tut's grass, papyrus sedge, paper reed, Indian matting plant, or bulrush, papyrus was one of the most important plants in ancient Egypt, used to produce paper, woven goods, food, and fragrance. Although sometimes referred to as Nile grass, papyrus is actually an aquatic reed, or sedge. These plants could possibly be the iconic "rushes" in which the infant Moses was found by the pharaoh's sister in the Bible story.

Today, this perennial is a popular landscape plant, particularly for water gardening. It's part of the genus Cyperus—representing more than 600 plants around the world—and is native to Africa and Madagascar. Although it is a graceful plant with tall, reedy, clumping stems, they are topped by somewhat comical, oversized, umbrella-like grassy rays. There is no denying its drama, however; a large urn of papyrus can stand alone as a focal point, and groupings can be used to effect in a mixed border.

GROWING PAPYRUS

Fast-growing papyrus is easy to cultivate. Although it will handle partial shade, it prefers full sun. The rhizomes are usually planted in pots filled with fertile soil that are then submerged in water. This makes papyrus an excellent candidate for a pond or naturalized bog. Papyrus will grow from either seed or division. Alas, the seeds do not readily germinate and can take a month or more to sprout, even in their native habitat.

SCIENTIFIC NAME: *Cyperus papyrus*

FAMILY: Cyperaceae

HEIGHT: 5 to 8 feet (1.5–2.4 m)

WIDTH: 2 to 4 feet (60 cm–1.2 m)

FOLIAGE COLOR: Green

SOIL pH: Slightly acidic to alkaline

LIGHT: Full sun to partial shade

CARING FOR THE PLANTS

Prune only to remove broken stems. A balanced fertilizer applied in spring will support growth of the huge stems. In most zones, papyrus is an annual or half-hardy perennial. It has no frost tolerance, so move it indoors for the winter. It has no damaging pests or diseases, except rust fungus, which can discolor the stems and foliage.

You can divide plants in spring. After the danger of frost has passed, unpot or dig up the plant, and cut the rhizomes into groups of two or three. Re-pot the new plants and grow them as usual or give them away.

The Bog Garden

If there is a wet or swampy area in your yard, consider creating a bog. This is an ideal place to grow semi-aquatic plants and establish a unique habitat that will attract beneficial insects, songbirds, hummingbirds, chipmunks, frogs, toads, salamanders, and even small reptiles. Or you can create an artificial bog by digging out a 2-foot (60 cm) pond, lining it, adding drainage holes 1-foot (30 cm) down, and then filling it with 30 percent coarse sand and 70 percent peat moss, compost, and native soil. Make sure it gets enough water to keep it . . . well, boggy. Plants that will flourish here include papyrus, flag iris, reeds, sedges, heather, turtle-head, jack-in-the-pulpit, and blue-eyed grass, as well as carnivorous species like Venus flytrap and pitcher plant.

Sweet Potato Vine

SCIENTIFIC NAME: *Ipomoea batatas*

FAMILY: Convolvulaceae

HEIGHT: 8 to 10 feet (2.4–3 m)

WIDTH: 6 to 12 inches (15–30 cm)

FOLIAGE COLOR: Chartreuse, gold, bronze, brown, red, purple, and nearly black

SOIL pH: Neutral to acidic

LIGHT: Full sun

Two varieties of ornamental sweet potato, one in chartreuse and the other in a purplish green-black, make a stylish display as they spill over the edges of terra-cotta pots.

Ornamental sweet potato vines, with their delicate cascading tendrils, are the ideal "spiller" plants, perfect for raised beds or container gardening. These fast-growing tender herbaceous perennials are native to tropical regions of the Americas and are cultivars of the same species as edible sweet potatoes. The ornamental varieties are too bitter to eat, however, and so are grown strictly for show. The leaves range in color from almost black to purple, bronze, and copper to bright chartreuse and display several different shapes. The small flowers are typically a deep pink.

These vines are also popular as houseplants and can be grown inside year-round or just during the cold-weather months. They are sure to add something extra to the home or patio. Like many rooting vines, sweet potatoes can be vigorous growers in the right conditions and might need frequent trimming to stay in check. Their toughness and drought tolerance make them great choices for mixed containers and hanging baskets. Or grow them as an annual ground cover in landscaped areas or flower beds. In containers they complement coleus, cordyline (especially purple varieties of the vine), and annual geranium, a classic pairing.

GROWING SWEET POTATO VINE

Ornamental sweet potato vines are easily propagated from either small rooted pieces from the eye buds of the tuber or by stem cuttings—so there are no plant seeds to fuss over as with their morning glory cousins. Place your sweet potato tuber in a glass of water, keeping the top third exposed by securing it in place with toothpicks. You can also place stem cuttings in water: rooting will then take place within a few weeks. The young vines are best planted outdoors in the spring once temperatures consistently stay about 50° F (10° C).

CARING FOR THE PLANTS

These ornamental vines enjoy a bright, sunny location outdoors, and they thrive in heat. Yet, they will also grow in partial shade and sometimes even in full shade. The more sun the plant gets, however, the more vibrant the leaf coloration will be.

They are prone to root rot, so give the plants well-draining soil whether you grow them in pots or in the ground. In containers, make sure there are adequate drainage holes. Although they are tolerant of drought, sweet potato vines prefer to be kept moist but not soggy. They are prolific growers, but if you want to fertilize them monthly, use a general all-purpose, water-soluble fertilizer.

Overgrown or leggy plants should be cut back to encourage bushier growth and to keep them under control. New plants can be started with these cuttings, giving you an endless supply year-round.

Editor's Picks

The are many varieties of ornamental sweet potato vine. Below are a few of the more popular cultivars you can choose from.

- **'Sweet Carolina Purple' features dark purple foliage and smaller tubers. A less-vigorous grower, it is suitable for small containers.**
- **'Blackie' features black foliage with deeply cut leaves.**
- **'Marguerite' has bold chartreuse green foliage with pretty heart-shaped leaves.**
- **'Tricolor' is a less-vigorous grower with small pointy leaves that are variegated in shades of green, pink, and white.**

A GALLERY OF
GROUND COVERS

Ground cover plants are valuable members of the landscape. They are often underappreciated, but they can provide color and interest to areas that may otherwise be dull or difficult to plant. Many will thrive under trees where few other plants will grow. They can also act as low-maintenance weed barriers, stabilize soil, fill in gaps between stepping stones, and provide a habitat for our pollinator friends. Flowering ground covers provide all of the above-mentioned benefits, along with added color from their blooms. Even when not in flower, many are evergreen and provide interest year-round.

ASIAN STAR JASMINE
Asian star jasmine *(Trachelospermum asiaticum)* is a vigorous twining vine with small, fragrant, creamy yellow flowers. Use this quick grower in the front of a border or as coverage on banks and slopes. It will also climb upward if given strong support.

BARRENWORT
Not only does barrenwort *(Epimedium)* have pretty heart-shaped flowers that float above the foliage, but it also has the ability to grow and thrive under the canopy of large shade trees, which makes it a superior ground cover.

BLUE STAR CREEPER
Blue star creeper *(Isotoma fluviatilis)* is a fast-growing ground cover for areas with foot traffic. It produces blue, star-shaped blooms in spring and early summer. Be careful to plant where its rambunctious nature won't be a problem.

BUGLEWEED
Ajuga reptans, also known as carpet bugleweed or just bugleweed, is a creeping evergreen shrub that quickly fills in empty areas, smothering out weeds and controlling erosion while adding exceptional foliage color and blooms.

BUNCHBERRY
Bunchberry *(Cornus canadensis)* is a good choice to edge a shady garden, for naturalized areas, or to plant beneath shrubs and trees. The deeply veined, rich green leaves are accented by showy Dogwood-type white flowers in late spring.

CATMINT
Catmint *(Nepeta)* is a good choice if you are looking for season-long blooms and aromatic foliage. This short, clumping perennial blooms most of the summer with superior deer and rabbit resistance, and it is also drought-tolerant.

Dig Deeper
READ MORE AT GARDENING KNOW HOW

Find out what makes the list as the top flowering ground covers by scanning the QR code or following the link below. You can also learn more about how to use ground covers by following the other links.

- "Top 10 Flowering Ground Covers" (URL = gkh.us/176160)
- "Part Sun and Shade Ground Cover for Every Garden" (URL = gkh.us/186151)
- "Planting Between Pavers — Using Ground Covers Around Pavers" (URL = gkh.us/80139)

CREEPING JUNIPER
The graceful, aromatic creeping juniper *(Juniperus horizontalis)* spreads to fill sunny areas, and it can be used as a foundation plant or accent in a flower border. The blue-green foliage will take on a plum-colored tint in winter.

DRAGON'S BLOOD STONECROP
Sedum spurium 'Dragon's Blood' is an attractive ground cover, spreading quickly in a sunny landscape. It awakens from dormancy in spring with green leaves and red flowers to follow.

DWARF MONDO GRASS
Dwarf mondo grass *(Ophiopogon japonicus)* is a good choice for full or partial shade, and it is one of the few plants you can grow near black walnuts. The varieties for planting between pavers grow only an inch or two (2.5–5 cm) tall and spread readily.

FORGET-ME-NOT
The perennial forget-me-not *(Myosotis)* spreads easily, freely self-seeding for more of the wildflower to grow and bloom in shady spots where the tiny seeds may fall. It grows best in a damp, shady area, but it can adapt to full sun.

IRISH MOSS
Irish moss *(Sagina subulata)* adds soft, spongy texture to paths in shady areas. Only a couple of inches tall, it doesn't create an obstruction. It's usually sold in flats like sod, which you can just cut to fit and lay where you want it to grow.

LILY-OF-THE-VALLEY
Lily-of-the-valley *(Convallaria)* is one of the most fragrant blooming plants in the spring and early summer. Its bell-like flowers peek from long green leaves, making a naturalistic ground cover that provides a carpet of sweet-scented beauty.

LILYTURF
Lilyturf *(Liriope muscari)* is a short clumping ornamental grass with wide, dark green strappy leaves and purple flowers that almost resemble grape hyacinths in late summer. It is perfect along paths and walkways or planted en masse in landscape beds.

PACHYSANDRA
Pachysandra is a favorite ground cover for hard-to-plant areas, such as under trees or in shady areas with poor or acidic soil. There are several varieties of pachysandra available to choose from, but be aware that many of these can be invasive.

PERENNIAL PEANUT
This isn't your average peanut. Instead, perennial peanut *(Arachis glabrata)* provides optimal ground cover in well-draining sites with full sun. Also called ornamental peanut, it is a high-quality forage plant, and it is also used for soil conservation.

SPOTTED DEADNETTLE
Spotted deadnettle *(Lamium maculatum)*, a shade-thriving plant with a wide range of soil and condition tolerance, grows as a spreading mat of herbaceous stems and leaves. Its small, speckled leaves gives the plant its name.

SWEET WOODRUFF
An often forgotten herb, sweet woodruff *(Galium odoratum)* can be a valuable addition to the garden. With its star-shaped whorls of leaves and lacy white flowers, it can add texture and spark to a deeply shaded part of the garden.

WILD VIOLET
Wild violet *(Viola odorata)* has heart-shaped leaves with purple-blue, white, or yellow flowers. It makes excellent instant ground cover in a woodland garden, but it will pop up unchecked if not controlled with some type of barrier.

Invasive Ground Covers

Although the chief purpose of ground covers is to spread out to fill an empty area of a garden or lawn, many can become invasive and quickly overflow their allotted space. Among the most invasive species are those listed below. If you have a choice, pick a cover that is less tenacious. If you do choose a potentially invasive species, check with your state extension before planting.

- Artichoke thistle
- Bishop's weed
- Bugleweed *(Ajuga)*
- Chameleon plant
- Creeping phlox
- Creeping thyme
- Cushion spurge
- English ivy
- German ivy
- Japanese pachysandra
- Mexican evening primrose
- Myrtle
- Periwinkle *(Vinca minor)*
- Stringy stonecrop

SUCCULENTS AND CACTI

Succulents and cacti, which are classified as succulents, have become true garden stars in the past few years. Suddenly, the appeal of designing a planting bed using textures and shapes seems to be equaling—or in some cases surpassing—the attraction of the classic flower garden.

SUCCULENTS

Botanically speaking, succulents are plants with parts that are thickened, fleshy, and engorged, usually to retain water in arid climates or soil conditions. These water-preserving plants are often found in habitats with high temperatures and low rainfall, such as deserts. Succulents can thrive on limited water sources, but they have also evolved other ways to survive dry terrain: a reduced number of stoma, or pores; waxy, spiny, or hairy surfaces that create a humid micro-habitat around the plant; an impervious outer skin; roots near the soil surface to collect even minute amounts of water; and stems as the main site of photosynthesis, rather than fragile leaves.

CACTI

Cacti appeal to gardeners, especially beginners, because they are so low-maintenance, offer such interesting contours, blend so well with one another, as well as with flowering plants, and are perfect specimens for xeriscaping. They are forgiving of neglect, adaptable to different climates, and will reward you with a "little touch of the desert" even in suburban or urban spaces.

Desert-inspired plantings featuring a variety of succulent and cactus species enliven a poolside garden created for a hot climate.

Dig Deeper

READ MORE AT GARDENING KNOW HOW

To learn more about succulents and cacti and to get suggestions about how you can incorporate them into your own garden, follow these links.

- **"Succulent Plant Info: Learn About Types of Succulents and How They Grow"** (URL = gkh.us/83147)
- **"A Succulent Garden Outside — How to Plant an Outdoor Succulent Garden"** (URL = gkh.us/14866)
- **"Exotic Showstoppers: Beautiful Succulents** (URL = gkh.us/129)
- **"Cactus Landscaping — Types of Cactus for the Garden** (URL = gkh.us/1661)
- **"Cacti for Beginners: Easy Cactus Varieties** (URL = gkh.us/150372)
- **"Xerophytic Garden Design: How to Use Xerophyte Desert Plants in the Landscape** (URL = gkh.us/50385)

From a gardener's viewpoint, succulents offer a fantasy of unusual geometric shapes, plump or fingerlike leaves, and rope-like tendrils, and a rainbow range of deep or pastel colors. Some produce surprisingly lush flowers.

Aeonium

SCIENTIFIC NAME: *Aeonium* spp.

FAMILY: Crassulaceae

HEIGHT: 2 inches to 5 feet (5 cm–1.5 m)

WIDTH: Variable

FOLIAGE COLOR: Various shades of green, purplish black; variegated white, red, yellow, and green

SOIL pH: Slightly acidic

LIGHT: Full sun to partial shade

***Aeonium arboreum,* also called tree houseleek and Irish rose, displays it waxy rosettes atop thick, branching netlike-patterned stems. The rosettes can be a solid color or variegated, making striking additions to rock and Mediterranean-themed gardens.**

The Aeonium genus includes about 35 succulent species. They are known for their glossy, waxy, fleshy leaves that grow in rosettes, a signature formation so precise that live plants are often mistaken for artificial specimens. Less notable are the clusters of small, star-shaped flowers. Aeoniums are native to the Canary Islands and Africa and are found in solid and variegated colors of white, red, yellow, and green and in varying heights and widths.

These plants look especially good when part of a cactus or succulent display. Consider combining them with aloe vera, agave cactus, or jade plants. An outdoor succulent garden could feature plants in the ground, those in containers, or a combination of both.

GROWING AEONIUMS

In warm areas with relatively few freezes, aeoniums are easy to grow. In regions with colder winters, they can be brought indoors and placed on a sunny windowsill. They prefer temperatures between 40 and 100° F (4–38° C). Like other succulents, aeoniums have evolved a special adaptive survival strategy for growing in hot, dry locations—fleshy leaves for storing moisture. Unlike many other succulents, however, aeoniums have shallow root systems and cannot be allowed to dry out completely. Only the top few inches (8 cm) of soil should be allowed to dry.

Aeoniums grow best in shallow pots that contain a mixture of cactus soil and peat that drains well. It helps to place a thin layer of inorganic mulch, such as ornamental rock or lava chips, around the base of your plants.

In cooler temperate zones, frost may kill the foliage and the rosette will fall off. If the plant is mulched, however, it may regrow in spring. Aeoniums can also be started from cuttings. Just snip off one rosette, and let the cut end dry out for a few days. Then set it in lightly moist peat moss. The piece will quickly root and produce a new plant.

CARING FOR THE PLANTS

Aeonium care is remarkably easy. Plants in containers require more frequent watering than those in the ground. Fertilize these once annually in spring when new growth commences. In-ground plants rarely need fertilizer. If applying mulch, be careful not to pile it up around the stem or rot might set in.

The most common problems are root rot and insect pests. Root rot is prevented by using clay pots with good drainage or checking soil percolation prior to planting. Keep the roots moist but never soggy. Good care also requires watching for mites and scale that may attack your plants. These can be combated with horticultural soaps or applications of neem oil. Be careful of overspraying, which can cause discoloration and lesions on the skin of your plant.

Aeonium Species

Aeonium species range in size from tiny, low-growing plants to ones that span several feet.

- ***A. arboreum,*** is a tall, branching variety that can reach 78 inches (2 m).
- ***A. holochrysum*** has bright green leaves with brown markings in rosettes that grow to about 4 inches (10 cm) in diameter.
- ***A. smithii*** branches to form a small shrub up to 2 feet (60 cm) with circles of rosettes with purple or brown dashes.
- ***A. tabuliforme,*** the flat-topped aeonium or saucer plant, only grows about 2 inches (5 cm) high, but can spread up to 18 inches (45 cm) in diameter.
- ***A. valverdense,*** has striking green rosettes with orange-pink-red coloring.

Agave

Sharp-pointed agave plants take center stage in a natural-style desert garden. Agaves are versatile plants that work well in a variety of climates and landscapes.

SCIENTIFIC NAME: *Agave* spp.

FAMILY: Asparagaceae

HEIGHT: 1 to 20 feet (30 cm–6 m)

WIDTH: 1 to 10 feet (30 cm–3 m)

FOLIAGE COLOR: Blue-green to gray-green; variegated green, white, or gold

SOIL pH: Acidic, neutral

LIGHT: Full sun

Agaves are dramatic succulents found in many types of landscaping and are known for their large, rosette-forming leaves that end in spiny tips. They are part of the Agavaceae family, along with dracaena, yucca, and ponytail palm. The *Agave* genus, which includes 270 species and a number of natural hybrids, offers a lot of variety. There are large, stiff specimens that can grow to 10 feet (3 m) or more, as well as small, dish-sized agaves. There are even a few with uncharacteristically soft leaves and no spines. Agave foliage tends toward a blue-green in hardier varieties and gray-green in the warm-climate varieties. Some are variegated with gold or white markings.

Many agaves are native to North America, Central America, and South America, and a number are adaptable to the colder climates of the Pacific Northwest and Canada. Almost every climate is capable of supporting agave—some are hardy down to single digits for short periods of time and with sufficient shelter.

Once in its lifetime, the plant produces a flower spire, displaying long-lasting, cup-shaped blossoms of white, yellow, or green. An agave in bloom can be quite the traffic stopper! Sadly, for most agave species, once the flowers produce berry seed pods, the plant dies, leaving behind its pups (offsets).

The century plant, one of the most noteworthy landscape agaves, produces a lovely inflorescence (flower). The warm-season American agave, or American aloe, has a white stripe running down the center of the leaves. Some other garden favorites include *A. parryi, A. ocahui, A. macroacantha,* and *A. gigantensis.*

GROWING AGAVES

This plant is drought tolerant and perennial, making it ideal for the arid garden. It's usually best to plant this slow-growing succulent in the spring or early autumn. Agaves have a large taproot and do not transplant well, so choose a permanent site before planting. Agaves need full sun and gritty soil that percolates easily. If planting in condensed soil or heavy clay, amend half the soil with sand or grit.

Diligently water the plant for the first week, and then cut it to half the amount of water the second week. Taper off until you are only watering once every week or two. The plants should be allowed to dry out before irrigation.

In spring, a granulated time-release fertilizer will provide nutrients for the season. After establishment, your "neglected" agave will be quite happy.

AGAVE PLANTS IN CONTAINERS

Agaves grown in unglazed pots require even more grit or pebbles in the soil and can actually be planted in a cactus potting mix. They will require more water than those in the ground and will need to be repotted every year to replenish the soil and prune the roots. Just remember to bring sensitive forms indoors when temperatures start to drop.

Note: The sap of the agave is toxic to both people and pets.

For agave varieties in which the parent plant doesn't die after flowering, use long-handled pruners to remove the tough spent bloom.

Aloe Vera

A row of aloe vera looks stunning in a patio container. Be sure to bring your aloes indoors if you live in a cool climate; these tropical succulents need warmth to survive.

Commonly grown as a houseplant, aloe vera is known for the soothing gel contained in its leaves, which is used on sunburns and other skin irritations. There are more than 300 species of aloe, the most common being *Aloe barbadensis* Miller. This tropical succulent originated in Africa; it features fleshy lance-shaped leaves with jagged edges that grow out from a basal rosette. Given the proper growing conditions, spiky flowers will appear on the end of stalks in shades of yellow, red, or orange. Young plants don't generally flower, and aloe grown as a houseplant can take years to produce flower stalks. Still, this fast-growing succulent will reach its mature size in three to four years and produces pups that can be repotted or given as gifts to other plant lovers. Easy peasy.

Although most people display these plants in their homes, there is no reason they cannot become happy outdoor campers during the warm months. Just make sure the chance of frost is over and your nighttime temperatures are well above freezing before leaving them outside. Aloes can travel to the garden or deck in their regular pot or container and make the journey back inside in the autumn.

GROWING ALOE VERA

Humans have been cultivating aloe vera plants for literally thousands of years. It is also one of the most widespread medicinal plants on the planet, formerly used in ancient Greece, Egypt, India, Mexico, Japan, and China. Egyptian queens Nefertiti and Cleopatra used it in their beauty regimens, while Alexander the Great and Christopher Columbus applied it to soldiers' wounds.

Aloes are succulents, and, like cacti, these plants do best in dry conditions. They should be planted in a cactus potting mix or regular potting soil amended with perlite or builder's sand. This step is to ensure good drainage. Also, make sure that the pot has plenty of drainage holes. Aloe vera cannot tolerate standing in water. Because they need bright light, they do best in south- or west-facing windows. To water them properly, wait until the soil is completely dry before supplying hydration. Drench the soil, but make sure it all drains freely. Most aloes die from overwatering or poor drainage.

If you decide to fertilize your aloe vera plant—which probably does not need it—do so once a year in spring. Use a phosphorus-heavy, water-based product at half strength.

Growing aloe vera is not only easy but can also provide your family with a plant that helps treat minor burns and skin rashes.

Note: Consuming the leaves of aloe is toxic for people, dogs, and cats.

SCIENTIFIC NAME: *Aloe* spp.

FAMILY: Asphodelaceae

HEIGHT: 12 to 36 inches (30 cm–1 m)

WIDTH: 6 to 12 inches (15–30 cm)

FOLIAGE COLOR: Vibrant green to grayish blue-green

SOIL pH: Acidic

LIGHT: Full to partial sun

READ MORE AT GARDENING KNOW HOW

Learn about the many kinds of aloe and how you can use them.

- **"Aloe Plant Types — Growing Different Aloe Varieties"** (URL = gkh.us/124663)
- **"Ways to Use Aloe: Surprising Aloe Plant Uses"** (URL = gkh.us/153385)
- **"Growing Plants for Cosmetics: Learn How to Grow a Beauty Garden"** (URL = gkh.us/101217)

GARDENING WITH CACTUS

Cacti make outstanding landscaping plants—they require little maintenance, thrive in a variety of climates, and are easy to care for and grow. Most will even tolerate neglect. These plants are also well adapted to containers. Cacti vary in size, color, shape, and growing habits. They may soar skyward in upright columns, spread in treelike clumps, or form compact spiny balls. They might cascade over large rocks or dangle in hanging baskets. Some varieties also produce stunning flowers. In spite of their desert origins, many will thrive in a number of growing conditions. This versatility makes cactus cultivation possible nearly anywhere.

Cacti are members of the Cactaceae family, which includes some 127 genera. The name derives from the ancient Greek, *kaktos*, meaning "spiny plant." Cacti evolved around 25 million years ago in the Western Hemisphere, possibly when uplifting in the Andes Mountains created areas of great aridity.

IDENTIFYING CACTUS

While all cacti are considered succulents, there are many succulents that are not cacti. Fortunately, a number of features can help you separate these two closely related plants.

- Cactus plants generally have few or no leaves.
- Cacti are distinguished from other succulents by the rounded indentations along their stems, which are modified buds called "areoles." From these spring the sharp spines (usually) for which cacti are best known.
- A wide variety of non-cactus succulents are native to different regions across the world. By contrast, almost all types of cacti are native only to the New World.

GROWING CACTUS OUTDOORS

Whenever possible, choose a sunny, sloped location for cacti to allow for better drainage, which is vital for these desert plants. Depending on the type of cacti, beds should be about 6 to 12 inches (15–30 cm) deep with well-drained soil specifically meant for cactus. This can be purchased or mixed yourself using two parts potting soil, two parts sand, and one part gravel. Cacti also enjoy a moderate layer of mulch such as pebbles, rocks, or similar inorganic substance. Once established, cacti require little maintenance and very little, if any, water.

Cacti that are popular for landscaping include the species shown on this page and the next.

BARREL CACTUS

The two genera, *Echinocactus*, with a fuzzy crown of fine spines, and ferocactus, with ferocious thorns, both resemble spine-covered barrels. They thrive in arid, sunny gardens and may be low and squat or reach 10 feet (3 m) in height. Barrel cacti aid lost desert travelers because they grow tilted to the southwest.

CANDELABRA CACTUS

Tall, branching *Myrtillocactus cochal* grows on hillsides, so planting on slopes gives it a natural look. It also works in xeriscape and rock gardens. It can reach 10 feet (3 m) tall and wide, with white, cup-shaped flowers that open by day and close at night. Always supply extra water during hot spells.

CHOLLA CACTUS

Part of the *Opuntia* genus, this jointed plant with thin, round stems and wicked spines makes an interesting landscaping option. There are more than 20 species, and the plants may be creepers, shrubs, or trees. Heights vary from 3 feet (1 m) to 15 feet (5 m). The flowers are green or orange.

CLARET CUP CACTUS

Echinocereus triglochidiatus, also called hedgehog, Mojave mound, and kingcup cactus, can reach 3 feet (1 m) high and 6 feet (1.8 m) wide. The juicy fruit tastes like strawberries and turns bright orange as it ripens. Consider blending claret cup with sage, poppies, yucca, penstemon, and native grasses.

CHRISTMAS CACTUS

Also known as Easter or crab cactus (*Schlumbergera* spp.), this native of Brazil loves bright, indirect light. The flat, leafless, segmented stems produce exotic blossoms in pink, red, or white. It is often grown indoors, as well as in warm-climate gardens. Temperate-zone gardeners should bring it inside in autumn.

GOLDEN BALL CACTUS

Parodia leninghausii (or *Notocactus leninghausii*) also goes by lemon ball cactus or yellow tower and rarely exceeds 3 feet (1 m). It starts out globular, then becomes more columnar; it also forms in clusters and is a smart choice for fire-resistant landscaping. It welcomes some shade during the hottest hours of the day.

MEXICAN FENCE POST

Lophocereus marginatus can reach 16 feet (4.8 m) in height, with stems 3 to 8 inches (7.5–20 cm) in diameter. It blooms in mid-to-late spring, with the blossoms evident along the ribs and down its sides. It appreciates frequent watering during hot spells. In warmer regions it is used as a living fence.

OLD MAN CACTUS

Cephalocereus senilis, often called Cousin It—after the *The Addams Family* TV show character, is identified by tall, columnar, or branching growth covered in long, woolly hair. It can reach heights of up to 40 feet (12 m), and its side stems will produce night blooms after it reaches 20 feet (6 m).

ORGAN PIPE CACTUS

Lemaireocereus thurberi, or pitayo dulce, grows in clusters that look similar to organ pipes or sausage links. These plants require sun and winter temperatures above freezing. They grow up to 30 feet (9 m) high with clumps equally wide. The spring flowers bloom at night and close at dawn.

PEANUT CACTUS

Echinopsis chamaecereus is a branched cactus with fingerlike stems that has a clustering and trailing habit. Low-growing and cylindrical, it reaches about 1 foot (30 cm) high. Its vase-shaped blooms appear from spring through summer. It grows well in rock gardens and xeriscapes.

PINCUSHION CACTUS

This drought-resistant cactus has tiny spines projecting from its ball-like shape. Small and squat, it rarely tops more than 6 inches (15 cm). Other members of the *Mammillaria* genus, which contains more than 200 species, also sport colorful names—crawling log, old lady, powder puff, and snowball cushion.

PRICKLY PEAR CACTUS

This drought-tolerant *Opuntia* has broad, flat, prickly stems, with tips that turn coral in bright sun. Ideal for the hottest garden spots, it bears fruit and large yellow or orange flowers. Heights range from a foot (30 cm) to 18 feet (5.5 m). Varieties include beavertail, bunny ears, cow's tongue, and the treelike Indian fig.

QUEEN OF THE NIGHT

Epiphyllum oxypetalum, also called Dutchman's pipe, orchid cactus, or princess of the night, rarely blooms and only at night; its flowers wilt before dawn. This profusely branched cactus can grow to 10 feet (3 m) in height and sometimes uses other plants for support. It does best in diffused sunlight.

SAGUARO

Carnegiea gigantea is a species of large, treelike cacti well known to fans of Western movies. Appearing like spiny swords stuck in the ground, they can be grown both indoors and outdoors. They require patience, however, as they usually take between 20 and 50 years to reach only 3 feet (1 m) in height.

SILVER TORCH CACTUS

Cleistocactus strausii, called silver torch of woolly torch cactus, grows in slender, clustering columns up to 8 feet (2.4 m) tall with long, tubular, blooms in deep red that protrude horizontally from columns. This gray-green cactus likes full sun and well-draining soil and looks good with lime or plum-colored succulents.

STAR CACTUS

Also called sand dollar, sea urchin, and star peyote cactus, *Astrophytum asterias* is small, round, and spineless, reaching 2 inches (5 cm) in height with a diameter of 2 to 6 inches (5–15 cm). The 7 to 10 ribbed segments contain rows of woolly aureoles. Often grown as a houseplant, this cactus produces a yellow flower.

STRAWBERRY HEDGEHOG CACTUS

This *Echinocereus* goes by strawberry cactus, saint's cactus, purple torch, or Engelmann's hedgehog cactus. It is small, with free-branching clusters or mounds of erect stems and a surplus of ornamental spines. It grows to about 28 inches (71 cm) tall and tolerates light shade.

TOTEM POLE CACTUS

Pachycereus schottii monstrosus is notable for its knobby limbs, which look quite sculptural in the right garden setting. Unlike most columnar cacti, the tall totem pole has neither spines nor ribs. It can reach impressive heights of 10 to 12 feet (3–3.7 m) and a width of 3 to 6 feet (1–1.8 m).

Echeveria

A grouping of echeveria shows the diversity of the rosette shapes and some of the many color varieties available. This succulent looks great planted en masse.

Low-maintenance echeverias are now one of the most popular succulents. Their distinct rosette shapes, plump leaves, and range of colors make them natural choices for succulent gardens, floral arrangements, terrariums, rock gardens, and even as wedding cake decorations. They are members of the Crassulaceae or stonecrop family, a diverse group of flowering plants characterized by succulent leaves, as well as a unique form of photosynthesis known as Crassulacean acid metabolism.

These plants form thick-leaved rosettes; the leaves are fleshy and have a waxy cuticle on the exterior. The leaves are often colored, and a firm touch can mar the skin and leave marks. The echeveria is slow growing and usually doesn't exceed a foot (30 cm) in height or spread. There are 150 cultivated varieties, making it easy to find just the right ones for your garden.

GROWING ECHEVERIAS

These plants are found from Texas south to Central America, and the domestic versions still prefer desert conditions. Yet, they will tolerate periods of moisture as long as they are allowed to dry out between waterings. If they are grown in unglazed clay pots, the water is able to evaporate. Otherwise, they need full sun and well-drained soil.

Succulent plants are easy for gardeners to love. Their simple care, sunny dispositions, and moderate growth habits make them perfect for warm seasons outdoors or well-lit home interiors. They thrive on brief periods of neglect, along with low water and nutrients.

They often produce offsets—baby plants—that nestle against the mother rosette. These offspring are easy to separate and grow. Just pull the little rosette away and replant in cactus potting mixture or a homemade blend of sand, topsoil, and compost. You can also start new plants from leaf cuttings. Place the leaf on the surface of the soil, and it will root within a few weeks. Soon a small rosette will appear next to the rooted leaf, which will dry up and crumble away.

The many varieties and colors of echeverias can provide wonderful tones and texture for mixed beds, succulent walls, and container arrangements. The sheer visual diversity of these plants means they lend themselves well to group displays, especially when mixed with other succulents and cacti. You can opt for contrasting or complementary plantings. Place the larger varieties in the center and the trailing or lower types at the edges.

SCIENTIFIC NAME: *Echeveria* spp.

FAMILY: Crassulaceae

HEIGHT: Maximum 12 inches (30 cm)

WIDTH: Maximum 12 inches (30 cm)

FOLIAGE COLOR: Blue-gray or gray-green; variegated green and purple

SOIL pH: Acidic

LIGHT: Bright, direct sun

CARING FOR THE PLANTS

The biggest issue is overwatering. Provide moderate amounts of water in the hot, dry season, and then let the soil dry out completely before you irrigate again. Potted plants should not be left in a wet saucer or soft rot or root issues may occur.

The only other problem of real concern is mealybugs, whose feeding behavior can seriously deplete the plants' vigor. T prevent weeds and conserve moisture, situate the plants in full sun and mulch around them. You may sometimes need to pinch off damaged or errant growth.

Learn more about just a few varieties of these lovely plants.

- **"Echeveria 'Lola' Info: Learn How to Care for a Lola Echeveria** (URL = gkh.us/127044)
- **"Care of Peacock Echeveria — Tips for Growing Peacock Echeveria** (URL = gkh.us/127056)
- **"Echeveria Pallida Plant Info: Growing Argentine Echeveria Succulents** (URL = gkh.us/135435)
- **"Painted Lady Echeveria: Tips for Growing a Painted Lady Plant Echeveria** (URL = gkh.us/124397)

Euphorbia

Massed *Euphorbia resinifera,* the resin spurge, decorates a rock garden. It is just one of the thousands of *Euphorbia* species. Its erect succulent stems have the appearance of spiny cactus and emit a thick, milky white sap known as latex when cut or damaged.

Euphorbia is a very large and diverse genus with more than 2,000 species. About 1,200 of them are succulents, some featuring bizarre shapes and wide, fleshy leaves; other examples look like cacti, including the spines. Members of this rather confusing genus, commonly referred to as spurge, can be annual, perennial, or biennial, as well as herbaceous plants or woody shrubs, and either deciduous or evergreen. One of the only things they have in common is a milky white sap that can be irritating to skin and eyes. Most varieties also produce weird and unusual flowers.

The euphorbias used as landscape elements or as houseplants are mainly succulents; many feature interesting shapes and foliage, such as the crown of thorns (*E. milii,* shown at right). A few are known for their floral displays, with that holiday staple, the poinsettia, being the most popular. Euphorbias occur naturally in many parts of the world, including Africa, Asia, Europe, and North and South America. This means a number of garden varieties are hardy in temperate climates.

These plants are almost impossible to kill, making them e a perfect choice for the novice gardener. Growing euphorbia is also a great propagation project for children, providing them a plant to share with a teacher or friend. Whether you want a giant thornless cactus-like specimen that tops 6 feet (1.8 m) tall or a creeping, sweetly flowering ground cover, consider adding euphorbia to your garden.

GROWING EUPHORBIAS

These succulents are easy to start from seeds- tr sowing them indoors in pots—or to propagate from cuttings. You can root stem cuttings in a pot filled with soil-less medium, such as peat. Mist them thoroughly, and enclose the pot in a zip-lock or other resealable bag to keep moisture in. Let the plants breathe once a day for an hour, so the soil does not become moldy. Once the cuttings have rooted, fill the container with regular soil or plant them outdoors in moderate climates. You can also propagate euphorbia by gathering up the "volunteers" around an established plant.

SCIENTIFIC NAME: *Euphorbia* spp.

FAMILY: Euphorbiaceae

HEIGHT: 6 to 36 inches (15 cm–1 m)

WIDTH: 6 to 36 inches (15 cm–1 m)

FOLIAGE COLOR: Various greens

SOIL pH: Neutral, acidic

LIGHT: Full sun

CARING FOR THE PLANTS

As a general rule, these plants require well-drained soil in full sun. A few tolerate shadier conditions, but none of the family is fussy about soil conditions. They even thrive in very poor soils and can tolerate periods of drought. Provide them light, moderate moisture, and watch for annoying pests like whitefly. Always water them under the plant's leaves to prevent powdery mildew. You will not need to fertilize them often—wait until the bottom leaves become yellow before supplying a water-soluble plant food. Prune only if the plant gets out of hand.

Note: Gardeners should be cautious when handling spurge, as the milky latex sap can be irritating or even poisonous to humans and pets.

When propagating new plants from cuttings, allow the stem to dry out for a few days before planting. This allows the sap to form a callus on the cut end and prevents rotting.

Haworthia

Haworthia fasciata, or the zebra plant, is just one of the fascinating forms of haworthia.

SCIENTIFIC NAME: *Haworthia* spp.

FAMILY: Asphodelaceae

HEIGHT: 3 to 20 inches (7.5–50 cm)

WIDTH: 3 to 5 inches (7.5–12.5 cm)

FOLIAGE COLOR: Various greens, red, and brown to nearly black

SOIL pH: Neutral

LIGHT: Full to partial sun

Known by names, depending on species, the haworthia has fat, juicy, translucent leaves and rich green interiors. Not all haworthia plants have the see-through leaves, however, but those that do are truly fascinating. All of these low-maintenance, hardy little succulents are easy to grow, and their care is similar to that of their cousins, the aloes.

For a very long time, plants of the *Haworthia* genus were placed in the large lily family, Liliaceae. But in the early 1800s a more thorough investigation of plant genera took place, and *Haworthia* was reassigned to the Asphodelcaceae family, which also includes the aloes.

These tiny succulents, native to southern Africa, come in many forms. In most, the leaves grow in rosettes from 1 to 12 inches (2.5–30 cm) in diameter. The varieties with see-through foliage usually feature thick triangular pads with an interior like the inside of a green gumdrop. Some species have a white band along the edge of the leaf, others have red tips, and still others are covered with white pearly warts.

No matter the species, haworthia care is minimal. And although they do very well in indoor containers, you can bring them outdoors in summer. Their delightful candy-like appearance becomes a definite inspiration when it's time to put together a grouping of container plants. And under exterior sunlight, it is easier to get a glimpse of their interiors—the luscious flesh that makes up these water-storing succulents.

GROWING HAWORTHIA

If you're lucky enough to live in a warm climate, plant your haworthia outside in full sun where soil is gritty and well-draining. For most gardeners, sadly, this species is limited to indoor growth.

Choose a container that has excellent drainage and use a cactus mix or half potting soil and half grit—sand or perlite. The container should be shallow, as the root system on window-leaved plants is not deep. Place the potted succulent in a bright area with some protection from the hottest rays of the day. Water weekly during the summer or once the top of the soil has dried out. In winter, cut watering back to once a month.

CARING FOR THE PLANTS

Haworthia is susceptible to no notable pests or diseases. When soil is kept too moist, soil gnats may become a problem. Fungal or rot issues also occur in plants that are kept in high humidity, dimly lit rooms, or overwatered. Overwatering is probably the biggest cause of failure to thrive with this plant.

For optimum growth, keep temperatures around 70 to 90° F (21–32° C). Fertilize once in autumn and once again in spring. If your haworthia is really content, you might even get one or two small white flowers. Repot plants every two to three years to keep the root system healthy and the soil at its peak.

Haworthia Species

There are many *Haworthia* species, all of them eye-catching, with unique formations.

- ***H. attenuata,*** known as the zebra plant, with short evergreen leaves in a rosette
- ***H. coarctata,*** with curvy, dark green foliage
- ***H. cooperi,*** or Cooper's haworthia, with glassy, green-tinted marble-like rosettes (shown at left)
- ***H. cymbiformis,*** called the cathedral window haworthia, with tiny pale green, gumdrop-shaped rosettes
- ***H. fasciata,*** also known as the zebra plant, with triangular shaped leaves in white-striped dark green
- ***H. limifolia,*** known as fairy washboard, with a tight spiral of ridged dark to light green, triangular-shaped leaves
- ***H. obtusa*** with plump, compact marble-like leaves
- ***H. retusa,*** called the star cactus, with shiny triangular leaves in a tight rosette
- ***H. truncata,*** known as horse's teeth, with bright green rectangular leaves.

Ice Plant

SCIENTIFIC NAME: *Delosperma* spp.

FAMILY: Aizoaceae

HEIGHT: 3 to 6 inches (7.5–15 cm)

WIDTH: 2 to 4 feet (60 cm–1.2 m)

FOLIAGE COLOR: Deep green to blue-green leaves with brilliant purple, pink, red, yellow, or white flowers

SOIL pH: Neutral

LIGHT: Full sun

The bright purple-pink flowers of *Delosperma cooperi,* or Cooper's ice plant, add to this succulent's appeal. Most succulents are grown for their interesting shapes and textures, but some, such as ice plants and portulaca, are cultivated for their stunning blooms.

If you are seeking a drought-tolerant, attractive flowering plant to fill a difficult spot in your garden, consider the ice plant. This hardy perennial succulent has narrow, fleshy green leaves and bears bright, bristly, daisy-like flowers. The name is not related to any degree of cold hardiness, however, but rather refers to the blooms and leaves, which seem to shimmer as though they were coated in frost or ice crystals. The plants rarely grow above 6 inches (15 cm) in height, but can widen to 4 feet (1.2 cm) or more. In form, they may range from a spreading ground cover to a bushy sub-shrub. Some popular varieties of ice plant *(Delosperma* spp.) include the Cooper's ice plant *(D. cooperi),* the most common variety, which has purple flowers; hardy yellow *(D. brunnthaleri),* which consists of lovely yellow flowers; Starburst *(D. floribundum),* which boasts mauve-rose flowers and a white center; and hardy white *(D. herbeau),* which has white flowers that offer exceptional beauty.

Ice plant foliage is typically evergreen, and because of this they make a great year-round filler, although there may be some die back of foliage in the winter. On the other hand, their vivid flowers will remain in bloom for most of the summer and into autumn. Ice plants typically form dense mats and can be used in sunny but sheltered xeriscapes, in rock gardens, on slopes, or as edging for flowering borders. They also work well as container plants that easily take over the upper space and soon spill merrily over the sides of the pot.

GROWING ICE PLANTS

These plants were originally native to Africa, so they naturally prefer a location with at least six hours of full sun. Sun-starved plants tend to get leggy, with weakened growth. Yet ice plants can also handle some occasional shade. They grow well in poor soil, but, like most succulents, they do not tolerate wet soil. In fact, wet soil, especially during the winter months, is likely to kill the plants. In areas where the soil stays consistently dry, this plant can become invasive, so you need to take that into consideration when deciding where to plant it.

Ice plants can be propagated by division, cuttings, or seeds. If you are propagating by division, it is best to divide the plants in the spring. Cuttings can be taken anytime in the spring, summer, or autumn. When using seeds, scatter them on the surface of the starter tray, but do not cover them, as they need light to germinate. Plants the seedlings 15 to 18 inches (28–45 cm) apart in fast-draining soil, and they will quickly spread to fill the empty spaces. Each spring, prune out any weather-beaten stems.

CARING FOR THE PLANTS

Once they are established, ice plants require little maintenance. As succulents, they need only occasional watering and thrive in drought-like conditions. In addition, these plants need little to no fertilizing. Simply pop your ice plant babies in the ground, and watch them grow!

Jade Plant

SCIENTIFIC NAME: *Crassula ovata*

FAMILY: Crassulaceae

HEIGHT: 3 to 6 feet (1–1.8 m)

WIDTH: 2 to 3 feet (60 cm–1 m)

FOLIAGE COLOR: Emerald green

SOIL pH: Neutral to acidic

LIGHT: Full sun

Jade plants *(Crassula ovata)* make lovely specimens for mixed succulent gardens. These succulents are also popular as potted houseplants because they are so easy to care for.

Crassula is a genus with 350 species, but perhaps the best known is the jade plant. This emerald green plant is also affectionately known as the friendship tree, the lucky plant, or even the money tree, because it is thought to bring good fortune to its owners. That is the reason these plants are often given as housewarming gifts. They are also known to live a long time.

These natives of South Africa are famously easy to grow and hard to kill, which accounts for their popularity. They resemble bonsai, or miniature trees, and many people enjoy displaying them in their homes and offices. Jades have the typical fleshy, oval-shaped leaves of the succulent and thick, woody stems that resemble small tree trunks. And with just a bit of care, your jade plant can grow into a jade tree between 3 and 6 feet (1–1.8 m) tall, but it will do so slowly, growing about 2 inches (5 cm) a year. Because they're typically grown indoors, jades can be brought home or started at any time, either from a commercial nursery or through propagation. They also do well on the deck or patio during the warm months but must come inside when the temperatures start to plummet.

GROWING JADE PLANTS

Plant jades in a commercial cactus mix or regular potting soil amended with perlite. These plants can become top-heavy, however, so be aware that as they mature they might need to be planted in a heavier sand that best anchors their short roots to keep them upright.

After soil, the most important factors to consider are water, light, temperature, and fertilizer. Never let a jade plant dry out completely. Yet, do not water a jade plant too often, because this can cause root rot. Jade plants do not require a watering schedule; simply water them when the top of the soil feels dry to the touch. If your jade plant is losing leaves or has leaf spots, this is most commonly caused by too little water.

Jade plants should be kept in full sun to prevent them from becoming stunted and leggy. They prefer daytime temperatures of 65 to 75° F (18°–24° C) but can tolerate nighttime temperatures of 50 to 55° F (10–13° C). That being said, if they get lots of sunlight, they will do fine in temperatures that are higher than this.

Fertilize your jade plant sparingly and only when there are signs of growth. This means applying a balanced, water-soluble fertilizer about once every six months. The best method is to water the plant normally first, and then water it with the fertilizer mix. That way the soil is nice and wet, and the fertilizer cannot damage the dry roots.

Note: Homeowners with pets should be careful about where they place a jade plant in their home or property—all parts of the plant are toxic to cats, dogs, and horses.

Kalanchoe

Delicate pale pink blooms tipped with darker pink is just one of the color combinations available with *Kalanchoe blossfeldiana.* These lovely plants will grace the indoors but can be kept in containers on a patio or deck to brighten the hot summer months.

The kalanchoe is a thick-leaved succulent that is often seen in florist shops or garden centers. *Kalanchoe blossfeldiana,* also known as flaming Katy, Christmas kalanchoe, florist kalanchoe, and Madagascar widow's-thrill, is the species most often grown, and a majority end up as potted houseplants. Yet, in areas that can mimic their native island of Madagascar, such as Florida or other warm-weather regions, they can be grown outdoors. For areas with colder winters, specimens need to come indoors before any chance of frost.

The plant produces an impressive bloom—clusters of tiny flowers in red, orange, pink, white, or yellow—held aloft on stems above the foliage. The starry flowers are long lasting and bloom from winter to spring. Many gardeners believe the plant's deep green, felted, scalloped leaves, which persist after blooming, are nearly as attractive as the flowers.

GROWING KALANCHOE

Kalanchoe plants are simple to grow from cuttings. The vegetative stems produce the best plants and root quickest. Take a 2- to 3-inch (5-7.5 cm) section, and strip off the bottom couple of leaves. Let the cutting sit out in a warm, dry location to form a callus on the end. Then plant the cutting in a pot with a pre-moistened peat and perlite mixture up to the first leaf. Enclose the pot in a plastic bag to conserve moisture, and place it in a window with indirect light. Cuttings will root in 14 to 21 days and are then ready to transplant. Kalanchoes require well-drained soil—60 percent peat moss and 40 percent perlite is ideal—and mild temperatures of at least 60° F (16° C).

Once kalanchoes are established, little maintenance is necessary—water the plant deeply, and then allow it to dry out completely before you give it further moisture. Fertilize once a month with houseplant food during the growing season. This succulent has few disease or pest problems, especially when grown indoors. Just be aware that strong, southern light can burn the tips of the leaves, so place pots in partial sun to light shade areas. Cut off spent flower stems, and pinch back leggy growth to force a compact plant.

SCIENTIFIC NAME: *Kalanchoe* spp.

FAMILY: Crassulaceae

HEIGHT: 6 to 18 inches (15–45 cm)

WIDTH: 6 to 18 inches (15–45 cm)

FOLIAGE COLOR: Various shade of green or variegated greens and red, with flowers in orange, pink, red, white, or purple

SOIL pH: Acidic

LIGHT: Full sun to partial shade

ENCOURAGE A SECOND BLOOM

Many people have received a kalanchoe as a gift, and, after that first lovely period of blooming, wondered why the flowers never came back. The trick is, this plant needs short winter-light periods to form new buds, so you must fool it into thinking it is experiencing winter. During October and early March, the day lengths are short enough to naturally force flower buds. You can also put the plant in a closet or dim room for most of the day. Bring it out only for morning light, and then put it away after a few hours. The plant needs six weeks of 12 to 14 hours of darkness to form spectacular new flowers. The best temperatures for the formation of flowers are 40 to 45° F (4–7° C) at night and 60° F (16° C) during the day.

Kalanchoe Species

Along with *K. blossfeldiana,* there are other members of the genus that can work in garden containers or in indoor pots.

- ***K. beharensis,*** known as elephant's ear kalanchoe or felt bush, is a dramatic olive green variety that can reach the height of 20 feet (6 m).
- ***K. thyrsiflora,*** known as the flapjack paddle plant, has a rosette of fleshy grayish green leaves with red margins, covered in a white powdery bloom.
- ***K. tomentosa,*** also known as pussy ears or panda plant, has many colorful cultivars.

Portulaca

The colorful flowers of portulaca can bloom in multiple colors on a single plant.

For a truly beautiful, low-growing ground cover–type of plant, consider the portulaca, sometimes known as the sun rose or moss rose. Portulacas are succulent annuals native to Brazil, Argentina, and Uruguay, and, needless to say, enjoy exposure to the sun. This plant was a favorite years ago in grandmother's garden, but like many other traditional species, it is making a comeback, riding on the coattails of the current "succulent revival."

Portulacas have a lot to recommend them. For starters they are extremely hardy, drought resistant, and very attractive. Their reddish stems have fleshy, needle-shaped, green leaves and bear flowers with ruffled petals that look like miniature roses. Colors include white, orange, yellow, pink, and red . . . often on the same plant.

These tenacious succulents have been used to beautify old structures, stone walkways, and driveways, as they grow well in the cracks where the winds have deposited just enough soil to support them. They look lovely in containers, as well as whiskey barrel planters and hanging baskets. The portulaca stems, with their twining leaves and bright blooms, will grow out and over the edges of the containers, making a grand display—like a party in a pot. They will also attract butterflies and hummingbirds to your yard.

GROWING PORTULACA PLANTS

When starting these succulents from seeds, do not cover the seeds with soil or cover them only very lightly, because they need the sunlight to sprout and grow.

Portulacas tolerate many types of soil but prefer sandy, well-drained beds. They don't require much water, because the foliage retains moisture so well. When watering them, keep it light, as the root zones are shallow. They have a high tolerance for heat and will self-seed, especially under hanging planters. Be aware that portulacas in open garden beds can spread easily, popping up where least expected.

Note: Gardeners should mind where they place portulacas in their landscape—all parts of the plant are toxic to dogs and cats.

SCIENTIFIC NAME: *Portulaca grandiflora*

FAMILY: Portulacaceae

HEIGHT: 3 to 9 inches (7.5–23 cm)

WIDTH: 6 to 12 inches (15–30 cm)

FOLIAGE COLOR: Medium-green leaves with flowers in shades of white, orange, yellow, pink, and red

SOIL pH: Neutral to acidic

LIGHT: Full sun

Healthful Purslane

One promising plant that many gardeners overlook is common purslane *(Portulaca oleracea)*, a relative of the portulaca. Also called pigweed, little hogweed, and fatweed, purslane is a succulent weed with paddle-shaped leaves and bright flowers. It also happens to be a vegetable and one of the most nutrient-dense foods on earth. It can be cooked or eaten raw in the same ways as spinach and lettuce, in salads and on sandwiches. The taste is slightly salty/sour, similar to spinach or watercress. It also has a long history as an alternative medicine, which is not surprising—it is known to supply substantial levels of omega-3 fatty acids, vitamins A and C, magnesium, potassium, iron, and calcium. Perhaps all pigweed really needs to put it on the garden map is a good PR person.

Sedum/Stonecrop

SCIENTIFIC NAME: *Sedum* spp. and *Hylotelephium* spp.

FAMILY: Crassulaceae

HEIGHT: 6 to 24 inches (15–60 cm)

WIDTH: 12 to 24 inches (30–60 cm)

FOLIAGE COLOR: Various shades of green, purple, and red, with flowers from white to bright pink

SOIL pH: Acidic, neutral

LIGHT: Full sun to partial shade

Showy 'Autumn Joy' stonecrop—formerly classified as *Sedum spectabile*—enlivens a flower bed with both pretty succulent foliage and clusters of tiny star-shaped blooms.

Few plants in your garden will be more tolerant of hot sun and bad soil than perennial sedums. They are perfect for the novice gardener and probably a favorite filler for the seasoned pro. Plus, there is such a large variety to select from, that finding specimens that work in your landscape will be a breeze. Sedum is also known as stonecrop, showy stonecrop, and order stonecrop—names reflecting a frequent gardener's joke that only stones require less care and live longer.

Sedums are divided into two categories: low-growing and upright. The smallest are just a few inches (8 cm) tall, and the tallest can be up to 3 feet (1 m). The great majority of sedum varieties are shorter, however, which is why they are often used as ground covers, in xeriscapes, and in rock gardens. In general, the plants have thick, fleshy leaves and tiny, star-shaped flowers that bloom late in the growing season.

There are numerous *Sedum* species, including *S. acre*, *S. album*, *S. reflexum*, *S. dasyphyllum*, *S. hispanicum*, *S. microcarpum*, *S. sexangulare*, and *S. spathulifolium* (shown below). A number of sedums have recently been reassigned new genera. One of the most popular sedum species cultivars, *Sedum spectabile* 'Autumn Joy', is now officially a stonecrop called *Hylotelephium spectabile* 'Autumn Joy'.

GROWING SEDUM

Sedum plants need very little attention or care; they thrive in conditions in which other plants do well, but will be just as happy in more challenging areas . . . like that part of your yard that gets too much sun or too little water to support anything else.

Plant sedum in the spring once the danger of frost is over, but before the stifling heat of summer arrives. For shorter varieties, the easiest method is laying your starter plants on the ground in the spots you have chosen. They will send out roots anywhere the stem is touching the ground. To further ensure the rooting process, you can cover the plants with a thin layer of soil. For taller sedum varieties, break off one of the stems and push it into the ground where you would like it to grow. The stem will root very easily, and a new plant will be established in a season or two.

CARING FOR THE PLANTS

Although sedum is extremely forgiving, it has a moderate growth rate, depending on species. Hardiness can also vary based on species; some will overwinter in temperate climates, others need warmth throughout the year. Even when planted in so-so soil, sedums need no additional water or fertilizer. In fact, overwatering and overfertilizing can actually harm your plants.

Editor's Picks

In addition to the widespread 'Autumn Joy' (now formally a stonecrop), gardeners can shop for a multitude of sedum cultivars, including the following.

- **'Dragon's Blood' is a ground cover with green leaves edged with wine and red buds that flower pink.**
- **'Purple Emperor' is an upright variety with dramatic deep purple leaves and rosy pink flowers.**
- **'Bronze Carpet' is a ground-hugging variety with bronze-red foliage and pink flowers.**
- **'Spurium Tricolor' is a small ground cover with green leaves dappled in pink and creamy white and bright pink flowers**
- **'Jaws' is a sort of 'Autumn Joy' with serrated, curled foliage and salmon-rose flowers.**

Sempervivum

Colorful sempervivum, more commonly known as hens and chicks, nestles in a rock crevice in an alpine garden. The genus name *Sempervivum* means "forever alive" in Latin.

SCIENTIFIC NAME: *Sempervivum* spp.

FAMILY: Crassulaceae

HEIGHT: 3 to 6 inches (7.5–15 cm)

WIDTH: 6 to 12 inches (15–30 cm)

FOLIAGE COLOR: Shades of green, often with red to purple tips

SOIL pH: Neutral

LIGHT: Full sun

Sempervivum is a genus of about 40 species, which originally proliferated from Morocco to Iran. Also known as hens and chicks, liveforever, house leeks, or roof leeks, these succulents offer unique forms and subtle beauty for very little effort. These low-growing evergreen perennials feature rubbery stems and thick, fleshy pads that form rosettes. The leaves are typically pointed; some grow in shades of red, others have purple tips, some are even shrouded with gossamer hairs.

The "hen" plant produces miniature rosette offsets known as "chicks," which are easily propagated. Star-shaped flowers in shades of mauve-pink, red, or yellow form at the tip of a thick, jagged stalk. The flower stalk may extend 8 to 12 inches (20–30 cm) before flowering, then shrinks back once the plant blooms and the mother plant dies.

Don't be afraid to plant hens and chicks in a hot, dry spot with rocky or gritty soil and low fertility. Not only will these hardy little succulents thrive in such sites, they will multiply and flower. They are also naturals for alpine settings, xeriscapes, or rock gardens. Or try gently wiring them on a vertical succulent wall or even on driftwood. For sheer diversity of form, size, and color, these plants prove themselves in a host of locations. They grow slowly, but most do well in colder climates, bouncing back each spring.

GROWING SEMPERVIVUMS

This plant's growing conditions are only limited by sunlight and good drainage. Sempervivums prefer full sun and well-draining compost mixed with 25 to 50 percent sand or other grit.

The easiest way to cultivate hens and chicks is to separate their offsets, which are clones of the mother. To grow from seed, however, you will need to know a few tricks.

First, sow the seeds in 2-inch (5 cm) pots, lightly pressing them into the soil. The seeds need light to germinate and temperatures of at least 70° F (21° C). If the seeds don't germinate in four or five weeks, put the pots in the refrigerator for another two to four weeks, and then repeat the sun and temperature conditions. In most cases, the seeds will germinate, and you will get tiny little rosettes.

Plant your seedlings in late spring, when there's no longer a chance of frost, and it's still not too hot outside. The majority of mature sempervivums are frost hardy, but if you grow a variety that is not, place it in a container and move it indoors for winter.

One more thing . . . sempervivums tend to hybridize quite easily, so when they grow from seed, the plants may not be true to form. Who knows? You may get something interesting or unusual, just not in the same form as the parent.

You can collect seeds from your sempervivums. Once the flowers are spent, a small, dry, seed-filled fruit is produced. Remove the pods and allow the fruit to dry completely before crushing it and removing the seeds. Refrigerate the seeds for four weeks before sowing.

Yucca

When in full bloom, the yucca displays masses of creamy white flowers rising high from a nest of swordlike leaves. Be sure to plant yucca in low-traffic areas—the sharp leaves can cut passers-by.

A native of the southwestern United States and the arid parts of Mexico and the Caribbean, the yucca is a warm-weather plant that looks great in xeriscapes. Because it can also withstand cold, it also works as a specimen plant in many other garden types—the yucca's swordlike leaves add a distinctive look to any landscape. It is a perennial evergreen shrub that comes in several species.

The most common garden species is *Y. filamentosa*, or Adam's needle. For an indoor plant, *Y. elephantipes*, or spineless yucca, is a good choice with foliage that won't cut you like its outdoor cousin. It also grows to a manageable size when used as a houseplant.

GROWING YUCCA

Although this is a popular houseplant species, you can also grow yucca outdoors. It thrives in soil that drains well and well tolerates full sun. It is also able to withstand temperatures as cold as 10° F (-12° C), so you can grow a yucca plant in many different climates. The creamy white, downward-facing bell-shaped flowers bloom best in full sun, during mid- to late summer, with some yucca growing as tall as 10 feet (3 m).

When landscaping with yuccas, it is best to keep them away from sidewalks and other high-traffic areas, as the leaves are extremely sharp and can cut someone if they should brush up against the plant.

Yucca is very forgiving when it comes to soil types, as long as the soil drains well. This is especially important during the first year, when the growing yucca plant needs time to adjust to the soil and local rainfall. Be sure to leave plenty of room to grow a yucca, as a mature plant can reach to 3 feet (1 m) across. They also have a fairly extensive root system, and another plant can appear a short distance away. Even if the plant is removed, it can be difficult to get rid of the entire root system, and the yucca will regrow from any root left in the ground.

At a Glance

SCIENTIFIC NAME: *Yucca* spp.

FAMILY: Asparagaceae

HEIGHT: 3 to 10 feet (1–3 m)

WIDTH: 3 feet (1 m)

FOLIAGE COLOR: Green, variegated green, and yellow, or green and white; white flowers

SOIL pH: Acidic, neutral, or alkaline

LIGHT: Full sun

CARING FOR THE PLANTS

Caring for yucca plants is fairly simple. When older leaves die on a mature yucca plant, simply cut them away, usually in the spring. This helps the rest of the plant look neater and allows the newer leaves to grow. When caring for yucca plants, it is a good idea to wear gloves to protect your hands from the sharp leaves.

After yucca has stopped flowering and the fruit has appeared, prune back the flower stalk clear to the ground.

When you decide to grow a yucca plant in your yard, you're adding a striking feature to your landscape. The good news is that caring for yuccas is easy. With a little care and maintenance, your yucca plant should thrive for years to come.

Dig Deeper

READ MORE AT GARDENING KNOW HOW

Learn about yucca plants and how you can use them both indoors and out.

- **"Caring for Yucca: Tips for Landscaping with Yuccas Outdoors"** (URL = gkh.us/629)
- **"Yucca Plant Varieties: Common Types of Yucca Plants"** (URL = gkh.us/59737)
- **"Yucca Houseplant Care: Tips for Growing Yucca in Containers"** (URL = gkh.us/18387)

CHAPTER SIX

THE KITCHEN GARDEN

The kitchen garden is a time-honored tradition, a centuries-old way to ensure that fresh fruits, vegetables, herbs, and seasonings are within easy reach of the cook's domain. Today's kitchen garden design takes notes from the past, but it adds modern growing and watering techniques, along with more whimsy and personality.

Whether you decide to cultivate a few raised beds or rototill a large space for your plants, the guidelines remain the same. Make sure that your garden has at least six hours of sunlight; rich, organic soil; adequate water; and is located in a spot that is convenient to your house. If you stick to those basics, after only one season of sowing and growing you'll be proudly proclaiming, "Let the harvest begin."

GROWING YOUR OWN FOOD

Homeowners with extensive properties can turn a large swath of their backyards into a dream kitchen garden with a variety of fruit and vegetable plots.

Grocery prices are going up. It's a fact of life we can't escape, and it's probably an ongoing trend. But you can substantially reduce those food bills if you have a flourishing kitchen garden. It is one of the better ways to ensure access to fresh produce, as well as knowing what chemicals, if any, are going into your food. It also allows you to enjoy the great outdoors as you tend your plot.

WHAT IS A KITCHEN GARDEN?

During the Middle Ages—possibly even going back to Greek and Roman times—housewives and husbandmen grew the vegetables or fruits they regularly ate—beans, maize, or berries, say—in small garden plots near their homes. They also cultivated the herbs that flourished in their region, along with the flowering plants that kept insect or animal pests away. These early kitchen gardens later transitioned into English cottage gardens and French *potagers*.

Because these gardens were located so near the home, they often acquired attractive trappings. Many featured charming elements like rail or picket fences, pebbled paths, stone benches, and ornamental sundials or dovecotes. They became places of refuge on occasion, where the cook/gardener could steal a moment of peaceful repose among nature's bounty.

That tradition has been carried on in the modern kitchen garden, which is a space focused on growing edible produce, but also one that offers a certain aesthetic appeal.

CREATING A KITCHEN GARDEN

Your garden design and plant choices will rely heavily upon what your family enjoys eating. If they love salads or vegetable dishes, your goal will be simple—sow and harvest fresh green produce. But some gardeners use a kitchen garden to fulfill most of their fruit and vegetable needs. Dwarf fruit trees, fruiting vines and canes, greens and root vegetables, and summer crops, such as corn and tomatoes, all feature prominently in such a garden. Still, even limited spaces can provide plenty of food if you sow successive crops, use vertical supports, and plant small amounts of diverse foods. The kitchen garden can be as basic as a raised bed or as ambitious as a large plot with room to expand.

Here are several tips to help you make the most of your kitchen.

- *Raised beds.* Consider starting off with one or two raised beds in a sunny spot. Typically, vegetables need at least six hours of sun—morning or afternoon or both—though eight hours is better. Any plants that require filtered sun can be protected by a length of shade cloth. Raised beds warm up quickly in spring, are easier to cultivate due to their elevation, and can handle a lot of plants if you use vertical supports for beans, cucumbers, and other climbers. Just fill the beds with quality organic soil and top dress with amendments each spring.
- *Plants.* When choosing how to stock a kitchen garden, keep in mind your growing season. Some plants, like tomatoes and peppers, require warm nights in addition to hot summer days. Other less-hardy plants, like lettuces and some herbs, may wilt in

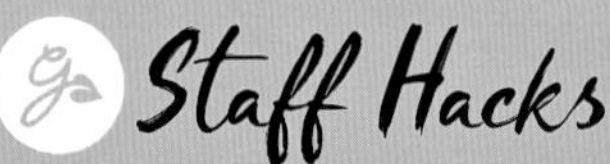

Heather Rhoades, GKH owner, offers her thoughts on the appeal of a keyhole garden. This type of raised garden bed is built from organic materials layered in a circle. At the center, a composting well funnels nutrients from food waste into the nearby soil, which results in lush plants and an abundant harvest. Rhoades notes, "I have several keyhole garden-style beds that I grow my vegetables in. I originally built one to test the style of garden bed for a GKH article, but after I tried the one, I loved it so much, I converted all my vegetable beds into keyhole gardens. They help deter critters and make composting a cinch."

the hot sun. Smart gardeners often start their vegetables indoors. Prime candidates include arugula, pole beans, bok choy, broccoli, brussels sprouts, cabbage, carrots, cauliflower, celeriac, celery, and collard greens.

- *Location.* The position of a kitchen garden should be chosen for convenience. If you have a 10-minute walk to get there, chances are greatly reduced that your garden will be properly weeded and watered, plus you may not harvest regularly and lose some produce.
- *Soil.* If you're down to a choice of two spots when creating a dug-in garden, pick the one with loamier soil. If the quality is right, the soil will bind together when you squeeze it but break apart easily when disturbed. Otherwise, most soils can be improved with organic matter, and if the soil is really bad, you can build raised beds.
- *Fertilizer.* Too much fertilizer, especially nitrogen (the first number on the fertilizer package) may promote plenty of lush green growth, but you'll end up with less fruit and a smaller harvest. Excessive fertilizing can also harm your plants and soil. Instead, incorporate organic compost, up to 20 percent of the total soil makeup, into your soil to supply the natural nutrients and living micro-organisms plants need to thrive. Remember, when you feed the soil, the soil feeds the plants.
- *Mulch.* Adding a 3-inch (7.5 cm) layer of organic mulch around your plants will insulate the soil, keeping it cooler in summer and warmer in autumn and winter. Mulch helps retain moisture, keeps weeds at bay, and forms a protective barrier against any plant diseases that might splash up from the soil.

Using your space wisely, with a variety of vegetable plots, some spread out and others using vertical supports, intermixed with fruit trees, ensures a bountiful and diverse harvest.

- *Water.* Most vegetables require 1 inch (2.5 cm) of water per week, including any natural rainfall. The most efficient and productive way to irrigate, however, is by using soaker hoses and drip lines. These deliver water slowly and on target, and they allow roots time to absorb the moisture and soil to adequately hydrate. This method also helps keep foliage dry. (Sopping wet foliage is prone to diseases.) Automatic timers are another way to take the effort and worry out of regular watering.
- *Drainage.* Plants can't grow in waterlogged soil, so the position of a vegetable garden should be somewhat elevated. If the location lies at the bottom of a hill or in an indentation in the ground, the soil will have a hard time drying out, and the plants will suffer.

Even apartment dwellers can grow fresh produce, such as container-friendly plants like tomatoes, on a balcony or terrace.

COMPLEMENTARY PLANTING AND ROTATING CROPS

There are a number of ways to keep your kitchen garden offering up masses of fresh, delicious vegetables. These include crop rotation, several types of succession planting, and using companion plants to protect your produce from pests.

RELAY SUCCESSION PLANTING

Don't you hate it when your vegetables have passed their prime, withered away, and left a bare, unproductive spot in your kitchen garden? The solution might be relay succession planting—seeding crops at intervals of 7 to 21 days. This method provides a consistent supply of veggies throughout the season and can double or even triple your garden's output.

If you want to grow spinach, say, plant a few seeds one week, and then one to three weeks later plant a few more, continuing in this manner for the whole season. After the first batch of spinach is picked, reuse the spot to plant more spinach seeds. Staggered sowing also works well with lettuce, beans, corn, carrots, radishes, beets, and greens.

MIXED CROP SUCCESSION PLANTING

Another form of succession planting utilizes different crops and takes advantage of your region's growing cycle. In a temperate climate, plant a short-season cool crop in spring, plant a longer-season warm-weather crop in summer, and finally, plant a short-season cool-weather crop in autumn. Each of these plantings would take place in the same spot after harvesting. For example, you could plant lettuce in spring, tomatoes in summer, and cabbage in autumn. This method works best for determinate crops, those that produce all their fruit (or edible material) at once.

In a more tropical area, where winters aren't cold, and summers are often too hot for many vegetables, a gardener could plant a short-season, cool-weather crop in winter; a long-season, warm-weather crop in spring; plant a heat-tolerant crop in midsummer; and then another long-season, warm-weather crop in autumn. An example would be spinach in winter, squash in spring, okra in summer, and tomatoes in autumn. This method takes full advantage of all of your garden space at all times during the growing season.

CROP ROTATION

Crop rotation refers to shifting annual vegetables to new areas of the garden each year. This practice prevents pests and diseases from continuously building up in the soil. If you move the crop, the pest or disease has no host on which to live. Crop rotation also allows the soil to replenish nutrients that one plant may have depleted.

The trick is to rotate families of plants away from the same spot each season. Ideally, a single vegetable family should grow in a repeat location only every three to four years. Heavy feeders, including corn, lettuce, broccoli, tomatoes, and cucumbers, use up a lot of nitrogen to produce flowers, fruit, and leaves. Give their beds a rest by next planting light feeders like carrots, potatoes, beets, or onions. Also, deeply rooted crops, such as tomatoes, carrots, or beets, break up the soil as they seek out minerals, bringing them up closer to the surface for other plants to use the following year.

Plant families

It helps to make a chart indicating where you plant these families each year.

- *Alliums:* Onions, shallots, scallion, leeks, chives, and garlic.
- *Brassicas:* Broccoli, cauliflower, kale, cabbages, brussels sprouts, turnip greens, radishes, collards, and mustard greens. These share pest issues and often need nets to block cabbage moths. They need nitrogen-rich soil. Rotate in after legumes.
- *Cucurbits:* Zucchini and summer squash, cukes, pumpkins and winter squash, melons (watermelon, cantaloupe), and gourds. All are heavy feeders that grow best in rich soil.
- *Legumes:* Green beans, green peas, southern peas, peanuts, and soybeans. Legumes are soil "fixers" that add nitrogen back to the soil.
- *Nightshades:* Tomatoes, eggplant, peppers, and potatoes. These are heavy feeders that need rich soil. They are affected by the same diseases. Never follow potatoes with tomatoes.
- *Umbellifers:* Carrots, parsnips, fennel, parsley, and dill.

Bonnie Grant, GKH Writer, offers this advice on growing vegetables: "Few things are more rewarding than growing your own food. And veggies are easy. Don't start with a grandiose plan or you might risk disappointing yourself. Stick with the basics until you get a feel for what you are doing, and then add in some new stuff as a challenge."

The Three Sisters

A trio of Native American staples—corn, beans, and squash—are known as the Three Sisters. They not only taste good when served together, they also nutritionally complement one another. Try planting them together: the corn stalks provide structures for the vining beans to climb, while the wide squash leaves spread over the ground, retaining moisture and deterring weeds. Bean roots host rhizobia, which absorb nitrogen from the air and transform it into usable nutrients for neighboring plants.

COMPANION PLANTING

Companion planting is simply growing two or more plants close together for the benefit of one or both. Benefits include pest control, pollination, providing habitats for beneficial insects, maximizing use of space, and otherwise increasing crop productivity. For almost every vegetable, there is a beneficial companion plant that will increase soil nutrients, chase away pests, and help you get the most out of your garden. Here is a sampling of plants and their garden friends and foes.

Tomato

- *Friends:* Basil helps tomatoes produce greater yields and repels flies and mosquitoes. Marigolds repel nematodes and other pests. Other friends include asparagus, carrots, celery, the onion family, lettuce, parsley, and spinach.
- *Foes:* Cabbage, cauliflower, broccoli, brussels sprouts, corn, beets, peas, fennel, dill, potatoes, and rosemary.

Peppers

- *Friends:* Basil helps repel aphids, spider mites, mosquitoes, and flies, and improves the pepper's flavor. Others include onions, spinach, and tomatoes.
- Foes: Bean vines can spread among pepper plants.

Lettuce

- *Friends:* Mint keeps away slugs; chives and garlic repel aphids. Others include asparagus, beans, beets, broccoli, carrots, corn, peas, radishes, and marigolds, which attract aphid-eating ladybugs.
- *Foes:* Parsley plants can crowd lettuce.

Radish

- *Friends:* Radishes attract cucumber beetles away from the cukes. Harvested before carrots, they loosen the soil as carrots start to take off. Also onions, beets, cabbage, kale, lettuce, spinach, and squash.
- *Foes:* Hyssop.

Universal Companions

There are some plants that go with just about any vegetable you might want to grow. Plant them liberally throughout—some add bright color and others lovely scents, while helping to reduce pests, increase crop yields, and improve flavor.

ANNUALS

Marigold

Basil

Borage

Calendula

Nasturtium

PERENNIALS

Mints

Thyme

ANNUAL FRUITS AND VEGETABLES

Annuals, such as plump eggplants, juicy red tomatoes, crisp cucumbers, crunchy carrots, and deep-green broccoli, are vegetable garden mainstays that not only taste delicious, but also help you to eat healthy while keeping down your grocery costs.

Most of the vegetables that we buy in the supermarket, the farmer's market, or the produce stand are annuals. As with flowering plants, annual vegetables complete their life cycles—from germination to flowering and fruiting to the production of seeds—within one growing season, and then they die. The length of the growing season or period in which these stages take place varies according to geographical location.

We all have our favorites veggies . . . perhaps butter lettuce, winter squash, or fresh garden peas. In fact, annuals make up the bulk of the vegetables in our modern diet—maize (corn), potatoes, tomatoes, peppers, soybeans, and spinach, along with grasses such as wheat, and rice. In regions with shorter growing seasons, certain vegetables will perform better under those restrictive conditions. These include beans, beets, broccoli, cabbage, cauliflower, carrots, cucumber, and ground cherries, little parcels that can be unwrapped and eaten raw, like cherry tomatoes.

A GARDEN DIARY

When planting annual vegetables and fruits, it is essential to start seeds or sow outdoors at the right time. It helps to keep a garden diary, indicating month-by-month when plants should go into the ground (often determined by the date of your last predicted frost). Depending on your local climate, correct planting dates will differ. If you are uncertain, contact the county cooperative extension or your regional agricultural bureau for planting information.

A raised bed packs together onion, lettuce, cucumber, and other veggies for a bountiful summertime harvest of fresh produce.

Follow this link or scan the QR code for several informative articles that will help you get the most from a vegetable garden.

- **Vegetable Growing Guide** (URL = gkh.us/160774)

To learn how you can thwart pests that endanger your crops, grow veggies in containers, or make your annuals last more than a season, follow these links.

- **"Common Pests in Vegetable Gardens — Tips on Treating Vegetable Pests"** (URL = gkh.us/50283)
- **"Patio Garden Plants — Small Fruits and Vegetables"** (URL = gkh.us/166338)
- **"Self Sowing Veggies: Reasons for Planting Vegetables That Self Seed"** (URL = gkh.us/131985)

Beet

SCIENTIFIC NAME: *Beta vulgaris*

FAMILY: Amaranthaceae

HEIGHT: 12 to 18 inches (30–45 cm)

WIDTH: 18 to 24 inches (45–60 cm)

SOIL pH: Acidic, neutral

LIGHT: Full sun to partial shade

HARVEST: Late spring or autumn

A gardener displays a good day's haul of beets. By staggering your crops, you can ensure that you have a steady supply of both roots and greens during harvest season.

The vegetable beet, one of several cultivated varieties of *Beta vulgaris* grown for its edible taproot and leaves, is called beetroot in British English and also known as the table beet, garden beet, red beet, dinner beet, or golden beet. This healthy and tasty veg has been cultivated since ancient times, and during its long history has been used as both a culinary and medicinal plant

The bulbous root can be served boiled, roasted, or raw, and the leafy portion, called beet greens, can be added raw to salads when young and boiled or steamed when mature. Pickled beetroot is a traditional food in many countries. As well as a culinary staple, the deep purple root is also used as a food colorant, adding its bright tones to tomato paste, desserts, jams, ice cream, candy, breakfast cereals, and other foods and beverages.

Along with the well-known purple-red beet, there are also golden, white and red-ringed varieties of this root vegetable. The golden and white beets have a sweeter taste than the earthier reds.

GROWING BEETS

These tasty red vegetables are easy to grow. When considering how to grow beets in your garden, remember that they do best in backyard or raised-bed gardens, because they don't require much room.

Your first consideration will be soil composition. Beets thrive in deep, well-drained soil. Sandy soil is best; clay is the worst because it is too heavy for large roots to grow. Clay soil should be mixed with organic matter to help soften it. Hard soil can cause the roots of the beet to be tough, but if you plant beets in autumn, use a slightly heavier soil to help protect against any early frost.

When to plant is another consideration. Beets can be grown all winter long in many southern areas, but in northern soils, you shouldn't put them in the ground until the temperature of the soil is at least 40° F (4° C). Beets like cool weather, and they grow well in the chillier temperatures of spring and autumn and do poorly in hot weather.

Plant the seeds in a row, spacing them 1 to 2 inches (2.5–5 cm) apart. Lightly cover the seeds with loose soil, and then sprinkle it with water. You should see the plants sprouting in 7 to 14 days. If you want a continuous supply, plant your beets in several plantings, about three weeks apart from one another.

You can plant beets in partial shade, but you want their roots to reach a depth of at least 3 to 6 inches (7.5–15 cm), so don't plant them under a tree where they might run into the tree's roots.

WHEN TO PICK BEETS

You can harvest beets seven to eight weeks after the planting of each group. When the taproots have reached the desired size, gently dig them up from the soil. Beet greens can be harvested as well: pick these while the beet is young and the root is small.

Editor's Tips

A root or earth cellar was once a common place to store vegetables like beets and potatoes long-term. Lacking one doesn't mean you can't preserve your surplus beet crop.

- **Keep beet greens in the refrigerator in a plastic bag for up to one week.**
- **Store beets in the crisper of your fridge for one to three weeks.**
- **Store in a cold, moist place (40 to 50°F, or 4 to 10°C, is ideal) for up to three months.**
- **Freeze beets for up to a year by first cutting off the leaves, cleaning off the soil, and then gently boiling them for 30 minutes. After cooling them in an ice bath, cut them into uniform pieces, and place in freezer bags.**

Bush Beans

A bush bean variety of green bean plants mass together in a kitchen garden. Also known as French beans, string beans, and snap beans, these are the young, unripe fruits of various cultivars of the common bean *(Phaseolus vulgaris).*

"Bean" is the common name for the seeds of several genera of the family Fabaceae, which are used for human or animal consumption. People have been planting beans, mostly *Phaseolus vulgaris* and its various cultivars, for centuries for use as either snap beans, shelling beans, or dry beans.

BUSH VERSUS POLE BEANS

There are two types of garden beans: bush beans and pole beans. Bush beans differ from pole beans in that bush beans, which grow to up to 2 feet tall (60 cm), don't need any kind of support to stay upright. Pole beans, on the other hand, can grow up to 12 feet (3.65 m) and need a pole or some other support to stay upright (for information on growing pole beans, *see* page 189).

In general, bush beans take less time than pole beans to produce a crop. Their seeds can be planted within 6 inches (15 cm) of other bush bean plants and will also take up less room in a garden. Some beans have varieties in both bush and pole categories, such as the green bean and pinto bean.

Bush beans can be further broken down into three types: snap beans (where the pods are eaten), green shelling beans (where the beans are eaten green), and dry beans, (where the beans are dried and then rehydrated before eating).

GROWING BUSH BEANS

Bush beans grow best in well-drained soil that is rich in organic material, and they need full sun to produce best. Before you start planting bush beans, you should consider amending the soil with bean inoculant, which contains bacteria that help the plants produce better. Your bush beans will still produce if you do not add inoculants to the soil, but it will help you get a more abundant crop.

Plant bush bean seeds about 1.5 inches (3.5 cm) deep and 3 inches (7.5 cm) apart. If you are planting more than one row, the rows should be 18 to 24 inches (45 to 60 cm) apart. You can expect beans to germinate in about one to two weeks. If you would like a continuous harvest of bush beans through the season, plant new bush bean seeds about once every two weeks.

Stringless Beans

Green snap beans may be the most familiar bean. These green beans with an edible pod used to be called "string" beans, but today's varieties have been bred to lack the tough, stringy fiber along the pod's seam. Now they easily "snap" in two. Some green snap beans are not green at all, but purple and, when cooked, become green. There are also wax beans, which are simply a variant of snap bean with a yellow, waxy pod.

SCIENTIFIC NAME: *Phaseolus vulgaris*

FAMILY: Fabaceae,

HEIGHT: Up to 2 feet (60 cm)

WIDTH: Up to 18 inches (45 cm)

SOIL pH: Neutral to slightly acidic

LIGHT: Full sun

HARVEST: Summer

CARING FOR THE PLANTS

Once bush bean plants have started growing, they need little care. Make sure that they get at least 2 to 3 inches (5 to 7.5 cm) of water a week, either from rainwater or a watering system. If you like, you can add compost or fertilizer after the beans have sprouted, but if you started out with organic-rich soil, they will not need it.

Bush beans do not normally have any issues with pests or disease, but on occasion they will suffer from bean mosaic, anthracnose, bean blight, and bean rust. Pests such as aphids, mealybugs, bean weevils, spider mites, and bean leaf beetles can be a problem too. Control is fairly uncomplicated. For example, if you see spider mites, use a hose to spray a hard stream of water on infested leaves. To control bean leaf beetles, it is best to delay planting until mid to late June. If beetles appear, handpick beetles off the beans and place in a pail of soapy water.

Carrot

Harvest-ready carrots break through the garden's soil. These super-healthful veggies offer a sweet taste with a crisp texture that's delicious whether eaten cooked or raw.

SCIENTIFIC NAME: *Daucus carota sativus*

FAMILY: Apiaceae

HEIGHT: 1 foot (30 cm)

WIDTH: 9 inches (23 cm)

SOIL pH: Slightly acidic

LIGHT: Full sun to partial shade

HARVEST: Summer to early winter

A domesticated form of the wild carrot (the European and southwestern Asian native *Daucus carota*), the garden carrot *(D. carota sativus)* is a root vegetable. Although we most often associate a bright orange color with this vegetable, purple, black, red, white, and yellow cultivars exist. Originally cultivated for its leaves and seeds, it is now most often harvested for its taproot, although the plant's stems and leaves are also edible. The carrots available today have been selectively bred to produce bigger, less woody, and tastier taproots than their wild progenitor.

The carrot is a biennial member of the umbellifer family, Apiaceae, which is most notably distinguished by the characteristic inflorescence of tightly aggregated flowers in an umbrella-like shape. The plant first appears as a rosette of leaves while it builds up an enlarged taproot. The carrot can mature as quickly as 90 days after sowing the seed or as long as 120 days. The mature taproot is prized for its high quantities of alpha- and beta-carotene, as well as its vitamin A, vitamin K, and vitamin B6 content.

GROWING CARROTS

Carrots grow best in cool temperatures, such as those that occur in early spring and late autumn. The night temperature should be dropping to about 55° F (13° C), and the daytime temperatures should be averaging 75° F (24° C) for optimum growth. Carrots grow in small gardens and even flower beds, and they can accept a little bit of shade as well.

Start out with soil that will help your carrots grow healthy. Before planting, soil surfaces should be cleared of trash, rocks, and large pieces of bark. Finer pieces of plant material can be mixed down into the soil for enrichment. The soil should be a sandy, well-drained loam. Heavy soils cause the carrots to mature slowly, and the roots will end up unattractive and rough. Remember that when you grow carrots, rocky soil leads to poor-quality roots.

Till or dig up the area to soften and aerate the ground to make it easier for the roots to grow long and straight. Fertilize the soil with 1 cup (128 g) of 10-20-10 for every 10 feet (3 m) of row you plant. You can use a rake to mix the soil and fertilizer.

Plant your carrots in rows that are 1 to 2 feet (30–60 cm) apart. Seeds should be planted about ½ inch (1 cm) deep and 1 to 2 inches (2.5–5 cm) apart. When deciding how many carrots to plant, assume you will get about 1 pound (0.5 kg) of carrots in each 1-foot (30 cm) row.

CARING FOR THE PLANTS

When the plants are 4 inches (10 cm) high, thin them to 2 inches (5 cm) apart. You might find that some of the carrots are already large enough to eat.

You will want to keep your plants free of weeds. This is especially important when they are small. The weeds will take nutrients away from the roots and will cause poor carrot development.

HARVESTING CARROTS

Carrots grow continuously after you plant them. They also don't take very long to mature. You can start the first crop in mid-spring, after threat of frost has passed, and continue to plant new seeds every two weeks for continuous harvest through the autumn.

You can begin to harvest when the taproots are finger sized. You can, however, allow them to stay in the soil until winter if you mulch the garden well. To check the size of your carrots, gently remove some dirt from the top of the root. To harvest, gently lift the carrot from the soil.

Parsnip *(Pastinaca sativa)*, another member of the carrot family, can be mistaken for a white carrot because of its similar size and shape. Consider growing this root veggie with your carrot crop. Often used in the same recipes, the spicy bite of the parsnip complements the sweeter taste of the carrot.

Corn

SCIENTIFIC NAME: *Zea mays*

FAMILY: Poaceae

HEIGHT: 6 to 8 feet (1.8–2.4 m)

WIDTH: 1 to 2 feet (30–60 cm)

SOIL pH: Acidic, neutral

LIGHT: Full sun

HARVEST: Summer

Young corn plants stand in a row at the edge of a kitchen garden, thriving in their sunny spot.

Corn *(Zea mays)*, also called maize, was first domesticated by indigenous peoples in southern Mexico about 10,000 years ago. Since then it has become a staple food in many parts of the world, and these days it is one of the most popular vegetables you can grow in your garden. Who doesn't love corn on the cob drizzled with butter on a hot summer day? Furthermore, it can be blanched and frozen, so you can enjoy fresh corn from your garden even in winter.

TYPES OF CORN

The two types are traditional corn and sweet corn. Traditional, or field, corn has a starchier flavor and a slightly harder cob than sweet corn, which is softer and has a pleasantly sweet taste. Sweet corn is a great choice for a home kitchen garden.

Sweet corn plants are definitely a warm-season crop and easy to grow. You can choose either sweet corn or super sweet corn plants, but don't grow them together; different varieties can cross-pollinate, resulting in starchy corn.

Corn can be ready for harvest at 60 days, 70 days, or 90 days. One of the methods for corn planting is to have a continuous growing season. To do this, plant several types of corn with varying maturation intervals: for example, plant an early variety near the beginning of the season, wait a couple weeks to plant another early variety, and then plant a third, later variety. You can also plant the same kind staggered by 10 to 14 days so that you have a continuous crop of fresh sweet corn to eat all summer long.

GROWING SWEET CORN

Corn enjoys growing in full sunshine. If you want to grow corn from seed, be sure you plant the seeds in well-drained soil, which will dramatically increase your yield. Make sure your soil has plenty of organic matter, and fertilize before you plant the corn. Good soil preparation is very important.

Wait until there have been plenty of frost-free days before putting the corn into the soil; otherwise, your crop will be sparse. It is best to plant sweet corn in soil that is warm—at least above 55° F (13° C). For super sweet corn, be sure the soil is at least 65° F (18° C), as super sweet corn prefers a warmer climate. Plant the seeds ½ inch (1 cm) deep in cool, moist soil and at least 1 to 2 inches (2.5–5 cm) deep in warm, dry soil. To protect plants from cross-pollination, plant the rows 12 inches (30 cm) apart with at least 30 to 36 inches (75–90 cm) between rows.

Mulch will help keep your corn weed-free and will retain moisture during hot, dry weather. You can cultivate the rows shallowly, so you do not injure the roots. Make sure you water the plants if there has been no rain so that they get enough moisture.

PICKING SWEET CORN

Picking sweet corn is an easy task. Each stalk should produce at least one ear of corn, which will be ready to pick about 20 days after you see signs of the first silk growing. You can then just grab the ear, twist, pull in a downward motion, and snap it off quickly. Some stalks will then grow a second ear.

Corn Varieties

There are many sweet corn varieties, from hybrids to heirlooms, which ripen at different times of the season in various colors. Here are just some of the best kinds of corn so you can get cracking on your summer garden planning.

- **Standard sweet corn.** This classic group is one of the most popular. The flavor and texture simply sing "summer," but the drawback is that they don't store for long. There are early- and late-maturing hybrids. Some of the standard varieties are the white Silver Queen, yellow Earlivee, and bicolor Utopia
- **Sugar-enhanced corn.** These varieties may have up to 18 percent more sugar content than the standard sugar types. They hold better than sugar varieties, but the skin around the kernels is more tender and sensitive to damage. Some of the better varieties are the golden Sweet Riser, the yellow Legend, and white Sweet Ice.
- **Supersweet corn.** Supersweet is also called shrunken corn due to the appearance of the dried kernels. It contains twice the amount of sugar as traditional sweet corn varieties. Because it converts sugar to starch much more slowly, it can be stored much longer. Common supersweet corn varieties include yellow Krispy King, bicolor Candy Corner, and yellow Sweetie.

Cucumber

Dozens of cucumbers, trained on a pole system, are ready for harvesting.

Cucumbers *(Cucumis sativus)* are warm-weather annuals believed to have originated on the Indian subcontinent and cultivated for at least 3,000 years. Technically fruit, their savory flavor often has them grouped with vegetables. They are now summer favorites, with a crisp refreshing taste and texture that is great for pickling, tossing in salads, or eating straight off the vine.

TYPES OF CUCUMBERS

There are two main types of cucumbers: slicing and pickling. The slicing types are long and usually grow to about 6 or 8 inches (15–20 cm) in length, while the pickling types are shorter, reaching around 3 to 4 inches (8–10 cm) once mature. Within these categories, there are hundreds of cultivars with various shapes, sizes, flavors, growing habits, and climate preferences.

GROWING CUCUMBERS

You can start your cucumbers indoors from seed, either purchased or saved and harvested from previous plants, in peat pots or small flats. Transplant to the garden a couple weeks thereafter, but only when all danger of frost has passed. Before you move them to the garden, harden off the plants in a protected location to lessen any stress that might occur during transplanting. During cool periods, cucumbers can be covered with plant protectors, as well.

Cucumbers like warm, humid weather and plenty of sunlight. Choose a sunny site that has adequate drainage and fertile soil. Good soil will have plenty of organic matter, such as compost. Adding compost to the soil will help get your cucumbers off to a good start, and applying an organic fertilizer, such as manure, will help give the plants nutrients during growth. When you begin preparing the soil, remove any rocks, sticks, or other debris, and then mix ample amounts of organic matter and fertilizer into the soil.

Cucumbers may be planted in hills or rows about 1 inch (2.5 cm) deep and thinned as needed. As a vine crop, cucumbers usually require a lot of space. In large gardens, the vines can spread throughout rows; within smaller gardens, you can train them for climbing on a fence or trellis. Training cucumbers on a support will reduce space and lift the fruit off the soil, while also giving your garden a neater appearance. The bush or compact varieties are quite suitable for growing in small spaces or even in containers.

SCIENTIFIC NAME: *Cucumis sativus*

FAMILY: Cucurbitaceae

HEIGHT: 24 inches to 8 feet (60 cm–2.4 m)

WIDTH: 1 to 3 feet (30 cm–1 m)

SOIL pH: Neutral

LIGHT: Full sun

HARVEST: Summer

CARING FOR THE PLANTS

Cucumbers will grow quickly with little care, other than adequate irrigation. Be sure the plants receive an inch of water every week. You can also regularly feed them with a water-soluble plant food that both feeds the plants and supplies them with beneficial microbes. You can apply it directly to the soil around plant stems or work a continuous-release fertilizer into the soil.

HARVESTING CUCUMBERS

Once the cumbers begin appearing, check your vines daily because the fruit can enlarge quickly. If you let them get too big, not only will they have a bitter taste, but the plant will also not continue producing. The more you harvest, the more fruit the vines will yield. To harvest, cut the stem above the cucumber, using a knife or clippers.

READ MORE AT GARDENING KNOW HOW

To find out the best time to harvest your cukes, just follow this URL or scan the QR code.

- **"Cucumber Harvest: Learn When and How to Harvest Cucumbers"** (URL = gkh.us/16215)

Eggplant

A purple eggplant ripens in the bright sunlight. Its self-pollinating flower is typical of the nightshade family, with a star shape in various shades of purple.

Eggplant *(Solanum melongena),* also known as the aubergine or brinjal, is a member of the nightshade family that is grown worldwide for its edible fruit. There are several varieties to choose from, with a range of sizes, shapes, and colors. The most familiar is the glossy, deep purple variety with its egg-shaped fruit that reveals creamy white flesh that has a spongy and "meaty" texture. White cultivars that are longer in shape are also available. Eggplant is classified botanically as a berry, but it is typically used as a vegetable in cooking.

Growing eggplants in the veggie garden can be so rewarding when the time comes to harvest these tasty, versatile plants. By understanding what eggplants need to grow and thrive, you can ensure a good harvest.

GROWING EGGPLANTS

Like their close cousins tomatoes, eggplants are hot-weather vegetables. They grow during short, hot seasons, so be aware of soil and air temperatures as you plan how and when to get eggplants started. If starting from seeds, make sure the soil is between 75° and 85° F (24–30° C). Use a heating mat if necessary. They'll need these warm temperatures and two to three weeks to germinate.

Start seeds in soil ¼ of an inch (0.6 cm) deep. Thin seedlings so they are 2 to 3 inches (5–7.5 cm) apart. You can move the young plants into the garden once temperatures stay reliably above 50° F (10° C). Knowing where to plant eggplant is important. Find a spot in the garden where they will get full sun. The soil should be fertile and well-drained. Amend if necessary to make sure the plants will get enough nutrients and will not be in standing water. Space the transplants about 18 inches (45 cm) from one another and in rows that are 36 inches (1 m) apart.

CARING FOR THE PLANTS

Eggplants do best when the soil has a consistent moisture level. Water regularly, especially when the plants are young so that they develop deep roots. Avoid overhead watering to prevent disease, but consider using mulch to keep the soil moist and warm and to keep weeds down. Generally, the plants should get an inch (2.5 cm) of rain or watering per week.

SCIENTIFIC NAME: *Solanum melongena*

FAMILY: Solanaceae

HEIGHT: 2 to 4 feet (60 cm–1.2 m)

WIDTH: 1 to 3 feet (30 cm–1 m)

SOIL pH: Acidic, neutral, alkaline

LIGHT: Full sun

HARVEST: Summer

HARVESTING EGGPLANT

You can wait until each eggplant is a mature size for its variety to harvest, but you can also pick those that are not fully mature. When smaller, the fruits will be tender in texture and flavor. Don't let eggplants stay on the plant past maturity; they will not retain their quality. To harvest eggplants, use shears or scissors. If you pull them off, you will most likely damage the plant, the fruit, or both.

Eggplants are always best eaten fresh, and when cut, oxidation will rapidly turn the flesh brown. They also don't keep well, so use your harvested fruits soon after picking, although you can store them uncut for about a week in the refrigerator. Pickling is possible, but other preservation methods don't result in good quality. For this reason, it makes sense to start picking the fruits when they are smaller and immature to extend the harvest period.

READ MORE AT GARDENING KNOW HOW

Flowers are key to an eggplant harvest. Follow these links to be sure your plants have the best chance of thriving.

- **"Can You Hand Pollinate an Eggplant: Tips for Pollinating Eggplants by Hand"** (URL = gkh.us/69285)
- **"What to Do for Eggplant Blossoms Drying Out and Falling Off"** (URL = gkh.us/447)

Garlic

Garlic plants grow throughout the winter, with heads ready for late-spring to midsummer harvesting. With proper curing and storage, the harvested heads can last a very long time, so that you can enjoy them for months longer than many other garden veggies.

SCIENTIFIC NAME: *Allium sativum*

FAMILY: Amaryllidaceae

HEIGHT: 12 to 18 inches (30–45 cm)

WIDTH: 6 to 12 inches (15–30 cm)

SOIL pH: Slightly acidic to neutral

LIGHT: Full sun

HARVEST: Spring to summer

Garlic *(Allium sativum),* a native of South Asia, Central Asia, and northeastern Iran, has thousands of years of history as a cultivated plant used as a food flavoring and as a traditional medicine.

This member of the genus *Allium*, which gives us so many flavorful vegetables, is a close relative of the onion, shallot, scallion, leek, chive, Welsh onion, and Chinese onion. It is just about essential to a kitchen garden—fresh garlic is a strongly flavored seasoning that crops up in cuisines from all around the world. An added plus is that garlic plants are easy to grow and require very little care once in the ground.

You can choose to plant either softneck or hardneck varieties, which get their names from their types of stalks. Softneck garlic has pliable stalks (which make attractive displays when braided for storage), and hardneck garlic has woody, stiff stalks.

GROWING GARLIC

Garlic plants need cool temperatures to thrive. As you would with many spring- or summer-flowering bulbs, you should plant garlic in the autumn. Where there are cold winters, you can plant four to six weeks before the ground freezes. In areas with mild winters, you can plant your garlic through winter but before February.

Before planting garlic, prepare the soil. Unless your soil is naturally loose, add a lot of organic matter like compost or well-aged manure to produce large, healthy heads.

Most gardeners grow garlic using the bulbs rather than seeds. Choose large, undamaged bulbs to plant; these will produce the biggest heads. Separate the bulbs into individual cloves (just as you do when cooking, but without peeling them), leaving the "paper" on them.

Plant each clove about an inch (2.5 cm) deep. The fatter end that was at the bottom of the bulb should be at the bottom of the hole. If your winters are colder, you can plant the pieces deeper. Space the cloves 2 to 4 inches (5–10 cm) apart in rows spaced 12 to 18 inches (30–45 cm) apart. If you want bigger garlic bulbs, you can try spacing cloves on a 6-by-12-inch (15 -30 cm) grid.

CARING FOR THE PLANTS

While the plants are green and growing, fertilize them, but stop fertilizing after they begin to "bulb-up." If you feed your garlic too late, your garlic won't go dormant.

If there isn't much rain in your area, water the plants while they are growing just as you would any other green plant in your garden.

HARVESTING AND CURING GARLIC

Garlic is ready to harvest once the leaves turn brown. You can start checking when five or six green leaves are left.

The harvested garlic will need to cure before you store it anywhere. Make sure to bundle eight to a dozen together by their leaves and hang them in a place to dry.

Editor's Picks

Garlic varieties are divided into two categories: softneck and hardneck. These lists give you a few ideas of cultivars you can try for either one.

Softneck varieties

- 'Early Italian'
- 'Inchelium Red'
- 'Silver White'
- 'Walla Walla Early'

Hardneck varieties

- 'Amish Rocambole'
- 'California Early'
- 'Chesnok Red'
- 'Northern White'
- 'Romanian Red'

To learn more about the differences between the two, scan the QR code or follow this link to "Softneck vs Hardneck Garlic — Should I Grow Softneck or Hardneck Garlic" (URL = gkh.us/157496).

THE ONION FAMILY

Onions belong to the Amaryllidaceae, or Amaryllis family—herbaceous, mostly perennial and bulbous flowering plants. Created in 1805, the family currently contains 1,600 species, with onions and chives falling into the subfamily Allioideae, with 18 genera. The leaves are typically linear with bisexual, symmetrical flowers arranged in umbels. The pungent odor associated with onions comes from the presence of allyl sulfide compounds. Onions are used to flavor sauces, gravies, soups, stews, curries, and casseroles, and as raw garnishes. Few ingredients add piquancy to salads, burgers, and sandwiches like raw onions; few add depth to cooked dishes like caramelized onions.

GROWING ONIONS

Most onion varieties are sold as seedlings in bare-root bundles; each plant will start growing within days after being planted. If you can't plant your onions right away, remove their bindings and place them in a bucket with 2 inches (5 cm) of moist soil in the bottom. Keep them in a cool, bright place but out of direct sunlight until you are ready to plant.

Staff Hacks

Did you know onion plants have pretty flowers, too? Amy Draiss, GKH Digital Community Manager, offers these instructions for making the most of these fabulous blooms. "Alliums are easy-care bulbs with large flower heads that rise above the foliage in varying shades of purple, white, pink, and blue. They only bloom for a short time between spring and summer. After you have enjoyed the early-season bloom and the flowers have turned brown, you can extend the life of these playful pom-poms with spray paint. Adding color back to the flower head will extend the show for a few more weeks. First, you will want to stake each individual flower, as the stem will quickly become fragile after the flower is spent. An inexpensive bamboo stake or plant support will do. While spraying the flower head the same color as the natural bloom seems like the obvious choice, you can choose any color (or colors) to add a bright pop of pigment. The possibilities are endless, as modern spray paint is available in a wide array of shades, including metallic and glittery options. To prevent overspray onto other plants or home surfaces, hold a piece of cardboard or a large paper plate behind the flower before you paint. Direct the nozzle at the flower, and apply an even coat. You may want to apply several coats to achieve the desired color. The paint is not harmful to the plant and the plant should return reliably the next spring."

Onion Diseases

A wet growing season is bad news for your onion crop. Many diseases, most of them fungal, invade the garden and ruin onions during warm, moist weather. Unfortunately, most onion diseases have similar symptoms, including spots and lesions on leaves and bulbs, areas that look water soaked, and browning foliage. There is no method of treating these diseases, so the best course is to focus on protecting next year's crop.

- Place your onion patch on a three- or four-year rotation. Grow other crops there in the intervening years, but avoid members of the onion family.
- Avoid fertilizing with nitrogen after midseason. It delays the development of bulbs and gives diseases more time to infest your crop.
- Discard culls and other organic debris promptly. Fungi overwinter in garden debris, and this includes onion plant matter.
- Be careful with cultivating tools: cuts in bulbs and foliage create entry points for disease spores.
- Buy seeds, plants, and sets that are certified disease-free whenever possible.
- Stop disease spores from invading onions after harvest by spreading them on a table or screen to dry, so the air circulates freely around them.
- Pull out and discard diseased bulbs. Disease spores spread by wind and by water splashing soil onto the plant; they are also carried on your hands, clothing, and tools.

Walla Walla onions are ready for harvest. The Walla Walla and the Vidalia are the most common varieties of sweet onions.

A Gallery of Onions

Bulb onions *(Allium cepa)* vary slightly in flavor, texture, and color, but most of these kinds of onions can be substituted for one another in recipes.

BERMUDA ONION
Large, flat, and mostly white, these sweet, mild onions were first brought to Bermuda in 1616 and soon became a staple crop. As onion shipments to the East Coast increased, Americans began to call Bermuda the "Onion Patch."

PEARL ONION
Also called baby onions, or creamers, these are actually a small, sweet variety of bulb onions. Rounded like white or yellow onions, their diameter ranges from ¼ to ½ inch (6.35–12.7 cm). Cocktail onions are pearl onions pickled in brine.

RED ONION
These medium-to-large cultivars, sometimes called purple onions, have purplish red skin and white flesh tinged with red. They are used in cooking and provide tangy, sharp flavor. They can also be eaten raw or pickled.

SWEET ONION
Their low sulfur and high water content mean these onions lack the pungency of other varieties. They are ideal for deep frying, making "blooming onions," and roasting, as well as for preparing French onion soup.

YELLOW ONION
This all-purpose variety, astringent and sweet, is used in numerous dishes. The size of a fist, with tough skin and meaty layers, this onion's harsh taste is softened by cooking. Spanish onions are a type of yellow onion, milder, and often eaten raw.

WHITE ONION
These thin-skinned, rounded onions are more tender and have a sharper, more pungent flavor than yellow onions. They can be cooked the same ways, as well as minced and added to raw salsas and chutneys.

Other *Alliums*

LEEK
Leeks *(A. porrum/A. ampeloprasum)* are cultivars of the broadleaf wild leek. The edible part of the plant is a bundle of leaf sheaths. Leeks are the national flower of Wales and, with their sweet oniony flavor, are often used in salads, soups, and as a side dish on is own.

EGYPTIAN WALKING ONION
Also called tree onions *(A. x proliferum)*, these plants have clusters of bulblets at the top where flowers would normally be. The name comes from the bulblets' habit of bending to the ground and taking root. Young plants are strongly flavored.

SCALLION
Sometimes called green onions, scallions *(A. cepa)* are young onions harvested early, before the bulbs form. The white stalks offer an intense oniony bite, while the leaves taste fresh and are milder. *Allium fistulosum*, or "bunching onions," are scallions that never form bulbs.

SHALLOT
Shallots *(A. ascalonium)* are small onions that have a distinctive tapered shape and skins of a coppery brown; the skins can also be reddish or gray. Their delicate flavor is unique among *Alliums*, so if a recipe calls for shallots, it's best not to substitute other varieties.

Okra

Long pods of okra are ready for picking. This warm-weather crop yields the green vegetable found in many world cuisines.

Okra *(Abelmoschus esculentus),* also called ladies' fingers or ochro, is a flowering plant in the mallow family. Its origins are uncertain, but it is now cultivated in tropical, subtropical, and warm temperate regions around the world. The edible green seed pods have become a signature ingredient in the cuisine of several areas, including the American South (where it is often used in gumbo), Cuba and Puerto Rico (where it is referred to as *quimbombó),* and India (where it is called *bhindi),* along with the Middle East, Brazil, and Sri Lanka.

Okra can be eaten cooked, pickled, or raw. Often disparaged for its slimy texture, the pods of the plant are mucilaginous, which results in the characteristic "goo" of cooked okra. A tried-and-true method of de-sliming okra is to cook it with acidic foods, such as tomatoes, which lessens some of the slime.

GROWING OKRA

The best time to plant okra is about two to three weeks after the last chance of frost has passed. Okra is a warm-season crop that requires a lot of sunshine, so find a place in your garden that doesn't get much shade. Also, when planting okra, be sure there is good drainage in your garden.

To prepare your garden area for planting, add 2 to 3 pounds (.9–.36 kg) of fertilizer for every 100 square feet (9.2 m^2) of garden space. Work the fertilizer into the ground about 3 to 5 inches (7.5–12.5 cm) deep. This will allow your growing plants the greatest chance of absorbing nutrients.

After fertilization, rake the soil to remove all rocks and sticks. Work the soil well, about 10 to 15 inches (25–38 cm) deep, so the plants can get the most nutrients from the soil around their roots. You can then plant rows spaced about 1 to 2 inches (2.5–5 cm) apart.

CARING FOR THE PLANTS

Once your growing okra is up and out of the ground, thin the plants to about 1 foot (30 cm) apart. When you grow this vegetable, it may be helpful to plant it in shifts so that you can get an even flow of ripe crops throughout the summer.

Water the plants every 7 to 10 days. The plants can handle dry conditions, but regular water is definitely beneficial. Carefully remove grass and weeds around your growing okra plants.

Editor's Tip

Because okra is self-pollinating, you can save some of the pods for seeds to plant the following year. This will make for a great crop the second time around. Instead of harvesting the young, tender pods, leave some pods on the plants, and then collect them when they become fully mature and almost dry. Leaving the pods on the plant to dry out does slow down the development of new pods, however, so wait until you have harvested all the okra you intend to use for the season before letting some of them mature.

At a Glance

SCIENTIFIC NAME: *Abelmoschus esculentus*

FAMILY: Malvaceae

HEIGHT: 6 to 8 feet (1.8–2.4 m)

WIDTH: 3 feet (1 m)

SOIL pH: Acidic

LIGHT: Full sun

HARVEST: Summer, autumn

HARVESTING OKRA

Okra matures quickly, especially if you have a summer of hot weather, which the plant prefers. The pods will be ready for harvest at about two months from planting. Harvesting can be tricky, however, because you have to harvest the pods before they become tough. It takes only about four days from the time of flowering to the time to pick okra, so harvest every other day to keep them producing as long as possible.

Picking okra should be done when the pods are 2 to 3 inches (5–7.5 cm) long. It is a simple task: just test the larger pods by cutting them open with a sharp knife. If they are too difficult to cut, they are too old and should be removed, as they will rob the plant of the nutrients it needs to produce new pods. If the pods are tender, use a sharp knife to cut the stem cleanly just below the okra pod.

Once you're done picking okra, store the pods in plastic bags in your refrigerator, where they will last about a week, or blanch and freeze the pods if you have too much to use right away. Once thawed, they are perfect for stews and soups.

Pea

Green pea pods are ready for harvest. Pea plants are easy to cultivate but have a limited growing season. As with other legumes, peas will fix nitrogen in the soil, making it available for other plants. This makes them a great companion plant.

SCIENTIFIC NAME: *Pisum sativum*

FAMILY: Fabaceae

HEIGHT: 12 to 18 inches (30–45 cm)

WIDTH: 6 to 12 inches (15–30 cm)

SOIL pH: Acidic, neutral

LIGHT: Full to partial sun

HARVEST: Late spring, summer

Peas are tasty, nutritious legumes that are quite easy to grow. Though there are many varieties of *Pisum sativus* (the type species of the *Pisum* genus) plants to be found, they can generally be sorted into three categories: garden peas and snow peas.

Garden peas, also known as English peas, are the most common type of pea. They have tough, inedible pods, and they are a great source of fiber and protein. Garden peas are also the fastest-growing type of edible pea. They are often served boiled or steamed.

Snow peas are part of the edible-pod, or sugar pea, category. These peas have thinner, edible pods, and they are generally sweeter than garden peas. Snow pea pods are delicate and almost completely flat, as are the peas inside. Their most common usage is in Chinese dishes, such as stir-fries, although they are also often eaten raw or steamed.

GROWING PEAS

Choose a sunny spot in your garden with rich, well-draining soil; pea plants need full sun, though they will tolerate light shade. They need less fertilizing than many other vegetables, so adding a little compost to the soil before planting is usually adequate. For climbing peas, choose a location where they can grow up a sturdy trellis or other stable support structure.

Peas are cool-weather plants; if you sow them too late in the spring, they may struggle in the hotter months. Instead, as soon as the ground is workable and thawed, start sowing peas directly outdoors. These will likely be one of the first plants you start each year. They tolerate cold well, so there is no need to start them inside. Sow the seeds to a depth of about 1 inch (2.5 cm).

CARING FOR THE PLANTS

Water your pea plants only when there is not enough rain to provide about an inch (2.5 cm) of water each week. Spring is usually wet, so some years you likely won't have to water at all. When you do water them, be sure to water the soil only at the base of the plant to avoid increasing the risk of disease and mildew.

HARVESTING PEAS

Harvesting your peas at the right time is essential. These plants grow very quickly, but they also overmature quickly and can become inedible. Once the pods start to flesh out with peas, check on them daily. Pick peas as soon as the pods have reached their maximum size. If you think the pods are ready, pick one, and try it; the peas inside should be thin-skinned, sweet, and tender.

The Snap Pea

A close cousin of the garden and snow pea is the snap pea *(Pisum macrocarpon).* Like the snow pea, the snap pea, or sugar snap pea, is part of the edible-pod, or sugar pea, category. It has rounder pods and a much sweeter flavor than other varieties. It is commonly eaten raw or served in salads.

Peppers

Ripening bell peppers. How long you keep them on the vine will determine their color at harvest.

Peppers (*Capsicum* spp.), native to Mexico, Central America, and northern South America, are members of the nightshade family, along with tomatoes and eggplants. The *Capsicum* genus includes thousands of cultivars that produce a wide array of heat levels, from the sweetly mild to the scorching hot. *C. annuum* includes bell peppers, cayennes, jalapeños, and serrano, while *C. chinense* includes fiery peppers, such as the habaneros, Scotch bonnets, and Carolina Reapers.

Like most gardeners, when you're planning your vegetable garden, you'll probably want to include some peppers. These easy-to-grow plants not only look great, they also produce right up until the first frost of autumn. Peppers are excellent in all sorts of dishes, raw and cooked. They can be pickled or frozen at season's end and enjoyed in dishes throughout the winter.

GROWING PEPPERS

Temperature is an important factor. Unless you live in a hot climate, always start pepper plant seedlings indoors. The seeds need warmth to germinate.

Fill a seed tray with seed starting soil or well-draining potting soil, placing one to three seeds in each container. Place the tray in a warm location or use a warming mat to keep them between 70 to 90° F (21–32° C)—the warmer the better.

You can cover the tray with plastic wrap. Water droplets will form on the underside of the plastic to let you know the baby seeds have enough water. If the drops stop forming, it's time to give them a drink. You should begin to see signs of plants popping up within a couple of weeks.

When your little plants get to be a few inches tall, gently transfer them separately into small pots. As the weather begins to warm, harden off the seedlings by putting them outside for a bit during the day. This, along with a little fertilizer now and then, will strengthen them in preparation for the garden. When the weather has warmed up and your young plants have grown to about 8 inches tall (20 cm), you can transfer them to the garden. They'll thrive in soil with a pH of 6.5 or 7.

Peppers thrive in the warm seasons, so wait for the nighttime temperatures in your region to rise to 50° F (10° C) or higher before transplanting them to the garden. A frost will either kill the plants altogether or inhibit pepper growth, leaving you with bare plants.

Placed the plants in the soil 18 to 24 inches (46–60 cm) apart. They'll enjoy being located near your tomatoes. The soil should be well drained and amended before you put them into the ground. Healthy pepper plants should produce peppers throughout late summer and even early autumn.

HARVESTING PEPPERS

Begin to pick the peppers once they are 3 to 4 inches (7.5 to 10 cm) long, and the fruit is firm and green. If they feel somewhat thin, the peppers aren't ripe. If they feel soggy, it means they've been left on the plant too long. After you harvest the first crop of peppers, feel free to fertilize the plants to give them the energy they need to form another crop.

If you are growing bell peppers and prefer the red, yellow or orange shades, allow them to stay longer on the vine to mature. They'll start out green, but you'll notice they have a thinner feel. Once they begin to take on color, the peppers will thicken and become ripe enough to harvest.

SCIENTIFIC NAME: *Capsicum* spp.

FAMILY: Solanaceae

HEIGHT: 6 inches to 3 feet (15 cm–1 m)

WIDTH: 1 to 3 feet (30 cm–1 m)

SOIL pH: Mildly acidic, neutral

LIGHT: Full sun

HARVEST: Summer, autumn

When choosing what kind of pepper to grow, remember that they vary in heat from just about nothing to scorching. Scoville heat units (SHU) measure this heat and are a good guide to help you choose the level you are comfortable with. Remember, the higher the number, the hotter the pepper.

SHU	Pepper Variety
800,000 to 3,200,000	• Pepper X • Carolina Reaper • Dragon's Breath
350,000 to 800,000	• Red Savina • Chocolate habanero
100,000 to 350,000	• Habanero • Scotch bonnet
10,000 to 100,000	• Malagueta • Cayenne • Serrano • Chipotle • Chile de arbol
1,000 to 10,000	• Guajillo • Poblano • Jalapeño • Ancho
100 to 1,000	• Banana pepper • Cubanelle
0 to 100	• Bell pepper • Pimiento

Pole Beans

The long vines of scarlet runner beans *(Phaseolus coccineus)*, a type of pole bean, grow upward on an arrangement of poles. Before harvest time, the bright red flowers of these plants will add interest and color to your kitchen garden.

SCIENTIFIC NAME: *Phaseolus* spp. and *Vigna unguiculata sesquipedalis*

FAMILY: Fabaceae

HEIGHT: Up to 10 feet (3 m)

WIDTH: 2 to 3 feet (60 cm–1 m)

SOIL pH: Acidic

LIGHT: Full sun

HARVEST: Spring, summer

Fresh, crisp beans are summer treats that are easy to grow in most climates. Beans may be pole or bush; pole beans include varieties of common beans *(Phaseolus vulgaris)*, runner beans *(P. coccineus)*, or yardlong beans *(Vigna unguiculata sesquipedalis)*.

Pole beans allow the gardener to maximize vertical planting space, and planting pole beans also ensures a longer crop period and may yield up to three times as many beans as the bush varieties (for more information on bush beans, *see* page 178). They do require some training onto a pole or trellis, but the height makes them easier to harvest, and the graceful flowering vines add dimensional interest to the vegetable garden.

GROWING POLE BEANS

Find a sunny spot in your kitchen garden to plant pole beans. Weather is also an important consideration. Sow the seeds when soil temperatures are around 60° F (16° C), and the ambient air has warmed to at least the same temperature. Most varieties require 60 to 70 days to first harvest and are normally harvested at least five times during the growing season. Beans in general do not transplant well and do best when directly sown into the garden.

Pole beans need well-drained soil and plenty of organic amendment to produce a large crop, but they need little fertilizer. If you do use fertilizer, add it to the soil before planting. Side dress with manure or mulch or use black plastic to conserve moisture, minimize weeds, and keep soil warm for increased yield.

Sow the seeds 4 to 8 inches (10–20 cm) apart in rows that are 24 to 36 inches (60cm–1 m) apart. Push down the seeds about 1 inch (2.5 cm), and then lightly brush soil over them. When planting them in hills, sow four to six seeds at even intervals around the hill. Water after planting until the top 2 to 3 inches (5–7.5 cm) of soil are damp. Germination should take place in 8 to 10 days.

CARING FOR THE PLANTS

These beans need a support structure at least 6 feet (2 m) high, and the vines can grow 5 to 10 feet (1.5–3 m) long. Beans need a little help climbing their support structure, especially when young. It's important to get them up off the ground early to prevent rot and loss of blooms. They will need at least an inch (2.5 cm) of water per week and should not be allowed to dry out, but they also cannot tolerate soggy soils.

HARVESTING POLE BEANS

A single plant can yield several pounds of beans. Harvesting them begins as soon as the pods are full and swollen. Pick them every three to five days to avoid harvesting older beans, which can be woody and bitter. The pods are best used fresh, but they can be lightly blanched and frozen for future use. Consistent harvesting will encourage new flowers and promote longer-living vines.

Editor's Picks

There are several varieties of these beans that have long proven to be kitchen garden winners.

- 'Asparagus Yardlong' (above) is a stringless, black-seeded variety that grows well in hot climates.
- 'Blue Coco', an heirloom variety, produces flat, bluish purple pods covering chocolate-colored seeds.
- 'Blue Lake' is an old-time favorite that produces large, disease-resistant beans with great flavor.
- 'Kentucky Wonder', a dark green heirloom variety, also called Old Homestead, is high yielding and one of the most popular of all pole beans.
- Kentucky Blue', a cross of Kentucky Wonder and Blue Lake, yields enormous pods that are straight, smooth, and plump, with dark green stems and light strings.
- 'Romano', also called the Italian flat bean, produces delicious, broad, flat beans with a stringless seam that reveals tiny, lime green to white-colored peas.

Potato

A gardener harvests a crop of potatoes. This staple and nutrient-dense veggie is easy to grow at home and can be prepared in countless ways.

Potatoes are one of the most important staple food crops in the world. These versatile, hardy vegetables are nutrient-dense, can be prepared in countless different ways, and are used in everything from fast food to haute cuisine.

Thousands of potato cultivars have been developed all over the world. Many of these varieties have been selectively bred for specific qualities of skin, color, flavor, and texture; red, white, yellow, blue, and purple potatoes exist in all shapes and sizes. Some of the most popular varieties include Yukon Gold, Russet Burbank, and All Blue.

All potato plant varieties may be planted in March or April. Care must be taken not to plant the seed potatoes too early, however, as the pieces may rot in overly damp soil. Likewise, if planted in March, they stand a chance of being frozen back by a late frost.

GROWING POTATOES

Potatoes can be started from seed or seed potatoes. Seed potatoes are generally recommended because they have been bred to resist disease and are certified. They will also provide you with the earliest and fullest harvest when compared to seed-started plants.

Seed potatoes can be planted whole or cut up so that there are one or two buds or "eyes" on each piece.

The conditions needed to grow potatoes vary only slightly by variety. As a general rule, potatoes require well-drained soil with plenty of organic matter incorporated into it. They need a lot of water, at least 1 inch (2.5 cm) per week, but the tubers will rot if allowed to soak in saturated, poorly draining soil.

Trenches are the most common way to plant potatoes. Dig trenches 4 inches (10 cm) deep and 2 to 3 feet apart (60 cm–1 m). Cut apart seed potatoes into sections that have at least two to three eyes, or growing points. Plant the pieces 12 inches (30 cm) apart with the majority of the eyes facing upward, and then lightly cover the pieces with soil. As they sprout, add more soil to cover the green growth until it matches soil level; potatoes will turn green and become toxic if exposed to sunlight.

Potatoes can also be grown in containers, compost heaps, or even piles of straw. A large planter or barrel is a common choice of container, but they will grow in just about anything; other popular choices include tires, garbage cans, and burlap sacks.

SCIENTIFIC NAME: *Solanum tuberosum*

FAMILY: Solanaceae

HEIGHT: 1 to 3 feet (30 cm–1 m)

WIDTH: 1 to 3 feet (30 cm–1 m)

SOIL pH: Acidic

LIGHT: Full sun

HARVEST: Autumn

A growing potato is an undemanding plant. They need very little other than mild temperatures, lots of water, and enough soil to keep them away from the sun.

HARVESTING POTATOES

When the flowers die and turn yellow, stop watering the potato plants, and wait one week. Then, carefully dig up the tubers with a trowel or dump them out of their container. Once the potatoes have been dug up from the soil, allow them to air dry in a cool, dry place before storing them.

Editor's Picks

The humble spud doesn't have to be boring with so many cultivars available. Here is a sampling of varieties well suited for home gardens.

- **'Daisy Gold' is a cheerful yellow, flaky, and moist all-purpose potato.**
- **'Kennebec' has smooth, thin skin and a creamy texture.**
- **'Magic Molly' is deep purple both inside and out.**
- **'Masquerade' has strikingly marbled purple and white skin and moist, white flesh.**
- **'Princess Laratte" is a French variety with a nutty taste**
- **'Red Gold' is a pretty potato with yellow flesh and raspberry-red eyes and offers a unique nutty flavor.**
- **'Swedish Peanut Fingerling' has waxy, firm yellow flesh and a rich heirloom flavor.**
- **'Yukon Gold' is an all-time favorite for roasting.**

Radish

SCIENTIFIC NAME: *Raphanus raphanistrum* subsp. *sativus*

FAMILY: Brassicaceae

HEIGHT: 6 to 18 inches (15–45 cm)

WIDTH: 3 to 14 inches (7.5 to 36 cm)

SOIL pH: Acidic, neutral

LIGHT: Full sun to partial afternoon shade

HARVEST: Summer, autumn

When radishes near maturity, the tops of their swollen roots will sometimes begin to emerge from the soil. One way to check on their progress is to pull up a sacrificial radish plant to see if the roots have reached a usable size. Watering the radishes well the night before harvesting them makes it far easier to pull them from the ground.

The origins of the radish *(Raphanus raphanistrum* subsp. *sativus)* are obscure, but we do know that this edible root vegetable has been cultivated for thousands of years. The radish is now grown and consumed throughout the world. It is mostly eaten raw, imparting a spicy, peppery flavor and crunchy texture to salads, and it provides a decorative accent on relish trays. When cooked, it maintains its flavor and texture, making it an excellent addition to roasted root vegetable medleys. As well as attractive and tasty, it is an excellent source of potassium, vitamin C, and folate. Plus, it is one of the easiest vegetables that you can cultivate in your vegetable garden.

There are five main varieties of radish, with hybrid types branching from these. Red Globe is an early, high-yielding variety producing uniform, bright red globes with crisp, tender, juicy, and mild white flesh. Black radish, a winter variety, is crisp and pungent, with spicy white flesh. California Mammoth, a large, round, white radish, has a mild, sweet flavor. Daikon is a crisp and juicy Chinese variety with a mild and tangy taste. 'Crisp White Icicles' radish is a long, white tapered variety with a rich, spicy flavor.

GROWING RADISHES

Radishes are generally grown from seed and grow best in cool weather. They require a loose soil for proper root formation. Composted manure, grass, and leaves can be added to improve soil fertility. Removing rocks, sticks, and inorganic debris from the planting site is recommended. The soil needs to be consistently moist. Heavy rains can compact soil and form a hard crust on the surface, which inhibits root formation. On the other hand, drought stress makes radishes tough and alters their mild flavor.

Sow seeds as soon as the soil can be worked in the spring or in late summer for an autumn crop. Spade or till the soil to a depth of 8 to 12 inches (20–30 cm). Using a hoe, make rows that are about an inch (2.5 cm) deep. Plant the radish seeds by hand, with a seeder, or use radish seed tape. Push the seeds into the ground to a depth of ½ inch (1.25 cm), spacing them 1 inch (2.5 cm) apart. Once you've filled up a row, cover the seeds with a loose layer of soil. When all rows are done, lightly sprinkle them with water, enough to settle things in, but not soaked to the point of becoming muddy. Watering too hard can wash the seeds right out of the soil they were just planted in.

Germination takes 4 to 6 days. For a steady harvest, use succession planting by sowing radish seeds every 7 to 10 days.

HARVESTING RADISHES

Radishes mature quickly, with most varieties ready for harvest in three to five weeks. They can be harvested at any usable size, but smaller radish roots tend to be zestier. As roots mature, they become tougher. If left in the ground too long, they will turn woody.

To harvest round types of radishes, firmly grasp the foliage and base of the plant and gently pull the root from the soil. For longer varieties, like daikon, use a shovel or fork to loosen the soil so the root doesn't break when pulling. Harvested radishes store well for several weeks in the refrigerator.

Editor's Tips

The following tips should help you harvest a good radish crop:

- **If the soil becomes crusty, lightly sprinkle the surface with water. Gently break up the surface using your hand or a small cultivator.**
- **As radish roots reach an edible size, harvest every other one to increase the space between remaining plants.**
- **Radishes need 1 inch (2.5 cm) of rain or supplemental water a week. Water radishes deeply, as they have large taproots and few horizontal roots.**
- **Growing radish plants in full sun gives the best yields, but radishes can also tolerate light shade.**
- **Plant several radish varieties for different colors, sizes, and flavors.**

GROWING LETTUCE IN THE GARDEN

Growing lettuce *(Lactuca sativa)* is an easy and inexpensive way to put fresh gourmet salad greens on the table. As a cool-season crop, lettuce grows well with the cool, moist weather available in spring and autumn. In cooler climates, the lettuce growing season can also be extended year-round using an indoor hydroponic system.

WHEN TO PLANT LETTUCE

The lettuce growing season begins in early spring and extends through autumn for northern climates. In warmer areas, lettuce can also be grown outdoors throughout the winter. Increasing daylight hours and hot temperatures stimulates lettuce to bolt, which makes growing lettuce more challenging during the summer months.

As a cool-season crop, lettuce can be direct-seeded into the garden as soon as the soil can be worked in the spring. If the ground is still frozen, wait until it thaws. Lettuce can also be started or grown indoors. Try succession planting and growing varieties of lettuce with differing maturity times to harvest plants throughout the growing season.

HOW TO GROW LETTUCE

Lettuce prefers moist, cool conditions, and you don't even have to worry about chilly weather because the seedlings can tolerate a light frost. In fact, these plants grow best when temperatures are between 45 and 65° F. (7–18° C.).

READ MORE AT GARDENING KNOW HOW

To learn how to take care of lettuce growing in water, just follow the first URL or scan the QR code. For other options, just follow the other links listed below.

- **"Regrowing Lettuce in Water: Caring for Lettuce Plants Growing in Water"** (URL = gkh.us/95353)
- **"Growing Lettuce in the Garden — How to Grow Lettuce Plants"** (URL = gkh.us/1613)
- **"Hanging Container Lettuce: How to Make a Hanging Lettuce Basket"** (URL = gkh.us/136790)

Lettuce tastes more flavorful and the leaves remain tender when it grows quickly. Prior to planting, work organic compost or high-nitrogen fertilizer into the garden soil to encourage rapid leaf growth. Lettuce prefers a soil pH between 6.2 and 6.8.

Due to its small seed size, it's better to sprinkle the seeds on top of fine soil, and then cover lightly with a thin layer of dirt. A small hand-held seeder or seed tape can also be used for proper spacing of plants. Avoid planting too deeply, as the plants require sunlight to germinate.

To avoid dislodging newly planted seed, water by gently misting the area with a fine spray until the soil is moist. When direct-seeding into the garden, consider using a plastic row cover, cold frame, or scrap window pane to protect the seed from being washed away by heavy rains. For optimal growth, lettuce requires 1 to 2 inches (2.5 to 5 cm) of rain or supplemental water per week.

Give lettuce plenty of room to mature by spacing plants 8 to 12 inches (20 to 30 cm) apart. Planting in full sun will generate faster leaf production, but it can encourage bolting during hot weather. Still, lettuce will actually thrive in a little bit of shade too, making it great for planting between taller crops, like tomatoes or corn, which will provide shade as the season progresses. This also helps save on space in smaller gardens.

TIPS FOR HARVESTING LETTUCE PLANTS

You will want to harvest your lettuce crops in the best way possible to ensure fresh, flavorful greens for your salads.

- For crisper lettuce, harvest in the morning. Wash leaves in cold water, and dry with a paper towel. Place lettuce in a plastic bag, and store in the refrigerator.
- Leaf lettuce can be harvested once the outer leaves reach a usable size. Picking the young, tender outer leaves will encourage the inner leaves to continue growing.
- Harvest romaine and leaf lettuce as baby greens by cutting straight across the plant 1 or 2 inches (2.5 to 5 cm) above the soil level. Be sure to leave the basal growing point for further leaf development.
- Harvest head lettuce (depending on the variety) when they've reached a suitable size. If you allow the lettuce to become too mature, you'll end up with bitter lettuce.
- Harvest iceberg when the head forms a tight ball and the outer leaves are pale green. Plants can be pulled or heads can be cut.
- Romaine (cos) types of lettuce can be harvested by removing tender outer leaves or waiting until a head is formed. When removing the head, cut the plant above the base to encourage regrowth or remove the entire plant if regrowth is not desired.

Lettuce Favorites and Other Garden Salad Greens

ARUGULA
Also known as rocket, Italian cress, Mediterranean rocket, and roquette, *Eruca vesicaria* has a peppery, spicy, and slightly tart flavor that adds zest to a salad. Another cool-weather crop, plant this with lettuces for a varied salad garden.

BUTTERHEAD
Also known as butter, Boston, and bibb lettuce, this delicate variety has a ruffled appearance, with a blanched heart and sweet, buttery flavor. Boston is a lighter green with softer leaves and big heads. Similar to butterhead, bibb has smaller heads.

CORAL LETTUCE
Also known as Lollo Rosso (red) and Lollo Bionda (pale green), these are curly-edged lettuces with a mild, slightly bitter flavor. The frilly leaves, produced loosely in a whole head, add color, texture, and volume to your salads.

CRESS
Also known as watercress, upland cress, curly cress, and land cress, *Nasturtium officinale* is a highly nutritious, dark leafy aquatic green with a crisp, peppery flavor that stands out in a mixed salad. You can also use it for dainty tea sandwiches.

CRISPHEAD
Also known as iceberg, Reine de Glace, and igloo lettuce, crisphead lettuce forms a large, dense head that resembles a cabbage. With a crispy, crunchy texture that holds up to shredding, it has sweet, mild flavor that makes it a salad favorite.

ENDIVE, ESCAROLE, AND FRISÉE
The genus *Cichorium* gives us these three salad favorites. Crisp endive has a sweet, nutty flavor with a bitter finish. Escarole is less bitter, while frisée's bitter, frilly outer leaves reveal a creamy yellow center.

KALE
Highly popular kale, often touted as a "superfood" is a dark, leafy crucifer you can eat raw or cooked. It can be dry and tough, but the crunchy leaves have an earthy flavor. Young kale is softer and thinner leaves, with a milder taste.

LOOSE LEAF
Also known as Batavia lettuce, leaf lettuce, green leaf lettuce, red leaf lettuce, and Redina, loose leaf lettuce is sweet and crisp. When you feel like having like a salad, you can cut off outer leaves, and the rest of the plant will continue to grow.

MÂCHE
Also known as field salad, lamb's lettuce, corn salad, field lettuce, and fetticus, tender *Valerianella locusta* is best eaten raw. It has a soft, velvety, and crisp texture, with a mild, herbal, and nutty flavor that pairs well with vinaigrette.

MUSTARD GREENS
Brassica juncea, the same plant that gives us the condiment mustard, can be served raw or cooked. This salad green is peppery, pungent, and a little bitter To avoid too much bitterness, harvest mustard greens while they are young.

OAK LEAF
Also known as royal oak and green oak lettuce, this easy grower is recognizable by the shape of its deeply lobed leaves. The soft, slightly frilled leaves of young oak leaf have a mild and gentle taste, with crunchy stems.

ROMAINE
Also known as cos lettuce, sweet, crisp Romaine has compact hearts of long, broad leaves. It is the centerpiece of Caesar salads, and the outer leaves can be used as wraps. In the garden, it requires higher fertility than loose-leaf types.

Spinach

The healthy, dark green leaves of 'Bloomsdale Long Standing' spinach are ready for a first harvest. This classic savoy variety with meaty leaves has a rich, nutty flavor. Savoy spinaches are tasty, but their crinkles and curls can make them hard to clean.

Spinach *(Spinacia oleracea)* has been cultivated for over 2,000 years, and it remains a great addition to any vegetable garden today. This common plant is easy to grow and extremely healthful; spinach is a great source of iron, calcium, and vitamins A, B, C, and K.

GROWING SPINACH

Spinach is a cool-weather crop that does best in the spring and autumn. It prefers well-draining, rich soil and a sunny location. In regions with higher temperatures, the crop will benefit from some light shade from taller plants.

The soil should have a pH of at least 6.0 but, ideally, it should be close to neutral—between 6.5 and 7.5. Before planting, amend the seed bed with compost or aged manure. Sow seeds when outdoor temperatures are at least 45 F° (7 °C). Space the seeds 3 inches (7.5 cm) apart in rows, and cover lightly with soil. For successive plantings, sow another batch of seeds every two to three weeks.

Spinach takes about six weeks to mature. For an autumn crop, sow seeds from late summer to early autumn, or as late as four to six weeks before the first frost date. If needed, provide a row cover or cold frame to protect the plants. Spinach can also be planted in containers. To grow spinach in a pot, use a container that is at least 8 inches (20 cm) deep.

CARING FOR THE PLANTS

Keep spinach consistently moist, not soggy. Water deeply and regularly, especially during dry periods, and keep the area around the plants weeded.

Feed the plant at midseason with compost, blood meal, or kelp to encourage rapid growth of new, tender leaves. Spinach is a heavy feeder, so if you do not incorporate or side dress with compost, incorporate a 10-10-10 fertilizer prior to planting.

SCIENTIFIC NAME: *Spinacia oleracea*

FAMILY: Amaranthaceae

HEIGHT: 6 to 12 inches (15–30 cm)

WIDTH: 6 to 12 inches (15–30 cm)

SOIL pH: Neutral

LIGHT: Full to partial sun

HARVEST: Spring to autumn

Leaf miners are a common pest associated with spinach crops. Frequently check the undersides of the leaves for eggs. When leaf miner tunnels are evident, destroy the leaves. Floating row covers can also help repel leaf miners.

HARVESTING SPINACH

You can begin harvesting spinach leave as soon as they are large enough to eat. Remove the outer leaves; this allows the center leaves to continue growing for another harvest.

Spinach Varieties

Spinach comes in three main varieties, categorized by the types of leaves they produce.

- **Smooth-leaf spinach.** The leaves of this type are smooth and flat, which makes it easy to rinse off any impurities from their surfaces. Most processed, commercial spinach is smooth leaf.
- **Savoy spinach.** The leaves of this variety are thick and deeply crinkled, which makes it hard to clean them of any sand and dirt. They keep longer and contain less oxalic acid than flat-leaf spinach.
- **Semi-savoy spinach.** The leaves are crinkled, but not as much as with savoy. Despite the crinkles, this variety is quite easy to clean because the leaves are partially straight. This is a popular variety for home gardens.

Squash/Pumpkin

SCIENTIFIC NAME: *Cucurbita* spp.

FAMILY: Cucurbitaceae

HEIGHT: 1 to 3 feet (30 cm–1 m)

WIDTH: 10 to 15 feet (3–4.5 m)

SOIL pH: Acidic to neutral

LIGHT: Full sun

HARVEST: Autumn

A bright orange pumpkin peeks out from its large, green leaves. The pumpkin is just one of the many varieties of winter squash. All have similar growth habits and requirements.

The *Cucurbita* genus is often referred to as simply "squash," but it includes almost all types of squash, pumpkin, and zucchini, as well as many gourds. All of the plants produced within these species can be grown as winter squash, though many varieties of *Cucurbita pepo,* in particular, are better treated as summer squash. Winter squashes are harvested and eaten (or stored) after they reach maturity, while summer squashes are harvested before maturity. Winter squashes are usually vine growers, while summer squashes tend to be bushier and don't cover as much ground.

Squashes as a whole are hugely popular and commonly grown garden vegetables, especially in the Americas. Some of the most well-known varieties in the genus include butternut squash, acorn squash, spaghetti squash, zucchini, and the traditional orange pumpkin, among many others.

GROWING SQUASH

As with other vine-growing crops, squash prefers heat, but it is often somewhat hardier than melons or cucumbers. Squash plants require full sun, fertile soil, and sufficient moisture. The use of well-composted material mixed into the soil is recommended, such as kitchen compost or decomposed manure. Many types of squash, especially pumpkins, require a large amount of space to grow; a minimum of 20 square feet (1.85 m2) is recommended for pumpkins.

Squashes can be sown directly into the garden or started indoors. Summer and winter squashes are commonly planted in hills about 1 inch (2.5 cm) deep. Sow seeds only after any danger of frost has ended and the soil has warmed. Usually, only four to five seeds per hill is plenty, thinning down to two or three of the healthiest plants per hill once the seedlings have developed their true leaves.

Hills and rows of summer squash should be approximately 3 to 4 feet (1–1.2 m) apart, while winter squash should be spaced approximately 4 to 5 feet (1.2–1.5 m) apart with 5 to 7 feet (1.5–2.1 m) between rows.

HARVESTING SQUASH

Check daily when harvesting squash plants, as these crops grow quickly, especially in hot weather. You should harvest squash frequently to encourage more production, and pick the fruits while still small. Squash that is overly ripe becomes hard and seedy and loses its flavor. The summer varieties should be gathered before the seeds have fully ripened and while the rinds are still soft. The winter varieties should not be picked until well matured.

Summer squash can be stored in cool, moist areas up to two weeks. They may also be canned or frozen. Winter squash can be stored in a cool, dry location for one to six months.

READ MORE AT GARDENING KNOW HOW

Learn more about squashes by following the links below.

- **"What a Female Flower and a Male Flower Look Like on a Squash Plant"** (URL = gkh.us/4174)
- **"Picking Squash Blossoms — How and When to Pick Squash Flowers"** (URL = gkh.us/14651)

Sweet Potato

A gardener digs up the soil to reveal a nice harvest of sweet potatoes. This flavorful root vegetable is a favorite in many autumn and winter recipes.

The sweet potato is the large, sweet-tasting tuberous root of the *Ipomoea batatas* plant. A native of the tropical regions of the Americas, it is the only major crop plant of the more than a thousand species of Convolvulaceae, or the morning glory family. Along with the starchy root, the young shoots and leaves of the plant are sometimes eaten as greens.

Sweet potatoes are warm-weather vegetables; they do not grow like regular potatoes, and in fact they aren't related to potatoes at all. Sweet potatoes grow on vines, require a long, frost-free growing season, and produce a sweet, bright orange-fleshed tuber that is an especially popular ingredient in autumn and winter dishes. Some varieties can be found that produce white, yellow, or purple sweet potatoes.

GROWING SWEET POTATOES

When growing sweet potatoes, start out with "slips." These are small pieces of tubers that are used to start the plants. They can also be started from sweet potatoes you buy from the grocery store, but purchased slips are quality-controlled to be disease-free. Plant these slips into the ground as soon as all chance of frost has passed, and the ground has warmed. Sweet potatoes require soil temperature of 70 to 80° F (21–27° C), so you should start them in early summer to midsummer. Otherwise, the soil won't be warm enough for these plants to grow.

Plant the slips 12 to 18 inches (30–45 cm) apart on a wide, raised ridge of soil that is about 8 inches (20 cm) high. Leave about 3 to 4 feet (1–1.2 m) between rows, so that there will be enough space to work between them when harvesting. Keep the soil moist during the growing season, but make sure it drains well to limit the chances of rot setting in. From the moment you plant the slips, it takes only six weeks for the sweet potatoes to be ready to harvest.

HARVESTING SWEET POTATOES

In order to harvest the growing sweet potatoes, just stick your shovel into the side of the ridge. You can feel around for the sweet potatoes and pull them out that way, being careful not to injure others still growing. They are generally ready around the first frost of autumn.

A standard crop of sweet potatoes will usually produce more tubers than you can eat right away. When stored in a cool, dry place, they can last for several weeks.

At a Glance

SCIENTIFIC NAME: *Ipomoea batatas*

FAMILY: Convolvulaceae

HEIGHT: 1 to 12 inches (2.5–30 cm)

WIDTH: 5 to 20 feet (1.5–6 m)

SOIL pH: Acidic

LIGHT: Full sun to partial shade

HARVEST: Autumn

Yams

Although the names "yam" and "sweet potato" are often used interchangeably, these are two different plants. They have many similarities—both are sweet, autumn-harvest tubers, for instance—but they are actually members of entirely separate families: yams are related to lilies and are members of the Dioscoreaceae family, while sweet potatoes are members of the morning glory family (Convolvulaceae). Yams grow best in tropical to subtropical climates, as they need up to a full year of frost-free temperatures to mature. They are commonly grown in Central and South America, the Caribbean, and Africa. They should be planted in early spring.

Tomato

SCIENTIFIC NAME: *Solanum lycopersicum*

FAMILY: Solanaceae

HEIGHT: 4 to 8 feet (1.2–2.4 m)

WIDTH: 2 to 4 feet (60 cm–1.2 m)

SOIL pH: Slightly acidic

LIGHT: Full sun

HARVEST: Summer

A pole system within a raised bed supports the growing vines of tomato plants. These plants are favorite with home gardeners and can be grown in containers for those with only small spaces to spare for a garden, such as an apartment balcony.

Nothing compares to the juicy taste of a red, ripe tomato straight out of the garden. These delectable fruits not only taste great but are quite easy to grow and mature quite early. They can grow in a variety of conditions, with the exception of the extreme cold, and they don't require a lot of space. You can start them from seed or transplant from seedlings, and they can thrive when planted straight in the ground or in containers. Some common varieties are cherry, heirloom, roma, main crop, and beefsteak tomatoes, but there are hundreds of types to choose from, depending on individual preferences.

STARTING TOMATO SEEDS

Tomatoes should usually be started indoors when growing from seeds, as they need a good deal of heat to germinate. Start about six to eight weeks before you plan on planting them out into your garden. For colder areas, plan to plant two to three weeks after your last frost, so you should start growing tomatoes from seed at four to six weeks before your last frost date.

Tomato seeds can be started in small pots of damp seed-starting soil, damp potting soil, or in moistened peat pellets. Plant two seeds in each container to increase your chances of developing a seedling in each, in case some of the seeds do not germinate. The tomato seeds should be planted about three times deeper than the size of the seed—roughly ⅛ to ¼ inch (3–6 mm) deep, depending on the tomato variety.

After the tomato seeds have been planted, place the seedling containers in a warm place. For fastest germination, temperatures of 70 to 80° F (21–27° C) are best, especially if heated from below. Many gardeners find that placing the planted tomato seed containers on top of the refrigerator or another appliance that generates heat while running works very well for germination. A heating pad on low, covered with a towel, will also work.

After planting, the tomato seeds should germinate in one to two weeks. Cooler temperatures will result in a longer germination time and warmer temperatures will make the tomato seeds germinate faster.

READ MORE AT GARDENING KNOW HOW

To get tips about growing the best, most flavorful tomatoes in containers, just follow this link or scan the QR code above for an informative video.

- **"Growing Tomatoes in Containers for Beginners"** (URL = gkh.us/188007)

PLANTING SEEDLINGS

Tomatoes can grow roots along their stems, so plant them deep; right up to the first set of leaves. If the plant is too long and unstable, dig a small trench, and lay the plant on its side, gently bending it into a right angle. Bury the stem in this position, leaving those first two leaves exposed. Allow for 3 feet (1 m) between the plants and 5 feet (1.5 m) between rows. They will need support as they grow, either from stakes or cages. Set the stakes in place when you plant the seedlings and loosely tie the plants to their stakes as they grow.

HARVESTING TOMATOES

Watch the bottom of the fruit carefully: this is where tomatoes begin to ripen. Lightly squeeze to test for firmness. Once the first bloom of red appears on the skin, it's harvest time. Grasp the fruit firmly, but gently, and pull from the plant by holding the stem with one hand and the fruit with the other, breaking the stalk just above the calyx. Store them indoors to continue to ripen. Store them at 55 to 70° F (13–21° C)—or cooler to slow the ripening and warmer to hasten it—and check routinely for ripeness. They may last from three to five weeks stored this way.

Watermelon

A round, green watermelon sits in the soil as it ripens. These melons have become synonymous with summertime. With their juicy, bright pink flesh and sweetly refreshing flavor, they make a perfect hot-weather snack or dessert for a picnic or barbecue.

Watermelons are part of the Cucurbitaceae family, making them a somewhat distant cousin of vegetables such as squash, pumpkin, and zucchini. These iconic summer fruits have been cultivated for thousands of years; they are believed to have originally been native to Africa before later spreading throughout the rest of the world.

Of the hundreds of varieties of watermelon that have been established, there are four basic categories: seedless, picnic, icebox, and yellow/orange fleshed.

- Seedless watermelons were created in the 1990s. These self-sterile hybrids are as sweet as seeded varieties, and they contain tiny, underdeveloped seeds that are more easily consumed that the larger black seeds found in traditional watermelon. They usually weigh 10 to 20 pounds (4.5-9 kg).
- Picnic watermelons tend to be larger, from 16 to 45 pounds (7.25-20 kg) or more, perfect for a picnic gathering. These are the traditional oblong or round melons with a green rind and sweet, red flesh.
- Icebox watermelons have been bred to feed just one person or a small family and, as such, are much smaller than their counterparts at only 5 to 15 pounds (2.25-7 kg). Watermelon plant varieties in this genre include the 'Sugar Baby' and the 'Tiger Baby'.
- Yellow/orange fleshed watermelons are typically spherical and can be both seedless and seeded. As the name implies, their flesh is a pretty yellow to orange in color, rather than the typical pink.

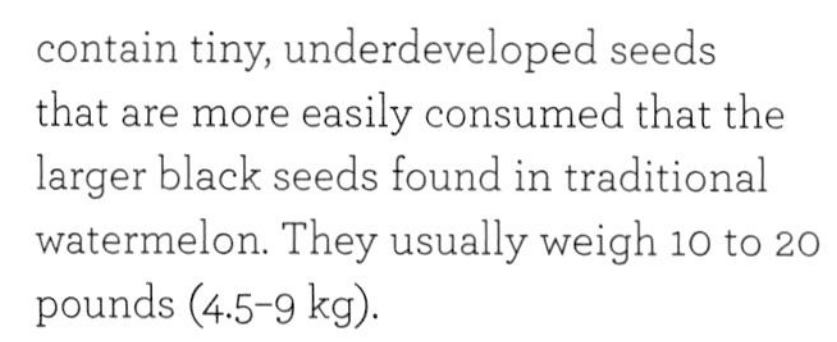

READ MORE AT GARDENING KNOW HOW

Follow the link below or scan the QR code to make sure you get the most from this delicious summertime favorite.

- **"How to Pick a Ripe Watermelon"** (URL = gkh.us/1935)

SCIENTIFIC NAME: *Citrullus lanatus*

FAMILY: Cucurbitaceae

HEIGHT: 9 to 18 inches (23–45 cm)

WIDTH: 10 to 15 feet (3–4.5 cm)

SOIL pH: Slightly acidic

LIGHT: Full sun

HARVEST: Summer

GROWING WATERMELONS

Watermelons take very little special attention to grow, especially in areas with hotter temperatures. They prefer sandy loam soil, full sun, and plenty of water. They also require a good amount of space to grow, as their vines tend to take up a lot of room.

Wait until the last frost has passed and soil temperatures reach at least 65 F° (18 C°). Plant watermelon seeds 1 inch (2.5 cm) deep in hills at least 3 feet (1 m) apart, with 7 to 10 feet (2.1–3 m) between rows. Keep the area free of weeds, and thin the plants when two or three leaves emerge from the seedlings. Using hot caps, floating row covers, or mulch with black plastic can help retain soil moisture and heat.

HARVESTING WATERMELONS

Watermelons take about 120 days to mature from start to finish. When they're ready to harvest, you'll notice that the little curly tendrils attached to each melon will turn brown and get a little crisp. The color of the watermelon will also get duller, and the skin will be hard and resistant to the penetration of your fingernail when you try to press it into the side. Another way to know if the watermelon is ripe is to pick one up and turn it over: if the bottom where it sits in the soil is yellow, the watermelon is probably ripe.

Zucchini

A green zucchini is ready for harvest. The most pertinent advice here is to harvest often and when the fruits are small.

Zucchini *(Cucurbita pepo)* has been a garden staple for centuries and has been cultivated since at least 5500 BCE. Today, zucchini, also called courgette or baby marrow, is a popular kitchen garden vegetable because it is a rapidly growing, prolific producer. A mature zucchini can grow to nearly 2 feet (1 m) in length, but it is typically harvested at about 6 to 10 inches (15–25 cm). The zucchini itself is a long and slender summer squash and is actually the fruit of the plant. In cookery, however, it is used as a vegetable, cooked and eaten as a savory main or side dish. The plant also produces female and male flowers; both are edible and are often used to garnish a meal.

The plants have two growth habits, vining and bush. Vining zucchini grow along the ground, requiring several feet of space between plants. You can also train this type to grow vertically on a very sturdy support. The bush variety is more compact. Try one of these if you have limited garden space—they can thrive in containers. Whether you choose vining or bush, resist the urge to grow too many; one plant will produce 6 to 10 pounds (3–4.5 kg) of fruit over the growing season.

There are a few varieties; the most popular is the basic green zucchini, which has a very mild, slightly sweet, grassy taste. The golden zucchini (not to be confused with yellow squash, a different variety of summer squash) is a bush type with brilliant yellow to almost orange fruit. The flavor is much the same as green zucchini, although some folks say it is sweeter.

GROWING ZUCCHINI

You sow zucchini as individual plants or group them on hills, making sure the location affords them at least 6 to 8 hours of full sun per day. Zucchini likes to start off in the area it will grow, but if you can't wait for soil temperatures to warm to direct sow into the garden, start seeds indoors three to six weeks before the last frost date. Be sure to harden off the seedlings for a week before transplanting them outdoors.

To start individual plants outside, be sure the chance of frost has passed and that soil temperatures have warmed and the air is close to 70° F (21° C). Prior to planting, work a few inches of compost or other organic matter into the soil. Space plants about 3 feet (1 m) apart to allow for space to grow, discourage disease, and allow for air flow. Plant each seed about an inch (2.5 cm) deep. Thin to one plant per spot once the seeds have sprouted and have grown their first set of true leaves.

If you are planting on a hill, mound up soil about 6 to 12 inches (15–30 cm) high and 12 to 24 inches (30–60 cm) wide. On the top of the hill, in a circle, plant three seeds. As the seedlings grow and get their first leaf, snip off the two weakest, leaving one strong seedling per hill.

CARING FOR THE PLANTS

Once seedlings are established, mulch around them to retain moisture and control weeds; as the plants grow, the large leaves will shade the soil and act as living mulch.

Make sure the plants get at least 2 inches (5 cm) of water a week. If you don't receive enough rainfall, supplement with manual watering. Use a soaker hose or another method to water the plants below their leaves, as watering with a sprinkler can cause the plants to develop powdery mildew.

Monitor the plants for pests. If early pests become a problem, cover the plants beneath a floating row cover. Drought-stressed plants are more susceptible to insect injury, as well as some diseases.

Zucchini are heavy feeders. If the leaves become pale or seem weak, side-dress the plants with well-aged compost or use a foliar spray of kelp or liquid fish fertilizer.

HARVESTING ZUCCHINI

Depending upon the variety, zucchini will be ready to harvest in 35 to 55 days from planting. Just cut the fruit from the plant, and use within three to five days, or store them in the refrigerator for up to two weeks.

SCIENTIFIC NAME: *Cucurbita pepo*

FAMILY: Cucurbitaceae

HEIGHT: 2 feet (60 cm)

WIDTH: 2 to 3 feet (60 cm–1 m)

SOIL pH: Slightly acidic to slightly alkaline

LIGHT: Full sun

HARVEST: Summer

Row Covers

Row covers are a great way to protect your prized plants from damaging cold or pests. Some of the best row covers include floating garden row covers, made of very lightweight woven material that allows light and water to penetrate, while insulating against the sudden drops in temperature common in many growing regions.

To learn more about floating row covers, scan the code or follow the link to "Row Covers for Garden Plants — How to Use Floating Row Covers in the Garden" (URL = gkh.us/16602).

PERENNIAL FRUITS AND VEGETABLES

Perennial vegetables and fruits, like perennial flowering plants, continue to produce for more than two years. These plants don't need to be started from scratch each year, and if well tended, they can provide years of harvesting. These perennials are generally eaten more in the form of fruit—such as berries, apples, and oranges, and so on—but there are also a number of perennial vegetables we enjoy on a regular basis.

Some of the better-known perennial vegetables found around the globe include asparagus, artichoke, and rhubarb. In the tropics staples like cassava, breadfruit, and taro are also grown as perennial crops. Perennial produce makes up an important part of many cultural diets around the world, and these foods are also a key factor in supporting the many self-employed subsistence farmers who live in the tropics.

In certain cases, perennials like potatoes are treated as annuals and sown anew each year in alternating locations to reduce pest pressure and the possibility of devastating disease.

The line between fruits and vegetables can be a bit blurry, at least in terms of how they are used. Some vegetables, such as rhubarb, are used in cooking as if they were fruits, including them in desserts and sweet foods like pies and jams.

READ MORE AT GARDENING KNOW HOW

Follow these links to informative articles that will help you get the most from a perennial vegetable garden.

- **"Perennial Vegetable Plants — How to Grow Perennial Vegetables** (URL = gkh.us/80195)
- **"Edible Perennial Plants — Growing a Perennial Food Garden"** (URL = gkh.us/166341)
- **"Cleaning the Garden in Autumn — Getting Your Garden Ready for Winter"** (URL = gkh.us/2523)

As more and more gardeners have begun exploring options for their kitchen gardens beyond the standard crops, wild foods, such as ramps (above) and Jerusalem artichokes are getting their space in home plots.

Asparagus

SCIENTIFIC NAME: *Asparagus officinalis*

FAMILY: Asparagaceae

HEIGHT: 6 to 12 inches (15–30 cm)

WIDTH: 1 to 3 feet (30 cm–1 m)

SOIL pH: Neutral

LIGHT: Full sun

HARVEST: Spring

New shoots of asparagus peek up from the soil. These shoots are a prized vegetable, served as an appetizer or side dish, often boiled or steamed and drizzled with Hollandaise sauce.

Asparagus *(Asparagus officinalis),* also called garden asparagus or sparrow grass, are the tender young shoots of a perennial flowering plant native to most of Europe and western temperate Asia. Formerly grouped in the lily family, since the early 2000s, the species has been classified in a family of its own, the Asparagaceae, along with yucca, bluebell, and hosta.

This is a long-lasting perennial—it is so long-lived, in fact, that some types of asparagus survive for as long as 20 to 30 years. Asparagus takes three years to grow before it is ready to harvest, but it can then be cultivated and harvested season after season for several decades.

Asparagus plants can be either male or female. There are some similarities between the two, but most farmers and gardeners choose to produce only male asparagus; male asparagus does not expend energy producing fruit, so it produces as many as three times more spears than female. Male asparagus also tends to live longer and start producing spears earlier in spring, making it generally more valuable.

GROWING ASPARAGUS

To start, buy one-year-old, healthy asparagus crowns. Dig a trench 8 to 10 inches (20–25 cm) deep and wide enough to accommodate the growing asparagus roots. If you're planting a larger crop with multiple rows, space the trenches 4 feet (1.2 m) apart.

Apply about 1 pound (.5 kg) of triple superphosphate (0-46-0) or 2 pounds (1 kg) of superphosphate (0-20-0) to the soil for every 50 feet (15 m) of trench. Place the crowns 18 inches (45 cm) apart, right on top of the fertilizer. Work liberal amounts of organic material into the dug soil, then use this soil to backfill the trench to a depth of 2 inches (5 cm).

As the asparagus grows, backfill with more soil every time you see another 2 inches (5 cm) of the tender new stalks. Care must be taken to protect these delicate shoots. Once the trench is filled, the bulk of the hard work is done. Weed the bed thoroughly in early spring to avoid competition for nutrients, and feed the growing asparagus annually with a 10-10-10 granular fertilizer.

READ MORE AT GARDENING KNOW HOW

Scan the QR code or follow this link to learn more about growing this vegetable.

- **"Planting Asparagus: How to Make an Asparagus Bed"** (URL = gkh.us/575)

HARVESTING ASPARAGUS

In the third year of growth, after planting one-year-old crowns, asparagus spears will be ready for harvesting. During this initial harvest year, spears should be harvested during the first month only. Removing the spears for more than a month during this important year of growth will weaken and possibly kill the plant.

Harvest spears that are 5 to 8 inches (12.5–20 cm) long and as big around as your finger. Asparagus that grows too long will quickly become woody and bitter; you will want to harvest it early enough in the season so that it is still tender, while allowing smaller spears to continue growing. Carefully cut or break the spears from the point closest to their attachment to the fibrous roots. Excessive disturbance of the area can result in damage to spears that have not yet broken ground.

A GALLERY OF

CRUCIFEROUS VEGETABLES

The cruciferous group of vegetables have recently generated a lot of interest in the health world due to the cancer-fighting compounds they contain. Subsequently, many gardeners began to wonder if they could grow them in their gardens. Good news! You probably already grow at least one type (and more likely several types) of crucifer.

These nutrient- and antioxidant-rich vegetables belong to the Cruciferae/Brassicaceae/mustard family, which is mainly made up of the *Brassica* genus, but which does include a few other genera. In general, cruciferous vegetables are cool-weather crops with flowers that have four petals, so that they resemble a cross. *Crucifer* means "cross-bearer" in Latin. In most cases, it is the leaves or flower buds of cruciferous vegetables that are eaten, but there are a few examples where the roots or seeds are also consumed.

As with most vegetables that belong to the same family, crucifers are susceptible to identical diseases and pests, so it's vital not to replant them in the same spot the following season. Allow at least two years before returning them to the original site. Diseases include anthracnose, bacterial leaf spot, black leaf spot, black rot, downy mildew, peppery leaf spot, root-knot, white-spot fungus, and white rust. Insect pests may include aphids, beet armyworm, cabbage looper, cabbage maggot, corn earworm, cutworm, diamondback moth, and nematodes.

TYPES OF CRUCIFEROUS VEGETABLES

This large family is made up of many popular vegetables . . . and then there is broccoli. An American president famously said he "hated it," and many people concurred. Yet it is one of the most versatile of vegetables, which can be steamed, roasted, grilled, riced, added to soups and stir-fries, and eaten raw. Some of broccoli's crucifer brethren are shown here.

Scan the QR code or follow the link to find out more about growing cruciferous vegetables.

- **"Types of Cabbage — Different Cabbages to Grow in Gardens "** (URL = gkh.us/134704)

BROCCOLI RABE
Broccoli rabe *(Brassica rapa)* is also known as rapini. This green vegetable's leaves, buds, and stems are all edible. Rapini is associated with Mediterranean cuisine, and it has a somewhat bitter taste. It is, however, a good source of vitamins A, C, and K, as well as the minerals potassium, calcium, and iron.

BRUSSELS SPROUTS
Brussels sprouts, part of the Gemmifera groups of *Brassica oleracea,* is a flavorful leaf vegetable grown for its edible buds, which can be steamed, grilled, roasted, or stir-fried. The sprouts resemble miniature cabbages. This is another veggie that people either adore or strenuously avoid.

CABBAGE
Cabbage *(Brassica oleracea)* is a round, compact, leafy green biennial grown as an annual vegetable. Smooth-leafed, firm-headed green cabbage is the most common, followed by smooth-leafed purple and crinkle-leafed savoy in both colors. Raw cabbage is a rich source of vitamins K and C and dietary fiber.

CAULIFLOWER
Cauliflower is part of the Botrytis group of *Brassica oleracea.* Its edible white flesh is often called "curd" due to its similarity to cheese curd. The head is composed of a white inflorescence meristem that also comes in hybrids of orange or purple. In the garden, cauliflower can be more demanding than its cousins.

CHINESE BROCCOLI
Part of the Alboglabra group of *Brassica oleracea,* Chinese broccoli is also known as gai lan, kai-lan, jie lan, or Chinese kale. It has thick, flat, glossy blue-green leaves with thick stems and florets similar to broccoli. The taste is strong and bitter. Broccolini, which has florets, is a hybrid between gai lan and broccoli.

CHINESE CABBAGE
Brassica rapa includes two cultivar groups of leaf vegetables used in Chinese cuisine: Pekinensis (napa cabbage) and Chinensis (bok choy). Napa cabbage has broad green leaves that form a compact head; bok choy has smooth, dark green leaf blades that form clusters similar to celery.

COLLARD GREENS

A member of the Viridis group of *Brassica oleracea*, this cultivar, with its large, slightly bitter, dark-green leaves, is eaten as a vegetable all over the world—and has been for 2,000 years. It contains substantial amounts of vitamins K, A, and C, as well as manganese and is a moderate source of calcium and vitamin B6.

DAIKON

Also called winter radish, daikon *(Raphanus sativus* var. *longipinnatus)* is a white root vegetable shaped like a large carrot, but flavored like a mild radish. It is grown in many Asian countries and is the most popular vegetable in Japan. The Chinese and Korean varieties are greenish in color.

HORSERADISH

Horseradish *(Armoracia rusticana)* is a perennial root vegetable used as a spice and condiment in many cuisines. When it is cut or grated, enzymes from within the plant cells digest sinigrin to produce volatile mustard oil—responsible for the piquant taste. For more information, *see* page 242.

KOHLRABI

A member of the Gongylodes group of *Brassica oleracea*, this stout cultivar of wild cabbage is also called German turnip. It was created by artificial selection resulting in a swollen, nearly spherical shape. The mild, sweet taste is similar to broccoli stem or cabbage heart. It can be eaten raw or cooked.

KOMATSUNA

Komatsuna *(Brassica rapa* var. *perviridis)* is a hardy leafy green vegetable grown commercially in Japan and Taiwan, China. A versatile cool-weather plant, it is eaten raw, pickled, stir-fried, boiled, and used fresh in salads or added to soups. Plus the leaves can be prepared at all stages of growth.

MIZUNA

Mizuna *(Brassica rapa* var. *niposinica)*—called Japanese mustard, spider mustard, or kyona—is an attractive crucifer with glossy, serrated, dark green leaves that are eaten cooked or raw. The mild mustard flavor is peppery like arugula and slightly bitter like frisée lettuce.

MUSTARD

The edible leaves, stems, and seeds of the brown mustard plant *(Brassica juncea)* appear in cuisines from around the world. Spicy brown mustard comes from this plant's seeds. The four main subgroups of this genus are *integrifolia, juncea, napiformis,* and *tsatsai,* distinguished by size, leaf shape, or color.

ROMANESCO BROCCOLI

This cool-season chartreuse-colored plant is recognized by the upright, spiraling fractals on its cauliflower-like head. The flavor, however, is similar to that of broccoli—mild, nutty, and sweet. It is actually an edible flower bud of *Brassica oleracea* that was first cultivated in 16th-century Italy.

RUTABAGA

This oblong root vegetable—known as a swede, Swedish turnip, neep, rwden/rwdins, and turnip—should not be confused with the related white turnip. Rutabaga *(Brassica napus)* originated as a hybrid between a cabbage and a turnip and has since become a winter favorite when boiled and cubed or mashed.

TURNIP

Also called white turnip, the turnip *(Brassica rapa* subsp. *rapa)* is a fleshy root vegetable grown in most temperate climates. Small, tender varieties are raised for human consumption, while larger varieties become livestock feed. It has white skin, except for the pink or green part that protrudes above the ground.

WASABI

Wasabi *(Eutrema japonicum* or *Wasabia japonica),* also called Japanese horseradish, is a bog plant found along stream beds in Japan's river valleys. The earliest record of its use as a food goes back to 700 CE. A green paste made from the ground rhizomes is a pungent condiment for sushi and other foods.

Editor's Tip

Broccoli may be a highly healthful vegetable for human consumption, but not all creatures will reap its many benefits. Be aware that there is a health risk associated with overfeeding broccoli to your pet dog. This crucifer contains compounds called isothiocyanates that can cause gastric irritation in some canines. So no slipping servings of this veggie under the table.

Celery

A row of healthy celery plants shows their bright green stalks and leaves. Celery is a finicky grower, however, and only thrives if all its exacting needs are met.

Celery *(Apium graveolens)* is generally considered to be a very challenging vegetable to grow. It has a very long growing season but a very low tolerance for both heat and cold, making it difficult to keep alive through changing seasons while protecting it from the elements. It has been cultivated for thousands of years, although it was first valued for medicinal rather than culinary uses.

GROWING CELERY

Because celery has such a long maturity time, unless you live in a location with long growing seasons, you need to start celery seeds indoors at least 8 to 10 weeks before the last frost date in your region.

Celery seeds are tiny and tricky to plant. If you have trouble handling them, try mixing them with sand and sprinkling the sand-seed mix over the potting soil. Cover the seeds with just a little bit of soil—celery seeds like to be planted very shallowly.

Once the celery seeds have sprouted and are large enough, either thin the seedlings or separate them out to their own pots.

Once the temperatures outside are consistently above 50 F° (10°C), you can begin transplanting your celery seedlings into the garden. Remember that celery is very temperature sensitive, so don't plant it out too early.

Plant your celery where it will get six hours of sun. In slightly warmer areas, however, it may also need to be shaded during the hottest hour of the day.

Celery should be planted in rich, well-draining soil. It also needs a lot of water; make sure to keep the soil consistently moist by watering deeply and frequently. Celery can't tolerate drought of any kind. If the ground isn't kept consistently moist, it will negatively affect the taste of the celery. Water the soil only at the base of the plant, however, to avoid risking mildew or fungal infection. You will also need to fertilize the plant regularly.

HARVESTING CELERY

Picking celery should begin when the lower stalks are at least 6 inches (15 cm) long from ground level to the first node. This will usually be three to five months after planting. The stalks should still be close together, forming a compact bunch or cone; the upper stalks should reach 18 to 24 inches (45–60 cm) in height and 3 inches (7.5 cm) in diameter when they are ready for harvest.

Harvesting celery is easily done by cutting the stalks below where they are joined together. You can also harvest the leaves for use as a flavoring in soups and stews. A few plants can be left to flower or go to seed, if desired, for use in recipes and propagation of future crops.

SCIENTIFIC NAME: *Apium graveolens*

FAMILY: Apiaceae

HEIGHT: 8 to 15 inches (20–38 cm)

WIDTH: 6 to 12 inches (15–30 cm)

SOIL pH: Neutral

LIGHT: Full sun

HARVEST: Autumn

Celeriac

A variant of celery, celeriac *(Apium graveolens* var. *rapaceum),* also called celery root, knob celery, and turnip-rooted celery, is cultivated for its edible stem and shoots. In cooking, it is treated as a root vegetable and can be roasted, stewed, blanched, and mashed. Sliced, it appears in soups, casseroles, and other savory dishes, adding a slightly nutty, green taste. The flavorful leaves are often used as a garnish. Growing this variety is basically the same as with celery.

Globe Artichoke

Lovely to look at and delicious to eat, the globe artichoke is a worthy addition to your kitchen garden. Simmered, steamed, or stuffed, it makes a delicate-flavored side dish.

Most often, gardeners grow plants either for their visual appeal in a garden or because they produce tasty fruits and vegetables. The globe artichoke is a rarity that is valued for both: not only is it a highly nutritious food, the plant is so attractive it is also often grown as an ornamental.

Globe artichokes (*Cynara cardunculus* var. *scolymus*) are an edible variety of thistle. The flower bud, the edible part of the plant, develops on a tall stem from the center of the plant. Green globe artichoke plants produce three to four buds, roughly 2 to 5 inches (5–12.5 cm) in diameter. If the artichoke bud is not harvested, it will open into an eye-catching purple thistle-like flower.

GROWING GLOBE ARTICHOKES

Globe artichoke plants require a 120-day growing season, so direct sowing of seeds in the spring is not recommended. Instead, you should start plants indoors between late January and early March. Use a planter that is about 3 or 4 inches (7.5–10 cm) and a nutrient-rich starting soil.

Artichokes are slow to germinate, so allow three to four weeks for the seeds to sprout. Warm temperatures in the range of 70 to 75° F (21–24° C) and slightly moist soil will improve germination speed. Once sprouted, keep the soil moist but not soggy. Artichokes are heavy feeders, as well, so you should apply a diluted fertilizer solution weekly. Once the seedlings are three to four weeks old, cull the weakest artichoke plants, leaving only one per pot.

Editor's Picks

There is a wealth of choices when it comes to choosing a variety of globe artichoke to plant. Here is a small sampling of some that work well in home gardens.

- **'Colorado Star' is a fast maturer with purple-green to deep purple buds.**
- **'Emerald' is a thornless variety with bright green buds.**
- **'Imperial Star' is an early-harvester variety with a sweet, mild flavor.**
- **'Purple Italian Globe' is an heirloom variety from Italy.**
- **'Tavor' is an early-maturing variety with purple-tipped green heads.**
- **'Violet de Provence' is a purple heirloom variety from France.**

SCIENTIFIC NAME: *Cynara cardunculus* var. *scolymus*

FAMILY: Asteraceae

HEIGHT: 3 to 6 feet (1–1.8 m)

WIDTH: 4 to 5 feet (1.2–1.5 m)

SOIL pH: Neutral

LIGHT: Full sun

HARVEST: Summer

When the seedlings are ready for transplanting into the garden, select a sunny location that has good drainage and rich, fertile soil. Prior to planting, test the soil and amend if necessary. Globe artichoke plants prefer a neutral soil pH between 6.5 and 7.5. When planting, space the plants a minimum of 4 feet (1.2 m) apart.

After transplanting, they need little extra maintenance. They do best with yearly applications of organic compost and a balanced fertilizer during the growing season. To overwinter in areas that receive heavy frost, cut back artichoke plants, and protect the crowns with a thick layer of mulch or straw.

HARVESTING GLOBE ARTICHOKES

Artichokes are usually ready to be harvested in mid to late summer and will continue well into the first frost. Buds are harvested once they reach full size, just before the bracts begin to spread open.

To harvest, simply cut off the bud, along with 3 inches (7.5 cm) of stem. After harvesting, continue to water and feed the plants. After several frosts, cut back the artichoke plant and mulch heavily.

Jerusalem Artichoke

The vegetable part of the Jerusalem artichoke, also known as the sunchoke, is just a lumpy tuber, but the plant makes a stunning garden display with its sunny yellow flowers.

Many vegetable gardeners are unfamiliar with Jerusalem artichoke plants, although they might know them by their common name, sunchoke. Jerusalem artichokes are native to North America and have little in common with the artichokes found in your local supermarket.

Jerusalem artichoke plants *(Helianthus tuberous)* are perennial relatives of the sunflower. The edible portions are the fat, misshapen tubers that grow belowground. Tubers are dug in the autumn. They can be cooked like a potato, either fried, baked, or boiled, or eaten raw—and they have a flavor and crunch similar to water chestnuts.

Jerusalem artichoke plants can grow 6 to 10 feet (1.8–3 m) high and are covered with flowers in late August and September. The flowers are a bright and cheerful golden yellow. The leaves are about 3 inches (7.5 cm) wide and 4 to 8 inches (10–20 cm) long.

GROWING JERUSALEM ARTICHOKES

Growing a Jerusalem artichoke begins with the soil. These plants grow and produce flowers in almost any type of soil, but yields are much more abundant when they are planted in loose, well-aerated, well-draining soil. An all-purpose fertilizer should be worked into the soil when planting.

Planting Jerusalem artichokes is much like planting potatoes. Plant small tubers (or pieces of tuber with two or three buds each) 2 to 3 inches (5–7.5 cm) deep and 2 feet apart (60 cm) in early spring. Start as soon as the ground has warmed enough that it can be worked. Water the area well after planting, and the tubers will sprout in two to three weeks.

HARVESTING JERUSALEM ARTICHOKES

Wait until the first frost to begin digging mature tubers out of the ground. When the plants begin to brown sometime in late summer or early autumn, this is usually a good sign that they're ready to harvest. Dig carefully, making sure not to injure the delicate skin of the plants, and harvest only what you need.

SCIENTIFIC NAME: *Helianthus tuberosus*

FAMILY: Asteraceae

HEIGHT: 6 to 10 feet (1.8–3 m)

WIDTH: 3 to 5 feet (1–1.5 m)

SOIL pH: Neutral

LIGHT: Full sun to partial shade

HARVEST: Summer to winter

Cut away the dying plants, but leave the remaining tubers in the ground. They can be harvested all winter until they begin to sprout in the spring. It should be noted, however, that any piece of tuber left to overwinter will almost certainly sprout, and your garden could be easily overrun with Jerusalem artichokes. On the other hand, if you assign a permanent corner of your garden to these plants, growing them can be even easier, because they will replenish themselves. Just give your patch a dose of fertilizer each spring.

Editor's Picks

For a veggie that is just hitting its stride in popularity, there are already numerous Jerusalem artichoke cultivars, including the following.

- 'Beaver Valley Purple' is a tan tuber heavily tinged with purple and striped with purplish brown bands.
- 'Clearwater' is a Maine-sourced heirloom with white skin and flesh.
- 'French Mammoth White" is a knobbier white variety.
- 'Passamaquoddy' is a purple-skinned variety.
- 'Skorospelka' has reddish skin with white flesh.
- 'Stampede' is a common, but delicious, yellow-skinned variety.
- 'White Fuseau' is white skinned.
- 'Wild White' is a large, smooth-skinned variety.
- 'Wild Red' is a small and elongated red tuber.

Radicchio

Growing radicchio shows its colors of green and red. As its common name implies, this vegetable is popular in Italy. In fact, varieties of radicchio are named after the Italian regions where they originate, such as radicchio di Chioggia and radicchio rosso di Treviso.

Radicchio is a member of the Asteraceae, or aster family, and is one of the chicories commonly found and utilized in many areas of Europe. Radicchio's popularity has more recently crossed the pond, and it is now commonly utilized in the Americas, as well. It is often served in salads, sautéed, or used as a garnish due to its ruby hue.

Radicchio has burgundy-colored leaves with white ribs, resembling a small cabbage head, and it is not to be confused with radichetta, another chicory type with similar red coloration but lacking the heading form. Radicchio's leaf texture is similar to that of the French endive, another popular heading chicory variety.

GROWING RADICCHIO

Radicchio may be grown as a spring, summer, or autumn vegetable, but the most common red-leaf heading radicchio does best when grown in cool temperatures. Radicchio is frost tolerant for a short period of time, and growing temperatures can fluctuate quite far, between 30 and 90° F (-1–32° C). Higher temperatures for any length of time, however, will burn the leaves of the radicchio, and they can only tolerate extreme cold for a little while.

This plant prefers plenty of sunlight, but it will tolerate shade in the garden, as well. Radicchio will grow in a variety of soil conditions, from sandy to clay-like loam, but it much prefers a neutral to alkaline soil pH of 7.5 to 8.0, excellent drainage, and plenty of water.

Radicchio can be directly sown into the ground or transplanted, depending on the time of year and what climate you live in. If transplanting, start the seeds indoors four to six weeks before you plan for transplantation. If you're starting from direct-sown seeds outside, you should wait to plant them until after the danger of frost has passed. Plants should be spaced 8 to 12 inches (20–30 cm) apart in rows.

Radicchio plants need a constant supply of water to their shallow roots and to encourage the growth of the tender shoots; consider using an automated watering system or irrigation if needed.

CARING FOR THE PLANTS

There are several concerns about caring for these plants. Radicchio plants are often attacked by the same types of pests as the cabbage family, such as aphids, many beetle types, thrips, and ants.

SCIENTIFIC NAME: *Cichorium intybus*

FAMILY: Asteraceae

HEIGHT: 6 to 12 inches (15–30 cm)

WIDTH: 6 to 18 inches (15–45 cm)

SOIL pH: Neutral to alkaline

LIGHT: Full sun

HARVEST: Autumn

Most of these radicchio pests can be countered by any number of chemical or biological deterrents. Consult with your local garden supply center about methods of control related to your specific insect invader, type of plant, and climate.

Radicchio can also be affected by a variety of fungal issues and powdery molds. These usually occur due to inadequate drainage and are most common in areas of the country with extremely wet conditions. Make sure each plant has well-draining soil and good air circulation to minimize the risk of mold, mildew, fungal infection, and rot.

HARVESTING RADICCHIO

Growing radicchio are green or reddish green until cold weather arrives; they will then take on a rich range of reds, from pink to dark burgundy. You can harvest radicchio almost any time during growth, as early as when leaves are just 2 to 3 inches (5–7.5 cm) long or after a head fully forms and feels firm to the touch. If you snip away the older leaves, the younger ones at the center will continue growing for later use.

Place your radicchio harvest in a perforated plastic bag, and store in a cold and moist place, such as your fridge's vegetable crisper. It will keep for about three to four weeks.

A GALLERY OF BERRIES

Berries can be some of the most rewarding plants to grow. When they are picked at their peak of ripeness, few fruits can rival them for sweetness and flavor. Technically, berries are small, pulpy, often edible fruit . . . juicy, rounded, brightly colored, with a sweet or tart flavor. They do not usually have a stone like a cherry or plum, but pips or small seeds may be present.

Wild berries were a key food source for humans since before the dawn of agriculture and still remain among the primary food sources of other primates. For thousands of years berries were a seasonal staple for hunter-gatherers, who soon learned to store them for the winter. They eventually began making them into fruit preserves or pemmican, a Native American mixture of berries with meat and fats. Blackberries and raspberries were first cultivated in Europe around the 17th century. Today the most widely grown commercial example is the strawberry, with a yearly yield of twice the amount of all other berries combined.

GROWING BERRIES

There are many varieties of berries, and most are simple to grow. Strawberries, blueberries, raspberries, and blackberries are typically the most popular garden choices, but there are also plenty of exotic or lesser-known examples that can be grown in containers as part of your edible landscape. Goji berry, black chokecherry, and honeyberry are some unusual candidates that will add interest to a backyard berry patch.

Whether you are planting the more traditional varieties or growing unusual berries in pots, place your beds or containers in a spot with plenty of direct sunlight. The needs of species vary, but most need at least six hours of sun a day to produce the most fruit. When you are growing berries in containers, irrigation is also important. Depending on the types of berries you select, you may have to water several times a week.

If you want to try growing berries in your garden, start with one or more of the examples shown on these pages, and discover how much flavor you will add to your life.

Please keep in mind that some berries are poisonous to humans—such as those found on deadly nightshade plants and pokeweed. Others, such as white mulberry, red mulberry, wonderberry, and elderberry, are poisonous when unripe, but completely edible when ripe.

BLACKBERRY
Easy-care, rambling blackberries (*Rubus* spp.)—whose fruit is described as an aggregate of drupelets—are members of the rose family. They like full sunlight and rich, sandy, well-draining soil. Some varieties do well in colder climates but almost every type is hardy in milder temperate regions.

BLUEBERRY
Homegrown blueberries (*Vaccinium* sect. *cyanococcus*) often seem more flavorful than those purchased at the store. To ensure a delicious crop, plant them in acidic, well-draining soil. Blueberries also prefer full to partial sunlight. The lower to the ground, the hardier the bush will be in colder planting regions.

BOYSENBERRY
This large maroon "bramble" fruit is a hybrid cross between loganberry, raspberry, dewberry, and blackberry. Boysenberry (*Rubus ursinus*) prefers to grow in full sun and well-draining, nutrient-dense soil. Ideal for making jam or juice, it is known to be hardy in temperate planting regions.

CHILEAN GUAVA
Chilean guava (*Ugni molinae*) is an evergreen shrub that reaches 3 to 6 feet (1–1.8 m) in height when mature. It requires a warm climate for outdoor planting, but as a container plant it can grow indoors when it gets cold. The fruit looks like reddish blueberries and has a slightly spicy flavor.

CHOKEBERRY
Also called aronias, chokeberries (*Aronia melanocarpa*) are part of the rose family. They enjoy full sun and their strong roots retain moisture. The dark purple fruit makes great jams, jellies, juice, tea, and wine, and it is rich in fiber, vitamin C, and powerful antioxidants that may have heart-healthy benefits.

CRANBERRY
Commercial cranberries (*Vaccinium macrocarpon*) grow in bogs, but these woody perennial vines will thrive in your backyard if you give them acidic soil and if your climate can trigger a dormant period—meaning at least three months with cool to cold temperatures between 32 to 45° F (1–7° C).

CURRANT

Clustering, pea-sized currants *(Ribes* spp.) come in several varieties—black, red, and white. With their sweet, bright, acidic flavor, they are popular berries and are delicious when eaten fresh or made into pies and jellies. These plants prefer to stay cool, so locate them in full sun to partial sun.

GOJI BERRY

Also called wolfberry, Goji berry *(Lycium barbarum)* is a popular "health" berry. It is the bright orange-red fruit of a shrub native to China. The shrub grows fairly tall in the wild, but in gardens will expand to fit the pot it is planted in, then stop. This berry is also remarkably tolerant of heat and cold.

GOOSEBERRY

Gooseberry is the common name for many species of fruit found in the genus *Ribes*. The smooth, rounded berries, which may be green, orange, red, purple, yellow, white, or black, have a grapelike flavor and are used to make jams and jellies. They love full sun and rich soil and are hardy in temperate regions.

GROUND CHERRY

Ground cherries *(Physalis* spp.), members of the Nightshade family and also called husk tomatoes or cape gooseberries, are low-lying plants, similar to the tomatillo. They grow inside a papery husk and taste like strawberries. Start them as seeds indoors, then transplant to a sunny location after any risk of frost.

HONEYBERRY

Also known by the names blue honeysuckle and fly honeysuckle or the Ainu name, *haskap*, Honeyberry *(Lonicera caerulea)* is a small, rectangular blue berry that grows on attractive, silver-green foliage that turns bright yellow in autumn. In containers, the shrubs do well in both sun or part shade.

HUCKLEBERRY

This is the name used in North America for plants in two closely related genera, *Vaccinium* and *Gaylussacia*. The berries may be red, black, or blue and have been used both as a food source and as a type of traditional medicine. Huckleberries need acidic soil, shade, and consistently damp soil.

LINGONBERRY

Lingonberries *(Vaccinium vitis-idaea)* are attractive, low-growing shrubs that thrive happily in the shade, producing brilliant red berries with a pleasing, tart flavor. They are popular in Scandinavian cooking, especially as a garnish for crepes and in sauces. They are also very high in powerful antioxidants.

LOGANBERRY

Loganberry *(Rubus* x *loganobaccus)*, a hybrid of the North American blackberry and the European raspberry, resembles the blackberry, but the fruit is a dark red and tastes similar to a raspberry. Eat them fresh or use them to make jam. The plants love full sun and do best in well-draining soil.

RASPBERRY

Raspberry *(Rubus* spp.), a thorny shrub that produces tart drupelets in red, white, yellow, and black, is used in juices, jellies, and pies. Some varieties produce in the spring, others in the autumn (these are easier to grow). Plant raspberry bushes in a spot with ample sun and well-draining soil.

SERVICEBERRY

The shadbush tree *(Amelanchier canadensis)* is often used as an ornamental for its showy white flowers, but its blueberry-like fruit makes tasty cobblers, wines, and jams. These trees do well in temperate zones and can handle partial shade; just make sure to plant them in well-draining acidic soil.

STRAWBERRY

These succulent red hybrid berries, famous for their taste and scent, are now a staple of American kitchens. Strawberries *(Fragaria* x *ananassa)* will grow in containers, hanging baskets, in the ground, or in raised beds provided they are placed in a sunny location with well-draining, nutrient-rich soil.

WINEBERRY

These red berries, which grow wild along fields and roads in many places, are still used as the breeding stock for hybrid raspberries. Wineberries *(Rubus phoenicolasius)* make tasty wine, jam, and baked desserts. Although they are not durable once picked, freezing them will make your harvest last longer.

Ramp

SCIENTIFIC NAME: *Allium tricoccum*
FAMILY: Amaryllidaceae
HEIGHT: 6 to 8 inches (cm)
WIDTH: 4 to 20 inches (10–50 cm)
SOIL pH: Neutral
LIGHT: Shade to partial shade
HARVEST: Spring

Ramps, or wild leeks. There is some dispute regarding the genesis of the name. Some folks say the name "ramp" is a shortened version of Aries the Ram, the zodiac sign for April and the month that growing ramps usually begin to appear. Others say "ramp" is derived from a similar English plant called "ramsons."

Once the province of foragers who would comb the woodlands in search of these wild leeks, ramps have increasingly entered the rows of many kitchen gardens. Ramps *(Allium tricoccum)* are native to the moist woodlands of the Appalachians in eastern North America, where they are commonly found in groups in rich, moist, deciduous forests. A member of the onion family, the ramp is a pungent vegetable that is enjoying a resurgence in popularity. These days, ramps can be found at many farmers' markets grown by local farmers. This is creating a demand for more ramps, which is exciting many a home gardener.

Ramps are easily identified by their foliage; usually two broad, flat leaves are produced from each bulb. The leaves are light, silvery green, 1 to 2½ inches (2.5–6 cm) wide and 5 to 10 inches (12.5–25 cm) long. As spring bloomers, the leaves wither and die by late spring or early summer, and a small cluster of white flowers is produced.

Ramps are harvested for their bulbs and leaves, which taste like pungent spring onions with a garlicky aroma. Both early colonists and American Indians prized ramps. They were an important early spring food source after months of no fresh vegetables and were considered a tonic. Today they are found sautéed in butter or olive oil in fine dining establishments.

Ramps and their relatives have been used medicinally to treat a host of ailments, and one of these traditional remedies has crossed over into the world of modern medicine. One of the most common uses of both garlic and ramps was to expel internal worms, and a concentrated form is now produced commercially. It's called allicin, which comes from the scientific name *Allium*, the genus for all onions, garlic, and ramps.

GROWING AND CARING FOR RAMPS

Ramps can be grown from seed or via transplants. Seeds can be sown at any time the soil isn't frozen, with late summer to early autumn the prime time. Seeds need a warm, moist period to break dormancy, followed by a cold period. If there is not sufficient warming after sowing, the seeds will not germinate until the second spring, meaning germination can take anywhere from 6 to 18 months.

Keep in mind that ramps naturally grow in a shaded area with rich, moist, well-draining soil high in organic matter. When preparing the soil, think damp forest floor. Incorporate plenty of the organic matter found in decaying forest soil, such as composted leaves or decaying plants. Remove weeds, loosen the soil, and rake to prepare a fine seed bed. Thinly sow the seeds on top of the ground, and then press them gently into the soil. Water and cover the ramp seeds with several inches (8 cm) of leaves to retain moisture.

If you are transplanting bulbs, plant in late winter to early spring. Set bulbs 3 inches (7.5 cm) deep and 4 to 6 inches (10–15 cm) apart. Water and mulch the bed with 2 to 3 inches (5–7.5 cm) of composted leaves.

With such a short growing time, these ephemeral plants will need little care once they are in the ground.

HARVESTING

You can harvest your ramps as soon as they leaf out, but be careful not to deplete your patch until it has had a chance to enlarge and fully establish itself. Ideally, you should leave a patch undisturbed for a few years. You can then harvest by thinning out the largest plants, carefully digging out the whole clump, including the bulb. You can then chop them to eat raw in salads, or fry or blanch them to flavor other dishes. Ramps can also be pickled or dried for later use.

Rhubarb

Rhubarb in the garden. The tart flavor of the ruby or green stems of this vegetable makes them suitable for use in recipes for pies, crumbles, jams, and sauces.

The origins of rhubarb's culinary usage are vague, although the plant is mentioned as far back as the third century CE in *The Herbal Classic of Shen Nong,* a Chinese compilation of oral traditions about medicinal herbal plants. It was not until the early 18th century that rhubarb appears as a vegetable crop in England and Scandinavia.

Rhubarb *(Rheum rhabarbarum)* is a perennial vegetable in the buckwheat family, harvested for its long stalks. The stalks have a sour flavor that works great in pies, sauces, and jellies. Rhubarb pairs especially well with strawberries, so you may want to plant both in your garden.

GROWING RHUBARB

Temperature should be your first consideration. Plant rhubarb where the winter temperatures go below 40° F (4° C), so that dormancy can be broken when it warms up in the spring. Summer temperatures below 75° F (24° C) on average will yield quite a nice crop.

Because rhubarb is a perennial, its care is a little different from that of many other vegetables. Choose a sunny spot with good drainage, and plant it along the edge of your garden, so that it doesn't disturb your other vegetable crops when it comes up each spring. You should purchase either crowns or divisions from your local garden center. Each of these crowns or divisions will require enough space to rise up from the soil and provide you with large, healthy leaves. This means planting them about 1 to 2 feet (30–60 cm) apart in rows that are spaced 2 to 3 feet (60 cm–1 m) apart. Each growing rhubarb plant requires about a square yard (1 m^2) of space.

Rhubarb plants prefer loamy soils, and because they are "heavy feeders" that take in large amounts of nutrients from the soil, you should amend the soil with either a balanced commercial fertilizer or rich compost, or both.

Once you have prepared the soil, take the crowns, and place them in the ground. Don't plant them deeper than 1 or 2 inches (2.5–5 cm) into the soil, or they won't come up. As flower stalks appear on the growing rhubarb, remove them right away so they don't rob the plant of nutrients. Make sure you water the plants during dry weather; rhubarb doesn't tolerate drought.

CARING FOR THE PLANTS

The care of established rhubarb plants doesn't require a whole lot from you. They pretty much just come up each spring and grow well on their own. Just remove any weeds from the area, and carefully cultivate around the stalks so that you don't injure the growing rhubarb.

At a Glance

SCIENTIFIC NAME: *Rheum rhabarbarum*

FAMILY: Polygonaceae

HEIGHT: 2 to 3 feet (60 cm–1 m)

WIDTH: 3 to 4 feet (1–1.2 m)

SOIL pH: Acidic, neutral

LIGHT: Full to partial sun

HARVEST: Spring to early summer

HARVESTING RHUBARB

Rhubarb is one of the first crops of the year, but don't harvest the first season after planting, as this will not allow your plant to expand to its fullest. Wait until the second year, and then begin picking stalks as soon as they have reached their full length—depending on the variety you've planted, this can be as short as 12 inches (30 cm) or as long as 2 feet (60 cm).

To pick rhubarb, avoid cutting the stalks with a knife. Instead, firmly grasp the stalk, and then pull and twist. After harvesting the stalks, use a knife to trim the leaves from the stalks, and immediately discard them. They are toxic, and leaving them on can speed up the wilting of the stalks.

You can use your rhubarb fresh or blanch and freeze it for later use.

Note: Rhubarb leaves and roots are toxic both to people and pets.

Dig Deeper

READ MORE AT GARDENING KNOW HOW

Scan the QR code or follow this link to learn more about harvesting rhubarb.

- **"When to Harvest Rhubarb and How to Harvest Rhubarb"** (URL = gkh.us/2231)

CHAPTER SEVEN

THE HERB GARDEN

An herb is any seed-bearing plant that does not have a woody stem and dies down to the ground after flowering. It is a widely distributed group of plants, generally easy to grow and care for. Renowned for centuries for their many beneficial qualities, they have been divided into three types: culinary herbs, medicinal herbs, and aromatic herbs. Culinary herbs can be eaten, used fresh or dried as seasonings, and were once valuable in the preservation of meats and other perishable foods. Medicinal herbs have a long history, going back to ancient Egypt, India, Greece, Rome, China, Japan, and other parts of the world. Even today there are still many popular herbal health supplements, while the chemical makeup of herbs continues to be scrutinized in relation to treating serious diseases. Aromatic herbs are used to calm the senses, sharpen the mind, enhance religious ceremonies and rituals, and in the practice of aromatherapy.

THE AURA OF HERBS

Herbs are among the most rewarding plants when it comes to stimulating our senses. They greet us with the sounds of buzzing bees, the sight of delicate butterflies, and the pungent, often-deep scents of both flowers and foliage. A number of them are fuzzy, sticky, velvety, or raspy to the touch. And so many of them are edible, which is no small benefit.

With so much to offer it is not surprising that over the passing centuries herbs have inspired wonderfully creative garden designs, which play upon their varied shapes, textures, and colors. Yet even if you are not quite so fancifully inclined as to start enclosing everything in sculpted boxwood, you will find that even a haphazard herb garden has a beauty—and creates a sensual aura—all its own.

If you favor a more formal or curated arrangement for your herbs, however, there are several imaginative styles to choose from.

- *Bee garden.* This includes many favorites of these tiny pollinators—basil, bee balm, borage, catnip, chamomile, fennel, germander, horehound, hyssop, lavender, lemon balm, marjoram, oregano, rosemary, sage, savory, and thyme.
- *Shakespeare garden.* This classic herb garden arrangement uses herbs popular in Elizabethan England—bay, burnet, calendula, carnation, chamomile, hyssop, johnny-jump-up, lavender, lemon balm, marjoram, mint, mustard, myrtle, parsley, pinks, rose, rosemary, savory, strawberry, and thyme.
- *Medieval garden.* These are herbs that were protected in walled monastery gardens of the Middle Ages—angelica, caraway, chives, iris, johnny-jump-ups, lavender, lemon balm, marjoram, mint, pinks, rose, rosemary, sage, santolina, and southernwood.
- *Gray -and-silver garden.* Make a statement by restricting your color choices in this stylish, modern herb bed; consider using apple mint, sage, gray lavender cotton, horehound, lamb's ear, lavender, silver thyme, and yarrow.
- *Wagon wheel garden.* Re-create the outer rim and spokes of a wheel with white pebbles or gravel—or use an actual wheel—and plant a different colorful variety of herb inside each segment; possibilities include purple basil, sage, dill, lavender, nasturtium, chamomile, catnip, and hyssop.

Most herbs will thrive in containers, which means you can have a movable garden that allows you to make the most of the available levels of sunlight that these plants need.

THE OPTIMUM GROWING SITE

When choosing a location for your herb garden, there are several important factors to consider. Foremost, you'll need to choose a site that receives at least six to eight hours of sunlight per day. Many herbs need plenty of sunshine in order to grow and reach their full potential. Herbs, like most sun-loving plants that don't receive their minimum daily allowance of sunlight, will end up leggy, awkward-looking, and unproductive, instead of lush, beautiful, and fertile.

But before you start digging, spend a day making note of all the sunny spots in your yard. Check on these spots at hourly intervals to see exactly how long the sun remains in any given space. Trees, bushes, building structures, and even tall flowers or vegetables can cast shade at different times during the day. Knowing the sunlight potential of these sites will make your garden planning easier.

Built at the site of Shakespeare's New Place home in Stratford-on-Avon, this Tudor-style knot garden includes culinary herbs, medicinal herbs, and edible flowers, with species such as thyme, hyssop, lavender, and oregano, along with flowers in blues, pinks, and yellows.

If sunlight in your yard seems in short supply, think about container gardening. By growing your herbs in portable containers, you will be able to easily move them to follow that much-needed light. Of course, there are some shade-loving herbs, such as parsley, mint, and chamomile, but finding them shadier locations should not be a problem. Again, these shade lovers can also be placed in portable containers.

Herbs should be planted in well-drained soil that is somewhat light and easy to till. You can check the quality of your soil by running a hose at the chosen location for several minutes. If the water puddles, you will need to amend the soil, possibly by adding sand, peat, or compost. Be careful when adding compost though. If you make the soil too rich, your herbs will become weak and more prone to diseases. (That's just how they roll.)

The ideal pH level for most herbs is 6.5, but they are frequently forgiving and can grow in soil that is slightly acidic or alkaline. For best results, stick to moderate fertilization.

Herb gardens are meant to be used and admired—that's why it's important to consider practicality when choosing a site. No one wants to traipse across a dark yard at dinner time to harvest a few leaves of basil or oregano for a single recipe. A location near your kitchen or outdoor food prep area will eliminate this problem. If the herb garden is right outside your back door, you can also enjoy the rich, savory scents that emanate from it. Choosing a garden site close to the house will also make it easier to water, prune, and tend to your herbs as needed.

Don't forget to include herbs among the plantings in your flower or vegetable garden. Flowers and herbs often look great together, and sometimes even benefit one another, but be sure the species all have similar growing requirements. For instance, you wouldn't plant a sun-loving herb like basil with shade plants, such as begonias. If you're looking for companions to rosemary, sage, thyme, or oregano, try echinacea, petunia, zinnia, marigold, bee balm, or black-eyed Susan.

The Medicinal Herb Garden

Herbs were likely some of the first medicinal substances used by early humans, employed to ease discomfort or soothe injuries long before they became food additives. Perhaps hunter-gatherers witnessed animals in distress chewing on certain stomach-easing plants, or they experimented with different plant species to stanch or heal wounds. Once these cures or health aids proved successful, the practice of utilizing them seems to have been adopted all over the globe. While some of the medicinal claims for herbs have been disproved in the modern era, quite a number of these plants are still recognized for their contributions to human wellness. Many culinary herbs are also lauded for their beneficial constituents, which include high levels of vitamins, minerals, and fiber, plus compounds known as antioxidants that inhibit the production of harmful free radicals that damage cells. Herbs also make a great savory substitute for salt in a restricted diet. Powerhouse herbs include parsley, peppermint, oregano, basil, thyme, dill, sage, cilantro, and rosemary.

The same heavenly scent that makes lavender so popular with humans brings butterflies to its blooms. You can plan an herb garden with these pollinators in mind.

EDIBLE HERBS

An edible herb garden, or culinary herb garden, is made up of herbs that are used mostly for adding flavor to your cooking and salads or for making teas. The edible herb garden is by far the most popular type of herb garden for the home gardener.

There are many varieties of different herbs, and some have stronger flavors than others. To be sure you're getting the flavor you desire, pinch off a leaf and taste it before purchasing the plants.

It's best to keep a culinary herb garden in close range of your kitchen, just outside your back door, for example, or even in a few pots on the kitchen windowsill. Whatever its location, the closer, the better, because no one wants to have to go clear across the yard to get a few fresh herbs while in the middle of preparing a favorite dish.

HOW TO HARVEST HERBS

Picking herbs might seem like an easy task, and it generally is, but there are right and wrong ways to do it. Time the harvest for best flavor, and pick the leaves, stems, or flowers in ways that ensure the plant will be able to continue growing and producing. Knowing how and when to harvest herbs for optimal flavor is important.

Your herb harvest will vary a bit by type of plant. There are also general guidelines for all herbs grown in the garden. Here are some important tips to maximize your harvest.

- Harvest leafy annual herbs, like basil, by pinching off leaves at the tips of stems.
- Harvest leafy perennials—such as sage, tarragon, thyme, and oregano—by removing longer stems of leaves.
- Harvest stemmed herbs—such as lavender, rosemary, and parsley—by cutting off stems at the base.
- When harvesting annual herbs, you can cut back half to three-quarters of the plant at one time.
- For perennial herbs, never take more than one-third at a time.
- If harvesting any kind of herbs for their flowers, be sure to remove the blooms before they are in full flower.

WHEN TO HARVEST HERBS

You can harvest herbs when they are large enough to sustain new growth. If you follow the guidelines discussed at left for annuals and perennials, the amount you get in one harvest will vary, but the plant should regenerate foliage.

Timing is essential for getting herbs at their peak flavor. The aim is to pick them when the aromatic and tasty oils in the plants are at their highest levels. This occurs in the morning, after the dew has dried but before it's hot outside. Another important aspect of timing is to pick leaves before the flowers develop. If you use them after the flowers appear, they will not taste as good. You can pinch flowers off as they begin to show to keep getting a harvest of leaves.

Snipping a bit of fresh rosemary in the early morning, before the day gets too hot, means that its aromatic oils will be at their peak of flavor.

SAVING EDIBLE HERBS

Most culinary herbs are best and at their most potently flavorful when picked fresh from your garden and used right away. Still, at the end of the growing season you may want to freeze or dry some of your surplus herb crop for use during the winter months.

You can keep dried herbs for months in airtight jars, well-sealed plastic containers, or zippered bags. Dried herbs do lose some of their flavor over time, so be sure to adjust your recipes accordingly, adding more if needed.

Choosing Edible Herbs

By choosing to grow the herbs you use most often, you'll save yourself a lot of money and a lot of time by not having to run out to the grocery store every time your recipe requires the use of fresh herbs. Your own perfect edible herb garden will consist of all the herbs that you use in your family's cooking. Different types of cuisine use different herbs.

For Italian foods:
- Basil
- Oregano
- Rosemary
- Parsley

For Asian dishes:
- Thai basil
- Lemongrass

For French cuisine:
- Tarragon
- Chervil
- Bay leaf
- Marjoram
- Fennel

For Mexican cooking:
- Cilantro (also known as coriander)
- Thyme
- Lemon verbena

For a tea garden:
- Chamomile
- Peppermint
- Spearmint

Other popular culinary herbs:
- Chives
- Sage
- Dill

Common Edible Herbs

BASIL

In Western cuisine, the generic term "basil" refers to the variety also known as sweet basil or Genovese basil. For more information, *see* page 220.

BAY LEAF

The leaves of this aromatic evergreen, called bay laurel, sweet bay, and true laurel, are a staple of Mediterranean regional cuisines. For more information, *see* page 237.

CHAMOMILE

The daisy-like flowers of this medicinal herb are used to make an herbal tea prized for its calming properties. For more information, *see* pages 226 and 251.

CHERVIL

Also called French parsley or garden chervil, this delicate herb with a subtle flavor is essential for cooking French cuisine. For more information, *see* page 223.

CHIVES

This allium family member looks great in a garden and also adds a light onion flavor to dishes without being overpowering. For more information, *see* page 239.

CILANTRO

Also known as coriander, Chinese parsley, dhania, and kothmir, this aromatic herb features in many Mexican recipes. For more information, *see* page 224.

DILL

Lending its flavor to the pickle named for it, this herb is found in many culinary traditions, including German and Scandinavian. For more information, *see* page 225.

FENNEL

Fennel's fresh, aromatic anise flavor can be used as a seasoning, or you can eat the root of this herb raw, sautéed, or roasted. For more information, *see* page 240.

LEMONGRASS

The star of many Asian cuisines, such as Thai, this lemony herb brightens the flavor of curry pastes, sauces, and salads. For more information, *see* page 227.

LEMON VERBENA

This versatile lemon-scented herb can add citrus flavor to dishes ranging from hearty roasts to sweet desserts and jams. For more information, *see* page 228.

MARJORAM

This savory herb is perfect to use in marinades for meats and fish, and it features in many Mediterranean dishes. For more information, *see* page 247.

OREGANO

These robust leaves are key ingredients in many Italian dishes and in dried form are part of the French herb mix *herbes de Provence*. For more information, *see* page 249.

PARSLEY

Not just a garnish on the side of a plate, this clean, slightly bitter herb can be a base for soups, broths, stews, and sauces. For more information, *see* page 232.

PEPPERMINT

Highly mentholated, almost hot, and full of flavor, this classic mint pairs well with chocolate and appears in many sweet recipes. For more information, *see* page 248.

ROSEMARY

This aromatic herb can flavor soups, casseroles, and stews, as well as meat, fish, and poultry. It also works well with veggies and salads. For more information *see* page 252.

SAGE

This strong herb has an earthy flavor that works well in pork and lamb recipes and makes a traditional holiday poultry stuffing. For more information, *see* page 253.

SPEARMINT

A mild and cool mint, spearmint works well in desserts and teas and also in savory dishes like couscous and tabbouleh. For more information, *see* page 248.

TARRAGON

Commonly used in French cuisine, it works well in fish recipes and is an essential ingredient in the classic béarnaise sauce. For more information, *see* page 255.

THAI BASIL

This Southeast Asian herb is slightly spicy, with an anise-like taste. It holds up to higher cooking temperatures than sweet basil. For more information, *see* page 220.

THYME

Thyme appears in many savory dishes and pairs well with meat, tomatoes, and beans, and can be used in savory baking. For more information *see* page 256.

Annual herbs, such as summer savory, complete their entire life cycle in a single season.

Biennial herbs take two years to complete their whole life cycle, producing leaves in the first season, flowers in the second, and then dying. Many biennials that don't like frost, such as dill, are treated as annuals.

ANNUAL AND BIENNIAL HERBS

Herbs fall into three hardiness categories: annual, biennial, and perennial. A number of herbs grown in temperate regions are tender perennials that are treated as annuals—plants that complete their life cycle, from germination to the production of seeds, within one growing season, and then die as the cold weather approaches. The bad news is that you will need to replant them again the next year, but the good news is that annual herbs are extremely easy to grow.

Certain herbs, such as rosemary and basil, can be placed in pots and overwintered indoors and then restored to the garden the following spring. Other herbs will simply die back. Smart gardeners dry these faded specimens indoors and then collect the seeds to create starter trays for the next growing season. Simply place the seeds in a marked container or zip-lock bag and store them in a dry, dark space. Biennial herbs will grow for two seasons before dying back. Their seeds can also be harvested.

LOCATION COUNTS

Two of the most familiar annual herbs—rosemary and oregano—originated in the semi-tropical Mediterranean, a key factor to guide the gardener when it comes to determining a location for planting. Hot and dry is the theme here. Other annuals, like basil and parsley, require a moister environment.

When it comes to harvesting annual herbs, you can safely cut back half to three-quarters of the plant at one time.

READ MORE AT GARDENING KNOW HOW

Follow these links to learn more about successfully growing herbs.

- **"Growing Herbs at Home: Making an Herb Garden in Your Yard"** (URL = gkh.us/3400)
- **"Try Something New This Spring — Grow Your Own Herbs"** (URL = gkh.us/454)
- **"General Care for Your Herb Garden"** (URL = gkh.us/26)
- **"Making Herbs Bigger Through Pinching and Harvesting"** (URL = gkh.us/338)

An herb garden needn't take up much space. Many annual herbs will thrive in containers, such as balcony window boxes or pots set on a patio or deck.

Anise

The anise plant's feathery leaves and the umbels of tiny white flowers, which resemble Queen Anne's lace, add a delicate touch to the look of an herb garden.

Anise *(Pimpinella anisum)* furnishes one of the strongest flavors available in nature. This Southern European and Mediterranean herb is renowned for a taste reminiscent of licorice. It is a member of the Apiaceae, a family of mostly aromatic flowering plants commonly known as the celery, carrot, or parsley family, or simply as umbellifers. The plant, which is cultivated as an ornamental bush, grows wild in northern regions of North America, sprawling across open prairie land and creating vast stretches of snowy-colored blossoms from June to September. Anise flowers are delicate, borne in umbels like Queen Anne's lace. The feathery leaves grow on slightly purple, erect, square stems that rise from thick rhizomes. The plants have a bushy, clumping growth habit. It grows to just under 2 feet (60 cm) tall and requires a warm growing season of at least 120 days.

Anise seeds, which resemble caraway or carrot seeds, are used for baking, seasoning sacory dishes, and flavoring liqueurs in many world cuisines.

Anise is widely cultivated in many European and Asian countries, and due its delightful appearance and fragrance, home gardeners are now growing this herb.

GROWING ANISE

Anise requires a fairly alkaline, well-drained soil, and although it will tolerate full sun with consistently moist soil, most varieties will prefer shade or part shade. Directly sow the seed into a prepared bed that is free of weeds, roots, and other debris. Maturing seedlings need regular water until the plants are established, and then can tolerate periods of drought.

Anise may be harvested in late summer to early autumn, when the flowers go to seed. Save the seed heads in a paper bag until they are dry enough for the seed to fall out of the withered flowers. Keep the seeds in a cool dark location until spring sowing.

These seeds are tiny, but they can be sown with a seed syringe for indoor starting or mixed in sand for outside planting.

A soil temperature of 60° F (15° C) is best for germination. Space the seeds in rows 2 to 3 feet (60 cm–1 m) apart at a rate of 12 seeds per foot (30 cm). Plant the seed ½ inch (1.25 cm) deep in well-cultivated soils. Water the plants after emergence twice a week until they are 6 to 8 inches (15–20 cm) high, and then gradually reduce irrigation.

Apply a nitrogen-rich fertilizer prior to flowering in June to July.

USES FOR ANISE

Anise has both culinary and medicinal properties. It is used as a digestive aid and to help respiratory illness. Its uses in foods and beverages span a wide range of international cuisines. Eastern Europeans have used it widely to flavor liqueurs such as Anisette.

The crushed seeds yield an aromatic oil that is used in soaps, perfume, and potpourris. Dry the seeds for future use in cooking and store them in a glass container with a tightly sealed lid. The many uses of the herb provide an excellent incentive to grow anise plants.

SCIENTIFIC NAME: *Pimpinella anisum*

FAMILY: Apiaceae

HEIGHT: 24 inches (60 cm)

WIDTH: 12 to 24 inches (30–60 cm)

BLOOMS: Midsummer to autumn

SOIL pH: Alkaline

LIGHT: Full sun to full shade

Caraway

Another member of the carrot family is caraway *(Carum carvi)*. With the same kind of finely divided, feathery leaves and tiny flowers, it resembles anise. With a distribution through most of Europe, it is no surprise that it has been incorporated into many of its culinary traditions. Its leaves, fruits, seeds, and roots are all edible and used in desserts, liquors, breads, and other foods.

Basil

This easy-to-grow herb can thrive in a garden bed or in a planter. It also comes in a wide range of varieties, such as the green 'Genovese' and the purple-black 'Dark Opal'. With so many pleasing colors available, basil also makes an attractive foliage plant.

Sweet basil *(Ocimum basilicum)* is one of the most popular herbs in kitchens worldwide and, happily, one of the easiest to grow. Often called the "king of herbs," it has been used in food preparation and for its medicinal properties for more than 5,000 years. This member of the mint family is closely identified with Italian cooking, although its origins range from Central Africa to Southeast Asia. The highly aromatic leaves offer a delightful variety of flavors, from the slightly lemony-mint of sweet basil to cinnamon and licorice. The highly popular 'Genovese' is a standard for Italian cookery, with its sweet-flavored leaves and soft texture.

This is a tall herb, with large, glossy green leaves in colors that range from rich green to deep purple, with smooth or crinkled surfaces. The flowers are insignificant but are very popular with bees. The flower buds are also edible. Bush basil *(Ocimum minimum)* is a dwarf variety that only grows to 6 inches tall (15 cm). Compact and sturdy, it may overwinter in milder climates.

GROWING BASIL

To grow basil from seeds, start them indoors about six weeks before your last spring frost. Choose a location with great drainage and plenty of sun exposure. Scatter the seeds over the bed, lightly cover them with dirt, and water thoroughly. Thin seedlings to 6 inches (15 cm) apart. Basil is ready for harvesting 60 to 90 days from seeding.

If you choose to grow nursery transplants, dig a small hole and tease out the root ball a bit before placing the basil in the ground. Water thoroughly. It is key to remember that basil is very sensitive to cold—even a light frost will kill it. Do not plant basil until all danger of frost has passed.

Basil's powerful fragrance makes it a popular pest-repelling plant for companion planting. Plus, this fast-growing herb thrives equally well in gardens and containers.

HARVESTING BASIL

Once your plants mature, harvest often. The more you harvest basil, the more the plant will grow. When you pinch off a stem above a pair of leaves, two more stems will grow back. And keep pinching off the flowers—once a basil plant flowers, the leaves will start to lose their flavor.

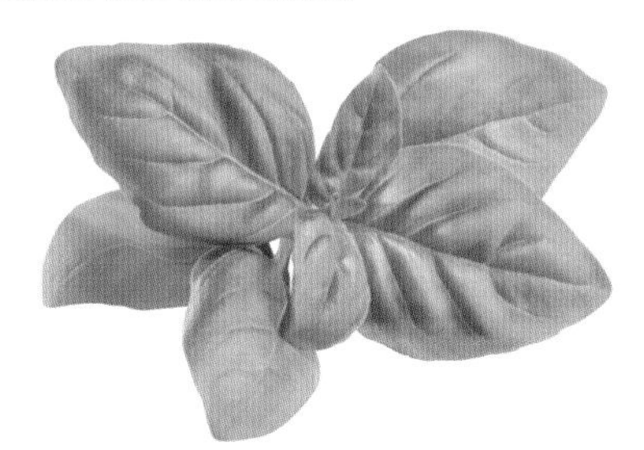

At a Glance

SCIENTIFIC NAME: *Ocimum basilicum*

FAMILY: Lamiaceae

HEIGHT: 18–24 inches (45–60 cm)

WIDTH: 18–24 inches (45–60 cm)

BLOOMS: Early summer to first frost

SOIL pH: Acidic to alkaline

LIGHT: Full sun to light shade

Editor's Picks

Most of us are familiar with the sweet basil varieties used in Italian cuisine, but many other types have culinary uses. Why not try one or more of the dozens of basil varieties and cultivars to add flavor to soups, sauces, salads, and exotic dishes? You could be in for a real taste treat. Here is a small sampling.

- 'Amethyst' *(O. basilicum var. purpurescens).* With striking deep purple—almost black—leaves, this garden stunner has a sweet, musky taste that goes great in salads.
- 'Cinnamon' *(O. basilicum).* This cultivar has a spicy aroma and leaves a warm feeling. Great for teas and baked goods.
- 'Dark Opal' *(O. basilicum).* With its pretty purple leaves, it is often grown as an ornamental.
- 'Mrs. Burns' Lemon' *(O. basilicum).* This large basil is a proven favorite, with a strong lemon aroma that works well in tart vinaigrettes, beverages, and desserts.
- 'Lesbos' *(O. x citriodorum).* This lemon basil has tasty, dark green leaves that are great in baked goods and teas.
- 'Napoletano' *(O. basilicum).* This Italian variety, popular for sauces and salads, has the typical aroma of licorice or anise with a spicy overtone of cinnamon and clove.
- 'Thai' *(O. tenuiflorum).* Commonly known as holy basil, this species has purple or green leaves with a delicate taste of cloves.

Borage

The shape of its brilliant blue blossoms gives this plant its alternate name, starflower. Bees love these blooms, which makes them a great choice for a pollinator garden.

Borage *(Borago officinalis)* is an attractive, old-fashioned herb that was originally native to the Middle East. In ancient times it was said to foster bravery and courage in soldiers during wartime. The Romans introduced it to Britain, where it is still found growing wild. In the modern garden it is easily cultivated as an annual herb with vivid blue flowers and the scent of cucumber. It can be somewhat gangly in habit, but the sight of the pretty, dangling, star-shaped blooms acts as a distraction. The oval leaves are hairy and rough with the lower foliage pushing 6 inches (15 cm) in length. The stems are a greenish gray and covered with a prickly fuzz, which can act to deter insects.

For many centuries the leaves and stems of this plant were considered edible: used in hot dishes, salads, and to make tea. The herb was also known for treating many ailments, from jaundice to kidney problems. But researchers have discovered that borage contains pyrrolizidine alkaloids (PAs), compounds that can be toxic to the liver and may contribute to cancer growth. So gardeners should take that into consideration if it is their habit to consume borage in any form.

Borage still has a lot to offer. It is often grown to lure pollinators like butterflies and honeybees into the vegetable garden. It is also considered a good companion plant for tomatoes, squash, and strawberries and may help increase your yield of fruit.

GROWING BORAGE

Borage may not be as common in plant nurseries as basil or thyme, but it is useful if you have a space that needs something reliable. It grows quickly and colonizes a corner of the garden by self-seeding and reappearing every year. Look for a spot that gets at least four hours of direct sunlight on most days, and avoid taller plants that might shade the borage as it matures. Borage also grows quite well in containers.

This herb can be started indoors in the early spring, or you can sow seeds directly into the ground after the last predicted frost. Prepare a bed with well-tilled, well-draining soil containing an average amount of organic matter. The plant is not fussy about the pH levels. If you opt for starting inside, make sure to harden off the seedlings before you transplant them by gradually acclimating them to outdoor conditions. When sowing the garden bed, plant seeds ¼ to ½ inch (6.35 mm–1.5 cm) under the soil in rows 12 inches (30 cm) apart. Thin the seedlings to at least 12 inches (30 cm) apart when the plants measure 4 to 6 inches (10–15 cm) tall. The appealing, small blue blooms will appear in June and July. The borage plant itself may expand to 12 inches (30 cm) or more wide, with a tall bushy habit.

Borage can be perpetuated by allowing the flowers to go to seed and self-sow. Pinching the terminal growth will result in a bushier plant but might sacrifice some of the flowers. If you are supporting your local honeybees, leave the flowers alone. Borage is known for producing an excellent honey.

Note: Although some people do eat the leaves, they are technically toxic both to people and pets.

At a Glance

SCIENTIFIC NAME: *Borago officinalis*

FAMILY: Boraginaceae

HEIGHT: 1 to 3 feet (30 cm–1 m)

WIDTH: 9 to 24 inches (23–60 cm)

BLOOMS: Summer

SOIL pH: Acidic, neutral, alkaline

LIGHT: Full sun to partial shade

Honey Plants

Beekeeping has become increasingly popular, an important endeavor as bee populations shrink. There are some plants well suited to plant near hives, which will help produce delicious honeys. Borage produces a light, almost clear honey with a delicate flavor. Other herbs, such as mints, sage, thyme, bee balm, basil, salvia, lavender, and lemon balm, are also "honey plants."

Calendula

SCIENTIFIC NAME: *Calendula officinalis*

FAMILY: Asteraceae

HEIGHT: 12 to 24 inches (30–60 cm)

WIDTH: 12 to 24 inches (30–60 cm)

BLOOMS: Spring, summer, autumn

SOIL pH: Neutral

LIGHT: Full sun to partial shade

Calendula, also known as pot marigold, bursts into bright summertime bloom. These cheerful flowers can be grown as an herb, but in flower beds, they look great massed together, and their golden colors can complement flowers in tones of blue and purple.

Calendula, also known as pot marigold, common marigold, or Scotch marigold, is a short-lived perennial that is typically grown as an annual in temperate climates. An old-fashioned favorite that is still popular for herb gardens, flower borders, cottage gardens, and containers, calendula differs from the common marigold. Yet it is also part of the Asteraceae family, along with daisies and chrysanthemums, and even has a daisy-like appearance.

The common name "pot marigold" originated in Renaissance times from the golden flowers that bloomed during festivals of the Virgin Mary—*Mary + gold = marigold.* Ancient cultures in Greece, Rome, the Middle East, and India employed this plant as a treatment for wounds, as well as a dye for fabrics, cosmetics, and foods like butter and cheese. When added to stews, soups, and salads, the petals have a spicy flavor said to resemble saffron. As a restorative herb, calendula is believed to stimulate the immune system. In the vegetable garden, these versatile plants will draw aphids away from your valuable produce.

Modern gardeners choose calendula for their cheerful flowers and profuse blooming habit. The most common varieties produce flowers in sunny yellows, oranges, and reds, but there are also cultivars in subtle shades of pink and cream.

GROWING CALENDULAS

Pot marigolds can be grown in beds or containers in full sun to light shade. They prefer cool temperatures, so flowers will last longer in filtered sun areas. If you sow the seeds in spring after the last frost, the plants should flower in six to eight weeks. Like most herbs, calendulas are adaptable and do not require a lot of maintenance—poor-to-average, well-draining soil and only occasional watering after plants are established will suffice. Roots will often confine themselves to the space provided. These plants are also frost tolerant and somewhat cold hardy.

If deadheaded frequently, these plants should bloom from spring through autumn and beyond. Regular pinching keeps the foliage bushy and prevents tall, spindly stalks. Best of all, calendula flowers readily reseed, so with luck you will have a new crop the following spring.

Marigold versus Pot Marigold

These two plants are a bit like cousins—they share the same family, Asteraceae, but marigolds belong to the *Tagetes* genus of at least 50 species, while calendula are members of the smaller *Calendula* genus, with only 15 to 20 species.

- Calendulas are edible; only some marigolds are edible.
- Marigolds are native to South America, southwestern North America, and tropical America; calendula is native to northern Africa and south-central Europe.
- Marigold petals are rectangular with rounded corners; calendula petals are long and straight.
- Marigold seeds are straight and black, with white paintbrush tips; calendula's are brown, curved, and bumpy.
- Marigolds range from 6 inches (15 cm) to 4 feet (1.2 m); calendulas rarely exceed 2 feet (60 cm).
- Marigolds have a strong, pungent odor (unpleasant to some); calendulas smell slightly sweet.

Chervil

SCIENTIFIC NAME: *Anthriscus cerefolium*

FAMILY: Apiaceae

HEIGHT: 12 to 24 inches (30–60 cm)

WIDTH: 6 to 12 inches (15–30 cm)

BLOOMS: Summer

SOIL pH: Alkaline

LIGHT: Full sun to partial shade

A lush chervil plant thrives in a balcony container, ready for harvesting. This herbal staple of French cuisine adds a delicate, faint anise taste to foods like poultry, seafood, young spring vegetables, soups, and sauces.

Sometimes called French parsley or garden chervil, this herb was once known as myrhis due to its volatile oil, which has an aroma similar to the resinous substance myrrh. The common name is Anglo Saxon and comes from the Latin *chaerephylla* or *choerephyllum,* for "leaves of joy."

Native to the regions of the Black Sea, the Caspian Sea, and western Asia, chervil *(Anthriscus cerefolium)* has been cultivated since the days of the Roman Empire. During the medieval era it was eaten as a spring tonic meant to cleanse the body of winter's impurities, especially during Lent.

Chervil looks like a slightly paler, more delicate, and more finely shaped flat-leaf parsley, but with frillier, daintier leaves that somewhat resemble carrot greens. Some bunches will have tightly closed leaves. If you harvest bunches that have blossoms, avoid those, because the herb itself will have turned bitter.

GROWING CHERVIL

Chervil can be grown in a small pot on your windowsill or you can directly plant it in a garden that gets a mixture of sun and shade. It can be grown from seed sown in the spring or late autumn. To keep crops coming, sow seeds through the season every three to four weeks. It is ready to harvest when the leaves are fully open and tender. You can air-dry the leaves and store them.

Transplanting chervil can be difficult, due to the long taproot. It prefers a cool and moist location; otherwise, it rapidly goes to seed (bolting). It is usually grown as a cool-season crop, like lettuce, and should be planted in early spring and late autumn or in a winter greenhouse. Regular harvesting of leaves also helps to prevent bolting. Once summer heats up, chervil will bolt, just like its parsley cousin. When it bolts, it develops bitter flavors, blooms, and goes to seed.

Slugs are often attracted to chervil and the plant is sometimes used to bait them.

USES OF CHERVIL

Chervil is one of the herbs used to make *fine herbes* (the others are parsley, tarragon, and chives), a delicate herb blend used extensively in French cooking. Chervil is particularly delicious with eggs—either added to an omelet or sprinkled on scrambled eggs. It can also bring a fresh kick when added to lightly dressed salads.

Chervil has had various uses in folk medicine. It was claimed to be useful as a digestive aid, for lowering high blood pressure, and, infused with vinegar, for curing hiccups. Besides its digestive properties, it is used as a mild stimulant.

Editor's Tip

Plant chervil in a vegetable garden. Because it is often used to deter veggie enemies like slugs and snails, chervil is a good companion for radishes, lettuces, and broccoli (as well as other cabbage family plants), protecting them from damage, while also improving the vegetables' growth and flavor. Chervil will tolerate shady conditions, so plant it thickly among the plants you want to protect. You can also cultivate it with parsley, chives, and tarragon so that you can create your own homegrown *fines herbes* mixture.

Cilantro/Coriander

A young *Coriandrum sativum* plant rises from the soil. You can grow this herb for both its leaves—called cilantro—which in cookery are used as an herb, or for its seeds—called coriander—which are used as a spice.

SCIENTIFIC NAME: *Coriandrum sativum*

FAMILY: Apiaceae

HEIGHT: 1 to 2 feet (30–60 cm)

WIDTH: 12 to 18 inches (30–45 cm)

BLOOMS: Spring, summer, autumn

SOIL pH: Acidic

LIGHT: Full sun to partial sun

This delicate herb *(Coriandrum sativum)*, with its fresh, piquant flavor, has long been used in Mexican and Thai cuisine but now has fans around the world. It is also an herb that many people dislike—the plant contains saponins, bitter-tasting plant-derived organic chemicals that can give the leaves a soapy or even a "dirty feet" flavor.

This species provides two separate culinary ingredients—the thin, green stems and flat, lacy leaves, which are best eaten fresh, are called cilantro. But under the name coriander, the seeds of this plant are used as a spice, especially in dishes of Indian, Middle Eastern, and Asian origin. The "seeds" are actually two cilantro seeds encased in a husk. The husk is hard, round, and light brown or gray in color. Before you plant them, you need to gently crush the husk while holding the two cilantro seeds together to increase the chances that they will germinate. Soak the seeds in water for 24 to 48 hours, remove from the water, and dry.

This plant, which originated in Europe, Asia, and Africa, is not enamored of hot weather. If temperatures get too warm, the plant will bolt—meaning it will grow flowers, and then go to seed. The ideal conditions for cilantro are sunny but cool. It grows best where it gets early-morning or late-afternoon sun, but is protected during the hottest part of the day.

GROWING CILANTRO

Once you have prepared the cilantro seeds, you can start plants indoors or outdoors. Place the seeds in the bed or starter tray about 2 inches (5 cm) apart and then cover them with about a ¼-inch (6.35 mm) layer of soil. Once the plants reach 2 inches (5 cm) in height, thin them to about 3 to 4 inches (7.5–10 cm) apart. It's best to grow cilantro in slightly crowded conditions because the leaves will shade the roots and help to keep the plant from stressing in hot weather.

When transplanting into the garden, place holes 3 to 4 inches (7.5–10 cm) apart and gently set the plants in them. Water thoroughly after transplanting. Cilantro also does well in containers, which can be moved if the midday sun is too intense.

A cilantro plant that goes to seed will likely grow again next year, or you can collect the seeds and use them as coriander in your cooking. Cilantro can be started in fall once temperatures start to cool. It grows quickly the following spring, often yielding leaves within 30 days.

Herb Combos

Try planting a mix of herbs with similar requirements in a large container. Or consider growing the ingredients for Italian or Mexican dishes in a single pot. Try the combinations below, or experiment with your own mix.

- **Sun loving:** marjoram, lavender, rosemary, sage, and oregano.
- **Moisture loving:** tarragon, cilantro, basil, and parsley
- **Aromatic:** lemon verbena, lemon thyme, and hyssop
- **Italian:** basil, oregano, parsley, and thyme
- **Mexican:** cilantro/coriander, oregano, and epazote *(Dysphania ambrosioides)*, a pungent leafy herb

Dill

The yellow flowers of the dill plant *(Anethum graveolens)* stand tall above feathery foliage. This herb allows you to waste no portion of it: its flowers, leaves, stems, and seeds are all edible. You can also dry the plant for later use in many recipes.

At a Glance

SCIENTIFIC NAME: *Anethum graveolens*

FAMILY: Apiaceae

HEIGHT: 3 to 5 feet (1–1.5 m)

WIDTH: 2 to 3 feet (60 cm–1 m)

BLOOMS: Late summer, early autumn

SOIL pH: Slightly acidic

LIGHT: Full sun

This popular culinary herb, with a distinctive flavor that's a cross between celery and fennel, is native to Europe and Asia. Cooks appreciate that both the leaves and seeds are edible. These are used to season a variety of foods such as breads, salads, soups, and party dips, and are sprinkled on potatoes, salmon and other fish dishes, as well as lamb and vegetables like peas, beets, and asparagus. Dill also plays a big role in seasoning pickled foods that will be jarred or canned and stored for the winter.

Dill's attractive feathery foliage makes it a nice addition to flower or vegetable beds, where it will attract bees and butterflies, especially the Eastern black swallowtail. It has a habit of self-seeding, however, so make sure you keep it in check by deadheading spent flowers before they go to seed.

Mature plants are multi-branched and upright with finely dissected leaves. Be aware that the wide, flat flowers can make the plant top-heavy, so some specimens might require staking. The entire plant is extremely fragrant—and although the foliage and seeds are most commonly thought of as seasonings, the flowers are also edible.

GROWING DILL

You can buy potted nursery specimens, but it's usually best to sow dill seeds directly in the ground—these plants develop a long taproot that doesn't like to be disturbed. Planting dill seed is easy—simply scatter the seeds in your desired location after the last frost, then lightly cover the seeds with soil. Water the area thoroughly. Dill will germinate best at soil temperatures between 60 and 70° F (15–21.° C).

The top chefs know that you can't beat fresh dill for its flavor. The best way to ensure the freshest dill possible is to provide a continuing harvest by sowing new seeds every two weeks.

Dill plants do best in full sun. Other than that proviso, dill will grow happily in both poor and rich soil or in damp or dry conditions. In spite of its delicate appearance, dill is actually a fairly cold-hardy plant. When started outdoors in spring, after the chance of frost has passed, it will grow quickly, with seedlings appearing in about 10 to 14 days.

HARVESTING DILL

You can harvest the leaves at any time until dill blooms, which occurs about eight weeks after sowing. To harvest the leaves, trim off the amount you desire for cooking—up to two-thirds of the plant is the rule of thumb for annuals, which should quickly grow back. Once the flowers develop, however, the plants focus on seed development rather than growing more leaves. Collect the seed pods as they begin to turn brown, and place them in a paper bag. Gently shake the bag, and the seeds will fall out. Use them fresh for cooking, or store them in the refrigerator for two to three weeks. Dill can also be frozen or dried for later use.

German Chamomile

German chamomile in full bloom rises alongside rosemary in an herb garden. These small, daisy-like flowers not only add a light touch to the garden, they also help to keep harmful insect pests from affecting its companions.

Originally native to Europe, North Africa, and Asia, this herb is also known as barnyard daisy, Hungarian chamomile, and wild chamomile. Unlike its sister plant, Roman chamomile, which is a perennial, German chamomile is an annual, growing for only one season. Gardeners will tell you, however, that the German variety self-seeds so readily, it's practically a perennial, as well.

The fragrant flowers form at the top of green, hairy stems and have white petals, surrounding vivid yellow centers. The leaves are very small, finely divided, and downy to the touch. They give off an apple-like aroma when they are crushed. These hardy plants can often be found growing wild in meadows and on cliff edges and coastal paths.

The herb is also believed to have medicinal properties. Its use goes back to the Middle Ages, when it was classed as a carminative, painkiller, diuretic, digestive aid, treatment for menstrual cramps, and a mild laxative with anti-inflammatory and bactericidal effects. Chamomile is still a source for herbal remedies, beverages, and skincare products. The plant is known to contain antispasmodic and anti-inflammatory constituents and is quite effective in treating stomach and intestinal cramps. The flowers contain beneficial polyphenol compounds, including apigenin, quercetin, patuletin, and luteolin. Research indicates the plant may have anti-anxiety properties as well. To make your own calming herbal tea from fresh or dried flowers, simply steep them in boiling water for five minutes. The plant is also used by a few craft brewers as a flavoring.

GROWING CHAMOMILE

Chamomile is best planted in the spring and can be started either from seeds or young nursery plants. Chamomile grows best in cool conditions and should be planted in partial shade, but will also manage under full sun. The soil should be dry. The plants mature quickly, reaching full bloom within 10 weeks or so. Once your chamomile is established, it needs very little care.

Like most herbs, chamomile prefers not being fussed over. Too much fertilizer will result in weakly flavored foliage and fewer flowers. Chamomile is drought tolerant and only needs to be watered during extended dry spells. For the most part, chamomile is not affected by many pests. A plant weakened by lack of water or other issues, however, may be attacked by aphids, mealybugs, or thrips. The herb is often recommended as a companion plant to place in the vegetable garden because its strong scent is known to keep pests away.

SCIENTIFIC NAME: *Matricaria chamomilla* or *M. recutita*

FAMILY: Asteraceae

HEIGHT: 18 to 24 inches (45–60 cm)

WIDTH: 8 to 12 inches (20–30 cm)

BLOOMS: Summer

SOIL pH: Acidic to alkaline

LIGHT: Full sun

Although mature plants can become a bit floppy, they work well as underplantings for an herb or vegetable garden, to soften the edges on rock walls, and in containers. For chamomile tea, harvest the flowers once they are fully open. After you dry the flowers and leaves, store them in a cool, dark spot in an airtight container or freeze them.

Note: Chamomile is likely unsafe for use during pregnancy. Its topical use for skin disorders may cause contact dermatitis.

Spotting the Difference

The closely related Roman chamomile *(Chamaemelum nobile)* is quite similar in appearance to this variety of chamomile. To tell the two apart, cut the flower receptacle—the portion of the flower that connects the bloom to the stalk—in half. If the receptacle has a solid interior, the plant is Roman. If the receptacle has a hollow interior, it is German chamomile.

Lemongrass

The thin blades of the lemongrass plant give this herb an attractive silhouette that works beautifully in borders, as well as in a warm-region herb gardens.

SCIENTIFIC NAME: *Cymbopogon citratus*

FAMILY: Poaceae

HEIGHT: 2 to 4 feet (60 cm–1.2 m)

WIDTH: 2 to 3 feet (60 cm–1 m)

BLOOMS: Not applicable

SOIL pH: Neutral

LIGHT: Full sun

For gardeners who ask something extra of their plants, lemongrass *(Cymbopogon citratus)* easily fulfills two roles. This fast-growing ornamental grass increases curb appeal, while offering a tasty herb for soups, stir-fries, and teas. Native to Sri Lanka and India, lemongrass is perennial in warm regions, but treated as an annual in temperate zones. It grows in abundance in areas that mimic its warm and humid habitat. Provide lots of heat, light, and moisture, and your lemongrass will grow and multiply quickly.

This herb is found in recipes throughout Southeast Asia, particularly in Thai and Indonesian dishes. As an herbal medicine, it has a history of use for treating digestive tract spasms, stomachache, high blood pressure, convulsions, pain, vomiting, cough, rheumatism, fever, the common cold, and exhaustion.

Lemongrass—also known as barbed wire grass, silky heads, Cochin grass, Malabar grass, oily heads, citronella grass, or fever grass—grows into a tall plant, with long, slender gray-green foliage that adds gorgeous reds and burgundies to autumn gardens. The plump stems, and sometimes the leaves, are used for cooking. All parts of the plant have a strong lemon flavor with hints of ginger. Lemongrass's fragrance also acts as a pest repellent—its oil seems to deter unwanted insects, such as mosquitoes.

GROWING LEMONGRASS

Lemongrass may not always be available in your local supermarket, so it makes sense to grow it yourself. For indoor cultivation, go to the grocery store, and buy the freshest lemongrass plants you can find. Trim a couple of inches (5 cm) off the top, and peel away anything that looks dead. Place the stalks in a glass of shallow water, and set it near a sunny window. In a few weeks, tiny roots should emerge. After they mature a bit, transfer the plant to a pot of soil with the crown just below the surface. This pot can stay indoors or go out on the deck or patio. Growing the plant indoors gives you easy access to the fresh herb when you need it. If you live in a warm climate, you can plant your lemongrass in the backyard in a bog or pond. Cool climate gardeners need to bring their plants indoors in autumn.

Outdoors, lemongrass is best planted from potted nursery specimens in spring, after all danger of frost has passed. Lemongrass grows best in full sun, at least six hours daily, even in tropical regions. Plants grown in the shade will be sparse and could attract pests. Lemongrass prefers moist soil—the standard 1-inch (2.5 cm) per week of water will allow it to thrive—yet once established, the herb has a tolerance for drought. A 3-inch (7.5 cm) layer of mulch can help conserve soil moisture and will enrich the soil. You can also supply a slow-release 6-4-0 fertilizer to feed your plants throughout the growing season. Manure tea will add important trace nutrients.

Note: Be aware that this plant contains cyanogenic glycosides and other oils that are mildly toxic to dogs, cats, and horses.

Editor's Picks

If you are purchasing a nursery-grown plant, you might have other lemongrass varieties to choose from.

- **East Indian *(C. flexuosus)* is an heirloom variety of lemongrass that contains potent essential oils with medicinal benefits.**
- **Palmarosa *(C. martinii)* yields a rich aromatic oil that is often used in aromatherapy.**
- **Citronella *(C. nardus)* is familiar to many as the source of the citronella oils used in candles and other mosquito repellents.**
- **Java citronella *(C. winterianus)* is a compact lemongrass with yellowish and reddish foliage.**

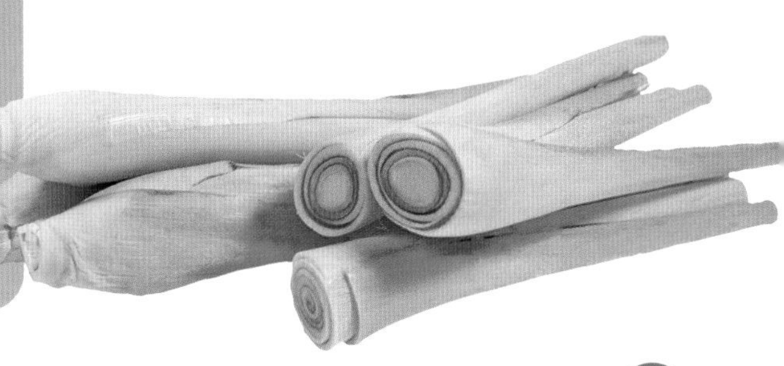

WEEDS OR WILDFLOWERS?

There is often a thin line between plants we consider desirable in the garden and those we label—and often dismiss—as wildflowers or weeds. Just imagine that as certain savvy people are out in the fields harvesting young dandelions and purslane for salads and St. John's wort for healing wounds, other gardeners are in their yards battling with hoes and herbicides to kill off these exact same plants.

Maybe it is time to re-evaluate the plants we think of as lawn nuisances and garden intruders and instead consider the positive uses and health aids they might provide. Beneficial weeds can accomplish a number of roles in the garden or yard, including fertilizing the soil, increasing moisture, providing shelter for tender seedlings, acting as living mulch, repelling pests, attracting beneficial insects, or serving as food or other resources for humans.

Foraging for wild rosehips. Overlooked plants can yield unexpected rewards. Rosehips, for example, have many health benefits and can be used to make, teas, jelly, and syrup or used to flavor soups, sauces, and desserts. They are easy to dry in baskets or paper bags. Always be sure to harvest from plants that have not been sprayed with herbicides, pesticides, or fertilizers.

A WELCOME FOR THE UNWANTED

According to the doctrines of permaculture—which seeks to integrate arrangements observed in flourishing ecosystems into land management and settlement design—weeds and other invasive plants actually do have a place in the ecological scheme of things. These plants often perform intensive and thankless jobs, such as rapidly repairing earth in degraded urban and suburban landscapes, attracting nutrients through prolific fruiting, supporting wildlife, building topsoil, and reintroducing nitrogen. In many parts of the world, it is necessary to augment commercial agriculture with wild food sources, and these include nuts, berries, fruits, and edible greens—much of the latter supplied by "weeds."

LET THE RIGHT ONES IN

These pages show some common garden invaders—and one example of ancient "dinosaur fodder"—that may have surprisingly positive qualities.

BURDOCK

The root of *Arctium lappa,* which originated in Japan, contains powerful antioxidants, including quercetin, luteolin, and phenolic acids. It removes toxins from the blood, may inhibit some types of cancer, and can treat skin issues. It also reduces inflammation and helps control blood sugar.

CHICORY

Cichorium intybus is a somewhat woody, perennial herb, usually with bright blue flowers. Native to the Old World, the fresh root is packed with the prebiotic fiber inulin. Chicory may aid bowel movements, improve blood sugar control, and support weight loss. For more information, *see* page 238.

CLOVER

Trifolium, like all legumes, hosts bacteria that fix beneficial nitrogen in the soil. Clover provides ground cover, helping retain water in the soil as a "living mulch," and protecting nearby crops from insect predation. It attracts pollinators and companions well with brassicas like cabbage and broccoli.

DANDELION

The tender young leaves of *Taraxacum* species are edible in salads, while the flowers are one of the first foods for hungry bees coming out of hibernation. It serves as a companion plant for most flowers and vegetables, attracting pollinators, and its deep taproot breaks up soil.

EVENING PRIMROSE
Oenothera biennis is a lovely wildflower not closely related to the garden primrose. A perennial plant of an upright habit, it bears buttercup yellow blooms. The seed-oil supplement, which contains the fatty acid gamma-linolenic acid (GLA), is taken to reduce pain and improve mobility.

GOLDENROD
Solidago, which is found in meadows and other open green spaces, is used to reduce pain and swelling, as a diuretic to increase urine flow, and to stop muscle spasms. It is also used for gout and joint pain, as well as skin conditions like eczema. Its young leaves are also edible and used in teas.

HORSETAIL
Equisetum is a "living fossil," the lone remainder of an ancient subclass. Dinosaurs definitely dined on early examples of this genus. Today the fertile stems of some species are eaten like asparagus. It is also used to provide invigoration, weight control, and skincare, as well as to boost hair and bone health.

JOE-PYE WEED
Members of the *Eutrochium* genus act as major lures for pollinators and predatory insects that feed on garden insect pests. This tall, spreading, somewhat gangly plant produces purple, pink, or white blooms in midsummer, furnishing the garden with pops of color when most other flowers are fading.

LAMB'S QUARTERS
Known as *Chenopodium album*, or white goosefoot, in Europe, *Chenopodium berlandieri*, or pitseed goosefoot, in North America, this edible plant is incredibly nutritious: high in fiber and protein and loaded with Vitamins A and C. Known to distract leaf miners from crops, it also prevents soil erosion.

MILK THISTLE
The prickly *Silybum marianum* plant contains silymarin, known for its antioxidant, antiviral, and anti-inflammatory properties. Herbal remedies derived from it are said to protect the liver and bones, boost breast milk production, help treat acne, lower blood sugar, and may prevent age-related brain decline.

MULLEIN
Verbascum, or figwort, is a flowering plant that acts as an expectorant, helping the body expel excess mucus in the throat or chest, typically by making coughs more productive. It is also a demulcent, creating a soothing anti-inflammatory coating over mucous membranes. For more information, *see* page 107.

NETTLE
Urtica dioica is known for its sting, but young plants are edible and can be used to make an herbal tea. Nettle serves as a great companion planting for broccoli, mint, valerian, and fennel, helping them to produce healthy yields. Once grown as a fiber crop, it is still used as a high-protein additive in animal feed.

ST. JOHN'S WORT
Hypericum perforatum, a lovely yellow flowering plant that grows wild in gardens and vacant lots, is used to treat kidney and lung ailments, insomnia, and to aid wound healing. It is also said to boost mood and provide relief from depression, but how this mechanism works is not yet understood.

WILD GARLIC
Allium vineale, or crow garlic, is considered a noxious weed by many. Yet, it can companion fruit trees, nightshades (tomatoes, peppers, potatoes, etc.), brassicas (cabbage, broccoli, kohlrabi, etc.) and carrots, and it repels slugs, aphids, carrot flies, and cabbage worms. It is sometimes eaten like chives.

WILD MUSTARD
Three species of wild Brassicaceae were combined to create the modern hybrid domesticated mustard. These plants make good companions for grape vines, radish, and other brassicas, like cabbage, cauliflower, and broccoli. The plant attracts ladybugs and traps aphids. The leaves and seeds are edible.

WILD ROSE
The *Rosa* genus includes the feral multiflora rose, which is used as root stock for domesticated roses and as a natural, thorny fence for livestock. Wild roses companion well with strawberries, grape, and garden roses, and are known for their healthful rosehips, which are used to make tea.

Lemon Verbena

The fragrant leaves of lemon verbena reach out over its pot. Plant this herb in containers near seating areas or well-used pathways—every time you brush past the plants you will be rewarded with a waft of its fresh, lemony aroma.

Lemon verbena *(Aloysia citriodora)* is yet another lemon-scented herb that is used in the kitchen. If you live in a region in a frost-free area with milder winters, the plant behaves as a perennial. It can grow into a valued landscape shrub about 6 feet tall by 8 feet wide (1.8-x-2.4 m), one that will release its refreshing citrus aroma as you brush by. In cooler climates, it is best to treat it as an annual, and bring potted specimens inside in the autumn.

Also known as lemon beebrush and vervain, this native of Chile and Argentina is a small, woody, delicate shrub with narrow glossy leaves and small white flowers. Due to its strong aroma it is often used to scent oils.

It is often presented as a garnish, because the leaves tend to be quite sharp in flavor. You can also add chopped leaves to sweet drinks and tea and use them to flavor desserts, jams, and alcoholic beverages. It can even be used as a substitute for fresh lemons or lemon zest. Lemon verbena is sometimes used in making perfumes and toilet waters. Medicinally, the flowers and leaves have been used to help with certain medical conditions and has been utilized as a fever reducer, sedative, and antispasmodic. The leaves can be used fresh, or you can dry them for future use. When dried as an ornamental, the sprigs hold their scent for many years to come.

Editor's Tip

Potpourri, a mixture of dried flowers, herbs, and spices, has been used for centuries. Whether set out in a dish or poured into sachets, it can add wonderful fragrance wherever you place it. Aromatic herbs like lavender and chamomile, as well as lemon verbena, are perfect for these mixes.

To learn how you can grow a selection of aromatic herbs and other plants to create your own signature blends, follow the link to "Potpourri Garden Plants: Creating a Potpourri Herb Garden" (QR = gkh.us/58830), or scan the QR code.

SCIENTIFIC NAME: *Aloysia citriodora*

FAMILY: Verbenaceae

HEIGHT: 18 inches to 6 feet (45 cm–1.8 m)

WIDTH: 18 inches to 4 feet (45–1.2 m)

BLOOMS: Late summer

SOIL pH: Slightly acidic

LIGHT: Full sun

GROWING LEMON VERBENA

Growing it isn't too difficult, but this herb can be sensitive, having a high water requirement. It can be propagated from either seeds or cuttings. The cuttings can be placed in a jar of water while you wait for new roots to form. Once they form, wait a few weeks for a good root structure to develop before planting them into soil. Set them out at the same time you plant tomatoes, coleus, and other heat lovers. Lemon verbena yields the most intense flavor in full sun.

To grow lemon verbena from seeds, scatter them in starter trays, and cover with a light layer of soil. Moisten well, and give them plenty of sunshine. Once the seedlings have grown several leaves, you can transplant them into the garden after first hardening them off with gradual exposure to outdoor temperatures. Space the plants 12 to 18 (30–45 cm) inches apart to give them room to spread out.

To encourage leaf production, feed regularly with a water-soluble plant food. In periods of bad weather, your plants might get a bit beat up. Revive a battered plant by trimming it back to one-third. It will come back even fuller and healthier.

You can harvest the leaves once they are large enough for your uses.

Note: This herb is edible by humans, but it is toxic to horses, dogs, and cats.

Nasturtium

Nasturtiums spill over the sides of a wooden planter. The colorful flowers, in vivid oranges and yellows, rise over the distinctive oval leaves of this herbaceous plant.

At a Glance

SCIENTIFIC NAME: *Tropaeolum majus*

FAMILY: Tropaeolaceae

HEIGHT: 1 to 10 feet (30 cm–3 m)

WIDTH: 1 to 3 feet (30 cm–1 m)

BLOOMS: Spring, summer, autumn

SOIL pH: Acidic, neutral, alkaline

LIGHT: Full sun

Nasturtiums have a lot going for them—lovely, jewel-toned flowers that peek out from dense foliage and large, beautifully shaped leaves that resemble a lotus; plus both the blossoms and leaves make tasty additions to salads and sandwiches. These plants are also quick to germinate and easy to grow. The humorous advice, "Be nasty to nasturtiums," is not far off the mark—they really do best with a little neglect.

The flowers of this South American native are funnel-shaped and trend toward the hot end of the color spectrum—with varying shades of yellow, orange, pink, and red. There are growing habits for almost every landscaping need: bushy plants for borders and edges; trailing specimens for walls and containers; and climbers that add dramatic height to the garden. They also do well in hangers, window boxes, and ground planters. Below are a few of the most popular cultivars.

- 'Alaska' is an heirloom variety with variegated foliage and multicolored blossoms. A bushy, dwarf plant, it reaches a compact spread of 8 inches (20 cm).
- 'Black Velvet' is a striking, deep red, almost black, with a bright yellow throat.
- 'Canary Creeper' is a trailing variety best planted near fences or trellises. Its unique yellow flowers spread out like canary wings.
- "Empress of India' is a bushy, dwarf heirloom cultivar with dark green foliage and scarlet blossoms.
- 'Jewel' grows 16 inches (40.6 cm) tall and flowers profusely in yellow, red, orange, mahogany, and rose. The flowers sometimes get lost under the foliage.
- 'Peach Melba' has flowers that taste like watercress and are yellow with maroon spots. This bushy dwarf reaches 10 inches (25 cm) in height and width.

Because nasturtium leaves and flowers are edible, with a peppery tang, the plants are often found in vegetable gardens. When planted alongside broccoli, cabbage, and cauliflower, they keep pests like aphids away.

Dig Deeper

READ MORE AT GARDENING KNOW HOW

Scan the QR code or follow this link to learn more about this edible flower.

- **"Picking Nasturtiums to Eat — Learn How to Harvest Edible Nasturtiums"** (URL = gkh.us/108628)

GROWING NASTURTIUMS

Nasturtiums can be either started from seeds or purchased in seedlings pots at nurseries. You may need to manipulate the seed coat for faster germination: either nick the seeds with a knife or soak them overnight in lukewarm water. Plant seedlings immediately in a container or sunny part of the garden that allows plenty of room for growth. These plants should be placed directly into their permanent location, as nasturtium flowers do not transplant well. If you must start seeds and then transplant them, use peat pots that can be placed in the ground without disturbing the seedling's roots. For climbing varieties you may want to set up a trellis near the planting site.

The seeds typically germinate quickly, and the plant will start blooming soon after. Once established, nasturtiums generally take care of themselves. Their watering needs are average and if the soil is too rich or you've added too much fertilizer, you will get lush foliage but few nasturtium flowers. Removing spent blooms is rarely necessary.

Parsley

Curly parsley ready for harvesting. Its dense foliage is tightly curled and has a slightly bitter taste compared to the flat-leaf varieties. Both are often used as a garnish.

This hardy herb is popular in both the garden and the kitchen. It occurs in a flat-leaf, also called Italian, variety and a curly leaf variety. Both are European in origin but have now spread around the globe. Parsley, with its bright, herbaceous flavor, is added to many savory dishes or used as a decorative garnish; its fern-like foliage is also high in vitamins. In the garden, parsley makes an attractive edging plant that is rarely affected by disease, though pests such as aphids, can occasionally present a problem. Parsley is considered a biennial, but is treated as an annual in colder climates. It can be grown in containers or in a bed and is generally established through seeds.

This plant grows in clumps with its lacy foliage reaching about a foot (30 cm) in height. It is the triangular, dark green leaves that make a good garnish or an aromatic addition to recipes. In summer, butterflies love the petite whitish yellow blossoms that form lacy flat-topped clusters in the classic umbel shape of its family.

Different varieties of parsley yield different flavors, so consider how you'd like to use the herb before choosing which to plant. For example, curly parsley can be a little bitter for some palates, while the less-robust taste of flat-leaf parsley is more in favor with today's cooks. The latter is available throughout the year.

GROWING PARSLEY

Parsley seeds can be started outdoors—sown directly in the garden as soon as the soil is manageable in spring—but the proven method is to sow them indoors in peat pots about six weeks before planting time. This step is helpful because parsley germinates very slowly, taking three weeks or more to sprout. Most varieties of parsley also grow fairly slowly, establishing maturity between 70 to 90 days after planting. Parsley seeds are quite small, so there is no need to cover them with soil. Simply sprinkle seeds on top of the soil and mist well with water. Once the seeds have sprouted, thin the seedlings down to only one or two plants per pot.

SCIENTIFIC NAME: *Petroselinum crispum*

FAMILY: Apiaceae

HEIGHT: 9 to 12 inches (23–30 cm)

WIDTH: 9 to 12 inches (23–30 cm)

BLOOMS: Summer

SOIL pH: Acidic, neutral

LIGHT: Full sun to partial shade

Although this herb tolerates poor soil and drainage, it's always preferable to situate plants in organic-rich, well-drained soil. A planting bed with full sun to partial shade is also recommended. Once established, this easy-care herb requires little maintenance, other than occasional watering or weeding. A decent layer of mulch around the bases, however, will reduce the need for both watering or weeding.

Parsley can be harvested throughout the year, even indoors during winter. You can start harvesting parsley once the leaves start to curl. For optimal flavor, pick parsley early in the morning when the plant's oil is strongest. Parsley is best used while fresh; however, it can be frozen until you need it. Freezing parsley is actually better than drying, which can cause the herb to lose some of its flavor.

Note: Parsley is technically toxic both to people and pets due to chemical compounds in it called furanocoumarins.

READ MORE AT GARDENING KNOW HOW

Scan the QR code or follow this link to learn how this plant can bring important pollinators to your culinary herb garden.

- **"Using Parsley for Butterflies: How to Attract Black Swallowtail Butterflies"** (URL = gkh.us/82393)

Scented Geranium

The deeply divided leaves of scented geranium give off a sharp citrus scent when crushed or bruised. The 'Citronella' cultivar has a heady citronella-like fragrance.

Scented geraniums pack a lot of punch into one plant and are a delight in any home or garden. Their varied and textured leaves, the bright hues of their flowers, the scented oils they produce, and the flavor they add to food and beverages appeal greatly to our senses.

Like their fellow hothouse cousins, zonal geraniums, scented geraniums are not true geraniums, but rather members of the *Pelargonium* genus. Although they are categorized as tender perennials, they are treated as annuals throughout most of Europe and the United States, while their beauty is appreciated all over the world. It's an added bonus that they are so easy to grow.

Scented geraniums, which are native to Africa, were found by early European explorers and brought back to Holland. From there, the popular houseplant migrated to England in the 1600s. They were particularly favored during the Victorian era, when the fragrant leaves were added to the finger bowls guests used to rinse their hands between courses at dinner.

From those original African plants, horticulturists developed more than a hundred varieties, with different shaped and textured leaves, flower colors, and aromas. The varieties are first categorized by their scent, which includes mint, rose, citrus, and spice. The leaves run the gamut from smoothly rounded to finely cut and lacy and from gray-green to dark viridian to lime. Furthermore, they have glands at the base of their leaf hairs where the scent is formed. The tiny flowers range from white to shades of lilac and pink to red, often combining colors on one bloom.

GROWING SCENTED GERANIUMS

Scented geranium care is fairly basic. You can grow them in pots, indoors or out, or in the ground. (In containers they make the perfect patio or balcony plant.) They prefer lots of sun, but may need some protection at midday. They aren't fussy about soil type, although they don't like wet feet. Fertilize them lightly and sparingly while they're actively growing. Before the first frost, dig up your plants to bring them inside, or take cuttings for winter growing. Keep them in a sunny window, water regularly, and fertilize very little.

Scented geraniums' biggest downside is they tend to get leggy and need to be trimmed back to encourage bushiness. Over-fertilization will only increase this problem.

At a Glance

SCIENTIFIC NAME: *Pelargonium graveolens*

FAMILY: Geraniaceae

HEIGHT: 1 to 3 feet (30 cm–1 m)

WIDTH: 1 to 2 feet (30–60 cm)

BLOOMS: Seasonal

SOIL pH: Slightly acidic

LIGHT: Full sun to partial shade

Don't throw those trimmings away: you can easily propagate scented geranium from cuttings to replace older plants or to give as gifts. You might want to line a driveway or path with plants grown from your cuttings.

Whether they are in containers or in the ground, locate scented geraniums where they will be touched or brushed against, because the leaves need to be bruised or crushed to release their aromatic oils. Not only do these plants offer textured leaves, lovely flowers, and exquisite scents, they're also edible! The leaves can be used to flavor teas, jellies, jams, or baked goods, and the aromatherapy is free for the taking.

Editor's Picks

It's worth exploring some of the delightfully fragrant cultivars of scented geranium.

- 'Apricot' has deep pink flowers and fruity-scented leaves.
- 'Attar of Roses', with pink flowers, gives off a heady rose fragrance.
- 'Chocolate Mint' has chocolate-colored leaves that smell like mint.
- 'Cinnamon' smells like the spice and has pink flowers.
- 'Fringed Apple' has white flowers and a sour apple aroma.
- 'Ginger' is softly scented of spice, with lavender blooms.
- 'Mrs. Taylor' is scented of musky woods and has deep red flowers.
- 'Nutmeg', with pink-accented white flowers, has a nutmeg scent.
- 'Prince Rupert', in variegated pink, has a lemony aroma.

Stevia

Stevia plants are rather plain, with bright green leaves and scentless flowers that are white with purplish accents. Stevia is a natural sweetener, which accounts for its common names of candyleaf, sweetleaf, and sugarleaf.

Stevia *(Stevia rebaudiana),* a natural sweetener with essentially no calories, is welcomed by people interested in both weight loss and those hoping to maintain a healthier diet. Its recent heyday arrived at a time when the safety of synthetic sweeteners was being questioned, and many people were looking for ways to eat more natural types of foods.

Stevia itself is a nondescript-looking plant with small, moderately broad green leaves; at maturity it reaches approximately 2 to 3 (60 cm–1 m) feet in height. It is native to Paraguay, where the indigenous people have used it for centuries, possibly millennia, as a sweetener. Indian women once used the plant, called *yerba dulce,* or "sweet herb," to make a contraceptive tea.

Stevia leaves are estimated to be anywhere between 10 to 300 times sweeter than traditional white refined sugar, yet they contain neither calories nor carbohydrates. This is because there are molecules in stevia called glycosides, essentially molecules with sugar attached to them, that give the leaves their sweet taste. Our bodies, however, cannot break apart the glycosides, meaning that the leaves have no calories when consumed by humans.

Stevia is used as a food additive in many countries; for example, it accounts for 40 percent of Japan's sweetening agents. It was banned as an additive in the United States for over a decade due to possible health risks, however, and only in 2008 was it allowed to be used again.

GROWING STEVIA

Stevia has been declared safe by the FDA and has been in continuous use internationally, so there's no reason not to grow your own plant as a sweetener . . . and great conversation piece. Stevia is a perennial in warmer areas like the American South, but in cooler regions it is treated like an annual and either brought indoors in autumn or allowed to die back.

Stevia care is not too intensive; simply place starter plants in loose, well-drained soil in full sun and water frequently but shallowly. Space stevia plants 18 inches (45 cm) apart or plant them in 12-inch (30 cm)containers. You can harvest the leaves to use as your own natural sweetener throughout the summer, but they're at their sweetest in autumn, just as they're getting ready to flower.

Pick the leaves—all of them if you're treating the plant as an annual—and dry them by placing them on a clean cloth in full sun for an entire afternoon. Save the leaves whole, or crush them into a powder in the food processor and store them in an airtight container.

At a Glance

SCIENTIFIC NAME: *Stevia rebaudiana*

FAMILY: Asteraceae

HEIGHT: 24 to 36 inches (60 cm–1 m)

WIDTH: 12 to 18 inches (30–45 cm)

BLOOMS: Early to mid-autumn

SOIL pH: Alkaline

LIGHT: Full sun

Nature's Other Sweetener

Stevia is just one of nature's sweeteners. For millennia, bees have furnished humans with another form of natural sweetener. These small wonders of the insect world are capable of converting the nectar they harvest from flowers into liquid gold—the sweet, viscous, amber back-up food of the hive, otherwise known as honey. After they collect nectar with their long tongues, enzymes in their stomachs make it stable for long-term storage. A honey's flavor is determined by the nectar source—typically flowers, herbs, and trees.

Summer Savory

Tiny lilac flowers have begun to appear in a bed of summer savory. Although they make for an attractive display, be sure to harvest any of the leaves you want to use for cooking before the flowers begin to bloom, otherwise much of the herb's taste will be gone.

Native to the eastern Mediterranean and the Caucasus, summer savory *(Satureja hortensis)* is an annual herb and part of the large mint family. It is sometimes used as a substitute—or in conjunction with—rosemary, thyme, or sage. Considered less bitter than its winter savory cousin, with its peppery notes, summer savory is thought to have the more superior flavor. It adds a piquant boost to meat recipes, as well as oil, butter, and vinegar infusions. Its flavor really comes to the fore in bean dishes, however, earning it the title the "bean herb."

Cultivated for at least 2,000 years, both summer and winter savory have a range of uses after harvesting and are worthy additions to any herb garden. Savory is a key addition to *herbes de Provence,* a famous blend of dried herbs intrinsic to southern French cuisine, alongside marjoram, rosemary, thyme, and oregano. While both species are edible, summer savory is much more common than its winter counterpart. Their names reflect the fact that summer savory is an annual plant (that only lives for one season) and winter savory is a perennial plant that returns year after year. Summer savory peaks between July and September.

This herb matures into a low-growing shrub with a mound-like formation that rarely exceeds 1 or 2 feet (30–60 cm) in height. The plant features many thin, branching stems with a purple cast that are covered in fine hairs. The gray-green, inch-long (2.5 cm) leaves are typically longer than they are wide. The tiny flowers bloom during the late summer in shades of pink, lilac, or white; they are edible, with a spicy flavor, and also have medicinal, aromatic, and decorative value.

GROWING SUMMER SAVORY

This tolerant herb likes rich, moist, well-drained soil and full sun. It also grows quickly and easily enough that it's not at all a hassle to start a new crop each spring. Summer savory plants can be sown as seed directly into the ground after all danger of frost has passed. Drop one to two seeds per inch (2.5 cm), and sow shallowly, as light is required for germination. The seeds will germinate in from 7 to 14 days. The seeds can also be started indoors about four weeks before the last frost, and then transplanted out in warmer weather. It can even be grown indoors during the winter. Once they are established, little plant care is necessary, other than watering.

Harvest your summer savory by cutting off the tops when buds are just beginning to form. Ideally, the stems should be around 6 to 8 inches (15–20 cm) long before harvesting, and they can be used either fresh or dried. Be aware that once the plant has started to flower, much of the aroma and flavor will be lost.

At a Glance

SCIENTIFIC NAME: *Satureja hortensis*

FAMILY: Lamiaceae

HEIGHT: 12 to 24 inches (30–60 cm)

WIDTH: 12 to 20 inches (30–50 cm)

BLOOMS: Summer

SOIL pH: Alkaline

LIGHT: Full sun

Editor's Tip

In order to guarantee access to summer savory all season long, sow new seeds once every week. This will furnish you with a constant supply of plants that are ready to harvest.

PERENNIAL HERBS

A savvy gardener demonstrates the most efficient way to water a rosemary plant. Watering from the bottom will encourage root growth and reduce the risk of overwatering, as well as discourage any mold forming on the soil and leaves. Use this method with all your herbs, both potted and garden specimens.

Growing herbs can get expensive, if the only ones you cultivate are annuals that need replacing every spring. Consider mixing in a number of perennial herbs, specimens that can survive for multiple growing seasons and rarely need replanting. Perennial herbs will give you lasting value—along with attractive garden interest—year after year.

True perennials will last for two years or more in the garden; most of them go dormant during the winter, and then return in spring. Tender perennials will also come back for many years when grown in warmer climates. In temperate areas, however, you will need to bring them indoors in pots during freezing weather.

In terms of flavor profile, perennial herbs are a force to be reckoned with—some aromatic plants offer piquant lemon, pine, or anise flavors. Other seasonings, such as oregano, marjoram, rosemary, tarragon, and thyme, are noted for their pungent and robust Mediterranean notes.

PRUNING FOR STRENGTH

When fall arrives, it's a good idea to cut your perennial herbs back to the base with pruners before applying a thick layer of mulch. You'll be surprised at how much bigger and stronger they will be the following spring. And when harvesting perennial herbs throughout the growing season, never take more than one-third of the plant at a time.

READ MORE AT GARDENING KNOW HOW

To learn more about growing and caring for your herb garden, follow these links.

- **"Dividing Perennial Herbs: Lean About Herb Plant Division** (URL = gkh.us/127377)
- **"Cold Hardy Herbs — Growing Herbs That Survive Winter** (URL = gkh.us/82447)
- **"Winterizing Your Herb Garden: How to Overwinter Herbs** (URL = gkh.us/83548)

Unlike most herbs that are harvested before the plant flowers, most people pick their lavender when it is in bloom so that they can dry it for use in cookery, floral arrangements, sachets, and a host of craft projects.

Bay Leaf

SCIENTIFIC NAME: *Laurus nobilis*

FAMILY: Lauraceae

HEIGHT: 10 to 60 feet (3–18 m)

WIDTH: 5 to 20 feet (1.5–6 m)

BLOOMS: Late spring to early summer

SOIL pH: Acidic to alkaline

LIGHT: Full sun to partial shade

The leaves of the bay laurel tree, native to the Mediterranean region, are used in many of the area's cuisines, including France and Italy. Although the tree can reach 60 feet (18 m), pruned container plants can be kept to a more manageable 4 to 6 feet (1.2–1.8 m).

Bay laurel, or sweet bay, is a medium-sized evergreen shrub or tree that is native to the Mediterranean. This member of the laurel family, which is made up of roughly 2,850 species, is used primarily as a culinary herb and is a component of the noted *bouquet garni,* a French seasoning blend. The dried leaves are added to sauces, soups, stews, and hearty meat and game dishes. The fresh leaves are used mainly in marinades and for preserving fish. Fresh leaves have a much stronger flavor than dried leaves.

For centuries the herb has been used medicinally for diseases and disorders such as rheumatism, sprains, indigestion, and earaches, and to enhance perspiration. Modern research reports that bay leaf may also be effective in treating diabetes and migraine headaches.

This herb is hardy in warmer regions, in cooler climates it may need to move indoors when temperatures dip. Fortunately, bay makes an excellent container plant. If you can grow it outdoors all year, it will mature into a tree. This can grow dozens of feet in height, but its size can be controlled by frequent pruning. Laurels are quite tolerant of clipping and can be trained into topiary shapes that look gorgeous with the tree's glossy green foliage.

GROWING BAY LAUREL

Gardeners typically purchase bay laurel seedlings from a nursery, but growing the plant from seeds is also possible, provided the grower has some patience—bay seed germination is a slow process. To improve your chances, never plant seeds that are dried out and order your seeds from a reputable purveyor. When they arrive, soak them in warm water for 24 hours, and then plant them immediately.

If you plan to harvest seeds from an existing plant, look for a female. Sweet laurels are dioecious, meaning male and female flowers are borne on separate plants. In the spring, inconspicuous pale yellow-green flowers bloom on mature female trees, followed by small, purplish black, oval berries. Each berry carries a single seed.

To start seeds indoors, fill a tray with a layer of moist, soil-less seed mix. Spread the seeds over the surface, about 2 inches (5 cm) apart, and gently press them down. Cover the seeds with a bit more moist mix. Lightly dampen the medium with a spray bottle; do not saturate it or the seeds will rot. Place the seed tray in a warm spot of around 70° F (21° C) with up to eight hours of sun per day. Keep the seeds moist to slightly on the dry side as they germinate. Be aware that it can take from 10 days to 6 months (!) for bay seeds to germinate. When leaves begin to appear, transplant the seedlings into pots or into the garden bed once the last chance of frost is over. Bay laurel roots are very shallow, so frequent watering might be necessary during dry periods.

Note: Bay laurel is toxic to dogs, cats, and horses.

Bouquet Garni

French for "garnished bouquet," a *bouquet garni* is a small bundle of herbs tied together with string, and sometimes wrapped in a porous cloth like cheesecloth. The bundle is dropped into sauces and soups to impart the herbs' flavors, and then is disposed of before serving. Bay leaves, along with parsley and thyme, are standard ingredients, but other herbs can be added, depending on the recipe.

Chicory

Common chicory, familiar to many as a roadside wildflower, makes a pleasing addition to an herb garden, with daisy-like flowers in soft periwinkle blues. The leaves have uses in the kitchen, including as a side dish, and the flowers make a pretty garnish.

Chicory *(Cichorium intybus)*, also known as common chicory, is a rather woody perennial herb that likes dry, stony soil and, as a result, is often seen growing on roadsides and in empty lots and scrublands. It is easy to cultivate in the garden as a cool-season crop that is grown for its leaves—which are tasty braised in butter and served over vegetables, while both the leaves and flowers can be used as a garnish. Another related species, *C. endivia*, produces curly endive and escarole, while radicchio, a form of leaf chicory, and pale Belgian endive, a forced delicacy, are varieties of *C. intybus*. (Yes, even botanists find the classification of chicory to be confusing.)

Common chicory still grows wild in its native Europe, and is now common in North America, China, and Australia, where it has become widely naturalized.

There are two types of chicory plant: root chicory is grown for the leaves and the large root *(C. intybus* var. *sativum)*, which can be baked, ground, and used as a coffee substitute and a food additive. In the 21st century, inulin, an extract from chicory root, has been used in food processing as a sweetener and source of dietary fiber. This variant can also be force-grown to create the tender white leaves known as Belgian endive, *witloof*, or *chicon*. Popular varieties to grow include 'Daliva', 'Flash', and 'Zoom'.

At a Glance

SCIENTIFIC NAME: *Cichorium intybus*

FAMILY: Asteraceae

HEIGHT: 3 to 5 feet (1–1.5 m)

WIDTH: 1 to 2 feet (30–60 cm)

BLOOMS: Early summer to first frost

SOIL pH: Neutral

LIGHT: Full sun

Radicchio *(C. intybus)* is the second type of chicory plant. It is a leafy vegetable grown for its tasty leaves (for more information, *see* page 207). Catalogna chicory *(C. intybus* var. *foliosum)*, popular in Italy, includes a whole subfamily. Chicory is also grown as a forage crop for livestock.

Common chicory resembles a dandelion plant, with a rosette of lobed or toothed, lance-shaped leaves 3 to 10 inches (7.5–25 cm) in length, which form around the base. The leaves are dark green with some red tones and bear fine hairs on both leaf surfaces. As a perennial, chicory produces only leaves during its first season. Tall stalks typically bear bright blue daisy-like flowers, rarely in white or pink, after that.

GROWING CHICORY

Seeds can be started indoors five to six weeks before they are moved outdoors. Plant the seeds ¼ inch (6.35 mm) deep in a prepared bed, 6 to 10 inches (15–25 cm) apart in rows 2 to 3 feet (60 cm–1 m) apart. If the plants grow too close together, thin them when the plants have three to four true leaves.

Cultivating chicory is similar to growing most lettuces or greens. Chicory requires well-drained soil with plenty of organic matter. It performs best when temperatures are below 75° F (24° C). Extended care requires vigilant weeding and mulching to prevent moisture loss and further weed growth. Chicory plants require 1 to 2 inches (2.5–5 cm) of water per week, or enough to keep the soil evenly moist. The herb can be fertilized with a quarter cup (60 mL) of nitrogen-based fertilizer (such as a 21-0-0) per 10 feet (3 m) of row. Apply this four weeks after transplanting or once the plants have been thinned.

Chives

The purple globes of chive flowers make this plant an attractive ornamental, as well as a prime addition to your culinary herb garden. Another bonus is that dried chive flowers are wonderful in an everlasting bouquet and keep much of their purple color.

SCIENTIFIC NAME: *Allium schoenoprasum*

FAMILY: Amaryllidaceae

HEIGHT: 10 to 15 inches (25–38 cm)

WIDTH: 10 to 15 inches (25–38 cm)

BLOOMS: Early summer

SOIL pH: Slightly acidic to neutral

LIGHT: Full sun to light shade

Cooks are always happy to have fresh chives on hand, and you should consider them an essential part of any culinary garden. Chives *(Allium schoenoprasum)*, native to Europe, Asia, and North America, grow in grass-like tufts that dry wonderfully for year-round use. The edible leaves, with their bright, mild flavor, are a favorite topping for omelets, deviled eggs, and baked potatoes and can adorn meats and cheeses, season breads and soups, and enhance a salad. Members of the onion family, they can substitute for other kinds of onions if you run out. The attractive, edible purple flowers can be added to salads or pickled in vinegar.

GROWING CHIVES

If there were an award for "easiest herb to grow," chives would win it. Learning to grow chives is so easy that even a child can do it, which makes this an excellent plant to introduce kids to gardening. Divisions are the most common way to cultivate these plants. Find an established clump of chives in early spring or mid-autumn. Gently dig up the clump, and pull away a smaller clump with at least 5 to 10 bulbs. Transplant this to the desired location in your garden.

To start your chives crop indoors, plant the seeds about ¼ inch (6 mm) deep in the soil. Water well, and then place the seeded tray in a dark spot with temperatures ranging from 60 to 70° F (15–21° C) until the seeds sprout. Once you see the sprouts, move the trays into the light. When the chives reach 6 inches (15 cm) in height, transplant them to the garden. If you're planting chive seeds directly outdoors, wait until after the last frost.

Chives prefer strong light and rich soil, but be sure to avoid soil that is too wet or too dry. Once the chives are about a foot (30 cm) tall, simply snip off what you need for a recipe with sharp scissors, up to half the plant.

COMPANION PLANTING WITH CHIVES

Chives have a sulfur-based oil that is the heart of the flavors we enjoy, but it can also act as a deterrent to many pests. The large, tufted, purple flower heads are a bee magnet that will draw pollinators to your garden and increase the yield in your veggie patch. With these positives, you will find that this herb makes a great companion to a variety of other kinds of plants, from rose bushes to fruit trees and more.

- Planting chives near roses helps repel black spot and enhances growth. Chives can also ward off Japanese beetles that attack roses and other ornamentals.
- When planted near apple trees, chives may prevent apple scab and deter borers. They also deter insect pests from attacking grapes and draw pollinators, increasing yields.
- In the vegetable garden, the oils in chives repel numerous insects, and the pollinators it attracts help increase yields. Chives can increase the length and flavor of carrots and repel aphids from celery, lettuce, and peas. They also repel destructive cucumber beetles, while tomatoes benefit from their oils and attractive flowers.

Note: Chive plants are toxic to dogs and cats.

Mix chives and water in a blender with a little dish soap for a solution that acts like a pest repellent on most plants and deters powdery mildew on vegetables.

Fennel

The fat white root of the fennel plant yields a tasty vegetable known as Florence fennel, or in Italy, *finocchio.* Fennel is an Italian staple and is one of the signature flavors of Italian sausage. For non-cooks, the plant also makes a pretty ornamental.

Fennel *(Foeniculum vulgare)* has a long and varied history. The ancient Egyptians and the Chinese used it strictly for medicinal purposes, and this lore was brought back to Europe by early traders. During the Middle Ages, the herb was believed to hold magical or protective qualities—people hung fennel over their doors to drive away evil spirits. Eventually, the crisp anise flavor established it as a culinary herb for seasoning eggs and fish. Today, every part of the plant is used in the kitchen—fennel seeds add a delicious anise-like taste to sauces, fish dishes, and many baked goods. The leaves are lovely in salads, soups, and stuffing. You can even eat the bulbs as a cooked or raw vegetable. Fennel belongs to the carrot and parsley family and is a cousin to other umbellifer herbs, such as caraway, dill, and cumin.

This aromatic plant's feathery, branching, yellow-green foliage and tall stature make it attractive in border plantings and cottage gardens. In butterfly gardens, swallowtail caterpillars use it as a food source and pupal site. The plant sports small yellow flowers in summer, followed by aromatic fruits that are commonly, though incorrectly, referred to as seeds. As a short-lived perennial it blooms best in the second year. Native to southern Europe, the herb is now naturalized throughout Europe, North America, and Australia and is found in gardens all over the world.

GROWING FENNEL

Plant your fennel in the spring, in a sunny location in slightly acidic soil at the back of a well-drained bed. There are two methods of propagation—division or seeds. Propagation isn't as easy as with other garden plants because fennel has a long taproot that doesn't like to be divided or moved. Planting fennel seeds is the much easier option.

Seeds can be sown as soon as the soil warms in the spring. Soaking the seeds for a day or two before sowing will ensure better germination. Keep the area moist until the seeds sprout, and then thin the seedlings to 12 to 18 inches (30–45 cm) apart when they reach 4 to 6 inches (10–15 cm) tall. Plants will begin flowering about 90 days after planting.

The fine-textured foliage has a fast growth rate and can reach up to 6 feet (1.8 m) tall, making it an excellent backdrop for flowers. It readily re-seeds and, while not considered invasive, it has certainly earned its reputation for an aggressive habit. Once established, fennel doesn't need much care. It appreciates the occasional dose of mild fertilizer and some additional water if the weather is hot and dry. In addition to its culinary contributions, fennel will attract beneficial insects to the garden.

Fennel can be cut back early in the season to encourage bushier growth and should be deadheaded for seed harvest and to prevent overseeding of new plants. Harvest and dry seeds as the flower heads fade. There's only one restriction on fennel: don't plant it near dill. Cross-pollination results in strangely flavored seeds for both plants.

SCIENTIFIC NAME: *Foeniculum vulgare*

FAMILY: Apiaceae

HEIGHT: 4 to 6 feet (1.2–1.8 m)

WIDTH: 1.5 to 3 feet (45 cm–1 m)

BLOOMS: Summer

SOIL pH: Acidic

LIGHT: Full sun

READ MORE AT GARDENING KNOW HOW

If your fennel isn't producing as it should, learn how to solve this problem. Just scan the QR code or follow this link.

- **"No Bulbs on Fennel: Getting Fennel to Produce Bulbs "** (URL = gkh.us/95653)

Ginger

Ginger plants grown in a container are getting ready for harvest. This spicy rhizome is often used in Asian cuisine. You can grow your own from grocery store gingerroot.

The rhizomes of the ginger plant *(Zingiber officinale)*—with their slightly peppery, sweet flavor—are the parts we typically turn to when preparing Asian recipes. The leaves can also be boiled and used in teas and will pair well with rice and pork dishes. This moderately tender perennial can be grown in many temperate regions, although in some locations the leaves will die in the winter. For really cold climates, ginger should be grown in a pot and brought indoors during winter.

Native to maritime Southeast Asia, the plant was carried to the Mediterranean by Arab traders. Ginger's knobby rhizomes grow tall pseudostems (false stems made of rolled leaf bases) bearing narrow green leaf blades and clusters of white and pink buds that bloom into yellow flowers. Ginger might seem like a difficult herb to grow—you often see the rhizome in grocery stores or Asian markets, but the plant is rarely found in a garden center. Yet the truth is, you can easily grow ginger at home.

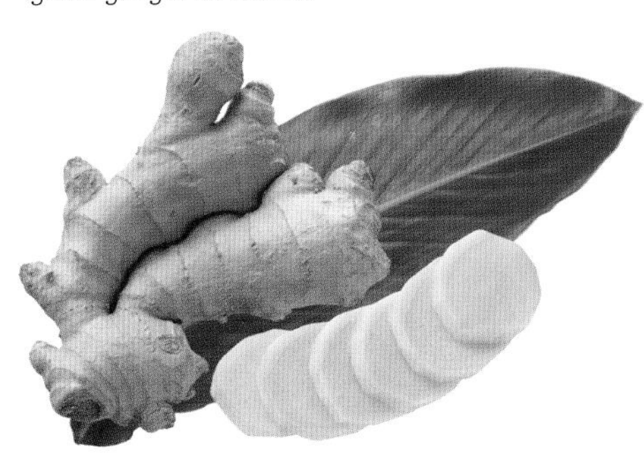

GROWING GINGER

Ginger dealers are available online, or you can simply head to your local grocery store and buy a gingerroot in the produce section. Choose a healthy, plump root about 4 to 5 inches (10–12.5 cm) long with at least a few "fingers." If possible, choose one upon which the tips of the fingers are greenish.

Ginger grows best in partial to full shade and likes rich, loose soil. It's a good idea to add lots of compost or rotted manure to the chosen spot. If you plan to grow in containers, use high-quality potting soil. Plant your gingerroot in the early spring, after all chance of frost has passed. Break off a finger that is 1 to 2 inches (2.5–5 cm) long and has at least one bud (a knob-like rounded point). To help prevent rot, dry the pieces for a day or two before putting them in the ground.

Plant the ginger sections in a shallow trench no more than 1 inch (2.5 cm) deep. If the growing root pushes back up through the top of the soil, this is okay and not uncommon. Plant one ginger plant per square foot (0.1 m^2), and then water thoroughly. When the leaves emerge, water sparingly, but deeply. The leaves can grow up to 4 feet (1.2 m) tall and are susceptible to wind damage, so consider staking them if violent storms are predicted.

At a Glance

SCIENTIFIC NAME: *Zingiber officinale*

FAMILY: Zingiberaceae

HEIGHT: Up to 4 feet (1.2 m)

WIDTH: Up to 2 feet (60 cm)

BLOOMS: Autumn

SOIL pH: Neutral, alkaline

LIGHT: Full sun to partial shade

Ginger takes 10 months to mature, so it will be ready for harvest the following spring, or you can let it grow through to the next summer for a larger harvest. To harvest, lift the ginger plant gently from the soil. If you'd like it to continue growing, break off a part that has foliage and carefully replant it. Snip off the foliage of the segment you are keeping, and wash the root, which can be broken into smaller pieces for easier use.

Wild Ginger

Although not the same as culinary ginger, most wild gingers *(Asarum* and *Hexastylis* species) can be eaten, and as their common name suggests, have a similar spicy, ginger-like aroma. The fleshy root (rhizome) and leaves of most wild ginger plants can be substituted in many Asian cuisines; however, some forms have an emetic property, so care should be taken when selecting and ingesting.

To read more about these plants, scan the QR code or follow this link to "Caring for Wild Ginger: How to Grow Wild Ginger Plants" (URL = gkh.us/42215).

Horseradish

The green leaves of a horseradish plant sprawl along a garden fence. This plant isn't a very attractive one, but its harvest makes it worthy of a space in your herb patch.

SCIENTIFIC NAME: *Armoracia rusticana* (also known as *Cochlearia armoracia)*

FAMILY: Brassicaceae

HEIGHT: 24 to 32 inches (60–81 cm)

WIDTH: 32 to 36 inches (81 cm–1 m)

BLOOMS: Summer

SOIL pH: Acidic, neutral

LIGHT: Full sun

Horseradish *(Armoracia rusticana)* is a clump-forming perennial that's categorized as both a vegetable and an herb. It is primarily grown for its pungent, yellow-white roots that are used to perk up a variety of savory dishes. It can be grated into salads and sauces or used to create mayonnaise-type dressings and sandwich spreads. The fiery, earthy flavor goes especially well with roast beef and fish.

Originally native to Asia and Europe, this plant is hardy in many colder regions. When mature, it features long, shiny, toothed, dark green leaves, and in summer it bears tiny, white, four-petal flowers on panicles. Horseradish is normally planted in the spring and will grow quickly enough for the roots to be ready to harvest by autumn. Once horseradish is firmly established, you will be harvesting the roots for many years to come.

GROWING HORSERADISH

A horseradish plant is typically grown from a root cutting. These can be ordered from a reputable nursery or you may be able to find someone locally who is raising horseradish and would be willing to share some with you. As soon as you get your root cutting in early spring, plant it in the ground. Dig a hole that is deep enough to stand up the root. While holding the root upright in the hole, backfill the hole until all but the crown of the root is covered in soil.

Once the root is planted, water your horseradish thoroughly, and then leave it alone. It actually does best if you plant it, and then ignore it. You don't need to fertilize or fuss over it. Horseradish grows to 18 to 24 inches (30–45 cm) tall and, sad to say, it is not the prettiest plant, but worth the effort for the zest the roots will add to dishes.

HARVESTING HORSERADISH

There are two schools of thought when it comes to harvesting this plant. The first one says that you should harvest horseradish in the autumn, right after the first frost. The other says that you should harvest horseradish in early spring, when the horseradish plants need to be divided anyway. Which method is best is up to you. Both are acceptable.

Dig down around the horseradish plant as far as you possibly can, and then with your spade, gently lift the root out of the ground. Break off some of the roots and replant them in the ground. The rest of the horseradish root can be processed into ground horseradish.

The leaves, which have a sharp, bitter taste, can be picked and dried any time.

Note: Horseradish roots are technically toxic to both people and pets.

Horseradish is known for spreading vigorously if steps are not taken to halt it, so keep in mind that when growing this spicy herb, you need to either give it lots of room or provide firm boundaries. If you do not want it to take over your garden, either grow it in a deep container or place a plastic tub around it in the ground to keep its roots in check.

Hyssop

***Hyssopus officinalis,* or hyssop, is an herbaceous flowering plant used in traditional medicine and cooking, as well as by beekeepers for the production of a rich, aromatic honey.**

This native of Southern Europe and the Middle East is a perennial, evergreen member of the mint family. Throughout history, hyssop *(Hysoppus officinalis)* has been a valued part of herbal medicine, relied on to relieve colds and sore throats. In modern times, penicillin has been made from the mold that grows on the leaves. The herb was also used for ceremonies of religious purification. Other common names include *herbe de Joseph, herbe sacrée, herbe sainte, hiope, hisopo, hissopo, hysope, jufa, rabo de gato,* and *ysop.* In the kitchen, pungent, aromatic hyssop leaves are combined with game and fish dishes or added to soups, stews, and salads. Hyssop leaves steeped in boiling water also make a soothing tea to treat a cold or sore throat.

Hyssop is also an attractive flowering shrub or sub-shrub. The woody stem supports upright branches with green, lance-shaped leaves. In summer, the plant produces pink, blue, purple, or, more rarely, white fragrant flowers, which are loved by winged pollinators. Hyssop makes a great edging plant or border specimen when massed in flower gardens. It can also be successfully grown in containers big enough to accommodate the large root system.

GROWING HYSSOP

Sow hyssop seeds indoors or directly in the garden about eight to 10 weeks before the last predicted frost. Plant them about ¼ inch (0.635 cm) deep and about 6 to 12 inches (15–30 cm) apart. Hyssop seeds usually take between 14 and 21 days to germinate; indoor seedlings can be transplanted outside after the last threat of frost. Heavily trim back established plants in early spring and again after flowering to prevent them from becoming too spindly. This also encourages bushier growth.

Once blooming has ceased and the seed capsules have completely dried, they can be collected and stored for producing hyssop the next season. In some areas, hyssop plants will readily self-seed. In addition, the plants can be divided in autumn.

HARVESTING AND PRUNING HYSSOP

In the kitchen, hyssop is best used fresh, but it can be dried or frozen and stored for later use. When harvesting hyssop, collect it in the morning once any dew has dried. Suspend the plants upside down in small bunches to dry in a dark, well-ventilated area. Or you can put the leaves in a plastic bag and place it in the freezer until ready to use.

Note: The essential oil includes the chemicals thujone and phenol, which give it antiseptic properties, but which can also cause seizures.

At a Glance

SCIENTIFIC NAME: *Hyssopus officinalis*

FAMILY: Lamiaceae

HEIGHT: 12 to 24 inches (30–60 cm)

WIDTH: 12 to 18 inches (30–45 cm)

BLOOMS: Spring to autumn

SOIL pH: Slightly alkaline

LIGHT: Full sun to partial shade

Which Hyssop?

Agastache, another genus in the mint family, is native to North America and includes several species with "hyssop" in their common names. *A. foeniculum* (above) is also known as anise hyssop; *A. mexicana* is sometimes called Mexican giant hyssop; and *A. rupestris* goes by threadleaf giant hyssop. It is easy to see why gardeners get the two genera confused. Anise hyssop leaves have a strong anise scent and can be used as a seasoning, a tea, and in salads.

Lavender

The tall spikes of lavender make a fetching display as they dip over a stone wall. Place this aromatic herb in a spot you pass often in order to take advantage of its calming scent.

Lavender is a popular Mediterranean herb renowned for its fragrant aroma and spikes of purple flowers. Used to flavor jams and vinegars, the flowers are also combined with savory herbs in soups and stews. When crystallized, they make a tasty dessert garnish. This easy-care member of the mint family enjoys hot, dry conditions, making it suitable for use in a variety of landscape settings and an excellent candidate for xeriscapes and areas prone to drought.

There are 47 species of lavender, with over 450 varieties, but the main types are English and French (or Spanish), Portuguese, and lavandin. The English and French types have different qualities and smells, and even differing appearances, habits, and needs.

English lavender *(Lavandula angustifolia)* is the common type, called "English" because it thrives in that climate. Hardier than other species, it provides a gentle, relaxing, and complex scent and the highest-quality oil. 'Hidcote' is one of the most popular English lavenders with long-lasting dark purple flowers. 'Alba Nana' is a dwarf variety that combines beautiful white blooms with a soothing scent. 'Munstead' has a compact habit and flowers of a light, rosy purple. 'Rosea' has a strong, calming scent and a profusion of pale pink flowers.

French Lavender *(L. stoechas)* is emblematic of France—in the south of France, you can literally smell lavender in the streets, not just in the beautiful fields with their long rows of perfumed flowers. It is known for having long, attractive, large petals (bracts) at the top of each spike, or inflorescence. Gardeners call them "ears." It has a more "resinous" scent than English lavender and is not usually used for oil. In the United States it is called Spanish lavender. 'Anouk' is a showy magenta variety of French lavender with very large ears. Stunning 'Ballerina' has short, plump spikes of deep violet flowers and large white ears. Elegant 'With Love' has unusual green foliage, plump, short spikes of cerise, and delicate pink ears with bright magenta veins.

Dig Deeper

READ MORE AT GARDENING KNOW HOW

To learn how to craft with this heavenly scented herb, scan the QR code or follow this link.

- **"Fresh Lavender Uses and Craft Ideas"** (URL = gkh.us/179909)

At a Glance

SCIENTIFIC NAME: *Lavandula* spp.

FAMILY: Lamiaceae

HEIGHT: 2 to 3 feet (60 cm–1 m)

WIDTH: 2 to 4 feet (60 cm–1.2 m)

BLOOMS: Summer

SOIL pH: Alkaline

LIGHT: Full sun

GROWING LAVENDER

Lavender seeds are slow to germinate, so purchasing seedlings makes the most sense. Although lavender is quite tolerant, it thrives best in warm, sunny conditions in well-drained soil. An alkaline soil rich in organic matter can encourage plant oil production, enhancing the fragrance.

As a native of arid regions, the plant will not tolerate overly wet conditions. Placing lavender in areas with adequate drainage will reduce the chance of root rot. They should be watered regularly early on, but established plants need little water. Regular pruning keeps them neat in appearance and helps to encourage new growth. Low-growing varieties can be cut back to new growth while larger types can be pruned to about a third of their height.

Lavender may take up to a year or more to be ready for harvesting. When your crop is ready, it's best to harvest the plants early in the day, picking flower spikes not fully opened. Gather the spikes in a bundle, and hang upside-down in a dry, dark space for one or two weeks. You can then use the dries lavender in cooking or crafts.

Lemon Balm

The lush leaves of lemon balm begin to spill over the edges of a raised-bed herb garden. Its fragrant, citrus-scented essential oil makes it a versatile herb in the kitchen and out.

Lemon balm *(Melissa officinalis)* was considered a sacred plant by the Greeks, but today it is one of the least commonly cultivated herbs. Although it may be a rare sight in modern herb gardens, it is highly therapeutic, with valuable medicinal, as well as culinary applications. Growing it will also attract bees and help restore our sadly dwindling bee population.

Lemon balm tends to be a pass-along plant that gardeners end up receiving during plant swaps. You may be wondering what to do with your lemon balm "gift," but it is a wonderful herb to have in your patch. Native to the eastern Mediterranean and western Asia, this citrus-scented herb has been grown for centuries for its medicinal value. The plant is rich in antibacterial, antiviral, antispasmodic, and antidepressant compounds. The leaves, stems, flowers, and oils have been used for easing anxiety, promoting sleep, increasing appetite, soothing indigestion, and reducing muscle tension caused by stress. Before the Middle Ages, it was often steeped in wine to produce a healing elixir that was consumed to improve the patient's mood and lower stress. Applied topically, the mixture was said to speed up the healing time of wounds and treat insect bites and stings. Today, the leaves are used in teas and potpourris; in cooking to add a lemony taste to salads, fruit dishes, teas, and poultry recipes; in making essential oils; and as an insect repellent.

A perennial member of the mint family, the plant grows into a bushy, leafy herb about 2 feet (60 cm) high. In the spring and autumn, it produces clusters of light yellow flowers. The crushed leaf is simultaneously sweet and tart in flavor, with the distinctive aroma of lemons.

GROWING LEMON BALM

Lemon balms are not picky about their environment. The soil needs to be rich in nutrients and organic matter and have ample drainage. They will thrive in full sunlight but can do well in partial shade. In dry climates, plant lemon balm in a spot with partial shade over one that gets full sun.

The herb can be easily propagated from seeds, cuttings, or by plant division. Start seeds indoors six to eight weeks before the last frost in your area. After all threat of frost has passed, move seedlings outside, spacing them 12 to 15 inches (30–38 cm) apart. Provide a deep watering to help ease the transition. Germination should occur between 12 to 21 days.

SCIENTIFIC NAME: *Melissa officinalis*

FAMILY: Lamiaceae

HEIGHT: 24 to 36 inches (60 cm–1 m)

WIDTH: 18 to 36 inches (45 cm–1 m)

BLOOMS: Summer

SOIL pH: Slightly acidic to neutral

LIGHT: Full sun to partial shade

CARING FOR LEMON BALM

Once established, lemon balm requires very little care. Trimming/harvesting is recommended to encourage healthy new growth, but never trim more than one-third of a plant at a time. Harvest larger, older leaves first. Watering by hand is especially important in extreme heat or drought—the soil should remain consistently moist.

These plants are aggressive reseeders, and if not carefully controlled, can quickly become invasive in the garden. Removing the flowers as soon as they appear will reduce this threat. This herb can be susceptible to whitefly, spider mites, thrips, and powdery mildew.

Editor's Tip

There are lots of uses for herbs outside the kitchen. Make a bug repellent from lemon balm oil, which can repel a variety of biting insects, as does a crushed basil leaf. Place lemon verbena near doorways or in windows to drive mosquitoes and other pests from your home. Lavender will repel flies and mosquitoes, or you can use it fresh or dried in closets or dresser drawers to deter moths; repel fleas by crumbling a bit onto your pet's bedding. Put some of those leftover bay leaves into your canisters of flour, pasta, or rice. The herb's bitter smell discourages many pests and can keep weevils from invading dried goods. The pungent aroma of rosemary will repel flies and will also keep cats from using your garden as a litter box. Mint and catnip repel flies, as well as ants and mice.

Lovage

Mature lovage plants form dense mounds of pretty green foliage. This plant is an all-around star when it comes to harvesting—the leaves, stalk, stems, and roots are all edible.

Lovage *(Levisticum officinale)* is a tall, perennial, culinary herb often grown for the celery-like flavor of its leaves, stems, roots, and seeds. This member of the carrot family is also known by the name love parsley. Originally found in western Asia, parts of the Middle East, and the Mediterranean region, lovage is cold hardy in most temperate regions but may need some protection where winters regularly reach temperatures below 0° F (-18° C).

All parts of lovage are edible and delicious, plus the plant can be included in any recipe that calls for parsley or celery. It has a high salt content, however, so a little will go a long way. The stalks and stems are best used in carbohydrate-based dishes, such as pasta and potato recipes. The young leaves are typically added to salads, and the root is dug up at the end of the season and used as a vegetable. Interestingly, the herb's seeds and stems provide a commonly used flavoring for confections. The seeds are also steeped to flavor oils and vinegars. Lovage is quite popular in Europe, where it is found in German and Italian cuisine.

The flower yields an aromatic essential oil used in perfumery, while the root and rhizome (stem) have medicinal properties and are used as "irrigation therapy" for pain and swelling of the lower urinary tract, for prevention of kidney stones, and to increase the flow of urine when urinary tract infections are present.

GROWING LOVAGE

Lovage plants shoot up like weeds and may grow to more than 5 feet (1.5 m). They bear thick, lacy green foliage and yellow flowers that form umbrella-shaped umbels and produce seeds of ½ inch (1 cm) in length. The base of the plant is composed of thick, celery-like stems with glossy green leaves that decrease in number as you move up the stalk. Sunlight and well-drained soils are the key to growing lovage, as well as soil with a pH of 6.5 and a sandy, loamy quality.

Start lovage seed indoors five to six weeks before the date of your last frost. Scatter them on the surface of the soil and dust with sand. You can also sow seeds outside in late spring when soil temperatures have warmed to 60° F (16° C).

Seedlings require consistent moisture until they are several inches (4–6 cm) tall, and then irrigation may diminish. Transplant lovage plants so they are spaced 8 inches (20 cm) apart in rows 18 inches (45 cm) away from one another. Lovage will bloom earlier when planted indoors. You can expect flowers on transplants in early summer that will last until late summer. You can harvest lovage leaves at any time, but they are best when young. Seeds will arrive late in summer or early spring.

Lovage has a reputation for being a good companion plant for potatoes and other tubers and root crops, such as asparagus and rhubarb. They also do well sharing space with other herbs like parsley, hyssop, and fennel. Leaf miners that feed on the leaves seem to be the primary pest of the plant.

HARVESTING LOVAGE

To harvest the tasty leaves, snip or pinch off as needed to use fresh. Harvesting when they are young and tender is optimal, but you can take the leaves and stalks any time during the growing season. Gathering them in the morning, just after any dew has dried, is best. If you intend to dry your harvest, be sure to gather the leaves before the plant has flowered. Roots should also be harvested just before the plants flower. Gently lift them out of the soil with a garden fork. You can also dry these by first cutting them into small pieces. In late summer you can harvest seeds when they have turned brown. To gather them, gently rub them off the plant, or place the seed heads in a paper bag, where they will drop as they ripen.

SCIENTIFIC NAME: *Levisticum officinale*

FAMILY: Apiaceae

HEIGHT: 5 feet (1.5 m)

WIDTH: 2 to 3 feet (60 cm–1 m)

BLOOMS: Early summer

SOIL pH: Slightly acidic

LIGHT: Full sun to partial shade

Marjoram

When tiny flowers cover the plant in summer, marjoram can be quite a pretty sight. Still, if you are growing it to use as a fresh herb, be sure to harvest before the blooms appear.

Also known as sweet marjoram and knotted marjoram, marjoram *(Origanum majorana)* is a perennial herb that is a close relative of oregano. Originally native to Europe, this small, low-growing plant has a mounded, shrubby appearance with aromatic, ovate, gray-green leaves that grow to about an inch (2.5 cm) in length. The tiny white or pink flowers bloom from mid- to late summer and, while pretty, are not especially showy. Best planted in the spring, marjoram grows slowly and eventually becomes a spreading ground cover.

Like its cousin oregano, marjoram has become a popular herb in kitchens around the globe. The leaves have a flavor that is both sweet and spicy; they can be used in making teas and do a great job of adding pizzazz to salads. The herb is often used in Italian cooking, as well as other Mediterranean-style cuisines.

Marjoram is said to be hardy in warmer temperate regions, but many gardeners swear they have overwintered the plants in colder areas. If your winters are particularly severe, grow marjoram as an annual in containers and bring it inside in the autumn.

GROWING MARJORAM

Marjoram is easy to cultivate, providing you offer it full sun with some midday shade and the usual well-drained soil. There are three varieties that are commonly grown: sweet marjoram, pot marjoram, and wild marjoram (also known as common oregano). All three types are popular for use as a kitchen seasoning, and they are also known for their enticing fragrance.

When growing marjoram, it's generally best to start the seeds indoors during late winter or early spring. Push seeds just below the soil surface in your starter tray. Seedlings with at least two sets of leaves can be transplanted outdoors once all threat of frost has passed.

Marjoram can also be grown indoors year round as a windowsill herb, as long as you give it light, provide a loose soil mixture, and don't overwater it. Keep the temperatures between 65° and 75° F (18–24° C). During mild weather, marjoram containers can be placed outside in a sunny area. They should, however, always be moved back indoors once frost is imminent.

Plants established in the garden require little care, other than occasional watering.

SCIENTIFIC NAME: *Origanum majorana*

FAMILY: Lamiaceae

HEIGHT: 12 to 24 inches (30–60 cm)

WIDTH: 12 to 24 inches (30–60 cm)

BLOOMS: Summer

SOIL pH: Acidic, neutral

LIGHT: Full sun

Because marjoram is tolerant of drought, it makes an exceptional plant for novice herb gardeners. If you forget to water it every now and then, that's okay. There's no need for fertilizer either with marjoram. It's hardy enough to basically care for itself.

HARVESTING AND DRYING MARJORAM

When harvesting marjoram for future kitchen use, pick the shoots just before flowers begin to open. This results in the best flavor, as fully opened blooms may produce a bitter taste. Bundle marjoram cuttings and hang them upside down in a dark, well-ventilated area. Once they are dried, place them in airtight containers and keep them in a cool dark spot. They can last from one to three years.

Note: Gastrointestinal irritants within marjoram make it technically toxic to humans, as well as to pets.

Dry some of your marjoram for use in culinary herb mixtures. Along with lavender, basil, rosemary, thyme, and fennel, it makes up the French herbes de Provence. For Middle Eastern dishes, combine it with oregano, thyme, sesame, and sumac to make your own za'atar.

Mint

Whichever of the many mints you choose, planting them in a container is a smart way to control spreading. These aggressive growers can take over a garden if left unchecked.

SCIENTIFIC NAME: *Mentha* spp.

FAMILY: Lamiaceae

HEIGHT: 12 to 18 inches (30–45 cm)

WIDTH: 18 to 24 inches (20–60 cm)

BLOOMS: Summer

SOIL pH: Alkaline

LIGHT: Full sun to partial shade

Widely distributed and found in many environments, especially in temperate and sub-temperate regions, the numerous species that make up the genus *Mentha* are aromatic, almost exclusively perennial herbs. Within the numerous species, there are also many recognized hybrids.

Their leaves can vary from lanceolate to oblong, in colors from pale yellow to dark green or gray-green to purple and blue. The flowers are white to purple.

Mint's reputation as an aggressive plant that will take over the garden is well deserved, yet growing it can be a rewarding experience if it is kept under control.

GROWING MINT

All mint varieties, except peppermint, can be grown from seed. Peppermint does not produce seeds; therefore, this type must be propagated only by taking root cuttings from established plants. All types of mint, however, can be grown by this method.

Taking a cutting is, in fact, one of the easiest methods. Simply pull or snip off a rooted piece of mint growing from the parent plant. Pot it up, and water. Large clumps can also be dug up and divided into smaller plants.

PLANTING MINT IN CONTAINERS

One of the best ways to grow mint in the garden without the threat of rampant spreading is by using containers. Merely sink the plant into the soil, leaving the top sticking out about an inch (2.5 cm) or so. You might also want to keep containers spaced at least a foot or two (30–60 cm) apart to prevent various types from cross-pollinating.

Although most varieties of mint are easy to grow in various settings, these plants thrive best when located in organically rich, moist, and well-drained soil. Full sun to partial shade is also acceptable.

As with most herbs, it is best to harvest leaves just before the plant begins to flower. You can simply pluck a leaf or two directly off the stems, if you need a small amount. If you wish to harvest for bulk storage or your recipe calls for a large quantity, cut whole stems with leaves using garden shears or a pair of sharp scissors. Whichever method, to ensure peak flavor, pick your mint in the morning, after dew has dried, when the essential oils are percolating.

COMMON PROBLEMS

Growing mint usually presents few problems other than aggressive spreading on the part of the plant itself, but pests can occasionally affect the plants. Some of the most common include aphids, spider mites, cutworms, and mint root borers. Mint can also be susceptible to diseases such as mint rust, verticillium wilt, and anthracnose.

Types of Mint

Numerous mint varieties exist, and all are worth cultivating. Mints are most often used for flavoring dishes or as garnishes, but many types are also grown for their unique aromas. Some of the most commonly grown plants include chocolate mint (above), apple mint, orange mint, pennyroyal, peppermint, and spearmint.

For more about mint types, scan the QR code or follow this link to "Mint Plant Varieties: Types of Mint for the Garden" (URL = gkh.us/35575).

Oregano

Lush oregano plants cascade over a slope in a rock garden. An essential member of an herb garden, oregano is sometimes referred to as the "pizza herb," because it is a main flavoring in pizza sauce. It goes brilliantly with tomato-based dishes and features in scores of Italian, French, and other Mediterranean recipes.

SCIENTIFIC NAME: *Origanum vulgare*

FAMILY: Lamiaceae

HEIGHT: 18 inches (45 cm)

WIDTH: 18 inches (45 cm)

BLOOMS: Summer

SOIL pH: Acidic, neutral

LIGHT: Full sun

No list of perennial herbs is complete without oregano, which continues to be one of the top kitchen seasonings. There are many varieties of oregano, including both Italian and Greek versions, and it is part of the French *bouquet garni* mixture that flavors soups and stews. It is used in tomato sauce recipes, especially for pizza.

The genus *Origanum*, part of the mint family, includes numerous perennial herbs and sub-shrubs that are native to western Asia and the Mediterranean. Some have even naturalized in North America. The most common species are popular culinary herbs, which include *O. vulgare* (oregano) and *O. majorana* (marjoram).

This herb's leaves are generally oval, dark green, and positioned in opposite pairs along the stems. Some varieties have fuzzy leaves. Oregano starts as a ground-hugging rosette of leaves, but it can easily reach 2 feet (60 cm) in height. The clusters of flowers are usually white or pink rose-purple.

Oregano is such an easy-care herb, it can be grown indoors or in regions prone to drought. As a companion in vegetable gardens, it repels the insects that plague beans and broccoli.

GROWING OREGANO

Oregano can be grown from seeds, cuttings, or purchased container plants. Seeds should be started indoors prior to your region's last predicted frost. There's no need to cover oregano seeds with soil—simply mist them with water and cover the seed tray or container with plastic wrap. Place them in a sunny window to germinate, which usually happens within a week or so. Once the seedlings have reached approximately 6 inches (15 cm) in height, the plants can be thinned to 1 foot (30 cm) apart.

Your plants can be transplanted into the garden once the risk of frost has passed.

Editor's Tip

To encourage healthy oregano plants, when harvesting from a dense specimen, instead of snipping off just the leaf ends, reach down and snip off the entire woody stem at the base. Trimming the lower, outer branches in sections all around the plant allows air to circulate in the interior. This promotes better growth.

Be sure to place oregano in areas with full sun for at least six hours a day and in well-drained soil. Oregano grows quickly, providing leaves suitable for harvesting almost immediately.

Established plants do not require much attention and need watering only during excessively dry periods. Oregano doesn't need to be fertilized either. For overwintering outdoors, plants should be cut back to the ground and covered with a layer of mulch. Container plants can also be grown indoors all year round or brought inside from the garden in the autumn.

For optimal flavor if you are growing oregano for kitchen use—or if you desire more compact plant growth—pinch back the flower buds before they bloom. Flavorwise, after the plant blooms, the leaves will either become milder or more bitter, depending on the variety.

The leaves and stems can be harvested anytime once they have reached 4 to 6 inches (10–15 cm) tall. It's best to pick the leaves in the morning hours once the dew has dried. The leaves can be stored whole, placed in freezer bags and frozen. They can also be bundled, hung up, and dried in a dark, well-ventilated area, and then stored in airtight containers until ready to use.

Note: Oregano is toxic to pets, so be mindful of where you plant it.

Pineapple Sage

Unlike the more familiar garden sage with gray-green foliage, pineapple sage has leaves of bright green. These edible leaves give off a delectable pineapple scent when crushed.

Although most gardeners are familiar with culinary sage *(Salvia officinalis)*, there are many different types of sage, or salvia, plants available. Some have medicinal or aromatic properties, or are grown purely for ornamental purposes. They may be perennial or annual, blooming or non-blooming; their foliage may occur in sage green, variegated purple and green, or variegated gold; the small blossoms can range from lavender to bright blue to cheery red. With so many varieties of sage, there's bound to be one or two to suit your landscaping needs. Nearly all types are hardy and easy to care for.

Pineapple sage, a popular ornamental variety, is a perennial native to Mexico and Guatemala, but in some temperate climates it may be treated like an annual. This semi-woody sub-shrub can reach 3 feet (1 m) in height, with red, tubular flowers that bloom in late summer to early fall. These flowers are a favorite of desirable pollinators like hummingbirds, butterflies, and bees. The crushed leaves smell like pineapple, hence the common name, but the strength of the scent differs depending on your region's climate. The leaves can also be dried and used to steep tea. The minty-flavored blossoms make a pretty garnish for salads and desserts, and are also used in jellies, jams, potpourris, and flower arrangements. The plant also has a history as a medicinal herb due to its antibacterial and antioxidant properties.

GROWING PINEAPPLE SAGE

Pineapple sage should be grown from seed indoors; the seeds will germinate within two weeks. Don't transplant seedlings outdoors until they are at least 8 inches (20 cm) tall and after any danger of frost has passed. Space the seedlings in the bed 18 to 24 inches (45–60 cm) apart.

Pineapple sage grows rapidly in a location that receives morning sun and afternoon shade. They like well-drained soil that is consistently moist, but established plants will tolerate drought conditions. If your winter temperatures go below freezing, locating the plant in a protected, sunny location with a layer of mulch will encourage it to return again in spring. This herb is known for its deer resistance and has relatively few insect pests.

SCIENTIFIC NAME: *Salvia elegans*

FAMILY: Lamiaceae

HEIGHT: Up to 5 feet (1.5 m)

WIDTH: Up to 3 feet (1 m)

BLOOMS: Summer to early autumn

SOIL pH: Neutral

LIGHT: Full sun to partial shade

Editor's Picks

In addition to pineapple sage, below are some other attractive choices among the many *Salvia* species.

- Grape-scented sage *(S. melissodora)*, which smells more like the flower freesia, can get quite tall at 6 to 8 feet (1.8–2.5 m). It is a late-bloomer that attracts hummingbirds. The leaves and flowers can be steeped to make tea.
- Mealycup sage *(S. farinacea)* attains a height of 2 to 3 feet (60 cm–1 m) and is punctuated with blue, purple, or white flower spikes. Check out 'Empire Purple', 'Strata', and 'Victoria Blue.'
- Mexican bush sage *(S. leucantha)* grows to 3 to 4 feet (1–1.2 m), is drought tolerant, and features purple or white flower spikes.
- Scarlet sage *(S. splendens)* is an annual that thrives in full sun and well-draining soil. Blossoms are scarlet in color and last from late spring through the first frost.

To learn more about sage varieties, scan the QR code or follow the link to "Sage Plants for Gardens: Learn About Different Types of Sage" (URL = gkh.us/95657).

Roman Chamomile

SCIENTIFIC NAME: *Chamaemelum nobile*

FAMILY: Asteraceae

HEIGHT: 3 to 6 inches (7.5–15 cm)

WIDTH: 9 to 12 (23–30 cm)

BLOOMS: Summer

SOIL pH: Alkaline

LIGHT: Full sun to partial shade

Roman chamomile has tiny daisy-like flowers. This low-growing plant can work as a fragrant ground cover that can take the place of high-maintenance turfgrass.

There are two types of chamomile—Roman chamomile, a perennial, and its close cousin German chamomile *(Matricaria recutita* or *M. chamomilla)*, an annual. The Roman variety is the true chamomile, but German chamomile is used in many of the same ways. Both are native to Europe and have been adorning herb gardens and lawns—and acting as companion plants for vegetables—for many centuries. The German variety has larger flowers, but the Roman's flowers offer more intense scents. And compared to German chamomile, this plant's morphology, properties, and chemical composition are distinctly different.

The word chamomile derives from the Greek *chamaimēlon,* meaning "earth-apple," so-called because of the plant's apple-like scent. Extracts or dried flowers of *Chamaemelum nobile* are used in hair and skin care products and in herbal teas, perfumes, and cosmetics and to flavor foods.

There is no scientific evidence that this plant has any therapeutic uses, despite its long history in folk medicine. Yet, according to aromatherapy practices, its essential oil, which is a stunning dark blue, is said to work as a calming agent that reduces stress and aids in falling asleep.

A creeping ground cover that grows like a mat, Roman chamomile has leaves that are feathery, finely dissected, and downy to smooth to the touch. The solitary, daisy-like flowerheads, rising little more than 6 inches (15 cm) above the ground, consist of prominent yellow disk flowers and silver-white ray flowers. Their fragrance is described as sweet, crisp, fruity, and herbaceous. The Roman variety is roughly the same height as normal turfgrass, so it can be used in the yard to create a fragrant chamomile lawn for those who want an easy-care and eco-friendly alternative to grass. This works especially well in spots where foot traffic is light or in places with little or no mower access.

GROWING ROMAN CHAMOMILE

Chamomile can be started from seeds or purchased as seedlings from a garden center. It appreciates cool conditions and should be planted in partial shade, but will also tolerate full sun. Once your chamomile is established, it needs very little care. Go easy on fertilizer, if you use it at all. Overfertilizing will result in lots of weak foliage and fewer flowers. And because chamomile is drought-tolerant, it only needs to be watered during extended dry periods. Healthy chamomile plants are not affected by many pests, but ailing specimens may be troubled with aphids, mealybugs, and thrips. Chamomile is often recommended as a companion plant in the vegetable garden because its strong scent keeps pests away.

Note: Any use of Roman chamomile is likely unsafe during pregnancy. Topical applications made from this herb may cause contact dermatitis.

An Herb of Many Names

This low-growing, aromatic herb is often found in dry fields and around gardens and cultivated areas throughout Europe, North America, and South America. Also known botanically as *Anthemis nobilis,* as well as *Chamaemelum nobile,* it has a number of common names, too. Depending on the region, Roman chamomile is also called English chamomile, garden chamomile, ground apple, low chamomile, sweet chamomile, mother's daisy, or whig plant.

Rosemary

Blossoming rosemary. Plant these evergreens near walkways to take advantage of their rich, pinewood scent. This scent pairs very well with other members of the mint family, and rosemary is often used in products like shampoos. Its scent is also said to enhance memory, making the Shakespeare quote "Rosemary for remembrance" particularly apt.

SCIENTIFIC NAME: *Salvia rosmarinus* (synonym *Rosmarinus officinalis*)

FAMILY: Lamiaceae

HEIGHT: 2 to 6 feet (60 cm–1.8 m)

WIDTH: 2 to 4 feet (60 cm–1.2 m)

BLOOMS: Spring, summer

SOIL pH: Acidic, neutral

LIGHT: Full sun to partial shade

Rosemary *(Salvia rosmarinus)* is an attractive, fragrant, perennial herb that grows into a rounded evergreen shrub. It features slender, needle-like, gray-green leaves on erect woody stems and produces clusters of small, blue-to-white flowers. They typically bloom in late spring to early summer, filling the garden with their piny fragrance for two seasons.

This herb's piquant taste has come to be associated with the cuisine of the Mediterranean and Middle Eastern regions. The leaves are used to flavor grilled meats, especially lamb, along with fish, chicken, potatoes, and other vegetables. They can even be added to fresh fruit. The edible flowers are sometimes used as a dessert garnish.

Here are some top contenders among the many cultivars of this herb.

- 'Arp' has light green foliage with a lemony scent; it's known for its cold tolerance.
- 'Golden Rain' stays compact at 2-to-3-feet (60 cm–1 m) high and wide, and it features yellow markings on its foliage.
- 'Albus' is a white-flowering variety.
- 'Prostratus' has a low, spreading growth habit at roughly 2-feet (50 cm) high and 2-to-3-feet wide.

GROWING ROSEMARY

Rosemary is most often propagated from cuttings because it can be tricky getting evergreen rosemary seeds to germinate. It seems success comes only when the seeds are very fresh and when they are planted in optimum growing conditions. To take cuttings, snip stems that are about 2 inches (5 cm) long, and remove the leaves on the bottom two-thirds of the cutting. Place the cuttings in a mixture of perlite and peat moss, spraying to keep them moist until roots begin to grow. After that, you can plant the cuttings directly into the garden after any threat of frost has passed. The shrub has a moderate growth rate and will reach its mature size and begin flowering in its second season.

In the garden, space rosemary seedlings or nursery plants at least 2 to 3 feet (60 cm–1 m) apart. Rosemary does best in well-drained soil and in a spot with six to eight hours of sunlight. Make sure no taller trees or shrubs are close enough to shade the bed. Although this herb is not a heavy feeder, mixing compost into the soil at planting time can ensure the shrub a healthy start. Providing a balanced liquid fertilizer will continue to encourage quality growth. Pruning the plant above the leaf joints will make it bushier, but don't harvest more than a third of the foliage for seasonings. Bundles of the herb can be dried in a cool, dry place and stored in airtight containers.

These perennials don't do well in temperatures below freezing. Fortunately, this versatile herb also grows well in containers—both outdoors and indoors—as long as it receives enough light. Rosemary plants are prone to becoming root-bound, however, and should be repotted at least once a year.

READ MORE AT GARDENING KNOW HOW

To learn more about the various rosemary types available, scan the QR code or follow this link.

- **"Rosemary Plant Types: Varieties of Rosemary Plants for the Garden"** (URL = gkh.us/95807)

Sage

Flanked by lemon balm and lemongrass, massed sage plants fill a corner of a raised bed. This herb is grown for its many culinary uses, but it makes an attractive ornamental, too.

If you enjoy making your own poultry stuffing, you'll be familiar with the savory scent and taste of *Salvia officinalis,* also known as garden sage, common sage, or culinary sage. This flavorful culinary herb is used either fresh or dried, and it especially complements rich meats like pork, game, and turkey. It also goes well with cheese dishes and makes a delicious herb-infused vinegar. Its medicinal properties include high levels of antioxidants like chlorogenic acid, caffeic acid, rosmarinic acid, ellagic acid, and rutin, which have all been linked to lower cancer risk, memory improvement, and improved brain function.

Originally native to the Mediterranean region, this pretty shrub is notable for its pale, velvet-soft, gray-green leaves. The small, camphor-scented flowers—in bluish lavender to pinkish lavender—grow in whorls on short, upright spikes. There are at least 900 species of *Salvia,* which is the largest genus of plants in the mint family, but this is the species most people mean when they refer to "sage."

GROWING SAGE

This perennial herb loves the full sun—but it will tolerate some light shade. It requires well-drained sandy or loamy soil, so avoid wet feet at all costs. Sage originally comes from a hot, dry climate and will grow best in similar conditions.

Start sage in the milder weather of spring or autumn. Sow seeds on the average date of the last spring frost. Indoors, scatter them over seed-starting soil and cover with ⅛ inch (3.2 mm) of soil. Keep the soil damp but not soaked. Sage seeds are slow to germinate so starting them requires patience—not all the seeds will germinate, and the ones that do may take six weeks to sprout. If using nursery plants, position them at the same depth as in their previous container. Space plants about 2 feet (60 cm) apart.

Sage is often grown from cuttings. In spring, take a softwood cutting from a mature plant, dip the cut tip in rooting hormone, then insert it into a small container of potting soil. Cover the plant with clear plastic, and keep it in indirect sunlight until new growth appears. You can then plant the cutting in your garden. Note that sage is one herb where flowering intensifies the flavor.

At a Glance

SCIENTIFIC NAME: *Salvia officinalis*

FAMILY: Lamiaceae

HEIGHT: 2 to 3 feet (60 cm–1 m)

WIDTH: 2 to 3 feet (60 cm–1 m)

BLOOMS: Summer

SOIL pH: Acidic, neutral

LIGHT: Full sun

Editor's Picks

Not all *Salvias* are edible, but the following examples of *S. officinalis* cultivars are favored by many chefs.

- 'Aurea'—or golden sage—is a creeping sage with gold and green variegated leaves.
- 'Berggarten' is similar to common sage except that it does not bloom, yet it does have the same lovely soft, silvery green leaves.
- 'Kew Gold' is a very pretty dwarf variety with yellow leaves.
- 'Minimum', or dwarf garden sage, has purplish blue flowers and offers the same robust flavors as its larger cousin.
- 'Purpurascens'—purple garden sage (above)—has purple foliage when young and is brimming with vitamins A and C.
- 'Tricolor' is a pungent sage with uneven variegations on the grayish green leaves, including white, pink, or purple marbling.
- 'Window Box' is small variety that is great for containers.

To learn how to bring your sage plants indoors, scan the QR code or follow this link to "Care of Potted Sage Herbs — How to Grow Sage Plant Indoors" (URL = gkh.us/15822).

Sorrel

The large leaves of garden sorrel *(Rumex acetosa)* can be used in salads or in sautéed vegetable dishes. Its cousin, French sorrel *(R. scutatus),* is also widely used in cookery.

Sorrel is a culinary herb that adds a tangy, lemon flavor to dishes. It is also known as sourwood, sorrel dock, sour dock, sour leek, and spinach dock. The two cultivated species are garden sorrel, *Rumex acetosa,* and French sorrel, *R. scutatus.* The main difference between the two is that French sorrel has smaller leaves and a subtler flavor than garden sorrel. This perennial herb also grows wild in many parts of the world.

Sorrel is an upright plant with leaves that look a lot like Swiss chard or spinach. The leaves grow 3 to 6 inches (7.5–15 cm) in length and can be plain green or veined in red and appear smooth or crinkled. If allowed to bloom, sorrel produces attractive whorled purple flowers.

This delicate herb is widely included in French cooking, but it is less well-known in the United States. Chefs often use sorrel leaves as the base of creamy sauces for eggs and fish dishes. It adds an interesting element to salads and cooked vegetables and is delicious when made into sorrel soup. Young leaves tend to have a more acidic taste and do well in salads; mature leaves are tasty sautéed as you would spinach.

GROWING SORREL

Sorrel seeds can be sown in the autumn or planted in spring after the soil has warmed up. (Sorrel can also be started by dividing the roots of a mature plant.) Prepare a bed in well-drained soil and full sun, and sow the seeds 6 inches (15 cm) apart, just barely under the surface of the soil. Keep the plants moderately moist until germination occurs, and then thin the seedlings once they are 2 inches (5 cm) in height. When you reach this stage, the needs of the two varieties will differ slightly. Garden sorrel needs damp soils and temperate conditions. French sorrel performs best when it is grown in dry, open areas with inhospitable soils. These plants have very deep and persistent taproots and grow well with little attention. Your garden sorrel, on the other hand, will require at least an inch (2.5 cm) of water every week.

Sorrel will usually bolt (flower) when temperatures begin to soar, usually in June or July. When this happens, you can enjoy the plant's lovely appearance, but flowering will slow the production of leaves. If you want to encourage larger leaves and more voluminous production, cut the flower stalk off, and the plant will give you a few more harvests. You can even cut it to the ground, and it will produce a full new crop of foliage.

HARVESTING SORREL

Sorrel can keep producing from late spring until autumn with proper management and providing you harvest only what you need from the plant. This herb is much like lettuce and greens, in that you can cut the outer leaves away, and the plant will continue to produce foliage. You can usually begin to harvest sorrel when the plants are 4 to 6 inches (10–15 cm) tall.

At a Glance

SCIENTIFIC NAME: *Rumex* spp.

FAMILY: Polygonaceae

HEIGHT: 12 to 18 inches (30–45 cm)

WIDTH: 18 to 24 inches (45–60 cm)

BLOOMS: Summer

SOIL pH: Acidic

LIGHT: Full sun

Wild Sorrel

It shares a common name with *Rumex* species, but wood sorrel (genus *Oxalis*) is not botanically related. Wood sorrel can be found growing wild throughout most of North America. Its three heart-shaped leaflets resemble clover, and the five-petaled flowers are usually white or yellow. All parts of wood sorrel are edible, including leaves, flowers, seed pods, and roots. Be aware, however, that those with gout, rheumatism, or kidney stones should avoid this plant because of its high oxalic acid content.

Tarragon

French tarragon in a terra-cotta planter adds a feathery feel to a container herb garden. Chopped fine, the fresh green leaves will add an anise-like kick to savory dishes. For winter use, you can also dry the leaves after a late-summer harvest.

Tarragon *(Artemisia dracunculus)*, also known as estragon, is a perennial herb that is part of the sunflower or daisy family. There are actually two types of tarragon—the French version is more widely available and has a stronger flavor than the Russian variety. The French variety (subspecies *sativa*) is the one being discussed here.

This plant grows erect and bears slender, often branching stems that bear long, needle-like leaves that are a glossy light green and very aromatic. The tiny flowers are yellow or a greenish hue. Just one plant is usually sufficient to supply a generous amount of leaves.

Tarragon is native to milder European regions, yet it is a very cold hardy perennial—surviving temperatures down to -20º F (-28.8º C). It does not do well in overly hot climates, however. In the garden it is easy to grow in well-drained soil when placed in a sunny or partially shaded spot that is protected from the wind.

Tarragon is commonly grown for its aromatic leaves with their peppery, licorice-like flavor. These are used for flavoring many dishes and are especially popular for flavoring vinegar. Tarragon is a valued seasoning in soups and stews and is delightful with chicken, fish, and game dishes. The herb is also part of the traditional French recipe for béarnaise sauce.

GROWING TARRAGON

French tarragon cannot be grown from seeds. This variety, which is prized for its superior anise-like flavor, must be propagated by cuttings or division only. Still, tarragon is worth the extra effort and can add a sophisticated culinary herb to your garden.

Space tarragon cuttings approximately 18 to 24 inches (45–60 cm) apart to ensure adequate air circulation. Ideally, they should be located in well-drained, fertile soil. Yet these hardy plants will endure and even thrive in areas with poor, dry, or sandy soil. Tarragon has a vigorous root system, making it quite tolerant of arid conditions. Established plants do not require frequent watering, except during extreme drought. Applying a thick layer of mulch in the autumn will help the plants through winter. Garden plants should be divided every three to five years.

SCIENTIFIC NAME: *Artemisia dracunculus*

FAMILY: Asteraceae

HEIGHT: 24 inches to 3 feet (60 cm–1 m)

WIDTH: 12 to 24 inches (30–60 cm)

BLOOMS: Summer

SOIL pH: Neutral

LIGHT: Partial sun to partial shade

Potted tarragon can also be grown indoors all year round as a houseplant or greenhouse plant or grown outside in warm weather, then moved inside in the autumn.

HARVESTING TARRAGON

Both the leaves and flowers of tarragon plants can be harvested. Harvesting usually takes place in late summer. Although best used fresh, tarragon can be frozen or dried by hanging the stems and leaves in bundles in a dark, dry spot, and then placing them in an airtight container until ready for use.

Although French tarragon is grown from cuttings or divisions, varieties like Russian tarragon can be propagated from seeds. These should be started indoors around April or before your area's last predicted frost. Sow about four to six seeds per pot using moist, composted potting soil. Cover the seeds lightly and keep them in low light at room temperature. Thin seedlings when they reach a couple of inches (7.5 cm) tall. You can then transplant them outdoors once temperatures have significantly warmed.

Thyme

Common thyme *(Thymus vulgaris)* fills the corner of stone garden bed. This hardy, drought-tolerant plant is great for use in xeriscapes in which water is at a premium.

Members of the mint family, plants of the genus *Thymus* are aromatic evergreen herbs. One of the most popular for culinary herb gardens, *T. vulgaris* is a low-growing, woody perennial of Mediterranean origin. Not surprisingly it performs quite well in dry, sunny locations. This beloved culinary herb, also known as common thyme, garden thyme, and English thyme, provides a distinctive earthy-minty-citrus taste, similar to a toned-down rosemary. The leaves can easily be stripped of the stems and added to recipes for stuffings, sauces, and soups, and it adds a delicious flavor to poultry, fish, seafood, and vegetable dishes. It blends well with other ingredients from its native region, such as garlic, olives and olive oil, and tomatoes.

Editor's Tip

The flavor of thyme will benefit from active neglect. Growing the herb in poor soil with little water will actually cause thyme to flourish, resulting in more strongly flavored leaves. For this reason, thyme is an excellent choice for xeriscaping or low-water landscapes.

This versatile herb is also lovely to look at and is often used as a decorative plant in the flower garden. It has a compact habit and stays fairly small, growing best in full sun and well-draining soil. Its tiny gray-green leaves remain evergreen, and the tiny, tubular pink, white, or lavender flowers grow at the top of the stems in a sphere shape. They typically bloom from May to September. Thyme flowers are edible by humans and also a favorite of bees.

Other species include Mediterranean thyme *(T. capitatus)*, a very fragrant type from southern Spain used in the preparation of olives. Wild thyme (*T. praecox*) is a pretty plant often cultivated as an ornamental. *T. citriodorus* includes various citrus-scented thymes. Caraway thyme *(T. herba-barona)* has a very strong caraway scent and is both a culinary herb and an effective ground cover. Woolly thyme (*T. pseudolanuginosus*) is strictly a ground cover, and creeping thyme *(T. serpyllum)* provides nectar for honeybees.

GROWING THYME

Thyme should be planted in spring after the chance of frost has passed. It will mature enough to allow for harvest within a few months, then will reliably return year after year. Most varieties are cold tolerant in regions where temperatures dip below freezing. A thick layer of mulch will offer protection during the winter, but be sure to remove it in the spring.

Thyme is typically grown from a division. In the spring or autumn, select a mature plant, and use a spade to gently lift a clump from the ground. Tear or slice a smaller clump from the main plant, making sure there is a root ball intact on the division. Replant the mother specimen, and plant the division in the location you have chosen.

Thyme can also be grown from seeds, but the seeds are difficult to germinate and can take a long time to sprout. To use this method, start by scattering seeds in a soil-filled tray, then gently cover the seeds with soil. Water the tray thoroughly with a sprayer, then cover it with plastic wrap, and place it in a warm location. Germination will occur from 1 to 12 weeks. Once the seedlings reach 4 inches (10 cm), they can be transplanted into your garden. Thyme is easy to care for once it's established, and it even tolerates drought conditions.

To harvest thyme, simply snip off the amount you need for your recipe. Once a thyme plant is established—in about a year—it's very hard to overharvest the leaves. For newer plants, however, cut back no more than one-third of the foliage.

At a Glance

SCIENTIFIC NAME: *Thymus* spp.

FAMILY: Lamiaceae

HEIGHT: 6 to 12 inches (15–30 cm)

WIDTH: 6 to 12 inches (15–30 cm)

BLOOMS: Summer

SOIL pH: Acidic to alkaline

LIGHT: Full sun

Winter Savory

Mounds of winter savory are both attractive and aromatic additions to an herb garden. This fragrant herb is often planted near beehives to lend its flavor to honey. The leaves maintain their rich, spicy scent even when dried, making them perfect for potpourris.

Unlike its annual cousin summer savory, winter savory *(Satureja montana)* is grown as a perennial in many temperate regions. It also has a more powerful flavor than the summer version, will grow in less-fertile soil, and is often used in dried form, whereas summer savory is typically consumed fresh. Winter savory also has higher nutritional value—the shoots and leaves are a rich source of vitamins C, A, and the B group and in minerals such as zinc, magnesium, calcium, and iron.

The plant is a hardy semi-evergreen with erect, woody, bushy stems that bear glossy, dark green oblong leaves with a pinelike scent. The small lilac or white flowers, arranged in terminal spikes, contain both types of reproductive organs and attract many bees. The fruit matures into four nutlets. This herb can be used as a companion plant for beans, where it is said to keep weevils away, and for roses, where it may reduce mildew and aphid infestations.

Winter savory is a native of the dry hillsides of southern Europe and the Mediterranean; it was Roman writer Pliny who named the genus *Satureja,* derived from "satyr," a creature half goat and half man who reveled in all savory delights. It was the ancient Romans who introduced the herb to England. Today, it is cultivated in culinary herb gardens worldwide.

Both savories have a strong peppery flavor, although winter savory is more pungent. It helps to enliven a variety of foods without the use of salt and pepper. In fact, winter savory is often paired with beans during cooking to prevent the addition of salt from toughening the beans. It perfectly combines with the taste of beef, pork, beans, and cheese and is frequently used to prepare potato salads, mushrooms, pasta, broths, seafood, and mayonnaise. It is also used to make infused vinegar, herb butter, and steeped tea, while the dried leaves are added to potpourri. The flavor of winter savory is at its best just before flowering, yet even when dried, it retains its full flavor.

GROWING WINTER SAVORY

Once it is established, care of winter savory is nominal. It can survive soil of poor quality, but like most herbs, it requires at least six hours of full sun and well-draining soil. Sow seeds in the spring in starter flats, and transfer the seedlings outdoors once the soil warms; be sure to space seedlings 10 to 12 inches (25–30 cm) apart in the garden.

At a Glance

SCIENTIFIC NAME: *Satureja montana*

FAMILY: Lamiaceae

HEIGHT: 6 to 12 inches (15–30 cm)

WIDTH: 8 to 12 inches (20–30 cm)

BLOOMS: Summer

SOIL pH: Alkaline

LIGHT: Full sun

Winter savory can also be propagated via cuttings. Collect cuttings—the tips of new shoots—in late spring and place them in pots of wet sand. When the cuttings root, transplant them to the garden.

Harvest winter savory in the morning when the essential oils are at their most potent. It can then be used fresh or dried. In temperate climates, winter savory will go dormant in the winter and put out new leaves in the spring. Older plants tend to get woody, so keep them pruned to encourage new green growth.

Herb-Infused Vinegars

A smart way to make the most of a surplus of fresh herbs like winter savory is to use them in infused vinegars. These make tangy additions to the kitchen condiment shelf, and they also make great gifts for a home cook, especially if presented in a pretty bottle.

To find out how to create these delicious herbal vinegars, scan the QR code or follow the link to "Herbal Vinegar Recipes — How to Infuse Vinegar with Herbs" (URL = gkh.us/146545).

CHAPTER EIGHT

GARDEN SHRUBS

As a design element, shrubs play the role of the "wallpaper" of gardens—often serving as attractive backdrops for fancy ornamentals or mass flower plantings. Yet, certain species can stand alone as showpieces that need no embellishment. With their variety of shapes, sizes, growth habits, colors, and textures, shrubs also combine splendidly in groupings. The variety of arrangements you can create is nearly endless. And although you might think the flowering species have it all going on, certain foliage shrubs can more than hold their own—just consider the sculptural quality of a mugo pine, the graceful drape of a false cypress, or the delightful whimsy of a yew-based topiary garden or an intricate privet maze. Whether you use shrubs to soften your home's foundation, obscure unsightly fixtures in the yard, or celebrate them in their own right, they offer something worthwhile to every garden.

PLANTING AND PRUNING SHRUBS

You've just come home from the garden shop with some attractive young shrubs, and now you must decide where to place them. But first you've got to determine the shrub's overall height and width at maturity, so you can leave adequate space. For instance, if a shrub is meant as a foundation planting, ensure that its mature growth will not block windows or obstruct walkways—or crush its neighbors on either side. This information can be furnished at the garden shop or researched online.

Also get some index cards or a small notebook or find a gardening app in which you can write down the name, the maintenance requirements, and the location of your new shrubs. That way you will always have an archive of what they are called, where they are planted, what sort of sunlight, pH and nutrient levels, and watering needs they have. These requirements are typically listed on the growers' tags, which can be stapled right to your info sheet or scanned into your app. Noting the cultivar names is important in case you love a shrub so much you want to add more of that variety the following year.

The wide selection at many garden centers can be intimidating. Be prepared when you go shrub shopping, researching your planting zone, soil types, available sun, and other factors to determine which plants will work for your needs. And never hesitate to ask the staff questions.

PLANTING PROPERLY

The best time to plant shrubs is typically in the autumn or, if necessary, early spring. This gives the roots plenty of time to become established, increasing their chances of survival. The most important element of planting any shrub or tree is the size of the hole. Again, the roots need room to adequately spread out to anchor the shrub or tree to the ground.

To prepare the site, clear away any mulch or debris around the intended planting area, and dig a hole twice as wide as but the same depth as the container. Pile the excess soil around the perimeter of the hole in at least two different spots—this makes it easier to backfill after planting. Check the depth with the shovel handle to make sure it matches the depth of the container. Once they match, remove the shrub from its container by thumping briskly all around the sides and the bottom to loosen the plant. Never try to pull out a plant by its stem or leaves. If it resists releasing, use garden pruners to cut away the plastic pot.

Place the plant in the hole to check that the top of the root ball is even with or slightly above the soil surface. Adjust the soil level until the plant sits at the proper depth. Next, carefully rough up the root ball with your fingers to loosen any wound-up roots, and then shake off soil from the smaller roots. Then determine which "face" of the plant you want to view from the front and pivot the plant in that direction as you finally set it in the hole. Backfill with the leftover soil, gently tamping the soil to eliminate air pockets. The top of the root ball should be covered with ½ inch (1.25 cm) of soil.

WATERING AND MULCHING

When you water your new shrub, make sure you thoroughly saturate the root ball and the surrounding soil. Try setting your hose on a very low flow and moving it around the plant a few times during the course of an hour or two. Keep your new shrub well watered—during the first season it should never completely dry out. Remember, it is expanding its roots that whole time, even if there is not a lot of growth up top. Typically, there is more vigorous growth during the second season.

Most shrubs benefit from a 2- to 3-inch (5–7.5 cm) layer of shredded bark mulch spread over the entire root zone to help cool the roots and conserve water.

PRUNING AND REJUVENATING SHRUBS

Regular pruning will keep shrubs looking their best—by helping them maintain a pleasing shape, removing dead or dying branches, and encouraging more blooms and robust foliage. Most shrubs need trimming every few years, otherwise they can become leggy and overgrown.

Some flowering shrubs, like lilacs and forsythia, set their buds soon after blooming, so it is key to prune them right after flowering. Others, like roses and crape myrtle, can be trimmed later in winter (never in the autumn), when the plant is dormant. One goal of pruning deciduous shrubs is to allow air into the crown. With certain evergreens

The first rule of planting a shrub is digging a hole to the proper size. It should sit so its top is at the soil level or a just bit higher.

Most shrubs will benefit from a layer of mulch or other barriers to help retain moisture and prevent the spread of weeds.

Hedge shrubs will need regular trimming to keep them well shaped. You can use an electric trimmer or manual shears.

Unruly shrubs might call for pruning. There is, of course, a right way to do this so that you encourage new growth.

like arborvitae, however, if you prune the foliage too deeply, the browned interiors will be revealed. The foliage of box and yew, on the other hand, can be cut into quite deeply, even right up to the trunk or branches.

Besides maintenance pruning, there is rejuvenation or renewal pruning for when you've let your shrubs grow wild for too long or if the yard in your new home is full of badly overgrown shrubs. Before calling someone to tear out the unruly plants, consider addressing the problem yourself. Use pruners, loppers, or a pruning saw to cut the oldest, heaviest stems as close to the ground as possible. This method stimulates the plant to produce new, thick growth just below the pruning cut. If you simply trim the tops off the shrubs, they will grow even leggier and taller.

Another option is to prune an overgrown, neglected shrub into a small tree. This is particularly effective if many of the branches are in poor condition. Prune out all upright stems except one, then remove lower branches on that stem for a trunk-and-canopy effect.

Cutting Techniques

Making the cleanest cut possible on greenwood branches will help the shrub recover from the cut by compartmentalizing, or walling off, the cut area. A jagged tear requires more energy to heal and can increase the risk of disease. Two different kinds of cuts are typically called for.

Heading cuts. Used on unruly stems and branches, heading cuts are made just outside a branch node with a bud; this stimulates the bud's growth and is commonly used to shape hedges and shrubs.

Thinning cuts. It is essential to cut out dense-growing branches to promote air circulation at the tree's center. Thinning cuts are made where the unwanted branch meets the base of the shrub.

LANDSCAPING WITH SHRUBS

Shrubs can be one of the best tools for providing form and structure in your garden. By incorporating different specimens in several sizes, along with flowering and non-flowering shrubs, you will also be adding visual variety. The trick is getting the balance right—assembling mass plantings, while choosing some stars to showcase.

Landscape shrubs can range in size from dwarf varieties to towering, treelike species. There are evergreen shrubs that retain their foliage—and color—throughout the year, and deciduous shrubs that eventually lose their foliage after putting on a colorful autumn show. If you are at all artistically inclined, it helps to sketch out your "goal garden," envisioning how the shrubs will look together after they have matured to full size.

The specimens you choose should be based on several factors—your existing plants, the size and shape of your space, what sort of effect you want to create, and, perhaps most important, the climate of your region. Like flowers and vegetables, shrubs are not hardy in all climates. Some do not do well in extended heat, while others can't survive in sub-freezing temperatures. So always check on a shrub's hardiness before purchasing it.

USING SHRUBS TO EFFECT

Shrubs have many practical uses within the landscape—foundation plantings, privacy hedges, boundary markers, and windbreaks. They can be used as backdrops, to enhance garden beds, or to simply add seasonal interest. Foliage differs from plant to plant, so look for leaf or needle colors that will create a subtle contrast to the other plants in your landscape. Autumn foliage colors in deciduous shrubs can range from deep orange and chartreuse to silver and gold, and variegated varieties can display red, purple, and dark green. Also, factor in the appearance of the shrub after its initial blooming period is over—the majority of shrubs are non-flowering most of the year.

Always bear in mind that native shrubs (or naturalized outsiders) are more accustomed to the growing conditions in your region than imports or exotics. They also provide a natural complement to any native trees and flowers.

Most will also lend themselves well to life in containers, and even the smallest patio or balcony can display a few examples. Container shrubs are also excellent paired in entryways, as garden focal points, and as screens.

Whatever it is you require of your shrubs, these landscaping workhorses will get the job done and look good while doing it. Whether you are using them for outlining boundaries, privacy screening, foundation plantings, or as specimen plants, the right shrubs will always enhance your landscape or garden.

DROUGHT-TOLERANT SHRUBS

Many evergreen shrubs with drought tolerance will thrive in all but the coldest growing conditions. One popular drought-tolerant evergreen is glossy abelia, which has shiny green leaves and frothy flowers and typically grows to 6 feet (1.8 m) in height. Boxwood is an excellent, dense shrub for edging and borders. Most types

Keep in mind that even flowering shrubs are usually green for most of the growing season, so choose a variety of shapes, sizes, textures, and colors to create year-round interest.

of juniper also handle drought with ease. Bottlebrushes are also drought-tolerant bushes that reach 10 feet (3 m). They need a sunny location to produce the red flowers that look a little like narrow scrub brushes.

Deciduous shrubs, those that lose their leaves in autumn, include one of the most popular drought-tolerant shrubs—the butterfly bush. Its vivid panicles of flowers really do bring butterflies to the yard. Another of the best deciduous shrubs for dry climates is beautyberry, a perennial that offers bright spring flowers followed by striking fall berries. This shrub is also pest and disease resistant.

SHRUBS FOR WETLANDS

Whether your yard has a bog, marsh, wetlands area, creek, or just a low-lying spot that collects a lot of water, you have to choose your shrubs carefully. These include varieties that are indigenous to marshy areas, along with plants that simply tolerate wet soil better than others. This is critical because most shrubs will rot and die in marshy ground. For the best results, choose species native to your area. Also make sure the plants you use are matched to the amount of sun available and the nutrient content of the soil.

Fortunately, there are a number of native and non-native plants that can thrive in marshy areas. Several types of dogwood grow in wet soil, including silky and red osier. Potentilla is a native shrub that grows in boggy soil.

Choose Wisely

Making a selection among all the types of shrubs available can be overwhelming. Here are some guidelines for how to create a pleasing effect with a limited "palette" of plants.

- **Don't buy one of everything.** As tempting as that may be, your garden could end up looking chaotic. Limit your choices to a handful of varied specimens with similar needs.
- **Plant in groups.** Don't just plop individual shrubs in the ground; create relationships.
- **Use repetition.** Planting the same shrub in several spots creates visual harmony.
- **Don't plant in rows.** Except for establishing borders or hedges, let the sizes flow in and out.
- **Consider every season.** Select shrubs with different seasonal features and interesting structures.

Combining shrubs with small trees and foliage plants of varying hues and shapes creates a soothing effect with pops of color.

So often taken for granted, shrubbery, arranged in thoughtful groupings, adds vital curb appeal to a home's landscape.

Easily the most famous of flowers, the rose is a prized shrub that comes in many forms, from lush bushes to climbers to small trees.

FLOWERING SHRUBS

Flowering shrubs play important roles in the landscape. They can be used as privacy hedges, borders, foundation plantings, or specimen plants. Adding some flowering shrubs to a new or an existing garden can add extra elegance to the landscape, along with the special surprise that blooming plants offer.

CHOOSING THE RIGHT SHRUB

For example, if you live in a coastal area, be sure to ask how the plant tolerates salt spray. If you hope to attract birds and pollinators, ask about this. If wildlife has a nasty habit of eating everything in your landscape, inquire about deer-resistant plants. Some shrubs are considered reliable, long bloomers in cold climates and warm climates alike. Certain varieties of these shrubs may just show better cold hardiness or heat tolerance than others.

FRAGRANCE AND COLOR

Flowering shrubs can offer both fragrance and color. What can beat the vibrant pop of yellow that a forsythia adds to the early spring landscape or the fragrant scent of lilacs as they paint the landscape in shades from creamy white to deep purple? Many flowering shrubs offer varieties in a range of colors, such as hydrangeas with it pom-poms of blooms available in pink to blue, including all shades of lavender to violet to purple, as well as green and white. Whatever your color and scent preferences, there is sure to be a flowering shrub to meet your requirements.

Flowering shrubs, such as the classic lilac, can add both color and scent to a garden.

READ MORE AT GARDENING KNOW HOW

Learn more about caring for these beautiful plants and get tips on how to choose colors to show off in your garden.

- **"Easy-to-Care-For Flowering Bushes** (URL = gkh.us/186350)
- **"Best Flowering Shrubs to Plant in Pots"** (URL = gkh.us/186010)
- **"Beautiful Purple Flowering Shrubs"** (URL = gkh.us/186266)
- **"10 Showy Pink Flowering Shrubs: Choosing a Bright Pink Flowering Bush"** (URL = gkh.us/175854)
- **"Planting Bushes in the Yard: Landscaping Shrubs for Nearly Any Purpose"** (URL = gkh.us/286)

Some flowering shrubs can bloom in more than one season. The dark crimson, bell-shaped flowers of weigela 'Bristol Ruby' usually appear in late spring and early summer, but in some climates can bloom all summer long.

Abelia

The white and pink flowers of *Abelia* x *grandiflora* attract pollinators to the garden. Its foliage is also a draw, changing colors from greens to bronzy purplish by autumn.

Abelia shrubs are known for their attractive foliage, and not just their flowers, making them a common choice in landscaping. This evergreen has a variety of foliage colors throughout the summer that transition to deeper and more brilliant hues as temperatures drop. The flowers offer several bursts of blooms, with clusters of fragrant and frilly pink or white tubular flowers. Native to eastern Asia and Mexico, the genus *Abelia,* which includes 30 species of deciduous and evergreen shrubs, is part of the honeysuckle family. The popular glossy abelia *(A.* x *grandiflora)* is considered semi-evergreen, as it may lose half its leaves in cold winters. Many gardeners are familiar, as least by sight, with the 'Edward Goucher' cultivar that has graced gardens since 1911. A cross between *A.* x *grandiflora* and *A. shumannii,* it features clusters of lavender-pink flowers from midsummer into autumn and glossy, dark green leaves that turn purplish bronze in autumn.

These hardy plants are very drought tolerant and rabbit and deer resistant. They are generally pest and disease free, and they don't exhibit invasive properties. As an added bonus, their lovely flowers attract butterflies, bees, and hummingbirds to the garden.

GROWING ABELIA

When planting abelia in your yard, choose a spot that gets as much full sun as possible. It can grow in partial shade, but full sun will allow it to bloom more vibrantly and produce healthier, more vividly colored foliage. Leave room for the plant to spread—abelia will sprawl out across large areas if given enough space.

It is an adaptable plant and grows in a variety of soil types, but generally responds best to fertile, well-draining soil amended with organic material. Once established, it requires very little in the way of care. Regular watering will keep it healthy, and some varieties should be pruned for the health of the plant, to control spreading, and for aesthetic reasons. Some cultivars are more compact and require little pruning, making them even less time consuming to care for. 'Lavender Mist,' for example, a hybrid of 'Edward Goucher' spreads only slightly, with gray-green foliage that turns a purplish red in autumn and a deep purple in winter. Blooms on these compact shrubs are lavender and white.

SCIENTIFIC NAME: *Abelia x grandiflora*

FAMILY: Caprifoliaceae

HEIGHT: 2 to 10 feet (60 cm–3 m)

WIDTH: 2 to 8 feet (60 cm–2.4 m)

BLOOMS: Spring, summer, autumn

SOIL pH: Acidic to neutral

LIGHT: Full to partial sun

Editor's Picks

Abelias offer a wealth of options, with a range of sizes, as well as flower and foliage colors. Here are some of the more common cultivars that are sure to add multi-season interest to your garden.

- 'Confetti' is a compact shrub with light green leaves with creamy white margins that turn a rosy hue in autumn.
- 'Kaleidoscope' is an abelia favorite, with subtly fragrant white flowers that last through autumn and with light green leaves with yellow margins than turn a darker green with reddish orange margins.
- 'Mardi Gras' has white flowers surrounded by variegated foliage that transitions from light green to creamy white with pink tips to a golden color in autumn.
- 'Plum Surprise' sports yellow-green leaves that turn emerald in summer and burgundy by autumn. It reddish stems bear single white flowers with a purple blush and a yellow throat.
- 'Rose Creek' leafs out in a pinkish foliage that matures to darker green in the summer and takes on a purple shade by winter. Fragrant white flowers bloom in clusters from pink sepals.
- 'Sunshine Daydream', with its slightly fragrant white flowers, is a striking tricolor, with leaves that turn from dark pink with green and white variegation to pale pink, golden yellow, and green.

Azalea

Azalea bushes in shades of white, salmon pink, magenta, and bright red create a riotous springtime display. You can mix and match these shrubs to create different effects.

These members of the *Rhododendron* genus are beautiful, rounded, perennial shrubs with vibrant flowers. They work well as stand-alone showpieces, in mass groupings, or when mixed with other shrubs and small trees. These easy keepers can be grown in almost any garden in temperate zones, adding bright hues to your spring blooms. Although evergreen azaleas originated in Japan, Korea, or Taiwan, China, today they can be found in many different regions. Be sure to select a shrub that is hardy for your particular region.

Azalea versus Rhododendron

Listed under the *Rhododendron* genus, the azalea is often confused with the shrub that goes by that name. However similar the two are at first glance, there are differences. Take note of the floral structure: the rhododendron's flowers have around 10 stamens, while azalea's flowers usually have 5 to 6. Their branches and leaves are similar, but the typically evergreen rhododendron has larger, leathery leaves. The azalea is usually deciduous, and it also blooms earlier than its cousin.

Also consider the needs of your landscape—do you want an evergreen azalea that retains its leaves in winter or a deciduous variety that typically offers larger blooms.

This shrub's wide array of colors range from pastel shades to vivid pinks, purples, reds, and oranges. Bloom times vary from late winter to early summer. Some recent varieties re-bloom again in the autumn. Also consider staggering your bloom times within the landscape. Azaleas look especially effective against a row of evergreen trees. They also do very well in containers.

GROWING AZALEAS

Azaleas perform best in soil amended with compost, peat moss, or pine bark to improve drainage, increase nutrient retention, and lower soil pH. The hole should be roughly 6 inches (15 cm) deeper and 12 inches (30 cm) wider than the root ball, allowing the root system to spread and establish itself. Transplanting a mature shrub in colder regions works best in the spring; in warmer regions, transplant in late summer or early autumn.

Azaleas have a shallow root system and require well-drained soil; they will not tolerate wet feet. They prefer a slightly shaded spot, with protection from hot afternoon sun. Conversely, too much shade can result in poor bloom production and weak growth.

SCIENTIFIC NAME: *Rhododendron* spp.

FAMILY: Ericaceae

HEIGHT: 3 to 20 feet (1–6 m)

WIDTH: 3 to 20 feet (1–6 m)

BLOOMS: Early spring to summer

SOIL pH: Acidic

LIGHT: Partial sun

CARING FOR THE PLANTS

Mulching can help retain moisture and control weeds. But be sure to keep mulch away from the main trunk and stems. Azaleas are typically not hungry plants, but a spring application of a general, balanced fertilizer or a product for acid-loving plants is beneficial. Water well after application.

Pruning is rarely necessary, but you may clip your plants to maintain size, create a better shape, or rejuvenate the specimen. Prune only as the flowers are fading or you risk cutting off next year's buds. To prepare your azaleas for winter, slow down, and eventually stop watering. Also, never fertilize after midsummer. A layer of mulch around the plant will help to prepare the shrub for freezing temps.

COMMON PROBLEMS

Azaleas are seldom plagued by pests and disease, but problems you might encounter include scale, lace bugs, root rot, and mineral deficiencies. Nutrient deficiencies cause yellowing leaves, dead branch tips, and stunted growth. Adding nutrients, such as iron, may help. If pests are found, apply an insecticide after the plant has bloomed to protect precious pollinators.

Beautyberry

Callicarpa bodinieri, **or Bodinier's beautyberry bush, produces clusters of eye-catching purple berries. Members of this striking genus of shrubs aren't really known for their floral displays, but the colorful berries are as pretty as any flower.**

Beautyberry shrubs bloom in late summer, but their flowers aren't much to look at. It is the jewel-like, purple or white berries that make these shrub true dazzlers. The berries usually last several weeks after the leaves drop—if hungry birds don't eat them all. The autumn foliage is an attractive yellow or chartreuse color.

Beautyberries live up to their common name, which comes from the botanical name *Callicarpa,* meaning "beautiful fruit." American beautyberry *(C. Americana),* also known as American mulberry, grows wild in woodland areas in the southeastern United States. Other types include the Asian natives Japanese beautyberry *(C. japonica),* Chinese purple beautyberry *(C. dichotoma),* and odinier's beautyberry *(C. bodinieri).*

GROWING BEAUTYBERRY

Beautyberry seeds should be started in late winter. Soak the seeds in water for at least a day before planting, and then plant them shallowly in small pots or seed-starting trays, about half a dozen seeds per pot. Keep the pots indoors and consistently moist, preferably near a brightly lit window or under a growing lamp. When the seeds have germinated and sprouted seedlings—which can take a few months—transplant the strongest seedlings outdoors.

Plant in a location with full sun exposure (or light shade if full sun isn't an option) and well-draining soil. If the soil quality is very poor, mix some compost with the fill dirt when you backfill the hole. Otherwise, wait until the following spring to feed the plant for the first time.

Young beautyberry shrubs need about an inch of rain per week. Give them a slow, deep watering when rainfall isn't enough. They will be drought-tolerant once established. They don't need a lot of fertilizer, but they will benefit from a shovelful or two of compost in spring.

It's best to prune beautyberry shrubs in late winter or very early spring. There are two methods of pruning. The simplest is to cut the entire shrub back to 6 inches (15 cm) above the ground. It grows back with a neat, rounded shape. This method keeps the shrub small and compact.

If you are concerned about leaving a gap in the garden while the shrub regrows, you can instead prune it gradually. Each year, remove one-quarter to one-third of the oldest branches close to the ground. Using this method, the shrub grows up to 8 feet (2.4 m) tall, and you will completely renew the plant every three to four years.

Note: Beautyberry shrubs reseed themselves readily, and several varieties are considered invasive in some areas.

At a Glance

SCIENTIFIC NAME: *Callicarpa* spp.

FAMILY: Lamiaceae

HEIGHT: 3 to 6 feet (1–1.8 m)

WIDTH: 3 to 6 feet (1–1.8 m)

BLOOMS: Spring, summer

SOIL pH: Acidic to neutral

LIGHT: Full to partial sun

Editor's Picks

Each of the *Callicarpa* species has a variety of cultivars. Here are a few.

- ***C. americana* 'Lactea' has milky white berries.**
- ***C. americana* 'Russell Montgomery' has attractive white berries.**
- ***C. bodinieri* 'Profusion' produces an abundance of violet fruit.**
- ***C. dichotoma* 'Early Amethyst' has small purple berries.**
- ***C. dichotoma* 'Albifructus' produces white berries.**
- ***C. dichotoma* 'Issai' has gorgeous violet-blue berries.**
- ***C. japonica* 'Leucocarpa' features white berries.**
- ***C. japonica* 'Luxurians' has large, showy fruit clusters.**

Blue Mist

Blue mist *(Caryopteris),* also known as bluebeard and blue spirea, offers late-summer flowering of a deep blue-violet color. The 'Heavenly Blue' variety features gray-green leaves with silvery reverse sides and clusters of small, hairy blooms in a delicate blue.

Caryopteris, also known as blue mist, bluebeard, and blue spirea, is an East Asian native of the mint family sometimes classified as a "sub-shrub." This plant has woody stems that partially die back in the winter or even entirely all the way to the crown of the plant. It forms an airy shrub with aromatic green, silvery green, yellow, or green-and-white foliage, depending upon the cultivar. Blue mist's prized feature, however, is the blue to purple blooms, which flower in late summer all the way up until the first heavy winter frost. These delicately pretty flowers are great attractors for pollinators, such as butterflies and bees.

GROWING BLUE MIST

Blue mist can be grown from seed, but it is much easier to propagate from cuttings of an already-established plant. To propagate, simply cut several 6-inch (15 cm) pieces of new stems from a mature shrub, strip the lowest leaves from the stems, and dip the cuttings in rooting hormone powder or solution. Plant the cuttings in pots until roots develop, making sure to give them lots of sunlight and water. Once the cuttings have developed healthy roots, they can be transplanted outdoors to the garden.

When planting blue mist from seed, collect seeds in the autumn, and place them in a plastic bag with some damp sphagnum moss. Chill them in the fridge for about three months. In late winter, plant the seeds indoors in pots, about ¼ inch (.635 mm) deep, and leave them to germinate somewhere with lots of sunlight. They should be ready to plant outside when spring arrives.

Caring for the shrubs is quite easy, as long as they get plenty of sunlight. They can tolerate partial shade, however, and they don't need very much fertilizer—in fact, overfertilizing will result in overgrown, unkempt plants. They are also drought tolerant and don't require constant watering.

At a Glance

SCIENTIFIC NAME: *Caryopteris* spp.

FAMILY: Lamiaceae

HEIGHT: 2 to 4 feet (60 cm–1.2 m)

WIDTH: 2 to 4 feet (60 cm–1.2 m)

BLOOMS: Summer

SOIL pH: Neutral

LIGHT: Full sun

Pruning of any deadened branches due to harsh winter and freezing should be postponed until the plant begins to leaf out in the spring. The entire shrub can be cut back to the ground in the spring, as this helps revitalize it and fosters a more attractive, evenly rounded shape. Flowering occurs on new growth.

Although blue mist is a pollinator attractor, it is not usually at risk from animal pests like deer and rabbits.

Editor's Picks

Here is just a minuscule sampling of stunning *Caryopteris* cultivars available for you to choose from for your home landscaping.

- **C. x *clandonensis* 'Beyond Midnight' features extremely dark, glossy foliage, a compact habit, and deep misty blue flowers.**
- **C. x *clandonensis* 'First Choice' has dark green leaves, dark purplish blue flowers, and a compact habit.**
- **C. x *clandonensis* 'Heavenly Blue' produces clusters of slightly fluffy, dark blue flowers that appear at intervals in late summer on long stems scattered among pointed, aromatic, gray-green leaves.**
- **C. x *clandonensis* 'Worcester Gold' has warm yellow to chartreuse foliage and blooms in fragrant lavender-blue flowers in late summer and early autumn.**
- **C. x *incana* 'Beyond Pink'd' has an abundance of blooms that provide a pop of dark pink flowers on a compact shrub.**

Butterfly Bush

SCIENTIFIC NAME: *Buddleja* spp.

FAMILY: Scrophulariaceae

HEIGHT: 3 to 12 feet (1–3.7 m)

WIDTH: 3 to 8 feet (1–2.4 m)

BLOOMS: Summer

SOIL pH: Acidic to neutral

LIGHT: Full sun

A gorgeous black swallowtail butterfly alights on a bright purple spike of a butterfly bush. Sometimes referred to as summer lilac for its resemblance to that spring-blooming shrub, these non-native plants have become increasingly popular in pollinator gardens.

The butterfly bush is prized for its long panicles of colorful flowers and its ability to attract butterflies. The genus *Buddleja* (also spelled *Buddleia*) comprises more than 140 species of flowering plants native to Asia, Africa, and the Americas. Most of these shrubs top out at less than 16 feet (4.6 m) tall. They bloom in spring and summer, but the naturally attractive shape of the shrub and evergreen foliage keep the bush appealing, even when it is not in bloom. They are amazingly tough plants, hardy to -20° F (-28 °C) and tolerant of far warmer climates.

GROWING BUTTERFLY BUSH

Planting a butterfly bush in the right location minimizes the time you'll spend on maintenance. Choose a sunny or partly shaded area where the soil is well-drained. Poorly draining soil that is constantly wet encourages rot. When planted in good-quality garden soil, a butterfly bush rarely needs fertilizer.

Give your butterfly bush plenty of room to grow, as most varieties can spread surprising distances. If you buy a starter plant from a garden center, the plant tag will tell you the mature size of the cultivar you have chosen. Although they tolerate severe pruning to maintain a smaller size, you can reduce the time you'll spend pruning by planting it in a location with plenty of room for the plant to develop its natural size and shape.

Once established, they are quite easy to care for. They are very tough plants, and you shouldn't have to do any special maintenance outside of regular watering and deadheading. Make sure to water the shrub slowly and deeply during prolonged dry spells so that the soil absorbs the water deep into the root area.

If needed, fertilize with a 2-inch (5 cm) layer of compost over the root area, or scratch in some general-purpose fertilizer. Cover the root zone with a 2-to-4-inch (5–10 cm) layer of mulch. This is particularly important in cold climates where the roots will need winter protection.

The most labor-intensive part of caring for butterfly bushes is deadheading. In spring and summer, promptly remove the spent flower clusters. Seed pods develop when the flower clusters are left on the plant. When the pods mature and release their seeds, weedy young plants emerge. The seedlings should be removed as soon as possible.

Young shrubs that are cut off at ground level may re-emerge, so remove the roots along with the top growth. Don't be tempted to transplant the seedlings into other parts of the garden; butterfly bushes are usually hybrids, and the offspring probably won't be as attractive as the parent plant.

Should You Plant Butterfly Bush?

Experts advise that you should think about your property as an important link in your local ecosystem, with each plant in your garden affecting the local food web. Planting non-native plants in your yard actually makes it harder for the local butterflies and birds to survive. Butterfly bush is considered a harmful, invasive plant in many regions. Check with your local extension office or other agricultural authority prior to planting to ensure that the plant is permitted in your area.

Buttonbush

Buttonbush *(Cephalanthus* spp.) makes an unusual addition to a garden—its distinctive flowers resemble spiky ping-pong balls, earning the plant several nicknames, including Spanish pincushion, honeyball, and little snowball.

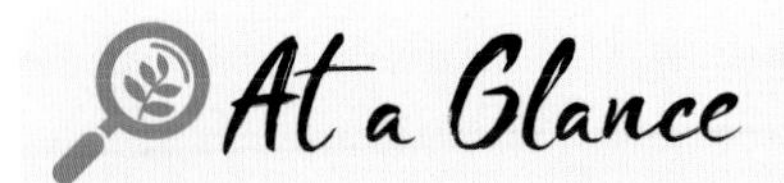

SCIENTIFIC NAME: *Cephalanthus* spp.

FAMILY: Rubiaceae

HEIGHT: 6 to 12 feet (1.8–3.7 m)

WIDTH: 6 to 12 feet (1.8–3.7 m)

BLOOMS: Summer

SOIL pH: Neutral

LIGHT: Full to partial sun

Cephalanthus, a genus of flowering plants in the coffee, madder, or bedstraw family, Rubiaceae, comprises six species that are commonly known as buttonbush. Native to the eastern United States and Canada, as well as tropical regions of the Americas, Africa, and Asia, these shrubs or small trees feature simple leaves arranged in opposite pairs or whorls of three. It is their dense, globe-like clusters of flowers, however, that make them so spectacular. Common buttonbush *(C. occidentalis)* is the species most found in cultivation. It is also known by a number of alternate names, including button willow, pond dogwood, swampwood, or button wood. The distinctive summer blooms, which look like spiky ping-pong balls, have also earned the plant the monikers of Spanish pincushion, globeflower, honeyball, and little snowball.

This unique plant thrives in moist locations. It loves ponds, riverbanks, swamps, or just about any site that is consistently wet, and it can tolerate water as deep as 3 feet (1 m). It is also a beneficial plant in many ways. Growing buttonbush along riverbanks or other riparian environments provides seeds for geese, ducks, and shorebirds, and songbirds also like to nest in the foliage. Deer do tend to snack on the twigs and leaves, however, which might put other plants in your garden at risk as well. Still, if you want to create a rain garden, buttonbush is a great option.

GROWING BUTTONBUSH

Buttonbush is relatively simple to grow; all it really needs is lots of moisture and sunlight. If you're planning to start from seed, sow them straight in the ground outside—no starter pots needed. Make sure the soil is consistently very moist, pull any nearby weeds, and cut back other plants that might compete for nutrients while the buttonbush seeds are still getting established.

Once established, it won't require any particular special care; this plant doesn't like to be fussed over and is best left to its own devices. The only real concern is making sure the soil is consistently moist. Planting in an area near water, such as by a pond, river, or in a rain garden, will usually take care of that for you. Buttonbush is a very hardy plant and is not particularly susceptible to any pests or diseases. It also doesn't require pruning, but if it becomes unruly you can cut it to the ground in early spring. It is a relatively fast-growing plant that will rebound quickly.

What Is a Rain Garden?

If a lot of rain ends up in one part of your yard, why not take advantage of it? You can create a rain garden by building a berm in that spot, and then using swales (stone channels) or plastic pipes to guide runoff from the gutters and higher parts of the yard to the garden. This also helps keeps the water from entering your basement or house. The water is then absorbed through a network of deep-rooted native plants, especially those adapted to your area and to the different water depths in your garden. Species possibilities include shrubs like buttonbush, as well as other plants like astilbe, liatris, sedge, daylily, lavender, sage, hosta, sedum, and foxglove.

Camellia

Blooming camellia looks lovely in a Chinese-style stone garden. These are dense, compact shrubs with brilliant foliage. They offer bright, long-blooming flowers that do well in containers, but they also serve as popular foundation and specimen plants.

SCIENTIFIC NAME: *Camellia* spp.

FAMILY: Theaceae

HEIGHT: 2 to 12 feet (60 cm–3.7 m)

WIDTH: 2 to 10 feet (60 cm–3 m)

BLOOMS: Late autumn to early spring

SOIL pH: Acidic

LIGHT: Partial sun

Camellias have long been admired for the beauty of their exquisite blooms. Members of the tea family, Theaceae, these flowers appear on glossy evergreen shrubs that bring color and life to gardens from autumn to spring. There are over 100 species of camellias, native to the Philippines, but most varieties stem from *Camellia japonica,* which originated in Japan. *C. sasanqua* is another common garden variety, which is hardier and tougher than the *japonicas,* better tolerating drought and resisting disease.

GROWING CAMELLIAS

Camellias have a reputation as demanding and picky plants, but if you properly plant them, however, the time spent on maintenance will be significantly reduced.

Choose a shady area with dappled sunshine, not in direct sun, and one protected from winds. Be sure the soil is well prepared. Camellias require acidic soil that drains well. Test the soil first to be sure the pH is between 5.5 and 6.5 before you put your plant in the ground. While you are digging, work in organic material to ensure the soil has adequate nutrients and drainage.

Bury your new shrub slightly higher than the surrounding soil to allow excess water to drain away from the center of the plant. Don't plant where it will have competition for nutrients; for example, don't plant it beneath a tree with shallow roots, such as a birch.

Young camellias are not very drought-resistant. When you are first growing one, it will require regular and generous irrigation. Water the young shrubs deeply to encourage the root system to spread downward. Once the shrub is mature, it needs less water. In time, and with enough regular rainfall, you might not have to water it at all.

Camellias do not do well with a lot of fertilizer, so don't overuse it. Once the shrub has finished blooming, spread a balanced fertilizer for acid-loving plants around the plant's drip line. Irrigate well.

Both *C. japonica* and *C. sasanqua* require a little pruning to maintain their beauty, but they should be pruned at different times. *Japonicas* bloom in early spring, so they should be pruned immediately after the flowers fade. *Sasanquas* flower in autumn, forming buds in spring. Prune them in early spring to avoid snipping off flowers.

COMMON PROBLEMS

Camellias are prey to several common problems, including scorched or yellowed leaf centers, which indicates too much sun. Burnt leaf edges indicates overfertilization. Shrubs planted in neutral or alkaline soil can develop a condition called chlorosis, which turns the leaves yellow. Watch out, too, for tea scale, which are tiny pests that present as minuscule brown or white specks. Two fungal diseases are common: camellia petal blight and camellia leaf gall. With petal blight, the flowers rapidly brown and fall off. Overwatering, summer drought, or sudden freezes can also cause bud drop.

Editor's Picks

These gorgeous flowers come in numerous varieties. Here is a tiny sampling of *C. japonica* cultivars.

- **'April Dawn' has large, showy white blooms shot through with pale to deep pink.**
- **'Australis' features show-stopping double rose-red blooms.**
- **'Bonomiana' blooms with tightly furled petals in pastel pink streaked in darker pink.**
- **'Debutante' features peony-form flowers in medium to deep pink**
- **'Elfin Rose' has bright candy pink double blooms.**
- **'Moonshadow' has creamy white double blooms edged in a fuchsia that fades to pale pink at the center.**
- **'Pink Perfection' is a pale shell pink**
- **'Yuletide' features pretty single flowers in vivid red.**

Daphne

The variegated pink blooms of *Daphne cneorum* 'Eximea' make this low-growing variety a garden showpiece. Also called garland or rose daphne, this fragrant evergreen beauty is native to rocky outcrops and the edges of pine woodlands.

Lovely to look at and enticingly fragrant, daphnes are a delightful landscape shrub. You can find daphne plant types to suit most any need, from shrub borders and foundation plantings to stand-alone specimens. The genus consists of over 70 broadleaf evergreen species native to Europe, Asia, and Africa.

The plants are quite visually appealing, thanks to their white or light pink tubular flowers, which bloom in spring or early winter in warmer climates. The flowers are followed by small red berries called drupes. In warm climates, the small ovular, light green foliage is yearlong, while in cooler climates, the shrub may experience leaf loss.

GROWING DAPHNES

Daphnes are hardy down to 14° F (-10° C) temperatures, but they should be treated as semi-evergreens or deciduous plants in colder environments. The shrubs can also survive high humidity levels, although they may become prone to fungal leaf spots.

Plant your specimens in a spot that receives full sun or partial shade. Varieties with variegated leaves will promise a striking display when grown in some shade. And be sure to choose your site well because daphnes do not like to be transplanted.

Well-drained soil is a must. Daphnes will do best in slightly acidic pH and a high content of compost. They also grow best when given a thick but light layer of mulch during summer months. This helps keep the roots cool and the soil moist.

It's best to water the shrub when rainfall is scarce. Ensure that it receives at least 1 inch (2.5 cm) of water per week, whether through rainfall, irrigation, or a combination. You should also fertilize the plant twice a year, using a granular balanced fertilizer.

Note: Be advised that the plant is poisonous. You should never plant daphne shrubs where pets or children play, because chewing on the flowers, foliage, or red berries can be fatal.

SCIENTIFIC NAME: *Daphne* spp.

FAMILY: Thymelaeaceae

HEIGHT: 1 to 5 feet (30 cm–1.5 m)

WIDTH: 2 to 6 feet (60 cm–1.8 m)

BLOOMS: Winter, spring, summer

SOIL pH: Slightly acidic

LIGHT: Full sun to partial shade

Daphne Varieties

One challenge of growing daphne is choosing a type. These are three of the most commonly grown and easily available varieties.

- ***D.* x *burkwoodii*** can be evergreen, semi-evergreen, or deciduous, depending on the climate zone. It grows 3 to 4 feet (1 m) tall and blooms in late spring, often followed by a second flush of flowers in late summer. The popular 'Carol Mackie' is a variegated variety.
- ***D. cneorum,*** or garland daphne, is a low grower that reaches heights of less than a foot (30 cm), making it ideal for rock gardens and edging pathways. The trailing branches spread about 3 feet (1 m). Aglow with flowers in the spring, you can cover the stems with mulch after the blooms fade to encourage rooting. The best varieties include 'Eximia', 'Pygmaea Alba', and 'Variegata'.
- ***D. odora,*** or winter daphne, is the variety of choice if you like a powerful fragrance. It can reach 6 feet (1.8 m) tall and has narrow, glossy leaves. It is, however, the type most likely to suffer from sudden death syndrome. The flowers bloom in late winter. 'Aureo-Marginata' is a popular winter daphne cultivar with variegated leaves.

Deutzia

SCIENTIFIC NAME: *Deutzia* spp.

FAMILY: Hydrangeaceae

HEIGHT: 1 to 20 feet (30 cm–6 m)

WIDTH: 2 to 15 feet (60 cm–4.6 m)

BLOOMS: Early spring to midsummer

SOIL pH: Acidic to alkaline

LIGHT: Partial sunlight

The lovely but often overlooked deutzia is finally coming into its own as a preferred flowering shrub for home landscaping. With its dainty fluffs of fragrant blooms in pretty pinks and whites, it makes an elegant border plant and, massed together, a low hedge.

If you are looking for a shrub that can bloom in shade, the graceful deutzia might be the plant for you. This shrub's abundant flowers and flexible growing conditions are definite pluses for many gardeners.

Deutzia is a genus of about 60 species, most of which are native to China and elsewhere in Asia, while a few originate from Europe and Central America. These mound-forming shrubs have long, arching branches that give them a weeping or cascading appearance.

They are members of the hydrangea family, and like hydrangeas, they produce small flowers that grow abundantly in clusters. Deutzia blossoms, however, look quite different from their relation, with the petals of some species elongated and gently drooping and others bell-shaped or open. These fragrant flowers are pure white or tinged with pink, and they appear for about two weeks in early spring to midsummer.

Deutzia produces deciduous, light-green leaves, and some varieties develop red leaves in fall. These shrubs are ornamental during the winter season too, with bark that peels back to reveal a reddish orange color underneath.

CHOOSING A VARIETY

Fuzzy deutzia *(D. scabra)* has been cultivated in Japan for hundreds of years and was especially popular in American gardens in the mid-to-late 1800s. Its clusters of small, white, often doubled flowers have the look of cotton balls covering the branches. This species grows up to 10 feet (3 m) tall and tolerates shade. Some gardeners report it can bloom even in full shade.

Another variety is slender deutzia *(D. gracilis)*, which is among the most popular species for ornamental plantings. It tolerates either full sun or partial shade. It can grow in a wide range of pH conditions, including alkaline soil, but it requires that the soil be moist and well drained. These plants generally grow to 2 to 4 feet (60 cm to 1.2 m) tall and wide. A 2-foot-tall (60 cm) cultivar known as 'Nikko' is available. Slender deutzia can tip root, meaning it develops roots where cascading branches touch the soil. This results in a plant that will spread if you let it.

Deutzia x *lemoinei* is a hybrid form with very abundant panicles of white flowers that cover the plant for weeks in late spring. It grows 5 to 7 feet (1.5 to 2.1 m) tall and wide.

CARING FOR DEUTZIAS

Deutzia care is generally quite simple. These plants are tolerant of a wide range of soil conditions and do not suffer from significant disease problems. The exception is that they can be damaged by excessive moisture from poorly drained soil or by drought. Water the plants regularly if rainfall is infrequent.

Most deutzia species prefer mid-cool to slightly warmer temperatures, but they can survive when it reaches as low as -4° F (-20° C.) Be sure to learn about your specific variety of deutzia. Information on different varieties is available from extension services and local nurseries.

Growing deutzia plants require regular pruning every year to look their best. Prune your shrubs immediately after they finish flowering for optimum results. Deutzias flower on second-year growth, so if you prune too late in the season, you risk removing the developing flower buds that will produce next year's blooms.

Elderberry

The foamy white flowers of the European elderberry make it a great choice for gardeners looking for an attractive flowering shrub, but for those who want to create a bird garden, American has it beat. *Sambucus canadensis* is one of the top bird-attracting plants

The elderberry is a large bush or shrub that is native to Central Europe and North America, where it is commonly found growing along the road, forest edges, and abandoned fields. It is classified as the *Sambucus* genus, which is made up of about 10 species of shrubs and small trees in the Adoxaceae family. These bushes produce fragrant bunches of small, waxy white flowers. Not only are they attractive plants, but they yield edible flowers and fruit high in vitamins A, B, and C. The shrub's bluish black berries are used in wines, juices, jellies, and jams. The fruits themselves are quite bitter, so they are rarely eaten alone.

The two most common types of *Sambucus* plants are *S. nigra*, the European elderberry (also called black elderberry or European elder), and *S. canadensis*, the American elderberry (also known the American black elderberry, Canada elderberry, or common elderberry). The American elderberry grows wild among fields and meadows and ranges between 10 and 12 feet (3–4 m). The European variety is less hardy, but significantly taller, climbing up to 20 feet (6 m) in height. All elderberry shrubs produce fruit; however, the American elderberry varieties are more successful than the European, which are better known for their lovely foliage.

There is also a red elderberry *(S. racemosa)*, which is similar to the American species but with one important difference: the brilliant berries it produces are poisonous.

Among these three types of elderberry plants, there are several varieties, which are bred for different ornamental characteristics. 'York,' for instance, is an American variety that produces the largest berries of all the elderberry shrubs. For pollinating purposes, it can be paired with 'Nova,' which has a large, sweet fruit.

Dig Deeper

READ MORE AT GARDENING KNOW HOW

To find out how to keep your elderberry in shape, scan the QR code or follow the link below.

- **"Trimming Elderberry Plants: Learn About Pruning an Elderberry"** (URL = gkh.us/70100)

At a Glance

SCIENTIFIC NAME: *Sambucus* spp.

FAMILY: Adoxaceae

HEIGHT: 6 to 10 feet (1.8–3 m)

WIDTH: 6 to 12 feet (1.8–4 m)

BLOOMS: Midsummer

SOIL pH: Acidic

LIGHT: Full sun to partial shade

GROWING ELDERBERRY

Make sure to undertake elderberry planting in early spring. Allow for cross-pollination by planting two or more cultivars near each other. Trees should be planted 3 feet (1 m) apart and in rows that are spaced 13 to 16 feet (4–5 m) apart. A well-draining, loamy soil is best. Sandy soils can be improved by adding a few inches (5–10 cm) of organic matter. After planting, abundantly water the plants so they get a good start.

Elderberry shrubs are tolerant of many conditions, but not drought. Remember that the bushes require about an inch or two (2.5–5 cm) of water each week.

You should weed once in a while, but do so carefully; you do not want to disturb the roots. Use mulch where it is necessary to prevent weed growth, and pluck weeds that manage to sneak through.

The first two years after planting elderberry bushes, let them grow wildly. Do not prune, and do not bother picking the berries. After that, you can prune the elderberry bushes in early spring by cutting them back and removing all the dead areas. This will optimize bush growth and the production of berries. Right around mid-August and mid-September, there is a 5- to 15-day ripening period. During this time, you should begin harvesting berries. Be sure to pick them before the birds do—elderberry bushes produce one of their favorite foods.

Forsythia

Vibrant forsythia contrasts with the still-bare trees of an early-spring landscape. The golden yellow blossoms of this shrub burst into bloom before most other flowering plants.

A forsythia plant can add dramatic flair to a yard in the early spring. The *Forsythia* genus consists of about 11 species, mostly native to eastern Asia, but one is native to southeastern Europe. These flowering shrubs belong to the Oleaceae, or olive family. They are recognized by brilliant and full yellow blooms. They provide a pleasant pop of color to gardens and can reach 10 feet (3 m) in height and spread. Forsythias are among the first plants of spring to burst forth in flower, so make sure to take care of them and get the most from their beautiful blooms.

There isn't much variety of color in the different types of forsythia. All are yellow, with only subtle variations in shade. There is a white forsythia, but that is a completely different plant belonging to a different botanical family. There are, however, differences in the size of the shrub and enough variation in bloom times that you can extend the season a couple of weeks by planting different varieties.

GROWING FORSYTHIA

Forsythia requires full sun, so make sure your shrub gets at least six hours of sunlight a day. While it can tolerate less than this, its ability to flower will be reduced.

They also need to be grown in well-draining soil with a high content of organic matter. Overly wet, marshy, or swampy soil will prevent the plant from growing well. Mulching around the shrub's base will ensure that the soil retains moisture, weeds are kept down, and new organic material can work its way into soil.

Forsythias like well-draining soil, but they should still be regularly watered. They require at least 2 inches (5 cm) of water a week. If there is inadequate rainfall, you can supplement with water from the hose; however, if you are worried about water conservation, rest assured that these plants can tolerate periods of decreased watering.

Additionally, you should use a balanced fertilizer to feed these plants. Do so once every two to three months in the spring and the summer, but do not fertilize in the autumn or wintertime.

It is also best to prune the plants yearly. Without pruning, they can quickly become overgrown. The best time to prune them is right after they've finished blooming. With proper forsythia shrub care, your forsythia plant will reward you with a brilliant display of welcoming yellow flowers in the spring.

SCIENTIFIC NAME: *Forsythias* spp.

FAMILY: Oleaceae

HEIGHT: 2 to 10 feet (60 cm–3 m)

WIDTH: 2 to 10 feet (60 cm–3 m)

BLOOMS: Early spring

SOIL pH: Neutral to slightly alkaline

LIGHT: Full sun to partial shade

Try planting one of the most popular varieties of forsythia, the 'Beatrix Farrand', a graceful, fountain-shaped shrub. This cultivar is one of the largest of the forsythias, measuring up to 10 feet (3 m) tall and wide. It also has some of the largest flowers, measuring in at about 2 inches (5 cm) in diameter. Other types are often compared to 'Beatrix Farrand,' because it is considered superior in habit and vigor, as well as flower color and size.

Fringe Flower

The frilly white bloom of massed fringe flower shrubs add a delicate touch to a privacy hedge. These versatile plants can be used as single ornamental specimens or planted in small groups. They are perfect for foundations, hedges, borders, and woodland gardens.

Next time you detect an intoxicating scent outside, look for an unassuming evergreen shrub decorated with frilly white or pink flowers. This would be the fringe flower, or *Loropetalum chinense*. These shrubs are easy to cultivate in most climates, although some varieties are hardier than others. After choosing the right cultivar of fringe flowers, learn how to care for them so their delightful fragrance can perfume your yard.

Fringe flowers are native to Japan, China, and the Himalayas. They may be as tall as 10 feet (3 m) but are usually small trees of only 5 feet (1.5 m) or so. Their leaves are oval and glossy green, set on stems with crinkly brown bark. Blooms appear in late winter to early spring and can last for up to two weeks. These frilly flowers measure about 1 to 1½ inches (2.5–4 cm) long and are made up of long and slender, strappy petals.

Most varieties are white or ivory, but there are some fringe flowers that come in bright pinks with purple leaves. An interesting feature of the plants is their longevity. In their native habitat there are specimens that are over 100 years old and 35 feet (11 m) tall.

GROWING FRINGE FLOWERS

Fringe flowers are low maintenance and not terribly fussy. They should be planted somewhere with partial sunlight and partial shade. These plants will do best if they receive dappled morning sun, but are not exposed to stronger midday rays. They should also be sited where they will be protected from strong winds.

They prefer rich soil, but fringe flowers can also grow in clay. If your soil is rich, make sure it is well-draining, with a pH between 4.5 and 6.5 and a high organic content.

Fringe flowers are tolerant of drought once established; nonetheless, water the plants more often during long, dry spells or extreme heat. A layer of mulch around their root zones will help reduce competitive weeds and conserve moisture.

You can prune a shrub to maintain a smaller size. Pruning is done in early spring, and a light application of slow-release fertilizer right around the same time will enhance the plant's health.

Pruning can also be used to manipulate how the plants grows. For instance, larger cultivars can assume the form of small trees when the lower limbs are removed. Adventurous gardeners might want to try to espalier these beautiful shrubs or even bonsai the plant for a pot-bound display. Alternatively, they make excellent and easy-to-grow borders and specimens.

SCIENTIFIC NAME: *Loropetalum chinense*

FAMILY: Hamamelidaceae

HEIGHT: 4 to 6 feet (1.2–1.8 m)

WIDTH: 4 to 6 feet (1.2–1.8 m)

BLOOMS: Early spring

SOIL pH: Acidic

LIGHT: Partial sun to partial shade

Editor's Picks

There are several cultivars of fringe flowers. Some of the most well known include the following.

- **'Hillier' has a spreading habit and small white flowers, which can be used as a ground cover.**
- **'Snow Muffin' is a dwarf plant, only 18 inches (45 cm) tall, with small leaves and abundant white flowers in early springtime.**
- **'Snow Dance' is a dense, compact shrub that produces snowy white flowers in the spring.**
- **'Razzleberri' is a 6 foot (1.8 m) shrub with showy, bright pinkish red fringe-like flowers and copper-burgundy foliage.**

Hibiscus

Hibiscus, also called rose or swamp mallow, features stunning blooms that supply food for nectar-feeding insects and birds. These wetland natives work well in bog gardens.

Hibiscus, classified under the scientific name *Hibiscus moscheutos,* is a fast-growing shrub that will add a tropical flair to your garden. When you know how to care for them, you will be rewarded with many years of lovely flowers. The large, trumpet-shaped flowers come in vibrant shades of white, pink, red, blue, orange, peach, yellow, and purple, and they range from 3 to 8 inches (7.5–20 cm) in diameter.

Hibiscus are native to Asia, where they flower continuously and can grow up to 24 inches (60 cm) each year. In colder climates, they are usually kept as container specimens, which can be brought inside during the colder months or grown annually.

GROWING HIBISCUS

Many people choose to grow hibiscus in a container, so they can easily be moved. Provide it with at least six hours of sunlight, especially if you want to optimize blooms. Although warm, humid conditions are ideal for tropical hibiscus, you may want to provide afternoon shade when it's overly hot.

Hibiscus also prefers a cozy fit when growing in a container. It should be slightly root-bound in the pot, and when you do decide to repot, give it only a little bit more room. Always make sure that the plant has excellent drainage.

The plant flowers best in temperatures between 60 to 90° F (16–32° C) and cannot tolerate temperatures below 32° F (0° C). In the summer, it can go outside, but once the weather starts to get near freezing, it's time to bring it back indoors.

Hibiscus Varieties

Among the various kinds of hibiscus are hardy and tropical specimens, native plants, annuals, and perennials. There are also related plants, like hollyhock, common mallow, and even okra. With so many options for growing hibiscus, every gardener in every setting can find a type that will grow and thrive while adding beauty to the garden. Some of the main types of hibiscus include the following.

- **Native hibiscus.** Also known as rose mallow, there are numerous species of this hibiscus that are native to the wetlands of the eastern United States northward to southern Ontario.
- **Hardy hibiscus.** These cold-tolerant, perennial shrubs can be just as beautiful as their tropical counterparts, with big showy blooms in a range of colors.
- **Tropical hibiscus.** These types of hibiscus have some overlap with the native species that grow in Florida and southern Louisiana. Tropical varieties can be very large and showy, with bright and rich color options.
- **Perennial hibiscus.** These are shrubs that can range from smaller, dwarf varieties to large, tree-like bushes.
- **Annual hibiscus.** Contrary to the name, these are not true annuals, but they are tropical and can be grown as annuals in slightly cooler climates.

SCIENTIFIC NAME: *Hibiscus moscheutos*

FAMILY: Malvaceae

HEIGHT: 3 to 7 feet (1–1.7 m)

WIDTH: 2 to 4 feet (60 cm–1.2 m)

BLOOMS: Spring to autumn

SOIL pH: Neutral to acidic

LIGHT: Full sun

When in its blooming stage, the plant requires daily watering. Once the weather cools, it needs far less water; water only when the soil is dry to the touch.

In the summer, use a high-potassium fertilizer. You can either use a diluted liquid fertilizer once a week, a slow-release fertilizer once a month, or add a high-potassium compost to the soil. In the winter, you don't need to fertilize at all.

THE GLORY OF ROSES

Over the passing centuries, roses have stolen the hearts of countless gardeners. These thorny ramblers produce flowers of such exquisite beauty and sublime colors that even many non-gardeners adore them. Throughout history they have been used as potent symbols for love, beauty, war, and politics.

Roses are shrubby plants that appeared in the fossil record 35 million years ago. They were first cultivated in China around 7,000 BCE. Early Romans admired them greatly, using their petals as confetti during celebrations. During the 17th century roses were so esteemed they were considered legal tender by royalty. Napoleon's wife, Empress Josephine of France, established an extensive collection of roses at Chateau de Malmaison, heightening the craze. In the late 18th century, cultivated, repeat-blooming roses from China were introduced to Europe. They became the darlings of hybridizers seeking hardiness and longevity . . . and were the ancestors of most modern roses. Today some 150 species grow throughout the Northern Hemisphere, including northern Africa.

TYPES OF ROSES

Roses are divided into three categories—wild roses, old roses, and modern roses. The latter two groups are further divided according to hybrid and lineage. Climbing roses are not a distinct type; they are named for their stiff upright canes that can be trained to grow upward or sideways and are found in both grandifloras and floribundas.

READ MORE AT GARDENING KNOW HOW

To learn more about caring for these glorious shrubs, follow these links.

- **"Starting a Rose Garden — Caring for Rose Bushes"** (URL = gkh.us/1896)
- **"Tips for How to Buy Rose Plants"** (URL = gkh.us/3431)
- **"Bare Root Roses Care and How to Plant Bare Root Rose Bushes "** (URL = gkh.us/3452)
- **"Planting Rose Bushes — Step by Step Instructions to Plant a Rose Bush"** (URL = gkh.us/3425)

The Parc de Bagatelle is an impressive rose garden in a corner of the enormous Bois de Boulogne in Paris. This magical place features hybrid tea roses arranged to create floral carpets near a 1775 chateau, while the heady scent of rambling roses forming tall arbors perfume the air.

Wild roses

Wildflower type, or "species" roses, lack the cross-breeding history and hybridization of modern varieties. Their five-petal, single-bloom flowers are almost always pink.

Old garden roses

Also known as "antique," "heritage," and "historic" roses, old roses have been around for millennia. Hardy and disease-resistant, they usually bear fragrant double flowers, but only bloom once per season. Examples include exotic China roses, with their lovely fragrance and compact, bushy blooms and the ancient, deeply scented damask roses and Gallica roses.

Modern garden roses

Bred after 1867—and often usurping old roses—modern roses offer larger, continuous blooms. They typically lack fragrance, however, and are less hardy and disease-resistant. Examples include long-stemmed hybrid tea roses, with bountiful, ornate blooms of 30 to 50 petals; continuous blooming floribunda roses with large flower clusters; grandiflora roses, a subgroup of hybrid tea roses with elegant, showy blooms that form clusters like hybrid teas and offer constant growth cycles like floribundas. Polyantha roses are similar to floribundas, but with smaller blooms. Miniature roses, a compact form of hybrid tea or grandiflora roses, are often grown indoors. Centifolia roses or "cabbage" roses have thin, overlapping petals. English/David Austin roses combine the best qualities of old and modern roses and offer hundreds of varieties.

'BLACK BACCARA'
High-centered and very full, the blooms of this scentless hybrid tea are a deep red-burgundy with a velvety texture set against glossy, dark green foliage.

'BROCÉLIANDE'
A show-stopping garden addition with its large and full blossoms in cerise red with creamy white stripes, this deeply fragrant shrubby hybrid tea typically blooms singly.

'CHARTREUSE DE PARME'
One of the most fragrant of modern roses, this Delbard hybrid tea emits a rich citrus perfume. The double blooms of vibrant magenta pink sit among dark green foliage.

'THE FAIRY'
Sprays of tiny, soft pink pom-pom flowers adorn this polyantha rose. One of the David Austin shrub roses, it is tough and reliable, with a spreading and fan-like growth habit.

'GERTRUDE JEKYLL'
This pretty pink climber, named for garden designer Gertrude Jekyll, is one of the most popular of the David Austin English roses. Fully doubled, it has a heady, old rose fragrance.

'GOLDEN CELEBRATION'
One of the largest flowered of the David Austin English roses, this showy cultivar bears rich yellow cup-shaped blooms that emit a strong tea fragrance.

'HOT COCOA'
This floribunda has ruffled, medium-large, cupped blooms in russet with a darker reverse, with some in variations of chocolate and orange colors. It has a fruity fragrance.

'JULIA CHILD'
Also known as the Absolutely Fabulous rose, this buttery yellow floribunda has an old-fashioned form and sweet licorice fragrance. It is named after chef Julia Child.

'LOVE AND PEACE'
A striking specimen rose with a fruity fragrance, this is a hybrid tea with lemon yellow petals edged in vibrant dark pink. The high-centered blooms are typically borne singly.

'NEIL DIAMOND'
This showy hybrid tea rose, named for the U.S. singer, is large, full, and strongly fragrant, with deep pink petals, adorned with white speckles and stripes.

'NOVALIS'
This old-fashioned floribunda rose bears clusters of large, full blooms in a unique mauve-lavender color. This fragrant cultivar makes a striking cut flower for floral arrangements.

'PEACE'
This beautiful hybrid tea, also called the Madame A. Meilland, is one of the world's most popular roses. Very large and full, it has pale yellow petals tipped with rose pink.

'PRINCESS OF WALES'
Compact, free-flowing, and mildly fragrant, with clusters of white blooms with creamy centers, this floribunda cultivar was named in honor of Diana, Princess of Wales.

'QUEEN AMBER'
Set against its dark green foliage, the amber color of this large, many-petaled floribunda shrub rose brightens a garden with sunny color. It has a mildly sweet fragrance.

'RED INTUITION'
This graceful hybrid tea rose has made its way from the florist's fridge to home gardens. It is prized for its unusual striping of rich cardinal red, with slashes of bright, clear red.

'THÉRÈSE BUGNET'
With the delicate beauty of a damask, this heirloom miniature full-blooming rugosa rose has old-fashioned, ruffled petals of lilac pink that emit a spicy scent.

Honeysuckle

Clusters of delicate yellow and white honeysuckle flowers dot the lush green foliage that tumbles over a wooden fence. When in bloom, their captivating scent fills the air.

Everyone recognizes the lovely fragrance of a honeysuckle and the sweet taste of its nectar. Honeysuckles are heat-tolerant and wildly attractive in any garden. This low-maintenance plant is a great addition to the landscape and will draw abundant wildlife with its sweet, yellow to bright red blossoms.

A member of the genus *Lonicera*, honeysuckles belong to a large family of hardy shrubs and vines that hail from North America, Europe, Asia, and the Mediterranean. There are more than 180 different varieties, which can be found as native or naturalized plants in these regions, growing beside forest edges and in semi-forested areas. Some are deciduous and some, in warmer regions, are evergreen. Because of their versatility and abundance, growing and caring for them is easy.

The different types include both shrubs and climbing vines. The vines climb by twining themselves around their supporting structure, but they can't cling to solid walls.

Trumpet honeysuckle *(L. sempervirens)* and Japanese honeysuckle *(L. japonica)* are two of the most ornamental varieties. In spring, trumpet honeysuckle produces deep red to coral, yellow-throated tubular blossoms. Japanese honeysuckle produces pink or red blossoms from summer through early autumn. Check with your local agricultural authorities before planting either trumpet or Japanese honeysuckle Both have escaped cultivation and are considered invasive in some areas.

When it comes to shrubs, winter honeysuckle *(L. fragrantissima)* is an excellent choice for informal hedges or screens. It also makes a nice potted plant with creamy white blossoms and a long blooming season. Sakhalin honeysuckle *(L. maximowiczii* var. *sachalinensis)* grows into shrubs similar in appearance and habit to winter honeysuckle, but the flowers are deep red. For those who find the fragrance of honeysuckle too strong, *L. korolkowii* 'Freedom' is the perfect shrub. It produces unscented, white blossoms with a blush of pink. Despite their lack of fragrance, they still attract bees and birds to the garden.

At a Glance

SCIENTIFIC NAME: *Lonicera* spp.

FAMILY: Caprifoliaceae

HEIGHT: 12 to 20 feet (3.7–6 m)

WIDTH: 3 to 6 feet (1–1.8 m)

BLOOMS: Spring, summer, autumn

SOIL pH: Neutral, acidic, alkaline

LIGHT: Dappled sunlight

GROWING HONEYSUCKLE

Honeysuckles can be grown as ground cover in suitable areas, but most do best with some type of support, either along a fence or on a trellis. Many varieties will also perform well in containers, as long as they receive regular water and an application of 10-10-10 plant food at the beginning of the growing season.

While honeysuckles prefer full sun, they will tolerate some shade. The plant is not fussy about soil types either, although it helps to site them in an area that has well-draining soil. You can amend the soil with organic matter, if necessary.

Regular shearing and shaping is a crucial component of caring for honeysuckles to keep them from growing out of control and becoming a tangled mass of vines. Vine species can also become invasive as a ground cover and require clipping to tame. Prune your plant in the autumn or winter, when it is dormant. This way, the plant will happily return each year, providing an abundance of blooms and sweet nectar for both you and wildlife.

Editor's Tip

It is easy to harvest honeysuckle nectar. Just pick a flower off the vine, and grasp in one hand. With the other, pinch just above the calyx, hard enough to break through the petal. Gently pull on the end of the flower until you see the style, which looks like a white string. Continue to slowly pull the style down the center of the flower until all the nectar pools at the end. Bring to your lips for a tiny sip of honey-like sweetness.

Hydrangea

Soil contents influences the color of a hydrangea's blooms, and some will show a variety of colors on a single plant. Here a *Hydrangea macrophylla* displays showy globes of pink to blue. To its left is a lacecap variety with tiny buds in the center of larger flowers.

Who can forget the beautiful and ever-changing blooms of the *Hydrangea* genus. These ornamental garden plants are rightfully some of the most popular, with blooms in various shades of white, blue, pink, maroon, red, and pale green. Of these plants, native to Asia and the Americas, some produce blue flowers when grown in acidic soil, while others are pink in soils with a higher content of lime. And then of course, there are the white hydrangeas, with blooms resembling large snowballs.

Not only are they easy to grow but they are also quite hardy and resistant to most pests and diseases, making it even easier to care for hydrangeas. With numerous varieties to choose from, you're certain to find one that's right for you.

All hydrangea varieties share ornamental flowers and ample foliage, but they offer an expansive range of physical characteristics and growth patterns. Learn about the various types of hydrangeas to find which best suits your preference.

Many people know bigleaf hydrangeas, which are the most popular hydrangeas, with their rounded inflorescences as big as grapefruits. These come in two varieties: the *H. macrophylla*—the more popular with full orbs of blossoms, and the *H. macrophylla normalis,* known as lacecap hydrangea—with flat disk-shaped blossoms and round "caps" of smaller flowers in the center surrounded by a fringe of showier flowers.

Smooth hydrangea *(H. arborescens)* is a popular and easy-to-grow understory plant, which prefers some shade and lots of moisture. The rounded shrub grows to 5 feet (1.5 m) high and wide, with huge white flower clusters. Oakleaf hydrangea *(H. quercifolia),* on the other hand, is one of the few hydrangea varieties to offer brilliant autumn color. Its lobed leaves turn to scarlet and burgundy, and the plant grows to 8 feet (2.4 m) tall. The large conical flowers are white when they first open, but will mature into a pinky mauve.

SCIENTIFIC NAME: *Hydrangea* spp.

FAMILY: Hydrangeaceae

HEIGHT: 1 to 20 feet (30 cm–6 m)

WIDTH: 2 to 12 feet (60 cm–3.7 m)

BLOOMS: Mid-summer through autumn

SOIL pH: Neutral, acidic, alkaline

LIGHT: Full sun to partial sun

GROWING HYDRANGEA

Although there are many types of hydrangeas, most can be grown in full sun or partial shade. Keep in mind, however, that most varieties do not like extremely hot conditions, so try to locate them in an area where they can enjoy some afternoon shade.

Hydrangea should be planted in spring once the threat of frost has passed. They can be grown in a wide range of soils, but they typically prefer rich, moist soil that drains easily. After planting, water thoroughly, and consider also adding a layer of mulch.

The shrubs will require deep watering at least once a week, especially in periods of dry weather. They will also benefit from an occasional boost of fertilizer once or twice a year in spring or summer.

They can be transplanted easily, but this should only be done during dormancy in autumn or winter. Be sure to dig up the entire root ball, and replant immediately. Flowers are produced on new growth, so you should prune hydrangeas once their blooming has ceased. Pruning time will differ between the different varieties.

To find out how to get the best from these showy, bright bloomers, scan the QR code or follow the link below.

- **"5 Tips for Happy Hydrangeas"** (URL = gkh.us/180331)

Japanese Kerria

The bright yellow blooms of Japanese kerria resemble small chrysanthemums or African marigolds (which accounts for one of its common names, Japanese marigold bush). Not only are these blooms pretty, they are also especially attractive to bees.

A native of China, Japan, and Korea, Japanese kerria *(Kerria japonica)* is also called Japanese rose, Japanese yellow rose, Japanese marigold bush, Japanese globeflower, or Easter rose. It gets the genus name *Kerria* from early-19th-century Scottish plant hunter William Kerr, who had been active in China and introduced the *Kerria* cultivar 'Pleniflora' to Europe.

Japanese kerria is a versatile shrub with arching, greenish yellow stems and masses of golden-yellow, chrysanthemum-like flowers that put on a show in spring. The bright green leaves turn yellow in fall, and the airy stems and branches provide color in the depths of winter, after the deciduous foliage is long gone. In spite of its graceful, delicate appearance, Japanese kerria is as tough as nails, is rarely bothered by pests, and tends to be deer resistant

GROWING JAPANESE KERRIA

Although you can propagate Japanese kerria by fresh-sown seed, softwood cuttings treated with hormone, or by division, most gardeners begin with a nursery-grown potted specimen, which will do best in moderately fertile, well-drained soil, and won't perform well in heavy clay. Although it tolerates full sunlight in cool climates, it generally prefers a site in afternoon shade. Too much sunlight causes the shrub to take on a bleached appearance, and the flowers will tend to fade quickly.

Japanese kerria care is not complicated. Basically, just regularly water your shrubs, being careful not to overwater. The plant is fairly drought-tolerant and doesn't do well in soggy soil. You can apply a single, light application of an organic fertilizer, such as seaweed extract or fish emulsion, in early spring. Be stingy though—if the soil is too rich, the plant's growth can be excessive, but it will produce fewer blossoms.

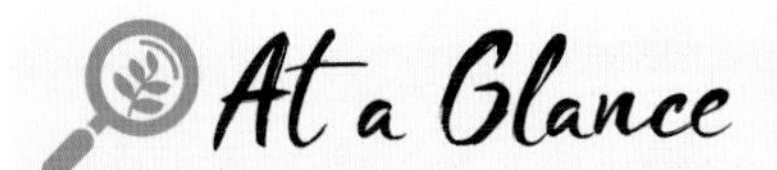

SCIENTIFIC NAME: *Kerria japonica*

FAMILY: Rosaceae

HEIGHT: 3 to 8 feet (1–2.4 m)

WIDTH: Up to 6 feet (1.8 m)

BLOOMS: Spring

SOIL pH: Acidic, neutral, alkaline

LIGHT: Partial sun to partial shade

Prune your shrub after blooming to maintain a tidy appearance and to promote blooms the following season. Seriously overgrown shrubs can be rejuvenated by cutting the plant to the ground, which improves blooming and creates a fuller, healthier plant. Regularly removing suckers can also keep the plant in check and prevent unwanted growth. Its spreading nature, however, makes Japanese kerria useful for erosion control, naturalized areas, and mass plantings, because its mounding growth habit is spectacular when it is grown in drifts.

Note: Although Japanese kerria is relatively well-behaved in most climates, it can become invasive in certain areas, particularly in the eastern and southeastern United States. If this is a concern, it's always a good idea to check with your local Cooperative Extension office before planting.

Editor's Picks

Japanese kerria's blooms vary from double to single in shades of yellow to almost white. Here is a selection.

- **'Albiflora' bears creamy pale yellow, almost white flowers.**
- **'Golden Guinea' is a prolific bloomer with large flowers, up to 2 inches (5 cm) or more across.**
- **'Pleniflora' bears double, nearly round, golden-yellow flowers that are 1 to 2 inches (2.5–5 cm) across. Also sold as 'Flora Pleno'.**
- **'Picta' is a heavy bloomer that produces single yellow flowers, but it is its gorgeous green leaves edged in white that are its big draw.**

Jasmine

Jasminum officinale, **sometimes called poet's jasmine, is one of the most fragrant types of jasmine. The intensely scented flowers bloom throughout the summer and into the autumn. Plant this vining type near a window or seating area to enjoy its beguiling scent.**

Thoughts of jasmine call to mind summer evenings scented with a heady, floral fragrance that seems to hang in the air. These widely cultivated flowers are part of the genus *Jasminum,* which includes approximately 200 species native Eurasia, Africa, and Oceania.

The plants may be vines or bushes and some are evergreen. Most jasmine plants are found in tropical to subtropical climates, although a few may thrive in temperate zones. Protection from cold temperatures is one of the most important aspects of jasmine plant care. Growing jasmine vines can create a perfumed shield over arbors, trellises, and fences. The bush types are excellent landscape specimens with starry pink, white, ivory, or even yellow scented blooms.

GROWING JASMINE

Jasmine plant care may require a bit of work, but the results are well worth the effort. Not all jasmine plants are fragrant, but the most common and hardy do produce a sweet, carrying fragrance. Common jasmine is a vine and has larger glossy green leaves than royal jasmine. Both can survive in temperate climates if they are planted in a sheltered area. Arabian jasmine is a small bush with evergreen leaves. There are many other varieties of jasmine plant, and adding one or two will add a striking visual and olfactory touch to the garden.

First, choose a warm, sheltered location. The vining varieties require a support structure, as some can reach 15 feet (4.6 m) tall. All jasmine plants prefer sun to light shade sites with well-draining and moderately fertile soil.

Jasmine is most commonly grown from nursery specimens. To plant, install the specimen in the ground at the same level it was growing in the nursery pot. Most plants are grafted onto the common jasmine rootstock because of their superior hardiness.

Once in the ground, this plant requires vigilance. The vines need to be trained early when they are young. You can use plant ties or just weave them through trellis sections. Fertilize the plant in spring just before new growth appears. Pinch off the tips of the vines in the second year to promote branching, which will fill the trellis with bushy growth. Vining jasmine plant is prone to spider mites, which can be combated with horticultural oil or neem oil.

SCIENTIFIC NAME: *Jasminum* spp.

FAMILY: Oleaceae

HEIGHT: 3 to 20 feet (1–6 m)

WIDTH: 3 to 15 feet (1–4.6 m)

BLOOMS: Winter, spring, summer, autumn

SOIL pH: Acidic, neutral

LIGHT: Full sun to light shade

INDOOR JASMINE CARE

Dwarf varieties of jasmine make excellent houseplants. They require a sunny location in the home and even more hydration than outdoor specimens. Vines can also be brought inside, and the height will be easy to manage with pruning or pinching in the dormant season. Potted plants don't have access to extra nutrients, so fertilize twice annually. Watch carefully for pests, and water from the bottom to prevent spotting on the glossy leaves. Your jasmine plant will flower in late spring into summer. Repot it before bloom time in early spring as needed.

You can also grow indoor plants from cuttings. Harvest tip cuttings in spring. Dip the cutting into a rooting hormone, and push the end into a soil-less medium, such as peat. Keep the cutting lightly moist. Once rooted, follow general jasmine care instructions.

READ MORE AT GARDENING KNOW HOW

To learn about the various species and varieties of this heavenly plant, scan the QR code or follow this link.

- **"Jasmine Plant Types: Common Varieties of Jasmine Plants"** (URL = gkh.us/61324)

Lilac

SCIENTIFIC NAME: *Syringa* spp.

FAMILY: Oleaceae

HEIGHT: 8 to 15 feet (2.4–4.6 m)

WIDTH: 6 to 12 feet (1.8–2.7 m)

BLOOMS: Spring

SOIL pH: Neutral

LIGHT: Full sun

In spring, common lilacs (*Syringa vulgaris*) burst into lush bloom with flowers in the color named for them. Lilacs have long been a garden favorite, with their intense, romantic scent.

A longtime favorite, the lilac, classified as *Syringa,* is grown for its intense fragrance and beautiful blooms. It is native to eastern Europe, particularly on the rocky hills of the Balkan peninsula, but has also been naturalized in parts of Europe, Asia, and North America. It is a member of the olive family (Oleaceae), along with ash trees, forsythia bushes, and privet hedges. Its flowers can range in color from pink to purple, and even white and yellow.

Lilacs add shade or privacy when planted as a hedgerow. They range from dwarf varieties, which grow up to 8 feet (2.4 m) tall, and larger ones that reach 30 feet (9 m) in height. With proper care, these lovely plants can grace your garden for decades.

Horticulturists have crossbred the 28 species of lilac so extensively that even the experts sometimes have trouble telling lilac types apart. Even so, some species have attributes that might make them better suited to your garden and landscape.

Common lilac *(S. vulgaris)* is the most familiar variety, with lilac-colored blossoms and a strong fragrance. They grow to a height of about 20 feet (6 m). Persian lilac *(S. persica)* grows 10 feet (3 m) tall, with pale lilac flowers about half the diameter of common lilacs. They are a good choice for an informal hedge. For those who want a smaller shrub, dwarf Korean lilac *(S. palebinina)* top out at only 4 feet (1.2 m) tall and make a good informal hedge plant.

For a large tree, there is the white-flowered tree lilac *(S. amurensis),* which reaches 30 feet (9 m). Its cultivar 'Japonica' blooms with unusual, very pale yellow flowers.

Chinese lilac *(S. chinensis),* one of the best varieties to use as a summer screen or hedge, is a cross between the common lilac and Persian lilac. It quickly reaches 8 to 12 feet (2.4–3.7 m). Himalayan lilac *(S. villosa),* also called late lilac, has rose-like blossoms. It grows as tall as 10 feet (3 m).

GROWING LILACS

Spring or autumn is the best time for planting a lilac bush. Situate the plant with its roots spread vertically in the ground, and dig the hole both deep and wide enough to accommodate it. If planting more than one bush, space them at least 5 feet (1.5 m) apart to prevent overcrowding, even if you plan to mass them together as hedges for privacy.

Choose an area with plenty of afternoon sun and well-drained soil in a slightly elevated area whenever possible. After planting, water thoroughly, and add a layer of loose mulch to keep out weeds and retain moisture.

Watered thoroughly, but not too often, because lilacs do not like their roots to become saturated. Frequent use of fertilizer is not necessary; however, fertilizing in early spring may help give blooms a boost, provided there is not too much nitrogen, which will result in insufficient flowering.

Pruning is perhaps the most crucial component of lilac care. Keeping them well-pruned will also prevent the chance of disease, such as powdery mildew.

READ MORE AT GARDENING KNOW HOW

To learn more about caring for fragrant and beautiful lilacs, follow the links below.

- **"Is Lilac a Tree or a Shrub: Learn About Types of Lilac Trees and Shrubs"** (URL = gkh.us/79872)
- **"Container Grown Lilacs: Learn How to Grow Lilac in a Pot "** (URL = gkh.us/98247)
- **"No Lilac Scent: Why a Lilac Tree Doesn't Have Fragrance"** (URL = gkh.us/3932)

Mahonia

The bright yellow flowers of *Mahonia aquifolium*, also known as Oregon grape holly, stand out against sharply delineated, dark green leaves. In autumn, the shrub will be covered with purplish blue-black berries that will draw hungry birds to the garden.

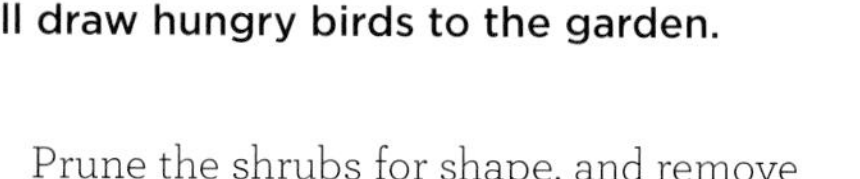

SCIENTIFIC NAME: *Mahonia* spp.

FAMILY: Berberidaceae

HEIGHT: 3 to 10 feet (1–3 m)

WIDTH: Up to 3 feet (1 m)

BLOOMS: Winter, spring

SOIL pH: Acidic, neutral, alkaline

LIGHT: Partial shade

With its large and dramatic foliage, a mahonia shrub can introduce a unique architectural element to a backyard landscape. The *Mahonia* genus is made up of woodland plants native to North America that feature fragrant golden-yellow late-winter or early-spring blooms. The plants offer an abundance of food to birds through their autumn berries, which are deep purple with a whitish bloom. The clusters of flowers are also appealing to beneficial pollinators like bees and butterflies.

GROWING MAHONIA

All mahonia plants are easy to care for. They are drought tolerant and only need watering during extended dry spells. Most varieties do well in any soil across a range of pH levels, as long as it is well-draining. A layer of organic mulch around the plants will help the soil retain moisture and reduce competition from weeds.

Depending on the variety of mahonia you are growing, your plant may prefer different conditions. For instance, Oregon grape hollies should be planted in a partially shaded area with moist, neutral to slightly acidic, well-draining soil. Creeping mahonia, on the other hand, likes full sun in cool climates and afternoon shade where summers are hot.

Prune the shrubs for shape, and remove suckers and seedlings as necessary to restrict them to the desired areas. Mahonias don't require regular fertilization, but they may benefit from a layer of compost over the root zone in springtime.

Mahonia Varieties

There are more than 70 species of *Mahonia* plants, and each of them has many cultivars and hybrids. Some of the most commonly grown include the following.

- ***M. aquifolium,*** or Oregon grape holly is a handsome, 3-to-6 foot (1–1.8 m) ornamental that can play a number of roles in the garden, making it a favorite with homeowners. The plant's appearance changes with the seasons. In spring, the branches bear long, hanging clusters of lightly fragrant yellow flowers that give way to dark blue berries in summer. New spring foliage is bronze in color, turning green as it matures. In autumn, the leaves take on a pleasing, purplish cast.
- ***M. fremontii,*** or Frémont's mahonia, has yellow blooms and reaches 8 feet (2.4 m) in height.
- ***M.* x *media* 'Charity'** is a tall, adaptable hybrid with striking green foliage. It is often used to create a natural privacy fence.
- ***M. repens,*** or creeping mahonia, is an excellent specimen or foundation plant. With foliage, flowers, and berries similar to the Oregon grape holly, it has all the features of the taller form in a compact plant that grows to only 9 to 15 inches (23–38 cm) tall. It spreads by means of underground rhizomes, and seedlings often emerge under the plant where berries fall to the ground. It also looks good in shrub groupings or borders. When closely planted, the prickly, holly-like foliage forms a barrier that few animals can penetrate. It can be planted as a ground cover in a variety of situations, as it stabilizes soil on slopes and hillsides, and is deer resistant.

Mock Orange

Philadelphus, **or mock orange, is an easy-to-grow shrub that flowers in late spring and early summer. This shrub possesses attractive white flowers that resemble orange blossoms and emit a wonderfully fragrant orange blossom–like scent.**

For a stunning citrus fragrance in the garden, you can't go wrong with the mock orange shrub. Classified as the *Philadelphus* genus, mock oranges consist of 60 species of shrubs native to North America, Central America, Asia, and southeast Europe. These late spring-blooming deciduous shrubs look great when placed as a border, used in groups as screening, or simply as a stand-alone specimen plant. Their blooms even make excellent cut flowers indoors.

Though it's not a true orange, its name supposedly derives from the fragrant white flowers, which in some varieties are thought to resemble those of orange blossoms. The showy, cup-shaped, four-petaled flowers bloom for only a week or two, but you can still enjoy the plant's dark green oval, serrated, foliage throughout the season.

GROWING MOCK ORANGE

Mock oranges thrive best in areas with full sun to partial shade and moist, well-drained soil. Adding compost to the soil will help improve most drainage issues.

Dig your planting hole deep enough to accommodate all of the roots. Be sure to spread the roots out and add soil halfway, tamping it down before adding in the remaining soil. Water well after planting.

A young shrub will require consistent moisture until it's established, and though it is somewhat drought tolerant, the bush prefers to be kept in moist conditions. Mulching the area around the shrub will help the soil retain moisture and minimize the time you spend watering it.

Mock oranges are not usually heavy feeders, though a water-soluble, all-purpose fertilizer can be used in late winter/early spring, as needed, if you notice that the plant is not growing as well as it should.

Annual pruning will keep your shrubs looking tidy and help with maintaining its shape. Since the shrub blooms on the previous year's growth, pruning needs to be done soon after the blooming period in early summer. Simply prune off the growth just above the outer-facing buds on stems that have finished flowering. Overgrown shrubs can be pruned back by a third, though this may reduce flowering next season.

SCIENTIFIC NAME: *Philadelphus* spp.

FAMILY: Hydrangeaceae

HEIGHT: 10 to 12 feet (3–3.7 m)

WIDTH: 10 to 12 feet (3–3.7 m)

BLOOMS: Spring, summer

SOIL pH: Acidic, neutral

LIGHT: Full sun to partial shade

Mock Orange Varieties

Mock orange bushes come in many varieties, ranging in height from 4 to 8 feet (1.2–2.4 m) or taller. They can vary in growth pattern, as well as physical appearance. Here are several popular varieties.

- ***P. coronarius*** includes two interesting cultivars: 'Aureus' is notable for its bold foliage, which progressively darkens from a vibrant gold color throughout the growing season. 'Variegatus' has variegated leaves with white edges and light green centers.
- ***P.* x *virginalis,*** or Minnesota snowflake, features large double flowers and a very pungent fragrance.
- ***P.* x *purpureomaculatus* 'Belle Etoile'** is a compact shrub with a long bloom period. Its large white blooms and yellow stamens appeal to flower lovers.
- ***P. lewisii,*** or wild mock orange, is the largest variety of mock orange and produces dramatic white blossoms

Ninebark

Ninebark is a popular flowering shrub that is known for its clusters of late-spring flowers, but also for the way the bark peels away as the plant matures. It is also known as common ninebark, eastern ninebark, and Atlantic ninebark.

SCIENTIFIC NAME: *Physocarpus opulifolius*

FAMILY: Rosaceae

HEIGHT: 3 to 10 feet (1–3 m)

WIDTH: 3-8 feet (1–2.4 m)

BLOOMS: Spring, summer

SOIL pH: Neutral

LIGHT: Full sun to partial shade

Ninebark is a deciduous flowering shrub commonly used in landscaping, as a hedge, along foundations, or to stabilize sloping areas and prevent erosion. Classified as the *Physocarpus opulifolius,* ninebark is named after its unique exfoliating quality, by which thin layers of bark peel back from the plant as it matures. The bush is native to North America and is coarse in texture, with yellow, green, or reddish leaves that grow from gracefully arching branches. Most varieties bloom in clusters of white or pink flowers in late spring and produce red fruit in late summer and autumn.

Caring for a ninebark shrub is simple once you determine the optimal location to site it on your property, as well as ensuring it is growing in the correct kind of soil. It usually prefers soil that is only slightly acidic and requires ample space to look its best. The plant pairs well with lilac and spiraea when used as a mixed border plant. It can be grown as a potted nursery plant or started from a bare-root or ball-and-burlap.

Because of this shrub's easy growing habit and cold hardiness, plant breeders have developed many cultivars with various foliage colors, textures, and sizes.

'Diablo' is an 8- to 10-foot-tall (2.4–3 m) shrub with burgundy foliage that flowers in late spring, and 'Dart's Gold' has bright yellow leaves that turn to deep chartreuse. 'Coppertina' is a very popular cultivar bred from the two. It produces copper-colored foliage in spring that matures to a deep maroon color on its arching stems. It is highly adaptable and easy to grow.

Some cultivars of the shrub are smaller and more compact. 'Seward Summer Wine' reaches only 5 feet (1.5 m) high and displays reddish purple foliage with light pink flowers. 'Little Devil' grows to around 3 to 4 feet (1–1.2 m), with deep burgundy foliage that complements pink blooms.

GROWING NINEBARK

To a nursery-grown ninebark shrub, dig a hole as deep as the plant's container and twice as wide. Make sure the crown is even with the top of the soil surrounding the planting area. After setting it in place, gently fill the hole with backfill, making sure there are no air pockets. Water the plant well until it is established.

These shrubs like a sunny to lightly shaded location. Allow room for this well-branching shrub to spread out in the landscape. Ninebark can reach 6 to 10 feet (1.8–3 m) in height with a 6 to 8 foot (1.8–2.4 m) spread. Most gardeners prefer to let them grow naturally, so no pruning is necessary.

Once established, the plants are very drought tolerant and can thrive with only occasional watering. During spring, you can add compost and organic food. Apply a balanced fertilizer specifically developed for shrubs and trees. Spread it in a thin layer starting a few inches from the plant's trunk.

As mentioned above, pruning is not required for the health or growth of ninebark shrubs. You can, however, shape the plant and thin inner branches as you desire. Refrain from pruning to allow for the plant's excellent winter display of peeling bark.

Editor's Tip

If the leaves of your ninebark start curling, turning brown, or dropping off, the culprit could be clay soil. This compacted soil makes it hard for the shrub to absorb nutrients and water. Try mixing manure or compost into the soil or adding fine gravel to increase drainage.

Pieris

Pieris japonica, **most commonly known as Japanese andromeda or lily of the valley shrub, is prized for the bell-like flowers that cascade gracefully amid its deep-hued evergreen foliage. This early spring bloomer is popular for its long flowering period, as well as its colorful flower buds and all-season interest.**

The *Pieris* genus consists of seven species of evergreen shrubs in the heather family, or Ericaceae. Common varieties used in home landscaping include *P. japonica, P. floribunda,* and *P. formosa*). They are native to mountainous regions of eastern and southern Asia, eastern North America, and Cuba. Most species are admired for their year-round interest. The foliage of these varieties changes color throughout the seasons. In late summer or autumn, they have long, dangling clusters of colorful flower buds. In spring, these buds open into dramatic blossoms.

Sometimes referred to as lily-of-the-valley shrubs, these plants feature spirals of lance- or oval-shaped leaves and bell-shaped flowers. They can be used in shrub groupings or as a foundation plant. It can also easily stand alone as a specimen plant that few other shrubs can rival.

GROWING PIERIS

It is best to grow pieris on a site with full to partial shade and rich, well-drained soil with plenty of organic matter and an acidic pH. If your soil isn't particularly rich, work in a thick layer of compost before planting. If necessary, amend the soil with an azalea or camellia fertilizer to add nutrients and to adjust the pH level. Pieris shrubs won't tolerate alkaline soil.

Plant pieris in spring or autumn. Set the plant in a hole at the depth at which it grew in its container, and press down with your hands as you backfill the planting hole to eliminate air pockets. Water immediately after planting. If you are planting more than one shrub, allow approximately 6 or 7 feet (1.8 to 2.1 m) between each of them to encourage good air circulation. These shrubs can be susceptible to a number of fungal diseases; good air circulation will go a long way toward preventing them.

Keep the soil lightly moist at all times. Water slowly, allowing the soil to soak up as much moisture as possible. Fertilize in winter and early summer with a fertilizer designed for acid-loving plants, such as azaleas or camellias.

SCIENTIFIC NAME: *Pieris* spp.

FAMILY: Ericaceae

HEIGHT: 9 to 12 feet (2.7–3.7 m)

WIDTH: 6 to 8 feet (1.8–2.4 m)

BLOOMS: Late winter, early spring

SOIL pH: Acidic, neutral

LIGHT: Full sun to partial shade

Pieris Varieties

There are three main species of this dramatic, spring-blooming shrub to choose from.

- ***P. floribunda***, or the mountain andromeda, is a dense and bushy shrub from the eastern United States. It provides winter interest with flower buds that stand upright throughout the season and abundant spring blooms of creamy white flowers.
- ***P. formosa,*** known as Chinese or Himalayan pieris, is a species native to Nepal, the eastern Himalayas, Assam in India, Myanmar, Vietnam, and central and southern China. The 'Wakehurst' cultivar of this species received an Award of Garden Merit by the Royal Horticultural Society as an ornamental shrub credited for attracting pollinators. It produces red leaves in early spring that turn green and pretty white flowers.
- ***P. japonica,*** also known as Japanese andromeda, lily of the valley shrub, and Japanese pieris, is perhaps the most well known of the *Pieris* genus. Some noteworthy cultivars of the species include 'Mountain Fire,' with brilliant red foliage, 'Variegata,' with leaves in a variety of colors before maturing, and 'Purity,' a compact shrub with extra-large, pure white flowers.

Potentilla

Bright yellow flowers cover this low-growing shrub from spring to late summer or early autumn. Cheerful potentilla is great to use for mass plantings or as hedging. You can also plant one as an ornamental specimen in a mixed border, rock garden, or container. The flowers are also an important food source for butterflies and other pollinators.

A member of the rose family, potentilla *(Dasiphora fruticosa)* gets its name from its former genus, *Potentilla*, a name you will still find it listed under at many gardening sites. Also called shrubby cinquefoil, golden hardhack, bush cinquefoil, shrubby five-finger, widdy, and kuril tea, this plant is native to the cool temperate and subarctic regions of the Northern Hemisphere in Canada, the United States, Europe, and Northern Asia, where it can be found growing wild in high-altitude areas.

Bright yellow saucer-shaped flowers cover potentilla from early summer until autumn. The shrub grows to only about 1 to 3 feet (30 cm–1 m) tall, but what it lacks in size it makes up in ornamental impact. Gardeners in cold climates will find many uses for this hardy little shrub. Use it as a foundation plant, an addition to borders, in mass plantings, and as a ground cover.

GROWING POTENTILLA

Plant potentilla during the cooler months of spring or autumn, although spring will give it the best chance to establish itself for a full growing season. Potentilla needs full sun or light shade. A little shade during the heat of the day will help keep the plant blooming longer. It prefers moist, fertile, well-drained soil, but it will tolerate clay, rocky, alkaline, dry, or even poor soils.

If you are planting container specimens, cover the soil with 2 inches (5 cm) of compost, and mix it into the soil to about 6 to 8 inches (15–20 cm) deep. Dig a hole one and half times larger than the root ball, spacing each hole 3 to 6 feet (1–1.6 m) apart for every specimen. Remove the plants from the containers, and gently loosen the roots before placing them in a hole so that the top of the root ball is just slightly higher than the soil surface. Gently tamp down soil around the base of each plant, and then water well.

CARING FOR THE PLANTS

Strong disease and insect resistance makes caring for potentilla quite easy. This shrub grows wild in boggy soils, so water it during prolonged dry spells. It will survive without consistent watering, but it thrives when it gets plenty of moisture.

Give your potentilla plants a shovelful of compost in late spring as the flower buds begin to swell, or fertilize it with a complete fertilizer. Use organic mulch to help the soil retain moisture and discourage weeds. Pull back the mulch before the first freeze, and then push it back around the plant when the ground is frozen. At the end of the flowering season, cut out the old branches at ground level, or rejuvenate the shrub by cutting the entire plant back to ground level and allowing it to regrow. After a few years, it takes on an awkward shape unless you cut it all the way back.

SCIENTIFIC NAME: *Dasiphora fruticosa* (formerly *Potentilla fruticosa)*

FAMILY: Rosaceae

HEIGHT: 3 inches to 4 feet (7.5 cm–1.2 m)

WIDTH: 6 inches to 5 feet (25 cm–1.5 m)

BLOOMS: Spring to autumn

SOIL pH: Mildly acid, neutral, mildly alkaline

LIGHT: Full sun to light shade

Editor's Picks

Although the main species' shrubs produce single yellow flowers, you'll find many cultivars with color variations and some with double flowers. Here are just a few.

- **'Abbotswood' is a very popular cultivar with single white flowers and bluish green leaves.**
- **'Primrose Beauty' blooms in a soft shade of buttery yellow and has silvery leaves.**
- **'Medicine Wheel Mountain' has bright yellow flowers with ruffled petals. It is shorter than most cultivars and spreads about 4 feet (1.2 m) wide.**
- **'Sunset' has bright orange flowers that fade to yellow during the heat of summer.**
- **'UMan' features bicolored bright red-and-orange flowers.**

Quince

Flowering quince *(Chaenomeles* spp.) is an Asian native that blossoms in early spring. Although its bloom time is brief, it vivid color is worth it. These thorny bushes make superb hedges that will shelter songbirds, as well as ensure your privacy.

Quince shrubs *(Chaenomeles* spp.) are heritage ornamental plants with brief, but memorably dramatic, floral displays. Members of the rose family, they are multi-stemmed deciduous shrubs that bloom a slightly haphazard clutter of red, orange, white, or pink flowers alongside dark green shiny leaves. The flowers remain for about 10 to 14 days before being followed by yellowish green fruits. This genus is an old one and has been cultivated in Asia for thousands of years, but it didn't arrive in the United States until the 1800s.

Flowering quince shrubs are often used by gardeners as a barrier or border planting, especially because of their thorny habit. The plants light up the spring with a blaze of colorful blooms. They are also a favorite on farms because of their edible fruit. It helps that the plant is easy to care for and won't use up much of a gardener's time.

Various species and cultivars of quince shrubs exist, but the common flowering quince are most often planted in home gardens. This venerable species has numerous cultivars readily available at nurseries, garden centers, and online. Most of the different varieties are a similar size of about 6 to 10 (1.8–3 m) feet tall and wide.

Chaenomeles speciosa 'Moerloosei' is one such frequently sold variety, appreciated for its several-week-long bloom period. It produces white and pink flowers during early spring. *C. speciosa* 'Geisha Girl' is a 4-to-5-foot (1.3–1.5 m) plant with light orange flowers. For brighter orange flowers, *C. speciosa* 'Orange Delight' offers a rewarding and dazzling show of vibrant double blooms.

There are also some hybrids of the species *C. speciosa* and *C. japonica*, or Japanese quince. Hybrid *C.* x *superba* cultivars include 'Jet Trail' that produces white blooms, 'Crimson and Gold' with deep crimson blooms, and 'Pink Lady' with rich pink flowers.

SCIENTIFIC NAME: *Chaenomeles* spp.

FAMILY: Rosaceae

HEIGHT: 3 to 10 feet (1–3 m)

WIDTH: 3 to 10 feet (1–3 m)

BLOOMS: Winter, spring

SOIL pH: Acidic, neutral

LIGHT: Full sun

GROWING QUINCE

Quince shrubs are generally low maintenance and highly tolerant of both urban conditions and drought stress. These tough and undemanding plants will grow in sun or partial shade. They will, however, produce a more abundant bloom when exposed to full sunlight.

They accept most well-draining soils. Use a slightly acidic or neutral soil for the best flower display. Apply mulch as a weed suppressant and to retain soil moisture.

These plants will also grow faster and bloom more abundantly if you provide irrigation during dry periods. Water the plants in the morning to encourage excess moisture evaporation. In early spring, apply an all-purpose, slow-release fertilizer or compost as a soil amendment.

Quince shrubs form compact and virtually impenetrable hedges. They are perfect territory for sheltering bird nests and the homes of other small wildlife. The most difficult task when caring for quince is pruning a bush planted in too small a location to accommodate its full, mature size. Nonetheless, this plant will withstand severe pruning without problem, so don't hesitate to cut it down to the size you want.

Editor's Tip

Flowering quince is a great plant to use in rows that can form an impenetrable hedge to provide a security barrier. Be sure, however, to position any of these shrubs away from high-traffic areas—the thorns can cut anyone passing too close.

Rhododendron

SCIENTIFIC NAME: *Rhododendron* spp.

FAMILY: Ericaceae

HEIGHT: 5 to 20 feet (1.5–6 m)

WIDTH: 3 to 10 feet (1–3 m)

BLOOMS: Spring to early summer

SOIL pH: Acidic

LIGHT: Filtered, dappled sunlight

Pink and red rhododendron put on a springtime show under the dappled sunshine of a garden path through a wooded area. These bright bloomers work well in border edgings, mass plantings, and container groupings. They can also create hedges and privacy screens and are at home in any garden, from the most formal to the most casual.

Rhododendron is a large genus of more than a thousand species of evergreen and deciduous shrubs. Most species are native to eastern Asia and the Himalayas, and others hail from other regions of Asia, North America, Europe, and Australia. These shrubs can make an attractive, blooming specimen in many landscapes. They require acidic soil like other members of the heath family, including heather, pieris, and mountain laurel. Many species feature large, leathery, evergreen leaves and brightly colored flowers.

GROWING RHODODENDRONS

Rhododendrons are fairly low maintenance when planted properly. Growing them successfully requires an appropriate location and adequate soil preparation. For the most part, soil should be prepared in autumn, and shrubs should be planted in spring.

Unlike many blooming plants, they do not like full morning sun in winter and do best when planted in dappled shade on the north side of a building. Growing rhododendrons are happiest in a location protected from the wind and not under the eaves of a building.

Rhododendrons should be planted in groupings in prepared beds, rather than in individual planting holes. The soil must be well-draining, loamy, and fertile, with the proper pH. Use a soil test to ensure that the pH is between 4.5 and 5.5. A 50% ratio of organic matter is encouraged as a soil amendment, because it provides aeration and drainage and will allow the plant to set higher. Agriculture sulfur can also be used, but avoid aluminum sulfate, which can be harmful to the plant.

The bushes will likely be purchased as a containerized plants or a balled and burlapped specimens. The root balls should be well moisturized prior to planting. Place each plant in a tub or bucket for a brief soaking until air bubbles disappear. Then situate in the ground so that its crown is at the same level as in the pot. Water thoroughly, and cover with an organic mulch, which will break down to supply nutrients as it decomposes. A pine bark covering applied at 2 inches (5 cm) is thought to inhibit fungi that cause root rot.

Rhododendrons require fertilization once a year following a hard freeze in autumn or early spring. Use a specialized fertilizer for acid-loving plants, such as organic cottonseed meal. The organic material you have worked into the soil previously will break down to provide some of the necessary nutrients.

Consistently moist soil is necessary, but too much water creates problems for the growing rhododendrons. Curling and twisting leaves indicate that water is needed immediately. The bush should not be allowed to go through the stress of wilting. You may wish to introduce shade-loving annuals as companion plants, which will indicate when water is needed.

Once established properly, your rhododendrons need only adequate watering, pruning, and deadheading of the flowers to encourage their abundant return.

Editor's Picks

There are a wealth of options when choosing a rhododendron. Here is just a small sampling.

- 'Black Satin' features deep pink flowers and coal black foliage.
- 'Blue Peter' has violet-blue flowers and mid-green leaves.
- 'Boule de Neige' has dense evergreen foliage with pink buds that open to white flowers.
- 'Bow Bells' has magenta buds that open to pale pink.
- 'Elviira' features cherry red flowers and dark evergreen foliage.
- 'Nova Zembla' features dark green foliage with scarlet flowers.
- 'Windsong' is an evergreen with citrus yellow blooms.

Rose of Sharon

SCIENTIFIC NAME: *Hibiscus syriacus*

FAMILY: Malvaceae

HEIGHT: 8 to 12 feet (2.4–3.7 m)

WIDTH: 6 to 10 feet (1.8–3 m)

BLOOMS: Summer, autumn

SOIL pH: Acidic, neutral

LIGHT: Full sun to partial shade

Rose of Sharon displays an abundance of big, showy flowers that come in various hues, including pink, purple, lavender, red, blue, and white, often with dark throats. Mass them together to create gorgeous privacy hedges or windbreaks or use singly as specimens.

Rose of Sharon *(Hibiscus syriacus)*, a native of Korea and south-central and southeast China, is a large deciduous flowering shrub in the mallow family, Malvaceae. Also known as shrub althea, Syrian ketmia, and rose mallow, it grows to about 9 to 12 feet (2.7–3.7 m) tall and often reaches a spread of 10 feet (3 m). With these impressive dimensions, it can work beautifully as a blooming privacy border or as a natural windbreak.

Flamboyant flowers appear in summer in shades of white, red, pink, and purple, adding long-lasting summer color with little fuss. The large, five-petaled blooms (3 inches, or 7.5 cm in diameter) attract birds, butterflies, and other beneficial pollinators.

Depending on the cultivar, its silhouette can vary. Some rose of Sharon varieties have attractive drooping branches, while others assume an upright silhouette. Care for this shrub can depend on the form taken by your specimen.

GROWING ROSE OF SHARON

Rose of Sharon is best planted into rich, slightly acidic soil in a full-sun to partial-shade location. It prefers moist, well-draining soil, although it will tolerate most soil conditions, except those that are soggy or extremely dry. A top dressing of organic compost or mulch can benefit the bush.

Because of a large, dense habit, it makes an excellent living wall when planted in rows. When left untended, though, it will drop its seeds close to the parent plant. In spring, these seeds will easily germinate and grow into new plants. This means it can quickly form colonies, which has caused it to be considered invasive in some areas. When including rose of Sharon in your landscape, consider this reseeding habit. Prepare to remove additional plants appearing in unwanted areas. These can be relocated to a more desirable location or shared with friends.

After planting, this attractive shrub can thrive even with neglect, other than some occasional pruning for shape. Flowers grow on the current year's growth, so early pruning before buds develop can keep it growing it in top form and keep the tree-like shrub in bounds.

COMMON PROBLEMS

Bud drop can be a problem. This can be caused in part when a rose of Sharon bush is under stressful conditions, so try to keep the shrub as happy as possible. Too little water or too much fertilization may contribute to bud drop. Monitor conditions on a growing shrub, and you will be rewarded with a long season of lovely single or double blooms.

READ MORE AT GARDENING KNOW HOW

To learn more about these vibrantly flowered shrubs, follow the links below.

- **"Rose of Sharon Seed Propagation: Harvesting and Growing Rose of Sharon Seeds"** (URL = gkh.us/96598)
- **"Rose of Sharon Winter Care: Preparing Rose of Sharon for Winter"** (URL = gkh.us/96603)
- **"Rose of Sharon Fertilizer Guide: Learn How to Feed an Althea Plant"** (URL = gkh.us/113493)
- **"Rose of Sharon Problems – Dealing with Common Althea Plant Issues"** (URL = gkh.us/113489)

Spiraea

SCIENTIFIC NAME: *Spiraea* spp.

FAMILY: Rosaceae

HEIGHT: 1 to 20 feet (30 cm–6 m)

WIDTH: 2 to 10 feet (60 cm–3 m)

BLOOMS: Spring, summer

SOIL pH: Neutral

LIGHT: Full sun to light shade

Bridal wreath spiraea *(Spiraea prunifolia)* features clusters of small white flowers that are traditionally made into wedding wreaths, which is where it gets its common name. No matter which spiraea variety you choose, these shrubs are sure to add interest and lasting beauty to your landscape for many years to come.

Novice and experienced gardeners alike love spiraea bushes for their eye-catching beauty, fast growth rate, hardiness, and ease of care. These deciduous shrubs can be divided into two categories: spring blooming and summer blooming. The spring-blooming spiraea has a delicate cascading habit with large clusters of white flowers poised on arching branches. The summer-blooming bush boasts beautiful pink, white, or red flowers atop upright branches. Both varieties are prized for their lovely shapes and flowers.

Native to the temperate Northern Hemisphere, spiraea (sometimes spelled "spirea" in common names) is also known as meadowsweet or steeplebush. The genus name *Spiraea* comes from the Greek word for "twisting" after the pod-like fruits that have a twisting appearance.

GROWING SPIRAEA

Hardy in just about any growing zone, spiraea is an easy shrub to grow. Nursery-grown specimens are available at most garden centers and should be planted during the spring or autumn for best results.

Depending on the variety, spirea bushes grow from 2 to 6 feet (60 cm–1.8 m) tall. Be sure to place your bush in a location that will accommodate its mature size. Spiraea bushes do very well as a focal plant in the landscape or as part of a larger grouping for a screen or border.

It does best when planted in full sun or light shade—full shade results in stunted growth and a reduction in the number and size of blooms. Position it in an area with well-drained soil: it does not like wet feet. Once planted, the care requires a minimal time investment.

Adding mulch around the base will help retain moisture, and regular summer watering will promote healthy blooms and growth.

Spiraea blooms consistently and profusely on new wood, but after some time the plant begins to look a bit bedraggled. Pruning it after a couple of years will rejuvenate it. Prune summer-blooming spiraea bushes during the winter or in the spring. Spring bloomers can be pruned right after the flowers are gone. Remove dead wood and trim canes of spring varieties to the ground. Trimming spiraea back, in many cases, will induce a second bloom.

Few problems bother these hardy shrubs. Aphids may become an issue, but they are rarely serious enough to warrant treatment.

Spiraea Varieties

Many types of spiraea will work well in your garden. Below are just a few popular choices available.

- ***S. betulifolia,*** or birchleaf spiraea, is best known for its autumn foliage, which dazzles in purple, orange, and red hues.
- ***S. billardii*** 'Triumphans' is prized for its summertime display of dark pink blossoms.
- ***S. densiflora*** is a spring-bloomer with bright pink flowers and attractive, long-lasting foliage.
- ***S. hunbergii,*** called early spiraea for its early-spring bloom, also puts on a show in autumn with brilliant purple, orange, burgundy, red, and yellow foliage.
- ***S. japonica,*** or Japanese spiraea, is popular for its wide array of sizes, forms, colors, and textures. Always check with your local agricultural authorities, however, before deciding to plant this species: it has been declared invasive in a variety of habitats.
- ***S. prunifolia***, known as bridal wreath spiraea, is a large species, with wide-arching branches dotted with romantic white flowers. During autumn, the foliage bursts into blazing reds, oranges, and yellows.

Sweetshrub

SCIENTIFIC NAME: *Calycanthus* spp.

FAMILY: Calycanthaceae

HEIGHT: 6 to 10 feet (1.8–3 m)

WIDTH: Up to 12 feet (3.7 m)

BLOOMS: Mid-spring to early summer

SOIL pH: Acidic, alkaline, neutral

LIGHT: Full sun to shade

Sweetshrub *(Calycanthus floridus)* displays dusky maroon blooms. Also known as Carolina allspice, this is an attractive shrub with flowers that emit a spicy, cinnamon-like fragrance. This fragrance attracts beetles, which are their key pollinators.

Calycanthus, most often called sweetshrub, is a genus of flowering plants in the family Calycanthaceae. There are species within this genus that are native to areas in both the western and eastern United States, where it grows in the understory of deciduous woodlands, as well as in eastern China. You don't often see sweetshrub in cultivated landscapes, possibly because the flowers are usually hidden beneath the outer layer of foliage. Whether you can see them or not, you'll enjoy the fruity fragrance when the maroon to rusty brown flowers bloom in mid-spring. A few of the cultivars have yellow or white flowers. The foliage is also fragrant when crushed.

Two sweetshrubs, *Calycanthus floridus* and *C. occidentalis*, are rarities in the plant world because their flowers are pollinated by beetles. This came about because the primitive flowers, which are formed from undifferentiated sepals and petals (tepals) arranged in a spiral, evolved before the advent of winged insects. Beetles, which are essential for their pollination, are attracted to the spicy scent of the flowers' volatile oils.

Because the flowers and leaves are both fragrant, they were once often placed in dresser drawers and trunks to keep clothes and linens smelling fresh. They are also great to add into potpourris. *Calycanthus* oils are used today in the perfume industry, and the plant is used as a traditional medicine by Native Americans.

Three particular species are often cultivated as ornamentals by nurseries, especially in the United States and England.

- *C. chinensis*, with white flowers, is native to China and known as Chinese sweetshrub and Chinese wax shrub. It is used extensively in the breeding of cultivars.
- *C. floridus* is native to the eastern United States, from New York south to Florida. Known as Carolina spicebush, Carolina allspice, and eastern sweetshrub, this species is often planted in gardens, as a specimen shrub, or massed as hedges.
- *C. occidentalis*, known as California spicebush and western sweetshrub, is often seen in traditional, native plant, and wildlife gardens.

GROWING SWEETSHRUB

Sweetshrubs are undemanding plants, adapting well to most soils and thriving in a variety of climates. They grow in any exposure, from full sun to shade. They aren't picky about the soil. Alkaline and wet soils aren't a problem, although they prefer good drainage. They also tolerate strong winds, making them useful as a windbreak.

Care of these shrubs is simple. Water then often enough to keep the soil moist, and a layer of mulch over the root zone will help the soil hold moisture and reduce watering.

The method of pruning a sweetshrub bush depends upon how you use it. It makes a good deciduous hedge and can be sheared to maintain the shape. In shrub borders and as specimens, thin sweetshrub bushes to several upright branches arising from the ground. If left untrimmed, expect a height of 9 feet (2.7 m) with a spread of 12 feet (3.7 m). The shrubs can be pruned to shorter heights for use as a foundation plant.

COMMON PROBLEMS

Part of sweetshrub care involves protection from disease issues. Watch for bacterial crown gall, which causes a warty growth at the soil line. Unfortunately, there is no cure and the plant should be destroyed to prevent the spread of the disease. Once a shrub is affected, the soil is contaminated, so don't replace another sweetshrub in the same location.

It is also susceptible to powdery mildew. The presence of the disease usually means that the air circulation around the plant is poor. Thin out some of the stems to allow air to move freely through the plant. If air is blocked by nearby plants, consider thinning them as well.

Note. The flowers and seeds of sweetshrub are poisonous.

Viburnum

Beautiful white balls of blooming *Viburnum opulus,* known as snowball viburnum, make a showy display in a spring garden. It is just one of the many gorgeous viburnum shrubs.

SCIENTIFIC NAME: *Viburnum* spp.

FAMILY: Adoxaceae

HEIGHT: 3 to 20 feet (1–6 m)

WIDTH: 3 to 12 feet (1–3.7 m)

BLOOMS: Early spring to midsummer

SOIL pH: Neutral, acidic

LIGHT: Full sun to partial shade

"A garden without a viburnum is akin to life without music or art," said renowned horticulturist, Dr. Michael Dirr. With over 150 species of *Viburnum* that can boast of interesting foliage, attractive and fragrant flowers, and showy berries, you'll have a hard time picking just one variety.

Native throughout the temperate Northern Hemisphere, viburnums are a group of large-flowering evergreen or deciduous shrubs and small trees. Many have either white or pink blooms in early spring. Also commonly referred to as cranberry bush, viburnums are often used as ornamental fixtures in the home landscape. They are also used in shrub borders or as hedges and screening. The larger varieties of viburnums also make excellent focal points as specimen plantings.

There are several different types. One of the more well-known species is the old-fashioned snowball viburnum *(V. opulus)* with beautiful globes of white blooms. Varieties popular for their intoxicating fragrance include the Asian hybrids Cayuga and Burkwood. There are also viburnums prized for their autumn foliage or berries, such as the southern arrowwood *(V. dentatum)* that produces attractive purplish red leaves. For lovely blue-green foliage, try tea viburnum *(V. setigerum).* Species with interesting berry color include those that change as they ripen from green to pink, yellow, or red to blue or black, such as blackhaw viburnum *(V. prunifolium)* that turns from red to black.

GROWING VIBURNUM

Most homeowners choose container-grown plants from a local nursery. When planting, pay attention to the individual needs of the particular species. Most viburnums prefer full sun, but many will also tolerate partial shade. While not particularly picky about their growing conditions, they generally prefer fertile, well-draining soil.

Plant in spring or fall. Gently remove the specimen from its container, and dig a hole as deep as the root ball but at least two to three times wider to ensure it has space to spread. Backfill with some of the soil, and then add water to the hole before filling in with the remaining dirt. If you are planting more than one, space them anywhere from 5 to 15 feet (1.5–4.6 m) apart, depending on their size at maturity and their use in the landscape.

Water the shrubs every 7 to 10 days during dry periods. It will also help to add a 2-inch (5 cm) layer of mulch to retain moisture. You can apply a slow-release fertilizer to viburnums, as well, but this isn't required.

Pruning is normally done for shaping purposes and to remove any dead, diseased, or broken branches. If you notice leggy shoots, trim them back in early summer to maintain the shrub's form. Be sure to prune only after a shrub is done blooming.

Viburnum has few pest issues, but the viburnum leaf beetle *(Pyrrhalta viburni)* can be a real threat. If you see these pests, remove egg-infested leaves. You can apply organic pesticides, but avoid synthetic pesticides that kill beneficial insects.

READ MORE AT GARDENING KNOW HOW

With so much variety, it may be hard to sort through the pros and cons of each viburnum. To find out more about some of its varieties, follow the links below.

- **"Judd Viburnum Care — How to Grow a Judd Viburnum Plant"** (URL = gkh.us/100526)
- **"Koreanspice Viburnum Care: Growing Koreanspice Viburnum Plant"** (URL = gkh.us/100573)
- **"Growing Dwarf Viburnums —Learn About Small Viburnum Shrubs"** (URL = gkh.us/134564)

Weigela

Weigela is an excellent spring-blooming shrub that can add flair and color to your spring garden. Its petite flowers will also attract hummingbirds and butterflies

This old-fashioned beauty is a member of the honeysuckle family, the Caprifoliaceae. Native to eastern Asia, it was first imported to Europe in the mid-1800s and went on to become a favorite ornamental. This dense, compact shrub blooms profusely in spring and sporadically through the summer with five-lobed white, pink, red, and sometimes yellow flowers surrounded by oblong leaves with serrated margins. The most popular variety is *Weigela florida,* which charms with its pretty pink flowers and striking variegated foliage. All varieties work well for shrub borders and foundation plantings. Because they are at their best when in flower, consider including them in mixed borders with other shrubs that provide different seasonal interest.

Dwarf cultivars are also available of various weigelas. Caring for these smaller plants involves less pruning, and they need less room for their growth. Dwarf varieties also grow well in containers. Just find a full sun area you would like to decorate with attractive blooms.

GROWING WEIGELA

A tough and hardy shrub, weigela needs little more than the right spot watering as necessary. Most are cultivated from nursery-grown specimens. As with any shrub planting, learn the mature size of the bush, and be sure to allow room in the landscape for its full growth. Leave the equivalent space when positioning your new plants.

Choose a location with moist, well-draining soil that receives full sun for the greatest show of springtime blooms. Weigela can also be planted in light shade, and blooms will appear, but flowering will not be as abundant.

Growing shrubs should be fertilized once a year. A regular, balanced plant food in late winter can promote more springtime blooms.

Pruning weigelas helps keep them looking healthy and beautiful. Mature bushes benefit from the removal of older interior branches in late winter to improve the shrub's vigor and bloom the next year. Following its spring bloom, you can give it a light pruning for shape. Trimming weigela bushes right after they bloom will keep you from inadvertently pruning off next year's flowers.

At a Glance

SCIENTIFIC NAME: *Weigela florida*

FAMILY: Caprifoliaceae

HEIGHT: 1 to 10 feet (30 cm–3 m)

WIDTH: 18 inches to 12 feet (45 cm–3.7 m)

BLOOMS: Spring, early summer

SOIL pH: Acidic

LIGHT: Partial to full sun

Editor's Picks

Once considered a bit passé, weigela is making a comeback, with innovative breeders creating exciting new cultivars. Here are just a few.

- 'Czechmark Trilogy' blooms in pink, red, and white in spring to early summer. It grows to heights of 3 to 4 feet (1–1.2 m) with a mounding habit that creates an equal spread.
- 'Eyecatcher' is a compact shrub that grows to 2 feet tall (60 cm) and wide. It displays bold, variegated foliage and produces deep red flowers in late spring.
- 'Magical Fantasy' grows to 4 feet (1.2 m) and has blooms ranging from pale pastel pink to deep rose and green and white foliage.
- 'Ghost' grows to about 4 to 5 feet (1.2–1.5 m) with deep red flowers and chartreuse foliage that pales to a shiny pale yellow in summer.
- 'Polka' reaches 5 feet (1.5 cm) tall and wide and features yellow-throated, pink flowers that bloom from early summer to early autumn.
- 'Red Prince' grows 5 to 6 feet tall (1.5–1.8 m) and displays bright red flowers on arching stems in late spring, then again in late summer.
- 'Sonic Bloom Pink' bursts into bright pink bloom in early spring and continues all summer long. It reaches 4 to 5 feet (1.2–1.5 m) tall with a matching spread.
- 'Wine and Roses' has deep, wine-colored foliage and pink rose-like booms. It grows to a height of 5 feet (1.5 m) with a similar spread.

Witch Hazel

Witch hazel is a beautiful flowering shrub that blooms in winter. Placing it near a cool-colored evergreen will help bring out its warm, golden hues.

The witch hazel bush *(Hamamelis virginiana)* is a small tree with fragrant yellow blooms. A member of the Hamamelidaceae family, it is closely related to the sweet gum. Witch hazel has many common names, but the generic name means "together with fruit," which refers to the fact that this is the only tree in North America to have flowers, ripe fruit, and next year's leaf buds on its branches at the same time.

The "witch" in its name does not refer to a woman with magical powers, but is instead derived from the Anglo-Saxon word *wych,* meaning "bend." Found in woody areas, witch hazel, also called water-witch, has flexible branches, which might have led to its use as a divining tool to dowse for underground sources of water and minerals. These days, witch hazel is commonly used to treat insect bites and sunburn and as a refreshing lotion for after shaving.

Witch hazel shrubs can reach 30 feet (9 m) high and 15 feet (4.6 m) wide at maturity, and this size mean that they are often referred to as a tree. The plant sets out fragrant yellow flowers that resemble dainty ribbons in the autumn.

Growing witch hazel shrubs is a favorite amongst gardeners looking for winter color and fragrance. Many people plant witch hazel in a location where they can enjoy not only its beauty but also its sweet aroma. These shrubs are excellent for use in borders and mixed hedges, or even alone as a specimen plant if given enough room to spread.

GROWING WITCH HAZEL

One of witch hazel's draws is that it flowers during the cold winter months and can thrive in thriving in both cold and hot temperatures, as long as humidity levels are moderate. It is possible to propagate witch hazel from seeds, but it can take up to two years to germinate, so most gardeners looking to add this plant to their landscaping choose to transplant a nursery-grown specimen.

Early spring or late autumn is the best time for planting. Look for a sunny location, and if you live in a hot climate, one that also gets a bit of afternoon shade. Even though they are considered understory plants, they will thrive in partial shade to full sun.

Witch hazel shrubs like likes rich, loamy, moist soil that is acidic to neutral, but they are adaptable to varying pH levels. If you need to enrich your soil add some compost. Be sure to keep an eye on rainfall—young plants need regular watering, especially during dry spells.

Care for established shrubs requires minimal time apart from regular watering the first season. You can also apply a well-balanced, liquid fertilizer once a month throughout the summer season. Because it thrives in the cold winter months, overwintering is typically no problem. Witch hazel is not bothered by any serious pests or disease and will tolerate some browsing deer. Some homeowners, who have a lot of deer, put netting around the base of young shrubs to keep the deer from munching.

If you want to preserve and accentuate its horizontal growth habit, prune regularly just after the plant finishes flowering. Then, in autumn, prune out suckers growing from the base of the shrub. You'll want to prune witch hazel back severely if the shrubs are old and need rejuvenation. Prune to rejuvenate them just after flowering.

SCIENTIFIC NAME: *Hamamelis virginiana*

FAMILY: Hamamelidaceae

HEIGHT: 10 to 30 feet (3–9 m)

WIDTH: Up to 15 feet (4.6 m)

BLOOMS: Autumn, winter

SOIL pH: Acidic, neutral, alkaline

LIGHT: Full sun to partial shade

To explore two other lovely witch hazel varieties, *Hamamelis x intermedia* 'Jelena' and Chinese witch hazel *(H. mollis),* follow the links below.

- **"How to Grow Jelena Witch Hazel"** (URL = gkh.us/112951)
- **"Chinese Witch Hazel Plant — How to Grow Chinese Witch Hazel "** (URL = gkh.us/144225)

FOLIAGE SHRUBS

A Eurasian blackcap munches on a bright red cotoneaster berry. Many foliage shrubs produce drupes and berries that feed birds in the autumn and winter.

Foliage shrubs are the backbones of home landscaping. These are the plants that camouflage unsightly aspects of a property, such as the house foundation, AC units, chain-link fences, or pool equipment. They create verdant backdrops for some of the showier garden plants, and evergreen varieties provide color in an otherwise barren wintertime landscape. For newly built houses, there are fast-growing varieties that will add almost-instant interest to a plain yard. Grouped together, they form privacy screens and windbreaks that provide protection from the elements.

Despite their utilitarian reputation, many are stunners in their own right. Greenery ranges in color from lime to deep hunter, and there are golden shrubs, blue-green ones, and others with a mix of hues. Some grow in cones, others in mounds, and still others as tall pyramids. Some have stiff branches; others gracefully droop. Shrubs like yew and boxwood can be trimmed into elegantly architectural or whimsically fantastical shapes in topiary gardens. Privet is often used to create intricate garden mazes and labyrinths. Foliage shrubs are only limited by your own imagination.

HOME FOR WILDLIFE

For nature lovers, one of the great things about these kinds of shrubs is that they can attract beneficial wildlife. Hollies and junipers, for example, produce colorful berries that birds love, and many shrubs have dense foliage that provides safe nesting sites and shelter from harsh weather.

Groupings of shrubs and small trees in a range of colors, from golden to deep green, create a private corner in a backyard for dining and relaxing.

Dig Deeper

READ MORE AT GARDENING KNOW HOW

Learn more about these plants that form the backbone of your landscaping plans.

- **"Full Sun Evergreens: Growing Sun Loving Evergreen Plants"** (URL = gkh.us/141007)
- **"Planting Near Your Home: Foundation Plants for the Front Yard"** (URL = gkh.us/1847)
- **"Dwarf Shrubs for Gardens — Choosing Bushes for Small Spaces"** (URL = gkh.us/104946)

Arborvitae

Tall cones of arborvitae make a natural hedge for privacy and are ideal for creating windbreaks. Novice gardeners will be particularly rewarded when planting these tall, conical shrubs, due to their low maintenance and uncomplicated growth patterns.

Arborvitae belongs to the genus *Thuja,* a classification of coniferous trees and shrubs in the cypress family. Of the five species in the genus, two are native to North America, with the other three originating in eastern Asia. A native tree can reach heights as high as 60 feet (18 m), but those used for home planting will never top a quarter of that.

Arborvitae, which means "tree of life" in Latin, is one of the most versatile and attractive trees or shrubs found in the landscape. It is useful as a hedge material, in pots, or as an interesting focal point for the garden. Planting an arborvitae hedge provides security and a beautiful screen for parts of a property better left hidden.

This easy-to-grow evergreen comes in a wide variety of sizes and colors, providing a solution for almost any landscape situation.

GROWING ARBORVITAE

Like most evergreen plants, for best results, arborvitaes are planted when they are not actively growing. Depending on where you live, they may be planted in late winter if soils are workable, or you might have to wait until early spring when the earth has thawed.

They are usually sold balled and burlapped, which means the root system is protected from harsh conditions and allows greater leeway on when to plant than with bare-root trees. They can also be established in the ground in late autumn if the base is covered with a thick layer of bark or organic mulch.

Location and soil conditions are the primary concerns. It prefers to be planted in moist, well-drained soil in a spot that gets full sun or even partial shade. Check drainage before planting, and add grit to a depth of 8 inches (20 cm) if your soil retains too much moisture. The best soil will have pH levels of 6.0 to 8.0, and it should have a good amount of organic material worked in to increase its structure and nutrient levels.

These scale-leaved evergreens have a broad, spreading root system, which tends to be near the surface. Dig the hole twice as wide and deep as the root ball to allow roots to spread as the tree becomes established.

Water frequently for the first few months, and then begin to taper off as the plants establish themselves. Irrigate deeply when you do water, and ensure that plants don't dry out in hot, punishing summer weather.

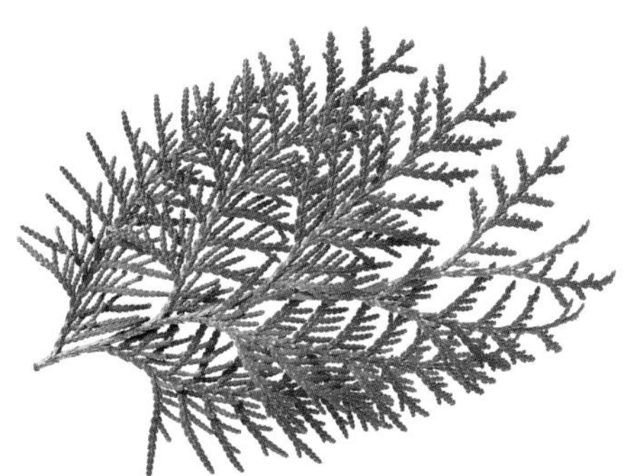

At a Glance

SCIENTIFIC NAME: *Thuja* spp.

FAMILY: Cupressaceae

HEIGHT: 12 inches to 15 feet (30 cm–4.6 m)

WIDTH: 3 to 8 feet (1–2.4 m)

FOLIAGE COLOR: Various shades of green

SOIL pH: Acidic, alkaline

LIGHT: Full to partial sun

CARING FOR THE PLANTS

Arborvitaes require very little pruning and have naturally graceful, pyramidal shapes. If you use them in formal hedges, you can shape them with hedge shears in early spring. Otherwise, just prune off any damaged branches, as needed. In spring, apply a 3-inch (7.5 cm) layer of mulch around the base of the tree and fertilize in spring with a good all-purpose landscape fertilizer.

Watch for spider mite infestations during hot, dry weather. Deep watering and spraying off the foliage can minimize these pests' presence.

Editor's Picks

There are several varieties of arborvitae that are particularly well suited for home planting.

- **'Brandon' is a classic conical evergreen and is mildly fragrant. It can reach a height of 15 feet (4.6 m) and a width of 8 feet (2.4 m).**
- **'Emerald Green' is a hedge plant favorite in a stunning bright green. It grows to 15 feet (4.6 m) tall and 4 feet wide (1.2 m).**
- **'Golden Globe' is a globe shape with yellow-green to golden foliage and sized about 4 feet tall by 4 feet wide (1.2 x 1.2 m).**
- **'North Pole' is a tall, narrow variety in bright green that is perfect for privacy hedges. It grows to 15 feet (4.6 m) tall and 5 feet (1.5 m) wide.**
- **'Tom Thumb' is a rounded miniature that stays tiny at 12 to 15 inches (30–38 cm) tall, making it great for containers or rock gardens.**

Boxwood

The dense evergreen foliage of the boxwood lends itself to shaping for hedges and topiaries, so this popular shrub is often planted in elegant and formal gardens.

Buxus is a genus of about 70 species in the family Buxaceae, which are spread across the globe, with species that are native to western and southern Europe; southwest, southern and eastern Asia; Africa; Madagascar; northernmost South America; Central America; Mexico; and the Caribbean. The majority are tropical or subtropical plants, but the European and some Asian species are frost-tolerant. Many boxwood varieties and cultivars exist. The varieties seen in so many gardens, called boxwood—or just "box"—are dense, evergreen shrubs that are often planted in elegant and formal landscapes. Boxwoods are grown for foliage, as their flowers are insignificant.

Growing boxwood in your home landscape allows you to create a formal hedge, a symmetrical border, or a matching pair of shrubs to balance an entryway. Boxwoods can also be planted as focal points or foundation plantings.

GROWING BOXWOOD

As slow-growing landscape plants, boxwoods are valuable and, consequently, they are expensive. Take time to carefully choose where to plant your boxwood. Make sure to plant them in a spot most appropriate for their needs. A full- or part-sun location is needed for optimum growth. They require well-drained soil, and although the plants prefer organic soil, their soil needs are adaptable.

When planting boxwoods, consider your year-round climate. If temperatures become extremely hot in summer, boxwoods will appreciate afternoon shade and regular watering. Water deeply, because frequent, shallow irrigation will not reach the root zone of the growing shrub. Until established, after about two years, boxwoods will need at least weekly watering.

Locate them in an area that is protected from winter wind to avoid a condition called winter bronzing. Plant at the same level they were planted at the nursery or in the container: planting too deeply can lead to stress and possibly death.

CARING FOR THE PLANTS

Water and mulch properly for a long-lived, vigorous specimen. Properly mulching the shallow-rooted boxwood helps retain moisture and keeps roots cool. Growing boxwoods should have a 2-to-3-inch (5–7.5 cm) layer of mulch extending 12 inches (30 cm) past the foliage. As with all shrub mulching, trunks should not be covered.

SCIENTIFIC NAME: *Buxus* spp.

FAMILY: Buxaceae

HEIGHT: 2 to 8 feet (60 cm–2.4 m)

WIDTH: 2 to 8 feet (60 cm–2.4 m)

FOLIAGE COLOR: Light to dark green

SOIL pH: Neutral, alkaline

LIGHT: Full to partial sun

Aside from watering and mulching, growing boxwood is a low-maintenance task, unless you wish to keep them as a sheared hedge. Shearing, or pruning, is the most time-consuming part of boxwood care, but you will be rewarded with a healthy, long-lasting hedge. Older boxwood care will include thinning limbs to allow sunshine to reach the inner foliage.

COMMON PROBLEMS

The boxwood leaf miner is the most common pest you will encounter. If foliage begins to yellow, treat it with organic oil or insecticidal sprays. Phytophthora root rot may result from soggy soils.

Yearly soil tests can determine if soil pH levels for boxwood is correct: between 6.5 and 7. It is best to test the soil before planting. The pH level can be raised with the addition of lime and lowered by sulfur.

READ MORE AT GARDENING KNOW HOW

Learn more about the different types of boxwood and how you can shape them.

- **"Common Boxwood Varieties: Learn About Different Types of Boxwoods "** (URL = gkh.us/84093)
- **"Best Topiary Shrubs — Choosing Shrub Topiary Varieties"** (URL = gkh.us/166786)

Cotoneaster

The herringbone pattern of the branches of rock cotoneaster *(Cotoneaster horizontalis)* creates an interesting basketweave effect on a wall or the ground. Birds flock to the bright red berries in autumn, and the neat pink flowers of summer are a magnet for bees.

SCIENTIFIC NAME: *Cotoneaster* spp.

FAMILY: Rosaceae

HEIGHT: 6 inches to 10 feet (15 cm–3 m)

WIDTH: 18 inches to 15 feet (45 cm–4.6 m)

FOLIAGE COLOR: Green to red

SOIL pH: Acidic, neutral, alkaline

LIGHT: Full sun to partial shade

Cotoneaster is a genus of flowering plants in the rose family native to temperate Asia, Europe, and North Africa. With its host of species, whether you're looking for a 6-inch (15 cm) ground cover or a 10-foot (3 m) privacy hedge, you are sure to find a cotoneaster that will meet your needs.

They vary in size, but the many species of cotoneaster all have a few things in common. They typically have a wide spread three times or more of their height, glossy leaves, and red or black fall and winter berries. Growing cotoneaster is a snap, as most species shrug off adverse conditions like drought, strong winds, salt spray, infertile soil, and variable pH levels.

GROWING COTONEASTER

You can propagate cotoneaster from seed or stem cuttings, but most people buy container or bare-root plants from garden centers and nurseries. Autumn is the time to transplant cotoneaster.

Cotoneaster care is easy if you plant in a good location. They need full sun or partial shade and thrive in fertile soils but tolerate any soil as long as it is well-drained. Most types of cotoneaster are hardy in areas with average extreme low temperatures of between 20° (-7° C) to -20° F (-29° C).

To transplant a nursery specimen, dig a hole twice the width and depth of the root ball. Mix in one to two shovelfuls of organic matter, such as aged compost, leaf mold, or well-rotted manure. Gently remove the plant from the container, and untangle any matted roots. Place so that the crown of the root ball is at ground level. Backfill with the removed soil, and firmly pat it into place. Regularly water gently during the first growing season.

Apply a thick layer of mulch around ground cover types soon after planting to suppress weeds. It's difficult to weed around the low-growing plants once they begin to spread.

CARING FOR THE PLANTS

Cotoneaster shrubs only need watering during prolonged dry spells and do fine without regular fertilization, but shrubs that don't seem to be growing might benefit from a light dose of a complete fertilizer.

Prune cotoneaster shrubs any time of year. Most types only need light pruning to remove wayward branches or to control disease. To keep the plants looking neat, cut out selected branches all the way to the base rather than shearing or shortening them.

Note: Cotoneaster berries are toxic to humans and animals.

Editor's Picks

Cotoneaster has many uses in the garden, depending on the species. Here is a list of common types.

- **Rock cotoneaster *(C. horizontalis)* is a branched variety with green leaves in the summer and scarlet berries in the fall. It is perfect for slopes, so use it for ground cover or hedges on hills.**
- **Hedge cotoneaster *(C. lucidus)* and many-flowered cotoneaster *(C. multiflorus)* are great for screening hedges. Hedge cotoneaster can be sheared as a formal hedge, but many-flowered cotoneaster develops a naturally rounded shape on its own.**
- **Cranberry cotoneaster *(C. apiculatus)* makes a good ground cover for erosion control, especially on slopes. Pink summer blossoms are followed by small, red berries in autumn, along with bronzy red foliage.**
- **Bearberry *(C. dammeri)*, a low-growing ground cover, has white flowers in spring, followed by red fruit in late summer and bronzy purple foliage in autumn.**
- **Spreading cotoneaster *(C. divaricatus)* is a bushy shrub with white summer flowers followed by yellow and red autumn colors and red berries. Use it as a hedge or a tall foundation plant.**

Dwarf Norway Spruce

The bright golden-tipped needles of *Picea abies* 'Little Gem' seem to give the garden a verdant glow. Try planting one of the dwarf Norway Spruce varieties in a rockery, along a path, or in a container with annual plants. The shrub is fragrant when needles are crushed and also useful on sloping ground and exposed, windy hillsides.

A dwarf Norway spruce (*Picea abies*) is one of the best small evergreen shrub species for the landscape. There are several varieties, all of which produce compact mounds of green foliage that complement any bed, foundation planting, container, or pathway edge. Because they are low-growing, with branches produced in horizontal layers that grow thickly on the shrub, they don't need facer plants in front of them to hide any unsightly trunks. The various varieties all tend to be slow growers, taking as many as 10 years to reach mature size, but they can live for 50 years or more.

GROWING DWARF NORWAY SPRUCE

These little shrubs prefer a sunny location, but some, such as the bird's nest spruce, can tolerate partial shade. The soil must be well-draining and evenly moist, with an acidic to moderately alkaline pH level. It will thrive in rocky soil, clay, or even sand.

They have the best growth if the soil is kept moist, but once mature plants are established, most can handle periods of drought. These are adaptable plants, and some cultivars, such as the 'Barryi' dwarf spruce, are highly tolerant of urban pollution, even thriving in inner-city environments. They tend to be cold-hardy, as well, and cultivars like 'Little Gem' can withstand temperatures below -20°F (-29° C).

CARING FOR THE PLANTS

These shrubs require little maintenance. Remove any diseased, broken, or damaged limbs any time of the year. If you wish to keep the plant in a diminutive habit, trimming is best done in late winter to early spring in the second year after planting. Feed the plant in spring with an all-purpose fertilizer applied just as new green growth appears. Water the plant weekly in summer.

They are susceptible to few diseases, and pests like rabbits or deer don't bother them.

SCIENTIFIC NAME: *Picea abies*

FAMILY: Pinaceae

HEIGHT: 2 to 6 feet (60 cm–1.8 m)

WIDTH: 2 to 6 feet (60 cm–1.8 m)

FOLIAGE COLOR: Various greens

SOIL pH: Acidic to moderately alkaline

LIGHT: Full sun to partial shade

Dwarf Norway Spruce Varieties

Among the many dwarf *Picea abies* cultivars, there are a few stand-outs.

- **'Little Gem'** is a brilliant emerald green that makes a stunning companion for plants with purple foliage. It grows to an equal height and width between 1 and 2 feet (30–60 cm).
- **'Barryi'** is a slow-growing variety that matures from a small globe to a broad pyramidal shape.
- **'Pumila'** has dark green foliage that emerges light green in spring.
- **'Nidiformis'** is better known as bird's nest spruce, so-called because of the small depression in the center of the mound. It grows to only 2 feet (60 cm) tall and about 4 feet (1.2 m) wide. New growth is a brilliant greenish yellow suspended in clusters at the tips of the stems, adding interest to the plant. At maturity the needles are short and grayish green.

To learn the particulars about this cultivar, scan the QR code or follow the link to "Bird's Nest Spruce Care: How to Grow Bird's Nest Spruce Shrubs" (QR = gkh.us/50883).

False Cypress

Golden threadleaf false cypress *(Chamaecyparis pisifera* 'Filifera Aurea Nana') is a small variety of false cypress that looks great as a specimen plant that adds a delicate touch to the landscape with its thread-like needles cascading from pendulous branches.

SCIENTIFIC NAME: *Chamaecyparis* spp.

FAMILY: Cupressaceae

HEIGHT: 5 to 70 feet (1.5–21 m)

WIDTH: 3 to 20 feet (1–6 m)

FOLIAGE COLOR: Various greens, golden yellow, blue-green, steel blue, and silvery green

SOIL pH: Acidic to neutral

LIGHT: Full sun to partial shade

False cypress *(Chamaecyparis* spp.), a native of Japan, is a medium to large evergreen shrub. In the wild, varieties of false cypress may grow 70 feet (21 m) tall and 20 to 30 feet (6–9 m) wide. For landscaping purposes, nurseries tend to grow only dwarf or unique varieties of *Chamaecyparis pisifera*. The "mop" or thread-leaf cultivars usually have pendulous threads of chartreuse to gold-colored scaly foliage. With a medium growth rate, these false cypress cultivars usually stay dwarf at about 5 feet (1.5 m) tall or shorter. 'Squarrosa' varieties of *C. pisifera* may grow to 20 feet (6 m), and certain cultivars like 'Boulevard' are grown specifically for their columnar habit. 'Squarrosa' false cypress trees have upright sprays of fine, sometimes feathery, silver-blue scaly foliage.

There are many benefits to growing false cypress trees and shrubs. The small thread-leaf varieties add bright evergreen color and unique texture as foundation plantings, borders, hedges, and accent plants. They obtained the common name "mops" from their foliage, which bears a resemblance to the strings of a mop, and the plant's overall shaggy, mop-like mounding habit. Topiary and pom-pom varieties are also available for specimen plants and can be used as a unique bonsai in a Zen garden. Oftentimes hidden by the pendulous foliage, the bark of false cypress plants has a reddish brown color with an attractive shredded texture. The taller blue-toned 'Squarrosa' varieties can be used as specimen plants and privacy hedges. These varieties tend to be slower growing than other false cypresses.

Whether you're looking for a low-growing foundation plant, dense hedge, or unique specimen plant, false cypress has a variety to fit your needs.

GROWING AND CARING FOR FALSE CYPRESS

False cypress grows best in full sun, but it can tolerate light shade. The gold varieties, however, need more sun to develop their brilliant color. In cooler climates, false cypresses can be prone to winter burn. This condition results in brownish needles that make it appear as if the shrub has been burned, but winter damage can be trimmed out in spring. Dead foliage may persist on larger false cypress varieties, making it necessary to annually trim out the plants to keep them tidy and healthy.

False cypresses grow in most soil types but prefer it to be slightly acidic. Young plants should be watered deeply as needed to develop healthy root systems. As low-maintenance plants, false cypress care is minimal. Established plants will become more drought and heat tolerant. Evergreen spikes or slow-release evergreen fertilizers can be applied in spring.

False cypress is rarely bothered by wildlife pests, such as deer and rabbits.

READ MORE AT GARDENING KNOW HOW

To find out how to grow and care for golden mop false cypress, scan the QR code or follow the link below.

- **"Golden Mop False Cypress: Information About Golden Mop Shrubs"** (URL = gkh.us/113667)

Holly

An English holly bush displays clusters of bright red berries and sharply delineated, deep green leaves. These hollies are frequently used as traditional Christmas decorations.

SCIENTIFIC NAME: *Ilex* spp.

FAMILY: Aquifoliaceae

HEIGHT: 15 to 30 feet (4.6–10 m)

WIDTH: 10 to 20 feet (3–6 m)

FOLIAGE COLOR: Green, variegated green and white or creamy gold

SOIL pH: Acidic

LIGHT: Full sun to partial shade

Ilex is the only genus in the Aquifoliaceae, but that doesn't mean it's a small family. There are more than 560 species of flowering plants in the genus, including evergreen and deciduous trees, shrubs, and climbers from tropic to temperate zones worldwide. The type species is *Ilex aquifolium,* the English holly so often associated with the Christmas holidays. Other common garden hollies are the American holly *(I. opaca),* Chinese holly *(I. cornuta),* Japanese holly *(I. crenata),* and Yaupon holly *(I. vomitoria).*

Holly is valued primarily for its glossy foliage and colorful berries (which are technically drupes), and it's a great wildlife plant. The drupes provide much needed nutrition for birds and other wildlife during the cold season, and the dense foliage is excellent for nesting.

Growing holly bushes in your yard can add structure and a splash of color in the winter and a lush, green backdrop for flowers in the summer. They range in size from small shrubs to large climbers, and though they all have similarly distinctive leaves, the shapes, textures, and colors can vary. They are often used as foundation plantings, and you can also clip them into bushes or hedges or mass several to create a privacy screen.

GROWING HOLLY BUSHES

The best time for planting holly is either in the spring or autumn. The relatively low temperatures combined with higher rainfall will make settling into the new location much less stressful for the bush.

The best location will have well-drained but not dry, slightly acidic soil. They prefer full sun, but most hollies are very tolerant of less than ideal locations and will grow well in part shade or dry or swampy soil.

If you are growing a holly bush for its bright berries, keep in mind that most holly varieties have male and female plants and that only the female holly shrub produces berries. You will need to plant a female variety with a male variety nearby. You can, too, try to find varieties that don't need a male plant in order to produce holly berries.

The initial care of holly is much like other trees and shrubs. Make sure that your newly planted bush is watered daily for the first week, twice a week for a month after that, and, if planting in spring, once a week for the remainder of summer.

There are several *Ilex* varieties to choose from. To find one for your garden, scan the QR code or follow the link below.

- **"Common Types of Holly Shrubs: Learn About Different Holly Plant Varieties"** (URL = gkh.us/53528)

CARING FOR THE PLANTS

After hollies are established care is easy. Fertilize once a year with a balanced fertilizer. They do not need to be watered in normal conditions, but if your area is experiencing a drought, you should give your hollies at least 2 inches (5 cm) of water per week. It also helps to mulch around the base of the shrub to help retain water in the summer and to even out the soil temperature in the winter.

Proper care for holly shrubs also calls for regular pruning to keep their natural growth in check. Pruning will ensure that they retain a nice compact form rather than becoming leggy and scraggly.

If you find that your holly shrubs are being damaged in the winter by snow and wind, you can wrap them in burlap to protect them from the weather.

Juniper

The deep lush green pyramids of juniper bushes add height to a corner of a front yard. Juniper's many varieties have long been popular shrubs for home landscaping.

Juniperus is a well-traveled genus, with species endemic across the Northern Hemisphere, making it one of the most widely distributed on the planet. There are more than 170 cultivated varieties of juniper, including low-growing ground covers, mid-sized shrubs, and tall trees. The shapes include narrow columns, tight pyramids, and rounded forms that spread as wide as their height or more. The fragrant foliage typically appears as either needles or overlapping scales, but some shrubs have both, with leaves that start out as needles that transition to scales as they mature.

Juniper shrubs are either male or female. The male flowers provide the pollen for the female flowers, and once pollinated, the females produce berries or cones. One male shrub can provide pollen for several females.

Juniper lends the landscape both a well-defined structure and a fresh fragrance that few other shrubs can match. Their care is easy because they never need pruning to maintain their attractive shapes, and they tolerate adverse conditions without complaint.

GROWING JUNIPERS

Plant junipers in a location with full sun or light shade. When they get too much shade, the branches spread apart in an effort to let more sunlight in, and the damage to their shape can't be repaired.

Junipers grow in any type of soil, as long as it is well drained. They do not like having their feet in wet mud, but tolerate most other types of soil. Many junipers make excellent street shrubs because they tolerate the spray from road salt and other urban pollution.

Consider the mature size before you plant. Many species grow so fast that they rapidly occupy the space allotted. You can prune upright junipers to keep them compact.

Plant container-grown junipers any time of year. Shrubs with balled and burlapped roots are best planted in autumn. Dig the planting hole as deep as the root ball and two to three times wider. Set the shrub in the hole so the soil line on the stem is even with the surrounding soil. Backfill with the soil removed from the hole without amendments. Press down firmly as you fill the hole to remove air pockets. Water deeply after planting, and add additional soil if it settles into a depression.

CARING FOR THE PLANTS

Water young shrubs during dry spells for the first two years. Afterward, the shrub is drought tolerant and can make do with what nature provides. Fertilize the shrub with 10-10-10 fertilizer in the spring of the year after planting and every other year thereafter.

Like all trees, junipers occasionally suffer from diseases. Phomopsis blight is the most serious disease that attacks them. You can identify it by looking for browning branch tips. Control this disease by spraying the new growth with a fungicide several times during the growing season.

SCIENTIFIC NAME: *Juniperus* spp.

FAMILY: Cupressaceae

HEIGHT: 6 inches to 15 feet (15 cm–4.6 m)

WIDTH: 1 to 12 feet (30 cm–4 m)

FOLIAGE COLOR: Various greens

SOIL pH: Acidic, neutral, alkaline

LIGHT: Full sun

Tree or Shrub?

Because shrubs are nothing more than short trees, the line between the two types of plants is a blurred one. Some cases are clearer than others. For example, California juniper *(J. californica)* is considered a low, coastal shrub, because it stays close to the ground, but western juniper *(J. occidentalis)* always presents as a tall tree sculpted by the wind. Then you have the ground cover species, such as creeping juniper *(J. horizontalis)* that features plume-like branches that extend horizontally. Categorizing a juniper as a tree or a shrub is sometimes more difficult. Pfitzer juniper *(J. chinensis* 'Pfitzerana'), perhaps the most popular cultivated juniper, grows to 5 feet (1.5 m) high and 10 feet (3 m) wide and is considered a small tree by some and a shrub by others. This is also the case with Hetz Chinese juniper *(J. chinensis* 'Hetzii'), which grows to 15 feet (4.5 m) tall.

Mirror Plant

The bright green and buttery yellow leaves of *Coprosma repens* light up a garden border planting. It's easy to understand why it is known as mirror plant, looking-glass plant, and creeping mirror plant, among other "shiny" names.

SCIENTIFIC NAME: *Coprosma* spp.

FAMILY: Rubiaceae

HEIGHT: 4 to 5 feet (1.2–1.5 m)

WIDTH: 3 to 4 feet (1–1.2 cm)

FOLIAGE COLOR: Green; variegated combinations of creamy white, lime green, bright pink, purple, gold, or soft yellow

SOIL pH: Neutral to acidic

LIGHT: Full sun to partial shade

Native to New Zealand, Australia, and some Pacific islands, the mirror plant *(Coprosma* spp.) is an evergreen shrub or small tree in the family Rubiaceae. It is named for its amazingly shiny, jewel-like leaves.

This is a fast-growing shrub that can reach mature heights of 10 feet (3 m). It tend to be low maintenance and will thrive even in difficult conditions—especially salty coastal environments. Mirror plant is available in several variegated forms and various combinations of creamy white, lime green, bright pink, purple, gold, or soft yellow. The colors intensify when cooler weather arrives in autumn. Dwarf varieties, which top out at 2 to 3 feet (60 cm–1 m), are also available. Look for clusters of inconspicuous white or greenish white blooms in summer or autumn followed by fleshy fruit that turns from shiny green to bright red or orange. Use it in shrub borders, rock gardens, and in containers. You can also use it for a hedge, privacy screen, or espalier; spreading forms make useful ground covers that can contain soil erosion on sloping banks.

GROWING MIRROR PLANTS

Mirror plants require moist, well-drained soil with a neutral or slightly acidic pH. They will tolerate partial shade but prefer full sunlight to reach their full potential.

Set nursery-grown plants in the garden in spring or autumn, spacing them 18 to 36 inches (45 cm–1 m) apart, depending on the variety. Regularly water the young plants until they are established. Once established, occasional watering is usually sufficient, although they benefit from watering during hot, dry weather. Be careful not to overwater: mirror plants like moist soil, but the roots are likely to rot if the soil remains muddy or soggy. Provide a regular, balanced fertilizer before new growth emerges in spring.

CARING FOR THE PLANTS

A neglected mirror plant can become scraggly. Twice-yearly pruning will keep it looking its best. Just trim the tree to any desired size and shape.

It is generally not susceptible to pests and diseases, but it can occasionally be damaged by root rot and scale insects.

Coprosoma Varieties

There are several species of this glossy plant to choose from.

- ***C.* x *kirkii.*** This ground cover variety grows 1 to 3 feet tall (30 cm–1 m), with yellow-green leaves and white fruits speckled red. The 'Variegata' cultivar is a bit smaller and has white-edged gray-green leaves and translucent white berries.
- ***C. petriei.*** This spreading, mounding plant grows 2 feet (60 cm) tall and has shiny, bright green leaves.
- ***C. repens.*** This fast grower can reach 10 feet (3 m) tall and 6 feet (1.8 m) wide, with a wide range of colors for its glossy leaves. 'Argentea' has green flecked with silvery white; 'Marble Queen' is creamy white splashed with green; 'Marble King' is cream speckled in lime green; 'Picturata' is green blotched in creamy yellow; 'Marginata' is green edged in creamy white; and 'Pink Splendor' is green with yellow edges that turn pink at maturity.
- ***Coprosma* hybrids.** There are several Coprosma hybrids. 'Coppershine' has bright green leaves shaded with shiny copper; 'Evening Glow' has glossy green leaves with gold variegation that turns orange-red in autumn and winter; 'Rainbow Surprise' is cream and pink with a red wash in autumn and winter; and 'Tequila Sunrise' has shiny green leaves edged with gold that turns bright red and orange in winter.

Mugo Pine

SCIENTIFIC NAME: *Pinus mugo*

FAMILY: Pinaceae

HEIGHT: 18 inches to 20 feet (45 cm–6 m)

WIDTH: 3 to 30 feet (1–9 m)

FOLIAGE COLOR: Pine green

SOIL pH: Acidic, neutral, alkaline

LIGHT: Full to partial sun

Pinus mugo **goes by many names: mugo pine, bog pine, creeping pine, dwarf mountain pine, scrub mountain pine, or Swiss mountain pine. This small species of conifer is great for home landscaping with its interesting foliage that produces upright "candles."**

Native to European mountain areas, such as the Alps, Carpathians, and Pyrenees, mugo pines *(Pinus mugo)* are great alternatives to junipers for gardeners who want something a bit different in the landscape. Like their towering cousins the pine trees, mugos have dark green color and a fresh pine smell year round, but in a much smaller package. Short, shrubby varieties are neat in appearance with branches that grow to within inches of the soil. It has a naturally spreading habit and tolerates light shearing.

These versatile, dense plants make good screens and barriers that can add privacy to the landscape and direct the flow of foot traffic. Use them to divide sections of the garden and create garden rooms. Low-growing varieties make excellent foundation plants. In spring, new growth shoots almost straight up at the tips of the horizontal stems to form "candles." Lighter in color than the older foliage, the candles form an attractive accent that rises above the shrub. Shearing off the candles results in dense growth the following season.

GROWING MUGO PINE

Mugo pines thrive in cool temperatures and high elevations. This group of evergreen trees grows to between 3 and 20 feet (1–6 m) in height, and they can spread to widths of between 5 and 30 feet (1.5–9 m). If you live in a region without particularly hot summers, you can easily grow these shrubs in your home landscape.

They adapt to a wide range of soil types, and they resist drought so well that they never need watering. All they ask for is full sun, perhaps with a little afternoon shade, and room to spread to their mature size.

If you have bought a container or burlapped plant, dig a large hole, and amend the removed soil with small gravel if you have clay soil or coconut coir if it is sandy. Remove the plant from the container, gently loosen the roots, and place in the hole, packing the amended soil around it. Gently tamp the soil, and, then water thoroughly. You can also mulch around the base to keep the new plant's roots cool.

PRUNING MUGO PINES

Pruning isn't always necessary, depending on the variety you plant. If you want a shorter, more compact shrub, with a smooth and rounded silhouette, the principal rule is to never prune in the autumn. Pines do not produce new buds from old growth, meaning growth will stop at any pruning points if you cut branches out of season. Instead, prune in spring, and only trim the new growth. Tender new growth on mugo pines appears as "candles" on the branch tips.

To keep the mugo pine from getting too tall, cut the candles in half in springtime. This reduces the size the new growth will achieve over the season. Done annually, this keeps the shrub to a reasonable size and makes its canopy thicker. If it gets too thick, you may want to remove some exterior candles.

Editor's Picks

These mugo pine varieties are available in nurseries or from mail order sources.

- **'Compacta' is labeled as growing 5 feet (1.5 m) tall and 8 feet (2.4 m) wide, but it usually grows a good bit larger.**
- **'Enci' grows very slowly to a height of only about 3 feet (1 cm). It has a flat top and a very dense growth habit.**
- **'Gnome' is the smallest of the mugos, forming a mound of dense foliage only 18 inches (45 cm) tall and 3 feet (1 m) wide.**
- **'Mops' grows 3 feet (1 cm) tall and wide and has a neat, round shape.**
- **'Pumilio' grows taller than Enci and Mops. It forms a shrubby mound up to 10 feet (3 m) wide.**

A GALLERY OF

GARDEN TREES

If shrubs add architectural shapes, framework, and height to a garden, just imagine what a few well-placed trees can do. In general, trees provide vistas, privacy, and splashes of autumn color, and can increase the value of your property. In a garden setting, trees may be practical, ornamental, or inspirational, deciduous or evergreen, flowering or non-flowering, plus many come in scaled-down varieties. When situated properly, trees will also shade vulnerable parts of the garden—flowers, herbs, or veggies that don't appreciate full sun.

OTHER BENEFITS

Trees have some other unique qualities that make them real garden assets.

- Trees are protective. A treeline at the border of your home or garden can reduce the effects of storms, making high winds less damaging.
- Tree roots actually draw water down into the soil, helping keep your plant roots moist.
- Trees improve soil. After absorbing CO_2 from the air, they turn that carbon it into a type of sugar that is excreted from their roots. Microorganisms in the soil feed on this, then breed and die, decaying into a rich soil called humus. Healthy soil means more absorbent soil, so less risk of wet feet for you or your plants.
- Trees can actually make soil. Soil is composed of water, air, minerals, and organic matter—every living and dead thing in the soil. Plant roots, living and decaying, make up the majority of organic matter in soil, and when those roots die, they feed the soil. After pruning your trees, some excess roots will die, resulting in increased organic matter in the soil—and you'll see a spurt of growth from the trees. In this way, trees create the ideal conditions needed for them to grow.
- Deciduous trees supply free mulch every autumn in the form of fallen leaves. Shred the leaves, and then spread them over the garden with a leaf blower.
- Trees draw birds and other wildlife to your yard.

DWARF FRUIT TREES

These diminutive versions of full-size orchard trees bear normal-size fruit, but occupy a smaller footprint in the garden. Make sure any trees you buy are self-fertile—meaning they don't rely on cross-pollination from another tree to bear fruit—and are grafted onto dwarf rootstock.

Landscaping Trees

CHASTE TREE
Height: 6 to 8 feet (1.8–2.4 m)
Chaste tree is a lesser-known, shrublike tree *(Vitex agnus-castus)* that can be pruned into a multi-trunk tree form. Spikes of striking lilac-purple flowers bloom in summer. A small, pretty tree in the South, up north it dies back in winter and regrows in spring.

CRABAPPLE
Height: 15 to 20 feet (4.6–6 m)
With its dense branches, dazzling, deep purplish flowers, and tiny fruit that can be made into a tart jelly, the cold-hardy crabapple *(Malus* spp.) is a favorite accent tree that also works in a border. The long-lasting fruit is an excellent source of food for birds in the winter.

CREPE MYRTLE
Height: 10 to 20 feet (3–6 m)
This Southern landscape star *(Lagerstroemia indica)* has dark bark, glossy leaves, vibrant fall colors, and showy, frilly flowers in nearly every shade. The mature tree tolerates heat, humidity, and drought. The name is spelled both "crepe" and "crape."

DOGWOOD
Height: 15 to 20 feet (4.6–6 m)
Huge pink, red, or white spring blossoms, showy red fruit, and impressive autumn color help to explain why the dogwood *(Cornus* spp.) is so popular. Gardeners may choose from many different varieties, including new disease-resistant hybrids.

EASTERN REDBUD
Height: 20 to 30 feet (6 –9 m)
The dramatic features of the eastern redbud *(Cercis canadensis)* provide year-round interest. It produces brilliant purplish pink flowers in early spring and pretty heart-shaped leaves in stunning red or gold in autumn. In winter, the bare branches make lovely patterns.

JAPANESE MAPLE
Height: 15 to 20 feet (4.6–6 m)
These eye-catching accent trees *(Acer* spp.) offer delicate foliage, interesting bark, and elegant, arching limbs. Foliage shades can range from pale green to deep burgundy, and many cultivars offer stunning autumn color. Most varieties prefer part shade.

Dwarf Fruit Trees

OLIVE TREE

Height: 10 to 40 feet (3.0–12.1 m)
Prized for its picturesque gnarled trunk, this soulful, Mediterranean evergreen *(Olea europaea)* does well in temperate regions, but should be pot grown and brought inside during cold weather in order to fruit. The shrub form is known as *O. europaea* 'Montra'.

SAUCER MAGNOLIA

Height: 20 to 30 feet (6–9m)
With its large, spring-blooming, pinkish purple flowers and shiny dark green leaves, the saucer magnolia *(Magnolia* x *soulangeana)* is a garden showstopper. Consider 'Grace McDade', which is said to bear the largest flowers, or 'Jurmag1', with its tight, dark flowers.

APPLE

Height: 10 to 12 feet (3–3.7 m)
Imagine the thrill of picking tasty, full-size apples *(Malus domestica)* in your own garden. Dwarf tree varieties include 'Cameron Select', a cultivar of the popular Honeycrisp apple, along with such tasty favorites as 'Gala', 'Jonagold', 'Cox', and 'Pink Lady'.

CHERRY

Height: 10 feet (3 m)
Cherry trees *(Prunus* spp.) are renowned for their spectacular spring blooms and sweet or sour fruit. Sweet cherries are perfect for snacking, while sour cherries are better for baking. Consider semi-dwarf, self-pollinating 'Stella' or 'Nanking', 'Lapins', 'Northstar', and 'Sunburst'.

SCARLET FIRETHORN

Height: 10 feet (3 m)
The durable semi-evergreen firethorn *(Pyracantha coccineas)* is characterized by dense foliage, thorny stems, and red berries that birds love. These berries offer blazing autumn color, and when the tree is planted in rows, the thick foliage forms a perfect privacy screen.

SHORE PINE

Height: 6 to 20 feet (1.8– 6 m)
This petite, sun-loving, evergreen *(Pinus contorta* 'Chief Joseph'), also known as lodgepole pine, has a slow growth rate that makes it perfect for the garden or for placing in a container. In autumn, the attractive green needles will transition into a bright golden hue.

LEMON

Height: 2 feet (60 cm)
For a small lemon tree, try the sweet Meyer lemon *(Citrus* x *meyeri)*, a hybrid cross between a lemon and a mandarin orange. This amazing dwarf tree is able to fruit at just 24 inches (60 cm). Grow one on your patio during the summer, then overwinter it indoors.

PEACH/APRICOT

Height: 8 to 10 feet (2.4–3 m)
If you live in a cold climate, grow your peach *(Prunus persica)* or apricot *(P. armeniaca)* tree in a pot that can move indoors during the chilly months. Dwarf varieties include heirloom 'Belle of Georgia', 'June Gold', 'Bonfire', 'Contender', 'Pix Zee', and 'Pixie-Cot' apricot.

WASHINGTON HAWTHORN

Height: 30 feet (9 m)
To attract birds and butterflies to your garden, consider planting a Washington hawthorn *(Crataegus phaenopyrum)*. This smaller deciduous tree offers fragrant flowers in the spring and then bears small red fruit that attracts wildlife. The autumn foliage is spectacular.

WEEPING CHERRY

Height: 20 to 30 feet (6–9 m)
For a touch of elegance in the garden, consider the weeping cherry *(Prunus pendula)*. In spring, before the green leaves emerge, the slender, cascading branches are festooned with double white or pink blossoms, making this graceful tree the highlight of any setting.

PEAR

Height: 4 to 8 feet (1.2–2.4 m)
A dwarf pear *(Pyrus* spp.) is a good option for those who want a small fruit tree. 'Conference' is a popular dwarf cultivar, sweet and juicy and self-fertile. Try 'Louise Bonne', a sweet dessert pear, or the ubiquitous Bartlett (Williams) variety. Dwarf pears grow well in pots.

PLUM

Height: 10 feet (3 m)
The hardy 'Johnson' cultivar is a dwarf plum *(Prunus domestica)* with red skin and sweet red flesh. It requires a second plum of a different variety for pollination. Or try an heirloom variety like 'Damson' *(Prunus institia)*, which is a self-fertile cultivar.

Privet

SCIENTIFIC NAME: *Ligustrum* spp.

FAMILY: Oleaceae

HEIGHT: 4 to 15 feet (1.2–4.6 m)

WIDTH: 4 to 10 feet (1.2–3 m)

FOLIAGE COLOR: Green or yellow

SOIL pH: Acidic, neutral, alkaline

LIGHT: Full sun to partial shade

Privet is one of the most popular hedge shrubs. It lends itself to shearing and shaping, so much so that it is a popular species for creating elaborate patterns, such as a leafy maze.

Privets (*Ligustrum* spp.) belong to a genus of erect, deciduous or evergreen shrubs native to Europe, North Africa, and Asia. They bloom in early summer with panicles of pungently fragrant white flowers, followed by bunches of black berries. These adaptable plants are among the easiest shrubs and small trees to grow, tolerating a wide range of conditions. Their versatility and undemanding nature has led to their extensive use in landscapes all over the world. Plant them as hedges, foundation plants, patio trees, or in shrub borders.

Suitable privet species for home landscapes include the following.

- Garden privet *(L. ovalifolium)*, also known as California, Korean, or oval-leafed privet, is a 15-foot (4.6 m) shrub that forms a nice hedge when closely planted. It requires frequent shearing and produces numerous seedlings that must be removed before they become established. Note that it is listed as an invasive species in several areas of the United States, and 46 states have it listed on their lists of noxious weeds. Check with your agricultural authority before planting this privet variety.
- Golden privet *(L. vicaryi)* grows 6 feet (1.8 m) high or taller and has golden yellow leaves. For best color, plant it in full sun and in a situation where it won't need frequent shearing.
- Glossy privet *(L. lucidum)* is an pretty evergreen tree that grows about 45 feet (13.5 m) tall or more, but you can grow it as a large shrub with frequent pruning. It produces large, showy flower clusters and a huge crop of purple-blue berries.
- Japanese privet *(L. japonicum)* grows to 10 feet tall (3 m) and 5 or 6 feet (1.5–1.8 m) wide. This variety is commonly used as a hedge or screen plant, and can be shaped into a small tree.

GROWING PRIVET

Privets thrive in full sun or partial shade. They tolerate most soil types, and with the exception of Chinese privets *(L. sinense)*, they tolerate moderate amounts of salt in the soil. Don't plant them near roadways that are treated with salt in the winter or on oceanfront property where the foliage is likely to be sprayed with salt. Privets also tolerate a moderate amount of urban pollution. You should avoid planting privets in poorly drained soil or areas where water accumulates. Avoid planting common privet *(L. vulgare)* because of its invasive nature. Common privet seeds are spread by birds that eat the berries. As a result, it has spread into wild areas where it crowds out native plants.

CARING FOR THE PLANTS

Privets withstand drought, but they grow best if irrigated during prolonged dry spells. Fertilize the plants in early spring and again in late summer or autumn. You can also fertilize in summer if the plants are growing rapidly or appear to need another feeding. Use 0.7 pounds (0.3 kg) of 15-5-10 or 15-5-15 fertilizer for each 100 square feet (9 m^2).

Privets begin forming the buds for the next year's flowers soon after the current season's blossoms fade. To avoid shearing off the young buds, prune the plants right after they flower. Prune to control the height and prevent the plant from overreaching its bounds. Don't worry about overdoing it: privets tolerate severe pruning.

Ligustrums **are very fast-growing shrubs. Japanese privets, for example, can add more than 24 inches (60 cm) of growth per year, and other varieties grow quickly, as well. This rapid growth rate means these shrubs need frequent pruning to keep them under control.**

To learn the best way to care for privets, follow the link to "Cutting Back Privet: How and When to Prune Privet Hedges" (URL = gkh.us/107877, or scan the QR code.

Smoke Tree

When the smoke tree blooms, it creates a uniquely dramatic effect, as if covered in clouds of smoke. The puffs of smoke that are the feathery, fuzzy flowers will last most of the summer before they start to fall off and fade for autumn foliage.

SCIENTIFIC NAME: *Cotinus* spp.

FAMILY: Anacardiaceae

HEIGHT: 10 to 15 feet (3–4.6 m)

WIDTH: 10 to 15 feet (3–4.6 m)

FOLIAGE COLOR: Green or purple, with smoky purplish pink blooms

SOIL pH: Acidic, alkaline

LIGHT: Full sun

Closely related to sumac, the *Cotinus* genus comprises seven species of flowering plants in the family Anacardiaceae. Two particular species are often used as landscaping shrubs: *C. coggygria,* the European smoke tree, and *C. obovatus,* the American smoke tree. Also known as the smoke bush, this plant charms with its gorgeous reddish brown or mauve flowers with feathery hairs that make appear from the distance as if it is smothered in clouds of smoke. This upright, slow-growing shrub features waxy green leaves, although there are cultivars in other colors, such as purple.

Planted singly, it can make for an unusual and attractive ornamental. Use it as a centerpiece tree similar to the Japanese maple in the front yard or as a pretty patio accent in the backyard. Planted in groups, smoke trees are great for creating shrub borders along property edges. This can be an excellent idea; this attractive border will separate your yard from your neighbor's in a way both of you will enjoy.

GROWING AND CARING FOR SMOKE TREES

Purchase a healthy tree from your local garden center. It will need well-drained soil and a location with full sun. It can grow in partial shade, but this will result in sparser foliage. Mulch a young shrub with a 2-inch (5 cm) layer of wood chips or bark mulch to keep weeds away, and keep the soil moist, being sure to leave an inch or two (2.5–5 cm) of space around its trunk. Deeply water the young plant about twice a week. Smoke trees need little feeding, and a layer of compost of fertilizer in the spring and an application of organic plant food once a year should suffice.

When handling the plant, be careful not to damage the thin bark. Use caution when performing your usual garden and lawn maintenance, never hitting the bark with the lawnmower or other gardening equipment. Weed whackers can also do harm, so again, use caution near your shrubs.

The plant will droop as it gets larger, so pruning is very important. Wait until late autumn or early spring, after the shrub is done blooming. This will ensure that your smoke tree grows up strong. Keeping the soil alkaline should also help your shrubs stay healthy and looking their best.

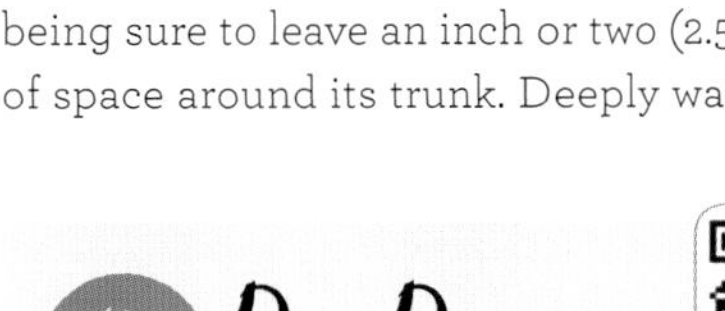

READ MORE AT GARDENING KNOW HOW

You can take these stunningly lovely shrubs indoors. To find out how, scan the QR code or follow the link below. To find out how to propagate these shrubs follow the bottom link

- **"Smoke Tree in Pots: Tips for Growing Smoke Trees in Containers"** (URL = gkh.us/79443)
- **"Smoke Tree Propagation Methods — How to Propagate a Smoke Tree"** (URL = gkh.us/112819)

COMMON PROBLEMS

There are a few issues you need to keep your eye on. The oblique-banded leafroller can be a problem with smoke trees. Keeping the soil well-drained is essential. If you notice brown leaves, this could be the result of verticillium wilt caused by the fungus *Verticillium.* Another fungal condition is leaf spot, which can happen in warmer weather. Stem canker and scabs are other problems to watch out for.

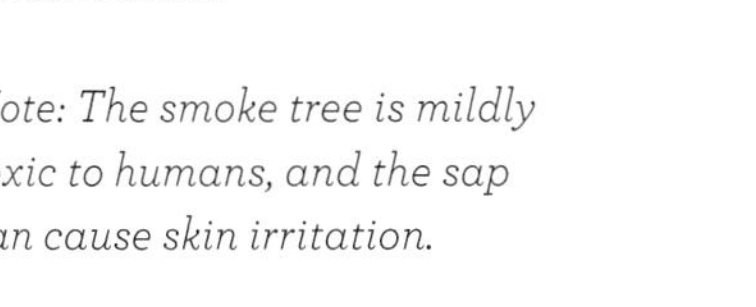

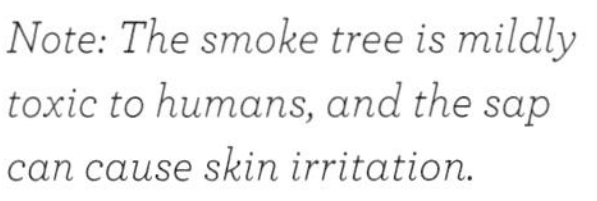

Note: The smoke tree is mildly toxic to humans, and the sap can cause skin irritation.

Wintercreeper

SCIENTIFIC NAME: *Euonymus fortunei*

FAMILY: Celastraceae

HEIGHT: Up to 70 feet (21 m) as a vine; 2 to 10 feet (30 cm–3 m) as a shrub

WIDTH: 2 to 10 feet (30 cm–3 m) as a shrub

FOLIAGE COLOR: Green; variegated yellow and green or green and white

SOIL pH: Acidic, neutral, alkaline

LIGHT: Full to partial sun

A shrub variety of wintercreeper *(Euonymus fortunei* 'Silver Queen') has been trimmed into a compact globe of white-tipped green leaves that stands out in a rocky border. Just one of the many species of *Euonymus,* it also has vining varieties.

The genus *Euonymus,* in the staff vine family, Celastraceae, includes about 175 different euonymus plants, from dwarf shrubs to vines and tall trees that are native around the globe, from Europe to East Asia and Australasia to North America, Madagascar, and China. They go by many names, depending on species, including wintercreeper, spindle, burning bush, strawberry-bush, wahoo, or simply euonymus. If you are looking for bushes, trees, or climbers, euonymus has them all. Gardeners choose these plants for their attractive foliage and stunning autumn color. Some also offer unique fruits and seed pods. They are available in a wide range of colors and sizes and include both evergreen and deciduous types. That gives you a good selection of different euonymus to choose from when you are looking for border plants, hedges, screens, ground cover, or specimen plants.

Wintercreeper *(E. fortunei),* native a China, is a popular choice for home plantings. It is an attractive, woody evergreen vine, also known as the spindle and Fortune's spindle. Numerous varieties are available, including those with a strong climbing habit. Some vines quickly reach heights of 40 to 70 feet (12–21 m), making pruning wintercreeper vines necessary to keep it under control. Be aware that in some areas is listed as an invasive spreader. Check your local agricultural authorities before planting.

GROWING WINTERCREEPER

Wintercreeper does best in regions without harsh winters or ones without intense temperature fluctuations. It will do well in full sun or partial shade, and it is not very particular about soil conditions. It does best, however, in an acid loam that is moist but not overly saturated.

Once the ground can be worked in spring, space plants 18 to 24 inches (45–60 cm) apart. Water young plants well until they are established. Once established, wintercreeper tolerates dry conditions and does not require extra water.

CARING FOR THE PLANTS

Once planted, wintercreeper requires minimal attention. In fact, once it is established in the landscape, the care of wintercreeper plants is simple. It also transplants well and can be used to fill in other garden areas once mature.

Although not necessary—unless it becomes unruly—pruning wintercreeper may be done to control growth and to cut tall sprouts if it is being for ground cover. Always use clean and sharp pruning shears when clipping.

Euonymus scale can be a problem and is fatal if not controlled. Check for scale insects on the underside of leaves and use an insecticidal soap or neem oil as directed.

Burning Bush

Another popular euonymus is burning bush *(E. alatus* 'Fire Ball'). This dramatic shrub gets its name from the brilliant red color of its leaves during autumn. It grows to about 3 feet (1 m) high and wide, but accepts trimming, shaping, and shearing.

To learn more about this fascinating variety, along with many others, scan the QR code or follow the link to read "Types of Euonymus — Choosing Different Euonymus Plants for Your Garden" (URL = gkh.us/108062).

Yew

The esteemed Longwood Gardens in Pennsylvania displays shaped yews in its Topiary Garden, demonstrating how well these shrubs can be shaped into whimsical forms.

At a Glance

SCIENTIFIC NAME: *Taxus* spp.

FAMILY: Taxaceae

HEIGHT: 4 to 60 feet (1.2–18 m)

WIDTH: 4 to 20 feet (1.2–6 m)

FOLIAGE COLOR: Various greens

SOIL pH: Neutral

LIGHT: Full sun to full shade

The yew shrub is part of the *Taxus* genus, belonging to the Taxaceae family. It is a medium-sized evergreen shrub native to Japan, Korea, and northeastern China. The yew has green foliage that sports bright scarlet berries in the autumn. The fruit lays hidden among the foliage of the female plant until September, wherein the short-lived arils turn the striking red shade. Yew is a great shrub for borders, entranceways, paths, specimen gardening, or mass plantings. In addition, yew shrubs tend to be drought resistant and tolerant of repeated shearing and pruning, making their care a relatively easy endeavor.

Taxine is the name of the toxin found in the *Taxus* yew and shouldn't be confused with taxol, which is a chemical extraction of the bark of the western yew *(T. brevifolia)* used in cancer treatment.

GROWING AND CARING FOR YEW BUSHES

This evergreen shrub flourishes in full sun to partial sun and in well-drained soil, but it is tolerant of most any exposure and soil makeup, with the exception of overly wet soil, which may cause root rot.

Yews mature to a height of 5 feet tall by 10 feet wide (1.5 x 3 m), although they are almost exclusively pruned into the size desired for a particular location. Slow growing, they can be heavily sheared into a variety of shapes and are often used as a hedge. They don't need annual pruning, but you should regularly remove dead, damaged, or diseased branches. You can rejuvenate an overgrown shrub with a bit of good pruning in late winter to early spring before the new foliage appears.

As mentioned previously, the yew can be susceptible to root rot and other fungal disease brought on by overly wet soil conditions. In addition, pests like black vine weevil and mites are also issues that can afflict the shrub.

Note: All portions of the Taxus *yew are toxic to animals and humans, with the exception of the fleshy portion of the arils (the name for the* Taxus *fruit).*

Editor's Picks

Many cultivars and types of yew shrubs are available, so gardeners interested in adding a yew or two to their landscaping will find a variety to choose from.

- ***Taxus* x *media* is notable for its long, dark green evergreen needles. Although an evergreen, this yew's foliage may suffer winter burn or turn brown in cold northern ranges, and it can melt out in warmer southern ranges. It will again return, however, to its green hue in early spring, at which time the male yew will shed dense pollen from its small white flowers.**
- **If you're looking for a *T.* x *media* that's rounded when young and spreads with age, 'Brownii', 'Densiformis', 'Fairview', "Kobelli', 'L.C.', 'Bobbink', 'Natorp', 'Nigra', and 'Runyanii' fit the bill.**
- **For a shrub that spreads more rapidly from the get-go, 'Berryhillii', 'Chadwickii', 'Everlow', 'Sebian', 'Tauntonii' and 'Wardii' are cultivars of this type. Another spreader, 'Sunburst', has golden yellow spring growth that fades to chartreuse green with a hint of gold in summer.**
- **For those needing a smaller variety, 'Repandens' is a slow-growing dwarf spreader that reaches about 3 feet (1 m) tall by 12 feet (3.5 m) wide with sickle-shaped, dark green needles at the ends of its branches.**
- **For upright column-like specimens, 'Citation', 'Hicksii', 'Stoveken' and 'Viridis' are excellent choices. 'Capitata' is an upright pyramidal form, which can attain a 20-to-40-feet (6–12 m) height by 5-to-10-feet (1.5–3 m) width. It is often limbed up to reveal striking purple, reddish brown bark, making it a stunning plant at entranceways, large foundations, and in specimen gardens.**

CHAPTER NINE

GARDEN DECOR

The more thought you put into customizing your garden space, the more time you will want to spend there. After all, the modern garden is not just a place for cultivation, it can also be a spot for reflection and relaxation. You could start by creating inviting walkways to make each part of the garden accessible, and then consider adding practical features like a shed, a pergola, trellises, or even a small greenhouse. Then carve out a seating or dining area with lawn or patio furniture. Finally, bring it all together with artwork, sculpture, lighting, small decorative items, and, the finishing touch, a water feature. All it takes is some time, a flexible budget, and the imagination to bring your dream garden to life.

CREATING GARDEN PATHS

Paths and walkways give the garden landscape some sense of structure. Garden paths can create a pleasing pattern in the garden; allow access for ease of harvest, pruning, and weeding; and protect grass or tender plants from being trampled upon. Many times, paths will lead the viewer from one area of the garden toward a distant destination, often another section of the garden containing a particular sculpture, seating area, plant specimen, water feature, or other focal point.

When designing a garden path, the choice of materials varies depending upon not only the budget, but also the intent or theme of the garden. For instance, is the garden formal or informal in nature? Is there a water feature or other point that can be accessed by the inclusion of a bridge? And, naturally, you must consider your working budget for overall landscape design and decide how much of that can be allotted for paths and walkways. Their cost can run the gamut from quite pricey to inexpensive do-it-yourself projects with recycled materials.

MAKING GARDEN PATHWAYS

Many suburban yards consist of a sprawling lawn, along with landscaped beds of flowers or produce, which can look nice, but also a bit boring. Adding a path, or several paths, not only creates some visual drama to enliven the garden, it also reduces the amount of irrigation needed for plants.

When considering path placement, it's helpful to sketch out a plan on paper that can be reworked and tweaked before investing in materials or randomly digging up sod. The location of the paths in the actual garden can then be marked out with twine, rope, special spray paint, or even a garden hose to best achieve the correct configuration. Determine which areas of the garden will benefit most from the construction of pathways—for instance, it makes sense to place a walkway near a vegetable patch that needs regular tending. You should also consider installing solar lights along the paths for nighttime viewing of the garden—the hours when the spectacular jumbo moths of summer are on view.

READ MORE AT GARDENING KNOW HOW

Paths and walkways help you to construct discrete garden spaces, lead you to entrances, and guide you through your property. Follow these links to learn more about using these to best advantage.

- **"Paths for Gardens: Tips for Designing a Garden Path"** (URL = gkh.us/51534)
- **"Sensory Walkway Ideas — Creating Sensory Garden Paths"** (URL = gkh.us/149380)
- **"Flagstone Walks: Tips for Installing a Flagstone Path"** (URL = gkh.us/315)
- **"DIY Mosaic Pebble Pathway: Tips for Making Pebble Walkways for Gardens"** (URL = gkh.us/135539)

If your property already has paths leading to the entryways or the garage, you might want to create garden paths in similar materials or materials that complement them. Paths should be wide enough for two people to stroll abreast, or at minimum wide enough for a wheelbarrow or other garden equipment to fit on—at least 4 feet (1.2 m) wide. The inclusion of a nook, bench, or other type of garden decor might dictate even wider proportions in that area. You might want to feature a wide central path with narrower, discrete paths veering off from it.

You won't mind being led up the garden path when it leads to a charming lattice-work archway with seating. Line your path with interesting objects and plants to keep all your senses engaged.

MATERIALS FOR GARDEN PATHS AND WALKWAYS

The purpose of your pathway will dictate your choice of construction materials. Is the path being built for strolling and admiring the garden or is it a utilitarian walkway, making it easier for you to access different areas for maintenance or harvesting?

- River rock, sand, gravel, brick, terra-cotta pavers, flagstone, or even broken-up concrete from the removal of an old sidewalk or patio can all create interesting pathways. Do consider, however, whether a brick, flagstone, or paving stone walk will become dangerously icy or slick in winter.
- Permeable surfaces that promote drainage—gravel or decomposed granite, for example—are smart options for walkways.
- You could choose a path composed of moss, grass, creeping thyme, or other plants that can handle foot traffic.
- Wooden walkways, such as those made of natural cedar wood, can create weather-resistant, all-season pathways. Pre-made, roll-out versions, both straight and curved, are available that are easy to lay out. Elevated boardwalks can also lead a path through a bog garden.
- The color of the material may play a role in your comfort, depending upon your climate. Lighter colors reflect light and tend to stay cool under foot, although they may create sun glare; dark colors absorb and retain the warmth of the sun.
- You can put down black plastic or landscape fabric after you lay out the pathway to discourage weed growth, and then cover it with bark mulch.
- The noise created on the path should also be considered; a covering such as gravel crunches underfoot, and it can sometimes be annoying; bark, on the other hand, is quiet and soothing underfoot.
- A turning in the path from which to view the "heart" of the garden, along with the addition of boulders, statuary, and other ornamental objects along the way can enhance your vision of the space.

A low picket fence lines a gravel path studded with stepping stones. Curving walkways create interest and surprise.

Terra-cotta pavers lead to a bloom-covered trellis that opens to a quiet and secluded spot in the garden.

A bark-covered path with wooden pavers takes you through a green garden. Be sure to line your path with lighting fixtures if you enjoy a nighttime stroll.

Flagstones laid out in a haphazard pattern cut a pathway across a green turfgrass lawn, letting visitors take in the beauty of the flower and foliage borders.

BUILDINGS AND STRUCTURES

There are many practical structures you can add to your garden that will still make a design statement, providing you integrate them into your overall visual scheme. Suppose you are hankering for a garden with that full farmhouse effect or one with a Western or Southwestern theme; or you crave a quirky bohemian paradise, a serene Asian haven, or a sleek modern retreat. Whatever your chosen style, you will likely be able to find structures to enhance your vision at online sites or big-box garden centers.

PRACTICAL ADDITIONS

Below are some structures you can choose to make your life a little easier and your garden a little more interesting. Remember that even practical features can serve a decorative purpose, so try to match any new additions to your existing structures as much as possible.

A utilitarian shed stores tools inside while the outside walls serve as pollinator stations, with rows of bee and insect houses, a birdhouse, and a hummingbird feeder.

Fences

Fences and gates have several uses in the garden: they can act as barriers or edging, afford privacy, create shade, and shelter your garden from high winds or other harsh conditions. There are different styles to choose from, and all can be acquired from garden centers or handmade from nearly any material. Whatever your choice, however, make sure it complements the rest of the house and garden. For instance, picket fencing is ideal for the cottage garden, while a rustic-looking iron or weathered wooden fence and gate combos can be perfect in a country or Western setting.

Sheds

Gardening requires a lot of equipment, and that equipment requires housing to keep it safely stowed and out of the elements. The solution most gardeners turn to is the shed—a smallish, sturdy, enclosed structure with a full-size door and sometimes a window or two. Sheds come in various sizes and materials, from small aluminum tool sheds to roomy wooden tractor sheds large enough to house all your hand and power tools. Some even provide a loft for storing holiday decor or other seasonal items.

Gazebos

These classic, airy, roofed lawn structures originated in ancient Egypt roughly 5,000 years ago. They then somehow cropped up independently in diverse places, as Japanese tea houses and Roman summerhouses and as part of ornate Persian gardens. In the 18th century, the traditional Chinese gazebo became all the rage for European estates. Today, these structures come in a variety of styles and materials and can be assembled on site by contractors or ordered as DIY projects. Nothing beats gathering with friends or family at dusk on a summer night and watching the sunset from your own private viewing pavilion—complete with a full bar set-up and selection of canapes, of course.

Greenhouses

If you are an avid gardener who wants to start plants early in spring, nurture plants late into the autumn, keep growing hardy veggies through the winter, or try your hand at some exotics, consider installing a heated greenhouse. Even smaller models can be pricey, but their impact in the garden is priceless. When furnished with a vintage rug, a few wicker chairs, and a flea market oil lamp, your "glass palace" also becomes a four-season haven.

The She-Shed

One current trend is converting the humble garden shed into a "she-shed," a haven for women similar in nature to the basement "man cave." The interior can be embellished with a few comfy chairs, a small sofa, and a desk. If the "she-shed" is also meant to focus on gardening, it will require a potting bench and shelves for pots and tools.

Bridges

Bridges make striking features in the garden . . . with or without water. If you lack a stream or water source, create a dry stream bed by arranging river rocks or white gravel in a formation that appears to "run" beneath the bridge. This technique is often seen in Asian gardens. Bridges are relatively easy to construct or you can purchase one and assemble it from a kit. The style of bridge is usually determined by the type of garden it's going into. For instance, in a traditional country garden, a white wooden bridge with handrails would be suitable. In a more modern garden, a simple arch of pale wooden planks would be very effective over a reflecting pool.

Trellises

These raised structures are intended to support climbing flowers like morning glories and viny vegetables, such as peas or pole beans. Simple trellises are easy to construct at home from leftover wood, but the ornate commercial ones at the garden shop offer a bit more swagger and style. These are typically made of wood or composite materials and can be painted any color to complement your other garden features.

Arches

These fanciful wooden or composite structures make charming entries to gardens and are also used to support heavy climbers, such as roses or wisteria. Some come with a bench installed on each side. If you already have fencing in your garden, try to match the color of the archway to the fence.

Pergolas

These shade-producing structures with spaced overhead slats are a tradition in Europe, where they reduce the effect of the sun's heat and rays on stone patios or graveled seating areas without blocking out the light. They also provide a stable support for any number of climbing plants—roses, clematis, honeysuckle, passion flower, jasmine, grape vine, wisteria, trumpet vine, ivy, bougainvillea, morning glory, kiwi, sweet pea, and golden hops.

Windmills

Nothing lends a farmhouse effect to a garden like the presence of a towering windmill, whether it works to draw water from a well or not. There are numerous kits for purely decorative windmills online, from the basic prairie-style to the more elaborate Dutch version. Even the smallest versions have their own charm. Miniature golf, anyone?

A small greenhouse is often a coveted structure for gardeners who want a place to nurture young or exotic plants.

A small pergola shades a pillow-bedecked swinging chaise that offers a place to read or nap while enjoying your outdoor space.

An arched entryway to a garden is flanked by sturdy trellises for roses to climb and topped by built-in planters for bright annuals.

THE "GETAWAY" GARDEN

For many of us, our outdoor spaces have become far more important to our lives than they once were. When long-term home-stays were mandated during the early days of the Covid pandemic, more and more people around the world began using their yards, patios, and gardens—even apartment balconies and terraces—as extensions of their family rooms, living rooms, or kitchens. Some even brought their laptops and cell phones outside and turned a small table and bench into an outdoor office. Imagine how nice it might have been, Zooming a meeting from your garden.

And so we still turn to our gardens for a multitude of uses. But what if your garden is not yet the charming place you'd like it to be? Creating a warm, welcoming backyard oasis in or around your garden doesn't have to be expensive or even very time-consuming. Sometimes just making subtle changes to the existing space and decor can perk up the ambiance and inspire you to spend more time outdoors.

FURNITURE OPTIONS

Your garden furniture can be as simple as a seating area to enjoy nature or as complicated as a complete outdoor cooking and dining area.

Outdoor kitchen

Imagine preparing the fresh vegetables that your kids gathered just a few feet away or grilling up some late-night burgers under the stars with your closest friends. Whatever your style of hospitality may be, outdoor kitchens—perhaps including prep surfaces, sinks, storage cupboards, grills, stove-tops, pizza ovens, and refrigerators—are one of the best ways to enjoy the garden with friends and family.

Dining area

What's the point of cooking or grilling outdoors if there is not a suitable place nearby to dine *al fresco*? Your garden could be the perfect spot to locate a dining table and chairs. Consider traditional redwood picnic tables, iron or resin umbrella table sets, two-seater cafe combos, or simply cover a folding table with a pretty cloth and add mix-and-match chairs and a vase with fresh-cut blossoms from your garden.

A complete outdoor kitchen, with a prep area, fridge, grill, and sink, has been installed on a stone terrace. The adjacent dining area is shaded by a cheerful striped umbrella.

Outdoor lighting

The right lighting can help make or break your evening ambiance. Outdoor lighting not only showcases interesting features throughout your space, but it also provides your yard and garden with additional beauty and security. Choose from white fairy lights, strings of Edison bulbs, Chinese paper lanterns, bamboo torches, individual pathway lights, landscape spotlights, pinpoint firework lights in white or colors, wax candles, flameless candles . . . the options are almost limitless. Be sure to look for the many solar lights available that require no electrical connections.

Fire pits

Fire pits are among the most useful features for people who enjoy being outside after the warm weather ends. Much like their predecessors, the campfire and the outdoor fireplace, fire pits act as a focal point for social gatherings and cookouts; the more ornate ones also work as landscape-design elements.

Outdoor seating

There really are endless possibilities when it comes to outdoor seating in and around the garden. From traditional iron or resin patio furniture to classic wooden Adirondack chairs, tree stumps, carved wood or stone benches, oversized pillows, poufs, ottomans, ceramic garden stools, and so on, your choice of garden seating is limited only by your entertaining needs and your budget. And don't forget to add a few throw pillows, which can easily alter the mood of a space simply with the use of color or pattern.

An ornate pedal organ gets a new lease on life upcycled as an outdoor planter. Combing the local flea markets is a creative way to add budget-friendly, one-of-a-kind decorations to your garden.

Garden as gallery

Don't be afraid to add artwork to the garden—paintings, wood carvings, tikis, statues, flags, mirrors, pottery animals, copper weather vanes—virtually anything that strikes your fancy. Just don't place a valuable piece of art in an unprotected area—weather will dampen cardboard backings and warp wooden frames. You can be more daring with metal or stone sculptures, treated wood pieces, terra-cotta, ceramics, or anything made of plastic or resin.

Flea market decor

There is now a widespread bohemian gardening subculture that proudly displays flea market or second-hand finds—old bicycles, crusty, paint-splattered wooden ladders, wicker planters, wire baskets, Victorian plant stands, even literal kitchen sinks. There are also the farmhouse fanatics who liberally festoon their gardens with found objects like rusty old tools as well as wagon wheels, oxen yokes, barn lanterns, and antique farming equipment. Search out your local charity shops, yard sales, flea markets, and other places to buy secondhand objects that you can upcycle into unique pieces of garden decor.

For additional creative upcycling tips, follow this link.

- **"Garden Upcycling Ideas: Learn About Upcycling in the Garden"** (URL = gkh.us/91999)

A quiet corner of a backyard has been transformed into a quirky spot for conversation with classic metal yard chairs painted in bright hues. A trellis is flanked by a white picket fence, while a painted birdhouse and other garden ornaments add a touch of whimsy.

Lounging zone

If your garden has enough space for a small patio, consider adding several loungers. These comfy chairs invite a quick nap after a few hours of reading the latest mystery. Zero-gravity loungers, which tip back effortlessly, offer the sensation of floating in mid-air. Another favorite option for lounging is a hammock, either strung between two trees or fastened to a metal frame. If your garden boasts a sturdy tree limb, consider adding a single-seater hammock chair as your own private sanctuary.

TREASURED OBJECTS

Just as many people fill their homes with the items they cherish, many gardeners fill their outdoor spaces with the decorative objects they love. These treasures might include artwork, metal sculpture or wall hangings, and yard art like gazing balls, wind chimes, concrete animals, or garden spinners.

Whether in front of a fireplace, a campfire, or a fire pit, who doesn't love the warm and welcoming ambiance of crackling flames? A fire pit, the newest entry in controlled fire, can be surrounded with comfy seating to give your family an inviting spot to gather in.

WATER FEATURES

Including a source of water in the garden is a tradition that goes back many centuries. Early Middle Eastern houses were often constructed around an open, central courtyard replete with exotic plants and cascading fountains. In Asia, gardens may have had spare plantings but usually showcased a small stream or koi pond. Today, the cooling sight and soothing sound of water continues to provide a refreshing addition to home gardens around the world.

A water feature is considered any landscape enhancement that uses water and other materials to bring beauty and tranquility to the environment. Water features can include ponds, waterfalls, and fountains. If you lack the space for a large water feature, opt for small features, such as solar fountains, container water gardens, or bubbling water urns. These fit easily into a garden or small patio, yet most still provide the pleasant sound of gurgling water. Locate your water feature away from areas where water runs off lawns or gardens; this run-off may contain bacteria, chemicals, or plant debris. Also locate your feature away from shrubs or trees that shed leaves or pine needles.

Stately purple irises line the stone edging of a diminutive artificial pond.

TYPES OF PLANTS

Be sure that the plants you include in or around your water feature don't mind wet feet. Bog plants that are tolerant of water covering their soil include umbrella palm, papyrus, pickerelweed, dwarf cattail, and colocasia.

Oxygenators that clean and add oxygen to water include fanwort, hornwort, and arrowhead. Surface floating plants include duckweed, water lettuce, water lily, water hyacinth, and water fern. Certain floating plants, such as water lilies, are known for their exquisite flowers. Eelgrass or pondweeds actually live under the water. Iris, canna, and taro do well planted adjacent to water.

TYPES OF WATER FEATURES

Even a simple birdbath is an attractive water feature, easily enhanced by surrounding it with plants or shrubs. But if you have something more dramatic in mind, consider the suggestions below.

Fountain

This large, multi-tiered water feature can be made of stone, resin, or concrete. Although new fountains are pricey, older ones can sometimes be picked up from online marketplaces. Even if they no longer work, replacing a pump and tubing is not a major deal. Just be sure you have a grounded outlet nearby.

Bubbler

This is a mid-sized ceramic pot fitted with a recycling pump that makes a pleasant burbling sound. A bubbler looks good on a base of white or orange pebbles. Consider pot colors that complement your plants—pale neutrals or rich earth tones will go with anything, while bright colors like royal blue, bright red, sunny yellow, neon pink, or vibrant orange will provide contrast.

Small fountain

This portable water feature is often powered by batteries or solar panels. You can use one in a birdbath or on a tabletop or collect several to add interest to a woodland garden or shady area.

Pond

A favorite backyard addition, a pond needs a circulation system to keep the water moving and a filtration system to keep the water clean. Ready-made pond liners, pump assemblies, and maintenance kits simplify the process. Livestock troughs and large plastic tubs make great ponds for smaller spaces.

Water Garden in a Barrel

One of the most engaging outdoor projects to share with children is the creation of a water garden in a half-barrel planter. The first step is to line the barrel with heavy plastic, then fill it halfway with water. Add water-loving plants like cattail or canna set on bricks, along with duckweed, water lily, or other floating plants. Be sure to drop in a "dunk," a large floating pellet of compressed grasses that keeps mosquitoes from breeding there. Your mini-pond will likely house a frog or two—providing another natural control for mosquitoes—and should receive daily visits from chipmunks, dragonflies, and maybe even hummingbirds.

READ MORE AT GARDENING KNOW HOW

To learn more about water features and how to add a DIY fountain to your garden, follow these links.

- **"What Is a Water Feature: Types of Water Features for Gardens"** (URL = gkh.us/60552)
- **"Upcycled Fountain Ideas: Tips for DIY Water Features"** (URL = gkh.us/123949)

Koi pond

These Asian-style ponds are adored by adults and children alike. (Some predators are equally thrilled, so be sure to protect your fish with fine netting.) The koi, an ancient type of carp, has now spread beyond Japan and can be found in much of the world. Koi or goldfish require a pond with a depth of 2 to 3 feet (60–90 cm). If your region has freezing winters, dig the pond even deeper. To maintain the health and safety of your fish, there needs to be a constant flow of water and overhangs where they can take cover if threatened.

Reflecting pool

These serene features are created in the same way as ponds, by excavating a substantial hole, lining it with heavy vinyl, and adding a recycling pump. Reflecting pools are generally more geometric than ponds, a simple rectangle or square edged in stone with a dark interior to provide reflections and create a captivating sense of mystery.

Stream

This is probably the most work-intensive type of water addition, but when you relax beside a moving, burbling brook that you created and watch all the wild creatures, birds, and insects that are drawn to the spot, it will feel totally worthwhile. Many gardeners take on the construction alone, but consider engaging a few cash-strapped teenagers or burly college kids to help out. Streams require the same system of recycling and filtering water as a pond.

Waterfall

This dramatic garden addition usually accompanies a fabricated stream or is included in the design of a pond. Waterfalls work particularly well if your property already has a slope, otherwise, soil and rock can be built up to provide a drop. Make sure to create a series of cascades in order to vary the sounds of splashing water.

Bog

Consider creating a bog in a low-lying area of lawn that might already be a bit marshy, where semi-aquatic flowering plants can flourish, pollinators will feed, and your local amphibious neighbors will be sure to explore.

A narrow terrace garden offers the best of a bog garden, koi pond, and stream-fed waterfall. Seating provides a perfect view of the tranquil scene, and water-loving plants offer the brightly colored fish a place to hide from any unwanted visitors.

A refreshing spray of water rises above the flowers from a classic, cherub-themed fountain that can also serve as a birdbath.

A bubbler urn can fit into a garden of just about any size. Here a bubbler tucked in among the flowers attracts thirsty butterflies.

CHAPTER TEN

WEEDS, GARDEN PESTS, AND DISEASES

It often feels as if gardens are magnets for problems. In spite of all the hard work you put into your cherished plots, some invader, pest, or disease is always just looming on the horizon. Gardeners once felt free to use toxic chemical sprays against these threats—often with dire ecological results. DDT, anyone? But now a new era of planetary stewardship is upon us, and we are much more careful about how we fight back, seeking out organic solutions before resorting to the chemical sprayer. Weeds can be controlled by pulling or using boiling water or white vinegar. Biological controls for insect pests include ladybugs, praying mantids, ground beetles, aphid midges, braconid wasps, damsel bugs, and green lacewings. Other safer solutions include neem oil, pyrethrin, and good old soapy water. Chamomile tea is a cure-all for fungal diseases, while baking soda and liquid soap protect roses from black spot. To thwart fungal, viral, and bacterial diseases, a mix of garlic cloves, water, and liquid soap does the trick.

CONTROLLING WEEDS

Weeds are a fact of life for most gardeners. They may pop up in cracks in a walkway or against the foundation . . . or in the heart of your garden, taking advantage of the healthy soil you created for your chosen plants.

A light-hearted definition of a weed is "any plant growing where you don't want it." Yet true weeds, based on human value judgment, are the most costly category of agricultural pests. Worldwide, they cause more yield loss and add more to farmers' production costs than insects, crop pathogens, nematodes, or warm-blooded pests. In the United States, they are formally categorized as *weed* (such as crabgrass), *noxious weed* (field bindweed), and *invasive weed* (kudzu or English ivy). Elsewhere, they might be classified by their gross morphological features as grasses, sedges, and broadleaf weeds or grouped by their life cycle as annual, biennial, and perennial.

Whatever the categories, these weeds need to be recognized and controlled. Yet, weeds aren't inherently bad: many weeds stabilize the soil, add organic matter, and recycle nutrients. Some are edible to humans and provide habitat and food for wildlife. There might also be cases where you keep a "visiting" species. You may be thrilled to see charming, albeit aggressive plants, such as columbine. Other plants that spring up are violas, ivy, foxglove, and lupine.

If you see a seedling you don't recognize, use an app or search online for a match. You can opt to wait and see if the adult plant is one you want to preserve. Unfortunately, by that time an objectionable plant might already be entrenched. If something is recognizable as a weed, remove it while it is young to prevent further spreading. Plants with deep taproots will also be easier to unearth when immature.

In general, you can minimize weeds with a thick layer of mulch around your plants, and any weeds that make it through are much easier to remove. Keep your garden clogs and weeding tools clean to prevent spreading any seeds. Be cautious with pre-emergence sprays, as these may prevent your veggie seeds from emerging. For an eco-friendly weed treatment, spread black plastic over an area in the autumn or early spring. Leave it for six to eight weeks to prevent weed seed germination.

Editor's Tip

You should turn to chemical control as a last resort only; the organic approach to weed control is far more environmentally friendly.

COMMON GARDEN INVADERS

Here are some of the most common weeds that crop up in home gardens, with tips on how to combat them.

Bindweed

This climber (*Convolvulus* spp.), often called wild morning glory, wraps thin threadlike vines around other plants. It has a large and hardy root system, so killing it may take several attempts. Start by pouring boiling water about 2 to 3 feet (60–90 cm) beyond the bindweed to reach as many roots as possible. Or heavily apply an herbicide, and re-apply when the plant reaches 12 inches (30 cm). Adding plants that spread densely will force bindweed out of the bed.

Common chickweed

This annual weed (*Stellaria media*) grows in moist areas; without competition from other plants, it can produce roughly 800 seeds and takes up to eight years to eradicate. Fight back by pulling young plants before they flower and keeping soil at a low pH (acidic).

Crabgrass

This frustrating nuisance (*Digitaria* spp.) is the bane of gardeners and lawn lovers. In early spring, a pre-emergent herbicide works well against crabgrass. For spot crabgrass treatment all year, say in flower beds or small areas of a lawn, a nonselective herbicide will work. Later in the year, after the seeds have germinated, use a crabgrass-selective herbicide. Be aware that mature crabgrass is better able to resist selective herbicides.

Dandelion

A selective broadleaf herbicide will kill young dandelions (*Taraxacum officinale*) but no other plants. Use a nonselective herbicide only for spot dandelion removal. Dig up the taproot when the seedlings first appear. (Try those young leaves in salads!) Or try applying a pre-emergent—a chemical that prevents seeds from germinating—in late winter. Ultimately, you need to stop dandelions early, before the fluffy seed heads appear.

Dig Deeper

READ MORE AT GARDENING KNOW HOW

Follow the links below for more information about weeds.

- **"What Is a Weed: Weed Info and Control Methods in Gardens"** (URL = gkh.us/270)
- **"Garden Weed Management: How to Control Weeds in Your Garden"** (URL = gkh.us/6947)
- **"Newspaper for Weeds — Does Newspaper Kill Weeds?"** (URL = gkh.us/187034)

Horsetail

Horsetail (*Equisetum* spp.), is a perennial, flowerless ditch weed that spreads by both spores and rhizomes, making it a very hard-to-kill pest. There are no specific horsetail herbicides, and most chemical options are not particularly effective. If you dig it up, all the roots must be removed, or the weed will reappear. Another option is smothering the plants with a sheet of plastic for at least one growing season.

Nutsedge

This perennial grasslike weed (*Cyperus* spp.) grows in wet or poorly drained areas. It can be very difficult to eradicate manually—yanking it out by hand stimulates more growth from the weed's underground nutlets. When applied properly, a selective herbicide will kill it without harming your other plants.

Pigweed

These highly troublesome weeds (*Amaranthus* spp.) can invade lawns and gardens. Pull out the red taproot early, before it can establish itself, and mulch in the winter to prevent sunlight from reaching the seeds.

Plantain

Plantago major (broadleaf plantain) has smooth, oval leaves, while *P. lanceolata* (narrow-leaf plantain) has ribbed, lance-shaped leaves. Prevent plantains with soil aeration and twice-a-year fertilization. Dig up the plants as they emerge, especially in sandy soil or soil softened by rain or irrigation. Or apply a post-emergent herbicide labeled for plantains in autumn or spring.

Purslane

Succulent *Portulaca oleracea* has fleshy red stems and small, paddle-shaped leaves that grow in circles close to the ground. Deal with this plant while young; at the seed stage it can throw seeds some distance away from the mother plant and infest other parts of your garden. Hand-pulling works, but the seeds will continue to ripen. Toss plants into the compost pile or the trash.

Scotch thistle

Onopordum acanthium has a terrible reputation, yet in a small garden, it can be controlled. If you cut it down while it's flowering, be sure to burn or bag the flowers, which can produce ripe seeds even after being severed from the stem. Preempt this weed when it's still a rosette with a thorough coating of weed killer. If you dig up Scotch thistle, be sure to wear thick gloves as protection from its sharp prickles.

Hand-pulling weeds from a border. Weeding is one of the more onerous chores of garden maintenance, but getting ahead of these invaders can ensure your wanted plants flourish.

Weed Control Methods

There are a number of weed control methods, depending on the weed and the gardener. Here are your options.

Cultural weed control. One of the easiest ways to control weeds is through cultural control, or, simply, prevention. Close planting in the garden can reduce weed growth by eliminating open space for them to take over. Cover crops are good for this, as well. Adding mulch will prevent light from getting to weed seeds and prevents growth.

Mechanical weed control. This can be accomplished through hand-pulling, hoeing, digging, or mowing (which slows growth and reduces seed formation). These methods are effective, but can be time consuming.

Chemical weed control. Many weeds, like dodder, ivy, and kudzu, can become aggressive to the point of taking over, so chemical control is sometimes necessary and used as a last resort. There are numerous herbicides available to help eliminate common weed plants.

Natural weed control. Invasive weeds are generally well worth the trouble of removal. Some weeds, however, can actually be quite attractive in the garden, so why not consider allowing them to stay? This more-natural weed control method results in a lush native environment when weeds are given their own designated spot. Some of these "good weeds" include Joe-pye weed, chicory, hawkweed, and Queen Anne's lace, which are all attractive plants in their own right. Of course, which weed goes and which weed stays depends on the preferences of an individual gardener, although a little bit of information on weed types and control methods makes this decision easier.

DISCOURAGING PESTS

Experts estimate that there are up to 30 million species of insects on the planet—some 200 million insects for every living human. It's no wonder that identifying garden pests can be tricky. But recognizing insect pests helps you distinguish between beneficial bugs and bug pests so that you can encourage the former and discourage the latter. It also allows you to tailor pest control to the particular culprits involved.

EVALUATING INSECT DAMAGE

If you actually see an insect on a plant, note its appearance and habit—size, color, body shape; flying or crawling; alone or in a group—plus the damage it did and the type of plant it targeted. Insects usually damage plants either by sucking or chewing. Sap-feeding pests insert slender, needle-like mouthparts into the leaves or stems of plants and suck out the sap. This results in browning or wilting, or a sticky substance called honeydew on the foliage. If the leaves are spotted, you likely have mesophyll feeders, sucking out individual plant cells of leaves and stems. Other pests chew holes in the leaves, trunks, or branches.

Eradicating insects

Following is a list of common insect pests and how to identify and treat them.

- Aphids are teensy pear-shaped bugs that suck the sap out of leaves and stems. Signs include sticky honeydew, wilted or yellowed leaves, or black sooty fungus residue. Treat them with a soapy water solution or upgrade to neem oil.

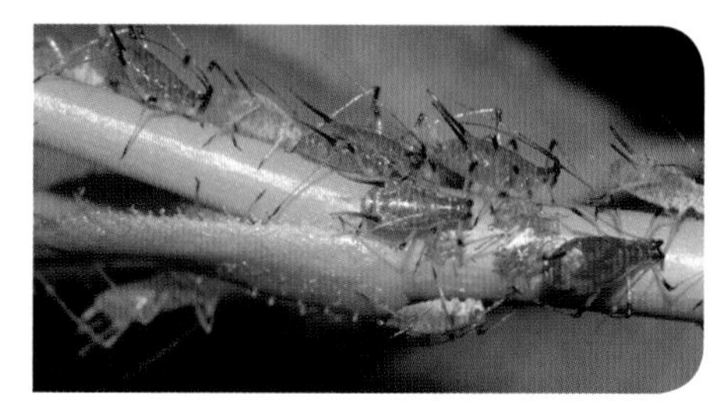

A swarm of aphids attack a rose stem.

- Cabbage maggot adults are tiny gray-brown flies. Females lay eggs at the roots of brassicas, and the larvae gorge themselves on the roots, killing the plants. Signs are wilting foliage and stunted growth. To treat, cover young cabbages with row covers until after egg-laying season; destroy any eggs you find.

Colorado potato beetles make a meal of the leaves of a potato plant.

- Colorado potato beetles enjoy all nightshade plants, including tomatoes, peppers, and eggplants. They eat foliage, cause stunted growth, and decimate young plants. Signs are feeding beetles and defoliated plants or leaves speckled with holes. Hand pick them off, and drown them in soapy water. Destroy any eggs.
- Cutworms look like grubs but are moth larvae that feed at night. They cut through stems of young plants and damage older plants. Collar stems with 4-inch (10 cm) segments of paper towel tubes, fitting them snugly into the ground. Diatomaceous earth or coffee grounds can also deter these pests.
- Flea beetles eat the foliage of broccoli, cabbage, cauliflower, kale, radish, tomato, eggplant, and pepper plants. The larvae feast on roots. Signs are small black beetles and small round holes in foliage. Dust leaves with talcum powder, or mix 1 part alcohol, 2½ parts water, and 1 teaspoon liquid dish soap.
- Japanese beetles voraciously eat foliage and flowers; their larvae eat plant roots. Signs are beetles on foliage and skeletonized leaves. Apply row covers, and hand pick beetles off plants, and drown. Treat grub spots in the lawn with milky spore bacteria.
- Mexican bean beetles look like ladybugs but more orange-yellow, with 16 black spots. Both the larvae grubs and adults devastate foliage. Fight back at the earliest stage—dust diatomaceous earth on foliage to kill the bright yellow eggs and larvae. And be sure to move your beans the following season.

A slug chomps through daisy leaves.

- Slugs feed at dusk and dine on your vegetable plants until dawn. Signs include jagged holes in leaves and slimy trails. Hand pick off or deter with diatomaceous earth, eggshells, or coffee grounds sprinkled around the plants. Do not use poison baits; other wildlife might eat the dead slugs.

Beneficial Insects

Some plants are wildly popular with the most beneficial insects for a garden.

To learn how to attract these helpers, scan the QR code or follow the link to "Creating Bug Gardens: Attracting Beneficial Insects for a Garden" (URL = gkh.us/99206).

A squash bug leaves browned foliage.

- Squash bugs, brown and slightly flattened, suck the sap from zucchini, summer squash, winter squash, and pumpkins, along with cucumbers and melons. Look for yellowing or browning leaves. Scrape eggs from the underside of leaves. Adults overwinter in vines so compost or burn any autumn garden debris.
- Thrips are minute, slender insects with fringed wings and asymmetrical mouthparts. They feed mostly on plants by puncturing and sucking up the contents. Look for tiny rice-like flecks on foliage, deformed growth, and discolored spots. Blast with a garden hose or saturate the plant with dish soap and water.
- Tomato hornworms are larval sphinx moths, an unusual moth that should be protected . . . but they do love to eat tomatoes. Signs are the larvae themselves, plus holes in the leaves. Do not kill them, but do remove them to a distant spot with lots of greenery.

The tomato hornworm is a fascinating creature to catch sight of, with coloration that blends perfectly with the tomato plants it eats. It is the larval stage of the beautiful sphinx moth, so rather than killing this voracious pest, remove any you find, and relocate to another spot.

ANIMAL PESTS

Hungry animals can be a menace to both the flower garden and the kitchen garden. They can threaten plants on two levels: below the ground and above the ground. Burrowing voles will eat roots, bulbs, and tubers. Browsing deer, along with rabbits, woodchucks, and other small mammals will eat foliage, flowers, or fruit—sometimes all three. One aspect of having a garden is enjoying the wildlife that comes into the space, but not when they decimate your tulips . . . or help themselves to your entire strawberry harvest.

Animal deterrents

Fortunately, gardeners have come up with a variety of ways to humanely foil these wily intruders.

- Place wire cloches over growing plants to protect their delicate leaves.
- Spray this hot pepper mixture on your plants. Mix 1 ounce of hot pepper sauce, 4 drops of natural dish soap, and 1 cup of aromatic marigold leaves. Add eggs and garlic for an extra ick factor.
- Plant species that animals dislike—marigolds keep rabbits away, and mint and lavender will keep small pests at bay.

Staff Hacks

Do you want to learn how to enjoy wildlife without compromising your garden? Nikki Tilley, GKH Archivist, offers her advice. "Inviting wildlife to your backyard might seem counterintuitive when planting a garden, especially vegetables, but you can actually enjoy them both. I always include extra veggie plants in addition to other known favorites to help discourage animals from visiting my other garden beds. While it's inevitable that a few plants will be lost here and there, overall, this is usually enough to keep the wildlife happy and my other plants intact. I'm still able to enjoy beautiful blooms and harvest plenty of vegetables each season, while welcoming wildlife to the garden. It's a win-win!"

Dig Deeper

READ MORE AT GARDENING KNOW HOW

To learn more about insects in the garden, follow these links.

- **"What Bug Is This — Basic Tips on Identifying Garden Pests"** (URL = gkh.us/134520)
- **"Getting Rid of Bad Bugs with Beneficial Insects"** (URL = gkh.us/261)

- Check out store-bought repellents geared to specific pests; these include predator urine for deer.
- Add a splash of milk and 4 drops of dish soap to the water in a spray bottle to keep deer away.
- Stop deer and squirrels from munching on young plants with bars of soap raised up on skewers.
- Offer critters alternative food sources, like bird seed in small buckets, away from the garden.
- Chicken wire or other fencing—sunk several inches into the ground and high enough to thwart deer—will safeguard the kitchen garden.
- Use noise to scare off shy animals like deer and rabbits. Place a large wind chime in the garden or leave a battery-operated radio on overnight tuned to classic rock.
- To keep birds away from newly seeded plots, you can always resort to a trusty scarecrow.

A scarecrow stands vigil over a garden. This traditional method keeps birds away.

PLANT DISEASES

Gardeners should take heart knowing that if their garden is flourishing, that means their plants are healthy—and healthy plants are better able to resist disease. Yet the cool moist spring and autumn weather in many temperate regions is ideal for the spread and development of plant diseases. This is why it's important to space plants properly and provide good air circulation to keep diseases at bay. Commercial disease-control products are all protectants, which means they must be applied before the problem occurs. Therefore, it pays to be vigilant throughout the growing season and frequently check leaves, stems, branches, bark, buds, flowers, and fruit for any signs of infection.

COMMON PLANT DISEASES

There are several common diseases.

- Black knot *(Apiosporina morbosa)* is a disfiguring fungal disease of native plum and cherry trees that leaves wart-like growths. New knots appear in midsummer on small twigs. The knots can grow up to 8 inches (20 cm) in diameter and turn black in the autumn. Control by planting the more resistant types. At the end of January prune out knots, cutting at least 4 inches (10 cm) beyond the knots, and bag them at once to prevent spores from spreading. Spraying with lime sulfur during the dormant season and wettable sulfur at full bloom and petal drop may reduce new infections.

Black knot appears as wart-like growths.

Black spot disfigures the leaves of a rose.

- Black spot is a common fungal disease of roses that causes circular, smudge-edged black spots with fringed margins. Leaves turn yellow, and bloom sizes may be reduced. Control by planting resistant varieties, dispose of infected leaves, and don't spray water on leaves. Pruning hard before spring growth will remove infected shoots. In spring and early summer, spray with sulfur- or copper-based fungicide, and then apply at one-to-two-week intervals through the growing season, occasionally alternating the fungicide.

When plants display symptoms of disease, it's a good idea to prune out the diseased, damaged, or dead plant tissue. Be aware, though, that disease pathogens can catch a ride on your pruners or other gardening tools, possibly infecting the next plant you use them on. Sterilizing tools between uses can help prevent the spread of diseases.

To find out how to keep your tools sterile, scan the code or follow the link to "Sterilizing Pruning Tools: Learn How to Sterilize Pruning Tools" (URL = gkh.us/121835)

Botrytis blight devastates a rose.

- Botrytis blight, also called gray mold, is a fuzzy fungus that develops on dead and dying plant tissue but spreads to healthy tissue in wet conditions. Infections appear as water-soaked spots on foliage, flower parts, and young stems. On flowering plants, woody ornamentals, and small fruit, it can cause flower, leaf, and shoot blights and stem and fruit rot. Susceptible plants include peonies, roses, hostas, strawberries, and raspberries. Control with disease-resistant cultivars, and discard garden debris and refuse in autumn. Grow susceptible, sun-loving plants in sunny areas with good air circulation. Water only at the base of plants. Remove infected leaves and fruit. Fungicides rarely control this disease.

Downy mildew browns pumpkin plants.

- Downy mildew grows in moist environments and attacks cold-season vegetables, such as brassicas and cucurbits, and might cause the loss of your whole harvest. Symptoms begin with irregular yellow patches on leaves, which then turn light brown. A fluffy white fungus will start to grow on the undersides of leaves. Cabbage, cauliflower, and broccoli can develop dark spots. Severe infections can kill young plants. Control with good air circulation and spacing and a copper fungicidal spray, and clean up garden debris where spores hide.

Late blight disease destroys tomatoes.

- Early and late blight are fungal diseases that attack nightshade members. Early blight *(Alternaria solani)* appears as dark brown or black leaf spots with concentric rings on stems and large, black, leathery, sunken spots on fruit. During wet years, infections occur in spring. Late blight *(Phytophthora infestans)* forms irregular greenish black blotches first on older leaves or stems, then quickly spreads to fruit. It may not appear until August in wet years, but can destroy entire plants overnight. Control early blight by spacing and pruning, avoid overhead watering, pick off infected leaves, and apply a copper spray every 7 to 10 days. For late blight, remove entire plants, and bag immediately. Do not compost. Apply a copper spray every 5 to 10 days.

Mosaic disease infects eggplant leaves.

- Mosaic is a group of viruses that affect numerous plants. The tomato mosaic virus affects tomatoes, peppers, potatoes, apples, pears, and cherries; the tobacco mosaic virus infects tobacco, tomatoes, peppers, cucumbers, beets, lettuce, and petunias. Symptoms include mottled yellow and green leaves, often curled and distorted; yellowing; stunted growth; malformed fruits; and reduced yield. No chemical solutions are available, so remove infected plants, right down to the roots, and destroy them; do not cultivate susceptible plants in the same area for two years.

- Powdery mildew is a garden threat caused by many different species of fungi in the order Erysiphales. It is very host-specific—mildew on cucumbers will not infect roses. Look for white, powdery growth on leaves and shoots that develops during warm days with cool nights. Targets include roses, maples, gooseberries, phlox, peonies, ninebark, lupines, lilacs, sage, squash, and cucumbers. Control by choosing disease-resistant varieties, and avoid planting in shady or crowded spots. Start a fungicide spray program before the disease is advanced. Destroy infected leaves. Prevention includes spraying a copper- or sulfur-based fungicide every 10 days from spring to autumn.

Powdery mildew attacks peony leaves.

- Rust refers to a large family of fungi, with each type infecting only specific plants. Most rust diseases begin as small orange, red, or brown spots on the underside of leaves that then turn brown in summer. Susceptible plants include hollyhock, heuchera, daylily, pear, rhododendron, zinnia, and juniper. Control with resistant cultivars, remove infected leaves, and spray every 10 days with a copper- or sulfur-based fungicide.

Rust disease takes over a zinnia leaf.

READ MORE AT GARDENING KNOW HOW

To learn how to spot a disease-free plant before you take it home, as well as other useful info on plant diseases, follow the links below.

- **"Choosing Healthy Plants: How to Tell If a Plant Is Healthy"** (URL = gkh.us/63048)
- **"Plant Disease Transmission to Humans: Can Virus and Plant Bacteria Infect a Human"** (URL = gkh.us/45209)
- **"Diseased Plant Disposal: What to Do with Infected Plants in the Garden"** (URL = gkh.us/17896)

Verticillium wilt infects basil seedlings.

- Verticillium wilt is a serious fungal disease that affects deciduous trees, herbaceous perennials, berries, flowering cherries, and vegetables. It invades roots, moving upward, plugging up the plant's transportation system. Symptoms start with yellowing, wilting, and dying of young twigs and branches, often on one side. It gets worse from year to year. Cutting into a woody stem can reveal black or brown streaks. Control is all prophylactic; there is no treatment for infected plants. Avoid drought stress or flooding of landscape trees. Remove dead and dying plants, infested roots, and soil; replant with resistant species. After pruning each tree, sterilize tools with rubbing alcohol, Lysol, or a 10% household bleach solution.

CHAPTER ELEVEN

WELCOMING POLLINATORS

We depend on pollinators for one out of every three bites of the food we eat. Just think about that for a minute. Nearly 80 percent of the 1,400 crop plants grown worldwide, those that produce our food and plant-based products, require pollination from bees, birds, butterflies, moths, fruit bats, and other creatures.

The world is finally realizing the debt we owe to these tiny laborers, and so individual gardeners have started creating havens for these busy helpers. We know from the news that honeybee colonies are collapsing, and each year gardeners report seeing fewer honeybees among their flowers. Fortunately, there are also pollinating solitary bees that we can draw to our yards. Monarch butterflies are again on the endangered list, so they also need support in the form of milkweed plants. Let us hope that a multitude of gardeners will begin doing their part to ensure the well-being of these most vulnerable pollinators.

SUPPORTING BEES

Bees play a vital role in our food chain. Not only do they pollinate the fruits and vegetables we eat, they also pollinate the clover, alfalfa, and corn consumed by dairy and market animals. Yet, due to loss of habitat and use of toxic pesticides—likely the root cause of the devastating phenomenon known as "colony collapse"—there has been a worldwide decline in bee populations.

Planting nectar-rich flowers one way to help. You can even establish a bee garden in planters if you don't have a lot of space. Anyone with a balcony or patio can grow container plants for bees. Not killing off spring dandelions, one of the first foods available to bees coming out of hibernation, is another way to support these garden friends.

CREATING A BEE GARDEN

There are a number of tricks to bring bees into your yard and to keep them coming back.

- Choose plants that attract them. These winged pollinators love native wildflowers, flowering herbs, flowering shrubs, and many flowering fruits and vegetables, especially berries.
- Group similar plants together. Bees will be attracted to clumps of the same plant, so allow at least a square yard (1 m^2) of space per species. If space is limited, grow a few wildflowers or herbs in a planter box as a foraging habitat for honeybees.
- Plant flowers with long blooming cycles. Another option is to plant flowers that will bloom in succession, one flowering just as another is fading. This system can furnish food well into two growing seasons.
- Allow your plants to flower. Some herbs lose their flavor or grow bitter after flowering, but if feeding bees is your intent, allow some of your herbs to bloom. After you harvest vegetable crops, some plants will continue to flower, perhaps the last food bees will find in the autumn.
- Add a water source to your bee garden. A shallow dish or a bird bath with pebbles in it, a small fountain, or even a dripping hose, will provide water for bees to sip. Large-leaf plants that retain droplets after watering offer another bee hydrating station.
- Do not use pesticides, herbicides, or other chemicals. This cannot be emphasized enough. Neonicotinoids used in commercial sprays have been linked to the problem of colony collapse, where a whole network of hives stops functioning. Many chemicals are toxic to bees and other pollinators, which defeats the whole point of drawing them to your yard.

Staff Hacks

GKH senior editor, Liz Baessler, offers her recipe for mead. "If you keep bees to harvest honey, you're probably looking for something to do with it all. My favorite thing is getting in touch with my inner Norse god and making mead. With 3 pounds (1.4 kg) of honey you can make 1 gallon (1.8 l)—or five wine bottles—of mead. You'll need a gallon jug, an air lock, and sanitizer, plus a sachet of wine yeast. Sterilize your jug, plop in your honey, and then fill it most of the way up with water. Cover the top with a sanitized hand, and shake thoroughly. Add the yeast, secure the sterilized air lock, and let the whole thing sit in a dark, out-of-the-way spot for a few months. The yeast will eat all the sugar, turning it into alcohol. Give the result a try. You might just discover your new favorite drink."

Types of Bees

A bee is not aggressive by nature. Its priority, when out and about, is to gather nectar and pollen before returning to the hive. In the temperate-climate garden you may encounter the following bees.

Bumblebee. These gentle feeders (genus *Bombus)* often nest in holes in the ground or under fallen logs. Bumblebees pollinate native flowers, tomatoes, peppers, and strawberries.

Carpenter bee. This dark bee (genus *Xylocopa),* with its shiny abdomen, burrows into hard plant material, such as dead wood. Considered solitary bees that do not form hives, they are important pollinators of shallow or open-faced flowers.

Honeybee. The small honeybee *(Apis mellifera)* has a largely hairless, striped abdomen. Many subspecies, ranging in color from nearly black to bright orange, are farmed by beekeepers.

Mason bee. The genus *Osmia* contains large, hairy bees that are great cross-pollinators because they are not picky about where they feed—fruit and nut orchards or berry patches. These solitary bees normally live in gaps between rocks, but can be drawn in the yard with bamboo nesting sites.

- Appreciate weeds and wildflowers. Dandelion, clover, loosestrife, milkweed, goldenrod, and other flowering weeds are important food sources for bees. If you encourage these plants to grow in your yard, the contented buzzing of feeding bees will soon become a fixture in your garden landscape.

Bee-Friendly Plants

BLACK-EYED SUSAN

Perennial *Rudbeckias*, with their golden yellow flowers and deep brown centers, are rich in nectar. For more information *see* page 90.

CATMINT

Bees love the purple flower spikes of catmint (*Nepata* spp.); look for species that won't self-seed and take over your garden.

CONEFLOWER

The nectar-rich composite flowers of traditional garden *Echinaceas* will attract bees in droves. For more information *see* page 97.

HYSSOP

An evergreen herb, *Hyssopus officinalis* is a mint family member grown for its aromatic leaves and flowers. For more information *see* page 243.

LAVENDER

This fragrant herb is a well-known lure for many types of pollinators; grow it in clumps to encourage bees. For more information *see* page 244.

LUPINE

The fat, pea-like flowers—in purple, pink, or white—of *Lupinus* species attract bumblebees and mason bees. For more information *see* page 106.

RED HOT POKER

This striking, fiery perennial plant, also known as torch lily (*Kniphofia* spp.), attracts bees, hummingbirds, and Baltimore orioles.

SALVIA

Salvias, or sages, which tolerate dry conditions and bloom "forever," are magnets for pollinators. For more information *see* pages 250 and 253.

SEDUM

The succulents in the large *Sedum* genus bear blossoms that many bees, butterflies, and flies find intoxicating. For more information *see* page 167.

SUNFLOWER

The tall, cheerful *Helianthus* annuals offer a bounty of nectar to bees, hoverflies, and small insects. For more information *see* page 81.

THYME

Thyme (genus *Thymus*) blooms in summer when populations of bees—and their hungry young—are at their peak. For more information *see* page 256.

VERBENA

The verbena flower (*Verbena* spp.) will grow until the first frost, offering food to bees and butterflies through the autumn.

ATTRACTING BUTTERFLIES

The concept of butterfly gardening—creating an environment that welcomes these winged beauties into your yard—has become a popular endeavor in recent years. Butterflies and other pollinators are finally being recognized for the important role they play in the planet's ecology, and, as a result, gardeners all over the world are creating safe habitats for them. With the right plants, you can create your own butterfly garden, one that offers not only nectar-bearing flowers that are butterfly favorites, but also host plants that support their caterpillars.

ATTRACTING BUTTERFLIES

To create a butterfly garden, you'll need to select an area in full sun that is sheltered from high winds. Designate this area as a butterfly-only zone, and do not include any birdhouses, bird baths, or bird feeders in it. Butterflies do, however, like to bathe themselves and drink from shallow puddles of water, so it helps to add a small, shallow dish filled with pebbles and water to serve as a butterfly bath. Butterflies also like "puddling," or taking up minerals by lapping wet soil, so offer them a wet spot on a patch of bare dirt, as well. They will also sun themselves on dark rocks or reflective surfaces, such as gazing balls. This helps heat up and dry out their wings so they can fly properly. The most important thing for butterfly health, though, is to never use pesticides in a butterfly garden.

There are many flowers, wildflowers, weeds, and even trees that attract butterflies. Butterflies have good vision and are drawn to large groups of brightly colored flowers. They are also attracted to strongly scented flower nectar. They tend to favor plants with clusters of blooms or large flowers that offer them a "landing deck" to rest on while drinking the sweet nectar.

Butterflies are active from spring until frost, so plant specimens with staggered bloom times so that they will able to enjoy nectar from your garden all season long.

SELECTING PLANTS FOR BUTTERFLY EGGS

It is not enough to just have plants that attract butterflies with their nectar. You will also need to include plants that support butterfly eggs and larvae in your butterfly garden.

Butterfly hosts are the specific plants that butterflies lay their eggs on or near so that their larvae can eat the plant before forming a chrysalis. These species are basically sacrificial plants that you add to the garden and allow the caterpillars to feast on so they will grow into healthy butterflies.

When a female butterfly is ready to lay her eggs, she will flit around to different plants, landing on different leaves and testing them out with her olfactory glands. Once she finds the right plant, she will lay her eggs, usually on the undersides of leaves but sometimes under loose bark or in mulch near the host plant.

After hatching from their eggs, caterpillars will spend their entire larval stage eating the leaves of their host plants until they are ready to make their chrysalises and morph into butterflies. Some butterflies lay their eggs in trees. In these cases, you can try planting dwarf varieties of fruit or flowering trees or simply locate your butterfly garden near one of these larger trees.

With the proper balance of plants that attract butterflies and those that host their young, you can create a welcoming and nurturing butterfly garden.

Butterfly Hosts

To help you choose plants to attract these winged beauties, here is a list of some common garden butterflies and their preferred host plants.

American lady: artemisia

Black swallowtail: carrots, rue, parsley, dill, fennel

Buckeye: snapdragon

Cabbage white: broccoli, cabbage, cauliflower

Common blue: legumes, bird's foot trefoil

Common hairstreak, checkered skipper: mallow, hollyhock

Dainty sulphur: sneezeweed *(Helenium),* marigold

Dogface: lead plant, false indigo *(Baptista),* prairie clover

Gorgone checkerspot: sunflower

Great spangled fritillary: violet

Monarch: milkweed

Mourning cloak: willow, elm

Orange sulphur: alfalfa, vetch, pea

Painted lady: thistle, hollyhock, sunflower, mallows

Pearl crescent, silvery checkerspot: aster

Pipevine swallowtail: azaleas, phlox, petunia, Dutchman's pipe

Red admiral: nettle

Red spotted purple: willow, aspen, poplar, black oak

Silver spotted skipper: American wisteria, black locust

Silvery blue: lupine

Tiger swallowtail: wild cherry, birch, ash, poplar, apple tree, tulip tree, sycamore

Viceroy: pussy willow, plum, cherry

Best Plants for Butterflies

BEE BALM
Monarda, a native North American plant often found in border gardens, is a favorite of bees and butterflies. For more information *see* page 89.

BUTTERFLY WEED
Asclepias tuberosa is a perennial milkweed with spectacular orange flowers that produce copious amounts of nectar.

COSMOS
The tall flowers of *Cosmos bipinnatus* attract a number of butterflies, including monarchs. For more information *see* page 68.

FLOWERING ALMOND
Prunus glandulosa, or Chinese bush cherry, has spring-blooming pink or white flowers that love full sun. Both butterflies and bees adore it.

GLOBE THISTLE
The purple flowers of this spiny upright thistle (*Echinops* spp.) are an important source of nectar for butterflies and bees.

MILKWEED
Asclepias is a genus of tall, herbaceous, flowering plants that are critical to the monarch butterfly life cycle and their sole host plant for caterpillars.

JOE-PYE WEED
Eutrochium purpureum is a tall perennial native with aromatic purple flowers; the foliage hosts several moth larvae.

LANTANA
Lantana produces scented flowers that form clusters (umbels) of red, orange, yellow, or blue-and-white florets. For more information *see* page 73.

PHLOX
Low-growing phlox bears multicolor flowers; the foliage supports lepidoptera larvae, including hawk moths. For more information *see* page 100.

SHASTA DAISY
This classic hybrid daisy, *Leucanthemum* x *superbum* bears summer blooms that pollinators love. For more information *see* page 101.

ZINNIA
These grassland natives brighten up gardens with their vivid color while attracting pollinators to the yard. For more information *see* page 85.

READ MORE AT
GARDENING KNOW HOW

Scan the QR code or follow the link below for more info.

- **"Butterfly Garden Design: Tips for Attracting Butterflies in Gardens"** (URL = gkh.us/13)

ENCOURAGING BIRDS

For some of us, the desire to attract birds and other native wildlife is among the top reasons we begin gardening. Though birds can frequently be found foraging through lawns and flitting about shrubbery, it's usually not until gardeners begin planting bird-friendly landscapes that they begin to notice a true difference in the various species that visit. Gardening for birds is just one way to bring more interest to your yard, as well as provide a valuable resource for our feathered friends.

One way to combine the enjoyment of birds with supporting your regional ecology is to encourage pollinating birds to visit your yard and garden. Most people are aware that bees, along with butterflies and moths, are considerable pollinators. Bees, especially, make headlines due to their declining numbers. And rightly so, because they play a big role in food production—and their loss would be devastating. But there is another player on that pollinator team—birds.

Birds predominantly pollinate wildflowers, which are not that critical from a food supply standpoint. In North America, no commercial food crops rely on birds for reproduction. Yet wildflowers are important as part of our native ecosystem. The destruction of wildflower habitat by commercial development harms the birds that pollinate these plants; subsequently, declines in bird populations impact several ecosystems.

HOW DO BIRDS POLLINATE?

The process of flower pollination by birds is known as ornithophily. Flowers attract birds with their bright colors and other lures. When a bird alights on a flower to eat nectar, sticky pollen attaches to its beak and feathers. That pollen-laden bird goes on to the next flower, dropping off pollen and picking up more. Through this process, they pollinate numerous flowers. Birds that pluck insects off flowers also contribute to the pollination process.

There are more than 2,000 species of pollinating birds, mostly nectar eaters, but also the insect-eating birds mentioned above. In North America, hummingbirds make up some of the most important pollinators. Orioles are also nectar eaters, but do most of their pollinating in the tropics, where they spend their winters. In other parts of the world pollinating birds include honeyeaters, honeycreepers, sunbirds, and some types of parrots.

Beneficial Bats

Most bats in the United States dine on insects, but in parts of the Southwest, fruit bats are major pollinators, as they are in many other regions of the world. Even so, insect-eating bats are also beneficial, consuming roughly 1,200 mosquitoes per hour, up to 6,000 per night. Considering mosquitoes transmit a number of serious illnesses, this is no small service to humans.

If you want to draw these birds to your garden, choose flowers with characteristics that appeal to them. The ones these birds feed from need to open during the day. Night-blooming plants will attract insect pollinators and bats.

- Tubular shapes
- Petals that curve back and down
- Bright colors, especially the color red for hummingbirds
- A place to land or perch
- A lack of odor

Never use pesticides or herbicides of any kind in or around the pollinator garden. Even organic pesticides can be potentially harmful, and herbicides can actually wipe out some of the most important food plants for pollinators.

HUMMINGBIRDS

Hummingbirds fascinate humans with their jewel-like colors, their darting and hovering behavior, and their brazen disregard for our presence. When it comes to feeding, hummingbirds prefer flowers in shades of red, fuchsia, and purple. The shape of a flower is also important—tubular flowers help lure pollinators with long beaks and tongues like hummingbirds.

In general, birds require three things in the garden, and these are also true for hummers: a food source, a water source, and a safe place to perch. A garden full of hummingbird-friendly plants, along with a few plastic nectar feeders, is a good start. A small fountain or shallow dish of water will also appeal to them for bathing or cooling off. Finally, make sure there are dense bushes or trees where these tiny gems can take refuge and rest. Once you have supplied these basic necessities, with an emphasis on food, you will be delighted when the first hummingbird stakes his claim to your garden. Before long, you will find yourself hanging up additional feeders to handle the overflow.

Flowers Hummingbirds Love

CARDINAL FLOWER
Bright red cardinal flowers *(Lobelia cardinalis)* depend on hummingbirds for fertilization. For more information, *see* page 74.

CORAL BELLS
The small flowers of the perennial shade plants in the *Heuchera* genus still manage to attract hummingbirds. For more information *see* page 142.

DELPHINIUM
A tall, summer-blooming, traditional garden flower, *Delphinium* is a hummingbird favorite. For more information *see* page 102.

FUCHSIA
Often found in hanging baskets, color-drenched fuchsia (genus *Fuchsia)* is a sure bet for bringing pollinators into the yard.

HOLLYHOCK
Towering, sun-loving hollyhocks (genus *Alcea)* attracts both hummingbirds and butterflies to the garden. For more information *see* page 104.

HONEYSUCKLE
Magnifica honeysuckle, *Lonicera sempervirens*, with its large, scarlet flowers, makes a perfect match for hummers. For more information *see* page 280.

JEWELWEED
Impatiens capensis goes by many names, including jewelweed and touch-me-not. Whatever it is called, hummingbirds love it.

RED COLUMBINE
The showy blooms of *Aquilegia canadensis* are timely for hummers returning north from their winter homes. For more information *see* page 96.

ROSE OF SHARON
Hibiscus syriacus is a late-blooming shrub with brilliant flowers that hummingbirds adore. For more information *see* page 292.

TRUMPET VINE
Campsis radicans produces reddish orange to salmon flowers that hummers love to dive into. For more information *see* page 112.

READ MORE AT
GARDENING KNOW HOW

Find tips on bird-friendly gardening, as well creating a garden haven for other beneficial wildlife.

- **"What Is a Bird Garden — Tips on Gardening for Birds"** (URL = gkh.us/157480)
- **"Hummingbird Garden Ideas: Best Flowers For Attracting Hummingbirds"** (URL = gkh.us/15620)
- **"Pollinators in Your Garden"** (URL = gkh.us/165602)
- **"Beneficial Garden Animals: What Animals Are Good for Gardens"** (URL = gkh.us/51791)
- **"How to Create a Wildlife Garden"** (URL = gkh.us/14520)

PART TWO

The Indoor Gardener

CHAPTER TWELVE

IDEAL PLANTS FOR INSIDE THE HOME

Houseplants have the power to evoke a feeling of joy in any room they grace. They represent the outdoors in an indoor setting and perhaps bring a bit of wild nature into our tame, domestic lives. The gratification one experiences after nurturing a plant through all four seasons, and then on into a new year, is remarkable. Houseplants benefit us by supplying a needed touch of greenery and even flowers in some cases during the monochromatic, often dreary, days of winter. They are also true "air conditioners," removing toxins from the air in the rooms where they are placed, taking in CO_2, and releasing oxygen. The portable nature of most houseplants makes them especially useful as decorative objects—traveling from the kitchen window to brightening up a dining or living room to cheering up a child's sickroom to providing the home office with a touch of feng shui.

HOUSEPLANT MAINTENANCE

Cultivating indoor plants requires its own specific skill set. Furthermore, it does not necessarily follow that someone who is a successful outdoor gardener is equally able to grow plants inside the home. In fact, the opposite is often true—the person blessed with the green thumb in the yard is often the individual cursed with the black thumb indoors. This disparity might occur because the needs of indoor plants differ from those of garden plants. They can be more finicky about watering, feeding, or daily doses of sunlight. Garden plants give us a broad canvas on which to express ourselves. Indoor plants, like intricate drawings, require more precise attention . . . and a more rapid response to potential problems.

Still, most indoor plants, especially the low-light specimens, require only a small amount of care each week once they are established. If they continue to grow in size, an occasional pot change will be in order. In temperate regions, certain species can even spend the summer outdoors and come back inside when the autumn weather turns cold. Even if you have had trouble in the past with houseplants, the examples listed here include a number of foolproof species that practically live on air. In fact, one of them actually does.

READ MORE AT GARDENING KNOW HOW

Save money by making your own plant food. Just scan the QR code to an informative video and article, or follow the link.

- **"No Waste Kitchen Garden: Homemade Plant Food"** (URL = gkh.us/175127)

An artificial light can supplement any natural sunlight. Windows that have reduced light or are blocked by buildings may need the additional light source.

CARE OF HOUSEPLANTS

The contributing factors for healthy growth are pretty much the same as with garden plants, but indoor specimens can be more delicate and react more quickly to alterations in environment.

Light

Sunlight is a key part of indoor plant care. In order to provide the right amount of light, check the tag on the plant when you purchase it. If the houseplant is a gift, check online for its light requirements. Houseplants generally need one of the following levels of light.

- Bright or direct light is strong light that shines through a window or screen. The brightest light will come from a south-facing window.
- Indirect light comes from a light bulb or is sunlight that has been filtered through something, such as a curtain.
- High-light houseplants will need five or more hours of bright light, preferably near a south-facing window. They need to be within 6 feet (1.8 m) of a window.
- Medium-light houseplants should be exposed to several hours of bright or indirect light daily. This light can come from a window or from overhead lighting.
- Low-light houseplants need very little light. Typically, they do well in rooms that have a light source but no windows. Still, they need light of some kind—if the room is kept mostly in darkness, they will not survive.

Water

Proper watering is essential. The general rule for most houseplants is to water them only if the top of the soil feels dry. A few plants, particularly succulents and cacti, should be watered only when the soil is completely dry. Still other plants may need to be kept constantly moist. These special watering needs should be marked on the plant's tag. If there are no special instructions for watering, then use the "dry to the touch" method.

For humidity-loving plants, such as the tropicals, a misting with tepid water will provide a bit of humidity to the foliage without directly splashing leaves.

Misting tropical plants is a great way to create the humid conditions they need.

Fertilizer

There are two types of fertilizer used for feeding houseplants—water soluble and slow release. You can add water-soluble fertilizer to your plants' water once a month in warm weather and once every two months in cooler weather. Or add a slow-release fertilizer to the soil once every two to three months.

Temperature

Most houseplants were originally tropical plants, so they cannot tolerate cold temperatures. The majority prefer to be kept in rooms that are between 65 and 75° F (18–21° C). In a pinch, many houseplants can tolerate temperatures as low as 55° F (13° C), but they will not thrive at temperatures this low for very long. The aspidistra is said to survive in temperatures just above freezing, but why take that chance?

An indoor gardener applies a slow-release fertilizer spike to a peace lily. Read your plant's tag or check online to find out what your plant needs to thrive.

Take note of the position of your houseplants in relation to any heating elements in your home. Most prefer warm temps, so set your thermostat accordingly.

Wiping down the leaves of your houseplants is part of home maintenance, and it also gives you a chance to check for any pests or other problems.

Propagating Houseplants

If you have a favorite plant that is growing well, you might consider propagating it. This can also fulfill your need to "grow something" during the winter, when outdoor gardening is on hold. There are many candidates for propagating via cuttings, offsets, or root division, most of them requiring very little in the way of equipment.

- Begonia, coleus, pothos, Tradescantia, umbrella plant, rosemary, philodendron, and prayer plant can all be propagated in water. Cut a stem just above a leaf node and place it in a glass vase, changing the water every three to five days. Once a proper root system has formed, the new plant can be potted up.
- Some succulents, like aloe vera, spider plant, or ponytail palm, produce offshoot "pups" that can be transplanted into their own pots. Spider plants are famous for sending out multiple stalks where baby spider plants grow; simply place the babies in a pot beside the mother plant, and trim the stem once the new plant takes root.
- Multi-stemmed plants, like snake plant, peace lily, and Boston fern, can be gently taken from their pots and the roots separated into several plants. Keep the repotted plants moist and out of bright light until they are established.
- African violets can be easily propagated from a single leaf. Snip off a healthy outer leaf and two inches (5 cm) of the stem, slicing the stem at an angle to maximize water absorption, and set it in a small pot filled with moist starter medium. Place the pot in a plastic bag, puff it up with your breath, and seal with a twist tie. Within six to eight weeks a new plant will appear at the base of the leaf.

A pothos cutting is prepared for potting.

DISPLAYING YOUR PLANTS

Houseplants make a statement wherever they are placed. They bring natural beauty into the kitchen, add charm to a nursery, provide a soothing element in the bedroom, bathroom, or yoga studio, perk up a dreary basement rec room, and add dramatic interest to the living room, dining room, and great room. They also detoxify the air and create a restful "green space" for the eyes.

You will also discover a host of products intended to increase the appeal of plants. You could start with the addition of colorful or textural pots. Whatever your decorating taste, from traditional to eclectic, lush bohemian pared-down mid-century modern, you will find containers to match your theme. Planters with built-in reservoirs work for a variety of species, while African violet pots have an inner liner that is porous enough to absorb the water fed into the outer pot, keeping delicate leaves dry. Fill large pots with empty water bottles before adding soil to keep them portable. And plant platforms on wheels are great for moving heavy specimens around your floor space.

As in the garden, use one outstanding plant as a focal point or create groupings that mix varieties of plants and pots of different materials. These can add an artful element to the fireplace mantel, dining table, or entryway. Never be afraid to experiment with plant placement—recall how random a field of wildflowers can be and, yet, how beautiful. You can achieve a similar effect indoors by thinking beyond the box.

Any houseplant display starts with the pots you choose to grow your plants in. There is sure to be one that coordinates with your decorating style, from industrial metals for a clean, urban feel, ornate porcelain for traditional interiors, hand-thrown containers for a bohemian or farmhouse style, or geometrics for a mid-century modern feel.

SPACE-SAVING SOLUTIONS

Homeowners—and especially apartment dwellers—often need ways to display their plants that don't take up extra space. Here are some helpful design solutions that elevate plants beyond the usual windowsill site.

- Install floating shelves to support clusters of small plants.
- Hang ceramic pockets or wall-mounted planters for spill-over plants like ivy, air plants, ferns, and trailing herbs.
- Place a metal trellis in the pot of a large climber, like a philodendron, and train the tendrils to grow upward rather than outward.
- Hang plants from the ceiling or upper window frame in metal planters with chains or pots in woven hangers.
- Install a towel bar in the kitchen and wire several galvanized metal "trough" planters to it for an instant farmhouse look.
- Place several small plants together in one planter to conserve space; this type of "dish garden" was once a popular housewarming gift.
- Run a copper or brass pipe between two bookcases or cabinets and suspend several plants from it at different heights.
- Consider a three-tiered serving stand in the kitchen for holding pots of cooking herbs and a small, healing aloe vera plant in case you accidentally burn your finger.
- Extend the depth of your windowsill with a wooden platform for larger plants, or, in the case of cat owners, attach a wooden flower box with high sides.
- Bump out a mini-greenhouse (or garden window) from an existing window, where you can establish your own indoor garden.

Feng Shui and Plants

According to the Asian philosophy of feng shui, living plants invite the energy of nature into the home and nourish your own personal energy. They also strengthen the effects of the element wood, which brings the vital energy of growth and action into the space. Wood inspires compassion, kindness, and flexibility; the color green represents rejuvenation. Purifying plants include areca palm and Boston fern; protective plants include snake plant; luck-producing plants include lucky bamboo, and money-producers include jade and money plants. Rounded leaves create gentle vibes, but it is best to avoid plants with spiky leaves or spines, like cacti, which can drain your energy. This is also true of browning or dying plants. Interestingly, fake plants can be used, but they must be so lifelike as to fool the eye.

LIGHTING OPTIONS

Most plants, even low-light specimens, require some proximity to windows, but this does not mean the inner areas of your rooms must remain plantless. There are a number of grow lights on the market that allow plants to flourish even in the darkest corners or in rooms without a single window. Many gardeners set up propagation stations in their basements with the aid of these lights.

Plants require certain colors from the light spectrum to stay healthy: blue light helps plants produce chlorophyll, the pigment they need to grow. It also encourages germination and root development in young plants and seedlings. Red light regulates plant growth and helps plants to produce flowers and fruit. Green light helps maximize photosynthesis, the process in which they use sunlight to turn water and carbon dioxide into nutrients.

Full-spectrum grow lights supply these three colors, and some even allow you to adjust the levels. You can also select between a warm or cool light, with warm colors offering more of a cozy glow to the room. How much light a bulb or fixture provides depends on its intensity. This is usually measured in lumens in the case of LEDs. The higher the number of lumens, the more light that bulb will produce–and the brighter it will appear.

A DIY woodworking project takes simple wood planks and creates a bespoke shelving unit to display cactus of various heights, along with a bottle collection. Include your favorite mementos when planning your houseplant display.

Types of grow lights

- LED, or light emitting diode, bulbs are the most effective at producing light and the most efficient to operate, lasting up to five times longer than many other bulbs. Choose a full-spectrum LED bulb for your grow fixture.
- Compact fluorescent bulbs are less efficient than LEDs, so more expensive to run. They have a shorter lifespan and may release mercury vapor if the bulb is broken. If you choose these bulbs, full spectrum will cover a broader range of plant needs.
- Halogen bulbs are not optimal for lighting plants, but brighter than incandescent bulbs. They also lack the blue light needed for growth. They can be effective if combined with other types of light, but can also get quite hot.
- Incandescent bulbs are not well suited to indoor plants—they are inefficient, they get hot, they cost more to operate, and they produce light farther along the red spectrum.

Gather plants of varying sizes and shapes to create instant interest. Here a variety of houseplants are displayed in different styles of containers, but all work together.

TROUBLESHOOTING PROBLEMS

Just like garden plants, indoor plants are subject to many pests and diseases. These can slow down or halt a plant's growth, impact flowering, or even physically distort parts of the plant. Yet all it takes to combat these potential threats is some familiarity with the pests and diseases in order to determine the best ways to defeat them.

COMMON PESTS

Pests that typically affect houseplants tend to be insects.

- *Aphids.* These tiny sucking insects cause yellowing and distorted leaves, stunted growth, and produce a sticky substance called honeydew that quickly grows sooty black mold. Aphids damage a wide range of plants and also spread viruses, many of which are incurable. Control them by swabbing them off with alcohol, using a stream of water, or applying insecticidal soap.
- *Mealybugs.* These pests leave a white, cottony residue on leaves and stems. This residue is either egg sacs or the pests themselves—small, flat, fuzzy, or powdery oval white spots. Mealybugs literally suck the life out of houseplants. Control by immediately isolating infested plants, then scraping away any white residue and spots on leaves. Mix one part alcohol to three parts water with some dish soap, and wash down the entire plant. Repeat a few days later. Neem oil will also work.

Turn to chemical control only as a last resort. Research organic approaches for your issue, which will be safer for you and your family and are more environmentally friendly.

A macro shot of a small grouping of recently hatched spider mites, which can soon devastate a houseplant.

- *Spider mites.* Spider mites are one of the more common houseplant pests, and elimination begins with detection—the three most frequent signs of spider mites are yellow, tan, or white spots on the leaves of your plant; very small white or red spots on the leaves that move, which are the mites; and white, cottony webbing on the underside of the leaves. If there is an infestation of spider mites, immediately isolate the plant, and then power spray the leaves and stems with a faucet wand. Repeat several times. You can also apply neem oil or a miticide directly on the insects.
- *Scale.* These insects suck sap from plants, robbing them of essential nutrients. Scale bugs are small, oval, and flat, with a protective brown shell-like covering. Scales generally target the undersides of leaves and leaf joints. There are three types: armored scale, soft scale, and mealybug *(see first column)*. Scales can be detected by placing double-stick tape on leaves. Scale-damaged plants look withered and sickly. If scale insects are not dealt with, their deadly effects will spread. Control them by scrubbing off leaves, swabbing with alcohol, washing with insecticidal soap, or applying neem oil for a month. Heavily infested plants should be discarded.

PREVENTING DISEASES

Diseases in houseplants, just like those in humans, can range between bacterial, viral, and fungal infections. There are also physiological disorders, not caused by pests or infections, that can cause a range of problems and undermine plant health. These include overwatering, underwatering, poor ventilation, and improper air temperature or sun exposure.

The first step in controlling most diseases is prevention. Always buy disease-free plants. Use clean soil when repotting and carefully scrub pots with a light bleach solution before reusing. Make sure all houseplants have adequate ventilation and plenty of room. Continually look for and remove spent flowers and foliage. Providing your houseplants with the proper growing conditions and checking them often for problems will significantly reduce the chances of disease. Below are listed some of the common diseases that affect houseplants.

Fungal diseases

Fungi are a very common cause of diseases in houseplants. Most of them can be attributed to overwatering, as most fungi need moisture to thrive.

- *Anthracnose.* Watch for leaf tips that become yellow, gradually turning into dark brown lesions. Plants eventually die. Control by removing and destroying infected leaves.
- *Botrytis.* Also called gray mold, this fuzzy gray fungus appears on foliage and stems. Control by promptly removing brown or dead leaves before it spreads.
- *Fungal leaf spots.* These include small brown spots with yellow margins or black spotting. Remove and destroy the affected houseplant. Control with neem oil.

- *Powdery mildew.* Look for a white powder-like coating on all parts of the plant. The disease is transmitted from decaying plant matter or airborne spores. Control with good ventilation and careful watering. Always destroy severely infected plants.
- *Root and stem rot.* This fungus is caused by poor drainage or overwatering—plant tissues become soft, turn brown, wilt, and die. Control by monitoring water and drainage.

Viral or bacterial diseases

Viral infections are not that common in houseplants, unless they are left outdoors. Those plants that are infected might then appear stunted, with crinkled leaves and mottled color. Most often, viral infections are caused by insects, such as aphids or nematodes.

Houseplants affected by bacterial dropsy, or edema, exhibit water-soaked spots with cork-like swellings along the leaf surface and stem. Plants may not fully recover, but repotting can improve their chances, along with improved drainage and ventilation. Otherwise, they should be destroyed.

Tips for Health

Health problems in houseplants can worsen without intervention. You need to remember that these plants are grown in artificial conditions. A lot of indoor plants come from tropical countries, and the natural pest controls found in tropical forests might not be available indoors. The growth that is produced in warm, indoor conditions with less-than-perfect light is often soft—an ideal target for fungus. Insect outbreaks also increase quickly indoors because of warm, sheltered conditions, the perfect environment for pests to thrive. Check your plants regularly so that you can act at the first signs of trouble.

- Keep your plants strong by making sure conditions are as close to their original habitat as possible. Healthy plants are better able to withstand an attack.
- Keep plants well ventilated but without drafts. Humid air, especially if it's cool, will cause fungal diseases to erupt.
- Do not overfeed your plants. Too much nitrogen causes plants to become soft and sappy, making them more vulnerable to pests and diseases.
- Isolate any new plants until you know they are free from pests and diseases.
- Give your houseplants regular check-ups, making sure to look under the leaves where the majority of health problems first start.

Repotting a Houseplant

Repotting not only gives a root-bound plant a chance to spread out, it can also improve its chances of avoiding disease. Just follow these simple steps to give your houseplant a new, healthy home.

1. Remove your plant from its current pot.

2. Gently loosen the roots.

3. Add pebbles to new pot for drainage.

4. Add new potting mix to the new pot.

5. Center plant on top of the fresh soil.

6. Tamp down the soil, and water well.

HOUSEPLANTS FOR HIGH TO MEDIUM LIGHT

Most houseplants are grown for their interesting foliage, rather than for their blooms. The sharply delineated, unique fenestrations of monstera's leaves, for example, add dramatic interest to a modern room.

Most plants need sunlight in order to perform photosynthesis. Yet the amount of light required varies from plant to plant. Many jungle-based houseplants grow in diffused light. Some plants, however, especially those native to South Africa and Australia, need ample sunshine to thrive. These high- to medium-light plants should receive between six and eight hours of direct sunlight each day. (Direct sunlight means an uninterrupted path of light from the sun directly to the plant.) These plants do best near a south-facing window, positioned no farther than six feet (1.8 m) away. Sun-loving indoor plants include succulents like cacti, jade, and aloe vera, as well as the colorful crotons and Persian shields. Some plants can do well in both high and low light, such as snake plants, which turn up on "best" lists for both categories.

REGULATING LIGHT LEVELS

Even though sunlight traveling through a glass window is diffused and reduced in intensity, bright light can still scorch these plants. Signs of overexposure include drooping, crisp, or wrinkled leaves; burnt patches on leaves in white, yellow, or brown; faded foliage colors; and dried-out soil. Conversely, signs that a plant is not receiving enough sunlight might be stretched or leggy growth, abnormally small leaves, pale green or yellow leaves, and slowed or stopped growth. Flowering plants may bloom only sparsely, and variegated plants may turn completely green.

READ MORE AT GARDENING KNOW HOW

Learn more about catering to the lighting needs of your indoor plants by following the links below.

- **"Rotating Houseplants — How Often Should I Turn a Houseplant**
  (URL = gkh.us/79194)
- **"Fluorescent Light and Plants: Lighting Options for Indoor Gardening**
  (URL = gkh.us/221)

Scan the QR code or follow the link below to find a host of informative articles about caring for your indoor plants.

- **All Things Houseplants**
  (URL = gkh.us/151859)

Placing plants near a window allows you to control their daily dose of direct sunlight. Even sun-loving species can benefit from periods of indirect light.

African Violet

Frilly and elegant African violets, long a favorite houseplant choice, line a windowsill. Pinch spent blooms: this will encourage the development of more flowers.

The delicate, fuzzy-leafed African violet is an agreeable plant that always lends a soft touch of color and coziness to any room with its bright blooms in shades from purple to white. Not surprisingly, it is native to Africa, where it thrives in the tropical rainforests of Tanzania and Kenya. Originally classified as *Saintpaulia,* it has recently been re-categorized under the genus *Streptocarpus.* Despite its common name, it is not related to the violet; the name instead comes from the plant's most common color.

GROWING AFRICAN VIOLETS

There are three ways to grow this plant, by seed, by leaf cuttings, and by division. Growing from seed requires light soil and a warm environment. To sprout the tiny seeds, use a light soil mixture of peat, vermiculite, and greensand. A bit of Epsom salt can help to lighten the soil even more. Make sure your room temperature is between 65 and 75° F (18–24° C), which is also the soil temp for optimal sprouting. The seeds should germinate in 8 to 14 days.

The far more popular—and successful—method of propagation is from leaf cuttings, best undertaken in spring. Using a sterile knife or scissors, remove a healthy leaf, along with its stem, from the plant's base. Trim the stem down to about 1 to 1.5 inches (2.5–3.8 cm). You can dip the tip of the stem into some rooting hormone, and then place the cutting in a 1-inch (2.5 cm) deep hole in potting soil. Press the soil firmly around it, and water thoroughly with tepid water.

Create a little greenhouse environment for your cutting by covering the pot with a plastic bag and securing it with a rubber band, being sure to occasionally give it some fresh air. Place the pot in a sunny location, keeping the soil just moist.

Roots will usually form in three to four weeks, and leaves should appear in six to eight weeks. You should see several plants form at the base of the cutting. Separate the small new plants by carefully pulling or cutting them apart. Each of these will give you a brand-new plant.

Separation, or division, is the third method of propagation. This technique involves cutting the crown from the plant or separating the pups, or suckers, making sure that each portion has a piece of the main plant's root system. This is especially effective if your African violet has grown too large for its pot. Each piece can be planted in its own pot with a suitable potting soil mix to instantly multiply your collection.

SCIENTIFIC NAME: *Streptocarpus* spp. (formerly *Saintpaulia*)

FAMILY: Gesneriaceae

HEIGHT: 2 to 12 inches (5–30 cm)

WIDTH: 2 to 6 inches (5–15 cm)

FOLIAGE COLOR: Shades of green with white, blue, pink, or purple flowers

SOIL pH: Acidic

LIGHT: Moderate to bright, indirect light

SPECIAL CARE

Small pots encourage bloom. Water with lukewarm or tepid water when the soil feels dry to the touch, and never let the plants stand in water or completely dry out. Water at the base of the plant, and never splash the foliage: just a drop can cause foliar spots and damage.

During the active growing season, fertilize every two weeks with African violet food or a food with a higher phosphorus number, such as 15-30-15. You can mix fertilizer at one-quarter strength and apply at every watering. Reduced flowering and paler leaf color indicate that growing plants are not receiving enough fertilizer.

African violets do best in medium-intensity light. Place pots 3 feet (1 m) from a south- or west-facing window for the right lighting. If this light cannot be maintained for eight hours, supplement with fluorescent lights. Plants with dark green foliage usually need somewhat higher light levels than those with pale or medium-green foliage. Regularly turn the pots to keep flowers from growing toward the light.

READ MORE AT GARDENING KNOW HOW

Scan the code or follow the link to learn how to keep your African violets hydrated and happy.

- **"African Violet Watering Guide: How to Water an African Violet Plant"** (URL = gkh.us/130334)

Air Plant

Two types of air plant, *Tillandsia argentea* (left and right) and *T. ionantha* (middle), are displayed in glass jars. Setting up an environment for these epiphytic plants to flourish depends on finding a proper base for them, such as small pieces of wood.

Air plants, which are classified under the genus *Tillandsia,* make up around 500 different species in the Bromeliaceae family. The foliage of these plants comes in a variety of colors, such as green, blue-green, crimson, pink, orange, and peach. All of these plants are naturally epiphytic, meaning their survival does not depend on soil. Instead, they grow by clinging to trees, rocks, or other plants and extracting excess nutrients and moisture from the air.

The plants can be found growing wild in areas of Mexico, the United States, and Argentina. They are, however, also popular as a rather low-maintenance indoor plant.

GROWING AIR PLANTS

Most species of *Tillandsia* should be mounted, rather than grown in pots. They thrive when mounted on solid substrates that do not retain liquid; only a few species can adapt to soil. The plants can be glued or wired to a base, such as shells, rocks, wood, coral, or slate. They should not be covered with moss, which could cause rotting. Choose a decorative mount to complement your indoor space, and consider arranging the plants in clumps.

Water the plants two to four times a week with a mister until they are fully saturated. Mist the plants daily if your environment is particularly dry. Most of the tropical plant varieties thrive between 70 and 80° F (21–27° C) and in high humidity.

The plants also should be kept in bright, indirect, or filtered sunlight from spring until autumn. Move them into direct light during the winter months. Monitor light levels: you might need to supplement winter sunlight with full-spectrum artificial lights for about 12 hours per day.

SPECIAL CARE

Although air plant care is minimal, the plant can sometimes begin to look sickly. If your plant isn't looking its best, especially if it's shriveled or brown, there's a good chance that it is extremely thirsty. Although misting them is often recommended, spritzing usually doesn't provide enough moisture to keep the plant healthy and hydrated.

An air plant can be returned to a healthy, well-hydrated state by soaking the entire plant in a bowl or bucket of lukewarm water. A 10-minute soak might be enough, but watch your plant closely to determine its particular needs. If the plant begins to look swollen, it's absorbing too much water, and it will benefit from a shorter bath.

Ensure your air plant receives adequate air circulation. If it is in a container, uncover it, and move it to an airy location. You can instead remove it from the container for a full day every week. Always shake off excess water after watering, and allow it to dry in a colander or on a layer of paper towels.

Use a bromeliad fertilizer twice a month. Alternatively, feed the plant with a low-copper liquid fertilizer diluted to one-quarter strength once a month.

SCIENTIFIC NAME: *Tillandsia* spp.

FAMILY: Bromeliaceae

HEIGHT: 6 to 24 inches (15–60 cm)

WIDTH: 6 to 24 inches (15–60 cm)

FOLIAGE COLOR: Gradated green, blue-green, crimson, pink, orange, and peach

SOIL pH: Not applicable

LIGHT: Bright, indirect light

Air Plant Species

There are several of the *Tillandsia* species to choose from.

- ***T. caput-medusae*** is a clumping species with twisting, silvery leaves growing from a bulbous base and a red flower stalk.
- ***T. cyanea,*** the most popular species, has pink quill-like bracts nestled among large, bright purple flowers and a mass of thin, curving green leaves in a rosette form.
- ***T. ionantha*** features a row of green leaves, with deep pink or red plume-like bracts, and violet-blue flowers
- ***T. plumosa*** forms a globe of fuzzy silver leaves.

Areca Palm

Dypsis lutescens, **also known as areca palm, golden cane palm, yellow palm, butterfly palm, and bamboo palm, is a tall, graceful plant that makes a statement in the home.**

The areca palm, classified under the name *Dypsis lutescens,* is one of the most widely used palms for bright interiors. These palms, native to Madagascar, are yet considered an endangered species. You would not know it, however, because they seem to cover the region. Areca palms resemble bamboo and are thus often grown as outdoor fencing. When grown as houseplants, these big, bold plants demand attention. Their tall golden trunks feature feathery, arching fronds, each with up to 100 bright green leaflets.

GROWING ARECA PALMS

A full-grown areca palm is quite expensive, so they are usually purchased as small, tabletop plants. They add 6 to 10 inches (15 to 25 cm) of growth per year until they reach a mature height of 6 or 7 feet (1.8 or 2.1 m.). Areca is one of the few palms that can tolerate trimming without serious harm, making it possible to keep mature plants indoors for their full lifespan of up to 10 years.

A well draining, peat-based potting mix can be used for indoor plants. Sand and peat moss can be used as organic soil amendments to improve porousness and lower soil pH. Take note that areca palms are sensitive to overwatering, as well as to fluoridated water. Allow the soil to dry out between waterings. Then, use distilled water or collected rainwater to rehydrate your plant.

Another key factor to successfully growing areca palms indoors is providing just the right amount of light. They need bright, filtered sunlight from a south- or west-facing window. The leaves turn yellowish green in direct sunlight. Leaves need not be pruned, however, unless they turn brown, because they can still carry out photosynthesis. The palms also thrive in high humidity, so keep the plants away from cold windows, air conditioners, and heat sources.

SPECIAL CARE

Fertilize your areca palm with a time-release fertilizer in spring. This gives the plant most of the nutrients it needs for the entire season. The fronds benefit from a micronutrient spray in summer. You can use a liquid houseplant fertilizer that contains micronutrients for this purpose. Make sure the product is labeled as safe for foliar feedings, and dilute it according to the label instructions. Do not feed areca palms in autumn and winter.

SCIENTIFIC NAME: *Dypsis lutescens*

FAMILY: Arecaceae

HEIGHT: 4 to 5 feet (1.2–1.5 m)

WIDTH: 6 to 7 feet (1.8–2.1 m)

FOLIAGE COLOR: Bright green with hints of yellow, silver, or gold

SOIL pH: Acidic, neutral

LIGHT: Bright, indirect light

Areca palms need repotting every two to three years. The plant likes a tight container, and crowded roots help limit its size. The main reasons for repotting are to replace the aged potting soil and to remove fertilizer salt deposits that build up in the soil and on the sides of the pot. Use a palm potting soil or a general-purpose mix amended with a handful of clean builder's sand. Take care to plant the palm in the new pot at the same depth as in the old pot, and do not spread apart the brittle roots.

Boston Fern

With its artfully flowing fronds, a Boston fern makes a perfect plant for a hanging basket. This plant will do well indoors, but it can also take a turn displayed on a porch or patio.

Boston fern, also known as *Nephrolepis exaltata,* is a fern species in the family Lomariopsidaceae. Native to forests and swamps, especially in South America, Mexico, Central America, Florida, the West Indies, Polynesia, and Africa, it is also a popular houseplant throughout North America. Also known as Boston swordfern, wild Boston fern, tuber ladder fern, and fishbone fern, this evergreen plant can reach as high as 5 feet (1.5 m), but most houseplants top out at no more than 3 feet (1 m) tall. Most of the species have erect fronds, but two popular cultivars, 'Bostoniensis' and 'Teddy Junior' feature gracefully arching fronds.

GROWING BOSTON FERNS

To properly care for a Boston fern you must first ensure that it is in the right kind of environment. Boston ferns should be grown in bright, indirect light, without too much shade. They can be placed on porches or patios for filtered morning sunlight and afternoon shade. These plants also prefer warm and humid conditions and dislike drafts or heating vents. It's a good idea to provide additional humidity for them, especially in the winter. Most homes are rather dry, even more so when heaters are running.

Mist your fern once or twice a week to help it get the humidity it needs. The leaves will turn yellow if the humidity is not high enough, so misting is particularly necessary if you live in a dry climate. For extra humidity care, try setting your fern's pot on a tray of pebbles filled with water.

Organically rich, loamy soil with good drainage prevents Boston ferns from rotting. For indoor plants, use a peat-based potting mix with added perlite to improve drainage. It is important to make sure that the fern's soil remains damp at all times. Check the soil daily, and water the plants if the soil feels at all dry.

SCIENTIFIC NAME: *Nephrolepis exaltata*

FAMILY: Lomariopsidaceae

HEIGHT: 2 to 3 feet (60 cm–1 m)

WIDTH: 2 to 3 feet (60 cm–1 m)

FOLIAGE COLOR: Bright green

SOIL pH: Acidic

LIGHT: Bright, indirect light

SPECIAL CARE

One of the lesser-known care tips for a Boston fern is that they do not need much fertilizer. Fertilizer should only be given to the plant a few times a year, during the spring and summer. Use a 20-10-20 liquid houseplant fertilizer at half strength

Boston ferns tend to be planted in potting mixtures that are high in peat moss, so it is a smart idea to soak the pot once a month or so to make sure the peat moss is fully hydrated. Be sure to let it drain thoroughly after this soaking.

For the most part, Boston ferns are only susceptible to pests, especially spider mites and mealybugs, when grown outside and neglected. If your plant becomes infested, make sure to treat it as quickly as possible to keep it healthy.

Boston fern care is as simple as making sure that the plant is placed in a suitable environment. If your fern is located in a sunny spot and properly watered, your plant will live for many years to come.

READ MORE AT GARDENING KNOW HOW

To learn about caring for ferns, both indoors and in baskets, follow these links.

- **"Fern in a Hanging Container: Care of Ferns in Hanging Baskets"** (URL = gkh.us/142665)
- **"Growing Ferns Indoors"** (URL = gkh.us/158)

Bromeliad

SCIENTIFIC NAME: Various genera

FAMILY: Bromeliaceae

HEIGHT: 1 to 3 feet (30 cm–1 m)

WIDTH: 1 to 3 feet (30 cm–1 m)

FOLIAGE COLOR: Solid or striped green (with flowers in pink, red, orange, and yellow.

SOIL pH: Acidic

LIGHT: Bright, indirect light

The *Guzmania* is just one of the many genera of the exotic bromeliads. Although this genus is epiphytic in its natural environment, you can successfully grow this red-blooming variety in a potting medium to use it as a houseplant.

Bromeliads, members of the Bromeliaceae family, provide the home with an air of the tropics. Native to tropical and subtropical regions of the Americas, these slow-growing plants come in myriad hues and textures. With solid or striped green foliage and stunning pink, red, orange, and yellow flowers, they will surely add an exotic touch to any indoor space. They might, however, take one to three years to become mature flowering plants, and they require specific conditions to do so.

It is prized for its thick foliage that grows in a natural rosette. Near the end of its life, a bromeliad might produce an inflorescence, or flower, whose form and color vary widely among each variety. The wide leaves are sword shaped or scoop-like and grow around a central "cup." This cup is used to catch water in the plant's natural habitat.

GROWING BROMELIADS

To ensure success, offer the appropriate humidity level, temperature, and water and feeding routine. Research what the genus and species you have will require, because these plants depend on a relatively specific environment to eventually bloom. New gardeners learning how to grow bromeliads will find that the plant doesn't need deep pots or dense potting soils. In fact, they do better in shallow pots and can grow in low-soil mediums, such as an orchid mix, which is a blend of bark, sphagnum moss, and other organic amendments.

Bromeliads need medium to bright indirect light as indoor specimens. After choosing an ideal location for the plant, set the pot in a saucer of gravel filled partially with water to increase humidity and help provide a moist atmosphere. Make sure the roots are not submerged in water or this might invite rot.

Water needs are easily met by filling the cup at the base of the leaves. Empty any water that collects in the pot weekly to remove debris and dead insects that stagnant water tends to lure into the cup.

SPECIAL CARE

Feed the plants with a half-strength fertilizer every month during the growing season.

Bromeliads may not live long, but they will produce offsets, called pups, that you can remove and start as new plants. Watch for pups at the base of the plant and nurture them until they are large enough to remove from the parent plant. Cut them, and then plant them in sphagnum moss or any well-draining medium. As soon as the pup forms a cub, it is important to keep it filled with water so the new plant receives adequate hydration.

Types of Bromeliads

Among the many bromeliad varieties, there are several standout genera.

- ***Aechmea.*** Called the urn plant, this diverse genus comes in many forms and colors with spiny-edged leaves in solid green, speckled, or bands with silver scales and various-colored blooms.
- ***Cryptanthus.*** Called the earth star, this terrestrial bromeliad grows almost flat against the ground, resembling a brightly colored starfish.
- ***Guzmania.*** Known as the air pine or living vase, this is a show-stopper when in bloom.
- ***Neoregelia.*** Called blushing bromeliad or fingernail plant, this features spectacular foliage in green, bronze, yellow, orange, red, purple, pink, and white
- ***Vrieseas.*** This large bromeliad displays soft, spineless foliage that can be patterned or solid green, with brightly colored winter-blooming flowers.

Croton

Crotons *(Codiaeum variegatum)* display a vast diversity of form, color, and size. With so much variety on offer, crotons make it easy to find one to fit into your home's decor.

SCIENTIFIC NAME: *Codiaeum variegatum*

FAMILY: Euphorbiaceae

HEIGHT: 3 to 8 feet (1–2.4 m)

WIDTH: 3 to 5 feet (1–1.5 m)

FOLIAGE COLOR: Variegated green with white, pink, orange, red, yellow, or purple

SOIL pH: Acidic

LIGHT: Bright, indirect light

Croton plants, known by the scientific name *Codiaeum variegatum,* have a reputation for their wonderful variety of leaf forms and foliage colors. Croton leaves can be short, long, twisted, thin, thick, and several of these combined. Colors range from green, variegated, yellow, red, orange, cream, pink, and black to a combination of all these. It is safe to say that if you look hard enough, you will find a croton that matches your decor.

The plants are native to India and Malaysia, where they grow in humid, warm conditions, with dappled light and plentiful water. When grown inside, crotons can be fussy, but if you know how to care for them properly, they can make for resilient plants. Pot-grown crotons are usually much smaller than the outdoor plants, which can reach 10 feet (3 m) in height. Indoor crotons grow relatively slowly, gaining no more than 12 inches (30 cm) per growing season.

GROWING CROTONS

A croton should be kept in a well-drained, moist soil that has been enriched with compost. It also thrives in humus-rich, acidic soil. Check the variety of crotons you have purchased to determine the light needs of your specific plant. Some varieties of crotons need high light, while others need medium or low light. As a general rule, the more variegated and colorful the croton plant, the more light it will need.

Because it is a tropical plant, crotons benefit from high humidity and minimal watering. Placing it on a pebble tray or regularly misting it will help keep the plant looking its best. Crotons growing in containers should only be watered when the top of the soil is dry to the touch. They should then be watered until water flows out of the bottom of the container.

Maintaining the ideal temperature is crucial for growing healthy plants indoors. Croton should be kept away from drafts and cold—it cannot tolerate temperatures below 60° F (15° C). If it is exposed to temperatures lower than this, the plant will lose leaves and could possibly die.

SPECIAL CARE

The croton's reputation for being fussy may be attributed to its tendency for bad first impressions. This plant does not like to be moved, and when it is moved, it can quickly go into shock, resulting in leaf loss. New plant owners are often discouraged as they watch their croton lose some or all of its foliage within the first days of buying it. This, however, is normal behavior for the plant. Avoid moving it as much as possible. If the plant is experiencing leaf loss, simply maintain proper care and regrowth will begin within a short period of time.

Crotons benefit from the application of slow-release pellets three times per growing season (early spring, mid-summer, and early autumn). Alternatively, liquid fertilizer can be used every other month during the growing season.

Editor's Picks

Here is a small selection of the many croton cultivars available.

- **'Lauren's Rainbow' has narrow leaves in shades of yellow, green, and deep purple.**
- **'Oakleaf' produces tri-lobed leaves in tones of burgundy, red, green, orange, and yellow.**
- **'Petra' features large, wide leaves in shades of yellow, green, orange, bronze, and burgundy red.**
- **'Red Iceton' has large yellow leaves that mature to striking shades of red and pink with bright veins.**
- **'Sunny Star' produces elliptical leaves in light green dashed in gold.**
- **'Victoria Gold Bell' has dangling leaves in orange, red, green, or red.**
- **'Zanzibar' has narrow leaves in red, green, purple, orange, and yellow.**

Dragon Tree

SCIENTIFIC NAME: *Dracaena* spp.

FAMILY: Asteraceae

HEIGHT: Up to 6 feet (1.8 m)

WIDTH: 3 to 10 feet (1–3 m)

FOLIAGE COLOR: Variegated combinations of green, red, and yellow

SOIL pH: Neutral to acidic

LIGHT: Bright, indirect light

There are many species of *Dracaena,* but *D. marginata*, with its sophisticated, sword-like leaves in red-edged green, is one of the most popular plants for growing indoors.

The dragon tree is a fantastic container plant that has earned a rightful place in many temperate-climate homes and tropical gardens. It is classified as a *Dracaena,* a genus of about 120 different species that come in a wide range of shapes and sizes. One of the most popular species is the *D. marginata,* which is native to Madagascar and features long sword-like leaves that are green in the center and red on both sides. "Dragon tree" usually refers to this species, which is easy to care for, drought tolerant, and practically indestructible.

You can plant these slow growers during any season. Although they can reach to about 20 feet (6 m) in warm outdoor climates, they are more commonly kept as indoor houseplants. Most houseplant owners prefer to prune potted dragon plants to 6 feet (1.8 m) or smaller.

Dragon trees are hardy in climates that are warm year-round, which means most gardeners keep them in pots that they bring inside during the winter. This is no problem, however, as the trees are extremely well suited to container life and indoor climates. In fact, they are some of the most popular houseplants out there, due to their tolerance for a range of temperatures.

GROWING DRAGON TREES

Plant a dragon tree in loose, well-draining soil, such as a loamy soil amended with peat moss. Use a pot large enough for the plant's sizable root system. Water frequently during its growing season. Fluoride can cause leaf discoloration, so it's best to use non-fluoridated water. To avoid overwatering, wait until the top half of the soil is dry before watering. Brown on the leaves signals that the plant has been overwatered, while yellow usually means it needs more water.

The plant can grow in a variety of light conditions, but it thrives in bright, indirect sunlight; in direct light, the foliage can burn. In lower light, the leaves won't grow as large and will appear less pigmented.

A dragon tree does best when temps are between 65 and 80° F (18–27° C)—the range most houses are already kept at. It can survive lower temperatures, but its growth will slow down severely. If your house is especially dry, consider lightly misting the plant every couple of days.

SPECIAL CARE

A dragon tree is remarkably tough, with a strong root system. Therefore, the plant can handle being potted and repotted at your will. The plant may need a larger pot, but it usually grows slowly enough that repotting is only necessary every second or third year. The potting soil can also be refreshed to replace any compacted parts of the mixture.

Dragon trees require little feeding and will thrive with just a regular slow-release fertilizer once in the spring and once again in the summer. Do not fertilize in the winter.

Note: Dracaena marginata *is harmless to humans when ingested, but be aware that it is extremely toxic to pets.*

Fluoride and Houseplants

Water is not always just water when it comes to hydrating your houseplants. Some plants are sensitive to fluoride, such as the dragon tree, peace lily, spider plant, and parlor palm. Over time, repeated watering with fluoridated tap water will cause the long, narrow foliage of these plants to brown at the tips. Use rainwater, bottled water, or distilled water, and if you have been using tap water, you can flush the soil with rainwater or bottled water to reduce any fluoride buildup already present.

Inch Plant

Tradescantia zebrina, or inch plant, is a type of spiderwort known for its attractive striped foliage. Common names include silver inch plant and wandering dude.

Many years ago, before raising plants for profit became a common business venture, everyone with houseplants knew how to grow inch plants. Gardeners would share cuttings from their inch plants with neighbors and friends, and the plants frequently traveled from place to place. Their popularity has really never waned.

Also known as spiderwort and classified under the scientific name *Tradescantia zebrina,* inch plants are native to Mexico, Central America, and Colombia, but can also be found on the Caribbean islands. They boast bushy hanging stems of purple foliage with green and white stripes. The flowers produced depend on the plant variety, but they can be white, purple, pink, or a range of other similar colors.

Inch plants are highly treasured houseplants because of their attractive appearance and low maintenance. With their signature trailing habit, they are often kept in hanging containers. They also don't grow very tall because the stems have downward growth habit. The plants can either be left to grow leggy and whimsical or pinched back regularly for a bushier look. They are not very fussy, as long as an adequate moisture level is maintained. They can be easily started and grown at any point during the year and may also be propagated from small stem cuttings.

GROWING INCH PLANTS

The only difficulty when caring for inch plants is reaching the balance between consistently moist but never overwatered. The plants can be initially placed in a typically humid area of the home, such as a bathroom or kitchen. They can be kept in normal potting soil or soil with good drainage. Mix in a small amount of sand to add drainage to a standard potting soil. They also require bright, indirect light. If the light is too dim, the distinctive purple leaf markings will fade.

Keep the soil slightly moist by misting frequently, but don't water directly into the crown as this will cause an unsightly rot. Be particularly careful not to let the plant become too dry during the winter months.

SCIENTIFIC NAME: *Tradescantia zebrina*

FAMILY: Commelinaceae

HEIGHT: 6 to 9 inches (15–23 cm)

WIDTH: 1 to 2 feet (30–60 cm)

FOLIAGE COLOR: Variegated striped green, white, and gray with purple underside

SOIL pH: Neutral to acidic

LIGHT: Bright, indirect light

SPECIAL CARE

An important part of growing inch plants is pinching back the long, vining tendrils. Pinch back about a fourth of the plant to encourage branching and increase fullness.

Inch plants have a relatively short lifespan, and do not age well. No matter how attentive you are to the plant's needs, before long it will lose its leaves at the base, while its long legs keep growing. This means it's time to renew your plant by taking cuttings and re-rooting them. Don't be surprised if it needs to be renewed once a year or so.

There are several ways to restart or grow an inch plant. The most efficient way is to cut off a dozen long legs and bury the cut ends in fresh potting soil. Keep the soil moist and within a few weeks you'll see new growth. The salt buildup in old soil is lethal to inch plants, so always make sure your soil is fresh.

Note: Inch plants are only very mildly toxic to pets and people, but their sap can cause contact dermatitis on the skin, especially in those with sensitive skin or those with allergies.

With so many houseplants being easy to propagate through cuttings, why not organize a plant swap? You don't need to be a member of a garden club to gather together some plant-loving compatriots to share cuttings with one another. It's a great, no-cost way to add to everyone's collection. And who knows? You might just land up with your new favorite species.

Money Tree

SCIENTIFIC NAME: *Pachira aquatica*

FAMILY: Balsaminaceae

HEIGHT: 6 to 8 feet (1.8–2.4)

WIDTH: 1 to 2 feet (30–60 cm)

FOLIAGE COLOR: Bright green

SOIL pH: Neutral to acidic

LIGHT: Bright, indirect light

A young money tree plant *(Pachira aquatica)* displays its intricately braided trunk. These lovely trees can start out small but will grow into, tall, imposing houseplants.

The money tree, or *Pachira aquatica,* is a popular houseplant that is said to bring positive energy and affluence to its owner—hence the common name. Also known as a Guiana chestnut, Malabar chestnut, or Saba nut, the tree is native to Central and South America. It features a long slender trunk, often braided into three, five, or seven stems, and attractive bright green foliage. The trees grow to impressive heights of up to 60 feet (18 m) in their native habitats but are more commonly kept as small, potted specimens or as taller, dramatic ornamentals.

Its name can be traced back to the 1980s when it became popularized as a houseplant in Taiwan, especially among those who practice feng shui. The money tree is considered to create positive *chi,* or energy, in the home. For this reason, the tree is frequently placed in offices, banks, and private homes.

In its native region, a money tree produces fruits that are oval green pods divided inside into five chambers. The seeds within the fruit swell until the pod bursts. The nuts, when roasted, taste a bit like chestnuts and can be ground into flour.

A money tree is a relatively low-maintenance houseplant that adds a tropical feel to artificially lit interior landscapes. Nurseries will usually have already trained a young tree's trunk to grow in a braided pattern, which enhances its decorative appeal. It will require no extra care to continue to growing this way as it matures. There are only a few specific conditions that must be kept up to adequately care for it.

GROWING MONEY TREES

A money tree can be placed in indirect light that maintains bright to medium levels or under fluorescent lighting. Keep it away from drafty areas, and move it outside during the summer to an area with dappled light.

The tree does best when planted in a well-draining, nutrient-rich potting soil. Consider using peat moss with some gritty sand for extra drainage.

It also prefers a moderately humid room and deep but infrequent watering. If your home is on the dry side, you can increase the humidity by placing the pot on a saucer filled with pebbles. Water your money tree until the water runs from the drainage holes, and then let the soil dry out between watering. Water it frequently during the spring and summer and less often during the autumn and winter.

SPECIAL CARE

You can use a basic fertilizer blend diluted to half strength to feed your money tree. The plant only requires fertilizer once a month throughout the spring and summer and every other month throughout the autumn and winter.

Taking off any damaged or dead plant material is helpful in encouraging new growth at the top of the plant. Prune the plant in order to control its size. It should also be repotted every two years in a clean peat mixture. Try not to move it around a lot; a money tree plant dislikes being moved and responds by dropping its leaves.

Braided Stems

Certain houseplants, such as the money tree and the lucky bamboo, are sold with the stems intricately braided. Most braiding is actually done by intertwining three individual plants, which gives a fuller, bushier look to the resulting specimen. As well as highlighting the plant's natural beauty, braiding provides structural support and often has cultural meaning.

Monstera

Big and bold, monsteras are powerful statement plants that add drama to any room they are placed in. The large, deeply cut leaves look as if they have holes in them, which has inspired one of the alternate common names, the Swiss cheese plant.

The monstera *(Monstera deliciosa),* also known as a Swiss cheese plant or split-leaf philodendron, is a houseplant. This striking beauty is an easy-to-grow, tropical plant with characteristic splits in its glossy, dark green leaves. It is a climbing evergreen native to the rainforests of Central America, but it is considered a designer plant in indoor spaces.

The plants thrive in most home interiors. In nature, the intricate aerial roots grow on other vegetation to provide support for the rest of the plant. As potted houseplants, the plant's thick-stemmed vines allow for plant growth of 1 to 2 feet (30–60 cm) per year and have leaves that can grow to 3 feet (1 m) long.

GROWING MONSTERA

This native of the tropics needs warm interior temperatures of at least 65° F (18° C) or warmer. Set its pot in an area exposed to bright, indirect sunlight. The plant's leaves might burn if it receives too much direct sunlight. Even so, bring the plant outdoors once or twice a year to encourage growth.

A monstera also needs moderately moist soil and high humidity. Choose a deep pot with many drainage holes, and use a well-draining peat-based potting soil. The aerial roots need something to hang on to, so place a wooden or moss-covered stake set into the middle of the pot for extra support. To increase humidity, mist the foliage with demineralized water or rainwater.

Water once every other week, and wait until excess water drains through the drainage holes. The soil should dry out slightly between waterings. Limit watering during the autumn and winter months.

SPECIAL CARE

Apply a balanced liquid 20-20-20 fertilizer every few weeks during the growing season. Fertilizer diluted to half strength can be used as a replacement for regular watering.

While the plant is still young, repot it once a year to encourage growth and freshen the soil. Go up in container size until you reach the largest pot you wish to use. Thereafter, the plant needs a fresh top-dress of rich soil annually, but will be content for several years at a time, even if it is root-bound.

Repot monstera in early spring before new leaves occur for the best results. Fill the bottom third of your new pot with soil mixture, and lightly set the stake into the center. Then, set the base of the plant into the container so the original soil line on the plant is a touch below where the new line will be. Next, fill in around the base roots and any aerial roots that reach into the soil. Firm up the potting mix around the stake, and use plant ties to attach the stem to the stake.

Trim aerial roots if they are beginning to look unkempt. They can also be tucked back into the pot. The stems and leaves can be trimmed without altering the growth of the plant and may also be used for propagation.

Note: Monstera is mildly toxic to humans and toxic to both dogs and cats.

At a Glance

SCIENTIFIC NAME: *Monstera deliciosa*

FAMILY: Araceae

HEIGHT: Up to 15 feet (4.6 m)

WIDTH: Up to 8 feet (2.4 m)

FOLIAGE COLOR: Glossy dark green

SOIL pH: Acidic, neutral

LIGHT: Bright, indirect light

Specialized Leaves

The development of leaves with jagged edges or holes allows the monstera to withstand the heavy rainfall of its tropical habitat. In the wild these plants produce a cone-shaped fruit that tastes like a combination of strawberry, passion fruit, mango, and pineapple. *Monstera deliciosa* owes its genus name to the leaves—*Monstera* is Latin for "strange"—and the species name refers to the delicious fruit.

Oyster Plant

The oyster plant *(Tradescantia spathacea)* is a spectacular plant that features several tiny white flowers nestled in the "boat" made by a pair of waxy purple bracts. This habit gives it the alternate names of boat lily or Moses-in-the-cradle.

SCIENTIFIC NAME: *Tradescantia spathacea*

FAMILY: Commelinaceae

HEIGHT: 6 to 12 inches (15–30 cm)

WIDTH: 1 to 2 feet (30–60 cm)

FOLIAGE COLOR: Dark green with purple undersides; variegated combinations

SOIL pH: Acidic, neutral

LIGHT: Bright, indirect light

The oyster plant, classified under the scientific name *Tradescantia spathacea,* is a small houseplant native to Central America. It is made up of long, lance-shaped leaves in glossy, dark green with vibrant purple undersides. Its dense clusters of leaves in variegated shades of green and purple make the plant an attractive, yet compact complement to indoor spaces. It can also feature small white or pink rosette-shaped flowers. The plant may also be found under the names boat lily or Moses-in-the-cradle.

GROWING OYSTER PLANTS

It grows quite quickly and should be planted in early spring. It is not difficult to care for and is a highly functional houseplant that rarely has serious issues with pests or diseases, although some common plant pests may be found on it. Special pruning is also not necessary for these plants, besides the removal of dead leaves if desired.

The oyster plant does best when grown in consistent temperatures between about 55 and 80° F (13– 27° C). Do not place it near drafty windows and doors, heating elements, or air-conditioning units. With its tropical origins, it may be beneficial to place a tray of water and pebbles beneath the plant's container to increase humidity. Alternatively, place the plant in a bathroom with windows, or plug in an electric humidifier nearby.

Bright, indirect light is ideal for this plant. It can survive in full sun or shade, but might then be vulnerable to sun damage or lack foliage vibrancy. Use a rich and well-draining soil with a slightly acidic to neutral soil pH. Regular houseplant potting mix should be adequate for its needs.

You should never let the soil fully dry out, but avoid overwatering at all costs. If the plant is watered too frequently it may die from root rot. Once established, an oyster plant does not have to be watered very often. From spring to autumn, feel the soil to determine whether it needs watering. During the winter, you can largely ignore the plant, only watering it every two weeks.

SPECIAL CARE

An oyster plant does not need fertilizer, but applying it may stimulate growth. Consider feeding the plant a regular fertilizer, but only use it during the growing season.

If your oyster plant starts to develop any issues, chances are that you have overwatered it. It may be advantageous to repot the plant in a well-draining soil. In the process of repotting the plant, check the roots for root rot damage. If you find suspected rot, trim off the affected roots to help keep the spread to a minimum.

Even if your plant shows no signs of improper care, repot it every two years or so, because the root system can become very dense. The container used should be larger than the plant's root ball and should have many drainage holes. After transplanting it, use plenty of water before returning to a normal watering schedule.

Persian Shield

The breathtaking beauty of the Persian shield *(Strobilanthes dyerianus)* comes from the purple-and-green leaves that seem to shimmer. These plants, also known as the royal purple plant, add amazing metallic color to any style of home decor.

Chances are fairly high that you have seen this attractive foliage plant at nurseries and garden centers. The bright leaves of the Persian shield are almost better than a flowering specimen, providing stunning color year-round. The plant's common name derives from the flashy, purple-and-silver iridescence of its foliage, which resembles small, pointed armor shields. It produces 4 to 7 inch (10–18 cm) long, slender leaves tipped with a point. They are slightly serrated and have deep green veins with purple to silver on the entire surface of the leaf.

Despite being named "Persian," this plant, classified under the scientific name *Strobilanthes dyerianus,* derives from Myanmar, where it adapts to both hot and cooler climates. In the hot and dry inter-monsoonal months and rainy monsoon months, the plant is an evergreen sub-shrub. During the winter, it can be grown as an annual plant or herbaceous perennial, making it suitable for life as a houseplant.

Persian shields are most commonly grown indoors or as a summer annual in cooler climates. Use these attractive plants to brighten up the home and create a tropical ambiance with ease of care. They are often planted from potted nursery plants in the spring after the soil has fully warmed. It will grow quite quickly in warm and humid conditions and can reach 2 feet (60 cm) tall within a couple of weeks.

GROWING PERSIAN SHIELDS

Persian shields perform well in containers with neutral or slightly acidic soil, facing full sunlight. Bright, indirect light and some direct sunlight will ensure the plant's foliage retains its signature vibrancy.

Provide high humidity and even moisture. The best way to provide extra humidity indoors is to place a thin layer of rocks in a saucer and balance the plant's pot on top. Keep the saucer full of water. This keeps the roots out of the water, but the evaporation of the water creates higher humidity in the air.

SPECIAL CARE

Fertilization is one of the most important Persian shield care instructions, especially for potted plants. Feed every two weeks with a half dilution of liquid plant food. Suspend feeding in autumn and winter.

SCIENTIFIC NAME: *Strobilanthes dyerianus*

FAMILY: Acanthaceae

HEIGHT: 3 to 4 feet (1–1.2 m)

WIDTH: 2 to 3 feet (60 cm–1 m)

FOLIAGE COLOR: Deep purple, lilac, and green overlaid with silvery highlights

SOIL pH: Acidic, neutral

LIGHT: Bright, indirect light

Pinch the stems back to make your plant bushier. You can also share this lovely plant easily with friends and family. Persian shield propagation is done through seed or cuttings. Take 2-to-3-inch (5–7.5 cm) sections from the tips of the plant, cutting just below a growth node. Strip the bottom leaves off, and insert the cutting into a non-soil medium, such as peat. Mist the medium, and place a bag over the cutting. Remove the bag for one hour daily to keep the cutting from molding. In a couple of weeks, the cutting will produce roots, and you can replant it in a potting mixture.

If you live in a warm climate, you can grow these dazzlers outdoors. Why not go for a "royal" garden of pretty purple plants, planting your Persian shield with plants in shades of violet, such as lilac-colored impatiens and purple sweet potato vines.

Ponytail Palm

The gracefully drooping leaves of the *Beaucarnea recurvata,* or ponytail palm, make an attractive addition to a covered porch. Its bulbous root, which sits partially above the soil, inspired another of its common names, the elephant's foot palm.

The ponytail palm has become a very popular houseplant in recent years, and it is easy to see why. With its sleek bulb-like trunk and long, lush, curly leaves, this tree is visually stunning. Not only that, it is also forgiving and simple to take care of.

Classified under the scientific name, *Beaucarnea recurvata,* the ponytail palm is native to arid regions in Central America, where it can grow up to 30 feet (9 m) in height. Indoors, on the other hand, it is often kept as a small desktop plant or as a taller ornamental that makes a bold statement.

Oddly enough, a ponytail palm is neither a palm nor a tree. In fact, it is a succulent member of the Asparagaceae family, which includes edible asparagus and agave. The small trees are often grown in shallow pots with a ponytail-like tuft of hanging dark green leaves. The plants do not require a great deal of attention, given they are provided with the right conditions. They may even grow as tall as 5 feet (1.5 m) if the plant is repotted over time into suitably sized containers. They are, however, slow-growing plants, so it may be best to leave yours as small, decorative plants.

GROWING PONYTAIL PALMS

Growing a ponytail palm in the home is easy. The plant likes full sun or bright, indirect light, but nonetheless, it is so forgiving that it will also be fine with bright light just half of the time. In fact, if you keep your plant in low-light conditions half of the year and provide bright light the other half of the year, it will still be perfectly happy. By the same token, if you keep your plant outdoors in the summer, it will tolerate any indoor light conditions throughout the winter.

The ponytail palm is a succulent, and therefore grows best in semi-dry conditions with temperatures above 60° F (15° C). It will, however, tolerate cooler temperatures as low as 50° F (10° C).

For its growing needs, use a cactus-succulent potting mix augmented with peat to improve its richness. Water the plant every 7 to 14 days, letting the soil dry out significantly in between waterings.

SPECIAL CARE

When repotting a ponytail palm, use a pot that is only an inch or two (2.5-5 cm) wider than the previous one. If the new pot is too large, the plant can get too much water at once, which can be damaging to its growth. Make sure the plant is root-bound before repotting it, because it thrives in dry soil.

Fertilize only two or three times a year. Use a liquid fertilizer during the growing season or a slow-release pellet fertilizer in the spring.

At a Glance

SCIENTIFIC NAME: *Beaucarnea recurvata*

FAMILY: Asparagaceae

HEIGHT: 6 to 8 feet (1.8–2.4 m)

WIDTH: 3 to 5 feet (1–1.5 m)

FOLIAGE COLOR: Dark green

SOIL pH: Neutral

LIGHT: Bright, indirect light

Ponytail Bonsai

The ponytail palm makes an excellent candidate to become a bonsai, a tree or plant grown in miniature form. This can be accomplished by keeping it in a small pot and trimming the roots by no more than one-quarter of their volume once every few years. The plant will not grow taller, but the trunk will thicken quite interestingly. Your bonsai will still require bright or partial sunlight and warm temperatures.

Pothos

The lush leaves of the pothos *(Epipremnum aureum)* make it a pretty addition to your houseplant collection, and its trailing habit makes it especially suitable for hanging baskets. This popular species goes by many names, including golden pothos, Ceylon creeper, hunter's robe, ivy arum, taro vine, and silver vine.

Pothos, classified under the scientific name *Epipremnum aureum,* is considered by many to be a great plant to introduce novice gardeners to the art of caring for indoor plants. Native to the Solomon Islands of the South Pacific, this plant is now a common feature across households all over the world. It can be recognized by a trailing vine of heart-shaped green leaves with pale green, white, or yellow striations on the top and undersides. Because pothos care is undemanding, this lovely plant provides a simple way to add a touch of green in your home. It can be introduced at any point during the year and is a very quick grower.

GROWING POTHOS

Pothos enjoys a wide range of environments. It does well in bright, indirect light or in low light, but it will not tolerate direct light. For this reason, a pothos plant makes a great addition to your bathroom or home office, where light levels tends to be low.

Light levels also affect the foliage's coloration. If your pothos is highly variegated—particularly if it has white striations—it might lose its variegation when the light is too low. Only the green parts of the leaves can produce energy for the plant, so they must receive enough light. If the plant is not exposed to sufficient light, its leaves will compensate by turning greener, and its growth will also slow down.

Its soil needs are flexible. The plant can be grown in dry soil or in vases of water. It will thrive in nutrient-rich soil, but it will do almost as well in nutrient-poor soil.

Water only when the soil has dried out completely. The plant risks root rot in consistently damp soil. Watch it leaves to determine if you are getting its water levels correct: if there are black spots on them, it has been overwatered, and if they are beginning to droop, it has been underwatered.

SCIENTIFIC NAME: *Epipremnum aureum*

FAMILY: Araceae

HEIGHT: 6 to 10 feet (1.8–2 m)

WIDTH: 3 to 6 feet (1–1.8 m)

FOLIAGE COLOR: Glossy medium green variegated with pale green underside

SOIL pH: Neutral to acidic

LIGHT: Bright, indirect light

SPECIAL CARE

You can fertilize your pothos plant about once every three months, and this will help it grow more quickly, but most people find that their plants grow quickly enough even without being fertilized.

Pothos is very popular due to the fact that it can be grown in water or in dry soil. Cuttings can be taken from a mother plant and rooted in water. If keeping the houseplant in a jug of water, place it in a hard-to-reach area, where it can remain untouched as long as water remains in the jug. Alternatively, pothos can be started in soil and will tolerate moderate periods of dry soil with little consequence. Note that cuttings started in one growing medium have a hard time switching to the other. So, a pothos plant started in soil will have a hard time thriving if moved to water, and a pothos cutting started in water will not do very well in soil, especially if it has spent a long period of time growing in water.

Note: Pothos plants are toxic to adults, children, and pets.

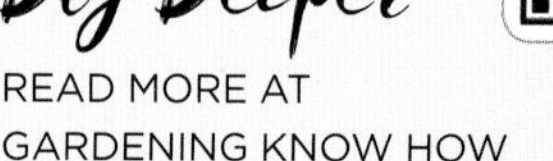

READ MORE AT GARDENING KNOW HOW

Not all houseplants are safe around your furry friends. To learn more about toxic plants, scan the code or follow this link.

- **"Is Pothos Pet Friendly — Learn About Pothos Pet Toxicity"** (URL = gkh.us/163476)

Prayer Plant

A particularly striking cultivar of the prayer plant is *Maranta leuconeura* var. *erythroneura* 'Fascinator'. Its unique tricolor herringbone plant pattern works well with modern decor.

SCIENTIFIC NAME: *Maranta leuconeura*

FAMILY: Moraceae

HEIGHT: 6 to 12 inches (15–30 cm)

WIDTH: 6 to 12 inches (15–30 cm)

FOLIAGE COLOR: Bicolor green shades and tricolor deep green with yellow splotches and red veining

SOIL pH: Neutral to acidic

LIGHT: Bright, indirect light

The prayer plant, classified under the scientific name *Maranta leuconeura,* is a low-growing plant native to Brazil. It can be recognized by its striking, decorative leaves, which come in tricolor and bicolor varieties of deep green shades with yellow splotches and red veins. The plant can eventually reach a foot tall (30 cm) in height, but it is a very slow grower. It is a common houseplant and can be planted and cared for indoors year-round, but it is not likely to sustain itself for multiple years.

GROWING PRAYER PLANTS

Although the prayer plant is somewhat tolerant of low-light conditions, it does best in bright, indirect sunlight. Hang or set your plant near a window, avoiding direct sunlight, which could scorch its leaves.

As a native of the rainforest, this plant thrives in high humidity. It can survive in a variety of soils, but opt for one that is well-draining. It should be kept constantly moist, but not soggy. Use warm water whenever the top layer of the plant becomes dry.

Ideal temperatures for the prayer plant are between 60 and 80° F (16–27° C). If temperatures are low for extended periods, it may experience leaf loss.

During winter dormancy, the soil should be kept drier. Keep in mind, however, that dry air can also be an issue in winter. Place your plant among several other houseplants, and mist them daily with warm water in order to create more humid conditions. Another method of increasing humidity is to place a bowl of water near the plant. Alternatively, set its container on top of a shallow dish of pebbles and water, but do not allow the plant to sit directly in the water.

SPECIAL CARE

Repot your prayer plant using an ordinary potting soil in early spring, when you can also easily propagate it. If you wish to propagate it, take stem cuttings from just below the nodes closest to the bottom of the stem. Cuttings can be placed in a mixture of moist peat and perlite and covered with plastic to retain moisture levels. You may want to poke a few air holes in the plastic to allow for adequate ventilation, as well. Place the cuttings in a sunny location. Because prayer plants are prone to pests such as spider mites, mealybugs, and aphids, it is a good idea to inspect new plants thoroughly before bringing them indoors. You may also want to occasionally check again when watering or feeding the plants.

Editor's Picks

With its big oval leaves in unique patterns and colorations, the prayer plant always makes a statement. Here are just a few of its cultivars.

- **'Fascinator' has deep green leaves edged in lighter green and marked by maroon veining and lime green highlights down the center.**
- **'Kim' has dramatic light-colored foliage with purple spots and streaks of creamy white.**
- **'Lemon Lime' features a prominent pattern in bright lime, medium, and dark green shades.**
- **'Silver Feather' combines light and deep green with faint, gray-blue markings between the veins.**

Rex Begonia

Rex begonias, also known as painted-leaf begonias or fancy-leaf begonias, are stunning plants that live up to their common names. There are many varieties, including ones in shades of red and others with leaves that swirl in snail-like formations.

SCIENTIFIC NAME: *Begonia rex-cultorum*

FAMILY: Begoniaceae

HEIGHT: 12 to 18 inches (30–45 cm)

WIDTH: 12 to 18 inches (30–45 cm)

FOLIAGE COLOR: Shades of green, red, silver, and even purple in solids and variegated color combinations

SOIL pH: Acidic

LIGHT: Bright, indirect light

Some might find it shocking that certain begonias are actually grown for their leaves, rather than their flowers. The rex begonia plant is one of those. Although it does flower, the main attraction is the beautiful and ornate foliage that it produces. Known under the scientific name *Begonia rex-cultorum,* this plant is admired for its large, variegated leaves, which come in a variety of green, red, silver, and even purple colors.

Rex begonia is in the rhizomatous group of the *Begonia* genus, meaning it has rhizomes, or thickened stems, from which colorful leaves emerge. This plant grows horizontally with leaves reaching 6 inches (30 cm) in length. Caring for it indoors can be a little tricky, but it is certainly possible to grow beautiful specimens if you understand the plant's needs.

GROWING REX BEGONIAS

A rex begonias thrive in bright, indirect light. Some direct sun is okay for short periods, especially if it is from an eastern-facing window with gentle morning sun exposure. During periods of the year when the sun is strongest, or if you live in an area where the sun is particularly strong, you will want to move the plant accordingly. Use sheer curtains to diffuse direct sun, or set the plant a few feet back from a very sunny window. Too much direct sun can burn the foliage.

Generally, rex begonias prefer relatively cool temperatures, moist soil, and humid conditions. Use an airy, light, and fast-draining soil and try to keep it evenly moist. Still, strike a balance since these plants are easily prone to root rot. A good rule of thumb is to allow the top inch or so (2.5 cm) to dry out before watering again. It is better to keep the soil on the slightly drier side, but never let the soil completely dry out, since this can quickly spell death for your plant. Letting the soil get too dry can cause rex begonias to quickly wilt.

SPECIAL CARE

As far as fertilizing goes, you can use a dilute solution about twice a month during the active growing season. Avoid fertilizing during the winter months when plant growth can come to a halt.

Prevent your plant's leaves from being wet for extended periods of time, especially at night, since this can encourage powdery mildew as well as bacterial leaf spot. Because rex begonias prefer conditions with high humidity, aim to increase the humidity, especially during the winter months. You can place the plant on a tray with wet pebbles, introduce a humidifier nearby, or place it in humid areas of the house, such as a bathroom. You can also group plants together, which will increase humidity through a natural process of transpiration.

If you'd like to propagate the plant, you can use leaf cuttings or cut sections of the rhizome for repotting. Choose a pot that is wider than it is deep since this is more appropriate for rhizomatous plants like rex begonias.

Note: Rex begonias are mildly toxic to humans, but can be deadly to cats, dogs, and horses.

Editor's Picks

Here is just a tiny sampling of stunning rex begonia varieties.

- **'China Curl' has a center band of silver edged in deep pink and a chocolate-brown edge.**
- **'Curly Fireflush' has deeply spiraled leaves of chocolate-lined chartreuse green.**
- **'Harmony's Red Robin' has a deep black center suffused with iridescent gray that's banded in a brilliant red and bordered with chocolate brown.**
- **'Regal Minuet' has dark rose leaves with silver banding, black leaf outlines, and dark centers.**

Snake Plant

A snake plant *(Dracaena trifasciata)* sits on a table near a curtained window. This species is most commonly known as the snake plant, but other monikers include Saint George's sword, mother-in-law's tongue, and viper's bowstring hemp. This low-maintenance species, with its boldly striped, upright foliage, is an ideal houseplant for beginners.

If a prize were available for the most tolerant plant, the snake plant would certainly be one of the front-runners. Classified under the scientific name *Dracaena trifasciata,* snake plants are native to rocky, dry habitats in tropical West Africa. It is one of the most popular and hardy species of houseplants, boasting stiff, sword-like leaves that vary in color. Most varieties have green-banded leaves with a yellow border.

Snake plant care is very straightforward. This plant can be neglected for weeks at a time; yet, with its strappy leaves and architectural shape, it will still look fresh. Increasing the plant's exposure to light will improve the growth rate, but it will also survive in darker corners of the house. Likewise, it is resilient in droughts and has few insect problems. NASA research has even shown that a snake plant is able to help keep the air inside your home clean, removing toxins, such as formaldehyde and benzene. In short, it is the perfect houseplant.

GROWING SNAKE PLANTS

Snake plants can grow well in both containers on the floor or as small tabletop plants. They prefer warm weather and can suffer in the cold. Position your plants somewhere with little draft. Indirect and steady light with some direct sun is also ideal. They can easily adapt to low light, however, so feel free to prioritize other plants in your collection.

To optimize growth, use a loose, well-draining potting mix that is sandier and low in peat content. All-purpose cactus potting soil works well. The plants are susceptible to overwatering, which can lead to root rot. Wait until the soil is dry to the touch to water your plants. During the winter, they require minimal watering, only monthly or when the soil is dry.

SPECIAL CARE

Use a mild cactus fertilizer during the growing season or a balanced liquid slow-release 10-10-10 fertilizer or a 20-20-20 fertilizer diluted to half strength. Do not fertilize the plant during winter months.

Pruning is advised to encourage new growth. Use sterile pruning shears, scissors, or a sharp knife to remove leaves at the soil line or cut off damaged or mature leaves.

SCIENTIFIC NAME: *Dracaena trifasciata* (formerly *Sanseviera)*

FAMILY: Asparagaceae

HEIGHT: 6 inches to 8 feet (15 cm–2.4 m)

WIDTH: 6 inches to 3 feet (25 cm–1 m)

FOLIAGE COLOR: Mottled and striped green centers with bright yellow margins

SOIL pH: Slightly acidic to slightly alkaline

LIGHT: Bright, indirect light

It is best to prune during the growing season in spring or summer. Pruning off-season can stress out a plant. If you wish to control the height of a snake plant, simply remove the tallest leaves.

Snake plants can also be easily grown from cuttings. The most important thing to remember is that they can rot, so a free-draining soil should be used. Rather than using leaf cuttings, a simpler way to propagate snake plants is by dividing. The roots produce rhizomes, which can simply be removed with a sharp knife and potted up. Again, these will need to go into a free-draining soil.

Note: Snake plants are poisonous if ingested.

Swedish Ivy

A young Swedish ivy will soon display the trailing habit that makes it a favorite for hanging containers. The variegated types are commonly grown as small houseplants. Non-toxic to cats and dogs, these petite plants make a great choice for pet lovers.

Swedish ivy, classified under the scientific name *Plectranthus,* is a popular hanging basket houseplant, native to northern Australia and the Pacific Islands. Also known as Swedish begonia and creeping Charlie, the plant is appreciated for its lovely trailing habit. It features cascades of thick stems and rounded glossy green leaves with white scalloped edges. The *P. australis* variety blooms with pretty white or pale lavender flowers in the late spring or early summer. Variants of *P. coleoides* can have striking pink edges. The plant grows a few feet downwards as its foliage drops. It can live from three to five years on average.

Many gardeners incorporate this ivy as an annual into containers or use it as a ground cover in the garden, as well as a houseplant. The easy care of Swedish ivy makes them great for even the most novice gardeners. The average room temperatures and humidity of indoor environments is perfect for these plants. They can also be moved outside in the summer or grown on decks or balconies.

GROWING SWEDISH IVY

Learning how to grow Swedish ivy is not at all difficult. Keep your plant somewhere that receives bright, indirect light all year long. If the leaves begin to droop, your plant may be getting too much light. It also thrives in temperatures from 60 to 75° F (18–21° C), which is average room temperature. Colder temperatures might kill the plant so keep this in mind when adjusting the thermostat.

The plant does best in a light and loamy potting mix with some perlite mixed in to help with drainage, although any good potting soil should be fine. The soil should be kept slightly moist at all times. Water the ivy once a week from the beginning of spring until autumn. Be sure to allow the soil to dry out slightly between waterings. Good drainage is necessary, so do not let the ivy sit in overflow water. During the winter, the plant can become prone to overwatering, so reduce watering frequency.

SCIENTIFIC NAME: *Plectranthus* spp.

FAMILY: Lamiaceae

HEIGHT: 10 to 12 inches (25–30 cm)

WIDTH: 15 to 20 inches (38–50 cm)

FOLIAGE COLOR: Solid green or green edge with creamy white

SOIL pH: Acidic to neutral

LIGHT: Bright, indirect light

SPECIAL CARE

During the growing season, feed the plant every few weeks with a balanced houseplant fertilizer, such as a 20-20-20. Never fertilize the plant during winter months. If the leaves are looking dull or droopy, consider upping its fertilizer intake. Do this only in moderation, however, because too much nitrogen fertilizer can hinder blooming.

Pinch off vine tips after flowering to keep the plant from becoming too leggy. Repot Swedish ivy every two or three years.

The best way for propagating the plant is through cuttings. Cut a healthy stem section with a crown of leaves on the end. Remove the lower ends of the foliage to expose a bare stem. Dip the cutting in rooting hormone and place it in a container prepared with potting medium.

For best root development, place the cuttings in indirect sunlight. Spray cuttings frequently with water or place clear plastic over the pot to retain moisture and humidity. Roots should form in three weeks with new plants forming from the base. Transplant individual plants and discard the old stem.

Hedera Ivy

Several other plants share the "ivy" common name, all in the *Hedera* genus, including English ivy, Irish ivy, and Russian ivy.

To learn more about these species, scan the QR code or follow the link to "Ivy Houseplants — Information on Caring for Ivy Plants" (URL = gkh.us/12945).

Weeping Fig

SCIENTIFIC NAME: *Ficus benjamina*

FAMILY: Moraceae

HEIGHT: 3 to 6 feet (1–1.8 m)

WIDTH: 1 to 2 feet (30–60 cm)

FOLIAGE COLOR: Dark to medium green with paler green underside and variegated green and white combinations

SOIL pH: Acidic to neutral

LIGHT: Bright, indirect light

A young weeping fig *(Ficus benjamina)* thrives in its spot on a windowsill, adding green color to an all-white interior. This lovely houseplant, with its lushly verdant foliage, can grow to become a statuesque statement piece.

Weeping figs, classified under the scientific name *Ficus benjamina,* are elegant trees with slender gray trunks and a profusion of dark to medium green leaves. Also known as ficus trees, these large broadleaf evergreens are native to tropical and subtropical climates of Asia and Australia. When grown indoors, they are usually pruned to about 3 to 6 feet (1–1.8 m) in height. Nurseries also commonly braid their trunks for aesthetic appeal.

These attractive container plants are grown in many homes and offices and are easy to care for. As indoor plants, they are slow-growing, so it is mostly a matter of selecting an appropriate location and establishing the plant with the correct soil.

GROWING WEEPING FIGS

Weeping figs thrive in indirect, bright sunlight. Ideally, locate the plant where it will be exposed to some direct morning sunlight and filtered light for the rest of the day. Sunny areas with some afternoon shade will also do the plant good.

Use any well-draining potting soil. The plants will not need nutrient-rich soil unless they are being repotted. It is best to have improved drainage when repotting.

Weeping figs require a consistent watering schedule. Allow the plant to dry between waterings, however, and be careful not to overwater. If the plant is watered too frequently or allowed to sit in water, its leaves will droop, and it may develop root rot.

In their natural environments, weeping figs have fluctuating temperatures from nighttime to daytime. Typically, they thrive when kept in 75 to 85° F (24–30° C) temperatures during the day and 65 to 70° F (18–21° C) temperatures at night. Avoid the use of heavy air conditioning during warmer months, and consider setting your thermostat to keep the house cooler at night.

Measures can also be taken to increase humidity indoors for the plants. A humidifier can be placed nearby to prevent the plant's leaves from shriveling and drying out. You can also mist the leaves to keep them hydrated.

SPECIAL CARE

Fertilizer is a must for weeping figs. At the beginning of the growing season, feed your plant with slow-release pellets. Throughout the rest of the growing season, use a liquid fertilizer relatively often. Feed the plants monthly during spring and summer and every other month during autumn and winter.

You may notice drooping leaves on your plants, even while maintaining the ideal indoor conditions for its success. If this occurs, try supplementing its soil with some magnesium and manganese.

Note: Weeping figs are toxic to humans and pets, so choose an appropriate spot to place it.

HOUSEPLANTS FOR LOW LIGHT

How much sun to give a houseplant is always a key consideration. Some, like the peace lily, need indirect light. Under the right conditions, these leafy specimens will produce elegantly tapered white to off-white flowers starting in the early summer that will continue to bloom throughout the year.

Many tropical plants grow in the understory of the rainforest, far below the canopy of trees and beneath more light-hungry plants. These same shade-tolerant plants are able to thrive indoors without a great deal of sunlight. The Victorians, in particular, enjoyed decorating their homes with oversized low-light plants in ornate pots that could be set down anywhere there was a bit of light, and then live for years. Plants that typically fall into the low-light category include ferns, philodendrons, begonias, lucky bamboo, and prayer plants.

CARING FOR LOW-LIGHT PLANTS

Most of these plants require infrequent watering, perhaps every two weeks, or when the soil feels dry to the touch. Overwatering causes yellowing leaves, brown tips, wilting despite wet soil, and also the start of root rot. Signs of underwatering include dry leaves, leaf drop, leaf curling, wilting, and brown tips. The soil will feel dry, but the plant will improve after watering. Indications your low-light plants are getting too much sun include drooping, crisp, or wrinkled leaves; burnt or scorched patches on leaves in white, yellow, or brown; faded pigments; and dried-out soil.

Undemanding low-light plants make excellent gifts for those acquaintances who swear they kill anything green, for children who might be a bit neglectful when caring for a plant, and for seniors who don't want anything high maintenance to fuss over.

Dig Deeper

READ MORE AT GARDENING KNOW HOW

Whether you love the look of lush houseplant foliage, which comes in colors from solid greens to fanciful variegations, or are searching for one that has lovely blooms, there is a plant for you. Follow the links below for some great ideas.

- **"What Plants Grow Indoors in Shade: Houseplants That Like Shade"** (URL = gkh.us/1920)
- **"Flowering Indoor Plants: Good Houseplants with Flowers for Low Light"** (URL = gkh.us/448)

Even houseplants that tolerate shade can light up a room. Some species have widely diverging varieties, such as the rex begonia that comes in a dazzling array of vibrant color combinations and leaf shapes.

Cast-Iron Plant

Aspidistras are long-time houseplant favorites and were nearly ubiquitous in early-20th-century homes. The common name of "cast-iron plant" attests to the fact that these plants will survive just about anything, including neglect and pollution.

The cast-iron plant, classified under the scientific name *Aspidistra elatior,* is an extremely hardy houseplant and a perennial favorite in some regions. Native to China and Japan, the plant is a member of the asparagus family. It produces small purple flowers that only appear near the soil surface and are usually hidden within its foliage. In fact, the blossoms are unlikely to appear at all when the plant is grown indoors. What this plant may lack in glitz, however, it makes up for with robust, arching, dark green, glossy leaves, which can reach almost 3 feet (1 m) in length and 4 inches (10 cm) in width.

Cast-iron plants are ideal for anyone who wants to grow houseplants but doesn't have a lot of time for plant care. The species can survive even the most extreme conditions in which other plants would shrivel and die. Growing cast-iron indoors is extremely easy and rewarding, but keep in mind it has a slow growth rate and will do best if introduced in the spring.

GROWING CAST-IRON PLANTS

The cast-iron plant has a reputation for being impossible to kill, but it still requires a few key conditions to thrive. The plant grows well in low light indoors and is not finicky about regular water, either. Although it is a slow grower, this reliable performer will live for many years.

Place your plant near a north-facing window, where it will receive indirect partial sunlight. If the window has a strong light source, slightly set the plant back to a spot where it will receive less direct light.

It can be planted in a variety of soils, but prefers ones with good drainage. Use a standard-quality potting mix or any rich soil with a slightly acidic to neutral soil pH.

SCIENTIFIC NAME: *Aspidistra elatior*

FAMILY: Asparagaceae

HEIGHT: 2 to 3 feet (60 cm–1 m)

WIDTH: Up to 4 inches (10 cm)

FOLIAGE COLOR: Dark green to reddish-purple and variegated

SOIL pH: Acidic, neutral

LIGHT: Partial shade

Cast-iron plants are tolerant of droughts, so let the soil dry out between watering. While the plants are young, water more frequently so the soil is always a bit moist. Although cast-iron plants will tolerate extreme conditions, it's always a good idea to provide it with regular watering, especially during the heat of summer.

SPECIAL CARE

This plant also responds well to organic soil and an annual dose of all-purpose fertilizer. Feed the plant once a month during spring and summer or use a slow-release fertilizer only during spring. Apply fertilizer after watering to prevent burning the roots.

Propagate cast-iron plants by division. Although new plants are slow to grow, with some patience and time, your new plant will thrive and flourish.

Don't forget your bathroom when deciding where to place your houseplants. These days, with more and more homeowners using their bathrooms as quiet retreats rather than as just utilitarian spaces, it makes sense to add a pretty plant or two. There are some plants that will actually benefit from placement in this kind of humid environment.

To find out more about plants for bathrooms, scan the QR code or follow this link to "Best Bathroom Plants: Growing Plants Near Showers and Tubs" (URL = gkh.us/107470)

Chinese Evergreen

Tropical *Aglaonema* 'Stripes', with long, leathery leaves displaying a silver-striped pattern, is just one of the many varieties of this beautiful houseplant to choose from.

SCIENTIFIC NAME: *Aglaonema* spp.

FAMILY: Araceae

HEIGHT: 1 to 2 feet (30–60 cm)

WIDTH: 1 to 2 feet (30–60 cm)

FOLIAGE COLORS: Various greens, red, and white and variegated combinations

SOIL pH: Acidic

LIGHT: Indirect light

The Chinese evergreen, classified under the scientific name *Aglaonema,* refers to various decorative plant species native to Asia. These varieties each are recognized by their large, narrow, and glossy oval leaves in various shades of green, red, and white, as well as variegated combinations. Older plants also produce flowers in spring or summer, which make the plants an attractive addition to your home decor.

Chinese evergreens can make even the novice indoor gardener look like an expert. This tropical foliage plant is one of the most durable houseplants you can grow, tolerating poor light, dry air, and drought. It is slow-growing and can be potted and cared for year-round.

GROWING CHINESE EVERGREENS

Although Chinese evergreens are tolerant of many growing conditions, following certain recommendations will yield greater results. This includes placing them in well-draining soil, preferably an equal mix of potting soil, perlite, and sand.

The plants thrive in medium-to-low-light conditions or indirect sunlight. Wherever you place yours in the home, you should make sure it receives warm temperatures and somewhat humid conditions. This flexible plant will, however, tolerate less-than-ideal conditions if necessary. It prefers temperatures no lower than 60° F (16° C) with average indoor temps ranging between 70 and 72° F (21–22° C) being most favorable, but it can tolerate temperatures around 50 and 55° F (10–13° C). Keep your Chinese evergreen away from drafts, which can cause browning of the foliage.

These plants also enjoy moderate watering—not too much, not too little. Allow your plant to dry out between watering. Overwatering will lead to root rot.

SPECIAL CARE

You should fertilize older plants once or twice yearly using a water-soluble houseplant fertilizer.

If your plant becomes too large or leggy, give it a quick trim. It's also possible to save cuttings during the process for propagating new plants. Cuttings will root easily in water.

Older plants will sometimes produce flowers reminiscent of calla or peace lilies. This occurs in spring to summer. Most people choose to cut the blooms prior to seed production, but you may choose to use them to try your hand at seed growing. Keep in mind, however, that this will take much longer than propagation.

To limit the accumulation of dust build-up, clean the plant's leaves occasionally by wiping them down with a soft, damp rag, or simply place them in the shower and allow them to air dry.

Chinese evergreens can also be affected by spider mites, scale, mealybugs, and aphids. Routinely checking the leaves for signs of pests will help limit problems later.

Editor's Picks

Here is just a tiny sampling of stunning *Aglaonema* varieties to try.

- **'Chocolate' has gorgeous dark, chocolaty green foliage with striking red veining.**
- **'Dalmatian' displays jade green splattered with pink spots.**
- **'Pictum Tricolor' has a camouflage pattern of mixed greens.**
- **'Prestige' has green leaves with splotches of red, pink, and cream.**

Dieffenbachia

Dieffenbachia, also called the leopard lily, is a tropical flowering plant that is widely cultivated as an ornamental. And no wonder—its buds unfurl into eye-catchingly lush leaves in variegated hues decorated with stripes, splotches, and spots or with colored veins in shades of green, yellow, white, or cream on the deep green base.

SCIENTIFIC NAME: *Dieffenbachia* spp.

FAMILY: Araceae

HEIGHT: 3 to 10 feet (1–3 m)

WIDTH: 2 to 3 feet (60 cm–1 m)

FOLIAGE COLOR: Dark green with white, cream, or yellow splotches and veining

SOIL pH: Slightly acidic

LIGHT: Partial shade or bright, indirect light

A Victorian-era favorite, the large and showy dieffenbachia can be the perfect living decoration for the modern home or office. Native to parts of the Caribbean and South America, plants of the *Dieffenbachia* genus are known for their pointed, ovate leaves, which come in various combinations of green, cream, and white. In nature, these plants can be as large as 20 feet (6 m) in height, with long leaves reaching 20 inches (50 cm) in length, When kept as houseplants, however, they are more likely to range between 3 and 5 feet tall (1–1.5 m).

When you learn how to care for it, you'll find the dieffenbachia to be very adaptable to different kinds of lighting and conditions in which you might not expect it to grow. They are popular indoor plants because they can thrive in shady conditions and are not too demanding.

GROWING DIEFFENBACHIA

Dieffenbachia is prone to a few problems that can be easily overcome in most situations. The most common problem, for example, is too much moisture. To avoid overwatering, plant your dieffenbachia in a fast-draining, well-aerated potting mix. Water lightly, keeping the soil consistently moist, but not soggy. Check the soil to make sure the top inch (2.5 cm) is dry before watering the plant.

Another common problem with dieffenbachias is improper lighting. Most varieties of this plant species do best in a filtered-light situation, where bright to moderate light shines through a sheer curtain or other filtering window cover. Filtered light is particularly important in the spring and summer, when the houseplant is producing new, tender leaves that are subject to sunburn if the light is too bright or shines directly on the plant.

SPECIAL CARE

Browning bottom leaves on a dieffenbachia is normal for the plant. Snip them off to keep the plant tidy. If leaves of the plant appear bleached with a webby substance on the underside, check the plant for spider mites, and treat with an insecticidal soap spray or neem oil. Don't use chemicals for this issue on the growing dieffenbachia, as it often makes the problem worse.

You may also notice that your plant produces water droplets. Do not be concerned. This is simply a by-product of the transpiration process, which is active in most plants. Keep in mind that dieffenbachias thrive in humid environments and can survive in low-light conditions, making them perfect choices to place in a bathroom.

Note: Dieffenbachia is highly toxic to humans, dogs, and cats.

Editor's Tip

Dieffenbachias were previously known as "dumb cane," a name that has largely been dropped due to its derogatory connotations. The leaves, if chewed or eaten, can cause swelling of the tongue and throat, leading to a temporary loss of speech (the origin of the older name). While this is usually not serious, it can cause suffocation. Avoid placing a dieffenbachia plant where curious children or pets might be tempted to taste it.

Fiddle-Leaf Fig

A young fiddle-leaf fig *(Ficus lyrata)* makes a bit of a statement displayed on a kitchen counter. Its distinctive oval-shaped leaves make this plant a conversation piece.

You may recognize the fiddle-leaf fig as a large and leafy tropical accent to well-lit offices or homes. Classified under the name *Ficus lyrata,* fiddle-leaf figs are evergreen trees with enormous, fiddle-shaped, dark green leaves that grow upright on a sleek trunk. Native to African rainforests, these plants can only survive outdoors in very warm, coastal areas. They will, however, serve as an attractive container plant to be kept indoors in cooler climates.

Often kept in floor-standing pots, the trees can grow to over 6 feet (1.8 m) tall. They grow relatively quickly and can be potted during any season. It can be a bit difficult, though, to replicate the steamy conditions of the plants' native habitat, so it is important to learn the appropriate methods of care.

GROWING FIDDLE-LEAF FIGS

Use a pot and potting soil that provide excellent drainage, because these trees won't survive wet soil. Any quality indoor plant potting soil should do the trick. Place the tree in a spot where it will get high, indirect light exposure. Be careful not to put the plant anywhere in the house where it might be exposed to hot afternoon sun; direct sunlight can burn the leaves. Very low light, on the other hand, will cause slow growth.

Fiddle-leaf figs do require a moderate amount of moisture, but it is better to underwater than overwater them. Don't add water until the top inch (2.5 cm) of soil is dry to the touch. When the plant is overwatered, it often loses leaves and suffers from root rot, which can eventually kill it. Water the plant slightly less during winter months when humidity levels are low.

SPECIAL CARE

Fiddle-leaf figs are not particularly demanding plants once you prepare the correct growing environment, but some extra steps of care are beneficial. If you start growing them in containers, you'll need to repot them every year. Move up one pot size when you see roots emerging from the pot.

The pots will also need to be rotated every few days to ensure that a different part of the plant faces the source of sunlight. This extra measure ensures that the plant does not begin to grow in the direction of the light source.

Dust the leaves with a damp cloth every week or two—not only to keep your house neat and tidy, but to also allow more light to hit the leaves, which will promote more efficient photosynthesis. There is also no harm in pruning any damaged or dead leaves, as well as the top of the main stem, because they will no longer benefit the plant.

Use high-nitrogen plant food or special fiddle-leaf fig fertilizer during the growing season. It is not necessary to use fertilizer on this plant over the winter months.

Note: Fiddle-leaf figs are toxic to cats and dogs.

SCIENTIFIC NAME: *Ficus lyrata*

FAMILY: Moraceae

HEIGHT: 6 to 10 feet (1.8–3 m)

WIDTH: 2 to 3 feet (60 cm–1 m)

FOLIAGE COLOR: Dull green with a paler green underside

SOIL pH: Slightly acidic

LIGHT: Partial shade

The Popularity of Plants

The popularity of certain houseplants rises and falls just as any other home decor trend will do. In the case of the fiddle-leaf fig, for example, it was a relatively obscure plant until 2010, when users of the then-new Pinterest website began uploading scores of beautiful shots of this fascinating plant. Since then it has become a top-seller with online merchants, big box retailers, and local garden centers and plant nurseries.

Fittonia

SCIENTIFIC NAME: *Fittonia* spp.

FAMILY: Acanthaceae

HEIGHT: 3 to 6 inches (7.5–15 cm)

WIDTH: 12 to 18 inches 3(0–45 cm)

FOLIAGE COLOR: Rich green with bright pink, red, or white veining

SOIL pH: Slightly acidic

LIGHT: Filtered indirect sun, partial shade

Fittonia, also known as the nerve plant, is an attractive, spreading evergreen perennial with densely patterned leaves in a variety of pretty color combinations.

The fittonia (*Fittonia* spp.), also known as the nerve plant, mosaic plant, or painted net leaf, is a tropical plant native to Peru and other areas of the South American rainforest. Named for its 19th-century discoverers, botanists Elizabeth and Sarah May Fitton, it is a member of the Acanthaceae, or acanthus family. It features striking foliage in primarily olive green with distinctive veining of pink, white, or red. For specific color characteristics, look for fittonia species such as *F. argyroneura,* with silver-white veins, or *F. pearcei,* a carmine pink–veined beauty.

The fittonia does indeed flower. The blooms, however, are insignificant reddish to white spikes that tend to blend in with the foliage. They are rarely seen when the plant is grown indoors.

As a tropical native, the fittonia craves high humidity, but doesn't do well with too much irrigation. It is a great plant for use in terrariums, hanging baskets, dish gardens, or even as a ground cover outdoors in the right climate. The foliage is low-growing and trailing, with oval-shaped leaves on rooting, mat-forming stems.

GROWING FITTONIA

Fittonia likes well-drained moist soil, but not too wet. Use a standard potting soil with a peat moss base. Water the plant moderately, and let it dry out between waterings. Use room temperature water to avoid shock. Finding the balance between over- and under-watering can be a challenge. If the fittonia is left to fully dry out, it might collapse, and repeated collapsing can be detrimental to its health. On the other hand, overwatering will cause leaves to yellow and become limp. Monitor your plants' behavior, and water accordingly.

Fittonia flourishes in warm, humid environments. Place your plant away from drafts in a warm spot. It will grow well in some shade but prefers indirect sunlight. Keep the plant under fluorescent lights or near a north-facing window with light coming in through a sheer curtain. Misting can imitate the humidity of a tropical setting.

SPECIAL CARE

Feed as recommended for tropical plants per the instructions of your fertilizer brand. During its growing season, a weak dose of liquid fertilizer, such as a balanced 5-5-5 diluted to half strength, can be applied weekly.

Its trailing nature can lead to a straggly appearance. Prune its tips to create a fuller, bushier plant. To propagate, divide rooted stem pieces or take tip cuttings.

Problems are few; however, avoid overwatering, which can lead to root rot. Xanthomonas leaf spot, which causes necropsy of the veins, and mosaic virus might also affect the plant. Pests might include aphids, mealybugs, and thrips.

READ MORE AT GARDENING KNOW HOW

To find out how to perk up a drooping fittonia, scan the QR code or follow this link.

- **"Fixing a Wilted Fittonia Plant: What to Do for Droopy Fittonias"** URL = gkh.us/133594)

Japanese Sago Palm

SCIENTIFIC NAME: *Cycas revoluta*

FAMILY: Cycadaceae

HEIGHT: 3 to 10 feet (1–3 m)

WIDTH: 3 to 10 feet (1–3 m)

FOLIAGE COLOR: Glossy dark green

SOIL pH: Acidic

LIGHT: Bright to low light

The sculptural quality of an elegant Japanese sago palm *(Cycas revoluta),* with its graceful upright fronds, lends itself to inclusion in a contemporary-design interior.

The Japanese sago palm, classified under the scientific name *Cycas revoluta,* is a popular houseplant known for its feathery foliage and ease of care. These plants are native to warm parts of Japan and southern China and feature long, glossy, dark green fronds. They are a great plant for beginners and make an unusual addition to nearly any room. The name might imply that it is a palm, but the plant is actually considered a cycad. Cycads are one the oldest groups of tropical and subtropical plants dating back to prehistoric times— hence the sago palm's hardiness. They often grow from trunks that don't branch out and produce nuts, but do not flower or fruit.

Cycads are fascinating, ancient plants that predate the age of dinosaurs. Some cycads you might consider cultivating are the blue-gray *Dioon edule,* which grows in bright light to part shade; *Stangeria eriopus,* a slow-growing fernlike plant; and the palmlike, shade-loving *Macrozamia,* a genus suited to temperate or subtropical regions.

Japanese sago palms make good houseplants in cooler climates, where they cannot survive outside. They are slow-growing and may only gain an inch or two (2.5–5 cm) and one new frond each year. Although they can become as tall as 10 feet (3 m) when grown outdoors, the houseplants usually range between 2 and 3 feet (50 cm–1 m).

GROWING JAPANESE SAGO PALM

Japanese sago palms are easy to care for, but do have special needs and preferences. Bright light is optimal, although they will tolerate low-light conditions. What they will not tolerate, however, is too much moisture. Sago palms prefer to be planted in well-drained soil, and like other cycads, they do not respond well to overwatering. In fact, too much water can quickly lead to root rot and eventual death. Therefore, it's best to allow the plant to dry out some between waterings.

SPECIAL CARE

Japanese sago palms also require regular fertilizing monthly to ensure vigorous health and encourage blooms. However, they might take 15 years before blooming in containers, (if at all), at which time the plant blooms only about every third year (on average). This often takes place in late spring.

While these plants are for the most part problem-free, you may encounter some signs of sickness on occasion. One of the most common issues is sago palm yellowing. However, as is the case with most cycads, this is a normal reaction to nutrient conservation—with older leaves turning yellow and then brown.

On the other hand, if sago palm yellowing occurs with new growth, this could signal a nutrient deficiency. Newly planted sago palms with yellowing leaves may be suffering from improper planting or poor drainage. For nutritional deficiencies, try feeding it houseplant fertilizer regularly, about once a month. If the plant has been improperly planted or has poor drainage, promptly repot it in suitable soil that is not too deep and has adequate drainage.

These plants are well known for harboring pests like scale bugs. If you notice scale infestations, try hand picking them off or moving the plants outdoors to allow their natural predators to help eliminate the problem.

Note: The Japanese sago palm is toxic to humans and pets.

Lucky Bamboo

SCIENTIFIC NAME: *Dracaena sanderiana*

FAMILY: Asparagaceae

HEIGHT: 1 to 3 feet (30 cm–1 m)

WIDTH: 1 to 2 feet (30–60 cm)

FOLIAGE COLOR: Green

SOIL pH: Acidic

LIGHT: Partial shade

A lucky bamboo makes a stylish statement when its stems are braided into an intricate pattern. In Chinese tradition, the number of stalks in an arrangement has meaning; for example, one stalk stands for truth or commitment, two stands for love, three for happiness, five for health, eight for abundance, and nine for good fortune and happiness.

Bamboo was once considered an exotic outdoor plant, but many gardeners have discovered that when cultivated to contain its spread, it is also a versatile and robust addition to the indoor garden. Classified under the botanical name *Dracaena sanderiana,* bamboo houseplants are known colloquially as lucky bamboo. Lucky bamboo is often shipped in from Taiwan, China, where it has been popularized for its favorable feng shui. In these cases, professionals train the stalks to grow in a variety of shapes by braiding, twisting, and curling them. The sculptural plants feature stiff decorative stalks with bright green, angled leaves. They are often found in offices, businesses, homes, and on desks, where they are thought to bring good luck and fortune to their owners. They are often given as gifts for this reason.

Bamboo houseplants are thought to be nearly indestructible. They do require proper light, water, potting media, fertilizer, and temperature control to be at their healthiest. You will find, however, that it is a challenge to kill these plants with neglect.

GROWING LUCKY BAMBOO

You might often see people growing lucky bamboo in low-light parts of their homes or offices. This is because lucky bamboo needs very little sun. It grows best in low, indirect light. That being said, when you grow lucky bamboo inside, it does need some light— it will not grow well in near darkness.

Use a well-drained, rich potting soil. The soil should be kept somewhat moist, but avoid overwatering. When you grow bamboo inside, you can also choose to transplant it into soil. Make sure that the container you will be growing it in has good drainage. Only use bottled or distilled water, because the plant is sensitive to chlorine and other chemicals commonly found in tap water.

Many lucky bamboo owners grow their plants in a vase filled with water. If you plan to do so, make sure to change the water every two to four weeks. The plant will need at least 1 to 3 inches (2.5 to 7.5 cm) of water before it grows roots. Once it has grown roots, you will need to make sure that the roots are covered by the water. As the plant grows, the amount of water in which it is kept should be increased. The higher up the stalk the water level is, the higher up the stalk the roots will grow. According to legend, the more roots the plant has, the more luck the top foliage will bring.

SPECIAL CARE

Try adding a small drop of liquid fertilizer when changing the water to encourage the plant to grow. Plants grown in water will only need to be fed every other month or so. Use a very weak liquid fertilizer if you plan on using this method.

Tied in Ribbons

Also called ribbon plant and friendship bamboo, this plant is a popular gift. The stems are often tied with a red ribbon, which in feng shui symbolizes fire, a representation of good luck and celebration. Other ribbon colors have other meanings: a green ribbon is for new and strong beginnings, a white ribbon is for confidence and purity; blue stands for calmness, serenity, healing, and relaxation; purple symbolizes spiritual awareness and mental healing; orange encourages creativity; yellow show cheerfulness and kind intentions; and pink makes a romantic statement.

A GALLERY OF

ORCHIDS

Indoor gardeners who are up for a challenge—and who relish producing some truly breathtaking flowers—should consider raising orchids. In the wild, these plants, with their graceful, sensuous blooms, grow in tropical rainforests and other warm, humid, wooded areas. Domesticated orchids, meanwhile, have been bred to be compact and to blossom under artificial light.

Orchids belong to one of the largest plant families, the Orchidaceae, with about 900 genera and 25,000 species. Varieties that grow on the surface of trees and take nourishment and moisture from air, rain, and debris, are called epiphytes or air plants.

Orchids do have a reputation for being finicky, but many are no harder to grow than the average houseplant. Start with an "easy" orchid to learn the basics of orchid husbandry, and you'll soon be addicted to these fascinating plants and seeking out more demanding examples. Most growers agree that *Phalaenopsis,* the moth orchid, performs well in the average home environment, making it perfect for beginners.

CARING FOR ORCHIDS

A healthy orchid has a strong, erect stem with dark green, leathery leaves. Never buy an orchid that looks brown or wilted. The exquisite flowers have three sepals, three petals, and a three-chambered ovary. One petal is usually highly modified, forming a "lip," or labellum. The flowers occur in a range of colors, shapes, and sizes, sometimes mimicking insects, animals, or birds.

Most orchids require moist, well-draining conditions and a specialized growing medium—redwood or fir bark, sphagnum peat moss, rocks, cork, charcoal, sand, or potting soil. Coarse perlite, fir bark, and sphagnum moss make a good home mix.

READ MORE AT GARDENING KNOW HOW

Find out more about these exotically beautiful plants.

- **"Orchid Growing Tips: How to Take Care of Orchid Plants Indoors** (URL = gkh.us/3697)
- **"Growing Orchids in Water: Caring for Orchids Grown in Water"** (URL = gkh.us/98717)

Many gardeners find that once they have success with one orchid plant, they can't help but keep adding more to their collection.

The grade of bark you choose is usually dependent on the type of orchid you're planting. *Phalaenopsis* grows in coarse bark, cattleyas in medium-grade bark, and young orchids in fine bark. Orchids also prefer shallow planting to keep their "feet" dry.

Light requirements depend on the type of orchid. Most prefer bright, indirect light from an east- or south-facing window or room. Moth orchids, however, prefer low lighting, such as a shaded window or a spot that receives morning sun and afternoon shade. You can also grow orchids under fluorescent lights. Warning signs of too much light are yellow or bleached-looking leaves; with too little light they become greener. Black or brown patches mean the plant is likely sun scorched and should be moved. The wrong light can also result in poor flowering.

Orchids tolerate cooler or warmer temperatures throughout their normal growing season, but they need to be about 15° F (8° C) cooler at night to bloom properly. Moving them to a cooler area of the home, like a basement, at night often works.

Orchids should be allowed to dry out a bit between waterings. Overwatering is the prime cause of orchid death, so if you are in doubt, don't water until the top two inches (5 cm) of soil feel dry to the touch. Water the orchid in the sink until water runs through the drainage hole, and then let it drain thoroughly. Decrease watering when blooming stops, then increase when new leaves appear. Indoor orchids need about 50 to 70 percent humidity. You can provide this by placing a tray of pebbles in water beneath plants, misting them daily, or using a humidifier.

While orchids are producing new growth, fertilize them weekly or bi-weekly with an orchid-specific product, and then decrease to monthly or bi-monthly once they mature. Discontinue feeding during dormant periods. Occasional orchid pests like mealybugs, scale, and aphids can usually be washed off or treated with insecticidal soap.

BRASSAVOLA NODOSA
The haunting lady of the night is named in part for its lovely evening fragrance. It often blooms multiple times a year—in autumn or winter and then again sporadically in spring. Grow in bright light and moderate temperatures.

***CATTLEYA* SPP.**
Known as the corsage orchid, this variety, familiar to most people, makes a wonderful indoor plant. The often-fragrant blooms range in color from white to pink, red, yellow, and orange. Place in medium or bright, indirect light.

***CYMBIDIUM* SPP.**
The easy-going boat orchid, a popular, evergreen indoor variety, features waxy, long-lasting flowers that appear in winter or early spring. *Cymbidiums* like bright light and will even grow outdoors in a shady spot in the summer.

***CYCNOCHES* SPP.**
The swan orchid produces elegant flowers that resemble a swan's neck. Its many cultivars come in a wide range of colors, including yellow, bronze, deep red, green, and white, as well as spotted varieties. Indoors they prefer diffused lighting.

***DENDROBIUM* SPP.**
Often found in florist bouquets, this Southeast Asian orchid offers gorgeous long-lasting blooms. Flower colors range from white to purple, pink, and even green. These plants prefer medium-to-bright light and moderate temperatures.

***MILTONIOPSIS* SPP.**
The friendly-faced pansy orchid with its bright, open blooms comes from the cool Brazilian cloud forests. It will flower for a month in spring, and possibly again in the autumn. Supply bright, diffused light and cooler temps.

***ODONTOGLOSSUM* SPP.**
A cousin of the *Oncidiums,* this genus of orchids produces clusters of large, long-lasting, spectacular flowers in shades of pink, red, orange, yellow, and white, often with splotches of other colors. It prefers medium or bright light.

***ONCIDIUM* SPP.**
Dancing lady orchids offer petite flowers in clusters of 50 or more; colors include yellow, purple, red, pink, and white, with flamboyant, contrasting markings. Cultivar 'Sharry Baby' smells of chocolate. Provide medium-to-bright light.

***PAPHIOPEDILUM* SPP.**
One of the most distinctive orchids, the tropical Venus slipper has large blooms composed of a hollow "pouch" backed by a sepal and two petals. Species with variegated foliage look lovely even when they're not flowering.

PHAIUS TANKERVILLEAE
The dramatic nun's orchid is actually easy to grow. In winter, it produces clusters of purple, brown, and white flowers on tall stems, with rich, green, corrugated leaves. It prefers medium-to-bright light and warmer temperatures.

***PHALAENOPSIS* SPP.**
Widely available and affordable, moth orchids are also long bloomers in all types of light. Flowers may be white, pink, red, green, yellow, orange, or purple. Two species, *P. gigantea* and *P. hieroglyphica,* are both especially stunning.

PROSTHECHEA COCHLEATA
The easy-growing clamshell orchid produces long-lasting, clam-shaped purple flowers with chartreuse sepals that reach out like tropical tentacles. The mature plant produces numerous blossoms. Provide it with low-to-bright light.

Parlor Palm

The parlor palm might be considered somewhat old-fashioned, often linked to stuffy, 19th-century rooms, but it is a refined plant that can fit well in modern-style interiors.

SCIENTIFIC NAME: *Chamaedorea elegans*

FAMILY: Arecaceae

HEIGHT: 2 to 6 feet (60 cm–1.8 m)

WIDTH: 2 to 3 feet (60 cm–1 m)

FOLIAGE COLOR: Light green

SOIL pH: Acidic to neutral

LIGHT: Bright, indirect light

SPECIAL CARE

If you're planting a parlor palm indoors, opt for mixing a few plants in the same container. Individual plants grow straight up and look more attractive and filled out in a group. Parlor palms have relatively weak root systems and don't mind crowding, so don't transplant more often than necessary.

You may need to repot once a year for the first few years if your plant is growing steadily, but after that point, top dressing should be enough to keep it healthy. Because parlor palms tend to be grouped together in one container, feed them a basic fertilizer every month or two to ensure the soil doesn't get sapped of nutrients.

The parlor palm is the quintessential houseplant—the proof is right in the common name. Classified under the scientific name *Chamaedorea elegans,* it is found in the rainforests of southern Mexico and Guatemala but has been brought into homes as an indoor plant. Its other often-used common name, the Victorian parlor palm, attests to the fact that it has a long history as a popular houseplant. It is admired for its clumps of deep green, textured foliage and thin trunk. A parlor palm is usually grown in stylish pots as a floor-standing shrub.

The fronds are sometimes used in flower arrangements, Palm Sunday decorations, and wreaths, because they can last for 40 days after being cut from the plant.

GROWING PARLOR PALMS

Growing a parlor palm indoors is ideal because it grows very slowly and thrives in low-light and cramped spaces. It's also an excellent air purifier. Cultivating it is very easy and gratifying. This houseplant prefers low light and may even suffer in direct sunlight, so there's no need to place it near your brightest windows. It will, however, do best if positioned by a window that receives some early-morning or late-afternoon light. It is often placed in a spot with northern exposure or an entrance foyer, where it can receive its light needs while also showing off its fine-textured leaves.

Your parlor palm will likely be able to survive completely away from windows if that's what your space requires—it just won't grow very fast. Even with sunlight, it is a slow grower, often taking years to reach its full height of 3 to 4 feet (1–1.2 m) tall.

Use a large pot and any high-quality peat-based potting mix. Water your plant sparingly—underwatering is better than overwatering. Allow the top inch (2.5 cm) of soil to begin to dry between waterings, and water it even less frequently in the winter. Monitor its appearance, though: if the fronds begin to yellow, it might need more water.

The Victorian Indoor Garden

Those with older homes might wish to recreate a Victorian feel with their houseplant collection. Parlor palms are a premier selection, as are cast-iron plants, Boston ferns, philodendrons, rex begonias, and crotons.

Peace Lily

SCIENTIFIC NAME: *Spathiphyllum* spp.

FAMILY: Araceae

HEIGHT: 1 to 3 feet (30 cm–1 m)

WIDTH: 1 to 3 feet (30 cm–1 m)

FOLIAGE COLOR: Dark green(with a white or yellow flower)

SOIL pH: Acidic

LIGHT: Partial shade

Rising about the glossy green foliage, the elegant white spathe of the peace lily shelters the yellow flower within. Although it is called a "lily," these plants are actually arums.

Peace lilies, classified under the genus *Spathiphyllum,* are also known as closet plants. Native to Central America and Asia, these tropical plants feature glossy, ovular, pointed leaves that emerge from the soil. They are named for their white and yellow flowers, which bloom twice a year. What most people think of as the flower is actually a specialized leaf bract that grows hooded over the flowers. Following the spring-blooming season, the elegant flower stalks remain for several months.

Peace lilies make excellent houseplants for the home or office. These lovely plants not only brighten up a living space, but are also excellent at cleaning the air of the room they are placed in.

When it comes to indoor plants, they are some of the easiest to care for. They can be purchased and introduced into the home year-round. Because these plants are used to tropical and subtropical environments, avoid exposure to cold temperatures while moving them in. Once provided with the right indoor environment, the plant will reach maturity within three years of planting.

GROWING PEACE LILIES

Like many popular indoor plants, peace lilies enjoy medium to low light. The type of light you need to provide will depend most on what you want your plant to look like. Those that are placed in ample light tend to more often produce the lovely white spathes and flowers, while ones kept in low light will bloom less and will look more like traditional foliage plants.

One of the most common mistakes when caring for a peace lily is overwatering. Never water on a schedule. Instead, check the soil once a week to judge whether or not watering is needed. If the soil is still at all damp, do not water the plant. Some people will go so far as to wait until their peace lily is starting to droop. Because they are very drought tolerant, this method will not harm the plants and sufficiently prevents overwatering.

SPECIAL CARE

Peace lilies do not need frequent fertilizing. Feeding the plant with a balanced fertilizer one to two times per year will be enough to keep it happy.

A peace lily also benefits from repotting or dividing when it outgrows its container. Watch for signs of overcrowding: if its leaves are drooping less than a week after being watered or if it has crowded, deformed leaf growth, it is time for a new home. Move the plant into a pot that is at least 2 inches (5 cm) larger than its current pot. If you are dividing, use a sharp knife to cut through the center of the root ball, and replant each half in its own container.

Note: Peace lilies are toxic to both pets and humans, so keep them out of reach from any dogs, cats, and babies.

READ MORE AT GARDENING KNOW HOW

To learn what to do if your peace lily lacks its trademark blooms, scan the QR code or follow this link.

- **"Peace Lily Not Blooming: Reasons a Peace Lily Never Flowers"** (URL = gkh.us/62301)

Peperomia

A pretty peperomia thrives in a window with indirect sunlight. These small, neat plants are great for windowsills, desktops, and other compact areas in the home.

A peperomia houseplant is an attractive addition to a desk, table, or mantelpiece. Its common name refers to the *Peperomia* genus of plants, which include more than 1,500 species from tropical and subtropical regions of Central and South America. The species vary in appearance, but the most well-known types are compact plants with rounded and slightly thick leaves, in dark green, white, yellow, red, and pink, as well as variegated combinations.

They are not especially hardy, which may explain why they are not among the most popular houseplants. They are, however, very tolerant plants with a compact form that lets them occupy a small space wherever you choose to place them. They are slow growing, low maintenance, and can be introduced at any time during the year.

Of the numerous *Peperomia* species that exist, not all are cultivated and grown for distribution to the public. Plant collectors might possess an unusual variety, as might arboretums or botanical gardens for indoor displays.

GROWING PEPEROMIA

When growing a peperomia, place the plant in medium to low light and away from direct sun. The plant will do best if situated near a window, where it will be exposed to bright, indirect sunlight. You may also grow it under fluorescent lighting.

Use a loose and well-draining soil with added peat moss, perlite, or coarse gravel. These amendments allow roots to receive the air circulation necessary for the health and development of your plant. If your peperomia is wilting, in spite of regular watering, it is likely not getting enough oxygen to the roots. In this case, repot it in a richer soil.

These houseplants should be watered sparingly. Allow the soil to dry as deep as 5 inches (13 cm) between waterings.

SPECIAL CARE

During the growing season, occasionally feed your peperomia with a diluted liquid fertilizer after watering. Leach the plant in summer by flushing with water to remove the salts left behind by fertilization.

Repot peperomias in spring, but keep pots small unless you are growing them as part of a container combination.

SCIENTIFIC NAME: *Peperomia* spp.

FAMILY: Piperaceae

HEIGHT: 6 to 12 inches (30–60 cm)

WIDTH: 6 to 18 inches (30–45 cm)

FOLIAGE COLOR: Dark green, white, yellow, red, and pink and variegated combinations

SOIL pH: Slightly acidic

LIGHT: Partial shade

Editor's Picks

Several types of peperomia can brighten your indoor displays. Following are some of the most widely available varieties.

- ***P. argyreia* 'Watermelon'. This peperomia has silver stripes with elliptical-shaped leaves. Both this variety and 'Emerald Ripple' reach only 8 inches (20 cm) in height and width if planted in a container large enough to allow for root development. It has a mounding habit with draping leaves.**
- ***P. caperata* 'Emerald Ripple'. Heart-shaped leaves and foliage texture similar to a waffle make growing this variety a pleasure. The attractive leaves and stems may have a silvery or burgundy tint peeking through the green.**
- ***P. obtusifolia.* Called the baby rubber plant, it has a more upright demeanor. Some of these types of peperomias have solid green, shiny leaves, while others are variegated with gold-and-white coloration.**
- ***P. obtusifolia* 'Minima'. This is a dwarf specimen, reaching about half the size of the standard.**

Philodendron

The heart-shaped leaves of a *Philodendron hederaceum hederaceum* have a velvety texture. The many Philodendron species display various leaf shapes, textures, and colors.

For generations, philodendrons have served as mainstays of interior gardens. The *Philodendron* genus consists of hundreds of species of foliage plants from Central and South America. Their leaves may be dark green, white, or yellow, as well as red and pink or other variegated combos. The most well-known species have large, green, glossy leaves, which introduce a tropical quality to indoor spaces. Some are vining and can grow several feet in length and are mounted on a support structure, such as a trellis, or allowed to trail in a basket. Non-climbing varieties, on the other hand, tend to be kept in containers in which they grow vertically.

GROWING PHILODENDRONS

A philodendron will tell you exactly what it needs. Even inexperienced houseplant owners will have no trouble growing this plants, which readily adapts to the conditions of the home. It thrives year-round without complaint, but will enjoy an occasional stay outdoors in a shady spot when the weather permits. Taking it outdoors also gives you a chance to flush the soil with plenty of fresh water and clean the leaves. Unlike most houseplants, a philodendron will not experience as much stress when moving from indoor to outdoor settings. Additionally, this plant is an excellent source of air purification inside the home.

Set the plant in a spot with indirect sunlight, such as near a window where the sun's rays never actually touch the foliage. It's normal for older leaves to yellow, but if several leaves yellow at the same time, the plant might be getting too much light. On the other hand, if the stems are long and leggy with lots of space between leaves, it probably isn't getting enough.

Use a loose and well-draining potting soil with a high content of organic matter. For a container plant, replace the soil every few years to avoid leaf browning or yellowing.

When growing philodendrons, allow the top inch (2.5 cm) of soil to dry out between waterings. The length of your index finger to the first knuckle is about this depth, so inserting your finger into the soil is a good way to check the moisture level. Droopy leaves can mean that the plant is getting too much or not enough water. But the leaves recover quickly when you correct the watering schedule. The non-climbing variety tends to have more drought tolerance than the vining variety.

At a Glance

SCIENTIFIC NAME: *Philodendron* spp.

FAMILY: Aroideae

HEIGHT: 1 to 4 feet (30 cm–1.2 m)

WIDTH: 1 to 5 feet (30 cm–1.5 m)

FOLIAGE COLOR: Various shades of solid green and silver and variegated combinations of green, pink, black, cream, and bronze

SOIL pH: Acidic

LIGHT: Indirect light

SPECIAL CARE

Feed philodendrons with a balanced liquid foliage houseplant fertilizer that contains macronutrients. Water the plant with the fertilizer once a month in spring and summer and every six to eight weeks in autumn and winter. Slow growth and small leaf size is the plant's way of telling you that it isn't getting enough fertilizer. Pale new leaves usually indicate that the plant isn't getting enough calcium and magnesium, which are essential micronutrients for philodendrons.

Philodendron Species

Here is a short list of common *Philodendron* varieties.

- ***P. bipennifolium.*** The fiddle-leaf philodendron has dark green, violin-shaped leaves.
- ***P. bipinnatifidum.*** The splitleaf philodendron has lacy, deeply lobed leaves.
- ***P. domesticum.*** The elephant ear philodendron has glossy green, spade-shaped leaves.
- ***P. erubescens.*** The red-leaf philodendron has coppery red leaves growing from reddish purple stems.
- ***P. hederaceum hederaceum.*** The velvet-leaf philodendron has velvety-textured leaves.
- ***P. hederaceum oxycardium.*** The heartleaf philodendron is a vining species.

Rubber Tree

With a simple swirl of greenery, a tall *Ficus elastica* makes an elegant addition to any room. This is a plant of many names, including rubber tree, rubber fig, rubber bush, and Indian rubber bush.

Rubber trees *(Ficus elastica)* are eye-catching plants native to the tropics of Southeast Asia. In their natural habitat, these trees can grow up to a soaring 100-feet (30 m) tall. As a houseplant, they are kept much smaller, but they are still somewhat of a tropical marvel, thanks to their oversized, oval-shaped leaves in rich greens.

While it is certainly not a beginner's houseplant, the rubber tree is relatively manageable and flexible when it is properly cared for. Starting with a young tree, rather than a mature one, will allow it to adapt to being an indoor plant. It can be introduced at any point during the year, and its size can be limited. It simply will need adequate light, moisture, and warmth, as it would receive in nature. Position your tree several feet away from a window with southern- or eastern-facing light, and it will provide an exotic addition to your indoor space.

GROWING RUBBER TREES

As with any plant, when it comes to care, the correct balance of water and light is crucial. Make sure it doesn't get too much of either. Remember it is your ability to control these conditions that will determine the success of the plant. The rubber tree can handle bright light but prefers indirect light or partial shade that isn't too hot. Some homeowners recommend positioning it near a window with sheer curtains. This allows plenty of light to come through, but not too much heat.

Keep the plant moist during the growing season, and water it at least once a week. It is also a good idea to regularly wipe off the large leaves using a damp cloth, or you can spritz them with water. If you notice the leaves turning yellow and brown or falling off, the plant is being overwatered. To promote new leaf growth, cut a slit in the node where a leaf fell off. This will allow a new leaf to grow more quickly.

During the dormant season, a rubber tree might only need to be watered once or twice a month. If leaves begin to droop, but not fall off, increase watering gradually until the leaves perk up again.

Dig Deeper

READ MORE AT GARDENING KNOW HOW

To find out how to keep your rubber tree in its best shape, follow the links below.

- **"Rubber Tree Branching Tips: Why Won't My Rubber Tree Branch Out"** URL = gkh.us/130433)
- **"Tips on How to Prune a Rubber Tree"** URL = gkh.us/2237)

At a Glance

SCIENTIFIC NAME: *Ficus elastica*

FAMILY: Moraceae

HEIGHT: 6 to 10 feet (1.8–3 m)

WIDTH: 1 to 3 feet (30 cm–1 m)

FOLIAGE COLOR: Dark green, deep maroon, or variegated with yellow, cream, pink, or white

SOIL pH: Acidic

LIGHT: Indirect light to partial shade

SPECIAL CARE

Use a weak liquid fertilizer throughout the growing season. When healthy, the plants are heavy feeders.

Once your rubber plant is healthy and you have mastered its proper care, you may wish to propagate it. There are a few methods for creating new rubber plant cuttings. The simplest is to take a small branch from a healthy tree, put it in good potting soil or water, and let it root. Air layering is an alternate method in which you make a cut in a healthy plant, put a toothpick in the hole, and then pack damp moss around the cut. After that, wrap it with plastic wrap to keep the moisture level higher. Once roots begin to appear, cut the branch off, and plant it.

Spider Plant

Chlorophytum comosum, **usually called spider plant due to its spider-like look, is also known as spider ivy and ribbon plant. Its trailing habit makes it perfect for hanging pots.**

SCIENTIFIC NAME: *Chlorophytum comosum*

FAMILY: Asparagaceae

HEIGHT: 1 to 2 feet (30–60 cm)

WIDTH: 1 to 2 feet (30–60 cm)

FOLIAGE COLOR: Green and white-striped or solid green

SOIL pH: Neutral

LIGHT: Indirect light to partial shade

The spider plant, classified under the scientific name *Chlorophytum comosum,* is considered one of the most popular and adaptable of houseplant choices. Native to tropical and southern Africa, it features long, thin leaves that are commonly variegated with white or cream striping.

The spider plant is so named because of its spider-like plantlets, or spiderettes, which dangle down from the mother plant like spiders on a web. Once the plants are well established, small, star-shaped blooms emerge from their long stems. Spiderettes replace these flowers when they fall off and can be divided for propagation.

GROWING SPIDER PLANTS

These plants tolerate lots of abuse, making them excellent candidates for newbie gardeners or those without a green thumb. Plant owners can follow specific measures to make household conditions mimic the plant's native environment. First, take note that they enjoy cooler temperatures—around 55 to 65° F (13–18° C). Make sure you have a suitable indoor climate, then choose a location with partial shade and indirect light.

Provide them with well-drained soil, and water them well, but do not allow the plants to become too soggy. Overwatering can lead to root rot, and the plants prefer to dry out a bit between waterings.

Spider plants can benefit from occasional pruning, cutting them back to the base. They also prefer a semi-potbound environment; repot them only when their large, fleshy roots are highly visible and watering becomes difficult.

SPECIAL CARE

Spider plants can be propagated by division of the mother plant or by rooting the plant babies. Spider plant babies can be planted in water or soil, but will generally yield more favorable results and a stronger root system when planted in soil.

As daylight increases in spring, spider plants should begin producing flowers, eventually developing into babies, or spiderettes. This may not always occur, however, as only mature plants with enough stored energy will produce spiderettes.

When rooting spiderettes, it is best to allow the plantlet to remain attached to the mother plant. Choose a spiderette to place in a pot of soil near the mother plant. Keep the plant well watered and once it roots, you can cut it from the mother plant.

Alternatively, you may cut off one of the plantlets, place it in a pot of soil, and water generously. Position the pot in a ventilated plastic bag and move it to a bright location. Once the spiderette is well rooted, remove it from the bag, and grow as usual.

Leaf browning is a common issue noticed by spider plant owners, but rest assured that it is normal and will not harm the plant. Browning is often the result of fluoride found in water, which causes salt buildup in the soil. To flush out excess salts, periodic leaching of the plants is advised. Give them a thorough watering, and allow the water to drain out, and then repeat as needed. It might also help to use distilled water or even rainwater on plants, instead of fluoridated water from the kitchen or outside spigot.

Spider plants are known for the numerous spiderettes they produce. Take advantage of these offshoots to increase your spider collection.

To find out more about propagating from this plant, scan the QR code or follow this link to "Propagating Spiderettes: Learn How to Root Spider Plant Babies" (URL = gkh.us/75597)

Staghorn Fern

An indoor gardener covers the base of a staghorn fern *(Platycerium bifurcatum)* with sheet moss to ready it for mounting on a wooden plank. Once firmly attached to the plank, it will be hung vertically so that its fronds can flow gracefully downward.

Staghorn ferns, which are classified under the scientific name *Platycerium bifurcatum*, have an out-of-this-world appearance. The plants feature two types of leaves, one of which is green and pronged, reaching up to 3 feet (1 m) in length. These leaves are responsible for the plant's name, as they are thought to resemble the antlers of a large deer or elk. The other, less-distinctive leaves, known as shield fronds, are small and flat and cover the root-ball structure, collecting water and nutrients for the plant. Shield fronds overlap onto a mounting surface and provide stability for the fern.

There are 17 species in the *Platycerium* genus, but only the staghorn fern can be grown as a house plant. It is epiphytic, growing on tree trunks in its natural habitats of Africa, Southeast Asia, and Australia; therefore, when grown indoors, the plant must be mounted on a substrate, rather than planted in soil. Its care relies on careful light, temperature, and moisture monitoring. It is considered somewhat difficult to grow, but its unique appearance makes the challenge a worthwhile and rewarding endeavor.

GROWING STAGHORN FERNS

The staghorn fern is a very attractive plant that adds an unusual visual element to the home. Not only is it uniquely decorative, it also has a good chance of thriving if you set up an indoor environment to mimic the plant's natural, subtropical conditions.

First and foremost, ensure that the plant will be exposed to partial sunlight. The staghorn fern is acclimated to the semi-shade of dappled sunlight, because it evolved to grow beneath the thick canopy of leaves in its rain-forest home. As a rain-forest denizen, it also thrives in high-humidity conditions. Consider placing yours in your bathroom or kitchen, which is typically a higher-humidity environment than other parts of the home.

A staghorn fern is usually grown mounted on a substrate, such as a piece of wood or bark slab or in a basket without any soil. Instead, it will need a little mound of compost, moss, or other organic matter piled underneath it. You can then secure the fern to the growing medium and substrate, using fishing line, wire, or plant strips tied around the wooden board or bark slab. The fronds of the plant will eventually conceal the fastening material.

This plant also requires ample moisture. Water it frequently, but allow the base to dry out in between. For thorough watering, the plant can be removed from its mounting or basket and soaked in a sink filled with water for about 10 to 20 minutes.

SCIENTIFIC NAME: *Platycerium* spp.

FAMILY: Polypodiaceae

HEIGHT: 2 to 3 feet (60 cm–1 m)

WIDTH: 2 to 3 feet (60 cm–1 m)

FOLIAGE COLOR: Light green

SOIL pH: Not applicable

LIGHT: Partial sun to semi-shade

SPECIAL CARE

You may wish to feed your staghorn fern to encourage growth. If you choose to do so, use a well-balanced, water-soluble fertilizer once a month during spring and summer.

The plant is prone to black spot, which is a fungal disease. To prevent the disfiguring spores, do not water over the foliage.

READ MORE AT GARDENING KNOW HOW

Staghorn ferns are epiphytes, meaning that they do not grow in soil and need a substrate to attach to. Scan the QR code or follow the link below for tips on mounting your staghorn fern, as well as other epiphytic houseplants, such as certain orchids and bromeliads.

- **"Epiphyte Mounting Tips: How to Mount Epiphytic Plants "** URL = gkh.us/68535)

Zebra Plant

A zebra plant *(Aphelandra squarrosa)* displays the trademark striping that inspired its common name. This tropical species prefers the dappled light and shade that occurs under the thick tree canopies of its native rainforest home.

SCIENTIFIC NAME: *Aphelandra squarrosa*

FAMILY: Acanthaceae

HEIGHT: 1 to 2 feet (30–60 cm)

WIDTH: 1 to 5 feet (30 cm–1.5 M0

FOLIAGE COLOR: Dark glossy green with whitish veining

SOIL pH: Neutral to acidic

LIGHT: Indirect sun to partial shade

The distinctively striped zebra plant is a member of the family Acanthaceae, which includes about 2,500 species of dicotyledonous flowering plants distributed in Indonesia and Malaysia, Africa, Brazil, and Central America. Classified under the scientific name *Aphelandra squarrosa,* this species is native to Brazilian rainforests, where it grows into a large, upright shrub that blooms profusely in the moist, tropical heat. As a houseplant, the zebra plant is known for its large, shiny leaves and dark green foliage, deeply veined in white or yellow, reminiscent of zebra stripes. Its brightly colored flowers and tall golden bracts make for a prized display that can last up to six weeks. It is usually small at the time of purchase, and many indoor gardeners consider them a short-lived friend. With propagation by stem cuttings, however, your original plant can last for decades!

GROWING ZEBRA PLANTS

A zebra plant should be placed in indirect light or partial shade, which replicates its native growth environment under tree canopies. Direct sunlight may burn the leaves, while full shade will prevent blooming.

Use a potting medium that drains well, and keep it moist, rather than wet. A multi-purpose potting mix will suffice in most cases. You can add sand to the soil in order to encourage draining.

Above all else, a zebra plant requires high humidity. It is crucial to set its pot on a tray filled with pebbles to increase humidity levels. Regular watering and misting is similarly important. A humidifier can also be used to improve moisture levels.

The plant may thrive in 40 to 80 percent humidity, but it despises wet feet. A common issue a zebra faces is drooping or falling leaves, which can usually be explained by overwatering. Water the plant every two weeks or when you notice the soil is drying. With each watering, you should make sure the soil is completely saturated.

Because it is tropical, a zebra plant prefers warm climates and will do well in households with an average daytime temperature of 70°F (20°C) and nighttime temperature of 60°F (15°C), as long as it is kept out of drafts.

SPECIAL CARE

If you want your zebra plant to bloom, you must understand the natural rhythm of the plant. First, purchase a plant whose bracts are just beginning to form. In early winter, your plant will go into semi-dormancy, and growth will be minimal. Don't let the soil completely dry out, but water a little less frequently. By late winter, begin watering and feeding the plant with a weak fertilizer solution every two weeks. Once side shoots develop and new flower heads can be seen, move your plant to the brightest possible area and water generously.

The plant will bloom in summer, and it is the bracts that provide the yellow, orange, or red-tinged "flower." The true flowers die within days, but the colorful bracts can remain for months. Once these begin to die, they should be removed and the plant cut back to allow room for future new growth.

There are some problems to look out for when growing a zebra plant. If grown in a damp climate, it might fall prey to fungal diseases. Keep an eye out for common bugs, such as mealybugs, aphids, scale, and spider mites. If you use any insecticidal soap, make sure none gets on the flowers.

Glossary

Aeration Loosening soil to introduce air and improve drainage. May refer to the act of tilling, turning, or physically aerating soil (including compost piles), or used in reference to the condition of existing soil. Perlite, pumice, sand, and earthworm activity also increase aeration in soil.

Annual A plant that completes its entire lifecycle (sprouts, fruits and/or flowers, and produces seed) in one year or fewer. Annuals must be re-planted each year. Most vegetable crops are annuals. If allowed, many annual flowers will self-seed and come back as volunteers the following year.

Bareroot A plant that is sold in a dormant state with its roots exposed (typically wrapped in burlap) as opposed to in a pot with soil. Bareroot fruit trees are a common sight at nurseries in the late autumn or early spring.

Beneficial insects Insects that play a helpful role in the garden, such as acting as pollinators or eating pest insects. Common examples include bees, ladybugs, parasitic wasps, green lacewings, and praying mantids. Encouraging or releasing beneficial insects is a common practice in organic gardening or part of an integrated pest management strategy.

Biodegradable A material that will eventually break down or naturally decompose under the right conditions—such as with the help of bacteria, fungi, and oxygen. Organic matter is biodegradable. Not to be confused with "compostable," because not all biodegradable materials are ideal for a home compost pile—including treated wood scraps, noxious weeds, animal carcasses, or pet waste.

Bolt This is when plants "go to seed"—when they begin to flower and eventually develop seeds. This typically happens at the end of the season, but environmental stress (extreme heat, inadequate sunlight) can cause plants to bolt early. Once they do, the eating quality, flavor, texture, and lifespan rapidly declines.

Botanical teas This homemade natural liquid fertilizer is made by "brewing" or steeping soil amendments such as alfalfa meal, kelp meal, and/or neem meal in water. The result is a nutrient-rich solution used to water and feed plants. Botanical teas may be passively steeped, or actively aerated (bubbled) to increase enzyme activity and potency. You can also use sprouted seeds, referred to as "sprouted seed tea."

Biennial A plant that lives for two years. Typically, biennials focus on establishing a strong root system and leafy growth in the first year of life, followed by fruiting/flowering, and going to seed the second year.

Brassicas These are members of the cabbage family, also known as "cole crops." They include cabbage, broccoli, cauliflower, bok choy, mustard greens, kohlrabi, Brussels sprouts, radish, turnips, and others. Brassicas are generally grown as cool-season crops, though many varieties are heat tolerant and can be grown in summer.

Chill hours The number of hours a plant or seed needs to be exposed to temperatures between 32 to 45° F (0–7° C) in order to break dormancy and either sprout, flower, or bear fruit. For instance, certain fruit trees need a range of 200 to 400 chill hours each winter in order to successfully bear fruit the following year. *See also* vernalization.

Chlorosis The yellowing of plant leaves due to insufficient chlorophyll. It can be caused by disease, damaged or bound plant roots, highly alkaline soil, inadequate drainage, and/or nutrient deficiencies.

Cold frame A small structure that covers plants, protecting them from very cold or freezing conditions. Like a greenhouse, cold frames have transparent roofs in glass or plastic to allow sunlight in but are built low to ground, more closely shrouding the plants.

Companion planting The practice of using specific combinations of plants growing near one another to provide various benefits, including attracting pollinators, deterring pests, encouraging healthy growth, adding nitrogen to the soil, or providing shade/support for one another.

Compost Decomposed organic matter considered a premium organic soil amendment that offers numerous benefits to soil and plant health. You can either buy compost or create homemade compost from collected leaves, straw, non-fatty kitchen scraps, and garden waste. With the right balance of biodegradable materials, a little time, and the aid of decomposers (microorganisms, fungi, worms, insects, etc.) raw materials break down into a nutrient-rich, soil-like material—finished compost.

Compost tea Natural liquid fertilizer made by "brewing" or steeping finished compost or worm castings in water. This mild but nutrient-rich solution is used to water and feed plants. Compost tea may be passively steeped or actively aerated (bubbled) to increase microbial activity.

Cool-season crops These vegetable crops prefer cooler soil and air temperatures to thrive, between 40 and 75° F (4.5–24° C). Most are very cold hardy and frost tolerant. They include the brassica family (cabbage, broccoli, cauliflower), leafy greens, and root vegetables (radishes, carrots, beets, turnips). These are best suited for the early spring or fall garden. Some cool season crops will tolerate temporary hot conditions, while others may bolt in heat.

Cover crops Fast-growing plants that are cultivated with the primary purpose of protecting or rejuvenating the soil between seasons or other edible crops. They may feed the soil by fixing nitrogen, or act as a living mulch by reducing erosion, compaction, and runoff. Ryegrass, fava beans, oats, clover, barley, alfalfa, and other legumes or cereal grains are common cover crops.

Crop A plant that is cultivated for harvest, like cutting flowers or vegetables.

Crop rotation The practice of routinely rotating the types of crops that are grown in each plot or garden bed. Good crop rotation can improve soil health and biodiversity, reduce the demand for fertilizer, and lessen disease and pest pressure by avoiding growing the same crops in the same location year after year.

Cut and come again A method used to continually harvest from a single plant over an extended period of time, rather than harvesting the entire plant at one time (which kills the plant). Most applicable to leafy greens, such as kale, romaine lettuce, or Swiss chard. Pick a few of the oldest, outermost leaves each week instead of cutting out the whole head.

Cultivar A species that was selected or bred by humans for a particular feature or characteristic. Cultivars carry a specific name in addition to the scientific name and/or common name, e.g., 'Love and Peace', 'Golden Celebration', and 'Princess of Wales' are all different cultivars (varieties) of roses.

Damping off This refers to when seedlings suddenly wilt and die. Their stems typically become very thin near the soil line, causing them to topple. Damping off can be attributed to a number of different fungal diseases, and it is most common when seedlings are overwatered, have inadequate air flow, or when old diseased garden soil is used to start new seeds.

Days to maturity The time from when seeds are sown until the plant should be ready to harvest. A plant description or seed packet will usually outline the specific varieties' expected growth timeline (also including days to germinate/sprout), though different care and growing conditions can lead to some variation.

Deadheading The practice of removing spent or dying flowers from plants once the blooms are past their prime. Regular deadheading creates a tidy appearance, reduces seed scatter, and also encourages more new flowers to bloom. If you intend to save seeds from annual flowers, however, it is best to allow the flower to become fully brown and dry while it is still on the plant before deadheading it.

Deciduous Plants that lose their leaves during the autumn to winter months and regrow them in spring. They are the opposite of "evergreen."

Determinate Determinate, which means "of limited time," is a growth habit in which a plant's main stem and branches will slow or halt growth once it begins to flower and bear fruit. In gardening, it is most often used to distinguish between types of tomatoes (determinate versus indeterminate), but also to describe the growth habits of bean plants and others. Determinate tomatoes and bush beans stay more compact and bear all their fruit over a shorter period of time. Indeterminate tomatoes and pole beans continue to grow and bear fruit on larger plants over a prolonged period of time (*see also* indeterminate).

Direct sow To plant seeds directly in the soil outdoors in their final growing location, as opposed to starting seeds in small containers (indoors or in a greenhouse) and transplanting them as seedlings later.

Dirt Your precious garden soil is not technically dirt! Dirt is devoid of the living organisms, nutrients, and well-balanced composition present in healthy soil—the things needed to successfully grow plants.

Espalier A plant pruning and training technique that forms a wide, flat structure of branches. Commonly used for fruit trees. Great for use in small spaces and against structures, fences, or walls to create a unique visual impact.

Evergreen Plants, trees, and shrubs that do not lose their leaves or needles in autumn.

Foliar feeding (foliar spray) The process of spraying plants, trees, or shrubs with a fine mist of liquid fertilizer (or other liquid amendment) from a sprayer. Plants have the ability to absorb nutrients more quickly through their leaves and vascular system than through their roots in the soil. Pesticides may also be applied through a foliar spray.

Frost date Used to describe either the average first date (autumn) or last date (spring) that your area receives frost. The days between last and first are your most robust growing season. Planting instructions commonly refer to these dates, such as "sow seeds outdoors two weeks before your last spring frost date," or "transplant seedlings six weeks before the first autumn frost date."

Fruit A seed capsule that emerges from a flower, such as a tomato or melon.

Full sun Generally refers to a minimum of six hours or more of direct sunlight.

Germination When a seed breaks dormancy and sprouts its first growth; the emergence of a new seedling from a seed.

GMO Stands for "genetically modified organism." Some plants and seeds are genetically modified by humans in a lab setting for select qualities, such as pesticide resistance. GMO "Roundup ready" corn and soy are prime examples. Generally frowned upon (and thought to be dangerous) by the organic farming and natural health communities.

Grafting A horticulture technique when a cut portion of a plant is joined or fused to another—to grow together as one plant. A common practice where a strong, disease-resistant, or otherwise ideal lower portion (the rootstock) is fused with various upper portions (the scion). For example, to graft a specific variety of apple onto a different hardy apple rootstock. The resulting plant will produce fruit true to the scion used.

Green manure Certain plants or crops that are grown exclusively to be turned into the soil or allowed to decompose on the soil surface as mulch to enrich the soil with nutrients. A few plants often grown as green manure include clover, oats, buckwheat, winter wheat, beans and peas. Similar benefits and uses as cover crops.

Hand pollination When humans aid in the pollination process by physically transferring pollen from one flower or plant to another. This can be done either using a small tool (paint brush, cotton swab) or with the flower itself.

Hardening off The process of readying tender seedlings that were raised indoors (or in other protected conditions) to be planted outside. Seedlings are gradually exposed to conditions such as wind, cold and/or direct sun over the period of 7 to 10 days, so they can become increasingly strong and resilient.

Hardiness The degree to which a plant can withstand cold temperatures or other climatic issues.

Hardiness Zone (USDA Hardiness Zones) In this system, created by the U.S. Department of Agriculture, areas in the United States are grouped and designated into particular planting or hardiness zones (3a through 11b) based on similar climatic conditions. The zones are used to define what plans grow best in what areas, as well as provide guidance on when to plant what. The system is mostly based around frost dates and cold temperatures but doesn't account for other variables between locations like average high temperatures, humidity, or precipitation.

Heirloom Refers to a plant or variety of vegetable that is at least 50 years old. Furthermore, the seeds must be either open-pollinated or self-pollinated to be considered heirloom, not a hybrid. An heirloom variety often has a meaningful story behind it—a history of being passed down within a community, culture, farm, or family, much like a family "heirloom" would.

Heat tolerance The ability to resist heat-triggered issues like poor pollination, bitterness, premature flowering, and lack of fruit-set.

Humus Another word for finished compost. Once natural organic materials such as leaves, food scraps, or other garden waste are fully decomposed, they're considered humus. Humus is dark, nutrient-rich, and improves the moisture retention and overall condition of soil.

Hybrid Seeds that are created through the cross-pollination between two different varieties or species of plants. Cross-breeding may happen naturally but is often done in a controlled setting or intentionally by humans with the goal of combining beneficial attributes from each plant. For example, for natural disease resistance or higher yield. Hybrid seeds are usually denoted as F1 or F2, which means Filial or "first children"—as in the first generation of seeds produced from breeding. Hybrids are not GMO and also different from open-pollinated seeds. Seeds produced from hybrid plants are not likely to "breed true" and therefore aren't great for seed-saving.

Indeterminate A plant that continues to grow in size and bear fruit over a longer period of time, as opposed to a determinate plant that is shorter lived with a more concentrated fruiting period. Most often used in reference to vining tomato varieties that will produce tomatoes throughout the entirety of the growing season (*see also* determinate).

Integrated pest management An approach to managing garden pests in an organic, sustainable manner that focuses on minimizing health, economic and environmental risks. It involves a hierarchy of decisions and actions, including identifying the pest, assessing the severity of the problem, and using a variety of preventative, biological, cultural, physical pest control measures before resorting to chemical intervention.

Leggy Describes overly tall, stretched-out seedlings. Leggy seedlings are not ideal, as they're usually weaker and prone to toppling. Prevent leggy seedlings by providing ample bright light. Seedlings stretch and become tall when they're in search of better light and will lean toward the strongest light they're provided. The stems of most leggy seedlings can be partially buried, once they're properly hardened off.

Loam The ideal type of soil for growing food and plants, loamy soil is a well-balanced mix of sand, silt, and clay. Therefore, it also possesses good moisture retention and drainage properties. Soil that contains too much clay or silt is often mixed with other soil or soil components (e.g., sand) to achieve a more loam-like consistency.

Macronutrients The elements nitrogen, phosphorous, potassium, calcium, magnesium, and sulfur are macronutrients that are essential to plant health and growth. These are usually added to the soil through amendments and/or cover crops. (*See* NPK.)

Medium In horticultural circles, a medium is the material plants grow in.

Microgreens Young, leafy vegetables or herbs that are harvested just above the soil line when the plants have their first pair of leaves, called cotyledons, and possibly the just-developing true leaves.

Micronutrients The elements boron, chlorine, copper, iron, manganese, molybdenum, and zinc are the seven micronutrients essential for healthy plant growth. These can be added to the soil through compost, organic matter, and rock dust.

Mild climate Regions without extremes—no freezing temperatures in winter and relatively temperate summers.

Mulch Any material that is placed on the surface of otherwise bare soil. Mulch is not only decorative, it also reduces erosion and runoff, suppresses weeds, increases moisture retention, and protects the soil and plant roots.

Mycorrhizae *Myco* means "fungus" and *rhizae* means "root." Mycorrhizae are specialized fungi that colonize the root system of plants to form a mutually beneficial or symbiotic relationship. They act as extensions of the root system, increasing the surface area and exchange of nutrients and water between the soil and the plant's roots. You can inoculate the soil around new plants with mycorrhizae by either lightly dusting the root ball or watering with a mycorrhizae solution after transplanting young seedlings.

Native This term refers to plants that are indigenous to a certain region; native varieties of plants adapt better to their home habitat better than imports or exotics.

Nightshades The Solanaceae plant family includes tomatoes, potatoes, peppers, and eggplant. Nightshade leaves are considered mildly toxic, so the leaves are not safe to eat, while most other common garden plants (brassicas, carrots, beets, radishes, turnips) have edible leaves.

Nitrogen-fixing When nitrogen is taken in from the atmosphere (air) and turned into stored nitrogen in soil, where plants can then utilize the nitrogen to support growth. The process is facilitated by specialized bacteria (rhizobia) that colonize plant roots. Legumes and other crops are particularly effective at fixing nitrogen, including peas, clover, alfalfa, vetch, fava beans, flax, lentils, ryegrass, and soybeans.

No-till gardening A gardening philosophy or style in which the soil is disrupted as little as possible and is not intentionally tilled or turned over every season as in traditional agriculture. Tilling soil leads to a loss of soil structure, compaction, increased runoff and erosion. In contrast, letting the soil go undisturbed preserves the living soil food web, and can increase soil fertility, plant health, and productivity. Also known as "no dig" gardening.

N-P-K These letters stand for "nitrogen," "phosphorus," and "potassium," which are three key macronutrients essential for plant health and growth. The "N-P-K ratio" is listed on fertilizer containers, such as 8-2-1 (a high-nitrogen fertilizer) or 4-4-4 (a well-balanced fertilizer). In general, nitrogen promotes robust leafy green growth, phosphorus is essential for flower and fruit development, and potassium plays a role in overall plant resilience, nutrient utilization, root growth, and photosynthesis. (*See also* macronutrients.)

Open pollinated Seed that will generally "breed true" (produce offspring roughly identical to the parent plant) when the plants are pollinated by another plant of the same variety. Good for seed-saving and consistency. Yet if open-pollinated plants are cross-pollinated by a similar plant of a different variety (e.g., two different types of squash), the saved seeds may not breed true.

Organic gardening A style of gardening that focuses on growing healthy plants in the most natural and safe means possible. Organic gardeners and farmers avoid the use of toxic, chemical, or otherwise synthetic fertilizers and pesticides. Instead, soil and plant health is supported with things like compost, manures, integrated pest management, beneficial insects, and natural soil amendments.

OMRI The Organic Materials Review Institute is a nonprofit organization that certifies whether certain agricultural inputs are safe to use in organic farming. If you see "OMRI-certified" on a gardening product, that means it is considered acceptable to use in an organic garden.

Part sun/part shade This refers to three-to-six hours of sunlight daily.

pH In chemistry, the pH scale is used to determine how acidic or alkaline something is. The number 7 represents a neutral pH. The lower the pH, the more acidic. The higher the pH number, the more alkaline. In gardening, the pH of soil is often considered (including tested or adjusted) to satisfy the ideal growing conditions of particular plants. Most common crops prefer a slightly acidic soil of 6.0 to 7.0.

Perennial Plants that can grow or live for more than two years. In freezing climates, perennials may appear to die back in the winter but will regrow in the spring.

Permaculture This principle focuses on the intentional, careful design and maintenance of agriculturally-productive ecosystems (including garden spaces) so that they mimic the diversity, stability, and resilience of natural ecosystems. Examples of permaculture principles include water harvesting, composting, re-wilding of spaces, regenerative agriculture, and community resilience.

Pollination The fertilization of a flower by wind, insect, birds, etc., where the male pollen reaches the female stigma, resulting in a seed, sometimes surrounded by an edible fruit like a pepper.

Pollinator Anything that aids in the transfer of pollen between plants or flowers, including bees, butterflies, birds, bats, insects, the wind, humans, or other animals. The vast majority of plants rely on pollinators to successfully reproduce—and produce the edible crops we rely on.

Polyculture The practice of growing many types of plants in one garden bed, container, or space—including a mix of companion plants. Growing a wide variety of plants creates biodiversity in your garden, attracts beneficial insects, and reduces the chances of widespread devastation by pests or disease that typically inflict the same kind of crop. It also helps to balance the nutritional demand placed on soil. Polyculture is in contrast to the monoculture we see (growing a huge swath of just one crop, such as corn) common in conventional or commercial farming operations.

Potting up The act of moving a plant from a smaller container into a larger one. Typically done with seedlings as they grow bigger to prevent the plant from becoming root bound and stunted. Also knoen as "repotting," ot applies to houseplants or other potted plants. *(See also* root bound)

Propagation The process of growing (creating) new plants through any variety of methods, including from seed, cuttings, grafts, or other plant parts.

Rhizome An underground stem that grows horizontally from nodes rather than vertically like most other plants. Ginger and turmeric are examples of edible rhizomes. Mint is a notoriously invasive plant because it spreads through vigorous underground rhizomes, also sometimes called "runners."

Root bound A plant, shrub, or tree that is growing in too small of a container that in turn restricts roots and stunts plant growth. Some rootbound plants can recover by being potted up into a larger container or the ground. Some severe cases, however, can leave the plant permanently stunted. *(See also* potting up.)

Row covers Fabric that is used to either exclude pests or raise temperatures of the area beneath it. "Remay" is a type of poly-spun row cover material commonly used in farm and garden settings and it comes in several different thicknesses. Row covers may or may not have hoops under it to create a low "tunnel."

Scarification The process of breaking through the hard outer covering of a seed to allow moisture to penetrate and enable the seed to germinate.

Scientific name/Latin name The name that is unique to a specific species (usually containting a genus and species name, such as *Lathyrus odoratus* for the sweet pea flower). Scientific names are consistent in any language, whereas a single species may have several common names that may vary by region or country.

Season extender Any structure or tool that protects plants from harsh conditions and thereby extends the growing season. Most commonly applied to shelters against frost but may also be used for things that deflect extreme heat and sun, such as shade cloth. Examples include cold frames, cloches, greenhouses, and hoops that support row covering materials like plastic or frost blankets.

Self-seed, or self-sow This occurs when a plant grows naturally from a seed that was dispersed or dropped by a parent plant without human intervention. If allowed to go to seed in the garden, most annual flowers will drop seeds around them, allowing new flowers to grow in the same vicinity the following year. *(See also* volunteer.)

Sheet mulch The process of mulching an area with wide and fairly solid sheets of material, such as cardboard, burlap, newspaper, rolls of painters paper, or synthetic materials like plastic or landscape fabric. Provides similar benefits as classic mulching but can be longer-lasting and even more effective at smothering weeds. Good for pathways, large open spaces, preparing the soil in a new garden space, covering a soil over winter, or smothering grass.

Slow-release fertilizer Fertilizer that will slowly degrade in the soil to make fresh nutrients available to plants over time instead of a strong boost of nutrients at once. Granular or dry "meal"-type fertilizers are usually slow release, often applied as a top-dressing and then watered in. These types of fertilizers generally pose less risk of "burning," or shocking, plants compared to liquid fertilizer.

Soil amendments Materials that are added to soil to increase the health, nutrient content, moisture retention, and/or soil structure. Natural soil amendments include things such as dried plant or animal material (e.g., alfalfa meal, kelp meal, neem meal, bone meal, or crustacean meal), compost, worm castings, lava rock or perlite, peat moss, greensand, granular fertilizers, and rock dust.

Soil food web The important and symbiotic relationship between soil and the network of living things within it. Members of the soil food web include beneficial microorganisms, fungi, protozoa, nematodes, earthworms, mycorrhizae, and other arthropods and creatures. In combination they break down organic matter, introduce nutrients, and improve soil aeration, drainage and moisture retention. Also known as "organic living soil."

South-facing For gardeners in the Northern Hemisphere, a south-facing garden—one that receives unobstructed sun from the south—will maximize sun exposure in all seasons and throughout the day. Planting a garden along the northern side of a house or fence is the opposite of south-facing.

Sprout Germinated seeds that are not grown in medium but instead rinsed in water and drained several times a day.

Stratification The process of subjecting seed to a moist and cold treatment to break dormancy, which occurs naturally when seed is sown outdoors in the autumn and experiences a winter period.

Succession sowing (succession planting) Continually planting new seeds or seedlings in a staggered timeframe over a growing season. The goal of succession planting is usually to offset harvest dates to provide a slower, continual harvest over many months instead of large crops maturing all at one time. This is especially effective with quick-developing vegetables like radishes, bush beans, or baby greens. Three ways to successively sow are: 1. Staggering sowings of the same crop 2. Sowing two varieties of the same crop with different maturing dates 3. Replacing one finished crop with a different crop.

Rooting hormone Substances that stimulate root growth on fresh cuttings during the propagation process, while also protecting the new cuttings from disease. These products can be purchased in a powder or gel form. Aloe vera and cinnamon powder are also effective at encouraging root growth in cuttings.

Tender perennial A warm-climate perennial that is not cold hardy in all temperate zones.

Terminal bud The portion of a plant where new growth originates from, most often in the center or top "leader." If the terminal bud is cut, it often causes the plant to stop or slow upward growth and can encourage branching instead. When harvesting leafy greens using the "cut and come again" method you want to avoid cutting the terminal bud. (*See also* cut and come again.)

Thinning Separating or reducing the number of plants in one space or container; for example, by cutting out or gently pulling apart extra seedlings that are too crowded. Proper thinning practices and spacing promotes fast and healthy growth.

Transplanting The process of relocating plants from one location to another. Most often used to describe when young seedlings are taken out of their starter containers and planted outside. Could also refer to planting a tree or potting a plant from a small container into a larger one.

Top dressing The act of applying amendments or fertilizer to the top of the soil, as opposed to tilling it in.

Untreated seed Seed that does not have a chemical treatment such as fungicide applied to it.

Vermicompost (vermicomposting) Composting with worms. This composting method is typically accomplished in a dedicated closed system, such as a worm bin or tiered worm farm. The worms are routinely fed garden waste or kitchen scraps in appropriate types and quantities to maintain a healthy worm bin. In turn, the compost worms eat the waste materials to produce one of the most wonderful forms of compost available—worm castings (aka, worm poop). (*See also* worms castings.)

Variegated Plants that display patches or streaks of varying colors, most often white and green. It rarely occurs in nature; most plants that routinely contain variegation have been bred or propagated by humans for this trait. Thought to be caused by a random genetic mutation and doesn't always carry on to future seeds.

Vernalization The process of exposing seeds or bulbs to a prolonged period of cold temperatures. The goal is to satisfy the plant's natural requirement for chilling in order to break dormancy and successfully sprout, flower, and/or bear fruit. Humans artificially perform vernalization by storing seeds or bulbs in refrigeration or freezers to imitate seasonal chilling hours. Many nut and fruit trees along with some varieties of garlic, milkweed, and flower bulbs require vernalization, which is also known as "chill hours." (*See also* chill hours.)

Volunteer A plant that germinates and grows with little to no help from the gardener. They typically grow from a plant that went to seed previously in the general vicinity; however, birds or other animals may also spread the seeds. (*See also* self-seed, or self-sow.)

Warm-season crops Vegetables that need consistently warm conditions to grow, will thrive when temperatures are about 75° F (24° C) or above, and do not tolerate frost or cold conditions unless they're protected. Plant warm season crops when the soil and air temperatures are above 50° F (10° C) and will be warmer for several months ahead as the plants mature. Warm season crops include tomatoes, melons, summer squash (zucchini), winter squash (butternut, pumpkin), beans, peppers, corn, sweet potato, cucumbers, and eggplant.

Worm castings Another word for vermicastings, or worm poop. When food passes through a worm's body (such as kitchen scraps in a worm compost bin), it is broken down into concentrated, highly-bioavailable nutrients and beneficial microbes for plants. Though potent, worm castings are very mellow, slow-release, and can't "burn" plants as other animal manure or fertilizer can. As a soil amendment, worm castings also increase soil's moisture retention abilities and improve drainage. Sometimes referred to as "black gold."

Xeriscaping The practice of landscape design that utilizes native, drought-tolerant plants that use little-to-no water aside from what the natural climate provides. It is most popular where the weather tends to be hot and dry. Xeriscaping also incorporates rock, stone, and other hardscaping features.

Index of Common Plant Names

Index of Latin Plant Names

Photo Credits

KEY

DT = Dreamstime.com

SS = Shutterstock.com

t = top m = middle c= center
b = bottom l - left r = right

COVER: tl quangpraha/GettyImages; tr Quadxeon/DT; bl sanddebeautheil/GettyImages; mr Schwirl52/GettyImages; br YinYang/GettyImages

BACK COVER: *From top to bottom:* Adinamn/DT; Nightunter/DT; Flibustier/DT; Andreaobzerova/DT; Mariokrpan72/DT

TITLE PAGE: Tobkatrina/DT

CONTENTS: Vilax/DT

FOREWORD: 6–7 Gardening Know How; 7, Backyard Stories photos featuring Birdsong Ranch project, Brad Cox Architect, Inc; photography by Mark Pinkerton at Virtual Imaging 360

INTRODUCTION: 8 Dprahl/DT; 9 Leeyiutung/DT

Part One: The Outdoor Gardener

10–11 Appalachianviews/DT

Chapter One: Learning the Basics

12 Lovelyday12/DT; 12–13 Andreaobzerova/DT; 14 box tl Varbenov/DT; 14 box tm Chernetskaya/DT; 14 box tr Fbxx71/DT; 14 box bl Vkph/DT; 14 box bm TatyanaL/SS; 14 box br Bertoldwerkmann/DT; 15 box Amenic181/DT; 15bl Tibor13/DT; 15mr Wellphotos/DT;16 Andreaobzerova/DT; 17t Mkistryn/DT; 17m Mccrainemercantile/DT; 17b Hannamariah/DT; 18bl Appalachianviews /DT; 18tr Amaranta/DT; 19 box Gstockstudio1/DT; 19b Mashiki/DT

Chapter Two: Garden Tools and Accessories

20 Dimasobko/DT; 20–21 Ivandzyuba/DT; 22tl Hhounen Kihan; 22tr F42pix/DT; 22bl Selena2009/DT; 22br christopher miles/Alamy Stock Photo; 23tl Bozenafulawka/DT; 23 ml Brookebecker/DT; 23bl Bonekot/DT; 23tm Alinamd/DT; 23ml Photokrolya/DT; 23bm Design56/DT; 23bl rburkholder/DT; 23mc GKH; 23tr Rawpixel; 24l Stuartbur/DT; 24ml Bruce Works/SS; 24tl hernetskaya/DT; 24tr Best Choice; 24ml Mrgreen/DT; 24mc Garden Claw; 24mr Gudella/DT; 24bl Photka/DT; 24bm Photka/DT; 24br Photka/DT; 25tl Stefan11/DT; 25ml Yanas/DT; 25bl Troy-Bilt; 25tr Pioneer111/DT; 25mrt Kunertus/DT; 25mrb Vitaga/DT; 25br Perutskyy29/DT; 26tl Chernetskaya/DT; 26ml zygotehasnobrain/DT; 26bl Seanlockephotography/DT; 26tr New Africa/SS; 26mr Fotosenmeer/DT; 26 box Gunold/DT; 27tl Celwell/DT; 27ml Tubtrug; 27bl Tomak/DT; 27tr AVN Photo Lab/SS; 27tm Suncast; 27bm Aguirre_mar/DT; 27mr Fpf/DT; 27br Dja65/DT; 28l Upixa2/DT; 28tr Photog2112/DT; 28mr Nito100/DT; 28br Kravcs/DT; 29tl Atlasfotoreception/DT; 29ml Alice love artwork/SS; 29bl Kate Nag/SS; 29tm Djeleva1/DT; 29bm Lammeyer/DT; 29tr Ergodyne; 29mr Junpinzon/DT; 29br OceanProd/DT

Chapter Three: Creating the Garden

30 Toa555/DT; 30–31 Andreaobzerova/DT; 32 Consuelo2002/DT; 33t Fabriceloyola9/DT; 33l Foxy/SS; 33 bix Lig23/DT; 34ml Littleny/DT; 34bl Nancykennedy/DT; 34tr Popova Valeriya/SS; 34mr meirion matthias/SS; 34br Crisfotolux/DT; 35tl Manfredxy/DT; 35ml Onepony/DT; 35bl Hannamariah/DT; 35tr Leesniderphotoimages/DT; 35mr Industryandtravel/DT; 35br Studioceja/DT; 36l Paulmaguire/DT; 36r Feldarbeit/DT; 37 Tonywoodhouse/DT; 38tl Gardens by Design/SS; 38bl Hanneseichinger/DT; 39 box Ozgur Coskun/SS; 40 Freshhouse/DT; 41tl Oleksiy Maksymenko Photography/Alamy Stock Photo; 41tml Helinloik/DT; 41tmr Mikolimpik/DT; 41tr Monikabaumbach/DT; 41 box BIOSPHOTO /Alamy Stock Photo; 42 John Trax/Alamy Stock Photo; 43tr Egis/DT; 43br Andreaobzerova/DT; 44 box tl LMPark Photos/SS; 44 box tm Beekeepx/SS; 44 box tr Ad Oculos/SS; 44 box bl ArieStudio/SS; 44 box bm Kayla Blundell/SS; 44 box br Olyjo3/DT; 44tr Tbintb/DT; 45 box Joandawn/DT; 46 Photos4967/DT; 47bl Cebas1/DT; 47tr Goodluz/DT

Chapter Four: The Flower Garden

48 Ivusakzkrabice/DT; 48–49 Junojess/DT; 50tr Andreaobzerova/DT; 50br Andreaobzerova/DT; 51 box Goncharukv/DT; 51tm Andreaobzerova/DT; 51tr Andreaobzerova/DT; 51mr Lvenks/DT; 51br Rigsby8131/DT; 52bl Public Domain; 52tr eurobanks/SS; 53 Mrdenpol/DT; 54 90024090germano/DT; 55 tr Olganikishina/DT; 55 box tl Sarah_Robson/DT; 55 box tml Lapandr/DT; 55 box tm Elenaseiryk/DT; 55 box tmr Shauna286/DT; 55 box tr Kimbobo/DT; 55 box bl Zigzagmtart/DT; 55 box bml Kagab4/DT; 55 box bm Onepony/DT; 55 box bmr Flatbox2/DT; 55 box br Wam1975/DT; 56 bl Public Domain; 56 tr oy6uca/DT; 56mr Artbankua/DT; 56br Appalachianviews/DT; 57tl Daveymad7/DT; 57ml Tupungato/DT; 57bl Mirekova/DT; 57tr Pleprakaymas/DT; 57br Vwalakte/DT; 58 Kristi Blokhin/SS; 59tl Joliephantasm/DT; 59ml Lukomskiprajzner/DT; 59bl Sanddebeautheil943/DT; 59tm T-Iva/SS; 59mc Maxopphoto/DT; 59bm GeorgeColePhoto/SS; 59tr Pavlobaliukh/DT; 59mr Sergbk/DT; 59br Gerry Bishop/SS; 60tl Doethion/DT; 60br Freshhouse/DT; 61tl Joliephantasm/DT; 61m Xuanmai2009/DT; 62tl Sillu654/DT; 62bl Haraldmuc/DT; 63tl Dimanchik/DT; 63mr Simicv/DT; 64tr Adinamnt/DT; 64bm Marty Kropp/SS; 65tl Dogfella/DT; 65bm Artpost2000/DT; 66tl Kamonrutm/DT; 66br Dole/DT; 67tl Solovki/DT; 67bl Mruckszio/DT; 67 box ClaudiaSchueth/DT; 68mr Dole/DT; 69 tl Mayaafzaal/DT; 69br Ksushsh/DT; 70tr David J. Stang/Creative Commons Attribution-ShareAlike 4.0 International; 70mr gardenlife/SS; 70br Mfomojola/DT; 71box tl Nickkurzenkokurzenkonv/DT; 71 box tm Larrymetayer/DT; 71 box tr Gerry Bishop/SS; 71 box bl Rickmcmillin/DT; 71box bm Sj347/DT; 71br Connerscott/DT; 71bl Public Domain; 71br Photohampster/DT; 2tl Onepony/DT; 72ml Joloei/DT; 72 box Augusthalem/DT; 73tl Sheila2002/DT; 73br Alisali/DT; 74tl AlenaBalotnik/SS; 74bl Scisetti Alfio/SS; 74 box Steven J. Baskauf/Creative Commons Attribution-ShareAlike 4.0 International; 75tl Zeljko225/DT; 75br Vilor/DT; 76mr Vilor/SS; 77tl Kj2kj9/DT;

77bl Anphotos/DT; 77tm Anphotos/DT; 77bm Joss/DT; 77tr Anphotos/DT; 78tl Severina74/DT; 78mr Tompet80/DT; 79tl Kurylo54/DT; 79br Olgapkurguzova/DT; 80tl Tanyki88/DT; 80bl Sgoodwin4813/DT; 81tl Erinkate25/DT; 81mr Tale/DT; 82tl IrynaL/SS; 82bl kamnuan/SS; 3tl Arfi Binsted/SS; 83mr Vilor/SS; 4tl Athapet/DT; 84bm Pannaraituk/DT; 84 box Alima007/DT; 5tl Alinamd/DT; 85b Gala_kan/DT; 86tl Elenathewise/DT; 86br Jianbinglee/DT; 87tl Anatolii57/DT; 87bl Ksushsh/DT; 88tl Terehinat4/DT; 88bl Voltan1/DT; 89tl Oseland/DT; 89br Martinao/DT; 90tl Sofiaworld/DT; 90br AN NGUYEN/SS; 91tl Ragsac19/DT; 91mr Verastuchelova/DT; 92tl Natalysavina/DT; 92br Sgoodwin4813/DT; 93tl Doethion/DT; 94bl Welcomia/DT; 94tr Wonderful Nature/SS: 95tl OLAYOLA/DT; 95tr Nancykennedy/DT; 95bl Chortenya/DT; 95br Aimful/DT; 96tl Cjchiker/DT; 96mr Kostiuchenko/DT; 97tl dragoncello/DT; 97bm Elenathewise/DT; 98tl Haraldmuc/DT; 98bl Ksena2009/DT; 99tl Agatchen/DT; 99mr Griffin024/DT; 100tl Redtbird02/DT; 100mr Dole/DT; 101br Elenathewise/DT; 101tl Gmeyerle/DT; 102tl Demamiel62/DT; 102bm Vilor/DT; 103tl Photodynamx/DT; 103 box gehapromo/DT; 103 br Vilor/DT; 104tl Verastuchelova/DT; 04 br Lijuan Guo/SS; 105tl Mariola Anna S/SS; 105m Sgoodwin4813/DT; 106tl Orestligetka/DT; 106mr Troichenko/DT; 107tl Berkshots/DT; 107bm Pipa100/DT; 108tl Sarka137/DT; 108 box Passenger Window/SS; 108br Neirfy/DT; 109tl hacohob/SS; 109bm New Africa/SS; 109mr New Africa/SS; 110tl Sannikovdmitry/DT; 110mb Marlonneke/DT; 111tl Boonsom/DT; 111mb Marlonneke/DT; 111 box Kazakovmaksim/DT; 112tl Thefutureis/DT; 112mr Kostiuchenko/DT; 113tl Info23144/DT; 113mb Emilio100/DT; 114tl Sampete/DT; 114ml Wilderwine/DT; 114bl Cbechinie/DT; 115tl Vnarong/DT; 115br Verastuchelova/DT; 116tl Aphichetc/DT; 116br Tamara_k/DT; 117tl Chiffanna/DT; 117b Topaz777/DT; 118br Dole/DT; 118tl Suradech/DT; 119tl Zigzagmtart/DT; 119 mb Artmim/DT; 119mr Robynmac/DT; 120tl Fallsview/DT; 120br Dole/DT; 121tl Bedo/DT; 121mr Vilor/DT; 122b Rozaliya/DT; 122tl Chingraph/DT; 123tl Onepony/DT; 123mr Toomler/DT; 124tl Onepony/DT; 124b Spirovo2010/DT; 125tl Casanowe/DT; 125mr Liligraphie/DT; 126tl Marsia16/DT; 126br Iropa/DT; 127tl Gitamaluo/DT; 127b Clicktrick/DT; 128tl Darkop/DT; 128b Vilax/DT; 129tl Olyas8/DT; 129bm Antonel/DT; 129 box Lumanproductions/DT; 130tl Aleoks/DT; 130mr Multik/DT; 131tl Sampete/DT; 131br Nerss/DT;

Chapter Five: The Foliage Garden

132 Zena1986/DT; 132–133 Bratty1206/DT; 134b Elenathewise/DT; 134t Mysikrysa/DT; 135 Demamiel62/DT; 136tl Kclarksphotography/DT; 136br Demamiel62/DT; 137tl Herreid/DT; 137br spline_x/SS; 138tl Augusthalem/DT; 138l Chfonk/DT; 138tm Chfonk/DT; 138tr Chfonk/DT; 138br Chfonk/DT; 139tl Xoﬀlowers/DT; 139l Digitalimagined/DT; 139m Digitalimagined/DT; 139r Digitalimagined/DT; 140 box Martinao/DT; 140tl Wirestock/DT; 40tr Photohampster/DT; 140ml Kozminov/DT; 140tr Rospoint/DT; 140bl Pilens/DT; 140br Jcaley/DT; 141tl Wklimek3/DT; 141tml Tpalexeeva/DT; 141tmr Rjcvanhees/DT; 141tr Ntrirata/DT; 141ml Simonapavan/DT; 141mcl Jeri52/DT; 141mcr Clearvista/DT; 141mr Jeri52/DT; 141bl Kathryn Roach/SS; 141bml Yorozu520/DT; 141bmr Poorvajnk/DT; 141br Ravennka/DT; 142tl Mashiki/DT; 142b Crannnk/DT; 143tl Joycegraceweb/DT; 143bm Newt96/DT; 144tl Romarti/DT; 144br Chfonk/DT; 145tl Wasnoch/DT; 145mr Kankulm/DT; 146tl Marcovarro/DT; 146tr Alohapattyaof/DT; 146ml G_r_B/SS; 146mr Shaowen1994/DT; 146bl Pxlman/DT; 146br guentermanaus/SS; 147tl Pxlman/DT; 147tml Pxlman/DT; 147tmr Keifer/DT; 147tr Woodpencil/DT; 147ml Henkwallays/DT; 147mcl Orestligetka/DT; 147mcr Birute/DT; 147mr Montreenanta/DT; 147bl guentermanaus/SS; 147bml Kwselcer/DT; 147bmr Troyka/DT; 147br Jukuraesamurai/DT; 148tl Apugach5/DT; 148br Juliasudnitskaya/DT; 149tl Marinodenisenko /DT; 149br Pstedrak/DT; 150tl Mariokrpan72/DT; 150bm Tevarak11/DT; 151tl Ijankovic854/DT; 151mr Natalia van D/SS; 152tl Pierwszy/DT; 152tr Nickkurzenkokurzenkonv/DT; 152ml Weisschr/DT; 152mcl Apugach5/DT; 152mcr Pilens/DT; 152mr Beekeepx/DT; 152bl youyuenyong budsawongkod/SS;152br Nahhan/DT; 153tl Nancyayumi/DT; 153tml Photoinsel/DT; 153tmr Dmf090987/DT; 153tr Phjlg/DT; 153ml Simonapavan/DT; 153mcl Mashiki/DT; 153mcr Steinebachmichael/DT; 153mr Evgeniymuhortov2/DT; 153bl Eyewave/DT; 153br Vadimzhakupov/DT; 154tl Studioceja/DT; 154br Studioceja/DT; 155tl Arttravelphoto/DT; 155bm Videowokart/DT; 156tl Dashark/DT; 156bl Masummerbreak/DT; 157tl Nevada31/DT; 157bm Levkr/DT; 158tl Oakovtun/DT; 158tr Nmessana/DT; 158ml Agap13/DT; 158mr Marcel6182/DT; 158bl Bozhenamelnyk/DT; 158br Sarayutwatchasit/DT; 159tl Nailotl/DT; 159tml Tracyimmordino/DT; 159tmr Tondafoto/DT; 159tr Khuruzero/DT; 159ml Aopsan/DT; 159mcl Sireagle/DT; 159mcr maristos/DT; 159mr Epantha/DT; 159bl Galumphinggalah/DT; 159bml Achompunuch/DT; 159bmr Ir717/DT; 159br Eutoch/DT; 160tl Kurylo54/DT; 160ml Chfonk/DT; 160b Chfonk/DT; 160tr Chfonk/DT; 161tl Tigrimohamed2016/DT; 161br toibkk/DT; 162tl 8thcreator/DT; 162bm Mraoraor/DT; 163tl Andreistanescu/DT; 163br Griffin024/DT; 164tl Unteroffizier/DT; 164br JaCrispy/DT; 165tl Kuarmungadd/DT; 165bm Grafvision/DT; 166tl Keifer/DT; 166bm Pannaraituk/DT; 166 boxBelokurov/DT; 167tl Kazakovmaksim/DT; 167mb Monikabaumbach/DT; 168tl Itlookslikemaik/DT; 168bl Griffin024/DT; 169tl Tepic/DT; 169bm Kav777/DT

Chapter Six: The Kitchen Garden

170 Subbotina/DT; 170–171 sirtravelalot/SS; 172 box Serge Mouraret/Alamy Stock Photo; 172tr Rixie/DT; 173tr Halfpoint/SS; 173br Fedecandoniphoto/DT; 75 box t Martin Kemp/SS; 175 box mtl Vvoevale/DT; 175 box mtr Lucagal/DT; 175 box bml Caseyjadew/DT; 175 box bmr Geografika/DT; 175 box bl Aurelielemoigne/DT; 175 box br Fotokate/DT; 176tl Piliphoto/DT; 176br Teyakp/DT; 177tl Idenviktor/DT; 177bm Photomaru/DT; 178tl Slowmotiongli/DT; 178 brMayakova/DT; 179tl Sergejsbelovs/DT; 179bm Saddako123/DT; 180tl Modfos/DT; 180mr Kkovaleva/DT; 181tl Somesense182/DT; 181br Boonchuay/DT; 182tl Wirestock/DT; 182bm Muslimovatv/DT; 183tl Garsya/DT; 183bm Volkop/DT; 184 Damatz/DT; 185tl agefotostock / Alamy Stock Photo; 185tm Slovegrove/DT; 185tr Midosemsem/DT; 185ml Wellesenterprises/DT; 185mc Ulphoto/DT; 185mr Davidgn/DT; 85bl Grazza23/DT; 185bml Olyas8/DT; 185bmr Artography/DT; 185br Atosan/DT; 186tl Boonsom/

DT; 186br Jjy8888/DT; 187tl Luschikovvv/DT; 187 box Captivatinglightphotos/DT; 187br Sikth/DT; 188tl Fortise/DT; 188bm Peterkozikowski/DT; 189tl Davidwatmough/DT; 189m Anny88stock/DT; 190tl Ahundov/DT; 190bm Igordutina/DT; 191bm Nbvf/DT; 191tl TasFoto/DT; 193tl Vaivirga/DT; 193tml Belliot/DT; 193tmr Kwangmoo/DT; 193tr Janecat11/DT; 193ml OLEG PIYAK TSYGANYUK/SS; 193mcl Rmorijn/DT; 193mcr Czalewski/DT; 193mr Pstedrak/DT; 193bl Brebca/DT; 193bcl Eugenesergeev/DT; 193bcr Moxumbic/DT; 193br Kwangmoo/DT; 194tl Petrarichli/DT; 194bl Elenaprost/DT; 195tl Richie0703/DT; 195br Draftmode/DT; 196tl Ahundov/DT; 196bl Philkinsey/DT; 196 box Mrdoomits/DT; 197tl Paulmaguire/DT; 197br Desuz/DT; 198tl Tchara/DT; 198bl Kkovaleva/DT; 199tl Nemesis2207/DT; 199bm Peterzijlstra/DT; 200tl Zigzagmtart/DT; 200br Bhofack2/DT; 201tl Natagolubnycha/DT; 201br Egal/DT; 202tl Bhofack2/DT; 202tr Orestligetka/DT; 202ml Mkos83/DT; 202mr Krungchingpixs/DT; 202bl Tonktiti/DT; 202br Thaninormai/DT; 203tl Jeedgot/DT; 203tml Sirisris/DT; 203tmr Mgrigorjevs/DT; 203tr Martingaalsk/DT; 203ml Yorozu520/DT; 203mcl Pawinp/DT; 203mcr Papava/DT; 203mr Marysalen/DT; 203bl Jackf/DT; 203bm Padufoto/DT; 203br Yorozu520/DT; 204tl Slogger/DT; 204bl Onairjiw/DT; 204 box Wraysk/DT; 205tl Kobeza/DT; 205br Boonchuay/DT; 206tl Wirestock/DT; 206bm Onlyfabrizio/DT; 207tl Rainer/DT; 207br Teamarbeit/DT; 208tl Saiko3p/DT; 208tr Studiobarcelona/DT; 208ml Pstedrak/DT; 208mr Zhukovsky/DT; 208bl Helgaf1/DT; 208br Insolite48/DT; 209tl Kslight/DT; 209tml Waldenstroem/DT; 209tmr Lianem/DT; 209tr Anantaradhika/DT; 209ml Zutosekale/DT; 209mcl Peachpappa/DT; 209mcr Sever180/DT; 209mr Visharo/DT; 209bl Slogger/DT; 209bcl Simonapavan/DT; 209bcr Mreco99/DT; 209br Photoweges/DT; 210tl Denny128/DT; 210br Juliedeshaies/DT; 211tl Debu55y/DT; 211mr pukao/SS

Chapter Seven
The Herb Garden

212 Corners74/DT; 212–213 Fotofix/DT; 214 Shaiith/DT; 215tl Nina Alizada/SS; 215br Romantiche/DT; 216 Alexraths/DT; 217 Row 1: l Olyaponomarenko/DT; ml Yorozu520/DT; m Maximfesenko/DT; mr Bebenjy/DT; r Eugenesergeev/DT;Row 2: l Suwanneeredhead/DT; ml Jlmcanally/DT; m Barmalini/DT; mr Banprik/DT; r SophieWalster/DT; Row 3: l Scisettialfio/DT; ml Nazzu/DT; m Elfthryth/DT; mr Mesocyclone70/DT; r Alicja13l/DT; Row 4: l Quadxeon/DT; ml Sagegardenherbs/DT; m Irinka7/DT; mr Juliedeshaies/DT; r As-design/DT; 218tl Lantapix/DT; 218ml Leptospira/DT; 218br Kayfochtmann/DT; 219tl Mruckszio/DT; 219bl Dole/DT; 219 box Ikeroesia/DT; 220tl Gorchittza2012/DT; 220bm Kkovaleva/DT; 221tl Zutosekale/DT; 221br Scisettialfio/DT; 222tl Lianem/DT; 222mr Ovydyborets/DT; 223tl Ljubov/DT; 223br Vvoevale/DT; 224tl Natalavilman/DT; 224mb Scisettialfio/DT; 224mr Maxsol7/DT; 225tl Cobalt70/DT; 225bl Olesh/DT; 225r Bikicav/DT; 226tl Erikapichoud/DT; 226mr Rbiedermann/DT; 227tl Valerygreen/DT; 227br Anny88stock/DT; 228tr Vitaliebaciu83/DT; 228br Evron/DT; 228bml Elen/DT; 228bmr Alexeybykov/DT; 228br Youths/DT; 229tl Innapol20/DT; 229tml Alatielin/DT; 229tr Meunierd/DT; 229tmr Evgeniymuhortov2/DT; 229ml Orestligetka/DT; 229mcl Elinkac/DT; 229mcr Lianem/DT; 229mr Stevanovicigor/DT; 229bl Weisschr/DT; 229bml Tommeaker26/DT; 229bmr Joellen_joli/DT;229br Zibedik/DT; 230tl Nancyayumi/DT; 230br Wirestock/DT; 231tl Corluc/DT; 231r Dole/DT; 232tl Slowmotiongli/DT; 232bl Pstedrak/DT; 233tl Westhimal/DT; 233bl Jpcprod/DT; 234tl Naramit/DT; 234bl Scisettialfio/DT; 235tl Martina Unbehauen/SS; 235br Maxsol7/DT; 236tl Bialasiewicz/DT; 236br Shkolnica123/DT; 237tl Lalalulustock/DT; 237mr Troichenko/DT; 238tl Mruckszio/DT; 238bl Otrokovice/DT; 239br Verastuchelova/DT; 239tl Darkop/DT; 240tl Barmalini/DT; 240bl Czuber/DT; 240mr Ilonai/DT; 241tl Allasravani/DT; 241bl Dole/DT; 241 box Carbonbrain/DT; 242tl Vbaleha/DT; 242br Ovydyborets/DT; 243tl Lanika137/DT; 243 box Kalebkroetsch/DT; 243br Scisettialfio/DT; 244tl Frizzantine/DT; 244br Antonel/DT; 245tl Snowboy234/DT; 245bm Kolesnikovserg/DT; 246tl Slowmotiongli/DT; 246br Enjoylife25/DT; 247tl Photohampster/DT; 247mr Misintatiana/DT; 248tl Paulmaguire/DT; 248mr Czuber/DT; 48box Hupeng/DT; 249tl Wertaw/DT; 249br Pipa100/DT; 250tl Kewuwu/DT; 250bl Pipa100/DT; 251tl Ikeroesia/DT; 251mr JPC-PROD/SS; 252tl Marinodenisenko /DT; 252br Khumthong/DT; 253tl Darkop/DT; 253bm Scisettialfio/DT; 253 box Zigzagmtart/DT; 254tl Siegi232/DT; 254bl Splinex/DT; 254 box Argenlant/DT; 255tl Paulmaguire/DT; 255br Enjoylife25/DT; 256tl Wklimek3/DT; 256br Pixelelfe/DT; 257tl Verastuchelova/DT; 257br Scisettialfio/DT

Chapter Eight:
Garden Shrubs

258 Chamillewhite/DT; 258–259 Fallsview/DT; 260 Chamillewhite/DT; 261tl Lianem/DT; 261tr Bialasiewicz/DT; 261bl Mturhanlar/DT; 261br Djem82/DT; 262 Fabriceloyola9/DT; 263tr Irynalastochka/DT; 263mr Lawcain/DT; 263br Olikzu/DT; 264tl Catarii/DT; 264br Marinodenisenko /DT; 265tl simona pavan/SS; 265bm Scisettialfio/DT; 266tl semper-scifi/SS; 266br MirasWonderland/SS; 267tl Tracyimmordino/DT; 267r Outeliermucha/DT; 268tl Beekeepx/DT; 268bm HJBecker/Creative Commons Attribution-ShareAlike Version 2.0 Generic; 269tl Candyspics/DT; 269mr Ivonnewierink/DT; 270tl Krisata/DT; 270bl James St. John/Creative Commons Attribution 2.0 Generic; 271tl Erizito/DT; 271mb Griffin024/DT; 272tl Yorozu520/DT; 272bl Robyn Mackenzie/SS; 273tl Thefutureis/DT; 273mb Sikth/DT; 274tl 02pveee/DT; 274bl Splinex/DT; 274tr Adam88x/DT; 275tl Ehrlif/DT; 275mr LiliGraphie/SS; 276tl Yorozu520/DT; 276mr Scisettialfio/DT; 277tl Adisa/DT; 277mr Quang Ho/SS; 278 Moskwa/DT; 279 Row 1: l Simonbizun/DT; ml Carmenhauser/DT; mr Photohampster/DT; r Caymia/DT; Row 2: l Salicyna/Creative Commons Attribution-ShareAlike Version 4.0 International; ml Olga18x27/DT; mr amomentintime/Alamy Stock Photo; r Ashahawkesworth/DT; Row 3: l Emeraldstudiopdx/DT; ml Humorousking207/DT; mr Krisata/DT; r Ioannaalexa/DT; Row 4: l Beibaoke1/DT; ml Pstedrak/DT; mr Marina Rose/SS; r Ulf Eliasson/Creative Commons Attribution-ShareAlike Version 3.0 Unported; 280tl Sophieso/DT; 280bl Nevinates/DT; 281tl Georgie225/DT; 281bm Simic Vojislav/SS; 282tl Visharo/DT; 282bl Kostiuchenko/DT; 283tl Shan 16899/SS; 283bm Scisettialfio/DT; 284tl Marinodenisenko /DT; 284bl Bat09mar/DT; 285tl Spotluda/DT; 285tr Luckymarinka/DT; 286tl Darkop/DT;

286bl Kaspri/DT; 287tl Tangsphoto/DT; 287br Pixabay; 288tl Yorozu520/DT; 288bl Griffin024/DT; 289tl Spotluda/DT; 289mr Dole/DT; 290tl Viktoriia Kolosova/SS; 290bl oksana2010/SS; 291tl Matewe/DT; 291mr naKornCreate/SS; 292tl jongholee/SS; 292bm Milart1964/DT; 293tl Macsstock/DT; 293r vilax/SS; 294tl Nick Pecker/SS; 294br Meister Photos/SS; 295tl Ihor Hvozdetskyi/SS; 295bm Olexandr Panchenko/SS; 296tl Marinodenisenko /DT; 296br Dole/DT; 297tl Shimofamy3223/DT; 297bm Lianem/DT; 298tl Alp2311/DT; 298br Sebcz/DT; 299tl Gorlovkv/DT; 299bm Gummy Bear/SS; 300tl Yarygin/SS; 300bm Scisetti Alfio/SS; 301tl Gabrielaberes/DT; 301r Maxopphoto/DT; 302tl Mashiki/DT; 302bm Scisettialfio/DT; 303tl Svetlanaaf/DT; 303r Splinex/DT; 304tl Enrouteksm/DT; 304r Madlen/SS; 305tl Ibalogh2010/DT; 305bm Natalyaa/DT; 306tl Goga18128/DT; 306r Humorousking207/DT; 307tl Tradeom/DT; 307mr Scisettialfio/DT; 308tl Botanic World/Alamy Stock Photo; 308tr LindaHarms/DT; 308ml JenningsSayre/DT; 308mr Lightfantastic/DT; 308bl Zhan1999/DT;308br Asterixvs/DT; 309tl Hbphotoart/DT; 309tml Romanoverko/DT; 309tmr Ustunibisoglu/DT; 309tr Gimbat/DT; 309ml Adrianasulugiuc/DT; 309mcl Tangsphoto/DT; 309mcr Nickkurzenkokurzenkonv/DT; 309mr Animaflora/DT; 309bl Peter Turner Photography/SS; 309bml Aaron90311/DT; 309bmr Mojkinairina/DT; 309br Agban99/DT; 310tl Chernetskaya/DT; 310bm Kostiuchenko/DT; 311tl Ironstuff/DT; 311br Imagetwelve/DT; 312tl Nataliapavlova369/DT; 312bm Anoushkatoronto/DT; 312 box Irynalastochka/DT; 313tl Leesnider photoimages/DT; 13bm Splinex/DT

Chapter Nine: Garden Decor

314 Doromonic/DT; 314–315 Micheb/DT; 316 Jamiehooper/DT; 317tl Photodynamx/DT; 317tr Hannamariah/DT; 317m Romeo1232/DT; 317b Mashiki/DT; 318bl Terra24/DT; 318 box Helo80808/DT; 319t Janeh15/DT; 319m Murmakova/DT; 319b Iperl/DT; 320 Oocoskun/DT; 321tl Amhaywald/DT; 321mr Trudywilkerson/DT; 321br Nadine123/DT; 322bl Alan64/DT; 322 box Daseaford/DT; 323t Lisaewing/DT; 323m Marilyngould/DT; 323b Thespeedybutterfly/DT

Chapter Ten: Weeds, Garden Pests, and Diseases

324 Philipsteuryphotography/DT; 324–325 Aleksandr Rybalko/SS; 326ml Denny128/DT; 326mb Furiarossa/SS; 326tr Bhupinder Bagga/SS; 326br Wojphoto/DT; 327tl Tamara_k/DT; 327tcl Kclarksphotography/DT; 327bcl Robert Flogaus-Faust/Creative Commons Attribution 4.0 International; 327b Anitabonita/DT; 327tr Pisotckii/DT; 327tcr Vnikitenko/DT; 327mcr Kjwells86/DT; 328bl Digitalg/DT; 328m Vitaserendipity/DT; 328r Septemberrain/DT; 329tl Stigsfoto/DT; 329bl Tabouleh/DT; 329br Okanakdeniz/DT; 330bl Bjphotographs/DT; 330tm Sasiwit/DT; 330tr Tj876648298/DT; 330mr Sasiwit/DT; 331tl Stefans42/DT; 331ml Sasiwit/DT; 331mc Idubert/DT; 331bm Thanapornpinp/DT; 331l She Homesteads/SS

Chapter Eleven: Welcoming Pollinators

332 Davide Bonora/SS; 332–333 Flyingdolphin/DT; 334l Palex66/DT; 334m Dr.alex/DT; 334r Tsekhmister/DT; 335 Row 1: l Katarinagondova/DT; m Wirestock/DT; r dragoncello/DT; 335 Row 2: l Nletson1/DT; m Meryll/DT; r Sumikophoto/DT; 335 Row 3: l Petesteele59/DT; m Criminalatt/DT; r Vrabelpeter1/DT; 335 Row 4: l Noonie/DT; m Ralfliebhold/DT; r Khuntuu1973/DT; 336bl Ambientideas/DT; 336tm Dvande/DT; 336m Jpsdk/DT; 337 Row 1: l Ionel.stoica/DT; m Ctmphotog/DT; r Ritam777/DT; Row 2: l Elviraspring/DT; m Inavanhateren/DT; r Cathykeifer/DT; Row 3: l Lburk895/DT; m Pimmimemom/DT; r Sidorovat/DT; Row 4: l jenwolfphoto/DT; m Suebmtl/DT; 338bl Stevebyland/DT; 338m Mtruchon/DT; 338 box Martinpel/DT; 338tr Mhryciw/DT; 339 Row 1: l Proedding77/DT; m Hopkora/DT; r Sandywoods8910/DT; Row 2: lmvramesh/SS; m Janet Griffin-Scott/Alamy Stock Photo; r Indish/DT; Row 3: l Kquinnferris/DT; m Wirestock/DT; Row 4: l Jldwrite/DT; m Kelly Colgan Azar/Creative Commons Attribution-NoDerivs 2.0 Generic

Part Two: The Indoor Gardener

340–341 Annu1tochka/DT

Chapter Twelve: Ideal Plants for Inside the Home

342 Jhernan124/DT; 342–343 Toyakis2/DT; 344tm Pomphotothailand/DT; 344br Rido/DT; 345m Helinloik/DT; 345tr Chernetskaya/DT; 345br Gballgiggs/DT; 345box Bilalphotos/DT; 346 Tebastien/DT; 347m Psisaa/DT; 347br Annu1tochka/DT; 348 Wollertz/DT; 349 box Irinayeryomina/DT; 350tl Ganzevayna/DT; 350br Tannjuska/DT; 351tl Anngirna/DT; 351bm Amradul/DT; 352tl Martinao/DT; 352mr Chernetskaya/DT; 353tl Serezniy/DT; 353r Elnur/DT; 354tl Kitti Gavinratchatarot/SS; 355tl MKiryakova/DT; 354bm Greenkiller/DT; 355bm Sdbower/DT; 356tl Honeyinside/DT; 356bm Andreadonetti/DT; 357tl JMP_Traveler/SS; 357bm Kav777/DT; 358tl jamaludinyusup/DT; 358bl Filmpoznan/DT; 359tl Tran Trung Designer/SS; 59bm funny face/SS; 360tl Photographee.eu/SS; 360bm Dewins/DT; 361tl Afiraz/SS; 361br Ksenia Lada/SS; 362tl Mariokrpan72/DT; 362mr Nidnotes/DT; 363tl Bilalphotos/DT; 363mr Rodrusoleg/DT; 364tl Alohapattyaof/DT; 364bl Aperturesound/DT; 365tl Maritxu22/DT; 365mr Monikabaumbach/DT; 366tl Bozhenamelnyk/DT; 366mb Dewins/DT; 366r Espoir2004/DT; 367tl Serezniy/DT; 367br Lenanet/DT; 368tl Gavran333/SS; 368bl cisetti Alfio/SS; 369tl Tynza1/DT; 369br trambler58/SS; 370tl Agneskantaruk/DT; 370br TY Lim/SS; 371tl Dyfrain/DT; 371bl Dyfrain/DT; 372tl Monikabaumbach/DT; 372br Chernetskaya/DT; 373tl Darkop/DT; 373mr Chernetskaya/DT; 374tl Jantaneeboonkhaw/DT; 374r Popjd149/DT; 375tl Duskbabe/DT; 375bl Feodorkorolevsky/DT; 376tl Africa Studio/Alamy Stock Photo; 376br Pannaraituk/DT; 377tl Mlharrisphotography/DT; 377r Sppepper/DT; 378 1265violet/DT; 379tl Anantkaset/DT; 379tcl Fotobym/DT; 379tcr Mjpower8/DT; 379tr Smitty411/DT; 379ml Kthanaphon3811/DT; 379mcl Genlady/DT; 379mcr pisces2386/DT; 379mr Espion/DT; 379bl Jomphong/DT; 379bcl Smitty411/DT; 379bcr Espion/DT; 379br Whiskybottle/DT; 380tl Wheatfieldmediastock/DT; 380mr Sabellopro/DT; 381tl Armifello/DT; 381mr Borojoint/DT; 382tl Serjshklyaev/DT; 382bm Matka_wariatka/DT; 383tl Monikabaumbach/DT; 383bm Chfonk/DT; 384tl Sasapin Kanka/SS; 384br Olesia_O/SS; 385tl Ellinnur/DT; 385mr TuktaBaby/SS; 386tl Ansyvan/DT; 386br joloei/SS; 387tl Westhimal/DT; 387br Artpost2000/DT